The
International Directory of *Little Magazines* & *Small Presses*
42nd Edition, 2006–2007

Len Fulton, Editor

★ **Dustbooks** ★

CONTENTS

If you have a press or magazine you would like to list in the Dustbooks directories simply go to our website at www.dustbooks.com, click on the Directory Listing Forms button and follow instructions.

PAPER: $37.95/copy ISBN 0-913218-38-3
    $135.00/4-year subscription
CLOTH: $55.00/copy ISBN 0-913218-39-1
    $145.00/4-year subscription

email: publisher@dustbooks.com

website: http://www.dustbooks.com

Published annually by Dustbooks, P.O. Box 100, Paradise, CA 95967, also publishers of the *Directory of Editors, Directory of Poetry Publishers* and the *Small Press Review/Small Magazine Review* (bimonthly). Systems design, typesetting format and computer programming by Neil McIntyre, 3135 Prince Henry Drive, Sacramento, CA 95833.

# Mountain Book Company

A VIRTUAL BOOK WHOLESALER

FACILITATING ELECTRONIC ORDERING FOR SELECTED SMALL PUBLISHERS

www.mountainbook.org

a member of Pubnet

Featured Publishers:

Ankh Books: A new publishing company in Canada that focuses on children's fantasy and adventure novels. First book is *Rafi's Song and the Stones of Erebus,* hardcover fiction, ranked the number one bestseller for young adults at McNally Robinson Booksellers in March 2006. www.ankhbooks.com

Clearwater Publishing: refreshing books since 1990. Funny, perennially bestselling books on dull subjects, including the books of Kenn Amdahl: *There Are No Electrons: Electronics for Earthlings, Algebra Unplugged, Calculus for Cats,* and *Joy Writing: Discover and Develop Your Creative Voice,* as well as *Economics for the Impatient,* by CA Turner and *The Barefoot Fisherman: a fishing book for kids* by Paul Amdahl. www.clearwaterpublishing.com

Devenish Press: Books and post card books featuring art-quality color photographs and stories of Ireland, by Tom Quinn Kumpf, including *Ireland: Standing Stones to Stormont* and *Children of Belfast.* www.devenishpress.com

FIA International LLC: Republishing the books of the late Warren Ziegler, including *Ways of Enspiriting* and *When Your Spirit Calls.* Mr Ziegler founded Futures-Invention Associates International and has a worldwide following. www.enspiriting.com

Privacy Journal: The authoritative journal on privacy issues since 1974 also publishes books, including *Ben Franklin's Website: Privacy and Curiosity from Plymouth Rock to the Internet,* by Robert Ellis Smith, *Compilation of State and Federal Privacy Laws, The Law of Privacy Explained, War Stories,* and *The Directory of Privacy Professionals.* www.privacyjournal.net

Media Visions Press: Publishes *Global Sense* by Judah Freed, an update of *Common Sense* by Thomas Paine, to renew hope in these times that try our souls. *Global Sense* shows how our global interactivity empowers us to change the world by changing ourselves. www.mediavisionspress.com

Table Mountain Press: Publishers of educational fiction. *The Path* is set in the time of Jesus. It follows a devout Jewish boy's adventurous life on the old Silk Road where he meets a Confucian cook, a Hindu guru, Buddhist monks, a Taoist, a Zoroastrian, and Jesus of Nazareth. www.thepathbook.com

Wisefool Press: The books of Jed McKenna including *Spiritual Enlightenment: The Damnedest Thing, Spiritually Incorrect Enlightenment,* and *Spiritual Warfare.* www.wisefoolpress.com

Typical terms are 45% discount for bookstore members of Pubnet.org, free shipping, non-returnable, net 30.

SAN 631922X   More info: sales@mountainbook.org

nine muses books nine muses mystery theatre

3541 kent creek road, winston oregon 97496   mw9muses@teleport.com
archive under development: ninemusesbooks.net

Carol Barth   Charlie Burks   Gary David   Louise Dovell   Stephen Fandrich   Jean Ferner   Martina Goodin   Larry Griffin   Glenda J. Guilmet & David Lloyd Whited   Michael Hureaux-Perez   Joseph F. Keppler   Josef Knoepfler   Marion Kimes   Maryrose Larkin   Ezra Mark   Gretchan Mattila   Tom Prince   Robbo   dan raphael   Judith Roche   Donna Sandstrom   Robin Schultz   Wally Shoup   Bill Shively   Willie Smith   Douglas Spangle   Roberto Valenza   margareta waterman   Don Wilsun

now celebrating

iteration: poems 1974-2004
margareta waterman

"she fills the cadences with enlivening and revelatory inflection…twists of her phrasings most reward those those who pay attention…voices of lovers and gods, protesters and travelers, those who suffer and those who triumph, may sing, yowl, whisper and harangue…"
　　　　　　　　　　—*Doug Nufer*

isbn 1-878888-45-5
232 pages, decorated in gold and red

photo:Michael Mendenhall

i am not a poet because i write poetry
i am a poet because
everything
is grist for the mill
that grinds me into illumination
so that only words are left

whether i like it or not

College Literature

Kostas Myrsiades, Editor

College Literature

210 E. Rosedale Avenue

West Chester University

West Chester, PA 19383

phone: 610.436.2901

fax: 610.436.2275

collit@wcupa.edu

College Literature is a quarterly journal of scholarly criticism serving the needs of college/university teachers by providing access to innovative ways of studying and teaching new bodies of literature and experiencing old literatures in new ways.

Special Issues; forthcoming

- Reading Homer in the 21st Century
- The Splendor of Arabic Belles-Lettres
- August Wilson (A Retrospective)
- The Literature and Medicine of Life, Death, and Disease

The MacGuffin

Originating in Victorian England, the moving force and sometimes the solution of a work of mystery fiction was referred to as a MacGuffin. Alfred Hitchcock used the term and stated that "No film is complete without a MacGuffin" because that's what " . . . everybody is after."

POETRY

CREATIVE
NON-FICTION

ART

FICTION

Schoolcraft College
The MacGuffin
www.macguffin.org

18600 Haggerty Rd.
Livonia, MI 48152
macguffin@schoolcraft.edu
Phone: (734) 462-4400 EXT. 5327

KUDOS

A great poet once said that art is not life because 'Art has its own dynamic. It is a runaway train which society either boards, or does not board.' Editor Maria Mazziotti Gillan decided from the beginning that the *Paterson Literary Review* would board that train and bring with it all voices, all people, not just a few—not only the dominant cultures, but each writer who has a genuine story to tell. We thank her for an all-inclusive literary magazine with a high degree of excellence—a journal that is global as well as deeply personal.
Grace Cavalieri
Producer, host: "The Poet and the Poem from the Library of Congress"

Paterson Literary Review is huge in every sense of the word...an anthology of poets and fiction writers both famous and unknown in every issue. Where else could a schlepp like me rub verbal elbows with the likes of Diane DiPrima, Marge Piercy, and Jim Daniels, as well as the occasional ex-girlfriend? It has the quality of a raucous and unwieldy wedding reception, where anything can happen and usually does—the drunken uncle as well as the five-year-old little darling in her step dance outfit, all of them welcome, all of them happily vital and fully alive.
Joe Weil, Poet, Editor
Black Swan Review

Powerful, provocative and profound. If Allen Ginsberg were alive and could only subscribe to one journal, he would pick *Paterson Literary Review.*
Vivian Shipley, Editor
Connecticut Review

"The *Paterson Literary Review*...Real poems for real people, poetry to enrich our everyday lives."
Leslie Heywood, Poet, Professor

PATERSON LITERARY REVIEW
Published by **The Poetry Center** at Passaic
County Community College
1 College Boulevard, Paterson, NJ 07505
Editor: Maria Mazziotti Gillan
www.pccc.edu/poetry

Diary of a Poet:
An Imaginary Life
by Karla Andersdatter

A Collection of New and Selected Work,
A Mosaic of Literary Art,
A Mystical Fictional Memoir,
A Book of Autobiographical Fiction
A Novel

In a limited, reserved, signed, numbered
hardback edition, 6X9, 418 pp. with color
dustjacket and photos of author's paintings.
Available to libraries on Sept 17, 2006 **$39.95**

*"Whether this poet's runes are read or unread, her love
notes refused or accepted, the solitude she enters is not a
world of depression or self-pity. She has too much fight in
her for that, too many tricks of self-invention. She turns
her poetry into narrative, her narrative into fable or
folktale, and ends with a trickster tale about a man who
fools both the devil and the Angel of God...
Coyote is her muse!"*

from the Introduction by David Shaddock

*"This may well be her very best collection, just as her
recent novel OF LOVE AND PROMISES was the best tale
telling I'd heard from her over all these years... how many
now? 35? She's just getting better and better."*

Steve Sanfield

ISBN 0-935430-21-0 IN BETWEEN BOOKS
P.O. Box 790, Sausalito, CA 94966
415 383-8447

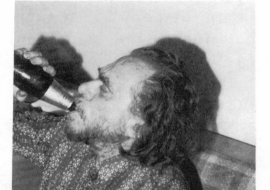

Key to Directory Listings

Listings are of two basic kinds: Those for **magazines** (periodicals, printed in all caps), and those for **presses** (book publishers).

A complete **magazine** listing would include, in following order: name of magazine, name of press (if any), name(s) of editors, address, phone number(s), fax number, email address, website address, founding year, type of material used, additional comments by editors including recent contributors, circulation, frequency of publication, number of issues published in 2005, expected in 2006 and 2007, one-year subscription price, single copy price, sample copy price, back issue price, discount schedules, average number of pages, length of reporting time on manuscripts, policy on simultaneous submissions, percentage of submissions published, payment rates, rights purchased and/or copyright arrangements, number of reviews published in 2005, areas of interest for review materials and advertising rates.

A complete **press** listing would include, in the following order: names of press, name of magazine published by that press, if any, name(s) of editor(s), address, phone number(s), fax, email and website information, founding year, type of material used, additional comments by editors including recent contributors, , average press run, number of titles published in 2005, expected in 2006 and 2007, discount schedules, average number of pages, length of reporting time on manuscripts, policy on simultaneous submissions, percentage of submissions published, payment or royalty arrangements, rights purchased and/or copyright arrangements.

New Feature – Subject indexing in main listings: Each publisher is listed in the Subject Index under those subjects that publisher has indicated. In addition, the subjects are listed at the end of each publisher's main listing. This should further help to characterize each publishing program.

A listing preceded by a bullet (•) is a new listing to this edition. A listing preceded by a double-dagger (‡) means that the publisher has not reported to us for some time – though we have reason to believe the press is still operating.

For those who wish to list a press or magazine in future editions of *The International Directory of Little Magazines & Small Presses* or the companion *Directory of Poetry Publishers*, special forms are available on the Dustbooks website www.dustbooks.com. Once you have registered, logged into the listing and filled out the data, a request for update is sent 1-3 months before the next editions go to press at the end of July. New editions are published on September 15th.

Keep Your Directory Updated!
With

Small Press Review

Bi-Monthly

The bi-monthly *Small Press Review* has two editorial sections, one for books, one for magazines. Each section contains news and notes on editorial needs and contests, reviews of new releases, guest editorials, listings of new publishers, letters, columns by Bob Grumman, Len Fulton, Michael Andre and others, and the popular "Free Sample Mart," offering free copies of some thirty books and magazines per issue. Published for 38 years and counting! You've invested in this directory, now keep it current!

DUSTBOOKS
THE LEADER IN THE SMALL PRESS INFORMATION FIELD
P.O. Box 100, Paradise, CA 95967–0100

A

A & U AMERICA'S AIDS MAGAZINE, David Waggoner, Editor-in-Chief & Publisher, 25 Monroe Street, Suite 205, Albany, NY 12210-2729, 518-426-9010, Fax 518-436-5354, mailbox@aumag.org. 1991. Poetry, fiction, articles, art, photos, cartoons, interviews, satire, criticism, reviews, music, letters, parts-of-novels, long-poems, collages, plays, news items, non-fiction. "Recent contributors: John Ashbery, Gwendolyn Brooks, Michael Lassell, Mark Doty, Mark O'Donnell, Edward Field, Eve Ensler, David Bergman, Walter Holland, Leslea Newman, Paula Martinac, Diamanda Galas, William Parker, Assoto Saint, etc." circ. 180M. 12/yr. Pub'd 12 issues 2005; expects 12 issues 2006, 12 issues 2007. sub. price $24.95, $80.00 Library; per copy $3.95; sample $5. Back issues: $10 for all back issues, except 1991 fall premiere $30.00. 40pp. Reporting time: 6 months to 1 year. Simultaneous submissions accepted: yes. Publishes 5% of manuscripts submitted. Payment: 5 complimentary copies and negotiable honorariums. Copyrighted, reverts to author. Pub's reviews: 60 in 2005. §Anything AIDS-related, especially the arts and AIDS. Ads: Back cover $32,010/full page $22,488/1/2 page $15,291, all rates for color. Subjects: AIDS, Arts, Avant-Garde, Experimental Art, Literature (General), Theatre, Visual Arts.

A Cappela Publishing, Inc., Patrika Vaughn, CEO, PO Box 3691, Sarasota, FL 34230-3691, phone: 941-351-2050 fax: 941-351-4735 email: acappub@aol.com website: www.acappela.com. 1996. Fiction, non-fiction. avg. press run 3M. Expects 5 titles 2006. Discounts: 5-9 copies 30%, 10-199 48%, 200+ 50%. 208pp. Reporting time: 3 months. Simultaneous submissions accepted: no. Publishes 20% of manuscripts submitted. Payment: 6% on sales, bi-yearly. Copyrights for author. Subjects: Autobiography, Business & Economics, Fiction, Guidance, Marketing, Memoirs, Mystery, Non-Fiction, Novels, Publishing, Romance, Self-Help, Writers/Writing, Young Adult.

AAIMS Publishers, Edward Torrey, 11000 Wilshire Boulevard, PO Box 241777, Los Angeles, CA 90024-0777, 213-968-1195, 888-490-2276, fax 213-931-7217, email aaims1@aol.com. 1969. avg. press run 4M. Pub'd 1 title 2005; expects 1 title 2006, 2 titles 2007. Discounts: 1 copy 30%, 2 35%, 3 40%, 4 41%, 15 45%, 30 47%, 45 49%, 200+ 50%. 250pp. Reporting time: 3 weeks. Copyrights for author. Subjects: African Literature, Africa, African Studies, Black, Family, Military, Veterans, Religion, Women.

Aardvark Enterprises (A Division of Speers Investments Ltd.), J. Alvin Speers, 204 Millbank Drive S.W., Calgary, Alberta T2Y 2H9, Canada, 403-256-4639. 1977. Poetry, fiction, articles, photos, cartoons, interviews, reviews, letters, news items, non-fiction. "Open to proposals." avg. press run varies. Pub'd 6 titles 2005; expects 6 titles 2006, 6 titles 2007. Discounts: inquiries invited - quantity discounts only. 100pp. Reporting time: fast, return mail usually. Publishes 50% of manuscripts submitted. Payment: by arrangement on individual project. Copyrights for author. Subjects: Canada, Ethics, Family, History, Politics, Religion, Storytelling.

Aardwolfe Books, Ray LeBlanc, PO Box 471, Aiea, HI 96701-0471, publisher@aardwolfe.com, www.aardwolfe.com. 2000. Fiction. "Recent title: *Khalifah,* by John Elray." avg. press run 5M-10M. Expects 1 title 2006, 1 title 2007. Discounts: 40-50%. 350pp. Reporting time: 2 months. Simultaneous submissions accepted: yes. Publishes 2% of manuscripts submitted. Payment: standard terms. Does not copyright for author. Subjects: Fiction, Satire.

•Aaron Communications III, Aaron Johnson, P.O. Box 63270, Colorado Springs, CO 80962-3270, 719-487-0342. 2005. Fiction, art, plays, non-fiction. "Aaron Communications III is purposeful in its mission of communicating to youth and young adults around the world a message of hope, Gods love, and divine purpose in life through faith and personal relationship with Jesus Christ. Our mission is accomplished by publishing contemporary books/subjects/topics and state of the art publications that are relevant to todays youth and young adults in light of current youth culture without compromising or deviating from sound scripture, the Holy Bible." avg. press run 1500. Expects 4 titles 2006, 8 titles 2007. Discounts: industry standards. 200pp. Reporting time: Six weeks minimum. Will immediately acknowledge receipt. Simultaneous submissions accepted: Yes. Publishes 10% of manuscripts submitted. Payment: t.b.d. Copyrights for author. Subjects: Arts, Autobiography, Biography, Children, Youth, Christianity, Fiction, Guidance, Inspirational, Juvenile Fiction, Motivation, Success, Non-Fiction, Non-Violence, Performing Arts, Prison, U.S. Hispanic.

AAS HISTORY SERIES, Univelt, Inc., Donald C. Elder, Series Editor, PO Box 28130, San Diego, CA 92198, 760-746-4005, Fax 760-746-3139, sales@univelt.com, www.univelt.com. 1977. Non-fiction. "History of Science (esp. Space Science and Technology). Science Fiction and Space Futures. An irregular serial. Standing orders accepted. Vols 1-26 published." circ. 400. Irregular. Pub'd 3 issues 2005; expects 2 issues 2006, 2 issues 2007. sub. price varies. Back issues: no. Discounts: 20% and more by arrangement; reduced prices for classroom use. 200-500pp. Reporting time: 90 days. Payment: 10% (if the volume author). Copyrighted, authors may republish material with appropriate credits given and authorization from publishers. Ads: none. Subjects: History, Science, Science Fiction, Space.

aatec publications, Christina Bych, PO Box 7119, Ann Arbor, MI 48107, 800-995-1470, Fax 734-995-1471, e-mail aatecpub@mindspring.com. 1980. Non-fiction. "We specialize in the sustainable energies, with an emphasis on photovoltaics. *aatec* books offer background and working knowledge to actual and aspiring renewable energy users." avg. press run 5M. Pub'd 1 title 2005; expects 2 titles 2006, 2 titles 2007. Discounts: contact for schedules. 200+pp. Reporting time: 2-3 weeks. Simultaneous submissions accepted: yes. Payment: 15% of monies received, annual. Copyrights for author. Subject: Energy.

AB, Holly Davis, PO Box 190-abd, Philomath, OR 97370. 2003. Articles, interviews, criticism, reviews, letters, news items, non-fiction. "*Ab* is a reader-written zine discussing how and where to live better and longer; including, how to steer clearer of increasingly-berserk political/economic/social/religious systems. *Ab* is an ab-apa: I prefer concise, *compact,* single-spaced, one-sided, two *full* pages ready to copy, text 6x10 inches (153x254mm). Disposable copies preferred. Authors may include small ads on their pages. Reviews should be mostly quotes or paraphrases of the most useful info in the book or article, not merely a description." circ. 400. 1/yr. Pub'd 1 issue 2005; expects 1 issue 2006, 1 issue 2007. sub. price $2; per copy $2; sample $2. Back issues: 6 for $10. 16pp. Reporting time: 1 month. Simultaneous submissions accepted: yes. Publishes 50% of manuscripts submitted. Payment: subscription/back issues or token cash. Not copyrighted. Pub's reviews: 2 in 2005. Subjects: Anthropology, Archaelogy, Aviation, Bicycling, Botany, Clothing, Health, How-To, Human Rights, Immigration, Lifestyles, Nutrition, Safety, Science, Technology, Transportation, Travel.

Abaton Book Company, Lauri Bortz, 100 Gifford Avenue, Jersey City, NJ 07304-1704, fax 201-369-0297. 1997. Art, photos, music, plays. "Unique limited edition projects." Pub'd 4 titles 2005; expects 4 titles 2006, 4 titles 2007.

ABBEY, White Urp Press, David Greisman, 5360 Fall River Row Court, Columbia, MD 21044-1910, e-mail at greisman@aol.com. 1971. Poetry, articles, art, interviews, criticism, reviews, letters. "*Abbey* recently was named the 351st best informalzine in America and still claims to be the Molson's Ale of Small Press rags. We published our 100th issue in March of 2004, continuing a standard for excellent poetry and artwork mixed with production values that the Amercian Association of Informalzines noted has remained embarassingly mediocre during the entirety of the rag's 34 year publication history. Recent contributors: Taylor Graham, Carol Hamilton, D.E. Steward, Luis Cuauhtemoc Berriozabal, John Elsberg, Edmund Conti, Richard Peabody, Harry Calhoun, Blair Ewing, Bill Kaul, Cheryl Townsend, Ruth Moon Kempher, Wayne Hogan, Joan Payne Kincaid, and Robin Merrill." circ. 200. 3-4/yr. Pub'd 4 issues 2005; expects 4 issues 2006, 4 issues 2007. sub. price $2; per copy 50¢; sample 50¢. Back issues: 50¢ for regular issues, $2 for Abbey #100 (while supplies last). 28pp. Reporting time: 2 minutes-2 years. Simultaneous submissions accepted: Not cool. Hold Abbey to a response deadline if you must, but show some respect, will ya? Payment: nothing. Copyrighted, reverts to author. Pub's reviews: None in 2005. §Poetry, baseball. Ads: $10/$5. Subject: Poetry.

Abbey Press, Northern Ireland, Adrian Rice, Courtenay Hill, Newry, Country Down BT34 2ED, United Kingdom, 01693-63142, Fax 01693-62514, Molly71Freeman@aol.com, www.geocities.com/abbeypress/. 1997. Poetry, fiction, interviews, satire, criticism, reviews, letters, long-poems, plays, non-fiction. "Recent publication - *A Conversation Piece: Poetry & Art,* edited by Adrian Rice and Angela Reid. 50 poets on 50 artworks from the collections of the National Museums and Galleries of Northern Ireland. Some poets include: Seamus Heaney, Michael Longley, Brendan Kennelly, Paul Muldoon, Tom Paulin, Medbh McGuckian, Ruth Padel, Paula Meehan, and John Montague." avg. press run 1000. Pub'd 4 titles 2005; expects 4 titles 2006, 4 titles 2007. 64pp. Simultaneous submissions accepted: yes. Copyrights for author. Subject: Poetry.

Abecedarian books, Inc., Alan Reese, 2817 Forest Glen Drive, Baldwin, MD 21013, 410-692-6777, fax 410-692-9175, toll free 877-782-2221, books@abeced.com, www.abeced.com. 2005. Poetry, fiction, photos, plays, non-fiction. avg. press run 1000. Expects 12 titles 2006, 25 titles 2007. 156pp. Reporting time: 2-3 weeks. Simultaneous submissions accepted: Yes. Copyrights for author. Subjects: Erotica, Fantasy, Fiction, Health, Humor, Mystery, Non-Fiction, Poetry, Science Fiction, Short Stories, T'ai Chi, Vegetarianism, Women, Young Adult, Zen.

Abernathy House Publishing, Sandra S. Walling Publisher, John W. Walling Editor, PO Box 1109, Yarmouth, ME 04096-1109, 207-838-6170, info@abernathyhousepub.com, www.abernathyhousepub.com. 2002. avg. press run 5000. Pub'd 2 titles 2005; expects 2 titles 2006, 3 titles 2007. Discounts: 40 to 55%. 36pp. Reporting time: 6 Weeks. Simultaneous submissions accepted: yes. Publishes 30% of manuscripts submitted. Payment: Royalty paid or flat fee. Author and Illustrator. Subjects: African-American, Aging, AIDS, Animals, Children, Youth, Family, Marine Life, Native American, Non-Violence, Reading, Relationships, Young Adult.

Abigon Press, Peter Stokes PhD., Editor; Christian Wilde, Author, Hidden Causes of Heart Attack and Stroke, Inflammation, Cardiology's Newest Frontier, 12135 Valley Spring Lane, Studio City, CA 91604, ascap@pacbell.net. 1991. Non-fiction. "Will review health related books and general non-fiction for publication, but prefer a synopsis or treatment form first." avg. press run 3,000-5,000.

ABLAZE Publishing, 2800 122nd Place NE, Bellevue, WA 98005-1520, 877-624-0230, Fax 509-275-5817, info@laugh-it-off.com, www.laugh-it-off.com. 2003. avg. press run 3M. Expects 2 titles 2006, 2 titles 2007. Discounts: 10 or more books, 40% discount with resale number. 120pp. Simultaneous submissions accepted: no. Publishes 1% of manuscripts submitted. Payment: determined on individual basis. Copyrights for author. Subjects: Audio/Video, Cartoons, Christianity, Classical Studies, Cooking, Handicapped, Health, Mental Health.

ABLE MUSE, Alex Pepple, Editor, 467 Saratoga Avenue #602, San Jose, CA 95129, www.ablemuse.com, editor@ablemuse.com. Poetry, fiction, art, photos, interviews, criticism, reviews, long-poems, concrete art, non-fiction. Pub's reviews. §Poetry Books, Poets.

ABOL TABOL, Sasabindu Chaudhuri, 7/1 d Kalicharan Ghosh Road, Kolkata, W. Bengal, India, 033-25571767, babychowin@yahoo.co.in. Poetry. "Translated 35 comedy poetry of a famous poet *Sukumar Roy* in German." 1/yr. Copyrighted, reverts to author. Pub's reviews. §Poetry and classical based songs.

•**ABRAMELIN: a Journal of Poetry and Magick,** Vanessa Kittle, Box 337, Brookhaven, NY 11719, 631 803-2211. 2006. Poetry, fiction, articles, art, photos, interviews, reviews, long-poems, non-fiction. "www.abramelin.net. What we want...Essays on Magick and Thelema. By magick I mean with a K if you know what I mean.Poetry that shows rather than tells. Poems that make me jealous of the writer. Poems that are inspired with wonderful language and imagery. In short literature.Poetry submissions needn't be about magick at all. I feel that real poetry is magick. In fact, poetry that is literally magickal in theme has to be twice as good. Please note that I hate rhyming poems. Very short fiction. But beware, I learned from the best. Thelemic artwork. How we want it. Words should be pasted into an email. Art should be attached to an email (please query first!). I will not open attachments from unknown senders. My address is: Nessaralindaran@aol.com. Please include a subject line (for example, poetry submission). Please send only 1 story or essay, and up to 3 poems. Feel free to include a bio if it is your will. Abramelin takes one-time rights. All other rights revert to author after publication. By submitting, author certifies it is her work, and holds Abramelin and me harmless from any legal concerns. Issues will be published when I feel a sense of completion. I expect this will be somewhere between 2 and 4 times a year." 3/yr. Expects 2 issues 2006. 93pp. Reporting time: A few days to a couple weeks. Simultaneous submissions accepted: No. Publishes 5% of manuscripts submitted. Pub's reviews. §Poetry books and books concerning magick. Subjects: Anarchist, Astrology, Astronomy, Avant-Garde, Experimental Art, Beat, Buddhism, Counter-Culture, Alternatives, Communes, Erotica, Human Rights, Literary Review, Magic, Philosophy, Poetry, Spiritual, Women.

ABRAXAS, Ingrid Swanberg, Editor-in-Chief; Warren Woessner, Senior Editor, PO Box 260113, Madison, WI 53726-0113, 608-238-0175, abraxaspress@hotmail.com, www.geocities.com/abraxaspress/. 1968. Poetry, articles, art, satire, criticism, letters, collages, concrete art. "Address for exchanges and large packages: 2518 Gregory Street, Madison, WI 53711. *Abraxas* is no longer considering unsolicited poetry except for special projects. We will announce submission policies as projects arise. See our website for reading periods. We are particularly interested in lyric poetry and contemporary poetry in translation. *Abraxas Press* has published an anthology of Jazz Poetry, *Bright Moments* ($4.00), and a translation of Cesar Vallejo's *Trilce*, based on the only authorized edition ($11). The most recent issue, #44/45, includes a previously unpublished long poem by d.a.levy. Inquiries should be sent to Ingrid Swanberg at above address. We have recently published T.L. Kryss, David Lincoln Fisher, Andrea Moorhead, prospero saiz." circ. 500+. Irregular. Expects 2 issues 2006, 2 issues 2007. sub. price $16/4 issues, $20/4 issues foreign, surface rate; $31/4 issues foreign airmail, pan American; $36/4 issues foreign airmail, overseas; per copy $4; sample $8 double issues, $4 single issue (please add $1.50 shipping for first copy, $1 for each additional copy). Back issues: catalog on request, SASE please. Discounts: 20% 1-4 copies; 40% 5-9 copies; 50% on orders of more than 10 copies. 60-80pp, 120-144pp double issues. Reporting time: 1 month to 2 years or longer. We currently have a *very* great backlog of unsolicited mss. Simultaneous submissions accepted: Yes; please inform us of acceptance elsewhere. Publishes 2% of manuscripts submitted. Payment: copies; 40% author's discount on additional copies. Copyrighted, reverts to author. Pub's reviews. Ads: none. Subjects: Avant-Garde, Experimental Art, Criticism, Graphics, Native American, Poetry, Satire, Translation.

Absey & Co., 23011 Northcrest Drive, Spring, TX 77389, 888-412-2739, Fax 281-251-4676, abseyland@aol.com.

ABSINTHE: New European Writing, Dwayne D. Hayes, P.O. Box 11445, Detroit, MI 48211-1445, www.absinthenew.com, dhayes@absinthenew.com. 2003. Poetry, fiction, art, interviews, reviews, letters, parts-of-novels, plays, non-fiction. "Absinthe: New European Writing introduces work (poetry and prose) by European writers who have not appeared widely in English. Recent contributors include Yuri Andrukhovych, Christa Wolf, Sandor Kanyadi, Saviana Stanescu, Juan Jose Millas, and Sophia Nikolaidou." circ. 500. 2/yr.

3

Pub'd 2 issues 2005; expects 2 issues 2006, 2 issues 2007. sub. price $12; per copy $7; sample $5. Back issues: $5. 108pp. Reporting time: 12-15 weeks. Simultaneous submissions accepted: No. Publishes 25% of manuscripts submitted. Payment: 2 copies and a subscription. Copyrighted, reverts to author. Pub's reviews: 1 in 2005. §Books by European writers in translation. Subjects: Danish, Europe, France, French, German, Greek, Ireland, Italy, Poland, Russia, Scandinavia, Scotland, Spain, Translation, U.S.S.R., Wales.

•ABZ A Magazine of Poetry, ABZ Poetry Press, John McKernan, John McKernan, Editor Marshall University, One John Marshall Drive, Huntington, WV 25755-2646. 2006. circ. 500. 1/yr. Expects 1 issue 2006, 1 issue 2007. price per copy $8.00; sample $8.00. Back issues: Please inquire. Discounts: 40%. 48pp. Reporting time: Submisions read only September 1 to December 31. 3-4 months. Simultaneous submissions accepted: Yes. Payment: Small amount per poem. Copyrighted, reverts to author. Pub's reviews: none in 2005. Ads: None. Subject: Poetry.

•ABZ Poetry Press (see also ABZ A Magazine of Poetry), John McKernan, PO Box 2746, Huntington, WV 25727-2746. Poetry. avg. press run 800. Expects 1-2 titles 2007. Discounts: 40%. 48-72pp. Reporting time: Magazine Submissions September 1-December 1 Yearly: Book Contest Submissions must have May 2007 postmark for 2007 Contest. Write for complete Guidelines and Official Entry Blank. Simultaneous submissions accepted: Yes. Payment: Standard Book Contract. Copyrights for author. Subject: Poetry.

AC Projects, Inc., 7376 Walker Road, Fairview, TN 37062-8141, 615-799-8104, Fax 615-799-2017. 1977. "Not accepting ms until further notice." avg. press run 3M-25M. Pub'd 1 title 2005; expects 1 title 2007. Discounts: inquire please. 44-691pp.

Academic Innovations, Mindy Bingham, 1386 Rio Virgin Dr., Washington, UT 84780, 800-967-8016, 800-967-4027. 1990. avg. press run 10000. Expects 1 title 2006. Subjects: Education, Family.

ACCCA Press, Milli Janz, 149 Cannongate III, Nashua, NH 03063-1953. 1978. Articles. *"Culture Without Pain or Money* is now in a new 2nd edition, and is being distributed in Haiti, Japan, The Philippines and Egypt. It is being used currently in many parts of the U.S. as a blueprint for initiating, developing and continuing cultural centers in communities. (Especially where art services are exchanged in lieu of money). Because the book is in a smaller edition, the price for the book and mailing will remain at $4 each. For the newest edition, $10 and $3 p/h = $13." Discounts: 10%. Payment: when other writers will join me, I will offer a per page fee.

•Accendo Publishing, Tammy McClure, 355 N Wolfe Road # 237, Sunnyvale, CA 94085, 408-406-6697 phone, 408-733-1444 fax. 2005. Fiction, art, photos, non-fiction. avg. press run 500. Expects 1 title 2006, 3 titles 2007. Discounts: 5-10 copies 20%11+ copies 30%. 300pp. Subjects: Alternative Medicine, Anthology, Autobiography, Energy, Erotica, Fiction, Global Affairs, Memoirs, Motivation, Success, Mystery, Non-Fiction, Picture Books, Relationships, Water, Women.

Accent On Music, LLC, Mark Hanson, PMB 252, 19363 Willamette Drive, West Linn, OR 97068, (503)699-1814, (503)699-1813(FAX), (800)313-4406, info@accentonmusic.com. Music. "Expanding to instructional DVDs in 2005. Please email request to submit before submitting any material for possible publication. Outside material rarely accepted." Pub'd 1 title 2005; expects 2 titles 2006, 2 titles 2007. Reporting time: 4 weeks. Simultaneous submissions accepted: No. Publishes 1% of manuscripts submitted. Payment: Negotiable. Copyrights for author.

ACM (ANOTHER CHICAGO MAGAZINE), Barry Silesky, Senior Editor, 3709 N. Kenmore, Chicago, IL 60613, 312-248-7665, www.anotherchicagomag.com. 1976. Poetry, fiction, articles, art, photos, cartoons, interviews, satire, criticism, reviews, long-poems. "Recent contributors have included Albert Goldbarth, Diane Wakoski, Wanda Coleman, Alan Cheuse, Perry Glasser, Sterling Plumpp, Stuart Dybek, and Nin Andrews. Send work from February 1st to August 31st." circ. 2.5M. 2/yr. Pub'd 2 issues 2005; expects 2 issues 2006, 2 issues 2007. sub. price $14.95; per copy $8; sample $8. Back issues: $8. Discounts: 10% on 10 or more. 220pp. Reporting time: 10 weeks. Simultaneous submissions accepted: yes. Publishes 2% of manuscripts submitted. Payment: copy + 1 year subscription, token honorarium when possible. Copyrighted, reverts to author. Pub's reviews: 20 in 2005. §Small press poetry, fiction, literary reviews or criticism. Ads: $250/$125. Subjects: Fiction, Photography, Poetry, Politics, Reviews.

ACME Press, PO Box 1702, Westminster, MD 21158, 410-848-7577. 1991. Fiction, satire. "Our basic requirement is that a work be funny. We prefer comic novels (60K-90K words)." avg. press run 5M. Pub'd 1 title 2005; expects 1 title 2006, 1 title 2007. Discounts: standard. 250pp. Reporting time: 4 weeks. Simultaneous submissions accepted: yes. Publishes less than 1% of manuscripts submitted. Payment: varies. Copyrights for author. Subjects: Fiction, Humor, Novels, Satire.

THE ACORN, J.K. Colvin, Harlon Stafford, Joy Burris, PO Box 1266, El Dorado, CA 95623, acorn@mail2world.com. 1993. Poetry, fiction, articles, satire, non-fiction. "We seek to publish quality fiction, non-fiction, essays, and poetry. No porn, erotica, or articles of prejudice. Our focus is on the western slope of the Sierra Nevada. Length: 4000 words maximum for prose; poems to 30 lines (shorter poems have a better chance)." circ. 250. 4/yr. Pub'd 5 issues 2005; expects 4 issues 2006, 4 issues 2007. sub. price $12; per copy $4; sample $4. Discounts: 5-9 20%, 10+ 40%. 48pp. Reporting time: 3 months (1 month after deadlines of 2/1, 5/1, 8/1, 11/1). We accept simultaneous submissions if so informed. Publishes 35% of manuscripts submitted. Payment: 2 free copies. Copyrighted, reverts to author. Ads: none. Subjects: California, Essays, Family, Fiction, Folklore, History, Homemaking, Memoirs, Nature, Non-Fiction, Poetry, Satire, Storytelling, The West.

Acorn Books, Jami Parkison, 7337 Terrace, Suite 200, Kansas City, MO 64114-1256, 816-523-8321, fax 816-333-3843, e-mail jami.parkison@micro.com, www.acornbks.com. 1997. Non-fiction. "Biographies for children about well-known midwesterners. Submissions through agents only." avg. press run 2M. Pub'd 2 titles 2005; expects 3 titles 2006, 3 titles 2007. Discounts: 20/40% (nonreturnable). 125pp. Subjects: Biography, Children, Youth, History, Midwest, The West.

Acrobat Books, Tony Cohan, PO Box 870, Venice, CA 90294, 310-578-1055, Fax 310-823-8447. 1975. Fiction, art, photos, non-fiction. "Non fiction books in the creative arts. *Kirsch's Handbook of Publishing Law* by Jonathan Kirsch; *Directing the Film* by Eric Sherman; *Nine Ships, A Book of Tales* by Tony Cohan; *Outlaw Visions* ed. by Tony Cohan/Gordon Beam; *Frame By Frame* by Eric Sherman." avg. press run 4M. Pub'd 3 titles 2005; expects 4 titles 2006, 5 titles 2007. Discounts: 1-5 copies 20%, 6-49 40%. 196pp. Reporting time: 60 days. Payment: negotiable. Copyrights for author. Subjects: Arts, Fiction.

Acting World Books (see also THE AGENCIES-WHAT THE ACTOR NEEDS TO KNOW; THE HOLLYWOOD ACTING COACHES AND TEACHERS DIRECTORY), Lawrence Parke, PO Box 3044, Hollywood, CA 90078, 818-905-1345, Fax 800-210-1197. 1981. "Publications and career guidance for the acting community. Publishes books and periodicals of career and acting methodology natures. Typical is the six-volume 'seminars to go' series on six different 'how to' topics involved in the actor's career building processes. In-house publishing and waiting." avg. press run 2M. Expects 1 title 2006, 2 titles 2007. Discounts: trade, 40% booksellers. 40pp. Payment: none. Copyrights for author. Subjects: Electronics, Entertainment, How-To, Theatre.

Actium Publishing, Inc., Dan Brown, 1375 Coney Island Avenue #122, Brooklyn, NY 11230, 718-382-2129, fax 718-621-0402, email home@actium1.com. 1996. avg. press run 5M. Pub'd 3 titles 2005. Discounts: 55% wholesalers, 20% stop orders. 250pp. Reporting time: 4-12 weeks. Simultaneous submissions accepted: yes. Publishes less than 1% of manuscripts submitted. Subjects: Business & Economics, How-To, Internet.

Acton Circle Publishing Company, Thomas E. Anderson, PO Box 1564, Ukiah, CA 95482, 707-463-3921, 707-462-2103, Fax 707-462-4942; actoncircle@pacific.net. 1992. Non-fiction. "The company was started to publish guides for starting and running popular small business enterprises. Although it will publish in other subject areas, that is the main thrust of its activity." avg. press run 3-5M. Pub'd 1 title 2005; expects 2 titles 2006, 2+ titles 2007. Discounts: dealers 1-2 net, 3-9 30%, 10-49 40%, 50-299 50%. 200pp. Reporting time: 2 months. Simultaneous submissions accepted: yes. Payment: 10%. Copyrights for author. Subjects: Business & Economics, Careers, Finances, Gardening, Management, Nature.

AD/VANCE, Vance Philip Hedderel, Editor-in-Chief, 1593 Colonial Terrace #206, Arlington, VA 22209-1430. 1992. Articles, interviews, music, letters, news items. 250. 3/yr. Pub'd 3 issues 2005; expects 3 issues 2006, 3 issues 2007. sub. price $5; per copy $2; sample $1. Back issues: negotiable, however back issues are not generally available. Discounts: none. 8pp. Reporting time: usually within 3 weeks. Simultaneous submissions accepted: no. Publishes less than 10% of manuscripts submitted. Payment: 2 sample issues. Not copyrighted. Pub's reviews: 4 in 2005. §Art, Brontes, Dada, surrealism, film, gays, poetry, music, lesbianism, London, Post Modernism, tapes and records. Ads: none. Subjects: Advertising, Self-Promotion, Avant-Garde, Experimental Art, Dada, Electronics, Gay, Music, Post Modern.

Adams-Blake Publishing, Paul Raymond, 8041 Sierra Street, Fair Oaks, CA 95628, 916-962-9296. 1992. Non-fiction. "We look for technology or management titles that we can sell direct to business and government for very high margins. For example, if we had a book titles "Quality Control in the Semiconductor Manufacturing Environment" we could sell about 800 a year for a few years... at $125 each. We do modified Print on Demand (we keep a low inventory) and only look for books that we can get top-dollar for... thus we are not trade publishers... so if you have a trade book (i.e. one sold via Borders or B&N) we are NOT for you. But if you have niche-market science or techology titles, do contact us." avg. press run 5M. Expects 7 titles 2006, 10 titles 2007. Discounts: 40-50% industry standard. 300pp. Reporting time: 3-4 weeks. Simultaneous submissions accepted: yes. Publishes 5% of manuscripts submitted. Payment: 10% net. Copyrights for author. Subjects: Business & Economics, Computers, Calculators, Consulting, Energy, Engineering, Management, Marketing, Medicine, Nursing, Physics, Real Estate, Technology, Textbooks.

Adams-Pomeroy Press, Catherine Blakemore, PO Box 189, Albany, WI 53502, 608-862-3645, Fax 608-862-3647, adamspomeroy@ckhnet.com.

Adastra Press, Gary Metras, 16 Reservation Road, Easthampton, MA 01027-1227, gmetras@rcn.com. 1978.

Poetry. "All books and chapbooks are hand-set letterpress printed and hand-sewn with flat spine paper wrapper. Each book is individually designed with the poetry in mind. I pay attention to the craft and art of printing and expect poets to pay attention to their art. Interested authors may query first but it is not necessary to do so. The poetry should have some bite to it and be grounded in experience. Poem cycles, thematic groups and long poems are always nice to produce in chapbook format. Manuscripts should have 12 to 18 pages; nothing longer; no full-length manuscripts will be considered, only chapbooks. Accepted authors can expect to help with publicity. Payment is copies. *Adastra Press* is a one man operation, paying for itself as it goes without grants of any kind, and I am always overworked and booked in advance. Chances of acceptance are slim, but there's no harm in trying. Some titles to date are: *Behind Our Memories* by Michael Hettich. *Raiding a Whorehouse* by Michael Casey. *Beautiful Wreckage: New and Selected Poems* by W.D. Ehrhart and *Festival Bone* by Karen Rigby. Send $8 for a sample chapbook." avg. press run 200. Pub'd 4 titles 2005; expects 4 titles 2006, 3 titles 2007. Discounts: bookstores 30%, distributors 40%, more than 1 copy, 20% on cl/signed editions. 18pp. Reporting time: up to 3 months. Simultaneous submissions accepted: yes. Publishes less than 1% of manuscripts submitted. Payment: usually percent of print run, but each arrangement made individually. Does not copyright for author. Subject: Poetry.

Addicus Books, Inc., Rod Colvin, Susan Adams, Jack Kusler, PO Box 45327, Omaha, NE 68145, 402-330-7493. 1994. "We publish high-quality non-fiction books with a focus on consumer health, self-help, business, and true crime." avg. press run 5, 000 to 10,000. Pub'd 7 titles 2005; expects 7 titles 2006, 10 titles 2007. Discounts: retailers 40%, wholesalers, distributors 55%. STOP 40%, plus shipping. 275pp. Reporting time: 1 month. Simultaneous submissions accepted: yes. Publishes 2-3% of manuscripts submitted. Payment: royalty contract based on list price. Copyrights for author. Subjects: Business & Economics, Crime, Drugs, Health, How-To.

ADIRONDAC, Adirondack Mountain Club, Inc., Neal S. Burdick, Editor, 814 Goggins Road, Lake George, NY 12845-4117, 518-668-4447, e-mail ADKinfo@adk.org. 1922. Poetry, articles, art, photos, interviews, reviews, letters, news items, non-fiction. "Avg. length: 1000-3000 words, with conservation, education, and recreation focus, representing different stances on issues of concern to the Adirondack and Catskill constitutionally-protected Forest Preserves. Contributors include ADK members, state authorities, Forest Preserve historians, outdoor recreationists, etc." circ. 20M. 6/yr. Pub'd 7 issues 2005; expects 6 issues 2006, 6 issues 2007. sub. price $20; per copy $2.95; sample $2.95. Back issues: $4.95. Discounts: retailers 40% (min. 10 copies); libraries $15/yr. 32pp. Reporting time: 3 months. Payment: none. Copyrighted, does not revert to author. Pub's reviews: approx. 24 in 2005. §Natural history, conservation, "muscle-powered" recreation, Adirondack or Catskill history and lore. Ads: Full page: $660; 1/2 page $345; 1/4 page $200. Classifieds $5.00 per line. Subjects: Adirondacks, Conservation, Earth, Natural History, Ecology, Foods, Environment, Sports, Outdoors.

Adirondack Mountain Club, Inc. (see also ADIRONDAC), Andrea Masters, Publications Director; Neal Burdick, Editor of Adirondac, 814 Goggins Road, Lake George, NY 12845-4117, 518-668-4447, FAX 518-668-3746, e-mail pubs@adk.org. 1922. Articles, non-fiction. "We publish guidebooks—hiking, canoeing, climbing, skiing, and biking guides—as well as natural and cultural histories about the Forest Preserve of New York State (which comprises the Adirondack and Catskill parks). We also publish a history of the Adirondack Park for young people (ages 10+), trail maps, and an annual calendar of Adirondack nature photography." avg. press run 3M. Pub'd 2 titles 2005; expects 3 titles 2006, 3 titles 2007. Discounts: retail 1-5 20%, 6-99 40%, 100+ 42%, STOP 40%; schools & libraries 25%; wholesalers, 10-49 40%, 50-99 46%, 100+ 50%, and free freight. 200pp. Reporting time: 3 weeks to 3 months (decided by Committee). We accept simultaneous submissions (must be disclosed). Publishes 1% of manuscripts submitted. Payment: typical is 7-1/2% royalty on gross. Copyrights for author. Subjects: Adirondacks, Children, Youth, Conservation, Earth, Natural History, Education, Nature, New York, Sports, Outdoors, Travel.

THE ADIRONDACK REVIEW, Black Lawrence Press, Colleen Ryor, 305 Keyes Avenue, Watertown, NY 13601-3731, publisher@blacklawrencepress.com, editor@adkreview.com, www.blacklawrencepress.com, www.adkreview.com. 2000. Poetry, fiction, articles, art, photos, cartoons, interviews, criticism, reviews, long-poems, non-fiction. "TAR publishes an eclectic mix of fresh voices in literature, as well as interviews, art, photography, and French and German translations. Poets whose work has appeared in the Review include: Denise Duhamel, Walt McDonald, Timothy Liu, D.C. Berry, Lee Upton, R.T. Smith, Bob Hicok, Lola Haskins, James Reidel, Ilya Kaminsky, as well as many newcomers." circ. 6000. 2/yr. Pub'd 4 issues 2005; expects 2 issues 2006, 2 issues 2007. sub. price free; per copy free; sample free. Back issues: free. Discounts: N/A (on-line). 50pp. Reporting time: same day to one year (depending on backlog and editorial load), but we try to respond within 2 months. Simultaneous submissions accepted: Yes. Publishes 3% of manuscripts submitted. Payment: none. Copyrighted, reverts to author. Pub's reviews: approx. 12 in 2005. §film, music, poetry and literary fiction. Ads: see website for current ad specs. Subjects: Adirondacks, Arts, Book Reviewing, Fiction, France, French, German, Literary Review, Literature (General), Poetry, Short Stories, Translation.

Admiral House Publishing, Michael Mueller, Publisher, 4281 7th Avenue SW, Naples, FL 34119-4029, email AdmHouse@swfla.rr.com. 1997. Fiction, interviews. "No unagented material read or returned." avg. press run 15M. Pub'd 2 titles 2005; expects 4 titles 2006, 6 titles 2007. Discounts: from 20% (short discount) to 55% (distributor). 300pp. Reporting time: 2 months. Simultaneous submissions accepted: no. Publishes 1% of manuscripts submitted. Payment: 10-15%. Copyrights for author. Subjects: Drama, Fiction.

ADOLESCENCE, Libra Publishers, Inc., 3089C Clairemont Dr., Suite 383, San Diego, CA 92117, 619-571-1414. 1960. Articles. circ. 3M. 4/yr. Pub'd 4 issues 2005; expects 4 issues 2006, 4 issues 2007. sub. price $115; per copy $25; sample free. Back issues: $25. Discounts: 10% to subscriber agents. 256pp. Reporting time: 6 weeks. Payment: none. Copyrighted, does not revert to author. Pub's reviews: 60 in 2005. §Behavioral sciences. Ads: $300/$175. Subjects: Psychology, Society.

Advanced Learning Press, Anne Fenske Mrs., 317 Inverness Way South, Suite 150, Englewood, CO 80112, 303-504-9312, 303-504-9417, 800-844-6599. 1992. Non-fiction. "Professional development for educators in the areas of standards, assessment, accountability, and leadership. Douglas B. Reeves, Ph.D. Larry Ainsworth." avg. press run 4000. Pub'd 2 titles 2005; expects 2 titles 2006, 6 titles 2007. Discounts: 40% for quantities of 1-49, 50% for quantities of 50 or more. 200pp. Reporting time: 2 weeks. Simultaneous submissions accepted: No. Publishes 80% of manuscripts submitted. Payment: 1-1,000 7.5%, 1001-3,000 10%, 3001+ 15%. Copyrights for author. Subjects: Education, Leadership.

ADVANCES IN THANATOLOGY, Center for Thanatology Research & Education, Inc., Austin H. Kutscher, Editor; Roberta Halporn, Executive Editor, 391 Atlantic Ave., Brooklyn, NY 11217-1708, 718-858-3026, 718-852-1846,no 800,rhalporn@pipeline.com, thanatology.org. 1970. Non-fiction. "Death & Dying, Grief and Recovery from Grief, Medical Education in Thanatology." circ. 500. 4/yr. Pub'd 3 issues 2005; expects 4 issues 2006, 4 issues 2007. sub. price $72; per copy $20.; sample Free. Back issues: $2-. Discounts: 20% none to institutions or classrooms, unless multiple copies of same issue. 120pp. Simultaneous submissions accepted: No. Copyrighted, does not revert to author. Pub's reviews. Ads: Fill page:$125.00Half page:$65.00. Subjects: Euthanasia, Death, Family.

ADVANCES IN THE ASTRONAUTICAL SCIENCES, Univelt, Inc., R.H. Jacobs, Series Editor, PO Box 28130, San Diego, CA 92198, 760-746-4005, Fax 760-746-3139, sales@univelt.com, www.univelt.com. 1957. "Space and related fields. An irregular serial. Publishers for the American Atronautical Society. Vols. 1-122 published. Standing orders accepted." circ. 400. Irregular. Pub'd 2 issues 2005; expects 4 issues 2006, 5 issues 2007. sub. price varies. Back issues: no. Discounts: normally 20% but more by arrangement; discounts for classroom use. 400-700pp. Reporting time: 60 days. Payment: none. Copyrighted, authors may republish material with appropriate credits given and authorization from publishers. Ads: none. Subjects: Engineering, Science, Space.

Advantage World Press, Tawana Bivins Rosenbaum, Editor; Lynnette Khalfani, Publisher, 1625 Nottingham Way, Mountainside, NJ 07092-1340, 973-324-0034, Fax 973-324-1951, info@advantageworldpress.com, www.advantageworldpress.com. 2003. Non-fiction. "Advantage World Press is an independent publisher specializing in nonfiction books, especially personal finance, investing and business titles. We also publish newsletters, pamphlets and other printed and audio materials. Our mission is to provide readers with timely, interesting information that will give them the upper hand in managing their increasingly complex personal and financial lives." avg. press run 10M+. Expects 1 title 2006, 3 titles 2007. Discounts: standard. 256pp. Reporting time: 4 weeks. Simultaneous submissions accepted: yes. Publishes less than 10% of manuscripts submitted. Payment: negotiable. Copyrights for author. Subjects: Business & Economics, Finances, Non-Fiction.

Adventure Books Inc., Dina J. Daniel, PO Box 5196, Fresno, CA 93755, 559-294-8781, adventure-books@juno.com. 2000. Poetry, fiction, long-poems, non-fiction. avg. press run 1M. Pub'd 1 title 2005; expects 3 titles 2006, 12 titles 2007. Discounts: 60% offered on bulk orders. 150pp. Reporting time: 1-2 months. Simultaneous submissions accepted: yes. Publishes 10% of manuscripts submitted. Payment: yes. Copyrights for author. Subjects: Fantasy, Fiction, Mystery, Non-Fiction, Poetry.

ADVENTURES, Pamela Smits, Editor, 6401 The Paseo, Kansas City, MO 64131, 816-333-7000. 1969. Fiction, articles, non-fiction. "Inspirational and character building for 6 to 8-year-old children focusing on learning features with Bible lesson." circ. 42M. 52/yr. Pub'd 52 issues 2005. sub. price $7.95; sample free with SASE. 4pp. Reporting time: 8-12 weeks. Simultaneous submissions accepted: no. Publishes 30% of manuscripts submitted. Payment: $25 per story (100-150 words). Copyrighted, we retain all rights. Subjects: Children, Youth, Religion.

Aegean Publishing Company, PO Box 6790, Santa Barbara, CA 93160, 805-964-6669. 1993. Non-fiction. "Technology-oriented popular books." avg. press run 5M. Expects 1 title 2006, 1 title 2007. Discounts: schedules available on request. 256pp. Reporting time: contact publisher. Payment: contact publisher. Copyrights for author. Subjects: Design, Engineering, Technology.

AERIAL, Rod Smith, PO Box 25642, Washington, DC 20007, 202-362-6418, aerialedge@aol.com. 1984. Poetry, fiction, articles, art, photos, cartoons, interviews, satire, criticism, reviews, music, letters, parts-of-novels, long-poems, collages, plays, concrete art, news items, non-fiction. "*Aerial #9*, just published, is a special issue on the work of Bruce Andrews." circ. 1M. Irregular. sub. price $25/2 issues; per copy varies; sample $15.00. Back issues: #6/7 is $15, #5 is $7.50. Discounts: 40% to retailers. 200pp. Reporting time: 1 week-6 months. Payment: contributors copies. Copyrighted, reverts to author. Pub's reviews. §Lit. mags, poetry, fiction, criticism, art. Ads: $100/$60/will consider exchanges. Subjects: Arts, Culture, Essays, Language, Literature (General), Poetry.

•**AE-TU Publishing,** GLADYS CROSS, P O Box 960246, Miami, FL 33296-0246, (305)408-3817, Fax on demand, aetupub@hotmail.com, www.aetupublishing.com. 2004. Non-fiction. avg. press run 1000. Expects 1 title 2006, 2-3 titles 2007. Discounts: 2-4 20%; 5-9 30%; 10-24 40%; 25-49 42%; 50-74 44%; 75-99 46%; 100-199 48%; 200 or more 50%. 240pp. Simultaneous submissions accepted: No. Does not copyright for author. Subjects: Biography, Book Reviewing, Civil Rights, Dreams, Engineering, Futurism, Sherlock Holmes, Human Rights, Metaphysics, Non-Fiction, Physics, Political Science, Publishing, Science, Science Fiction.

AFFABLE NEIGHBOR, Affable Neighbor Press, Joel Henry-Fisher, Editor in Chief; Leigh Chalmers, Poetry Editor; Marshall Stanley, Assistant Editor, 43 Margaret Street, Whitmore Lake, MI 48189-9502. 1994. Poetry, fiction, articles, art, photos, cartoons, interviews, satire, criticism, reviews, music, letters, parts-of-novels, collages, concrete art, news items, non-fiction. "*Affable Neighbor* has no set format, so it is hard to generalize. Most issues are unsuitable for children, nudity, graphic language, etc. But also has contained puzzles, 'serious' literature, etc., 'arts of all kinds.' Recently published a 'Weak Stomach' issue that was suitable for children." circ. 25-1M. Irregular. Pub'd 6 issues 2005. sub. price $20 (includes prizes and extras); per copy $2 (or less). Back issues: #1-3 $2, #4 $1, #5-7 $2, #6 $1.50. Discounts: selective trades, otherwise individually bargained. 50pp. Reporting time: as soon as we get around to it. Simultaneous submissions accepted: yes. Payment: free copies. Not copyrighted. Pub's reviews. §Unique, outspoken, offensive, stretching the definitions of magazines and censorship "art " too. Ads: $1,000/$500/all negotiable. Subjects: Absurdist, Agriculture, Americana, Anarchist, Arts, Avant-Garde, Experimental Art, Beat, Cartoons, Celtic, Counter-Culture, Alternatives, Communes, Creativity, Cults, Culture, Dada, Drugs.

Affable Neighbor Press (see also AFFABLE NEIGHBOR), Joel Henry-Fisher, Editor-in-Chief; Leigh Chalmers, Poetry Editor; Marshall Stanley, Assistant Editor, 110 Felch St., Ann Arbor, MI 48103-3330. 1994. Poetry, fiction, articles, art, photos, cartoons, interviews, satire, criticism, reviews, music, letters, parts-of-novels, long-poems, collages, plays, concrete art, news items, non-fiction. "Normally geared only for small self runs, although open to anything." avg. press run 100. Pub'd 1 title 2005. Pages vary. Reporting time: as soon as we get around to it. Simultaneous submissions accepted: yes. Payment: per individual. Does not copyright for author. Subjects: Absurdist, Agriculture, Americana, Anarchist, Arts, Avant-Garde, Experimental Art, Beat, Cartoons, Celtic, Counter-Culture, Alternatives, Communes, Creativity, Cults, Culture, Dada, Drugs.

THE AFFILIATE, Reveal, Peter Riden, Publisher, Conceptor, Editor, 777 Barb Road, #257, Vankleek Hill, Ontario K0B 1R0, Canada, 613-678-3453. 1987. Poetry, articles, art, photos, cartoons, interviews, reviews, music, letters, news items, non-fiction. "To be an Affiliate means the scope is universal. The desire is to be a participant to a global dialogue with others of the same scope. The attitude is one of reciprocity and understanding. Traveling distances by way of correspondence or hosting one another. A requisite for excellence in conduct and expression. An aim at cleaning up our act for our planet Earth. The recognition of one's talent(s) in their achievements, be it music, art and all other laudable efforts. An obvious open mind through the desire to pride rather than shame our body. A communal strength in our international friendship. If this is part of what you feel deep inside—join in! Subscribe! Become an *Affiliate*." circ. as requested, can be as much as 10M. 6/yr. Pub'd 6 issues 2005; expects 6 issues 2006, 6 issues 2007. sub. price $75 US/North America, $100 anywhere else; per copy $10 N. America, $15 elsewhere; sample $10 N. America, $15 elsewhere. Back issues: as collectors items they may turn to be more costly than originally priced. Discounts: complimentary to contributors and traders. 52-60pp. Reporting time: must be received prior to the 15th preceding the current issue. Simultaneous submissions accepted: yes. Publishes 20% of manuscripts submitted. Payment: complimentary issue and undeniably an opportunity to become better known. Copyrighted, rights revert to author by mutual agreement if to be reprinted. Pub's reviews: few in 2005. §We definitely have an extended section for the most pioneering and cohesive publications. Ads: Contact for ad rates. Subjects: Advertising, Self-Promotion, Anarchist, Arts, Astrology, Birth, Birth Control, Population, Book Arts, Celtic, Civil Rights, Communication, Journalism, Community, Computers, Calculators, Conservation, Cults, Drugs, Ecology, Foods.

Affinity Publishers Services, A. Doyle, Founder, c/o Continuous, PO Box 416, Denver, CO 80201-0416, 303-575-5676, email: mail@contentprovidermedia.com. 1981. avg. press run 55. Expects 2 titles 2007. Discounts: standard. 70pp. Subjects: Biography, Business & Economics, Consumer, Crafts, Hobbies, Gardening, Homemaking, How-To, How-To, Newsletter, Reference, Tapes & Records, Vegetarianism.

Affirmative Publishing LC, Catina Bridges, Patty Holmes, Ruth Reynolds, 104 Colton Street, Upper

Marlboro, MD 20774. 1999. Fiction, parts-of-novels, plays, non-fiction. avg. press run 5M. Expects 5 titles 2006, 10 titles 2007. Discounts: distributors, wholesalers, bookstores, churches. 200pp. Simultaneous submissions accepted: yes. Publishes 10% of manuscripts submitted. Payment: 20%, 80% to authors. Copyrights for author. Subjects: Leadership, Self-Help, Sex, Sexuality, Singles, Spiritual, Supernatural, Young Adult.

African American Images, Jawanza Kunjufu, 1909 West 95th Street, Chicago, IL 60643-1105, 312-445-0322, Fax 312-445-9844. 1980. Non-fiction. avg. press run 5M. Pub'd 10 titles 2005. Discounts: 5-100 40%, 101-199 46%, 200+ 50%. 125pp. Reporting time: 2 months. Publishes 10% of manuscripts submitted. Payment: 10% net. Copyrights for author. Subjects: Black, Education, Family, Sociology.

AFRICAN AMERICAN REVIEW, Joycelyn Moody Ph.D., Editor; Aileen Keenan, Managing Editor, Saint Louis University, Humanities 317, 3800 Lindell Boulevard, St. Louis, MO 63108-3414, 314-977-3688, FAX 314-977-1514, moodyjk@slu.edu, keenanam@slu.edu, http://aar.slu.edu. 1967. Poetry, fiction, articles, art, photos, interviews, criticism, reviews, long-poems, collages, non-fiction. "As the official publication of the Division on Black American Literature and Culture of the Modern Language Association, the quarterly journal *African American Review* promotes a lively exchange among writers and scholars in the arts, humanities, and social sciences who hold diverse perspectives on African American literature and culture." 4/yr. Pub'd 4 issues 2005; expects 4 issues 2006, 4 issues 2007. sub. price $40 individuals, $80 institutions (foreign add $15); per copy $12, $24 institutions (no foreign single issues); sample $12. Back issues: $12. 200pp. Reporting time: 3 months. Simultaneous submissions accepted: no. Publishes 12% of manuscripts submitted. Payment: 1 copy and 5 offprints; honorarium. AAR holds copyright on entire issue, author on individual article or poem. Pub's reviews: 31 in 2005. §African-American literature. Ads: $200/$120. Subjects: African Literature, Africa, African Studies, Black, Book Reviewing, Community, Criticism, Dance, Education, Fiction, History, Literary Review, Men, Music, Poetry, Theatre, Women.

THE AFRICAN BOOK PUBLISHING RECORD, Hans M. Zell, Editor; Cecile Lomer, Ass. Editor (US office), PO Box 56, Oxford 0X13EL, England, +44-(0)1865-511428; fax +44-1865-311534. 1975. Articles, interviews, criticism, reviews, news items. "Largely a bibliographic tool, providing information on new and forthcoming African published materials; plus 'Notes & News', 'Magazines', 'Reports', 'Reference Sources' sections and interviews; normally one major article on aspects of publishing and book development in Africa per issue. Major book review section. (Ca. 40-60 reviews per issue). US Office, PO Box 50408, Columbia, SC 29250-0408." circ. 500. 4/yr. Pub'd 4 issues 2005; expects 4 issues 2006, 4 issues 2007. sub. price £175/$290 institution; £87.50/$145 individual; sample gratis. Discounts: 15% to adv. agents/10% to subs. agents. 84pp. Reporting time: 6-8 weeks. Simultaneous submissions accepted: no. Publishes 25% of manuscripts submitted. Payment: none. Copyrighted. Pub's reviews: 192 in 2005. §Books published in Africa only, with an emphasis on scholarly books, creative writing, reference tools, and children's books. Ads: £250 ($400)/£175 ($280)/£300 ($480). Subjects: African Literature, Africa, African Studies, Bibliography, Publishing.

THE AFRICAN HERALD, Good Hope Enterprises, Inc., Dr. Richard O. Nwachukwu, PO Box 132394, Dallas, TX 75313-2394. 1989. Articles, photos, interviews, news items, non-fiction. "Additional address: 4300 N. Central Expressway, Suite 201, Dallas, TX 75206." circ. 15M. 12/yr. Pub'd 12 issues 2005; expects 12 issues 2006, 12 issues 2007. sub. price $15 corps, libraries; $12 individuals; per copy $1; sample free. Back issues: $1.50. Discounts: 30% to 40%. 32pp. Publishes 95% of manuscripts submitted. Payment: none. Copyrighted, does not revert to author. Pub's reviews: 6 in 2005. §African/African-American Books. Ads: $1365/$725/$475/$295/$155 business card size.

African Ways Publishing, Lynn D. Casto, Publisher, 3112 Estates Drive, Fairfield, CA 94533-9721, 925-631-0630, Fax 925-376-1926. 1996. Non-fiction. "Publish history, political, biographical books about Africa." avg. press run 3M. Pub'd 1 title 2005; expects 1 title 2006, 1 title 2007. Discounts: retail 1-2 books 20%, 3-4 30%, 5+ 40%; wholesale 55%. 300pp. Reporting time: 6 weeks. Payment: trade standard. Copyrights for author. Subjects: African Literature, Africa, African Studies, African-American, Biography, History, Memoirs, Politics.

AFRO-HISPANIC REVIEW, Marvin A. Lewis, Edward J. Mullen, Romance Languages, Univ. of Missouri, 143 Arts & Science Building, Columbia, MO 65211, 573-882-5040 or 573-882-5041. 1982. Poetry, fiction, articles, interviews, criticism, reviews, letters, news items. "We also publish translations." circ. 500. 2/yr. Pub'd 2 issues 2005; expects 2 issues 2006, 2 issues 2007. sub. price $15 indiv., $20 instit.; per copy $7.50; sample $7.50. Back issues: $10. Discounts: 40%. 60pp. Reporting time: 60 days. Simultaneous submissions accepted: no. Publishes 40% of manuscripts submitted. Payment: 3 copies of issue containing contribution. Copyrighted, does not revert to author. Pub's reviews: 3 in 2005. §Afro-Hispanic history, literature and sociology. Ads: $100/$50/50¢. Subjects: Black, Latin America.

•**AFTERIMAGE, Visual Studies Workshop,** Karen vanMeenen, 31 Prince Street, Rochester, NY 14607, 585/442.8676, fax 585.442.1992, afterimage@vsw.org, www.vsw.org/afterimage/. 1972. Articles, art, photos,

9

interviews, criticism, reviews, concrete art, news items. "Afterimage features critical articles about the visual arts, photography, independent film and video, alternative publishing, and multimedia, also covering important issues and debates within art history and sociology, cultural studies, communication studies, and related fields." 6/yr. Pub'd 6 issues 2005; expects 5 issues 2006, 6 issues 2007. sub. price $33; per copy $5.50; sample free. Back issues: $5 + SH. Discounts: distributors & bookstores 50% discount.Afterimage in the classroom 50% discount. 60pp. Reporting time: 4-6 weeks. Simultaneous submissions accepted: No. Publishes 15% of manuscripts submitted. Payment: 5 cents per word after publication. Pub's reviews. Ads: $750 front cover inside (full color)/$700 back cover inside (full color)/ $800 back cover (full color)/$500 full page/ $300 1/2 page/$200 1/4 page/ $125 bottom runner/$25 highlighted notice. Subjects: Arts, Audio/Video, Avant-Garde, Experimental Art, Book Arts, Criticism, Culture, Photography, Visual Arts.

AFTERTOUCH: New Music Discoveries, Ronald A. Wallace, 1024 West Willcox Avenue, Peoria, IL 61604-2675, 309-685-4843. 1984. Articles, art, interviews, music. circ. 10,000. 2/yr. Pub'd 1 issue 2005; expects 1 issue 2006, 2 issues 2007. sub. price $10; per copy $2.50; sample $2.50. Discounts: none. 36pp. Publishes 0% of manuscripts submitted. §Music. Ads: Yes. Subject: Music.

Agathon Books, Allen A. Huemer, PO Box 630, Lander, WY 82520-0630, 307-332-5252, Fax 307-332-5888, agathon@rmisp.com, www.rmisp.com/agathon/. 1998. "Issues in philosophy and related areas, using a clearly-reasoned, good-spirited approach." avg. press run 3M. Expects 3 titles 2006, 4+ titles 2007. Discounts: trade 40%, colleges and libraries 25%, bulk and jobber 60% max. 300pp. Reporting time: 6 months. Simultaneous submissions accepted: yes. Publishes 25% of manuscripts submitted. Payment: arranged individually. Copyrights for author. Subjects: Myth, Mythology, Philosophy, Poetry.

Ageless Press, Iris Forrest, 3759 Collins St., Sarasota, FL 34232-3201, 941-365-1367, irishope@comcast.net. 1992. Fiction, articles, non-fiction. "First book is an anthology of experiences of dealing with computers. Fiction & nonfiction." avg. press run 5M. Expects 1 title 2006, 1 title 2007. 160pp. Reporting time: 2 weeks. Simultaneous submissions accepted: Yes. Payment: negotiable. Does not copyright for author. Subjects: Artificial Intelligence, Computers, Calculators, Fiction, Health, Humor, Mystery, Non-Fiction, Short Stories.

THE AGENCIES-WHAT THE ACTOR NEEDS TO KNOW, Acting World Books, Lawrence Parke, PO Box 3044, Hollywood, CA 90078, 818-905-1345. 1981. "Articles in every issue by and or about subject material people, orgns, currently recommended procedures, etc." circ. 1.5M. 12/yr. Pub'd 12 issues 2005; expects 12 issues 2006, 12 issues 2007. sub. price $50; per copy $10. Back issues: not available. Discounts: 40% bookstore. 56pp. Reporting time: 2 weeks. Payment: as and if negotiated. Copyrighted, reverts to author. Ads: $500 1/2 page/special 6 months in both pub's, rate $800. Subjects: Electronics, Entertainment, How-To, Theatre.

Agityne Corp, PO Box 690, Upton, MA 01568, 508-529-4135, www.agityne.com/. 2002. Non-fiction. Expects 2 titles 2006, 3 titles 2007. 200pp. Simultaneous submissions accepted: No. Copyrights for author.

Aglob Publishing, Angela Waiters-Eniola, PO Box 4036, Hallandale, FL 33008, 954-456-1476, Fax 954-456-3903, aglobpubl1@aol.com. 2000. Non-fiction. avg. press run 500-50M. Pub'd 25 titles 2005; expects 45 titles 2006, 70 titles 2007. Discounts: agent, trade, bulk. 100-300pp. Reporting time: 8-16 weeks. Simultaneous submissions accepted: yes. Payment: negotiable. Subjects: African-American, AIDS, Alcohol, Alcoholism, Alternative Medicine, Health, How-To, Non-Fiction.

AGNI, Sven Birkerts, Editor; William Pierce, Senior Editor, Boston University Writing Program, 236 Bay State Road, Boston, MA 02215, 617-353-7135, agni@bu.edu. 1972. Poetry, fiction, non-fiction. "We look for the honest voice, the idiosyncratic signature, experimental where necessary but not willfully so. Writing that grows from a vision, a perspective, and a passion will interest us, regardless of structure or approach. Recent contributors include Harvey Blume, Keith Gessen, Nicholas Montemarano, Vivek Narayanan, Maureen Howard, Christopher Benfey, Margot Livesey, Howard Norman, Peter LaSalle, and George Scialabba. We strongly encourage you to buy a sample copy before submitting your work." circ. 3,000. 2/yr. Pub'd 2 issues 2005; expects 2 issues 2006, 2 issues 2007. sub. price $17, $20 institutions; per copy $9.95; sample $9.95 for issue 57 or later (spring 2003). Back issues: see https://www.bu.edu/agni/order/back-issues/index.html. Discounts: $31 for 2 years and free back issue, $44 for 3 years and 2 back issues (for individuals only). 200-270pp. Reporting time: 2-4 months. Reading period is September 1st to May 31st only (check www.bu.edu/agni/about for changes). Simultaneous submissions encouraged. Publishes ~1% of manuscripts submitted. Payment: $10 per page ($150 max, $20 minimum). Copyrighted, reverts to author. Ads: $500/$350. Subjects: Essays, Fiction, Memoirs, Poetry, Translation.

AGRICULTURAL HISTORY, University of California Press, Claire Strom, Editor, University of California Press, 2000 Center Street, Suite 303, Berkeley, CA 94704-1223, 510-643-7154. 1926. Articles, reviews, non-fiction. "Editorial address: Department of History, Minard Hall, North Dakota State University, Fargo, ND 58105-5075. Copyrighted by Agricultural History Society." circ. 957. 4/yr. Pub'd 4 issues 2005; expects 4 issues 2006, 4 issues 2007. sub. price $47 indiv., $158 instit., $22 students; per copy $12 indiv.; $42 instit., $12 students. Back issues: $12 indiv.; $42 instit., $12 students. Discounts: foreign subs. agent 10%, one-time orders 10+ 30%. 128pp. Reporting time: 2-3 weeks. Payment: varies. Copyrighted, does not revert to author. Pub's reviews: 100 in 2005. §Agricultural history and economics. Ads: $295/$220. Subject: Agriculture.

THE AGUILAR EXPRESSION, Xavier F. Aguilar, 1329 Gilmore Avenue, Donora, PA 15033, 724-379-8019, www.wordrunner.com/xfaguilar. 1986. Poetry, fiction, art, reviews, letters. circ. 150. 2/yr. Pub'd 2 issues 2005; expects 2 issues 2006, 2 issues 2007. sub. price $15; per copy $8; sample $8. 8-16pp. Reporting time: 1 month. Simultaneous submissions accepted: no. Publishes 10% of manuscripts submitted. Payment: 2 free copies, byline. Not copyrighted. Pub's reviews: 2 in 2005. §Poetry books and short story collections. Ads: by request. Subjects: Fiction, Poetry.

Ahsahta Press, Janet Holmes, Director, Boise State University, Department of English, Boise, ID 83725-1525, 208-426-2195, ahsahta@boisestate.edu, http://ahsahtapress.boisestate.edu. 1975. Poetry. "We run the Sawtooth Poetry Prize competition annually." avg. press run 1000. Pub'd 5 titles 2005; expects 5 titles 2006, 5 titles 2007. Discounts: 40% to trade, bulk, jobber, classroom; distributed by Small Press Distribution. 100pp. Reporting time: 3 months, submit only March 1-May 30. Simultaneous submissions accepted: yes. Publishes 1% of manuscripts submitted. Payment: copies of book; 8% for first 1,000 sold, 10% for next 1,000 sold, 12% thereafter. Copyrights for author. Subject: Poetry.

AIM MAGAZINE, Ruth Apilado, Editor; Myron Apilado, Managing Editor, PO Box 1174, Maywood, IL 60153-8174. 1973. "*AIM* is a national magazine that uses the written word to help purge racism from the human bloodstream. A consistent theme that winds its way through the prose poetry of the magazine is one that depicts how people from one ethnic group, usually through some personal experience, come to realize the common humanity of all ethnic groups. We're looking for compelling, well-written pieces with lasting social significance. The story should not moralize. Maximum length is 4,000 words." circ. 7M. 4/yr. Pub'd 4 issues 2005; expects 4 issues 2006, 4 issues 2007. sub. price $12; per copy $4; sample $5. Back issues: $6. Discounts: 30%. 48pp. Reporting time: 2 months. Simultaneous submissions accepted: yes. Publishes 70% of manuscripts submitted. Payment: $15-$25 articles and stories. Not copyrighted. Pub's reviews: 2 in 2005. §Black and Hispanic life. Ads: $250/$150/$90 1/4 page. Subjects: African Literature, Africa, African Studies, Black, Book Reviewing, Fiction, Socialist, Sociology.

Aircraft Owners Group (see also CESSNA OWNER MAGAZINE; PIPERS MAGAZINE), Jodi Lindquist, Editor, PO Box 5000, Iola, WI 54945, 800-331-0038, e-mail cessna@aircraftownergroup.com or piper@aircraftownergroup.com. 1974. Articles, photos, interviews, reviews, letters. avg. press run 3M-5M.

Airplane Books, Barbara Richter, 831 Ridge Road, Highland Park, IL 60035-3835. 1994. Art, cartoons, non-fiction. "*Eat Like A Horse* treats the serious subject of dieting in a light-hearted and humorous fashion. 150 recipes, 80 of which are vegetarian. Each recipe original and tested." Pub'd 1 title 2005; expects 3 titles 2006, 5 titles 2007. Discounts: standard. 192pp. Subjects: Arts, Cooking, How-To, Yoga.

•AIS Publications (see also GENRE: WRITER AND WRITINGS), Alexis James, PO Box 42603, Indianapolis, IN 46242-0603, Office: (317) 856-8942, Cell: (317) 292-2615. 1996. Poetry, photos, parts-of-novels, non-fiction. "To publish biographies, reporting as near as factual as possible and to offer opportunities to up and coming writers in varoius genre. Recently we have T. Chandler, A. Skriloff, N. Yelton, M. Kondritz and R.Ciras who have contributed works in their individual genre." Expects 2 titles 2006, 3 titles 2007. Reporting time: 3 months. Simultaneous submissions accepted: Yes. Publishes 10% of manuscripts submitted. Payment: No advances at this time. Payment in copies of author's works. Copyrights for author. Subjects: Autobiography, Biography, Business & Economics, Civil Rights, Haiku, Holocaust, Human Rights, Humanism, Indigenous Cultures, Mental Health, Native American, Non-Fiction, Poetry, Prison, Quotations.

AK Press, Ramsey Kanaan, PO Box 40682, San Francisco, CA 94140, 415-864-0892, FAX 415-864-0893, akpress@org.org. 1994. Fiction, art, criticism, long-poems, non-fiction. "Most of what we publish is solicited. However we have published the occasional unsolicited work. We largely publish non-fiction of a radical nature, in the fields of anarchism, art & culture." avg. press run 2M-10M. Pub'd 15 titles 2005; expects 18 titles 2006, 25 titles 2007. Normal discounts to trade, depending on whether it's to a retailer, distributor, library, etc. 100-400pp. Reporting time: a couple of months. Publishes 2% of manuscripts submitted. Payment: usually 10% of net sales, no advance. Subjects: Anarchist, Arts, Biography, Dada, Entertainment, Environment, Feminism, Fiction, History, Literature (General), Non-Fiction, Philosophy, Political Science, Sex, Sexuality, Surrealism.

Akashic Books, Johnny Temple, Publisher; Johanna Ingalls, Managing Editor, PO Box 1456, New York, NY 10009, 212-433-1875, 212-414-3199, Akashic7@aol.com, www.akashicbooks.com. 1997.

ALABAMA HERITAGE, University of Alabama Press, Donna Cox, Box 870342, 500 Margaret Drive, Tuscaloosa, AL 35487-0342, 205-348-7434, www.AlabamaHeritage.com.

‡ALABAMA LITERARY REVIEW, Theron E. Montgomery III, Editor; James G. Davis, Fiction Editor; Ed Hicks, Poetry Editor; Steve Cooper, Prose Editor, Smith 253, Troy State University, Troy, AL 36082,

334-670-3307, Fax 334-670-3519. 1987. Poetry, fiction, articles, art, photos, cartoons, interviews, criticism, reviews, parts-of-novels, long-poems, plays. "No bias against style or length of poetry, fiction or drama. First issue included Eve Shelnutt and Elise Sanguinetti." circ. 800+. 1/yr. Pub'd 1 issue 2005; expects 1 issue 2006, 1 issue 2007. sub. price $10; per copy $10; sample $5. 100pp. Reporting time: 2-3 months. Publishes 5-10% of manuscripts submitted. Payment: copies and honorarium when available; $5-10 per printed page. Copyrighted, reverts to author. Pub's reviews: 5 in 2005. §All kinds, particularly poetry and fiction by new authors and/or smaller presses. Ads: $25. Subjects: Book Reviewing, Criticism, Fiction, Photography, Poetry.

Alamo Square Press, Bert Herrman, 103 FR 321, Tajique, NM 87016, 503-384-9766, alamosquare@earthlink.net. 1988. Non-fiction. "Book length, gay, non-pornographic, social or spiritual importance only." avg. press run 5M. Pub'd 1 title 2005; expects 1 title 2006. Discounts: 40% retail, 55% distributor. 144pp. Reporting time: 2 weeks. Simultaneous submissions accepted: no. Publishes 20% of manuscripts submitted. Payment: negotiable. Copyrights for author. Subjects: Gay, Lesbianism, Occult, Psychology, San Francisco, Spiritual, Zen.

Alan Wofsy Fine Arts, Milton J. Goldbaum, Zeke Greenberg, Adios Butler, PO Box 2210, San Francisco, CA 94126, 415-292-6500, www.art-books.com, alanwolfsyfinearts@art-books.com. 1969. Art, cartoons. "Art reference books only." avg. press run 500. Pub'd 4 titles 2005; expects 4 titles 2006, 5+ titles 2007. Discounts: 20-40. 300pp. Payment: varies. Copyrights for author. Subjects: Arts, Comics, Reference, Reprints.

ALARM CLOCK, Allen Salyer, PO Box 1551, Royal Oak, MI 48068, 248-442-8634. 1990. Music. "Women in Music." circ. 200. 4/yr. Pub'd 5 issues 2005; expects 4 issues 2006, 4 issues 2007. sample price $2. 32pp. Payment: contributor's copy. Copyrighted, reverts to author. Pub's reviews: 10-15 per issue in 2005. §Music, science fiction, fashion, women's issues. Subject: Music.

Alaska Geographic Society, Penny Rennick, Editor, PO Box 93370, Anchorage, AK 99509, 907-562-0164, Fax 907-562-0479, e-mail info@akgeo.com. 1968. Photos, news items, non-fiction. "Alaska Geographic, an award-winning series of books published four times a year, presents the places, people, and wonder wonder of Alaska to the world." avg. press run 10M. Pub'd 4 titles 2005; expects 4 titles 2006, 4 titles 2007. Discounts: library 20%, wholesalers 40%+. 112pp. Reporting time: 1 month. Simultaneous submissions accepted: no. Publishes 20% of manuscripts submitted. Payment: purchase 1 time rights to publish. Does not copyright for author. Subjects: Anthropology, Archaelogy, Aviation, Biography, Birds, Canada, Conservation, Earth, Natural History, Education, History, Native American, The North, Pacific Northwest, Photography, Reference, Sports, Outdoors.

Alaska Native Language Center, Tom Alton, University of Alaska, PO Box 757680, Fairbanks, AK 99775-7680, 907-474-7874, Fax 907-474-6586. 1972. Non-fiction. "We publish materials in or about Alaska Native languages only." avg. press run 500-1M. Pub'd 2 titles 2005; expects 5 titles 2006, 6 titles 2007. Discounts: wholesalers 40% on 5 each or more; 20% on fewer than 5 each. 300pp. Sometimes copyrights for author—joint copyright or ANLC alone. Subjects: Alaska, Autobiography, Bilingual, Culture, Education, Folklore, Genealogy, How-To, Indians, Language, Memoirs, Native American, Non-Fiction, Storytelling, Women.

Alaska Northwest Books, Tim Frew, Executive Editor; Tricia Brown, Acquisition Editor, PO Box 10306, Portland, OR 97296-0306, 503-226-2402, Fax 503-223-1410, editorial@gacpc.com. 1959. Non-fiction. "We do not want to receive unsolicited manuscripts—query letters and proposals only, please. We publish primarily regional nonfiction in the following subject areas: nature and the environment, travel, Native heritage, cooking, essays of place, regional history, and adventure literature. Our books are centered on Alaska and the Pacific Northwest. We publish some children's books, most of which are targeted to the geographic regions and subject areas in which we publish books for an adult audience. Some recent authors are Loretta Outwater Cox (*The Winter Walk*) and Kaylene Johnson (*Portrait of the Alaska Railroad*). Manuscript submission guidelines available with SASE. No poetry please." avg. press run 8M. Pub'd 8 titles 2005; expects 8 titles 2006, 10 titles 2007. Discounts: standard discounts described in catalog. Reporting time: 3-6 months. Simultaneous submissions accepted: no. Publishes 3% of manuscripts submitted. Payment: royalty on net; payments twice annually. Copyrights for author. Subjects: Alaska, Animals, Cooking, Earth, Natural History, Gardening, Native American, Non-Fiction, Pacific Northwest, Transportation.

ALASKA QUARTERLY REVIEW, Ronald Spatz, Fiction Editor, Executive Editor, University of Alaska-Anchorage, 3211 Providence Drive, Anchorage, AK 99508, 907-786-6916. 1981. Poetry, fiction, parts-of-novels, long-poems, plays, non-fiction. "We are looking for high quality traditional and unconventional fiction, poetry, short plays, and literary nonfiction. Unsolicited manuscripts welcome between August 15 and May 15." circ. 2.7M. 2/yr. Pub'd 2 issues 2005; expects 2 issues 2006, 2 issues 2007. sub. price $10; per copy $6.95; sample $6. Back issues: $6 and up. 250pp. Reporting time: 6-15 weeks. Publishes less than 1% of manuscripts submitted. Payment: 1 contributor's copy and a one-year subscription; additional payment depends on terms of grants. Copyrighted, reverts to author. Subjects: Drama, Essays, Fiction, Literary Review,

Literature (General), Memoirs, Non-Fiction, Novels, Poetry, Prose, Short Stories, Writers/Writing.

ALBERTA HISTORY, Historical Society of Alberta, Hugh A. Dempsey, 95 Holmwood Ave NW, Calgary Alberta T2K 2G7, Canada, 403-289-8149. 1953. Articles, reviews, non-fiction. "3.5M to 5M word articles on Western Canadian History." circ. 1.6M. 4/yr. Pub'd 4 issues 2005; expects 4 issues 2006, 4 issues 2007. sub. price $25; per copy $5.50; sample free. Back issues: $5.50. Discounts: 33%. 28pp. Reporting time: 2 months. Simultaneous submissions accepted: no. Publishes 50% of manuscripts submitted. Payment: nil. Copyrighted. Pub's reviews: 12 in 2005. §In our field-Western Canadian History. No ads. Subjects: History, Native American.

Albion Press, 14100 Tamiami Trail E., Lot 348, Naples, FL 34114-8485, 314-962-7808 phone/Fax, e-mail albionpr@stlnet.com.

Alcatraz Editions, Gary Young, 3965 Bonny Doon Road, Santa Cruz, CA 95060. 1978. Poetry, fiction, articles, art, photos, cartoons, satire, criticism, reviews, music, long-poems, collages. "See *Alcatraz 3* for current biases. No new books until further notice." avg. press run 500. Pub'd 1 title 2005. Discounts: 40% to trade on orders of 3 or more. 80-120pp. Subject: Translation.

Alegra House Publishers, Robert C. Peters, Managing Editor; Linda Marado, Co-Editor; Edward Amicucci, Co-Editor, PO Box 1443-D, Warren, OH 44482, 216-372-2951. 1985. Non-fiction. "Major goals/objectives: 1) Provide self-help adult and childrens' books(divorce, war, learning, relaxation), 2) self-help cassette tape (divorce, learning, relaxation)." avg. press run 5M. Pub'd 4 titles 2005; expects 6 titles 2006, 6 titles 2007. Discounts: bookstores 40%, distributors 50%, 20% STOP. 224pp. Reporting time: 3 months. Simultaneous submissions accepted: yes. Publishes 2% of manuscripts submitted. Payment: negotiable. Does not copyright for author. Subjects: Children, Youth, Drugs, Family, Psychology.

‡**THE ALEMBIC,** Department of English, Providence College, Providence, RI 02918-0001. 1920. Poetry, fiction, articles, art, photos, interviews, reviews, long-poems, collages, plays, concrete art. "Recent contributors include Mark Rudman, James Merrill, Ai, C.D. Wright, Jane Lunin Perel, Martha Collins, William Matthews, Bruce Smith. Looking for exploratory poetry, fiction, art in black and white, and reviews." circ. 4M. 1/yr. Pub'd 1 issue 2005; expects 1 issue 2006, 1 issue 2007. sub. price $15/2 years; per copy $8. 200pp. Reporting time: 4 months. Simultaneous submissions accepted: no. Publishes 15% of manuscripts submitted. Payment: copies. Copyrighted, reverts to author. Pub's reviews: 5 in 2005. §Poetry, fiction, literary criticism. Ads: $75. Subjects: Drama, Gay, Music, Poetry, Prose, Reviews, Short Stories.

Aletheia Publications, Inc., Carolyn D. Smith, Publisher; Guy J. Smith, Managing Editor, 46 Bell Hollow Road, Putnam Valley, NY 10579-1426, 845-526-2873, Fax 845-526-2905. 1993. Non-fiction. "Short-run (1M-2M) paperbacks for tightly targeted markets, especially works dealing with the attitudes and experiences of expatriate and repatriate Americans and with running a freelance business." avg. press run 1M. Pub'd 5 titles 2005; expects 2 titles 2007. Discounts: 4-5 25%, 6-99 40%, 100+ 50%. 150-250pp. Reporting time: 2-3 months. Simultaneous submissions accepted: yes. Publishes a very small % of manuscripts submitted. Payment: 10%. Copyrights for author. Subjects: Editing, Government, How-To, Psychology, Sociology.

Al-Galaxy Publishing Corporation, Martin Mathias, PO Box 2591, Wichita, KS 67201, 316-651-0464, Fax 316-651-0461, email: sales@algalaxypress.com. 1994. Reviews, non-fiction. avg. press run 100M. Pub'd 1 title 2005; expects 3 titles 2006, 5 titles 2007. Discounts: 2-4 books 20%, 5-9 30%, 10-24 40%, 25-49 42%, 50-74 44%, 75-99 46%, 100-199 48%, 20-499 50%, 500+ 52%. 180pp. Reporting time: 60 days. Simultaneous submissions accepted: yes. Publishes 10% of manuscripts submitted. Payment: 8-10% of net (agreed fraction paid in advance). Copyrights for author unless he/she requests otherwise. Subjects: New Age, Physics, Religion, Self-Help, Sex, Sexuality.

Alice James Books, April Ossmann, Executive Director, University of Maine at Farmington, 238 Main Street, Farmington, ME 04938-1911, 207-778-7071 phone/Fax, ajb@umf.maine.edu. 1973. Poetry. "Alice James Books is a nonprofit cooperative poetry press. Named after Alice James—the sister of novelist Henry James and philosopher William James—whose fine journal and gift for writing were unrecognized within her lifetime, the press seeks out and publishes the best contemporary poetry by both established and beginning poets, with particular emphasis on involving poets in the publishing process. Since 1994, the press has been affiliated with the University of Maine at Farmington. The cooperative selects manuscripts for publication through both regional and national competitions: the New England/New York Award, and the Beatrice Hawley Award. Winners of regional awards become active cooperative members, judging future contests and participating in editorial and executive decisions. National awards do not carry a cooperative work commitment. Known for its commitment to emerging and early career poets, AJB has published books by Jane Kenyon, Jean Valentine, B.H. Fairchild, Forrest Hamer, Richard McCann, Matthea Harvey, Donald Revell, Sarah Manguso, and Larissa Szporluk." avg. press run 1.5M. Pub'd 6 titles 2005; expects 5 titles 2006, 6 titles 2007. 80pp. Reporting time: 2-4 months. We accept simultaneous submissions if notified. Publishes 1% of manuscripts submitted. Payment: no royalties; author receives cash award as part of cooperative's contract with author. Copyrights for author.

Subjects: Poetry, Women.

•ALIMENTUM - The Literature of Food, Paulette Licitra, Publisher-Editor; Peter Selgin, Editor; Cortney Davis, Poetry Editor, P. O. Box 776, New York, NY 10163, info@alimentumjournal.com www.alimentumjournal.com. 2005. Poetry, fiction, art, interviews, parts-of-novels, long-poems, non-fiction. ''We publish original ficiton, poetry, and creative nonfiction all relating to a food theme. Recent contributors have included Oliver Sacks, Mark Kurlansky, Cortney Davis, Carly Sachs, Esther Cohen, Clifford A. Wright, Janna MaMahan.'' 2/yr. Expects 2 issues 2006, 2 issues 2007. sub. price $18; per copy $10; sample $10. Back issues: $10. Discounts: 20-55%. 128pp. Reporting time: 3 months. Simultaneous submissions accepted: Yes. Payment: contributor copies. Copyrighted, reverts to author. Subjects: Cooking, Food, Eating.

all nations press, Catherine McCormick, po box 601, White Marsh, VA 23183, 757-581-4063, www.allnationspress.com. 2002. Poetry, non-fiction. ''All Nations Press publishes quality poetry and non-fiction from new and established writers. We pride ourselves in the top quality of the writing and the presentation of the book.'' avg. press run 1000. Pub'd 4 titles 2005; expects 5 titles 2006, 5 titles 2007. Discounts: 50% discount to all distributors and bookstores, etc.. 150pp. Reporting time: one month. Simultaneous submissions accepted: Yes. Publishes 10% of manuscripts submitted. Payment: varies. Copyrights for author. Subjects: Absurdist, African-American, Memoirs, Non-Fiction, Poetry, Post Modern, Russia, Travel.

ALL ROUND, Tilke Elkins, PO Box 10193, Eugene, OR 97440-2193, 541-431-3390, nathen@allroundmagazine.com, www.allroundmagazine.com. 1999. Fiction, articles, art, photos, cartoons, interviews, reviews, letters, collages, non-fiction. ''ALL ROUND is a full-color, lavishly hand-illustrated magazine for children. Theme issues feature carefully researched and unusual facts on subjects like Trees, Being Born and Music. Introduces children to the intricate nature of the universe. Printed on 100% post-consumer recycled paper and ad-free. Each issue features 50 drawings by readers based on its theme. Before sending us anything, call or email for information on the theme of the upcoming magazine and to find out what we're currently looking for. What we usually use are hand-illustrated two page spreads with total dimensions of 16" wide by 10" high. Subjects are approached with a sustainable and non-ageist perspective.'' circ. 3M. 2/yr. Pub'd 2 issues 2005; expects 2 issues 2006, 2 issues 2007. sub. price $19/18 months, $36/3 years; per copy $6.95; sample $6.95. Back issues: $9. 48pp. Simultaneous submissions accepted: yes. Payment: no. Copyrighted, reverts to author. Pub's reviews: 1 in 2005. §Call our office for the upcoming theme. Subjects: Arts, Aviation, Birds, Children, Youth, Comics, Counter-Culture, Alternatives, Communes, Ecology, Foods, Energy, Games, Gardening, Humor, Music, Pacific Northwest, Science, Transportation.

THE ALLEGHENY REVIEW, Beata Gomulak, Senior Editor, Box 32, Allegheny College, Meadville, PA 16335, 814-332-6553. 1983. Poetry, fiction, art, photos, criticism, long-poems, plays, non-fiction. ''Editorial staff changes yearly. Publish work by undergraduate college students only, from across the country. *The Allegheny Review* has been used as a classroom text. National edition founded 1983; a local version under similar names has been published since 1983.'' circ. 100+. 1/yr. Pub'd 1 issue 2005; expects 1 issue 2006, 1 issue 2007. sub. price $4; per copy $4; sample $4. Back issues: $3. Discounts: 25 copies, $2 each for use in classroom. 100pp. Reporting time: 4 months after deadline. Simultaneous submissions accepted: no. Publishes 5% of manuscripts submitted. Payment: 1 copy, $150 to contest winners (best submission each genre; poetry, fiction, nonfiction, art). Copyrighted, rights revert to author upon request. Ads: none. Subjects: Drama, Fiction, Literary Review, Photography, Poetry.

Glen Allen Press, Craig Biddle, Sarah Peyton, 4036-D Cox Road, Glen Allen, VA 23060, 804-747-1776, Fax 804-273-0500, mail@glenallenpress.com, www.glenallenpress.com. 2002. Art, non-fiction. ''We publish non-fiction books aimed at helping customers to pursue, protect, and enjoy their life-serving values. Philosophically, we stand for rational self-interest, individual rights, and laissez-faire capitalism. In a word, we advocate Objectivism, the philosophy of Ayn Rand, and we are dedicated to publishing titles that demonstrate or apply the principles of this philosophy.'' avg. press run 3M. Pub'd 1 title 2005; expects 1 title 2006, 2 titles 2007. 160pp. Reporting time: 8 weeks. Simultaneous submissions accepted: yes. Payment: varies. Copyrights for author. Subjects: Arts, Ethics, Non-Fiction, Parenting, Philosophy, Politics.

Allworth Press, Tad Crawford, Publisher, Nicole Potter, 10 East 23rd Street, Suite 510, New York, NY 10010, 212-777-8395, Fax 212-777-8261, Pub@allworth.com, www.allworth.com. 1989. Art, photos, criticism, music, non-fiction. ''Allworth Press publishes business, legal, career guidance, and self-help books for creative individuals in the visual, performing, writing and fine arts as well as collections of criticism in aesthetics and graphic design. Allworth also publishes books for the general public on business, law and personal finance. Helios Press, an imprint of Allworth's parent company, Allworth Communications, Inc., features new and re-issued works in psychology, spirituality, and current affairs.'' avg. press run 5M. Pub'd 30 titles 2005; expects 30 titles 2006, 30 titles 2007. 225pp. Reporting time: varies. Simultaneous submissions accepted: yes. Publishes 2% of manuscripts submitted. Copyrights for author. Subjects: Arts, Cartoons, Comics, Communication, Journalism, Crafts, Hobbies, Design, Desktop Publishing, Graphic Design, How-To, Law,

Music, New Age, Photography, Visual Arts, Writers/Writing.

Ally Press, Paul Feroe, 524 Orleans St., St. Paul, MN 55107, 651-291-2652, pferoe@comcast.net. 1973. Poetry. "The Ally Press is a publisher and distributor of books and tapes by Robert Bly. It will seek to maintain a blacklist of all Bly material in print through its mail-order service. In addition it publishes a quarterly newsletter detailing Bly's current reading schedule. Those desiring these free mailings can write care of the press. Ally Press is not accepting any manuscripts at this time." avg. press run 1.5M. Expects 2 titles 2007. Discounts: 1-4 20%, 4-49 40%. 60pp. Payment: in copies. Copyrights for author. Subject: Poetry.

ALMOST NORMAL COMICS and Other Oddities, W. E. Elliott, Almost Normal Comics, PO Box 12822, Ft. Huachuca, AZ 85670, flesh_on_bone@yahoo.com, http://almostnormalcomics.tripod.com. 2001. Fiction, art, cartoons, interviews, letters. "Almost Normal Comics and Other Oddities is an anthology of alternative comics and weird stories showcasing the talents of artists and writers working in the small press." circ. 2000. 1/yr. Pub'd 1 issue 2005; expects 1 issue 2006, 1 issue 2007. price per copy $5.50; sample $3.50. Back issues: $3.50. Discounts: 5 copies 50%. 88pp. Reporting time: 3 to 4 weeks. Simultaneous submissions accepted: Yes. Publishes 80% of manuscripts submitted. Payment: Complimentary copies of the issue work appears in. Copyrighted, reverts to author. No ads. Subjects: Comics, Zines.

Alms House Press, Alana Sherman, Lorraine S. DeGennaro, PO Box 218, Woodbourne, NY 12788-0218. 1985. Poetry. "16-24 pages of poetry that works as a collection. We seek variety and excellence in many styles. Each year we publish one or two chapbooks. Costs: $9 handling/reading fee. Chapbook sent to each contributor. Recent winners include Lenore Balliro, and William Vernon." avg. press run 200. Pub'd 4 titles 2005; expects 3-4 titles 2006, 3-4 titles 2007. Discounts: 50% bookstores; $10 set of five. 20pp. Reporting time: 4 months. We do not accept simultaneous submissions. Payment: 15 copies to the author. Copyrights for author. Subject: Poetry.

ALONE TOGETHER, Raven Publishing, Inc., Janet Hill, Editor, PO Box 2885, Norris, MT 59745, 406-685-3545, Fax 406-685-3599, at@ravenpublishing.net, toll free: 866-685-3545. 1997. Poetry, fiction, articles, art, photos, cartoons, interviews, satire, criticism, reviews, letters, collages, news items, non-fiction. "A bi-monthly newsletter/forum for survivers of child abuse." 6/yr. Pub'd 6 issues 2005; expects 6 issues 2006, 6 issues 2007. sub. price $18, $32/2 years, $45/3 years; per copy $3; sample $3. Back issues: $3. 20pp. Reporting time: 30 days. Simultaneous submissions accepted: yes. Publishes 85% of manuscripts submitted. Payment: free copy of issue in which work is published. Copyrighted, reverts to author. Pub's reviews: 2 in 2005. §Books on child abuse, trauma-based disorders, recovery methods, therapy. Ads: $6.50/$4. Subjects: Alcohol, Alcoholism, Alternative Medicine, Birth, Birth Control, Population, Family, Feminism, Gender Issues, Non-Violence, Occult, Poetry, Prison, Religion, Self-Help, Sex, Sexuality, Sexual Abuse, War.

Alpha Beat Press (see also ALPHA BEAT SOUP), Dave Christy, Ana Christy, 806 East Ridge Ave., Sellersville, PA 18960-2723. 1987. Poetry, fiction, articles, art, photos, interviews, long-poems. avg. press run 300. Pub'd 24 titles 2005. Broadside. Reporting time: immediately. Simultaneous submissions accepted: yes. Publishes 35% of manuscripts submitted. Payment: copies. Copyrights for author. Subjects: Beat, Jack Kerouac, Poetry.

•ALPHA BEAT SOUP, Alpha Beat Press, Dave Christy, 806 E. Ridge Avenue, Sellersville, PA 18960, 215,534,9409, dave421165@verizon.net.

Alpine Guild, Inc., PO Box 4848, Dillon, CO 80435, Fax 970-262-9378, information@alpineguild.com. 1977. Non-fiction. "Publish books only, aimed at specific identifiable, reachable audiences. The book must provide information of value to the audience." Pub'd 3 titles 2005; expects 5 titles 2006, 3 titles 2007. Discounts: standard. Reporting time: within 30 days. Payment: depends on book, audience, etc. Copyrights for author. Subjects: Disabled, Education, Handicapped, Health, Leadership, Management, Medicine, Psychology, Publishing.

Alpine Press, S.F. Achenbach, PO Box 1930, Mills, WY 82644, 307-234-1990. 1985. Non-fiction. "*How To Be Your Own Veterinarian (Sometimes)*, by Ruth B. James, D.V.M. We do not read unsolicited manuscripts." avg. press run 15M. Pub'd 2 titles 2005; expects 1 title 2006, 2 titles 2007. Discounts: 1-2 copies 20%, 3-9 25%, 10+ 30%, freight paid with prepaid orders. 300pp. Reporting time: long. Payment: negotiated individually on merits of book. Copyrights for author. Subject: Agriculture.

Alpine Publications, Inc., Betty McKinney, Managing Editor, 225 S. Madison Avenue, Loveland, CO 80537, 970-667-9317, Fax 970-667-9157, alpinepubl@aol.com, www.alpinepub.com. 1975. Non-fiction. "We publish nonfiction hardback & trade paperback how-to books for the dog, horse, and pet markets. About half of our sales are by mail order. Our books are high quality, in-depth, thorough coverage of a specific subject or breed. Authors must know their field and be able to provide useful, how-to information with illustrations." avg. press run 2M. Pub'd 7 titles 2005; expects 10 titles 2006, 10 titles 2007. Discounts: 1-4 20%, 5-20 35%, 21-74 40%, 75-99 42%, 100-149 45%. 200pp. Reporting time: 8-12 weeks. Payment: royalty. Copyrights for author.

Subjects: Animals, Earth, Natural History.

Alta Research, Reed White, 131 NW 4th Street #290, Corvallis, OR 97330-4702, 877-360-ALTA, 541-929-5738, alta@alta-research.com. 1983. Photos, non-fiction. "Desire write-ups and information on recreation within easy access of airports in the western states." avg. press run 10M. Pub'd 4 titles 2005; expects 3 titles 2006, 3 titles 2007. Discounts: 2 books 20%, 3-25%, 6-30%, 12-35%, 24-40%, 48-50%. 500pp. Reporting time: 30 days. Payment: negotiable. Does not copyright for author. Subjects: Aviation, The West.

Altair Publications, Edmond Wollmann, PO Box 221000, San Diego, CA 92192-1000, 858-453-2342, e-mail altair@astroconsulting.com. 1995. Art, photos, interviews. "Mostly academically oriented texts." avg. press run 5M. Pub'd 1 title 2005; expects 2 titles 2006, 3 titles 2007. Discounts: 40%. 300pp. Reporting time: 6-8 weeks. Simultaneous submissions accepted: no. Payment: negotiated. Copyrights for author. Subjects: Astrology, Metaphysics, Psychology, Spiritual, Theosophical.

AltaMira Press, Mitchell Allen, Publisher, 1630 N. Main Street #367, Walnut Creek, CA 94596, 925-938-7243, Fax 925-933-9720. 1995. Non-fiction. "AltaMira Press, a division of Rowman & Littlefield Publishers Inc., entered into a publishing agreement with the American Association for State and Local History Press in September, 1995. Under this agreement, AltaMira has assumed marketing, publishing, distributing, and selling of all book titles previously published by American Association for State and Local History Press." avg. press run 2M. Pub'd 40 titles 2005; expects 50 titles 2006, 60 titles 2007. Discounts: AASLH members 20%; trade 20%-40%. 200-300pp. Reporting time: 3-4 months. Payment: every 12 months. Copyrights for author. Subjects: Education, History.

Altamont Press, Inc. (see also FIBERARTS), Rob Pulleyn, Publisher, 67 Broadway Street, Asheville, NC 28801-2919, 704-253-0468. 1973. Art, photos. "Looking for a broad spectrum of high quality crafts/arts books." avg. press run 7.5M. Pub'd 50 titles 2005; expects 50 titles 2006, 50 titles 2007. Discounts: all depend on volume, college and university bookstores, foreign; all other wholesale books through Sterling Publishing Co. 150+pp. Reporting time: 1-2 months. Simultaneous submissions accepted: yes. Publishes 10% of manuscripts submitted. Payment: 5%+. Copyrights for author. Subjects: Arts, Crafts, Hobbies, Fashion, How-To, Quilting, Sewing, Visual Arts, Weaving.

ALTERNATIVE EDUCATION RESOURCE ORGANIZATION, Jerry Mintz, 417 Roslyn Road, Roslyn Heights, NY 11577, 516-621-2195, Fax 516-625-3257, jerryaero@aol.com. 1989. Articles, photos, interviews, satire, reviews, letters, news items, non-fiction. "Covers the latest developments and news in alternative education." circ. 700. 4/yr. Pub'd 3 issues 2005; expects 3 issues 2006, 4 issues 2007. sub. price $18.50; per copy $4.50. Back issues: $4.50. 24pp. Payment: none. Pub's reviews: 12 in 2005. §Only alternative education. Ads: subscription. Subject: Education.

ALTERNATIVE HARMONIES LITERARY & ARTS MAGAZINE, New Dawn Unlimited, Inc., Jerri Hardesty, 1830 Marvel Road, Brierfield, AL 35035, 205-665-7904, Fax 205-665-2500, e-mail wytrabbit1@aol.com. 1997. Poetry, fiction, art, photos, cartoons, long-poems, plays, non-fiction. "Any length is fine. Recent contributors: Errol Miller, Susan S. Hahn, Iris Schwartz." circ. 300. 4/yr. Pub'd 4 issues 2005; expects 4 issues 2006, 4 issues 2007. sub. price $15; per copy $4; sample $3. Back issues: $2 or free if one sends postage ($1). Discounts: $1 each for 20 or more. Also considers this rate for worthwhile causes. 40pp. Reporting time: 3-6 months. Simultaneous submissions accepted: yes. Publishes 15% of manuscripts submitted. Payment: copies. Not copyrighted, rights remain with author. Ads: trade only.

ALTERNATIVE PRESS INDEX, Julie Adamo, Co-Editor; Charles D'Adamo, Co-Editor; Erin Hall, Co-Editor; Caroline Nappo, Co-Editor; Abigail Anzalone, Co-Editor; Elissa Thomas, Co-Editor, Alternative Press Center, Inc., PO Box 33109, Baltimore, MD 21218, 410-243-2471, altpress@altpress.org. 1969. "The *Alternative Press Index* is a quarterly subject index to over 300 newspapers, magazines, and journals from around the world that focus on social theory and movements." circ. 700. 4/yr. Pub'd 4 issues 2005; expects 4 issues 2006, 4 issues 2007. sub. price $400 libraries, $75 individuals; sample free. Back issues: 50% discount if 3 or more back volumes are purchased. Discounts: $75 individuals, high schools, movement groups. 200+pp. Copyrighted, reverts to author. No ads accepted. Subject: Indexes & Abstracts.

ALTERNATIVE PRESS REVIEW, Jason McQuinn, Allan Antliff, Thomas Wheeler, PO Box 6245, Arlington, VA 22206. 1993. Articles, art, photos, cartoons, interviews, satire, criticism, reviews, music, letters, collages, news items, non-fiction. "Reprints from alternative press magazines, tabloids, newsletter & zines, plus original material covering the entire alternative press/alternative media scene, with an emphasis on periodical reviews & other media reviews." circ. 8M. 4/yr. Pub'd 2 issues 2005; expects 4 issues 2006, 4 issues 2007. sub. price $16; per copy $4.95; sample $6. Discounts: wholesale 5-19 copies 20%, 20-59 40%, 60-99 45%, 100-249 50%, 250+ 55%. 68pp. Reporting time: 2-3 months. Simultaneous submissions accepted: yes. Publishes 5% of manuscripts submitted. Payment: 5¢/word for original contributions, or 2.5¢/word for reprints. Not copyrighted. Pub's reviews: 200 in 2005. §Alternative press, alternative media, alternative social issues & movements, critiques of mainstream media. Ads: $300/$187.50/$135 1/4 page/$120 1/6 page. Subjects: Communication,

Journalism, Counter-Culture, Alternatives, Communes, Magazines, Reprints, Reviews.

ALT-J: Association for Learning Technology Journal, University Of Wales Press, Grainne Conole, Editor; Jane Seale, Deputy Editor; Martin Oliver, Deputy Editor, 10 Columbus Walk, Brigantine Place, Cardiff CF10 4UP, Wales, 044-029-2049-6899, Fax 44-029-2049-6108, press@press.wales.ac.uk, www.wales.ac.uk/press. 1993. "An international journal devoted to research and good practice in the use of learning technologies within higher education." 2/yr. sub. price £90 institutions, £60 individuals. Discounts: 10%. 80pp. Subjects: Computers, Calculators, Education.

Always Productions, PO Box 33836, San Diego, CA 92163.

Amadeus Press, Carol Flannery, Gail Siragusa, 512 Newark Pompton Tpke., Pompton Plains, NJ 07444, 973-835-6375 x204, fax 973-835-6504, www.amadeuspress.com. 1987. avg. press run 3000. Pub'd 10 titles 2005; expects 22 titles 2006, 22 titles 2007. Discounts: 1-4; 20%5-100; 47%100+; 50%. 300pp. Reporting time: 4-6 weeks. We do not usually accept simultaneous submissions. Publishes 10% of manuscripts submitted. Payment: Generally 7-1/2% for paperback, 10% cloth. Does not copyright for author. Subject: Music.

Amador Publishers, Adela Amador, Proprietor; Harry Willson, Editor-in-Chief, 607 Isleta Blvd. SW, Albuquerque, NM 87105-3827, 505-877-4395, 800-730-4395, Fax 505-877-4395, harry@nmia.com, www.amadorbooks.com. 1986. Fiction. "Not open for submissions of new material until after 2000." avg. press run 3M. Pub'd 2 titles 2005; expects 2 titles 2007. Discounts: bookstores 40%, wholesalers 50%. 176-250pp. Reporting time: varies. Publishes less than 1% of manuscripts submitted. Payment: varies. Copyrights for author. Subjects: Autobiography, Cooking, Fantasy, Fiction, Health, Romance, Southwest.

AMBIT, Martin Bax, 17 Priory Gardens, London, N6 5QY, England, 0181-340-3566. 1959. Poetry, fiction, art, photos, reviews, long-poems. "Always looking for material which excites and interests. Suggest contributors read the magazine before they submit." circ. 3M. 4/yr. Pub'd 4 issues 2005; expects 4 issues 2006, 4 issues 2007. sub. price £24 UK, £26 ($52) USA and overseas; per copy £6 UK, £8 overseas; sample £6 UK, £8 overseas. Back issues: recent back nos. £6 UK, £8 overseas; Archival issues £10. Discounts: bookstores 1-11 25%, 12+ 33%. 96pp. Reporting time: 4 months. Publishes less than 5% of manuscripts submitted. Payment: by arrangement. Copyrighted, reverts to author. Pub's reviews: 30+ in 2005. §Poetry. Ads: b&w: £325/£190/£115 1/4 page;colour £500/£280; serial ad discount 20% for 4 issues. Subjects: Fiction, Poetry.

AMBIT : JOURNAL OF POETRY AND POETICS, furniture_press, Christophe Casamassima, 19 Murdock Road, Baltimore, MD 21212, 410.718.6574. 2003. Poetry. circ. 200. 2/yr. Pub'd 1 issue 2005; expects 1 issue 2006, 2 issues 2007. sub. price 15; per copy 8; sample 8. Back issues: 8 and 20. 60pp. Reporting time: 4 months. Simultaneous submissions accepted: Yes. Publishes 10% of manuscripts submitted. Payment: one copy. Copyrighted. Pub's reviews: none in 2005. §experimental poetry, chapbooks, magazines, zines, pamphlets, books. Ads: 25 whole page15 half page10 quarter page. Subjects: Poetry, Reviews.

AMERICA, 106 West 56th Street, New York, NY 10019, 212-581-4640. 1909. Poetry, articles, cartoons, interviews, reviews, letters, non-fiction. "*America* is a journal of opinion that publishes about 10 poems a year selected from over 1,000 submissions." circ. 40M. 41/yr. Pub'd 41 issues 2005; expects 41 issues 2006, 41 issues 2007. sub. price $43; per copy $2.25; sample $2.25. Back issues: $2.25. Discounts: call for details. 32pp. Reporting time: 3 weeks. Simultaneous submissions accepted: no. Payment: yes. Copyrighted, shared rights. Pub's reviews: 200+ in 2005. §General interest. Ads: call for ad brochure or ads@americapress.org.

America West Publishers, George Green, PO Box 2208, Carson City, NV 89702, 800-729-4131. 1985. Non-fiction. "New Age, new science & technology, new spirituality, metaphysics. Some recent contributors: Dr. Taki Anagoston, Dr. Eva Snead, and John Coleman, PhD." avg. press run 5M. Pub'd 14 titles 2005; expects 10 titles 2006. Discounts: bookstores 40%, distributors 50-60%, bulk (over 500) 50%, libraries 20%. 250pp. Reporting time: 4-6 weeks. Publishes 1% of manuscripts submitted. Payment: twice yearly—10% of wholesale net, 5% of retail price. Copyrights for author. Subjects: Earth, Natural History, Geology, Medicine, Politics, Psychology, Religion, Spiritual.

American & World Geographic Publishing, Barbara Fifer, Special Projects Editor, PO Box 5630, Helena, MT 59601, 406-443-2842. 1970. Photos, non-fiction. "We are now emphasizing packaging." avg. press run 7.5M. Pub'd 16 titles 2005; expects 18 titles 2006, 15 titles 2007. Discounts: available upon request. 104pp. Reporting time: 12 weeks. We accept simultaneous submissions if marked as such. Publishes 5% of manuscripts submitted. Payment: varies, we have photo-editorial mix. Does not copyright for author. Subjects: Midwest, Photography, Travel, The West.

American Book Publishing (see also Bedside Books), PO Box 65624, Salt Lake City, UT 84165, 801-486-8639, Fax 801-382-0881, nospam@american-book.com, www.american-book.com. Fiction, non-fiction. "Please submit electronically only, we are ecology minded and you can obtain our submission information at our website." Pub'd 70 titles 2005; expects 75 titles 2006, 75 titles 2007. 250pp. Reporting time: 30 days. Copyrights for author.

AMERICAN BOOK REVIEW, Charles Harris, Publisher; Charlie Alcorn, Managing Editor; Jeffrey Di Leo, Executive Editor; John Tytell, Executive Editor, Illinois State University, Campus Box 4241, Normal, IL 61790-4241, 309-438-3026, Fax 309-438-3523. 1977. Reviews. "Length: ideally, 750-1.5M words. Reviewers should be primarily writers. Contributors: Marjorie Perloff, Michael Joyce, Steve Tomasula, Alicia Ostriker, Lance Olsen, Brian Evenson, etc." circ. 5M. 6/yr. Pub'd 6 issues 2005; expects 6 issues 2006, 6 issues 2007. sub. price $30 libraries & institutions, $35 foreign, $24 individuals, $40/2 years individuals; per copy $4; sample $4. Back issues: $4 (check w/office). 33pp. Reporting time: 1-2 months. Payment: $50 honorarium per review, or subscription. Copyrighted. Pub's reviews: 205 in 2005. §Literary or closely allied fields. Ads: check w/advertising manager. Subject: Literary Review.

American Canadian Publishers, Inc., Arthur Goodson, Editorial Director; Herman Zaage, Art Director, PO Box 4595, Santa Fe, NM 87502-4595, 505-983-8484, Fax 505-983-8484. 1972. Poetry, fiction, articles, art, photos, interviews, satire, criticism, reviews, music, letters, parts-of-novels, long-poems, collages, plays, concrete art, news items, non-fiction. "We are categorically against realism in the novel simply because it is by now a bankrupt form. We reject orthodox "story" because it generally tortures the truth to fit the formula. We support the novel that investigates "inner consciousness," that is multi-dimensional and open-structured in language and thought. Interested? Send SASE for free Catalog full of new examples. *No unsolicited manuscripts*. Thanks!" avg. press run 1.5M-3M. Pub'd 2 titles 2005; expects 2 titles 2006, 6 titles 2007. Discounts: 40% to dealers; 50% bulk-class adoptions: rates negotiable. 200pp. Payment: negotiable. Copyrights for author. Subjects: Arts, Criticism, Dada.

American Carriage House Publishing (see also LIFETIME MAGAZINE), Louann Carroll, P.O. Box 1130, Nevada City, California, CA 95959, 530.470.0720. 2003. Articles, news items, non-fiction. "Our mission is to educate the public on adoption, family and children's issues. Recent contributors are: Mardie Caldwell, Louann Carroll, and Heather Feathestone. l." avg. press run 3500. Expects 3 titles 2006, 5 titles 2007. Discounts: Family, children, self-help, adoption. 410pp. Reporting time: 6 months. Simultaneous submissions accepted: No. Publishes 6% of manuscripts submitted. Payment: We are not accepting new submissions at this time. Copyrights for author. Subjects: Adoption, Children, Youth, Family.

THE AMERICAN DISSIDENT, G. Tod Slone, 1837 Main Street, Concord, MA 01742-3811, todslone@yahoo.com. 1998. Poetry, articles, art, cartoons, satire, criticism, reviews, non-fiction. "One page max. for poems, 750 words max. for essays. Material should be WRITTEN ON THE EDGE WITH A DASH OF RISK AND PERSONAL EXPERIENCE AND INVOLVEMENT. Suggested areas of critique include, though not exclusively, corruption in academe, poet laureates paid for by the Library of Congress, sell-out beatniks and hippies, artistes non-engags, politically-controlled state and national cultural councils, media whores, Medicare-bilking doctors, boards of wealthy used-car-salesperson trustees of public institutions, justice-indifferent lawyers, autocratic judges, thug cops, other dubious careerists, the happy-face culture of extreme denial and aberrant rationalization, the democratic sham masking the oligarchic plutocracy and, more generally, the human veil of charade placed upon the universe. If you are a professor, for example, send something critical of your college, not the President of the USA. Submissions should be negative, controversial, and confrontational with a strong dose of visceral indignation." circ. 200. 2/yr. Pub'd 2 issues 2005; expects 2 issues 2006, 2 issues 2007. sub. price $16; per copy $8; sample $8. Back issues: $8. Discounts: 10 copies for $70. 64pp. Reporting time: 1 week - 2 months. Simultaneous submissions accepted: yes. Publishes 4% of manuscripts submitted. Payment: 1 copy. Copyrighted, reverts to author. Pub's reviews: 2 in 2005. §Criticism, parrhesia, dissidence, poetry. Ads: $40/$20. Subjects: Absurdist, Anarchist, Arts, Beat, Bilingual, Cartoons, Counter-Culture, Alternatives, Communes, Education, Essays, Ethics, Literary Review, Literature (General), Magazines, Poetry, H.D. Thoreau.

THE AMERICAN DRIVEL REVIEW, Tara Blaine, 1425 Stuart Street #1, Longmont, CO 80501, 720-494-8719 info@americandrivelreview.com www.americandrivelreview.com. 2004. Poetry, fiction, articles, art, photos, cartoons, interviews, satire, criticism, reviews, letters, parts-of-novels, long-poems, collages, plays, concrete art, news items, non-fiction. "The American Drivel Review: A Unified Field Theory of Wit "Humor [is] the gaiety that death teaches."—Russell Edson The American Drivel Review seeks within its humble pages to: Probe the function of humor in the arts and the lives of ladies and gentlemen! Reject the base generalities of universalism in favor of a worldview that constructs reality as in Mr. Edisons Amazing Kaleido-Scopic Lenses! Capture mad-cap antics! Provoke the collusion of the reading public! Knock the pristine white satin top-hat from the crown of the monocled crowd! Affirm the existence of gorgons, ape-men, and Mr. Schrdingers unfortunate tabby-cat! Potential contributors, please post up to five pages of fiction, essay, drama, poetry, letters to the editor, reviews, illustration, advertisements, hybrid works, memoir, found art, collage, screen-plays, lyrics, academic papers, photo-graphs, journal entries, or scientific studies via United States Postal Service or Mr. Gores Magical E-Lectronic Wire Transfer. Recently published gentlefolk include Laird Hunt, Jack Collom, Willie Smith, Junior Burke, Andrew Wille, and Richard Froude." circ. 500. 4/yr. Pub'd 4 issues 2005; expects 4 issues 2006, 4 issues 2007. sub. price $20; per copy $3.50; sample $3.50. Back issues: $3.50. Discounts: 2-10 copies 50%. 70pp. Reporting time: 1-3 months. Simultaneous submissions accepted: No. Publishes 35% of manuscripts submitted. Payment: 2 contributor copies. Copyrighted, reverts to author. Pub's reviews: none in 2005. §Humor, scientific studies, abstract concepts. Subjects: Absurdist, Anarchist, Arts, Cartoons, Comics, Dada, Entertainment, Experimental, Humor, Literature (General), Non-Fiction, Poetry, Prose, Reviews, Short Stories.

AMERICAN FORESTS, Michelle Robbins, Editor, PO Box 2000, Washington, DC 20013, 202-737-1944. 1895. Articles, art, photos, interviews, reviews, news items, non-fiction. "We are looking for factual articles that are well written, well illustrated, and will inform, entertain, and perhaps inspire. *We do not accept fiction and rarely accept poetry.* We welcome informative news stories on issues of interest to American Forests readers—look for topics that touch on projects or issues in which we have been involved. Articles should be neither too elementary nor too technical. A written or e-mailed query is required; we cannot accept phone queries. Include SASE with submissions." circ. 20M. 4/yr. Pub'd 4 issues 2005; expects 4 issues 2006, 4 issues 2007. sub. price $25 membership; per copy $3; sample $2 postage w/SASE. 48pp. Reporting time: 12-16 weeks. Simultaneous submissions accepted: yes. Payment: full length feature articles, *with photo or other illustrative support* ranges from $300 to $1,800; cover photos $400. Copyrighted, reverts to author. Pub's reviews: 6 in 2005. §Trees, forests, forest policy, nature guides, forestry. Ads: available on request. Subjects: Conservation, Earth, Natural History, Ecology, Foods, Nature.

AMERICAN HARMONICA, 104 Highland Avenue, Battle Creek, MI 49015.

AMERICAN HIKER, American Hiking Society, Gwyn Hicks, 1422 Fenwick Lane, Silver Spring, MD 20910-2160, 301-565-6704. 1977. Articles, photos, cartoons, interviews, reviews, news items. circ. 10M. 6/yr. Pub'd 6 issues 2005; expects 6 issues 2006, 6 issues 2007. sub. price $25; sample $2. Back issues: $4 if available. 32pp. Reporting time: 6 weeks. Publishes 5-10% of manuscripts submitted. Payment: $25-$50 for briefs, $75-$125 for lectures. Pub's reviews: 20 in 2005. §Books on the outdoors. Subjects: Cities, Conservation, Earth, Natural History, Environment, Sports, Outdoors.

American Hiking Society (see also AMERICAN HIKER), Darren Schwartz, 1422 Fenwick Lane, Silver Spring, MD 20910-2160, 301-565-6704. 1977. Articles, photos, interviews, reviews, news items. avg. press run 10M. Pub'd 6 titles 2005; expects 6 titles 2006, 6 titles 2007. Discounts: please inquire. 28pp. Reporting time: 6 weeks. Publishes 5% of manuscripts submitted. Payment: none. Does not copyright for author. Subjects: Conservation, Earth, Natural History, Environment, Sports, Outdoors.

American Homeowners Foundation Press, Bruce Hahn, 6776 Little Falls Road, Arlington, VA 22213, 703-536-7776, www.americanhomeowners.org. 1984. Non-fiction. "Booklets through books." avg. press run 3-10M. Pub'd 2 titles 2005; expects 3 titles 2006, 3 titles 2007. Discounts: standard. 160pp. Reporting time: varies. Payment: varies. We can copyright for author.

AMERICAN INDIAN CULTURE AND RESEARCH JOURNAL, American Indian Studies Center, Duane Champagne, 3220 Campbell Hall, Box 951548, Los Angeles, CA 90095-1548, 310-825-7315, Fax 310-206-7060, www.sscnet.ucla.edu/esp/aisc/index.html. 1972. Poetry, fiction, articles, criticism, reviews. "*AICRJ* is a multidisciplinary journal that focuses on historical and contemporary issues as they pertain to American Indians. Some poetry and fiction are also published." circ. 1.2M. 4/yr. Pub'd 4 issues 2005; expects 4 issues 2006, 4 issues 2007. sub. price $25 individuals, $60 institutions; per copy $12. Back issues: $7 (varies by year). Discounts: bookstores and jobbers 20%, 40% if 10+. 300pp. Reporting time: 4 months (articles are refereed). Simultaneous submissions accepted: no. Publishes 10% of manuscripts submitted. Payment: none. Copyrighted, rights don't revert to author, but authors have permission to reprint free. Pub's reviews: 80 in 2005. Ads: $150/$75. Subjects: Essays, Native American, Poetry.

American Indian Studies Center (see also AMERICAN INDIAN CULTURE AND RESEARCH JOURNAL), Duane Champagne, 3220 Campbell Hall, Box 951548, UCLA, Los Angeles, CA 90095-1548, 310-825-7315, Fax 310-206-7060, www.sscnet.ucla.edu/esp/aisc/index.html. 1969. Poetry, fiction, articles, non-fiction. "AISC publishes books of interest to scholars and the general public that address contemporary and historical issues as they pertain to American Indians in addition to the quarterly *American Indian Culture and Research Journal.*" avg. press run 1M-2M. Pub'd 1 title 2005; expects 4 titles 2006, 2-3 titles 2007. Discounts: bookstores and jobbers 20%, 10+ 40%. 300pp. Reporting time: 6 months. Simultaneous submissions accepted: no. Publishes 5% of manuscripts submitted. Payment: varies per project. Does not copyright for author. Subjects: Essays, Fiction, Native American, Poetry.

AMERICAN JONES BUILDING & MAINTENANCE, Missing Spoke Press, Von G. Binuia, Editor, 15 Maple St., #2, Concord, NH 03301-4202, Tel:206-218-5437; Email: vonb1@excite.com. 1997. Poetry, fiction, art, photos, interviews, satire, parts-of-novels, long-poems, non-fiction. "No line limits. No word limits. Send query with or regarding works of 9,000 or more words. Poetry, short fiction, essays, and interviews that address the interests and concerns of the working class in *American Jones Building & Maintenance.*" circ. 200. 2/yr. sub. price $12; per copy $6; sample $3. Back issues: $6. 128pp. Reporting time: 3-4 months. Simultaneous submissions accepted: yes. Publishes 2% of manuscripts submitted. Payment: various and 2 copies.

Copyrighted, reverts to author. Pub's reviews: none in 2005. §Poetry. Subjects: Americana, Charles Bukowski, Community, Conservation, Bob Dylan, Essays, Fiction, Human Rights, Labor, New England, New Hampshire, Poetry, Short Stories, Washington (state), Worker.

AMERICAN JUROR (formerly FIJACTIVIST, 1989-2004), Iloilo Marguerite Jones, PO Box 5570, Helena, MT 59604-5570, 406-442-7800. 1989. Articles, art, photos, cartoons, interviews, reviews, letters, news items, non-fiction. "Mostly in-house, but we have arranged to publish relevant articles." circ. 3M. 4/yr. Pub'd 4 issues 2005; expects 4 issues 2006, 4 issues 2007. sub. price $25; sample free info. package; sample FIJActivist $3. Discounts: $15/$10; 20 + $1 each. 12pp. Payment: none. Not copyrighted. Pub's reviews: 2 in 2005. §Law. Ads: none. Subject: Law.

American Legacy Media, William Wood D., 1544 W 1620 N STE 1-G, Clearfield, UT 84015-8243, 801-774-5472, info@americanlegacymedia.com, http://americanlegacymedia.com. 2004. Non-fiction. "Welcome to American Legacy Media Telling the stories of the American legacyWe specialize in publishing biographies, autobiographies, historic, military compilations and essays focusing on historic review." avg. press run 3000. Pub'd 2 titles 2005; expects 2 titles 2006, 2 titles 2007. Exclusive Distributor: IPG (Independent Publishers Group. Standard discount rates apply. 300pp. Reporting time: 2-3 weeks. Simultaneous submissions accepted: Yes. Publishes 10% of manuscripts submitted. Payment: Standard royalty arrangments apply. Copyrights for author. Subjects: Autobiography, Biography, History, Memoirs, Military, Veterans, Mormon, Non-Fiction, Utah, World War II.

AMERICAN LETTERS & COMMENTARY, Anna Rabinowitz, Publisher and Executive Editor, David Ray Vance; Catherine Kasper, Co-Editors, P.O. Box 830365, San Antonio, TX 78283, amerletters@satx.rr.com, www.amleters.org. 1988. Poetry, fiction, articles, art, criticism, reviews, long-poems, non-fiction. "AL&C is an eclectic literary magazine featuring innovative and challenging writing in all forms. Past contributors include Barbara Guest, Paul Hoover, Christine Hume, Amy England, Ann Lauterbach, Donald Revell, C.D. Wright, Clauda Rankine and Susan Wheeler. Particularly interested in hybrid-genre works and experimental poetics. Open to new and lively voices in all genres." circ. 1.5M. 1/yr. Pub'd 1 issue 2005; expects 1 issue 2006, 1 issue 2007. sub. price $8, $12/2 years; per copy $8; sample $6. Back issues: $6. 200pp. Reporting time: 2 - 5 months. We accept simultaneous submissions if advised. Payment: copies. Copyrighted, reverts to author. Pub's reviews: approx. 3 in 2005. §Poetry, literary fiction and nonfiction. Ads: $50/$30/exchange ads. Subjects: Essays, Experimental, Fiction, Literary Review, Poetry, Prose, Short Stories.

American Literary Press, Joe Cooney, Managing Editor, 8019 Belair Road #10, Baltimore, MD 21236, 410-882-7700, Fax 410-882-7703, amerlit@americanliterarypress.com, www.americanliterarypress.com. 1991. Poetry, fiction, long-poems, non-fiction. avg. press run 500-1M. Pub'd 50 titles 2005; expects 60 titles 2006, 70 titles 2007. Discounts: 1-5 40%, 6-25 43%, 26-50 46%. 200pp. Reporting time: 3-4 weeks. Simultaneous submissions accepted: yes. Publishes 20% of manuscripts submitted. Payment: 40%-50%. Copyrights for author. Subjects: African-American, Autobiography, Christianity, Fantasy, Feminism, Fiction, How-To, Humor, Inspirational, New Age, Novels, Peace, Poetry, Women.

AMERICAN LITERARY REVIEW, John Tait, Editor; C. L. Elerson, Managing Editor, PO Box 311307, University of North Texas, Denton, TX 76203-1307, 940-565-2755. 1990. Poetry, fiction. "Recent contributors: Nancy Eimers, Nance Van Winckel, Eric Pankey, Kathleen Peirce, William Olseon, Jesse Lee Kercheval, Andrew Feld, G.C. Waldrep, Michael Czyzniejewski, Dulcie Leimbach, Danit Brown, George Rabosa, William Pierce, Sandra Jacobs, Kurt Rheinheimer, Neela Vaswani." circ. 900. 2/yr. Pub'd 2 issues 2005; expects 2 issues 2006, 2 issues 2007. sub. price $14 individual, $25 institution; per copy $7 + $1 for shipping and handling; sample $7 + $1 for shipping and handling. Back issues: $6, if available. Discounts: standard. 128pp. Reporting time: 8-12 weeks. We accept simultaneous submissions if indicated. Publishes 5% of manuscripts submitted. Payment: 2 copies. Copyrighted, reverts to author. Pub's reviews: 2 in 2005. §Contemporary poetry, short story collections, creative nonfiction essays and memoirs. Ads: $150/$75/$50 must be camera ready. Subjects: Essays, Poetry, Short Stories.

•**American Poet,** Dan Brady, Managing Editor, The Academy of American Poets, 584 Broadway, Suite 604, New York, NY 10012, 212-274-0343, fax 212-274-9427, www.poets.org. "American Poet is the journal of the Academy of American Poets."

THE AMERICAN POETRY JOURNAL, J.P. Dancing Bear, PO Box 2080, Aptos, CA 95001-2080, editor@americanpoetryjournal.com, www.americanpoetryjournal.com. 2003. Poetry, articles, criticism, reviews. "The APJ seeks to publish work using poetic device, favoring image, metaphor and good sound. We like alliteration, extended metaphors, image, movement and poems that can pass the 'so what' test. The APJ has in mind the reader who delights in discovering what a poem can do to the tongue and what the poem paints on the cave of the mind. The APJ wants to provide the poems published within its pages the best possible focus and seeks to further promote them through reviewers and literary websites as well as by nominating works to the Pushcart Prize. The APJ also offers the American Poet Prize. Please send submissions of no more than five poems. Please enclose a self-addressed, stamped envelope (SASE) for our response, or the submission will not be read. Envelopes which are too small or have insufficient postage for a manuscripts return will only get a response, and the manuscript will be recycled. A cover letter is a nice way to break the ice but not necessary, however, be sure to include contact information such as: name, address, phone, and email on the page of each poem. Send submissions in standard #10 envelopes. Please limit your non-contest submissions to twice per reading period unless you have been invited to do otherwise or you are a subscriber (1 year or more)." 2/yr. Expects 2 issues 2006, 2 issues 2007. sub. price $10; per copy $6. 60pp. Reporting time: 6 weeks. Simultaneous submissions accepted: yes. Publishes 1% of manuscripts submitted. Payment: 1 copy. Copyrighted, reverts to author. Subject: Poetry.

AMERICAN POETRY REVIEW, Stephen Berg, David Bonanno, Arthur Vogelsang, 117 S. 17th Street, Ste. 910, Philadelphia, PA 19103-5009, 215-496-0439. 1972. Poetry, fiction, articles, art, photos, cartoons, interviews, satire, criticism, reviews, music, letters, parts-of-novels, long-poems, collages, plays, concrete art, news items, non-fiction. circ. 17,000. 6/yr. Pub'd 6 issues 2005; expects 6 issues 2006. sub. price $19; per copy $3.95; sample $3.95. Back issues: $5. Discounts: through Ingram for stores and newsstands. 56pp. Reporting time: 10 weeks. Simultaneous submissions accepted: no. Publishes less than 1% of manuscripts submitted. Payment: $1/line for poetry; $60/tabloid page for prose. Copyrighted, reverts to author. Pub's reviews: 30 in 2005. §Literary. Ads: $950/$575. Subject: Poetry.

American Research Press (see also SMARANDACHE NOTIONS JOURNAL), Joanne McGray, Box 141, Rehoboth, NM 87322, m_l_perez@yahoo.com, www.gallup.unm.edu/~smarandache/eBooks-otherformats.htm and www.gallup.unm.edu/~smarandache/eBooksLiterature.htm. avg. press run 10.

AMERICAN ROAD, Mock Turtle Press, Thomas Repp MFA, Executive Editor, PO Box 46519, Mont Clemens, MI 48046, Orders 1-877-285-5434. General information 425-774-6135, fax 586-468-7483, sales@mockturtlepress.com, www.mockturtlepress.com, General Manager Becky Repp 206-369-5782. 2003. "Writers should request a copy of our guidelines and become familiar with American Road magazine prior to submitting queries. E-mail queries preferred. Be sure to include information on photographic support." circ. 10M. 4/yr. Pub'd 3 issues 2005; expects 4 issues 2006, 4 issues 2007. sub. price $15.95 (US), Canadian orders add $12/yr s/h, foreign orders add $22/yr s/h; per copy $4.95; sample $5 (includes s/h) for authors. Back issues: $4.95 + $2.50 s/h per issue or 2-4 issues $3.85 s/h. Discounts: 2-4 copies 30%, 5+ 40%; also distributed by Prestige. 68pp. Reporting time: 6 months average. Simultaneous submissions accepted: no. Publishes 1% of manuscripts submitted. Payment: 13¢/word. Pub's reviews: 6 in 2005. §Historic highways. Ads: $1694/$990. Subjects: Americana, History, Non-Fiction, Transportation, Travel.

•**American Short Fiction,** Stacey Swann, Editor; Jill Meyers, Managing Editor; Rebecca Bengal, Contributing Editor, PO Box 301209, Austin, TX 78703, 512.538.1305 (voice), 512.538.1306 (fax), web: americanshortfiction.org, email: editors@americanshortfiction.org, subscriptions@americanshortfiction.org. 1991-1998; Re-launched in 2006. "American Short Fiction is a quarterly magazine of new fiction and, occasionally essays and artwork that re-launched in Winter 2006. During its first run from 1991 to 1998, the magazine was a a two-time finalist for the National Magazine Award in Fiction. American Short Fiction has published some of the finest writers working in the form, including Joy Williams, Desmond Hogan, Reynolds Price, Gina Berriault, Louise Erdrich, Dagoberto Gilb, Andrea Barrett, Antonya Nelson, Joyce Carol Oates, Charles Baxter, Ursula K. Le Guin, and Dan Chaon, among many others. Four times a year, the magazine's editors select and publish short stories and novel excerpts by established and new writers. It is our goal to discover and publish new fiction in which transformations of language, narrative, and character occur swiftly, deftly, and unexpectedly. Authors wishing to submit short stories to American Short Fiction should read an issue of the magazine, which is available in bookstores and at http://www.americanshortfiction.org. Complete submission guidelines are also available on our Web site. Please note that we do not accept submissions by email, and we only read unsolicited fictionmeaning, we do not accept unsolicited submissions of essays or artwork." avg. press run 3000. Expects 4 titles 2006, 4 titles 2007. Simultaneous submissions are fine as long as they are clearly marked as such, and the author notifies the editors immediately if the submission is accepted elsewhere. Payment is competitive but varies.

AMERICAN TANKA, Laura Maffei, PO Box 120-024, Staten Island, NY 10312-0024, editorsdesk@americantanka.com, www.americantanka.com. 1996. Poetry. "This journal is dedicated exclusively to English-language tanka poetry." circ. 150. Annual. Pub'd 1 issue 2005; expects 1 issue 2006, 1 issue 2007. sub. price $20; per copy $12; sample $12. Back issues: 3 for $20. 96pp. Reporting time: 12-16 weeks. Simultaneous submissions accepted: no. Publishes 10% of manuscripts submitted. Copyrighted, reverts to author. Ads: none. Subject: Poetry.

•**The American Zen Association (see also HERE AND NOW),** 5500 Prytania St., #20, New Orleans, LA 70115.

Americans for the Arts (see also ARTSLINK), Vanessa Vozar, Director of Publication Sales; Anne

Canzonetti, Communications Coordinator; Randy Cohen, VP of Research & Information, 1000 Vermont Ave. NW, Washington, DC 20005, To order publications, call 1.800.321.4510. For information on Americans for the Arts and membership, call 202.371.2830. 1996. Articles, news items. "Interested in material on arts administration/management, legislation affecting all the arts, news on all art forms, fundraising/resource development for the arts, arts research & policy studies. ArtsLink is a newsletter for members of Americans for the Arts. We publish Monographs several times per year on various issues of interest to arts professionals. If you would like Monograph guidelines, e-mail Randy Cohen at rcohen@artsusa.org or write him at Americans for the Arts, 1000 Vermont Ave. NW, Washington, DC 20005." avg. press run 3M. Pub'd 5 titles 2005; expects 5 titles 2006, 5 titles 2007. Discounts: Members of Americans for the Arts receive discounts on publications. We also offer discounts for quantity orders. Call 1.800.321.4510 for information. Monographs are usually 12-24pp. Payment: varies. Does not copyright for author. Subjects: Arts, Awards, Foundations, Grants, Cities, Community, Creativity, Culture, Management, Marketing, Multicultural, Performing Arts, Public Affairs, Research, Technology, Theatre, Visual Arts.

Amethyst & Emerald, Cathyann Ortiz, Editor-Publisher, 1556 Halford Avenue, Suite 124, Santa Clara, CA 95051-2661, 408-244-6864, Fax 408-249-7646. 1997. Poetry, non-fiction. avg. press run 500. Pub'd 1 title 2005; expects 3 titles 2006, 3 titles 2007. 150pp. Reporting time: 2 months. Simultaneous submissions accepted: yes. Subjects: New Age, Poetry, Prose, Self-Help, Spiritual, Women.

Amherst Media, Inc., Craig Alesse, P.O. Box 586, Amherst, NY 14226, 716-874-4450; www.amherst-media.com. 1976. "We publish how-to photography books." avg. press run 15M. Expects 25 titles 2006. Discounts: 40% stores, 20% schools. 128pp. Reporting time: 6 weeks. Publishes 40% of manuscripts submitted. Payment: negotiable. Copyrights for author. Subjects: How-To, Photography.

Amherst Writers & Artists Press, Inc. (see also PEREGRINE), Pat Schneider, Editor; Nancy Rose, Assistant Editor, PO Box 1076, Amherst, MA 01004, 413-253-7764 phone/Fax, awapress@aol.com, www.amherstwriters.com. 1981. Poetry, fiction, reviews. avg. press run 800-1M. Pub'd 3 titles 2005; expects 3 titles 2006, 3 titles 2007. 100+pp. Simultaneous submissions accepted: yes. Copyrights for author. Subjects: Children, Youth, Dance.

Ammons Communications, Amy Garza Ammons, 29 Regal Ave, Amy, Sylva, NC 28779-2877, v.ammons@mchsi.com. 1985. Poetry, fiction, art, photos, plays, non-fiction. "Ammons Communications believes everyone has a story they could tell. Our mission is to give the writer a voice and suggestions as how to to best market his/her work. Much of what we publish is based on heritage or is something the author feels strongly about and has first hand knowledge that will benefit the reader. We are a cooperative publishing house. We take a manuscript and do all the work necessary for the author to have a book in his/her hand, and charge for our preparatory work only one time, giving the author full rights for his/her book. We find the most economical printer, and author pays for the printing. Free Estimates. Recent: Memories of Merritt Island by Gail Briggs Nolen, White Feather by Nancy M. Pafford." avg. press run 1000. Pub'd 5 titles 2005; expects 4 titles 2006. Discounts: 2-10 30%. 250pp. Reporting time: Upon receipt, we send a letter stating our terms. Publishing is in the hands of the writer. Simultaneous submissions accepted: Yes. Publishes 90% of manuscripts submitted. Payment: We are co-operative publishers. Authors have full rights for their work. Copyrights for author. Subjects: Americana, Appalachia, Arts, Family, Fiction, Folklore, History, Inspirational, North Carolina, Novels, Performing Arts, Photography, Picture Books, Poetry, Storytelling.

Amnos Publications, Ann Lampros, 2501 South Wolf Road, Westchester, IL 60154, 312-562-2744. 1984. Non-fiction. "We publish historical studies of the early Christian Church, based upon the teachings of the Eastern Orthodox Church." avg. press run 7M. Pub'd 2 titles 2005; expects 2 titles 2006, 2 titles 2007. Discounts: trade. 175pp. Does not copyright for author. Subject: Religion.

Amsterdam University Press, Saskia de Vries, Prinsengracht 747-751, 1017 JX, Amsterdam, The Netherlands, T 0031 (0)20 4200050, F 0031 (0)20 4203412, www.aup.nl.

Anacus Press, An Imprint of Finney Company (see also Finney Company, Inc.), Alan Krysan, President, 8075 215th Street West, Lakeville, MN 55044, (952) 469-6699, Fax: (952) 469-1968, (800) 326-9272, Fax: (800) 330-6232 feedback@finney-hobar.com, www.anacus.com. 1995. Non-fiction. "This imprint of Finney Company offers bicycling guides and bicycling narratives for hard-core bike riding enthusiasts and leisure riders. We have a Ride Guide Series and a Bed, Breakfast and Bike Series." avg. press run 5000. Expects 1 title 2006, 1-3 titles 2007. Discounts: 1-9 copies 20%10-49 copies 40%50 or more copies 50%. 112-400pp. Reporting time: 8-10 weeks. Simultaneous submissions accepted: Yes. Payment: varies. Subjects: Bicycling, Great Lakes, Leisure/Recreation, Non-Fiction, Pacific Northwest, Transportation, Travel.

Anagnosis, Aris Karey, Deliyianni 3, Maroussi 15122, Greece, +302106254654, Fax:+302106254089, www.anagnosis.gr. 2002. Non-fiction. "Anagnosis is a publishing house based in Athens, Greece. We publish and sell books in the English and Greek languages. We specialize in books on: Greek Life, History and Culture; and Educational Books (including texts for the International Baccalaureate)." Pub'd 4 titles 2005; expects 4 titles 2006, 5 titles 2007. Discounts: 35% to bookstores, retailers, to schools depending upon size of order. Reporting time: 1 month. Payment: to be discussed. Copyrights for author. Subjects: Anthropology, Archaelogy, Folklore, Greek, History, Philosophy, Travel.

Anancybooks, Beresford McLean, PO Box 28677, San Jose, CA 95159-8677, 408-286-0726, Fax 408-947-0668, info@anancybooks.com, www.anancybooks.com. Expects 1 title 2006. 503pp. Publishes 100% of manuscripts submitted. Copyrights for author.

ANARCHY: A Journal of Desire Armed, Lawrence Jararch, PO Box 3448, Berkeley, CA 94703, editors@anarchymag.org. 1980. Poetry, fiction, articles, art, photos, cartoons, satire, criticism, reviews, letters, collages, news items, non-fiction. "Features: 1,000 to 4,500 words. Reviews: 200-750 words (unless previously queried-up to 1,500 words)." circ. 7M. 2/yr. Pub'd 2 issues 2005; expects 2 issues 2006, 2 issues 2007. sub. price $8 3rd class/$12 first class; per copy $4.95; sample $6. Back issues: $6 for 1st, $4 each for additional back issues. Discounts: 10-19 copies 20%, 20-59 40%, 60-99 45%, 100-249 50%, 250+ 55%. 84pp. Reporting time: 2-3 months. Simultaneous submissions accepted: yes. Publishes 5-10% of manuscripts submitted. Payment: free subscriptions for now and/or multiple copies. Not copyrighted. Pub's reviews: 20 Books, 60 Magazines in 2005. §Anarchist, libertarian/anti-authoritarian books, sexual liberation, feminism, ecology, radical history, atheism. No ads. Subjects: Anarchist, Libertarian.

•**Anchor Cove Publishing, Inc.,** Thomas McEwen, PO Box 270588, Littleton, CO 80128, Tel 303-972-0099, Fax 303-265-9119. 2005. Non-fiction. "Primary focus is books on recreational boating." avg. press run 5000. Expects 1 title 2006. Discounts: Bookstores and retailers 40%, Distributors 55%. 800pp. Reporting time: 2 to 3 weeks. Simultaneous submissions accepted: Yes. Publishes 5% of manuscripts submitted. Does not copyright for author. Subjects: Leisure/Recreation, Sports, Outdoors.

Ancient City Press, Mary A. Powell, President; Marta Weigle, Secretary-Treasurer, Editor, 3101 Old Pecos Trail, Unit 244, Santa Fe, NM 87505-9088, 505-982-8195. 1961. Non-fiction. "Booklets through book-length." avg. press run 2M-5M. Pub'd 5 titles 2005; expects 6 titles 2006, 5 titles 2007. Discounts: 1 book 0%, 2 or more 43%, prepayment required. 48pp booklet, 300pp book. Reporting time: 1-4 months. Payment: contracts negotiated individually, royalties paid once a year. Copyrights for author. Subjects: Airplanes, Americana, Anthropology, Archaelogy, Architecture, Autobiography, Children, Youth, Crafts, Hobbies, Folklore, Native American, New Mexico, Non-Fiction, Real Estate, Reprints, Southwest, U.S. Hispanic.

ANCIENT PATHS, Skylar Hamilton Burris, PO Box 7505, Fairfax Station, VA 22039, ssburris@msn.com http://www.editorskylar.com. 1998. Poetry, fiction, art, reviews, parts-of-novels. "Prose to 2,500 words, poetry to 60 lines - formal or free verse, rhymed or unrhymed. Christian themes, images, and values preferred. No preaching. Nothing didactic. We've published poetry by Ida Fasel, Walt McDonald, and Giovanni Malito. Prose by Lynn Terrel and Ronald Mackinnon Thompson. Always looking for quality black and white artwork. Email as a .gif or .jpeg attachment. No email submissions [except for artwork and outside the U.S.]." circ. 100-200. biennial (January of odd years). Pub'd 2 issues 2005; expects 1 issue 2006, 1 issue 2007. sub. price $10 (if ordered at least 1 mo. prior to publication); per copy $5 (Issue 13) / $12 (Issue 14); sample $5. Back issues: $5 (Issue 13 only). Discounts: $1 off multiple copies of the same issue. 80pp. Reporting time: initial response in 4-5 weeks. We accept simultaneous submissions and reprints. Publishes 10-15% of manuscripts submitted. Payment: 1 copy and $2 per poem, $6 per story, $6 per artwork. Not copyrighted. Pub's reviews: 3 in 2005. §Christian literary magazines, Judeo-Christian poetry chapbooks. Ads: $35 one-half page. Subjects: Christianity, Fiction, Literature (General), Poetry, Prose, Religion, Short Stories.

RC Anderson Books (see also Redgreene Press), RC Anderson, PO Box 22322, Pittsburgh, PA 15222.

Andmar Press, John M. Gist, PO Box 217, Mills, WY 82644, e-mail fjozwik@csi.com; www.andmar-press.com. 1982. Articles, non-fiction. avg. press run 5M. Expects 4 titles 2006, 4 titles 2007. Discounts: contact for guidelines. 300pp. Reporting time: 1 month. Simultaneous submissions accepted: yes. Publishes 5% of manuscripts submitted. Copyrights for author. Subjects: Fiction, Gardening, Horticulture, The West, Wyoming.

Androgyne Books, Ken Weichel, 930 Shields, San Francisco, CA 94132, 415-586-2697. 1971. Poetry, fiction, articles, art, photos, criticism, collages, plays. "Please contact press before sending mss.See our website at: www.androgynebooks.org." avg. press run 500. Pub'd 2 titles 2005; expects 4 titles 2006. Discounts: 40% bookstores, 50% wholesalers. 200pp. Reporting time: 3 weeks. Payment: 10% of press run. Copyrights for author. Subjects: Avant-Garde, Experimental Art, Beat, Biography, California, Dada, Fiction, Literature (General), Poetry, Prose, Reviews, San Francisco, Short Stories, Surrealism.

Andros Books, Susanne L. Bain, Kevin R. Bain, P. O. Box 2887, Mesa, AZ 85204, androsbks@aol.com. 1999. Fiction, non-fiction. "Nonfiction relating to home school. Gentle women's fiction with a positive attitude. Printed length approximating 200 pages (ms. 300 pages). We are a new publisher and are looking for fresh, positive works. Nothing erotic or violent. We can only return ms. mailed with SASE (w/adequate postage)."

avg. press run 1K. Pub'd 1 title 2005; expects 2 titles 2006, 3-4 titles 2007. 200pp. Reporting time: 30-60 days. We accept simultaneous submissions, but notify us of status. Payment: 7%, no advance. Does not copyright for author. Subjects: Education, Parenting, Women.

ANGEL FACE POETRY JOURNAL, Mary Agnes Dalrymple, PO Box 102, Huffman, TX 77336, MaryAnkaPress@cs.com, www.maryanka.com. 2004. Poetry. "*Angel Face* seeks free-verse poetry to be arranged according to the pattern of the rosary (the mysteries). Editor's goal is to bring the rosary "into life." Open to all faiths. Poets need not be Catholic or Christian. Editor tends to select secular/spiritual works that come from the poet's life, but will also consider works written from the biblical source material for the mysteries. Links to rosary information can be found on website. Editor will consider any well-written poem but prefers not to see rhyming poetry or didactic verse. Also, nothing negative or derogatory. For guidelines, please visit *www.maryanka.com*. Or send SASE to above address." 1/yr. Expects 1 issue 2006, 1 issue 2007. price per copy $6. 50pp. Reporting time: 6 months. Simultaneous submissions accepted: yes. Publishes 10% of manuscripts submitted. Payment: 1 copy. Copyrighted, reverts to author. Subjects: Poetry, Religion.

Angel Power Press, PO Box 3327, Oceanside, CA 92051, 760-721-6666. 1999. Non-fiction. "Publish books on parenting and family issues." avg. press run 5M. Expects 1 title 2006, 1 title 2007. Discounts: booksellers 1-2 copies 20%, 3-4 30%, 5+ 40%; wholesale discounts for stocking orders 55%. 224pp. Reporting time: 6 weeks. Payment: negotiable. Copyrights for author. Subjects: Children, Youth, Family, Parenting.

Angst World Library, Thomas Carlisle, Kathleen Carlisle, PO Box 593, Selma, OR 97538-0593. 1974. Fiction, parts-of-novels, non-fiction. "Please query prior to submitting ms. and *always* enclose SASE. *Tragedy of the Moisty Morning* by Jessica Salmonson." avg. press run 100-500. Expects 2 titles 2006, 3 titles 2007. Discounts: 40% on purchases over 5 copies; 40% to retailers. Pages vary. Reporting time: 1-2 months. Payment: 25% of net profit + 5 copies, and/or outright purchase. Copyrights for author. Subjects: Fiction, Futurism, Science Fiction.

Anhinga Press, Rick Campbell, Director; Lynne Knight, President, PO Box 10595, Tallahassee, FL 32302, 850-442-1408, Fax 850-442-6323, info@anhinga.org, www.anhinga.org. 1973. Poetry. "The Anhinga Prize is open to all poets writing in English who have not yet published a second full-length book of poetry, carries an award of $2000 plus publication, requires an entry fee of $20US, and is judged anonymously. See our web site or send SASE for complete details. Aside from the contest, we publish three or four additional manuscripts per year." avg. press run 1200. Pub'd 4 titles 2005; expects 4 titles 2006, 4 titles 2007. Discounts: 40%. 96pp. Reporting time: varies greatly, contest submissions 10 months. Simultaneous submissions accepted: yes. Publishes 1% of manuscripts submitted. Payment: varies. Copyrights for author. Subjects: Literature (General), Poetry.

ANIMAL PEOPLE, Merritt Clifton, Editor; Kim Bartlett, Publisher, PO Box 960, Clinton, WA 98236-0960. 1992. News items, non-fiction. "*Animal People*, published for people who care about animals enough to try to help them, is the leading independent newspaper and electronic information service covering animal protection worldwide. We emphasize original investigative reporting, both from the field and in hot pursuit of paper trails, on topics ranging from animal care-and-control in your own home town to zoological conservation in the middle of nowhere. We document problems and spotlight effective responses, with verifiable statistics; cut through the hyperbole of fundraising appeals to show who is really doing what with the money; and take seriously the late humane advocate William Randolph Hearst's maxim that the purpose of news media should be to 'Comfort the afflicted, afflict the comfortable, print the news and raise hell.' We have no alignment or affiliation with any other entity. Our policy is simply, 'Be kind to animals'; our interest is in all the many ways that may be done." circ. 15M. 10/yr. Pub'd 10 issues 2005; expects 10 issues 2006, 10 issues 2007. sub. price $24; per copy $3; sample send free sample on request. Back issues: $3. 24pp. Reporting time: 1 week maximum. Simultaneous submissions accepted: no. Payment: none for opinion pieces; 15¢ a word for features. Copyrighted, reverts to author. Pub's reviews: 40 in 2005. §Animals. Ads: $1,155/$578/50¢ per word classified. Subject: Animals.

THE ANNALS OF IOWA, Marvin Bergman, 402 Iowa Avenue, Iowa City, IA 52240, 319-335-3931, fax 319-335-3935, e-mail marvin-bergman@uiowa.edu. 1863. Articles, reviews. circ. 1M. 4/yr. Pub'd 4 issues 2005; expects 4 issues 2006, 4 issues 2007. sub. price $20; per copy $6; sample none. Discounts: 20% for resale. 120pp. Reporting time: 90 days. Simultaneous submissions accepted: no. Publishes 25% of manuscripts submitted. Payment: none. Copyrighted, does not revert to author. Pub's reviews: c. 80 in 2005. §History of Iowa and the Midwest; other relevant state and local history. Subjects: Biography, Book Reviewing, History, Iowa, Midwest.

Annedawn Publishing, Don Langevin, PO Box 247, Norton, MA 02766-0247, 508-222-9069. 1992. Non-fiction. "I now accept unsolicited manuscripts, both of a horticultural and birdwatching nature, from writers in search of publishers." avg. press run 10M. Pub'd 3 titles 2005; expects 3 titles 2006, 4 titles 2007. Discounts: 1-4 20%, 5-23 40%, 24+ 45%. 128pp. Reporting time: 1 month. Publishes 10% of manuscripts submitted. Payment: credit card. Copyrights for author. Subjects: Birds, Gardening, How-To.

Annick Press Ltd., Rick Wilks, Colleen MacMillan, 15 Patricia Avenue, Toronto, ON M2M 1H9, Canada, 416-221-4802, Fax 416-221-8400, annickpress@annickpress.com. 1975. Fiction, non-fiction. "We cannot accept unsolicited manuscripts any longer." avg. press run 10M. Pub'd 23 titles 2005; expects 26 titles 2006, 30 titles 2007. Discounts: order from Firefly Books Ltd., 66 Leek Cr, Richmond Hill,Ont. L4B 1H1, or your favorite supplier. 24-400pp. Reporting time: 3 months. Payment: twice a year. Copyrights for author. Subjects: Children, Youth, Young Adult.

ANQ: A Quarterly Journal of Short Articles, Notes, and Reviews, Elizabeth Foxwell, Managing Editor, 1319 18th Street NW, Washington, DC 20036, 202-296-6267 x275, Fax 202-293-6130, www.heldref.org. 1988. Articles, criticism, reviews. "*ANQ*, formerly titled *American Notes and Queries*, is a medium of exchange for bibliographers, biographers, editors, lexicographers, and textual scholars. From sources and analogues to the identification of allusions, from variant manuscript readings to previously neglected archives, from Old English word studies to *OED* supplements, from textual emendations to corrections of bibliographies and other scholarly reference works, *ANQ* provides a needed outlet for short factual research concerning the language and literature of the English-speaking world. We publish signed reviews of critical studies, new editions, and recently published bibliographies. Manuscripts offering only explication de textes are not appropriate. Manuscript length should not exceed 1,600 words in length; must be accompanied by loose stamps and a self-addressed envelope for the return mailings; and must follow the MLA documentation style that includes parenthetical citations in the text and an alphabetized list of Works Cited as described in *The MLA Style Manual*. Authors are responsible for reading and correcting proofs." circ. 500. 4/yr. Pub'd 4 issues 2005; expects 4 issues 2006, 4 issues 2007. sub. price $52 individual, $96 institution; per copy $24; sample same. Back issues: contact publisher for back issue prices. 64pp. Reporting time: 1 month. Simultaneous submissions accepted: no. Payment: 2 copies of the issue in which the author's contribution appears. Copyrighted, rights revert to author only upon request. Pub's reviews: 18 in 2005. §Bibliographies, new scholarly editions of the major poets, novelists, essayists, and men-of-letters of the English-speaking world, critical studies. Ads: $155. Subjects: Bibliography, Biography, Book Reviewing, Drama, English, Fiction, Literary Review, Literature (General), Theatre.

ANT ANT ANT ANT ANT, Chris Gordon, PO Box 3158, Eugene, OR 97403. 1994. Poetry. "*ant ant ant ant ant* is a journal of contemporary haiku which emphasizes originality and innovation while remaining rooted in tradition. Each issue features the work of five poets who are contributing to the development of the form or whose past work has gone largely unnoticed. Interested participants should send 100 haiku per submission that represent the range and depth of their work. Unpublished material is preferable but some reprinted material is acceptable. Translations are of interest as well. If your manuscript is chosen, 30 of your haiku will appear in an upcoming issue. Please include a SASE with all your correspondence." circ. 200. 1/yr. Pub'd 1 issue 2005; expects 1 issue 2006, 1 issue 2007. sub. price $8; per copy $8; sample $8. 44pp. Reporting time: 1-3 months. Simultaneous submissions accepted: yes. Publishes 5% of manuscripts submitted. Payment: none. Not copyrighted. Subjects: Haiku, Poetry.

ANTHILLS, Centennial Press, Charles Nevsimal, Editor, PO Box 170322, Milwaukee, WI 53217-8026, www.centennialpress.com, chuck@centennialpress.com. 2000. Poetry. "Firm in our resolve to provide only the best poesy available in this (or any) hemisphere, Centennial Press is prepared to elicit a new era of quality in what we have christened: the language of the heart. Past issues have included words by A.D. Winans, William Taylor Jr., Antler, Gunther C. Fogle, John Sweet, Matt Cook, Susan Firer, justin.barrett, Hugh Fox, Alex Carlson, Glenn W. Cooper, and other substantial small press poets and underdog writers." Simultaneous submissions accepted: Yes. Payment: One (1) copy per contributor. Copyrighted, reverts to author.

THE ANTHOLOGY OF NEW ENGLAND WRITERS, Frank Anthony, Editor in Memoriam (1922-2006); Susan Anthony, Editor; John Kenneth Galbraith, Honorary Advisor, PO Box 5, Windsor, VT 05089-0005, 802-674-2315, newvtpoet@aol.com, www.newenglandwriters.org. 1989. Poetry, fiction. "Each issue a contest issue: *AnthNEW* includes three Robert Penn Warren Awards ($300, $200, $100) and ten each, Honorable Mentions, Commendables, Editor's Choice. Guidelines: Free Verse: Open to ALL poets (not just New England); reading fee $5 for each set of 3 poems (6 poems/$10: one year NEW membership; 9 poems/$15: membership and anthology); unpublished, original poems 30 lines or less; type each poem with title: one page/no name, address; include a 3x5 card with your name, address and poem titles. SASE for winner's list only, poems are not returned. Annual postmark date: June 15. Winners announced at New England Writers Conference, third Saturday of July. Published in November. Indexed in *The American Humanities Index* and *Index of American Periodical Verse*. Also Short Short Fiction Contest for original unpublished work (no more than 1,000 words) open to all. Postmark date June 15, $5 fee per entry, $300 Marjory Bartlett Sanger Award. Winner published in *The Anthology of New England Writers*. Winners announced at NEW Conference. Mail entries for both contests to Dr. Frank Anthony, New England Writers Contest, PO Box 5, Windsor, VT 05089-0005." circ. 400. 1/yr. price per copy $5.00. 56pp. Simultaneous submissions accepted: Notify if published elsewhere. Publishes 5% of manuscripts submitted. Payment: 1 copy. Copyrighted, reverts to author. Subjects: Fiction, Poetry, Short Stories.

Anthony Publishing Company, Inc., Carol K. Anthony, Hanna Moog, 206 Gleasondale Road, Stow, MA 01775-1356, 978-897-7191. 1980. "Certain work on the subject of I Ching only." avg. press run 5M. Pub'd 7 titles 2005. Discounts: 1-4 30%, 5+ 40%. 250pp. Reporting time: 1 week. Simultaneous submissions accepted: no. Publishes 1% of manuscripts submitted. Payment: yearly. Copyrights for author. Subjects: Asia, Indochina, Philosophy, Psychology.

Anti-Aging Press (see also SO YOUNG!), Julia Busch, Box 142174, Coral Gables, FL 33114, 305-662-3928, 305-661-2802, Fax 305-661-4123, julia2@gate.net. 1992. Poetry, articles, cartoons, reviews, non-fiction. "Additional address: 4185 Pamona Avenue, Coconut Grove, FL 33133. Committed to erasing wrinkles on all levels—mental, emotional, physical via books, cassettes, newsletters. Imprint Kosmic Kuprints for spiritual, metaphysical, New Age titles." avg. press run 3M-5M. Pub'd 1 title 2005; expects 2 titles 2006, 2 titles 2007. Discounts: 1-2 copies 20%, 3-4 30%, 5-199 40%, 200+ 50%; payment with order; returns. 128-256pp. Payment: royalty on wholesale, or outright buy. We copyright for author, but depends on individual arrangement. Subjects: Acupuncture, Aging, Book Reviewing, Health, How-To, Newsletter, Non-Fiction, Poetry, Self-Help.

ANTIETAM REVIEW, Philip Bufithis, Executive Editor; Ethan Fischer, Senior Editor; Paul Grant, Poetry Editor; Benita Keller, Photography Editor; Mary Jo Vincent, Managing Editor, 14 West Washington St., Hagerstown, MD 21740-5512, 301-791-3132. 1982. Poetry, fiction, photos, interviews, reviews. "*AR* accepts well-crafted literary short stories and creative fiction with no more than 5,000 words. (ONE submission per contributor), up to three poems with no more than 30 lines (we discourage inspirational verse, doggerel and haiku), and up to three B & W photography prints (please e-mail us for specifications of submitting). Payment: 2 copies of AR, $50 for prose, $25 for poetry, $25 for photography. Reading period is from Sept. 1 through Dec. 1. Simultaneous submissions accepted. Include SASE for response only. Literary Contest reading period: May 1 through Sept. 1. Same guidelines as above. Story Prize $150, Poetry Prize $100. Include SASE for response only. Reading fee for contest: $15 (fee is for one mss., and up to three poems)." circ. 1,000. 1/yr. Pub'd 1 issue 2005; expects 1 issue 2006, 1 issue 2007. sub. price $8.40; per copy $8.40. Back issues: $6.30. 75pp. Reporting time: 2 to 4 months. Simultaneous submissions accepted: yes. Publishes 3% of manuscripts submitted. Copyrighted, reverts to author. Pub's reviews: 3 in 2005. Subjects: Fiction, Photography, Poetry.

THE ANTIGONISH REVIEW, Jeanette Lynes, Co-Editor; Gerald Trites, Co-Editor, St Francis Xavier University, PO Box 5000, Antigonish, Nova Scotia B2G 2W5, Canada. 1970. Poetry, fiction, articles, art, interviews, criticism, reviews. "All submissions from U.S. must be accompanied by Postal Reply Coupons; submissions accompanied by U.S. postage will not be returned." circ. 900. 4/yr. Pub'd 4 issues 2005; expects 4 issues 2006, 4 issues 2007. sub. price $24 in Canada; $30 (US funds) outside of Canada; per copy $8; sample $6 accompanied by postage. Back issues: $6. plus postage. Discounts: 20%. 144pp. Reporting time: 4-6 months. Simultaneous submissions accepted: no. Publishes 20% of manuscripts submitted. Payment: 2 copies for poetry; $50 for fiction and reviews; $100 for articles and essays. Copyrighted. Pub's reviews: 26 in 2005. §Literary, biographies and autobiographies of poets, writers, artists. Ads: none. Subjects: Book Reviewing, Criticism, Fiction, Literary Review, Poetry.

THE ANTIOCH REVIEW, Robert Fogarty, Editor; Judith Hall, Poetry Editor, PO Box 148, Yellow Springs, OH 45387, 937-769-1365. 1941. Poetry, fiction, articles, criticism, long-poems, non-fiction. "Recent contributors: Katherine Vaz, Bruce Jay Friedman, Sheila Kohler, Daniel Harris, Rick DeMarinis, Barbara Sjoholm. No unsolicited reviews accepted." circ. 4M. 4/yr. Pub'd 4 issues 2005; expects 4 issues 2006, 4 issues 2007. sub. price $40 ($52 foreign), $76 institutional ($88 foreign); per copy $9.50; sample $7. Back issues: $7. Discounts: 10% to agents. 200pp. Reporting time: fiction 3-4 months, poetry 2-3 months. We do not read fiction from June 1 to September 1. We do not read poetry from May 1 to September 1. Simultaneous submissions accepted: no. Publishes 2% of manuscripts submitted. Payment: $15 per page (approx. 425 words). Copyrighted, reverts to author. Pub's reviews: 50 in 2005. §No unsolicited reviews considered. Ads: $250/$150. Subjects: Fiction, Poetry, Public Affairs.

Anvil Press (see also SUB-TERRAIN), Brian Kaufman, Publisher, 278 East First Avenue, Vancouver, B.C. V5T 1A6, Canada, 604-876-8710, info@anvilpress.com, www.anvilpress.com. 1988. Fiction, photos, plays, non-fiction. "We publish literary trade titles in all genres, plus occasional broadsheets and pamphlets. Submissions should be accompanied by a sample chapter and outline with query letter. Canadian authors *only*." avg. press run 1M. Pub'd 7 titles 2005; expects 8 titles 2006, 10 titles 2007. Discounts: bookstores 40% on orders of 4+ books; 20% to libraries/institutions. 100-200pp. Publishes 2% of manuscripts submitted. Payment: 15%. Copyrights for author.

Anvil Publishers, Inc., Lee Xavier, Editor, PO Box 2694, Tucker, GA 30085-2694, 770-938-0289, Fax 770-493-7232, anvilpress@aol.com, www.anvilpub.com. 2001. Non-fiction. "History, biography, how-to." avg. press run 2M. Expects 3 titles 2006, 3 titles 2007. Discounts: retailers 1-2 books 0%, 3-4 20%, 5-24 30%,

25-99 40%, 100+ 45%, libraries and schools 1-24 20%, 25+ 25%. 300pp. Reporting time: 2 months. Simultaneous submissions accepted: yes. Payment: 5% first 1,000, 10% thereafter. Copyrights for author. Subjects: Americana, History, South.

APEX SCIENCE FICTION & HORROR DIGEST, Jason Sizemore, PO Box 2223, Lexington, KY 40588, 859-312-3974, http://www.apexdigest.com, submission@apexdigest.com. 2004. Fiction, articles, art, interviews, non-fiction. "Brings & binds & offers up an international collection of science horror from the dark corners of the world. The glossy cover, book reviews, and genre interviews add leavening to the brew, but make no mistake: Apex Digest straddles the genre world with one foot in blood and the other in Strontium." circ. 1500. 4/yr. Pub'd 4 issues 2005; expects 4 issues 2006, 4 issues 2007. sub. price $20; per copy $6; sample $6. Back issues: $5. Discounts: 2-10 copies 10%11 copies 15%. 112pp. Reporting time: 14 days. Simultaneous submissions accepted: No. Publishes 5% of manuscripts submitted. Payment: 1.5 cents per word + 2 contributor copies. Copyrighted, reverts to author. Ads: $35 1/2 Page - $60 Full interior page - $80 Inside Front Cover Right Flap - $80 Inside back cover left flap - $110 Inside Front Cover Left Flap (Full Color) - $110 Inside back cover right flap (Full Color) - $150 Back cover (full color). Subjects: Fiction, Horror, Science Fiction.

The Apostolic Press, Terri Neimann, Associate Editor, 547 NW Coast Street, Newport, OR 97365, 541 264-0452. 1992. Non-fiction. "We are seeking material for either books or a quarterly newsletter consisting of Biblical Greek subject matter only." avg. press run 1M. Pub'd 1 title 2005; expects 4 titles 2006, 1 title 2007. Discounts: trade. 224pp. Publishes 0% of manuscripts submitted. Does not copyright for author. Subject: Religion.

APOSTROPHE: USCB Journal of the Arts, Sheila Tombe, Managing and Poetry Editor; Ellen Malphrus, Fiction Editor, 801 Carteret Street, Beaufort, SC 29902, 843-521-4158, sjtombe@gwm.sc.edu. 1996. Poetry, fiction, art, interviews, criticism, reviews, letters, parts-of-novels, plays. "'Eclectic excellence required.' Recent contributors: James Dickey, Lyn Lifshin, and Virgil Suarez. If books are submitted for review, we might review them." circ. 700. 1/yr. Pub'd 1 issue 2005; expects 1 issue 2006, 1 issue 2007. sub. price $10; per copy $10; sample $3. Back issues: $5. Discounts: student $5 per copy. 70pp. Reporting time: no deadlines; replies (as soon as) when can. Simultaneous submissions accepted: yes. Publishes 10% of manuscripts submitted. Payment: 2 copies. Rights revert to author. Pub's reviews: none in 2005. §Outstanding fiction, criticism, or poetry. Subjects: Arts, Classical Studies, Design, Drama, English, Fiction, Literary Review, Literature (General), Poetry, Shakespeare.

APPALACHIA JOURNAL, Appalachian Mountain Club Books, Sandy Stott, 5 Joy Street, Boston, MA 02108, 617-523-0636. 1877. Poetry, fiction, articles, art, photos, interviews, reviews, letters, news items, non-fiction. "Most pieces in Appalachia are between 1,500-4,000 words. Poetry rarely exceeds 45 lines. Bias against 'I came, I saw, I conquered...' Interested in historical considerations of land, mountains, rivers and the people who sought them. Also interested in contemporary stories of relationships with landscapes. Recent contributors: Diane Morgan, Reg. Saner, Lynn Rogers, Guy and Laura Waterman, Justin Askins, Doug Peacock." circ. 13M. 2/yr. Pub'd 2 issues 2005; expects 2 issues 2006, 2 issues 2007. sub. price $10; per copy $5; sample $5. Back issues: $5. Discounts: 10+ copies 20%. 160pp. Reporting time: 1-3 months. Simultaneous submissions accepted: no. Payment: copies. Copyrighted, reverts to author. Pub's reviews: 20 in 2005. §Mountaineering, conservation, canoeing, walking, backpacking, cycling. Subjects: Adirondacks, Appalachia, Conservation, Earth, Natural History, Ecology, Foods, Geography, Poetry, Reviews, Sports, Outdoors, Weather.

Appalachian Consortium Press, A 14-member publications committee acts as editorial board, University Hall, Appalachian State University, Boone, NC 28608, 704-262-2064, fax 704-262-6564. 1971. Poetry, fiction, articles, art, photos, interviews, criticism, music, non-fiction. "We publish occasional works of poetry but, most often, *non-fiction* relating to the Appalachian region." avg. press run 2M. Pub'd 3 titles 2005; expects 5 titles 2006, 4 titles 2007. Discounts: on purchases for resale, 1-3 books 0%, 4+ 20%. 150pp. Reporting time: at least 6 months. Payment: a negotiable 5-10% of sales. Copyrights for author. Subjects: Appalachia, Bibliography, Biography, History, Literature (General), Photography, Reference, Sociology, South.

APPALACHIAN HERITAGE, George Brosi, CPO 2166, Berea, KY 40404-3699, 859-985-3699, 859-985-3903, george_brosi@berea.edu, www.berea.edu/appalachianheritage. 1973. Poetry, fiction, articles, art, photos, interviews, non-fiction. "Usually under 1,500 words. Material must have Southern Appalachian author or focus." circ. 500. 4/yr. Pub'd 4 issues 2005; expects 4 issues 2006, 4 issues 2007. sub. price $18; per copy $6; sample $6. Back issues: $6. 100pp. Reporting time: 4-6 weeks. Simultaneous submissions accepted: no. Publishes 10% of manuscripts submitted. Payment: 3 copies. Copyrighted, reverts to author. Pub's reviews: 28 in 2005. §Appalachian subjects. Ads: none. Subject: Appalachia.

Appalachian Mountain Club Books (see also APPALACHIA JOURNAL), Beth Krusi, Editor & Publisher, 5 Joy Street, Boston, MA 02108, 617-523-0636. 1897. Photos, non-fiction. "We publish nonfiction books and maps focusing on guidebooks for the Northeast and recreational how-to books. We usually contract authors for projects but we welcome unsolicited proposals." avg. press run 5M. Pub'd 6 titles 2005; expects 6 titles 2006, 8 titles 2007. Discounts: 10-24 books 40%, 25-49 42%, 50-74 43%, 75-149 44%, 150-249 45%, 250-799 46%, 800+ 47%. 256pp. Reporting time: 1-4 months. Simultaneous submissions accepted: yes. Payment: varies. Copyrights for author. Subjects: Earth, Natural History, Sports, Outdoors.

•**APPLE VALLEY REVIEW: A Journal of Contemporary Literature,** Leah Browning, Editor, c/o Queen's Postal Outlet, Box 12, Kingston, Ontario K7L 3R9, Canada, http://www.applevalleyreview.com/. 2005. Poetry, fiction, non-fiction. "Each issue features a collection of beautifully crafted poetry, short fiction, and essays. We prefer work that has both mainstream and literary appeal. Prose submissions may range from 100 to 3000 words. Shorter pieces stand a better chance of being published, but you may query the editor if you have an exceptional longer piece. Preference is given to short (under two pages), non-rhyming poetry. We accept submissions only via e-mail and do not accept simultaneous submissions. All work must be original, previously unpublished, and in English. Translations are welcome if permission has been granted. Please do not send us genre fiction (e.g., horror, science fiction, mysteries); erotica, work containing explicit language, or anything else you wouldn't want your grandmother to read; work that is scholarly or critical, inspirational, or intended for children; or anything that is violent or more than a little depressing. Please note that these are purely editorial preferences. Work that is not a good fit here may be perfect for another market. Recent contributors include Hal Sirowitz, David Thornbrugh, Anna Evans, Louie Crew, Arlene L. Mandell, Janet Zupan, Thomas D. Reynolds, Jeanpaul Ferro, Steve Klepetar, Davide Trame, Clay Carpenter, Peter Dabbene, J. D. Nelson, Tania de Souza, Lynn Strongin, and Corey Mesler." 2/yr. Expects 2 issues 2006, 2 issues 2007. price per copy $0; sample free. Back issues: $0/in archive. 50pp. Reporting time: 1 week to 3 mos. Simultaneous submissions accepted: No. Publishes 2% of manuscripts submitted. Copyrighted, reverts to author. Subjects: Appalachia, Essays, Family, Folklore, Gender Issues, Marriage, Memoirs, Multicultural, Parenting, Poetry, Relationships, Short Stories, South, Southwest, Women.

Apples & Oranges, Inc., Gene S. Kira, PO Box 2296, Valley Center, CA 92082. 1988. Non-fiction. "Publish titles on sports." avg. press run 5M. Expects 3 titles 2006, 5 titles 2007. Discounts: please inquire, 1-3 20%, 4-39 40%, etc. 320pp. Copyrights for author. Subjects: Non-Fiction, Sports, Outdoors.

APPLESEEDS, Cobblestone Publishing Company, Susan Buckley, Editor; Barbara Burt, Editor, 30 Grove Street, Suite C, Peterborough, NH 03458, 603-924-7209, Fax 603-924-7380, custsvc@cobblestone.mv.com. 1998. 9/yr. Pub'd 9 issues 2005; expects 9 issues 2006, 9 issues 2007. sub. price $29.95 (USA); per copy $4.95; sample $4.95. Back issues: $4.95. 36pp. Simultaneous submissions accepted: yes. Ads: none.

Applied Probability Trust (see also MATHEMATICAL SPECTRUM), D. W. Sharpe, School of Mathematics and Statistics, University of Sheffield, Sheffield S3 7RH, England, tel: +44 (0)114 222-3920; fax: +44 (0)114 272-9782; email: apt@sheffield.ac.uk; web: http://www.appliedprobability.org. 1968. Articles, reviews, letters. Subjects: Education, Mathematics.

AQUARIUS, Eddie S. Linden, Flat 4, Room B, 116 Sutherland Avenue, Maida-Vale, London W9, England. 1968. Poetry, fiction, articles, reviews. "Special all Irish issue forthcoming with Seamus Heaney. 1992 *Aquarius* will publish in late summer a special issue on women and women writers. It will contain poetry, fictional prose, essays, interviews and reviews. Hilary Davies is the guest editor and we are seeking contributions that will reflect the best of women's writing today. They may be sent to Hilary Davies, 70 Wargrave Avenue, Stanford Hill, London N15-6UB, England. Postage cost must be sent to cover the return of material. Special issue in celebration of the 80th birthday of John Heath-Stubbs - *Aquarius* 23/24 English lost 5 pounds. Published - 1998 - also published Heath-Stubbs - collected 'literary essay' 1998 - Carcanet Press - Manchester, England." circ. 1.5M. 2/yr. sub. price $40; per copy $6; sample £5 - $12. Back issues: $5. Discounts: 33% trade. 120pp. Payment: special issues only. Pub's reviews: 40 in 2005. §Poetry, biography. Ads: £80/£40. Subject: Poetry.

AQUATERRA, METAECOLOGY & CULTURE, Jacqueline Froelich, 5473 Highway 23N, Eureka Springs, AR 72631. 1986. Poetry, articles, art, cartoons, letters, news items. "Water-related information particularly compost toilet information and innovative conservation." circ. 3M. 1/yr. price per copy $9.95; sample $9.95. Back issues: $9.95. Discounts: inquire. 140pp. Reporting time: varies. Simultaneous submissions accepted: yes. Publishes 50% of manuscripts submitted. Payment: none. Copyrighted, reverts to author. Pub's reviews: 1 in 2005. §Submissions related to technical and/or spiritual experiences with water articles, research, interviews, ceremonies, prose, poetry, artwork, summaries of water organizations. Ads: inquire. Subjects: Conservation, Earth, Natural History, Ecology, Foods, Education, Energy, Engineering, Networking, Newsletter, Water.

Ara Pacis Publishers, PO Box 1202, Des Plaines, IL 60017-1202. 1998. Poetry, fiction, non-fiction. Expects 3 titles 2006, 3 titles 2007.

Aran Press, Tom Eagan, 1036 S. Fifth Street, Louisville, KY 40203, aranpres@aye.net. 1983. "Publish *plays* for community, professional, college, university, summer stock and dinner theatre markets. No children's plays. No other submissions - look *only* at plays. Also publishing novellas and play collections." avg. press run Not looking for new material. Pub'd 1 title 2005; expects 1 title 2006, 1 title 2007. Discounts: 50%. 90pp.

Simultaneous submissions accepted: no. Payment: yes. Copyrights for author. Subject: Performing Arts.

ARARAT, Leo Hamalian, 55 E 59th Street, New York, NY 10022-1112. 1960. Poetry, fiction, articles, art, criticism, reviews, parts-of-novels. "We prefer material in some way pertinent to Armenian life and culture." circ. 2.2M. 4/yr. Pub'd 4 issues 2005; expects 4 issues 2006, 4 issues 2007. sub. price $24; per copy $7; sample $4. Back issues: $4. Discounts: 15%. 74pp. Reporting time: 4 months. Payment: $10 a printed page (roughly). Copyrighted, reverts to author. Pub's reviews: 30 in 2005. §Ethnic Armenian. Ads: $250/$125. Subject: Armenian.

•Arbutus Press, Susan Bays, 2364 Pinehurst Trail, Traverse City, MI 49686, phone 231-946-7240, FAX 231-946-4196, editor@arbutuspress.com, www.Arbutuspress. 1998. Fiction, non-fiction. avg. press run 3000. Pub'd 2 titles 2005; expects 5 titles 2006, 6 titles 2007. 200pp. Subjects: Great Lakes, Travel.

ARC, Mordechai Beck, Co-editor, Issue 19; Jeffrey M. Green, Co-editor, Issue 19, PO Box 39385, Tel Aviv 61393, Israel, iawe_mailbox@yahoo.com. 1982. Poetry, fiction, interviews, satire, criticism, parts-of-novels, non-fiction. "Arc prints works by Israeli residents who write in English, prints translations from Israelis who write in other languages, and occasionally prints works by Israeli writers who reside elsewhere. Arc is the showcase of the Israel Association of Writers in English." circ. 500. 1/yr. Pub'd 1 issue 2005; expects 1 issue 2006, 1 issue 2007. 64pp. Reporting time: up to 1 year. Payment: none. Copyrighted, reverts to author. Subjects: Anthology, Arts, Avant-Garde, Experimental Art, Culture, Judaism, Literary Review, Literature (General), Middle East, Poetry, Prose.

ARCATA ARTS, Gordon Inkeles, P.O.B. 800, Bayside, CA 95524, 707 822 5839, 707 826 2002, 888 687 8962, pub@arcata-arts.com, http://arcata-arts.com. 1998. Non-fiction. "We publish a line of massage books, card decks and videos by Gordon Inkeles." Pub'd 1 title 2005; expects 1 title 2006, 1 title 2007. Discounts: 1—case quantities 45%, Contact us for case quantity discounts. 172pp. Simultaneous submissions accepted: No. Publishes 0% of manuscripts submitted. All our published material is copyrighted. Subject: Health.

Archer Books, John Taylor-Convery, Rosemary Tribulato, PO Box 1254, Santa Maria, CA 93456, 805-878-8279 phone, email: jtc@archer-books.com, web site: www.archer-books.com. 1998. Non-fiction. "Serious commercial work only. Politics, history, biography. Also provide editing, typesetting and book design services for other publishers." avg. press run 3M. Pub'd 4 titles 2005; expects 4 titles 2006, 6 titles 2007. Discounts: Titles available from Midpoint Trade Books, Ingram, Baker & Taylor, SPD, et al. Quantity discounts to 55%, STOP orders accepted. 250pp. Reporting time: 1 month. Simultaneous submissions accepted: yes. Publishes 5% of manuscripts submitted. Payment: percentage of net sales receipts. Copyrights for author. Subjects: Biography, Culture, Current Affairs, Human Rights, Latino, Memoirs, Non-Fiction, Political Science, Politics, Public Affairs, U.S. Hispanic.

ARCHIPELAGO, Katherine McNamara, PO Box 2485, Charlottesville, VA 22902-2485, editor@archipe-lago.org, www.archipelago.org. 1997. Poetry, fiction, articles, art, photos, interviews, criticism, reviews, music, letters, parts-of-novels, long-poems, plays, concrete art, non-fiction. "Emphasis is on writing, not subject. Strong interest in international writers, Americans abroad or with critical (literary) insight, non-academic fiction and poetry. Recent contributors: Frederic Tuten, Anna Marie Ortese, Benjamin H. Cheever, K. Callaway, Maria Negroni, Hubert Butler, Larry Woiwode, Sandor Kanyade, Daniela Fischerova, Zuyin Ding, Dannie Abse, Jaroslav Seifert, Susan Garrett, and 'Institutional Memory,' conversations with distinguished publishers, editors, booksellers from the old world of publishing books." circ. via the world wide web - 17,000+ unique visitors/mo. 4/yr. Expects 3 issues 2006, 4 issues 2007. free to all; donations gladly accepted. Back issues: available in Archive. 100-150pp. Reporting time: 4-6 months. Simultaneous submissions accepted: will consider; editor must be notified if simultaneous submission. Publishes a small % of manuscripts submitted. Payment: none. Copyrighted, reverts to author. Pub's reviews. Subjects: Essays, Fiction, Journals, Literary Review, Magazines, Non-Fiction, Poetry, Prose, Reading, Reviews, Short Stories, Visual Arts, Writers/Writing.

Arctos Press (see also RUNES, A Review of Poetry), CB Follett, Editor; Susan Terris, Editor, PO Box 401, Sausalito, CA 94966-0401, 415-331-2503, Fax 415-331-3092, runes@aol.com, http://members.aol.com/runes. 1996. Poetry. "Anthologies, theme oriented, send only in response to call for submissions. Looking for quality poems. Recent contributors: Lucille Clifton, Li Young Lee, David St. John, Richard Wilbur, Jane Hirshfield, Shirley Kaufman, Philip Levine, W. S. Merwin." avg. press run 1200. Pub'd 4 titles 2005; expects 2 titles 2006, 3 titles 2007. Discounts: usual. 150pp. Reporting time: 4 months. We accept simultaneous submissions if notified. Publishes 1% of manuscripts submitted. Payment: in copies. Copyrights for author. Subject: Poetry.

Arden Press, Inc., Susan Conley, Editor, PO Box 418, Denver, CO 80201, 303-697-6766. 1980. Non-fiction. "We are actively pursuing women's topics of either historical or contemporary significance, reference works, nonfiction works including practical guides in all subject areas. No autobiographical works or memoirs are considered." avg. press run 3M. Pub'd 3 titles 2005; expects 4 titles 2006, 5 titles 2007. Discounts: 1-4 copies 20%, 5-49 40%, 50+ 50%, to trade. 250pp. Reporting time: 1 month. Simultaneous submissions accepted: yes. Payment: 8-15% according to number of copies sold; annual payments. Copyrights for author. Subjects:

Bibliography, Biography, History, How-To, Motivation, Success, Non-Fiction, Politics, Reference, Self-Help, Women, Writers/Writing.

ARETE, 8 New College Lane, Oxford OX1 3BN, England.

Argo Press (see also CHARLTON SPOTLIGHT), Michael E. Ambrose, PO Box 4201, Austin, TX 78765-4201, charspot01@austin.rr.com. 1972. Fiction. "All submissions are by solicitation only." avg. press run 500. Pub'd 1 title 2005. Discounts: 5 or more 40%. 200pp. Reporting time: varies. Simultaneous submissions accepted: no. Publishes a variable % of manuscripts submitted. Payment: individual terms. Copyrights for author. Subjects: Comics, Fantasy, Science Fiction.

Argonne House Press (see also WORDWRIGHTS MAGAZINE), R.D. Baker, 1620 Argonne Place NW, Washington, DC 20009-5901, 202-328-9769, www.wordwrights.com, publisher@wordwrights.com. 1993. Poetry, fiction, satire, parts-of-novels, long-poems, non-fiction. "We only consider chapbook or book length manuscripts from authors published in *WordWrights Magazine*. For a FREE SAMPLE COPY of the magazine, contact us by letter or e-mail." avg. press run 500. Pub'd 12 titles 2005; expects 12 titles 2006, 12 titles 2007. Discounts: 50%. 60pp. Reporting time: 6 months. Simultaneous submissions accepted: yes. Publishes 50% of manuscripts submitted. Payment: Royalty on copies sold. Copyrights for author.

ARIEL, A Review of International English Literature, University of Calgary Press, Pamela McCallum, The University of Calgary, 2500 University Drive NW, Calgary, Alberta T2N 1N4, Canada, 403-220-4657, Fax 403-289-1123, ariel@ucalgary.ca, www.english.ucalgary.ca/ariel/. 1970. Articles, reviews. "*Ariel* is a refereed journal devoted to the critical and scholarly study of the new and the established literatures in English around the world. It welcomes particularly articles on the relationships among the new literatures and between the new and the established literatures. It publishes a limited number of original poems in each issue." circ. 950. 4/yr. Pub'd 4 issues 2005; expects 4 issues 2006, 4 issues 2007. sub. price $60 institution, $28 individual (orders outside Canada to be paid in US funds, Visa or Mastercard); per copy $15; sample G.S.T. Canada. Back issues: $35 indiv., $50 instit., payable in Cdn. funds, add G.S.T. in Canada; discount on 5 or more volumes. Discounts: $1 for agents, claim period is 6 months ($2 on p/h claims). 150pp. Reporting time: 3 months. Simultaneous submissions accepted: no. Payment: none. Copyrighted, contact editor regarding rights reverting to author. Pub's reviews: 12-14 in 2005. §English literature. Ads: write for info. Subjects: Literary Review, Literature (General).

Ariko Publications, Jonathan Musere, 8513 Venice Blvd #201, Los Angeles, CA 90034. 1998. Articles, non-fiction. "We primarily deal with translation, oral, literary and field research work associated with personal names and proverbs from the central, Southern and Eastern African region." Pub'd 3 titles 2005; expects 2 titles 2006, 3 titles 2007. Discounts: 60%. 200pp. Reporting time: 1 month. Simultaneous submissions accepted: yes. Payment: 10% on retail price copies. Copyrights for author. Subjects: African Literature, Africa, African Studies, Black, Culture, Folklore, Language, Non-Fiction, Reference, Textbooks, Translation.

•**Aristata Publishing,** Craig Elliott, 16429 Lost Canyon Rd., Santa Clarita, CA 91387, Ph (661) 600-5011, Fx (661) 299-9478, general@aristatapublishing.com, www.aristatapublishing.com. 2003. Art. "Aristata creates projects that enable artists to bring their artwork to the public in a creative an innovative way." avg. press run 5000. Pub'd 1 title 2005; expects 3 titles 2006, 2 titles 2007. Discounts: 50%. 150pp. Reporting time: One Month. Simultaneous submissions accepted: Yes. Publishes 1% of manuscripts submitted. Payment: On Per Book Basis. Does not copyright for author. Subject: Arts.

Arizona Master Gardener Press, Cathy L. Cromell, 4341 E. Broadway Road, Phoenix, AZ 85040-8807, 602-470-8086 ext. 312, Fax 602-470-8092. 1996. Non-fiction. "We publish books that educate the public about appropriate plants and maintenance for arid, low-desert gardening. Non-fiction, any length." avg. press run 3M. Pub'd 1 title 2005; expects 1 title 2006, 1 title 2007. 150pp. Subjects: Gardening, Horticulture.

Arjuna Library Press (see also JOURNAL OF REGIONAL CRITICISM), Count Prof. Joseph A. Uphoff Jr., Executive Director, 1025 Garner St., D, Space 18, Colorado Springs, CO 80905-1774, Email address pfuphoff@earthlink.net Website address http://home.earthlink.net/~pfuphoff/. 1983. Fiction, art, photos, long-poems, non-fiction. "The current debate is regarding the use of meaning versus deliberate meaningless images. The language poets draw pictures without meaningful implication. They work with fragments and irrational splicing, Surrealist Fragmentation. The metaphorical poets use words as other meanings versus using words in other contexts. The message poets determine literal comprehension. Thus, there are three kinds of logic, rhetorical, cryptic, and definitive. There are two kinds of irony, dramatic and journalistic. There are two kinds of reality, fictional and factual. We are looking for examples of these including those in visual poetics. The universe we employ is complex with a fictional context in virtual reality and a factual context in forensics (Forensic surrealism). The Free Syntagma of the Surrealist Collage in Virtual Space, including the Internet, is being used to orchestrate online galleries where Visual Poetics can be supplemented by the presentation of literary frames. The Mail Art movement includes the opportunity for cost effective use of color illustration and large collections." 30pp. Reporting time: indefinite. Payment: dependent on market, profit sharing. Does not copyright for author. Subjects: Anthropology, Archaelogy, Arts, Avant-Garde, Experimental Art, Communication, Journalism, Criticism, Dada, Drama, Martial Arts, Mathematics, Metaphysics, Myth, Mythology, Photography, Poetry, Surrealism.

The Ark, Geoffrey Gardner, 51 Pleasant Street, Marlborough, NH 03455-2532, 603-876-4160, anarkiss@mindspring.com. 1970. Poetry, long-poems. "This is a highly selective press. Publication is now primarily by invitation and occasional as economies allow. We will consider poetry of any form or style. Depth, power and excellence are what we want. We are especially interested in new translation of poetry from all languages and periods. Query before submission. Stringent finances have made it very unlikely that we will be able to take on any new publishing ventures over the next several years. We will continue to read all that comes to us. It is less likely than ever we will accept any new, unsolicited work for publication." avg. press run 1.5M+. Pub'd 1 title 2005; expects 1 title 2006, 2 titles 2007. Discounts: 40% to bookstores only. 116pp. Reporting time: at once to 3 months. Payment: unique to each project and by arrangement with each author. Copyrights for author. Subjects: Poetry, Translation.

Armadillo Publishing Corporation, Lawrence Simpson, PO Box 2052, Georgetown, TX 78627-2052, 512-863-8660. 1997. Poetry, fiction, art, non-fiction. "Publishing, co-publishing, and self-publishing production services for authors on all topics. We produce 70-400 page paperback books in runs of 25-200; archive electronic files for future runs. Over 40 titles, including Patsy McCleery/nonfiction, Don Snell/art & poetry, Larry Simpson/fiction, Lucas Adams/nonfiction, and George Neuvirth/nonfiction, history." avg. press run +/- 100. Pub'd 7 titles 2005; expects 8 titles 2006, 12 titles 2007. Discounts: 1-10 books 25%, 10+ 40%. 175pp. Reporting time: 1 week. Simultaneous submissions accepted: no. Publishes 75% of manuscripts submitted. Payment: co-publishing 15%. Does not copyright for author.

ARNAZELLA, Woody West, Advisor, 3000 Landerholm Circle SE, Bellevue, WA 98007, 206-641-2373. 1976. Poetry, fiction, art, photos, cartoons, satire, parts-of-novels, plays, non-fiction. circ. 300. 1/yr. Pub'd 1 issue 2005; expects 1 issue 2006, 1 issue 2007. price per copy $10; sample $10. Back issues: $3. 80pp. Reporting time: spring. Payment: copies. Copyrighted, reverts to author. Subjects: Arts, Avant-Garde, Experimental Art, Cartoons, Fiction, Non-Fiction, Photography.

ARSENIC LOBSTER MAGAZINE, Susan Yount, Editor, lobster@magere.com. Est.2000. Poetry, art, photos, criticism, reviews. "*Arsenic Lobster* seeks eloquent emotion, articulate experiment; the charlie-horse hearted, heavily quirked, the harrowing. Honed lyricism, stripped narrative... Be compelled, *compulsed, MOVED*, to write. INCLUDE ALL SUBMISSIONS IN BODY OF EMAIL (no attachments please). 3-5 POEMS, ANY LENGTH. (Lobster art/photos by PDF attachment only). PLEASE WRITE FIRST INITIAL, LAST NAME, DATE & SUBMISSION CATEGORY IN SUBJECT LINE (Example: J. Doe 1/29/05 Review). Address checks/other correspondence to: S. Yount, 1608 S. Paulina St., Chicago, IL 60608-1915." circ. approx.300. 2/yr. sub. price $10; per copy $5; sample $5. Back issues: #'s 5 & 6 available. 30pp. Reporting time: varies. Simultaneous submissions accepted: Yes. Publishes .5% of manuscripts submitted. Payment: 1 copy. Pub's reviews: 2 in 2005. §Intelligent, guttural poetry. Ads: none. Subject: Poetry.

ART BUREAU, Bert Benson, Gigi Conot, Jason Martin, PO Box 225221, San Francisco, CA 94122, 415-759-1788, info@artbureau.org, www.artbureau.org. 2002. Articles, art, photos, cartoons, letters, collages, plays, concrete art, news items, non-fiction. "*Art Bureau* is a black and white offset publication with 32 pages of artwork, interviews and information about the art and design community. Stickers, postcards and other keepsakes are included with each issue.*P*." circ. 500. 3/yr. Pub'd 2 issues 2005; expects 3 issues 2006, 3 issues 2007. sub. price $10; per copy $3.50; sample $3.50. Discounts: publisher's discount $3 each copy, no trades. 32pp. Reporting time: 30 days. Simultaneous submissions accepted: yes. Publishes 40% of manuscripts submitted. Payment: contributor copies. Copyrighted, reverts to author. Ads: $10 1/2 page. Subject: Arts.

ART CALENDAR, Carolyn Blakeslee Proeber, Publisher, PO Box 2675, Salisbury, MD 21802, 410-749-9625, Fax 410-749-9626, carolyn@artcalendar.com, www.artcalendar.com. 1985. Articles, art, photos, interviews, news items. "Marketing and career management journal for visual artists. Articles on marketing, art law, psychology of creativity; interviews with dealers, curators. Professional listings: grants, residencies, juried shows, museums, etc., reviewing portfolios." circ. 22M. 11/yr. Pub'd 11 issues 2005; expects 11 issues 2006, 11 issues 2007. sub. price $33; per copy $5; sample $5. Back issues: $5 each subject to availability (includes s/h). Discounts: inquire. 56pp. Reporting time: varies. We accept simultaneous submissions if disclosed as such. Publishes 10% of manuscripts submitted. Payment: yes. Copyrighted, reverts to author. Ads: inquire. Subjects: Arts, Avant-Garde, Experimental Art, Awards, Foundations, Grants, Book Arts, Crafts, Hobbies, Culture, Design, Electronics, Festivals, Law, Photography, Psychology, Public Relations/Publicity, Visual Arts, Weaving.

THE ART HORSE, Epona Publishing, Kathleen M. Wermuth, 2 Mason Street, Gloucester, MA 01930-5902, http://kathywer.homepage.com/index.html. 1999. Fiction, articles, art, reviews, long-poems, non-fiction. "*The Art Horse* is a small newsletter written from a personal view. Subjects cover new pieces of art by equine artist

Kathleen Gorman Wermuth. As well as covers subjects about horse art, books and writings. I completely write it as for now." circ. 30-50. 4/yr. Expects 2 issues 2006, 4 issues 2007. sub. price $4; per copy $1.25; sample free. Back issues: none at this time. Discounts: at this time not available. 5pp. Reporting time: 1 month, LSASE for return of manuscript. Simultaneous submissions accepted: yes. Payment: free advertising in one issue unless otherwise stated. Pub's reviews. §Horse art and books. Subjects: Advertising, Self-Promotion, Animals, Arts, How-To, Poetry, Short Stories.

THE ART OF ABUNDANCE, Pellingham Casper Communications, Paula Langguth Ryan, 1121 Annapolis Road, Suite 120, Odenton, MD 21113, 800-507-9244; 208-545-8164 (fax), www.ArtOfAbundance.com. 1999. Articles, reviews. "Our mission is to help people heal their relationship with money and create the life they truly desire. Recent contributors include Paula Langguth Ryan, William Deitrich, Catherine Ponder, Steve Rhode, Anita Law, Janet Hall, Alan Cohen." circ. 3336. 12/yr. Pub'd 12 issues 2005; expects 12 issues 2006, 12 issues 2007. sub. price $0; per copy $0; sample $0. Back issues: $0. Discounts: magazine is delivered electronically only at this time. 10pp. Reporting time: 3-6 months, send electronically, with article in body of email, will not accept attachments. Simultaneous submissions accepted: Yes. Publishes 10% of manuscripts submitted. No payment made. We provide links to your website, and contact info if readers wish to contribute directly to author of article. Copyrighted, reverts to author. Pub's reviews: approx 10 in 2005. §personal finance, self-help, inspirational, metaphysical, new age. Ads: do not currenty accept advertising. Subjects: Aromatherapy, Careers, Finances, Guidance, Inspirational, Mentoring/Coaching, Metaphysics, Philosophy, Physics, Psychology, Reading, Relationships, Sociology, Spiritual.

ART PAPERS, Dr. Charles Reeve, Editor-in-Chief; Dr. Jerry Cullum, Senior Editor, PO Box 5748, Atlanta, GA 31107-5748, 404-588-1837, Fax 404-588-1836, editor@artpapers.org, www.artpapers.org. 1977. Articles, art, photos, interviews, criticism, reviews, news items, non-fiction. "Features: 2,000-3,000 words. Reviews: 600-800 words. *Art Papers* is primarily interested in reviews of contemporary and experimental artists' exhibitions in all media (painting, sculpture, architecture, digital art, film, photography, performance, video, music, dance). For writers' guidelines e-mail or write (no phone calls). *Art Papers Magazine* - a non-profit arts publication providing diverse and independent perspectives on international contemporary art and culture for over 25 years." circ. 135M. 6/yr. Pub'd 6 issues 2005; expects 6 issues 2006, 6 issues 2007. sub. price $35; per copy $7; sample $1.75. Back issues: $10 per copy. Discounts: Group subscriptions to groups of 10 or more. 72pp. Reporting time: 6 weeks. Simultaneous submissions accepted: no. Publishes unsolicited submissions 30% of manuscripts submitted. Payment: copies, fees range from $50 to $325. Copyrighted, reverts to author. Pub's reviews: approx. 10 book reviews; do not review magazines in 2005. §Contemporary visual arts, dance, new music, theater, performance, video, film. Ads: contact for rates. Subjects: Architecture, Arts, Avant-Garde, Experimental Art, Book Arts, Electronics, Multicultural, Performing Arts.

ART TIMES, Raymond J. Steiner, PO Box 730, Mount Marion, NY 12456-0730, 845-246-6944, info@arttimesjournal.com, www.arttimesjournal.com. 1984. "Other address: 16 Fite Road, Saugerties, NY 12477. *Art Times* is a monthly journal and resource for all of the arts. Although the bulk is written by Staff members, we solicit poetry and short stories from free-lancers around the world (we are listed in *Writer's Market, Literary Market, Poet's Market,* etc). Fiction: short stories up to 1,500 words. No excessive sex, violence or racist themes. High literary quality sought. Poetry: up to 20 lines. All topics; all forms. High literary quality sought. Readers of *Art Times* are generally over 40, affluent and art conscious. Articles in *Art Times* are general pieces on the arts written by staff *and are not solicited.* General tone of paper governed by literary essays on arts—no journalistic writing, press releases. *Always include SASE.* Guidelines: business size envelope, 1 first-class stamp." circ. 28M. 10/yr. Pub'd 10 issues 2005; expects 10 issues 2006, 10 issues 2007. sub. price $15, $30 foreign; sample SASE + 3 first class stamps. Back issues: same. Discounts: bundles (25-100 copies) sent free to preforming art centers, galleries, museums and similar distribution points. 20pp. Reporting time: 6 months (24-48 months for publication). Simultaneous submissions accepted: yes. Publishes .01% of manuscripts submitted. Payment: poetry 6 free issues + 1 yr. sub.; short stories $25 + 1 yr. sub. Copyrighted, reverts to author. Pub's reviews: 75-100 in 2005. §We only review art books. Ads: $1360 full/$700 half /$377 1/4 page/Classified $29 for 1st 15 words, 50¢ each additional word for classifieds. Subject: Arts.

ART VISIONARY MAGAZINE, Damian P. Michaels, Editor, GPO Box 1536, Melbourne, Victoria 3001, Australia, artvisionary@optusnet.com.au. "International art of the Fantastic, Visionary & Surreal."

ART:MAG, Peter Magliocco, Editor, PO Box 70896, Las Vegas, NV 89170, 702-734-8121. 1984. Poetry, fiction, art, photos, cartoons, interviews, satire, parts-of-novels, long-poems. "Subscribers receive chapbooks & 'surprises' now and then." circ. 100+. 1/yr. Pub'd 2 issues 2005; expects 1 issue 2006, 1 issue 2007. sub. price $8; per copy $5; sample $3. Back issues: query. Discounts: none. 35-90pp. Reporting time: 1-3 months. Simultaneous submissions accepted: yes. Publishes 25% of manuscripts submitted. Payment: 1 copy of magazine. Not copyrighted. Pub's reviews: 1-2 in 2005. §Poetry, fiction. Ads: exchange only. Subjects: Arts, Essays, Fiction, Poetry, Satire, Short Stories.

Arte Publico Press, Nicolas Kanellos, Publisher, University of Houston, Houston, TX 77204-2090,

713-743-2841, fax 713-743-2847. 1980. Poetry, fiction, art, photos. avg. press run 3M. Pub'd 22 titles 2005; expects 20 titles 2006, 20 titles 2007. Discounts: 40% trade. 120pp. Reporting time: 4 months. Payment: varies per type of book. Copyrights for author. Subjects: Chicano/a, Drama, Fiction, Poetry.

ARTELLA: the waltz of words and art, Marney Makridakis, P.O. Box 78, Johnson, NY 10933, www.ArtellaWordsandArt.com. Poetry, fiction, articles, art, photos, parts-of-novels, long-poems, collages, non-fiction. "Artella focuses on publishing works that combine words and art, with a heavy emphasis on fostering collaborations among writers and artists. Our Web site, www.ArtellaWordsAndArt.com, includes a "Projects Seeking Partners" list, where artists and writers can connect with one another to create works for publication. The magazine often includes a multimedia component, such as CDs with music and audio interviews. Artella magazine alternates between full-color print issues and PDF e-issues that are distributed to subscribers online. The latter also includes resources and articles relevant to writers and artists, in addition to the creative pairings of writing and art." circ. 2500. 6/yr. Pub'd 6 issues 2005; expects 6 issues 2006, 6 issues 2007. sub. price $39; per copy $15; sample free electronic copy. Back issues: $15. Discounts: over 10 copies - 50% discount. 40pp. Reporting time: 30 days. Simultaneous submissions accepted: Yes. Publishes 40% of manuscripts submitted. Payment: pays in complimenary copies. Authors/artists retain copyright of their original work. Pub's reviews: approx 10 in 2005. §materials relevant to the creative life. Subjects: Abstracts, Arts, Avant-Garde, Experimental Art, Book Arts, Community, Crafts, Hobbies, Creativity, Experimental, Fiction, Poetry, Prose, Storytelling, Visual Arts, Writers/Writing, Zines.

ARTFUL DODGE, Daniel Bourne, Editor; Philip Brady, Poetry Editor; Marcy Campbell, Fiction Editor; Carolyne Wright, Translations Editor; Leonard Kress, Creative Non-Fiction Editor, Department of English, College of Wooster, Wooster, OH 44691, www.wooster.edu/artfuldodge. 1979. Poetry, fiction, art, photos, cartoons, interviews, satire, criticism, reviews, parts-of-novels, long-poems, collages, plays, non-fiction. "Contributors of fiction include Dan Chaon, Bob Shacochis, Mark Axelrod, Lynne Sharon Schwartz, Joan Connor, Robert Mooney, William S. Burroughs, Sarah Willis. Poets include Gary Gildner, Julia Kasdorf, Charles Simic, Gregory Orr, Alfred Corn, Madeline DeFrees, Beth Ann Fennelly, Diane Glancy, Cynthia Hogue, William Pitt Root, John Kinsella, E. Ethelbert Miller, Lynn Powell, Daniel Tobin, Roger Weingarten, Denise Duhamel, Mong-Lan, H. L. Hix, Nin Andrews, Margaret Gibson, Venus Khoury-Ghata (translated by Marilyn Hacker), Horace (translated by William Matthews), Tim Seibles, Yannis Ritsos, Maj Ragain, Christopher Howell, Kate Fetherston, Stuart Dybek, John Haines. According to *Library Journal,* our interviews (Borges, Sarraute, Milosz, Merwin, Michael Dorris, Lee Smith, William Matthews, Stanislaw Baranczak, Tim O'Brien, Vaclav Havel, Charles Simic, William Least Heat-Moon, Tess Gallagher, William Heyen, George Bruce, Gregory Orr, James Laughlin, John Haines, Jim Daniels, Gwendolyn Brooks) are 'much more perceptive and informative than most.' Translations are heartily encouraged; we like to print special sections of contemporary writing beyond America's extensive, though not infinite, linguistic/cultural borders. We also do a 'poet as translator' series, featuring the original poetry and translations of such prominent and emerging practitioners as William Stafford, Tess Gallagher, Pablo Medina, Khaled Mattawa, Nicholas Kolumban, Len Roberts, Mary Crow, Karen Kovacik, Orlando Ricardo Menes, etc." circ. 1M. 1 double issue/yr. Pub'd 1 issue 2005; expects 1 issue 2006, 1 issue 2007. sub. price indiv. $7, instit. $10; Current issues $7. Back issues $5. Discounts: at least 20%—please query. 180pp. Reporting time: 6 months or longer. We accept simultaneous submissions, as long as we are immediately notified of publication elsewhere. Publishes less than 1% of manuscripts submitted. Payment: 2 copies, plus at least $5 per page honorarium, thanks to Ohio Arts Council. Copyrighted, reverts to author. Pub's reviews. §Poetry, fiction, translation, creative nonfiction (especially work centered on place). Ads: $100/$60. Subjects: Fiction, Poetry, Translation.

Artisan Studio Design (see also EROSHA; VLQ (Verse Libre Quarterly)), C.E. Laine, PO BOx 185, Falls Church, VA 22040-0185, Fax 703-852-3906, editor@vlqpoetry.com, http://VLQpoetry.com.

ARTISTAMP NEWS, Ed Varney, 4426 Island Hwy S, Courtenay, BC V9N 9T1, Canada. 1991. Articles, art, criticism, reviews, letters, news items. "This newsletter's objective is to present current news of events and editions and history of artist use of the stamp format as a print medium, profiles of artists, and articles about techniques used in producing stamp art. Includes section of mail-art show & project listings, reviews of related books and publications." circ. 400. 1/yr. Pub'd 1 issue 2005; expects 1 issue 2006, 1 issue 2007. sub. price $10/2 years; per copy $5; sample $4. Back issues: $4 each; not all issues available. Discounts: no wholesale. 12pp. Reporting time: 12 months. Publishes 75% of manuscripts submitted. Payment: 10 copies. Copyrighted, reverts to author. Pub's reviews: 23 brief-description in 2005. §Books or periodicals either about or utilizing stamps by artists or sheets of stamps by artists. Ads: 45¢/word. Subjects: Biography, Book Reviewing, Counter-Culture, Alternatives, Communes, History, Newsletter, Philately, Visual Arts.

•**ARTISTIC RAMBLINGS, Red Tiger Press,** A.D. Beache, P.O. Box 2907, Thomasville, NC 27361, PH: 832-634-7012, Fax: 530-323-8251, email: ArtisticRamblings@gmail.com. 2005. Poetry, fiction, articles, art, photos, interviews, music, letters, long-poems, non-fiction. 4/yr. Expects 4 issues 2007. sub. price $22; per copy $5.95; sample $5.95. Back issues: inquire. Discounts: 3-10 copies 25%. 48pp. Reporting time: 2-6 weeks.

Simultaneous submissions accepted: Yes. Payment: 1 contributor's copies of the magazine. Copyrighted, reverts to author. Pub's reviews: none in 2005. §Fiction, poetry, essays, creative non-fiction, etc. Subjects: Book Arts, Creativity, Fantasy, Fiction, Futurism, Horror, Humor, Interviews, Occult, Photography, Poetry, Prose, Quotations, Science Fiction, Short Stories.

Arts & Letters Press, Gunnar Dennis McIlnay, 826 Walnut Street, Hollidaysburg, PA 16648.

ARTS & LETTERS: Journal of Contemporary Culture, Martin Lammon, Georgia College & State University, Campus Box 89, Milledgeville, GA 31061-0490, 478-445-1289, al@gcsu.edu, http://al.gcsu.edu. 1998. Poetry, fiction, interviews, reviews, plays, non-fiction. *"Arts & Letters* strives to publish a range of literary works that express the vital force of contemporary culture as opposed to popular culture. We represent a wide variety of voices and genres: poetry, fiction, drama, creative nonfiction, translations, and book reviews. Recent contributors include Margaret Gibson, Ernest Gaines, Maxine Kumin, W.S. Merwin, Michael Waters, Dinty W. Moore, Brad Barkley, Jean Valentine, Donald Hall, Judith Ortiz Cofer, Bret Lott, Debra Marquart, Virgil Suarez, Janice Eidus, Laurie Lamon, and Daniel Wallace. Regular submission period is September 1 to March 1. *Arts & Letters* also sponsors a poetry, fiction, creative nonfiction, and drama competition every spring. Prizes are publication and $1,000 for each genre. Postmark deadline for the contest is March 15. A $15 entry fee includes a year's subscription. Visit our web site or send SASE or email for guidelines." circ. 1.5M. 2/yr. Pub'd 2 issues 2005; expects 2 issues 2006, 2 issues 2007. sub. price $15; per copy $8; sample $5. Back issues: $25 for Issue #1, $5 for others. Discounts: 25% off cover price for bookstores ($6 per copy). 184pp. Reporting time: 4-8 weeks. Simultaneous submissions accepted: Yes, if we are notified immediately that the work has been accepted elsewhere. Publishes less than .5% of manuscripts submitted. Payment: $10 per published page, $50 minimum. Copyrighted, reverts to author. Pub's reviews: 4 in 2005. §Reviews are assigned only. Ads: $100 full page trade. Subjects: Arts, Culture, Drama, Essays, Fiction, Literature (General), Multicultural, Non-Fiction, Poetry, Translation.

Arts End Books (see also NOSTOC MAGAZINE), Marshall Brooks, Editor, PO Box 441, West Dover, VT 05356-0441, marshallbrooks.com. 1979. Poetry, fiction, music, parts-of-novels, long-poems, non-fiction. "Send a SASE for our catalog describing our subscription package program. No submissions please; queries okay." avg. press run varies. Pub'd 2 titles 2005; expects 2 titles 2006, 2 titles 2007. Discounts: on request. Pages vary. Reporting time: a few weeks. Simultaneous submissions accepted: no. Publishes 1-5% of manuscripts submitted. Payment: worked out on an individual basis with each author, for each project. Copyrights for author. Subjects: Bibliography, Book Reviewing, Poetry.

ARTSLINK, Americans for the Arts, Susan Gillespie, Managing Editor, 1000 Vermont Avenue NW, 6th Floor, Washington, DC 20005, 202-371-2830. 1997. Articles. circ. 2.5M. 4/yr. Pub'd 4 issues 2005; expects 4 issues 2006, 4 issues 2007. sub. price with Americans for the Arts membership only. 8pp. Payment: none. Copyrighted, does not revert to author. Ads: please call 202-371-2830. Subjects: Arts, Avant-Garde, Experimental Art, Business & Economics, Dance, Drama, Education.

Artwork Publications, LLC, Arthur W. Wilson, 8335 SW Fairway Drive, Portland, OR 97225-2755, 503-297-2045, Fax 503-297-5163, artwilsn@easystreet.com. 1995. "Korean War, military history." avg. press run 5M. Expects 2 titles 2006, 1 title 2007. Discounts: wholesaler 55%, bookstore 25%. 488pp. Publishes 5% of manuscripts submitted. Payment: author pays print costs, Artwork Publications has 1/2 interest after print costs are amortized; sales costs are shared. Copyrights for author. Subjects: History, Military, Veterans.

Arx Publishing LLC (see also Evolution Publishing; THE TARPEIAN ROCK), Claudio R. Salvucci, PO Box 1333, Merchantville, NJ 08109, 856-486-1310, Fax 856-665-0170, info@arxpub.com, www.arxpub.com. 2001. Fiction. "Fantasy, sci-fi, action/adventure, allegorical and satirical novels. Preference for historical fiction focusing on ancient, classical Greco-Roman, Medieval, Church, Renaissance or Early American history." avg. press run 1M-1.5M. Pub'd 1 title 2005; expects 2 titles 2006, 2 titles 2007. Discounts: trade 40%. 250pp. Reporting time: 6-8 weeks. Simultaneous submissions accepted: yes. Publishes less than 1% of manuscripts submitted. Payment: varies by contract. Copyrights for author. Subjects: Fantasy, Fiction, Novels, Science Fiction.

Ascension Publishing, Betsy Thompson, 920 East Cedar Avenue, Burbank, CA 91501-1528, 818-848-8145. 1990. "Approx. 190 pages. Work is generally concerned with proposing new possibilities for coping with modern living through ideas that offer greater serenity." avg. press run 3M. Expects 1 title 2006, 2 titles 2007. Discounts: bookstore 40%; other 3-199 40%, 200-499 50%, 500+ 65%. 190pp. Copyrights for author. Subjects: Inspirational, Metaphysics, New Age, Parenting, Self-Help, Spiritual.

ASCENT, W. Scott Olsen, Department of English, Concordia College, Moorhead, MN 56562, E-mail Ascent@cord.edu. 1975. Poetry, fiction, letters, parts-of-novels, long-poems, non-fiction. circ. 500. 3/yr. Pub'd 3 issues 2005; expects 3 issues 2006, 3 issues 2007. sub. price $12; per copy $5; sample $5. Back issues: $5. 100pp. Reporting time: 1 week to 3 months. Simultaneous submissions accepted: yes. We accept 60 manuscripts out of 2,600 submitted each year. Payment: none. Copyrighted, reverts to author. Subject:

Literature (General).

ASCENT, Timeless Books, Clea McDougall, 837 Rue Gilford, Montreal, QC H2J 1P1, Canada, 514-499-3999, Fax 514-499-3904, info@ascentmagazine.com, www.ascentmagazine.com. 1999. Articles, art, photos, interviews, reviews, music, letters, concrete art, non-fiction. "Additional address: *Ascent*, 334 Cornelia Street #519, Plattsburgh, NY 12091. Contact magazine for submissions and advertising. Recent contributors: David Suzuki, Arundhati Roy, Geeta Iyengar, Sharon Gannon, Krishna Das, Tias Little and Richard Rosen." circ. 7000. 4/yr. Pub'd 4 issues 2005; expects 4 issues 2006, 4 issues 2007. sub. price $15.95; per copy $4.95; sample $7.00. Back issues: $7.00. Discounts: contact distributors or magazine. 72pp. Simultaneous submissions accepted: no. Payment: 20¢ per published word. Copyrighted, reverts to author. Pub's reviews: 24 in 2005. §Spirituality, social action, yoga, Buddhism, environment. Subjects: Arts, Book Reviewing, Canada, Counter-Culture, Alternatives, Communes, Humanism, India, Inspirational, Interviews, Philosophy, Photography, Religion, Spiritual, Vegetarianism, Visual Arts, Zen.

Ash Lad Press, Bill Romey, PO Box 294, East Orleans, MA 02643, 508-255-2301 phone/Fax. 1975. Non-fiction. "No unsolicited submissions accepted." avg. press run 1.5M. Pub'd 1 title 2005; expects 2 titles 2006. Discounts: trade 40% for orders of over 5, 20% for 1-4, texts 20%, libraries 25%. 150pp. Payment: cooperative sharing of costs and income. Copyrights for author. Subjects: Education, Psychology, Travel.

Ash Tree Publishing, Susun Weed, PO Box 64, Woodstock, NY 12498, 845-246-8081. 1986. Non-fiction. "Women's health, women's spirituality." avg. press run 15M. Pub'd 1 title 2005; expects 2 titles 2006, 2 titles 2007. Discounts: 20% 1-2 copies, 30% 3-9, 40% 10-51, 40% S.T.O.P. orders, 45% 1 case, 50% 2-4 cases, 55% 5 cases. 240pp. Reporting time: 2-6 months. Publishes 1% of manuscripts submitted. Payment: standard. Copyrights for author. Subjects: Ecology, Foods, Health, Spiritual, Translation, Women.

The Ashland Poetry Press, Stephen H. Haven, Editor, Ashland University, Ashland, OH 44805, 419-289-5110, FAX 419-289-5329. 1969. Poetry. "Thematic anthologies and occasional individual books of poems by a single poet; series of lectures by AU annual writer-in-residence. Annual Richard Snyder publication Competition for full-length collection of poetry." avg. press run 1M. Pub'd 1 title 2005; expects 2 titles 2006, 2 titles 2007. Discounts: 40% to book companies. 85pp. Reporting time: solicited manuscripts mainly; Annual Snyder publication competition. We accept solicited simultaneous submissions. Payment: 10%. Does not copyright for author. Subject: Poetry.

ASIA FILE, Pan, PO Box 277193, Sacramento, CA 95827-7193, E-mail asiafile@earthlink.net, www.EroticTravel.com. 1994 Print / 1998 Online. Articles, photos, interviews, criticism, reviews, letters, news items, non-fiction. circ. 1M. 3-4/yr. Pub'd 3 issues 2005; expects 3 issues 2006, 3 issues 2007. sub. price $39; sample $15. Back issues: contact us. 12-20pp. Reporting time: 1 month. Simultaneous submissions accepted: no. Publishes 50% of manuscripts submitted. Payment: trade for subscription/back issues. Copyrighted, reverts to author. Pub's reviews: 3 in 2005. §Prostitution, nightlife, sex. Ads: contact us. Subjects: Anarchist, Asia, Indochina, Cuba, Libertarian, Men, Newsletter, Sex, Sexuality, Travel.

ASIAN ANTHROPOLOGY, The Chinese University Press, Chee-Beng Tan Prof., Editor; Gordon Mathews Prof., Editor, The Chinese University of Hong Kong, Sha Tin, New Territories, Hong Kong, Hong Kong, 852-26096508, 852-26037355. 2002. 1/yr. Pub'd 1 issue 2005; expects 1 issue 2006, 1 issue 2007. sub. price US$20 (Institution)/US$12 (Individual). 200pp. Reporting time: 30 days. Simultaneous submissions accepted: No. Pub's reviews: 5 in 2005. §culture and anthropology. Subjects: Abstracts, Anthropology, Archaeology.

ASIAN JOURNAL OF ENGLISH LANGUAGE TEACHING, The Chinese University Press, Gwendolyn Gong Prof., Editor; George S. Braine Prof., Editor, The Chinese University of Hong Kong, Sha Tin, New Territories, Hong Kong, Hong Kong, 852-26096508, 852-26037355, cup@cuhk.edu.hk, www.chineseupress.com. 1990. 1/yr. Pub'd 1 issue 2005; expects 1 issue 2006, 1 issue 2007. sub. price US$21.5 (Institution), US$11.5 (Individual); per copy US$21.5 (Institution), US$11.5 (Individual). Simultaneous submissions accepted: No. Pub's reviews: 3 in 2005. Subject: Language.

THE ASIAN PACIFIC AMERICAN JOURNAL, Hanya Yanagihara, 16 West 32nd Street, Suite 10A, New York, NY 10001-3814, 212-494-0061. 1992. Poetry, fiction, art, photos, parts-of-novels, long-poems, plays, non-fiction. circ. 2M. 2/yr. Pub'd 2 issues 2005; expects 2 issues 2006, 2 issues 2007. sub. price $45, includes membership to the Asian American Writers' Workshop; per copy $10; sample $12. Back issues: $12. Discounts: call for special prices. 200pp. Reporting time: 3 months. We accept simultaneous submissions but please let us know. Publishes 20% of manuscripts submitted. Payment: 2 free copies. Copyrighted, reverts to author. §Asian or Asian American. Ads: $250/$120/quarter page $60. Subject: Asian-American.

ASIAN SURVEY, University of California Press, Lowell Dittmer, Editor; David Fraser, Managing Editor; Bonnie Dehler, Assistant Editor, University of California Press, 2000 Center Street, Suite 303, Berkeley, CA 94704-1223, 510-643-7154. 1960. Non-fiction. "Editorial address: Institute of East Asian Studies, 6701 San Pablo Avenue, Room 408, Marchant Bldg., Oakland, CA 94608." circ. 2031. 6/yr. Pub'd 6 issues 2005; expects

6 issues 2006, 6 issues 2007. sub. price $75 indiv., $230 instit., $45 students ($20 air freight); per copy $16 indiv., $42 instit., $16 student; sample free. Back issues: $16 indiv., $42 instit., $16 student. Discounts: 10% foreign agents, 30% 10+ one time orders, standing orders (bookstores): 1-99 40%, 100+ 50%. 196pp. Reporting time: 1-2 months. Payment: varies. Copyrighted, does not revert to author. Ads: $295/$220. Subject: Asia, Indochina.

•**Aspen Mountain Publishing,** Thomas Smith J, 5885 Cumming Highway Suite 108, PMB 254, Sugar Hill, GA 30518, www.aspenmtnpublishing.com. 2006. Fiction, non-fiction. Expects 2 titles 2006, 2 titles 2007. Discounts: Wholesalers and Bookstores 50%. 204pp. Reporting time: 30 days. Simultaneous submissions accepted: Yes. Publishes 5% of manuscripts submitted. Payment: No advances, increasing % to authors over three years, quarterly payments. Does not copyright for author. Subjects: Americana, Business & Economics, Careers, Employment, Humor.

Aspermont Press, Roger Scott, 1249 Hayes Street, San Francisco, CA 94117, 415-863-2847.

ASPHODEL, Martin Itzkowitz, Department of Composition & Rhetoric, Rowan University, Glassboro, NJ 08028. 2000. Poetry, fiction, articles, satire, parts-of-novels, long-poems, non-fiction. "We focus on literary fiction, creative non-fiction, poetry. If experimental fiction is sent, please have a literary angle to the work. No science fiction, true crime, horror, or romance. Translations of fiction or poetry are considered." circ. 500. 1/yr. Pub'd 1 issue 2005; expects 1 issue 2006, 1 issue 2007. sub. price $7.50; per copy $7.50; sample $3.50. Back issues: inquire. Discounts: no trade discounts. 150pp. Reporting time: about six months. Simultaneous submissions accepted: Yes. Publishes 10% of manuscripts submitted. Payment: copies of publication. Copyrighted, reverts to author. No ads. Subjects: Essays, Experimental, Feminism, Fiction, Haiku, Humor, Non-Fiction, Poetry, Short Stories.

Aspicomm Media, Renee Flagler, Susan Herriott, PO Box 1212, Baldwin, NY 11510, Phone (516) 642-5976, Fax (516) 489-1199, www.aspicomm.com. 2001. Fiction, non-fiction. "Aspicomm Books missioin is to provide readers with exceptional quality and substance and create boundless opportunities for talented aspiring writers of all literary styles." Expects 2 titles 2006, 3 titles 2007. Discounts: 2-50 copies 25%50-100 Copies 40%over 100 copies 55%. 240pp. Reporting time: 3 months. Simultaneous submissions accepted: Yes. Does not copyright for author. Subjects: African-American, Black, Caribbean, Family, Fiction, Mystery, Relationships, Singles.

ASSEMBLAGE: A Critical Journal of Architecture and Design Culture, Alicia Kennedy, K. Michael Hays, 1140 Washington St. Apt. 6, Boston, MA 02118-4502, email assmblag@gsd.harvard.edu. 1986. Articles, art, photos, interviews, criticism, reviews, letters, non-fiction. "Send editorial correspondence and books for review to Alicia Kennedy, PO Box 180299. Send subscriptions and address changes to MIT Press Journals, 5 Cambridge Center, Suite 4, Cambridge MA 02142-1493. *Assemblage*'s project is the theorization of architecture—its histories, its criticisms, and its practices—along cultural fault lines. Cutting across disciplines, we promote experiments with forms of exegesis, commentary, and analysis. Among the journal's recurring sections, 'The Strictly Architectural' raises the question of what 'properly' belongs to architecture, 'New Babylons' charts out an urbanism of ideas, 'Re:view' engages books and conferences as jumping off points for longer investigations, and 'Re:assemblage' sends trajectories into previous issues and out toward emerging debates." circ. 2.3M. 3/yr. Pub'd 3 issues 2005; expects 3 issues 2006, 3 issues 2007. sub. price $62 individuals, $130 institutions $40 students; per copy $22; sample free to libraries for review. Back issues: $22 for individuals, $44 for institutions. Discounts: trade—under 5 copies 25%, 5+ 40%; agency 10%. 114pp. Reporting time: 2 months. Simultaneous submissions accepted: no. Publishes 10% of manuscripts submitted. Payment: none, contributors receive 2 copies of the journal. Copyrighted, does not revert to author. Pub's reviews: 6 in 2005. §Avant-garde/experimental art and architecture, cultural criticism. Ads: $350/$250/$625 2-page spread/agency discount 15%. Subjects: Architecture, Arts, Avant-Garde, Experimental Art, Cities, Criticism, Culture, Design, Visual Arts.

The Association of Freelance Writers (see also FREELANCE MARKET NEWS), A Cox, Sevendale House, 7 Dale Street, Manchester, M1 1JB, England, 0161-228-2362, Fax 0161-228-3533. 1968. "We use articles of interest to freelance writers." Pub'd 11 titles 2005; expects 11 titles 2006, 11 titles 2007. 16pp. Reporting time: 1 month. Simultaneous submissions accepted: no. Publishes 50% of manuscripts submitted. Payment: £50 per 1000 words. Does not copyright for author.

Asylum Arts (see also Leaping Dog Press / Asylum Arts Press), Jordan Jones, Editor and Publisher, c/o Leaping Dog Press, PO Box 3316, San Jose, CA 95156-3316, Phone/fax: (877) 570-6873 E-mail: editor@leapingdogpress.com, Web: www.leapingdogpress.com, Chapbooks and ephemera: www.cafe-press.com/ldp/. 1990. Poetry, fiction, art, photos, criticism, letters, long-poems, collages, plays, non-fiction. "Manuscripts by invitation only, and only during the months of May-July. Asylum Arts publishes high-quality literary titles—fiction, plays, translations, essays, and poetry—in attractive trade paperback format. Recent books by Gerard de Nerval, Robert Peters, Charles Baudelaire, Kenneth Bernard, Geoffrey Clark, Cynthia

Hendershot, Eric Basso, Richard Martin, and Samuel Appelbaum." avg. press run 1000. Pub'd 10 titles 2005; expects 4 titles 2006, 3 titles 2007. Distributed to the book trade by Biblio Distribution, 4501 Forbes Blvd., Suite 200, Lanham, MD 20706, Phone (301) 459-3366, Fax (301) 429-5746. 128pp. Reporting time: 3-6 months. Simultaneous submissions accepted: no. Payment: varies from book to book. Copyrights for author. Subjects: Arts, Avant-Garde, Experimental Art, Dada, Drama, Dreams, Erotica, Essays, Fiction, Literature (General), Novels, Post Modern, Prose, Short Stories, Surrealism, Translation.

AT THE LAKE MAGAZINE, Anne Frohna, Editor; Barb Krause, General Manager, 93 West Geneva St., P.O. Box 1080, Williams Bay, WI 53191, phone 262-245-1000; fax 262-245-2000; toll free 800-386-3228; e-mail media@ntmediagroup.com; web www.ntmediagroup.com. 1997. Articles, photos, non-fiction. "Regional magazine focusing on Southeastern Wisconsin." circ. 30M. 4/yr. Pub'd 4 issues 2005; expects 4 issues 2006, 4 issues 2007. sub. price $16.95; per copy $4; sample free. Back issues: $4. 84pp. Reporting time: 6 weeks. Simultaneous submissions accepted: yes. Publishes 10% of manuscripts submitted. Payment: $0.25/word. Not copyrighted. Ads: $1700 FP color. Subject: Wisconsin.

•**Athanata Arts, Ltd.,** Peter Arcese, P.O. Box, Garden City, NY 11530-0321. 2001. Poetry. "Publishers of the NYQ Poetry Series." avg. press run 1500. Expects 3 titles 2006, 5 titles 2007. Discounts: 55% wholesale, 40% retail, 20% STOP. 92pp. Reporting time: Does not accept unsolicited manuscripts. Simultaneous submissions accepted: No. Payment: Advance & royalty negotiated on individual basis. Copyrights for author. Subjects: Arts, Audio/Video, Creativity, Design, Drama, Education, Law, Liberal Arts, Literature (General), Music, Poetry, Theatre, Visual Arts, Zen.

Athanor Books (a division of ETX Seminars), Bruce Schaffenberger, P.O.Box 22201, Sacramento, CA 95820, 916-424-4355. 1993. Non-fiction. "We publish exclusively non-fiction books on spiritual and mystical topics such as sacred sites and truelife stories of otherworldly encounters. The works we publish are handbooks, directories, course manuals, and case studies." avg. press run 5M. Pub'd 1 title 2005; expects 3 titles 2006, 4 titles 2007. Discounts: 2-4 copies 20%, 5-99 40%, 100+ 50%. 300pp. Reporting time: 4-6 weeks. Simultaneous submissions accepted: yes. Publishes 2% of manuscripts submitted. Payment: 8% to 500 copies; 10% over. Copyrights for author. Subjects: Bibliography, New Age, Occult, Spiritual.

Athena Press, 5956 W 16th Ave, Hialeah, FL 33012-6814.

Athena Press, Queen's House, 2 Holly Road, Twickenham TW1 4EG, United Kingdom, www.athena-press.com.

AT-HOME DAD, Peter Baylies, 61 Brightwood Avenue, North Andover, MA 01845, athomedad@aol.com, www.athomedad.com. 1994. Articles, satire, letters, news items, non-fiction. "First-hand experiences of being an at-home dad preferred; plus experiences of running a home business while caring for children. The At-Home Dad Newsletter is now a free online publication." circ. 100,000 hits per year on website. Weekly/ bi weekly as posted. Pub'd 4 issues 2005; expects 4 issues 2006, 4 issues 2007. sub. price Free; per copy free. Simultaneous submissions accepted: yes. Publishes 20% of manuscripts submitted. Payment: plus media exposure website is read by most all national news/parent media. Copyrighted, reverts to author. Pub's reviews: 10 in 2005. §Any on fatherhood, parenting, recipes, kid publications or products, home business. Ads: none. Subjects: Birth, Birth Control, Population, Book Reviewing, Business & Economics, Children, Youth, Family, Humor, Men, Metaphysics, Parenting.

ATLANTA REVIEW, Daniel Veach, PO Box 8248, Atlanta, GA 31106. 1994. Poetry, art, interviews. "Quality poetry of genuine human appeal, interviews with poets. Does not publish fiction, reviews or criticism. *Atlanta Review* has published Seamus Heaney, Derek Walcott, Billy Collins, Maxine Kumin, Charles Simic, Naomi Shihab Nye, Stephen Dunn, Rachel Hadas, and Charles Wright. Each spring issue features a new country or region: Asia, Africa, Ireland, England, Australia, the Caribbean, Greece, Spain, Turkey, etc. Art in black and white." circ. 3M. 2/yr. Pub'd 2 issues 2005; expects 2 issues 2006, 2 issues 2007. sub. price $12; per copy $6; sample $5. Back issues: $5. Discounts: negotiable. 128pp. Reporting time: 1 month. Simultaneous submissions accepted: yes. Publishes 1% of manuscripts submitted. Payment: 2 free copies. Copyrighted, reverts to author. Subject: Poetry.

Atlantic Path Publishing, PO Box 1556, Gloucester, MA 01931-1556, 978-283-1531, Fax 866-640-1412, contactus@atlanticpathpublishing.com, www.atlanticpathpublishing.com. 2002. Non-fiction. "Our titles include *Writing and Developing Your College Textbook* (2003), *Self-Publishing Textbooks and Instructional Materials* (2004), and *Writing and Developing College Textbook Supplements* (2005). We are interested in book proposals, which can be made via email to me.lepionka@verizon.net. Atlantic Path publishing specializes in books on writing and publishing for scholars, academics, instructors, teachers, publishers and editors."

Atlantic Publishing Group, Inc., 1210 SW 23rd Place, Ocala, FL 34474-7014, 800-555-4037, Fax 352-622-5836, sales@atlantic-pub.com, www.atlantic-pub.com. 1986. Non-fiction. "Publishes in the area of food service management and culinary arts only." avg. press run 4M. Pub'd 17 titles 2005; expects 20 titles

2006, 25 titles 2007. 250pp. Copyrights for author. Subject: Food, Eating.

ATLANTIS: A Women's Studies Journal/Revue d'etudes sur les femmes, Meg Luxton, Editor; Linda Kealey, Editor; June Corman, Editor, Institute for the Study of Women, Mt. Saint Vincent University, Halifax, N.S. B3M 2J6, Canada, 902-457-6319, Fax 902-443-1352, atlantis@msvu.ca, www.msvu.ca/atlantis. 1975. Articles, art, interviews, satire, criticism, reviews. circ. 1M. 2/yr. Pub'd 2 issues 2005; expects 2 issues 2006, 2 issues 2007. sub. price individual $25 + $1.75 GST Can, $30 US, $35US overseas; institution $45 + $3.15 GST Can, $50 US, $55US overseas; student $15 + $1.05 GST Can., $20 US, $25US overseas; per copy $12 + p/h; sample same. Back issues: same. 200pp. Reporting time: 6-8 months. Simultaneous submissions accepted: no. Publishes 35-40% of manuscripts submitted. Payment: 1 complimentary issue. Copyrighted, does not revert to author. Pub's reviews: 15 in 2005. §Women's studies, feminism, interdisciplinary research, creative work on the topic of women. Ads: $250/$125. Subjects: Biography, Education, English, Feminism, History, Humanism, Humor, Lesbianism, Literary Review, Political Science, Politics, Psychology, Science, Society, Women.

Atrium Society Publications, Fanta Plessl, Assistant Director, PO Box 816, Middlebury, VT 05753, 802-462-3900, fax 802-462-2792, e-mail atrium@atriumsoc.org, www.atriumsoc.org. 1984. Art. "We focus exclusively on understanding conflict in its many forms (internal, interpersonal, international) and helping readers—particularly young readers—learn to resolve their differences nonviolently. We publish no unsolicited written material but are often interested in seeing samples of illustrative work for our non-fiction children's books." avg. press run 5M. Pub'd 4 titles 2005; expects 2 titles 2006, 2 titles 2007. 150pp. Payment: none. Subjects: Peace, Psychology.

ATS Publishing, Robert Jay Bentz, 996 Old Eagle School Road, Suite 1105, Wayne, PA 19087, 610-688-6000. 1989. Non-fiction. avg. press run 2M. Pub'd 1 title 2005; expects 1 title 2006, 1 title 2007. Discounts: available upon request. 160pp. Copyrights for author. Subjects: Communication, Journalism, How-To.

AUDIO EXPRESS, Edward T. Jr. Dell, PO Box 876, Peterborough, NH 03458, 603-924-9464, www.audioxpress.com. 1988. Articles, photos, interviews, reviews, letters, news items. circ. 8.5M. 6/yr. Pub'd 6 issues 2005; expects 6 issues 2006, 6 issues 2007. sub. price $28; per copy $6; sample free trial issue available. Discounts: 50% bulk, 20% agent off institutional rates. 64pp. Reporting time: 4 weeks. Simultaneous submissions accepted: no. Publishes 8% of manuscripts submitted. Payment: yes. Copyrighted, reverts to author. Pub's reviews: 6 in 2005. §Vacuum tubes, do-it-yourself audio equipment. Ads: $525/$340/$1 per word. Subjects: Audio/Video, Engineering, How-To.

August Press LLC, Wayne Dawkins, President; Rob King, Art Director, 108 Terrell Road, PO Box 6693, Newport News, VA 23606, wdawkins4bj@aol.com, www.augustpress.net. 1992. Pub'd 1 title 2005; expects 1 title 2006, 1 title 2007. Discounts: distributors 50-55 percent, wholesalers 50 percent, retailers 40 percent. Special discounts for institutions, classrooms and remainder buyers. 203pp.

Aunt Lute Books, Joan Pinkvoss, Senior Editor; Shay Brawn, Managing Editor, PO Box 410687, San Francisco, CA 94141, 415-826-1300; FAX 415-826-8300. 1978. Fiction, criticism, plays, non-fiction. "We publish multicultural, women's literature. Recent authors: Audre Lorde, Gloria Anzaldua, Melanie Kaye-Kantrowitz, Cherry Muhanji. Aunt Lute Books is part of the Aunt Lute Foundation, which is the non-profit entity that grew out of the work of Spinsters/Aunt Lute Book Co." avg. press run 3M-5M. Pub'd 2 titles 2005; expects 3 titles 2006, 5 titles 2007. Discounts: bookstores 20% on 1+ books, distributors 45-55%, no rate for single orders (unless bought at selected conferences). Reporting time: 3 months. Copyrights for author. Subjects: Feminism, Lesbianism, Third World, Minorities, Women.

AURA LITERARY ARTS REVIEW, Christopher Giganti, Editor-in-Chief; Daniel Robbins, Assistant Editor-in-Chief; Russell Helms, Editor, David Good, Steven Smith, HUC 135, 1530 3rd Avenue South, Birmingham, AL 35294, 205-934-3216. 1974. Poetry, fiction, articles, art, photos, interviews, reviews, plays. circ. 500. 2/yr. Pub'd 2 issues 2005; expects 2 issues 2006, 2 issues 2007. sub. price $12; per copy $6; sample none. Back issues: none. 140pp. Reporting time: asap, within 2 months usually. Simultaneous submissions accepted: no. Publishes 5-10% of manuscripts submitted. Payment: 2 copies. Copyrighted, reverts to author. Pub's reviews: none in 2005. §Fiction, poetry. Ads: $100/$50. Subjects: Literary Review, Literature (General), Poetry.

Auromere Books and Imports, 2621 W. US Highway 12, Lodi, CA 95242-9200, 800-735-4691, 209-339-3710, Fax 209-339-3715, books@auromere.com, www.auromere.com. 1974. "Sri Aurobindo Books, classical Indian Spiritual Texts, Children's Books, and Health books, including Ayurveda. We also have a few horticultural books. Also carry a number of side lines including imported bookmarks and incense. We are the exclusive U.S. representative of a number of publishers from India and their titles are significantly more in number. Including: Ganesh & Co.; National Book Trust of India; Hemkunt Books; All India Press; Children's Book Trust of India. In addition we also represent Sri Aurobindo Books Distribution Agency and here in the U.S., list has over titles. We do not accept submissions, as we publish existent classical texts. A free catalog of our books is available on request." avg. press run 5M-10M. Pub'd 1 title 2005; expects 3 titles 2006, 5 titles

2007. Discounts: trade 40%, $50 minimum order after discount; jobbers, distributors by arrangement. 200pp. Payment: variable. Does not copyright for author. Subjects: Children, Youth, Occult, Philosophy, Spiritual.

THE AUROREAN, Cynthia Brackett-Vincent, PO Box 187, Farmington, ME 04938, 207-778-0467. 1995. Poetry. "Please note that as of 2006, we publish biannually (Spring/Summer and Fall/Winter) and that our address has changed as of 2005! One of 12 'Insider Reports' in 1999 *Poet's Market*, recommended by *Small Press Review*. Request guidelines or sample! Approx. 36 lines max. I always send proofs; I always acknowledge receipt of manuscript. One Poet-of-the-Quarter each issue receives 10 copies, 100 word bio. and 1 year subscription. No e-mail submissions. Please do not fold poems individually. Also publishes *The Unrorean* twice yearly - editor's alter ego. You may submit solely to *Unrorean* or, unless otherwise requested, poems will be considered for both. *Unrorean* is 11x17, laser printed; $2 each; pays 1 copy per poem. New: judge picks 'Best Poem' for each *Aurorean*; winner receives $20. Also, send quotes for 'Poetic Quote of the Season' - 4 lines max. from not too obscure poet; cannot be acknowledged or returned; winner receives 2 free issues of *Aurorean*. As well: editor picks one chapbook to recommend each issue (not a review); send recently published chaps; cannot be returned or acknowledged." circ. 500. 2/yr. Pub'd 4 issues 2005; expects 2 issues 2006, 2 issues 2007. sub. price $21, $25 international (two issues); per copy $11, $12 international: current 2 issues. Back issues: quarterlies over one year old: $3 each (U.S. only); biannuals over one year old (after May '07): $7 each (U.S. only). Reporting time: 3 months maximum. Simultaneous submissions accepted if noted up front; I discourage them as we always reply in stated time. Publishes 15% of manuscripts submitted. Payment: 2 copies per poem, up to 5 total copies per issue. Copyrighted, reverts to author. Ads: will do ad and subscription exchanges with other journals; send a sample with request. Subjects: Haiku, Inspirational, New England, Self-Help.

Ausable Press, Chase Twichell, 1026 Hurricane Road, Keene, NY 12942, 518-576-9273, 518-576-9227 fax, www.ausablepress.org. 1999. Poetry. "Ausable's mission is to publish poetry that investigates and expresses human consciousness in language that goes where prose cannot. We do not publish anthologies, light verse, illustrated poetry, inspirational poetry, or poetry for children. We rarely publish translations. We're open to all styles and subjects, but are paticularly interested in work that deals with contemporary life in contemporary language. We also have a strong interest in work by new poets." avg. press run 1500. Pub'd 4 titles 2005; expects 5 titles 2006, 5 titles 2007. Discounts: distributors 55%bookstores 40%retailers 40%. 100pp. Reporting time: 3—4 months. Simultaneous submissions accepted: Yes. Publishes 1% of manuscripts submitted. Payment: $1,000 advance; 10% royalties on all books. Copyrights for author. Subject: Poetry.

Autelitano Media Group (AMG) (see also BEACHCOMBER MAGAZINE), Phil Autelitano Jr., 1036 Dean St., Schenectady, NY 12309-5720, 561-350-1923, Fax 561-276-0931, Autelitano@aol.com, www.Auteli-Media.com. 1992. Non-fiction. "Small business, marketing, management, and self-help." avg. press run 5M. Pub'd 1 title 2005; expects 2 titles 2006, 2 titles 2007. Discounts: 35% to retailers, 55% to distributors. 144pp. Reporting time: 1 month. Simultaneous submissions accepted: yes. Publishes 1% of manuscripts submitted. Payment: negotiable. Copyrights for author. Subjects: Advertising, Self-Promotion, Business & Economics, Management, Marketing.

Authors of Unity Publishing, Genie O'Malley, 575 Madison Ave., 10th Floor, New York, NY 10022, 212 605 0407 or 646 286 0166. 2002. Non-fiction. "Personal Development, Self-Help, Spirituality, Religious, RelationshipsLife's a Smelling Success, Dear Dinah, Complete Earthly Woman, The Gent's Prayer, Be Nice (Or Else!)." avg. press run 8000. Pub'd 3 titles 2005; expects 5 titles 2006, 10 titles 2007. Discounts: distributors 60%wholesalers 55%bookstores 55%retailers 55%jobbers 55%institutions and classrooms2-10 copies 25%, 10-30 35% over 30 copies 55%55% all. 200-250pp. Reporting time: 2-3 weeks. Simultaneous submissions accepted: Yes. Publishes 1% of manuscripts submitted. Payment: 7-10% of retail $1000-$5000 advance. Copyrights for author. Subjects: Metaphysics, New Age, Psychology, Relationships, Religion, Self-Help, Spiritual, Supernatural.

AuthorsOmniscient Publishers, Olga Kellen, 11325 SW 1st Street, Coral Springs, FL 33071, (954)340-8845, authors@authors-sell-book.com, http://www.authors-sell-book.com. 2004. Fiction, non-fiction. "*A Temporary New Wife*, a contemporary novel by Malcolm Goodway: http://www.authors-sell-book.com/a-temporary-new-wife.html ; *American International Adoption Agencies: How to Choose One That's Right for Your Family*, a how-to guide for prospective adoptive parents by Olga Kellen: http://www.authors-sell-book.com/international-adoption-agencies.html ." Expects 3 titles 2006, 5-10 titles 2007. Discounts: 40%-60%. 50-300pp. Reporting time: 1 week. Simultaneous submissions accepted: Yes. Publishes 20% of manuscripts submitted. Payment: contract, no advances. Copyrights for author. Subjects: Fiction, Gender Issues, Guidance, How-To, Humor, Literature (General), Non-Fiction, Novels, Relationships, Self-Help, Senior Citizens, Sex, Sexuality, Singles, Translation, Writers/Writing.

Autonomedia, Inc. (see also SEMIOTEXT(E)), Jim Fleming, Lewanne Jones, PO Box 568, Brooklyn, NY 11211, 718-936-2603, e-Mail autonobook@aol.com. 1983. Fiction, criticism, non-fiction. "Essays. Post-Marxist theory, post-structuralist theory, philosophy, politics and culture." avg. press run 5M. Pub'd 7 titles 2005; expects 7 titles 2006, 10 titles 2007. Discounts: trade 40%, distributors 50%. 300pp. Reporting time: 6 weeks. Payment: arranged per title for royalties. Copyrights for author. Subjects: African Literature, Africa, African Studies, Anarchist, Arts, Asia, Indochina, Avant-Garde, Experimental Art, Communication, Journalism, Communism, Marxism, Leninism, Computers, Calculators, Criticism, Culture, Electronics, Feminism, History, Language, Latin America.

Autumn House Press, Michael Simms, P.O. Box 60100, Pittsburgh, PA 15211, 412-381-4261, www.autumnhouse.org. 1998. Poetry. ''Autumn House authors include Gerald Stern, Andrea Hollander Budy, Ed Ochester, Julie Suk, Jo McDougall, Sue Ellen Thompson, Samuel Hazo and others.'' avg. press run 1500. Pub'd 4 titles 2005; expects 5 titles 2006, 6 titles 2007. Discounts: 5 or more copies 40%. 64-432pp. Reporting time: Contest deadline June 30 each year. Winner announced in September. See website for guidelines. www.autumnhouse.org. Simultaneous submissions accepted: Yes. Publishes 1% of manuscripts submitted. Payment: $2,500 for Prize winner and 7% royalty. Copyrights for author. Subject: Poetry.

•**Avari Press,** Adam Barkafski, Managing Editor; Anthony Verrecchia, President and Publisher, P.O. Box 11325, Lancaster, PA 17605, editor@avaripress.com, http://www.avaripress.com. Fiction, non-fiction. ''Avari Press is a publishing company devoted entirely to producing literary works of high fantasy.'' avg. press run 5000. Expects 3-5 titles 2007. 300-500pp. Reporting time: One month or less. Simultaneous submissions accepted: Yes. Payment: Varies, but usually 10% of retail. Copyrights for author. Subjects: Fantasy, Fiction, Gay, History, Medieval, Mystery, Non-Fiction, Novels, Renaissance, J.R.R. Tolkien, Young Adult.

Avery Color Studios, Wells Chapin, 511 D Avenue, Gwinn, MI 49841, 800-722-9925. 1956. Fiction, photos, non-fiction. ''History, folklore, shipwrecks, pictorials. Contributors: Frederick Stonehouse, Joan Bestwick, Neil Moran, Cully Gage, Wes Oleszewski.'' avg. press run 5M. Pub'd 2 titles 2005; expects 4 titles 2006, 2 titles 2007. Discounts: 40% trade. 185pp. Reporting time: 30 days. Payment: negotiable. Copyrights for author. Subjects: Americana, Animals, Cooking, Fiction, Folklore, History, Michigan, Midwest, Native American, Non-Fiction, Photography, Reprints, Sports, Outdoors, Sports, Outdoors.

Aviation Book Company, Nancy Griffith, 7201 Perimeter Road South, Seattle, WA 98108-2999. 1964. Non-fiction. ''Aviation only.'' avg. press run 3M. Expects 3 titles 2006. Discounts: distributor, dealer, school, public library. 192pp. Reporting time: 90 days. Payment: usually 10% of list price. Copyrights for author. Subject: Aviation.

Avisson Press, Inc., M.L. Hester, 3007 Taliaferro Road, Greensboro, NC 27408, 336-288-6989 phone/FAX. 1995. Non-fiction. ''Book-length only; history, serious nonfiction. Looking too for experts in cuting edge nutrition or supplements. Also young adult (age 12-18) biographies of famous people or historical period. PLEASE DO NOT SEND YOUR OWN LIFE STORY OR INSPIRATIONAL HOW-I-OVERCAME MY MISERABLE CHILDHOOD, ETC. type manuscripts.Additional address: PO Box 38816, Greensboro, NC 27438.'' avg. press run 1M-3M. Pub'd 7 titles 2005; expects 6 titles 2006, 7 titles 2007. Discounts: 20-40%. 144pp. Reporting time: 2-4 weeks. Simultaneous submissions accepted: yes. Publishes 3% of manuscripts submitted. Payment: standard royalty (6-10%). Copyrights for author. Subjects: Biography, Young Adult.

Avocet Press Inc., Melanie Kershaw, Cynthia Webb, 19 Paul Court, Pearl River, NY 10965, 212-754-6300, oopc@interport.net, www.avocetpress.com. 1997. Poetry, fiction. ''Publishers of Renee Ashley's second book of poetry *The Various Reasons of Light*.'' avg. press run 3M. Pub'd 1 title 2005; expects 3 titles 2006, 6 titles 2007. Reporting time: 6 months. Simultaneous submissions accepted: yes. Publishes 1% of manuscripts submitted. Copyrights for author. Subjects: Fiction, Mystery, Poetry.

Avocus Publishing, Inc., Claire Pyle, Managing Editor, 1223 Potomac Street NW, Washington, DC 20007, 202-333-8190. 1989. Non-fiction. ''Avocus publishes books on educational and social issues. Each book offers a collection of personal accounts - real people speaking candidly about timely social issues. 'Learn from other people's experience' is the company motto. Avocus books are reader-friendly. Neither technical nor clinical, they appeal to a large and varied audience. Most important, Avocus books are not an end in themselves, but provide the foundation for discussion and informed decisions. Upcoming Avocus projects include collections of essays dealing with date rape, censorship in the arts, women's experiences with birth control, adoption and infertility.'' avg. press run 4M. Pub'd 2 titles 2005; expects 6 titles 2006, 10 titles 2007. Discounts: standard. 200pp. Reporting time: 4-8 weeks. Payment: 10-60% of profit, no advance. Copyrights for author. Subjects: Adoption, Education, Essays, Family, Feminism, Health, Non-Fiction, Parenting, Textbooks.

AXE FACTORY REVIEW, Cynic Press, Joseph Farley, PO Box 40691, Philadelphia, PA 19107. 1986. Poetry, fiction, articles, art, photos, cartoons, interviews, satire, criticism, reviews, music, letters, parts-of-novels, long-poems, collages, plays, concrete art, news items, non-fiction. ''Poetry, black and white art, and book reviews have the best shot. Also read short stories. Currently overstocked in all areas but art. Recent contributors include Louis McKee, Taylor Graham, John Sweet, A.D. Winans, Xu Juan, Arthur Winfield Knight. Indexed in *Index of American Periodical Verse* and the *American Humanities Index*. It is recommended that writers read an issue or two before submitting. Samples back issues available for $8. All checks to "Cynic

Press.".'' circ. 200. 2-3/yr. Pub'd 2 issues 2005; expects 2 issues 2006, 2 issues 2007. sub. price $15/2 issues (all checks to Cynic Press); per copy $9; sample $8. Back issues: $8. Discounts: none. Pages vary. Reporting time: immediately. Simultaneous submissions accepted: yes. Publishes 10% of manuscripts submitted. Payment: 1 copy; more for featured poet. Copyrighted, reverts to author. Pub's reviews: 35 in 2005. §Poetry, sci-fi, martial arts, Asian literature and history, fiction, short stories, American history, Medieval history, sex, art history. Ads: $50/$25/trade. Subjects: Asia, Indochina, Book Reviewing, Cartoons, Erotica, Essays, Fantasy, Fiction, Horror, Interviews, Non-Fiction, Poetry, Satire, Science Fiction.

AXES & ALLEYS, Scott Birdseye, Jeremy Rosen, 25-26 44th Street #A1, Astoria, NY 11103, 718-204-0313, jeremy@danielbester.com. 2003. Fiction, articles, art, photos, cartoons, interviews, satire, criticism, reviews, music, letters, news items, non-fiction. circ. 40,000. 12/yr. Pub'd 12 issues 2005; expects 12 issues 2006, 12 issues 2007. sub. price free. 30pp. Reporting time: 3. Simultaneous submissions accepted: no. Copyrighted, reverts to author. Pub's reviews: 1 in 2005. §music, fiction. Subject: Experimental.

Axiom Information Resources, Terry Robinson, PO Box 8015, Ann Arbor, MI 48107, 734-761-4824. 1987. Non-fiction. avg. press run 10M. Pub'd 1 title 2005; expects 4 titles 2006, 4 titles 2007. Discounts: 10 or more copies 40%. 182pp. Copyrights for author. Subjects: Electronics, Entertainment, Reference.

AXIOS, Axios Newletter, Inc., Daniel John Gorham, 30-32 Macaw Avenue, PO Box 279, Belmodan, Belize, 501-8-23284. 1981. Articles, art, photos, interviews, criticism, reviews, letters, parts-of-novels, non-fiction. ''*Axios* is published for the purpose of explaining the world-wide Orthodox Catholic faith and religious practices to those who would wish to have a better understanding of it. *Axios* carries articles that help to give a religious solution to world and personal problems. We criticize the half-stupid ideas put forth by the 'reasonable men of this world'! Now read in 32 countries.'' circ. 8,462. 10/yr. Pub'd 12 issues 2005; expects 10 issues 2006, 6 issues 2007. sub. price $10; per copy $2; sample $2. Back issues: $2. Discounts: 40%. 24pp. Reporting time: 2-4 weeks. Payment: varies. Copyrighted. Pub's reviews: 15 in 2005. §Religion, all types! (Our book reviews are well read in religious book stores.). Ads: $85/$55. Subjects: Public Affairs, Religion.

Axios Newletter, Inc. (see also AXIOS; GORHAM; ORTHODOX MISSION; Orthodox Mission in Belize; THE VORTEX), Daniel John Gorham, Joseph T. Magnin, 16 Maxi Street, PO Box 90, Santa Elena, Cayo, Belize, 501-8-23284. 1981. Articles, art, photos, cartoons, interviews, satire, criticism, reviews, letters, parts-of-novels, news items, non-fiction. ''We publish Orthodox Christian books, art and pamphlets, also philosophy and historical books. Republish old out-of-print books, in some cases—would like to see some religious history of Russia, Greece, Albania, Bulgaria, Finland, Rumania, and also America, if it pertains to the Orthodox Christian.'' avg. press run varies. Pub'd 3 titles 2005; expects 5 titles 2006. Discounts: 40% trade. 355pp. Reporting time: 2-4 weeks. Payment: negotiated. Copyrights for author. Subjects: History, Libertarian, Religion.

THE AZOREAN EXPRESS, Seven Buffaloes Press, Art Coelho, PO Box 249, Big Timber, MT 59011. 1985. Poetry, fiction, art, photos, cartoons, collages. ''Although I have a strong focus on rural America and working people, I also consider non-rural material and everything of literary value. Spotlight is on poetry and fiction. Prefer fiction to be 5 or 6 double-space pages. Will accept stories up to 10 double-space pages.'' circ. 500. 2/yr. Pub'd 1 issue 2005; expects 2 issues 2006, 2 issues 2007. sub. price $11.75; per copy $11.75; sample $11.75. Back issues: $11.75. 80pp. Reporting time: 1 day to 2 weeks. Payment: copies. Copyrighted, reverts to author. Subjects: Agriculture, Appalachia, California, Fiction, Folklore, Great Plains, Poetry.

•**Azreal Publishing Company,** Nicole Perkins, 1226 High Road, Tallahassee, FL 32304-1833, (850) 222-7425, www.azrealpublishing.com, info@azrealpublishing.com. 2004. Fiction, non-fiction. ''Azreal Publishing Company was created in the spring of 2001 with the goal of publishing Christian books for children, teens, and young adults that would introduce them to the Gospel by incorporating performance elements with the reading of literature. On January 1, 2004 Azreal Publishing Company officially became a business owned by publisher/writer, Nicole Perkins. Our mission is to publish childrens picture books that are beautifully illustrated, and contain powerful messages and stories that celebrate the great diversity among Gods people. In our Juvenile and YA divisions we will publish fiction and non-fiction books that are enjoyable to read and socially relevant to the challenges faced by todays youth. We also plan to release Spanish and Braille versions of all our books.'' avg. press run 3000. Pub'd 1 title 2005; expects 1-3 titles 2007. Discounts: 2-10 copies 25%11-30 copies 35%31-70 copies 45%2-5 boxes (70 per box) 50%6 or more boxes (70 per box) 55%. 32pp. Reporting time: Response in 1-2 months. Simultaneous submissions accepted: Yes. Payment: Royalites are set at 10% and are paid against any advance given. Does not copyright for author. Subjects: African-American, Asian-American, Bilingual, Biography, Children, Youth, Christianity, Disabled, Drama, Inspirational, Juvenile Fiction, Latino, Multicultural, Non-Fiction, Picture Books, Spiritual.

Azro Press, PMB 342, 1704 Llano Street B, Santa Fe, NM 87505, gae@nets.com, www.azropress.com. 1997. avg. press run 1K-2.5K. Pub'd 2 titles 2005; expects 8 titles 2006, 5 titles 2007. Discounts: 40% to 55%. 32pp. Reporting time: 6 months. Simultaneous submissions accepted: yes. Publishes 10% of manuscripts submitted.

Payment: 5-10%. Copyrights for author. Subject: Children, Youth.

AZTLAN: A Journal of Chicano Studies, UCLA Chicano Studies Research Center Press, Chon A. Noriega, Editor; Wendy Belcher, Managing Editor, University of California-Los Angeles, 193 Haines Hall, Los Angeles, CA 90095-1544, 310-825-2642, press@chicano.ucla.edu, www.chicano.ucla.edu. 1970. Articles, criticism, reviews, news items. "*Aztlan* is the oldest continuously published journal focusing on the Chicano experience in the U.S. and Mexico. It is the journal of record in the field." circ. 1M. 2/yr. Pub'd 2 issues 2005; expects 2 issues 2006, 2 issues 2007. sub. price $30 individuals, $195 libraries & institutions. Back issues: $15.00 indiv., $95 instit. Discounts: classroom use. 300pp. Reporting time: 3 months. Simultaneous submissions accepted: no. Publishes 25% of manuscripts submitted. Payment: books in quantity. Copyrighted, does not revert to author. Pub's reviews: 9 in 2005. §Chicano studies. Ads: $225/$125. Subjects: Chicano/a, Society.

B

The B & R Samizdat Express, Barbara Hartley Seltzer, Vice-President; Richard Seltzer, Publisher; Robert Richard Seltzer, Vice-President; Heather Katherine Seltzer, Vice-President; Michael Richard Seltzer, Vice-President; Timothy Seltzer, Vice-President, 33 Gould Street, West Roxbury, MA 02132, 617-469-2269, seltzer@samizdat.com, main content site http://www.samizdat.com online store http://store.yahoo.com/samizdat. 1974. "We publish books on CD and DVD—plain text books, organized for ease of use. We have over 150 offerings (including our "Complete Book DVD" which includes the full text of over 10,000 classic books). We do not solicit manuscripts. You can see the tables of contents of all our CDs and DVDs at our Yahoo store http://store.yahoo.com/samizdat." Pub'd 40 titles 2005; expects 40 titles 2006, 60 titles 2007. Our books are in electronic form, hence they have no "pages".pp. Reporting time: We do not read manuscripts. Copyrights for author. Subjects: African Literature, Africa, African Studies, Anthropology, Archaeology, Children, Youth, Classical Studies, Drama, Fiction, History, Humor, Native American, Occult, Philosophy, Poetry, Political Science, Psychology, Religion.

BABEL MAGAZINE, Sisyphus Press, PO Box 10495, State College, PA 16805-0495, www.babelmagazine.com.

BABYSUE, BABYSUE MUSIC REVIEW, Don W. Seven, PO Box 3360, Cleveland, TN 37320-3360. 1985. Poetry, cartoons, interviews, satire, reviews, music. "We mainly feature bizarre adult cartoons, although we feature poetry, interviews, and reviews as well." circ. 5M. 2/yr. Pub'd 2 issues 2005; expects 2 issues 2006, 2 issues 2007. No subscriptions; price per copy $5; sample $5. Back issues: $5. 32pp. Reporting time: 1 month. Simultaneous submissions accepted: yes. Publishes 5% of manuscripts submitted. Payment: 1 free copy of magazine in which work appears. Copyrighted, reverts to author. Pub's reviews: 500 in 2005. §Cartoons, music magazines, cassettes, CDs and vinyl. We do not accept advertisements. Subjects: Comics, Humor, Magazines, Music, Poetry, Satire.

BABYSUE MUSIC REVIEW, BABYSUE, Don W. Seven, S. Fievet, PO Box 3360, Cleveland, TN 37320-3360. 1985. Photos, cartoons, interviews, music, news items. "*Babysue Music Review* consists mostly of music reviews. We review all types of music on all formats (vinyl, CD, cassette)." circ. 5M. 4/yr. Pub'd 4 issues 2005; expects 4 issues 2006, 4 issues 2007. price per copy $5; sample $5. Back issues: $5. Discounts: varies. 32pp. Reporting time: 3 months. Payment: each contributor recieves 1 copy of the issue in which their contribution appears. Copyrighted, reverts to author. Pub's reviews: 500 in 2005. §Anything related to music. We do not accept advertisements. Subjects: Arts, Comics, Music.

The Bacchae Press, Robert Brown, c/o The Brown Financial Group, 10 Sixth Street, Suite 215, Astoria, OR 97103-5315, 503-325-7972; FAX 503-325-7959; 800-207-4358; E-mail brown@pacifier.com. 1992. Poetry, fiction. "We publish mostly poetry. In 1993, we published 5 books of poetry: 2 anthologies of local poets, 1 full-length collection of poetry, and two chapbooks. All of our books are professionally printed on high-quality paper. Chapbook contest deadline is April 15." avg. press run 500. Pub'd 3 titles 2005; expects 4 titles 2006, 4 titles 2007. Discounts: 40%. 70pp. Reporting time: 3 months. Simultaneous submissions accepted: yes. Publishes less than 1% of manuscripts submitted. Payment: 10%. Copyrights for author. Subjects: Fiction, Ohio, Poetry.

Back House Books (see also CAFE NOIR REVIEW), Philip Henderson, 1703 Lebanon Street, Adelphi, MD 20783. 1999. Poetry, fiction, articles, photos, cartoons, interviews, satire, criticism, reviews, letters, parts-of-novels, long-poems, plays, non-fiction. "We are looking for well-written, quality material. No neo-conservatives/far-rightists, please." avg. press run 300. Pub'd 1 title 2005; expects 1-2 titles 2006, 2-3 titles

2007. Pages vary. Reporting time: 1-3 months. Simultaneous submissions accepted: no. Publishes 1-2% of manuscripts submitted. Payment: 10% of sales on books. Copyrights for author. Subjects: African Literature, Africa, African Studies, Arts, Asian-American, Black, Chicano/a, Communism, Marxism, Leninism, Gay, Lesbianism, Literary Review, Poetry, Race, Society, Third World, Minorities, Women, Worker.

Backbeat Press, Tazz Richards, Jenni Morrison, 123 E San Carlos # 306, San Jose, CA 95112, 408-464-6715, tazz@backbeatpress.com, www.backbeatpress.com. 1999. Fiction, articles, photos, interviews, criticism, reviews, music, news items, non-fiction. ''Not accepting unsolicited manuscripts at this time.'' avg. press run 10K. Expects 1 title 2006, 2 titles 2007. Discounts: call or e-mail. 200pp. Simultaneous submissions accepted: yes. Payment: inquire. Copyrights for author. Subjects: African Literature, Africa, African Studies, Anthology, Arts, Biography, Careers, Clothing, Crafts, Hobbies, Dance, Feminism.

Backcountry Publishing, Michelle Riley, Editor; Matt Richards, Editor, 3303 Dick George Road, Cave Junction, OR 97523-9623, 541-955-5650. 1997. Non-fiction. ''Books and booklets (40-600 pages); Only interested in authors who want to take strong role in publicizing, publishing their own books. We are a publishing co-op that supports, shares and directs authors through collective publishing. Topics limited to primitive skills, wilderness living, and simple living. Backcountry Publishing is distributed by Partners Publishers Group.'' avg. press run 5K. Pub'd 1 title 2005; expects 3 titles 2006. Discounts: 3-20 40%, 20-199 40% + free shipping, 200-499 50%, 500+ 55%. 180pp. Reporting time: 4-6 weeks. Simultaneous submissions accepted: yes. Payment: individual basis. Does not copyright for author. Subjects: Crafts, Hobbies, How-To, Native American, Sports, Outdoors.

BACKWARDS CITY REVIEW, Gerry Canavan, Tom Christopher, Don Ezra Cruz, Patrick Egan, Jaimee Hills, P.O. Box 41317, Greensboro, NC 27404-1317. 2004. Poetry, fiction, art, photos, cartoons, parts-of-novels, long-poems, plays, non-fiction. ''Check guidelines at www.backwardscity.net. We no longer read work year-round. Looking for work from both new and established writers. Fiction and poetry contest in current issue. Recent contributors include Michael Parker, Adam Berlin, Cory Doctorow, Jim Rugg, Peter S. Conrad, Tony Tost, Greg Williamson, Erica Bernheim, Gabriel Gudding, Arielle Greenberg, Ander Monson, Jonathan Lethem, and Kurt Vonnegut.'' circ. 300. 2/yr. Pub'd 1 issue 2005; expects 2 issues 2006, 2 issues 2007. sub. price 12; per copy 7; sample 5. Back issues: 5. Discounts: 2-10 copies 20%10+ copies 30%. 144pp. Reporting time: approximately 4 months. Simultaneous submissions accepted: Yes. Payment: Usually copies; cash prizes for contest winners. Copyrighted, reverts to author. Ads: $100 full page. Subjects: Arts, Cartoons, Comics, Essays, Experimental, Fiction, Non-Fiction, Novels, Photography, Poetry, Prose.

The Backwaters Press, Greg Kosmicki, Editor; Rich Wyatt, Editor, 3502 North 52nd Street, Omaha, NE 68104-3506, 402-451-4052e-mail: gkosmicki@cox.net..comWebsite: www.thebackwaterspress.homes-tead.com. 1997. Poetry. ''The Backwaters Press no longer offers any contests. We read year-round for Open Submissions; poets should note in the cover letter and on the mailing address "Open Submissions" when submitting. Send SASE for open submission details, or e-mail to gkosmicki@cox.net with the subject line "Open Submissions Guidelines;" or go to the website at www.thebackwaterspress.homestead.com. No deadlines; we read all year.'' avg. press run 300-600. Pub'd 8 titles 2005; expects 12 titles 2006, 12 titles 2007. Discounts: libraries and bookstores, please query, newest titles available through Ingram and Baker&Taylor. 80pp. Reporting time: Reports in one to two months for open submissions. Simultaneous submission OK, please note in cover letter. Publishes less than 1% of manuscripts submitted. Payment: Poets published under open submissions will receive 10% of the press run as payment, as well as generous discounts on their titles. Copyrights for author. Subject: Poetry.

BAD POETRY QUARTERLY, PO Box 6319, London E11 2EP, England.

Bad Press (see also BAD PRESS SERIALS), Jow Lindsay Mr, 21 Portland Rise, Finsbury Park, London, United Kingdom, Email: badpress@gmail.com Web: http://badpress.infinology.net. Poetry, fiction, articles, art, photos, cartoons, interviews, satire, criticism, reviews, music, letters, parts-of-novels, long-poems, collages, plays, concrete art, news items, non-fiction. Subjects: Absurdist, Arthurian, Artificial Intelligence, Communism, Marxism, Leninism, Counter-Culture, Alternatives, Communes, Feminism, Fiction, Gay, Global Affairs, Media, Philosophy, Political Science, Post Modern, Shipwrecks, Sociology.

BAD PRESS SERIALS, Bad Press, Jow Lindsay Mr, 21 Portland Rise, Finsbury Park, London, United Kingdom, Email: badpress@gmail.com Web: http://badpress.infinology.net. Pub's reviews.

THE BADGER STONE CHRONICLES, Seven Buffaloes Press, Art Coelho, PO Box 249, Big Timber, MT 59011. 1987. Poetry. ''This literary newsletter is dedicated to the life and artistic times of the late Michael Lynn Coelho—pen name: Badger Stone. Each issue special theme. #2 issue, Family Farm.'' 2/yr. sub. price $5. 8pp. Subject: Poetry.

BAGAZINE, X-Ray Book Co., Johnny Brewton, Po Box 2234, Pasadena, CA 91102. 2005. Poetry, art, photos, satire, reviews, music, letters, parts-of-novels, collages, plays, concrete art. ''Bagazine is an assemblage magazine in a bag. Contributors are asked to submit 126 pieces per guidelines for assembly. We do not print your stuff. Silkscreen, Gocco, Letterpress, Xerox, Potato Prints, Photography, rubberstamp, chapbooks, comics, poems, CDs etc... www.bagazine for guidelines and more information." circ. 126. 6/yr. Expects 2 issues 2006, 6 issues 2007. price per copy $55. Back issues: inquire. Discounts: inquire. 40pp. Reporting time: 10 Days. Simultaneous submissions accepted: No. Publishes 35% of manuscripts submitted. Payment: (1) copy. Copyright reverts to Artist or Author with permission to reprint in collected works book. §Jazz, Assemblage, D.I.Y., Novels, CDs and LPs, Film. Ads: Inquire. Subjects: Abstracts, Avant-Garde, Experimental Art, Book Arts, Crafts, Hobbies, Experimental, Futurism, Music, Photography, Poetry, Postcards, Zines.

Walter H. Baker Company (Baker's Plays), Deirdre Shaw, Managing Director, PO Box 699222, Quincy, MA 02269-9222, 617-745-0805, Fax 617-745-9891, www.bakersplays.com. 1845. Plays. "Seeking one-act, full length, musicals, chancel and children's plays." avg. press run 1M. Expects 18 titles 2006, 25 titles 2007. Discounts: 20-40%. 50pp. Reporting time: 3-4 months. Payment: varies, 50/50 split amateur rights; 80/20 split professional rights; 10% book royalty. Copyrights for author. Subjects: Drama, Theatre.

Balanced Books Publishing, Robin Mastro, PO Box 14957, Seattle, WA 98144, 206-328-3995, fax 206-328-1339, toll free 877-838-4858, info@balancedbookspub.com, www.balancedbookspub.com. 2003. Non-fiction. "Balanced Books is a small press nestled in the heart of the Pacific Northwest. We chose the pristine beauty of this corner of the world to establish our business because it inspires us to seek balance between the outer world of activity and the inner world of peace. We at Balanced Books support ideas, concepts, and philosophies that encourage personal growth, inspire creative change, and bring joy into people's lives. The mission of Balanced Books is to inform, uplift, and support personal and planetary growth by offering beneficial techniques and philosophies through books that promote health, prosperity, positive relationships, and happiness. We are not accepting submissions at this time." avg. press run 5000. Expects 1 title 2006, 2 titles 2007. Discounts: Please check website - www.balancedbookspub.com. 200pp. Reporting time: We are not accepting submissions at this time. Subjects: Health, New Age, Non-Fiction, Self-Help, Spiritual.

Balcony Media, Inc., 512 E. Wilson Avenue, Suite 213, Glendale, CA 91206, 818-956-5313(T), 818-956-5904(F), web: www.laarch.com, email: diana@balconypress.com. 1994. Art, non-fiction. "Prefer art and architecture submissions with a focus on cultural importance as opposed to analytical or reference material. Authors must be able to provide all images and illustrations with permissions." avg. press run 5M. Pub'd 1 title 2005; expects 4 titles 2006, 5 titles 2007. Discounts: varies depending on quantity. 150pp. Reporting time: 1 month. Simultaneous submissions accepted: No. Publishes 10% of manuscripts submitted. Payment: 10% net, paid annually. Copyrights for author. Subjects: Architecture, Arts, Culture, Design, Los Angeles, Southwest.

Ballena Press, Katherine Siva Saubel, Chairman, Founder, Lowell John Bean, Thomas C. Blackburn, Lynn Gamble, Sylvia Vane, PO Box 578, Banning, CA 92220, (951)849-7289, Fax (951)849-3549, E-mail: malkipress@aol.com, www.malkimuseum.com. 1973. Non-fiction. "We publish works on the anthropology of the western United States, especially California and the Southwest. We are interested only in books demonstrating the highest level of scholarship. Unsolicited manuscripts are not used and will not be returned to the author." avg. press run 1M. Pub'd 1 title 2005; expects 2 titles 2006. Discounts: 40% wholesale, 20% educational, 20% membership. 100-400pp. Reporting time: 1 month to 1 year. Simultaneous submissions accepted: no. Publishes a variable % of manuscripts submitted. Payment: varies. Copyrights for author. Subjects: Anthropology, Archaelogy, California, Folklore, Native American, Pacific Northwest, Religion, Southwest, The West.

•BALLISTA, Mucusart Publications, Paul Neads, 6 Chiffon Way, Trinity Riverside, Gtr Manchester M3 6AB, England, +4407814570441, paul@mucusart.co.uk, www.mucusart.co.uk/press.htm. 2002. Fiction. "BALLISTA is the new short fiction magazine from Mucusart Publications, bringing you new and original writing exploring the realms of the supernatural, paranormal, horror, Gothick, psychological, occult & macabre - even SF, dark fantasy or just the downright bizarre will be considered through open submissions.Ballista will be published twice a year from October 2006. Issue 1 features the work of John Light, Rosie Lugosi, H.Ann Dyess, Dermot Glennon, Andrew Myers, Paul Tristram & Neil Deadman amongst others." circ. 100. 2/yr. Expects 1 issue 2006, 2 issues 2007. sub. price 7.00; per copy 3.50; sample 3.50. Back issues: 2.00. Discounts: 10-19 copies 10%, 20+ copies 15%. 52pp. Reporting time: 4-8 weeks. Simultaneous submissions accepted: No. Publishes 5% of manuscripts submitted. Payment: GB5.00 + complimentary copy. Copyrighted, reverts to author. Subjects: Fantasy, Fiction, Folklore, Horror, Myth, Mythology, New Age, Occult, Science Fiction, Short Stories, Spiritual, Supernatural.

BALLOT ACCESS NEWS, Richard Winger, PO Box 470296, San Francisco, CA 94147, 415-922-9779, fax 415-441-4268, e-Mail ban@igc.apc.org, www.ballot-access.org. 1985. News items. "Bias in favor of voter's right to vote for the party of his or her choice. Bias against laws which interfere with this right." circ. 1M. 12/yr. Pub'd 12 issues 2005; expects 12 issues 2006, 12 issues 2007. sub. price $13; per copy free; sample free. Back issues: $1 per issue. 6.25pp. Publishes 25% of manuscripts submitted. Payment: none. Not copyrighted.

44

Pub's reviews: 3 in 2005. §Political parties. Ads: none. Subjects: Civil Rights, Political Science, Politics.

THE BALTIMORE REVIEW, Susan Muaddi Darraj, PO Box 36418, Towson, MD 21286, www.BaltimoreReview.org. 1996. Poetry, fiction, interviews, reviews, parts-of-novels, long-poems, non-fiction. "Annual Fiction, Poetry, and Creative Nonfiction Contests. See our website for details." 2/yr. Pub'd 2 issues 2005; expects 2 issues 2006, 2 issues 2007. sub. price $15; per copy $8; sample $10. Back issues: $10. Discounts: distributors 55%retailers 50%. 144pp. Reporting time: 4 months. Simultaneous submissions accepted: Yes. Publishes 10% of manuscripts submitted. Payment: 2 contributor copies. Copyrighted, reverts to author. Pub's reviews: 10 in 2005. §Fiction, poetry, and nonfiction by small, independent, or university presses. Ads: Full page only $150 per issue (discounts with more than one issue). Discount for non-profits or arts organizations. Subjects: Arts, Book Reviewing, Essays, Fiction, Interviews, Literary Review, Non-Fiction, Novels, Poetry, Prose, Reviews, Short Stories.

Bamboo Ridge Press (see also BAMBOO RIDGE, Journal of Hawai'i Literature and Arts), Eric Chock, Darrell H.Y. Lum, PO Box 61781, Honolulu, HI 96839-1781, 808-626-1481 phone/Fax, brinfo@bambooridge.com. 1978. Poetry, fiction, plays. "Particular interest in island writers and writing which reflects the multi-ethnic culture of Hawaii." avg. press run 1M. Pub'd 2 titles 2005; expects 2 titles 2006, 2 titles 2007. Discounts: 40%. 125-200pp. Reporting time: 6 months. Simultaneous submissions accepted: no. Copyrights for author. Subjects: Asian-American, Hawaii, Literature (General).

BAMBOO RIDGE, Journal of Hawai'i Literature and Arts, Bamboo Ridge Press, Eric Chock, Darrell H.Y. Lum, PO Box 61781, Honolulu, HI 96839-1781. 1978. Poetry, fiction, articles, parts-of-novels, plays, non-fiction. "Particular interest in literature reflecting the multi-ethnic culture of the Hawaiian islands." circ. 600-1M. 2/yr. Pub'd 2 issues 2005; expects 2 issues 2006, 2 issues 2007. sub. price $20 individual, $25 institutions; per copy $8-18; sample $10. Back issues: varies. Discounts: 40%. 125-200pp. Reporting time: 6 months. Simultaneous submissions accepted: no. Payment: usually $10/poem, $20/prose piece. Copyrighted, reverts to author. Ads: $100/$60. Subjects: Asian-American, Hawaii, Literature (General).

Banana Productions (see also INTERNATIONAL ART POST), Anna Banana, RR 22, 3747 Highway 101, Roberts Creek, BC V0N 2W2, Canada, 604-885-7156, Fax 604-885-7183. 1988. Art, photos. "This is a cooperatively published periodical. Contributors pay and get 1/2 the edition." avg. press run 1M. Pub'd 1 title 2005; expects 1 title 2006, 1 title 2007. Discounts: 40% on consignment, 50% wholesale. 1 page. Reporting time: acknowledgement within 1 week of receipt of deposit (50% up front). Simultaneous submissions accepted: yes. We publish 100% of art or photos submitted. Payment: they receive 500 copies of the stamp(s). Copyrights for author. Subjects: Advertising, Self-Promotion, Arts, Design, Graphics, Philately, Photography.

BANANA RAG, Anna Banana, RR 22, 3747 Hwy. 101, Roberts Creek, B.C. V0N 2W2, Canada, 604-885-7156. 1971. Articles, art, photos, cartoons, letters, collages, news items. "The Banana Rag is a long-time "zine" reflecting my connection with the International Mail-art Network (IMAN), and publishes material sent in by the network correspondents, along with an update on what's happening in my art life. (for example, the current issue contains a listing of all participants in my Sticker Tree project, along with reproductions of a number of the cards returned.) Subscriptions are $15/2 issues whenever they come out; $40 for deluxe edition accompanied by a signed and numbered limited color print by editor A. Banana. New ISSN 1715-1341 for issue #33. Had a previous one, but in 1991-96, I changed the title and focus to Artistamp News, publishing a 12 page newsletter about artists postage-like stamps. Then in 2002, after a few issues of the Banana Bulletin, I returned to the Banana Rag title and format." circ. 200. 1/yr. Pub'd 1 issue 2005; expects 1 issue 2006, 1 issue 2007. sub. price $15/2 issues; $40 for deluxe edition that includes signed and numbered ltd. edition color print by A. Banana.; per copy $15/2 issues; $40 for deluxe edition that includes a signed and numbered, limited edition color print by editor, A. Banana.; sample $5. Back issues: inquire. Discounts: nada. 4-8pp. Reporting time: usually within a year! Simultaneous submissions accepted: No. No payments given. Not copyrighted. §BANANA RELATED art, postcards information, articles, jokes, music, news-stories, products, photos, "slanguage," etc. etc. No ads. Subjects: Absurdist, Agriculture, Arts, Avant-Garde, Experimental Art, Botany, Cartoons, Conservation, Cooking, Dada, Entertainment, Experimental, Food, Eating, History, Humor, Postcards.

Bancroft Press, Bruce Bortz, Publisher, PO Box 65360, Baltimore, MD 21209-9945, 410-358-0658, Fax 410-764-1967. 1991. Fiction, non-fiction. "We are a general interest trade publisher specializing in books by journalists. However, submissions are welcome from all serious writers." avg. press run 3,000. Pub'd 4 titles 2005; expects 5 titles 2006, 4-6 titles 2007. Discounts: standard discounts apply. 300pp. Reporting time: varies. Simultaneous submissions accepted: yes. Publishes 1-5% of manuscripts submitted. Payment: yes. Copyrights for author. Subjects: African-American, Anthology, Arts, Biography, Book Reviewing, Current Affairs, Electronics, Essays, Fiction, Finances, Humor, Literary Review, Memoirs, Non-Fiction, Parenting.

Bandanna Books, Sasha "Birdie" Newborn, 1212 Punta Gorda Street #13, Santa Barbara, CA 93103-3568, 805-899-2145 phone/Fax. 1975. Fiction, art, interviews, parts-of-novels, non-fiction. "Bandanna Books serves the college market online as a general college bookstore. We publish college and college prep materials for the humanities and world languages, including teacher and self-study guides. As a sideline, BBooks also does book production for self-publishing writers at competitive rates. Inquire at *bandanna@cox.net.*" avg. press run 1M. Expects 2 titles 2006, 2 titles 2007. Discounts: Credits on textbooks 1-4 copies 0%, 5 or more copies 20%. Credit for returned resaleable copies expires after 2 years. 80pp. Reporting time: 2 months. Simultaneous submissions accepted: yes. Publishes 1% of manuscripts submitted. Payment: by agreement. Copyrights for author. Subjects: African Literature, Africa, African Studies, Classical Studies, Culture, Drama, Education, English, France, French, Greek, History, Language, Liberal Arts, Literature (General), Religion, Shakespeare, Visual Arts.

Bandido Books, 9806 Heaton Court, Orlando, FL 32817, 407-657-9707, Fax 407-677-9796, publish@bandidobooks.com, www.bandidobooks.com. 1999. Non-fiction. "Publisher of technical and literature of interest to nurses and nursing students." avg. press run 10M. Pub'd 5 titles 2005; expects 6 titles 2006, 7 titles 2007. Discounts: 10-55% depending on quantity. 58pp. Reporting time: 4 weeks. Simultaneous submissions accepted: yes. Subjects: Education, Inspirational, Nursing.

Banks Channel Books, 2314 Waverly Drive, Wilmington, NC 28403-6040, Order phone 1-800-2229796, E-mail bankschan@ec.rr.com. 1993. Fiction, art, photos, non-fiction. "We publish Carolina authors only." avg. press run 1M-5M. Expects 2 titles 2006. Discounts: retailers 1-2 copies 20%, 3 or more 40%, 10+ prepaid, nonreturnable 45%. 200pp. Simultaneous submissions accepted: no. Payment: 10% of gross receipts. Copyrights for author. Subjects: Fiction, Gardening, Immigration, Non-Fiction, North Carolina, Novels.

THE BANNER, CRC Publications, John Suk, 2850 Kalamazoo SE, Grand Rapids, MI 49560, 616-224-0819. 1865. Poetry, fiction, articles, photos, cartoons, interviews, reviews, letters, news items, non-fiction. "Religion-in the Reformed-Presbyterian tradition." circ. 25M. 12/yr. Pub'd 26 issues 2005; expects 18 issues 2006, 12 issues 2007. sub. price $36.95; per copy $2.50. Back issues: $2.50. 64pp. Reporting time: 2 weeks. Simultaneous submissions accepted: no. Copyrighted, reverts to author. Pub's reviews: 20 in 2005. §Religion. Ads: $1410/$805/$65 per column inch. Subject: Religion.

Banshee Press (see also ONE TRICK PONY), Louis McKee, PO Box 11186, Philadelphia, PA 19136-6186. 1997. Poetry. "Recently published a book by Tom Devaney, chapbooks by Harry Humes and Joyce Odam, and a limited edition letterpress broadside, "No War," by Stephen Berg, and more." avg. press run 350. Pub'd 1 title 2005; expects 2 titles 2006, 1 title 2007. pp varies. Reporting time: query first. Payment: copies. Copyrights for author. Subject: Poetry.

Banta & Pool Literary Properties, Gary Pool, Executive Editor; Frank Banta, Publisher, 1020 Greenwood Avenue, Bloomington, IN 47401, writerpool@aol.com. 1995. Poetry, fiction, non-fiction. avg. press run 2500 copies. Discounts: 40% discount to the trade, 20% to libraries. Payment: 2% 10, net 30 days. Copyrights for author. Subjects: Biography, Cooking, Gay, Immigration, Indiana, Literature (General), Poetry, Politics, U.S. Hispanic.

Bard Press (see also WATERWAYS: Poetry in the Mainstream), Richard Spiegel, Editor, 393 St. Pauls Avenue, Staten Island, NY 10304-2127, 718-442-7429. 1974. Poetry, art, long-poems. "Chapbooks containing the work of one poet, most recently Ida Fasel and Joy Hewitt Mann. Most poets come to us through our magazine *Waterways*. Publication by invitation only." avg. press run 300. Pub'd 2 titles 2005; expects 2 titles 2006, 2 titles 2007. Discounts: 40% to booksellers. 32pp. Simultaneous submissions accepted: no. Payment: in copies. Copyrights for author. Subject: Poetry.

‡**BARDIC RUNES,** Michael McKenny, 424 Cambridge Street South, Ottawa, Ontario K1S 4H5, Canada, 613-231-4311. 1990. Poetry, fiction, art. "*Traditional and high fantasy only.* Prefer short stories but use some poems. Setting must be pre-industrial, either historical or of author's invention. Length: 3,500 words or less. Art: only illustrations of stories, usually contracted from Ottawa fantasy artists." circ. 500. 2/yr. Pub'd 2 issues 2005; expects 3 issues 2006, 3 issues 2007. sub. price $10/3 issues; per copy $4; sample $4. Back issues: $3.50. 64pp. Reporting time: normally within 2 weeks. Payment: on acceptance, 1/2¢ per word. Copyrighted, reverts to author. Ads: none. Subject: Fantasy.

Bardsong Press, Ann Gilpin, PO Box 775396, Steamboat Springs, CO 80477, 970-870-1401, Fax 970-879-2657, bard@bardsongpress.com, www.bardsongpress.com. 1997. Fiction. "We specialize in historical fiction, especially Celtic/Medieval/Britain." avg. press run 2M. Expects 1 title 2006. Discounts: 40% to stores, 55% to wholesalers. 400pp. Reporting time: 4 months. Simultaneous submissions accepted: yes. Publishes 1% of manuscripts submitted. Payment: varies. Copyrights for author. Subjects: Celtic, Fiction, Novels.

Barefoot Press, Kent Bailey, Director, 1012 Danny Drive, Sarasota, FL 34243-4409, 941-751-3200, fax 941-751-3244. 1987. Fiction, art, photos, cartoons. "We are concerned with publishing high quality, *lasting* graphics (posters and cards) and children's books. As such, we print on acid free paper wherever possible (as in our *California Girls* poster). Sorry, we do not accept submissions of any kind." avg. press run 5M. Subjects:

Graphics, Photography, Picture Books, Postcards.

Barney Press, Donna Litherland, 3807 Noel Place, Bakersfield, CA 93306, 805-871-9118. 1982. "How to books on speed reading, imaging, Jungian psychology, changing human energy patterns, development of women's consciousness. Books designed to help students with study habits." avg. press run 500. Pub'd 1 title 2005; expects 1 title 2006, 1 title 2007. Discounts: 40/60, $5 for examination copy to schools. 128pp. Reporting time: 6 weeks. Simultaneous submissions accepted: yes. Publishes 5% of manuscripts submitted. Payment: 40%. Copyrights for author. Subjects: Cities, How-To, Novels, Spiritual.

BARNWOOD, The Barnwood Press, Tom Koontz, 10553 2nd Ave. NW, Seattle, WA 98177-4805. 1980. Poetry. "Online only, since 2002; poems added as accepted; submissions read only September 1 through May 31; see editorial statement at barnwoodpress.org." Back issues: $10. Reporting time: 1 month. Simultaneous submissions accepted: yes. Publishes 1% of manuscripts submitted. Payment: $25/poem. Copyrighted, reverts to author. Subject: Poetry.

The Barnwood Press (see also BARNWOOD), Tom Koontz, 10553 2nd Ave. NW, Seattle, WA 98177-4805. 1975. Poetry. "Our organization is a nonprofit cooperative in support of contemporary poetry. Criterion is artistic excellence. Web site at *barnwoodpress.org*. Recent authors include: Bly, Carter, Friman, Goedicke, Herz, Jerome, Robinson, Ronnow, Stafford, Watts." avg. press run 1M. Pub'd 2 titles 2005; expects 2 titles 2006, 2 titles 2007. Discounts: 50% to indie bookstores, 40% to other stores, 50% to members and for desk copies. 80pp. Reporting time: 1 to 3 weeks. Simultaneous submissions accepted: yes. Publishes 1% of manuscripts submitted. Payment: 10% of run, additional copies available at cost. Copyrights for author. Subject: Poetry.

BARROW STREET, Barrow Street Press, Patricia Carlin, Peter Covino, Lois Hirshkowitz, Melissa Hotchkiss, PO Box 1831, Murray Hill Stn., New York, NY 10156, 212-937-1970, www.barrowstreet.org. 1999. Poetry. circ. 1.5M. 2/yr. Pub'd 2 issues 2005; expects 2 issues 2006, 2 issues 2007. sub. price $15; per copy $8; sample $8. Discounts: trade and bulk 40%. 110pp. Reporting time: 6 months. Simultaneous submissions accepted: yes. Publishes 2% of manuscripts submitted. Payment: 2 copies. Copyrighted, reverts to author. Pub's reviews: 3 in 2005. §Poetry. Ads: none. Subject: Poetry.

Barrow Street Press (see also BARROW STREET), Patricia Carlin, Peter Covino, Lois Hirshkowitz, Melissa Hotchkiss, PO Box 1831, Murray Hill Stn., New York, NY 10156, 212-937-1970, info@barrowstreet.org, www.barrowstreet.org. 1999. Poetry. avg. press run 1250. Pub'd 3 titles 2005; expects 2 titles 2006, 2 titles 2007. Discounts: trade 40%. 80pp. Reporting time: 6 months. Simultaneous submissions accepted: yes. Publishes 2% of manuscripts submitted. Payment: as per contract. Copyrights for author. Subject: Poetry.

Barrytown/Station Hill Press, Kate Schapira, Managing Editor, 124 Station Hill Road, Barrytown, NY 12507, 845-340-4300, fax: 845-339-0780, web: www.stationhill.org, email: publisher@stationhill.org. 1978. Poetry, fiction, art, photos, satire, criticism, music, letters, long-poems, collages, plays, concrete art, non-fiction. "Publisher of international literature & visual and performing arts, emphasizing the contemporary & innovative, yet excluding neither the ancient nor the traditional, presented with a commitment to excellence in book design and production. Prose fiction by Maurice Blanchot, Rosemarie Waldrop, Franz Kamin, Lydia Davis, Spencer Holst; poetry by John Cage, Jackson Mac Low, Kenneth Irby, Robert Kelly, Paul Auster, Armand Schwerner, Charles Bernstein, Norman Weinstein, etc.; discourse by James Hillman, Ed Sanders, Blanchot, Porphyry, etc; visual arts by Russian avant-garde, Wolf Kahn, Thomas Dugan, etc. Other imprints and series include: *Artext, Contemporary Artist Series, Open Book,* and *P-U-L-S-E Books*." avg. press run 1.5M-3M. Pub'd 12 titles 2005; expects 20 titles 2006, 20 titles 2007. Discounts: 50% distributor, 20% on single orders, escalating with qty. 64-200pp. Reporting time: no guarantee except by written arrangement. Payment: usually 10% of edition in copies or 10% of gross. Copyrights for author. Subjects: Arts, Classical Studies, Criticism, Fiction, France, French, James Joyce, Literature (General), Music, Occult, Philosophy, Photography, Poetry, Psychology, Spiritual, Tapes & Records.

BASALT, Jodi Varon, David Axelrod, School of Arts and Sciences, Eastern Oregon University, La Grande, OR 97850, 541-962-3633. 1981. Poetry, art, photos, interviews, reviews, long-poems, non-fiction. "Basalt, formerly Calapooya, is especially interested in contemporary translations from any language. Please include originals and premissions to translate from the author. Prose poems are also welcome. Recent contributors include Amy Newman, Greg Glazer, Sandra Alcosser, Minor White, and Kay Walkingstick." circ. 1M. 1/yr. Pub'd 1 issue 2005; expects 1 issue 2006, 1 issue 2007. sub. price $5; per copy $7; sample $5. Back issues: $5. 44pp. Reporting time: 1-4 months. Simultaneous submissions accepted: no. Publishes 3% of manuscripts submitted. Payment: copies. Copyrighted, reverts to author. Pub's reviews: 1 in 2005. §Contemporary Poetry books and chapbooks, especially from writers and presses in the Pacific Northwest. Ads: gratis ads. Subjects: Literature (General), Poetry, Translation.

BATHTUB GIN, Pathwise Press, Christopher Harter, PO Box 178, Erie, PA 16512, pathwisepress@hot-mail.com. 1997. Poetry, fiction, art, photos, interviews, satire, criticism, reviews, letters, parts-of-novels, collages, plays. "No strict length limits, prose around 2,500 words preferred. Looking for work that has the kick of bathtub gin (could be strong imagery, feeling within the work, or attitude). No trite rhymes. Recent issues featured Todd Moore, G. Tod Slone, Mark Terrill, Kell Robertson and Lindsay Wilson. Submission time: June1 to September 15." circ. 250-300. 2/yr. Pub'd 2 issues 2005; expects 2 issues 2006, 2 issues 2007. sub. price $8; per copy $5; sample $5. Back issues: $3.50. Discounts: sliding scale. 60pp. Reporting time: 1-2 months. Simultaneous submissions accepted: yes. Publishes 5% of manuscripts submitted. Payment: 2 contributer's copies, plus discount on extra copies. Copyrighted, reverts to author. Pub's reviews: 6 in 2005. §Poetry chapbooks and broadsides, works from small presses. Ads: 2.5 x 4 inches $15/issue or $25/year; 2.5 X 2 $10/issue or $17/year; 2.25 X 1 $7/issue or $12/year. Subjects: Absurdist, Avant-Garde, Experimental Art, Drama, Essays, Literature (General), Photography, Poetry.

The Battery Press, Inc., PO Box 198885, Nashville, TN 37219, 615-298-1401; E-mail battery@aol.com. 1976. "We reprint scarce military unit histories. Inquire for a list of reprints. No new projects at this time." avg. press run 1M. Pub'd 22 titles 2005; expects 22 titles 2006, 18 titles 2007. Discounts: 1-4 copies 20%, 5+ 40%. 350-500pp. Simultaneous submissions accepted: no. Payment: varies. Copyrights for author. Subjects: History, Military, Veterans.

William L. Bauhan, Publisher, William L. Bauhan, PO Box 443, Dublin, NH 03444-0443, 603-563-8020. 1959. Poetry, art. "Specialize in New England regional books, plus arts and Americana." avg. press run 1.5M-2.5M. Pub'd 6 titles 2005; expects 8 titles 2006, 8 titles 2007. Discounts: 40% off on 5 or more copies, flat 20% off on textbooks, ltd. editions. 150pp. Reporting time: a month or so. Payment: 10% of list price; less on poetry & small editions. Copyrights for author. Subjects: Arts, History.

Bay Area Poets Coalition (see also POETALK), Maggie Morley, POETALK, PO Box 11435, Berkeley, CA 94712-2435, poetalk@aol.com, www.bayareapoetscoalition.org. 1974. Poetry. "Poetry - under 35 lines preferred." avg. press run 400. Pub'd 2 titles 2005; expects 2-3 titles 2006, 2-3 titles 2007. 36pp. Reporting time: 2-6 months. Simultaneous submissions accepted: yes. Publishes 20-30% of manuscripts submitted. Payment: copy. Rights revert to authors. Subject: Poetry.

Bay Press, Kimberly Barnett, Sally Brunsman, 1411 4th Avenue, Suite 830, Seattle, WA 98101-2225, 206-284-5913. 1981. Criticism. "Contemporary cultural criticism." avg. press run 7M. Pub'd 2 titles 2005; expects 2 titles 2006, 2 titles 2007. Discounts: trade 20-50%. 192pp. Reporting time: 6 weeks. Simultaneous submissions accepted: yes. Publishes 1% of manuscripts submitted. Payment: net receipts, payable bi-annually. Copyrights for author. Subjects: AIDS, Architecture, Arts, Criticism, Culture, Gay, Media, Non-Fiction, Photography, Politics.

Bay Tree Publishing, David Cole, 721 Creston Road, Berkeley, CA 94708, telephone 510-526-2916, fax 510-525-0842. 2002. Non-fiction. "Bay Tree publishes nonfiction in the areas of current affairs, business and psychology." avg. press run 4000. Expects 2 titles 2006, 2 titles 2007. Discounts: 1-4 copies 20%, 5+ copies 45%. 300pp. Reporting time: 1 month. Simultaneous submissions accepted: Yes. Publishes 5% of manuscripts submitted. Payment: Occasionally offer an advance up to $1500. Graduated royalties 10-12% of net sales. Copyrights for author. Subjects: Advertising, Self-Promotion, Aging, Business & Economics, Communication, Journalism, Community, Consumer, Environment, Finances, Immigration, Insurance, Marketing, Multicultural, Politics, Psychology, Public Affairs.

BAY WINDOWS, Rudy Kikel, Poetry Editor, 631 Tremont Street, Boston, MA 02118, 617-266-6670, X211. 1983. Poetry. "We're looking for short poems (1-36 lines) on themes of interest to gay men or lesbians." circ. 60M. 51/yr. Pub'd 51 issues 2005; expects 51 issues 2006, 51 issues 2007. sub. price $50; per copy 50¢; sample $3 (includes p/h). Back issues: not available. 80pp. Reporting time: 2-3 months. We accept simultaneous submissions if so advised. Publishes 10% of manuscripts submitted. Payment: copies. Copyrighted, reverts to author. Pub's reviews: 51+ in 2005. §Gay or lesbian—fiction, non-fiction, poetry. Ads: $716.10/$346.50/ $173.25 1/4 page/$92.40 1/8 page. Subjects: Gay, Lesbianism.

Bayhampton Publications, Kelly Smith, Director of Marketing and Sales, 54 Mozart Crescent, Brampton, ON L6Y 2W7, Canada, 905-455-7331, Fax 905-455-0207, www.bayhampton.com. 1995. Fiction, non-fiction. "Publishing for Professionals", see website. Contact *before* sending submissions." avg. press run 5M. Expects 1 title 2006, 1 title 2007. Discounts: available on request; bookstores, 40%; libraries, 20%. 250pp. Copyrights for author. Subjects: Education, Non-Fiction, Novels, Parenting, Psychology, Self-Help.

BAYOU, Reginald Shepherd, Department of English, University of West Florida, Pensacola, FL 32514, 850-474-2900. 2002. Poetry, fiction, non-fiction. "Bayou seeks sophisticated, intelligent, well written poetry, fiction, and non-fiction that takes full advantage of the resources of the English language and literary tradition; besides that, we have no particular stylistic biases. We do not want vague, clichd, amateurish, or preachy work. Recent contributors have included Marilyn Hacker, Brenda Hillman, Timothy Liu, and Cole Swensen." circ. 300. 2/yr. Pub'd 2 issues 2005; expects 2 issues 2006, 2 issues 2007. sub. price $10; per copy $5; sample $5. Back issues: $2.95. Discounts: 2-10 copies 25%. 96pp. Reporting time: three months; we do not read over the

48

summer. Simultaneous submissions accepted: Yes. Publishes 5% of manuscripts submitted. Payment is in copies. Copyrighted, reverts to author. Ads: We don't currently carry ads.

BAYOU, Laurie O'Brien, Editor, The University of West Florida/English Dept., 11000 University Parkway, Pensacola, FL 32514-5751, 904-474-2923. 1976. Poetry, fiction. *"The Panhandler* is a magazine of contemporary poetry and fiction. We want poetry and stories rooted in real experience of real people in language with a strong colloquial flavor. Works that are engaging and readable stand a better chance with us than works that are self-consciously literary. Recent contributors: Walter McDonald, Malcolm Glass, Enid Shomer, David Kirby, Joan Colby, Victor Gischler.'' circ. 500. 2/yr plus chapbook. Pub'd 3 issues 2005; expects 3 issues 2006, 3 issues 2007. sub. price $10 includes yearly chapbook; per copy $5; sample $5. Back issues: $4.50. Discounts: 10 or more 40%. 70pp. Reporting time: 4-6 months. Please inform us of simultaneous submissions and acceptance elsewhere. Publishes 5% of manuscripts submitted. Payment: copies. Copyrighted, reverts to author. Ads: $50/$25. Subjects: Fiction, Poetry.

Beach & Company, Box 303, Cherry Valley, NY 13320.

BEACHCOMBER MAGAZINE, Autelitano Media Group (AMG), Phil Autelitano Jr., PO Box 2255, Delray Beach, FL 33445, 561-734-5428, Fax 561-276-0931, Autelitano@aol.com, www.AuteliMedia.com. 1985. Poetry, fiction, articles, art, photos, cartoons, interviews, reviews, letters, news items, non-fiction. ''We prefer anything with a South Florida slant, primarily lifestyle-related. We also like anything 'beachy' - that is, poetry, fiction, nonfiction related in some way to the ocean, coastal living, etc.'' circ. 35M. 10/yr. Pub'd 10 issues 2005; expects 10 issues 2006, 10 issues 2007. sub. price $24.95; per copy $2.95; sample $2.95 w/full-color cover. Back issues: $2. 32pp. Reporting time: 2 weeks. Simultaneous submissions accepted: yes. Publishes 10% of manuscripts submitted. Payment: varies ($10 to $100). Copyrighted, reverts to author. Pub's reviews: 10 in 2005. §Small business, poetry, nonfiction, anything South Florida or coastal lifestyle/affluent related. Ads: $600/$330/$220. Subjects: Arts, Communication, Journalism, Entertainment, Florida, Leisure/Recreation.

Beacon Light Publishing (BLP), Lynda Keena, PO Box 1612, Thousand Oaks, CA 91358, 805-583-2002, toll free 888-771-1197. 1999. Art, photos, criticism, music, plays, non-fiction. avg. press run 3.5M. Expects 1-2 titles 2006, 3-5 titles 2007. Discounts: for over 20 books 40% to bookstores, schools, colleges, universities. 180pp. Reporting time: 1 month. We usually accept simultaneous submissions, but it depends on the subject. Publishes 1-2% of manuscripts submitted. Copyrights for author. Subjects: Christianity, Civil War, Electronics, France, French, Inspirational, Men, Photography, Religion.

Beacon Press, 25 Beacon Street, Boston, MA 02108, 617-742-2110. 1854. Non-fiction. ''No original fiction, poetry inspirational books, or memoirs accepted. We publish books on scholarly topics that have an interest for the general reader, and trade books with potential scholarly uses. Subjects: women's studies, environmental studies, religious studies, gay and lesbian studies, African-Americanm Asian-American, Jewish, Latino, and Native American studies, anthropology, politics and current affairs, legal studies, child and family issues, Irish studies, history, philosophy, education. Submit 2 sample chapters (typed double-spaced) with table of contents, synopsis, and curriculum vitae.'' avg. press run varies widely. Pub'd 60 titles 2005; expects 50 titles 2006, 60 titles 2007. Discounts: trade, nonreturnable and returnable special bulk, text...all different. Reporting time: 6-8 weeks. Simultaneous submissions accepted: yes. Publishes less than 1% of manuscripts submitted. Payment: negotiated separately. Copyrights for author. Subjects: Buddhism, Christianity, Civil Rights, Conservation, Earth, Natural History, Ecology, Foods, Ethics, Feminism, Gay, Human Rights, Ireland, Judaism, Lesbianism, Literature (General), Men.

THE BEACON: Journal of Special Education Law & Practice, Harbor House Law Press, Inc., Pamela Wright, PO Box 480, Hartfield, VA 23071, 804-758-8400, Fax 202-318-3239, info@harborhouselaw.com, www.harborhouselaw.com. *"The Beacon* is a new electronic journal of special education law and practice. We publish articles and essays for attorneys and advocates who represent children with disabilities and others who are interested in special education legal topics.'' circ. 3.5M. 4/yr. Pub'd 2 issues 2005; expects 4 issues 2006, 4 issues 2007. sub. price free; sample free. Simultaneous submissions accepted: yes. Publishes 30% of manuscripts submitted. Not copyrighted. Subjects: Education, Law, Parenting.

Beagle Bay Books, Jacqueline Simonds, Robin Simonds, 3040 June Meadow Road, Reno, NV 89509, 775-827-8654, Fax 775-827-8633, info@beaglebay.com, www.beaglebay.com. 1999. Fiction, non-fiction. ''Fiction: Historical Adventure aimed at women. We are not accepting any new fiction manuscripts at this time. Non-fiction: Personal development and travel (non-guidebook). Additionally, Beagle Bay Books is a distributor of small press non-fiction titles.'' avg. press run 5k. Pub'd 3 titles 2005; expects 3 titles 2006, 3 titles 2007. Discounts: generous to trade, usual to wholesalers and distributors. 300pp. Reporting time: up to 6 months. Simultaneous submissions accepted: no. Publishes 1% of manuscripts submitted. Payment: industry standard. Copyrights for author. Subjects: Fiction, Self-Help, Travel.

Bear & Company, One Park Street, Rochester, VT 05767-0388, Tel: 802-767-3174, Toll Free:

1-800-246-8648, Fax: 802-767-3726, Email: info@innertraditions.com. 1981. Art, music, non-fiction. Pub'd 60 titles 2005; expects 60 titles 2006, 60 titles 2007. 300pp. Reporting time: 8 weeks SASE only. Publishes 1% of manuscripts submitted. Payment: 8%-10% of net. Copyrights for author. Subjects: Americana, Anthropology, Archaelogy, Astrology, Autobiography, Biography, Catholic, Community, Conservation, Counter-Culture, Alternatives, Communes, Ecology, Foods, Feminism, Health, Men, Metaphysics, Myth, Mythology.

THE BEAR DELUXE, Thomas L. Webb, Editor, PO Box 10342, Portland, OR 97296, 503-242-1047, Fax 503-243-2645, bear@orlo.org. 1993. Poetry, fiction, articles, art, photos, cartoons, interviews, satire, criticism, reviews, music, letters, parts-of-novels, plays, news items, non-fiction. "Send most unique environmental story ideas in well-developed one-page query letter. Send clips and letter as initial contact. Follow-up with phone call and have patience. Non-fiction ideas are reviewed and assigned. Fiction, poetry and essay considered under open submission policy. Ideal word limit is 2,500 (up to 4,000 accepted)." circ. 20M. 4/yr. Pub'd 3 issues 2005; expects 3 issues 2006, 4 issues 2007. sub. price $16/4 issues; per copy $3; sample $3. Back issues: $5 if available. Discounts: possible trades. 48pp. Reporting time: 6 months. We accept simultaneous submissions, but must be noted. Publishes 5% of manuscripts submitted. Payment: 5¢/word, copies; $30 photographs, subscription, contributor copies and invitations to events. Copyrighted, reverts to author. Pub's reviews: 16 in 2005. §Environmental, social justice, media, popular culture. Ads: $750/$450/$30 and up. Subjects: Arts, Book Reviewing, Conservation, Environment, Fiction, Literature (General), Non-Fiction, Poetry, Short Stories.

Bear House Publishing (see also LUCIDITY POETRY JOURNAL), Ted O. Badger, Editor, 14781 Memorial Drive #10, Houston, TX 77079-5210. 1985. Poetry, articles, criticism. "Contract Publication of chapbooks, write for prices and parameters." avg. press run 100-300. Pub'd 4 titles 2005; expects 6 titles 2006, 6 titles 2007. Discounts: negotiable. 30-50pp. Reporting time: 30 days or less. Publishes 90% of manuscripts submitted. Payment: primarily a press for self-publishing, but we do some promotion. Inserts copyright notice but does not register. Subjects: Poetry, Prose.

Bear Star Press, Beth Spencer, 185 Hollow Oak Drive, Cohasset, CA 95973, 530-891-0360, www.bearstarpress.com. 1996. Poetry. "Poets/poetry from Western and Pacific states with no restrictions as to form. Annual contest—rules change year to year. Not for profit! Currently not publishing chapbooks." avg. press run 500-1,000. Pub'd 3 titles 2005; expects 2 titles 2006, 2-3 titles 2007. Discounts: varies, stores usually take 40%. Chapbooks 35-40pp, other books 60-80pp. Reporting time: 3-5 months. Simultaneous submissions accepted: yes. Payment: cash and copies to authors. We can copyright for author but usually do not. Subjects: Poetry, Short Stories.

The Bear Wallow Publishing Company, Jerry Gildemeister, 809 South 12th Street, La Grande, OR 97850, 541-962-7864, bearwallow@uwtc.net, www.bear-wallow.com. 1976. Art, photos, non-fiction. "Primarily, Bear Wallow is for in-house publishing projects; however, we work with authors wishing to self-publish; and consider special projects that fit our style. Specialize in one-of-a-kind, limited edition printing." avg. press run 1M-10M. Pub'd 1 title 2005; expects 1 title 2006, 1 title 2007. Discounts: school & library 20% - 50%; trade 40% from suggested retail. 96-208pp. Reporting time: promptly. Payment: 5-10%, quarterly. Copyrights for author. Subjects: Arts, Aviation, History, Non-Fiction, Old West, Photography, The West, Wyoming.

BearManor Media, Ben Ohmart, PO Box 750, Boalsburg, PA 16827, ben@ritzbros.com, www.bearmanor-media.com. 2001. Non-fiction. "We are mostly interested in: Old time radio, voice actors, biographies of old movie stars, directors, writers, composers; books on the golden age of entertainment (between 200 and 350 pages). No fiction or non-entertainment books, please. Our previous releases include biographies on Paul Frees (voice actor), The Great Gildersleeve (radio program), Alias Smith and Jones (tv biography), Agnes Moorehead biography, Guy Williams biography, Albert Salmi (character actor), Hollywood's Golden Age by Edward Dmytryk. Upcoming biographies include The Doris Day Show Book, Dolores Fuller (Ed Wood's girlfriend), George Raft, Alan Young, Don Ameche, Verna Felton, the little people of films, and many radio subjects." avg. press run 1M, then reprints. Pub'd 4 titles 2005; expects 25 titles 2006, 30 titles 2007. Discounts: 40% to libraries, distributors, bulk resellers. 205pp. Reporting time: 1 month. Simultaneous submissions accepted: yes. Payment: 20%. Copyrights for author. Subjects: Arts, Autobiography, Biography, Broadcasting, Disney, Non-Fiction, North America, Radio.

BEATLICK NEWS, Joseph Speer, 940 1/2 W Van Patten, Las Cruces, NM 88005, 505-496-8729. 1988. Poetry, fiction, articles, art, photos, cartoons, interviews, criticism, reviews, letters, parts-of-novels, non-fiction. "The mission of Beatlick News is to network with poets and writers around the world. We seek to serve the writing community by distributing news about chapbooks, events, talented writers, and literary opportunities. We publish the highest caliber of literature that we can find.Recent contributors: Thom the World Poet, Barry Alfonso, James C. Floyd, Michael White, Bill Peach, Emma Wisdom, Anita Sinclair, Duane Locke..." 4/yr. Pub'd 4 issues 2005; expects 4 issues 2006, 4 issues 2007. sub. price $12.00; per copy free; sample free. Back issues: not available. Discounts: No discounts. 16pp. Reporting time: two weeks. Simultaneous submissions accepted: Yes. Publishes 60% of manuscripts submitted. No payment, free copies. Copyrighted, reverts to author. Pub's reviews: approx 15 in 2005. §the books or our friends and books from the 1920's. Ads: We do not advertise. Subjects: Absurdist, African-American, Arts, Beat, Bilingual, Essays, Literary Review, Literature (General), New Mexico, Non-Fiction, Short Stories, Travel, Zines.

•**BEATLICK NEWS POETRY & ARTS NEWSLETTER,** Joe Speer, 940 1/2 Van Patten Ave., Las Cruces, NM 88005-2222, 505-496-8729.

Beaver's Pond Press, Inc., 7104 Ohms Lane, Suite 216, Edina, MN 55439-2129, 952-829-8818, email: BeaversPondPress@integra.net, www.beaverspondpress.com. 1998.

Beckham Publications Group, Barry Beckham, PO Box 4066, Silver Spring, MD 20914, phone: 301-384-7995; fax: 413-702-5632; editor@beckhamhouse.com, jv@beckhamhouse.com; www.beckham-house.com. 1996. Poetry, fiction, satire, plays, non-fiction. avg. press run 1,000.

Bedside Books (see also American Book Publishing), 325 East 2400 South, Salt Lake City, UT 84115, info@american-book.com, www.american-book.com.

Beekman Books, Inc., Michael Arthur, 300 Old All Angels Hill Road, Wappingers Falls, NY 12590, 845-297-2690. 1972. Art, music, non-fiction. "Beekman is a distributor of titles published in North America, England and other European countries. We do not accept unsolicited manuscripts. Beekman publishes a small number of non-fiction and gift books. We are known for our music, homoeopathic, business & finance, medical and other technical lines. No unsolicated mss." Pub'd 5 titles 2005; expects 10 titles 2006, 20 titles 2007. Discounts: 20%. 300pp. Reporting time: 6 months. Payment: 8-10%. Copyrights for author. Subjects: Agriculture, Architecture, Arts, Aviation, Biography, Business & Economics, Children, Youth, Communication, Journalism, Communism, Marxism, Leninism, Ecology, Foods, Education, Health, History, Labor, Literature (General).

BEGINNINGS - A Magazine for the Novice Writer, Jenine Killoran, PO Box 214-R, Bayport, NY 11705-0214, 631-472-1143, jenineb@optonline.net, www.scbeginnings.com. 1998. Poetry, fiction, articles, cartoons, long-poems, non-fiction. "3,000 words max. for short stories. Children's section written or drawn by children. Need articles by published writers - how to get published, write better fiction, etc. Looking for poetry, 30 lines max. Serves as a showcase for beginning writers and poets only. Photos and artwork which accompany submissions may also be accepted. Send SASE for detailed guidelines. We also feature four contests per year with cash prizes for fiction and poetry. We also need writing related cartoons. Pays five dollar per cartoon." circ. 2,500. 3/yr. Pub'd 3 issues 2005; expects 3 issues 2006, 3 issues 2007. sub. price $14, $15 includes free back issue; per copy $6.00; sample $5. Back issues: $3. 54pp. Reporting time: 8-12 weeks. Simultaneous submissions accepted: yes. Publishes 30% of manuscripts submitted. Payment: copy in which work appears. Copyrighted, reverts to author. Ads: $200/$75/$25/ business card. Subjects: Fiction, Humor, Mystery, Poetry, Romance, Spiritual, Supernatural.

Behavioral Sciences Research Press, Inc., 12803 Demetra Drive, Ste. 100, Dallas, TX 75234, 972-243-8543, Fax 972-243-6349. 1979. Non-fiction. avg. press run 5K-25K. Pub'd 1 title 2005; expects 2 titles 2006, 4 titles 2007. 350pp. Reporting time: 60 days. Simultaneous submissions accepted: yes. Payment: by contract. Copyrights for author. Subjects: Business & Economics, Management, Motivation, Success, Psychology, Self-Help.

Belfry Books (see also Toad Hall, Inc.), A.P. Pinzow, RR 2 Box 2090, Laceyville, PA 18623, 717-869-2942; Fax 717-869-1031. 1995. "We primarily are consultants for book-length works only. Send a query letter first. Will read and provide written analysis of first 3 chapters plus synopsis of a manuscript or the complete self-published book for $50. Will work with self-publishers before and after publication. Belfry specializes in New Age and the Paranormal." avg. press run 4M. Pub'd 1 title 2005; expects 2 titles 2006, 2 titles 2007. 224pp. Reporting time: 3 months. Payment: We publish by co-op arrangement only. Copyrights for author.

Believe! Publishing, Susan O'Hanlon CPRW, PO Box 55, Norwood, PA 19074-0055, 717-917-1399, Fax 419-781-7170, info@believepublishing.com, www.believepublishing.com. 2002. Fiction, non-fiction. "Publisher of Illustrated Gift Books & Children's Books." avg. press run 5-10M. Expects 1 title 2006, 2 titles 2007. Discounts: call or email for details - wholesale dist. through B&T. 64pp. Reporting time: 2-3 months. Publishes 2% of manuscripts submitted. Payment: call or email for details. Copyrights for author. Subjects: Careers, Inspirational, Nursing.

•**Bellevue Literary Press (see also BELLEVUE LITERARY REVIEW),** Erika Goldman, Editorial Director; Jerome Lowenstein, Publisher, Dept. of Medicine, NYU School of Medicine, 550 First Avenue OBV 612, New York, NY 10016, 212-263-7802, FAX:212-263-7803, egoldman@BLReview.org. 2005. Fiction, non-fiction. "The Bellevue Literary Press will feature original authoritative and literary works, both fiction and nonfiction, in the sciences, social sciences and arts. It is the natural outgrowth of the *Bellevue Literary Review*, founded in 2000 as 'a journal of humanity and human experience...a well-regarded magazine featuring fiction, nonfiction and poetry by Bellevue's doctors and well-established writers.' (*Washington Post*) The *BLR* has published work by Rick Moody, Abraham Verghese, Julia Alvarez, Philip Levine, Rafael Campo, Sharon Olds, and David

51

Lehman. As with the *Bellevue Literary Review*, the Press's authors will focus on relationships to the human body, illness, health and healing." avg. press run 2000. Expects 4 titles 2006, 8 titles 2007. 200-500pp. Simultaneous submissions accepted: Yes. Copyrights for author. Subjects: Fiction, Medicine, Non-Fiction, Public Affairs, Science.

BELLEVUE LITERARY REVIEW, Bellevue Literary Press, Danielle Ofri MD, PhD, Editor-in-Chief; Jerome Lowenstein MD, Nonfiction Editor; Ronna Wineberg JD, Fiction Editor; Frances Richey, Poetry Editor; Corie Feiner, Poetry Editor; Stacy Bodziak, Managing Editor, NYU School of Medicine, Dept. of Medicine, 550 First Avenue, OBV-A612, New York, NY 10016, www.BLReview.org, info@BLReview.org. 2000. Poetry, fiction, non-fiction. "Recent contributors include Amy Hempel, Stephen Dixon, Sheila Kohler, and James Tate. The Editors invite submissions of previously unpublished works of fiction, creative nonfiction, and poetry that touch upon relationships to the human body, illness, health, and healing. We encourage creative interpretation of these themes. Submit online at www.BLReview.org." 2/yr. Pub'd 2 issues 2005; expects 2 issues 2006, 2 issues 2007. sub. price $12; per copy $7; sample $7. Back issues: $7. Discounts: negotiable. 160pp. Reporting time: 3-5 months. Simultaneous submissions accepted: yes. Publishes 2-5% of manuscripts submitted. Payment: copies, one-year subscription + one-year gift subscription. Copyrighted, reverts to author. Ads: trades. Subjects: Disease, Fiction, Humanism, Literary Review, Medicine, Non-Fiction, Poetry, Prose.

BELLINGHAM REVIEW, Signpost Press Inc., Brenda Miller, Editor-in-Chief, Mail Stop 9053, WWU, Bellingham, WA 98225, 360-650-4863, bhreview@cc.wwu.edu. 1977. Poetry, fiction, non-fiction. "No prose over 9,000 words." circ. 2000. 2/yr. Pub'd 2 issues 2005; expects 2 issues 2006, 2 issues 2007. sub. price $14/2 issues, $27/4 issues, $40/6 issues; per copy $7; sample $7. Back issues: $7. 150pp. Reporting time: 1-4 months. Simultaneous submissions accepted: yes. Publishes 5% of manuscripts submitted. Payment: varies. Copyrighted, reverts to author. Ads: exchange with other non-profits. Subjects: Essays, Fiction, Literary Review, Non-Fiction, Poetry.

BELLOWING ARK, Bellowing Ark Press, Robert R. Ward, Editor, PO Box 55564, Shoreline, WA 98155, 206-440-0791. 1984. Poetry, fiction, art, photos, letters, parts-of-novels, long-poems, plays, non-fiction. "*Bellowing Ark* publishes high-quality literary works that affirm the fact that life has meaning. We are interested in poetry, fiction, essays and work in other forms that extends the philosophical ground established by the American Romantics and the transcendentalists. Our belief is that the techniques developed in the last 80 years (and particularly the last 30) are just that, technique; for us polish is a secondary consideration and work in the "modern" vein need not apply (i.e. stories should have a plot; poetry should contain a grain of universal truth). Our desire is to expand the philosophical and literary marketplace of ideas, not to be its arbiters—but we have very definite ideas about what our mission entails. Please write for a sample copy or subscription if you have any doubts. While form is generally not a consideration for selection we have one occasional feature, "Literal Lives", which presents well-developed autobiographical stories. Other work particularly featured in the past have been serializations and sequences; long and narrative poems; stories of childhood; and love, nature and erotic poetry. Our contributors over the past year have included Jacqueline Hill, Bill Roberts, E.R. Romaine, Teresa Noelle Roberts, James Hobbs, Len Blanchard, Tom Cook, and Tanyo Ravicz." circ. 1M+. 6/yr. Pub'd 6 issues 2005; expects 6 issues 2006, 6 issues 2007. sub. price $18; per copy $4; sample SASE (9-1/2 X 12-1/2 please) with $1.29 postage, or $4. Back issues: varies: Some back issues are now quite rare, quotes on request. Discounts: negotiable. 32pp. Reporting time: 6-10 weeks. Simultaneous submissions accepted: no. Publishes less than 1% of manuscripts submitted. Payment: in copy at present. Copyrighted, reverts to author on publication. Pub's reviews: 1 in 2005. §No unsolicited reviews. We review volumes of poetry that interest us. None. Subjects: Biography, Fiction, Poetry.

Bellowing Ark Press (see also BELLOWING ARK), Robert R. Ward, Editor-in-Chief, PO Box 55564, Shoreline, WA 98155, 206-440-0791. 1987. "As we are just beginning book publishing, we are not currently able to consider unsolicited manuscripts; however, we are interested in any work with a philosophical bent as described under the listing for the magazine we publish, *Bellowing Ark*. At this time the best approach would be to submit work to *Bellowing Ark* with a cover letter describing the complete project; also, *BA* has in the past published chapbook-length poetry manuscripts and has serialized complete book-length works." avg. press run 1M. Pub'd 4 titles 2005; expects 5 titles 2006, 5 titles 2007. Discounts: will negotiate. 48-192pp. Payment: negotiable (currently 10% of net). Copyrights for author. Subjects: Fiction, Poetry.

Bellywater Press, Sara Billups ', P.O. Box 95125, Seattle, WA 98145-2125, www.bellywaterpress.com. 2003. Poetry, art, non-fiction. "The two writers and two designers that formed Bellywater Press give a hearty nod to the connection between visual and verbal. We specialize in both hand-bound, illustrated, and printed books, as well as small-run perfect bound anthologies, travel writing, and other non-fiction." avg. press run 1000. Pub'd 4 titles 2005; expects 4 titles 2006, 4 titles 2007. 130pp. Reporting time: 3 months. Simultaneous submissions accepted: Yes. Publishes 5% of manuscripts submitted. Payment: 10% of wholesale cost per copy. Copyrights for author. Subjects: Arts, Book Arts, Christianity, Community, Creativity, Culture, Design, Essays, Literature (General), Non-Fiction, Picture Books, Religion, Travel, Writers/Writing.

BELOIT FICTION JOURNAL, Clint McCown, Editor-in-Chief; Heather Skyler, Managing Editor, Box 11, Beloit College, Beloit, WI 53511, 608-363-2308. 1984. Fiction. "We publish new contemporary short fiction. Theme and subject matter open, except we will not print pornography, political propaganda, or religious dogma. Length of stories ranges from about three to thirty pages. Recent contributors include Tony Ardizzone, Maura Stanton, Gary Fincke, Erin McGraw, Alvin Greenberg, Scott Russell Sanders, T.M. McNally, Rick Bass, A. Manette Ansay." circ. 700. 1/yr. Pub'd 1 issue 2005; expects 1 issue 2006, 1 issue 2007. sub. price $15; per copy $15; sample $15. Back issues: $6 singles; $14 doubles, all issues available. 232pp. Reporting time: varies, 2 weeks to 2 months. Simultaneous submissions accepted: yes. Publishes 1% of manuscripts submitted. Payment: in copies. Copyrighted, reverts to author. Subjects: Fiction, Short Stories.

BELOIT POETRY JOURNAL, John Rosenwald, Editor; Lee Sharkey, Editor; Marion Stocking, Reviews Editor, P.O. Box 151, Farmington, ME 04938, (207)778-0020, sharkey@maine.edu, www.bpj.org. 1950. Poetry, reviews. "We publish the best of the poems submitted. No biases as to length, form, subject, or school. Occasional chapbooks on special themes, most recently a chapbook of Poets Under 25. Some recent contributors: Margaret Aho, Lucille Clifton, Bei Dao, Patricia Goedicke, Albert Goldbarth, Garth Greenwell, Lola Haskins, Janet Holmes." circ. 1.3M. 4/yr. Pub'd 4 issues 2005; expects 4 issues 2006, 4 issues 2007. sub. price $18; per copy $5; sample $5. Back issues: $5 and up. Discounts: for classroom adoption. 48pp. Reporting time: immediately to 4 months. Simultaneous submissions accepted: no. Publishes .5% of manuscripts submitted. Payment: 3 copies. Copyrighted, reverts to author. Pub's reviews: 4 in 2005. §Books by and about poets, mags with poetry. All reviews written by reviews editor. No ads. Subjects: Poetry, Reviews.

Benchmark Publications Inc., Alice McElhone, PO Box 1594, New Canaan, CT 06840-1594, 203-966-6653, Fax 203-972-7129, www.benchpress.com. 1995. Non-fiction. "Books and tools for business, education and the public interest." avg. press run 5-10K. Pub'd 2 titles 2005; expects 3 titles 2006, 2 titles 2007. 320pp. Reporting time: 3 months. Simultaneous submissions accepted: no. Payment: to be determined. Rights are assigned to BPI for specific edition. Subjects: Business & Economics, Computers, Calculators, Government, How-To, Management, Non-Fiction, Politics.

R.J. Bender Publishing, R.J. Bender, J.R. Angolia, D. Littlejohn, H.P. Taylor, PO Box 23456, San Jose, CA 95153, 408-225-5777, Fax 408-225-4739, order@bender-publishing.com. 1967. Non-fiction. avg. press run 5M. Expects 4 titles 2006, 4 titles 2007. Discounts: 33%-55%. 400pp. Reporting time: 1-2 years. Payment: variable. Copyrights for author. Subjects: Airplanes, German, History, Military, Veterans, Non-Fiction, World War II.

Benecton Press, W. R. Klemm, 9001 Grassbur Road, Bryan, TX 77808, 979-589-2665. 2004. Non-fiction. avg. press run 1000. Expects 1 title 2006, 1 title 2007. Discounts: 30-45%, depending on other terms, such as shipping, consignment, etc. 312pp. Subjects: Non-Fiction, Research, Science.

The Benefactory, Inc., 2 Klarides Village Drive, Seymour, CT 06483-2737. 1991. "Children's book publisher: true animal stories from The Humane Society of the United States with accompanying audio tape narrated by Tom Chapin and plush animal bringing a character to life for the child. Published in 1997: *Cheesie, The Travelin' Man, Chocolate, A Glacier Grizzly, Caesar: On Deaf Ears, Condor Magic*. 1998: *Buster, Where Are You?* and *Rico's Hawk.*" avg. press run 7.5M. Pub'd 5 titles 2005; expects 4 titles 2006, 6 titles 2007. Discounts: yes. 32pp. Simultaneous submissions accepted: yes. Publishes 10% of manuscripts submitted. Payment: yes. Copyrights for author. Subjects: Animals, Children, Youth, Environment.

Bereshith Publishing, Vincent Harper, Executive Editor, PO Box 2366, Centreville, VA 20122-2366, 703-222-9387, Fax 707-922-0875, info@bereshith.com. 1998. Poetry, fiction, art. "Two imprints: ShadowLands Press and Final Frontier Books. Publishing schedule full until 2002." avg. press run 500-1.5M. Pub'd 2 titles 2005; expects 2 titles 2006, 3 titles 2007. 375pp. Reporting time: 2-3 months. Simultaneous submissions accepted: yes. Payment: advance and royalties for novels. Copyrights for author. Subjects: Fantasy, Science Fiction.

THE BERKELEY REVIEW OF BOOKS, H.D. Moe; Florence Windfall, Publisher & Managing Editor, 1731 10th Street, Apt. A, Berkeley, CA 94710. 1988. Poetry, fiction, articles, art, photos, interviews, satire, criticism, reviews, music, letters, parts-of-novels, long-poems, collages, plays, concrete art, non-fiction. "We want reviews (200-300 words) of what isn't reviewed; art, poems, fiction that couldn't have been possibly written or drawn. Open to any kind of books, very interested in experimental writing, art (*not* the language prose/poetry sponsored by the university presses—'Our American professors like their literature clear, cold and very dead'—Sinclair Lewis). Recent contributors: Jenifer Stone, Ivan Arguelles, Lisa Chang, D. McNaughton, Larry Eigner, Mary Rudge, Hadassal Haskale, David Meltzer, Denise du Roi, Norman Moser." circ. 500-1M. 1/yr. Pub'd 1 issue 2005; expects 1 issue 2006, 1 issue 2007. sub. price $35; per copy $35; sample $35. Back issues: $35 + $3 p/h. Discounts: 30%-70%. 400-450pp. Reporting time: 3-4 months. Simultaneous submissions accepted: yes. Publishes 10% of manuscripts submitted. Payment: none as of now. Copyrighted, reverts to author. Pub's reviews: 50 in 2005. §All subjects. Ads: $100/$60/$40 1/4 page/$25 1/8 page.

Berry Hill Press, Doris Bickford, Douglas Swarthout, 2349 State Route 12-B, Deansboro, NY 13328,

315-821-6188 phone/fax; dls@berryhillbookshop.com. 1995. "Subjects: gardening, history, cinema, women authors and artists." avg. press run 5M. Expects 1 title 2006, 1 title 2007. Copyrights for author.

The Bess Press, Reve' Shapard, 3565 Harding Avenue, Honolulu, HI 96816, 808-734-7159. 1979. Non-fiction. "The Bess Press is a regional, educational and trade publisher seeking manuscript materials for the el-hi, college and trade markets. We are actively seeking regional materials, including Asian/Pacific history texts, and cookbooks, humor, and children's books dealing with Hawaii." avg. press run 5M. Pub'd 12 titles 2005; expects 12 titles 2006, 12 titles 2007. Discounts: standard. 200pp. Reporting time: usually less than 4-6 weeks. Simultaneous submissions accepted: yes. Publishes 3% of manuscripts submitted. Payment: standard 10%. Copyrights for author. Subjects: Asian-American, Cooking, Crafts, Hobbies, Dictionaries, Dining, Restaurants, How-To, Humor, Native American, Non-Fiction, Pacific Region, Elvis Presley, Reference, Travel, Young Adult.

Betelgeuse Books, David Pelly, Publisher; Glenna Munro, Associate Publisher, Suite 516, 3044 Bloor St. West, Toronto Ontario M8X 2Y8, Canada, betelg@idirect.com. 1980. Fiction, non-fiction. "We are a small press specializing in 'northern wilderness literature.' No unsolicited manuscripts." avg. press run 3M. Discounts: 40% trade, 20% library. 192pp. Payment: varies. Subjects: Canada, History, The North.

Between The Lines, Paul Eprile, Editorial Co-ordinator, 720 Bathurst Street, Suite 404, Toronto, Ontario M5S 2R4, Canada, 416-535-9914, fax 416-535-1484, btlbooks@web.ca. 1977. Photos, interviews, criticism, non-fiction. "Popular non-fiction, national and international history, economics, politics, theory and practice, women, enviroment, Third World." avg. press run 2M. Pub'd 7 titles 2005; expects 11 titles 2006, 11 titles 2007. Discounts: for university bookstore course orders 20%, trade stores 5+ copies 40%, 20% libraries, except to library services. 240pp. Reporting time: 2-3 months. Payment: variable. Copyrights for author. Subjects: Canada, Civil Rights, Communication, Journalism, Culture, Education, Feminism, Gay, History, Labor, Native American, Political Science, Politics, Socialist, Society, Third World, Minorities.

Beynch Press Publishing Company, Alyce P. Cornyn-Selby, 1928 S.E. Ladd Avenue, Portland, OR 97214, 503-232-0433. 1986. Non-fiction. avg. press run 5M. Pub'd 2 titles 2005; expects 4 titles 2006, 4-6 titles 2007. 100pp. Reporting time: 1 month. Simultaneous submissions accepted: no. Payment: each is different, money and number of copies. Copyrights for author. Subjects: How-To, Psychology.

Beyond Words Publishing, Inc., Cynthia Black, Editor, 20827 NW Cornell Road, Ste. 500, Hillsboro, OR 97124-9808, 503-531-8700, Fax 503-531-8773, www.beyondword.com. 1983. Non-fiction. "Hardcover and softcover titles 200 pages of text. Children's picture books approx. 30-50 words of text and illustrations. Children's authors must be willing to do school and other programs." avg. press run 7K. Pub'd 15 titles 2005; expects 15 titles 2006, 15 titles 2007. Discounts: bookstore standard 40%-high volume up to 45%. 200pp. Reporting time: 90 days. Simultaneous submissions accepted: yes. Publishes .5% of manuscripts submitted. Payment: 10% royalty and up. Copyrights for author if requested. Subjects: Children, Youth, Health, Inspirational, Metaphysics, Non-Fiction, Parenting, Psychology, Self-Help, Spiritual.

Biblio Press, Doris B. Gold, Editor & Publisher, PO Box 20195, London Terrace Stn., New York, NY 10011-0008, 212-989-2755, bibook@aol.com. 1979. Non-fiction. "Jewish women's studies, (non-fiction) and significant reprint fiction; bibliographies, and reference materials on Jewish women. No poetry. Authors should not submit mss. Query first. Distributors: H & M Distribution, Trumbull, CT; New Leaf Distribution, Lithia Springs, GA. All Biblio books (since 1997) now in Holmes & Meier, NYC catalog for ordering, (212) 374-0100." avg. press run 1M-3M. Expects 2 titles 2006, 1 title 2007. Discounts: Women's bookstores get 40% plus other special discounts off; jobbers 25% or more, Judaica & religion bookstores 20% and up; our distributors generously discount. 150pp. Reporting time: 3 weeks for queries. Simultaneous submissions accepted: yes. Publishes 5% of manuscripts submitted. Payment: flat fee for ms and limited royalty arrangement. Copyrights for author. Subjects: Judaism, Reference, Religion, Women.

BIBLIOPHILOS, Dr. Gerald J. Bobango, 200 Security Building, Fairmont, WV 26554, 304-366-8107. 1982. Poetry, fiction, articles, art, photos, cartoons, satire, criticism, reviews, letters, non-fiction. "Query first - Unsolicited material not considered or answered. Scholarly nonfiction feature articles, 1500-3000 words, 750-1000 word book reviews; fiction, uses 7-8 per year, 1500-3000 words. Documentation Turabian/Chicago Style Manual only. Poetry submitted in batches of 5. We want nothing that Ann Landers or Erma Bombeck would publish. Recent contributors: G. James Patterson, Mardelle Fortier, and Patricia Fain Hutson." circ. 300-400. 6/yr. Pub'd 6 issues 2005; expects 6 issues 2006, 6 issues 2007. sub. price $18, $35/2 years; per copy $5.25; sample $5.25. Back issues: $5 + $1 p/h. 72pp. Reporting time: 30 days. Simultaneous submissions accepted: no. Publishes 20% of manuscripts submitted. Payment: $5-$25, complimentary issue. Copyrighted, we retain 1st N. American serial rights only. Pub's reviews: 25 in 2005. §History, literature, literary criticism, language and linguistics, art, music, book collecting. Ads: $35/$20/yearly rates available. Subjects: Americana, Appalachia, Autobiography, Bibliography, Book Arts, Book Collecting, Bookselling, Book Reviewing, Classical Studies, Emily Dickinson, Fiction, History, Italian-American, Literature (General), Medieval,

Romanian Studies.

BIBLIOTHEQUE D'HUMANISME ET RENAISSANCE, Librairie Droz S.A., A. Dufour, M. Engammare, Librairie Droz S.A., 11r.Massot, 1211 Geneve 12, Switzerland. 1934. Articles, criticism, reviews. "History of 16th century." circ. 1M. 3/yr. Pub'd 3 issues 2005; expects 3 issues 2006. sub. price 100 SW.FR ($73)-yr (indiv.); 140 SW.FR ($94)-yr (institutions); per copy 40 SW.FR. ($24). 300pp. Pub's reviews: 100 in 2005. §15th and 16th Centuries. Subjects: Book Reviewing, Criticism, History.

The Bieler Press, Gerald Lange, 4216-1/4 Glencoe Avenue, Marina del Rey, CA 90292. 1975.

BIG BRIDGE: A Webzine of Poetry and Everything Else, Michael Rothenberg, 16083 Fern Way, Guerneville, CA 95446, www.bigbridge.org. 1997. Poetry, fiction, articles, art, photos, cartoons, interviews, satire, criticism, reviews, letters, parts-of-novels, long-poems, collages, plays, concrete art, non-fiction. "We think walls are good for keeping out the cold and rain. And for displaying some art. They're useless in the creation and propagation of art. We don't care if Language poetry appears next to sonnets, or haiku next to spoken word and workshop poetry beside agit-smut. Our tastes are catholiceven though we're Jews and pagans and Buddhists and libertines and run-of-the-mill Christians. We don't care how art is shapedround like moon, flat like roadkill, angular like love, twisted like political promises. We hear many voices (even when we're taking our meds) and are guided by whimsy and passion and urgency. We want more.Recent contributors include Philip Whalen, Joanne Kyger,David Meltzer,Ira Cohen, Jack Collom, Anselm Hollo. Louise Landes Levi, John Brandi, Anne Waldman, Bill Berkson, Lyn Hejinian, Renee Gregorio." 40,000 hits monthly. 1/yr. sub. price free online. Back issues: free archives online. 300 pages. Simultaneous submissions accepted: OK. Payment: none. Pub's reviews.

BIG HAMMER, Iniquity Press/Vendetta Books, David Roskos, Editor, Dave Roskos, PO Box 54, Manasquan, NJ 08736, 732-295 9920, iniquitypress@hotmail.com www.iniquitypress.com (no email submissions). 1988. Poetry, art, photos, cartoons. "Looking for poems & prose about working for a living, class antagonism, raising children, factories, relationships between labor & management, the environment, antiwar,antigovt,antibush, etc. also poems about fleamarkets. Send poems about ANYTHING, if I can't use em, I'll mail em back. No yuppies, prudes, mfa/workshop bullshit. Not looking for state-sanctioned poetry." circ. 250. 1/yr. Pub'd 1 issue 2005; expects 1 issue 2006, 1 issue 2007. sub. price $6; per copy same; sample $6. Back issues: same. Discounts: 60/40. 56-100pp. Reporting time: 1 day to 6 months. Simultaneous submissions accepted: yes. Publishes 30% of manuscripts submitted. Payment: 1 or 2 copies. Copyrighted, reverts to author. Pub's reviews: 5 in 2005. §Poetry, DIY publishing, zines. Ads: some, so far always in trade. Subjects: Absurdist, AIDS, Anarchist, Civil Rights, Crime, Disabled, Drugs, Editing, Gender Issues, Labor, Music, Surrealism, Tapes & Records, War, Zines.

Big Mouth Publications, Joan Frank, 560 Concho Dr., Sedona, AZ 86351-7957. 1992. Music, non-fiction. "Big Mouth Publications publishes motivational audiotapes featuring dynamic narration teams, music and sound effects." avg. press run 5M. Pub'd 1 title 2005; expects 1 title 2006. Discounts: 55% wholesalers. Subjects: Audio/Video, How-To, Humor, Motivation, Success, New Age, Non-Fiction, Self-Help.

BIG MUDDY: Journal of the Mississippi River Valley, Southeast Missouri State University Press, Susan Swartwout, MS 2650, One University Plaza, Cape Girardeau, MO 63701, (573) 651-2044, fax (573)651-5188, upress@semo.edu, www6.semo.edu/universitypress. 2001. Poetry, fiction, articles, art, interviews, reviews, letters, non-fiction. "Recent contributors and authors include Linda Busby Parker, Virgil Suarez, Elaine Fowler Palencia, Philip Kolin, David Radavich, Colleen McElroy, John Cantey Knight." circ. 300. 2/yr. Pub'd 2 issues 2005; expects 2 issues 2006, 2 issues 2007. sub. price $20; per copy $10; sample $6. Back issues: inquire. Discounts: 40%classrooms 50%. 150pp. Reporting time: 8 - 12 weeks. Simultaneous submissions accepted: Yes. Publishes 10% of manuscripts submitted. Payment: 2 copies. Copyrighted, reverts to author. Pub's reviews: 30 in 2005. §particularly small press or general-interest university press books. Ads: $50 or approved exchange. Subjects: African-American, Americana, Conservation, Essays, Fiction, History, Interviews, Literary Review, Midwest, Native American, Non-Fiction, Novels, Poetry, Short Stories, South.

BIG SCREAM, Nada Press, David Cope, 2782 Dixie S.W., Grandville, MI 49418, 616-531-1442. 1974. Poetry, fiction, art. "We include 2-5 pages of each writer publ.- some longpoems tend to have imagist bias; prefer *personal* poems. Contributors: David Cope, Andy Clausen, Anne Waldman, Marcia Arrieta, Jim Cohn, Antler, Jeff Poniewaz. Poets and writers *must* include SASE with their submissions." circ. 100. 1/yr. Pub'd 1 issue 2005; expects 1 issue 2006, 1 issue 2007. sub. price $10; per copy $10; sample $10. Back issues: $10. 50pp. Reporting time: 1-3 months. Simultaneous submissions accepted: yes. Publishes 02% of manuscripts submitted. Payment: 1 copy, more if requested. Subjects: Fiction, Poetry.

Big Valley Press, Charlie Knower, S2104 Big Valley Road, La Farge, WI 54639, 608 489 3525. 2005. Non-fiction. avg. press run 3000. Expects 1 title 2006, 3 titles 2007. 100pp. Subjects: Adolescence, Family, Fiction, Inspirational, Libraries.

BIGFOOT TIMES, Daniel Perez, 10926 Milano Avenue, Norwalk, CA 90650, www.bigfoottimes.net. 1979. Articles. "Manuscripts not accepted." circ. 550. 12/yr. Pub'd 12 issues 2005; expects 12 issues 2006, 12 issues 2007. sub. price $12; per copy $1.50; sample free. Back issues: $1.50/copy. 4pp. Simultaneous submissions accepted: yes. Publishes 0% of manuscripts submitted. Payment: check/paypal/money order. Copyrighted, reverts to author. Pub's reviews: 4 in 2005. §Bigfoot books. Ads: $50 full page.

BIGNEWS MAGAZINE, 484 West 43rd St., Apt. 24D, New York, NY 10036-6341, 212-679-4535, Fax 212-679-4573, bignewsmag@aol.com, www.mainchance.org. 2000. Fiction, articles, art, photos, cartoons, interviews, parts-of-novels, non-fiction. "We generally represent the 'outcast' point of view." circ. 15M. 12/yr. Pub'd 9 issues 2005; expects 9 issues 2006, 12 issues 2007. sub. price $25; per copy $2; sample $2 (free on website). Back issues: When available, $2. Otherwise, back content on website. 16pp. Reporting time: 4 weeks. Simultaneous submissions accepted: yes. Publishes 2% of manuscripts submitted. Payment: $35-$65. Copyrighted, reverts to author. Pub's reviews: 8 in 2005. §The 'outcast' or 'outsider' point of view. Ads: Full Page $2,500 Half Page $1,500. Subjects: Arts, Literature (General).

Bilingual Review Press (see also BILINGUAL REVIEW/Revista Bilingue), Gary D. Keller, General Editor; Karen S. Van Hooft, Executive Editor, Hispanic Research Center, Arizona State Univ., Box 875303, Tempe, AZ 85287-5303. 1973. Poetry, fiction, articles, criticism, plays. "We publish U.S. Hispanic creative literature (fiction, poetry, drama), art books, scholarship, and collections of articles in the following areas: U.S. Hispanic language and literature, Chicano and Puerto Rican studies, contemporary methods of literary analysis." avg. press run 1M cloth, 2M paper. Pub'd 4 titles 2005; expects 9 titles 2006, 9 titles 2007. Discounts: 20% for textbooks; trade—1-4 copies 20%, 5-24 42%, 25-99 43%, 100+ 44%. 256pp. Reporting time: 8-10 weeks. Payment: varies from author subsidy with repayment to author from royalties on copies sold, to standard 10% royalty with no subsidy, depending on commercial prospects of book. We copyright in our name. Subjects: Bilingual, Chicano/a, Criticism, Drama, Fiction, Language, Poetry.

BILINGUAL REVIEW/Revista Bilingue, Bilingual Review Press, Gary D. Keller, Editor; Karen S. Van Hooft, Managing Editor, Hispanic Research Center, Arizona State Univ., Box 872702, Tempe, AZ 85287-2702. 1974. Poetry, fiction, articles, interviews, criticism, reviews. "Research and scholarly articles dealing with bilingualism, primarily but not exclusively Spanish-English; U.S.-Hispanic literature; English-Spanish contrastive linguistics; fiction, poetry, etc., concerning Hispanic life in the US." circ. 1M. 3/yr. Pub'd 3 issues 2005; expects 3 issues 2006, 3 issues 2007. sub. price $40 institutions, $25 individuals; per copy $14 institutions, $8 individuals; sample $14 institutions; $8 individuals. Back issues: depends on issue. Discounts: none. 96pp. Reporting time: 6-8 weeks. Payment: 2 complimentary copies of issue. Copyrighted, does not revert to author. Pub's reviews: 9 in 2005. §Books dealing with our primary areas of interest: bilingualism, U.S. Hispanic literature. Ads: $150/$90/2-pg spread $250, back cover $200, inside back cover $175. Subjects: Bilingual, Chicano/a, Education, Language, Latino, U.S. Hispanic.

Biographical Publishing Company, John R. Guevin, 35 Clark Hill Road, Prospect, CT 06712-1011, 203-758-3661, Fax 253-793-2618, biopub@aol.com. 1991. Poetry, non-fiction. avg. press run 100-1M. Pub'd 4 titles 2005; expects 6 titles 2006, 8 titles 2007. Discounts: wholesale 55%, stores 40%. 120pp. Reporting time: 2 weeks. Simultaneous submissions accepted: yes. Publishes 25% of manuscripts submitted. Payment: author gets all profits less printing, distribution, and shipping costs. Does not copyright for author. Subjects: AIDS, Animals, Autobiography, History, India, Inspirational, Non-Fiction, Pets, Poetry, Short Stories, Surrealism, Weddings, Women.

BIOLOGY DIGEST, Plexus Publishing, Inc., Mary Suzanne Hogan, 143 Old Marlton Pike, Medford, NJ 08055, 609-654-6500. 1977. Non-fiction. "*Biology Digest* is an abstracting journal with subject and author indexes. Each issue also contains a full-length original feature article on some life science subject of particular timely interest. We also publish an annual cumulative index." circ. 2M. 9/yr. Pub'd 9 issues 2005; expects 9 issues 2006, 9 issues 2007. sub. price $149; per copy only sold by volume year. Back issues: same. Discounts: call for pricing. 170pp. Reporting time: 60 days. Payment: feature article varies. Copyrighted, reverts to author. Pub's reviews: 4 books in 2005. §Biology, life sciences, medicine, health, ecology. Subject: Science.

Birch Brook Press, Tom Tolnay, PO Box 81, Delhi, NY 13753, phone/fax orders & sales inquiries 607-746-7453, email birchbrook@usadatanet.net, www.birchbrookpress.info. 1982. Poetry, fiction, art. "Birch Brook Press prefers inquiries with samples from manuscript, SASE a must if writer wants a reply. BBP has its own complete letterpress print shop and uses monies from designing, printing, typesetting books for other publishers to do original, theme-oriented anthologies on a project-by-project basis, soliciting material for each. Becaus of our antique methods of production, BBP is not a good market for full-length novels. Among our most recent anthologies are *Tales for the Trail, The Suspense of Loneliness, Baseball & The Lyrical Life, Fateful Choices, Romance of the Book, Magic & Madness in the Library.* (These projects are now completed.) We sometimes do handcrafted books of unusual merit by individual writers on a co-op basis. While popular culture is our primary interest, we publish two/three books of literary poetry/fiction each year. Recent titles include *Daimonion Sonata* by Steven Owen Shields; *The Architect, The Physician, & The Poet* by Rolf Sigford;

Shadows in the Stream by Robert J. Romano, Jr.; *The Hungarian Sea* by Hollace Gruhn; *Rome Burning* by Helen Barolini; *Synesthetics* by Harry Smith & Stanley Nelson; *Contemporary Martyrdom* by John Popielaski; *Longing for Laura* by AM Juster; *A Punk in Gallows America* by PW Fox; *Walking the Perimeters of the Plate Glass Window Factory* by Jared Smith; *White Buffalo* by Peter Skinner. Some of our books are crafted entirely by hand, are signed and numbered, and these are sold as Limited Editions." avg. press run 500-1.5M. Pub'd 4 titles 2005; expects 4 titles 2006, 4 titles 2007. Discounts: 1 copy 32%, 2-4 36%, 5-9 38%, 10-15 40%; these discounts do not apply to limited editions which are discounted to shops/wholesalers at 32% regardless of quantity. 56-128pp. Reporting time: 6-8 weeks. We accept simultaneous submissions if indicated. Payment: modest, varies. Copyrights for author. Subjects: Culture, Fiction, Literature (General), Poetry, Sports, Outdoors.

BIRD DOG, Sarah Mangold, 1535 32nd Avenue, Apt. C, Seattle, WA 98122, www.birddogmagazine.com. 2000. Poetry, art, interviews, criticism, reviews, letters, long-poems, collages, concrete art, non-fiction. "Bird Dog: A dog used to retrieve game birds. To follow a subject of interest with persistent attention. A scout...Bird Dog: a journal of innovative writing and art: collaborations, interviews, collage, poetry, poetics, long poems, reviews, graphs, charts, non-fiction, cross-genre. Recent contributors include: Brigitte Byrd, Karen Ganz, Noah Eli Gordon & Sara Veglahn, Camille Guthrie, Bob Harrison, Christine Hume, Brenda Iijima, Julie Kizershot, Drew Kunz, John Latta, Michael Leddy, Corey Mead, Joseph Noble, Kristin Palm, David Pavelich, Heidi Peppermint, Kerri Sonnenberg, Jane Sprague, Donna Stonecipher, Stacy Szymaszek, Mark Tardi, Steve Timm, Hung Q. Tu, Dana Ward." circ. 150. 2/yr. Pub'd 2 issues 2005; expects 2 issues 2006, 2 issues 2007. sub. price $15; per copy $8; sample $8. Back issues: inquire. 75pp. Reporting time: Two weeks to three months. Simultaneous submissions accepted: Yes. Payment: Pays Contributor Copy. Copyrighted, reverts to author. Pub's reviews: 2 in 2005. §Innovative/experimental poetry and poetics. Subjects: Arts, Avant-Garde, Experimental Art, Book Arts, Criticism, Culture, Experimental, Interviews, Performing Arts, Poetry, Prose, Reviews, Translation, Visual Arts, Writers/Writing.

Birdalone Books, Viola Roth, 2212 32nd St., San Diego, CA 92104-5602, Fax 812-337-0118. 1988. Poetry, fiction, criticism, music, long-poems, non-fiction. "Primary interest is in the facsimile reprinting, via offset lithography, of obscure out-of-print literature (e.g. William Morris) and music. Specialty is in high-*quality* production, encompassing paper selection, design, and binding. Any volume is also available in half- or full-leather (goat or calf), completely hand-sewn and hand-bound, with authentic, *sewn* silk headbands. All acid-free papers and boards; skins are pared by hand (no bonded leather!). Bindery will also do repairs and restoration of customers' other books, at competitive prices. No unsolicited mss, please." avg. press run 750. Pub'd 1 title 2005; expects 1 title 2006, 1 title 2007. Discounts: 1 copy: 10%, 2-5: 20%, 6-9: 30%, 10+: 40%. 400pp. Payment: 5% of net sales. Copyrights for author. Subjects: Arts, Fiction, Music, Music, Philosophy, Translation.

Birdsong Books, Nancy Carol Willis, 1322 Bayview Road, Middletown, DE 19709, 302-378-7274, Fax 302-378-0339, birdsongbooks@delaware.net. 1998. Art, non-fiction. "Birdsong Books publishes natural science picture books for children with beautiful, scientifically-realistic illustrations and well-researched, age appropriate text. Our mission is teaching kids to care for the Earth and all living things. Contact by mail with a complete submissions package. Do your homework - read our books. Include a competitive analysis and tell me why your manuscript is better/unique and why you are qualified to write it. . Do not phone, fax or email. Include SASE." avg. press run 4M. Pub'd 1 title 2005; expects 1 title 2006, 1 title 2007. Discounts: contact for specific rates. 32pp. Reporting time: 1-3 months. Will accept simultaneous submissions if stated as such. Payment: varies. Copyrights for author. Subjects: Animals, Birds, Children, Youth, Earth, Natural History, Nature, Non-Fiction, Picture Books.

BIRMINGHAM POETRY REVIEW, Robert Collins, Co-Editor; Tina Harris, Co-Editor, English Department HB 205 UAB, 1530 3rd Ave. S., Birmingham, AL 35294, 205-934-8573. 1987. Poetry. circ. 600. 2/yr. Pub'd 2 issues 2005; expects 2 issues 2006, 2 issues 2007. sub. price $5; per copy $2; sample $2.50. Back issues: $2.50. 64pp. Reporting time: 3-6 months. Simultaneous submissions accepted: no. Publishes 1% of manuscripts submitted. Payment: 2 copies, plus a one year subscription. Copyrighted, reverts to author. Pub's reviews: 6 in 2005. §Contemporary poetry. Ads: none. Subject: Poetry.

Birth Day Publishing Company, PO Box 7722, San Diego, CA 92167. 1975. Poetry, articles, art, photos, interviews, reviews, letters, non-fiction. "We publish material dealing with spirituality in general and, in particular, the life and teachings of an Indian holy man named Sri Sathya Sai Baba. Published material has been book length, non-fiction. Recent contributors include Samuel H. Sandweiss, M.D., Dr. John S. Hislop, Ph.D, and Howard Murphet. Ms by invitation only." avg. press run 5M. Pub'd 2 titles 2005; expects 3 titles 2006, 3 titles 2007. Discounts: book trade 40%, bulk 50%, classroom/library 40%, jobber 50%. 225pp. Payment: usually none. Copyrights for author. Subjects: Psychology, Religion, Spiritual.

BIRTHKIT NEWSLETTER, Midwifery Today, Jan Tritten; Cheryl K Smith, Managing Editor, PO Box 2672, Eugene, OR 97402, 503-344-7438. 1994. "Birth information for midwives, childbirth educators and interested consumers. Photos, experiences, technical and non-technical articles." circ. 650. 4/yr. Expects 4 issues 2006, 4 issues 2007. sub. price $20; per copy $5; sample $3.50. Discounts: none. 12pp. Reporting time: 6 weeks. Simultaneous submissions accepted: no. Publishes 85% of manuscripts submitted. Copyrighted, . Ads: none.

BITTER OLEANDER, Paul B. Roth, 4983 Tall Oaks Drive, Fayetteville, NY 13066-9776, Fax 315-637-5056, info@bitteroleander.com, www.bitteroleander.com. 1974. Poetry, fiction, interviews, long-poems. "We strive to preclude the conventional issues and sentiments on which mainstream poetry thrives, with a poetry not only rich in its imagination but one that treats words as sacred rather than vehicles to the same place over and over again. Some recent contributors are Duane Locke, Alan Britt, Anne Coray, Anthony Seidman, Christine Boyka Kluge, Silvia Scheibli, Rob Cook, George Kalamaras and Carol Dine. We also welcome translations of living poets and the short fiction of all writers as a way of widening our imaginative base. Our annual *Frances Locke Memorial Poetry Award* offers a winning prize of $1000, publication in *The Bitter Oleander* and 5 copies of the Award issue for the most imaginative poem entered. Contact us for guidelines or click on our web-site." circ. 1500. 2/yr. Pub'd 2 issues 2005; expects 2 issues 2006, 2 issues 2007. sub. price $15; per copy $8; sample $8. Back issues: $8. Discounts: We offer 20% discounts to Public and University libraries. 128pp. Reporting time: Within 1 month. Simultaneous submissions accepted: Yes. Publishes less than .50% of manuscripts submitted. Payment: 1 copy. Copyrighted, reverts to author. Ads: $200/$125. Subjects: Essays, Experimental, Fiction, Interviews, Poetry, Short Stories, Surrealism.

BkMk Press, Robert Stewart, Editor-in-Chief; Ben Furnish, Managing Editor, University of Missouri-Kansas City, 5101 Rockhill, University House, Kansas City, MO 64110, 816-235-2558, FAX 816-235-2611, bkmk@umkc.edu. 1971. Poetry, fiction, non-fiction. "*BkMk Press* ordinarily publishes non-commercial materials of high quality & cultural significance, poetry, fiction and essay collections. Check www.umkc.edu/bkmk for details on the annual John Ciardi Prize for Poetry and G. S. Sharat Chandra Prize for Short Fiction." avg. press run 750. Pub'd 5 titles 2005; expects 4 titles 2006. Discounts: trade 40%. 75pp. Reporting time: 6 months. Simultaneous submissions accepted: yes. Payment: 10% royalty. Copyrights for author. Subjects: Essays, Fiction, Literature (General), Multicultural, Poetry, Prose, Short Stories.

Black Bear Publications (see also BLACK BEAR REVIEW), Ave Jeanne, 1916 Lincoln Street, Croydon, PA 19021-8026, bbreview@earthlink.net, www.blackbearreview.com. 1984. Poetry, articles, art, reviews. "Chapbook publications depends upon funding at present times. Usually no more than 3 per year. Manuscripts should reflect Black Bear image. Contributors should have a good knowledge of Black Bear and have worked with us before. Send complete manuscript. We have recently published *Tracers*, by Gerald Wheeler. We receive numerous chapbook submissions, so be prepared for competition. Follow guidelines. Samples available for $5 ppd. in the US and Canada. Illustrators receive cash payment on acceptance for illustrating our chapbooks. Query for current titles. Our main objective is to get more poets into print and off the streets. Enclose a $5 reading fee and SASE. Subsidy considered." avg. press run 500. Pub'd 3 titles 2005; expects 3 titles 2006, 3 titles 2007. 34pp. Reporting time: 2 weeks. Simultaneous submissions accepted: no. Publishes 5% of manuscripts submitted. Payment: in copies. Copyrights for author. Subject: Poetry.

BLACK BEAR REVIEW, Black Bear Publications, Ave Jeanne, Poetry & Art Editor, Black Bear Publications, 1916 Lincoln Street, Croydon, PA 19021, bbreview@earthlink.net, www.blackbearreview.com. 1984. Poetry, art, reviews, collages. "We like to see poetry that is pulssant, and explosive, reflecting social concern. Forms used are avant-garde, free verse and haiku. No line limit. We would like to see artwork in black & white, (4x6—no larger, signed by author. Cover illustrations, cash on publication. Poets published: John Elsberg, Sherman Alexie, Ivan Arguelles, Andrew Gettler, John Grey, Jon Daunt, A. D. Winans. Artists published: Nancy Glazer, Mark Z., Kathryn DiLego, Ruth Richards, Walt Phillips, Ristau. E-mail submissions only. No attached files please." circ. 500. 2/yr. Pub'd 2 issues 2005; expects 2 issues 2006, 2 issues 2007. sub. price $12; per copy $6; sample $6. Back issues: $5. Discounts: 40%. 64pp. Reporting time: 1 week. Simultaneous submissions accepted: no. Publishes 5% of manuscripts submitted. Payment: contributor copy. Copyrighted, reverts to author. Ads: $45/$25—barter. Subjects: Avant-Garde, Experimental Art, Haiku, Poetry.

BLACK BOUGH, Charles Easter, 188 Grove Street #1, Somerville, NJ 08876. 1991. Poetry, art. "We publish haiku, senryu, tanka, haibun, longer poems in the haiku or Japanese tradition. Accept news items about haiku. SASE required for return. Recent contributors include Emily Romano, Jim Kacian, and Michael Dylan Welch. Our name is taken from Pound's 'In a station at the Metro,' arguably one of the earliest haiku-like pooems in English. We emphasize haiku and related forms that exemplify the use of the eastern form in the western idiom and milieu." circ. 200. 3/yr. Pub'd 3 issues 2005; expects 3 issues 2006, 3 issues 2007. sub. price $16.50; per copy $6; sample $6. Back issues: $6. Discounts: none. 30pp. Reporting time: 1-3 months. Simultaneous submissions accepted: no. Publishes 5% of manuscripts submitted. Payment: $1 for each verse, up to $4 for sequence/longer poem. No contributor's copies, except in cases of financial hardship. Copyrighted, reverts to author. Pub's reviews: 10 in 2005. §Haiku and related poetry. Exchanges with similar magazines. Subject: Haiku.

Black Buzzard Press (see also VISIONS-INTERNATIONAL, The World Journal of Illustrated Poetry),

Bradley R. Strahan, 3503 Ferguson Lane, Austin, TX 78754. 1979. Poetry, art. *"No unsolicited manuscripts!"* avg. press run 250-850. Expects 1 title 2006, 1 title 2007. Discounts: 20 or more 40%. 32pp. Reporting time: 2 weeks to 2 months. Payment: by arrangement. Copyrights for author. Subject: Poetry.

Black Diamond Book Publishing, N. Earle, PO Box 492299, Los Angeles, CA 90049-8299, 800-962-7622, Fax 310-472-9833, nancy_shaffron@compuserve.com. 1994. Fiction. "Books: New Age, healing, and visionary fiction. Submissions are not accepted at present." avg. press run 5M. Pub'd 1 title 2005; expects 1 title 2006, 1 title 2007. Discounts: wholesale/distributors discounts available; contact publisher. 200+pp. Simultaneous submissions accepted: no. Payment: available upon request. Copyrights for author. Subjects: Fiction, New Age, Self-Help, Sexual Abuse, Spiritual, Supernatural.

Black Dome Press Corp., 1011 Route 296, Hensonville, NY 12439, 518-734-6357, Fax 518-734-5802. 1990. Non-fiction. avg. press run 3M. Pub'd 5 titles 2005; expects 4 titles 2006, 5 titles 2007. Discounts: 40%. 200pp. Reporting time: 3 months. Simultaneous submissions accepted: yes. Publishes 5% of manuscripts submitted. Payment: varies per contract. Copyrights for author. Subjects: Adirondacks, Architecture, Arts, Biography, Earth, Natural History, Folklore, Geology, History, Native American, New York, Non-Fiction, Sports, Outdoors.

Black Dress Press (see also SPINNING JENNY), C.E. Harrison, P.O. Box 1373, New York, NY 10276-1373, www.blackdresspress.com. 1994. Poetry, fiction, long-poems, plays. avg. press run 1M. Pub'd 1 title 2005; expects 1 title 2006, 1 title 2007. Discounts: refer to DeBoer Distributors. 96pp. Reporting time: 1-4 months. Simultaneous submissions accepted: no. Publishes less than 5% of manuscripts submitted. Payment: complimentary copies. Copyrights for author. Subjects: Arts, Drama, Fiction, Literary Review, Literature (General), Music, Poetry.

Black Forest Press, Julie Knox, CEO; Jan Knox Ph.D., CFO; Warren Knox, VP Marketing; Dahk Knox Ph.D, Publisher, Belle Arden Run, 490 Mountain View Drive, Mosheim, TN 37818, 800-451-9404; FAX 619-482-8704; E-mail: inquiries@blackforestpress.com. 1991. Poetry, fiction, satire, plays, non-fiction. "Kinder Books is an imprint for children's books. Black Forest Press is a small press which focuses on the publications of new authors who have difficulty obtaining large press publishers, but whose work has merit and is marketable. BFP also publishes books on professional growth and career development; spiritual religious books (Segen Books/imprint); Civil War and World War II books (Abenteuer Books/imprint); psychology and educational books; Kinder Books/imprint for Children's Books; Dichter Books/imprint for ethnic and poetry books and Abentenuer Books/imprint for Drama and Adventure books; Sonnenschein Books/imprint for visionary and contemporary books." avg. press run 2M-5M. Pub'd 101 titles 2005; expects 100+ titles 2006, 100+ titles 2007. Discounts: 20% to educational institutions who order quantities of 50 books/sets of books at a time; 15% on orders of 21-49; 10% on orders of 1-20; distributors/wholesalers regular discounts; 40% to bookstores. 200-250pp. Reporting time: 2 weeks. Simultaneous submissions are accepted, but no more than two by any one author at a time. Publishes 10% of manuscripts submitted. Payment: varies with promotion's agreement and terms. Copyrights for author. Subjects: Education, Employment, Fiction, Guidance, Networking, Newsletter, Non-Fiction, Poetry, Reference, Self-Help, Short Stories, Tapes & Records, Textbooks, Worker, World War II.

Black Heron Press, Jerry Gold, PO Box 95676, Seattle, WA 98145. 1984. Fiction. "May do something other than fiction, if it appeals to us." avg. press run 1.2M. Pub'd 4 titles 2005; expects 4 titles 2006, 4 titles 2007. Discounts: trade 40% regardless of # of copies, 42% if order prepaid. 200pp. Reporting time: 4-6 months. Simultaneous submissions accepted: yes. Publishes .003% of manuscripts submitted. Payment: 8% of retail price of book, payment semiannually. Copyrights for author. Subjects: Fiction, Literature (General), Novels, Short Stories.

BLACK JACK & VALLEY GRAPEVINE, Seven Buffaloes Press, Art Coelho, Box 249, Big Timber, MT 59011. 1973. Poetry, fiction, art, photos, interviews, reviews, parts-of-novels, long-poems, collages. *"Black Jack*: rural poems & stories from anywhere in America, especially the West, the Appalachias, Oklahoma, and the Ozarks. Work that tells a story, a craft that shows experience, not only of the head (technique), but of the heart (passion and compassion). I'm more than prejudiced against poems that are made up or forced, even when they are concocted out of the supposed wisdom of some established school. A 'school' is nothing more than a group of individuals sitting in one communal literary lap. Give me a loner on his foggy mountaintop; at least the fog is from the mountain, not from his song or his tale to tell. *Valley Grapevine* takes material native to Central California...the San Joaquin and Sacramento Valleys. Especially want work from small town farming communities, but will look at non-rural city work too.Focus on Okies, hoboes, ranch life, migrant labor, the Dustbowl era, and heritage and pride. Want writers and poets who write predominately of the valley of their birth. Contributors: Gerry Haslam, Wilma McDaniel, Richard Dokey, Dorothy Rose, Morine Stanley, Frank Cross, William Rintoul." circ. 750. 1/yr. Pub'd 1 issue 2005; expects 1 issue 2006, 1 issue 2007. price per copy $11.75 P.P.; sample $11.75 P.P. Back issues: none. Discounts: 1-4, 0%; 5 copies or over, 40%. 80pp. Reporting time: within a week, often a day or two. Payment: copies, often other free copies. Copyrighted, reverts to author. No ads. Subjects: Agriculture, Appalachia, Fiction, Poetry.

BLACK LACE, BLK Publishing Company, Alycee J. Lane, PO Box 83912, Los Angeles, CA 90083, 310-410-0808, fax 310-410-9250, e-mail newsroom@blk.com. 1991. Poetry, fiction, articles, art, photos, interviews, satire, criticism, reviews, letters, news items, non-fiction. "Erotic black lesbian magazine. *Black Lace* is currently on hiatus. Atlanta address: 4300 Flat Shoals Road #1910, Union City, GA 30291, 770-964-7247, Fax 770-969-7857, jay2hatl@aol.com." circ. 9M. 4/yr. Expects 4 issues 2006, 4 issues 2007. sub. price $20; per copy $5.95; sample $7. Back issues: $7. Discounts: none. 48pp. Reporting time: 4 weeks. Simultaneous submissions accepted: yes. Publishes 10% of manuscripts submitted. Payment: varies. Copyrighted, rights reverting to author varies. Pub's reviews: 1 in 2005. §Black lesbian community. Ads: $420. Subjects: African-American, Black, Gay, Lesbianism, Sex, Sexuality.

Black Lawrence Press (see also THE ADIRONDACK REVIEW), Colleen Ryor, 305 Keyes Avenue, Watertown, NY 13601-3731, publisher@blacklawrencepress.com, editor@adkreview.com, www.blacklawrencepress.com, www.adkreview.com. 2003. Poetry, fiction, non-fiction. "Black Lawrence Press is an independent press specializing in books of contemporary literature (poetry and fiction), politics, and modern culture and society. Black Lawrence will also publish the occasional translation." avg. press run 500. Expects 3 titles 2006, 4 titles 2007. 80pp. Reporting time: from one month to up to six months, but we try to respond sooner, usually within two months. Simultaneous submissions accepted: Yes. Publishes 2% of manuscripts submitted. Payment: negotiable, but usually either 100 copies or 7% royalties. Author's work is copyrighted. Subjects: Culture, Current Affairs, Fiction, France, French, German, Literature (General), Movies, Music, Non-Fiction, Novels, Poetry, Political Science, Politics, Short Stories, Translation.

Black Light Fellowship, PO Box 5369, Chicago, IL 60680, 773-826-7790, Fax 773-826-7792. 1976. Non-fiction. "Street address: Black Light Fellowship, 2859 W. Wilcox Street, Chicago, IL, 60612." avg. press run 6M. Pub'd 2 titles 2005; expects 2+ titles 2006. Discounts: 20% short, 40% trade, 50% distributors. 200pp. Payment: yes. Subjects: Black, Religion.

Black Mountain Press, PO Box 18912, Asheville, NC 28814, Tel; 828-350-8484,email. BlackMtnPress@aol.com. Poetry, fiction, art, photos, interviews, criticism, music, long-poems, collages, plays, non-fiction. "We publish only works related to the former students and teachers of Black Mountain College, or related work." Pub'd 1 title 2005; expects 1 title 2006, 1 title 2007.

Black Oak Press, Tom Jennings, May Richards, PO Box 4663, University Place Stn., Lincoln, NE 68504, 402-467-4608. 1978. Poetry, fiction, art, parts-of-novels, long-poems, plays. "38 titles in print. Publish chapbooks besides hardcover and trade paperbacks. We solicit most of our material and prefer query letters to unsolicited manuscripts." avg. press run 1M. Pub'd 3 titles 2005; expects 3 titles 2006, 4 titles 2007. Discounts: negotiable. 64pp. Reporting time: 2 months for mss, 2 weeks for query letters. Simultaneous submissions accepted: yes. Publishes 1% of manuscripts submitted. Payment: negotiable. Copyrights for author. Subjects: Dada, Novels, Poetry, Satire.

Black Pearl Enterprises LLC, Tanya Bates, PO Box 14304, Lansing, MI 48901, 517-204-4197, 18884829797, 5174829522, www.divineblackpearls.com. 2002. Poetry, fiction, non-fiction. avg. press run 250. Pub'd 1 title 2005; expects 3 titles 2006, 5 titles 2007. Discounts: Distributed by Baker & Taylor, Amazon.com, BarnesandNoble.com, Borders.com, Waldenbooks.com, www.divineblackpearls.com. 75pp. Simultaneous submissions accepted: No. Does not copyright for author. Subjects: African-American, Bisexual, Book Collecting, Bookselling, Book Reviewing, Feminism, Fiction, Peace, Psychiatry, Relationships, Self-Help, Spiritual.

Black Rose Books Ltd., D. Roussopoulos, C.P. 1258, Succ. Place du Parc, Montreal, Quebec H2X 4A7, Canada, 514-844-4076, Fax 514-849-4797, blakrose@web.net, http://www.web.net/blackrosebooks. 1970. Non-fiction. "USA address: 2250 Military Road, Tonawanda, NY 14150, (716) 683-4547. Published over 250 books." avg. press run 3M. Pub'd 10 titles 2005; expects 10 titles 2006, 10 titles 2007. Discounts: regular trade. 200pp. Reporting time: 6 months. Simultaneous submissions accepted: yes. Publishes 10% of manuscripts submitted. Payment: 10% of list price. Copyrights for author. Subjects: Anarchist, Book Reviewing, Business & Economics, Canada, Cities, Community, Ecology, Foods, Feminism, Humanism, Labor, Philosophy, Sociology.

THE BLACK SCHOLAR: Journal of Black Studies and Research, Robert Chrisman, Editor; Robert L. Allen, Senior Editor, PO Box 2869, Oakland, CA 94609, 510-547-6633. 1969. Poetry, articles, art, photos, interviews, criticism, reviews, music. "Manuscripts for full-length articles may range in length from 2M to 5M words, include brief biographical statement, typewritten, double spaced. Articles may be historical and documented, they may be analytic and theoretical; they may be speculative. However, an article should not simply be a 'rap'; it should present a solid point of view convincingly and thoroughly argued. Recent Contributors: Jesse Jackson, Manning Marable, Jayne Cortez, Sonia Sanchez, Henry Louis Gates." circ. 10M. 4/yr. Pub'd 4 issues 2005; expects 4 issues 2006. sub. price $30 individual, $85 institution; per copy $6. Back issues: $6. Discounts: publishers 10% off above rates. 80pp. Reporting time: 1-2 months. Payment: in contributors copies of magazine and 1 year subscription. Rights become property of the *Black Scholar*. Pub's reviews: 22 in 2005. §The black experience or black related books. Ads: $1,200/$725/$550 1/4 page/classified $200 for 50 words or less, over 50 words add $22 per line per 7 words. Subjects: African Literature, Africa, African Studies, Black.

BLACK SHEETS MAGAZINE, Bill Brent, 33-3313 Moku St., Pahoa, HI 96778-8305, 415-431-0173; Fax 415-431-0172; blacksheets@blackbooks.com. 1993. Fiction, articles, art, photos, reviews, letters, non-fiction. circ. 6M. 3/yr. Pub'd 3 issues 2005; expects 3 issues 2006, 3 issues 2007. sub. price $20; per copy $6; sample $6. 60pp. Reporting time: 6 months. Simultaneous submissions accepted: yes. Publishes 5% of manuscripts submitted. Payment: minimal. Copyrighted, reverts to author. Pub's reviews: 50 in 2005. §Alternative sexuality. Ads: $250/$140/inquire. Subjects: Music, Reviews, Sex, Sexuality.

Black Spring Press (see also BLACK SPRING REVIEW), John Gallo, 63-89 Saunders Street #6G, Rego Park, NY 11374. 1997. Poetry, fiction, articles, plays. ''We are looking to publish poetry/fiction that takes risks. We want work that isn't afraid to push the envelope - writing that is expressive rather than fancy. We are especially encouraging young writers - ignore the workshop mentality.'' avg. press run 100-250. Pub'd 5 titles 2005; expects 7 titles 2006, 7-10 titles 2007. 64pp. Reporting time: 3-6 months. Simultaneous submissions accepted: yes. Publishes 5% of manuscripts submitted. Payment: percentage of press run. Does not copyright for author. Subject: Literature (General).

BLACK SPRING REVIEW, Black Spring Press, John Gallo, 63-89 Saunders Street #6G, Rego Park, NY 11374. 1997. Poetry, fiction, articles, plays. ''We are looking for writing that comes from the guts. As we see it, there are two kinds of writers: what we call 'expressionists' and 'craftsmen'. We prefer the former.'' circ. 100. 4-5/yr. Pub'd 4 issues 2005; expects 4 issues 2006, 4-5 issues 2007. sub. price $20; per copy $5; sample $5. 28pp. Reporting time: 3-6 months maximum. Simultaneous submissions accepted: yes. Publishes 40% of manuscripts submitted. Payment: 1 copy. Copyrighted, reverts to author. Ads: free, space permitting. Subject: Literature (General).

Black Thistle Press, Hollis Melton, 165 Wiswall Hill Road, Newfane, VT 05345-9548, 212-219-1898. 1990. Poetry, fiction. ''We are no longer publishing new work, only selling books published.'' avg. press run 1M-5M. Discounts: 1-5 20%, 5+. 200pp. Payment: individual arrangements made. Copyrights for author. Subjects: Fiction, Non-Fiction, Poetry.

BLACK WARRIOR REVIEW, Molly Dowd, Editor; Alissa Nutting, Managing Editor; Jennifer Ridgeway, Poetry Editor; Andrew Farkas, Fiction Editor; Colin Rafferty, Nonfiction Editor, PO Box 862936, University of Alabama, Tuscaloosa, AL 35486-0027, 205-348-4518. 1974. Poetry, fiction, art, photos, cartoons, interviews, parts-of-novels, long-poems, non-fiction. ''Publishes the freshest contemporary fiction, poetry, and nonfiction along with art and comics in each issue. Recent contributors include Bob Hicok, Rachel Zucker, Joshua Beckman, Renee Ashley, Douglas Trevor, Paul Maliszewski, and Amy Gustine.Holds annual fiction and poetry contests, each with a prize of $1000 and publication in the spring issue. The contest opens May 1, 2006 and closes October 1, 2006. Please send up to 3 poems or prose up to 7500 words per entry along with a $15 reading fee (includes 1-year subscription) and SASE.'' circ. 2K. 2/yr. Pub'd 2 issues 2005; expects 2 issues 2006, 2 issues 2007. sub. price $16; per copy $10; sample $10. Back issues: $8. Discounts: none at present. 180pp. Reporting time: 4 weeks to 5 months. Accepts simultaneous submissions; note on cover letter. Publishes 1% of manuscripts submitted. Payment: one-year subscription and honorarium. Copyrighted, reverts to author. Ads: $150/$90. Subjects: Arts, Cartoons, Essays, Fiction, Non-Fiction, Poetry.

•**BlackBerry Literary Services,** Sandra Peoples, 2956 Mackin Road, Flint, MI 48504, 810-234-0899, fax: 810-234-8593, toll-free:1-877-266-5705, web:www.bblit.bravehost.com, email:bblit@bravehost.com. 2005. Poetry, fiction, interviews, parts-of-novels, long-poems, plays, non-fiction. ''Recently published new author C. Lynn. The mission of BlackBerry Literary Services is to empower writers with the tools they need to become successful authors. We guide our authors through the entire self publishing process, from proofreading and editing to the actual printing. We do not purchase any manuscripts, and we do not collect a royalty. We simply help authors to see their dream work in print. Authors decide how many books they believe they can sell, and therefore determine their own initial print run. BlackBerry Literary Services will not consider assisting with pieces that deal with hate, pornography, or pieces that are poorly written.'' avg. press run 200. Pub'd 2 titles 2005; expects 10 titles 2006, 20 titles 2007. Discounts: 2-10 copies, 25%consider up to 55% for bookstores. 120pp. Reporting time: 2-4 weeks. Simultaneous submissions accepted: Yes. Publishes 75% of manuscripts submitted. Payment: Authors keep 100% of all profits they make from their work. BlackBerry does not charge a royalty. Does not copyright for author. Subjects: Advertising, Self-Promotion, African-American, Family, Fiction, Finances, Food, Eating, Non-Fiction, Novels, Parenting, Picture Books, Poetry, Prison, Prose, Publishing, Religion.

BLACKBIRD, David Stone, PO Box 16235, Baltimore, MD 21210, e-mail chocozzz2@aol.com. 1997. Poetry, art, photos, cartoons, interviews, criticism, long-poems, collages, concrete art. ''Anthology of visual poetry, experimental poetry, art, photography, textual poetry and narrative that is theme related. Query by e-mail. Submit original for publication by mail with SASE. Recent contributors: Eric Basso, Guy Beining, Dave Chirot, Harry Burrus, Guido Vermeulen (Belgium). Experimental, Holocaust, visual poetry, political, blackbird art and myth, Paul Celan, international, new voices. Submission quantity: 1-10. Do not e-mail submissions." circ. 200. 1/yr. Pub'd 1 issue 2005; expects 1 issue 2006, 1 issue 2007. sub. price $30; sample $30w/postage US, $35 foreign (US dollars). Back issues: none. Discounts: none. 200pp. Reporting time: ASAP with SASE. We prefer exclusive submissions, not simultaneous submissions. Publishes 30% of manuscripts submitted. Payment: 1 copy. Copyrighted, reverts to author. Ads: none. Subjects: Avant-Garde, Experimental Art, Holocaust, Visual Arts.

BLACKBOOK PRESS, THE POETRY ZINE, Kyle Van Heck, 1608 Wilmette Avenue, Wilmette, IL 60091, 847-302-9547, krvanheck@noctrl.edu. 2004. Poetry, fiction, articles, art, photos, cartoons, interviews, criticism, reviews, letters, collages, plays, news items, non-fiction. "Prose/poetry should be no longer than 2 pages. Any photos, artwork, or cartoons should be black and white. Always include a SASE, state if you want your manuscript returned. Any work not accompanied by SASE will be recycled. NO NATURE POETRY, RELIGIOUS VERSE OR GREETING CARD VERSE. Promotional stickers available 2 for $1." circ. under 50. 12/yr. Pub'd 6 issues 2005; expects 12 issues 2006, 12 issues 2007. sub. price $10; per copy $2; sample $2. Back issues: selected issues available, please ask via e-mail or mail. 20pp. Reporting time: ASAP. or 1 and 2 months. Simultaneous submissions accepted: if notified. Publishes about 70% of manuscripts submitted. Payment: 1 copy of issue containing work. Not copyrighted. Pub's reviews: 2 in 2005. §Poetry, music, concerts, books. Ads: Yes. Full page $10. All ads must be copy ready. Subjects: Anarchist, Atheism, Avant-Garde, Experimental Art, Chicago, Civil Rights, Counter-Culture, Alternatives, Communes, Cults, Euthanasia, Death, Fiction, Government, Illinois, Interviews, Poetry, Prose, Zines.

BLACKFIRE, BLK Publishing Company, Alan Bell, PO Box 83912, Los Angeles, CA 90083, 310-410-0808, fax 310-410-9250, e-mail newsroom@blk.com. 1992. Poetry, fiction, articles, art, photos, interviews, long-poems, non-fiction. circ. 12M. 6/yr. sub. price $30; per copy $5.95; sample $7.00. Back issues: $7.00. 48pp. Reporting time: 4 weeks. Simultaneous submissions accepted: yes. Payment: varies. Copyrighted, rights reverting to author varies. §Black gay community. Ads: $1800. Subjects: African-American, Black, Gay, Interviews, Sex, Sexuality.

BLACKFLASH, Annie Gauthier, Co-managing Editor; Diana Savage, Co-managing Editor, 12-23rd Street East, 2nd Floor, Saskatoon, Saskatchewan S7K 0H5, Canada, 306-374-5115, Fax 306-665-6568, editor@blackflash.ca. 1983. Articles, art, photos, interviews, criticism, reviews. circ. 1,700. 3/yr. Pub'd 3 issues 2005; expects 3 issues 2006, 3 issues 2007. sub. price Individuals: $22 Canadian; $24 USD for American Subscribers; $32 USD for international; Institution: $32 Canadian; $36 USD for American institutions; $42 USD for international institutions; per copy $8; sample $5. Back issues: $5. Discounts: bulk. 48pp. Reporting time: 2 months. Simultaneous submissions accepted: no. Publishes 25% of manuscripts submitted. Copyrighted, reverts to author. Pub's reviews: 5 in 2005. §Contemporary visual arts, contemporary photography and critical writing on contemporary photography. Subjects: Arts, Photography.

Blackwater Publications, James P. Gannon, 80 Laurel Oaks Lane, Castleton, VA 22716-2523, 540/987-9536; www.blackwaterpublications.com. 2004. Criticism, non-fiction. "Our mission is to publish quality non-fiction with emphasis on biography, autobiography, political commentary, journalism, local and regional history." avg. press run 500-1000. Expects 3 titles 2006, 3 titles 2007. Discounts: Bookstores: one copy, 20%; 2-4 copies, 35%; 5 or more copies, 40%; carton quantity, 50%.Wholesalers: 55%Classrooms: 25%. 140-200pp. Reporting time: 30 days. Simultaneous submissions accepted: Yes. Publishes 10% of manuscripts submitted. Payment: Negotiable. Does not copyright for author. Subjects: Americana, Biography, Book Collecting, Bookselling, Catholic, Celtic, Civil War, Communication, Journalism, History, Iowa, Ireland, Midwest, Minnesota, Politics, Presidents, Public Affairs.

BLADES, Francis Poole, Poporo Press, 335 Paper Mill Road, Newark, DE 19711-2254. 1977. Poetry, fiction, art, satire, letters, collages, news items. "*Blades* is a tiny magazine, so send short poems (15 lines=one page). Occasionally we publish longer ones, 3 or 4 pages. We publish surrealism (drawings too), satire, humor, linguistically interesting work. Very short stories, dreams, and cultural documents also sought; prose should be short. We are interested in non-English poems, also. Editors like imagery and poems that examine the strange natural world." circ. 175. 2-3/yr. Pub'd 2 issues 2005; expects 2 issues 2006, 2 issues 2007. sub. price $5 or exchange of publications and SASE, libraries $35/year; per copy $1 with SASE; sample $1, or for exchange enclose SASE. Back issues: $2. 36pp. Reporting time: 2 months. Payment: copies. Copyrighted, reverts to author. Pub's reviews: none in 2005. §Poetry, film, art, music (rock, blues, jazz, world). Ads: exchange ads free. Subjects: Dada, Humor, Poetry, Transportation, Visual Arts.

John F. Blair, Publisher, Carolyn Sakowski, 1406 Plaza Drive, Winston-Salem, NC 27103, 336-768-1374. 1954. Fiction, non-fiction. Pub'd 17 titles 2005; expects 20 titles 2006, 23 titles 2007. Discounts: wholesalers 50%, libraries and schools 50%, trade schedule is according to quantity of books ordered; non-returnable - 50%

for retail, 55% wholesale. 100-300pp. Reporting time: 6-8 weeks. Simultaneous submissions accepted: yes. Publishes less than 1% of manuscripts submitted. Payment: % of net sales, bi-annual payments. Copyrights for author. Subjects: Civil War, Folklore, Non-Fiction, North Carolina, South, Sports, Outdoors, Transportation.

•**Blanket Fort Publishing,** Sarah Phelan, 117 Lakeview Avenue, Lynn, MA 01904, 781-632-1824. 2005. Fiction. "To provide intelligent, realistic fiction for women." avg. press run 3000. Expects 1-3 titles 2006, 2-4 titles 2007. Discounts: traditional 40%. 200-450pp. Reporting time: 1 month. Simultaneous submissions accepted: Yes. Publishes 5% of manuscripts submitted. Does not copyright for author. Subjects: Novels, Women.

BLAST, Bill Tully, Craig Cormick, PO Box 134, Campbell, ACT 2612, Australia. 1987. Poetry, fiction, articles, art, cartoons, satire, criticism, reviews, music, letters, parts-of-novels, collages, news items, non-fiction. circ. 1M. 4/yr. Pub'd 3 issues 2005; expects 4 issues 2006, 4 issues 2007. sub. price $A30; per copy $A2; sample free. Back issues: $A3. Discounts: 40%. 30pp. Reporting time: 3-10 months. Simultaneous submissions accepted: no. Payment: if we are subsidized. Copyrighted, reverts to author. Pub's reviews: 4 in 2005. Ads: $A80/$A40.

Bleak House Books, an imprint of Diversity Incorporated, Benjamin LeRoy, Editor-in-Chief; Julie Kuczynski, Editor; Alison Janssen, Editor, 923 Williamson St., Madison, WI 53703-3549, Fax: 608.259.8370 , info@bleakhousebooks.com www.bleakhousebooks.com, www.diversityincorporated.com. 1995. Fiction. "Bleak House Books, an imprint of Diversity Incorporated publishes crime and dark literary fiction. We enjoy stories that are creative in their use of language, setting, character, and tone. We are very interested in adding women mystery writers to our catalog. Our 2004/5 frontlist includes work from Marshall Cook, *Murder at Midnight*; John Galligan, *The Blood Knot*; Paul A. Toth, *Fizz*; Adam Gittlin, *The Men Downstairs*; Shane Brolly, *You'd Think There Would be More Suicides Around Here*; Suzanne Burns, *The Flesh Procession*; Nathan Singer *A Prayer for Dawn*; Michael Lister *Blood of the Lamb*. We will take a chance on an underdog project if it is of high quality or has some mark of distinction that sets it apart from the competition. Authors must be willing and determined to help promote his/her own cause. As a company, we have a DIY attitude, and we ask that our authors do, too. The author's work does not end with the publishing of the book. Email queries will be deleted. Do not call to pitch, tell, sell, bitch about anything. Writers write. Send query letter and synopsis to us before sending any part of your manuscript. Edit, edit, edit. We get too many books that aren't done or are "done" but are filled with plenty of mistakes. We, like every other publisher, are only going to take you seriously the first time. Step forward with your best foot, and do it once. This is a business." avg. press run 5000. Expects 8 titles 2006, 14 titles 2007. 240pp. Reporting time: 3 months. We accept simultaneous submissions, but please note as such. Publishes 1% of manuscripts submitted. Payment: Standard Royalties and Advance based on author's history and scope of project. Copyrights for author. Subjects: Crime, Fiction, Mystery.

THE BLIND MAN'S RAINBOW, The Blind Press, Melody Sherosky, Editor, PO Box 1190, Troy, MT 59935-1190, editor@theblindpress.com, www.theblindpress.com. 1993. Poetry, articles, art, interviews, criticism, reviews, letters. "All forms of poetry and b&w art are welcome. No restriction on poem length. See or website for additional guidelines. Current needs: interviews with artists and writers; reviews of fiction, poetry collections, and books pertaining to writing; travel articles on literary happenings." circ. 500-700. 4/yr. Pub'd 4 issues 2005; expects 4 issues 2006, 4 issues 2007. sub. price $14 US, $18 foreign; per copy $4 US, $5 foreign; sample $4 US, $5 foreign. Back issues: $1 US, $2 foreign. Discounts: contact us for discounts for 5 issues or more. 28pp. Reporting time: 1-6 months. Simultaneous submissions accepted: yes. Publishes 8% of manuscripts submitted. Payment: 1 contributor's copy. Copyrighted, reverts to author. Pub's reviews: 56 in 2005. §We review small press magazines and chapbooks. All subject matter welcome, though literary publications are what we review most. Ads: Contact us for information on advertising in our pages, in mailings, or on our website. Subjects: Arts, Interviews, Literary Review, Photography, Poetry, Reviews, Zines.

•**The Blind Press (see also THE BLIND MAN'S RAINBOW),** Melody Sherosky, Editor, PO Box 1190, Troy, MT 59935.

BLINK & Blink Chapbooks, Blink Chapbooks, Margaret Rabb, PO Box 95487, Seattle, WA 98145-2487, rabbm@u.washington.edu. 2001. Poetry. "BLINK is "a little little magazine of little poems." We publish between four and six very short poems in each issue." 6/yr. sub. price $6; per copy $1; sample $1. 4pp. Reporting time: Varies. Payment: Contributors' copies. Copyrighted, reverts to author.

Blink Chapbooks (see also BLINK & Blink Chapbooks), Margaret Rabb, CB #3520, Greenlaw Hall, UNC, Chapel Hill, NC 27599-3520.

Bliss Publishing Company, Inc., Stephen H. Clouter, PO Box 920, Marlboro, MA 01752. 1989. Non-fiction. "Booklength manuscripts." avg. press run 2M. Expects 4 titles 2006, 4 titles 2007. Discounts: 40% trade. 220pp. Reporting time: 8 weeks. Payment: negotiated. Copyrights for author. Subjects: Arts, Classical Studies, Conservation, Earth, Natural History, Ecology, Foods, English, Music, New England, Reprints, Sports,

Outdoors.

BLITHE SPIRIT, Caroline Gourlay, Hill House Farm, Knighton, Powys LD7 1NA, United Kingdom, 0154-752-8542, Fax 0154-752-0685. 1991. Poetry. "Haiku, senryu, renku, tanka and articles on these, normally from members of British Haiku Society only. Recent contributors: James Kirkup, Dee Evetts, David Cobb, Kohjin Sakamoto, Jim Norton, George Marsh, Jackie Hardy, and Brian Tasker." circ. approx. 400-500. 4/yr. Pub'd 4 issues 2005; expects 4 issues 2006, 4 issues 2007. sub. price £12 Britain, £16 elsewhere; per copy £4; sample £4. Back issues: £3. Discounts: none. 64pp. Reporting time: 1 month. Simultaneous submissions accepted: no. Publishes 30% of manuscripts submitted. Payment: none. Copyrighted, reverts to author. Pub's reviews: 24 in 2005. §Haiku, senryu, renku, tanka, haibun. Ads: none. Subjects: Haiku, Poetry, Zen.

BLK, BLK Publishing Company, Alan Bell, PO Box 83912, Los Angeles, CA 90083, 310-410-0808, fax 310-410-9250, e-mail newsroom@blk.com. 1988. Articles, photos, cartoons, interviews, criticism, reviews, music, letters, news items, non-fiction. circ. 22M. 12/yr. Pub'd 12 issues 2005; expects 12 issues 2006, 12 issues 2007. sub. price $18; per copy $4; sample $2.95. Back issues: all $2.95 except #1 which is $10. Discounts: none. 60pp. Reporting time: 4 weeks. Simultaneous submissions accepted: yes. Payment: varies. Copyrighted, rights reverting to author varies. Pub's reviews: none in 2005. §Black lesbian and gay community. Ads: $1800/$1170/.40¢. Subjects: African-American, AIDS, Black, Book Reviewing, Cartoons, Civil Rights, Electronics, Entertainment, Fashion, Gay, Interviews, Lesbianism, Men, Race, Women.

BLK Publishing Company (see also BLACK LACE; BLACKFIRE; BLK; KUUMBA), PO Box 83912, Los Angeles, CA 90083, 310-410-0808, Fax 310-410-9250, newsroom@blk.com. 1988. "Atlanta address: 4300 Flat Shoals Road, Suite 1910, Union City, GA 30291, 770-964-7247, Fax 770-969-7857."

BLOODJET LITERARY MAGAZINE, New World Press, Noni Howard Ph.D, Publisher, 20 Driftwood Trail, Half Moon Bay, CA 94019-2349, 650-726-5939; Fax 415-921-3730. 1974. Poetry, fiction, art, photos, letters, parts-of-novels, long-poems, collages. "Length 100-200 pages, women preferred but will consider men, Jennifer Stone is a recent contributor. Persons able to write grants or obtain other funding especially considered. Please send nothing by mail without calling my phone or fax number for a personal inquiry. Each is devoted to the work of one person." circ. 1.2M. 1-2/yr. Expects 2 issues 2006, 2 issues 2007. price per copy $10; sample $10. Back issues: $7.50. Discounts: 40% to bulk or educational institutions. 100pp. Reporting time: 60-90 days. Publishes less than 10% of manuscripts submitted. Payment: free copies. Copyrighted, reverts to author. Subjects: Literature (General), Poetry.

THE BLOOMSBURY REVIEW, Marilyn Auer, Publisher, Editor-in-Chief, 1553 Platte Street, Suite 206, Denver, CO 80202-1167, 303-455-3123, Fax 303-455-7039. 1980. Poetry, fiction, articles, art, photos, interviews, criticism, reviews, letters, long-poems, non-fiction. "We do not publish original fiction at this time." circ. 50M. 6/yr. Pub'd 6 issues 2005; expects 6 issues 2006, 6 issues 2007. sub. price $18; per copy $3; sample $5. Back issues: $5. Discounts: inquiries about distribution are welcome. 24pp. Reporting time: 3 months. Payment: $10 per review, $5 poetry, $20 features. Copyrighted, reverts to author. Pub's reviews: 900 in 2005. §Literature, history, biography, poetry, autobiography, politics-All subject areas. Ads: $3,550/$1,800/$40 first 25 words, $1 each additional word. Subjects: Agriculture, Anthropology, Archaelogy, Architecture, Arts, Biography, Book Reviewing, Chicano/a, Children, Youth, Conservation, Earth, Natural History, Ecology, Foods, Folklore, History, Labor, Latin America.

•**Blowtorch Press,** Elizabeth Dearborn, 55 Lark Street, Buffalo, NY 14211, webmaster@blowtorchpress.com. 2005. Fiction, non-fiction. Expects 1 title 2006, 5 titles 2007. Discounts: Standard trade discount 55%. 644pp. Subjects: Fiction, Medicine, Non-Fiction, Reference.

BLUE COLLAR REVIEW, Partisan Press, Al Markowitz, Mary Franke, PO Box 11417, Norfolk, VA 23517, 757-627-0952, redart@pilot.infi.net. 1997. Poetry, fiction, art, photos, interviews, reviews, long-poems, non-fiction. "Poetry and writing of high quality with a progressive working class perspective. Abroad range of work, not polemic or screed. We have published work by Martin Espada, Robert Edwards, Tom McGrath, Sonia Sanchez. Please put name and address on every page, SASE for return of manuscript. For best results, see a sample issue." circ. 253. 4/yr. Pub'd 4 issues 2005; expects 4 issues 2006, 4 issues 2007. sub. price $15 - make checks to Partisan Press; per copy $5; sample $5. Discounts: $3 in quantity. 40-60pp. Reporting time: 3-6 weeks. Simultaneous submissions accepted: yes. Publishes 25% of manuscripts submitted. Payment: copies. Copyrighted, reverts to author. Pub's reviews: 1 in 2005. §Working class issues or perspectives in fiction, novels, films...poetry. Ads: $60/$40. Subjects: Communism, Marxism, Leninism, Culture, Feminism, Labor, Multicultural, Peace, Race, Socialist, Society, Worker.

Blue Cubicle Press (see also THE FIRST LINE), David LaBounty, P.O. Box 250382, Plano, TX 75025-0382, 972 824 0646. 2003. Fiction, plays. "Blue Cubicle Press is an independent publisher dedicated to giving voice to writers who realize their words may never pay the mortgage but who are too stubborn to stop trying. We're here to support the artists trapped in the daily grind." avg. press run 500. Pub'd 1 title 2005; expects 1-2 titles 2006, 4-5 titles 2007. 200pp. Reporting time: 3 months. Simultaneous submissions accepted: Yes. Copyrights for author. Subjects: Travel, Worker, Zines.

Blue Dolphin Publishing, Inc., Paul M. Clemens, PO Box 8, Nevada City, CA 95959, 530-265-6925. 1985. Non-fiction. "We publish books on comparative spiritual traditions, personal growth, self-help, and health. We offer high resolution computer output from our ECRM and accept both IBM and Macintosh. Call for price list. 10% discount to Dustbooks' users." avg. press run 3M-5M. Pub'd 20 titles 2005; expects 22 titles 2006, 24 titles 2007. Discounts: 40-55%. 200+pp. Reporting time: 3-6 months, bids 1 week. Simultaneous submissions accepted: yes. Publishes less than 1% of manuscripts submitted. Payment: 10%. Copyrights for author. Subjects: Aging, Anthropology, Archaelogy, Astrology, Christianity, Cooking, Danish, Ecology, Foods, Education, Energy, Feminism, Gardening, How-To, Humor, Italy, Marriage.

Blue Dove Press, Jeff Blom, 4204 Sorrento Valley Blvd, Ste. K, San Diego, CA 92121, 858-623-3330, orders 800-691-1008, FAX 858-623-3325, mail@bluedove.org, www.bluedove.org. 1993. Non-fiction. "No unsolicited manuscripts, queries only. Please look at our catalog (free upon request) before making submissions." avg. press run 5M. Pub'd 2 titles 2005; expects 6 titles 2006, 6 titles 2007. Discounts: 40%, more in large quantities. 200pp. Reporting time: 4 weeks. Simultaneous submissions accepted: no. Publishes 0% of manuscripts submitted. Payment: negotiated on a case by case basis. Copyrights for author. Subjects: Buddhism, Christianity, India, Inspirational, Judaism, Religion, Spiritual, Sufism.

BLUE HORSE, Blue Horse Publications, Jacqueline T. Bradley, Editor & Publisher; Eugenia P. Mallory, Graphics Editor, P.O. Box 6061, Augusta, GA 30906, 706-798-5628. 1964. Poetry, fiction, satire. *"Blue Horse* is a magazine of satire, misanthropy and scurrilous language without regard to sex, religion, age, race, creed, or I.Q. *Blue Horse* is the periodical of Blue Horse Movement which recognizes the folly of human life and the inutility of politics. *Blue Horse* sees writers as the victims of their own art. Currently publishing only solicited chapbooks." circ. 500. Irregular. Expects 1 issue 2007. price per copy $3.50; sample $2. Back issues: $4 except Vol. l, $8. Discounts: prisoners pay postage only. 36pp. Reporting time: 30-60 days. Simultaneous submissions accepted: no. Payment: copies. Copyrighted. Exchange ads. Subjects: Dada, Fiction, Humor, Poetry, Satire.

Blue Horse Publications (see also BLUE HORSE), Jacqueline Bradley, Editor & Publisher, PO Box 6061, Augusta, GA 30906, 706-798-5628. 1964. Poetry, fiction, satire. avg. press run 500. Expects 1 title 2007. Discounts: 25%. 36pp. Reporting time: 30-60 days. Simultaneous submissions accepted: no. Payment: mutual agreement. Does not copyright for author. Subjects: Dada, Fiction, Humor, Poetry, Satire.

Blue Hot Books, Lisa Wolters, 5818 Wilmington Pike #320, Dayton, OH 45459-7004, 937-416-2475, Fax 937-767-9933, www.bluehotbooks.com. 1995. Fiction. "Since 1995, Blue Hot Books has published "substantive fiction," books which delve deeper into character and plot than the usual fare." Expects 1 title 2006, 6 titles 2007. Discounts: New Leaf DistributorsGreenLeaf DistributorsIngramBaker & TaylorAmazon.comBarnesandnoble.com. 300pp. Reporting time: 4 months, from agents only. Simultaneous submissions accepted: Yes. Payment: Advances plus royalties. Copyrights for author. Subjects: Fiction, Novels.

BLUE MESA REVIEW, Julie Shigekuni, Editor, Creative Writing Center/Univ. of New Mexico, MSCO3-2170, Humanities 274, Albuquerque, NM 87131-0001, 505-277-6347, fax 505-277-0021, bluemesa@unm.edu, www.unm.edu/~bluemesa (web). 1989. Poetry, fiction, interviews, reviews, non-fiction. "New foreign translations and local venues sections in Fall 2006 issue." circ. 1,000. 2/yr. Pub'd 1 issue 2005; expects 2 issues 2006, 2 issues 2007. sub. price $24; per copy $12; sample $12. Discounts: please contact UNM Press, 800-249-7737. 225pp. Reporting time: 3-4 months. Simultaneous submissions accepted: yes. Publishes 5-10% of manuscripts submitted. Payment: 2 copies. Copyrighted, reverts to author. Pub's reviews: 4 in 2005. §fiction, poetry, creative non-fiction. Subjects: Fiction, Literary Review, New Mexico, Non-Fiction, Poetry, Reviews.

THE BLUE MOUSE, Swan Duckling Press, Mark Bruce, PO Box 586, Cypress, CA 90630. 1998. Poetry. "Poems about personal experience have the best chance." circ. 300. 4/yr. Pub'd 4 issues 2005; expects 4 issues 2006, 4 issues 2007. sub. price $6; per copy $2; sample $2. Back issues: $2. Discounts: none. 24pp. Reporting time: 6 months. Simultaneous submissions accepted: no. Publishes 20% of manuscripts submitted. Payment: 2 copies. Not copyrighted, author keeps copyright. Ads: $30/$15.

Blue Mouse Studio, Rex Schneider, Chris Buchman, 26829 37th Street, Gobles, MI 49055, 616-628-5160; fax 616-628-4970. 1980. Cartoons. "No unsolicited manuscripts." avg. press run 2M. Pub'd 1 title 2005; expects 1 title 2006, 1 title 2007. Discounts: wholesalers 50%; retailers 40%. 80pp. Subjects: Americana, Children, Youth, Humor.

Blue Planet Books Inc., Monique Johnson, 4619 W. McRae Way, Glendale, AZ 85308, Fax 623-780-0468, www.blueplanetbooks.net. 2000. Fiction. "Submit only first chapter and synopsis - standard manuscript format. Only work ready for publication, 25 pages max., clean copy double-spaced. Anything less will not be considered. Professional presentation a must." avg. press run varies from 5M-50M. Pub'd 2 titles 2005; expects 2 titles 2006, 2 titles 2007. Discounts: 50% off cover price, add shipping and handling. 320pp. Reporting time:

1 month. Simultaneous submissions accepted: no. Publishes .1% of manuscripts submitted. Payment: standard contract, very small advance and royalty. Copyrights for author. Subjects: Fantasy, Medieval, Novels, Romance, Science Fiction.

Blue Poppy Press, Bob Flaws, Honora Lee Wolfe, 5441 Western Avenue #2, Boulder, CO 80301-2733, 800-487-9296. 1981. Non-fiction. "A division of Blue Poppy Enterprises, Inc. Material is mostly translations from Chinese medical source texts." avg. press run 1M-5M. Expects 3 titles 2006. Discounts: 55% consignment to distributors; 40% to stores, other. 100-600pp. Reporting time: 3 weeks. Publishes 5-7% of manuscripts submitted. Payment: 7-10% of all sales, paid biannually. Copyrights for author. Subjects: Health, Women.

Blue Raven Press, Barbara Gislason, 219 S.E. Main St., Suite 506, Minneapolis, MN 55414, 612-331-8039, 612-331-8115, www.blueravenpress.com.

Blue Raven Publishing, Frances Colbert, 9 South Wenatchee Avenue, Wenatchee, WA 98801-2210, 509-665-8353. 1983. Photos. avg. press run 5M. Expects 1 title 2006. Discounts: all books are 40% off the retail price. 176pp. Payment: author fee. Does not copyright for author. Subjects: Arts, Visual Arts.

Blue Scarab Press, Harald Wyndham, PO Box 4966, Pocatello, ID 83205-4966. 1984. Poetry, fiction. "Blue Scarab Press does not accept unsolicited manuscripts." avg. press run 350 to 500. Expects 1 title 2006, 1 title 2007. Discounts: 40% to booksellers or wholesalers, discounts for volume. 50-150pp. Publishes 100% of those we solicit% of manuscripts submitted. Payment: copies and royalty after recuperation of costs. Copyrights for author. Subject: Poetry.

Blue Sky Marketing Inc., Vic Spadaccini, Editor, PO Box 21583, Saint Paul, MN 55121-0583, 651-687-9835. 1982. "We are no longer accepting outside submissions for the indefinate future while we focus on internally produced publications." avg. press run 5M. Discounts: distributed by Adventure Publications. 116pp. Simultaneous submissions accepted: yes. Publishes .1% of manuscripts submitted. Payment: negotiable. Copyrights for author on request.

Blue Star Press, Deborah Ann Baker, 5333 71st Way NE, Olympia, WA 98516-9199. 1995. Poetry, fiction. "Poetry: 60 pages max., poems 22 lines max. Fiction: Children's picture book, easy readers. Recently published *Forbidden Crossings* by Deborah Ann Baker, Diamond Homer Trophy Winner." avg. press run 500-2.5M. Pub'd 1 title 2005; expects 1 title 2006, 1+ titles 2007. Discounts: 1-4 0%, 5-9 30%, 10+ 40%, prepaid orders we pay postage. 60pp. Reporting time: 3 months. Simultaneous submissions accepted: yes. Payment: individual (copies). We send forms to authors to copyright in author's name. Subjects: Inspirational, Poetry.

•**Blue Tiger Press,** Robert Kokan, 2016 Hwy 67, Dousman, WI 53118, 262-965-2751. 2005. Poetry. avg. press run 300. Expects 1 title 2006. Discounts: 15%. 85pp. Reporting time: 3 months. Simultaneous submissions accepted: Yes. Publishes 1% of manuscripts submitted. Payment: flexible. Copyrights for author. Subject: Poetry.

BLUE UNICORN, Ruth G. Iodice, John Hart, Fred Ostrander, 22 Avon Road, Kensington, CA 94707, 510-526-8439. 1977. Poetry, art. "*Blue Unicorn* is a journal looking for excellence of the individual voice, whether that voice comes through in a fixed form or an original variation or in freer lines. We publish poets who are established and those who are less known but deserve to be known better, and we are also proud to welcome new talent to our pages. We like poems which communicate in a memorable way whatever is deeply felt by the poet, and we believe in an audience that is delighted, like us, by a lasting image, a unique twist of thought, and a haunting music. We also use a limited number of expert translations. Among recent contributors to our tri-quarterly are: Rosalie Moore, Charles Edward Eaton, James Schevill, John Ditsky, Don Welch, Barbara A. Holland, Lawrence Spingarn, A.D. Winans, William Dickey, Adrianne Marcus, Stuart Silverman. Please send only unpublished poems." circ. 500. 3/yr. Pub'd 3 issues 2005; expects 3 issues 2006, 3 issues 2007. sub. price $18; add $6 mailing for foreign subscriptions; per copy $7; add $2 mailing for copies sent abroad; sample $7; add $2 mailing for copies sent abroad. Back issues: $5. 40pp. Reporting time: 1-3 months. Simultaneous submissions accepted: no. We publish 5% or less of manuscripts submitted. Payment: 1 copy. Copyrighted, reverts to author. Ads: none. Subjects: Arts, Poetry.

Blue Unicorn Press, Inc., Wanda Z. Larson, Publisher, PO Box 40300, Portland, OR 97240-0300, 503-957-5609. 1990. Poetry, art, letters. avg. press run 200-1M. Pub'd 1 title 2005; expects 4 titles 2006, 2+ titles 2007. Discounts: 2-4 books 20%, 5-99 40%, 100+ 50%. 64-350pp. Reporting time: 1 month to 1 year. Simultaneous submissions accepted: yes. Publishes 5% of manuscripts submitted. Payment: to be worked out. Copyrights for author. Subjects: Anthropology, Archaelogy, Biography, History, Medieval, Minnesota, Poetry.

BLUELINE, Richard Henry, Editor, State University College, English Dept., Potsdam, NY 13676, 315-267-2043. 1979. Poetry, fiction, articles, art, reviews, parts-of-novels, plays, non-fiction. "We are interested in material that has some relationship to the Adirondack mountain region or to similar regions. Short fiction and essays should be no more than 3.5M words, poems 75 lines or less. Recent contributors include

66

Ginnah Howard, Joan Connor, Maggie Mitchell, M.J. Iuppa, Sandra L. Graff, Robert Schuler.'' circ. 600. 1/yr. Pub'd 1 issue 2005. sub. price $10; per copy $10; sample $10. Back issues: $6. Discounts: $7 per copy to distributors. 180-200pp. Reporting time: by February 1. Simultaneous submissions accepted: no. Publishes 5% of manuscripts submitted. Payment: copies. Copyrighted, reverts to author. Pub's reviews: 10 in 2005. §Short fiction, novels, poetry, essays about the Adirondacks, and ecocriticism. No ads. Subjects: Adirondacks, Fiction, Poetry.

BLUELINES, Lois Peterson, #202, 7027-134 Street, Surrey, BC V3W 4T1, Canada, 604-596-1601, lpwordsolutions@hotmail.com; www.lpwordsolutions.com. ''*Bluelines* is a print newsletter 'exploring the relationship between writers and readers and the words that connect them.' Looking for articles, short columns, essays on a range of topics to do with reading and writing. Complete guidelines are available on our website.'' sub. price $15.

Blueprint Books (see also CKO UPDATE), Bette Daoust Ph.D., PO Box 10757, Pleasanton, CA 94588, 925-425-9513, Fax 1-800-605-2914, 1-800-605-2913, editor@blueprintbooks.com, blueprintbooks.com. 2004. Articles, interviews, reviews, non-fiction. avg. press run 10000. Pub'd 3 titles 2005; expects 5 titles 2006, 12 titles 2007. Discounts: 3 - 299: -40%300 - 499: -50%500 - up: -55%. 256-398pp. Reporting time: 2 to 4 weeks. Simultaneous submissions accepted: Yes. Publishes 35% of manuscripts submitted. Payment: percentage of net (generally 30%). Copyrights for author. Subjects: Advertising, Self-Promotion, Biography, Book Reviewing, Business & Economics, Consulting, Management, Newsletter, Non-Fiction, Pacific Region, Public Relations/Publicity, Publishing, Reviews, Speaking, Writers/Writing, Zines.

Bluestocking Press, Jane A. Williams, PO Box 1014, Dept. D, Placerville, CA 95667-1014, 530-622-8586, Fax 530-642-9222, 1-800-959-8586 (orders only), website: www.bluestockingpress.com. 1987. Fiction, non-fiction. ''UPS address: 3333 Gold Country Drive, El Dorado, CA 95623 Query with SASE for reply. Not accepting any new submissions.'' avg. press run 5M. Pub'd 4 titles 2005; expects 2 titles 2006, 2 titles 2007. Quantity discounts available to booksellers, wholesalers, retailers—query for schedule. 175pp. Simultaneous submissions accepted: no. Payment: by agreement. Does not copyright for author. Subjects: Business & Economics, Careers, Current Affairs, Finances, Government, History, Thomas Jefferson, Law, Libertarian, Middle East, Non-Fiction, Political Science, World War II.

BOA Editions, Ltd., Thom Ward, Editor; Peter Conners, Associate Editor, 260 East Avenue, Rochester, NY 14604, 585-546-3410, www.boaeditions.org. 1976. Poetry. ''Authors include: W.D. Snodgrass, Anthony Piccione, Michael Waters, Dorianne Laux, Peter Makuck, Carolyn Kizer, Lucille Clifton, Li-Young Lee, Anne Hebert, Yannis Ritsos, David Ignatow, Ray Gonzalez, Laure-Anne Bosselaar, Debra Kang-Dean, and Russell Edson.'' avg. press run 500 cloth, 2M paper. Pub'd 10 titles 2005; expects 12 titles 2006, 10 titles 2007. 96pp. Reporting time: 3 months. Simultaneous submissions accepted: yes. Payment: advance and royalty. Copyrights for author. Subjects: Poetry, Translation.

Bob & Bob Publishing, Robert O. Owolabi, Bob & Bob Associates, Inc., P.O. Box 10246, Gaithersburg, MD 20898-0246, 301-518-9835, Fax 301-515-0962, bobandbobinc@comcast.net, www.bobandbob.com. 1995. Simultaneous submissions accepted: yes. Publishes 85% of manuscripts submitted. Copyrights for author.

Bogg Publications (see also BOGG: A Journal of Contemporary Writing), John Elsberg, George Cairncross, Sheila Martindale, Wilga Rose, 422 North Cleveland Street, Arlington, VA 22201. 1968. Poetry, fiction. ''Only solicited mss considered from writers who have appeared in *Bogg* magazine.'' avg. press run 300. Pub'd 1 title 2005; expects 3 titles 2006, 2 titles 2007. 24pp. Reporting time: varies. Simultaneous submissions accepted: no. Payment: 25% of print run (in copies). Copyrights for author; author has to register. Subjects: Comics, Humor, Poetry.

BOGG: A Journal of Contemporary Writing, Bogg Publications, John Elsberg, US Editor; Sheila Martindale, Canadian Editor; Wilga Rose, Australian and NZ Editor, 422 N Cleveland Street, Arlington, VA 22201. 1968. Poetry, fiction, articles, art, interviews, satire, reviews, letters, plays, concrete art. ''Canadian address: 36114 Talbot Line, Shedden, Ontario NOL 2EO. Australian address: 13 Urara Road, Avalon Beach, NSW 2107. Poetry, experimental poetry (to include visual poetry), modern haiku and tanka, prose poems and very short innovative/wry prose, interviews, plus essays on British and American small press history and experience; mainly short reviews. Some recent contributors include Ann Menebroker, Guy Beining, Hugh Fox, John M. Bennett, Miriam Sagan, Richard Peabody, Todd Moore, Kathy Ernst, Martin Galvin, John Millett, Gerald England, Michael Dylan Welch, Kyle Laws, Harriet Zinnes, J. Wesley Clark, Leroy Gorman, and Ruth Moon Kempher. The magazine puts out a series of free (for postage) pamphlets of poetry. Bogg is largely a journal of U.S. writers, but it includes a leavening of British, Canadian, Australian, New Zealand, and South African work. ISSN 0882-648X.'' circ. 850. 2/yr. Expects 2 issues 2006, 3 issues 2007. sub. price $15/3 issues; per copy $6.00; sample $4.00. Back issues: negotiable. Discounts: 40% 10 copies or more, or additional copies bought by contributors. 56pp. Reporting time: 1 week. Simultaneous submissions accepted: no. Publishes 1% of manuscripts submitted. Payment: 2 copies of issue. Copyrighted, reverts to author. Pub's reviews. §Small press publications, U.K., Commonwealth, and U.S. Subjects: Experimental, Fiction, Haiku, Interviews, Poetry, Post Modern, Prose, Reviews.

The Bold Strummer Ltd., Nicholas Clarke, Publisher, 110-C Imperial Avenue, PO Box 2037, Westport, CT 06880-2037, 203-227-8588, toll free 866-518-9991 (orders only),Fax 203-227-8775, theboldstrummer@msn.com, www.boldstrummerltd.com. 1974. Cartoons, interviews, music. "The Bold Strummer publishes books on guitars and related instruments and equipment. Also importer and distributor of books of same. A leading publisher of boosk about flamenco." avg. press run 1M. Pub'd 6 titles 2005; expects 8 titles 2006, 4 titles 2007. Discounts: 20-50%. 130pp. Reporting time: approx. 6 months (if this means from contest to publication). Simultaneous submissions accepted: yes (20% as most are not our subject). Publishes 60% of manuscripts submitted. Payment: royalty 10% of retail. We copyright for author if required. Subject: Music.

Bollix Books, Staley Krause, 1609 W. Callender, Peoria, IL 61606, 309-453-4903, Fax 309-676-6557, editor@bollixbooks.com, www.bollisbooks.com. 2002. Fiction. "Unsolicited submissions are not currently accepted. However, queries can be sent by email. Authors wishing to send a query should carefully review the Writer's Guidelines, making certain that the work which they wish to submit is consistent with the needs of the editor. All queries should include name, e-mail and phone number as well as a short summary of the work and a sample paragraph. E-mail queries will be responded to within 3 weeks and will almost always consist of a form response that will either request the complete project by mail, or reject it. If you wish to submit artwork or an illustrated manuscript, your query should include a single PDF file of the art that you wish to submit as well as name, telephone and e-mail address. Bollix Books is a small, family-owned fiction publisher of literary, quirky and unusual children's picture books, and chapter books. Please don't confuse quirky or unusual with scatological; Captain Underpants is the last thing we want to publish. Bollix is not interested in stories about puppies or kitties or things cute or fuzzy. Bollix publishes stories that challenge young people to think about things they've never thought of in ways they've never thought of, using characters that clearly distinguish themselves as substantive and unique. In general, Bollix does not publish rhyming books unless they are at the level of a Seuss or a Bill Peet. The literary quality of submissions should be high and if authors have had their work rejected by other publishing houses because it is 'too literary' Bollix might be a good house to consider. Bollix believes that any media to which children are exposed must be considered carefully. As such, stories that tackle social issues and incorporate moral themes that are relevant but not overdone are especially interesting to Bollix.. Bollix believes strongly in the benefits of collaboration and prides itself in working closely with authors and illustrators through every step of the publishing process. Nonfiction is not being considered at this time. The format for Bollix books is artistic, bold and whimsical." Pub'd 1 title 2005; expects 2 titles 2006, 6 titles 2007. Discounts: Our wholesale terms are 52% off of retail value, no minimum, customer pays freight, net 60; retail: 1-10 books 20%, 11+ 46% (can mix titles), customer pays freight, net due in 30 days. 32pp. Reporting time: 4-5 months. Simultaneous submissions accepted: yes. Publishes 2-5% of manuscripts submitted. Payment: quarterly statements, small/no advance. Copyrights for author. Subject: Children, Youth.

Bolton Press, Denton VanDerWeele, President, 3600 Oak Manor Lane, Apt. #42, Largo, FL 33774-1220, 727-489-3628. 1987. Fiction, non-fiction. "Hardbound and softbound books." avg. press run 5M. Pub'd 1-2 titles 2005. Discounts: 40% trade, 50% jobber. 250pp. Reporting time: 6 weeks. Payment: negotiated. Copyrights for author. Subjects: Family, Literature (General).

BOMB MAGAZINE, Betsy Sussler, Editor-in-Chief; Rachel Kushner, Senior Editor, 80 Hanson Place #703, Brooklyn, NY 11217-1505, 212-431-3943, Fax 212-431-5880. 1981. Poetry, fiction, art, photos, interviews, parts-of-novels. circ. 60M. 4/yr. Pub'd 4 issues 2005; expects 4 issues 2006, 4 issues 2007. sub. price $18; per copy $4.95; sample $6 (includes p/h). Discounts: trade 40%, classroom 30%. 112pp. Reporting time: 3 months unsolicited. Simultaneous submissions accepted: yes. Publishes 5% of manuscripts submitted. Payment: yes. Copyrighted, reverts to author. Pub's reviews: 20 in 2005. §Art, literary fiction, poetry. Ads: $1,485/$795/$605 1/4 page. Subjects: Arts, Drama, Electronics, Fiction, Science Fiction, Theatre, Visual Arts.

Bombshelter Press (see also ONTHEBUS), Jack Grapes, P.O Box 481266, Bicentennial Station, Los Angeles, CA 90048, 310-651-5488, jgrapes@bombshelterpress.com, http://www.bombshelterpress.com. 1975. Poetry. "We publish books of California poets, most specifically poets from the Los Angeles area. Poets should not send manuscripts without sending a query letter first. Recent books by Macdonald Carey, Doraine Poretz, Michael Andrews, John Oliver Simon, Lee Rossi, Ko Wan, Jack Grapes, Bill Mohr, James Krusoe, and an anthology of *New Los Angeles Poets*. *Onthebus* is a biannual literary magazine—open to submissions from anyone." avg. press run 800. Pub'd 3 titles 2005; expects 3 titles 2006, 3 titles 2007. Discounts: 40% consignment to bookstores, etc., 50% to distributors. 72pp. Reporting time: 3-4 months. Simultaneous submissions accepted: no. Payment: free copies (usually 50) plus 10% of profits from sales. Copyrights for author. Subject: Poetry.

Bonanza Publishing, PO Box 204, Prineville, OR 97754, bonanza@ricksteber.com.

Bone World Publishing, John Berbrich, Editor, 3700 County Road 24, Russell, NY 13684.

Bonus Books, Inc., 1223 Wilshire Blvd., #597, Santa Monica, CA 90403-5400, www.bonusbooks.com. 1985. Non-fiction. avg. press run 5M-10M. Pub'd 25 titles 2005; expects 28 titles 2006, 30 titles 2007. Discounts: please inquire. 240pp. Reporting time: 2 months (send SASE). Simultaneous submissions accepted: yes. Publishes less than 5% of manuscripts submitted. Payment: standard scale. Copyrights for author. Subjects: Advertising, Self-Promotion, Aging, Autobiography, Biography, Broadcasting, Communication, Journalism, Current Affairs, Fundraising, Health, How-To, Non-Fiction, Nursing, Sports, Outdoors, Textbooks.

THE BOOK ARTS CLASSIFIED, Tom Bannister, PO Box 1209, Beltsville, MD 20704-1209, 800-821-6604, Fax 800-538-7549, pagetwo@bookarts.com, www.bookarts.com. 1993. "Free classified ads! We also publish the *Book Arts Directory* online." sub. price $16. Discounts: none. 12pp. Payment: none. Not copyrighted. Ads: $225/$125/25¢ per word classified, discounts for multiple submissions. Subjects: Book Arts, Book Collecting, Bookselling, Calligraphy, Printing.

•**Book Coach Press,** Blais Sabine Miss, 14 Moorside Private, Ottawa, Ontario K2C 3P4, Canada, (613) 226-4850, 1-877-GGR-RUNE, www.gentlegiantrunes.com, gentlegiantrunes@sympatico.ca. 2005. 216pp.

BOOK DEALERS WORLD, North American Bookdealers Exchange, Al Galasso, Editorial Director; Russ von Hoelscher, Associate Editor, PO Box 606, Cottage Grove, OR 97424-0026. 1979. Articles, news items, non-fiction. "Articles of interest to self-publishers, writers, and mail order book dealers and information sellers. 1000-2000 words length." circ. 20M. 4/yr. Pub'd 4 issues 2005; expects 4 issues 2006, 4 issues 2007. sub. price $40; per copy $10; sample $3. Back issues: 2 for $8. Discounts: 35% off 1 yr. sub. 32pp. Reporting time: 2 weeks. Publishes 30% of manuscripts submitted. Payment: ad space in exchange for contributions or $20 to $50 for articles depending on length. Copyrighted, reverts to author. Pub's reviews: 100+ in 2005. §Money-making and money-saving books of all types, how-to, male-female relationships, health & diet, computer-related, business, internet. Ads: $400/$220/$16-20 words. Subjects: Book Collecting, Bookselling, Printing.

Book Faith India, Chaitanya Nagar, Mgr. Editor, 414-416 Express Tower, Azadpur Commercial Complex, Delhi 110033, India, 91-11-713-2459, Fax 91-11-724-9674 and 724-9664, e-mail pilgrim@del2.vsnl.net.in. 1993. Non-fiction. avg. press run 1.5-3M. Pub'd 60 titles 2005; expects 20 titles 2006. Discounts: 40%. 350pp. Reporting time: 60 days. Simultaneous submissions accepted: yes. Publishes 15% of manuscripts submitted. Payment: 10% annually in July. Does not copyright for author. Subjects: Asia, Indochina, Buddhism, Non-Fiction, Religion, Third World, Minorities, Transportation.

•**Book Marketing Solutions,** Thomas White, 10300 E. Leelanau Court, Traverse City, MI 49684, p. 231-939-1999, f. 231-929-1993, info@bookmarketingsolutions.com. 2003. Poetry, fiction, photos, non-fiction. Pub'd 6 titles 2005; expects 15 titles 2006, 20 titles 2007. 196pp. Reporting time: 7-14 days. Simultaneous submissions accepted: Yes. Copyrights for author. Subjects: Business & Economics, Children, Youth, Christianity, Consulting, Fiction, Holocaust, Indigenous Cultures, Leadership, Non-Fiction, Picture Books, Poetry, Self-Help, Speaking, Textbooks, Young Adult.

BOOK MARKETING UPDATE, Open Horizons Publishing Company, John Kremer, PO Box 205, Fairfield, IA 52556-0205, 641-472-6130, Fax 641-472-1560, e-mail johnkremer@bookmarket.com. 1986. Articles, art, photos, cartoons, interviews, reviews, letters, news items, non-fiction. "News, stories, and resources to help other publishers market their books more effectively." circ. 3M. 26/yr. Pub'd 26 issues 2005; expects 26 issues 2006, 26 issues 2007. sub. price $197; per copy $6; sample $6. 4-6pp. Reporting time: 1 week. Payment: none. Copyrighted, reverts to author. Pub's reviews: 3-4 in 2005. §Book publishing, marketing, direct mail, graphics, printing, publicity, directories. Ads: none. Subjects: Advertising, Self-Promotion, Book Arts, Book Collecting, Bookselling, Book Reviewing, Business & Economics, Graphics, Magazines, Media, Newspapers, Printing, Publishing, Radio, Reviews, Television, Writers/Writing.

BOOK NEWS & BOOK BUSINESS MART, Premier Publishers, Inc., Neal Michaels, Owen Bates, PO Box 330309, Fort Worth, TX 76163, 817-293-7030. 1971. Articles, reviews, news items. "Recent contributors: Lee Howard, author and president of *Selective Books*; Galen Stilson, consultant and publisher of *The Direct Response Specialist*. Character of circulation: distributed to mail order dealers, suppliers to mail order firms, new entrants to mail order and new opportunity seekers. Doubles as advertising forum for mail order distributors, news magazine and wholesale catalog." circ. 50M. 3/yr. Pub'd 3 issues 2005; expects 3 issues 2006, 3 issues 2007. sub. price $8; per copy $3; sample $3. 80pp. Payment: negotiable. Copyrighted, reverts to author. Pub's reviews: 8 in 2005. §Self-improvement, do-it-yourself, how-to, success oriented how-to, or instruction manual how-to. Ads: $500/$275/$1. Subjects: Book Collecting, Bookselling, Business & Economics, How-To, Printing.

THE BOOK REPORT: The Magazine for Secondary School Library Media & Technology Specialists, Linworth Publishing, Inc., Marlene Woo-Lun, Publisher, 480 East Wilson Bridge Road #L, Worthington, OH 43085-2372. 1982. Articles, reviews, news items. circ. 15M. 5/yr. Pub'd 5 issues 2005; expects 5 issues 2006, 5 issues 2007. sub. price $49 US, $65 Canada; per copy $11; sample no charge. Back issues: $11. Discounts: 5%. 96pp. Payment: honorarium and copies of magazine in which article appears. Copyrighted, does not revert to author. Pub's reviews: 750 in 2005. §Books, CD-ROMS, videos and online resources suitable for school libraries, grades 6-12. Ads: $1230/$895/$685 1/3 page (b/w); 1 time rate-add $875 for color. Subjects: Book Reviewing, Education, Libraries.

BOOK/MARK SMALL PRESS REVIEW, Mindy Kronenberg, PO Box 516, Miller Place, NY 11764-0516, 631-331-4118, cyberpoet@msn.com, www.writernetwork.com. 1994. Reviews, non-fiction. "Reviews run 600-1000 wds avg.. We look for objective assessments of books by writers who are empathetic with their material and connected to the genre of literature (poets, novelists, essayists, artists, serious hobbyists) or have experience/interest in the subject/field of the books reviewed. Recent contributors include Thomas Fink, Michael McIrvin, Jodee Stanley, Thaddeus Rutkowski, and Richard Kostelanetz." circ. 800. 4/yr. Pub'd 4 issues 2005; expects 4 issues 2006, 4 issues 2007. sub. price $12; per copy $3.50 ppd.; sample $3 ppd. Back issues: $2 ppd. 12pp. Reporting time: immediately, 3 weeks max. Simultaneous submissions accepted: yes. Publishes 60-80% of manuscripts submitted. Payment: copies/subscription, sometimes gratis ads. Copyrighted, reverts to author. Pub's reviews: 47-50 in 2005. §Poetry, fiction, the arts, sciences, popular culture, history—we're eclectic. Ads: $250/$135/$75 1/4 page; also on an exchange-basis. Subjects: Arts, Book Arts, Book Reviewing, Criticism, Culture, Current Affairs, Literary Review, Literature (General), Multicultural, Reviews, Writers/Writing.

Bookhaven Press, LLC, Erin Taylor, Victor Richards, Preston James, Dennis Damp, 249 Field Club Circle, McKees Rocks, PA 15136-1034, 412-494-6926, Fax 412-494-5749, bookhaven@aol.com, http://federal-jobs.net. 1985. Articles, non-fiction. "Looking for new career and job search titles from computer literate authors." avg. press run 5M. Pub'd 2 titles 2005; expects 2 titles 2006, 2 titles 2007. Discounts: 1-4 20%, 5-9 30%, 10-24 40%, 25-49 42%, 50-74 44%, 75-99 46%, 100-199 48%, 200+ 50%; S.T.O.P. orders earn 40% discount CWO + $2 s/h. 288pp. Reporting time: 8 weeks. Simultaneous submissions accepted: yes. Publishes 1% of manuscripts submitted. Payment: negotiable. Copyrights for author. Subjects: Business & Economics, Careers, Employment, Environment, Government, How-To, Military, Veterans.

Bookhome Publishing/Panda Publishing, Scott Gregory, PO Box 5900, Navarre, FL 32566, E-mail bookhome@gte.net; www.bookhome.com. 1996. Non-fiction. "Nonfiction ms./proposals in areas of business, lifestyles, writing, publishing." avg. press run 2M. Pub'd 1 title 2005; expects 5 titles 2006, 7 titles 2007. 225pp. Reporting time: 6-8 weeks. Simultaneous submissions accepted: no. Publishes 2% of manuscripts submitted. Payment: varies. We file the copyright in the name of the author. Subjects: Business & Economics, Careers, Lifestyles, Non-Fiction, Publishing, Writers/Writing.

The Bookman Press, Barbara Wersba, PO Box 1892, Sag Harbor, NY 11963, 631-725-1115. 1994. Poetry, fiction, criticism, letters. "No unsolicited manuscripts. Work only with established authors and books in the public domain. Signed, limited editions aimed at collectors, universities, and special bookstores." avg. press run 300. Expects 1 title 2006, 3 titles 2007. Discounts: will sell through direct mail only. Copyrights for author.

BookPartners, Inc., Thorn Bacon, Editor-in-Chief; Ursula Bacon, Publisher; Ross Hawkins, President, 3739 SE 8th Ave. #1, Portland, OR 97202-3701, bpbooks@teleport.com, www.bookpartners.com. 1992. Non-fiction. "BookPartners, Inc. is a small publisher whose objective in trade book publishing is to earn a reputation that lives up to the responsibility that Eugene Fitch Ware innocently placed upon publishers when he wrote: 'Man builds no structure that outlives a book.' BookPartners occupies a unique middle ground in American trade book publishing with its partnership approach. It collaborates with authors in book development, preparation, marketing, financing and sales to provide more intense cooperation and equitable profit sharing. One rule of excellence governs the selection of BookPartner books. They must have the potential to be lifetime books that gain prestige as they develop reputation." avg. press run 2.5M-3M. Pub'd 15 titles 2005; expects 40 titles 2006, 40 titles 2007. Discounts: 45%. 175pp. Reporting time: 3 weeks. Simultaneous submissions accepted: yes. Publishes 25% of manuscripts submitted. Payment: quarterly. Copyrights for author. Subjects: Autobiography, Cooking, Health, History, Pacific Northwest, Self-Help.

Books for All Times, Inc. (see also EDUCATION IN FOCUS), Joe David, PO Box 202, Warrenton, VA 20188, 540-428-3175, staff@bfat.com. 1981. Fiction, non-fiction. "Currently seeking articles on important education issues for an upcoming book. Will only consider (always query) material of lasting quality (non-fiction). We have no fiction needs at this time. When we seek fiction, we want modern classics of mentally healthy and efficacious characters achieving. Example: *Dodsworth* by Sinclair Lewis." avg. press run 1M. Pub'd 3 titles 2005; expects 1 title 2006, 1 title 2007. Discounts: 20% libaries; 30% bookstores; 40% wholesalers and distributors; write publisher for details. 250pp. Reporting time: query always, 4 weeks at the most. Payment: to be negotiated. Copyrights for author. Subjects: Education, Fiction, Libertarian, Non-Fiction.

BOOKS FROM FINLAND, Jyrki Kiiskinen, Editor-in-Chief; Hildi Hawkins, Editor; Soila Lehtonen, Editor, PO Box 259, FI-00171 Helsinki, Finland, 358 (0) 201 1313451357942, booksfromfinland@finlit.fi , www.finlit.fi/booksfromfinland. 1967. Poetry, fiction, articles, photos, interviews, satire, criticism, reviews, parts-of-novels, plays, news items, non-fiction. circ. 3M. 4/yr. Pub'd 4 issues 2005; expects 4 issues 2006, 4 issues 2007. sub. price Fim120 Finland & Scandinavia, Fim160 other countries; per copy Fim30. Back issues: Fim20/copy. 80pp. Reporting time: 2 months. Payment: approx Fim200 per page. All rights belong to authors/translators. Pub's reviews: 17 in 2005. §History, politics, arts, nature, folklore. Ads: Fim3500 full page. Subjects: Book Reviewing, Fiction, Literary Review, Poetry, Prose.

BOOKS OF THE SOUTHWEST, Dr. Francine K. Ramsey Richter, Publisher; Rawlyn W. Richter, Editor, 2508 Garner Field Road, Uvalde, TX 78801-6250, e-mail richter@hilconet.com. 1957. Reviews. circ. 500. 4/yr. Pub'd 4 issues 2005; expects 4 issues 2006, 4 issues 2007. sub. price $28 indiv., $36 instit., $60 foreign; per copy available on-line at www.geocities.com/booksofthesouthwest; sample available on-line. Back issues: ask for quote. Discounts: none. 30pp. Payment: none. Not copyrighted. Pub's reviews: 600 in 2005. §Anything Southwest Americana. Ads: none. Subject: Southwest.

•**BOOKS TO WATCH OUT FOR,** Carol Seajay, PO Box 882554, San Francisco, CA 94188-2554, 415-642-9993, editor at BooksToWatchOutFor dot com, www.BooksToWatchOutFor.com. 2003. Interviews, reviews, news items. "Three subscription-based monthly book reviews - More Books for Women, The Lesbian Edition, The Gay Men's Edition - briefly review a wide range of 25-30 books in each issue, with news from the publishing world, occasional interviews and short features. The staff of Women & Children First bookstore compiles More Books for Women; Carol Seajay, former publisher of Feminist Bookstore News, compiles More Books for Women; and Richard Labonte compiles The Gay Men's Edition." circ. 5000. 10/yr. Pub'd 10 issues 2005; expects 10 issues 2006, 10 issues 2007. sub. price $30 via email; $42 via post; discounted combination packages available; per copy $5 print; sample $3 print. 16pp. Pub's reviews: 500 plus in 2005. §feminist, lesbian, gay, queer books. Ads: issue sponsorships available. Subjects: Bisexual, Feminism, Gay, Gender Issues, Lesbianism, Women.

THE BOOKWATCH, Diane C. Donovan, Editor, 12424 Mill Street, Petaluma, CA 94952, 415-437-5731. 1980. Reviews. "*The Bookwatch* publishes short (approx. 100 words) reviews, bias towards titles which would appeal to a general readership. Reviews outline the scope of each title with notations on how it compares to similar publications. Only titles which are recommended are reviewed. The bulk of *The Bookwatch* lies in nonfiction, but other major sections include science fiction and fantasy and young adult fiction. A section is also devoted to audiocassettes." circ. 5M. 12/yr. Pub'd 12 issues 2005; expects 12 issues 2006, 12 issues 2007. sub. price $12; per copy $1.50; sample $1.50. Back issues: $1.50 each. Discounts: 40% bookstores. 12pp. Reporting time: 4-6 weeks. Payment: 1 copy of issue in which review appears. Copyrighted, reverts to author. Pub's reviews: 800+ in 2005. §General-interest nonfiction (science, history/culture, health, travel), SF and Fantasy, Young adult fiction. Ads: $504/$327.60/write for smaller size rates. Subjects: Book Reviewing, Children, Youth, Computers, Calculators, Consumer, Earth, Natural History, Ecology, Foods, Fantasy, Newsletter, Science, Science Fiction.

THE BOOMERPHILE, Old Stage Publishing, Dan Culberson, Editor, Publisher, PO Box 17446, Boulder, CO 80308-0446, 303-444-3363, www.forums.delphiforums.com/boomer. 1992. Articles, interviews, satire, criticism, reviews, music, letters, news items, non-fiction. "Additional address: 6359 Old Stage Road, Boulder, CO 80302. *The BoomerPhile* is for and about Baby Boomers, to counteract all the negative publicity they have received all their lives, to talk about things that interest them today (health, old age, mortgages, kids in college, nostalgia, music, etc.), and to allow them to make fun of themselves, for a change." circ. 150. 12/yr. Pub'd 12 issues 2005; expects 12 issues 2006, 12 issues 2007. sub. price $20; per copy $2.50; sample $1. Back issues: $5. Discounts: standard rates. 8pp. Reporting time: 1-2 months. Simultaneous submissions accepted: yes. Publishes 25-50% of manuscripts submitted. Payment: 1 copy for items of interest; 2 copies for original work. Copyrighted, reverts to author. Pub's reviews: 1 in 2005. §Americana, arts, entertainment, humor, politics, sex, singles, society, baby boomers, history. Subjects: Americana, Business & Economics, Civil Rights, Counter-Culture, Alternatives, Communes, Culture, Entertainment, Erotica, Family, Feminism, Health, History, Humor, Jack Kerouac, Politics, Elvis Presley.

Borden Publishing Co., Michele Reyes, 300 Carlsbad Village Drive, Suite 108A #110, Carlsbad, CA 92008, 760-594-0918, Fax 760-967-6843, bordenpublishing@sbcglobal.net, www.bordenpublishing.com. 1939. Art, non-fiction. "Art, non-fiction, reference, occult, metaphysical, local histroy." avg. press run 2M-4M. Discounts: trade 1-4 books 25%, 5+ 40%. Payment: 10% royalty. Copyrights for author. Subjects: Arts, California, Collectibles, Hypnosis, Metaphysics, Occult.

BORDERLANDS: Texas Poetry Review, Jack Brannon, Editor; Robert Ayres, Editor, PO Box 33096, Austin, TX 78764, borderlandspoetry@sbcglobal.net, www.borderlands.org. 1992. Poetry, art, photos, interviews, reviews. "*Borderlands* provides a venue for contemporary American poetry that shows an awareness of the historical, social, political, ecological and spiritual. We have a special interest in poets of the southwest and bi-lingual poets. Past contributors include: William Stafford, Pattiann Rogers, Naomi Shihab Nye, David Romtvedt, Walter McDonald, James Ulmer, Wendy Barker." 2/yr. Pub'd 2 issues 2005; expects 2 issues 2006, 2 issues 2007. sub. price $24 includes p/h; per copy $12 includes p/h or $10 retail; sample same. Back issues: same. 125pp. Reporting time: varies up to 4 months. Simultaneous submissions accepted: NO. Publishes 3% of manuscripts submitted. Payment: 1 copy. Copyrighted, reverts to author. Pub's reviews: 4 in 2005. §Southwest and Texas writing, political poetry or poetry that addresses our general interests, multicultural poets, outwardly-directed poetry. Ads: exchange only. Subjects: Arts, Book Reviewing, Criticism, Essays, Journals, Literature (General), Poetry, Politics, Reviews, Society, Southwest, Texas, Third World, Minorities.

BORDERLINES: Studies in American Culture, University Of Wales Press, Phil Melling, Jon Roper, 6 Gwennyth Street, Cathays, Cardiff CF24 4YD, Wales, 44-029-2023-1919, Fax 44-029-2023-0908, press@press.wales.ac.uk. 1994. Articles. circ. 400. 4/yr. sub. price £25.20 individuals, £36 institutions. Discounts: 10%. 220pp. Pub's reviews. Subject: Americana.

Bordighera, Inc., Anthony Julian Tamburri, Fred Gardophe, Paolo Giordano, PO Box 1374, Lafayette, IN 47902-1374, 818-205-1266, via1990@aol.com. 1990. Poetry, fiction, interviews, criticism, reviews, plays, non-fiction. avg. press run 500. Pub'd 3 titles 2005; expects 3 titles 2006, 3 titles 2007. Discounts: agents and jobbers 1-4 copies 30%, 5-9 35%, 10-25 40%, 26-50 45%, 51+ 50%. 35pp. Reporting time: 3 months. Accepts simultaneous submissions on occasion. Publishes 25% of manuscripts submitted. Payment: yes. Copyrights for author. Subjects: Americana, Communism, Marxism, Leninism, Essays, Feminism, Gay, Immigration, Italian-American, Italy, Lesbianism, Literature (General), Novels, Theatre, Third World, Minorities, Women, Writers/Writing.

Borealis Press Limited (see also JOURNAL OF CANADIAN POETRY), Frank Tierney, Glenn Clever, 110 Bloomingdale Street, Ottawa, Ont. K2C 4A4, Canada, 613-798-9299, Fax 379-897-4747. 1972. Poetry, fiction, criticism, plays, non-fiction. "With few exceptions, publish only material Canadian in authorship or orientation. Query first." avg. press run 1M. Pub'd 10 titles 2005; expects 10 titles 2006, 8 titles 2007. Discounts: 40% to retail; 20% to jobbers. 150pp. Reporting time: 6 months. Simultaneous submissions accepted: no. Publishes 2-3% of manuscripts submitted. Payment: 10% once yearly. Does not copyright for author. Subjects: Canada, Children, Youth, Criticism, Culture, Drama, English, Fiction, Folklore, Government, History, Literature (General), Native American, Poetry, Public Affairs, Society.

A. Borough Books, Evan Griffin, Editorial Director, 3901 Silver Bell Drive, Charlotte, NC 28211, 704-364-1788, 800-843-8490 (orders only), humorbooks@aol.com. 1994. Non-fiction. "Non-fiction book proposals only (no manuscripts), 200 pages or less. Topics: recent history, how-to, humor." avg. press run 1M-3M. Pub'd 2 titles 2005; expects 2 titles 2006, 2 titles 2007. Discounts: 20% library (2 or more), 20% academic (10 or more), 40% bookseller (5 or more), 55% jobber. 128pp. Reporting time: 2 months. Simultaneous submissions accepted: yes. Publishes 30% of manuscripts submitted. Payment: negotiable. Does not copyright for author. Subjects: History, How-To, Humor, World War II.

BOTH SIDES NOW, Free People Press, Elihu Edelson, Editor, 10547 State Highway 110 North, Tyler, TX 75704-3731, 903-592-4263; web site: www.bothsidesnow.info. 1969. Poetry, fiction, articles, art, cartoons, interviews, satire, criticism, reviews, music, letters, news items, non-fiction. "'A Journal of Lightworking and Peacemaking.' Articles on current events and thinkpieces with emphasis on alternatives which have implicit spiritual content. Unique spiritual/political synthesis related to such concepts as 'New Age politics' and 'the Aquarian conspiracy.' Editorial concerns include nonviolence, pacifism, decentralism, green politics, human rights, social justice, alternative lifestyles & institutions, healing, economics, appropriate technology, organic agriculture, philosophy, prophecy, psychic phenomena, the occult, metaphysics, and religion. Reprints of important material which deserves wider circulation." circ. 200. 4 double issues/year (quarterly). Pub'd 3 issues 2005; expects 4 issues 2006, 4 issues 2007. sub. price $9/10 issues, $6/6 issues; per copy $2 (double issue); sample $2 (double issue). Back issues: listed in current issue and on web site. Discounts: 30% on 10 or more copies. 20-22pp. Reporting time: erratic. Simultaneous submissions accepted: yes. Payment: subscription. Copyrighted, reverts to author. Pub's reviews: approx. 10 in 2005. §'New Age', spirituality, pacifism, anarchism, religion, the occult and metaphysics, radical and 'Green' politics, general alternatives. Ads: $50 (7-1/2 X 10)/smaller sizes pro-rated/classifieds 20¢/word. Subjects: Anarchist, Astrology, Counter-Culture, Alternatives, Communes, Metaphysics, New Age, Occult, Philosophy, Politics, Religion, Reprints, Spiritual.

BOTTLE, Bottle of Smoke Press, Bill R. Roberts, 50 Loch Lomond St., Bear, DE 19701-4714, bill@bospress.net, www.bospress.net. 2002. Poetry, fiction, art, long-poems, concrete art. "Charles Bukowski, Charles Plymell, Dan Fante, Henry Denander, David Barker, A.D. Winans, Gerald Locklin, Michael Madsen, Marc Snyder, S.A. Griffin, Gary Aposhian, Neeli Cherkovski, Ann Menebroker, and Bradley Mason Hamlin." circ. 126. 1/yr. Expects 2 issues 2006, 1 issue 2007. price per copy $35; sample $35. 25pp. Reporting time: 2 months. Simultaneous submissions accepted: yes. Payment: contributors copies. Copyrighted, reverts to author. Subjects: Charles Bukowski, Poetry.

Bottle of Smoke Press (see also BOTTLE), Bill R. Roberts, 902 Wilson Drive, Dover, DE 19904-2437, bill@bospress.net, www.bospress.net. 2002. Poetry, fiction, long-poems. "Limited edition, signed chapbooks by writers and poets including: Charles Bukowski, Gerald Locklin, A.D. Winans, t.l. kryss, Henry Denander, S.A. Griffin, David Barker, Adrian Manning, justin.barrett, Owen Roberts & Bradley Mason Hamlin, Kent

Taylor, d.a. levy, Soheyl Dahi, Christopher Cunningham, Marc Snyder.'' avg. press run 226. Pub'd 7 titles 2005; expects 10 titles 2006, 10 titles 2007. Discounts: bulk available, please inquire. 36-40pp. Reporting time: 2 months. Simultaneous submissions accepted: no. Payment: contributors copies only. Copyrights for author. Subjects: Beat, Bibliography, Book Collecting, Bookselling, Charles Bukowski, Fiction, Literature (General), Poetry.

Bottom Dog Press, Larry Smith, PO Box 425, Huron, OH 44839, 419-433-5560, x20784 http://members.aol.com/lsmithdog/bottomdog. 1984. Poetry, fiction, parts-of-novels, long-poems. ''We do books of poetry,fiction, personal essays and national anthologies on a theme. A book of poetry should be 65-100 poems with a unifying themes and forms. We are particularly interested in the work of Midwest writers. Our Series include: Midwest Writers—Working Lives—Paul Laurence Dunbar—Harmony Series. We expect the writer to work with us on the book. Our slant is towards writing that is direct and human with clean, clear images and voice. We prefer the personal, but not the self-indulgent, simple but not simplistic, writing of value to us all. Our bias is towards sense of place writing—being who you are, where you are, and towards working class writing. Authors we've published: Robert Flanagan, Ed Sanders, Jim Ray Daniels, Ray McNiece, Daniel Thompson, Scott Sanders, David Shevin, Chris Llewellyn, Annabel Thomas, Kenneth Patchen, Todd Davis, Allen Frost. We also do some audio and CD books & DVD Exs. SONGS OF THE WOODCUTTER: ZEN POEMS OF WANG WEI AND TAIGU RYOKAN and D.A.LEVY AND THE MIMEOGRAPH REVOLUTION. Query first,$10 reading fee on POETRY manuscript submissions, $20 for a book of fiction; you'll get a full response. No e-mail submissions, though you might query on-line.'' avg. press run 650 poetry, 1M fiction. Pub'd 4 titles 2005; expects 7 titles 2006, 5 titles 2007. Discounts: 1-4 30%, 5-9 copies 35%, 40% 10+ copies. 160pp. Reporting time: 1-6 months, query first. Simultaneous submissions accepted: We'll consider simultantious submissions as long as we are notified. Payment: either through royalties, copies, or co-op arrangement. Copyrights for author. Subjects: Community, Fiction, Poetry, Zen.

BOULDER HERETIC, Old Stage Publishing, Dan Culberson, PO Box 17446, Boulder, CO 80308-0446, 303-444-3363, danculberson@juno.com. 1999. Articles, interviews, satire, criticism, reviews, non-fiction. circ. 25-30. 12/yr. Pub'd 3 issues 2005; expects 5 issues 2006, 12 issues 2007. sub. price $20; per copy $1; sample $1. Back issues: $5. Discounts: $10/year. 6pp. Reporting time: 1 week. Simultaneous submissions accepted: yes. Publishes 33% of manuscripts submitted. Payment: 2 copies. Copyrighted, reverts to author. Pub's reviews: none in 2005. §Atheism, religion, philosophy, freethinking, Agnosticism, etc. Ads: none. Subjects: Atheism, Buddhism, Catholic, Christianity, Cults, Euthanasia, Death, Humanism, Judaism, Mormon, Myth, Mythology, Philosophy, Politics, Psychology, Religion, Mark Twain.

BOULEVARD, Richard Burgin, Editor, 6614 Clayton Road, PMB 325, Richmond Heights, MO 63117, 314-862-2643. 1985. Poetry, fiction, articles, art, photos, cartoons, interviews, criticism, music, parts-of-novels, long-poems, plays, non-fiction. ''Contributors: John Barth, W.S. Merwin, John Updike, Tess Gallagher, Kenneth Koch, Tom Disch, Allen Ginsberg, Joyce Carol Oates, Alice Adams, David Mamet, Donald Hall, John Ashbery, Phillip Lopate. *Boulevard* is committed to publishing the best of contemporary fiction, poetry, and non-fiction.'' circ. 3.5M. 3/yr. Pub'd 3 issues 2005; expects 3 issues 2006, 3 issues 2007. sub. price $15 for three issues, $22 for six issues, $25 for nine issues.; per copy $8; sample $8 plus five first class stamps. Back issues: $10. Discounts: 50% agency. 200-225pp. Reporting time: 12 weeks. Simultaneous submissions accepted: yes. Publishes 1% of manuscripts submitted. Payment: $25-$300 (poetry), $50-$300 (fiction), plus one contributor's copy. Extra contributor's copies available at 50% discount. Copyrighted, reverts to author. §Fiction, poetry, lit. criticism, art/music criticism. We have a short fiction contest yearly with a $1500 prize and publication in Boulevard. Ads: $150/$500 for back cover. Subjects: Arts, Criticism, Fiction, Literature (General), Poetry.

Boulevard Books, Inc. Florida, Barbara Mulligan, Kay Judah, 1016 Buena Vista Boulevard, Panama City, FL 32401-2157. 1992. Fiction, art. ''We presently have nine freelance writers and illustrators who will be developing material for publication in the next two years. Our primary market will be supplement readers for alternative reading programs in public schools. Two titles are 'paired' to be marketed at one time; one title geared for the middle school interest level and one for the senior high school level where teachers need new approaches in their reading programs. We have twelve titles already developed for this market. The design of the books and format is new; i.e. we have not found anything like them in the marketplace. Several of our writers are certified public school educators. We also have planned a series of easy reading adult mystery novels of about 320 pages in 6 X 9 format.'' avg. press run 1M. Expects 6 titles 2007. Discounts: 20% short or terms offered by a large distributor. Pages vary. Payment: to be negotiated. Copyrights for author. Subjects: Children, Youth, Fantasy, Fiction, Mystery, Novels, Short Stories.

Box Turtle Press (see also MUDFISH), Jill Hoffman, Poetry Editor, 184 Franklin Street, New York, NY 10013. 1983. avg. press run 1.2M. Pub'd 1 title 2005; expects 1 title 2006, 1 title 2007. Discounts: 1983. 200pp. Reporting time: immediately to 6 months. Simultaneous submissions accepted: no. Publishes 5% of manuscripts submitted. Payment: 1 copy.

The Bradford Press (see also Toad Hall, Inc.), RR 2 Box 2090, Laceyville, PA 18623, 717-869-2942; Fax 717-869-1031. 1995. Fiction. "We primarily are consultants for book-length works only. Send a query letter first. Will read and provide written analysis of first 3 chapters plus synopsis of a manuscript or the complete self-published book for $50. Will work with self-publishers before and after publication. The Bradford Press publishes fiction only." avg. press run 4M. Pub'd 1 title 2005; expects 2 titles 2006, 2 titles 2007. 224pp. Reporting time: 3 months. Payment: We publish by co-op arrangement only. Copyrights for author. Subjects: Science Fiction, Short Stories.

•**BRADY MAGAZINE,** Krissy Brady, 165 Old Muskoka Road, Suite 306, Gravenhurst, Ontario P1P 1N3, Canada, 705-687-3963 [phone], 705-687-8736 [fax], editor@bradymagazine.com [e-mail], http://www.brady-magazine.com [website]. 2003. Articles. "Brady Magazine is an online writer's trade directory that is updated on a daily basis. We accept article submissions from writers at any stage in their career, and working in any genre. Articles submitted must always be related to the writing field. Articles must be between 1,000 and 2,500 words. No typical article topics (such as How to Defeat Writer's Block) unless consisting of an interesting twist. No query is needed, just send us your work. Submissions must be sent to us using our online form, which can be found at http://www.bradymagazine.com/forms/subform.html. Any submissions sent to us not using our online form will be deleted immediately. We pay $20CDN for first electronic rights, and $10CDN for reprint rights. If sending us an article that has been previously published, please let us know where and when it was published. Payment is made upon acceptance. We no longer accept success stories, writing tips, or book reviews." Reporting time: 1-2 months. Simultaneous submissions accepted: Yes. Publishes 30% of manuscripts submitted. Payment: On acceptance. Copyrighted, reverts to author. Ads: Text Advertising- Website$30.00 weekly (7 days)$75.00 monthly (30 days)$135.00 bi-monthly (60 days)Text Advertising- Newsletters$10.00 per 4 (four)-line ad$30.00 per solo ad (unlimited lines). Subject: Writers/Writing.

Branch Redd Books (see also BRANCH REDD REVIEW), William Sherman, 9300 Atlantic Avenue, Apt. 218, Margate City, NJ 08402-2340. 1976. Poetry. "No unsolicited contributions please." avg. press run 400. Pub'd 1 title 2005; expects 1 title 2006. Discounts: none. Pages vary. Copyrights for author. Subject: Poetry.

BRANCH REDD REVIEW, Branch Redd Books, William David Sherman, 9300 Atlantic Ave, Apt 218, Margate City, NJ 08402-2340. 1976. Poetry. "No unsolicited contributions, please." circ. 400. Irregular. Expects 1 issue 2006. sub. price No subscriptions available; per copy $10; sample none. Discounts: none. Pages vary. Payment: copies. Copyrighted, reverts to author. Subject: Poetry.

BRANCHES, Uccelli Press, Toni La Ree Bennett, PO Box 85394, Seattle, WA 98145-1394, 206-240-0075, Fax 206-361-5001, editor@branchesquarterly.com, www.branchesquarterly.com. 2001. Poetry, fiction, art, photos, interviews, satire, criticism, reviews, parts-of-novels, long-poems, collages, non-fiction. "Seeking an eclectic, sophisticated mix of poetry, short prose, art, photos, fiction, essays, translations. Preferred method of submission is to e-mail work in body of message to submit@branchesquarterly.com. Send art/photos as jpeg attachments." 4/yr. Pub'd 4 issues 2005; expects 4 issues 2006, 4 issues 2007. sub. price $8; per copy $8; sample $8. Reporting time: 6 months. Copyrighted, reverts to author. Pub's reviews: 1 in 2005. §poetry.

BRANCHES, Elsa F. Kramer, PO Box 30348, Indianapolis, IN 46230, 317-255-5594, editor@branches.com, www.branches.com. 1988. Poetry, articles, art, photos, cartoons, interviews, letters, news items, non-fiction. "600 to 1,000 words written to the state theme; author must be current or former resident of Indiana or writing about a person or event in Indiana. Electronic submissions only." circ. 20M. 6/yr. Pub'd 6 issues 2005; expects 6 issues 2006, 6 issues 2007. sub. price $20; per copy $4; sample $4 web offset. 32pp. Reporting time: 2-3 weeks. Simultaneous submissions accepted: no. Publishes 50% of manuscripts submitted. Payment: none. Copyrighted, reverts to author. Ads: $800/$480/$50. Subjects: Alternative Medicine, Dreams, Metaphysics, New Age, Peace, Religion.

Branden Books, Adolph Caso, PO Box 812094, Wellesley, MA 02482, 781-235-3634, Fax 781-790-1056, branden@brandenbooks.com, www.brandenbooks.com. 1909. Fiction, art, music, letters, long-poems, plays, non-fiction. "See our latest catalogue. No manuscripts accepted, only queries with SASE." avg. press run 5M. Pub'd 15 titles 2005; expects 10 titles 2006, 15 titles 2007. Discounts: from 1 copy 10% to 101+ copies 48%. 215pp. Reporting time: 1 week. Simultaneous submissions accepted: no. Publishes 1% of manuscripts submitted. Payment: 5%-10% net on monies from sales; 50% on monies from sales of rights. Copyrights for author. Subjects: Americana, Arts, Bilingual, Biography, Book Arts, Classical Studies, Drama, Education, Fiction, Health, History, Literature (General), Peace, Political Science, Religion.

Brandylane Publishers, Inc. (see also PLEASANT LIVING), R.H. Pruett, 5 S. 1st St., Richmond, VA 23219-3716, 804-644-3090, Fax 804-644-3092. 1985. Poetry, fiction, non-fiction. "We publish fiction, non-fiction, poetry. Especially interested in working with unpublished writers." avg. press run 1.5M. Pub'd 14 titles 2005; expects 12 titles 2006, 12 titles 2007. Discounts: standard 40%, 55% distributors, 30% STOP orders. 200pp. Reporting time: 4-8 weeks. Simultaneous submissions accepted: yes. Publishes 10% of manuscripts submitted. Payment: varies. Copyrights for author.

Brason-Sargar Publications, Sondra Anice Barnes, Publisher, PO Box 872, Reseda, CA 91337, 818-994-0089, Fax 305-832-2604, sonbar@bigfoot.com. 1978. Poetry, art. "We are primarily interested in gift books which express psychological truths. Must use as few words as possible. We publish thoughts, observations or statements expressing human truths written in a style which visually looks like poetry but is not poetry per se. If the poet reads our books *Life Is The Way It Is* or *We Are The Way We Are* and can write in this style, then we are interested and will negotiate payment." avg. press run 2M 1st printing, up to 20M subsequent printings. Pub'd 1 title 2005; expects 4 titles 2006, 6 titles 2007. Discounts: 40% bookstores, 50% distributers. 96pp. Reporting time: 30 days. Payment: to be negotiated. Copyrights for author. Subjects: New Age, Philosophy, Psychology, Quotations, Self-Help, Spiritual.

BRAVADO, Jenny Argante, Coordinating Editor; Sue Emms, Fiction Editor; Owen Bullock, Poetry Editor, PO Box 13-533, Grey Street, Tauranga 3001, New Zealand, 07 576 3040, fax:07 570 2446. "New magazine publishing poetry, fiction." 2/yr. sub. price $15; per copy $10.

Brave Ulysses Books, Cecil L. Bothwell III, 54 Fulton St., Asheville, NC 28801-1807, 828-713-8840, cecil@braveulysses.com, www.braveulysses.com. 1996. Satire, non-fiction. "Three titles in print, two collected essays and city guide *Finding your way in Asheville* (NC). Will soon publish first children't title. We are a micro press and are unlikely to publish more than one title per year." avg. press run 2M. Pub'd 1 title 2005; expects 1 title 2006, 1-2 titles 2007. Discounts: 70% to all resellers. 110pp. Reporting time: 1 month, inquire first (1 week on inquiries). We accept simultaneous submissions, but inquire first. Publishes a small % of manuscripts submitted. Payment: negotiable. Does not copyright for author. Subjects: Environment, Essays, Humor, Politics, Short Stories.

BRAZOS GUMBO, Samuel Pittman II, P.O. Box 12290, College Station, TX 77842, Brazos-Gumbo@yahoo.com. 2004. Poetry, art, photos. "Brazos Gumbo is a regional journal of poetry and art showcasing the work of residents, present and past, of the Brazos Valley region of Texas. The journal publishes original, unpublished poems of any kind. Poets from the Brazos Valley should submit no more than 4 typed pages of unpublished poetry, include all contact information on each page and include a S.A.S.E. Brazos Gumbo accepts email submissions." 4/yr. Expects 2 issues 2006, 4 issues 2007. sub. price $28; per copy $10; sample $7. Back issues: inquire. 48pp. Reporting time: 2 weeks to 1 month. Simultaneous submissions accepted: Yes. Publishes 35% of manuscripts submitted. Payment: Contributors recieve 1 free copy of the issue their work appears in, and 50% any copies of that same issue. Ads: 1/4 page: $25; 1/2 page: $50; Full page: $100. Subjects: Family, Fantasy, Humor, Texas.

BRB Publications, Inc. (see also Facts on Demand Press), Michael Sankey, PO Box 27869, Tempe, AZ 85285-7869, 800-929-3811, Fax 800-929-4981, brb@brbpub.com, www.brbpub.com. 1989. Non-fiction. avg. press run 2.5 m. Pub'd 5 titles 2005; expects 7 titles 2006, 7 titles 2007.

THE BREAD AND BUTTER CHRONICLES, Seven Buffaloes Press, Art Coelho, PO Box 249, Big Timber, MT 59011. 1986. Art, photos, news items. "Special three-page feature in every issue entitled 'Rural American Hall of Fame'; inductees taken from poets, writers, and artists in rural and working people. There's a farm column by Frank Cross where he covers rural American literature at large. I list contests, mags looking for special materials, special anthologies being sought. New publications just born. Events, etc. *New focus* is on *rural essays.*" circ. 500. 2/yr. Expects 2 issues 2006, 2 issues 2007. sub. price $6.75; per copy $4.75; sample $4.75. Back issues: none available. 8pp. Reporting time: 1 day to 2 weeks. Payment: copies. Copyrighted, reverts to author. Subjects: Arts, Newsletter, Photography.

Breakout Productions, Michael Hoy, President; Gia Cosindas, Editorial Liason, PO Box 1643, Port Townsend, WA 98368, 360-379-1965, Fax 360-379-3794. 1998. Non-fiction. "We specialize in 'how-to' books on outrageous subjects written in an authoritative style, and books about obscure-but-useful technologies. Our books are controversial and unusual. Manuscripts that we accept are usually at least 200 pages long." avg. press run 2M. Pub'd 15 titles 2005; expects 15 titles 2006, 15 titles 2007. Discounts: 5-9 20%, 10-49 40%, 50-99 45%, 100-199 50%, 200+ 55%. 120pp. Reporting time: 3 months. Simultaneous submissions accepted: yes. Publishes 5% of manuscripts submitted. Payment: negotiable. Copyrights for author. Subjects: Anarchist, Counter-Culture, Alternatives, Communes, Crime, How-To, Non-Fiction.

Brenner Information Group, Robert C. Brenner, Editor-in-Chief; Jenny Hanson, Editor, PO Box 721000, San Diego, CA 92172-1000, 858-538-0093. 1988. Non-fiction. "50-300 pages published. How-to subjects (business)." avg. press run 2M. Pub'd 15 titles 2005; expects 8 titles 2006, 10 titles 2007. Discounts: 0-55%. 300pp. Reporting time: 4-6 weeks. Simultaneous submissions accepted: yes. Publishes 10% of manuscripts submitted. Payment: 10%-12%. Copyrights for author. Subjects: Business & Economics, Computers, Calculators, Consumer, Design, Editing, Graphics, How-To, Internet, Labor, Marketing, Printing, Reference, Research, Self-Help, Technology.

Brentwood Christian Press, Jerry L. Luquire, 4000 Beallwood Avenue, Columbus, GA 31904. 1982. Fiction, articles, long-poems, non-fiction. "Also publishes religious and educational material." avg. press run 300-500.

Pub'd 200 titles 2005; expects 200 titles 2006, 200 titles 2007. Discounts: 30%. 120pp. Reporting time: 2 days. Simultaneous submissions accepted: yes. Publishes 60% of manuscripts submitted. Copyrights for author. Subjects: Christianity, History, Poetry, Religion.

THE BRIAR CLIFF REVIEW, Tricia Currans-Sheehan, 3303 Rebecca St., Sioux City, IA 51104, 712-279-1651. 1988. Poetry, fiction, articles, art, photos, interviews, satire, criticism, reviews, concrete art, non-fiction. "The Briar Cliff Review is an eclectic literary and cultural magazine focusing on, but not limited to, Siouxland writers. We are looking for quality poetry, fiction, humor/satire, Siouxland history, thoughtful nonfiction, book reviews and art." circ. 750. 1/yr. Pub'd 1 issue 2005; expects 1 issue 2006, 1 issue 2007. sub. price $12; per copy $12; sample $12. Back issues: $9. Discounts: 40% discount = $7.20 a copy. 90pp. Reporting time: 3-6 months. Simultaneous submissions accepted: Yes. Payment: two free copies. All rights return to the author, with acknowledgment to The Briar Cliff Review. Pub's reviews: 3 in 2005. §Poetry/short story collections novels and creative nonfiction. No advertising. Subjects: Arts, Fiction, History, Interviews, Iowa, Literary Review, Literature (General), Midwest, Minnesota, Native American, Nebraska, Non-Fiction, Photography, Poetry, Prose.

Briarwood Publications, Inc., Barbara Turner, 150 West College Street, Rocky Mount, VA 24151, 540-483-3606; website www.briarwoodva.com. 1998. Poetry, fiction, non-fiction. Pub'd 6 titles 2005; expects 6 titles 2006, 6 titles 2007. Discounts: max 40%; short 20%. 250pp. Simultaneous submissions accepted: yes. Publishes 2% of manuscripts submitted. Does not copyright for author.

BRICK, A Literary Journal, Michael Redhill, Publisher, Editor; Michael Helm, Editor; Michael Ondaatje, Editor; Esta Spalding, Editor; Linda Spalding, Editor, Box 537, Station Q, Toronto, ON M4T 2M5, Canada, www.brickmag.com, info@brickmag.com, orders@brickmag.com, submissions@brickmag.com. 1977. Articles, photos, interviews, non-fiction. "*Brick* does not accept unsolicited poetry or fiction submissions." 2/yr. Pub'd 2 issues 2005; expects 2 issues 2006, 2 issues 2007. sub. price US$41/2 years; per copy US$12 + shipping. Back issues: Please see website, www.brickmag.com. Discounts: institutions may subscribe for one year at a cost of US$28. 160pp. Copyrighted, reverts to author. Ads: Full page: US$800; half-page: US$475.

BrickHouse Books, Inc., Clarinda Harriss, Editor-in-Chief, 306 Suffolk Road, Baltimore, MD 21218, 410-235-7690, 410-704-2869. 1970. Poetry. "BrickHouse Books averages 500-1000 copies of poetry or prose. New Poets Series, formerly the corporate name as well as its premier imprint, is for first collections only. Poetry by authors with previous books, as well as fiction (55-90 pages), goes directly to BrickHouse Books. Stonewall is specifically for mss. with a gay/lesbian perspective." avg. press run 500. Pub'd 6 titles 2005; expects 6 titles 2006, 6 titles 2007. Discounts: 40% to bookstores; $10-15 retail depending on # of pages. 80pp. Reporting time: 3-6 months. Simultaneous submissions accepted: yes. Publishes 5% of manuscripts submitted. Payment: all cash revenue from sales goes to publish the next issue; 25 copies free to author. Author holds own copyright. Subjects: Fiction, Graphics, Poetry.

BRIDAL CRAFTS, Clapper Publishing Co., Barbara Sunderlage, 2400 Devon, Suite 375, Des Plaines, IL 60018, 847-635-5800. 1951. circ. 300M. 1/yr. Pub'd 1 issue 2005; expects 1 issue 2006, 1 issue 2007. price per copy $3.95-$4.95. 106pp. Reporting time: 3 months. Simultaneous submissions accepted: yes. Payment: yes. Copyrighted, does not revert to author. Pub's reviews. §Craft books. Subject: Crafts, Hobbies.

BRIDGES: A Journal for Jewish Feminists and Our Friends, Jessica Stein, Poetry Editor, Rosa Maria Pegueros; Clare Kinberg, Managing Editor; Faith Jones, Yiddish Editor, PO Box 1206, Ann Arbor, MI 48106-1206, 888-359-9188, E-mail clare@bridgesjournal.org. 1990. Poetry, fiction, articles, art, photos, cartoons, interviews, reviews, music, letters, parts-of-novels, long-poems, plays, news items, non-fiction. "*Bridges* seeks works of relevance to Jewish feminists which combines identity and social/political activism." circ. 3M. 1/yr. Pub'd 1 issue 2005; expects 1 issue 2006, 1 issue 2007. sub. price $18; per copy $9; sample free. Back issues: $9. Discounts: must order through ubiquity. 128pp. Reporting time: 6 months. Simultaneous submissions accepted: no. Payment: 5 issues. Copyrighted, reverts to author. Pub's reviews: 10 in 2005. §Feminism, multi-cultural alliances, Jewish identity. Subjects: Feminism, Judaism.

BRIDGES: An Interdisciplinary Journal of Theology, Philosophy, History, and Science, Robert S. Frey, Editor-Publisher, PO Box 3075, Oakton, VA 22124-3075, 703-281-4722, Fax 703-734-1976, E-mail Bridges23@aol.com. 1988. Articles, photos, reviews. "Each issue of "Bridges" provides a forum for interdisciplinary reflection on themes that share the common focus of values, humaneness, ethics, and meaning. Affiliated with Lebanon Valley College of Pennsylvania." circ. 650. 2/yr. Pub'd 2 issues 2005; expects 2 issues 2006, 2 issues 2007. sub. price $45 institutions, $30 individuals, $15 students; foreign: $50 instit., $35 indiv., $20 students; per copy $15 (US); sample $15 (US). Back issues: prices upon request. 175pp. Reporting time: 1 month. Simultaneous submissions accepted: no. Publishes 80% of manuscripts submitted. Payment: none, complimentary copies of particular issue. Copyrighted, does not revert to author. Pub's reviews: 40 in 2005. §Theology, philosophy, history, science, cultural criticism, Holocaust. Ads: $50/$25. Subjects: Book Reviewing, Culture, History, Holocaust, Philosophy, Religion, Science.

Bright Hill Press, Bertha Rogers, Editor, PO Box 193, Treadwell, NY 13846-0193, 607-829-5055, fax 607-829-5054, wordthur@stny.rr.com. web: www.brighthillpress.org. 1992. Poetry, fiction, art, photos, cartoons, criticism, parts-of-novels, long-poems, collages, plays, non-fiction. "We have 2 competitions per year: a chapbook (poetry) and a full-length poetry book competition - both national. Full-length poetry book competition judged by nationally-known poets. We also publish anthologies with a theme. We publish an anthology periodically and call for mss. periodically." avg. press run 500-1000. Pub'd 10 titles 2005; expects 10 titles 2006, 10 titles 2007. Discounts: trade 40%, bulk 40%, classroom 20-40%, agent 20%, jobber 40-55%. 70pp. Reporting time: 3-6 months. We accept simultaneous submissions, with notification if accepted elsewhere. Publishes 2% of manuscripts submitted. Payment: prize winnings and copies. Does not copyright for author. Subjects: Book Arts, Graphics, Native American, Poetry.

Bright Mountain Books, Inc., Cynthia Bright, 206 Riva Ridge Drive, Fairview, NC 28730-9764, booksbmb@charter.net. 1983. Non-fiction. "Length of material: booklength. Biases: regional, Southern Appalachians, Carolinas, nonfiction. Imprint: Historical Images." avg. press run 2M. Pub'd 2 titles 2005; expects 4 titles 2006, 4 titles 2007. Discounts: 40% trade, 20% libraries on 1-5 copies, 40% on 6+. 200pp. Reporting time: 2 months. Simultaneous submissions accepted: yes. Publishes 10% of manuscripts submitted. Payment: 10% of retail price on actual sales, paid quarterly. Copyrights for author. Subjects: Appalachia, Autobiography, Aviation, Civil War, Cooking, History, Horticulture, Humor, Memoirs, Myth, Mythology, Native American, Non-Fiction, North Carolina, South, Travel.

Bright Ring Publishing, Inc., MaryAnn F. Kohl, PO Box 31338, Bellingham, WA 98228-3338, 800-480-4278, www.brightring.com. 1985. Non-fiction. "We no longer accept unsolicited manuscripts. We are looking for material for teachers using learning centers, individualized classrooms, and creative thinking. Preferrably early childhood and primary. Should transfer easily to use at home. Creative, independent, open-minded. First contribution, *Scribble Art And Other Independent Creative Art Experiences for Children*, 144 pages, black line drawings (120), 11 X 8-1/2, suitable for teachers, parents, children, and others who work with children ages 2-forever. We do not publish poetry, fiction, picture books, or books with fill-ins or coloring. Books must closely mirror our format and design which can be viewed on our website. If it doesn't follow our format, we can't consider it. Thank you for your consideration." avg. press run 5M. Pub'd 1 title 2005; expects 1 title 2006, 1 title 2007. Discounts: bulk. 150pp. Reporting time: 4 weeks. We are not accepting manuscripts unless they specifically follow our art "recipe", of materials, steps, and variations...on the subject of art only...and in this venue, simultaneous submissions are acceptable. Payment: 4% of net, quarterly. Copyrights for author. Subjects: Children, Youth, Crafts, Hobbies, Education, Family, How-To, Parenting.

Brighton Publications, Inc., Sharon E. Dlugosch, PO Box 120706, St. Paul, MN 55112-0706, 651-636-2220. 1977. Non-fiction. "We're developing party themes, games, celebration themes. We need authors who can convey their enthusiasm and knowledge of a subject, as well as willing to rewrite." Expects 3 titles 2006, 5 titles 2007. 160pp. Reporting time: 3 months. Payment: 10% of net. Copyrights for author. Subjects: Business & Economics, Consumer, Homemaking, How-To, Marriage.

BRILLIANT CORNERS: A Journal of Jazz & Literature, Sascha Feinstein, Lycoming College, Williamsport, PA 17701, 570-321-4279. 1996. Poetry, fiction, art, photos, interviews, criticism, reviews, music, parts-of-novels, long-poems, collages, plays, non-fiction. "BRILLIANT CORNERS publishes jazz-related poetry, fiction, and nonfiction. It features a four-color cover and occassionally publishes art and photography within the issue (black-and-white reproduction only). Recent contributors include Yusef Komunyakaa, Sonia Sanchez, Amiri Baraka, Philip Levine, Hayden Carruth, and Gary Giddins." circ. 700. 2/yr. Pub'd 2 issues 2005; expects 2 issues 2006, 2 issues 2007. sub. price $12; per copy $7; sample $7. Back issues: $7. Discounts: Ingram Periodicals (distributor). 90pp. Reporting time: 2 to 4 months. Simultaneous submissions accepted: No. Publishes 4% of manuscripts submitted. Payment: 2 copies of the issue. Copyrighted, reverts to author. Pub's reviews: 2 in 2005. §Jazz-related literature. Ads: $125/full-page ad. Subjects: African-American, Arts, Essays, Fiction, Interviews, Memoirs, Music, Non-Fiction, Performing Arts, Poetry, Prose.

BRILLIANT STAR, Amethel Darel-Sewell, Managing Editor; Ramzia Duszynski, Fiction Editor, Baha'i National Center, 1233 Central Street, Evanston, IL 60201. 1969. Poetry, fiction, articles, art, photos, cartoons, interviews, music, plays, non-fiction. "Material should not generally exceed 500 words. We do publish unpublished writers. Prefer articles & fiction which reflect racial and cultural diversity. Stories with moral or religious theme should not be 'preachy' or heavy-handed in conveying a lesson. No Christmas material will be accepted. Send for guidelines, 2 year theme list and informational material on the Baha'i Faith." circ. 3M. 6/yr. Pub'd 6 issues 2005; expects 6 issues 2006, 6 issues 2007. sub. price $18; per copy $3.50; sample $3 with 9 X 12 SASE with postage for 5 oz. Back issues: $3.50. Discounts: Bulk (5 or more) $2.50. 32pp. Reporting time: 8-12 weeks. Simultaneous submissions accepted: yes. Publishes 10% of manuscripts submitted. Payment: 2 copies. Copyrighted, rights revert to author if they specify that they are retaining copyright. Ads: none. Subjects: Asian-American, Black, Children, Youth, Literature (General), Native American, Spiritual, Third World, Minorities, Women.

Britton Road Press, Jay E. Frances, PO Box 044618, Racine, WI 53404, Fax 262-633-5503. 1998. Fiction, non-fiction. "Recently published *Flight: When Someone Disappears*, by Genevieve Sesto." avg. press run 3M. Pub'd 1 title 2005; expects 1 title 2006, 2 titles 2007. Discounts: we are distributed by Century Book Distribution. 325pp. Reporting time: 6 months. Simultaneous submissions accepted: yes. Publishes 10% of manuscripts submitted. Payment: standard. Does not copyright for author. Subjects: Children, Youth, Fiction, Graphic Design, Midwest, Non-Fiction.

Broken Jaw Press (see also NEW MUSE OF CONTEMPT), Joe Blades, PO Box 596 Stn A, Fredericton, NB E3B 5A6, Canada, ph/fax 506-454-5127, jblades@nbnet.nb.ca, www.brokenjaw.com. 1985. Poetry, fiction, cartoons, criticism, non-fiction. "Focus on Canadian, especially Canadian authors and/or subjects." avg. press run 700. Pub'd 12 titles 2005; expects 10 titles 2006, 12 titles 2007. Discounts: direct trade 40%, trade in U.S./Canada by General Distributions Services, e-book distribution by Publishing Online. 80pp. Reporting time: 4-6 months. Simultaneous submissions accepted: no. Publishes 1% of manuscripts submitted. Payment: 10% of list price. Copyrights for author. Subjects: Bisexual, Canada, Gay, Ernest Hemingway, History, Lesbianism, Literature (General), Poetry, Self-Help, Short Stories.

BROKEN PENCIL, Hal Niedzviecki, PO Box 203 Station P, Toronto, ON M5S 2S7, Canada, 416-538-2813, E-mail editor@brokenpencil.com. 1995. Fiction, articles, cartoons, interviews, criticism, reviews, music, letters, parts-of-novels, collages, news items, non-fiction. "We use anything on the subject of alternative culture in Canada. Fiction by Canadians only. Our main capacity is as a review journal of Canadian zines." circ. 2.5M. 2-3/yr. Pub'd 2 issues 2005; expects 3 issues 2006, 3 issues 2007. sub. price $12/3 issues; per copy $5; sample $5. 88pp. Reporting time: 2-3 months. Simultaneous submissions accepted: no. Payment: copy/$25-$200. Copyrighted, reverts to author. Pub's reviews: hundreds in 2005. §Anything published in Canada on an independent/small press basis. Ads: $200/$100. Subjects: Canada, Comics, Communication, Journalism, Counter-Culture, Alternatives, Communes, Culture, Fiction, Literature (General), Politics, Publishing, Zines.

Broken Rifle Press, Gerald R. Gioglio, Publisher, 33 Morton Drive, Lavallette, NJ 08735-2826, 732-830-7014, jerrkate@erols.com. 1987. Non-fiction. "Focus on peace, antiwar movements, non-violent resistance." avg. press run 3.5M. Discounts: 1-5 20%, 6-32 40%, 33-64 43%, 65-98 46%, 99+ 48%. Reporting time: Not Accepting Manuscripts at this time. Payment: standard. Copyrights for author. Subjects: History, Military, Veterans, Non-Fiction, Non-Violence, Peace, Sociology, Third World, Minorities.

Broken Shadow Publications, Gail Ford, 472 44th Street, Oakland, CA 94609-2136, 510 594-2200. 1993. Poetry, fiction, non-fiction. "Material we publish is honest, accessible, and deeply felt. Contributing authors place an emphasis on communication, and participate in regular peer reviews to ensure the clarity and power of their work. BSP does not accept unsolicited manuscripts." avg. press run 500. Expects 1 title 2006, 1 title 2007. 75pp. Simultaneous submissions accepted: no. Copyrights for author. Subjects: Essays, Poetry, Short Stories.

Bronze Girl Productions, Inc., Christine Mitchell, Publisher, 1341 Helmsman Way, Sacramento, CA 95833-3419, fax 916-922-1989, bronzegirl.com,. 2005. Poetry, fiction, non-fiction. "Query first. We accept poetry manuscripts, cookbooks, children fiction and non-fiction, self-help, and how-to's. No adult fiction. MS should be typed, double-spaced, clean, title of work on each page." avg. press run 2000. Expects 3 titles 2006, 6 titles 2007. Discounts: 1 copy 0%2-4 copies 25%5-99 copies 40%100+ copies 55%. 200pp. Reporting time: 2-4 months. Simultaneous submissions accepted: Yes. Publishes 10% of manuscripts submitted. Payment: Semi-annually payment of royalties. Royalties range from 7 1/2% to 15% based on sales. Copyrights for author. Subjects: African-American, Aging, Chicano/a, Children, Youth, Cooking, How-To, Juvenile Fiction, Motivation, Success, Non-Fiction, Parenting, Pets, Poetry, Relationships, Religion, Self-Help.

Brooding Heron Press, Samuel Green, Co-Publisher; Sally Green, Co-Publisher, Bookmonger Road, Waldron Island, WA 98297, 360-420-8181. 1984. Poetry. "No unsolicited manuscripts. Work by James Laughlin, Olav Hauge, Hayden Carruth, Donald Hall, Jane Hirshfield and Ted Kooser." avg. press run 300. Pub'd 1 title 2005; expects 1 title 2006, 1 title 2007. Discounts: 30% to bookstores for trade copies. 36-54pp. Reporting time: 1-2 weeks. Simultaneous submissions accepted: no. Publishes 1% of manuscripts submitted. Payment: copies, 10% of run. Copyrights for author. Subjects: Literary Review, Poetry.

Brook Farm Books, Jean Reed, PO Box 246, Bridgewater, ME 04735, 506-375-4680. 1981. Fiction, cartoons, satire, non-fiction. "Especially interested in home-school material. Canadian address: Box 101, Glassville, NB Canada E7L 4T4." avg. press run 5M. Pub'd 1 title 2005; expects 1 title 2006, 1 title 2007. Discounts: 1-9 40%, 10-49 45%, 50+ 50%, 40% STOP. 80-480pp. Reporting time: 2 months. Simultaneous submissions accepted: no. Payment: 10%, no advance. Copyrights for author. Subjects: Education, Humor.

Brook Street Press, James Pannell, PO Box 20284, St. Simons Island, GA 31522, 912-638-0264, Fax 912-638-0265, info@brookstreetpress.com, www.brookstreetpress.com. 2002. Fiction. "Brook Street Press is a publisher committed to an ongoing partnership with its writers, one that allows them the time to develop their craft. And it is willing to accept the risk and make the commitment to a supportive working relationship. While traditional publishers focus on bestseller candidates and short-term results, Brook Street Press is structured in a manner that allows us to accept works based upon our view of their literary merit. We have no illusions that we can predict the next blockbuster book. While we would certainly welcome bestseller status we are focused on works that deserve publication and an ability to build an audience over time, not just the first six months after release. We believe that this patient approach is not only sound artistically, but also good business. We will only publish a limited number of titles each year. We believe in 'paying for performance.' When a book sells, the author, the agent, and the publisher should all share in the rewards. Our contracts are structured to minimize risk to all parties and share in the rewards of a successful title." avg. press run 2M. Expects 3 titles 2006, 7 titles 2007. Discounts: 40-50%. 300pp. Reporting time: 3-6 months. Simultaneous submissions accepted: yes. Publishes 0.25% of manuscripts submitted. Payment: negotiable. Copyrights for author. Subject: Fiction.

Brooke-Richards Press, Brooke Sosa, Editor, 15030 Ventura Blvd., #19-415, Sherman Oaks, CA 91403, 818-205-1266, fax: 818-906-7867. 1989. "Supplementary textbooks. Not accepting submissions at the present time." avg. press run varies. Pub'd 2-3 titles 2005. Discounts: 40%. 96pp. Subjects: Biography, History.

Brookline Books, Milt Budoff, 34 University Rd, Brookline, MA 02445, 617-834-6772. 1978. Poetry, fiction. avg. press run 5000. Pub'd 6 titles 2005; expects 6 titles 2006, 6 titles 2007. Discounts: bookstores 20%. 175pp. Reporting time: 2 months. Simultaneous submissions accepted: Yes. Publishes 1% of manuscripts submitted. Payment: varies. Copyrights for author. Subjects: AIDS, Alternative Medicine, Animals, Arts, Avant-Garde, Experimental Art, Disabled, Education, History, Interviews, Literature (General), Novels, Poetry, Psychiatry, Psychology, Textbooks.

Brooks Books (see also MAYFLY), Randy Brooks, 3720 N. Woodridge Drive, Decatur, IL 62526, (217) 877-2966. 1976. Poetry. "Brooks Books, formerly High/Coo Press, publishes English-language haiku books, chapbooks, online collections and Mayfly magazine. Founded in 1976 by Randy and Shirley Brooks, our goal is to feature the individual haiku as a literary event, and to celebrate excellence in the art through collections by the best contemporary writers practicing the art of haiku.Brooks Books is a private publisher of English-language haiku publications. Our publications include Mayfly, a small biannual magazine, clothbound books such as Almost Unseen: Selected Haiku of George Swede, dual-language trade paperback books of haiku by contemporary Japanese and English-language haiku writers, chapbooks, and haiga web collections. Brooks Books promotes the well-crafted haiku, with sensory images that evoke an immediate emotional response as well as a long-lasting, often spiritual, resonance in the imagination of the reader. Brooks Books exists to publish appreciated books and magazine issues of excellent haiku in English.Brooks Books is the sponsor of the English-language Haiku web site available online at:http://www.brooksbookshaiku.comThe web site features individual English-language haiku, haiku poets, online web collections of haiku, online collections of haiga, new books related to haiku, haiku magazines, a catalog of related books for sale and news about upcoming haiku events. We welcome submissions and encourage you to become a reader and writer of haiku." avg. press run 1000. Pub'd 2 titles 2005; expects 2 titles 2006, 2 titles 2007. Discounts: bookstores - 5 or more copies 40%distributors - 10 or more coies 50%. 128pp. Reporting time: 3-4 months. Simultaneous submissions accepted: No. Publishes 2% of manuscripts submitted. Payment: 10% of the press run OR equivalent wholesale value of 10% of the press run. For example, with a press run of 1000 the author may receive 100 copies or 50% of the retail price value for 100 copies. Copyright is returned to author who registers and own copyright. Subjects: Haiku, Poetry, Zen.

Brookview Press, David Lee Drotar, 901 Western Road, Castleton-on-Hudson, NY 12033, 518-732-7093 phone/Fax, info@brookviewpress.com, www.brookviewpress.com. 2000. Non-fiction. "Brookview Press is a small independently owned publisher located in Castleton-on-Hudson, about 2 hours north of New York City. We publish unique, quality paperback books about nature and the environment." avg. press run 2.5M. Pub'd 1 title 2005; expects 1 title 2006, 2 titles 2007. Discounts: trade 1-10 copies 40%, 10+ non-returnable 50%; bulk, classroom, wholesaler 10+ copies 50%. 300pp. Reporting time: 4 months. Simultaneous submissions accepted: yes. Publishes 1% of manuscripts submitted. Payment: royalties annually. Copyrights for author. Subjects: Environment, Essays, Leisure/Recreation, Literature (General), Nature, Non-Fiction.

Brown Books Publishing Group, Kathryn Grant, 16200 N. Dallas Parkway, Suite 170, Dallas, TX 75248-2616, 972-381-0009, fax: 972-248-4336, publishing@brownbooks.com, www.brownbooks.com.

Brown Fox Books, Mark Godfrey, 1090 Eugenia Place, Carpinteria, CA 93013, 805-684-5951, Fax 805-684-1628, Manager@Brownfoxbooks.com, www.Brownfoxbooks.com. 1985. Non-fiction. "We publish books of interest to automotive and motor sports enthusiasts." avg. press run 3M. Pub'd 1 title 2005; expects 2 titles 2006, 4 titles 2007. Discounts: 20-55% based on quantity. 288pp. Simultaneous submissions accepted: no. Copyrights for author. Subjects: Autos, Biography, Transportation.

Brunswick Publishing Corporation, 1386 Lawrenceville Plank Road, Lawrenceville, VA 23868, 434-848-3865; Fax 434-848-0607; brunswickbooks@earthlink.net. 1973. Poetry, fiction, long-poems, plays, non-fiction. "Most categories apply. We accept or reject upon examination on individual basis." avg. press run 500-5M. Pub'd 12 titles 2005; expects 15 titles 2006, 18 titles 2007. Discounts: jobber 40% trade books, 20%

textbooks. 300pp. Reporting time: 2 weeks. Simultaneous submissions accepted: yes. Publishes 5% of manuscripts submitted. Payment: send for statement of philosophy and purpose. Copyrights for author. Subjects: African Literature, Africa, African Studies, Autobiography, Biography, Fiction, Non-Fiction, Novels, Poetry, Political Science, Psychology, Reference, Religion, Spiritual, Sports, Outdoors, Virginia, World War II.

BRUTARIAN, Dominik Salemi, 9405 Ulysses Court, Burke, VA 22015-1605. 1991. Poetry, fiction, articles, art, photos, cartoons, interviews, satire, criticism, reviews, music, letters, parts-of-novels, long-poems, collages, plays, concrete art, news items, non-fiction. ''Quality not quantity is the philosophy here. We have contributors who work for highbrow publications like Sally Ekhoff of the *Village Voice*, artists like Jarrett Huddleston whose paintings routinely fetch five figures and writers like myself (Salemi the editor) whose work has appeared primarily in underground publications.'' circ. 3M. 4/yr. Pub'd 4 issues 2005; expects 4 issues 2006, 4 issues 2007. sub. price $12; per copy $4; sample $6. Back issues: $7 (cheap for works of such unsurpassed genius). Discounts: $2 per if order 10 copies or more. 84pp. Reporting time: 30 days. Simultaneous submissions accepted: no. Publishes 10% of manuscripts submitted. Payment: features fetch 5¢/word, reviews $20, art $40 a page, cover illustration $100, 10¢/word for stories from established writers and for features. Copyrighted, reverts to author. Pub's reviews: 50+ in 2005. §Any area dealing with pop culture or offbeat controversial subject matter. Ads: $90/$50/$30/$175 inside cover/$500 back cover.

BRYANT LITERARY REVIEW, Tom Chandler, Faculty Suite F, Bryant University, Smithfield, RI 02917, website http://bryant2.bryant.edu/~blr/. 2000. Poetry, fiction. ''Contributors: Michael S. Harper, Denise Duhamel, and Baron Wormser.'' circ. 1M+. 1/yr. Pub'd 1 issue 2005; expects 1 issue 2006, 1 issue 2007. sub. price $8; per copy $8; sample $8. 120pp. Reporting time: approx. 3 months. Publishes 5% of manuscripts submitted. Payment: 2 copies. Copyrighted, reverts to author. Subjects: Fiction, Poetry.

•**BTW Press, LLC,** Mary Jo Sherwood, PO Box 554, Chanhassen, MN 55317, 1-866-818-8029, www.btwpress.com. 2005. Non-fiction. avg. press run 5000. Pub'd 1 title 2005; expects 5 titles 2006, 10 titles 2007. Discounts: 2-5 copies 20%6-24 copies 40%25+ copies 45%. 200pp.

BUCKLE &, Bernhard Frank, PO Box 1653, Buffalo, NY 14205. 1998. Poetry. ''No inspirational verse. Send 3-5 poems or poetry translations. No previously published poems, please.'' circ. 200. 2/yr. Pub'd 2 issues 2005; expects 2 issues 2006, 2 issues 2007. sub. price $9; per copy $5; sample $5. 56pp. Reporting time: 2 weeks for first submissions, 2 months for repeat submissions. Simultaneous submissions accepted: no. Publishes maybe 5% of manuscripts submitted. Payment: 1 year subscription. Copyrighted, reverts to author. Ads: none. Subjects: Poetry, Translation.

Buddhist Text Translation Society, Dharma Realm Buddhist Assn., 1777 Murchison Drive, Burlingame, CA 94010-4504, (707) 468-9112, e-mail EileenHu@drba.org. 1970. Poetry, articles, art, photos, interviews, non-fiction. ''The Buddhist Text Translation Society (BTTS) began publishing in 1970 with the goal of making the principles of Buddhism available to an English-reading audience in a form that can be put directly into practice. BTTS translators are both scholars and practicing Buddhists. Translations are accompanied by contemporary commentary. To date, the following have been published, classics such as the *Shurangama Sutra*, the *Lotus Sutra,* and the *Vajra Sutra*; esoteric works such as the *Earth Store Bodhisattva Sutra* and the *Shurangama Mantra;* books on informal instruction in meditation; and books that have grown out of the American Buddhist experience. Bilingual Chinese/English scriptures are also available including chapters from the *Avatamsaka Sutra, The Heart Sutra* and the *Brahma Net Sutra*. Extensive commentaries accompany each of these works in both languages. Limited material is available in Spanish, Vietnamese and French.'' avg. press run 2M. Pub'd 6 titles 2005; expects 8 titles 2006, 10 titles 2007. Discounts: retail stores 2-4 books 20%, 5-30 40%, Call for 31 plus books. Distributed by New Leaf Distributors. 200pp. Payment: none, Non-profit organization. Copyrights for author.

•**Buenos Books America,** Guy Bayard, 1133 Broadway, Suite 706, New York, NY 10010, www.buenos-books.us. Non-fiction. ''academic publishing: philosophy of law, international law, philosophy of scienceElectronic submissions only authors must hold a Ph. D in the field.'' Reporting time: one week. Simultaneous submissions accepted: Yes. Publishes 50% of manuscripts submitted. Does not copyright for author. Subjects: History, Law, Non-Fiction, Philosophy, Research, Science, U.S. Hispanic.

BUFFALO SPREE, Elizabeth Licata, 6215 Sheridan Drive, Buffalo, NY 14221-4837, 716-634-0820, fax 716-810-0075. 1967. Articles, photos, interviews, criticism, reviews, news items, non-fiction. ''We have stopped publishing poetry and fiction, and are now a city/regional magazine. We normally assign articles and do not encourage unsolicited material, though we will review it.'' circ. 25M. 8/yr. sub. price $20; per copy $4.50; sample $4.50. Discounts: none. 225pp. Reporting time: 1 month. Simultaneous submissions accepted: no. Payment: varies, payment upon publication. Copyrighted, authors must request permission for rights to revert. Pub's reviews: 8 in 2005. §Biography, art, music, health, fitness, food. Subjects: Fiction, Non-Fiction, Short Stories.

‡**BULLETIN OF HISPANIC STUDIES, Liverpool University Press,** Dorothy Sherman Severin, James

Higgins, Dept. Of Hispanic Studies, The University, PO Box 147, Liverpool L69 3BX, England, 051 794 2774/5. 1923. Articles, reviews. "Specialist articles on the languages and literatures of Spain, Portugal and Latin America, in English, Spanish, Portuguese and Catalan." circ. 1M. 4/yr. Pub'd 4 issues 2005; expects 4 issues 2006, 4 issues 2007. sub. price inland (European community) indiv. £29, instit. £75, overseas indiv. US $50, instit. US $155; per copy £20. Back issues: £40 per volume. 112pp. Reporting time: 3 months max. Payment: none. Not copyrighted. Pub's reviews: 200 in 2005. §Languages and literatures of Spain, Portugal and Latin America. Ads: £250/£150/£80 1/4 page. Subject: Language.

The Bunny & The Crocodile Press/Forest Woods Media Productions, Inc, Grace Cavalieri, President, Editor; Colleen Fellows, Vice Pres.; Cynthia Comitz, Senior Editor, Chief of Production; Kenneth Flynn, Treasurer, Editor, 1821 Glade Court, Annapolis, MD 21403-1945, 304-754-8847. 1976. Poetry. "Other address: Suite 1102, 4200 Cathedral Ave. NW. Manuscripts by invitation only, no unsolicited mss." avg. press run 500-1M. Pub'd 2 titles 2005; expects 10 titles 2006, 10 titles 2007. Discounts: 10% for orders of 12+. 77-100pp. Simultaneous submissions accepted: no. Payment: to date authors obtain grants to publish, get 80% of sales; publisher supplies 20% funding. Author owns copyright. Subject: Poetry.

Burd Street Press, Harold E. Collier, Acquisitions Editor, PO Box 708, 73 W. Burd Street, Shippensburg, PA 17257, 717-532-2237, Fax 717-532-6110. 1992. Fiction, non-fiction. "Burd Street Press brings military history to the novice reader." avg. press run 1M-2M. Pub'd 4 titles 2005; expects 10 titles 2006, 15 titles 2007. Discounts: available on request. 150-250pp. Reporting time: 30 days for proposals, 90 days for full manuscripts. Simultaneous submissions accepted: yes. Publishes 25% of manuscripts submitted. Payment: twice yearly. Copyrights for author. Subjects: Aviation, Biography, Civil War, Diaries, History, Non-Fiction, War, World War II.

Burning Books, Melody Sumner Carnahan, Michael Sumner, PO Box 2638, Santa Fe, NM 87504, Fax 505-820-6216, brnbx@nets.com, burningbooks.org. 1979. Poetry, fiction, art, interviews, music. "Burning Books has published books of and about contemporary music, literature, and art since 1979. We are artists and writers who publish books that extend possibilities in literature, music, art, and ideas. We use volunteer labor, donated professional services, income from previous publications and advance sales to create our books." avg. press run 1M-3M. Pub'd 1 title 2005; expects 2 titles 2006, 2 titles 2007. Discounts: 40/60. 84-450pp. Reporting time: 6 weeks. Simultaneous submissions accepted: yes. Publishes 0% of manuscripts submitted. Payment: varies. We sometimes copyright for author. Subjects: Arts, Avant-Garde, Experimental Art, Fiction, Literature (General), Music, Philosophy, Short Stories, Visual Arts.

Burning Bush Publications (see also IN OUR OWN WORDS), Amanda Majestie, Acquisitions, PO Box 9636, Oakland, CA 94613-0636, 510-482-9996, www.bbbooks.com, editors@bbbooks.com. 1996. Poetry, fiction, photos, non-fiction. "Burning Bush is a press committed to social and economic justice." avg. press run 1M. Pub'd 1 title 2005; expects 1 title 2006, 2 titles 2007. Discounts: 40% to bookstores, 50% for 100 or more copies. 160pp. Reporting time: 3 months. Simultaneous submissions accepted: yes. Payment: negotiable. Copyrights for author. Subjects: African-American, Asian-American, Chicano/a, Diaries, Gay, Immigration, Journals, Judaism, Lesbianism, Literature (General), Multicultural, Native American, Women.

Burning Deck Press, Keith Waldrop, Rosmarie Waldrop, 71 Elmgrove Avenue, Providence, RI 02906. 1962. Poetry. "Order from Small Press Distribution." avg. press run 500-1M. Expects 4 titles 2006, 3 titles 2007. Discounts: see schedule of Small Press Distribution. 64-80pp. Reporting time: 2 months. Payment: 10% of edition (copies). Does not copyright for author. Subjects: Fiction, Poetry.

BURNSIDE REVIEW, Sid Miller, P.O. BOX 1782, Portland, OR 97207, sid@burnsidereview.org, www.burnsidereview.org. 2004. Poetry, fiction, art, photos, criticism, reviews, long-poems. "Published poetry, interviews and reviews. Reads poetry year round. Past contributors include Dorianne Laux, Virgil Suarez, Paul Guest and Robyn Art. We like the narrative, but would like to see more of a movement to the lyrical. See our website for complete guidelines, samples, and contest info." circ. 250. 2/yr. Expects 1 issue 2006, 2 issues 2007. sub. price $10.00; per copy $8.00; sample $8.00. Back issues: $4.00. Discounts: n/a. 68pp. Reporting time: 1-3 months. Simultaneous submissions accepted: Yes. Publishes 5% of manuscripts submitted. Payment: one copy. Copyrighted, reverts to author. Pub's reviews: 2 in 2005. §poetry chapbooks and full poetry books. Ads: negotiable. Subjects: Arts, Liberal Arts, Oregon, Poetry.

BUSINESS SPIRIT JOURNAL, The Message Company, James Berry, Richard Auer, 4 Camino Azul, Santa Fe, NM 87508, 505-474-7604, Fax 505-471-2584, message@bizspirit.com, www.bizspirit.com. 1997. Articles, photos, cartoons, interviews, criticism, reviews, letters, news items, non-fiction. "We cover business topics: vision, values, leadership, spirituality in business, sustainability, integrity, etc." circ. 50M. 12/yr. Pub'd 12 issues 2005; expects 12 issues 2006, 12 issues 2007. sub. price free online; sample free. Back issues: $5 hardback issues. 12pp. Reporting time: 30 days. Simultaneous submissions accepted: yes. Publishes 50% of manuscripts submitted. Payment: none. Copyrighted, reverts to author. Pub's reviews: 24 in 2005. §Science, business, leadership, creativity. Ads: call for rates. Subjects: Business & Economics, Cosmology, Creativity,

Ethics, Leadership, Management, Physics, Religion, Science.

•BUST DOWN THE DOOR AND EAT ALL THE CHICKENS: A Journal of Absurd and Surreal Fiction, Bradley Sands, 57 Cherry Street, Northampton, MA 01060, (413) 320-4173/ http://www.absurdistjournal.com. Fiction, satire. "We are seeking stories of an absurdist or surrealist nature that are within the range of 2000 to 5000 words. They should not fit comfortably within any genre. We have peculiar tastes and recommend that you read an issue before sending in your work.Please see website for more detailed guidelines and an online sample issue: www.absurdistjournal.comRecent contributors include Steve Aylett, D. Harlan Wilson, Kenji Siratori, John Edward Lawson, Kevin L. Donihe, Vincent W. Sakowski, and Alyssa Sturgill." circ. 200. 2/yr. Pub'd 2 issues 2005; expects 2 issues 2006, 2 issues 2007. sub. price $16; per copy $5 ($1.25 for shipping); sample $5. Back issues: issue 3 ($5). Discounts: 30%. 80pp. Reporting time: 2 weeks or longer. Simultaneous submissions accepted: Yes. Publishes 10% of manuscripts submitted. Payment: $5 and one contributor's copy. Copyrighted, reverts to author. Ads: trade. Subjects: Absurdist, Avant-Garde, Experimental Art, Dada, Experimental, Fantasy, Fiction, Horror, Humor, Kafka, Literature (General), Prose, Satire, Science Fiction, Surrealism.

Butcher Shop Press, David Greenspan, Publisher Editor-in-Chief; H NGM N, Editor, 529 Beach 132nd St., Rockaway Park, NY 11694-1413. 1999. Poetry, fiction, articles, art, photos, interviews, criticism, reviews, long-poems, non-fiction. *"We consider ourselves to be everything that is right with poetry. We live through our art and our lives are our art. . .while some continue to Howl against the system we take it outside and beat it."* Our Chapbooks usually run between 100-200 copies. The Butcher's Block runs anywhere above 500 copies. Payment: cash, checks money orders.

BUTTON, Sally Cragin, PO Box 77, Westminster, MA 01473, sally@moonsigns.net, www.moonsigns.net. 1993. Poetry, fiction, art, cartoons, music, parts-of-novels. "We like wit, brevity, the cleverly-conceived of essay/recipe, poetry that might have a rhyme scheme, but isn't a rhyme scheme that's abab or aabb or anything really obvious, true moments carefully preserved. We don't like whining, cheap sentimentality, egregious profanity, vampires, neuroses for neuroses' sake, most song lyrics passing as poetry, anything overlong, overdull or overreaching. Recent contributors include: Mary Campbell, Sven Birkerts, Stephen Sandys, They Might Be Giants, Brendan Galvin, Diana Der-Hovanessian. Sample material can be viewed on our website." circ. 1M. 1/yr. Pub'd 1 issue 2005; expects 1 issue 2006, 1 issue 2007. sub. price $10 for 6 issues; $40 for lifetime subscription.; per copy $2; sample $2. Back issues: same. Discounts: none - our prices are low, low, low; stores are 60/40 split. 28pp. Reporting time: 9 weeks, we return manuscripts only if we comment on them; otherwise, response only. Simultaneous submissions accepted: no. Publishes 5-10% of manuscripts submitted. Payment: subscriptions for writer + 1 friends + honorarium. Copyrighted, reverts to author. Pub's reviews: 1 in 2005. §Fiction, fashion, poetry, manuals. Ads: $100/$60/$25 minimum. Subjects: Cartoons, Crafts, Hobbies, Fiction, Music, Poetry.

BUZZWORDS, Zoe King, David King, www.buzzwordsmagazine.co.uk, editor@buzzwordsmagazine.co.uk. 1999. Fiction. "We are now an online only publication - paper publication ceased September 2003." 6/yr. Pub'd 6 issues 2005; expects 6 issues 2006, 6 issues 2007. Reporting time: 2-3 months. We prefer not to accept simultaneous submissions. Publishes 10% of manuscripts submitted. Copyrighted, reverts to author. Subjects: Book Reviewing, Fiction, Literary Review, Literature (General), Short Stories, Writers/Writing.

BWALO: A Forum for Social Development, S. Khaila, C. Hickey, M. Tsoka, PO Box 278, Zomba, Malawi, 265-524-916, Fax 265-524-578. 1997. *"Bwalo* is an annual independent expression of considered yet controversial opinion on a broad range of human and social development issues. Articles are informed by professional interdisciplinary research, and where not, by judicious speculation and advocacy on the basis of fundamentals." circ. 500. 1/yr. Pub'd 1 issue 2005; expects 1 issue 2006, 1 issue 2007. sub. price US$25; per copy US$25. 164pp. Reporting time: 3-4 months. Simultaneous submissions accepted: no. Payment: none. Copyrighted. Ads: negotiable. Subjects: African Literature, Africa, African Studies, Government.

BYLINE, Marcia Preston, Editor & Publisher; Sandra Soli, Poetry Editor; Carolyn Wall, Fiction Editor, PO Box 5240, Edmond, OK 73083-5240, 405-348-5591. 1981. Poetry, fiction, articles, interviews, non-fiction. circ. 3M. 11/yr. Pub'd 11 issues 2005; expects 11 issues 2006, 11 issues 2007. sub. price $24; per copy $5; sample $5. Back issues: $5 (incl. p/h). 36pp. Reporting time: 6-8 weeks. We accept simultaneous submissions except for poetry. Publishes 1% of manuscripts submitted. Payment: varies by department, approx. 5¢/word. Copyrighted, reverts to author. Ads: $350/$200/$1 per word. Subjects: Fiction, How-To, Non-Fiction, Poetry, Writers/Writing.

Byte Masters International, Bernard H. Browne Jr., PO Box 3805, Clearwater, FL 33767, 727-593-3717, FAX 727-593-3605, Email BernieByte@aol.com. 1991. Non-fiction. "Authored and published the America Online and Best Web Site book series (version 3 & 4) judged to have been one of the best computer books ever published as far as both design and content! New book series in progress which will be published some time year year or early next year." avg. press run 5K. Pub'd 1 title 2005; expects 1 title 2006, 1 title 2007.

82

Discounts: trade, bulk and other. 500pp. Simultaneous submissions accepted: no. Copyrights for author. Subjects: Business & Economics, Computers, Calculators, How-To.

C

C & G Publishing, Inc., Cyndi Duncan, Georgie Patrick, 2706 West 18th St. Rd, Greeley, CO 80634-5772, 970-356-9622, ccgcook@aol.com. 1989. Poetry, non-fiction. avg. press run 5M 1st, 2.5M subsequent. Pub'd 1 title 2005; expects 2 titles 2006, 1 title 2007. Discounts: 40% trade. Pages vary. Simultaneous submissions accepted: no. Payment: yes. Copyrights for author. Subjects: Cooking, Poetry.

C & M Online Media Inc., Nancy McAllister, 3905 Meadow Field Lane, Raleigh, NC 27606-4470, www.cmonline.com, cm@cmonline.com. 1976. Fiction, art. "We publish about 12 titles a year on our website. Our imprint is Boson Books. (Not publishing at this time under the New South Company, but New South titles are still available.) We have e-book distribution primarily through cyberread.com, mobipocket.com, contentreserve.com, powells.com, amazon.com and netlibrary.com. Selected titles are published as trade paperbacks. Several of our books recently published in both electronic and paper formats are: Belaset's Daughter by Feona Hamilton, Chinese Business Etiquette and Culture by Kevin Bucknall, and A Ship's Tale by N. Jay Young." Pub'd 12 titles 2005; expects 12 titles 2006, 12 titles 2007. 300pp. Reporting time: 3-4 weeks. Simultaneous submissions accepted: no. Publishes 1% of manuscripts submitted. Payment: 25% Boson Books online, 50% Boson Books trade paper. Does not copyright for author. Subjects: Drama, Fiction, Non-Fiction, North Carolina, Numismatics, Poetry, Post Modern, Science Fiction.

C & T Publishing, Lynn Koolish, Managing Editor; Amy Marson, Production Director; Liz Aneloski, Editor, 1651 Challenge Drive, Concord, CA 94520-5206, 925-677-0377. 1983. Non-fiction. "We publish how-to quilting books, most of which are softcover with an average of 112 pages. Most books are all color." avg. press run 15M. Pub'd 15 titles 2005; expects 18 titles 2006, 28 titles 2007. Discounts: Total retail amount: $50 or less 20%, $51-300 40%, $301-600 45%, $601+ 50%. 112pp. Reporting time: 8 weeks. Simultaneous submissions accepted: yes. Publishes 10% of manuscripts submitted. Payment: 10% on net, quarterly. Copyrights for author. Subjects: Antiques, Arts, Collectibles, Crafts, Hobbies, How-To, Internet, Quilting, Sewing.

Caddo Gap Press (see also EDUCATIONAL FOUNDATIONS; EDUCATIONAL LEADERSHIP & ADMINISTRATION; INTERNATIONAL JOURNAL OF EDUCATIONAL POLICY, RESEARCH, AND PRACTICE; ISSUES IN TEACHER EDUCATION; JOURNAL OF CURRICULUM THEORIZING; JOURNAL OF THOUGHT; MULTICULTURAL EDUCATION; NOTES AND ABSTRACTS IN AMERICAN AND INTERNATIONAL EDUCATION; SCHOLAR-PRACTITIONER QUARTERLY; SUMMER ACADEME: A Journal of Higher Education; TABOO: Journal of Education & Culture; TEACHER EDUCATION QUARTERLY; VITAE SCHOLASTICAE: The Journal of Educational Biography), Alan H. Jones, Publisher, 3145 Geary Boulevard, Suite 275, San Francisco, CA 94118, 415-666-3012 telephone,415-666-3552 fax,caddogap@aol.com,www.caddogap.com. 1989. "Caddo Gap Press is primarily a publisher of educational books and journals, with particular interest in the fields of teacher education and the social foundations of education." avg. press run 2M. Pub'd 5 titles 2005; expects 5 titles 2006, 5 titles 2007. Discounts: 20% to educational institutions; 40% to bookstores; other discounts based on quantity. 150pp. Reporting time: 1 month. Simultaneous submissions accepted: yes. Publishes 10% of manuscripts submitted. Payment: to be arranged, usually 10%. Copyrights for author. Subject: Education.

CADENCE: The Review of Jazz & Blues: Creative Improvised Music, Robert D. Rusch, Cadence Building, Redwood, NY 13679, 315-287-2852, Fax 315-287-2860. 1975. Articles, photos, interviews, criticism, reviews, music, news items. "We run about 24 interviews or oral histories a year. Have covered more than 44,000 record releases (reviews) since 1976. We also publish a yearly index." circ. 10M+. 12/yr. Pub'd 12 issues 2005; expects 12 issues 2006, 12 issues 2007. sub. price $30; per copy $3; sample $3. Back issues: $5 each. Discounts: Distributors only 5-10 $2.09; 11-15 $1.92; 16-20 $1.86; 20-49 $1.74; 50 $1.61; 100 or more $1.50. 144pp. Reporting time: 2 weeks. Payment: varies. Shared copyrights. Pub's reviews: 1.6M in 2005. §Jazz, blues and related areas, creative improvised music. Ads: $200/$125/75¢. Subjects: Entertainment, Music.

CADENZA, John Ravenscroft, Zoe King, 2 Coastguard Cottages, Shore Road,Freiston Shore, Boston, Lincs PE22 0LZ, United Kingdom, eds@cadenza-magazine.co.uk. 2000. Poetry, fiction, articles, interviews, reviews, letters, news items. "Recent issues have included interviews with Monica Ali, Joanne Harris, and Jim Crace. We're looking for cutting edge fiction and poetry. Full details on our website at: www.cadenza-magazine.co.uk." 2/yr. Pub'd 4 issues 2005; expects 2 issues 2006, 2 issues 2007. 86pp. Reporting time: two to three months. Simultaneous submissions accepted: No. Publishes 10% of manuscripts submitted. Payment:

Copies only at present. Copyrighted, reverts to author. Pub's reviews: approx 10 in 2005. §Fiction, biography.

Cadmus Editions, Jeffrey Miller, PO Box 126, Belvedere-Tiburon, CA 94920-0126, 707-762-0510. 1979. Poetry, fiction, music, parts-of-novels. "Do not send unsolicited mss." avg. press run 1500. Pub'd 3 titles 2005; expects 3 titles 2006, 3 titles 2007. Discounts: Trade editions distributed by Publishers Group West. 250pp. Reporting time: 30 days. Simultaneous submissions accepted: no. Publishes .001% of manuscripts submitted. Payment: negotiable; paid annually. Copyrights for author. Subjects: Fiction, Poetry.

Caernarvon Press, Terry Hertzler, Publisher, 4435 Marlborough Ave. #3, San Diego, CA 92116, (619) 284-0411, terryh@cts.com. 1985. Poetry, fiction, long-poems, non-fiction. "Publishes poetry and short fiction, rarely unsolicited work. Poets published include Steve Kowit, LoVerne Brown, Brandon Cesmat and Karen Stromberg." avg. press run 300-2000. Discounts of up to 50%. Write for pricing list. 25-100pp. Subjects: Fantasy, Fiction, Poetry, Vietnam.

CAFE NOIR REVIEW, Back House Books, Philip Henderson, 1703 Lebanon Street, Adelphi, MD 20783. 1990. Poetry, fiction, articles, cartoons, interviews, satire, criticism, reviews, parts-of-novels, long-poems, plays. "Length of material: fiction, 2,500 words; poetry, no limits. Want good strong politically-oriented material. Will accept anything which is dangerous, erotic, even pornographic. We especially are looking for young black writers who are otherwise 'unpublishable.' We're just starting, but we intend to grow. Please, no trash. We demand *quality* poetry and fiction, nevertheless." circ. 250. Irregular. Pub'd 1 issue 2005; expects 1 issue 2006, 2-3 issues 2007. sub. price $16; per copy $4; sample $4. Back issues: $5. Discounts: 40%. 50pp. Reporting time: 3 weeks to 2 months. Payment: contributor copies. Copyrighted, reverts to author. Pub's reviews: 1 in 2005. §Fiction, race relations, music, general culture, world politics. Ads: $100/$50/$15 1/4 page/$7 1/8 page. Subjects: Anarchist, Black, Erotica, Fiction.

THE CAFE REVIEW, Steve Luttrell, Editor-in-Chief; Wayne Atherton, Editor; Alex Fisher, Editor, c/o Yes Books, 589 Congress Street, Portland, ME 04101, cafereweditors@mailcity.com, www.thecafereview.com. 1989. Poetry, art, photos, interviews, criticism. "Send $1 handling fee per submission and SASE (very important)." circ. 300-500. 4/yr. Pub'd 4 issues 2005; expects 4 issues 2006, 4 issues 2007. sub. price $28; per copy $7.95 newsstand; sample $8 includes p/h. Back issues: $5 includes p/h. Discounts: none. 60-70pp. Reporting time: 2-4 months. Simultaneous submissions accepted: no. Publishes 10% of manuscripts submitted. Payment: 1 copy. Copyrighted, reverts to author. Pub's reviews: a few in 2005. §Small press poetry and visual art (photography). Subject: Beat.

THE CAIMAN (formerly THE WEIRD NEWS), Donald F. Busky, 7393 Rugby Street, Philadelphia, PA 19138-1236, caimans@yahoo.com. 1989. Cartoons, satire. circ. 100. 4/yr. Pub'd 4 issues 2005; expects 4 issues 2006, 4 issues 2007. sub. price free; per copy free; sample free. Back issues: free. Discounts: free trades. 4pp. Reporting time: 1 week. Simultaneous submissions accepted: yes. Payment: none. Not copyrighted. Pub's reviews: none in 2005. §Political commentary. Ads: none. Subjects: Anarchist, Arts, Beat, Civil Rights, Communism, Marxism, Leninism, Counter-Culture, Alternatives, Communes, Education, Essays, Fantasy, Futurism, Government, History, Judaism, Liberal Arts, Worker.

•**CAIRN: The New ST. ANDREWS REVIEW, St. Andrews College Press,** Thomas Heffernan, Managing Editor; Ron Bayes, Consulting Editor; Kemp Gregory, Consulting Editor, St. Andrews Prebytery College, 1700 Dogwood Mile, Laurinburg, NC 28352, 910-277-5000, 910-277-9925. "Each issue will have a guest editor. *Cairn* is especially interested in fiction and poetry by new writers. We have no particular editorial biases, but in general we do not accept genre work, childrens lit , or literary criticism. Recent contributors include Dana Gioia, Robert Creeley, and Virgil Suarez. Submissions are read between June 1 and November 1, and *Cairn* is published in late spring."

CAKETRAIN, Caketrain Press, Donna Weaver, 174 Carriage Drive, North Huntingdon, PA 15642, www.caketrain.org, caketrainjournal@hotmail.com. Poetry, fiction, reviews, long-poems, non-fiction. "Caketrain is a new journal out of Pittsburgh, PA, and is dedicated to fresh and daring literature, placing no limits on length or genre. Recent contributors include: David Baratier, Jim Daniels, Sean Thomas Dougherty, Sue William Silverman, Virgil Suarez, Simon Perchik and others." circ. 500. 2/yr. Expects 2 issues 2006, 2 issues 2007. sub. price $16.00; per copy $8.00; sample $7.50. Back issues: $6.00 or inquire. 150pp. Reporting time: two weeks to three months. Simultaneous submissions accepted: Yes. Publishes 15% of manuscripts submitted. Payment: Payment is one copy of issue contributors work appears in. Copyrighted, reverts to author. Pub's reviews: none in 2005. §poetry, fiction, non-fiction. Ads: Full page: $100Half Page: $75Quarter Page: $50. Subjects: Fiction, Non-Fiction, Poetry, Prose.

Caketrain Press (see also CAKETRAIN), Donna Weaver, 174 Carriage Drive, North Huntingdon, PA 15642, www.caketrain.org, caketrainjournal@hotmail.com. 2003. Poetry, fiction, art, photos, interviews, long-poems, non-fiction. "Caketrain is a new journal out of Pittsburgh, PA, and is dedicated to fresh and daring literature, placing no limits on length or genre. Issue One (available Summer 2004) contributors include: Jim Daniels, Corie Feiner, Sue William Silverman, David Baratier and others. Issue Two (Available Fall 2004) contributors include Virgil Suarez, Simon Perchik, Sean Thomas Dougherty, Camille Dungy and Ben Miller." avg. press run 250. Expects 2 titles 2006, 2 titles 2007. 150-175pp. Reporting time: Two weeks to three months. Simultaneous submissions accepted: Yes. Publishes 15% of manuscripts submitted. Payment: Payment is one copy of issue contributor appears in. Does not copyright for author. Subjects: Fiction, Literature (General), Memoirs, Mental Health, Multicultural, Non-Fiction, Poetry.

California Bill's Automotive Handbooks, Howard W. Fisher, Publisher, PO Box 91858, Tucson, AZ 85752-1858, 520-547-2462, Fax 888-511-1501, web: www.californiabills.com www.goodyearbooks.com www.nononsenseguides.com. 1987. Non-fiction. "Our focus is on automotive and outdoor recreation titles. Please do *not* send manuscripts; send letter of inquiry plus an outline. We require releases before reviewing manuscripts." avg. press run 10M first printing. Pub'd 1 title 2005; expects 3 titles 2006, 2 titles 2007. Discounts: retail, wholesale, mail order - upon request. 160pp. Reporting time: 1-2 months. Payment: upon request. Copyrights for author. Subject: Autos.

CALIFORNIA EXPLORER, Kay Graves, 1135 Terminal Way, Suite 209, Reno, NV 89502. 1978. Articles, photos. "Articles of interest to beginner and advanced hikers & RVers. Places to visit primarily in California." circ. 5M. 6/yr. Pub'd 6 issues 2005; expects 6 issues 2006, 6 issues 2007. sub. price $28.50; per copy $5.95; sample free. Back issues: $4. Discounts: 20%. 12pp. Reporting time: 2 months. Simultaneous submissions accepted: no. Publishes 90% of manuscripts submitted. Payment: $75-$175. Copyrighted, reverts to author. Ads: $350 1/3 page/$275 1/4 page. Subjects: Nature, Travel.

CALIFORNIA QUARTERLY (CQ), Kate Ozbirn, Editor, CSPS/CQ, 21 Whitman Court, Irvine, CA 92617, 949-854-8024, jipalley@aol.com. 1973. Poetry. "For submissions and subscriptions send to: CSPS/CQ, PO Box 7126, Orange, CA 92863." circ. 400. 4/yr. Pub'd 4 issues 2005; expects 4 issues 2006, 4 issues 2007. sub. price $25.00; per copy $7.50; sample $7.50. Back issues: $2-3. Discounts: 50/50. 64pp. Reporting time: 6-8 months. Simultaneous submissions accepted: yes. Publishes 2-5% of manuscripts submitted. Payment: 1 copy of magazine. Copyrighted, reverts to author. Pub's reviews: 6 in 2005. §Books of poetry, in separate publication. Subject: Poetry.

Callawind Publications / Custom Cookbooks / Children's Books, 2059 Hempstead Turnpike, PMB 355, East Meadow, NY 11554-1711, 514-685-9109, Fax 514-685-7952, info@callawind.com. 1995. Non-fiction. "Cookbook publisher, cookbook packager, children's book packager. Queries only; please do not send manuscripts." Pub'd 2 titles 2005; expects 2 titles 2006, 2 titles 2007. 125pp. Subjects: Children, Youth, Cooking, Dining, Restaurants, Lifestyles, Picture Books, Travel.

CALLBOARD, Belinda Taylor, 870 Market Street #375, San Francisco, CA 94102, 415-430-1140; www.theatrebayarea.org. 1976. Articles, photos, interviews. "Open to short articles (750-2,000 words) related to theatre. No reviews. Essays, features, interviews with theatre personalities. Emphasis on San Francisco Bay Area." circ. 10M. 12/yr. Pub'd 12 issues 2005; expects 12 issues 2006, 12 issues 2007. sub. price $40; per copy $5.50; sample $8. Back issues: $8. 44pp. Reporting time: 2 months. Simultaneous submissions accepted: no. Most ms. are assigned, unsolicited ms. are occasionally published. Payment: $150/article; $100/cover art. Copyrighted, reverts to author. Pub's reviews: 10 in 2005. §Theatre: production, administration, playwriting, plays, acting, how to articles, etc. Ads: $720/$445/$1 per word classified. Subject: Theatre.

Calliope Press, Eileen Wyman, PO Box 2408, New York, NY 10108-2408, 212-564-5068. Fiction, non-fiction. avg. press run 2 M. Subject: Biography.

CALLIOPE: Exploring World History, Cobblestone Publishing Company, Rosalie F. Baker, Editor, 30 Grove Street, Suite C, Peterborough, NH 03458, 603-924-7209, Fax 603-924-7380, custsvc@cobblestone.mv.com. 1990. Poetry, articles, art, photos, reviews, non-fiction. "The magazine will accept freelance articles related to themes covered. Write for guidelines." circ. 10.5M. 9/yr. Pub'd 9 issues 2005; expects 9 issues 2006, 9 issues 2007. sub. price $29.95 + $8 foreign, Canadian subs add 7% GST; per copy $4.95; sample $4.95. Back issues: $4.95. Discounts: 15% for sub. agencies, bulk rate 3+ $17.95/year sub. each. 52pp. Reporting time: queries sent well in advance of deadline may not be answered for several months. Go-aheads usually sent 5 months prior to publication date. Payment: on publication. Copyrighted, *Calliope* buys all rights. Pub's reviews: 39 in 2005. §Books pertaining to the issues' themes, and written for children ages 8-14. Ads: none. Subject: History.

Calyx Books (see also CALYX: A Journal of Art and Literature by Women), Margarita Donnelly, Director; Beverly McFarland, Senior Editor, PO Box B, Corvallis, OR 97330, 541-753-9384, Fax 541-753-0515, calyx@calyxpress.com, www.calyxpress.com. 1986. Poetry, fiction, non-fiction. "Until future notice, Calyx Books is not accepting book manuscripts at this time." avg. press run 3.5M. Pub'd 2 titles 2005; expects 1 title 2006, 2 titles 2007. Discounts: trade schedule as per Consortium Book Sales & Dist. Poetry 110pp; fiction & prose 200pp. Reporting time: 6-12 months. Simultaneous submissions accepted: yes. Publishes 1-2% of manuscripts submitted. Payment: individually contracted. Copyrights for author. Subjects: Fiction, Homelessness, Literature (General), Multicultural, Poetry, Women.

CALYX: A Journal of Art and Literature by Women, Calyx Books, Beverly McFarland, Senior Editor, PO Box B, Corvallis, OR 97339, 541-753-9384, Fax 541-753-0515, calyx@calyxpress.com, www.calyxpress.com. 1976. Poetry, fiction, art, photos, reviews, parts-of-novels, non-fiction. *"Calyx* is the Major West Coast publication of its kind. Recently reviewed as 'undoubtedly...one of the best literary mags in the U.S.'—New Pages Press. (128 pages). Manuscript queries and submissions must be accompanied by a SASE. The journal is no longer open to submissions all year round. Open reading dates for journal submissions are 10/1-12/31 annually. Be sure to include brief bio statement with all submissions. Since 2001 *Calyx Journal* has sponsored an annual poetry contest, The Lois Cranston Memorial Poetry Prize. Winner receive $300 and publication in *Calyx Journal.* Submit up to 3 unpublished poems between March 1 and May 31 (inclusive) with a $15 reading fee. Please see *www.calyxpress.com* for guidelines." circ. 3.5M. 2/yr. Pub'd 2 issues 2005; expects 2 issues 2006, 2 issues 2007. sub. price $21 indiv., institutional & library $27 (subs are 3 issues but take 18 months to complete); International postaage add $21 per volume, Canada/Mexico postage add $11 per volume; per copy $9.50; sample $9.50 + $2 p/h. Back issues: send for list. Discounts: trade 3 copies 30%, 4-5 35%, 6+ 40%. 128pp. Reporting time: 6-12 months. Simultaneous submissions accepted: yes. Publishes 4-5% of manuscripts submitted. Payment: in copies and subscriptions, possible modest cash payment. Copyrighted, reverts to author. Pub's reviews: 15 in 2005. §Feminist criticism, reviews of books & films by women, autobiographies, literary or art books by woman. Ads: $550/$285/$150 1/4 page/75¢ classified. Subjects: Fiction, Literature (General), Poetry, Women.

CAMBRENSIS: THE SHORT STORY QUARTERLY MAGAZINE OF WALES, Arthur Smith, 41 Heol Fach, Cornelly, Bridgend, Mid-Glamorgan, CF334LN South Wales, United Kingdom, 01656-741-994. 1987. Fiction, art, cartoons. "Uses only short stories, under 2,500 words, by writers born or resident in Wales; no poetry used; cartoons/black & white artwork sharp-contrast used." circ. 500. 4/yr. Pub'd 4 issues 2005; expects 4 issues 2006, 4 issues 2007. sub. price £6; per copy £1.50; sample IRC. Back issues: £1.25. Discounts: 20%. 72pp. Reporting time: by return. Payment: none at present time, copies given. Copyrighted, reverts to author. Pub's reviews: 30 in 2005. §literary. Ads: £40/£20/£10 1/4 page.

Cambric Press dba Emerald House, Joel Rudinger, Publisher, 208 Ohio Street, Huron, OH 44839-1514. 1975. Poetry, fiction, non-fiction. "Self-publishing, book manufacturer." avg. press run 500-1M+. Pub'd 2 titles 2005; expects 2 titles 2006, 2 titles 2007. Discounts: 40% on bulk orders over 10; 30% under 10. 64-96pp. Reporting time: 4 weeks. Simultaneous submissions accepted: yes. Publishes 10% of manuscripts submitted. Payment: 100% to author first printing. Copyrights for author. Subjects: Biography, Futurism, Great Lakes, Novels, Poetry, Science Fiction.

Camel Press (see also DUST (From the Ego Trip)), James Hedges, Editor, Box 212, Needmore, PA 17238, 717-573-4526. 1984. Poetry, fiction, articles, non-fiction. "Autobiography, 1,000-2,500 words." avg. press run 700. Pub'd 1 title 2005; expects 1 title 2006, 1 title 2007. Discounts: on request. 20pp. Reporting time: 2 weeks. Simultaneous submissions accepted: yes. Publishes 5% of manuscripts submitted. Payment: 50 free copies, page charges may be requested from author. Copyrights for author. Subjects: Biography, History, Public Affairs.

CAMERA OBSCURA: Feminism, Culture, and Media Studies, Amelie Hastie, Editor; Constance Penley, Editor; Sasha Torres, Editor; Sharon Willis, Editor; Lynne Joyrich, Editor; Patricia White, Editor; Molly Moloney, Managing Editor, c/o Department of Film Studies, University of California, Santa Barbara, CA 93106-9430, 805-893-7069; fax 805-893-8630; e-Mail cameraobscura@filmstudies.ucsb.edu. 1976. Articles, photos, interviews, criticism, reviews, letters, non-fiction. "Duke University Press." circ. 3M. 3/yr. Pub'd 3 issues 2005; expects 3 issues 2006, 3 issues 2007. sub. price individual $30, student $20, institution $100 (print-only or e-only), institution $111 (print-plus-electronic), foreign postage: Canada add $9 plus GST; outside US/Canada + $12); per copy $33 institutions, $12 individuals. Back issues: volumes: $100 (institutions), single issues: $33 (institutions), $12 (individuals). Discounts: 40% bookstores. 200pp. Reporting time: 3-5 months. Simultaneous submissions accepted: no. Payment: none. Copyrighted, does not revert to author. Pub's reviews. §Film criticism. Ads: check with Duke University Press, Journals Division. Subjects: Electronics, Feminism, Gender Issues, Media, Race, Sex, Sexuality, Women.

Camino Bay Books, Ann Adams, 331 Old Blanco Road, Kendalia, TX 78027-1901, 830-336-3636, 800-463-8181. 1997. Non-fiction. avg. press run 5M. Expects 1-2 titles 2006, 1-2 titles 2007. Discounts: 1-4 books 20%, 5-99 40%, 100+ 50%. 250pp. Reporting time: 6 weeks. Payment: negotiable. Does not copyright for author. Subjects: Animals, Earth, Natural History, Philosophy.

Camp Colton, Kathleen Lundstrom, 30000 S Camp Colton Dr., Colton, OR 97017, 503-824-2267. 1983. Art, concrete art, non-fiction. "So far only in house, will consider outside material; glass art subjects." avg. press run 15M. Discounts: 33% booksellers, 50% distributors. 140pp. Reporting time: 1-2 months. Payment: negotiable. Copyrights for author. Subjects: Arts, Avant-Garde, Experimental Art, Crafts, Hobbies, How-To.

CANADIAN CHILDREN'S LITERATURE, Canadian Children's Press, Andrew Reimer, Dept. of English, University of Winnipeg, 515 Portage Ave., Winnipeg MB R3B 2E9, Canada, 519-824-4120 ext.

53189, Fax 519-837-1315, ccl@uoguelph.ca, http://www.uoguelph.ca/ccl/. 1975. Articles, interviews, criticism, reviews. "*CCL* publishes critical articles and in-depth reviews of Canadian books and other media for children and adolescents." circ. 900. 4/yr. Pub'd 4 issues 2005; expects 4 issues 2006, 4 issues 2007. sub. price $29 indiv., schools; $36 Postsecondary & other instit. (plus $10 postage outside Canada); per copy $10; sample $10 (plus $2.50 postage outside Canada). Back issues: prices available upon request. Discounts: none. 96pp. Reporting time: 6 months. Simultaneous submissions accepted: no. Publishes 40% of manuscripts submitted. Payment: 1 copy of issue. Copyrighted, reverts to author. Pub's reviews: 110 in 2005. §Canadian books, plays and videos written for children and adolescents. Ads: $250/$150/$85 1/4 page/$295 OBC/$275 IFC/20% discount for 4 consecutive ads. Subjects: Canada, Children, Youth, Criticism.

Canadian Children's Press (see also CANADIAN CHILDREN'S LITERATURE), 4th Floor, MacKinnon Building, University of Guelph, Guelph, Ontario N1G 2W1, Canada. 1975. Articles, interviews, criticism, reviews. avg. press run 1M. Discounts: none. 150pp. Reporting time: 6 months. Simultaneous submissions accepted: no. Publishes 10% of manuscripts submitted. Payment: negotiable.

Canadian Committee on Labour History (see also LABOUR/LE TRAVAIL), Bryan D. Palmer, Arts Publications, FM 2005, Memorial University, St. John's, NL A1C 5S7, Canada, 709-737-2144. 1971. Non-fiction. "Recent contributors: John Stanton, Cy Gonick, Ian McKay, Doug Smith, Gil Levine, D.P. Stephens, Margaret Hobbs, Joan Sangster, Errol Black, Tom Mitchell, and Bryan D. Palmer." avg. press run 750. Pub'd 1 title 2005; expects 2 titles 2006, 2 titles 2007. Discounts: 20% on orders over 5. 150-300pp. Reporting time: 6 months. Simultaneous submissions accepted: no. Publishes 25% of manuscripts submitted. Payment: variable. Does not copyright for author. Subjects: History, Labor.

Canadian Educators' Press, S. Deonarine, 100 City Centre Drive, PO Box 2094, Mississauga, ON L5B 3C6, Canada, 905-826-0578. 1995. Non-fiction. avg. press run 800. Pub'd 2 titles 2005; expects 5 titles 2006, 5 titles 2007. Discounts: depends on quantity. 250pp. Reporting time: 3 months. Simultaneous submissions accepted: no. Payment: 10% net sale. Copyrights for author. Subjects: Canada, Education, Management, Sociology, Textbooks, Textbooks.

CANADIAN JOURNAL OF COMMUNICATION, Kim Sawchuk, Editor; Richard K. Smith, Publisher, Canadian Centre for Studies in Publishing, Simon Fraser Univ., 515 West Hastings St., Vancouver BC V6B 5K3, Canada, (604) 291-5116. 1974. Articles, reviews. "3M words on communication and mass media." circ. 400 (plus online). 4/yr. Pub'd 4 issues 2005; expects 4 issues 2006. sub. price Individuals: print and online $60Can, $60US; online only $30Can, $30US; Institutions: print $100Can, $100US; online $90Can, $90US; print and online $125Can, $125US; per copy $25; sample $20. Back issues: $20. Discounts: none. 120-140pp. Reporting time: 3 months. Simultaneous submissions accepted: no. Publishes 35% of manuscripts submitted. Payment: none. Copyrighted, does not revert to author. Pub's reviews: 40 in 2005. §All areas of communication. Ads: write for information. Subjects: Canada, Communication, Journalism.

CANADIAN JOURNAL OF COUNSELLING, University of Calgary Press, Vivian Lalande, Editor, University of Calgary Press, 2500 University Drive NW, Calgary, AB T2N 1N4, Canada, 613-237-1099, toll-free 877-765-5565, Fax 613-237-9786, info@ccacc.ca, www.ccacc.ca/. 1967. Non-fiction. "*The Canadian Journal of Counselling* is a refereed, bilingual journal published quarterly for the Canadian Counselling Association. Published articles are of interest to counsellor educators as well as to practitioners working in private practice or in schools, community agencies, university and college counselling centres, and other institutions in which counselling psychology is practiced. Article topics include research reports, conceptual papers, innovative practices, professional issues commentaries, and critical summaries of research." circ. 2,350. 4/yr. Pub'd 4 issues 2005; expects 4 issues 2006, 4 issues 2007. sub. price $50 CAD individual Canadian nonmembers, $50 USD individual international nonmembers, $85 CAD Canadian institutions, $85 USD international institutions; per copy $15. 100pp. Pub's reviews. Ads: contact association for details.

CANADIAN JOURNAL OF LATIN AMERICAN AND CARIBBEAN STUDIES/Revue canadienne des etudes latino-americaines et caraibes, University of Calgary Press, V. Armony, Editor, CALACS, CCASLS SB-115, Concordia University, 1455 de Maisonneuve Ouest, Montreal, QC H3G 1M8, Canada, calacs@concordia.ca. 1976. Articles, reviews. "*The Canadian Journal of Latin American and Caribbean Studies* is published for the Canadian Assn. for Latin American and Caribbean Studies. *CJLACS* is a multidisciplinary, refereed journal. Articles are accepted in four languages - English, French, Spanish, and Portuguese." circ. 400. 2/yr. Pub'd 2 issues 2005; expects 2 issues 2006, 2 issues 2007. sub. price $40 individual, $23 student, $60 institutions. 150pp. Publishes 25% of manuscripts submitted. Payment: none. Copyrighted, does not revert to author. Pub's reviews: 9 in 2005. §All fields of scholarly Latin American and Caribbean studies. Ads: write for details. Subjects: Caribbean, Latin America.

CANADIAN JOURNAL OF PHILOSOPHY, University of Calgary Press, M. Stingl, Administrative Editor, University of Calgary Press, Univ. of Calgary, 2500 University Dr. N.W., Calgary, Alberta T2N 1N4, Canada, 403-220-3514, Fax 403-282-0085, ucpmail@ucalgary.ca. 1971. Articles, reviews. "Publishes philosophical work of high quality in any field of philosophy." circ. 900. 5/yr. Pub'd 5 issues 2005; expects 5 issues 2006, 5 issues 2007. sub. price $25 indiv., $50 instit., $15 student, add GST in Canada; outside Canada, prices in US dollars; per copy $9. Back issues: back volume of 4 issues $30. 150pp. Reporting time: 2 months. Payment: none. Copyrighted, does not revert to author. Pub's reviews: 4 in 2005. §Philosophy. Ads: write for info. Subject: Philosophy.

CANADIAN JOURNAL OF PROGRAM EVALUATION, University of Calgary Press, B. Cousins, Editor, Canadian Evaluation Society, 1485 Laperriere Avenue, Ottawa, ON K1Z 7S8, Canada, 613-725-2526, Fax 613-729-6206, ces@thewillowgroup.com. 1986. Articles, criticism, reviews. "Publishes all aspects of the theory and practice of evaluation including research and practice notes." circ. 1.8M. 2/yr plus occasional special issue. Pub'd 3 issues 2005; expects 2 issues 2006, 3 issues 2007. sub. price Indiv. $110 Canada; outside Canada price in U.S. dollars; libraries $145 Canada, outside Canada price in US dollars, $40 full time students, seniors (60+) $57.50; GST included; per copy $11 + G.S.T. Canada. 150pp. Reporting time: 2 months. Payment: none. Copyrighted, does not revert to author. Pub's reviews: 6 in 2005. §Evaluation of programs in all fields. Ads: write for info. Subject: Public Affairs.

Canadian Library Association (see also FELICITER), Beverly A. Bard, 328 Frank Street, Ottawa, Ontario K2P 0X8, Canada, 613-232-9625 X322, fax: 613-563-9895, www.cla.ca. 1946. Non-fiction. avg. press run 250. Expects 2 titles 2006, 2 titles 2007. Discounts: bulk only. 200pp. Reporting time: 6 months. Simultaneous submissions accepted: no. Publishes 75% of manuscripts submitted. Payment: 10%. Copyright varies. Subject: Libraries.

CANADIAN LITERATURE, E.M. Kroller, University of British Columbia, Buchanan E158, 1866 Main Mall, Vancouver, B.C. V6T 1Z1, Canada, 604-822-2780, fax 604-822-5504. 1959. Poetry, criticism, reviews. "Criticism and reviews focus primarily on Canadian writers. All publication press releases can be sent to cl.reviews@ubc.ca." circ. 1.5M. 4/yr. Pub'd 3 issues 2005; expects 4 issues 2006, 4 issues 2007. sub. price indiv. $45, institution $60 plus $20 postage (outside Canada); per copy $15; sample $15-25. Back issues: may be obtained from Journal. Discounts: $2 for agencies. 192-208pp. Reporting time: 3 months. Publishes 10% of manuscripts submitted. Payment: none. Copyrighted, copyright remains with journal. Pub's reviews: 100-120 in 2005. §Canadian writers and writing. Ads: $300/$400/$250. Subjects: Canada, Criticism, Literary Review, Poetry.

CANADIAN MONEYSAVER, Dale L. Ennis, Box 370, Bath, Ontario K0H 1G0, Canada, www.canadian-moneysaver.ca, moneyinfo@canadianmoneysaver.ca. 1981. Articles, interviews, non-fiction. circ. 32.8M. 9/yr. Pub'd 10 issues 2005; expects 9 issues 2006, 9 issues 2007. sub. price Canada $21.35, Elsewhere $75, online $21.35; per copy $3.95; sample $3.95. Back issues: $3.95. Discounts: up to 50% off for large orders (100+). 44pp. Reporting time: 3 weeks. Publishes 95% of manuscripts submitted. Payment: negotiable. Copyrighted, reverts to author. Pub's reviews: 25-30 in 2005. §Finance, money management, investment, consumer savings, tax planning, financial and retirement planning. Ads: US$4,000/$3,000. Subjects: Business & Economics, Consumer, Finances, Real Estate, Self-Help, Taxes.

CANADIAN REVIEW OF AMERICAN STUDIES, Marie Corrigan, University of Toronto Press, 5201 Dufferin Street, North York, ON M3H 5T8, Canada. 1970. Articles, criticism, reviews, non-fiction. "The journal publishes essays, review essays and shorter reviews whose purpose is the multi- and inter-disciplinary analysis and understanding of the culture, both past and present, of the United States - and of the relations between the cultures of the U.S. and Canada." circ. 475. 3/yr. Pub'd 3 issues 2005; expects 3 issues 2006, 3 issues 2007. 230pp. Reporting time: 2 months. Copyrighted, does not revert to author. Pub's reviews: 29 in 2005. §All fields of American studies. Ads: write for information. Subjects: Americana, History, Politics, Sociology.

CANADIAN WOMAN STUDIES/les cahiers de la femme, Luciana Ricciutelli, Editor-In-Chief, 212 Founders College, York Univ., 4700 Keele Street, Toronto, Ontario M3J 1P3, Canada, 416-736-5356, fax 416-736-5765, e-mail cwscf@yorku.ca. 1978. Poetry, fiction, articles, art, photos, cartoons, interviews, reviews, non-fiction. "We do not publish sexist, racist, homophobic, or any other discriminatory material. Length of articles: 10 typed, double-spaced pages." circ. 3M. 4/yr. Pub'd 4 issues 2005; expects 4 issues 2006, 4 issues 2007. sub. price $38.52 indiv. (Cdn), $53.50 instit. (Cdn), add $20 outside Canada; per copy $10; sample $5. Back issues: usually $5 per issue unless out of print. 156pp. Reporting time: 6 months. Simultaneous submissions accepted: no. Publishes 10% of manuscripts submitted. Payment: complimentary copy of issue in which work appears. Copyrighted, reverts to author. Pub's reviews: 50 in 2005. §Women's studies, women's issues, feminism, literary works and criticism. Ads: contact for rates. Subjects: Feminism, Women.

CANDELABRUM POETRY MAGAZINE, Red Candle Press, M.L. McCarthy, 1 Chatsworth Court, Outram Rd., Southsea PO5 1RA, England, tel: 02392 753696, rcp@poetry7.fsnet.co.uk, www.members.tri-pod.com/redcandlepress. 1970. Poetry. "CPM is a formalist poetry magazine, but good quality free verse is not excluded. Authors keep the copyright. We send the usual British copyright copies." circ. 1M. 2/yr. Pub'd 2 issues 2005; expects 2 issues 2006, 2 issues 2007. Subscription to Volume 12 (2005-7) £15: Us $30. US subscription in bills only, to avoid the bank charge; price per copy £3, US$6 in bills. 40pp. Reporting time: 1-2 months. Simultaneous submissions accepted: no. Payment: 1 free copy, no cash payment. Copyrighted, reverts to author. Ads: £20/£10 (US $40/$20 in bills) for A5 flysheet insertion. Subject: Poetry.

Candlestick Publishing, David Alter, PO Box 39241, San Antonio, TX 78218-1241. 1988. Non-fiction. Pub'd 2 titles 2005; expects 2 titles 2006, 1 title 2007. Discounts: library editions 30%, paperbacks 50%. Simultaneous submissions accepted: yes. Publishes 10% of manuscripts submitted. Subjects: Christianity, History, Human Rights, Libertarian.

THE CANNON'S MOUTH, Greg Cox, 22 Margaret Grove, Harborne, Birmingham B17 9JH, United Kingdom, [+44] 121 449 3866. Poetry, articles, art, photos, interviews, criticism, reviews, long-poems. "The Cannon's Mouth is the quarterly journal of the Cannon Poets who meet monthly at the mac, Cannon Hill Park, Birmimgham, UK. We publish poetry submitted by members and non members. We welcome original material that we think our readership will find useful, amusing and/or of interest. Regular contributors include John Allcock and Don Barnard [current poet Laureate of Birmingham UK] We regret that we are not usually able to pay for material published." circ. 1200. 4/yr. Pub'd 4 issues 2005; expects 4 issues 2006, 4 issues 2007. sub. price £10.50; per copy £3.00; sample free. Back issues: £3.00. Discounts: over 10 copies £2.50 per copy plus plus cost of delivery. 56pp. Reporting time: up to 3 months. Simultaneous submissions accepted: Yes. Publishes 25% of manuscripts submitted. Payment: Usually nil. Copyrighted, reverts to author. Pub's reviews: approx. 10 in 2005. §Anything related to poetry. Ads: quarter A5 5/Half A5 10/Full A5 15/Double A5 25/ Back Cover 30. Subjects: Creativity, Criticism, England, English, Haiku, Humor, Inspirational, Poetry, Writers/Writing.

Canonymous Press, Daniel Smith, PO Box 1478, Las Cruces, NM 88004-1478, e-mail press@canon-ymous.com, www.canonymous.com. 1992. avg. press run 100-400. Pub'd 3 titles 2005.

•**Cantadora Press (see also COGNITIO: A Graduate Humanities Journal),** Russell James, 5406 Persimmon Hollow Rd., Milton, FL 32583-6700. 2002. Articles, non-fiction. "Publisher of masters theses, local history books, genealogy books related to Florida, military history books, and peer-reviewed English-language hardcopy academic humanities journals." avg. press run 100. Expects 6 titles 2006, 10 titles 2007. Discounts: 10% discount to distributors, agents, jobbers, bookstores, wholesalers, retailers. 50pp. Reporting time: 1 day. Simultaneous submissions accepted: No. Publishes 90% of manuscripts submitted. Payment: 15%. Copyrights for author. Subjects: African-American, The Americas, Bibliography, Catholic, Civil Rights, Classical Studies, English, Ethics, Florida, Genealogy, Military, Veterans, Native American, Non-Fiction, Philosophy, Political Science.

•**Cantarabooks LLC,** Cantara Christopher, 204 East 11th Street 171, New York, NY 10003, 917.674.7560, editor@cantarabooks.com, www.cantarabooks.com. 2005. Poetry, fiction, satire, criticism, letters, plays, non-fiction. "Cantarabooks: n, pl. Playful-serious works of fiction, nonfiction and poetry that explore the dark and light of human relationships. Our authors for 2006: John Edward Gill, Michael Matheny, Vicki Miller, Jason Shamai, Stephen Gyllenhaal." avg. press run 500. Expects 3 titles 2006, 7 titles 2007. Discounts: 30-50% "Reading Group" discount in lots of 10 on selected titles. Includes reading guide and author Q&A. For 2006-2007: Inquire for Quality Time by Michael Matheny and Claptrap by Stephen Gyllenhaal. Reporting time: 2 months. Simultaneous submissions accepted: Yes. Publishes 2% of manuscripts submitted. Payment: 40% of net after production/distribution costs on third-party sales; 40% of retail on direct website sales of ebooks. Does not copyright for author. Subjects: Cities, Counter-Culture, Alternatives, Communes, Essays, Fiction, Gender Issues, Global Affairs, Humanism, Memoirs, Movies, Novels, Relationships, Short Stories, Theatre.

•**Capalo Press,** Carone Sturm, 3705 Arctic PMB 2571, Anchorage, AK 99503, 907-322-7105. Non-fiction. "The kind of work we publish is mainly alternative, evidence-based treatments dealing with substance abuse. The editorial mission is to get this crucial research out to the public, who unfortunately, are largely unaware of most of their options. Some of our recent contributors our Roberta Jewell, author of My Way Out, and Melanie Solomon, author of AA-Not the Only Way; Your One Stop Resource Guide to 12-Step Alternatives." Subjects: Alcohol, Alcoholism, Alternative Medicine, Hypnosis, Self-Help.

THE CAPE ROCK, Harvey Hecht, English Dept, Southeast Missouri State Univ., Cape Girardeau, MO 63701, 314-651-2500. 1964. Poetry, photos. "Our criterion for selection is the quality of the work, not the bibliography of the author. We consider poems of almost any style on almost any subject and favor poems under 75 lines. Each submission should have the author's name and complete address, preferably in the upper right hand corner. A self-addressed, stamped envelope (SASE) is required to guarantee return. We do not read submissions April through August. We feature the work of a single photographer in each issue; submit 20-25 thematically organized 5 x 7 B & W glossies. Submissions, subscriptions, and queries should be addressed to *The Cape Rock*, Harvey Hecht, Editor." circ. 600. 2/yr. Pub'd 2 issues 2005; expects 2 issues 2006. sub. price $10; per copy $6; sample $4. Back issues: $5. Discounts: 25% off on orders of 20 or more (our cost plus postage). 64pp. Reporting time: 2-4 months. Payment: $100 for photography in each issue; other payment in copies. Copyrighted, rights to contents released to authors and artists upon request, subject only to their giving credit to *The Cape Rock* whenever and wherever else the work is placed. *The Cape Rock* retains reprint rights. No ads. Subjects: Photography, Poetry.

THE CAPILANO REVIEW, Sharon Thesen, Editor; Carol Hamshaw, Managing Editor, 2055 Purcell Way, North Vancouver, B.C. V7J 3H5, Canada, 604-984-1712. 1972. Poetry, fiction, art, photos, interviews, criticism, parts-of-novels, long-poems, collages, plays, concrete art. circ. 1M. 3/yr. Pub'd 3 issues 2005; expects 3 issues 2006, 3 issues 2007. sub. price $25; per copy $9; sample $9. Back issues: $7 for regular back issues, $10-20 for special issues. Discounts: 25% to bookstores. 120pp. Reporting time: 4 months. Simultaneous submissions accepted: no. Publishes 3% of manuscripts submitted. Payment: $50-200 maximum. Copyrighted, reverts to author. Ads: $150/$75/$50 1/3 page. Subjects: Arts, Avant-Garde, Experimental Art, Canada, Experimental, Literary Review, Poetry, Post Modern, Race, Translation, Visual Arts, Writers/Writing.

Card Publishing, Gary Grossman, 3450 Sacramento Street #405, San Francisco, CA 94118-1914, cardpublishing.com. 2002. Non-fiction. avg. press run 5000. Pub'd 1 title 2005; expects 2 titles 2006, 4 titles 2007. 300pp. Copyrights for author.

Career Advancement Center, Inc., Arthur VanDam, PO Box 436, Woodmere, NY 11598-0436, 516-374-1387, Fax 516-374-1175, caradvctr@aol.com, www.smallbusinessadvice.com. 1991. Non-fiction. "Personal finance, business and career development, mass market appeal, user-friendly, marketing and sales." avg. press run 2M. Pub'd 1 title 2005; expects 3 titles 2006, 3 titles 2007. Discounts: competitive, 40% STOP order. 100pp. Reporting time: 3 months. Simultaneous submissions accepted: yes. Publishes 5% of manuscripts submitted. Payment: 6-10% of retail price. Copyrights for author. Subjects: Business & Economics, Finances, How-To.

THE CARETAKER GAZETTE, Thea K. Dunn, PO Box 4005, Bergheim, TX 78004-4005, 830-336-3939, www.caretaker.org. 1983. Articles, photos, cartoons, interviews, reviews, letters, news items, non-fiction. "Articles about property caretaking, homesteading, estate management, RV living, caretaker profiles." circ. 12M. 6/yr. Pub'd 6 issues 2005; expects 6 issues 2006, 6 issues 2007. sub. price $29.95; per copy $6; sample $6. Back issues: $6. Discounts: none. 16pp. Reporting time: 1 month. Simultaneous submissions accepted: yes. Publishes 40% of manuscripts submitted. Payment: no. Copyrighted, reverts to author. Pub's reviews: 6 in 2005. §Conservation, environment, property caretaking, RV living. Ads: 65¢ per word classifieds. Subjects: Agriculture, Employment, Environment.

Caribbean Books-Panama, Warren White A, Publisher; Frankie White Ann, Editor, Apdo. 0301-01249, Colon, Republic of Panama, +507-433-0349, http://www.caribbeanbookspub.com, publisher@caribbeanbooks-pub.com. 2003. Fiction, non-fiction. "Caribbean Books is looking for well written books in most genre. The well crafted story or non fiction is more important than the genre." Pub'd 2 titles 2005; expects 12 titles 2006, 24 titles 2007. Discounts: 30%. 300-400pp. Reporting time: 1week-1 month. Simultaneous submissions accepted: Yes. Payment: negotiable. Copyrights negotiable. Subjects: Current Affairs, Earth, Natural History, Fantasy, Fiction, Indigenous Cultures, Mystery, Myth, Mythology, Non-Fiction, Novels, Political Science, Politics, Religion, Science Fiction, Shipwrecks, Storytelling.

THE CARIBBEAN WRITER, Marvin Williams, University of the Virgin Islands, RR 1, Box 10,000, Kingshill, St. Croix, VI 00850, Phone: 340-692-4152, Fax: 340-692-4026, e-mail: qmars@uvi.edu, website: www.TheCaribbeanWriter.com. 1987. Poetry, fiction, interviews, reviews, parts-of-novels, plays, non-fiction. "*The Caribbean Writer* is an international literary anthology with a Caribbean focus. The Caribbean should be central to the work or the work should reflect a Caribbean heritage, experience or perspective." circ. 1.2M. 1/yr. Pub'd 1 issue 2005; expects 1 issue 2006, 1 issue 2007. sub. price $25 + p/h (2 Year Individual), $40 + p/h (2 Year Institutional); per copy $15 + $4 p/h; sample $7 + $4 p/h. Back issues: same. Call for discount information. 304pp. Reporting time: authors of accepted mss are notified within 3 months. Simultaneous submissions accepted: yes. Publishes 20% of manuscripts submitted. Payment: 2 copies. Copyrighted, reverts to author. Pub's reviews: 30 in 2005. §Caribbean fiction, poetry, or related reference materials. Ads: $250 (Full Page) / $150 (Half Page) / $100 1/4 page. Subject: Caribbean.

Carnegie Mellon University Press, Sharon Dilworth, Carnegie Mellon University, English Department, Pittsburgh, PA 15213, 412-268-6446.

Carnifex Press, Armand Rosamilia, PO Box 1686, Ormond Beach, FL 32175, armand@carnifexpress.net, http://www.carnifexpress.net. 2004. Fiction. "small press publisher of Epic Fantasy and Horror. Publishes novella-length (20,000 - 50,000 word) trade paperbacks and chapbooks." avg. press run 2000. Pub'd 3 titles 2005; expects 9 titles 2006, 9 titles 2007. 132pp. Reporting time: 6-8 weeks. Simultaneous submissions accepted: No. Publishes 5% of manuscripts submitted. Payment: 5 cents per word for themed anthologies; 10% royalty (no advance) on novellas. Copyrights for author. Subjects: Comics, Fantasy, Fiction, Horror, H.P. Lovecraft, Myth, Mythology, Short Stories, J.R.R. Tolkien, Zines.

Carolina Academic Press, Keith Sipe; Bob Conrow, Acquisitions Editor; Taylor Arnold, Acquisitions Editor, 700 Kent Street, Durham, NC 27701, 919-489-7486, fax:919-493-5668. 1976. "Legal, medical, and scholarly titles." avg. press run 1.5M. Pub'd 28 titles 2005; expects 30 titles 2006. Discounts: sliding scale for retailers. 450pp. Reporting time: 6 months. Payment: various. Copyrights for author. Subject: Medicine.

THE CAROLINA QUARTERLY, Amy Weldon, General Editor, CB# 3520 Greenlaw Hall, Univ of N. Carolina, Chapel Hill, NC 27599-3520, 919-962-0244, Fax 919-962-3520. 1948. Poetry, fiction, art, photos, reviews, long-poems. "Looking for well-crafted poems and stories. We do not read during May-July. Wood Award ($500) is given to author of best short story or poem *The Carolina Quarterly* publishes each year. Only writers without major publications are eligible for Award." circ. 900. 3/yr. Pub'd 3 issues 2005; expects 3 issues 2006, 3 issues 2007. sub. price $12 indiv., $15 instit.; per copy $5; sample $5 (postage paid). Back issues: $5. Discounts: 20% local stores, agent 10%. 88-100pp. Reporting time: 4-6 months. Simultaneous submissions accepted: no. Publishes 1% of manuscripts submitted. Payment: 3 copies. Copyrighted, reverts to author. Pub's reviews: 8 in 2005. §Fiction, poetry, non-fiction. Ads: $80/$40. Subjects: Fiction, Literature (General), Poetry.

Carolina Wren Press/Lollipop Power Books, Andrea Selch, President; Veronica Noechel, Vice President; Lesley Landis, Art Director, 120 Morris Street, Durham, NC 27701, 919-560-2738; www.carolinawren-press.org. 1976. Poetry, fiction, letters, non-fiction. "Our goal is to publish high-quality, non-stereotyping literature for adults and children that is both intellectually and artistically challenging. Our publishing priorities are: works which are written by women and/or minorities, works which deal with issues of concern to those same groups, works which are innovative. Please send a sample of writing (20pp.), not whole mss. or query letters. Include SASE." avg. press run 1000 copies. Pub'd 1 title 2005; expects 2 titles 2006, 1 title 2007. Discounts: 40% to bookstores after 5 copies, (1-4 20%). 150pp. Reporting time: 6 months for regular submissions; longer for contests. Simultaneous submissions are accepted; please indicate status and let us know immediately if your work is accepted elsewhere. Publishes .1% of manuscripts submitted. Payment: l0% of printrun. Copyright may stay with author. Subjects: Asian-American, Black, Chicano/a, Children, Youth, Disease, Fiction, Gay, Lesbianism, Mental Health, Multicultural, Native American, Poetry, Prose, U.S. Hispanic, Women.

Carousel Press, Carole T. Meyers, Editor & Publisher; Gene Meyers, Sales Manager, PO Box 6038, Berkeley, CA 94706-0038, 510-527-5849, carous4659@aol.com, www.carousel-press.com. 1976. Non-fiction. "We are interested in general round-up travel guides, 200-300 pages." avg. press run 5-10M. Pub'd 1 title 2005; expects 1 title 2006, 1 title 2007. Discounts: trade, bulk, jobber 40% 5-12 books; 41% 13-24; 42% 25-49; 43% 50-99; library 10% prepaid; STOP orders 20% disc. + $3.50 shipping prepaid. 350pp. Reporting time: 4 weeks, include return postage; or via e-mail. Simultaneous submissions accepted: no. Publishes 1% of manuscripts submitted. Payment: royalties. Copyrights for author. Subjects: California, Cities, Co-ops, Europe, Family, Games, Reprints, San Francisco.

Carpe Diem Publishing, William A. Conner, Jessica E. Griffin, 1705 E. 17th Street, #400, The Dalles, OR 97058, 541-296-1552, waconner@aol.com. 1993. Fiction. avg. press run 3M-10M. Expects 1 title 2006, 6 titles 2007. Reporting time: 3 months to 1 year. Simultaneous submissions accepted: yes. Payment: negotiable, upon acceptance. Copyrights for author. Subjects: Anarchist, Arthurian, Atheism, Birth, Birth Control, Population, Celtic, Comics, Computers, Calculators, Counter-Culture, Alternatives, Communes, Creativity, Magic, Martial Arts, Music, Pacific Northwest, Sex, Sexuality, Tarot.

Carrier Pigeon Press, Ramon Sender Barayon, PO Box 460141, San Francisco, CA 94146-0141, 415-821-2090. 1992. Non-fiction. "Books about intentional communities, religious sects, experimental social groups, memoirs of members and ex-members of such groups." avg. press run 600. Expects 4 titles 2006, 4 titles 2007. Discounts: 40% trade or jobber. 350pp. Reporting time: 6 weeks. Simultaneous submissions accepted: no. Publishes 1% of manuscripts submitted. Payment: 10-12%. Subjects: Autobiography, Christianity, Community, Counter-Culture, Alternatives, Communes, Cults, Sociology, Women.

Carol Anne Carroll Communications, Carol Anne Carroll, PO Box 410333, San Francisco, CA 94141-0333, 415-839-6310, WritingandBeyond@aol.com. 1998. Non-fiction. "Started in 1998, Carol Anne Carroll Communications expanded into publishing in 2001. Books published to date cover home business and real estate. CACC publishes very few manuscripts, and to date, all have been based on personal referrals. Unsolicited materials will not be returned and be destroyed. BRIEF email queries will be responded to as appropriate.CACC's primary focus remains helping other authors self-publish, and providing the writing, editing, marketing, and administrative support needed to achieve self-publishing goals." avg. press run varies, 500+. Expects 2 titles 2006, 2 titles 2007. Discounts: based on quantity, contact publisher. 150-200pp. Reporting time: varies. Payment: varies, % to outright purchase. Copyrights for author. Subjects: Business & Economics, Careers, Real Estate, Reference.

Cascada Corporation / Scherf Books, MegaGrace Books, Dietmar Scherf, Executive Editor, PO Box 80180, Las Vegas, NV 89180-0180, ds@scherf.com, www.scherf.com, www.megagrace.com, www.cascada.cc. 1990.

Non-fiction. "All materials have to be of sound moral character and in essence need to be based on the biblical Pure Grace message (you can find some basic information and explanations regarding the Pure Grace message at www.megagrace.com). DOES NOT ACCEPT UNSOLICITED queries/submissions at this time. Publishes first-time authors. Solid and sound grammar is important." avg. press run 2M-5M. Pub'd 1-2 titles 2005; expects 1-2 titles 2006, 1-2 titles 2007. Discounts: 55% (free s/h within USA) if bought directly from MegaGrace, (single copy orders welcome-same discount); prepayment required. Cloth 224pp, paper 396pp. Reporting time: up to 6 months. Simultaneous submissions accepted: yes. Publishes less than 0.1% of manuscripts submitted. Payment: varies (approx. 5-8% of sold books). Does not copyright for author. Subjects: Christianity, Inspirational, Non-Fiction.

•**Casperian Books LLC,** Kimberley Bernhardt, PO Box 161026, Sacramento, CA 95816-1026. 2006. Fiction. "Most types of fiction, with particular interest in contemporary realism, family saga, historical fiction (especially stories set in the ancient world), satire, science fiction, dystopian fiction, alternate histories, edgy urban fiction, ethnic/multicultural fiction, gay/lesbian fiction, gen x/noir, and books that have strong race/class/politics/religion/sexuality/gender themes. Not interested in children's picture books. Will consider non-fiction that is both accessible and at least marginally falls within our general interests, which include in no particular order and without stating on which side of the fence we're sitting: (ancient) history, punk rock, popular/street culture, gay/lesbian issues, drug policy, social policy, sociology, psychology, anthropology/archaeology, philosophy/critical theory, film, and religion." Expects 2 titles 2006, 4 titles 2007. Reporting time: 2 weeks. Simultaneous submissions accepted: Yes. Payment: 66% of net receipts. Does not copyright for author. Subjects: Beat, Brontes, Charles Bukowski, Bob Dylan, Fiction, James Joyce, Kafka, Jack Kerouac, Literature (General), Henry Miller, Novels, Prose, Satire, Science Fiction.

Cassandra Press, Inc., Fred Rubenfeld, President, PO Box 228, Boulder, CO 80306, 303 444 2590. 1985. Non-fiction. "We publish New Age and metaphysical and political tyranny and holistic health books. I like to see the full manuscript before making a final decision, although this isn't necessarily true with an established author. We are now actively looking for new titles to expand next year. We are not accepting novels or children's books." avg. press run 8M-12M. Pub'd 3 titles 2005. Discounts: 40% to stores, 1-3 copies 20%. 150-230pp. Reporting time: 1-2 months. Payment: varies. Copyrights for author if asked. Subjects: Astrology, Birth, Birth Control, Population, Counter-Culture, Alternatives, Communes, Ecology, Foods, Health, How-To, Occult, Politics, Spiritual.

CATAMARAN SAILOR, Ram Press, Mary Wells, Rick White, PO Box 2060, Key Largo, FL 33037, 05-451-3287, Fax 305-453-0255, rick@catsailor.comt, www.catsailor.com. 1995. Articles, photos, cartoons, interviews, satire, criticism, reviews, letters, news items, non-fiction. "40-60 pages - newsprint." circ. 20M. 10/yr. Pub'd 10 issues 2005; expects 10 issues 2006, 10 issues 2007. sub. price $10; per copy $1; sample free. Back issues: $1. Discounts: none. 60pp. Reporting time: 60 days. Simultaneous submissions accepted: yes. Publishes 90% of manuscripts submitted. Payment: none. Copyrighted, reverts to author. Pub's reviews: 3 in 2005. §Catamaran, multihull sailing. Ads: $150$90/$75 1/3 page/$60 1/4 page/$25 business card/$10 classified. Subject: Sports, Outdoors.

Cattpigg Press, Cal Beauregard, Joedi Johnson, PO Box 565, Billings, MT 59103, 406-248-4875, e-mail starbase@mcn.net, website www.mcn.net/~starbase/dawn. 1994. Photos, non-fiction. avg. press run 1-2M. Pub'd 1 title 2005; expects 2 titles 2006, 1 title 2007. 100pp. Reporting time: 3-5 weeks. Publishes 10% of manuscripts submitted. Copyrights for author. Subjects: Antiques, Collectibles, Crafts, Hobbies.

•**Cavalier Press,** Michelle De La Rosa, P O Box 6437, Falls Church, VA 22040, http://www.cavalierpress.com. 2002. Fiction. "Cavalier Press grew out of a conviction that Gays, Lesbians, Bisexuals, and Transgendered people need a source of quality fiction." avg. press run 1000. Pub'd 5 titles 2005; expects 8 titles 2006, 8 titles 2007. Discounts: 40-55%. 400pp. Reporting time: Acknowledge submission within 24 hours and decision to publish or not in 60 days. Simultaneous submissions accepted: Yes. Subjects: Drama, Fantasy, Fiction, Gay, Lesbianism, Mystery.

Cave Books, Richard Watson, Editor, 2870 Sol Terra Lane, Missoula, MT 59803-1803, 314-862-7646. 1980. Fiction, non-fiction. "Only prose (adult non-fiction, fiction) concerning caves, karst, and speleology. Must be authentic, knowledgable, and realistic." avg. press run 1.5M. Pub'd 4 titles 2005; expects 4 titles 2006, 4 titles 2007. Discounts: 40% trade. 200pp. Reporting time: 3 months. Simultaneous submissions accepted: yes. Publishes 5% of manuscripts submitted. Payment: 10%. Copyrights for author. Subjects: Anthropology, Archaelogy, Autobiography, Biology, Caves, Conservation, Fiction, Geology, New Mexico, Non-Fiction, Novels, Sports, Outdoors.

‡**Wm Caxton Ltd,** Kubet Luchterhand, PO Box 220, Ellison Bay, WI 54210-0220. 1986. Poetry, criticism, letters, non-fiction. "We have 25 titles in print, 2 more in press now, and a total of 4 more in various stages of editing/typesetting/proofing. We publish book-length manuscripts, and reprint some books (9 of our titles so far); most titles so far are non-fiction, though we have published 4 books of poetry and are looking for more

good poetry. We're especially interested in northern mid-West material of all kinds; we have two philosophy titles; one book about theatre technique (*Chamber Theatre* by Robert Breen); a reprint of a classic Wisconsin economic history book (*Empire In Pine* by Robert Fries). In a phrase, we will consider publishing any book that is actually *about* something.'' avg. press run 700-2M. Pub'd 2 titles 2005; expects 6 titles 2006, 6 titles 2007. Discounts: Trade bookstores 40%, returnable for credit only; textbooks 20% returnable for credit only for orders of five copies or more; returns must be in saleable condition, unmarked in any way, returned within 6 months of invoice date. 230pp. Reporting time: 1-6 months, depending upon season. Payment: varies widely; prefer subvention coupled with much higher than average royalty structure on first printing, guarantee to keep in print for 5 years, high but not as high as original on later printings. Copyrights for author. Subjects: Midwest, Non-Fiction.

The Caxton Press, Wayne Cornell, General Editor, 312 Main Street, Caldwell, ID 83605, 208-459-7421. 1895. Non-fiction. ''Books around 40,000 words up, unless largely photo.'' avg. press run 5M. Pub'd 5 titles 2005; expects 6 titles 2006, 6 titles 2007. Discounts: 1-24 40% 25+ 45%. 236pp. Reporting time: 60-90 days. Simultaneous submissions accepted: yes. Payment: 10% of list. Copyrights for author. Subjects: Americana, Non-Fiction.

CC. Marimbo, Randy Fingland, PO Box 933, Berkeley, CA 94701-0933. 1996. Poetry. ''CC. Marimbo is currently publishing minichaps which are 5-1/2 X 4-1/4, handsewn, with a unique cover design/package. The object is to publish/promote underpublished writers in an accessible and artistic format.'' avg. press run 26-150. Pub'd 1 title 2005; expects 2 titles 2006, 2 titles 2007. Discounts: 1 copy, no discount; 2-5 copies, 30%; 6 or more copies, 40%. Wholesale terms available upon request. 40pp. Reporting time: 4-6 weeks. Simultaneous submissions accepted as long as it's up front. Publishes 5% of manuscripts submitted. Payment: yes, generally 10% of cover price. Copyrights for author. Subject: Poetry.

Cedar Hill Books (see also CEDAR HILL REVIEW), Maggie Jaffe, Senior Editor; Esther Rodriguez, Assistant Editor, 3730 Arnold Avenue, San Diego, CA 92104, www.cedarhillbooks.org. 1987. Poetry, fiction, art, reviews, concrete art, non-fiction. ''We have suspended all book projects.'' avg. press run 500. Pub'd 2 titles 2005; expects 3 titles 2006, 3 titles 2007. Discounts: 40%-55%. 100pp. Reporting time: 3-6 months. Simultaneous submissions accepted: Yes. Publishes 10% of manuscripts submitted. Payment: Author receives 250 copies of the initial print run. Copyrights for author. Subjects: Arts, Book Reviewing, California, Fiction, Latin America, Literary Review, Native American, Poetry, Politics, Prison, Prose, Short Stories, Translation, Vietnam, War.

CEDAR HILL REVIEW, Cedar Hill Books, Maggie Jaffe, 3730 Arnold Avenue, San Diego, CA 92104, www.cedarhillbooks.org. 1987. Poetry, fiction, art, reviews, concrete art. ''We have suspended Cedar Hill Review.'' circ. 400. 2/yr. Expects 1 issue 2006, 1 issue 2007. sub. price $40; per copy $15; sample $15. Back issues: inquire. Discounts: 40-55%. 100pp. Reporting time: 3-6 months. Simultaneous submissions accepted: Yes. Publishes 10% of manuscripts submitted. Payment: 1 conpy. Copyrighted, reverts to author. Pub's reviews. §Poetry, Short Stories, and Concrete-Art. Ads: Full page=$150/Half page=$80. Subjects: Anthology, Arts, California, Fiction, Latin America, Literary Review, Native American, Non-Fiction, Novels, Poetry, Prison, Prose, Reviews, Writers/Writing.

CELEBRATION, Prospect Press, William Sullivan, 2707 Lawina Road, Baltimore, MD 21216-1608, (410) 542-8785. 1975. Poetry. circ. 100. 1/yr. Expects 1 issue 2006, 1 issue 2007. price per copy $3.00; sample $3.00. Back issues: $3.00. 25pp. Simultaneous submissions accepted: No. Publishes 5% of manuscripts submitted. Copyrighted. Pub's reviews: none in 2005. Subject: Poetry.

Celebrity Profiles Publishing, Richard Grudens, Madeline Grudens, PO Box 344, Stonybrook, NY 11790, 631-862-8555, Fax 631-862-0139, celebpro4@aol.com, rgrudens1@aol.com. 1995. Interviews, music, non-fiction. avg. press run 5M. Pub'd 1 title 2005; expects 2 titles 2006, 2 titles 2007. Discounts: 55%. 300pp. Reporting time: 3 months. Simultaneous submissions accepted: yes. Publishes 30% of manuscripts submitted. Payment: by agreement. Copyrights for author. Subjects: Biography, Collectibles, Entertainment, Interviews, Music.

CELLAR, CONTEMPORARY GHAZALS, R.W. Watkins, PO Box 111, Moreton's Harbour, NL A0G 3H0, Canada. 2003. Poetry, articles, art, photos, cartoons, interviews, criticism, reviews, letters, news items. ''*Cellar* publishes essays and reviews focusing on novelist/playwright/screenwriter Laird Koenig, the early and/or darker films of Jodie Foster, and the point at which these two themes intersect: Koenig's 1974 novel/Foster's 1976 film *The Little Girl Who Lives Down The Lane* (the life and work of director Nicolas Gessner may receive future exploration as well). Each issue also features poetry (especially haiku, sijo, and other Eastern forms) connected in some way to Foster and/or Koenig, based on *Down The Lane*, or related to said tale in theme and/or mood. Contributors, recent and forthcoming, include Jena Von Brucker, Rynn Jacobs, Robin Tilley, G.B. Jones, and R.W. Watkins.'' circ. 100+. 2/yr. Expects 1 issue 2006, 1 issue 2007. sub. price $6US outside Canada; per copy $3US outside Canada; sample same. 24pp. Reporting time: shortly after receipt. Simultaneous submissions accepted: yes, provided you inform us. Publishes 75% of manuscripts submitted. Payment: free copy. Not copyrighted. Pub's reviews. §Anything regarding Laird Koenig, Jodie Foster, Nicolas Gessner (director), and their artistic output, related poetry or fiction, suspense, etc. Subjects: Disney, Electronics, Fantasy, Haiku, Movies, Mystery, Poetry.

Celo Valley Books, Diana M. Donovan, 160 Ohle Road, Burnsville, NC 28714, 828-675-5918. 1989. Poetry, fiction, non-fiction. avg. press run 50-3M. Pub'd 5 titles 2005; expects 5 titles 2006, 5 titles 2007. 176pp. Reporting time: 1 month. Payment: all our titles are paid for by the author. Copyrights for author. Subjects: Autobiography, Biography, Dictionaries, Fiction, Novels, Poetry, Psychology, Sports, Outdoors.

Celtic Heritage Books, PO Box 770637, Woodside, NY 11377-0637, Tel/Fax: 718-478-8162; Toll Free: 877-785-2610 (code 0236). 1985. Non-fiction. "Desired works are approximately 150 pages." Expects 1 title 2006, 1 title 2007. Discounts: 30%. 90pp. Reporting time: 3 weeks. Payment: varies with each contributing author. Copyrights for author. Subjects: Anthropology, Archaelogy, Celtic, Folklore, Gaelic, History, Ireland, Religion, Scotland.

Centennial Press (see also ANTHILLS), Charles Nevsimal, Editor, PO Box 170322, Milwaukee, WI 53217-8026.

THE CENTENNIAL REVIEW, R.K. Meiners, Editor; Cheryllee Finney, Managing Editor, 312 Linton Hall, Mich. State Univ., E. Lansing, MI 48824-1044, 517-355-1905. 1955. Articles. "Topics cover English literature, soc. sci, sciences, humanities, 3M words, double-spaced. Contributors: Joseph Needham, Susan Fromberg Schaeffer." circ. 1M. 3/yr. Pub'd 3 issues 2005; expects 3 issues 2006. sub. price $12; per copy $6; sample $6. Back issues: $6. 200pp. Reporting time: 3-6 months. Publishes 10% of manuscripts submitted. Payment: year's free subscription. Copyrighted, reprint rights granted on request of the author. Ads: $75/$50. Subjects: Arts, Biography, Emily Dickinson, English, Ernest Hemingway, Non-Fiction, Religion, Science, Women.

Center for Japanese Studies, Bruce E. Willoughby, Executive Editor, 105 S. State St. #1085, Ann Arbor, MI 48109-1285, 734-647-8885, Fax 734-647-8886. 1947. Poetry, fiction, criticism, non-fiction. "We publish scholarly monographs, symposia, bibliographic and reference aids, language aids, literature in translation, and poetry on and about Japan." avg. press run 500-1M. Pub'd 9 titles 2005; expects 5 titles 2006, 8 titles 2007. 250pp. Reporting time: 2-6 months. Simultaneous submissions accepted: no. Payment: varies with series and book. We hold copyright. Subjects: Anthropology, Archaelogy, Bibliography, Buddhism, Business & Economics, Criticism, Fiction, History, Japan, Language, Poetry, Reference, Religion, Reprints, Theatre, Translation.

Center for Literary Publishing (see also COLORADO REVIEW), Stephanie G'Schwind, Director & Editor, Colorado Review / Dept of English, Colorado State University, Fort Collins, CO 80523, 970-491-5449, creview@colostate.edu, http://coloradoreview.colostate.edu. 1992. Poetry, long-poems. "The Center for Literary Publishing publishes the Colorado Prize for Poetry book series, an annual contest for a book-length manuscript of poems. Poets interested in submitting should obtain complete guidelines at our website." avg. press run 750 to 1,000. Pub'd 1 title 2005; expects 1 title 2006, 1 title 2007. Discounts: Book orders should be directed to University of Oklahoma Press, our distributor. Subscriptions to and sample issues of Colorado Review should be directed to the Center for Literary Publishing. 64-128pp. Simultaneous submissions accepted: Yes. Publishes 1% of manuscripts submitted. Payment: The Colorado Prize offers $1,500 honorarium against royalties. Copyrights for author. Subject: Poetry.

Center For Self-Sufficiency, A.C. Doyle, Founder, PO Box 416, Denver, CO 80201-0416, 305-575-5676. 1982. "www.centerforselfsufficiency.org." avg. press run 2M. Discounts: 25% to libraries & bookstores. 60pp. Subjects: Business & Economics, Consumer, Crafts, Hobbies, Gardening, Homemaking, How-To, Newsletter, Reference, Tapes & Records, Vegetarianism.

Center for Thanatology Research & Education, Inc. (see also ADVANCES IN THANATOLOGY), Roberta Halporn, 391 Atlantic Ave., Brooklyn, NY 11217-1708, 718-858-3026, 718-852-1846,no 800,rhalporn@pipeline.com, thanatology.org. 1980. Poetry, art, photos, non-fiction. "We are book publishers as well as journal publishers. We have two separate lines: 1 on straight death & dying and 1 on gravestone studies. Oddly enough most people think they have nothing to do with each other. Our customers are more concerned with treatment of the terminally ill and funerals. As a bookseller of all publishers relating to this subject, I can tell you it has become a hot item. I produce a separate list (from our own publications) listing the books available from all publishers that are relevant. The list has grown from 2 sides of an 81/2 x 11 sheet, to 3 sides of an 81/2 x 14 sheet." avg. press run 800. Pub'd 2 titles 2005; expects 5 titles 2006. Discounts: 1-4=20%, 5up=40,90up=52. 80-200pp. Reporting time: 1-2 months. Simultaneous submissions accepted: Yes. Does not copyright for author. Subjects: African-American, Arts, Asian-American, Children, Youth, Education, Euthanasia, Death, Feminism, Folklore, Grieving, History, Nursing, Poetry, Psychology, Self-Help, Visual Arts.

The Center Press, Susan Artof, PO Box 6936, Thousand Oaks, CA 91361, 818-889-7071, Fax 818-889-7072.

94

1991. "Looking for clear writing and good concept. Electronic query ok. Will consider IBM-PC 5-3/4'' disk on MSWORD or WordPerfect." avg. press run 3M. Pub'd 2 titles 2005; expects 3 titles 2006, 5 titles 2007. Discounts: 2-19 books 38%, 20 books 40%, 21-100 42%, up to 55% if over 4 case orders; average distributors 55%, payment 60 days. 176-224pp. Reporting time: 4-6 weeks. Publishes 10% of manuscripts submitted. Payment: to be arranged. Copyrights for author. Subjects: Children, Youth, Humor, Psychology, Satire, Sports, Outdoors, Travel, Writers/Writing.

CENTER: A Journal of the Literary Arts, Brian Barker, Managing Editor; Liz Langemak, Poetry Editor; Nicky Beer, Nonfiction Editor; Nathan Oates, Fiction, 202 Tate Hall, Columbia, MO 65211, 573-884-7775. 2000. Poetry, fiction, interviews, reviews, non-fiction. "We are looking for the highest quality fiction, poetry, nonfiction and interviews. *Center* is a literary publication for writers and general readers." circ. 500. 1/yr. Pub'd 1 issue 2005; expects 1 issue 2006, 1 issue 2007. price per copy $6; sample $3. Back issues: $3. 125pp. Reporting time: 3 months. Simultaneous submissions accepted: yes. Publishes 10% of manuscripts submitted. Payment: 2 copies. Copyrighted, reverts to author. Pub's reviews. §Literary books. Ads: none. Subjects: Fiction, Literary Review, Non-Fiction, Poetry.

Central Avenue Press, John Oelfke, Editor; Scott Oelfke, Editor, PO Box 144, 2132-A Central SE, Albuquerque, NM 87106, (505) 323-9953 www.centralavepress.com. 2001. Poetry, non-fiction. "Central Avenue Press is a small, independent press that publishes fiction, poetry, literary nonfiction and writing/reference. We publish two or three manuscripts each year. Current year titles: *Growing Great Characters* (Writing/Reference) Martha Engber, November 2006 *20 Things You Must Know to Write a Great Screenplay* (Writing/Reference) Rick Reichman, November 2006." avg. press run 2000. Pub'd 1 title 2005; expects 2 titles 2006, 2 titles 2007. Discounts: All titles distributed to the trade by Biblio and Quality Books / Web site sales - 10 or more copies 10%. 200pp. Reporting time: six months. Simultaneous submissions accepted: Yes. Publishes 5% of manuscripts submitted. Payment: Advance on first 1000 copies. Standard trade paperback royalty of 7-10% of cover price, payable semi-annually. Copyrights for author. Subjects: Anthology, Catholic, Fantasy, Fiction, Literature (General), Mystery, Non-Fiction, Novels, Poetry, Science, Science Fiction, Short Stories, Travel, Writers/Writing, Young Adult.

Century Press, PO Box 298, Thomaston, ME 04861, 207-354-0998, cal@americanletters.org, www.american-letters.org. 1997. avg. press run 500. Pub'd 2 titles 2005; expects 3 titles 2006, 3 titles 2007. Discounts: 1-4 0%, 5-24 2% PER BOOK ORDERED, 25+ BOOKS ORDERED, 50% HARDCOVER DISCOUNT SAME BUT WITH MAXIMUN DISCOUNT OF 20%. 200pp. Reporting time: 2-3 weeks. Simultaneous submissions accepted: yes. Publishes a very high % of manuscripts submitted. Payment: 10% of amount received on first 2500 copies, then 15%. Copyrights for author.

Ceres Press, David Goldbeck, Nikki Goldbeck, PO Box 87, Woodstock, NY 12498, tel/fax: 845-679-5573, web: www.HealthyHighways.com. 1977. "Unsolicited mss. cannot be returned unless S.A.S.E." avg. press run 5M. Pub'd 1 title 2005; expects 1 title 2006. Discounts: normal trade. Reporting time: 2 months. Payment: as agreed. Subjects: Birth, Birth Control, Population, Design, Environment.

•Cervena Barva Press, Gloria Mindock, P. O. Box 440357, West Somerville, MA 02144-3222, editor@cervenabarvapress.com, http://www.cervenabarvapress.com. 2005. Poetry, fiction, interviews, long-poems, plays. "I look for work that has a strong voice, is unique, and takes risks with writing. Writers must query by e-mail only. I usually only solicit but am willing to look at 2 poems in the body of an e-mail. I hold one open poetry and fiction chapbook contest a year. My website interviews writers monthly by invitation only. The website is updated regularly and has information about the press, contests, workshops, and readings. I have a newsletter that I send out monthly. This is open for anyone to sign up for. I have published Rane Arroyo, Catherine Sasanov, Gary Fincke, Eric Pankey, Simon Perchik, Susan Tepper, Roberta Swann, Dzvinia Orlowsky, David Ray, Gian Lombardo, Michael Burkard, Diane Wald, David Breeden, Barry Casselman, John Minczeski, John Bradley, William James Austin, John M. Bennet, Loredana Brugnaro, and Ed Cates in a postcard series. Chapbooks forthcoming in 2006 by Judy Ray, Ian Randal Wilson, Ed Miller, Richard Kostelanetz, Susanne Morning, and others. Full-length books by CL Bledsoe, UK playwright Michael Nash and Flavia Cosma. I also publish a postcard series yearly. I am open to queries from writers around the world and encourage writers from Central and Eastern Europe to query and contact me." avg. press run 300. Pub'd 1 title 2005; expects 7 titles 2006. 24-80pp. Simultaneous submissions accepted: No. Payment: Author gets 30% royalty on full-length books, 25 copies, review copies, and acknowlegement copies for editors who have supported their work. Chapbook authors receive 25 copies. Copyrights for author. Subjects: Avant-Garde, Experimental Art, Fiction, Poetry, Prose, Short Stories, Theatre.

CESSNA OWNER MAGAZINE, Aircraft Owners Group, Jodi Lindquist, Editor, PO Box 5000, Iola, WI 54945, 715-445-5000; E-mail cessna@aircraftownergroup.com. Articles, photos, interviews. "Aimed at owners and pilots of Cessna aircraft." circ. 6.3M. 12/yr. Pub'd 12 issues 2005; expects 12 issues 2006, 12 issues 2007. sub. price $42, includes membership in Cessna Owner Organization; per copy $4; sample free on request. Back issues: $3. Discounts: subscription only. 64pp. Reporting time: varies. Payment: 5¢/word and up, on publication; one-time rights + 30 days. Copyrighted, rights revert to author after 30 days. Pub's reviews: 6 in 2005. §Aviation, pilot's skills and experiences. Ads: call for media kit. Subjects: Airplanes, Aviation.

•CESUM MAGAZINE, Adam Moore, 1903 Merner Avenue, Cedar Falls, IA 50613, 319-210-0951, cesiummagazine@gmail.com, www.cesium-online.com. 2005. Fiction, articles, art, photos, cartoons, interviews, reviews, music, letters, collages, non-fiction. "Our editorial mission statement is simple: art. media. culture. politics. We publish works with a hip vantage point, that are edgy and relevant to intelligent, plugged-in readers from 18-30. We emphasize giving unrepresented authors exposure, and especially love essays and non-fiction exploring various cultures and ideas." circ. 300. 4/yr. Pub'd 1 issue 2005; expects 4 issues 2006, 4 issues 2007. sub. price $18; per copy $4.95; sample $4.95. Back issues: inquire. Discounts: Bookstores sell for 2.00 a copy; order of 3-10 copies receives 25% off. 40pp. Reporting time: less than two weeks. Simultaneous submissions accepted: Yes. Publishes 50% of manuscripts submitted. Payment: two contributor copies. Copyrighted, reverts to author. Pub's reviews: none in 2005. §movies, music, artists, bands,. Ads: please contact us or see the website. Subjects: Americana, Anarchist, Arts, Fashion, Gay, Gender Issues, Government, Human Rights, Politics, Post Modern, Presidents, Prose, Religion, Reviews, Sex, Sexuality.

CHALLENGING DESTINY, David M. Switzer, R.R. 6, St. Marys, ON N4X 1C8, Canada, csp@golden.net, http://challengingdestiny.com, Available in PDF and other electronic formats. 1997. Fiction, art. "2,000-10,000 words. Recent contributors: Hugh Cook, K.G. McAbee, E.L. Chen, Ian Creasey, Uncle River, A.R. Morlan, Fraser Sherman, and Ken Rand." circ. 200. 2/yr. Pub'd 2 issues 2005; expects 2 issues 2006, 3 issues 2007. price per copy $4.98. Reporting time: 1-4 weeks. Simultaneous submissions accepted: yes. Publishes 3% of manuscripts submitted. Payment: 1¢ Canadian per word. Copyrighted, reverts to author. Pub's reviews: 14 (more on web) in 2005. §Science fiction and fantasy. Subjects: Fantasy, Science Fiction.

Chandler & Sharp Publishers, Inc., E. J. Barrett, 11 Commercial Blvd.Suite A, Novato, CA 94949, 415-883-2353, FAX 415-440-5004, www.chandlersharp.com. 1972. "College-level books in the social sciences with particular emphasis on anthropology, sociology and political science." avg. press run 3-5M. Pub'd 3 titles 2005; expects 4 titles 2006, 6 titles 2007. Discounts: textbooks 20%. 300pp. Reporting time: 6-8 weeks. Simultaneous submissions accepted: yes. Payment: royalties. Copyrights for author on request. Subjects: Anthropology, Archaelogy, Asian-American, Cities, Culture, Government, Indigenous Cultures, Political Science, Politics, Public Affairs, Sociology, Textbooks, Women.

CHANTEH, the Iranian Cross-Cultural Quarterly, Saideh Pakravan, 7229 Vistas Lane, McLean, VA 22101, saideh_pakravan@yahoo.com, www.saideh-pakravan.com. 1992. Poetry, fiction, articles, art, photos, cartoons, interviews, satire, criticism, music, letters, non-fiction. "Going online starting January 1, 2003. No longer hard copy. Open to writers of all nationalities interested in the multicultural experience, in exile and adaptation to new environments. Any and all writing, including political. The only criteria are relevance and excellence in writing." Reporting time: 4 weeks. We accept simultaneous submissions when notified. Payment: 2 copies. Copyrighted, reverts to author. Pub's reviews: 12 in 2005. §The exile and multicultural experience, culture shock, travel, politics in the Middle East. Ads: $350/$175. Subjects: Arts, Essays, Fiction, Poetry, Religion.

CHAPMAN, Joy M. Hendry, Editor; Edmund O'Connor, Assistant, 4 Broughton Place, Edinburgh EH1 3RX, Scotland, 0131-557-2207. 1970. Poetry, fiction, articles, art, interviews, criticism, reviews, long-poems. "Literary material, philosophical orientation, Scottish bias, but *not* exclusive. High standards." circ. 2000. 3/yr. Pub'd 3 issues 2005; expects 3 issues 2006, 3 issues 2007. sub. price £20 (£25 overseas, US$48); per copy £5.50 ($13) + 70p ($2) postage; sample £3.30 ($8) + 70p ($2) postage. Back issues: list available. Discounts: variable. 144pp. Reporting time: 2 months. Simultaneous submissions accepted: no. Publishes 1% of manuscripts submitted. Payment: copies of magazine. Copyrighted. Pub's reviews: 70 in 2005. §Literature (general), politics, culture. Ads: £75/£40. Subjects: Essays, Fiction, Literary Review, Magazines, Non-Fiction, Poetry.

Chapultepec Press, David Garza, 4222 Chambers, Cincinnati, Ohio 45223, OH 45223, chapultepecpress@hot-mail.com http://www.tokyoroserecords.com.

THE CHARIOTEER, Pella Publishing Co., Carmen Capri-Karka, 337 West 36 Street, New York, NY 10018, 212-279-9586. 1960. Poetry, fiction, articles, art, criticism, reviews, letters, plays. "Purpose: to bring to English-speaking readers information on, appreciation of, and translations from modern Greek literature, with criticism and reproductions of modern Greek art and sculpture." circ. 1M. 1/yr. Pub'd 1 issue 2005; expects 1 issue 2006, 1 issue 2007. sub. price $15 US indiv., $20 US instit., $20 foreign indiv., $25 foreign instit.; per copy $15; sample free. Back issues: $9-single; $15-double. Discounts: jobbers 20%, bookstores 20%. 160pp. Reporting time: 1 year. Payment: 20 offprints. Copyrighted, rights revert to author if requested. Pub's reviews: none in 2005. §Modern Greek Literature & Poetry. Ads: $125/$75/Outside Back Cover-$250/Inside Covers-$200. Subjects: Culture, Greek.

CHARITON REVIEW, Jim Barnes, Brigham Young University, Department of English, Provo, UT 84602,

801 422-1503, jim_barnes@byu.edu, www.jimbarnes.org. 1975. Poetry, fiction, art, photos, reviews. "We try to keep open minds, but admit a bias to work that relies more on strong imagery than talkiness. We are very interested in translation, particularly translations of modern poets and especially those from languages other than French or Spanish though we have used numerous translations from those two languages. Recent contributors include Gordon Weaver, Steve Heller, Elizabeth Moore, Lynn Thorsen, Lucien Stryk, Brian Bedard, Beryl Schlossman, Lewis Horne, David Ray, Quinton Duval, Ivy Dempsey, Paul Zarzyski, translations of Belli, Koteski, Huchel, Paulovski, Sabines, Aleixandre, Elytis, Nick. No xerox or carbons or dot matrix." circ. 650+. 2/yr. Pub'd 2 issues 2005; expects 2 issues 2006. sub. price $12 one year (2 issues), $20 two years (4 issues); per copy $7; sample $7. Back issues: Vol. 1 #1 $500, Vol. 1 #2 $100, Vol. 2 #1 $100; Vol. 2 #2 $100; others $5. Discounts: on request. 104pp. Reporting time: 1 month or less. Publishes 1% of manuscripts submitted. Payment: $5/page up to $50 and 1 copy. Copyrighted, rights returned to author on request. Pub's reviews: 1 in 2005. §Modern poetry, fiction, translation, mags. Ads: $200/$100. Subjects: Fiction, Literary Review, Poetry, Translation.

Deborah Charles Publications, B.S. Jackson, 173 Mather Avenue, Liverpool L18 6JZ, United Kingdom, fax 44-151-729-0371 from outside UK. 1986. Non-fiction. "Mainly legal theory. Legal semiotics monographs." avg. press run 300. Discounts: 5% subscription agents, 25% bookshops. 250pp.

CHARLTON SPOTLIGHT, Argo Press, Michael E. Ambrose, PO Box 4201, Austin, TX 78765-4201, charspot01@austin.rr.com. 2000. Articles, art, photos, cartoons, interviews, criticism, reviews, letters, news items, non-fiction. "The magazine focuses on the history and creators of the Charlton Comics Group. Potential contributors should have deep knowledge of Golden Age, Silver Age, and Bronze Age comic books and of particular comics creators, like Steve Ditko, Pat Boyette, Tom Sutton, Dick Giordano, et al. We specialize in an "oral history" approach to the Charlton Comics story, featuring in every issue personal memoirs by the writers, editors, and artists who were there, along with detailed checklists and analytical commentary." circ. 1,800. Annual. Pub'd 1 issue 2005; expects 1 issue 2006, 1 issue 2007. sub. price $14/2 issues ppd. USA, $16 Canada, $28 foreign; per copy $7.95; sample $7.95. Back issues: inquire. Discounts: inquire. 76pp. Reporting time: varies. We don't consider simultaneous submissions; almost all submissions are by special arrangement/ solicitation. Publishes a variable % of manuscripts submitted. Payment: varies. Copyrighted, reverts to author. Pub's reviews: 20 in 2005. §Charlton Comics or associated comics-related pubs. Ads: inquire. Subject: Comics.

Chase Publishing, Anne C. Chase, PO Box 1200, Glen, NH 03838-1200, 603-383-4166, Fax 603-383-8162, achase@chasepublishing.com, www.chasepublishing.com. 1991. Poetry, fiction, non-fiction. "Publishers of *Moments, Undertones,* and *The Head of the Bull* by Philip E. Duffy (short story collections), the *Cafe Chimes Cookbook* by Kathleen Etter (vegetarian cookery), and *The Litter of Leaving: Collected Poems* by E.M. Beekman (2003 release)." avg. press run 1-2M. Expects 1 title 2007. Discounts: trade 1-4 copies 25%, 5-99 40%. 175pp. Reporting time: 4 weeks. Simultaneous submissions accepted: no. Payment: determined separately for each book. Copyrights for author. Subjects: Fiction, Non-Fiction, Poetry.

CHASQUI, David William Foster, Dept of Languages and Literature, Arizona State University, Tempe, AZ 85207-0202, 480-965-3752, fax: 480-965-0135, web: www.public.asu.edu/~atdwf. 1971. Articles, interviews, criticism, reviews. circ. 500. 2/yr. Pub'd 2 issues 2005; expects 2 issues 2006, 2 issues 2007. sub. price $15. Discounts: none. 180pp. Reporting time: 3 months. Simultaneous submissions accepted: no. Publishes 30% of manuscripts submitted. Payment: none. Copyrighted, reverts to author. Pub's reviews: 65 in 2005. §Brazilian and Spanish American literature, literary criticism, theory, film, photography. Ads: none. Subjects: Latin America, Literary Review.

Chatoyant, PO Box 832, Aptos, CA 95003, 831-662-3047 phone/Fax, books@chatoyant.com, www.chatoyant.com. 1997. Poetry, art. "Chatoyant publishes a small number of books per year. We cannot accept any unsolicited material at this time. Unsolicited materials will not be returned." avg. press run 1M. Pub'd 1 title 2005; expects 1 title 2006, 1 title 2007. Discounts: please contact us. 80pp. Simultaneous submissions accepted: no. Publishes 0% of manuscripts submitted. Copyrights for author. Subjects: Arts, Poetry.

THE CHATTAHOOCHEE REVIEW, Marc Fitten, Editor; Jo Ann Yeager Adkins, Managing Editor, Georgia Perimeter College, 2101 Womack Road, Dunwoody, GA 30338-4497, 770-274-5145. 1980. Poetry, fiction, articles, art, photos, interviews, reviews, parts-of-novels, non-fiction. "We publish a number of Southern writers, but *CR* is not by design a regional magazine. We prefer fiction marked by a distinctive voice and powered by innovative language, not gimmicks, which invites the reader's imagination to work along side of well-wrought characters. Recent contributors: William Gay, George Singleton, and Ignacio Padilla. In poetry we look for vivid imagery, unique point of view and voice, freshness of figurative language, and attention to craft. Recent contributors: Robert Dana, Ron Rash, Wendy Bishop, A.E. Stallings, and George Szirtes. All themes, forms, and styles are considered as long as they impact the whole person: heart, mind, intuition, and imagination." circ. 1200. 4/yr. Pub'd 4 issues 2005; expects 4 issues 2006, 4 issues 2007. sub. price $20/yr or $30/2 yrs; per copy $6; sample $6. Back issues: $6. Discounts: 50% to retailers, free ads. 120pp. Reporting time: 3-4 months. Simultaneous submissions accepted: yes, with notification. Publishes 1% of manuscripts submitted. Payment: See Website for guidelines and payment: www.chattahoochee-review.org. Copyrighted, reverts to author. Pub's reviews: 10 in 2005. §Poetry, fiction, plays, creative nonfiction. Ads: $250. Subject: Literary Review.

Chatterley Press International, 19 Dorothy Street, Port Jefferson Station, NY 11776, 631-928-9074 phone/Fax, info@chatterleypress.com. 2000. Fiction. "www.chatterleypress.com." avg. press run 150. Pub'd 7 titles 2005; expects 7 titles 2006, 7 titles 2007. Discounts: 55%. 200-250pp. Reporting time: 6 months. Simultaneous submissions accepted: yes. Publishes less than 1% of manuscripts submitted. Payment: Copies. Does not copyright for author. Subjects: Emily Dickinson, English, Fiction, Journals, D.H. Lawrence, Literature (General), Anais Nin, Renaissance, Women.

CHECKER CAB MAGAZINE - THE LITTLE 'ZINE THAT COULD! Fiction That Takes The Long Way Home, Katy Lawson, P. O. Box 1464, North Highlands, CA 95660-1464, checkercab@sbcglobal.net, www.checkercabmagazine.com. 2005. Poetry, fiction, articles, photos, cartoons, interviews, criticism, reviews, letters, parts-of-novels, non-fiction. "Our mission is to entertain, and to give writers a vehicle for publication. We love good fiction. Bring it on! Please avoid profanity, sex, and violence unless they are necessary to the story. *Please include SASE if you want your manuscript returned. Without adequate return postage, it will be recycled. Thank you.*" circ. 400. 4/yr. Expects 3 issues 2006, 4 issues 2007. sub. price $20; per copy $6; sample $6. Back issues: $6 *while supplies last.* 40pp. Reporting time: 1 week to 1 month *SASE with postage or no reply.* Simultaneous submissions accepted: Yes. Publishes 50% of manuscripts submitted. Payment: $10 per story, poem, or graphic. Copyrighted, reverts to author. Pub's reviews: none in 2005. §Books (fiction and non), magazines, writing programs. Ads: Full page $200/ Hallf page $100 / Quarter page $50 / Business card size $25 / Classified 50 cents per word. All advertising content subject to approval by staff. Subjects: Advertising, Self-Promotion, Dictionaries, Essays, Fiction, Hawaii, Motivation, Success, Non-Fiction, Pacific Region, Reviews, Short Stories, Storytelling, Travel, Writers/Writing, Zines.

CHELSEA, Alfredo de Palchi, Editor; Robert McPhillips, Fiction Editor; Emanuel di Pasquale, Poetry Editor; Michael Tyrell, Book Review Editor; Michal Lando, Assistant Editor, PO Box 773, Cooper Station, New York, NY 10276-0773. 1958. Poetry, fiction, art, photos, interviews, reviews, parts-of-novels, long-poems, plays, non-fiction. "Send prose of no more than 25-30 typed double-spaced pages. Send SASE with all correspondence. Correspondence, queries, mss without SASE will be destroyed unread. No phone calls or emails. Reading period: September to June. Authors who familiarize themselves with the magazine, follow submissions and contest guidelines, and who demonstrate a high level of literary skill have the best chance of publication. We encourage you to read an issue before submitting. Annual fiction contest deadline is June 15 (postmark). Pays $1,000 plus publication. Send SASE for guidelines." circ. 2200. 2/yr. Pub'd 2 issues 2005; expects 2 issues 2006, 2 issues 2007. sub. price $16/2 consecutive issues as published or one double issue, $20 foreign; per copy $10; sample $8. Back issues: prices range from $15 to $25 if rare. Discounts: agency 30%, bookstores 30%. 224pp. Reporting time: 2 to 4 months. Simultaneous submissions accepted: no. Publishes less than 2% of manuscripts submitted. Payment: 1 copy. Copyrighted, reverts to author. Pub's reviews: 15 in 2005. §We review only small press/independently published books and have some lists of those we would like to see reviewed, though we are open to suggestions. Interested writers should send SASE to book review editor Michael Tyrell. Ads: Exchange. Subjects: Book Reviewing, Essays, Fiction, Poetry, Translation.

Chelsea Green Publishing Company, Morris Stephen, Publisher, PO Box 428, White River Junction, VT 05001-0428, 802-295-6300. 1984. Non-fiction. "Emphasis on non-fiction: nature, environment, outdoors. Books for sustainable Living." avg. press run 5M. Pub'd 7 titles 2005; expects 10 titles 2006, 12 titles 2007. Discounts: under 5 35% prepaid, 5+ 45% returnable, 10+ 50% non-returnable. 200pp. Reporting time: 2-3 months. Payment: varies. Copyrights for author. Subjects: Animals, Biography, Birds, Conservation, Earth, Natural History, Ecology, Foods, Essays, Gardening, History, How-To, New England, New York, Non-Fiction, Politics, Society.

Cherokee Publishing Company, Alexa Selph, PO Box 1730, Marietta, GA 30061, 404-467-4189. 1968. "Additional address: 764 Miami Circle NE #206, Atlanta, GA 30324." avg. press run 3M. Pub'd 5 titles 2005; expects 5 titles 2006. Discounts: 1-4 books 35%, 5-24 40%, 25-199 42%, 200+ 45%, STOP 40%. Pages vary. Reporting time: 3 months. Simultaneous submissions accepted: yes. Publishes 1% of manuscripts submitted. Payment: usually 10% of net. Copyrights for author. Subjects: Americana, Biography, Civil War, History, Reprints, South.

THE CHEROTIC (r)EVOLUTIONARY, Frank Moore, Editor; Linda Mac, Editor; Michael LaBash, Art Editor, PO Box 11445, Berkeley, CA 94712, 510-526-7858, FAX 510-524-2053, fmoore@eroplay.com. 1991. Poetry, fiction, articles, art, photos, cartoons, interviews, satire, criticism, reviews, music, letters, parts-of-novels, long-poems, collages, plays, concrete art, news items, non-fiction. "Recent contributors: Annie Sprinkle, LaBash, John Seabury, Carol A. Queen, Frank Moore, Jesse Beagle, Veronica Vera, James David Audlin, Linda Montano, Robert W. Howington, JoAnna Pettit, Ana Christy, H.R. Giger, and Mapplethorpe." circ. 500. Irregular. Pub'd 1 issue 2005; expects 1 issue 2007. price per copy $5; sample $5. Back issues: $5.

Discounts: trade ok, consignment 40%. 28pp. Reporting time: 1-2 months. Simultaneous submissions accepted: yes. Publishes 10% of manuscripts submitted. Payment: free copy of issue. Copyrighted, reverts to author. Ads: inquire for rates. Subjects: Anarchist, Arts, Avant-Garde, Experimental Art, Beat, Cartoons, Community, Counter-Culture, Alternatives, Communes, Culture, Dada, Erotica, Essays, Ethics, Feminism, Fiction, Gay.

Cherry Valley Editions, Elizabeth Plymell, PO Box 303, Cherry Valley, NY 13320, cveds@cherryvalley.com. 1974. avg. press run 200. Discounts: 1 copy 15%; 2-4 copies 20%; 5+ 40%. 100pp. Reporting time: 1 month. Simultaneous submissions accepted: No. Publishes 1% of manuscripts submitted. Payment: varies per author. Copyrights for author. Subjects: Fiction, Philosophy, Poetry.

Cheshire House Books, Attn: Joanna Rees, PO Box 2484, New York, NY 10021, 212-861-5404 phone/Fax, publisher@samthecat.com.

CHESS LIFE, U.S. Chess Federation, Glenn Petersen, United States Chess Federation, 3054 NYS Route 9W, New Windsor, NY 12553, 914-562-8350; Fax 914-236-4852; cleditor@uschess.org. 1939. Articles, photos, cartoons, interviews, reviews, news items, non-fiction. ''Incorporates *Chess Review*; until 1960 name was *Chess Life & Review*. Chess must be central to all material submitted. Very little fiction used.'' circ. 61M. 12/yr. Pub'd 12 issues 2005; expects 12 issues 2006, 12 issues 2007. sub. price $40; per copy $3.75; sample free with req. for writer guidelines. 84pp. Reporting time: 1 month. Payment: on publication. Copyrighted, does not revert to author. Pub's reviews: 8-10 in 2005. Ads: $3520/$1950/$1 per word, min. $15. Subjects: Crafts, Hobbies, Games.

CHICAGO REVIEW, Joshua Kotin, Editor, 5801 South Kenwood, Chicago, IL 60637. 1946. ''please read the magazine (buy a copy or visit your library) to see what *CR* publishes.'' circ. 2900. 4/yr. Pub'd 3 issues 2005; expects 3 issues 2006, 3 issues 2007. sub. price $22 individuals, $42 institutions (plus overseas postage—see website); per copy $10; sample $8. Back issues: yes, on inquiry; see website. Discounts: agency 15% subscription. 144pp. Reporting time: Three to five months. Check website. Simultaneous submissions accepted: Very strongly discouraged. Publishes 1% of manuscripts submitted. Payment: Three free copies plus year subscription. Copyrighted, rights revert to author only on request. Pub's reviews: 35 in 2005. §Literature. Ads: $150/$75. Subjects: Arts, Literary Review.

Chicago Review Press, Gerilee Hundt, Managing Editor, 814 North Franklin Street, Chicago, IL 60610, 312-337-0747. 1973. Art, interviews, non-fiction. avg. press run 5M-7.5M. Pub'd 25 titles 2005. Discounts: distributed by Independent Publishers Group. 200pp. Reporting time: 1-2 months (if submission includes SASE). Simultaneous submissions accepted: yes. Publishes 5% of manuscripts submitted. Payment: royalty 7.5%-10% of retail price is our standard. Copyrights for author. Subjects: Adoption, Arts, Chicago, Children, Youth, Cooking, Crafts, Hobbies, Gardening, How-To, Illinois, Midwest, Politics, Science, Sports, Outdoors.

Chicago Spectrum Press, Dorothy Kavka, Senior Editor, 4824 Brownsboro Center, Louisville, KY 40207-2342, 502-899-1919; Fax 502-896-0246; evanstonpb@aol.com. 1993. avg. press run 2M. Pub'd 20 titles 2005; expects 25 titles 2006, 25 titles 2007. Discounts: 2-4 20%, 5-99 40%, 100+ 50%. 224pp. Reporting time: 1 month. Simultaneous submissions accepted: no. Publishes 10% of manuscripts submitted. Payment: standard small press agreement. Copyrights for author. Subjects: African Literature, Africa, African Studies, Biography, Book Collecting, Bookselling, Civil War, Cooking, Desktop Publishing, How-To, Judaism, Kentucky, Literature (General), Non-Fiction, Poetry, Printing, Self-Help, Textbooks.

Chicken Soup Press, Inc., Margaret S. Campilonga, PO Box 164, Circleville, NY 10919-0164, 845-692-6320, Fax 845-692-7574, poet@hvc.rr.com. 1995. avg. press run 2.5M. Pub'd 3 titles 2005; expects 2 titles 2006, 2 titles 2007. Discounts: industry standard. Young adult 160pp, children's 32pp. Simultaneous submissions accepted: no. Payment: 10%. Copyrights for author. Subjects: Children, Youth, Young Adult.

Chicory Blue Press, Inc., 795 East Street North, Goshen, CT 06756, 860-491-2271, Fax 860-491-8619. 1987. Poetry, fiction, art, interviews, letters, parts-of-novels, non-fiction. ''Chicory Blue Press specializes in writing by women, with a current focus on women poets past 65.'' avg. press run 500-1M. Pub'd 1 title 2005; expects 1 title 2006. Discounts: 3-199 40%, 200-499 50%, 500+ 55%. Reporting time: 3-5 months. Simultaneous submissions accepted: yes. Publishes 2-3% of manuscripts submitted. Payment: negotiable. Copyrights for author. Subjects: Communication, Journalism, Feminism, Fiction, Memoirs, Poetry, Women.

The Chicot Press, Randall P. Whatley, Box 53198, Atlanta, GA 30355, 770-640-9918, Fax 770-640-9819, info@cypressmedia.net. 1978. Non-fiction. avg. press run 2M. Discounts: 1-4 copies 20%, 5-9 30%, 10-99 40%, 100-499 45%, 500+ 50%. 100pp. Reporting time: 60 days. Payment: percentage of profits. Copyrights for author. Subjects: Agriculture, Bilingual, Business & Economics, France, French, Gardening, How-To, Language, Louisiana.

•**A Child Called Poor,** Ayasha Banks, P O Box 5716, Albany, GA 31706, 229-291-7556, 229-439-9061, ACHILDCALLEDPOOR.COM. 2003. avg. press run 1000. Expects 1 title 2006, 2 titles 2007. Discounts: 5-15 copies 10%16-24 copies 25%. 224pp.

Children Of Mary (see also FIDELIS ET VERUS), Jack Law, PO Box 350333, Ft. Lauderdale, FL 33335-0333, 954-583-5108 phone/fax, mascmen8@bellsouth.net, www.catholicbook.com. 1981. Non-fiction. "Orthodox Roman Catholic views reflected in commentary apparitions of Jesus and Mary in Bayside, NY (1970-85) are completely recorded in two volumes *Roses* and also published in *Fidelis et Verus*, a Catholic quarterly newspaper, $10/yr." avg. press run 2M (newspaper) and 15K for books. Pub'd 3 titles 2005; expects 4 titles 2006, 4 titles 2007. Discounts: 40% trade, bulk, classroom, agent, jobber, etc. 300pp. Reporting time: 3 months. Payment: voluntary. Does not copyright for author. Subjects: Birth, Birth Control, Population, Book Collecting, Bookselling, Book Reviewing, Christianity, Communism, Marxism, Leninism, Electronics, Government, Newspapers, Non-Fiction, Philosophy, Politics, Religion, Socialist, Spiritual, Textbooks.

CHILDREN, CHURCHES AND DADDIES, A Non Religious, Non Familial Literary Magazine, Scars Publications, Janet Kuypers, Attn: Janet Kuypers, 829 Brian Court, Gurnee, IL 60031-3155, ccandd96@scars.tv, http://scars.tv. 1993. Poetry, fiction, art, photos, letters, long-poems, non-fiction. "cc&d is a magazine for contemporary poetry, short prose/prose/stories, art and even essays for our philosophy sections. I'm a computer artist, and a feminist specializing in acquaintance rape education. Anything about pertinent issues will be given attention (including anything astronomy related, or anything political in nature). We don't want rhyme. Try under 5 pp per poem, under 10 for prose, but since email submissions are what we prefer, you can always send us submissions, and we can consider anything reasonable in length. No racist/sexist/homophobic material. Include editor's name on address on emvelope. SASE necessary. I primarily accept work on disk (Mac Preferred, but email submissions are preferred. Submit as many pieces as you like, but no originals. Select accepted pieces go into annual collection books (both paperback and hardcover), so if we choose your work for an annual collection book, we will notify you. cc&d also ran book, chapbook, and calender contests, and currently runs contests to appear in books. Contact cc&d for more information. Issues available in print (paid only), electronic format, and on the internet for free at the above address. Email contact is preferred and any information about cc&d magazine is only a click away at http://scars.tv." circ. varies. Issue timelines vary. Pub'd 12 issues 2005; expects 12 issues 2006, 12 issues 2007. sub. price none, pay for individual books with *cc&d* materials. Individual issues of *cc&d* magazine sell for $6.00 American each ($5.00 for the issue, plus $1.00 shipping and handling).; per copy $14.00 for a book, $6.00 for an issue.; sample $14.00 for a book, $6.00 for an issue. Back issues: $13.23 for a book, $6.00 for an issue. Pages vary (on average, 200 pages in a collection book, 40 to 48 pages in an issue of cc&d. Reporting time: I'll get back to you in a week if there is a SASE; otherwise, you'll never hear from me. Simultaneous submissions accepted: yes. Publishes 40% of manuscripts submitted. Payment: none. The magazine logo is copyrighted, but the individual work of each author is always theirs. Ads: contact CC&D. Subjects: Arts, Chicago, Counter-Culture, Alternatives, Communes, Culture, Dada, Feminism, Fiction, Graphics, Journals, Literature (General), Magazines, Midwest, Photography, Poetry, Women.

Children's Book Press, Harriet Rohmer, 2211 Mission Street, San Francisco, CA 94110-1811, 415-995-2200, FAX 415-995-2222, cbookpress@cbookpress.org. 1975. "We prefer for authors to write to us for our editorial guidelines, rather than inquire by phone. We publish legends, folklore and contemporary stories of the different peoples who live in America today. Most of our books are bilingual in Spanish, Chinese, Korean or Vietnamese. We do not solicit manuscripts." avg. press run 7.5M. Pub'd 2 titles 2005; expects 6 titles 2006, 8 titles 2007. Discounts: 40% trade, other rates on request. 32pp. Reporting time: up to 4 months. Simultaneous submissions accepted: yes. Payment: yes. Copyrights for author. Subjects: Folklore, Third World, Minorities.

China Books & Periodicals, Inc., Greg Jones, Editor, 360 Swift Ave., Suite #48, South San Francisco, CA 94080-6220, 800-818-2017 [tel], 650-872-7808 [fax], email: orders@chinabooks.com, website: www.china-books.com. 1960. Fiction, photos, non-fiction. "China Books publishes only books relating to China, including history, language, culture, children, art, music, and other topics. We are less interested in Chinese American topics, but will consider the right books for our market. Recent authors include Peter Uhlmann, Jeannette Faurot, Stefan Verstappen, Tony Gallagher, and Elizabeth Chiu King. We also distribute books for other publishers to bookstores around the world, have an active web site, and retail bookstore." avg. press run 3M-5M. Pub'd 5 titles 2005; expects 6 titles 2006, 10 titles 2007. Discounts: trade 1-4 20%, 5-50 40%, 51-100 42%, 101-250 43%. 250pp. Reporting time: 1-3 months. Simultaneous submissions accepted: yes. Publishes 3% of manuscripts submitted. Payment: negotiable. Copyrights for author. Subjects: Acupuncture, Agriculture, Antiques, Architecture, Arts, Asia, Indochina, Asian-American, Autobiography, Bilingual, Biography, Birth, Birth Control, Population, Buddhism, Business & Economics, Calligraphy, China.

CHINA REVIEW INTERNATIONAL, Roger T. Ames, Executive Editor; Daniel Tschudi, Managing Editor, Center for Chinese Studies, Univ of Hawaii, 1890 East-West Road, Rm. 417, Honolulu, HI 96822-2318, 808-956-8891, Fax 808-956-2682. 1994. Reviews. "For subscriptions, contact: University of Hawaii Press Journals Department, 2840 Kolowalu Street, Honolulu, HI 96822, telephone (808) 956-8833. Reviews are commissioned, generally; however, unsolicited reviews are occasionally accepted." circ. 500. 2/yr. Pub'd 2 issues 2005; expects 2 issues 2006, 2 issues 2007. sub. price $30 individuals, $50 institutions, $18 students; per copy $20. Discounts: for one-time orders: 20% on 10-19 copies, and 30% on 20 or more. 300pp. Reporting time: 1 month. Simultaneous submissions accepted: no. Payment: complimentary copy of book that is reviewed to reviewers and tearsheets of published review. Copyrighted, does not revert to author. Pub's reviews: 125 in 2005. §Any field in Chinese studies. Ads: $200/$125. Subject: China.

THE CHINA REVIEW: AN INTERDISCIPLINARY JOURNAL ON GREATER CHINA, The Chinese University Press, Shaoguang Wang Prof., Editor, The Chinese University of Hong Kong, Sha Tin, New Territories, Hong Kong, Hong Kong, 852-26096508,852-26037355, cup@cuhk.edu.hk,www.chineseupress.com. 2001. 2/yr. Pub'd 2 issues 2005; expects 2 issues 2007. sub. price US$60 (Institution), US$35 (Individual); per copy US$33 (Institution), US$17.5 (Individual). 250pp. Simultaneous submissions accepted: No. Pub's reviews: 4 in 2005. §China related issues. Subject: China.

‡**CHINESE LITERATURE, Chinese Literature Press,** He Jingzhi, 24 Baiwanzhuang Road, Beijing 100037, People's Republic of China, 892554. 1951. circ. 50M. 4/yr. Pub'd 4 issues 2005; expects 4 issues 2006, 4 issues 2007. sub. price $10.50. 200pp. Copyrighted. Pub's reviews: 4 in 2005. §Chinese literature and art areas.

‡**Chinese Literature Press (see also CHINESE LITERATURE),** Tang Jialong, 24 Baiwanzhuang Road, Beijing 100037, People's Republic of China. 1951. avg. press run 50M. Pub'd 4 titles 2005; expects 4 titles 2006, 4 titles 2007. 200pp. Payment: in Chinese and foreign currency. Copyrights for author. Subjects: Asia, Indochina, Literature (General).

The Chinese University Press (see also ASIAN ANTHROPOLOGY; ASIAN JOURNAL OF ENGLISH LANGUAGE TEACHING; THE CHINA REVIEW: AN INTERDISCIPLINARY JOURNAL ON GREATER CHINA; HONG KONG JOURNAL OF SOCIOLOGY; JOURNAL OF PSYCHOLOGY IN CHINESE SOCIETIES; QUEST: AN INTERDISCIPLINARY JOURNAL FOR ASIAN CHRISTIAN SCHOLARS), Steven K Luk Dr., Director; Esther Tsang Ms., Project Editor; Wai-keung Tse Mr., Project Editor; Shelby Chan Ms., Project Editor; Wendy Yau Ms., Project Editor, The Chinese University of Hong Kong, Sha Tin, New Territories, Hong Kong, 852-26096508,852-26037355. 1977. Plays. "Chinese culture and China studies." avg. press run 1000. Pub'd 55 titles 2005; expects 60 titles 2006, 60 titles 2007. Discounts: 30%. 300pp. Reporting time: 6 months. Simultaneous submissions accepted: No. Publishes 100% of manuscripts submitted. Copyrights for author. Subjects: Asia, Indochina, Bilingual, Calligraphy, Classical Studies, Dictionaries, Education, Language, Politics, Psychology, Social Work, Translation.

Chistell Publishing, 2500 Knights Road, Suite 19-01, Bensalem, PA 19020. 1998. Pub'd 1 title 2005. 250pp. Reporting time: 1 week. Simultaneous submissions accepted: yes. Publishes 5% of manuscripts submitted.

CHRISTIAN CONNECTION PEN PAL NEWSLETTER, VISIONHOPE NEWSLETTER, Annagail Lynes, PO Box 45305, Phoenix, AZ 85064-5305, 602-852-9774, christpals@netzero.net, www.angelfire.com/az/ChristianPals/. 1997. Articles, reviews, non-fiction. 6/yr. Pub'd 6 issues 2005; expects 6 issues 2006, 6 issues 2007. sub. price $15; per copy $3; sample $3. Back issues: $3. 12pp. Reporting time: 1 month. Simultaneous submissions accepted: yes. Publishes 50% of manuscripts submitted. Payment: complimentary copy, byline and free ad space. Copyrighted, reverts to author. Pub's reviews: 6 in 2005. §Christian books. Ads: Classified Ads - 1st 50 words - $1, .10/word for every word thereafter. Subjects: Christianity, Cooking, Family, Poetry, Religion.

THE CHRISTIAN LIBRARIAN, Anne-Elizabeth Powell, Editor-in-Chief, Ryan Library, PLNU, 3900 Lomaland Drive, San Diego, CA 92106. 1957. Articles, interviews, reviews, letters, non-fiction. "1,500-3,500 words. Looking for articles of Christian interpretation of librarianship; philosophy, theory, and practice of library science; bibliographic essays." circ. 800. 3/yr. Pub'd 3 issues 2005; expects 3 issues 2006, 3 issues 2007. sub. price $30 domestic, $35 foreign; per copy $8.50; sample same. 36pp. Reporting time: 2 weeks. Simultaneous submissions accepted: yes. Publishes 80% of manuscripts submitted. Payment: none. Not copyrighted. Pub's reviews: 51 in 2005. §Library science, reference, religion. Ads: none. Subjects: Bibliography, Book Reviewing, Communication, Journalism, Computers, Calculators, Indexes & Abstracts, Libraries, Networking, Reference, Religion.

Christian Traditions Publishing Co., 7728 Springborn Road, Casco, MI 48064-3910, 810-765-4805; searcher@in-gen.net. 1997. Non-fiction. avg. press run 1M. Expects 1 title 2006. 276pp.

CHRISTIAN*NEW AGE QUARTERLY, Catherine Groves, PO Box 276, Clifton, NJ 07015-0276, www.christiannewage.com, info@christiannewage.com. 1989. Articles, art, cartoons, reviews, letters, non-fiction. "*Christian*New Age Quarterly* is a lively forum exploring the similarities and distinctions between Christianity and the New Age movement. Essentially a vehicle for communication—to draw the two ideological groups into genuine dialogue—articles must quickly cut through superficial divisions to explore the substance of our unity and differences. Pertinent controversy is fine. Garbage thinking (ie., 'I'm right - you're wrong') makes the editor frown. Submissions should sparkle with both insight and creativity. Article lengths vary from 400 to 1500 words (longer pieces accepted if excellent). Guidelines available, for more info see website." 4/yr. Pub'd 3 issues 2005; expects 3 issues 2006, 4 issues 2007. sub. price $12.50 USA/$18.50 outside USA; per copy $3.50 USA/$5.00 outside USA; sample $3.50 USA/$5.00 outside USA. Back issues: $3.50 USA/$5.00 outside USA. Discounts: prepaid orders only; on 5 or more copies, 30%. Averages 20pp. Reporting time: 6 weeks (and we always respond, if SASE enclosed). Simultaneous submissions accepted: no. Publishes 20% of manuscripts submitted. Payment: in subscription or copies (depending on nature of article). Copyrighted, reverts to author. Pub's reviews: 3 in 2005. §Books which address both Christian and New Age issues. Before sending review copies, write for reviewer's address or see "A Message to Book Publishers" on website. Ads: $45/$35/$25 1/4 page/$15 1/6 page/cheap classifieds! Subjects: Christianity, New Age, Religion, Spiritual.

Christoffel & Le Cordier, 401 Langham House, 302 Regent Street, London W1B 3HH, England, christoffel@regent-st.com, www.christoffel.co.uk.

Chrysalis Reader, Carol S. Lawson, Editor, Box 4510, Route 1, Dillwyn, VA 23936, 1-434-983-3021. 1985. Poetry, fiction, non-fiction. "The Chrysalis Reader is an annual anthology of original, never-before-published poetry, short stories, and essays based on a spiritual theme. Contact the editor for a list of upcoming themes: chrysalis@hovac.com." avg. press run 1,000 copies per year. Pub'd 1 title 2005; expects 1 title 2006, 1 title 2007. 192pp. Publishes 20% of manuscripts submitted. Payment: $25 for poetry; $100—$150 for short story or essay. Copyright belongs to Chrysalis Reader.

CHRYSANTHEMUM, Goldfish Press, Koon Woon, 202 6th Avenue South #1105, Seattle, WA 98104-2303, 206-682-3851, nooknoow@aol.com. 1990. Poetry. "*Chrysanthemum* is a forum for all persuasions of the world community to communicate in a friendly manner through the art of poetry.We are not interested in academic exercises needing another publication credit. Rather, we are interested in poets who have mulled long and hard about things. We provide shelter to ordinary folks who also happen to love poetry,who are human first and "poet" second. We seek a multicultural mix and minorities of all types. Some recent contributors are Betty Priebe, Marjorie Pepper, Bob Holman, Norm Davis, Jim Cohn, Jack Foley and Mary-Marcia Casoly, and Cathy Ruiz." circ. 300. 4/yr. Pub'd 1 issue 2005; expects 4 issues 2006, 4 issues 2007. sub. price $20; per copy $5; sample $4, xerox. Back issues: none. Discounts: none. 44pp. Reporting time: 2 weeks. Simultaneous submissions accepted: no. Publishes 2% of manuscripts submitted. Payment: 1 copy. Copyrighted, reverts to author. Subject: Poetry.

CIMARRON REVIEW, E.P. Walkiewicz, Editor, 205 Morrill Hall, Oklahoma State University, Stillwater, OK 74078-4069, (405) 744-9476, cimarronreview@yahoo.com, http://cimarronreview.okstate.edu. 1967. Poetry, fiction, art, photos, interviews, reviews, parts-of-novels, long-poems, non-fiction. "Read an issue or two before submitting to get a feel for what we publish. Recent contributors include Nona Caspers, Catherine Brady, Boyer Rickel, Kim Addonizio, Gary Fincke, James Harms and Brian Henry. We read year round; no electronic submissions." circ. 600. 4/yr. Pub'd 4 issues 2005; expects 4 issues 2006, 4 issues 2007. sub. price $24 ($28 in Canada), $65/3 years ($72 Canada); per copy $7; sample $7. Back issues: $7. Discounts: Back issues more than one year old are $5. 96-128pp. Reporting time: One to six months. Simultaneous submissions accepted: Yes. Publishes 5% of manuscripts submitted. Payment: Two copies and a year's subscription. Copyrighted, reverts to author. Pub's reviews: 4 in 2005. §Poetry, fiction and non-fiction. Ads handled on individual basis. Subjects: Arts, English, Essays, Fiction, Literature (General), Non-Fiction, Photography, Poetry, Prose, Reviews, Short Stories, Writers/Writing.

CINEASTE MAGAZINE, Gary Crowdus, Editor-in-Chief; Dan Georgakas, Consulting Editor; Roy Grundmann, Contributing Editor; Cynthia Lucia, Editor; Richard Porton, Editor; Leonard Quart, Contributing Editor; Barbara Saltz, Advertising Rep., 243 Fifth Ave., #706, New York, NY 10016-8703, 212-366-5720, Fax 212-366-5724. 1967. Articles, photos, interviews, satire, criticism, reviews, letters. "Offers a social & political perspective on the cinema—everything from the latest hollywood flicks & the American independent scene to political thrillers from Europe and revolutionary cinema from the Third World. Query before submitting." circ. 11M. 4/yr. Pub'd 4 issues 2005; expects 4 issues 2006, 4 issues 2007. sub. price $20 (institutions $35); per copy $6; sample $6. Back issues: $4 to subscribers/$5 to others. Discounts: 25%. 68pp. Reporting time: 2-3 weeks. Payment: reviews $50, articles $100 and up. Copyrighted. Pub's reviews: 60 in 2005. §Social, political perspective on all aspects of movies. Ads: $400/$300. Subjects: Criticism, Electronics, History, Politics, Sociology.

•**CineCycle Publishing,** Darren Alff, P.O. Box 982216, Park City, UT 84098. 2006. Non-fiction. "CineCycle Publishing works to create Film Industry and Outdoor Related (bicycling, hiking, canoeing, etc.) products." avg. press run 1000. Expects 2 titles 2006. Discounts: Education/Institution/Classroom Discount - 15%Distributor/Bookstore/Wholesaler/Retailer Discount - 35%. 192pp. Reporting time: 2 weeks. Simultaneous submissions accepted: Yes. Copyrights for author. Subjects: Arts, Audio/Video, Bicycling, How-To, Media, Movies, Non-Fiction, Sports, Outdoors, Television.

CIRCLE INC., THE MAGAZINE, Circle of Friends Books, Tommy W. Lee, PO Box 670096, Houston, TX 77267-0096, 281-580-8634. 2004. Fiction, articles, interviews, satire, reviews, non-fiction. "We publish all types of material that is geared towards uplifting the reader. Our literature should bring change, inspire positive development.'' Reporting time: 2 months. Simultaneous submissions accepted: yes. Subjects: African-American, Crime, Fiction, Spiritual.

THE CIRCLE MAGAZINE, Penny Talbert, 173 Grandview Road, Wernersville, PA 19565, 610-823-2707, Fax 610-670-7017, circlemag@aol.com, www.circlemagazine.com. 1996. Poetry, fiction, articles, art, photos, cartoons, interviews, satire, criticism, reviews, music, collages, non-fiction. circ. 2M+. 4/yr. Pub'd 4 issues 2005; expects 4 issues 2006, 4 issues 2007. sub. price $15; per copy $4; sample $4. Back issues: none. 52pp. Reporting time: 3-4 months. Simultaneous submissions accepted: yes. Publishes 1% of manuscripts submitted. Payment: copy. Copyrighted, reverts to author. Pub's reviews: 20-30 in 2005. §Everything but religious. Ads: $110/$65. Subject: Literature (General).

Circle of Friends Books (see also CIRCLE INC., THE MAGAZINE), Tommy W. Lee, PO Box 670096, Houston, TX 77267-0096, 281-580-8634. 2004. Fiction, articles, interviews, satire, reviews, non-fiction. ''We publish all types of material that is geared towards uplifting the reader. Our literature should bring change, inspire positive development.'' avg. press run 10M. Pub'd 1 title 2005; expects 3 titles 2006, 5 titles 2007. Discounts: bookstores 40%, distributors 50-55%, (all) qty: 2-4 20%, 5-99 40%, 100+ 50%. 280pp. Reporting time: 2 months. Simultaneous submissions accepted: yes. Publishes 25% of manuscripts submitted. Payment: $500-$1,500. Copyrights for author. Subjects: African-American, Crime, Fiction, Spiritual.

Circlet Press, Inc., Cecilia Tan, 1770 Mass Avenue #278, Cambridge, MA 02140, 617-864-0492, Fax 617-864-0663, circlet-info@circlet.com. 1992. Fiction. ''We publish anthologies of short stories of erotic science fiction and fantasy. We accept manuscripts only between April 15 and August 31. Jan. 1 each year we announce specific anthology topics. Write for complete, very specific guidelines. *No horror! No novels!* We have added an imprint of erotic nonfiction and sex how-to books also. Writer/SASE for query instructions.'' avg. press run 2000. Pub'd 4 titles 2005; expects 4 titles 2006, 4 titles 2007. Discounts: retail 40%-48%, short 20%. 192pp. Reporting time: 6-24 months. Simultaneous submissions accepted: yes. Publishes 5% of manuscripts submitted. Payment: varies by book. Copyrights for author. Subjects: Bisexual, Erotica, Fantasy, Gay, Science Fiction, Sex, Sexuality.

City Life Books, LLC, Suzette Barclay, P.O. Box 371136, Denver, CO 80237, 303-773-9353. 2003. Poetry, fiction, non-fiction. ''We publish books that fit our motto "Books About Life : Books For Life" that supports a positive outlook and uplifting message. As long as the subject matter is in this vein, we are open to various art and writing forms.'' avg. press run 3000. Pub'd 1 title 2005; expects 3 titles 2006, 5 titles 2007. Discounts: Wholesaled through Baker & Taylor, bulk discounts to retailers 1-5 copies 40%, 5 and up copies 50%. 150pp. Reporting time: 6-8 weeks. Simultaneous submissions accepted: Yes. Publishes 15% of manuscripts submitted. Payment: Each contract will be individually negotiated. Copyrights for author. Subjects: Animals, Christmas, Colorado, Family, Feminism, Fiction, Grieving, Inspirational, Motivation, Success, Novels, Pets, Poetry, Relationships, Women, Writers/Writing.

City Lights Books, Lawrence Ferlinghetti, Nancy J. Peters, Robert Sharrard, Elaine Katzenberger, Attn: Bob Sharrard, Editor, 261 Columbus Avenue, San Francisco, CA 94133, 415-362-8193. 1955. Poetry, fiction, articles, non-fiction. avg. press run 3M. Pub'd 5 titles 2005; expects 5 titles 2006. 100pp. Reporting time: 4 weeks. Payment: varies. Copyrights for author. Subjects: Anarchist, Ecology, Foods, Fiction, Libertarian, Literature (General), Poetry, Politics.

CKO UPDATE, Blueprint Books, Bette Daoust Ph.D., PO Box 10757, Pleasanton, CA 94588, 925-425-9513, Fax 1-800-605-2914, 1-800-605-2913, editor@blueprintbooks.com, blueprintbooks.com. 2005. Articles, interviews, reviews, non-fiction. 6/yr. Expects 5 issues 2006, 6 issues 2007. sub. price $19.95; per copy $3.95; sample free. Back issues: inquire. Discounts: 3 - 299: -40%300 - 499: -50%500 - up: -55%. 80pp. Reporting time: 5 - 10 business days. Simultaneous submissions accepted: Yes. Publishes 40% of manuscripts submitted. Payment upon acceptance. Copyrighted. Pub's reviews. §Business, Consulting, Business Self-Help. Subjects: Audio/Video, Book Reviewing, Business & Economics, Communication, Journalism, Consulting, Desktop Publishing, Finances, Government, Non-Fiction, Public Affairs, Public Relations/Publicity, Quotations.

CLACKAMAS LITERARY REVIEW, Amanda Coffey, Kate Gray, James Grabill, Andy Mingo, Trevor Dodge, 19600 South Molalla Avenue, Oregon City, OR 97045. 1996. Poetry, fiction, interviews, satire, reviews, non-fiction. ''The *Clackamas Literary Review* is a nationally distributed magazine that publishes quality literature with a fresh voice. It is an annual magazine produced at Clackamas Community College under the direction of the English Department. *CLR* promotes the work of emerging writers and established writers of fiction, poetry, and creative nonfiction. Send poetry and prose separately. Submissions are limited to 6 poems, 1 story (7,000 words), or 1 essay per submission. Please include a SASE for response. We have previously published work by Ron Carlson, Naomi Shihab Nye, Denise Chavez, Pamela Uschuk, George Kalamaras, Christopher Howell, H. Lee Barnes, and Greg Sellers.'' circ. 1M. 1/yr. Pub'd 1 issue 2005; expects 1 issue 2006, 1 issue 2007. sub. price $10; per copy $10. Back issues: $5. 220pp. Reporting time: 30 weeks. Simultaneous submissions okay, please inform us if accepted elsewhere. Fiction and poetry contests ($15. entry fee) are held each spring. 2005 judges are Hannah Tinti and Elizabeth Woody. Prizes of $500 each. Publishes 4-5% of manuscripts submitted. Payment: copies. Pub's reviews: 2 in 2005. §Poetry, fiction, CNF. Ads: trade space.

•**Cladach Publishing,** Catherine Lawton, P.O. Box 336144, Greeley, CO 80633, 970-371-9530 phone, 970-351-8240 fax, info@cladach.com, www.cladach.com. 1999. Fiction, non-fiction. avg. press run 1000. Pub'd 2 titles 2005; expects 2 titles 2006, 2 titles 2007. Discounts: Wholesale 55%, Retail 40-45%. 200pp. Simultaneous submissions accepted: Yes. Payment: 7-10% net proceeds. Copyrights for author. Subjects: Christianity, Christmas, Colorado, Cooking, Fiction, Gardening, Health, Inspirational, Juvenile Fiction, Marriage, Memoirs, Non-Fiction, Novels, Parenting, Relationships.

Claitor's Law Books & Publishing Division, Inc., Robert G. Claitor, 3165 S. Acadian, PO Box 261333, Baton Rouge, LA 70826-1333, 225-344-0476; FAX 225-344-0480; claitors@claitors.com; www.claitors.com. 1922. Non-fiction. "Unsolicited manuscripts not desired." avg. press run 1M. Pub'd 100 titles 2005; expects 110 titles 2006, 120 titles 2007. Discounts: trade 1 copy 20%, 2-4 33%, 5+ 40%. 500pp. Reporting time: 90 days. Simultaneous submissions accepted: no. Publishes 1% of manuscripts submitted. Payment: 6-10%. Copyrights for author. Subjects: Law, Louisiana, Taxes, Textbooks.

CLAMOUR: A Dyke Zine, Renee Gladman, 144 Albion Street, San Francisco, CA 94110.

Clamp Down Press, Joshua Bodwell, PO Box 7270, Cape Porpoise, ME 04014-7270, 207-967-2605. 1997. Poetry, fiction, long-poems. "Recently published book of poems by Christopher Locke. The book was letterpress printed, silk-screened with original artwork and handbound in a paper and cloth edition. All Clamp Down Press books are handcrafted, limited editions, using different formats and binding techniques. Upcoming projects: back-to-back book by Fred Voss/Joan Jobe Smith,slaughter house poems by Dave Newman, a short poem seqence on death by David Mason Heminway.Almost all Clamp Down Press books and broadsides are illustrated. The broadside series includes work by Philip Levine, Billy Collins, Galway Kinnell, James Wright, Ed Ochester, David Mason Heminway and Tom Sexton." avg. press run 200-500. Pub'd 2 titles 2005; expects 4 titles 2006, 4 titles 2007. Discounts: Offer traditional trade discounts to dist., wholesalers, etc. 32 to 100pp. Reporting time: varies. Simultaneous submissions accepted: yes. Payment: No advances. Payment schedules vary with each author and project. Copyrighting for author varies. Subjects: Book Arts, Fiction, Literature (General), Miniature Books, Poetry, Wood Engraving/Woodworking.

Clamshell Press, D.L. Emblen, 160 California Avenue, Santa Rosa, CA 95405. 1973. "We do not read unsolicited book mss." avg. press run 250-500. Pub'd 1 title 2005; expects 2 titles 2006, 2 titles 2007. 48pp. Copyrights for author. Subjects: Arts, Criticism, Language, Poetry, Translation.

Clapper Publishing Co. (see also BRIDAL CRAFTS; CRAFTS 'N THINGS; THE CROSS STITCHER; PACK-O-FUN; PAINTING), Barbara Sunderlage, 2400 Devon, Suite 375, Des Plaines, IL 60018, 847-635-5800, 800-444-0441.

CLARA VENUS, Red Hand Press, Marie Kazalia, Attn: Marie Kazalia, PO BOX 422344, San Francisco, CA 94142, E-mail: RedHandPress@hotmail.com, http://ClaraVenus.BlogSpot.com, http://RedHandPress.BlogSpot.com. 2004. Poetry, fiction, art, photos, collages. "Clara Venus inaugural Issue Spring 2K5 contributors: Lyn Lifshin, Michael Rothenberg, Duane Locke, Sue Mayfield-Geiger, Francis Poole, Cheryl Townsend,Viola Lee,Reginald Sinclair Lewis, Alison Carb Sussman, Austin Alexis, Nikki Thompson, Christopher Mulrooney, Paul Valery, Elizabeth Brunazzi, Tina Butcher, Tsaurah Litzky, H D Moe, Kit Kennedy,Belladonna, Julie L. Andrews, Dorothy Bates,Laura Elrick, Deborah Rothchild, Oliver Cutshaw,Lala,Cynthia Liang,Graham Nunn,Jacqueline K. Powers, Suellen Wedmore. In 2005 Red Hand Press begins publishing 3 new literary annuals—Clara Venus, fulva flava, and Defect Cult—in print and on-line versions. Small Press poets, writers and artists may submit their work for consideration. One submission opens you to consideration for all three publications—unless your (optional) cover letter indicates a preference. SUBMIT: Poetry: all forms and styles, prose poems Prose: flash (500 words or less) fiction, memoir, creative nonfiction Artwork: Send your high contrast color and b&w graphics, drawings, prints, collages, paintings and photographs for consideration. By mail: submit clear clean photocopies of original images. Via e-mail: send JPEGs. Keep in mind the openness of these publications and the any stated themes when submitting artwork. Clara Venus (Spring 2K5) http://ClaraVenus.blogspot.com. The name of this publication taken from Rimbauds poetry—his description of a lady emerging from her bath—*her buttocks engraved with the words Clara Venus ... hideously beautiful...*The focus of Clara Venus literary annual—the female outside roles and beyond descriptions shes commonly been written into. Let*s eradicate the last vestiges of those hackneyed stereotypes. You tell us in your words what they are/were and go beyond... Theme(s) for Issue 2(expected publication date April 2006) INFERENCES. (from the Editor) Statistically the entire world population is 52% female and 48% male. According to the interactive on-line project Word Count at www.wordcount.org, that tracks the 86,800 most frequently used English words ranked in order of commonness and *giving a barometer of relevance*, the top 6 words used: *the* (1) *of* (2) *and *(3) *to* (4) *a* (5) *in *(6) Accordingly some word usage in relation to

104

gender.... *he* (ranked 14) *his* (ranked 27) *man*(ranked 142) (Remember, the higher the number the *less* frequently used the word) *she* (ranked 30) *her* (ranked 36) *woman* (ranked 393) Some common names (and euphemisms) for gender specific parts: dick (5366) cock (10870) penis (10871) all much more frequently used than the female: vagina (16307) cunt (18636) pussy (21548) Thinking on the above may bring various inferences to mind, and these may be construed as themes for writing to be submitted to the editor for consideration for Issue 2 of Clara Venus. Deadline April 2K6.'' circ. 350. 1/yr. Expects 1 issue 2006, 1 issue 2007. sub. price $15. for one issue of each annual (3); per copy $6.99; sample $3.95. Back issues: inquire. 50pp. Reporting time: weeks to months. Simultaneous submissions accepted: Yes. Publishes 34% of manuscripts submitted. Payment: copies. ISSN: 1553-7285. Subjects: Absurdist, Arts, Asia, Indochina, Asian-American, Avant-Garde, Experimental Art, Beat, Bisexual, Dreams, Erotica, Feminism, Fiction, India, San Francisco, Women.

Clarity Press, Inc., Diana G. Collier, Editorial Director, 3277 Roswell Road NE, Suite 469, Atlanta, GA 30305, Editorial: 877-613-1495 Fax 877-613-7868, clarity@islandnet.com, editorial: claritypress@usa.net, www.claritypress.com. 1984. Fiction, non-fiction. ''Prefer nonfiction on human rights, foreign policy and social justice issues.'' avg. press run 3M. Pub'd 4 titles 2005; expects 4 titles 2006, 4 titles 2007. Discount schedule established by distributor, SCB Distributors, Gardena, California. 220pp. Reporting time: 2 months—send query letter first (we will respond only if interested, so SASE not necessary). Simultaneous submissions accepted: yes. Payment: negotiable. Copyrights for author. Subjects: African-American, Black, Civil Rights, Current Affairs, Human Rights, Middle East, Native American, Political Science, Socialist, Third World, Minorities.

Arthur H. Clark Co., Robert A. Clark, PO Box 14707, Spokane, WA 99214, 509-928-9540. 1902. ''Documentary source material and non-fiction dealing with the history of the Western U.S.'' avg. press run 750-1.5M. Pub'd 7 titles 2005; expects 10 titles 2006, 9 titles 2007. Discounts: 1-2 copies 15%, 3-4 25%, 5-25 40%, 26+ 45%. 300pp. Reporting time: 2 months. Publishes 20% of manuscripts submitted. Payment: 10% generally. Copyrights for author. Subject: History.

CLARK STREET REVIEW, Ray Foreman, PO Box 1377, Berthoud, CO 80513, clarkreview@earthlink.net, http://home.earthlink.net/~clarkreview/. 1990. Poetry, fiction. ''Narrative poetry and (short shorts max. length 800 words) by previously published writers. Accepts previously published work. Recent contributors: Errol Miller, Ray Clark Dickson, Laurel Speer, and Lamar Thomas. Look for work that is clear, tuned to the mother tongue and above all, interesting to writer/readers.'' circ. 100. 8/yr. Pub'd 7 issues 2005; expects 8 issues 2006, 8 issues 2007. sub. price $10/10 issues; per copy $2; sample $2. Back issues: $2. Discounts: none. 20pp. Reporting time: 2 weeks. Simultaneous submissions accepted: yes. Publishes 20% of manuscripts submitted. Payment: 1 copy. Copyrighted, reverts to author. Subjects: Poetry, Prose.

CLASSICAL ANTIQUITY, University of California Press, Mark Griffith, Editor, Univ of California Press, 2000 Center Street, Suite 303, Berkeley, CA 94704-1223, 510-643-7154. 1981. Non-fiction. ''Editorial address: Department of Classics, 7233 Dwinelle Hall 2520, Univ. of CA, Berkeley, CA 94720.'' circ. 592. 2/yr. Pub'd 2 issues 2005; expects 2 issues 2006, 2 issues 2007. sub. price $40 indiv.; $128 instit. (+ $15 air freight); $22 students; per copy $22 indiv.; $65 instit.; $22 students; sample free. Back issues: $22 indiv.; $65 instit.; $22 students. Discounts: 10% foreign subs., 30% one-time orders 10+, standing orders (bookstores): 1-99 40%, 100+ 50%. 176pp. Reporting time: 3 months. Payment: none. Copyrighted, does not revert to author. Ads: $295/$220. Subject: Classical Studies.

THE CLASSICAL OUTLOOK, Mary English C., Editor, Department of Classics and General Humanities, Dickson Hall, Montclair State University, Upper Montclair, NJ 07043. 1923. Poetry, articles, criticism, reviews. circ. 4M. 4/yr. Pub'd 4 issues 2005; expects 4 issues 2006, 4 issues 2007. sub. price $45 ($47 Canada, $50 overseas); per copy $10; sample $10. Back issues: same. 40pp. Reporting time: 6 months. Simultaneous submissions accepted: no. Publishes 19% of manuscripts submitted. Payment: 2 complimentary copies. Copyrighted, does not revert to author. Pub's reviews: 59 in 2005. §Latin, classical Greek, classical studies, pedagogy. Ads: $320/$250/$150 1/4 page. Subjects: Anthropology, Archaelogy, Book Reviewing, Classical Studies, Education, Language.

Clearbridge Publishing, PO Box 33772, Shoreline, WA 98133, 206-533-9357, Fax 206-546-9756, beckyw@clearbridge.com, www.clearbridge.com.

ClearPoint Press, Christiane Buchet, PO Box 170658, San Francisco, CA 94117, 415-386-5377 phone/Fax. 1991. Non-fiction. ''We publish books on meditation and spiritual development. We do not accept unsolicited material.'' avg. press run 3M. Expects 1 title 2006, 1 title 2007. Discounts: standard industry. 136pp. Payment: 10%. Does not copyright for author. Subject: Buddhism.

Clearwater Publishing Co., PO Box 778, Broomfield, CO 80038-0778, 303-436-1982, fax 917-386-2769, e-mail kenn@clearwaterpublishing.com OR wordguise@aol.com. 1990. ''Readable, entertaining introductions to subjects taught in schools, like algebra and electronics. Primarily a vehicle for publishing books by Kenn

Amdahl, who owns the company. Because we've been doing this for a while, we get submissions from hopeful authors which we have so far resisted. Our first title, There Are No Electrons: Electronics for Earthlings, was rejected 89 times before Kenn formed Clearwater. He did not intend to become a "publishing company," it just sort of happened. Self publishing was a good option for us, we suggest you investigate it as well. Sadly, Clearwater just isn't a very likely publisher for other authors. Growing would mean Kenn might have to actually work. More info on the company at www.clearwaterpublishing.com. And please turn our titles cover-out in book stores when you find them. It saves the manager time. Thanks." Pub'd 1 title 2005; expects 2 titles 2006, 1 title 2007. 260pp. Subjects: Business & Economics, Education, Fiction, Mathematics, Music, Physics, Science, Spiritual, Sports, Outdoors, Textbooks, Writers/Writing.

Cleis Press, Frederique Delacoste, Acquisitions Editor; Felice Newman, Marketing Director, PO Box 14684, San Francisco, CA 94114-0684, cleis@cleispress.com; www.cleispress.com. 1980. Fiction, non-fiction. "Full-length book manuscripts only. Please include SASE w/complete ms. or sample chapter(s). Welcome manuscripts or query letters from progressive women and men writers. Cleis Press is committed to publishing progressive nonfiction and fiction by women and men, especially gay and lesbian." avg. press run 5M. Pub'd 5 titles 2005; expects 7 titles 2006, 7 titles 2007. Discounts: standard bookstore & distributor, please write for terms. 150-300pp. Reporting time: 2-3 months. Payment: please write us for information on royalty. Copyrights for author. Subjects: Feminism, Fiction, Latin America, Lesbianism, Novels, Women.

Cleveland State Univ. Poetry Center, Ted Lardner, Co-Director; Ruth Schwartz, Co-Director; David Evett, Editorial Committee; Rita Grabowski, Coordinator; Bonnie Jacobson, Editorial Committee, 1983 East 24th Street, Cleveland, OH 44115-2400, 216-687-3986; Fax 216-687-6943; poetrycenter@popmail.csuohio.edu. 1962. Poetry, concrete art. "1 local (Ohio) poetry series—51 published since 1971, 24-100pp. 2 national series, 61 published since 1971, most 72-120pp. Other additional titles also published. Among authors published: David Breskin, Jared Carter, Chrystos, Beckian Fritz Goldberg, Marilyn Krysl, Robert Hill Long, Frankie Paino, Caludia Rankine, Tim Seibles, Sandra Stone, Anthony Vigil, Judith Vollmer, Jeanne Murray Walker. Submit only Nov. 1st-Feb. 1st, $20 reading fee for national series, $1,000 prize for best booklength ms. (50-100pp). Send SASE for complete guidelines, $2 for 64 page catalogue." avg. press run 600 local series, 1.3M-1.5M national series. Pub'd 4 titles 2005; expects 4 titles 2006, 4 titles 2007. Discounts: 40% to retail bookstores, 50% to wholesalers/jobbers. Distributed through Partners Book Distributing (800-336-3137) and Ingram (615-793-5000) and Spring Church Book Co., PO Box 127, Spring Church, PA 15686. 32-100pp. Reporting time: 5-7 months. We accept simultaneous submissions, but identify as such. Publishes .5% of manuscripts submitted. Payment: local series 100 copies, national series 50 copies + $300. Copyrights for author. Subject: Poetry.

THE CLIFFS "sounding", The Vertin Press, Kilgore Splake T., P.O. Box 7, 220 Sixth Street, Calumet, MI 49913, 906-337-5970. 2005. Poetry, fiction, art, photos, interviews, satire, criticism, reviews, letters, parts-of-novels, long-poems, collages, plays, non-fiction. circ. 150. 4/yr. Expects 4 issues 2006, 4 issues 2007. sub. price $28; per copy $6; sample $7. Back issues: $7. Discounts: 20%. 40pp. Reporting time: within 4 weeks. Simultaneous submissions accepted: No. Payment: complimentary copy. Copyrighted, reverts to author. Pub's reviews. §Poetry.

THE CLIMBING ART, Ron Morrow, Editor, 6390 E. Floyd Dr., Denver, CO 80222-7638. 1986. Poetry, fiction, articles, art, photos, cartoons, interviews, satire, criticism, reviews, letters, parts-of-novels, long-poems, collages, news items, non-fiction. "We will consider material of any length, and will even serialize book-length mss. We publish only material that is well written and of interest to those who live in, travel in, or climb mountains. Recent contributors include Reg Saner, David Craig and Grant McConnell." circ. 1M. 1/yr. Pub'd 1 issue 2005; expects 1 issue 2006, 1 issue 2007. sub. price $18; per copy $4.50; sample free. Back issues: inquire. Discounts: 1-4 copies 20%, 5-24 40%, 25-49 43%, 50-99 46%, 100+ 50%; jobbers up to 55%. 144-160pp. Reporting time: 2 months. Simultaneous submissions accepted: yes. Publishes 20% of manuscripts submitted. Payment: up to $200. Copyrighted, reverts to author. Pub's reviews: 20 in 2005. §The mountains, mountaineering and rock-climbing, mountain-area histories, biographies of figures associated with the mountains. Ads: $100/$50/$30. Subjects: Adirondacks, Alaska, Appalachia, Book Reviewing, California, Maine, New England, Pacific Northwest, Sports, Outdoors, H.D. Thoreau, The West.

Clover Park Press, Geraldine Kennedy, Publisher; Martha Grant, Acquisitions Editor, PO Box 5067, Santa Monica, CA 90409-5067, 310-452-7657, info@cloverparkpress.com, http://www.cloverparkpress.com. 1990. Non-fiction. "Non-fiction, send letter or email query first. Interested in science for non-scientists, literary travel, biography, California history, excellent writing that illuminates life's wonders and wanderings. Book length. All production details customized to individual book and market. See web site for guidelines and updated information. NO personal stories of abuse, addiction, mental illness, or incarceration." Expects 2 titles 2006, 5 titles 2007. Discounts: upon request. Reporting time: 4-6 weeks. Simultaneous submissions accepted: yes. Payment: as per contract. Copyrights for author. Subjects: African Literature, Africa, African Studies, Architecture, Biography, California, Cities, Earth, Natural History, Los Angeles, Nature, Science, Travel, The

West, Women, Yosemite.

Cloverfield Press, Matthew Greenfield, 429 North Ogden Drive, Apt.1, Los Angeles, CA 90036-1730, submissions@cloverfieldpress.com, www.cloverfieldpress.com. 2004. Fiction. "Currently publishing only individual works of short fiction, with each short story as its own book. Each book has a hand-printed letterpress dust jacket and endpapers. We are not publishing collections of short stories or longer works of fiction or non-fiction. Recent authors and illustrators have included Haruki Murakami, Justus Ballard, Henry Baum, Miranda July, Mary Rechner, Laurence Dumortier, Carol Treadwell, Ann Faison, Michiko Yao, Elinor Nissley, Eric Ernest Johnson, Emma Hedditch, Nava Lubelski and Lecia Dole-Recio." Pub'd 2 titles 2005; expects 4 titles 2006, 4-6 titles 2007. Reporting time: Six months. Simultaneous submissions accepted: Yes.

•**Coach House Books,** Stan Bevington, Publisher; Alana Wilcox, Senior Editor; Christina Palassio, Managing Editor; Bill Kennedy, Web Editor, 401 Huron, on bpNichol Lane, Toronto, ON M5S 2G5, Canada, t: 800-367-6360, f: 416-977-1158, website: www.chbooks.com. "Located in a crumbling old coach house on bpNichol Lane, in the heart of Toronto's Annex neighborhood, Coach House has been publishing literary fiction, poetry, drama and artists' books for over forty years. Since its inception, the press has produced an impressive list of innovative and challenging literature by some of Canada's finest authors, including Margaret Atwood, Christian Bok, Nicole Brossard, Anne-Marie MacDonald, Anne Michaels and Michael Ondaatje."

COALITION FOR PRISONERS' RIGHTS NEWSLETTER, Mara Taub, PO Box 1911, Santa Fe, NM 87504, 505-982-9520. 1976. Articles, cartoons, interviews, letters, news items, non-fiction. "Length of material: 250+/- words. Politically progressive. Half of each issue is excerpts of letters from prisoners." circ. 7M+. 12/yr. Pub'd 12 issues 2005; expects 12 issues 2006, 12 issues 2007. sub. price $12 individuals, $25 to institutions, free to prisoners and their families; per copy free; sample free. Back issues: free if available. 8pp. Reporting time: 6 weeks. We accept simultaneous submissions from prisoners. Publishes (from prisoners) less than 20% of manuscripts submitted. Payment: none. Not copyrighted. Ads: none. Subjects: African-American, Civil Rights, Crime, Human Rights, Prison.

•**Coastal 181,** Cary Stratton, Jim Rigney, 29 Water Street, Newburyport, MA 01950, 978-462-2436, 978 462-9198 (fax), 877-907-8181, www.coastal181.com. 2000. Non-fiction. "Focus on motorsports, particularly driver autobiographies, auto racing history." avg. press run 4000. Pub'd 2 titles 2005; expects 4 titles 2006, 6 titles 2007. Discounts: 40% wholesale. 272pp. Reporting time: 3 - 6 weeks. Simultaneous submissions accepted: Yes. Publishes 20% of manuscripts submitted. Payment: Varies with author. Varies with book. Subjects: Autobiography, Autos, Biography, History, Sports, Outdoors, Transportation.

Cobblestone Publishing Company (see also APPLESEEDS; CALLIOPE: Exploring World History; COBBLESTONE: Discover American History; FACES: People, Places, and Culture; FOOTSTEPS: African American History; ODYSSEY: Adventures in Science), Lou Waryncia, Managing Editor, 30 Grove Street, Suite C, Peterborough, NH 03458, 603-924-7209, Fax 603-924-7380, custsvc@cobblestone.mv.com. 1980. avg. press run 22M. Pub'd 55 titles 2005; expects 55 titles 2006, 50 titles 2007. 52pp. Reporting time: queries sent well in advance of deadline may not be answered for several months. Go-aheads usually sent 5 months prior to publication date. Simultaneous submissions accepted: yes. Publishes a variable % of manuscripts submitted. Payment: upon publication. We own copyright.

COBBLESTONE: Discover American History, Cobblestone Publishing Company, Margaret E. Chorlian, Editor, 30 Grove Street, Suite C, Peterborough, NH 03458, 603-924-7209, Fax 603-924-7380, custsvc@cobblestone.mv.com. 1980. Poetry, fiction, articles, art, photos, interviews, reviews, music, plays, non-fiction. "Material must be written for children ages 8-14. Most articles do not exceed 1M words, write Editor for guidelines as we focus each issue on a particular theme." circ. 36M. 9/yr. Pub'd 9 issues 2005; expects 9 issues 2006, 9 issues 2007. sub. price $29.95 + $8/yr for foreign and Canada, Canadian subs add 7% GST; per copy $4.95; sample $4.95. Back issues: $4.95, annual set $48.95, includes slipcase and cumulative index. Discounts: 15% to agency, bulk rate 3 subs @ $17.95 each/year. 52pp. Reporting time: queries sent well in advance of deadline may not be answered for several months. Go-aheads usually sent 5 months prior to publication date. Payment: on publication. Copyrighted, *Cobblestone* buys all rights. Pub's reviews: 89 in 2005. §History books for children, ages 8-14, American history related only. No ads. Subjects: Children, Youth, History.

CODA: The Jazz Magazine, Bill Smith, PO Box 1002, Station O, Toronto, Ont. M4A 2N4, Canada, 416-465-9093. 1958. Articles, photos, interviews, criticism, reviews, news items. "Our emphasis is on the art rather than the commerce of the music (i.e. we concentrate on non-commercialism) and we cover jazz of all styles and areas." circ. 3M. 6/yr. Expects 6 issues 2006. sub. price $24 Canada & US, elsewhere $36 Can.; per copy $4; sample $4. Back issues: $15 for 10. Discounts: agency discount (subscriptions only) 20%. 40pp. Reporting time: 1 month to 2 years. Payment: small. Rights revert to author on publication. Pub's reviews: 22 in 2005. §Jazz, blues. Ads: $300/$160/75¢ (min. $15). Subjects: Black, Music.

COE REVIEW, Gordon Mennenga, 1220 1st Ave NE, Cedar Rapids, IA 52402. 1972. Poetry, fiction, art.

"Poetry is read September-November and fiction is read January-March." circ. 500. 2/yr. Pub'd 2 issues 2005; expects 2 issues 2006, 2 issues 2007. sub. price $5; per copy $5; sample $5. Back issues: $5. 125pp. Simultaneous submissions accepted: No. Publishes 50% of manuscripts submitted. Payment: Free Copy. Copyrighted.

Coffee House Press, Allan Kornblum, Publisher; Christopher Fischbach, Senior Editor, 27 N. 4th Street, Minneapolis, MN 55401, 612-338-0125, Fax 612-338-4004, fish@coffeehousepress.org, www.coffeehouse-press.org. 1984. Poetry, fiction, art, long-poems. "Books may be ordered directly from publisher." avg. press run 3M. Pub'd 12 titles 2005; expects 12 titles 2006, 12 titles 2007. Discounts: retail 1-4 copies 20%, 5-24 425, 25-99 43%, 100-249 44%, 250-499 45%, 500-750 46%, 750+ 47%; libraries, standing orders 10%. Reporting time: up to 5 months. Simultaneous submissions accepted: no. Publishes 1% of manuscripts submitted. Payment: 8% of list for trade books. Copyrights for author. Subjects: Essays, Fiction, Iowa, Literature (General), Novels, Poetry, Short Stories.

•**COFFEESPOONS,** David Moore L, 1104 E. 38th Place, Tulsa, OK 74105, 918-712-9278. 2006. Monthly. Expects 3 issues 2006, 12 issues 2007. sub. price $20; per copy $3.25; sample $3. 60pp. Reporting time: 4-8 weeks. Simultaneous submissions accepted: Yes. Publishes 5% of manuscripts submitted. Payment: Two contributors copies. Copyrighted, reverts to author. Pub's reviews.

•**COGNITIO: A Graduate Humanities Journal, Cantadora Press,** Russell James, 5406 Persimmon Hollow Rd., Milton, FL 32583-6700. 2002. Articles, non-fiction. circ. 100. 2/yr. Expects 1 issue 2006, 2 issues 2007. sub. price $10; per copy $10; sample $10. Back issues: $10. Discounts: 10%. 50pp. Reporting time: 1 day. Simultaneous submissions accepted: No. Publishes 90% of manuscripts submitted. Payment: 15% royalties on books payable every quarter, no compensation to journal authors. Copyrighted, reverts to author. Pub's reviews: none in 2005. §Humanities books. Ads: $10 per half-page, will trade for advertising space in other journals. Subjects: African-American, The Americas, Catholic, English, Ethics, Florida, Genealogy, History, Military, Veterans, Non-Fiction, Political Science, Research, Reviews.

The Colbert House, Jerry Jerman, Larry Colbert, 1005 N. Flood Avenue, Suite 138, PO Box 150, Norman, OK 73069, 405-329-7999,FAX 405-329-6977, 800-698-2644, customerservice@greatbargainbooks.com, www.greatbargainbooks.com. 1995. Fiction, non-fiction. avg. press run 3M. Expects 3 titles 2006, 5 titles 2007. Discounts: trade 2-4 books 20%, 5-24 40%, 25-49 45%, 50-99 46%, 100+ 50%. 192pp. Reporting time: 3 months. Simultaneous submissions accepted: no. Publishes less than 8% of manuscripts submitted. Payment: no royalties, profit division. Copyrights for author. Subjects: African-American, Children, Youth, Fiction, Religion.

COLD-DRILL, Cold-Drill Books, Mitch Wieland, Faculty Editor, 1910 University Drive, Boise, ID 83725, 208-426-3862. 1970. Poetry, fiction, articles, art, photos, cartoons, parts-of-novels, plays, concrete art, non-fiction. "Submission deadline: December 1st for March 1 issue. Send xerox, SASE (we notify by Jan. 15 only if accepted). Open to literary and innovative forms of high quality." circ. 500. 1/yr. Pub'd 1 issue 2005; expects 1 issue 2006, 1 issue 2007. sub. price $15 (inc. p/h); per copy $15 (inc. p/h); sample $15 (inc. p/h). Back issues: same. Discounts: none. 150pp. Reporting time: by January 1 of each year. Payment: copy of magazine. Copyrighted, reverts to author. Subjects: Fiction, Idaho, Literature (General), Poetry, Short Stories.

Cold-Drill Books (see also COLD-DRILL), Tom Trusky, Dept. of English, Boise State University, Boise, ID 83725. 1980. "Prior publication in *Cold-Drill Magazine* required. Interested in multiple artist's books editions." avg. press run 50-1M. Pub'd 1 title 2005; expects 1 title 2006. Discounts: 40%, no returns. Pages vary. Reporting time: 4 months. Payment: 25% on third printing. Copyrights for author. Subjects: Book Arts, Diaries, Family, Idaho, The West, Women.

•**Colgate Press,** Jack Lohman, P.O.Box 597, Sussex, WI 53089, 414-477-8686. 2005. Discounts: Retailers: 1 Book- 20% discount 2-3 Books- 30% 4 or more- 40% Wholesalers: 1-2 Books- 30% discount 3-4 Books- 40% 5 or more- 50% Quantity Stocking Orders- %55 Libraries, Universities, Companies, and Institutions: 1-2 Books- None 3-4 Books- 20% 5 or more- 30%. 272pp. Copyrights for author.

Collectors Press, Inc., Lisa Perry, Operations Manager; Jennifer Weaver-Neist, Editorial Manager, PO Box 230986, Portland, OR 97281, 503-684-3030, Fax 503-684-3777. 1992. Art, photos, non-fiction. "Collectors Press, Inc. is an award-winning pop culture publisher and is currently accepting manuscripts and proposals for books on the following topics: cooking, pop culture, fashion, art, crafts, hobbies, and advertising. Content should be visual in nature." avg. press run 7.5M. Pub'd 12 titles 2005; expects 13 titles 2006, 13 titles 2007. Trade discounts. 150pp. Reporting time: standard. Simultaneous submissions accepted: yes. Publishes 5% of manuscripts submitted. Payment: confidential. Copyrights for author.

COLLEGE ENGLISH, Jeanne Gunner, Dept. of English, U Mass/Boston, Santa Clara University, Santa Clara, CA 95053. 1939. Articles, criticism, reviews, letters. "*College English* no longer publishes poetry. Instead, we invite articles on the theory and pedagogy of creative writing. This change has enabled the journal to cover more genres of creative writing than poetry alone." circ. 13M. 6/yr. Pub'd 6 issues 2005; expects 6 issues 2006, 6 issues 2007. sub. price $25; per copy $6, $5 members; sample $6, $6.25 from NCTE in Urbana, IL. Back issues: $6. 100pp. Reporting time: 16 weeks. Simultaneous submissions accepted: no. Publishes 9% of manuscripts submitted. Payment: none. Copyrighted, reverts to author. Pub's reviews: 9 in 2005. §Literary theory, linguistic theory, theory of learning and pedagogy, history of English studies, studies of works of literature, rhetoric-composition. Ads: phone NCTE for most recent rates (800-369-6283). Subject: English.

COLLEGE LITERATURE, Kostas Myrsiades Ph.D., 210 East Rosedale Avenue, West Chester University, West Chester, PA 19383, 610-436-2901, fax 610-436-2275, collit@wcupa.edu, www.collegeliterature.org. 1975. Articles, reviews. circ. 500. 4/yr. Pub'd 4 issues 2005; expects 4 issues 2006, 4 issues 2007. sub. price $40.00; per copy $10.00; sample free. Back issues: inquire. Discounts: 10%. 212pp. Reporting time: usually 4 months. Simultaneous submissions accepted: No. Publishes 40% of manuscripts submitted. Payment: none. Copyrighted, does not revert to author. Pub's reviews: approx. 20 in 2005. §comparative literature and pedagogy; teaching literature. Ads: $150 full page only, B/W. Subjects: African Literature, Africa, African Studies, Book Reviewing, Feminism, Gender Issues, Indexes & Abstracts, Indigenous Cultures, Language, Literature (General), Multicultural, Post Modern, Race, Reading, Reviews, Third World, Minorities.

COLOR WHEEL, Frederick Moe, Brad Marion, 36 West Main Street, Warner, NH 03278, info@colorwheeljournal.net www.colorwheeljournal.net. 1990. Poetry, fiction, articles, art, photos, criticism, letters, long-poems, collages, non-fiction. "*Color Wheel* seeks to publish high quality writing and artwork that stimulates thoughtful discussion and dialogue. We prefer themes that focus on ecological and spiritual concerns, or counterculture musings. We encourage contributions from New England writers and artists in general and New Hampshire writers are highly encouraged." circ. 400. 2/yr. Pub'd 2 issues 2005; expects 2 issues 2006, 2 issues 2007. sub. price $24 for three issues; per copy $12; sample $9. Back issues: $9. Discounts: to contributors. 114pp. Reporting time: 1 to 2 months. Simultaneous submissions accepted: no. Publishes 20% of manuscripts submitted. Payment: 1 or more copies of issue in which work appears. Copyrighted, reverts to author. Pub's reviews: 2 in 2005. §planning on including reviews of small press books, artists books, indie music, zines, etc. Ads: no ads. Subjects: Arts, Environment, Humanism, New England, New Hampshire, Peace, Poetry, Spiritual.

COLORADO REVIEW, Center for Literary Publishing, Stephanie G'Schwind, Editor; Donald Revell, Poetry Editor; Jorie Graham, Poetry Editor, Colorado Review / Dept of English, Colorado State University, Fort Collins, CO 80523, 970-491-5449, creview@colostate.edu, http://coloradoreview.colostate.edu. 1956. Poetry, fiction, reviews, parts-of-novels, long-poems, non-fiction. "Colorado Review publishes both new and established writers of contemporary short fiction, poetry, and creative nonfiction. Recent contributors include Kent Haruf, Mark Spragg, Ann Hood, Bret Lott, Jacob Appel, Paul Mandelbaum, Floyd Skloot, Jonis Agee, Kathleen Lee, Joyelle McSweeney, Alice Notley, G. C. Waldrep, Dan Beachy-Quick, Martha Ronk, Joanna Klink, Aaron McCollough, Lucie Brock-Broido, Tomaz Salamun, and Sophie Cabot Black." circ. 1100. 3/yr. Pub'd 3 issues 2005; expects 3 issues 2006, 3 issues 2007. sub. price $24; per copy $10.00; sample $10.00. Back issues: $10.00. Discounts: Discount to distributors is 50%. Bookstore discount is 30% on three or more copies. 200pp. Reporting time: Two months. Simultaneous submissions accepted: Yes. Publishes 1% of manuscripts submitted. Payment: $5 per page plus two copies of the issue in which author is published. Copyrighted, reverts to author. Pub's reviews: 13 in 2005. §Poetry, literary fiction, and creative nonfiction. Book reviews are normally solicited. Ads: Full page is $150; half page is $75. Subjects: Essays, Fiction, Memoirs, Non-Fiction, Poetry.

COLORLINES, Tram Nguyen, 4096 Piedmont Avenue, PMB 319, Oakland, CA 94611, 510-653-3415, Fax 510-653-3427, colorlines@arc.org, www.colorlines.com. 1998. Articles, art, photos, cartoons, interviews, criticism, reviews, music, news items, non-fiction. "Recent contributors: Angela Davis, Robin D.G. Kelley, Mike Davis, Gloria Anzaldua, William 'Upski' Wimsatt, Michael Omi, June Jordan, Angela Oh. Material: 3,000-4,000 words per article. Biases: welcome articles with race angle or community organizing/activism angle and investigative pieces." circ. 20M. 4/yr. Pub'd 4 issues 2005; expects 4 issues 2006, 4 issues 2007. sub. price $16; per copy $6 publisher, $3.95 newsstand; sample free. Back issues: $6. Discounts: please contact publisher for bulk prices; trades are free. 45pp. Reporting time: 1-2 months. Simultaneous submissions accepted: yes. Publishes 10% of manuscripts submitted. Payment: 10¢ per word up to a maximum of $250. Copyrighted, rights negotiable. Pub's reviews: 5 in 2005. §Politics, race/ethnicity non-fiction/fiction, sociology, gender/feminist studies. Ads: $1,025/$700/$1.25 per word (min. 25 words). Subjects: Civil Rights, Culture, Immigration, Labor, Politics, Race, Sociology.

Columbia Alternative Library Press, Jason McQuinn, PO Box 1446, Columbia, MO 65205-1446, 573-442-4352 jmcquinn@calpress.org. 1989. avg. press run 2M. Expects 4 titles 2006, 4 titles 2007. Discounts: 10-19 copies 20%, 20-59 40%, 60-99 45%, 100-249 50%, 250+ 55%. 200pp. Reporting time: 2-3 months. Simultaneous submissions accepted: yes. Publishes 5-10% of manuscripts submitted. Payment: royalties = 5% of gross sales. Does not copyright for author. Subjects: Anarchist, Libertarian.

COMBAT, the Literary Expression of Battlefield Touchstones, Editorial Staff, PO Box 3, Circleville, WV 26804-0003, majordomo@combat.ws, www.combat.ws/. 2002. Poetry, fiction, articles, art, photos, cartoons, satire, parts-of-novels, non-fiction. "Theme: ramifications of wartime insights and experiences by combatants, noncombatants, and their families." circ. online. 4/yr. Expects 4 issues 2006, 4 issues 2007. sub. price free. Simultaneous submissions accepted: no. Copyrighted. Pub's reviews. Subject: Military, Veterans.

THE COMICS JOURNAL, Fantagraphics Books, Gary Groth, 7563 Lake City Way, Seattle, WA 98115. 1976. Articles, cartoons, interviews, criticism, reviews, letters, news items. "*The Comics Journal* is a monthly magazine devoted to news and reviews of the comic book trade, both mainstream and independent publishing." circ. 10M. 10/yr. Pub'd 10 issues 2005; expects 10 issues 2006, 10 issues 2007. sub. price $35 USA; per copy $4.95; sample $4.95. 120pp. Reporting time: 1-2 months. Simultaneous submissions accepted: yes. Publishes 1% of manuscripts submitted. Payment: 1-1/2¢ per word. Copyrighted, reverts to author. Pub's reviews: 100 in 2005. §Comics, comics-related publications and products. Ads: $200/$120. Subject: Comics.

COMICS REVUE, Manuscript Press, Rick Norwood, PO Box 336 -Manuscript Press, Mountain Home, TN 37684-0336, 432-926-7495. 1984. Cartoons. "We publish syndicated comic strips: Rick O'Shay, Buz Sawyer, Alley Oop, Tarzan, Krazy Kat, Little Orphan Annie, Steve Canyon, Modesty Blaise, The Phantom, Gasoline Alley, and Flash Gordon. We are not interested in looking at submissions unless they are better than what is available from the syndicates. No submissions can be returned. Submissions are discouraged, but if you must submit a comic strip, send xerox copies only and include a SASE for a reply." circ. 1200. 12/yr. Pub'd 12 issues 2005; expects 12 issues 2006, 12 issues 2007. sub. price $45; per copy $9; sample same. Back issues: $9 for single copies, $45 for 12 copies, current or old. Discounts: 10-99 copies 40% off, 100-499 copies 50% off, 500+ copies 60% off. 64pp. Reporting time: indefinite. Simultaneous submissions accepted: no. Publishes 0% of manuscripts submitted. Payment: $5 per page. Copyrighted, reverts to author. Pub's reviews: 10-12 in 2005. §Comic strip reprints. Ads: $125/$70. Subject: Comics.

Command Performance Press, Contee Seely, 1755 Hopkins St., Berkeley, CA 94707-2714, 510-524-1191. 2005. Photos. "Our first and only book is a book of photos of millinneum-era Berkeley, California, with historical and sociological commentary. The future is an open book." Expects 1 title 2006. 216pp. Simultaneous submissions accepted: No. Copyrights to be determined. Subjects: Americana, California, History, Picture Books.

Common Boundaries, Debra J. Gawrych, Sherry Roberts, 2895 Luckie Road, Weston, FL 33331-3047, 954-385-8434, Fax 954-385-8652, www.commonboundaries.com, info@commonboundaries.com. 2001. Fiction, non-fiction. "Published: *The Seven Aspects of Sisterhood: Empowering Women Through Self-Discovery* by Debra J. Gawrych. Next book: *The Art of Consulting -.*" avg. press run 2M. Expects 1 title 2006, /1-2 titles 2007. Pages vary. Reporting time: 3-6 months. Simultaneous submissions accepted: yes. Publishes 10% of manuscripts submitted. Does not copyright for author. Subjects: Adolescence, Leadership, Psychology, Self-Help, Spiritual, Women.

Common Courage Press, Greg Bates, Flic Shooter, Box 702, Monroe, ME 04951, 207-525-0900, 800-497-3207, Fax 207-525-3068. 1991. Non-fiction. "Politics, alternative, social justice, feminism, race and gender issues, ecology, economics." avg. press run 5K. Pub'd 12 titles 2005; expects 12 titles 2006, 12 titles 2007. Discounts: trade 1-10 25%, 20+ 40%. 250pp. Reporting time: 30 days. Simultaneous submissions accepted: yes. Publishes 5% of manuscripts submitted. Payment: 10% net. Copyrights for author. Subjects: African-American, Anarchist, Disabled, Ecology, Foods, Environment, Feminism, Gay, Humanism, Hunger, Lesbianism, Mexico, Non-Fiction, Peace, Politics, Race.

Communication Creativity, Ann Markham, 425 Cedar, PO Box 909, Buena Vista, CO 81211, 719-395-8659, Marilyn@CommunicationCreativity.com, www.communicationcreativity.com. 1977. Non-fiction. "Communication Creativity books are designed to be both entertaining and informational. They deal primarily with subjects in the fields of business. Not soliciting submissions." avg. press run 5M. Pub'd 3 titles 2005; expects 3 titles 2006, 4 titles 2007. Discounts: from 20% to 50%. 224pp. Subjects: Advertising, Self-Promotion, Business & Economics, Communication, Journalism, Consumer, Fiction, Finances, History, How-To, Non-Fiction, Printing, Publishing, Real Estate, Self-Help, Women, Writers/Writing.

The Communication Press, Randall Harrison, PO Box 22541, San Francisco, CA 94122, 415-386-0178. 1977. Cartoons. "Our focus is on humorous how-to, such as our *How To Cut Your Water Use—and Still Stay Sane and Sanitary.* We also are interested in art, psychology and communication. We're probably a poor market for freelancers as we already have as many projects as we can handle for the next few years; and we hope to stay small and quality oriented." avg. press run 5M. Pub'd 1-2 titles 2005. Discounts: 40% trade. 96-128pp. Reporting time: 6-8 weeks. Payment: variable. Copyrights for author. Subjects: How-To, Humor.

Communicom Publishing Company, Donna Matrazzo, 19300 NW Sauvie Island Road, Portland, OR 97231, 503-621-3049. 1984. Non-fiction. "We publish and distribute books (and other items) related to business communications, specializing in writing and audio visual work. Title published: *The Corporate Scriptwriting*

Book, Donna Matrazzo.'' avg. press run 5M. Discounts: 20% to schools, bookstore discount varies by volume. 250pp. Reporting time: no specification. Payment: arrangements made on book-by-book basis. Copyrights for author. Subjects: Communication, Journalism, Electronics, How-To, Textbooks.

COMMUNITIES, Diana Christian, Editor, 1025 Camp Elliott Road, Black Mountain, NC 28711, 828-669-9702, communities@ic.org, www.ic.org, store.ic.org. 1972. Articles, art, photos, interviews, reviews, letters. ''Bias: limited to contributions relating to aspects of intentional communities and cooperative living.'' circ. 3K. 4/yr. Pub'd 5 issues 2005; expects 4 issues 2006, 4 issues 2007. sub. price US$20/4 issues within USA, US$24/4 issues to Canada, US$26/4 issue to other countries; per copy $6; sample $6. Back issues: full available set (approx. 120) $350. Discounts: 3-4 copies 25%, 5-9 30%, 10-24 35%, 25-49 40%, 50+ 50%. 76pp. Reporting time: 60 days. Simultaneous submissions accepted: yes. Payment: free copies, or 1 year subscription. Copyrighted, reverts to author. Pub's reviews: 12 in 2005. §Intentional communities, alternative culture, worker-owned co-ops, student co-ops. Ads: $250/$145/proportionals. Subjects: Community, Counter-Culture, Alternatives, Communes, Lifestyles, New Age.

Community Service, Inc. (see also NEW SOLUTIONS), PO Box 243, Yellow Springs, OH 45387-0243, 937-767-2161, www.smallcommunity.org. 1940. Articles, interviews, criticism, reviews, letters, news items, non-fiction. avg. press run 900. Pub'd 2 titles 2005; expects 1 title 2006, 1 title 2007. Discounts: write for schedule, 40% off for 10. 35pp. Reporting time: 4-6 weeks. Simultaneous submissions accepted: yes. Publishes 66% of manuscripts submitted. Payment: none. Does not copyright for author. Subjects: Biography, Business & Economics, Community, Education, Family, Newsletter, Philosophy, Society, Sociology.

Compact Clinicals, 7205 NW Waukomis Drive, Kansas City, MO 64151, 816-587-0044 or 800-408-8830, Fax 816-587-7198. 1996. Non-fiction. ''Psychology books - condensed reviews of assessment and treatment of mental disorders. A series produced for mental health professionals and educated lay public. Please contact before submitting.'' avg. press run 2M. Pub'd 2 titles 2005; expects 4 titles 2006, 6 titles 2007. Discounts: Retail: 1-3 0%, 4+ 20%; wholesalers/distrib. up to 24 books 35%, 25+ 50%. 96pp. Simultaneous submissions accepted: yes. Payment: 7% royalty. Does not copyright for author. Subjects: Mental Health, Psychiatry, Psychology.

A COMPANION IN ZEOR, Karen MacLeod, 1622-B Swallow Crest Drive, Sunrise Villas Apartments, Edgewood, MD 21040-1751, Fax 410-676-0164, Klitman323@aol.com, cz@simegen.com www.simegen.com/ sgfandom/rimonslibrary/cz/. 1978. Poetry, fiction, art, cartoons, interviews, letters, news items. ''Contributions based on the universes of Jacqueline Lichtenberg, and Jean Lorrah. Any and all universes they have created or worked in. Preferred, nothing obscene—no homosexuality unless relevant to story line. Science-fiction oriented. Limited only to creations based on Lichtenberg and Lorrah works. None other considered. Issues now produced for the website. Paper production is now secondary market, but available.'' circ. 100. Irregular. Expects 1 issue 2006, 2 issues 2007. price per copy issues are different prices, SASE list on line, can negotiate for free issues on occasion; sample See price lists on line, with issue availability—http://www.simegen.com/marketplace/ emporium/czordfor.html. Back issues: See website price list for available issues and costs—http:/ /www.simegen.com/marketplace/emporium/czordfor.html. Discounts: willing to discuss and arrange. 60pp. Reporting time: 1 month. Payment: contributor copy, possibly more than one if arranged. Copyrighted, rights revert to author after 5 years to the contributor. Pub's reviews: 1 in 2005. §Almost anything but romance type, science fiction preferred for my own reading. Subject: Science Fiction.

Comparative Sedimentology Lab., R.N. Ginsburg, University of Miami, RSMAS/MGG, 4600 Rickenbacker Cswy., Miami, FL 33149. 1972. Pub'd 1 title 2005. Discounts: 10% on orders of 10 copies or more of any one issue. Subjects: Caribbean, Environment, Florida, Geology, History, Science.

The Compass Press, W.D. Howells, Box 9546, Washington, DC 20016, 202-333-2182, orders 212-564-3730. 1988. Articles, interviews, non-fiction. ''Contemporary history with special interest in institutional biography and generational change. Current public and political affairs with special interest in decision process.'' avg. press run 3M. Pub'd 2 titles 2005; expects 4 titles 2006, 4 titles 2007. Discounts: standard. 300pp. Payment: possible, modest advance for completed mss only 15% net. Copyrights for author. Subjects: Anthropology, Archaelogy, Biography, History, Political Science, Politics, Public Affairs, Sociology.

COMPASS ROSE, David Crouse, Jennifer Monroe, 40 Chester Street, Chester, NH 03036, 603-887-7428, compassrose@chestercollege.edu, http://compassrose.chestercollege.edu. 1990. Poetry, fiction, articles, art, photos, interviews, satire, parts-of-novels, long-poems, non-fiction. ''We are looking for intelligent work with an attention to craft. We have no real length biases and our tastes range from the experimental to the traditional. Please see our website for more information about our publishing schedule and writing contests.'' circ. 800. 1/yr. Pub'd 1 issue 2005; expects 1 issue 2006, 1 issue 2007. sub. price $10; per copy $10; sample $10. Back issues: $8. 100pp. Reporting time: 2-3 months. Simultaneous submissions accepted: yes. Publishes 5% of manuscripts submitted. Payment: copies. Copyrighted, reverts to author. Subject: Literature (General).

THE COMPLEAT NURSE, Dry Bones Press, J. R.N. Rankin, 3615 Villa Serena Circle, Rocklin, CA

95765-5547, www.drybones.com. 1991. Poetry, fiction, articles, cartoons, interviews, satire, criticism, reviews, letters, news items, non-fiction. "*TCN* only became monthly in late 1992. A 4 pager, occasionally longer. Any matter of interest to nurses, their patients or colleagues. Great interest in law, social policy affecting health care/health care delivery. Support single-payer health care. Welcome idea pieces, controversial pieces to trigger discussion." circ. 500. 12/yr. Pub'd 12 issues 2005; expects 12 issues 2006, 12 issues 2007. sub. price $12; per copy offering; sample SASE. Back issues: SASE, if available. Discounts: Bulk arrangement, usually cost of printing and shipping extra amount requested. 4-6pp. Reporting time: we will respond briefly at once. Simultaneous submissions accepted: yes. Payment: copies, diskette in desired format, glory, being published. Copyrighted, reverts to author. Pub's reviews: 3 in 2005. §Nursing, patient-authored books, economics, arts and letters, health care. Ads: $50/$30/$10 per column inch, $10 business card. Subjects: Computers, Calculators, Disease, Health, Medicine, Nursing, San Francisco.

Comrades Press, Verian Thomas, Editor, 23 George Street, Stockton, Southam, Warwickshire CV47 8JS, England, editor@comrade.org.uk, www.comrade.org.uk/press. 2000. Poetry, fiction, photos, long-poems, non-fiction. "Comrades Press uses print on demand technology for hardback and paperback books and also publishes handmade chapbooks of poetry." avg. press run 50. Pub'd 3 titles 2005; expects 6 titles 2006, 6 titles 2007. 100pp. Reporting time: 3 months. Simultaneous submissions accepted: no. Publishes 3% of manuscripts submitted. Payment: 10 copies of chapbooks. Copyrights for author. Subjects: Experimental, Fiction, Non-Fiction, Poetry.

Comstock Bonanza Press, 18919 William Quirk Drive, Grass Valley, CA 95945-8611, 530-263-2906. 1979. Non-fiction. avg. press run 1.5M. Pub'd 1 title 2005; expects 1 title 2006, 1 title 2007. Discounts: 40% trade and wholesale, 15% schools and libraries. 120-400pp. Reporting time: 45 days. Simultaneous submissions accepted: yes. Publishes 5% of manuscripts submitted. Payment: 10%. Copyrights for author. Subjects: Asian-American, Biography, California, Government, History, Memoirs, Native American, Non-Fiction, Politics, Race, Transportation, The West, Women.

THE COMSTOCK REVIEW, John M. Bellinger, Managing Editor; Peggy Sperber Flanders, Assoc. Managing Editor, Comstock Writers' Group, Inc., 4956 St. John Drive, Syracuse, NY 13215, www.comstockreview.org. 1987. Poetry. "Formerly *Poetpourri.*" circ. 500. 2/yr. Pub'd 2 issues 2005; expects 2 issues 2006, 2 issues 2007. sub. price $16/2 issues, $28/4 issues; per copy $9; sample $6 through year 2003. Back issues: $4 for Poetpourri. 108pp. Reporting time: 6 weeks after end of reading periods (Jan. 1-Mar. 15 yearly at present). Simultaneous submissions discouraged. Publishes less than 10% of manuscripts submitted. Payment: contributor's copy only. Copyrighted, reverts to author. Pub's reviews: approx.40 on website in 2005. §poetry only. Ads: none. Subject: Poetry.

CONCHO RIVER REVIEW, Mary Ellen Hartje Dr., General Editor; Jerry Bradley Dr., Poetry Editor; Charlie McMurtry Dr., Fiction Editor; Jennifer DiJulio Ms., Nonfiction Editor; Brad Butler Dr., Layout Editor, English Department, Angelo State University, San Angelo, TX 76909, 915-942-2269, me.hartje@angelo.edu. 1987. Poetry, fiction, articles, criticism, reviews, non-fiction. "Fiction and non-fiction: 1500-5000 words; poetry open, book reviews. We read and consider all submissions. Circulation office: English Department, Angelo State University, Box 10894 ASU Station, San Angelo, TX 76909." circ. 300. 2/yr. Pub'd 2 issues 2005; expects 2 issues 2006, 2 issues 2007. sub. price $14; per copy $8; sample $5. Back issues: $5. Discounts: query. 115pp. Reporting time: 2-6 months. Simultaneous submissions accepted: yes. Publishes 10-15% of manuscripts submitted. Payment: copies. Copyrighted, reverts to author. Pub's reviews: 10 in 2005. §Fiction, poetry, nonfiction by writers of Texas and the Southwest or about Texas and the Southwest. Ads: query. Subjects: Southwest, Texas.

•**CONCRETE JUNGLE JOURNAL, Concrete Jungle Press,** D. Wayne Dworsky, 163 Third Avenue #130, New York, NY 10003, 718-465-8573 URL: www.concretejunglepress.com. 2006. Poetry, fiction, articles, art, photos, cartoons, interviews, satire, reviews, parts-of-novels, long-poems, news items, non-fiction. "The theme of Concrete Jungle Journal is nature in the city." circ. 100. 200/yr. Expects 200 issues 2006, 800 issues 2007. sub. price One year is $10/Two years is $18; per copy $3; sample $2. Back issues: $2. Discounts: 40% agents; 60%wholesalers, 40%retailers, 40%institutions, classrooms and bookstores. 16pp. Reporting time: within three months. Simultaneous submissions accepted: Yes. Payment: At the moment payment is in contributor copies. Copyrighted, reverts to author. Pub's reviews. §nature books, books for walks in the city, nature in the city. Ads: full page $50/half page $30/quarter page $20/text (20 words)$10. Subjects: Birds, Botany, Cities, Fiction, Haiku, Handicapped, Interviews, Maps, Nature, New York, Novels, Poetry, Reviews, Satire, H.D. Thoreau.

Concrete Jungle Press (see also CONCRETE JUNGLE JOURNAL), D. Wayne Dworsky, Editor; Lynette Perez, Editor; Stavreula Kristofkorski, Editor, 163 Third Avenue #130, New York, NY 10003, Tel: 718-465-8573, Fax: 718-468-3007, URL: www.concretejunglepress.com. 2004. Poetry, fiction, parts-of-novels, long-poems, non-fiction. avg. press run 1000. Pub'd 3 titles 2005; expects 1 title 2006, 1 title 2007. Discounts: Wholsalers 60%/retailers, stores, schools, institutions 40%. 43-200pp. Reporting time: Reports in 3 months. Simultaneous submissions accepted: Yes. Copyrights for author. Subjects: Nature, New York, Novels, Poetry,

Young Adult.

Concrete Wolf Press, Brent Allard, Lana Ayers, Martha D. Hall, PO Box 730, Amherst, NH 03031-0730, editors@concretewolf.com, http://concretewolf.com. 2001. Poetry, art, photos. "Concrete Wolf is a chapbook-only press now via our annual contest. We have suspended publication of the quarterly journal." avg. press run 250-1000. Pub'd 2 titles 2005; expects 1 title 2006, 1 title 2007. Discounts: Author and school discounts. 40pp. Reporting time: 6-12 months. Simultaneous submissions accepted: yes. Publishes 0.5% of manuscripts submitted. Payment: Contest prize $100 plus 50 copies. Copyrights for author. Subject: Poetry.

CONDUIT, William D. Waltz, 510 Eighth Avenue NE, Minneapolis, MN 55413, www.conduit.org, info@conduit.org. 1993. Poetry, fiction, art, photos, cartoons, interviews, reviews, letters, non-fiction. "Past contributors: Mary Jo Bang, Gillian Conoley, Russell Edson, Alice Fulton, Bob Hicok, Noelle Kocot, Geoffrey G. O'Brien, Tomaz Salamun, Cole Swensen, James Tate, Dean Young. Prose: 2,500-3,500 words maximum. Poetry: any length." circ. 1000. 2/yr. Pub'd 2 issues 2005; expects 2 issues 2006, 2 issues 2007. sub. price $15 individuals, $25 institutions; per copy $8; sample $6. Back issues: $6. Discounts: none. 80pp. Reporting time: 9 weeks-9 months. Simultaneous submissions accepted: no. Publishes 1% of manuscripts submitted. Payment: copies. Copyrighted, reverts to author. Ads: none. Subjects: Arts, Avant-Garde, Experimental Art, Literature (General), Philosophy, Poetry, Science.

CONFLUENCE, Wilma Acree, Editor; Dr. Beverly Hogue, Fiction Editor; Joan Stewart, Fiction Editor; Janet Bland, Fiction Editor; Carol Steinhagen, Poetry Editor, PO Box 336, Belpre, OH 45714-0336, 304-295-6599, wilmaacree@charter.net. 1989. Poetry, fiction, art, photos, interviews, satire, criticism, reviews, parts-of-novels, non-fiction. "Poetry of any length or general literary style. Fiction shouldn't exceed 5,000 words; no dot matrix due to scanner equipment; SASE required. Prefer no simultaneous submissions. Work displays knowledge of language, its flexibilities. Contributors include T.M.Bemis, R.G. Cantalupo,Mark Mansfield, Herbert Woodward Martin." circ. 1M. 1/yr. Pub'd 1 issue 2005; expects 1 issue 2006, 1 issue 2007. sub. price $5 + $1.50 S&H; per copy $5 + $1.50 S&H; sample $5 + $1.50 S&H. Back issues: $3 + $1.50 S&H. Discounts: 5 or more 20%. 128pp. Reporting time: 1-9 months if submitted Sept. 1-Jan.31. Simultaneous submissions accepted: no. Publishes 4-6% of manuscripts submitted. Payment: copies. Copyrighted, reverts to author. Ads: dna. Subjects: Essays, Fiction, Literature (General), Poetry, Short Stories.

CONFRONTATION, Martin Tucker, English Department, C.W. Post of Long Island Univ., Greenvale, NY 11548, 516-299-2720. 1968. Poetry, fiction, articles, interviews, parts-of-novels, long-poems, plays. circ. 2M. 2/yr. Expects 2 issues 2006. sub. price $10; per copy $7; sample $3. Back issues: $5 to $10 for special and rare editions. Discounts: 20% on orders of 10 or more copies. 325pp. Reporting time: 6-8 weeks. We accept simultaneous submissions, but not preferred. Publishes 10-15% of manuscripts submitted. Payment: $20-$150 stories, $10-$75 poetry. Copyrighted, reverts to author. Pub's reviews: 40 in 2005. §Fiction, poetry, criticism. Subjects: Literary Review, Magazines.

CONJUNCTIONS, Bradford Morrow, Editor, 21 East 10th Street #3E, New York, NY 10003-5924, Phone: 845-758-1539, fax: 845-758-2660, e-mail: conjunctions@bard.edu, URL: www.conjunctions.com. 1981. Poetry, fiction. "Contributing editors include: Walter Abish, Chinua Achebe, John Ashbery, Martine Bellen, Mei-mei Berssenbrugge, Mary Caponegro, Elizabeth Frank, William H. Gass, Peter Gizzi, Jorie Graham, Robert Kelly, Ann Lauterbach, Norman Manea, Rick Moody, Howard Norman, Joanna Scott, Peter Straub, William Weaver, JohnEdgar Wideman. Among most recently published authors are: William T. Vollmann, Joyce Carol Oates, Can Xue, John Sayles, Lois-Ann Yamanaka, John Ashbery, Carole Maso, John Barth, William H. Gass, Rae Armantrout, Brian Evenson, and Kelly Link." circ. 7.5M. 2/yr. Pub'd 2 issues 2005; expects 2 issues 2006, 2 issues 2007. sub. price $18 indiv., $35 instit. and overseas; $32/2 yrs indiv., $70/2 yrs instit. and overseas; per copy $12; sample $12. Back issues: $12. Discounts: special rates to distributors. 400pp. Reporting time: solicited mss. immediately, unsolicited 4-6 weeks. Simultaneous submissions accepted: no. Publishes 3-5% of manuscripts submitted. Payment: $125 plus copies. Copyrighted, reverts to author. Ads: $350 full page. Subjects: Arts, Experimental, Fiction, Futurism, Humor, Interviews, Literature (General), Myth, Mythology, Non-Fiction, Poetry, Post Modern, Prose, Satire, Short Stories.

THE CONNECTICUT POET, Hanover Press, Faith Vicinanza, Editor; John Jeffrey, Editor, PO Box 596, Newtown, CT 06470-0596, 203-426-3388, Fax 203-426-3398, hanoverpress@faithvicinanza.com, www.poetz.com/connecticut. 1995. Poetry, articles, reviews. "This is an online poetry newsletter. Poetry, calls for submissions, calendar, websites, quotes are published monthly." circ. 1-100M. 12-24/yr. sub. price free. 20pp. Reporting time: 60 days. Simultaneous submissions accepted: yes. Publishes 1% of manuscripts submitted. Payment: none. Not copyrighted, rights revert to author on publication. Pub's reviews: 5 in 2005. §Poetry only. Ads: none. Subjects: Newsletter, Poetry.

THE CONNECTICUT POETRY REVIEW, J. Claire White, Co-Editor; Harley More, Co-Editor, PO Box 818, Stonington, CT 06378. 1981. Poetry, interviews, satire, criticism, reviews. "Reviews: 700 words. Poems: 10-40 lines. But we do make exceptions. We look for poetry of quality which is both genuine and original in content. That is all we seek. We will consider any new and interesting book of poems mailed to us for a review. Some past and recent contributors: Cornelia Veenendaal, Nikki Giovanni, Walter MacDonald, Laurel Speer, John Updike, Dona Stein, James Sallis, Celia Gilbert, Diane Wakoski, Stuart Friebert, Felice Picano, Joseph Bruchac, W.D. Ehrhart, Joel Chace, Anna Maxwell, James Chichetto, Marge Piercy, Steve Abbott, Rochelle Ratner, Dan Duffy, A.R. Ammons, Mark Johnson, Jefferson Peters, Greg Kuzma, Diane Kruchkow, Daniel Langton, M. Marcuss Oslander, Robert Peters, Philip Fried, Emily Glen, Andrew Holleran, Edwin Honig, Rudy Kikel, F.D. Reeve, Dennis Cooper, Richard Kostelanetz, Charles Edward Eaton, Clifton Snider, Wm. Virgil Davis, John Tagliabue, Edward Butscher, Allen Ginsberg, Margaret Randall, Barry Spacks, J. Kates, Eugenio de Andrade, Susan Fromberg Schaeffer, Claudia Buckholts, Simon Perchik, Odysseus Elytis, Peter Wild, Gabriela Mistral, and William Reichard.'' circ. 400. 1/yr. Pub'd 1 issue 2005; expects 1 issue 2006, 1 issue 2007. sub. price $3.50; per copy $3.50; sample $3.50. Back issues: $25 first issue. Discounts: none. 40-45pp. Reporting time: 3 months. Payment: $5 per poem, $10 per review. Copyrighted, reverts to author. Pub's reviews. §Poetry, poetry, poetry. Subjects: Literary Review, Poetry.

CONNECTICUT REVIEW, Dr. Vivian Shipley, SCSU, 501 Crescent Street, New Haven, CT 06515, 203-392-6737, Fax 203-392-5748. 1967. Poetry, fiction, articles, art, photos, interviews, non-fiction. ''SASE for reply only. We do not return ms. 2000-4000 words, put word count on work; 3-5 poems, black and white/color photograph and art work. Send 2 copies of typed work, send 1 copy of poems. Recent contributors: Maxine Kumin, Sherod Santos, Todd Jokl, Lawrence Ferlinghetti, John Searles, and Colette Inez.'' circ. 3M. 2/yr. Pub'd 2 issues 2005; expects 2 issues 2006, 2 issues 2007. sub. price $16; per copy $8; sample $8. 208pp. Reporting time: 2-4 months. Simultaneous submissions accepted: no. Publishes 10% of manuscripts submitted. Payment: 2 copies. Copyrighted, reverts to author. Ads: none. Subjects: Essays, Fiction, Poetry, Translation.

CONNECTICUT RIVER REVIEW: A National Poetry Journal, Sue Holloway, Editor, PO Box 4053, Waterbury, CT 06704, http://pages.prodigy.net/mmwalker/cpsindex.html. 1978. Poetry. ''Submission period: Oct 1 - April 15. *CRR* is currently published once a year in July/August. Looking for original, honest, diverse, vital, well-crafted poetry. Poetry, poetry translations. No simultaneous submissions. Recent contributors: Claire Zoghb, Faith Vicinanza, Ruth Holzer, Geri Radasci, and Lance Lee.'' circ. 350. 1/yr. Pub'd 1 issue 2005; expects 1 issue 2006, 1 issue 2007. sub. price $14, $25/2 years; per copy $12; sample $12. Back issues: $12. 124-148pp. Reporting time: 8-12 weeks. Simultaneous submissions accepted: no. Publishes 15% of manuscripts submitted. Payment: 1 copy. Copyrighted, reverts to author. Ads: none. Subject: Poetry.

CONNEXIONS DIGEST, Connexions Information Services, Inc., Ulli Diemer, 489 College Street, Suite 305, Toronto, Ontario M6G 1A5, Canada, 416-964-1511, www.connexions.org. 1976. Articles, art, photos, cartoons, interviews, criticism, reviews, letters, news items. ''A digest linking groups working for social justice—we are interested in materials that include reflection, analysis, report on action.'' circ. 1.2M. 4/yr. Pub'd 4 issues 2005; expects 4 issues 2006, 4 issues 2007. sub. price $15.50 Canada, $18 foreign; per copy $30 for directory issue; sample $1. Back issues: $1. Discounts: 40% for resale; other negotiable. 48pp. Reporting time: 3 months maximum. Payment: none. Not copyrighted. Pub's reviews: 200 in 2005. §Social justice struggles/analysis. Ads: $175/$100/25¢. Subjects: Canada, Indexes & Abstracts, Networking, Reference.

Connexions Information Services, Inc. (see also CONNEXIONS DIGEST), Ulli Diemer, Managing Editor, 489 College Street, Suite 305, Toronto, Ontario M6G 1A5, Canada, 416-964-1511, www.connexions.org. 1975. avg. press run 2M. Pub'd 1 title 2005; expects 2 titles 2006. 224pp. Subjects: Canada, Indexes & Abstracts, Networking, Reference.

CONSCIENCE: The Newsjournal of Catholic Opinion, David Nolan, Catholics for a Free Choice, 1436 U Street NW #301, Washington, DC 20009-3997, 202-986-6093, Fax 202-332-7995, conscience@catholicsfor-choice.org, www.conscience-magazine.org. 1980. Articles, interviews, reviews, letters, news items. ''Published by Catholics for a Free Choice, we publish in-depth coverage of the topics central to our mission, including women's rights in society and in religions, reproductive rights, sexuality and gender, feminist theology, social justice, US politics, church and state issues, and the role of religion in formulating public policy. We are especially interested in items related to prochoice Catholicism.'' circ. 15,000. 4/yr. Pub'd 4 issues 2005; expects 4 issues 2006, 4 issues 2007. sub. price $15; per copy $5; sample free. Back issues: $6.50 depending on availability. Discounts: trade 33%, bulk by arrangement. 56pp. Reporting time: 1 month. Simultaneous submissions accepted: No. Publishes approx. 10% of manuscripts submitted. Payment: c. $200 for a 1,500 word article. Copyrighted, reverts to author. Pub's reviews: 10 in 2005. §Women's studies, Catholic church, abortion/family planning, sexuality, church/state issues. Ads: Rates on request. Subjects: AIDS, Biotechnology, Birth, Birth Control, Population, Catholic, Current Affairs, Feminism, Gender Issues, Politics, Public Affairs, Religion, Sex, Sexuality, Women.

Conservatory of American Letters (see also NORTHWOODS JOURNAL, A Magazine for Writers), Robert Olmsted, Executive Director; Richard S. Danbury III, Senior Editor; S.M. Hall III, Fiction Editor, PO Box 298, Thomaston, ME 04861-0298, 207-354-0998, cal@americanletters.org, www.americanletters.org. 1986. ''CAL is the owner of Dan River Press, Northwoods Press and Century Press, who offer publication of poetry, fiction, local history. We use anything *not* seditious, pornographic or evangelical.'' avg. press run 500. Pub'd 4 titles 2005; expects 5 titles 2006, 5 titles 2007. Discounts: 2% 5 or more paperback books ordered to maximum of 50% for 25 or more, 5 or more hardcovers 2% per book to maximum of 20%. 150pp. Reporting time: 1 week to 1 month. Simultaneous submissions accepted: yes. Publishes a high % of manuscripts submitted. Payment: 10% of amount received royalties from first 2500 copies then 15%. Copyrights for author.

Consumer Press, Joseph Pappas, 13326 SW 28th Street, Ste. 102, Fort Lauderdale, FL 33330-1102, 954-370-9153, info@consumerpress.com. 1989. Non-fiction. avg. press run 5M. Pub'd 2 titles 2005; expects 2 titles 2006, 3 titles 2007. Discounts: trade, bulk, jobber. 200pp. Reporting time: varies. Publishes 10% of manuscripts submitted. Payment: standard. Copyrights for author. Subjects: Construction, Consumer, Drugs, Health, How-To, Medicine, Mental Health, Non-Fiction, Nutrition, Parenting, Psychiatry, Psychology, Real Estate, Women.

Contemax Publishers, Warren R. Freeman, Karin R. Griebel, 17815 24th Ave N., Suite 100, Minneapolis, MN 55447. 1995. ''We publish how to books.'' Expects 2 titles 2006. 170pp. Subjects: Careers, How-To, Motivation, Success, Self-Help.

CONTEMPORARY GHAZALS, CELLAR, R.W. Watkins, PO Box 111, Moreton's Harbour, NL A0G 3H0, Canada. 2003. Poetry, articles, art, interviews, criticism, reviews, letters. ''The ghazal is a type of poetry featuring repetition and inner rhyme, and which finds its origin in 7th Century Arabia. *Contemporary Ghazals* publishes a) English-language ghazals, preferably written in the correct Persian style as introduced/popularized in the West by the late Agha Shahid Ali; b) English translations/adaptations (from the original Persian, Arabic, Urdu, etc.) of ancient ghazals; c) articles and book reviews focusing on ghazals, ghazal collections, and their authors; and d) related artwork or photographs. Contributors, as of recent or forthcoming, include Agha Shahid Ali, Denver Butson, Marcyn Del Clements, Teresa M. Pfeifer, Daniel Hales, Barbara Little, J.W. McMillan, I. H. Rizvi, R.W. Watkins, and Bill West.'' 2-3/yr. Expects 2 issues 2006, 2-3 issues 2007. sub. price $12US outside of Canada; per copy $4US outside of Canada; sample $4US outside of Canada. Back issues: same. 20pp. Reporting time: almost immediately. Simultaneous submissions accepted: yes. Publishes 80% of manuscripts submitted. Payment: free copy. Not copyrighted. Pub's reviews. §Ghazals, original or translated. Ads: $65/$40; other $55/$20. Subjects: Classical Studies, India, Medieval, Middle East, Poetry, Religion, Sufism.

CONTEMPORARY VERSE 2: the Canadian Journal of Poetry and Critical Writing, Clarise Foster, 207-100 Arthur Street, Winnipeg, Manitoba R3B 1H3, Canada, (204) 949-1365, cv2@mb.sympatico.ca, www.contemporaryverse2.ca. 1975. Poetry, articles, interviews. ''Contemporary Verse 2 strives to bring the best poetry from around the world into the spotlight. Each issue features interviews with established and emerging poets, a selection of new poems, reviews and/or articles, and coming soon, a new section of French poetry.'' 4/yr. Pub'd 4 issues 2005; expects 4 issues 2006, 4 issues 2007. sub. price $25.00; per copy $7.00; sample $7.00. Back issues: $5.00 or inquire. 95pp. Simultaneous submissions accepted: No. Payment: Please visit our web site for details. Copyright remains with author. Pub's reviews: approx. 4 in 2005. §New collections of poetry. Ads: $150 (full page)/$100 (2/3 page)/$75 (half page)/$50 (1/3 page).

CONTEMPORARY WALES, University Of Wales Press, Richard Wyn Jones, 10 Columbus Walk, Brigantine Place, Cardiff CF10 4UP, Wales, 44-029-2049-6899, Fax 44-029-2049-6108, press@press.wales.ac.uk, www.wales.ac.uk/press. 1987. Articles. circ. 500. 1/yr. Pub'd 1 issue 2005; expects 1 issue 2006, 1 issue 2007. sub. price £6.50; per copy £7.50; sample £7.50. Discounts: booksellers 10%. 100pp. Payment: none. Copyrighted. Ads: £75/£37.50. Subject: Sociology.

CONTEXTS: UNDERSTANDING PEOPLE IN THEIR SOCIAL WORLDS, University of California Press, Claude Fischer, Editor; Scott Savitt, Managing Editor, University of California Press, 2000 Center St., Suite 303, Berkeley, CA 94704-1223, 510-643-7154. 2002. Photos, reviews, non-fiction. ''Editorial Office: Department of Sociology, University of California, Berkeley, CA 94720-1980. Copyrighted by the American Sociological Association.'' circ. 2858. 4/yr. Pub'd 4 issues 2005; expects 4 issues 2006, 4 issues 2007. sub. price $45 indiv., $139 inst.; per copy $12 indiv., $37 inst.; sample same as single copy. Discounts: foreign subs. agents 10%, 10+ one-time orders 30%, standing orders (bookstores): 1-99 40%, 100+ 50%. 72pp. Reporting time: varies. Copyrighted, does not revert to author. Pub's reviews: approx. 20 in 2005. §sociology and related fields. Ads: $295/$220. Subjects: Culture, Sociology.

Continuing Education Press, Alba Scholz, Portland State University, Continuing Education Press, PO Box 1394, Portland, OR 97207-1394, www.cep.pdx.edu. 1981. Non-fiction. avg. press run 10,000. Pub'd 1 title 2005; expects 1 title 2006, 1 title 2007. 100pp. Payment: contract terms by arrangement. Can copyright for author. Subjects: Education, Handwriting/Written, Non-Fiction, Pacific Northwest, Public Affairs, Science.

CONTROLLED BURN, Daniel Crocker, Editor; Carol Finke, Fiction Editor, KCC, 10775 N. St. Helen Road, Roscommon, MI 48653, 989-275-5000, Fax 989-275-8745, crockerd@kirtland.edu. 1994. Poetry, fiction, photos, reviews, long-poems, non-fiction. circ. 275. 1/yr. Pub'd 1 issue 2005; expects 1 issue 2006, 1 issue

2007. price per copy $6.00; sample $5. Back issues: $4.00. 120pp. Reporting time: 2 months. We prefer not to accept simultaneous submissions. Publishes 5% of manuscripts submitted. Payment: 2 copies. Copyrighted, reverts to author. Pub's reviews: 3 in 2005. Subject: Literary Review.

COOKING CONTEST CHRONICLE, Karen Martis, PO Box 10792, Merrillville, IN 46411-0792. 1985. circ. 2.5M. 12/yr. Pub'd 12 issues 2005; expects 12 issues 2006, 12 issues 2007. sub. price $19.95; per copy $3; sample $3. Back issues: $3. Discounts: none. 6pp. Not copyrighted. Pub's reviews: 12 in 2005. §Cookbooks. Ads: $100/$75/must be food related and approved by editor. Subjects: Cooking, Creativity, Homemaking, Newsletter.

Cooper Hill Press, Donna Presnell, General Manager, 1440 Whalley Avenue #232, New Haven, CT 06515, 203-387-7236 phone/Fax, editor@cooperhill.com, www.cooperhill.com. 1999. "Imprint: American Language Sourcebooks. We publish books by educators. Our latest publications are: The Cooper Hill Stylebook: a Guide to Writing and Revision, by Gregory Heyworth, PhD. The Cooper Hill College Application Essay Bible, edited by Rosette Liberman, EdD." avg. press run 2.5M. Pub'd 1 title 2005; expects 1 title 2006, 2 titles 2007. Discounts: wholesalers/distributors 55%, bookstores 40%, libraries 20%. 464pp. Reporting time: 8-10 weeks. Simultaneous submissions accepted: yes. Publishes no set % of manuscripts submitted. Payment: negotiable. Copyrights for author. Subjects: Editing, Education, English, Reference.

Copper Beech Press, M.K. Blasing, Director; Randy Blasing, Editor, P O Box 2578, English Department, Providence, RI 02906, 401-351-1253. 1973. Poetry, fiction, long-poems. avg. press run 1M. Pub'd 4 titles 2005; expects 3 titles 2006, 3 titles 2007. Discounts: bookstores, jobbers, etc. 1-5 20%; 6-9 33%; 10+ 40%. 64pp. Reporting time: ASAP, usually within 1 month. Payment: copies, 5%. Does not copyright for author. Subjects: Fiction, Poetry, Translation.

Copper Canyon Press, Michael Wiegers, Managing Editor; Joseph Bednarik, Marketing Director, PO Box 271, Port Townsend, WA 98368, poetry@coppercanyonpress.org, www.coppercanyonpress.org, 360-385 4925 (tel). 1972. Poetry, long-poems. "Copper Canyon Press publishes poetry, poetry in translation, and letterpress broadsides. Authors include Ted Kooser, W.S. Merwin, Hayden Carruth, Carolyn Kizer, Pablo Neruda, C.D. Wright, Ruth Stone, Jim Harrison, Antonio Machado, Han Shan, James Galvin, and Olga Broumas. The editors no longer consider unsolicited manuscripts; queries should include SASE. Copper Canyon books are distributed to the trade by Consortium, 1045 Westgate Drive, St. Paul, MN 55114-0165, 800-283-3572." avg. press run 2.5M. Pub'd 14 titles 2005; expects 16 titles 2006, 16 titles 2007. Discounts: standard 40%, returnable, short 20% on cloth. 120pp. Reporting time: 4 months. Simultaneous submissions accepted: no. Publishes less than 1% of manuscripts submitted. Payment: standard 7% royalty rate. Copyrights for author. Subject: Poetry.

Cornell Maritime Press, Inc., Marci Andrews, Managing Editor, PO Box 456, Centreville, MD 21617, 410-758-1075, www.cmptp.com. 1938. "We publish books for the merchant marine, recreational boating books, regional adult nonfiction, children's regional fiction and nonfiction, and knots and leather handicraft books." avg. press run 3M. Pub'd 10 titles 2005; expects 12 titles 2006, 12 titles 2007. Discounts: on request. 224pp. Reporting time: 1 month. Simultaneous submissions accepted: no. Copyrights for author.

CORNERSTONE, Jon Trott, Editor-in-Chief; Eric Pement, Senior Editor; Dawn Mortimer, Editorial Director; Chris Wiitala, Music Editor, 939 W. Wilson Avenue, Chicago, IL 60640, 773-561-2450 ext. 2080, Fax 773-989-2076. 1972. Poetry, fiction, articles, art, photos, cartoons, interviews, satire, criticism, reviews, music, letters, news items, non-fiction. "Call publication." circ. 38M. 3-4/yr. Pub'd 2 issues 2005; expects 3 issues 2006, 4 issues 2007. sub. price donation; per copy donation; sample SASE with 5 first class stamps. Back issues: call publication. Discounts: call for info. 64-72pp. Reporting time: 3-6 months, respond only if we wish to use work. Simultaneous submissions accepted: yes. Publishes 2% of manuscripts submitted. Payment: varies. Copyrighted, reverts to author. Pub's reviews: 14 in 2005. §Religious, social, political. Ads: $1,300/$840/50¢ classified. Subjects: Christianity, Religion.

•**Cornerstone Publishing,** 100 Leverington Avenue, Suite 2, Philadelphia, PA 19127, 267-975-7676, books@cornerstonepublishing.com, www.cornerstonepublishing.com. 1992. Poetry, non-fiction. "Our Vision: Cornerstone Publishing, our vision is "to take the message and the messenger to the masses." Our Mission: With a clarity of purpose and a focused vision, inspired authors from numerous walks of life have come together to join the Cornerstone family over the years with a united purpose: to inspire, motivate, educate and impact the lives of those who read their words.Has God called you to "write the vision"...?" avg. press run 2000. Pub'd 5 titles 2005; expects 10 titles 2006, 15 titles 2007. 150pp. Reporting time: 2-8 weeks. Simultaneous submissions accepted: Yes. Publishes 25% of manuscripts submitted. Payment: 50-50. Copyrights for author. Subjects: African-American, Children, Youth, Family, Multicultural, Non-Fiction, Parenting, Publishing, Relationships, Young Adult.

CORONA, Lynda Sexson, Co-Editor; Michael Sexson, Co-Editor; Sarah Merrill, Managing Editor, Dept. of Hist. & Phil., Montana State Univ., PO Box 172320, Bozeman, MT 59717-2320, 406-994-5200. 1980. Poetry, fiction, articles, art, photos, cartoons, satire, music, collages, plays, non-fiction. "Journal of arts and ideas;

116

imaginative treatment of cultural issues. Looking particularly for work that transcends categories. We are interested in everything from the speculative essay to recipes for the construction or revision of things; we publish art and ideas that surprise with their quality and content. Recent contributors: Frederick Turner, William Irwin Thompson, James Hillman, Rhoda Lerman, Philip Dacey, Ivan Doig, Donald Hall, A.B. Guthrie, Jr., Richard Hugo, William Matthews, Stephen Dixon, James Dickey, Rayna Green, Fritjof Capra, Wendy Battin, Charles Edward Eaton, Nick Johnson.'' circ. 2M. Occasional. Expects 1 issue 2007. sub. price $10; per copy $10; sample $10. Back issues: $10. Discounts: trade, classroom, 20% (orders of 10 or more). 130pp. Reporting time: 1 week to 6 months. Payment: nominal honorarium, 2 copies. Copyrighted. Pub's reviews: 10 in 2005. §All aspects of current thought, technology & the imagination, metaphor, art, religion. Ads: $150/$95/$65/back cover (inside) $200. Subjects: Arts, Culture.

CORRECTION(S): A Literary Journal for Inmate Writing, Correction(s), Editorial Board, PO Box 1326, Boone, NC 28607-1326. 2001. Poetry, fiction, art, parts-of-novels, long-poems. ''Please submit 4-6 poems or up to 8 pages (for fiction) of your work with a brief bio. *Correction(s)* is a biannual journal dedicated to the poetics and vision of incarcerated, American writers. Please proofread carefully before sending manuscript. Typed and handwritten manuscripts acceptable. Please print as neatly as possible. We do not accept previously published work. Also accepts artwork for front cover designs. Send SASE if you want your work returned. Acquires first rights.'' 2/yr. Expects 2 issues 2006, 2 issues 2007. sub. price $5 inmates, $15 everyone else; per copy $3 inmates, $8 everyone else. Discounts: for those that buy in bulk (20 or more): 10% (more if intended for use in a prison); please inquire. 30-40pp. Reporting time: 4-6 weeks. Simultaneous submissions accepted: yes. Payment: 1 copy. Not copyrighted. Subject: Prison.

CORRECTIONS TODAY, Susan Clayton, Managing Editor, American Correctional Association, 206 North Washington Street, Suite 200, Alexandria, VA 22314, 703-224-0000. 1938. Fiction, articles, art, photos, interviews, reviews, letters, news items, non-fiction. ''We accept manuscripts from members of the American Correctional Association on topics related to the field of corrections. Manuscripts should be submitted to the attention of Susan Clayton at the above address and should be no longer than 10 double-spaced, typed pages. We accept well-written pieces on new and informative programs and issues that would be of interest to our members.'' circ. 20M. 7/yr. Pub'd 7 issues 2005; expects 7 issues 2006, 7 issues 2007. sub. price free sub. with membership to the American Correctional Assn.; per copy $6.00; sample free. Back issues: $6.00 per issue. 200pp. Reporting time: 4-6 weeks. Payment: none, we are a non-profit organization. Copyrighted, does not revert to author. Pub's reviews: 25 in 2005. §Anything related to the corrections field of on criminal justice issues. Ads: b/w $1,233/b/w $960/2-color and 4-color fees apply, call for rates, frequency rates available. Subjects: Crime, Education, Employment, Fiction, Literary Review, Non-Fiction, Prison, Psychology, Reviews.

•**Corvus Publishing Company,** Dennis Padovan, 6021 South Shore Road, Anacortes, WA 98221-8915, 360-293-6068, DP@CorvusBooks.com, www.CorvusBooks.com. Non-fiction. ''Publication of book length manuscripts dealing with wildlife health or disease.'' Simultaneous submissions accepted: Yes. Subjects: Animals, Birds, Wildlife.

Costa Rica Books, Christopher Howard, PO Box 025216, Suite 1, SJO 981, Miami, FL 33102-5216, 619-461-6131, crbooks@racsa.co.cr, www.costaricabooks.com. Non-fiction. Simultaneous submissions accepted: yes. Publishes a very small % of manuscripts submitted. Payment: none, because author prints his own books. Copyrights for author. Subjects: How-To, Latin America, Taxes, Travel.

Coteau Books, Geoffrey Ursell, Publisher; Edna Alford, Editor; Barbara Sapergia, Juvenile Fiction editor, 2517 Victoria Ave., Regina, Sask. S4P 0T2, Canada, 306-777-0170, e-mail coteau@coteaubooks.com. 1975. Poetry, fiction, art, criticism, long-poems, plays, non-fiction. ''Coteau Books was established to publish prairie and Canadian writing: poetry, fiction, songs, plays, children's books and literary criticism. We do *not* consider manuscripts from non-Canadian writers. Coteau Books is committed to publishing the work of new as well as established writers and two series of books are devoted to new writers' work.'' avg. press run 1.5M. Pub'd 18 titles 2005; expects 16 titles 2006, 16 titles 2007. Discounts: See Fitzhenry & Whiteside (our distributor) for detailed discount schedule. 80-325pp. Reporting time: 2-6 months. Simultaneous submissions accepted: no. Publishes 4% of manuscripts submitted. Payment: normally 10% royalties. Subjects: Adolescence, Anthology, Arts, Autobiography, Biography, Canada, Children, Youth, Culture, Literature (General), Multicultural, Myth, Mythology, Native American, Nature, Poetry, Prose.

Cotsen Institute of Archaeology Publications, Julia Sanchez, Director of Publications, Univ. of California-Los Angeles, A210 Fowler, Los Angeles, CA 90095-1510, 310-825-7411. 1975. Non-fiction. avg. press run 500. Pub'd 4 titles 2005; expects 8 titles 2006, 4 titles 2007. Discounts: 20% to agencies. 200pp. Reporting time: Immediate follow-up; 60 day review period. Simultaneous submissions accepted: no. Payment: none. Does not copyright for author. Subjects: Anthropology, Archaeology, History.

Cottontail Publications (see also THE PRESIDENTS' JOURNAL), Ellyn R. Kern, 79 Drakes Ridge, Bennington, IN 47011-1802, 812-427-3921, cot202@netscape.net. 1979. Articles, news items, non-fiction. avg.

press run 1M. Pub'd 2 titles 2005; expects 1 title 2006, 1 title 2007. Discounts: 2-50 40%, short discount under $10 cover price. 90pp. Reporting time: 6 weeks or less. Payment: to be negotiated. Copyrights for author. Subjects: Americana, Collectibles, Crafts, Hobbies, Genealogy, History.

COTTONWOOD, Cottonwood Press, Tom Lorenz, Editor; Tom Lorenz, Fiction Editor; Philip Wedge, Poetry Editor; Denise Low, Review Editor, Room 400, Kansas Union, 1301 Jayhawk Blvd., University of Kansas, Lawrence, KS 66045, 785-864-2528 (Lorenz), 785-864-3777 (Wedge). 1965. Poetry, fiction, art, photos, interviews, reviews. "We publish a wide variety of styles of poetry, fiction, and nonfiction. Poetry submissions should be limited to the five best, fiction to one story. Past issues have included interviews with William Burroughs, Gwendolyn Brooks and Scott Heim. We have published recent work by Gerald Early, Wanda Coleman, Patricia Traxler, William Stafford, Jared Carter, Victor Contoski, Robert Day, W.S. Merwin, Antonya Nelson, Connie May Fowler, Oakley Hall, and Luci Tapahonso. We welcome submissions of photos, graphics, short fiction, poetry, and reviews from new as well as established writers." circ. 500-600. 2/yr. Pub'd 1 issue 2005; expects 2 issues 2006, 2 issues 2007. sub. price $15, $18 overseas; per copy $8.50; sample $5. Back issues: $4. Discounts: 30% trade, bulk negotiable. 112pp. Reporting time: 2-5 months. Simultaneous submissions accepted: Yes (fiction only). Publishes 1% of manuscripts submitted. Payment: 1 copy, eligibility for yearly Alice Carter Awards in poetry and fiction. Copyrighted. Pub's reviews: 2 in 2005. §national, midwest poetry or fiction chapbooks. Ads: none. Subjects: Arts, Biography, Black, Book Reviewing, Fiction, Kansas, Literary Review, Photography, Poetry, Translation.

Cottonwood Press (see also COTTONWOOD), Tom Lorenz, Editor, 400 Kansas Union, Box J, Univ. of Kansas, Lawrence, KS 66045, 785-864-2528. 1965. "We generally solicit material for the press." avg. press run 500-1M. Pub'd 1 title 2005; expects 1 title 2006, 1 title 2007. Discounts: 30% to bookstores. 80pp. Copyrights for author. Subjects: Arts, Biography, Black, Book Reviewing, Fiction, Kansas, Literary Review, Photography, Poetry, Translation.

Cottonwood Press, Inc., Cheryl Thurston, 109-B Cameron Drive, Fort Collins, CO 80525, 970-204-0715. 1986. Non-fiction. "We are interested primarily in practical books for language arts teachers, grades 5-12." avg. press run 2M. Pub'd 3 titles 2005; expects 3 titles 2006, 3-5 titles 2007. Discounts: available upon request. 100pp. Reporting time: 2-4 weeks. We accept simultaneous submissions only if notified. Payment: royalties of 10% of net sales. Copyrights for author. Subjects: Colorado, Drama, Education, English, History, How-To, Humor, Media, Poetry.

Michael E. Coughlin, Publisher (see also THE DANDELION), Michael E. Coughlin, PO Box 205, Cornucopia, WI 54827. 1978. avg. press run 600. Pub'd 4 titles 2005; expects 2 titles 2006, 1 title 2007. Discounts: 40% to bookstores ordering 3 or more copies. 200pp. Reporting time: 2 months. Payment: negotiated. Copyrights for author. Subjects: Anarchist, Libertarian.

Council For Indian Education, Hap Gilliland, President and Editor; Sue A. Clague, Assistant and Bus. Mgr., 1240 Burlington Avenue, Billings, MT 59102-4224, 406-248-3465 phone, 1-5 pm Mtn.time, FAX: (406)-248-1297 www.cie-mt.org., cie@cie-mt.org. 1963. Fiction, non-fiction. "Book ordering address: 1240 Burlington Avenue, Billings, MT 59102-4224. Books on themes related to authentic Native American life and culture, for all students, both fiction and non-fiction, also Indian crafts, and books on teaching Native American students." avg. press run 1M. Pub'd 4 titles 2005; expects 2 titles 2006, 2 titles 2007. Discounts: 1 20%, 2-9 30%, 10+ 40% to bookstores only. avg. 100pppp. Reporting time: 2-8 months. Simultaneous submissions accepted: yes. Publishes 3% of manuscripts submitted. Payment: 10% of wholesale price or 2¢ per word. We furnish author with copyright forms. Subjects: Alaska, Children, Youth, Crafts, Hobbies, Education, Folklore, Native American.

COUNTER CULTURE, Third Way Publications Ltd., PO Box 1243, London SW7 3PB, England, 44(0)20-7-373-3432 phone/Fax, thirdway@dircon.co.uk, www.thirdway.org. 1992. Articles, art, photos, cartoons, interviews, criticism, reviews, music, letters. "750-1,000 words of decentralist, green, radical, alternative comment." circ. 200. 4/yr. Pub'd 4 issues 2005; expects 4 issues 2006, 4 issues 2007. sub. price UK £5, EU £6, rest of world (air) £9, $15US; per copy £1, $2US; sample £1.25, $3US. Back issues: none. Discounts: none. 8pp. Simultaneous submissions accepted: no. Publishes 30% of manuscripts submitted. Payment: none. Copyrighted, reverts to author. Pub's reviews: 17 in 2005. §Alternative politics, arts, analysis of popular culture, anti-commercialist, etc. Ads: on application. Subjects: Arts, Avant-Garde, Experimental Art, Counter-Culture, Alternatives, Communes, Internet.

COUNTERPOISE: For Social Responsibilities, Liberty and Dissent, Charles Willett, Founding Editor, 1716 SW Williston Road, Gainesville, FL 32608-4049, 352-335-2200. 1997. Articles, criticism, reviews, letters. "Review journal for alternative books, magazines and videos." circ. 200. 4/yr. Pub'd 4 issues 2005; expects 4 issues 2006, 4 issues 2007. sub. price $40 individual; $60 institution; per copy $12 + $5 S&H; sample free. Back issues: $12 + $5 S&H. Discounts: none. 67pp. Payment: none. Copyrighted, does not revert to author. Pub's reviews: 150 in 2005. §Alternative press. Ads: Full page $300; half-page $180. Subjects: Audio/Video,

Bibliography, Book Reviewing, Counter-Culture, Alternatives, Communes, Criticism, Human Rights, Libraries, Magazines, Publishing, Reference, Reviews.

Country Messenger Press, Edna Siniff, 78D Cameron Lake Loop Road, Okanogan, WA 98840, siniff@ncidata.com. 1986. Non-fiction. "Feature senior citizen stories and documentaries." avg. press run 1M. Expects 1 title 2006, 1 title 2007. Discounts: standard. 80pp. Reporting time: 2 months. We occasionally accept simultaneous submissions. Publishes 10% of manuscripts submitted. Payment: quarterly payments. Copyrights arranged with each author. Subjects: History, Non-Fiction, Senior Citizens, Storytelling.

Coyote Books, James Koller, PO Box 629, Brunswick, ME 04011. 1964. avg. press run varies 200-5000. Expects 1 title 2006. Discounts: 40% to retail. 100-300pp. Reporting time: varies. Query before sending simultaneous submissions. Publishes a small % of manuscripts submitted. Payment: copies - percentage. Copyright varies.

CRAB CREEK REVIEW, Emily Bedard, Heather Blasch, Stacy Carlson, Eleanor Lee, PO Box 85088, Seattle, WA 98145-1088, editors@crabcreekreview.org, www.crabcreekreview.org. 1983. Poetry, fiction, art, satire, non-fiction. "*CCR* is a biannual publication that publishes a diverse mix of energetic poems, free or formal, and remains more interested in powerful imagery than obscure literary allusion. We like work that reads well aloud, has an authentic voice, presents clear and effective images, and poems that display a sense of wit and word-play. Recent contributors include: Derek Sheffield, Kathleen Flenniken, Will Holman, Alice Derry and Kevin Miller. Translations are welcome—please submit with a copy of the poem in its original language, if possible. Send up to 5 poems. Simultaneous submissions are accepted when clearly indicated in the cover letter, and must be withdrawn immediately if accepted elsewhere. *CCR* also seeks submissions of short fiction. We accept stories up to 6,000 words, with an admitted predilection for dynamic prose of distinct voice and strong images. Offer a compelling view of the world in which we live and let us revel in your telling of it. Recent fiction from Justin Courter, Bill Teitelbaum, Daniel Bartlett, and Tom Juvik. Art is cover only." circ. 1000. 2/yr. Pub'd 1 issue 2005; expects 2 issues 2006, 2 issues 2007. sub. price $12/$20 (libraries); per copy $7; sample $5; $3 for anniversary anthology (1994). Back issues: $5. 100pp. Reporting time: 12-20 weeks. Simultaneous submissions accepted: no. Publishes 5% of manuscripts submitted. Payment: 2 copies. Copyrighted, rights revert to author but request mention of *Crab Creek Review* with subsequent printings. Subjects: Fiction, Literature (General), Poetry, Short Stories, Translation.

CRAB ORCHARD REVIEW, Jon Tribble, Managing Editor; Allison Joseph, Editor & Poetry Editor; Carolyn Alessio, Prose Editor, SIUC Dept. of English - Mail Code 4503, 1000 Faner Drive, Carbondale, IL 62901, 618-453-6833, www.siu.edu/~crborchd. 1995. Poetry, fiction, parts-of-novels, long-poems, non-fiction. "Journal of creative works publishing fiction, poetry, creative non-fiction, interviews, novel excerpts, and book reviews. Recent contributors include Donna Hemans, Lee Ann Roripaugh, Ned Balbo, A. Van Jordan, Jesse Lee Kercheval. Considers submissions for our Winter/Spring general issue from February through April. From August through October, we only consider submissions for our Summer/Fall special issue (theme announced on web site). Annual Poetry, Fiction, and Nonfiction contests held February 1 through April 1." circ. 2M. 2/yr. Pub'd 2 issues 2005; expects 2 issues 2006, 2 issues 2007. sub. price $15; per copy $10; sample $8. Back issues: $6. 280pp. Reporting time: 3 weeks to 7 months. We encourage simultaneous submissions, but do like to be informed. Publishes 2% of manuscripts submitted. Payment: $50 min. for poetry, $100 min. for prose, $20 per published page, plus a year's subscription and 2 copies. Copyrighted, reverts to author. Pub's reviews: 10 in 2005. §Small press and university press titles only (poetry, fiction, creative nonfiction); book reviews are done in-house by staff. Writers may send books for review to the Managing Editor. Ads: none. Subjects: Fiction, Interviews, Literary Review, Non-Fiction, Poetry, Short Stories.

CRAFTS 'N THINGS, Clapper Publishing Co., Barbara Sunderlage, 2400 Devon, Suite 375, Des Plaines, IL 60018, 847-635-5800. 1951. circ. 230M. 10/yr. Pub'd 10 issues 2005; expects 10 issues 2006, 10 issues 2007. price per copy $3.95-$4.95. 106pp. Reporting time: 3 months. Simultaneous submissions accepted: yes. Payment: yes. Copyrighted, does not revert to author. Pub's reviews. §Craft books. Subject: Crafts, Hobbies.

Craftsman Book Company, Gary Moselle, Publisher; Laurence Jacobs, Editor, 6058 Corte Del Cedro, Carlsbad, CA 92011, 760-438-7828. 1952. Non-fiction. "Craftsman Book Company publishes *practical references for professional builders*. Craftsman books are loaded with step-by-step instructions, illustrations, charts, reference data, checklists, forms, samples, cost estimates, rules of thumb, and examples that solve actual problems in the builder's office or in the field. Every book covers a limited construction subject fully, becomes the builder's primary reference on that subject, has a high utility-to-cost ratio, and will help the builder make a better living in his profession. Length is variable but should be at least 500 manuscript pages including illustrations and charts. We seek queries and outlines and will consider material in nearly all construction areas and trades, including electrical, heating and air conditioning, lath and plaster, painting, prefab housing construction, heavy construction, estimating, and costing." avg. press run 5M. Pub'd 10 titles 2005; expects 12 titles 2006, 12 titles 2007. Discounts: trade 1-4 copies 33%, 5-49 copies 40%, 50+ copies 45%. 297pp. Reporting time: 3 weeks. Simultaneous submissions accepted: yes. Publishes 10% of manuscripts submitted.

119

Payment: 12-1/2% of net of all books sold, 7-1/2% for discounts of 50% or more. Copyrights for author. Subjects: Architecture, Business & Economics.

Crandall, Dostie & Douglass Books, Inc., 245 West 4th Avenue, Roselle, NJ 07203-1135, Phone: 908.241.5439, Fax: 908.245.4972, Email: Publisher@CDDbooks.com, www.CDDbooks.com. 2002. "Lifting the White Veil: An Exploration of White American Culture in a Multiracial Context." Expects 1 title 2006, 1 title 2007. Subjects: Current Affairs, How-To, Human Rights, Multicultural, Non-Violence, Public Affairs, Race, Society.

•**Crane Press,** Kurt DuNard, P.O. Box 680367, Franklin, TN 37068, 615-599-2017, fax 615-599-2018, 800-745-6273, Info@CranePress.com. Fiction, non-fiction. "Any fiction or non-fiction which will uplift and motivate the reader to live a better life." Discounts: 4299: -40%300499: -50%500up: -55%. Reporting time: 30 days. Simultaneous submissions accepted: No. Payment: Industry standard. Does not copyright for author. Subjects: Autobiography, Bibliography, Business & Economics, Careers, Fiction, Futurism, How-To, Inspirational, Non-Fiction, Philosophy, Self-Help, Speaking, Tennessee.

CRANKY LITERARY JOURNAL, Amber Curtis, Editor-in-Chief; Amy Schrader, Poetry Editor; Erin Malone, Associate Editor, 322 10th Avenue E. C-5, Seattle, WA 98102, 206.328.4518. 2004. Poetry, fiction, interviews, reviews, non-fiction. "*Cranky* publishes poetry and fiction with a fresh edge. The journal appears tri-annually and aspires to include an array of work from many styles and schools. Our only standard for selection is the quality of the work and our own aesthetic. The editors particularly enjoy writing which displays music, wit, and a fondness for language and word play. Writers we admire? Anne Carson, Frank O'Hara, Heather McHugh, Mary Szybist, Alice Munro, Lorrie Moore, and Lydia Davis, to name a few. Recent contributors are Ilya Kaminsky, Richard Kenney, Rebecca Brown, Matthew Zapruder, Julie Larios, and Kary Wayson." circ. 500. 3/yr. Expects 3 issues 2006, 3 issues 2007. sub. price $20; per copy $8; sample $8. Back issues: inquire. Discounts: We sell to retailers at 60% of cost—$4.20 per copy. 92-100pp. Reporting time: 6-8 weeks. Simultaneous submissions accepted: Yes. Payment: One contributor copy. Copyrighted, reverts to author. Pub's reviews: 6 in 2005. §poetry and novels. No advertising. Subjects: Experimental, Fiction, Poetry.

CRANNOG, Tony O'Dwyer, Roscam, Galway, Ireland, editor@crannogmagazine.com, www.crannogmagazine.com. 2002. Poetry, fiction, parts-of-novels, plays. "We publish quality material with strong, fresh imagery. While we welcome submissions from all over the world we feel a loyalty to our local community of writers ie Ireland, particularly Galway and more particularly Galway Writers' Workshop.Recent contributors have included Moya Cannon (former editor Poetry Ireland), Patricia Burke Brogan (Eclipsed), Rita Ann Higgins (Sunny Side Plucked), Joan McBreen (An Bhilleog Ban, The White Page), John Arden (British Playwright and poet now Galway resident)." circ. 200. 3/yr. Pub'd 3 issues 2005; expects 3 issues 2006, 3 issues 2007. sub. price 15; per copy 5; sample 5. Back issues: 3. Discounts: 20-25%. 70pp. Reporting time: 4-6 weeeks. Simultaneous submissions accepted: Yes. Publishes 60% of manuscripts submitted. Payment: copy of magazine. Copyrighted, reverts to author. Subjects: Fiction, Literature (General), Poetry.

THE CRAPSHOOTER, Leaf Press, Larry Edell, Andrea Foote, PO Box 421440, San Diego, CA 92142, larryedell@aol.com. 1995. Articles, cartoons, non-fiction. "Gambling material *only*." circ. 2M. 4/yr. Pub'd 4 issues 2005; expects 4 issues 2006, 4 issues 2007. sub. price $25; per copy $7; sample $7. Back issues: 5 for $30 ppd. Discounts: 50% for subscription agents. 4pp. Reporting time: immediate. Simultaneous submissions accepted: yes. Publishes 50% of manuscripts submitted. Payment: varies. Copyrighted, reverts to author. Pub's reviews: 4 in 2005. §Gambling with emphasis on casino craps. Ads: none. Subject: Games.

CRAZED NATION, TRANSCENDENT VISIONS, David Kime, 251 S. Olds Boulevard #84-E, Fairless Hills, PA 19030-3426. "We print essays about mental illness issues."

The Crazy Pet Press, 231 Market Place #283, San Ramon, CA 94583, 888-877-7737, Fax 925-242-0199, mail@crazypetpress.com, www.crazypetpress.com. 2003. Cartoons. "Dog and cat related only, pet/child interactive cartoons aimed at children only, humorous and fun only, must have credentials in pet industry (I.e. vet, groomer, pet shop owner, pet sitter, breeder)." avg. press run 10M. Pub'd 1 title 2005; expects 1 title 2006, 1 title 2007. Discounts: trade. 64pp. Reporting time: varies. Payment: buy out only. Does not copyright for author.

Crazy Woman Creek Press, Penny Wolin, 3073 Hanson, Cheyenne, WY 82001, 707-829-8568, www.jewsofwyoming.org. 1998. Photos, interviews. "Subject matter to be primarily photographic in nature and dealing with cultures in the American west." avg. press run 3M. Expects 1 title 2006. Discounts: trade 50%, no returns. 200pp. Reporting time: 2 months. Simultaneous submissions accepted: no. Payment: yes. Copyrights for author. Subjects: Americana, Genealogy, Photography, Picture Books, The West.

CRAZYHORSE, Garrett Doherty, Editor; Carol Ann Davis, Editor; Anthony Varallo, Fiction Editor, Dept. of English College of Charleston, 66 George Street, Charleston, SC 29424, crazyhorse@cofc.edu, http://crazyhorse.cofc.edu. 1960. Poetry, fiction, art, interviews, criticism, long-poems, non-fiction. circ. 1800.

2/yr. Pub'd 2 issues 2005; expects 2 issues 2006, 2 issues 2007. sub. price $15; per copy $8.50; sample $5. Back issues: $5. Discounts: please inquire. 160pp. Reporting time: 3-4 months. Simultaneous submissions accepted: Yes. Publishes 3% of manuscripts submitted. Payment: $20 per page for all. Copyrighted, reverts to author. Ads: $125 full page. Subjects: Fiction, Literature (General), Non-Fiction, Poetry, Prose.

CRC Publications (see also THE BANNER), Patricia Nederveld, Director, Faith Alive Department; Robert DeMoor, Banner Editor; Emily Brink, Reformed Worship Editor, 2850 Kalamazoo SE, Grand Rapids, MI 49560. 1979. Fiction, articles, art, photos, cartoons, interviews, criticism, reviews, music, letters, news items, non-fiction. "Religion-in the Reformed-Presbyterian tradition." Pub'd 40 titles 2005; expects 50 titles 2006, 60 titles 2007. Discounts: 15-50% to qualified bookstores/distributors. Pages vary. Reporting time: varies. Does not always copyright for author. Subject: Religion.

THE CREAM CITY REVIEW, Phong Nguyen, Editor-in-Chief; Zeke Jarvis, Managing Editor, PO Box 413, English Dept, Curtin Hall, Univ. of Wisconsin, Milwaukee, WI 53201, 414-229-4708. 1975. Poetry, fiction, art, photos, interviews, criticism, reviews, parts-of-novels, long-poems, non-fiction. "We publish a variety of writers and writings, offering a range of perspectives, styles, and contents from new and well-known writers. We prefer prose of 25 pages or less, though we'll consider longer pieces. Please submit no more than one work of prose, or up to five poems. Short, small press book reviews and creative nonfiction are especially welcome, as are b/w camera-ready art and photos. Recent contributors: Marge Piercy, Maxine Kumin, Ted Kooser, Stuart Dybek, Amy Clampitt, Tess Gallagher, Lawrence Ferlinghetti, Denise Levertov, Alicia Ostriker, Cathy Song, Russell Edson, William Kittredge, Audre Lorde, Donald Hall, Albert Goldbarth, Adrienne Rich, Diane Glancy, Adrian C. Louis, Kate Braverman, William Stafford, and Gary Soto." circ. 2M. 2/yr. Pub'd 2 issues 2005; expects 2 issues 2006, 2 issues 2007. sub. price $22 for 1 year, $41 for 2 years; per copy $12; sample $7. Back issues: $7, double issues $12. Discounts: schools send SASE for rates. 200pp. Reporting time: 6-8 months, we read from Sept. 1st - April 1st only. Simultaneous submissions acceptable with notification. Publishes 5-7% of manuscripts submitted. Payment: 1 year subscription. Copyrighted, reverts to author. Pub's reviews: 5 in 2005. §Poetry, fiction, creative nonfiction, art. Ads: $100/$50/no classified word rate. Subjects: Chicano/a, Environment, Essays, Fiction, Gay, Interviews, Lesbianism, Literary Review, Memoirs, Native American, Non-Fiction, Poetry, Reviews, Short Stories, Translation.

Creative Arts Book Company, Paul Samuelson, George Samsa, Lissa Fox, 833 Bancroft Way, Berkeley, CA 94710, staff@creativeartsbooks.com. 1968. Poetry, fiction, criticism, music, letters, non-fiction. avg. press run 2.5M-5M. Pub'd 40 titles 2005; expects 70 titles 2006, 70 titles 2007. Reporting time: 6 weeks. Simultaneous submissions accepted: yes. Payment: yes. Copyrights for author. Subjects: Adoption, Autobiography, Black, California, Crime, Erotica, Fiction, Handicapped, Holocaust, Juvenile Fiction, Jack Kerouac, Literature (General), Memoirs, Music, Mystery.

The Creative Company, PO Box 227, Mankato, MN 56002.

Creative Guy Publishing, Pete Allen, 206-7600 Moffatt Rd, Richmond, BC V6Y 3V1, Canada. 2003. Fiction, satire. "We publish an annual anthology of humorous speculative fiction novellas called the Amityville House of Pancakes, (trade paperback, ebook). We will look at proposals for other works, but presently are primarily interested in our own projects. Outside this, we also publish novellas in ebook, chapbook and audiobook formats on an individual basis, and are primarily interested in genre fiction. Humour is good. We DO NOT publish novel length mss. Please check our website for specific and updated guidelines. Query BY EMAIL ONLY (submissions@creativeguypublishing.com). Any unsolicited hard copy mss. will be recycled unread." Pub'd 6 titles 2005; expects 6 titles 2006, 6 titles 2007. Discounts: Distributed through Ingram, 50% wholesale, any number. Also available directly from publisher, 50%. Returnable. 180-200pp. Reporting time: Query first, generally 2-3 months. Query BY EMAIL ONLY. Any unsolicited hard copy mss will be recycled unread. Simultaneous submissions accepted: Yes. Publishes 10% of manuscripts submitted. Payment: 65% royalty on net, 20% for AHOP title (per author), no advance. Does not copyright for author. Subjects: Absurdist, Canada, Fantasy, Fiction, Humor, Satire, Science Fiction.

CREATIVE NONFICTION, Lee Gutkind, 5501 Walnut Street #202, Pittsburgh, PA 15232-2329, 412-688-0304, fax 412-683-9173. 1993. Interviews, reviews, non-fiction. circ. 4.5M. 3/yr. Pub'd 3 titles 2005; expects 3 issues 2006, 3 issues 2007. sub. price $29.95/4 issues; per copy $10; sample $10. Back issues: $10. 164pp. Reporting time: 3-5 months. Simultaneous submissions accepted: yes. Publishes 1% of manuscripts submitted. Payment: varies. Copyrighted, does not revert to author. Pub's reviews: 8 in 2005. §Creative nonfiction. Ads: $275/$200. Subjects: Book Reviewing, English, Essays, Journals, Literature (General), Non-Fiction.

Creative Roots, Inc., Lloyd deMause, 140 Riverside Drive, New York, NY 10024, 212-799-2294. 1975. Non-fiction. "Book publishing." avg. press run 2M. Pub'd 1 title 2005; expects 2 titles 2006, 5 titles 2007. Discounts: 2 or more-20%. 350pp. Reporting time: 1 month. Payment: variable. Copyrights for author. Subjects: History, Psychology.

Creative With Words Publications (CWW) (see also THEECLECTICS), Brigitta Geltrich, Editor & Publisher; Bert Hower, Nature Editor, PO Box 223226, Carmel, CA 93922-3226, Fax: 831-655-8627; e-mail: cwwpub@usa.net; http://members.tripod.com/~creativewithwords. 1975. Poetry, fiction, cartoons, satire. "On any topic, written by all ages (poetry and prose)." Pub'd 12 titles 2005; expects 12-14 titles 2006, 12 titles 2007. Discounts: schools & libraries 10%; authors receive 20% off on orders 1-9 copies; 30% off on orders 10-19 copies and 40% off on orders of 20 copies and more. There are no free copies. Pages vary (approx. 60+pp). Reporting time: 1 month for inquiries, SASE is always a must; if a seasonal anthology, reporting time is 2 months after set deadline. Simultaneous submissions accepted: no. Publishes 90% of manuscripts submitted. Payment: 20% reduction of regular cost to participants, no payment in copies; small fee for guest artists, readers, and guest editors. Copyrights for author. Subjects: Children, Youth, Folklore, Poetry, Senior Citizens.

Creative Writing and Publishing Company, Cheryl Britt, PO Box 511848, Milwaukee, WI 53203-0311, (414)447-7810, same for fax, creatwritpub.com. 1995. Non-fiction. "Creative Writing and Publishing contributes to exciting the imagination of young children. One of our missions is to put reading back in first place." avg. press run 250. Pub'd 1 title 2005; expects 2 titles 2006, 1 title 2007. Discounts: 3 to 12 copies 25%. 24pp. Reporting time: Right now not accepting any manuscripts. Simultaneous submissions accepted: No. Does not copyright for author. Subjects: African-American, Arts, Cartoons, Children, Youth, Family, Fantasy, Food, Eating, Health, Juvenile Fiction, Pets, Picture Books, Poetry, Publishing, Television, Theatre.

CREATIVITY CONNECTION, Marshall J. Cook, Room 622 Lowell Hall, 610 Langdon Street, Madison, WI 53703, 608-262-4911. 1990. Articles, interviews, reviews, letters, news items, non-fiction. "We publish articles of interest to writers and small press publishers." circ. 500. 4/yr. Pub'd 4 issues 2005; expects 4 issues 2006, 4 issues 2007. sub. price $21 for one year$15 for one year pdf edition; sample on request. Discounts: A buck an issue for classroom sets or subscriptions of five or more copies for writers' groups. 20pp. Reporting time: 2 weeks or less. Simultaneous submissions accepted: yes. Publishes 25% of manuscripts submitted. Payment: 3 copies; more on request. Copyrighted, reverts to author. Pub's reviews: 50 in 2005. §Creativity, writing (how-to), writers (auto & bio), small presses/ publishers. Ads: none. Subjects: Creativity, Fiction, Non-Fiction, Publishing, Self-Help, Writers/Writing.

CREEPY MIKE'S OMNIBUS OF FUN, Michael Ruspantini, PO Box 401026, San Francisco, CA 94140-1026, creepymike@hotmail.com. 1995. Art, photos, cartoons, interviews, reviews, music. "*CMOOF* does fairly short reviews of comics, zines, music and interviews (humorous) of comics creators, music figures, interesting characters. Also review videos. Likes alt. comics, punk/noise music and weird news plus funny stories from my own wacky life!" circ. 1M+. 3/yr. Pub'd 3 issues 2005; expects 3 issues 2006, 3 issues 2007. sub. price n/a; per copy $2; sample $2. Back issues: $2. Discounts: selective trades, bulk/agent rates available on request. 36pp. Simultaneous submissions accepted: no. Publishes 0% of manuscripts submitted. Payment: courtesy copies. Not copyrighted. Pub's reviews: 7 in 2005. §Punk/noise music, comix/mini-comics, alternative/underground/psychotronic movies/videos, zines and small press publications. Ads: $40/$20/$75 back cover/$10 1/4 page. Subjects: Cartoons, Comics, Entertainment, Magazines, Movies, Music, Reviews, Tapes & Records, Television.

CREOSOTE: A Journal of Poetry and Prose, Ken Raines, Mohave Community College—Dept. of English, 1977 W. Acoma Blvd., Lake Havasu City, AZ 86403, 928-505-3375. 2000. Poetry, fiction, satire, parts-of-novels, long-poems, non-fiction. "Our mission is to publish the best poetry and prose we can find. There is a slight editorial bias toward more traditional poetic forms and prose styles. However, we have published a wide variety of materials. Recent contributors include Barry Ballard, Robert Parham, Simon Perchik, Ruth Moose, Paul Sohar, Ryan G. Van Cleave, and William Wilborn." circ. 400. 1/yr. Pub'd 1 issue 2005; expects 1 issue 2006, 1 issue 2007. sub. price $4; per copy $4; sample $2. Back issues: $2. Discounts: 1-100 copies 40%. 48pp. Reporting time: 3-6 months. Simultaneous submissions accepted: Yes. Payment: 2-3 copies. Copyrighted, reverts to author. Ads: $200-full page/$140-half page. Subjects: Americana, Essays, Fiction, Humor, Literature (General), Non-Fiction, Novels, Poetry, Prose, Satire, Short Stories.

Crescent Moon (see also PAGAN AMERICA; PASSION), Jeremy Robinson, Cassidy Hughes, PO Box 393, Maidstone, Kent ME14 5XU, United Kingdom. 1988. Poetry, articles, art, photos, interviews, criticism, reviews, music, letters, parts-of-novels, news items. "We prefer a letter and sample first, not a whole manuscript. Return postage and envelope. We are open to many ideas for books." avg. press run 100-200. Pub'd 15 titles 2005; expects 15 titles 2006, 20 titles 2007. Discounts: Trade: single order 20%, 2+ 35%, add $1.50 postage. 120pp. Reporting time: 2 months. Simultaneous submissions accepted: yes. We publish 5% or less of manuscripts submitted. Payment: to be negotiated. Copyrights for author. Subjects: Arts, Biography, Book Reviewing, Creativity, Criticism, Culture, Emily Dickinson, Electronics, Feminism, Interviews, D.H. Lawrence, Literary Review, Literature (General), Magic, Media.

CRICKET, Marianne Carus, Editor-in-Chief; Deborah Vetter, Executive Editor; Tracy Schoenle, Associate Editor; Adam Oldaker, Assistant Editor; Heather Delabre, Contributing Editor, PO Box 300, Peru, IL 61354,

815-224-5803, ext. 656, Fax 815-224-6615, mmiklavcic@caruspub.com. 1973. Poetry, fiction, articles, art, photos, interviews, music, plays, non-fiction. "Word limit for fiction: 2000 words; for non-fiction: 1500 words. SASE is required for response." circ. 74M. 12/yr. Pub'd 12 issues 2005; expects 12 issues 2006, 12 issues 2007. sub. price $35.97; per copy $5; sample $5. Back issues: $5. 64pp. Reporting time: approximately 3 months. Please indicate that it's a simultaneous submission. Publishes 1% of manuscripts submitted. Payment: stories and articles up to 25¢ per word (2000 max), poems up to $3 per line. Copyrighted, does not revert to author. Pub's reviews: 60 one-paragraph in 2005. §Any good children's or young adult books: fiction or non-fiction. Subjects: Children, Youth, Literature (General), Magazines.

Crime and Again Press, Bill Gluck, 245 Eighth Avenue, Ste. 283, New York, NY 10011, 212-727-0151; crimepress@aol.com. 1998. Fiction. "40,000 to 75,000 words. Mystery only, will consider true crime." avg. press run 3M-5M. Expects 3 titles 2006, 3-5 titles 2007. Discounts: 20%-55%. 240pp. Reporting time: 4-6 months. Simultaneous submissions accepted: no. Payment: negotiable. Copyrights for author. Subjects: Fiction, Mystery.

CRIMINAL JUSTICE ABSTRACTS, Richard S. Allinson, 2455 Teller Road, Thousand Oaks, CA 91320. 1968. circ. 1M. 4/yr. Pub'd 4 issues 2005; expects 4 issues 2006, 4 issues 2007. sub. price $200; per copy $50. 180pp. Reporting time: 2 months. Simultaneous submissions accepted: no. Payment: none. Copyrighted, reverts to author. Ads: $350 full page. Subjects: Abstracts, Crime, Law, Sociology.

Criminal Justice Press (see also Willow Tree Press, Inc.), Richard S. Allinson, PO Box 249, Monsey, NY 10952, Fax 845-362-8376. 1983. Pub'd 6 titles 2005; expects 13 titles 2006, 10 titles 2007. Subjects: Abstracts, Crime, Law, Sociology.

THE CRIMSON CRANE, James R. III Bauman, 11301 Mountain Lake Drive, Anchorage, AK 99516-4608, theguy@qci.net. 2001. Poetry, fiction, non-fiction. "Poetry: 1 page max. Fiction and nonfiction: 20 pages max. We accept submissions from present or graduate students or alumni of Antioch University. We are the literary journal of Antioch University-Los Angeles." circ. 200+. 2-4/yr. Pub'd 2 issues 2005; expects 2 issues 2006, 3 issues 2007. price per copy $4.70; sample $4.70. Back issues: $4.70. 25pp. Reporting time: we don't report; if we accept, we will ask permission to publish. Simultaneous submissions accepted: yes. Publishes 10-15% of manuscripts submitted. Payment: 1 copy. Copyrighted, reverts to author. Subject: Literary Review.

•**CRITICAL INQUIRY, University of Chicago Press,** W.J.T. Mitchell, University of Chicago, Wieboldt Hall 202, 1050 East 59th Street, Chicago, IL 60637, Telephone: (773) 702-8477; Fax: (773) 702-3397, http://www.journals.uchicago.edu/CI/home.html. 1974. "Founded 30 years ago, *Critical Inquiry* is an interdisciplinary journal devoted to publishing the best critical thought in the arts and humanities. Combining a commitment to rigorous scholarship with a vital concern for dialogue and debate, the journal presents articles by eminent and emerging critics, scholars, and artists on a wide variety of issues central to contemporary criticism and culture. In *CI* new ideas and reconsideration of those traditional in criticism and culture are granted a voice. The wide interdisciplinary focus creates surprising juxtapositions and linkages of concepts, offering new grounds for theoretical debate. In *CI*, authors entertain and challenge while illuminating such issues as improvisations, the life of things, Flaubert, and early modern women's writing. *CI* comes full circle with the electrically charged debates between contributors and their critics." 4/yr.

CRITICAL REVIEW, Jeffrey M. Friedman, 32-26 35th Street, Astoria, NY 11106-1102, 203-270-8103; fax 203-270-8105; e-mail info@criticalreview.com. 1987. Articles, reviews. "Uniquely, *Critical Review* offers its contributors the opportunity to explore, develop and criticize neo-liberal political and social theory at length. It welcomes extended scholarly essays and review essays that conform to its style sheet (available on request). Of particular interest are developments and criticisms of ideas informed by classical liberalism, including public choice theory, Austrian-school economics, and spontaneous order analysis. *CR* is the only journal in the world that confronts such ideas in every field with the most sophisticated scholarship drawn from other intellectual traditions." circ. 3M. 4/yr. Pub'd 4 issues 2005; expects 4 issues 2006, 4 issues 2007. sub. price $29, libraries $59; per copy $7.25; sample $7.25. Back issues: $10-$20, indiv/$15-$30 libraries. 160pp. Reporting time: 2 months. Payment: none. Copyrighted, rights revert to author if arranged. Pub's reviews: 14 in 2005. §Economics, anthropology, jurisprudence, political science, history, philosophy, sociology. Ads: $75 full page. Subjects: Middle East, Philosophy, Political Science, Politics, Sociology.

CRONE CHRONICLES: A Journal of Conscious Aging, Glenda Martin, 319 West 3rd St., Laurel, MT 59044. 1989. Poetry, articles, art, photos, cartoons, interviews, reviews, letters, collages, news items, non-fiction. circ. 6M. 4/yr. Pub'd 4 issues 2005; expects 4 issues 2006, 4 issues 2007. sub. price $21 in US; per copy $6.95; sample $6.50. Back issues: $6 per issue, order 3 issues get 1 free. Discounts: On contract, case by case. 80pp. Reporting time: varies. Simultaneous submissions not desirable. Publishes 30% of manuscripts submitted. Payment: none at this time. Copyrighted, reverts to author. Pub's reviews: 20-30 in 2005. §Aging, metaphysics, consciousness, community, spirituality. Ads: $300/$150/$1 word classified. Subjects: Aging, Astrology, Autobiography, Biography, Book Reviewing, Community, Counter-Culture, Alternatives,

Communes, Creativity, Culture, Dreams, Essays, Ethics, Euthanasia, Death, Psychology, Religion.

Crones Unlimited, Mary Fogarty, Managing Editor, PO Box 433, Peralta, NM 87042, M5799@cronesunlimited.com, www.cronesunlimited.com. 1998. Poetry, fiction, art. "Request submission guidelines via e-mail, website or primary address; send SASE." avg. press run 2.0M. Pub'd 2 titles 2005; expects 2 titles 2006, 2 titles 2007. 175pp. Reporting time: 2 months. Simultaneous submissions accepted: yes. Payment: 15% of retail sales. Copyright reverts back to author 6 months after printing. Subjects: Animals, Children, Youth, Family, Humor, Inspirational, Men, Nature, Poetry, Prose, Short Stories, Spiritual, Women.

CROSS CURRENTS, Kenneth Arnold, Editor; Joseph Cunneen, Founding Editor; Shelley Schiff, Managing Editor, College of New Rochelle, New Rochelle, NY 10805-2339, 914-235-1439, Fax 914-235-1584, aril@ecunet.org. 1950. Poetry, articles, interviews, reviews, letters, non-fiction. "Relation of religion and ethics to contemporary intellectual, political, cultural, philosophical questions. Published by the Association for Religion and Intellectual Life." circ. 4.5M. 4/yr. Pub'd 4 issues 2005; expects 4 issues 2006, 4 issues 2007. sub. price $40, libraries $50, outside US $5 additional postage; per copy $7.50; sample $7.50. Back issues: $7.50. 144pp. Reporting time: 1 month. Payment: none. Copyrighted, reverts to author. Pub's reviews: 52 in 2005. §Theology, philosophy, world politics, literature, and arts. Ads: $400/$250/$150 1/4 pg. Subject: Religion.

THE CROSS STITCHER, Clapper Publishing Co., Barbara Sunderlage, 2400 Devon, Suite 375, Des Plaines, IL 60018, 847-635-5800. 1951. circ. 107M. 10/yr. Pub'd 10 issues 2005; expects 10 issues 2006, 10 issues 2007. price per copy $3.95-$4.95. 106pp. Reporting time: 3 months. Simultaneous submissions accepted: yes. Payment: yes. Copyrighted, does not revert to author. Pub's reviews. §Craft books. Subject: Crafts, Hobbies.

•**Cross-Cultural Communications,** Stanley H. Barkan, Publisher, 239 Wynsum Ave., Merrick, NY 11566-4725, Tel: 516-868-5635 Fax: 516-379-1901 E: cccpoetry@aol.com, www.cross-culturalcommunications.com. 1971. Poetry, fiction, art, photos, music, parts-of-novels, plays, non-fiction. "Focus: bilingual poetry from traditionally neglected languages and cultures. Recent contributors: Stanley Kunitz, Joan Alcover, John Amen, Fuad Attal, Bohdan Boychuk, Mia Barkan Clarke, Vince Clemente, Aleksey Dayen, Kristine Doll, Arthur Dobrin, Charles Fishman, John Gery, Isaac Goldemberg, Theofil Halama, Joan Carole Hand, Peter Thabit Jones, Dariusz Tomasz Lebioda, Beverly Matherne, Bill Negron, Biljana D. Obradovic, Stanislao G. Pugliese, Clementine Rabassa, Kyung-nyun Kim Richards, Steffen F. Richards, Youngju Ryu, Nat Scammacca, Ignazio Silone, Gerald Stern, Adam Szyper, Henry Taylor, Stoyan "Tchouki" Tchoukanov, Tino Villanueva, A. D. Winans, Yang Guija, Yun Humyong." avg. press run 1,000. Pub'd 15 titles 2005; expects 15 titles 2006, 15 titles 2007. Discounts: Wholesalers, Jobbers, Retailers: 40% Distributors: 50%/55%Authors: 40%. Copyrights for author. Subjects: Anthology, Asia, Indochina, Bilingual, Eastern Europe, France, French, Holocaust, Italy, Judaism, Latin America, Multicultural, Native American, Poetry, Scandinavia, Translation, Women.

CROSSCURRENTS, Bob Fink, 516 Ave K South, Saskatoon, Sask. S7M 2E2, Canada, Fax 306-244-0795, green@webster.sk.ca—www.webster.sk.ca/greenwich/xc.htm. 1975—. Art, satire, criticism, music, non-fiction. "*Crosscurrents* is a musicolgy newsletter on issues of ancient music, origins, archaeology. It also deals (less often) with the arts, society, ecology and history. Under our imprint are new and recent books and essays as well: *On the Origin of Music—Readings and Essays* (http://www.webster.sk.ca/greenwich/readings.htm) ; Oldest known musical instrument: *Neanderthal Flute* (http://www.webster.sk.ca/greenwich/fl-compl.htm) and more. See our URL: http://www.webster.sk.ca/greenwich/fulllist.htm for the full list of our webpages." *Circ: 500-5M depending on subject and reprints.* Quarterly, irregular, includes reprints and *Extras.* Pub'd 4 issues 2005; expects 4 issues 2006, 4 issues 2007. Subscription $15 U.S.; price per copy $1.50 U.S.; sample $1.50 (postpaid). Back issues: *$5 for any 10, 1975 to present + $2 postage.* 4-8pp. Copyrighted. Pub's reviews: 1 in 2005. §Arts and musicology. Subjects: Anthropology, Archaelogy, Arts, Criticism, Environment, History, Human Rights, Music, Science.

Crossway Books, Allan Fisher, Vice President of Editorial, 1300 Crescent Street, Wheaton, IL 60187, 630-682-4300. 1979. Fiction, non-fiction. "A division of Good News Publishers. Publish books with an evangelical Christian perspective, including novels, contemporary issues, theology, and the family." avg. press run 7M. Pub'd 90 titles 2005; expects 85 titles 2006, 75 titles 2007. Discounts: trade, jobber. 192pp. Reporting time: 6 months. Simultaneous submissions accepted: yes. Publishes 2-3% of manuscripts submitted. Payment: based on net receipts. Copyrights for author. Subjects: Christianity, Fiction, Non-Fiction.

R.L. Crow Publications, William S. Gainer, P.O. Box 262, Penn Valley, CA 95946, Fax and Message: (530) 432-8195, info@rlcrow.com. 2003. Poetry. "R.L. Crow Publications is a small publishing house, publishing from one to five books and several limited edition broadsides per year. We are currently focusing on contemporary poetry and prose. Though we are not limited to publishing one type or form of writing we do look for material that is written with a clarity of language, boldness of expression and uses an honesty of experience as its platform. We do lean toward the Meat and Street styles of writing. R.L. Crow believes that poetry is an expressive literary art form of which each poem is a stand-alone piece of art and that the best way to express this art is through the directness of the short poem. We appreciate an economy of language.R.L. Crow Publications' mission is to challenge contemporary poets and writers to work with a clarity of language and boldness of expression that leaves the reader with a new understanding of the familiar. It is R.L. Crow Publications' business to showcase and publish the best of these efforts.Please read our current back list: Roxy: Todd Cirillo, W. S Gainer, Will Staple; Leaning Against Time, Neeli Cherkovski; tiny teeth - the Woormwood Review poems, Ann Menebroker.'' avg. press run 1000+. Pub'd 2 titles 2005; expects 1 title 2006, 2 titles 2007. Discounts: We generally work though our distributors: Small Press Distribution or Baker and Taylor. We do sell direct to booksellers, with retail seller permits, at 45% discount with the buyer paying shipping for 20 units or less. 60-100pp. Reporting time: Please review our website (rlcrow.com) before submitting. Simultaneous submissions accepted: No. Publishes 1% of manuscripts submitted. Payment: Negotiated indiviually. Copyrights for author. Subject: Poetry.

CRUCIBLE, Terrence L. Grimes, Office of the Vice President for Academic Affairs, Barton College, Wilson, NC 27893, 252-399-6344. 1964. Poetry, fiction. ''Short stories should not exceed 8,000 words.'' circ. 300. 1/yr. Pub'd 1 issue 2005; expects 1 issue 2006, 1 issue 2007. sub. price $7; per copy $7; sample $7. Back issues: $7. Discounts: none. 70pp. Reporting time: 2-4 months. Simultaneous submissions accepted: no. Publishes 10% of manuscripts submitted. Payment: 2 complimentary copies of issue. Copyrighted, reverts to author. Subjects: Fiction, Literary Review, Literature (General), Poetry.

Crystal Clarity, Publishers, Sean Meshorer, 14618 Tyler Foote Road, Nevada City, CA 95959, 1-800-424-1055; 530-478-7600; fax 530-478-7610. 1969. Subjects: Autobiography, Cooking, Counter-Culture, Alternatives, Communes, New Age, Religion, Spiritual, Yoga.

•**Crystal Dreams Publishing,** Sarah Schwersenska, W1227 East County Rd A, Berlin, WI 54923, 920-361-0961. 2000. Poetry, fiction, non-fiction. ''We publish most genres, are looking for How-To and CHildren's books and also love to publish poetry.'' avg. press run 100. Pub'd 6 titles 2005; expects 20-30 titles 2006, 50-60 titles 2007. Discounts: 30% discount to bookstores, wholesalers, retailers, schools, libraries. 200-400pp. Reporting time: up to 60 days. Simultaneous submissions accepted: Yes. Payment: Currently 25% royalties, paid quarterly. Does not copyright for author. Subjects: Children, Youth, Horror, How-To, Humor, Memoirs, New Age, Non-Fiction, Poetry, Romance, Science Fiction, Self-Help, Sex, Sexuality, Short Stories, War, Young Adult.

Crystal Press, John Baxter, 4212 E. Los Angeles Avenue # 42, Simi Valley, CA 93063-3308, 805-527-4369, Fax 805-527-3949, crystalpress@aol.com. 1992. Fiction, non-fiction. ''We publish books that give readers greater insight into business or education, and we wish to review Northwest fiction.'' avg. press run 1M. Pub'd 1 title 2005; expects 2 titles 2006, 2 titles 2007. 200pp. Reporting time: 60 days. Simultaneous submissions accepted: yes. Payment: by arrangement. Copyrights for author. Subjects: Business & Economics, Education, Futurism, New Hampshire.

Crystal Publishers, Inc., Frank Leanza, 3460 Lost Hills Drive, Las Vegas, NV 89122, 702-434-3037 phone/Fax. 1985. Music. avg. press run 5M. Pub'd 2 titles 2005; expects 2 titles 2006, 5 titles 2007. Discounts: 46-55% wholesaler. 224pp. Reporting time: 6-8 weeks. Payment: semi-annual. Copyrights for author. Subjects: Music, Textbooks.

CULTURE CHANGE, Eve Gilmore; Jan Lundberg, Publisher, PO Box 4347, Arcata, CA 95518, 707-826-7775. 1993. Articles, art, photos, cartoons, interviews, reviews. ''Max: 2,000 words; average: 1,000 words. Our name says it all (re: bias).'' circ. 10M. 4/yr. Pub'd 4 issues 2005; expects 4 issues 2006, 4 issues 2007. sub. price $30 includes membership to the Alliance for a Paving Moratorium; per copy $4; sample free. Back issues: $4. Discounts: 50% off cover price for distributors. 38pp. Reporting time: maximum 1 month. Simultaneous submissions accepted: yes. Publishes 70% of manuscripts submitted. Payment: none, yet. Copyrighted, reverts to author. Pub's reviews: 4 in 2005. §Alternative transporation, alternatives to automobile and sprawl. Ads: contact office for quotes. Subjects: Autos, Bicycling, Energy, Environment.

CULTUREFRONT, Mel Rosenthal, Photography Editor; Philip Katz, Associate Editor, 150 Broadway, Room #1700, New York, NY 10038-4401, 212-233-1131, fax 212-233-4607, e-mail hum@echonyc.com. 1992. Poetry, fiction, articles, photos, interviews, reviews, letters, non-fiction. ''Articles are generally commissioned.'' circ. 2M. 4/yr. Pub'd 4 issues 2005; expects 3 issues 2006, 3 issues 2007. sub. price $15; $25 for libraries; per copy $5; sample $5. Back issues: $7 per issue. Discounts: contact publisher for discounts. 48-52pp. Reporting time: 3 weeks. Simultaneous submissions accepted: no. Payment: authors donate their articles. Copyrighted, *Culturefront* retains copyright unless other arrangements are made. Pub's reviews: 18 in 2005. §The humanities, the production and interpretation of culture. Ads: $750/$400/$250 1/4 page; back cover $1250/inside cover $1000/1/3 page $325/1-6 page $175. Subjects: Arts, Book Reviewing, Culture, Electronics, History, Humanism.

Culturelink Press, Diane Asitimbay, P.O. Box 3538, San Diego, CA 92163, Tel. (619) 501-9873, www.culturelinkpress.com; Fax purchase and school orders: Tel(619) 501-1369. 2004. Criticism, news items, non-fiction. "Culturelink Press is a small publishing house that is committed to publishing titles that inform readers of cultural differences among people within the United States as well as increase cultural awareness in the international community. *What's Up America?* is a cultural handbook for foreigners and Americans alike. It answers questions foreigners often ask Americans. Plans are underway to publish a collection of cultural essays, and a volume of short fiction on cultural themes for 2005-2006." avg. press run 1000. Expects 1 title 2006, 3 titles 2007. Discounts: Distributors - 25%Wholesalers - 55-65%Retailers - 40%Classrooms -Multiple orders discount. 200-300pp. Reporting time: Not accepting manuscript submissions at this time. Simultaneous submissions accepted: No. Does not accept manuscript submissions at this time. Subjects: Americana, The Americas, Culture, Current Affairs, Essays, Non-Fiction, Short Stories, Travel.

CUNE MAGAZINES, Cune Press, Scott C. Davis, PO Box 31024, Seattle, WA 98103, Fax (206) 782-1330; www.cunemagazines.com; www.cunepress.net; magazines@cunepress.com. 1995. Articles, art, photos, cartoons, interviews, satire, news items, non-fiction. "Cune (from "cuneiform") is devoted to publishing thoughtful nonfiction and literary fiction by talented new writers. Many of our authors are based in the Pacific Northwest or on the West Coast and are represented in our anthology, An Ear to the Ground (www.cunepress.net). Writers who wish to publish with us should study the writing in this volume (available in most libraries or we can provide the book to potential Cune Press contributors at half price: etg@cunepress.com) Equally important, we publish work across the East-West (Islamic-Western) divide. Our Bridge between the Cultures Series includes writing by Arabs, Arab-Americans, and Americans who are engaged with the Arab / Islamic world. (See www.bridgebetweenthecultures.com) We invite queries for submissions to the Cune Magazines. Please visit the site (www.cunemagazines.com) and gauge your submission to a specific magazine in the Cune Magazines group, including the following: ProphetwithoutHonor.com (vigorously stated opinion, expose, and analysis); Troas.com (East-West and North-South issues; archaeology and the origin of the species; serious writing for the lay public); Literary Entrepreneurs (Writer's vision and craft collide with the book publishing industry; how to forge a career as a writer); GreekandLatinRoots.com (using Greek and Latin root words to learn vocabulary, spelling, word usage, and the "rules" of English). Send submissions to magazines@cunepress.com." Payment: At this time submissions to Cune Magazines are pro bono.

Cune Press (see also CUNE MAGAZINES), Scott C. Davis, PO Box 31024, Seattle, WA 98103, Fax 206-782-1330, www.cunepress.net, www.cunemagazines.com, cune@cunepress.com. 1994. Fiction, articles, art, cartoons, non-fiction. "Cune Press (from "cuneiform") is devoted to publishing thoughtful nonfiction and literary fiction by talented new writers. Many of our authors are based in the Pacific Northwest or on the West Coast and are represented in our anthology, *An Ear to the Ground* (www.cunepress.net). Writers who wish to publish with us should study the writing in this volume (available in most libraries or we can provide the book to potential Cune Press contributors at half price: etg@cunepress.com). Equally important, we publish work across the East-West (Islamic-Western) divide. Our Bridge between the Cultures Series includes writing by Arabs, Arab-Americans, and Americans who are engaged with the Arab / Islamic world(see www.bridgebetweentheCultures.com). We invite queries for submissions to the Cune Magazines. Please visit the site (www.cunemagazines.com) and gauge your submission to a specific magazine in the Cune Magazines group, including the following: *ProphetwithoutHonor.com* (vigorously stated opinion, expose, and analysis); *Troas.com* (East-West and North-South issues; archaeology and the origin of the species; serious writing for the lay public); *Literary Entrepreneurs* (Writer's vision and craft collide with the book publishing industry; how to forge a career as a writer); *GreekandLatinRoots.com* (using Greek and Latin root words to learn vocabulary, spelling, word usage, and the "rules" of English). Send submissions to magazines@cunepress.com." avg. press run 2M. Pub'd 2 titles 2005; expects 4 titles 2006, 4 titles 2007. Discounts: trade 40%. 256pp. Reporting time: 3 months. Simultaneous submissions accepted: We are not accepting book length manuscripts for publication at this time. Typically, we publish books by writers who have first gotten to know us by: 1) volunteering 2)publishing in our online magazines 3)publishing in our anthology An Ear to the Ground. Publishes 2% of manuscripts submitted. Payment: 5% royalty on cover price. Copyrights for author.

CURL MAGAZINE, Marie President, Demetra Burrs, 39270 Paseo Padre Parkway #142, Fremont, CA 94538-1616, 877-854-3850, Fax 510-429-9659, bayareafitness@excite.com, www.CurlMagazine.com. 2002. Articles, photos, interviews, satire, reviews, letters. circ. 5M. 4/yr. Pub'd 1 issue 2005; expects 4 issues 2006, 4 issues 2007. sub. price $22; per copy $5.99; sample free. Back issues: $5.99. 44pp. Reporting time: 2 weeks. Simultaneous submissions accepted: yes. Publishes 75% of manuscripts submitted. Payment: per scale. Copyrighted. Pub's reviews: 1 in 2005. §Bodybuilding, fitness travel. Ads: $350/$200. Subjects: Lifestyles, Sports, Outdoors, Women.

CURRENTS: New Scholarship in the Human Services, University of Calgary Press, P. Miller, Editor; M. Rothery, Editor, Faculty of Social Work, Univ. of Calgary, 2500 University Drive NW, Calgary, AB T2N 1N4, Canada, 403-220-7550, Fax 403-282-7269, currents@ucalgary.ca, www.uofcpress.com/journals/currents. 2002. Articles, reviews. "*Currents* is a refereed electronic journal that publishes critical and research work by current graduate students in the Human Services as well as articles by guest scholars." Approx. 10 articles per volume year. Expects 1 issue 2006, 1 issue 2007. sub. price free access. Reporting time: 2 months or less. Publishes 50% of manuscripts submitted. Payment: none. Copyrighted, does not revert to author. Ads: email for information. Subjects: Adolescence, Adoption, Children, Youth, Family, Gender Issues, Mental Health, Sexual Abuse, Social Security, Social Work.

CUTBANK, English Dept., University of Montana, Missoula, MT 59812. 1973. Poetry, fiction, articles, art, photos, interviews, criticism, reviews, long-poems. ''All correspondence should be addressed to 'editor(s)-in-chief'. All submissions should be addressed to either the 'poetry editor' or the 'fiction editor. Recent contributors include James Tate, Mary Blew, Dara Wier, Jim Harrison, Norman Dubie, James Welch.'' circ. 600. 2/yr. Pub'd 2 issues 2005; expects 2 issues 2006, 2 issues 2007. sub. price $12; per copy $6.95; sample $4. Back issues: write for current information. Discounts: trade rates for bulk orders. 120+pp. Reporting time: 8-12 weeks. Simultaneous submissions accepted: yes. Publishes 1% of manuscripts submitted. Payment: 2 issues. Copyrighted, rights revert to author with provision that *CutBank* is credited. Pub's reviews: none in 2005. §Poetry, fiction. Ads: $90/$45. Subjects: Book Reviewing, Fiction, Literary Review, Montana, Poetry, Short Stories.

•**CUTTHROAT, A JOURNAL OF THE ARTS,** Pamela Uschuk, Editor-In-Chief; William Pitt Root, Poetry Editor; Donley Watt, Fiction Editor, P.O. Box 2414, Durango, CO 81302, 970-903-7914, www.cutthroat-mag.com, cutthroatmag@gmail.com. 1995. Poetry, fiction, reviews, long-poems. ''Our editorial mission is to publish the best in well-crafted literary poetry and short fiction. We do not publish genre writing (i.e. no romance, sci-fi, mystery writing, horror, etc.). We have no regional, gender or racial biases. In 2006, we hope to expand our palette to include a couple of book reviews. We offer two prizes—$1250 first/$250 second places each—The Joy Harjo Poetry Award and The Rick DeMarinis Short Fiction Award. 2006 judges are Naomi Shihab Nye and Robert Olen Butler. Reading fee is $15 and contest deadline is October 1st. Our contributors included Fred Chappell, Dorianne Laux, Rebecca Seiferle, Joy Harjo, Rick DeMarinis, Marvin Bell, Naomi Shihab Nye, Richard Jackson, Jeffrey Franklin, Kelly Cherry, BJ Buckley and Tehihla Lieberman. Go to our website or email us for complete guidelines.'' 1/yr. Pub'd 1 issue 2005; expects 1 issue 2006, 1 issue 2007. sub. price 2 issues/$22; per copy $15; sample $15. Discounts: Trade discounts—5-10 copies 40%. 130pp. Reporting time: 12 weeks. Simultaneous submissions accepted: but authors must inform us of acceptances elsewhere. Payment is in contributors copies, except for the prize money distributions. Pub's reviews: none in 2005. §Short story and poetry collections. Ads: full page: $125/half page: $75/no classifieds. Subjects: The Americas, Environment, Experimental, Family, Fiction, Poetry, Politics, Short Stories.

CYBERFICT, Martin Kich, Editor, English Department, Wright State Univ - Lake Campus, 7600 State Routem 703, Celina, OH 45822, www.wright.edu/~martin.kich/. 2003. ''*Cyberfict* is an online journal devoted to computer-related fiction of all kinds, including but not restricted to cyberpunk and other futuristic fiction, fiction published on the internet or on CD-ROM, the use or influence of hypertext in fiction, and fiction-related internet sites and software. We will consider any approach to this broad topic, including criticism of individual or multiple works, profiles of or interviews with authors, descriptions of pedagogical approches or issues, theoretical studies, interdisciplinary studies, bibliographical articles, notes, book reviews, and reports on related cultural phenomena. We are very open to submissions by graduate students and, as a special feature, professors may submit groups of undergraduate essays/book reviews (500-700 words each). We welcome graphics with any submission. Submissions: 500-10,000 words; read year round. The journal is published when we receive enough creditable material for a new issue. Email submissions to martin.kich@wright.edu. Prefer submission to be attached as an rtf file, but Wordperfect, Word or html files accepted. SASE required for paper submissions. Inquiries welcome.'' Reporting time: within 90 days. Subject: Fiction.

CYNIC BOOK REVIEW, Cynic Press, Joseph Farley, PO Box 40691, Philadelphia, PA 19107. 2001. Reviews. ''Make checks out to Cynic Press for samples. Zine on hiatus indefinitely.'' 2/yr. Pub'd 1 issue 2005; expects 2 issues 2006, 2 issues 2007. sub. price $20/6 issues; per copy $5; sample $4. 20pp. Reporting time: 3 weeks. Simultaneous submissions accepted: yes. Publishes 15% of manuscripts submitted. Payment: 1 year subscription. Copyrighted for Cynic Press. Pub's reviews: 40 in 2005. §Poetry, short stories, novels, archeology, biography, Asia, prehistory, history. Ads: $20/$10. Subject: Reviews.

Cynic Press (see also AXE FACTORY REVIEW; CYNIC BOOK REVIEW; HOLY ROLLERS; LOW BUDGET ADVENTURE; LOW BUDGET SCIENCE FICTION), Joseph Farley, PO Box 40691, Philadelphia, PA 19107. 1996. Poetry, fiction, articles, art, photos, cartoons, interviews, satire, criticism, reviews, music, letters, parts-of-novels, long-poems, collages, plays, concrete art, news items. ''Books are by invitation or contest. Unsolicited book manuscripts require a $15 reading fee, check made out to Cynic Press.'' avg. press run varies. Pub'd 1 title 2005; expects 4 titles 2006, 5 titles 2007. Pages vary. Reporting time: immediate to five weeks. Simultaneous submissions accepted: yes. Publishes 1% of manuscripts submitted. Payment: copies or special arrangement. Copyrights for author. Subjects: Asia, Indochina, Asian-American, China, Essays, Fiction, Lapidary, Poetry, Religion, Sex, Sexuality, Tapes & Records, Translation.

Cypress House, Joe Shaw, Editor, 155 Cypress Street, Fort Bragg, CA 95437, 707-964-9520, Fax

707-964-7531, publishing@cypresshouse.com. 1986. Fiction, art, non-fiction. "Cypress House titles focus on biography, autobiography, self-help and how-to books. Our current list also includes quality fiction and poetry titles." avg. press run 2M. Pub'd 5 titles 2005; expects 5 titles 2006, 5 titles 2007. Discounts: 1-2 books 0%, 3-5 33%, 6+ 40%. 224pp. Reporting time: 3 months. Simultaneous submissions accepted: yes. Copyrights for author. Subjects: Biography, Fiction, Health, History, How-To, Literature (General), Memoirs, Self-Help, Women, World War II.

D

D.B.A. Books, Diane M. Bellavance, Editor, 291 Beacon Street #8, Boston, MA 02116, 617-262-0411. 1980. Non-fiction. avg. press run 5M. Pub'd 3 titles 2005; expects 4 titles 2006, 4 titles 2007. Discounts: 2-5 10%, 6-9 15%, 10+ 20%, also 10% for prepayment. 100pp. Reporting time: 2 weeks. Payment: by contract. Does not copyright for author. Subjects: Advertising, Self-Promotion, Broadcasting, Business & Economics, Communication, Journalism, Education, How-To, Marketing, Media, Public Relations/Publicity, Self-Help.

Dablond Publishing, Danielle Holloway, 6733 Colgate Avenue, Los Angeles, CA 90048, dablondpublish@aol.com. 2000. Non-fiction. "We currently are not reading unsolicited work." avg. press run 3M-5M. Expects 1 title 2006, 3 titles 2007. Discounts: 40% to bookstores, 55% to distributors. 96pp. Reporting time: 12 weeks. Simultaneous submissions accepted: no. Payment: no advance, 10% royalties. Does not copyright for author. Subjects: Drama, New Age, Non-Fiction.

Daedal Press, Dorothy Keesecker, Ernest Walters, 257 Foster Knoll Drive, Joppa, MD 21085-4756. 1968. Fiction, art. "High literary merit fiction. Works about art and artists a plus. Must be suitable (sellable) to a strong targeting audience with direct mail. No present use of distributors or bookstores except with advance purchases or author's locale. Highly selected original artist made printmaking (lithos, etchings, acquatint, reduction relief)." avg. press run 2M. Pub'd 1 title 2005; expects 3-5 titles 2006, 3-5 titles 2007. Discounts: 10-50% by number bought, returns acceptable if perfect. 265pp. Reporting time: 1 month or less, query and 1-page synopsis. Simultaneous submissions accepted: yes. Payment: 10-20% on net sale. Copyrights for author.

DAILY WORD, Unity House, Colleen Zuck, 1901 NW Blue Parkway, Unity Village, MO 64065, 816-524-3550, fax 816-251-3553. 1924. Poetry, articles, photos, non-fiction. "Types of materials presented spiritual, Christian, motivational. Daily affirmations and lessons. Not seeking submissions at this time." circ. 1.5K. 12/yr. Pub'd 12 issues 2005; expects 12 issues 2006, 12 issues 2007. sub. price $10.95; per copy $1.75; sample free. 48pp. Reporting time: 6 weeks. Simultaneous submissions accepted: no. Payment: upon acceptance. Copyrighted, reverts to author. Ads: none. Subjects: Health, History, Motivation, Success, Non-Fiction, Religion, Self-Help, Spiritual.

Dakota Books, 2801 Daubenbiss #1, Soquel, CA 95073, 831-477-7174. 1992. Non-fiction. "On recovery." avg. press run 2M. Expects 1 title 2006, 2 titles 2007. Discounts: 40%. 64pp. Reporting time: 1 month. Payment: 10% royalties, paid semi-annually. Copyrights for author. Subject: Self-Help.

THE DALHOUSIE REVIEW, Ronald Huebert, Editor, Dalhousie University, Halifax, Nova Scotia B3H 3J5, Canada, 902-494-2541, fax 902-494-3561, email dalhousie.review@dal.ca. 1921. Poetry, fiction, articles, criticism, reviews. "Authors change with each issue." circ. 500. 4/yr. Pub'd 4 issues 2005; expects 4 issues 2006, 4 issues 2007. sub. price institutional: $32.10 within Canada, outside $40 includes GST; individual: $22.50 within Canada, $28 outside; per copy $10 + mailing, handling (double issue $12); sample $10 + mailing and handling ($12 double issue). Back issues: vary from $10 to $25. Discounts: none. 144pp. Reporting time: 1-3 months. Simultaneous submissions accepted: yes. Publishes 10% of manuscripts submitted. Payment: 2 complimentary copies of issue and 10 offprints. Copyrighted, rights are held by both publisher and author. Pub's reviews: 30-40 in 2005. §All areas would be examined. Ads: $300/$150. Subjects: Anthropology, Archaeology, Arts, Book Reviewing, Classical Studies, Criticism, Criticism, English, Fiction, History, Indexes & Abstracts, Literary Review, Philosophy, Poetry, Political Science, Theatre.

Dalkey Archive Press (see also THE REVIEW OF CONTEMPORARY FICTION), John O'Brien, ISU Campus Box 8905, Normal, IL 61790-8905, 309-438-7555. 1984. Fiction. "No unsolicited manuscripts." avg. press run 6k. Pub'd 27 titles 2005; expects 25 titles 2006, 25 titles 2007. Discounts: 45% to bookstores with a minimum of 5 units. 200pp. Reporting time: 1 month. Payment: 10%. Copyrights for author. Subjects: Fiction, Literature (General).

Dan River Press (see also NORTHWOODS JOURNAL, A Magazine for Writers), Richard S. Danbury III, Editor, PO Box 298, Thomaston, ME 04861-0298, 207-354-0998, cal@americanletters.org, www.americanletters.org. 1978. Fiction. "See website for guidelines." avg. press run 500. Pub'd 4 titles 2005; expects 4 titles 2006, 4 titles 2007. Discounts: 5-24 copies 2% per copy paperbacks, maximum 50% for 25 or more copies. hardcovers 5 or more copies 2% per copy to maximum of 20%. 145-180pp. Reporting time: 1-4 weeks. Simultaneous submissions accepted: yes for books, NO to Dan River Anthology (year). Publishes anthology 40% of manuscripts submitted. Payment: 10% of amount received royalties from first 2500 copies then 15%. Copyrights for author. Subjects: Fiction, Literature (General).

Dancing Bridge Publishing, Elizabeth Rodenz, 370 Central Park West, Ste. 610, New York, NY 10025, 212-749-0029, Fax 212-280-4177, Erodenz@worldnet.att.net. 2003. Fiction, non-fiction. "Specializing in adult and childrens books that uplift and build bridges in people's lives." avg. press run 5M. Expects 2 titles 2006, 3 titles 2007. 320pp. Reporting time: 1 month. Simultaneous submissions accepted: yes. Publishes 10% of manuscripts submitted. Payment: varies. Copyrights for author. Subjects: Children, Youth, Psychology, Self-Help.

THE DANDELION, Michael E. Coughlin, Publisher, Michael E. Coughlin, PO Box 205, Cornucopia, WI 54827. 1977. Articles, cartoons, satire, criticism, reviews, letters. *"The Dandelion* is an occasional journal of philosophical anarchism which welcomes a wide variety of articles, cartoons, reviews, satire, criticism and news items. Prefers shorter articles, but will consider major pieces if appropriate. A sample copy is available for $2 to prospective authors." circ. about 400. 0/yr. Pub'd 1 issue 2005; expects 2 issues 2006, 1 issue 2007. sub. price $8/4 issues; per copy $2.00; sample $2.00. Back issues: $2.00. Discounts: 25% off listed price for bulk orders. 28pp. Reporting time: 1 month. Payment: copies of the magazine. Not copyrighted. Pub's reviews: none in 2005. §Anarchist/libertarian history, biographies, philosophy. Ads: none. Subjects: Anarchist, Libertarian.

DANDELION ARTS MAGAZINE, Fern Publications, Joaquina Gonzalez-Marina, Casa Alba, 24 Frosty Hollow, E. Hunsbury, Northants NN4 0SY, England, 01604-701730. 1978. Poetry, articles, art, photos, interviews, criticism, reviews, music, collages. *"Dandelion Arts Magazine* is an international publication and therefore the material submitted must have international appeal and not to offend anyone." circ. 1M. 2/yr. Pub'd 2 issues 2005; expects 2 issues 2006, 2 issues 2007. sub. price £9 UK, £18 Europe incl. postage + packing, £20 USA and the rest of the world (money could be sent in dollars but add extra for transaction); per copy £5 UK, £10 Europe incl. postage + packing, £10 USA and the rest of the world; sample £5 UK, £10 Europe incl. postage + packing, £10 USA and the rest of the world. Back issues: £5 UK, £10 Europe incl. postage + packing, £10 USA and the rest of the world. 20-30pp. Reporting time: by return of post provided an International Reply Coupon is attached or cheque in sterling payable to J. Gonzalez-Marina. Simultaneous submissions accepted: yes. Publishes 30% of manuscripts submitted. Payment: it is an international non-profit magazine. Copyrighted, reverts to author. Pub's reviews: 22 in 2005. §Nature, history, travel, arts, poetry, music biographies, short stories, etc. Ads: £50/£25/£15 1/4 page. Subjects: Arts, Autobiography, Bilingual, Biography, Book Arts, History, Poetry, Short Stories.

DARK ANIMUS, James R. Cain, PO Box 750, Katoomba, NSW 2780, Australia, skullmnky@hotmail.com, www.darkanimus.com. 2002. Poetry, fiction, art. "Publishes dark pulp fiction, art and poetry, showcasing the work of emerging and established writers. Contributors include Mike Arnzen, Tim Curran, Graham Masterton, Hertzan Chimera, Paul Haines and Robert Hood." 4/yr. Expects 1 issue 2006, 4 issues 2007. sub. price $25; per copy $5; sample $5. Back issues: $5. Discounts: 40% for bulk orders. 80pp. Reporting time: 8 weeks. Simultaneous submissions accepted: no. Publishes 10% of manuscripts submitted. Payment: 1 contributor copy. Copyrighted, reverts to author. Pub's reviews: none in 2005. §f/sf/h books. Subjects: Fiction, Magazines, Poetry.

Dash-Hill, LLC, Andrew Stewart, Editor, 3540 W. Sahara Avenue #O94, Las Vegas, NV 89102-5816, 212-591-0384, www.dashhillpress.com. 2000. Non-fiction. "We publish only 2-3 titles per year. We do not want unsolicited manuscripts at this time. We have enough finished manuscripts for 2006-2007." avg. press run 3M. Pub'd 2 titles 2005; expects 2 titles 2006, 2 titles 2007. 246pp. Reporting time: 1-3 months. Publishes 8% of manuscripts submitted. Payment: royalty variable, payment quarterly. Copyrights for author. Subjects: Business & Economics, Crime, Health, How-To, Management, Marketing, Reference, Safety, Self-Help.

Datamaster Publishing, LLC, Brigitte A. Thompson, PO Box 1527, Williston, VT 05495, 802-288-8040, Fax 802-288-8041, datamaster@surfglobal.net, www.DatamasterPublishing.com. 1995. Non-fiction. "We publish books in the field of early childhood education for parents, daycare providers, therapists, and preschool teachers." avg. press run 1M. Pub'd 2 titles 2005; expects 5 titles 2006, 5 titles 2007. Discounts: 20% for resale, larger for bulk orders. 120pp. Reporting time: 1 month. Simultaneous submissions accepted: yes. Publishes 30% of manuscripts submitted. Payment: yes. Copyrights for author. Subjects: Business & Economics, Family, Non-Fiction, Parenting.

DAVID McCALLUM UPDATES, http://davidmccallum.org, http://www.davidmcallum.org. "Keep informed on what David McCallum is doing now career wise as well as getting a reminder when a television show or movie will be on or a live theater play that he appears in. Contact address: Mr. David McCallum, NCIS, c/o

Belisarius Productions, Sunset Gower Studios, 1438 N. Gower Street, Building 35, 4th Floor, Los Angeles, CA 90028.'' Copyrighted, reverts to author. Subjects: Entertainment, Performing Arts, Television.

Dawn Publications, 12402 Bitney Springs Rd., Nevada City, CA 95959, 530-274-7775, toll free 800-545-7475, fax 530-274-7778, nature@dawnpub.com. 1979. Fiction, non-fiction. avg. press run 10M. Pub'd 6 titles 2005; expects 6 titles 2006, 6 titles 2007. Discounts: 5-99 books returnable 45%, 5-99 books non-returnable 50%. 32pp. Reporting time: 2 months. Simultaneous submissions accepted: yes. Publishes less than 1/10% of manuscripts submitted. Payment: yes. Copyrights for author. Subjects: Animals, Children, Youth, Cosmology, Earth, Natural History, Education, Environment, Nature, Non-Fiction, Picture Books, Science.

Dawn Sign Press, Joe Dannis, 6130 Nancy Ridge Drive, San Diego, CA 92121-3223. 1983. Fiction, parts-of-novels, plays, non-fiction. ''We are a specialty publisher of instructional sign language and educational deaf culture materials for both children and adults, deaf and hearing.'' avg. press run 5M-20M. Pub'd 5 titles 2005; expects 5 titles 2006, 5 titles 2007. Discounts: write for details. 100pp. Reporting time: 120 days. Payment: varies. Copyrights for author. Subjects: Arts, Bilingual, Children, Youth, Culture, Drama, Education, Games, Humor, Multicultural, Photography, Reference, Self-Help.

•**DayDream Publishing,** Laney Dale, 808 Vincent ST, Redondo Beach, CA 90277, www.daydreampub-lishers.com. 2006. Poetry, fiction, photos, music, non-fiction. avg. press run 3000. Expects 15 titles 2006, 75 titles 2007. 250pp. Reporting time: 60 days. Simultaneous submissions accepted: Yes. Publishes 10% of manuscripts submitted. Copyrights for author.

dbS Productions, Bob Adams, PO Box 1894, University Station, Charlottesville, VA 22903-0594, 800-745-1581, Fax 434-293-5502, info@dbs-sar.com, www.dbs-sar.com. 1990. Non-fiction. ''Outdoor skill related, first-aid, survival; biology skills; video production.'' avg. press run 10M. Pub'd 3 titles 2005; expects 4 titles 2006, 5 titles 2007. Discounts: 20% bulk, 40% retail. 60pp. Reporting time: 1 month. Payment: 10% biannual. Copyrights for author. Subjects: Biology, Electronics, Medicine, Scouting, Sports, Outdoors.

DEAD FUN, Kelli, PO Box 752, Royal Oak, MI 48068-0752. 1998. Poetry, fiction, art, photos, reviews, music, collages, non-fiction. ''Please limit short stories to 2000 words, anything above that relates to gothic or horror genre, need pen and ink art contributions badly.'' 2/yr. Pub'd 2 issues 2005; expects 2 issues 2006, 2 issues 2007. price per copy $3.75. Discounts: Will trade single copy and give discounts on bulk. 48pp. Reporting time: 2-4 weeks. Simultaneous submissions accepted: yes. Publishes 50% of manuscripts submitted. Payment: 1 copy. Not copyrighted. Pub's reviews: 6 in 2005. §gothic, horror. Ads: $13/$8/ 1/4 pg $5. Subject: Zines.

December Press, Curt Johnson, Box 302, Highland Park, IL 60035. 1958. Fiction, non-fiction. ''Publishes special issues for December Press, which see: publishes them as books. Can still be subscribed for these at $40/4 issues. Has suspended publication as a magazine of shorter pieces.'' avg. press run 1M. Pub'd 3 titles 2005; expects 1 title 2006, 1 title 2007. Discounts: 20% 1-5; 40% 6+. 256pp. Reporting time: 12 weeks. Simultaneous submissions accepted: no. Publishes .025% of manuscripts submitted. Payment: 10% net. Copyrights for author. Subjects: Fiction, History, Literature (General), Memoirs, Movies, Short Stories, Short Stories.

deep cleveland press, Mark S. Kuhar, PO Box 14248, Cleveland, OH 44114-0248, 216-706-3725, press@deepcleveland.com, www.deepcleveland.com. 2003. Poetry, fiction, art, photos, satire, parts-of-novels, long-poems, collages, plays, concrete art. avg. press run on-demand. Pub'd 1 title 2005; expects 5 titles 2006, 5-10 titles 2007. Discounts: bookstores 1-4 30%, 5-9 35%, 10+ 40%. 76pp. Reporting time: 1-6 months. Simultaneous submissions accepted: yes. Publishes 10% of manuscripts submitted. Payment: 10% after costs. Copyrights for author. Subject: Poetry.

DeerTrail Books, Jack Campbell, 637 Williams Court, Gurnee, IL 60031-3136, 847-367-0014. 1988. Non-fiction. ''Interested in non-fiction m.s.—books only—of approx. 40-100,000 words. Subjects are open, but no poetry, religious tracts, personal life philosophies, autobiographies, and other subjects of interest only to the writer. We *don't* want to see a ms. first. Write a one-page letter (if you can) describing your subject, your reader, and your thrust and treatment. We are currently interested only in subjects that are aimed to fill the needs of a specific audience. An audience hot on a readily - identified subject. In other words, a book that might sell well to a group through mailorder promotion. We are getting good at reaching narrow - interest audiences.'' avg. press run 2M-5M. Pub'd 1 title 2005; expects 3-4 titles 2006, 4-5 titles 2007. Discounts: standard trade. 124-150pp. Reporting time: 90 days. Simultaneous submissions accepted: no. Payment: negotiable. Copyrights for author. Subjects: Celtic, Design, Genealogy, History, Scotland, Senior Citizens, Sociology.

THE DEFENDER - Rush Utah's Newsletter, Eborn Books, Rush Utah, Bret Brooks, Eborn Books, Box 559, Roy, UT 84067. 1993. Poetry, fiction, articles, art, photos, cartoons, satire, criticism, reviews, letters, news items, non-fiction. ''Defends Mormonism against anti-Mormon claims.'' circ. 5M. 4/yr. Pub'd 4 issues 2005; expects 4 issues 2006, 4 issues 2007. sub. price $14.95; per copy $4.95; sample $4.95. 20pp. Payment: none.

130

Not copyrighted. Pub's reviews: 8 in 2005. §Anti-Mormon. Ads: $100/$75. Subject: Mormon.

Defiant Times Press (see also Regent Press), Wendy-O Matik, 6020-A Adeline, Oakland, CA 94608, defianttimespress@lycos.com. 1/2/4. avg. press run 500. Pub'd 1 title 2005; expects 3 titles 2006, 3 titles 2007. Discounts: standard. 100pp. Reporting time: 2 months. Simultaneous submissions accepted: yes. Payment: 10%. Does not copyright for author. Subject: Relationships.

•Delaney Day Press, Rhonda Oveson, 14014 North 64th Drive, Glendale, AZ 85306-3706, Tel:623-810-7590, Fax:623-878-2084, books@delaneydaypress.com, www.delaneydaypress.com. 2005. Fiction, non-fiction. "Currently we are publishing nonfiction inspirational and children's health books. Three children's fiction books are planned for fall/winter 2006." avg. press run 3000. Expects 3-4 titles 2007. Discounts: Trade 2-4 books 20%offdiscounts 5-9 books 30%off 10-24 books 40%off 25-199 books 46% 200 Or more books 50%offWholesale discount 50%Library discount 30%Nontradesales 45% nonreturnable. 200pp. Reporting time: 30-60 days. Simultaneous submissions accepted: Yes. Payment: Royalty rate for hardcover is 10% list price for first 5,000 sold, 12.5% for 5,000-10,000, 15% for over 10,000; Softcover is 7.5% list price. Copyrights for author. Subjects: Children, Youth, Christianity, Family, Health, Inspirational, Juvenile Fiction, Memoirs, Mental Health, Non-Fiction, Nursing, Nutrition, Parenting, Self-Help, Spiritual, Young Adult.

Delta Press, 27460 Avenue Scott, Valencia, CA 91355, Fax 661-294-2208. 1999. Poetry, art, photos, long-poems. avg. press run 500. Expects 1 title 2006, 2 titles 2007. Discounts: trade 25-99 20%, 100-299 40%, 300-499 45%, 500-999 50%, STOP 20-40%. 64pp. Reporting time: 4-6 weeks. Simultaneous submissions accepted: no. Publishes 10% of manuscripts submitted. Payment: royalty payments are per stated in contract, agreed % of the price per copy sold, an advance installment against royalties also apply. Copyrights for author. Subjects: Arts, Poetry.

Delta-West Publishing, Inc., John van Geldern, President, 507 Casazza Drive, Suite D, Reno, NV 89502-3346, 775-828-9398, 888-921-6788 (outside of NV), fax 775-828-9163, info@deltawest.com. 1990. Fiction, satire, non-fiction. "We prefer full-length novels which have unusual story lines and characters and in which there is a strong philosophical message. We also entertain non-fiction book-length writings and political satire. Presently 3 years backlogged." avg. press run 15M. Pub'd 3 titles 2005. Discounts: conventional quantity trade discounts, STOP orders and wholesale distributor discounts. 300pp. Reporting time: 60 days. Publishes 1% of manuscripts submitted. Payment: industry standard but we encourage author participation in pub. work for greater royalties. Copyrights for author. Subjects: Fiction, Non-Fiction, Satire.

The Denali Press, Alan Edward Schorr, Editorial Director and Publisher, PO Box 21535, Juneau, AK 99802, 907-586-6014, Fax 907-463-6780, denalipress@alaska.com. 1986. Non-fiction. "Firm publishes only reference and scholarly publications oriented toward library (academic and public) market, with modest sales directly to stores and individuals. Principally interested in: directories, guides, handbooks, indexes/abstracts as well as scholarly academic works, principally in the area of cultural diversity, ethnic and minority groups as well as occasional titles on Alaskana. Emphasis on books about ethnic groups and refugees. Exclusive distributor in US for Hull University Press, Libris, and Meridian Books. Recent titles include national resource directories for Hispanics and refugees/immigrants, as well as books on Jewish refugee children, US policy in Micronesia, Southern social justice organizations." avg. press run 2M. Pub'd 3 titles 2005; expects 4 titles 2006, 3 titles 2007. Discounts: 20%. 320pp. Reporting time: 1 month. Simultaneous submissions accepted: yes. Publishes 1% of manuscripts submitted. Payment: 10%. Does not copyright for author. Subjects: Alaska, Anthropology, Archaelogy, Bibliography, Biology, Book Reviewing, Chicano/a, Counter-Culture, Alternatives, Communes, Geography, History, Indexes & Abstracts, Libraries, Native American, Public Affairs, Reference, Science.

Denlinger's Publishers Ltd., Gustav Postreich, Executive Editor; Marcia Buckingham, Senior Editor, PO Box 1030, Edgewater, FL 32132-1030, 386-416-0009, 386-236-0517 (fax), editor@thebookden.com, acquisitions@thebookden.com, www.thebookden.com. 1926. Fiction, non-fiction. "We do not publish text books, erotica, poetry or illustrated works. Unpublished and published author are welcome. We are dedicated to expanding the opportunities of authors through the use of technology. Submissions are accepted ONLY electronically via disk or email. Please see our guidelines at www.thebookden.com/guide.html. Careful compliance will significantly improve your submission experience." Pub'd 50 titles 2005; expects 24 titles 2006, 24 titles 2007. Discounts: bookstores 1-4 books 25%, 5+ 40%. 225pp. Reporting time: 3-6 months. Simultaneous submissions accepted: yes. Publishes less than 2% of manuscripts submitted. Payment: 10% print, 50% other rights. Contract can be viewed at www.thebookden.com/agree.html. Does not copyright for author. Subjects: Alcohol, Alcoholism, Aviation, Civil War, Fiction, History, How-To, Humor, Inspirational, Memoirs, Military, Veterans, Psychology, Science Fiction, Self-Help, Sexual Abuse, Women.

DENVER QUARTERLY, Bin Ramke, Editor; Danielle Dutton, Associate Editor, University of Denver, Denver, CO 80208, 303-871-2892. 1966. Poetry, fiction, articles, interviews, satire, criticism, reviews, parts-of-novels, long-poems, non-fiction. "Poems: John Ashbery, Christine Hume, James Tate, Benjamin Ivry, Jane Miller, Ann Lauterbach, Paul Hoover. Essays: John Felstiner, Daniel Tiffany, David Wojahn, Lee Upton,

Malinda Markham. Fiction: Kass Fleisher, Charles Baxter, special fiction issues edited by Paul Maliszewski..."
circ. 1,700. 4/yr. Pub'd 4 issues 2005; expects 4 issues 2006, 4 issues 2007. sub. price $24/institutions,
$20/individuals; per copy $10; sample $10. Back issues: cost is based on rarity of the individual issue; usually
$10. Discounts: individual: 1 yr $20, 2 yrs $37, 3 yrs $50. 136pp. Reporting time: 2-4 months. We accept
simultaneous submissions if told. Publishes 5% of manuscripts submitted. Payment: $10 per page. Copyrighted,
reverts to author. Pub's reviews: 6 in 2005. §Literature of last 100 years and contemporary fiction and poetry.
Subjects: Arts, Poetry.

Department of Romance Languages, Floyd Gray, University of Michigan, 4108 MLB, Ann Arbor, MI
48109-1275, 734-764-5344; fax 734-764-8163; e-mail kojo@umich.edu. 1980. Articles. "We publish literary
criticism in the Romance Languages. Manuscripts by invitation only." avg. press run 500. Discounts: 20% off
to book wholesalers. 250pp. Simultaneous submissions accepted: no. Copyrights for author. Subjects:
Caribbean, Criticism, Europe, France, French, Italy, Language, Latin America, Literature (General), Spain.

DESCANT, Dave Kuhne, English Department, TCU, Box 297270, Fort Worth, TX 76129, 817-257-6537.
1957. Poetry, fiction. "*Descant* does not publish poetry volumes or essays. We offer the Frank O'Connor
Award, $500 for best story in an issue. Also the Gary Wilson Award for an outstanding story ($250), and the
$500 Betsy Colquitt Poetry Award for the best poem in an issue, and the $250 Baskerville Publishers Award for
an outstanding poem in an issue. There are no submission fees or entry forms, just submit your work with a
SASE. Copyright is returned to authors upon request. We accept submissions from September 1 through April
1." circ. 500. 1 issue published each summer. Pub'd 1 issue 2005; expects 1 issue 2006, 1 issue 2007. sub. price
$12, $18 foreign; per copy $12; sample $6. Back issues: $6. 150pp. Reporting time: 6 weeks. Simultaneous
submissions accepted: yes. Publishes .5% of manuscripts submitted. Payment: in copies. We return copyright to
author upon request. No ads. Subjects: Fiction, Poetry.

DESCANT, Karen Mulhallen, PO Box 314, Station P, M5S 2S8, Toronto, ON, Canada, phone: 416 593 2557,
fax: 416 593 9362, email general: info@descant.on.ca, email subscriptions/back issues: circulation@des-
cant.on.ca, web: www.descant.on.ca. 1970. Poetry, fiction, articles, art, photos, interviews, long-poems, plays,
non-fiction. circ. 1M. 4/yr. Pub'd 4 issues 2005; expects 4 issues 2006, 4 issues 2007. sub. price individuals:
$25/1 year, $40/2 years; institutions: $35/1 year, $70/2 years; add $6 per year outside Canada; per copy $15;
sample $8.50. Back issues: $8.50 plus $2 postage in Canada and $4 shipping/handling outside Canada. 200pp.
Reporting time: 9-12 months. Simultaneous submissions accepted: no. Publishes 2% of manuscripts submitted.
Payment: $100. Copyrighted, reverts to author. Ads: Full Page Ad 21 x 14 cm / 9 x5 inches = $300.00, Half
Page Ad 10.5 x 7 cm / 4.5x2.5 inches = $150.00, Quarter Page Ad 5 x 3.5 cm / 2x1 inches = $75.00. Ad
exchanges considered also. Subjects: Arts, Canada, Criticism, Culture, Drama, Fiction, Literary Review,
Literature (General), Photography, Poetry.

Desert Bloom Press, Newton Sanders, PO Box 670, Cortaro, AZ 85652-0670, 520-572-1597 phone/Fax,
dbpress@dakotacom.net, www.dakotacom.net/~dbpress. 1989. Fiction, non-fiction. "Not currently accepting
submissions. Publishes young adult fiction, adult suspense, and literary criticism dealing with Italian culture."
avg. press run 500 (+ print-on-demand capability). Pub'd 2 titles 2005; expects 1 title 2006. Discounts: 1: 0%,
2-4: 20%, 5-9: 40%, 10-99: 50%, 100-up:55%, STOP orders: 40% discount plus $3.95 for priority mail. 250pp.
Reporting time: 1 month. Simultaneous submissions accepted: no. Publishes 2% of manuscripts submitted.
Payment: negotiable. Copyrights for author. Subjects: Fiction, Italy, Young Adult.

The Design Image Group Inc., The Editorial Committee, 7000 South Adams St., Suite 111, Willowbrook, IL
60527-7565, 630-789-8991, Fax 630-789-9013. 1998. Fiction. avg. press run 3M-9M. Expects 6 titles 2006, 6
titles 2007. Discounts: 50/free ship. 262pp. Reporting time: 60 days. Simultaneous submissions accepted: yes.
Publishes 1-2% of manuscripts submitted. Payment: competitive advances and royalties. Copyrights for author.
Subjects: Fantasy, Fiction, Novels, Short Stories.

DESIRE, Eros Books, Mary Nicholaou, 463 Barlow Avenue, Staten Island, NY 10308, 718-317-7484,
marynicholaou@aol.com, www.geocities.com/marynicholaou/classic_blue.html. 1999. Fiction, articles, art,
cartoons, criticism, reviews, letters, parts-of-novels, non-fiction. "*Desire* is a postmodern magazine of literary
fiction and nonfiction. We provide a forum for experiments in open forms that interrogate the canon and lead to
transformation and redescription. Accepts any length and multiple submissions of literary merit." 4/yr. Pub'd 2
issues 2005; expects 4 issues 2006, 4 issues 2007. sub. price $20; per copy $5.00; sample $4. Back issues: $4.
Discounts: 40%. 60pp. Reporting time: 8 weeks. Simultaneous submissions accepted: yes. Publishes 10% of
manuscripts submitted. Payment: one year free subscription. Copyrighted, reverts to author. Pub's reviews: 1 in
2005. §Postmodern fiction (romance) and nonfiction. Ads: $10/$5. Subjects: Biography, Criticism, Culture,
Education, Essays, Fiction, Gender Issues, Language, Lifestyles, Literary Review, Literature (General),
Memoirs, Multicultural, Mystery, Myth, Mythology.

DESIRE STREET, Dr. Beau Boudreaux, Editor; Andrea S. Gereighty, President, New Orleans Poetry Forum,
257 Bonnabel Boulevard, Metairie, LA 70005-3738, 504-835-8472 (Andrea), 504-467-9034 (Jeanette), Fax

504-834-2005, ager80@worldnet.att.net, Fax 504-832-1116, neworleanspoetryforum@yahoo.com. 1984. Poetry. circ. 1.2M. 4/yr. Pub'd 4 issues 2005; expects 4 issues 2006, 4 issues 2007. sub. price $30, also entitles subscribers to one free critique of one 1-page original poem and all 50 weekly Weds. night 3-hour workshops when/if in New Orleans, LA, or send poems to workshop and we'll critique and return to you; per copy $10; sample $5. Back issues: $5 + 66¢ p/h. 55pp. Reporting time: 6 months. Simultaneous submissions accepted: yes. Publishes 45% of manuscripts submitted. Payment: seeing their work in publication and 1 copy. Copyrighted, reverts to author. Pub's reviews. §Books of poetry. Ads: $100/$75. Subjects: Louisiana, Poetry.

•**Devenish Press,** Jan Bachman, P.O. Box 17007, Boulder, CO 80308-0007, 303-926-0378 phone/fax, books@devenishpress.com, www.devenishpress.com. 1999. Art, photos, non-fiction. ''Devenish Press has published books about Ireland by author and photographer Tom Quinn Kumpf. Topics have included The Troubles in Northern Ireland and Irish culture, including legends, myths, and the Otherworld.'' avg. press run 3000. Discounts: Any amount 50%. 150pp. Reporting time: Two weeks. Simultaneous submissions accepted: No. Payment: Terms have varied according to author preference. Does not copyright for author. Subjects: Book Arts, Charles Bukowski, Indigenous Cultures, Ireland, Non-Fiction, Wyoming.

Devi Press, Inc., Ethan Walker III, 126 W. Main, Norman, OK 73069, (405) 447-0364. 2003. Poetry, non-fiction. ''Publisher of books about spirituality.'' avg. press run 5000. Pub'd 2 titles 2005; expects 1 title 2006, 1 title 2007. Discounts: 40%. 250pp. Reporting time: Not accepting submissions. Simultaneous submissions accepted: Yes. Publishes 1% of manuscripts submitted. Payment: Undetermined. Does not copyright for author. Subjects: Metaphysics, New Age, Spiritual.

DEVIL BLOSSOMS, John C. Erianne, PO Box 5122, Seabrook, NJ 08302. 1997. Poetry, fiction. ''No upward limit for poetry, 2500 words for short stories. I like works which focus on the dark side of human nature. Recent contributors include Patricia Garfinkel and A.D. Winans.'' circ. 500. 1-2/yr. Expects 2 issues 2006, 1-2 issues 2007. sub. price $8/3 issues; checks payable to John C. Erianne; per copy $3; sample $3. Discounts: 1-25 copies 35%, 26+ 45%. 24pp. Reporting time: 1-2 weeks. Simultaneous submissions accepted if so stated. Publishes 1% of manuscripts submitted. Payment: 1 copy. Copyrighted, reverts to author. Subjects: Fiction, Poetry.

Devil Mountain Books, Clark Sturges, PO Box 4115, Walnut Creek, CA 94596, 925-939-3415, Fax 925-937-4883, cbsturges@aol.com. 1984. Fiction, articles, non-fiction. avg. press run 1.5M. 100-300pp. Copyrights for author. Subjects: Alcohol, Alcoholism, Americana, Autobiography, Biography, California, Drugs, Essays, Medicine, San Francisco, Short Stories, The West.

Dharma Publishing (see also GESAR-Buddhism in the West), Tarthang Tulku, President; Rima Tamar, Publisher's Contact, 2910 San Pablo Avenue, Berkeley, CA 94702, 510-548-5407 ext. 20, fax: 510-548-2230, web:dharmapublishing.com. 1972. Articles, art, photos, interviews, reviews, news items. ''91 titles currently in print; over 200 reproductions of Tibetan art in full color. Sepcializes in books on Buddhism. We have our own photo-typesetting and offset printing facilities.'' avg. press run 5M. Pub'd 4 titles 2005; expects 10 titles 2006, 10 titles 2007. Discounts: bookstores 1 book 0%, 2-4 20%, 5-25 40%, 26+ 45%; 40% maximum on returnable books; distributors by contract; libraries 20%; class adoptions 20%. 32-400pp. Reporting time: do not accept submissions. Publishes very small % of manuscripts submitted. Payment: subject to individual arrangement. Copyright is held by Dharma Publishing. Subjects: Buddhism, Children, Youth, Health, History, Humanism, Inspirational, Metaphysics, Philosophy, Psychology, Religion, Spiritual.

DIALOGOS: Hellenic Studies Review, Michael Trapp, David Ricks, Dept. of Byzantine & Modern Greek, Attn: David Ricks, King's College, London WC2R 2LS, United Kingdom, fax 020-7848-873-2830. 1994. Poetry, articles, reviews. ''*Dialogos* considers any material related to the Greek world and Greek culture, of any period. Articles max. 8000 words, review articles max. 3500 words. Previous contributors include Edmund Keeley, Oliver Taplin, Robin Osborne, Stephen Halliwell and G.E.R. Lloyd. Translations from Greek literature of any period are particularly welcome.'' circ. 500. 1/yr. Pub'd 1 issue 2005; expects 1 issue 2006, 1 issue 2007. sub. price $59.50 cloth, $29.50 paper; per copy $59.50 cloth, $29.50 paper; sample $59.50 cloth, $29.50 paper. Back issues: apply to publisher. Discounts: none. 150pp. Reporting time: average 3 months. Simultaneous submissions accepted: yes. Publishes 10% of manuscripts submitted. Payment: none. Copyrighted, reverts to author. Pub's reviews: 1 in 2005. §Greek world and Greek culture from ancient times to the present. Ads: inquire. Subjects: Anthropology, Archaelogy, Classical Studies, Drama, Fiction, Greek, Literature (General), Poetry, Religion.

The Dibble Fund for Marriage Education, Catherine M. Reed, PO Box 7881, Berkeley, CA 94707-0881, 800-695-7975, Fax 510-528-1956, e-mail dibblefund@aol.com, www.buildingrelationshipskills.org. 1991. Non-fiction. ''We focus exclusively on materials which help adolescents learn relationship skills.'' avg. press run 1M+. Pub'd 1 title 2005; expects 1 title 2007. Discounts: 40% trade. 100pp. Reporting time: 2 months. Simultaneous submissions accepted: no. Payment: negotiable. Copyrights for author. Subjects: Adolescence, Marriage, Relationships.

DIFFERENT KIND OF PARENTING, KotaPress, Kara L.C. Jones, PO Box 514, Vashon Island, WA

98070-0514. 2001. "This is a zine aimed at bereaved parents after the death of a child; those who have other living childen, those who do not, those who may someday have others. Focus is mainly grief, healing, and transformation in the parents lives after death of a child." 4/yr. Back issues: Full archive of back issues soon to be available online at KotaPress.com for free as PDF files. Sometime in 2006. Simultaneous submissions accepted: yes. Payment: Free author copy with limited reproduction rights. Copyrighted, reverts to author. Pub's reviews: approx. 4 in 2005. §Anything with a grief and healing bent to it—based on real experiences with death of a child. Grief of this kind is hard enough, so we are not interested in materials that make up stories about it for entertainment.

Paul Dilsaver, Publisher, 2802 Clydesdale Court, Fort Collins, CO 80526-1155. 1974. Poetry, fiction. "Have published limited edition chapbooks under the imprints of Blue Light Books, Rocky Mountain Creative Arts, Academic & Arts Press. Authors published include Pulitzer winner Yusef Komunyakaa, John Sweet, John Garmon, Clifton Snider, Elinor Meiskey, John Calderazzo, Howard McCord, Victoria McCabe, Bim Angst, Kirk Robertson, R.P. Dickey, Richard F. Fleck, and many others. Most current imprint: Scrooge's Ledger. New titles by Richard Houff, Joseph Shields, and Peter Magliocco. Submissions by open call for specific projects only." avg. press run 100-150. Pub'd 1 title 2005; expects 2 titles 2006, 2 titles 2007. Pages vary. Payment: copies. Does not copyright for author. Subjects: Fiction, Poetry.

Dimi Press, Dick Lutz, 3820 Oak Hollow Lane, SE, Salem, OR 97302, 503-364-7698, Fax 503-364-9727. 1981. Non-fiction. "We are presently not accepting submissions." avg. press run 1.5M. Pub'd 1 title 2005; expects 2 titles 2006, 3 titles 2007. Discounts: 1-4 20%, 5+ 40%; libraries 20%, 10+ 50%. 130pp. Payment: 10% royalties, no advance. Copyrights for author. Subjects: Animals, Biology, Birds, Caves, Earth, Natural History, Travel.

DINER a journal of poetry, Eve Rifkah, Michael Milligan, P.O. Box 60676, Greendale Station, Worcester, MA 01606, 508-853-4143, www.spokenword.to/diner. 2000. Poetry, art, photos, interviews, criticism, reviews, long-poems. "We look for work that take risks with language, that understands the music of poetry not necessarily sweet.We feature 2 poets each issue with 10 pages of poetry and a 2-3 page interview. We have or will publish Sandra Kohler, Jeffrey Levine, Annie Finch, Gray Jacobik, Michael Casey." circ. 450. 1/yr. Pub'd 2 issues 2005; expects 1 issue 2006, 1 issue 2007. sub. price $14; per copy $14; sample $5. Back issues: $5 all available. Discounts: 2-10 copies 30%11 plus copies 40%. 250pp. Reporting time: not more than 6 months. Simultaneous submissions accepted: Yes. Payment: pay by copy. Copyrighted, reverts to author. Pub's reviews: 2 in 2005. §poetry books or chapbooks published within last 2 years. Ads: $250- full, $125 - half, $75 - quarter.

Dionysia Press Ltd. (see also UNDERSTANDING MAGAZINE), Denise Smith, Thom Nairn, 127 Milton Road West, 7, Duddingston House Courtyard, Edinburgh, EH15 1Jg, United Kingdom, 0131-6611153 [tel/fax, 0131 6614853 [tel]. 1989. Poetry, fiction, articles, criticism, reviews, plays. avg. press run 500. Pub'd 10-20 titles 2005; expects 10 titles 2006, 10 titles 2007. Discounts: 5 (poetry collections) £15 + postage. 150pp. Reporting time: 8 months. Simultaneous submissions accepted: no. Publishes 10% of manuscripts submitted. Payment: free copies. Does not copyright for author.

THE DIRTY GOAT, Host Publications, Inc., Elzbieta Szoka, Joe W. Bratcher III, 2717 Wooldridge, Austin, TX 78703, 512-482-8229, jbratcher3@aol.com. 1988. Poetry, fiction, art, photos, interviews, criticism, parts-of-novels, long-poems, plays. "Maximum length 20 pages. Will consider anything. Recent contributors: Mel Clay, David Ohle, Alfred Leslie, Gerald Nicosia. Artwork done in b/w and color." circ. 500. 2/yr. Pub'd 4 issues 2005; expects 2 issues 2006, 2 issues 2007. sub. price $20; per copy $10; sample $2. Back issues: none. Discounts: 1 copy 20%, 2-9 30%, 10-24 40%, 25-49 43%. 100pp. Reporting time: indeterminate. Payment: free copy. Copyrighted, reverts to author. Ads: none. Subjects: African Literature, Africa, African Studies, The Americas, Arts, Avant-Garde, Experimental Art, Beat, Bilingual, Criticism, Culture, Dada, Drama, English, Erotica, Essays, Europe, Fiction.

DIRTY LINEN, Paul Hartman, Editor-Publisher, PO Box 66600, Baltimore, MD 21239-6600, 410-583-7973, Fax 410-337-6735. 1983. Articles, photos, interviews, reviews, music, news items, non-fiction. "Folk, world music. Record and concert reviews: preferably 200-300 words, max. 400 words. Feature articles and interviews: 1,000-2,000+ words depending on topic. No unsolicited manuscripts." circ. 11M. 6/yr. Pub'd 6 issues 2005; expects 6 issues 2006, 6 issues 2007. sub. price $22; per copy $5; sample $4. Back issues: $4 plus postage. Discounts: distributors 55%, retail stores 40%. 100pp. Simultaneous submissions accepted: no. Publishes 0% of manuscripts submitted. Payment: $100 for major articles. Copyrighted, rights revert to author upon request. Pub's reviews: approx. 60 in 2005. §Folk/World Music. Ads: b&w: $1050 full page; $585 1/2 page; $325 1/4 page; $440 1/3 page; $220 1/6 page; $100 business card; color: $1590 full page; $945 half page; $530 1/4 page. Frequency discounts available. Subjects: Celtic, Music, Tapes & Records.

DISC GOLF WORLD, Rick Rothstein, Editor-Publisher, 509 E 18th St, Kansas City, MO 64108-1508, 816-471-3472, fax 816-471-4653, email info@discgolfworld.com. 1984. Articles, photos, cartoons, interviews, reviews, letters, news items, non-fiction. circ. 9.1m. 4/yr. Pub'd 4 issues 2005; expects 4 issues 2006, 4 issues

2007. sub. price $20 US ($30 1st class), $28 Can., $41 Europe, $44 Australia & Japan; per copy $6N. America, $8 rest; sample same. 96pp. Reporting time: 1-2 weeks. Simultaneous submissions are not usually accepted. Publishes 50-60% of manuscripts submitted. Payment: sometimes, in kind (merchandise). Copyrighted, reverts to author. Pub's reviews: 1 in 2005. §New sports and games, psychology of individual sports (especially golf), flying disc subjects. Ads: $635-$385/$390-235 Full(color-bw)/1/2. Subjects: Games, Sports, Outdoors.

DIVIDE Creative Responses to Contemporary Social Questions, Ginger Knowlton, Univ. of Colorado, Boulder / UCB 317, Boulder, CO 80309, www.colorado.edu/journals/divide.

Dixon-Price Publishing, Kendall Hanson, PO Box 1360, Kingston, WA 98346-1360, 360-297-8702, Fax 360-297-1620, dixonpr@dixonprice.com, www.dixonprice.com. 1999. Fiction, non-fiction. "Query first. We are ONLY considering nautical/maritime material related to Puget Sound boating or beachcombing." avg. press run 500. Pub'd 1 title 2005; expects 3 titles 2006, 3 titles 2007. Discounts: 2-4 copies 25%, 5-25 35%, 26-49 45%, 50+ 55%. 220pp. Simultaneous submissions accepted: no. Publishes 1-5% of manuscripts submitted. Copyrights for author. Subjects: Animals, How-To, Marine Life, Reprints, Sports, Outdoors, Travel.

THE DMQ REVIEW, Sally Ashton, Editor; Sarah Busse, Assistant Editor; Marcelle Kube, Assistant Editor, editors@dmqreview.com, www.dmqreview.com. 1997. Poetry, art. "Please read guidelines on website completely before submitting." 4/yr. Pub'd 4 issues 2005; expects 4 issues 2006, 4 issues 2007. Reporting time: 2 months. We accept simultaneous submissions with notification. Publishes less than 1% of manuscripts submitted. Copyrighted, rights revert to author, but we require first rights. Ads: contact us for quotes. Subjects: Arts, Poetry.

Doctor Jazz Press, A.J. Wright, 119 Pintail Drive, Pelham, AL 35124. 1979. Poetry, art. "DJ Press continues to issue poetry broadsides. No submissions, please; I am still overstocked. Until next time, this is Doctor Jazz signing off." avg. press run 100. Pub'd 2 titles 2005; expects 8 titles 2006. 1 page. Reporting time: less than a month. Payment: 25 copies. Copyrights for author. Subject: Poetry.

•DOLLS UNITED INTERACTIVE MAGAZINE, Kathleen Chrisman, 6360 Camille Drive, Mechanicsville, VA 23111, http://www.dollsunited.com, 804-339-8579, editor@dollsunited.com. 2002. Articles, art, photos, interviews, reviews. "Dolls United Interactive Magazine is a multi-media magazine for cloth art doll makers, artists, and enthusiasts. We publish artcies about doll making in all mediums: beading, clay, sewing, designing, painting, sculpting, embossing, fabric manipulation, and more. We also like to publish articles that apply to doll making as a business: tax information, branding, web design, photo editing, and more. Issues often contain one-two interviews with doll makers, and conference coverage. Each issue follows a specific "theme" and we try to apply our articles and dolls to that theme. In the past we have done such themes as "Asian Influence", "Winter Romance", "Stage & Screen", "Mystical", and more." circ. 200. 4/yr. Pub'd 4 issues 2005; expects 4 issues 2006, 4 issues 2007. sub. price $24; per copy $7; sample free. Back issues: $7. 115pp. Reporting time: Within a week. Simultaneous submissions accepted: Yes. Pub's reviews: 2 in 2005. §Anything related to dollmaking. Ads: $100 - full page$50 - half page$30 - quarter page. Subjects: Arts, Avant-Garde, Experimental Art, Business & Economics, Color, Crafts, Hobbies, Creativity, Design, How-To, Internet, Interviews, Marketing, Photography, Quilting, Sewing, Textiles, Visual Arts.

DOPE FRIENDS, Emmett Taylor, Ivy Shields, Ballagh, Bushypark, Galway, Ireland, e-mail mmtaylor@iol.ie. 1998. Art, cartoons, reviews, letters. "Ongoing comic book series." Pub'd 2 issues 2005; expects 4 issues 2006, 4 issues 2007. price per copy $2. Discounts: 5-10 copies $1.80; 11-19 copies $1.65; 20 or more $1.50. 24pp. Simultaneous submissions accepted: no. Pub's reviews: 3 in 2005. §comics, subculture magazines. Ads: $20/$14/ 1/4 pg $7.50. Subjects: Adolescence, Alcohol, Alcoholism, Cartoons, Comics, Drugs, Humor, Ireland.

Doral Publishing, Luana Luther, Editor-in-Chief; Beverly Black, Editor; Michelle O'Hagen, Graphic Design; Alvin Grossman, Publisher; Gwen Henson, Editor; Lynn Grey, Marketing Manager; Lisa Liddy, Graphic Artist, 16080 West Wildflower Drive, Surprise, AZ 85374-5053, (623) 875-2057, (623) 875-2059, (800) 633-5385. 1986. Non-fiction. "Doral publishes books for the purebred dog market. We specialize in breed books and show pertaining to purebred dogs in general. Hardback books average some 300 pages in length. We also publish dog-related books for children." avg. press run 3M-5M. Pub'd 4 titles 2005; expects 4 titles 2006, 5 titles 2007. Discounts: 1-3 books - 10%, 4-9 books - 25%, 10-24 books - 40%, 25-49 books - 45%, 50-99 books - 50%, 100+ books - 55%. 285pp. Reporting time: 3-4 weeks. Simultaneous submissions accepted: yes. Publishes 10% of manuscripts submitted. Payment: 10% 1st book - paid January & July. Copyrights for author. Subject: Animals.

DOTLIT: The Online Journal of Creative Writing, Craig Bolland, Nike Bourke, Stuart Glover, Helen Klaebe, Philip Neilsen, Angela Slatter, Glen Thomas, Queensland University of Technology, Creative Industry Facul, PO Box 2434, Kelvin Grove, QLD 4059, Australia, (07)3864 2976, FAX (07)3864 1810, http://www.dotlit.qut.edu.au. 2000. "Fiction: max 4,000, poetry: up to two poems, creative non-fiction: max 4,000, reviews: multiple titles max 4,000; single titles max 2,000, hypertexts, digital storytelling: max 2 minutes, and scholarly articles about the practice of creative writing: max 7,000 words. Unsolicited material and only unpublished works accepted. Turnaround can be up to 6 months." 2/yr. Expects 2 issues 2006, 2 issues 2007. Back issues: http://www.dotlit.qut.edu.au. on line journal, variable no of pages. Reporting time: 3-6 months. Copyrighted, reverts to author. Pub's reviews. §Particularly interested in reviewing fiction or creative non-fiction that develops the craft of writing and new writing about writing. Subjects: Fiction, Literature (General), Non-Fiction, Novels, Poetry, Short Stories.

DOUBLE ROOM: A Journal of Prose Poetry & Flash Fiction, Peter Conners, Founding Editor; Mark Tursi, Founding Editor; Cactus May, Associate Editor; Michael Neff, Publisher, double_room@hotmail.com, www.webdelsol.com/double_room. 2002. Poetry, fiction, art, photos, criticism, reviews. "In addition to publishing prose poetry and flash fiction, we ask each contributor to write roughly 250 words regarding one or both of the forms. Our goal is to not only present the best writing possible, but to advance the discussion regarding these forms. We have two open submission periods per year which are posted on our web site. Recent contributors include Rosmarie Waldrop, Cole Swenson, Daryl Scroggins, Ron Silliman, Holly Iglesias, Russell Edson, Bin Ramke, and Sean Thomas Dougherty." circ. online publication with unlimited circulation. 2/yr. Expects 2 issues 2006, 2 issues 2007. sub. price free; sample online. Back issues: free. 40pp. Reporting time: 1-4 months. Simultaneous submissions accepted: Yes. Payment: none. Copyrighted, reverts to author. Pub's reviews: 10 in 2005. §Books of prose poetry, flash fiction, or critical work regarding those forms. Ads: none.

DOVETAIL: A Journal by and for Jewish/Christian Families, Mary Rosenbaum, Editor; Carol Weiss Rubel, Review Editor, 775 Simon Greenwell Ln., Boston, KY 40107, 502-549-5440, Fax 502-549-3543, 800-530-1596, DI-IFR@Bardstown.com, carolw44@aol.com, www.dovetailinstitute.org. 1992. Articles, photos, cartoons, interviews, reviews, letters, news items, non-fiction. "Articles are 800-1,000 words, run with 2- or 3-sentence bio. We look for a wide variety of ideas and opinions on interfaith marriage." circ. 1M. 4/yr. Pub'd 6 issues 2005; expects 6 issues 2006, 4 issues 2007. sub. price $39.95 US, $39.95 International; per copy $5.50; sample $5.50. Back issues: $5.50. Discounts: call for quote. 16pp. Reporting time: 2-4 months. We accept simultaneous submissions if notified. Publishes 25% of manuscripts submitted. Payment: $25/article. Copyrighted, does not revert to author. Pub's reviews: 9 in 2005. §Interfaith marriage, life cycle ceremonies, family rituals. Ads: $200/$125/$50 1 inch. Subjects: Christianity, Family, Judaism, Marriage, Multicultural, Parenting, Relationships, Religion, Self-Help, Spiritual.

DOWN IN THE DIRT LITERARY MAGAZINE, the prose & poetry magazine revealing all your dirty little secrets, Scars Publications, Alexandria Rand, Editor, Scars Publications, 829 Brian Court, Gurnee, IL 60031-3155, AlexRand@scars.tv, http://scars.tv. 1999. Poetry, fiction, art, photos, letters, long-poems, collages, non-fiction. "*down in the dirt* looks for new writers, so that new voices be heard. We publish print and internet issues of writings, preferring email submissions over letters (to avoid typing errors in reproduction), but select accepted writings, along with accepted writings from the literary magazine, *children, churches and daddies*, will appear in annual books (both paperback and hardcover), so if we choose your work for an annual collection book, we will notify you. Issues available in print (paid only), and on the internet for free at http://scars.tv. Email contact is preferred and any information about *down in the dirt* magazine is only a click away at http://scars.tv." circ. varies, usually always on internet, but can appear in collection books. Frequency varies. sub. price $50.00 American/year; per copy around $13.23 for books, $6.00 for a single print issue; sample around $13.23 for books, $6.00 for a single print issue. Back issues: around $13.23 for books, $6.00 for a single print issue. In print form, *Down in the Dirt* appears with *Children, Churches and Daddies* acceptances into a collection book, which on average is 200-300 pages. Reporting time: electronic requests receive responses within 3 days, you will hear from us within a week if you enclose a SASE, otherwise you will never hear from us. Simultaneous submissions accepted: Yes. Publishes 75% of manuscripts submitted. Payment: appearance of your work in text and e-books on the internet. Not copyrighted. Subjects: Arts, Chicago, Counter-Culture, Alternatives, Communes, Culture, Feminism, Fiction, Graphics, Language, Literary Review, Magazines, New Age, Photography, Poetry, Women.

Down The Shore Publishing, Ray Fisk, PO Box 100, West Creek, NJ 08092, 609-978-1233; fax 609-597-0422. 1984. Fiction, non-fiction. "We are primarily a regional publisher, producing trade and gift books for the NJ shore and mid-atlantic." avg. press run varies. Pub'd 3 titles 2005; expects 5 titles 2006, 5 titles 2007. Discounts: 1-2 books 0%, 3-5 20%, 6-11 40%, 12+ 42%. Pages vary. Reporting time: 1-3 months. Simultaneous submissions accepted: yes. Publishes 1% of manuscripts submitted. Payment: varies. We sometimes copyright for author. Subjects: Americana, Fiction, History, Literature (General), Nature.

Down There Press, Leigh Davidson, 938 Howard St., #101, San Francisco, CA 94103-4100, 415-974-8985 x 205, fax 415-974-8989, 800-289-8423, downtherepress@excite.com, www.goodvibes.com/dtp/dtp.html. 1975. Fiction, photos, non-fiction. "We publish sexual health books for children, women and men. Our books are sex-positive, innovative, lively, and practical, providing basic physiological information and realistic, non-judgmental techniques for strengthening sexual communication.We also publish award-winning erotica, both literary and photographic, for adults.Recent and best-selling titles include The Big Book of Masturbation, Photo Sex, Herotica 6, Anal Pleasure & Health, Exhibitionism for the Shy, A Kid's First Book About Sex."

avg. press run 4000. Pub'd 4 titles 2005; expects 1 title 2007. Discounts: Distributed to the trade by SCB Distributors, Gardena CA, 800-729-6423. 200pp. Reporting time: 3 months. Simultaneous submissions accepted: Yes. Publishes 1% of manuscripts submitted. Payment: we pay small advances, and royalties based on net sales. Copyrights for author. Subjects: Counter-Culture, Alternatives, Communes, Culture, Fiction, Gay, Gender Issues, Health, Lesbianism, Photography, Psychology, Relationships, Self-Help, Senior Citizens, Singles, Visual Arts, Women.

Downeast Books, Karin Womer, Chris Cornell, PO Box 679, Camden, ME 04843, 207-594-9544, Fax 207-594-0147, books@downeast.com, www.downeastbooks.com, www.countrysportpress.com. 1967. Fiction, art, photos, non-fiction. "Maine or New England subject matter." avg. press run 3-5M. Pub'd 30 titles 2005; expects 30 titles 2006, 30 titles 2007. Discounts: trade 1-4 20%, 5-14 40%, 15-49 42%, 50-79 43%, 80-99 44%, 100+ 45%; call for cataloguer discounts. 165pp. Reporting time: 6-8 weeks. Simultaneous submissions accepted: yes. Publishes 2% of manuscripts submitted. Payment: varies. Copyrighting for author varies. Subjects: Antiques, Architecture, Arts, Biography, Children, Youth, Conservation, Crafts, Hobbies, Earth, Natural History, Fiction, Gardening, History, How-To, Humor, Literature (General), Newsletter.

DOWNSTATE STORY, Elaine Hopkins, 1825 Maple Ridge, Peoria, IL 61614, 309-688-1409, email ehopkins@prairienet.org, http://www.wiu.edu/users/mfgeh/dss. 1992. Fiction, art. "2000 word maximum, mainstream fiction." 1/yr. Pub'd 1 issue 2005; expects 1 issue 2006, 1 issue 2007. price per copy $8; sample $8. Back issues: $5. Discounts: yes. 65pp. Reporting time: varies. Simultaneous submissions accepted: yes. Publishes 10% of manuscripts submitted. Payment: $50. Copyrighted, reverts to author. Ads: negotiable. Subject: Short Stories.

DOWNTOWN BROOKLYN: A Journal of Writing, Wayne Berninger, English Department; Long Island Univ., Brooklyn Campus, 1 University Plaza, Brooklyn, NY 11201. 1992. Poetry, fiction, art, photos, parts-of-novels, long-poems, plays, concrete art, non-fiction. "Submissions only accepted from current and former students, faculty, and staff of the Brooklyn Campus of Long Island University." circ. 2000 copies. 1/yr. Pub'd 1 issue 2005; expects 1 issue 2006, 1 issue 2007. sub. price free first come first served; per copy free first come first served; sample free first come first served. Back issues: available in LIU/Brooklyn library and at library at U of Wisconsin/Madison. 175pp. Reporting time: deadline first Monday in December; response in following April. Payment: none. Copyrighted, reverts to author.

The Dragon Press, Richard Wills, Cynthia Harlan, 4230 Del Rey Avenue, Marina del Rey, CA 90292, 1-877-907-5400, Fax 626-398-7450. 1986. Articles, photos, news items, non-fiction. avg. press run 1000-2500. Pub'd 2 titles 2005; expects 2-3 titles 2006, 2-3 titles 2007. Discounts: trade 2-49 books 20%, 50-99 45%, 100+ 50%. 140pp. Reporting time: 30 days or less. Simultaneous submissions accepted: yes. Publishes 10% of manuscripts submitted. Payment: varies according to project. Copyrights for author. Subjects: Advertising, Self-Promotion, Crime, How-To, Marketing.

•**DRAMA GARDEN, New Creature Press,** Joseph Verrilli, PO Box 1158, Bridgeport, CT 06601-1158, 203-455-7285. 2006. Poetry, fiction, articles, art, photos, cartoons, satire, reviews, letters, collages, non-fiction. "Recent contributors: Marie Kazalia, Ana Christy, Laurel Speer, Lyn Lifshin, Colin Cross, D.J. Weston, Jonathan K. Rice, Laura Stamps, and Mark Sonnenfeld." circ. 50. 3/yr. Expects 3 issues 2006, 3 issues 2007. sub. price $10; per copy $4; sample $4. 21pp. Reporting time: 1 week. Simultaneous submissions accepted: yes. Publishes 95% of manuscripts submitted. Payment: contributor copy. Not copyrighted. Pub's reviews. §Poetry, prose on any subject. Subjects: Relationships, Religion, Society.

Dramaline Publications, Courtney Marsh, 36851 Palm View Road, Rancho Mirage, CA 92270-2417, 760-770-6076, FAX 760-770-4507, drama.line@verizon.net. 1983. Plays. "We publish scene-study books for actors. Monologues and scenes. The original monologues and scenes must be of no longer than a three minute duration, must embrace contemporary points of view, be written in modern language." avg. press run 2M. Pub'd 3 titles 2005; expects 4 titles 2006, 4 titles 2007. Discounts: 1-99 books 40%, 100-199 43%, 200+ 45%. 64pp. Reporting time: 1 month. Simultaneous submissions accepted: no. Publishes 5% of manuscripts submitted. Payment: 10% of cover price paid yearly. Does not copyright for author. Subject: Drama.

THE DRAMATIST, Gregory Bossler, The Dramatists Guild of America Inc., 1501 Broadway Suite 701, New York, NY 10036. 1964. Articles, photos, interviews, letters, news items, non-fiction. circ. 7M. 6/yr. Pub'd 6 issues 2005; expects 6 issues 2006, 6 issues 2007. sub. price $25; per copy $5 (Canada $8). 48pp. Reporting time: 6 months. Simultaneous submissions accepted: Yes. Payment: $25 for under 250 words, $50 for 250-499, $75 for 500-999, $100 for 1,000-1,499, $150 for 1,500-2,499, $200 for 2,500 or more. Copyrighted, reverts to author. Ads: full page color $675, full page B&W $500, half page B&W $325, classified $40 for 40 words 75¢ each addional word. Subjects: Interviews, Theatre, Writers/Writing.

Dream Catcher Publishing, Dwan Hightower, President, 3260 Keith Bridge Road #343, Cumming, GA 30041-4058, 770-887-7058, fax 888-771-2800, dcp@dreamcatcherpublishing.net, www.dreamcatcherpublishing.net. 2001. Poetry, fiction, non-fiction. avg. press run 5000. Pub'd 6 titles 2005; expects 8 titles 2006, 8 titles

2007. Discounts: 40%. 250pp. Simultaneous submissions accepted: no. Publishes 90% of manuscripts submitted. Copyrights for author. Subjects: Fantasy, Fiction, Native American, Non-Fiction, Picture Books, Poetry.

DREAM FANTASY INTERNATIONAL, Chuck Jones, Editor-in-Chief & Publisher, 411 14th Street #H1, Ramona, CA 92065-2769. 1980. Poetry, fiction, articles, art, cartoons, satire, non-fiction. "All prose to above address. All poetry submissions to Senior Poetry Editor Carmen M. Pursifull, 809 W. Maple, Champaign, IL 61820-2810. Length of prose material accepted: 1,000-2,000 words. *Not commonly accepted*: sexually explicit material or use of vulgar or 'four-letter' words. Basic type of subject accepted: anything relating to dreams; dream fragments, fiction, poetry, non-fiction, haiku, etc. Articles on precognition, astral projection, etc. Mss will not be returned unless so requested at time of submission. Also fantasy pieces, fiction, prose and poetry. Checks/money orders and overseas drafts must be made payable to Charles Jones rather than DIQ. Send prose to Editor-in-Chief, Chuck Jones." circ. 65-80. 1-2/yr. Pub'd 2 issues 2005. sub. price US $56 (domestic rate); per copy $14 ppd. (Domestic), guidelines $2 for LSASE with 2 1st class stamps; sample Outside US: $12. Consult US Editor for postage and handling costs. Back issues: $15 each. 99-111pp. Reporting time: 8-10 weeks. Simultaneous submissions accepted: yes. Publishes 40% of manuscripts submitted. Payment: in the form of complimentary copy upon receipt of $4.50 for s/h. Copyrighted, reverts to author. Ads: $57/$35/$10. Subjects: Dreams, Fantasy, Fiction, Haiku, Poetry, Prose, Psychology, Satire, Science Fiction, Short Stories, Spiritual.

Dream Horse Press, J.P. Dancing Bear, PO Box 2080, Aptos, CA 95001-2080, dreamhorsepress@yahoo.com, www.dreamhorsepress.com. 1997. Poetry. "DHP publishes two manuscripts a year: one from our chapbook contest, Dream Horse Press Annual National Chapbook Contest series, deadline May 31; and The Orphic Poetry Book Prize, deadline October 31. See website for further details and guidelines." avg. press run 500. Pub'd 2 titles 2005; expects 2 titles 2006, 2 titles 2007. Reporting time: 3 months. Simultaneous submissions accepted: yes. Publishes 1% of manuscripts submitted. Copyrights for author. Subject: Poetry.

DREAM NETWORK, Roberta Ossana, Editor & Publisher, PO Box 1026, Moab, UT 84532-3031, 435-259-5936; Publisher@DreamNetwork.net http:dreamnetwork.net http://DreamNetwork.com. 1982. Poetry, articles, art, photos, interviews, reviews, letters. "Articles: 1500-2000 words. Full color covers, reproducible black and white original art and high quality photos (can be submitted via email as .jpg scanned at 300dpi or .pdf files) are preferred. We receive articles from some of the finest Dreamworkers in the country, both lay and professional, such as Arnold Mindell, Stanley Krippner, Gayle Delaney, Montague Ullman, Deborah Hillman, David Feinstein, with emphsis on people like you! Questions & experiential sharing of dream-related experience invited. Contributing artists include Deborah Koff-Chapin, Susan Boulet, Susan St. Thomas, etc. Spiritual, psychology, New Age. Exploration of the meaning of dreams and the evolution of relevant mythologies in our time." circ. 4M. 4/yr. Pub'd 4 issues 2005; expects 4 issues 2006, 4 issues 2007. sub. price $25 USA; $35 Canada, Mexico, libraries; $45 foreign airmail. Available Online in .pdf format an exact replica of the print publication. $16 Worldwide; per copy $7; sample $7. Back issues: $7. Discounts: 50% jobbers, agents, distributors, etc. 52pp. Reporting time: maximum 1-2 months. We accept simultanous submissions occassionaly. Publishes 50-75% of manuscripts submitted. Payment: 10 copies of issue in which their work is published and 1-year subscription. Copyrighted, rights revert to author if requested. Pub's reviews: 20 in 2005. §Books on dreams, mythology, dream education—anything dream or myth related, vidoes, CD's, Cassette tapes. Ads: $700/$400/classified $10/20 words or $35 per year. Subjects: Anthropology, Archaelogy, Book Reviewing, Dreams, Education, Human Rights, Interviews, Journals, Magazines, Motivation, Success, Myth, Mythology, Native American, New Age, Poetry, Psychology, Reviews.

Dream Publishing Co., G. Robert Lyles III, 1304 Devonshire, Grosse Pointe Park, MI 48230, 313-882-6603, Fax 313-882-8280. 1999. Fiction. "A new media company that creates a children's picture book series on health that empowers kids to overcome adversity and live healthier lives. Acceptance, tolerance and diversity are key elements. Multicultural and fun characters show kids that they are not alone with these health issues. Approved by the Dept. of Education for California." avg. press run 1-3M. Pub'd 2 titles 2005; expects 2 titles 2006. Discounts: standard. 32pp. Simultaneous submissions accepted: no. Publishes 0% of manuscripts submitted. Copyrights for author. Subjects: African-American, Children, Youth, Education, Family, Health, Inspirational, Latino, Multicultural, Nursing, Nutrition, Picture Books.

Dream Street Publishing, Del Kyger, PO Box 65355, Tucson, AZ 85728-5355, Fax 520-529-3911. 1998. "Metaphysically oriented material that help us better understand and accept our relationship with God. Childrens stories (fables) that contain insights on living a full, rich, joyful and loving life." avg. press run 5M. Pub'd 1 title 2005; expects 1 title 2006, 3 titles 2007. Discounts: 40-55%. Simultaneous submissions accepted: no. Payment: varies. Copyrights for author. Subjects: Channelling, Children, Youth, Metaphysics, Spiritual.

DREAMS AND NIGHTMARES, David C. Kopaska-Merkel, 1300 Kicker Road, Tuscaloosa, AL 35404, 205-553-2284, e-Mail dragontea@earthlink.net. 1986. Poetry, art, cartoons. "Contributors: Charlee Jacob, Bruce Boston, Robert Frazier, Ann K. Schwader, Keith Daniels, Cathy Buburuz. Generally poems should fit, single-spaced, on 8-1/2 X 11 paper. I print some longer ones. Don't like gory or trite poems, but gore and sex ok if not gratuitous. *Any* format is fine. I also publish prose poems and a small amount of short-short fiction." circ. 200. 3/yr. Pub'd 3 issues 2005; expects 3 issues 2006, 3 issues 2007. sub. price $12/6 issues inside N. America and $15/6 issues elsewhere.; per copy $3; sample $3. Discounts: on a case-by-case basis. 24pp. Reporting time: 2-8 weeks, average 3 weeks. Simultaneous submissions accepted: no. Publishes less than 5% of manuscripts submitted. Payment: $5 per contribution on acceptance plus 2 contributor's copies. Copyrighted, reverts to author. Ads: $10 for 8-1/2 X 11 insert. Subjects: Fantasy, Poetry, Science Fiction.

•**dreamslaughter,** dreamslaughter dreamslaughter, PO Box 571454, Tarzana, CA 91357, 8183216708, http://www.dreamslaughter.com. 2005. Non-fiction. "progressive politics." avg. press run 2000. Pub'd 1 title 2005; expects 2 titles 2006, 3 titles 2007. 200pp. Simultaneous submissions accepted: Yes. Publishes 100% of manuscripts submitted. Copyrights for author. Subjects: Education, Multicultural, Non-Fiction, Non-Violence, Philosophy, Political Science, Politics, Quotations, Reference, Self-Help, Sociology, Spiritual.

THE DROOD REVIEW OF MYSTERY, J. Huang, Editor & Publisher; B. Thoenen, Managing Editor; J. Jacobson, Managing Editor; H. Francini, Managing Editor, 484 E. Carmel Drive #378, Carmel, IN 46032, Fax 317-705-1402, info@droodreview.com, www.droodreview.com. 1982. Articles, art, cartoons, interviews, criticism, reviews, news items, non-fiction. "Short reviews 50-500 words. Articles 1,500-5,000 words." circ. 1.7M. 6/yr. Pub'd 6 issues 2005; expects 6 issues 2006, 6 issues 2007. sub. price $20; per copy $3.50; sample same. Discounts: Standing order bookseller customers in the US earn a 45% discount and free freight on orders of 5 or more copies per issue, non-returnable. Higher discounts available for larger quantities; contact us for details. Discounts are also available for library customers who take five or more copies sent together to a single address; contact us for details. 24pp. Reporting time: 2-6 weeks. Simultaneous submissions accepted: no. Payment: none. Copyrighted, does not revert to author. Pub's reviews: 180 in 2005. §Mystery & detective fiction. Ads: Base page rage is $225. Discounts available for frequency and to booksellers who sell Drood in their stores. "Ride-Along" program allows advertisers to have their materials included in our mailings; contact us for details. Subjects: Book Reviewing, Criticism, Literary Review, Mystery.

DRT Press, Adrienne Bashista, PO Box 427, Pittsboro, NC 27312-0427, 1-919-542-1763 (phone/fax), editorial@drtpress.com, www.drtpress.com. 2004. Fiction, non-fiction. "DRT Press published books about adoption and families. Our focus is on books for children, but we will also consider manuscripts for adults as long as they are within our parameters. We are a very small press and very selective. We can only publish books that do not compete with other items in print. Please check our website (www.drtpress.com) to see if we are accepting unsolicited manuscripts at any given time." avg. press run 5000. Expects 1 title 2006, 2 titles 2007. Discounts: 5-20 copies, 40%; closed case (30 copies), 50%. We encourage adoption non-profits to contact us for use of our books as fundraising items. 38pp. Reporting time: 3 months. Simultaneous submissions accepted: Yes. Payment: Standard advance against royalties. Copyrights for author. Subjects: Adoption, Family.

DRUMVOICES REVUE, Eugene B. Redmond, Southern Illinois University, English Dept., Box 1431, Edwardsville, IL 62026-1431, 618-650-2060; Fax 618-650-3509. 1990. Poetry, fiction, articles, art, photos, interviews, criticism, reviews, letters, non-fiction. "Prefer poems of no more than 3 pages. Multicultural-gender inclusive. Recent contributors: Maya Angelou, Gwendolyn Brooks, John Knoepfle, Carlos Cumpian, Rohan B. Preston, Derek Walcott, Amiri Baraka, Allison Funk, and Janice Mirikitani." circ. 1.5M. 1-2/yr. Pub'd 1-2 issues 2005; expects 2 issues 2006, 2 issues 2007. sub. price $10; per copy $10; sample $5. Discounts: 40%. 132pp. Reporting time: seasonal. Simultaneous submissions accepted: yes. Publishes 50% of manuscripts submitted. Payment: 2 copies. Copyrighted, reverts to author. Pub's reviews. §Anthologies, clusters of chapbooks or volumes of poetry, novels. Ads: $200/$100/others negotiable. Subjects: African Literature, Africa, African Studies, African-American, Literature (General), Midwest.

Paul Dry Books, Paul Dry, 117 S. 17th Street, Suite 1102, Philadelphia, PA 19103, 215-231-9939, fax:215-231-9942, website: www.@pauldrybooks.com.

THE DUCKBURG TIMES, Dana Gabbard, Editor, 3010 Wilshire Blvd., #362, Los Angeles, CA 90010-1146, 213-388-2364. 1977. Articles, art, photos, cartoons, interviews, criticism, reviews, letters, news items, non-fiction. "Our sole criterion for the acceptance of material is that it in some way relate to the works of Walt Disney and associates. We run quite a lot on famed comic book artist Carl Barks, but are also interested in material on other Disney artists, the studio, Disney animation, the theme parks, etc. If in doubt, contact us first. Especially on the lookout for material from overseas fans. We have special guidelines to follow when running Disney copyrighted art available upon request. Always open to the unusual and critical." circ. 1.4M. 1/yr. sub. price $12; per copy inquire; sample $3. Back issues: inquire. 28pp. Reporting time: ASAP. Payment: copy of issue material appears in. Copyrighted, rights revert to author upon written request. Pub's reviews: none in 2005. §Walt Disney, animation, Carl Barks, comics, theme parks, and related. Classified free to subscriber if under 50 words, Disney-related. Subjects: Comics, Disney.

Duende Press, Larry Goodell, Box 571, Placitas, NM 87043, 505-867-5877. 1964. Poetry. avg. press run 500.

Discounts: 40% plus mailing. Subjects: Avant-Garde, Experimental Art, Southwest, Tapes & Records.

Dufour Editions Inc., Christopher May, President & Publisher; Brad Elliott, Creative Director, PO Box 7, Chester Springs, PA 19425-0007, 610-458-5005, Fax 610-458-7103. 1949. Poetry, fiction, articles, criticism, reviews, long-poems, plays, non-fiction. "Dufour Editions publishes, co-publishes, and exclusively distributes selected titles of British or Irish origin. We also publish some works of American origin." avg. press run 500-3000. Pub'd 4 titles 2005; expects 4 titles 2006, 4 titles 2007. Discounts: trade 1-4 20%, 5-14 40%, 15-24 41%, 25-49 42%, 50-99 43%, 100+ 44%; short discounted titles: 20% any quantity. SCOP & STOP 30%; libraries 10%. Pages vary. Reporting time: 1-6 months. Simultaneous submissions accepted: yes. Publishes 1% of manuscripts submitted. Payment: negotiated. Copyrights for author. Subjects: Celtic, Children, Youth, Classical Studies, Fiction, German, History, Humanism, Ireland, Literature (General), Non-Fiction, Philosophy, Poetry, Politics, Scotland, Socialist.

DUFUS, RD Armstrong, Lummox, PO Box 5301, San Pedro, CA 90733-5301, www.geocities.com/lumoxraindog/index.html. 2003. Poetry, art, photos, reviews, long-poems. "Dufus wishes to raise the bar of Internet poetry." 2-3/yr. Pub'd 2 issues 2005; expects 2 issues 2006, 2 issues 2007. sub. price Free; per copy Free; sample Free. Back issues: Free. Discounts: It's all free - duh it's online? Reporting time: 2-4 months. Simultaneous submissions accepted: Yes. Publishes 3% of manuscripts submitted. Payment: Seeing your poem online. Not copyrighted. Pub's reviews: a few in 2005. §Poetry books and chapbooks. Ads: None. Subjects: Essays, Poetry, Reviews.

‡**Duke University Press (see also THEATER),** Box 90660, Durham, NC 27708-0660, 919-687-3600; Fax 919-688-4574, www.dukeupress.edu. "Street address: 905 W. Main Street, Durham, NC 27701."

Dumouriez Publishing, Tawan Chester, Torquemada Harrell, PO Box 12849, Jacksonville, FL 32209, 904.536.8910, http://www.dpublishing1.com ,admin@dpublishing1.com, tocca@dpublishing1.com. 2005. Art, photos, letters, non-fiction. "Publish traditional and electronic books and reprints. Nonfiction: motvational,inspirational, self-help,religious/spiritual in nature Recent Titles: An Intimate Walk-The Ultimate Relationship, WOMEN(With Open Minds Eternally Nurtured), One Day of Overcoming-A Lifetime of Living." avg. press run 3000. Expects 3 titles 2006, 3 titles 2007. Discounts: STOP copy 20%, 2-10 copies 25%, 11-20 copies 35%, 21-30 copies 45%, 31+ copies 55%, 2+ Non returnable copies 65%(no FOB). 200pp. Reporting time: Responds 1 month after recieving query or proposal pkg with SASE. No phone calls accepted. Simultaneous submissions accepted: No. Publishes 2% of manuscripts submitted. Payment: Pays 5-10% royalty on net receipts. Prefer author to handle copyrighting but will consider it on a case by case basis. Subjects: Arts, Culture, Grieving, Hypnosis, Inspirational, Motivation, Success, Non-Fiction, Parenting, Publishing, Religion, Reprints, Spiritual, Travel, Women, Writers/Writing.

Dunamis House, Bette Filley, 19801 SE 123rd Street, Issaquah, WA 98027, 425-255-5274, fax 425-277-8780. 1991. Non-fiction. "Additional address: PO Box 321, Issaquah, WA 98027." avg. press run 3.5M. Pub'd 1 title 2005; expects 1 title 2006, 1-2 titles 2007. Discounts: 40% trade, 55% distributors. 264pp. Reporting time: 6 weeks. Payment: varies. Copyrights for author. Subjects: Aging, Christianity, How-To, Non-Fiction, Pacific Northwest, Religion, Senior Citizens, Sports, Outdoors, Washington (state).

DUST (From the Ego Trip), Camel Press, James Hedges, Editor, Box 212, Needmore, PA 17238, 717-573-4526. 1984. Poetry, fiction, articles, non-fiction. "Contributions of good literary quality are welcome; manuscripts should be between 1M and 2.5M words in length." circ. 700. Irregular. Expects 1 issue 2006, 1 issue 2007. sub. price $1-3 per issue on standing order; per copy $1-3; sample $1. Discounts: on request. 20pp. Reporting time: 2 weeks. Simultaneous submissions accepted: yes. Publishes 5% of manuscripts submitted. Payment: 50 free copies. Copyrighted, rights revert to author if requested. No ads. Subjects: Biography, History, Public Affairs.

Dustbooks (see also THE SMALL PRESS REVIEW/SMALL MAGAZINE REVIEW), Len Fulton, PO Box 100, Paradise, CA 95967-0100, 530-877-6110, 1-800-477-6110, Fax 530-877-0222, email: publisher@dustbooks.com, Website: http://www.dustbooks.com. 1963. "We have a small general trade list: poetry, novels, anthologies, non-fiction prose, how-to, etc. But our real expertise & commitment is small press/magazine information. We do three annuals: this Directory you're holding (now in its forty second annual edition); its companion volume, the *Directory of Small Press/Magazine Editors and Publishers*, and the *Directory of Poetry Publishers*, which, by the way, contains our annual Sweepstakes—a listing of the dozen or so poets most popular with editors. We do a bi-monthly, the *Small Press Review/Small Magazine Review* (see separate listing). NOTE: To be listed in this directory or any of our other reference titles go to our website at dustbooks.com and click on the Directory Listing Forms button." avg. press run 1M-2M. Pub'd 5 titles 2005; expects 5 titles 2006, 5 titles 2007. Discounts: 2-10 25%, 11-25 40%, 26+ 50% (bookstores), distributors by arrangement, jobbers 20-25%. Returns only after six months but before one year; returns are for credit ONLY. 300-1,000pp. Reporting time: 3-6 months. Simultaneous submissions accepted: yes. Publishes 1% of manuscripts submitted. Payment: royalty (15%). Copyrights for author. Subjects: Bibliography, Biography,

How-To, Publishing, Reference.

DWAN, Donny Smith, 915 West Second St. #7, Bloomington, IN 47403, e-mail dwanzine@hotmail.com. 1993. Poetry, interviews, reviews, letters, parts-of-novels, long-poems, non-fiction. "We want queer writing, accept material in Spanish or English. Recent contributors: Fabian Iriarte, Lisa B. Falour, Susana Cattaneo." circ. 75. Irregular. Pub'd 3 issues 2005; expects 3 issues 2006, 3 issues 2007. price per copy varies ($0 to $5); sample $2. Discounts: free to prisoners. 38pp. Reporting time: 1-36 weeks. Simultaneous submissions accepted: no. Publishes 5% of manuscripts submitted. Payment: copies. Copyrighted, reverts to author. Pub's reviews: 10 in 2005. §Queer history, feminism, sex. Subjects: Bilingual, Bisexual, Gay, Gender Issues, Lesbianism, Libraries, Poetry, Sex, Sexuality, Translation, Zines.

DWELLING PORTABLY, Light Living Library, Po Box 190—DB, Philomath, OR 97370. 1980. Articles, reviews, letters. "Helpful suggestions about portable dwelling, long comfortable camping, low-cost light-weight living. How to save money, energy, weight, space, land, live and travel more imaginatively. Simultaneous, photocopy submission recommended." circ. 2M. 2/yr. Pub'd 2 issues 2005; expects 3 issues 2006, 3 issues 2007. sub. price $3; per copy $1. Back issues: some tiny-type reprints, 5/$2. Discounts: 6/$5 (back issues). 12pp. Simultaneous submissions accepted: yes. Publishes 75% of manuscripts submitted. Payment: subscriptions or ads; token $5 if requested. Not copyrighted. Pub's reviews: 2 in 2005. Ads: 25¢ per word. Subjects: Bicycling, Conservation, Consumer, Counter-Culture, Alternatives, Communes, Crafts, Hobbies, Ecology, Foods, Energy, Environment, Food, Eating, How-To, Lifestyles, Miniature Books, Pacific Northwest, Sports, Outdoors, Transportation.

E

E & D Publishing, Inc., Ellington, Daniels, PO Box 740536, San Diego, CA 92174, edpub@pacbell.net, www.eandpublishing.com. 2000. Fiction. avg. press run 3-5M. Expects 2 titles 2006, 5-6 titles 2007. Discounts: bulk, trade. 300pp. Reporting time: within 6 weeks. Simultaneous submissions accepted: yes. Publishes 40% of manuscripts submitted. Payment: negotiated. Copyrights for author. Subjects: Fiction, Inspirational, Novels, Self-Help.

E & E Publishing, Eve Heidi Bine-Stock, 1001 Bridgeway, No. 227, Sausalito, CA 94965, Tel: 415-331-4025, Fax: 415-331-4023, www.EandEGroup.com/Publishing. 2001. Poetry, fiction, art, cartoons, criticism, non-fiction. "We publish children's picture books and non-fiction for adults. For children's books, we like to see an artist's large body of non-published artwork dealing with a common theme, around which we can develop a storybook or concept book. For adults, our best-selling title is HOW TO WRITE A CHILDREN'S PICTURE BOOK." Pub'd 3 titles 2005; expects 5 titles 2006, 5 titles 2007. Reporting time: 4-6 weeks. Simultaneous submissions accepted: Yes. Publishes 2% of manuscripts submitted. Payment: Author: 5% of Retail Cover Price; Illustrator: 5% of Retail Cover Price; No Advance; Pay Royalty from First Copy Sold. While we do not copyright for the author, we do provide two free copies of the book for the author to send to the Copyright Office. Subjects: Animals, Arts, Children, Youth, Picture Books.

E. S. Publishers & Distributors, H. A. Enob, Adam Otokiti, P.O. Box 75074, Washington, DC 20013, 202 302-7211. 2005. Poetry, fiction, photos, satire, parts-of-novels, plays, non-fiction. "ESPD is interested in compelling writing with an international flair, particularly weaving threads of stories from England, another European countries or Australia, with Nigeria or any other African or Caribbean country, and the United States of America or Canada." Expects 3-5 titles 2006, 5-8 titles 2007. Subjects: Adoption, African Literature, Africa, African Studies, African-American, The Americas, Autobiography, Biography, Caribbean, England, Europe, Fiction, India, Multicultural, Non-Fiction, The West, Women.

Eagle's View Publishing, Monte Smith, Publisher-Editor; Denise Knight, Editor, 6756 North Fork Road, Liberty, UT 84310, 801-393-4555 (orders), editorial phone 801-745-0905. 1982. Non-fiction. "We also publish a line of frontier clothing patterns." avg. press run 10M. Pub'd 1 title 2005; expects 4 titles 2006, 4 titles 2007. Discounts: standard for trade and jobber. 112pp. Reporting time: 12 months. Simultaneous submissions accepted: yes. Publishes 10% of manuscripts submitted. Payment: varies. Copyrights for author. Subjects: Americana, Children, Youth, Clothing, Crafts, Hobbies, Great Plains, History, How-To, Indians, Jewelry, Gems, Native American, Non-Fiction, Quilting, Sewing, Reprints, The West.

Eakins Press, PO Drawer 90159, Austin, TX 78709-0159, www.eakinpress.com, sales@eakinpress.com.

Earth Star Publications (see also THE STAR BEACON), Ann Ulrich Miller, Publisher, PO Box 117, Paonia, CO 81428, 970-527-3257, earthstar@tripod.net, http://earthstar.tripod.com/. 1987. Fiction, non-fiction. "Open to any subject matter and length. Recent titles have included fiction, self-help, children's, and metaphysical and New Age subjects. New releases include *The Light Being* (sci fi) by Ann Carol Ulrich and *That Crazy Lady Down the Road* (UFO/autobiography) by Judy Messoline. In 2004, we published *Black Pearls*, a historical novel by DJ McMurry and *Stranded On Earth: The Story of a Roswell Crash Survivor*, an autobiography by Commander Sanni Emyetti Ceto, which is in its fourth printing. Earth Star is a self-publishing service. Authors pay for the publishing of their work." avg. press run 500. Pub'd 3 titles 2005; expects 5 titles 2006, 5 titles 2007. Discounts: 40% to retailers. 180pp. Reporting time: 6 weeks. Simultaneous submissions accepted: yes. Payment: 100% to author; publisher collects one-time fee; open to other arrangements. Copyrights for author. Subjects: Biography, Fiction, Science Fiction, Spiritual.

Earth-Love Publishing House LTD, Laodeciae Augustine, Senior Editor, 3440 Youngfield Street #353, Wheatridge, CO 80033, 303-233-9660. 1990. Fiction, non-fiction. "Interested in minerals/mineralogical themes. Publishes book an average of 8 months after acceptance." avg. press run 15M. Pub'd 1 title 2005; expects 2 titles 2006, 1 title 2007. Discounts: Available only through distributors. 500+pp. Reporting time: 3-4 months. Simultaneous submissions accepted: yes. Payment: 8% royalty on wholesale sales. Does not copyright for author. Subject: Reference.

•**Earthly Muse Publishing,** Alana Thompson, 615-974-2340, inquiry@earthlymuse.com, www.earthly-muse.com. 2006. Poetry, fiction, non-fiction. "Online submissions only. At Earthly Muse Publishing it is our mission to provide a catalogue of texts that focus on the education, empowerment, and enlightenment of women in the world. We are committed to discovering, publishing, and promoting manuscripts that reflect this goal. We are looking for works by, for, and about women." Expects 2-3 titles 2007. Discounts: standard. Reporting time: 6-8 weeks. Simultaneous submissions accepted: Yes. Payment: No advances at this time. Can be negotiated, but we prefer that authors copyright their own work.

EARTH'S DAUGHTERS: Feminist Arts Periodical, Kastle Brill, Co-Editor; Joan Ford, Co-Editor; Bonnie Johnson, Co-Editor; Robin Willoughby, Co-Editor; Ryki Zuckerman, Co-Editor; Joyce Kessel, Co-Editor; Pat Colvard, Co-Editor, PO Box 41, Central Park Station, Buffalo, NY 14215-0041, 716-627-9825, http://bfn.org/~edaught. 1971. Poetry, fiction, art, photos, satire, parts-of-novels, long-poems, collages, plays. "We are a feminist arts periodical. Format varies with preannounced themes. Most issues are flat-spined, digest-sized issues. Poetry can be up to 40 lines (rare exceptions for exceptional work). free form, experimental—we like unusual work. All must be strong, supportive of women in all their diversity. We like work by new writers. Rarely publish rhyme. Recent contributors: Diane DiPrima, Janine Pommy Vega, Lyn Lifshin, Joseph Bruchak, and Susan Fantl Spivack." circ. 1M. 2-3/yr. Pub'd 2 issues 2005; expects 2 issues 2006, 2-3 issues 2007. sub. price $18/3 issues, instit. $22/3 issues; per copy $6; sample $6. Back issues: collectors set (issues 1-53) $300. Discounts: libraries only. 60pp. Reporting time: 4-5 months. Simultaneous submissions accepted if notified immediately when published elsewhere. Publishes 30% of manuscripts submitted. Payment: 2 issues complimentary and reduced prices on further copies. Copyrighted, reverts to author. Ads: none. Subjects: Fiction, Literature (General), Poetry, Women.

Earthwinds Editions, Elizabeth Doran, P.O. 505319, Chelsea, MA 02150, 617-889-0253. 2005. Poetry, art. "OF ALTAIR, THE BRIGHT LIGHT- 2005—Ifeanyi Menkiti is the author of two previous collections of poetry, Affirmations (1971) and The Jubilation of Falling Bodies (1978). Other poems have appeared in journals and periodicals such as the Sewanee Review, Ploughshares, New Directions, New Letters, the Massachusetts Review. In 1975, he was honored with a fellowship in poetry from Massachusetts Council on the Arts and Humanities through the Artists Foundation, followed in 1978 by an award from the National Endowment for the Arts. Menkitis poetry has also been aired on National Public Radio and he has given public readings in the New York City public schools under the auspices of the Academy of American Poets as well as for radio stations WBAI (NYC) and WGBH (Boston).About Menkitis WritingIfeanyi Menkiti writes from a world perspective as well as from the perspective of a long time resident of the United States. The editors of Earthwinds Press, have found his poetry fresh, engaging and full of surprises. The poems are tough, serious, and often come at you with a whimsical twist or a biting satire. The reader is struck by the energy of the poems, as well as by their unwavering historical sense. This is poetry that moves, poetry that will not stand still, and we expect our readers will really enjoy this book." avg. press run 750. Expects 1 title 2006, 1 title 2007. Discounts: 5-10 copies 25%11-25 copies 30%25-50 copies 45%libraries-10%. 100pp. Copyrights for author. Subjects: African Literature, Africa, African Studies, African-American, Avant-Garde, Experimental Art, Book Arts, Book Collecting, Bookselling, History, Reviews, Travel, Visual Arts.

THE EAST VILLAGE INKY, Ayun Halliday, 122 Dean Street, Brooklyn, NY 11201, inky@erols.com. 1998. Articles, art, cartoons, criticism, reviews, music, letters, non-fiction. "I do not accept unsolicited materials for publication though some extraordinary letters are published as articles." circ. 1M. 4/yr. Pub'd 4 issues 2005; expects 4 issues 2006, 4 issues 2007. sub. price $8; per copy $3; sample $2. Back issues: $3 (subject to availability). Discounts: 50/50 split in advance with independent distro's and booksellers. 40pp. Simultaneous submissions accepted: no. Publishes 0% of manuscripts submitted. Copyrighted, reverts to author. Pub's

142

reviews: 30 in 2005. §Childcare, childrearing philosophy, literature, autobiography, women's (feminist), zines. Subjects: Autobiography, Book Reviewing, Feminism, Humor, Movies, New York, Parenting, Reviews.

East West Discovery Press, Icy Smith, Editorial Director, PO Box 2393, Gardena, CA 90247, 310-532-1115, Fax 310-768-8926, info@eastwestdiscovery.com, web www.eastwestdiscovery.com. 2000. Photos, non-fiction. "East West Discovery Press is an independent publisher and distributor of multicultural and bilingual books, and teaching resources with an emphasis on history, culture and social justice." Pub'd 1 title 2005; expects 2 titles 2006, 2 titles 2007. Discounts: 40% to book trade. 200pp. Copyrights for author. Subjects: Asian-American, Bilingual, California, Children, Youth, Culture, Education, Games, History, Immigration, Los Angeles, Multicultural, Parenting, Photography, Trivia, Young Adult.

EASTGATE QUARTERLY REVIEW OF HYPERTEXT, Eastgate Systems Inc., Diane Greco, 134 Main Street, Watertown, MA 02472, 617-924-9044, info@eastgate.com, www.eastgate.com. Poetry, fiction, articles, art, photos, interviews, satire, criticism, parts-of-novels, long-poems, collages, non-fiction. "Electronic submissions only; send disks, not paper. Please see our submission guidelines on our website. Works should be in some way 'hypertextual' (loosely construed). Recent contributors include Kathryn Cramer, Robert Kendall, Edward Falco, and Judith Kerman." Expects 1-2 issues 2006, 1-2 issues 2007. sub. price $49.95; per copy $19.95. Discounts: site licenses available, call for details. Reporting time: 6-8 weeks. Simultaneous submissions accepted: yes. Copyrighted, reverts to author. Subjects: Essays, Fantasy, Fiction, Literature (General), Science Fiction.

Eastgate Systems Inc. (see also EASTGATE QUARTERLY REVIEW OF HYPERTEXT), Diane Greco, 134 Main Street, Watertown, MA 02472, 617-924-9044, info@eastgate.com, www.eastgate.com. Poetry, fiction, articles, art, photos, satire, criticism, long-poems, non-fiction. "Electronic submissions only. Send disks or URLs, *not* paper. Works should be in some way 'hypertextual' (loosely construed). Please visit our website or view our catalogue before submitting; familiarity with our publications will give a good sense of what we're looking for. As a part of Eastgate Systems, the Reading Room is a showcase for World Wide Web-based work." avg. press run 1M-1.5M. Pub'd 2 titles 2005; expects 4 titles 2006, 4 titles 2007. Discounts: call for details. Reporting time: 6-8 weeks, longer submissions require more time. Simultaneous submissions accepted: yes. Publishes 1-2% of manuscripts submitted. Payment: varies, usually 15% of sales. Copyrights for author.

EbonyEnergy Publishing, Inc. (NFP), Cheryl Katherine Wash, P.O. Box 43476, Chicago, IL 60643-0476, 773-851-5159. 1999. Poetry, fiction, articles, art, photos, cartoons, interviews, satire, criticism, reviews, music, letters, parts-of-novels, long-poems, collages, plays, concrete art, news items, non-fiction. "EbonyEnergy Publishing, Inc. (NFP) is a division of The GEM Group. EbonyEnergy is a publishing house with a mission to spread universal themes and messages to a wide and diverse audience. EbonyEnergy belives in publishing real voices by real people by way of fiction, non-fiction, prose, poetry, novels, plays, audio, video. EbonyEnergy welcomes all voices from all cultures and economics. EbonyEnergy is positive energy and we want your voice to be heard." avg. press run 1000. Pub'd 5 titles 2005; expects 10-15 titles 2006, 15-20 titles 2007. Discounts: Negotiable. Volume, trade, distributors, school. Discounts Available. 200pp. Reporting time: 3 - 6 months. Simultaneous submissions accepted: Yes. Publishes 75% of manuscripts submitted. Payment: Negotiable. We will copyright for author upon request. Subjects: African Literature, Africa, African Studies, Antiques, Arts, Bibliography, Biography, Black, Book Collecting, Bookselling, Book Reviewing, Business & Economics, Children, Youth, Classical Studies, Comics, Communication, Journalism, Communism, Marxism, Leninism, Community.

Eborn Books (see also THE DEFENDER - Rush Utah's Newsletter), Bret Eborn, Cynthia Eborn, 3601 S. 2700 W. B120, West Valley City, UT 84119, 801-965-9410, ebornbk@doitnow.com. 1988. Pub'd 10 titles 2005; expects 10 titles 2006, 10 titles 2007. 20pp. Subjects: Americana, Anthropology, Archaelogy, Arizona, Christianity, Mormon, Newsletter, Religion.

EcceNova Editions, Alex Allen, Assistant Editor, 308-640 Dallas Road, Victoria, BC V8V 1B6, Canada, Fax: 250-595-8401 email: info@eccenova.com URL: www.eccenova.com. 2003. Non-fiction. "We accept NON-FICTION submissions from credentialed (academic or professional)researchers in most fields of RELIGION and SCIENCE. Keen to increase our list in Ufology, Science Speculation, Biblical Interpretation, Quantum Mechanics, Cosmology, NDEs, Mythology. Recent works include a Fatima/UFO trilogy by Portuguese historians Dr. Joaquim Fernandes & Fina d'Armada, and "Jesus, Mary, and Child: Biblical Precedence for The Da Vinci Code" by Janet Tyson, MA.; We do not accept fiction, children's books, "how to" guides, or spiritual testimonies. Tell us about your bacground in this field, why the book adds something new to the world of information (we like submissions that challenge the status quo or provide new insights), and provide some ideas on how you might help promote your work. Queries and proposals can be sent by email or post. Please supply a SASE, email address, or International Reply Coupon if not in Canada. Visit our website and read our up-to-date information on the "Submissions" page before sending your query." Reporting time: 1 month. Simultaneous submissions accepted: Not officially, but we understand that time issues are a concern for authors...if you must do this, just advise us. Payment: 15% on wholesale. Copyrights for author. Subjects:

Ancient Astronauts, Artificial Intelligence, Cosmology, Euthanasia, Death, Metaphysics, Myth, Mythology, Non-Fiction, Occult, Religion, Science, Space, Supernatural, Theosophical.

Eckankar, Attn: John Kulick, PO Box 27300, Minneapolis, MN 55427-0300, 952-380-2300, Fax 952-380-2395. 1965. Non-fiction. Pub'd 3-5 titles 2005; expects 3-5 titles 2006, 3-5 titles 2007. Copyrights for author.

Eco Images (see also THE WILD FOODS FORUM), Vickie Shufer, P.O. Box 61413, Virginia Beach, VA 23466-1413, 757-421-3929, 757-421-3929, wildfood@infionline.net, http://wildfood.home.infionline.net. 1985. Articles, non-fiction. "The Wild Foods Forum is a quarterly newsletter that provides information on how to identify and use wild plants for food, medicine and crafts. Dr. James Duke, former Economic Botanist with the USDA, is a regular contributor as well as Christopher Nyerges, Peter Gail and other leading herbalists and outdoor teachers. Other publications include nature-related books, paddling guides, and adventure travel experiences." avg. press run 1000. Pub'd 2 titles 2005; expects 3 titles 2006, 2 titles 2007. Discounts: 2 copies 10%3-4 copies 20%5 copies 30%More than 5 40%. 150pp. Reporting time: 1-2 months. Simultaneous submissions accepted: Yes. Payment: individual arrangements. Does not copyright for author. Subjects: Alternative Medicine, Botany, Food, Eating, Gardening, Nature, Newsletter, Non-Fiction.

Ecopress, An Imprint of Finney Company (see also Finney Company, Inc.), Alan Krysan, President, 8075 215th Street West, Lakeville, MN 55044, Phone: 952-469-6699 or (800) 846-7027, Fax: 952-469-1968 or (800) 330-6232, ecopress@peak.org, www.ecopress.com. 1993. Non-fiction. avg. press run varies. Pub'd 1 title 2005; expects 2 titles 2006, 4 titles 2007. Discounts: variable. Reporting time: 2-4 months. Simultaneous submissions accepted: yes. Publishes 5% of manuscripts submitted. Payment: negotiable. Copyrights for author. Subjects: Environment, Nature, Non-Fiction, Sports, Outdoors.

ECOTONE: Reimagining Place, David Gessner, UNCW Dept. of Creative Writing, 601 South College Road, Wilmington, NC 28403-3297, 910-962-3070. 2005. Poetry, fiction, art, photos, interviews, parts-of-novels, long-poems, non-fiction. "The journal Ecotone emphasizes the deep importance of place in contemporary writing. We hope to break across genres, and across disciplines, to discover writing that is new, dangerous, and refuses to stay safely in a single place. Our goal is an ambitious one: to reclaim landscapes, to remap and reimagine place in writing that is vital, thorny, and alive. We publish high-quality works of creative nonfiction, fiction, and poetry, as well as interviews with new and established authors about the idea of place in literature." circ. 3000. 2/yr. Expects 1 issue 2006, 2 issues 2007. sub. price $18; per copy $9.95; sample $10. Back issues: $10. No discounts. 200pp + 8 page art insert. Reporting time: 3 months. Simultaneous submissions accepted: Yes. Publishes 5-10% of manuscripts submitted. Payment: 2 copies. Copyrighted, reverts to author. Ads: Free on exchange. Subjects: Appalachia, Conservation, Creativity, Culture, Environment, Essays, Fiction, Literature (General), Moving/Relocation, Nature, Poetry, Prose, Short Stories, Travel, Visual Arts.

Ecrivez!, Nancy Hill McClary, Chief Operating Officer, PO Box 247491, Columbus, OH 43224-2002, 614-253-0773, Fax 614-253-0774. 1996. Fiction, non-fiction. "Publishing will be *affordable*, seeking individuals with *allowances in their budget.*" Pub'd 1 title 2005. Discounts: negotiable. 250pp. Simultaneous submissions accepted: yes. Does not copyright for author. Subjects: African-American, Bibliography, Children, Youth, Fiction, How-To, Juvenile Fiction, Men, Mystery, Non-Fiction, Race, Relationships, Reprints, Science Fiction, Self-Help, Short Stories.

THE EDGE CITY REVIEW, T.L. Ponick, Editor-in-Chief, 10912 Harpers Square Court, Reston, VA 20191, E-mail terryp17@aol.com, www.edge-city.com. 1994. Poetry, fiction, articles, cartoons, interviews, satire, criticism, reviews, music, letters, parts-of-novels, long-poems, non-fiction. "Read guidelines on our website." circ. 500+. 3/yr. Pub'd 3 issues 2005; expects 3 issues 2006, 3 issues 2007. sub. price $17; per copy $6; sample $6 ppd. Back issues: varies. Discounts: none currently. 48pp. Reporting time: 5 months. We accept simultaneous submissions if the author lets us know. Publishes 10% of manuscripts submitted. Payment: 2 contributor's copies. Copyrighted, reverts to author. Pub's reviews: 20 in 2005. §University Presses, non-vanity published poetry, fiction, literary criticism, music. Ads: $50 1/4 page. Subjects: Arts, Book Reviewing, Celtic, Communication, Journalism, Current Affairs, England, English, Essays, Fiction, Ireland, Literary Review, Literature (General), Music, Poetry, Prose.

EDGE Science Fiction and Fantasy Publishing, PO Box 1714, Calgary, AB T2P 2L7, Canada, 403-254-0160. 1996. Fiction. "We publish all types of science fiction and fantasy hardcover and trade paperback book-length literature from 70,000 to 100,000 words." avg. press run 2-3M. Pub'd 5 titles 2005; expects 6 titles 2006, 6 titles 2007. Discounts: trade 40%, bulk 42%, wholesale 50%, distribution 52% (minimums in effect). 350-375pp. Reporting time: 4-6 weeks. Simultaneous submissions accepted: no. Publishes 3-5% of manuscripts submitted. Payment: advance plus royalty. Copyrights for author. Subjects: Fantasy, Science Fiction.

Edgewise Press, Richard Milazzo, Howard B. Johnson Jr., Joy L. Glass, 24 Fifth Avenue #224, New York, NY 10011, 212-982-4818, Fax 212-982-1364. 1995. Poetry, articles, art, photos, interviews, criticism, letters.

"Edgewise Press is dedicated to publishing quality paperback books of verse, essays, and other forms of writing." avg. press run 1M-2M. Pub'd 1 title 2005; expects 3 titles 2006, 4 titles 2007. Discounts: 60/40. 64pp. Publishes 0% of manuscripts submitted. Payment: 7-10%. Does not copyright for author. Subjects: Arts, Criticism, Essays, Poetry, Visual Arts.

EDGZ, Blaine R. Hammond, Editor; Debra Brimacombe, Assistant Editor, Edge Publications, PO Box 799, Ocean Park, WA 98640-0799. 2000. Poetry, art, photos, collages, concrete art. "Poetry and visual art only. Poetry must have some reference or application beyond the personal—struggling with issues of life and meaning. Want all sorts of voices and styles except disengaged, vague, abstract or dense language poetry. Also want cover and interior graphics. SASE for guidelines. I use recycled paper." circ. 300. 2/yr. Pub'd 2 issues 2005; expects 2 issues 2006, 2 issues 2007. sub. price $13; per copy $7; sample $4.00. Back issues: $4.00. Discounts: $3.50 to retail outlets. Pages vary. Reporting time: 1 week to 6 months. We accept simultaneous submissions if they promise not to withdraw anything once we've accepted it. Publishes 15% of manuscripts submitted. Payment: 1 copy, discount on extras. Copyrighted, reverts to author. Ads: $50/$30/$20 2-3", one free ad per year for subscribers. Subjects: Graphics, Poetry.

Edin Books, Inc., Linda S. Nathanson, Publisher and Editor, 102 Sunrise Drive, Gillette, NJ 07933-1944. 1994. Non-fiction. avg. press run 7.5M. Expects 1 title 2007. Discounts: 40%. 277pp. Simultaneous submissions accepted: no. Publishes 0% of manuscripts submitted. Copyrights for author. Subjects: Interviews, Metaphysics, New Age.

Edition Gemini, Gernot U. Gabel, Juelichstrasse 7, Huerth-Efferen D-50354, Germany, 02233/63550, Fax 02233/65866. 1979. Criticism, letters, non-fiction. avg. press run 150-300. Pub'd 3 titles 2005; expects 3 titles 2006. Discounts: trade 30%. 70pp. Reporting time: 1 month. Payment: yes. Copyrights for author. Subjects: Bibliography, History, Literature (General), Philosophy.

THE EDITORIAL EYE, EEI Press, Linda Jorgensen, 66 Canal Center Plaza, Suite 200, Alexandria, VA 22314, 703-683-0683. 1978. Articles, reviews. "*The Editorial Eye* focuses on editorial standards and practices. Its purpose is to help its readers produce high quality publications. Information on content, usage, style, language, software, and production tips." circ. 2.5M. 12/yr. Pub'd 12 issues 2005; expects 12 issues 2006, 12 issues 2007. sub. price $99, Canadian subs add $10 per year, overseas $119 year prepaid, US funds; per copy $12; sample free. Back issues: $12. Discounts: 10% to subscription agencies. 12pp. Reporting time: 30 days, query. Payment: $25-$100. Copyrighted, does not revert to author. Pub's reviews: 25 in 2005. §Editorial matters, style guides, proofreading, editing, software, production info. Ads: no advertising. Subjects: Editing, English, Newsletter, Publishing.

Editorial Research Service, Laird M. Wilcox, 1009 East Layton Drive, Olathe, KS 66061-2933, 913-829-0609. 1978. Articles, interviews, reviews, letters, news items. "Publications include: *Guide to the American Right* 1999, 1,500 entries; *Guide to the American Left* 1999, 1,500 entries." avg. press run 410. Pub'd 3 titles 2005; expects 8 titles 2006. Discounts: 10% single copies, 25% 5 or more copies; prepayment required. 108pp. Reporting time: 30 days. Payment: flat fee. Does not copyright for author. Subjects: Politics, Public Affairs.

EduCare Press, Kieran O'Mahony, PO Box 17222, Seattle, WA 98127, 206 706-4105. 1988. Poetry, fiction, letters, non-fiction. avg. press run 2M. Pub'd 2 titles 2005; expects 3 titles 2006, 2 titles 2007. Discounts: usual. 200pp. Copyrights for author. Subjects: Aging, Children, Youth, Education, Fiction, Geography, Greek, History, Non-Fiction, Novels, Philosophy.

THE EDUCATION DIGEST, Prakken Publications, Kenneth Schroeder, Managing Editor, PO Box 8623, Ann Arbor, MI 48107, 734-975-2800 ext. 207, Fax 734-975-2787, kschroeder@eddigest.com. 1935. Articles, cartoons, reviews, news items. "*Education Digest* does not accept original manuscripts, prior publication required. Selected by editorial staff. 'Outstanding Articles condensed for quick review'" circ. 15M. 9/yr. Pub'd 9 issues 2005; expects 9 issues 2006, 9 issues 2007. sub. price $48; per copy $6; sample free on request. Back issues: $6. Discounts: agent 10%, individual multi-year rates: 2 yr $86, 3 yr $124. 80pp. Payment: honorarium possible for rights. Copyrighted, does not revert to author. Pub's reviews: 40 in 2005. §Education. Ads: $775/$510/$50 per col. inch. Subjects: Education, Reference.

EDUCATION IN FOCUS, Books for All Times, Inc., Joe David, Editor, PO Box 2, Alexandria, VA 22313, 703-548-0457. "A semi-annual newsletter which provides an *in focus* look at education from a rational and humane viewpoint." 2/yr. Pub'd 2 issues 2005; expects 2 issues 2006, 2 issues 2007. price per copy $3. 6pp. Reporting time: 4 weeks. Payment: varies. Copyrighted, we buy rights to use in newsletter, book, and on Internet. Pub's reviews: none in 2005. §Education. Ads: $75 for 2-1/4 X 4-1/2/$25 for 2-1/4 X 1-1/2. Subject: Education.

EDUCATIONAL FOUNDATIONS, Caddo Gap Press, Darrell Cleveland, Editor, 3145 Geary Boulevard, Suite 275, San Francisco, CA 94118, 415-666-3012. 1986. Articles. "*Educational Foundations* seeks manuscripts of 20-25 double-spaced typewritten pages on issues, themes, research, and practice in the social foundations of education. Most contributors are scholars in the various social foundations disciplines." circ. 700. 4/yr. Pub'd 4 issues 2005; expects 4 issues 2006, 4 issues 2007. sub. price $50 individuals, $100 institutions; per copy $25. Discounts: agency 15%. 96pp. Reporting time: 1-2 months. Publishes 25% of manuscripts submitted. Payment: none. Copyrighted, rights revert to author if desired. Ads: $200 full page. Subject: Education.

EDUCATIONAL LEADERSHIP & ADMINISTRATION, Caddo Gap Press, Elizabeth O'Reilly, Editor, 3145 Geary Boulevard #275, San Francisco, CA 94118, 415-392-1911. 1988. Articles. "Annual journal of the California Association of Professors of Educational Administration." circ. 200. 1/yr. Pub'd 1 issue 2005; expects 1 issue 2006, 1 issue 2007. sub. price $50 individuals, $100 institutions; per copy $50. 96pp. Reporting time: 2 months. Publishes 25% of manuscripts submitted. Payment: none. Copyrighted, reverts to author. Ads: $200 per page. Subject: Education.

The Edwin Mellen Press (see also Mellen Poetry Press), Herbert Richardson, PO Box 450, Lewiston, NY 14092, 716-754-2266. 1974. "United Kingdom Division: The Edwin Mellen Press, Ltd., Lampeter, Dyfed, Wales SA48 7DY. Canadian Division: The Edwin Mellen Press-Canada, PO Box 67, Queenston, Ontario L0S 1L0. We now have a poetry series (Mellen Poetry Press Series). These are small softcover/paper books including works by first published poets. The price range is $15-$30. By the way, we pay NO royalties at all on ANY books, but also require NO subsidies. We also require camera-ready copy to our specifications." avg. press run 300. Pub'd 300 titles 2005; expects 300 titles 2006, 350 titles 2007. Discounts: 20% to resellers, special discounts for quantity orders, text prices for all books. 300pp. Reporting time: 2 months. Simultaneous submissions accepted: no. Payment: 5 free copies to the author/editor. We deposit 2 copies of the published book, copyrighted in the author's name, with the Copyright Office, and 1 copy with the Cataloging Division. Subjects: Black, Classical Studies, Counter-Culture, Alternatives, Communes, German, History, Judaism, Music, Philosophy, Poetry, Religion, Society, Translation, Women.

EEI Press (see also THE EDITORIAL EYE), Linda Jorgensen, 66 Canal Center Plaza #200, Alexandria, VA 22314, 703-683-0683. 1972. Articles, interviews, reviews, news items. "We publish *The Editorial Eye* and 7 titles for professional publications people." Expects 1 title 2006, 1 title 2007. Discounts: inquire. newsletter 12pp; books 100-300pppp. Reporting time: 1 month or less. Payment: inquire. EEI Press copyright. Subjects: Book Arts, Broadcasting, Communication, Journalism, Graphic Design, Internet, Language, Magazines, Newsletter, Paper, Photography, Publishing, Reading, Research, Reviews, Writers/Writing.

Wm.B. Eerdmans Publishing Co., Jon Pott, Editor-in-Chief, 255 Jefferson Avenue, S.E., Grand Rapids, MI 49503, 616-459-4591. 1911. Photos, non-fiction. avg. press run 3M. Pub'd 106 titles 2005; expects 120 titles 2006, 130 titles 2007. Discounts: 40% trade. 250pp. Reporting time: 4-6 weeks. Simultaneous submissions accepted if so noted. Publishes 5% of manuscripts submitted. Payment: 7-10% of retail. Copyrights for author. Subjects: Children, Youth, Christianity, Ethics, Great Lakes, History, Michigan, Non-Fiction, Religion.

EFG, Inc., Elaine Floyd, 2207 South 39th Street, St. Louis, MO 63110-4019, 314-647-6788, FAX 314-647-1609. Subjects: Advertising, Self-Promotion, Newsletter, Publishing.

EFRYDIAU ATHRONYDDOL, University Of Wales Press, J.I. Daniel, W.L. Gealey, 10 Columbus Walk, Brigantine Place, Cardiff CF10 4UP, Wales, 44-029-2049-6899, Fax 44-029-2049-6108, press@press.wales.ac.uk, www.wales.ac.uk/press. Articles. "Philosophical material." circ. 350. 1/yr. Pub'd 1 issue 2005; expects 1 issue 2006, 1 issue 2007. sub. price £6.50; per copy £6.50; sample £6.50. Back issues: £5. Discounts: trade 10%. 80pp. Payment: none. Copyrighted, does not revert to author. Pub's reviews: none in 2005. §Philosophical. Subject: Philosophy.

The Eighth Mountain Press, Ruth Gundle, 624 Southeast 29th Avenue, Portland, OR 97214, 503-233-3936, ruth@eighthmountain.com. 1985. Poetry, fiction, non-fiction. "We publish only women writers." avg. press run 4M. Pub'd 2 titles 2005; expects 2 titles 2006, 2 titles 2007. Discounts: books are distributed to the trade by Consortium of St. Paul & subject to their discount schedule. 200pp. Reporting time: 3 months. Simultaneous submissions not usually accepted; please notify if so. Publishes .01% of manuscripts submitted. Payment: 7% paper, 10% cloth usually. Copyrights for author. Subjects: Essays, Feminism, Fiction, Judaism, Lesbianism, Poetry, Prose, Transportation, Women.

Eighth Sea Books, Lori Hall Steele, PO Box 1925, Traverse City, MI 49685-1925, 231-946-0678, info@8thSeaBooks.com, www.8thSeaBooks.com. 2003. Poetry, fiction, articles, photos, news items, non-fiction. avg. press run 5000. Expects 3 titles 2006, 5 titles 2007. Reporting time: 6 months. Simultaneous submissions accepted: yes. Copyrights for author.

88: A Journal of Contemporary American Poetry, Hollyridge Press, Ian Randall Wilson, Managing Editor, PO Box 2872, Venice, CA 90294, 310-712-1238, Fax 310-828-4860, t88ajournal@aol.com, guidelines at www.hollyridgepress.com. 2001. Poetry, criticism, reviews, long-poems. "Will consider all types. No translations at this time. Contributors include: Roger Weingarten, Kathleene West, William Trowbridge, Richard Gabriel, Gail Wronsky, and Dean Young.'' 1/yr. Pub'd 1 issue 2005; expects 1 issue 2006, 1 issue 2007. price per copy $13.95. Available to bookstores through Ingram and Baker & Taylor at a short discount. 176pp. Reporting time: 3-6 months. Simultaneous submissions accepted: no. Publishes 2% of manuscripts submitted. Payment: contributor copies. Copyrighted, reverts to author. Pub's reviews: 4 in 2005. §Poetry and poetics. Ads: $300/$175/$100 1/4 page. Subjects: Criticism, Poetry, Reviews.

EKPHRASIS, Frith Press, Laverne Frith, Editor; Carol Frith, Editor, PO Box 161236, Sacramento, CA 95816-1236, http://hometown.aol.com/ekphrasisl. 1997. Poetry. ''A poetry journal focusing on the growing body of verse based on individual works from any artistic genre. Recent contributors: Peter Meinke, David Hamilton, William Greenway, Virgil Suarez, Linda Nemec Foster, Terry Blackhawk, Philip Dacey and Annie Finch. Visit our website for a link to guidelines for the Ekphrasis Prize.'' circ. 150+. 2/yr. Pub'd 2 issues 2005; expects 2 issues 2006, 2 issues 2007. sub. price $12; per copy $6; sample $6. Discounts: none. 50pp. Reporting time: 1 month - 6 months. Simultaneous submissions accepted: no. Publishes 5%-7% of manuscripts submitted. Payment: 1 copy. Copyrighted, reverts to author. Ads: none. Subjects: Arts, Poetry.

Elderberry Press, LLC, David W. St. John, 1393 Old Homestead Drive, Second Floor,, Oakland, OR 97462, 541-459-6043 phone/Fax, editor@elderberrypress.com, www.elderberrypress.com. 1996. Poetry, fiction, articles, photos, cartoons, satire, letters, plays, non-fiction. ''We are always looking for good politically incorrect fiction and nonfiction. All subjects considered excepting racist, hateful, ultra-violent or pornographic. Give me a call or drop me an email and let's discuss your MS. If I do ask for it in hard copy I'll get back to you in 21 days or less. I'm sorry, but I don't accept proposals, partially completed MSS, or agented MSS. New writers welcome.'' avg. press run 1M. Pub'd 18 titles 2005; expects 18 titles 2006, 18 titles 2007. Discounts: 50%. 250pp. Reporting time: 21 days. Simultaneous submissions accepted: yes. Publishes 10% of manuscripts submitted. Payment: varies. Copyrights for author. Subjects: Agriculture, Conservation, Criticism, Electronics, English, Fiction, Folklore, Language, Libertarian, Jack London, Medieval, Religion, Science Fiction, Socialist, Transportation.

ELECTRONIC GREEN JOURNAL, Maria Anna Jankowska, Editor; Bill Johnson, Managing Editor, University of Idaho Library, Moscow, ID 83844-2360, 208-885-6631, e-mail majanko@uidaho.edu, www.egj.lib.uidaho.edu/index.html. 1994. Articles, reviews, non-fiction. ''Contribution from authors on topics related to sources of information on environmental protection, conservation, management of natural resources, and ecologically balanced regional development. The international journal also seeks articles dealing with environmental issues specific to libraries, publishing industries, and information sciences. Our goal is to provide information in articles, essays, reports, annotated bibliographies and reviews that will be of interest to librarians, environmental educators, information consultants, publishers, booksellers, environmentalists, researchers, regional planners and students all over the world.'' circ. varies. 2/yr. Pub'd 2 issues 2005; expects 2 issues 2006, 2 issues 2007. sub. price free; per copy free; sample free. Back issues: free. 84pp. Reporting time: 6-8 weeks. Simultaneous submissions accepted: no. Publishes 60% of manuscripts submitted. Payment: none. Copyrighted, reverts to author. Pub's reviews: 25 in 2005. §Environmental protection, policy, science, nature/wildlife, global environment, conservation, environment information sources. Ads: $75/$50/$25 1/4 page. Subjects: Conservation, Environment.

•**ELEMENTS,** Bernard Washington, 2260 W. Holcombe Blvd., Ste. 418, Houston, TX 77030, 713-747-4934, bwashington53@hotmail.com. 1979. Poetry, fiction, articles, art, photos, cartoons, interviews, satire, criticism, reviews, music, letters, news items, non-fiction. ''We don't accept long stories or narratives.'' circ. 1K. 6/yr. Pub'd 6 issues 2005; expects 6 issues 2006, 6 issues 2007. sub. price $30; per copy $9.50; sample $9.50. Back issues: $9 each. Discounts: price varies on amount of order. 50pp. Reporting time: 1 week. Simultaneous submissions accepted: yes. Publishes 100% of manuscripts submitted. Payment: none. Copyrighted, reverts to author. Pub's reviews: 4 in 2005. §Music, politics, current events, movies, historic events, nonfiction. Ads: $75/$35/$20 (prices per year). Subjects: Advertising, Self-Promotion, African-American, Arts, Bibliography, Book Reviewing, Children, Youth, Communication, Journalism, Crystals, History, Interviews, Writers/Writing.

THE ELEVENTH MUSE, Steven D. Schroeder, PO Box 2413, Colorado Springs, CO 80901, poetrywest@yahoo.com, http://www.poetrywest.org/muse.htm. 1982. Poetry, articles, art, photos, interviews, criticism, reviews. ''Submit via e-mail. Annual poem contest with December 1st deadline. $5 for one poem, $10 for up to 3, $15 for up to 6. $200 first prize.'' circ. 250. 1/yr. Pub'd 1 issue 2005; expects 1 issue 2006, 1 issue 2007. sub. price $8; per copy $8; sample $5. Back issues: $5. 60-90pp. Reporting time: 1 to 2 months. Simultaneous submissions accepted: Yes. Publishes 5% of manuscripts submitted. Payment: 1 contributor copy plus discount on additional copies. Copyrighted, reverts to author. Pub's reviews: Ads: $250+ for Benefactors, $100 for Patrons, $50 for Sponsors, $25 for Friends. Subject: Poetry.

ELIXIR, Elixir Press, Dana Curtis, PO Box 27029, Denver, CO 80227, www.elixirpress.com. 2000. Poetry, fiction. ''Recent contributors: Donald Revell, Claudia Keelan, R.T. Smith, Sandra Kohler, Adrian Matejka. Reading period May 15 - Sept. 1. Interested in poetry and fiction.'' 2/yr. Pub'd 2 issues 2005; expects 2 issues

2006, 2 issues 2007. sub. price $8; per copy $5; sample $3. Back issues: $3. 120pp. Reporting time: 3-4 months. Simultaneous submissions accepted: yes. Publishes 1% of manuscripts submitted. Copyrighted, reverts to author. Subjects: Avant-Garde, Experimental Art, Experimental, Fiction, Poetry, Post Modern.

Elixir Press (see also ELIXIR), Dana Curtis, PO Box 27029, Denver, CO 80227-0029, www.elixirpress.com. 2000. Poetry, fiction. "Currently, we only consider unsolicited full-length and chapbook poetry and fiction manuscripts through our contests. Recent contributors: Tracy Philpot, Michelle Mitchell-Foust,Jay Snodgrass, Sarah Kennedy, Jim McGarrah, Jane Satterfield, Duriel E. Harris, Samn Stockwell,and Jake Adam York." avg. press run 1M. Pub'd 3 titles 2005; expects 5 titles 2006, 5 titles 2007. 100pp. Reporting time: 6 months. Simultaneous submissions accepted: yes. Publishes 1% of manuscripts submitted. Copyrights for author. Subjects: Fiction, Poetry.

Ellis Press, PO Box 6, Granite Falls, MN 56241, Fax 507-537-6815. 1978.

ELT Press (see also ENGLISH LITERATURE IN TRANSITION, 1880-1920), Robert Langenfeld, English Dept., Univ of N. Carolina, PO Box 26170, Greensboro, NC 27402-6170, 336-334-5446, Fax 336-334-3281, langenfeld@uncg.edu. 1988. Criticism, non-fiction. "ELT Press publishes the 1880-1920 British Author Series. We print books which make available new critical, biographical, bibliographical and primary works on 1880-1920 British authors. Cloth-bound and original paperback books." avg. press run 500. Pub'd 2 titles 2005; expects 2 titles 2006, 2 titles 2007. Discounts: 20% to jobbers, agents. 300pp. Reporting time: 2-3 months. Simultaneous submissions accepted: no. Publishes 10% of manuscripts submitted. Payment: none. Copyrights for author. Subjects: Bibliography, Biography, Criticism, Fiction, Literature (General), Poetry.

Emerald Wave, 13828 White Oak Circle #R, Fayetteville, AR 72704-8422, 479-575-0019, Fax 479-575-0807, emeraldwave33@aol.com. 1985. Non-fiction. "Emerald Wave began as a self-publisher and is now actively working with other New Age oriented books." avg. press run 5M. Expects 4 titles 2006, 1 title 2007. Discounts: 1-3 copies 20%, 4-9 30%, 10+ 40%, wholesalers 55%+/-. 200pp. Reporting time: 4 months average. Simultaneous submissions accepted: yes. Publishes .02% of manuscripts submitted. Payment: 7-10% gross, no advance. Does not copyright for author. Subjects: Birth, Birth Control, Population, Channelling, Health, Metaphysics, New Age, Psychology, Self-Help.

EMERGING, LP Publications (Teleos Institute), Diane K. Pike, 7119 East Shea Blvd., Suite 109, PMB 418, Scottsdale, AZ 85254, 480-948-1800, Fax 480-948-1870, teleosinst@aol.com. 1972. Articles, photos, letters. circ. 125. 2/yr. Pub'd 2 issues 2005; expects 2 issues 2006, 2 issues 2007. sub. price $50; sample free. Discounts: none. 36pp. Payment: none. Not copyrighted. No ads. Subjects: Humanism, Metaphysics, Occult, Spiritual.

Empire Publishing Service, PO Box 1344, Studio City, CA 91614-0344. 1960. Fiction, music, plays, non-fiction. avg. press run 2M-10M. Pub'd 30 titles 2005; expects 20 titles 2006, 40 titles 2007. Discounts: 20%-45%. 150pp. Reporting time: 3-12 months. Simultaneous submissions accepted: no. Payment: varies. Copyrights for author. Subjects: Arts, Drama, Education, Entertainment, Shakespeare, Storytelling, Theatre.

EMRYS JOURNAL, Emrys Press, L.B. Dishman, PO Box 8813, Greenville, SC 29601, www.emrys.org. 1983. "This annual spring publication of poetry, short stories, and essays attracts hundreds of submissions from the United States and abroad. It is sponsored by the Emrys Foundation which promotes excellence in the arts, especially literary, visual, and musical works by women and minorities. READING PERIOD IS FROM AUGUST 1 THROUGH NOVEMBER 1 ONLY. Submissions recieved at other times will be returned unread." circ. 200. 1/yr. Pub'd 1 issue 2005; expects 1 issue 2006, 1 issue 2007. sub. price $12; per copy $12; sample $12. Back issues: inquire. Discounts: 40% to wholesale and retail only. 120pp. Reporting time: 2 months. Simultaneous submissions accepted: Yes. Publishes 10% of manuscripts submitted. Payment: 5 complimentary copies. Copyrighted, does not revert to author. Subjects: Fiction, Non-Fiction, Poetry.

Emrys Press (see also EMRYS JOURNAL), L.B. Dishman, PO Box 8813, Greenville, SC 29601, www.emrys.org. 1983. Poetry, fiction, non-fiction. "We are looking for poetry, contemporary fiction and creative non fiction not to exceed 5000 words. Submit no more than 2 stories or essays and 5 poems per author. Please do not send any religious, romance, or science fiction. Also no gore, cliches, television dramas, or anything that would make our readers want to dump the entire work in the trash. READING PERIOD IS FROM AUGUST 1 through NOVEMBER 1 each year. We do not accept anything other than during that time." avg. press run 500. Pub'd 1 title 2005; expects 1 title 2006, 1 title 2007. Discounts: 40% to wholesale and retail only. 120pp. Reporting time: 2 months. Simultaneous submissions accepted: Yes. Publishes 10% of manuscripts submitted. Payment: Emrys has first rights, authors paid in contibutor's copies, no monetary payment at this time. Awards for best poetry, fiction and essay one per edition currently in the sum of $250. Does not copyright for author. Subjects: Dance, Essays, Fiction, Memoirs, Non-Fiction, Poetry.

Encounter Books, Peter Collier, 900 Broadway, Ste.400, New York, NY 10003-1239, 415-538-1460, Fax 415-538-1461, read@encounterbooks.com, www.encounterbooks.com. 1997. Non-fiction. "Quality non-fiction, serious books about history, culture, politics, religion, social criticism, public policy. Authors include William Kristol, Roger Kimball, Robert Spencer, Victor Davis Hanson, William McGowan." avg. press run 5M cl; 10M pa. Pub'd 12 titles 2005; expects 14 titles 2006, 14 titles 2007. Discounts: text 20%; trade 1-5 40%; 6-24 45%; 25-249 50%; 250 or more 55% and free freight. 240pp. Reporting time: 3 months. Simultaneous submissions accepted: yes. Publishes 2% of manuscripts submitted. Payment: 7% of list, advances vary. Copyrights for author. Subjects: Biography, Business & Economics, Criticism, Culture, Current Affairs, Politics, Religion.

END OF LIFE CHOICES, David Goldberg, PO Box 101810, Denver, CO 80250-1810, Fax 303-639-1224, davidgoldberg@endoflifechoices.org, www.endoflifechoices.org. 1980. Articles, photos, interviews, reviews, letters, news items. "Previously *Hemlock Timelines*." circ. 25M. 4/yr. Pub'd 4 issues 2005; expects 4 issues 2006, 4 issues 2007. sub. price $35; per copy $5; sample free. Back issues: $3. Discounts: none. 16pp. Reporting time: 3 weeks. Simultaneous submissions accepted: yes. Publishes 40% of manuscripts submitted. Payment: none. Copyrighted, does not revert to author. Pub's reviews: 4 in 2005. §Assisted suicide, euthanasia. Ads: $2000/$1000/10¢ per word. Subjects: Aging, Cartoons, Ethics, Euthanasia, Death, Guidance, Human Rights, Humanism.

ENGLISH LITERATURE IN TRANSITION, 1880-1920, ELT Press, Robert Langenfeld, English Department/U of North Carolina, P.O. Box 26170, Greensboro, NC 27402-6170, 336-334-5446, Fax 336-334-3281; langenfeld@uncg.edu. 1957. Articles, criticism, reviews, letters, non-fiction. "*ELT* publishes essays on fiction, poetry, drama, or subjects of cultural interest in the 1880-1920 period of British literature. We do not print essays on Joyce, Conrad, Lawrence, Yeats, Virginia Woolf, or Henry James unless these authors are linked with minor figures in the period. 20-25 double-spaced pages is customary length for an essay." circ. 800. 4/yr. Pub'd 4 issues 2005; expects 4 issues 2006, 4 issues 2007. sub. price $32 US Inst./ $18 Indiv.; per copy $10; sample free. Back issues: single-copy rate, discounts for run of 2 years or more. No discounts on regular issues. 128pp. Reporting time: 2-3 months. Simultaneous submissions accepted: no. Publishes 10% of manuscripts submitted. Payment: none. Copyrighted, does not revert to author. Pub's reviews: 60 in 2005. §Books related to the 1880-1920 period of British literature. Ads: $100 full-page; $150 for two ads. Subjects: Bibliography, Biography, Biography, Book Reviewing, Criticism, Drama, Sherlock Holmes, Rudyard Kipling, Literature (General), Reviews, G.B. Shaw.

Enlighten Next (see also WHAT IS ENLIGHTENMENT?), Andrew Cohen, PO Box 2360, Lenox, MA 01240-5182, 413-637-6000, Fax 415-637-6015, info@enlightennext.org. 1989. Photos, non-fiction. avg. press run 10K. Pub'd 1 title 2005; expects 3 titles 2006, 2 titles 2007. Discounts: 40%. 130pp. Payment: none. Copyrighting for author depends. Subjects: Religion, Spiritual.

Enlightened Living Publishing, LLC, Racina Stollings, P O Box 7291, Huntington, WV 25775-7291, telephone 304-486-9000, fax 304-486-5815, toll free 866-896-2665, e-mail: info@enlightenedlivingpublishing.com, www.enlightenedlivingpublishing.com. 2004. Non-fiction. "It is Enlightened Living Publishing, LLC's goal to publish authors that write, not from theory, but from extensive personal experience in the field addressed in their books." Expects 8 titles 2006, 12 titles 2007. Reporting time: 3 months. Simultaneous submissions accepted: Yes. Copyrights for author. Subjects: Business & Economics, Health, Sex, Sexuality.

THE ENTERTAINMENT REVIEW OF THE SUSQUEHANNA VALLEY, Barbara Crouse Fish, PO Box 964, Williamsport, PA 17703-0964, 800-747-0897. 1992. Art, photos, reviews, music, plays, non-fiction. "This publication promotes the cultural and recreational opportunities of 10 counties in northcentral PA. Focus on travel and historical sites." circ. 10M. 6/yr. Pub'd 6 issues 2005; expects 6 issues 2006, 6 issues 2007. sub. price $11; per copy $2; sample free. Back issues: $2. 24pp. Reporting time: 6 weeks. Simultaneous submissions accepted: yes. Publishes 50% of manuscripts submitted. Payment: 5¢ per word. Copyrighted, does not revert to author. Ads: $600/$475/$320 1/3 page. Subject: Travel.

Envirographics, Lisa Hagenauer, Editor-in-Chief; John A. Harant, Editor & Publisher, 98 Levan Dr., Painesville, OH 44077-3324, 440-352-8135. 1986. Non-fiction. avg. press run 10M. Pub'd 1 title 2005; expects 1 title 2006, 1 title 2007. Discounts: dealers 4-40%, 100-45%, 200-50%, 500+ 55%. 250pp. Does not copyright for author. Subjects: Conservation, Environment, Health, How-To, Nature, Self-Help, Water.

ENVIRONMENTAL & ARCHITECTURAL PHENOMENOLOGY NEWSLETTER, David Seamon, 211 Seaton Hall, Architecture Dept., Kansas State University, Manhattan, KS 66506-2901, 913-532-1121. 1990. Poetry, articles, art, criticism, reviews, letters, news items, non-fiction. "Articles and other materials focusing on the nature of environmental and architectural experience. Also, the question of what places are, why they are important in peoples' lives, and architecture as place making." circ. 200. 3/yr. Pub'd 3 issues 2005. sub. price $10 US; $12 non-US payable in dollars; sample free. Back issues: $10/volume (1990-1999). 16pp. Reporting time: 2 months. Simultaneous submissions accepted: no. Publishes 25% of manuscripts submitted. Payment: none, we're entirely non-profit. Not copyrighted. Pub's reviews: 15 in 2005. §Architecture as place making, environmental ethics, phenomenology, nature of place. Subjects: Architecture, Arts, Cities, Design, Ecology, Foods, Environment.

•**Ephemera Bound Publishing,** Derek Dahlsad, 719 9th St N, Fargo, ND 58102, 701-306-6458. 2005. Fiction, articles, satire, non-fiction. "Our mix of books hopefully catches the works left behind by other publishers, either books that have fallen off the end of backlists or books from new or unproven authors. In earlier days, pulp magazines and novels were the domain of new and unproven authors, who developed their craft before expanding into so-called 'real' books. The cheaper nature of the pulps made them 'ephemera,' something that's used and discarded. Our goal is to redevelop the pulpy genre, bringing back the kind of books that were once dominated by writers missed by the big publishers." avg. press run 2000. Pub'd 4 titles 2005; expects 8 titles 2006, 18 titles 2007. Discounts: 40% off cover price for direct sales; also available through Ingram & Baker & Taylor at standard discounts. Rates subject to change; check our website for current information. 200pp. Reporting time: One To Two Weeks. Simultaneous submissions accepted: Yes. Publishes 20% of manuscripts submitted. Payment: 10%-15% of wholesale price. Does not copyright for author. Subjects: Erotica, Fantasy, Feminism, Fiction, Gender Issues, History, Horror, Lesbianism, Literature (General), Non-Fiction, Novels, Occult, Religion, Romance, Sex, Sexuality.

EPICENTER: A LITERARY MAGAZINE, Jeffery Green, PO Box 367, Riverside, CA 92502, www.epicentrermagazine.org. 1994. Poetry, fiction, articles, art, photos, satire, criticism, reviews, long-poems, collages, concrete art, non-fiction. "Epicenter is a literary magazine. We publish poetry, short stories, creative non-fiction, and artwork. Our magazine is not clutered with adds, just literature. We have printed work by Stephen Pyle, Guy R Beining, Zdravka Evtimova, Virgil Suarez, Brad Maxfield, B.Z. Niditch, Egon H.E. Lass, and Elizabeth Hopp. We are open to a wide variety of styles and subjects and appreciate the non-depressing. Send us work with vivid imagery and fresh ideas. Any style is acceptable." circ. 500. 2/yr. Pub'd 2 issues 2005; expects 2 issues 2006, 2 issues 2007. sub. price $24.00; per copy $7.00; sample $1.00 PDF file. Back issues: $7.00. Discounts: More than 5 copies, $5.50. 120pp. Reporting time: one month. Simultaneous submissions accepted: Yes. Publishes 3% of manuscripts submitted. Payment: Copies of the magazine. Copyrighted, reverts to author. Pub's reviews: none in 2005. §Literary works. Ads: We do not print advertisments. Subjects: Absurdist, African Literature, Africa, African Studies, Anarchist, Arts, Essays, Experimental, Fiction, Literature (General), Non-Fiction, Philosophy, Poetry, Politics, Prose, Reviews, Satire.

EPOCH MAGAZINE, Michael Koch, Editor, 251 Goldwin Smith Hall, Cornell University, Ithaca, NY 14853-3201, 607-255-3385, Fax 607-255-6661. 1947. Poetry, fiction, articles, art, cartoons, long-poems. "We are interested in the work of both new and established writers. Recent contributors include: Antonya Nelson, Jhumpa Lahiri, Yusef Komunyakaa, Heidi Jon Schmidt, Dan Chaon, Jim Daniels, Kevin Canty, many other fine writers, some of whom are not yet well known. Submissions received between April 15 and Sept. 21 will be returned unread." circ. 1M+. 3/yr. Pub'd 3 issues 2005; expects 3 issues 2006, 3 issues 2007. sub. price $11; per copy $6.50+; sample $5. Back issues: varies. 128pp. Reporting time: 4-6 weeks. Simultaneous submissions accepted: no. Payment: $5-$10 per printed magazine page, sometimes more, depending on our funding. Copyrighted, reverts to author. Ads: $180 (full cover); $160 (full page); $90 (half-page). Subjects: Fiction, Poetry.

Epoch Press, Joyce R. Green, Editor; Lucy Knapp, Editor, 8356 Olive Boulevard, St. Louis, MO 63132-2814, Phone: 314-991-8758, Fax: 314-997-1788, Web Site: www.epoch-press.net, E-Mail: whgreen@inlink.com, lucyknapp@whgreen.com. 1986. Poetry, fiction, satire, criticism, long-poems, non-fiction. "Recent contributors: *Absolute Art* by Andrew Kagan, PhD; *American Art: Thoughts of a Collector* by A. Everette James, MD; and *Science and Moral Choice* by Ronald Icenogle; *Lawyers, Litigants and Whores* by Donald I. Peterson, M.D.; *Life's Little Annoyances* by Arthur Cook; *Still Waters Run Deep: A Healthcare Novel* by Suzanne Knoebel, M.D.; *The Aristeia* by Henri Novalis." avg. press run 1M. Pub'd 22 titles 2005; expects 25 titles 2006, 20-30 titles 2007. Discounts: libraries 10%, bookstore 20%, wholesalers and distributors 35%-40%. 200pp. Reporting time: varies. Simultaneous submissions accepted: yes. Publishes approx. 75% of manuscripts submitted. Payment: up to 3,500 copies: 40% of retail price, over 3,500: 25% of retail price, outside of US sales: 25% of retail price. Copyrights for author. Subjects: Acupuncture, Alternative Medicine, Arts, Bisexual, Civil War, Collectibles, Ethics, Finances, Gay, Gender Issues, Non-Fiction, Philosophy, Self-Help, Society.

Epona Publishing (see also THE ART HORSE), Kathleen M. Wermuth, 6208 Hackberry Lane, Maryville, TN 37801-1160. 1999. Poetry, fiction, art, long-poems, non-fiction. "Although I am self-publishing my first book about horses for children, due the first of the year, I would accept submissions from other authors. Horse related subjects preferred. Also look for subjects relating to other animals, historical and geared for children. As well as subjects relating to art and miniatures." Expects 1 title 2006, 2 titles 2007. Discounts: currently working on price guides for bulk rate. 35pp. Reporting time: 1 month, LSASE for return of material. Simultaneous submissions accepted: yes. Payment: may be subsidary (I'm a small pub.). Will copyright for author for a fee. Subjects: Animals, Children, Youth, Magazines, Miniature Books, Picture Books.

EquiLibrium Press, Susan Goland, 10736 Jefferson Blvd. #680, Culver City, CA 90230, 310-417-8217, Fax 310-417-8122, equipress@equipress.com. 1998. Non-fiction. "'Books that inform and inspire.'(R) Nonfiction women's health and wellness. **Not accepting submissions until further notice. See website for updates.**."

avg. press run 3M. Pub'd 1 title 2005. Discounts: upon request. Pages vary. Reporting time: 45 days. Simultaneous submissions accepted: yes. Payment: varies. Copyrights for author. Subject: Women.

Equine Graphics Publishing Group: New Concord Press, SmallHorse Press, Parallel Press, Toni Leland, 7270 Forest Lane, Nashport, OH 43830-9045, 800-659-9442, 740-588-0181, fax 740-588-0183, writer-one@newconcordpress.com, http://www.newconcordpress.com. 1985. Poetry, fiction, non-fiction. avg. press run 2000. Pub'd 7 titles 2005; expects 7 titles 2006. Discounts: wholesalers: 55%, returnsbookstores, retailers: 1-4 copies 20%, 5+ copies 40%. 250-450pp. Reporting time: queries: 1-2 weeks, manuscript: 1-2 months. Simultaneous submissions accepted: No. Publishes 2% of manuscripts submitted. Subjects: Animals, Fantasy, Fiction, Poetry, Romance, Self-Help, Senior Citizens.

ERASED, SIGH, SIGH, Via Dolorosa Press, Hyacinthe L. Raven, 701 East Schaaf Road, Cleveland, OH 44131-1227, ViaDolorosaPress@sbcglobal.net, www.angelfire.com/oh2/dolorosa/erased.html. 1994. Poetry, fiction, long-poems. "We do not accept submissions by phone, fax or e-mail. Send for submission guidelines or view them at www.angelfire.com/oh2/dolorosa/crusade.html We definitely recommend you read a couple issues prior to submitting; we have a particular style and tone of work that we print, and we ONLY print work that is about death, particularly suicide. Include SASE for response; we do not reply by email. Do not send disks." circ. 1M. 2/yr. Pub'd 2 issues 2005; expects 2 issues 2006, 2 issues 2007. sub. price $8 US, $10 foreign (checks/money orders drawn on a US bank made payable to Via Dolorosa Press); per copy $3.50 + postage; sample $4.25 (includes postage). Back issues: same as current issue prices. Discounts: rates available upon request for bookstores. 36pp. Reporting time: 2 months. Simultaneous submissions accepted: yes. Publishes 25% of manuscripts submitted. Payment: 1 copy. Not copyrighted. Ads: trades ad space with appropriate publications. Subjects: Euthanasia, Death, Grieving.

Erespin Press, David L. Kent, Copy Editor, 6906 Colony Loop Drive, Austin, TX 78724-3749. 1980. Poetry, satire, non-fiction. "Particularly interested in historical translations." avg. press run 200. Pub'd 1 title 2005; expects 4 titles 2006, 4 titles 2007. 50pp. Reporting time: 1 week. Payment: by arrangement. Copyrights for author. Subjects: Classical Studies, History, Humanism, India, Medieval, Poetry, Satire, Translation.

Eros Books (see also DESIRE; PSYCHE), Mary Nicholaou, 463 Barlow Avenue, Staten Island, NY 10308, 718-317-7484. 1997. Fiction, articles, art, cartoons, interviews, criticism, reviews, letters, parts-of-novels, non-fiction. "We accept only postmodern, literary fiction and nonfiction. We expose the culture's effect on our soulful existence hoping to resurrect our psyche's true desire. Any length that has literary merit. Send SASE for reply." avg. press run 500. Pub'd 4 titles 2005; expects 4 titles 2006, 6 titles 2007. Discounts: 40%. 130pp. Reporting time: within 8 weeks. Simultaneous submissions accepted: yes. Publishes 50% of manuscripts submitted. Payment: 50% on net, negotiated. Copyrights for author. Subjects: Biography, Fiction, Gender Issues, Language, Literature (General), Memoirs, Non-Fiction, Novels, Philosophy, Post Modern, Research, Romance, Short Stories, Translation.

EROSHA, Artisan Studio Design, C.E. Laine, PO Box 185, Falls Church, VA 22040-0185, Fax 703-852-3906, editor@erosha.net, http://erosha.net. 2001. Poetry, fiction, articles, art, photos, interviews, satire, criticism, reviews, letters, long-poems, non-fiction. "*Erosha* looks for quality poetry of any length or style (except rhymed poetry). Prose submissions should be under 5,000 words. All material should in some way express human sexuality or romantic relations. Art and photography is also eligible for publication. Past contributors include Janet Buck, Lyn Lifshin, kris t kahn, Michael Meyerhofer, Dorothy Doyle Mienko, Rae Pater, Dan Sicoli, Debrah Kayla Sterling, Dan Tompsett and contributing editors Donna Hill and C.E. Laine. *Erosha* nominates for the Pushcart Prize." circ. electronic, POD. 8/8/8. price per copy free; sample $1. 20pp. Reporting time: 60 days. Simultaneous submissions accepted: yes. Publishes 5% of manuscripts submitted. Payment: none. Not copyrighted. Subjects: Avant-Garde, Experimental Art, Erotica, Essays, Experimental, Gender Issues, Photography, Poetry, Prose.

Eryon Press (see also TIFERET: A Journal of Spiritual Literature), Cynthia Brown, PO Box 659, Peapack, NJ 07977-0659, 908-781-2556. 2004. avg. press run 1000. Expects 2 titles 2006, 4 titles 2007. 350pp.

ESPERANTIC STUDIES, Jason M. Clark, Editor; Mark Fettes, Editor, 8888 University Drive, Faculty of Education, Burnaby, BC, V5A 1S6, Canada, Off: 604-291-4489, Fax: 604.434.2624, jclark@esperantic.org, www.esperantic.org. 1991. Articles, reviews, non-fiction. "We publish Esperantic Studies in a print edition and also post it online at www.esperantic.org." circ. 12M. 2/yr. Pub'd 2 issues 2005; expects 2 issues 2006, 2 issues 2007. sub. price free. Back issues: free for SASE. 4pp. Payment: none. Not copyrighted. Pub's reviews: 1 in 2005. §Language problems (international, cross-cultural). Ads: none. Subjects: Communication, Journalism, Language, Sociology.

Etaoin Shrdlu Press (see also PABLO LENNIS), John Thiel, Fandom House, 30 N. 19th Street, Lafayette, IN 47904. 1976. Poetry, fiction, articles, art, photos, criticism, reviews, letters, non-fiction. "Science fiction, fantasy and science only." avg. press run 100. Expects 1 title 2006. 90pp. Reporting time: 2 weeks or less. Simultaneous submissions accepted: no. Publishes 80% of manuscripts submitted. Payment: none. Does not copyright for author.

ETC Publications, James Berry, 1456 Rodeo Road, Palm Springs, CA 92262, 760-325-5352, fax 760-325-8841. 1972. "Considers timely topics in all non-fiction areas." avg. press run 2.5M. Pub'd 10 titles 2005; expects 12 titles 2006. Discounts: usual trade. 256pp. Reporting time: 4 weeks. Payment: standard book royalties. Copyrights for author. Subjects: Biography, Business & Economics, Crafts, Hobbies, Earth, Natural History, Ecology, Foods, Education, How-To, Native American, Psychology, Society, Sports, Outdoors.

Ethos Publishing, Harold Lewis Malt, 4224 Spanish Trail Place, Pensacola, FL 32504-8561. Fiction, art, non-fiction. avg. press run 3M. Expects 2 titles 2006, 2 titles 2007. Discounts: bookstores 40%, wholesalers 55%. 250pp. Reporting time: 1 month. We accept simultaneous submissions, but query first. Publishes 10% of manuscripts submitted. Payment: negotiated. Subjects: Aging, Arts, Fiction, How-To.

Etruscan Press, Youngstown State University, English Department, Youngstown, OH 44555.

THE EUGENE O'NEILL REVIEW, Zander Brietzke, Editor; Ingrid Strange, Publication Coordinator, Department of English, Suffolk University, Boston, MA 02114-4280, 617-573-8272. 1977. Articles, art, photos, cartoons, interviews, criticism, reviews, letters, plays, news items, non-fiction. "*The Review's* aim is to serve as a meeting ground for O'Neill enthusiasts of academe and those of the Theatre. So it tries to blend critical articles of a scholarly sort, with news and reviews of current productions and publications. Articles of all sizes—from pithy notes to lengthy analyses—are welcome. Over-long articles are serialized. ISSN 1040-9483." circ. 550. 1/yr. Pub'd 2 issues 2005; expects 2 issues 2006, 2 issues 2007. sub. price $35 for individuals in US + Canada, and all institutions; per copy $35; sample free. Back issues: $15 per copy. Discounts: none. 200pp. Reporting time: 2-6 months, frequently sooner. Simultaneous submissions accepted: yes. Publishes 60% of manuscripts submitted. Payment: none. Copyrighted, permissions to reprint (with acknowledgement) are never refused. Pub's reviews: 8 in 2005. §Any books or articles devoted to Eugene O'Neill (in whole or in part) or to 20th century drama and any film or stage performance of O'Neill's work. Ads: $200/$100. Subjects: Drama, Newsletter, Theatre.

EUPHONY, Jesse Raber, 5706 S University Ave, Room 001, Chicago, IL 60615. 2000. Poetry, fiction, articles, criticism, reviews, music. "About 20% of our material is University of Chicago student writing. The other 80% is supplied by amateurs and professionals from around the nation (and beyond)." circ. 2500. 2/yr. Pub'd 2 issues 2005; expects 2 issues 2006, 2 issues 2007. sub. price $0; per copy $0; sample free. Back issues: inquire. 125pp. Reporting time: 3 months. Simultaneous submissions accepted: Yes. Publishes 4% of manuscripts submitted. Payment: no payment. Copyrighted, reverts to author. Pub's reviews: 2 in 2005. §new books of poetry, fiction, or literary criticism. Ads: about $100 full page—negotiable. Subjects: Absurdist, Experimental, Fiction, Non-Fiction, The North.

Eurotique Press, Janet L. Przirembel, Kevin P. Grieco, 3109 45th Street, Suite 300, West Palm Beach, FL 33407-1915, 561-687-0455; 800-547-4326. 1995. Fiction, art, cartoons, non-fiction. avg. press run 1.5M-2M. Pub'd 1 title 2005; expects 4 titles 2006, 7-8 titles 2007. Discounts: bookstores 20%. Reporting time: 2-3 months. Payment: worked out individually. Copyrights for author. Subjects: Erotica, Fiction, Non-Fiction.

EVANSVILLE REVIEW, Denis Illige-Saucier, Editor-in-Chief, Univ. of Evansville, English Dept., 1800 Lincoln Avenue, Evansville, IN 47722, 812-488-1042. 1991. Poetry, fiction, interviews, satire, parts-of-novels, plays, non-fiction. "Nothing longer than 15 pages, please. We publish many undiscovered writers along with established writers. Please query with nonfiction and interviews. Recent contributors include Marge Piercy, David Ignatow, Lucian Stryk, John Updike, Felix Stefanile, Willis Barnstone, Charles Wright, and Tess Gallagher. All manuscripts are recycled, not returned. Please include SASE for reply. A brief bio or list of previous publications is appreciated as we print contributors notes." circ. 3M. 1/yr. Pub'd 1 issue 2005; expects 1 issue 2006, 1 issue 2007. price per copy $5; sample $5. Back issues: $5. Discounts: negotiable. 200pp. Reporting time: We notify in late March. Manuscripts are not read between January and August and must be received by early December. We accept simultaneous submissions with notification. Publishes 3% of manuscripts submitted. Payment: 2 copies. Not copyrighted. Ads: none. Subjects: Bilingual, Drama, Essays, Fiction, Interviews, Literary Review, Literature (General), Poetry, Prose, Satire, Short Stories, Translation.

EVENT, Billeh Nickerson, Editor; Ian Cockfield, Managing Editor; Christine Dewar, Fiction Editor; Elizabeth Bachinsky, Poetry Editor, Douglas College, PO Box 2503, New Westminster, B.C. V3L 5B2, Canada, 604-527-5293, Fax 604-527-5095, event@douglas.bc.ca, http://event.douglas.bc.ca. 1971. Poetry, fiction, reviews, long-poems, non-fiction. "Although we are devoted to those who are writing high-quality work but are not yet established, we feature prominent authors as well. Previous contributors include Leon Rooke, Susan Musgrave, Patricia Young and Tim Bowling. We do not accept e-mail submissions." circ. 1.2M. 3/yr. Pub'd 3 issues 2005; expects 3 issues 2006, 3 issues 2007. sub. price US$24.95, US$39.95/2 years, US$89.95/5 years; per copy US$9.95; sample current US$10. Back issues: US$7. Discounts: subscription agencies 25%. 136pp. Reporting time: 1-6 months. Simultaneous submissions accepted: yes. Publishes 2% of manuscripts submitted. Payment: honorarium, $22/page upon publication. Copyrighted, reverts to author. Pub's reviews: 12 in 2005.

§Poetry, short fiction, novels. Ads: $200/$100. Subjects: Fiction, Non-Fiction, Poetry.

Event Horizon Press, Barbora Cowles, Publisher, PO Box 2006, Palm Springs, CA 92263, 760-329-3950. 1990. Poetry, fiction, art, photos, long-poems, plays, non-fiction. "Not presently accepting submissions." avg. press run 250-5M. Pub'd 2 titles 2005; expects 2 titles 2006, 2 titles 2007. Discounts: offered to distributors, bulk purchases and libraries. 48-352pp. Publishes less than .05% of manuscripts submitted. Payment: contracts set up with each author. Copyrights for author. Subjects: Fiction, History, Humor, Law, Science Fiction.

Everflowing Publications, Shonnese C.L. Coleman, PO Box 191536, Los Angeles, CA 90019, 323-993-8577, everflowing@nycmail.com. 2000. Poetry, art, long-poems. avg. press run 1M. Expects 1 title 2006, 1-2 titles 2007. Discounts: 40% to bookstores, some bulk orders, agents, etc. 96pp. Reporting time: 3-6 months. Simultaneous submissions accepted: yes. Publishes 3% of manuscripts submitted. Payment: to be determined. Does not copyright for author. Subjects: African-American, Avant-Garde, Experimental Art, Black, Culture, Dance, Drama, Performing Arts, Poetry.

Evolution Publishing (see also Arx Publishing LLC), Claudio R. Salvucci, PO Box 13333, Merchantville, NJ 08109, 856-486-1310, Fax 856-665-0170, info@evolpub.com, www.evolpub.com. "An imprint of Arx Publishing. Monographs in Native American language, Native American history, Early Colonial history, North American dialectology, classical history, classical linguistics, philology, and archaeology." avg. press run 500-1M. Pub'd 5 titles 2005; expects 12 titles 2006, 15 titles 2007. Discounts: standard 20%. 150pp. Reporting time: 6-8 weeks. Simultaneous submissions accepted: yes. Publishes less than 10% of manuscripts submitted. Payment: varies by contract. Copyrights for author. Subjects: Classical Studies, History, Language, Native American, Non-Fiction.

Excelsior Cee Publishing, J.C. Marshall, PO Box 5861, Norman, OK 73070, 405-329-3909, Fax 405-329-6886, ecp@oecadvantage.net, www.excelsiorcee.com. 1989. Non-fiction. "Nonfiction publisher and distributor of some independently published books." avg. press run 3M. Discounts: available on request. 200pp. Reporting time: 6 weeks. Simultaneous submissions accepted: yes. Payment: negotiable. Copyrights for author. Subjects: Family, How-To, Humor, Inspirational, Non-Fiction, Self-Help, Women.

EXCEPTIONALITY EDUCATION CANADA, Judy Lupart, Christina Rinaldi, Department of Educational Psychology, 6-102 Education North, University of Alberta, Edmonton, AB T6G 2G5, Canada, Telephone: (780) 492-2198/7471, Fax: (780) 492-1318, E-mail: eecj@ualberta.ca, judy.lupart@ualberta.ca, christina.rinaldi@ualberta.ca. 1991. Articles. "The journal is intended to provide a forum for scholarly exchange among Canadian professionals in education and related disciplines who work with students across the spectrum of exceptionality. The purpose is to present current research and theory and to identify emerging trends and visions for the education of students with exceptionalities." circ. 225. 3/yr. Pub'd 3 issues 2005; expects 3 issues 2006, 3 issues 2007. sub. price Inst. $60, Indiv. $40, Student $25; in Canada add GST, outside Canada price is in US dollars $55/2 years (indiv.); per copy $10 + GST in Canada; outside Canada in US dollars. 108pp. Reporting time: 2 months. Copyrighted, reverts to author. Pub's reviews: 1 in 2005. §Education of students with exceptionalities. Ads: none. Subjects: Children, Youth, Education.

EXECUTIVE EXCELLENCE, Executive Excellence Publishing, Ken Shelton, 1366 E. 1120 S., Provo, UT 84606, 800-304-9782; editorial@eep.com; www.eep.com. 1984. Articles, reviews, non-fiction. "Generally one-page articles directed toward pesonal and organizational development. Contributors include Stephen Covey, Ken Blanchard, Brian Tracy, Charles Garfield, Warren Bennis, Peter Senge and many more." circ. 25M. 12/yr. Pub'd 12 issues 2005; expects 12 issues 2006, 12 issues 2007. sub. price $129; sample complimentary. Back issues: $10 each. Discounts: $109 each for 6-25, $99 each for 26-99. 20pp. Reporting time: 2 months. Simultaneous submissions accepted: yes. Publishes 10-15% of manuscripts submitted. Payment: none. Copyrighted, does not revert to author. Pub's reviews: 60 in 2005. §Business, leadership, self-help, management, success. Ads: none. Subjects: Business & Economics, Careers, Leadership, Management, Motivation, Success, Self-Help.

Executive Excellence Publishing (see also EXECUTIVE EXCELLENCE; PERSONAL EXCELLENCE), Ken Shelton, 1806 N. 1120 W., Provo, UT 84604-1179, 800-304-9782; editorial@eep.com; www.eep.com. 1984. Articles, non-fiction. "Recent titles include: *Winning the Information War* by Tim Timmerman, *Monkey Business* by William Oncken, *The Philosophy of Winning for Women* by Denis Waitley, *Old Dogs, New Tricks* by Warren Bennis, *Success is a Journey* by Brian Tracy, and *Leadership from the Inside Out* by Kevin Cashman." avg. press run 5-10K. Pub'd 10 titles 2005; expects 10 titles 2006, 10 titles 2007. Discounts: trade 40%. 250pp. Reporting time: 1 month. Simultaneous submissions accepted: yes. Publishes 10% of manuscripts submitted. Payment: negotiable. Copyrights for author. Subjects: Business & Economics, Careers, Leadership, Management, Motivation, Success, Self-Help.

EXIT 13 MAGAZINE, Tom Plante, Editor, PO Box 423, Fanwood, NJ 07023, Exit13magazine@yahoo.com (no attachments). 1987. Poetry, photos. "Previously published *Berkeley Works Magazine* (1981-1985). I seek manuscripts of poetry with a view of the terrain familiar to the writer. *Exit 13 Magazine* prefers a geographic bent and uses work from all over the U.S. and occasional contributions from outside these borders. Fresh faces and views are welcome. Back issues are available. Photos of Exit 13 road signs earn a free magazine. ISSN 1054-3937." circ. 500. 1/yr. Pub'd 1 issue 2005; expects 1 issue 2006, 1 issue 2007. price per copy $8; sample $8. Discounts: 40% for 5 or more copies of any one issue, prepaid. 76pp. Reporting time: 4 months. Simultaneous submissions accepted: yes. Publishes 10% of manuscripts submitted. Payment: copy of issue containing author's work. Copyrighted, rights revert to author but *Exit 13 Magazine* keeps anthology rights. Ads: $45 camera ready/$25/$13 1/4 page camera ready. Subjects: Americana, The Americas, Earth, Natural History, Folklore, Geography, Ireland, Poetry, Travel.

Expanded Media Editions, Pociao, Prinz Albert Str. 38, 53113 Bonn, Germany, 0228/22 95 83, FAX 0228/21 95 07. 1969. Poetry, fiction, art, photos, interviews, criticism, music, collages. "Recent contributors: W. S. Burroughs, Jurgen Ploog, Claude Pelieu-Washburn, Allen Ginsberg, Gerard Malanga, Paul Bowles." avg. press run 2M. Pub'd 3 titles 2005; expects 2 titles 2006, 4 titles 2007. Discounts: 1-5 copies 25%, 6-20 30%, 21-50 40%, 50+ 50%. 100pp. Payment: 10% per sold book. Copyrights for author. Subjects: Fiction, Poetry.

EXPERIMENTAL FOREST, jeanette trout, kevyn knox, 2430 North 2nd St. #3, Harrisburg, PA 17110-1104, 717-730-2143, xxforest@yahoo.com, www.geocities.com/paris/salon/9699. 1999. Poetry, fiction, articles, art, cartoons, interviews, satire, criticism, reviews, letters, parts-of-novels, long-poems, plays, news items, non-fiction. "Experimental and avant-garde stuff. Recent contributors: Richard Kostelanetz, John Taggart, Kerry Keys, Rick Kearns, Jack Veasey, Marty Esworthy, Gene Hosey, Deborah Ryder, Snow, and stevenallenmay." circ. 250+. 6/yr. Pub'd 3 issues 2005; expects 6 issues 2006, 6 issues 2007. sub. price $18; per copy $4; sample $4. Back issues: $7 each. 60pp. Reporting time: 2-4 months. Simultaneous submissions accepted: no. Publishes 10% of manuscripts submitted. Payment: 1 copy (and discount on extra copy). Copyrighted, reverts to author. Pub's reviews: 2 in 2005. §Poetry, essays, politics. Ads: $50/$25. Subjects: Absurdist, Avant-Garde, Experimental Art, Beat, Buddhism, Charles Bukowski, Communism, Marxism, Leninism, Current Affairs, Dada, Bob Dylan, Essays, Global Affairs, Government, Human Rights, James Joyce, Jack Kerouac.

Explorer Press, Terry Collins, 1501 Edgewood Drive, Mount Airy, NC 27030-5215, 336-789-6005, Fax 336-789-6005, E-mail terryleecollins@hotmail.com. 1993. avg. press run 10M. Pub'd 2 titles 2005; expects 1 title 2006, 1 title 2007. Discounts: inquire. 200pp. Reporting time: 3 months. Simultaneous submissions accepted: yes. Payment: inquire. Copyrights for author. Subjects: Biography, Comics, North Carolina, Television.

EZ Nature Books, Ed Zolkoski, Owner, PO Box 4206, San Luis Obispo, CA 93403. 1983. Photos, non-fiction. avg. press run 3M-5M. Pub'd 3 titles 2005; expects 3 titles 2006, 2 titles 2007. Discounts: 40% to retailers, other by negotiation. 128pp. Publishes 5-10% of manuscripts submitted. Payment: 10% paid quarterly. Does not copyright for author. Subjects: Animals, Bicycling, Biography, California, Catholic, Cooking, Earth, Natural History, History, Indians, Native American, Nature, Whaling, World War II.

F

Face to Face Press, Sheryl Levart, 3419 Fillmore St., Denver, CO 80205-4257, slevart@face2facepress.com, www.face2facepress.com. 1999. Poetry, fiction, articles, art, photos, interviews, satire, criticism, reviews, parts-of-novels, long-poems, collages, plays, news items, non-fiction. avg. press run 1.5M. Expects 1 title 2006, 2 titles 2007. Discounts: 40%. 120pp. Reporting time: 2 months. Simultaneous submissions accepted: yes. Payment: 10% net sales. Copyrights for author. Subject: Multicultural.

FACES: People, Places, and Culture, Cobblestone Publishing Company, Elizabeth Crooker Carpentiere, Editor, 30 Grove Street, Suite C, Peterborough, NH 03458, 603-924-7209, Fax 603-924-7380, custsvc@cobblestone.mv.com. 1984. Articles, art, photos, reviews, non-fiction. "*Faces* is designed to expose young people to other peoples and cultures of the world; to help them realize that no country is any better than any other; to learn and understand how other people live and do things; to see the world in new ways and to help them reflect on how they assign importance to things, ideas and people in their own lives. Material must be written for children ages 8-14. Write for guidelines as we focus each issue on a particular theme." circ. 13.5M. 9/yr. Pub'd 9 issues 2005; expects 9 issues 2006, 9 issues 2007. sub. price $29.95; add $8 for foreign mail, Canadian subs add 7% GST; per copy $4.95; sample $4.95. Back issues: $4.95. Discounts: 15% for sub. agencies, bulk rate 3 or more $17.95/year sub. each. 52pp. Reporting time: queries sent well in advance of deadline may not be answered for several months. Go-aheads usually sent 5 months prior to publication date. Payment: on publication. Copyrighted, Cobblestone Publishing buys all rights. Pub's reviews: 81 in 2005.

§Books for children, age 8-14, related to themes covered. No ads. Subjects: Anthropology, Archaelogy, Culture.

Facts on Demand Press (see also BRB Publications, Inc.), PO Box 27869, Tempe, AZ 85285-7869, 800-929-3811, Fax 800-929-4981, brb@brbpub.com, www.brbpub.com. 1996. avg. press run 5M. Pub'd 12 titles 2005; expects 10 titles 2006. Discounts: available through National Book Network.

Faded Banner Publications, Don Allison, PO Box 101, Bryan, OH 43506-0101, 419-636-3807,419-63603807 (fax), 888-799-3787, fadedbanner.com. 1997. Non-fiction. ''We specialize in Civil War and local history titles.'' avg. press run 1150. Pub'd 1 title 2005; expects 1 title 2006, 2 titles 2007. Discounts: 5-99 copies 40%, 10 or more copies non-returnable 50%, 100 or more copies 50%. 290pp. Reporting time: 1 month. Simultaneous submissions accepted: Yes. Publishes 5% of manuscripts submitted. Payment: To be determined. Does not copyright for author. Subjects: Anthropology, Archaelogy, Civil War, Military, Veterans, Ohio, Wisconsin.

C.H. Fairfax Co., Inc., PO Box 7047, Baltimore, MD 21216, www.yougetpublished.com.

Falcon Publishing, LTD, David L Fey Jr., P O Box 6099, Kingwood, TX 77345-6099, 713-417-7600,281-360-8284,sales@falconpublishing.com,www.falconpublishing.com. 2004. Fiction. ''The mission of Falcon Publishing, LTD is to assist new authors in the publication of their work. We provide complete pre-publication and publishing services that include, ISBN, LCCN, copyright, content editing, typesetting, cover design, illustrations, printing, marketing and sales through the Falcon Publishing web site and affiliates.Falcon Publishing does not publish pronographic material.'' avg. press run 2000. Expects 3 titles 2006, 1 title 2007. Discounts: 25-99 copies 20%100-499 copies 40%500-1000 copies 50%1000+ copies 60%. 300pp. Reporting time: Two weeks. Simultaneous submissions accepted: Yes. Payment: 40% for books sold by Falcon Publishing. $1.00 per book sent directly to author. Copyrights for author. Subjects: Children, Youth, Christianity, Fiction, Leadership, Mystery, Self-Help, Storytelling.

Fall Creek Press, Helen Wirth, PO Box 1823, Bisbee, AZ 85603-2823, 520-432-4774. 1991. Fiction. ''Publishes only books on spontaneous theatre.'' avg. press run 3M. Expects 1 title 2007. 192pp. Does not copyright for author. Subjects: Drama, Theatre.

•**Falls Media,** David Smith, 1 Astor Place, PH K, New York, NY 10003, 917-667-2269, www.wouldyour-ather.com. 2004. ''Humorous, pop-culture driven books & games.'' avg. press run 40000. Pub'd 2 titles 2005; expects 2 titles 2006, 3 titles 2007. Discounts: retailers, wholesalers - 40-60%. 120pp. Subjects: Absurdist, Culture, Games, Humor, Young Adult.

Famaco Publishers (Qalam Books), D.A. Miller, PO Box 440665, Jacksonville, FL 32244-0665, 904-434-5901, Fax 904-777-5901, famapub@aol.com. 1996. Non-fiction. ''At least 50,000 words. Recent contributors: Mukhtar Muhammad and Dewayne E Moore.'' avg. press run 2.5M. Pub'd 2 titles 2005; expects 2 titles 2006. Discounts: available on request. 500pp. Reporting time: variable. Simultaneous submissions accepted: yes. Publishes 20% of manuscripts submitted. Payment: specific arrangement. Copyrights for author. Subjects: How-To, Leadership, Management, Religion.

Family Learning Association, Inc. (see also PARENT TALK NEWSLETTER), Carl B. Smith, Director, 3925 Hagan Street, Suite 101, Bloomington, IN 47401, 812-323-9862, 1-800-759-4723, Fax 812-331-2776. 1990. Non-fiction. ''Materials to enhance learning in schools and in the home.'' avg. press run 5M. Pub'd 12 titles 2005; expects 8 titles 2006, 10 titles 2007. 100-250pp. Reporting time: 4-8 weeks. Payment: negotiable, usually royalty of 6-12% of money received. Subjects: Children, Youth, Education, Language, Parenting, Reading, Reference, Speaking.

FAMILY THERAPY, Libra Publishers, Inc., Martin Blinder, Editor, 3089C Clairemont Dr., Suite 383, San Diego, CA 92117, 619-571-1414. 1960. Articles. circ. 1.5M. 3/yr. Pub'd 3 issues 2005; expects 3 issues 2006, 3 issues 2007. sub. price $75; per copy $25; sample free. Back issues: $25. Discounts: 10% to subscriber agents. 128pp. Reporting time: 3 weeks. Payment: none. Copyrighted. Pub's reviews. §Behavioral sciences. Ads: $150/$85. Subjects: Psychology, Society.

Fantagraphics Books (see also THE COMICS JOURNAL), Gary Groth, (Comics Journal), 7563 Lake City Way, Seattle, WA 98115. 1976. Articles, art, cartoons, interviews, criticism, reviews, news items. ''Fantagraphics publishes the widest variety of classic and contemporary comics and cartoons of any publisher, including the works of Robert Crumb, Jules Feiffer, E.C. Segar, Winsor McCay, Harold Gray, Hal Foster, Gilbert and Jaime Hernandez, Peter Bagge, Dan Clowes, Ralph Steadman, Spain Rodriguez, Kim Deitch, Rick Geary, Jose Munoz, and Carlos Sampayo.'' avg. press run 6M. Pub'd 30 titles 2005; expects 35 titles 2006, 35 titles 2007. Comics 32pp, books 150pp. Reporting time: 1-2 months. Simultaneous submissions accepted: yes. Publishes 1% of manuscripts submitted. Payment: on publication, royalties vary. Copyrights for author. Subject: Comics.

Fantail, PO Box 462, Hollis, NH 03049-0462, http://www.fantail.com, mail@fantail.com, phone: (603) 880-3539. 1996. Art, photos, non-fiction. avg. press run 2.5M. Expects 1 title 2007. Discounts: 2-3 20%, 4-9

30%, 10-199 40%, 200+ 50%. 205pp. Simultaneous submissions accepted: yes. Copyrights for author. Subjects: African Literature, Africa, African Studies, Cooking, History, Transportation.

FAQs Press, Linda Resnik, Dee Brock, PO Box 130115, Tyler, TX 75713, 903-565-6653 phone/Fax, www.FAQsPress.com. 2000. Non-fiction. ''FAQs Press publishes consumer reference books answering frequently asked questions about specific topics. We will accept written proposals for reference-type books on popular topics written for general audiences.'' Expects 4-6 titles 2007.

Farcountry Press, Lisa Juvik, 2222 Washington Street, Helena, MT 59604, lisa.juvik@farcountrypress.com.

FARMER'S DIGEST, Sandy Simonson, 1003 Central Avenue, Fort Dodge, IA 50501-0624, 800-673-4763. 1938. Reviews. circ. 10M. 10/yr. Pub'd 10 issues 2005; expects 10 issues 2006, 10 issues 2007. sub. price $19.95; per copy $3.50; sample $3.50. Back issues: $3.50. 100pp. Reporting time: none. Simultaneous submissions accepted: no. Payment: none. Copyrighted, does not revert to author. Pub's reviews: 10 in 2005. §Agriculture, nostalgia. Subjects: Agriculture, Book Reviewing.

FARMING UNCLE, Louis Toro, Editor & Publisher, c/o Toro, PO Box 427, Bronx, NY 10458-0711. 1977. Articles, reviews, non-fiction. circ. 1M. 4/yr. Pub'd 4 issues 2005; expects 4 issues 2006, 4 issues 2007. sub. price $10; per copy $3; sample $3. Back issues: $3 each. 24pp. Reporting time: immediate. Simultaneous submissions accepted: yes. Publishes 90% of manuscripts submitted. Payment: .05¢. Copyrighted, reverts to author. Pub's reviews: 4 in 2005. §Agriculture, small farms, gardening, animal husbandry, etc. Ads: $47.50/$27.50/$10 1 inch. Subjects: Agriculture, Animals, Environment, Gardening.

R. E. FARRELLBOOKS, LLC, P.O. Box 6507, Peoria, AZ 85385-6507, (623) 640-7915. 2004. Fiction. avg. press run 5500. Expects 1 title 2006, 1 title 2007. 272pp. Subject: Science Fiction.

•Fast Foot Forward Press, Jane Booth, 7 West 41st Ave, #302, San Mateo, CA 94403-5105, 650-483-7007, info@fastfootforwardpress.com, www.fastfootforwardpress.com. 2006. Non-fiction. ''We focus on publishing books with a stong sports theme. These include practical, how-to books on sport-related topics such as nutrition and sports psychology; personal experience - the passion for sport, the transformation that sport works on body and soul; biographies; humor. Our first title, Transformed by Triathlon: The Making of an Improbable Athlete, is a humorous, uplifting book recounting the transformation of a fortysomething woman who long ago traded physical exercise for food into an athlete capable of completing an olympic-distance triathlon.'' Expects 2 titles 2007. 300pp. Reporting time: One month. Simultaneous submissions accepted: Yes. Subjects: Autobiography, Bicycling, How-To, Memoirs, Non-Fiction, Self-Help, Sports, Outdoors.

FAT TUESDAY, F.M. Cotolo, Editor-in-Chief; B. Lyle Tabor, Associate Editor-Emeritus; Thom Savion, Associate Editor; Lionel Stevroid, Associate Editor; Kristen Cotolo, Managing Editor, 560 Manada Gap Road, Grantville, PA 17028, 717-469-7159. 1981. Poetry, fiction, art, satire, parts-of-novels, collages. ''As *Fat Tuesday* rolls through the new millennium, the publishing of small press editions becomes more difficult than ever. Money continues to be a major problem, mostly because small press seems to play to the very people who wish to be published in it. Sadly, the cast makes up the audience, and more people want to be in *Fat Tuesday* than want to buy it. Our audio-theater edition was a 40-plus-minute stereo cassette called *Fat Tuesday's Cool Noise*. It featured original music, poetry readings, sound collage and more by 20 artists. And next, Fat Tuesday released a few stereo-audio-cassette collections of original "musical poetry" by Frank Cotolo. "Fat" has also produced the ever-popular folk trio, Henry Morgan and The High Grass Boys' CDs. As far as what we want to publish when we receive financing to do so—send us shorter works. *Crystals of thought and emotion which reflect your individual experiences. As long as you dig into your guts and pull out pieces of yourself. Your work is your signature...Like time itself, it should emerge from the penetralia of your being and recede into the infinite region of the cosmos,* to coin a phrase. Certainly, perusing any of the issues we have published in the last decade will let you know how we admire in an author's work, an artist's stroke. However, all of those editions are now out of print. Also, join us at our website community, Fat Tuesday at YAHOO!. The club is free and features many writers and readers. You can post poetry, prose, editorials, etc. We often answer unsolicited submissions with personal comments, opinions, howdayados and the like. So, write to us, send us pieces of yourself, buy our products to keep our commercial-free policies intact (and keep this in mind for all other small presses, too), and please use SASEs and remember *Fat Tuesday* is mardi gras—so fill up before you fast. Bon soir.'' circ. 350-500. irreg. Expects 1 issue 2007. price per copy $5 (cassettes, zines and CDs), plus $1 postage; sample $5. Back issues: In-print issues are out of print. Cassette presentation and CDs available, but CDs are only for various artists. Inquire with a SASE about all product, old, new and projected. Discounts: inquire. 45pp. Reporting time: have patience, but we're usually quick! Simultaneous submissions accepted: no. Publishes 5% of manuscripts submitted. Payment: 1 complimentary copy in which work appears. Copyrighted, reverts to author. Ads: $100/$50/25¢ per classified word. Subjects: Comics, Dada, Fiction, Humor, Philosophy, Poetry, Satire, Zen.

Fathom Publishing Co., Constance Taylor, PO Box 200448, Anchorage, AK 99520-0448, 907-272-3305. 1978. Non-fiction. avg. press run 3M-5M. Pub'd 2 titles 2005; expects 1 title 2006. 500pp. Reporting time: 1

month. Simultaneous submissions accepted: yes. Publishes 1% of manuscripts submitted. Payment: varies. Copyrights for author. Subjects: Alaska, Law, Non-Fiction, Textbooks.

FEDERAL SENTENCING REPORTER, University of California Press, Doug Berman, Editor, University of California Press, 2000 Center Street, Suite 303, Berkeley, CA 94704-1223, 510-643-7154. 1988. "Editorial address: 233 Broadway, New York, NY 10279." circ. 2.5M. 5/yr. Pub'd 5 issues 2005; expects 5 issues 2006, 5 issues 2007. sub. price $225 indiv., $241 inst., add $20 air freight, $116 academics; per copy $50; sample free. Back issues: $50. 72pp. Ads: none.

Feel Free Press (see also OPEN WIDE MAGAZINE), James Quinton, 'The Flat', Yew Tree Farm, Sealand Road, Chester, Cheshire, CH1 6BS, United Kingdom. 2001. Poetry, fiction. "Feel Free Press publishes the work of those poets and writers who have made a mark in Open Wide Magazine." avg. press run 75. Expects 7 titles 2006, 14 titles 2007. 100pp. Reporting time: 1 month. Simultaneous submissions accepted: No. Publishes 25% of manuscripts submitted. Payment: Feel Free Press authors receive 10 copies of their book/broadside/chapbook. Copyrights for author. Subjects: Fiction, Folklore, Haiku, History, Humanism, Lesbianism, Literature (General), Philosophy, Photography, Poetry, Politics, Printing, Religion, Science Fiction, Tapes & Records.

FELICITER, Canadian Library Association, Elizabeth Morton, Editor, 328 Frank Street, Ottawa, Ontario K2P 0X8, Canada, 613-232-9625, ext. 322. 1956. Articles, photos, cartoons, interviews, reviews, letters. circ. 3M. 6/yr. Pub'd 6 issues 2005; expects 6 issues 2006, 6 issues 2007. sub. price $95 Cdn.; per copy $9.50 Cdn.; sample free. 56pp. Reporting time: 3 months. Simultaneous submissions accepted: no. Publishes 75% of manuscripts submitted. Payment: none. Copyrighted, does not revert to author. Pub's reviews: 15 in 2005. §Library and information science, Canadian reference. Ads: $1,239 Cdn./$889 Cdn. Subject: Libraries.

FEMINIST COLLECTIONS: A QUARTERLY OF WOMEN'S STUDIES RESOURCES, Women's Studies Librarian, University of Wisconsin System, Phyllis Holman Weisbard, JoAnne Lehman, 430 Memorial Library, 728 State Street, Madison, WI 53706, 608-263-5754. 1980. Articles, interviews, criticism, reviews, non-fiction. "Publishes book and video reviews on a variety of topics, plus news of Internet, periodical, and other resources for feminist research and teaching. Contributors are drawn from the University of Wisconsin System and elsewhere. Submissions are solicited from women's studies scholars." circ. 1.1M. 4/yr. Pub'd 4 issues 2005; expects 4 issues 2006, 4 issues 2007. sub. price $30 individuals and women's programs, $55 institutions (includes subscriptions to *Feminist Collections, Feminist Periodicals,* and *New Books On Women & Feminism*) Please inquire about special rates in Wisconsin; per copy $3.50; sample $3.50. Back issues: $3.50. 40pp. Reporting time: 1-2 weeks. Simultaneous submissions accepted: no. Payment: we are unfortunately unable to pay contributors. Copyrighted. Pub's reviews: 100 in 2005. §Any feminist or women-related books or magazines are of interest and help us stay current; we particularly note feminist reference works. Subjects: Bibliography, Book Reviewing, Feminism, Lesbianism, Libraries, Printing, Wisconsin, Women.

FEMINIST PERIODICALS: A CURRENT LISTING OF CONTENTS, Women's Studies Librarian, University of Wisconsin System, Phyllis Holman Weisbard, Ingrid Markhardt, 430 Memorial Library, 728 State Street, Madison, WI 53706, 608-263-5754. 1981. "Designed to increase public awareness of feminist periodicals, this publication reproduces table of contents pages from over 120 periodicals on a quarterly basis. An introductory section provides bibliographic background on each periodical." circ. 1.1M. 4/yr. Pub'd 4 issues 2005; expects 4 issues 2006, 4 issues 2007. sub. price $30 individuals and women's programs, $55 institutions (includes subscriptions to *Feminist Periodicals, Feminist Collections,* and *New Books On Women & Feminism*) Please inquire about special prices in Wisconsin; per copy $3.50; sample $3.50. Back issues: $3.50. 160pp. Copyrighted. Subjects: Bibliography, Feminism, Indexes & Abstracts, Lesbianism, Libraries, Magazines, Women.

The Feminist Press at the City University of New York (see also WSQ (formerly WOMEN'S STUDIES QUARTERLY)), Florence Howe, Publisher; Anjoli Roy, Assistant Editor, The Graduate Center, 365 Fifth Avenue, Suite 5406, New York, NY 10016, 212-817-7915, Fax 212-817-1593, www.feministpress.org. 1970. Fiction, non-fiction. "We do not accept submissions. Queries may be sent to the publisher via e-mail." avg. press run 3000. Pub'd 11 titles 2005; expects 18 titles 2006, 18 titles 2007. Discounts: See Consortium, our distributor; or our catalog on line at www.feministpress.org. 300-400pp. Reporting time: If we request a manuscript, we are relatively quick responding; no more than a month. Simultaneous submissions accepted: Yes. Publishes 2% of manuscripts submitted. Payment: Normal professional contract. Copyrights for author. Subjects: African Literature, Africa, African Studies, African-American, Autobiography, Biography, Black, Chicano/a, Education, Feminism, History, Lesbianism, Literature (General), Non-Fiction, Reprints, Third World, Minorities, Women.

FEMINIST REVIEW, Collective, Women's Studies, Univ. of N. London, 116-220 Holloway Road, London N7 8D8, United Kingdom. 1979. Articles, criticism, reviews. "A socialist *feminist* journal." circ. 4M. 3/yr.

Pub'd 3 issues 2005; expects 3 issues 2006, 3 issues 2007. sub. price (institutions) £123 UK, (individuals) £24 U.K., £30 overseas, $42 U.S.; per copy £9.99, North America $12.95. Back issues: apply to publisher. 128pp. Reporting time: 16-20 weeks. Simultaneous submissions accepted: no. Publishes 5-10% of manuscripts submitted. Payment: none. Copyrighted, reverts to author. Pub's reviews: 4-8 per issue in 2005. §Women: theory, politics, fiction, research. Ads: £110/£70/£55 1/3 page/£45 1/4 page. Subjects: Politics, Women.

FEMINIST STUDIES, Claire G. Moses, Editorial Director, 0103 Taliaferro, University of Maryland, College Park, MD 20742-7726, 301-405-7415, Fax 301-405-8395, creative@feministstudies.org; www.feministstudies.org. 1972. Poetry, fiction, articles, art, photos, cartoons, interviews, criticism, reviews, parts-of-novels, long-poems. 6M. 3/yr. Pub'd 3 issues 2005; expects 3 issues 2006, 3 issues 2007. sub. price $212 institutions, $35 individuals; per copy $77 inst., $17 indiv.; sample $77 inst., $17 indiv. Back issues: $77 inst., $17 indiv. Discounts: none. 200-250pp. Reporting time: 4 months. Simultaneous submissions accepted: no. Publishes 7% of manuscripts submitted. Payment: none. Copyrighted, does not revert to author. Pub's reviews: 3 in 2005. §All fields of women's studies, on feminism, on sexuality, on family, on human relations, on psychology, significant works by women authors. Ads: $360. Subjects: Criticism, Feminism, Global Affairs, History, Human Rights, Lesbianism, Philosophy, Sex, Sexuality, Sociology, Women.

Fern Publications (see also DANDELION ARTS MAGAZINE), Joaquina Gonzalez-Marina, Casa Alba, 24 Frosty Hollow, E. Hunsbury, Northants NN4 0SY, England, 01604-701730. 1978. avg. press run 1M per title. Pub'd 2 titles 2005. 20-30pp. Reporting time: about 2 weeks. Simultaneous submissions accepted: yes. Publishes 40% of manuscripts submitted. Payment: none. Copyrights for author. Subjects: Arts, Autobiography, Bilingual, Biography, Book Arts, History, Poetry, Short Stories.

FERRY TRAVEL GUIDE, Dan Youra Studios, Inc., Dan Youra, Editor, PO Box 1169, Port Hadlock, WA 98339-1169. 1984. Articles, photos, non-fiction. ''We purchase interesting articles and photos on NW ferries.'' circ. 110M. 3/yr. Pub'd 2 issues 2005; expects 3 issues 2006, 3 issues 2007. sub. price $6, including shipping; per copy $1.95; sample $1. Back issues: $1.50 plus shipping. Discounts: 3-12 40%, 13-50 45%, 51-150 50%, 151+ 55%. 48pp. Reporting time: fast. Payment: yes. Copyrighted, reverts to author. Pub's reviews: 3 in 2005. §Northwest travel. Ads: $3,000/$1500/$10. Subjects: Pacific Northwest, Sports, Outdoors, Transportation.

FIBERARTS, Altamont Press, Inc., Sunita Patterson, 67 Broadway Street, Asheville, NC 28801-2919, 704-253-0468. 1973. Articles, art, interviews, criticism, reviews, news items, non-fiction. circ. 24M. 5/yr. Pub'd 5 issues 2005; expects 5 issues 2006, 5 issues 2007. sub. price $22; per copy $5.50; sample $5.50. Back issues: $4.50. Discounts: shops 35% US, 35% Canadian, 50% foreign + postage. 80pp. Reporting time: 3 weeks. Simultaneous submissions accepted: no. Publishes 10% of manuscripts submitted. Payment: yes, depends on length, content, etc. Copyrighted, does not revert to author. Pub's reviews: 20 in 2005. §Arts, textiles, basketry. Ads: $800/$450/$1.10. Subjects: Arts, Crafts, Hobbies, Fashion, How-To, Quilting, Sewing, Visual Arts, Weaving.

FICTION, Mark Jay Mirsky, Editor; Nyshie Perkinson, Managing Editor, c/o Dept. of English, City College, 138th Street & Convent Ave., New York, NY 10031, 212-650-6319. 1972. Fiction, parts-of-novels. ''We are a journal of new directions for the novel and short story. *Fiction* has brought the unknown and the famous together in handsome pages to an international and discriminating audience of readers for 20 years. We represent no particular school of fiction, except the innovative, and in that sense our pages have been a harbor for many writers often at odds with each other. As a result of our willingness to publish the difficult and experimental, to look at the unusual and obscure, while not excluding the well known, *Fiction* has won a unique reputation in the U.S. and abroad, including in recent years, O.Henry Award, Pushcart Prize, and Best of the South.'' circ. 3M. 2/yr. Pub'd 2 issues 2005; expects 2 issues 2006, 2 issues 2007. sub. price $38/4 issues; per copy $10; sample $5. Back issues: $8. 200pp. Reporting time: 3+ months. Simultaneous submissions accepted: yes. Publishes 1% of manuscripts submitted. Payment: $75 + copies. Copyrighted, reverts to author. Subjects: Fiction, Literature (General).

Fiction Collective Two (FC2), Brenda L. Mills, Managing Editor, Dept. of English, Florida State University, Tallahassee, FL 32306-1580, 850-644-2260, Fax 850-644-6808. 1974. Fiction. ''Novels and collections of short stories. Members are authors we have published or are about to publish. Distribution through University of Alabama Press, Chicago Distribution Center, 11030 South Langley Avenue, Chicago, IL 60628. Please read our submissions guidelines at http://fc2.org/queries.htm before submitting.'' avg. press run 2.2M. Pub'd 6 titles 2005; expects 7 titles 2006, 7 titles 2007. Discounts: 1-4 books 20%, 5-24 40%, 25-49 41%, 50-74 42%, 75-124 43%, 125-199 44%, 200-299 45%, 300+ 46%. 200pp. Reporting time: 6 months to 1 year. Reading period: Sept.-Jan. Simultaneous submissions accepted: yes. Publishes 2% of manuscripts submitted. Payment: 10% royalties, 80% of subsidiary rights sales. Copyrights for author. Subjects: Avant-Garde, Experimental Art, Fiction, Literature (General).

The Fiction Works, Ray Hoy, 2070 SW Whiteside Drive, Corvallis, OR 97333, 541-730-2044, 541-738-2648, fictionworks@comcast.com, http://www.fictionworks.com. 1997. Fiction, non-fiction. ''We are closed to submissions until 2007 due to a long production queue.'' avg. press run 5000. Pub'd 25 titles 2005; expects 20 titles 2006, 25 titles 2007. Discounts: Bookstores: 30% (no minimum order)Distributors: 55% (no minimum order)Libraries: 20% (no minimum order). 245pp. Reporting time: One week (when we are open to submissions). Simultaneous submissions accepted: Yes. Publishes 5% of manuscripts submitted. Payment: 10% of the retail (or promotional) price paid by the customer. Does not copyright for author. Subjects: Audio/Video, Drama, Fantasy, Fiction, Horror, Mystery, Newsletter, Non-Fiction, Old West, Reference, Romance, Science Fiction, Supernatural, Textbooks, Young Adult.

FICTION WRITER'S GUIDELINE, Blythe Camenson, 2511 Schell Court NE, Albuquerque, NM 87106-2531, 505-352-9490, bcamenson@aol.com, www.fictionwriters.com. 1993. Articles, cartoons, interviews, reviews, news items, non-fiction. ''500-1000 word articles covering 'how-to' write fiction topics, interviews with agents, editors, and well-known authors. New markets for fiction. Recent contributors: Betty Wright, Stephanie Krulik, and Sara Goodman.'' circ. 1M. 6/yr. Pub'd 6 issues 2005; expects 6 issues 2006, 6 issues 2007. sub. price $48 (free to members of Fiction Writer's Connection); per copy $3.50; sample SASE/55¢. Back issues: $3.50. 8pp. Reporting time: 1 month. Simultaneous submissions accepted: yes. Publishes 70% of manuscripts submitted. Payment: $1-$25. Copyrighted, reverts to author. Pub's reviews: 5 in 2005. §Books on the craft and business of writing. Ads: $18 business card and run mimimum 3 issues. Subjects: Fiction, Writers/Writing.

THE FIDDLEHEAD, Ross Leckie, Managing Editor; Lynn Davies, Poetry Editor; M.A. Jarman, Fiction Editor, Campus House, PO Box 4400, University of New Brunswick, Fredericton, NB E3B 5A3, Canada, 506-453-3501. 1945. Poetry, fiction, art, reviews, parts-of-novels, long-poems, plays. circ. 1.1M. 4/yr. Pub'd 4 issues 2005; expects 4 issues 2006, 4 issues 2007. sub. price $20 Canada, U.S. $20US + $6 postage; per copy $8 Can.; sample $8 + postage Can. and US. Back issues: $5-8. Discounts: 10% on purchases of 10 copies or more; bookstores 33-1/3%. 128-200pp. Reporting time: 10-30 weeks, include SASE with Canadian stamp, IRC, or cash. Simultaneous submissions accepted: no. Publishes 1% of manuscripts submitted. Payment: $10 printed page. Copyrighted. Pub's reviews: 30-40 in 2005. §Canadian literature. Ads: $100/$52. Subjects: Literary Review, Poetry.

FIDDLER MAGAZINE, Mary E. Larsen, PO Box 101, N. Sydney, NS B2A 3M1, Canada, 650-948-4383. 1994. Articles, interviews, reviews, music, non-fiction. ''Recent Contributors: Jay Ungar, John Hartford, Lindajoy Fenley, Craig Mishler, Stacy Phillips.'' circ. 3M. 4/yr. Pub'd 4 issues 2005; expects 4 issues 2006, 4 issues 2007. sub. price $20; per copy $6; sample $6. Back issues: varies. 60+pp. Reporting time: 2 weeks to 1 month. Publishes 50% of manuscripts submitted. Payment: $10-200, depending on length & whether or not feature article. Copyrighted. Pub's reviews: 5 in 2005. §Music, must be related to fiddling. Ads: $300/$200/$110 1/4/$60 1/8/$45/50¢ per word classified. Subject: Music.

FIDELIS ET VERUS, Children Of Mary, Jack Law, PO Box 350333, Ft. Lauderdale, FL 33335-0333. 1985. News items. ''Traditional/Orthodox Roman Catholic items that are news plus doctrine (Catholic).'' circ. 2M. 6/yr. Pub'd 6 issues 2005; expects 6 issues 2006, 6 issues 2007. sub. price $10 for 10 issues; per copy $1; sample $1. Back issues: $1. Discounts: 10¢ per copy in bulk. 10pp. Reporting time: bi-monthly. Simultaneous submissions accepted: yes. Publishes 5% of manuscripts submitted. Payment: submit cost of article. Not copyrighted. Pub's reviews: 2 in 2005. §Only traditional Roman Catholic books/magazines. Ads: $100/$55/$10 per column inch (2 column page); columns 3-3/8 wide. Subjects: Birth, Birth Control, Population, Book Reviewing, Christianity, Communism, Marxism, Leninism, Electronics, Government, Magazines, Newsletter, Newspapers, Non-Fiction, Philosophy, Politics, Religion, Socialist, Textbooks.

FIELD: Contemporary Poetry and Poetics, Oberlin College Press, David Walker, Editor; David Young, Editor; Martha Collins, Editor-at-Large; Pamela Alexander, Associate Editor; DeSales Harrison, Associate Editor; Warren Liu, Associate Editor, 50 N. Professor St., Oberlin, OH 44074-1091, 440-775-8408, Fax 440-775-8124, oc.press@oberlin.edu. 1969. Poetry, long-poems. ''Also essays on poetry and translations of poetry.'' circ. 1.5M. 2/yr. Pub'd 2 issues 2005; expects 2 issues 2006, 2 issues 2007. sub. price $14, $24/2 years; per copy $7 ppd.; sample $7 ppd. Back issues: $12, all backs, except most recent year. Discounts: 40% bookstores (minimum order 5 copies), 15% subscription agencies. 100pp. Reporting time: 6-8 weeks. Simultaneous submissions accepted: no. Publishes .25%-.50% of manuscripts submitted. Payment: $15 per page. Copyrighted, reverts to author. Pub's reviews: 7 in 2005. §new books of contemporary poetry and poetry in translation. Ads: none. Subjects: Poetry, Translation.

Nicolin Fields Publishing, Inc., Linda Chestney, 861 Lafayette Rd Unit 2A, Hampton, NH 03842-1232, 603-758-6363, Fax 603-758-6366, nfp@rcn.com. 1994. Poetry, non-fiction. avg. press run 1.5-6M. Pub'd 5 titles 2005; expects 4 titles 2006, 3-4 titles 2007. Discounts: 40% retail stores (bike shops) and specialty stores, distributors 50-67%. 200pp. Reporting time: 1-2 months. Simultaneous submissions accepted: yes. Publishes 10% of manuscripts submitted. Payment: varies/standard. Copyrights for author. Subjects: Bicycling, Cooking, Health, Inspirational, New England, New Hampshire, Non-Fiction, Quotations, Self-Help, Sports, Outdoors.

Fieldstone Alliance, Vincent Hyman, 60 Plato Boulevard East, Suite 150, St. Paul, MN 55107, 800-274-6024, Fax 651-556-4517, books@fieldstonealliance.org, www.fieldstonealliance.org. 1990. Non-fiction. "Publishes practical, easy-to-use books for nonprofit organizations on topics such as nonprofit management, community building, and violence prevention." avg. press run 5M. Pub'd 5 titles 2005; expects 4 titles 2006, 4 titles 2007. 130pp. Payment: contact editor. Copyrights for author.

FIFTH ESTATE, Collective Staff, PO Box 201016, Ferndale, MI 48220-9016. 1965. Articles, photos, criticism, reviews, letters, non-fiction. "We don't encourage unsolicited mss." circ. 5,000. 4/yr. Pub'd 4 issues 2005; expects 4 issues 2006, 4 issues 2007. sub. price $10 domestic, $20 foreign, $20 institutions; per copy $3.00; sample free. Back issues: $4. Discounts: none. 32pp. Payment: none. Not copyrighted. Pub's reviews: 25 in 2005. §Ecology, politics, anarchism, feminism. Ads: not accepted. Subject: Politics.

•**5th Street Books,** Patricia Turner, Manager, 1691 Norris landing Drive, Suite A, Snellville, GA 30039-0028, 770-483-0431, www.5thstreetbooks.com. 2005. Fiction. avg. press run 5000. Expects 3 titles 2006, 5 titles 2007. Discounts: undecided. 200pp. Simultaneous submissions accepted: Yes. Publishes 5% of manuscripts submitted. Copyrights for author.

•**FIGHT THESE BASTARDS, Platonic 3way Press,** Oren Wagner, Co-Editor; Steve Henn, Co-editor; Don Winter, Co-editor, P.O. Box 844, Warsaw, IN 46581, 317-457-3505 email address for publication: evilgenius@platonic3waypress.com web site address: Platonic3WayPress.com. 2005. Poetry, fiction, art, criticism, reviews. "Mission and biases: We are looking for poetry of revolt, against the Academy, against the poetic mainstream. We are looking for poetry accessible beyond the ivory towers of academia and outside the bounds of religious or politically correct restrictions. We enjoy poetry that celebrates honesty and humor. We enjoy poetry with some bite to it. We enjoy poetry that claims to represent the interests, views, or tastes of the common person, particularly as distinct from those of the rich and powerful. Recent contributers: Linda McCarriston, Lyn Lifshin, Fred Voss, Gerald Locklin, Mike Kriesel, Robert L. Penick." circ. 250. 2/yr. Expects 1 issue 2006, 2 issues 2007. sub. price $10 for a 3-issue subscription; per copy $4; sample $4. Back issues: $4. No discounts. 35-40pp. Reporting time: 2 weeks to 2 months. Simultaneous submissions accepted: Yes. Publishes 2% of manuscripts submitted. Payment: 1 contributer's copy. Copyrighted, reverts to author. Pub's reviews: 3 in 2005. §books of poetry, chapbooks of poetry. Ads: queery for. Subjects: Abstracts, Alcohol, Alcoholism, Americana, Anarchist, Avant-Garde, Experimental Art, Criticism, Feminism, Gay, Homelessness, Post Modern, Satire, Sex, Sexuality, Worker.

Filibuster Press, Kyle Hannon, 5 Kim Ct., Elkhart, IN 46514-4009, 574-266-6622, publisher@filibuster-press.com, www.filibusterpress.com. 1994. Fiction. "We focus on self-reliant stories with libertarian themes and capitalist heros. Mid-western base." avg. press run 1M. Pub'd 1 title 2005; expects 1 title 2006, 1 title 2007. Discounts: 2-4 copies 35%, 5-9 40%, 10-24 45%, 25-99 50%. 270pp. Reporting time: 1-4 months. Simultaneous submissions accepted: yes. Publishes 10% of manuscripts submitted. Payment: varies. Copyrights for author. Subjects: Environment, Fiction, Politics.

The Film Instruction Company of America, Henry C. Landa, 5928 W. Michigan Street, Wauwatosa, WI 53213-4248, 414-258-6492. 1960. Non-fiction. "We seek manuscripts and do not accept unsolicited works." avg. press run 800-3M. Pub'd 1 title 2005; expects 2 titles 2006, 2 titles 2007. Discounts: 40% to retailers and brokers, 50% to true wholesalers. 150+pp. Simultaneous submissions accepted: no. Payment: 15%-25%. Copyrights for author. Subjects: Airplanes, Aviation, Energy, Politics, Solar.

FILM QUARTERLY, University of California Press, Ann Martin, University of California Press, 2000 Center Street, Suite 303, Berkeley, CA 94704-1223, 510-643-7154. 1945. Interviews, criticism, reviews. circ. 4550. 4/yr. Pub'd 4 issues 2005; expects 4 issues 2006, 4 issues 2007. sub. price $30 indiv., $120 instit. (+ $20 air freight), $30 student; per copy $8 indiv., $35 instit., $8 student; sample free. Back issues: same as single copy price. Discounts: foreign subs. agents 10%, 10+ one-time orders 30%, standing orders (bookstores): 1-99 40%, 100+ 50%. 64pp. Reporting time: 2-3 weeks. Payment: 2¢ per word. Copyrighted, does not revert to author. Pub's reviews: about 100 in 2005. §Film. Ads: $430/$315.

Film-Video Publications/Circus Source Publications, Alan Gadney, Editor, 7944 Capistrano Avenue, West Hills, CA 91304. 1974. "Current books are *Gadney's Guide to 1,800 International Contests, Festivals, and Grants in Film and Video, Photography, TV-Radio Broadcasting, Writing, Poetry, Playwriting and Journalism, Updated Address Edition* awarded 'Outstanding Reference Book of the Year' by the American Library Association (5-1/2 x 8-1/2, 610 pages, $15.95 for softbound, $23.95 for hardbound, plus $1.75 each postage & handling)." avg. press run 5M. Pub'd 2 titles 2005; expects 4 titles 2006, 8 titles 2007. Discounts: bookstores 1-5 assorted copies 20%, 6+ 40%; wholesale up to 55%. 300pp. Reporting time: 6 weeks. Payment: trade standard. Copyrights for author. Subjects: Arts, Awards, Foundations, Grants, Business & Economics, Electronics, Entertainment, Festivals, Media, Movies, Photography, Reference, Television.

FINANCIAL FOCUS, Jack W. Everett, 2140 Professional Drive Ste. 105, Roseville, CA 95661-3734, 916-791-1447, Fax 916-791-3444, jeverett@quiknet.com. 1980. Non-fiction. circ. 5M. 12/yr. Pub'd 12 issues

2005; expects 12 issues 2006, 12 issues 2007. sub. price $39.97; sample free. Discounts: call for info. 8pp. Reporting time: 1 month. Simultaneous submissions accepted: yes. Copyrighted, reverts to author. Pub's reviews: 1 in 2005. §Financial. Ads: none. Subject: Business & Economics.

FINE BOOKS & COLLECTIONS, Scott Brown, PO Box 106, Eureka, CA 95502, 707-443-9562, Fax 707-443-9572, scott@finebooksmagazine.com, www.finebooksmagazine.com. 2002. Articles, photos, cartoons, interviews, criticism, reviews, news items, non-fiction. ''We publish articles and essays related to book collecting. Recent contributors include Larry McMurtry, Paul Collins, Dana Gioia, Amy Stewart, and Roy Parvin.'' circ. 2.5M. 6/yr. Pub'd 6 issues 2005; expects 6 issues 2006, 6 issues 2007. sub. price $25. Discounts: standard trade. 76pp. Reporting time: 6 weeks. Simultaneous submissions accepted: yes. Publishes 10% of manuscripts submitted. Payment: $200-$600, depending on length and difficulty. Copyrighted, reverts to author. Pub's reviews: 20 in 2005. §Books and magazines about books, book arts, collecting. Ads: $400/$200. Subjects: Book Arts, Book Collecting, Bookselling.

Fine Edge Productions, Reanne Douglass, 13589 Clayton Lane, Anacortes, WA 98221-8477, 360-299-8500, Fax 360-299-0535, office@FineEdge.com. 1987. ''We publish outdoor guidebooks for nautical and bicycling; recreational topographical maps; some adventure/travel. Imprints: FineEdge.com and Mountain Biking Press.'' avg. press run 5M. Pub'd 7 titles 2005; expects 9-10 titles 2006. Discounts: 40% wholesalers. 98-500pp. Reporting time: 3-6 months. Publishes 3% of manuscripts submitted. Payment: varies according to title. We sometimes copyright for author. Subjects: Bicycling, Sports, Outdoors.

FINE MADNESS, Sean Bentley, John Malek, Anne Pitkin, Judith Skillman, David Edelman, Sherry Rind, PO Box 31138, Seattle, WA 98103-1138, www.finemadness.org, finemadness@comcast.net. 1982. Poetry, art, long-poems. ''Writers we have recently published include Albert Goldbarth, Caroline Knox, Peter Wild, Pattiann Rogers, and Melinda Mueller. We want to see evidence of minds at work. As T.S. Eliot wrote, '*The poet must become more and more comprehensive, more allusive, more indirect, in order to force, to dislocate if necessary, language into its meaning.*' We read email submissions only from poets outside the U.S. Postal submissions must include a SASE.'' circ. 800. 1/yr. Pub'd 1 issue 2005; expects 1 issue 2006, 2 issues 2007. sub. price $12USD/2 issues (U.S.); $14USD outside the U.S.; per copy $7USD (U.S.); $8USD outside U.S.; sample $4. Back issues: Volume 1 Number 1 $10. Discounts: 40% trade, libraries 2/$14; outside U.. 2/$14, 1/$8. 64pp. Reporting time: 4 months. Simultaneous submissions accepted: no. Publishes 5% of manuscripts submitted. Payment: none; we have annual contests, however. Copyrighted, reverts to author. Ads: none. Subjects: Absurdist, Arts, Avant-Garde, Experimental Art, Dada, Experimental, Humor, Literary Review, Literature (General), Pacific Northwest, Peace, Poetry, Reading, Satire, Translation, Writers/Writing.

Fine Tooth Press, JJ Sargent, PO Box 11512, Waterbury, CT 06703, kolchak@snet.net, http://www.finetoothpress.com. 2004. Poetry, fiction, criticism, parts-of-novels, non-fiction. ''Fine Tooth Press presents books by authors on the same page - perhaps at different corners and along the edges, but certainly off center! Our publications challenge genre specifications, erode boundaries and motivate readers to interact with texts that many times defy rational explanation or description. You wont find smarmy or meek prose here. These books are "in your face" and will stick with you for a very long time. We publish personal and intuitive poetry, bold speculative fiction with an edge, scholarly criticism with a hearty attitude, and more.'' avg. press run 500. Expects 8 titles 2006, 8 titles 2007. Retail discounts placed through publisher: 2-10 copies 20%, 11-24 copies 25%, 25+ copies 30%; Retail distribution via Ingram: 40-55%. 200pp. Reporting time: 2 months. Simultaneous submissions accepted: No. Publishes 25% of manuscripts submitted. Payment: 12-15%; no advance; bi-annual dispersement. We copyright for author by request. Subjects: Anarchist, Anthropology, Archaeology, Arts, Asian-American, Biography, Comics, Criticism, Ecology, Foods, English, Fiction, Humanism, Latin America, Lesbianism, Medieval, Men.

Fingerprint Press, Nathan Lewis Sr., PO Box 278075, Sacramento, CA 95827, 877-807-4509, info@fingerprintpress.com, www.fingerprintpress.com. 1998. Poetry, fiction, art, interviews, parts-of-novels, long-poems, non-fiction. ''We are an independent publishing company specializing in biography, memoir, inspirational fiction, real romance, and poetry.'' avg. press run 250-1000. Pub'd 2 titles 2005; expects 3 titles 2006, 3 titles 2007. Discounts: see website. 200pp. Reporting time: 3 weeks. Simultaneous submissions accepted: no. Publishes 10% of manuscripts submitted. Copyrights for author. Subjects: African-American, Autobiography, Black, California, Catholic, Christianity, Family, Inspirational, Memoirs, Parenting, Poetry, Religion, Sacramento.

Finishing Line Press, CJ Morrison, Founding Editor; Leah Maines, Senior Editor; Kevin Murphy Maines, Production and Graphic Design Editor; Beth Dungan, Editorial Assistant; Elizabeth Cordell, Production Assistant, PO Box 1626, Georgetown, KY 40324, 859-514-8966, finishingbooks@aol.com, www.finishingline-press.com. 1998. Poetry. ''Some of our titles have won book awards and have been included in anthologies—including the San Diego Book Award for Poetry, and (anthology) Billy Collins' 180 MORE.'' avg. press run 500. Expects 50 titles 2006, 75/82 titles 2007. Discounts: 40% to booksellers. 30pp. Reporting time: 3 months. Please don't call or email us every week to see what we have decided on your manuscript. We

161

need 3 months to decide and then we will send you a letter with our decision. If you have not heard from us after 3 months, then please contact us via email or letter. Simultaneous submissions accepted: yes. Publishes 4% of manuscripts submitted. Payment: 10% of press run in copies. Copyrights for author. Subject: Poetry.

Finney Company, Inc. (see also Anacus Press, An Imprint of Finney Company; Ecopress, An Imprint of Finney Company; Hobar Publications, A Division of Finney Company; Windward Publishing, An Imprint of Finney Company), Alan Krysan, President, 8075 215th Street West, Lakeville, MN 55044, (952) 469-6699, Fax: (952) 469-1968, (800)846-7027, Fax: (800) 330-6232, feedback@finney-hobar.com, www.finney-hobar.com. 1958. Non-fiction. "Finney Company continues to expand, covering such areas as career development and exploration, school-to-work, tech prep, placement, and on the job. We publish the Occupational Guidance Series and our most recent release is Planning My Career." avg. press run 5000. Pub'd 1 title 2005; expects 2-3 titles 2006, 2-3 titles 2007. Discounts: 1-9 copies 20%10-49 copies 40%50 or more copies 50 %. Reporting time: 8-10 weeks. Simultaneous submissions accepted: Yes. Payment: varies. Subjects: Careers, Consulting, Education, Employment, Interviews, Leadership, Management, Mentoring/Coaching, Motivation, Success, Networking, Non-Fiction, Speaking, Worker, Young Adult.

FIRE, Jeremy Hilton, Field Cottage, Old Whitehill, Tackley, Kidlington OXON OX5 3AB, United Kingdom. 1994. Poetry, fiction, art, long-poems, collages, concrete art. "Long poems welcome, but prose, especially fiction, should be *short*. Some bias towards experimental, alternative writing but not exclusively. Only minimal space for art/collage etc." circ. 250+. 3/yr. Pub'd 3 issues 2005; expects 3 issues 2006, 3 issues 2007. sub. price £7; per copy £4. Back issues: #1 £2, #2 £1, #4 £2, #5 £3. 150pp. Reporting time: 6-8 weeks. Simultaneous submissions accepted: yes. Payment: none. Not copyrighted.

The Fire!! Press, Thomas H. Wirth, 241 Hillside Road, Elizabeth, NJ 07208-1432, 908-289-3714 phone/Fax, fire.press@verizon.net. 1981. Poetry, fiction, art. "Not soliciting manuscripts at this time." avg. press run 2M. Discounts: 40%. Subjects: African-American, Black, Gay.

FIREBREEZE PUBLISHING, Helena Hanley, 11666 N. 28th. Dr. #255, Phoenix, AZ 85029-5625, 602-547-3946. 2005. Fiction, satire. "Ethnic/multicultural, regional, humor/satire, literary fiction dealing with communities and culture, Central/South American, Caribbean, African, African-American, Asian/Asian-American and other minorities. Well crafted narrative and dialogue important. Will accept submissions for poetry on a continual basis. No gimmicky writing, Horror, religious inspiration, science fiction, genre fiction, children, young adult, western, thematic specialties or pornographic material. Always looking for new material." circ. 300. Expects 2 issues 2006, 2 issues 2007. Discounts: 2-10 copies 20%. 32-48pp. Reporting time: 2 months. Simultaneous submissions accepted: No. Publishes 5% of manuscripts submitted. Payment: Pays one contributors copy; additional copies by negotiations. Not copyrighted. Subjects: African Literature, Africa, African Studies, African-American, Asia, Indochina, Asian-American, Caribbean, Chicano/a, China, Cuba, Fiction, Latin America, South America.

firefall editions, Robinson Joyce Jr., 3213 Arundel Ave., Alexandria, VA 22306, 5105492461, www.firefallmedia.com. 1974. Art, photos, music, long-poems. "To create the visual novel, realistically imaged, without cartoons: to create a new american idiom: to be the penthouse of the imagination." avg. press run 5000. Pub'd 3 titles 2005; expects 5 titles 2006, 7 titles 2007. Discounts: distributors - 50%; educational - 25%. 200pp. Reporting time: 3 months or more. Simultaneous submissions accepted: No. Publishes 3% of manuscripts submitted. Payment: 50-50 split on net revenue. Copyrights for author. Subjects: Americana, Calligraphy, Cults, Medicine, New Mexico, Photography, Robotics, San Francisco, Science, U.S.S.R., Wyoming.

THE FIREFLY (A Tiny Glow In a Forest of Darkness), Jane Kirby, Jon Lurie, 211 7th Street East #503, Saint Paul, MN 55101-2390. 1990. Poetry, fiction, articles, art, photos, cartoons, interviews, satire, criticism, reviews, music, letters, parts-of-novels, long-poems, collages, news items, non-fiction. "Submissions should be limited to 1500 words. We want to recieve letters, articles, poetry, B&W artwork, from people interested in revolutionary change. This revolutionary change focusing on children, families and communities. We seek information on obtaining and using technology for the good of humankind and the Earth. We seek stories of injustices done to Americans by other Americans and the government." circ. 500. 4/yr. Pub'd 6 issues 2005; expects 2 issues 2006, 4 issues 2007. sub. price $10/6 issues; per copy $1+stamp; sample $1+stamp. Back issues: $1 if available, $5 if we must reprint. Discounts: Free to prisoners and AFDC families, trades encouraged. 8-12pp. Reporting time: 30-60 days. Simultaneous submissions accepted: yes. Publishes less than 50% of manuscripts submitted. Payment: free copies for family and friends. Not copyrighted. Pub's reviews: 1 in 2005. §Politics, history, children's history, Afro-American history, Native American history, women's issues, revolutionary parenting and community life. Ads: please inquire.

Firelight Publishing, Inc., Mark Anderson, Box 444, Sublimity, OR 97385-0444, 503-767-0444, Fax 503-769-8950, editor@firelightpublishing.com, www.firelightpublishing.com. 2001. Fiction, non-fiction. "Recent publications include Bone Walk: The Journey of Thomas Shepard (medieval fantasy) and The

Economic Gang: One Man's Battle Against Japan, Inc. (biography/business). Forthcoming books include Tribunal (medical thriller) and the second volume of the Bone Walk trilogy. We are a small press so while we are very open to new authors, we also have very high standards. Any submissions should meet our criteria of "Simply Enjoyable Books" (tm): books that a person can get lost in, unforgettable characters, intriguing plots—books that a person would love to curl up with in front of a crackling fire. *Always* query - it's unprofessional not to do so. Don't be afraid to submit, we don't bite.'' avg. press run 3M. Pub'd 2 titles 2005; expects 2 titles 2006, 3 titles 2007. Discounts: 40-45% retailers, 55% wholesalers. 350pp. Reporting time: 6 - 8 weeks. Simultaneous submissions accepted: Yes but please indicate that it's a simultaneous submission. To not do so is rude and we'll curse you for all eternity. Publishes 5% of manuscripts submitted. Payment: varies. Copyrights for author. Subjects: Consulting, Creativity, Editing, Fantasy, Fiction, Folklore, Humor, Literature (General), Mystery, Myth, Mythology, Novels, Oregon, Pacific Northwest, Science Fiction, The West.

Fireweed Press, PO Box 75418, Fairbanks, AK 99707-2136, 907-452-5070 or 907-488-5079. 1976. ''Publishes anthologies and prize-winning works by contemporary Alaskan authors. Submissions accepted only for projects in progress; no unsolicited manuscripts read. 1983: ''Hunger and Dreams, The Alaskan Women's Anthology'', 22 contributors including Sheila Nickerson, Mary TallMountain, Donna Mack, Jean Anderson; edited by Pat Monaghan. 1984: ''A Good Crew'' Anthology of men's writings about relationships in the north, edited by Larry Laraby and Roland Wulbert; ''The Compass Inside Ourselves'' by Nany Lord, winning short-story collection chosen by Stanley Elkin.'' avg. press run 1M. Discounts: 40% to bookstores, orders of 5 or more. 130pp. Reporting time: 1 month. Payment: varies. Copyrights for author. Subject: Alaska.

First Books, Jeremy Solomon, President, 6750 SW Franklin, # A, Portland, OR 97223-2542, 503,968,6777. 1988. Poetry, fiction, non-fiction. Discounts: 50%. Simultaneous submissions accepted: No. Subjects: Animals, Arts, Cooking, Fiction, Humor, Mathematics, Memoirs, Moving/Relocation, Non-Fiction, Novels, Parenting, Poetry, Real Estate, Weddings, Young Adult.

FIRST CLASS, Four-Sep Publications, Christopher M., PO Box 86, Friendship, IN 47021, christopherm@four-sep.com, www.four-sep.com. 1996. Poetry, fiction, photos, long-poems, plays. ''Prefer short fiction. Cover letter preferred. Desires good, thought-provoking, graphic, uncommon pieces. Recent: John Bennett, Gerald Locklin, Errol Miller, Greg Fitzsimmons, Alan Catlin, B.Z. Niditch.'' circ. 200-400. 2/yr. Pub'd 3 issues 2005; expects 3 issues 2006, 2 issues 2007. sub. price $11/2 issues; per copy $6 ppd.; sample $1 sampler, $6 issue. Back issues: inquire. Discounts: inquire, offer, selective trades, 60-40 for distributors. 60pp. Reporting time: 1 week initial response, 5 months accept./reject. Simultaneous submissions accepted: yes. Publishes 10-15% of manuscripts submitted. Payment: 1 copy. Copyrighted, reverts to author. Pub's reviews: 100 in 2005. §Short fiction and non-traditional poetics. Ads: inquire. Subjects: Absurdist, Counter-Culture, Alternatives, Communes, Literature (General), Poetry, Post Modern.

FIRST INTENSITY, First Intensity Press, Lee Chapman, PO Box 665, Lawrence, KS 66044-0665, e-mail leechapman@aol.com. 1993. Poetry, fiction, art, photos, parts-of-novels. ''Short stories: no more than 15 mss. pages (double-spaced). Poetry: no book-length mss. Recent contributors: Gustaf Sobin, Paul West, John Taggart, Nathaniel Tarn, Theodore Enslin, Barry Gifford, Kenneth Irby, Diane diPrima, John Yau, Duncan McNaughton, Etel Adnan, Carol Moldaw, Maxine Chernoff, Phillip Foss.'' circ. 300. 1/yr. Pub'd 1 issue 2005; expects 1 issue 2006, 1 issue 2007. sub. price $28; per copy $14; sample $7. Back issues: $7. 200pp. Reporting time: 3 months. Simultaneous submissions accepted: no. Payment: 1 copy. Copyrighted, reverts to author. Pub's reviews. Ads: full page $150. Subjects: Fiction, Poetry, Short Stories.

First Intensity Press (see also FIRST INTENSITY), Lee Chapman, PO Box 665, Lawrence, KS 66044, e-mail leechapman@aol.com. 1993. ''Do not accept unsolicited book mss.'' avg. press run 300. Pub'd 2 titles 2005. 40-70pp.

THE FIRST LINE, Blue Cubicle Press, David LaBounty, Jeff Adams, PO Box 250382, Plano, TX 75025-0382, 972-824-0646, submission@thefirstline.com, www.thefirstline.com. 1999. Fiction, non-fiction. ''Word Limit: 300-3,000. Fiction: General, but must begin with the first line provided on website. Nonfiction: Essays about books with interesting/memorable first lines.'' circ. 500. 4/yr. Pub'd 4 issues 2005; expects 4 issues 2006, 4 issues 2007. sub. price $10; per copy $3.50; sample $3.50. Back issues: $4. 60pp. Reporting time: 6 weeks. Simultaneous submissions accepted: yes. Publishes 25% of manuscripts submitted. Payment: $20 for fiction, $10 for essay. Copyrighted, negotiable. Subject: Literature (General).

FIRSTHAND, Don Dooley, Editor, PO Box 1314, Teaneck, NJ 07666, 201-836-9177. 1980. Fiction, articles, art, photos, cartoons, reviews, letters, parts-of-novels, news items, non-fiction. ''Must appeal to a male homosexual audience.'' circ. 60M. 13/yr. Pub'd 13 issues 2005; expects 13 issues 2006, 13 issues 2007. sub. price $47.97; per copy $4.99; sample $5. Back issues: $5. 132pp. Reporting time: 4-6 weeks. Simultaneous submissions accepted: no. Publishes 10% of manuscripts submitted. Payment: $150 for 10-20 pages typed double-spaced. Copyrighted, rights reverting to author can be discussed. Pub's reviews: 39 in 2005. §Homosexual-related items. Ads: $600/$300/no classified. Subjects: Gay, Men.

FISH DRUM MAGAZINE, Suzi Winson, PO Box 966, Murray Hill Station, New York, NY 10156, www.fishdrum.com. 1988. Poetry, fiction, articles, art, photos, cartoons, interviews, criticism, reviews, music, letters, long-poems, collages, non-fiction. "*Fish Drum* prefers West Coast poetry, the exuberant 'continuous nerve movie' that follows the working of the mind and has a relationship to the world and the reader. Philip Whalen's work, for example, and much of *Calafia, The California Poetry*, edited by Ishmael Reed. Also magical-tribal-incantatory poems, exemplified by the future/primitive *Technicians of the Sacred*, ed. Rothenberg. *Fish Drum* has a soft spot for schmoozy, emotional, imagistic stuff. Literate, personal material that sings and surprises, OK? We've published poetry by Philip Whalen, Ira Cohen, Miriam Sagan, Leslie Scalapino, Alice Notley, John Brandi, Joanne Kyger and Leo Romero, all of whom have books around worth finding and reading. We're looking for New Mexico authors, also prose: fiction, essays, what-have-you, and artwork, scores, cartoons, etc. - just send it along, with SASE. *Fish Drum* is being produced in memory of and to honor Robert Winson (April 28, 1959 - October 20, 1995) the founder, editor and publisher." circ. 2M. 1-2/yr. Pub'd 2 issues 2005; expects 2 issues 2006, 2 issues 2007. sub. price $24/4 issues; sample $6. Discounts: 40%. 80pp. Reporting time: 2-6 months. Simultaneous submissions accepted: no. Publishes 2-5% of manuscripts submitted. Payment: 2 or more copies. Copyrighted, reverts to author. Pub's reviews: 4 in 2005. §mostly Poetry, sometimes fiction, natural history, or Zen. Ads: exchange only. Subjects: Animals, Comics, Fiction, Literature (General), Poetry, Religion, Science Fiction, Southwest, Tapes & Records, Visual Arts, Zen.

FISH PISS, Box 1232, Place d'Armes, Montreal, QB H2Y 3K2, Canada. 1996. "Postal Code (equivalent of Zip Code in U.S., absolutely necessary for mailing!): H2Y 3K2." circ. 3000. Irregular, about 2x per year. sample price $4.00 (US except when ordered from Canada) plus $3.00 postage (worldwide). 148pp. Publishes 50% of manuscripts submitted. Pub's reviews: 25 in 2005. §Comics, graphic novels, zines, essays. Ads: Full page, $250.00. Half page, $140.00. Quarter page, $75.00.

Fithian Press, John Daniel, Editor, PO Box 2790, McKinleyville, CA 95519-2790, 805-962-1780, Fax 805-962-8835, dandd@danielpublishing.com. 1985. Poetry, fiction, non-fiction. "We are open to anything but we specialize in memoir, fiction, poetry, and social issures. In addition to our general catalogue we issue annual catalogs in California and World War II books." avg. press run 1M. Pub'd 20 titles 2005; expects 20 titles 2006, 20 titles 2007. Discounts: trade 1-4 20%, 5+ 47%; wholesale 1-9 20%, 10+ 50%; library 20%. 160pp. Reporting time: 6-8 weeks. Simultaneous submissions accepted: yes. Publishes 5% of manuscripts submitted. Payment: author pays production costs and receives 60% net royalty. Copyrights for author. Subjects: Fiction, Literature (General), Memoirs, Novels, Poetry, Short Stories.

Fitness Press, Phyllis Rogers, P O Box 4912, Marietta, GA 30061, 770-578-8207; Fax 770-973-2154. 2000. Non-fiction. "Mission is to publish health and fitness information for older adults." avg. press run 3000. Expects 1 title 2006, 1 title 2007. Discounts: 1-2 books no discount 3-4—20% off 5-9—30% off 10-199—40% off 200-499—50% off 500+ - 55% off. 150pp. Reporting time: 30 days. Simultaneous submissions accepted: Yes. Publishes 1% of manuscripts submitted. Payment: TBD. Copyrights for author. Subjects: Aging, Alternative Medicine, Health, How-To, Senior Citizens.

Five Bucks Press (see also RAGMAG DIGEST), J.D. Scheneman, PO Box 31, Stacyville, IA 50476-0031, 641-710-9953, fivebuckspress@omnitelcom.com, www.fivebuckspress.com. "See website for writer guidelines and deadlines for various publication opportunities or request details by snail mail, include #10 SASE for reply."

580 SPLIT, Erika Staiti, Mills College, P.O. Box 9982, Oakland, CA 94613-0982. 1999. Poetry, fiction, art, photos, cartoons, music, parts-of-novels, long-poems, collages, plays, non-fiction. "Not far from our office at Mills College in Oakland, California, the 580 Split is a risky jumble of ramps, overpasses, and interchanges, where highways cross, merge, intersect, and branch out in every direction. 580 Split, an annual journal of arts and literature, is both the convergence and divergence of many roads: a place of risk and possibility. We publish innovative prose and poetry and are open to well-crafted experimental approaches. Recent contributors have included Bruce Andrews, Mary Burger, Edwin Torres. Featured interview with William T. Volmann. Please see our website for complete list of contributors, submission guidelines, contact information, and contest guidelines." circ. 650. 1/yr. Pub'd 1 issue 2005; expects 1 issue 2006, 1 issue 2007. sub. price 7.50; per copy 7.50; sample 7.50. Back issues: inquire. Discounts: Beginning in 2005, we will offer subscription rates to institutions, bookstores, and other retailers. Inquire via email. 120pp. Reporting time: 4-6 months. Simultaneous submissions accepted: Yes. Publishes 2% of manuscripts submitted. Payment: 2 contributor copies. Copyrighted, reverts to author. §Innovative and experimental prose, poetry, and art. We do not accept advertising for the journal; however, we are interested in link swaps for our website. Subjects: Arts, Experimental, Fiction, Journals, Photography, Poetry.

Five Fingers Press (see also FIVE FINGERS REVIEW), Jaime Robles, PO Box 4, San Leandro, CA 94577-0100. 1984. Fiction, interviews, non-fiction. avg. press run 1M. Pub'd 1 title 2005; expects 1 title 2006, 1 title 2007. Discounts: subs. $16/2 issues, 40% consignment; 50% outright sale. 200pp. Reporting time: 3-5 months. Payment: 2 copies of magazine, cash payment depends upon funding. Does not copyright for author.

Subjects: Avant-Garde, Experimental Art, Culture, Essays, Fiction, Literary Review, Multicultural, Poetry, Short Stories, Translation.

FIVE FINGERS REVIEW, Five Fingers Press, Jaime Robles, PO Box 4, San Leandro, CA 94577-0100. 1984. Poetry, fiction, interviews, non-fiction. *"Five Fingers Review* seeks to publish fresh, innovative writing and artwork that is not necessarily defined by the currently 'correct' aesthetic or ideology. *Five Fingers Review* welcomes work that crosses or falls between genres. In addition to new fiction and poetry, *Five Fingers Review* presents essays, interviews, and translations. Past published writers include Norman Fischer, Peter Gizzi, Lyn Hejinian, Fanny Howe, Jaime Robles, Keith Waldrop, Rosmarie Waldrop. Each issue explores a theme; 2006 theme is: Foreign Lands and Alternate Universes. We have an annual contest as well. More information may be found at www.fivefingersreview.org." circ. 1M. 1/yr. Pub'd 1 issue 2005; expects 1 issue 2006, 1 issue 2007. sub. price $18/2 issues; sample $7.00. 224pp. Reporting time: We read from June 1 to August 30. Decisions are mailed in January. Submissions are returned outside of reading submission period. Annual contest deadline is June 1. Simultaneous submissions accepted: yes. Payment: 2 copies, cash payment depends upon funding. Copyrighted, reverts to author. Pub's reviews. Ads: $125 (4-1/2 X 7-1/2)/$75 (4-1/2 X 3-1/2)/$50 1/4 page (2 X 3). Subjects: Avant-Garde, Experimental Art, Culture, Essays, Fiction, Literary Review, Multicultural, Poetry, Short Stories, Translation.

FIVE POINTS, David Bottoms, Editor; Megan Sexton, Executive Editor, P.O. Box 3999, Georgia State University, Atlanta, GA 30302-3999, 404-463-9484, Fax 404-651-3167. 1996. Poetry, fiction, art, photos, interviews, parts-of-novels, long-poems, non-fiction. "Recent contributors:Ann Beattie, Philip Levine, Naomi Shihab Nye, Peter Davison, Phillip Booth, Rick Bass, and Tess Gallagher." circ. 6M. 3/yr. Pub'd 3 issues 2005; expects 3 issues 2006, 3 issues 2007. sub. price $20; per copy $8; sample $6. Back issues: $6. Discounts: classroom. 170pp. Reporting time: 3-4 months. Simultaneous submissions accepted: no. Payment: $50 per poem, $15 per prose page. Copyrighted, reverts to author. Ads: $200/$100/$50 1/4 page. Subjects: Arts, Fiction, Interviews, Non-Fiction, Poetry.

FIVE WILLOWS MAGAZINE, Koon Woon, 202 6th Avenue South #1105, Seattle, WA 98104-2303, 202-682-3851. 2004. Poetry. circ. 300. 4/yr. Expects 2 issues 2006, 4 issues 2007. sub. price $20; per copy $5; sample $4. Back issues: none. Discounts: inquire. 44pp. Reporting time: 2 weeks. Simultaneous submissions accepted: no. Publishes 10% of manuscripts submitted. Payment: copy. Copyrighted, reverts to author. Ads: $100/$50. Subjects: Asian-American, Poetry.

5:AM, Box 205, Spring Church, PA 15686.

FLASH!POINT, Frances LeMoine, PO Box 540, Merrimack, NH 03054-0540, flashpointlit@yahoo.com. 1998. Poetry, fiction, articles, art, photos, long-poems, plays. "Recent contributors: RD Armstrong, Edward Boccia, B.Z. Niditch, Doug Holder, Corey Mesler, Judith Henschmeyer, Doug Paugh. Send best." circ. 500. 3/yr. Pub'd 2 issues 2005; expects 3 issues 2006, 4 issues 2007. sub. price $30; per copy $10; sample $6. Back issues: $6. Discounts: classroom. 100pp. Reporting time: 5 days to 1 year. We accept simultaneous submissions if noted. Publishes 5% of manuscripts submitted. Payment: 1 copy. Copyrighted, reverts to author. Pub's reviews: 2 in 2005. §Poetry, short fiction collections. Ads: none.

Floating Bridge Press, Peter Pereira, Kathleen Flenniken, Jeff Crandall, Ted McMahon, Ron Starr, John Pierce, Susan Rich, C/O Richard Hugo House, 1634 - 11th Avenue, Seattle, WA 98122, www.scn.org/arts/floatingbridge; email floatingbridgepress@yahoo.com. 1994. Poetry. "We publish at least 1 poetry chapbook and 1 poetry anthology per year, from manuscripts submitted to our annual competition. We are committed to producing a high-quality book, printed on acid-free, archival-quality paper, with cardstock cover and engaging cover art. We also produce a local reading for the winning poet(s). Send SASE for guidelines; $10.00 ppd. for sample book. We have a variety of tastes, but tend to prefer manuscripts that hold together thematically as a collection. We sometimes publish broadsides, and recently produced an audio CD." avg. press run 200-400 chapbook; 500-1000 anthology. Pub'd 2 titles 2005; expects 3 titles 2006, 2 titles 2007. Discounts: bookstores and libraries 40%. Chapbooks 24-32pp, anthologies 80-150pppp. Reporting time: 3-6 months. Simultaneous submissions accepted: yes. Payment: honorarium plus copies. Copyrights for author. Subject: Poetry.

Floreant Press, Barbara Baer, 6195 Anderson Rd, Forestville, CA 95436, 7078877868. 1995. Poetry, fiction, non-fiction. "First two books were collections of regional women's writing from northern California of an environmental shade but not programmatic. Fiction, essays, poetry, artwork included. Third book, a volume of poetry by Fionna Perkins, also from the north coast of California. Fourth book, another collection with theme of tea, with color photographs. Fifth book this year: collection of travel essays by Maxine Rose Schur with illustrations. Sixth book will be collection of essays on pomegranates translated from Russian by Grigory Levin." avg. press run 3000. Expects 1 title 2006, 1 title 2007. Discounts: 2-10 copies 25%. 250pp. Reporting time: Does not accept unsolicited manuscripts. Publishes only when material or author intrigues the publisher. Simultaneous submissions accepted: No. Publishes 0% of manuscripts submitted. Payment: Varies—if it's a collection, a small honorarium; single authors receive more. Copyrights for author. Subjects: Fiction, Travel,

The West, Women.

•Floreant Press, Barbara Baer ms, 6195 Anderson Rd, Forestville, CA 95436, 707 887 7868. 1995. Fiction, non-fiction. "Collections of regional (north coast of California) women's writing; travel; memoir." avg. press run 3000. Pub'd 1 title 2005; expects 1 title 2006. 200pp. Reporting time: only solicited manuscripts read; all others returned if SASE enclosed. Simultaneous submissions accepted: No. Publishes 1% of manuscripts submitted. Copyrights for author.

Florida Academic Press, Max Vargas, PO Box 540, Gainesville, FL 32602-0540, 352-332-5104, Fax 352-331-6003, FAPress@gmail.com, web: www.FloridaAcademicPress.com. 1997. "Non-fiction: scholarly and how-to; Africa; Middle East; politics and history." avg. press run 2M. Pub'd 3 titles 2005; expects 1 title 2006, 2 titles 2007. Discounts: 20% to distributers; bookstores to 3 20% on STOPS, 4+ 40%. 300pp. Reporting time: 2-3 months if submission meets specifications, 1 week if it doesn't. Simultaneous submissions accepted: no. Publishes 5-10% of manuscripts submitted. Payment: end of year 8% paperback/hardcover. Copyrights for author. Subjects: African Literature, Africa, African Studies, Asia, Indochina, Government, History, Judaism, Middle East, Non-Fiction, Political Science, Third World, Minorities.

THE FLORIDA REVIEW, Jeanne Leiby, Editor, English Department, University of Central Florida, Orlando, FL 32816-1346, 407-823-2038. 1972. Poetry, fiction, art, cartoons, reviews, parts-of-novels, long-poems, non-fiction. "We look for fiction (up to 7,500 words) and poetry (any length). We are especially interested in new writers. We publish fiction of high quality—stories that delight, instruct, and aren't afraid to take risks, and we welcome experimental fiction, so long as it doesn't make us feel lost or stupid. Also, we look for clear, strong poems—poems filled with real things, real people, real emotions, poems that might conceivably advance our knowledge of the human heart. Some of our recent contributors include Billy Collins, David Huddle, Dionisio Martinez, Wendell Mayo, Judy Copeland, and Fleda Brown." circ. 1,500. 2/yr. Pub'd 2 issues 2005; expects 2 issues 2006, 2 issues 2007. sub. price $15; per copy $8; sample $8. Back issues: $5. Discounts: Please inquire. 160pp. Reporting time: 15 weeks. Simultaneous submissions accepted: yes. Publishes 2% of manuscripts submitted. Payment: occasional honoraria; 2 copies. Copyrighted, reverts to author. Pub's reviews: 6 in 2005. §Fiction, poetry, and nonfiction books and collections from small press publishers (such as Sarabande, Livingston Press, etc.). Subjects: Experimental, Fiction, Literary Review, Literature (General), Non-Fiction, Poetry, Prose, Reviews, Short Stories, Travel, Writers/Writing.

Flowerfield Enterprises, LLC, Nancy Essex, 10332 Shaver Road, Kalamazoo, MI 49024, 269-327-0108, www.wormwoman.com. 1976. "Flowerfield Enteprises continues to celebrate the energizing power of self-sufficiency by publishing books and videos which help people regain control over their own lives. Major focus is on composting organic wastes with earthworms (*Worms Eat My Garbage* has sold over 180,000 copies to date). *Worms Eat Our Garbage: Classroom Activities for a Better Environment* uses earthworms in a non-invasive manner to teach interested learners science, math, writing and other disciplines. *The Worm Cafe: Mid-Scale vermicomposting of Lunchroom Wastes* describes larger-scale recycling of food wastes in schools." avg. press run 10M. Pub'd 1 title 2005; expects 2 titles 2007. Discounts: 1-9 copies 20%, 10+ 40%. 150pp. Payment: royalties negotiated. Copyrights for author. Subjects: Animals, Audio/Video, Biology, Children, Youth, Disease, Earth, Natural History, Ecology, Foods, Education, Health, How-To, Medicine, Science, Young Adult.

FLUENT ASCENSION, Warren Norgaard, c/o FIERCE Concepts, PO Box 6407, Glendale, AZ 85312, submissions@fluentascension.com, www.fluentascension.com. 2002. Poetry, fiction, articles, art, photos, satire, criticism, reviews, music, letters, parts-of-novels, long-poems, collages, non-fiction. "We look for new innovative work in all genres from new, as well as established, writers, artists, poets, and photographers. If unsure about 'appropriateness' please query. Please note that while we do accept simultaneous submissions, we will not consider previously published material." 2/yr. Pub'd 2 issues 2005; expects 2 issues 2006, 2 issues 2007. sub. price free. Back issues: Back Issues Available on CD-ROM for $5 each, which includes all back issues. Pages vary. Reporting time: 2-4 months. Simultaneous submissions accepted: yes. Payment: none. Copyrighted, reverts to author. Pub's reviews: 2 in 2005. §Poetry, innovative fiction, art, satire, essay, nonfiction. Ads: varies, please contact for information. Subjects: Arts, Avant-Garde, Experimental Art, Bilingual, Buddhism, Essays, Fiction, Gay, Journals, Non-Fiction, Poetry, Prose, Satire, Sex, Sexuality, Short Stories, Visual Arts.

Flume Press, Casey Huff, California State University, Chico, 400 W. First Street, Chico, CA 95929-0830, 530-898-5983. 1984. Poetry, fiction. "We are a small not-for-profit press devoted to publishing the work of newer poets and fiction writers. We are interested in poetry with clear, strong images, a freshness, and an ability to excite in us a definite and strong reaction. We have few biases about form, although we do appreciate writing that shows craft and control in its form. We are interested in serious literary fiction, contemporary work that is well-crafted and emotionally engaging. Chapbooks are chosen from an annual competition—poetry in even years, fiction in odd years. Prize: $500 and 25 copies. Fee: $20 (each entrant receives a copy of winning chapbook). Deadline: Dec. 1. See our Website (www.csuchico.edu/engl/flumepress) for more details." avg.

press run 500. Pub'd 1 title 2005; expects 1 title 2006, 1 title 2007. Discounts: 2-9 20%, 10-19 30%, 20+ 40%. 32-40pp. Reporting time: 16 weeks. Simultaneous submissions accepted: yes. Publishes 1% of manuscripts submitted. Payment: $500 + 25 copies. Does not copyright for author. Subjects: Fiction, Poetry, Short Stories.

Flying Pencil Publications, Madelynne Diness Sheehan, 33126 SW Callahan Road, Scappoose, OR 97056, 503-543-7171, fax: 503-543-7172. 1983. Non-fiction. "Fishing is our subject-specialty. New edition of *Fishing in Oregon* now out." avg. press run 5M. Pub'd 1 title 2005; expects 1 title 2006, 1 title 2007. Discounts: 40% to retailers, 55% to distributors. 365pp. Reporting time: 30 days. Simultaneous submissions accepted: yes. Payment: variable. Copyrights for author. Subjects: Oregon, Pacific Northwest, Sports, Outdoors, The West.

FLYWAY, Stephen Pett, 206 Ross Hall, Iowa State University, Ames, IA 50011, 515-294-8273, FAX 515-294-6814, flyway@iastate.edu. 1995. Poetry, fiction, non-fiction. "*Flyway* is open to a range of poetry, fiction, and nonfiction. Recent contributors include Jane Smiley, Madison Smartt Bell, Ted Kooser, Neal Bowers, William Trowbridge, Ray A. Young Bear, Mary Swander, and Michael Martone. Reads submissions from September 15 to May 1." circ. 600. 3/yr. Pub'd 3 issues 2005; expects 3 issues 2006, 3 issues 2007. sub. price $18; per copy $8; sample $8. Back issues: $8. 120pp. Reporting time: 4 weeks to 2 months. Simultaneous submissions accepted: no. Publishes 1-2% of manuscripts submitted. Payment: 2 copies free, additional copies at cost. Copyrighted, reverts to author. Pub's reviews: 2 in 2005. §Poetry, fiction, literary, non-fiction. Ads: exchange. Subjects: Fiction, Non-Fiction, Poetry.

•FMA Publishing, Donna Ann Marshall, 1920 Pacific Ave, #16152, Long Beach, CA 90746, (T)310-438-3483, (F)310-438-3486, (E)info@fmapublishing.com, www.fmapublishing.com. 2002. Poetry, fiction, non-fiction. "Our Mission is to introduce books that promote positive change, self and educational awareness, compassion, effective discipline and a commitment to the betterment of self through the understanding that change starts with a solid foundation centered in God. Our Vision is to layout a foundation through our books for growth and development, inspiration and too discover that salvation comes from Jesus Christ and that walking daily in the power of God through the Holy Spirit will effectively change lives." avg. press run 2000. Pub'd 1 title 2005; expects 1 title 2006, 4 titles 2007. Discounts: 1-100 copies 50%101-Above copies 55%. 192pp. Reporting time: 4-6 weeks. Simultaneous submissions accepted: No. Payment: Varies. Copyrights for author. Subjects: Crime, Fiction, Mystery, Non-Fiction, Self-Help, Women.

Focus Publications, Inc., Jan Haley, Barbara Smith, PO Box 609, Bemidji, MN 56601, 218-751-2183; focus@paulbunyan.net. 1994. Fiction, non-fiction. "Publications are primarily Christian (religion) and children. *No unsolicited manuscripts; send proposal.*" avg. press run 1M-10M. Pub'd 1 title 2005; expects 3-4 titles 2006, 3 titles 2007. Discounts: 40-50%. 150pp. Reporting time: 60 days. Simultaneous submissions accepted: no. Payment: 7.5%. Copyrights for author. Subjects: AIDS, Aviation, Children, Youth, Health, Religion, Women.

Focus Publishing/R. Pullins Co., Ron Pullins, PO Box 369, Newburyport, MA 01950, 800-848-7236, Fax 978-462-9035, pullins@pullins.com, www.pullins.com. 1987. Non-fiction. "Focus Publishing is a small, independent college and high school textbook publisher in the Classics, Philosophy, Political Science, Public Administration and Modern Languages. We accept proposals and finished manuscripts of any length in these areas of study by reputable scholars, professors and instructors." avg. press run 2M. Pub'd 12 titles 2005; expects 25 titles 2006, 25+ titles 2007. Discounts: textbook plan, library wholesaler and distributors plan, trade stores and agency plan, trade megastores, distributor and web giant plan. 200pp. Reporting time: 1 month. Simultaneous submissions accepted: yes. Publishes 20% of manuscripts submitted. Payment: negotiable. Copyrights for author. Subjects: Classical Studies, Greek, Horticulture, Language, Myth, Mythology, Non-Fiction, Philosophy, Political Science, Textbooks, Translation.

FOLIO: A Literary Journal of American University, Editors change yearly, Dept. of Literature, American University, Washington, DC 20016, NO PHONE CALLS PLEASE, folio_editors@yahoo.com, www.foliojournal.org. 1984. Poetry, fiction, photos, interviews, parts-of-novels, non-fiction. "Recent contributors include: E. Ethelbert Miller, Nathalie Handal, Henry Taylor, Maureen Seaton, Amy Bloom as well as new writers. Quality fiction, poetry, translations, essays, and photography. Please limit poetry submissions to batches of five; prose to 2,500 words. We read from September 1 to March 1." circ. 500. 2/yr. Pub'd 2 issues 2005; expects 2 issues 2006, 2 issues 2007. sub. price $12; per copy $6 (includes postage); sample $6. Back issues: $6. 64pp. Reporting time: 3-5 months. Simultaneous submissions accepted: yes. Publishes 4% of manuscripts submitted. Payment: 2 contributors copies. Copyrighted, reverts to author. Ads: Limited ad exchanges with other journals only. Subjects: Essays, Fiction, Interviews, Literature (General), Non-Fiction, Photography, Poetry, Prose, Short Stories, Translation, Visual Arts, Washington, D.C.

FOLK ART MESSENGER, Ann Oppenhimer, PO Box 17041, Richmond, VA 23226, 804-285-4532, 1-800-527-3655, fasa@folkart.org. 1987. Articles, art, photos, interviews, criticism, reviews, news items. "2,000 words or less. Subject: contemporary folk art. Rarely select unsolicited manuscripts. Contributors: Minhazz Majumdar, Bill Swislow, Carol Crown, Bud Goldstone, Chuck Rosenak, Willem Volkersz, Tony

Rajer, Lynne Browne, David Whaley, Jeffrey Hayes, Georgine Clarke, Betty-Carol Sellen.'' circ. 1.2M. 3/yr. Pub'd 3 issues 2005; expects 3 issues 2006, 3 issues 2007. sub. price $35, $60 overseas; per copy $15; sample $15. Back issues: $15. No discounts. 40pp. Reporting time: 30 days. Simultaneous submissions accepted: no. Payment: none. Copyrighted, rights revert to author after one year. Pub's reviews: 20 in 2005. §Folk art, contemporary self-taught art, Appalachia, outsider art. Ads: none. Subjects: Collectibles, Visual Arts.

Follow Me! Guides, Hillary Davis, PO Box 525, Peterborough, NH 03458, 1-800-862-5042 ext. 23, hillarydavis@mac.com. 2001. Non-fiction. Pub'd 1 title 2005; expects 2 titles 2006, 4 titles 2007. 288pp. Subjects: Cooking, New England, New Hampshire, New York, Travel.

Fontanel Books, Alan S. Gintzler, 4106 Saline St., Pittsburgh, PA 15217-2716, 505-471-4102, Fax 505-471-4202, fontanelbooks@earthlink.net, www.fontanelbooks.com. 2001. Poetry, fiction, non-fiction. avg. press run 3M. Expects 1 title 2006, 2 titles 2007. Discounts: 40% to bookstores, 55% to wholesalers. 207pp. Simultaneous submissions accepted: no. Does not copyright for author. Subjects: Children, Youth, Cosmology, Fiction, Judaism, Juvenile Fiction, Literature (General), Metaphysics, Myth, Mythology, New Age, Novels, Poetry, Prose, Short Stories, Spiritual, Young Adult.

Food First Books, Sal Glynn, Managing Editor, 398 60th Street, Oakland, CA 94618, 510-654-4400, FAX 510-654-4551, foodfirst@foodfirst.org. 1975. Non-fiction. ''Publications are progressive. Recent books include *Alternatives to the Peace Corps: A Directory of Third World and U.S. Volunteer Opportunities, Views From the South: The Effects of Globalization and the WTO on Third World Countries, America Needs Human Rights, The Future in the Balance: Essays on Globalization and Resistance*.'' avg. press run 3M. Pub'd 2 titles 2005; expects 2 titles 2006, 3 titles 2007. 150pp. Reporting time: 3-6 months. Simultaneous submissions accepted: yes. Publishes 5% of manuscripts submitted. Payment: yes. Copyrights for author. Subjects: Agriculture, Ecology, Foods, Global Affairs, Human Rights, Hunger.

•**Foodnsport Press,** Gail Davis, 609 N Jade Drive, Key Largo, FL 33037, 541-688-8809, www.foodnsport.com. 2005. Non-fiction. avg. press run 3000. Pub'd 2 titles 2005; expects 2 titles 2006, 5 titles 2007. Discounts: STOP orders 40%. Subjects: Health, Nutrition.

•**Footsteps Media,** Jillian Robinson, #621, 6929 N. Hayden Road, Suite C4, Scottsdale, AZ 85250, footstepsadventures@cox.net.

FOOTSTEPS: African American History, Cobblestone Publishing Company, Charles F. Baker III, Editor, 30 Grove Street, Suite C, Peterborough, NH 03458, 603-924-7209, Fax 603-924-7380, custsvc@cobblestone.mv.com. 1999. 5/yr. Pub'd 3 issues 2005; expects 5 issues 2006, 5 issues 2007. sub. price $23.95 (USA); per copy $4.95; sample $4.95. Back issues: $4.95. 52pp. Simultaneous submissions accepted: yes.

Fordham University Press, Tartar Helen, 2546 Belmont Avenue, University Box L, Bronx, NY 10458, 718-817-4781. 1907. Poetry, photos, letters, non-fiction. avg. press run 500. Pub'd 22 titles 2005; expects 24 titles 2006, 23 titles 2007. Discounts: Retail Trade Discount Titles (T)1 - 25%2-9 - 40%10-24 42%25-49 44%50+ - 46%Short discount titles (S)1 - 25%2-9 - 40%10+ - 20%Wholesale Trade discount titles (T)1-24 - 44%25-49 - 48%50+ - 50%Short discount titles (S)35% (any quantity). 250-300pp. Reporting time: 1 month. Simultaneous submissions accepted: Yes. Payment: Standard. Copyrights for author.

Foremost Press, Mary Holzrichter, 7067 Cedar Creek Rd., Cedarburg, WI 53012, 262.377.3180,mary@foremostpress.com, http://foremostpress.com. 2001. Fiction, non-fiction. ''Our objective is to build a fine library of books readers will enjoy. Both in hard copy and an electronic version. We are committed to great books of fiction and non-fiction. And above all else, to quality work that never lets you, the reader, down.While we prefer working with previously published authors, people who know the rules and what is expected of them, we will consider manuscripts from unpublished authors. But the work must be the equivalent of what a professional produces. By taking this position, we assure our readers quality books. And the added exposure we offer authors may lead to publication with a major house.'' Pub'd 6 titles 2005; expects 6 titles 2006, 6 titles 2007. Discounts: 40%. 225pp. Reporting time: When your manuscript is received, we respond within 7-10 working days. Simultaneous submissions accepted: No. Publishes 10% of manuscripts submitted. Payment: 20% on hard copy sold through our website at retail.10% on wholesale orders, as from a bookstore.On sales of electronic versions, we hold $0.97 as the transaction cost, then split the balance received with you, 50-50. Copyrights for author. Subjects: Biography, Fiction, Horror, How-To, Memoirs, Mystery, New Age, Non-Fiction, Novels, Romance, Science Fiction, Self-Help.

FORESIGHT MAGAZINE, John W.B. Barklam, Judy Barklam, 44 Brockhurst Road, Hodge Hill, Birmingham B36 8JB, England, 021-783-0587. 1970. Articles, reviews, letters, news items. ''Articles of approx. 1000 words welcomed. A bias towards philosophy as related to life. Dealing also in mysticism, occultism, UFOs and allied subjects. Aims are to help create peace and encourage spiritual awareness and evolution in the world.'' circ. 1.1M. 4/yr. Pub'd 4 issues 2005; expects 4 issues 2006, 4 issues 2007. sub. price £5.20 - $9.00; per copy £1.25-2.25; sample £1.25-2.25. Back issues: 50p - $1. Discounts: none. 20pp. Reporting time: immediate. Payment: none. Copyrighted, rights revert to author if requested. Pub's reviews: 40 in 2005. §Health, philosophy, psychic phenomena, UFOs, prediction, occult, spiritualism, and allied fiction. Ads: £9 ($16.25)/£5 ($9)/4p (8¢). Subjects: Book Reviewing, Health, Spiritual.

FORUM, Polebridge Press, Daryl Schmidt, Editor, PO Box 6144, Santa Rosa, CA 95406, 707-532-1323, fax 707-523-1350. 1981. Articles, criticism, reviews. "*Forum* is published by Polebridge Press on behalf of the Westar Institute and its seminars. The Westar Institute conducts research on biblical and American traditions and is devoted to improving biblical and religious literacy. A journal of the foundations and facets of Western culture." circ. 1.2M. 2/yr. Pub'd 2 issues 2005; expects 2 issues 2006, 2 issues 2007. sub. price $30; per copy $15; sample $15. 220pp. Copyrighted. Pub's reviews. §Religious studies, especially critical biblical scholarship, and American cultural studies. Subject: Religion.

FotoArt International, 5 Courtney Way, Red Bank, NJ 07701-0770, fotoart@usamailbox.com. 2003.

Fotofolio, Inc., Martin Bondell, Juliette Galant, Evan Schoninger, 561 Broadway, 2nd Floor, New York, NY 10012-3918, 212-226-0923. 1975. Art, photos, cartoons. "Publishers of art and photographs in poster, postcard, notecard, book and boxed gift formats. Recent contributors: Andre Kertesz, Edward Gorey, Gary Baseman, Robert Mapplethorpe, Duane Michals, Man Ray, Brassai, William Eggleston, Lauren Greenfield, Berenice Abbott, Herb Ritts, Georgia O'Keeffe, Helen Frankenthaler, The Quilts of Gee's Bend, William Wegman, Annie Leibovitz, Wolfgang Tillmans, David La Chapelle, Mark Rothko." avg. press run 6M. Pub'd 300 titles 2005. Subjects: African-American, Americana, Animals, Arts, Children, Youth, Comics, Entertainment, Fashion, History, Humor, Movies, New York, Non-Violence, Photography, Postcards.

FOTOTEQUE, Timson Edwards, Co., PO Box 55-0898, Jacksonville, FL 32255-0898, 904-705-6806, htpp://www.fototeque.com (must inquire prior to adding portfolios). 1995. Articles, photos, criticism, reviews. "We prefer work by new and emerging fine art photographers, particularly those using view cameras. Need exhibit reviews from all over the world, guidelines with SASE. Annual photo contest and free artist listings for directory section." 2/yr. Pub'd 4 issues 2005; expects 4 issues 2006, 2 issues 2007. sub. price $12.00 / $24.00 / $48.00 - a 9X12 version will soon be available. We only publish black and white work.; per copy $15 + p/h; sample same. Back issues: $20 + p/h. Discounts: request in writing on company letterhead, 40% off multiples of 10. 48pp. Reporting time: 12-18 weeks. Simultaneous submissions accepted: yes. 80% of the material we get, we publish. We only ask that it is presented in a professional manner. If you want your materials returned, please send enough postage and packing materials for their return. Payment: We publish portfolios and rarely pay cash for the photos we feature. We sometimes buy cover photos and the payment does vary widely. Normally though we pay with 4 copies for the artist and lots of exposure. We don't publish for a profit at this point in the magazine's life. Copyrighted, reverts to author. Pub's reviews: 4 in 2005. §Books and mags about photography only, fine art, commercial, anything, fine art and documentary; we only require that the review be well written. As if you were going for a Pulitzer. There is nothing more annoying than bad grammer and mispelled words. Send us a query first and make sure that photos are captioned. Do not send us a review of your own work, we usually know. Ads: We have an exchange program where we publish other service ads in exchange for ads in our magazine. Our rates range from $400/Full $225/Half $150/Quarter page. We also feature complimentary classified / directory ads. Subjects: Photography, Picture Books.

Foundation Books, Duane Hutchinson, Stephen K. Hutchinson, PO Box 22828, Lincoln, NE 68542-2828, 402-438-7080, Fax 402-438-7099, www.foundationbooks.com. 1970. Poetry, non-fiction. "History, biography and storytelling are our main areas of interest. The format of the paperback books is 5-1/2 X 8-1/2. The binding is Smythe-sewn for added strength and alkaline-based paper stock is used which meets the requirements of the American National Standard for Information Sciences - Permanence of Paper for Printed Library Materials, ANSI Z39.48-1984. The books are copyrighted by Foundation Books and Library of Congress Cataloging-in-Publication Data is included. Expanded bar codes are used on the back covers." avg. press run 1M-3M. Pub'd 4 titles 2005; expects 3 titles 2006, 4 titles 2007. Discounts: booksellers: 1 20%, 2-4 33%, 5-49 40%, 50-99 41%, 100-249 42%, 250+ 43%. 125-200pp. Reporting time: acknowledge receipt, 1 week; reading 2-6 months. Payment: to be arranged with individual author. Copyright for author by special arrangement. Subjects: Airplanes, Americana, Animals, Aviation, Biography, Folklore, History, Iowa, Midwest, Religion, Speaking, Storytelling, Supernatural, Treasure, The West.

The Foundation for Economic Education, Inc. (see also THE FREEMAN: Ideas On Liberty), Sheldon Richman, 30 South Broadway, Irvington, NY 10533, 914-591-7230; Fax 914-591-8910; E-mail freeman@fee.org. 1946. Articles, photos, criticism, reviews, non-fiction. "Publish single-author and anthologized works in political-economic philosophy and history. Titles must be written from consistent free-market, private-property, limited-government philosophical perspective. Ideas for books should be queried first, with outline." avg. press run 2-3M. Pub'd 12 titles 2005; expects 5 titles 2006, 4 titles 2007. Discounts: Trade - normal distributor terms. Direct/mail order: 2-4 20%, 5-49 40%, 50-499 50%, 500+ 60%. 250pp. Reporting time: 2-4 weeks. Payment: negotiated. Copyrights negotiated. Subjects: Business & Economics, Current Affairs, Government, History, Human Rights, Libertarian, Political Science, Public Affairs, Reviews,

Social Security.

Fountainhead Productions, Inc., James G. Fennessy III, 514 Morristown Road, Matawan, NJ 07747-3580, 732-583-2211; Fax 732-583-4123; topgun@skyweb.net. 1999. Fiction, non-fiction. "Writers should submit query with synopsis (1-3 pages). *Please note that while our National Writing Contest is being held we publish few manuscripts from other sources. Details on the Writing Contest may be obtained on our website at www.fountainheadpub.com.*" avg. press run 5M. Expects 10 titles 2006, 25 titles 2007. Discounts: up to 55%. 175-350pp. Reporting time: 30-90 days. Simultaneous submissions accepted: yes. Payment: 5% of list price. Copyrights for author. Subjects: Arts, Catholic, Celtic, Crime, Drugs, Entertainment, Fiction, Finances, Gaelic, Games, How-To, Ireland, Non-Fiction, Science, Science Fiction.

Fouque Publishers, Thomas Thornton, Thomas Stoelger, 244 5th Avenue #M220, New York, NY 10001-7604, 646-486-1061, Fax 646-486-1091, fouquepublishers@earthlink.net. 1999. Poetry, fiction, interviews, satire, music, letters, plays, non-fiction. avg. press run 1M. Expects 10 titles 2006, 25 titles 2007. Discounts: 40-45%, 10% (for 10+), 10%, wholesalers 50%. 200pp. Reporting time: 6 weeks. Simultaneous submissions accepted: yes. Publishes 5% of manuscripts submitted. Payment: 8-30%. Copyrights for author. Subjects: Autobiography, Drama, Fiction, History, Memoirs, Music, Non-Fiction, Novels, Poetry, Self-Help, Short Stories, Translation.

Four Continents Press, Sandy Sanderson, 256 S. Robertson #3194, Beverly Hills, CA 90211-2898, 310-276-6525, Fax 310-276-6595, fourcontpress@hotmail.com. 1999. Non-fiction. "Recent books are on international business and foreign adventures. Other titles include biographies." avg. press run 1M. Pub'd 3 titles 2005; expects 2 titles 2006, 2 titles 2007. Discounts: 1 book 0%, 2-4 25%, 5-9 30%, 10-24 40%, 25-75 44%, 76-99 47%, 100+ 50%. 250pp. Reporting time: 30 days. Simultaneous submissions accepted: no. Publishes 10% of manuscripts submitted. Payment: 8%-12%, 30 day payment. Does not copyright for author.

Four Seasons Publishers, Frank Hudak, PO Box 51, Titusville, FL 32781, phone 321-632-2932,fax 321-632-2935,fseasons@bellsouth.net. 1996. Poetry, fiction, music, non-fiction. avg. press run 10M. Pub'd 3 titles 2005; expects 12 titles 2006, 18 titles 2007. Discounts: 40-50%. 250pp. Reporting time: 2-4 weeks. Publishes 10% of manuscripts submitted. Payment: 10-15%. Copyrights for author. Subjects: Alcohol, Alcoholism, Americana, Christianity, Fantasy, Fiction, How-To, Inspirational, Literature (General), Non-Fiction, Poetry, Romance, Science Fiction, Self-Help, Spiritual.

Four Walls Eight Windows, 245 West 17th St., Apt. 11, New York, NY 10011-5373, e-mail edit@4w8w.com, www.4w8w.com. 1987. Fiction, non-fiction. avg. press run 4M. Pub'd 28 titles 2005; expects 30 titles 2006, 30 titles 2007. Discounts: write for details. 240pp. Reporting time: 3 months. Simultaneous submissions accepted: yes. Publishes 1% of manuscripts submitted. Payment: varies. Copyrights for author. Subjects: African Literature, Africa, African Studies, Arts, Biography, Culture, Feminism, Fiction, Health, History, How-To, Literature (General), New York, Politics, Science Fiction.

Four Way Books, Martha Rhodes, PO Box 535, Village Station, New York, NY 10014, www.fourway-books.com four_way_editors@yahoo.com. 1993. Poetry, fiction. "We seek to publish highest quality poetry and short fiction collections. We sponsor yearly poetry competitions. Past judges: Robert Pinsky, Stephen Dobyns, Gregory Orr, Heather McHugh. As well, we read poetry and fiction manuscripts in June of every year. We do charge a small reading fee for this service. Please go to our web site as deadlines and submissions guidelines may change." avg. press run 1500. Pub'd 8 titles 2005; expects 8 titles 2006, 8 titles 2007. Discounts: standard. Pages vary. Reporting time: ASAP. Simultaneous submissions accepted: Yes. Payment: standard. Copyrights for author. Subjects: Poetry, Short Stories.

4AllSeasons Publishing, S Goss M, P.O. Box 6473, Shreveport, LA 71136, 504-715-3094. 2001. Fiction. avg. press run 10000. Pub'd 1 title 2005; expects 1 title 2006, 1 title 2007. Discounts: Distributors standard 55 percent.Bookstores 40 percent. 275pp. Simultaneous submissions accepted: No. Publishes 1% of manuscripts submitted. Subjects: African-American, Romance, Women.

4AM POETRY REVIEW, Maria Thibodeau, 13213 Oxnard #7, Van Nuys, CA 91401, fourampoetryre-view@gmail.com http://fourampoetryreview.i8.com. 2004. Poetry. "Conceived with the lofty belief that poetry is a form of condensed energy, that language holds power and, though it assumes different forms, one of its possibilities is to alter those who encounter it, *4AM* exists to give space to emerging and established poets who write because they cant not and to be the mere vessel through which carefully-wrought words are spread like a medicine against the eroding forces of cultural vacuity. *4AM* seeks poetry that is accessible without being shallow, rather, poems whose meaning isn't so oblique as to be irrelevant but whose language makes a visceral impact, leaves you shaken, your mind replaying the sounds over as you turn in sleep. We want: Imagery, language used in powerful and surprising ways, a careful interplay of sound and meaning. [Brand names we admire, among others: Neruda, Piercy, Atwood, Roethke, Hass, Rilke, Sexton, Hecht, Bedient, etc.] *4AM* 2005 included: matt robinson, Susan Case-Gray, Anthony Robinson, Sarah Blackman, Simon Perchik, Rebecca Loudon, Barbara Fletcher, Lyn Lifshin, Alex Stolis, Judson Simmons, Kimberley Fu, Juan Carlos Vargas, Michael Meyerhofer, Mark DeCarteret, Carine Topal, Arlene Ang, Gerry McFarland, Davide Trame, others.We

170

do not want: first drafts, prose with line breaks, free-form gabble, obtrusive rhymes." circ. 200. 1/yr. Expects 1 issue 2006, 1 issue 2007. sub. price $5; per copy $5; sample $5. Back issues: $5. 50pp. Reporting time: 6 weeks. Simultaneous submissions accepted: Yes. Publishes 5% of manuscripts submitted. Payment: 2 copies. Copyrighted, reverts to author. No ads. Subject: Poetry.

Four-Sep Publications (see also FIRST CLASS), Christopher M., PO Box 86, Friendship, IN 47021, christopherm@four-sep.com, www.four-sep.com. 1996. Poetry, fiction, photos, long-poems, plays. "Prefer short fiction. Cover letter preferred. Desires good, thought-provoking, graphic, uncommon pieces." avg. press run 250-400. Pub'd 3 titles 2005; expects 3 titles 2006, 2 titles 2007. Discounts: inquire. 55-65pp. Reporting time: 1 week initial response. Simultaneous submissions accepted: yes. Publishes 10-15% of manuscripts submitted. Payment: varies, personal. Copyrights for author. Subjects: Absurdist, Counter-Culture, Alternatives, Communes, Literature (General), Poetry, Post Modern.

FOURTEEN HILLS: The SFSU Review, Creative Writing Dept., SFSU, 1600 Holloway Avenue, San Francisco, CA 94132, 415-338-3083, fax 415-338-0504, E-mail hills@sfsu.edu. 1994. Poetry, fiction, interviews, criticism, parts-of-novels, long-poems, plays, non-fiction. "*Fourteen Hills* is an entirely graduate-student run literary review dedicated to high-quality, innovative creative literary work. Submissions should include the writer's name, address, phone number and the name of the piece. Maximum 5 poems or 1 story, drama or creative non-fiction submission per writer. Maximum word length: 5,000. Recent contributors: Gina Ochsner, Dorothy Allison, Amy Gerstler, Amiri Baraka, Paul Hoover, Bernadette Mayer, C.D. Wright, Leslie Scalapino, Terese Svoboda, Anne Marie Aubin, Renee Gladman, and Ray Bradbury." circ. 600. 2/yr. Pub'd 2 issues 2005; expects 2 issues 2006, 2 issues 2007. sub. price $17; per copy $9; sample $5-$7. 160pp. Reporting time: 2-4 months. Simultaneous submissions accepted: yes. Publishes 15% of manuscripts submitted. Payment: 2 contributor copies. Copyrighted, reverts to author. Ads: $120/$60/$30 business card/$500 cover 2/$400 cover 3, will trade. Subjects: Fiction, Literature (General), Poetry, Prose, Short Stories.

FOURTH GENRE: EXPLORATIONS IN NONFICTION, Michigan State University Press, David Cooper, Editor; Michael Steinberg, Editor, Dept. of Writing, Rhetoric, & American Cultures, 229 Bessey, Michigan State University, East Lansing, MI 48824, 517-432-2556; fax 517-353-5250; e-mail fourthgenre@cal.msu.edu. 1999. Non-fiction. "Seeking reflective personal essays, memoirs, literary journalism, and personal critical essays up to 8000 words, as well as interviews, book reviews, and photos. Reading periods March 15-June 15 and Sept. 15-Dec. 15 only. For submission guidelines and other information see our website at *www.msupress.msu.edu/FourthGenre* or email fourthgenre@cal.msu.edu. Recent contributors: Brent Lott, Floyd Skloot, Kim Barnes, Stuart Dybek, and Brenda Miller." circ. 300. 2/yr. Pub'd 2 issues 2005; expects 2 issues 2006, 2 issues 2007. sub. price $30; per copy $18; sample $18. Back issues: $18. Discounts: 5% agent discount. 200pp. Reporting time: 3-4 months. Simultaneous submissions accepted: yes. Publishes 5% of manuscripts submitted. Payment: none. Copyrighted, reverts to author. Pub's reviews: 20 in 2005. §All books of creative nonfiction. Ads: $250/$150. Subjects: Book Reviewing, Essays, Memoirs.

THE FOURTH R, Polebridge Press, Culver H. Nelson, Editor, PO Box 6144, Santa Rosa, CA 95406, 707-523-1325, fax 707-523-1350. 1981. Articles, interviews, criticism, reviews. "*The Fourth R* is published by Polebride Press on behalf of the Westar Institute and its seminars. The Westar Institute conducts research on biblical and American traditions and is devoted to improving biblical and religious literacy. An advocate for biblical and religious literacy, *The Fourth R* addresses a broad range of questions about religion, past and present." circ. 1.5M. 6/yr. sub. price $25; per copy $4.50; sample $4.50. 24pp. Copyrighted. Pub's reviews. §Religious studies, especially critical biblical scholarship, and American cultural studies. Subject: Religion.

FOURTH WORLD REVIEW, John Papworth, 26 High Street, Purton, Wiltshire SN5 9AE, England, 01793-772214. 1966. Articles, interviews, criticism, reviews, letters, news items, non-fiction. "Any material bearing on human scale concepts—politics and economics." circ. 2M international. 5/yr. Pub'd 5 issues 2005; expects 5 issues 2006, 5 issues 2007. sub. price according to self-assessed income status; per copy £1; sample £1. Back issues: £2. Discounts: 50%. 32pp. Payment: none. Pub's reviews: 18 in 2005. §Economics, politics, ecology. Ads: on application. Subjects: Environment, Human Rights, Humanism, Political Science, Politics, Public Affairs, Society, Third World, Minorities.

FPMI Solutions, Inc., Kevin Wilson, Editor, 101 Quality Circle NW, Suite 110, Huntsville, AL 35806-4534, 256-539-1850. 1985. Articles, interviews, non-fiction. "We publish short books of interest to federal government employees and managers." avg. press run 5M. Pub'd 4 titles 2005; expects 6 titles 2006, 6 titles 2007. Discounts: discounts to re-sellers; also discounts based on volume to all purchasers. 75pp. Reporting time: 60 days. Payment: varies depending upon nature of submission and subject matter. Does not copyright for author. Subject: Government.

FRAN MAGAZINE, Andrew Hume, Sam Kuhlmann, PO Box 291459, Los Angeles, CA 90029, 213.250.3788. 2002. Fiction, articles, photos, interviews, satire, criticism, reviews, music, plays, news items, non-fiction. "Fran is primarily a humor magazine. We're sometimes abrasive, sometimes self-depricating, sometimes lovable. We feature music and film coverage primarily. We have childish games like MASH; Henry Rollins wordfinders (w/ words like "caring", "punking", and "muscles"; DIY articles about prison wine and sex, lurking and cooking dogs; interviews with musicians and filmmakers; photoshopped nude celebrities (Ben Affleck with nude lady's legs); etc. We like to think that we're equal parts pointed social satire and serious social concern. We don't generally like to receive "rants" or tales of college debauchery. We're often looking for more New Journalism or gonzo journalism style articles. Potential contributors, please make us shit our pants with glee." 4/yr. Pub'd 4 issues 2005; expects 4 issues 2006, 4 issues 2007. sub. price $10; per copy $2.50; sample $1.50. Back issues: inquire. Discounts: generally 40%, inquire. 46pp. Reporting time: 1-3 weeks. Simultaneous submissions accepted: Yes. Payment: $30 per article (hopefully more soon). Copyrighted, reverts to author. Pub's reviews. §music, concerts, stage, clothing, films, various products. Ads: $500/$225/$150(inquire for rear and inside covers and color pricing). Subjects: Absurdist, Alcohol, Alcoholism, Americana, Arts, Avant-Garde, Experimental Art, Communication, Journalism, Culture, Drugs, Experimental, F. Scott Fitzgerald, Humor, Interviews, Non-Fiction, Satire, Whaling.

THE FRANK REVIEW, Lindsay Wilson, Nathan Graziano, Lindsay Wilson & Nathan Graziano, P.O. Box 3193, Moscow, ID 83843-1907, frankreview@excite.com. Articles, art, cartoons, interviews. "A very irregular digest-size triquarterly review magazine seeking submissions in essays, features on writing, interviews, b&w artwork and photography, reviews of chapbooks, magazines, books, exhibits, theater, modern dance, online journals and spoken word CDs. Please send books, chaps and magazines in for review consideration. *Always* seeking unsolicited reviews with SASE or sent via email. First issue of every year is a year in review issue with an extra four pages. *We do not accept poetry,* our contest has been canceled! We simply want to help promote writers, magazines, and presses and to help create more of a community within the Little Magazine scene. Send all questions to the editors, e-mail address above." 3/yr. Pub'd 3 issues 2005; expects 3 issues 2006, 3 issues 2007. sub. price $4; per copy $1 + stamp; sample $1 + stamp. Back issues: none. Discounts: write for info. 24-28pp. Reporting time: 3 weeks to 3 months. Simultaneous submissions accepted: no. Publishes 15% of manuscripts submitted. Payment: 1 copy. Not copyrighted. Pub's reviews: 40 in 2005. §Small press, chapbooks, online journals, magazines, books, spoken word CDs. Ads: $10 1/2 page/$6 1/4 page. Subjects: Book Reviewing, Cartoons, Dada, Essays, Internet, Literary Review, Pacific Northwest, Photography, Post Modern, Reviews, Satire, Society, Writers/Writing, Wyoming, Zines.

FRANK: AN INTERNATIONAL JOURNAL OF CONTEMPORARY WRITING AND ART, David Applefield, Editor-Publisher, 32 rue Edouard Vaillant, 93100 Montreuil Sous Bois, France, (33) 1 48596658, e-mail david@paris-anglo.com. 1983. Poetry, fiction, art, photos, interviews, parts-of-novels, collages, plays. "All texts should be under 20 double-spaced typed pages—absolutely open to all styles, techniques, visions, genres, languages, but we are particularly interested in work with international and cross-cultural content. We also encourage literary work Recent contributors include: Jean Lamore, Billy Collins, Lewis Lapham, Gabriel Garcia Marquez, Aim Cesaire, Leopold Senghor, President Jacques Chirac, George Plimpton, Octavio Paz, Jim Morrison, Vaclav Havel, W.S. Merwin, Gennadi Aigi, Maurice Girodias, Rita Dove, Frederick Barthelme, Samuel Beckett, Duo Duo, Stephen Dixon, A.I. Bezzerides, Dennis Hopper, John Sanford, Bukowski, Hubert Selby, Italo Calvino, Breyten Breytenbach, Paul Bowles, Derek Walcott, Tom Waits, John Berger, Edmond Jabes, E.M. Cioran, Robert Coover, Edmund White, Henry Miller, Nancy Huston, C.K. Williams, and special feature on English-language writing in Paris today! 40 Philippino protest poets, Congolese fiction, the best of Swiss writing, and unpublished Burroughs. And plenty of lesser known talent." circ. 4M. 2/yr. Pub'd 2 issues 2005; expects 2 issues 2006, 2 issues 2007. sub. price $38 (4 issues), $60 instit.; per copy $10; sample $9. Back issues: issues 1-5 pack for $70. Discounts: 40% for bookstores and orders over 6 copies. 224pp. Reporting time: 12 weeks. Simultaneous submissions accepted: yes. Publishes 5% of manuscripts submitted. Payment: 2 copies plus $5/printed page. Copyrighted, reverts to author. Pub's reviews: §Literature, poetry, politics, art, translation, interviews. Ads: $1,000/$500/$3500 back cover. Subjects: Arts, Avant-Garde, Experimental Art, Fiction, France, French, Jack Kerouac, Literary Review, Magazines, Poetry, Translation.

Franklin-Sarrett Publishers, 3761 Vineyard Trace, Marietta, GA 30062, 770-578-9410, Fax 770-973-4243, info@franklin-sarrett.com, www.franklin-sarrett.com. 1992. Non-fiction. avg. press run 3M. Pub'd 1 title 2005; expects 1 title 2006, 2 titles 2007. Discounts: write for details. 110pp. Reporting time: 30 days. Payment: write for details. Copyrights for author. Subjects: Business & Economics, Non-Fiction.

FREE INQUIRY, Paul Kurtz, Editor-in-Chief; Tom Flynn, Editor, Council For Secular Humanism, PO Box 664, Amherst, NY 14226-0664, 716-636-7571. 1980. Articles, cartoons, interviews, criticism, reviews, letters, non-fiction. "Recent contributors: Francis Crick, Camille Paglia, Martin Gardner, Wendy Kaminer, Marilyn French, Albert Ellis, Richard Dawkins, E.O. Wilson, Peter Ustinov, and Richard Rorty." circ. 25M. 4/yr. Pub'd 4 issues 2005; expects 4 issues 2006, 4 issues 2007. sub. price $31.50; per copy $6.95; sample same. Back issues: 20% discount on 10 or more copies. Discounts: agency remits—40% 1st year, 20% 2nd year and after. 68pp. Reporting time: varies. Simultaneous submissions accepted: no. Publishes 10% of manuscripts submitted. Payment: we do not pay for feature editorial. Copyrighted, does not revert to author. Pub's reviews: 25 in 2005. §Philosophy, religion, morality, humanism, science. Ads: none. Subjects: Atheism, Birth, Birth Control,

Population, Education, Ethics, Human Rights, Humanism, Philosophy, Religion, Science.

FREE LUNCH, Ron Offen, PO Box 717, Glenview, IL 60025-0717, www.poetsfreelunch.org. 1988. Poetry, news items. "Please limit to three poems per submission between 9/1 and 5/31 *only*. Do not want ponderous, abstract, philosophic work with pithy observations, nicey-nice religious poems with tacked-on morals, greeting card love, nature, animal verse or haiku. Lately I've grown a bit weary of the rambling personal lyric, poem-as-therapy verse, and flat-footed prose chopped up into lines to look like a poem. I am not partial to literary poems: poems about poems, poets, writing poems, poetry readings, etc. I want figurative language: similes, metaphors, alliteration, images, etc. Sympathetic to new poets, experimental work. Not opposed to form per se. Want to give all 'serious' U.S. poets a free subscription (based on submissions). Recent contributors: Billy Collins, Philip Dacey, Lisel Mueller, David Wagoner, and Charles Harper Webb. Always try to comment on submissions. Must have SASE with *all* submissions, inquiries, etc." circ. 1.1M. Irregular. Pub'd 2 issues 2005; expects 2 issues 2006, 2 issues 2007. sub. price 3 issues/$12 US, $15 foreign; per copy $5 US, $6 foreign; sample $5 US, $6 foreign. Back issues: query. 32pp. Reporting time: 1-4 months. Simultaneous submissions accepted: yes. Publishes 5-10% of manuscripts submitted. Payment: 1 copy of appearance issue and free subscription. Copyrighted, does not revert to author. Query. Subject: Poetry.

Free People Press (see also BOTH SIDES NOW), Elihu Edelson, 10547 State Hwy 110 N, Tyler, TX 75704-3731. 1974. "The main function of Free People Press is to publish *Both Sides Now*. It also publishes a few saddle-stitched booklets, both original and reprints." Reporting time: varies. Payment: copies. Author retains copyright. Subjects: Fiction, Metaphysics, New Age, Non-Violence, Occult, Peace, Philosophy, Politics, Religion, Reprints.

Free Reign Press, Inc., 502 Valley Stream Circle, Langhorne, PA 19053, 215-891-8894 phone, www.freereignpress.com. 2000. Fiction, articles, cartoons, satire, reviews, non-fiction. avg. press run 5M. Expects 2 titles 2006, 3-4 titles 2007. Discounts: trade varies with quantity, ranges from 20%-55%. 207pp. Reporting time: not currently accepting unsolicited manuscripts. Simultaneous submissions accepted: yes. Publishes an unknown % of manuscripts submitted. Payment: approx. 10% royalty, varies. Copyrights for author. Subjects: Absurdist, Atheism, Humor, Libertarian, Novels, Philosophy, Politics, Satire, Science Fiction, Short Stories.

FREEBIES MAGAZINE, Gail M. Zannon, Publisher, PO Box 21957, Santa Barbara, CA 93121-1957, freebies@aol.com. 1977. "All materials produced by in-house staff. We do not solicit or accept freelance materials." circ. 450M. 6/yr. Pub'd 6 issues 2005; expects 6 issues 2006, 6 issues 2007. sub. price $7.95/5 issues; per copy $3; sample $3. Back issues: not available. Discounts: 20% off on bulk/agency purchases. 24pp. Copyrighted. Ads: classified $5.50/word ($15 minimum).

FREEDOM AND STRENGTH PRESS FORUM, Scars Publications, Gabriel Athens, Scars Publications, 829 Brian Court, Gurnee, IL 60031-3155, Editor@scars.tv, http://scars.tv. 1999. Poetry, fiction, art, photos, letters, long-poems, collages, non-fiction. "You can't be strong or free if you don't speak up. A lot of people have very good ideas and most do not feel as if their voice can be heard. We want to make sure you have your space and your opportunity to be heard. All postings to our boards are considered 'published'; if you are interested in having your essays or input published in print form you can e-mail, asking about your work being added on to Scars Publications' collection books (with *children, churches and daddies* and *down in the dirt* magazines as well). We want people to be heard when it feels like no one is there to listen, because no one should be stopped from thinking and expressing their ideas." circ. usually always on internet, but can appear in collection books. Frequency varies. Pub'd around $12 for books issues 2005. price per copy around $13.23 for books Freedom and Strength writing appears in; sample around $13.23 for books Freedom and Strength writing appears in. Back issues: around $13.23 for books Freedom and Strength writing appears in. 200-300pp. Reporting time: work can be posted directly to the website, so response is immediate. Simultaneous submissions accepted: Yes. Publishes 100% of manuscripts submitted. Payment: appearance of your work in text and e-books on the internet. Not copyrighted. Subjects: Arts, Chicago, Counter-Culture, Alternatives, Communes, Culture, Feminism, Fiction, Graphics, Journals, Language, Magazines, Midwest, Photography, Poetry, Women.

THE FREEDONIA GAZETTE: The Magazine Devoted to the Marx Brothers, Paul G. Wesolowski, Editor-in-Chief, 335 Fieldstone Drive, New Hope, PA 18938-1224, 215-862-9734. 1978. Fiction, articles, photos, cartoons, interviews, satire, criticism, reviews, letters, plays, news items, non-fiction. "Articles range from 1 typewritten page (double-spaced) to 15 pages. We deal mainly with articles on the Marx Brothers and people associated with them, reviews of books on these topics, reviews of stage shows impersonating them, interviews with people who worked with the Marxes and with impersonators. We're especially in need of artwork, either drawings or caricatures of the Marxes. We have a strong reputation for well-researched articles which turn up facts not known to most fans and fanatics. U.K. subscriptions/submissions: Dr. Raymond D. White, 137 Easterly Road, Leeds LS8 2RY England." circ. 500. 2/yr. Pub'd 2 issues 2005; expects 2 issues 2006, 2 issues 2007. sub. price $10; per copy $5; sample $5. Back issues: $5 when available (#1-#4,#8 currently sold-out). Discounts: 10 or more of the same issue (current or back issues) $4.50 each; 50 or more (mix and match current and/or back issues) $4 each. 20pp. Reporting time: maximum 1 month. Simultaneous submissions accepted: yes. Publishes 75% of manuscripts submitted. Payment: sample copy of issue the work appears in. yes/no. Pub's reviews: 4 in 2005. §Marx Brothers, humor, classic film comedy. Subjects: Biography, Humor, Movies, Television, Theatre.

FREEFALL, Micheline Maylor, Editor; Lynn Fraser, Managing Editor, Alexandra Writers Centre Society, 922 9th Avenue S.E., Calgary, AB T2G 0S4, Canada, Fax 403-264-4730, awcs@telusplanet.net, www.alexandraw-riters.org. 1990. Poetry, fiction, articles, art, photos, cartoons, interviews, criticism, reviews, long-poems, non-fiction. "Interviews must be with writers, publishers or those in the business of writing. Prose: maximum 3,000 words. Poetry: 2-5 poems, 6 pages maximum. Photos: must be glossy and black and white. Art work: black ink drawings. Non fiction: writing related topics or creative non fiction. Postcard stories maximum of 3." circ. 300. 2/yr. Pub'd 2 issues 2005; expects 2 issues 2006, 2 issues 2007. sub. price $20 Canada; $25 US; sample $10.00 Canada; $9.00 US. Back issues: $10.00 Canada; $8.00 US. 40pp. Reporting time: 2 months from deadline. Simultaneous submissions accepted: no. Publishes 30% of manuscripts submitted. Payment: $5 per printed page upon publication and 1 copy of *Freefall*. Copyrighted, reverts to author. Pub's reviews: none in 2005. §all categories are welcome. Ads: $100 full/half(upper or lower)$50/Quarter range $20-$30. Subjects: Arts, Book Reviewing, Canada, Criticism, Dada, Diaries, English, Fiction, Folklore, Haiku, Interviews, Literary Review, Literature (General), Poetry, Postcards.

FREELANCE MARKET NEWS, The Association of Freelance Writers, Angela Cox, Editor, Sevendale House, 7 Dale Street, Manchester, M1 1JB, England, 0161-228-2362, Fax 0161-228-3533. 1968. "Provides market information telling writers, poets and photographers where to sell. World-wide circulation." 11/yr. Pub'd 11 issues 2005; expects 11 issues 2006, 11 issues 2007. sub. price overseas £29; per copy £2.50; sample £2.50. 16pp. Reporting time: 1 month. Simultaneous submissions accepted: no. Publishes 50% of manuscripts submitted. Payment: £40 per 1000 words. Ads: classified: 35p per word.

FREELANCE WRITER'S REPORT, Dana K. Cassell, PO Box A, North Stratford, NH 03590, 603-922-8338, fwr@writers-editors.com, www.writers-editors.com. 1977. Articles, interviews, news items, non-fiction. circ. 400. 12/yr. Pub'd 12 issues 2005; expects 12 issues 2006, 12 issues 2007. sub. price $39; per copy $3 current issue; sample free with 9X12 SASE with 60¢ p/h. Back issues: $3. 8pp. Reporting time: 1 month. Simultaneous submissions accepted: yes. Publishes 25% of manuscripts submitted. Payment: 10¢/word. Copyrighted, reverts to author. Pub's reviews: 25 in 2005. §Freelance writing and editing, home business. Ads: 50¢ per word with discount for multiple insertions. Subject: Communication, Journalism.

THE FREEMAN: Ideas On Liberty, The Foundation for Economic Education, Inc., Sheldon Richman, Editor; Beth Hoffman, Managing Editor, 30 South Broadway, Irvington, NY 10533, 914-591-7230; Fax 914-591-8910; E-mail freeman@fee.org. 1946. Articles, criticism, reviews, letters. "Solicits articles and book reviews from standpoint of a free-market, private-property, limited government philosophy. Length typically between 1000-2000 words. Columnists include Richard M. Ebeling, Sheldon Richman, Lawrence W. Reed, Walter Williams, Robert Higgs, Stephen Davies, Donald Boudreaux, Burton Folsom, Charles Baird, and Russell Roberts." circ. 8M+. 10/yr. Pub'd 12 issues 2005; expects 12 issues 2006, 12 issues 2007. sub. price $40; per copy $3.50; sample free. Discounts: $10 per carton (100+ copies) of back issues for classroom use. 48pp. Reporting time: 1 week. Simultaneous submissions accepted: no. Publishes 20% of manuscripts submitted. Payment: 10¢ per word. Copyright to FEE unless author retains. Pub's reviews: 40 in 2005. §Political theory, history, biography & economics, from free-market perspective. Ads: $800/$500. Subjects: Business & Economics, Current Affairs, Government, History, Human Rights, Libertarian, Political Science, Public Affairs, Reviews.

FREETHOUGHT HISTORY, Fred Whitehead, Box 5224, Kansas City, KS 66119, 913-588-1996. 1992. Poetry, articles, reviews, non-fiction. "A newsletter providing a center for exchange of information on research in the history of agnosticism, atheism, philosophical and religious controversy, also with attention to topics of freethought culture including poetry, art, music, etc. Features description and listing of work in progress, short biographies of freethinkers, notes and queries, reports on conferences and historic sites, and essays on the interpretation of intellectual history." circ. 200. 4/yr. Expects 4 issues 2006, 4 issues 2007. sub. price $10; per copy $3; sample $3. Discounts: none. 12pp. Reporting time: 1 week. Payment: in copies. Copyrighted, reverts to author. Pub's reviews. §Atheism, freethought, intellectual and philosophical history. Subjects: Philosophy, Religion.

•**French Bread Publications (see also PACIFIC COAST JOURNAL),** Stillson Graham, P.O. Box 56, Carlsbad, CA 92018. 1992. Poetry, fiction. "Solely prints books authored by Stillson Graham. Does not accept manuscripts for book or chapbook publishing." avg. press run 300. Expects 1 title 2006, 1 title 2007. No discounts. 320pp. Subjects: Fiction, Poetry.

Mike French Publishing, 1619 Front Street, Lynden, WA 98264, 360-354-8326.

FRESH GROUND, White Eagle Coffee Store Press, Paul Andrew E. Smith, PO Box 383, Fox River Grove, IL 60021, 708-639-9200. 1993. Poetry. circ. 300+. 1/yr. Expects 1 issue 2006, 1 issue 2007. sub. price $5.95; per copy $5.95; sample $5.95. Discounts: $3 each in tens. 30pp. Reporting time: 6 weeks. Payment: 1 copy. Copyrighted, reverts to author. Subject: Poetry.

FRESHWATER, Edwina Trentham, 170 Elm Street, Enfield, CT 06082-3873, 860-253-3105, freshwater@acc.commnet.edu, www.acc.commnet.edu/freshwater.htm. 2000. Poetry. "No length limit, but we are looking for originality and craft. Submit up to five poems with name, address, and e-mail on each poem. Recent conributors include Cortney Davis, Katharyn Howd Machan, Charles Rafferty. SASE for notification only." circ. 500. 1/yr. Pub'd 1 issue 2005; expects 1 issue 2006, 1 issue 2007. sub. price $6; per copy $6; sample $6. 70pp. Reporting time: 2-3 months. We accept simultaneous submissions if indicated and notified if accepted elsewhere. Publishes 5% of manuscripts submitted. Payment: 2 copies. Copyrighted, reverts to author. Ads: none. Subject: Poetry.

Fretwater Press, Brad Dimock, 1000 Grand Canyon Avenue, Flagstaff, AZ 86001, 520-774-8853, fax 520-779-9552, e-mail braddimock@fretwater.com, website www.fretwater.com. 1998. Non-fiction. avg. press run 6M. Pub'd 2 titles 2005; expects 2 titles 2006, 2 titles 2007. Discounts: bookstores 40%. 300pp. Reporting time: 1 month. Simultaneous submissions accepted: no. Publishes 1% of manuscripts submitted. Payment: negotiable. Does not copyright for author. Subjects: Arizona, Environment, Idaho, Non-Fiction, Old West, Oregon, Southwest, The West.

Friendly Oaks Publications, James D. Sutton, 227 Bunker Hill, PO Box 662, Pleasanton, TX 78064-0662, 830-569-3586, Fax 830-281-2617, E-mail friendly@docspeak.com. 1990. Non-fiction. avg. press run 5-7M. Pub'd 4 titles 2005; expects 6 titles 2006, 3 titles 2007. Discounts: bulk. 200pp. Reporting time: 6 weeks. Simultaneous submissions accepted: yes. Publishes 5-10% of manuscripts submitted. Payment: negotiable. Copyrights for author. Subjects: Consulting, Education, Family, Inspirational, Psychology.

FRIENDS OF PEACE PILGRIM, Bruce Nichols, Editor, PO Box 2207, Shelton, CT 06484. 1987. "Our newsletter focuses on the life of Peace Pilgrim and how her 28 year pilgrimage for peace and message continues to inspire people today. We are interested in current pilgrims and walkers who are traveling for peace and in stories and issues that enhance and inspire the lives of our readers to create more peace in their own lives, families, and communites. Friends of Peace Pilgrim is an all-volunteer non-profit organization. Our newsletter is distributed freely. We do not offer compensation for articles." circ. 6000. 3/yr. Pub'd 3 issues 2005; expects 3 issues 2006, 3 issues 2007. sub. price free; per copy free; sample free. Back issues: free. 8pp. Payment: none. Not copyrighted. Ads: none. Subjects: Community, Environment, Human Rights, Non-Violence, Peace, Spiritual.

Friends United Press, Barbara Mays, 101 Quaker Hill Drive, Richmond, IN 47374, 765-962-7573. 1969. Non-fiction. "Non-fiction books (average length 100-180 pages) relating to Quaker (Society of Friends) history, biography, faith experience, and religious practice." avg. press run 1M. Pub'd 5 titles 2005; expects 6 titles 2006, 6 titles 2007. Discounts: 40% to bookstores on orders over 5 copies. 150-175pp. Reporting time: 2 to 4 months. Simultaneous submissions accepted: yes. Publishes 8% of manuscripts submitted. Payment: 7-1/2% of our income on each title after production costs are met. Copyrights for author. Subjects: Biography, Christianity, History, Non-Violence, Peace, Religion, Reprints, Spiritual, Women.

Frith Press (see also EKPHRASIS), Laverne Frith, Editor; Carol Frith, Editor, PO Box 161236, Sacramento, CA 95816-1236, http://hometown.aol.com/ekphrasisl. 1995. Poetry. "After 2003, we are suspending our annual chapbook competition until further notice. We will continue to publish chapbooks from time to time by invitation only." avg. press run 200. Pub'd 1 title 2005; expects 1 title 2006, 1 title 2007. 32pp. Does not copyright for author. Subject: Poetry.

THE FROGMORE PAPERS, The Frogmore Press, Jeremy Page, 42 Morehall Avenue, Folkestone, Kent CT19 4EF, United Kingdom. 1983. Poetry, fiction. "Short stories of more than 2,000 words are unlikely to be chosen. Recent contributors: Pauline Stainer, John Latham, Roger Elkin, Myra Schneider, R. Nikolas Macioci, George Gott, John Harvey, Linda France, Tobias Hill, Judi Benson, Tamar Yoseloff, Elizabeth Garrett." circ. 500. 2/yr. Pub'd 2 issues 2005; expects 2 issues 2006, 2 issues 2007. sub. price $20; per copy $10; sample $5 (dollar bills only). Back issues: $10 for special 50th issue. Discounts: none. 40pp. Reporting time: 3 months. Simultaneous submissions accepted: no. Publishes 2-3% of manuscripts submitted. Payment: 1 copy. Not copyrighted. Pub's reviews: approx. 20 in 2005. §Mostly poetry collections/anthologies. Ads: not available. Subjects: Fiction, Poetry, Short Stories.

The Frogmore Press (see also THE FROGMORE PAPERS), Jeremy Page, 42 Morehall Avenue, Folkestone, Kent. CT19 4EF, United Kingdom. 1983. Poetry. "Collections published tend to be by writers previously published in *The Frogmore Papers*. Recent titles have been *New Pastorals* by Robert Etty and *Bush Klaxon Has a Body Like a Trio Sonata* by Bob Mitchell. *Mongoose on His Shoulder* by Geoffrey Holloway appeared in October. Please write for details. Do not send unsolicited manuscripts." avg. press run 250. Pub'd 2 titles 2005; expects 2 titles 2006, 2 titles 2007. Discounts: none. 44pp. Reporting time: 3 months. Simultaneous submissions accepted: no. Publishes 3% of manuscripts submitted. Payment: 12 complimentary copies. Copyrights for author. Subject: Poetry.

FROGPOND: Quarterly Haiku Journal, Haiku Society of America, John Stevenson, Editor, PO Box 122, Nassau, NY 12123-0122, ithacan@earthlink.net. 1978. Poetry, articles, art, criticism, reviews. "Publish haiku, haiku sequences, haibun, some renku, some translations, brief essays and book reviews. Material should show familiarity with modern developments in North American haiku; not interested in 'pretty nature pictures' or philosophical constructs; poems should focus on the 'suchness' of the here-and-now moment, avoiding cliches, simile and overt metaphor. Traditional and experimental haiku in 1-4 lines. Recent contributors: Tom Clausen, Carolyn Hall, Peggy Willis Lyles, Philip Rowland, Ruth Yarrow. Publish 3 regular issues and occasional supplements." circ. 800. 3/yr. Pub'd 3 issues 2005; expects 3 issues 2006, 3 issues 2007. sub. price $33 USA, $35 Canada and Mexico, $45 elsewhere; per copy $8 USA, $10 Canada, $12 elsewhere; sample $8 USA, $10 Canada, $12 elsewhere. Back issues: same. Discounts: none. 96pp. Reporting time: 2 weeks. Simultaneous submissions accepted: no. Publishes less than 1% of manuscripts submitted. Payment: $1/item accepted. Copyrighted, reverts to author. Pub's reviews: 20 in 2005. §Books and chapbooks of contemporary haiku, senryu, new translations of Japanese and other haiku. Ads: none. Subject: Haiku.

From Here Press (see also XTRAS), William J. Higginson, Penny Harter, PO Box 1402, Summit, NJ 07902-1402. 1975. Poetry, criticism, long-poems, non-fiction. "Not reading unsolicited work. *XTRAS* is a series title." avg. press run 200-1M. Expects 1 title 2006, 1 title 2007. Discounts: 40% to trade (5 mixed titles). 40-120pp. Payment: varies. Copyrights for author. Subjects: Criticism, Haiku, Poetry.

Front Row Experience, Frank Alexander, 540 Discovery Bay Boulevard, Discovery Bay, CA 94514, 925-634-5710. 1974. Art, cartoons, non-fiction. "One page letter of inquiry first, submit manuscript only when requested. Submitted manuscripts should include self-addressed-stamped-return envelopes and should be typed double space of about 200 8-1/2 X 11 size pages. They should be lesson plans or guidebooks for *teachers* from preschool to 6th Grade. We are not interested in areas other than 'perceptual-motor development', 'movement education', 'special education.' Some recently published books are: *Funsical Fitness, School Based Home Developmental P.E. Program, Dimondball Games.*" avg. press run 500. Discounts: 1+ 20%, 5+ 45%, 100+ 50%. 100pp. Reporting time: 1 week for letter of inquiry, 1 month for manuscript (include SASE), and only send manuscript when requested to do so. Simultaneous submissions accepted: yes. Publishes 10% of manuscripts submitted. Payment: all authors 10% royalty. Copyrights for author. Subjects: Children, Youth, Education, Family, Games, Health, Non-Fiction, Sports, Outdoors, Textbooks.

THE FRONT STRIKER BULLETIN, Bill Retskin, The Retskin Report, PO Box 18481, Asheville, NC 28814-0481, 828-254-4487. 1986. Articles, photos, letters, news items, non-fiction. "The American Matchcover Collecting Club. Articles relating to matchcover collecting in America, and the matchbook industry in America, only." Back issues: $1 each plus S/H. (Minimum order 5). Payment: personal check or money order. Copyrighted, reverts to author. §Matchcover collecting-hobbies. Subject: Crafts, Hobbies.

Frontline Publications, Ernie Hernandez, PO Box 1104, Lake Forest, CA 92609, 949-837-6258. 1982. Articles, non-fiction. "Books about lawyers, management, science, and computers. Am seeking manuscripts on computer technology—particularly 'how-to' guidebooks; also books about lawsuit abuse." avg. press run 5M. Expects 1 title 2006, 2 titles 2007. Discounts: trade-none, wholesaler-50%, college classrooms-10% (on verified orders: instructor desk copies-free). 279pp. Payment: 10-15% of net. Copyrights for author. Subjects: Business & Economics, Computers, Calculators, Internet, Law, Management, Politics, Research, Science, Society, Sociology, Technology.

FROZEN WAFFLES, Frozen Waffles Press/Shattered Sidewalks Press; 45th Century Chapbooks, Bro. Dimitrios, David Wade, Rick Fox, The Writer's Group, 329 West 1st St., Apt. 5, Bloomington, IN 47403-2474, 812-333-6304 c/o Rocky. 1976. Poetry, fiction, articles, art, interviews, reviews, collages, concrete art. "Additional address: c/o Rocky, Apt. #5, 329 W. 1st St., Bloomington, IN 47403-2474. Want poems using the magic of the banal, subreal, 'everyday' (cf Prevert, Zen poetry, D. Wade & Richard Gombar's poems in *Stoney Lonesomes* No. 4 & 5, Spike Jones writing about Stravinsky's shoes squeaking, etc.) or the magic of the 'meta-real' (cf Breton, Neruda, Bly, the school of Duane Locke at it's best, etc.) Frags from diaries (names changed to protect the guilty), anecdotes, weird observations, fresh interviews, art work (India ink only!) will also be appreciated. Ditto: book & mag reviews (short!). Would like black India ink sketches of poets accepted by us. Preferably self-portraits: or by fellow-artists of poets. We have been delayed until funding problems stabilize. *Zen Events, Banal Episodes* has been superseded by *Hungry Horse in a Blank Field* by Dimitrios/Wade. One copy of *Death of a Chinese Paratrooper* by David Wade may still be available at the rare (unsalable) price of $115. Three deaths in our family in a short time period, etc. But we continue to work toward publication. Plan to print special issues of a single poet, also. Actually, *Frozen Waffles* is the *anthology* of poetry and art work and short fiction, etc. which will appear irregularly until funding permits us to function on an annual basis. Are filled up totally! Will let you know in this directory when to submit again. Are re-organizing and will remain silent until finished! Please NO more unsolicited material until notified!'' circ. 200-400. Irregular. sub. price will vary; per copy about $7.50 to rise to the occasion each year as inflation nibbles away; sample none. Back issues: $6 each (after 2 years: $10 each). Discounts: 10% off 5 or more. 36-80pp. Reporting time: 2 weeks-2 months; if no reply, you had no SASE, or material was lost in the mail. Payment: 1 copy. Copyrighted. Pub's reviews. §Poetry, poetics, bios of poets. No ads, not yet, anyway. Subjects: Asian-American, Book Reviewing, Dada, Fiction, Haiku, Native American, Photography, Poetry, Third World, Minorities, Translation, Zen.

Frozen Waffles Press/Shattered Sidewalks Press; 45th Century Chapbooks (see also FROZEN WAFFLES), David Wade, Bro. Dimitrios, Rick Fox, The Writer's Group, 329 West 1st Street #5, Bloomington, IN 47403-2474. 1980. Poetry, art, interviews, reviews, parts-of-novels, long-poems. ''Address for packages: c/o Writer's Group, PO Box 1941, Bloomington, IN 47402. Poetry, prose poems; almost any kind of short work (plays, aphorisms, parables [modern], fantasy, Si Fi, futureworlds, etc.). Oral & visual qualities to be expressed in cassettes, post cards, poster poems, etc. Please NO more unsolicited material until notified in this directory! 'Poetry videos' in the future are a possibility! Would like *input* on this.'' avg. press run varies. Discounts: hope to give breaks to people over 40; mental institutions, prisons, etc. 22-45pp, 85-125pp. Reporting time: 5 seconds to 5 days; if you don't hear from us, we probably never got your material. Simultaneous submissions accepted: no. Percentage of manuscripts published depends on quality. Payment: at least one free copy of your work(s); money later, much money much later; inflation has bloated our poverty. Copyrights for author. Subjects: Beat, Buddhism, Dada, Fiction, Haiku, Indiana, Jack Kerouac, Native American, Poetry, Third World, Minorities, Translation, Zen.

FUCK DECENCY, Andrew Roller, 5960 S. Land Park Drive #253, Sacramento, CA 95822, www.asstr.org/~roller/index.html, ftp://ftp.asstr.org/pub/authors/roller/. 1986. Poetry, fiction, articles, art, photos, cartoons, interviews, satire, criticism, reviews, music, letters, parts-of-novels, news items, non-fiction. ''Send only a few poems.'' circ. Internet only. 50/yr. Pub'd 10 issues 2005; expects 50 issues 2006, 50 issues 2007. sub. price Free; per copy Free; sample Free. Back issues: free. Discounts: free. 1 page. Reporting time: 4 weeks or longer. Simultaneous submissions accepted: yes. Publishes 50% of manuscripts submitted. Payment: free over the internet. Copyrighted, reverts to author. Ads: sponsored by Ad: $100. Subject: Erotica.

FUGUE, Ron McFarland, Faculty Advisor, Brink Hall, Room 200, Engl. Dept., University of Idaho, Moscow, ID 83844-1102, 208-885-6156. 1989. Poetry, fiction, articles, art, photos, interviews, satire, criticism, long-poems, non-fiction. circ. 250. 2/yr. Pub'd 2 issues 2005; expects 2 issues 2006, 2 issues 2007. sub. price $14; per copy $8; sample $8. Back issues: issue #13+ $5; others inquire. 100pp. Reporting time: 12 weeks. Simultaneous submissions accepted: yes. We publish 2% or less of manuscripts submitted. Payment: up to $50 for prose and $25 for poetry as funds allow. Copyrighted, reverts to author. Subjects: Criticism, Fiction, Non-Fiction, Poetry.

Fugue State Press, James Chapman, PO Box 80, Cooper Station, New York, NY 10276, 212-673-7922. 1990. Fiction. ''We publish experimental novels, nothing else. We are looking for emotional, vulnerable experimental writing, not technically dazzling writing. By experimental we mean something so personal and idiosyncratic that it doesn't seem to belong in the world. Please don't send detective novels, science fiction, etc., nor ordinary literary fiction. Please query first, and please only contact by email (info@fuguestatepress.com). Please don't send mss. by regular mail...thanks.'' avg. press run 1M. Pub'd 3 titles 2005; expects 3 titles 2006, 3 titles 2007. Discounts: 40%. 200pp. Reporting time: Immediate response (usually the same day) by email. By snail mail, it'll take months and months...don't use snail mail to query or submit to us! Simultaneous submissions accepted: but only submit by email after a query. Do not submit or query by snail mail. Publishes .3% (3/10ths of 1%) of manuscripts submitted. Payment: Minimal advance, sometimes paid in copies. The royalty rate is usually 10% of the cover price. Copyrights for author. Subject: Fiction.

Fulcrum, Inc., Robert C. Baron, Publisher, 16100 Table Mountain Pkwy #300, Golden, CO 80403-1672, 303-277-1623. 1984. Non-fiction. ''Non-fiction only: gardening (including the Xeriscape Series and the Survival Guide Series,)outdoors and nature (including the Front Range Living Series and an extensive list of Colorado titles), travel and outdoor recreation, Native American culture (including the Keepers Series and Vine Deloria's God is Red), the American West (including Notable Westerners Series and Notable Western Women Series), western culture, American history, memoirs and literature, the environment, teacher resources and childrens literature.'' avg. press run 4-6M. Pub'd 40 titles 2005; expects 50 titles 2006, 50 titles 2007. Discounts: bookstore 42% for 5, 45% for 25; non returnable 50%, libraries 20%. 230pp. Reporting time: 6 weeks. Simultaneous submissions accepted: yes. Publishes 2% of manuscripts submitted. Payment: negotiable. Copyrights for author. Subjects: Asian-American, Biography, Children, Youth, Conservation, Earth, Natural History, Education, Folklore, Gardening, History, Humor, Native American, Public Affairs, Self-Help, Sports, Outdoors, Women.

FULLOSIA PRESS, Thomas Dean, RPPS, PO Box 280, Ronkonkoma, NY 11779, deanofrpps@aol.com, http://rpps_fullosia_press.tripod.com. 1971. Poetry, fiction, articles, art, photos, cartoons, interviews, satire, criticism, reviews, letters, parts-of-novels, plays, news items, non-fiction. "*FP* is right/conservative in orientation but accepts the other point of view. Likes Arthurian legend Keltic themes. Special issues for Christmas, St. Patrick's Day, Independence Day, Labor Day. Recently published Peter Vetrano, Dr. Kelley White, Laura Stamps, Michael Ceraolo, John Grey, Charles P Reiss, Awesome David Lawrence. Short stories should be to the point, no more than 5 pages. *Submit by email*, text in message (no downloads); mail-ins must be accompanied by disk." circ. 500. 12/yr. Pub'd 14 issues 2005; expects 12 issues 2006, 12 issues 2007. sub. price $20; per copy $5; sample $5 e-publication. Back issues: $10. Discounts: free online. Reporting time: 1 week. Simultaneous submissions accepted: no. Publishes 30% of manuscripts submitted. Payment: none. Copyrighted, reverts to author. Pub's reviews: 15 in 2005. §Keltic issues, American Revolution. Ads: none. Subjects: Christianity, Civil War, Crime, Culture, English, H.L. Mencken, Military, Veterans, Movies, Native American.

THE FUNNY PAPER, F.H. Fellhauer, 615 NW Jacob Drive #206, Lees Summit, MO 64081-1215, felix22557@aol.com. 1985. Poetry, fiction, articles, cartoons, non-fiction. "SHORT - 500 to 1000 words - 16 line poem. NO FEE, contests pay $25 to $100." circ. varies. 4/yr. Pub'd 4 issues 2005; expects 4 issues 2006, 4 issues 2007. price per copy $2; sample $2. 10pp. Reporting time: most entries not returned. Simultaneous submissions accepted: yes. Payment: prizes and awards; $5/25/100. Copyrighted, reverts to author. §Humor. Ads: $3 per column inch. Subjects: Cartoons, Humor, Poetry.

THE FUNNY TIMES, Ray Lesser, Susan Wolpert, PO Box 18530, Cleveland Heights, OH 44118, 216-371-8600, Fax 216-371-8696, www.funnytimes.com, info@funnytimes.com. 1985. Fiction, cartoons, interviews, satire, reviews. "Prefer anything humorous, political (liberal), or satirical; mainly dealing with politics, relationships, animals, environment, and basic slice-of-life nonsense." circ. 74M. 12/yr. Pub'd 12 issues 2005; expects 12 issues 2006, 12 issues 2007. sub. price $23; per copy $2.95; sample $3. Back issues: $3 per issue. Discounts: available for newsstand distributors. 28pp. Reporting time: 6-8 weeks. Simultaneous submissions accepted: yes. Publishes 5% of manuscripts submitted. Payment: $160 per tabloid size (10 X 16'') page, divided accordingly. Copyrighted, reverts to author. §Humor books, compilations of humor and/or political cartoons. Ads: none. Subjects: Humor, Politics, Short Stories.

THE FURNACE REVIEW, Ciara LaVelle, 905 Michigan Ave., Apt. 3, Miami Beach, FL 33139-5352, submissions@thefurnacereview.com, http://www.thefurnacereview.com. 2004. Poetry, fiction, photos. "Online-only. Accepts only previously unpublished work. Recent contributors: Sarah Lynn Knowles, Matt Alberhasky, Ben Berman, Jill Holtz, Jillian Foster Knight, Allison Landa, Kelly N. Patterson, Luivette Resto-Ometeotl. Contact editor@thefurnacereview.com with questions, and see us online at www.thefurnacereview.com." 4/yr. Pub'd 2 issues 2005; expects 4 issues 2006, 4 issues 2007. Reporting time: 4 months. Simultaneous submissions accepted: Yes. Publishes 15% of manuscripts submitted. Copyrighted, reverts to author. §poetry, prose, fiction and photography from emerging writers and artists. Ads: $50/link, no text; $75/banner ad.

furniture_press (see also AMBIT : JOURNAL OF POETRY AND POETICS), Christophe Casamassima, 19 Murdock Road, Baltimore, MD 21212, 410.718.6574. 2002. Poetry, criticism, reviews, long-poems. avg. press run 100-200. Pub'd 6 titles 2005; expects 12-15 titles 2006, 12-15 titles 2007. 16-60pp. Reporting time: within the week for pamphlets, within 6 months for Ambit. Simultaneous submissions accepted: Yes. Publishes 10% of manuscripts submitted. Payment: 5 copies for pamphlets, 10 copies for chapbooks, 1 copy for Ambit. Copyrights for author. Subjects: Poetry, Zines.

Future Horizons, Inc., 721 West Abram Street, Arlington, TX 76013-6995, 817-277-0727, 1-800-4890727, Fax 817-277-2270, info@futurehorizons-autism.com. 1990. "Future Horizons specializes in autism/PDD information for families, employers, child care providers, and children. Although most our projects are first selected by our editor, we will accept outside proposals and manuscripts." avg. press run 5M. Pub'd 10 titles 2005; expects 5 titles 2006, 5 titles 2007. Discounts: 50-555. 256pp. Reporting time: 2 months. Publishes 2-3% of manuscripts submitted. Payment: 5-8%. Does not copyright for author. Subjects: Children, Youth, Disabled, Electronics, Family, Health, Medicine, Parenting, Safety, Self-Help.

THE FUTURIST, Edward S. Cornish, World Future Society, 7910 Woodmont Avenue, Suite 450, Bethesda, MD 20814-3032, 301-656-8274. 1966. Articles, art, photos, letters, news items, non-fiction. "A journal of forecasts, trends, and ideas about the future. *The Futurist* does not normally encourage freelance writers. Most of our articles are written by experts in their field who are not writers by profession. Similarly, we do not publish books from outside our staff." circ. 30M. 6/yr. Pub'd 9 issues 2005; expects 10 issues 2006, 6 issues 2007. sub. price $45; per copy $4.95; sample $4.95 + $3 postage. 60pp. Reporting time: 8 weeks. Payment: author's copies (10). Copyrighted, does not revert to author. Pub's reviews: 35 in 2005. §Future studies. Ads: $1250/$750/$2. Subject: Futurism.

G

Gabriel's Horn Publishing Co., Inc., James H. Bissland, Box 141, Bowling Green, OH 43402, 419-352-1338, fax 419-352-1488. 1981. "We do not consider unsolicted submissions. We prefer to recruit authors according to our editorial plans." avg. press run 3M. Pub'd 1 title 2005. Discounts: Different schedules for retailers, wholesalers, schools, and libraries. 160pp. Subjects: Americana, Cooking, Midwest, Ohio.

Gain Publications, Al Sheahen, Editor, PO Box 2204, Van Nuys, CA 91404, 818-981-1996. 1982. Non-fiction. avg. press run 5M. Discounts: 40%. 240pp. Subjects: Business & Economics, Politics, Public Affairs, Sociology.

The P. Gaines Co., Publishers, Phillip Williams, PO Box 2253, Oak Park, IL 60303. 1979. Non-fiction. "We are now concentrating on self-help, business and legal guidebooks. Current publications: *How to Form Your Own Illinois Corporation Before the Inc. Dries!*, *The Living Will and the Durable Power of Attorney Book, With Forms*, and *Naming Your Business and Its Products and Services.*" avg. press run 1M-5M. Expects 3 titles 2006. Discounts: standard. 150-200pp. Reporting time: 4 weeks. Payment: advances negotiable. Copyrights for author. Subjects: Business & Economics, How-To, Law.

Galaxy Press, Lance Banbury, 71 Recreation Street, Tweed Heads, N.S.W. 2485, Australia, (07) 5536-1997. 1979. Poetry, art, satire, criticism, long-poems, plays, non-fiction. "So far, only self-written (self aggrandizing? no) material, due to lack of real personal collaboration and ongoing contact in cases where material submitted was desirable. Traditional modes preferred with an emphasis on international contexts. Recent contributor: Sheila Williams." avg. press run 150. Pub'd 5 titles 2005; expects 5 titles 2006, 3 titles 2007. Discounts: 40%. 14pp. Reporting time: 2 weeks. Simultaneous submissions accepted: yes. Publishes 10% of manuscripts submitted. Payment: copies. Copyrights for author. Subjects: Australia, Christianity, Criticism, English, Poetry, Prose, Religion.

Galde Press, Inc., Phyllis Galde, David Godwin, PO Box 460, Lakeville, MN 55044, telephone: 952-891-5991, email: phyllis@galdepress.com web: www.galdepress.com. Poetry, fiction, non-fiction. avg. press run 1.5M. Pub'd 11 titles 2005; expects 8 titles 2006, 10 titles 2007. Discounts: 1-2 copies 20%, 3-4 30%, 5-99 43%, 100+ 50%. 200pp. Reporting time: 1-2 months. Simultaneous submissions accepted: yes. Publishes 20% of manuscripts submitted. Payment: 10% on collected monies. Copyrights for author. Subjects: Anthropology, Archaelogy, Biography, Children, Youth, Fiction, Folklore, Health, History, Metaphysics, Military, Veterans, Minnesota, Non-Fiction, Occult, Religion, Spiritual, Supernatural.

Galen Press, Ltd., M.L. Sherk, Jennifer Gilbert, PO Box 64400, Tucson, AZ 85728-4400, 520-577-8363, Fax 520-529-6459. 1993. Non-fiction. "We publish non-clinical, health related books directed towards both health professionals and the public. Current publication areas include biomedical ethics and guides for health profession students and educators. We concentrate on publishing books for which there is a defined need not currently being met." avg. press run 15M. Pub'd 3 titles 2005; expects 4 titles 2006, 4 titles 2007. Discounts: call. 448pp. Reporting time: 5 weeks. Simultaneous submissions accepted: no. Publishes 10% of manuscripts submitted. Payment: negotiable. Copyrights for author. Subjects: Careers, Civil War, Employment, Ethics, Euthanasia, Death, Forensic Science, Grieving, Health, Medicine, Non-Fiction, Nursing, Reference, Textbooks, Vietnam.

The Galileo Press Ltd., Julia Wendell, Editor-in-Chief, 3637 Black Rock Road, Upperco, MD 21155-9322. 1980. Poetry, fiction, long-poems, non-fiction. "Prints collections of poetry, short fiction, novellas, non-fiction and children's literature. It is best to query first before submitting." avg. press run 1M. Pub'd 3 titles 2005; expects 6 titles 2006, 5 titles 2007. Discounts: 40% to all bookstores; 40% to all classroom orders of 8 or more; 20%-55% wholesale; 10% courtesy library. 80pp. Reporting time: 3-6 months. Payment: 10% royalties plus author's copies. Copyrights for author. Subjects: Children, Youth, Fiction, Literature (General), Non-Fiction, Novels, Poetry, Short Stories.

Gallaudet University Press, John V. Van Cleve, Director and Editor-in Chief, 800 Florida Avenue NE, Washington, DC 20002-3695, 202-651-5488. 1980. Fiction, non-fiction. "Gallaudet University Press is a scholarly publisher specializing in work related to deafness, speech pathology, audiology, and related fields. The Press has a children's imprint called Kendall Green Publications that publishes children's texts and literature with a relation to hearing impairment, and an imprint called Clerc Books for instructional materials." avg. press run 3M-5M. Pub'd 12 titles 2005; expects 17 titles 2006, 13 titles 2007. Discounts: trade 40%, text 25%. 250pp. Reporting time: 2 months. Payment: 7.5% of net. Copyrights for author. Subjects: Autobiography,

Biography, Children, Youth, Education, English, Fiction, History, Language, Mental Health, Non-Fiction, Parenting, Sociology, Textbooks, Trade, Young Adult.

Gallery West Associates, James Parsons, Philip Bareiss, PO Box 1272, El Prado, NM 87529, 505-751-0073. 1980. Articles, art, non-fiction. "Writers must query. We are a very small art gallery press. *The Art Fever* is our first book publication." avg. press run varies. Pub'd 1 title 2005; expects 1 title 2006, 1 title 2007. Discounts: regular trade. Payment: by agreement. Usually copyrights for author. Subjects: Americana, Arts, Southwest.

Gallopade International, Michele Yother, President, 665 Highway 74 South #600, Peachtree City, GA 30269-3036. 1979. "We are not seeking submissions; do welcome inquiries about our writing/publishing books and workshops; as we begin developing CD-ROM titles, we will be looking for one freelance photographer in each state (video experience helpful); may hire one freelance writer in each state with Macintosh & who's willing to do work-for-hire following our guidelines. We also provide 3 month internships (non-paid) which include all aspects of our publishing company. Send resume and SASE for consideration." avg. press run based on demand. Pub'd 1200 titles 2005; expects 1000 titles 2006, 1000 titles 2007. Discounts: 1-9 20%, 10+ 50% non-returnable, all pre-paid; or returnable 1-4 20% FOB, 5-19 43% FOB, 20-49 45% FOB, 50+ 45% free freight. 36+pp. Subjects: Americana, Book Collecting, Bookselling, Business & Economics, Children, Youth, Cities, Communication, Journalism, Computers, Calculators, Drama, Education, English, Family, Fiction, Futurism, Games, Gardening.

Galt Press, Mark Warda, PO Box 186, Lake Wales, FL 33859-0186, 863-678-0011, galt@galtpress.com, www.galtpress.com. 1983. avg. press run 3M. Pub'd 1 title 2005; expects 2 titles 2006, 4 titles 2007. Discounts: 1-4 20%, 5+ 42%. 190pp. Reporting time: 90 days. Simultaneous submissions accepted: yes. Copyrights for author. Subjects: Collectibles, Divorce, Law, Politics.

•**GAMBARA MAGAZINE,** Scott Johnson, PO Box 3887, Santa Cruz, CA 95063-3887, editor@gambara.org. 2006. Poetry, fiction, articles, art, photos, satire, criticism, reviews, parts-of-novels, plays, non-fiction. "We will publish whatever we find interesting, under the presumption that others will find it interesting too. We have no specific mission beyond that. The content could be described broadly as 'literary,' but we resolutely avoid the soporific tales of quiet desperation that many associate with that word. See http://gambara.org for a full sampling of our delights. All pieces are first published on the website, and the best pieces from each year are collected in an annual print version near the beginning of the year, including a selection of visual art. The first print issue will come out January/February 2007." circ. 1500. 1/yr. sub. price $12; per copy $12; sample free online. Back issues: inquire. Discounts: 2-10 copies 20%. 250pp. Reporting time: 2-3 weeks. Simultaneous submissions accepted: Yes. Publishes 10% of manuscripts submitted. Payment: Compensation, at first, will consist of the rapture of creation. However, when the magazine goes to print, contributors will receive free copies. Copyrighted, reverts to author. Pub's reviews. §Out-of-the-way fiction, poetry, and non-fiction; overlooked but intriguing work generally. Subjects: Airplanes, Amish Culture, Bicycling, Drugs, Finances, Food, Eating, Galapagos Islands, Lighthouses, North Carolina, Numismatics, Elvis Presley, Reading, Satire, Scouting, Weather.

Garden House Press (see also OUT OF LINE), Sam Longmire, P.O. Box 321 Trenton, Ohio 45067, Trenton, OH 45067, 513-988-7183. 2003. Poetry, fiction, articles, interviews, non-fiction. "GARDEN HOUSE PRESS (GHP) is interested in writing that promotes peace, social justice, tolerance, diversity, freedom, healthy relationships, environmental justice, creativity, and sprituality. GHP publishes OUT OF LINE, an annual anthology of writings with underlying themes of peace and justice. Recent contributors include Michael Casey, Maureen Tolman Flannery, CB Follett, Paula Friedman, Lyn Lifshin, Karen Malpede, and Liza Lowitz. GHP is also publishing the anthology, GARDENING AT A DEEPER LEVEL, a collection of writings about the significance of gardening for the individual and the community. GHP has a liberal and progressive perspective. No hate literature." avg. press run 750. Pub'd 1 title 2005; expects 2 titles 2006, 3 titles 2007. Discounts: 2-5 copies 5%. 200pp. Reporting time: Two months for reporting. Simultaneous submissions accepted: Yes. Payment: Contributors receive 2 free copies and the opportunity to purchase additional copies at a reduced cost. Copyrights for author. Subjects: Biography, Black, Community, Conservation, Ecology, Foods, Education, Fiction, Gardening, Gay, Health, History, Humanism, Latin America, Lesbianism, Libertarian.

Gardenia Press, P. Elizabeth Collins, President; Robert L. Collins, Vice President, 17 Cale Circle, Newport News, VA 23606-3733, 866-861-9443, Fax 414-463-5032, pressgdp@gowebway.com, www.gardenia-press.com. 1999. Fiction, satire, non-fiction. "Gardenia Press specializes in fiction from first-time novelists. We started our non-fiction imprint (Hearthside Book Publishing) in 2001." avg. press run 2M. Expects 4 titles 2006, 4 titles 2007. Discounts: 45-55%. 300pp. Reporting time: 12-15 weeks. Simultaneous submissions accepted: yes. Publishes 2% of manuscripts submitted. Payment: 10.5%-12%. Copyrights for author. Subjects: Ancient Astronauts, Anthropology, Archaelogy, Biography, Fantasy, Fiction, History, Humor, Metaphysics, Motivation, Success, New Age, Non-Fiction, Romance, Science Fiction, Women.

GARGOYLE, Paycock Press, Richard Peabody, Co-Editor; Lucinda Ebersole, Co-Editor, 3819 North 13th

Street, Arlington, VA 22201-4922, Phone/Fax 703-525-9296, hedgehog2@erols.com, gargoylemagazine@comcast.com, www.gargoylemagazine.com. 1976. Poetry, fiction, articles, art, photos, interviews, satire, reviews, music, parts-of-novels, collages, non-fiction. "We only read submissions during the summer months. As we are celebrating our 30th anniversary with the release of issue #51 in 2006, we'll be taking this year off. Next reading period begins June 2007. Contributors: Kathy Acker, Gail Galloway Adams, Roberta Allen, Naomi Ayala, Doreen Baingana, Nicole Blackman, Marie-Claire Blais, Neil Boyack, Kate Braverman, Tiffany Lee Brown, Laura Chester, Jan Clausen, Paula Coomer, Lucy Corin, Quinn Dalton, Trevor Dodge, John Dufresne, Bruce Fleming, Thaisa Frank, Abby Frucht, Kate Gale, Steve Gillis, Elizabeth Hand, Nik Houser, Lida Husik, Christine Japely, Pagan Kennedy, Jesse Lee Kercheval, Nathan Leslie, Michael Martone, C. M. Mayo, Richard McCann, Pat MacEnulty, Kat Meads, Rick Moody, Thylias Moss, Eileen Myles, Susan Smith Nash, Susan Neville, Hal Niedzvicki, Naomi Shihab Nye, Lance Olsen, Toby Olson, Elizabeth Oness, David Petersen, Kit Reed, Kevin Sampsell, Lynda Schor, Julianna Spallholz, Megan Staffel, Patricia Storms, Elizabeth Swados, Todd Swift, Eileen Tabios, Venus Thrash, Angel Threatt, Jessica Treat, Paul West, Dallas Wiebe, and Lidia Yuknavitch." circ. 1.5M. 1/yr. Pub'd 2 issues 2005; expects 1 issue 2006, 2 issues 2007. sub. price $30 individuals (2 issues) $40 universities (2 Issues); per copy $18.95; sample $10. Back issues: inquire/limited. 350pp. Reporting time: 1-3 months. Simultaneous submissions accepted: no. Publishes 10% of manuscripts submitted. Payment: 1 copy and 50% off on additional copies. Copyrighted, reverts to author. Ads: $100/$60. Subjects: Fiction, Poetry.

Garrett County Press, Harvey Wallbanger, Editor, 828 Royal Street #248, New Orleans, LA 70116, 504-598-4685, www.gcpress.com. 1997. Fiction, articles, art, photos, cartoons, satire, letters, non-fiction. "The GCPress is pre-anti-ist." avg. press run 5M. Expects 3 titles 2006, 3 titles 2007. 200pp. Reporting time: 3 months. Simultaneous submissions accepted: no. Publishes 2% of manuscripts submitted. Payment: good. Does not copyright for author. Subjects: Sex, Sexuality, Worker.

Garrett Publishing, Inc., Arnold S. Goldstein, 2500 N. Military Trail, Suite 260, Boca Raton, FL 33431-6320, 561-953-1322, Fax 561-953-1940. 1990. Non-fiction. "Garrett Publishing, Inc. publishes mostly financially-based books, i.e. on asset protection and offshore financing, with the exception of *Dr. Amarnick's Mind Over Matter Pain Relief Program* and *Don't Put Me In A Nursing Home!*" avg. press run 5M. Pub'd 2 titles 2005; expects 5 titles 2006, 5 titles 2007. Discounts: U.S. book retailers, foreign accounts please inquire for schedule and terms. 300pp. Publishes 1% of manuscripts submitted. Payment: to be determined. Subject: Finances.

Gaslight Publications, PO Box 1344, Studio City, CA 91614-0344. 1950. Fiction, satire, parts-of-novels, plays, non-fiction. "Related to Sherlock Holmes only." avg. press run 5M. Pub'd 20 titles 2005. Discounts: 20%-40%. 176pp. Reporting time: query 3 weeks, mss. 3-12 months. Simultaneous submissions accepted: no. Payment: varies. Subjects: Mystery, Non-Fiction.

GASTRONOMICA: The Journal of Food and Culture, University of California Press, Darra Goldstein, 2000 Center Street, Suite 303, Journals Division, Berkeley, CA 94704-1223, 510-643-7154, Fax 510-642-9917, journals@ucpress.edu. 2001. Articles, art, photos, cartoons, reviews. "Send all editorial correspondence and submissions to Darra Goldstein, Editor, *Gastronomica*, Weston Hall, 995 Main Street, Williams College, Williamstown, MA 01267. *Gastronomica* is a vital forum for ideas, discussion, and thoughtful reflection on the history, literature, representation, and cultural impact of food. We welcome articles from any field touching on the history, production, uses, and depictions of food. Articles should generally not exceed 8,000 words. Each submission should be accompanied by a cover letter with the author's name, address, phone number and e-mail address, as well as a brief biographical statement, a 100-word abstract, and a word count. Since submissions are refereed anonymously, the author's name should appear only on the cover sheet. Send 3 copies. Manuscripts must be prepared according to the Chicago Manual of Style, with double-spaced notes at the end of the text. Artwork may be submitted as transparencies, JPEGS, or in clear photocopied form. Submissions will be returned only if accompanied by an SASE." circ. 10,332. 4/yr. Pub'd 4 issues 2005; expects 4 issues 2006, 4 issues 2007. sub. price $42 indiv., $175 inst., $30 student; per copy $10 indiv., $46 inst., $10 student. Back issues: $10 indiv., $46 inst., $10 student. Discounts: foreign subs. agents 10%, 10+ one-time orders 30%, standing orders (bookstores): 1-99 40%, 100+ 50%. 128pp. Reporting time: 4-6 weeks. Simultaneous submissions accepted: no. Payment: yes. Copyrighted, copyrights revert to author if requested. Pub's reviews. §Food studies, gastronomy, cookbooks, food and culture. Ads: $894/$600/$541 1/4 page. Subjects: Arts, Culture, Ecology, Foods.

Gateways Books And Tapes, Iven Lourie, Senior Editor; Linda Corriveau, Associate Editor; Matthias Schossig, Associate Editor, Box 370, Nevada City, CA 95959-0370, 530-477-8101, fax 800-869-0658, info@gatewaysbooksandtapes.com, www.gatewaysbooksandtapes.com. 1972. "Length-varied, spiritual, metaphysical bias. E.J. Gold. Labyrinth trilogy. Publishers of Robert S. de Ropp (The Master Game), Reb Zalman Schachter-Shalomi (The Dream Assembly), Michael Hutchison (The Book of Floating), Dr. Claudio Naranjo (The Enneagram of Society), and others. We will read query letters and proposals, and we will let authors know if their books fit our list. Email via info@gatewaysbooksandtapes.com or write to our P.O. Box." avg. press run

1M-5M. Pub'd 5 titles 2005; expects 6 titles 2006, 6 titles 2007. Discounts: 25/40% trade, 50% wholesalers (negotiable). 200pp. Reporting time: 3 months maximum. Payment: negotiable. Subjects: Arts, Games, Humor, Metaphysics, Non-Fiction, Psychology, Science Fiction, Spiritual.

A GATHERING OF THE TRIBES, Amy Ouzoonian, Associate Editor; Cynthia Lowen, Associate Editor; Cynthia Kane, Associate Editor; Jack Tilton, Visual Editor; Steve Cannon, Editor-in-Chief; Renee McManus, Managing Editor, PO Box 20693, Tompkins Square, New York, NY 10009, 212-674-3778, Fax 212-674-5576, info@tribes.org, www.tribes.org. 1991. Poetry, fiction, articles, art, photos, cartoons, interviews, criticism, reviews, parts-of-novels, long-poems, collages. *"Tribes* is a multicultural literary magazine of the arts. Recent contributors are Ishmael Reed, Jessica Hagedorn, Quincy Troupe, Victor Hernandez Cruz, Jayne Cortez, Paul Beatty, Karen Yamashita, and David Hammons. We are interested in non-traditional, non-academic work only, accept few unsolicited contributions and will only return work with SASE." circ. 3M. 2/yr. Pub'd 1 issue 2005; expects 2 issues 2006, 2 issues 2007. sub. price $20; per copy $12.50; sample $12.50. Back issues: sold out except 1993. 96pp. Reporting time: 3 months. Simultaneous submissions accepted: yes. Publishes 10% of manuscripts submitted. Payment: copies of magazine. Copyrighted, reverts to author. Pub's reviews: 1 in 2005. §Art, literature, culture. Ads: $495/$395/$175 1/4 page/$100 business card. Subject: Multicultural.

Gauntlet Press (see also GAUNTLET: Exploring the Limits of Free Expression), 5307 Arroyo Street, Colorado Springs, CO 80922-3825, info@gauntletpress.com, www.gauntletpress.com.

GAUNTLET: Exploring the Limits of Free Expression, Gauntlet Press, Barry Hoffmann, 309 Powell Road, Springfield, PA 19064, 610-328-5476. 1990. Fiction, articles, art, photos, cartoons, interviews, satire, reviews, letters, news items, non-fiction. "Looking for material dealing with censorship - prints both sides of the issue. Also looking for censored work (with history of censorship), and censored art. Length 1000-2500 words. *No taboos.* Contributors include Ray Bradbury, Isaac Asimov, George Carlin, artist Rubert Williams, Douglas Winter, William F. Nolan, Henry Slesar and Harlan Ellison. *No unsolicited submissions. Query with SASE. No exceptions."* circ. 8M. 2/yr. Pub'd 2 issues 2005; expects 2 issues 2006, 2 issues 2007. sub. price $16 postage included; per copy $6.95 + $2 p & h; sample $6.95 + p & h. Back issues: $9.95 + $2 p & h. Discounts: 30% bookstores, 20% libraries, 50-60% distributors, 20-30% for bulk purchases for classroom (10 or more). 112pp. Reporting time: 3-5 weeks. Publishes 10% of manuscripts submitted. Payment: 1/4¢ a word for text (up to 1¢), $2-$5 for art. Copyrighted, reverts to author. Pub's reviews: 20 in 2005. §Censored or controversial material, horror, fantasy or mystery. Ads: $400/$250/$175 1/4 page. Subjects: Civil Rights, Comics, Electronics, Essays, Fantasy, Fiction, Movies, Music, Mystery, Non-Fiction, Reviews, Satire.

Gay Sunshine Press, Inc., Winston Leyland, PO Box 410690, San Francisco, CA 94141, 415-626-1935; Fax 415-626-1802. 1970. Poetry, fiction, interviews, criticism, reviews, music, letters, non-fiction. *"Gay Sunshine* was founded in 1970 to publish cultural, literary, political material by gay people. During the first five years of its existence it published only the tabloid cultural journal, *Gay Sunshine,* which ceased publication in 1982. Since 1975 it has been publishing chapbooks and books. Publishes only books now." avg. press run 5M. Pub'd 2 titles 2005; expects 2 titles 2006, 2 titles 2007. Discounts: distributors to the Book Trade: Book People Distributors and Bookazine, Koen, (N.J.) Alamo Square San Francisco (at 40% discount). No discounts to individuals or libraries. Discounts to book jobbers & specialty shops. 192pp. Reporting time: 1 month. Payment: royalties. Copyrights for author. Subjects: Black, Erotica, Essays, Fiction, Gay, History, Interviews, Latin America, Literature (General), Poetry, Psychology, Sex, Sexuality, Third World, Minorities, Translation, Walt Whitman.

GAYELLOW PAGES, Frances Green, Box 533 Village Station, New York, NY 10014-0533, 646-213-0263 http://gayellowpages.com, gayellowpages@earthlink.net. 1973. "Directory of organizations, businesses, publications, bars, AIDS resources, churches, etc., of interest to gay women and men in USA & Canada. No charge to be listed; self-addressed stamped #10 envelope for details." Print on demand, CD, online edition, mailing lists. Please see website for details. 1/yr. Pub'd 1 issue 2005; expects 1 issue 2006, 1 issue 2007. sub. price $25; per copy $25; sample $25 by mail. Discounts: 40% consigned, 50% prepaid. 554pp. §Gay-related topics, gay-supportive feminist. Ads: Contact for details. Subjects: Bisexual, Feminism, Gay, Lesbianism, Lifestyles, North America, Women.

Gazelle Publications, T.E. Wade Jr., 11560 Red Bud Trail, Berrien Springs, MI 49103, 269-471-4717, info@gazellepublications.com, www.gazellepublications.com. 1976. Poetry, non-fiction. "We consider juvenile material that is not fantasy, material suitable for classroom use, or how-to material. Brochure available showing current titles. Query first. We are not currently using unsolicited material." avg. press run 4M. Pub'd 1 title 2005; expects 1 title 2006, 1 title 2007. Discounts: trade and library 20% to 48% or more. 150pp. Reporting time: 1 week. Payment: open, depends on market potential. Copyrights for author. Subjects: Children, Youth, Education, How-To, Poetry.

Gearhead Press, Bruce Rizzon, Co-Editor; Barbara Rizzon, Co-Editor, Attn: Bruce Rizzon, 53 Nash Street, Sparta, MI 49345-1217. 1975. Poetry, long-poems. "Our favorite poet right now is Bruce Rizzon. Write for free list of our titles. *A Walk in the Spring Rain, Vol. 2*, Fall 1981, $1.00. Also expect *A Desolate Angel. Blood on the Moon* $2.00 and *Ninth Street, Five Raindrops* in 82 or 83, *Diamonds And Rust Poems, For Sale Poems, Dean Lake Poems* $1.00, *Asphalt Shadows Poems* $1.50, *Osiris Rising Poems, I Am The Lonely Sea* $6.00, *Dago Red, The Road* $2.50, and *The Blues*, all by Bruce Rizzon. Make all checks/money orders payable to Bruce Rizzon." avg. press run 10M. Pub'd 3 titles 2005; expects 5 titles 2006, 5 titles 2007. Discounts: none. 26-60pp. Reporting time: 4 minutes to 4 years? maybe. SASE on all submissions. We will read all manuscripts sent to us. Give us time before we return any unused mss or unwanted mss. Copyrights for author. Subjects: Philosophy, Poetry.

Geekspeak Unique Press (see also PLOPLOP), John Clark, ploplopt@yahoo.com. 1991. Poetry, fiction, art, concrete art. "Recent books by Fielding Dawson, John Clark, Deb Sellers, J.T. Whitehead and Kit Andis." avg. press run 100. Pub'd 2 titles 2005; expects 6 titles 2006, 6 titles 2007. Discounts: 20%. 25-30pp. Reporting time: 6-8 weeks. Simultaneous submissions accepted: yes. Publishes 5% of manuscripts submitted. Payment: negotiable. Sometimes copyrights for author. Subject: Poetry.

GEM Literary Foundation Press, Cheryl Katherine Wash, P.O. Box 43476, Chicago, IL 60643-0476, 773-445-4946. 2002. Poetry, fiction, articles, art, photos, cartoons, interviews, satire, criticism, reviews, music, letters, parts-of-novels, long-poems, collages, plays, concrete art, news items, non-fiction. Copyrights for author. Subjects: Advertising, Self-Promotion, African Literature, Africa, African Studies, African-American, AIDS, Alcohol, Alcoholism, Festivals, Fiction, Novels, Picture Books, Poetry, Sex, Sexuality, Sexual Abuse.

Gemini Publishing Company, Don Diebel, 3102 West Bay Area Blvd., Suite 707, Friendswood, TX 77546, Phone: 281-316-4276, Fax: 281-316-1024, email:getgirls@getgirls.com, website: http://www.getgirls.com. 1978. Non-fiction. avg. press run 2M-3M. Expects 1 title 2007. Discounts: 1-24 50%, 25-49 55%, 50-99 60%, 100-199 65%, 200+ 70%. 200pp. Reporting time: 1 month. Simultaneous submissions accepted: yes. Payment: 5-10%. Copyrights for author. Subjects: Cities, How-To, Men, Women.

Gemstone House Publishing, Suzanne P. Thomas, PO Box 19948, Boulder, CO 80308, sthomas170@aol.com. 1998. Plays. "Current emphasis on real estate titles and personal finance. Recent title *Rental Houses for the Successful Small Investor, Second Edition.* Also looking at doing a series of romances set in Colorado at some point in the future. Prefer e-mail queries, mail queries okay. Unsolicited submissions will be recycled, not returned even if postage is included." avg. press run 3-6M. Expects 1 title 2006, 1 title 2007. Discounts: orders for 5+ books 40% if returnable, 50% if non-returnable. 304pp. Reporting time: 3 months max. Simultaneous submissions accepted: yes. Payment: varies-competitive. Copyrights for author. Subjects: Business & Economics, Finances, Publishing, Real Estate, Romance.

GemStone Press, Stuart M. Matlins, LongHill Partners, Inc., PO Box 237, Woodstock, VT 05091, 802-457-4000. 1987. Non-fiction. "Gemology, jewelry, education." avg. press run 10M. Pub'd 8 titles 2005; expects 2 titles 2006, 4 titles 2007. Discounts: 1-4 copies 20%, 5-4 40%, 15-24 42%, 25-49 44%, 50-99 46%, 100+ 48%. 304pp. Reporting time: 2 months. Simultaneous submissions accepted: yes. Publishes 5% of manuscripts submitted. Payment: depends on title and author. Copyrights for author. Subjects: Antiques, Collectibles, Consumer, Crafts, Hobbies, Design, Fashion, Geology, How-To, Jewelry, Gems, Lapidary, Visual Arts.

Genesis Publishing Company, Inc., Trudy Doucette, 36 Steeple View Drive, Atkinson, NH 03811-2467. 1994. Non-fiction. "General trade books on science, philosophy, and religion." avg. press run 3M. Expects 4 titles 2006, 4 titles 2007. Discounts: bookstores 30%, 10-24 40%, agents 11-50 40%, 51- 50%. 180pp. Reporting time: 3 weeks. Simultaneous submissions accepted: no. Publishes 5% of manuscripts submitted. Payment: 10%. Copyrights for author. Subjects: Biology, Christianity, Ethics, Fiction, Philosophy, Physics, Religion, Science, Textbooks.

•**GENIE: POEMS: JOKES: ART,** David Rogers, 1753 Fisher Ridge, Horse Cave, KY 42749. 2005. Poetry, fiction, art, cartoons, satire. "Be funny! Erotica is fine but not porn (there is a difference)." circ. 100. 2/yr. Pub'd 1 issue 2005; expects 2 issues 2006, 2 issues 2007. sub. price $5; per copy $2.50; sample $2.50. 50pp. Reporting time: 3 months. Simultaneous submissions accepted: yes, but only if writer promises not to withdraw. Payment: 1 copy. Copyrighted, reverts to author. Subjects: Erotica, Satire.

•**GENRE: WRITER AND WRITINGS, AIS Publications,** Alexis James, PO Box 42603, Indianapolis, IN 46242-0603, Office: (317) 856-8942, Cell: (317) 292-2615. "To offer a venue for writers in their various genre. The work, eventualy, will vary. This is a start up publication, therefore we are looking for contributors. We intend to offer contests, where we will read the submitted works and also, where we do not read submitted works. We accept queries and proposals for articles, columns, i.e., various subject matter. Standaard query letters and proposals are accepted." Reporting time: 2 months. Simultaneous submissions accepted: Yes, at this time we will accept simultaneous submissions, however, we would need to keep abreast of the status with your other submissions of the same manuscript. Publishes 10% of manuscripts submitted. Payment: Magazine copies with Author's article. in the process of copywriting publication. Pub's reviews: none in 2005. §We will review the reviews of books and magazines in most genres at this time. They must be clear, concise and contain no slander. Ads: Ads are accepted, however rates are in the works and soon to be published. Look for updates in the next 3 months. Subjects: Biography, Business & Economics, Euthanasia, Death, Finances, Forensic Science, Haiku, Holocaust, Human Rights, Humanism, Indigenous Cultures, Mental Health, Native American, Non-Fiction, Poetry.

THE GEORGIA REVIEW, Stephen Corey, Acting Editor; David Ingle, Assistant Editor; Mindy Wilson, Managing Editor, 012 Gilbert Hall, University of Georgia, Athens, GA 30602-9009, 706-542-3481. 1947. Poetry, fiction, art, photos, criticism, reviews, letters, non-fiction. "An international journal of arts and letters, past winner of the National Magazine Award in Fiction. Contributors range from previously unpublished to the already famous. Nonfiction preferences: thesis-oriented essays, *not* scholarly articles. Fiction and poetry selections are especially competitive. Translations and novel excerpts are *not* desired. Between May 15 and August 15,unsolicited manuscripts are not considered (and will be returned unread)." circ. 4M. 4/yr. Pub'd 4 issues 2005; expects 4 issues 2006, 4 issues 2007. sub. price $30 in US, $38 outside US; per copy $10; sample $7. Back issues: $10. Discounts: agency sub. 10% ads 15%. 208pp. Reporting time: 2-3 months. Simultaneous submissions accepted: no. Publishes less than .5% of manuscripts submitted. Payment: $40 per page for prose; $3 per line for poetry; plus copies and one-year subscription. Copyrighted, reverts to author. Pub's reviews: 61 in 2005. §General humanities and arts, poetry, fiction, essays, interdisciplinary studies, cultural criticism, biography. Ads: $425 inside front/back covers / $350 full page / $225 half page. Subjects: Criticism, Culture, Essays, Fiction, Literary Review, Non-Fiction, Poetry, Reviews, Short Stories.

GERMAN LIFE, Mark Slider, 1068 National Highway, LaVale, MD 21502-7501, 301-729-6190, Fax 301-729-1720, editor@germanlife.com. 1994. Articles, art, photos, interviews, reviews, letters, news items. "We publish articles from newsbriefs to feature length in size. For editorial guidelines and a sample of *German Life*, please send $4.95 to the attention of the Editor at above address." circ. 40M. 6/yr. Pub'd 6 issues 2005; expects 6 issues 2006, 6 issues 2007. sub. price $22.95; per copy $4.95; sample $4.95. Back issues: $5.95. Discounts: bulk 50%. 64pp. Reporting time: 8-10 weeks. Simultaneous submissions accepted: yes. Publishes 20% of manuscripts submitted. Payment: varies. Copyrighted. Pub's reviews: 15+ in 2005. §German culture, history, travel, German-Americana. Ads: $2575/$1675/$1110-1/3 page. Subjects: Europe, German, History, Travel.

GERTRUDE, Eric Delehoy, Editor; Justus Ballard, Fiction Editor; Steven Rydman, Poetry Editor, 7937 N Wayland Ave, Portland, OR 97203, www.gertrude-journal.com. 1998. Poetry, fiction, art, photos, interviews, parts-of-novels, concrete art, non-fiction. "Gertrude is a quality literary journal featuring the creative talents of gay, lesbian, bisexual, transgender, and straight supportive writers and artists. We strive to provide a positive forum in which to share these voices and visions, free of commercial advertising. Work is open to all subject matter and authors need not be GLBT but should be supportive of the community. Recent authors published: Casey Charles, Stephen Kopel, Carol Guess, Ronda Stone, Henry Alley, Francisco Aragon, Janell Moon, Noah Tysick, Janet Buck, Deanna Kern Ludwin, and Elizabeth Howkins." circ. 300. 1/yr. Expects 1 issue 2006, 1 issue 2007. sub. price $6.00; per copy $6.95; sample $6.95. Back issues: inquire. Discounts: Contributor discounts on copies and subscriptions. 72pp. Reporting time: 3-6 months. Simultaneous submissions accepted: Yes. Publishes 5-7% of manuscripts submitted. Payment: One copy of magazine in which author/artist's work appears. Copyrighted, reverts to author. Ads: Occasionally trades advertising with other literary journals. Subjects: AIDS, Bisexual, Feminism, Fiction, Gay, Gender Issues, Lesbianism, Literature (General), Multicultural, Non-Fiction, Poetry, Prose, Short Stories, Visual Arts.

•**GERTRUDE, Gertrude Press,** Eric Delehoy, PO Box 83948, Portland, OR 97283, www.gertrudepress.org. 1997. Poetry, fiction, art, photos, parts-of-novels, concrete art, non-fiction. "Gertrude is the biannual literary publication of Gertrude Press. Gertrude Press is a non profit 501(c)3 (status pending) organization showcasing and developing the creative talents of lesbian, gay, bisexual, trans, queer-identified, and allied individuals." circ. 150. 2/yr. Pub'd 1 issue 2005; expects 2 issues 2006, 2 issues 2007. 64pp. Reporting time: 3 months. Simultaneous submissions accepted: Yes. Publishes 3% of manuscripts submitted. Payment: Contributor Copies. Not copyrighted. Pub's reviews: none in 2005. §Beginning in 2006 we will publish 1-2 per issue. Ads: No advertising. Subjects: AIDS, Avant-Garde, Experimental Art, Bisexual, Feminism, Fiction, Gay, Lesbianism, Multicultural, Non-Fiction, Poetry, Prose, Short Stories.

•**Gertrude Press (see also GERTRUDE),** Eric Delehoy, PO Box 83948, Portland, OR 97283, www.gertrudepress.org. 1997. Poetry, fiction, art, photos, interviews, parts-of-novels, collages, concrete art, non-fiction. "Gertrude Press is a nonprofit 501(c)3 (status pending) organization showcasing and developing the creative talents of lesbian, gay, bisexual, trans, queer-identified, and allied individuals. We publish the biannual literary and arts journal, Gertrude, and limited edition poetry and fiction chapbooks." avg. press run 259. Pub'd 1 title 2005; expects 3 titles 2006, 4 titles 2007. 64pp. Reporting time: 3 months. Simultaneous submissions accepted: Yes. Payment: Literary Journal pays contributor copy, Chapbooks pay $50 plus 50 copies. Copyrights for chapbooks only; for journal, rights revert to author upon publication. Subjects: AIDS,

Arts, Avant-Garde, Experimental Art, Bisexual, Experimental, Feminism, Fiction, Gay, Gender Issues, Interviews, Lesbianism, Multicultural, Non-Fiction, Poetry, Short Stories.

GESAR-Buddhism in the West, Dharma Publishing, 2910 San Pablo Avenue, Berkeley, CA 94702, 415-548-5407. 1973. Poetry, art, photos, interviews, reviews, news items. circ. 3.5M. 4/yr. Expects 4 issues 2006, 4 issues 2007. sub. price $12; per copy $3.50; sample $2. Back issues: $2/copy. No discount for subscription. 48pp. Reporting time: 2 months. Payment: none. Copyrighted, does not revert to author. Pub's reviews. §Currenty, in-house creation by Gesar staff and Nyingma students. No ads accepted. Subjects: Buddhism, Philosophy.

Gesture Press, Nicholas Power, 623 Christie St., #4, Toronto, Ontario M6G 3E6, Canada. 1983. Poetry, art, photos, long-poems, collages, concrete art. "We are currently *not* accepting submissions. (We're interested in expansive poems with new formal concepts or unique lexicons. The content will determine the form of publication, completing the gesture)." avg. press run 100-250. Discounts: trade-40%, short-30%, agents-10%, libraries-full price. 1-40pp. Reporting time: 3 months. Publishes 5% of manuscripts submitted. Payment: percentage of print run (usually 10%). Copyrights for author. Subjects: Fiction, Photography, Poetry, Postcards, Visual Arts.

THE GETTYSBURG REVIEW, Peter Stitt, Editor, Gettysburg College, Gettysburg, PA 17325, 717-337-6770. 1988. Poetry, fiction, articles, art, photos, satire, criticism, parts-of-novels, long-poems, collages, non-fiction. "Suggested length for essays and fiction: 3,000-7,000 words. Recent contributors include: Sidney Wade, Reginald Shepherd, Rebecca McClanahan, Robert Wrigley, Alice Friman, James Tate, Debora Greger, Linda Pastan, and Robert Bly. We publish essay-reviews that treat books in broader context. Reading period Sept-May. Include SASE for reply." circ. 4M. 4/yr. Pub'd 4 issues 2005; expects 4 issues 2006, 4 issues 2007. sub. price $24, $32 foreign; per copy $6 + $1 p/h; sample $6 + $1 p/h. Back issues: $6 + $1 p/h. Discounts: bookstores 40% with option to return unsold copies. 184pp. Reporting time: 1-6 months. Simultaneous submissions accepted: yes. Publishes approx. 2% of manuscripts submitted. Payment: $2.50 per line for poetry, $30 per page for prose. Copyrighted, reverts to author. Pub's reviews: 2 books reviewed in 2005. §all. Ads: $225. Subjects: Essays, Fiction, Literature (General), Poetry.

Ghost Pony Press, Ingrid Swanberg, Editor, PO Box 260113, Madison, WI 53726-0113, 608-238-0175, ghostponypress@hotmail.com, www.geocities.com/abraxaspress, www.thing.net/~grist/l&d/dalevy/dalevy.htm, www.thing.net/~grist/ld/saiz/saiz.htm. 1980. Poetry, art, photos, interviews, long-poems, collages, concrete art. "We are interested in lyric poetry and prose-poems. Open to all forms. Considerable emphasis on the lyric mode. Books, chapbooks, pamphlets, broadsides. Past & upcoming contributors: Peter Wild, d.a.levy, Ivan Arguelles, Connie Fox, W.R. Rodriguez, Gerald Locklin, prospero saiz. Forthcoming: a retrospective collection of the black-and-white photography of Leslie Haber." avg. press run 500. Expects 2 titles 2007. Discounts: 20% 1-4 copies; 40% 5-9; 50% on orders of 10 and more copies. 120pp. Reporting time: 3 months or longer, we currently have a very great backlog of submissions (please send inquiries, not mss!). Simultaneous submissions accepted: yes. Publishes 2% of manuscripts submitted. Payment: copies. Copyrighting for author varies. Subjects: Avant-Garde, Experimental Art, Photography, Poetry.

Gibbs Smith, Publisher, Madge Baird, V.P. Managing Editor; Suzanne Taylor, V.P. Development Editor; Linda Nimori, Editor; Monica Weeks, Editor; Holly Venables, Editorial Assistant; Melissa Mikesell, Editorial Assistant, PO Box 667, Layton, UT 84041, 801-544-9800, Fax 801-544-5582, info@GibbsSmith.com. 1969. Poetry, fiction, art, criticism, non-fiction. "Additional address: 1877 E. Gentile Street, Layton, UT 84040. Books on architecture, arts, reprints, guide books, natural environment, poetry, children's, inspirational, cookbooks, nonfiction." avg. press run 5M-7M. Pub'd 45 titles 2005; expects 36 titles 2006. Discounts: 49.5% average. 144-160pp. Reporting time: 12 weeks. Simultaneous submissions accepted: yes. Publishes 1% of manuscripts submitted. Payment: 10% on net. Copyrights for author. Subjects: Animals, Architecture, Arts, Biography, California, Collectibles, Earth, Natural History, Environment, Fiction, New York, Novels, Short Stories, Southwest, Textbooks, Utah.

Gifted Education Press/The Reading Tutorium, Maurice D. Fisher, PO Box 1586, 10201 Yuma Court, Manassas, VA 20109-1586, 703-369-5017, giftededpress@comcast.net, www.giftededpress.com. 1981. Non-fiction. "Our books present clear and rigorous techniques for teaching gifted children in grades K-12 based upon using educational theory and practice. We are mainly interested in books on teaching the humanities, the sciences, and mathematics to the gifted. They are sold primarily by direct mail to school districts, libraries and universities across the nation. Some of our books are: (1) *Applying Multiple Intelligences to Gifted Education* by Holt & Holt; (2) *Technology Resource Guide* by O'Neill & Coe; (3) *The Philosophy of Ethics Applied to Everyday Life* by James Logiudice & Michael E. Walters; (4) *Humanities Education for Gifted Children* by M. Walters; (5) *How to Increase Gifted Students' Creative Thinking and Imagination* by W. Wenger; and (6) *Teaching Shakespeare to Gifted Children* by M. Walters. We are actively seeking manuscripts of 50 to 70 pages on educating gifted students and how to use computers with the gifted. We are also actively searching for field representatives to sell our books across the USA through workshops and inservice training. *Will not accept* *unsolicited manuscripts*—they will be returned to the author without being read! *Send 1 page letter of inquiry first*—this is all we need to determine if we're interested in your book.'' avg. press run 500. Pub'd 3 titles 2005; expects 5 titles 2006, 5 titles 2007. Discounts: 20% to jobbers & bookstores. 65pp. Reporting time: 3-4 months. Simultaneous submissions accepted: yes. Payment: 10% of retail price. Copyrights for author. Subjects: Children, Youth, Education, Philosophy, Psychology.

Gilgal Publications, Judy Osgood, Executive Editor, PO Box 3399, Sunriver, OR 97707, 541-593-8418. 1983. Non-fiction. ''We are currently publishing a series of 12 books on coping with stress and resolving grief. This is our Gilgal Meditation series. The contributors to each book are individuals who have lived through the experience they are talking about. For example, our first book was *Meditations For Bereaved Parents*. Some of the contributors to it were Paula D'Arcy, Meg Woodson & Joyce Landorf. The meditations are all 1 to 2 pages long and are written in what we call a ''sharing tone''. The authors aren't claiming to have all the answers. They are saying, ''this is what helped me; maybe it will help you too''. Our latest book released in Dec 1993 was *Meditations for Alcoholics and Their Families*. We ask that all potential contributors get our guidelines before they write a word for us.'' avg. press run 3M+. Discounts: for resale—40% off list. 72pp. Reporting time: 2 weeks - 2 months. Simultaneous submissions accepted: no. Publishes 5% of manuscripts submitted. Payment: on acceptance. Copyrights for author. Subjects: How-To, Psychology, Religion.

GIN BENDER POETRY REVIEW, T.A. Thompson, PO Box 150932, Lufkin, TX 75915-0932, ginbender@yahoo.com, www.ginbender.com. 2002. Poetry, fiction, photos, interviews, reviews. ''*Gin Bender Poetry Review* is a literary webzine whose goal is not to replace the print journal, but supplement it. We look for writers who practice their craft. We have an annual poetry contest.'' 3/yr. Pub'd 1 issue 2005; expects 3 issues 2006, 3 issues 2007. sub. price free online. 20pp. Reporting time: 4-6 weeks. Simultaneous submissions accepted: no. Publishes 10% of manuscripts submitted. Payment: 1 copy of newsletter. Copyrighted, reverts to author. Pub's reviews. §Poetry books and chapbooks. Ads: none. Subjects: Fiction, Haiku, Nature, Poetry, Prose, Short Stories, Zines.

Gingerbread House, Maria Nicotra, 602 Montauk A Highway, West Hampton Beach, NY 11978, 631-288-5119, Fax 631-288-5179, ghbooks@optonline.net, www.gingerbreadbooks.com. 1999. Fiction. ''At this time we cannot accept unsolicited mss. and will return mss. unopened. Will advise when this changes. Our launch list consists of revised reprintings of three modern classic children's picture books: *Grandpa Loved; Grandma's Scrapbook* and *Shh! The Whale is Smiling*.'' avg. press run 6M. Expects 3 titles 2006, 5 titles 2007. Discounts: industry standards. 32pp. Simultaneous submissions accepted: no. Publishes 0% of manuscripts submitted. Payment: competitive with industry standard. Copyrights for author. Subjects: Catholic, Children, Youth, Family.

GINOSKO, Robert Paul Cesaretti, PO Box 246, Fairfax, CA 94978, GinoskoEditor@aol.com. 1993. Poetry, fiction, parts-of-novels, collages. ''ghin-*oce*-ko: to perceive, understand, recognize, come to know; the knowledge that has an inception, a progress, an attainment; recognition of truth be personal recognition. Writing that lifts up the grace and apprehensions of human frailities yet carries with it the strength and veracity of humility, compassion, belief.'' circ. 1M. 1/yr. sub. price $12/copy; per copy $8; sample free. Back issues: $5. Discounts: none. 50-70pp. Reporting time: 4-8 weeks. Simultaneous submissions accepted: Yes. Payment: copy. Not copyrighted.

GIRLFRIENDS MAGAZINE, Heather Findlay, Editor-in-Chief, PMB 30, 3101 Mission St., San Francisco, CA 94110-4515, 415-648-9464, fax 415-648-4705, e-mail staff@girlfriendsmag.com, website www.girlfriends-mag.com. 1994. Fiction, articles, art, photos, cartoons, interviews, satire, criticism, reviews, letters. ''Submissions should have something to do with lesbian culture, politics, or entertainment. Recent contributors include Betty Dodson and Pat Califia; interviews: Camryn Manheim and Ani Difranco.'' circ. 30M. 12/yr. Pub'd 12 issues 2005; expects 12 issues 2006, 12 issues 2007. sub. price $29.95; per copy $4.95. Back issues: $9-15. 48pp. Reporting time: 8-12 weeks. Simultaneous submissions accepted: yes. Publishes 5% of manuscripts submitted. Payment: 10¢ per word. Copyrighted, reverts to author. Pub's reviews: 50 in 2005. §Lesbian, lesbian icon, feminist, gay, transgender. Ads: $2000/$1000/$800 1/3 page. Subjects: Bisexual, Culture, Feminism, Gay, Lesbianism, Relationships, San Francisco, Women.

Gival Press, Robert L. Giron, PO Box 3812, Arlington, VA 22203, 703-351-0079 phone, gival-press@yahoo.com, www.givalpress.com. 1998. Poetry, fiction, criticism, long-poems, plays, non-fiction. ''An imprint of Gival Press, LLC. We publish in English, French, and Spanish.'' avg. press run 500. Pub'd 5 titles 2005; expects 6 titles 2006, 6 titles 2007. Discounts: varies. 100pp. Reporting time: 3-5 months. We accept simultaneous submissions only if told that it is. Publishes 20% of manuscripts submitted. Payment: varies. Copyrights for author. Subjects: Essays, Fiction, Gay, Non-Fiction, Poetry, Textbooks.

Glad Day Books, Grace Paley, PO Box 112, Thetford, VT 05074.

GLASS ART, Shawn Waggoner, PO Box 260377, Highlands Ranch, CO 80163-0377, 303-791-8998. 1985. Articles, art, photos, letters. circ. 7M. 6/yr. Pub'd 6 issues 2005; expects 6 issues 2006, 6 issues 2007. sub. price

$30; per copy $6; sample $6. Back issues: $6. 64-80pp. Copyrighted. Pub's reviews.

GLASS TESSERACT, Michael Chester, Editor; Thomas Neuburger, Consulting Editor, editor@glasstesseract.com. 2001. Poetry, fiction. "Email only, no surface mail. Fiction up to 2,000 words, poetry of less than epic length. Eclectic in styles from traditional to experimental. The magazine is free online as a PDF file (for viewing, printing, or saving) at www.glasstesseract.com, accounting for most of our circulation. A comb-bound issue on linen paper, with color frontispiece and cover art is also available. A rotating selections menu on the site presents material from past, present, and future issues. All submissions & orders are by email." circ. 500. 2/yr. Pub'd 2 issues 2005; expects 2 issues 2006, 1 issue 2007. price per copy Not for sale. Bound copy free to author and selected complimentary copies. Sends pdf files, free to authors and others. 48pp. Reporting time: 4 months. Simultaneous submissions accepted: yes. Publishes 2% of manuscripts submitted. Payment: 1 bound copy & 1 pdf file of the magazine. Copyrighted, reverts to author. Subjects: Experimental, Fiction, Poetry, Prose, Short Stories.

GLB Publishers, W.L Warner, Editor & Publisher, 1028 Howard Street #503, San Francisco, CA 94103-2868, 415-621-8307, www.GLBpubs.com. 1990. Poetry, fiction, long-poems. "A press for books of fiction, nonfiction and poetry by gay, lesbian, and bisexual authors. Both explicit and non-explicit. Also PO Box 78212, San Francisco, CA 94107. Large GLB Internet presence for print books and e-books (downloading). Also a separate Division (Personal Publishing) for publishing assistance to self-publishers (see http://www.perspublishing.com)." avg. press run 3M. Pub'd 4 titles 2005; expects 6 titles 2006, 6 titles 2007. Discounts: 55%. 200pp. Reporting time: 2 months. Simultaneous submissions accepted: no. Publishes 30% of manuscripts submitted. Payment: variable. Copyrights for author. Subjects: Bisexual, Erotica, Feminism, Fiction, Gay, Human Rights, Lesbianism, Men, Non-Fiction, Parenting, Poetry, Psychology, Sex, Sexuality, Society, Women.

Glenbridge Publishing Ltd., James A. Keene, Editor-in-Chief & Vice-President, 19923 E. Long Avenue, Centennial, CO 80016-1969, 720-870-8381, fax: 720-870-5598, website: www.glenbridgepublishing.com, email: glenbridge@qwest.net. 1986. Non-fiction. "Currently have 5 additional titles in process, all of which are appropriate for all types of libraries (university, historical, college, community college, public, reference, etc.), the trade market and use as auxiliary text/text material for college, university, and community college as well as for business (management, sales, etc.)." avg. press run 2.5-7.5M. Pub'd 6 titles 2005; expects 7 titles 2006, 7 titles 2007. Discounts: jobber 20%, trade: 1-2 books 20%, 3-9 30%, 10-49 40%, 50-99 42%, 100-299 44%, 300-499 46%, 500-999 48%, 1000 50%. 200-300pp. Reporting time: 6-8 weeks. Payment: hard cover, 10%, pay once yearly. Copyrights for author. Subjects: Americana, Anthropology, Archaelogy, Arts, Biography, Business & Economics, Health, How-To, Music, Philosophy, Political Science, Politics, Psychology.

The Glencannon Press, R.B. Rose, Publisher, PO Box 1428, El Cerrito, CA 94530-4428, 707-745-3933, fax 707-747-0311. 1993. Fiction, non-fiction. "All ms. must relate to maritime history or subjects. We will consider non-maritime fiction for our Palo Alto Books imprint." avg. press run 1.5M. Pub'd 4 titles 2005; expects 4 titles 2006, 4 titles 2007. Discounts: 40% to retailers. Cloth 500pp, paper 200+pp. Reporting time: 2 months. Simultaneous submissions accepted: yes. Publishes 10% of manuscripts submitted. Payment: negotiable. Copyrights for author. Subjects: Christianity, Fiction, History, Non-Fiction, Sports, Outdoors, Transportation, War, The West, World War II.

Glimmer Train Press, Inc. (see also GLIMMER TRAIN STORIES), Linda Swanson-Davies, Co-editor; Susan Burmeister-Brown, Co-editor, 1211 NW Glisan St., Suite 207, Portland, OR 97209, Ph: 503/221-0836 Web site address: www.glimmertrain.org. 1990. Fiction. "Literary short fiction. We look for work that is extraordinarily well written and emotionally significant. Recent contributors include Pulitzer Prize winners and just-emerging writers." avg. press run 12000. Pub'd 4 titles 2005; expects 4 titles 2006, 4 titles 2007. Discounts: Distributors: 100+ copies, 50% discount. All others, prepaid and shipped to same address, 5+ copies, 40% discount. 250pp. Reporting time: Varies by category. See our writing guidelines at www.glimmertrain.org. Please don't make simultaneous submissions to our competitions. DUSTBOOKS, IF YOU MUST SIMPLIFY HERE, JUST STICK WITH "NO." THANKS! Payment: Payment ranges by category, from $700 - $2,000 for an accepted piece. See guidelines. We buy 1st-pub rights. When we print story, we list author name, year, and copyright symbol. Subjects: Fiction, Literature (General).

GLIMMER TRAIN STORIES, Glimmer Train Press, Inc., Linda Swanson-Davies, 1211 NW Glisan St., Suite 207, Portland, OR 97209, Ph: 503/221-0836 Web site address: www.glimmertrain.org. 1990. Fiction. "We publish new literary short stories by big names (Robert Olen Butler, Ann Beattie, William Trevor, Junot Diaz, Joyce Carol Oates), and by unpublished or lightly published writers. We look for great writing with emotional significance. New authors are especially welcome. Please make all submissions via our online submission procedure. Visit our site: www.glimmertrain.org." circ. 12000. 4/yr. Pub'd 4 issues 2005; expects 4 issues 2006, 4 issues 2007. sub. price $36; per copy $12; sample $12. Back issues: $13. Discounts: 100+ copies to distributors, 50% discount.All others, 5+ copies, prepaid, 40% discount. 250pp. Reporting time: Depends on category. See writing guidelines: www.glimmertrain.org. Simultaneous submissions accepted: No. Publishes 1% of manuscripts submitted. Payment: $700 upon acceptance. Copyrighted, reverts to author. §Literary short stories. Subjects: Fiction, Literature (General).

•**GLOBAL ONE TRAVEL & AUTOMOTIVE MAGAZINE, Knowledge Concepts Publishing,** Ella Patterson, P. O. Box 3084, Cedar Hill, TX 75105-3084, 972-223-1558. 2003. Articles, photos, cartoons, interviews, reviews, letters, news items. "Mission: To disseminate information on auto, travel, cuisine, hotels, resorts." Pub'd 4 issues 2005; expects 4 issues 2006, 4 issues 2007. sub. price $12; per copy $1.00; sample $1.00. Back issues: inquire. Discounts: 2-10 copies 10%11-20 copies 15%20-above copis 20%. 32pp. Reporting time: 7 to 10 days. Simultaneous submissions accepted: No. Payment: 10 cents per word. Copyrighted, does not revert to author. Pub's reviews: 10 in 2005. §automotive, travel. hotels, resorts, cuisine. Ads: Full page 2000Half page 15001/4 page 10001/3 page 500. Subjects: Airplanes, Autos, Aviation, Careers, Family, Fashion, How-To, Humor, Insurance, Lifestyles, Nutrition, Performing Arts, Photography, Real Estate, Safety.

Global Options (see also SOCIAL JUSTICE: A JOURNAL OF CRIME, CONFLICT, & WORLD ORDER), Gregory Shank, PO Box 40601, San Francisco, CA 94140, 415-550-1703. 1974. Articles, interviews, reviews. "Send editorial material and ordering information: Social Justice, PO Box 40601, San Francisco, CA 94140." avg. press run 3M. Pub'd 4 titles 2005; expects 4 titles 2006, 4 titles 2007. Discounts: Distribution handled through DeBoer, Ingram, Ubiquity. 200pp. Reporting time: 1-3 months. Simultaneous submissions accepted: no. Publishes 40% of manuscripts submitted. Payment: varies. Copyrights for author. Subjects: Book Reviewing, Civil Rights, Community, Crime, Drugs, Human Rights, Labor, Law, Prison, Socialist, Society, Sociology, Tapes & Records, Third World, Minorities.

Global Sports Productions, Ltd., Ed Kobak, 1223 Broadway, Suite 102, Santa Monica, CA 90404, 310-454-9480, Fax 253-874-1027, globalnw@earthlink.net, www.sportsbooksempire.com. 1980. avg. press run 15M. Pub'd 5 titles 2005; expects 5 titles 2006, 6 titles 2007. Discounts: 20% to bookstores and distributors. 505pp. Simultaneous submissions accepted: no. Publishes 0% of manuscripts submitted. Does not copyright for author. Subjects: Careers, Communication, Journalism, Crafts, Hobbies, Employment, Reference, Sports, Outdoors.

GLOBAL VEDANTA, Swami Bhaskarananda, Allen R. Freedman, Stafford Smith, 2716 Broadway Avenue East, Seattle, WA 98102-3909, 206-323-1228, Fax 206-329-1791, global@vedanta-seattle.org, www.vedanta-seattle.org. 1996. Poetry, fiction, articles, art, photos, cartoons, interviews, satire, reviews, letters, news items, non-fiction. "1,500 to 1,700 words. Recent contributors:Swami Adiswarananda, Swami Akhilananda, Swami Asitananda, Russell Atkinson, Swami Atmajayananda, Elias Augustinho, Pravrajika Ajayaprana, Swami Ashokananda, Ila Basu, Swami Bhaktimayananda, Swami Bhaskarananda, Dr. Kidoor Bhat, Scott Cantrell, Arindam Chakrabarti, Dr. Malay Chakrabarti, Sujit Chakrabartty, Biswaranjan Chakraborty, Ramananda Chatterjee, Asim Chaudhuri, Swami Chetanananda, Sheldon Douglass, Richard Engstrom, Allen Freedman, Devra Freedman, Dr. Amit Goswami, Umesh Gulati, Terry Jang, John Kloeck, Dipak Lakhani, Dr. Peeyush K. Lala, Mrs. Angelica Landreani, Marion Lee, Pravrajika Madhavaprana, Swami Manishananda, Charles Mathias, Swami Medhasananda, Mrs. Runu Midy, Amita Modi, Luiz Antonio Souto Monteiro, Prabhat K Mukherjee, Swami Nikhilananda, Dr. Thillayvel Naidoo, Swami Nihsreyasananda, Henrique de Souza Nunes, Bahut Pagal, William Page, Vijai Pasricha, Joseph Peidle, Swami Prabhananda, Bhaskar Puri, Mrs. Charlene Ratcliffe, Carmen Lucia Reis, Dr. Bob Rice, Mithra Sankrithi, Swami Sarvatmananda,.Swami Satprakashananda, Swami Shraddhananda, Stafford Smith, Dr. Anil Sookdeo, Swami Sunirmalananda, Dr. Mohini Sindwani, Joao Trevisan, Pravrajika Varadaprana, Pravrajika Vidyaprana, Swami Vidyatmananda, Brahmachari Vimuktachaitanya, John Yale." circ. 800. 4/yr. Pub'd 4 issues 2005; expects 4 issues 2006, 4 issues 2007. sub. price $10, $12 Canada & Mexico, $15 Central & South America & Europe, $17 all other countries; per copy $3; sample free. Back issues: $3. Discounts: none on subscriptions, otherwise 40% on individual copies for resale or bulk purchase. 16pp. Reporting time: a few days. Simultaneous submissions accepted: yes. Publishes 50% of manuscripts submitted. Payment: none. Copyrighted, reverts to author. Pub's reviews: 6 in 2005. §Broad-minded religious books of any tradition. Ads: none. Subject: Religion.

Gloger Family Books, Yehoshua Gloger, 2020 NW Northrup Street #311, Portland, OR 97209-1679. 1989. avg. press run 2M. Pub'd 1 title 2005; expects 1 title 2006, 1 title 2007. Discounts: 40%. 250pp. Reporting time: 1 month. Simultaneous submissions accepted: yes. Publishes 10% of manuscripts submitted. Payment: 50% net profit. Does not copyright for author. Subjects: Judaism, Religion, Spiritual.

Goats & Compasses, Peter Mittenthal, PO Box 524, Brownsville, VT 05037, 802-484-5169. 1991. Poetry, long-poems, plays. avg. press run 500. Pub'd 2 titles 2005; expects 2 titles 2006. Discounts: none. 26pp. Reporting time: 3 months. Simultaneous submissions accepted: no. Publishes 1% of manuscripts submitted. Payment: percentage of copies. Copyrights for author. Subjects: Poetry, Translation.

Gold Standard Press, Corporate Service Center, 5190 Neil Road, Suite 430, Reno, NV 89502-8535, contact@kokobono.com.

Golden Door Press, Keith Walker, 6450 Stone Bridge Road, Santa Rosa, CA 95409, (707) 538-5018. 1994. Fiction, non-fiction. Expects 1 title 2006. Discounts: All copies 40%. 250pp. Copyrights for author.

GOLDEN ISIS MAGAZINE, Golden Isis Press, Gerina Dunwich, Al B. Jackter, PO Box 4263, Chatsworth, CA 91313-4263, 775-417-0737 phone/Fax, golden.isis@prodigy.net. 1980. Articles, art, interviews, reviews, letters, news items, non-fiction. "The main focus of the publication is on New Age, Pagan spirituality, magick, and the metaphysical. Recent contributors: Maria Gladstone, RuneRaven, J.H. Grayson, Hugh Henderson, Jon Remmet, Barbara Hastings." circ. 4M. 4/yr. Pub'd 4 issues 2005; expects 4 issues 2006, 4 issues 2007. sub. price $20; per copy $5; sample $5. Discounts: none. 100pp. Reporting time: 1-2 months. Simultaneous submissions accepted: yes. Publishes 10-15% of manuscripts submitted. Payment: free subscription. Copyrighted, reverts to author. Pub's reviews: 96 in 2005. §New Age, paganism, witchcraft, wicca, occult, metaphysics, magick, shamanism, paranormal, astrology, divination, crystals, tarot, palmistry, numerology, runes, herbs, alternative healing, UFOs, poetry. Ads: $100/$50. Subjects: Astrology, Book Reviewing, Metaphysics, New Age, Non-Fiction, Occult, Reviews, Supernatural, Tarot.

Golden Isis Press (see also GOLDEN ISIS MAGAZINE), Gerina Dunwich, PO Box 4263, Chatsworth, CA 91313. 1980. Poetry, fiction, art, satire, long-poems, non-fiction. "A one-time reading fee of $10 (refunded upon publication of the work) plus return postage is required with each chapbook submission. Maximum length for manuscripts (including artwork, diagrams, etc.) is 80 pages. Query first with SASE or send complete manuscript with brief cover letter and reading fee. Simultaneous, photocopied and reprint submissions O.K. We also accept computer printout submissions. Sample chapbooks are available for $9.95 (postpaid)." avg. press run 1M. Expects 1 title 2006. 52pp. Reporting time: 1-2 months. Simultaneous submissions accepted: yes. Publishes 10% of manuscripts submitted. Payment: 10% royalties on all copies sold for as long as the book remains in print; we also offer 10 free copies of the book. Copyrights for author. Subjects: Astrology, Feminism, Gay, Haiku, Lesbianism, Metaphysics, Myth, Mythology, Native American, New Age, Non-Fiction, Occult, Poetry, Spiritual, Supernatural, Tarot.

Golden Quill Press, 102 Keswick Farm Road, Troutville, VA 24175-7130, 845-627-0386, thewritesource@pobox.com, www.thewritesource.homestead.com www.tellittothefuture.homestead.com, www.writersint.homestead.com. 1988. Poetry, fiction, non-fiction. "Only do cooperative publishing." avg. press run 1M. Pub'd 3 titles 2005; expects 5 titles 2006, 5 titles 2007. Discounts: 20-40%. 200pp. Simultaneous submissions accepted: no. Copyrights for author. Subjects: Fiction, History.

Golden West Books, Donald Duke, PO Box 80250, San Marino, CA 91118-8250, 626-458-8148. 1961. Photos. avg. press run 4M-5M. Expects 2 titles 2006, 2 titles 2007. Discounts: 40%. 265pp. Reporting time: 3 weeks. Payment: 10% royalties. Copyrights for author. Subjects: Health, History, Transportation.

GoldenHouse Publishing Group, Greg Roadifer, 290 Energy Boulevard, Billings, MT 59102-6806, 406-655-1224, groadifer@msn.com. 1998. Non-fiction. "Very selective with self-help emphasis. Recent/current project: The Golden Guru Book Series." avg. press run 5M. Pub'd 1 title 2005; expects 1 title 2007. 144pp. Simultaneous submissions accepted: no. Publishes 1% of manuscripts submitted. Payment: variable. Does not copyright for author. Subjects: Health, Management, Marketing, Self-Help.

GoldenIsle Publishers, Inc., Tena Ryals, Laura Dykes, 2395 Hawkinsville Highway, Eastman, GA 31023, 478-374-5806(5841), Fax 478-374-9720. 1998. "Novels (hardcover) Writers: Don Johnson, Fern Smith-Brown, Jack P. Jones, and Clifford Moody. Novels are 224-500 pages in length. One nonfiction and one novel scheduled for publication in 2005." avg. press run 1M. Expects 2 titles 2007. Discounts: 10-55%. 224pp. Reporting time: not accepting any at present, except by invitation. Payment: Industry standard. Copyrights for author. Subjects: Fiction, Humor, Medicine, Novels.

Goldfish Press (see also CHRYSANTHEMUM), Koon Woon, 202 6th Avenue South #1105, Seattle, WA 98104-2303, 206-682-3851, nooknoow@aol.com. 1989. Poetry, fiction, articles, satire, criticism, parts-of-novels, non-fiction. "Interested in works that combine literature with philosophy and socially-conscious." avg. press run 500. Expects 1 title 2006, 2 titles 2007. Discounts: negotiable. 200pp. Reporting time: 3 months. Payment: negotiable. Copyrights for author. Subjects: Asian-American, Black, Native American, Philosophy, Poetry, Third World, Minorities.

Good Book Publishing Company, Dick B., PO Box 837, Kihei, HI 96753-0837, 808-874-4876, dickb@dickb.com, www.dickb.com/index.shtml. 1991. Non-fiction. "Publishing company formed to enable books to be written and published and sold to members of Alcoholics Anonymous, Twelve Step programs, recovery centers and workers, the religious community, historians, archivists, and scholars. Titles should relate to the Biblical and spiritual roots of A.A. and to the history of the basic ideas A.A. derived from the Bible and Christian sources. Exclusive distributor of Paradise Research Publications, Inc." avg. press run 3M. Pub'd 3 titles 2005; expects 5 titles 2006, 6 titles 2007. Discounts: 20% individual, 40% volume. 400pp. Reporting time: 1 week. Simultaneous submissions accepted: yes. Payment: 10%, no advance. Does not copyright for author. Subjects: Alcohol, Alcoholism, Biography, Christianity, Health, History, Inspirational, Non-Fiction, Reference, Religion, Spiritual.

GOOD GIRL, Nikko Snyder, Candis Steenbergen, 837 rue Gilford, Montreal, QB H2J 1P1, Canada,

514-288-5626, Fax 514-499-3904, info@goodgirl.ca, www.goodgirl.ca. 2002. Poetry, articles, art, photos, cartoons, interviews, satire, criticism, reviews, music, letters, collages, concrete art, news items, non-fiction. ''See writers guidelines on our website.'' circ. 750. 3-4/yr. Pub'd 2 issues 2005; expects 3 issues 2006, 4 issues 2007. sub. price $19.95; per copy $5.50; sample $7. Back issues: $7. 32pp. Reporting time: 2-4 months. Simultaneous submissions accepted: no. Payment: none. Copyrighted, reverts to author. Pub's reviews: 15 in 2005. §Social justice, pop culture, environment, gender, race, feminism. Ads: $500/$200/$100. Subjects: African-American, AIDS, Alternative Medicine, Anarchist, Arts, Avant-Garde, Experimental Art, Birth, Birth Control, Population, Community, Feminism, Gay.

Good Hope Enterprises, Inc. (see also THE AFRICAN HERALD), Dr. Richard O. Nwachukwu, PO Box 132394, Dallas, TX 75313-2394, 214-823-7666, fax 214-823-7373. 1987. Non-fiction. ''The company published *The Dark and Bright Continent: Africa in the Changing World, The Agony: The Untold Story of the Nigerian Society.*'' avg. press run 5M. Pub'd 1 title 2005; expects 2 titles 2006, 2 titles 2007. Discounts: 35% to 55%. 200pp. Reporting time: 3 months. Payment: based on sales. Copyrights for author. Subjects: African Literature, Africa, African Studies, Business & Economics, Politics.

Good Life Products, Martha Fernandez, PO Box 170070, Hialeah, FL 33017-0070, 305-362-6998, Fax 305-557-6123. 1986. Non-fiction. ''We specialize in the field of Cosmetology. We publish books on haircutting, coloring and permanent waving. Also produce videotapes. We also publish in Spanish. Not accepting submissions at this time.'' avg. press run 5M. Pub'd 2 titles 2005; expects 2 titles 2006, 4 titles 2007. Discounts: 4-9 20%, 10-19 30%, 20-39 40%, 40+ 50%. 200pp. Copyrights for author. Subject: How-To.

Good News Publishing Ministries, 690 Mount Airey Church Road, Columbus, MS 39701-9712, 662-245-1376, 1-877-59-GOODNEWS, Fax 662-245-1343, dapoet1@bellsouth.net, www.dgoodnews.com.

Good Times Publishing Co., Dorothy Miller, 2211 West 2nd Avenue #209, Vancouver, B.C. V6K 1H8, Canada, 604-736-1045. 1989. Non-fiction. ''Most recent publication: *Food For Success*, by Dr. Barbarah Tinskamper. At present we limit ourselves to self-help books only. In particular, nutrition and psychology. The author should have a university education of a reputable institution and have several years of experience in the field that he/she is writing about. The book should be geared to the general public; the style and format should be easy and fun to read.'' avg. press run 5M. Pub'd 3 titles 2005; expects 1 title 2006, 2 titles 2007. Discounts: 55% wholesale, 40% bookstores. 140pp. Reporting time: 2 months. Payment: 2-4%. Copyrights for author. Subject: How-To.

GOODIE, Panther Books, Romy Ashby, Editor; Foxy Kidd, Publisher, 197 7th Avenue #4C, New York, NY 10011, www.goodie.org, romy@goodie.org, foxy@goodie.org. 1999. price per copy $5. Discounts: 30% for magazines; 40% for books. 20pp.

Goose River Press, Deborah J. Benner, 3400 Friendship Road, Waldoboro, ME 04572, Telephone & Fax: 207-832-6665, e mail: gooseriverpress@adelphia.net, web:www.gooseriverpress.com. 2000. Poetry, fiction, plays, non-fiction. avg. press run 500. Expects 5 titles 2006, 5 titles 2007. Discounts: to be negotiated. 100pp. Reporting time: 2 weeks. Simultaneous submissions accepted: no. Publishes 10% of manuscripts submitted. Payment: to be negotiated. Copyrights for author. Subjects: Adolescence, Children, Youth, Christianity, Cooking, Fiction, Inspirational, Non-Fiction, Poetry, Short Stories.

GORHAM, Axios Newletter, Inc., David Gorham, 30-32 Macaw Avenue, PO Box 279, Belmopan, Belize, 501-8-23284. 1981. Poetry, articles, art, photos, interviews, reviews, letters, parts-of-novels, news items, non-fiction. ''A continuing journal of genealogy and history of all the various branches of the Gorham family. Need historical articles, on places named after the Gorhams, obscure Gorham pioneers, how to trace your ancestors, interviews of well-known persons involved in genealogy; new products about innovations in capturing, storing, indexing and retrieving data-personal opinion (must be in-depth and scholarly dealing with the Gorham genealogy and history); *Profiles of Present Day Gorham's.*'' circ. 3M. 4/yr. Pub'd 4 issues 2005; expects 4 issues 2006. sub. price $15; per copy $2; sample $2. Back issues: $2. Discounts: 40%, write for further information. 24pp. Reporting time: 6-8 weeks. Payment: $10 to $100 depending on article (sometimes 2¢ a word). Copyrighted, reverts to author. Pub's reviews: 25 in 2005. §Genealogy and history. Ads: $320/$175/30¢. Subject: History.

Gorilla Convict Publications, DK Schulte, Ben Osborne, PO Box 492, St. Peters, MO 63376, www.gorillaconvict.com. 2004. Fiction, photos, non-fiction. ''Gorilla Convict Publications was formed to give a voice to the convict. Its anthology series, "Prison Stories", is looking for the most real, violent, and bizarre stories from the belly of the beast. Seth M. Ferranti, the Gorilla Convict writer, penned the first Prison Stories title.'' avg. press run 10M. Expects 4 titles 2006, 5 titles 2007. Discounts: wholesale $7.50 for bulk to bookstores. 268pp. Reporting time: 3 months. Simultaneous submissions accepted: yes. Publishes 25% of manuscripts submitted. Payment: varies. Copyrights for author. Subjects: African-American, Black, Crime, Prison, Short Stories.

190

Gothic Press, Gary Crawford, 1701 Lobdell Ave. No. 32, Baton Rouge, LA 70806, 225, 925, 2917 www.gothicpress.com gothicpt12@aol.com. 1979. Poetry, fiction, criticism, long-poems. "Horror, Gothic, or dark fantasy." avg. press run 300. Pub'd 1 title 2005; expects 1 title 2006, 1 title 2007. Discounts: 40%. 50pp. Reporting time: 1 month. Simultaneous submissions accepted: No. Publishes 5% of manuscripts submitted. Payment: 10% royalty. Copyrights for author. Subjects: Criticism, Fantasy, Fiction, Horror.

Bruce Gould Publications, Bruce Gould, PO Box 16, Seattle, WA 98111. 1976. Non-fiction. "Publish books in the field of finance (business, stock and commodity markets)." avg. press run 10M. Expects 2 titles 2006. Discounts: 40% to bookstores, 55% to wholesalers. 200pp. Reporting time: 30 days. Payment: 10-20%. Copyrights for author. Subject: Business & Economics.

GRAIN MAGAZINE, Saskatchewan Writers Guild, Kent Bruyneel, Editor, PO Box 67, Saskatoon, SK S7K 3K1, Canada, 306-244-2828, grainmag@sasktel.net. 1973. Poetry, fiction, art, satire, parts-of-novels, long-poems, plays. "Only queries are accepted via e-mail; submissions are made in hard copy. Submissions will be considered only if accompanied by an SASE with sufficient Canadian postage or int'l reply coupon, or by an e-mail address. We publish only the best literary art. Length—flexible, though preferably not more than 8 pages of poetry and 30 pages of prose or drama. Fiction and poetry are the main focus; we also consider creative non-fiction, songs, and produced one-act plays or excerpts from produced full-length plays. Please look at a recent issue before submitting." circ. 1M. 4/yr. Pub'd 4 issues 2005; expects 4 issues 2006, 4 issues 2007. sub. price CND $29.95; USA $29.95 p/h $6.00; Foreign $29.95 p/h $10.00.; per copy $9.95; sample $13.00. Back issues: $13.00. 128pp. Reporting time: 3 months. Simultaneous submissions accepted: no. Publishes 5% of manuscripts submitted. Payment: $50/page up to $225, $50 visual art, $100 cover art, plus 2 copies of the issue. Copyrighted, reverts to author. Ads: $350/$225 CDN funds. Subjects: Arts, Drama, Fiction, Language, Poetry.

GRAND LAKE REVIEW, Martin Kich, Wright State University-Lake Campus, 7600 State Route 703, Celina, OH 45822, 419-586-0374, Fax 419-586-0368, martin.kich@wright.edu, www.wright.edu/~martin.kich/. 1997. Poetry, fiction, art, photos, cartoons, interviews, long-poems, collages, plays. "Now published only online, the Grand Lake Review was published for five years as an annual, paper publication, presenting the work of students and faculty at the Lake Campus, the work of writers in the communities the campus serves, and the invited work of selected writers from throughout the rest of Ohio. In 2004-2005, we published two online issues. Due to the volume of submissions that we have received, the Grand Lake Review will be published monthly beginning in September 2005. There are no geographical or any other kinds of restrictions on submissions. We are willing to consider all poetry, regardless of subject, form, or style (though we are not likely to publish work written mechanically in strict meter and rhyme schemes, work expressing greeting-card sentiments, or religious work that proselytizes). We are also very interested in receiving short stories, short plays, creative nonfiction, photos, and artwork. There is no submission fee and no payment. Published work will remain online." circ. online. 12/yr. Pub'd 2 issues 2005; expects 5 issues 2006, 12 issues 2007. Reporting time: 3-4 months. Simultaneous submissions accepted: yes. Payment: none. Copyright remains with author, although we do reserve the right to include work that we have published in future special collections. Subject: Literary Review.

Grand River Press, Michael Maran, PO Box 1342, East Lansing, MI 48826, 517-332-8181. 1986. Non-fiction. "We specialize in legal self-help publications for use in Michigan." avg. press run 3M. Pub'd 2 titles 2005; expects 2 titles 2006, 2 titles 2007. Discounts: 40% trade. 300pp. Reporting time: 3 months. Simultaneous submissions accepted: yes. Publishes 10% of manuscripts submitted. Payment: negotiable. Copyrights for author. Subjects: Law, Michigan.

Grand Slam Press, Inc., 2 Churchill Road, Englewood Cliffs, NJ 07632. 1995. Non-fiction. "Not accepting manuscripts at this time." avg. press run 3M. Pub'd 1 title 2005; expects 3 titles 2006. Discounts: bookstores 2-4 books 20%, 5-99 40%, 100+ 50%; wholesalers 25-49 50%, 50-99 52%, 100-999 55%, 1000+ 57%; schools and libraries 20% on orders of 5 or more. 168pp. Subjects: Children, Youth, Sports, Outdoors.

Granite Publishing Group, Pamela Meyer, Brian Crissey, PO Box 1429, Columbus, NC 28722, 828-894-8444, Fax 828-894-8454, GraniteP@aol.com, www.5thworld.com. 1988. Articles, art, photos, interviews, music, letters, news items, non-fiction. avg. press run 3M. Pub'd 6 titles 2005; expects 6 titles 2006, 12 titles 2007. Discounts: trade 40%. 220pp. Reporting time: 6 weeks. Simultaneous submissions accepted: yes. Publishes 1% of manuscripts submitted. Payment: 10%. Copyrights for author. Subjects: Alternative Medicine, Ancient Astronauts, Astrology, Astronomy, Botany, Buddhism, Edgar Cayce, Channelling, Conservation, Cosmology, Counter-Culture, Alternatives, Communes, Creativity, Crystals, Ecology, Foods, Native American.

GRASSLANDS REVIEW, Laura B. Kennelly, PO Box 626, Berea, OH 44017. 1989. Poetry, fiction, photos. "Shorter pieces of fiction fare better. Editors' Prize Contest semi-annually (even-numbered years). In *FF5* #43 we are described as 'a litmag which consistently publishes an interesting mix of work, some good old-fashioned stories plus stuff from the more experimental (but still solid) edge.' Authors published include John E. White, Don Shockey, Jennifer Gomoll, Zan Gay, William Bedford Clark, J.E. McCarthy, Barry Brummett, Greg

191

Jenkins, Brian Collier, Marlene Tilton, Christoph Meyer. Only material postmarked in October or March will be considered." circ. 300. 2/yr. Pub'd 2 issues 2005; expects 2 issues 2006, 2 issues 2007. sub. price $12 individual, $20 libraries; per copy $6 (recent); sample $5. Discounts: none. 80pp. Simultaneous submissions accepted: yes. Publishes 10% of manuscripts submitted. Payment: 1 copy with special rate for extra copies. Copyrighted, reverts to author. Subjects: Poetry, Short Stories.

GRASSLIMB, Valerie E. Polichar, P.O. Box 420816, San Diego, CA 92142-0816, valerie@grasslimb.com, www.grasslimb.com. 2002. Poetry, fiction, art, cartoons. "Contributors include Taylor Graham, Richard Kostelanetz, James Sallis, Leonard Cirino, Simon Perchik, Josey Foo. Although general topics are welcome, we're less likely to select work regarding romance, sex, the elderly, parents and children. Fiction in an experimental, avant-garde or surreal mode is often more interesting to us than a traditional story. Include word count in fiction; nothing over 2500 words can be read, prefer 1500." 2/yr. Pub'd 2 issues 2005; expects 2 issues 2006, 2 issues 2007. sub. price $5; per copy $2.50; sample $2. Back issues: $2.50. Discounts: wholesalers 65%. 8pp. Reporting time: 4 months. Simultaneous submissions accepted: yes. Payment: $5-$60 plus 2 copies. Copyrighted, reverts to author. Pub's reviews: 1 in 2005. Subjects: Crime, Experimental, Fiction, Literature (General), Poetry, Prose, Science Fiction, Short Stories, Surrealism.

GRASSROOTS FUNDRAISING JOURNAL, Kim Klein, Publisher; Stephanie Roth, Editor, 1904 Franklin St Ste 705, Oakland, CA 94612, 510-452-4520, Fax 510-452-2122, info@grassrootsfundraising.org, www.grassrootsfundraising.org. 1981. Articles, non-fiction. "Grassroots fundraising for social justice causes. Contributors: Kim Klein, Stephanie Roth, and others." circ. 4M. 6/yr. Pub'd 6 issues 2005; expects 6 issues 2006, 6 issues 2007. sub. price $39 for organizations with budgets under $250,000; $48 for organizations with budgets between $250,000 and $1 million; $56 for organizations with budgets over $1 million; per copy $5; sample free. Back issues: $5. Discounts: 25% for 10+ subs ordered at one time, discounts for bulk back issues. 20pp. Reporting time: 2 months. Simultaneous submissions accepted: yes. Publishes 20% of manuscripts submitted. Payment: $75. Copyrighted, reverts to author. Pub's reviews: 2 in 2005. §Fundraising, economics, organizational development. Ads: full-page display $1150/half-page display $500/other sizes available/price varies by size and frequency. Subject: Fundraising.

Gravity Presses (Lest We All Float Away), Inc. (see also NOW HERE NOWHERE), Michael J. Barney, Paul Kingston, 27030 Havelock, Dearborn Heights, MI 48127, 313-563-4683, e-mail mikeb5000@yahoo.com. 1998. Poetry, art, photos, long-poems. avg. press run 250. Pub'd 3 titles 2005; expects 4 titles 2006, 4 titles 2007. Discounts: negotable. 48pp. Reporting time: 3-6 months. Simultaneous submissions accepted: yes. Publishes 10% of manuscripts submitted. Payment: of the 250 copies the author gets 200, we get 50 to sell. Does not copyright for author. Subject: Poetry.

GRAY AREAS, Netta Gilboa, 4212 West Cactus Rd. #1110, PMB 195, Phoenix, AZ 85029-2902, www.grayarea.com. 1991. Articles, photos, cartoons, interviews, reviews, music, letters, news items, non-fiction. "*Gray Areas* is dedicated to examining the gray areas of life. We specialize in subject matter which is illegal, potentially illegal, immoral and/or controversial. Recent topics include: UFO's, adult films, drug testing, computer crimes, bootleg tapes, sampling, prank phone calls, etc. We also review books, movies, CDs, comics, concerts, magazines, catalogs, software, live video and audio tapes." circ. 10M. Irregular, 1-2/yr. Pub'd 1 issue 2005. sub. price $23, $32 1st class for 4 issues when published; per copy $6.95; sample $8. Back issues: $8 while available. Discounts: wholesaler and retail store available. 164pp. Reporting time: 1 month or less. Simultaneous submissions accepted if notified as such. Publishes 25% of manuscripts submitted. Payment: masthead listing, byline, copies. Copyrighted, rights reverting to author negotiable. Pub's reviews: 150+ per issue in 2005. §Virtually everything received—over 60 pages of reviews per issue. Ads: $600/$300/$150 1/4 page/$75 1/8 page $40. Subjects: Anarchist, Book Reviewing, Computers, Calculators, Counter-Culture, Alternatives, Communes, Crime, Drugs, Bob Dylan, Interviews, Law, Magazines, Music, Reviews, Sex, Sexuality, Sociology, Tapes & Records.

Grayson Books, Ginny Connors, Editor, PO Box 270549, W. Hartford, CT 06127, 860-523-1196 phone/Fax, GraysonBooks@aol.com, www.GraysonBooks.com. 1999. Poetry, non-fiction. "We are a small press publishing only a couple of titles each year. Focus on excellent contemporary poetry and issues related to family and education. Not actively seeking manuscripts at this time." Pub'd 2 titles 2005; expects 2 titles 2006, 2 titles 2007. Discounts: standard discounts given to wholesalers, retailers and institutions that order in bulk. Copyrights for author. Subjects: Family, Poetry.

Graywolf Press, Fiona McCrae, Publisher & Editorial Director, 2402 University Avenue #203, St. Paul, MN 55114, 651-641-0077, 651-641-0036. 1974. Poetry, fiction, criticism, long-poems, non-fiction. avg. press run 3.5M-15M. Pub'd 16 titles 2005; expects 20 titles 2006, 24 titles 2007. 60-300pp. Reporting time: 12 weeks. Simultaneous submissions accepted: yes. Publishes less than 1% of manuscripts submitted. Payment: negotiable. Copyrights for author. Subjects: Criticism, Fiction, Literature (General), Non-Fiction, Poetry, Prose, Short Stories.

THE GREAT AMERICAN POETRY SHOW, A SERIAL POETRY ANTHOLOGY, The Muse Media, Larry Ziman, P.O. Box 69506, West Hollywood, CA 90069-0506, 1-323-969-4905. ''See specifics under The Muse Media.''

THE GREAT BLUE BEACON, Andy J. Byers, 1425 Patriot Drive, Melbourne, FL 32940, ajircc@juno.com. 1996. Poetry, fiction, articles, cartoons, reviews, non-fiction. ''Short—up to 800 words. Material is for assisting all writers of all genres and skill levels in improving their writing skills. Sal Amica M. Buttaci, prize-winning poet and fiction author, is a frequent contributor. Short-short story and poetry contests sponsored periodically. E-mail for guidelines.'' circ. 150+. 4/yr. Pub'd 4 issues 2005; expects 4 issues 2006, 4 issues 2007. sub. price $10, $8 students, $14 out of U.S.; per copy $4; sample $1. 8pp. Reporting time: 2-3 weeks. Simultaneous submissions accepted: yes. Publishes 10% of manuscripts submitted. Payment: copies. Copyrighted, reverts to author. Pub's reviews: 6-8 in 2005. §Writing—all genres. Ads: none. Subjects: Biography, Book Reviewing, Cartoons, Communication, Journalism, Desktop Publishing, Editing, Fiction, Literary Review, Magazines, Newsletter, Non-Fiction, Poetry, Prose, Publishing, Reviews.

Great Elm Press, Walt Franklin, 1205 County Route 60, Rexville, NY 14877. 1984. avg. press run 300. Pub'd 5 titles 2005; expects 2 titles 2006, 2 titles 2007. 40pp. Reporting time: 1 week. Subjects: Appalachia, Earth, Natural History, Ecology, Foods, Literature (General), Poetry.

The Great Rift Press, Katherine Daly, 1135 East Bonneville, Pocatello, ID 83201, 208-232-6857, orders 800-585-6857, Fax 208-233-0410. 1987. Non-fiction. ''We also sell publishing business software.'' avg. press run 3M. Pub'd 1 title 2005; expects 2 titles 2006, 2 titles 2007. Discounts: resalers 25%=1; 40%=2-10; 42%=11-20; additional 5% discount and FREE shipping on pre-paid orders of 2 or more. 288-352pp. Reporting time: 1 month. Simultaneous submissions accepted: yes. Payment: negotiable. Subjects: Bibliography, Biography, Idaho, Montana, Non-Fiction, Sports, Outdoors, Wyoming.

GREAT RIVER REVIEW, Robert Hedin, Richard Broderick, PO Box 406, Red Wing, MN 55066, 651-388-2009, info@andersoncenter.org, www.andersoncenter.org. 1977. Poetry, fiction, articles. ''Poetry, fiction, essays, translations. Some authors recently published: Philip Levine, Maggie Anderson, Linda Pastan, Marvin Bell, Olga Broumas, and Ted Kooser.'' circ. 500. 2/yr. Pub'd 2 issues 2005; expects 2 issues 2006, 2 issues 2007. sub. price $14; per copy $6; sample $6. Back issues: $6. 120pp. Reporting time: 1-4 months. Publishes 5% of manuscripts submitted. Payment: copies. Copyrighted, reverts to author. Pub's reviews: 12 in 2005. §Poetry, fiction, non-fiction, translations. Ads: none. Subjects: Fiction, Poetry.

Greekworks, 337 West 36th St., New York, NY 10018-6401.

GREEN ANARCHIST, John Conner, BM 1715, London WC1N 3XX, United Kingdom. 1984. Articles, cartoons, interviews, reviews, music, letters, news items, non-fiction. ''No unsolicited poetry.'' circ. 3M. 4/yr. Pub'd 4 issues 2005; expects 4 issues 2006, 4 issues 2007. sub. price £4; per copy £1; sample free. Back issues: 50p/issue. Discounts: 33% for s/r, streetsell is £5 for a bundle of 10, £20 four a 50-issue bulk order, no s/r. 24pp. Reporting time: deadline approx. 1 month before publication. Publishes 75% of manuscripts submitted. Payment: none. Not copyrighted. Pub's reviews: 24 in 2005. §Green/anarchist, radical politics, animal liberation, environmental protest, parapolitics. Ads: £60/£30/6p per word for small ads. Subjects: AIDS, Anarchist, Ecology, Foods, England, Environment, Global Affairs, Politics, Vegetarianism, War, Women, Zines.

GREEN ANARCHY, John Zerzan, PO Box 11331, Eugene, OR 97440, collective@greenanarchy.org, www.greenanarchy.org. 1999. Poetry, fiction, articles, art, interviews, criticism, reviews, letters, non-fiction. circ. 5000. 3/yr. Pub'd 4 issues 2005; expects 3 issues 2006, 3 issues 2007. sub. price $18/5 issues; per copy $4; sample $4 or free review copies. Back issues: $4 or $50 for #9-21. Discounts: inquiries welcome. 80pp. Simultaneous submissions accepted: yes. Publishes 40% of manuscripts submitted. Payment: none. Not copyrighted. Pub's reviews: 32 in 2005. §Politics, history, culture, technology. Ads: none. Subjects: Anarchist, Cities, Culture, Current Affairs, Earth, Natural History, Environment, Essays, Gender Issues, Non-Fiction, Politics, Prison, Reviews, Technology, War, Zines.

Green Bean Press, Ian Griffin, PO Box 237, New York, NY 10013, 718-965-2076 phone/Fax, ian@greenbeanpress.com, www.greenbeanpress.com. 1995. ''We are not currently seeking new manuscripts, so please do not query at this time.'' Discounts: 1 40%, 2-10 43%, 11-25 47%, 26+ 50%. Simultaneous submissions accepted: no. Does not copyright for author. Subjects: Literature (General), Novels, Poetry.

THE GREEN HILLS LITERARY LANTERN, Adam Brooke Davis, Managing Editor; Joe Benevento, Co-editor (poetry); Jack Smith, Co-editor (prose), Truman State University, Division of Language and Literature, McClain Hall, Kirksville, MO 63501-4221, 660-785-4487, adavis@truman.edu, jksmith@grm.net, jbeneven@truman.edu, ll.truman.edu/ghllweb. 1990. Poetry, fiction, interviews, reviews, non-fiction. ''GHLL will be shifting to electronic publication with #XVII (July 2006). While we will maintain the same exacting standards, the new medium may permit us to increase frequency of publication. Send mss to Green Hills

Literary Lantern, Truman State University, McClain Hall, Kirksville, MO 63501. Please direct fiction mss to Adam Brooke Davis, poetry to Joe Benevento. Fiction up to 7,000 words. No religious or genre fiction. No haiku, limericks, or poems over 2 pages. We're open to new writers. Recent contributors include DeWitt Henry, Karl Harshbarger, Gary Fincke, Doug Rennie, Grant Tracey, Walter Cummins, Ian MacMillan, Edmund de Chasca, Mark Wisniewski, Virgil Suarez, Jim Thomas, James Doyle, and Francine Marie Tolf.'' circ. 500. 1/yr. Pub'd 1 issue 2005; expects 1 issue 2006, 1 issue 2007. sub. price $10; per copy $10; sample $10. Back issues: $7. 288pp. Reporting time: 3 - 4 months. Simultaneous submissions accepted: Yes. Publishes 2-10% of manuscripts submitted. Payment: none. Copyrighted, reverts to author. Pub's reviews: 3 in 2005. §Novels, short story collections, poetry collections. Subjects: Interviews, Literary Review, Non-Fiction, Poetry, Reviews.

Green Hut Press, Janet Wullner-Faiss, 1015 Jardin Street East, Appleton, WI 54911, 920-734-9728, janwfcloak@uspower.net. 1972. Poetry, fiction, art, interviews, non-fiction. "We publish the writing and art work of the late German-American artist Fritz Faiss (1905-1981) *exclusively*. Limited editions. Mail order, except for a few selected bookstores. Library discount. Inquiries welcome. SASE please. Prices range between $9 and, for a hand-colored-by-artist edition, $200.'' avg. press run 200. Discounts: libraries 20% postpaid when accompanied by cash payment. 75pp. Subjects: Arts, Color, Creativity, German, Humanism, Non-Fiction, Poetry, Psychology, Textbooks, Visual Arts.

GREEN MOUNTAINS REVIEW, Neil Shepard, General Editor & Poetry Editor; Leslie Daniels, Fiction Editor, Johnson State College, Johnson, VT 05656, 802-635-1350. 1987. Poetry, fiction, articles, art, interviews, criticism, reviews, parts-of-novels, long-poems, non-fiction. circ. 1.7M. 2/yr. Pub'd 2 issues 2005; expects 2 issues 2006, 2 issues 2007. sub. price $15; per copy $9.50; sample $7. Back issues: $7. Discounts: 40% off for store buyers. 192pp. Reporting time: 3-6 months (we read Sept. 1-March 1). Simultaneous submissions accepted: yes. Publishes 2% of manuscripts submitted. Payment: 2 copies + 1 year subscription. Copyrighted, reverts to author. Pub's reviews: 2 in 2005. §Poetry, fiction, creative non-fiction, literary essays, interviews, book reviews. Ads: $150/$75. Subjects: Book Reviewing, Criticism, Culture, Fiction, Poetry.

GREEN PRINTS, "The Weeder's Digest'', Pat Stone, PO Box 1355, Fairview, NC 28730, 828-628-1902, www.greenprints.com, patstone@atlantic.net. 1990. Poetry, fiction, articles, art, non-fiction. "Shares the human, *not* the how-to, side of gardening through fine stories and art.'' circ. 13M. 4/yr. Pub'd 4 issues 2005; expects 4 issues 2006, 4 issues 2007. sub. price $19.97; per copy $6.00; sample $6.00. Discounts: 1/2 price, min. order 6. 80pp. Reporting time: 1-3 months. Simultaneous submissions accepted: yes. Publishes 10% of manuscripts submitted. Payment: $50-200. Copyrighted, reverts to author. Ads: $400 1/2 page. Subject: Gardening.

Green River Press, Nancy A. Robinson, PO Box 6454, Santa Barbara, CA 93160, 805-964-4475, Fax 805-967-6208, narob@cox.net. 1999. Poetry, fiction, non-fiction. avg. press run 3.5M. Pub'd 1 title 2005; expects 1 title 2006, 1 title 2007. Discounts: trade 55%. 350pp. Reporting time: 6 months. Simultaneous submissions accepted: yes. Publishes 60% of manuscripts submitted. Payment: copies and 40% discount. Copyright arrangements vary per book. Subjects: Adoption, Autobiography, Fiction, Non-Fiction, Parenting, Poetry.

Green River Writers, Inc./Grex Press, Mary E. O'Dell, 103 Logsdon Court, Louisville, KY 40243-1161, 502-245-4902. 1993. Poetry. "Solicited manuscripts only.'' avg. press run 1M. Expects 2 titles 2006, 1 title 2007. Discounts: 40% to booksellers. 60pp. Payment: on individual basis. Subject: Poetry.

Green Stone Publications, Joe Devine, PO Box 22052, Seattle, WA 98122-0052, 206-524-4744. 1987. Fiction. avg. press run 2M. Pub'd 1 title 2005; expects 1 title 2007. Discounts: 2-4 20%, 5-9 30%, 10-24 40%, 25-49 42%, 50-74 44%, 75-99 46%, 100-199 48%, 200+ 50%. 280pp. Subjects: Education, English, Humor.

The Greenfield Review Press, Joseph Bruchac III, Editor; Carol Worthen Bruchac, Editor; James Bruchac, Assistant Director, PO Box 308, Greenfield Center, NY 12833-0308, (518) 583-1440. 1970. Poetry. "Our main interests have been Native American poetry and short fiction and traditional storytelling from a number of cultures. WE ARE NOT ACCEPTING ANY MANUSCRIPTS AT PRESENT.'' avg. press run 2M. Pub'd 1 title 2005. Discounts: trade: 1-5 copies, 25%; 5 or more copies, 40%; distributed to the trade by Talman Co. 80pp single author, anthologies 300pp. Payment: 2% of press run, $250 advance on royalties of 10% retail price on each copy sold. Copyrights for author. Subject: Poetry.

GREENHOUSE REVIEW, Greenhouse Review Press, Gary Young, 3965 Bonny Doon Road, Santa Cruz, CA 95060.

Greenhouse Review Press (see also GREENHOUSE REVIEW), Gary Young, 3965 Bonny Doon Road, Santa Cruz, CA 95060-9706, 831-426-4355. 1975. Poetry, parts-of-novels, long-poems. "Greenhouse Review Press publishes a tradebook, chapbook and broadside series. Titles: *The Fugitive Vowels* by D.J. Waldie; *The Dreams of Mercurius* by John Hall; *House Fires* by Peter Wild; *Thirteen Ways of Deranging An Angel* by Stephen Kessler; *Looking Up* by Christopher Budkley; *Any Minute* by Laurel Blossom; *Yes* by Timothy

Sheehan; *By Me, By Any, Can and Can't Be Done* by Killarney Clary; *Begin, Distance* by Sherod Santos; *Jack the Ripper* by John Hall, *Unselected Poems* by Philip Levine." avg. press run varies. Pub'd 3 titles 2005; expects 4 titles 2006. Discounts: 30% to bookstores. Pages vary. Reporting time: 4 weeks. Payment: copies. Copyrights for author. Subject: Poetry.

THE GREENSBORO REVIEW, Jim Clark, Editor, PO Box 26170, Dept. of English, Univ. of North Carolina-Greensboro, Greensboro, NC 27402-6170, 336-334-5459, Fax 336-256-1470, jlclark@uncg.edu, www.uncg.edu/eng/mfa. 1966. Poetry, fiction. "We like to see the best being written regardless of subject, style or theme. We publish new talent beside established writers, depending on quality. No restrictions on length of poetry; short stories should be 7,500 words or less. Recent contributors include Robert Morgan, Peter Ho Davies, Stephen Dobyns, Dale Ray Phillips, Thomas Lux, Jill McCorkle, George Singleton, Kelly Cherry, Stanley Plumly, and Julianna Baggott. Submissions accepted between August 15 and February 15 (deadlines for the two issues: September 15 and February 15 each year). Literary Awards guidelines for SASE. SASE with mss. Stories anthologized in editions of *The Best American Short Stories, Prize Stories: The O. Henry Awards*, *The Pushcart Prize*, and in *New Stories from the South.*" circ. 800. 2/yr. Pub'd 2 issues 2005; expects 2 issues 2006, 2 issues 2007. sub. price $10; per copy $5; sample $5. Back issues: $1.50-$4/according to price on cover. Discounts: none. 128pp. Reporting time: 3-4 months. Simultaneous submissions accepted: no. Publishes 1.6% of manuscripts submitted. Payment: 3 copies. Copyrighted, rights revert to author upon request. Subjects: Fiction, Poetry.

Grip Publishing, Stacy Nelson, PO Box 091882, Milwaukee, WI 53209, 414-807-6403. 2004. Fiction. "Grip Publishing's mission is to provide literature to all genres of the reading populatation interested in urban fiction. Grip Publishing is interested in various forms of work. Work submitted for publishing should be sent at any time. Unsolicited work is acceptable. Queries and proposals are acceptable." avg. press run 2000. Expects 1 title 2006, 2 titles 2007. Discounts: 2-10 copies15%10-20 copies 20%20 or more copies 25%. 200pp. Reporting time: Two weeks. Simultaneous submissions accepted: Yes. Payment: Must be discussed. Copyrights for author. Subjects: African-American, Bisexual, Black, Fiction, Gay, Novels.

The Groundwater Press, Rosanne Wasserman, Eugene Richie, PO Box 704, Hudson, NY 12534, 516-767-8503. 1974. Poetry. "We're a nonprofit press, dependent upon grants. Unsolicited material not returned. We contact our own authors 99% of the time. Last titles: *Common Preludes* by Edward Barrett; *Double Time* by Star Black; *Every Question But One* by Pierre Mantory, translation by John Ashbery; *Mecox Road* by Marc Cohen; *The History of Rain* by Tomoyuki Iino; *The Necessary Boat* by Susan Baran." avg. press run 500. Pub'd 2 titles 2005; expects 1-2 titles 2006, 1-2 titles 2007. Discounts: 60/40, 50/50 wholesalers. 32-80pp. Reporting time: 1 year. Simultaneous submissions accepted: no. Payment: varies according to grants and donations. Copyrights for author. Subject: Poetry.

THE GROVE REVIEW, Matt Barry, 1631 NE Broadway, PMB #137, Portland, OR 97232, editor@thegrovereview.org, www.thegrovereview.org. 2004. Poetry, fiction, art, photos, interviews, letters, parts-of-novels, long-poems, plays. "The Grove Review offers a first-rate venue for unknown to renowned artists to publish their craft. We work to foster a vibrant artistic community. Recent contributors include author Ursula K. Le Guin and photographer Michael Kenna." 2/yr. Expects 1 issue 2006, 2 issues 2007. sub. price $20; per copy $11; sample $11. Back issues: inquire. Discounts: inquire. 160pp. Reporting time: Please allow 3 - 4 months prior to inquiring. Typically responds much sooner. Simultaneous submissions accepted: No. Publishes 1% of manuscripts submitted. Payment: $50 + 2 copies. Copyrighted, reverts to author. Ads: full page $500; half page $300; qtr. page $200.

THE GROWING EDGE MAGAZINE, New Moon Publishing, Inc., Tom Weller, Editor, PO Box 1027, Corvallis, OR 97339-1027, 514-757-8477. 1980. "Indoor and outdoor gardening for today's high-tech grower. Covers hydroponics, controlled environments, greenhouses, drip irrigation, organic and sustainable gardening, water conservation aquaponics, aquaculture and more." circ. 39,500. 6/yr. Pub'd 6 issues 2005; expects 6 issues 2006, 6 issues 2007. sub. price $37.95 1st class mail, $26.95 3rd class mail, $79.50 international; per copy $4.95 + $1.50 p/h; sample $4.95 + $1.50 p/h. Back issues: same. 96pp. Reporting time: 2 months. Simultaneous submissions accepted: yes. Publishes 50%-75% of manuscripts submitted. Payment: 20¢ per word/photos negotiable. Copyrighted, 1st and reprint rights to publisher then reverts back to author. Pub's reviews: 36-48 in 2005. §Hydroponic, greenhouse, and aquaculture. Ads: Full: b+w $1758, color $2563; half: b+w $1168, color $1975; marketplace ad $250, retailers club $50. Subjects: Agriculture, Counter-Culture, Alternatives, Communes, Gardening.

GROWING FOR MARKET, Lynn Byczynski, PO Box 3747, Lawrence, KS 66046, 785-748-0605, 800-307-8949, growing4market@earthlink.net, www.growingformarket.com. 1992. Articles. "*Growing for Market* is a practical, hands-on journal for farmers who direct-market produce and flowers. Therefore, writers must be knowleddeable about growing on a commercial scale." circ. 3M. 12/yr. Pub'd 12 issues 2005; expects 12 issues 2006, 12 issues 2007. sub. price $30; per copy $3; sample $3. Discounts: none. 20pp. Reporting time: 6 months. Simultaneous submissions accepted: no. Publishes 75% of manuscripts submitted. Payment:

$75/printed page, $200 maximum. Copyrighted, reverts to author. Pub's reviews: 12 in 2005. §Small-scale farming, flower gardening, herbs, dried flowers. Ads: $400/$240/$68 1/3 page/$120 1/4 page/$90 1/6 page. Subject: Gardening.

Gryphon Books (see also HARDBOILED; PAPERBACK PARADE), Gary Lovisi, PO Box 209, Brooklyn, NY 11228-0209. 1983. Fiction, articles, art, interviews, satire, criticism, reviews, parts-of-novels, non-fiction. "A small press publisher that (in addition to publishing the magazines *Hardboiled* and *Paperback Parade*) publish numerous books on a variety of subjects dealing with paperback collecting, pulp magazines, detective fiction, science fiction, and fantasy, Sherlock Holmes—in fiction and non-fiction. Please Note: *Do not send mss, on anything over 3,000 words-send only* query letter about the story/novel, *with SASE.* Material received without SASE will not be returned. Writers can send letter with SASE for guidelines. It is suggested you order a recent copy of our magazines or books to get an idea of what I am looking for." avg. press run 500-1M. Pub'd 5 titles 2005; expects 4 titles 2006, 5 titles 2007. Discounts: 40% on 5 or more of the same item/issue ordered. 50-200pp. Reporting time: 3-6 weeks. Simultaneous submissions accepted: no. Publishes 5% of manuscripts submitted. Payment: varies. Copyrights for author. Subjects: Bibliography, Book Arts, Book Collecting, Bookselling, Collectibles, Crime, Fantasy, Fiction, Sherlock Holmes, H.P. Lovecraft, Magazines, Mystery, Non-Fiction, Science Fiction, Writers/Writing, Zines.

Gryphon House, Inc., Kathy Charner, PO Box 207, Beltsville, MD 20704-0207, 301-595-9500. 1971. Non-fiction. "We publish books of activities for use by pre-school teachers and parents." Pub'd 13 titles 2005; expects 10 titles 2006, 11 titles 2007. Discounts: available upon request. 256pp. Reporting time: 3 weeks. Simultaneous submissions accepted: no. Publishes 5% of manuscripts submitted. Payment: 8-10-12.5% on net sales. Copyrights for author. Subjects: Children, Youth, Education.

Guarionex Press Ltd., William E. Zimmerman, Chief Editor & Publisher, 201 West 77th Street, New York, NY 10024, 212-724-5259. 1979. Non-fiction. "The goal of *Guarionex Press* is to publish books that help people articulate their thoughts and feelings. Our books affirm the power of the human spirit and imagination to overcome life's problems. Our first book is *How to Tape Instant Oral Biographies.* The book teaches youngsters and grownups how to interview family members and friends and use the tape or video recorder to capture their life stories, memories and traditions on tape. Great family, school and vacation activity. Its second book is a new form of diary/journal called *A Book of Questions to Keep Thoughts and Feelings*; it helps people keep a diary. The third book is *Make Beliefs*, a gift book to spark the imagination. A new activity both for youngsters and adults. Our fourth is *Lifelines*; a book of hope to get you through the tough times of life." avg. press run 5M. Expects 1-2 titles 2006, 1-2 titles 2007. Discounts: 10-50% depending on volume. 112pp. Reporting time: 3 months. Payment: fair arrangement negotiable. Copyrights for author. Subjects: Children, Youth, Communication, Journalism, Consumer, Crafts, Hobbies, Education, Family, Games, Genealogy, How-To, New Age, New Age, Senior Citizens, Spiritual.

Guernica Editions, Inc., Antonio D'Alfonso, Editor & Publisher, 11 Mount Royal Avenue, Toronto, Ontario M6H 2S2, Canada, 416-658-9888, Fax 416-657-8885, guernicaeditions@cs.com. 1978. Poetry, fiction, photos, criticism, long-poems, plays, non-fiction. "Guernica Editions publish works of literature, criticism or culture. We specialize in translations and we focus on writing dealing with pluricultural realities. USA distributors: Paul and Company." avg. press run 1M. Pub'd 30 titles 2005; expects 39 titles 2006, 25 titles 2007. Discounts: 40% to bookstores, 40% to jobbers and wholesalers, 46% for 10+ to library wholesalers. 50-400pp. Reporting time: 3-6 months; if we're definitely not interested, the answer is faster—within 2-4 weeks. We do not accept simultaneous submissions. Payment: authors receive about 10 copies and 10% royalty; copyright is shared by author and publisher for the duration of the edition. Does not copyright for author. Subjects: Literature (General), Politics.

Guilford Publications, Inc. (see also SCIENCE & SOCIETY), 72 Spring Street, New York, NY 10012.

•**GULF & MAIN Southwest Florida Lifestyle,** Dominik Goertz, 2235 First St., Suite 217, Fort Myers, FL 33901, 239-791-7900, 239 791-7974, www.gulfandmain.net. 2000. Articles, art, photos, interviews. "luxury lifestyle magazine with local freelance journalists and fashion photographers." circ. 275000. 6/yr. Pub'd 6 issues 2005; expects 6 issues 2006, 6 issues 2007. sub. price $19.95; per copy $3.95; sample $3.95. Back issues: inquire. Discounts: inquire. 72pp. Simultaneous submissions accepted: No. Publishes 5% of manuscripts submitted. Copyrighted. Pub's reviews: 2 in 2005. §trendy topics, luxury lifestyle. Ads: inquire. Subjects: Arts, Audio/Video, Autos, Avant-Garde, Experimental Art, Business & Economics, Consumer, Dining, Restaurants, Fashion, Health, Jewelry, Gems, Lifestyles, Massage, Performing Arts, Real Estate.

GULF COAST, Sasha West, Managing Editor; David Ray Vance, Associate Editor, Dept. of English, University of Houston, Houston, TX 77204-3013. 1987. Poetry, fiction, art, photos, interviews, reviews, parts-of-novels, long-poems, non-fiction. "Reading period: 8/15-5/1. Contest held in March/April. See website for details. No electronic submissions. Recent contributors include: Terrance Hayes, Anne Carson, Dana Levin, Billy Collins, Linda Bierds, C, Dale Young, Sabrina Orah Mark, Joe Meno, G. C. Waldrep, Rick Barot, Robert

Hass, Josip Novakovich, Michael Collier, Martha Ronk, Denise Duhamel, Matthea Harvey, Cate Marvin, Sarah Messer, Tomaz Salamun, R. T. Smith." circ. 2300. 2/yr. Pub'd 2 issues 2005; expects 2 issues 2006, 2 issues 2007. sub. price $14; per copy $8; sample $7. Back issues: Barthelme issue, $12; regular back issue, $7. 300pp. Reporting time: 4-6 months. Simultaneous submissions accepted: yes. Publishes 5% of manuscripts submitted. Payment: copies, $50 per poem, $100 per story. Copyrighted, reverts to author. Pub's reviews: 9 in 2005. §Poetry, fiction, nonfiction. Subjects: Fiction, Interviews, Literary Review, Literature (General), Non-Fiction, Poetry, Short Stories, Translation, Visual Arts.

Gurze Books, Lindsey Hall, Editor; Leigh Cohn, Publisher, PO Box 2238, Carlsbad, CA 92018, 760-434-7533, Fax 760-434-5476, gurze@aol.com. 1980. Non-fiction. "Self-help, health/psychology." avg. press run 7.5M-10M. Pub'd 2 titles 2005; expects 3 titles 2006, 2 titles 2007. Discounts: trade distribution through PGW, B&T, Ingram. 176pp. Reporting time: 2 months. Publishes 1% of manuscripts submitted. Payment: varies. Copyrights for author. Subjects: Alcohol, Alcoholism, Health, Parenting, Psychology, Women.

The Gutenberg Press, Fred Foldvary, Editor in Chief; Janet Schweiss, Assistant Editor, c/o Fred Foldvary, 1920 Cedar Street, Berkeley, CA 94709, 510-843-0248, e-mail gutenbergpress@pobox.com. 1980. Non-fiction. "Recent authors: Tertius Chandler, Fred Foldvary, John Hospers. Mostly publish books on social issues, social philosophy, and ancient history. Titles include: *The Soul of Liberty*, by Fred Foldvary. *The Tax We Need*, by Tertius Chandler. *Remote Kingdoms* and *Godly Kings and Early Ethics* by Tertius Chandler, *Anarchy or Limited Government?* by John Hospers. One art book also published." avg. press run 600. Pub'd 1 title 2005; expects 1 title 2006, 1 title 2007. Discounts: 40% bookstores and 52% jobbers. 300pp. Reporting time: within 1 month. Simultaneous submissions accepted: ok. Publishes 10% of manuscripts submitted. Payment: after costs are met, profits are split 50/50. Copyrights for author. Subjects: History, Philosophy.

H

HA!, Writers' Haven Press, Sharon E. Svendsen, Poetry Editor, Circulation Manager; Nancy Ryan, Prose, Cartoons, and Art Editor, P. O. Box 368, Seabeck, WA 98380-0368, (360)830-5772. 2004. Poetry, fiction, art, cartoons, satire, parts-of-novels, non-fiction. "HA! publishes only humorous material. We aren't prudes, but we don't want dirty jokes. If you send us anything that is political, it needs to be satirical. If it makes us laugh, we like it." circ. 230. 4/yr. Expects 3 issues 2006, 4 issues 2007. sub. price $18; per copy $5; sample $5 plus $1.50 postage. Back issues: $5. Discounts: 10 copies or more copies 15%. 48pp. Reporting time: three to six months. Simultaneous submissions accepted: Yes. Publishes 70% of manuscripts submitted. Payment: $5 per published piece. Copyrighted, reverts to author. §Humorous material only. Ads: $100/$55/$30/$20. Subject: Humor.

HAIGHT ASHBURY LITERARY JOURNAL, Alice Rogoff, Indigo Hotchkiss, Gail Mitchell, Cesar Love, 558 Joost Avenue, San Francisco, CA 94127. 1980. Poetry, fiction, art, photos. "Recent contributors: Julia Vinograd, Will Walker, Laura del Fuego, Marci Blackman, Edgar Silex. Biases: culture and milti-cultural themes; street life, prison; feminist issues; political issues; family, crime, children, love and other visions." circ. 2M. 1-3/yr. Pub'd 2 issues 2005; expects 2 issues 2006, 2 issues 2007. sub. price $40 lifetime, includes 6 back issues and future issues, $8 for 2 issues, $16 for 4 issues; per copy $2; sample $3 (with postage). Back issues: *This Far Together* (anthology) $15 (with postage), journals $3 (with postage). Discounts: $13 for 10. 16pp. Reporting time: 3-6 months. Simultaneous submissions accepted: yes. Publishes 5% of manuscripts submitted. Payment: 3 copies if mailed, more copies per writer if picked up in person, "center" writers paid, some fiction paid. Copyrighted. Ads: $40 large/$30+/$20. Subjects: Literature (General), Poetry.

Haight-Ashbury Publications (see also JOURNAL OF PSYCHOACTIVE DRUGS), David E. Smith MD, Executive Editor; Richard B. Seymour, Editor in Chief, 856 Stanyan Street, San Francisco, CA 94117, 415-752-7601, Fax 415-933-8674. 1967. Articles, art, photos, reviews, non-fiction. avg. press run 1.5M. Pub'd 1 title 2005; expects 1 title 2006, 1 title 2007. We provide quantity discounts for our books; price list available. 100pp. Reporting time: 60 days. Simultaneous submissions accepted: no. Publishes 33% of manuscripts submitted. Payment: none. Does not copyright for author. Subjects: Alcohol, Alcoholism, Drugs, Health, Mental Health, Sociology.

Haiku Society of America (see also FROGPOND: Quarterly Haiku Journal), John Stevenson, Editor, PO Box 122, Nassau, NY 12123, 518-766-2039. 1978. Poetry. "Haiku and related material only." avg. press run 1M. 96pp. Reporting time: 1-2 weeks. Simultaneous submissions accepted: no. Publishes less than 1% of manuscripts submitted. Payment: $1 honorarium for each piece/poem accepted. Copyrights for author. Subjects: Haiku, Poetry.

Hailey-Grey Books, Jennifer Jackson, 2569 Fairmount Blvd, Cleveland Heights, OH 44106, 216-932-3235.

1993. Fiction. "Action-adventure, thrillers." avg. press run 20000. Pub'd 1 title 2005; expects 2 titles 2006, 4 titles 2007. Discounts: 1-3 books 30%4-10 books 40% off11 or more 50%. 450pp. Reporting time: two months. Simultaneous submissions accepted: No. Publishes 4% of manuscripts submitted. Payment: variable depending on work required to prepare work for publication. Copyrights for author. Subjects: Fiction, D.H. Lawrence.

Halbar Publishing (see also SHARING & CARING), Bill Halbert, Mary Barnes, 309 VZ County Road 3224, Wills Point, TX 75169-9732. 1994. Poetry, fiction, articles, art, photos, cartoons, interviews, satire, criticism, reviews, music, letters, parts-of-novels, long-poems, collages, plays, concrete art, news items, non-fiction. "No libel, no porn, no limit to length. We publish comb bound or perfect bound in the full letter size or the half letter size and perfect bound paperbacks trimmed slightly smaller in either size. We publish books for Memo-It Books out of Elkhart, Illinois and personal chapbooks for writers, color available. Also have musical consultant. We furnish books as needed, 5 or more per order once we have the master, furnish proof copy." avg. press run varies. Pub'd 20 titles 2005; expects 30 titles 2006, 40 titles 2007. 100pp. Reporting time: 2 weeks. Simultaneous submissions accepted: yes. Publishes 90% of manuscripts submitted. Payment: commensurate. Copyright for author if wanted.

Haley's, Marcia Gagliardi, PO Box 248, Athol, MA 01331, marcia@haleysantiques.com, www.haleysantiques.com. 1989. Poetry, fiction, photos, interviews, non-fiction. "Looking for material that will appeal to readers in our region." avg. press run 1M. Pub'd 9 titles 2005; expects 8 titles 2006, 8 titles 2007. Discounts: 40% trade. 100pp. Reporting time: 6 weeks. Accepting simultaneous submissions depends on prior arrangement. Publishes 10% of manuscripts submitted. Payment: varies. Copyrights for author. Subjects: Fiction, Non-Fiction, Poetry.

Hallard Press, Bernard Gadd, 43 Landscape Rd, Papatoetoe, Auckland 1701, New Zealand, 64 09 2782731, 64 09 2782731. 1981. Poetry. "Mainly New Zealand poetry, ocassionally fiction, and usually of invited writers." avg. press run 100. Pub'd 1 title 2005; expects 3 titles 2006, 4 titles 2007. Discounts: 40%. 60-70pp. Reporting time: 1 week. Simultaneous submissions accepted: No. Payment: nil. Copyrights for author.

Hamster Huey Press, Paul R Spadoni, 7627 84th Avenue Ct. NW, Gig Harbor, WA 98335-6237, Phone 253-851-7839 http://www.hamsterhueypress.com. 2004. Fiction. "We are not seeking additional manuscripts at this time." avg. press run 3000. Pub'd 1 title 2005; expects 1 title 2007. Discounts: Hamster Huey and the Gooey Kablooie1-2 copies: $6.95 for 3-99 copies: $4.50 for 100-199: $4.00 for 200-499: $3.50 for 500+: $3.15. 8pp. Simultaneous submissions accepted: No. Publishes 1% of manuscripts submitted. Copyrights for author.

HAND PAPERMAKING, Tom Bannister, Mina Takahashi, PO Box 77027, Washington, DC 20013-7027, 800-821-6604, Fax 301-220-2394, info@handpapermaking.org. 1986. Articles, interviews, criticism, reviews. "Dedicated to advancing traditional and contemporary ideas in the art of hand papermaking." circ. 1.5M. 2/yr. Pub'd 2 issues 2005; expects 2 issues 2006, 2 issues 2007. sub. price $45; per copy $18; sample $18. Back issues: $18 each, $15 for subscribers. Discounts: none. 40pp. Reporting time: 2 months. Simultaneous submissions accepted: no. Publishes 25% of manuscripts submitted. Payment: $50-$150. Copyrighted, does not revert to author. Pub's reviews: 4 in 2005. §Paper and book arts. Ads: $270/$200/75¢. Subjects: Book Arts, Visual Arts.

Hands & Heart Books (see also Toad Hall, Inc.), RR 2 Box 2090, Laceyville, PA 18623, 717-869-2942; Fax 717-869-1031. 1995. Non-fiction. "We primarily are consultants for book-length works only. Send a query letter first. Will read and provide written analysis of first 3 chapters plus synopsis of a manuscript or the complete self-published book for $50. Will work with self-publishers before and after publication. Hands & Heart Books publishes non-fiction how-to books for crafters and hobbyists." avg. press run 4M. Pub'd 1 title 2005; expects 2 titles 2006, 1 title 2007. 224pp. Reporting time: 3 months. Payment: We publish by co-op arrangement only. Copyrights for author. Subjects: Arts, Cooking, Crafts, Hobbies, How-To.

Handshake Editions, Jim Haynes, Atelier A2, 83 rue de la Tombe-Issoire, Paris 75014, France, 4327-1767. 1971. Poetry, fiction, articles, photos, cartoons, parts-of-novels. "Only personal face-to-face submissions solicited. Handshake mainly publishes Paris-based writers. Small print-runs, but we attempt to keep everything in print (i.e., frequent re-prints). Libertarian bias. Writers recently published include Ted Joans, Sarah Bean, Michael Zwerin, Jim Haynes, Elaine J. Cohen, Ken Timmerman, Judith Malina, Lynne Tillman, Samuel Brecher, Suzanne Brogger, Jayne Cortez, Amanda P. Hoover, Echnaton, Yianna Katsoulos, William Levy, and Barry Gifford." avg. press run 1M. Pub'd 3 titles 2005; expects 12 titles 2006. Discounts: 1/3 prepaid; all cheques payable to Jim Haynes. Payment: copies of the book. Does not copyright for author. Subjects: Libertarian, Philosophy.

HandyCraft Media Productions, Fred Nishperly A, P.O. Box 222, Republic, MO 65738-0222, 417-234-8373. 2004. Photos, non-fiction. "Currently seeking video submissions from independent producers on arts and craft, how-to and special intersrt topics. We work primarily with the library, educational and catalog markets producing specialized prgrams on video (DVD and VHS), e-books, streaming media and other formats. We work directly with artists and crafters to produce a finished progam for resale and distribution. We also have

198

in-house capability for video production for authors and artitst with a viable, marketable concept that can be created in an A/V medium. Contact us with your ideas.some of our recent titles include: Gourd Artistry (Melynda Lotven), Introduction to Pewter Smithing (Tom and Pat Hooper), Turning Wood into Art, JewelryMaking with Nena (Nena Galloway Potts)." avg. press run 1000. Pub'd 2 titles 2005; expects 12 titles 2006, 15 titles 2007. Discounts: Educational Discount: 20% on 10+ copiesWholesale: 20-50 copies 50%, 51-100 copies 55%, 101+ copies 60%. 220pp. Reporting time: Reports on submissions within 4-6 weeks of receipt. Simultaneous submissions accepted: Yes. Publishes 10% of manuscripts submitted. Payment: Negotiated on a case by case basis. Copyrights for author. Subjects: Audio/Video, Construction, Crafts, Hobbies, How-To, Jewelry, Gems, Marketing, Photography, Real Estate, Speaking, Wood Engraving/ Woodworking.

HANG GLIDING, Gil Dodgen, U.S. Hang Gliding Assoc., Inc., PO Box 1330, Colorado Springs, CO 80901-1330, 719-632-8300, fax 719-632-6417. 1974. Articles, photos, cartoons, interviews, reviews, letters, news items. "Information pertaining to hang gliding and soaring flight." circ. 8M. 12/yr. Pub'd 12 issues 2005; expects 12 issues 2006, 12 issues 2007. sub. price $35; per copy $3.95; sample same. Back issues: prior 1982 $1.50, 1982-1990 $2, 1991+ $2.50. Discounts: newsstand 50%. 64pp. Reporting time: 2 months. Simultaneous submissions accepted: yes. Publishes 70% of manuscripts submitted. Payment: limited, cover photo $50, feature story. Copyrighted. Pub's reviews: 2 in 2005. §Aviation, outdoor recreation. Ads: b/w: $615/$365/50¢ per word classified. Subjects: Aviation, Sports, Outdoors.

HANGING LOOSE, Hanging Loose Press, Robert Hershon, Dick Lourie, Mark Pawlak, Ron Schreiber (1934-2004); Donna Brook, Associate Editor; Marie Carter, Associate Editor, 231 Wyckoff Street, Brooklyn, NY 11217, www.hangingloosepress.com. 1966. Poetry, fiction. "Emphasis remains on the work of new writers—and when we find people we like, we stay with them. Among recent contributors: Kimiko Hahn, Paul Violi, Donna Brook, D. Nurkse, Sherman Alexie, Ron Overton, Gary Lenhart, Sharon Mesmer, Charles North. We welcome submissions to the magazine, but artwork & book mss. are by invitation only. We suggest strongly that people read the magazine before sending work." circ. 2M. 3/yr. Pub'd 3 issues 2005; expects 3 issues 2006. sub. price $22.00/3 issues (individuals); per copy $9.00; sample $11.00 (incl. postage). Back issues: prices on request, including complete sets. Discounts: 40% to bookstores, 20% to jobbers. 128pp. Reporting time: 2-3 months. Simultaneous submissions accepted: no. Payment: 2 copies + small check. Copyrighted, does not revert to author. §Poetry. No ads. Subjects: Fiction, Poetry.

Hanging Loose Press (see also HANGING LOOSE), Robert Hershon, Dick Lourie, Mark Pawlak, Ron Schreiber; Emmett Jarrett, Contributing Editor; Donna Brook, Contributing Editor; Marie Carter, Editorial Associate, 231 Wyckoff Street, Brooklyn, NY 11217, www.hangingloosepress.com. 1966. Poetry, fiction. "Book mss by invitation only." avg. press run 2M. Pub'd 6 titles 2005; expects 6 titles 2006, 6 titles 2007. Discounts: bookstores, 40% (more than 4 copies), 20%, 1-4 copies; STOP orders 30%. 96-120pp. Payment: yes. Copyrights for author. Subjects: Fiction, Poetry.

Hannacroix Creek Books, Inc, Submissions Editor, 1127 High Ridge Road, #110, Stamford, CT 06905-1203, 203-321-8674, Fax 203-968-0193, hannacroix@aol.com. 1996. Poetry, fiction, non-fiction. "Not open to unsolicited manuscripts at this time." avg. press run 1M-3M; also POD (Print-on-Demand). Expects 4 titles 2006, 4-6 titles 2007. Pages vary. Payment: negotiable. Copyrights for author. Subjects: Children, Youth, Poetry, Self-Help.

Hanover Press (see also THE CONNECTICUT POET; THE UNDERWOOD REVIEW), Faith Vicinanza, Linda Yuhas, PO Box 596, Newtown, CT 06470-0596, 203-426-3388, Fax 203-426-3398, hanoverpress@faith-vicinanza.com. 1995. Poetry, fiction, art, photos, criticism, parts-of-novels, long-poems, non-fiction. avg. press run 1M. Pub'd 3 titles 2005; expects 3 titles 2006, 3 titles 2007. 80pp. Reporting time: 6-9 months. Simultaneous submissions accepted: yes. Publishes 3% of manuscripts submitted. Payment: 10% of press run for single author books. Does not copyright for author. Subjects: Beat, Creativity, Erotica, Essays, Fiction, Gay, Haiku, Journals, Lesbianism, Literary Review, Myth, Mythology, Newsletter, Non-Fiction, Poetry, Short Stories.

HAPPENINGNOW!EVERYWHERE, Happening Writers' Collective, P.O. Box 45204, Somerville, MA 02145, happeningmagazine@yahoo.com, www.happeningnoweverywhere.com. 2005. Poetry, fiction, articles, art, photos, cartoons, interviews, satire, criticism, reviews, music, letters, parts-of-novels, long-poems, collages, plays, concrete art, news items, non-fiction. "A magazine for young people written and edited by their peers, under 18 years of age. Original submissions are welcome for the editors' consideration. Contributors must be under 18 years of age, no minimum age. SASE must accompany mailed submissions. E-mailed submissions are OK." circ. 250. 4/yr. Expects 2 issues 2006, 4 issues 2007. sub. price $12.00; per copy $3.00; sample $3.00. Back issues: $3.00. Discounts: 30%. 24pp. Simultaneous submissions accepted: No. Publishes 40% of manuscripts submitted. Payment: 1 copy of magazine. Discount on purchase of more copies in which contributor appears. Copyrighted, reverts to author. Pub's reviews. §Anything of interest to young people under age 18. No ads. Subjects: Adolescence, Children, Youth, Fiction, Media, Movies, Music, Poetry, Prose,

Reviews.

Happy About, Mitchell Levy, 21265 Stevens Creek Blvd, Suite 205, Cupertino, CA 95014, 408-257-3000, dustbooks-publisher@happyabout.info, http://www.happyabout.info. 1992. Satire, criticism, news items, non-fiction. "Our books contain wisdom. Looking for business related topics that contain war stories, test cases testimonials from people that have been there and done that. Our books are typically 80-130 pages and are published in tradebook, eBook and podbook formats." avg. press run varies. Pub'd 1 title 2005; expects 2 titles 2006, 3 titles 2007. Discounts: please inquire. 80-130pp. Payment: 50% of profit. Copyrights for author. Subjects: Advertising, Self-Promotion, Business & Economics, Computers, Calculators, Consulting, Consumer, Finances, Internet, Interviews, Libraries, Management, Marketing, Publishing, Quotations, Real Estate, Research.

Harbor House, Carrie McCullough, Publisher; E. Randall Floyd, Founder; Michael Hunley, Assistant to the Publisher; Nathan Elliott, Creative Director, 111 Tenth Street, Augusta, GA 30901, 706-738-0354(phone), 706-823-5999(fax), harborhouse@harborhousebooks.com, www.harborhousebooks.com. 1997. Fiction, non-fiction. "Founded in 1997, Harbor House seeks to publish the best in original adult fiction and non-fiction. Our current collection of titles includes contemporary non-fiction (social commentary, memoirs, biographies), thrillers, Civil War fiction and The Unexplained. BatWing Press is our new imprint which launched in 2005. BatWing is dedicated to publishing the finest in horror fiction.The Civil War Classics series premiers Civil War fiction inspired by true events.In June 2004, Harbor House began renovation of an 1879 cottage in the heart of downtown Augusta near the Savannah River. The cottage now serves as the corporate headquarters of Harbor House." Pub'd 15 titles 2005; expects 12 titles 2006, 15 titles 2007. Simultaneous submissions accepted: yes. Publishes 5% of manuscripts submitted. Payment: 7 percent to 10 percent royalty of net retail price. Royalty reports twice per year. Advances vary based on topic, exposure and experience. Copyrights for author. Subjects: Americana, Autobiography, Biography, Civil War, Folklore, Horror, H.P. Lovecraft, Non-Fiction, Novels, Occult, Religion, South, South Carolina, Spiritual, Supernatural.

Harbor House Law Press, Inc. (see also THE BEACON: Journal of Special Education Law & Practice), PO Box 480, Hartfield, VA 23071, 804-758-8400, Fax 202-318-3239, info@harborhouselaw.com, www.harborhouselaw.com. 1999. Articles, non-fiction. "Our mission is to publish special education legal and advocacy information for parents, advocates, educators, and attorneys. Our goal is to ensure that children with disabilities have equality of opportunity, full participation, independent living, and economic self-sufficiency. We welcome inquiries from professionals who seek a publisher for their manuscripts." avg. press run 5M. Pub'd 1 title 2005; expects 2 titles 2006, 3 titles 2007. Discounts: bulk 50%, bookstore 40%. 390pp. Reporting time: 3-6 months. Publishes 10% of manuscripts submitted. Copyrights for author. Subjects: Education, Law, Parenting, Self-Help.

Hard Press, Jeff Wright, 632 East 14th Street, #18, New York, NY 10009, 212-673-1152. 1976. Poetry, art, photos, cartoons, music, letters, collages. "To date Hard Press has published 80 different *post cards*, generally poetry of two to twenty lines, sometimes accompanied by art-work, but sometimes just original art work, cartoons, collages, photos, by themselves. Contributors include: Kathy Acker, Amiri Baraka, Ted Berrigan, Robert Creeley, Allen Ginsberg, Anselm Hollo, Phillip Lopate, Alice Notley, Maureen Owen, Pedro Pietri, Anne Waldman, Jeff Wright. Also three books to date." avg. press run 500. Pub'd 4 titles 2005; expects 4 titles 2006, 4 titles 2007. Discounts: 40%. 1 page. Reporting time: 8 weeks. Payment: 10% of copy. Copyrights for author. Subjects: Arts, Poetry.

HARDBOILED, Gryphon Books, Gary Lovisi, PO Box 209, Brooklyn, NY 11228. 1988. Fiction, articles, interviews, letters, non-fiction. "Previously *Detective Story Magazine* and *Hardboiled Detective*. Publish the hardest, cutting-edge crime fiction, stories full of impact, action, violence. Also reviews, articles, interviews on hardboiled topics. Please Note: The best way to write for *Hardboiled* is to *read Hardboiled* and see *exactly* what we're after!" circ. 1M. 4/yr. Pub'd 4 issues 2005; expects 4 issues 2006, 4 issues 2007. sub. price $35/4 issues domestic, $55/4 issues outside USA; per copy $10 + postage; sample $10 + postage. Back issues: #1-9 $29, or $6 each, (only for the 9 early issues of *Detective Story Magazine*). Discounts: 40% on 5 or more of each issue. 100-110pp. Reporting time: 2-6 weeks. Simultaneous submissions accepted: no. Publishes 3% of manuscripts submitted. Payment: $5-$50 depending on quality and length, + 2 free copies on publication. Copyrighted, reverts to author. Pub's reviews: 18 in 2005. §Hardboiled, crime-fiction, mystery, suspense. Ads: $50/$25. Subjects: Crime, Mystery, Short Stories.

Harlan Publishing Company; Alliance Books; Diakonia Publishing (Christian Books), P.O. Box 397, Summerfield, NC 27358, 336-643-5849, harlan@northstate.net, www.harlanpublishing.com. 1999. avg. press run 5M. Expects 3 titles 2006, 5 titles 2007. Discounts: 1-4 30%, 5-23 40%, 24+ 45%, wholesale/distributor 55%. 350pp. Reporting time: 6-8 weeks. Simultaneous submissions accepted: yes. Payment: standard book contract (negotiable). Copyrights for author. Subjects: Biography, Christianity, Fiction, Inspirational, Marriage, Mentoring/Coaching, Mystery, Parenting, Politics, Relationships, Religion, Reprints, Spiritual, Supernatural.

Shannon D. Harle, Publisher (see also PANIC STRIPS; ROTTEN PEPPER; T.V. HEADS), 329 Merrills Cove Rd., Asheville, NC 28803-8527.

HARMONY: Voices for a Just Future, Sea Fog Press, Rose Evans, Managing Editor, PO Box 210056, San Francisco, CA 94121-0056, 415-221-8527. 1987. Poetry, articles, cartoons, interviews, criticism, reviews. "*Harmony Magazine* publishes articles on reverence for life—for animal rights, disabled rights, gay rights, peace, justice, ecology—against war, capital punishment, abortion, euthanasia, covert action, etc." circ. 1.4M. 6/yr. Pub'd 6 issues 2005; expects 6 issues 2006, 6 issues 2007. sub. price $12; per copy $2; sample $2. Back issues: $2. Discounts: 10+ copies 40%. 28pp. Reporting time: 3-8 weeks. Simultaneous submissions accepted: yes. Publishes .03% of manuscripts submitted. Payment: copies only. Copyrighted, reverts to author. Pub's reviews: 10 in 2005. §War & peace, social justice, hunger, abortion, death penalty. Ads: $100/$50/10¢ per word. Subjects: Non-Violence, Peace, Politics.

Harobed Publishing Creations, Deborah Tillman, P.O.Box 8195, Pittsburgh, PA 15217-0915, 412-243-9299 fax/phone(if beeps redial fax in use). 2004. Poetry, art, reviews, long-poems. "Harobed Publishing Creations publishes selected books of poetry. Prefers "personal" free verse, ryhtm or prose, regardless of style, form, and genre." We offer Poetry books (60-90 pages), slim volumes (44-55 pages)and chapbooks (20-30 pages),with full-color cover,perfect-binding,and ISBN. Press run 200-1000 copies. Send material for review consideration to Deborah Tillman, editor." Pub'd 1 title 2005; expects 3 titles 2006, 10 titles 2007. Reporting time: 30 days. Simultaneous submissions accepted: No. Does not copyright for author. Subjects: Book Collecting, Bookselling, Book Reviewing, Fashion, Literary Review, Literature (General), Newsletter, Performing Arts, Picture Books, Postcards, Printing, Prose, Visual Arts.

HARP-STRINGS, Madelyn Eastlund, Editor; Sybella Beyer Snyder, Associate Editor, PO Box 640387, Beverly Hills, FL 34464. 1989. Poetry. "Recent contributors: Barry Ballard, Robert Cooperman, Taylor Graham, Ruth F. Harrison, Howard F. Stein. No short poems (under 14 lines), maximum lines 80. Looking for '*poems to remember.*' Looking for narratives 'good story poems' ballads, patterned poetry. Annual contest: The Edna St. Vincent Millay Harp-Weaver Poetry Contest, *as well as three other quarterly contests—change each year.* Read only February, May, August, November. Each reading is to plan the following issue—no files are kept. Poems kept only for current issue." circ. 100. 4/yr. Pub'd 4 issues 2005; expects 4 issues 2006, 4 issues 2007. sub. price $14; per copy $4.00; sample $4.00. Back issues: a few for most recent years. 20 - 24pp. Reporting time: end of reading month. No simultaneous submissions read. Publishes 5% of manuscripts submitted. Payment: copy. Copyrighted, reverts to author. Subject: Poetry.

HARPUR PALATE, J. D. Schraffenberger, Editor; Kathryn Henion, Associate Editor, English Dept., PO Box 6000, Binghamton University, Binghamton, NY 13902-6000, http://harpurpalate.binghamton.edu. 2000. Poetry, fiction, art, photos, non-fiction. "Past contributors have included Ruth Stone, Lydia Davis, Lee K. Abbott, Marvin Bell, B. H. Fairchild, Jack Ridl, Sascha Feinstein, Jamie Wriston Colbert, Sean Thomas Dougherty, and Ryan G. Van Cleave. *Harpur Palate* has no restrictions on subject matter or form. Quite simply, send us your highest-quality fiction and poetry. We do not accept submissions via e-mail. Fiction: Length should be between 250 and 8,000 words; ONE submission per envelope. Poetry: Send 3-5 poems, no more than 10 pages total per author. Reading periods: We accept submissions all year around. The deadline for the Winter issue is October 15 and the deadline for the Summer issue is March 15. Mail us a copy of your manuscript, a cover letter, and SASE for our response. Manuscripts without SASEs will be discarded unread. Copies of manuscripts will NOT be returned. *Harpur Palate* also sponsors the Milton Kessler Memorial Prize for Poetry in the fall and the John Gardner Memorial Prize for Fiction in the spring. See website or send SASE for info." circ. 700. 2/yr. Pub'd 2 issues 2005; expects 2 issues 2006, 2 issues 2007. sub. price $16 (Institutions add $4; outside U.S. add $6). Send check or money order. Make sure the check is drawn on a U. S. bank and is made out to *Harpur Palate*; per copy $10. Back issues: $5. 180pp. Reporting time: 4 to 6 months. We accept simultaneous submissions if stated as such in cover letter. If your work is accepted elsewhere, please let us know immediately. Publishes 1% of manuscripts submitted. Payment: 2 contributor's copies per author. Copyrighted, reverts to author.

Harrington Park Press, Bill Palmer, 10 Alice Street, Binghamton, NY 13904-1580, Tel.:(607) 722-5857, Fax (607)722-8465, Web: http://www.HaworthPress.com. 1978. Fiction, non-fiction. ". . . the umbrella imprint of The Haworth Press, focusing on gay, lesbian, bisexual, transgender and other gender studies. Harrington Park Press is the alternative press of The Haworth Press, Inc. Harrington titles are devoted to gay and lesbian studies, bisexuality, and related areas. Harrington Park Press had originally published only nonfiction but it now offers literary/fiction works under the Southern Tier Editions (gay male) book series and Alice Street Editions (lesbian). Harrington Park Press also includes several internationally known journals that are leaders in their fields. -Journal of Homosexuality -Journal of Lesbian Studies -Harrington Gay Men's Fiction Quarterly -Harrington Lesbian Fiction Quarterly -Journal of Bisexuality -Journal of Gay & Lesbian Politics (new) -Journal of Gay Lesbian Issues in Education (new) -Journal of Gay & Lesbian Psychotherapy: the official journal of the Association of Gay & Lesbian Psychiatrists -Journal of Gay & Lesbian Social Services -Journal of GLBT Family Studies (new) -Journal of GLBT Issues in Counseling (in development) -Journal of GLBT

Community & Public Health (in development) -International Journal of Transgenderism: the official journal of the Harry Benjamin International Gender Dysphoria Association (new)." avg. press run 1200. Pub'd 40 titles 2005; expects 40 titles 2006, 40 titles 2007. Discounts: Retail Bookstore Discount Schedule:1-4 books 25%, 5-49 books 42%, 50-99 books 44%, 100+ books 46%. Bookstores & Distributors; 33 1/3% on hardbound copies. Discount Notes: 1. Classroom adoption orders receive 20% discount; a. All orders identifiable as adoption orders. b. Orders for 5 copies or more 2. Wholesale discount: 20% on orders for less than 50 copies and 50% on orders for 50 copies or more. 275pp. Reporting time: Haworth will contact the author in eight to ten weeks after submission. Simultaneous submissions accepted: No. Publishes 30% of manuscripts submitted. Copyrights for author. Subjects: Bisexual, Family, Fantasy, Feminism, Fiction, Gay, Gender Issues, Health, Journals, Lesbianism, Lifestyles, Political Science, Sex, Sexuality, Women, Young Adult.

Hartley & Marks, Publishers, Rodger Reynolds, Managing Editor, PO Box 147, Point Roberts, WA 98281, (800) 277-5887.

THE HARVARD ADVOCATE, Casey Cep, President; Daniel Mach, Publisher, 21 South Street, Cambridge, MA 02138, Fax 617-496-9740, contact@theharvardadvocate.com. 1866. Poetry, fiction, articles, art, photos, cartoons, interviews, criticism, reviews, long-poems, collages, plays, non-fiction. *"The Harvard Advocate* publishes work from Harvard undergraduates, affiliates, and alumni. We regret that we cannot read manuscripts from other sources." circ. 4M. 4/yr. Pub'd 4 issues 2005; expects 4 issues 2006, 4 issues 2007. sub. price $25 for 4 issues; per copy $8; sample $5. Back issues: price varies. Discounts: none. 60pp (16 color)pp. Reporting time: 4-6 weeks. Simultaneous submissions accepted: yes. Publishes 10% of manuscripts submitted. Payment: none. Copyrighted, does not revert to author. Pub's reviews: 12 in 2005. §fiction, poetry, features, film/animation, art,. Ads: $200-$1400. Subjects: Literary Review, Literature (General).

Harvard Common Press, Bruce Shaw, Publisher, 535 Albany Street, Boston, MA 02118, 617-423-5803; 888-657-3755. 1976. Photos, non-fiction. avg. press run 7.5-50M. Pub'd 8 titles 2005; expects 15 titles 2006, 15 titles 2007. Discounts: 12-299 50% retail dicount. 220pp. Reporting time: 2-4 months. Simultaneous submissions accepted: yes. Copyrights for author. Subjects: Adoption, Birth, Birth Control, Population, Business & Economics, Careers, Cooking, Employment, Family, How-To, Nature, Parenting, Transportation, Women.

HARVARD REVIEW, Christina Thompson, Lamont Library, Harvard University, Cambridge, MA 02138, 617-495-9775. 1992. Poetry, fiction, interviews, reviews, plays, non-fiction. "We publish writers at all stages of their careers, from the very well-known to the never-before-published. We are interested in most literary genres and styles (except sci-fi, horror, etc). Recent contributors include: Arthur Miller, Joyce Carol Oates, Jorie Graham, Jim Crace, Seamus Heaney, Alice Hoffman, Lyn Hejinian, Lan Samantha Chang, John Ashbery and Robert Creeley." circ. 2500. 2/yr. Pub'd 2 issues 2005; expects 2 issues 2006, 2 issues 2007. sub. price $16; per copy $10; sample n/a. Back issues: $10 inquire for availability. 256pp. Reporting time: 3-6 months. Simultaneous submissions accepted: Yes. Payment: no payment. Copyrighted, reverts to author. Pub's reviews: approx. 50 in 2005. §fiction, poetry, essays, creative non-fiction. Ads: 1/2 page $350, full page $500. Subjects: Drama, Essays, Fiction, Literary Review, Poetry, Prose.

HARVARD WOMEN'S LAW JOURNAL, Lisa Westfall, Editor-in-Chief, Publications Center, Harvard Law School, Cambridge, MA 02138, 617-495-3726. 1978. Articles, reviews. "We are a law review; all submissions are generally law related; however, legal histories, literary and sociological perspectives on the law as it affects women and feminism are welcomed." circ. 900. 1/yr. Pub'd 1 issue 2005; expects 1 issue 2006, 1 issue 2007. sub. price $17 US, $20 foreign; per copy $17; sample not available. 350pp. Reporting time: varies. Copyrighted, does not revert to author. Pub's reviews: 7 in 2005. §Law related, legal histories and sociological literary perspectives on the law as it affects women and feminism. Ads: none. Subjects: Family, Feminism, Law, Sex, Sexuality, Women.

Harvest Hill Press, Sherri Eldridge, PO Box 55, Salisbury Cove, ME 04672, 207-288-8900; fax 207-288-3611. 1994. Non-fiction. "Cookbooks only." avg. press run 7M. Pub'd 7 titles 2005; expects 4 titles 2006, 8 titles 2007. 160pp. Simultaneous submissions accepted: no. Publishes 0% of manuscripts submitted. Subjects: Children, Youth, Cooking.

Harvest Shadows Publications, PO Box 378, Southborough, MA 01772-0378, Prefer contact by email. dbharvest@harvestshadows.com, www.harvestshadows.com. 2003. Fiction, non-fiction. Pub'd 1 title 2005; expects 2 titles 2006, 2 titles 2007. Discounts: Discounts available. Contact for more info. 224-320pp. Copyrights for author. Subjects: Fiction, Horror, Supernatural, WICCA.

Hastings Art Reference, Peter Hastings Falk, PO Box 833, Madison, CT 06443, 203-245-2246, Fax 203-245-5116, pfalk@cshore.com, www.falkart.com. 1985. Art, non-fiction. "Publisher of the biographical dictionary, *Who Was Who In American Art,* and monographs on American artists in conjunction with museum or gallery exhibitions." avg. press run 2M. Pub'd 3 titles 2005; expects 3 titles 2006, 3 titles 2007. Discounts: varies by title. 250-1,750pp. Reporting time: 2 weeks. Simultaneous submissions accepted: yes. Payment:

negotiable. Copyrights for author. Subjects: Arts, Reference.

•**Haunted Rowboat Press,** Patrick Shawn Bagley, 162 Longley Road, Madison, ME 04950. 2005. Poetry, fiction, interviews, reviews. ''For complete guidelines, please send a #10 SASE to Haunted Rowboat Press 162 Longley Road Madison, Maine 04950.'' avg. press run 150. Expects 2 titles 2006, 4-5 titles 2007. Discounts: Bookstores: 1-4 copies 25%5+copies 40%. 30-40pp. Reporting time: 1 month. Simultaneous submissions accepted: Yes. Publishes 30% of manuscripts submitted. Payment: Payment is two copies of the issue in which your work appears. Does not copyright for author. Subjects: Fantasy, Fiction, Literary Review, Mystery, Poetry, Reviews, Translation.

HAWAI'I REVIEW, Clint Frakes, Editor; Lisa Ottiger, Managing Editor; Christopher Kelsey, Fiction Editor; Clint Frakes, Poetry Editor, c/o Dept. of English, 1733 Donaghho Road, Honolulu, HI 96822, 808-956-3030. 1973. Poetry, fiction, art, photos, cartoons, satire, music, parts-of-novels, long-poems, plays, non-fiction. ''Accept works of visual art, poetry, fiction, and non-fiction, including plays, short-short stories, essays, humor, cartoons. Publish all forms of literature including, but not limited to, works which focus on Hawai'i and the Pacific. Submissions *must* include SASE w/sufficient postage for return of material with reply.'' circ. 1M. 2/yr. Pub'd 2 issues 2005; expects 2 issues 2006, 2 issues 2007. sub. price $20, $30/2 years; per copy $10; sample $10. Back issues: $5. 150-250pp. Reporting time: 3-5 months. Simultaneous submissions accepted: yes. Publishes 5% of manuscripts submitted. Payment: 4 copies. Copyrighted, reverts to author. Ads: call for prices. Subjects: Arts, Asian-American, Avant-Garde, Experimental Art, Biography, Essays, Fiction, Hawaii, Indigenous Cultures, Multicultural, Non-Fiction, Pacific Region, Poetry, Prose, Theatre, Translation.

HAWAII PACIFIC REVIEW, Patrice Wilson, Editor, 1060 Bishop Street, Hawai'i Pacific University, Honolulu, HI 96813, 808-544-1108. 1987. Poetry, fiction, satire, reviews, parts-of-novels, long-poems, non-fiction. ''The *Hawaii Pacific Review* is looking for poetry, short fiction, and personal essays that speak with a powerful and unique voice. We encourage experimental narrative techniques and poetic styles. While we occasionally accept work form novice writers, we publish only work of the hightest quality. We will read one submission per contributor consisting of one prose piece of up to 5000 words or 5 poems. Please include a cover letter with a 5-line bio and an SASE. Experimental works, translations and long poetry (up to 100 lines) are all welcome. Our reading period is Sept. 1 to Dec. 31.'' circ. 500-750. 1/yr. Pub'd 1 issue 2005; expects 1 issue 2006, 1 issue 2007. sub. price $8.95; per copy $8.95; sample $5. Back issues: $7. Discounts: bulk $4 per copy. 100pp. Reporting time: 12-15 weeks. Simultaneous submissions accepted, but they must be indicated in the cover letter. Publishes 5% of manuscripts submitted. Payment: 2 copies. Copyrighted, reverts to author. Pub's reviews: 5 in 2005. §Poetry, fiction, essays. Ads: exchange. Subjects: Essays, Fiction, Poetry, Satire, Short Stories.

Hawk Publishing Group, Inc., 7107 S. Yale Avenue, PMB 345, Tulsa, OK 74136-6308, 918-492-3677, Fax 918-492-2120, www.hawkpub.com. 1999. ''Please read the submission guidelines on our website before sending materials to Hawk.'' Pub'd 15 titles 2005; expects 12 titles 2006, 12 titles 2007. Reporting time: 3 months. Simultaneous submissions accepted: yes. Copyrights for author.

The Haworth Press, Bill Palmer, Vice President and Publications Director, 10 Alice Street, Binghamton, NY 13904-1580, Tel.: (607)722-5857, Fax: (607)722-8465, Web: http://www.HaworthPress.com. 1978. Fiction, non-fiction. ''The Haworth Press is an independent publisher of academic and professional books and journals on a wide range of subjects focusing on contemporary issues. For a list of all topics go to www.HaworthPress.com.'' avg. press run 1400. Pub'd 220 titles 2005; expects 250 titles 2006, 200 titles 2007. Discounts: Retail Bookstore Discount Schedule for Titles in the Haworth Trade Catalog: 1-4 books 25%, 5-49 books 42%, 50-99 books 44% 100+ books 46% Bookstores & Distributors; 33 1/3% on hardbound copies Discount Notes:1. Classroom adoption orders receive 20% discount; a. All orders identifiable as adoption orders. b. Orders for 5 copies or more 2. Wholesale discount: 20% on orders for less than 50 copies and 50% on orders for 50 copies or more. 350pp. Reporting time: Haworth will contact the author in eight to ten weeks after submission. Simultaneous submissions accepted: No. Publishes 30% of manuscripts submitted. Copyrights for author. Subjects: Agriculture, Children, Youth, Disabled, Fiction, Gender Issues, Journals, Libraries, Marketing, Medicine, Mental Health, Political Science, Reference, Sex, Sexuality, Social Work, Textbooks.

HAYDEN'S FERRY REVIEW, Salima Keegan, Managing Editor, Box 871502, Arizona State University, Tempe, AZ 85287-1502, 480-965-1243. 1986. Poetry, fiction, art, photos, interviews. ''Publishes approximately 25 poems, 5 short stories. Past contributors: Raymond Carver, Rick Bass, Joy Williams, John Updike, T.C. Boyle, Rita Dove, Maura Stanton and Joseph Heller.'' circ. 1M. 2/yr. Pub'd 2 issues 2005; expects 2 issues 2006, 2 issues 2007. sub. price $14; per copy $6.00; sample $7.50. Back issues: $7.50. 128pp. Reporting time: 8-10 weeks after deadline. We accept simultaneous submissions with notification. Payment: in copies (2), $25/page max. $100. Copyrighted, reverts to author. Subjects: Fiction, Poetry.

Health Plus Publishers, Paula E. Clure, PO Box 1027, Sherwood, OR 97140, 503-625-0589, Fax 503-625-1525. 1965. Non-fiction. ''We publish books on health, particularly holistic health, nutrition, and fitness. We are publishers of Dr. Paavo Airola's books, including *How to Get Well, Everywoman's Book*, and *Are You Confused?* Other publications include: *Change Your Mind/Change Your Weight*, by Dr. James McClernan, and *Exercise For Life*, by Mark L. Hendrickson and Gary J. Greene. Query first.'' avg. press run 7.5M-10M. Pub'd 1 title 2005; expects 2 titles 2006, 1 title 2007. Discounts: inquire. 250pp. Reporting time: 3-6 months. Payment: no advance, royalties negotiable. Copyrights for author. Subject: Health.

Health Press, K. Frazier, PO Box 37470, Albuquerque, NM 87176-7470, goodbooks@healthpress.com. 1988. Non-fiction. "Books related to cutting-edge health topics, well-researched, geared to general public. Require outline with 3 chapters for submission—prefer complete manuscript. Authors must be credentialed (MD, PhD) or have credentialed professional write intro/preface. Controversial topics desired.'' avg. press run 5M. Pub'd 4 titles 2005; expects 4 titles 2006, 4 titles 2007. Discounts: bookstore 40%+, library 10%, (depending on quantity). 250pp. Reporting time: 8-10 weeks. Simultaneous submissions accepted: yes. Payment: standard royalty. Copyrights for author. Subjects: Drugs, Health, Medicine, Psychology, Self-Help.

Health Yourself, Ken Davis MD, 1617 Cafe Dumonde, Conroe, TX 77304, 936 7608558. 2003. Non-fiction. avg. press run 3000. Pub'd 1 title 2005; expects 1 title 2006, 1 title 2007. Discounts: 20%. 130pp. Reporting time: N/A. Copyrights for author. Subjects: Health, Medicine, Nutrition.

HEALTHY WEIGHT JOURNAL, Frances M. Berg, Editor, 402 South 14th Street, Hettinger, ND 58639, 701-567-2646, Fax 701-567-2602, e-mail fmberg@healthyweight.net. 1986. "Publishing office: 4 Hughson Street South, Hamilton, ON Canada L8N 3K7, 800-568-7281, e-mail info@bcdecker.com.'' circ. 1.5M. 6/yr. Pub'd 6 issues 2005; expects 6 issues 2006, 6 issues 2007. sub. price US & Canada: $65 individuals, $95 institutions, $32.50 students; elsewhere: $85 individual, $125 institutions, $45 students (U.S. funds only); per copy $19 US & Canada, $25 elsewhere; sample free. Back issues: $19 US & Canada, $25 elsewhere. Discounts: agents 5%. 20pp. Payment: none. Copyrighted, does not revert to author. Pub's reviews: 12-16 in 2005. §Obesity, weight management, Nutrition, eating disorders. Ads: contact Bob Sutherland at Canadian address above. Subjects: Health, Medicine.

Heartland Publishing, Jo Moon, PO Box 402, Seymour, MO 65746-0402, Tel. (417) 848-7946, Tel/Fax (417) 935-9146, www.goheartland.com. 2005. Poetry, long-poems, non-fiction. "Emphasis on memoir and short story collections. Will consider how-to books for a sustainable future.'' avg. press run 2000. Pub'd 1 title 2005; expects 1 title 2006, 2 titles 2007. Discounts: 2-6 copies: 30%6+ copies: 40%Distributors: standard contract price. 200pp. Reporting time: 1-2 months. Simultaneous submissions accepted: Yes. Payment: No advances, royalties to be negotiated. Copyrights for author. Subjects: Civil War, Community, Environment, Ethics, Missouri, Native American, Nebraska, New Age, New Mexico, Old West, Spiritual, The West.

HEARTLANDS: A Magazine of Midwest Life and Art, Larry Smith, Managing Editor, Firelands College, Huron, OH 44839, 419-433-5560 X20784, lsmithdog@aol.com, www.theheartlandstoday.net. 2003. Poetry, fiction, articles, art, photos, reviews, non-fiction. "This is a magazine format for the older *The Heartlands Today* (12 volumes). We are distinctly Midwest in focus, with a theme of Midwest Art and Live. Check our homepage. Magazine format is 8-1/2 x 11 with lots of photos and art. We look for good clear writing in the Midwestern vein. Say what you mean and show it rather than telling about it. We do fiction, poetry, personal essays, and querried articles.'' circ. 700. 1/yr. Pub'd 1 issue 2005; expects 1 issue 2006, 1 issue 2007. sub. price $7; per copy $7. Discounts: 30% to trade. 96pp. Reporting time: seasonal. Simultaneous submissions accepted: yes. Publishes 20% of manuscripts submitted. Payment: $10-$20 plus 2 copies. Copyrighted, reverts to author. Pub's reviews. Ads: $300 1/2 page/$150 other. Subjects: Community, Fiction, Folklore, Leisure/Recreation, Lifestyles, Ohio, Poetry, Writers/Writing.

•**HEARTLODGE: Honoring the House of the Poet,** Andrea L. Watson, Editor; Cheryl Loetscher, Editor; Shirley Sullivan, Editor; Leta McDonald, Editor; Tricia DuBois, Editor, P.O. Box 370627, Denver, CO 80237, heartlodgepoets@gmail.com. 2005. Poetry. "As five poets, editors, and publishers who founded HeartLodge, our mission is to welcome to our poetry journal both established and emerging writers, with an emphasis on poems containing unique voice, imagery, and sense of place. We value the writing of kindred spirits and receive high quality poems from all over the world. OUR READING PERIOD IS SEPTEMBER 1-JANUARY 31. Please submit up to 3 poems with brief Bio and SASE. Recent Contributors: Lyn Lifshin, Simon Perchik, Paul Hostovsky, Carol Aronoff, Barry Ballard, Jim Ciletti, Kathleen Cain, David Breeden.'' 1/yr. Pub'd 1 issue 2005; expects 1 issue 2006, 1 issue 2007. 68pp. Reporting time: 3 months. Simultaneous submissions accepted: Yes, but notify editors if accepted elsewhere. Publishes 5% of manuscripts submitted. Payment: Contributor's copy upon publication. Copyrighted, reverts to author. Ads: None.

Hearts That Care Publishing, 888 West X Street, Washougal, WA 98671-7432.

Heartsome Publishing, PO Box 129, Norfolk, MA 02056.

Heartsong Books, PO Box 370, Blue Hill, ME 04614-0370, publishers/authors phone: 207-266-7673, e-mail maggie@downeast.net, http://heartsongbooks.com. 1993. Fiction, non-fiction. "We are not accepting submissions at this time. The Heartsong vision is one of kinship. We trust that our books will help young people - all people - understand and respect the interconnectedness of all life and inspire them to act on that understanding in compassionate, powerful, and celebratory ways - for the good of Earth and for the good of generations to come. We at Heartsong express our kinship vision not only in the books we publish, but through gifts of money, outreach and opportunity." avg. press run 2M-4M. Pub'd 1 title 2005; expects 1 title 2007. Discounts: trade, bulk, classroom. Pages vary. Subjects: Children, Youth, Culture, Earth, Natural History, Education, Environment, Futurism, History, Inspirational, Metaphysics, Native American, Non-Fiction, Non-Violence, Occult, Peace, Spiritual.

Heat Press, Christopher Natale Peditto, Publisher & General Editor; Barbara Romain, Associate Editor; Teresa D'Ovido, Art Director; Harold Abramowitz, Associate Editor, PO Box 26218, Los Angeles, CA 90026, 213-482-8902, heatpresseditions@yahoo.com. 1993. Poetry, long-poems. "Heat Press's roots are in Philadelphia, PA. Current series of published poets, Open Mouth Poetry Series (originally the name of an open poetry series in Philly), features poets close to the Beat Generation in their coming out and oral word sensibilities. Allied interests include the culture of jazz, 'Black' and pan-African cultures, the 'road' and nomadic cross-cultural traditions (versewinds), street poets of the oral tradition, and miscegenated-polyglottal-mouth-music poetry texts. Currently not accepting unsolicited manuscripts, but inquires are welcomed. Recent authors include Eric Priestley (*Abracadabra*), Charles Bivins (*Music in Silence*), Elliott Levin (*does it swing?*) and Will Perkins (*!Scat*)." avg. press run 1.5M. Expects 1 title 2006, 1 title 2007. 100pp. Payment: negotiable. Copyrights for author. Subject: Poetry.

The Heather Foundation, Spencer H. MacCallum, 713 W. Spruce #48, Deming, NM 88030, 915-261-0502, sm@look.net. 1973. Non-fiction. "The Heather Foundation is dedicated to furthering understanding of society as an evolving, spontaneously ordered cooperation among free-acting individuals. Taxation and other institutionalized coercions are viewed as something to be outgrown. The Foundation sponsors research, lectures and publications. It also preserves and administers the intellectual estates of persons such as E.C. Riegel and Spencer Heath who contributed notably to the humane studies. Areas of interest include philosophy of science, the inspirational content of religion and the aesthetic arts, non-political money, and the multi-tenant income property as a model and forerunner of non-political communities. Interested persons are invited to request the Foundation's booklist, '*Creative Alternatives in Social Thought*.'" avg. press run 2M. Pub'd 1 title 2005; expects 1 title 2006, 1 title 2007. Discounts: 50% to bookstores, ppd. provided they supply name and address of customer. 175pp. Reporting time: 30 days. Simultaneous submissions accepted: yes. Copyrights for author. Subjects: Anarchist, Anthropology, Archaelogy, Business & Economics, Christianity, Community, Creativity, Inspirational, Libertarian, Peace, Philosophy, Political Science, Real Estate, Science, Society, Sociology.

HEAVEN BONE MAGAZINE, Heaven Bone Press, Steven Hirsch; Gordon Kirpal, Contributing Editor, 62 Woodcock Mt. Dr., Washingtonville, NY 10992-1828, 845-496-4109. 1986. Poetry, fiction, articles, art, photos, cartoons, interviews, satire, criticism, reviews, music, long-poems, collages, plays, concrete art. "Recent contributors: Anne Waldman, Kirpal Gordon, Diane D'Prima, Antler, Janine Pommy Vega, David Chorlton, Stephen-Paul Martin, Fielding Dawson, Jack Collom, Cynthia Hogue, Joseph Donahue. We like work that is deeply rooted in nature and image yet inspired by cosmic visions and spiritual practice. Current issues tending toward the surreal and eidetic. Editor loves work of Rilke. "Where are his followers?" Nothing turns us off more than artificially forced end-line rhyming; however, rhymed verse will be considered if obviously excellent and showing careful work. We would like to see more short stories and essays on various literary and esoteric topics. Reviews also being considered, but query first. SASE please." circ. 2.5M. 1/yr. Pub'd 1 issue 2005; expects 1 issue 2006, 1 issue 2007. sub. price $10; per copy $10; sample $10. Discounts: 40% to bookstores, 50% to distributors. 96-144pp. Reporting time: 3-36 weeks. Publishes 3% of manuscripts submitted. Payment: Free copy, 30% off additional copies. Copyrighted, reverts to author. Pub's reviews: 20 in 2005. §Literary, spiritual, experimental, metaphysical, music, spoken audio, spoken literature. Ads: $240/$130/$90 1/4 page. Subjects: Arts, Avant-Garde, Experimental Art, Book Reviewing, Buddhism, Essays, Fiction, Language, Metaphysics, New Age, Poetry, Spiritual.

Heaven Bone Press (see also HEAVEN BONE MAGAZINE), Steven Hirsch, 62 Woodcock Mtn. Dr., Washingtonville, NY 10992, 845-496-4109. 1986. Poetry, fiction, articles, art, photos, cartoons, interviews, satire, criticism, reviews, music, long-poems, collages, plays, concrete art. "We publish a bi-annual poetry chapbook contest winner and 2-4 poetry and/or fiction titles. Recently published: *Things*, visual writing by Stephen-Paul Martin; *Walking the Dead*, poems by Lori Anderson; *Red Bracelets*, poems by Janine Pommy Vega; *Down With the Move*, by Kirpal Gordon; *Bright Garden at World's End*, by David Dahl; *Terra Lucida*, by Joseph Donahue; and *Fountains of Gold* by Wendy Vig and Jon Anderson." avg. press run 500. Pub'd 3 titles 2005; expects 2 titles 2006, 5 titles 2007. Discounts: 40% bookstores, 50% distributors. 40pp. Reporting time: 6-36 weeks. Payment: varies; set fee or individual percentage of sales. Copyrights for author. Subjects: Arts, Avant-Garde, Experimental Art, Book Reviewing, Buddhism, Essays, Fiction, Language, Metaphysics, New Age, Poetry, Spiritual.

HECATE, Hecate Press, Carole Ferrier, Editor, School of English, Media Studies & Art History, The University of Queensland, St. Lucia, Queensland 4072, Australia, phone: 07 336 53146, fax: 07 3365 2799, web: www.emsah.uq.edu.au/awsr, email: c.ferrier@mailbox.uq.edu.au. 1975. Poetry, fiction, articles, art, criticism, plays. "Incorporates *Hecate's Australian Women's Book Review.* Articles on historical, sociological, literary, etc. topics. Aspects of women's oppression and resistance. Some interviews and reviews. Some creative writing. Please make all payments in equivalent in Australian currency if possible. We almost never run American poets." circ. 2M. 2/yr. Pub'd 3 issues 2005; expects 3 issues 2006, 3 issues 2007. sub. price $25/yr (ind), $100 (inst), please pay in Australian $; per copy $6 (Ind); $30 (Inst); sample $6 (ind); $10 (inst). Back issues: $8 volume (Ind); $100 (Inst); concession price *may* be negotiated for runs. Discounts: 33% for bookshops. 180pp. Reporting time: varies. Publishes 6% of manuscripts submitted. Payment: $40 poem, $60 story, $90 article. Copyrighted. Pub's reviews: 30 in 2005. §Socialist, feminist. Ads: negotiable, exchange. Subject: Women.

•**Hecate Press (see also HECATE),** Carole#Editor Ferrier, School of English, Media Studies and Art History, The University of Queensland, St. Lucia, Queensland 4072, Australia. 1975. Fiction, articles, cartoons, interviews, criticism, reviews, parts-of-novels, long-poems, non-fiction.

HEELTAP/Pariah Press, Pariah Press, Richard D. Houff, c/o Richard D. Houff, 604 Hawthorne Ave. East, St. Paul, MN 55101-3531. 1996. Poetry. "I like short, up to 32 lines, blank, free, post-beat, narrative, hit the mark and have something to say poems. Tom Clark, Dave Etter, and Paul Dickinson are recent contributors. The magazine is made from government trash bins materials." circ. 500. 2/yr. Pub'd 2 issues 2005; expects 2 issues 2006, 2 issues 2007. sub. price $18/4 issue sub.; per copy $5; sample $5. Back issues: $5. Discounts: none as yet. 48pp. Reporting time: 2 weeks to 1 month. Simultaneous submissions accepted: yes. Publishes 5% of manuscripts submitted. Payment: copies. Copyrighted, reverts to author. Pub's reviews: one in 2005. §poetry. Ads: none as yet. Subjects: Anarchist, Avant-Garde, Experimental Art, Beat, Dada, Humor.

Heidelberg Graphics, Larry S. Jackson, 2 Stansbury Court, Chico, CA 95928-9410, 530-342-6582. 1972. "Heidelberg Graphics publishes manuscripts by invitation only. For all others we offer complete services for self-publishing. Stansbury Publishing is an imprint of Heidelberg Graphics. Recent books include *Chronicles of the Clandestine Knights: Hyacinth Blue* (Tony Nunes), *Annie Kennedy Bidwell: An Intimate History* (Lois H. McDonald), *The Chaining of the Dragon: A Commentary on the Book of Revelation* (Ralph Schreiber), *Around the World in 52 Words: Ritual Writing for this New Millennium* (Rob Burton), and *The Plains Beyond* (L D Clark). Visit www.HeidelbergGraphics.com for more information. We also invite unpublished publishable manuscripts for free posting in Forum on our Web site." avg. press run 600-6M. Pub'd 3 titles 2005; expects 3 titles 2006, 3 titles 2007. Discounts: write for prices or see ABA Book Buyers Handbook. 200pp. Reporting time: 8-16 weeks. Simultaneous submissions accepted: no. Publishes .01% of manuscripts submitted. Payment: negotiable. Copyrights for author. Subjects: Biography, Christianity, Fiction, History, How-To, Magazines, Native American, Newsletter, Non-Fiction, Poetry, Religion, Reprints, World War II.

Helicon Nine Editions, Gloria Vando-Hickok, Editor-in-Chief, Box 22412, Kansas City, MO 64113, 816-753-1095, Fax 816-753-1016, helicon9@aol.com, www.heliconnine.com. 1977. Poetry, fiction. "We are publishing high quality volumes of fiction, poetry and/or essays. Please query before sending ms." avg. press run 1M-2.5M. Pub'd 2 titles 2005; expects 2 titles 2006, 2 titles 2007. Discounts: 40% bookstores, distributors. 55-512pp. Reporting time: varies. We accept but do not encourage simultaneous submissions. Payment: varies with individual writers. Copyrights for author. Subjects: Arts, Avant-Garde, Experimental Art, Bilingual, Essays, Fiction, Poetry, Short Stories, Visual Arts, Women.

HELIOTROPE, A JOURNAL OF POETRY, Susan Sindall, Co-Editor; Laurel Blossom, Co-Editor; Barbara Elovic, Co-Editor; Victoria Hallerman, Associate Editor, Website Editor, P.O Box 456, Shady, NY 12409, www.heliopoems.com. 2001. Poetry. "Founded by four women poets, Heliotrope agrees with Coleridge, that poems are, "...the best words in their best order." We publish an eclectic mix of style and form, and our poets are from all over the world. Recent contributors include: Billy Collins, Heather McHugh, Jean Valentine, D. Nurkse, Stephen Dunn, Carl Dennis, Rachel Hadas, among many others. Visit www.heliopoems.com to sample the magazine, subscribe, or access the guidelines for submission. We urge all poets to visit the guidelines before submitting, and, if possible, to purchase a sample copy of the magazine, which will give you a better sense of the kinds of poems we publish." circ. 450. 1-2/yr. Pub'd 1 issues 2005; expects 2 issues 2006, 2 issues 2007. sub. price $8.00; per copy $8.00; sample $6.00. Back issues: $8.00. 70pp. Reporting time: 6-8 months; *read Sept-April only.* Simultaneous submissions accepted: Yes. Payment: 2 copies of the magazine; additional copies available at a discount. Copyrighted, reverts to author. Subject: Poetry.

HELIOTROPE: A Writer's Summer Solstice, Iris Gribble-Neal, Tom Gribble, PO Box 9938, Spokane, WA 99209-9938, e-mail gribneal@comcast.net. 1997. Poetry, fiction, art, interviews, satire, criticism, reviews, long-poems, non-fiction. circ. 200. 1/yr. Pub'd 1 issue 2005; expects 1 issue 2006, 1 issue 2007. sub. price $8.50; per copy $8.50; sample $8.50. Back issues: $8.50. 125pp. Reporting time: 30 days after cutoff date of Sept. 21. Simultaneous submissions accepted: no. Publishes 20% of manuscripts submitted. Payment: copy.

Copyrighted, reverts to author. Pub's reviews: 1 in 2005. §Poetry, short stories, creative nonfiction. Ads: $25 a page, some ad exchanges arranged.

Helm Publishing, Dianne Helm, 3923 Seward Ave., Rockford, IL 61108-7658, work: 815-398-4660, dianne@publishersdrive.com, www.publishersdrive.com. 1995. Poetry, fiction, photos, interviews, reviews, parts-of-novels, news items, non-fiction. Pub'd 2 titles 2005; expects 3 titles 2006, 3 titles 2007. Discounts: 40% trade, 25% classroom, 15% agent, 10% jobber, 30% bulk. 200pp. Reporting time: 2-4 months. Simultaneous submissions accepted: yes. Payment: Payments of Royalties June 30th and Dec.31st. Copyrights for author. Subjects: African Literature, Africa, African Studies, Agriculture, Antiques, Arts, Aviation, Bibliography, Biography, Book Collecting, Bookselling, Book Reviewing, Business & Economics, Children, Youth, Cities, Comics, Communication, Journalism, Community.

HERE AND NOW, The American Zen Association, Jeffrey Cantin, Richard Collins, 5500 Prytania St #201, New Orleans, LA 70130, info@nozt.org, www.nozt.org. 1991. Articles, photos, interviews, criticism, letters, news items, non-fiction. *"Here and Now* is the newsletter of the American Zen Association." circ. 200. 1/yr. sub. price $14. 8pp. Reporting time: 1 month. Payment: copies. Not copyrighted. Subject: Zen.

Heritage Books, Inc., Leslie Towle, 65 E. Main Street, Westminster, MD 21157-5026, 301-390-7708, Fax 301-390-7153, info@heritagebooks.com. 1978. Non-fiction. "Subject matter of interest includes local and regional histories pertaining to eastern U.S. and source records of interest to historians and genealogists." avg. press run 200-300. Pub'd 60 titles 2005; expects 100 titles 2006, 120 titles 2007. Discounts: 1-5 assorted titles 20%, 6+ 40%; free shipping on both. 250pp. Reporting time: 1 month. Simultaneous submissions accepted: yes. Publishes 80% of manuscripts submitted. Payment: 10% of sales, paid semi-annually. Does not copyright for author. Subjects: Americana, Genealogy, History, Reprints.

Heritage Global Publishing, J.V. Goldbach, 908 Innergary Place, Valrico, FL 33594, 813-643-6029. 1998. Non-fiction. "Book released early 1999: *Help Your Child Avoid Multiple Sclerosis: A Parenting Decision."* avg. press run 3-5M. Expects 1 title 2006, 2-3 titles 2007. Discounts: standard trade. 250pp. Simultaneous submissions accepted: yes. Publishes 2% of manuscripts submitted. Payment: flexible. Copyrights for author. Subjects: Health, Parenting, Religion.

Heritage House Publishers, PO Box 194242, San Francisco, CA 94119, 415-776-3156. 1990. Non-fiction. "Not currently accepting submissions. Heritage House Publishers specializes in regional/city guidebooks and in California history and biography. Our first title, published October 1991, is *Historic San Francisco: A Concise History and Guide* by Rand Richards. Heritage House Publishers is currently distributed to the trade by Great West Books, PO Box 1028, Lafayette, CA 94549." avg. press run 3K. Pub'd 1 title 2005; expects 1 title 2007. Discounts: 1-4 books 20% (prepaid), 5-24 42%, 25-49 44%, 50-99 46%, 100+ 48%. 400pp. Subjects: Biography, California, Cities, History, San Francisco, Transportation.

Heritage West Books, Thomas A. McDannold, 54977 Hunting Road, Bend, OR 97707-2632, 661-823-1941, Fax 661-823-1888, buckeye@lightspeed.net. 1989. Non-fiction. "History, ethnography, biography." avg. press run 1M-3M. Pub'd 2 titles 2005; expects 3 titles 2006, 3 titles 2007. Discounts: trade-jobber, classroom: 1-4 20%, 5-24 40%. Reporting time: 3 weeks. Payment: yes. Copyrights for author. Subjects: Asian-American, Biography, California, History, Senior Citizens.

Hermes House Press (see also KAIROS, A Journal of Contemporary Thought and Criticism), Richard Mandell, Alan Mandell, 113 Summit Avenue, Brookline, MA 02446-2319, 617-566-2468. 1980. Poetry, fiction, parts-of-novels, long-poems, plays. "Unsolicited manuscripts currently not being read. Experimental works, translations and artwork are encouraged; copy price and number of pages vary. Recent work: *The Deadly Swarm*, short stories by LaVerne Harrell Clark; *The Bats*, a novel by Richard Mandell; *Three Stories*, by R.V. Cassill; *Going West*, poetry by Stanley Diamond; *Bella B.'s Fantasy*, short stories by Raymond Jean; *Crossings*, a novel by Marie Diamond; *O Loma! Constituting a Self* (1977-1984), writings by sociologist Kurt H. Wolff; *Thinking, Feeling, and Doing*, critical essays by Emil Oestereicher." avg. press run 1M. Pub'd 1 title 2005. Discounts: available upon request. Pages vary. Reporting time: 4-8 weeks. Payment: copies plus an agreed percentage after cost. Copyrights for author. Subjects: Fiction, Poetry.

Hermitage (Ermitazh), Igor Yefimov, Marina Yefimov, PO Box 578, Schuylkill Haven, PA 17972, 570-739-1505, fax 570-739-2383, e-mail yefimovim@aol.com, web www.hermitagepublishers.com. 1981. Poetry, fiction, articles, art, criticism, non-fiction. "We publish mostly books in Russian language or books in English dealing with Russian topics: literary criticism, history, translations from Russian, Russian culture, travel into Russia." avg. press run 1M. Pub'd 15 titles 2005; expects 15 titles 2006, 16 titles 2007. Discounts: 40% with 10 copies or more; 30% for jobbers if less than 10; no returns; no discount for libraries. 200pp. Reporting time: 2 months. Payment: negotiable. Subjects: Fiction, History, Literature (General).

HEROES FROM HACKLAND, Mike Grogan, 1225 Evans St., Arkadelphia, AR 71923, 870-246-6223. 1995. Poetry, fiction, articles, photos, cartoons, interviews, satire, criticism, reviews, letters, non-fiction. "Length:

anything from one line to 1,500 words. We do not like crudities or improper language. We don't like religious dogma - we look for imagery and coherence. Recent contributors: Hazel Guyol, William Michael Fagan.'' circ. 175. 3/yr. Pub'd 3 issues 2005; expects 3 issues 2006, 3 issues 2007. sub. price $10.50; per copy $3.50; sample $3.50. Discounts: none. 52pp. Reporting time: 10 days. Simultaneous submissions accepted: no. Publishes 75% of manuscripts submitted. Payment: $5 for each essay, photo, cartoon. Copyrighted, reverts to author. Pub's reviews: 1 in 2005. §We look at anything for review. Ads: no ads. Subjects: Cartoons, Comics, Disney, Movies, Television.

THE HERON'S NEST, Christopher Herold, Editor-in-Chief; Ferris Gilli, Associate Editor; Paul MacNeil, Associate Editor; Peggy Willis Lyles, Associate Editor; Robert Gilliland, Associate Editor, 816 Taft Street, Port Townsend, WA 98368, www.theheronsnest.com. 1999. Poetry. ''Quarterly Journal on-line with an annual print edition that includes the all issues of the previous year and the Readers' Choice Awards for that year. Over 100 Haiku in each quarterly issue, 1 quarterly award and 2 Editors' Choice Runners-Up. Commentary included with winning poem. Most of the best writers of English language haiku submit their works.'' Read regularly by thousands, including the vast majority of the English-speaking global haiku community. 4 quarterly issues and Readers' Choice Awards issue (on-line) ; 1 perfect-bound, annual paper edition. Pub'd 13 issues 2005; expects 5 issues 2006, 5 issues 2007. sub. price $15 US, $16 Canada and Mexico, $17 international. Back issues: Volumes I,II, and III: $1.25 in U.S.; $1.50 in Canada and Mexico; & $1.75 elsewhereVolumes IV, V, and VI: $1.50 in U.S.; $1.75 in Canada and Mexico; & $2.00 elsewhereVolume VII: No back issues as yet. Discounts: none. Reporting time: less than 6 weeks. Simultaneous submissions accepted: no. Publishes 10% of manuscripts submitted. Payment: none. Copyrighted, reverts to author. Ads: none. Subject: Haiku.

Herrmann International, Ned Herrmann, 794 Buffalo Creek Road, Lake Lure, NC 28746, Fax 704-625-9153. 1981. Non-fiction. ''Ned Herrmann's first book, *The Creative Brain*, is a book that is geared toward individuals who want to gain full access to their mental capabilities and learn how this can be a very creative process. The author has been a trainer of trainers in a corporate setting for over 20 years. Basing his work on brain dominance theory, the author has developed a model of thinking styles which can be used in training or for an individual's quest to know more about him or herself.'' avg. press run 5M. Pub'd 1 title 2005; expects 1 title 2007. Discounts: trade 2-7 35%, 8-48 40%, 49-104 50%, 105+ 55%, STOP 25%. 480pp. Copyrights for author. Subjects: Careers, Creativity, Education, Relationships, Self-Help, Textbooks.

Hexagon Blue, Mary Jesse, 19301 SE 16th Street, Sammamish, WA 98075, 425-890-5351, info@hexagonblue.com, www.hexagonblue.com. ''We are currently soliciting manuscripts to begin publishing other authors' works.''

Heyday Books (see also NEWS FROM NATIVE CALIFORNIA), Jeannine Gendar, Managing Editor; Malcolm Margolin, Publisher, PO Box 9145, Berkeley, CA 94709, 510-549-3564, Fax 510-549-1889. 1974. Poetry, art, photos, non-fiction. ''Books on California history and literature, California Indians, women of California, natural history, and regional guidebooks, fiction and poetry.'' avg. press run 4M. Pub'd 14 titles 2005; expects 16 titles 2006, 20 titles 2007. Discounts: retail 1-4 copies 20%, 5-24 40%, 25-49 43%, 50-99 45%, 100+ 46%. 320pp. Reporting time: 6 weeks. Simultaneous submissions accepted: yes. Publishes 1% of manuscripts submitted. Payment: comparable to what's offered by major publishers, in fact modeled on their contracts. Copyrights for author. Subjects: Alaska, Bicycling, California, Earth, Natural History, Europe, History, Indians, Literature (General), Myth, Mythology, Native American, Politics, Sports, Outdoors, Third World, Minorities, Women.

The Heyeck Press, Robin R. Heyeck, 25 Patrol Court, Woodside, CA 94062, 650-851-7491, Fax 650-851-5039, heyeck@ix.netcom.com. 1976. Poetry, long-poems, non-fiction. ''Books on paper marbling. All books are printed letterpress.'' avg. press run 500. Pub'd 1 title 2005; expects 2 titles 2006, 2 titles 2007. Discounts: fine editions, book dealers only 30%; letterpress paper wrappers (trade) 1-3 copies 20%, 4+ 40%. 80pp. Reporting time: 90 days. Simultaneous submissions accepted: no. Publishes 1-2% of manuscripts submitted. Payment: percentage of sales paid in cash. Copyrights for author. Subjects: Fiction, Literature (General), Poetry.

HIDDEN OAK POETRY JOURNAL, Louise Larkins, Editor, 402 South 25th St, Philadelphia, PA 19146-1004, hidoak@att.net. 1999. Poetry, art, photos. ''Accepts submissions on any subject, 25 lines or less. Send not more than 4 at a time. Include brief bio.'' circ. 100. 2 or 3/yr. Pub'd 3 issues 2005; expects 2 issues 2006, 2 issues 2007. sub. price $12 (3 issues); per copy $5; sample $4. 65pp. Reporting time: 2 weeks. Simultaneous submissions accepted: no. Publishes 40% of manuscripts submitted. Payment: 1 free copy. Not copyrighted.

Higganum Hill Books, Richard C. DeBold, Editor, PO Box 666, Higganum, CT 06441, rcdebold@connix.com. 1999. Poetry, non-fiction. avg. press run 500. Pub'd 1 title 2005; expects 2 titles 2006, 2 titles 2007. Discounts: standard universal schedule. 72pp. Reporting time: 1 week. Simultaneous submissions accepted: yes. Publishes 10% of manuscripts submitted. Payment: standard. Does not copyright for author. Subjects: Counter-Culture,

Alternatives, Communes, Education, Poetry.

HIGH COUNTRY NEWS, Paul Larmer, Publisher; Greg Hanscom, Editor, PO Box 1090, Paonia, CO 81428, 970-527-4898, editor@hcn.org. 1970. Articles, art, photos, cartoons, interviews, criticism, reviews, letters, news items. ''We're after hard-hitting, but fairly-reported environmental journalism with a regional slant. We cover Montana, Wyoming, Colorado, California, Utah, Idaho, Nevada, Arizona, New Mexico, Oregon and Washington.'' circ. 25,000. 24/yr. Pub'd 24 issues 2005; expects 24 issues 2006, 24 issues 2007. sub. price $37 indiv., $47 instit.; per copy $3.00; sample free. Back issues: $3.00 (incl. p/h) single copy; bulk rates available on request. Discounts: sell in bulk to schools, libraries, organizations. 24pp. Reporting time: 4 weeks. Simultaneous submissions accepted: no. Payment: 25¢ per word, $50-$100 per published B & W photo. Copyrighted, reverts to author. Pub's reviews: 50 short blurbs in 2005. §Conservation, natural resources, wildlife, energy, land use, growth, unions and the rural economy, and other western community issues. Ads: Text ads: $.86/word for both print & web ads per issue;Display Ad sizes: 1/16, 1/8, 1/4 pages (1/2 page ad-1/issue on first-come/first-served basis). Advance insertion orders accepted.Visit www.hcn.org/advertising.jsp then select *Download Our Media Kit* for pricing, acceptable formats, issue dates/deadlines. Subjects: Conservation, Energy, Environment, Native American, The West.

High Plains Press, Nancy Curtis, Box 123, 539 Cassa Road, Glendo, WY 82213, 307-735-4370, Fax 307-735-4590, 800-552-7819. 1984. Poetry, non-fiction. ''Specializes in Wyoming and the West.'' avg. press run 3M. Pub'd 4 titles 2005; expects 4 titles 2006, 4 titles 2007. Discounts: bookstores 1-4 20%, 5+ 40%, wholesales more. 200pp. Reporting time: 2 months. Simultaneous submissions accepted: yes. Publishes 3% of manuscripts submitted. Payment: based on material, usually 10% net sales. Copyrights for author. Subjects: History, Old West, Poetry, The West, Wyoming.

Higher Ground Press, Debi Morigeau, P.O. Box 650, Summerland, British Columbia, Canada V0H 1Z0, Canada, Tel 250-496-6802, 866-496-6802, hgt@uniserve.com. 2003. Fiction. ''Higher Ground Press is committed to publishing New Age fiction.'' Pub'd 1 title 2005. Discounts: 35%. 200pp. Reporting time: Two months. Simultaneous submissions accepted: Yes. Publishes 1% of manuscripts submitted. Payment: 7% royalties. Does not copyright for author. Subjects: Fiction, Inspirational, Metaphysics, New Age, Spiritual.

Highsmith Press, Matt Mulder, Director; Nancy Knies, Managing Editor; Virginia Harrison, Copy Editor; Patti Kressin, Sales & Marketing Coordinator, PO Box 800, Ft. Atkinson, WI 53538, 920-563-9571, Fax 920-563-4801, hpress@highsmith.com, www.hpress.highsmith.com. 1991. ''We publish books with creative ideas and activities for the library or classroom. Subjects include: library skills, Internet resources and activities, reading activities, storytelling and professional library handbooks.'' avg. press run 2M-3M. Pub'd 20 titles 2005; expects 20 titles 2006, 20 titles 2007. Discounts: 20-50% jobber; booksellers (please contact Patti Kressin). 80-120pp. Reporting time: 30 days. Simultaneous submissions accepted: yes. Publishes 1% of manuscripts submitted. Payment: 10-12% of net. Copyrights for author. Subjects: Education, Internet, Libraries, Reading, Storytelling.

HILL AND HOLLER, Seven Buffaloes Press, Art Coelho, Box 249, Big Timber, MT 59011. price per copy $11.75 P.P.; sample $11.75 P.P.

Hill Country Books, J.O. Walker, PO Box 791615, San Antonio, TX 78279, 830-228-5424. 1994. Non-fiction. ''Prefer mss. under 400pp. Will consider any good non-fiction. Especially interested in Texas or Southwest material; also health and recovery subjects.'' avg. press run 5M. Pub'd 1 title 2005; expects 2 titles 2006, 3 titles 2007. Discounts: averages 40%. 200pp. Reporting time: 2 weeks. Simultaneous submissions accepted: yes. Publishes 20% of manuscripts submitted. Payment: co-publishing arrangements. Copyrights for author. Subjects: Health, History, Southwest, Sports, Outdoors.

HILL COUNTRY SUN, Allan C. Kimball, PO Box 1482, Wimberley, TX 78676, 512-847-5162, allan@hillcountrysun.com, www.hillcountrysun.com. 1990. Articles, photos, interviews, reviews, non-fiction. ''Only material focused on the Central Texas hill country.'' circ. 30M. 11/yr. Pub'd 11 issues 2005; expects 11 issues 2006, 11 issues 2007. sub. price $18; per copy free; sample free. Back issues: $2 each. 32pp. Reporting time: return mail. Simultaneous submissions accepted: yes. Publishes 30% of manuscripts submitted. Payment: $40 per article. Copyrighted, reverts to author. Pub's reviews: 2 in 2005. §Texas travel. Ads: $800 full page. Subjects: Arts, Music, Texas, Travel.

Hilltop Press, Steve Sneyd, 4 Nowell Place, Almondbury, Huddersfield, West Yorkshire HD5 8PB, England.

Himalayan Institute Press, Laura Brownell, Marketing Manager; Jesse Litchman, Marketing Associate, 630 Main St Suite 350, Honesdale, PA 18431, 570-647-1531, fax 570-647-1552, 800-822-4547, hibooks@himalayaninstitute.org, www.HimalayanInstitute.org. 1971. Non-fiction. ''The Himalayan Institute Press publishes books, audio and video products regarding philosophy, spirituality, psychological health, self-help, inspiration, holistic health, Ayurveda, meditation and yoga.'' avg. press run 3000. Expects 8 titles 2006, 10 titles 2007. Discounts: Retail discount: Orders between $100.00 and $499.99 receive a 40% discount; Orders over $500.00

receive a 47% discount. Library and school orders receive a 20% discount. 150-300pp. Reporting time: Two to four months. Simultaneous submissions accepted: Yes. Publishes 70% of manuscripts submitted. Payment: Each arrangement is unique and tailored to the individual project. Copyrights for author. Subjects: Alternative Medicine, Astrology, Autobiography, Biography, Health, Inspirational, Metaphysics, New Age, Non-Violence, Philosophy, Psychiatry, Psychology, Religion, Self-Help, Spiritual.

HIMALAYAN PATH, Yes International Publishers, Theresa King, 1317 Summit Ave., St. Paul, MN 55105, 651-645-6808,fax 651-645-7935,yes@yespublishers.com, www.yespublishers.com. "Authoritative, comprehensive, holistic, multilevel teachings in the Himalayan yoga tradition." 4/yr. sub. price $18/USA, $22/Canada, $25/Europe,India,Asia,So.Am.; per copy $5. Back issues: $5. 32pp.

Hippopotamus Press (see also OUTPOSTS POETRY QUARTERLY), Roland John; B.A. Martin, Business Manager, Mansell Pargitter, 22 Whitewell Road, Frome, Somerset BA11 4EL, England, 0373-466653. 1974. Poetry, long-poems. "Size, number of pages, cost will vary with the material. Against: concrete, typewriter, neo-surrealism and experimental work. For: competent poetry in recognisable English, a knowledge of syntax and construction, finished work and not glimpses into the workshop, also translations. Recent books include G.S. Sharat Chandra (U.S.A.), Edward Lowbury (Canada), Stan Trevor (S. Africa) Shaun McCarthy, Peter Dale, William Bedford, Humphrey Chucas, Debjani Chatterjee, Peter Dent." avg. press run 750 paper, 250 cloth. Pub'd 2 titles 2005; expects 5 titles 2006. Discounts: 35% off singles, 45% off bulk orders. 80pp. Reporting time: 1 month. Payment: by arrangement/royalty. Standard UK copyright, remaining with author. Subjects: Criticism, Poetry.

HIRAM POETRY REVIEW, Willard Greenwood, Box 162, Hiram, OH 44234, 330-569-5331, Fax 330-569-5166, poetryreview@hiram.edu. 1967. Poetry, articles, art, photos, interviews, satire, criticism, reviews, letters, long-poems, collages, plays, concrete art. "We seek to discover the best new poets in America. Send 3-5 poems of your best work." circ. 500. 1/yr. Pub'd 1 issue 2005; expects 1 issue 2006, 1 issue 2007. sub. price $9, $23 for 3 years; per copy $9; sample $5. Back issues: No. 1 unavail.; others vary; send for info. Discounts: 60-40 to subscription agencies; 60-40 to retail bookstores. Reporting time: 1-3 months. Simultaneous submissions accepted: yes. Publishes 1-5% of manuscripts submitted. Payment: 2 copies. Copyrighted, rights revert to author by request. Pub's reviews: 2 in 2005. §Poetry, books, some little magazines. No ads. Subject: Poetry.

Historical Resources Press, 2104 Post Oak Court, Corinth / Denton, TX 76210-1900, 940-321-1066, fax 940-497-1313, www.booksonhistory.com. 1994. Non-fiction. "The Mission of Historical Resources Press is: Seeking to find the truth about what really happened! We seek to publish the true story about HISTORY made YESTERDAY and TODAY as RESOURCES for TOMORROW! The truth is not always easy to find, but we believe, with much research, is possible, even these days after so much of real HISTORICAL importance has been, and is being, destroyed. We have published some of the truth, not all of it. We have published a history of photography during the Civil War, *Photographer .. Under Fire* by Jack C. Ramsay, Jr.; history of a POW of WWII, *Patton's Ill-Fated Raid* by Harry Thompson; and an autobiography, *Angel Kisses And My Beating Heart, My Life and Near-Death Experiences* by Jack C. Ramsay. This year we are planning to publish a booklet of experiences and encouragement by *One Suddenly Blind Patient, One Caretaker And One Little Dog*." Simultaneous submissions accepted: no. Subjects: Autobiography, Biography, Civil War, History, Military, Veterans, Non-Fiction, Photography, Texas, World War II.

Historical Society of Alberta (see also ALBERTA HISTORY), Hugh A. Dempsey, 95 Holmwood Ave. NW, Calgary, Alberta T2K 2G7, Canada. 1907. Articles, reviews, non-fiction. "3,500 to 5,000 word articles on western Canadian history." avg. press run 1.6M. Pub'd 1 title 2005; expects 1 title 2006, 1 title 2007. Discounts: 33%. 28pp. Reporting time: 2 months. Simultaneous submissions accepted: no. Publishes 50% of manuscripts submitted. Payment: none. Does not copyright for author. Subjects: History, Native American.

HISTORICAL STUDIES IN THE PHYSICAL & BIOLOGICAL SCIENCES, University of California Press, J.L. Heilbron, Editor; Diana Wear, Managing Editor, University of California Press, 2000 Center Street, Suite 303, Berkeley, CA 94704-1223, 510-643-7154. 1970. Non-fiction. "Editorial address: Office for History of Science & Technology, 470 Stephens Hall, Univ. of CA, Berkeley, CA 94720." circ. 566. 2/yr. Pub'd 2 issues 2005; expects 2 issues 2006, 2 issues 2007. sub. price $32 indiv., $107 instit. (+ $15 air freight), $20 student; per copy $16 indiv., $55 instit., $16 student; sample free. Back issues: same as single copy price. Discounts: foreign subs. agent 10%, one-time orders 10+ 30%, standing orders (bookstores): 1-99 40%, 100+ 50%. 200pp. Reporting time: 1-2 months. Copyrighted, does not revert to author. Ads: $295/$220. Subject: History.

History Compass, LLC, Lisa Gianelly, Jeff Levinson, 25 Leslie Rd., Auburndale, MA 02466, www.historycompass.com, 617 332 2202 (O), 617 332 2210 (F). 2005. Plays, non-fiction. "Non-fiction. Primary source-based U.S. history materials for classrooms and historic site/museums. Publish books, plays, and teacher guides." Reporting time: 8 weeks, to queries only. Simultaneous submissions accepted: Only if notified. We occasionally copyright for author. Subjects: Biography, Black, Children, Youth, Education, History, Labor, Military, Veterans, Native American, Politics, Science, Transportation, Women.

HISTORY OF INTELLECTUAL CULTURE, L. Panayotidis, Editor; P. Stortz, Editor, Faculty of Education, EDT 722, Univ. of Calgary, 2500 Univ. Drive NW, Calgary, AB T2N 1N4, Canada, 403-220-6296, Fax 403-282-8479, elpanayo@ucalgary.ca, pjstortz@ucalgary.ca, www.ucalgary.ca/hic/. 2001. Articles, reviews. 1/yr. Pub'd 1 issue 2005; expects 1 issue 2006, 1 issue 2007. sub. price free access. Reporting time: 6 months. Simultaneous submissions accepted: no. Publishes 25% of manuscripts submitted. Payment: none. Copyrighted, both author and journal hold copyright. Pub's reviews: 5 in 2005. §Intellectual history and history in general. Ads: email for information. Subjects: Culture, History.

H-NGM-N, H_NGM_N B_ _KS, Nate Pritts, Matt Dube, 715 College Avenue, Natchitoches, LA 71457, nathanpritts@hotmail.com. 2000. Poetry. "Each issue of *H-NGM-N* will physically ape an earlier influential journal - our way of keeping the old revolutions alive. Issue One (due in Oct. 2001) is our homage to *C*, Ted Berrigan's magazine from the '60s. Future issues will pattern on *Something, Black Mt. Review* and *Fuck You: a journal of the arts.*" 2/yr. Expects 1 issue 2006, 2 issues 2007. price per copy $2 + 1s; sample $2 + 1s. Pages vary. Reporting time: quick, 1 month tops. Simultaneous submissions accepted: no. Payment: copies. Copyrighted, reverts to author. Ads: we'll do trade ads. Subject: Poetry.

H_NGM_N B_ _KS (see also H-NGM-N), Nate Pritts, EIC.; Matt Dube, Fiction Ed., NSU/Dept. of Language & Communication, Natchitoches, LA 71497, editor@h-ngm-n.com. 2000. Poetry, fiction, art, cartoons, criticism, non-fiction. "Online magazine, 2X year: http://www.h-ngm-n.com : Chapbooks - varies, see site for details." Pub'd 4 titles 2005; expects 4 titles 2006, ? titles 2007. 25-32pp. We accept simultaneous submissions, but let us know ASAP if something happens elsewhere. Payment: copies and huge support. Does not copyright for author.

Ho Logos Press, Karen Pulley, Manager of Marketing & Sales; Robert Hougland, Managing Editor, 7007 W Tonto Dr, Glendale, AZ 85308-5535, 877-407-7744,623-566-6104,fax 623-566-6105, hlpressmarketing@yahoo.com, www.hlpress.com. 1999. Fiction, plays, non-fiction. "We call our publishing approach "New, Great Themes!", themes concerning the major issues the world faces, the West in particular. Issues such as terrorism, abortion, education, the military-industrial complex and more. The mission of the Press is to deconstruct these major issues to an origin where their essence can be presented to enlighten human life.Recent publications include "The Restoration" by David J. Bean and "Quote This!!!" by Vincent Fu. Our upcoming authors include Rene Cortes "USA 911: Terrorism: Terror Terrifies Terrorist" (part one of a 3 part essay)and Paul Stein "The Glass Forest" (fiction). We also represent author Robert Hougland (two plays - "Gold Rush" and "Who's Afraid of the Big Blair Witch" (on abortion)." avg. press run 4000. Pub'd 1 title 2005; expects 2 titles 2006, 2 titles 2007. Discounts: 50%, or upon agreement, higher. 300-400pp. Reporting time: 2-4 weeks. Simultaneous submissions accepted: Yes. Publishes 5% of manuscripts submitted. Subjects: Airplanes, Christianity, Current Affairs, Global Affairs, Government, History, Old West, Philosophy, Politics, Reference, Religion, Spiritual, Theosophical, War, World War II.

Hobar Publications, A Division of Finney Company (see also Finney Company, Inc.), Alan Krysan, President, 8075 215th Street West, Lakeville, MN 55044, (952) 469-6699, Fax:(952) 469-1968, (800)846-7027, Fax: (800) 330-6232, feedback@finney-hobar.com, www.finney-hobar.com. 1964. Non-fiction. "This division of Finney Company offers instructional material for career and technical educators. Recent titles include Horsemanship Handbook, Forest Management Digest and Concrete and Concrete Masonry." avg. press run 5000. Pub'd 2 titles 2005; expects 3-5 titles 2006, 3-5 titles 2007. Discounts: 1-9 copies 20%10-49 copies 40%50 or more copies 50%. 128-500pp. Reporting time: 8-10 weeks. Simultaneous submissions accepted: Yes. Payment: varies. Subjects: Agriculture, Animals, Biology, Biotechnology, Birds, Business & Economics, Conservation, Construction, Co-ops, Crafts, Hobbies, Gardening, Nature, Non-Fiction, Technology, Wood Engraving/Woodworking.

HOBART, Aaron Burch, PO Box 1658, Ann Arbor, MI 48103, info@hobartpulp.com, submit@hobartpulp.com, http://www.hobartpulp.com. 2001. Fiction. "Hobart is a literary journal featuring entertaining, inventive fiction with a particular fondness for stories involving truckers, vagabonding, entomology and mathematics. Current print issue, edited by Ryan Boudinot, features stories by Rick Moody, Aimee Bender, Stephen Elliott and Stephany Aulenback. Website updates monthly with short shorts. www.hobartpulp.com." circ. 700. 2/yr. Pub'd 2 issues 2005; expects 2 issues 2006, 2 issues 2007. sub. price $17; per copy $10; sample $6. Back issues: $7. 200pp. Reporting time: 1-3 months. Simultaneous submissions accepted: Yes. Publishes 10% of manuscripts submitted. Payment: 2 contributor copies, plus a 1 year (2 issue) subscription. Copyrighted, reverts to author. Subjects: Experimental, Fiction.

Hobblebush Books, Sidney Hall Jr., 17-A Old Milford Road, Brookline, NH 03033, Ph./Fax: 603-672-4317, E-mail: hobblebush@charter.net, Web: www.hobblebush.com. 1993. *"Publishes literary and non-literary books that present a unique voice and make a difference. Book design services to authors and other publishers.*

See website.'' avg. press run 3M. Pub'd 4 titles 2005; expects 4 titles 2006, 5 titles 2007. 150pp. Reporting time: 3 weeks. Simultaneous submissions accepted: yes. Copyrights for author. Subjects: Autobiography, Humor, Literature (General), Poetry.

Hochelaga Press, Raymond Beauchemin, Denise Roig, 8140 Ogilvie, LaSalle, QC H8P 3R4, Canada, 514-366-5655, Fax 514-364-5655, hochelaga@sympatico.ca. 1995. Poetry, fiction, non-fiction. avg. press run 500-1M. Pub'd 1 title 2005; expects 1 title 2007. Discounts: bookstore 40%, wholesale 50%. Reporting time: 4-6 months. Simultaneous submissions accepted: yes. Payment: yes. Copyrights for author.

HOGTOWN CREEK REVIEW, Michael Martin, Editor; Elisa Maranzana, Editor, 4736 Hummingbird Lane, Valdosta, GA 31602-6701, tel:229-219-1122, www.hogtowncreek.org. 1999. Poetry, fiction, articles, art, photos, cartoons, interviews, criticism, reviews, letters, parts-of-novels, long-poems, non-fiction. *''Hogtown Creek Review* is a magazine weaving literary art and popular culture. Based in Florida, we welcome submissions from all over the map. Publishing imaginative writing and artwork in an inventive, accessible format. Looking for inspired fiction, poetry, creative non-fiction, reviews and artwork. Recent contributors include: Jack Butler, Elizabeth McCracken, Miller Williams, Bill Manhire, Matthew Stevenson, Moira Crone, Dean Paschal, Michael McFee, Margaret Luongo, Tina Mullen, Rootman, Pat Wolfe, Lola Haskins. Please acknowledge simultaneous submissions. Limit one story and five poems; SASE.'' circ. 1000. annual;. Pub'd 1 issue 2005; expects 1 issue 2006, 1 issue 2007. price per copy $10; sample $5. Back issues: $5. 85pp. Reporting time: 1-3 months. Simultaneous submissions accepted: yes. Payment: 2 copies. Copyrighted. Pub's reviews: 4 in 2005. §Fiction, poetry, non-fiction, essays, creative non-fiction. Ads: $100/$50/$25 1/4 page.

Holbrook Street Press, PO Box 399, Cortaro, AZ 85652-0399, 520-616-7643, fax 520-616-7519, holbrookstpress@theriver.com, www.copshock.com. 1998. Non-fiction. avg. press run 5M. Expects 2 titles 2006, 2 titles 2007. 400pp. Reporting time: 4 weeks. Simultaneous submissions accepted: yes. Publishes 2% of manuscripts submitted. Subjects: Crime, Mental Health, Non-Fiction, Psychiatry, Psychology, Self-Help.

Hole Books, Dolly Sen, Editor, 2 Hailsham Avenue, London SW2 3AH, England, (0) 208 677 3121, fax (0) 208 677 3121, email holebooks@yahoo.co.uk, web www.holebooks.com. Established 2002. Poetry, fiction, non-fiction. ''Underground, alternative writings.'' Pub'd 3 titles 2005; expects 3 titles 2006, 3 titles 2007. Discounts: on request. 100pp. Reporting time: 6 weeks. Simultaneous submissions accepted: yes. Publishes 3% of manuscripts submitted. Copyrights for author. Subjects: African-American, Anarchist, Beat, Biography, Experimental, Fiction, Novels, Poetry, Psychiatry.

THE HOLLINS CRITIC, R.H.W. Dillard, Editor; Amanda Cockrell, Managing Editor, PO Box 9538, Hollins University, VA 24020. 1964. Poetry, criticism, reviews. ''Essay on particular work of one author; several poems. Essay approximately 5000 words, no footnotes. No unsolicited essay or review mss. Essays by prior commitment only. Short poems are published in every issue. We read poetry from September to December only. Other features are a cover picture of the author under discussion, a checklist of author's writing and a brief sketch of career, plus book reviews. Recent essayists: Lewis Turco, Henry Taylor, Howard Nelson, George Garrett.'' circ. 400. 5/yr. Pub'd 5 issues 2005; expects 5 issues 2006, 5 issues 2007. sub. price $8 U.S.; $9.50 elsewhere; per copy $2 U.S.; sample $1.50 U.S. Back issues: $2 U.S. ($3 elsewhere). 24pp. Reporting time: 2 months. Simultaneous submissions accepted with an SASE. Publishes 4% of manuscripts submitted. Payment: $25 for poems. Copyrighted, poetry rights revert to auther. Pub's reviews: 15 in 2005. §Mainly current fiction and poetry and critical works. Subjects: Literary Review, Literature (General).

Hollyridge Press (see also 88: A Journal of Contemporary American Poetry), Ian Randall Wilson, Managing Editor, PO Box 2872, Venice, CA 90294, 310-712-1238, Fax 310-828-4860, hollyridge-press@aol.com, http://www.hollyridgepress.com. 2000. Poetry, fiction. ''Publishes literary fiction: novels, short story collections, novella collections. Also publishes poetry annual and chapbook series.'' Pub'd 12 titles 2005; expects 2 titles 2006, 4 titles 2007. Discounts: available through Ingram and Baker & Taylor. Payment: up to 15% hardcover. Copyrights for author. Subjects: Fiction, Literature (General).

THE HOLLYWOOD ACTING COACHES AND TEACHERS DIRECTORY, Acting World Books, Lawrence Parke, PO Box 3044, Hollywood, CA 90078, 818-905-1345. 1981. ''Occasional articles by and or about subject material people, orgns, currently recommended procedures, etc.'' circ. 1.2M. 4/yr. Pub'd 4 issues 2005; expects 4 issues 2006, 4 issues 2007. No subscriptions available; price per copy $15. Back issues: not available. Discounts: none except to bookstores (40%). 55pp. Copyrighted, reverts to author. Ads: $400 1/2 page/special 6 months in both pub's, rate $800. Subjects: Electronics, Entertainment, How-To, Theatre.

Hollywood Creative Directory, Jeff Black, 5055 Wilshire Blvd., Los Angeles, CA 90036, 800-815-0503, 323-525-2369, Fax 323-525-2393, www.hcdonline.com. 1987. ''The many directories that make up the Hollywood Creative Directory catalogue, commonly known as "the phone books to Hollywood," offer the most comprehensive, up-to-date information available, listing the names, numbers, addresses and current titles of entertainment professionals from the film, television and music industries. For almost twenty years this "insider's guide to the insiders" has been a must-have for anyone working in the professional entertainment industry. The current catalogue includes the Hollywood Creative Directory, the Hollywood Representation Directory, the Hollywood Distributors Directory, and the Hollywood Music Industry Directory. All print directories are available in one searchable online database. The Hollywood Creative Directory is released three times a year in print. The company is also co-publishing The Hollywood Reporter Blu-Book Production Directory, the premier guide for below-the-line production services." avg. press run 5M. Pub'd 8 titles 2005; expects 8 titles 2006, 8 titles 2007. Discounts: 1-4 20%, 5-9 30%, 10-24 47%,. 400pp. Reporting time: 8 weeks. Payment: 5-10% monthly payment. Copyrights for author. Subjects: Arts, Media, Music, Performing Arts, Reference, Television, Theatre, Visual Arts.

Hollywood Film Archive, D. Richard Baer, Editor, 8391 Beverly Boulevard, PMB 321, Hollywood, CA 90048-2633. 1972. "HFA compiles and publishes film reference information. In addition to our own books, we are interested in high-quality comprehensive reference information on film or television. Please inquire before submitting material. Those submitting unsolicited material must include a self-addressed stamped envelope in order to have it returned. Our Cinema Book Society book club considers books of other publishers for sale to members, libraries, the film and TV industries, and the general public. We distribute motion picture reference books for other publishers, including *American Film Institute Catalogs, Screen World*, and the complete reprint of *Variety Film Reviews 1907-1996*, and *Variety Obituaries 1905-1994*." avg. press run 5M. Pub'd 2 titles 2005; expects 4 titles 2006. Discounts: 1-4 copies, 20% to bona fide booksellers, wholesalers, jobbers, etc., 5 or more 40%; large quantities, inquire. Reporting time: 3-4 weeks. Subjects: Electronics, Movies, Reference, Visual Arts.

Holmes House, S.J. Holmes, 530 North 72nd Avenue, Omaha, NE 68114. 1999. Poetry. "We are committed to 4 poets but will look at other submissions. Always send for guidelines first." avg. press run 400. Pub'd 2 titles 2005; expects 2 titles 2006, 3-4 titles 2007. Discounts: 40% stores, 50% libraries. 40pp. Reporting time: 2 months. Simultaneous submissions accepted: no. Publishes 20% of manuscripts submitted. Payment: 25 copies to poet. Does not copyright for author. Subjects: Gay, Nebraska, Poetry, Spiritual.

Holy Cow! Press, Jim Perlman, PO Box 3170, Mount Royal Station, Duluth, MN 55803, 218-724-1653 phone/Fax. 1977. Poetry, fiction, articles, parts-of-novels, long-poems. "Holy Cow! Press is a Midwestern independent publisher that features new work by both well-known and younger writers. Besides single author collections, we try to tastefully assemble anthologies centered around important themes. We are supportive of first books by younger writers; PLEASE query before submitting manuscripts." avg. press run 1.5M. Pub'd 5 titles 2005; expects 4 titles 2006, 5 titles 2007. Discounts: 40% off to classrooms, bulk, institutions, bookstores. 96pp. Reporting time: 2-4 months. We accept simultaneous submissions if informed. Publishes 2% of manuscripts submitted. Payment: negotiable with each author. Copyrights for author. Subjects: Literature (General), Poetry.

Holy Macro! Books, Bill Jelen, 13386 Judy Avenue NW, PO Box 82, Uniontown, OH 44685-9310, 330-715-2875, Fax 707-220-4510, consult@MrExcel.com, www.HolyMacroBooks.com. 2002. Non-fiction. "Books, e-Books or CD-ROM's on Microsoft Office products." avg. press run 2M. Pub'd 3 titles 2005; expects 5 titles 2006, 5 titles 2007. Discounts: trade. 300pp. Reporting time: 4 weeks. Simultaneous submissions accepted: yes. Publishes 10% of manuscripts submitted. Payment: negotiable. Copyrights for author. Subject: Computers, Calculators.

HOLY ROLLERS, Cynic Press, PO Box 40691, Philadelphia, PA 19107. 2001. Poetry. "Checks made out to Cynic Press. Final issue due out in 2007." circ. 50. 2/yr. Pub'd 1 issue 2005; expects 1 issue 2006, 1 issue 2007. sub. price $20/6 issues; per copy $7; sample $5. Back issues: $5. 12pp. Reporting time: 3 weeks. Simultaneous submissions accepted: okay. Publishes 15% of manuscripts submitted. Payment: 2 copies. Copyrighted for Cynic Press. Ads: $20/$10. Subjects: Poetry, Religion, Spiritual.

Homa & Sekey Books, Shawn X. Ye, PO Box 103, Dumont, NJ 07628, 201-384-6692, Fax 201-384-6055, info@homabooks.com, www.homabooks.com. 1997. Fiction, art, non-fiction. "A member of PMA (Publishers Marketing Association) and AAS (Association for Asian Studies), Homa & Sekey Books is one of the few U.S. publishers of fine books on Asia, especially on China and Korea. Founded in 1997, Homa & Sekey Books was initially engaged in helping US and UK publishers sell translation rights to Asian publishing houses. The company soon grew into book publishing. Currently, our publishing focuses are fiction, art, business, biography, history and culture primarily on Asian topics. We will soon expand to include travel and juvenile books, among others. Journal publications are also on our drawing table. Under our English publishing program, we not only publish books translated from Asian languages, especially from Chinese and Korean, but also books written originally in English. We pride ourselves on this publishing endeavor aiming to help Western readers better understand and appreciate the East Asian cultures that are often too far away and somewhat mystified. We have a special program under which we publish, sometimes co-publish, highly selected titles in the Chinese language. Meanwhile, we serve as an international literary agency helping sell translation rights of American and British titles to Asian publishers. We also distribute, to the U.S. and Europe markets, books and journals published by Asian publishing houses." avg. press run 3M. Pub'd 6 titles 2005; expects 8 titles 2006, 10 titles 2007.

Discounts: from 20% to 55%. 256pp. Reporting time: 2-6 weeks. Simultaneous submissions accepted: yes. Payment: yearly or by contract. Can copyright for author if necessary. Subjects: Arts, Asia, Indochina, Asian-American, Fiction, History, Literature (General), Romance, Short Stories.

HOME EDUCATION MAGAZINE, Mark Hegener, Editor; Helen Hegener, Editor, PO Box 1083, Tonasket, WA 98855, 509-486-1351, hem-editor@home-ed-magazine.com. 1984. Poetry, articles, art, photos, cartoons, interviews, satire, criticism, reviews, letters, news items. *"Home Education Magazine* is for families who choose to teach their children at home. Please write for editorial guidelines, include SASE. Please no fiction or poetry." circ. 12.5M. 6/yr. Pub'd 6 issues 2005; expects 6 issues 2006, 6 issues 2007. sub. price $32; per copy $6.50; sample $6.50. Back issues: $6.50. Discounts: write for info, include SASE. 68pp. Reporting time: 6 weeks. Simultaneous submissions accepted: no. Publishes 25% of manuscripts submitted. Payment: $50-$100 per article. Copyrighted, reverts to author. Pub's reviews. §Homeschooling, education, child development, alternative education, family. Ads: $1250/$750/65¢ per word classified (min. $10/issue). Subjects: Children, Youth, Education, Family.

HOME PLANET NEWS, Home Planet Publications, Donald Lev, Editor, PO Box 455, High Falls, NY 12440, 845-687-4084, homeplanetnews@yahoo.com. 1979. Poetry, fiction, articles, art, photos, cartoons, interviews, criticism, reviews, letters, parts-of-novels, long-poems, news items. "We like lively work of all types and schools. Poetry should run about a page. (Need shorter ones right now.) For articles, reviews, etc., please query first. Some recent contributors include: Richard Kostelanetz, Andrew Glaze, Tuli Kupferberg, Gerald Locklin, Lyn Lifshin, Frank Murphy, Hal Sirowitz, David Gershator, Barry Wallenstein, Bob Holman, Andy Clausen, A D. Winans, Linda Lerner, William Doreski, Enid Dame, Edward Sanders, Janine Pommy Vega, Peter Lamborn Wilson and Robert Kelly.." circ. 3M. 1-3/yr. Pub'd 2 issues 2005; expects 3 issues 2006, 3 issues 2007. sub. price $10; per copy $4; sample $4. Back issues: $4. Discounts: 40% consignment, 50% cash, 25% agents. 24pp. Reporting time: 3 months. Simultaneous submissions accepted: no. Publishes 10% of manuscripts submitted. Payment: copies & 1 year gift subscription. Copyrighted, reverts to author. Pub's reviews: 13 books, 9 magazines in 2005. §Poetry, fiction. Ads: $150/$75. Subjects: Book Reviewing, Criticism, Fiction, Literary Review, Literature (General), Poetry, Theatre, Visual Arts.

Home Planet Publications (see also HOME PLANET NEWS), Donald Lev, PO Box 455, High Falls, NY 12440, 845-687-4084, homeplanetnews@yahoo.com. 1971. Poetry. "Home Planet Publications publishes occasional books of poetry, but does not consider unsolicited manuscripts and is presently inactive. For our magazine, *Home Planet News,* see listing above." avg. press run 400. Discounts: 50% cash to stores; 40% consignment; 25% agents. 60pp. Payment: negotiable. Copyrights for author. Subjects: Literary Review, Poetry.

HOME POWER, Home Power, Inc., Linda Pinkham, Managing Editor; Ian Woofenden, Senior Editor; Joe Schwartz, Technical Editor, PO Box 520, Ashland, OR 97520, Order line 800-707-6585, 541-512-0201, Fax 541-512-0343. 1987. Articles, photos, reviews, letters, news items, non-fiction. "Length of material 400 to 2,500 words. All articles must contain hard, hands-on information about the use of renewable energy in home settings." circ. 40M. 6/yr. Pub'd 6 issues 2005; expects 6 issues 2006, 6 issues 2007. sub. price $22.50; per copy $6.95; sample Free online in PDF. Back issues: Most available in print (prices vary). All available individually in PDF ($5 ea.) or batched on CD-ROM ($29 ea.). Discounts: bulk, agent 50% off cover. 148pp. Reporting time: 8 weeks. Simultaneous submissions accepted: no. Publishes 33% of manuscripts submitted. Payment: none. Copyrighted, rights revert if author so desires. Pub's reviews: 4 in 2005. §Renewable energy, ecology. Ads: Full: $2350, Half: $1292, Quarter $713. Multiple insertion discounts. Subjects: Energy, Technology.

Home Power, Inc. (see also HOME POWER), Richard Perez, PO Box 275, Ashland, OR 97520, 916-475-3179. 1987. Non-fiction. "Our first book went to press May 1991, *The Battery Book.* Compendium of Home Power Magazine - available on CD ROM. CD ROM Solar 2- available issues 1-42, CD ROM Solar 3 issues 43-60 - available 6/98. The new electric Vehicles C available 4/15/96, *2nd Revised edition Heavan's Flame available* 6/98, Solar 4 6/99 on CD, Solar 5 6/00 on CD." avg. press run 5M. Pub'd 2 titles 2005. Discounts: 40%. 100-400pp. Reporting time: 3-4 months. Payment: small advance, 16% of net sales 0-10K, 20% of net sales 10K+ - contract. Copyrights for author if so desired. Subject: Energy.

Homecourt Publishers, Ben Bache, 2435 East North Street #245, Greenville, SC 29615-1442, 864-232-7108 phone/Fax, info@homecourtpublishers.com, www.homecourtpublishers.com. 2003. Non-fiction. "Recent release: *What Made Them Say That?* - a quotation book with a twist. Instead of the ordinary list of clever sayings, it provides the reader with history's greatest quotations and the stories behind them." Expects 3 titles 2006. 250pp. Copyrights for author.

HONG KONG JOURNAL OF SOCIOLOGY, The Chinese University Press, Siu-kai Lau, The Chinese University of Hong Kong, Sha Tin, New Territories, Hong Kong, 852-26096508,852-26037355, cup@cuhk.edu.hk, www.chineseupress.com. 2000. Non-fiction. circ. 200. 1/yr. Pub'd 1 issue 2005; expects 1 issue 2006, 1 issue 2007. sub. price $20; per copy $20; sample free. Back issues: $20. 190pp. Simultaneous submissions accepted: No. Payment: NIL. Copyrighted. Pub's reviews: 3 in 2005. §Books in Sociology. Subject: Sociology.

Honors Group, Martin Wasserman, Adirondack Community College, SUNY, Queensbury, NY 12804. 1997. Articles, criticism, non-fiction. "We are looking for research articles, essays, and even poetry on the life and work of Franz Kafka. Contributions should be no longer than 15 pages. Send submissions with SASE. At this time, our press is only publishing anthologies and we will not look at book-length manuscripts." avg. press run 500. Expects 1 title 2006, 2 titles 2007. 150pp. Reporting time: 1 month. Simultaneous submissions accepted: yes. Publishes 50% of manuscripts submitted. Payment: authors receive free books. Copyrights for author. Subjects: Essays, Kafka.

Hoover Institution Press, Patricia A. Baker, Executive Editor, Stanford University, Stanford, CA 94305-6010, 650-723-3373, e-mail baker@hoover.stanford.edu. Non-fiction. "Subjects usually published are: economics, political science, public policy, studies of nationalities in Central and Eastern Europe, Asian Studies, international studies." avg. press run 1M. Pub'd 8 titles 2005; expects 8 titles 2006, 6 titles 2007. Discounts: wholesale: 1-4 copies 20%, 5-24 42%, 25-49 45%, 50-99 48%, 100+ 50%; Retail 1-2 copies 20%, 3-24 40%, 25-49 42%, 50-249 44%, 250+ 46%. 200pp. Reporting time: varies, 2-4 months. Payment: individually arranged. Copyrights for author. Subjects: Asia, Indochina, Bibliography, Business & Economics, Communism, Marxism, Leninism, Education, History, Latin America, Middle East, Non-Fiction, Political Science, Politics, Public Affairs, U.S.S.R.

Hope Publishing House, Faith Annette Sand, Publisher, PO Box 60008, Pasadena, CA 91116, 626-792-6123; fax 626-792-2121. 1983. Criticism, non-fiction. "We deal with religious and educational topics and like to facilitate getting women and minorities into print, although we publish men, too. We are a nonprofit publishing venture, a program unit of the So. Calif. Ecumenical Council and concentrate on subjects of import to the faith community like human rights and related issues for the Palestinians and Israelis. We are currently interested in concerns for the church and faith society, as well as ecology, health and justice issues." avg. press run 3M-5M. Pub'd 6 titles 2005; expects 6 titles 2006, 6 titles 2007. Discounts: as required to trade and bulk buyers. 228pp. Reporting time: 2 months. Payment: royalties are arranged, payments are made biannually. Copyrights for author. Subjects: Alcohol, Alcoholism, Biography, Christianity, Culture, Environment, Family, Feminism, Global Affairs, Health, Inspirational, Latin America, Non-Violence, Religion, South America, Spiritual.

Horned Owl Publishing, Rob Von Rudloff, J. Bryony Lake, 4605 Bearwood Court, Victoria, BC V8Y 3G1, Canada, fax 250-414-4987; e-mail hornowl@islandnet.com. 1992. Fiction, non-fiction. "We publish scholarly books in the field of Pagan Studies and Pagan Children's Literature. We prefer submissions of at least 25,000 words for the former." avg. press run 4000. Discounts: trade 40%, distributor 55%. 200pp, children's literature 40pp. Reporting time: 2 months. Simultaneous submissions accepted only when identified as such. Publishes 2% of manuscripts submitted. Payment: advance based on anticipated production run; royalty 10% (less for foreign sales, etc.). Copyrights for author. Subjects: Anthropology, Archaelogy, Celtic, Children, Youth, Classical Studies, Greek, History, Magic, Metaphysics, Myth, Mythology, Religion, Scandinavia, WICCA.

Horse & Buggy Press, Dave Wofford, 2016 Englewood Avenue, Durham, NC 27705-4113, 919-828-2514. 1996. Poetry, fiction, articles, art, photos, criticism, letters, non-fiction. "All of our books are letterpress printing by hand, hand-bindings, hand papermaking, and limited editions." avg. press run 250. Pub'd 2 titles 2005; expects 2 titles 2006, 2 titles 2007. Discounts: 30% off for bookstores, dealers. (Orders of 5 books minimum, can be mix and match). 48pp. Copyrights for author. Subjects: Poetry, Short Stories.

Horse Creek Publications, Inc., Suzanne H. Schrems, Edward L. Schrems, 4500 Highland Hills Drive, Norman, OK 73026, 405-364-9647, schrems@worldnet.att.net. 2002. Fiction, non-fiction. "History, nonfiction and historical fiction. Book length manuscripts designed for a 'good read.'" avg. press run open. Expects 3 titles 2006, 3 titles 2007. 200pp. Reporting time: 3 months. Simultaneous submissions accepted: yes. Payment: 10%. Copyrights for author. Subjects: History, Montana, Non-Fiction, Politics, The West, Women.

HOR-TASY, Daniel Betz, PO Box 158, Harris, IA 51345. 1980. Fiction. "We are looking for psychological horror & pure fantasy (eg: faeries, trolls, sword & sorcery, myths, legends). The horror we want is based on or in the mind, so we don't really want the over-used haunted houses, monsters, hexes, ghosts, etc. We'd like to get one issue out each year. We are not interested in science fiction." circ. 400. Expects 1 issue 2006, 1 issue 2007. price per copy $4. 72pp. Reporting time: immediately to 3 weeks. Payment: copies. Copyrighted, reverts to author. Subjects: Fantasy, Fiction.

HORTIDEAS, Greg Williams, Pat Williams, 750 Black Lick Road, Gravel Switch, KY 40328, 859-332-7606. 1984. Articles, reviews, news items, non-fiction. "Short articles on vegetable, flower, and fruit growing, directed to amateur gardeners; including abstracts from the technical horticultural literature, new product reviews, and book reviews." circ. 1M. 12/yr. Pub'd 12 issues 2005; expects 12 issues 2006, 12 issues 2007. sub. price $25; per copy $2.50; sample $2.50. Back issues: $2.50. Discounts: none, mailorder only. 12pp. Reporting time: 1 month. Payment: free issue. Copyrighted, does not revert to author. Pub's reviews: 28 in

2005. §Gardening, horticulture, agriculture, botany, forestry. No ads. Subjects: Agriculture, Gardening, Indexes & Abstracts.

The Hosanna Press, Cathie Ruggie Saunders, 203 Keystone, River Forest, IL 60305, 708-771-8259. 1974. Poetry, fiction, art, concrete art. "Limited edition fine printings from foundry type on rag & unique handmade papers, w/ original graphics. Innovative concepts of book, paper, and print pursued." avg. press run 25-100. Expects 1 title 2006, 1 title 2007. Pages vary. Reporting time: 3-6 weeks. Payment: 10% of edition. Copyrights for author. Subjects: Arts, Book Arts, Graphics, Poetry, Visual Arts.

Host Publications, Inc. (see also THE DIRTY GOAT), Elzbieta Szoka, Joe W. Bratcher III, 2717 Wooldridge, Austin, TX 78703-1953, 512-482-8229, Fax 512-482-0580, jbratcher3@aol.com. 1988. Poetry, fiction, art, photos, interviews, criticism, parts-of-novels, long-poems, plays. "Poetry books average 100 pages with illustrations. Drama books average 300 pages. Recent authors: Anna Frajlich, Gerald Nicosia, Urszula Koziol, Layle Silbert. Prefer to publish books by authors with some reputation. Other material, by less established artists, considered for *The Dirty Goat.*" avg. press run 1M-1.5M. Pub'd 3 titles 2005; expects 3 titles 2006, 4 titles 2007. Discounts: 1 copy 20%, 2-9 40%, 10+ 55%. 150pp. Reporting time: indeterminate. Payment: advance up front with no payments later. Does not copyright for author. Subjects: African Literature, Africa, African Studies, The Americas, Arts, Avant-Garde, Experimental Art, Beat, Bilingual, Criticism, Culture, Dada, Drama, English, Erotica, Essays, Europe, Fiction.

•**Hot Box Press / Southern Roots Publishing,** Joe Gaston, PO Box 161078, Mobile, AL 36616, 251-645-9018, info@hotboxpress.com. 2000. Non-fiction. "As a small company we look for titles that will cater to a specific or specialized market. The Hot Box Press side of the company deals specifically with books for the railroad enthusiast. The Southern Roots side is open to any topic with a specific niche in mind. We work closely with our authors in developing a marketing strategy that can be implemented by both parties. We prefer receiving queries as to unsolicited manuscripts. All queries should describe the subject matter and for non-railroad books, data on the specific market the book is targeting would be very helpful. All queries should be addressed to Joe Gaston." avg. press run 1000. Expects 1 title 2006, 2 titles 2007. Discounts: 1-2 copies no discount3-199 copies 40%200-up 50%. 160pp. Simultaneous submissions accepted: yes. Payment: Negotiable. Copyrights for author. Subjects: Biography, History, Non-Fiction, Transportation.

Hot Pepper Press, Taylor Graham, Hatch Graham, PO Box 39, Somerset, CA 95684. 1991. Poetry. "Not currently reading for chapbooks."

HOTEL AMERIKA, David Lazar, Editor; Jean Cunningham, Managing Editor, 360 Ellis Hall, Ohio University, Athens, OH 45701, 740-597-1360, editors@hotelamerika.net, www.hotelamerika.net. 2002. Poetry, fiction, photos, satire, parts-of-novels, long-poems, non-fiction. "Hotel Amerika seeks to find and define a diverse constituency of writers and readers. Work we publish ranges from the utterly accessible writing that speaks to readers directly with subtle literary qualities whose effects may be profound to work that challenges the most sophisticated readers in our audience. Work we publish cuts across all genres, including poetry, fiction, essay, and translations. We have recently published John Ashbery, Maxine Kumin, Charles Wright, Leonard Kriegel, Guy Davenport. Work published in Hotel Amerika has been selected for Best American Poetry, Pushcart Prize, and named as notable in Best American Essays. Contest guidelines available on website." circ. 1200. 2/yr. Pub'd 1 issue 2005; expects 2 issues 2006, 2 issues 2007. sub. price $18; per copy $9; sample $9. Back issues: $5. 130pp. Reporting time: 2-4 months. Simultaneous submissions accepted: No. Copyrighted, reverts to author. Ads: Full page $150 one time; $100 two or more times.Half page $100 one time; $75 two or more times.Hotel Amerika participates in ad exchanges with interested publications.

House of Hits, Inc., Dan McKinnon, North American Airlines Bldg 75, Suite 250, JFK International Airport, Jamaica, NY 11430, 718-656-2650. 1973. "We're basically interested in aviation and current history involving the Middle East." avg. press run 2M-10M. Pub'd 2 titles 2005; expects 3 titles 2006, 4 titles 2007. Discounts: libraries 20%, retailers 40%, wholesalers 50%. 200pp. Reporting time: 12 months. Publishes 2% of manuscripts submitted. Payment: negotiated. Copyrights for author. Subjects: Aviation, Middle East.

Emma Howard Books, Attn: Armando H. Luna, PO Box 385, Planetarium Stn., New York, NY 10024-0385, 212-996-2590 phone/Fax, emmahowardbooks@verizon.net, www.eelgrassgirls.com. 1994. Fiction. "Children's and Young Adult books." avg. press run 3M. Pub'd 1 title 2005; expects 2 titles 2006, 3 titles 2007. Discounts: 40%. 30pp. Reporting time: 1 month. Simultaneous submissions accepted: no. Publishes so far 50% of manuscripts submitted. Payment: individual arrangements. Copyrighting for author varies.

•**Howling Dog Press / Brave New World Order Books (see also OMEGA),** Michael Annis, P.O. Box 853, Berthoud, CO 80513-0853, WritingDangerously@msn.com, www.howlingdogpress.com, www.howlingdog-press.com/OMEGA. 1981. Poetry, fiction, art, long-poems, non-fiction. "Recent and forthcoming contributors: Antler, Jim Corbett, Gregory Greyhawk, Will Inman, Heller Levinson, Oswald LeWinter, Mike Palecek, David Ray, Kenneth Rosen, Y St. Michel-Anon. We don't publish books for the hell of it; we don't slaughter trees for precious egos. Time is short, so don't waste yours sending us work that everyone else is doing. We are never convinced or persuaded by convention, by one's past, or what someone else may think of your work or your necktie. We care nothing about who you studied under or from what school, or if you shook hands with the poet laureate. Most of them will teach you the fine art of mediocrity. We notice crimes against criteria, cloning, and theft. Every manuscript must stand on its own in the present, regardless of all the accolades and votes of confidence you may have already received. Write as if it's the last opportunity you'll ever have to say something substantial and of actual importance, since it very well may be. If you have a statement you want to leave for posterity, come here. If you are interested in plug-and-play publishing, go somewhere else—far away. (And, absolutely NO right wing screed propaganda! NO Limbaughese, NO Dobson pontifications, NO save-me-from-myself-and-the-devil.) "Draw blood ... write a poem.".'' Pub'd 2 titles 2005; expects 5 titles 2006, 7 titles 2007. Discounts: Bookstores, retailers: 1-4 copies = 30%, 5-9 copies = 40%, 10 or more = 45%. Classrooms: 30%. Howling Dog Press does NOT consign books, broadsides, tapes, or CDs. All books are on a purchase basis. Returns are allowed on merchandise in very good condition, preferably wrapped, if wrapped when shipped initially. Credit is given for future merchandise; $-refunds on wrapped merchandise only. Shipping and postage: Howling Dog Press pays for shipment of books to the outlet. It is expected that the outlet will pay any shipping charges for any items returned. Outlets are given wholesale prices. 208pp. Reporting time: Generally, we are not fooled. We respond as soon as we open it. Simultaneous submissions accepted: No. Publishes 5% of manuscripts submitted. Payment: There is not a "usual royalty." We craft contracts individually to fit the situation. Copyrights for author.

Howling Wolf Publishing, Kirby Jonas, PO Box 1045, Pocatello, ID 83204, 208-233-2708 phone e-mail kirby@kirbyjonas.com. 1997. Fiction. avg. press run 2500. Pub'd 1 title 2005; expects 1 title 2006, 1 title 2007. Discounts: 20% short, 40%, 57% maximum. 290pp. Reporting time: 4 months. Simultaneous submissions accepted: yes. Payment: 10% royalty. Copyrights for author. Subject: Fiction.

Howln Moon Press, Betty A. Mueller, 7222 State Highway 357, Franklin, NY 13775-3100, 607-829-2187 (office), 888-349-9438 (ordering), email: bmueller@hmpress.com. 1993. Art, photos, cartoons, non-fiction. ''We publish books about dogs and dog training. Books with a 'new' point of view or fresh ideas get our attention. Query with outline or sample chapter first. No unsolicited manuscripts please.'' Pub'd 2 titles 2005; expects 2 titles 2006, 3-4 titles 2007. Discounts: 20% prepaid STOP orders, Small Retailers Program. Pages vary. Reporting time: one month. Simultaneous submissions accepted: no. Publishes 50% of manuscripts submitted. Payment: to be arranged. Does not copyright for author. Subjects: Animals, Health, How-To, Non-Fiction, Pets, Psychology, Reference.

HUBBUB, Lisa Steinman, Jim Shugrue, 5344 S.E. 38th Avenue, Portland, OR 97202, 503-775-0370. 1983. Poetry. ''*Hubbub* publishes poetry reviews by invitation only, but accepts submissions of all kinds of poetry: excellence is our only criterion.'' circ. 350. 1/yr. Pub'd 1 issue 2005; expects 1 issue 2006, 1 issue 2007. sub. price $5; per copy $5; sample $3.35. Back issues: $3.35. Discounts: 40%. 60pp. Reporting time: 1-3 months. Simultaneous submissions accepted: no. Publishes .05% of manuscripts submitted. Payment: 2 contributor copies. Copyrighted, reverts to author. Pub's reviews: 1 in 2005. §Poetry. Ads: $50/$25/will swap with other literary magazines in some cases. Subject: Poetry.

THE HUDSON REVIEW, Paula Deitz, Editor, 684 Park Avenue, New York, NY 10021, 212-650-0020, Fax 212-774-1911. 1948. Poetry, fiction, articles, criticism, reviews, parts-of-novels, long-poems, non-fiction. ''Although we have developed a recognizable group of contributors who are identified with the magazine, we are always open to new writers and publish them in every issue. We have no university affiliation and are not committed to any narrow academic aim, nor to any particular political perspective.'' circ. 4.5M. 4/yr. Pub'd 4 issues 2005; expects 4 issues 2006, 4 issues 2007. sub. price $32 domestic, $36 foreign; per copy $9; sample $9. Back issues: varies. Bulk rates and discount schedules on request. 176pp. Reporting time: 12 weeks maximum. Simultaneous submissions accepted: no. Payment: 2-1/2¢ per word for prose, 50¢ per line for poetry. Copyrighted, rights revert to author under 1978 law on request. Pub's reviews: 80 in 2005. §Literature, fine and performing arts, sociology and cultural anthropology. Ads: $300/$200. Subjects: Arts, Literary Review.

Hug The Earth Publications (see also HUG THE EARTH, A Journal of Land and Life), Kenneth Lumpkin, 42 Greenwood Avenue, Pequannock, NJ 07440. 1980. Poetry, art, criticism, reviews, letters, long-poems. ''We publish broadsides, chapbooks, calendars, and a one-time only journal on land & life.'' avg. press run 500-1M. Pub'd 2 titles 2005; expects 1 title 2006. 40pp. Reporting time: 6-8 weeks. Copyrights for author.

HUG THE EARTH, A Journal of Land and Life, Hug The Earth Publications, Kenneth Lumpkin, 42 Greenwood Avenue, Pequannock, NJ 07440. ''Features Charles Olson, Gary Snyder, Flavia Alaya, Ken Lumpkin, E. Durling Merrill, et al. Poems and prose on environment and place in literature.'' 24pp. Simultaneous submissions accepted: yes. Publishes 50% of manuscripts submitted. Copyrighted. §Myth, land, Magick.

THE HUMANIST, Frederick Edwords, Editor and Managing Editor; Karen Ann Gajewski, Editorial Assistant and Production Manager; Valerie White, Consulting Editor; Marian Hetherly, Copy Editor, 1777 T st. NW, Washington, DC 20009-7125, 800-837-3792, 202-238-9003 fax, www.americanhumanist.org, aha@american-humanist.org. 1941. Articles, art, photos, cartoons, interviews, criticism, reviews, letters, non-fiction. "Nonfiction articles addressing ethical, cultural, social, philosophical or political concerns from a humanist or politically progressive perspective are most likely to be published." circ. 16M. 6/yr. Pub'd 6 issues 2005; expects 6 issues 2006, 6 issues 2007. sub. price $24.95; per copy $4.75; sample same. Back issues: $5.50. Discounts: 40% bulk. 48pp. Reporting time: 2-3 months. Payment: 10 free copies. Copyrighted, reverts to author. Pub's reviews: 42 in 2005. §Church-state separation, feminism, ethics, science, humanism, education, politics, popular culture, literature. Ads: $700/$350. Subjects: Biotechnology, Birth, Birth Control, Population, Education, Euthanasia, Death, Futurism, Humanism, Philosophy, Religion.

HUNGER MOUNTAIN, The Vermont College Journal of Arts & Letters, Caroline Mercurio, Managing Editor, Vermont College, 36 College Street, Montpelier, VT 05602, 800-336-6794 x8633, Fax 802-828-8649, hungermtn@tui.edu, www.hungermtn.org. 2002. Poetry, fiction, art, photos, parts-of-novels, long-poems, non-fiction. "Please read submission guidelines at website before submitting. No submissions in February or March." circ. 1,500. 2/yr. Pub'd 2 issues 2005; expects 2 issues 2006, 2 issues 2007. sub. price One-year $17; Two-year $32; Four-year $60; Lifetime $400; per copy $10; sample $10. Back issues: $10. 175pp. Reporting time: 3 months. Simultaneous submissions accepted: yes. Publishes 5% of manuscripts submitted. Payment: $5 per page, minimum $30. Copyrighted, reverts to author. Ads: negotiable.

Hungry Tiger Press, David Maxine, Eric Shanower, 5995 Dandridge Lane, Suite 121, San Diego, CA 92115-6575. 1994. Fiction, art, cartoons. avg. press run 1.8M. Pub'd 2 titles 2005; expects 2 titles 2006, 2 titles 2007. Discounts: 20-50% depending on quantity ordered. 128pp. Reporting time: 1-2 months. Simultaneous submissions accepted: no. Publishes 20% of manuscripts submitted. Payment: advance against royalties or one-time fee, plus free copies, discount on further copies. Does not copyright for author. Subjects: Children, Youth, Fantasy, Juvenile Fiction.

Hunter House Inc., Publishers, Kiran Rana, Publisher; Jeanne Brondino, Acquisitions Editor; Alexandra Mummery, Editor, PO Box 2914, Alameda, CA 94501, 510-865-5282, Fax 510-865-4295, info@hunter-house.com, www.hunterhouse.com. 1978. Non-fiction. "We publish in the areas of health, women's health, fitness, sexuality and violence prevention." avg. press run 5M. Pub'd 17 titles 2005; expects 17 titles 2006, 18 titles 2007. Discounts: retailers/wholesalers: 1 10%, 2+ 20%, 6+ 40%, 100+ 45%; libraries: 2+ 10%, 6+ 20%. 288pp. Reporting time: 3-6 months. Simultaneous submissions accepted: yes. Publishes 25% of manuscripts submitted. Payment: 12% of net up to 15% pa; 12% of net up to 15% on cl; report and pay twice a year. Copyrights for author. Subjects: Adolescence, Alternative Medicine, Birth, Birth Control, Population, Children, Youth, Divorce, Education, Games, Guidance, Health, Men, Nutrition, Psychology, Relationships, Self-Help, Women.

Hunter Publishing, Co., Diane Thomas, PO Box 9533, Phoenix, AZ 85068, 602-944-1022. 1975. "We have published 5 books and one anthology on Ojo Books, one anthology on Japanese silk flower making, *The Challengers, 100 Years of Hot Air Ballooning, The Southwest Indian Detours: The Fred Harvey-Santa Fe Railway Adventures in the SW Country*. Interested in undertaking publishing venture for good craft-oriented ideas—resale to craft & hobby shops, book stores, museum gift stores, etc." avg. press run 10M-20M+. Pub'd 2 titles 2005; expects 3 titles 2006. Discounts: 40-50% retail; higher discount to distributors. 24-52pp. Reporting time: 4 weeks. Payment: negotiable. Copyrights for author. Subjects: Crafts, Hobbies, History, How-To.

Huntington Library Press, Susan Green, 1151 Oxford Road, San Marino, CA 91108, 626-405-2172, Fax 626-585-0794, e-mail booksales@huntington.org. 1920. Non-fiction. avg. press run 1M. Pub'd 6 titles 2005; expects 6 titles 2006, 6 titles 2007. Discounts: 20% average. 200pp. Reporting time: varies. Simultaneous submissions accepted: no. Publishes 1% of manuscripts submitted. Payment: generally no royalties paid. Copyrights for author. Subjects: Americana, Arts, California, History, Horticulture, Literature (General).

HUNTINGTON LIBRARY QUARTERLY, University of California Press, Susan Green, Editor, University of California Press, 2000 Center St., Suite 303, Berkeley, CA 94704-1223, 626-405-2174. 1931. Non-fiction. "*The Huntington Library Quarterly* publishes articles that primarily relate to the Huntington Collections of 16th-18th century art, history and literature of Great Britain and America." circ. 740. 4/yr. Pub'd 4 issues 2005; expects 4 issues 2006, 4 issues 2007. sub. price $36 indiv., $127 inst.; per copy $10 indiv., $40 inst.; sample free to libraries. Back issues: same as single copy. Discounts: agents 20%. 150pp. Reporting time: varies. Simultaneous submissions accepted: no. Publishes 15% of manuscripts submitted. Payment: none. Copyrighted, does not revert to author. Pub's reviews: 12 in 2005. §Literary history, history, art history. Ads: $295/$220. Subjects: Arts, History, Literature (General).

Huntington Press, Anthony Curtis, Deke Castleman, 3665 S. Procyon Avenue, Las Vegas, NV 89103, 702-252-0655; Fax 702-252-0675; editor@huntingtonpress.com; http://www.huntingtonpress.com; http://www.lasvegasadvisor.com. 1983. Non-fiction. avg. press run 5M-10M. Pub'd 5 titles 2005; expects 6 titles

2006, 6 titles 2007. Discounts: trade 20%-50%. 218pp. Reporting time: 60 days. Simultaneous submissions accepted: yes. Payment: negotiable. Copyrights for author. Subjects: Games, Mathematics, Travel.

HURRICANE ALICE, Meureen T. Reddy, Executive Editor; Meg Carroll, Book Review Editor; Joan Dagle, Submissions, Dept. of English, Rhode Island College, Providence, RI 02908. 1983. Poetry, fiction, articles, art, photos, cartoons, interviews, satire, criticism, reviews, letters, parts-of-novels, collages, non-fiction. "Emphasis on feminist re-view of 1)books 2)performance 3)visual art 4)everything. Recent contributors include Mary Sharratt, Susan Koppelman, and Judith Arcana." circ. 1M. 4/yr. Pub'd 4 issues 2005; expects 4 issues 2006, 4 issues 2007. sub. price $12; per copy $2.50; sample $2.50. Back issues: $2. 16pp. Reporting time: 6 months. Simultaneous submissions accepted if indicated on ms. Publishes poetry 10%, others 30% of manuscripts submitted. Payment: in issues (6). Copyrighted, reverts to author. Pub's reviews: 16 in 2005. §Any work viewed critically. Ads: $235 1/2 page/$35 for business card (camera-ready). Subjects: Culture, Feminism, Literature (General), Women.

HYPATIA: A Journal of Feminist Philosophy, Hilde Lindemann, 503 South Kedzie Hall, Michigan State University, East Lansing, MI 48824. 1986. Articles, reviews, non-fiction. "Address business and subscription correspondence to: Journals Manager, Indiana University Press, 601 N.Morton Street, Bloomington, IN 47404." circ. 1.5M. 4/yr. Pub'd 4 issues 2005; expects 4 issues 2006, 4 issues 2007. sub. price $40 individual domestic (USA); $54 individual foreign; $110 institutional; per copy $15.00 individual; $30.00 institution. Back issues: $15. individual; $30 institution. Discounts: bulk 40% for 5 or more. 250pp. 4 months. Simultaneous submissions accepted: no. Publishes 15% of manuscripts submitted. Payment: none. Copyrighted, does not revert to author. Pub's reviews: 40 in 2005. §Feminist philosophy. Ads: $325 full page /$200 half page. Subjects: Ethics, Feminism, Gender Issues, Philosophy, Sex, Sexuality, Women.

I

IAMBS & TROCHEES, William F. Carlson, 6801 19th Avenue #5H, Brooklyn, NY 11204, 718-232-9268. 2001. Poetry, articles, reviews, long-poems. "Metrical verse only. Recent contributors: Dick Allen, X.J. Kennedy, Paul Lake, and Timothy Murphy." 2/yr. Expects 2 issues 2006, 2 issues 2007. sub. price $15; per copy $8; sample $8. Back issues: $8. 64-128pp. Reporting time: 2 months. Simultaneous submissions accepted: no. Payment: 1 copy. Copyrighted, reverts to author. Pub's reviews. §Metrical verse only. Ads: none. Subjects: Essays, Poetry, Reviews, Translation.

IBBETSON ST. PRESS, Ibbetson St. Press, Doug Holder, Richard Wilhelm, Dianne Robitaille; Robert K. Johnson, Submissions Editor; Linda Conte, Website Manager & Consulting Editor, 25 School Street, Somerville, MA 02143, dougholder@post.harvard.edu. 1998. Poetry, articles, art, criticism, reviews. "Recent contributors: Ed Galing, Alexander L. Kearn, Tim Gager and Rufus Goodwin." circ. 200. 2/yr. Pub'd 2 issues 2005; expects 2 issues 2006, 2 issues 2007. sub. price $10; per copy $5; sample $5. 40-50pp. Reporting time: 2-6 months. Simultaneous submissions accepted: No. Publishes 20% of manuscripts submitted. Payment: 1 copy. Copyrighted, reverts to author. Pub's reviews: 4-8 in 2005. §Poetry. Ads: $5 classified. Subject: Poetry.

Ibbetson St. Press (see also IBBETSON ST. PRESS), Doug Holder, Dianne Robitaille, Dick Wilhelm, Robert K. Johnson, Dorian Brooks, Linda Conte, 25 School Street, Somerville, MA 02143-1721, dougholder@post.harvard.edu. 1999. Poetry, articles, art, criticism, reviews. "Recent Contributors: Lo Galluccio, Jennifer Matthews, Joanna Nealon, Susie Davidson, Ann Carhart, Philip Burnham, Jr, Harris Gardner, Tomas O'Leary, Deborah M. Priestly, Timothy Gager, Marc Goldfinger." avg. press run 200. Pub'd 3 titles 2005; expects 3 titles 2006, 3 titles 2007. 40pp. Reporting time: 2-3 months. Simultaneous submissions accepted: no. Publishes 20% of manuscripts submitted. Does not copyright for author. Subject: Poetry.

IBEX Publishers, Inc., Farhad Shirzad, Publisher, PO Box 30087, Bethesda, MD 20824, toll free 888-718-8188, 301-718-8188, Fax 301-907-8707. 1979. Poetry, fiction, news items, non-fiction. "We publish books about Iran and in the Persian language." avg. press run 2M-3M. Pub'd 5 titles 2005; expects 9 titles 2006, 12 titles 2007. Discounts: 1 copy 20%, 2-4 30%, 5+ 40%. Copyrights for author. Subjects: Language, Middle East, Poetry, Sufism.

•**Ibexa Press,** Dawn Devine, P.O. Box 611732, San Jose, CA 95161, www.ibexa.com, info@ibexa.com. 1997. Non-fiction. "Ibexa Press is devoted to publishing instructional guides for the design, history and construction of costumes. We currently specialize in the costume arts of Middle Eastern belly dance." avg. press run 3000. Pub'd 1 title 2005; expects 3 titles 2006, 3 titles 2007. Discounts: 25% discount on orders of 6-23. 50% discount on orders of 24 pieces. Titles can be mixed within an order. More detailed ordering information is available on our website. 200pp. Reporting time: 90 days. Simultaneous submissions accepted: No. Publishes 1% of manuscripts submitted. Payment: No advances, quarterly payment, royalties are calculated based on production costs and vary. Details are stipulated in each contract. Subjects: Clothing, Crafts, Hobbies, Dance, Design, Fashion, How-To, Multicultural, Non-Fiction.

Icarus Press, David Diorio, Non-fiction Editor, 1015 Kenilworth Drive, Baltimore, MD 21204, 410-821-7807, www.icaruspress.com. 1980. Poetry, non-fiction. avg. press run 1M. Pub'd 3 titles 2005; expects 3 titles 2006, 3 titles 2007. Discounts: 20-40%. 80pp. Payment: will vary depending on type. Subjects: Biography, History, Poetry.

Ice Cube Press, S.H. Semken, 205 North Front Street, North Liberty, IA 52317, 1-319-626-2055, fax 1-413-451-0223, steve@icecubepress.com, www.icecubepress.com. 1993. Fiction, non-fiction. "Publish an annual book on Midwest environment and spirituality. Midwest biographies, stories as well as being a book producer and designer for memoirs and family histories." avg. press run 500. Pub'd 6 titles 2005; expects 7 titles 2006, 8 titles 2007. Discounts: 45%, FF. 150pp. Reporting time: 1-2 months. Publishes 1% of manuscripts submitted. Payment: negotiable. Copyrights negotiable. Subjects: Americana, Community, Environment, Folklore, Memoirs, Nature, Psychology.

ICON, Dr. Michael Lynch, Advisor, Kent State University/ Trumbull campus, 4314 Mahoning Ave., Warren, OH 44483, 330-847-0571. 1966. Poetry, fiction, art, photos, non-fiction. "700 word limit on submissions. Limit of 6 prose, 6 poems, 6 artwork per issue. Typed or word processed only. Recent contributors: James Doyle, Barry Ballard, David Sapp, Richard Dinges, Jr. R.G. Cantalupo, Lyn Lifshin. Photos and art: color or black/white; will accept high quality reproductions; best size 5x7 inches. Deadlines: October 15, March 5. Press dates: early May and mid-December." 2/yr. Pub'd 2 issues 2005; expects 2 issues 2006, 2 issues 2007. sub. price $8; per copy $4. Back issues: some are available. Discounts: none. 48pp. Publishes 40% of manuscripts submitted. Payment: 1 copy. Not copyrighted, rights revert to author. Ads: none. Subjects: Essays, Fiction, Literature (General), Non-Fiction, Ohio, Photography, Poetry.

THE ICONOCLAST, Phil Wagner, 1675 Amazon Road, Mohegan Lake, NY 10547-1804. 1992. Poetry, fiction, art, parts-of-novels, non-fiction. "Up to 3,000 words. Please: no stories or poems about characters unable or unwilling to improve their conditions. Likes fiction to have a beginning, middle, and end, all in the service of a noteworthy event or realization." circ. 600-3M. 6/yr. Pub'd 6 issues 2005; expects 4 issues 2006, 5 issues 2007. sub. price $16/8 issues; per copy $5; sample $3. Back issues: $3.50. Discounts: 5+/10%, 10+/20%, 15+/30%, 20+/40%. 96pp. Simultaneous publication is not acceptable. Publishes 2% of manuscripts submitted. Payment: 1-3 copies, 40% discount on additional copies, 1¢/word or $2-5/poem on publication for first N.A. serial rights (there is no cash payment for contributors outside North America). Copyrighted, reverts to author. Pub's reviews: 50 in 2005. §Works of intelligence and craft. Ads: $100/$60/$35 1/4 page. Subjects: Book Reviewing, Essays, Fiction, Literary Review, Literature (General), Magazines, Poetry, Short Stories.

Iconoclast Press, Jack Haas, 3495 Cambie Street, Suite 144, Vancouver, BC V5Z 4R3, Canada, 604-682-3269 X8832, admin@iconoclastpress.com. 2002. Poetry, art, photos, non-fiction. "Query by email only please." Pub'd 3 titles 2005; expects 4 titles 2006, 4 titles 2007. 240pp. Reporting time: 2 months. Simultaneous submissions accepted: yes. Publishes 10% of manuscripts submitted. Payment: negotiable. Does not copyright for author. Subjects: Biography, California, Dreams, India, Libertarian, Occult, Pacific Northwest, Philosophy, Photography, Poetry, Religion, Spiritual, Sports, Outdoors, Women, Zen.

•**Idaho Center for the Book,** 1910 University Drive, Boise, ID 83725-1525, 208-426-1999, Fax 208-426-4373, www.lili.org/icb. 1994. Non-fiction. "*James Castle: His Life & Art*, our most recent publication, Idaho Library Association "Book of the Year" award-winner (2005)." avg. press run 1K. Pub'd 1 title 2005; expects 1 title 2006, 1 title 2007. Discounts: 30-40%. 150pp. Reporting time: 1-3 months. Simultaneous submissions accepted: yes. Publishes 1% of manuscripts submitted. Payment: 10%/annual. Copyrights for author. Subjects: Book Arts, Idaho.

THE IDAHO REVIEW, Mitch Wieland, Boise State University, 1910 University Drive/English Dept., Boise, ID 83725, 208-426-1002, http://english.boisestate.edu/idahoreview/. 1998. Poetry, fiction, interviews, parts-of-novels, long-poems, non-fiction. "No word limit. Recent contributors: Richard Bausch, Ann Beattie, Rick Bass, Joy Williams, Madison Smartt Bell, and Ron Carlson. Work featured in *Best American Short Stories, O. Henry, Pushcart* and *New Stories From the South*." circ. 1M. 1/yr. Pub'd 1 issue 2005; expects 1 issue 2006, 1 issue 2007. sub. price $10.00 per year.; per copy $10.00; sample $5. Back issues: $6.95. 200pp. Reporting time: 3-5 months. Simultaneous submissions accepted: yes, if noted. Publishes 5% of manuscripts submitted. Payment: average $10 per page, $100 max. Copyrighted, reverts to author. Pub's reviews. §Fiction. Ads: $150/$75. Subjects: Fiction, Literary Review, Poetry.

•**IDM Press,** Otto Laske PhD, PsyD, Editor in Chief; Nancy Moynihan M.Sc., Assistant Editor, 51 Mystic St, Medford, MA 02155-3643, 781.391.2361. 2005. Music, non-fiction. "IDM Press specializes in social science based text- and handbooks for the college and adult education market. A recent contributor is Dr. Otto Laske, a well-known social scientist and psychologist writing on coaching and process consultation. As to music, we publish musicology texts, especially those focusing on musical cognition and music theory. We occasionally publish poetry, mostly bilingual." avg. press run 1000. Expects 2 titles 2006, 5 titles 2007. Discounts: 55%. 300-500pp. Reporting time: 4 weeks at most. Simultaneous submissions accepted: No. Publishes 10% of manuscripts submitted. Payment: We typically expect print ready texts. Does not copyright for author. Subjects: Consulting, Education, Ethics, Management, Sociology, Textbooks.

Idylls Press, Debra Murphy, PO Box 3566, Salem, OR 97302-3566, 503-363-3601, 503-345-0890, info@idyllspress.com, www.idyllspress.com. 2004. Fiction, non-fiction. "We intend to publish some non-fiction and perhaps even poetry, if something particularly exciting comes along, but our main aim at Idylls Press is to publish quality literary, mainstream, and genre fiction with Catholic themes." avg. press run 3000. Expects 1 title 2006, 2 titles 2007. Discounts: distributors/wholesalers 55%, retailers/bookstores 40%, libraries/institutions 20%. 200-400pp. Reporting time: 4-6 weeks. Simultaneous submissions accepted: Yes. Payment: Advances: small or none. Royalties: 10-15%. Copyrights for author. Subjects: Arthurian, Catholic, Fantasy, Fiction, Literature (General), Mystery, Non-Fiction, Novels, Religion, Romance, Science Fiction, J.R.R. Tolkien.

Igneus Press, Peter Kidd, 310 N. Amherst Road, Bedford, NH 03110, 603-472-3466. 1990. Poetry. "Poetry books 50-150 pages. Recent authors: W.E. Butts, P.J. Laska, William Kemmett." avg. press run 500. Pub'd 1 title 2005; expects 4 titles 2006, 2-4 titles 2007. Discounts: 40%. 75pp. Reporting time: 1 month. Payment: 10% of run to author. Does not copyright for author. Subject: Poetry.

Ignite! Entertainment, Jeff Krell, P.O. Box 641131, Los Angeles, CA 90064-1980, ignite-entertainment@earthlink.net. 1996. Cartoons. "Current biases: Gay-positive entertainment, cartoons, humor." avg. press run 2M. Expects 2 titles 2006, 2 titles 2007. Discounts: 50%. 96pp. Reporting time: 2 months. Simultaneous submissions accepted: yes. Payment: 5-10% cover price. Copyrights for author. Subjects: Cartoons, Comics, Gay, German, Humor.

•**Ika, LLC,** Zachary Harris, 4630 Sansom Street, 1st Floor, Philadelphia, PA 19139-4630, 215-327-7341. 2005. Poetry, photos, satire, non-fiction. "The bulk of our focus are works that deal with any aspect of men in love and relationships. Anything from self-helf and psychology to satirical. Also, photo-essay works." avg. press run 3000. Pub'd 1 title 2005; expects 3 titles 2006. Discounts: 2-5 books - 25%, 6-10 books - 30%, 11-25 books - 40%, 26-49 books - 42%,50-74 books- 44%, 75-99 books 48%, 100+ books 50%. 200pp. Simultaneous submissions accepted: No. Publishes 1% of manuscripts submitted. Does not copyright for author. Subjects: Adolescence, African-American, Anthology, Culture, Food, Eating, Men, Multicultural, New Age, Non-Fiction, Non-Violence, Picture Books, Romance, Wine, Wineries, Women, Zen.

Ikon Inc., 151 First Ave. #46, New York, NY 10003. 1982. Poetry, fiction, non-fiction. "We are not accepting unsolicited manuscripts." avg. press run 1000. Pub'd 3 titles 2005; expects 4 titles 2006, 4 titles 2007. Discounts: 40%. Copyrights for author.

THE ILLUMINATA, Tyrannosaurus Press, Bret M. Funk, Garrie Keyman, Doug Roper, Terry Crotinger, PO Box 8337, New Orleans, LA 70182-8337, Illuminata@tyrannosauruspress.com, www.TyrannosaurusPress.com. 2002. Fiction, articles, interviews, satire, criticism, reviews, parts-of-novels, news items, non-fiction. "THE ILLUMINATA is the free speculative fiction (science fiction and fantasy) webzine of Tyrannosaurus Press. We publish SF-related articles, reviews, and original fiction. All submissions must be electronic. Visit our website for submission instructions." 12/yr. Pub'd 12 issues 2005; expects 12 issues 2006, 12 issues 2007. sub. price Free to download. Back issues: Available on website. 15pp. Simultaneous submissions accepted: yes. Payment: As a free publication, the Illuminata cannot compensate its contributors at this time. Interested parties must be content with gaining international exposure for their work. We require nonexclusive publication rights, but authors retain all rights to their articles/reviews/etc. and are free to seek placement for them elsewhere. Pub's reviews. §The Illuminata includes reviews of science fiction or fantasy related books, movies, comics, television, etc. Reviews should be approximately 500-750 words and should be honest and fair. Subjects: Fantasy, Science Fiction.

Illumination Arts, John Thompson, PO Box 1865, Bellevue, WA 98009, 425-644-7185. 1987. Fiction. "We publish inspiring/uplifting children's picture books with world-class artwork." Pub'd 4 titles 2005; expects 2 titles 2006, 2 titles 2007. Discounts: Normal trade discounts. 32pp. Reporting time: 2 months. Simultaneous submissions accepted: Yes. Payment: varies. Copyrights for author. Subjects: Children, Youth, Inspirational, Juvenile Fiction, Multicultural.

ILLUMINATIONS, Simon Lewis, English Dept., 66 George Street, College of Charleston, Charleston, SC 29424-0001, Tel: 843-953-1920, Fax: 843-953-1924, Web: www.cofc.edu/illuminations. 1982. Poetry, fiction, cartoons, interviews, letters, parts-of-novels, long-poems. "*Illuminations* is devoted to promoting the work of new writers by publishing their work within the context of the work of established figures. Bias: Serious writers; we mostly publish poetry—will consider short fiction or short extracts. Recent contributors: Carole Satyamurti,

Dennis Brutus, Jeremy Cronin, Lam Thi My Da, Virgil Suarez, Sandor Kanyadi, Marcus Rediker, Geri Doran, Gabeba Baderoon; interviews with Tim O'Brien and Athol Fugard. Issues 9 and 10 were anthologies of East and South African writing. Issue 13 dedicated to Stephen Spender, Issue 14 to Southern African writing, Issue 16 to Vietnamese poetry, Issue 17 to Cuban and Latin-American poetry.'' circ. 500. 1/yr. Pub'd 1 issue 2005; expects 1 issue 2006, 1 issue 2007. sub. price $15/2 issues; per copy $10; sample $10. Back issues: negotiable. Discounts: 33-1/3 commission. 80pp. Reporting time: 2-3 months minimum. Simultaneous submissions accepted: no. Publishes 5% of manuscripts submitted. Payment: none. Copyrighted, reverts to author. Ads: $150/$75/$40 1/4 page. Subjects: Avant-Garde, Experimental Art, Fiction, Literature (General), Novels, Poetry, Reviews, Translation.

THE ILLUSTRATOR COLLECTOR'S NEWS, Denis C. Jackson, PO Box 6433, Kingman, AZ 86402-6433, 360-452-3810; ticn@olypen.com. 1983. Art, cartoons, reviews, news items, non-fiction. ''Our publication caters to collectors and dealers and antique people who buy and sell old magazines, calendars, prints, and illustrated paper of all kinds.'' circ. 1,000. 6/yr. Pub'd 6 issues 2005; expects 6 issues 2006, 6 issues 2007. sub. price $18; per copy $3.50; sample $3.50. Back issues: $3.50. Discounts: 20%-50% on guide/books only - no discount on *the Illustrator Collector's News* The Bi-monthly Publication. 24pp. Reporting time: 30 days. We sometimes accept simultaneous submissions. Publishes 25-50% of manuscripts submitted. Payment: $25 per article and illustrations. Copyrighted, does not revert to author. Pub's reviews: 5 in 2005. §Collectibles and antiques, antiquarian books, paper, and illustrations. Ads: $64/$32/20¢. Subjects: Antiques, Arts, Book Arts, Book Collecting, Bookselling, Collectibles, Magazines.

IMAGE: ART, FAITH, MYSTERY, Gregory Wolfe, 3307 Third Avenue West, Seattle, WA 98119, phone 206-281-2988, fax 206-281-2335. 1989. Poetry, fiction, art, interviews, reviews, non-fiction. ''IMAGE is a unique forum for the best writing and artwork that are informed by—or grapple with—Judeo-Christian religious faith. We have never been interested in art that merely regurgitates dogma or falls back on easy answers or didacticism. Instead, our focus has been on writing and visual artwork that embody a spiritual struggle, that seek to strike a balance between tradition and a profound openness to the world.'' circ. 4500. 4/yr. Pub'd 4 issues 2005; expects 4 issues 2006, 4 issues 2007. sub. price $39.95; per copy $12. 128pp. Reporting time: 12 weeks. Simultaneous submissions accepted: Yes. Publishes 2% of manuscripts submitted. Payment: $10/page (for prose) or $2/line (for poetry) plus four copies of the journal; payment is upon publication. Copyrighted, reverts to author. Pub's reviews: approx. 8 in 2005. §reviews poetry, fiction, memoir. Ads: $600 full page (b+w)/$360 half page (b+w)/$1,200 back cover (color). Subjects: Arts, Dance, Fiction, Memoirs, Movies, Music, Non-Fiction, Performing Arts, Photography, Poetry, Religion, Spiritual, Theatre, Visual Arts, Writers/Writing.

Images Unlimited and Snaptail Press, a Division of Images Unlimited Publishing, Ms. Lee Jackson, PO Box 305, Maryville, MO 64468, 660-582-4279, Fax 775-871-7829, info@imagesunlimitedpub.com, www.imagesunlimitedpub.com. 1981. Non-fiction. ''Publishes books for parents and children, cookbooks, and apple lovers.'' avg. press run 2M. Pub'd 1 title 2005; expects 1 title 2006, 1 title 2007. Discounts: 20% for 2-5, 40% for 6-99, 50% for 100+. 130pp. Reporting time: 2 months. Simultaneous submissions accepted: no. Publishes 1% of manuscripts submitted. Payment: to be arranged. Copyrights for author. Subjects: Children, Youth, Cooking, Family, Food, Eating, How-To, Juvenile Fiction, Parenting, Picture Books.

Imago Press, Leila Joiner, 3710 East Edison Street, Tucson, AZ 85716, 520-327-0540, ljoiner@dakotacom.net, www.ImagoBooks.com. 2002. Poetry, fiction, non-fiction. ''Not accepting unsolicited manuscripts at this time.'' Pub'd 2 titles 2005; expects 3 titles 2006, 3 titles 2007. Discounts: 40%-50%. 300pp. Reporting time: 1 month. Simultaneous submissions accepted: yes. Publishes 25% of manuscripts submitted. Payment: none at present. Copyrights for author. Subjects: Aging, Anthology, Education, Essays, Fantasy, Fiction, Memoirs, Mystery, New Age, Non-Fiction, Novels, Poetry, Reading, Science Fiction, Short Stories.

Immediate Direction Publications (see also MIDNIGHT STREET), Trevor Denyer, 7 Mountview, Church Lane West, Aldershot, Hampshire GU11 3LN, England, tdenyer@ntlworld.com, www.midnightstreet.co.uk.

IMOCO Publishing, Paul Brodsky, President, PO Box 471721, Tulsa, OK 74147-1721, 208-978-2261, imoco@officefunnies.com, www.officefunnies.com. 1997. Fiction, cartoons, satire. avg. press run 4M. Pub'd 1 title 2005; expects 2 titles 2007. Discounts: Trade discounts available, contact for details. Less than 100pp. Copyrights for author. Subjects: Business & Economics, Humor, Self-Help.

Impact Publishers, Inc., Robert E. Alberti, Editor-in-Chief, PO Box 6016, Atascadero, CA 93423-6016, 805-466-5917, Fax 805-466-5919, info@impactpublishers.com, www.impactpublishers.com. 1970. Non-fiction. ''Self-help, popular psychology, personal development, divorce recovery, relationships, families, health, 'Little Imp' books for children.'' avg. press run 5M-10M. Pub'd 8 titles 2005; expects 8 titles 2006, 8 titles 2007. Discounts: bookstores: up to 4 copies, 25% prepaid; 5-49 copies 40%; 50 plus copies, contact Impact re terms; libraries paper 10%; cloth 15%; wholesale distributors: contact Impact re terms. 200-300pp. Reporting time: 6-8 weeks minimum. Simultaneous submissions accepted: yes. Publishes less than 1% of manuscripts submitted. Payment: standard royalty contract. Copyrights for author. Subjects: Children, Youth, Divorce, Family,

Grieving, Guidance, Health, Marriage, Non-Fiction, Parenting, Psychology, Relationships, Self-Help, Sex, Sexuality, Tapes & Records, Women.

Impassio Press, Olivia Dresher, Publisher & Editor, PO Box 31905, Seattle, WA 98103, 206-632-7675, Fax 775-254-4073, books@impassio.com, www.impassio.com. 2001. Fiction, interviews, letters, collages, non-fiction. "We publish fragmentary writing that's insightful, daring, and original, including: journals/diaries/ notebooks; letters; philosophical essay-fragments; aphorisms; poetic prose fragments; vignettes; fiction in diary or letter form." avg. press run 1M. Pub'd 1 title 2005; expects 1 title 2006, 1 title 2007. Discounts: 40% bookstores. 150pp. Reporting time: 4-6 weeks. Simultaneous submissions accepted: yes. Publishes 2% of manuscripts submitted. Payment: 5%. Copyrights for author. Subjects: Autobiography, Diaries, Essays, Fiction, Interviews, Journals, Literature (General), Memoirs, Non-Fiction, Philosophy, Prose, Quotations, Translation, Writers/Writing.

Implosion Press, Cheryl A. Townsend, Editor-in-Chief, 4975 Comanche Trail, Stow, OH 44224, 216-688-5210 phone/Fax, E-mail impetus@aol.com. 1984. Poetry, art, cartoons, interviews, reviews, letters, collages, news items. "Quarterly magazine takes in above listed items. Annual All Female issues take above items pertaining only to the gender of issue. Chapbooks series (usually 4-6 per year) is by invitation only, but will look at material sent in. Broadsides are also printed. Have published chapbooks by Gerald Locklin, Lyn Lifshin, Lonnie Sherman, Ron Androla, Bill Shields, amongst others." avg. press run 1M. Pub'd 4 titles 2005; expects 4 titles 2006, 4 titles 2007. Discounts: free for review. 100pp. Reporting time: within 4 months. Simultaneous submissions accepted: no. Publishes 5% of manuscripts submitted. Payment: 1 copy upon publication. Copyrights for author. Subjects: Avant-Garde, Experimental Art, Poetry.

IMPress, Madeleine Rose, 26 Oak Road, Withington, Manchester M2O 3DA, England, +44(0)161-2837636, info@impressbooks.fsnet.co.uk, www.impressbooks.fsnet.co.uk. 2000. Fiction, articles. "Titles include *Burning Worm* by Carl Tighe, shortlisted for the UK Awards - 2001 Whitbread First Novel Award and winner of Authors' Club Best First Novel. We do not accept unsolicited manuscripts." Expects 1 title 2006, 1 title 2007. Trade orders from Gardners Wholesalers in UK. Subjects: Essays, Fiction, Novels, Science Fiction, Short Stories.

In Between Books, Chris Swanberg, Kathleen Hughart, Mary Turnbull, PO Box 790, Sausalito, CA 94966, 415 383-8447. 1972. Poetry, fiction, long-poems. "Please send inquiries before sending MS. You can email us at*inbetweenbooks.com.*" avg. press run up to 1200, but can vary. Pub'd 4 titles 2005; expects 2 titles 2006, ? titles 2007. Discounts: 40% to stores, 20% to libraries. Pages vary. Reporting time: 2-4 weeks by UPS. 2-7 days by email *inbetweenbooks.com.* We prefer not to accept simultaneous submissions. Publishes a variable % of manuscripts submitted. Payment: varies. Copyrights for author. Subjects: Diaries, Dreams, Literature (General), Myth, Mythology, Novels, Poetry, Short Stories, Writers/Writing.

IN OUR OWN WORDS, Burning Bush Publications, PO Box 9636, Oakland, CA 94613, www.bbbooks.com. 2000. Poetry, fiction, articles, satire, non-fiction. "Online publication only." 2/yr. Pub'd 2 issues 2005; expects 2 issues 2006, 2 issues 2007. Simultaneous submissions accepted: yes. Publishes 5% of manuscripts submitted. Ads: free listings to editors for calls for submissions. Subjects: Poetry, Women.

•**IN OUR OWN WORDS,** Abby Bogomolny, P. O. Box 4658, Santa Rosa, CA 95402, http:/ /www.bbbooks.com. 2000. Poetry, fiction, articles, cartoons, satire, reviews, non-fiction. "Inspirational writing whose goal is to create a better, kinder world." 2/yr. Pub'd 2 issues 2005; expects 2 issues 2006, 2 issues 2007. Discounts: Online ezine only. 25pp. Reporting time: 5 months. Simultaneous submissions accepted: Yes. Publishes 25% of manuscripts submitted. Payment: publication only. Copyrighted, reverts to author. Subjects: African-American, Alternative Medicine, California, Chicano/a, Civil Rights, Current Affairs, Fiction, Florida, Gay, Health, Judaism, New York, Peace, Poetry, Women.

In Print Publishing, Tomi Keitlen, S, PO Box 20765, Sedona, AZ 86341, 928-284-5298, Fax 928-284-5283. 1991. Fiction, non-fiction. "We are an eclectic publisher." avg. press run 3M-5M. Pub'd 1 title 2005; expects 3 titles 2006. Discounts: inquire. 200-350pp. Reporting time: 6-8 weeks. Simultaneous submissions accepted: yes. We publish 1 out of 50 books submitted. Payment: 6%-8% depending on book. Copyrights for author. Subjects: Anthology, Autobiography, Biography, How-To, Inspirational, Metaphysics, New Age, Religion, Spiritual, Tapes & Records.

THE INCLUSION NOTEBOOK, Pennycorner Press, Gayle Kranz, Publisher; Kathleen Whitbvead, Editor, PO Box 8, Gilman, CT 06336, 860-873-3545; Fax 860-873-1311. 1996. Articles, photos, interviews, reviews, non-fiction. circ. 1000. 4/yr. Pub'd 4 issues 2005; expects 4 issues 2006, 4 issues 2007. sub. price $14.95; per copy $5. Back issues: Vol. I & II $35. 12-16pp. Publishes 1% of manuscripts submitted. Payment: negotiated. Copyrighted, reverts to author. Pub's reviews: 6-8 in 2005. §School inclusion. Subjects: Disabled, Education.

INDEFINITE SPACE, Marcia Arrieta, PO Box 40101, Pasadena, CA 91114. 1992. Poetry, art, photos. "Prefer poems not to exceed two pages. Does not accept previously published poems. Open to: modern, imagistic, abstract, philosophical, natural, surreal, and experimental creations." circ. 2M. 1/yr. Pub'd 1 issue 2005; expects 1 issue 2006, 1 issue 2007. sub. price $10/2 issues; per copy $6; sample $6. 36pp. Reporting time: 3 months or sooner. Publishes an unknown % of manuscripts submitted. Payment: 1 copy. Subjects: Photography, Poetry.

THE INDENTED PILLOW, Ronald K. Jones, PO Box 3502, Camarillo, CA 93011, rjones@mymailstation.com. 2002. Poetry, art. "Want poems reflecting the practices and experiences of tantra or achieving oneness with the cosmos through sexual bliss. Also accepts black and white line drawings separately or to accompany poems." circ. small. 1/yr. Expects 1 issue 2006, 1 issue 2007. sub. price $3; per copy $3.50; sample $3.50. Discounts: 40%. 20pp. Reporting time: 1 month. Simultaneous submissions accepted: yes. Publishes 50% of manuscripts submitted. Payment: copies. Copyrighted, reverts to author. Subjects: Erotica, Sex, Sexuality, Spiritual.

The Independent Institute (see also THE INDEPENDENT REVIEW: A Journal of Political Economy), Robert Higgs, 100 Swan Way, Oakland, CA 94621-1428, 510-632-1366, fax 510-568-6040, email info@independent.org, www.independent.org. 1986. Articles, reviews, non-fiction. "Critical analysis of government policy, past and present. Articles should not exceed 7,500 words and should be submitted in triplicate, typed doublespaced with author's name, address and phone number (abstract of no more than 150 words should be included). Authors should be prepared to submit article on 3.5 inch computer disk in a recent Macintosh Word or WordPerfect for Macintosh or DOS/Windows. Book manuscripts should be similarly prepared. Recent authors: Thomas Szasz, Stanley Engerman, Anna Schwartz, William Niskanen, Irving Horowitz, Leland Yeager, E.G. West." avg. press run 5M. Pub'd 10 titles 2005; expects 10 titles 2006, 10 titles 2007. Discounts: Returnable: 1-4 20%, 5-9 40%, 10-24 41%, 25-49 42%, 50-99 43%; Non-returnable: 1-4 25%, 5-9 42%, 10-24 43%, 25-49 44%, 50+ 45%. 250pp. Reporting time: 1-2 months. Simultaneous submissions accepted: no. Payment: negotiated. Does not copyright for author. Subjects: Agriculture, Anarchist, Anthropology, Archaeology, Biography, Book Reviewing, Business & Economics, Education, Environment, Global Affairs, Government, Human Rights, Immigration, Journals, Law, H.L. Mencken.

INDEPENDENT PUBLISHER ONLINE, Jim Barnes, Executive Editor, 1129 Woodmere Ave., Ste. B, Traverse City, MI 49686, 231-933-0445, Fax 231-933-0448, jimb@bookpublishing.com, www.independent-publisher.com. 1993. Poetry, fiction, articles, interviews, satire, criticism, reviews, letters, news items. "*Independent Publisher* reviews approx. 600 books from small presses each year." circ. 35M online subscribers. 11/yr. Pub'd 11 issues 2005; expects 11 issues 2006, 11 issues 2007. sub. price free; per copy free; sample free. 80pp. Simultaneous submissions accepted: no. Publishes 10% of manuscripts submitted. Payment: varies, $50-$150. Copyrighted, reverts to author. Pub's reviews: 500+ in 2005. §Books only - nonfiction. Ads: none. Subjects: Book Collecting, Bookselling, Book Reviewing, Libraries, Literary Review, Publishing, Reviews.

THE INDEPENDENT REVIEW: A Journal of Political Economy, The Independent Institute, Robert Higgs, 100 Swan Way, Oakland, CA 94621-1428, 510-632-1366, fax 510-568-6040, email review@independent.org, www.independent.org/review. 1996. Articles, reviews, non-fiction. "Critical analysis of government policy, past and present. Articles: should not exceed 7,500 words and should be submitted in triplicate, typed double spaced with author's name, address and phone number (abstract of no more than 150 words should be included). Authors should be prepared to submit articles on 3.5 inch computer disk in a recent Macintosh Word or WordPerfect for Macintosh or DOS/Windows." circ. 5M. 4/yr. Pub'd 4 issues 2005; expects 4 issues 2006, 4 issues 2007. sub. price $28.95; per copy $7.50; sample $7.50. Back issues: $7.50. Discounts: agent 10%, classroom 20%, bulk 20%, jobber 20%, distributors negotiated. 160pp. Reporting time: 1 month. Simultaneous submissions accepted: no. Payment: none. Copyrighted, does not revert to author. Pub's reviews: 50 in 2005. §Economics, history, political science, philosohpy, law (inquiries first before submission). Ads: $775/$350 1/4 page. Subjects: Biography, Business & Economics, Education, Environment, Global Affairs, Government, History, Human Rights, Immigration, Law, Libertarian, H.L. Mencken, Non-Violence, Philosophy, Political Science.

THE INDEPENDENT SHAVIAN, Dr. Richard Nickson, Douglas Laurie, Patrick Berry, The Bernard Shaw Society, PO Box 1159 Madison Square Stn., New York, NY 10159-1159, 212-982-9885. 1962. Poetry, articles, photos, cartoons, interviews, satire, criticism, reviews, letters, news items. "Publication deals with items concerning Bernard Shaw, his circle and his world: theatre, politics, music, etc." circ. 500 worldwide. 3/yr. Pub'd 3 issues 2005; expects 3 issues 2006, 3 issues 2007. sub. price $30 USA, $30 outside USA (airmail included); per copy $2; sample $2. Back issues: $2. Discounts: 13% for subscription agencies. single issues: 28pp; double issues: 48pp. Reporting time: none. Payment: none. Not copyrighted. Pub's reviews: 8 in 2005. §Anything pertaining to Bernard Shaw. Ads: none. Subject: G.B. Shaw.

INDEX TO FOREIGN LEGAL PERIODICALS, University of California Press, Thomas H. Reynolds, Editor; Kevin Durkin, Managing Editor, University of California Press, 2000 Center Street, Suite 303, Berkeley, CA 94704-1223, 510-643-7154. 1960. Non-fiction. "Editorial address: L250A Boalt Hall, Berkeley, CA 94720.

Copyrighted by The American Association of Law Libraries." circ. 600. 3/yr. Pub'd 3 issues 2005; expects 3 issues 2006, 3 issues 2007. sub. price $746 (+ $25 air freight); per copy $746. Back issues: $746. 250pp. Copyrighted, does not revert to author. Ads: none accepted. Subject: Law.

INDIA CURRENTS, Arvind Kumar, Box 21285, San Jose, CA 95151, 408-274-6966, Fax 408-274-2733, e-Mail editor@indiacurrents.com. 1987. Fiction, articles, art, photos, cartoons, interviews, satire, criticism, reviews, music, letters, parts-of-novels, collages, news items, non-fiction. "Between 300-1500 words. We look for insightful approach to India, its arts, culture, people. Recent contributors: Sandip Roy-Chowdhury, Rajeev Srinivasan, Laxmi Hiremath, Prasenjit Ranjan Gupta, Sukumar Ramanathan, Sarita Sarvate." circ. 24M. 11/yr. Pub'd 11 issues 2005; expects 11 issues 2006, 11 issues 2007. sub. price $19.95; per copy $1.95 + $1 s/h; sample same. Back issues: $3. 104pp. Reporting time: 3 months. Publishes 20% of manuscripts submitted. Payment: $50 for 1000 words. Copyrighted, reverts to author. Pub's reviews: 18 in 2005. §India and Indians, colonialism, immigration, multiculturalism, assimilation, racism. Ads: $690/$380/60¢. Subjects: Asia, Indochina, Asian-American, Buddhism, Sri Chinmoy, Immigration, India, Multicultural, Third World, Minorities, Vegetarianism, Yoga.

INDIANA REVIEW, Tracy Truels, Editor, Ballantine Hall 465, Indiana University, 1020 E. Kirkwood Avenue, Bloomington, IN 47405-7103, 812-855-3439. 1976. Poetry, fiction, art, photos, interviews, reviews, parts-of-novels, long-poems, plays, non-fiction. "*Indiana Review* is a magazine of poetry, fiction, nonfiction, and book reviews. We prefer writing that shows both an awareness of language and of the world. We publish 6-8 stories and about 40-60 pages of poetry per issue. We like writers who take risks. Recent contributors have included Marilyn Hacker, Kwame Dawes, Bob Hicok, Marilyn Chin, Denise Duhamel, Roy Jacobstein, Dan Kaplan, Timothy Liu, Aimee Nezhukumatathil, Lucia Perilllo, Terese Svoboda, Maureen Seaton, Stuart Dybek, Rick Moody and Michael Martone. We also sponsor poetry, fiction, and short-short/prose-poem prizes judged by leading writers. Award $1,000 to each winner as well as publication. Deadlines in March (poetry), June (short-short/prose-poem) and October (fiction). Send SASE or visit our website (www.indiana.edu/~inreview) for guidelines." circ. 2000. 2/yr. Pub'd 2 issues 2005; expects 2 issues 2006, 2 issues 2007. sub. price Individual $17, institutions $20, please add $12 for overseas ($7 for Canada); per copy $9; sample $9. Back issues: Based on availability. Discounts: trade 60/40% split; 50-50 to distributors. 180pp. Reporting time: 3 - 4 months. Please consult website for reading periods. Simultaneous submissions accepted: yes. Publishes less than 1% of manuscripts submitted. Payment: $5 per page poem, $5 per page story, $10 minimum. Copyrighted, reverts to author. §Recent collections of poetry or fiction; novels and poetry collections by new and established writers, especially from small presses; books of criticism or literary theory, both for literary works and the visual arts. Ads: $300/$150. Subjects: Comics, Fiction, Literary Review, Non-Fiction, Poetry, Prose, Reviews.

THE INDIE, Pasckie Pascua, Editor; Pasckie Pascua, Publisher; Marta Kay Osborne, AssociatePublisher; Matthew Mulder, ContributingWriter, 61 Dunwell Ave., Asheville, NC 28806-3431, 828-225-5994, raindance60@hotmail.com. 1999. Poetry, articles, art, cartoons, interviews, criticism, reviews, music, news items, non-fiction. "The Indie is an independent monthly newsmagazine published in Asheville, NC and distributed in Western North Carolina, choice downtown Manhattan, New York City and north New Jersey outlets, Fells Point and Hampden communities of Baltimore, and Washington DC." circ. 2000. 12/yr. Pub'd 10 issues 2005; expects 12 issues 2006, 12 issues 2007. sample price $2. Back issues: $2. Simultaneous submissions accepted: no. Copyrighted, reverts to author. Pub's reviews: 20 in 2005. §poetry, essays, creative non-fiction. Ads: Full page: $100, Half page: $60, 1/4 page: $40, Business card size: $10, Classified line rates: Up to 25 words: $5, Each additional line: $0.50, Photographs, logos, or a frame: $2. Subjects: Book Reviewing, Communication, Journalism, Culture, Essays, Global Affairs, Interviews, Movies, Multicultural, Music, Non-Fiction, Non-Violence, Peace, Performing Arts, Public Affairs, Spiritual.

•INDUSTRY MINNE-ZINE, Tricia Heuring, 12 Vincent Avenue South, Minneapolis, MN 55405, 612.308.2467. 2003. Poetry, articles, art, photos, cartoons, interviews, satire, criticism, reviews, music, long-poems, collages, concrete art, news items, non-fiction. "A publication that focuses on music, art, fashion & culture in the Twin Cities and the Midwest." circ. 20000. 6/yr. Pub'd 6 issues 2005; expects 6 issues 2006, 12 issues 2007. sub. price 20; sample free. Back issues: inquire. 135pp. Reporting time: 2 days. Simultaneous submissions accepted: No. Publishes 0% of manuscripts submitted. Payment: 0-$150 per article. Not copyrighted. Ads: $1000. Subjects: Arts, Avant-Garde, Experimental Art, Cartoons, Clothing, Community, Creativity, Design, Fashion, Graphic Design, Graphics, Minnesota, Performing Arts, Photography, Poetry, Politics.

INDY MAGAZINE, Jeff Mason, Editor-in-Chief; Chris Waldron, Senior Editor, 503 NW 37th Avenue, Gainesville, FL 32609-2204, 352-373-6336, jmason@gator.net, www.indyworld.com. 1993. Articles, photos, cartoons, interviews, criticism, reviews, letters, news items. "*Indy Magazine* covers the world of alternative comic books and independent film." circ. 8M-12M. 5/yr. Pub'd 5 issues 2005; expects 5 issues 2006, 5 issues 2007. sub. price $15; per copy $2.95; sample $3. Back issues: $3. Discounts: 1-9 copies 50%, 10-24 55%, 25+ 60%. 72pp. Simultaneous submissions accepted: no. Publishes 75% of manuscripts submitted. Payment:

2¢/word. Copyrighted, reverts to author. Pub's reviews: 250 in 2005. §Comic books, comix, film, anime, cartoons, TV. Ads: $150/$75/$40 1/4 page. Subjects: Book Collecting, Bookselling, Book Reviewing, Cartoons, Comics, Counter-Culture, Alternatives, Communes, Humor, Magazines, Movies.

Infinite Corridor Publishing, Joe Wolosz, Editor-in-Chief, 6633 Yount St., Youtville, CA 94599-1280, 415-292-5639; Fax 415-931-5639; E-mail corridor@slip.net. 1996. "Hotel and Hospitality related texts. All matter relates to the operations of the hospitality industry." avg. press run 3M. Expects 1 title 2006, 2 titles 2007. 176pp. Reporting time: 1 month. Simultaneous submissions accepted: no. Payment: 10% of net, paid every month. Copyrights for author. Subject: Marketing.

Infinite Possibilities Publishing Group, Inc., Shelley Parris, PO Box 150823, Altamonte Springs, FL 32715-0823, (407) 699-6603 office (407) 331-3926 fax. 2002. Poetry, fiction, non-fiction. avg. press run 2000. Pub'd 4 titles 2005; expects 10-15 titles 2006, 20-25 titles 2007. Discounts: 40%. 150pp. Reporting time: 6-8 weeks. Simultaneous submissions accepted: Yes. Publishes 3% of manuscripts submitted. Copyrights for author. Subjects: African Literature, Africa, African Studies, African-American, Anthology, Careers, Family, Fiction, Finances, How-To, Non-Fiction, Nutrition, Psychology, Public Affairs, Reference, Relationships, Young Adult.

The Infinity Group, Genie Lester, Publisher; Anne Nichandros, Editor, 22516 Charlene Way, Castro Valley, CA 94546, 510-581-8172; kenandgenie@yahoo.com. 1987. Poetry, fiction, art, photos, cartoons, parts-of-novels, long-poems, plays, non-fiction. "We are not interested in submissions at this time, although we are always happy to hear from people we previously published in our magazine, *Infinity Limited*." Pub'd 3 titles 2005; expects 2 titles 2006, 3 titles 2007. Simultaneous submissions accepted: no. Copyrights for author. Subjects: Anthology, Arts, Fiction, Poetry.

Infinity Publishing, 1094 New Dehaven St, Suite 100, West Conshohocken, PA 19428, info@infinitypublishing.com. 1997. Poetry, fiction, articles, art, photos, cartoons, interviews, satire, criticism, reviews, music, letters, parts-of-novels, long-poems, collages, plays, concrete art, news items, non-fiction. "We can publish any book in a matter of a few months. We have a bookstore return policy that stores love, and provide an easy way for authors to reach the masses. Our free publishing guide is also a sample of our printing quality." avg. press run print on demand. Pub'd 250 titles 2005; expects 400 titles 2006, 400 titles 2007. Discounts: 40% provided on quantities of 5 or more (1-4, for retailers, get 20%). 237pp. Reporting time: indefinite. Simultaneous submissions accepted: yes. Publishes 95% of manuscripts submitted. Payment: 30% on retail sales. Does not copyright for author.

Info Net Publishing, Herb Wetenkamp, 21142 Canada Road #1C, Lake Forest, CA 92630-6714, 949-458-9292, Fax 949-462-9595, herb@infonetpublishing.com. 1986. Articles, art, photos, interviews, reviews, news items, non-fiction. "How to, business, retailing, specialty sports, women's issues, small business, home business, SoHo." avg. press run 10M-20M. Pub'd 2 titles 2005; expects 2 titles 2006, 2 titles 2007. Discounts: 55% distributor, 40% retailer. 200+pp. Reporting time: 1-2 months. Simultaneous submissions accepted: yes. Publishes 5% of manuscripts submitted. Payment: please inquire. Copyrights for author. Subjects: Advertising, Self-Promotion, Bicycling, Business & Economics, Cooking, History, How-To, Magazines, Marketing, Public Relations/Publicity, Sports, Outdoors, Women.

INGLESIDE NEWS ZINE, IsaBelle Bourret, 5591 St-Laurent, Levis, QC, G6V 3V6, Canada, ingleside_news_zine@yahoo.com, www.geocities.com/ingleside_news_zine. 1998. Fiction, articles, art, photos, cartoons, interviews, satire, criticism, reviews, music, letters, parts-of-novels, collages, concrete art, news items, non-fiction. "perzine/ in english or french!!" circ. variable. 3-4/yr. Pub'd 2 issues 2005; expects 4 issues 2006, 4 issues 2007. sub. price 6 issues -$10Cdn in Canada, $10US in US, $20US int'l; per copy $2Cdn in Canada, $2US in US, $4US int'l; sample $2Cdn in Canada, $2US in US, $4US int'l. Back issues: $2Cdn in Canada, $2US in US, $4US int'l. Discounts: trades welcome—distro wholesale price is 1$, provided you sell the zine 2$. 40pp. Reporting time: I check email daily. Simultaneous submissions accepted: yes. Payment: we're not that rich yet. Copyrighted, reverts to author. Pub's reviews: 15 in 2005. §Mostly nonfiction, personal, experiences, unusual. Ads: we could do ad trades, but not too many—we advertize the distros that distro us. Subjects: Anarchist, Antiques, Architecture, Arts, Bibliography, Biography, Book Collecting, Bookselling, Book Reviewing, Cities, Communication, Journalism, Computers, Calculators, Conservation, Crafts, Hobbies, Criticism, Dance.

Iniquity Press/Vendetta Books (see also BIG HAMMER), David Roskos, PO Box 54, Manasquan, NJ 08736, 732 295 9920, iniquitypress@hotmail.com. 1988. Poetry, fiction, criticism. "Chapbooks are done by solicitation only; can't read unsolicited chap-mss(no time/$; focusing on mag). Published 2 in 04, & 2 in 05. Writers published include Andrew Gettler, Harvey Pekar, Ken Greenley, Joe Weil, Donald Lev, Hal Sirowitz, Lamont Steptoe, Bertha Sanchez Bello & Michael Pingarron." avg. press run 300-1M. Pub'd 2 titles 2005; expects 2 titles 2006, 3 titles 2007. Discounts: 60/40. 40pp. Reporting time: 1 month. Payment: author gets 100-150 copies. Copyrights for author. Subjects: Absurdist, Alcohol, Alcoholism, Anarchist, Crime, Culture,

Dada, Dreams, Drugs, Essays, Music, Poetry, War, Zines.

INKWELL, Alex Lindquist, Editor-in-Chief; Christine Adler, Editorial Consultant, Manhattanville College, 2900 Purchase Street, Purchase, NY 10577, www.inkwelljournal.org. 1995. Poetry, fiction, art, photos, interviews, parts-of-novels, non-fiction. ''A literary journal published semiannually in the spring and fall, Inkwell is dedicated to providing a forum for emerging writers and publishing high quality poems and short stories. Inkwell also features non-fiction, artwork, essays, memoir and interviews on writing by established figures, and yearly competitions in poetry and fiction.'' 2/yr. Pub'd 2 issues 2005; expects 2 issues 2006, 2 issues 2007. sub. price $15; per copy $8; sample $6. Back issues: $6. 185pp. Reporting time: 4-6 months. Simultaneous submissions accepted: Yes. Publishes 3% of manuscripts submitted. Payment: $10-100. Copyrighted, reverts to author. §Short fiction (5,000 words or less), poetry, creative non-fiction, memoir. Ads: $100 full/$50 half (display). Subjects: Literature (General), Non-Fiction, Poetry, Prose.

INKY TRAIL NEWS, Wendy Fisher, 50416 Schoenharr #111, Shelby Twp., MI 48315, e-mail inkytrails@comcast.net. 1993. Poetry, fiction, articles, art, photos, letters, news items, non-fiction. ''Newspaper dedicated to womens friendship, penpals, correspondence.'' circ. 1M. 6/yr. Pub'd 6 issues 2005; expects 6 issues 2006, 6-12 issues 2007. sub. price $20; per copy $3; sample $3. Discounts: please write and inquire. 24 tabloid-sized pagespp. Reporting time: 6-month subscription, a $10 value. Simultaneous submissions accepted: yes. Publishes 80% of manuscripts submitted. Payment: copies only. Copyrighted, reverts to author. Pub's reviews. §Women, correspondence, seniors, journals, memories, crafts, how-to, gardening, collectors/antiques. Ads: $5 includes the issue (short ads). Subjects: Antiques, Collectibles, Crafts, Hobbies, Culture, Essays, Gardening, Genealogy, Newsletter, Newspapers, Postcards, Psychology, Short Stories, Travel, Women, Writers/Writing.

Inner City Books, Daryl Sharp, Victoria Cowan, Box 1271, Station Q, Toronto, ON M4T 2P4, Canada, 416-927-0355, FAX 416-924-1814, icb@inforamp.net. 1980. Non-fiction. ''We publish *only* studies in Jungian psychology by Jungian analysts. Now 91 titles by 42 authors. Over a million books sold worldwide; over 200 other language editions. No unsolicited manuscripts.'' avg. press run 3M. Pub'd 6 titles 2005; expects 5 titles 2006, 6 titles 2007. Discounts: trade 40%/60 days or 50% prepaid; surface post, 10% of net. 160pp. Copyrights for author. Subject: Psychology.

Inner City Press (see also INNER CITY PRESS), Matthew Lee, P.O. Box 580188, Mount Carmel Station, Bronx, NY 10458, Web: InnerCityPress.org Tel: 718-716-3540. 1987. Fiction, satire, news items, non-fiction. ''Inner City Press / Community on the Move is a non-profit organization headquartered in the South Bronx of New York City since 1987. It began with a mimeographed newspaper, morphed into organizing the homesteading of long-abandoned buildings, then to fighting for fair access to finance, using the Community Reinvestment Act and combating predatory lending. While the work has gone nationwide, Inner City Press remains in and of The Bronx; its weekly Bronx Report goes online every Monday at www.innercitypress.org/ bxreport.html ICP covers human rights, including beyond the U.S.. ICP's 2004 tome, "Predatory Bender," has been noted in The Times of London, the Washington Post, and elsewhere. A sequel is forthcoming.'' avg. press run 6000. Pub'd 3 titles 2005; expects 4 titles 2006, 5 titles 2007. Discounts: standard. 400pp. Reporting time: depends. Simultaneous submissions accepted: Yes. Payment: depends. Copyright depends. Subjects: African Literature, Africa, African Studies, Asian-American, Chicago, Chicano/a, China, Cities, Civil Rights, Human Rights, Latin America, Puerto Rico, South America, Tennessee, Washington, D.C.

INNER CITY PRESS, Inner City Press, Matthew Lee, P.O. Box 580188, Mount Carmel Station, Bronx, NY 10458, Web: InnerCityPress.org Tel: 718-716-3540. 1987. News items, non-fiction. ''Inner City Press / Community on the Move is a non-profit organization headquartered in The Bronx since 1987. It began with a mimeographed newspaper, morphed into organizing the homesteading of long-abandoned buildings, then to fighting for fair access to finance, using the Community Reinvestment Act and combating predatory lending. While the work has gone nationwide, Inner City Press remains in and of The Bronx. Its weekly Reports (on community reinvestment, bank beat, the bronx, environmental justice, etc.) come out each week, and go online every Monday at www.innercitypress.org.'' 52/yr. Pub'd 52 issues 2005; expects 52 issues 2006, 52 issues 2007. Discounts: standard. 32pp. Reporting time: depends. Simultaneous submissions accepted: Yes. Payment: depends. depends. Pub's reviews: approx. 20 in 2005. §books about consumer issues, human rights, The Bronx, globalization, etc. Ads: depends / sliding scale. Subjects: Cities, Civil Rights, Human Rights, New York, Nicaragua.

Innisfree Press, Marcia Broucek, 908 Wolcott Ave., St. Joseph, MI 49085-1717, 215-518-6688, Fax 215 247-2343, InnisfreeP@aol.com. 1982. Non-fiction. avg. press run 5M. Pub'd 5 titles 2005; expects 5 titles 2006, 5 titles 2007. Discounts: 1-4 20%, 5-249 45%, 250-499 46%, 500+ 47%. 160pp. Reporting time: 2 months. Simultaneous submissions accepted: yes. Payment: 10% net receipts. Copyrights for author. Subjects: Careers, Christmas, Community, Creativity, Dreams, Feminism, Health, Inspirational, Psychology, Relationships, Religion, Self-Help, Spiritual, Storytelling, Women.

227

INNOVATING, Harold S. Williams, The Rensselaerville Institute, Rensselaerville, NY 12147, 518-797-3783. 1963. Articles, interviews, reviews, letters, non-fiction. "Publication is dedicated to enabling people to lead change by example. The quarterly includes innovation assumptions, paradigms, research and examples. While the focus is on the public and voluntary sector, the content is also relevant to business and other kinds of organizations." circ. 2M. 4/yr. Pub'd 4 issues 2005; expects 4 issues 2006, 4 issues 2007. sub. price Call; per copy $8; sample free. Back issues: $8. Discounts: according to volume. 70pp. Reporting time: 6 weeks prior to publication date. Simultaneous submissions accepted: yes. Percentage of manuscripts received that are published varies. Payment: yes if they have a track record. We will publish first time writers if it fits. Copyrighted, reverts to author. Pub's reviews: none in 2005. §Innovation/creativity, entrepreneur, management, education, outcome funding, outcome management, due diligence. Ads: none. Subjects: Community, Education, Essays, Finances, Government, Interviews, Management, Non-Fiction, Reviews.

Inspiring Teachers Publishing, Inc., Emma McDonald, Senior Editor; Dyan Hershman, Acquisitions Editor, 12655 N. Central Expressway, Suite 810, Dallas, TX 75243, 877-496-7633 (toll-free), 972-496-7633, Fax 972-763-0355, info@inspiringteachers.com, www.inspiringteachers.com. 1998. Articles, non-fiction. "We publish professional development and practical how-to books for teachers, specializing in materials for beginning educators." avg. press run 5M. Pub'd 4 titles 2005; expects 4 titles 2006, 4 titles 2007. Discounts: 40% for bookstores, Special Discounts for schools, districts, and other educators. Please call for details. 200pp. Reporting time: 6 months. Simultaneous submissions accepted: no. Payment: Typical royalties are 10% with no advance payment. Royalty payments are generally made 30 days after the end of each Quarter. Copyrights for author. Subject: Education.

Institute for Contemporary Studies, Melissa Stein, 3100 Harrison Street, Oakland, CA 94611-5526. 1972. Articles, news items. "Books on domestic and international public policy issues." avg. press run 3M. Pub'd 8-10 titles 2005; expects 8-10 titles 2006, 12 titles 2007. Discounts: on request. 300pp. Reporting time: 1-3 months. Payment: works for hire and royalty arrangements. Copyrights for author. Subjects: Business & Economics, Public Affairs.

Institute of Healing Arts & Sciences, 2 Wintonbury Mall, Bloomfield, CT 06002-2466, healing@anguillanet.com.

The Institute of Mind and Behavior (see also THE JOURNAL OF MIND AND BEHAVIOR), Raymond Russ Ph.D., PO Box 522, Village Station, New York, NY 10014, 212-595-4853. 1980. Criticism, reviews, non-fiction. "Send manuscripts to Raymond Russ, Ph.D., Department of Psychology Room 301, 5742 Little Hall, University of Maine, Orono, ME 04469-5742. We are interested in scholarly manuscripts, with interdisciplinary thrust, in the areas of: the mind/body problem in the social sciences; the philosophy of experimentalism and theory construction; historical perspectives on the course and nature of scientific investigation; and mind/body interactions and medical implications." avg. press run 2M. Pub'd 1 title 2005; expects 1 title 2006, 1 title 2007. Discounts: 18% on orders of 10 copies or more. 350pp. Reporting time: 10-19 weeks. Simultaneous submissions accepted: yes. Publishes 14% of manuscripts submitted. Payment: no fees to authors. Does not copyright for author. Subjects: Literature (General), Philosophy, Psychology, Society, Sociology.

INSURANCE, Chris Tokar, Kostas Anagnopoulos, 132 N. 1st Street #11, Brooklyn, NY 11211, ctokar@hotmail.com. 1999. Poetry, fiction, satire, parts-of-novels, long-poems, non-fiction. "Prefer to read at least 6 pages for submission; rarely take work more than 2,500 words (usually shorter). We take only previously unpublished work, lean toward experimental." 1/yr. Pub'd 1 issue 2005; expects 1 issue 2006, 1 issue 2007. sub. price $10; per copy $10. Back issues: $8. Reporting time: 1-6 months. Simultaneous submissions accepted: yes, but require notification immediately of submitted work accepted elsewhere. Publishes 5-10% of manuscripts submitted. Payment: $40 plus 2 copies of issue. Copyrighted, reverts to author. Ads: none. Subjects: Literature (General), Poetry, Prose.

Integra Press, A. Greenberger, Publisher, 1702 W. Camelback Road, Suite 13, PMB 119, Phoenix, AZ 85015, 602-841-4911, Fax 602-242-5745, info@integra.com. 1988. avg. press run 5-10M. Expects 1 title 2007. Discounts: 40%. 288pp.

Intelligenesis Publications, Sue Hansen, Richard King, Karen Lushbaugh, Pat Wright, 6414 Cantel Street, Long Beach, CA 90815, 562-598-0034, www.bookmasters.com/marktplc/00337.htm. 1998. "Shipping address: PO Box 545, Seal Beach CA 90740." avg. press run 3-5M. Pub'd 1 title 2005; expects 3 titles 2006, 3 titles 2007. Discounts: trade 1-2 full price; bulk, agent, jobber 40%; wholesaler 50%. 536pp. Reporting time: 3-6 months. Simultaneous submissions accepted: no. Publishes 5% of manuscripts submitted. We copyright as requested. Subjects: Astrology, History, Philosophy.

Intelligent Technologies, Inc., Jodee D. Bray, 10906 NE 39th St., #A4, Vancouver, WA 98682-6789, Fax 360-254-4151.

Interalia/Design Books, G. Brown, PO Box 404, Oxford, OH 45056-0404, 513-523-1553 phone/Fax. 1989. Art, non-fiction. "It is the goal of Interalia/Design Books to make meaningful contributions to the art of the book as a container of knowledge—the textual manifestation of a culture's evolution—and to the book as an object by promoting the dissemination of quality design through an editorial focus on architecture, design/crafts, art criticism, art of the book, facsimiles of out-of-print primary sources on architecture, design/crafts and art criticism. Also by promoting quality in the art of bookmaking by experimenting with alternative structures for the production of books as objects, including alternative printing and binding methods, encouraging limited editions of experimental books and of books for the bibliophile, encouraging artist/writer/printer/binder collaborations." avg. press run 1M. Pub'd 1 title 2005; expects 1 title 2006, 4 titles 2007. Discounts: 40% for orders of 10+. 100pp. Reporting time: 4-6 weeks. Payment: varies. Copyrights for author. Subjects: Architecture, Arts, Book Arts, Criticism, Design, Visual Arts.

INTERCHANGE, English Dept., Univ. of Wales, Hugh Owen Bldg., Penglais, Aberystwyth, Ceredigion SY23 3DY, United Kingdom.

Intercultural Press, Inc., Patricia A. O'Hare, Publisher; Erika Heilman, Editorial Director, 100 City Hall Plaza, Suite 501, Boston, MA 02108-2105, 617.523.3801, e-mail books@interculturalpress.com. 1980. Non-fiction. "Books on intercultural communication, intercultural education and cross-cultural training, especially practical materials for use in teaching and training; other areas: diversity, multicultural education, orientation for living abroad. Shipping address: 374 U.S. Route One, Yarmouth, ME 04096." avg. press run 2M. Pub'd 10 titles 2005; expects 12 titles 2006, 12 titles 2007. 200pp. Simultaneous submissions accepted: yes. Publishes 2% of manuscripts submitted. Payment: royalty. Copyrights for author. Subjects: Business & Economics, Communication, Journalism, Culture, Education, Moving/Relocation, Multicultural, Travel.

INTERCULTURE, Robert Vachon, Editor, Intercultural Institute of Montreal, 4917 St-Urbain, Montreal, Quebec H2T 2W1, Canada, 514-288-7229, FAX 514-844-6800. 1968. Articles, reviews, non-fiction. "Printed in two separate editions: *Interculture* (English edition ISSN 0828-797X); *Interculture* (French edition ISSN 0712-1571). Length of material: 28M words average (each issue devoted to a particular theme). Material: cross-cultural understanding - themes include education, medicine, spirituality, communication, politics and law in an intercultural perspective. Recent titles: *The Shaman and the Ecologist, Dissolving Uniot Society Through Education and Money, Beyond Global Democracy, Africa-India: Contemporary Alternative Esocophies.* Recent contributors: Peter Raine, Derek Rasmussen, Ashis Nandy, John Clammer, Robert Vachon, Martinus L. Daneel, Cosmas Gonese and Vinay Lal." circ. 1M. 2/yr. Pub'd 2 issues 2005; expects 2 issues 2006, 2 issues 2007. sub. price $20 individuals, $35 institutions in Canada; outside Canada $25 individuals, $40 institutions; per copy $9, instit. $11 including taxes for Canada or shipping outside Canada. Back issues: $4.50 older issues, $9 newer, instit. $11. Discounts: subscription agencies receive 15%. 60pp. Reporting time: 3 months. Copyrighted. §Cross-cultural issues. Subjects: Anthropology, Archaelogy, Community, Culture, Education, Human Rights, Immigration, Multicultural, Native American, Philosophy, Religion, Social Work, Society, Sociology, Third World, Minorities.

Interlink Publishing Group, Inc., Michel Moushabeck, Pam Thompson, 46 Crosby Street, Northampton, MA 01060, 413 582 7054 tel, 413 582 7057 fax, www.interlinkbooks.com, info@interlinkbooks.com. 1987. Art, photos, non-fiction. "We specialize in world travel, world literature (translated fiction), world history, ethnic cooking, and children's books from around the world." avg. press run 10M. Pub'd 50 titles 2005; expects 50 titles 2006, 50 titles 2007. Discounts: trade 40% & up. 160pp. Reporting time: We aim to reply in 4-6 months. Simultaneous submissions accepted: Yes. Payment: annually, royalty varies. Copyrights for author. Subjects: African Literature, Africa, African Studies, Arts, Bilingual, Children, Youth, Culture, Feminism, Fiction, History, Latin America, Middle East, Non-Fiction, Political Science, Sociology, Travel.

INTERLIT, Kim Pettit, Cook Communications Ministries International, 4050 Lee Vance View, Colorado Springs, CO 80918-7100, 719-536-0100, Fax 719-536-3266. 1964. Articles, interviews, letters, news items, non-fiction. "Trade journal for Christian publishers around the world." circ. 2.5M. 4/yr. Pub'd 4 issues 2005; expects 4 issues 2006, 4 issues 2007. sub. price $16; per copy $4; sample free. Back issues: $1.50 each. 24pp. Reporting time: 1 month. Payment: varies. Copyrighted, does not revert to author. Subjects: Book Collecting, Bookselling, Communication, Journalism, Desktop Publishing, Editing, Publishing, Third World, Minorities, Translation, Writers/Writing.

InterMedia Publishing, Inc., 2120 Southwest 33 Avenue, Ft. Lauderdale, FL 33312-3750, intermedia-pub@juno.com. 1996. Fiction, art, cartoons, non-fiction. "Query first." Expects 5 titles 2006, 35 titles 2007. Reporting time: 2 weeks. Simultaneous submissions accepted: yes. Copyrights for author.

INTERNATIONAL ADDICTION, University of Calgary Press, N. el-Guebaly, Editor, Addiction Centre, Foothills Hospital, 1403 29th Street NW, Univ. of Calgary, Calgary, AB T2N 2T9, Canada, 403-670-2025, Fax 403-670-2056, nady.el-guebaly@crha-health.ab.ca, http://ahdp.lib.ucalgary.ca/IA/. 2000. Articles, reviews. "*IA* is a referred electronic journal that is committed to the prevention and management of addiction worldwide."

1/yr. Pub'd 1 issue 2005; expects 1 issue 2007. sub. price free access. Reporting time: 2 months. Publishes 50% of manuscripts submitted. Payment: none. Copyrighted, does not revert to author. Pub's reviews: none in 2005. §Addiction. Ads: email for information. Subjects: Alcohol, Alcoholism, Drugs, Medicine, Psychiatry.

INTERNATIONAL ART POST, Banana Productions, Anna Banana, RR 22, 3747 Highway 101, Roberts Creek, BC V0N 2W2, Canada. 1988. Art, photos. "ISSN 0843-6312. *IAP* is a cooperatively published periodical of stamps by artists (Artistamps), printed in an edition of 700 copies in full color on gummed, glossy paper. Editions go to press as sufficient art and money accumulate to cover costs. After payment to participants, Banana Productions distributes the rest of the edition (approx. 400 sheets) through gallery and stationery shops, or uses them in promotional mailings." circ. 700. 1/yr. Pub'd 1 issue 2005; expects 1 issue 2006, 1 issue 2007. sub. price $30; per copy $15; sample $16. Back issues: write for order form, it varies from issues to issue. Discounts: 50% wholesale. 2-7 blocks of stamps. Reporting time: 3-6 months, depending on how quickly a space or press sheet is sold. Simultaneous submissions accepted: yes. Payment: 500 copies their own stamp(s), 3 copies of the sheet on which it is printed, and 1 copy of any other sheet(s) in the edition. Copyrighted. Ads: none. Subjects: Arts, Counter-Culture, Alternatives, Communes, Graphics, Philately, Photography, Visual Arts.

INTERNATIONAL ELECTRONIC JOURNAL FOR LEADERSHIP IN LEARNING, University of Calgary Press, K. Donlevy, Editor, Faculty of Education, Univ. of Calgary, 2500 University Drive NW, Calgary, AB T2N 1N4, Canada, 403-220-5675, Fax 403-282-3005, www.ucalgary.ca/~iejll/. 1997. Articles, reviews. "*IEJLL* is a refereed electronic journal that promotes the study and discussion of substantive leadership issues that are of current concern in education communities." 15-20 articles per volume year published as available. sub. price free access. Reporting time: 2 months. Publishes 40% of manuscripts submitted. Payment: none. Copyrighted, rights revert to author after 10 months. Pub's reviews: 3 in 2005. §Education. Ads: email for information. Subject: Education.

THE INTERNATIONAL FICTION REVIEW, Dr. Christoph Lorey, Culture & Language Studies, UNB, PO Box 4400, Fredericton, N.B. E3B 5A3, Canada, 506-453-4636, Fax 506-447-3166, e-mail ifr@unb.ca. 1973. "The *IFR* is an annual periodical devoted to international fiction. Mss are accepted in English and should be prepared in conformity with the *MLA Handbook for Writers of Research Papers*; articles: 10-20 typewritten pages; reviews: 600-800 words; spelling, hyphenation, and capitalization according to *Webster*." circ. 600. 1/yr. Pub'd 1 issue 2005; expects 1 issue 2006, 1 issue 2007. sub. price $25 instit., $20 indiv.; per copy $15; sample $15. Back issues: $15. Discounts: 20% for agents and jobbers. 128pp. Reporting time: 6 weeks - 3 months. Simultaneous submissions accepted: NO. Publishes 20% of manuscripts submitted. Payment: none. Copyrighted. Pub's reviews: 25 in 2005. §Contemporary fiction and scholarly works on fiction. Subjects: Criticism, Fiction.

International Jewelry Publications, Louise Berlin, Beverly Newton, PO Box 13384, Los Angeles, CA 90013-0384, 626-282-3781, Fax 626-282-4807. 1987. Photos, interviews, non-fiction. "*Gemstone Buying Guide, Diamond Ring Buying Guide*, 6th edition, *Pearl Buying Guide*, 4th edition, *Gold & Platinum Jewelry Buying Guide, Ruby, Sapphire & Emerald Buying Guide* by Renee Newman. *Gem & Jewelry Pocket Guide,Diamond Handbook*." avg. press run 6M. Pub'd 2 titles 2005; expects 2 titles 2006, 2 titles 2007. Discounts: 2-4 copies 30%, 5-11 40%, 12-24 42%, 25-49 45%, 50+ 48%. 160pp. Reporting time: 1 month, but call first before submitting manuscript. Copyrights for author. Subject: Jewelry, Gems.

•**INTERNATIONAL JOURNAL OF AMERICAN LINGUISTICS, University of Chicago Press,** Keren Rice, University of Toronto, 130 St. George Street, Department of Linguistics, Toronto, Ontario M5S 3H1, Canada, http://www.journals.uchicago.edu/IJAL/home.html. 1917. "*International Journal of American Linguistics* is a world forum for the study of all the languages native to North, Central, and South America. Inaugurated by Franz Boas in 1917, *IJAL* concentrates on the investigation of linguistic data and on the presentation of grammatical fragments and other documents relevant to Amerindian languages." 4/yr. Pub's reviews.

INTERNATIONAL JOURNAL OF EDUCATIONAL POLICY, RESEARCH, AND PRACTICE, Caddo Gap Press, Marianne Bloch, Co-Editor; Gaile Cannella, Co-Editor, 3145 Geary Blvd. PMB 275, San Francisco, CA 94118, 415-666-3012, fax 415-666-3552, caddogap@aol.com, www.caddogap.com. 2000. Articles. circ. 200. 4/yr. Pub'd 4 issues 2005; expects 4 issues 2006, 4 issues 2007. sub. price $75 individuals; $175 institutions; per copy $30; sample free. Back issues: $20. Discounts: 15% to agents. 96pp. Reporting time: 3 months. Simultaneous submissions accepted: No. Publishes 25% of manuscripts submitted. No payment. Copyrighted, reverts to author. Ads: $200 per page. Subject: Education.

INTERNATIONAL POETRY REVIEW, Mark Smith-Soto, Dept of Romance Languages, Univ. of North Carolina, Greensboro, NC 27402-6170, 336-334-5655. 1975. Poetry, art. "Our emphasis is on English translation of contemporary poets, presented in bilingual format. About a third of each issue is dedicated to original work in English. Some recent contributors are Alexis Levitin, Ana Istaru, Fred Chappell, Coleman Barks, Jorge Teillier, Mary Crow, Jascha Kessler, Bernhard Frank, Sarah Lindsay. Our reading period runs between September 1 and April 30. Beginning with the Spring 2006 issue, the magazine will be available online through EBSCO.'' circ. 300. 2/yr. Pub'd 2 issues 2005; expects 2 issues 2006, 2 issues 2007. sub. price $12 individuals; $20 libraries, institutions; per copy $6; sample $6. Back issues: varies. 100pp. Reporting time: 3-6 months. Simultaneous submissions accepted, but must be indicated. Publishes 2% of manuscripts submitted. Payment: copies. Copyrighted, reverts to author. Pub's reviews: 2 in 2005. §Poetry translation, poetry. Ads: $100/$50. Subjects: African Literature, Africa, African Studies, Armenian, Asia, Indochina, Bilingual, France, French, German, Greek, India, Language, Latin America, Literary Review, Poetry, Portugal, Spain, Translation.

International Publishers Co. Inc., Betty Smith, 239 West 23 Street, New York, NY 10011, 212-366-9816, Fax 212-366-9820. 1924. Non-fiction. avg. press run 1M-4M. Pub'd 5 titles 2005; expects 4 titles 2006, 5 titles 2007. Discounts: trade and short discount. 200-400pp, some 96-150pp. Reporting time: 1 week to 2 months. Simultaneous submissions accepted: yes. Publishes 5% of manuscripts submitted. Payment: royalties. Copyrights for author. Subjects: African Literature, Africa, African Studies, Americana, Biography, Black, Business & Economics, Communism, Marxism, Leninism, Labor, Peace, Politics, Public Affairs, Socialist, Women, Worker.

International University Line (IUL), Gary Flint, PO Box 2525, La Jolla, CA 92038, Tel 858-457-0595, Fax 858-581-9073, email info@iul-press.com, http://www.iul-press.com. 1992. Non-fiction. avg. press run 3M. Pub'd 2 titles 2005; expects 1 title 2006, 2 titles 2007. Discounts: up to 40%. 400pp. Reporting time: 6 months. Payment: 5% royalty. Does not copyright for author. Subjects: Biotechnology, Non-Fiction, Psychology, Science.

INTERNATIONAL WOMEN'S WRITING GUILD, Elizabeth Julia Stoumen, Box 810, Gracie Station, New York, NY 10028, 212-737-7536, Fax 212-737-9469, iwwg@iwwg.org, www.iwwg.org. 1976. Interviews, reviews, news items. ''A network for women who write, great variety of listings on where to submit work. New information every 2 months. Successes and questions of members. Lots more.'' circ. 3M. 6/yr. Pub'd 6 issues 2005; expects 6 issues 2006, 6 issues 2007. sub. price $45 (included in IWWG membership); sample $1. 32pp. Pub's reviews. Ads: $50 1/8 page. Subjects: Networking, Newsletter.

THE INTERPRETER'S HOUSE, Merryn Williams, 38 Verne Drive, Ampthill, MK45 2PS, United Kingdom, 01525-403018. 1996. Poetry, fiction. ''Stories up to 2000 words.'' circ. 150. 3/yr. Pub'd 3 issues 2005; expects 3 issues 2006, 3 issues 2007. sub. price £8.50; per copy £2.95; sample £2.95. Back issues: £2.95. 74pp. Reporting time: 1 month. Simultaneous submissions accepted: yes. Publishes 10% of manuscripts submitted. Payment: free copy. Not copyrighted, rights remain with author. Subjects: Poetry, Short Stories.

INTO THE TEETH WIND, Rimantos Ungalys, Laura Bradshaw, College of Creative Studies, University of California, Santa Barbara, Santa Barbara, CA 93106, www.ccs.ucsb.edu/windsteeth. 1999. Poetry, art. ''We accept poetry and artwork (for cover). SASE must be included with submissions. Contributors receive one free copy in which their work appears. The editors reserve the right to publish poetry and artwork on the publication's website.'' 4/yr. Pub'd 4 issues 2005; expects 4 issues 2006, 4 issues 2007. sub. price $20; per copy $5.50; sample $5.50. Discounts: contributors $5 or $10 for a double-issue. 60pp. Reporting time: 1-3 months. Simultaneous submissions accepted: no. Publishes 5% of manuscripts submitted. Payment: 1 copy. Copyrighted, reverts to author. Subject: Poetry.

The Intrepid Traveler, Sally Scanlon, Editor-in-Chief, PO Box 531, Branford, CT 06405, 203-488-5341, Fax 203-488-7677, admin@intrepidtraveler.com. 1990. Non-fiction. ''We publish travel guidebooks and books on travel marketing.'' avg. press run 5M. Pub'd 7 titles 2005; expects 5 titles 2006, 7 titles 2007. Discounts: per National Book Network, Inc. terms. 224-400pp. Reporting time: averages 3 months. Query before sending simultaneous submissions. Publishes 1% of manuscripts submitted. Copyrights for author. Subjects: Business & Economics, Dining, Restaurants, Disney, Florida, New Mexico, Non-Fiction, Travel, Trivia.

INVESTMENT COLUMN QUARTERLY (newsletter), NAR Publications, Nicholas A. Roes, PO Box 233, Barryville, NY 12719, 914-557-8713. 1977. Articles, criticism, reviews, news items. 4/yr. Pub'd 10 issues 2005; expects 10 issues 2006, 4 issues 2007. sub. price $75; per copy $20; sample $20. Back issues: $20. 2-4pp. Copyrighted. Pub's reviews: 2 in 2005. §Investments. Subject: Business & Economics.

The Invisible College Press, LLC, Paul Mossinger, Business Manager; Phil Reynolds, Editor-in-Chief, PO Box 209, Woodbridge, VA 22194-0209, 703-590-4005, editor@invispress.com, www.invispress.com. 2002. Fiction, non-fiction. ''The Invisible College Press is a small, independent publisher dedicated to bringing you literary-quality works in the fields of UFOs, Conspiracies, Secret Societies, the Paranormal, Anarchism, and other non-traditional, subversive topics that are underrepresented by mainstream, corporate media. Our titles are a blend of new, original fiction, and reprints of hard-to-find classics.'' avg. press run 1000. Pub'd 12 titles 2005; expects 12 titles 2006, 12 titles 2007. Simultaneous submissions accepted: Yes. Copyrights for author.

IODINE POETRY JOURNAL, Jonathan K. Rice, Editor, PO Box 18548, Charlotte, NC 28218-0548. 2000. Poetry. ''Summer broadside: Open Cut,free with no.10 SASE.'' circ. 350. 2/yr. Pub'd 2 issues 2005; expects 2

231

issues 2006, 2 issues 2007. sub. price $10 one year, $18 two years; per copy $6. Back issues: $5. 62pp. Reporting time: 1 to 2 months. Simultaneous submissions accepted: no. Publishes 10% of manuscripts submitted. Payment: 1 copy. Copyrighted, reverts to author. Subject: Poetry.

Ion Imagination Publishing, Ion Imagination Entertainment, Inc., Keith Frickey, Program Director, PO Box 210943, Nashville, TN 37221-0943, 615-646-3644, 800-335-8672, Fax 615-646-6276, flumpa@aol.com, www.flumpa.com. 1994. Fiction, art, photos, music, non-fiction. "Children's only, science related topics ONLY. No unsolicited materials. Specifically looking for illustrators, *not* authors, for ongoing, already established series. We are also a children's music publisher - please DO NOT sent any queries that are not elementary science related - we will not read them. Queries only with SASE for return." avg. press run 10M+. Pub'd 2 titles 2005; expects 2 titles 2006, 2 titles 2007. Discounts: please call for info. 40pp. Reporting time: 1 month to review. Simultaneous submissions accepted: no. Subjects: Animals, Audio/Video, Biology, Children, Youth, Science, Tapes & Records.

IOTA, Ragged Raven Press, Bob Mee, Janet Murch, 1 Lodge Farm, Snitterfield, Stratford-on-Avon, Warks CV37 0LR, England, 44-1789-730320, iotapoetry@aol.com, www.iotapoetry.co.uk. 1987. Poetry, reviews. "No line limit (but no room for epics), bias towards modern/contemporary." circ. 350. 4/yr. Pub'd 4 issues 2005; expects 4 issues 2006, 4 issues 2007. sub. price UK£18 for outside Europe inc p/h.Sterling only or credit card via website.; per copy UK£4.50 inc. p/h.; sample UK£4.50 inc. p/h. Back issues: UK£4.50 inc. p/h. 60pp. Reporting time: 1 month. Simultaneous submissions accepted: no. Publishes 15-20% of manuscripts submitted. Payment: 1 free copy. Copyrighted, reverts to author. Pub's reviews: 43 in 2005. §Poems and books about poetry. Ads: none. Subjects: Poetry, Reviews.

IOWA HERITAGE ILLUSTRATED, Ginalie Swaim, State Historical Society of Iowa, 402 Iowa Avenue, Iowa City, IA 52240, 319-335-3916, Fax 319-335-3935, ginalie-swaim@uiowa.edu. 1920. Articles, art, photos, interviews, letters, non-fiction. "*Iowa Heritage Illustrated* is Iowa's popular history magazine. It publishes manuscripts and edited documents on the history of Iowa and the Midwest that may interest a general reading audience. Submissions that focus on visual materials (photographs, maps, drawings) or on material culture are also welcomed. Originality and significance of the topic, as well as quality of research and writing, will determine acceptance. Manuscripts should be double-spaced, footnoted, and roughly 5-20 pages. Photographs or illustrations (or suggestions) are encouraged." circ. 2M. 4/yr. Pub'd 4 issues 2005; expects 4 issues 2006, 4 issues 2007. sub. price $50; per copy $9; sample free. Back issues: 1920-1972—50¢, 1973-June '84—$1, July '84-Dec. '86—$2.50, 1987—Summer '89 $3.50, fall 89 - winter 95 $4.50. Discounts: retailers get 40% off single issue cover price. 48pp. Reporting time: 3 months. Simultaneous submissions accepted: no. Publishes 35% of manuscripts submitted. Payment: 10 complimentary copies + $50-$500. Copyrighted, does not revert to author. Subjects: History, Iowa.

THE IOWA REVIEW, David Hamilton, Editor; Hugh Ferrer, Fiction Editor; Lynne Nugent, Managing Editor, 308 EPB, Univ. Of Iowa, Iowa City, IA 52242, 319-335-0462. 1970. Poetry, fiction, interviews, reviews, non-fiction. "With the advent of our recent contest, The Iowa Awards, we have changed our reading periods. Now we welcome open submissions through the fall semester only, from Labor Day until early December. During the second semester we concentrate on contest entries." circ. 2.5M. 3/yr. Pub'd 3 issues 2005; expects 3 issues 2006, 3 issues 2007. sub. price $24 (+$3 outside US); per copy $8.95; sample $8 for most recent issue. Discounts: 10% agency, 30% trade. 192pp. Reporting time: 2-4 months. Simultaneous submissions accepted: yes. Publishes 5% of manuscripts submitted. Payment: $25 for the first page, $15 for each subsequent page in all genres. Copyrighted, reverts to author. Pub's reviews: 4 in 2005. §Poetry, fiction, literary culture, nonfiction. Ads: $200/$100. Subjects: Book Reviewing, Criticism, English, Essays, Fiction, Literary Review, Literature (General), Non-Fiction, Poetry, Prose.

•Iris Publishing Group, Inc (Iris Press / Tellico Books), Robert Cumming B, 969 Oak Ridge Turnpike, # 328, Oak Ridge, TN 37830-8832, Ph: 865-483-0837, Fx: 865-481-3793, rcumming@irisbooks.com, www.iris-books.com. 1975. Poetry, fiction, criticism, long-poems, non-fiction. "Of our two book imprints, Iris Press is tho older and focuses on literary material (Poems literary fiction and other literary prose.) Our other imprint, Tellico Books is broader in scope and more flexible in its approach." avg. press run 1500. Pub'd 4 titles 2005; expects 7 titles 2006, 7 titles 2007. Discounts: distributors & wholesalers: 55%Bookstores, retailers, institutions, classrooms : 40%. 120pp. Reporting time: 2 months. Simultaneous submissions accepted: Yes. Publishes 1% of manuscripts submitted. Payment: Varies according to the type of material. Copyrights for author. Subjects: Appalachia, Essays, Fiction, History, Kentucky, Language, Latin America, Nature, Non-Fiction, Peace, Poetry, Prose, Puerto Rico, South Carolina, Tennessee.

IRIS: A Journal About Women, Kimberley Roberts, Coordinating Editor, PO Box 800588, University of Virginia, Charlottesville, VA 22904, 434-924-4500, Fax 434-982-2901, iris@virginia.edu, http://womens-center.virginia.edu/iris.htm. 1980. Poetry, fiction, articles, art, photos, interviews, reviews, music, long-poems, non-fiction. "We are a magazine for twenty-something women who want to make a difference in the world around them. We welcome submissions of high quality poetry, fiction, art, nonfiction, and reviews. We prefer submissions that represent a woman's experience or viewpoint. We also have features, which include 'Cool Women Profile' - Profiles of women young and old making a difference in their communities, but unknown to most; FYI - resource guide; 'Ask Iris' - A forum style discussion on an issue; 'Girl on the Street' - Composing a poll on a common issue/question. We do not accept email submissions. For sumission guidelines see http://iris.virginia.edu." circ. 2.5M. 2/yr. Pub'd 2 issues 2005; expects 2 issues 2006, 2 issues 2007. sub. price $9; per copy $5; sample $5. Back issues: $5. Discounts: 20% for trade or bulk. 70pp. Reporting time: 2-3 months. Simultaneous submissions accepted: yes. Publishes 5% of manuscripts submitted. Payment: a determined number of issues. Copyrighted, reverts to author. Pub's reviews: 4 in 2005. §Books about women or that are written by women and feminist theory, prefer nonfiction. Ads: $200/$140/$90 1/4 page. Subjects: African-American, Autobiography, Birth, Birth Control, Population, Bisexual, Black, Book Reviewing, Chicano/a, Community, Creativity, Education, Family, Feminism, Fiction, Food, Eating, Gender Issues.

IRISH FAMILY JOURNAL, Irish Genealogical Foundation, Michael C. O'Laughlin, Box 7575, Kansas City, MO 64116. 1978. Articles, art, photos, interviews, letters, news items, non-fiction. "Short articles, highlights, Irish American personalities, informal, tradition/history oriented. Time period: A) 1800's, B) current time for genealogy. Photos of Irish family castles, immigrants, lifestyle—1800's. Family names." circ. 2.5M+. 6 or 12/yr (12 issues to gold members). Pub'd 12 issues 2005; expects 12 issues 2006, 12 issues 2007. sub. price $59/$114; sample n/c. 8pp. Reporting time: 30 days. Payment: inquire. Copyrighted, reverts to author. Pub's reviews: 50 in 2005. §Irish genealogy, history, folklore, tradition. Ads: $1,000/$600. Subjects: Book Reviewing, Celtic, Genealogy, Ireland.

Irish Genealogical Foundation (see also IRISH FAMILY JOURNAL), Michael C. O'Laughlin, Box 7575, Kansas City, MO 64116, 816-454-2410, mike@irishroots.com. 1969. Articles, art, photos, interviews, letters, non-fiction. avg. press run 2M. Pub'd 10 titles 2005; expects 10 titles 2006, 10 titles 2007. Discounts: bulk purchases 40%-60%. 200pp. Reporting time: 30 days. Simultaneous submissions accepted: no. Payment: none. Does not copyright for author. Subjects: Celtic, Genealogy, Ireland, Reprints.

IRISH LITERARY SUPPLEMENT, Robert G. Lowery, Editor-Publisher; Maureen Murphy, Features Editor, 2592 N Wading River Road, Wading River, NY 11792-1404, 631-929-0224. 1982. Interviews, criticism, reviews, parts-of-novels, non-fiction. "Published in association with Boston College. All work assigned." circ. 4.5M. 2/yr. Pub'd 2 issues 2005; expects 2 issues 2006, 2 issues 2007. sub. price $6, $7.50 libraries, $12 foreign; per copy $3; sample $3. Back issues: $4. Discounts: only with subscription agencies. 32pp. Reporting time: varies. Payment: copies and book for review. Copyrighted, reverts to author. Pub's reviews: 140 in 2005. §Irish material. Ads: $500/$300. Subjects: Book Reviewing, Celtic, Criticism, Drama, Folklore, Ireland, Literary Review, Poetry, G.B. Shaw, Theatre.

IRON HORSE LITERARY REVIEW, Jill Patterson, Editor; William Wenthe, Poetry Editor, Texas Tech University, English Dept., PO Box 43091, Lubbock, TX 79409-3091, 806-742-2500 X234. 1999. Poetry, fiction, photos, interviews, reviews, non-fiction. "Accepts literary fiction, poetry, and creative nonfiction as well as b&w photographs. We prefer not to publish commercial genres, including fantasy, science fiction, romance, horror, erotica, etc. No short-shorts." circ. 500. 2/yr. Expects 2 issues 2006, 2 issues 2007. sub. price $12; per copy $6; sample $5. 180pp. Reporting time: 3 months. Simultaneous submissions accepted: yes. Publishes 1% of manuscripts submitted. Payment: $100 for fiction, $40 per poem. Copyrighted, reverts to author. Pub's reviews. §Literary fiction, poetry, creative nonfiction. Ads: $250/$150/$100 1/4 page. Subjects: African-American, Chicano/a, Fiction, Literary Review, Native American, Non-Fiction, Poetry, Texas.

Ironweed Press, Jin Soo Kang, Rob Giannetto, PO Box 754208, Parkside Station, Forest Hills, NY 11375, Ph 718-544-1120 Fax 718-268-2394. 1996. Fiction. avg. press run 2M. Pub'd 2 titles 2005; expects 3 titles 2006, 3-4 titles 2007. Discounts: 1-25%; 2-4-40%; 5-9-42%; 10-100-46%; 100+50%. Copyrights for author. Subjects: Biography, Criticism, Fiction, History, Music, Reprints, Writers/Writing.

Island Press, Barbara Dean, Executive Editor; Dan Sayre, Editor-In-Cheif; Chuck Savitt, Publisher, 1718 Connecticut Avenue NW #300, Washington, DC 20009, 202-232-7933; FAX 202-234-1328; e-mail info@islandpress.org; Website www.islandpress.org. 1978. Non-fiction. "Additional address: Box 7, Covelo, CA 95428. Books from original manuscripts on the environment, ecology, and natural resource management." avg. press run 3M. Pub'd 44 titles 2005; expects 48 titles 2006, 50 titles 2007. Discounts: trade 1-9 40%, 10-49 43%, 50-99 44%, 100-249 45%, 250+ 46%. 275pp. Reporting time: 3 weeks, sometimes less. Simultaneous submissions accepted: yes. Publishes 15% of manuscripts submitted. Payment: standard contracts, graduated royalties. Copyrights for author. Subjects: Biology, Conservation, Earth, Natural History, Ecology, Foods, Energy, Environment, Non-Fiction, Science, Water.

Island Publishers, Thelma Palmer, Co-Publisher; Delphine Haley, Co-Publisher, PO Box 201, Anacortes, WA 98221-0201, 360-293-5398. 1985. Poetry, non-fiction. avg. press run 5M. Pub'd 2 titles 2005; expects 1 title 2006. Discounts: 1-4 20%, 5-49 40%, 50+ 41%. 200pp. Reporting time: 1 month. Payment: inquire. Copyrights for author. Subjects: Animals, Cooking, History, Pacific Northwest, Poetry, Science.

Island Style Press, Michael Dougherty, 6950 Hawaii Kai Drive Apt. 403, Honolulu, HI 96825-4149. 1992. Non-fiction. avg. press run 5M. Discounts: 25%. 250pp. Reporting time: 30 days. Simultaneous submissions accepted: no. Publishes 5% of manuscripts submitted. Payment: 10%. Does not copyright for author. Subjects: Hawaii, History.

Islewest Publishing, Mary Jo Graham, 4242 Chavenelle Drive, Dubuque, IA 52002, 319-557-1500, Fax 319-557-1376. 1994. Non-fiction. avg. press run 1M-10M. Pub'd 2 titles 2005; expects 8 titles 2006, 15 titles 2007. Discounts: market norm. Reporting time: two weeks. Simultaneous submissions accepted: yes. Publishes 15% of manuscripts submitted. Copyrights for author. Subjects: Alcohol, Alcoholism, Gender Issues, Grieving, How-To, Men, Parenting, Psychology, Relationships, Self-Help, Sexual Abuse, Social Work, Vietnam.

ISOTOPE: A Journal of Literary Nature and Science Writing, Christopher Cokinos, Department of English, 3200 Old Main Hill, Logan, UT 84322-3200, 435-797-3697, fax 435-797-3797, http://isotope.usu.edu. 2003. Poetry, fiction, art, photos, non-fiction. "We are interested in lyric and short narrative essays, short stories, microfiction, prose poems, poetry and artwork that engages in and meditates on the varied complex relations among the human and non-human worlds, with a special interest in moving beyond merely laudatory descriptions of natural beauty and elegies on loss of the same. We are interested in *the beauty of things*—to use Robinson Jeffers's phrase—but seek to complicate typical modes of nature writing with a wider range of emotion and subject. We are especially interested in work engaging in fields, subjects and concerns that move beyond traditional nature writing—including urban ecosystems, astronomy, physics, chaos theory, genetic engineering, artificial intelligence, restoration ecology, earth sciences, cartography, sexuality, medicine and the body." circ. 900. 2/yr. Pub'd 2 issues 2005; expects 2 issues 2006, 2 issues 2007. sub. price $10; per copy $5; sample $5. Back issues: $5. Discounts: 20%. 52pp. Reporting time: 3-9 months. Simultaneous submissions accepted: Yes. Copyrighted, reverts to author.

ISSUES, Sue Perlman, PO Box 424885, San Francisco, CA 94142-4885, 415-864-4800 X136. 1978. Poetry, fiction, articles, art, photos, interviews, satire, reviews, non-fiction. "Messianic." circ. 40M. 6/yr. Pub'd 6 issues 2005; expects 6 issues 2006, 6 issues 2007. sub. price free; per copy free; sample 50¢. Back issues: 75¢ each. 8-12pp. Reporting time: 3-5 weeks. Payment: 10¢/word, minimum $25. Copyrighted, rights reverting to author is decided by contract. Pub's reviews: 5 in 2005. §Religion, Judaica, philosophy, Christianity. Ads: none. Subjects: Book Reviewing, Christianity, Interviews, Judaism, Poetry, Religion.

ISSUES IN TEACHER EDUCATION, Caddo Gap Press, Margaret Olebe, 3145 Geary Blvd. PMB 275, San Francisco, CA 94118, 415 666-3012. twice a year. sub. price $40 for individuals; $80 for institutions. 96pp. Subject: Education.

IT GOES ON THE SHELF, Purple Mouth Press, Ned Brooks, 4817 Dean Lane, Lilburn, GA 30047-4720, nedbrooks@sprynet.com. 1984. Art, reviews. "Art only, I write the text myself." circ. 350 paper, also at home.sprynet.com/~nedbrooks/home.htm. 1/yr. Pub'd 1 issue 2005; expects 1 issue 2006, 1 issue 2007. Discounts: trade, etc. 20pp. Reporting time: 1 week. Payment: copy. Not copyrighted, will copyright art if author wishes. Pub's reviews: 75 in 2005. §Science fiction, fantasy, typewriters, oddities. Subjects: Book Arts, Fantasy, Science Fiction.

ITALIAN AMERICANA, Carol Bonomo Albright, Editor; Bruno A. Arcudi, Associate Editor; John Paul Russo, Review Editor; Michael Palma, Poetry Editor, University of Rhode Island, 80 Washington Street, Providence, RI 02903-1803. 1974. Poetry, articles, reviews. "*Italian Americana*, a multi-disciplinary journal concerning itself with all aspects of the Italian experience in America, publishes articles, short stories, poetry, memoirs and book reviews. It is published in cooperation with the American Italian Historical Association. Submissions of 20 double-spaced pages maximum, following the latest MLA Style Sheet, are invited in the areas of Italian American history, sociology, political science, literature, art, folk art, anthropology, music, psychology, etc., and short stories. Book reviews of 1,000 words are assigned and poetry of no more than three pages is accepted. Submissions by historians, social scientists, literary critics, etc., of Italian are encouraged when related to Italian American studies. Comparative analysis is welcome when related to Italian American issues. Please submit materials in triplicate with an SASE. All submissions will be reviewed by the editor and two readers. Name should appear on the first page only with article title on subsequent pages. For poetry, one copy of each poem is acceptable." circ. 2.5M. 2/yr. Pub'd 2 issues 2005; expects 2 issues 2006, 2 issues 2007. sub. price $20 indiv., $25 instit., $15 student, $35 foreign; per copy $8.50; sample $7. Back issues: $7 for issues starting Fall 1990; no copies available for Spring/Summer '93. Discounts: $35/2 years, $54/3 years. 150pp. Reporting time: 1-2 months. Simultaneous submissions accepted: no. Publishes 15% of manuscripts submitted. Payment: $500 for best historical article published each year and $1000 poetry prize annually, $250 for best fiction or memoir published each year. Copyrighted, reverts to author. Pub's reviews: 28 in 2005. §Significant books, films, plays, and art about Italian-American experience. Ads: $190/$100. Subjects: Anthropology, Archaelogy, Arts, History, Italian-American, Literature (General), Music, Philosophy, Political Science, Psychology, Short Stories, Sociology.

Italica Press, Inc., Ronald G. Musto, Eileen Gardiner, 595 Main Street, #605, New York, NY 10044, 212-935-4230; fax 212-838-7812; inquiries@italicapress.com. 1985. Poetry, fiction, art, letters, long-poems, plays, non-fiction. "We specialize in English translations of Italian and Latin works from the Middle Ages to the present. Primary interests are in history, literature, travel, and art. Published titles include Petrarch's *The Revolution of Cola di Rienzo*, the poet's letters to the revolutionary; *The Marvels of Rome*, a medieval guidebook to the city; and Theodorich's *Guide to the Holy Land*, written c. 1172; *The Fat Woodworker* by Antonio Manetti, a comic Renaissance tale about Brunelleschi and his circle; and new translations from Italian of twentieth-century novels, *Cosima* by Grazia Deledda and *Family Chronicle* by Vasco Pratolini, *The Wooden Throne* by Carlo Sgorlon, *Dolcissimo* by Guiseppe Bonaviri, and *Woman at War* by Dacia Maraina. Our audience is the general reader interested in works of lasting merit." avg. press run 1.5M. Pub'd 6 titles 2005; expects 8 titles 2006, 8 titles 2007. Discounts: trade single copy 20%, 25% 2 copies, 30% 3-4, 35% 5-9, 40% 10-25, 43% 26-50, 50% 100+; classroom 25% on adoptions of 5 or more; others are negotiable. 200pp. Reporting time: 6 weeks. Simultaneous submissions accepted: yes. Publishes 10% of manuscripts submitted. Payment: approx. 10% of net sales. Copyrights for author. Subjects: Architecture, Arts, Bilingual, Biography, Cities, Fiction, History, Italy, Literature (General), Medieval, Non-Fiction, Novels, Renaissance, Translation, Transportation.

Ithuriel's Spear, James Mitchell, 730 Eddy St., #304, San Francisco, CA 94109, (415) 440-3204 / http://www.ithuriel.com. 2004. Poetry, fiction, art, non-fiction. "We are open to all proposals which concern the literary arts." avg. press run 1000. Expects 4 titles 2006, 4 titles 2007. Discounts: 2-10 copies 25%. 84pp. Reporting time: Less than 30 days. Simultaneous submissions accepted: Yes. Publishes 7% of manuscripts submitted. Payment: Variable, please contact publisher. Does not copyright for author. Subjects: Arts, Buddhism, Fiction, Gay, Literature (General), Poetry, San Francisco, Zen.

Ivy House Publishing Group, Janet Evans, Publisher; Benjamin Kay, Acquisitions Editor, 5122 Bur Oak Circle, Raleigh, NC 27612, 919-782-0281. 1993. Poetry, fiction, long-poems, non-fiction. "For more information, please visit *www.ivyhousebooks.com*." avg. press run 1000. Pub'd 40 titles 2005; expects 60 titles 2006, 70 titles 2007. Discounts: 1-4 35%, 5-99 40%, 100+ 45%. 200pp. Reporting time: 4-6 weeks. Simultaneous submissions accepted: Yes. Publishes 50% of manuscripts submitted. Payment: quarterly. Copyrights for author.

IWAN: INMATE WRITERS OF AMERICA NEWSLETTER, Michael D. Navton, Robert E. Plant, Theresa L. Johnson, Box 1673, Glen Burnie, MD 21060, e-mail inwram@netscape.com. 1998. Poetry, fiction, articles, art, cartoons, interviews, satire, criticism, reviews, news items, non-fiction. "Material should not exceed 3000 words. All submissions will be read beginning to end." circ. 120. 6/yr. Pub'd 2 issues 2005; expects 6 issues 2006, 6 issues 2007. sub. price $14; per copy $3; sample $3. Back issues: none. 16pp. Reporting time: 2 weeks. Simultaneous submissions accepted: no. Publishes 50% of manuscripts submitted. Payment: $5-10. Copyrighted, reverts to author. Pub's reviews: 3 in 2005. §Writings from inmates or former inmates, how-to, and good writings in general. Ads: $22/$15/ 1/4 page $7. Subjects: Arts, Literature (General), Prison, Publishing.

J

J & J Consultants, Inc. (see also NEW ALTERNATIVES), Walter Jones Jr., 603 Olde Farm Road, Media, PA 19063, 610-565-9692, Fax 610-565-9694, wjones13@juno.com, www.members.tripod.com/walterjones/. 1997. Poetry, articles, reviews, non-fiction. "Writers needed for magazine *New Alternatives*." avg. press run 250. Pub'd 1 title 2005; expects 1 title 2006. Discounts: 20% trade, 40% wholesale, 50% regional wholesale, 50% jobbers. 112pp. Reporting time: 2 months. Simultaneous submissions accepted: yes. Publishes 50% of manuscripts submitted. Payment: royalty 5% list price/flat fee. Does not copyright for author. Subjects: African-American, Non-Fiction, Poetry, Psychology.

J&W Publishers, Inc., Barbara Peterson, Editor, PO Box 7238, Marietta, GA 30065, (770) 374-2990. 1991. Poetry, fiction, non-fiction. "J&W Publishers publishes paperback originals. Publishes up to 10 titles per year. Royalties vary by project. Publishes book 18 months after acceptance. Responds in 2 months. Specifically, we are interested in innovative, appealing nonfiction subjects such as women's issues, inspirational, self-help, how-to and business." avg. press run 5000. Pub'd 3 titles 2005; expects 4 titles 2006, 10 titles 2007. Discounts: 1 book no discount2-4 books 20% off5-9 books 30% off10-24 books 40% off25-49 books 42% off50-74 books 44% off100-199 books 48% off200 or more books 50% off. 250pp. Reporting time: 2 months. Simultaneous submissions accepted: No. Payment: No advance - 6-15% royalty on wholesale price. Does not copyright for author. Subjects: African-American, Business & Economics, Careers, Communication, Journalism, Divorce,

Family, Gender Issues, How-To, Inspirational, Leadership, Management, Parenting, Relationships, Religion, Self-Help.

J. Mark Press (see also VACATION PLACE RENTALS), Barbara Morris Fischer, PO Box 24-3474, Boynton Beach, FL 33424, www.worldtv3.com/jmark.htm. 1963. Poetry. "3-16 lines, maximum 95 words. Stirring messages, picturesque phrases. No vulgarity. Prefer poets see prize-winning poems on our website. If you have no computer, ask your librarian to get it on the screen. Poems must be accompanied by a SASE or they won't be read and will be disposed of." avg. press run 500. Pub'd 3 titles 2005; expects 6 titles 2006, 6 titles 2007. Discounts: 40%. 82pp. Reporting time: 1 week. Simultaneous submissions accepted: yes. Publishes 40% of manuscripts submitted. Payment: prizes. Copyrights for author. Subjects: Anthology, Family, Haiku, Internet, Poetry, Romance, Spiritual.

JACK MACKEREL MAGAZINE, Rowhouse Press, Greg Bachar, PO Box 23134, Seattle, WA 98102-0434. 1994. Poetry, fiction, articles, art, photos, interviews, criticism, reviews, music, letters, parts-of-novels, long-poems, collages, news items. "Recent contributors: Ann Paiva, William D. Waltz, John Rose, David Berman, Katie J. Kurtz." circ. 500-1M. 4/yr. Pub'd 4 issues 2005; expects 4 issues 2006, 4 issues 2007. sub. price $12; per copy $5; sample $5. Back issues: $5. 40-60pp. Reporting time: 2-4 weeks. Payment: copies. Copyrighted, reverts to author. Pub's reviews: 8 in 2005. §Fiction, poetry, art, artists, photography, physics. Ads: $25/$15/$5 1/4 page. Subjects: Arts, Biography, Book Reviewing, Comics, Dada, Dance, Electronics, Fiction, History, Holography, Language, Literature (General), Mental Health, Music, Philosophy.

Jackson Harbor Press, William H. Olson, RR 1, Box 107AA, 845 Jackson Harbor Road, Washington Island, WI 54246-9048. 1993. Poetry, fiction, non-fiction. "We intend to do primarily regional works (Door County, Wisconsin), but are unable to accept unsolicited manuscripts at this time." avg. press run 1M. Pub'd 3 titles 2005; expects 2 titles 2006, 2 titles 2007. Discounts: 2-4 20%, 5-9 30%, 10+ 40%. 64pp. Reporting time: 2 weeks. Payment: each arrangement will be individually negotiated. Copyrights for author. Subjects: Cooking, Great Lakes, Haiku, History, Novels, Poetry, Wisconsin.

JAFFE INTERNATIONAL, Jaffe Publishing Management Service, Kunnuparambil P. Punnoose, Kunnuparambil Buildings, Kurichy, Kottayam 686549, India, 91-481-430470; FAX 91-481-561190. 1975. Interviews, criticism, reviews. "*Jaffe International* is a book promotion journal specialising in promoting American small press books and magazines in India and other Asian countries." circ. 3M. 4/yr. Pub'd 4 issues 2005; expects 4 issues 2006, 4 issues 2007. sub. price $10; per copy $2.50; sample same. Back issues: not available. Discounts: 15% on the annual subscription price. 48pp. Reporting time: 3 months. Payment: in copies. Copyrighted, reverts to author. Pub's reviews: 200 in 2005. §All subjects of human interest. Ads: $200/$125. Subjects: Book Collecting, Bookselling, Publishing.

Jaffe Publishing Management Service (see also JAFFE INTERNATIONAL), Nicy Jacob, Kunnuparambil Buildings, Kurichy, Kottayam 686549, India, phone/fax 91-481-430470. 1985. "Jaffe specializes in publishing reports, manuals, directories, group catalogs, etc. for the book and magazine publishing industry." avg. press run 1.1M. Pub'd 2 titles 2005; expects 2 titles 2006, 2 titles 2007. Discounts: 25%. 96pp. Reporting time: 3 months. Payment: 10% on the published price on copies sold, payment annually. Copyrights for author. Subjects: Book Collecting, Bookselling, Publishing.

Jako Books, Gablewoods South, PO Box VF665, Vieux Fort, St. Lucia, West Indies, 758-454-7839, info@jakoproductions.com, www.jakoproductions.com. 1999. Poetry, fiction, articles, art, photos, cartoons, interviews, criticism, reviews, music, letters, long-poems, news items, non-fiction. avg. press run 1000. Pub'd 1 title 2005; expects 2 titles 2006, 2 titles 2007. Simultaneous submissions accepted: yes. Subjects: African Literature, Africa, African Studies, Arts, Black, Book Reviewing, Caribbean, Criticism, Culture, Current Affairs, Fiction, Literary Review, Literature (General), Multicultural, Non-Fiction, Poetry, Short Stories.

Jalmar Press/Innerchoice Publishing, Cathy Winch, Editor; Susanna Palomares, Editor, PO Box 370, Fawnskin, CA 92333, Fax 909 866 2961 Email: info@jalmarpress.com. 1973. Non-fiction. "Affiliated with B.L. Winch Group, Inc. Primarily interested in activity driven materials for school counselors, school psychologists and other child care givers to use with children to develop their social, emotional, and ethical skills. Topics include: Self Esteem, Conflict Resolution, Anger Management, Character Development, Emotional Intelligence, etc. Have four series: 1) *Transactional Analysis for Everybody*, Warm Fuzzy Series, 2) *Conflict Resolution Series*, 3) *Right-Brain/Whole-Brain Learning Series*, 4) *Positive Self-Esteem Series*. Titles in *TA for Everybody Series*: Freed, Alvyn M. *TA for Tots (and Other Prinzes)*; Freed, Alvyn & Margaret *TA for Kids (and Grown-ups, too)*, 3rd edition newly revised and illustrated. Freed, Alvyn M. *TA for Teens (and Other Important People)*; Freed, Alvyn M. *TA for Tots Coloring Book. TA for Tots* Vol. II - Alvyn M. Freed. Steiner, Claude *Original Warm Fuzzy Tale; Songs of the Warm Fuzzy* cassette (all about your feelings)." avg. press run 1.5M. Pub'd 5 titles 2005; expects 6 titles 2006, 8 titles 2007. Discounts: trade 25-45%; agent/jobber 25-50%. 192pp. Reporting time: 4 weeks. Simultaneous submissions accepted: yes. Publishes 1% of manuscripts submitted. Payment: 7.5%-12.5% of net receipts. Copyrights for author. Subjects: Adolescence, Alcohol,

Alcoholism, Children, Youth, Divorce, Drugs, Education, Ethics, Grieving, Guidance, Motivation, Success, Non-Fiction, Non-Violence, Parenting, Sexual Abuse, Young Adult.

JAM RAG, Tom Ness, Box 20076, Ferndale, MI 48220-0076, 248-336-9243. 1985. Articles, photos, cartoons, interviews, satire, criticism, reviews, music, letters, news items. circ. 12M. 12/yr. Pub'd 12 issues 2005; expects 12 issues 2006, 12 issues 2007. sub. price $23; sample $1. Back issues: $1. Discounts: $5 per 100. 40pp. Simultaneous submissions accepted: yes. Publishes 20% of manuscripts submitted. Payment: varies. Not copyrighted, rights revert to author on publication. Pub's reviews: 10-15 in 2005. §Political, music, arts, philosophy. Ads: $648/$360/up to 30% disc./class $2/10 words. Subjects: Entertainment, Environment, Human Rights, Michigan, Music, Politics, Tapes & Records.

Jamenair Ltd., Peter K. Studner, PO Box 241957, Los Angeles, CA 90024-9757, 310-470-6688. 1986. Non-fiction. ''Books and software related to job search and career changing.'' avg. press run 10M. Discounts: depends on quantity. 352pp. Reporting time: 30 days. Payment: open, depends on material. Copyrights for author. Subjects: Business & Economics, Computers, Calculators, Education, Employment, How-To, Textbooks.

John James Company, George Keller, 79 Worth Street, New York, NY 10013, 212-431-3235, Fax 212-625-9823, jjpublishing@msn.com. 2000. Fiction. avg. press run 3M. Pub'd 2 titles 2005; expects 3 titles 2006, 3 titles 2007. Discounts: wholesalers 50%, bookstores min. qty. (6) 50%. 350pp. Simultaneous submissions accepted: no. Publishes 1% of manuscripts submitted. Payment: varies. Copyrights for author. Subjects: Fiction, France, French, History, Memoirs.

JAMES DICKEY NEWSLETTER, William Thesing, Editor, University of South Carolina, English Department, Columbia, SC 29208, 803-777-7073. 1984. Poetry, articles, interviews, reviews, long-poems. ''Mss. of all lengths are considered. All material should concern James Dickey/his work and includes comparative studies. We publish a few poems of *very* high caliber. Recent: Linda Roth, Gordon Van Ness, and John Van Peenen.'' circ. 200. 2/yr. Pub'd 2 issues 2005; expects 2 issues 2006, 2 issues 2007. sub. price $12 USA individuals, $14 institutions, outside USA: $12 indiv., $15 instit.; per copy $8; sample $8. Back issues: $8. Discounts: 25% to jobbers. 50pp. Reporting time: one month. Simultaneous submissions accepted: no. Publishes a variable % of manuscripts submitted. Payment: 2 copies. Copyrighted, reverts to author. Pub's reviews: 2-4 in 2005. §Modern American, work of or about James Dickey only. Ads: full page flyer inserted $100—one time. Subject: James Dickey.

JAMES JOYCE BROADSHEET, Pieter Bekker, Editor; Richard Brown, Editor-in-Chief; Alistair Stead, Editor, School of English, University of Leeds, West Yorkshire LS2 9JT, England, 0113-233-4739. 1980. Poetry, articles, art, photos, cartoons, criticism, reviews, letters, news items. circ. 800. 3/yr. Pub'd 3 issues 2005; expects 3 issues 2006, 3 issues 2007. sub. price £7.50 Europe (£6 for students)/$18 ($15 for students elsewhere); per copy £2 plus 50p postage Europe ($6 including postage elsewhere); sample £2/$4. Back issues: at current annual subscription rate. Discounts: 33-1/3% to bookshops only. 4-6pp. Reporting time: 6 months-1 year. Payment: none. Copyrighted. Pub's reviews: 15 in 2005. §Modern literature, James Joyce, contemporary criticism. Ads: Please inquire. Subjects: Book Reviewing, Criticism, Ireland, James Joyce, Literary Review, Literature (General), Reviews, Translation, Visual Arts.

JAMES JOYCE QUARTERLY, University of Tulsa, Sean Latham, Editor; Carol Kealiher, Managing Editor, University of Tulsa, 600 S. College, Tulsa, OK 74104, phone 918-631-2501, fax 918-631-2065, www.utulsa.edu/JJoyceQtrly. 1963. Articles, criticism, reviews. ''Academic criticism of Joyce's works; book reviews, notes, bibliographies; material relating to Joyce and Irish Renaissance and Joyce's relationship to other writers of his time. Articles should not normally exceed 20 pp. Notes should not excceed 6 pp. Please consult the Chicago Manual of Style and the "Special Note to Contributors" that appears on inside back cover of each issue of the *JJQ* regarding style and preparation of manuscript.'' circ. 1500. 4/yr. Pub'd 4 issues 2005; expects 4 issues 2006, 4 issues 2007. sub. price $22 U.S., $24 foreign; per copy $15.00; sample $15.00. Back issues: for back issues, write Swets & Zeitlinger, Heereweg 347b, Lisse, The Netherlands. 150pp. Reporting time: 4-5 months. Simultaneous submissions accepted: no. Publishes 40% of manuscripts submitted. Payment: contributors' copies & offprints. Copyrighted, does not revert to author. Pub's reviews: approx. 50 in 2005. §Joyce studies, modernism. Ads: $200. Subjects: James Joyce, Literary Review.

J'ECRIS, Jean Guenot, BP 101, Saint-Cloud 92216, France, (1) 47-71-79-63. 1987. ''Specialized on technical data concerning creative writing for French writers.'' circ. 2M. 4/yr. Pub'd 4 issues 2005; expects 4 issues 2006, 4 issues 2007. sub. price $47; per copy $12; sample free. Back issues: $10. 32pp. Payment: yes. Copyrighted, reverts to author. Pub's reviews: 15 in 2005. §Only books dealing with creative writing techniques. No ads. Subjects: Fiction, Literature (General), Printing, Writers/Writing.

Jessee Poet Publications (see also POETS AT WORK), Jessee Poet, PO Box 232, Lyndora, PA 16045. 1985. Poetry, long-poems. ''Chapbook publisher, send SASE for price. National contests (poetry) sponsor, send SASE for details.'' Reporting time: 2 weeks. Simultaneous submissions accepted: yes. Publishes 100% of manuscripts submitted. Payment: none. Does not copyright for author. Subject: Printing.

Jetbak Publishing, 1258 S. Fenway Street, Casper, WY 82601-4022.

JetKor, Sherri Del Soldato, PO Box 33238, Reno, NV 89533, 775-846-1185, Fax 775-746-4649, sdelsol@gbis.com, www.jetkor.com. 1999. Poetry, fiction, art, photos, cartoons, satire, non-fiction. "Currently we are only publishing in eBook format and the New StoriBook CD format. We are looking for young adult and children titles at this time. However, all submissions will be considered." avg. press run unlimited with eBooks, 2M for all other. Pub'd 3 titles 2005; expects 8 titles 2006, 16 titles 2007. Pages vary. Reporting time: 90 days. Simultaneous submissions accepted: yes. Publishes 65% of manuscripts submitted. Payment: royalties vary and quarterly payments. We assist with the copyright process. Subjects: Children, Youth, Earth, Natural History, Fiction, Gardening, Humor, Nature, Novels, Physics, Picture Books, Poetry, Romance, Science, Short Stories, Weather, Yoga.

‡**JEWISH CURRENTS,** Lawrence Bush, Editor, 45 E 33 Street 4th floor, New York, NY 10016, 212-889-2523, Fax 212-532-7518. 1946. Poetry, fiction, articles, art, photos, interviews, satire, criticism, reviews, letters, news items, non-fiction. "Articles of Jewish interest, progressive politics, Black-Jewish relations, 2M-3M words; reviews of books, records, plays, films, events, 1.8M-2M words; lively style, hard facts, secular p.o.v., pro-Israel/non-Zionist." circ. 14M. 6/yr. Pub'd 6 issues 2005; expects 6 issues 2006, 6 issues 2007. sub. price $30; per copy $5; Free sample. Back issues: $5. Discounts: 40% retail/25% subscription agency. 40pp—except Dec., 60pp (average). Reporting time: 2 months. Simultaneous submissions accepted: no. Publishes 30% of manuscripts submitted. Payment: 6 copies + subscription. Copyrighted. Pub's reviews: 30 in 2005. §Jewish affairs, political & cultural, feminism, civil rights, labor history, Holocaust resistance, Black-Jewish relations, Yiddish culture, Mideast peace process. Ads: $250/180/120/50 - for 2 col. inch (greetings and memorials); $1000/800/750/450/400/300 2-1/2 col. inch (commercial ads). Subjects: History, Judaism, Middle East, Politics, Socialist.

Jewish Publication Society, Ellen Frankel Dr., CEO; Rena Potok Dr., Senior Acquisitions Editor, 2100 Arch Street, Philadelphia, PA 19103-1308, 215-802-0600, Fax 215-568-2017. 1888. Art, photos, cartoons, non-fiction. avg. press run 3M. Pub'd 10 titles 2005; expects 15 titles 2006, 12 titles 2007. Discounts: normal trade. 350pp. Reporting time: 6-9 months. Simultaneous submissions accepted: yes. Publishes less than 10% of manuscripts submitted. Payment: modest advance and royalties. Copyrights for author. Subject: Judaism.

JEWISH WOMEN'S LITERARY ANNUAL, Henny Wenkart, National Council of Jewish Women NY Section, 820 Second Ave., New York, NY 10017-4504, 212-687-5030 ext.33/fax212-687-5032. 1994-95. "Poetry, fiction, art by Jewish women. No deadlines, we read continuously." 1/yr. sub. price $18 three issues; per copy $7.50. Back issues: available. 200pp. Simultaneous submissions accepted: yes. Payment: $15min., $5add.p.

Jireh Publishing Company, Janice Holman, P.O. Box 1911, Suisun City, CA 94585-1911, (510) 276-3322, (FAX: 425-645-0423), www.jirehpublishing.com. 1995. Fiction, non-fiction. "Supply readers with thought-provoking and character-building Christian books and study materials that will affect a change in their lives forever. Our focus is on general non-fiction works, such as Prayer, Health, Single's Issues, How-to's, Charismatic. Fiction genres: Suspense, Romance/Suspense, and mystery." avg. press run 500. Pub'd 2 titles 2005; expects 3 titles 2006, 4 titles 2007. Discounts: 10-25 copies 30%26-50 copies 35%51-100 copies 42%101-200 copies 45%201+ copies 50%. 325pp. Reporting time: 4 to 6 weeks. Simultaneous submissions accepted: Yes. Publishes 2% of manuscripts submitted. Payment: No advances. Royalty 12%. Copyrights for author. Subjects: Christianity, Fiction, Health, How-To, Non-Fiction, Self-Help, Singles, Trade.

JLA Publications, A Division Of Jeffrey Lant Associates, Inc., Dr. Jeffrey Lant, President, 50 Follen Street #507, Cambridge, MA 02138, 617-547-6372, drjlant@worldprofit.com, www.worldprofit.com and www.jeffreylant.com. 1979. Non-fiction. "We are interested in publishing books of particular interest to small businesses, entrepreneurs and independent professionals. To get an idea of what we publish, simply write us at the above address and request a current catalog. Up until now our titles have been all more than 100,000 words in length and are widely regarded as the most detailed books on their subjects. Recent books include Lant's *Multi Level Money*, Jeffrey Lant's Revised Third Edition of *Money Talks: The Complete Guide to Creating a Profitable Workshop or Seminar in any Field* and Lant's book *Cash Copy: How to Offer Your Products and Services So Your Prospects Buy Them...Now!* We are now open, however, to shorter (though still very specific and useful) books in the 50,000-75,000 word length and titles in human development as well as business development. We are different because we pay royalties *monthly* and get our authors very involved in the publicity process. We do not pay advances for material but do promote strenuously." avg. press run 4M-5M. Pub'd 7 titles 2005; expects 2 titles 2006, 5 titles 2007. Discounts: 1-9 copies 20%, 10-99 40% (you pay shipping); thence negotiable up to 60% discount on major orders. 300+pp. Reporting time: 30-60 days. Payment: 10%, monthly. Copyrights for author. Subjects: Business & Economics, Communication, Journalism, How-To, Printing.

238

Joelle Publishing, Norman Russell, PO Box 91229, Santa Barbara, CA 93190, 805-962-9887. 1987. Non-fiction. avg. press run 5M. Expects 2 titles 2006, 3 titles 2007. Discounts: trade 40%, jobber 55%, library 20%. 140pp. Reporting time: 3 weeks. Simultaneous submissions accepted: yes. Payment: to be arranged. Copyrights for author. Subjects: Health, Psychology.

JONES AV, Paul Schwartz, 88 Dagmar Av, Toronto, Ontario M4M 1W1, Canada, www.interlog.com/~oel. 1994. Poetry, art, photos, concrete art. "We are a chap book size poetry journal. All styles, but no rhymed poetry unless it is really, really good." circ. 100. 4/yr. Pub'd 4 issues 2005; expects 4 issues 2006, 4 issues 2007. sub. price $12 for Canada and US. Please query for other countries.; per copy $3 for Canada and US. Please query for other countries.; sample $3 for Canada and US. Please query for other countries. Back issues: $2 or $3 (as per original price) for Canada and US. Please query for other countries. 24pp. Reporting time: 3 months. Simultaneous submissions accepted: No. Publishes 50% of manuscripts submitted. Payment: contributor's copy. Copyrighted, reverts to author. Pub's reviews: approx 16 in 2005. §poetry. Subjects: Arts, Poetry.

THE JOURNAL, Kathy Fagan, Michelle Herman, OSU Dept. of English, 164 W. 17th Avenue, 421 Denney Hall, Columbus, OH 43210-1370, 614-292-4076, fax 614-292-7816, thejournal@osu.edu. 1973. Poetry, fiction, interviews, reviews, parts-of-novels, long-poems, non-fiction. "We are looking for quality poetry, fiction, nonfiction, and reviews of poetry collections." circ. 1.6M. 2/yr. Pub'd 2 issues 2005; expects 2 issues 2006, 2 issues 2007. sub. price $12; per copy $7; sample $7. Back issues: $3. 140pp. Reporting time: 3 months. Simultaneous submissions accepted: yes, if informed. Publishes 5% of manuscripts submitted. Payment: $30. Copyrighted, reverts to author. Pub's reviews: 4 in 2005. §Poetry. Ads: $100/$50. Subjects: Essays, Fiction, Interviews, Ohio, Poetry, Reviews.

THE JOURNAL (once "of Contemporary Anglo-Scandinavian Poetry"), Original Plus, Sam Smith, 18 Oxford Grove, Flat 3, Devon. EX34 9HQ, England, 01271862708; e-mail smithsssj@aol.com. 1994. Poetry, reviews. "We publish all types and length of poetry, from a ten page narrative poem by Genista Lewes in #5 to occasional haiku." circ. 150. 3/yr. Pub'd 3 issues 2005; expects 3 issues 2006, 3 issues 2007. sub. price $11 US, £7 UK; per copy $5US, £2.50 UK; sample £3. Back issues: £2. Discounts: 25%. 40xA4pp. Reporting time: 2-4 weeks. Simultaneous submissions accepted: no (but will consider previously published material). Publishes 2% of manuscripts submitted. Payment: 1 copy. Copyrighted, reverts to author. Pub's reviews: 35 in 2005. §contemporary poetry.

JOURNAL FRANCAIS, Anne Prah-Perochon, France Precourt, 944 Market Street, Suite 210, San Francisco, CA 94102, 415-981-9088 ext. 705, Fax 415-981-9177, fprecourt@journalfrancais.com, www.journal-francais.com. Articles, interviews, reviews. circ. 15.000/month. 12/year. Pub'd 12 issues 2005; expects 12 issues 2006, 12 issues 2007. sub. price $45; per copy $4.25. Back issues: $4.25 + $2 p/h. 32pp. Pub's reviews: 30 in 2005. §Any books or products having a link to France or French culture.

JOURNAL OF AESTHETICS AND ART CRITICISM, Susan Feagin, Editor, Dept of Philosophy, Anderson Hall, 7th Floor, Temple University, Philadelphia, PA 19122, 502-852-0458, FAX 502-852-0459, email jaac@blue.temple.edu. 1940. "JAAC is the journal of The American Society for Aesthetics, an interdisciplinary society which promotes study, research, discussion and publication in aesthetics." circ. 2.7M. 4/yr. Pub'd 4 issues 2005; expects 4 issues 2006, 4 issues 2007. sub. price $60. 130pp. Reporting time: less than 3 months. Simultaneous submissions accepted: no. Publishes 10% of manuscripts submitted. Payment: none. Copyrighted, does not revert to author. Pub's reviews: 50 in 2005. §Aesthetics, literature, and the arts. Subjects: Arts, Creativity, Criticism, Culture, Dada, Drama, Electronics, English, Fiction, Folklore, Humor, Music, Philosophy, Post Modern, Visual Arts.

THE JOURNAL OF AFRICAN TRAVEL-WRITING, Amber Vogel, PO Box 346, Chapel Hill, NC 27514. 1996. Poetry, fiction, articles, art, photos, interviews, reviews, letters, non-fiction. circ. 600. 1/yr. Pub'd 2 issues 2005; expects 1 issue 2006, 1 issue 2007. sub. price $10; per copy $6; sample $6. 192pp. Reporting time: 4-6 weeks. Simultaneous submissions accepted: no. Publishes 5% of manuscripts submitted. Payment: copies. Copyrighted, reverts to author. Pub's reviews: 6 in 2005. §Africa, travel. Subjects: African Literature, Africa, African Studies, Book Reviewing, Essays, Geography, Non-Fiction, Reviews, Short Stories, Transportation, Travel.

JOURNAL OF ASIAN MARTIAL ARTS, Via Media Publishing Company, Michael A. DeMarco, 821 West 24th Street, Erie, PA 16502, 814-455-9517; fax 814-526-5262; e-mail info@goviamedia.com; website www.goviamedia.com. 1991. Articles, art, photos, interviews, reviews, non-fiction. "Article length and topic is open to anything dealing with Asian martial arts. Author must be very familiar with the subject and the history and culture discussed." circ. 12M. 4/yr. Pub'd 4 issues 2005; expects 4 issues 2006, 4 issues 2007. sub. price $32; per copy $10; sample $10. Discounts: regular discounts offered. 124pp. Reporting time: 1-2 months. Simultaneous submissions accepted: no. Publishes 10% of manuscripts submitted. Payment: $75 to $500 for feature articles. Copyrighted, reverts to author. Pub's reviews: 14 in 2005. §Asian martial arts and related topics. Ads: $1,950; $590; $395 1/4 page. Subjects: Asia, Indochina, Martial Arts, Sports, Outdoors, T'ai Chi.

•JOURNAL OF BRITISH STUDIES, University of Chicago Press, Anna Clark, University of Minnesota, Dept. of History, 614 Soc Sci Tower, 267 19th Ave., S., Minneapolis, MN 55445, http://www.journals.uchicago.edu/JBS/home.html. 1961. "The *Journal of British Studies* is the premier journal devoted to the study of British history and culture. Our editors and board give the journal an unparalleled sweep from the medieval to the early modern, eighteenth-century, Victorian and twentieth-century periods, and provide a new interdisciplinary range. Its extensive book review section and review essays also make it the journal of record for reviews." 4/yr. Pub's reviews.

THE JOURNAL OF CALIFORNIA AND GREAT BASIN ANTHROPOLOGY, Malki Museum Press, Debra Jenkins Garcia, P.O. Box 578, Banning, CA 92220, 951-849-7289,951-849-3549, malkipress@aol.com, malkimuseum.org. 1974. Articles, interviews, non-fiction. "Quality articles dealing with ethnography, ethno history, languages, arts, archeology and prehistory of the Native peoples of Alta and Baja California and the Great Basin region." circ. 500. 2/yr. Pub'd 2 issues 2005; expects 2 issues 2006, 2 issues 2007. sub. price 40.00; per copy 20.00; sample 20.00. Back issues: 20.00. Discounts: 20% Museum Members. 270pp. Reporting time: 30-90 daus. Simultaneous submissions accepted: No. Publishes 90% of manuscripts submitted. Copyrighted, does not revert to author. Pub's reviews: 4 in 2005. §Anthropolgy, Archeology, Native American culture, lingusitics, ethnobotanicals, history. Ads: Full page $134.00, Half page $90.00, Quarter page $45.00. Subjects: Agriculture, Animals, Anthropology, Archaelogy, Language, Myth, Mythology, Native American, Weaving.

JOURNAL OF CANADIAN POETRY, Borealis Press Limited, Frank M. Tierney, Advertising Editor; W. Glenn Clever, Business Editor; David Staines, General Editor, 110 Bloomingdale Street, Ottawa, Ont. K2C 4A4, Canada, 613-797-9299, Fax 613-798-9747. 1976. Criticism, reviews. "Concerned solely with criticism and reviews of Canadian poetry. Does *not* publish poetry per se; we are a critical journal." circ. 500. 1/yr. Pub'd 1 issue 2005; expects 1 issue 2006, 1 issue 2007. sub. price $22.20 Canada, $20.95 others; $41.30/2 years Cdn., $39 others, $56.97/3 years Cdn. $53 others; per copy $12.95; sample $5. Back issues: $5. Discounts: book wholesalers 20%. 150pp. Reporting time: 4 months. Payment: none. Copyrighted, reverts to author. Pub's reviews: 40 in 2005. §Poetry only (Canadian). Ads: inquire. Subjects: Criticism, Poetry.

JOURNAL OF CELTIC LINGUISTICS, University Of Wales Press, David Cram, Editor; Donal O Baoill, Editor; Erich Poppe, Editor; David Thorne, Editor; James Fife, Editor, 10 Columbus Walk, Brigantine Place, Cardiff CF10 4UP, Wales, 44-029-2049-6899, Fax 44-029-2049-6108, press@press.wales.ac.uk, www.wales.ac.uk/press. Articles, reviews. circ. 500. Pub'd 1 issue 2005. price per copy £20.00. Discounts: 10%. 128pp. Payment: none. Copyrighted, reverts to author. Pub's reviews. §Linguistics. Ads: £75/£37.50. Subject: Language.

JOURNAL OF CHILD AND YOUTH CARE, Gerry Fewster, Editor; Thom Garfat, Editor, Malaspina University-College, Human Services, 900 5th Street, Nanaimo, BC V9R 5S5, Canada, 250-753-3245 X2207, Fax 250-741-2224, conlin@mala.bc.ca. 1981. Poetry, fiction, articles, art, photos, reviews, non-fiction. "This journal is primarily intended for child and youth care workers and all individuals who assume the responsibility for the well being of children." circ. 375. 4/yr. Pub'd 4 issues 2005; expects 4 issues 2006, 4 issues 2007. sub. price $49.50 indiv., $71.50 instit., in Canada add GST, outside Canada, price in U.S. dollars; per copy $18 + GST in Canada, outside Canada in US dollars. Back issues: $18 + GST in Canada, outside Canada in US dollars. 106pp. Reporting time: 8 months. Simultaneous submissions accepted: yes. Payment: none. Copyrighted, does not revert to author. Pub's reviews: 1 in 2005. §Child and youth care theory and practice. Ads: write for information. Subjects: Children, Youth, Community, Family, Sexual Abuse, Social Work.

THE JOURNAL OF COMMONWEALTH LITERATURE, John Thieme, Geraldine Stoneham, Bowker-Saur, Windsor Court, East Grinstead House, E. Grinstead, W. Sussex RH19 1XA, England, +44(0)1342-336122, Fax +44(0)1342-336197. 1965. Articles, interviews, non-fiction. "Maximum length for articles: 4M words. Oxford style. Style guide available on request. Published by: Bowker-Saur part of Reed Business Information." 3/yr. Pub'd 3 issues 2005; expects 3 issues 2006, 3 issues 2007. sub. price £105 ($170); per copy negotiable; sample inquire, at publisher's discretion. Back issues: negotiable. 128-256pp. Reporting time: 6 months. Simultaneous submissions accepted: no. Payment: £10 a page for bibliographers; no payment to other contributors. Copyrighted, does not revert to author. Subjects: Bibliography, Literary Review.

JOURNAL OF COURT REPORTING, National Court Reporters Association Press, Peter Wacht, Editor, 8224 Old Courthouse Road, Vienna, VA 22182, 703-556-6272, fax 703-556-6291, email pwacht@ncrahq.org. 1899. Cartoons, interviews, reviews, letters, news items, non-fiction. "Focus should be on stenographic court reporting and its various aspects such as ethics, technology, business. 500-2,000 words. Recent contributors: Richard Lederer, Rita Henley Jensen." circ. 30M. 10/yr. Pub'd 10 issues 2005; expects 10 issues 2006, 10 issues 2007. sub. price $49; per copy $5. Back issues: $5. Discounts: none. 132pp. Reporting time: 1-2 months. Accepts simultaneous submissions depending on where other submissions are sent. Publishes 50%-75% of manuscripts submitted. Payment: varies. Copyrighted, reverts to author. Pub's reviews: 15-30 in 2005. §Business, reference, law or medical related. Ads: $1,300/$815/varies. Subjects: Book Reviewing, Business & Economics, Language, Law, Management, Marketing.

JOURNAL OF CURRICULUM THEORIZING, Caddo Gap Press, Marla Morris, 3145 Geary Boulevard, PMB 275, San Francisco, CA 94118. Articles, art, photos, criticism, reviews. "Articles, commentary, art, opinion related to curriculum theory and practice." circ. 500. 4/yr. Pub'd 4 issues 2005; expects 4 issues 2006, 4 issues 2007. sub. price $75 ind., $150 inst.; per copy $20. Back issues: $20. Discounts: 15% to subscription agencies. 160pp. Reporting time: 2 months. Simultaneous submissions accepted: no. Publishes 50% of manuscripts submitted. Payment: none. Copyrighted, reverts to author. Pub's reviews. §Curriculum theory. Ads: $200 full page. Subject: Education.

THE JOURNAL OF DESIGN AND TECHNOLOGY EDUCATION, Trentham Books, Richard Kimbell, Westview House, 734 London Road, Oakhill, Stoke-on-Trent, Staffordshire ST4 5NP, England, 01782-745567, Fax 01782-745553. 1966. Articles, photos, cartoons, interviews, criticism, reviews, letters, concrete art, news items. "Prints articles on new developments in the whole field of design and technology education ranging from art through to applied science and technology." circ. 5M. 3/yr. Pub'd 2 issues 2005; expects 2 issues 2006, 3 issues 2007. sub. price £45 UK, £55 ROW; per copy £18; sample £18. Back issues: £18. Discounts: 10% series disc/w ads. 92pp. Reporting time: max. 1 month, usually 2 weeks. Payment: none. Copyrighted, rights held by magazine. Pub's reviews: 66 in 2005. §Craft, art, design, education. Ads: £400 full page back cover/£350 full page inner cover/£110 1/2 page/£55 1/4 page/£30 1/8 page. Subjects: Crafts, Hobbies, Education.

THE JOURNAL OF HISTORICAL REVIEW, Mark Weber, PO Box 2739, Newport Beach, CA 92659, 949-631-1490, ihr@ihr.org. 1979. Articles, reviews, non-fiction. "We specialize in historical material, notably from the Second World War, with an emphasis on revisionist viewpoints, especially of the 'Holocaust.'" circ. 1.5M. 6/yr. Pub'd 6 issues 2005; expects 6 issues 2006, 6 issues 2007. sub. price $40; per copy $7.50; sample $7.50. Back issues: $7.50. Discounts: 20% on books we distribute, 40% on books we publish (for booksellers). 40pp. Reporting time: varies. Simultaneous submissions accepted: no. Publishes 5% of manuscripts submitted. Payment: varies. Copyrighted. Pub's reviews: 10+ in 2005. §19th & 20th century history. Ads: $500/$300. Subjects: Europe, History, Holocaust, Middle East, World War II.

JOURNAL OF MENTAL IMAGERY, Akhter Ahsen Ph.D., c/o Brandon House, PO Box 240, Bronx, NY 10471. 1977. Articles, reviews. circ. 6.3M in USA, 9.6M in foreign countries. 4/yr. Pub'd 4 issues 2005. sub. price $50; per copy $25; sample free. Back issues: same as current prices. Discounts: none. 92pp. Reporting time: 2 months. Payment: none. Copyrighted, reverts to author. Pub's reviews: 4 in 2005. §Mental imagery. Subject: Psychology.

THE JOURNAL OF MIND AND BEHAVIOR, The Institute of Mind and Behavior, Raymond Russ, Editor, PO Box 522, Village Station, New York, NY 10014, 212-595-4853. 1980. Articles, criticism, reviews, letters, non-fiction. "*The Journal Of Mind And Behavior* (*JMB*) is an academic journal dedicated to the interdisciplinary approach within psychology and related fields—building upon the assumption of a unified science. The editors are particularly interested in scholarly work in the following areas: the psychology, philosophy, and sociology of experimentation and the scientific method; the relationship between methodology, operationism, and theory construction; the mind-body problem in the social sciences, literature, and art; issues pertaining to the ethical study of cognition, self-awareness, and higher functions of consciousness in animals; mind-body interactions and medical implications; philosophical impact of a mind-body epistemology upon psychology; historical perspectives on the course and nature of science. All manuscripts *must* follow style and preparation of the *Publication Manual of the American Psychological Association* (fourth edition, 1994) and be submitted in quadruplicate for review to: Dr. Raymond Russ, Department of Psychology, 5742 Little Hall, University of Maine, Orono, ME 04469-5742." circ. 1.2M. 4/yr. Pub'd 4 issues 2005; expects 4 issues 2006, 4 issues 2007. sub. price individual $46/yr, $85/2 yrs, $130/3 yrs, institutional $130/yr, $262/2 yrs, $390/3 yrs; per copy $18; sample free. Back issues: $130/3 yrs. individual; $390/3 yrs. institution (special package available upon request). Discounts: 15% on order of 10 copies or more. 145pp. Reporting time: 10-15 weeks. Publishes 12% of manuscripts submitted. Payment: none. Copyrighted, does not revert to author. Pub's reviews: 18 in 2005. §Psychology (both thoeretical and experimental), philosophy, history of science, medicine, art. Ads: $230/$130/discounts on multiple runs. Subjects: Literature (General), Philosophy, Psychology, Society, Sociology.

JOURNAL OF MUSIC IN IRELAND (JMI), Toner Quinn, Edenvale, Esplanade, Bray, Co Wicklow, Ireland, 00-353-1-2867292 phone/Fax, editor@thejmi.com, www.thejmi.com. 2000. Articles, interviews, satire, criticism, reviews, music, letters, news items, non-fiction. "800-7,000 word articles. Articles by Ireland's most respected composers and musicians." circ. 6000. 6/yr. Pub'd 6 issues 2005; expects 6 issues 2006, 6 issues 2007. sub. price 35 euro; per copy 4.95 euro. Back issues: 5 euro plus postage. 44pp. Reporting time: 2 weeks. Simultaneous submissions accepted: yes. Publishes 50% of manuscripts submitted. Payment: negotiated. Copyrighted, reverts to author. Pub's reviews: 12 in 2005. §Music—contemporary/classical, jazz, folk/tradition.

Subjects: Ireland, Music.

JOURNAL OF MUSICOLOGY, University of California Press, John Nadas, Editor, University of California Press, 2000 Center Street, Suite 303, Berkeley, CA 94704-1223, 510-643-7154. 1972. Articles, reviews, non-fiction. "Editorial address: CB #3320, Hill Hall, University of North Carolina, Chapel Hill, NC 27599-3320." circ. 651. 4/yr. Pub'd 4 issues 2005; expects 4 issues 2006, 4 issues 2007. sub. price $42 indiv., $141 instit., $27 students (+ $20 air freight); per copy $16 indiv., $40 instit., $16 students (+ $20 air freight); sample free. Back issues: same as single copy price. Discounts: foreign subs. agent 10%, one-time order 10+ 30%, standing orders (bookstores) 1-99 40%, 100+ 50%. 128pp. Reporting time: 1-2 months. Payment: varies. Copyrighted, does not revert to author. Pub's reviews: 8-10 in 2005. Ads: $295/$220. Subject: Music.

JOURNAL OF NARRATIVE THEORY, James A. Knapp, Co-Editor; Laura George, Co-Editor, Eastern Michigan University, 614J Pray-Harrold Hall, Eng. Dept., Ypsilanti, MI 48197, 734-487-3175, Fax 734-483-9744, website www.emich.edu/public/english/JNT/JNT.html. 1971. Criticism. "Since its inception in 1971, as the *Journal of Narrative Technique*, the *JNT* has provided a forum for the theoretical exploration of individual narrative texts. The *Journal of Narrative Theory* publishes essays that address the intersections between narrative, history, technology, ideology, and culture. The editors are particularly interested in essays that rethink narrative theory. Contributors should follow the MLA Handbook (5th ed.). Articles of fewer than 3,000 words or greater than 12,000 words are not considered for publication. Recent contributors: Abigail Lynn Coykendall "Bodies Cinematic, Bodies Politic: The 'Male' Gaze and the 'Female' Gothic in De Palma's *Carrie*" 30.3 (Fall 2000) Winner of the Florence Howe Award for Outstanding Feminist Scholarship. Jan Baetens "Going to Heaven: A Missing Link in the History of Photonarrative?" 31.1 (Winter 2001). M. Kellen Williams "'Where All Things Sacred and Profane Are Turned Into Copy': Flesh, Fact, and Fiction in Joseph Conrad's *The Secret Agent*" 32.1 (Winter 2002). Katerina Clark "M. M. Bakhtin and 'World Literature'" 32.3 (Fall 2002)." circ. 600. 3/yr. Pub'd 3 issues 2005; expects 3 issues 2006, 3 issues 2007. sub. price $25 libraries and institutions, $20 individuals, $10 postal surcharge outside the US; per copy $8; sample free. Back issues: $8. Discounts: 20% to subscription agents. 130pp. Reporting time: 1-4 months. Simultaneous submissions accepted: no. Publishes 10-15% of manuscripts submitted. Payment: offprints and copies only. Copyrighted, does not revert to author. Ads: Full page, 4 x 7 inches, $175. Half page horizontal, 4 x 3 inches, $150. Half page vertical, 2 x 7 inches, $150. Cover, 34 x 7 inches, $250. Subjects: Asian-American, Communism, Marxism, Leninism, Criticism, English, Fiction, Gay, History, Lesbianism, Literary Review, Literature (General), Politics, Post Modern, Race, Religion, Socialist.

JOURNAL OF NEW JERSEY POETS, Sander Zulauf, Editor; North Peterson, Associate Editor; Debra DeMattio, Associate Editor; Sharon Nolan, Editorial Assistant; Ellen Bastante, Layout Editor, County College of Morris, 214 Center Grove Road, Randolph, NJ 07869-2086, 973-328-5471, szulauf@ccm.edu. 1976. Poetry, articles, reviews. "Open to submission of poetry from present and past residents of New Jersey; no biases concerning style or subject. Reviews of books by New Jersey poets.*Special 30th Anniversary Issue # 43, 2006.*" circ. 1M. 1/yr. Pub'd 1 issue 2005; expects 1 issue 2006, 1 issue 2007. sub. price $10/issue, $16/2 issues, $16/issue libraries and institutions; per copy $10. Back issues: limited availability, details on request. Discounts: 50% booksellers. 72-80pp. Reporting time: 1 year. We accept simultaneous submissions with notice of same and notification of acceptance elsewhere. Publishes 3% of manuscripts submitted. Payment: 4 copies plus 2 issue subscription. Copyrighted, reverts to author. Pub's reviews: 9 in 2005. Ads: upon request. Subject: Poetry.

JOURNAL OF PALESTINE STUDIES, University of California Press, Hisham Sharabi, Editor; Linda Butler, Managing Editor, University of California Press, 2000 Center St., Suite 303, Berkeley, CA 94704-1223, 510-643-7154. 1971. Articles, reviews, news items, non-fiction. "Editorial address: Institute for Palestine Studise, 3501 M St. NW, Washington DC 20007. Copyrighted by the Institute for Palestine Studies." circ. 2965. 4/yr. Pub'd 4 issues 2005; expects 4 issues 2006, 4 issues 2007. sub. price $45 indiv., $136 inst., $25 student; per copy $12 indiv., $38 inst., $12 student; sample same as single copy. Discounts: foreign subs. agents 10%, 10+ one-time orders 30%, standing orders (bookstores): 1-99 40%, 100+ 50%. 208pp. Copyrighted, does not revert to author. Pub's reviews: approx. 40 in 2005. Ads: $295/$220. Subjects: Middle East, Political Science.

JOURNAL OF POLYMORPHOUS PERVERSITY, Glenn C. Ellenbogen, PO Box 1454, Madison Square Station, New York, NY 10159-1454, 212-689-5473, info@psychhumor.com, www.psychhumor.com. 1984. Satire. "The *Wall Street Journal* (12/20/84) called *JPP* '...a social scientist's answer to Mad Magazine.' *JPP* is a humorous and satirical journal of psychology (and psychiatry and the closely allied disciplines). Materials submitted should relate to psychology, psychiatry, mental health, or mental health research. First and foremost, the article *must* be humorous and/or satirical. Manuscripts should be no longer than 8 double-spaced (4 typeset) pages. Articles are reviewed for consideration by one or more of 18 Associate Editors, each representing a specialty area. Recent contributions include 'Psychotherapy of the Dead,' 'New Improved Delusions,' 'A Modern Day Psychoanalytic Fable,' 'Nicholas Claus: A Case Study in Psychometrics,' and 'The Etiology and

Treatment of Childhood.' We do not ever consider poems. The best way to get a clear idea of what we are looking for is read a real psychology or psychiatry journal. Then write a spoof of it. Vist our website to see example excerpts.'' circ. 4.2M. 2/yr. Pub'd 2 issues 2005; expects 2 issues 2006, 2 issues 2007. sub. price $14.95; per copy $7; sample $7 includes postage. Back issues: $7 per issue. 24pp. Reporting time: 4-6 weeks. Simultaneous submissions accepted: no. Publishes 3% of manuscripts submitted. Payment: 2 free copies. Copyrighted, does not revert to author. §Psychology, psychiatry, and medicine. Ads: $525/$625 back cover. Subjects: Humor, Medicine, Psychology, Satire, Science.

JOURNAL OF PROCESS ORIENTED PSYCHOLOGY, Lao Tse Press, Ltd., Leslie Heizer, Kate Jobe, 2049 NW Hoyt Street, Portland, OR 97209-1260, 503-222-3395. 1992. Articles, art, photos. "Work on process-oriented psychology only.'' circ. 1M. 2/yr. Pub'd 2 issues 2005; expects 2 issues 2006, 2 issues 2007. sub. price $20; per copy $10; sample $5. Back issues: $5. Discounts: classroom 35%, trade 1-4 20%, 5-9 40%, 10-24 42%, 25-49 43%. 90pp. Reporting time: 3-6 months. Simultaneous submissions accepted: yes. Publishes 50% of manuscripts submitted. Payment: copy. Copyrighted, reverts to author. Pub's reviews: none in 2005. §only about process work. Ads: NWAPB, NAPRA. Subject: Psychology.

JOURNAL OF PSYCHOACTIVE DRUGS, Haight-Ashbury Publications, David E. Smith MD, Executive Editor; Richard B. Seymour, Editor in Chief, 612 Clayton Street, San Francisco, CA 94117, 415-565-1904, Fax 415-864-6162. 1967. Articles, art, photos, non-fiction. "The *Journal of Psychoactive Drugs* is a multidisciplinary forum for the study of drugs, every issue features a variety of articles by noted researchers and theorists. ISSN 0279-1072.'' circ. 700. 4/yr. Pub'd 4 issues 2005; expects 6 issues 2006, 6 issues 2007. sub. price $90 (indiv.), $160 (instit.), + $20/yr surface postage outside U.S., + $40/yr airmail postage outside U.S. ($15/ $35 Canada only); per copy $40; sample $10. Back issues: $200 while supplies last of Vol.5-33. Discounts: 5% subscription agency. 100pp. Reporting time: 60-90 days on articles; 30 days on art for cover or book reviews. Simultaneous submissions accepted: no. Payment: $50 for cover photo/art. Copyrighted, does not revert to author. Pub's reviews: 4 in 2005. §Alcohol and other drug-related topics. Ads: $350/$275. Subjects: Alcohol, Alcoholism, Drugs, Health, Mental Health, Psychiatry, Psychology, Self-Help, Social Work, Sociology.

THE JOURNAL OF PSYCHOHISTORY, Psychohistory Press, Lloyd deMause, 140 Riverside Drive, New York, NY 10024, 212-799-2294. 1973. Articles, reviews. "Psychohistory of individuals and groups, history of childhood and family.'' circ. 4M. 4/yr. Pub'd 4 issues 2005; expects 4 issues 2006. sub. price $54 individual, $129 organization; per copy $13; sample $13. Back issues: $13. 110pp. Reporting time: 2 weeks. Payment: none. Copyrighted, does not revert to author. Pub's reviews: 40 in 2005. §Psychology & history. Ads: $200/$100. Subjects: History, Psychology.

JOURNAL OF PSYCHOLOGY IN CHINESE SOCIETIES, The Chinese University Press, Charles C. Chan Prof., Editor; Mike Cheung Prof., Managing Editor, The Chinese University of Hong Kong, Sha Tin, New Territories, Hong Kong, Hong Kong, 852-26096508, 852-26037355, cup@cuhk.edu.hk, www.chineseu-press.com. 2000. 2/yr. Pub'd 2 issues 2005; expects 2 issues 2006, 2 issues 2007. sub. price $40 (Institution), US$24 (Individual); per copy $20 (Institution), US$12 (Individual). Back issues: $20 (Institution), US$12 (Individual). Simultaneous submissions accepted: No. Pub's reviews: 3 in 2005. §psychology. Subject: Psychology.

Journal of Pyrotechnics (see also JOURNAL OF PYROTECHNICS), Bonnie Kosanke, Publisher; Kenneth Kosanke, Managing Editor, 1775 Blair Rd, Whitewater, CO 81527, 970-245-0692. 1995. Articles, reviews, non-fiction. "The Journal of Pyrotechnics publishes peer-reviewed, technical literature. We have three different types of publications. The *Journal of Pyrotechnics* is a peer-reviewed, technical journal published twice a year with articles in the area of pyrotechnics, including fireworks, pyrotechnic special effects, rocketry and propellants, and civilian pyrotechnics. The Journal is dedicated to the advancement of pyrotechnics through the sharing of information.The Pyrotechnic Reference Series are technical books on various pyrotechnic topics. The current titles include *The Illustrated Dictionary of Pyrotechnics*, *Lecture Notes for Pyrotechnic Display Practices*, *Lecture Notes for Pyrotechnic Chemistry*, and *Pyrotechnic Chemistry*.The Pyrotechnic Literature Series are technical books that are collections of articles by a single author on a group of articles by several articles on a single topic. There are five in the series *Pyrotechnic Publications by K. L. and B. J. Kosanke*, and there are 4 in the series *Pyrotechnic Publications by Dr. Takeo Shimizu*.'' avg. press run 1000. Pub'd 2 titles 2005; expects 2 titles 2006, 2 titles 2007. Discounts: 40%. 80-400pp. Reporting time: 1 to 10 days. Simultaneous submissions accepted: No. Publishes 75% of manuscripts submitted. Payment: This is quite flexible, depending on the type of publication. Some are gratis, others receive a percentage of the profits. Does not copyright for author. Subjects: Abstracts, Book Reviewing, Forensic Science, Research, Science, Textbooks.

JOURNAL OF PYROTECHNICS, Journal of Pyrotechnics, Bonnie Kosanke, Publisher, Kenneth Kosanke; Tom Smith, Managing Editor, 1775 Blair Rd, Whitewater, CO 81527, 970-245-0692. 1995. Articles, non-fiction. "The Journal of Pyrotechnics is dedicated to the advancement of pyrotechnics through the sharing of information. We have had authors from around the world contribute to our publication. Additionally, the journal is distributed to many countries around the world." circ. 1000. 2/yr. Pub'd 2 issues 2005; expects 2 issues 2006, 2 issues 2007. sub. price $36; per copy $35; sample $3 - US; $6 all other countries. Back issues: $21 per issue - currently all back issues are available. Discounts: 40% off cover price. 80pp. Reporting time: 1 to 10 days. Simultaneous submissions accepted: No. Publishes 75% of manuscripts submitted. Payment: Articles are submitted gratis. There is no payment for articles. Copyrighted, reverts to author. Pub's reviews: approx 6 in 2005. §literature on pyrotechnics. Ads: We don't offer advertising. However, we do have "sponsors" that pay $70 per issue, and they receive 2 complimentary copies of the issue along with the name and contact information for their business. Subjects: Experimental, Forensic Science, Non-Fiction, Physics, Research, Science.

JOURNAL OF REGIONAL CRITICISM, Arjuna Library Press, Count Prof. Joseph A. Uphoff Jr., Director, 1404 East Bijou Street, Colorado Springs, CO 80909-5520. 1979. Poetry, art, photos, criticism, parts-of-novels, long-poems, plays, news items, non-fiction. "The processes of Experimental Surrealism derive Free Surrealism as a parameter that applies to Objects, Annotations, and Measures such that Experimental Philosophy limits the subject to Ethical Surrealism by the Adventure. This journal is an ongoing development of mathematical theories, with associated works, presented as the Contemporary Fine Arts. It is published as a xerox manuscript copy. We cannot, at this time, pay contributors except by enhancing their reputations, but we have plans for the future that include a fair return on the investment made by a literary or artistic career. we are not directing writers and artists to compete but to compose. Thus, it is not necessary to malpractice technical focus to emulate popular, economic misconceptions. The creation of beautiful images and essays should be a sufficient accomplishment to stand on its own merits. Previous contributions are considered on a priority basis. We present criticism by quotation or annotation. In the context of performance art and choreography, various manifestations are being documented with illustrative contributions that advance the system used to graph poetic and dynamic action. The ongoing focus is upon the Eshkol-Wachman System of Movement Notation. In reference to the concepts of Douglas Davis (Art In America, 2005) there are three kinds of curatorial potential, stable antiquity, transient production, and virtual projection. The fossils of our aspiration will become the valuable relics exhibited from museum storage and archives." circ. open. 6-12/yr. Pub'd 12 issues 2005; expects 12 issues 2006, 12 issues 2007. sample price at cost. Back issues: at current cost. 4pp. Reporting time: indefinite. Payment: none. Copyrighted, reverts to author. Subjects: Arts, Criticism, Dada, Mathematics, Metaphysics, Philosophy, Photography, Physics, Surrealism.

JOURNAL OF SCIENTIFIC EXPLORATION, Dr. Bernhard Haisch, Editor-in-Chief; Marsha Sims, Executive Editor, 810 E. 10th Street, Lawrence, KS 66044-3018, e-mail sims@jse.com. 1987. "Publishes original multi-disciplinary research aimed at scientific advance and the expansion of human knowledge in areas falling outside the established scientific disciplines. It is a refereed journal, providing a neutral, professional forum for discussion and debate of anomalous phenomena." circ. 3M. 4/yr. Pub'd 4 issues 2005; expects 4 issues 2006, 4 issues 2007. sub. price $50 individuals, $55 foreign; $100 institutions; sample $13.74. Back issues: Complete back issues available. 140pp. Simultaneous submissions accepted: no. Publishes 25-50% of manuscripts submitted. Payment: none. Copyrighted, does not revert to author. Pub's reviews: 24 in 2005. §Science. Ads: exchanges. Subjects: Medicine, Philosophy, Physics, Science.

JOURNAL OF SOCIAL BEHAVIOR AND PERSONALITY, Select Press, Roderick P. Crandall, PO Box 37, Corte Madera, CA 94925, 415-209-9838. 1986. "Academic research, psychology, speech, business, sociology, etc." 4/yr + extras. Pub'd 7 issues 2005; expects 6 issues 2006, 6 issues 2007. sub. price $65; per copy $15; sample free. 200pp. Reporting time: 4 weeks. Copyrighted, does not revert to author.

JOURNAL OF THE AMERICAN MUSICOLOGICAL SOCIETY, University of California Press, Joseph H. Auner, Editor; Catherine Gjerdingen, Assistant Editor, University of California Press, 2000 Center St., Suite 303, Berkeley, CA 94704-1223, 510-643-7154. 1947. Articles, reviews. "Editorial office: JAMS, Department of Music, The State University of NY at Stony Brook, Stony Brook NY 11794-5475. Copyrighted by the American Musicological Association." circ. 3045. 3/yr. Pub'd 3 issues 2005; expects 3 issues 2006, 3 issues 2007. sub. price $100 indiv., $100 inst.; per copy $34 indiv., $34 inst.; sample same as single copy. Discounts: foreign subs. agents 10%, 10+ one-time orders 30%. 180pp. Copyrighted, does not revert to author. Pub's reviews: 15 in 2005. §musicology, music history, related fields. Ads: $405/$305. Subject: Music.

JOURNAL OF THE HELLENIC DIASPORA, Pella Publishing Co., A. Kitroeff, 337 West 36th Street, New York, NY 10018, 212-279-9586. 1974. Fiction, articles, art, photos, cartoons, interviews, satire, criticism, reviews, music, parts-of-novels, long-poems, collages, plays. "The magazine is concerned with the entire spectrum of scholarly, critical, and artistic work that is based on contemporary Greece." circ. 1M. 2/yr. Pub'd 2 issues 2005; expects 2 issues 2006, 2 issues 2007. sub. price Individual: domestic $20, foreign $25; Institutions: domestic $30, foreign $35; per copy $12; sample free. Back issues: $15. Discounts: jobbers & bookstores-20%. 96-112pp. Reporting time: 12 weeks. Payment: 30 offprints for articles. Copyrighted, reverts to author. Pub's reviews: 8 in 2005. §Modern Greek studies and affairs. Ads: $125/$75. Subject: Greek.

244

JOURNAL OF THOUGHT, Caddo Gap Press, Douglas J. Simpson, 3145 Geary Boulevard #275, San Francisco, CA 94118, 415-392-1911. 1965. Articles. "*Journal of Thought* is an interdisciplinary scholarly journal focusing on educational philosophy, featuring articles by scholars and researchers." circ. 500. 4/yr. Pub'd 4 issues 2005; expects 4 issues 2006, 4 issues 2007. sub. price $50 individuals, $100 institutions; per copy $15. 96pp. Reporting time: 2 months. Publishes 25% of manuscripts submitted. Payment: none. Copyrighted, reverts to author. Ads: $200 per page. Subject: Education.

Journey Books Publishing, Edward Knight, Editor; Donnie Clemons, Editor, 3205 Highway 431, Spring Hill, TN 37174, 615-791-8006. 1997. Poetry, fiction. "We are dedicated to publishing quality Science Fiction and Fantasy as well as speculative poetry. We currently publish anthologies of short story and novella length works. All anthologies are themed and we do have reading periods. Submissions received outside the reading periods will be returned unread. Please read our guidelines on our website before submitting." Pub'd 1 title 2005; expects 3 titles 2006, 3 titles 2007. Trade discounts are available. Reporting time: 3 months. We publish 20% of the short story submissions made to us. Payment: Short story submissions are paid at a set price per word Poetry will be paid a flat rate per poem. Copyrights for author. Subjects: Fantasy, Fiction, Juvenile Fiction, Novels, Science Fiction.

J-Press Publishing, Sid Jackson, 4796 126th St. N., White Bear Lake, MN 55110, 651-429-1819, 651-429-1819 fax, 888-407-1723, sjackson@jpresspublishing.com, http://www.jpresspublishing.com. 1998. Fiction, non-fiction. "j-Press Publishing is an independent publisher of books of both fiction and non-fiction. Our goal is to bring to the reading public the best of both fictional and non-fictional works by top-notch authors. j-Press Publishing has been in business since 1998. We publish 1-3 books a year. We have published in a variety of subject-categories: history, biography, art, psychology, mystery,literary fiction, and we've even published a cookbook. Our books are distributed nationally through all the major wholesalers to bookstores, libraries, gift shops, etc., and we also sell to the academic community (colleges and universities). We publish our books under the imprint of j-Press. We invite you to browse through our listing of books shown on our web site." avg. press run 1000. Pub'd 1 title 2005; expects 1-2 titles 2006, 1-2 titles 2007. Discounts: 40% bookstores55-60% wholesalers20% classrooms. 250-350pp. Reporting time: 2-3 wks. Simultaneous submissions accepted: No. Payment: contractual. Copyrights for author. Subjects: Fiction, Mystery.

JPS Publishing Company, Janice Brown, 1141 Polo Run, Midlothian, TX 76065, 214-533-5685 (telephone), 972-775-5367 (fax), info@jpspublishing.com. 1998. Fiction, non-fiction. "Primarily a self-help publisher for women." avg. press run 20000. Pub'd 1 title 2005; expects 1 title 2006, 3 titles 2007. Discounts: 40% bookstores, 67% distributor, 55% online bookstore. 250pp. Reporting time: 3 months. Simultaneous submissions accepted: Yes. Publishes 1% of manuscripts submitted. Copyrights for author. Subjects: Alternative Medicine, Literature (General), Non-Fiction, Self-Help, Singles, Vegetarianism.

JUBILAT, Robert Casper, Publisher; Jen Bervin, Editor; Terrance Hayes, Editor, English Dept., Bartlett Hall, University of Massachusetts, Amherst, MA 01003-0515, jubilat@english.umass.edu, www.jubilat.org. 2000. Poetry, art, interviews, letters, non-fiction. circ. 2000. 2/yr. Pub'd 2 issues 2005; expects 2 issues 2006, 2 issues 2007. sub. price $14/yr.; per copy $8; sample $6. Back issues: $6. 170pp. Reporting time: 3-6 months. We accept simultaneous submissions with notification. Publishes 2% of manuscripts submitted. Payment: 2 copies plus 1 year subscription. Copyrighted, reverts to author. Ads: $200 full page. Subjects: Arts, Interviews, Literature (General), Non-Fiction, Poetry, Reprints, Visual Arts.

Judah Magnes Museum Publications, Rebecca Fromer, Editor; Paula Friedman, Editor; Nelda Cassuto, Editor, 2911 Russell Street, Berkeley, CA 94705. 1966. Art, non-fiction. "Consideration of new volumes is suspended through 2002. Primarily art, Judaica, Western Americana, and related. Query first." avg. press run 1M. Pub'd 3 titles 2005; expects 2 titles 2006, 2 titles 2007. Discounts: upon request - contact Order Department at address above. 150-200pp. Reporting time: 6 months. Simultaneous submissions accepted: no. Publishes 15% of manuscripts submitted. Payment: varies. We do not usually copyright for author, this may change ff. 2002. Subjects: Judaism, Middle East, Poetry.

juel house publishers and literary services, Laura Williams, P.O.Box 415, Riverton, IL 62561, (217)629-9026 juelhouse@familyonline.com. 2004. Fiction, reviews. "To offer opportunity to new voices wishing to be heard, so that they may realize their potential and goals. Our prime directive is to give the world a reason to smile. We accept women's and young adult fiction short stories or novels. Recent contributors include small businesses in Rochester, Illinois." avg. press run 100. Pub'd 1 title 2005; expects 3 titles 2006, 5 titles 2007. Discounts: 10 -20 copies 40% 5-10 copies 15%. 80pp. Reporting time: 60 days to 90 days. Simultaneous submissions accepted: Yes. Publishes 10% of manuscripts submitted. Payment: 10% upon acceptance,advance negotiable. Does not copyright for author. Subjects: Book Reviewing, Entertainment, Family, Fiction, Humor, Interviews, Juvenile Fiction, Literary Review, Publishing, Reviews, Satire, Short Stories, Women, Young Adult.

Jullundur Press, Aram T. Armenian, 1001 G St., Suite 301, Sacramento, CA 95814, 866-449-1600, fax

Junction Press, Mark Weiss, PO Box F, New York, NY 10034-0246, 212-942-1985. 1991. Poetry. "Modernist or postmodernist poetry, non-academic. Long, even book length poems welcomed. Recent books by Mervyn Taylor, Richard Elman, Susie Mee, Stephen Vincent, Ira Beryl Brakner, Rochelle Owens, Armand Schwerner, Gloria Gervitz (bilingual), and *Across the Line/ Al otro lado: The Poetry of Baja California*, a bilingual anthology. Increasingly interested in Latin American poetry." avg. press run 1M. Pub'd 3 titles 2005; expects 2 titles 2006, 3 titles 2007. Discounts: bookstores 40%, standing orders 20%. 96pp. Reporting time: 3 months. Simultaneous submissions accepted: no. Payment: 10% paid in copies of first print, 8% thereafter. Copyrights for author. Subject: Poetry.

JUNIOR STORYTELLER, Storycraft Publishing, Vivian Dubrovin, PO Box 205, Masonville, CO 80541, 970-669-3755 phone/Fax, vivdub@aol.com, www.storycraft.com. Fiction, articles, non-fiction. "Shipping address: 8600 Firethorn Drive, Loveland, CO 80538. Newsletter/activity guide for young storytellers, age 9-12, in schools, libraries, camps and youth organizations. Each issue on theme, see website (Welcome Page) for upcoming themes. Purchased Pony Papers (for horse issue) and Meet the Fuzzybodies (for draw & tell) from Bea Caidy; Tandem Tale from Carol Rehme." circ. 500. 4/yr. Pub'd 4 issues 2005; expects 4 issues 2006, 4 issues 2007. sub. price $11.95; per copy $3.25; sample $3.25 + 55¢ p/h. Back issues: see website for availability (bottom of Join Page). Discounts: subscription discount for class and clubs 20%, single copy bulk rate (15+) $2. 8pp. Reporting time: query for assignment. Simultaneous submissions accepted: no. Payment: varies. Copyrighted, reverts to author. Pub's reviews: 2 in 2005. §Books for young readers on storytelling or related topics; no adult or teacher materials. Ads: do not currently use ads, but would be interested in storytelling products kids can use. Subjects: Children, Youth, Crafts, Hobbies, Education, Storytelling, Young Adult.

Juniper Creek Press, Virginia Castleman, Bill Cowee, Ellen Hopkins, 208 Glen Vista Drive, Dayton, NV 89403, 775-246-3427, junipercreekpres@aol.com. 2002. Fiction, articles, cartoons, interviews, news items, non-fiction. "We are a publisher of children's books, a children's newspaper and a producer of writer's conferences." Expects 1 title 2006, 3 titles 2007. 48pp. Simultaneous submissions accepted: yes. Payment: contract and work for hire. Does not copyright for author.

Juniper Creek Publishing, Inc., Ellen Hopkins, P.O. Box 2205, Carson City, NV 89702, 775 849-1637 (voice), 775 849-1707 (fax), jcpi@junipercreekpubs.com, www.junipercreekpubs.com. 2002. avg. press run 3500. Pub'd 1 title 2005; expects 2 titles 2006, 3 titles 2007. Discounts: retail discount 40%classroom, library discount 20%. 64pp.

Jupiter Scientific Publishing, Gezhi Weng, Stewart Allen, c/o Weng, 415 Moraga Avenue, Piedmont, CA 94611-3720, 510-420-1015, admin@jupiterscientific.org, www.jupiterscientific.org. 1996. Non-fiction. "Jupiter Scientific Publishing specializes in popular science books. For additional information check the website." avg. press run 2M. Expects 1 title 2006, 1 title 2007. Discounts: 2-3 20%, 4-7 25%, 8-11 30%, 12-15 35%, 16-47 40%, 48+ 45%. 300pp. Reporting time: 1 month. Simultaneous submissions accepted: yes. Publishes 2% of manuscripts submitted. Payment: 10%. Copyrights for author. Subject: Science.

JUST WEST OF ATHENS, Victoria Oswald, 6624 Hidden Woods Court, Roanoke, VA 24018-7489, submissions@westofathens.net, http://westofathens.net. 2004. Poetry, fiction, articles, art, photos, interviews, criticism, letters, long-poems, plays, non-fiction. "JUST WEST OF ATHENS was conceived in May 2004 in a slop bucket of ideas, with Victoria Oswald and Rachael Bloom at the helm. The magazine was designed to be a more thorough and fully developed version of the old literary journal For The Good Guys, with the sole purpose of showcasing the work of the most exceptional writers and artists of the time. WEST OF ATHENS' first issue debuted in late July 2004. The issue carried such writers as Lyn Lifshin, Tom Blessing, and Jill Chan, amongst many. The issue, like the magazine as a whole, was aimed at diversity; the writers who contributed came from many walks of life and many different areas of the world. Paul Adrian Mabelis once said in regards to education: "We worry more about how far along the line we are than whether we are actually ON the line [the line being knowledge]." This metaphor took on another meaning; the comparison between the intent of internet magazines and what they end up compromising on. WEST OF ATHENS is a magazine that does not claim to want your writing for reasons other magazines cannot also claim. We simply do not want literature to tarnish like a mind that has twiddled its thumbs for far too long." 4/yr. Pub'd 2 issues 2005; expects 4 issues 2006. Reporting time: It usually takes the editors 2 weeks or so to respond to a submission via e-mail, a little longer if the submission is sent through the postal service. Simultaneous submissions accepted: Yes. Payment: Unfortunately, Just West of Athens does not have the means to pay their contributors a monetary amount at this time. Copyrighted, reverts to author. Pub's reviews. §small press poetry chapbooks, slams, concerts, books; basically, anything of literary interest. Subjects: Abstracts, Arts, Internet, Interviews, Literary Review, Literature (General), Non-Fiction.

K

K.T. Publications, Kevin Troop, 16, Fane Close, Stamford, Lincs., PE9 1HG, England, (07180) 754193. 1987. Poetry, fiction, art, plays. "Up to 40 lines for poets; up to 2,000 words for fiction. Separate books or volumes of poetry. Naturally vary in length and style—"each book is different"." avg. press run varies. Pub'd 6 titles 2005; expects 6 titles 2006, 6 titles 2007. Discounts: please contact with details, requests, numbers. 40-50pp. Reporting time: as quickly as humanly possible. Simultaneous submissions accepted, but not keen, really. Publishes up to 10% of manuscripts submitted. Payment: none. Copyrights for author. Subjects: Education, Fiction, Poetry.

KABBALAH, Yenuda Berg, Michael Berg, Esther Sibilia, 1062 S. Robertson Boulevard, Los Angeles, CA 90035, 310-657-5404, Fax 310-657-7774, kabmag@kabbalah.dymp.com, www.kabbalah.com. 1996. Fiction, articles, photos, interviews, criticism, reviews, letters, news items, non-fiction. "Regular contributors are: Paul William Roberts, Mitch Sisskind, Kerry Madden-Lunsford, Barbara Einzig, and Ann Hirsch." circ. 8M. 4/yr. Pub'd 4 issues 2005; expects 4 issues 2006, 4 issues 2007. sub. price $12; per copy $5; sample free. Back issues: none. Discounts: available. 42pp. Simultaneous submissions accepted: no. Publishes 10% of manuscripts submitted. Payment: yes. Copyrighted, does not revert to author. Pub's reviews: 3 in 2005. §Spiritual, anti-aging medicine, immortality. Ads: $684/$363/$219 1/4 page/$164 1/8 page. Subjects: Business & Economics, Family, Motivation, Success, Relationships, Reviews, Self-Help, Spiritual, Women.

KAIROS, A Journal of Contemporary Thought and Criticism, Hermes House Press, Alan Mandell, Richard Mandell, 113 Summit Avenue, Brookline, MA 02446-2319. 1981. Poetry, fiction, articles, art, photos, interviews, criticism, reviews, long-poems, concrete art, non-fiction. "Not currently reading unsolicited material. Volume I, No. 3 focused on the meaning and experience of learning. Vol. I, No. 4 focused on German culture and society in America. Vol. II, No. 1 focused on the writings of Ernest Becker. Vol. II, No. 2 included materials on technology and poetry-in-translation. Poetry, fiction and artwork are encouraged. Please include SASE." circ. 500. 2/yr. Pub'd 2 issues 2005; expects 2 issues 2006, 2 issues 2007. sub. price $11 individual, $15 institutions; per copy $6 + $1 p/h; sample $6 + $1 p/h. Discounts: available upon request. 120pp. Reporting time: 4-8 weeks. Payment: copies. Copyrighted, reverts to author. Pub's reviews: 2 in 2005. §See past issues for tone, scope and direction. Ads: on exchange basis only. Subjects: Philosophy, Sociology.

KAJ-MAHKAH: EARTH OF EARTH, Natasha Martin, St. Louis, MO 63110, http://geocities.com/kajmahkah/. 2004. Poetry, fiction, art, photos, satire, criticism, reviews, plays, non-fiction. "Submissions open June 1st through September 1st only for this annual literary journal, which publishes prose, poetry, drama, and black-and-white art. For more information please go to http//:geocities.com/kajmahkah/ or email the Editor at kajmahkah@yahoo.com." sample price free. 20pp. Reporting time: Expect a response in 14 business days, usually faster. Simultaneous submissions accepted: No. Payment: $0, free biographies printed about each artist and writer. The writer/artist retains all rights; by submitting those parties agree to a one time publication under the company's name. The magazine will not tolerate any of those that plagarize and does not tolerate those that make use of the company's namesake, TrunkSpace, without explicit permission from the Editor and/or cofounders. Pub's reviews: none in 2005. §General fiction, children's/young adult, literary fiction, Romance, non-fiction, and poetry. Subjects: Arts, Drama, Fiction, Haiku, Literary Review, Multicultural, Non-Fiction, Photography, Poetry, Short Stories.

KALDRON, An International Journal Of Visual Poetry, Karl Kempton, Karl Young, Harry Polkinhorn, Klaus Peter Dencker, Thalia, PO Box 7164, Halcyon, CA 93421-7164, 805-489-2770, www.thing.net/~grist/l&d/kaldron.htm. 1976. Poetry. "*KALDRON* is North America's longest running visual poetry magazine. Its on-line version opened on Bastille Day, 1997. Sections include 1) Selections from the Kaldron Archive: Number 21/22 and First Visualog Show, 1979; 2) Volume Two Continuing on-line issue of the magazine: samples from Fall, 1997 for Kaldron Wall Archives; 3) A Kaldron Wall Ancestor: Chumash Rock Painting showing a solar eclipse. 4) SURVEYS: A - Individual Poets: Avelino de Araujo; Doris Cross; Klaus Peter Dencker; Scott Helms; d.a.levy (includes visual poetry, book art, paintings, lexical poetry: a - holistic approach to this major figure); Hassan Massoudy; bpNichol (includes a wide variety of poems, continuation of TTA project, and commentary); Kenneth Patchen; Marilyn R. Rosenberg; Alain Satie; Carol Stetser; thalia; Edgardo Antonio Vigo (first instalments of a joint memorial to this great and typically unrecognized) Argentine polymath, shown in conjunction with Postypographika; B - Group Surveys: Lettriste Pages; A Collective Effort of Australian Visual Poets; A Workshop with Hungarian Visual Poets; U.S. and Canadian Pages for Nucleo Post Arte's VI Biennial; Festival of Experimental Art and Literature, Mexico City, November, 1998; FREE GRAPHZ: Meeting place for graffiti art and visual poetry. Much more including numerous essays by Karl

Young who is also the site Webmaster." circ. web-www. sub. price donations accepted; per copy $10; sample all back issues are $10 each, limit of 4 per order. Back issues: limited number of sets available, contact publisher. Reporting time: 2 weeks to 1 month. Simultaneous submissions accepted: yes. Publishes 2% of manuscripts submitted. Payment: none. Copyrighted, reverts to author. Pub's reviews. §Visual poetry, language art publications, art and poetry. No ads. Subjects: Arts, Avant-Garde, Experimental Art, Book Arts, Communication, Journalism, Criticism, Culture, Dada, Design, Futurism, Graphics, Language, Literary Review, Literature (General), Poetry, Visual Arts.

KALEIDOSCOPE: Exploring the Experience of Disability through Literature & the Fine Arts, Gail Willmott, Editor-in-Chief, United Disability Services, 701 S. Main Street, Akron, OH 44311-1019, 330-762-9755, 330-379-3349 (TDD), Fax 330-762-0912, mshiplett@udsakron.org, pboerner@udsakron.org, www.udsakron.org. 1979. Poetry, fiction, articles, art, photos, interviews, satire, reviews, parts-of-novels, non-fiction. "We publish fiction, poetry, and visual arts that capture and reflect the experience of disability. Also critical essays and book reviews, photo essays, interviews, personal experience narratives. Established writers/artists featured along with new promising writers. *Kaleidoscope* presents works that challenge stereotypical perceptions of people with disabilities by offering balanced realistic images." circ. 2M. 2/yr. Pub'd 2 issues 2005; expects 2 issues 2006, 2 issues 2007. sub. price $10 indiv., $15 instit., add $8 Int'l and $5 Canada; per copy $6 ($8 International, payable in US currency); sample $6 to cover p/h. Back issues: $6. Discounts: none. 64pp. Reporting time: acknowledgment of manuscripts within 2 weeks; status of manuscripts within 2 weeks of deadline dates, March 1 and August 1. Simultaneous submissions accepted: yes. Publishes 10% of manuscripts submitted. Payment: contributors receive two complimentary copies and $10-$25 and up to $150 for commissioned work. Copyrighted, reverts to author. Pub's reviews: none in 2005. §Disability-related short story, poetry, visual art, books. Subjects: Book Reviewing, Criticism, Disabled, Essays, Fiction, Humor, Non-Fiction, Poetry, Prose, Reviews.

Kali Press, Cynthia A. Bellini, Managing Director, PO Box 5324, Eagle, CO 81631-5324, sales@kalipres.com. 1990. Poetry, fiction, art, photos, interviews, non-fiction. avg. press run 20-25M. Pub'd 2 titles 2005; expects 3 titles 2006, 4 titles 2007. Discounts: open for discussion. 100pp. Reporting time: 45 days. Simultaneous submissions accepted: yes. Publishes 5% of manuscripts submitted. Payment: open for discussion. Copyrights for author. Subjects: Australia, Disease, Environment, Health, How-To, Medicine, Non-Fiction, Pets, Reference, Water.

KALLIOPE, A Journal of Women's Literature and Art, Mary Sue Koeppel, Editor, FCCJ - South Campus, 11901 Beach Blvd., Jacksonville, FL 32246, 904-646-2081, www.fccj.org/kalliope. 1979. Poetry, fiction, articles, art, photos, interviews, criticism, reviews, plays. "*Kalliope* devotes itself to women in the arts by publishing their work and providing a forum for their ideas and opinions. Besides introducing the work of many new writers, *Kalliope* has published the work of established writers such as Marge Piercy, Denise Levertov, Susan Fromberg Schaffer, Kathleen Spivak, Enid Shomer, and Ruth Moon Kempher. Most issues include an interview with a prominent woman in the arts. Recent interviewees with *Kalliope* are Joyce Tenneson, Joy Harjo, Rosemary Daniell, Ruth Stone, and Eavan Boland. We have featured the photographs of Diane Farris, Joanne Leonard, Layle Silbert, and Anna Tomczak; the sculpture of Margaret Koscielny and Ella Tulin; the ceramics of Marilyn Taylor and Patti Warashina; and paintings and drawings by a large number of artists including Renee Faure, Marcia Isaacson, Mary Nash, Susan Zukowsky, and Mary Joan Waid. Theme issues have been devoted to women over 60; women under 30; women with disabilities; translations; Florida writers and artists; humor; women portraying men; the spiritual quest; women's body images; family; secrets; men speak to women; prose poetry and flash fiction; desire." circ. 1.6M. 2/yr. Pub'd 3 issues 2005; expects 2 issues 2006, 2 issues 2007. sub. price $16; per copy $7 recent issues before 2002; sample $4 pre-1987 issues, $7 issues (before 2002), $9 after 2002. Back issues: $7 recent, $4 pre-1987. Discounts: 40% to bookstores and distributors. 120pp. Reporting time: 3-6 months. Simultaneous submissions accepted: no. Publishes 10% of manuscripts submitted. Payment: copies or subscription, when possible, a small payment. Copyrighted, rights revert to author if requested for purposes of republication. Pub's reviews: 20 in 2005. §Books of poetry, novels, short stories. No ads. Subjects: Arts, Feminism, Women.

Kallisti Publishing, Anthony Michalski, 332 Center Street, Wilkes-Barre, PA 18702, 877-444-6188. 2000. Non-fiction. ""The Books You Need to Read to Succeed" - Kallisti Publishing specializes in the personal development books, e-books, and audio programs." avg. press run 2000. Pub'd 4 titles 2005; expects 8 titles 2006, 8 titles 2007. Discounts: 40% discount to retailers. 250pp. Reporting time: Two weeks. Simultaneous submissions accepted: Yes. Publishes 20% of manuscripts submitted. Payment: 0 - advance; 15% royalty. Copyrights for author. Subjects: Philosophy, Psychology, Self-Help.

KANTIAN REVIEW, University Of Wales Press, Howard Williams, Graham Bird, 10 Columbus Walk, Brigantine Place, Cardiff CF10 4UP, Wales, 44-029-2049-6899, Fax 44-029-2049-6108, press@press.wales.ac.uk, www.wales.ac.uk/press. 1997. Articles. circ. 300. 1/yr. Pub'd 1 issue 2005; expects 1 issue 2006, 1 issue 2007. sub. price £15 individuals, £30 institutions. Discounts: 10%. 160pp. Pub's reviews.

Subject: Philosophy.

KARAMU, Olga Abella, Department of English, Eastern Illinois Univ., Charleston, IL 61920, 217-581-6297. 1966. Poetry, fiction, collages, non-fiction. "Poems should be no longer than 3 pages; short stories no more than 3500 words. Submit no more than 5 poems or 1 story or essay at a time. We are looking for material that will interest a sophisticated, college-educated audience. We advise aspiring contributors to purchase and examine a sample issue ($8, $6) to see what kind of material we like. Some recent contributors, poetry: Jen Garfield, George Wallace, William Jolliff, Julie Price, Glen Sheldon, Natasha Marin. Prose: Pinky Feria, Martin McGowan, Sybil Smith, Donna Steiner, Aaron Sanders." circ. 500. 1/yr. Pub'd 1 issue 2005; expects 1 issue 2006, 1 issue 2007. sub. price $8.00; per copy $8.00; sample $8.00. Back issues: 2/$6. Discounts: $70 for 10 copies of current issue. 145pp. Reporting time: initial screening 4-6 months, promising material may be held up to 8 months for final decisions. We do get behind, so please be patient! Simultaneous submissions no longer accepted. Publishes 7% of manuscripts submitted. Payment: 1 contributor's copy, pre-publication discount on additional copies. Copyrighted, reverts to author. Subjects: Essays, Fiction, Poetry.

KARAWANE, Laura Winton, 402 S. Cedar Lake Road, Minneapolis, MN 55405, 612-381-1229, karawane@prodigy.net, www.karawane.org, www.karawane.homestead.com. 1996. Poetry, fiction, art, criticism, reviews, long-poems, plays, news items. "We serve the Spoken Word community. All contributors must perform their poetry in public. Slams, reading, open mics., etc." circ. 500. 2/yr. Pub'd 1 issue 2005; expects 2 issues 2006, 2 issues 2007. sub. price $5/2 issues; per copy $3; sample $2. Back issues: $2. Discounts: 50% to distributors and stores; ask me about bulk orders. 24pp. Reporting time: 6 months. Simultaneous submissions accepted: yes. Publishes 10% of manuscripts submitted. Payment: 5-10 free copies, more upon request. Copyrighted, reverts to author. Ads: $125/$75/$50 1/4 page/$35 business card. Subjects: Absurdist, Avant-Garde, Experimental Art, Fiction, Performing Arts, Poetry, Storytelling, Writers/Writing.

Kar-Ben Publishing, Inc., Judyth Groner, Madeline Wikler, c/o Lerner Publishing Group, 241 First Avenue North, Minneapolis, MN 55401, 800-4KARBEN (in USA). 1975. "A division of Lerner Publishing Group. Juveniles on Jewish themes—fiction, holiday stories and texts, preschool and primary level." avg. press run 10M. Pub'd 6 titles 2005; expects 6 titles 2006, 6 titles 2007. Discounts: 40% to trade; 25% on quantity orders to schools; up to 50% to major distributors. 32-48pp. Reporting time: 4-6 weeks. Simultaneous submissions accepted: yes. Publishes 1% of manuscripts submitted. Payment: royalty based on net sales, split between author/illustrator; sometimes small advance. Copyrights for author. Subjects: Children, Youth, Cooking, Folklore, Judaism, Religion.

•Kedzie Press, Jessica Sanchez, 2647 N. Western Ave., Ste #8042, Chicago, IL 60647-2034, (773)252-7220, www.kedziepress.com, info@kedziepress.com. 2006. Fiction, non-fiction. "Along with our commitment to publish extraordinary literature, we make every attempt to operate our business in the most environmentally-friendly manner possible. All of our titles are printed on 100% recycled post-consumer, chlorine free processed paper." avg. press run 4500. Expects 1 title 2006, 3 titles 2007. Special discounts available for higher qty. purchase, please email for qty. specific quote. 200-400pp. Subject: Literature (General).

THE KELSEY REVIEW, G. Robin Schore, Mercer County Community College, PO Box B, Trenton, NJ 08690, 609-586-4800 ext. 3326, kelsey.review@mccc.edu. 1988. Poetry, fiction, articles, art, cartoons, interviews, satire, criticism, parts-of-novels, long-poems, plays, non-fiction. "2,000 words maximum. Annual contributors limited to people who live or work in Mercer County, New Jersey." circ. 2M. 1/yr. Pub'd 1 issue 2005; expects 1 issue 2006, 1 issue 2007. sub. price free. Back issues: free, if available. 90pp. Reporting time: 30 days. Simultaneous submissions accepted: no. Publishes 10% of manuscripts submitted. Payment: 5 copies of journal. Copyrighted, reverts to author. Pub's reviews: none in 2005. §Open. No ads. Subjects: Fiction, Literary Review, Non-Fiction, Poetry.

Kelsey St. Press, Rena Rosenwasser, Editor; Hazel White, Editor; Patricia Dientsfrey, Editor; Tanya Erzen, Webmaster, Erin Morrill, 2824 Kelsey St., Berkeley, CA 94705, 510-845-2260, Fax 510-548-9185, info@kelseyst.com, www.kelseyst.com. 1974. Poetry, fiction, art, non-fiction. "Special guidelines for submission." avg. press run 1M. Pub'd 3 titles 2005; expects 4 titles 2006, 4 titles 2007. Discounts: 40% to the trade. 48pp. Reporting time: 4 months. Payment: in copies or 10% of the gross price. Copyright retained by author unless otherwise agreed. Subjects: Arts, Asian-American, Avant-Garde, Experimental Art, Fiction, Greek, Literature (General), Poetry, Women.

Kelton Press, Maria B. Orlowoski, PO Box 4236, Jackson, MI 49204, 517-788-8542; 888-453-5880.

The Kenneth G. Mills Foundation, Angela Wingfield, Mary Joy Leaper, 65 High Ridge Road, Suite 103, Stamford, CT 06905, 800-437-1454, fax: 905-951-9712, email: info@kgmfoundation.org, www.kgmfoundation.org. 1975. Poetry, art, photos, interviews, reviews, music, long-poems, non-fiction. "Home office: PO Box 790, Station F, Toronto, Ontario M4Y 2N7, Canada, Tel: 416-410-0453, Fax 905-951-9712. Philosophical, educational. Primarily the works of Canadian philosopher, poet, composer and conductor, artist Kenneth George Mills. Prose, poetry, and spoken-word recordings. Poetry of Rolland G. Smith. Not currently accepting submissions." avg. press run 2M. Pub'd 6 titles 2005; expects 8 titles 2006, 9 titles 2007. Discounts: 40% to trade. 260pp. Subjects: Inspirational, Metaphysics, New Age, Non-Fiction, Philosophy, Philosophy, Poetry, Prose, Spiritual.

The Kent State University Press, Will Underwood, PO Box 5190, 307 Lowry Hall, Kent, OH 44242-0001, 330-672-7913, 330-672-3104. 1965. Non-fiction.

Kenyette Productions, Kenyette Adrine-Robinson, 20131 Champ Drive, Euclid, OH 44117-2208, 216-486-0544. 1976. Poetry, art, photos. "Permanent address: 4209 E. 186th Street, Cleveland, OH 44122 (216) 752-4069. Past president, Urban Literary Arts Workshop (ULAW). Member: Verse Writers Guild of Ohio. Board member: Poets' & Writers' League of Greater Cleveland; past Treasurer of the Writers Center of Greater Cleveland 1999-2000." avg. press run 750. Expects 1 title 2006, 2 titles 2007. Discounts: non-profit organizations, bookstores, warehouses, vendors, public schools, artists, retail outlets. 48pp. Reporting time: 2 months. Simultaneous submissions accepted: yes. Publishes 10% of manuscripts submitted. Payment: negotiable. Copyrights for author. Subjects: African Literature, Africa, African Studies, Autobiography, Children, Youth, Haiku, Ohio, Photography, Poetry, Religion, Women.

THE KENYON REVIEW, David Lynn, Editor; David Baker, Poetry Editor; Nancy Zafris, Fiction Editor; John Kinsella, International Editor, 104 College Drive, Gambier, OH 43022, 740-427-5208, Fax 740-427-5417, kenyonreview@kenyon.edu. 1939. Poetry, fiction, interviews, criticism, reviews, parts-of-novels, long-poems, plays, non-fiction. "We *strongly* discourage 'blind' submissions from writers who have not read a recent issue of the magazine. Bookstore distributors are Ingram and Media Solutions. Issue dates are Dec. (Winter), March (Spring), June (Summer), and Sept. (Fall). Reading period is September 1-January 31 each year. Submissions must be sent using KR's online program at www.kenyonreview.org. Do not send submissions via email. Please note that unsolicited submissions will *not* be accepted through regular mail." circ. 6,500. 4/yr. Pub'd 4 issues 2005; expects 4 issues 2006, 4 issues 2007. sub. price $30 individuals, $35 libraries; per copy $10 single, $12 double issue. Shipping/handling extra for single copies. Back issues may be purchased online.; sample $12 includes postage. Back issues: Visit www.kenyonreview.org to purchase back issues. Discounts: agency 15%. 200pp. Reporting time: 3-4 months. Simultaneous submissions accepted: no. Publishes 3% of manuscripts submitted. Payment: $30 prose, $40 poetry (per printed page). Copyrighted, reverts to author. Pub's reviews: 3 in 2005. §Literature, criticism. Ads: $250 for half-page; $375 full-page; $450 for inside front or inside back cover. Frequency discounts available. 15% discount on ads for agencies and university presses. Subjects: Criticism, Culture, Drama, Essays, Experimental, Fiction, Interviews, Literary Review, Literature (General), Multicultural, Non-Fiction, Poetry, Reviews, Short Stories, Translation.

Keokee Co. Publishing, Inc. (see also SANDPOINT MAGAZINE), Billie Jean Plaster, Editor, PO Box 722, Sandpoint, ID 83864, 208-263-3573, www.keokeebooks.com. 1990. Articles, art, photos, cartoons, interviews, news items, non-fiction. "Accept manuscripts. Interested in non-fiction, history, regional, outdoors, recreation guides. No fiction or poetry." avg. press run 5M. Discounts: STOP orders 40% retail 40%, wholesale/jobbers 50%. 224pp. Reporting time: 2 months. Simultaneous submissions accepted: yes. Publishes 1% of manuscripts submitted. Payment: depends, negotiable. Copyrights for author. Subjects: Conservation, Environment, History, Idaho, Montana, Non-Fiction, Pacific Northwest, Sports, Outdoors, Transportation.

KEREM: Creative Explorations in Judaism, Gilah Langner, Sara R. Horowitz, 3035 Porter Street, NW, Washington, DC 20008, 202-364-3006, langner@erols.com, www.kerem.org. 1992. Poetry, articles, art, photos, interviews, non-fiction. circ. 2M. 1/yr. Pub'd 1 issue 2005; expects 1 issue 2006, 1 issue 2007. sub. price $8.50; per copy $8.50; sample $8.50. 128pp. Reporting time: 3-5 months. Simultaneous submissions accepted: yes. Publishes 20% of manuscripts submitted. Payment: none. Copyrighted, reverts to author. Ads: $100/$50. Subjects: Ethics, Judaism, Literature (General), Religion, Spiritual.

THE KERF, Ken Letko, 883 W. Washington Boulevard, Crescent City, CA 95531, 707-465-2360, Fax 707-464-6867. 1995. Poetry. "The editors especially encourage themes related to humanity and/or environmental consciousness, but are open to diverse subjects. Poems: 1-2 pages, no more than 7 pages accepted. Contributors: George Keithley, John Bradley, Philip Dacey, Susan Clayton-Goldner, Meg Files, Ray Gonzalez, and Susan Thomas." circ. 300-400. 1/yr. Pub'd 1 issue 2005; expects 1 issue 2006, 1 issue 2007. sub. price $5; per copy $5; sample $5. Back issues: $5. Discounts: none. 54pp. Reporting time: 2 months. Simultaneous submissions accepted: no. Publishes 3% of manuscripts submitted. Payment: 1 copy. Copyrighted, reverts to author. Ads: none. Subjects: Environment, Poetry.

KESTREL: A Journal of Literature and Art, Mary Dillow Stewart, Editor; John Hoppenthaler, Poetry Editor; Jack Hussey, Fiction Editor; Marian Hollinger, Art Editor; Erica Henson, Student Editor, Fairmont State University, 1201 Locust Avenue, Fairmont, WV 26554-2451, 304-367-4815, Fax 304-367-4896, e-mail kestrel@mail.fscwv.edu. 1993. Poetry, fiction, art, photos, interviews, parts-of-novels, long-poems, plays, non-fiction. "We are interested in presenting a substantial selection of a contributor's work—3-7 poems; 6-8 pages of artwork; a selection from a novel, so long as it has thematic and structural integrity. We also ask that contributors write a brief preface to their work. What we hope to establish is a forum in which contributors may address issues, experiences, and insights that may draw artist and audience closer together." circ. 600. 2/yr. Pub'd 2 issues 2005; expects 2 issues 2006, 2 issues 2007. sub. price $18.00; per copy $10.00; sample $10.00. Back issues: $5.00. 150pp. Reporting time: 6-12 months. Simultaneous submissions accepted: no. Payment: 3 copies of issue. Copyrighted, reverts to author. Ads: none. Subjects: Appalachia, Autobiography, Biography, Diaries, Essays, Fiction, Folklore, Interviews, Non-Fiction, Photography, Poetry, Short Stories, Translation, Visual Arts.

Kettering Foundation Press (see also KETTERING REVIEW), 200 Commons Road, Dayton, OH 45459-2799, 937-434-7300. 1983. Articles. avg. press run 8M. Pub'd 1 title 2005; expects 3 titles 2006, 3 titles 2007. 64pp. Reporting time: 2 months. Copyrights for author. Subjects: Education, Politics, Society.

KETTERING REVIEW, Kettering Foundation Press, Robert J. Kingston, Editor-in-Chief, 200 Commons Road, Dayton, OH 45459-2799, 937-434-7300. 1983. "Designed for the intelligent lay public with special interest in deliberative democracy and the relationships between peoples and their governments, individuals and their communities and civic institutions. Non-fiction only. Requirements: Manuscripts of approx. 3M words from those working in public politics and education who can address ideas of national and international importance in an interdisciplinary and popularly readable fashion. Read a sample before submitting. Articles must be exceptionally well-written; issues usually organized around a theme. Uses 5-6 articles per issue. No footnotes. Mss. must be accompanied by SASE. No responsibility is assumed for the return of unsolicited manuscripts." circ. 8M. 2/yr. Pub'd 1 issue 2005; expects 2 issues 2006, 3 issues 2007. price per copy $7; sample $7. 64pp. Payment: copies. Copyrighted, reverts to author. Subjects: Communication, Journalism, Community, Education, Government, Media, Newspapers, Political Science, Politics, Public Affairs, Society, Sociology.

Key Publications, PO Box 1064, Santa Monica, CA 90406, 818-613-7348. 1990. Non-fiction. "First book: *Parenting Your Aging Parents - How to Guarantee and Protect Their Quality of Life, and Yours!.* Second book: *Out on Your Own - Everything You Need to Know Before, During, and After Leaving the Nest.*" avg. press run as needed. Expects 1 title 2006, 1 title 2007. Discounts: negotiable. 300pp. Reporting time: 4 weeks with SASE. Simultaneous submissions accepted: no. Publishes 1% of manuscripts submitted. Payment: negotiable. Copyrights for author.

THE KIDS' STORYTELLING CLUB WEBSITE, Storycraft Publishing, Vivian Dubrovin, PO Box 205, Masonville, CO 80541, 970-669-3755 phone/Fax, vivdub@aol.com, www.storycraft.com. 1996. "Designed for young storytellers, age 9-12, in language arts or computer classes, home schooling, computer camps, etc. Check website for upcoming themes (bottom of Welcome Page). Won the 2001 Pegasus Award for 'exemplary resource for young storytellers and for those working with youth.'" circ. 2.5M. 12/yr. Pub'd 12 issues 2005; expects 12 issues 2006, 6 issues 2007. sub. price free (online). Back issues: no longer available. Discounts: none. 7pp. Reporting time: query for assignment. Simultaneous submissions accepted: no. Payment: varies by contract. Not copyrighted. Ads: would be interested in talking to companies with storytelling products. Subjects: Children, Youth, Crafts, Hobbies, Education, Storytelling, Young Adult.

King Publishing, 1801 Bush Street, Suite 300, San Francisco, CA 94109, Fax 415-563-1467.

Kings Estate Press, Ruth Moon Kempher, 870 Kings Estate Road, St. Augustine, FL 32086, 800-249-7485, rmkkep@bellsouth.net. 1993. Poetry, fiction, art, long-poems. "No longer accepting unsolicited manuscripts, until further notice. Have published Wayne Hogan, Michael Hathaway, Joan Payne Kincaid, John Elsberg, among others; two anthologies." avg. press run 200-300. Pub'd 2 titles 2005; expects 3 titles 2006, 2 titles 2007. 50-80pp. Payment: negotiated. Copyrights for author. Subjects: Poetry, Short Stories.

KISS MACHINE, POB 108, Station P, Toronto, ON M5S 2S8, Canada.

Kiva Publishing, Inc., Stephen W. Hill, Editor, 21731 East Buckskin Drive, Walnut, CA 91789, 909-595-6833, fax 909-860-5424. 1992. Poetry, fiction, art, non-fiction. "Strong emphasis on Southwest Native American painting and themes." avg. press run 7.5M. Pub'd 4 titles 2005; expects 8 titles 2006, 8 titles 2007. Discounts: 1-4 30%, 5-25 40-45%, 25+ call for rates. Pages vary. Reporting time: 3 months. Simultaneous submissions accepted: yes. Payment: to be arranged. Copyrights for author. Subjects: Jewelry, Gems, Native American, New Mexico, Southwest, Visual Arts.

Kivaki Press, Fred A. Gray, 96 Paa Ko Drive, Sandia Park, NM 87047-0501, 828-274-7941, info@kivakipress.com, www.kivakipress.com. 1992. Non-fiction. "Kivaki Press is devoted to publishing books that cover topics within three interwoven themes: restoring our damaged ecosystems and wilderness areas; renewing our communities' economic and cultural vitality; and healing our bodies naturally and sustainably. We seek compelling narratives, essays, and demonstrations of successes in these areas of ecosystem, community, and body revitalization. We are a small press, which means that our authors realize higher quality relationships with Kivaki and to their published works. Recent works include: *Igniting The Sparkle...an Indigenous Science*

251

Education Model and *On The Trail of Beauty*, a book on the work of one indigenous artist.'' avg. press run 25M. Pub'd 1 title 2005; expects 2 titles 2006, 3 titles 2007. Discounts: distributors 45%; resellers, libraries 1-3 (or S.T.O.P.) 25%, 4-11 40%, 12-23 42%, 24+ 45%. Reporting time: 4-8 weeks. Payment: 8-12% of cover price on net copies sold, depending on author's willingness to help market titles, payable quarterly. Copyrights for author. Subjects: Community, Conservation, Culture, Ecology, Foods, Family, Health, Parenting, Philosophy, Sex, Sexuality, Spiritual.

KLIATT, Claire Rosser, Paula Rohrlick, Jean Palmer, 33 Bay State Road, Wellesley, MA 02481, 781-237-7577 phone/fax, kliatt@aol.com. 1967. Articles, reviews. *"Kliatt* publishes reviews of paperback books and hardcover young adult fiction, audiobooks, and educational software recommended for libraries and classrooms serving young adults. Each issue includes an article on a topic relevant to young adult librarians and teachers, and the last issue of the year (November) includes an index.'' circ. 2.3M. 6/yr. Pub'd 6 issues 2005; expects 6 issues 2006, 6 issues 2007. sub. price $39 (add $2 for Canada, in U.S. funds); per copy $6; sample free. Back issues: none. Discounts: $2.50 agency discount; 2 years $68. 64pp. Payment: none. Copyrighted, does not revert to author. Pub's reviews: 1200+ in 2005. §New paperbacks and hardcover fiction for young adults, audiobooks, educational software. Ads: $250/$190/other sizes available; discounts for 3- and 6-time advertisers. Subjects: Book Reviewing, Children, Youth, Libraries, Reviews.

KMT, A Modern Journal of Ancient Egypt, Dennis Forbes, PO Box 1475, Sebastopol, CA 95473, 707-823-6079 phone/Fax. 1990. Articles, art, photos, interviews, reviews, collages. "Focus is *Ancient Egypt:* history, art, archaeology and culture.'' circ. 15M. 4/yr. Pub'd 4 issues 2005; expects 4 issues 2006, 4 issues 2007. sub. price $32; per copy $8; sample $9.50 (incl. p/h). Back issues: same. Discounts: distributor 40%-50%. 88pp. Reporting time: 60 days. Payment: $50-$400. Copyrighted, reverts to author. Pub's reviews: 16-20 in 2005. §History, culture, archaeology and art of Egypt. Ads: 4-color ads: $1,290/$795/$1,500 inside cover/$1,000 2/3 page/$620 1/3 page/$420 1/4 page/$350 1/6 page; black/white ads: $920/$545/$1,300 inside cover/$690 2/3 page/$420 1/3 page/$275 1/4 page/$230 1/6 page; discounts for multiple insertions. Subjects: Anthropology, Archaelogy, Arts, Culture, History, Middle East.

Knife in the Toaster Publishing Company, LLC, PO Box 399, Cedar, MN 55011-0399, 763-434-2422, Fax 763-413-1181, ericmjs@aol.com. 2002. Expects 1 title 2006, 3 titles 2007.

Allen A. Knoll Publishers, Abby Schott, 200 W. Victoria Street, 2nd Floor, Santa Barbara, CA 93101-3627, 805-564-3377, Fax 805-966-6657, bookinfo@knollpublishers.com. 1990. Fiction, photos, non-fiction. "Not looking for new submissions at this time.'' avg. press run 3-10M. Pub'd 3 titles 2005; expects 3 titles 2006, 3 titles 2007. Discounts: standard. 300pp. Payment: percentage different for each book. Copyrights for author. Subjects: California, Children, Youth, Fiction, Gardening, History, Humor, Literature (General), Los Angeles, Mystery, Newspapers, Novels, Photography, Reprints, Short Stories, Visual Arts.

•Knowledge Concepts Publishing (see also GLOBAL ONE TRAVEL & AUTOMOTIVE MAGAZINE), Ella Patterson, P. O. Box 3084, Cedar Hill, TX 75105-3084, 972-223-1558. 1991. Articles, interviews, reviews, news items. "Magazines: To disseminate information to automotive manufacturers, suppliers and the consumer.Books: To provide all people with common knowledge about women issues.'' Pub'd 4 titles 2005. Discounts: 5- 10 copies 20%11-25 copies 25%26 and above 40%. 255pp. Reporting time: approximately 7 to 10 days. Simultaneous submissions accepted: No. Publishes 8% of manuscripts submitted. Payment: 15%. Copyrights for author. Subjects: Advertising, Self-Promotion, Aromatherapy, Comics, Education, Feminism, Food, Eating, How-To, Motivation, Success, Newsletter, Newspapers, Parenting, Peace, Self-Help, Sex, Sexuality, Women.

KNUCKLE MERCHANT - The Journal of Naked Literary Aggression, Lost Prophet Press, Christopher Jones, 221 Stanford Drive SE #2, Albuquerque, NM 87106-3586, 505.256.4589 knucklemerchant@hotmail.com. 2001. Poetry, fiction, articles, art, photos, interviews, satire, criticism, reviews, non-fiction. circ. 500. 2/yr. Pub'd 2 issues 2005; expects 2 issues 2006, 2 issues 2007. sub. price $20; sample $5. Reporting time: 1 month. Simultaneous submissions accepted: yes. Publishes 1% of manuscripts submitted. Payment: 1-2 copies. Not copyrighted. Pub's reviews. Ads: $50/$25/$15. Subjects: Arts, Charles Bukowski, Celtic, Fiction, Poetry, Visual Arts.

Kobalt Books, Cedric Mixon, P.O. Box 1062, Bala Cynwyd, PA 19004, 314-503-5462. 2003. Poetry, fiction, non-fiction. "Journals.'' avg. press run 150. Pub'd 6 titles 2005; expects 3 titles 2006, 5 titles 2007. Discounts: 50% discount. 120pp. Reporting time: immediately. Simultaneous submissions accepted: Yes. Publishes 20% of manuscripts submitted. Payment: 50% net receipts. Does not copyright for author. Subjects: Advertising, Self-Promotion, African Literature, Africa, African Studies, African-American, Anthology, Biography, Motivation, Success, Public Relations/Publicity, Publishing, Religion, Romance.

KOBISENA, Prakalpana Literature, P40 Nandana Park, Calcutta 700 034, W.B., India. 1/yr. Pub'd 1 issue 2005; expects 1 issue 2006, 1 issue 2007. price per copy 1 IRC. 8pp.

Kodiak Media Group, Grabenhorst Rhonda, Contact Person, PO Box 1029-DB, Wilsonville, OR 97070, Fax 503-625-4087. 1989. Non-fiction. "Specializing in deafness, disability, deaf education, deaf culture, parents of deaf children, ASL and sign language." avg. press run varies. Pub'd 1 title 2005; expects 2 titles 2006, 2 titles 2007. Discounts: 1-3 0%, 5+ 30%, 10+ 40% (non returnable) FOB Wilsonville, OR. 112pp. Reporting time: varies. Payment: negotiable. Copyrights are negotiable. Subjects: Culture, Disabled, Education, Newsletter, Parenting, Sexual Abuse.

KOJA, Mikhail Magazinnik, Editor, PO Box 140083, Brooklyn, NY 11214. 1996. Poetry, fiction, art, collages, plays, concrete art. "This is the magazine of experimental writing/art exploring Russian/American avant crossroads. Some contributers are: R. Kostelanetz, Eileen Myles, William James Austin, Spencer Selby, Raymond Federman, Bruce Andrews. Unsolicited submissions must be accompanied by $7 for a sample copy. Submissions w/o $7 will be returned unread." circ. 200. 1-2/yr. Pub'd 1 issue 2005; expects 1 issue 2006, 2 issues 2007. sub. price not available; per copy $7; sample $7. 64pp. Reporting time: 6-9 months. Simultaneous submissions accepted: no. Publishes a variable % of manuscripts submitted. Payment: single copy. Copyrighted, reverts to author. Ads: $60/$40. Subjects: Absurdist, Avant-Garde, Experimental Art, Fiction, Poetry, Poetry, Post Modern, Prose, Short Stories, Translation, Visual Arts.

•**KOKORO,** Rebecca Knowlton, 454 N. Chugach, Palmer, AK 99645, http://www.kokoro-press.com. 2005. Fiction, articles, photos, cartoons, interviews, non-fiction. "Kokoro is targetted to the non-competition martial artist, specifically Shotokan karate, regardless of age, gender or organizational affiliation. Kokoro is interested in information specifically about the role of martial arts in every day life, health, stretching, and balance between mind, body and spirit." circ. 1000. 4/yr. Expects 4 issues 2006, 4 issues 2007. sub. price $20; per copy $5.00; sample free. Back issues: inquire. Discounts: not yet known. 12pp. Pub's reviews: none in 2005. §any material directly related to martial arts; specifically Shotokan Karate. Ads: not yet known.

Kosmos Books, 991 St. Andrews Drive, Ste. 138, Upland, CA 91784, ellesawatzky@earthlink.net.

KotaPress (see also DIFFERENT KIND OF PARENTING; KOTAPRESS ONLINE JOURNALS), Kara L.C. Jones, PO Box 514, Vashon Island, WA 98070-0514, editor@kotapress.com, www.kotapress.com. 1999. Poetry, articles, art, interviews, long-poems, non-fiction. "*We take e-mail submissions only*. We do not open any email attachments, so don't bother sending those. Please note, first and foremost, we are most interested in works (poetry included) written by parents after the death of a child. But not interested in religious oriented "make it better" takes on the experience. 1) For KotaPress Online Loss Journal, please see www.kotapress.com for current issues, full guidelines and archive. Please note that the Loss Journal publishes *non-fiction* poetry, essays, articles, short stories, etc. Please read current issue at least to make sure you really want to be published with us. 2) For our "Different Kind of Parenting: a zine for parents whose children have died" we are also looking for *non-fiction* works. This zine comes out in PDF format for email subscribers. Please query via email to editor@kotapress.com with "DIFF PARENT" in the subj line of your note for more information. Thanks!" Pub'd 12 titles 2005; expects 12 titles 2006, 12 titles 2007. 160-250pp. Reporting time: 1-6 months. Simultaneous submissions accepted: no. Publishes 25% of manuscripts submitted. Payment: Free access to e-book anthologies, online journals, and free author copies for print publication. One time electronic rights w/archive rights under Kota Press, then rights revert to author. Please note we ask for archive rights—this means we do not take down materials from the website after they are published, so don't ask us to do that for you! Subjects: Book Arts, Grieving, Literary Review, Anais Nin, Non-Violence, Pacific Northwest, Peace, Poetry.

KOTAPRESS ONLINE JOURNALS, KotaPress, Kara L. C. Jones, PO Box 514, Vashon Island, WA 98070-0514. 1999. "Email submissions only. We've archived all Journals except Loss Journal. Looking for works coming from real life grief, healing, loss, transformation experiences. Real death, dying, and grief are hard enough to deal with, so please don't send fictional pieces made up for entertainment purposes!" 6 to 12/y. sub. price free online. Back issues: Full archive available at KotaPress.com. Simultaneous submissions accepted: Yes. Copyrighted, reverts to author. Pub's reviews: approx. 4 in 2005. §Works about grief and healing based on real experiences.

Kotzig Publishing, Inc., Susan McCabe, 109 NW 16th St., Delray Beach, FL 33444-3029, 800-589-7989, Fax 561-819-0207, susan@kotzigpublishing.com, www.kotzigpublishing.com. 2001. avg. press run 5000. Pub'd 5 titles 2005; expects 3 titles 2006, 3 titles 2007. Discounts: start at 30% depending on volume.

KRAX, Andy Robson, 63 Dixon Lane, Leeds, Yorkshire LS12 4RR, England. 1971. Poetry, fiction, articles, art, photos, cartoons, interviews. "Prefer whimsical and amusing work by both writers and artists." 1/yr. Pub'd 1 issue 2005; expects 1 issue 2006, 1 issue 2007. sub. price £3.50 ($7) incl. Postage; per copy £3.50 ($7) incl. postage; sample $1. Back issues: on request. Discounts: trade 40%. 72pp. Reporting time: 6-8 weeks. Simultaneous submissions accepted: no. Publishes 8% of manuscripts submitted. Payment: cover design only £10 ($20). Copyrighted, reverts to author. Pub's reviews: 124 in 2005. §Light-hearted poetry. Subjects: Humor, Poetry.

Kriya Yoga Publications, 196 Mountain Road, PO Box 90, Eastman, Quebec J0E 1P0, Canada. 1989. avg. press run 3M. Pub'd 6 titles 2005. 250pp. Simultaneous submissions accepted: yes. Payment: 10% of net revenue.

KT Publishing, 111 West Ocean Blvd., 10th Floor, Long Beach, CA 90801.

Kumarian Press, Inc., Sondhi Krishna, Publisher-President; Erica Flock, Head of Marketing and Production; Jim Lance, Associate Publisher and Editor; Becky McRoberts, Controller, 1294 Blue Hills Avenue, Bloomfield, CT 06002, 860-243-2098, FAX 860-243-2867, ordering 1-800-289-2667, kpbooks@kpbooks.com, www.kpbooks.com. 1977. Non-fiction. ''We are an independent publisher of scholarly works that promote international engagement and an awareness of global connectedness. Our books look at current global issues, their social, ethical, cultural, political and economic context, and ways to overcome the problems they pose. Our publications deal with globalization, poverty, environment, health, the economy, and human rights. Please consult our website www.kpbooks.com for manuscript submission guidelines.'' avg. press run 1.5M-3M. Pub'd 13 titles 2005; expects 16 titles 2006, 20 titles 2007. Discounts: short/bookstores 10% on 1-2 mixed titles STOP orders, 15% on 3-4, 20% on 5+; wholesale and jobber 11+-30%. 288pp. Reporting time: 30-60 days. Simultaneous submissions accepted: yes. Copyrights for author in some instances. Subjects: Agriculture, Anthropology, Archaelogy, Business & Economics, Conservation, Environment, Gender Issues, Global Affairs, Government, Hunger, Immigration, Peace, Political Science, Politics, Sociology, Third World, Minorities.

KUMQUAT MERINGUE, Christian Nelson, PO Box 736, Pine Island, MN 55963-0736, Telephone 507-367-4430, moodyriver@aol.com, www.kumquatcastle.com. 1990. Poetry, fiction, art, photos, satire, reviews. ''Recent contributors: Lynne Douglass, Mark Weber, Ianthe Brautigan, Denise Duhamel, Eugene McCarthy, and Lyn Lifshin. Mostly use short poetry, rare pieces of short prose. Looking for writings that 'remind' us of the same feeling we get from reading Richard Brautigan. Also like to read things 'about' Richard Brautigan. Never any reading fees or 'contests'.'' circ. 600. Irregular. Expects 1 issue 2006, 1 issue 2007. sub. price $12/3 issues; per copy $6; sample $6. Back issues: usually sold to collectors at high prices. 40pp. Reporting time: 30-120 days. Simultaneous submissions accepted, but please let us know. Publishes Less than 1% of manuscripts submitted. Payment: 1 copy for each issue they appear in. Copyrighted, reverts to author. Subjects: Beat, Ernest Hemingway, Sherlock Holmes, Humor, Indians, Japan, Minnesota, Montana, New Mexico, Poetry, Sex, Sexuality, Southwest.

KUUMBA, BLK Publishing Company, Mark Haile, PO Box 83912, Los Angeles, CA 90083, 310-410-0808, fax 310-410-9250, e-mail newsroom@blk.com. 1991. Poetry, long-poems. ''Poetry journal for black lesbians and gay men. Atlanta address: 4300 Flat Shoals Road #1910, Union City, GA 30291, 770-964-7247, Fax 770-969-7857, jay1hatl@aol.com.'' circ. 1M. 2/yr. Expects 2 issues 2006, 2 issues 2007. sub. price $7.50; per copy $4.50; sample $5.50. Back issues: $5.50. 48pp. Reporting time: 4 weeks. Simultaneous submissions accepted: yes. Publishes 30% of manuscripts submitted. Payment: none. Copyrighted, rights reverting to author varies. Pub's reviews: 2 in 2005. §Black lesbian and gay community. Ads: $260. Subjects: African-American, Black, Gay, Lesbianism, Poetry.

KWC Press, Edmund August, Editor, 851 S. 4th Street #207, Louisville, KY 40203, eaugust@insightbb.com. 2002. Poetry, fiction, parts-of-novels, long-poems, non-fiction. ''We publish three chapbooks each year:one in poetry, one in fiction, and one in creative non-fiction. All of the chapbooks are chosen through contests hosted by the Kentucky Writers' Coalition. www.kentuckywriters.org.'' Copyrights for author.

L

L D A Publishers, 42-46 209 Street, Suite B-11, Bayside, NY 11361, 718-224-9484, Fax 718-224-9487, 888-388-9887. 1974. Non-fiction. avg. press run 1M. Pub'd 3 titles 2005; expects 3 titles 2006, 3 titles 2007. Discounts: 10% over 24 copies. 300pp. Copyrights for author. Subjects: Libraries, Reference.

La Alameda Press, J.B. Bryan, 9636 Guadalupe Trail NW, Albuquerque, NM 87114, 505-897-0285, www.laalamedapress.com. 1991. Poetry, fiction, non-fiction. ''We are a small press with an emphasis on literature: poetry, fiction, and creative non-fiction. Kate Horsley won the ''1996 Western States Book Award for Fiction'' for *A Killing in New Town*, which is now in its second printing. Several other titles are also in further editions. We are distributed by the University of New Mexico Press and Small Press Distribution. We do not accept unsolicited manuscripts becuase of our committment to regional writers and kindred spirits we know and work with. This simply happens to be our mission.'' avg. press run 1M. Pub'd 6 titles 2005; expects 6 titles 2006. Discounts: 40% bookstores, 55% distributors, 10% libraries or schools. 100-300pp. Simultaneous submissions accepted: no. Publishes 0% of manuscripts submitted. Payment: in books (10% of print run).

Copyrights for author. Subjects: Agriculture, Culture, Ecology, Foods, Feminism, Fiction, Gardening, Haiku, Health, Literature (General), Native American, New Mexico, Non-Fiction, Poetry, Southwest, Zen.

Labor Arts Books, Emanuel Fried, 215 East Hazeltine Ave.., Kenmore, NY 14217-2828, 716-873-4131. 1975. Fiction, plays. "For the moment not seeking submissions. Still working on distribution of present publications: *The Dodo Bird, Drop Hammer, Meshugah and Other Stories, Elegy for Stanley Gurski, Big Ben Hood, The Un-American.*" avg. press run 5M. Expects 1 title 2006. Discounts: write for information. 32-520pp. Payment: individual arrangement. Copyrights for author. Subjects: Drama, Labor, Theatre.

LABOUR/LE TRAVAIL, Canadian Committee on Labour History, Bryan D. Palmer, Arts Publications, FM 2005, Memorial University, St. John's, NF A1C 5S2, Canada, 709-737-2144. 1976. Articles, reviews, non-fiction. "Articles 20-60 pages, reviews 1000 words. Alvin Finkel, History, Athabasca University." circ. 1M. 2/yr. Pub'd 2 issues 2005; expects 2 issues 2006, 2 issues 2007. sub. price $25CDN, $30 US; per copy $20 CDN, $20 US; sample free. Back issues: Complete set $960 (48 issues, new subscribers $540). Discounts: 5 or more 20%. 400pp. Reporting time: 4 months. Simultaneous submissions accepted: no. Publishes 40% of manuscripts submitted. Payment: none. Copyrighted, does not revert to author. Pub's reviews: 100 in 2005. §Labour, history, especially social. Ads: $200/$150. Subjects: History, Labor.

LADYBUG, the Magazine for Young Children, Marianne Carus, Editor-in-Chief; Paula Morrow, Executive Editor, 315 5th Street, PO Box 300, Peru, IL 61354, 815-224-5803, ext. 656, Fax 815-224-6615, mmiklavcic@caruspub.com. 1990. Poetry, fiction, art, music, non-fiction. "Fiction: 300-800 words. Poems: 20 lines maximum. Crafts/activities/games: 1-4 pages. Original finger plays (12 lines max.) and action rhymes (20 lines max.). *Ladybug* is for children ages 2-6 and their parents and caregivers. SASE is required for a response." circ. 130M. 12/yr. Pub'd 12 issues 2005; expects 12 issues 2006, 12 issues 2007. sub. price $35.97; per copy $5; sample $5. Back issues: $5. 36pp. Reporting time: 12 weeks, SASE required. Simultaneous submissions accepted: yes, please indicate. Publishes 1% of manuscripts submitted. Payment: 25¢/word (fiction); $3/line (poetry). Copyrighted. Rights vary. Ads: none.

LadyePress USA, LLC, 230 West Laurel Street #705, San Diego, CA 92101-1467. 2001. avg. press run 5M. Discounts: standard. 145pp. Reporting time: 3 months. Simultaneous submissions accepted: yes. Payment: standard. Copyrights for author. Subjects: Biography, Gay, History.

Ladyslipper Press, Victoria Brehm, 15075 County Line Road, Tustin, MI 49688, 231-775-9455, www.ladyslipperpress.com. 2000. Fiction, articles, interviews, letters, non-fiction. "Ms. must be concerned with the Great Lakes. Submission requirements posted on the website." avg. press run 5M. Expects 1 title 2006, 2-3 titles 2007. Reporting time: 30 days. We accept simultaneous submissions, with notification. Payment: standard. Copyrights for author. Subject: Great Lakes.

•**Laguna Wilderness Press,** Ronald Chilcote, Founding Editor; Jerry Burchfield, Founding Editor, P.O. Box 149, Laguna Beach, CA 92652, Phone: 951-827-1571, Fax: 951-827-5685, info@lagunawildernesspress.com, www.lagunawildernesspress.com. 2002. Art, photos, collages, non-fiction. "Laguna Wilderness Press is a non-profit press dedicated to publishing books about the presence, preservation and importance of wilderness environments. In an effort to increase public awareness of these issues, Laguna Wilderness Press publishes books that feature the work of concerned artists, photographers, and environmentalists. Our books move in two directions: (1) to depict nature and pristine wilderness areas through photography and essay; (2) to focus on changing landscape and the impact of urban growth, technology, and development on natural beauty and resources. Recent titles include the works of Ronald Chilcote, Jerry Burchfield, Paul Paiement, and Robert Hansen." avg. press run 2500. Pub'd 2 titles 2005; expects 1 title 2006, 1 title 2007. Discounts: Distributors: 50%, Retailers: 40%. 112pp. Reporting time: 2 Weeks. Simultaneous submissions accepted: No. Copyrights for author. Subjects: Animals, Anthropology, Archaelogy, Avant-Garde, Experimental Art, Biology, Botany, Conservation, Earth, Natural History, Environment, Essays, Midwest, Native American, Nature, Photography, Wyoming, Yosemite.

Lahontan Images, Tim I. Purdy, PO Box 1592, Susanville, CA 96130-1592, 530-257-6747. 1986. Non-fiction. "Primarily interested in the history and related topics of eastern California and Nevada. First title is Eric N. Moody's *Flanigan: Anatomy of a Railroad Ghost Town.*" avg. press run 2M. Expects 2 titles 2006, 4 titles 2007. Discounts: 5 or more 40%. 150pp. Reporting time: 1 month. Payment: percentage of sales. Copyrights for author. Subjects: Agriculture, California, History, The West.

Lake Claremont Press, Sharon Woodhouse, 4650 N. Rockwell Street, Chicago, IL 60625, 773-583-7800, Fax 773-583-7877, lcp@lakeclaremont.com, www.lakeclaremont.com. 1994. Non-fiction. "Recent titles: *A Cook's Guide to Chicago; The Politics of Place: A History of Zoning in Chicago; A Field Guide to Gay and Lesbian Chicago; Today's Chicago Blues; A Chicago Tavern: A Goat, A Curse, and the American Dream.* Lake Claremont Press always welcomes book proposals for regional/nonfiction histories and guidebooks. Our focus is the Chicagoland area. If you have a query that fits these qualifications, we ask that you submit the following: 1)Book proposal/cover letter 2)Book outline 3)Author credentials 4)Brief marketing analysis 5)1-2 sample chapters (if not available send samples of previous writing) Please do not send a full manuscript until it is requested. Visit www.lakeclaremont.com for more information on our titles and authors.'' avg. press run 3M-6M. Pub'd 4 titles 2005; expects 6 titles 2006, 7 titles 2007. Discounts: 1-49 40%, 50-99 50%, 100+ 55%. 300pp. Reporting time: 3 weeks to 3 months. Simultaneous submissions accepted: yes. Publishes 5-20% of manuscripts submitted. Payment: royalties 10-15% net, paid monthly. Copyrights for author. Subjects: Chicago, Cities, Entertainment, Folklore, Food, Eating, Great Lakes, History, Illinois, Movies, Non-Fiction, Reference, Supernatural, Travel.

LAKE EFFECT, George Looney, Editor-in-Chief, Penn State Erie, 5091 Station Road, Erie, PA 16563-1501, 814-898-6281. 2001. Poetry, fiction, long-poems, non-fiction. 1/yr. sub. price $6; per copy $6. 150pp. Reporting time: 1-4 months. Simultaneous submissions accepted: yes. Publishes 5% of manuscripts submitted. Payment: two copies. Subjects: Absurdist, Arts, Avant-Garde, Experimental Art, Criticism, Experimental, Fiction, Folklore, Gender Issues, Non-Fiction, Philosophy, Poetry, Post Modern, Short Stories.

•LAKE STREET LIT: Art and Words from the Bottom of Lake Bonneville, Meredith Rae Nelson, P.O. Box 581438, Salt Lake City, UT 84158-1438, www.lakestreetlit.com. 2005. Poetry, fiction, art, photos, cartoons, music, parts-of-novels, long-poems, collages, plays, concrete art, non-fiction. ''The publication highlights musings relevant to Salt Lake City with themes local yet universal: church and state, alien and clique, tolerance and acceptance, homeland and war. Featured writers and artists have something to say literally and figuratively about our people, culture, and influences. Or, they want to contribute to our mythology.'' circ. 400. 2/yr. Expects 2 issues 2006, 2 issues 2007. price per copy $0; sample free. Back issues: inquire. 76pp. Reporting time: 1 month or less. Simultaneous submissions accepted: Yes. Payment: contributors are not paid. Copyrighted, reverts to author. Subjects: Arts, Avant-Garde, Experimental Art, Community, Creativity, Culture, Literature (General), Memoirs, Non-Fiction, Poetry, Religion, Sex, Sexuality, Society, Storytelling, Utah, Visual Arts.

LAKE SUPERIOR MAGAZINE, Lake Superior Port Cities Inc., Paul L. Hayden, Associate Publisher; Konnie LeMay, Editor, Lake Superior Port Cities Inc., P.O. Box 16417, Duluth, MN 55816-0417, 218-722-5002, fax 218-722-4096, www.lakesuperior.com, e-mail: edit@lakesuperior.com. 1979. Fiction, articles, photos, cartoons, interviews, reviews, letters, news items, non-fiction. ''We are a high-quality, glossy consumer magazine. We prefer manuscripts, but well-researched queries are attended to. We actively seek queries from writers in Lake Superior communities. Provide enough information on why the subject is important to the region and our readers, or why and how something is unique. We want details. The writer must have a thorough knowledge of the subject and how it relates to our region. We prefer a fresh, unused approach to the subject which provides the reader with an emotional involvement. Average 800-1,500 words, graphics/photos important.'' circ. 20M. 7/yr. Pub'd 7 issues 2005; expects 7 issues 2006, 7 issues 2007. sub. price $21.95; per copy $3.95 + p/h; sample same. Back issues: all issues $10, except current year—list available. 80pp. Reporting time: 3-5 months. Accept simultaneous submissions, but must know it is the case. Payment: up to $600, pix $20 (B&W), $50 (color), cover $125. Copyrighted, first rights for 90 days after publication. Pub's reviews: 12 in 2005. §Must be regional (Lake Superior) in topics covered. Ads: Full page $2,238 color; Full Page $1,790 B&W; Half page $1,500 color; Half Page $1,110 B&W. Subjects: Antiques, Arts, Book Reviewing, Business & Economics, Culture, Environment, Folklore, Gardening, Great Lakes, History, Native American, Photography, Shipwrecks, Travel, Water.

Lake Superior Port Cities Inc. (see also LAKE SUPERIOR MAGAZINE), Paul L. Hayden, Associate Publisher; Konnie LeMay, Editor, P.O. Box 16417, Duluth, MN 55816-0417, 888-244-5253, 218-722-5002, FAX 218-722-4096, www.lakesuperior.com, reader@lakesuperior.com. 1979.

Lakepointe Publishing, PO Box 767, Enid, OK 73702-0767.

Lamp Light Press, A.C. Doyle, Founder, Publishing Division, PO Box 416, Denver, CO 80201-0416, 303-575-5676, Fax 303-575-1187. 1983. avg. press run 600. Discounts: distributed by Prosperity & Profits Unlimited, PO Box 416, Denver, CO 80201. 60pp. Reporting time: 6 weeks. Subjects: Alternative Medicine, Business & Economics, Cooking, Creativity, Education, Family, Food, Eating, Health, How-To, Inspirational, Motivation, Success, Poetry, Publishing, Spiritual, Textbooks.

Lancer Militaria, Box 1188, Mt. Ida, AR 71957-1188, 870-867-2232; www.warbooks.com. 1978. ''Specialize in reference type material for military collectors/historians.'' avg. press run 3M. Pub'd 2 titles 2005; expects 3 titles 2006. Discounts: 40-50% depending on quantity. 112pp. Copyrights for author. Subject: Military, Veterans.

Land Yacht Press, Jay Richiuso, 504 Holt Valley Road, Nashville, TN 37221-1602, 615-646-2186 phone/Fax, landyachtpress@mindspring.com. 1995. Non-fiction. ''We publish books on history, local history, genealogy, and photographs, both as new books and reprints.'' avg. press run 200-1.5M. Pub'd 1 title 2005; expects 2 titles 2006, 2 titles 2007. Discounts: 1-5 books 20%, 6+ 40%. 260pp. Reporting time: 2 months. Simultaneous submissions accepted: yes. Publishes 50% of manuscripts submitted. Payment: 10% of net receipts, quarterly.

Depending on situation, we may/not allow author to hold copyright. Subjects: Genealogy, History, New York, Photography, Tennessee.

THE LANGSTON HUGHES REVIEW, Valerie Babb, Editor; R. Baxter Miller, Executive Editor, Department of English, 254 Park Hall, Univ. of Georgia, Athens, GA 30602-6205, 706-542-1261. 1982. Articles, interviews, criticism, reviews, news items. "Publishes articles on Langston Hughes, specifically, his cultural milieu and American modernism more generally. Also publishes special issues. Peer-reviewed." circ. 300-325. 2/yr. Pub'd 1 issue 2005; expects 2 issues 2006, 2 issues 2007. sub. price $20 ($25 foreign); per copy $14. Back issues: $9. 40-60pp. Reporting time: 6-8 weeks. Simultaneous submissions accepted: no. Publishes 3% of manuscripts submitted. Payment: none. Copyrighted, rights do not revert to author, but on request of author rights are assigned. Pub's reviews: 1 in 2005. §Langston Hughes and his contemporaries; African American literature and culture. Subject: Literary Review.

•**LANGUAGEANDCULTURE.NET,** Liz Fortini, 4000 Pimlico Drive, Ste. 114-192, Pleasanton, CA 94588, 925-462-0490 info@languageandculture.net. 2001. Poetry. "Languageandculture.net, an online poetry journal, welcomes original poetry and their English translation in the following languages: Spanish, French, German, Russian, Italian and the Slavic languages. Other languages are under review. We accept translations of known writers: please include the original language. Languageandculture.net also accepts original poetry in English. Please check online for submission guidelines, send 3-5 poems and a short bio and address inquiries to info@languageandculture.net. We also offer an annual Chapbook Series." 2/yr. Pub'd 35 issues 2005; expects 40 issues 2006. sample price 0. 40pp. Reporting time: 3 weeks. Simultaneous submissions accepted: Yes. Publishes 30% of manuscripts submitted. Payment: there is no paymnet. Copyrighted, reverts to author. Pub's reviews: none in 2005. §poetry. Subject: Poetry.

Lao Tse Press, Ltd. (see also JOURNAL OF PROCESS ORIENTED PSYCHOLOGY), Kate Jobe, Leslie Heizer, 2049 NW Hoyt Street, Portland, OR 97209-1260, 503-222-3395; fax 503-222-3778. 1995. Non-fiction. avg. press run 3-5M. Pub'd 2 titles 2005; expects 2 titles 2006, 4 titles 2007. Discounts: trade 1-4 20%, 5-9 40%, 10-24 42%, 25-49 43%. 300pp. Reporting time: 1-3 months. Simultaneous submissions accepted: yes. Publishes 90% of manuscripts submitted. Payment: yes. Copyrights for author. Subjects: Dreams, Health, New Mexico, Psychology.

The Larcom Press (see also LARCOM REVIEW), Susan Oleksiw, Rae Francover, Cliff Post, Natalie Greenburg, Eleanor Lodge, PO Box 161, Prides Crossing, MA 01965, 978-927-8707, Fax 978-927-8904, amp@larcompress.com, www.larcompress.com. 1998. Fiction, art, photos, reviews, non-fiction. "Mystery novels 60-80,000 words." avg. press run 1.5M. Pub'd 4 titles 2005; expects 6 titles 2006, 6-8 titles 2007. Discounts: 55% distributors, 40% bookstores. 200-265pp. Simultaneous submissions accepted: no. Publishes 10% of manuscripts submitted. Copyrights for author. Subjects: Book Reviewing, Fiction, Mystery, Non-Fiction, Photography.

LARCOM REVIEW, The Larcom Press, Susan Oleksiw, Rae Francover, Cliff Post, Natalie Greenburg, Eleanor Lodge, PO Box 161, Prides Crossing, MA 01965, 978-927-8707, Fax 978-927-8904, amp@larcompress.com, www.larcompress.com. 1998. Poetry, fiction, articles, art, photos, reviews, non-fiction. "Length of short stories and essays: 3,000 words. Recent contributors: Robert Chute, Robert Crawford, Holly Iglesias, Rhina Espaillat." circ. 300. 2/yr. Pub'd 2 issues 2005; expects 2 issues 2006, 2 issues 2007. sub. price $20; per copy $12; sample $7. Discounts: 40% to stores, 55% wholesalers. 250pp. Reporting time: none. Simultaneous submissions accepted: no. Payment: $25 story, poem, photo; $300 cover photo and special project. Copyrighted, reverts to author. Pub's reviews: a few in 2005. §Books on the new landscape and its people. Ads: none. Subjects: Book Reviewing, Fiction, Non-Fiction, Photography, Poetry.

Laredo Publishing Co., Inc./Renaissance House, 9400 Lloydcrest Drive, Beverly Hills, CA 90210-2528. 1991. "Children's/youth books." avg. press run 2M. Pub'd 15 titles 2005. Discounts: 40-45%. 32pp. Reporting time: 2-3 weeks. Simultaneous submissions accepted: yes. Publishes 20% of manuscripts submitted. Payment: 7%. Copyrights for author. Subject: Children, Youth.

THE LAS VEGAS INSIDER, Donald Currier, Good 'n' Lucky, PO Box 1185, Chino Valley, AZ 86323-1185. 1974. Articles, criticism, reviews, news items. circ. 5.1M. 12/yr. Pub'd 12 issues 2005; expects 12 issues 2006, 12 issues 2007. sub. price $45; sample $4. Back issues: $50 per 12 issues (any) 52. 8pp. Reporting time: 1 week. Payment: yes. Copyrighted, reverts to author. Pub's reviews: 10-15 in 2005. §Gaming, travel, finance. Ads: none. Subjects: Electronics, Transportation.

LATERAL MOVES, Alan White, Nick Britton, 5 Hamilton Street, Astley Bridge, Bolton BL1 6RJ, United Kingdom, (01204) 596369. 1994. Poetry, fiction, articles, art, cartoons, interviews, satire, reviews, letters, collages, news items, non-fiction. "A non-profitmaking magazine published by a voluntary arts organization. Recent contributors include: Morgan Kenney, Giovanni Malito, Sam Smith, Dave Ward, Andy Darlington, Neily Henderson, DF Lewis, Matthew Firth, Geoff Lowe, Brendan McMahon, David Price, Dee Rimbaud, Geoff Stevens and Ben Wilensky. The magazine features a strong element of down-to-earth humour and is politically incorrect. *Later Moves* networks extensively with other magazines." circ. 150. 6/yr. Pub'd 6 issues 2005; expects 6 issues 2006, 6 issues 2007. sub. price £18, $30 US; per copy £3.85, $6.50 US; sample £3.85, $6.50 US. Back issues: prices vary, SAE for details. Discounts: by negotiation. 48-52pp. Reporting time: 3 months. Simultaneous submissions accepted: no. Publishes 30% of manuscripts submitted. Payment: free copy of magazine. Copyrighted, reverts to author. Pub's reviews: 12 in 2005. §Small press publications and magazines, fiction. Ads: £20, $33 US/£10, $17 US/ £5, $8.50 US 1/4 page. Subjects: Arts, Avant-Garde, Experimental Art, Fiction, Literature (General), Magazines, Poetry.

Latham Foundation (see also THE LATHAM LETTER), Hugh H. Tebault III, Latham Plaza, 1826 Clement Avenue, Alameda, CA 94501-1397, 510-521-0920, www.latham.org. 1918. Non-fiction. "Publisher of educational books in the field of humane education. Teaching respect toward animals, and showing respect for each other are core values carried in all the works." Pub'd 4 titles 2005; expects 4 titles 2006, 4 titles 2007. Discounts: Std distribution schedule, special discounts for allied organizations. 64pp. Reporting time: varies.

THE LATHAM LETTER, Latham Foundation, Latham Found., Latham Plaza Bldg., 1826 Clement Avenue, Alameda, CA 94501-1397, 415-521-0920, www.latham.org. 1918. Poetry, articles, cartoons, interviews, reviews, letters, non-fiction. circ. 4M. 4/yr. Pub'd 4 issues 2005; expects 4 issues 2006, 4 issues 2007. sub. price $15, $25/2 years; per copy $2.50. Back issues: special rates. Discounts: contact Latham Foundation. 24pp. Reporting time: 30 days next issue, if appropriate as to time frame. Copyrighted, rights revert to author, but authorization to republish is rarely withheld. Pub's reviews: 14 in 2005. §Human/companion animal bond, pet-facilitated therapy, humane welfare, child protection, domestic violence, promotion of respect for all life through education. Subjects: Animals, Biology, Children, Youth, Conservation, Ecology, Foods, Education, Humanism.

LATIN AMERICAN LITERARY REVIEW, Latin American Literary Review Press, Yvette E. Miller, PO Box 17660, Pittsburgh, PA 15235-0860, 412-824-7903, www.lalrp.org, latinreview@hotmail.com. 1972. Fiction, articles, photos, interviews, criticism, reviews, music, non-fiction. "Length of article varies from 10-20 pages in special issues. Some recent contributors: Roberto Gonzales Echevarria, Jose J. Arrom, Guillermo Cabrera Infante, John Updike, Alistair Reid, Robert Coles, Jorge de Sena, Harold de Campos, Joaquin de Sousa Andrade et al. Articles published in English, Spanish & Portuguese." circ. 1M. 2/yr. Pub'd 2 issues 2005; expects 2 issues 2006, 2 issues 2007. sub. price $47; per copy $25; sample $25. Back issues: $14. Discounts: 10% for subscription agencies. 150pp. Reporting time: within 12 weeks. Simultaneous submissions accepted: no. Copyrighted. Pub's reviews: 10 in 2005. §Recent Latin American Fiction, poetry, theatre, criticism. Ads: $250/$145/$100. Subjects: Latin America, Literature (General).

Latin American Literary Review Press (see also LATIN AMERICAN LITERARY REVIEW), Yvette E. Miller, PO Box 17660, Pittsburgh, PA 15235-0860, 412-824-7903, www.lalrp.org, latinreview@hotmail.com. 1980. Fiction, photos, criticism, plays, non-fiction. "English translations of works by prominent L.A. writers." avg. press run 1.5M. Pub'd 8 titles 2005; expects 10 titles 2006, 10 titles 2007. Discounts: negotiable. 160pp. Reporting time: 4 months. Simultaneous submissions accepted: no. Publishes 1% of manuscripts submitted. Payment: varies. Copyrights for author. Subjects: Bilingual, Latin America, Latino, Literary Review, Literature (General), Spain.

LATIN AMERICAN PERSPECTIVES, Ronald H. Chilcote, Managing Editor, PO Box 5703, Riverside, CA 92517-5703, 951-827-1571, fax 951-827-5685, laps@mail.ucr.edu, www.latinamericanperspectives.com. 1974. Articles, art, photos, interviews, reviews. "Obtain subscriptions through: Sage Publications, 2455 Teller Road, Thousand Oaks, Ca 91320." circ. 2M. 6/yr. Pub'd 6 issues 2005; expects 6 issues 2006, 6 issues 2007. sub. price Individual Subscription: $74 , Student Subscription: $25, Institutions Combined (Print & E-Access): $519, Institutions E-Access Only: $494, Institutions Print Only: $499; per copy $16; sample free on request. Back issues: $11. Discounts: 25% (5-10 copies) 30% (11-20 copies) 40% (21-40 copies) classroom & university bookstores. 128pp. Reporting time: 6-9 months. Simultaneous submissions accepted: no. Publishes 25% of manuscripts submitted. Payment: none. Copyrighted. Pub's reviews: 10 in 2005. §Latin America, radical theory, political economy. Ads: 1 Full Page Ad: $415, 3-5 Full Page Ads: $380, 6 or More Full Page Ads: $340, 1 Half Page Ad: $295, 3-5 Half Page Ads: $270, 6 or More Half Page Ads: $250. Subjects: Business & Economics, Latin America, Politics.

The Latona Press, Marion K. Stocking, 24 Berry Cove Road, Lamoine, ME 04605. 1978. Non-fiction. "We are not looking for further manuscripts at the present time." avg. press run 1.5M. Discounts: To bookstores and wholesalers: 1-4 copies 20%, 5 or more 40%. Postage and shipping extra. No discount on orders not paid for in 30 days. 200pp. Payment: royalties. Copyrights for author. Subjects: Biography, Biology, Conservation, Earth, Natural History, Ecology, Foods, History, Maine, New England.

LAUGHING BEAR NEWSLETTER, Tom Person, Editor, 1418 El Camino Real, Euless, TX 76040-6555, e-mail editor@laughingbear.com, www.laughingbear.com. 1976. "*LBN* has been serving the small press community with news, information, and inspiration since 1976. *LBN* is for small press writers and publishers.

The emphasis is on limited budget publishing: design and strategies, alternative marketing techniques, and resources. The newsletter is being phased out and will cease publication with issue 150 (probably in 2006). However, our website will continue to offer articles and resources for independent publishers. *LBN* does NOT publish poetry, fiction or any other literary works, and will not consider submission of articles. We will also not be taking on any new subscribers - downloadable copies of the newsletter issues are immediately available on the web site." 4pp. Copyrighted, reverts to author. Pub's reviews: 30+ in 2005. §Small press publications of all kinds; publishing how-to especially. Subjects: How-To, Newsletter, Publishing, Reviews.

THE LAUGHING DOG, SUBSYNCHRONOUS PRESS, Hillary Lyon, Warren Andrle, #326, 4729 E. Sunrise, Tucson, AZ 85718, LaughingDogAZ@cs.com. 2000. Poetry. "Submit 3 poems at a time, maximum 30 lines each. No religious, political or pornographic poetry, please. No rhyming poems either. Recent contributors include: David Ray, Will Inman, and Gary Mex Glazner." circ. 150. 2/yr. Pub'd 2 issues 2005; expects 2 issues 2006, 2 issues 2007. price per copy $3; sample $3. Back issues: none. Discounts: contributors get additional copies for $1 each. 26pp. Reporting time: 3 weeks to 3 months. Simultaneous submissions accepted: no. Publishes 20% of manuscripts submitted. Payment: 1 free copy, plus discount on additional copies. Copyrighted, reverts to author. Ads: none. Subject: Poetry.

LAUNDRY PEN, Andree Kirk, Shelly Gill, 3132 Harrison St.,, Oakland, CA 94611, laundrypen@yahoo.com, www.geocities.com/laundrypen. 2002. Fiction. "*Laundry Pen* is on hiatus as of March 2005, and we are not currently accepting any submissions. Issue one is available for $3 cash including shipping, issue two is sold out. Thank you for your interest." 1/yr. 75pp. Reporting time: 3 months. Simultaneous submissions accepted: no. Publishes 25% of manuscripts submitted. Payment: copies. Copyrighted. Subjects: Experimental, Fiction.

Laureate Press, Lance Lobo, Editor, PO Box 8125, Bangor, ME 04402-8125, 800-946-2727. 1994. Non-fiction. avg. press run 5M. Pub'd 2 titles 2005; expects 2 titles 2006, 2 titles 2007. Trade Discount: 30%. 400pp. Copyrights for author. Subject: Sports, Outdoors.

THE LAUREL REVIEW, William Trowbridge, Associate Editor; David Slater, Associate Editor; Amy Benson, Editor; Nancy Mayer, Editor; Randall R. Freisinger, Associate Editor; Jeff Mock, Associate Editor; Leigh Allison Wilson, Associate Editor; Ann Cummins, Associate Editor, Department of English, Northwest Missouri State University, Maryville, MO 64468, 816-562-1265. 1960. Poetry, fiction, art, parts-of-novels, long-poems, non-fiction. "We read September through May. We have no regional, political, ethnic, or religious bias. We seek well-crafted poems, stories, and creative non-fiction accessible to a wide range of serious readers. Recent contributors: Nancy Van Winckel, Gary Finke, Albert Goldbarth, Charles Harper Webb, Katherine Soniat, Jonis Agee, Brendan Galvin, William Kloefkorn, Jim Daniels, Karla J. Kuban, Heather Ross Miller, Ian McMillan, Jonathan Holden." circ. 900. 2/yr. Pub'd 2 issues 2005; expects 2 issues 2006, 2 issues 2007. sub. price $10; per copy $7; sample $5. Back issues: $5. Discounts: 40%. 136pp. Reporting time: 1 week to 4 months. Simultaneous submissions accepted: no. Publishes less than 1% of manuscripts submitted. Payment: 2 copies, plus free one-year subsciption. Copyrighted, reverts to author. Pub's reviews: 2 in 2005. Ads: $80/$40. Subjects: Essays, Fiction, Non-Fiction, Poetry.

LAW AND LITERATURE, University of California Press, Peter Goodrich, Editor, University of California Press, 2000 Center St., Suite 303, Berkeley, CA 94704-1223, 510-643-7154. 1989. Articles. "Editorial address: Cardozo School of Law, Brookdale Center, 55 Fifth Avenue, New York, NY 10003. Copyrighted by the Cardozo School of Law, Yeshiva University." circ. 446. 3/yr. Pub'd 3 issues 2005; expects 3 issues 2006, 3 issues 2007. sub. price $37 indiv., $149 inst., $27 student; per copy $15 indiv., $54 inst., $15 student; sample same as single copy. Discounts: foreign subs. agents 10%, 10+ one-time orders 30%. 168pp. Copyrighted, does not revert to author. Ads: $295/$220. Subjects: Law, Literature (General).

Lawrence & Wishart, Thomas V. Cahill, 10 High Street, Knapwell, Cambridge CB3 8NR, United Kingdom, aj@erica.demon.co.uk. 1993. Pub'd 2 titles 2005; expects 2 titles 2006, 2 titles 2007. Discounts: trade terms - less 5% for cash with order, or payment before start of year of publication. 96pp. Reporting time: 3 months. Simultaneous submissions accepted: no. Publishes 25% of manuscripts submitted. Payment: none. Copyrights for author. Subject: Anarchist.

LAYALAMA ONLINE MAGAZINE, Pushpa Ratna Tuladhar, 320 Phurkesalla Marg, Dhimelohan Swoyambhu,, P. O. Box 5146, Kathmandu, Nepal, Kathmandu 71100, Nepal, Tel: + 977 1 4274815, Fax: + 977 1 4274815, email:layalama@layalama.com, Website: http://www.layalama.com. 2002. Poetry, fiction. circ. 500. 4/yr. Pub'd 4 issues 2005; expects 4 issues 2006, 4 issues 2007. sub. price $16; per copy US$4.00; sample free. Back issues: inquire. Discounts: 25 copies - 30%. 16pp. Reporting time: Within 2-4 weeks. Simultaneous submissions accepted: Yes. Publishes 50% of manuscripts submitted. Payment: No contribution. Copyrighted, reverts to author. Ads: On request.

Lazywood Press (see also MY TABLE: Houston's Dining Magazine), Teresa Byrne-Dodge, 1908 Harold Street, Houston, TX 77098-1502, 713-529-5500, mytable@aol.com, www.my-table.com. 1994. Non-fiction. "We publish only 1 or 2 new titles per year, in addition to a bimonthly magazine. All publications have a regional emphasis." avg. press run 6M. Pub'd 2 titles 2005; expects 1 title 2006, 2 titles 2007. Discounts: please call for schedule. Pages vary. Reporting time: 1-2 months. Simultaneous submissions accepted: yes. Publishes a very small % of manuscripts submitted. Payment: varies. Copyrights for author. Subjects: Cooking, Dining, Restaurants, Food, Eating, Humor, Texas.

Leadership Education and Development, Inc., Donna Harrison, Joy Rhodes, 1116 West 7th Street, PMB 175, Columbia, TN 38401, 931-379-3799; 800-659-6135, www.leadershipdevelopment.com. 1987. Non-fiction. "Biases: ethical management. Recent contributor: Fred A. Manske, Jr., CEO of Purolator Courier." avg. press run 5-10M. Expects 1-2 titles 2006, 2-3 titles 2007. Discounts: distributors 50%, bookstores 40-45%, quantity retail discounts up to 35%. 200pp. Reporting time: 2-3 months. Copyrights are negotiable. Subjects: Business & Economics, Inspirational, Leadership.

Leaf Press (see also THE CRAPSHOOTER), Larry Edell, Andrea Foote, PO Box 421440, San Diego, CA 92142, leafpress@aol.com. 1995. Non-fiction. "Gambling only." avg. press run 5M. Pub'd 2 titles 2005; expects 1 title 2006, 2 titles 2007. Discounts: 50% for distributors. 120pp. Reporting time: immediate. Simultaneous submissions accepted: yes. Publishes 20% of manuscripts submitted. Payment: varies. Copyright for author if requested. Subject: Games.

Lean Press, Michael Ryder, PO Box 80334, Portland, OR 97280-1334, 503-708-4415, Fax 503-626-9098, mike@leanpress.com, www.leanpress.com. 2002. Poetry, fiction, art, cartoons, non-fiction. avg. press run 3M. Expects 6 titles 2006, 12 titles 2007. 200pp. Reporting time: 8 weeks. Simultaneous submissions accepted: yes. Publishes 30% of manuscripts submitted. Payment: 10-15% net. Copyrights for author. Subjects: Fiction, Non-Fiction.

Leapfrog Press, Ira Wood, Donna Szeker, PO Box 1495, Wellfleet, MA 02667-1495, 508-349-1925, fax 508-349-1180, email books@leapfrogpress.com, www.leapfrogpress.com. 1996. Fiction, non-fiction. "Our list is eclectic and represents quality fiction, poetry, audiobooks, non-fiction and memoir—books that are referred to by the large commercial publishers as mid-list, but which we regard to be the heart and soul of literature. Please submit a query letter telling us about your publishing experience and no more than 40 pages from the beginning of the book. Manuscript to be returned must be accompanied by a SASE. Authors published include Martin Espada, Marge Piercy, Theodore Roszak, Maureen McCoy, Toni Graham, Lev Raphael, and Pagan Kennedy. We are distributed by Consortium Book Sales & Distribution." avg. press run 3-5M. Pub'd 4 titles 2005; expects 4 titles 2006, 4 titles 2007. 200-300pp. Reporting time: 6 - 9 months. Simultaneous submissions accepted: no. Publishes less than 1% of manuscripts submitted. Payment: varies according to book. Copyrights for author. Subjects: Fiction, Literature (General), Memoirs, Poetry.

Leaping Dog Press / Asylum Arts Press (see also Asylum Arts), Jordan Jones, Editor and Publisher, PO Box 3316, San Jose, CA 95156-3316, Phone/fax: (877) 570-6873 E-mail: editor@leapingdogpress.com, Web: www.leapingdogpress.com, Chapbooks and ephemera: www.cafepress.com/ldp/. 1990. Poetry, fiction, art, photos, criticism, letters, long-poems, collages, plays, non-fiction. "Manuscripts by invitation only, and only during the months of May-July. Leaping Dog Press publishes high-quality literary titles—fiction, plays, translations, essays, and poetry—in attractive trade paperback format. Recent books by Marie Redonnet, Eric Paul Shaffer, Greg Boyd, Mark Wisniewski, and Norberto Luis Romero. We are most interested in striking, clear, entertaining contemporary work and works in translation, especially from French and Spanish." avg. press run 1000. Pub'd 1 title 2005; expects 4 titles 2006, 5 titles 2007. Distributed to the book trade by Biblio Distribution, 4501 Forbes Blvd., Suite 200, Lanham, MD 20706, Phone (301) 459-3366, Fax (301) 429-5746. 144pp. Reporting time: 3-6 mos. Simultaneous submissions accepted: Yes. Publishes 2% of manuscripts submitted. Payment: in copies. Copyrights for author. Subjects: Absurdist, Arts, Avant-Garde, Experimental Art, Fiction, Poetry, Surrealism, Translation.

The Leaping Frog Press (see also Timson Edwards, Co.), Marlene McLauglin, Alex Gonzalez, PO Box 55-0898, Jacksonville, FL 32255-0898, Write to us (we all still write letters right?) PO Box 55-0898 Jacksonville, FL 32255-0898. http://www.short-fiction.com, www.timsonedwards.com, publisher@bell-south.net if you need to send email, do not send attachments, we will request the attachment. 1996. Fiction, photos. "Strictly limited to short (max. 2,500 words) fiction. Has 'Best Of' S.E., N.E. Midwest, S.W., N.W., regional anthologies competition for new and emerging writers held each year. All correspondence must have a SASE for return of anything sent or wanted. Currently seeking essays of up to 200 words regarding reading and windows, two separate topics and books. Also publishing poetry gift books illustrated with b/w photography." avg. press run Depending on the project, we will print as few as 200 to as many as 5M. Our magazine prints 500 and our anthologies will print about 1200 copies. Please enter our competitions and subscribe, this is how we manage to continue publishing the work of new writers... Pub'd 1 title 2005; expects 2 titles 2006, 5 titles 2007. Discounts: minimum 40% up to 50 + 20% with quantities and no returns. 128pp. Reporting time: 12 weeks minimum. Simultaneous submissions accepted: yes. Publishes 60% of manuscripts submitted. Payment: by prior arrangements. Does not copyright for author. Subjects: Christianity, Culture, Dreams, Essays, Family, Fiction, Humor, Inspirational, Literature (General), Mental Health, Motivation, Success, Mystery, Photography,

Satire, Spiritual.

THE LEDGE, Stacey Knecht, 8011 CE, Zwolle, The Netherlands, info@the-ledge.com, www.the-ledge.com. 2005. Poetry, fiction, articles, photos, interviews, music, letters, parts-of-novels, long-poems, plays, non-fiction. "The Ledge is a literary website, based in the Netherlands but aimed at an international audience. On the site, which can be viewed in both English and Dutch, visitors can read in-depth interviews with writers from around the world and hear them reading from their latest work, while reading along from 'a book'. There is also a built-in, ever-expanding reading guide: books to read 'before' and 'after'. The idea is, in time, to construct a worldwide-web of literature and a library/ archive of international, literary interviews. Visitors to the site can contribute to the database: comments, ideas for new 'before' and 'after' books, corrections, all suggestions are reviewed by the editors and, wherever possible, added to the site." Subjects: Anthology, Autobiography, Biography, Essays, Fiction, Interviews, Juvenile Fiction, Literature (General), Non-Fiction, Novels, Philosophy, Poetry, Reading, Short Stories, Zines.

THE LEDGE POETRY & FICTION MAGAZINE, Timothy Monaghan, Editor-in-Chief & Publisher, 40 Maple Avenue, Bellport, NY 11713-2011, www.theledgemagazine.com. 1988. Poetry, fiction. "*The Ledge Poetry & Fiction Magazine* is committed to the publication of new and exciting work by an eclectic range of contemporary poets and writers. Each issue of The Ledge is typeset and perfect-bound and features a wide range of poems and stories by contributors of all backgrounds and persuasions. The Ledge is open to all styles and schools of writing. We seek work that relates to the human experience, work that is provocative and not afraid to take risks or challenge the reader with a new perspective. We appreciate well-crafted work and structure and form as well as free verse. We seek compelling work by both established and emerging poets and writers; memorable poems and stories that utilize language in imaginative and innovative ways. We realize how difficult it is to articulate or to define exactly what we mean when describing the poems and stories we prefer, and simply encourage poets and writers to send us their best work. We also believe that superior work appeals to a wider audience than most journals endeavor to reach, and consider The Ledge a truly democratic publication in that regard. *The Ledge* sponsors an annual fiction awards competition, an annual poetry awards competition, and an annual poetry chapbook competition. Please e-mail us at: info@theledgemagazine.com or tkmonaghan@aol.com or send SASE for competition guidelines. You may also visit us on the web at www.theledgemagazine.com for complete guidelines and additional information about our publication." circ. 1.5M. 1/yr. Pub'd 1 issue 2005; expects 1 issue 2006, 1 issue 2007. sub. price $18/2 issues or $32/4 issues or $42/6 issues. For subscriptions outside North America, please add $5 per issue.; per copy $10; sample $10. Reporting time: 3 months. Simultaneous submissions accepted: yes. Publishes 3% of manuscripts submitted. Payment: 1 contributor's copy. Copyrighted, reverts to author. Subjects: Fiction, Poetry.

Leete's Island Books, Peter Neill, Box 1, Sedgewick, ME 04676, 212-748-8678; e-mail PNeill@compuserve.com. 1977. "Fiction, essays, interesting reprints; for the moment, because of time, no unsolicited manuscripts accepted." avg. press run 2.5M. Pub'd 2 titles 2005; expects 3 titles 2006, 4 titles 2007. Discounts: 40%, distributed by: Independent Publishers Group, Chicago Review Press, 814 N. Franklin, 2nd FL., Chicago, Illinois 60610, 312-337-0747. 250pp. Payment: varies with title. Copyrights for author. Subjects: Literature (General), Translation.

LEFT BUSINESS OBSERVER, Doug Henwood, 38 Greene Street, 4th Floor, New York, NY 10013-3505, phone 212-219-0010, fax 212-219-0098, dhenwood@panix.com, www.leftbusinessobserver.com. 1986. Articles, interviews, reviews, letters, news items, non-fiction. "Pieces range from 100-3,000 words. Most written by editor, but occasional outside contributions." circ. 4K. 11/yr. Pub'd 11 issues 2005; expects 11 issues 2006, 11 issues 2007. sub. price $22 indiv., $55 instit.; per copy $2.50; sample $2.50. Back issues: 4/$7.50, complete set 93 issues $90. Discounts: classroom up to 50%, bookstores 40%. 8pp. Reporting time: 1 week. Payment: varies, up to 10¢/word. Copyrighted, does not revert to author. Pub's reviews: 2 in 2005. §Economics, politics, feminism, social sciences. Ads: none. Subjects: Book Reviewing, Business & Economics, Communism, Marxism, Leninism, Media, Politics, Public Affairs.

LEFT CURVE, Csaba Polony, Editor; Jack Hirschman, Associate Editor, P.J. Laska, Des McGuinness, Agneta Falk, Richard Olsen, Scott Thompson, John Hutnyk, E. San Juan Jr., PO Box 472, Oakland, CA 94604, E-mail editor@leftcurve.org. 1974. Poetry, fiction, articles, art, photos, interviews, criticism, reviews, music, letters, long-poems, collages, non-fiction. "*Left Curve* is an artist produced journal addressing the crises of modernity from an integrative social-historical context by publishing original visual and verbal art, as well as critical articles." circ. 2M. Irregular. Pub'd 1 issue 2005. sub. price $30 indiv, $45 instit (3 issues); per copy $10 indiv., $15 instit.; sample $10. Back issues: $10. Discounts: 30% trade. 144pp. Reporting time: max. 6 months. Simultaneous submissions accepted: no. Publishes 5% of manuscripts submitted. Payment: 2-5 copies dependent on length. Copyrighted. Pub's reviews: 2 in 2005. §Contemporary art, poetry, cultural politics, literature, cultural. Ads: $200/$125/$15 min; $1 per word. Subjects: Arts, Avant-Garde, Experimental Art, Criticism, Culture, Essays, Literature (General), Media, Photography, Poetry, Politics, Post Modern, Short Stories, Socialist, Third World, Minorities, Visual Arts.

Left Hand Books, Bryan McHugh, Publisher, 85A Fairmont Avenue, Kingston, NY 12401, 845-340-9892, lefthandb@ulster.net. 1990. Poetry, art, photos, long-poems, plays. "Left Hand publishes poetry and artists' books in stunningly designed editions." avg. press run 1M. Pub'd 2 titles 2005; expects 2 titles 2006, 2 titles 2007. Discounts: contact Small Press Distribution. 74pp. Payment: arrangements vary. Author holds copyright. Subjects: Arts, Drama, Poetry.

LegacyForever, Porsha Starks J., 4930 Capri Avenue, Sarasota, FL 34235-4320, 941-358-3339. 2004. Poetry, fiction, music. Expects 2 titles 2006, 2 titles 2007. Discounts: 25 copies: 10%. 350pp. Reporting time: six weeks. Simultaneous submissions accepted: Yes. Publishes 50% of manuscripts submitted. Payment: Based upon work of author. Copyrights for author. Subjects: Fiction, Florida, Humor, Movies, Music, Mystery, Non-Fiction, Occult.

LEGAL INFORMATION MANAGEMENT INDEX, Elyse H. Fox, Legal Information Services, 6609 Glen Forest Drive, Chapel Hill, NC 27514, 919-419-8390. 1984. Articles, reviews. "Indexes articles, and reviews appearing in periodicals relating to legal information management and law librarianship. Payments must be made in U.S. funds." 7/yr. Pub'd 7 issues 2005; expects 7 issues 2006, 7 issues 2007. sub. price $148 U.S., $115 Canada & Mexico, $170 others (air mail); sample free on request. Back issues: $40. 32pp. Copyrighted. Subjects: Indexes & Abstracts, Law, Libraries.

Lekon New Dimensions Publishing, PO Box 504, Yonkers, NY 10702, 914-965-5181, rcnfyle@aol.com. 2000. Fiction. "Street address: 38 Centre Street, Yonkers, NY 10701. 2-3 novels per year, 250-360 pages. First novel *The Diamonds* by J. Sorie Couteh. Aims at mainstreaming authentic African writing of high quality into the general American market. Titles available from Baker & Taylor, etc." avg. press run 3M. Expects 1 title 2006, 2-3 titles 2007. Quantity discounts to 55%. 300pp. Reporting time: up to 3 months. Simultaneous submissions accepted: yes. Publishes a variable % of manuscripts submitted. Payment: standard royalty, 50% foreign royalties. Copyrights for author. Subjects: African Literature, Africa, African Studies, African-American, Biography, Fiction, Literature (General), Novels, Short Stories.

Lemieux International Ltd., William Lemieux, PO Box 170134, Milwaukee, WI 53217, 414-962-2844, FAX 414-962-2844, lemintld@msn.com. 1985. Fiction, non-fiction. avg. press run 1-3M. Pub'd 1 title 2005; expects 1 title 2006, 3 titles 2007. Discounts: trade. 200-300pp. Reporting time: 3 weeks. Simultaneous submissions accepted: yes. Publishes a variable % of manuscripts submitted. Payment: TBA. Copyrights for author. Subjects: Biography, Cooking, Fantasy, Gay, Health, History, How-To, Humor, Mental Health, Military, Veterans, Mystery, Spiritual, Travel.

Lemon Shark Press, Darcy Mobraaten, 1604 Marbella Drive, Vista, CA 92081-5463, 760-727-2850, lemonsharkpress@yahoo.com, www.lemonsharkpress.com. 2003. Fiction, non-fiction. "Publishing literary novels set in Hawaii." avg. press run 1M. Expects 1 title 2006, 3 titles 2007. Discounts: 40% for bookstores. 300pp. Reporting time: 3 months. Simultaneous submissions accepted: no. Publishes 1% of manuscripts submitted. Payment: private. Copyrights for author. Subject: Literature (General).

LEO Productions LLC., Linda E. Odenborg, PO Box 1333, Portland, OR 97207, 360-601-1379, Fax 360-210-4133. 1992. Fiction, art, letters, long-poems, plays, non-fiction. avg. press run 5M-10M. Pub'd 2 titles 2005; expects 3 titles 2006, 3 titles 2007. Discounts: yes. Reporting time: 3 months. Publishes 0% of manuscripts submitted. Payment: varies. Subjects: Arts, Bilingual, China, Diaries, Drama, Family, Fiction, France, French, History, Medieval, Oregon, Short Stories, Spiritual, Theatre, Young Adult.

•Les Figues Press, Teresa Carmody, PO Box 35628, Los Angeles, CA 90035, trose@olywa.net. 2005. Poetry, fiction, art, parts-of-novels, long-poems, plays. "Les Figues Press is the publisher of TrenchArt, an annual subscription series of novella-size books of literary prose and poetry. Each TrenchArt series publishes work the editors see existing in a conversation. We are looking for work that is unconventional and rigorous in its aesthetic integrity; each writer must also write an aesthetic essay or poetics for publication as part of the conversation. We suggest you look on our website or at the essays in *TrenchArt: Material* or *TrenchArt: Casements* for a better idea of what we mean by aesthetic essay. Recent and forthcoming publications include *Dies: A Sentence* by Vanessa Place, *A Story of Witchery* by Jennifer Calkins, *For Love Alone, Christina'S tead: +I'm'S-pace* by the Society of CumIn' Linguistics, and *Tribulations of a Westerner in the Western World* by Vincent Dachy. Additional information about Les Figues Press and TrenchArt can be found on our website at www.lesfigues.com." avg. press run 500. Pub'd 4 titles 2005; expects 4 titles 2006, 5 titles 2007. Discounts: Wholesale: 30% off. 80-200pp. Reporting time: 3-6 months. Simultaneous submissions accepted: Yes. Publishes 10% of manuscripts submitted. Does not copyright for author. Subjects: Arts, Experimental, Fiction, Literature (General), Poetry, Prose.

Lessiter Publications, Frank Lessiter, Editor & Publisher, PO Box 624, Brookfield, WI 53008-0624, 262-782-4480, Fax 262-782-1252. 1983. Photos, cartoons, interviews. avg. press run 2.5M. Pub'd 3 titles 2005; expects 5 titles 2006, 5 titles 2007. Discounts: trade, bulk. 150pp. Reporting time: 45 days. Simultaneous submissions accepted: no. Payment: yes. Copyrights for author. Subjects: Agriculture, Photography.

LETTER ARTS REVIEW, Rose Folsom, PO Box 9986, Greensboro, NC 27429, 800-369-9598, 336-272-6139, Fax 336-272-9015, lar@johnnealbooks.com. 1982. Articles, art, reviews. circ. 5M. 4/yr. Pub'd 4 issues 2005; expects 4 issues 2006, 4 issues 2007. sub. price $42 USA, $45 Canada, $62 all other countries; per copy $12.50; sample $12.50. Back issues: varied. Discounts: 60/40 for outlets, others negotiable. 64pp. Reporting time: 8 weeks or less. Publishes 60% of manuscripts submitted. Payment: on publication. Copyrighted, reverts to author. Pub's reviews: 10+ in 2005. §Calligraphy, graphic arts, typography, book arts, computer fonts. Ads: $550/$400/$25 classified/all one time/4x rate available. Subjects: Book Arts, Calligraphy.

•**LETTER X,** Amy Christian, Publisher, Editor; Nicole Lowman, Co-Editor, Seattle, WA 98102, submit@letterxmag.com, www.letterxmag.com. 2004. Poetry, fiction, articles, art, cartoons, non-fiction. "Letter X is a quarterly Creative Writing magazine independently published. We don't have a mission statement. We only want to make everyone's day a little better. Recent contributors include: Jason Ashbaugh, Steve Barker, Jeremy Giles, Jill James, Steve Lohse, Nicole Lowman, Rocco Lungariello, Brian McGuigan, Amy Muldoon, Jeb Obrian & Phil Vas." circ. 8000. 4/yr. Pub'd 4 issues 2005; expects 4 issues 2006, 4 issues 2007. sub. price $10. Back issues: inquire. 24pp. Reporting time: 1-2 months. Simultaneous submissions accepted: Yes. Payment: Contributor's Copies. Not copyrighted.

•**Level 4 Press,** William Roetzheim Jr., 13518 Jamul Drive, Jamul, CA 91935-1635, 619-669-3100, 619-374-7311 fax, sales@level4Press.com, www.level4press.com. 2005. Poetry. "Poetry books and poetry audio performance CDs. THE GIANT BOOK OF POETRY is our flagship product, an anthology with hundreds of authors from ancient through contemporary. Poems must be compatible with our "Level 4 Poetry Manifesto" as published in the introduction to THE GIANT BOOK OF POETRY. We are generally looking for longer collections of shorter poems." avg. press run 5000. Expects 12 titles 2006, 5 titles 2007. 150-750pp. Reporting time: Query prior to submission. Simultaneous submissions accepted: Yes. Subjects: Audio/Video, Poetry.

Lexicus Press, Jacqueline Stewart, P.O. Box 1691, Palo Alto, CA 94301, 6507995602. 2003. Non-fiction. "Travel books with an emphasis on history and ecology. Undiscovered gems of nature. Color photographs on every page." Pub'd 1 title 2005; expects 1 title 2007. Discounts: 1-5 copies 20%10+ copies 40%. 186pp. Reporting time: na. Does not copyright for author. Subject: Travel.

Lexikos, Mike Witter, PO Box 1289, Nevada City, CA 95959. 1980. Non-fiction. "In 1988 *Lexikos* combined with *Don't Call it Frisco Press.* We will continue to publish under both imprints and pursue much the same editorial policies as before." avg. press run 4M. Pub'd 1 title 2005; expects 1 title 2006, 2 titles 2007. Discounts: 50-55% to wholesalers; retail 1-4 20%, 5-9 40%, 10-24 42%, 25-49, 43%; 50+, 45%. 200pp. Reporting time: 1 month or less. Simultaneous submissions accepted: yes. Publishes 1% of manuscripts submitted. Payment: negotiable; innovative publishing programs are being developed. Copyrights for author. Subjects: Americana, California, Conservation, Ecology, Foods, Folklore, Geography, History, How-To, Reference, San Francisco, Transportation.

Leyland Publications, Winston Leyland, PO Box 410690, San Francisco, CA 94141, 415-626-1935. 1984. Fiction, cartoons, interviews, letters, non-fiction. avg. press run 7M. Pub'd 10 titles 2005; expects 6 titles 2006, 7 titles 2007. Distributed to the booktrade: Koen (N.J.), Alamo Square (Sacramento), Ingram, Last Gasp. 192pp. Reporting time: 1 month. Simultaneous submissions accepted: no. Payment: royalties or outright purchase. Copyrights for author. Subjects: Autobiography, Comics, Counter-Culture, Alternatives, Communes, Electronics, Erotica, Fiction, Gay, Military, Veterans, Music, Non-Fiction, Novels, Prison, Science Fiction, Sex, Sexuality, Short Stories.

Liaison Press, Allen Pete, 206-7600 Moffatt Rd, Richmond, BC V6Y 3V1, Canada. 2003. Fiction, satire, non-fiction. "Liaison Press is an imprint of Creative Guy Publishing. We offer ebook distribution for other small presses, (having cooperated with Beach House Books and Project M already) and as well we publish satire and farce on our own (in ebook and print, check for titles "You're Not Very Important" (sociopolitical satire of self-help), etc.).We are also particularly interested in previously published Canadian works that have fallen out of print. Query BY EMAIL ONLY (submissions@creativeguypublishing.com). Any unsolicited hard copy mss will be recycled unread. Please check the website for updated/specific guidelines." Pub'd 3 titles 2005; expects 3 titles 2006, 3 titles 2007. Discounts: Print distrbuted through Ingram, 50%Available through publisher, 50%Any amount - returnable. 200-300pp. Reporting time: query first, 2-3 months. Query BY EMAIL ONLY. Any unsolicited hard copy mss will be recycled unread. Simultaneous submissions accepted: Yes. Publishes 5% of manuscripts submitted. Payment: 65% royalty on net, no advance. Does not copyright for author. Subjects: Absurdist, Canada, Humor, Satire.

•**Libellum,** Vincent Katz, 211 West 19th Street, #5, New York, NY 10011-4001, libellum@el.net. 2004. Poetry, art, criticism, parts-of-novels, long-poems. "Libellum was founded to publish smaller-scale complete works, such as long poems or lectures, that might have a hard time getting published otherwise." avg. press run 500. Pub'd 1 title 2005; expects 1 title 2006, 2 titles 2007. Discounts: case sensitive. 50pp. Reporting time: I usually commission texts. Payment: Payment is in copies; authors share set of beliefs with publisher. Copyright is stated but not registered by publisher. Subjects: Anarchist, Anthropology, Archaelogy, Architecture, Chicago, Classical Studies, Essays, Experimental, F. Scott Fitzgerald, Non-Violence, Performing Arts, Poetry.

THE LIBERATOR, R.F. Doyle, 17854 Lyons Street, Forest Lake, MN 55025, 651-464-7663, Fax 651-464-7135, E-mail rdoyle@mensdefense.org. 1968. Articles, photos, interviews, news items. "Gender issues material." circ. 2M. sub. price $24; per copy $3; sample $3. Back issues: $3 (some $5). Discounts: 40%. 28pp. Simultaneous submissions accepted: yes. Publishes 40% of manuscripts submitted. Payment: seldom. Copyrighted, rights reverting to author conditional. Pub's reviews: 50 in 2005. §Gender issues. Ads: Write for ad schedule. Subjects: Civil Rights, Divorce, Men.

THE (LIBERTARIAN) CONNECTION, Erwin S. Strauss, 10 Hill Street #22-L, Newark, NJ 07102, 973-242-5999. 1968. Poetry, fiction, articles, art, photos, cartoons, interviews, satire, criticism, reviews, music, letters, parts-of-novels, long-poems, collages, plays, concrete art, news items, non-fiction. "Each subscriber is entitled to submit up to four pages of material to be printed in each issue. Additional pages run (unedited) for the cost of printing and mailing. Contributors you may have heard of include Bob ('The Abolition of Work') Black, Ace ('Twisted Image') Backwords, Robert ('Illuminatus!') Shea, Gerry ('Neutron Gun') Reith, Mike ('Loompanics') Hoy, Mike ('Factsheet Five') Gunderloy, Pat ('Salon') Hartman, Lev ('Anarchy') Chernyi, R.W. ('Liberty Magazine') Bradford." circ. 30. 8/yr. Pub'd 8 issues 2005; expects 8 issues 2006, 8 issues 2007. sub. price $20; per copy $2.50; sample $2.50. Back issues: $2.50. Discounts: none. 50pp. Reporting time: none. Simultaneous submissions accepted: yes. Publishes 100% of manuscripts submitted. Payment: none. Copyrighted, reverts to author. Pub's reviews: about 2 dozen in 2005. §Each contributor makes his/her own choices; works of socialist theory and of objectivist philosophy have been popular recently. Ads: ads may be submitted by subscribers as their four free pages, or as paid extra pages (current charge: $7 per extra page). Subjects: Anarchist, Counter-Culture, Alternatives, Communes, Libertarian, Philosophy, Politics.

Libertarian Press, Inc./American Book Distributors, Robert F. Sennholz, Lyn M. Sennholz, PO Box 309, Grove City, PA 16127-0309, 724-458-5861. 1952. Non-fiction. "LP publishes books and booklets on free market economics and political science. ABD is more diversified." avg. press run 2.5M-5M. Pub'd 2 titles 2005; expects 2 titles 2006, 4 titles 2007. Discounts: up to 60%, based on quantity, larger discounts available on booklets. 300pp. Reporting time: 30 days. Payment: negotiable. Copyrights depend on contract. Subjects: Biography, Business & Economics, Children, Youth, Libertarian, Philosophy, Political Science, Reprints.

LIBERTY, R.W. Bradford, Editor and Publisher, PO Box 1181, Port Townsend, WA 98368, 360-379-0242. 1987. Poetry, fiction, articles, art, cartoons, interviews, satire, criticism, reviews, non-fiction. "News and analysis, reviews, humor. Review of culture and politics from a classical liberal or libertarian perspective." circ. 10,000. 12/yr. Pub'd 11 issues 2005; expects 12 issues 2006, 12 issues 2007. sub. price $29.50; per copy $4; sample $4. Back issues: $4 each, up to $8 for select/rare issues. Discounts: 50%, minimum draw 10, fully returnable. 56pp. Reporting time: 2-4 weeks. Simultaneous submissions accepted: no. Payment: negotiable; most contributors write without remuneration. *Liberty* retains first print and cyberspace serial rights; copyright reverts to author on publication. Pub's reviews: 43 in 2005. §Current events, public policy, history, philosophy, economic theory, political theory, psychology, literature, etc. Ads: $300 full page, $163 half page, other sizes. Discounts: 5% for 3 insertions, 10% for 6, 15% for 12. Subjects: Anarchist, Business & Economics, Ethics, Human Rights, Libertarian, Philosophy, Political Science, Society.

Liberty Publishing Company, Inc., Jeffrey B. Little, Publisher, PO Box 4248, Deerfield Beach, FL 33442-4248, 561-395-3750. 1977. Non-fiction. "Nonfictn, business, horseracing, travel, computer software, video." avg. press run 5M-20M. Pub'd 3 titles 2005; expects 3 titles 2006, 3 titles 2007. Discounts: 40% - 5 or more assorted titles. 180pp. Reporting time: 6 weeks. Payment: 6-12% semi-annual. Will copyright only on request. Subjects: Business & Economics, Consumer, Cooking, Games, How-To, Non-Fiction, Sports, Outdoors, Travel.

Libra Publishers, Inc. (see also ADOLESCENCE; FAMILY THERAPY), William Kroll, President, 3089C Clairemont Dr., Suite 383, San Diego, CA 92117, 619-571-1414. 1960. Poetry, fiction, articles, art, photos, cartoons, interviews, satire, criticism, reviews, music, letters, parts-of-novels, long-poems, collages, plays, concrete art, news items. "Most interested in books in the behavioral sciences." avg. press run 3M. Pub'd 15 titles 2005; expects 20 titles 2006, 22 titles 2007. Discounts: 1-4 copies, 33-1/3%; 5 or more, 40%. 160pp. Reporting time: 4 weeks. Simultaneous submissions accepted: yes. Payment: 10% of retail price. Copyrights for author. Subjects: Psychology, Society.

Librairie Droz S.A. (see also BIBLIOTHEQUE D'HUMANISME ET RENAISSANCE), A. Dufour, 11r.Massot, 1211 Geneve 12, Switzerland. 1934. Articles, criticism, reviews. "History of the 16th century." Pub'd 3 titles 2005; expects 3 titles 2006.

LIBRARIANS AT LIBERTY, Charles Willett, 1716 SW Williston Road, Gainesville, FL 32608, 352-335-2200. 1993. Articles, criticism, reviews, letters, news items. "Short articles critical of mainstream publishing and librarianship. Focus on progressive or anarchist alternatives. Contributors: Jason McQuinn, Earl

Lee, Chris Atton, Sanford Berman, James Danky, James Schmidt, Kevin Larson." circ. 100. 2/yr. Pub'd 2 issues 2005; expects 2 issues 2006, 2 issues 2007. sub. price $15; per copy $10 + $3; sample free. Back issues: $5 + $3. 16pp. Payment: none. Not copyrighted. Subjects: Book Collecting, Bookselling, Book Reviewing, Counter-Culture, Alternatives, Communes, Libraries, Publishing.

LIBRARY HI TECH, MCB University Press, Dr. Michael Seadle, MCB University Press, 60/62 Toller Lane, Bradford, W. Yorkshire BD8 9BY, England, 01274-777700, Fax 01274-785200 or 785201, www.mcb.co.uk. 1983. Articles, reviews. "Library/reference, library technology and automation." 4/yr. Pub'd 4 issues 2005; expects 4 issues 2006, 4 issues 2007. sub. price $169; per copy $42; sample free. 96pp. Reporting time: 4 weeks. Simultaneous submissions accepted: no. Payment: none. We request that authors assign copyright to publisher. Ads: none. Subjects: Libraries, Reference.

LIBRARY HIGH TECH NEWS, MCB University Press, Ken Wachsberger, MCB University Press, 60/62 Toller Lane, Bradford, W. Yorkshire BD8 9BY, England, 01274-777700, Fax 01274-785200 or 785201, www.mcb.co.uk. 1984. Articles, reviews, news items. "Library/reference, library news, technology and automation." 10/yr. Pub'd 10 issues 2005; expects 10 issues 2006, 10 issues 2007. sub. price $199; per copy $20; sample free. 32pp. Reporting time: 4 weeks. Simultaneous submissions accepted: no. Payment: none. We request that authors assign copyright to publisher. Ads: none. Subjects: Libraries, Reference.

•THE LIBRARY QUARTERLY, University of Chicago Press, John Carlo Bertot, Wayne A. Wiegand, Florida State University, School of Information Studies, 101 Shores Building, Tallahassee, FL 32306-2100. 1931. "Since it began publishing in 1931, *The Library Quarterly* has maintained its commitment to informed research in all areas of librarianship—historical, sociological, statistical, bibliographical, managerial, and educational. Combining traditional patterns of investigation with newer, interdisciplinary approaches, the *Quarterly* seeks to interpret relevant issues and current research for the librarian, educator, administrator, and others involved with the collection and history of books." 4/yr. Pub's reviews.

Library Research Associates, Elma Van Fossen, PO Box 32234, San Jose, CA 95152-2234, Fax 408-926-2207. 1999. Non-fiction. avg. press run 3M. Expects 1 title 2006, 2 titles 2007. Discounts: 20%/40%/55%. 187pp. Reporting time: 1 month. Simultaneous submissions accepted: yes. Payment: 10-15%. Does not copyright for author. Subjects: Ecology, Foods, Health, Medicine, Science.

Library Research Associates, Inc., Matilda A. Gocek, Dianne D. McKinstrie, 254 Nininger Road, Monroe, NY 10950-3977, 914-783-1144. 1968. Fiction, non-fiction. avg. press run 3.5M. Pub'd 7 titles 2005; expects 4 titles 2006. Discounts: 40% to booksellers; 1-9 books 30%, 10-49 books 40%, 50-99 books 45%, 100+ books 50%. 250pp. Reporting time: 3 weeks. Simultaneous submissions accepted: no. Publishes 1% of manuscripts submitted. Payment: 10% royalties. Copyrights for author. Subjects: Bibliography, Biography, Fiction, History, Politics.

LIBRARY TALK: The Magazine for Elementary School Library Media & Technology Specialists, Linworth Publishing, Inc., Marlene Woo-Lun, Publisher, 480 East Wilson Bridge Road #L, Worthington, OH 43085-2372, 614-436-7107, fax 614-436-9490. 1988. Articles, reviews, news items. "We publish article manuscripts only *about* the management of the school library *by* authors who have been or are elementary school librarians." circ. 10M. 5/yr. Pub'd 5 issues 2005; expects 5 issues 2006, 5 issues 2007. sub. price $49 US, $65 Canada; per copy $11; sample complimentary copies free. Back issues: $11. Discounts: 5% classroom and subscription agency. 64pp. Payment: honorarium and copies of issue in which article appears. Copyrighted, does not revert to author. Pub's reviews: 625 in 2005. §Materials suitable for elementary school libraries, grades 1-6. Ads: $1230/$895 (1x b/w)/$685 1/3 page b/w; 1 time rate add $875 for color. Subjects: Book Reviewing, Education, Libraries.

LICHEN Arts & Letters Preview, The Editorial Board, 234-701 Rossland Road East, Whitby, Ontario L1N 9K3, Canada, info@lichenjournal.ca,www.lichenjournal.ca. 1999. Poetry, fiction, art, photos, interviews, reviews, plays, non-fiction. "LICHEN...Bringing you the best of new writing and art, first. LICHEN emphasizes the role of the literary magazine as a preview—for the reader—of new work by writers they may have heard of, and of work by writers who are new to everyone. LICHEN also includes special features: "Focus" which showcases the invited work of established writers—work that might be in-progress, experimental, or a departure for them; "Perspective" which features an interview with a new author who is in that transition between having signed a publishing contract and the release of the book; and "Depth of Field" which offers guest authors' views on the world of the written word. We hope to offer new perspectives to our community and beyond, by bringing important, sometimes unknown, but just as often solidly established writers and artists to the widest possible audience. We look for work that entertains our readers, that plays to their intelligence and willingness to be engaged. This doesn't mean that everything in 'LICHEN' is an easy go; it does mean that we value clarity as the means to the payoff in a story, poem, or picture. We strive to present new stories, poems, and art that challenges but also respects the reader. It should invite many readings, but also be satisfying the first time it's read. 'LICHEN' has published work by George Elliott Clarke, Steven Heighton,

Robyn Sarah, John Barton, Brian Bartlett, Jonathan Bennett, Sharon McCartney, Ken Howe, Stuart Ross, Margaret Christakos, Brad Smith, and Mark Anthony Jarman. Each year we hold the "Tracking A Serial Poet" poetry competition, as well as a short fiction competition." circ. 1000. 2/yr. Pub'd 2 issues 2005; expects 2 issues 2006, 2 issues 2007. sub. price $19; per copy $12; sample $12. Back issues: $12. Discounts: 20+ copies 40% (distributors only). 144pp. Reporting time: 3-6 months. Simultaneous submissions accepted: No. Publishes 8% of manuscripts submitted. Payment: 1 copy of issue in which work is published, and a 1-year subscription. Cash honorarium when finances allow. Copyrighted, reverts to author. Pub's reviews: 1 in 2005. §Literary fiction, poetry. Ads: Full $200/Half $110/Quarter$60. Subjects: Arts, Book Reviewing, Canada, Drama, English, Fiction, Literary Review, Non-Fiction, Photography, Poetry, Prose, Reviews, Visual Arts.

THE LICKING RIVER REVIEW, P. Andrew Miller, Faculty Advisor, Department of Literature and Language, Northern Kentucky University, Highland Heights, KY 41099. 1989. Poetry, fiction. "We welcome crafted work that leaves a memorable impression. Recent contributors include Joni Lang, Judi A. Rypma, Rhonda Pettit, Bill Garten, Kenneth Pobo. Poems under 75 lines, fiction under 5,000 words." circ. 1-1.5K. 1/yr. Pub'd 1 issue 2005; expects 1 issue 2006, 1 issue 2007. sub. price $5; per copy $5; sample $5. Back issues: $5. Discounts: please inquire. 96pp. Reporting time: 1-9 months. Simultaneous submissions accepted: no. Publishes 13% of manuscripts submitted. Payment: 2 contributor's copies. Copyrighted, reverts to author. Ads: none. Subjects: Kentucky, Literary Review, Midwest, Poetry, Short Stories.

LIFE 101, Neil White, 1739 University Avenue, Oxford, MS 38655, 662-513-0159, Fax 662-234-9266, neilwhite@elife101.com, www.nautiluspublishing.com. 1994. Articles, photos, non-fiction. "Editorial geared to college-bound high school seniors." circ. 125M. 14/yr. Pub'd 14 issues 2005; expects 14 issues 2006, 14 issues 2007. sub. price offered free to high schools in most states. 8pp. Reporting time: months. Simultaneous submissions accepted: yes. Publishes 10% of manuscripts submitted. Payment: varies. Copyrighted, reverts to author. Ads: none.

Life Energy Media, 15030 Ventura Blvd, Suite 908, Sherman Oaks, CA 91403, 818-995-3263. 1975. "Publishes and produces print, audio, and video materials on life energy concepts in the areas of organizations, massage, therapy, movement and dance, expressive arts, yoga, martial arts, spiritual evolution and other related areas." avg. press run 500-5M. Pub'd 3 titles 2005; expects 3 titles 2006, 3 titles 2007. Discounts: trade, quantity, conferences, classroom, jobbers. 20-350pp. Reporting time: initial interest 1 month. Payment: negotiable. We can copyright for author. Subjects: Business & Economics, Dance, Health, Psychology, Spiritual.

LIFE LEARNING, Life Media, Wendy Priesnitz, PO Box 112, Niagara Falls, NY 14304-0112, (416) 260-0303, email: publisher@lifelearningmagazine.com, Website: www.lifelearningmagazine.com. 2002. Articles, photos. "Additional address: 508-264 Queens Quay W, Toronto ON M5J 1B5. About self-directed learning and 'unschooling.' Guidelines for writers are on website." circ. 35M. 6/yr. Expects 6 issues 2006, 6/6 issues 2007. sub. price $24; per copy $4.95; sample $4.95. 44pp. Reporting time: 2 months. Simultaneous submissions accepted: no. Publishes 25% of manuscripts submitted. Payment: none at this time. Copyrighted, reverts to author. Ads: $1200 full page, see website for complete rates. Subjects: Education, Family, Parenting.

Life Lessons, Mary Frakes, PO Box 382346, Cambridge, MA 02238, 617-576-2546, fax 617-576-3234, e-mail walkingwm@aol.com, website www.mindwalks.com. 1997. Non-fiction. "Will consider authors interested in building a brand compatible with existing publications. Query first, no ms." avg. press run 3M-10M. Pub'd 1 title 2005; expects 2 titles 2006, 3 titles 2007. Discounts: bulk to trade. 256pp. Reporting time: 1 month. Simultaneous submissions accepted: yes. Publishes 2% of manuscripts submitted. Payment: negotiable. Copyrights for author. Subjects: Cooking, Crafts, Hobbies, Lifestyles, Motivation, Success, Self-Help.

Life Media (see also LIFE LEARNING; NATURAL LIFE), Wendy Priesnitz, 508-264 Queens Quay W, Toronto, Ontario M5J 1B5, Canada, 416-260-0303, email publisher@lifemedia.ca, web www.lifemedia.ca. 1976. Articles, letters, news items, non-fiction. "*NL* focuses on sustainable living and self-reliance issues and the environment and health. *LL* is a deschooling magazine. Books to date deal with home business and homeschooling. See websites for guidelines." Pub'd 3 titles 2005; expects 3 titles 2006, 3 titles 2007. Discounts: retail 40%. 150pp. Reporting time: 1 month. Simultaneous submissions accepted: no. Publishes 2% of manuscripts submitted. Payment: varies. Does not copyright for author. Subjects: Cooking, Co-ops, Ecology, Foods, Education, Energy, Environment, Family, Gardening, Society, Solar, Vegetarianism.

Life Untangled Publishing, Polina Skibinskaya, Toronto, Ontario, Canada, http://www.lifeuntangled.com. 2005. Collages, news items, non-fiction. "Life Untangled Publishing is a young, progressive Canadian publisher specializing in non-fiction." avg. press run 1000. Expects 20-30 titles 2006, 50 titles 2007. 200pp. Reporting time: 1 month. Simultaneous submissions accepted: Yes. Publishes 20% of manuscripts submitted. Payment: royalties on a case by case basis. Copyrights for author. Subjects: Anarchist, Anthropology, Archaeology, Biography, Business & Economics, Communication, Journalism, Communism, Marxism, Leninism, Community, Conservation, Criticism, Education, Gay, Graphics, History, How-To, Humanism.

266

LifeCircle Press, Melissa Mosley, PO Box 805, Burlington, IA 52601, www.lifecircleent.com. 2001. Poetry, articles, art, photos, cartoons, letters, news items, non-fiction. "Poetry concerning caregiving and elderly issues. Articles should be concerning 50+ issues. Photos and cartoons for family and 50+ issues. Interested in subjects and formats not already published." Pub'd 2 titles 2005; expects 2 titles 2006, 2 titles 2007. Discounts: 40% wholesale/retail. 60pp. Reporting time: 2 months. Simultaneous submissions accepted: no. Publishes 10% of manuscripts submitted. Payment: 10% of retail price. Copyrights for author. Subjects: Adolescence, Aging, Alternative Medicine, Cartoons, Community, Cooking, Crafts, Hobbies, Creativity, Culture, Education, Family, Finances, Global Affairs, Government, Senior Citizens.

LifeQuest Publishing Group, PO Box 760, Hana, HI 96713-0760, fax 425-392-1854, e-mail lifequest@usa.net. 1994. Music, non-fiction. avg. press run 30M. Expects 7 titles 2006, 12 titles 2007. Discounts: available upon request. 240pp. Reporting time: 60 days. Simultaneous submissions accepted: yes. Payment: yes. Copyrights for author. Subjects: Audio/Video, Hypnosis, Mental Health, Motivation, Success, New Age, Non-Fiction, Occult, Psychology, Yoga, Zen.

LifeSkill Institute, Inc., Sandra Spaulding Hughes, President; Mary Anne Mills, Editor, P.O. Box 302, Wilmington, NC 28402, 910-251-0665,910-763-2494,800-570-4009,lifeskill@earthlink.net,www.lifeskillinstitute.org. 2001. Non-fiction. "Prefer self-improvement/personal development titles." avg. press run 4000. Pub'd 1 title 2005; expects 3 titles 2006, 4 titles 2007. Discounts: Distributors/Wholesalers - 55%Bookstores/retailers - 40%Institutions/Classrooms - 5 or more 25%. 200pp. Reporting time: 60 days. Simultaneous submissions accepted: Yes. Publishes 25% of manuscripts submitted. Payment: 10%, pay semi-annual, advance on cases by case basis. Does not copyright for author. Subjects: Metaphysics, New Age, Psychology, Self-Help.

LifeThread Publications, Susan M. Osborn, President, 7541 Wooddale Way, Citrus Heights, CA 95610-2621, 916-722-3452, E-mail sosborn@ix.netcom.com. 1996. Non-fiction. "Accept materials related to system theory; systems perspectives on business & psychological issues." avg. press run 3M. Expects 1 title 2006, 1 title 2007. Negotiable. 200pp. Reporting time: 2 months. Simultaneous submissions accepted: yes. Payment: negotiable. Copyrights for author. Subjects: Business & Economics, Lifestyles, Politics.

LIFETIME MAGAZINE, American Carriage House Publishing, Louann Carroll, Editor; Jodie Lucas, Assistant Editor, P.O. Box 1130, Nevada City, California, CA 95959, 530.470.0720. 1995. Articles, news items, non-fiction. "Articles can be used on the websites and/or in the magazine or adoption anthalogies." circ. 500. 4/yr. Pub'd 1500 issues 2005; expects 2000 issues 2006, 2500 issues 2007. sub. price 25.00; per copy 5.99; sample 3.00. Back issues: Inquire. Discounts: 50% discount to the trade/distributors/agents, etc. 108pp. Reporting time: 6 months. Simultaneous submissions accepted: No. Publishes 10% of manuscripts submitted. Payment: net 30. Copyrighted. Pub's reviews: 20 in 2005. §Adoption Stories. Ads: 250.00 1/2 page175.00 1/4 page150.00 dqc. Subject: Adoption.

LIFTOUTS, Preludium Publishers, Barry Casselman, 520 5th Street SE #4, Minneapolis, MN 55414-1628, (612) 321-9044 barcass@mr.net. 1983. Poetry, fiction, criticism, reviews, parts-of-novels. "*Liftouts* is devoted primarily to reviews of new books and critical essays. Some short fiction and poetry is published, with an emphasis on translated works by foreign authors who have not previously been published in English. *Unsolicited submissions are not considered at this time.* Any inquiries should be accompanied by SASE. Translations of stories by Clarice Lispector, Luiz Vilela, Hans Christoph Buch, Sergio Sant'Anna and others have appeared in previous issues." circ. 5M. 1/yr. Expects 1 issue 2007. price per copy $5; sample $5. Back issues: $5. Discounts: negotiable. 40-75pp. Payment: varies. Copyrighted, reverts to author. Pub's reviews. §Poetry, fiction, plays, literary criticism, all literature in translation. Ads: $495/$275/$7.50 per column inch. Subjects: Book Reviewing, Criticism, Fiction, Poetry, Translation.

Light of New Orleans Publishing, Joshua Clark, 828 Royal Street #307, New Orleans, LA 70116, 504-523-4322, Fax 504-522-0688, editor@frenchquarterfiction.com, www.frenchquarterfiction.com. 2001. Fiction. "Published *French Quarter Fiction: The Newest Stories From America's Oldest Bohemia*, an anthology of the best works by living writers on the heart of New Orleans. Published Judy Conner's *Southern Fried Divorce* and Barry Gifford's *Back in America* in 2004." avg. press run 15,000. Pub'd 1 title 2005; expects 2 titles 2006, 2 titles 2007. 350pp. Payment: varies. Does not copyright for author. Subjects: Anthology, Fiction, Literature (General), Short Stories.

Light, Words & Music, Dan Polin, 19630 Sunnyside Drive N, Apt. M108, Shoreline, WA 98133-1209, 206-546-1498, Fax 206-546-2585, sisp@aol.com. 1995. "This press specializes in 'fusion of the arts' books." avg. press run 5M. Pub'd 1 title 2005; expects 1 title 2006, 1 title 2007. 150pp. Subjects: Alaska, Arts, Birds, Earth, Natural History, English, Florida, Hawaii, Inspirational, Music, Pacific Northwest, Photography, Quotations, Spiritual, Tapes & Records, Washington (state).

LIGHT: The Quarterly of Light Verse, John Mella, Lisa Markwart, PO Box 7500, Chicago, IL 60680, 800-285-4448 (Charge Orders only), 708-488-3188 (voice), www.lightquarterly.com (no submissions via fax or e-mail). 1992. Poetry, fiction, articles, art, cartoons, interviews, satire, criticism, reviews, letters, news items.

"*Light* is the only magazine in the United States that publishes light verse exclusively. Write for guidelines. Contributors include John Updike, X.J. Kennedy, Donald Hall, Michael Benedikt, and Tom Disch. We also publish cartoons, satire, reviews, and humor. Fax by prior arrangement." circ. 1M. 4/yr. Pub'd 4 issues 2005; expects 4 issues 2006, 4 issues 2007. sub. price $22/4 issues, $34/8 issues, $38/4 issues international; per copy $5 + $2 1st class mail; sample $4 + $2 1st class mail. Back issues: same. Discounts: jobber 10%. 64pp. Reporting time: 1-6 months. Simultaneous submissions accepted: no. Publishes 8% of manuscripts submitted. Payment: copies. Copyrighted, reverts to author. Pub's reviews: 60 in 2005. §Light verse, satire, cartoons. Ads: Write for ad card. Subjects: Cartoons, Comics, Essays, Fiction, Graphics, Literature (General), Poetry, Prose, Reviews.

The Lighthouse Press, Ron Richard, Publisher, PO Box 910, Deerfield Beach, FL 33443-0910, thelighthousepress@attbi.net, www.lighthouseedition.com, fax:954-360-9994.

LightLines Publishing, 12 Wilson Street, Farmington, NH 03835-3428, 603-755-3091, Fax 603-755-3748, lightlinespublishing@yahoo.com, www.lightlinespublishing.com. 1996. Non-fiction. avg. press run 10M. Pub'd 2 titles 2005; expects 2 titles 2006, 4 titles 2007. Discounts: 40% to retailer, 55% to distributors. 175pp. Reporting time: variable. Simultaneous submissions accepted: no. Publishes 10% of manuscripts submitted. Payment: variable. Copyrights for author. Subjects: Alternative Medicine, Metaphysics, Self-Help, Spiritual.

LIGHTWORKS MAGAZINE, Charlton Burch, Designer and Editor; Andrea Martin, Managing Editor, PO Box 1202, Birmingham, MI 48012-1202, 248-626-8026, lightworks_mag@hotmail.com. 1975. Articles, art, photos, interviews, collages, concrete art. "Illuminating new and experimental art. A tribute issue devoted to the life and art of Ray Johnson has been recently released." circ. 2M. Irregular. Pub'd 1 issue 2005; expects 1 issue 2006, 1 issue 2007. sub. price $20 (4 future issues) individuals, $25 institutions; per copy price varies; sample $5. Back issues: #10 $2, #14/15, #16, #17, #18 $4 each, #13 $3, #5 $1, all orders must add $2 to cover postage costs, #19, #20/21 $5 each, #22 Ray Johnson issue, $13 includes audio CD. Discounts: 30% on minimum orders of 12 copies of one issue. 64pp. Reporting time: usually quick. Publishes 50% of manuscripts submitted. Payment: none, other than a couple copies. Copyrighted. Pub's reviews: 60 in 2005. §Books, periodicals, and recordings which explore alternative & intermediate artforms, and artists' publications. No ads. Subjects: Arts, Avant-Garde, Experimental Art, Book Arts, Book Reviewing, Communication, Journalism, Counter-Culture, Alternatives, Communes, Creativity, Dada, Electronics, Graphics, Music, Networking, Photography, Visual Arts.

LILIES AND CANNONBALLS REVIEW, Daniel Connor, P.O. Box 702, Bowling Green Station, New York, NY 10274-0702, info@liliesandcannonballs.com, www.liliesandcannonballs.com. 2004. Poetry, fiction, art, photos, cartoons, interviews, satire, letters, parts-of-novels, long-poems, collages, plays, non-fiction. "LCR seeks to create a space for the synthesis of contrary elements: aesthetically driven and socially conscious literature and art; traditional and experimental forms; crazy-man conservative and bleeding liberal views. Recent contributors include James Doyle, Julio Cortazar, Albert Mobilio, Noah Eli Gordon, Jim Murphy, Ross Simonini, Lynn Crawford, and Lee Rowland." circ. 400. 2/yr. Pub'd 2 issues 2005; expects 2 issues 2006, 2 issues 2007. sub. price $23; per copy $12; sample $12. Back issues: inquire. Discounts: inquire. 96pp. Reporting time: 1 to 6 months, give or take. Simultaneous submissions accepted: Yes. Publishes 5% of manuscripts submitted. Payment: 1 copy. Copyrighted, reverts to author. Ads: inquire.

LILITH, Susan W. Schneider, Editor-in-Chief, 250 West 57th, #2432, New York, NY 10107, 212-757-0818. 1976. Poetry, fiction, articles, art, photos, interviews, criticism, reviews, letters, parts-of-novels, long-poems, plays, news items, non-fiction. "The 'Jewish Woman's Quarterly'." circ. 10M. 4/yr. Pub'd 4 issues 2005; expects 4 issues 2006, 4 issues 2007. sub. price $18; per copy $4.50; sample $6, includes postage. Back issues: $6 for in-print back issues. Out-of-print $50. Discounts: through distributors: DeBoer's, Ingram, Koens, small changes, desert moon. 48pp. Reporting time: 3 months. Simultaneous submissions accepted, as long as we are told when another publication accepts. Payment: negotiable. Copyrighted, rights reverting to author negotiable. Pub's reviews: 20 in 2005. §Pertaining to the Jewish, female experience, history, biography/autobio., feminist, fiction, poetry. Ads: on request. Subjects: Judaism, Women.

LILLIPUT REVIEW, Don Wentworth, Editor, 282 Main Street, Pittsburgh, PA 15201. 1989. Poetry. "All poems must be 10 lines or *less*. All styles and forms considered. SASE or in the trash, period. 3 poems maximum per submissions. Any submission beyond the maximum will be returned unread." circ. 250-350. Irregular. Pub'd 8 issues 2005; expects 8 issues 2006, 8 issues 2007. sub. price $12; per copy $1; sample $1 or SASE. Back issues: $1. Discounts: Individuals only: 6 issues=$5; 15 issues=$10. 16pp. Reporting time: 1-16 weeks. Simultaneous submissions accepted: no. Publishes 5% of manuscripts submitted. Payment: 2 copies. Copyrighted, reverts to author. Subjects: Haiku, Poetry, Translation.

Limberlost Press, Rick Ardinger, Editor; Rosemary Ardinger, Editor, 17 Canyon Trail, Boise, ID 83716. 1976. Poetry, fiction, interviews, reviews. "*Limberlost Press* is devoted to the publication of fine, letterpress-printed, limited edition poetry chapbooks. Established in 1976 as a literary magazine, the magazine, *The Limberlost*

Review, was suspended in the 1980s, when we began to letterpress chapbooks by individual authors. Since then, we have averaged three to four titles a year. Limberlost publishes work by nationally known writers, as well as established and emerging writers from the West (mostly). Noted writers in the Limberlost canon include Sherman Alexie, Edward Dorn, Lawrence Ferlinghetti, Gary Snyder, Gary Gildner, John Updike, Jim Harrison, Ed Sanders, Allen Ginsberg, John Haines, Jennifer Dunbar Dorn, Hayden Carruth, and others. Other poets include, Margaret Aho, William Studebaker, Judith Root, Nancy Takacs, Greg Keeler, Gino Sky, Chuck Guilford, Keith Wilson, Gary Holthaus, and others. Our books are printed on archival-quality papers, and sewn by hand in wrappers. A limited number of each title is bound by hand into cloth and boards as special signed/numbered editions. We try to keep the books affordable, typically between $15 to $25 (with signed copies priced higher). Occasionally, we publish full-length commercially printed books that are not letterpress printed, such as *Waltzing with the Captain: Rememebing Richard Brautigan*, a memoir by Montana writer Greg Keeler, *Coyote in the Mountains*, a collection of short stories by Idaho writer John Rember. Most of the time, we solicit manuscripts; however, sometimes a manuscript just arrives in the mail that just seems right for the canon. Because our methods are labor intensive, however, prospective contributors should be familiar with our books before considering. They should have held our books in their hands to truly understand what a Limberlost book is, and thus submit a collection for consideration that they feel is appropriate. A current list of titles in print is on our website at www.Limberlostpress.com." avg. press run 500. Pub'd 4 titles 2005; expects 4 titles 2006, 4 titles 2007. Discounts: 40% for 5 or more. 36pp. Reporting time: 1-2 months. Payment: in copies. Copyrights for author. Subjects: Literary Review, Poetry.

Limelight Editions, John Cerullo, Publisher, 512 Newark Pompton Turnpike, Pompton Plains, NJ 07444, 718-381-0421, 973-835-6375, fax 973-835-6504, info@limelighteditions.com, www.limelighteditions.com. 1984. Non-fiction. avg. press run 4M. Pub'd 10 titles 2005; expects 12 titles 2006, 14 titles 2007. Discounts: 1-4: 20%; 5-100: 47%; 100+: 50%. 300pp. Reporting time: 4-6 weeks. We do not usually accept simultaneous submissions. Publishes 10% of manuscripts submitted. Payment: generally 7-1/2% for paperback, 10% cloth. Does not copyright for author. Subjects: Autobiography, Biography, Criticism, Dance, Bob Dylan, Electronics, Music, Non-Fiction, Performing Arts, G.B. Shaw, Theatre.

LIMESTONE: A Literary Journal, Stacey Floyd, English Dept., Univ. of Kentucky, 1215 Patterson Office Tower, Lexington, KY 40506-0027, 859-257-6981, www.uky.edu/AS/English/Limestone. 1976. Poetry, fiction, art, photos, cartoons, interviews, plays, concrete art. "Since 1976, Limestone: A Literary Journal, ISSN 0899-5966, has published creative writing and art from around the world. We recently published Paul Muldoon, Seamus Heaney, Evan Boland, and friends in a special Irish Poets issue. We accept only previously unpublished manuscripts from August to Dec. Final decisions are made by March. Please see our web site for jourbnal information." circ. 500-1M. 1-2/yr. Pub'd 1 issue 2005; expects 2 issues 2006, 1 issue 2007. sub. price $12; per copy $6; sample $6. Back issues: $4. 150pp. Reporting time: 6 months. Simultaneous submissions accepted: yes. Publishes 10% of manuscripts submitted. Payment: copy of the journal. Copyrighted, reverts to author. Pub's reviews: 2 in 2005. §We are most interested in reviews of works by Kentucky authors (or regional) - either poetry or fiction. Ads: $100/$50. Subject: Literature (General).

Lincoln Springs Press, 40 Post Avenue, Hawthorne, NJ 07506-1809. 1987. Poetry, fiction, photos. "We have ceased accepting unsolicited poetry and fiction manuscripts for the time being." avg. press run 1M. Expects 4 titles 2006, 4 titles 2007. Discounts: 1-5 20%, 5-10 30%, 10+ 40%. 80pp. Reporting time: 6 months. Payment: 15% royalty. Copyrights for author. Subjects: Literature (General), Photography, Poetry, Prose.

LINQ, Dr. Dosia Reichardt, General Editor, School of Humanities, James Cook Univ.-North Queensland, Townsville 4811, Australia, e-mail jcu.linq@jcu.edu.au. 1971. Poetry, fiction, articles, interviews, criticism, reviews, parts-of-novels, long-poems, plays. "Critical articles about 3M words. Reviews 1M words." circ. 350. 2/yr. Pub'd 2 issues 2005; expects 2 issues 2006, 2 issues 2007. sub. price $30 indiv.; $40 instit. including postage, Australian, Overseas $50 Australian; per copy $15, Australian (including postage), $20 Australian overseas. Back issues: $3 prior to 1980. 140pp. Reporting time: 2 months. Simultaneous submissions accepted: yes. Payment: poetry $20 per poem, short fiction $50, reviews $30, articles $50 Australian dollars. Copyrighted, reverts to author. Pub's reviews: 8 in 2005. §Any area of contemporary interest, political, sociological, literary. Subjects: Arts, Bibliography, Book Reviewing, Criticism, Drama, Fiction, Literary Review, Poetry, Women.

Lintel, Naomi May Miller, Publisher, 24 Blake Lane, Middletown, NY 10940, 845-342-5224. 1978. Poetry, fiction, art, long-poems. "Not currently accepting unsolicited manuscripts." Discounts: 40% to bookstores; 45% on 25 copies or more; 55% to wholesalers.

Linworth Publishing, Inc. (see also THE BOOK REPORT: The Magazine for Secondary School Library Media & Technology Specialists; LIBRARY TALK: The Magazine for Elementary School Library Media & Technology Specialists), Carol Simpson, Editor; Marlene Woo-Lun, Publisher, 480 East Wilson Bridge Road #L, Worthington, OH 43085-2372, 614-436-7107, FAX 614-436-9490. 1982. Articles, reviews, news items. Discounts: 5%. Subjects: Book Reviewing, Education, Libraries.

Lion Press, Norma L. Leone, PO Box 92541, Rochester, NY 14692, phone 585-381-6410; fax 585-381-7439; for orders only 800-597-3068. 1985. Non-fiction. avg. press run 1M-5M. Pub'd 3 titles 2005. Discounts: 20-50%. 1-200pp. Simultaneous submissions accepted: no. Publishes 0% of manuscripts submitted. Copyrights for author. Subjects: Computers, Calculators, Health, How-To, Transportation, Women.

Liquid Paper Press (see also NERVE COWBOY), Joseph Shields, Jerry Hagins, PO Box 4973, Austin, TX 78765, www.eden.com/~jwhagins/nervecowboy. 1995. Poetry. "Recent books published by Liquid Paper Press include *The Active Ingredient, and Other Poems* and *The Back East Poems* by Gerald Locklin, *Sunday Ritual* by Ralph Dranow, *Picking the Lock on the Door to Paradise* by Joan Jobe Smith, *Notes of a Human Warehouse Engineer* by Belinda Subraman, *E Pluribus Aluminum* by Thomas Michael McDade, and *Hoeing in High Heels* by Wilma Elizabeth McDaniel. We do not accept unsolicited manuscripts." avg. press run 150. Pub'd 4 titles 2005; expects 4 titles 2006, 4 titles 2007. Discounts: 40% on purchase of 3 or more copies. 32pp. We currently only accept solicited chapbook manuscripts, with the exception of our annual chapbook. Payment: 30 complimentary copies. Copyrights for author. Subject: Poetry.

LISTEN, Anita Jacobs, Editor, 55 West Oak Ridge Drive, Hagerstown, MD 21740. 1948. Articles, art, cartoons, interviews, non-fiction. circ. 40M. 9/yr. Pub'd 9 issues 2005; expects 9 issues 2006, 9 issues 2007. sub. price $26.95, $33.45 foreign; per copy $2; sample $2. Back issues: 40¢. 32pp. Reporting time: 60 days. Simultaneous submissions accepted: yes. Publishes 50% of manuscripts submitted. Payment: $50-$250. Copyrighted, reverts to author. Ads: none. Subjects: Education, Health, Young Adult.

THE LISTENING EYE, Grace Butcher, Editor; Joanne Speidel, Co-Ass't Editor; James Wohlken, Co-Ass't Editor, KSU Geauga Campus, 14111 Claridon-Troy Road, Burton, OH 44021, 440-286-3840, grace_butcher@msn.com. 1970. Poetry, fiction, art, photos, non-fiction. "5 x 7 vertical format, black & white or color." circ. 250. 1/yr. Pub'd 1 issue 2005; expects 1 issue 2006, 1 issue 2007. sub. price $4; per copy $4; sample $4. Back issues: $4. Discounts: N/A. 60pp. Reporting time: 4 months max, sometimes sooner. Simultaneous submissions accepted: no. Publishes maybe 20% of manuscripts submitted. Payment: 2 free copies. Copyrighted, reverts to author. Subjects: Essays, Fiction, Photography, Poetry, Short Stories, Sports, Outdoors.

LITERALLY HORSES/REMUDA, Laurie A. Cerny, 208 Cherry Hill Street, Kalamazoo, MI 49006-4221, 616-345-5915, literallyhorses@aol.com. 1999. Poetry, fiction, cartoons, reviews, music, parts-of-novels, long-poems. "Poems should be under 50 lines. Fiction (short story) under 3,500 words. All material should have a horse/rider, or western lifestyle theme. Recent contributors: Richard Wheeler, Maria Bailey, Rod Miller and Emery Mehok." circ. 1M. 2/yr. Pub'd 4 issues 2005; expects 4 issues 2006, 2 issues 2007. sub. price $7.95; per copy $2.25; sample $2.50. Back issues: $2.50. Discounts: none. 46pp. Reporting time: 1 month. Simultaneous submissions accepted: yes. Publishes 50% of manuscripts submitted. Payment: contributor's copy/subscription. Copyrighted, reverts to author. Pub's reviews: 15 in 2005. §Topics must pertain to horses,showing of various disciplines like racing, rodeo, dressage, etc., cowboys, western lifestyle. Ads: none. Subjects: Animals, Fiction, Old West, Poetry, Prose, The West.

LITERARY IMAGINATION: The Review of the Association of Literary Scholars and Critics, Sarah Spence, Dept. of Classics, 221 Park Hall, University of Georgia, Athens, GA 30602-6203, 706-542-0417, Fax 706-542-8503, litimag@uga.edu, www.bu.edu/literary. 1999. Poetry, fiction, articles, interviews, criticism, reviews, parts-of-novels. circ. 2,133. 3/yr. Pub'd 3 issues 2005; expects 3 issues 2006, 3 issues 2007. sub. price $25 individuals, $60 US institutions, $66.75 Institutions in Canada/Mexico, $73.50 international institutions; per copy $8.95 + p/h; sample free. Back issues: $8.95 + p/h. 180pp. Reporting time: to 90 days. Simultaneous submissions accepted: no. Publishes 20% of manuscripts submitted. Payment: not usually. Copyrighted, reverts to author. Pub's reviews: 1 in 2005. Ads: $350/$225/$375 cv. Subjects: Criticism, Essays, Fiction, Literary Review, Literature (General), Poetry, Translation.

LITERARY MAGAZINE REVIEW, Jenny Brantley, Editor; Brian Fitch, Assistant Editor, Univ. of Wisconsin-River Falls, English Dept., 410 S. 3rd Street, River Falls, WI 54022, email: jennifer.s.brantley@uwrf.edu, web site: http://www.uwrf.edu/lmr/. 1981. Articles, criticism, reviews. "*LMR* is devoted to providing critical appraisals of the specific contents of small, predominantly literary periodicals for the benefit of readers and writers. We print reviews of about 1.5M words that comment on the magazines' physical characteristics, on particular articles, stories, and poems featured, and on editorial preferences as evidenced in the selections. Recent contributors include John Pennington, D.E. Steward, Phil Miller, Kevin Prufer, Steve Heller, Maria Melendez, Stella Pope Duarte, and John McNally. We would be happy to entertain queries offering disinterested reviews and omnibus notices and pieces describing, explaining, or examining the current literary magazine scene. Subscription exchange inquiries are welcome." circ. 300. 4/yr. Pub'd 4 issues 2005; expects 4 issues 2006, 4 issues 2007. sub. price $16; per copy $5; sample $5. Back issues: $7 an issue. Discounts: 10% to subscription agencies. 48-52pp. Payment: copies. Copyrighted, rights revert on author's request. Pub's reviews: 70 in 2005. §Literary magazines. We are interested in magazines that publish at least some fiction, poetry, literary nonfiction, or all three. Ads: none. Subjects: Criticism, Literary Review,

LITERARY RESEARCH/RECHERCHE LITTERAIRE, Prof. Calin-Andrei Mihailescu, Editor, Dept. of Modern Languages & Lit., University of Western Ontario, London, ON N6A 3K7, Canada, 519-661-3196, 519-661-2111 X85862, Fax 519-661-4093, cmihails@uwo.ca, http://collection.nlc-bnc.ca/100/201/300/literary_research-ef, or www.uwo.ca/modlang/ailc. 1983. "The review publishes articles, review-articles, and reviews of recent publications in various fields of comparative literature; it reflects books and journals published throughout the world. Prints materials in English, French, and occasionally in German, Italian, Portuguese, and Spanish." circ. 500. 1/yr. Pub'd 2 issues 2005; expects 2 issues 2006, 2 issues 2007. sub. price distributed to members of the ICLA at no cost; per copy individuals: $25/year, $40/2 years; libraries: $75/year, $140/2 years; sample $15. Back issues: $15/issue. Discounts: none. 500pp. Reporting time: 1 month. Simultaneous submissions accepted: yes. Publishes 60% of manuscripts submitted. Payment: none. Copyrighted, does not revert to author. Pub's reviews: 80 in 2005. §Comparative literature, literary and critical theory. Ads: none.

THE LITERARY REVIEW, Rene Steinke, Editor-in-Chief; Walter Cummins, Editor Emeritus; Harry Keyishian, Editor; Martin Green, Editor; John Becker, Editor; William Zander, Editor, Fairleigh Dickinson University, 285 Madison Avenue, Madison, NJ 07940, 973-443-8564, Fax 973-443-8364. 1957. Poetry, fiction, articles, interviews, criticism, reviews, long-poems. "We consider fiction and poetry submissions of any type and of any length (within reason) from new and established writers. We welcome critical articles on contemporary American and international literature and are eager to have submissions of essays that are written for a general literary audience rather than the academic quarterly market. *TLR* has always had a special emphasis on contemporary writing abroad (in translation) and we welcome submissions from overseas, and new translations of contemporary foreign literature. We are particularly interested in receiving translations of and essays on ethnic writing abroad." circ. 2M-2.5M. 4/yr. Pub'd 4 issues 2005; expects 4 issues 2006, 4 issues 2007. sub. price $18 U.S., $21 foreign; per copy $7 U.S., $8 foreign; sample $7 recent issues. Back issues: varies. Discounts: negotiable. 180-200pp. Reporting time: 4-5 months. Simultaneous submissions accepted: yes. Publishes 3% of manuscripts submitted. Payment: 2 free copies, additional copies at discount. Copyrighted, reverts to author. Pub's reviews: 10 in 2005. §Contemporary fiction, poetry, literary theory, US and world literature (contemporary). No ads. Subject: Literary Review.

LITRAG, Derrick Hachey, A.J. Rathbun, PO Box 21066, Seattle, WA 98111-3066, www.litrag.com. 1997. Poetry, fiction, art, photos, cartoons, interviews, criticism, reviews, long-poems. "Recent contributors include Mark Halliday, J. Robert Lennon, Edward Skoog, Derick Burleson and Malena Morling." circ. 1M. 3/yr. Pub'd 3 issues 2005; expects 3 issues 2006, 3 issues 2007. sub. price $12; per copy $3; sample $3. Discounts: available upon request. 40pp. Reporting time: 6-8 weeks. Simultaneous submissions accepted: yes. Publishes 5% of manuscripts submitted. Payment: 2 copies, special gift, per diam when possible. Copyrighted, reverts to author. Pub's reviews: 4 in 2005. §Well crafted original works. Ads: upon request. Subjects: Arts, Fiction, Photography, Poetry, Reviews.

Little Leaf Press, Beth E. Koch, CEO, Publisher, 5902 Hummingbird Road, Braham, MN 55006-2742, 304-638-0173, Fax 304-523-7212, littleleaf@maxminn.com, www.littleleafpress.com. 1998. Fiction, art, photos, reviews, non-fiction. "Delivery address: 5 Hilltop Road, Lavalette, WV 25535. Co-publishing books for children, history, hobby, academic." avg. press run 1-3M. Pub'd 3 titles 2005; expects 2-3 titles 2006, 3-5 titles 2007. Discounts: libraries 1-4 books 25%, free shipping; bookstores/online 45%, free shipping. 140pp. Reporting time: within 30 days. Simultaneous submissions accepted: yes. Publishes 5% of manuscripts submitted. Payment: 100% net sales. Copyrights for author. Subjects: Children, Youth, Crafts, Hobbies, History, Picture Books, Textbooks.

THE LITTLE MAGAZINE, Alifair Skebe, Michael Peters, Department of English, State Univ. of New York, University of Albany, Albany, NY 12222, website www.albany.edu/~litmag. 1965. Poetry, fiction. "*The Little Magazine* is an old literary journal revived under the editorship of UAlbany's faculty and graduate student writers. *TLM* is now a multi-media based journal published on the web and CD-ROM in effort to promote and display the creative opportunites that exist amongst literature, art, and new media. *We have no set guidelines.* We prefer work that lends itself to hypermedia/hypertext production. We like poetry and fiction that foregrounds language and is innovative in form, pushing its own limits and the limits of genre through sound, text, image. We'd like to see more work from minority writers. We do not read from May through August. Some recent contributors: Charles Bernstein, Raymond Federman, Christy Sheffield Sanford, Mark Amerika, Eduardo Kac, Juliana Spahr, Richard Kostelanetz. TLM can be found on line at www.albany.edu/~litmag." circ. 2M. 1/yr. Pub'd 2 issues 2005; expects 2 issues 2006, 2 issues 2007. sub. price $15 (for the CD-Rom); per copy $15 (for the CD-Rom); sample $15 (for the CD-Rom). Back issues: $6. Discounts: see website for details. Reporting time: 3 months. Simultaneous submissions accepted: yes. Publishes 20% of manuscripts submitted. Payment: 1 copy. Copyrighted, reverts to author. Ads: please inquire. Subjects: Fiction, Poetry.

•**Little Pear Press,** Martha Manno, PO Box 343, Seekonk, MA 02771, Martha@LittlePearPress.com, www.LittlePearPress.com. 2003. Poetry, fiction, non-fiction. "Poetry anthologies on themes, poetry by individuals, anthologies of women writers, short story collections, children's literature." avg. press run 1000. Expects 2 titles 2006, 2 titles 2007. Discounts: 40% discount 1+. 100pp. Reporting time: 6-8 weeks. Simultaneous submissions accepted: Yes. Copyrights for author. Subjects: Anthology, Autobiography, Experimental, Fiction, Humor, Juvenile Fiction, Memoirs, Non-Fiction, Novels, Poetry, Short Stories, Young Adult.

Little Poem Press, C. E. Laine, Editor, PO Box 185, Falls Church, VA 22040-0185, www.celaine.com/ LittlePoemPress. 2003. Poetry, fiction, long-poems. "We publish e-books and printed chapbooks (not to exceed 50 pages). No electronic submissions. Must include hardcopy and electronic file on disk/cd (.rtf/.doc/.txt only). Finished and polished manuscripts only. Please include author bio and acknowledgements. SASE required for returned work." avg. press run unlimited. Pub'd 4 titles 2005; expects 20 titles 2006, 30 titles 2007. Discounts: 10%. 50pp. Reporting time: 90 days. Simultaneous submissions accepted: no. Publishes 5% of manuscripts submitted. Payment: 50-50 split after expenses. Author retains copyright. Subject: Poetry.

LITURGICAL CATECHESIS, Resource Publications, Inc., Kathi Scarpaci, 160 E. Virginia Street #290, San Jose, CA 95112-5876, 408-286-8505, Fax 408-287-8748. 2001. Art, photos, reviews, non-fiction. "Bi-monthly publication devoted to creative ideas for building a unified, parish-wide catechetical effort." circ. 1.1M. 6/yr. Pub'd 1 issue 2005; expects 6 issues 2006, 6 issues 2007. sub. price $30; per copy $5; sample $5. Back issues: $6. Discounts: standard trade. 32pp. Reporting time: 6 weeks. Simultaneous submissions accepted: no. Publishes 10% of manuscripts submitted. Payment: $1-$100. Copyrighted, does not revert to author. Pub's reviews: 8 in 2005. §Religious education, catechesis. Ads: $1197/$961/$1 per word. Subjects: Arts, Catholic, Dance, Drama, Education, Religion, Spiritual.

•**LITVISION, LITVISION PRESS,** Patrick Simonelli, 7711 Greenback Lane #156, Citrus Heights, CA 95610.

The Live Oak Press, LLC, David M. Hamilton, Editor-In-Chief, PO Box 60036, Palo Alto, CA 94306-0036, 650-853-0197, info@liveoakpress.com, www.liveoakpress.com. 1982. Non-fiction. "We publish regional books about California including California literary history. We also copublish Genny Smith Books titles." avg. press run 1M. Pub'd 1 title 2005; expects 1 title 2006, 2 titles 2007. Discounts: 40% 3 or more. 96-250pp. Reporting time: 3 months. Simultaneous submissions accepted: yes. Publishes 10% of manuscripts submitted. Payment: Royalties on a sliding scale. No advances. Copyrights for author. Subjects: California, Jack London, San Francisco, Travel, Yosemite.

‡**Liverpool University Press (see also BULLETIN OF HISPANIC STUDIES),** Dorothy Sherman Severin, Professor; James Higgins, Professor, Dept. of Hispanic Studies, The University, PO Box 147, Liverpool L69 3BX, England, 051 794 2774/5. 1923. Articles, reviews. "Specialist articles on the languages and literatures of Spain, Portugal and Latin America, in English, Spanish, Portuguese, and Catalan." avg. press run 1.2M. Expects 4 titles 2006. 112pp. Reporting time: 3 months. Payment: none. Does not copyright for author. Subject: Language.

LIVING CHEAP NEWS, Larry Roth, PO Box 8178, Kansas City, MO 64112, 816-523-0224, livcheap@aol.com, www.livingcheap.com. 1992. "Usually, this is written in house, but we consider contributions (free), product recommendations, etc., from readers." circ. 2M. 10/yr. Pub'd 10 issues 2005; expects 10 issues 2006, 10 issues 2007. sub. price $12; per copy $1.20; sample $1.20. 4pp. Reporting time: varies. Payment: none. Copyrighted, does not revert to author. Pub's reviews: 30 in 2005. §Cheap and meaningful cooking, products, lifestyles, etc. Ads: none. Subject: Self-Help.

LIVING FREE, Jim Stumm, Box 29, Hiler Branch, Buffalo, NY 14223. 1979. Articles, cartoons, reviews, letters, news items, non-fiction. "We are pro-individual, pro-private property. Discuss ways for individuals, families, and small groups to live freer, more self-reliant lives. Not interested in politics, or mass movements for social change. By publishing mostly unedited letters, we provide a forum for freedom-seekers, survivalists, libertarians, homesteaders, anarchists, and other outlaws." circ. 200. 4-6/yr. Pub'd 7 issues 2005; expects 6 issues 2006, 8 issues 2007. sub. price $12 for 6 issues; per copy $2; sample $2. Back issues: $2 each, discounts for 10 or more. Discounts: 40% for 5 or more copies of 1 issue to 1 address, no returns, also applies to subscriptions. 8pp. Simultaneous submissions accepted: yes. Payment: none. Not copyrighted. Pub's reviews: 6 in 2005. §Non-fiction: self-reliance, enhancing freedom, living cheap, avoiding govt. restrictions. Ads: unclassified advertising; 25¢/word, $5 minimum/display advertising $20 for 1/4 page. Subject: Libertarian.

Livingston Press (see also Swallow's Tale Press), Joe Taylor, Tina Jones, Station 22, University of West Alabama, Livingston, AL 35470, www.livingstonpress.uwa.edu. 1984. Fiction. "Literary works only." avg. press run 1.5M. Pub'd 10 titles 2005; expects 10 titles 2006, 11 titles 2007. Discounts: 48% trade for 10 or more copies. 180pp. Reporting time: 6 months. Simultaneous submissions accepted: yes, encouraged in fact. Publishes 1/2% of manuscripts submitted. Payment: 10% of press run, royalty after sales of 1500. Copyrights for author.

LLEN CYMRU, University Of Wales Press, Gruffydd Aled Williams, 10 Columbus Walk, Brigantine Place, Cardiff CF10 4UP, Wales, 44-029-2049-6899, Fax 44-029-2049-6108, press@press.wales.ac.uk, www.wales.ac.uk/press. 1950. Articles. "Journal of various aspects of Welsh literature, printed in the Welsh language." circ. 300. 1/yr. Pub'd 1 issue 2005; expects 1 issue 2006, 1 issue 2007. sub. price £6.50; per copy £6.50; sample £6.50. Back issues: £6.50. Discounts: 10%. 143pp. Payment: none. Not copyrighted. Pub's reviews: 4 in 2005. §Welsh literature. Subject: Celtic.

Llumina Press, Deborah Greenspan, 7915 W. McNab Road, Tamarac, FL 33321, 954 726-0902. 1997. Poetry, fiction, photos, cartoons, satire, criticism, reviews, long-poems, plays, non-fiction. "We publish anything that is well written and carefully edited." avg. press run 1000. Pub'd 370 titles 2005; expects 500 titles 2006, 800 titles 2007. Discounts: 35% to 55%. 200pp. Reporting time: one to two weeks. Simultaneous submissions accepted: Yes. Payment: 10% of list to 30% of list. Copyrights: We can but we prefer that the author do it. Subjects: Advertising, Self-Promotion, Anthology, Autobiography, Experimental, Fantasy, Fiction, Finances, Food, Eating, Novels, Nutrition, Occult, Parenting, Philosophy, Picture Books, Romance.

LO STRANIERO: The Stranger, Der Fremde, L'Etranger, Ignazio Corsaro, Piazza Amedeo 8, Naples 80121, Italy, ITALY/81/426052. 1985. Poetry, articles, art, photos, interviews, satire, criticism, letters, collages, concrete art. circ. 10M. 2/yr. Pub'd 2 issues 2005; expects 2 issues 2006, 2 issues 2007. sub. price $50; per copy $25; sample $20. Back issues: $30. Discounts: distributor = $1/copy (at the order). 32pp. Payment: none. Registered at the Tribunal of Naples, Italy. §Politics, culture, sociology, avant gard/art, Italy, visual art. Ads: $200/$100/$20 ("spot" in the *network*). Subjects: Avant-Garde, Experimental Art, Culture, Italy, Politics, Sociology, Visual Arts.

Lockhart Press, Inc., Russell A. Lockhart, Editor; Franklyn B. Lockhart, Editor, 1717 Wetmore Avenue, Everett, WA 98201, 425-252-8882, ral@ralockhart.com, www.ralockhart.com. 1982. Poetry, fiction, long-poems, non-fiction. "Our aim is to publish books devoted to the direct expression of the psyche's restless search for place and value in our time. Our books will be crafted by hand in every particular: printing by handpress from handset type on handmade paper and handbound in limited editions. Inqiries invited. Inaugural Publication *Midnight's Daughter*, poems by Janet Dallett, winner of Letterpress Prize, Festival of the Arts, Seattle, 1983. New paperback editions began in 1991. Electronic editions began in 2000." avg. press run 120-200. Pub'd 1 title 2005; expects 1 title 2006, 1 title 2007. Discounts: 20% to distributors & subscribers to the press on handmade; standard discounts on paperbacks. 80pp. Reporting time: 2 months. Simultaneous submissions accepted: yes. Payment: 15% after direct cost recovery. Does not copyright for author. Subjects: Folklore, Poetry, Psychology.

Locks Art Publications, 600 Washington Square South, Philadelphia, PA 19106, 215-629-1000. 1968. Art. avg. press run 600 copies. Pub'd 4 titles 2005; expects 7 titles 2006, 5-7 titles 2007. Discounts: 1-4 copies 20%, 5+ 40%. 32pp. Reporting time: 3-4 months. Payment: variable. Copyrights for author. Subject: Arts.

LOGIC LETTER, Tom Ross, Sigrid Young, 13957 Hall Road, #185, Shelby Twp., MI 48315. Articles, criticism, reviews, letters, news items. "Logic Letter is a publication of the "truth society." LL shows how society (and often the individual) is going wrong. For example, few follow the axiom: "The solution begins where the problem began." Support to axioms (themes) often are taken from current news, from history and general experience. Please keep submissions to about 100 words." circ. 50. 12/yr. Pub'd 12 issues 2005; expects 8 issues 2006, 12 issues 2007. sub. price $6; sample $1. Back issues: $1. 2pp. Reporting time: 2 weeks. Copyrighted, reverts to author. Pub's reviews: 1 in 2005. §how-to, cats. Subjects: Criticism, Humanism, Psychology, Public Affairs, Society.

LONDON REVIEW OF BOOKS, Mary-Kay Wilmers, 28-30 Little Russell Street, London WC1A 2HN, England, 020-7209-1141, fax 020-7209-1151. 1979. Poetry, fiction, articles, art, photos, criticism, reviews, letters, non-fiction. circ. 34.9M. 24/yr. Pub'd 24 issues 2005; expects 24 issues 2006, 24 issues 2007. sub. price $42; per copy $3.95; sample $3.95 + postage. Back issues: $5 + postage. Discounts: 20% agency. 40pp. Payment: negotiable. Not copyrighted. Pub's reviews: 692 in 2005. Ads: £1835/£1045/classified £5.10/line (average 6 words).

LONE STARS MAGAZINE, Milo Rosebud, 4219 Flinthill, San Antonio, TX 78230-1619. 1992. Poetry, art. "Recent contributors: Terry Lee, Emily Moore, Ralph Martin, Violet Wilcox, Jan Brevet, Joseph Verrilli, Steven Duplij, Sheila Roark." circ. 200. 3/yr. Pub'd 4 issues 2005; expects 3 issues 2006, 3 issues 2007. sub. price $18; per copy $5; sample $5. Back issues: when available, in-print. Discounts: if possible. 24pp. Reporting time: 4-6 weeks. Simultaneous submissions accepted: yes. Publishes 60-80% of manuscripts submitted. Payment: none. Copyrighted, reverts to author. Ads: $20 per 1/4 page with 3 issues. Subjects: Poetry, Prose.

Lone Willow Press, Fredrick Zydek, PO Box 31647, Omaha, NE 68131-0647, 402-551-9=0343. 1994. Poetry. "We publish chapbooks. Usually by invitation only. We will, however, give a fair reading to all typescripts that meet our guidelines. Poems must reflect a single theme." avg. press run 350 first edition, 300 second edition.

Pub'd 27 titles 2005. Discounts: standard to bookstores (40%). 45-50pp. Reporting time: 2 months. Simultaneous submissions accepted: no. Publishes 3% of manuscripts submitted. Payment: 25 copies + 25% royalty once expenses are met, poets get 50% off additional copies. Copyrights for author. Subjects: AIDS, Gay, Nebraska, Poetry, Religion.

Long & Silverman Publishing, Inc., Rebecca Stein, 800 North Rainbow Boulevard, Suite 208, Las Vegas, NV 89107, Phone (702) 948-5073, Fax (702) 447-9733, www.lspub.com. 2003. Non-fiction. "Long & Silverman Publishing, Inc. is a highly regarded independent press committed to producing the very best in business, personal finance, and self-improvement books." avg. press run 5000. Pub'd 3 titles 2005; expects 3 titles 2006, 9 titles 2007. Discounts: See lspub.com for latest information. 250pp. Reporting time: 8 weeks for materials submitted by literary agent. Simultaneous submissions accepted: Yes. Publishes 5% of manuscripts submitted. Copyrights for author. Subjects: Business & Economics, Finances, Inspirational, Marketing, Motivation, Success, Real Estate, Self-Help, Taxes.

THE LONG ARC, RESOURCES FOR RADICALS, Laurel Smith, Editor; Matthew Behrens, Editor, PO Box 73620, 509 St. Clair Avenue West, Toronto, ON M6C 1C0, Canada, 416-651-5800, tasc@web.ca. 1997. *"The Long Arc* deals with non-violent political action and civil disobedience, both the theory and the practical expression. A key focus is news reports on a wide range of movements that use non-violent resistance and civil disobedience but are often seen in isolation. Contact editors about possible story ideas. No poetry or fiction." 6/yr. Pub'd 6 issues 2005; expects 6 issues 2006, 6 issues 2007. sub. price $15 (or more), free to prisoners. 20pp. Payment: in copies.

LONG SHOT, Daniel Shot, Nancy Mercado, Andy Clausen; Lynn Breitfeller, Art Editor, Magdalena Alagna, Koyuki Smith, PO Box 6238, Hoboken, NJ 07030, www.longshot.org. 1982. Poetry, fiction, articles, art, photos, cartoons, non-fiction. circ. 2M. 2/yr. Pub'd 2 issues 2005; expects 2 issues 2006, 2 issues 2007. sub. price $12; per copy $8; sample $8. Back issues: $6. 192pp. Reporting time: 10-12 weeks. Simultaneous submissions accepted: yes. Publishes 2% of manuscripts submitted. Payment: copies. Copyrighted, reverts to author. Ads: $150/$90. Subjects: Erotica, Lesbianism, Elvis Presley, Storytelling.

THE LONG STORY, R. Peter Burnham, Editor, 18 Eaton Street, Lawrence, MA 01843, 978-686-7638, rpburnham@mac.com, http://homepage.mac.com/rpburnham/longstory.html. 1982. Fiction. "Stories of 8,000-20,000 words, for serious educated literary people. We have very specific tastes and look for stories about common folk and committed fiction. Since we are the only journal devoted strictly to long stories, we do not close the door or anything completely (except detective fiction, sci-fi, romance and other forms of popular fiction). But the best way to save yourself time and postage is to be familiar with us. Sample copies are $6, and writers are strongly urged to buy a copy before submitting (orders are filled on the same day that they are received). No multiple submissions. No parts of novels; please note that we are a journal devoted to long stories, a literary form with a beginning, middle, and an end. Best length is 8,000-12,000 words since we are very unlikely to print a 20,000 word story unless it conforms exactly to our literary tastes. We are not particularly interested in the usual produce of the writing programs—stories that are merely about relationships without any reaching after higher significance, stories with a psychological core as opposed to a thematic, moral core, stories that are thinly disguised autobiography, stories about writers, etc." circ. 1000. 1/yr. Pub'd 1 issue 2005; expects 1 issue 2006, 1 issue 2007. sub. price $13 (2 issues); per copy $7; sample $7. Back issues: $6. Discounts: 50% to bookstores. 160pp. Reporting time: 1-2 months, sometimes longer. Simultaneous submissions accepted if notified. Publishes 2-3% of manuscripts submitted. Payment: 2 copies and gift subscription. Copyrighted, reverts to author. No ads. Subject: Fiction.

THE LONG TERM VIEW: A Journal of Informed Opinion, Dean Lawrence R. Velvel, Editor-in-Chief; Holly Vietzke, Associate Editor, Massachusetts School of Law, 500 Federal Street, Andover, MA 01810, 978-681-0800. 1992. Articles, interviews. "Each issue is devoted to a balanced discussion of a single topic (usually one that has not received adequate/in-depth coverage in the mainstream press). Contributors range from academics to professionals, have included Eugene McCarthy, Alfred Malabre of the *Wall Street Journal*, Eliot Janeway, John Anderson, Harvey Mansfield, Alexandra Astin, Martha Nussbaum." circ. 5M. 3/yr. Pub'd 2 issues 2005; expects 2 issues 2006, 3 issues 2007. sub. price $10; per copy $4.95; sample free. Back issues: $3.95. Discounts: negotiable. 100pp. Reporting time: 3-5 weeks. Simultaneous submissions accepted: yes. Publishes (solicited) 75% of manuscripts submitted. Payment: none. Copyrighted, reverts to author. Subjects: Business & Economics, Education, Government, Interviews, Law, Political Science, Politics, Public Affairs, Society.

Longhouse, Bob Arnold, 1604 River Road, Guilford, VT 05301, poetry@sover.net, www.sover.net/~poetry. 1973. Poetry, long-poems, concrete art. "Under the Longhouse imprint we have published 35 books of poetry including: *3*: poems by Bob Arnold, David Giannini and John Levy. *Scout* imprint has published booklets and folders by Theodore Enslin, Gerald Hausman, George Evans, David Huddle, Cid Corman, Jean Pedrick, Lyle Glazier, James Koller, Barbara Moraff, Bill Bathurst, Ian Hamilton Finlay, Jane Brakhage, Lorine Niedecker, Marcel Cohen, Janine Pommy Vega, Catherine Walsh, David Miller, Billy Mills, Bill Deemer, Keith Wilson,

Andrew Schelling, Tim McNulty, Mike O'Conner. Mss. solicited. All books from *Longhouse* are limited to 100-250 print run, offset with letterpress wraps. A complete listing of publications may be obtained from our bookshop and catalog services: *Longhouse*: publishers and bookseller; same address.'' avg. press run 150-300. Pub'd 4 titles 2005; expects 4 titles 2006, 4 titles 2007. 8-75pp. Payment: copies. Subjects: Poetry, Translation.

Longleaf Press, Michael Colonnese, Managing Editor; Robin Greene, Editor; Shannon Williams, Assistant Editor, Methodist College, English Dept., 5400 Ramsey Street, Fayetteville, NC 28311, 910-822-5403. 1997. Poetry. ''A non-profit college press dedicated to publishing poetry chapbooks from writers in the Southeast. Annual chapbook contest deadline: January 31, 2007. Contest open to NC, SC, TN, FL, GA, VA and AL residents who have not yet published a full length collection of poetry. Write for guidelines.'' avg. press run 500. Pub'd 1 title 2005; expects 2 titles 2006, 2 titles 2007. Discounts: none. 30pp. Reporting time: 4 months. Simultaneous submissions accepted: yes. Publishes 2% of manuscripts submitted. Payment: honorarium to author. Copyrights for author.

Loom Press, Paul Marion, Box 1394, Lowell, MA 01853. 1978. Poetry. avg. press run 500-1M. Expects 1 title 2006, 1 title 2007. Discounts: trade 40%, libraries 20%. Pages vary. Reporting time: 60-90 days. Payment: individual negotiations. Copyrights for author. Subject: Poetry.

•**Loonfeather Press,** Betty Rossi, P.O. Box 1212, Bemidji, MN 56619, 218-444-4869 www.loonfeather-press.com. 1979. Poetry, fiction, non-fiction. ''Loonfeather Press publishes good writing by new and emerging writers as well as established writers. Most of our authors are regional, but we also publish writers from beyond our region. We are particularly interested in the work of Ojibwe authors. Recent contributors include Lynn Levin, Kimberly Blaeser, Louise Erdrich, Sharon Chmielarz, Greg Bernard, Robert Treuer.'' avg. press run 700. Pub'd 4 titles 2005; expects 4 titles 2006, 4 titles 2007. Discounts: bookstores: 5 or more copies 40%institutions: 5 or more copies 40%classrooms: 5 or more copies 40% distributors: 55%. 115pp. Reporting time: Three months. Simultaneous submissions accepted: Yes. Publishes 25% of manuscripts submitted. Payment: 10% royalty paid semi-annually. Copyrights for author. Subjects: Fiction, Gardening, Juvenile Fiction, Native American, Nature, Novels, Poetry, Reprints, Short Stories.

Lord John Press, Herb Yellin, 19073 Los Alimos Street, Northridge, CA 91326, 818-360-5804. 1977. ''Work only with established authors - our primary market is collectors and universities. Do not want unsolicited manuscripts. Published authors: John Updike, Norman Mailer, Robert B. Parker, Ray Bradbury, Ursula K. Le Guin, John Barth, Raymond Carver, Stephen King, Dan Simmons.'' avg. press run 300-500. Pub'd 3 titles 2005; expects 3 titles 2006. Discounts: trade 40%. 50pp. Subjects: Criticism, Fiction.

LORE AND LANGUAGE, J.D.A. Widdowson, National Centre for Eng. Cultural Tradition, The University, Sheffield S10 2TN, England, Sheffield 0114-2226296. 1969. Poetry, articles, reviews, letters. ''Articles and items for those interested in language, folklore, cultural tradition and oral history.'' circ. 300. 1/yr. Pub'd 1 issue 2005; expects 1 issue 2006, 1 issue 2007. sub. price £12 indiv, £50 institutions. Back issues: price dependent on issue required; apply to National Centre for English Cultural Tradition. Discounts: none. 128pp. Reporting time: variable. Payment: none. Copyrighted, does not revert to author. Pub's reviews: 140 in 2005. §Language, folklore, cultural tradition, oral history. Ads: £95/£70/£40 1/4 page. Subjects: Folklore, Language.

Lorien House, David A. Wilson, Attn: David Wilson, PO Box 1112, Black Mountain, NC 28711, 828-669-6211, LorienHouseA1@aol.com. 1969. ''Right now I'm full into 2003 and do not need to see anything.'' avg. press run 100-500. Pub'd 2 titles 2005; expects 2 titles 2006, 2 titles 2007. Discounts: 5 copies 40%. 140pp. Reporting time: 1 week to 1 month. Simultaneous submissions accepted: no. Publishes 1/10 of 1% of manuscripts submitted. Payment: individually determined. We do not copyright for author, only assist author with copyright. Subjects: History, Poetry, Science, Solar.

LOS, Virginia M. Geoffrey, Editor; I.B. Scrood, Managing Editor; P.N. Bouts, Art Editor; M. Peel, Poetry Editor; M. Hardy, Editor-at-large, 150 N. Catalina St., No. 2, Los Angeles, CA 90004, website: http://home.earthlink.net/~lospoesy, email: lospoesy@earthlink.net. 1991. ''contemporary poesy & art.''

Lost Coast Press, Cynthia Frank, President; Joe Shaw, Editor, 155 Cypress Street, Fort Bragg, CA 95437, 800-773-7782, fax 707-964-7531, www.cypresshouse.com, joeshaw@cypresshouse.com. 1985. Poetry, fiction, art, non-fiction. ''See listing for Cypress House.'' Simultaneous submissions accepted: Yes.

LOST GENERATION JOURNAL, Deloris Gray Wood, Route 5 Box 134, Salem, MO 65560, 314-729-2545, Fax 314-729-2545. 1973. Poetry, fiction, articles, art, photos, cartoons, interviews, criticism, reviews, letters, news items, non-fiction. ''*LGJ* topics deal with Americans in Europe, chiefly Paris, between 1919 and 1939. Primary emphasis is placed on Americans who began making a name for themselves in literature, graphic and performing arts such as Pound, Stein and Hemingway. Article length can vary, but we prefer pieces between 800 and 2,500 words. Poetry should be 20 lines or less. Good photographs and art should relate to the theme in time and place as should the articles and poetry. Scholars must document their work with footnotes and bibliography. Lost Generation people (those who started in Paris) must state when they were abroad and supply evidence of their qualifications or cite references for confirmation. Authors should supply a passport-size photograph of themselves and a 200-word biographical blurb. Recent contributors: Mark Bassett, Robin Dormin, Mark Orwoll, John McCall, Jerry Rosco." circ. 400. 1/yr. Pub'd 1 issue 2005; expects 1 issue 2006, 1 issue 2007. sub. price $10; per copy $10; sample $10. Back issues: $10. Discounts: $9.50 per year to subscription agency. 32pp. Reporting time: 6 weeks, SASE earlier. Payment: 1¢ per word or 3 copies of issue article appears in. Copyrighted. Pub's reviews: 4 in 2005. §Twentieth Century literature, bibliography, biography, Americans in Paris, Hemingway, Pound, Stein, Miller. Ads: $150/$125/$85/$5 an inch. Subjects: African Literature, Africa, African Studies, Agriculture, Bibliography, Biography, Communication, Journalism, Dada, F. Scott Fitzgerald, France, French, Graphics, Ernest Hemingway, Literature (General), Magazines, Anais Nin, Photography, Printing.

Lost Horse Press, Christine Holbert, Publisher, 105 Lost Horse Lane, Sandpoint, ID 83864, 208-255-4410, Fax 208-255-1560, losthorsepress@mindspring.com. 1998. Poetry, fiction. avg. press run 500-2.5M. Pub'd 5 titles 2005; expects 4 titles 2006, 4 titles 2007. 125pp. Reporting time: 6 to 9 months. Simultaneous submissions accepted: yes. Publishes 5% of manuscripts submitted. Does not copyright for author. Subjects: Essays, Fiction, Pacific Northwest, Poetry, Prose, Writers/Writing.

Lost Prophet Press (see also KNUCKLE MERCHANT - The Journal of Naked Literary Aggression; THIN COYOTE), Christopher Jones, 221 Stanford Drive SE #2, Albuquerque, NM 87106-3586, 505.256.4589. 1992. Poetry, fiction, art, photos, long-poems, collages, plays. avg. press run 200. Pub'd 2 titles 2005; expects 3 titles 2006, 4 titles 2007. Discounts: on request. 30pp. Reporting time: 1 month. Simultaneous submissions accepted: yes. Publishes 1% of manuscripts submitted. Payment: 1/4 run in contributor copies. Does not copyright for author. Subjects: Fiction, Photography, Poetry.

Lotus Press, Inc., Naomi Madgett, Editor, PO Box 21607, Detroit, MI 48221, 313-861-1280, fax 313-861-4740, lotuspress@aol.com. 1972. Poetry. "Annual Naomi Long Madgett Poetry Award for an outstanding book-length manuscript by an African Americans. Submissions from January 2 to March 31. Visit www.lotuspress.org for guidelines." avg. press run 500-2M. Pub'd 2 titles 2005; expects 3 titles 2006, 2 titles 2007. Discounts: 30-40%; 50% for wholesalers. 80pp. Reporting time: 6-8 weeks. Simultaneous submissions accepted: no. Publishes 1% of manuscripts submitted. Payment: Free copies plus discounts. Copyrights for author. Subjects: African Literature, Africa, African Studies, Black, Literature (General), Literature (General), Poetry, Poetry, Third World, Minorities, Women.

THE LOUISIANA REVIEW, Dr. Maura Gage, Editor; Barbara Deger, Associate Editor; Dr. Susan LeJeune, Associate Editor; Joann Quillman, Art Editor, Liberal Arts Div. PO Box 1129, Louisiana State Univ., Eunice, LA 70535. 1999. Poetry, fiction, art, photos, parts-of-novels, plays. "*The Louisiana Review* seeks to publish the best poetry, fiction, reviews, and plays it can get. While Louisiana writers and poets as well as those associated with or connected to the state in some way are always welcome to submit their work, the journal is becoming more national in scope. We like imagistic and metaphoric poetry as well as poetry with surprising language and excellent craft. Recent contributors include Gary Snyder, Antler, Marge Piercy, Gerald Locklin, Dana Gioia, Errol Miller, Don Hoyt, David Cope, Jim Cohn, and many others. Submit work between October - March 31." circ. 300-600. 1/yr. Pub'd 1 issue 2005; expects 1 issue 2006, 1 issue 2007. sub. price $5; per copy $5; sample $5. 120-200pp. Reporting time: between 6-12 weeks. Accept simultaneous submissions if noted. Publishes 5% of manuscripts submitted. Payment: 1-2 copies in which their work appears. Not copyrighted, author retains all rights. Pub's reviews: 2 in 2005. §Creative books, fiction and poetry. Subjects: Drama, Fiction, Louisiana, Poetry.

Louisiana State University Press, PO Box 25053, Baton Rouge, LA 70894-5053, 225-578-6294, Fax 225-578-6461. 1935.

THE LOUISVILLE REVIEW, Sena Jeter Naslund, Co-Editor; Karen Mann, Managing Editor; Kathleen Driskell, Associate Editor, Spalding University, 851 S. 4th Street, Louisville, KY 40203, 502-585-9911 ext. 2777, louisvillereview@spalding.edu, www.louisvillereview.org. 1976. Poetry, fiction, parts-of-novels, long-poems, plays, non-fiction. "We do not accept electronic submissions. Include a SASE for reply; submissions recycled. Some recent contributors: Maura Stanton, Wendy Bishop, Ursula Hegi, Maureen Morehead, Jhumpa Lahiri, Robin Lippincott, Virgil Suarez, Tony Hoagland, David Brendan Hopes, Greg Pape, and Claudia Emerson." circ. 500. 2/yr. Pub'd 2 issues 2005; expects 2 issues 2006, 2 issues 2007. sub. price $14; per copy $8; sample $5. Back issues: $5 each (postpaid). 128pp. Reporting time: 4-6 months. Simultaneous submissions accepted: yes. Publishes 5% of manuscripts submitted. Payment: 2 complimentary copies. Copyrighted, reverts to author. Swap ads. Subjects: Essays, Fiction, Non-Fiction, Poetry.

The Love and Logic Press, Inc., Nancy M. Henry, Publisher, 2207 Jackson Street, Golden, CO 80401, 303-278-7552. 1993. Non-fiction. "The Love and Logic Press, Inc. is a subsidiary of Cline/Fay Institute, Inc. CFI was founded in 1983 as a mail order publisher of audio and video tapes and books by Jim Fay and Foster W. Cline, M.D., internationally-recognized authorities on parenting, education and child psychiatry. CFI currently carries over 65 titles, available exclusively through mail order and catalog, www.loveandlogic.com. The Love and Logic Press, Inc. was started to publish audio, video and book titles for the general trade beginning in Fall 1994. LLPI will concentrate on titles dealing with parenting, psychology and current social trends." avg. press run 10M. Expects 12 titles 2006, 18 titles 2007. Discounts: 1 copy 20% prepaid, 2-4 20%, 5-24 40%, 25-99 42% free freight, 100-249 43%, 250-499 44%, 500+ 45%; 25 or more copies include free freight. 256pp. Reporting time: 90 days. Simultaneous submissions accepted: yes. Publishes 4% of manuscripts submitted. Payment: advance against royalties; 5-7.5% on net sales; royalties paid twice yearly. Copyrights for author. Subjects: Children, Youth, Family, Parenting, Psychology, Self-Help, Sociology.

LOVING MORE, Mary Wolf, Ryam Nearing, PO Box 4358, Boulder, CO 80306, 303-543-7540, lmm@lovemore.com. 1995. Articles, art, photos, cartoons, interviews, reviews, letters, news items, non-fiction. "Under 1,000 words." circ. 2M. 4/yr. Pub'd 4 issues 2005; expects 4 issues 2006, 4 issues 2007. sub. price $24; per copy $6; sample $6. Back issues: $6. Discounts: 55% to bookstores. 40pp. Reporting time: varies. Simultaneous submissions accepted: no. Publishes 50% of manuscripts submitted. Payment: copies. Copyrighted, reverts to author. Pub's reviews: 10 in 2005. §New paradigm relationships, community. Ads: $350/$125/17¢ per word. Subjects: Family, Futurism, New Age, Relationships, Sex, Sexuality.

LOW BUDGET ADVENTURE, Cynic Press, PO Box 40691, Philadelphia, PA 19107. 2003. "Short stories and artwork - adventurous (western, mystery, spy, martial arts). Overstocked except for art." circ. 100. Pub'd 1 issue 2005; expects 1 issue 2006, 1 issue 2007. sub. price $20/6 issues; per copy $7; sample $6. 32pp. Reporting time: 3 weeks. Simultaneous submissions accepted: yes. Publishes 15% of manuscripts submitted. Payment: 1 year subscription. Copyrighted, reverts to author. Ads: $20/$10. Subjects: Audio/Video, Fiction, Martial Arts, Military, Veterans, Mystery, Old West.

LOW BUDGET SCIENCE FICTION, Cynic Press, Joseph Farley M., Editor, PO Box 40691, Philadelphia, PA 19107. 2002. Fiction, art, cartoons. "Make all checks to "Cynic Press". Currently overstocked." circ. 100. 2-4/yr. Expects 2 issues 2006, 2 issues 2007. sub. price $20/4 issues; per copy $7; sample $7. Back issues: $7. 32pp. Reporting time: 3 weeks. Simultaneous submissions accepted: yes. Publishes 15% of manuscripts submitted. Payment: 1 year subscription. Copyrighted, buys all rights unless otherwise specified. Ads: $20/$10. Subjects: Arthurian, Cartoons, Fantasy, Fiction, Horror, Science Fiction, Supernatural.

Low Fidelity Press, Bradley Armstrong, Editor; Tobin O'Donnell, Editor; Jeff Parker, Editor; Andrew Vernon, Editor, 1912 16th Ave South, Birmingham, AL 35205-5607. 2001.

LP Publications (Teleos Institute) (see also EMERGING), Diane K. Pike, 7119 East Shea Boulevard, Suite 109, PMB 418, Scottsdale, AZ 85254, 480-948-1800, Fax 480-948-1870. 1972. Fiction, non-fiction. avg. press run 100. Expects 2 titles 2006, 1 title 2007. Discounts: available upon request. 250pp. Reporting time: variable. Copyrights for author. Subjects: Humanism, Metaphysics, Occult, Spiritual.

LPD Press (see also TRADICION REVISTA), Barbe Awalt, Paul Rhetts, 925 Salamanca NW, Los Ranchos de Albuquerque, NM 87107-5647, 505-344-9382, Fax 505-345-5129, info@nmsantos.com. 1994. Art, photos, non-fiction. "Actively seeking material on Southwestern Hispanic artists and arts. Ideal length of finished product with illustrations is 160-280pp. Recent contributions by Diana Pardue, Heard Museum, Rey Montez, Paul Pletka, Carmella Padilla, Father Thomas Steele, S.J., Dr. Charles Carrillo." avg. press run 8M. Pub'd 5 titles 2005; expects 2 titles 2006, 2 titles 2007. Discounts: Library/school 25%, 1-9 40%, 10+ 45%. 250pp. Reporting time: 2-3 months. Simultaneous submissions accepted: yes. Publishes 25% of manuscripts submitted. Payment: negotiable. Copyrights for author. Subjects: Americana, The Americas, Arizona, Arts, Catholic, Christianity, Christmas, Colorado, Culture, Latino, New Mexico, Religion, Southwest, Texas, U.S. Hispanic.

LrnIT Publishing Div. ICFL, Inc., Philip N. Baldwin Jr., Dawn B. Barrett, Adalene Baldwin, Peggy Broussard, 1122 Samuel Pt., Colorado Springs, CO 80906-6310, 800-584-1080, Fax 925-476-0707, icfl@lrnit.org, www.lrnit.org. 1999. Non-fiction. "Additional address: 3305 W. Spring Mountain Road #60, Las Vegas, NV 89102. Recent contributors: Dr. Robert S. Reimers, Prof. at Tulane University, and Phil Baldwin Jr." avg. press run 2M. Pub'd 2 titles 2005; expects 1 title 2006, 2 titles 2007. Discounts: trade (-55%), bulk (-65%), agent/jobber (-60%), classroom (-65%), all FOB shipped. 230pp. Reporting time: 6 weeks. Simultaneous submissions accepted: yes. Publishes 15% of manuscripts submitted. Payment: negotiated. Copyrights for author. Subjects: Education, Engineering, Environment, Mathematics, Motivation, Success, Quotations, Textbooks.

LUCIDITY POETRY JOURNAL, Bear House Publishing, Ted O. Badger, 14781 Memorial Drive #10, Houston, TX 77079-5210, 281-920-1795, tedbadger1@yahoo.com. 1985. Poetry. "Seeking lucid poems about people and human relationships in understandable English without vulgarity. Page format limits lines and spaces to 36. Payments are given for most poems used but there is a small entry/reading fee for such submissions. Email or SASE will provide full guidelines." circ. 245. 2/yr. Pub'd 2 issues 2005; expects 2 issues 2006, 2 issues 2007. sub. price $7; per copy $3.50; sample $2. Back issues: $2. Discounts: none. 72pp. Reporting time: 6-18 months. Simultaneous submissions accepted: yes. Publishes 20% of manuscripts submitted. Payment: from $15 to $1 per poem. Copyrighted, reverts to author. No ads. Subject: Poetry.

Lucky Press, LLC, Janice M. Phelps, Editor-in-Chief, 126 S. Maple Street, Lancaster, OH 43130, Phone: 740-689-2950, Fax: 740-689-2951, Website: www.luckypress.com, Email: books@luckypress.com. 1999. Non-fiction. "Query first by MAIL with 1 page synopsis, author bio, 1 page marketing plan, Table of Contents. Unsolicited manuscripts will be disposed of." Pub'd 4 titles 2005; expects 5 titles 2006, 6 titles 2007. Discounts: Book wholesalers 50%; Bookstores 45%; Libraries 30%. No minimum. Returnable within 1 year. Net 30. Fax orders to 740-689-2951. 224pp. Reporting time: 1 month. Simultaneous submissions accepted: yes (after query). Payment: varies. Copyrights for author. Subjects: Alternative Medicine, Animals, Appalachia, Aviation, Birds, Disabled, Fiction, History, Ohio, Pets, Philosophy, Publishing, Young Adult.

Ludlow Press, Jun Da, Senior Editor; Jane Watson, Acquisitions Editor, PO Box 2612, New York, NY 10009-9998, FAX: 1 (212) 937-3625, editor@LudlowPress.com, www.ludlowpress.com. 2002. Fiction, satire. "Ludlow Press is a New York based independent, non-corporate publisher, and online magazine and resource center dedicated to publishing and promoting the very best fiction, poetry, and art of its time. For submission guidelines, go to our website. Our first Original Trade Paperbacks include: THE LOSERS' CLUB by Richard Perez {ISBN: 0971341591} and WILL@epicqwest.com by Tom Grimes {ISBN: 0971341575}." avg. press run 3000. Pub'd 2 titles 2005; expects 4 titles 2006, 6 titles 2007. 200pp. Reporting time: 6 months. Simultaneous submissions accepted: yes. Publishes 2% of manuscripts submitted. Payment: 50/50 royalty split. Copyrights for author. Subject: Novels.

LULLABY HEARSE, Sarah Ruth Jacobs, 45-34 47th St. Apt. 6AB, Woodside, NY 11377, editor@lullabyhearse.com, www.lullabyhearse.com. 2002. Poetry, fiction, art, photos, cartoons, reviews, collages, concrete art. "Query for fiction over 6,000 words. Traditional horror themes, mystery, crime, and melodrama stand very little chance next to contemporary horror and dark experimental fiction subs. Approximately 5% of all subs are used, and short fiction must be exceptionally sharp since it pays the same flat fee as full length." circ. 200. 4/yr. Pub'd 1 issue 2005; expects 4 issues 2006, 4 issues 2007. sub. price $18; per copy $5; sample $4. 20pp. Reporting time: 4-6 weeks. Simultaneous submissions accepted: yes. Publishes 3% of manuscripts submitted. Payment: no payment. Copyrighted, reverts to author. Subjects: Avant-Garde, Experimental Art, Charles Bukowski, Creativity, Experimental, Horror, Poetry, Prose, Supernatural.

LULLWATER REVIEW, Rotating editors, Box 22036, Emory University, Atlanta, GA 30322, 404-727-6184. 1990. Poetry, fiction, art, photos, interviews, parts-of-novels, long-poems, plays. "*The Lullwater Review* is a trade-size journal for the literary arts, dedicated to presenting its readers with a wide variety of forms, styles, and perspectives in fiction, drama, and poetry. Recent contributors include: James Cushing, Denise Duhamel, Colette Inez, Aurel Rau, Josephine Humphreys (interview), Greg Grummer, Cindy Goff, Eve Shelnutt, and Charles Edward Eaton." circ. 2M-3M. 2/yr. Pub'd 2 issues 2005; expects 2 issues 2006, 2 issues 2007. sub. price $12; per copy $5; sample $5. Back issues: $5 per copy. Discounts: none. 110pp. Reporting time: 3-5 months, on average (longer during the summer). Simultaneous submissions accepted if we are notified upon submission and the event that the work is published elsewhere. Payment: 3 copies of the issue in which author's work appears. Copyrighted, reverts to author. No ads. Subjects: Arts, Counter-Culture, Alternatives, Communes, Creativity, Culture, English, Fiction, Journals, Language, Literary Review, Literature (General), Novels, Poetry, Prose, Short Stories, Writers/Writing.

Luminous Epinoia Press, Edward Hunt, P O Box 10188, Virginia Beach, VA 23450-0188, (435)867-9045 www.luminousepinoia.com. 2004. Non-fiction. "The concept is to encourage those writings that promote empowerment of the reader (soulfully, healthfully, creatively, emotionally, physically). Luminous Epinoia is Lighting Creative Consciousness!" avg. press run 5000. Expects 1 title 2006, 2 titles 2007. Discounts: see distributors. 250pp. Reporting time: 2-3 weeks. Simultaneous submissions accepted: Yes. Payment: Sliding scale as books sell, (more commission to author). Copyrights for author. Subjects: Alternative Medicine, Children, Youth, Creativity, Dreams, Energy, Humanism, Inspirational, Nutrition, Parenting, Relationships, Self-Help, Sex, Sexuality, Theosophical, Women, Young Adult.

LUMMOX JOURNAL, Lummox Press, RD (Raindog) Armstrong, PO Box 5301, San Pedro, CA 90733-5301, 562-331-4351, e-mail raindog@lummoxpress.com http://www.lummoxpress.com. 1995. Poetry, fiction, articles, art, photos, cartoons, interviews, criticism, reviews, music, letters, news items. "The Lummox Journal publishes commentaries on creativity and the process that makes it possible, as well as biographies, reviews, essays, poetry and artwork—Contributors welcome." circ. 200. 6/yr. Pub'd 12 issues 2005; expects 6 issues 2006, 6 issues 2007. sub. price $22 US; $37 World; per copy $3; sample $3 or trade. Back issues: $2. Discounts: trade for subscription. 28pp. Reporting time: 1-3 months. We accept simultaneous submissions but need to know if work has been published elsewhere (so we can give credit where credit is due). Publishes 75% essays, poetry 2%, interviews 80% of manuscripts submitted. Payment: none, free copy. Copyrighted, reverts to author. Pub's reviews: 70 in 2005. §Poetry, music, fiction. Ads: $45-full/$30-half. Subjects: Arts, Beat, Biography, Book Arts, Book Reviewing, Communication, Journalism, Criticism, Education, Erotica, Essays, Los Angeles, Music, Poetry, Prose, Reviews.

Lummox Press (see also LUMMOX JOURNAL), Raindog, PO Box 5301, San Pedro, CA 90733-5301, 562-439-9858, email: lumoxraindog@earthlink.net, http://home.earthlink.net/~lumoxraindog/ http://www.geo-cities.com/lumoxraindog/dufus.html. 1994. Poetry, fiction, art, photos, concrete art. "Books are handmade and as such are unique in each design." 100 - 300 copies per print run. Pub'd 3 titles 2005; expects 8 titles 2006, 8/ titles 2007. 48pp. Reporting time: 6-8 months. Simultaneous submissions accepted: no. Publishes 5% of manuscripts submitted. Payment: initially 10% of run, after 2nd printing 10% of net profit. Copyrights for author. Subjects: Arts, Book Arts, Book Reviewing, Communication, Journalism, Criticism, Erotica, Essays, Latino, Los Angeles, Music, Occult, Poetry, Prose, Reviews, Tapes & Records.

LUNA, Ray Gonzalez, Editor, Dept. of English, Univ. of Minnesota, 207 Lind Hall, 207 Church St., Minneapolis, MN 55455.

Luna Bisonte Prods, John M. Bennett, 137 Leland Ave, Columbus, OH 43214, 614-846-4126. 1974. Poetry, art, cartoons, satire, letters, collages, concrete art. "Interested in exchanges. We print broadsides and labels, chapbooks, poetry products, and books. Would like to see more material in Spanish." avg. press run 250. Pub'd 4 titles 2005; expects 4 titles 2006, 4 titles 2007. Discounts: 40% for resale. 56pp. Reporting time: 2 weeks. Publishes 5% of manuscripts submitted. Payment: copies. Copyrighted to author, but author must do own registering for copyright. Subjects: Arts, Avant-Garde, Experimental Art, Dada, Folklore, Graphics, Poetry, Visual Arts.

Lunar Offensive Publications, Stephen Fried, 1910 Foster Avenue, Brooklyn, NY 11230-1902. 1994. Poetry, fiction, art, photos, cartoons, parts-of-novels, collages, plays. "Doing a one-time book of violently erotic/erotically violent short short stories, graphics (line or halftone and color for 2 covers) poems or parts of poems under 100 lines, and short screenplays, as for a video under 15 minutes. No pedophiles, no torture. SASE required. We're not using work by anyone we know. Include email address of you have one. We've published books by Elliot Richman, John Wheatcroft, Joi Brozek, Susan Brennan and Letta Neely but this is something different. Deadline uncertain and if the input is disappointing the project dies. Surprise me." avg. press run 1600. Pub'd 1 title 2005; expects 2 titles 2006, 1 title 2007. Discounts: 10% on orders of 12 or more (+ $5 shipping + 10 copies). 100pp. Reporting time: 3 months with SASE. Simultaneous submissions accepted. Simultaneous submissions accepted: yes. Payment: 30 copies from first run, sales split 50/50 on agreed book price. Does not copyright for author. Subjects: Dada, Dreams, Erotica, Euthanasia, Death, Fantasy, Fiction, Photography, Poetry, Politics, Reviews, Sex, Sexuality, Surrealism, War, Weapons, Women.

LUNGFULL! MAGAZINE, Brendan Lorber, Editor-in-Chief, 316 23rd Street, Brooklyn, NY 11215-6409, lungfull@rcn.net. 1995. Poetry, fiction, articles, art, photos, cartoons, interviews, criticism, reviews, letters, parts-of-novels, long-poems, collages. "We print the rough drafts of contributor's work in addition to the final version so the readers can witness the creative process in action." circ. 1,000. 1/yr. Pub'd 1 issue 2005; expects 1 issue 2006, 1 issue 2007. sub. price $19.90/2 ISSUES $39.80/4 ISSUES; per copy $9.95; sample $11.50. Back issues: see http://www.lungfull.org for updated list. 200pp. Reporting time: 4-12 months. We accept simultaneous submissions with notification. Publishes 2% of manuscripts submitted. Payment: 2 copies. Copyrighted, reverts to author. §Poetry, experimental writing, fiction, essays. Ads: $100/$60/$35 1/4 page. Subjects: Essays, Experimental, Fiction, Literature (General), Poetry.

Luthers Publishing, Gary Luther, Alan Luther, 1009 North Dixie Freeway, New Smyrna Beach, FL 32168-6221, 386-423-1600 phone/Fax, www.lutherspublishing.com. 1988. "We are private publishers, specializing in limited-run books. Unless partnership arrangements have been made, the author pays to publish his/her work. We offer expertise in design, editing, art, and typography to produce a quality paperback/hardcover book. Marketing support includes copyright, generally registered in author's name. ISBN and Library of Congress number/CIP secured. UPC bar code provided as appropriate. Title entered into numerous indexes and data bases, as well as the Internet. News release/book review media package developed." avg. press run 500-1M. Pub'd 10 titles 2005; expects 7 titles 2006, 8 titles 2007. Discounts: 40% trade. 100+pp. Reporting time: 10 working days. Copyrights for author.

Lycanthrope Press, Rev. Victor C. Klein, Rev. Laurence Talbot, PO Box 9028, Metairie, LA 70005-9028, 504-866-9756. 1993. Poetry, fiction, criticism, plays, news items, non-fiction. "We are the publishing arm of Ordo Templi Veritatis. As such, our interest is theology, occult, etc." avg. press run 15M+. Pub'd 2 titles 2005; expects 6 titles 2006, 12 titles 2007. Discounts: as per fair market/industry standard. 150+pp. Reporting time: 1 month; solicited only; letter. Simultaneous submissions accepted: yes. Publishes 10% of manuscripts submitted. Payment: standard. Copyrights for author. Subjects: Astrology, Atheism, Christianity, Erotica, Euthanasia, Death, Folklore, Humanism, Libertarian, Metaphysics, Myth, Mythology, New Age, Occult, Philosophy, Religion, Theosophical.

Lyceum Books, Inc., David Follmer, President, 5758 S. Blackstone, Chicago, IL 60637, 773-643-1902, Fax 773-643-1903, lyceum@lyceumbooks.com, www.lyceumbooks.com. 1989. Non-fiction. "Social Work is our only discipline." avg. press run 2M. Pub'd 6 titles 2005; expects 10 titles 2006, 10 titles 2007. Discounts:

bookstores, wholesalers 20%. 300pp. Reporting time: 2 months. Simultaneous submissions accepted: yes. Payment: 10% net. Copyrights for author. Subject: Social Work.

Lynx House Press, Christopher Howell, 420 West 24th, Spokane, WA 99203. 1972. Poetry, fiction. "Lynx House Press publishes only highly literary material: books commercial presses would consider too literary. Authors include Yusef Komunyakaa, Patricia Goedicke, Madeline DeFrees, Vern Rutsala, Gillian Conoley, Bill Tremblay, Carolyne Wright, Valerie Martin, Carlos Reyes, James Grabill, Robert Abel, and Carole Oles." avg. press run 1.5M. Pub'd 6 titles 2005; expects 6 titles 2006, 6 titles 2007. Discounts: 1 book 10%, 2 20%, 3 30%, 4+ 40%, libraries 20%. 80pp. Reporting time: 3-6 months. Simultaneous submissions accepted: yes. Publishes 1% of manuscripts submitted. Payment: sometimes pay 10%, often copies. Copyrights for author. Subjects: Fiction, Poetry.

•Lyons Publishing Limited, Judy Powell, 2704 Jerring Mews, Mississauga, Ontario L5L 2M8, Canada, info@judypowell.com. 2005. Fiction. "Area of focus: Romance novels, which must be written by African or Caribbean authors, or be set in an African or Caribbean country, or include African or Caribbean characters. May be written by writers of any culture or from any country, as long as there is some kind of link with Africa, the Caribbean or black people of the Third World." avg. press run 5000. Expects 2 titles 2006, 4 titles 2007. 260-320pp. Subjects: Black, Caribbean, Fiction, Jamaica, Novels, Romance.

THE LYRIC, Jean Mellichamp Milliken, Editor; Nancy Mellichamp Savo, Assistant Editor, PO Box 110, Jericho, VT 05465-0110. 1921. Poetry. "Rhymed verse in traditional forms preferred, about 40 lines maximum. We print poetry only. No Contemporary political or social themes; we do not seek to shock, confound, or embitter. Poems must be original, unpublished, and not under consideration elsewhere. Send SASE for reply." circ. 650. 4/yr. Pub'd 4 issues 2005; expects 4 issues 2006, 4 issues 2007. sub. price $12, $22/2 years $30/3 years, Canada and other foreign add $2 per year postage; per copy $3; sample $3. Back issues: depends on availability. 36pp. Reporting time: 2 months. Simultaneous submissions accepted: yes, grudgingly. Publishes 5% of manuscripts submitted. Payment: contributors receive complimentary copy of issue with their poem; quarterly and annual prizes for poetry published; $50 quarterly, $800 (total) annually. Copyrighted, reverts to author. No ads. Subject: Poetry.

M

MacAdam/Cage Publishing Inc., Patrick Walsh, Editor; Anika Streitfeld, Nonfiction Editor, 155 Sansome Street, Ste. 550, San Francisco, CA 94104-3615, 415-986-7502, Fax 415-986-7414, info@macadamcage.com. 1999. Fiction, non-fiction. "MacAdam/Cage publishes quality retail hardcover fiction and narrative nonfiction such as memoirs, nonfiction that reads like fiction." avg. press run 10M. Pub'd 6 titles 2005; expects 10 titles 2006, 10-20 titles 2007. Discounts: retail 1-9 copies 42% + freight, 10+ 46% + freight, 50% nonreturnable and free freight, no minimum. 300pp. Reporting time: 3-4 months. Simultaneous submissions accepted: yes. Payment: negotiated. Copyrights for author. Subjects: Fiction, Memoirs, Non-Fiction.

MacDonald/Sward Publishing Company, Catherine Snyder, 120 Log Cabin Lane, Greensburg, PA 15601, 724-832-7767. 1986. Fiction, articles, art, criticism, long-poems, plays, non-fiction. "Accepting no manuscripts at this time due to heavy schedule. We use historical material. Proceeds used for education. Now focusing on essays - mostly concerning Iraq invasion and occupation, and peace against torturous wars and torturous regimes." avg. press run 500-1M, also print on demand. Expects 2 titles 2007. Discounts: 1-5 books 20%; 6+ 40%. 250pp. Publishes less than 19% of manuscripts submitted. Payment: varies. Does not copyright for author. Subjects: Civil War, Essays, History, Race, Religion, War.

THE MACGUFFIN, Steven Dolgin, Editor; Nausheen Khan, Managing Editor; Elizabeth Kircos, Fiction Editor; Carol Was, Poetry Editor, Schoolcraft College, 18600 Haggerty Road, Livonia, MI 48152, (734) 462-4400 Ext. 5327, Fax: (734) 462-4679, Email: macguffin@schoolcraft.edu, Website: www.macguffin.org. 1984. Poetry, fiction, art, photos, parts-of-novels, long-poems, non-fiction. "*The MacGuffin* is whatever everybody is after...*The MacGuffin* is where you find it... we are eclectic and holistic. We will print the best of everything with no biases. Contributors include Jim Daniels, Stuart Dybek, Michael Steinberg, Dawn McDuffie, Linda Nemec Foster, and Terry Blackhawk." circ. 600. 3/yr. Pub'd 1 issue 2005; expects 3 issues 2006, 3 issues 2007. sub. price $22; per copy varies on issue/ current issue $9.00; sample $6. Back issues: varies. Discounts: varies. 160+pp. Reporting time: 12-16 weeks. Notify us regarding simultaneous submissions. Publishes 20% of manuscripts submitted. Payment: 2 contributor's copies, occasional honoraria. Copyrighted, reverts to author. Subjects: Arts, Fiction, Non-Fiction, Poetry.

B.B. Mackey Books, Betty Mackey, PO Box 475, Wayne, PA 19087-0475, www.mackeybooks.com. 1985.

Non-fiction. "Not seeking submissions at this time." avg. press run 2M. Pub'd 2 titles 2005; expects 1 title 2006, 2 titles 2007. Discounts: Any 1-49 books 40%,Any 50 or more 50%. 180pp. Payment: royalty, small advance on royalty. Does not copyright for author. Subjects: Florida, Horticulture, Memoirs.

MACROBIOTICS TODAY, George Ohsawa Macrobiotic Foundation, Carl Ferre, Editor, PO Box 3998, Chico, CA 95927-3998, 530-566-9765, Fax 530-566-9768, foundation@gomf.macrobiotic.net. 1970. Articles, interviews, reviews, non-fiction. "Length: 5-12 pages; double-spaced. Articles on macrobiotics, health, and nutrition accepted. Recent contributors include Verna Varona, David Briscoe, Meredith McCarty, and Julia Ferre." circ. 5M. 6/yr. Pub'd 6 issues 2005; expects 6 issues 2006, 6 issues 2007. sub. price $30; per copy $5.50; sample $1 ppd. Back issues: cover price. Discounts: 5-9 35%, 10-49 45%, 50+ 55%. 40pp. Reporting time: 6 weeks. Publishes 40% of manuscripts submitted. Payment: up to $50. Copyrighted, does not revert to author. Pub's reviews: 4 in 2005. §Macrobiotics, health, nutrition. Ads: $475/$270/$145 1/3 page/$90 1/6 pg/classifieds 50¢/frequency discounts. Subjects: Ecology, Foods, Health, Philosophy.

Macrocosm USA, Inc., Sandi Brockway, Editor & President, PO Box 185, Cambria, CA 93428, 805-927-2515, e-Mail brockway@macronet.org, www.macronet.org. 1989. Non-fiction. "Reviews and articles focused on social changes and solutions. Supplemental update on our website. Currently Internet based directory only." Expects 1 title 2006, 1 title 2007. Online searchable addable self serve directory. Reporting time: 60 days. Publishes 10% of manuscripts submitted. Payment: all works are loaned or contributed to Macrocosm USA, a nonprofit corporation. Does not copyright for author. Subjects: Arts, Civil Rights, Conservation, Consumer, Co-ops, Counter-Culture, Alternatives, Communes, Crime, Culture, Ecology, Foods, Labor, New Age, Parenting, Politics, Solar, Vegetarianism.

THE MAD HATTER, Ron Watson, 320 S. Seminary Street, Madisonville, KY 42431, 270-825-6000, Fax 270-825-6072, rwatson@hopkins.k12.ky.us, www.hopkins.k12.us/gifted/mad_hatter.htm. 1998. Poetry, art, photos, cartoons. "*The Mad Hatter* is an annual journal of creativity by students in grades four through 12. Established in 1998, TMH has featured distinguished work by students from across the United States and from around the world. Send copies only, including public, private, or home-school affiliation and a SASE. Recent contributors include Banah Gadbian, Kristy Chu, Amanda Wengert, Wan Chong Kim, Dong Gun Yoo, Zeke Pederson, Naomi Wolf, and others." circ. 600. 1/yr. Pub'd 1 issue 2005; expects 1 issue 2006, 1 issue 2007. sub. price $8; per copy $8; sample $8. Back issues: $8. Discounts: Classroom sets of 30, incased by pine bookracks that are hand-made and custom-decorated by students from Madisonville, Kentucky: Price: free to all secondary schools in Hopkins County District; $300 postage paid for schools outside of district. 60pp. Reporting time: 1 month. Simultaneous submissions accepted: yes. Publishes less than 10% of manuscripts submitted. Payment: 1 copy, additional copies for $8, postage paid. Copyrighted, reverts to author. Ads: none. Subjects: Adolescence, Lewis Carroll, Children, Youth, Education, Humor, Photography, Poetry, Visual Arts, Young Adult.

MAD POETS REVIEW, Eileen D'Angelo, Camelia Nocella, PO Box 1248, Media, PA 19063-8248. 1990. Poetry. "Anxious for work with 'joie de vivre' that startles and inspires, *MPR* places no restrictions on subject matter, form, or style, but assumes no responsibility for submissions received without adequate return postage. Submit original, unpublished work, limit 6 poems. We read submissions from Jan. 1 to June 1." 1/yr. Pub'd 1 issue 2005; expects 1 issue 2006, 1 issue 2007. price per copy $10; sample $11.50. Back issues: $8 if available, add $1.50 for postage/handling. Discounts: negotiable. 120-150pp. Reporting time: 3 to 12 weeks. Although we try to respond as quickly as possible, we receive bags of mail weekly for the magazine. Please be patient. Simultaneous submissions accepted: yes. Payment: copy of issue that work appears in. Copyrighted, reverts to author. Ads: none.

Mad River Press, Barry Sternlieb, Maureen Sternlieb, State Road, Richmond, MA 01254, 413-698-3184. 1986. Poetry, long-poems. "Manuscripts always solicited. Recent contributors: Gary Snyder, Linda Gregg, Cortney Davis, Richard Wilbur, W.S. Merwin, Hayden Carruth, Samuel Green, Tom Sexton, and Will Lane." avg. press run 125-500. Pub'd 3 titles 2005; expects 3 titles 2006, 3 titles 2007. 20-28pp. Payment: 10%-20% of press run. Copyrights for author. Subject: Poetry.

THE MADISON REVIEW, Meagan Walker, Managing Editor; Hillary Schroeder, Fiction Editor; Jason Harkleroad, Fiction Editor; Hannah Baker-Sority, Poetry Editor, Dept of English, H.C. White Hall, 600 N. Park Street, Madison, WI 53706, 263-3303. 1978. Poetry, fiction, art, photos, parts-of-novels, long-poems. "Short, short stories welcome." circ. 800. 2/yr. Pub'd 2 issues 2005; expects 2 issues 2006, 2 issues 2007. sub. price $8; per copy $5; sample $2.50. Back issues: $2.50. Discounts: $2/book for bulk orders be happy to trade copies. 80-150pp. Reporting time: replies given by Dec. 15th for Fall issue and by April 15th for Spring issue. Simultaneous submissions accepted: yes. Publishes 6% of manuscripts submitted. Payment: 2 copies. Copyrighted, reverts to author. §All subjects. Subjects: Fiction, Poetry.

The Madson Group, Inc., Madeline Bright Ogle, Editor; Stephen A. Mart, Editor, 13775 A Mono Way, Suite 224, Sonora, CA 95370, 360-446-5348, fax 360-446-5234, email madsongroup@earthlink.net, www.petgroomer.com. 1987. Articles, non-fiction. "Business, career, vocation, education, pets, dog grooming, pet grooming." avg. press run 1M minimum. Expects 1 title 2006, 3 titles 2007. 300pp. Reporting time: 30 days. Simultaneous submissions accepted: yes. Copyrights for author. Subjects: Animals, Business & Economics, Careers, Education, Management.

Magic Circle Press, Valerie Harms, PO Box 1123, Bozeman, MT 59771. 1972. Fiction, art, photos, criticism, non-fiction. "Focus is now on book packaging for clients." avg. press run 2M. Expects 1 title 2006. Discounts: 40% trade, 15% library. 150pp. Reporting time: 2 months. Payment: depends. Copyrights for author. Subjects: Children, Youth, Diaries, Journals, Anais Nin, Poetry, Theatre, Women.

MAGICAL BLEND/NATURAL BEAUTY & HEALTH/TRANSITIONS, MB Media, Inc., Michael Peter Langevin, Publisher; Susan Dobra Ph.D., Editorial Director; Anna Harris, Senior Editor, PO Box 600, Chico, CA 95927-0600, 888-296-2442, Fax 530-893-9076, editor@magicalblend.com. 1980. Articles, art, photos, interviews, reviews, letters, non-fiction. "Assess our style by looking at our magazine or see our websites at www.magicalblend.com, www.nbhonline.com, and www.transitionsmag.com. Length: approx 1,500 words average. Bias: We print material which is of a positive, uplifting cultural or spiritual nature. We hope to make our readers feel better about themselves and the world and help them get a better perspective on the context and significance of their lives." circ. 100M. 9/yr. Pub'd 6 issues 2005; expects 6 issues 2006, 9 issues 2007. sub. price $19.95; per copy $3.99 US, $4.99 elsewhere; sample same. Back issues: $250 for full set. Discounts: 100 or more, 50% retail. 72pp. Reporting time: 6 months. Simultaneous submissions accepted: yes. Publishes 4% of manuscripts submitted. Payment: copies and sometimes cash. Copyrighted, reverts to author. Pub's reviews: 150 in 2005. §Psychic/spiritual, positive, music, health. Ads: $2775/$2475/$295 column inch. Subjects: Celtic, Sri Chinmoy, Counter-Culture, Alternatives, Communes, Dreams, Bob Dylan, Ecology, Foods, Energy, Inspirational, Magic, Occult, Senior Citizens, Spiritual, T'ai Chi, Theosophical, Zen.

MAGNET MAGAZINE, Eric T. Miller, 1218 Chestnut Street, Suite 508, Philadelphia, PA 19107, 215-413-8570, fax 215-413-8569, magnetmag@aol.com. 1993. circ. 35M. 6/yr. Pub'd 6 issues 2005; expects 6 issues 2006, 6 issues 2007. sub. price $14.95; per copy $3.50; sample $4. Back issues: $4. 128pp. Reporting time: varies. Simultaneous submissions accepted: no. Publishes 0% of manuscripts submitted. Payment: varies. Copyrighted, does not revert to author. Pub's reviews: 10-12 in 2005. §Music and music criticism. Ads: $3,000/$2,100. Subjects: Criticism, Music.

Magnolia Publishing, Steve Keegan, PO Box 5537, Magnolia, MA 01930. 1993. avg. press run 10M. Pub'd 1 title 2005; expects 1 title 2006. Discounts: on request. 32pp. Subject: Children, Youth.

Magnus Press Imprint: Canticle Books, Warren R. Angel, PO Box 2666, Carlsbad, CA 92018, 760-806-3743, Fax 760-806-3689, toll free 800-463-7818, magnuspres@aol.com www.magnuspress.com. 1996. Non-fiction. avg. press run 5M. Pub'd 2 titles 2005; expects 3 titles 2006, 4 titles 2007. Discounts: 1-24 45%, 25-249 50%, 250+ 55%. 145pp. Reporting time: 1-4 weeks. Simultaneous submissions accepted: yes. Publishes 3% of manuscripts submitted. Payment: graduating on retail price. Copyrights for author. Subject: Christianity.

MAIN CHANNEL VOICES: A Dam Fine Literary Magazines, Nancy Kay Peterson, Co-founder and Co-editor; Carol Borzyskowski, Co-founder and Co-editor, P.O. Box 492, Winona, MN 55987-0492, http://www.mainchannelvocies.com. 2004. Poetry. "We have eclectic tastes and are looking for accessible poetry that triggers an "Aha!" response in the reader. We take rhymed verse, free verse, prose poems and experimental forms. We are not looking for greeting card verse or pornography. See our web site for samples of the kind of work we publish." circ. 100. 4/yr. Expects 4 issues 2006, 4 issues 2007. sub. price $25; per copy $7.50; sample $5. Back issues: $5. 38pp. Reporting time: 3 months. Simultaneous submissions accepted: Yes. Publishes 5% of manuscripts submitted. Payment: One copy. Copyrighted, reverts to author. Subject: Poetry.

Main Street Arts Press, PO Box 100, Saxtons River, VT 05154, 802-869-2960, msa@sover.net.

MAIN STREET RAG, M. Scott Douglass, Publisher, Poetry Editor & Managing Editor; Bill Wesse, Fiction Editor, 4416 Shea Lane, Charlotte, NC 28227-8245, 704-573-2516, editor@mainstreetrag.com. 1996. Poetry, fiction, articles, art, photos, cartoons, interviews, satire, criticism, reviews, letters, collages, non-fiction. "Any style or subject, we're eclectic, but we prefer things with an edge (even humor). Our submission guidelines will change starting in 2007. We will always read subscribers' manuscripts year round, but in 2007, we will have a restricted reading period for unsolicited poetry and short fiction. Please visit our website for current needs and submission guidelines before submitting." circ. 800. 4/yr. Pub'd 4 issues 2005; expects 4 issues 2006, 4 issues 2007. sub. price $20, $35/2 years; per copy $7; sample $7. Back issues: prices vary—available online. 96pp. Reporting time: 3-6 weeks. Simultaneous submissions accepted: absolutely not—acceptance isn't finalized until a *publishing agreement* is signed. Publishes less than 10% of manuscripts submitted. Payment: 1 contributor's copy (and sometimes more). Copyrighted, reverts to author. Pub's reviews: 35 in 2005. §Mostly collections, small press productions that don't get enough attention; must be recent. Ads: mostly swap. Subjects: Americana, Essays, Global Affairs, Humor, Internet, Interviews, Non-Fiction, Poetry, Politics, Reviews, Short

Stories.

THE MAINE EVENT, Liz Chandler, Janet Murphy, Rusheen, Firies, Co. Kerry, Ireland, 066-9763084 phone/Fax, maineevent@eircom.net, www.maineevent.net. 1999. Poetry. "Broad range of poetry considered." circ. 6M. 12/yr. Pub'd 12 issues 2005; expects 12 issues 2006, 24 issues 2007. sub. price E24; per copy E2.50; sample none. Back issues: none. 10pp. Simultaneous submissions accepted: yes. Payment: none. Copyrighted, reverts to author. Pub's reviews: 1 in 2005. Ads: E155/E90/E60 1/4 page. Subject: Poetry.

MAINE IN PRINT, PO Box 9301, Portland, ME 04104-9301, 207-386-1400, Fax 207-386-1401, www.mainewriters.org. 1975. Articles, interviews, reviews, letters, news items. "Published bi-monthly, *Maine In Print* is the newsletter of Maine Writers & Publishers Alliance, a non-profit literary organization. Each issue contains feature articles about writers and their craft; a calendar of statewide literary events; submissions, contests and grant opportunities; profiles of Maine authors and publishers; reviews of new Maine books; and more." circ. 3M. 6/yr. Pub'd 6 issues 2005; expects 6 issues 2006, 6 issues 2007. sub. price $35; sample free. 16pp. Reporting time: 6 weeks. Simultaneous submissions accepted: yes. Payment: $50 lead article. Copyrighted. §Writing craft, desktop and small press publishing, Maine literature. Ads: $450/$250/.20¢. Subjects: Book Arts, Literature (General), Maine, Publishing, Writers/Writing.

Maisonneuve Press, Robert Merrill, Dennis Crow, P.O. Box 2980, Washington, DC 20013-2980, 301-277-7505, Fax 301-277-2467. 1987. Photos, criticism, non-fiction. "Not accepting new manuscripts or proposals after May 1, 2006. We will be reorganizing and moving." Expects 4 titles 2006, 6 titles 2007. Discounts: see the discount schedule from our distributor—Independent Publishers Group (Chicago). 800-888-4741. www.ipgbook.com. 814 N. Franklin Street, Chicago, IL 60610. 280pp. Simultaneous submissions accepted: yes. Publishes 2-3% of manuscripts submitted. Payment: no advance, 5% of sales. Copyrights for author. Subjects: Cities, Criticism, Earth, Natural History, Education, History, Humanism, Labor, Literary Review, Literature (General), Philosophy, Political Science, Prison, Public Affairs, Socialist, Women.

Malafemmina Press, Rose Sorrentino, 4211 Fort Hamilton Parkway, Brooklyn, NY 11219. 1990. Poetry, plays. "Malafemmina Press is publishing a series of poetry chapbooks by Italian-American women on Italian-American themes. When ordering make checks payable to Rose Sorrentino." avg. press run 200. Pub'd 1 title 2005; expects 3 titles 2006. 20pp. Reporting time: 3 months. Simultaneous submissions accepted: no. Payment: 50 copies and 50% discount. Copyrights for author. Subjects: Italian-American, Women.

THE MALAHAT REVIEW, Marlene Cookshaw, Editor, PO Box 1700, Stn. CSC, Victoria, British Columbia V8W 2Y2, Canada. 1967. Poetry, fiction, art, photos, interviews, criticism, parts-of-novels, long-poems, plays. "Short works preferred. Index available 1967-1977, $3.95; $4.95 overseas." circ. 1.2M. 4/yr. Pub'd 4 issues 2005. sub. price $30 in Canada, $40 other; per copy $10, special issues $12; sample $10. Back issues: $8. Discounts: 33-1/3%, agents and bookstores only, no returns policy. 128pp. Reporting time: 4-12 weeks. Simultaneous submissions accepted: no. Publishes approx. 3% of manuscripts submitted. Payment: $30 per magazine page, prose and poetry. Copyrighted. Pub's reviews: 20 in 2005. §Poetry, fiction (Canadian). Ads: full page: $150 single issue, $500 four consecutive issues, half page: $100 single issue, $300 four consecutive issues, quarter page: $50 single issue, $160 four consecutive issues. Subject: Literary Review.

Maledicta Press (see also MALEDICTA: The International Journal of Verbal Aggression), Reinhold A. Aman, Editor & Publisher, PO Box 14123, Santa Rosa, CA 95402-6123, Phone: (707) 795-8178 E-mail: aman@sonic.net Web site: http://www.sonic.net/maledicta/. 1975. Articles. "Material of 100 pp typed minimum for books, must deal with verbal aggression. Glossaries monolingual or bilingual, are preferred to other material. Backlog of 4 years. No cloth binding available." avg. press run 4M. Pub'd 1 title 2005; expects 1 title 2006, 1 title 2007. Discounts: booksellers 20-40%, jobbers 40%. 160pp. Reporting time: 1 week. Simultaneous submissions accepted: no. Publishes 10% of manuscripts submitted. Payment: 10% paid annually, no advance. Copyrights for author. Subjects: Dictionaries, Folklore, Language, Reference.

MALEDICTA: The International Journal of Verbal Aggression, Maledicta Press, Reinhold A. Aman, Editor & Publisher, PO Box 14123, Santa Rosa, CA 95402-6123, Telephone: 707-795-8178 E-mail: aman@sonic.net Web site: http://www.sonic.net/maledicta/. 1975. Articles. "See any issue. 'Style Sheet' available. 25 pages maximum length of articles; must deal with verbal aggression. Glossaries in any languages preferred. Backlog 3 years." circ. 2M. 1/yr. Expects 1 issue 2006, 1 issue 2007. sub. price $20; per copy $20; No sample copies available. Back issues: Price varies per volume. Discounts: booksellers 20-40%, jobbers 40%. 160pp. Reporting time: 1 week. Simultaneous submissions accepted: no. Publishes 10% of manuscripts submitted. Payment: 10 free offprints. Copyrighted, reverts to author. Pub's reviews: none in 2005. §Verbal aggression (insults, curses, slang, etc.). No ads. Subjects: Folklore, Humor, Language, Sex, Sexuality.

Malki Museum Press (see also THE JOURNAL OF CALIFORNIA AND GREAT BASIN ANTHROPOLOGY), Lynn H. Gamble, Editor; Thomas C. Blackburn, Associate Editor; Lowell John Bean, Associate Editor, P.O. Box 578, Banning, CA 92220, 951-849-7289, Fax 951-849-3549, E-Mail:

malkipress@aol.com, www.malkimuseum.org. 1964. Poetry, articles, interviews, non-fiction. "Malki publishes books on Native American culture, linguistics (Native language dictionaries), ethnobotanicals, mythology, archeology, anthropology and some autobiographical text and poetry. Our mission is to preserve culture and linguistics." avg. press run 1500. Pub'd 2 titles 2005; expects 5 titles 2006, 5 titles 2007. Discounts: Wholesale 40%%Educational 20%Musuem Members 20%. 275pp. Reporting time: Editorial Board meets twice yearly. Simultaneous submissions accepted: Yes. Publishes 85% of manuscripts submitted. Payment: Decided on an individual basis. Malki retains most copyrights. Subjects: Agriculture, Animals, Anthropology, Archaelogy, Astronomy, Dictionaries, Earth, Natural History, Ecology, Foods, Horticulture, Indigenous Cultures, Language, Myth, Mythology, Native American, Nature, Non-Fiction, Storytelling.

Mama Incense Publishing, Lillian Powers, PO Box 4635, Long Beach, CA 90804-9998, 310-490-9097, www.mamaincense.com. 2004. Poetry, fiction, music, long-poems, non-fiction. "The goal of Mama Incense Publishing is to put informative, meaningful and entertaining works in the hands of the people. Whether it be poetry, children's literature, or fiction - if it has the possibility to change people's lives in a positive way, Mama Incense Publishing wants to assist in getting the message heard. Our first sponsored work "girl Child (The Transition - In Poetic Form)", by author/poet lily is a poetry collection detailing the trials many women go through in becoming a woman. It is a book of empowerment, of learning to love oneself before seeking love in the arms of another. Currently Mama Incense Publishing acts as a sounding board and a provider of information for first time self-publishers." avg. press run 3000. Expects 1 title 2006, 1 title 2007. Discounts: 1 copy: no discount2-5 books: 15% 6-20 books: 25% 21-50 books: 40%51-100 books: 45%101+: 50%. 64-200pp. Reporting time: 30 days. Simultaneous submissions accepted: Yes. Publishes 25% of manuscripts submitted. Does not copyright for author. Subjects: Advertising, Self-Promotion, African Literature, Africa, African Studies, African-American, Children, Youth, Family, Feminism, Fiction, Music, Non-Fiction, Novels.

Mammoth Books, Antonio Vallone, President-Publisher; Robert McGovern, Editor, 7 Juniata Street, DuBois, PA 15801, avallone@psu.edu. 1998. Poetry, fiction, articles, long-poems, non-fiction. "We are not accepting manuscripts at this time." avg. press run 300 copies, but digital printing allows us to easily reprint. Discounts: 30%. Payment: copies.

Mandala Publishing, Vrindaranya Devidasi, 17 Paul Drive, Suite 104, San Rafael, CA 94903-2043, 415.526.1380; 800.688.2218; Fax: 415.532.3281; info@mandala.org; www.mandala.org. 1995. Poetry, articles, art, photos, interviews, criticism, music, non-fiction. "We specialize in East Indian traditions and philosophy with an emphasis on Vedantic tradition. Vegetarian cookbooks would also be a priority." avg. press run 3M. Pub'd 2 titles 2005; expects 5 titles 2006, 7 titles 2007. Discounts: trade 60% (distributors) 45% (bookstores) 60% libraries. 200pp. Simultaneous submissions accepted: yes. Payment: none as of yet. Copyrights for author. Subjects: Arts, Asia, Indochina, Biography, Children, Youth, Classical Studies, Counter-Culture, Alternatives, Communes, Culture, India, Inspirational, Yoga.

•**MANDORLA: New Writing from the Americas / Nueva escritura de las Americas,** Kristin Dykstra, ISU, Dept. of English, Campus Box 4240, Normal, IL 61790-4240, Publications Unit tel (309) 438-3025, Fax (309) 438-5414, email to mandorla-magazine@ilstu.edu, website at http://www.litline.org/Mandorla/. 1991. Poetry, fiction, articles, art, photos, criticism, parts-of-novels, long-poems, plays. "First published in Mexico City in 1991, Mandorla emphasizes innovative writing in its original language—most commonly English or Spanish—and high-quality translations of existing material. Visual art and short critical articles complement this work. The name of the magazine—mandorla , describing a space created by two intersecting circles—alludes to the notion of exchange and imaginative dialogue that is necessary now among the Americas.Some of our recent contributors include Jay Wright, Carlos Aguilera, Vera Kutzinski, Tamara Kamenszain, Eleni Sikelianos, Jaime Saenz, Jose Kozer, Eduardo Milan, Antonio Jose Ponte, Reina Maria Rodriguez, Jorge Guitart, Paul Vanouse, Maria Negroni, Forrest Gander, Esther Allen, Giannina Braschi, Rosmarie Waldrop, Consuelo Castaneda, Rosa Alcala, Michael Davidson." circ. 900-1000. 1/yr. Pub'd 1 issue 2005; expects 1 issue 2006, 1 issue 2007. sub. price $10; per copy $10; sample $10. Back issues: $10. Discounts: Bookstores 50% off.Different prices apply for Latin America: please inquire. 225pp. Copyrighted, reverts to author. Ads: Full page $500.Half page $250. Subjects: The Americas, Arts, Avant-Garde, Experimental Art, Experimental, Fiction, Latino, Literature (General), Multicultural, North America, Photography, Poetry, Prose, Translation, U.S. Hispanic, Visual Arts.

MANGROVE MAGAZINE, Dept. of English, Univ. of Miami, PO Box 248145, Coral Gables, FL 33124, 305-284-2182. 1994. Poetry, fiction, articles, art, interviews, parts-of-novels, long-poems. "The annual '98 issue contains poetry by Campbell McGrath and interviews with Dale Peck and Campbell McGrath. Authors should submit work August 1 through December 1. We report December through April, sometimes sooner." circ. 500. 1/yr. Pub'd 1 issue 2005; expects 1 issue 2006, 1 issue 2007. sub. price $6; per copy $6; sample $6. Back issues: $6. Discounts: 10 for $40, 25 for $80. 125pp. Reporting time: 1-6 months. Simultaneous submissions accepted: yes. Publishes 3% of manuscripts submitted. Payment: 2 free copies. Copyrighted, reverts to author. Pub's reviews. §Poetry books and fiction. Ads: none. Subjects: Fiction, Interviews, Memoirs,

Poetry, Prose, Short Stories, Writers/Writing.

THE MANHATTAN REVIEW, Philip Fried, Founder and Editor, c/o Philip Fried, 440 Riverside Drive, #38, New York, NY 10027, 212-932-1854, phfried@aol.com. 1980. Poetry, articles, interviews, criticism, long-poems. "'My only prejudice is against those who lack ambition, believing there is no more to writing than purveying superficial ironies, jokes, or shared sentiments; or those who dedicate themselves to the proposition that poetry of a word, by a word and for a word shall not perish from this earth. A poem is not purely a verbal artifact. It must speak to and for human concerns. I welcome experiments, but poetry must ultimately communicate to an audience. It is not an unobserved wave in the vast ocean of language.' (quoted from preface to 1st issue). ISSN 0275-6889. In recent issues: Christopher Bursk, Peter Redgrove, Penelope Shuttle, Baron Wormser, D. Nurkse, Jeanne Marie Beaumont, Venus Khoury-Ghata, and Claire Malroux." circ. 500. 1/yr. Pub'd 1 issue 2005; expects 1 issue 2006, 1 issue 2007. sub. price 1 volume (2 issues) $10 individuals (U.S. and Canada), $15 libraries (U.S. and Canada), $19 libraries elsewhere; per copy $5 individuals, $7.50 libraries; sample $5 individuals, $7.50 libraries. Back issues: same, with 6 X 9 envelope and $1.60 postage. 64pp. Reporting time: 12-14 weeks. Simultaneous submissions accepted: no. Publishes .015% of manuscripts submitted. Payment: 2 copies. Copyrighted, reverts to author. Pub's reviews: none in 2005. §Poetry. Ads: $150/$75. Subjects: Literature (General), Poetry.

Manifold Press, Carol Frome, 102 Bridge Street, Plattsburgh, NY 12901, editormanifoldpress@msn.com, www.manifoldpress.com. 2003. Poetry, articles, art, interviews, criticism, long-poems. "We lean towards well-crafted free-verse poetry, but don't mind considering formal verse if it's handled in a fresh manner and does not rely only on rhyme. No doggerel, limericks, haiku, or language poetry. Also, we consider art, chapbooks, and essays for our website." avg. press run 1M. Expects 1 title 2007. 70pp. Reporting time: 3-4 months. Simultaneous submissions accepted: yes. Publishes 2-3% of manuscripts submitted. Payment: $500 advance for books (not e-chapbook). Copyrights for author. Subject: Poetry.

MANOA: A Pacific Journal of International Writing, Frank Stewart, Editor; Pat Matsueda, Managing Editor; Brent Fujinaka, Associate Editor, Univ. of Hawaii English Department, 1733 Donaghho Road, Honolulu, HI 96822, 808-956-3070, Fax 808-956-3083, mjournal-l@hawaii.edu, manoajournal.hawaii.edu. 1988. Poetry, fiction, interviews, non-fiction. "Manoa publishes contemporary writing from Asia, the Pacific, and the Americas. In general, each issue is devoted to a single country. Past issues have presented new work from such places as China, Tibet, Indonesia, Korea, Japan, PNG, Malaysia, Viet Nam, the Philippines, Australia, New Zealand, Pacific island nations, Mexico, South American nations, Nepal, Taiwan, Cambodia, and French Polynesia. US contributors have included Arthur Sze, Nguyen Qui Duc, Barry Lopez, W.S. Merwin, and Ha Jin. Manoa has also published interviews with Kenzaburo Oe, Ma Yuan, Xue Di, Soth Polin, and other writers of international stature." circ. 2.5M. 2/yr. Pub'd 2 issues 2005; expects 2 issues 2006, 2 issues 2007. sub. price $22; per copy $16; sample $12. Discounts: agency 10%, multiple orders: 10-19 20%, 20+ 30%. 220pp. Simultaneous submissions accepted: yes. Publishes 1% of manuscripts submitted. Payment: competitive, depends on material and length. Copyrighted, reverts to author. Ads: $200/$125. Subjects: Arts, Asia, Indochina, Asian-American, Autobiography, Earth, Natural History, Environment, Fiction, Hawaii, Literature (General), Non-Fiction, Novels, Poetry, Short Stories, Translation, Visual Arts.

Manuscript Press (see also COMICS REVUE), Rick Norwood, PO Box 336, Mountain Home, TN 37684-0336, 423-926-7495. 1976. "Comic strips." avg. press run 1000. Pub'd 1 title 2005; expects 1 title 2006, 1 title 2007. Discounts: 40% on 5 or more, 55% on 100 or more. 100-200pp. Reporting time: slow. Simultaneous submissions accepted: no. Publishes 0% of manuscripts submitted. Payment: by arrangement. Copyrights for author. Subjects: Comics, Science Fiction.

MANY MOUNTAINS MOVING, Naomi Horii, Editor-in-Chief; Debra Bokur, Poetry Editor; Steven Church, Essay Editor; David Rozgonyi, Book Review Editor, 1136 South University Blvd., Denver, CO 80210-1907, 303-545-9942, Fax 303-444-6510. 1994. Poetry, fiction, articles, art, photos, cartoons, interviews, satire, reviews, letters, parts-of-novels, long-poems, non-fiction. "We invite fiction, poetry and essays from writers of all cultures. Contributors include Sherman Alexie, Isabel Allende, Amiri Baraka, Robert Bly, Lorna Dee Cervantes, Marge Piercy, Luis Urrea and many others. Poems have appeared in Best American Poetry and Pushcart. We are starting a poetry book contest and will print one book of poems per year." circ. 3M. 5/yr. Pub'd 3 issues 2005; expects 3 issues 2006, 6 issues 2007. sub. price $16/2 issues; per copy $9; sample $6. Back issues: $6. Discounts: negotiable. 80pp. Reporting time: usually within 1 month, but up to 4 months occasionally. Simultaneous submissions accepted: yes. Publishes .1% of manuscripts submitted. Payment: contributors' copies. Copyrighted, reverts to author. Pub's reviews: 2 in 2005. §fiction, poetry, creative nonfiction. Ads: $200/$100/no classifieds. Subjects: Essays, Feminism, Fiction, Poetry, Short Stories.

Mapletree Publishing Company, David A. Hall, 6233 Harvard Lane, Highlands Ranch, CO 80130-3773, 800-537-0414, mail@mapletreepublishing.com, www.mapletreepublishing.com. 2002. Fiction, non-fiction. "We publish books about homeschooling and parenting, and some quality fiction. Our mission is to publish excellent books that gently promote religious values." avg. press run 2-5M. Pub'd 5 titles 2005; expects 7 titles

2006, 10 titles 2007. Discounts: 2-4 copies 20%; 5-35 copies 40%; even case quantities 50%. 300pp. Reporting time: 6-8 weeks. Simultaneous submissions accepted: yes. Publishes 2-5% of manuscripts submitted. Payment: 9-20% of wholesale, paid quarterly. Copyrights for author. Subjects: Education, Fiction, Parenting.

Marathon International Book Company, Jim Wortham, Publisher, Department SPR, PO Box 40, Madison, IN 47250-0040, 812-273-4672 phone/Fax, jwortham@seidata.com. 1969. "We are considering non-fiction and self help manuscripts. We are interested in considering other publishers' books for distribution. Please mail a sample copy of any title(s) you wish us to consider for distribution. We are also interested in purchasing small publishing companies. Contact us by mail or fax, please." avg. press run 3M. Pub'd 5 titles 2005; expects 5 titles 2006, 5 titles 2007. Discounts: 40% to trade; write for quantity and wholesale schedule. 64-300pp. Reporting time: 2-3 weeks. Simultaneous submissions accepted: yes. Publishes 5% of manuscripts submitted. Payment: 10% royalty or an outright purchase of the book rights. Copyright in author's name. Subjects: Drama, Poetry.

Peter Marcan Publications, Peter Marcan, PO Box 3158, London SEI 4RA, Great Britain, (020) 7357 0368. 1978. Non-fiction. "Has several titles in print including *The Lord's Prayer in Black & White, Music for Solo Violin* [a catalogue of published and unpublished works from the 17th century to 1989 with a 1997 supplement], and the *Marcan Visual Arts Handbook* [where to go for British contacts, expertise and specialty]." avg. press run 350-1M. Pub'd 1 title 2005; expects 2 titles 2006, 2 titles 2007. Discounts: 35% to book trade for two or more copies. 62-120pp. Subjects: Arts, Bibliography, Book Collecting, Bookselling, Cities, History, London, Music, Reference, Religion.

March Street Press (see also PARTING GIFTS), Robert Bixby, 3413 Wilshire Drive, Greensboro, NC 27408-2923, www.marchstreetpress.com. 1988. Poetry, fiction. "Currently reading. I hope to publish at least 3 books of poetry and one book of short stories per year. Reading fee: $20." avg. press run 50. Pub'd 15 titles 2005; expects 15 titles 2006, 15 titles 2007. Discounts: write. 40pp. Reporting time: 2-3 months. Payment: 10 free copies, 15% of sales. Does not copyright for author. Subjects: Fiction, Poetry.

Margaret Media, Inc., Mary Gehman, 425 Manasses Place, New Orleans, LA 70119, using cell phone temporarily: (601)918-8240, orders@margaretmedia.com. 1981. Non-fiction. "We are interested only in non-fiction about Louisiana and New Orleans." avg. press run 3M. Pub'd 1 title 2005; expects 1 title 2006, 2 titles 2007. Discounts: 40% to wholesalers. 150pp. Reporting time: 2 weeks. We accept simultaneous submissions, but query first. Publishes a variable % of manuscripts submitted. Payment: varies. Copyrighting for author depends on contract. Subjects: African-American, Biography, Children, Youth, Culture, Feminism, Folklore, History, Language, Leisure/Recreation, Louisiana, Multicultural, Race, South, Women.

MARGIN: Exploring Modern Magical Realism, Tamara Kaye Sellman, 321 High School Road NE, PMB #204, Bainbridge Island, WA 98110, magicalrealismmaven@yahoo.com, www.magical-realism.com. 1999. "UPDATE FOR 2007: *Reading period closed. Margin*'s format has changed. While the anthology itself remains accessible and completely archived on the web, it has suspended publication of new material. Instead, the staff is focusing its energy, time and resources on several new projects, including its new interactive community with newsletter and newsblog, new online writers workshops and mentorships, a print edition slated for *Margin*'s tenth anniversary, an online book discussion litblog, and the continued publication of its print zine, *Periphery* (www.angelfire.com/wa2/margin/periphery.html). Site reformatting for easier navigation is also in progress. Complete information about all new services and features associated with *Margin* can be found at www.magical-realism.com." Payment: all contributors 2000-2006 are in the process of being compensated. Copyrighted, reverts to author. Subject: Internet.

Markowski International Publishers, Marjorie L. Markowski, Editor, Michael A. Markowski, 1 Oakglade Circle, Hummelstown, PA 17036-9525, 717-566-0468, Fax 717-566-6423. 1981. Non-fiction. "Formerly Ultralight Publications, Inc. Publishes hardcover and trade paperback originals. Book catalog and ms guidelines for #10 SAE with two first class stamps. Publishes book on average of one year after acceptance. Simultaneous submissions OK. Primary focus is books on, human development, self-help, personal growth, sales and marketing, leadership training, network marketing, motivation and success. We are interested in how-to, motivational and instructional books of short to medium length that will serve recognized and emerging needs of society. Query or submit outline and three sample chapters. Reviews artwork/photos as part of ms package. Tips: 'We're very interested in publishing best sellers!'" avg. press run 5-50M. Pub'd 5 titles 2005; expects 10 titles 2006, 10 titles 2007. Discounts: 1-10, 2-4-20%, 5-9=30%, 10-24-40%, 25-49-42%, 50-74-45%, 75-99-47%, 100-499-50%, 500-999-55%, 1000 and up 60%. 108-192pp. Reporting time: 2 months. Simultaneous submissions accepted: yes. Publishes 1% of manuscripts submitted. Payment: 10%-12% royalty on wholesale price. Copyrights for author. Subjects: Motivation, Success, Psychology, Self-Help.

THE MARLBORO REVIEW, Ellen Dudley; Ruth Anderson Barnett, Poetry; Margaret Kaufman, Fiction; Helen Fremont, Fiction, PO Box 243, Marlboro, VT 05344, www.marlbororeview.com. 1995. Poetry, fiction, interviews, criticism, reviews, parts-of-novels, long-poems, non-fiction. "Longpoems okay, translations and reviews welcome. Recent contributors: Brenda Hillman, Yehuda Amichai, Stephen Dobyns, Heather McHugh, Dionision Martinez. No deadlines.'' circ. 1M. 2/yr. Pub'd 2 issues 2005; expects 2 issues 2006, 2 issues 2007. sub. price $16; per copy $8 + $1.30 postage; sample $8 + $1.30 postage. Back issues: none. Discounts: bookstores 40%. 100pp. Reporting time: 2-3 months. Simultaneous submissions accepted if notified. Publishes 6% of manuscripts submitted. Payment: copies. Copyrighted. Pub's reviews: 8 in 2005. §Poetry, fiction, and nonfiction. Ads: $150/$75/none. Subjects: Fiction, Interviews, Poetry, Reviews, Translation.

Marmot Publishing, Steven Laurens, 4652 Union Flat Creek Road, Endicott, WA 99125-9764, 509-657-3359, editor@marmotpublishing.com, www.marmotpublishing.com. 1993. Non-fiction. ''Please send queries only. We do not have the staff to read unsolicited manuscripts. Almost all general adult non-fiction subjects are welcome. Political material must be of a conservative or libertarian viewpoint. No pro-feminism or pro-multiculturalism.'' avg. press run 2M. Expects 1 title 2006, 1 title 2007. Discounts: bookstores-40%, distributor-55%. 300pp. Reporting time: 2 months. Simultaneous submissions accepted: yes. Payment: no advances, royalty negotiable. Copyrights for author. Subject: Non-Fiction.

MARQUEE, Steve Levin, York Theatre Building, 152 N. York Road, Suite 200, Elmhurst, IL 60126, 630-782-1800, Fax 630-782-1802, thrhistsoc@aol.com. 1969. Articles, photos, interviews, criticism. ''Historical research on American Theatre buildings contributed by members. Recent article Metropolitan Opera House, Philadelphia and current article-history of Atlantic City theatres w/vintage pictures. Comprehensive study Chicago Theatre, Chicago, IL. Theatre Draperies Issue—1983 - Color issue - Fifth Avenue Th. Seattle, Washington. Special issue - 1984 - Preservation of OLD Theatres. 1985 Theatre Acoustics. 1976 Mastbaum Th. - Phila Pa; Earle Theatre, Philadelphia issue-1986; Al Ringling Th. Baraboo, WI - 1991. Michigan Thr, Detroit, 1995.'' circ. 1M. 5/yr. Pub'd 5 issues 2005; expects 5 issues 2006, 5 issues 2007. sub. price $45; per copy $6.50; sample $6.50. Back issues: $6.50. Discounts: library rate $35. 30pp. Reporting time: 3 months. Publishes 85% of manuscripts submitted. Copyrighted, reverts to author. Pub's reviews: 6 in 2005. §Theatre architecture. Ads: $200/$125. Subjects: Architecture, Theatre.

Marsh Hawk Press, Editorial Collective; Sandy McIntosh, Managing Editor, PO Box 206, East Rockaway, NY 11518-0206, Fax 212-598-4353, marshhawkpress@cs.com, www.marshhawkpress.org. 2001. Poetry. ''We like poets who have assimilated modern and postmodern traditions but expand from them, particularly toward connectons with the visual arts. Marsh Hawk Press currently accepts submissions only through its annual competition: the Marsh Hawk Press Prize. (However, all submitted contest manuscripts are eligible for publication. See website for more information.).'' avg. press run 1000. Expects 6 titles 2006, 6 titles 2007. Discounts: standard 40% to wholesalers. 96pp. Copyrights for author. Subject: Poetry.

Marsh River Editions, M233 Marsh Road, Marshfield, WI 54449.

Martinez Press, 769 Mosswood Ave., South Orange, NJ 07079-2440, raymond@flatironsystems.com, www.flatironsystems.com. 1999. Fiction, non-fiction. ''East Coast Latin press: tech, bio's, historic fiction by Latin American writers.'' Expects 2 titles 2006, 4 titles 2007. Simultaneous submissions accepted: yes. Publishes 20% of manuscripts submitted. Copyrights for author. Subjects: Biography, Cities, Computers, Calculators, Cuba, Fiction, History, Internet, Latin America, Latino, Networking, Nicaragua.

Maryland Historical Press, Vera Rollo, 2364 Sandell Drive, Dunnwoody, GA 30338, 770-671-0740. 1964. Non-fiction. ''We publish only non-fiction: histories, US history, US Presidential history, biographies, aviation law, aviation biographies, aviation histories.'' avg. press run 1000. Expects 2 titles 2006, 2 titles 2007. Discounts: 33%. 200pp. Reporting time: Month. Simultaneous submissions accepted: No. Publishes 10% of manuscripts submitted. Payment: After costs recouped, 10% royalties, paid every 6 months. Copyrights for author. Subjects: Airplanes, Americana, Anthropology, Archaelogy, Aviation, Biography, Government, History, Indians, Indigenous Cultures, Interviews, Thomas Jefferson, Native American, North America, Philosophy, Religion.

Marymark Press, Mark Sonnenfeld, 45-08 Old Millstone Drive, East Windsor, NJ 08520, 609-443-0646. 1994. Poetry, fiction, art, photos, cartoons, music, collages. ''I prefer submissions that are in the experimental genre. Recent contributors are Spiel, Thomas Hays, Richard Kostelanetz, Jose Roberto Sechi, and Melanie Monterey.'' avg. press run 300-350+. Pub'd 50-75 titles 2005; expects 50-75 titles 2006, 50-75 titles 2007. Pages vary. Reporting time: 2 weeks maximum. Simultaneous submissions accepted: yes. Publishes 80-90% of manuscripts submitted. Payment: contributor's copies. Does not copyright for author. Subjects: Avant-Garde, Experimental Art, Beat, Poetry, Surrealism.

THE MASSACHUSETTS REVIEW, Corwin Ericson, Managing Editor, Editor; David Lenson, Editor; Ellen Watson, Editor, South College, University of Massachusetts, Amherst, MA 01003-7140, 413-545-2689. 1959. Poetry, fiction, articles, art, photos, interviews, satire, criticism, letters, long-poems, plays, non-fiction. ''*A SASE must accompany each manuscript + query*. No fiction or poetry mss considered from June 1 to Oct 1.'' circ. 2M+. 4/yr. Pub'd 4 issues 2005; expects 4 issues 2006, 4 issues 2007. sub. price $25; per copy $8; sample $8. Back issues: $7-$14. Discounts: 15% on ads for adv. agencies; 40% bookstores; $50 full page ad for univ.

and small presses. 172pp. Reporting time: 6-12 weeks. Publishes 10% of manuscripts submitted. Payment: $50 prose, $10 min. poetry, 35¢ per line. Copyrighted, rights revert to author on request. Ads: $125 full page. Subject: Literary Review.

MASSEY COLLECTORS NEWS—WILD HARVEST, Keith Oltrogge, Box 529, Denver, IA 50622, 319-984-5292. 1981. Articles. "Newsletter for collectors of Wallis, Ferguson, Massey Harris and Massey Ferguson tractors and farm equipment." circ. 2M. 6/yr. Pub'd 6 issues 2005; expects 6 issues 2006, 6 issues 2007. sub. price $24; per copy $4; sample same. Back issues: $3. 32pp. Reporting time: 30 days. Publishes 90% of manuscripts submitted. Payment: subscription extensions. Not copyrighted. Ads: $75/$40/$20 1/4 page/classifieds are free. Subjects: Agriculture, Antiques.

Massey-Reyner Publishing, Sandy Tayler, PO Box 323, Wallace, CA 95254, phone/fax 209-763-2590, e-mail learning@goldrush.com. 1996. Non-fiction. "We do not solicit manuscripts." avg. press run 5M. Pub'd 1 title 2005; expects 1 title 2006, 1 title 2007. Discounts: 2-5 books 25%; 6-15 30%; 16-300 40%; 301-499 45%; 500 + up 50%. 150pp. Reporting time: 2 months. Simultaneous submissions accepted: no. Payment: bi-annual payment. Copyrights for author. Subjects: Autobiography, Disabled, Education, Handicapped, Motivation, Success, Non-Fiction, Religion.

Master's Plan Publishing, 2727 NW Ninth Street, Corvallis, OR 97330, 541-758-3456, Fax 541-757-8250, mastersplanpublishing@earthlink.net, www.mastersplanpublishing.com. 2002. Non-fiction. "Health, medical, self-help." avg. press run 3,000. Expects 1 title 2006, 1 title 2007. Discounts: retailers 1-2 books 20%, 3-4 30%, 5+ 40%, wholesalers/distributors 1-2 books 30%, 3-4 40%, 5+ 50%, libraries, universities, companies 1-2 books 0%, 3-4 20%, 5+ 30%. 240pp. Simultaneous submissions accepted: no. Does not copyright for author. Subjects: Health, Medicine, Self-Help.

THE MATCH, Fred Woodworth, PO Box 3488, Tucson, AZ 85722. 1969. Fiction, articles, cartoons, interviews, criticism, reviews, letters, parts-of-novels, reviews. "Recent articles include 'Who the Police Beat,' 'Freedom Eclipsed,'. Not seeking contributions." circ. 2M. 4/yr. Pub'd 1 issue 2005; expects 3 issues 2006, 4 issues 2007. sub. price $12/4 issues; per copy $2.50; sample $2. Discounts: 50%, payable on receipt of copies. 60pp. Pub's reviews: 17 in 2005. §Anarchism, government. No ads. Subjects: Anarchist, Book Reviewing.

MATCHBOOK, Debrie Stevens, 240 Edison Furlong Road, Doylestown, PA 18901-3013, Fax 215-340-3965. 1995. Poetry, reviews, long-poems. "Eclectic. Suggest reviewing sample copy before submitting." circ. internet. 2/yr. Pub'd 2 issues 2005; expects 2 issues 2006, 2 issues 2007. sub. price on internet. Discounts: inquire. 64-128 web pages. Reporting time: 2-4 weeks. Simultaneous submissions accepted if noted. Publishes 5% of manuscripts submitted. Copyrighted, reverts to author. Pub's reviews: 10-12 reviews in 2005. §Chapbooks, small press magazines featuring poetry. Ads: $50/$25 per banner on website. Subjects: Poetry, Reviews, Translation.

MATHEMATICAL SPECTRUM, Applied Probability Trust, D.W. Sharpe, School of Mathematics and Statistics, University of Sheffield, Sheffield S3 7RH, England, tel: +44 (0)114 222-3920, fax: +44 (0)114 272-9782, email: apt@sheffield.ac.uk, web: http://www.appliedprobability.org. 1968. Articles, reviews, letters. circ. 2000. 3/yr. Pub'd 3 issues 2005; expects 3 issues 2006, 3 issues 2007. Subscription: £12.50 (or $24 US or $31 Aus); free sample copy on request. Back issues: on request. Contact s.c.boyles@sheffield.ac.uk for details of discounts. 24pp. Simultaneous submission *not* accepted. Payment: Prizes awarded annually for best student contributions. Copyrighted, does not revert to author. Pub's reviews: 12 in 2005. §Books on mathematics suitable for senior students in schools and beginning undergraduates in colleges and universities. Ads: on request. Subjects: Education, Mathematics.

Maui arThoughts Co., Victor C. Pellegrino, PO Box 967, Wailuku, HI 96793-0967, 808-244-0156 phone/Fax, booksmaui@hawaii.rr.com, www.booksmaui.com. 1987. Poetry, fiction, non-fiction. avg. press run 5M-25M. Pub'd 2 titles 2005; expects 2 titles 2006, 2 titles 2007. Discounts: 10% libraries and schools, 20% college bookstores, 40% retail, 40-55% major distributors. 160-220pp. Reporting time: 2 weeks. Simultaneous submissions accepted: no. Publishes 5% of manuscripts submitted. Payment: to be arranged. Copyrights for author. Subjects: Fiction, Non-Fiction, Poetry.

Maupin House Publishing, Inc., PO Box 90148, Gainesville, FL 32607, 1-800-524-0634, Fax 352-373-5546. 1988. avg. press run 3M. Pub'd 4 titles 2005; expects 5 titles 2006, 7 titles 2007. Discounts: industry standard. Pages vary. Reporting time: 2 months. We accept simultaneous submissions with notice. Publishes 5-10% of manuscripts submitted. Payment: negotiable. Copyrights for author. Subjects: Communication, Journalism, Education, English, Reading.

Maverick Books, Josh Greene, Box 897, Woodstock, NY 12498, 866-478-9266 phone/Fax, maverick-books@aol.com. 1998. Fiction, art, photos, reviews, non-fiction. avg. press run 1-2M. Expects 1 title 2006, 2 titles 2007. Discounts: varies on circumstance. 250-375pp. Reporting time: 3 months. Simultaneous submissions accepted: yes. Publishes 1% of manuscripts submitted. Payment: varies. Author obtains own copyright. Subjects: Arts, Biography, Feminism, Fiction, Romance, Women.

Mayapple Press, Judith Kerman, Editor-Publisher, 408 N. Lincoln St., Bay City, MI 48708, 989-892-1429 (voice/fax), jbkerman@mayapplepress.com, www.mayapplepress.com. 1978. Poetry, fiction, art, parts-of-novels, long-poems. "$10 reading fee, payable by check or PayPal on website. *Please* number multi-page works and include TOC. Email submissions OK with PayPal reading fee. Clear xeroxes OK, with name and address on every page; no snailmail returns or responses without SASE. We have a special interest in writing by women, Great Lakes regional writing, the Caribbean, translations, the immigrant experience, science fiction poetry, atypical Judaica - all sorts of things that cross typical category boundaries - as well as book arts and art/fine crafts. We have published poetry collections by Conrad Hilberry, Dennis Hinrichsen, Margo Solod, Susan Azar Porterfield, Gerry LaFemina, Pamela Miller, Hugh Fox, Judith Minty as well as an anthology of science fiction/fantasy poetry by leading genre authors and a multi-genre book about the Michigan cherry industry. *Please read the guidelines on our website before sending material.* No free advice. We expect authors, especially poets, to take a major hand in distribution (terms are negotiable, but concept is, alas, inevitable!)." avg. press run 400. Pub'd 7 titles 2005; expects 12 titles 2006, 12 titles 2007. Discounts: 1-5 copies to bookstores, jobbers & libraries 20%; 6 or more (mixed or same title) 30% consignment; 40% cash/returns; 50% no returns; 55% to wholesale distributors. Additional 5% discount for prepaid orders; include $2 for postage and handling per copy for first 3 copies, 75¢ per copy for additional copies. 50pp. Reporting time: up to 6 months. Simultaneous submissions accepted: OK - please inform us. We recommend sending an inquiry with sample section first. Payment: for poetry/fiction, 5% of run in lieu of royalties (minimum 10 copies) plus 50% discount on purchase of copies; for other projects, negotiable. Copyrights for author. Subjects: Book Arts, Caribbean, Great Lakes, Immigration, Judaism, Latin America, Literature (General), Michigan, Midwest, Poetry, Science Fiction, Translation, Women.

MAYFLY, Brooks Books, Randy Brooks, 3720 N. Woodridge Drive, Decatur, IL 62526, (217) 877-2966. 1986. Poetry. "Mayfly is a small, square (5.5" X 5.5") haiku magazine published two times a year. Our goal is to be very selective, but then publish each haiku with dignity. In our opinion, haiku is best savored in small servings. We will publish only the very best, the most evocative haiku. Mayfly was first published in 1986 as a new approach to publishing haiku. We wanted to feature the individual haiku above all else, without embellishment nor distractions. To avoid any recurring mayfly haiku submissions, we opened with a mayfly contest, which resulted in the following winning haiku published in the first issue. a mayfly taps the screen warm beets slip their skins—Peggy LylesWe have not published another mayfly haiku since.We feel it is the duty of editors and writers to make careful selection and proper presentation of only the very best, the most evocative, the truly effective haiku. We publish only 14 or 15 haiku per issue, but each haiku is printed on its own page. The writer is paid $10.00 per haiku.We continue to strive for excellence in selective editing and publication design, and we hope that you enjoy each issue.Submissions to Mayfly are limited to five poems per issue. We screen submissions and place maybes on our kitchen counter where they are read and re-read over a period of time. Those haiku which continue to move us with repeated reading are selected for publication.We accept submissions by snail mail only." circ. 350. 2/yr. Pub'd 2 issues 2005; expects 2 issues 2006, 2 issues 2007. sub. price $8; per copy $4; sample $4. Back issues: $4. Discounts: none. 16pp. Reporting time: 6 months. Simultaneous submissions accepted: No. Publishes 2% of manuscripts submitted. Payment: $10 per poem. Copyrighted, reverts to author. Subject: Haiku.

Mayhaven Publishing, Doris R. Wenzel, PO Box 557, 803 Buckthorn Circle, Mahomet, IL 61853-0557, 217-586-4493; fax 217-586-6330. 1990. Poetry, fiction, art, photos, cartoons, interviews, satire, letters, non-fiction. "We like variety in topic and style." avg. press run 2000. Pub'd 5 titles 2005; expects 14 titles 2006, 10 titles 2007. Discounts: Provided. 100-300pp. Reporting time: asap - many new submissions. Simultaneous submissions accepted: yes. Publishes less than 1% of manuscripts offered. Payment: Royalties: based on contract for: Traditional, Co-op or Annual Awards for Fiction. Copyrights for author. Subjects: Christmas, Earth, Natural History, Fiction, History, Literature (General), Memoirs, Miniature Books, Movies, Mystery, Nature, Non-Fiction, Romance, Satire, Trivia, Young Adult.

MB Media, Inc. (see also MAGICAL BLEND/NATURAL BEAUTY & HEALTH/TRANSITIONS), Michael Peter Langevin, Publisher; Susan Dobra Ph.D., Senior Editor, PO Box 600, Chico, CA 95927, 888-296-2442, Fax 530-893-9076, editor@magicalblend.com. 1980. Articles, art, photos, interviews, reviews, letters, non-fiction. "We publish writing that informs readers about alternative health practices, holistic living, cultural creativity, transformational ideas, and spiritual or paranormal knowledge. Transpersonal psychology, new age thought, spiritual exploration, health, transformation of society." avg. press run 100M. Pub'd 6 titles 2005; expects 7 titles 2006, 9 titles 2007. Discounts: 100+ copies 50% & shipping, 5+ copies 33% & shipping. 72pp. Reporting time: 6 months. Simultaneous submissions accepted: yes. Publishes 3% of manuscripts submitted. Payment: copies and sometimes cash. Copyrights for author. Subjects: Counter-Culture, Alternatives, Communes, Creativity, Environment, Health, Humor, Inspirational, Interviews, Music, Occult, Philosophy, Religion, Spiritual, Tarot, Vegetarianism, Zen.

MBA Publications, Myers Barnes, Publisher, PO Box 50, Kitty Hawk, NC 27949, 252-261-7611. 1996. "Some books are: *Closing Strong: The Super Sales Handbook, Reach the Top in New Home and Neighborhood Sales,* and *Red Neck Roundup* (photography book)." avg. press run 3M. Pub'd 1 title 2005; expects 1 title 2006, 1 title 2007. Discounts: 1-2 copies 20%, 3-4 30%, 5+ 40%, wholesale 50%. 250pp. Reporting time: 6 weeks. Payment: negotiable. Copyrights for author. Subjects: Americana, Business & Economics, Marketing, Photography, Real Estate.

MCB University Press (see also LIBRARY HI TECH; LIBRARY HIGH TECH NEWS; REFERENCE SERVICES REVIEW), 60/62 Toller Lane, Bradford, W. Yorkshire BD8 9BY, England.

McBooks Press, Inc., Alexander G. Skutt, Owner, Publisher; Jackie Swift, Editorial Director, I. D. Booth Bldg, 520 North Meadow Street #2, Ithaca, NY 14850-3229, 607-272-2114, FAX 607-273-6068, mcbooks@mcbooks.com, www.mcbooks.com. 1979. Fiction, non-fiction. "The bulk of our publishing is historical fiction, especially military and naval series. We can accept *no* unsolicited manuscripts. Letters of inquiry are welcome. We publish a very few books and we make the decision to publish on the basis of both commercial potential and literary merit. We are also interested in seeing inquiries about books on vegetarianism and regional books on upstate New York." avg. press run 4M. Pub'd 19 titles 2005; expects 19 titles 2006, 28 titles 2007. Discounts: standard terms are available to bookstores, wholesalers, etc. 320pp. Reporting time: 2 months on query letters. Simultaneous submissions accepted: yes. Publishes less than 1% of manuscripts submitted. Payment: usual royalty basis with an advance. Copyrights for author. Subjects: Fiction, New York, Sports, Outdoors, Vegetarianism.

McGavick Field Publishing, Phyllis McGavick, Acquisitions, Anne Field, 118 North Cherry, Olathe, KS 66061, 913-782-1700, Fax 913-782-1765, fran@abcnanny.com, colleen@nationwidemedia.net, www.abc-nanny.com. 1996. Articles, non-fiction. avg. press run 30-50M. Pub'd 1 title 2005; expects 4 titles 2006, 8 titles 2007. Discounts: trade, bulk and jobber. 145pp. Reporting time: 6 months. Simultaneous submissions accepted: yes. Publishes 10% of manuscripts submitted. Payment: to be determined on individual basis. Copyrights for author. Subjects: Employment, Parenting, Women.

MCM Entertainment, Inc. Publishing Division, 2040 S. Alma School Rd, # 218, Chandler, AZ 85248-2075. 1990. Non-fiction. 500pp. Publishes 100% of manuscripts submitted. Copyrights for author. Subjects: Biography, California, Catholic, Divorce, Drama, Family, History, Italian-American, Italy, Los Angeles, Marriage, Music, Non-Fiction, Romance, World War II.

McPherson & Company Publishers, Bruce R. McPherson, PO Box 1126, 148 Smith Avenue, Kingston, NY 12402, 845-331-5807, toll free order #800-613-8219. 1973. Fiction, art, criticism, non-fiction. "Other imprints: Documentext, Treacle Press. Distributor of Saroff Editions. No unsolicited mss. Query. See www.mcpher-sonco.com before making query." avg. press run 2M. Pub'd 5 titles 2005; expects 5 titles 2006, 7 titles 2007. Discounts: 1 copy 20%, 2-4 30%, 5-25 40%, 26-99 42%, 100-199 copies 43%, 200+ copies 45%; prepaid STOP, 30%; non-returnable 50% 5+ copies; course adoptions 20% returnable; library discount 20% for orders $75+; shipping additional for all classes except library. 200pp. Reporting time: 2 weeks-3 months. Publishes 1% of manuscripts submitted. Payment: royalties and copies. Copyrights for author. Subjects: Anthology, Arts, Avant-Garde, Experimental Art, Criticism, Essays, Fiction, Literature (General), Music, Novels, Performing Arts, Post Modern, Reprints, Satire, Short Stories.

MCT - MULTICULTURAL TEACHING, Trentham Books, Gillian Klein, Editor, Westview House, 734 London Road, Oakhill, Stoke-on-Trent, Staffordshire ST4 5NP, England, 01782-745567, Fax 01782-745553. 1982. "For professionals in schools and community. It is concerned with all aspects of teaching and learning in a multicultural society. It is equally concerned with the wide range of social work serving young people, their families, and communities. It is, therefore, an inter-professional journal that focuses on practices of teachers and social and community workers in their day to day work with young people of all ethnic groups. Each issue consists of case studies of professional practice, discussion of its aims and purposes and examples of its achievements. There are also reviews of important new books and resources and information about courses, conferences, and events of professional interest to readers." 3/yr. Pub'd 3 issues 2005; expects 3 issues 2006, 3 issues 2007. sub. price £35 ROW, £24 UK; per copy £10; sample £10. Back issues: £10. Discounts: 10% series disc. w/ ads. 64pp. Reporting time: max 1 month, usually 2 weeks. Copyrighted. Pub's reviews: 47 in 2005. §Multi ethnic education, anti racist education. Ads: £200/£100/£.50. Subjects: Education, Race.

ME MAGAZINE, Pittore Euforico, Carlo Pittore, PO Box 182, Bowdoinham, ME 04008, 207-666-8453. 1980. Poetry, art, criticism, reviews, collages, concrete art. "Important article on Maine's mighty artist, Bern Porter. Also, artwork-profusely illustrated. *An Artburst From Maine* by Carlo Pittore. ISSN 0272-5657." circ. 2M. Published at editor's discretion. Expects 5 issues 2006. sub. price $20; per copy $5; sample $5. Back issues: $5, $7.50 for ME IV (Audio Cassette). Discounts: 40%. 8pp. Reporting time: 2 months. Payment: copies. Not copyrighted. §Art movements, art, mail art. Ads: $140/$75. Subjects: Arts, Poetry.

•**MEAT FOR TEA: THE NORTHAMPTON REVIEW,** Meaty Gonzales, 23 Orchard Street, Northampton,

MA 01060, 413-585-5795, 323-547-4101. 2006. Poetry, fiction, art, photos, cartoons, interviews, satire, criticism, reviews, music, long-poems, collages, plays. "Meat for Tea: The Northampton Review was created to provide a non-academically affiliated forum in which the plethora of talented local artists and musicians can publish their work. In this part of Massachusetts there is an active art, music, and literary scene but practically no publishing opportunities outside academe. We have filled this void. We seek to showcase new talent, but also publish more established authors, like Jon Mandel and Dorion Sagan. In each issue is an EP length CD featuring the work of local bands. We're Meat for Tea—giving the F.U. to P.C. everywhere." circ. 150. 4/yr. Expects 4 issues 2006, 4 issues 2007. sub. price $25; per copy $6; sample $6. Back issues: $7. Discounts: 2-10 copies 30%. 65pp. Reporting time: one week—max. Simultaneous submissions accepted: Yes. Publishes 60% of manuscripts submitted. Payment: Free copy of the magazine. Copyrighted. Pub's reviews: none in 2005. §Films, Music, Restaurants in Northampton, Books, Magazines. Ads: $75/$50/$25/$15. Subjects: Absurdist, Advertising, Self-Promotion, Aromatherapy, Avant-Garde, Experimental Art, Beat, Book Reviewing, Lewis Carroll, Cartoons, Experimental, Fiction, Horror, Humor, Post Modern, Sex, Sexuality, Short Stories.

MEAT: A Journal of Writing and Materiality, Jacqueline Rhodes, Co-Editor; Jonathan Alexander, Co-Editor; Brian Bailie, Associate Editor, http://www.meatjournal.com. 2004. Poetry, fiction, articles, art, photos, cartoons, interviews, satire, criticism, reviews, music, letters, long-poems, collages, plays, concrete art, non-fiction. "In the rush toward digital space, what often gets left behind is the meat, the flesh, the working/breathing/paying-bills bodies that write.All of the folks responsible for the MeatJournal idea, have been (or still are) serious cyber-junkies, but all of us also worry that there's never enough critical attention to writing bodies, as those bodies are variously constructed/viewed/ interpreted/performed. The journal focuses less on high theory and practice and more on the people doing it. In each issue, we run a critical feature focusing on writers of various stripes and how they view their respective fields construction of their own body (flesh and body of work); think- (and feel-) pieces on new trends and possible consequences of those trends in writing; authors personal stories of how lack of money, time, and access have affected their own working theories and practices; poetry, prose, and digital performance art; and occasional rants and raves from different points on the political spectrum. Recent contributors: Erika Lpez, Ellen M. Gil-Gmez, Brian Bailie, Christi Rucker, Barclay Barrios, John Garcia." circ. 500. 4/yr. Pub'd 1 issue 2005; expects 2 issues 2006, 3 issues 2007. sub. price $0; per copy $0; sample Free. Back issues: inquire. Discounts: Online journal—it's all free! 25pp. Reporting time: 4 weeks. Simultaneous submissions accepted: No. Publishes 20% of manuscripts submitted. Copyrighted, reverts to author. Pub's reviews: approx. 2 in 2005. Subjects: Abstracts, African-American, Bisexual, Counter-Culture, Alternatives, Communes, Criticism, Essays, Experimental, Games, Gender Issues, Graphics, Philosophy, Politics, Post Modern, Reviews, Sex, Sexuality.

MEDIA SPOTLIGHT, Albert James Dager, Editor & Publisher, Po Box 290, Redmond, WA 98073. 1977. Articles, art, photos, cartoons, interviews, criticism, reviews, music, letters, news items, non-fiction. "Any unsolicited submissions might not be returned!" circ. 3M. 4/yr. Pub'd 4 issues 2005; expects 4 issues 2006, 4 issues 2007. sub. price any tax-deductible donation, preferably at least $25; per copy any tax-deductible donation; sample any tax-deductible donation. Back issues: for those available (some only by photocopy), any tax-deductible donation. 20pp. Reporting time: 4 weeks to 4 months. Simultaneous submissions accepted: no. Payment: copies. Copyrighted, reverts to author. Pub's reviews: 5 in 2005. §Media, Culture, Christian Lifestyle, Biblical analysis of media. Subjects: Arts, Christianity, Communication, Journalism, Culture, Electronics, Entertainment, Games, Literature (General), Magazines, Religion, Spiritual, Theatre, Visual Arts.

MEDICAL HISTORY, Wellcome Institute for the History of Medicine, Caroline Tonson-Rye, Welcome Trust Centre for the History of Medicine at UCL, 210 Euston Road, London NW1 2BE, England, +44 (0)20 7679 8107, fax +44 (0)20 7679 8194. 1957. Articles, reviews, news items. circ. 900. 4/yr. Pub'd 4 issues 2005; expects 4 issues 2006. sub. price individuals worldwide £34/$54.50 USA, institutions (worldwide) £69, $107 USA; per copy £12. Back issues: £9 if available. 120pp. Reporting time: 3-4 months. Simultaneous submissions accepted: no. Publishes 35% of manuscripts submitted. Payment: none. Copyright The Trustee, The Wellcome Trust. Pub's reviews: 92 in 2005. §All aspects of history of medicine and allied sciences. Ads: £540/£370/£240. Subjects: Alternative Medicine, Disease, Health, History, Medicine, Nursing, Society.

Medi-Ed Press, Sherlyn Hogenson, Director, 523 Hunter Boulevard, Lansing, MI 48910, 800-500-8205, fax 517-882-0554. Medi.EdPress@verizon.net; www.Medi-EdPress.com. 1986. avg. press run 3M. Pub'd 2 titles 2005; expects 2 titles 2006. Discounts: bookstores and wholesalers 1-4 copies 20%, 5-9 30%, 10-49 40%, 50+ 50%. 350pp. Simultaneous submissions accepted: no. Publishes 20% of manuscripts submitted. Subjects: Medicine, Music, Science.

Medusa Press, PO Box 458, San Carlos, CA 94070, info@medusapress.net, www.medusapress.nes. 1998. Fiction. "Currently, we are not accepting submissions, but are expected to by late 2004." avg. press run 1,000. Expects 1 title 2006, 2-3 titles 2007. 350pp. Simultaneous submissions accepted: no. Copyrights for author. Subjects: Horror, Supernatural.

MEDUSA'S HAIRDO, Beverly Moore, 2631 Seminole Avenue, Ashland, KY 41102, 606-325-7203, medusashairdo@yahoo.com. 1995. Poetry, fiction, art. "'The magazine of modern mythology.' 4000 word limit." circ. 50. 2/yr. Pub'd 2 issues 2005; expects 2 issues 2006, 2 issues 2007. sub. price $8.70; per copy $4.50; sample $4.50. Back issues: $4/copy for issues 1 & 3. Discounts: 2-5 copies $4.35 each, 6-9 $4.15 each, 10+ $4 each. 16-24pp. Reporting time: 4 weeks. Accepts simultaneous submissions if so noted. Publishes 2% of manuscripts submitted. Payment: 1 copy. Copyrighted, reverts to author. Ads: by arrangement. Subjects: Literature (General), Myth, Mythology, Poetry.

Mehring Books, Inc., PO Box 48377, Oak Park, MI 48237-5977, 248-967-2924, 248-967-3023, sales@mehring.com. News items, non-fiction. "Mehring Books, Inc. publishes 2-5 books and 5-10 pamphlets a year." Expects 3 titles 2006, 3 titles 2007. Discounts: trade 40%, library 20%, minimum order for discounts 5 titles/copies. Subjects: Anthropology, Archaelogy, Arts, Communism, Marxism, Leninism, Culture, History, Labor, Literary Review, Politics, Russia, Socialist, Third World, Minorities, U.S.S.R., Worker.

Mellen Poetry Press (see also The Edwin Mellen Press), Herbert Richardson, Director, PO Box 450, 415 Ridge Street, Lewiston, NY 14092-0450, 716-754-2266, Fax 716-754-4056, mellen@wzrd.com, www.mellen-press.com. 1974. Poetry, long-poems. avg. press run 200. Pub'd 34 titles 2005; expects 40 titles 2006, 45 titles 2007. Discounts: bookstore 40% pre-publication on 10+ copies, 20% post-publication. 64-72pp. Reporting time: 2-4 months. We prefer not to accept simultaneous submissions. Publishes 30-50% of manuscripts submitted. Payment: 5 free copies to the author, no royalties. We deposit 2 copies of published book with copyright office; book is listed in C.P. with Library of Congress. Subjects: Drama, Poetry, Translation.

A Melody from an Immigrant's Soul, Dora Klinova, 5712 Baltimore Dr. #461, La Mesa, CA 91942, (619) 667-0925 E-mail: dorishka1@sbcglobal.net. 2004. Poetry, photos, satire, non-fiction. "Klinova, Dora is an Award Winning Writer. The International Society of Poets awarded Dora by inscribed Silver Cup and a Medal "Poet of Merit Award". Klinova won several contests in newspapers. The theaters of San Diego, CA performed her stories. "The San Diego Union Tribune" and "The San Diego Jewish Times" published Klinova's articles many times. Also her stories were published in New York. The appearance of the book "A Melody from an Immigrant's Soul", written by Dora Klinova, a Russian-Jewish Immigrant, who recently came to America almost without any English, is an outstanding event. All readers who are interested in life itself, regardless of age, will be surprisingly pleased." avg. press run 500. Pub'd 1 title 2005; expects 1 title 2006, 1-2 titles 2007. Discounts: 2-10 copies 25%. 310pp. Reporting time: 2-3 weeks is enough for reprintng. Payment: payment by check or money order. Copyrights for author. Subjects: Cooking, Hawaii, Immigration, Inspirational, Nature, Parenting, Poetry, Sex, Sexuality, Short Stories, Spiritual, Tarot, U.S.S.R., World War II, Writers/Writing.

Menard Press, Anthony Rudolf, 8 The Oaks, Woodside Avenue, London N12 8AR, England. 1969. Poetry. "No new manuscripts can be considered for time being. Nuclear politics, poetry, poetics, translated poetry. The press's poetry books are distributed in the USA by Small Press Distribution Inc., Berkeley CA." avg. press run 1.5M. Expects 5 titles 2007. Discounts: usual. Poetry 56pp, politics 24pp. Subjects: Anthropology, Archaelogy, Criticism, Literature (General), Poetry, Politics, Translation.

Menasha Ridge Press, Russell Helms, Acquisitions Editor, 2204 1st Ave. S. #102, Birmingham, AL 35233-2331, 205-322-0439, rhelms@menasharidge.com. 1982. Non-fiction. avg. press run 5M. Pub'd 23 titles 2005; expects 18 titles 2006, 28 titles 2007. Discounts: per catalogue. 200+pp. Reporting time: 90 days. Simultaneous submissions accepted: yes. Publishes 2-5% of manuscripts submitted. Payment: 10% royalty based on net. Copyrights for author. Subjects: Bicycling, Reference, Sports, Outdoors, Travel.

Mercer University Press, Marc Jolley, Director, 1400 Coleman Ave., Macon, GA 31207, (478) 301-2880, (478) 301-2585 fax. 1979. Fiction, art, criticism, letters, non-fiction. Pub'd 40 titles 2005; expects 40 titles 2006, 40 titles 2007. Discounts: Retail (returnable) - short - 30% / trade - 40% Retail(nonreturnable)- short - 40% Retail(nonreturnable)-trade - 45% 1-99 /50% 100+. 300pp. Subjects: African Literature, Africa, African Studies, African-American, Biography, Civil War, Culture, History, Immigration, Memoirs, Multicultural, Philosophy, Political Science, Politics, Religion, Mark Twain, War.

Meridien PressWorks, Lydia Powell, Editor, J. Powell, PO Box 640024, San Francisco, CA 94164, 415-928-8904. 1996. Poetry, fiction, art, photos, non-fiction. "Poets and writers in California primarily. No unsolicited manuscripts." avg. press run 200-500. Pub'd 4 titles 2005; expects 3 titles 2006, 3 titles 2007. Discounts: mailing costs waived for bookstores. 40-100pp. Reporting time: 90 days. Simultaneous submissions accepted: yes. Publishes 10% of manuscripts submitted. Payment: all profits to authors. Copyrights for author. Subjects: Arts, Fiction, Photography, Poetry.

The Merion Press, Inc., PO Box 144, Merion Station, PA 19066-0144, 610-617-8919, Fax 610-617-8929, rjstern@merionpress.com, www.merionpress.com. 2001. Fiction. "We publish out-of-print, classic British detective stories." avg. press run 250. Pub'd 1 title 2005; expects 1 title 2006, 1 title 2007. 240pp. Does not copyright for author. Subject: Mystery.

Merkos Publications, Yechiel Goldberg, Editor, 291 Kingston Ave., Brooklyn, NY 11213, 718-778-0226, fax:

718-778-4148, email: orders@kehotonline.com.

•**Merl Publications,** Cuauhtemoc Gallegos, 1658 N Milwaukee Ave # 242, Chicago, IL 60647, (708)445 8385 contact@merlpublications.com www.merlpublications.com. 1995. Non-fiction. "Publisher of Bilingual Legal dictionaries and glossaries." avg. press run 1000. Expects 2 titles 2006, 4 titles 2007. Discounts: 20%Bookstores25%-40%Distributors40%-50%Wholesalers. Subjects: Bilingual, Language, Latino, Law, Non-Fiction.

Merrimack Books, Wayne Edwards, PO Box 231229, Anchorage, AK 99523-1229, we21011@earthlink.net. 1989. avg. press run 1M+. Expects 2 titles 2007. Discounts: 1-9 30%, 10-49 40%, 50 + 50%. 200-300pp. Reporting time: 4 weeks. Simultaneous submissions accepted: no. Publishes .01% of manuscripts submitted. Payment: varies. Does not copyright for author. Subjects: Fantasy, Fiction, Horror, Literature (General), Poetry.

Merwood Books, Heather Dunne, 237 Merwood Lane, Ardmore, PA 19003, 215-947-3934, Fax 215-947-4229. 1997. Poetry, fiction, music. "Contemporary fiction and poetry with literary bent." avg. press run 1M. Pub'd 1 title 2005; expects 2 titles 2006, 2 titles 2007. Discounts: negotiable. 250-375pp. Reporting time: 3-6 months. Simultaneous submissions accepted: yes. Publishes 10% of manuscripts submitted. Payment: negotiable. Does not copyright for author. Subjects: Fiction, Music, Poetry.

The Message Company (see also BUSINESS SPIRIT JOURNAL), James Berry, 4 Camino Azul, Santa Fe, NM 87508, 505-474-0998, Fax 505-471-2584. 1994. Non-fiction. "We publish full length perfect bound books, videos, and audio tapes." avg. press run 3M. Pub'd 4 titles 2005; expects 8 titles 2006, 1 title 2007. Discounts: Stop 20% + free shipping, bookstores/resellers 50% + free shipping, distributors 55% + free shipping. 200pp. Reporting time: 30-60 days. Simultaneous submissions accepted: yes. Publishes 1% of manuscripts submitted. Payment: 5-8%. Copyrights for author. Subjects: Energy, Science.

Metacom Press, William Ferguson, Nancy Ferguson, 1 Tahanto Road, Worcester, MA 01602-2523, 508-757-1683. 1980. Poetry, fiction. "Booklets have ranged from 16 to 28 pages. Titles so far are by John Updike, William Heyen, Ann Beattie, James Tate, James Wright, Diane Wakoski, Raymond Carver, James Merrill, John McPhee, Edward Gorey. All titles to date have been published in a limited-edition format, using imported papers and hand-binding. Our intention is to establish ourselves financially with the limited editions and then to move to a more democratic, less exclusive type of publication. No unsolicited manuscripts." avg. press run 150-300. Discounts: 30% to dealers, 10% to libraries. 20pp. Payment: 10% of list value of the edition. Copyrights for author. Subjects: Fiction, Poetry.

METAL CURSE, Ray Miller, PO Box 302, Elkhart, IN 46515-0302, email: cursed@sbinet.com. 1989. Fiction, articles, art, photos, cartoons, interviews, reviews, music, letters, news items. "Mostly reviews of Underground bands (all types), and interviews. Plus anti-censorship news, and other free-thought stuff. Biases, none that I know of, except for mainstream life." circ. 5M. 2/yr. Pub'd 2 issues 2005; expects 3 issues 2006, 4 issues 2007. price per copy $5; sample $5. Back issues: Sold out of 1-7, #8, #9 $3 each, #10, #11 $5 each. Discounts: Trades possible. Write first. Wholesale: 10-25 copies - $3 each, 26-50 copies - $2.75, 51-100 copies - $2.50, 100+ copies - $2 each. 52pp. Reporting time: 1 month. Simultaneous submissions accepted: yes. Payment: copy of issue with contribution. Not copyrighted. Pub's reviews: 60 in 2005. §Music, poetry, anti-censorship movements, almost anything out of the ordinary. Ads: $300/$180/$110 1/4 page. Subjects: Advertising, Self-Promotion, Arts, Avant-Garde, Experimental Art, Creativity, Criticism, Dreams, Drugs, Electronics, Entertainment, Human Rights, Humanism, Humor, Interviews, H.P. Lovecraft, Magazines.

Metallo House Publishers, Helene Andorre Hinson Staley, 170 E. River Road, Moncure, NC 27559-9617, 919-542-2908, Fax 919-774-5611. 1997. avg. press run 1M. Pub'd 1 title 2005. Discounts: available to libraries, bookstores, and direct from the publisher. 224pp. Reporting time: 2-3 months. Simultaneous submissions accepted: yes. Copyrights for author. Subjects: Law, Parenting, Sexual Abuse.

MeteoritePress.com, Russell Blackstone, Acquisitions Editor, 1730 New Brighton Blvd. #104-271, NE Minneapolis, MN 55413, meteoritepress@aol.com, www.meteoritepress.com. 2001. Art, satire, non-fiction. "Please send SASE with letter of inquiry only." avg. press run 2.5M. Expects 3 titles 2006, 3+ titles 2007. 144pp. Reporting time: 3 weeks. Simultaneous submissions accepted: yes. Does not copyright for author. Subjects: Counter-Culture, Alternatives, Communes, Humor, Non-Fiction, Satire.

METROPOLITAN FORUM, Thomasina, PO Box 582165, Minneapolis, MN 55458, 612-328-4177, info@metropolitanforum.com, www.metropolitanforum.com. 1977. Poetry, fiction, articles, art, photos, cartoons, interviews, satire, criticism, reviews, music, letters, news items, non-fiction. "Adult oriented weekly press looking for contributors. Articles can be about any adult subject. Open to all forms." circ. 6M. 52/yr. Pub'd 52 issues 2005; expects 52 issues 2006, 52 issues 2007. price per copy Free; sample $1.00 Postage. 12pp. Reporting time: 4 weeks. Simultaneous submissions accepted: yes. Publishes 95% of manuscripts submitted. Payment: free copies. Not copyrighted. §Adult Business, Sex Industry, Strip Clubs. Ads: Display Ads starting at $50/week. Full Page = $500/week. Subjects: Advertising, Self-Promotion, AIDS, Alcohol, Alcoholism, Arts,

Bisexual, Erotica, Fantasy, Gay, Gender Issues, Humor, Lesbianism, Marriage, Poetry, Sex, Sexuality, Women.

MEXICAN STUDIES/ESTUDIOS MEXICANOS, University of California Press, Jaime E. Rodriguez, Editor; Carla Duke, Editorial Assistant, University of California Press, 2000 Center Street, Suite 303, Berkeley, CA 94704-1223, 510-643-7154. 1985. Non-fiction. "Editorial address: 240 Krieger Hall, Univ. of CA, Irvine, CA 92697-3275." circ. 1350. 2/yr. Pub'd 2 issues 2005; expects 2 issues 2006, 2 issues 2007. sub. price $30 indiv., $107 instit., $18 students (+ $15 air freight); per copy $24 indiv. $55 instit., $24 students (+ $15 air freight); sample free. Back issues: $24 indiv.; $55 instit., $24 student (+ $15 air freight). Discounts: foreign subs. agent 10%, one-time orders 10+ 30%, standing orders (bookstores): 1-99 40%, 100+ 50%. 208pp. Copyrighted, does not revert to author. Ads: $295/$220. Subjects: Chicano/a, Political Science.

MGW (Mom Guess What) Newsmagazine, Jeffry Davis, Executive Publisher, 1123 21st St., Suite 200, Sacramento, CA 95814-4225, 916-441-6397, fax:916-441-6422, info@mgwnews.com, www.mgwnews.com. 1978. Poetry, articles, art, photos, cartoons, interviews, satire, criticism, reviews, music, letters, plays, news items. circ. 15,000 Bi-Monthly. 24/yr. Pub'd 24 issues 2005; expects 24 issues 2006, 24 issues 2007. sub. price $30; per copy Free; sample Free. Back issues: $1. Discounts: 5-25%. 32pp. Reporting time: 1 week. Simultaneous submissions accepted: yes. Publishes 25% of manuscripts submitted. Payment varies on submission type and length. Copyrighted, does not revert to author. Pub's reviews: 60 in 2005. §Politics, gay & human rights, civil rights, music, fiction, non-fiction, childrens issues. Ads: Full Page - $1400, Half Page - $700, Quarter - $350, Eighth - $175. Subjects: Anarchist, Arts, Book Reviewing, Children, Youth, Civil Rights, Community, Computers, Calculators, Crafts, Hobbies, Gay, Lesbianism, Movies, Music, Sex, Sexuality, Social Work, Sports, Outdoors.

Mho & Mho Works, Lolita Lark, Editor, Box 16719, San Diego, CA 92176, 619-280-3488. 1969. Non-fiction. "We do books on communications arts, on occult sexual practices, and family therapy. We are also interested in material having to do with the physically handicapped (one title was *The Cripple Liberation Front Marching Band Blues*)—not the usual miracle-cure , but real and honest essays and book-length reports on the affect and effect of being physically handicapped in a Pepsi Generation World. Most of our books are of normal length. We require that any submissions be accompanied by self addressed stamped envelope—otherwise, the manuscripts will go into our scratch paper file. We wouldn't discourage any submissions, but they must be honest and direct." avg. press run 5M-10M. Pub'd 3 titles 2005; expects 3 titles 2006, 3 titles 2007. Discounts: 40% to bookstores; 20% to libraries. 200-400pp. Reporting time: 6 weeks. Payment: we pay ourselves back for cost of publication out of earliest proceeds; then, we split 50/50 with author. Copyrights for author. Subjects: Disabled, Gay, Media, New Age.

Miami University Press, Keith Tuma, Editor, English Dept., Miami University, Oxford, OH 45056, 513-529-5221, Fax 513-529-1392, E-mail tumakw@muohio.edu. 1992. Poetry, fiction. "Miami University Press has begun a second series featuring collections of short fiction and books of poetry. The first book of stories is Marianne Villanueva's *Mayor of the Roses*, edited by Brian Roley, and the first book of poems, edited by Keith Tuma, will be an anthology of poems (and essays) from the Diversity in African American Poetry Festival of fall 2003: *"Bessie, Bop, or Bach": An Anthology of Poems and Essays from the Diversity in African American Poetry Festival*. The new series will emphasize multicultural and international writers, among others. Editorship will rotate among members of the creative writing faculty at Miami University." avg. press run 1M. Expects 2 titles 2006, 2 titles 2007. Discounts: 20% short, 40% full. 140pp. Reporting time: 3 months. Simultaneous submissions accepted: yes. Publishes 1% of manuscripts submitted. Payment: 10%. Copyrights for author. Subjects: African-American, Asian-American, Experimental, Fiction, Ireland, Latino, Native American, Poetry.

Mica Press - Paying Our Dues Productions, J.W. Grant; John F. Eastman, Fiction Editor; Chuck Miller, Poetry Editor, 1508 Crescent Road, Lawrence, KS 66044-3120, Only contact by E-mail jgrant@bookzen.com; website www.bookzen.com. 1990. Poetry, cartoons, reviews, non-fiction. "Do not submit manuscripts. Submit description only. As a service to small press authors and publishers we provide free space on our website (www.bookzen.com) to display books." avg. press run 2M. Pub'd 1 title 2005; expects 2 titles 2006, 2 titles 2007. 250-640pp. Payment: yes. Copyrights for author. Subjects: Cartoons, Jack Kerouac, Non-Fiction, Poetry, Reviews.

Micah Publications Inc., Robert Kalechofsky, Roberta Kalechofsky, 255 Humphrey Street, Marblehead, MA 01945, 617-631-7601. 1975. Fiction, articles, criticism. "Micah Publications publishes prose: scholarly, fictional, lyrical; a prose that addresses itself to issues without offending esthetic sensibilities, a prose that is aware of the esthetics of language without succumbing to esthetic solipsism. Three books a year. No unsolicited mss. Author must submit camera-ready copy of text - we'll do designs and illustrations. Author must also be involved in publicity." avg. press run 400. Pub'd 2 titles 2005; expects 4 titles 2006, 2-3 titles 2007. Discounts: 2-5 20%, 6-9 30%, 10-49 40%, 50+ 50%. 280pp. Reporting time: 3 months. Simultaneous submissions accepted: yes. Publishes 5% of manuscripts submitted. Payment: 10% to authors after primary expenses of printing and advertising is met from sale of books. Copyrights for author. Subjects: Animals, Fiction, Judaism,

Vegetarianism.

MICHIGAN FEMINIST STUDIES, 1122 Lane Hall, Univ. of Michigan, 204 South State Street, Ann Arbor, MI 48109-1290, 734-761-4386, Fax 734-647-4943, e-mail mfseditors@umich.edu. 1978. Poetry, articles, art, photos, cartoons, interviews, reviews, news items. "A journal produced in conjunction with the Women's Studies Program at the University of Michigan." circ. 250. 1/yr. Pub'd 1 issue 2005; expects 1 issue 2006, 1 issue 2007. sub. price $25 institutions, $10 individuals; per copy same; sample same. Back issues: $75 for full print run (1987-present). 150pp. Reporting time: 2 months. Simultaneous submissions accepted: yes. Publishes 10% of manuscripts submitted. Payment: none. Copyrighted, reverts to author. Pub's reviews: none in 2005. §Current feminist scholarship. Ads: ad exchange. Subject: Feminism.

MICHIGAN QUARTERLY REVIEW, Laurence Goldstein, 3574 Rackham, University of Michigan, 915 E. Washington St., Ann Arbor, MI 48109-1070, 734-764-9265. 1962. Poetry, fiction, articles, art, interviews, criticism, reviews, letters, parts-of-novels, long-poems. "We are not solely a literary magazine. In addition to poetry, fiction, and reviews, we include essays on a variety of topics in the humanities, arts & sciences. Writers are advised to refer to a sample back issue before submitting." circ. 1.8M. 4/yr. Pub'd 4 issues 2005; expects 4 issues 2006, 4 issues 2007. sub. price $25; per copy $7; sample $4. Back issues: $4 for regular issues, cover price for special issues. Discounts: agency rates - $30 for institution subscription; 15% for agent. 160pp. Reporting time: 6 weeks. Simultaneous submissions accepted: no. Publishes 1-2% of manuscripts submitted. Payment: $10/page of poetry, $10/page essays. Copyrighted, reverts to author. Pub's reviews: 14 in 2005. §Humanities, sciences, arts, literature. Ads: $100/$50. Subjects: Literary Review, Literature (General).

Michigan State University Press (see also FOURTH GENRE: EXPLORATIONS IN NONFICTION), 1405 S. Harrison Road, #25, East Lansing, MI 48823-5202, 517-355-9543; fax 517-432-2611; E-mail msp07@msu.edu.

Microdex Bookshelf, Chris Brozek, Christopher Fara, 1212 N. Sawtelle, Suite 120, Tucson, AZ 85716, 520-326-3502. 1989. Non-fiction. "Microdex Bookshelf specializes in creating common-sense manuals, tutorials and reference books for computer users. Absolutely no tech-jargon, but no condescending either; concise; don't belabor the obvious, yet include all details. Unsolicited manuscripts not accepted; inquire by letter, include SASE." avg. press run 500-5M. Expects 2 titles 2006, 2 titles 2007. Discounts: retail 40%, bulk 50-55%, libraries, teachers and S.C.O.P. 25%. 150pp. Reporting time: 30 days, include SASE, no returns unless prepaid. Payment: negotiable but typical 10% of list price. Copyrights negotiable. Subjects: Computers, Calculators, How-To, Non-Fiction, Reference, Textbooks.

MICROWAVE NEWS, Louis Slesin, PO Box 1799, Grand Central Station, New York, NY 10163, 212-517-2800. 1981. Articles, reviews, letters, news items. "A bimonthly report on non-ionizing radiation (from such sources as cellular phones, power lines, radar microwave transmitters, radio transmitters, VDTs etc.). Including the latest research, legislation, litigation, regulations." circ. 1M. Pub'd 3 issues 2005. sub. price $350; per copy $60; sample $10. Back issues: $100 a calendar year; bound volumes available. Discounts: by arrangement with publisher. 20pp. Copyrighted, does not revert to author. Pub's reviews: 25-30 in 2005. §Non-ionizing radiation, epidemiology, medical application. Ads: $2000/$1450-1150/$700 1/4 page/$425 1/8/$275 1/16.

MID-AMERICAN REVIEW, Karen Craigo, Editor-in-Chief and Poetry Editor; Michael Czyzniejewski, Editor-in-Chief; Karen Babine, Associate Editor and Nonfiction Editor; George Looney, Translations Editor; Ashley Kaine, Fiction Editor; Erik E. Eskilsen, Reviews Editor, Dept of English, Bowling Green State University, Bowling Green, OH 43403-0191, 419-372-2725, www.bgsu.edu/midamericanreview. 1980. Poetry, fiction, articles, criticism, reviews, parts-of-novels, long-poems, non-fiction. "Recent Contributors: Billy Collins, Ai, Sydney Lea, David Kirby, Lee Ann Roripaugh, Robin Becker, Joe Meno, Michelle Richmond,." circ. 2,200. 2/yr. Pub'd 2 issues 2005; expects 2 issues 2006, 2 issues 2007. sub. price $14; per copy $9; sample $5. Back issues: $10 for rare issues. Discounts: 20%/40%. 208pp. Reporting time: 1-4 months. Simultaneous submissions accepted: Yes, but please withdraw IMMEDIATELY if accepted elsewhere. Publishes 1% of manuscripts submitted. Payment: $10 per page up to $50 (when funding permits). Copyrighted, reverts to author. Pub's reviews: 24 in 2005. §Fiction, poetry, nonfiction, and criticism of contemporary literature. Ads: $85/$45/will exchange. Subjects: Book Reviewing, Criticism, Essays, Fiction, Literary Review, Literature (General), Non-Fiction, Ohio, Poetry, Prose, Reviews, Short Stories, Translation.

The Middle Atlantic Press, Blake Koen, Publisher, 10 Twosome Drive, Box 600, Moorestown, NJ 08057, 856-235-4444, orders 800-257-8481, fax 800-225-3840. 1968. "We are a trade book and educational materials publisher. Our material is oriented to the Middle Atlantic region, but all of our books are sold nation-wide. We accept unsolicited submissions with SASE." avg. press run varies. Pub'd 2 titles 2005; expects 4 titles 2006, 4-6 titles 2007. Pages vary with title. Reporting time: 1-2 months. Simultaneous submissions accepted: yes. Payment: 8% royalty on hardcover books, 5% + 10% on paperbacks to author, paid annually. Copyrights for author. Subjects: Folklore, Native American.

295

Middle Passage Press, Barbara Bramwell, 5517 Secrest Drive, Los Angeles, CA 90043, 213-298-0266. 1986. Non-fiction. avg. press run 5M. Pub'd 2 titles 2005; expects 2 titles 2006, 3 titles 2007. Discounts: 10-25%. 200pp. Reporting time: 3 months. Simultaneous submissions accepted: yes. Publishes 1% of manuscripts submitted. Payment: 10% retail, yes advances. Copyrights for author. Subject: Black.

Middlebury College Publications (see also NEW ENGLAND REVIEW), Stephen Donadio, Editor, Middlebury College, Middlebury, VT 05753, 802-443-5075, Fax 802-443-2088, E-mail nereview@middlebury.edu. 1978. Poetry, fiction, articles, interviews, criticism, reviews, parts-of-novels, long-poems. "Fiction, poetry, essays and reviews of the highest quality." avg. press run 2M. Pub'd 4 titles 2005; expects 4 titles 2006, 4 titles 2007. Discounts: 25% classroom. 184pp. Reporting time: 12 weeks. Simultaneous submissions accepted, if indicated. Payment: competitive. Does not copyright for author. Subjects: Literary Review, Literature (General).

Middleway Press, David McNeill, Managing Editor; Jason Henninger, Asst Book Editor, 606 Wilshire Boulevard, Attention: Mwende May, Marketing Associate, Santa Monica, CA 90401-1502, (310) 309-3208 ofc, (310) 260-8910 fax, middlewaypress@sgi-usa.org, www.middlewaypress.com. 2000. Non-fiction. "Religions—Nichiren Buddhist publisher. No unsolicited manuscripts." avg. press run 5M. Pub'd 3 titles 2005; expects 3 titles 2006, 3 titles 2007. Discounts: via Independent Publishers Group. 250pp. Reporting time: 2 months. Subjects: Buddhism, Culture, Education, Inspirational, Peace, Self-Help.

The Midknight Club, Faith Ann Hotchkin, Editor-in-Chief; Michael Szul, Submissions Assistant, PO Box 25, Browns Mills, NJ 08015, info@midknightclub.net, www.midknightclub.net. 1999. Fiction, non-fiction. "Recently published (Jan. 2000) *Out the In Door: New Technique in Lucid Dreaming.*" avg. press run 2M. Expects 7 titles 2006, 3 titles 2007. Discounts: volume discount plateau for trade. Reporting time: 3 months. Simultaneous submissions accepted: yes. Payment: 10% net. Copyrights for author. Subjects: Anthology, Dreams, Fiction, Folklore, Magic, Myth, Mythology, New Age, Non-Fiction, Occult, Philosophy, Religion, Science Fiction, Spiritual, Supernatural.

Mid-List Press, Lane Stiles, Publisher, 4324 12th Avenue South, Minneapolis, MN 55407-3218, 612-822-3733, Fax 612-823-8387, guide@midlist.org, www.midlist.org. 1989. Poetry, fiction, non-fiction. "Please write or visit our website for guidelines before submitting. Since 1990 we have sponsored the First Series Awards in Poetry, the Novel, Short Fiction, and Creative Nonfiction for writers who have yet to publish a book-length work in that category. Notable authors include Alfred Corn and Dr. William Nolen." avg. press run 500-2.5M. Pub'd 6 titles 2005; expects 4 titles 2006, 5 titles 2007. Discounts: wholesale 3-4 books 20%, 5-9 30%, 10-50 40%, 50+ 50%. Poetry 80pp, others 200-300pp. Reporting time: 1-6 months. Simultaneous submissions accepted: yes. Publishes less than 1% of manuscripts submitted. Payment: by contract. Copyrights for author. Subjects: Fiction, Literature (General), Non-Fiction, Poetry, Reprints, Short Stories.

Midmarch Arts Press, Judy Seigel, Editor, 300 Riverside Drive, New York City, NY 10025, 212-666-6990. 1975. Art, photos, criticism, long-poems, non-fiction. avg. press run 2M-3M. Pub'd 4 titles 2005; expects 3 titles 2006, 3 titles 2007. Discounts: 20% for Institutional L.P, 20% for Jobber L.P. for single copies; 20% for 3-5 copies; 30% 6-9; 40% 10 and over, plus postage. 100-318pp. Reporting time: 4 weeks. Publishes 35% of manuscripts submitted. Payment: royalties to authors. Copyrights for author. Subjects: Architecture, Arts, Biography, California, Crafts, Hobbies, Drama, Electronics, New England, Photography, Poetry, Post Modern, South, Texas, Visual Arts, Women.

MIDNIGHT SHOWCASE: Romance Digest, Erotic-ahh Digest, Special Digest, Twin Souls Publications, Jewel Adams, P.O. Box 726, Lusk, WY 82225, 307-334-3165, 727-848-5962, publisher@midnightshowcase.com, http://www.midnightshowcase.com.

MIDNIGHT STREET, Immediate Direction Publications, Trevor Denyer, Editor, 7 Mountview, Church Lane West, Aldershot, Hampshire GU11 3LN, England. 2004. Poetry, fiction, articles, interviews, reviews, non-fiction. "MS publishes horror, dark fantasy, science fiction and slipstream stories. It is currently open to submissions. Not accepting poetry at this time. MS is 52 pages, A4, stapled with full colour cover. Full details, including prices and writer guidelines, can be found on the website: www.midnightstreet.co.uk." 3/yr. 52pp. Reporting time: 3 months average. Simultaneous submissions accepted: No. Publishes 2% of manuscripts submitted. Payment: £2.50 per 1,000 words + contributor's copy. Poetry, illustrations and interviews are different. Check: www.midnightstreet.co.uk. Copyrighted, reverts to author. Pub's reviews: 3 in 2005. §Fiction, short stories.

MIDWEST ART FAIRS, James W. Schiller, Publisher, PO Box 72, Pepin, WI 54759, 715-442-2022. 1990. "Bi-annual listing of art fairs and craft festivals with listings of organizations, businesses, services, suppliers." circ. 7.5M. 2/yr. Pub'd 2 issues 2005; expects 2 issues 2006, 2 issues 2007. sub. price $15.95; per copy $10.95; sample $10.95. Back issues: $10.95. 120pp. Reporting time: 4 weeks. Payment: none. Copyrighted, reverts to author. Ads: $575/$285. Subjects: Arts, Crafts, Hobbies, Iowa, Jewelry, Gems, Minnesota, Quilting, Sewing, Wisconsin.

MIDWEST POETRY REVIEW, Pariksith Singh, 7443 Oak Tree Lane, Spring Hill, FL 34607-2324. 1980. Poetry. circ. 246. 4/yr. Pub'd 4 issues 2005; expects 4 issues 2006, 4 issues 2007. sub. price $20; per copy $5; sample $6. Back issues: $6 (when available). 40pp. Reporting time: 4-6 weeks. Simultaneous submissions accepted: no. Publishes 10%-15% of manuscripts submitted. Payment: $5 to $20; contests $25 to $500. Copyrighted, reverts to author. Pub's reviews. §Poetry, literature. Ads: $100 full page. Subject: Poetry.

THE MIDWEST QUARTERLY, James B.M. Schick, Editor; Stephen Meats, Poetry; Tim Bailey, Book Reviews, Pittsburg State University, History Department, Pittsburg, KS 66762, 620-235-4369. 1959. Poetry, articles, interviews, criticism, reviews, non-fiction. "Scholarly articles on history, literature, the social sciences (especially political), art, music, the natural sciences (in non-technical language). Most articles run 4M to 5M words. Can use a brief note of 1M to 2M words once in a while. Chief bias is an aversion to jargon and pedantry. Instead of footnotes we use a minimum of parenthetical documentation. Reviews and interviews are assigned. Contributors: Walter McDonald, Jeanne Murray Walker, Lyn Lifshin, Charles Bukowski, William Kloefkorn, among others, have been represented in our pages. Will consider all poems submitted." circ. 1M. 4/yr. Pub'd 4 issues 2005; expects 4 issues 2006. sub. price $15 within U.S., otherwise $20; per copy $5; sample $5. Back issues: $5. Discounts: 10% to agencies. 110pp. Reporting time: 3-6 months. Simultaneous submissions accepted: no. Publishes 15% of manuscripts submitted. Payment: copies only, varies 3 usually. Copyrighted, reverts to author. Pub's reviews: 12 in 2005. §Poetry, non-fiction. No ads. Subjects: Criticism, History, Literary Review, Poetry, Society.

Midwest Villages & Voices, Gayla Ellis, PO Box 40214, St. Paul, MN 55104, 612-822-6878 or e-mail: midwestvillages@yahoo.com (e-mail preferred). 1981. "We are a publishing group and cultural organization for Midwestern writers and visual artists. Submission by invitation only. Unsolicited submissions not returned." Discounts: 40% for bookstores; 50% for nonprofits. Subjects: Literature (General), Poetry.

Midwestern Writers Publishing House, PO Box 8, Fairwater, WI 53931.

MIDWIFERY TODAY, Midwifery Today, Jan Tritten, Editor-in-Chief, Box 2672, Eugene, OR 97402, 541-344-7438. 1985. "Birth information for midwives, childbirth educators and interested consumers. Photos, experiences, technical and non-technical articles." circ. 3M. 4/yr. Pub'd 4 issues 2005; expects 4 issues 2006, 4 issues 2007. sub. price $50; per copy $12.50; sample $12.50. Back issues: $10. 72pp. Reporting time: 6 weeks. Simultaneous submissions accepted: no. Payment: subscription. Copyrighted, reverts to author. Pub's reviews: 25 in 2005. §Midwifery, pregnancy, birth, childbirth education, breastfeeding. Ads: $700/$1.25 per word classified, 10-word minimum. Subject: Medicine.

Midwifery Today (see also BIRTHKIT NEWSLETTER; MIDWIFERY TODAY), Jan Tritten, Editor-in-Chief; Cheryl K. Smith, Managing Editor, PO Box 2672, Eugene, OR 97402, 541-344-7438; Fax 541-344-1422; editorial@midwiferytoday.com, www.midwiferytoday.com. 1986. Poetry, articles, interviews, letters, non-fiction. "Two books per year on the subject of midwifery which include articles on specialized topics such as shoulder dystocia, hemorrhage, normal birth. Query us first." avg. press run 1.5M. Pub'd 2 titles 2005; expects 2 titles 2006, 2 titles 2007. Discounts: send for information. 150pp. Reporting time: 1-6 months. Simultaneous submissions accepted: no. Publishes 50% of manuscripts submitted. Payment: send for information. We retain copyright. Subjects: Alternative Medicine, Birth, Birth Control, Population, Health, Medicine, Nursing.

Miles & Miles, Matthew Miles, Aida Gonzalez-Miles, 3420 M Street, Eureka, CA 95503-5462. 1992. Non-fiction. avg. press run 3.2M. Expects 1 title 2006, 1 title 2007. Discounts: normal trade. 168pp. Reporting time: 8 weeks. Payment: small advance against 10% royalty. Copyrights for author. Subjects: Arts, California, Crafts, Hobbies, Criticism, English, History, Humor, Literature (General), Quilting, Sewing, Quotations.

Milk Mug Publishing, 9190 W. Olympic Blvd., Ste. 253, Beverly Hills, CA 90212, info@milkmugpublishing.com, www.thehoopsterbook.com.

Milkweed Editions, H. Emerson Blake, Editor in Chief; Ben Barnhart, Assistant Editor, 1011 Washington Ave. S., Ste. 300, Minneapolis, MN 55415, 612-332-3192, Fax 612-215-2550, www.milkweed.org. 1984. Poetry, fiction, non-fiction. "Milkweed Editions publishes in each of its genres with the intention of making a humane impact on society. Please familiarize yourself with our books before submitting manuscripts or queries." avg. press run 3M-5M. Pub'd 14 titles 2005; expects 17 titles 2006, 21 titles 2007. 250pp. Reporting time: 6 months. Simultaneous submissions accepted: yes. Publishes 1% of manuscripts submitted. Payment: advance against royalties, royalties payment varies by author. Copyrights for author. Subjects: Earth, Natural History, Environment, Fiction, Literature (General), Non-Fiction, Poetry, Prose.

Mille Grazie Press, David Oliveira, 967 Clover Lane, Hanford, CA 93230-2255. 1992. Poetry. "The focus of Mille Grazie Press is to publish the fine poets who live and work along California's Central Coast. Poets selected for publication are invited by the editors to submit manuscripts. No unsolicited manuscripts will be considered. The primary consideration for selection is the skillful use of language and strong vision of the poet.

Mille Grazie Press publishes perfect bound chapbooks, from 24 to 40 pages. Current offerings include work by Glenna Luschei, Wilma Elizabeth McDaniel, and Will Inman.'' avg. press run 100. Pub'd 3 titles 2005; expects 4 titles 2006, 1 title 2007. 40pp. Payment: copies. Copyrights for author. Subject: Poetry.

Millennium Vision Press, Charles C. Hagan Jr., 401 West Main St., Suite 706, Louisville, KY 40202-2937, phone 502 5892607 fax 502 5896123. 2004. Poetry, non-fiction. ''Millennium Vision Press is eagerly looking for inspirational and religious poetry submissions. We are also interested in non-ficiton works for the legal and business community:Recent contributors: NOT GUILTY EVERY TIME Keys To Courtoom Victory If I Could Only Write A Line: The Religious and Inspirational Poetry of Mary Southers.'' avg. press run 2000. Expects 4 titles 2006, 4 titles 2007. Discounts: national distributors 65% off listwholesalers 50 to 60% off listretail bookstores 45%college bookstores 25% off listlibraries 20% if requested3-199 copies -40%200-499 -50%500 and up -40%, -25%. 175-325pp. Reporting time: 30 days. Simultaneous submissions accepted: Yes. Publishes 5% of manuscripts submitted. Payment: 6 to 10% royalty on net. Copyrights for author. Subjects: African-American, Black, Civil Rights, Inspirational, Law, Motivation, Success, Poetry, Self-Help.

Millennium Workshop Production, Tina Krivorotova, 11501 Maple Ridge Road, Reston, VA 20190, 703-925-0610 phone/Fax, vkrivorotov@yahoo.com, www.george-the-dragonslayer.com, www.lifemaker.net. 2000. Fiction, art, non-fiction. ''Take a look at *On Earth*, Book One of our flagship series George the Dragonslayer and His Friends. It gives a good idea about our house. We publish only lavishly illustrated exciting books of general interest that have high educational value.'' Expects 3 titles 2006. Discounts: 10+ copies 30%, 50 units (case) 40%, 100 units (2 cases) 45%, 500 (10 cases) 50%, 1000 55%, 2000 60%. 300pp. Simultaneous submissions accepted: no. Publishes 1% of manuscripts submitted. Copyrights for author. Subjects: Fantasy, Humor, Juvenile Fiction, Picture Books.

Mills Custom Services Publishing, Vicki Mills, Owner, Editor; Richard Mills, Owner, Editor, P.O. Box 866, Rancho Mirage, CA 92270, 760-250-1897, fax 760-406-6280, vamills@aol.com, www.aonestopmall.com, www.buybookscds.com. 2003. Poetry, fiction, satire, letters, non-fiction. ''We have published self-help and instructional books on beginning use and success and enjoyment with computers. We have books in English and also have Spanish translations. With clear and basic, bold directions and illustrations, even the brand new beginning user can step into the computer age with confidence. We have four authors we are working with to produce their books by early January 2005. One is a twice published author who is having us redo her book in a smaller and different format than her first. Another is working with us to abridge her first book and create a new format. A third is having us translate her current book into Spanish, and then will follow up with a workbook in Spanish. A fourth is in an in house creation in collaboration with an out-of-state author.'' avg. press run 150. Pub'd 1 title 2005; expects 1 title 2006, 5 titles 2007. Discounts: 40%. 190pp. Reporting time: 3 business days for initial response and confirmation of receipt. Simultaneous submissions accepted: Yes. Publishes 50% of manuscripts submitted. Payment: Varies depending on the amount of collaboration necessary and contractual agreement specifications. Initial consultation is done gratis to see how we can best serve the client's needs. We can do either, depends on client's preferences. Subjects: Adoption, Biography, Communication, Journalism, Computers, Calculators, Education, Family, Fiction, Libertarian, Libraries, Literary Review, Romance.

Mind Power Publishing, Henry Kabaaga, 57 Elsinge Road, Enfield, London, EN1 4NS, England, +44(0)1992851158. 2004. Fiction, non-fiction. ''Works of encouragement (motivational) for both adults and children. Works of mystery and adventure for children (fiction), all ages. Self help. Business, promoting entrepreneurship.'' avg. press run 3000. Expects 1 title 2006, 2 titles 2007. Discounts: 10-100 copies 10%100+ copies 25%. 150pp. Reporting time: 4 weeks. Simultaneous submissions accepted: Yes. This depends on the individual's piece of work. Subjects: Business & Economics, Careers, Children, Youth, Creativity, Education, English, Ethics, Finances, Guidance, Inspirational, Leadership, Literature (General), Management, Philosophy, Self-Help.

THE MINDFULNESS BELL, Barbara Casey, Editor, 645 Sterling Street, Jacksonville, OR 97530, e-mail mindbell@internetcds.com. 1990. Poetry, articles. ''Short poems and articles on the integration of mindful awareness, social responsibility, and daily practice of mindfulness in the Buddhist tradition.'' circ. 3M. 3/yr. Pub'd 3 issues 2005; expects 3 issues 2006, 3 issues 2007. sub. price $18; per copy $6; sample $6. Back issues: $6. Discounts: not available at this time. 40pp. Reporting time: 3-4 months. Simultaneous submissions accepted: yes. Publishes 25% of manuscripts submitted. Payment: none. Not copyrighted. Subjects: Buddhism, Non-Violence, Peace, Zen.

MINESHAFT, Everett Rand, Gioia Palmieri, P. O. Box 1226, Durham, NC 27702. 1999. Poetry, fiction, articles, art, photos, cartoons, interviews, satire, criticism, reviews, letters, parts-of-novels, news items, non-fiction. ''*Mineshaft* is a small independent international art magazine or zine. It features underground comics, sketchbook drawings, letters, fiction, poetry, photos & lots more! Many of the magazine's contributors are outsiders and they speak for all of us, such as R. Crumb, who designed our logos & is a regular contributor, Kim Deitch, Frank Stack, Billy Childish, Bill Griffith, Aline Kominsky-Crumb, Andrei Codrescu, Justin Green, Simon Deitch, Spain, Carol Tyler, Robert Armstrong, and many other amazing artists. Submissions are welcome. The mag was started in 1999, is published 2 times a year, and is printed on offset press. To find out more about *Mineshaft* & what it's all about check out the website at: www.mineshaftmagazine.com.'' circ. 1,500. 2/yr. Pub'd 2 issues 2005; expects 2 issues 2006, 2 issues 2007. sub. price $17.50; per copy $6.95; sample $6.95. Back issues: Please inquire for details or check out the website. Discounts: 40% to bookstores. 60pp. Reporting time: 1 to 3 months. Simultaneous submissions accepted: yes. Payment: contributor copies. Copyrighted, reverts to author. Pub's reviews: several in 2005. Generally no paid ads. Subjects: Cartoons, Comics, Essays, Fiction, Humor, Literary Review, Non-Fiction, Photography, Poetry, Prose, Reviews, Short Stories, Travel.

MINIATURE DONKEY TALK INC, Bonnie Gross, 1338 Hughes Shop Road, Westminster, MD 21158, 410-875-0118, Fax 410-857-9145, minidonk@qis.net, www.miniaturedonkey.net. 1987. Non-fiction. circ. 5.5M. 4/yr. Pub'd 6 issues 2005; expects 4 issues 2006, 4 issues 2007. sub. price $25; per copy $5; sample $5. Back issues: $5. 70pp. Simultaneous submissions accepted: yes. Publishes 80% of manuscripts submitted. Copyrighted, reverts to author. Ads: $220/$125/$65 1/4 page. Subjects: Agriculture, Animals, Non-Fiction, Pets.

MINISTRY & LITURGY, Resource Publications, Inc., William Burns, Publisher; Denise Anderson, Editor, 160 East Virginia Street, #290, San Jose, CA 95112-5876, 408-286-8505, Fax 408-287-8748, E-mail mleditor@rpinet.com, www.rpinet.com. 1973. Poetry, fiction, articles, art, photos, cartoons, criticism, reviews, music, letters, plays, concrete art, non-fiction. ''In-house graphics and typography. Formerly entitled *Modern Liturgy.*'' circ. 16M. 10/yr. Pub'd 10 issues 2005; expects 10 issues 2006, 10 issues 2007. sub. price $50; per copy $5; sample $5. Back issues: $6. Discounts: 40% trade & bulk, 10% for prepaid agency subscriptions. 48pp. Reporting time: 6 weeks. Simultaneous submissions accepted: no. Publishes 5% of manuscripts submitted. Payment: $1 to $100. Copyrighted, does not revert to author. Pub's reviews: 187 in 2005. §Religious arts, music, religious education, worship resources, symbol, myth, ritual. Ads: $1287/$1033/$1 per word. Subjects: Architecture, Arts, Catholic, Dance, Drama, Education, Music, Non-Violence, Religion, Spiritual.

Minnesota Historical Society Press (see also MINNESOTA HISTORY), Gregory M. Britton, Director; Ann Regan, Managing Editor, 345 Kellogg Blvd. West, St. Paul, MN 55102-1906, 651-297-2221. 1849. avg. press run 2M-8M. Pub'd 24 titles 2005; expects 22 titles 2006, 22 titles 2007. Discounts: 40% 1-9 books; 45% 10+ books. Reporting time: 3 months. Payment: negotiated. Copyrights for author. Subjects: African-American, Anthropology, Archaelogy, Architecture, Autobiography, Bibliography, Biography, Dictionaries, History, Indians, Minnesota, Native American, Non-Fiction, Women.

MINNESOTA HISTORY, Minnesota Historical Society Press, Anne Kaplan, Minnesota Historical Society Press, 345 Kellogg Blvd., St. Paul, MN 55102, 1651-297-2221.

MINNESOTA LITERATURE, Diane Wilson, 3723 Glendal Terrace, Minneapolis, MN 55410-1340, mnlit@aol.com. 1973. Articles, news items. ''All material is written by editor and staff—all is news-oriented (information about Minnesota literature—publications, events, opportunities, opinions, essays by other writers).'' circ. 750. 10/yr. Pub'd 10 issues 2005; expects 10 issues 2006, 10 issues 2007. sub. price $10; sample $1. Back issues: $1 if available. Discounts: we will arrange special classroom and group rates. 8pp. Reporting time: 1-2 months. Payment: $50 for essays related to creative writing. Not copyrighted. Ads: $15 column inch (3-1/2''). Subject: Literature (General).

THE MINNESOTA REVIEW, Jeffrey J. Williams, Dept. of English, Carnegie Mellon University, Baker Hall 259, Pittsburgh, PA 15213-3890, editors@theminnesotareview.org. 1960. Poetry, fiction, articles, art, photos, cartoons, interviews, satire, criticism, reviews, letters, parts-of-novels, long-poems, collages, non-fiction. ''A journal of committed writing. We have a long tradition of publishing politically engaged work that deals with cultural politics. Our aim now is to publish the work of engaged younger critics and writers, such as Marc Bousquet, Robin Sowards, Katie Hogan, and Rita Felski in criticism; and Stefano Benni, Aimee Labrie, May Hall, and Amy Wilkinson in poetry and fiction. Many of our future issues will be organized around a special topic, such as our Fall 2004 issue on 'Smart Kids' and recent issues on 'The Legacy of Michael Sprinker' and '50s Culture.' In each issue, our aim is to present new writing that is *daring* and encroaches bounds, whether they be stylistic or conceptual. Theory's a good word here.'' circ. 1.5M. 2/yr. Pub'd 2 issues 2005; expects 2 issues 2006. sub. price $30/2yr individual, $52 institutions and/or overseas; per copy $15; sample $15. Back issues: $15. Discounts: 10%. 180-260pp. Reporting time: 1-3 months. Simultaneous submissions accepted: yes. Publishes 5% of manuscripts submitted. Payment: 2 copies. Copyrighted, reverts to author. Pub's reviews: 11 in 2005. §Poetry, fiction, very interested in Left literary & cultural criticism (feminist, marxist, poststructural, postcolonial), literary theory. Ads: $100/pg. Subjects: Feminism, Literature (General).

MIP Company, PO Box 27484, Minneapolis, MN 55427, 763-544-5915, Fax 612-871-5733, mp@mipco.com, www.mipco.com. 1984. Poetry, fiction, non-fiction. Pub'd 3 titles 2005. Discounts: 40% when 10 or more copies purchased. Simultaneous submissions accepted: yes. Copyrights for author. Subjects: Erotica, Fiction, Poetry, Russia, Sex, Sexuality, Short Stories, U.S.S.R.

Missing Man Press, Wayne Wirs, 1313 S. Military Trail, #193, Deerfield Beach, FL 33442, 954 263-5416, mmp@missingmanpress.com, http://missingmanpress.com. 2004. Photos, non-fiction. "Missing Man Press is a small, independent publishing house whose goal is to produce high quality books, greeting cards, and calendars which are centered around inspirational themes of expanded consciousness." avg. press run 3000. Expects 2 titles 2006, 4 titles 2007. Discounts: 6-299 copies: 40%, 300-499 copies: 50%, 500+ copies: 55%. 170pp. Reporting time: We are not currently accepting submissions. Subjects: Inspirational, Photography, Spiritual.

Missing Spoke Press (see also AMERICAN JONES BUILDING & MAINTENANCE), Von G. Binuia, PO Box 1314, Concord, NH 03302, 603-724-4010, Email:vonb1@excite.com. 1997. Poetry, fiction, art, photos, interviews, satire, parts-of-novels, long-poems, non-fiction. "Working class words for middle-class consumption." avg. press run 300. 125pp. Reporting time: 3-4 months. Simultaneous submissions accepted: yes. Publishes 2% of manuscripts submitted. Payment: various and copies. Copyrights for author. Subjects: Americana, Community, Conservation, Essays, Fiction, Inventing, Labor, Nebraska, New Hampshire, Poetry, Socialist, Dylan Thomas, Worker.

Mission Press, Lynda Kennedy, Kathy Wittert, PO Box 9586, Rancho Santa Fe, CA 92067, e-mail MissionPress@compuserve.com. 1998. Photos, news items, non-fiction. avg. press run 2M. Expects 3 titles 2006, 4 titles 2007. Discounts: 20-60%. 150pp. Reporting time: 60 days. Simultaneous submissions accepted: yes. Publishes 30% of manuscripts submitted. Payment: flat fee or graduated royalties. Copyrights for author. Subjects: Science, Sports, Outdoors, Technology.

MISSISSIPPI REVIEW, Frederick Barthelme, Editor; Rie Fortenberry, Managing Editor, 118 College Dr., #5144, Hattiesburg, MS 39406-0001, 601-266-5600, www.mississippireview.com. 1971. Poetry, fiction, interviews, satire, parts-of-novels, long-poems, plays. "Because we only publish 2 issues/year, we do not accept unsolicited manuscripts, except under the guidelines of the annual MR Prize: We award $1000 each in fiction and poetry; winners and finalists are published in print issue. Entry fee is $15 per entry and includes a complimentary copy of the prize issue. Deadline is October 1. Send entries to MR Prize, 118 College Dr., #5144, Hattiesburg, MS 39406. For more information e-mail contest coordinator at rief@mississippireview.com or visit our Web site, www.mississippireview.com." circ. 1.5M. 2/yr. Pub'd 2 issues 2005; expects 2 issues 2006, 2 issues 2007. sub. price $15; per copy $12; sample $8. Back issues: $8 and as offered. Discounts: none. 150-225pp. Simultaneous submissions accepted: yes. Payment: copies. Copyrighted, reverts to author. Ads: $100/$50/ Will consider trade-out. Subjects: Fiction, Poetry.

THE MISSOURI REVIEW, Speer Morgan, Editor; Hoa Ngo, Managing Editor; Evelyn Somers, Associate Editor; Bern Mulvey, Poetry Editor; Kristine Somerville, Promotions and Circulation, 1507 Hillcrest Hall, University of Missouri-Columbia, Columbia, MO 65211, 573-882-4474, Fax 573-884-4671, umcastmr@mis-souri.edu. 1978. Poetry, fiction, articles, art, cartoons, interviews, reviews, parts-of-novels, non-fiction. circ. 6.5M. 3/yr. Pub'd 3 issues 2005; expects 3 issues 2006, 3 issues 2007. sub. price $22, $38/2 years, $48/3 years, $25 foreign yearly; per copy $8; sample $8. Back issues: call. Discounts: none. 208pp. Reporting time: 10-12 weeks. We accept simultaneous submissions with notification. Publishes 5% of manuscripts submitted. Payment: $30/page to $750. Copyrighted, author can reprint material without charge if author acknowledges mag. Pub's reviews: 50 in 2005. §Poetry, fiction, literary biography, history, memoir, general nonfiction. Ads: $400 or exchange. Subject: Literary Review.

The MIT Press, Ellen Faran, 55 Hayward Street, Cambridge, MA 02142-1315, 617-253-5646, 617-258-6779, 800-405-1619. 1932. Pub'd 230 titles 2005; expects 240 titles 2006, 240 titles 2007. Discounts: Trade discount to bookstores: 46%.

MND Publishing, Inc., 573 Marina Road, Deatsville, AL 36022-4431, mnd@mndbooks.com, www.mndbooks.com. 1987. avg. press run 2-5M. Pub'd 1 title 2005; expects 1 title 2006, 1 title 2007. Discounts: 20% single, 40% trade, 50% distributor. 100pp. Reporting time: 2 weeks. Simultaneous submissions accepted: no. Copyrights for author. Subjects: Health, Nutrition, Politics.

MOBILE BEAT: The DJ Magazine, Robert Lindquist, Editor; Daniel Walsh, Managing Editor, PO Box 309, East Rochester, NY 14445, 585-385-9920, Fax 585-385-3637, webmaster@mobilebeat.com. 1991. Articles, photos, interviews, reviews, music, letters, news items. circ. 18M. 6/yr + 1 buyers guide. Pub'd 6 issues 2005; expects 6 issues 2006, 6 issues 2007. sub. price $23; per copy $4.95; sample $5. Back issues: $5. Discounts: libraries 25%, wholesales/distributors. 116pp. Publishes 80% assigned, unassigned 20% of manuscripts submitted. Payment: varies. Copyrighted, reverts to author. Pub's reviews: 4 in 2005. §Music, sound/lighting equipment, performing, broadcasting. Ads: b/w $2195/$1460/$55 per inch. Subjects: Advertising, Self-Promotion, Entertainment, Music, Tapes & Records.

Mock Turtle Press (see also AMERICAN ROAD), Thomas Repp, Executive Editor, PO Box 46519, Mount Clemens, MI 48046, Orders 1-877-285-5434. General information 586-468-7299, fax 586-468-7483, sales@mockturtlepress.com, www.mockturtlepress.com. 1998. "Writers should request a copy of our guidelines and become familiar with American Road magazine prior to submitting queries. E-mail queries preferred. Be sure to include information on photographic support." Pub'd 1 title 2005; expects 1 title 2007. Wholesale discounts available on books—call publisher, Retail discount on books: Quantities: 1-2 @ 20%, 3-4 @ 30%, 5+ @ 40%. Shipping charges apply, American Road magazine is distributed by Disticor. 200pp. Reporting time: 6 months. Simultaneous submissions accepted: no. Publishes 1% of manuscripts submitted. Payment: 13¢ per word. Subjects: Americana, History, Non-Fiction, Transportation, Travel.

MODERN HAIKU, Charles Trumbull, Editor; Lidia Rozmus, Art Editor; Randy M. Brooks, Web Editor; Paul Miller, Book Review Editor; David Burleigh, Associate Editor, PO Box 7046, Evanston, IL 60204-7046. 1969. Poetry, articles, reviews. "'Best haiku magazine in North America'—Museum of Haiku Literature, Tokyo. International circulation. Good university and public library subscription list. Publishes haiku only, plus related book reviews and articles. No restrictions on article length. Contributors should enclose self-addressed, stamped return envelope." circ. 700. 3/yr. Pub'd 3 issues 2005; expects 3 issues 2006, 3 issues 2007. sub. price $23 in US; per copy $10; sample $10. Back issues: inquire. 100pp. Reporting time: 2 weeks. Simultaneous submissions accepted: no. Publishes 5% of manuscripts submitted. Payment: $1 for each haiku; $5 page for articles. Copyrighted, reverts to author. Pub's reviews: 40 in 2005. §Haiku, senryu, haibun. No ads. Subjects: Book Reviewing, Haiku.

THE MODERN LANGUAGE JOURNAL, Sally S. Magnan, Editor, University of Wisconsin, Department of French and Italian, Madison, WI 53706-1558, 608-262-5010. 1916. Articles, reviews, news items. "Sally S. Magnan, Editor, *The Modern Language Journal* (1994-present)." circ. c. 5000. 4/yr. Pub'd 4 issues 2005; expects 4 issues 2006, 4 issues 2007. sub. price $38 indiv, $102 instit; per copy $12; sample free (indiv.). Back issues: $17 indiv., $23 instit. 150pp. Reporting time: 1-3 months. Simultaneous submissions accepted: no. Publishes 15-20% of manuscripts submitted. Payment: 2 copies of issue in which article appears. Copyrighted, does not revert to author. Pub's reviews: 138 in 2005. §Subjects of interest to language teachers and researchers. Ads: $375/$265/175 1/4 page. Subject: Language.

•MODERN PHILOLOGY, University of Chicago Press, Richard Strier, University of Chicago, Wieboldt Hall 106, 1050 E. 59th Street, Chicago, IL 60637, 773-702-7600 (main #), 773-702-0694 (fax), http://www.journals.uchicago.edu/index.html. 1903. "Founded in 1903, *Modern Philology* continues to set a high standard for investigations in literary scholarship, history, and criticism. Although *Modern Philology* publishes articles only in English (with rare exceptions), it welcomes innovative and scholarly work on literature in all modern languages, worldwide. Reviews of recent books appear in every regular issue; review articles, and archival notes and documents are also featured." 4/yr. Pub's reviews.

MOMMY AND I ARE ONE, Jessica Hundley, Publisher & Editor, 2218 Princeton Ave., Los Angeles, CA 90026-2014, 323-960-0358, jjcrashcourse@hotmail.com. 1994. Fiction, articles, art, photos, cartoons, interviews, satire, criticism, reviews, music, letters, non-fiction. "Outside of the mainstream." circ. 10M. 2/yr. Pub'd 3 issues 2005. sub. price $12/4 issues plus postage; per copy $3 plus postage; sample $3. Back issues: $5/$10. 70pp. Reporting time: 2 months. Simultaneous submissions accepted: yes. Publishes 20% of manuscripts submitted. Payment: none yet. Copyrighted, reverts to author. Ads: $400/$200/$100 1/4 page. Subjects: Arts, Avant-Garde, Experimental Art, Essays, Fiction, Humor, Interviews, Movies, Music.

THE MONIST: An International Quarterly Journal of General Philosophical Inquiry, Barry Smith, Editor; Sherwood J.B. Sugden, Managing Editor, 315 Fifth Street, Peru, IL 61354, (815)224-6651,(815)223-4486,philomon1@netscape.net,http//monist.buffalo.edu. 1890. Articles, non-fiction. "THE MONIST, first published in 1890, is an international quarterly journal of general philosophical inquiry. Each issue (typically eight articles) is devoted to a single general topic in epistemology, metaphysics, aesthetics, or ethics selected by the Editor in advance. Recent contributors: Professors John Haldane (St. Andrews), John Hyman (The Queen's College, Oxford), Dominic Lopes (U. of British Columbia), Mark DeBellis (New York U.), Noel Carroll (U. of Wisconsin), Grace Yee (Monash U. Australia), Jennifer Church (Vassar), Mark Siebel (University of Leipzig). Editor: Barry Smith (SUNY)." circ. 1600. 4/yr. Pub'd 4 issues 2005; expects 4 issues 2006, 4 issues 2007. sub. price $30; per copy $12; sample $12. Back issues: $12. Discounts: Individual subscription: $30; institutional subscription: $50. 176pp. Reporting time: 3 months. Simultaneous submissions accepted: No. Publishes 40% of manuscripts submitted. Payment: copies and off-prints of article. Copyrighted, does not revert to author. §We list full bibliographic data as "Books Received" in philosophy, religion, science. Ads: Full page: $150Half-page: $80. Subjects: Philosophy, Religion.

MONKEY'S FIST, Robin Merrill, P.O. Box 316, Madison, ME 04950. 2001. Poetry. "Open reading period Jan 1 - Feb 28 ONLY. Send 3 poems ONLY. Include SASE. Make checks payable to Robin Merrill." 1/yr. sub. price $6; sample $6. 32pp. Reporting time: 2 months. Simultaneous submissions accepted: yes. Publishes 3% of manuscripts submitted. Payment: 1 copy.

Monkfish Book Publishing Company, Paul Cohen, 27 Lamoree Road, Rhinebeck, NY 12572, 845-876-4861, www.monkfishpublishing.com. 2002. Fiction, non-fiction. "Monkfish publishes books that combine spiritual and literary merit. Monkfish books range from memoirs to sutras, from fiction to scholarly works of thought.

Monkfish also publishes Provenance Editions, an imprint devoted to elegant editions of spiritual classics." avg. press run 3000. Pub'd 5 titles 2005; expects 9 titles 2006, 6-10 titles 2007. Discounts: See Consortium Book Sales and Distribution's trade schedule. 275pp. Reporting time: Varies but can take up to 6 months. Simultaneous submissions accepted: Yes. Publishes 5% of manuscripts submitted. Payment: Industry standard royalties. Copyrights for author. Subjects: Biography, Celtic, Sri Chinmoy, Classical Studies, Ecology, Foods, Folklore, India, Literature (General), Native American, Occult, Philosophy, Psychology, Religion, Reprints, Spiritual.

Monroe Press, Dorothy Towvim, 362 Maryville Avenue, Ventura, CA 93003-1912. 1985. Non-fiction. "Manuscripts relating to family issues, parenting, communication, relationships, adolescents and children. Recent contribution: *Why Do Kids Need Feelings? - A Guide to Healty Emotions,* by Dr. Monte Elchoness." avg. press run 5M. Expects 2 titles 2007. Discounts: available upon request. 200pp. Reporting time: 4 weeks. Payment: industry standard. Copyrights for author. Subjects: Children, Youth, Education, Family, Non-Fiction, Parenting, Psychology, Self-Help.

Monsoon Books, 106 Jalan Hang Jebat #02-14, 139527, Singapore, tel: (+65) 6476 3955, Fax: (+65) 6476 8513, email: sales@monsoonbooks.com, web: www.monsoonbooks.com.sg.

Montemayor Press, Edward Myers, Publisher, PO Box 526, Millburn, NJ 07041, 973-761-1341, Fax 973-378-9749, mail@montemayorpress.com, montemayorpress.com. 1999. Fiction, plays, non-fiction. "Montemayor Press specializes in 1) middle-grade and young-adult fiction; 2) literary fiction and drama by Latino authors; and 3) literary fiction and nonfiction of a more general nature. No submissions accepted at this time." avg. press run 2M. Pub'd 3 titles 2005; expects 3 titles 2006, 4 titles 2007. Discounts: bookstores 40%, schools 25%. 180pp. Publishes 0% of manuscripts submitted. Payment: standard. Copyrights for author. Subjects: Colorado, Fantasy, Fiction, Mexico, Multicultural, Non-Fiction, Novels, Poetry, South America, Women, Young Adult.

Montfort Publications (see also QUEEN OF ALL HEARTS), J. Patrick Gaffney, 26 South Saxon Avenue, Bay Shore, NY 11706, 516-665-0726, FAX 516-665-4349. 1947. avg. press run 5M. Pub'd 1 title 2005; expects 1 title 2006, 1 title 2007. Does not copyright for author.

THE MONTHLY INDEPENDENT TRIBUNE TIMES JOURNAL POST GAZETTE NEWS CHRONICLE BULLETIN, T.S. Child, Editor; Denver Tucson, Assistant Editor, 80 Fairlawn Drive, Berkeley, CA 94708-2106. 1983. Fiction, art, cartoons, satire, collages, non-fiction. "Due to our small size, the absolute maximum for any written piece is 1,200 words; the shorter the better. What we want is humor. No limitations as to form or topic. Send us things that will make us call an ambulance. Cartoons and drawings also welcome, but please no smarmy poetry. We will respond within a month." circ. 500. 1/yr. Pub'd 1 issue 2005; expects 1 issue 2006, 1 issue 2007. sub. price $6; per copy 50¢ (or 2 first class stamps); sample same. Back issues: same. Discounts: will trade issues with any magazine. 8pp. Reporting time: 1-4 weeks. Payment: 3 contributors copies. Not copyrighted. Ads: $60/$30. Subjects: Absurdist, Ancient Astronauts, Euthanasia, Death, Humor, Insurance, Romanian Studies, Satire, Sufism, Supernatural, Surrealism.

Moody Street Irregulars, Inc. (see also MOODY STREET IRREGULARS: A Jack Kerouac Magazine), Joy Walsh, Tim Madigan, Lisa Jarnat, 2737 Dodge Road, East Amherst, NY 14051-2113. 1977. Poetry, articles, art, photos, cartoons, interviews, criticism, reviews, music, letters, plays, news items. "Moody Street Irregulars will print poetry, and material pertaining to Kerouac and the Beats." avg. press run 1M-2.5M. Pub'd 2 titles 2005; expects 3 titles 2006. Discounts: 40% to bookstores. 50pp. Reporting time: 1-3 months. Payment: copies. Copyrights for author. Subjects: Literature (General), Newsletter, Poetry.

MOODY STREET IRREGULARS: A Jack Kerouac Magazine, Moody Street Irregulars, Inc., Joy Walsh, Tim Madigan, Lisa Jarnat, 2737 Dodge Road, East Amherst, NY 14051-2113. 1977. Poetry, articles, art, photos, cartoons, interviews, criticism, reviews, music, letters, plays, news items. "*Moody Street Irregulars* is a Kerouac newsletter. We are looking for material on Kerouac and other Beat writers. The magazine will always retain the spirit of Jack Kerouac. Recent contributors: George Dardess, Joy Walsh, Ted Joans, John Clellon Holmes, Tetsuo Nakagami, Gerld Nicosia, Dennis McNally, Janet Kerouac, Jack Kerouac, George Montgomery, Bill Gargan, Ben Walters." circ. 500-1M. 2-3/yr. Pub'd 2 issues 2005; expects 3 issues 2006. sub. price $10; per copy $5; sample $5. Back issues: $5. Discounts: 40% to bookstores. 50pp. Reporting time: 1-3 months. Payment: copies. Copyrighted, reverts to author. Pub's reviews: 3-9 in 2005. §Books on Kerouac and the Beats. Will accept contributions. Inquire as to ads; we now accept them. Subjects: Literature (General), Newsletter, Poetry.

Mo'omana'o Press, Vicki Draeger, 3030 Kalihi St., Honolulu, HI 96818, 808-843-2502; (fax) 808-843-2572; email: clear@maui.net. 2004. Fiction, non-fiction. ""Mo'omana'o" is Hawaiian for "the recording of thoughts." The editors of Mo'omana'o Press are all educators. Our regional interest publications have an educational component to promote intellectual, physical, and spiritual development. We are interested in material that preserves Hawaiian culture, tradition and values from a Christian perspective. Mo'omana'o Press is dedicated to publishing books for schools, churches, children and families." avg. press run 500. Expects 2 titles 2007. Discounts: 10 or more copies, 20%. 100pp. Reporting time: manuscripts submitted by invitation only; 3-4 months. Simultaneous submissions accepted: Yes. Payment: pays in contributors copies. Copyrights for author. Subjects: Adolescence, Children, Youth, Christmas, Community, Divorce, Ecology, Foods, Fiction, Folklore, Hawaii, Parenting, Relationships, Religion, Science, Women, Young Adult.

Moon Lake Media, 16519 S. Bradley Road, Oregon City, OR 97045-8734, info@moonlakebooks.com, www.moonlakebooks.com. 1994. Pub'd 2 titles 2005; expects 2 titles 2006, 2 titles 2007. 250pp.

Moon Mountain Publishing, PO Box 188, West Rockport, ME 04865-0188, www.moonmountainpub.com. 1999. "Moon Mountain Publishing will be closed during 2006. Please do not send manuscripts or art samples."

Moon Pie Press, Alice Persons, Nancy A. Henry, 16 Walton Street, Westbrook, ME 04092, www.moonpiepress.com. 2003. Poetry. "We are a small press in Maine publishing poetry chapbooks. Books are generally 25 to 30 pages long, and we prefer poems no longer than two pages. The poets we have published so far are Nancy A. Henry, Alice Persons, Ted Bookey, Michael Macklin, Ellen M. Taylor, Jay Davis, Darcy Shargo, David Moreau, Jay Franzel, Robin Merrill, Ed Rielly, Eva M. Oppenheim, Thomas Edison (yes, him!), Marita O'Neill, Dennis Camire, Patrick Hicks, Kevin Sweeney, Don Moyer, and Tom Delmore. Our poets generally have at least 6 poems accepted for publication in journals and magazines before they put together a manuscript. We work with poets to help edit and design the chapbooks, which are stapled, not bound, of high quality. NOTE: We also have a perfect bound anthology of 11 Moon Pie Press Poets, called A MOXIE AND A MOON PIE: THE BEST OF MOON PIE PRESS, Volume I, $10. See our website for details and ordering." avg. press run 100. Pub'd 4 titles 2005; expects 7 titles 2006, 7 titles 2007. Discounts: 2-10 copies 20%. 30pp. Reporting time: a month if we can. Simultaneous submissions accepted: Yes. Publishes 75% of manuscripts submitted. Payment: This varies, but we help the poets with the expense of the books, and help market books. Email us for our submission guidelines. Copyright on book belongs to us; contents belong to poet. Subjects: Animals, Autobiography, Feminism, Gardening, Language, Maine, Newspapers, Peace, Pets, Poetry, Relationships, Translation, Travel, Women, Writers/Writing.

Moondance Press, Shari Maser, 4830 Dawson Drive, Ann Arbor, MI 48103, 734-426-1641, maser@mac.com, http://www.blessingway.net. 2004. Non-fiction. "Moondance Press publishes innovative non-fiction books about pregnancy, childbirth, and girlhood." avg. press run 5000. Expects 1 title 2006. 272pp. Subjects: Family, Non-Fiction, Parenting, Women.

Morgan Quitno Corporation, Kathleen O'Leary Morgan, Scott Morgan, PO Box 1656, Lawrence, KS 66044, 785-841-3534, 800-457-0742, mqpr@midusa.net.

Morgen Publishing Incorporated, M. Jean Rawson, PO Box 754, Naples, FL 34106, Fax 239-263-8472. 2000. Poetry, non-fiction. "Recent publications: *A Manual of Special Education Law* and *Mercy Me! Cancer Prayers, Poems, and Psalms.*" Pub'd 1 title 2005; expects 1 title 2006, 1 title 2007. Discounts: contact for rates. 100-300pp. Reporting time: 3 months. Simultaneous submissions accepted: yes. Payment: negotiated. Copyrights for author. Subjects: Education, Law, Spiritual.

Morris Publishing, PO Box 2110, Kearney, NE 68848, 800-650-7888. Simultaneous submissions accepted: yes. Copyrights for author.

MOTHER EARTH, Third Way Publications Ltd., PO Box 1243, London SW7 3PB, England, 44(0)70-7-373-3432 phone/Fax, thirdway@dircon.co.uk, www.thirdway.org. 1992. Articles, art, photos, cartoons, interviews, criticism, reviews, music, letters. "750-1,000 words of decentralist, green, radical comment." circ. 200. 4/yr. Pub'd 4 issues 2005; expects 4 issues 2006, 4 issues 2007. sub. price UK £5, EU £6, rest of world (air) £9, $15US; per copy £1, $2US; sample £1.25, $3US. Back issues: none. Discounts: none. 8pp. Simultaneous submissions accepted: no. Publishes 30% of manuscripts submitted. Payment: none. Copyrighted, reverts to author. Pub's reviews: 15 in 2005. §Green issues, ethical investment/consumerism, Third World debt, boycott campaigns, animal rights. Ads: on application. Subjects: Book Reviewing, Environment, New Age, Political Science.

MOTHER EARTH JOURNAL: An International Quarterly, Herman Berlandt, Editor, Publisher; Katherine Gallagher, Co-Editor; Rob Tricato, Assistant Editor, 934 Brannan St., San Francisco, CA 94103, 415-868-8865, 415-552-9261, info@internationalpoetrymuseum.org. 1990. Poetry. "*Mother Earth* is an international journal presenting the poet's perspective on the current political and ecological global crisis. Here poetry from six continents is represented in fine English translations. 'Let the voice of the poet be heard throughout the world' is our slogan. Among our contributors are Robert Bly, Gary Snyder, Anabel Torres, Marianne Larsen, Seamus Heaney, Kofi Awoonor, Wole Soyinka, Bei Dao, Mahmoud Darwish, Lawrence Ferlinghetti, etc." circ. 1M. 4/yr. Pub'd 4 issues 2005; expects 4 issues 2006, 4 issues 2007. sub. price $15; per copy $5; sample $3. Back issues: $3.50 each. Discounts: 50%. 40pp. Reporting time: 3 months. Simultaneous submissions accepted: yes. Publishes 15% of manuscripts submitted. Payment: 2 copies. Not copyrighted, rights revert to author on publication. Ads: $150/$100/$60 1/4 page. Subjects: Finances, Poetry.

•**MOTHERVERSE: A Journal of Contemporary Motherhood,** Melanie Mayo-Laakso, Editor-in-Chief, 2663 Hwy 3, Two Harbors, MN 55616, website www.motherverse.com, email editor@motherverse.com, submissions email submissions@motherverse.com, ordering email order@motherverse.com, advertising email ads@motherverse.com. 2005. Poetry, fiction, articles, art, photos, cartoons, interviews, satire, reviews, music, letters, parts-of-novels, long-poems, concrete art, news items, non-fiction. "MotherVerse prints smart, insightful and bold works of literature and art that explore and challenge mainstream ideals and reflect honest images of motherhood. We encourage the exploration of motherhood across geographical, political and cultural lines and reflect this by printing material from women around the globe. Recent contributers include Eugenia Chao, Sarojni Mehta-Lissak, Kate Haas, Suzanne Kamata and Bronmin Shumway. All submissions should be made electronically." 4/yr. Pub'd 2 issues 2005; expects 4 issues 2006, 4 issues 2007. sub. price Print $12, Digital $5; per copy Print $3.50; sample Print $2.25(free by special request), Digital Free. Back issues: Print $3, Digital Free. Bulk discounts available on orders of 3 or more issues or subscriptions. Free issues for review provided when available by special request. Contact order@motherverse.com. 52pp. Reporting time: 2-3 months. Simultaneous submissions accepted: Yes. Publishes 15% of manuscripts submitted. Payment: 2 contributer copies or 1 year subscription. Copyrighted, reverts to author. Pub's reviews. §Books, Magazines, Journals and Portfolios that examine contemporary or historical motherhood issues. We do not review material which could be considered parenting advice or instruction. Ads: Limited ad space available, rates vary.Contact ads@motherverse.com or visit www.motherverse.com/advertise.html. Subjects: Arts, Birth, Birth Control, Population, Family, Feminism, Gender Issues, Global Affairs, History, Homemaking, Human Rights, Interviews, Lesbianism, Literature (General), Multicultural, Parenting, Women.

•**Motom,** Thomas Barber, 76 West 2100 South, Salt Lake City, UT 84115, (801)499-6021. 2005. Non-fiction. "As a new publisher we don't have an elaborate existing library, but we aim to. Currently, we are promoting, "Kick the Dealer...Not the Tires!" by Mark Marine. This non-fiction book takes the reader behind the scenes of the car buying process and and teaches them all they need to know in order to protect themselves when they buy a car." avg. press run 5000. Expects 1 title 2006, 3 titles 2007. Discounts: 1-5 33%6-49 40%50-99 45%100 or more 50%. 200pp. Reporting time: 1 week. Simultaneous submissions accepted: Yes. Publishes 25% of manuscripts submitted. Payment: Negotiable. Copyrights for author. Subjects: Abstracts, Absurdist, Adolescence, Advertising, Self-Promotion, Children, Youth, Christmas, Ethics, Fiction, How-To, Inspirational, Non-Fiction, Novels, Photography, Poetry, Zen.

MOTORBOOTY MAGAZINE, Mark Dancey, PO Box 02007, Detroit, MI 48202. 1987. Fiction, articles, art, photos, cartoons, interviews, satire, criticism, reviews, music, parts-of-novels, non-fiction. "This magazine promises 'attitude with an attitude'." circ. 15M. Sporadic. Pub'd 1 issue 2005; expects 2 issues 2006, 3 issues 2007. sub. price $16; per copy $6; sample $6. Back issues: $4. Discounts: trade with other publishers. 100pp. Copyrighted, reverts to author. Pub's reviews. §Satire, comics, music. Ads: $400/$200. Subjects: Comics, Humor, Music, Satire.

Mount Ida Press, Diana S. Waite, 152 Washington Avenue, Albany, NY 12210-2203, Tel: 518-426-5935, Fax: 518-426-4116. 1984. Non-fiction. "Award-winning historical research, writing, editing, and indexing." avg. press run 1.5M-2M. Pub'd 1 title 2005; expects 2 titles 2006, 2 titles 2007. Discounts: 40% trade. 144pp. Reporting time: 2 months. Payment: royalty. Copyrights for author. Subjects: Architecture, Cities, History, Thomas Jefferson, New York, Textiles.

Mount Olive College Press (see also MOUNT OLIVE REVIEW), Pepper Worthington, Editor, Mount Olive College, 634 Henderson Street, Mount Olive, NC 28365. 1990. "The Mount Olive College Press accepts letters of inquiry year-round. If the Press is interested, the editor will request a complete manuscript." avg. press run 500-800. Pub'd 5-7 titles 2005; expects 5-7 titles 2006, 5-7 titles 2007. Poetry 70-110pp, others 30-210pp. Reporting time: 6 months to 1 year. Simultaneous submissions accepted: no. Publishes 5% of manuscripts submitted. Payment: negotiated. Copyrights for author.

MOUNT OLIVE REVIEW, Mount Olive College Press, Pepper Worthington, Editor, Department of Language and Literature, 634 Henderson Street, Mount Olive, NC 28365, 919-658-2502. 1987. Poetry, art, reviews, non-fiction. "Future themes include topics of travel, film, and metaphor in literature as well as a focus on North Carolina writers and major American writers. Recent contributors: Janet Lembke, Joseph Bathanti, Gladys Owings Hughes, James L. Abrahamson. Length of literary criticism as it relates to theme 1M-6M words. MLA style appropriate. Length of creative genres flexible." Publish 1 every 2 years. sub. price $25; per copy $25; sample $25. 394pp. Reporting time: varies, 6-10 months. Simultaneous submissions accepted: no. Publishes 20% of manuscripts submitted. Payment: none. Copyrighted, reverts to author. Pub's reviews. §Interviews, essays.

THE MOUNTAIN ASTROLOGER, Tem Tarriktar, PO Box 970, Cedar Ridge, CA 95924-0970, 530-477-8839, www.mountainastrologer.com. 1988. Poetry, articles, art, photos, cartoons, interviews, satire, reviews, letters, news items. "Any length; must have astrology content. Send SASE for return of materials." circ. print run 27M. 6/yr. Pub'd 6 issues 2005; expects 6 issues 2006, 6 issues 2007. sub. price $36 bulk rate, $48 1st class, $36US Canada; per copy $7 postpaid in U.S./Canada; sample $7 postpaid in U.S./Canada. Back issues: $6 postpaid in U.S./Canada and shipping charges. Discounts: available through distributors; write for a list of distributors. 132pp. Reporting time: varies. Simultaneous submissions accepted: no. Publishes 30% of manuscripts submitted. Payment: varies. Copyrighted, reverts to author. Pub's reviews: 30 in 2005. §Astrology only. Ads: $745/$395/subject to change. Subjects: Astrology, New Age, Philosophy.

Mountain Automation Corporation, Claude Wiatrowski, 6090 Whirlwind Dr, Colorado Springs, CO 80918-7560, 719-598-8256, Fax 719-598-8516, Order 800-345-6120, Order Fax 970-493-8781, Order Email mac@intrepidgroup.com, Order Web http://www.railwayshop.com/mountain.shtml, Order Address POB 2324 Ft Collins CO 80522-2324. 1976. Art, photos, music, non-fiction. "We currently publish promotional books and videos, especially tourist souvenirs for specific attractions." avg. press run 5M. Expects 1 title 2007. Discounts: 50%. 24pp. Reporting time: 1 month. Simultaneous submissions accepted: yes. Payment: determined individually. Copyrights for author. Subjects: Alaska, Arizona, Arkansas, Canada, Children, Youth, Colorado, Hawaii, History, The North, Ohio, Religion, Transportation, The West.

Mountain Meadow Press, Borg Hendrickson, PO Box 447, Kooskia, ID 83539, phone 208-926-7875; fax 208-926-7579; email: mmp@cybrquest.com. 1987. Non-fiction. "Adult nonfiction, Pacific Northwest history and travel." avg. press run 4M. Expects 1 title 2006, 2 titles 2007. Discounts: STOP 40%, 5+ copies 40%, 50+ copies 44%, 100+ copies 46%, 400+ copies 47% freight free, saleable returns accepted with permission; nonreturnable 25+ copies 48%. 235pp. Publishes 0% of manuscripts submitted. Subjects: History, Idaho, Indians, Montana, Native American, Non-Fiction, Old West, Pacific Northwest, Travel, Washington (state), The West.

Mountain Media, Wayne Murray, Kat Farmer, Rick Tompkins, 3172 N. Rainbow Boulevard, Suite 343, Las Vegas, NV 89108, voice 702-656-3285, publisher@TheLibertarian.us, Web site http://www.LibertyBook-Shop.us. 1999. Fiction, non-fiction. "We publish a small number of libertarian and free-market titles in both fiction and non-fiction." avg. press run 5,000. Pub'd 1 title 2005; expects 2 titles 2007. Discounts: bookstore single-copy "STOP" 25 percent; 8-12 copies 30 percent plus shipping; 13-19 copies 40 percent plus shipping; 20-39 copies 50 percent plus shipping; 40+ copies 50 percent, free shipping. 600pp. Reporting time: 60-90 days. Simultaneous submissions accepted: Yes. Payment: negotiable. Copyrights for author. Subjects: Anarchist, Drugs, Fantasy, Fiction, Libertarian, Novels, Politics, Science Fiction, Southwest, The West.

Mountain Press Publishing Co., Rob Williams, Business Manager; John Rimel, Publisher; Jeannie Nuckolls, Production Coordinator, Roadside Geology Series Editor; Gwen McKenna, History Editor; Jennifer Carey, Natural History Editor, PO Box 2399, Missoula, MT 59806, 406-728-1900. 1948 (became full time publisher in mid-70's - printing company prior to that). Non-fiction. "We publish primarily non-fiction. Besides our successful *Roadside Geology* series, we are publishing regional nature/outdoor guides such as *Wildflowers of Wyoming*. We also publish quality western history and western Americana. We also publish topical science books such as *Finding Fault in California*." avg. press run 5M. Pub'd 12 titles 2005; expects 12 titles 2006, 12 titles 2007. Discounts: bookstores 2-14 copies 40%, $3.50 shipping, 15+ 45% free freight. 150-360pp. Reporting time: 2-6 months. Payment: twice a year; royalty of 10-12% based on the amount the publisher receives from sales of the book. Copyrights for author. Subjects: Americana, Animals, Birds, Earth, Natural History, Geology, Montana, Reprints, Sports, Outdoors, Transportation, The West.

Mountain Publishing, PO Box 12720, Chandler, AZ 85248-0029, 800-879-8719, fax: 480-802-5644, email: info@mountainpublishingusa.com. 1989. Non-fiction. "Manuscripts: book-length dealing with business." avg. press run 5M. Pub'd 1 title 2005; expects 2 titles 2006, 1 title 2007. 449pp. Reporting time: 60 days. Payment: negotiable. Copyrights for author. Subject: Business & Economics.

Mountain State Press, 2300 MacCorkle Avenue SE, Charleston, WV 25304-1099, 304-357-4767, mspl@newwave.net. 1978. Poetry, fiction, satire, criticism, plays. "We specialize in regional materials: Appalachian subjects and authors, primarily. We publish book-length mss. of fiction, nonfiction, and poetry. Book must either be written by a West Virginian or having to do with West Virginia." avg. press run 1.5M. Pub'd 1 title 2005; expects 1 title 2006, 1 title 2007. Discounts: 40% to bookstores, 25% gift shops, 10% libraries, schools and churches. 250pp. Reporting time: 2 months or more. Simultaneous submissions accepted: Yes, if informed. Publishes 2% of manuscripts submitted. Payment: negotiable. Copyrights for author. Subjects: Appalachia, Essays, Fiction, History, Novels, Short Stories.

The Mountaineers Books, Helen Cherullo, Publisher; Cassandra Conyers, Acquisitions Editor, 1001 SW Klickitat Way, Suite 201, Seattle, WA 98134-1161, 206-223-6303. 1961. Non-fiction. "We have over 350 titles in print, all having to do with the outdoors - how to, where to, history, climbing, hiking, skiing, snowshoeing, bicycling, mountaineering & expeditions. Must relate to mountaineering or self-propelled, non-commercial, non-competitive outdoor activities; mountain and/or NW history; conservation of natural resources." avg. press run 3M-5M. Pub'd 30 titles 2005; expects 30 titles 2006, 30 titles 2007. Standard book trade discounts. 240pp. Reporting time: 1-2 months. Simultaneous submissions accepted: yes. Publishes 5-10% of manuscripts submitted. Payment: negotiated royalties on net sales paid twice yearly. Copyrights for author. Subjects: Alaska, Biography, California, Conservation, Earth, Natural History, Ecology, Foods, Environment, Europe, Florida, How-To, Idaho, New England, Pacific Northwest, Sports, Outdoors, Transportation.

Mountainside Press, Alex Sophian, Publisher, PO Box 407, Shaftsbury, VT 05262, 802-447-7094, Fax 802-447-2611. 1991. "Focus on popular culture." avg. press run 500. Expects 1 title 2006, 2/3 titles 2007. Discounts: 2-4 40%, 5-25 42%, 26-49 46%, 50+ 50%. 288pp. Reporting time: 3 weeks. Simultaneous submissions accepted: yes. Publishes 20% of manuscripts submitted. Payment: 7%. Subjects: Americana, Arts, Culture, Leisure/Recreation, Performing Arts.

Mountaintop Books, Milton Forbes, 21708 Eastman Road, Glenwood, IA 51534-6221. 1989. Criticism, non-fiction. "Humanism, free thought, Biblical studies. Query only, SASE. Length 30,000-60,000 words. No poetry." Expects 1 title 2007. Discounts: Cost to bookstores and wholesalers is 50% of retail price plus shipping. 250pp. Reporting time: 3 months. Payment: royalty 10% of retail price. Does not copyright for author. Subjects: Christianity, Humanism, Judaism, Religion.

MOUSEION, Journal of the Classical Association of Canada/Revue de la Societe Canadienne des Etudes Classiques, University of Calgary Press, M. Joyal, Editor; J. Butrica, Editor; N. Kennell, Editor, University of Calgary Press, Univ. of Calgary, 2500 University Dr. N.W., Calgary, Alberta T2N 1N4, Canada, 403-220-3514, Fax 403-282-0085, ucpmail@ucalgary.ca. 1957. Articles, photos, reviews. "Formerly *Echoes du Monde Classique/Classical Views*. Reports on activities of Canadian classical archaeologists and articles on archaeological subjects, as well as articles and book reviews on classical history and literature." circ. 750. 3/yr. Pub'd 3 issues 2005; expects 3 issues 2006, 3 issues 2007. sub. price Instit. $40 + GST Canada, $40US outside Canada; indiv. $25 + GST Canada, $25US outside Canada; per copy $10 + GST. Back issues: Vol. 26-28 issues are $10 each and $15 per volume. Vol. 29 to present cost $10 each, $27/volume. 150pp. Reporting time: 6 weeks. Copyrighted, does not revert to author. Pub's reviews: 31 in 2005. §Classical studies. Ads: write for information. Subjects: Anthropology, Archaelogy, Classical Studies.

MOUTH: Voice of the Dis-Labeled Nation, Lucy Gwin, Mouth Magazine, 4201 SW 30th Street, Topeka, KS 66614-3203, Fax 785-272-7348. 1989. Articles, photos, cartoons, interviews, letters, news items, non-fiction. "(Send SASE for publishing schedule and guidelines. Only subscribers will be published.) *Mouth* speaks for 58 million Americans who are dis-labeled in one way or another. *Mouth* is known for its flaming exposes of charity's high rollers and bureaucracy's log jammers, for its consumer testing of deadening drugs and behavior modifiers, for its pride, its anger, its humor. *Mouth* is a crash course for Americans on the disability rights movement." circ. 4.2M. 6/yr. Pub'd 6 issues 2005; expects 6 issues 2006, 6 issues 2007. sub. price $16-32-48; per copy $5; sample $3. Back issues: $5. Discounts: bulk: bundles of 100 $165. 40pp. Reporting time: 21 days. Simultaneous submissions accepted: yes. Publishes 5% of manuscripts submitted. Payment: Editor is unpaid, occasionally we pay $50-75 for items. Copyrighted, reverts to author. §Do-gooderism, eugenics, mercy killing and other helping professional euphemisms. De-institutionalization—or does that make freedom sound too complicated? Ads: none. Subjects: Bigotry, Civil Rights, Disabled, Disease, Euthanasia, Death, Human Rights, Law, Medicine, Politics, Resistance, Social Movements, Sociology.

Moving Parts Press, Felicia Rice, 10699 Empire Grade, Santa Cruz, CA 95060-9474, 408-427-2271. 1977. Poetry, fiction, art, letters, parts-of-novels, long-poems, collages. "*COSMOGONIE INTIME An Intimate Cosmogony*a French/English collaboration between Yves Peyre, Elizabeth R. Jackson, Ray Rice and Felicia Rice, limited edition artists' book published in 2006. *Codex Espangliensis: From Columbus to the Border Patrol* a bilingual collaboration between Enrique Chagoya, Guillermo Gomez-Pena and Felicia Rice, limited editon published by Moving Parts Press in 1998 and trade edition published by City Lights Books in 2000. Much more information at www.movingpartspress.com." avg. press run 75. Discounts: 30%. 45pp. Reporting time: 1-2 months. Payment: 10% copies. Copyrights for author. Subjects: Poetry, Politics.

•**Mucusart Publications (see also BALLISTA; THE UGLY TREE),** Paul Neads, Andrew Myers, 6 Chiffon Way, Trinity Riverside, Gtr Manchester M3 6AB, England, +4407814570441, paul@mucusart.co.uk, www.mucusart.co.uk/press.htm. 2002. "Mucusart Publications aims to provide a voice and forum for stranded bards whilst not discriminating between the written and the spoken word. Mucusart explores the synergy between both through its performance poetry nights in the UK, its poetry magazine The Ugly Tree (three times a year), and its occasional single-poet pamphlet. 2006 sees the lauch of its twice yearly short fiction magazine, Ballista, featuring new writing on the supernatural." avg. press run 100. Pub'd 2 titles 2005; expects 4 titles 2006, 6 titles 2007. Discounts: 10-19 copies 10%, 20+ copies 15%. 48pp. Reporting time: 4-8 weeks. Simultaneous submissions accepted: No. Publishes 5% of manuscripts submitted. Payment: One off variable payment to authors for collected works; payment of GB5.00 + complimentary copy to authors featured in Ballista. Copyrights for author. Subjects: English, Fantasy, Horror, Myth, Mythology, Occult, Poetry, Science Fiction, Short Stories, Spiritual, Supernatural, Zines.

306

MUDFISH, Box Turtle Press, Jill Hoffman, Editor; Jennifer Belle, Associate Editor; Doug Dorph, Associate Editor; Stephanie Emily Dickinson, Associate Editor; Rob Cook, Associate Editor; Lawrence Applebaum, Associate Editor; Paul Wuensche, Associate Editor; Marina Rubin, Associate Editor; Matthew Keuter, Associate Editor; Michael Montlack, Associate Editor, 184 Franklin Street, New York, NY 10013, 212-219-9278. 1983. Poetry, art, photos. "Mudfish inividual poet's series: 1-5; Mudfish #15 forthcoming. Annual Mudfish Poetry Prize - inquire." circ. 1.2M. 1/yr. Pub'd 1 issue 2005; expects 1 issue 2006, 1 issue 2007. sub. price $20 for 2 year subscription; per copy $12 + $2.50; sample $12 + $2.50. All back issues $10 plus postage. 200pp. Reporting time: immediately to 6 months. Simultaneous submissions accepted: no. Publishes 5% of manuscripts submitted. Payment: 1 copy of magazine. Copyrighted, reverts to author. Ads: $250/$125. Subject: Poetry.

MUDLARK, William Slaughter, English Department, University of North Florida, Jacksonville, FL 32224-2645, mudlark@unf.edu, www.unf.edu/mudlark. 1995. Poetry, interviews, criticism, long-poems. *"Mudlark* is 'never in and never out of print.' As our full name, *Mudlark: An Electronic Journal of Poetry & Poetics,* suggests, we will consider accomplished work that locates itself anywhere on the spectrum of contemporary practice. We want poems, of course, but we want essays, too, that make us read poems (and write them?) differently somehow. Although we are not innocent, we do imagine ourselves capable of suprise. *Mudlark* has an ISSN (1081-3500), is refereed, copyrighted, archived and distributed free on the World Wide Web. Some recent contributors: Ian Randall Wilson, Jesse Lee Kercheval, Michael Ruby, Sheryl Luna, and Garin Cycholl." 5M discrete visitors per month. Irregular but frequent. sub. price free (online); per copy free; sample free. Back issues: free. Pages vary. Reporting time: no less than one day, no more than one month. We'd rather not accept simultaneous submissions because our turn-around time is short, but we will if notified with submission. Payment: In *Mudlark* poetry is free. Our authors give us their work and we, in turn, give it to our readers. What is the coin of poetry's realm? Poetry is a gift economy. One of the things we can do at *Mudlark* to pay our authors for their work is point to it here and there, wherever else it is. We can tell our readers how to find it, how to subscribe to it, and how to buy it if it is for sale. Copyrighted, reverts to author. Subjects: Criticism, Essays, Interviews, Poetry, Translation.

MULTICULTURAL EDUCATION, Caddo Gap Press, Alan H. Jones, Editor; Heather L. Hazuka, Editor, 3145 Geary Boulevard, Ste. 275, San Francisco, CA 94118, 415-392-1911. 1993. Articles, art, photos, interviews, reviews, letters, news items, non-fiction. *"Multicultural Education* features articles, reviews, listings of resources, and a variety of other materials geared to assist with multicultural education programs in schools and with development and definition of the field." circ. 5M. 4/yr. Pub'd 3 issues 2005; expects 4 issues 2006, 4 issues 2007. sub. price $50 individuals, $100 institutions, $40 students; per copy $15; sample free. Back issues: $10. Discounts: can be arranged. 40pp. Reporting time: 2 months. Publishes 25% of manuscripts submitted. Payment: only for solicited materials. Copyrighted, reverts to author. Pub's reviews: 12 in 2005. §Anything involved with multicultural education. Ads: $500/$300/$400 2/3 page/$200 1/3 page/$150 1/6 page/$50 1 inch. Subject: Education.

Multi-Media Publications Inc., R.R. #4B, Lakefield, ON K0L 2H0, Canada, 905-721-1540 phone/Fax, info@mmpubs.com, www.mmpubs.com. 1988. Photos, non-fiction. "Business topics. Currently producing a series of books on project management." Pub'd 20 titles 2005; expects 20 titles 2006, 20 titles 2007. Standard trade discounts for retailers and wholesalers. Non-book trade resellers work on a more granular discount schedule. 200-300pp. Reporting time: 2 weeks. Simultaneous submissions accepted: yes. Payment: Negotiable. Standard 20% of net revenues. Copyrights for author. Subjects: Audio/Video, Business & Economics, Careers, Consulting, Leadership, Management, Motivation, Success, Speaking.

Multnomah Publishers, Inc., Larry Libby, Rod Morris; David Webb, Editorial Director, David Kopp, 601 N. Larch St., Sisters, OR 97759-9320, 541-549-1144, Fax 541-549-8048. 1987. Fiction, non-fiction. "Imprints: Multnomah, Multnomah Gift, Multnomah Fiction." avg. press run 15M. Pub'd 100 titles 2005; expects 100 titles 2006, 100 titles 2007. Discounts: 40%. 225pp. Reporting time: 6 weeks. Simultaneous submissions accepted: yes. Publishes 1% of manuscripts submitted. Payment: varies. Copyrights for author. Subjects: Christianity, Fiction, Religion.

Munchweiler Press, Theo E. Lish, Publisher, 13940 Okesa Road, Apple Valley, CA 92307-7220, 760-245-9215, Fax 760-245-9418, tedlish@munchweilerpress.com, www.munchweilerpress.com. 1999. Fiction, art, photos, cartoons. "Specialize in picture books." avg. press run 10M. Expects 1 title 2006, 4 titles 2007. Discounts: available on request. 32pp. Reporting time: 1 month. Simultaneous submissions accepted: yes. Publishes 10-20% of manuscripts submitted. Payment: 2-1/2% to 10% based on cover price. Copyrights for author. Subject: Children, Youth.

Munsey Music, T. Munsey, Box 511, Richmond Hill, Ontario L4C 4Y8, Canada, 905-737-0208; www.pathcom.com/~munsey. 1970. "Include SASE if return of submission is required. Only accept fantasy/science fiction." avg. press run 5M. Pub'd 1 title 2005; expects 2 titles 2006, 4 titles 2007. Discounts: 1-4 copies no discount, 5-10 20%, 11-20 30%, 21-40 35%, 41+ 40%. 250pp. Reporting time: 6-12 months.

Simultaneous submissions accepted: yes. Payment: industry. Copyrights for author. Subjects: Fantasy, Fiction, Inspirational, Science Fiction, Spiritual, Young Adult.

MuscleHead Press, 3700 County Route 24, Russell, NY 13684.

The Muse Media (see also THE GREAT AMERICAN POETRY SHOW, A SERIAL POETRY ANTHOLOGY), Larry Ziman, PO Box 69506, West Hollywood, CA 90069, 323-969-4905, www.tgaps.com. 2002. Poetry. "Recent contributors: Lauren Seligman, Ronald Douglas Bascombe, Heidi Nye, Dennis Saleh, Lauren Young, Doug Draime, Carolyn J. Fairweather Hughes, Alan Britt, Sarah Brown Weitzman and Hector E. Estrada. We need to see a lot of poetry to find what we want to publish. So flood us with poems. We publish poems not poets. We'll accept good poems from new as well as established poets." avg. press run 1000. Pub'd 1 title 2005; expects 1 title 2007. Discounts: 40% for bookstores, retailers; 15% for agents, jobbers; wholesalers, distributors negotiable. 150pp. Reporting time: 1-8 weeks. Simultaneous submissions accepted: Yes. Publishes 2% of manuscripts submitted. Payment: Each contributor receives one copy of each issue he/she appears in. Does not copyright for author. Subject: Poetry.

Muse World Media Group, Roan Kaufman, PO Box 55094, Madison, WI 53705, 608-238-6681. 1990. Poetry, fiction, articles, interviews, news items, non-fiction. "We are actively seeking new titles. We also do subsidary publishing and co-publishing. In the past few years we've published books on commodity trading, business trade books, novels, and relationship books. So, we're open to publishing a variety of materials." avg. press run 2M - 10,000. Pub'd 2 titles 2005; expects 10 titles 2006. 150-250pp. Reporting time: 2 months. Simultaneous submissions accepted: yes. Publishes 10% of manuscripts submitted. Payment: 25% royalty. Copyrights for author. Subjects: Anarchist, Avant-Garde, Experimental Art, Engineering, How-To, Humor, Music, Novels, Nutrition, Occult, Reference, Relationships, Science, Sex, Sexuality, Writers/Writing.

Museon Publishing, PO Box 17095, Beverly Hills, CA 90209-2095, 310-788-0228. 1996. Non-fiction. "Travel material related to museums and art only. Accept proposals only." avg. press run 5M. Pub'd 1 title 2005; expects 2 titles 2006, 3 titles 2007. Discounts: 2-4 20%, 5-9 40%, 10-49 42%, 50-99 44%, 100+ 46%. 270pp. Reporting time: 1 month. Simultaneous submissions accepted: no. Payment: varies. Does not copyright for author. Subject: Travel.

Music City Publishing, P. Hunter, P.O. Box 41696, Nashville, TN 37204-1696, www.musiccitypublish-ing.com. 1987. Non-fiction. "Music City Publishing promotes Free Enterprise, Personal Responsibility, and Business Ownership. We support the Constitution of the United States and the Holy Bible, and publish works that promote them." Expects 1 title 2006, 3 titles 2007. Discounts: 25-99 35% discount. 100-499 45% discount. 500+ 55% discount. 272pp. Reporting time: One month. Simultaneous submissions accepted: Yes. Publishes 5% of manuscripts submitted. Payment: No advances. Author royalties: 15% of retail price. Quarterly payments. Copyrights for author. Subjects: Americana, Autobiography, Biography, Family, Finances, Humor, Inspirational, Memoirs, Mentoring/Coaching, Non-Fiction, Quotations, Relationships, Self-Help, Speaking, Storytelling.

MUSIC NEWS, David Island, 5536 NE Hassalo, Portland, OR 97213, 503-281-1191. 1896. Articles, art, photos, cartoons, music, news items, non-fiction. "2 pages double spaced typed maximum." circ. 55M. 3/yr. Pub'd 3 issues 2005; expects 3 issues 2006, 3 issues 2007. sub. price controlled circulation; per copy SASE; sample SASE. Back issues: none. 8pp. Reporting time: 1 month. Publishes 10% of manuscripts submitted. Payment: varies. Copyrighted, reverts to author. Pub's reviews: 8 in 2005. §Music. Ads: none. Subjects: Catholic, Children, Youth, Christianity, Music, Religion.

MUSIC PERCEPTION, University of California Press, Lola L. Cuddy, Editor; Katie Spiller, Managing Editor, Univ of CA Press, 2000 Center Street, Suite 303, Berkeley, CA 94704-1223, 510-643-7154. 1983. Reviews, music, non-fiction. "Editorial address: Department of Psychology, Humphrey Hall, 62 Arch St., Room 232, Queen's University, Kingston, Ontario, K7L 3N6 Canada." circ. 699. 4/yr. Pub'd 4 issues 2005; expects 4 issues 2006, 4 issues 2007. sub. price $58 indiv., $233 instit., $35 student (+ $20 air freight); per copy $21 indiv., $63 instit., $21 student; sample free. Back issues: same as single copy price. Discounts: foreign subs. agents 10%, one-time orders 10+ 30%, standing orders (bookstores): 1-99 40%, 100+ 50%. 128pp. Copyrighted, does not revert to author. Pub's reviews: 20 in 2005. §Music, physical psychology, psychology of perception. Ads: $295/$220. Subjects: Mathematics, Music, Psychology.

MUSIC THEORY SPECTRUM, University of California Press, Brian Alegant, Editor; Brian Hyer, Reviews Editor, University of California Press, 2000 Center St., Suite 303, Berkeley, CA 94704-1223, 510-643-7154. 1978. Articles, reviews. "Editorial address: Oberlin College Conservatory, 77 West College Street, Oberlin, OH 44074-1449. Copyrighted by the Society for Music Theory." circ. 1458. 2/yr. Pub'd 2 issues 2005; expects 2 issues 2006, 2 issues 2007. sub. price $45 indiv., $104 inst., $20 student; per copy $32 indiv., $59 inst., $20 student; sample same as single copy. Discounts: foreign subs. agents 10%, 10+ one-time orders 30%. 144pp. Copyrighted, does not revert to author. Pub's reviews: approx. 8 in 2005. §musicology: aesthetics, the history of theory, linear analysis, atonal theory, networks, and narratology. Ads: $320. Subject:

Music.

My Heart Yours Publishing, Tanya Davis, Jeannine Nyangira, PO Box 4975, Wheaton, IL 60187, (630) 452-2809, www.myheartyours.com, tanya@myheartyours.com, jeannine@myheartyours.com. 2004. Fiction, non-fiction. "Our purpose is to share our hearts in order to help form a wave of people walking in the Truth. As we truthfully deal with our inner beings and then share our hearts with others, both parties are then healed. Then those people will desire Truth on the inside, be healed, and then share with someone else. Eventually, this will create a healing wave—emotionally, spiritually, mentally, and physically. So far we have worked with memoir, fiction, and creative nonfiction. Our first book, *May I Please Speak with my Father,* was written by Tanya Davis and explores how women's relationships with their dads impacts their relationship with their heavenly Father. Several women contributed to this project, including editor Jeannine Nyangira." avg. press run 1800. Expects 2 titles 2006, 5 titles 2007. Discounts: 2-4 copies 20%, 5-9 copies 30%, 10-24 copies 40%, 25-49 copies 42%, 50-74 copies 44%, 100-199 copies 48%, 200+ copies 50%. 100-160pp. Reporting time: 2 months. Simultaneous submissions accepted: Yes. Publishes 70% of manuscripts submitted. Payment: To be discussed. Copyrights for author. Subjects: Children, Youth, Christianity, Essays, Family, Fiction, Journals, Memoirs, Non-Fiction, Religion, Spiritual.

MY TABLE: Houston's Dining Magazine, Lazywood Press, Teresa Byrne-Dodge, 1908 Harold Street, Houston, TX 77098-1502, 713-529-5500, teresabyrnedodge@my-table.com, www.my-table.com. 1994. Articles, art, criticism, reviews, non-fiction. "We are region-specific (i.e. we write about food, wine and restaurants of interest to readers in greater Houston area)." circ. 16M. 6/yr. Pub'd 6 issues 2005; expects 6 issues 2006, 6 issues 2007. sub. price $24; per copy $4.50; sample $7. Back issues: $7 each. Discounts: please call for schedule. 64-72pp. Reporting time: 2-3 weeks. Simultaneous submissions accepted: yes. Publishes 25% of manuscripts submitted. Payment: yes. Copyrighted, reverts to author. Pub's reviews: 25 in 2005. §Cookbooks, books on food, wine, and being at table. Ads: $1,980/$400. Subjects: Cooking, Dining, Restaurants, Essays, Food, Eating, Humor, Wine, Wineries.

Myriad Press, Gloria Stern, 12535 Chandler Blvd. #3, N. Hollywood, CA 91607, 818-508-6296. 1993. Fiction, parts-of-novels. Pub'd 2 titles 2005. Volume discounts. 200pp. Reporting time: 10-12 weeks. Simultaneous submissions accepted: yes. Payment: via contract. Does not copyright for author. Subjects: Adolescence, Criticism, Culture, Family, Fiction, Novels, Publishing, Writers/Writing.

Myrtle Hedge Press, PO Box 705, Kernersville, NC 27285.

MYSTERIES MAGAZINE, Phantom Press Publications, Kim Guarnaccia, 13 Appleton Road, Nantucket, MA 02554-2705. 1989. "Will consider any length material - always include an SASE with submission." circ. 17M. 4/yr. Pub'd 4 issues 2005; expects 4 issues 2006, 4 issues 2007. 90pp. Reporting time: 3-6 weeks. Simultaneous submissions accepted: no. Publishes 10% of manuscripts submitted. Payment: 5¢ per word and contributors copies. Subjects: Ancient Astronauts, Astronomy, Military, Veterans, Mystery.

MYSTERY ISLAND MAGAZINE, Mystery Island Publications, Bradley Mason Hamlin, Publisher; Nicky Hamlin, Editor, Mystery Island, 384 Windward Way, Sacramento, CA 95831-2420, blacksharkpress@mysteryisland.net www.mysteryisland.net. 2004. Poetry, fiction, articles, art, cartoons, interviews, criticism, reviews, music, non-fiction. "Mystery Island Magazine is a Pop Culture Literary venue, publishing themed issues, such as "the blues issue" or "the Hunter S. Thompson tribute issue." See our website for current open issues and specific guidelines: www.mysteryisland.net We prefer email submissions. Recent publications include: Tough Company by singer/songwriter Tom Russell, including previously unpublished letters and interviews with Charles Bukowski." circ. 500. 4/yr. Expects 4 issues 2006, 4 issues 2007. sub. price $25.00; per copy $5.99; sample $4.99. Back issues: see website. Discounts: See subscription price. 24pp. Reporting time: 1 week to 1 month. Simultaneous submissions accepted: No. Payment: Pays in contributor copies. Copyrighted, reverts to author. Pub's reviews. Ads: $150 full page/$90 three quarters/$75 half page/$50 quarter page/$25 business card display. Subjects: Crime, Cults, Entertainment, Essays, Fiction, Horror, Literature (General), Metaphysics, Movies, Mystery, Non-Fiction, Poetry, Science Fiction, Short Stories, Supernatural.

Mystery Island Publications (see also MYSTERY ISLAND MAGAZINE), Brad Hamlin, 384 Windward Way, Sacramento, CA 95831-2420, blacksharkpress@mysteryisland.net www.mysteryisland.net. 2003. Poetry, fiction, articles, art, interviews, non-fiction. "Mystery Island Publications publishes three ongoing series: Monster Zipper, a metaphysical crime series created and written by Bradley Mason Hamlin (looking for art based on characters in the series, see website to order issues: www.mysteryisland.net/monster), Mystery Island Magazine (each issue different theme for poetry, short stories, and articles, see website: www.mysteryisland.net/magazine), and Mystery Island Double Feature (genre based short stories, publishing two writers/two stories each issue, see webiste: www.mysteryisland.net/double)." avg. press run 500. Pub'd 3 titles 2005; expects 10 titles 2006, 10 titles 2007. Discounts: 2 or more copies 20%. 20-24pp. Reporting time: Response time: 1 week to 1 month. Simultaneous submissions accepted: No. Payment: Mystery Island Double Feature pays $10.00 per short story + contributor copies. Copyright remains with author. Subjects: Anarchist,

California, Comics, Cults, Fiction, Folklore, Haiku, Rudyard Kipling, Music, Occult, Poetry, Prison, Psychology, Religion, Science Fiction.

MYSTERY READERS JOURNAL, Janet A. Rudolph, PO Box 8116, Berkeley, CA 94707-8116, 510-845-3600, www.mysteryreaders.org. 1985. Articles, art, interviews, criticism, reviews, news items. "Each issue deals primarily with specific themes in mystery. 2001: New England Mysteries, Partners in Crime, Oxford, Cambridge. 2002: Pacific Northwest Mysteries, Culinary Crime, Southern Mysteries, Music and Mystery." circ. 2M. 4/yr. Pub'd 4 issues 2005; expects 4 issues 2006, 4 issues 2007. sub. price $28 everyone in US/Canada, $40 elsewhere; per copy $7; sample $7. Back issues: $9/issue. 64pp. Reporting time: 2 months. Simultaneous submissions accepted: yes. Publishes 80% of manuscripts submitted. Payment: free issue. Copyrighted, does not revert to author. Pub's reviews: 600 in 2005. §Mystery fiction, literary review magazines. No ads. Subjects: Book Collecting, Bookselling, Book Reviewing, Literary Review, Mystery.

THE MYSTERY REVIEW, Barbara Davey, PO Box 233, Colborne, Ont. K0K 1S0, Canada, 613-475-4440, Fax 613-475-3400, mystrev@reach.net, www.themysteryreview.com. 1992. Poetry, articles, art, interviews, criticism, reviews, letters. "Magazine content is geared to the interests of mystery readers, reviews of mystery and suspense titles, interviews with mystery authors, word games and puzzles related to mystery." circ. 7M. 4/yr. Pub'd 4 issues 2005; expects 4 issues 2006, 4 issues 2007. sub. price $25 US in the United States; per copy $6.95; sample $7.50 (including p/h). Back issues: $5 + p/h charges (see website for details). 76pp. Reporting time: 1 month. Simultaneous submissions accepted: no. Payment: honorarium only. Copyrighted, does not revert to author. Pub's reviews: 50 in 2005. §Mystery, suspense, thrillers, adult. Ads: contact magazine (see website). Subjects: Crime, Sherlock Holmes, Interviews, Literary Review, Mystery, Reviews.

Mystic Toad Press, Gail McAbee, PO Box 401, Pacolet, SC 29372-0401, 864-948-1263, mystictoad-books@yahoo.com. 2004. Poetry, fiction. "We publish genre fiction, currently sf/fantasy and mystery. We also publish children's fiction, including the recent Eppie and Ariana winner THE THING IN THE TUB AND OTHER POEMS." avg. press run 1000. Pub'd 3 titles 2005; expects 4 titles 2006, 4 titles 2007. Discounts: 45% for bulk amounts. For less than 10 copies, 20% plus free shipping. 275pp. Reporting time: We are not currently open to submissions. We expect that to change next year. Simultaneous submissions accepted: Yes. Publishes 10% of manuscripts submitted. Payment: Royalties paid yearly. Does not copyright for author. Subjects: Comics, Egypt, Fantasy, Fiction, Sherlock Holmes, Humor, Indians, Medieval, Movies, Mystery, Science Fiction, Scotland, Space.

N

N: NUDE & NATURAL, Lee Baxandall, Founder; Judi Ditzler, Editor, PO Box 132, Oshkosh, WI 54903, 920-426-5009. 1981. Poetry, fiction, articles, art, photos, cartoons, letters, news items. "Must relate to body acceptance and nude recreation." circ. 25M. 4/yr. Pub'd 4 issues 2005; expects 4 issues 2006, 4 issues 2007. sub. price $45; per copy $7 plus s/h; sample same. Back issues: same. Discounts: 40%, inquire. 124pp. Reporting time: 1 week. Simultaneous submissions accepted: no. Publishes 50% of manuscripts submitted. Payment: small. Copyrighted, reverts to author. Pub's reviews: 8 in 2005. §Issues on nudity. Ads: $975 4CP/$490 4C 1/2 page/$625 BWP/$350 bw 1/2 page. Subjects: Health, History, Lifestyles, New Age, Photography, Travel.

Nada Press (see also BIG SCREAM), David Cope, 2782 Dixie S.W., Grandville, MI 49418, 616-531-1442. 1974. Poetry, fiction, art. "Poets and writers *must* include SASE with their submissions and make sure there's enough postage on the envelope." avg. press run 100. Pub'd 1 title 2005; expects 1 title 2006, 1 title 2007. 50pp. Reporting time: 1-3 months. Simultaneous submissions accepted: yes. Publishes 2% of manuscripts submitted. Payment: copies. Subjects: Fiction, Poetry.

NAMBLA BULLETIN, Joe Power, PO Box 174, Midtown Station, New York, NY 10018, 212-631-1194, arnoldschoen@yahoo.com. 1979. Poetry, fiction, articles, art, photos, cartoons, interviews, satire, criticism, reviews, letters, parts-of-novels, collages, news items, non-fiction. circ. 2.2M. 4/yr. Pub'd 4 issues 2005; expects 4 issues 2006, 4 issues 2007. sub. price $35 US & Canada, $50 international; per copy $5; sample $5. Back issues: $5. Discounts: 50%. 24pp. Simultaneous submissions accepted: yes. Publishes 25% of manuscripts submitted. Payment: none. Copyrighted, reverts to author. Pub's reviews: 15 in 2005. §Gay, youth liberation, man/boy love. Subjects: Adolescence, Current Affairs, Gay, Politics, Sex, Sexuality, Young Adult.

NANNY FANNY, Lou Hertz, 008 Pin Oak Court, Indianapolis, IN 46260-1530, email: nightpoet@prodigy.net. 1998. Poetry, art. "Prefer 30 lines or less, prefer upbeat poems about people or events based on external observations, not through introspection. Takes mostly free verse. Formal poetry should be light and clever.

Love poems should focus on the lover, not the poet. Art: B&W only, for cover, possibly inside." circ. 150. 3/yr. Pub'd 3 issues 2005; expects 3 issues 2006, 3 issues 2007. sub. price $10; per copy $4; sample $4. Back issues: please write for info. Discounts: none. 40pp. Reporting time: 1-2 months. We accept simultaneous submissions if they are labelled as such. Publishes 7-10% of manuscripts submitted. Payment: contributor's copy. Not copyrighted. Pub's reviews: 5 in 2005. §Poetry, including anthologies. Subjects: Humor, Literary Review, Poetry.

Nanticoke Books, Hal Roth, Box 333, Vienna, MD 21869-0333, 410-376-2144. 1995. Fiction, photos, satire, non-fiction. "Regional - Chesapeake Bay/Delmarva history and folklore." avg. press run 3M. Pub'd 1 title 2005; expects 1 title 2006, 1 title 2007. Discounts: 40-50%. 224pp. Reporting time: We do not solicit manuscripts.

NAR Publications (see also INVESTMENT COLUMN QUARTERLY (newsletter)), Nicholas A. Roes, Ed Guild, PO Box 233, Barryville, NY 12719, 914-557-8713. 1977. Articles, criticism, reviews, news items. "We publish educational, consumer, and general interest books. Titles have been plugged on Nat'l (Network) TV, wire services, radio, etc. Only 5 titles chosen yearly but given well co-ordinated PR campaign." avg. press run 5M. Pub'd 2 titles 2005; expects 3 titles 2006, 5 titles 2007. Discounts: 25% library, classroom; 40% bookstore; special requests considered. 125pp. Reporting time: 3 months. Payment: by arrangement. Copyrights for author. Subjects: Education, Non-Fiction.

The Narrative Press, Vickie Zimmer, Editor; Michael Bond, Publisher, PO Box 145, Crabtree, OR 97335, 541-259-2154, Fax 541-259-2154, service@narrativepress.com, www.narrativepress.com. 2001. Non-fiction. "The Narrative Press publishes true first person accounts of adventure and exploration." avg. press run 250. Expects 3 titles 2006, 4 titles 2007. Discounts: trade/classroom 20%. 300pp. Reporting time: 2-4 months. Simultaneous submissions accepted: yes. Publishes a variable % of manuscripts submitted. Payment: varies. Copyrights for author. Subjects: Autobiography, Earth, Natural History, History, Marine Life, Military, Veterans, Nature, Non-Fiction, Travel.

THE NARROW ROAD: A Haibun Journal, Alan Mietlowski, 73 Constance Lane, Buffalo, NY 14227-1361, kujira@buffalo.com. 2000. Poetry, art. "Poetry: haibun only. Art: haiga and sumi-e only. No limit on length. Looking for haibun, especially travel and nature diaries, from all over the world. Guidelines available for SASE. Deadline schedule: Feb. 20, May 21, Aug. 22, Nov. 21. Please enclose SASE with all submissions." circ. 100+. 4/yr. Expects 4 issues 2007. sub. price $18 US, $18 overseas (surface mail) or $25 (airmail); per copy $5; sample $5. Discounts: 1-2 copies 0%, 3-10 20%, 10+ 30%. 32pp. Reporting time: 1 week to 1 month. Simultaneous submissions accepted: yes. Publishes 50-75% of manuscripts submitted. Payment: 1 copy. Not copyrighted. Pub's reviews. §Haibun only. Ads: $15/$10/$5 1/4 page/$20 inside covers, discounts on multiple issues. Subjects: Haiku, Japan, Poetry.

Nateen Publishing, Eileen Shapiro, Publisher, 730 North Naomi Street, Burbank, CA 91505, 818-567-1987, Fax 818-567-0829. 1999. Non-fiction. "Current title is *Tutoring as a Successful Business: An Expert Tutor Shows You How*." avg. press run 5M. Pub'd 1 title 2005; expects 1 title 2006, 1 title 2007. Discounts: 1-2 copies 20%, 3-4 30%, 5+ to booksellers 40%, wholesale 55%. Reporting time: 6 weeks. Payment: negotiable. Copyrights for author. Subjects: Business & Economics, Careers, Education.

National Court Reporters Association Press (see also JOURNAL OF COURT REPORTING), Peter Wacht, Editor, 8224 Old Courthouse Road, Vienna, VA 22182, 703-556-6272, fax 703-556-6291, email pwacht@ncrahq.org. 1899. Non-fiction. "Focus should be on stenographic court reporting or language. References, such as dictionaries or glossaries, are always of interest." avg. press run 3M. Pub'd 6 titles 2005; expects 7 titles 2006, 6 titles 2007. Discounts: varies. 250pp. Reporting time: 1-2 months. Simultaneous submissions accepted: yes. Publishes 50% of manuscripts submitted. Payment: varies. Will copyright if requested. Subjects: Language, Law, Reference.

•**National Economic Research Associates, Inc.,** Gregory Leonard, Lauren Stiroh, 50 Main Street, 14th Floor, White Plains, NY 10606, 617-621-6289. 1961. avg. press run 3000. Pub'd 1 title 2005; expects 1 title 2006, 1 title 2007. Discounts: 10+ copies 25%. 300pp.

NATIONAL MASTERS NEWS, Jerry Wojcik, Editor; Suzy Hess, Publisher, PO Box 50098, 2791 Oak Alley Suite 5, Eugene, OR 97405, 541-343-7716, Fax 541-345-2436, natmanews@aol.com. 1977. Articles, art, photos, interviews, satire, criticism, reviews, letters, news items, non-fiction. "The *National Masters News* is the bible of the Masters Athletics Program. It is the only national publication devoted exclusively to track & field, race walking and long distance running for men and women over age 30. An official publication of USA Track & Field, each month it delivers 32-48 pages of results, schedules, entry blanks, age records, rankings, photos, articles, training tips. Columns are about 1M words; anything of interest to over-age-30 performer/individual. Recent contributors: Mike Tymn, Hal Higdon, Dr. John Pagliano." circ. 8M. 12/yr. Pub'd 12 issues 2005; expects 12 issues 2006, 12 issues 2007. sub. price $28; per copy $3.00. Back issues: $3.00 plus $2.00 for each order. Discounts: http://www.nationalmastersnews.com. 37pp. Reporting time: 15-30 days.

Simultaneous submissions accepted: yes. Publishes 60% of manuscripts submitted. Payment: none. Copyrighted, reverts to author. Pub's reviews: 3 in 2005. §Athletics for over-age-30 performer in track & field, long distance running, and racewalking. Ads: $630/$420/$2. Subject: Sports, Outdoors.

National Poetry Association Publishers (see also POETRY USA), Herman Berlandt, Editor, 934 Brannan Street, 2nd Floor, San Francisco, CA 94103, 415-776-6602, Fax 415-552-9271, www.nationalpoetry.org. 1985. Poetry. "The National Poetry Association is primarily a literary presenting organization, with weekly programs and the annual National Poetry Week Festival and Poetry-Film Festival. We are, however, occasional book publishers. Our last title was *Peace or Perish: A Crisis Anthology* (1983) with over 80 poets represented, including Creeley, Bly, Everson, Levertov, Kaufman, McClure, Mueller, etc. The anthology was edited by Neeli Cherkovski and Herman Berlandt. A forthcoming new title will be *The Living Word: A Tribute Anthology* of poets, writers and artists who have died of AIDS, edited by Jeffrey Lilly." avg. press run 1M. Expects 1 title 2006, 4 titles 2007. Discounts: 50%. 124pp. Reporting time: 3 months. Simultaneous submissions accepted: yes. Publishes 5% of manuscripts submitted. Payment: 2 copies. Does not copyright for author. Subject: Poetry.

THE NATIONAL POETRY REVIEW, C.J. Sage, Editor; Hailey Leithauser, Assistant Editor, PO Box 4041, Felton, CA 95018-1196, nationalpoetryreview@yahoo.com, www.nationalpoetryreview.com. 2002. Poetry, art, criticism, reviews. "TNPR READS UNSOLICITED SUBMISSIONS ONLY DURING JUNE, JULY, & AUGUST. CURRENT SUBSCRIBERS MAY SUBMIT OUTSIDE THE READING PERIOD SO LONG AS THEY DO NOT ABUSE THAT PRIVILEGE. Please write *your own* address in the return address area of the SASE as well as in the address area. Recent contributors include Jennifer Michael Hecht, Ted Kooser, A. E. Stallings, Bob Hicok, C. Dale Young, Reginald Shepherd, Bruce Bond, Margot Schilpp, Lynne Knight, Diane Thiel, Maurya Simon, et cetera. TNPR YEARLY OFFERS THE ANNIE FINCH PRIZE FOR POETRY AND THE LAUREATE PRIZE FOR POETRY. See website for complete guidelines." 2/yr. Expects 2 issues 2006, 2 issues 2007. sub. price $12; per copy $7; sample $7. Discounts: for benefactors. 64pp. Reporting time: Approximately six weeks to eight weeks. Simultaneous submissions accepted: Yes, with note to that effect in cover letter and immediate notice if work is accepted elsewhere. Publishes Less than 1% of manuscripts submitted. Payment: One copy, and, when funds are available, a small honorarium. Also offers the Finch Prize for Poetry and The Laureate Prize for Poetry. Please refer to website for guidelines and rules. Copyrights. TNPR acquires first serial rights; reprint rights, with acknowledgment to The National Poetry Review, revert to author on publication. Pub's reviews. §Books of poetry may be submitted to TNPR for short review consideration. Subject: Poetry.

National Woodlands Publishing Company, John D. Schultz, Joanne C. Schultz, 8846 Green Briar Road, Lake Ann, MI 49650-9532, 231-275-6735, phone/Fax, nwoodpc@chartermi.net. 1979. Fiction, articles, photos, interviews, reviews, letters, non-fiction. avg. press run 5M. Expects 1 title 2007. Discounts: 1 copy 0%, 2-4 20%, 5-99 40%, 100-499 50%, 500+ 55% (same for all wholesale buyers). Pages vary. Reporting time: 1 month. Simultaneous submissions accepted: no. Publishes 10% of manuscripts submitted. Payment: negotiable. Copyrights for author. Subjects: Indians, Native American, Nature, Non-Fiction, Reference.

National Writers Press, Anita E. Whelchel, Manager, 17011 Lincoln Ave., #421, Parker, CO 80134, 720-851-1944, Fax 303-841-2607, www.nationalwriters.com. 1970. Fiction, non-fiction. avg. press run 1M. Pub'd 2 titles 2005; expects 10 titles 2006, 12 titles 2007. Discounts: 55% for bulk orders. 150pp. Reporting time: 1 week. Simultaneous submissions accepted: yes. Publishes 90% of manuscripts submitted. Payment: none. Copyrights for author. Subjects: Alcohol, Alcoholism, Current Affairs, Fiction, How-To, Non-Fiction.

Native West Press, Yvette A. Schnoeker-Shorb, Editor; Terril L. Shorb, Editor, PO Box 12227, Prescott, AZ 86304, 928-771-8376, nativewestpres@cableone.net, www.nativewestpress.com. 1996. Poetry, art, photos, interviews, non-fiction. "We irregularly publish small collections that help to enhance awareness of natural biodiversity and particularly of noncharismatic creatures native to the American West. Poets and essayists are from the arts, sciences, social sciences, and education. Queries only. Include SASE. (Or see our website.) Unsolicited manuscripts for anthologies are read only in response to our Calls for Submissions in either *Small Press Review* or *Poets & Writers Magazine*. Recent contributors include Jeffrey A. Lockwood, Joanne E. Lauck, Robert Michael Pyle, Elisavietta Ritchie, Kenneth Pobo, Carol N. Kanter, Antler, CB Follett, Philip Miller, and Sara Littlecrow-Russell." avg. press run 1M. Pub'd 1 title 2005; expects 1 title 2006, 1 title 2007. Discounts: 40% trade (5+ copies), libraries 25%. 90pp. Reporting time: 6 months. Simultaneous submissions accepted: no. Publishes 2% of manuscripts submitted. Payment: contributor copies. Copyrights for author. Subjects: Animals, Anthology, Earth, Natural History, Nature, The West.

NATURAL BRIDGE, Kenneth E. Harrison Jr., Editor; Steven Schreiner, Editorial Board; Howard Schwartz, Editorial Board; Mary Troy, Editorial Board; Eamonn Wall, Editorial Board; Jennifer McKenzie, Editorial Board; Nanora Sweet, Editorial Board; John Dalton, Editorial Board, English Dept., Univ. of Missouri, One University Blvd., St. Louis, MO 63121, natural@umsl.edu, www.umsl.edu/~natural. 1999. Poetry, fiction, non-fiction. "Submit only during these two periods: July 1-August 31, and Nov. 1-Dec. 31. No electronic submissions." 2/yr. Pub'd 2 issues 2005; expects 2 issues 2006, 2 issues 2007. sub. price $15; per copy $8;

312

sample $8. 200pp. Reporting time: 5 months. Simultaneous submissions accepted: yes. Publishes 5% of manuscripts submitted. Payment: two copies & 1 year subscription. Copyrighted, reverts to author. Ads: $100/$50/exchange. Subjects: Essays, Fiction, Non-Fiction, Poetry, Prose, Short Stories, Translation.

NATURAL LIFE, Life Media, Wendy Priesnitz, Box 112, Niagara Falls, NY 14304-0112, 416-260-0303, email: natural@life.ca, web: www.NaturalLifeMagazine.com. 1976. ''An environmental lifestyles magazine that circulates in USA and Canada.'' circ. 25M. 6/yr. Pub'd 6 issues 2005; expects 6 issues 2006, 6 issues 2007. sub. price $24 (+ GST in Canada); per copy $4.95; sample $4.95. Back issues: $4.95. 44pp. Simultaneous submissions accepted: no. Publishes 10% of manuscripts submitted. Payment: none. Ads: $1200/page, no classifieds. Subjects: Business & Economics, Children, Youth, Community, Cooking, Ecology, Foods, Education, Solar.

NATURE SOCIETY NEWS, Karen E. Martin, PO Box 390, Griggsville, IL 62340-0390, 217-833-2323, Fax 217-833-2123, natsoc@adams.net, www.naturesociety.org. 1966. 12/yr. Pub'd 12 issues 2005; expects 12 issues 2006, 12 issues 2007. sub. price $15, $20 US funds in Canada; sample no charge. Back issues: $2 (depends on availability). Discounts: 40% to agencies and catalogs. 32pp. Payment: only to regular staff contributors. Copyrighted, reverts to author. Pub's reviews: 24 in 2005. §Birds, nature (special emphasis: home-related; eastern North America). No ads. Subjects: Animals, Earth, Natural History.

Naturegraph Publishers, Barbara Brown, PO Box 1047, 3543 Indian Creek Road, Happy Camp, CA 96039, 530-493-5353, 530-493-5240, 1-800-390-5353. nature@isqtel.net, www.naturegraph.com. 1946. Non-fiction. avg. press run 2500. Expects 5 titles 2006, 2 titles 2007. Discounts: 1-4 copies 20%, 5-24 copies 40%, 25 - 49 copies 42%, 50-99 copies 43%, 100 copies 44%. 144pp. Reporting time: Within a week to up to two months depending on time and/or interest. Simultaneous submissions accepted: Yes. Publishes 1% of manuscripts submitted. Payment: No advances. Pays royalties once a year,. 10% of wholesale generally and 8% if bookis sold at discounts of 50% and up. Copyrights for author. Subjects: Americana, Anthropology, Archaelogy, Astronomy, Birds, Botany, Crafts, Hobbies, Earth, Natural History, Gardening, Indigenous Cultures, Marine Life, Multicultural, Native American, Nature, Quilting, Sewing, Southwest.

THE NAUTILUS, J.H. Leal, PO Box 1580, Sanibel, FL 33957, 941-395-2233, Fax 941-395-6706, jleal@shellmuseum.org. 1886. Articles, non-fiction. ''Original scientific research in malacology (mollusks).'' circ. 800. 4/yr. Pub'd 4 issues 2005; expects 4 issues 2006, 4 issues 2007. sub. price $35 (individuals), $56 (institutions), foreign postage $5, airmail $15. Back issues: $20 each where available. Discounts: $3 to agents on institutional rate ($56 per year). Cost to agent $53. 50pp. Reporting time: 9 months. Simultaneous submissions accepted: no. Publishes 50% of manuscripts submitted. Payment: charge page-charges, $60/page. Copyrighted, does not revert to author. Pub's reviews: 2 in 2005. §Only on mollusks. Subjects: Biology, Earth, Natural History.

NBM Publishing Company, Terry Nantier, 555 8th Avenue, Ste. 1202, New York, NY 10018-4364, 212-643-5407, Fax 212-643-1545. 1976. Cartoons. ''We publish *graphic novels* high-quality *comics* in book form.'' avg. press run 5M. Pub'd 25 titles 2005; expects 25 titles 2006, 25 titles 2007. Discounts: wholesale 50% returnable 1 year, 60% non-returnable; retail 40%-48% returnable 1 year, 50% non-returnable. 80pp. Reporting time: 2-4 weeks. Simultaneous submissions accepted: yes. Publishes 1% of manuscripts submitted. Payment: 8-12% of sales (retail). Copyrights for author. Subject: Comics.

N-B-T-V, D.B. Pitt, Narrow Bandwidth Television Association, 1 Burnwood Dr., Wollaton, Nottingham, Notts NG8 2DJ, England, 0115-9282896. 1975. Articles, photos, cartoons, interviews, criticism, reviews, letters, news items, non-fiction. ''Normal maximum length of article 1K words. Longer articles would be serialised. Bias is towards projects on a low budget which readers can carry out at home/school/college etc.'' circ. 200. 4/yr. Pub'd 4 issues 2005; expects 4 issues 2006, 4 issues 2007. sub. price £5, $12 US; per copy £1.50; sample 75p (Annual sub - £3 to non-earners). Back issues: bound volumes II + III (one book) £3. Discounts: under review, please inquire. 13pp. Reporting time: 1 week. Simultaneous submissions accepted: yes. Publishes 75% of manuscripts submitted. Payment: none. Copyrighted, copyright normally held on behalf of author but negotiable. Pub's reviews: 3 in 2005. §Television, hobby electronics, history of television. Ads: £10/£6/small ads free to subscribers, otherwise negotiable. Subjects: Crafts, Hobbies, Dining, Restaurants, Electronics, Engineering, How-To, Science.

NEBO, Andrew Geyer, Fiction Editor; Michael Ritchie, Poetry Editor, Department of English, Arkansas Tech University, Russellville, AR 72801, 479-968-0256. 1982. Poetry, fiction, articles, art, criticism, reviews, long-poems, non-fiction. ''We are interested in quality poetry and fiction by both new and established writers. In fiction we are open to a wide range of styles. We seek poems whose rhythms are as compelling and memorable as their diction and images, and as a result we print a large number of formal poems (poems using meter and rhyme). We have published poems by Howard Nemerov, Timothy Steele, Julia Randall, Dana Gioia, Brenda Hillman, Turner Cassity, R. L. Barth, and many other excellent poets, many previously unknown to us. In addition, we are interested in well-written reviews and criticism of English language poetry. We encourage poetic translations from contemporary writers and personal essays about travel in other parts of the world." circ. 300. 1-2/yr. Pub'd 1 issue 2005; expects 2 issues 2006, 2 issues 2007. sub. price $10; per copy $6; sample $5. Back issues: $5. 48-60pp. Reporting time: 2 weeks to 4 months; between Aug 1 and Feb 1, issue is put together. Reporting time is March for year's submissions. Payment: 1 copy. Copyrighted, reverts to author. Pub's reviews: 6 in 2005. §Poetry, fiction, literature in translation. Ads: $75/$45. Subjects: Fiction, Poetry.

THE NEBRASKA REVIEW, Zoo Press, James Reed, Fiction; Coreen Wees, Poetry; John Price, Creative Nonfiction, FA 212, University of Nebraska-Omaha, Omaha, NE 68182-0324, 402-554-3159. 1972. Poetry, fiction, reviews. "Dedicated to the best contemporary fiction, essays and poetry. Previous contributors include Kelly Cherry, Jack Myers, Rebecca Seiferle, Tom Franklin, Stewart O'Nan, Cris Mazza, Patricia Goedicke, Leslie Pietrzyk, Jonis Agee, DeWitt Henry, Elaine Ford, Richard Jackson. Prefer fiction and poetry which shows control of form and an ear for language, and which transcends mere competence in technique. Closed April 30 - August 30." circ. 1M. 2/yr. Pub'd 2 issues 2005; expects 2 issues 2006, 2 issues 2007. sub. price $15; per copy $8; sample $4.50. Discounts: bookstores 60/40, distributors 55/45. 108pp. Reporting time: 3-6 months. Payment: 2 copies and 1 yr. subscription. Copyrighted, reverts to author. Ads: $100/$60. Subjects: English, Fiction, Poetry.

•NEO: Literary Magazine, John Starkey, Editor, Departamento de Linguas e Literaturas, Universidade dos Acores, 9500 Ponta Delgada, Portugal, www.neomagazine.org. 2002. Poetry, fiction, interviews, parts-of-novels, non-fiction. "NEO, an international magazine of poetry, fiction, and creative nonfiction, is published in association with the Department of Modern Languages and Literature, University of the Azores (Azores, Portugal). North American contributors include Peter Makuck, Mark Levine, Mark Cox, Frank Gaspar, Katherine Vaz, Paulo da Costa, William Trowbridge, Patricia Goedicke, and Colette Inez (among others). Some established European contributors include David Albahari, Luisa Villalta, Jose Martins Garcia, Pedro da Silveira, Urbano Bettencourt, Alamo Oliveira, Ivo Machado, and Pedro Javier Castaneda Garcia. Approximately half of the submissions are from Luso-American or Azorean authors. Works are generally published in their original languages (predominantly English or Portuguese)." circ. 1000. 1/yr. Pub'd 1 issue 2005; expects 1 issue 2006, 1 issue 2007. sub. price $16/2 issues; per copy $10; sample $10. Back issues: $10. Discounts: 2-10 copies 20%, 11 or more 30%. 128pp. Reporting time: 3 to 5 months. Simultaneous submissions accepted: Yes. Publishes 5% of manuscripts submitted. Payment: in copies. Copyrighted, reverts to author. Subjects: Essays, Fiction, Interviews, Journals, Literary Review, Literature (General), Magazines, Memoirs, Multicultural, Non-Fiction, Novels, Poetry, Portugal, Short Stories, Travel.

THE NEO-COMINTERN, Joel Katelnikoff, 97 Maxwell Crescent, Saskatoon, Sask. S7L 3Y4, Canada, www.neo-comintern.com. 1998. Poetry, fiction, articles, art, cartoons, satire. circ. ~700. 2/yr. Pub'd 2 issues 2005; expects 2 issues 2006, 2 issues 2007. sub. price $10; per copy $4 ppd; sample $4 ppd. Back issues: $4 ppd. Discounts: $10 for 4 copies, $20 for 10 copies. 20pp. Simultaneous submissions accepted: no. Publishes 50% of manuscripts submitted. Payment: contributors receive complimentary copies. Copyrighted, reverts to author. Ads: none. Subjects: Absurdist, Creativity, Dada, Entertainment, Philosophy, Politics, Post Modern, Socialist.

NEONATAL NETWORK: The Journal of Neonatal Nursing, NICU Ink, Charles Rait, Editor-in-Chief, 2270 Northpoint Parkway, Santa Rosa, CA 95407-7398, www.neonatalnetwork.com. 1981. Non-fiction. circ. 12M. 8/yr. Pub'd 8 issues 2005; expects 8 issues 2006, 6 issues 2007. sub. price $44; per copy $8; sample free. Back issues: $8 each. Discounts: none. 72pp. Reporting time: 6 months-1 year. Simultaneous submissions accepted: no. Publishes 50% of manuscripts submitted. Copyrighted, does not revert to author. Pub's reviews. §Neonatal nursing only. Ads: b&w: $1750/$1275/$865 1/4 page.

NEROUP REVIEW, Michael LaPointe, 202 Spencer St., Apt. #5, Monterey, CA 93940-1859, www.neroupreview.com, submissions@neroupreview.com. 2004. Poetry, articles, art, photos, interviews, criticism, reviews, music, letters, long-poems, concrete art, non-fiction. "The Neroup Review publishes innovative science articles and poetry in the format of a Fine Arts magazine. Check the website for examples of our magazine. www.neroupreview.com." circ. 250. 4/yr. Expects 4 issues 2006, 4 issues 2007. sub. price $35; per copy $10; sample $10. Back issues: inquire. 100pp. Reporting time: 1 month. Simultaneous submissions accepted: Yes. Publishes 30% of manuscripts submitted. Payment: Copies. Copyrighted, reverts to author. Pub's reviews: none in 2005. §All Science minus science fiction, Cultural, Poetry, Fine Arts. No advertising. Subjects: Agriculture, Anarchist, Anthropology, Archaeology, Architecture, Arts, Biography, Book Reviewing, Classical Studies, Community, Computers, Calculators, Criticism, Dada, Earth, Natural History, Ecology, Foods, Energy.

NERVE COWBOY, Liquid Paper Press, Joseph Shields, Jerry Hagins, PO Box 4973, Austin, TX 78765, www.onr.com/user/jwhagins/nervecowboy.html. 1995. Poetry, fiction, art. "Open to all forms, styles and subject matter preferring writing that speaks directly and minimizes literary devices. Fiction (up to 5 pages), poetry, and black & white artwork submissions are welcome year round. Recent contributors include Gerald Locklin, Wilma Elizabeth McDaniel, Jennifer Jackson, Michael Estabrook, and Christopher Cunningham." circ. 250. 2/yr. Pub'd 2 issues 2005; expects 2 issues 2006, 2 issues 2007. sub. price $8; per copy $5; sample $5.

314

Back issues: $4. Discounts: selected trades, 40% on 6 or more copies (bookstores). 64pp. Reporting time: 2 months. Simultaneous submissions accepted: no. Publishes 5% of manuscripts submitted. Payment: 1 copy. Copyrighted, reverts to author. Ads: trade ads with other small magazines. Subjects: Arts, Literature (General), Poetry.

Neshui Publishing, Neshui, neshui62@hotmail.com—online email. 1993. Poetry, fiction, art, cartoons, interviews, satire, music, letters, long-poems, plays, non-fiction. "neshui also produces films... neshui-flims.com—titles: dictatorship of taste, 9 toes in monte carlo, mosquite king, romeo and julliet, dirty cowboy dress(western)." avg. press run 100. Pub'd 3 titles 2005; expects 3 titles 2006, 3 titles 2007. Discounts: 55% wholesalers. 200pp. Reporting time: thirty two secounds. Simultaneous submissions accepted: yes. Publishes 1% of manuscripts submitted. Payment: zero cash payment—75 copies. Copyrights for author. Subjects: Fiction, Young Adult.

NEW ALTERNATIVES, J & J Consultants, Inc., Walter Jones, 603 Ole Farm Road, Media, PA 19063, 610-565-9692, Fax 610-565-9694, wjones13@juno.com, www.members.tripod/walterjones. 1993. Poetry, fiction, articles, cartoons, music, non-fiction. "Short: 100-200 words." circ. 250. 6/yr. Pub'd 6 issues 2005; expects 6 issues 2006, 6 issues 2007. sub. price $12; per copy $3. 8pp. Reporting time: 2 months. Simultaneous submissions accepted: yes. Publishes 75% of manuscripts submitted. Payment: none. Copyrighted, reverts to author. Pub's reviews. §Parenting, childcare. Subjects: Adolescence, Children, Youth, Mental Health, Poetry.

NEW AMERICAN IMAGIST, Michael McClintock, General Editor; Jean George, Special Assignments Editor; Val Cho, Copyeditor, PO Box 124, South Pasadena, CA 91031-0124. 2001; formerly Seer Ox, founded in 1971. Poetry, art, long-poems. "The New American Imagist is interested in neo-Imagist and post-modern impressionist poetry written in contemporary idiom, grounded in contemporary experience. We are not interested in still-life poetry in dead language or work that merely imitates the Imagist movement of the early twentieth century. Our special six-panel collector's editions are intended to be representative of a poet's finest work, and have included Alan Catlin, Cor van den Heuvel, Luis Cuauhtemoc Berriozabal, Leonard J. Cirino, Robert Edwards, and Akitsu Ei. We read all work submitted continuously, from both known and unknown poets; our editorial process can be lengthy for final selections; reporting time can vary from two weeks to several months; work accepted into the final selection phase receives regular updates back to the poet. It is always best to submit 10-20 poems at a time; poetry may be any length up to 200 lines for a single poem. All work accepted and published as part of The New American Imagist series will be anthologized in book form (about each five years), published by Hermitage West, a private foundation based in California." circ. Varies with each edition, from 200 to 1500. Currently ranges from 4 to 9 issues per year. sub. price $12 for 8 issues.; per copy $1.50; sample $1.50. Back issues: All editions remain in print indefinitely. Discounts: Generous discounts on copies are offered to published poets and to libraries. Reporting time: Varies greatly from two weeks to several months. Publishes 1% of manuscripts submitted. Payment: 30 copies to the poet. Copyrighted, reverts to author. Subjects: Arts, Asia, Indochina, Asian-American, Celtic, Chicano/a, Criticism, Gaelic, Haiku, Libraries, Philosophy, Poetry, Psychology, Religion, Reprints, Translation.

New American Publishing Co., 3033 Waltham Way, McCarran, NV 89434, napc@pocketmail.com.

NEW AMERICAN WRITING, Paul Hoover, Maxine Chernoff, 369 Molino Avenue, Mill Valley, CA 94941, 415-389-1877, Fax 415-384-0364. 1971. Poetry, fiction, articles, criticism. "August to January submissions encouraged. Work by Ann Lauterbach, Nathaniel Mackey, Robert Coover, John Ashbery, Charles Bernstein, Charles Simic, Lyn Hejinian, Clark Coolidge, Wanda Coleman, Jorie Graham, Robert Creeley and others. Special issues: #4 Australian Poetry, #5 Censorship and the Arts, #9 New British Poetry, #18 Brazilian Poetry, #19 Clark Coolidge, #20 Russian Absurdist Poetry of the 1930s, #21 Poets Respond to Gerhard Richter, Poetry of Picasso, #22 Asian Poetry, Peret's Political Poems. Covers by prominent artists." circ. 4M. 1/yr. Pub'd 1 issue 2005; expects 1 issue 2006, 1 issue 2007. sub. price $12 per issue individuals; see EBSCO, SWETS, and others for libraries; $6 postal surcharge per issue foreign mail.; per copy $15 domestic, $22 Canada; sample $15. Back issues: varies, please inquire. Discounts: 60/40 to bookstores. 175pp. Reporting time: 1-6 months. Simultaneous submissions accepted: Yes. Publishes 1-5% of manuscripts submitted. Payment: 2 copies. Copyrighted, reverts to author. Ads: $250. Subjects: Fiction, Poetry, Translation.

New Atlantean Press, Nathan Wright, Publisher, PO Box 9638, Santa Fe, NM 87504, 505-983-1856 phone/Fax, global@thinktwice.com, www.thinktwice.com. 1992. "Send for a free catalog or visit our website." avg. press run 5M. Pub'd 2 titles 2005; expects 2 titles 2006, 2 titles 2007. Discounts: 5+ 40%, 30+ 45%, case purchases 50%, higher discounts possible. 128pp. Reporting time: 3 weeks. Simultaneous submissions accepted: yes. Payment: yes. Copyrights for author. Subjects: Health, Parenting, Philosophy, Spiritual.

NEW BOOKS ON WOMEN & FEMINISM, Women's Studies Librarian, University of Wisconsin System, Phyllis Holman Weisbard, Linda Fain, 430 Memorial Library, 728 State Street, Madison, WI 53706, 608-263-5754. 1979. "A subject-arranged, indexed bibliography of new titles in women's studies, listing books and periodicals.'' circ. 1.1M. 2/yr. Pub'd 2 issues 2005; expects 2 issues 2006, 2 issues 2007. sub. price $30 individuals and women's programs, $55 institutions (includes subscriptions to *New Books On Women & Feminism, Feminist Collections*, and *Feminist Periodicals*) Please inquire about special prices in Wisconsin; per copy $3.50; sample $3.50. Back issues: $3.50. 75pp. Copyrighted. Subjects: Bibliography, Feminism, Indexes & Abstracts, Lesbianism, Libraries, Women.

New Canaan Publishing Company Inc., Kathy Mittelstadt, PO Box 752, New Canaan, CT 06840, 203-966-3408 phone,203-548-9072 fax. 1995. Poetry, fiction, non-fiction. ''Publisher of children's books with strong educational and/or moral content.'' avg. press run 5M. Pub'd 2 titles 2005; expects 5 titles 2006, 4 titles 2007. Discounts: please call for rates. Pages vary. Reporting time: 3-4 months (not guaranteed). Simultaneous submissions accepted: yes. Publishes approx. 1% of manuscripts submitted. Payment: percentage royalty (4-10% depending on material). Copyrights for author. Subjects: Children, Youth, Christianity, Education.

New Community Press, Robert L. Batcheller, 2692 Madison Road N-1, #263, Cincinnati, OH 45208, 513-509-9352, newcommunitypress@cinci.rr.com. 2002. Non-fiction. avg. press run 15M. Pub'd 1 title 2005; expects 10 titles 2006, 10 titles 2007. Discounts: to be determined. 200pp. Reporting time: 30 days. Simultaneous submissions accepted: yes. Publishes 25% of manuscripts submitted. Payment: negotiable. Copyrights for author. Subjects: Construction, Consumer, Cooking, How-To, Internet, Real Estate.

New Concept Press, Norman Beim, 425 West 57th Street Suite 2J, New York, NY 10019, 212-265-6284, Fax: 212-265-6659. 1993. Fiction, plays. ''LiteratureNorman Beim.'' avg. press run 1000. Pub'd 1 title 2005; expects 1 title 2006, 1 title 2007. Discounts: 40%. 250-630pp. Subjects: Autobiography, Biography, Drama, Holocaust, Judaism, Literature (General), Memoirs, Novels, Performing Arts, Religion, Theatre.

•New Creature Press (see also DRAMA GARDEN), Joseph Verrilli, PO Box 1158, Bridgeport, CT 06601-1158, 203-455-7285. 2006. Poetry, articles, art, photos, cartoons, satire, reviews, letters, long-poems, collages, non-fiction. ''Some recent contributors: Marie Kazalia, Ana Christy, Laurel Speer, Lyn Lifshin, Colin Cross, D.J. Weston, Jonathan K. Rice, Laura Stamps, and Mark Sonnenfeld.'' avg. press run 50. Expects 3 titles 2006, 3 titles 2007. 21pp. Reporting time: 1 week. Simultaneous submissions accepted: yes. Publishes 95% of manuscripts submitted. Does not copyright for author. Subjects: Relationships, Religion, Society.

New Dawn Unlimited, Inc. (see also ALTERNATIVE HARMONIES LITERARY & ARTS MAGAZINE), Jerri Hardesty, 1830 Marvel Road, Brierfield, AL 35035, 205-665-7904; fax 205-665-2500; e-mail wytrabbit1@aol.com. 1997. Poetry, fiction, art, photos, cartoons, long-poems, plays, non-fiction. ''Always accepting submissions! Annual theme issues. Please send 5-10 pieces! Also, for Annual Chapbook competition-send 20-50 pages/manuscript with a $10 entry fee. Pays 100-200 copies, services, advertising, and artistic input. PLEASE SEE NEWDAWNUNLIMITED.COM.'' avg. press run 500. Pub'd 3 titles 2005; expects 6-8 titles 2006, 6-8 titles 2007. Discounts: $2 each for 20 or more; will consider this price for any good cause. 40-50pp. Reporting time: Varies with volume; 3 months after deadline for chapbooks. Simultaneous submissions fine, except on chapbooks. Publishes 5% of manuscripts submitted. Payment: 1-2 copies magazines; 100-200 copies Annual Chapbook winner. Does not copyright for author.

NEW DELTA REVIEW, Anna Hirsch, Fiction Editor; Bobbie Perry, Fiction Editor, New Delta Review, Louisiana State University, Department of English, 249 Allen Hall, Baton Rouge, LA 70803, 225-578-4079. 1984. Poetry, fiction, art, photos, interviews, reviews, non-fiction. *''New Delta Review* publishes new and established writers of poetry and fiction. We also accept literary interviews, reviews, essays, and art. For more information, please visit our Website: http://www.english.lsu.edu/journals/ndr.'' circ. 500. 2/yr. Pub'd 2 issues 2005; expects 2 issues 2006, 2 issues 2007. sub. price $12; per copy $7; sample $5 issue, $10 for 3. Back issues: $7 for any issue prior to the current one. 150pp. Reporting time: 3-5 months. Simultaneous submissions accepted: Yes, if noted in cover letter. We also ask that the author notify us if their work is accepted elsewhere. Publishes 1% of manuscripts submitted. Payment: 2 contributors' copies. Copyrighted, reverts to author. Pub's reviews: 7 in 2005. §Contemporary poetry, fiction and literary essays, popular culture, works on contemporary authors. Ads: $75/$40, one year contract (2 issues) $100/$60; mostly ad trades. Subjects: Essays, Fiction, Interviews, Poetry, Reviews.

New England Cartographics, Inc., Christopher J. Ryan, President; Valerie Vaughan, Editor, PO Box 9369, North Amherst, MA 01059-9369, 413-549-4124, toll free 888-995-6277, Fax 413-549-3621, email: geolopes@crocker.com URL: www.necartographics.com. 1986. Non-fiction. ''Specialize in outdoor recreation maps and guidebooks; hiking, backpacking, bicycling, mountain biking, paddling, rail-trails principally of areas in the North Eastern United States.'' avg. press run 3M-5M. Pub'd 2 titles 2005; expects 3 titles 2006, 4 titles 2007. Discounts: trade 40-45% retail, 45-55% wholesale/distributors. 178pp. Reporting time: 1 month. Simultaneous submissions accepted: yes. Publishes 25% of manuscripts submitted. Payment: 5-10% of cover price. Copyrights for author. Subjects: Adirondacks, Bicycling, Birds, Conservation, Geography, History, Leisure/Recreation, Maine, Maps, Nature, New England, New Hampshire, New York, Sports, Outdoors, Water.

THE NEW ENGLAND QUARTERLY, Linda Smith Rhoads, Editor, c/o Massachusetts Historical Society,

1154 Boylston St., Boston, MA 02215, 617-646-0543, fax: 617-859-0074, website: www.newenglandquarterly.org. 1928. Articles, criticism, reviews. *"The New England Quarterly*, a Historical Review of New England Life and Letters, publishes articles in the fields of literature, history, art, and culture; short memoranda and documents; and book reviews." circ. 2.5M. 4/yr. Pub'd 4 issues 2005; expects 4 issues 2006, 4 issues 2007. sub. price $35, individual; $25, student; $70, institution; per copy $10. Back issues: $12. 176pp. Reporting time: 6-8 weeks. Simultaneous submissions accepted: no. Publishes 20% of manuscripts submitted. Payment: 1-year free subscription. Copyrighted, does not revert to author. Pub's reviews: 45 in 2005. §American literature (with some connection to New England), New England history, art, culture, biography (all with some connection to New England). Ads: $200/$125. Subjects: Arts, Criticism, Culture, English, Feminism, History, Music, Native American, New England, Politics, Reviews, Sociology.

NEW ENGLAND REVIEW, Middlebury College Publications, Stephen Donadio, Editor; Carolyn Kuebler, Managing Editor; C. Dale Young, Poetry Editor, Middlebury College, Middlebury, VT 05753, 802-443-5075, fax 802-443-2088, e-mail nereview@middlebury.edu, http://go.middlebury.edu/nereview. 1978. Poetry, fiction, articles, photos, interviews, criticism, reviews, parts-of-novels, long-poems. "Submissions accepted must be postmarked between Sept.1 and May 31 only." circ. 2M. 4/yr. Pub'd 4 issues 2005; expects 4 issues 2006, 4 issues 2007. sub. price $25 individual, $40 institution; per copy $8; sample $8. Back issues: $4. Discounts: 2 years $45, 3 years $62; 20% classroom. 210pp. Reporting time: 3-4 months. Simultaneous submissions accepted, if indicated as such. Publishes 2% of manuscripts submitted. Payment: $10 per page, $20 minimum, plus 2 copies. Copyrighted. Pub's reviews: 4 in 2005. §Contemporary fiction, poetry, biography, autobiography, non-fiction. Ads: $200/$125/discounts for featured authors and books reviewed. Subjects: Fiction, Literary Review, Literature (General), Poetry.

NEW ENVIRONMENT BULLETIN, Harry Schwarzlander, 270 Fenway Drive, Syracuse, NY 13224, 315-446-8009. 1974. Articles, interviews, reviews, letters, news items. "Contains reports of activities of The New Environment Association, as well as articles and news items relating to the concerns of the Association, which are personal and social changes needed to achieve a sustainable society, and the creation of new communities which are humanly and environmentally sound. Content is contributed primarily by members and other readers." circ. 140. 10-11/yr. Pub'd 11 issues 2005; expects 10-11 issues 2006, 10-11 issues 2007. sub. price $12 (North America); sample free. Back issues: $5 for 2-year series (even-to-odd years). 6pp. Reporting time: not specified. Payment: none. Not copyrighted. Pub's reviews: 1 in 2005. §See above. Ads: none. Subjects: Agriculture, Community, Counter-Culture, Alternatives, Communes, Ecology, Foods, Energy, Environment, Futurism, Nature, New Age, Non-Violence, Peace.

New Falcon Publications, Frank Martin, 1739 E. Broadway Road, Suite 1-277, Tempe, AZ 85282, 602-708-1409 (phone),602-708-1410 (fax),info@newfalcon.com (email),http://www.newfalcon.com (website). 1982. Fiction, satire, criticism, plays, non-fiction. Pub'd 8 titles 2005; expects 8 titles 2006, 8 titles 2007. Discounts: 20% single copy, 30% 2-4 mix or match, 40% 5+ mix or match. Reporting time: 60-90 days. Simultaneous submissions accepted: yes. Publishes 3% of manuscripts submitted. Copyrights for author. Subjects: Anarchist, Biography, Criticism, Fiction, Folklore, Gay, Health, Lesbianism, Libertarian, Occult, Philosophy, Political Science, Psychology, Religion, Science Fiction.

THE NEW FORMALIST, The New Formalist Press, Leo Yankevich, Editor; David Castleman, Editor, P.O. Box 251, Dayton, WA 99328, thenewformalist@lycos.com http://www.newformalist.com. 2000. Poetry, fiction, reviews. "We publish metrical poetry along with occassional essays, reviews, and stories. Recent contributors include Jared Carter, Moore Moran, Richard Moore, Tom Riley, and Joseph S. Salemi." circ. 1000. 1/yr. Pub'd 2 issues 2005; expects 2 issues 2006, 2 issues 2007. sub. price $20; per copy $10; sample $10. Back issues: inquiries welcome. 90pp. Reporting time: One week to one year. Publishes 1% of manuscripts submitted. Payment: copies. Copyrighted, reverts to author. Pub's reviews: 50 in 2005. §Most things except temporary enthusiasms. Ads: inquire. Subjects: Anthology, Arts, Essays, Ethics, Novels, Poetry, Storytelling, Dylan Thomas.

The New Formalist Press (see also THE NEW FORMALIST), Leo Yankevich, David Castleman, Lamon Cull, Box 251, Dayton, WA 99328-0251, thenewformalist@lycos.com. 1990. Poetry, fiction, articles, interviews, satire, criticism, reviews, parts-of-novels, long-poems, non-fiction. "We appreciate the expansive humors of love, doubt, and joy, and we appreciate a conscionable belief. We appreciate laughter, and an intelligent responsibility. We appreciate the individual existence within the blessedness of continuity." avg. press run 250. Pub'd 2 titles 2005; expects 2 titles 2006, 2 titles 2007. 90pp. Reporting time: variable. Simultaneous submissions accepted: yes. Publishes 1% of manuscripts submitted. Payment: inquire. Copyrights for author. Subjects: Arts, Ethics.

NEW GERMAN REVIEW: A Journal of Germanic Studies, Claire Whitner, Editor; Victor Fusilero, Editor; Jens Priwitzer, Editor, Dept of Germanic Languages, UCLA, 212 Royce Hall, Los Angeles, CA 90095-1539, 310-825-3955. 1985. Articles, interviews, criticism, reviews. "Manuscripts should be prepared in accordance with the 1999 *MLA Handbook* (5th Edition) (paranthetical documentation) and not exceed 30 typed pages including documentation. Unsolicited book reviews are accepted." circ. 250. 1/yr. Pub'd 1 issue 2005; expects 3 issues 2006, 2 issues 2007. sub. price $8 students; $11 individuals; $14 institutions; per copy $8; sample free. 120pp. Reporting time: 3 months after submission deadline. Simultaneous submissions accepted: no. Publishes 50% of manuscripts submitted. Payment: none. Copyrighted, does not revert to author. Pub's reviews: 2 in 2005. §German literature, German culture, German theory, German visual arts and culture. Ads: $60 full page/on exchange basis. Subjects: Criticism, German, Literature (General).

NEW GRAFFITI, Renee Angers, Ontario, Canada, newgraffiti@hotmail.com. 2002. Poetry, fiction, articles, interviews, criticism, reviews, long-poems, non-fiction. "Currently, New Graffiti is a free on-line alternative literary zine, but we have plans on expanding into print in the near future. Our URL is: http://brainpanpublishing.0catch.com/newgraffiti/cover/NewGraffitiCover.htm.We publish short fiction, non-fiction, and poetry, as well as reviews and interviews. Where most "literary" zines intimidate with a somewhat cold and pretentious feel, we take a more light-hearted, fearless approach to literature.Recent contributors include John Martin of Black Sparrow Press: publisher responsible for discovering and publishing Charles Bukowski, and Steve Albini: guitarist for infamous punk band Big Black, as well as the producer on albums for bands such as Nirvana, NIN, and The Pixies." 4/yr. Pub'd 4 issues 2005; expects 4 issues 2006, 4 issues 2007. sub. price $0; per copy $0; sample free. Back issues: inquire. 20pp. Reporting time: 2 weeks. Payment: NG does not currently pay contributors. Authors/writers that agree to be published by NG, do so for exposure. Pub's reviews. §books, magazines, film, music. Subjects: Book Reviewing, Literary Review, Literature (General), Non-Fiction, Poetry.

THE NEW HAMPSHIRE REVIEW: A Journal of Poetry & Politics, Virginia Heatter, P.O. Box 322, Nashua, NH 03060-0322, www.newhampshirereview.com. 2005. Poetry, articles, art, reviews. "The New Hampshire Review is an online, quarterly journal of poetry and politics. We are interested in poetry from a variety of school and styles. Quality is our first concern, and we look for work which contemplates the human condition in interesting, fresh and meaningful ways. We also publish timely political essays written from a progressive point-of-view." 4/yr. Expects 4 issues 2006, 4 issues 2007. 150pp. Reporting time: 8-12 weeks. Simultaneous submissions accepted: Yes. Payment: no payment. First North American Serial Rights. Pub's reviews. §poetry collections. Subjects: Poetry, Politics.

NEW HOPE INTERNATIONAL REVIEW, New Hope International, Gerald England, 20 Werneth Avenue, Gee Cross, Hyde, Cheshire SK14 5NL, United Kingdom, www.geraldengland.co.uk. 1986. Reviews, music, letters. "Reviews of poetry books pamphlets and magazines. Unsolicited reviews not required but U.K. subscribers who can write fluently are welcome to join the reviewing team." circ. 1M. Continuously updated. Pub'd 2 issues 2005; expects 2 issues 2006, 2 issues 2007. price per copy $10 (includes postage) cash only. Back issues: $5 cash. 500pp. Simultaneous submissions accepted: no. Publishes (solicited only) 90% of manuscripts submitted. Payment: copies. Not copyrighted. Pub's reviews: 1000 in 2005. §Poetry, literary criticism. Ads: none. Subjects: Avant-Garde, Experimental Art, Beat, Biography, Book Reviewing, Haiku, Literary Review, Literature (General), Magazines, Poetry, Reviews, Tapes & Records, Textiles, Translation, Writers/Writing.

New Horizons Publishing, Jennifer Bishop, 5830 NW Expressway, Suite 225, Oklahoma City, OK 73132-5236, 405-823-9538, Fax 405-848-8118,. 2001. Poetry, fiction, non-fiction. Expects 1 title 2006, 3 titles 2007. Discounts: contact for rates. 125pp. Reporting time: 3-4 months. Simultaneous submissions accepted: yes. Publishes 1-3% of manuscripts submitted. Does not copyright for author.

NEW INTERNATIONAL A magazine of Marxist politics and theory, Pathfinder Press, Mary-Alice Waters, P.O. Box 162767, Atlanta, GA 30321-2767, www.pathfinderpress.com.

New Issues Poetry & Prose, Marianne Swierenga, Managing Editor; Nancy Eimers, Advisory Editor; Mark Halliday, Advisory Editor; William Olsen, Advisory Editor; J. Allyn Rosser, Advisory Editor; J.D. Dolan, Advisory Editor; Stuart Dybek, Advisory Editor; Richard Katrovas, Advisory Editor, Western Michigan University, 1903 W. Michigan Avenue, Kalamazoo, MI 49008-5331, 269-387-8185, Fax 269-387-2562, new-issues@wmich.edu, www.wmich.edu/newissues. 1996. Poetry. "New Issues Poetry Prize, $2,000 and publication for a first book of poems. Deadline: Nov. 30. Judge to be named. The Green Rose Prize in Poetry, $2,000 and publication for a book of poems by an established poet. Deadline: Sept. 30. Send SASE for complete guidelines or visit our website. We do not read unsolicited manuscripts." avg. press run 1.5M. Pub'd 12 titles 2005; expects 12 titles 2006, 6-12 titles 2007. Discounts: individuals order through Amazon.com or www.spdbooks.com; bookstores may order through distributor, Partners 800-336-3137 or through Small Press Distribution: www.spdbooks.com. 72pp. Reporting time: 6 months. Simultaneous submissions accepted: yes. We publish 1 out of 250 manuscripts submitted for publication. Payment: poet receives 10% of press run in lieu of royalties. Copyrights for author. Subjects: Fiction, Poetry.

•**THE NEW JERSEY POETRY RESOURCE BOOK, THE PATERSON LITERARY REVIEW,** Maria Mazziotti Gillan, The Poetry Center at Passaic County Community College, One College Blvd., Paterson, NJ

318

07505-1179, (973) 684-6555. 1979. "Written to help New Jersey Area poets, presenters, and individuals who love poetry locate useful resources." circ. 1000. 1/yr. Expects 1 issue 2006, 1 issue 2007. sub. price 10.00; per copy 10.00; sample 10.00. Discounts: 5 or more 40%. 65pp. Subjects: Poetry, Publishing.

THE NEW LAUREL REVIEW, Lee Meitzen Grue, Editor; Andy Young, Poetry Editor; Lewis Schmidt, Managing Editor, 828 Lesseps Street, New Orleans, LA 70117, 504-947-6001. 1971. Poetry, fiction, articles, art, photos, reviews, non-fiction. "We want fresh work; shy away from dry academic articles with footnotes, and from poems with the guts cut out. Recently published: Julie Kane, P.B. Parris, James Nolan, Arthur Pfister III, Len Roberts, Marilyn Coffey, Billy Marshall-Stoneking, Dave Brinks, and Jared Carter." circ. 500. 1/yr. Pub'd 1 issue 2005. sub. price $12 individuals, $15 institutions, $15 foreign; per copy double issue $9; sample $8. Back issues: $8. Discounts: 5 copies for $40. 125pp. Reporting time: varies, longer time for interesting work; somewhat crowded with fiction & poetry—about 6 weeks; do not read in summer. We prefer to be informed of simultaneous submissions, but simultaneous submissions not good practice; must have immediate notification upon another acceptance. Publishes maybe 10% of manuscripts submitted. Payment: 1 copy of the magazine in which their work appears. Copyrighted. Pub's reviews: none in 2005. §Poetry and books about poets and related matter, collections of short fiction. Ads: none. Subjects: Literature (General), Poetry.

NEW LETTERS, Robert Stewart, Univ. of Missouri - Kansas City; University House, 5101 Rockhill Road, Kansas City, MO 64110, 816-235-1168, Fax 816-235-2611, www.newletters.org. 1971 (Predecessor, *University Review,* 1934). Poetry, fiction, articles, art, photos, satire, parts-of-novels, long-poems. "The best in contemporary fiction, poetry, personal essay, art, interviews, book reviews, and photography. Contributors include Nye, Alexie, Woodrell, Doyle, Gildner, Bly, Gallagher, Oates, Price, Harrison, Levertov, Kumin. Special issues on Jack Conroy, the writer in politics, New S. African Writing, the writer and religion, the new inferno, writing on baseball." circ. 2.5M. 4/yr. Pub'd 3 issues 2005; expects 4 issues 2006, 4 issues 2007. sub. price $22; per copy $8-10, varies on length of issue; sample $10.00. Back issues: $7-$12, rare issues $20. Discounts: 25% on contract of 4 ads. 140pp. Reporting time: 2-4 months. Simultaneous submissions accepted: yes. Publishes 2-5% of manuscripts submitted. Payment: small, upon publication. Copyrighted, reverts to author. Pub's reviews: 9 in 2005. §Collections of poetry, essays, and short stories. Ads: half page $250 / full page $450. Subjects: Arts, Fiction, Interviews, Non-Fiction, Poetry.

NEW MILLENNIUM WRITINGS, PO Box 2463, Knoxville, TN 37901, mark@mach2.com, www.mach2.com.

New Moon Publishing, Inc. (see also THE GROWING EDGE MAGAZINE), Tom Alexander, Executive Editor; Tom Weller, Editor, PO Box 1027, Corvallis, OR 97339-1027, 514-757-8477. 1980. Discounts: 40% to bookstores, newstands. 96pp. Subject: Drugs.

NEW MUSE OF CONTEMPT, Broken Jaw Press, Joe Blades, Box 596 Stn A, Fredericton, NB E3B 5A6, Canada, www.brokenjaw.com. 1987. Fiction, reviews, concrete art. "Experimental literary, mail art, culture mag. *New Muse of Contempt* publishes a wide range of new and established writers and visual artists from Canada and beyond. It has become a semiannual international forum for correspondence art and interesting creative writings. Submissions of pithy poetry (esp. visual/concrete poetry, found poetry and homolinguistic text translations), short fiction, essays, book reviews welcome by post if accompanied by a SASE with Canadian postage (not USA postage) or International Postal Reply Coupons. Contributions of correspondence art - from collage and rubber stamps, stickers, photos and drawings, to project and exhibition announcements are always welcome." circ. 200-500. 2/yr. Pub'd 2 issues 2005; expects 2 issues 2006, 2 issues 2007. sub. price $12; per copy $6; sample $6. 52pp. Reporting time: 2-6 months. Simultaneous submissions accepted: no. Publishes 5% of manuscripts submitted. Payment: copies. Copyrighted, reverts to author. Pub's reviews: 4 in 2005. §Poetry and art. Ads: $100/$50. Subjects: Canada, Dada, Fiction.

New Native Press, Thomas Rain Crowe, Publisher; Nan Watkins, Managing Editor, PO Box 661, Cullowhee, NC 28723, 828-293-9237. 1979. Poetry, art. "No unsolicited manuscripts considered." avg. press run 1M. Pub'd 2 titles 2005; expects 1 title 2006, 1 title 2007. Discounts: $7.50 for 10 or more. 80pp. Payment: varies (usually 1/3 of run), 50% discount on additional copies. Copyrights for author. Subjects: Metaphysics, Myth, Mythology, Native American, Poetry, Post Modern, Spiritual, Surrealism.

NEW ORLEANS REVIEW, Christopher Chambers, Editor, Box 195, Loyola University, New Orleans, LA 70118, 504-865-2475. 1968. Poetry, fiction, articles, art, photos, cartoons, interviews, satire, criticism, reviews, non-fiction. "Past contributors include Walker Percy, Pablo Neruda, Hunter S. Thompson, Alain Robbe-Grillet, Christopher Isherwood, Annie Dillard, William Matthews, Gordon Lish, William Kotzwinkle, Julio Cortazar, Michael Harper, Yusef Komunyaaka, Ed Skoog, and Michael Martone. Check us out and send your best work. We privilege the language." circ. 1M. 2/yr. Pub'd 2 issues 2005; expects 2 issues 2006, 2 issues 2007. sub. price 2 issues - domestic $12 indiv, $20 instit, foreign $20; per copy $8 domestic, $10 foreign; sample $5 domestic, $10 foreign. Back issues: $5; inquire for availability. Discounts: none. 200pp. Reporting time: 4 months. Simultaneous submissions accepted: yes. Publishes 3% of manuscripts submitted. Payment: $25-$50

+copies. Copyrighted, reverts to author. Pub's reviews: 6 in 2005. §fiction, poetry, New Orleans. Subjects: Arts, Experimental, Fiction, Journals, Literary Review, Literature (General), Louisiana, Movies, Non-Fiction, Photography, Poetry.

New Orphic Publishers (see also THE NEW ORPHIC REVIEW), Ernest Hekkanen, Margrith Schraner, 706 Mill Street, Nelson, BC V1L 4S5, Canada, 250-354-0494, Fax 250-352-0743. 1995. Poetry, fiction, criticism, plays, non-fiction. "Recent contributors: Hillel Wright, Ed Roy, Margrith Schraner, Ernest Hekkanen. We don't look at unsolicited material." avg. press run 1.5M. Pub'd 5 titles 2005; expects 5 titles 2006, 4 titles 2007. Discounts: 40%. 150-350pp. Simultaneous submissions accepted: no. Publishes 1% of manuscripts submitted. Payment: 10%. Copyrights for author. Subjects: Fiction, Literary Review, Novels, Poetry.

THE NEW ORPHIC REVIEW, New Orphic Publishers, Ernest Hekkanen, Editor-in-Chief; Margrith Schraner, Associate Editor, 706 Mill Street, Nelson, BC V1L 4S5, Canada, 250-354-0494, Fax 250-352-0743. 1998. Poetry, fiction, articles, interviews, criticism, parts-of-novels, plays. "Stories, articles, and novel excerpts up to 10,000 words. I'm a harsh judge of poetry. Only send the best. Recent contributors: W.P. Kinsella, Jack Cady, Jana Harris, Catherine Owen, Chad Norman, and Michael Bullock." circ. 500. 2/yr. Pub'd 2 issues 2005; expects 2 issues 2006, 2 issues 2007. sub. price $25 USD; per copy $15 USD; sample $15 USD. Back issues: we always sell out. Discounts: 30% break. 120pp. Reporting time: up to 4 months. Simultaneous submissions accepted: yes. Publishes 20% of manuscripts submitted. Payment: 1 complimentary copy. Copyrighted, reverts to author. Pub's reviews. §Fiction. Ads: $150/$75. Subjects: Fiction, Literary Review, Novels, Poetry.

New Paradigm Books, John Chambers, 22491 Vistawood Way, Boca Raton, FL 33428, 561-482-5971, 800-808-5179, Fax 561-852-8322, darbyc@earthlink.net, www.newpara.com. 1997. Non-fiction. "We publish 'New Age' books, but with a broader-than-usual literary and historical character, e.g. *The Chinese Roswell*, by Hartwig Hausdorf (ufology), *Conversations with Eternity: The Forgotten Masterpiece of Victor Hugo*, (channeling), *Father Ernetti's Chronovisor*, by Peter Krassa (time travel). We have expanded into wider areas of health and spirituality with titles on multiple sclerosis and Sufism." avg. press run 5,000. Expects 1 title 2006, 2 titles 2007. Copyrights negotiable. Subjects: Aging, Animals, Channelling, Inspirational, Literature (General), Medicine, Metaphysics, New Age, Occult, Philosophy, Self-Help, Spiritual, Sufism, Theosophical.

THE NEW RENAISSANCE, an international magazine of ideas & opinions, emphasizing literature & the arts, Louise T. Reynolds, Editor-in-Chief; Frank Finale, Poetry Editor; Pamela Rosenblatt, Assistant Editor, Patti J. D. Michaud, Olivera Sajkovic; James E. A. Woodbury, Consulting Editors, 26 Heath Road #11, Arlington, MA 02474-3645. 1968. Poetry, fiction, articles, photos, interviews, criticism, long-poems. "Since April 1995, our policy for fiction & poetry has required an entry fee, as both are tied to our award programs: $16.50 per submission for non-subscribers US; $11.50 per submission for subscribers US. Foreign submitters: $13.50 subscribers, $18.50 non-subscribers. Unless a fiction ms is 4 pp or less, only one ms per submission. Ficton: mss from 2 to 36 pp. Poetry: 3-6 one-page poems; 2-4 two- page poems; only one long poem. Translations are welcome (Include originals) EACH submission requires entry fee. Mss without the fee will be returned *unread*. The fourth awards will be announced in the Fall 2006. Submitting periods: January 2-June 30, & Sept. 1-Oct. 31 for fiction and nonfiction; poetry from Jan. 2-June 30. Only work published in a 3-issue *tnr* volume is eligible. All writers published in *tnr* receive a nominal payment, as well as a copy of the issue they're in. Independent judges. Fiction Awards: 1st place: $500; 2nd $250; 3rd $100; one honorable mention $50. *tnr* Poetry Awards: 1st place - $250; 2nd - $125; 3rd - $60; three or four honorable mentions - $25 ea. Send mss with entry fees. Current subscibers extend their subscription by an issue. Non-subscribers receive a recent issue. For those submitting non-fiction, ms must be accompanied by $10 for a recent issue. Non-fiction may be on a variety of topics—literature, cinema, theatre, etc. Submitting periods—nonfiction: January 2 - November 30th each year. We are looking for writing that has something to say, says it with style or grace, & speaks in a personalized voice. All submissions MUST be accompanied by a SASE or IRC. All queries re guidelines, questions about submissions, etc., *must* be accompanied by a SASE, IRC. Fiction submissions take 5-8 months; poetry 4-7 months; non-fiction 2-5 months. Writers recently published: Ann Struthers, M. E. McMullen, R. Tagore (trans. Wendy Barker, S. Tagore), Barbara Honigmann (trans. Lauren Hahn), Judy Rowley, Myrna Stone, Karen Braucher, and Laura Weeks." circ. 1.3M. 2/yr. Pub'd 1 issue 2005; expects 2 issues 2006, 2 issues 2007. sub. price individuals $38/3 issues USA, $42/3 issues Canada (air mail); all others $52/3 issues (air mail); institutions $42/3 issues USA, $45 Canada (air mail), $55 all others (air mail); per copy $14.50 USA, $16.00 Canada, $18.50 all others; sample $10.50 USA, $12.00 Canada, $14.00 all others. Discounts: subscription agents, etc. 20%; 20 or more copies for classroom use 25%, 35+ 30%; bookstores 33-1/3%, advance payment. 144-184pp. Reporting time: poetry 4-5 months, prose 5-8 months. Simultaneous submissions accepted: Reluctantly. Publishes up to 12-20+% of manuscripts submitted. Payment: $17-$55 poems, $48-$85 fiction, $65-$175 non-fiction, $20-$25 per drawing. Copyrighted, reverts to author after publication. Ads: $170/$95. Subjects: Criticism, Current Affairs, Essays, Fiction, Graphics, Literature (General), Poetry, Politics, Reviews, Short Stories, Theatre, Translation, Visual Arts.

New Rivers Press, Inc., c/o MSUM, 1104 7th Avenue South, Moorhead, MN 56563-0178, contact@newriverspress.org, www.newriverspress.org. 1968. Poetry, fiction, art, photos, long-poems, concrete art. "We publish new writing of merit and distinction—poetry, combinations of poetry and prose, short fiction, memoirs, and translations (mostly poetry). We are also involved in publishing such regional programs as the Minnesota Voices Project and the Many Minnesotas Project. The press is in a transitional state. Check our website for updates. Currently not accepting submissions." avg. press run 1M-2.5M. Pub'd 10 titles 2005. Discounts: 1-5 copies 20%, 6+ 40% trade; 50% for outright purchases 1-4 20%, 5-24 42%, 24-99 43%, 100-249 44%, 250-499 45%, 500-750 46%, 750+ 47%. Bookstores order through Consortium Book Sales and Distribution 1045 Westgate Dr, Suite 90 St.Paul, MN 55114-1065, phone 800-283-3572, fax 612-221-0124. 96-300pp. Simultaneous submissions accepted: no. Copyrights for author. Subjects: African-American, Asian-American, Book Arts, Fiction, Literature (General), Poetry, Prose, Short Stories, Translation.

New Sins Press, Rane Arroyo, Co-Publisher; Glenn Sheldon, Co-Publisher; Dan Nowak, Editor; Melanie Dusseau, Editor, 3925 Watson Avenue, Toledo, OH 43612-1113. 1985. Poetry. "New Sins Press used to publish poetry chapbooks. Some of our authors were: Barbara Hamby, Mark Magiera, Julie Parson-Nesbitt and Richard Collins. We published one full-length poetry collection by Amy Yanity. Beginning in 2006, we will publish one full-length poetry collection annually through a poetry competition (deadline: May 1st)." avg. press run 500-1000. Expects 1 title 2006, 1 title 2007. 70pp. Reporting time: 1-2 months. Payment: in copies. Copyrights for author. Subjects: Avant-Garde, Experimental Art, Bisexual, Drama, Experimental, Gay, Health, Latino, Lesbianism, Race.

NEW SOLUTIONS, Community Service, Inc., Pat Murphy, Editor, PO Box 243, Yellow Springs, OH 45387, 937-767-2161, info@communitysolution.org. 1940. Articles, reviews, letters, non-fiction. circ. 250. 4/yr. Pub'd 4 issues 2005; expects 4 issues 2006, 4 issues 2007. sub. price $25 includes membership; per copy $3.50; sample free. Back issues: $2. Discounts: write for schedule, 40% on 10 or more. 7pp. Reporting time: 2 weeks. Simultaneous submissions accepted: yes. Publishes 66% of manuscripts submitted. Payment: copies. Copyrighted, reverts to author. §Community, alternatives in community, society, local economy, education, land trusts and land reform, ecological concerns, family, simple living, sustainability issues, peak oil. Exchange ads. Subjects: Biography, Business & Economics, Community, Education, Family, Newsletter, Philosophy, Society, Sociology.

New Star Books Ltd., Rolf Maurer, Publisher, #107, 3477 Commercial Street, Vancouver, B.C. V5N 4E8, Canada, 604-738-9429, Fax 604-738-9332. 1970. Non-fiction. "*New Star* is an independent press specializing in history, politics, environment, social issues, and literary titles." avg. press run 2M-3M. Pub'd 6 titles 2005; expects 6 titles 2006, 8 titles 2007. Discounts: 50% non-returnable (booksellers). 200pp. Reporting time: 6-8 weeks. Simultaneous submissions accepted: yes. Publishes 1-2% of manuscripts submitted. Payment: varies with contract. Copyrights for author. Subjects: British Columbia, Canada, Environment, Fiction, Gay, History, Labor, Native American, Politics.

NEW STONE CIRCLE, Mary Hays, Karen Singer, 1185 E 1900 N Road, White Heath, IL 61884. 1994. Poetry, fiction, art, photos, interviews, satire, parts-of-novels, long-poems, non-fiction. circ. 100. 1-2/yr. Pub'd 1 issue 2005; expects 2 issues 2006, 2 issues 2007. sub. price $8; per copy $4.50; sample $4.50. Back issues: $4.50. 50pp. Reporting time: 3-6 months. We accept simultaneous submissions, but let us know. We don't for contests. Publishes 5% of manuscripts submitted. Payment: 1 copy. Copyrighted, reverts to author. Subjects: Fiction, Poetry.

THE NEW SUPERNATURAL MAGAZINE, Ray Allen Morris, PO Box 3641, Page, AZ 86040-3641, MorrisPublish2@aol.com, http://hometown.aol.com/morrispublish2/. 1963. Poetry, fiction, articles, art, photos, cartoons, interviews, satire, criticism, reviews, music, letters, parts-of-novels, long-poems, collages, plays, concrete art, news items, non-fiction. "We publish All New and Beginner Writers." circ. 5.5M. 12/yr. Pub'd 12 issues 2005; expects 12 issues 2006, 12 issues 2007. sub. price $19.95 non-contributors, $9.95 contributors; per copy $1.75; sample computer. Back issues: $2.25. Discounts: stores 20%. 50pp. Reporting time: 1 month. Simultaneous submissions accepted: yes. Publishes 100% of manuscripts submitted. Payment: free copy your story's in, $9.95/year. Copyrighted, does not revert to author. Pub's reviews: 25 in 2005. §Horror, erotic, romance, teenagers, children, advertising, self-promotion, aging, agriculture, alcoholism/alcohol, experimental, family, fantasy. Ads: none. Subjects: Adolescence, Advertising, Self-Promotion, Aging, Agriculture, Alaska, Alcohol, Alcoholism, Experimental, Family, Fantasy, Feminism, Festivals, Fiction, Florida, Folklore, Hawaii.

NEW THOUGHT, Dr. Blaine C. Mays, Editor-in-Chief, International New Thought Alliance, 5003 East Broadway Road, Mesa, AZ 85206, 480-830-2461. 1913. Articles, interviews, reviews, news items. "*New Thought* is a self-help, metaphysical publication with articles designed to increase the creative fulfilling, and healing energies in each one of us. Material written from a philosophical and religious point of view is used in the magazine. Emphasis is always upon the positive, constructive, and inspirational." circ. 4M. 4/yr. Pub'd 4 issues 2005; expects 4 issues 2006, 4 issues 2007. sub. price $20; per copy $5; sample $5. Back issues: not offered. 56pp. Reporting time: 3-4 weeks. Payment: contributors' copies only. Copyrighted, reverts to author. Pub's reviews: 20 in 2005. §Metaphysics, spiritual enlightenments, self help. Ads: $737/$369/$32 column inch.

Subjects: Philosophy, Religion, Spiritual.

NEW UNIONIST, Jeff Miller, 1301 Cambridge St., Ste. 102, Hopkins, MN 55343-1925, 651-646-5546, nup@minn.net. 1975. Articles, photos, cartoons, reviews, letters, news items. "No outside manuscripts." circ. 9M. 12/yr. Pub'd 12 issues 2005; expects 12 issues 2006, 12 issues 2007. sub. price 12 issues $7; per copy 30¢; sample free. Discounts: 15¢ each. 8pp. Payment: copies only. Not copyrighted. Pub's reviews: 4 in 2005. §Socialism, labor, politics, current affairs. Subjects: Labor, Socialist.

NEW VERSE NEWS, THE, James Penha, c/o Penha, Jakarta International School, PO Box 1078JKS, Jakarta 12010, Indonesia, editor@newversenews.com. 2005. Poetry. "*The New Verse News* is an online journal [www.newversenews.com] that solicits and publishes poetry on topical issues and current events. It's a sort of poetic newspaper. Although the editor and thus the site have a clearly liberal political bias, we welcome contrary views and verse. Recent contributors: Rochelle Ratner, Simon Perchik, A.D. Winans, Rochelle Owens, Bill Costley. GUIDELINES: Submit previously unpublished poems to editor@newversenews.com for possible posting. Paste poems in the body of your email (no attachments) and write 'Verse News Submission' as the subject line. Send a brief bio too." Continually updated. Reporting time: 1-21 days. Simultaneous submissions accepted: Yes. Publishes 25% of manuscripts submitted. Payment: No payment. Copyrighted, reverts to author. Subjects: Current Affairs, Poetry, Politics, Writers/Writing.

New Victoria Publishers, Claudia Lamperti, PO Box 27, Norwich, VT 05055, 802-649-5297. 1976. Fiction. "Non-profit." avg. press run 3M. Pub'd 7 titles 2005; expects 6 titles 2006, 6 titles 2007. Discounts: distributed by BOOKWORLD, Sarasota, Florida. 800-444-2524. 200pp. Reporting time: 1 month. We'll possibly accept simultaneous submissions. Publishes 2-3% of manuscripts submitted. Payment: 10% of net. Copyrights for author. Subjects: Humor, Lesbianism, Literature (General), Mystery, Novels, Science Fiction, Women.

New Vision Publishing, Nicolette V. Phillips, 5757 Westheimer Road, PMB 3-362, Houston, TX 77057-5749, Fax 480-563-0675, newvisionpub@aol.com. 1996. "We're not a self-publisher, but do not accept unsolicited manuscripts." avg. press run 3M. Expects 3 titles 2006, 4 titles 2007. Discounts: 1 copy 20%, 2-4 30%, 6+ 40%. 300pp. Does not copyright for author. Subjects: Metaphysics, Spiritual.

New Voices Publishing, Rita Schiano, Executive Editor, PO Box 560, Wilmington, MA 01887, 978-658-2131, Fax 978-988-8833, rschiano@kidsterrain.com, www.kidsterrain.com. 2000. Fiction. "Children's picture books." avg. press run 3M. Pub'd 3 titles 2005; expects 2 titles 2007. Discounts: 40-55%. 28pp. Reporting time: 6-8 weeks. Simultaneous submissions accepted: yes. Publishes 25% of manuscripts submitted. Payment: 10%; 12-1/2%, 15% net. Copyrights for author. Subjects: Children, Youth, Picture Books.

New Win Publishing, Arthur Chou, 9682 Telstar Ave. Suite 110, El Monte, CA 91731, 626-448-3448, 626-602-3817, info@academiclearningcompany.com, www.newwinpublishing.com. 1978. Non-fiction. avg. press run 5,000. Pub'd 20 titles 2005; expects 25 titles 2006, 30 titles 2007. Discounts: 40-55%. Reporting time: 1month. Simultaneous submissions accepted: Yes. Publishes 10% of manuscripts submitted. Payment: 10%. Copyrights for author. Subjects: Business & Economics, Careers, Collectibles, Crafts, Hobbies, Employment, Health, How-To, Leisure/Recreation, Nature, Nutrition, Parenting, Self-Help, Sports, Outdoors, Wood Engraving/Woodworking.

New World Library, Marc Allen, Publisher, 14 Pamaron Way, Novato, CA 94949-6215. 1978. Fiction, non-fiction. avg. press run 15M. Pub'd 29 titles 2005; expects 32 titles 2006, 32 titles 2007. Discounts: 50-55% to distributors, 10% to individual consumers ordering 5 or more titles. 260pp. Reporting time: 15 weeks. Publishes less than 1% of manuscripts submitted. Payment: 12-16% of net royalty to authors, paid semi-annually. Copyrights for author. Subjects: Business & Economics, Creativity, Health, Inspirational, Metaphysics, Native American, New Age, Parenting, Psychology, Religion, Self-Help, Self-Help, Spiritual, Tapes & Records, Women.

New World Press (see also BLOODJET LITERARY MAGAZINE), Noni Howard Ph.D, Publisher, 20 Driftwood Trail, Half Moon Bay, CA 94019-2349, 650-726-5939; Fax 415-921-3730. 1974. Poetry, fiction, art, photos, letters, parts-of-novels, long-poems, collages. "Length is 100 pages plus, prefer women writers, Jennifer Stone, Adrian Marcus and Evelyn Hickey are recent contributors. Persons able to write grants or obtain other funding especially considered. Telephone and leave number before writing." avg. press run 1.2M. Expects 2 titles 2006, 1-3 titles 2007. Discounts: 40% bulk or to educational institutions, schools, etc. 100-200pp. Reporting time: 60 days. Simultaneous submissions accepted: yes. Publishes less than 10% of manuscripts submitted. Payment: 200 free copies. Copyrights for author. Subjects: Literature (General), Poetry.

•**New World Press, Inc,** Steven Thedford, 5626 Platte Dr., Ellenwood, GA 30294, (404)512-6760. 1994. Poetry, fiction, non-fiction. avg. press run 750. Expects 1 title 2006, 2 titles 2007. Discounts: 2-10 25%. 50pp. Reporting time: 6 months. Simultaneous submissions accepted: Yes. Publishes 10% of manuscripts submitted. Payment: Industry Standard. Does not copyright for author. Subjects: African Literature, Africa, African Studies, African-American, Autobiography, Children, Youth, Education, Egypt, Essays, Internet, Mystery.

THE NEW WRITER, Suzanne Ruthven, PO Box 60, Cranbrook, Kent TN17 2ZR, England, 01580-212626 admin@thenewwriter.com www.thenewwriter.com. 1996. Poetry, fiction, articles, interviews, reviews, letters, news items. "Monthly email News free of charge with annual subscription." 6/yr. Pub'd 6 issues 2005; expects 6 issues 2006, 6 issues 2007. sub. price £33.00; sample 6 IRCs for free sample. Discounts: negotiable. 56pp. Reporting time: 2-3 weeks. Simultaneous submissions accepted: yes. Publishes 5% of manuscripts submitted. Payment: varies. Copyrighted, reverts to author. Pub's reviews: 30 in 2005. §Short stories and writing techniques (but only if available in England). Ads: £150/£85/£50 1/4 page. Subjects: Fiction, Poetry, Writers/Writing.

THE NEW YORK QUARTERLY, Raymond Hammond, Editor, PO Box 693, Old Chelsea Station, New York, NY 10113, info@nyquarterly.com, www.nyquarterly.com. 1969. Poetry, interviews. "*The New York Quarterly* is a magazine devoted to the craft of poetry. The editors are interested in seeing poems of any style or persuasion, so long as they are well-intentioned and well-written. Recent contributors include W. D. Snodgrass, David Lehman, Timothy Liu, Franz Wright and Charles Bukowski. Writers are strongly encouraged to read recent issues of *NYQ* before submitting." circ. 1000. 3/yr. Pub'd 3 issues 2005; expects 3 issues 2006, 3 issues 2007. sub. price $20, $28 institutions, foreign orders add $10; per copy $8; sample $8. Back issues: $15. 176pp. Reporting time: 3 months. Simultaneous submissions accepted: yes. Publishes 5% of manuscripts submitted. Payment: issue copies. Copyrighted, reverts to author. Ads: $250/$150. Subjects: Interviews, Poetry.

Newmark Publishing Company, PO Box 603, South Windsor, CT 06074. 1986. Fiction, non-fiction. "*The Surgical Arena* by Peter Grant, M.D., published March 1994. *Destination 2020 White House* by Pete Grant, *The Medical Supreme Court* by Pete Grant, published in 2001, *Final Review for Malpractice Cases.*" avg. press run 7.5M. Expects 3 titles 2006, 5 titles 2007. Discounts: on request. 200pp. Reporting time: 3 months. Payment: individual contracts, negotiable. Copyrights for author. Subjects: Fiction, Health, Non-Fiction.

NewPages (see also NEWPAGES: Alternatives in Print & Media), PO Box 1580, Bay City, MI 48706. "We are interested in publishing books of value to librarians, booksellers, writers, readers, and publishers, including 'how-to', directories, bibliographies. Query first."

NEWPAGES: Alternatives in Print & Media, NewPages, Casey Hill, Publisher; Denise Hill, Editor, PO Box 1580, Bay City, MI 48706, 989-671-0081, www.newpages.com. 1979. Articles, art, photos, cartoons, satire, criticism, reviews, news items. "Published online. NewPages is the Portal of Independents! News, information and guides to independent bookstores, independent publishers, literary periodicals, alternative periodicals, independent record labels, alternative newsweeklies and more." 52/yr. Pub'd 52 issues 2005; expects 52 issues 2006, 52 issues 2007. Reporting time: 3-4 weeks. Copyrighted, reverts to author. Pub's reviews: §Consider all materials rec'd. Ads: inquire. Subjects: Book Reviewing, Communication, Journalism, Communication, Journalism, Literary Review, Magazines, Printing.

NEWS FROM NATIVE CALIFORNIA, Heyday Books, Malcolm Margolin, Publisher; Margaret Dubin, Managing Editor, PO Box 9145, Berkeley, CA 94709, 510-549-3564; FAX 510-549-1889. 1987. Articles, art, photos, interviews, criticism, reviews, letters, news items, non-fiction. "We are interested in material related to California Indians, past and present." circ. 10M. 4/yr. Pub'd 4 issues 2005; expects 4 issues 2006, 4 issues 2007. sub. price $19; per copy $4.95; sample $1. Back issues: range from $4 to $20. Discounts: 40% trade, call for other schedules. 56pp. Reporting time: 3 weeks. Simultaneous submissions accepted: yes. Payment: up to about $50/article. Copyrighted, does not revert to author. Pub's reviews: 5-10 in 2005. §Native American: culture, history, art, politics, literature. Ads: $545/$280/send for rate card. Subjects: Arts, Culture, History, Literature (General), Native American, Politics.

NewSage Press, Maureen Michelson, Publisher, PO Box 607, Troutdale, OR 97060-0607, 503-695-2211 www.newsagepress.com info@newsagepress.com. 1985. Non-fiction. "We are interested in publishing quality tradebooks—in content as well as production. NewSage only publishes nonfiction, specializing in books on grief and death, the animal/human bond, and social issues related to women, the environment, animals." avg. press run 7.5M. Pub'd 3 titles 2005; expects 4 titles 2006, 4 titles 2007. Discounts: For bookstores, purchase our books through our distributor for the U.S. and Canada, Publishers Group West (800-788-3123). All others may contact NewSage Press directly. On purchases of less than 12 books (mixed titles OK), there is a 20% discount. On orders of 12 books or more (mixed titles OK), discount is 40%. 190pp. Reporting time: 4 to 6 months. Simultaneous submissions accepted: yes. Publishes 10% of manuscripts submitted. Payment: Royalties paid, usually standard. Copyrights for author. Subjects: Animals, Environment, Euthanasia, Death, Feminism, Grieving, Marine Life, Memoirs, Multicultural, Non-Fiction, Non-Violence, Peace, Pets, Whaling, Women.

•NEWWITCH, Kenaz Filan, P.O. Box 641, Point Arena, CA 95468, Phone:888-724-3966, Fax:707-882-2793, website http://www.newwitch.com. 2002. Poetry, fiction, articles, art, photos, interviews, reviews, music, letters, non-fiction. 4/yr. Pub'd 4 issues 2005; expects 4 issues 2006, 4 issues 2007. sub. price $20. Back issues: inquire. Simultaneous submissions accepted: No. Copyrighted, reverts to author. Pub's reviews. Subjects: Counter-Culture, Alternatives, Communes, Magic, Multicultural, Myth, Mythology, Native American, Nature,

New Age, Non-Fiction, Religion, Spiritual, Supernatural, Tarot, WICCA, Women.

Next Decade, Inc., Barbara Brooks Kimmel, 39 Old Farmstead Road, Chester, NJ 07930-2732, 908-879-6625, Fax 908-879-2920. 1990. "Publish nonfiction reference books (legal, financial, health and retirement) and sold to the trade, universities, corporations and libraries." avg. press run 5M-10M. Pub'd 2 titles 2005; expects 2 titles 2006, 2 titles 2007. Discounts: 50% on distribution arrangements. 80-300pp. Reporting time: 1 month. Simultaneous submissions accepted: yes. Publishes 1% of manuscripts submitted. Payment: varies. Copyrights for author. Subject: Reference.

Nicholas Lawrence Books, Larry Thomas Ward, 932 Clover Avenue, Canon City, CO 81212, 719-276-0152, Fax 719-276-0154, icareinc@webtv.net. 1993. Photos, non-fiction. "We publish primarily celebrity biographies, autobiographies, and history." avg. press run 5,000. Pub'd 2 titles 2005; expects 3 titles 2006, 3 titles 2007. Discounts: 40% trade, etc. 175pp. Reporting time: 30 days. Simultaneous submissions accepted: yes. Publishes 50% of manuscripts submitted. Payment: $500 - $2000 advance, 10% royalty. Copyrights for author. Subjects: Autobiography, Biography.

Nicolas-Hays, Inc., B. Lundsted, PO Box 1126, Berwick, ME 03901-1126. 1976. Music, non-fiction. "We publish philosophy, music, psychology, alternative healing. We have recently published *Jung and the Alchemical Imagination,* by Jeffrey Raff and *Eros and Chaos* by Veronia Goodchild. We look to publish the author's life work - the books that have great meaning." avg. press run 5M-7.5M. Pub'd 2 titles 2005; expects 3 titles 2006, 6 titles 2007. Discounts: Normal trade discounts apply; write for account information; distributed by WeiserBooks, Inc. at Box 612, York Beach, ME 03910. 256pp. Reporting time: 3 months. Simultaneous submissions accepted: yes. Publishes 10% of manuscripts submitted. Payment: royalties, information available on request. Copyrights for author. Subjects: Health, Music, Philosophy, Psychology, Spiritual.

NICU Ink (see also NEONATAL NETWORK: The Journal of Neonatal Nursing), Charles Rait, Editor-in-Chief, 2270 Northpoint Parkway, Santa Rosa, CA 95407-7398, 888-642-8465, www.neonatalnetwork.com. 1986. Non-fiction. "Medical books." avg. press run 3M. Pub'd 2 titles 2005; expects 2 titles 2006, 2 titles 2007. Discounts: to bookstores and on quantity orders. 300-700pp. Reporting time: 4 months. Simultaneous submissions accepted: no. Publishes 50% of manuscripts submitted. Copyrights for author. Subjects: Medicine, Parenting.

Night Horn Books, John Spilker, Co-Publisher; Robert Anbian, Co-Publisher, Editor, PO Box 424906, San Francisco, CA 94142-4906, 415-440-2442; nighthornb@aol.com. 1978. Poetry, articles, art, photos, interviews, satire, long-poems, collages. "Books can be purchased directly at www.protestworks.com/nighthorn.html. Also vailable from Amazon.com and other outlets. In-print poetry titles include Tomorrow Triumphant by Otto Rene Castillo, WE Parts 1 & 2 by Robert Anbian, plus work by Jack Hirschman, Katerina Gogou. Also distributes selected book titles by Ruddy Duck Press, War&Peace Press, and other small presses. Does not currently accept unsolicited mss." Pub'd 1 title 2005; expects 1 title 2006, 1 title 2007. Discounts: 40% to the trade direct or through distributions; 50% off for 9 or less copies, 55% off 10 or more to jobbers, wholesalers. 100-125pp. Reporting time: 8-12 weeks. Payment: negotiable. Copyrights for author. Subjects: Arts, Literature (General), Poetry.

Night Howl Productions, PO Box 1, Clay Center, NE 68933.

NIGHT TRAIN, Rusty Barnes, Editor; Alicia Gifford, Fiction Editor, 212 Bellingham Ave., #2, Revere, MA 02151-4106, rustybarnes@nighttrainmagazine.com, www.nighttrainmagazine.com. 2002. Fiction, parts-of-novels. "*Night Train* (ISSN 1540-5494) welcomes submissions of flash fiction, short fiction, or self-contained novel excerpts in traditional or experimental styles. We do not consider poetry, criticism, book reviews or reprints. Please read *Night Train* to understand what we're all about. Visit our web site to see the latest information on submission guidelines, which can change. We're available through our website, at a growing number of independent book stores, and soon in some chains. Recent contributors: Robert Boswell, Steve Almond, Roy Kesey, Pia Ehrhardt, Jay Merill, DeWitt Henry, Terri Brown-Davidson." 2/yr. Pub'd 1 issue 2005; expects 2 issues 2006, 2 issues 2007. sub. price $17.95; per copy $9.95; sample $9.95. Back issues: $7. Discounts: 40%. 192pp. Reporting time: 3-6 months. Simultaneous submissions accepted: yes. Publishes 1-2% of manuscripts submitted. Payment: Pays in copies. Copyrighted. Ads: none. Subject: Literature (General).

Nightboat Books, Kazim Ali, Publisher; Jennifer Chapis, Editor, PO Box 656, Beacon, NY 12508, editor@nightboat.org, www.nightboat.org. 2003. Poetry, fiction. "Forthcoming in Fall 2006, "Radical Love," by Fanny Howe, five novels in one volume. Founded in 2003, Nightboat Books is a small, nonprofit publishing company dedicated to printing original books of poetry and prose, and bringing out-of-print treasures back to life. Nightboat seeks to publish cherished contemporary writers, as well as emerging and previously unknown poets and authors. Part of our inspiration comes from a desire to showcase new writers whose work may be otherwise underappreciated or misunderstood by the mainstream. Our mission is simple: distribute and promote beautifully crafted work that resists convention and transcends boundaries, books rich with poignancy, intelligence, and risk." avg. press run 1500. Pub'd 2 titles 2005; expects 2 titles 2006, 2 titles 2007. Discounts:

Author's Discount. 100pp. Reporting time: 2 mos. for prose queries, 4 mos. for poetry manuscripts via contest. Simultaneous submissions accepted: Yes. Payment varies depending on project. Copyrights for author.

NightinGale Resources, Lila Teich Gold, PO Box 322, Cold Spring, NY 10516, 212-753-5383. 1982. Non-fiction. "We publish fine editions of quality books and original cookbooks, directories, children's books, travel, facsimiles of out of print books." avg. press run 10M. Expects 3 titles 2006. Discounts: on request. Does not copyright for author. Subjects: Anthropology, Archaelogy, Biography, Children, Youth, Cooking, Crafts, Hobbies, Culture, Ecology, Foods, England, Europe, Family, Folklore, France, French, History, Judaism, Religion.

•**Nightjar Press (see also NIGHTJAR REVIEW),** Jeremy Rendina, P.O. Box 583, New York, NY 10002. 2005.

•**NIGHTJAR REVIEW, Nightjar Press,** Jeremy Rendina, Michael Klausman, P.O. Box 583, New York, NY 10002. 2005. Poetry, fiction, art, photos, long-poems, concrete art. "The featured writer of the inaugural issue is Lionel Ziprin, a legendary figureand lifelong resident of the Lower East Side whose curious body of writingincludes the one-thousand page epic poem, 'Sentencial Metaphrastic', as well as the highly off-kilter children's poems that make up 'Songs for Schizoid Siblings'. The Nightjar Review has excerpted the most ample selection from 'Songs' to date, which were composed in the mid 1950s at a time when Ziprin ran a greeting card company that employed such future luminaries as Bruce Conner, Jordan Belson, and Harry Smith. The 'Songs' were composed in the manner of Mother Goose rhymes and are infused with his own rendering of alchemy and the Kaballah. The first issue of The Nightjar Review is 144 pages perfect bound, with a silkscreened dust jacket featuring a new drawing by the artist Bruce Conner. Additonal contributions come from Anja Buechele, Dante Carfagna, Diane Cluck, inoli, Shannon Ketch, Michael Klausman, Angus MacLise, Peter Relic, Jeremy Rendina, John Fell Ryan, Dave Tompkins, and Yvonne." circ. 500. 2/yr. Expects 1 issue 2006, 2 issues 2007. sub. price $25; per copy $15. Discounts: 40% for 5 or more copies. 144pp. Reporting time: 1 month. Simultaneous submissions accepted: Yes. Payment: negotiable. Copyrighted, reverts to author. Subjects: Avant-Garde, Experimental Art, Photography, Poetry, Prose.

NIGHTLIFE MAGAZINE, Martine Desjardins, Publisher and Fashion Editor; Yann Fortier, Editor; Oliver Lalande, Music Editor; Sarah Levesque, Urban Culture Editor, 4200, Boulevard St. Laurent, Suite 1470, Montreal, Quebec H2W 2R2, Canada, 514.278.3222. 1999. Articles, art, photos, interviews, reviews, music, collages, news items. "Reference of activities and trends for Montrealers." circ. 40000. 10/yr. Pub'd 10 issues 2005; expects 10 issues 2006, 10 issues 2007. sub. price $35; per copy free; sample free. Back issues: $3,50. 100pp. Copyrighted. §Cosmetics and CDs. Ads: $2000 full page. Subjects: Arts, Bilingual, Canada, Dining, Restaurants, Entertainment, Fashion, Festivals, Music, Society, Visual Arts, Young Adult.

NIGHTSUN, Gerry LaFemina, Department of English, Frostburg State University, Frostburg, MD 21532-1099, nightsun@frostburg.edu. 1981. Poetry, fiction, criticism, long-poems. circ. 300. 1/yr. Expects 1 issue 2006, 1 issue 2007. sub. price $15; per copy $9; sample $5. Back issues: $3 per issue. Discounts: 10-19 copies 10%20-29 copies 20%30 + copies 40%. 100pp. Reporting time: 2 months. Simultaneous submissions accepted: No. Payment: small honorarium when possible; 2 copies of journal. Copyrighted, reverts to author. Ads: Full page: $120half page: $75quarter page: $40. Subject: Literary Review.

Nightsun Books, Ruth Wiley, 823 Braddock Road, Cumberland, MD 21502-2622, 301-722-4861. 1987. Poetry, fiction, cartoons, criticism, plays, non-fiction. "Please inquire before submitting manuscripts!" avg. press run 200-1M. Pub'd 5 titles 2005; expects 1 title 2006, 1 title 2007. Discounts: 1 0%, 2-4 20%, 5-24 40%, 25-49 43%, 50-99 46%, 100+ 50%. 30-200pp. Reporting time: varies. Payment: varies—inquire. Subjects: Anthology, Drama, Fiction, How-To, Philosophy, Philosophy, Poetry, Psychology, Visual Arts.

NIMROD INTERNATIONAL, Francine Ringold, 600 South College Avenue, Tulsa, OK 74104-3126. 1956. Poetry, fiction, articles, art, photos, interviews, parts-of-novels, long-poems, plays. "Recent contributors: Sarah Flygare, Jennifer Ward, Ruth Schwartz, Lucia Getsi, George O'Connell, Mary Sojourner, Patricia Traxler, William Losinger. Annual *Nimrod/Hardman* Awards: in poetry (Pablo Neruda Prize), in fiction (Katherine Anne Porter Prize). 1st prize in each category $2000, 2nd prize $1000. Submissions are accepted between January 1 and April 30 each year. Recent past judges include Mark Doty, Ron Carlson, Henry Taylor, and Anita Shreve. Please send business-size SASE for awards and guidelines." circ. 2,500. 2/yr. Pub'd 2 issues 2005; expects 2 issues 2006. sub. price $17.50/yr; $30/2 yrs.; outside US - $19/$33; per copy $10; sample $10. Back issues: varies; list of back issues available from *Nimrod*. Discounts: 10% orders over 20. 200pp. Reporting time: 3 months. Simultaneous submissions accepted: yes. Publishes 1% of manuscripts submitted. Payment: 2 copies of issue in which work is published and reduced cost on extra issues. Copyrighted, reverts to author. Ads: Exchange. Subjects: Fiction, Poetry.

nine muses books, margareta waterman, Publisher, 3541 Kent Creek Road, Winston, OR 97496, 541-679-6674, mw9muses@teleport.com. 1987. Poetry, fiction, parts-of-novels, long-poems. "nine muses is an artists' collective for the author-owned production of books and tapes. At this time 15 serious writers, highly esteemed by their colleagues, make up the list. a prime feature of nine muses books, in addition to the advantage of author ownership, is the design, which is done, not to a standard format, but with particular attention to each book as a work of art, so that illustration, color of paper and ink, balance of composition on each page, and so on, are fitted to the content and meaning of the book. submissions are by invitation.'' avg. press run 500. Pub'd 3 titles 2005; expects 4 titles 2006, 4 titles 2007. Discounts: trade to bookstores, bulk to libraries, etc. single orders no discount, prepay on first orders. 65pp. Payment: nine muses is an author's collective; see comments above. author owns books. Author owns copyrights and books. Subjects: Buddhism, Language, Literature (General), Magic, Myth, Mythology, Occult, Performing Arts, Poetry, Politics, Tapes & Records.

9N-2N-8N-NAA NEWSLETTER, G.W. Rinaldi, Robert R. Rinaldi Jr., PO Box 275, East Corinth, VT 05040-0275, www.n-news.com. 1985. Articles, art, photos, cartoons, interviews, criticism, reviews, letters, news items. ''Magazine consists of 36-40 pages/3 columns, several photos, column pages, small print, equal to 50 in larger print.'' circ. 9M. 4/yr. Pub'd 4 issues 2005; expects 4 issues 2006, 4 issues 2007. sub. price $20 US, $23 Canada, $26 foreign; per copy $6.50; sample $6.50 + $1 p/h. Back issues: send for order form. Discounts: none. 36-40pp. Reporting time: 1 month. Publishes 80% of manuscripts submitted. Payment: none. Copyrighted, does not revert to author. Pub's reviews: 6-8 in 2005. §Agriculture, old tractors, farm memorabilia, farm equipment, farm lifestyle. Ads: free non-commercial classifieds for members; commercial: 90¢/word, display rates: POR.

19TH-CENTURY LITERATURE, University of California Press, Joseph Bristow, Editor; Thomas Wortham, Editor, University of California Press, 2000 Center Street, Suite 303, Berkeley, CA 94704-1223, 510-643-7154. 1946. Reviews, non-fiction. ''Editorial address: Dept. of English, Box 951530, Rolfe Hall, Room 2225, 405 Hilgard, University of California, Los Angeles, CA 90095-1530.'' circ. 1913. 4/yr. Pub'd 4 issues 2005; expects 4 issues 2006, 4 issues 2007. sub. price $40 indiv., $112 instit., $25 students (+ $20 air freight); per copy $15 indiv., $33 instit., $15 students; sample free. Back issues: $15 indiv., $33 instit., $15 students. Discounts: foreign subs. agents 10%, one-time orders 10+, standing orders (bookstores): 1-99 40%, 100+ 50%. 144pp. Reporting time: 1-2 months. Copyrighted, does not revert to author. Pub's reviews: 4 in 2005. §19th-century literature, American and English. Ads: $295/$220. Subject: Literature (General).

19TH-CENTURY MUSIC, University of California Press, Larry Kramer, Editor; James Hepokoski, Editor; Christina Acosta, Managing Editor, University of California Press, 2000 Center Street, Suite 303, Berkeley, CA 94704-1223, 510-643-7154. 1977. Criticism, reviews, non-fiction. ''Editorial address: Dept. of Music, One Shields Avenue, University of California, Davis, CA 95616.'' circ. 1326. 3/yr. Pub'd 3 issues 2005; expects 3 issues 2006, 3 issues 2007. sub. price $40 indiv., $139 instit., $25 student (+ $20 air freight); per copy $21 indiv.; $53 instit. (+ $20 air freight), $21 student; sample free. Back issues: same as single copy price. Discounts: foreign subs. agents 10%, one-time orders 10+ 30%, standing orders (bookstores): 1-99 40%, 100+ 50%. 96pp. Reporting time: 1-3 months. Copyrighted, does not revert to author. Pub's reviews: 3 in 2005. §19th-century music. Ads: $295/$220. Subject: Music.

Ninety-Six Press, Gilbert Allen, William Rogers, Furman University, 3300 Poinsett Highway, Greenville, SC 29613, 864-294-3152/6. 1991. Poetry. ''Ninety-Six Press publishes books of poetry by authors from its region. The press reviews manuscripts only by invitation. No unsolicited manuscripts.'' avg. press run 500. Pub'd 1 title 2005; expects 1 title 2006, 1-2 titles 2007. Discounts: 40%. 50-70pp. Payment: copies. Copyrights for author. Subjects: Poetry, South.

NINTH LETTER, Jodee Stanley, Editor, 234 English Bldg., University of Illinois, 608 S. Wright St., Urbana, IL 61801, (217) 244-3145, fax (217)244-4147, www.ninthletter.com, ninthletter@uiuc.edu. 2004. Poetry, fiction, art, interviews, non-fiction. ''Recent contributors include Ann Beattie, Robin Hemley, Steve Stern, David Kirby, Lucia Perillo, T. R. Hummer, Ron Carlson, Sheryl St. Germain, and Robert Olen Butler.'' circ. 2000. 2/yr. Pub'd 2 issues 2005; expects 2 issues 2006, 2 issues 2007. sub. price 19.95; per copy 12.95; sample 8.95. Back issues: 8.95. 176pp. Reporting time: 6-8 weeks. Payment: $25 per page, plus 2 copies, on publication. Copyrighted, reverts to author.

Nip & Tuck Publishing, 736 Wilson Avenue, Kelowna, BC V1Y 6X9, Canada, 250-762-7861, nipandtuck@shaw.ca,. 1995. Non-fiction. avg. press run 1M. Pub'd 1 title 2005; expects 2 titles 2006, 5 titles 2007. Discounts: industry standard. 200pp. Simultaneous submissions accepted: no. Copyrights for author. Subjects: Biography, History, Immigration, Non-Fiction, The West, Women.

NMD Books, 2828 Cochran Street, Ste. 285, Simi Valley, CA 93065.

No Starch Press, William Pollock, 555 De Haro Street, Suite 250, San Francisco, CA 94107-2365, 415-863-9900. 1994. Non-fiction. ''Computer books for non-computer people. Books generally about 300 pages in length, we try to avoid long tomes at all costs. We will not publish cookie-cutter, how-to-use software type books. Prefer authors with writing experience, especially journalistic. Bias toward authors with nationally syndicated columns or who are regular contributors to major computer magazines. Interest in computer humor, non-traditional computer books for average people. Recent contributors: Owen Linzmayer (*Mac Addict,* columnist), and Wally Wang (author of *Visual Basic for Dummies*).'' avg. press run 7.5M. Pub'd 12 titles 2005; expects 15 titles 2006, 15 titles 2007. Standard trade discount schedule through O'Reilly. 300pp. Reporting time: 3-4 weeks. Simultaneous submissions accepted: yes. Publishes 10% of manuscripts submitted. Payment: 15% on all cash received from all sales. Copyrights for author. Subjects: Children, Youth, Computers, Calculators, Crafts, Hobbies, Family, Gardening, Humor, Judaism.

Noble Porter Press, Roger Karshner, 36-851 Palm View Road, Rancho Mirage, CA 92270, 760-770-6076, fax 760-770-4507. 1995. Non-fiction. "Not soliciting manuscripts." avg. press run 5M. Discounts: trade 40%. 200pp. Payment: 10% cover. Does not copyright for author.

NOBODADDIES, Doug Rice, 2491 State Route 45 South, Salem, OH 44460, E-mail rice@salem.kent.edu. 1994. Fiction, articles, art, photos, cartoons, interviews, criticism, reviews, letters, parts-of-novels, collages, non-fiction. "Recent contributors: Ray Federman, Larry McCaffery, Takyuki Tassumi, Steven Shaviro, Cris Mazza, Lance Olsen, Mark Amerika, Derek Pell. Biases: Literary texts that explode genres, that put pressure on the boundaries of discipline, that engage in nomadic narratives." circ. 500. 1/yr. Expects 1 issue 2006, 1 issue 2007. sub. price $10; per copy $10; sample $5. Back issues: $30 for issue #1, $5 all other issues. Discounts: 40%. 56pp. Reporting time: 2 weeks to 2 months. Simultaneous submissions accepted: no. Publishes 10% of manuscripts submitted. Payment: 1 copy. Copyrighted, reverts to author. Pub's reviews: 20 in 2005. §Alternative fiction, avant garde, photography, cultural theory. Ads: $150/$80/$45 1/4 page. Subjects: Avant-Garde, Experimental Art, Electronics, Fiction, James Joyce, Literary Review, Post Modern.

Noemi Press, Carmen Gimenez Smith, Publisher; Evan Lavender-Smith, Editor, P.O. Box 1330, Mesilla Park, NM 88047. 2002. Poetry, fiction, art. "Noemi Press is a not-for-profit publisher of innovative poetry and fiction chapbooks. We primarily publish new and emerging writers with the hope of creating greater exposure for their work. In both poetry and fiction we look for work that tends toward linguistic, syntactic, and formal experimentation without sacrificing allegiance to audience and beauty. Recent authors include Rebecca Stoddard, John Chavez, Karla Kelsey, and Kevin McIlvoy. www.noemipress.org." avg. press run 500. Pub'd 2 titles 2005; expects 6 titles 2006, 8 titles 2007. Discounts: 2-10 copies 20%. 18-40pp. Reporting time: 3-5 months. Simultaneous submissions accepted: Yes. Publishes 5% of manuscripts submitted. Payment: Author's copies. Copyrights revert to author upon publication. Subjects: Experimental, Fiction, Poetry.

THE NOISE, T Max, Publisher and Editor; Francis Dimenno, Senior Associate Editor; Lexi Kahn, Associate Editor; Joe Coughlin, Associate Editor; Steve Gisselbretch, Associate Editor; Robin Umbley, Associate Editor; Kier Byrnes, Associate Editor, 74 Jamaica Street, Jamaica Plain, MA 02130, 617-524-4735, tmax@thenoise-boston.com. 1981. Articles, photos, cartoons, interviews, reviews, music, news items. "Interviews and articles - 1600 words. Live reviews (of bands) - 150 words per band. Reviews of LPs - 200 words. Reviews of singles - 150 words. Our bias is away from commercial rock and roll, focusing on underground music from New England." circ. 5M. 10/yr. Pub'd 10 issues 2005; expects 10 issues 2006, 10 issues 2007. sub. price $18; per copy $4.50; sample $4.50. Back issues: $4.50-$50. Discounts: none. 48pp. Reporting time: 1 month. Simultaneous submissions accepted: no. Publishes 95% of manuscripts submitted. Payment: none. Copyrighted, reverts to author. Pub's reviews: 2 in 2005. §New England based rock 'n' roll books. Ads: Biz rates: $340 (full), $200 (half), $125 (quarter), $75 (eighth)Band rate: $222 (full), $133 (half), $88 (quarter), $55 (eighth). Subjects: Arts, Cartoons, Music, New England, Radio.

NOLA-MAGICK Press, Keith Nicholson, CEO, Author, Bartender & Ne'er-do-well; Barnabas Collins, Senior Editor, 828 Royal Street # 214, New Orleans, LA 70116, 504-301-1080, (fax) 504-309-9004, info@nolamagick.org, www.nolamagick.org. 2004. Fiction, criticism, reviews, non-fiction. "We are a nonprofit, occult publishing house. We also publish restaurant and nightclub reviews, concentrating on one city at a time." avg. press run 5000. Expects 2 titles 2006, 5 titles 2007. Discounts: 40-55%. Reporting time: 1 month. Simultaneous submissions accepted: Yes. Publishes 50% of manuscripts submitted. Payment: 40% minus production expenses. Copyrights for author. Subjects: Autobiography, Christianity, Dining, Restaurants, Fiction, Food, Eating, Louisiana, Magic, Metaphysics, New Age, Occult, Religion, Spiritual, Theosophical, Travel, WICCA.

Nolo Press, Ralph Warner, Publisher; Stephen Elias, Associate Publisher, 950 Parker Street, Berkeley, CA 94710, 510-549-1976, Fax 510-548-5902. 1971. Non-fiction. "Our books are of a special nature: they are how-to guides for laypeople, instructive in various legal procedures, and are frequently (at least every 12-18 months) updated to keep up with changes in the law. This means that our backlist books are often among our bestsellers and new editions are treated as new books - complete with a new press release. We cover business, retirement, immigration, intellectual property, estate planning, and more!" avg. press run 12M. Pub'd 45 titles 2005; expects 50 titles 2006, 55 titles 2007. Discounts: 50% to distributors, 40-46% bookstores. 300pp. Reporting time: 4-8 weeks. Publishes 1% of manuscripts submitted. Payment: 7-10% of retail, quarterly payment. Copyrights for author. Subjects: Business & Economics, Law, Reference.

Nolo Press Occidental, Charles Sherman, Owner; Joseph A. Cosentino Jr., General Manager, 501 Mission

Street, Suite 2, Santa Cruz, CA 95060, 831-466-9922, 800-464-5502, Fax: 831-466-9927, E-mail: inbox@nolotech.com, Website: http://www.nolotech.com. 1971. Non-fiction. avg. press run 10M. Pub'd 4 titles 2005; expects 3 titles 2006, 5 titles 2007. Discounts: 10-19 20%, 20-99 40%, 100+ 50%. 200pp. Payment: 10% of retail paid quarterly. Copyrights for author. Subjects: California, Divorce, Family, How-To, Law, Marriage, Non-Fiction, Reference, Relationships, Self-Help, Texas.

Nonetheless Press, Marie-Christine Ebershoff, Acquisitions, 20332 W. 98th Street, Lenexa, KS 66220-2650, 913-254-7266, Fax 913-393-3245, info@nonethelesspress.com. 2002. Non-fiction. ''Nonetheless Press imprint Looking Glass Press reviews memoirs, poetry, and fiction submissions. Contact person is Marcia Schutte.'' avg. press run 3M. Expects 10 titles 2006, 4/4 titles 2007. Reporting time: within 3 months. Simultaneous submissions accepted: yes. Publishes +/-5% of manuscripts submitted. Copyrights for author. Subjects: Arts, Autobiography, Biography, Business & Economics, Careers, Children, Youth, Consulting, Consumer, Current Affairs, Family, Fiction, Gardening, Global Affairs, Guidance, Health.

THE NONVIOLENT ACTIVIST, Judith Mahoney Pasternak, War Resisters League, 339 Lafayette Street, New York, NY 10012, 212-228-0450, fax 212-228-6193, e-Mail wrl@igc.apc.org. 1984. Articles, cartoons, interviews, reviews, news items. ''News of interest to the nonviolence movement; special focus on activities of the War Resisters League.'' circ. 8M. 6/yr. Pub'd 6 issues 2005; expects 6 issues 2006, 6 issues 2007. sub. price $25 institutions, $15 individuals; per copy $1.50; sample $1. 24pp. Simultaneous submissions accepted, but we want to know about it. Payment: none. Not copyrighted, all rights revert to author on publication. Pub's reviews: 12 in 2005. §Nonviolence, organizing ideas/skills, war/peace. Ads: $400/$220. Subjects: Non-Violence, Peace, Politics.

NOON, Diane Williams, 1369 Madison Avenue, PMB 298, New York, NY 10128, noonannual@yahoo.com. 2000. Fiction, articles, art, interviews. circ. 2M. 1/yr. Pub'd 1 issue 2005; expects 1 issue 2006, 1 issue 2007. sub. price $9; per copy $9. Back issues: none. Discounts: 55% distributor. 110pp. Reporting time: 1-2 months. Simultaneous submissions accepted: yes. Publishes 10% of manuscripts submitted. Payment: 2 copies of issue. Copyrighted, reverts to author. Ads: reciprocal ads with other magazines. Subjects: Arts, Fiction.

Noontide Press, PO Box 2719, Newport Beach, CA 92659, 949-631-1490, e-mail editor@noontidepress.com. 1962. Non-fiction. ''Noontide Press sells a wide variety of special-interest books, including many that are 'politically incorrect.''' avg. press run 4M. Pub'd 10 titles 2005; expects 10 titles 2006. Discounts: 40% for book sellers. Pages vary. Reporting time: 4 weeks. Simultaneous submissions accepted: yes. Publishes 1% of manuscripts submitted. Payment: standard. Copyrights for author. Subjects: Americana, History, Holocaust, Middle East, Public Affairs, World War II.

North American Bookdealers Exchange (see also BOOK DEALERS WORLD), Al Galasso, Editorial Director; Russ von Hoelscher, Associate Editor, PO Box 606, Cottage Grove, OR 97424-0026. 1979. Articles, interviews, news items, non-fiction. ''Manuscripts should be about making or saving money, self-publishing, mail order or book marketing. Will also accept titles relating to sexual communication, new diets, and health. Recent title: *Book Dealers' Dropship Directory*.'' avg. press run 1M. Pub'd 2 titles 2005; expects 2 titles 2006, 2 titles 2007. Discounts: 50%-75% on larger wholesale orders. 40pp. Reporting time: 2 weeks. Payment: outright purchase. Does not copyright for author. Subjects: Business & Economics, How-To, Publishing.

NORTH AMERICAN REVIEW, Grant Tracey, Editor; Vince Gotera, Editor; Ron Sandvik, Managing Editor, University Of Northern Iowa, 1222 W. 27th Street, Cedar Falls, IA 50614-0516, 319-273-6455. 1815. Poetry, fiction, articles, satire, reviews, non-fiction. ''We are especially interested in writing on the environment, race, ethnicity, gender, and class. The James Hearst Poetry Prize deadline (postmark) is October 31. The Kurt Vonnegut Fiction Prize deadline (postmark) is December 31. The Annual Student Cover Art Competition Deadline (postmark) is November 31. (Please visit our website for detailed entry information and required cover sheets at: http://webdelsol.com/NorthAmReview/NAR/) Please, no simultaneous or multiple submissions.'' circ. 2500. 5/yr. Pub'd 5 issues 2005; expects 5 issues 2006, 5 issues 2007. sub. price $22; per copy $5; sample $5. Back issues: $5. Discounts: agent 20%, bulk (10 or more) 30%. 56pp. Reporting time: 4 months. Simultaneous submissions accepted: no. Publishes 1-2% of manuscripts submitted. Payment: $5 per 350 words of prose, $1 a line for poetry ($20 minimum, $100 maximum). Copyrighted, reverts to author. Pub's reviews: 11 in 2005. §Drama, fiction, nonfiction, poetry, and popular culture. Ads: $125 and up. Subjects: Fiction, Non-Fiction, Poetry.

North Atlantic Books, PO Box 12327, Berkeley, CA 94712, 800-337-2665, 510-559-8277, fax 510-559-8272, www.northatlanticbooks.com. 1974. ''We don't want poetry or fiction submissions - don't publish enough.'' avg. press run 3-5K. Pub'd 50 titles 2005; expects 50 titles 2006, 50 titles 2007. Discounts: trade 1-4 books 20%, 5+ 40%. 200pp. Reporting time: 4-8 weeks. Simultaneous submissions accepted: yes. Publishes .5-1% of manuscripts submitted. Payment: by contract. Only automatic copyrighting by publication.

NORTH CAROLINA LITERARY REVIEW, Margaret Bauer, English Department, East Carolina University, Greenville, NC 27858, 252-328-1537; Fax 252-328-4889. 1991. Poetry, fiction, articles, art, photos, interviews, satire, criticism, reviews, letters, plays, concrete art, news items, non-fiction. "Past contributors: Fred Chappell, Lee Smith, Janet Lembke; A.R. Ammons, Linda Beatrice Brown, James Applewhite, Charles Wright, Margaret Maron, Alan Shapiro. Length: 1,000-6,000 words. Biases: critical and historical essays about NC writers, usually directed to theme of special feature section; interviews with NC writers; contemporary creative work by NC writers; comprehensive essay reviews of recent books by NC writers; MLA style when appropriate." circ. 500. 1/yr. Pub'd 1 issue 2005; expects 1 issue 2006, 1 issue 2007. sub. price $20/2 years, $36/4 years; per copy $15; sample $10-$20 depending on issue. Back issues: $10-$50. 200pp. Reporting time: 2-3 months. Simultaneous submissions accepted: no. Publishes 25% of manuscripts submitted. Payment: $25-$250 and/or subscriptions, extra copies, back issues. Copyrighted, rights revert to author on request. Pub's reviews: 5 in 2005. §North Carolina writers, literature, culture, history ONLY. Ads: $200/$125/$75 1/4 page. Subjects: Appalachia, Biography, Book Reviewing, Essays, Fiction, Food, Eating, Graphic Design, Literary Review, Non-Fiction, North Carolina, Photography, Poetry, Short Stories.

North Country Books, Inc., M. Sheila Orlin, 311 Turner Street, Utica, NY 13501, 315-735-4877. 1965. Photos, non-fiction. "NY State, history, biography, nostalgia, heavy accent on Adirondacks and upstate." avg. press run 3M-5M. Pub'd 8 titles 2005; expects 5 titles 2006, 10 titles 2007. Discounts: 1-4 20%, 5 40%. 200pp. Reporting time: 3-6 months. Simultaneous submissions accepted: yes. Publishes 5% of manuscripts submitted. Payment: 8% retail price, 20% withheld against returns. Copyrights for author. Subjects: Adirondacks, Autobiography, Biography, Children, Youth, Crime, Environment, Folklore, History, Native American, Nature, New York, Non-Fiction, Photography, Supernatural, Tapes & Records.

NORTH DAKOTA QUARTERLY, UND Press, Robert W. Lewis, Editor; Elizabeth Harris Behling, Fiction Editor; Donald Junkins, Poetry Editor, University of North Dakota, PO Box 7209, Grand Forks, ND 58202, 701-777-3322. 1910. Poetry, fiction, articles, art, photos, interviews, criticism, reviews, long-poems, non-fiction. "Recent contributors include Debra Marquart, Kim Chinquee, Scott Randall, and David Warfield." circ. 700. 4/yr. Pub'd 4 issues 2005; expects 4 issues 2006, 4 issues 2007. sub. price $25 individual, $30 institutional, $20 students and seniors; per copy $8 and $12 for special; sample $8. Back issues: $8 and $12 for special. Discounts: 20%. 175pp. Reporting time: 1-4 months. Simultaneous submissions only for fiction and essays (if noted in cover letter), not for poetry. Publishes 5% of manuscripts submitted. Payment: in copies. Copyrighted, reverts to author. Pub's reviews: 60 in 2005. §Native American studies, Canadian studies, northern plains literature. Ads: $150/$100. Subjects: Book Reviewing, Criticism, Culture, Great Plains, Ireland, Literary Review, Literature (General), Native American.

North Star Books, PO Box 589, Pearblossom, CA 93553-0589, 661-944-1130, NorthStarBooks@avradion-et.com. 1992. Non-fiction. "North Star Books, in business since 1992, publishes quality titles that TOUCH THE WORLD, ONE FAMILY AT A TIME. For the past decade health-related titles on dementia, caregiving, and Alzheimer's was the theme with proceeds donated worldwide. Today, North Star Books is adding other themes (wilderness trekking and investing). Authors must have a passion for their message and a platform from which to impact the marketplace with their passion." avg. press run 2-3M. Pub'd 1 title 2005; expects 1 title 2006, 1 title 2007. Discounts: 50-55% wholesaler, 50% for fundraising and premiums (case orders only), 20-40% retail, 20% S.T.O.P. orders. 160-300pp. Reporting time: 4-8 weeks. Simultaneous submissions accepted: No. Copyrights for author. Subjects: Aging, Business & Economics, California, Finances, Health, How-To, Humor, Memoirs, Motivation, Success, Nature, Non-Fiction, Nursing, Psychology, Self-Help, Sociology.

North Stone Editions (see also THE NORTH STONE REVIEW), PO Box 14098, Minneapolis, MN 55414. 1971. Poetry, fiction, criticism, reviews, letters. "At this point, these are the genres we're working with. More genres later, perhaps." avg. press run 1M-2M. Pub'd 1 title 2005; expects 1 title 2006, 2 titles 2007. Discounts: query, please, with proposal. Pages vary. Reporting time: 1 month to 6 weeks. Simultaneous submissions accepted: no. Publishes a small % of manuscripts submitted. Payment: after costs, yes. Copyrights for author. Subjects: Book Reviewing, Criticism, Dada, England, Fiction, Literary Review, Poetry, Reviews, Writers/Writing.

THE NORTH STONE REVIEW, North Stone Editions, James Naiden, Editor; Anne Duggan, Associate Editor; Sigrid Bergie, Contributing Editor; Richard Fournier, Contributing Editor; Eugene McCarthy, Contributing Editor; Michael Tjepkes, Contributing Editor; Jack Jarpe, Assistant Editor, PO Box 14098, Minneapolis, MN 55414. 1971. Poetry, fiction, articles, art, photos, interviews, reviews, long-poems, non-fiction. "Leslie Miller, Robert Bly, John Rezmerski, George T. Wright, Sigrid Bergie, etc., are among recent contributors." circ. 1.5M. 1+. Pub'd 1 issue 2005; expects 1 issue 2006, 1 issue 2007. sub. price $28/2 issues; per copy $14; sample $14. Back issues: query first. Discounts: depends—query first. 200-300+pp. Reporting time: 2-6 weeks or less. Simultaneous submissions accepted: no. Publishes 2-3% of manuscripts submitted. Payment: 2 copies. Copyrighted, reprint permission on written request. Pub's reviews: 15 in 2005. §Poetry, fiction, literary biography and theory, literary essay. Ads: $60/$35/$25 1/4 page, query first.

Northern Illinois University Press, Sarah Atkinson, Marketing Manager; Melody Herr, Acquisitions Editor;

Mary Lincoln, Director, 310 N. Fifth Street, DeKalb, IL 60115, (815) 753-1826 phone; (815) 753-1845 fax. 1965. Criticism, letters, non-fiction. avg. press run 1000. Pub'd 16 titles 2005; expects 14 titles 2006, 15 titles 2007. Discounts: 1-4 copies 25%5-49 copies 40%50-99 copies 42%100 + copies 45%Text orders 25%. 230pp. Subjects: Chicago, Civil War, Eastern Europe, Illinois, Indigenous Cultures, Law, Literature (General), Political Science, Religion.

NORTHERN PILOT, Peter M. Diemer, Publisher, PO Box 220168, Anchorage, AK 99522, 907-258-6898, Fax 907-258-4354, info@northernpilot.com. 1998. *"Northern Pilot* is seeking first-person stories and photographs. We want text with an authentic, powerful, unique voice. Our features cover the Northwest, Rocky Mtn. States, Canada, and Alaska. We publish only work of the highest quality. Technical features run 3,000-3,500 words; fiction or nonfiction 1,100-3,000 words. Please query with SASE and 5-line bio stressing personal aviation experience/expertise.'' circ. 40M. 6/yr. Pub'd 6 issues 2005; expects 6 issues 2006, 6 issues 2007. sub. price $19; per copy $3.99; sample $5.50. Back issues: $5.50. 48pp. Reporting time: 8-12 weeks. Simultaneous submissions accepted: yes. Payment: $200-$400 on publication. Copyrighted, reverts to author. Pub's reviews: none in 2005. §Aviation. Ads: call for rates. Subjects: Airplanes, Alaska, Aviation, California, Canada, Fiction, Humor, Non-Fiction, Oregon, Pacific Northwest, Pacific Region, Transportation, Washington (state).

Northern Publishing, Tony Russ, PO BOx 871803, Wasilla, AK 99687, 907-376-6474, 907-373-6474, tony@TonyRuss.com, www.TonyRuss.com. 1994. Non-fiction. ''Additional address: 574 Sarahs Way, Wasilla, AK 99654.'' avg. press run 3M. Pub'd 2 titles 2005; expects 3 titles 2006, 4 titles 2007. Discounts: 40%, 50%, 55%. 256pp. Reporting time: 1 month. Simultaneous submissions accepted: yes. Publishes 30% of manuscripts submitted. Payment: 10%. Copyrights for author. Subjects: Alaska, Biography, Sports, Outdoors, Travel.

Northland Publishing/Rising Moon/Luna Rising, Claudine Randazzo, Managing Editor, Northland; Theresa Howell, Managing Editor, Rising Moon, PO Box 1389, Flagstaff, AZ 86002-1389, 800-346-3257, Fax 800-257-9802, info@northlandpub.com, www.northlandpub.com. 1958. Art, photos, non-fiction. ''Northland publishing was founded in 1958, and is now recognized as an award-winning publisher of finely crafted books that capture the spirit of the West. Northland specializes in non-fiction titles with American West and Southwest themes, including Native American arts, crafts, and culture; regional cookery; lifestyle; interior design and architecture. Rising Moon and Luna Rising, Northlands children's imprints, publish southwestern picture books and is now focused on acquiring titles with wide appeal and universal themes for the national market. We publish heartwarming titles that challenge boundaries, incorporate lifes lessons, and provide hours of endless laughter. Luna Rising publishing bilingual titles (Spanish/English) for the National market.'' avg. press run 7500 to 15000. Pub'd 18 titles 2005; expects 16 titles 2006, 16 titles 2007. Discounts: 1-4 30% prepaid, S.T.O.P.; 5+ 42% returnable; 5+ 50% non-returnable. 144pp. Reporting time: 8 weeks. Simultaneous submissions accepted: Simultaneous submissions accepted. Publishes 2% of manuscripts submitted. Payment: 8-10% net receipts first printing softcover, 10-12% net receipts first printing hardcover. Copyrights for author. Subjects: Anthropology, Archaelogy, Arizona, Arts, Bicycling, Birds, Children, Youth, Construction, Cooking, Culture, Earth, Natural History, Health, Indians, Latino, Photography, Picture Books.

NORTHWEST REVIEW, John Witte, Editor; Jan MacRae, Fiction Editor, 369 P.L.C., University of Oregon, Eugene, OR 97403. 1957. Poetry, fiction, art, photos, reviews, parts-of-novels, long-poems, plays. ''Recent contributors: Raymond Carver, Hans Magnus Enzensberger, Olga Broumas, Barry Lopez, Morris Graves, Joyce Carol Oates, Ursula Le Guin. Bias: Quality in whatever form. No other predisposition.'' circ. 1M. 3/yr. Pub'd 3 issues 2005; expects 3 issues 2006. sub. price $22; per copy $8; sample $4. Back issues: $8 all except double issues or specially priced issues. Discounts: bookstore/agencies 40% wholesale. 140pp. Reporting time: 8-10 weeks average. Simultaneous submissions accepted: no! Publishes 1.5% of manuscripts submitted. Payment: 3 copies and whatever fame clings to publication. Copyrighted, rights reassigned upon request for inclusion in a book. Pub's reviews: 15 in 2005. §Literature, poetry, fiction, small press publications. Ads: $160 full page only. Subjects: Book Reviewing, Fiction, Poetry.

Northwestern University Press (see also TRIQUARTERLY), Susan Betz, 629 Noyes Street, Evanston, IL 60208-4170, (847) 491-2046; fax (847)491-8150; www.nupress.northwestern.edu. 1893. Poetry, fiction, criticism, plays, non-fiction. ''Northwestern University Press publishes in several disciplines including philosophy, Slavic studies, literature-in-translation, contemporary fiction and poetry, avant-garde and modernism studies, English-language Latino ficiton and memoirs, and theater and performance studies.'' Pub'd 40 titles 2005; expects 50 titles 2006, 50 titles 2007. Discounts: contact our sales department for discount schedule. Reporting time: Varies according to discipline. Simultaneous submissions accepted: No. Publishes 10% of manuscripts submitted. Payment: We pay royalties once a year. Copyrights for author. Subjects: Autobiography, Avant-Garde, Experimental Art, Biography, Chicago, Drama, Eastern Europe, Fiction, Latino, Literature (General), Non-Fiction, Performing Arts, Poetry, Theatre.

NORTHWOODS JOURNAL, A Magazine for Writers, Conservatory of American Letters, Dan River Press, Northwoods Press, Robert Olmsted, Editor; S.M. Hall III, Fiction Editor, PO Box 298, Thomaston, ME

04861-0298, 207-345-0998, cal@americanletters.org, www.americanletters.org. 1986. Poetry, fiction, articles, art, interviews, satire, criticism, reviews, letters, news items. circ. 200. 4/yr. Pub'd 4 issues 2005; expects 4 issues 2006, 4 issues 2007. price per copy $10.00 ppd.; sample $10.00 ppd. Back issues: if available $13.50 ppd. Discounts: 10+ copies, $3.30 each, plus shipping. 40pp. Reporting time: 48 hours to 2 weeks after deadline (90 days max.). Simultaneous submissions accepted: no. Publishes 5-20% fiction, poetry 85-90% of manuscripts submitted. Payment: cash for all acceptances, except letters, approx. $4+ per page depending on quality, relevancy, etc. Copyrighted, does not revert to author. Pub's reviews: 4-5 in 2005. §Small press and self-published only. Ads: $60/$42/$28 1/4 page. Subjects: Adirondacks, Americana, Appalachia, Book Reviewing, Conservation, Erotica, Family, Fantasy, Folklore, History, Literature (General), Maine, New England, Occult, Poetry.

Northwoods Press (see also NORTHWOODS JOURNAL, A Magazine for Writers), Robert W. Olmsted, Publisher, PO Box 298, Thomaston, ME 04861-0298, 207-354-0998, cal@americanletters.org, www.american-letters.org. 1972. Poetry, fiction, news items. "See our website or send SASE for guidelines." avg. press run 100-150. Pub'd 3 titles 2005; expects 4 titles 2006, 4 titles 2007. Discounts: 5-24 paperbacks 2% per book ordered to a maximum of 50% for 25 or more books. Hardcovers 5 or more 2% per book ordered to a maximum of 20%. 116pp. Reporting time: 1-4 weeks. Simultaneous submissions accepted: yes for books, no for anthologies. Payment: 10% of amount received royalties from first 2500 copies then 15%. Copyrights for author. Subjects: Fiction, Poetry.

NORTHWORDS, Angus Dunn, The Stable, Long Road, Avoch, Ross-shire IV9 8QR, Scotland, e-mail northwords@demon.co.uk. 1991. Poetry, fiction, articles, art, criticism, reviews, long-poems. circ. 500. 3/yr. Pub'd 3 issues 2005; expects 3 issues 2006, 3 issues 2007. sub. price £9 UK, £12 overseas; per copy £3 UK, £4 overseas; sample £3 UK, £4 overseas. Back issues: £2 UK, £3 overseas. Discounts: 33-1/2% discount. 64pp. Reporting time: 8 weeks. Simultaneous submissions accepted: no. Publishes 10% of manuscripts submitted. Token payment. Copyrighted, reverts to author. Pub's reviews: 20 in 2005. §Poetry, fiction, Scottish, Irish. Ads: £50/£30/no classifieds. Subjects: Gaelic, Poetry, Reviews, Scotland, Short Stories.

Norton Coker Press, Edward Mycue, PO Box 640543, San Francisco, CA 94164-0543, 415-922-0395. 1988. Poetry, fiction, art, satire, criticism, reviews, music, letters, plays, news items. avg. press run 150. Pub'd 22 titles 2005; expects 15 titles 2006, 10 titles 2007. Discounts: 5+ copies 40%. 44pp. Reporting time: 1-4 weeks. Payment: in copies. Copyrights for author. Subjects: Arts, Bibliography, Electronics, Literature (General), Music, Tapes & Records, Translation, Visual Arts.

NOSTOC MAGAZINE, Arts End Books, Marshall Brooks, Editor, PO Box 441, West Dover, VT 05356-0441. 1973. Poetry, fiction, articles, criticism, reviews, parts-of-novels. "A copy of our catalogue - detailing our past publications and describing our subscription package program is available upon request (please enclose a SASE). We read unsolicited mss. between October and December only. Sample copies of our publications available if you send a large SASE, plus a self-portrait of yourself (preferably hand-drawn); OR A portrait of your personal library, OR hall closet, OR garden. Vote. Support freedom of the presses." circ. 300. 2/yr. Pub'd 2 issues 2005; expects 2 issues 2006, 2 issues 2007. sub. price $10/4 issues; per copy $5; sample $5. Back issues: rates on request. Discounts: on request. 40pp. Simultaneous submissions accepted: no. Publishes 5% of manuscripts submitted. Payment: modest payment upon acceptance. Copyrighted, reverts to author. Pub's reviews: 5 in 2005. §Small press history, poetry, fiction & politics, bibliography. Ads: rates on request. Subjects: Bibliography, Book Reviewing, Poetry.

NoteBoat, Inc., Tom Serb, PO Box 6155, Woodridge, IL 60517, 630-697-7229,630-910-4553. 1998. Music. "Educational works for guitar." avg. press run 3500. Pub'd 1 title 2005; expects 1 title 2006, 2 titles 2007. Discounts: 1-2 copies 20%3-4 copies 30%5-12 copies 40%13-34 copies 45%35+ copies 50%. 110pp. Reporting time: 4-8 weeks. Simultaneous submissions accepted: No. Payment: 8% on net sales. Copyrights for author. Subject: Music.

NOTES AND ABSTRACTS IN AMERICAN AND INTERNATIONAL EDUCATION, Caddo Gap Press, Alan H. Jones, Editor, 3145 Geary Boulevard #275, San Francisco, CA 94118, 415-392-1911. 1961. Articles. "A semi-annual bulletin featuring information, news, research, and abstracts in the social foundations of education." circ. 100. 2/yr. Pub'd 2 issues 2005; expects 2 issues 2006, 2 issues 2007. sub. price $30 indiv., $60 instit.; per copy $15. 24pp. Reporting time: 2 months. Publishes 25% of manuscripts submitted. Payment: none. Copyrighted, reverts to author. Ads: none. Subject: Education.

NOTRE DAME REVIEW, Kathleen Canavan, Executive Editor; William O'Rourke, Fiction Editor; John Matthias, Poetry Editor; Steve Tomasula, Senior Editor, 840 Flanner Hall, University of Notre Dame, Notre Dame, IN 46556, 574-631-6952, Fax 574-631-4795. 1995. Poetry, fiction, interviews, reviews, parts-of-novels. "Recent contributors: Edward Falco, Seamus Heaney, Richard Elman, Denise Levertov, and Czeslaw Milosz. Manuscripts submitted April-August will be returned to sender unread." circ. 2M. 2/yr. Pub'd 2 issues 2005; expects 2 issues 2006, 2 issues 2007. sub. price $15 individuals, $20 institutions; per copy $8; sample $6.

Discounts: 10% for subscription agencies. 150pp. Reporting time: 3-4 months. Simultaneous submissions accepted: yes. Publishes 8% of manuscripts submitted. Payment: variable. Copyrighted, reverts to author. Pub's reviews: 7 in 2005. §Fiction, poetry, literary criticism/history. Ads: $165/$90/$75 1/3 page. Subjects: Fiction, Interviews, Literary Review, Literature (General), Poetry, Reviews.

NOTTINGHAM MEDIEVAL STUDIES, Michael Jones, Professor, School of History, University Park, Nottingham NG7 2RD, England, +44 115-9-515929, fax +44 115-9-515948, e-mail michael.jones@nottingh-am.ac.uk. 1957. Articles. "Articles on medieval language, literature, history, etc., concerning the whole of Europe making up to some 200pp of print @ 550 words per page." circ. 400. 1/yr. Pub'd 1 issue 2005; expects 1 issue 2006, 1 issue 2007. sub. price £20 sterling only; per copy £20 or $24; sample £20. Back issues: £10. Discounts: £17.50; back numbers before 2000 at greater discount. 200pp. Reporting time: 2 months. Simultaneous submissions accepted: yes. Publishes 30-50% of manuscripts submitted. Payment: none. Copyrighted. Pub's reviews: 4 in 2005. §Review-articles rather than reviews. Ads: none. Subject: Medieval.

NOVA EXPRESS, Lawrence Person, PO Box 27231, Austin, TX 78755, E-mail lawrenceperson@jump.net. 1987. Poetry, fiction, articles, art, interviews, satire, criticism, reviews, letters, non-fiction. "We cover cutting edge science fiction, fantasy, horror, and slipstream literature, with an emphasis on post cyberpunk works." circ. 850. 2/yr. Pub'd 2 issues 2005; expects 2 issues 2006, 2 issues 2007. sub. price $12/4 issues; per copy $4; sample $4. Back issues: $4. Discounts: starts at 40% for 25 issues, write for rates. 48pp. Reporting time: 1-3 months, sometimes less. Simultaneous submissions accepted: no. Publishes 10% freelance, assigned 90% of manuscripts submitted. Payment: 2 contributor copies and 4-issue subscription. Copyrighted, reverts to author. Pub's reviews: 55 in 2005. §Science fiction, fantasy, horror, slipstream. Ads: $100/$60/$35 1/4 page. Subjects: Bibliography, Book Reviewing, Criticism, Fantasy, Fiction, Futurism, Interviews, Literary Review, H.P. Lovecraft, Science Fiction.

Nova House Press, Tim Gavin, 470 North Latch's Lane, Merion, PA 19066. 1998. Poetry. "Nova House Press concerns itself with publishing the best possible poetry without regard to school, form, or content. We are interested in not only what is being said, but in how it is being said. The how and what of poetry are important to use; therefore, we search for poetry the employs a range of poetic elements to support the content of the chapbook. The poets whose work we have published include, Margaret Holley, R. T. Smith, Lou McKee, Marcia Harlow, Jenn Bryant, Len Roberts, Ken Fifer, and David St. John. We only accept solicited manuscripts." avg. press run 100. Pub'd 1 title 2005; expects 2 titles 2006, 2 titles 2007. Discounts: 50% discount to all institutions interested in a chapbook. 28pp. Reporting time: Varies depending on the number of manuscripts reviewed. Simultaneous submissions accepted: Yes. Publishes 5% of manuscripts submitted. Payment: Author receives 1/2 of the press run; however, if the author desires more copies, he or she can cover the cost of printing. Does not copyright for author. Subject: Poetry.

Nova Press, Jeff Kolby, 11659 Mayfield Ave, Suite 1, Los Angeles, CA 90049, 310-207-4078, E-mail novapress@aol.com. 1993. "We publish only test prep books for college entrance exams such as the GRE, LSAT, SAT, GMAT, and MCAT, or closely related books such as college guides and vocabulary improvement." avg. press run 3M. Pub'd 5 titles 2005; expects 5 titles 2006, 10 titles 2007. Discounts: 40%. 550pp. Payment: 10%-22.5% royalty. Subject: Education.

NOVA RELIGIO, University of California Press, Rebecca Moore, Editor; Catherine Wessinger, Editor, University of California Press, 2000 Center St., Suite 303, Berkeley, CA 94704-1223, 510-643-7154. 1997. Articles, reviews. "Editorial address: Dept. of Religious Studies, San Diego State University, 5500 Campanile Dr., San Diego, CA 92182-8143. Copyrighted by the Regents of the University of California." circ. 250. 3/yr. Pub'd 3 issues 2005; expects 3 issues 2006, 3 issues 2007. sub. price $47 indiv., $107 inst., $25 student; per copy $23 indiv., $42 inst., $23 student; sample same as single copy. Discounts: foreign subs. agents 10%, 10+ one-time orders 30%. 132pp. Copyrighted, does not revert to author. Pub's reviews: aprox. 30 in 2005. §Religious studies, history, literature, cultural studies, and sociology. Ads: $295/$220. Subjects: Culture, History, Literature (General), Religion, Sociology.

NOW AND THEN, Jane Harris Woodside, Editor-in-Chief; Nancy Fischman, Managing Editor; Linda Parsons, Poetry Editor; Sandra Ballard, Reviews Editor; Jo Carson, Poetry Editor, PO Box 70556, East Tennessee State University, Johnson City, TN 37614-0556, 423-439-5348; fax 423-439-6340; e-mail woodsidj@etsu.edu. 1984. Poetry, fiction, articles, art, photos, interviews, criticism, reviews, letters. "*Now and Then* is the publication of the Center for Appalachian Studies and Service of East Tennessee State University. Each issue is divided between expository and imaginative material: studies of Appalachian nature and culture on the one hand, and visual art, imaginative writing on the other. Issues always have a thematic focus; for example, recent issues focused on food in Appalachia and photography. Each issue features juxtaposed visuals of an Appalachian locale now (present) and then (past). Photos, graphics, critical studies of Appalachian nature and culture, personal essays, poetry, fiction are welcomed for consideration on a continuing basis. 'Appalachia' is considered to cover the mountain region from New Yord State to Georgia. We'd like people to send for a free listing of upcoming issues and writer's guidelines." circ. 1.5M. 3/yr. Pub'd 3 issues 2005; expects 3 issues

2006, 3 issues 2007. sub. price $20; per copy $7; sample $5. Back issues: $4.50. 44pp. Reporting time: 4 months. We accept simultaneous submissions, but we must be notified where else it's been submitted. Payment: $15-$75 generally for articles and fiction; $10 per poem and per review + copies of the magazine. Copyrighted, does not revert to author. Pub's reviews: 12 in 2005. §Appalachian arts, history, culture, ecology. Subjects: Appalachia, Fiction, Poetry.

NOW HERE NOWHERE, Gravity Presses (Lest We All Float Away), Inc., Paul Kingston, L.A. Beach, Patt Trama, 27030 Havelock, Dearborn Heights, MI 48127, 313-563-4683, e-mail kingston@gravitypresses.com. 1998. Poetry, fiction, art, photos. ''We have no formal guidelines for either form or contest; we've published sonnets, sestinas, language poetry and other experiments. However, we have high standards, so don't submit junk.'' circ. 150. 4/yr. Pub'd 2 issues 2005; expects 4 issues 2006, 4 issues 2007. sub. price $20; per copy $5.50; sample $5.50. Back issues: $6 (including p/h). Discounts: negotiable. 48pp. Reporting time: 3-6 months. Simultaneous submissions accepted: yes. Publishes 30% of manuscripts submitted. Payment: $1-5 per issue + one copy. Copyrighted, reverts to author. Ads: $40/$25/ 1/4 page $15. Subjects: Fiction, Poetry.

NSR Publications, Merry L. Gumm, 1482 51st Road, Douglass, KS 67039, 620-986-5472, e-mail: nsrpublications@englishthrough.com, website: nsrpublications.com. 2004. Fiction, non-fiction. ''Our primary focus is non-fiction for pre-kindergarten through young adult and educational books for primary grades. Our first published book titled "Help! I'm In Middle School...How Will I Survive?" is a lighthearted approach to the serious problems middle school children face in those tough pre-teen/teen years. For 2005 we have added "Let It Grow", a plant activity book, and "Dizzy Duck", a children's book.'' avg. press run 3000. Pub'd 1 title 2005; expects 3 titles 2006, 5 titles 2007. Discounts: 3-9 copies 20%10-29 copies 30%30-99 40%100 or more 45%. 80pp. Reporting time: 3 weeks. Simultaneous submissions accepted: No. Publishes 1% of manuscripts submitted. Payment: Authors provide the cost of printing up front. Fees for typesetting and cover design vary with each book. Does not copyright for author. Subjects: Adolescence, Children, Youth, Education, Family, Fiction, Non-Fiction, Young Adult.

Nunciata, A.C. Doyle, Publishing Division, PO Box 416, Denver, CO 80201-0416, 303-575-5676, Fax 303-575-1187. 1989. ''Formerly Assoc. Advertisers Services.'' avg. press run 1.5M. Pub'd 3 titles 2005; expects 10 titles 2006. Discounts: standard to libraries + bookstores. 60pp. Subjects: Advertising, Self-Promotion, Business & Economics, Education, Homemaking, How-To, Self-Help, Singles, Textbooks.

NUTHOUSE, Ludwig von Quirk, Chief of Staff, c/o Twin Rivers Press, PO Box 119, Ellenton, FL 34222. 1993. Poetry, fiction, articles, cartoons, interviews, satire, non-fiction. ''Humorous essays, stories, poetry and other amusements, preferably of 1,000 words or less. Recent contributors include Michael Fowler, Cornelia Snider Yarrington, John M. Floyd, Dale Andrew White.'' circ. 100+. 4-6/yr. Pub'd 4 issues 2005; expects 4 issues 2006, 4 issues 2007. sub. price $5 for 4 issues or $10 for 9 issues, checks must be payable to Twin Rivers Press; per copy $1.25; sample $1.25. Back issues: $1.25. 12pp. Reporting time: 1 month. Simultaneous submissions accepted: yes. Publishes 25% of manuscripts submitted. Payment: contributor's copy. Not copyrighted, all rights revert to author upon publication. Pub's reviews: approx. 4 in 2005. §humor, all genres. Ads: trade; classifieds free for subscribers. Subject: Humor.

NWI National Writers Institute, Maria Valentin, Publisher, PO Box 305, Palmyra, NJ 08065-0305, E-mail cust@top100online.com. 1996. Fiction, art, plays, non-fiction. ''We accept unsolicited mss. of 50 pages or more, specifically non-fiction, plays and fiction. All submitted work must be done entirely with SASE.'' avg. press run 3M. Pub'd 10 titles 2005; expects 25 titles 2006, 25+ titles 2007. Discounts: 45-55% bookstores, 40-45% libraries. 120-176pp. Reporting time: 2 weeks, turnaround from inquiry to publication 6 weeks. Simultaneous submissions accepted: yes. Publishes 80% of manuscripts submitted. Payment: 50% royalty of list, net price. Copyrights for author. Subjects: Arts, Computers, Calculators, Drama, Fantasy, Fiction, History, Humor, Literature (General), Movies, Non-Fiction, Novels.

Nystrom Publishing Co., Alex Jones, Mardi Nystrom, PO Box 378, Issaquah, WA 98027, 425-392-0451. 1985. Articles, photos, reviews. avg. press run 30M. Pub'd 2 titles 2005; expects 2 titles 2006, 2 titles 2007. 208pp. Reporting time: 30 days. Simultaneous submissions accepted: no. Publishes 0% of manuscripts submitted. Payment: individually arranged. Copyrights for author. Subject: Travel.

O

O!!Zone (see also O!!ZONE, A LITERARY-ART ZINE), Harry Burrus, Editor & Publisher, Mexico. 1993. Poetry, fiction, articles, art, photos, interviews, criticism, reviews. avg. press run 50-300. Discounts: none. 40-80pp, visual poetry anthologies 180pp. Reporting time: ASAP. Simultaneous submissions accepted: yes.

Payment: copies. Does not copyright for author. Subjects: Poetry, Surrealism.

O!!ZONE, A LITERARY-ART ZINE, O!!Zone, Harry Burrus, Editor & Publisher, Mexico. 1993. Poetry, fiction, art, photos, collages. *"O!!Zone* currently is in a dormant period. Future publication dates are uncertain. It will eventually resurface in some form. *O!!Zone* is not for prudes, the politically correct, ultra conservatives, the judgmental - those who believe they can decide what is right and proper for others. If easily offended by unusual lifestyles, nudity & provocative words...don't bother. *O!!Zone* is an international publication featuring poetry, visual poetry, reviews, interviews, manifestos, and art. I am particularly intrigued by poets who also do photography, college (or draw or paint or do line drawings). We welcome artists & visual poets. Send work that isn't taught in schools, words that lack in oral history, unspoken on any reading circuit. Time is a tyranny to be abolished. The writer expresses; the writer does not communicate - that's up to the reader. We are interested in D-I-S-C-O-V-E-R-Y and self-transcendence. Get Nakid! Submissions. *Do A Cover Letter.* Always include SASE or sufficient international coupons for return of work. No religious or when I was 12 poems or if you lack the energy of Isidore Ducasse. Poetry=2-4 poems; *expose yourself! Hit us! Bleed!* Photographic Submissions= 5 X 7 or 8 X 10 black and white prints. Desire nudes, surrealism, collage, & nude self-portraits. Yes, art brut. Liberate yourself. Do the unusal. *Can you shock? Enhance your chances!* Create & don't look over your shoulder. Inform your curious friends about *O!!Zone.* Share the word. Transform, mutate...SOAR! ...tempus edax rerum. *Rock us, don't bore.''* Sporadic. Pub'd 10 issues 2005; expects 5 issues 2006, 4 issues 2007. price per copy $25; sample varies, depends on what is available. Back issues: depends. Discounts: none. 80-128pp. Reporting time: ASAP. Simultaneous submissions accepted: yes. Payment: copy. Copyrighted, reverts to author. Pub's reviews: 2 in 2005. §Poetry books, art, photography. Subjects: Avant-Garde, Experimental Art, Fiction, Poetry, Surrealism, Visual Arts.

Oak Knoll Press, 310 Delaware Street, New Castle, DE 19720-5038, 800-996-2556, 302-328-7232, fax 302-328-7274, oakknoll@oakknoll.com, www.oakknoll.com. 1976. avg. press run 2-3M. Pub'd 30 titles 2005; expects 35 titles 2006, 40 titles 2007. Discounts: 1-4 20%, 5-25 40%, 26-99 45%, 100+ 50%, can mix titles. Pages vary. Reporting time: 1 month. Payment: 10% of income, quarterly payments. Copyrights for author. Subjects: Antiques, Arts, Bibliography, Biography, Book Collecting, Bookselling, Conservation, Crafts, Hobbies, Graphics, History, Indexes & Abstracts, Libraries, Literary Review, Literature (General), Printing, Reference.

Oak Tree Press, Billie Johnson, Publisher, 140 E. Palmer St., Taylorville, IL 62568, 217-824-6500, Fax 217-824-2040, oaktreepub@aol.com, www.oaktreebooks.com. 1998. Fiction, non-fiction. "Three annual contests (mystery, law enforcement professional and romance) Winning entry in each is published." avg. press run 1M. Pub'd 3 titles 2005; expects 10 titles 2006, 10 titles 2007. Discounts: request schedule from publisher. 250pp. Reporting time: 1-3 months. Simultaneous submissions accepted: yes. Publishes less than 1% of manuscripts submitted. Payment: negotiable. Copyrights for author. Subjects: Business & Economics, Fiction, How-To, Humor, Marriage, Mystery, Romance, Self-Help.

OASIS, Oasis Books, Ian Robinson, 12 Stevenage Road, London SW6 6ES, United Kingdom. 1969. Poetry, fiction, reviews, non-fiction. "Each issue is usually 24 pages long. Poetry: No long poems (45-50 lines max.). Fiction: 1200 max. usually, but exceptions are made. No biases." circ. 500. 3/yr. Pub'd 6 issues 2005; expects 3 issues 2006, 3 issues 2007. sub. price $30; per copy $5; sample $5. Back issues: $5. Discounts: goes to subscribers only. 16pp. Reporting time: 1 month max. We do not usually accept simultaneous submissions. Publishes 2% of manuscripts submitted. Payment: copies only. Copyrighted, reverts to author. Pub's reviews: 3 in 2005. §Poetry and fiction. Ads: none. Subjects: Essays, Fiction, Poetry, Reviews.

Oasis Books (see also OASIS), Ian Robinson, 12 Stevenage Road, London, SW6 6ES, United Kingdom. 1969. Poetry, fiction, long-poems, non-fiction. "No biases as to length or contributors, though we prefer short fiction. Contributors: Roy Fisher, Gustaf Sobin, Christopher Middleton, John Ash, De Stewart, Peter Dent, Ken Edwards, Andrea Moorhead, Vladimir Holan, Tomas Transtromer, Robin Fulton, Anna Akhmatova, and Douglas Gunn. Oasis Books is UK Distributor for S-Editions. No books planned for 2004/2005." avg. press run 200-600. Expects 3 titles 2006. Discounts: 25% over 1 copy, 33-1/3% 2+ (trade only). 30-50pp. Reporting time: 1 month max. Payment: copies only, usually. Copyrights for author. Subjects: Agriculture, Essays, Fiction, Graphics, Literature (General), Non-Fiction, Poetry, Prose.

Oberlin College Press (see also FIELD: Contemporary Poetry and Poetics), David Young, Co-editor; David Walker, Co-editor, 50 N. Professor St., Oberlin, OH 44074-1091, 440-775-8408, Fax 440-775-8124, E-mail oc.press@oberlin.edu. 1969. Poetry, long-poems. "Also essays on poetry and translations of poetry." avg. press run 1. Pub'd 3 titles 2005; expects 4 titles 2006, 2 titles 2007. Discounts: 1 copy 20%, 2+ 30%, bookstores and agencies. 100pp. Reporting time: 6-8 weeks. Simultaneous submissions accepted: yes. Publishes 0.25%- 0.50% of manuscripts submitted. Payment: $1,000 FIELD Poetry Prize Winner; royalty payments. Copyrights for author. Subjects: Poetry, Translation.

OBSCURITY UNLIMITED, Ian Shires, Kathy Shires, 1884 Meadows Road, Madison, OH 44157-1835.

1999. circ. 500+. 10/yr. Pub'd 10 issues 2005; expects 10 issues 2006, 10 issues 2007. sub. price $36; per copy $3.50; sample $3.50. 48pp. Reporting time: 1 week via e-mail, 2 weeks via snail mail. Simultaneous submissions accepted: yes. We publish most of the manuscripts submitted. Payment: copy. Copyrighted, reverts to author. Pub's reviews: over 200 in 2005. §Anything small press. Ads: $25/$15/free.

Obsessive Compulsive Anonymous, PO Box 215, New Hyde Park, NY 11040, 516-739-0662, Fax 212-768-4679, www.hometown.aol.com/west24th. 1988. Non-fiction. "12-step program for obsessive compulsive disorder." avg. press run 5M. Pub'd 1 title 2005; expects 1 title 2006, 1 title 2007. Discounts: distributor—Hazelden (800) 328-9000. 125pp. Subjects: Psychology, Self-Help.

OBSIDIAN III: Literature in the African Diaspora, Thomas Lisk, Editor, Dept. of English, Box 8105, NC State University, Raleigh, NC 27695-8105, 919-515-4150. 1975. Poetry, fiction, articles, interviews, criticism, reviews, letters, parts-of-novels, long-poems, plays, news items. "Founded in 1975 by Alvin Aubert as *Obsidian: Black Literature in Review,* the journal was transferred to North Carolina State University in 1986 as *Obsidian II.* The journal publishes creative works in English by Black writers worldwide, or writers addressing black issues. with scholarly critical studies by all writers on Black literature in English. Contributors to *Obsidian* and *Obsidian II* (both creative and scholarly) have included Michael S. Harper, Jay Wright, Gayl Jones, Houston A. Baker, Jr., Eugenia Collier, Lloyd W. Brown, Gerald Early, Wanda Coleman, Jerry W. Ward, Nikki Grimes, Raymond R. Patterson, Akua Lezli Hope, Gary Smith, Bu-Buakei Jabbi, Yusef Komunyakaa, Jane Davis, Philip Royster." circ. 400. 2/yr. Pub'd 2 issues 2005; expects 2 issues 2006, 2 issues 2007. sub. price $22; per copy $10; sample $10. Back issues: $10. Discounts: 40% bookstores. 130pp. Reporting time: 3 months. Simultaneous submissions accepted: no. Publishes 15% of manuscripts submitted. Payment: 2 copies. Copyrighted, reverts to author. Pub's reviews: 2 in 2005. §Creative works by Black writers or writers who address black issues (poetry, fiction, drama); scholarship and criticism on same. Ads: $225 full page/$165 half page. Subjects: African Literature, Africa, African Studies, Black, Book Reviewing, Drama, Fiction, Poetry, Third World, Minorities.

•**Ocean Publishing,** Frank Gromling, P.O. Box 1080, Flagler Beach, FL 32136-1080, 386-517-1600, Fax 386-517-2564, oceanpublisher@cfl.rr.com, www.ocean-publisher.com. 2002. Poetry, fiction, non-fiction. "Authors include Kay Day, Victor DiGenti, Dorothy K. Fletcher, Pete Davey, H. Steven Robertson, Jan Atchley Bevan, Alfred Nicol." avg. press run 2000. Pub'd 5 titles 2005; expects 7 titles 2006, 5 titles 2007. Discounts: bookstores: up to 40%, distributors/wholesalers: up to 55%, institutions/schools/corporations: 20%-30%. 200pp. Reporting time: 30-45 days. Simultaneous submissions accepted: Yes. Publishes 5% of manuscripts submitted. Payment: 8-10% of retail, small advances, six month payment cycles. Most often copyrights for publisher; specific cases may allow for author copyright. Subjects: Children, Youth, Conservation, Fiction, Florida, History, Juvenile Fiction, Marine Life, Memoirs, Non-Fiction, Picture Books, Poetry, Young Adult.

•**OCEAN YEARBOOK, University of Chicago Press,** Aldo Chircop, Moira McConnell, Dalhousie Law School, 6061 University Avenue, Halifax, Nova Scotia B3H 4H9, Canada, 902-494-2955 (main #), 902-494-1316 (fax), http://www.journals.uchicago.edu/OY/home.html. 1978. "Since 1978, the *Ocean Yearbook* has published original, peer-reviewed articles and reference materials for students and practitioners of international law, ocean development, coastal zone management, foreign policy, and strategic studies. Coverage includes the global management of marine resources, international law, and environmental policy." 1/yr.

Odysseus Enterprises Ltd., Joseph H. Bain, E. Angelo, PO Box 1548, Port Washington, NY 11050-0306, 516-944-5330, Fax 516-944-7540. 1984. avg. press run 100M. Pub'd 1 title 2005; expects 1 title 2006. Discounts: trade 40%, jobbers 50%, distributors 55%. 600pp. Copyrights for author. Subject: Gay.

ODYSSEY: Adventures in Science, Cobblestone Publishing Company, Elizabeth E. Lindstrom, Editor, 30 Grove Street, Suite C, Peterborough, NH 03458, 603-924-7209, Fax 603-924-7380, custsvc@cobblestone.mv.com. 1979. Fiction, articles, art, photos, interviews, reviews, letters, non-fiction. "The magazine will accept freelance articles related to themes covered; write editor for guidelines." circ. 23M. 9/yr. Pub'd 9 issues 2005; expects 9 issues 2006, 9 issues 2007. sub. price $29.95 + $8 foreign, Canadian subs add 7% GST; per copy $4.95; sample $4.95. Back issues: $4.95. Discounts: 15% to agencies, bulk rate—3 subs $17.95 each/yr. 52pp. Reporting time: queries sent well in advance of deadline may not be answered for several months. Go-aheads usually sent 3 months prior to publication date. Simultaneous submissions accepted: yes. Payment: on publication. Copyrighted, *Odyssey* buys all rights. Pub's reviews: 10 in 2005. §Science, math, technology, space, astronomy, earth and physical sciences. Ads: none. Subjects: Astronomy, Space.

OFF OUR BACKS, Editorial Collective, 2337B 18th Street NW, 2nd Floor, Washington, DC 20009-2003, 202-234-8072. 1970. Articles, art, photos, cartoons, interviews, criticism, reviews, letters, news items, non-fiction. "Consider ourselves a radical feminist *news* journal, with complete coverage of national and international news about women. Free to prisoners." circ. 22M. 6/yr. Pub'd 11 issues 2005; expects 6 issues 2006, 6 issues 2007. sub. price $25 indiv., $50 institutions (inc. libraries), $26 Canadian, $33 foreign, contributing subscription $35; per copy $3.95 newstand price; sample $5. Back issues: $5. Discounts: 40% for 5 or more copies monthly; billed/paid quarterly. 64pp. Reporting time: 6 months. Simultaneous submissions accepted: no. Publishes 50% of manuscripts submitted. Payment: copies. Copyrighted, reverts to author. Pub's reviews: 50 in 2005. §Women. Ads: $400/$210/40¢ (prepaid). Subjects: Birth, Birth Control, Population, Feminism, Gay, Health, Labor, Lesbianism, Politics, Third World, Minorities, Women.

•**Off the Grid Press,** Henry Braun, P.O. Box 84, Weld, ME 04285, www.offthegridpress.net. 2006. Poetry, art. "Off the Grid Press was founded in the Fall of 2005 as a writers' cooperative to provide a forum for older poets who have been overlooked by the current marketplace. For those, however innovative, who honor the work of Keats, Yeats, Stevens, Dickinson, Whitman, Williams and Reznikoff, as well as Szymborska, Neruda, Rilke and Akhmatova, we invite your submissions. Those who wish to submit work should have a manuscript of 60 pages or more ready for publication, but should submit only 6-10 poems for first reading. Those whose poems meet this first screening will be asked to send the entire manuscript. Manuscripts are read by the founding members of the press, Henry Braun, Bert Stern and Tam Lin Neville. There are no contests, entrance fees, or prescreening by graduate students. Send a self-addressed stamped envelope for return of manuscripts. Mail to: Off the Grid Press, P.O. Box 84, Weld, Maine 04285 Note: Starting date for submissions: July, 2006 Submission Guidelines: Those sending manuscripts should be over 60 years old and have already published at least one book of poems or five or more poems in nationally distributed literary magazines. Please include a resume. Those chosen can produce their book under the imprint of Off the Grid Press, but at this point must be able to finance the design, publication and distribution costs of the book themselves. For one thousand copies of a sewn and glued paperback of 128 acid free pages with a color cover, for instance, your cost would most likely be about $2800. You may choose your own designer (fees vary) as long as the design is consistent with the quality of our other books. Once published, the author automatically becomes a member of the board and joins in future editorial decisions, if he or she wishes." avg. press run 1000. Expects 4 titles 2006, 4 titles 2007. 60-125pp. Reporting time: one month. Simultaneous submissions accepted: No. Publishes 1% of manuscripts submitted. Payment: At this point we are a publishing collective; the selected author is responsible for the costs of publishing the book and recieves all profits. Copyrights for author. Subject: Poetry.

OFFICE NUMBER ONE, Carlos B. Dingus, 2111 Quarry Road, Austin, TX 78703, 512-445-4489. 1989. Poetry, fiction, articles, cartoons, satire, letters. "*Office Number One* is a zine of satire. I need short (100 - 300 words) satirical news items, strange essays, or fiction. Poetry is limericks or haiku. Satire should have an upbeat point and make sense. Once in a while I print more serious words—400 or less on philosophy or religion—but it's got to be good." circ. 2M. 2/yr. Pub'd 2 issues 2005; expects 2 issues 2006, 2 issues 2007. sub. price $8.84/6 issues; per copy $2; sample $2. Discounts: 24 copies $12 postpaid (minimum order). 12pp. Reporting time: 6-12 weeks. Simultaneous submissions accepted: yes. We publish less than 10% of manuscripts submitted (so many submitted are poorly written!). Payment: contributor's copies. Copyrighted, reverts to author. §Reviews of other dimensions of existence are interesting. Ads: call for rates. Subjects: Cartoons, Christianity, Cults, Essays, Fiction, Fiction, Humor, Metaphysics, New Age, Philosophy, Religion.

Ogden Press, 105 Greenway Place, Huntington, WV 25705-2205, Telephone # 304/733-3576. Pub'd 1 title 2005; expects 1 title 2006, 1 title 2007. 248pp.

‡**Ohio State University Press,** 1050 Carmack Road, Columbus, OH 43210, 614-292-6930. 1957.

Ohio University Press/Swallow Press, David Sanders, The Ridges, Building 19, Athens, OH 45701, 740-593-1157, www.ohio.edu/oupress. 1964. Poetry, fiction, criticism. "We consider unsolicited poetry only through our annual Hollis Summers Poetry Prize competittion. We publish a little short fiction and practically no long fiction. As a scholarly press, we have special strengths in regional works including the Midwest, Appalachia, and Ohio; African studies; Victorian studies, as well as a number of specialized series." avg. press run 1000. Pub'd 50 titles 2005; expects 50 titles 2006, 55 titles 2007. Discounts: Retail trade discount is 1-2 copies 20%; 3-49, 40%; 50-99, 41%; 100-250, 43%; 250 or more, 46%; short discount books, 1-2, 20%; 3 or more, 40%. 250pp. Reporting time: four months. Simultaneous submissions accepted: No. Payment: 7% royalty on net sales. Copyrights for author. Subjects: African Literature, Africa, African Studies, Americana, Appalachia, Civil War, Feminism, Fiction, Great Lakes, History, Literature (General), Midwest, Ohio, Old West, Philosophy, Poetry, Poland.

OHIO WRITER, Mark Kuhar, Editor, 12200 Fairhill Road, Townhouse #3A, Cleveland, OH 44120-1058, website: www.pwlgc.com. 1987. Articles, interviews, reviews. "Only service pieces published: interviews of writers, focus on aspect of writing in Ohio, reviews of books, writer's conferences. Major piece 2,000 words; focus piece 1,500 words; column 800 words; book review 400-500 words. Annual writing contest for poetry, fiction, nonfiction and writers on writing, open to Ohio residents. Published by the Poets' & Writers' League of Greater Cleveland." circ. 1M. 6/yr. Pub'd 6 issues 2005; expects 6 issues 2006, 6 issues 2007. sub. price $15, $18 institutions; per copy $2.50; sample $3. Back issues: $3. 16-20pp. Reporting time: 3 months. Simultaneous submissions accepted: yes. Publishes 5% of manuscripts submitted. Payment: $5-$50 depending on what. Copyrighted, reverts to author. Pub's reviews: 30 in 2005. §Books or magazines published in Ohio or by Ohio writers. Ads: $25 1/2/$35 1/9 page. Subjects: Book Reviewing, Communication, Journalism, Literary Review, Magazines, Newsletter, Ohio, Printing, Writers/Writing.

OHIOANA QUARTERLY, Kate Templeton Fox, Editor, 274 E. First Avenue, Columbus, OH 43201, 614-466-3831, Fax 614-728-6974, e-mail ohioana@sloma.state.oh.us. 1958. Articles, criticism, reviews, news items, non-fiction. "Published by the Ohioana Library Association. Reviews by staff and guest reviewers. Length of review varies from 40 to 800 words. Ohio authors or books on Ohio only. Articles on Ohio authors, music, other arts in Ohio, up to 2M words." circ. 2.5M. 4/yr. Pub'd 4 issues 2005; expects 4 issues 2006, 4 issues 2007. sub. price $25 (membership); per copy $6.50; sample gratis. Back issues: $6.50. Discounts: $25 to libraries. 112pp. Reporting time: 2-4 weeks. Simultaneous submissions accepted: no. Publishes 75% of manuscripts submitted. Payment: copies only. Copyrighted, rights do not revert to author, but we grant permission for full use by author. Pub's reviews: 400 in 2005. §Books about Ohio or Ohioans, books by Ohioans or former Ohioans. Ads: none. Subjects: Arts, Book Reviewing, Literary Review.

George Ohsawa Macrobiotic Foundation (see also MACROBIOTICS TODAY), Carl Ferre, Editor, PO Box 3998, Chico, CA 95927-3998, 530-566-9765, Fax 530-566-9768, foundation@gomf.macrobiotic.net. 1970. Articles, non-fiction. "Articles about macrobiotics and health. Books of at least 90 pages on macrobiotics, health, diet and nutrition. Special interest in cookbooks. Recent contributors include Julia Ferre, Natalie Buckley Rowland, Margaret Lawson, Rachel Albert, and Pam Henkel." avg. press run 3M-5M. Expects 1 title 2006, 1 title 2007. Discounts: 1 20%, 2-4 30%, 5+ 40%; distributors discount available. 192pp. Reporting time: 6 weeks. Publishes 10% of manuscripts submitted. Payment: 5% of gross retail sales, or 10% of net sales. Copyrights for author. Subjects: Cooking, Ecology, Foods, Health, Philosophy.

THE OLD RED KIMONO, Nancy Applegate, Faculty Advisor; Kimberly Yarborough, Editor; Derrick Lepard, Art Editor, Social & Cultural Studies,, Floyd College, Rome, GA 30162, 706-368-7623. 1972. Poetry, fiction. "*ORK* is looking for submissions of 1-5 short poems or one very short story (2,000 words max). A variety of literary styles are considered; free verse poems and short short stories are preferred. Recent contributors include Peter Huggins, John Cantey Knight, Ruth Moon Kempher, Al Braselton, Jessica Lindberg, and Matt Sunrich. Mss read September 1 - March 1." circ. 1400. 1/yr. Pub'd 1 issue 2005; expects 1 issue 2006. price per copy $4; sample $4. 72pp. Reporting time: 2 months. Simultaneous submissions accepted: Yes. Payment: 2 copies. Copyrighted, reverts to author. Subjects: Fiction, Poetry.

Old Sport Publishing Company, PO Box 2757, Stockbridge, GA 30281, 770-914-2237, Fax 770-914-9261, info@oldsportpublishing.com, www.oldsportpublishing.com. 2004. avg. press run 4M. Expects 1 title 2006, 2-4 titles 2007. Discounts: call for schedule. 536pp. Reporting time: 6 weeks (prefer detailed query letter; will not return unsolicited manuscripts). Simultaneous submissions accepted: yes. Publishes an unknown % of manuscripts submitted. Payment: negotiable. Will copyright for author upon request. Subjects: South, Sports, Outdoors.

Old Stage Publishing (see also THE BOOMERPHILE; BOULDER HERETIC; TOUCHSTONE), Dan Culberson, PO Box 17446, Boulder, CO 80308-0446, 303-444-3363, danculberson@juno.com. 1992. Articles, satire, criticism, reviews, news items, non-fiction. Pub'd 3 titles 2005; expects 3 titles 2006, 3 titles 2007. Reporting time: 1 week. Payment: 2 copies of issue for original work, 1 copy for reprinted work. Author retains all copyrights.

The Old Stile Press, Catchmays Court, Llandogo, Monmouthshire NP5 4TN, United Kingdom.

The Olivia and Hill Press, Inc., Jacqueline Morton, Brian N. Morton, PO Box 7396, Ann Arbor, MI 48107, 734-663-0235 (voice), Fax 734-663-6590, theOHPress@aol.com, www.oliviahill.com. 1979. Non-fiction. "We began with *English Grammar for Students of French* in 1979, and have added editions in Spanish, German, Italian, Latin, Russian and Japanese; the first two have now come out in fourth editions. German is presently in third edition. All $12.95. We distribute foreign language cassettes (novels, plays and poetry) imported from France. We also distribute cassette + book packages (fairy tales and stories) for children in French. We publish two anecdotal street guides: *Americans in Paris* and *Americans in London*. Both are paperback, 350 pages, 60 photos, $12.95 each. Our new product is *French Slang and Publicities* for the first and second year French student. We are interested in receiving unsolicited manuscripts in our area of interest. We also publish an ESL version, Gramatica espanola pana estudiantes de ingles $12.95. Visit our website." avg. press run 10M. Pub'd 2 titles 2005; expects 1 title 2006, 1 title 2007. Discounts: 20% to bookstores. 200pp. Payment: standard. Copyrights for author. Subjects: Bilingual, Language, Transportation.

Olympic Mountain School Press, Jana Bourne, P.O. Box 1114, Gig Harbor, WA 98335, 253-858-4448. 2004. Photos, non-fiction. "We only publish photography books. Nearly all of our planned titles are how-to books. Authors include Rod Barbee, David Middleton, Carolyn Wright and Scott Bourne, all well-known photographers or experts in their fields." avg. press run 3000. Expects 2 titles 2006, 5 titles 2007. Discounts: Standard industry discounts available for wholesale buyers representing bookstores. Other bulk discounts are 2-10 copies 25% off 11-20 copies 35% off 21-30 copies 45% off. 128-180pp. Reporting time: six months.

Simultaneous submissions accepted: Yes. Publishes 5% of manuscripts submitted. Payment: We negotiate royalty rates on a case by case basis. Copyrights for author. Subject: Photography.

Oma Books of the Pacific, Rachel Fischer Gladson, PO Box 9095, San Pedro, CA 90734-9095, publisher@omabooks.com, www.omabooks.com. 2003. Poetry, fiction. "Oma Books is not accepting unsolicited materials at this time." avg. press run 2,500. Expects 1 title 2006, 1 title 2007. 64pp. Simultaneous submissions accepted: no. Copyrights for author. Subjects: Family, Multicultural, Poetry.

•OMEGA, Howling Dog Press / Brave New World Order Books, Michael Annis, P.O. Box 853, Berthoud, CO 80513-0853, WritingDangerously@msn.com, www.howlingdogpress.com, www.howlingdogpress.com/ OMEGA. 2002. Poetry, fiction, articles, art, photos, cartoons, interviews, satire, reviews, parts-of-novels, long-poems, collages, plays, non-fiction. "Go online: www.howlingdogpress.com/OMEGA This will tell you everything you need to know. We are very open to many forms of expression, but we are closed to clones, imposters, and other crimes against criteria. The war, the imposter in office, and proselytizing through propaganda disgust us. Plagiarism will be prosecuted." 2-3/yr. Pub'd 2 issues 2005; expects 2 issues 2006, 2 issues 2007. sample price free online. Back issues: free archived. 120pp. Reporting time: Weeks to months. Simultaneous submissions accepted: Yes. Publishes 20% of manuscripts submitted. Payment: Online publication—non paying. Copyrighted, reverts to author. Pub's reviews. §poetry, philosophy, non-fiction, fiction, novels, progressive political works. Ads: Links/advertising, negotiable, trades.

•OmegaRoom Press, Radley Drew, 4041 Louisiana St #1, San Diego, CA 92104, omegaroom@yahoo.com. 2006. Fiction, cartoons. "Omega Room Press has two imprints: Omega Room Books specializes in Science Fiction and Fantasy (but will consider any fiction)and Omega Room Comics specializes comics and graphic novels. Please see www.omegaroom.com for more information and submission guidelines." Expects 10-15 titles 2006, 10-15 titles 2007. We offer a discount to retailers. For paper backs, we offer a 35% discount. For comics, we offer a 50% discount. 250-500pp. Reporting time: 1 week. Simultaneous submissions accepted: Yes. Does not copyright for author. Subjects: Fantasy, Fiction, Science Fiction.

Omni Books, K. Green, 2342 Shattuck Avenue, Berkeley, CA 94704.

Omonomany, James Weeks, Editor, 5050 Poplar Avenue Suite 1510, Memphis, TN 38157, 901-374-9027, Fax 901-374-0508, jimweeks12@msn.com. "www.omonomany.com." Subjects: Fiction, Memoirs, Military, Veterans.

ON EARTH, Douglas Barasch, Editor-in-Chief; Brian Swann, Poetry Editor, 40 West 20th Street, New York, NY 10011, 212-727-2700. 1979. Poetry, articles. "We are a quarterly environmental magazine of ideas." circ. 175M. 4/yr. Pub'd 4 issues 2005; expects 4 issues 2006, 4 issues 2007. sub. price $10; per copy $2.95; sample $5. Back issues: $5. Discounts: none. 48pp. Reporting time: 2-3 months. Simultaneous submissions accepted: no. Publishes prose 10%, poetry 2% of manuscripts submitted. Copyrighted, reverts to author. Pub's reviews: 10 in 2005. §Environment, energy, pollution: water, air; land conservation. Ads: none. Subjects: Conservation, Poetry.

ON PARAGUAY, Lynn Van Houten, 1724 Burgundy Court, Petaluma, CA 94954, 707-763-6835; E-mail paraguay@wco.com. 1994. Non-fiction. "Short articles relating to the culture, art, plants, animals and environment of Praguay and South America." circ. 250. 4/yr. Pub'd 4 issues 2005; expects 4 issues 2006, 4 issues 2007. sub. price $25; per copy $6.25. Back issues: $6.25. 8pp. Simultaneous submissions accepted: yes. Pub's reviews: 3 in 2005. §South America, Paraguay, children's folktales. Subject: South America.

ON SPEC, Diane Walton, Susan MacGregor, Barry Hammond, Peter Watts, Derryl Murphy, Steve Mohn, PO Box 4727, Edmonton, AB T6E 5G6, Canada, 403-413-0215, onspec@onspec.ca. 1989. Poetry, fiction. circ. 1.75M. 4/yr. Pub'd 4 issues 2005; expects 4 issues 2006, 4 issues 2007. sub. price $24CDN, $24US; per copy $5.95 Cdn.; sample $7CDN, $7US. Back issues: same as sample copies. Discounts: bookstore 40%. 112pp. Reporting time: 4-6 months. We accept simultaneous submissions, but please let us know. Publishes 5% of manuscripts submitted. Payment: $100-$180 depending on word count. Copyrighted, reverts to author. Ads: $175/$125. Subjects: Fantasy, Science Fiction.

One Eyed Press, Caroline Smith, 272 Road 6Rt, Cody, WY 82414, one_eyed_press@yahoo.com, www.one-eyed-press.com. 1998. Poetry, fiction. "Accepts highest quality mainstream fiction and poetry-no genre or traditional poems. No simultaneous submissions. Query with S.A.S.E." avg. press run 3-5M. Pub'd 1 title 2005; expects 1 title 2006, 2 titles 2007. Discounts: complete schedule available by calling 1-800-247-6553. Pages vary. Reporting time: 6-8 weeks. Simultaneous submissions accepted: no. Publishes 1-2% of manuscripts submitted. Payment: negotiable. Copyrights for author. Subjects: Fiction, Poetry.

ONE Health Publishing, LLC, PO Box 31073, St. Louis, MO 63131-1073, www.onehealthpublishing.com, publishers@onehealthpublishing.com, phone: 314-822-3774, fax: 314-821-5463. 2002. Non-fiction. Pub'd 2 titles 2005; expects 2 titles 2006, 2 titles 2007. Simultaneous submissions accepted: Yes.

338

One Horse Press/Rainy Day Press, Mike Helm, 1147 East 26th, Eugene, OR 97403, 503-484-4626. 1978. "History and culture of the Pacific Northwest is the prime concern of Rainy Day Press. The Oregon Country Library is indicative of our emphasis. The first four volumes were written by Fred Lockley in the 1920's. They are conversations with Oregon Country pioneers, previously published in the *Oregon Journal*, an oral history of life on the Oregon Trail and in the civilization building at its western end. The fifth, by Mike Helm, is a collection of ghost stories and other local legends taken from towns throughout Oregon. The sixth, in the framework of a contemporary journal, tells of a search for the mythical and historical soul of Oregon. Though I refer to Rainy Day Press as 'we', it is still a one-horse show, and I am the horse. As I have a million ideas of my own for writing and publishing projects, I am not yet seeking manuscript submissions. Instead, send money." avg. press run 4M. Discounts: 1 book 0%, 2-5 10%, 6-24 40%, 25-49 42%, 50-74 44%, 75-99 46%, 100-149 48%, 150 or more 50%. 300+pp. Subjects: Folklore, How-To.

One Less Press (see also ONE LESS: Art on the Range), Nikki Widner, 6 Village Hill Road, Williamsburg, MA 01096-9706, (413) 586-7921, onelessartontherange@yahoo.com, onelessmag.blogspot.com. 2004. Poetry, fiction, art, photos, cartoons, interviews, letters, parts-of-novels, collages, plays, concrete art, non-fiction. "We publish a collection of artistic works that challenge and engage in vision, concept, and constuction. Each issue is designated a specific theme which contributors respond to in some way with open interpretations. One Less evolves through its contributors building expression and discourse over a new theme. Recent contributors include: Debra Schulkes, Randall Stoltzfus, Sergio Vucci, Kyle Kaufman, Teresa Sparks, Mara Leigh Simmons, Ellen Baxt, Sharon Rogers, Sawako Nakayasu, Megan Breiseth, Jesse Morse, Gina Washington, sara larsen, Derek White, Louise Weinberg, captain snowdon, Pamela Matsuda-Dunn, Anne Waldman, Douglas Newton, Chris Mazura, Michael Robins, Brian Strang, Ellen Redbird, Christopher Gauthier, Bob Doto, Noah Eli Gordon, Sara Veglahn, Sarah Rosenthal, Amy E. Brandt, Matthew Langley, Chris Vitiello, Nick Moudry, Alexandra Hidalgo, Simone Sandy, Jessea Perry, Jennifer Ryan, and John Sullivan." avg. press run 200. Expects 2 titles 2006, 3 titles 2007. Discounts: 2-10 copies 25%. 150pp. Reporting time: one month. Simultaneous submissions accepted: No. Publishes 30% of manuscripts submitted. Payment: complimentary copy of the magazine. Copyrights revert back to authors/artists upon publication. Subjects: Avant-Garde, Experimental Art, Fiction, Non-Fiction, Photography, Poetry, Prose, Short Stories, Visual Arts.

ONE LESS: Art on the Range, One Less Press, Nikki Widner, 6 Village Hill Road, Williamsburg, MA 01096-9706, 413-268-7370, onelessartontherange@yahoo.com, onelessmag.blogspot.com. 2004. Poetry, fiction, art, photos, cartoons, letters, parts-of-novels, collages, plays, concrete art, non-fiction. circ. 300. 2/yr. Expects 2 issues 2006, 2 issues 2007. sub. price $18; per copy $10; sample $10. Back issues: $5. Discounts: 2-10 copies 25%. 150pp. Ads: $50 (full page)/$25 (half page)no classifieds.

1+1=3 Publishing, esynergy@pacbell.net, www.SynergyLifeMastery.com.

ONE TRICK PONY, Banshee Press, Louis McKee, 8460 Franford Ave., Philadelphia, PA 19136-2031. 1997. Poetry, art, photos, interviews, criticism, reviews, collages. "Health problems disrupted some of this year's plans, but things are now returning to normal. Recent contributors include: Denise Duhamel, Harry Humes, Afaa M. Weaver, Karla Huston, Naomi Shihab Nye, Len Roberts." circ. 400. irregular. Pub'd 2 issues 2005; expects 2 issues 2006, 2 issues 2007. sub. price $12/3 issues; per copy $5; sample $5. 84pp. Reporting time: 3-6 weeks. Simultaneous submissions accepted: no. Payment: copies. Copyrighted, reverts to author. Pub's reviews: 4-5 in 2005. §Poetry or poetry-related. Subjects: Criticism, Poetry, Reviews.

Online Training Solutions, Inc., PO Box 951, Bellevue, WA 98009-0951, 425-885-1441, Fax 425-881-1642, quickcourse@otsiweb.com. 1987. Non-fiction. "Formerly Online Press Inc. Online Training Solutions publishes the Quick Course and Practical Business Skills computer training books and online products. Quick Course books are for people with limited time to learn today's most popular software programs. Training oriented, Quick Course books teach the software while showing how to create documents people can use in their business. Quick Course books are used by schools, universities, business, training, companies, and corporations both for classroom instruction and for self-training. New in 2001, Practical Business Skills books and online training products are the next generation in the quick course family: PBS products include pre- and post-test materials, advanced hands-on exercises, and Mous coverage where applicable." avg. press run 10M+. Pub'd 12 titles 2005; expects 15 titles 2006, 15 titles 2007. Discounts: volume discounts are available. 160-256pp. Subject: Computers, Calculators.

ONTARIO REVIEW, Ontario Review Press, Raymond Smith, Editor, 9 Honey Brook Drive, Princeton, NJ 08540.

Ontario Review Press (see also ONTARIO REVIEW), Raymond Smith, Editor, 9 Honey Brook Drive, Princeton, NJ 08540.

ONTHEBUS, Bombshelter Press, Jack Grapes, Bombshelter Press, P.O. Box 481266, Bicentennial Station, Los Angeles, CA 90048, http://www.bombshelterpress.com or http://www.jackgrapes.com. 1989. Poetry, fiction, art, interviews, reviews. "*ONTHEBUS* is a literary journal that includes work from poets and writers throughout the U.S. Guidelines for submission on copyright page of each issue. Editor expects those submitting work to have read a copy of our magazine and to be familliar with our guidelines printed on copyright page." circ. 3M. 1/yr. Pub'd 1 issue 2005; expects 1 issue 2006, 1 issue 2007. sub. price $30 for 2 double issues; $35 for 2 double issues to institutions; per copy $15; sample $15.00. Back issues: $13.50 for double issues #6/7, #8/9, #10/11; $11 for issues #12, #13, #14. $15.00 for double issues 15/16, 17/18, 19/20;. Discounts: 40% bookstores. Double Issues have 332 pages. Single issues have 275 pages. Reporting time: 1-12 months. Simultaneous submissions accepted: yes. Publishes 5% of manuscripts submitted. Payment: 1 copy, $ if available. Copyrighted, reverts to author. Pub's reviews: 14 in 2005. §Books of poetry. Ads: $300/$200/$125 1/4 page.

Oolichan Books, Hiro Boga Ms, Managing Editor; Ron Smith Mr, Publisher, PO Box 10, Lantzville, B.C., V0R 2H0, Canada, 250-390-4839, oolichanbooks@telus.net, www.oolichan.com. 1975. Poetry, fiction, non-fiction. "Oolichan Books publishes books of poetry, creative non-fiction and fiction by Canadian writers only. See our website for submission guidelines. Query with sample writing and SASE. We attempt to maintain a balance between established and newer authors. Generally we are not interested in the mass market book, but rather in serious fiction and poetry which indicates how the writer sees through language. We produce books of excellent quality in content and design, and many of our authors have won prestigious awards. Recent contributors include: Bill New, Keith Harrison, Joanna Streetly, Rhona McAdam, Miranda Pearson and Michael Elcock." Pub'd 8 titles 2005; expects 8 titles 2006, 8 titles 2007. Discounts: trade: 40%. Reporting time: 1-3 months. Simultaneous submissions accepted: yes. Publishes 1% of manuscripts submitted. Copyrights for author. Subjects: Canada, Children, Youth, Fiction, Indigenous Cultures, Non-Fiction, Picture Books, Poetry.

Open Court Publishing Company, David Ramsay Steele, 140 South Dearborn St., #1450, Chicago, IL 60605-5203, 312-939-1500, Fax 312-939-8150. 1887. Non-fiction. "Our order dept. address: c/o Book Masters, PO Box 388, 1444 State Rt. 42, Ashland OH 44805 800-815-2280." avg. press run 3M. Pub'd 13 titles 2005; expects 13 titles 2006, 13 titles 2007. 300pp. Reporting time: 2-6 months. We will look at simultaneous submissions, but we give preference to exclusive submissions. Payment: varies. Copyrights for author. Subjects: Asia, Indochina, Education, Philosophy, Psychology, Religion, Sociology.

Open Hand Publishing LLC, Richard A. Koritz, PO Box 20207, Greensboro, NC 27420, 336-292-8585, Fax 336-292-8588, 866-888-9229; info@openhand.com; www.openhand.com. 1981. Non-fiction. "Open Hand is a literary/political press publishing multicultural books which will help to promote social change. We are not accepting unsolicited manuscripts at this time." avg. press run 2.5M. Pub'd 1 title 2005; expects 2 titles 2006, 2 titles 2007. Discounts: 40% to bookstores. 250pp. Reporting time: 4 weeks. Simultaneous submissions accepted: yes. Publishes 1% of manuscripts submitted. Copyrights for author. Subjects: African-American, Biography, British Columbia, Children, Youth, Civil Rights, History, Ireland, Labor, Multicultural, Pacific Northwest, Political Science, Theatre, War, Weaving, Women.

Open Horizons Publishing Company (see also BOOK MARKETING UPDATE), John Kremer, PO Box 205, Fairfield, IA 52556-0205, 641-472-6130, Fax 641-472-1560, e-mail johnkremer@bookmarket.com. 1983. Articles, art, photos, cartoons, interviews, reviews, letters, news items, non-fiction. "Books on marketing, publishing, publicity, and anything that strikes the publisher's fancy. Jay Frederick Editions is an imprint." avg. press run 3M-5M. Pub'd 3 titles 2005; expects 3 titles 2006, 3 titles 2007. Discounts: 40%. 288pp. Reporting time: 2 weeks. Payment: 10% of list price. Copyrights for author. Subjects: Advertising, Self-Promotion, Bibliography, Book Arts, Book Collecting, Bookselling, Business & Economics, Children, Youth, Communication, Journalism, Entertainment, How-To, Language, Media, Motivation, Success, Movies, Publishing, Quotations.

OPEN MINDS QUARTERLY, Dinah Laprairie, Editor-Publisher, 680 Kirkwood Drive, Bldg. 1, Sudbury, ON P3E 1X3, Canada, 705-675-9193 ext. 8286, Fax 705-675-3501, openminds@nisa.on.ca, www.nisa.on.ca. 1998. Poetry, fiction, articles, reviews, letters, parts-of-novels, non-fiction. "*OMQ* publishes writing by mental health consumer/survivors (i.e. individuals who live with mental illness). We accept poetry, short fiction, book/movie reviews, and first-person accounts of living with mental illness. Submission guidelines available upon request." circ. 750. 4/yr. Pub'd 4 issues 2005; expects 4 issues 2006, 4 issues 2007. sub. price Individuals: $35 Canada, $28.25 US/foreign; Organizations (two copies/issue): $50 Canada, $39.50 US/foreign; Consumer/survivor/student: $20 Canada, $17 US/foreign.; sample $5 Cdn. Back issues: $5.00 Cdn. Discounts: negotiable. 28pp. Simultaneous submissions accepted: yes. Publishes 60% of manuscripts submitted. Payment: Complimentary copies. Copyrighted, reverts to author. Pub's reviews: 4-6 in 2005. §Mental health-related, recent fiction or nonfiction, novels, films, etc. Ads: $350/$200/$100 1/4 page/$60 1/8 page (funds in Canadian). Subjects: Autobiography, Disease, Essays, Mental Health, Non-Fiction, Poetry, Psychiatry, Short Stories, Social Work, Sociology.

Open University of America Press, Mary Rodgers, Dan Rodgers, 3916 Commander Drive, Hyattsville, MD 20782-1027, 301-779-0220 phone/Fax, openuniv@aol.com. 1965. Poetry, articles. "We publish literary work in our interests: poetry, the Catholic Italian-American experience, and distance learning using the latest information technologies. We prefer short pieces which we publish as collections, generally buying the writer's ms outright for preservation in our Literary Trust after one-time dissemination. English only. SASE required with query and submission. Recent contributor: Lucille Columbro, *Aurora Farm Revisited*, 1997 (Italian-American experience)." avg. press run 250. Pub'd 4 titles 2005; expects 4 titles 2006, 4 titles 2007. Discounts: 40%. 150pp. Reporting time: 3-4 weeks. Simultaneous submissions accepted: no. Publishes 1% of manuscripts submitted. Payment: by contract. We copyright for author if necessary. Subjects: Catholic, Education, Italian-American, Poetry, Technology.

OPEN WIDE MAGAZINE, Feel Free Press, James Quinton, 'The Flat', Yew Tree Farm, Sealand Road, Chester, Cheshire, CH1 6BS, United Kingdom. 2001. Poetry, fiction, articles, interviews, satire, criticism, reviews, music, parts-of-novels, long-poems, news items, non-fiction. "Open Wide Magazine is a bi-monthly publication of 80 A5 pages packed full of high octane writing, poetry, reviews and interviews. Open Wide is something to treasure, something to keep on your bookshelf to be read and re-read at anytime and anywhere.Visit www.openwidemagazine.co.uk." circ. 600. 6/yr. sub. price Six issue subscription £15/$36 Three issue subscription £9/$18Single issues £3/$6Postage and packaging free.; Single issue price £3/$6. Back issues: Single issue price £3/$6. 80pp. Reporting time: It takes between one and two months for a submission to be considered. Simultaneous submissions accepted: No simultaneous submissions accepted or previously published works either. Publishes 10% of manuscripts submitted. Payment: Open Wide Magazine is self funded, non-profit and 100% independent. Money made from each issue is put back into the production of the next issue. So, unfortunately we are unable to provide contributors with a free copy of the magazine. Copyrighted. Pub's reviews: 6 in 2005. §Music review both live gig reviews and album reviews. Film reviews, book reviews and theatre/play reviews. Subjects: Arts, Avant-Garde, Experimental Art, Beat, Charles Bukowski, Erotica, Feminism, Jack Kerouac, Libertarian, Media, Henry Miller, Movies, Music, Non-Fiction, Reviews, Writers/Writing.

ORACLE POETRY, Rising Star Publishers, Obi Harrison Ekwonna, PO Box 7413, Langley Park, MD 20787. 1989. Poetry, fiction, criticism, reviews, long-poems. "Only well-made poems with meanings will be considered. No lesbian and gay materials accepted." circ. 500. 4/yr. Pub'd 1 issue 2005; expects 2 issues 2006, 4 issues 2007. sub. price $50, $70 institutions; per copy $10; sample $10. Back issues: $10 plus $2.50 p/h. Discounts: 30%, but may consider 40% bulk orders. 50pp. Reporting time: 2 months. Simultaneous submissions accepted: no. Publishes 50% of manuscripts submitted. Payment: in copies. Copyrighted, does not revert to author. Pub's reviews: 1 in 2005. §Any kind or genre, especially poetry. Ads: $500/$300/others on request. Subject: Poetry.

Oracle Press, C. Sawall, PO Box 5491, Chicago, IL 60680. 1979. Poetry, fiction. "Published books by Paris Smith, Delbert Tibbs, Tracey Young, Rick Laveau. No biases." avg. press run varies. Pub'd 3 titles 2005; expects 3 titles 2006, 3 titles 2007. 100-150pp. Reporting time: 4-6 weeks. Simultaneous submissions accepted: yes. Payment: open for discussion. Copyrights for author. Subjects: Fiction, Poetry.

ORACLE STORY, Rising Star Publishers, Obi Harrison Ekwonna, PO Box 7413, Langley Park, MD 20787. 1989. Fiction, criticism, reviews, long-poems. "Only well-made short stories with meanings will be considered. No lesbian and gay materials accepted." circ. 500. 4/yr. Pub'd 1 issue 2005; expects 2 issues 2006, 4 issues 2007. sub. price $50, $70 institutions; per copy $10; sample $10. Back issues: $10 + $2.50 p/h. Discounts: 30%, but may consider 40% bulk orders. 50pp. Reporting time: 2 months. Simultaneous submissions accepted: no. Publishes 50% of manuscripts submitted. Payment: in copies. Copyrighted, does not revert to author. Pub's reviews: 1 in 2005. §Any kind or genre, especially short stories or short novels. Ads: $500/$300/others on request. Subjects: African Literature, Africa, African Studies, Short Stories.

Orage Publishing, Nannette Schmitt, 1460 Wren Ct, Punta Gorda, FL 33950, p-941-639-6144, fax-941-639-4144. 2003. Fiction. "historical novels." avg. press run 2000. Pub'd 1 title 2005; expects 1 title 2006, 2 titles 2007. Discounts: distributors-55%bookstore -40%wholesalers-55%retailers -40%. 200-300pp. Simultaneous submissions accepted: No. Does not copyright for author. Subject: History.

ORAL HISTORY REVIEW, University of California Press, Andrew Dunar, Editor, University of California Press, 2000 Center St., Suite 303, Berkeley, CA 94704-1223, 510-643-7154. 1973. Articles, reviews. "Editorial address: Department of History, University of Alabama, Huntsville AL, 35899. Copyrighted by the Oral History Association." circ. 1057. 2/yr. Pub'd 2 issues 2005; expects 2 issues 2006, 2 issues 2007. sub. price $65 indiv., $119 inst., $35 student; per copy $30 indiv., $67 inst., $30 student; sample same as single copy. Discounts: foreign subs. agents 10%, 10+ one-time orders 30%. 198pp. Copyrighted, does not revert to author. Pub's reviews: approx. 24 in 2005. §genealogy, cultural preservation, history. Ads: $295/$220. Subjects: Genealogy, History.

ORANGE COAST MAGAZINE, Nancy Cheever, 3701 Birch Street, Suite 100, Newport Beach, CA 92660-2618, 949-862-1133. 1974. Fiction, articles, interviews, reviews, music, letters, parts-of-novels, non-fiction. "*Orange Coast* provides its affluent, educated readers with local insight. Articles range from in-depth investigations (local politics, crimes, etc) to consumer guides, calendar of events and personality profiles. Articles must have relevance to Orange County." circ. 40M. 12/yr. Pub'd 13 issues 2005; expects 13 issues 2006, 13 issues 2007. sub. price $19.95; per copy $3.50; sample same. Back issues: $5 if available. Discounts: contact marketing coordinator. 260pp. Reporting time: 3 months. Payment: $100-$300. Copyrighted, reverts to author. Pub's reviews: 24 in 2005. §Film, music, restaurants, books. Ads: B/W $3300/$1860; color $4230/$2850, singles classified—$5.50/word. Subject: California.

ORBIS, Carole Baldock, Editor, 17 Greenhow Avenue, West Kirby, Wirral CH48 5EL, England, +44 (0)151 625 1446; e-mail carolebaldock@hotmail.com. 1968. Poetry, fiction, articles, art, interviews, criticism, reviews, letters, news items. "Some longer poems, but mostly 40 lines. Prose: 500-1000 words. All types of material considered, and it should be the best it can be. 3 IRCs must be included with submissions overseas - *not* US-stamped addressed envelopes. NB, maximum of 4 poems per submission. 2 via email; no attachments. Brief covering letter preferred to CVs, press releases etc. Also Editor of *Competitions Bulletin*, which includes a growing Overseas Section. Details of 50+ UK contests for poetry; about 40 for short stories; around $200,000 in prizes each issue. $7 per issue; $40/6 pa." circ. 600. 4/yr. Pub'd 4 issues 2005; expects 4 issues 2006, 4 issues 2007. sub. price $38; per copy $11; sample varies. Discounts: 30% to trade. 84pp. Reporting time: aim is within the month for initial submissions. Simultaneous submissions accepted: no objection, providing I am kept informed. Publishes 1% of manuscripts submitted. Payment: Each issue, £50/$88: Featured Writer; 3-4 poems or 2000 words. Plus Readers Award: £50/$88 for piece receiving the most votes and four winners selected for submission to Forward Poetry Prize, Single Poem Category; £50/$88 split between four, or more, runners-up. Copyrighted, reverts to author. Pub's reviews: 80 in 2005. §Mainly collections of poetry; some short stories. Also books of interest to writers. Magazine reviews appear in the Poetry Index Section. Ads: $100/$50. Subjects: Essays, Fiction, Humor, Literary Review, Myth, Mythology, Poetry, Prose, Translation, Women, Young Adult.

ORCHID: A Literary Review, Keith Hood, Senior Executive Editor; Amy Sumerton, Executive Editor, P.O. BOX 131457, Ann Arbor, MI 48113-1457. 2002. Fiction, interviews, satire, reviews, parts-of-novels. "WE DON'T ACCEPT SUBMISSIONS IN MAY OR JUNE. PLEASE READ OUR WEBSITE FOR ADDITIONAL INFORMATION: WWW.ORCHIDLIT.ORG." Biannual. Pub'd 1 issue 2005; expects 2 issues 2006, 2 issues 2007. sub. price $16/1 YR., $30/2 YRS., $42/3 YRS.; per copy $8; sample $8. Back issues: $5. 200pp. Reporting time: 3 MONTHS. Simultaneous submissions accepted: Yes. Payment: 3 CONTRIBUTOR COPIES AND THE JOY OF SEEING YOUR STORY IN PRINT. Copyrighted, reverts to author. Pub's reviews: none in 2005. §FICTION. Subject: Fiction.

Orchises Press, Roger Lathbury, PO Box 20602, Alexandria, VA 22320-1602, 703-683-1243. 1983. Poetry, fiction, articles, concrete art. avg. press run 1M. Pub'd 4 titles 2005; expects 4 titles 2006, 5 titles 2007. Discounts: 40% on no-return items to bookstores with some exceptions, distributors and jobbers; 20% if a return privilege is wanted; items under $20 shipped no return unless otherwise stipulated. 80pp. Reporting time: 1 month. Publishes .05% of manuscripts submitted. Payment: 36% royalty after costs recouped, generous free copy policy. Copyrights for author. Subjects: Fiction, Memoirs, Poetry, Science.

Oregon State University Press, Karen Orchard, Director; Mary Elizabeth Braun, Acquisitions Editor, 500 Kerr Administration Building, Corvallis, OR 97331-2122, 541-737-3166, OSU.Press@oregonstate.edu, http://oregonstate.edu/dept/press. 1961. Non-fiction. "We publish scholarly and general interest books about the history, cultures, literature, environment, and natural resources of the state and region. No fiction, no poetry. Author guidelines available upon request." Pub'd 15 titles 2005; expects 18 titles 2006, 25 titles 2007. Discounts: 20-50% depending on quantity. Reporting time: 1-3 months. Simultaneous submissions accepted: no. Payment: varies. Copyrights for author. Subjects: Americana, Biography, Biology, Conservation, Earth, Natural History, Ecology, Foods, History, Indians, Myth, Mythology, Native American, Nature, Pacific Northwest, Reprints, Water, The West.

Origin Press, Byron Belitsos, PO Box 151117, San Raphael, CA 94915. 1996. Non-fiction. "Favored subject matter: spiritual, psychology, ufology, integral studies, global politics, esoterica, Urantia Book studies, and philosophy." avg. press run 3M. Expects 2-4 titles 2006, 2-4 titles 2007. Discounts: trade 20-40%, others negotiable. 250pp. Reporting time: 10 weeks. Simultaneous submissions accepted: yes. Publishes 2% of manuscripts submitted. Payment: 6% of list paid biannually. Copyrights for author. Subjects: Christianity, Culture, Global Affairs, Government, Health, Inspirational, Lifestyles, Metaphysics, Occult, Peace, Philosophy, Psychology, Religion, Self-Help, Spiritual.

Original Plus (see also THE JOURNAL (once "of Contemporary Anglo-Scandinavian Poetry")), Sam Smith, 18 Oxford Grove,Flat 3,, England, 01271862708; e-mail smithsssj@aol.com. 1998. Poetry, fiction, articles, art, reviews, parts-of-novels, long-poems, plays, non-fiction. "13 poetry collections to date." avg. press run 250. Pub'd 1 title 2005; expects 3 titles 2006, 1 title 2007. Discounts: 25%. 72pp. Payment: 10%. Copyrights for author.

ORNAMENT, Robert K. Liu, Co-Editor; Carolyn L.E. Benesh, Co-Editor, PO Box 2349, San Marcos, CA 92079, 760-599-0222, Fax 760-599-0228. 1974. Art, interviews, satire, criticism, letters, parts-of-novels, collages, news items. "Formerly published under the name of *The Bead Journal* which terminated with volume 3, #4. As of Volume 4, #1 published under the name of *Ornament*." circ. 50M. 4/yr. Pub'd 4 issues 2005; expects 4 issues 2006, 4 issues 2007. sub. price $23 domestic, $27 foreign; per copy $5.75; sample $5.75. Back issues: write for information. Discounts: 40% on wholesale orders. 100pp. Reporting time: 8-12 weeks. Simultaneous submissions accepted: yes. Payment: copies of the magazine in which article appears, number depends on length of article; also per page payments. Copyrighted, reverts to author. Pub's reviews: none in 2005. §Jewelry, ancient, ethnic, contemporary, forms of personal adornment, costume, clothing, beads, textiles. Write for rates. Subjects: Arts, Clothing, Collectibles, Crafts, Hobbies, Jewelry, Gems, Jewelry, Gems, Native American, Textiles, Weaving.

THE ORPHAN LEAF REVIEW, James Paul Wallis, 26 Grove Park Terrace, Fishponds, Bristol, BS16 2BN, United Kingdom, www.orphanleaf.co.uk orphanleaf@jpwallis.co.uk. 2004. Poetry, fiction, art, photos, cartoons, interviews, music, letters, parts-of-novels, long-poems, collages, plays, non-fiction. "An "orphan leaf" is a single page written to appear as though it's been taken from a book. It can be from any kind of book (prose, poetry, non-fiction, music manuscript, illustration etc.) and from any part of a book. Each leaf is a different size, paper and design, hand cut and assembled. The magazine aims to engage its readers as much with the visual and tactile qualities as with the writing." circ. 200. 3/yr. Pub'd 1 issue 2005; expects 3 issues 2006, 3 issues 2007. sub. price $24; per copy $10. Back issues: $8. 35pp. Reporting time: 1-3 months. Simultaneous submissions accepted: Yes. Publishes 20% of manuscripts submitted. Payment: Complimentary copy. Copyrighted, reverts to author. Subjects: Biography, Cooking, Diaries, Essays, Fiction, Indexes & Abstracts, Interviews, Literature (General), Maps, Non-Fiction, Novels, Poetry, Prose, Short Stories, Textbooks.

Orpheus Press, Richard Hanson, 3221 Tara Gale Drive, Louisville, KY 40216. 2000. Fiction. avg. press run 2M. Expects 4-6 titles 2007. 320-420pp. Reporting time: 3 months. Simultaneous submissions accepted: yes. Publishes 2% of manuscripts submitted. Payment: standard. Copyrights for author. Subjects: English, Fiction, Textbooks.

ORTHODOX MISSION, Axios Newletter, Inc., Father Daniel, 30-32 Macaw Avenue, Belmopan, Belize, 011-501-8-23284. 1973. Articles, art, interviews, reviews, parts-of-novels, news items, non-fiction. circ. 3.5M. 12/yr. Pub'd 12 issues 2005; expects 12 issues 2006, 12 issues 2007. sub. price $10; per copy $2; sample $2. 6pp. Reporting time: 2 months. Payment: $25 plus copies. Copyrighted, reverts to author. Pub's reviews: 3 in 2005. §Moral issues, politics, philosophy. Subjects: The Americas, Book Collecting, Bookselling, Book Reviewing, Christianity, Peace.

Orthodox Mission in Belize (see also Axios Newletter, Inc.), Father Daniel, 30-32 Macaw Avenue, PO Box 279, Belmopan, Belize, 501-8-23284, fax 501-8-23633. 1973. Articles, art, interviews, criticism, reviews, letters, parts-of-novels, news items, non-fiction. Pub'd 1 title 2005; expects 1 title 2006. 175pp. Reporting time: 2 months. Payment: open. Copyrights for author. Subjects: The Americas, Book Collecting, Bookselling, Book Reviewing, Christianity, Peace.

•Oscura Press, Lucero Don, PO 835, Tijeras, NM 87059-0835, 505-384-2792, press@thewestern.net, books.thewestern.net. 2006. Fiction. "It is not the mission of the Oscura Press to make money. Let the US Treasury make money; the mission for this publishing house the mission for any company, in fact is to create culture. The Oscura Press strives to run itself as a nonprofit, for zero profitability. We aim to revitalize reading, which we feel is declining in this age of iPods and on-demand TV. Were looking to publish the works of original authors, and to get those works into the reading publics hands. To this end, we only publish works of literary fiction, or other original works of literary merit. Recent works include "Necktie for a Two-Headed Tadpole: a modern-day alchemy book" by Jason Murk." avg. press run 5000. Expects 2 titles 2006, 3 titles 2007. Discounts: 3+ copies 40%. 400pp. Reporting time: 1 week. Simultaneous submissions accepted: Yes. Publishes 10% of manuscripts submitted. Copyrights for author. Subjects: Fiction, Literature (General).

OSIRIS, Andrea Moorhead, Box 297, Deerfield, MA 01342-0297. 1972. Poetry, interviews, long-poems. "*Osiris* is an international multi-lingual journal publishing contemporary poetry. English and French appear without translation. Poetry from other languages such as Spanish, Danish and Hungarian often appear with facing English translation. Recent contributors: Madeleine Gagnon (Quebec), Annemette Andersen (Denmark), George Moore, Gunter Kunert (Germany), and Ingrid Swanberg (USA)." circ. 1M. 2/yr. Pub'd 2 issues 2005; expects 2 issues 2006, 2 issues 2007. sub. price $18 individuals and institutions; per copy $9.00; sample $4.00. 48pp. Reporting time: 4 weeks. Simultaneous submissions accepted: no. Publishes 15% of manuscripts submitted. Payment: 5 copies. Copyrighted, rights revert to author, with credit line to *Osiris*. Ads: query. Subjects: France, French, Language, Literary Review, Poetry.

Osric Publishing (see also WHITE CROW), Christopher Herdt, 235 South 15th St., Apt 202, Philadelphia, PA 19102-5026. 1993. Poetry, fiction, art, photos, satire, letters, parts-of-novels, collages, non-fiction.

"Submissions should be made via e-mail; see Web site at www.wcrow.com for details." avg. press run 200. Pub'd 1 title 2005; expects 1 title 2007. 32pp. Reporting time: 6 months. Simultaneous submissions accepted: yes. Publishes 5% of manuscripts submitted. Payment: negotiable, contributors copies. Copyright for author upon request. Subjects: Fiction, Poetry.

THE OTHER ISRAEL, Adam Keller, Beate Zilversmidt, PO Box 2542, Holon 58125, Israel, Israel, 972-3-5565804 phone/Fax. 1983. Articles, interviews, reviews, letters, news items, non-fiction. circ. 4M. in principle 6/yr, but double issues. Pub'd 6 issues 2005; expects 6 issues 2006, 6 issues 2007. sub. price $30 individual, $50 institution; $15 students, unemployed; per copy $5; sample free on request. Discounts: 33%. 14-28pp. Payment: none. Not copyrighted. Pub's reviews: 1 in 2005. §Middle East politics, Economics, society, peace movement, conflict resolution. Ads: $100/$60. Subjects: Anarchist, Asia, Indochina, Civil Rights, Counter-Culture, Alternatives, Communes, History, Public Affairs, Third World, Minorities.

OTHER VOICES, Gina Frangello, Executive Editor; JoAnne Ruvoli, Assistant Editor, Univ. of Illinois, English Dept., 601 S. Morgan Street, M/C 162, Chicago, IL 60607, 312-413-2209, othervoices@list-serv.uic.edu. www.othervoicesmagazine.org. 1985. Fiction, interviews, letters, parts-of-novels, plays. "A prize-winning, independent market for quality fiction, we are dedicated to original, fresh, diverse stories and novel excerpts by new, as well as recognized, talent. No taboos, except ineptitude and murkiness. 6,000 word maximum preferred. SASE required. Winner of 19 Illinois Arts Council Literary Awards, inclusion in Best American Short Stories of the Century, Pushcart anthologies. Reading period is October 1 to April 1 *only*." circ. 1,700. 2/yr. Pub'd 2 issues 2005; expects 2 issues 2006, 2 issues 2007. sub. price $26/4 issues, institutions $30/4 issues, add $8 per sub. for outside the U.S.; per copy $9; sample $9 (inc. postage). Back issues: $7 (inc. postage) when available. Discounts: 20% classroom, 40% trade, 50% general distributor. 150pp. Reporting time: 10-12 weeks. Simultaneous submissions accepted: yes. Payment: copies, small cash gratuity. Copyrighted, reverts to author. Pub's reviews: 8 in 2005. Ads: $100/$60/exchange with non-profit lit mags. Subjects: Fiction, Literary Review, Literature (General), Magazines, Short Stories.

•**OTTN Publishing,** James Gallagher, 16 Risler Street, Stockton, NJ 08559, 609-397-4005, 609-397-4007 (fax), inquiries@ottnpublishing.com, www.ottnpublishing.com. 1998. Non-fiction. "We publish series nonfiction for juvenile/YA readers, which is primarily marketed to schools and libraries." avg. press run 2000. Expects 5 titles 2006, 5-10 titles 2007. Discounts: 30% wholesale (returnable) or 40% (nonreturnable). 64pp. Reporting time: 4-6 months. Simultaneous submissions accepted: Yes.

Our Child Press, Carol Perrott, PO Box 4379, Philadelphia, PA 19118-8379, 610-308-8988. 1980. Fiction, non-fiction. "Adoption related materials." avg. press run 2000. Pub'd 1 title 2005; expects 2 titles 2006, 2 titles 2007. 32pp. Reporting time: 6 months to a year. Simultaneous submissions accepted: Yes. Publishes 1% of manuscripts submitted. Payment: 5% net sales. Does not copyright for author. Subjects: Adoption, Family.

OUR SCHOOLS/OUR SELVES, Erika Shaker, Editor; Satu Repo, Editor, Canadian Centre for Policy Alternatives, 410-75 Albert Street, Ottawa, ON K1P 5E7, Canada, 416-463-6978 phone/Fax, web: www.policyalternatives.ca. "Subscripers to OS/OS get 4 issues a year. Topics: education and labour, social justice, anti-racism, feminism, socialism, 'A magazine for Canadian education activists.'" circ. 1M. 4/yr. Pub'd 4 issues 2005; expects 4 issues 2006, 4 issues 2007. sub. price $48 (Canada), $60 Canadian (outside Canada); per copy $12; sample $12. Back issues: $9. 160pp. Simultaneous submissions accepted: yes. Publishes 50% of manuscripts submitted. Payment: none. Pub's reviews: at least 2 per issue in 2005. §Education. Ads: $350/$190. Subjects: Education, Labor.

OUT OF LINE, Garden House Press, Sam Longmire, P.O. Box 321 Trenton, Ohio 45067, Trenton, OH 45067, 513-988-7183. 1998. Poetry, fiction, articles, non-fiction. "OUT OF LINE is an annual anthology of poetry, fiction, and nonficition with underlying themes of peace and justice. We look for works that deal with serious human issues such as tolerance, diversity, freedom, peace, healthy relationships, environmental justice, personal growth, and spirituality. Recent contributors include Michael Casey, Maureen Tolman Flannery, CB Follett, Paula Friedman, Lyn Lifshin, Karen Malpede, and Leza Lowitz OOL leans toward writers who bring a progressive and liberal perspective to their work. No hate literature." circ. 400. 500/yr. Pub'd 1 issue 2005; expects 1 issue 2006, 1 issue 2007. sub. price $12.50; per copy $12.50; sample free. Back issues: $5, all available. Discounts: 2-6 copies %5. 200pp. Reporting time: Two months. Simultaneous submissions accepted: Yes. Payment: Two free copies and the opportunity to purchase additional copies at cost. Copyrighted, reverts to author. No advertisements. Subjects: Alcohol, Alcoholism, Biography, Black, Community, Conservation, Ecology, Foods, Fiction, Gay, Humanism, Lesbianism, Poetry, Political Science, Politics, Religion, Spiritual.

OUT YOUR BACKDOOR: The Magazine of Do-It-Yourself Adventure and Homegrown Culture, Jeff Potter, 4686 Meridian Road, Williamston, MI 48895, 517-347-1689; jeff@outyourbackdoor.com; outyourback-door.com. 1989. Poetry, fiction, articles, art, photos, cartoons, interviews, satire, criticism, reviews, music, letters, parts-of-novels, long-poems, collages, concrete art, news items, non-fiction. "*OYB* is about thrifty, independent culture and exploration, the interface of art, action and hobby. *OYB* is an everyman's *Outside*—but

344

it's a refreshing antidote to the elite fantasy consumerist aspect of that mag. I cover hard-to-find, quality, cultural, affordable projects, as presented by aficionados. With an emphasis on: boats, bikes, XC skis, unbestseller books, owner-operated restaurants and much else in indy-culture. I fight against fragmentation, go for sustainability, practical harmony and cross-training of the brain. I often use reprints that won't see the mainstream to achieve our tasty blend. Truly indy media is so rare that one has to see *OYB* to understand it. The paper mag only comes out annually, but I put up new web stories several times a week. The web is a likely place for an outside submission to appear. 90% of *OYB* is by me!'' circ. 5M. 1/yr. Pub'd 1 issue 2005; expects 1 issue 2006, 2 issues 2007. sub. price $5/1 issue; per copy $5; sample $5. Back issues: $5. Discounts: retail 1-10 40%, wholesalers 30+ 50%. 48-64pp. Reporting time: Eventually, with SASE. Simultaneous submissions accepted: yes. Publishes 10% of manuscripts submitted. Payment: Usually nothing, but *OYB* is growing so payment may not be far off. Copyrighted, reverts to author. Pub's reviews: 40 in 2005. §Alternative, subculture, unusual, bikes, boats, equipment, hunting, fishing, travel, culture, thrifty lifestyles, inside info on places/things. Ads: $200 full / $150 half / $100 quarter. Subjects: Architecture, Bicycling, Book Collecting, Bookselling, Community, Conservation, Counter-Culture, Alternatives, Communes, Crafts, Hobbies, Culture, Design, Ecology, Foods, Gardening, Homemaking, Networking, Reprints, Sports, Outdoors.

OUTER-ART, Dr. Florentin Smarandache, University of New Mexico, 200 College Road, Gallup, NM 87301, smarand@unm.edu, www.gallup.unm.edu/~smarandache/a/outer-art.htm. 2000. Articles, art, photos, interviews, criticism, reviews, collages, concrete art. "Outer-Art is a movement set up by the editor in the 1990s (as a protest against random modern art, where anything could mean...art!) and consists of making art as ugly as possible, as wrong as possible, or as silly as possible, and generally as impossible as possible! It is an upside-down art!... to do art in the way it is not supposed to be done." 1/yr. Pub'd 1 issue 2005; expects 1 issue 2006, 1 issue 2007. Reporting time: 1 month. Simultaneous submissions accepted: yes. Copyrighted, reverts to author. Subjects: Arts, Avant-Garde, Experimental Art, Criticism, Essays, Multicultural, Post Modern, Visual Arts.

OUTLANDER, Robert Seaver Gebelein, PO Box 1546, Provincetown, MA 02657. 1994. "My bias is new civilization." Irregular. Expects 1 issue 2006, 1 issue 2007. sub. price $10 for 10 issues; per copy $1; sample $1. Back issues: $1. Discounts: make me an offer. 10pp. Reporting time: not set. Publishes 0% of manuscripts submitted. Payment: none. Copyrighted, reverts to author.

OUTPOSTS POETRY QUARTERLY, Hippopotamus Press, Howard Sergeant, Founder, Editor; Roland John, Editor, 22, Whitewell Road, Frome, Somerset BA11 4EL, United Kingdom. 1943. Poetry, articles, criticism, reviews. "*Outposts* is the longest-lived independent poetry magazine in the UK. It was founded to provide a satisfactory medium for those poets, recognised or unrecognised, who are concerned with the potentialities of the human spirit, and who are able to visualize the dangers and opportunites which confront the individual and the whole of humanity. Although recent contributors have included famous poets like Ted Hughes, Peter Porter, Roy Fuller, Vernon Scannell, Blake Morrison, Seamus Heaney, etc., the magazine makes a special point of introducing the work of new and unestablished poets to the public." circ. 1.9M. 4/yr. Pub'd 4 issues 2005; expects 4 issues 2006, 4 issues 2007. sub. price £14 or $24 (postage paid) for 1 year, £26 or $50 (postage paid) for 2 years; per copy £3.50, $7; sample $7. Back issues: price varies from £2-£10. Discounts: 35%. 80pp. Reporting time: 2 weeks, 4 weeks non-U.K. Simultaneous submissions accepted: yes. Payment: depends on length of poem. Copyrighted, reverts to author. Pub's reviews: 30 in 2005. §Poetry, criticism of poetry. Ads: £90 $120/£45 $70. Subjects: Criticism, Poetry.

Outrider Press, Phyllis I. Nelson, President, 2036 Northwinds Drive, Dyer, IN 46311-1874, 708-672-6630, Fax 708-672-5820, outriderPr@aol.com, www.outriderpress.com, 800-933-4680 code 03. 1988. Poetry, fiction, art. "Produces handmade, handbound, blank page books, 50-300 pp, suitable for journals or personal poetry as well as archival manuscript boxes. Our 2006 anthology will accept short fiction and creative nonfiction (to 2,500 words) and poetry (single-spaced up to 28 lines) on the theme of "vacations - the good, the bad and the ugly." Send SASE for guidelines and entry forms. We offer $2,000 in cash prizes - $1,000 in poetry and $1,000 in prose as determined by independent judges.Deadlines for manuscripts: Feb. 28, 2006." avg. press run 12M-13M. Pub'd 1 title 2005; expects 3 titles 2006, 4 titles 2007. Discounts: bookstores 60/40; others up to 50% off, depending upon # ordered. 232-288pp. Reporting time: 1-2 months. Simultaneous submissions accepted: yes. Publishes a variable % of manuscripts submitted. Payment: negotiable. Copyrights for author. Subjects: Animals, Cooking, Counter-Culture, Alternatives, Communes, Essays, Family, Fiction, Nature, Occult, Pets, Poetry, Romance, Women.

Outskirts Press, Inc., 10940 S. Parker Road - 515, Parker, CO 80134, 1-888-OP-BOOKS, info@outskirts-press.com, www.outskirtspress.com. 2000. Poetry, fiction, articles, art, interviews, satire, criticism, reviews, letters, parts-of-novels, long-poems, plays, non-fiction. "Recognize that publishing a book is only the first part of being an author. Self-promotion and marketing are equally important." avg. press run print-on-demand. Pub'd 50 titles 2005; expects 100 titles 2006, 500 titles 2007. 150pp. Reporting time: 5-10 days. Simultaneous submissions accepted: yes. Publishes 80% of manuscripts submitted. Payment: author determines their own profit. Copyrights for author. Subjects: Anthology, Autobiography, Biography, Experimental, Fiction, Genealogy, How-To, Non-Fiction.

Over the Wall Inc. Publishing & Productions, Craig Farris, Rodger Noe, Steven Lange, 1035 Jackson Street, Red Bluff, CA 96080, 888-267-1418. 2004. Fiction, non-fiction. "Kendall Publishing was sold to Over the Wall Inc. in 2004." avg. press run 5K. Pub'd 7 titles 2005. Discounts: 25% schools at 100 units, 25% libraries. 270+ pages. Reporting time: 60-90 days. Simultaneous submissions accepted: yes. Payment: 15%, advances negotiable. Copyrights for author. Subjects: Alcohol, Alcoholism, Crime, Drugs, Parenting, Psychology.

OVERLAND JOURNAL, Robert Clark, Oregon-California Trails Association, PO Box 1019, Independence, MO 64051-0519, 816-252-2276, Fax 816-836-0989, octa@indepmo.org. 1983. Articles, photos, reviews, non-fiction. "Articles concerning the covered wagon migration to the American West in the 19th century: Oregon Trail, gold rush (various routes)." circ. 2.5M. 4/yr. Pub'd 4 issues 2005; expects 4 issues 2006, 4 issues 2007. sub. price $35; per copy $6.25; sample free to public libraries. Back issues: $6.25. Discounts: none. 36pp. Reporting time: 30 days. Simultaneous submissions accepted: no. Publishes 75% of manuscripts submitted. Payment: none. Copyrighted, reverts to author. Pub's reviews: 25 in 2005. §Covered wagon migration to the American West in the 19th century, gold rush. Ads: $250/$150/$85 1/4 page. Subjects: Book Reviewing, Diaries, Great Plains, Health, The West.

The Overlook Press, Tracy Carns, Publishing Director, 141 Wooster Street #4, New York, NY 10012-3163, 914-679-8571. 1971. "We are distributed by Penguin USA, although special sales are based in Woodstock, NY. Fiction: Literary fiction, *some* fantasy and sci-fi, and foreign literature in translation. Non-fiction: Art, architecture, design, history, film, biography, homestyle, children's, martial arts and Hudson Valley regional." Pub'd 75 titles 2005; expects 75 titles 2006, 75 titles 2007. Reporting time: 6-8 weeks. Copyrights for author. Subjects: Arts, Calligraphy, Design, Literature (General), Martial Arts.

The Overmountain Press, Jason Weems, Acquisitions Editor; Sherry Lewis, Senior Editor; Daniel Lewis, Managing Editor, 325 West Walnut Street, PO Box 1261, Johnson City, TN 37605, 800-992-2691, Fax 423-232-1252, www.overmountainpress.com. 1970. avg. press run 2M. Pub'd 30 titles 2005; expects 30 titles 2006, 30 titles 2007. Discounts: 1-4 20%, 5-24 40%, 25-99 42%, 100-249 43%, 250-999 44%, 1000+ 45%. Pages vary. Reporting time: 6-8 months. Simultaneous submissions accepted: yes. Publishes 3% of manuscripts submitted. Payment: subject to negotiations. Does not copyright for author. Subjects: African-American, Appalachia, Aviation, Biography, Celtic, Civil War, Genealogy, History, Kentucky, Mystery, Native American, Non-Fiction, Novels, Elvis Presley, South.

OWEN WISTER REVIEW, PO Box 3625, Laramie, WY 82071-3625, 307-766-4027; owr@uwyo.edu. 1978. Poetry, fiction, art, photos, interviews, satire, parts-of-novels, non-fiction. "100% freelance written publication. Submissions are considered from Aug 1-Dec 15 All submissions must be accompanied by a short biographical statement and SASE. Photocopied and computer-printout submissions will be accepted, but dot-matrix is discouraged. Prose submission poets submit no more than 5 poems. Artists between 5-20 35 mm slides; black and white or color artworks and graphics in any media, any size will be considered." circ. 300-500. 1/yr. Pub'd 1 issue 2005; expects 1 issue 2006, 1 issue 2007. sub. price $8.20; per copy $6.95 + $1.25 postage; sample $5. Back issues: $5. Discounts: none. 120pp. Reporting time: 1-4 months. Simultaneous submissions accepted: yes. Publishes 10-20% of manuscripts submitted. Payment: 1 complimentary copy and 10% discount on any additional copies. Copyrighted, reverts to author. Subjects: Arts, Literature (General).

Owl Creek Press, Rich Ives, 2693 S. Camano Drive, Camano Island, WA 98282. 1979. Poetry, fiction, articles, long-poems. avg. press run 500-2M. Pub'd 4 titles 2005; expects 4 titles 2006, 4 titles 2007. Discounts: standard. Reporting time: 3-6 months. Simultaneous submissions accepted: yes. Payment: varies. Subjects: Fiction, Poetry.

The Owl Press, Albert Flynn DeSilver, PO Box 126, Woodacre, CA 94973-0126, 415-438-1539, asisowl@mindspring.com, www.theowlpress.com. 1997. Poetry, art, long-poems, concrete art. "Recent and forthcoming authors include Frank O'Hara, John Ashbery, Anne Waldman, Alice Notley, Joanne Kyger, Bill Berkson, Clark Coolidge, Bernadette Mayer, Anselm Berrigan, Edmund Berrigan, Brenda Coultas, Brendan Lorber, Lisa Jarnot and others." avg. press run 750. Pub'd 2 titles 2005; expects 3 titles 2006, 2 titles 2007. Discounts: 50-55%. 100pp. Reporting time: 1 month. Simultaneous submissions accepted: yes. Publishes .001% of manuscripts submitted. Payment: books. Copyrights for author. Subjects: Poetry, Prose.

THE OXFORD AMERICAN, Marc Smirnoff, Lisa Dixon, Bess Reed, J.E. Pitts, Sally Ann Cassady, 201 Donaghey Ave., #107, Conway, AR 72035-5001, www.oxfordamericanmag.com. 1992. Poetry, fiction, articles, art, photos, criticism, reviews, music, non-fiction. "*The Oxford American* is a general interest magazine covering all cultural aspects of the American South. *The Oxford American* is published by novelist John Grisham." circ. 50M+. 4/yr. Pub'd 6 issues 2005; expects 4 issues 2006, 4 issues 2007. sub. price $19.95; per copy call for rates; sample same. Back issues: varies, see website. Discounts: if you purchase 4 gift subscriptions, you receive the 5th one free of charge. 100+pp. Reporting time: 3-4 weeks, (high volume time) 3 months. We accept simultaneous submissions, but please notify of such. Publishes 10% of manuscripts submitted. Payment: varies, arrangements made after acceptance. Copyrighted, reverts to author. Pub's reviews: 30+ in 2005. §Books of fiction, poetry, nonfiction (Southern topics). Ads: contact our ad staff. Subjects: Fiction, Music, Non-Fiction, Poetry, Travel.

Oyez, Robert Hawley, 212 Colgate Avenue, Kensington, CA 94708-1122. 1964. Poetry, criticism. "Books usually designed by Graham McIntosh. Usually report promptly but not reading at this time. In 1997 we published a checklist of our publications - now out of print. In 2004 we will publish only a holiday keepsake. No other firm plans for the future." avg. press run 500-1M. Pub'd 3 titles 2005; expects 3 titles 2006. 60-80pp. Payment: 10% royalties and copies. Copyrights for author. Subjects: African Literature, Africa, African Studies, Criticism, Poetry.

•**OYEZ REVIEW,** Janet Wondra, Dept. of Literature & Languages, 430. S. Michigan Ave, Chicago, IL 60605, www.roosevelt.edu/oyezreview. 1965. Poetry, fiction, art, photos, non-fiction. "There are no restrictions on style, theme, or subject matter. With our rotating editorial staff, each issue has new energy and offers a fresh aesthetic experience. Though we consider it a large part of our mission to publish undiscovered writers, we also have a strong tradition of publishing some of today's best writers, including Charles Bukowski, James McManus, Carla Panciera, Sandra Kohler, and Saul Bennett." 1/yr. Pub'd 1 issue 2005; expects 1 issue 2006, 1 issue 2007. price per copy 5; sample 5. Back issues: inquire. Discounts: inquire. 100pp. Reporting time: 1-2 months after our Aug 1- Oct 1 reading period closes. Simultaneous submissions accepted: No. Payment: Pays with two contributor's copies. Subjects: Fiction, Non-Fiction, Photography, Poetry.

OYSTER BOY REVIEW, Damon Sauve, Fiction Editor; Jeffery Beam, Poetry Editor; Chad Driscoll, Editor, PO Box 299, Pacifica, CA 94044, email@oysterboyreview.com, www.oysterboyreview.com. 1994. Poetry, fiction, art, photos, reviews. "We're interested in the ignored, the misunderstood, and the varietal. We'll make some mistakes." circ. 250. 3/yr. Pub'd 3 issues 2005; expects 3 issues 2006, 3 issues 2007. sub. price $12; per copy $4; sample $4. Back issues: $4. Discounts: 30% libraries and bookstores. 60pp. Reporting time: 1-2 months. Simultaneous submissions accepted: no. Publishes 1% of manuscripts submitted. Payment: 2 copies. Copyrighted, reverts to author. Pub's reviews: 10 in 2005. §First books, chapbooks, poetry collections, novels. Ads: $60/$30/$15 1/4 page/$20 1/3 page. Subjects: Fiction, North Carolina, Poetry, Reviews.

Oyster River Press, Cicely Buckley, Publisher, 36 Oyster River Road, Durham, NH 03824-3029, 603-868-5006, oysterriverpress@comcast.net, www.oysterriverpress.com. 1989. Poetry. "A cooperative press, editors, writers, and illustrators, working together. Average of 2 publications per year, suitable for a broad audience. Initially submit 6-10 poems or 2 chapters, page numbers, synopsis, and a brief bio. This years publication is a collection of poems on war and peace, world conflicts; accepting submissions through April 15." avg. press run 1000. Pub'd 1 title 2005; expects 1 title 2006, 1 title 2007. 80-150pp. Reporting time: 1-6 months. Simultaneous submissions accepted: no. 7% of submitted manuscripts published. Translations a specialty; often bilingual presentation. Payment: Royalties 10% after production expenses are paid. Copyrights for author. Subjects: Bilingual, Creativity, English, Experimental, Fiction, Inspirational, Language, Literature (General), New England, New Hampshire, Non-Fiction, Peace, Photography, Short Stories, Writers/Writing.

P

P.R.A. Publishing, Yadira Payne, P.O. Box 211701, Martinez, GA 30917-1701, (706) 855-6173, (630) 597-0548, fax(s)(706) 855-8794, (425)669-3833 www.prapublishing.com, submissions@phoenixrisin-garts.com. 2000. Poetry, articles, art, reviews. "Will be adding titles for children's books and improving your chances in the creative arts world(business)." avg. press run 500. Pub'd 2 titles 2005; expects 3-5 titles 2006, 3-5 titles 2007. Discounts: Contact for more information. 115pp. Reporting time: 3-4 months. Simultaneous submissions accepted: Yes. Will provide forms for author to complete. Subjects: African-American, Anthology, Bilingual, Careers, Family, Literary Review, Picture Books, Poetry, Psychology, Public Relations/Publicity, Reviews.

PABLO LENNIS, Etaoin Shrdlu Press, John Thiel, Editor, Fandom House, 30 N. 19th Street, Lafayette, IN 47904. 1976. Poetry, fiction, articles, art, photos, criticism, reviews, letters, non-fiction. "Material should be very short, due to space. Open policy. Material is most apt to be rejected if it would look more in place in some other publication, and the addresses of these are given the author when known. Recent well-known contributors include many directory responders. The contents of *Pablo Lennis* are extraordinarily reportative of modern life. Don't be surprised if the world of our writers in some way turns out to be yours." circ. 100. 12/yr. Pub'd 12 issues 2005; expects 12 issues 2006, 12 issues 2007. sub. price $20-$25 overseas; per copy $2; sample $2. Back issues: none available. 26pp. Reporting time: 2 weeks or less. Simultaneous submissions accepted: no. Publishes 80% of manuscripts submitted. Payment: 1 copy of the issue plus copies of any commentary on the work. Not copyrighted. Pub's reviews: 42 in 2005. §Science fiction, fantasy, science. Ads: micro-ads 10¢ a word. Subjects: Fantasy, Science, Science Fiction.

PACIFIC COAST JOURNAL, French Bread Publications, Stillson Graham, Editor; Stephanie Kylkis, Fiction Editor, PO Box 56, Carlsbad, CA 92018-0056, e-mail paccoastj@frenchbreadpublications.com. 1991. Poetry, fiction, articles, art, interviews, satire, criticism, reviews, parts-of-novels, plays, non-fiction. "We publish experimental and semi-experimental work that furthers the cause of artistic insolence. The best work will entertain as well as confuse. Query e-mail submissions, unsolicited regular mail submissions OK." circ. 200. 3-4/yr. Pub'd 3 issues 2005; expects 4 issues 2006, 4 issues 2007. sub. price $12; per copy $3; sample $2.50. Back issues: $2.50. Discounts: none. 40pp. Reporting time: 6-9 months, sometimes longer. Simultaneous submissions accepted if they let us know. Payment: 1 copy. Copyrighted, author retains all rights. Pub's reviews: 3 in 2005. §Fiction, sciences, philosophy—no poetry please. Ads: $35/$20 or will trade with other publications. Subjects: Avant-Garde, Experimental Art, Essays, Poetry, Reviews, Short Stories, The West.

PACIFIC HISTORICAL REVIEW, University of California Press, David Johnson, Editor; Carl Abbot, Editor, Univ of California Press, 2000 Center Street, Suite 303, Berkeley, CA 94704-1223, 510-643-7154. 1931. Reviews, non-fiction. "Editorial address: Dept. of History, Portland State University, PO Box 751, Portland, OR 97207-0751." circ. 1448. 4/yr. Pub'd 4 issues 2005; expects 4 issues 2006, 4 issues 2007. sub. price $34 indiv., $123 instit., $22 students (+ $20 air freight); per copy $14 indiv., $36 instit., $14 students (+ $20 air freight); sample free. Back issues: $14 indiv., $36 instit., $14 students (+ $20 air freight). Discounts: foreign subs. agents 10%, one-time orders 10+ 30%, standing orders (bookstores): 1-99 40%, 100+ 50%. 170pp. Reporting time: 3 months. Payment: none. Copyrighted, does not revert to author. Pub's reviews: 100 in 2005. §Asia, American West, history, diplomatic history. Ads: $295/$220. Subjects: Asia, Indochina, Asian-American, The West.

Pacific Isle Publishing Company, Ronald W. Parkhurst, PO Box 827, Makawao, HI 96768, 808-572-9232 phone, books@bromes.com, www.bromes.com. 2000. Fiction, art, photos, cartoons, non-fiction. Pub'd 1 title 2005; expects 1 title 2006, 1 title 2007. Discounts: industry standard/negotiable. 216pp. Reporting time: 30 days. Simultaneous submissions accepted: yes. Publishes 50% of manuscripts submitted. Payment: negotiable. Copyrights for author. Subject: Horticulture.

THE PACIFIC REVIEW, James Brown, Faculty Editor, Department of English, Calif State University, San Bernardino, CA 92407. 1982. Poetry, fiction, parts-of-novels, long-poems, plays, non-fiction. "While the *PR* attempts to reflect its unique geographic region—Southern California—material is not limited to the area; the *PR* invites excellence in poetry, fiction, drama, and essay. Do not submit more than three poems at a time, and please also include a short biographical statement with your entry." circ. 1M. 1/yr. Pub'd 1 issue 2005; expects 1 issue 2006, 1 issue 2007. sub. price $7; per copy $5; sample $5 (libraries $6.50). Back issues: $2. Discounts: 40%. 104pp. Reporting time: 3 months (mss are not read Feb.-Aug.). Simultaneous submissions accepted: yes. Publishes 20% of manuscripts submitted. Payment: in copies. Copyrighted, reverts to author. Ads: $150/$100. Subjects: Arts, Drama, Fiction, Literary Review, Literature (General), Poetry.

Pacific View Press, Pam Zumwalt, PO Box 2897, Berkeley, CA 94702, Fax 510-843-5835, pvp@mindspring.com. 1992. Non-fiction. avg. press run 3-5M. Pub'd 3 titles 2005; expects 3 titles 2006, 2-3 titles 2007. 250pp. Simultaneous submissions accepted: yes. Payment: royalty. Copyrights for author. Subjects: Acupuncture, Asia, Indochina, Children, Youth, Health.

PACK-O-FUN, Clapper Publishing Co., Barbara Sunderlage, 2400 Devon, Suite 375, Des Plaines, IL 60018, 847-635-5800. 1951. circ. 105M. 10/yr. Pub'd 10 issues 2005; expects 10 issues 2006, 10 issues 2007. price per copy $3.95-$4.95. 106pp. Reporting time: 3 months. Simultaneous submissions accepted: yes. Payment: yes. Copyrighted, does not revert to author. Pub's reviews. §Craft books. Subject: Crafts, Hobbies.

PAGAN AMERICA, Crescent Moon, Jeremy Robinson, Cassidy Hughes, PO Box 393, Maidstone, Kent ME14 5XU, United Kingdom. 1992. Poetry. "*Pagan America* is a bi-annual collection of poetry from North America and Canada. Many poets are unknown, others are well-established. One book each year features women's love poetry." circ. 200. 2/yr. Pub'd 2 issues 2005; expects 2 issues 2006, 2 issues 2007. sub. price $17; per copy $8.50; sample $6. Back issues: $6 for 1, $5 for 2+. Discounts: Trade: 20% single order, 35% 2+. 80pp. Reporting time: 3 months. We publish 5% or less of manuscripts submitted. Payment: to be negotiated. Copyrighted, reverts to author. Ads: $20/$10/$5 1/4 page. Subjects: Arts, Culture, Feminism, Literature (General), Myth, Mythology, Poetry, Prose, Religion, Sex, Sexuality, Women.

Pagan Press, John Lauritsen, 11 Elton St., Dorchester, MA 02125-1412, 617-282-2133, john_lauritsen@post.harvard.edu. 1982. Articles, photos, interviews, non-fiction. "Founded to publish books of interest to intelligent gay men. Send query letter before submitting manuscript." avg. press run 2M. Expects 1 title 2006, 1 title 2007. 150pp. Does not copyright for author. Subject: Gay.

348

PageFree Publishing, Inc., Kim Blagg D, 109 South Farmer Street, Otsego, MI 49078, 269-692-3926. 1998. Poetry, fiction, cartoons, interviews, criticism, music, parts-of-novels, long-poems, plays, non-fiction. "We publish for a variety of authors, particularly those targeting niche readers." avg. press run 1000. Pub'd 300 titles 2005; expects 600 titles 2006, 1000 titles 2007. Discounts: 30-55%. 250pp. Reporting time: 2 days. Simultaneous submissions accepted: Yes. Publishes 90% of manuscripts submitted. Payment: 7% royalty. Does not copyright for author.

PAINTING, Clapper Publishing Co., Barbara Sunderlage, 2400 Devon, Suite 375, Des Plaines, IL 60018, 847-635-5800. 1951. circ. 67M. 10/yr. Pub'd 10 issues 2005; expects 10 issues 2006, 10 issues 2007. price per copy $3.95-$4.95. 106pp. Reporting time: 3 months. Simultaneous submissions accepted: yes. Payment: yes. Copyrighted, does not revert to author. Pub's reviews. §Craft books. Subject: Crafts, Hobbies.

PAJ NTAUB VOICE, Mai Neng Moua, Hmong American Institute for Learning (HAIL), 2654 Logan Avenue North, Minneapolis, MN 55411, Phone (651) 214-0955, Fax (612) 588-1534, mainengmoua@mn.rr.com. 1994. Poetry, fiction, art, photos, interviews, satire, criticism, letters, parts-of-novels, long-poems, plays, non-fiction. circ. 1000. 2/yr. sub. price $20 individual US, $30 individual international, 40 institution US, $50 institution international; per copy $10. Back issues: $5-$10 Loss and Separation; Becoming American; WAR; Art & Religion; Dating, Sex & Marriage; Visions for the Future; Gender & Identity; Silence. 80pp. Payment: $25 for publication, $25-$50 for reading at the public readings. Copyrighted, reverts to author. Subjects: Arts, Asia, Indochina, Asian-American, Fiction, Literature (General), Non-Fiction, Poetry.

Paladin Enterprises, Inc., Peder C. Lund, President and Publisher; Jon Ford, Editorial Director, Gunbarrel Tech Center, 7077 Winchester Circle, Boulder, CO 80301, 303-443-7250, Fax 303-442-8741, www.paladin-press.com. 1970. Non-fiction. "Non-fiction manuscripts on military related subjects are given first consideration. These include weaponry technology, police science, military tactics, martial arts, self-defense, espionage, survival. When accompanied with photos, mss are reviewed and returned within six weeks." avg. press run 1M-2M. Pub'd 40 titles 2005; expects 40 titles 2006, 40 titles 2007. Discounts: $50-$100 retail value - 20% all titles except supplementary list; $100-$500 40%; $500-$1000 45%; $1000-$5000, 50% both all titles except supplementary list. Over $5000 55% except supplementary list. 175pp. Reporting time: 6 weeks. Simultaneous submissions accepted: yes. Publishes 2% of manuscripts submitted. Payment: standard 10%, 12% & 15%. Copyrights for author. Subjects: Anarchist, Computers, Calculators, Counter-Culture, Alternatives, Communes, Crime, Drugs, History, How-To, Humor, Martial Arts, Military, Veterans, Non-Fiction, Reprints, Sports, Outdoors, War, Weapons.

Palanquin Press, Phebe Davidson, English Department, University of South Carolina-Aiken, Aiken, SC 29801, 803-648-6851 x3208, fax 803-641-3461, email phebed@aiken.edu, email scpoet@scescape.net. 1988. Poetry. "Sponsers 1 chapbook contest annually, fall and spring. Recently published: Lois Marie Harrod, Stuart Bartow, Laura Lee Washburn, Gay Brewer. Palanquin began its life publishing six pamphlets annually, each featuring a single poet, and then expanded its operation to include a spring chapbook contest. Currently, the press publishes three or four chapbooks annually with occasional longer titles. There are no restrictions on form or content, although Palanquin generally avoids sentimental, religious, and consciously academic work. Honest, well-crafted, accessible poems serve writers and readers alike to good advantage. Annual spring and fall chapbook contests: 20-25 pages of poetry plus bio and acknowledgements, $10 reading fee (includes copy of winning chapbook—checks payable to Palanquin Press), postmark deadline October 15 annually. SASE results only. Winner recieves $100 and 50 copies. Non-contest queries: include 3-5 poems with query letter." avg. press run Chapbooks 300, Full length 1M. Pub'd 4 titles 2005; expects 4 titles 2006, 5 titles 2007. 30pp. Reporting time: 2-3 months. Simultaneous submissions accepted: yes. Publishes 5% of manuscripts submitted. Payment: copies. Copyrights for author. Subject: Poetry.

Palari Publishing, David Smitherman, PO Box 9288, Richmond, VA 23227-0288, phone/fax 866-570-6724, info@palaribooks.com, www.palaribooks.com. 1998. Fiction, non-fiction. Pub'd 2 titles 2005; expects 4 titles 2006, 6 titles 2007. Discounts: 2-4 copies 20%, 5-99 40%, 100+ 50%. 200pp. Reporting time: 1 month. Simultaneous submissions accepted: No simultaneous submissions accepted. Publishes 2% of manuscripts submitted. Payment: varies. Copyrights for author. Subjects: African-American, Bibliography, Business & Economics, Fiction, Gay, Health, Lifestyles, Non-Fiction.

Palladium Communications, Carol Shepherd, Publisher, 320 South Main Street, PO Box 8403, Ann Arbor, MI 48107-8403, 734-668-4646; FAX 734-663-9361. 1991. Poetry, fiction, articles, interviews, satire, music, long-poems, plays, non-fiction. "We are a *special-interest-only* mixed media house for pan-American works which 'speak to the deep relationship of person to place, and communicate landscape and culture similarities and differences, to other people in other places on the planet.' Examples: plays, fiction, poetry on exile/diaspora/immigration/Nueva Onda experience; travel journals from unusual perspectives; bilingual editions; linguistic, jargon, and language accessibility and preservation works; involvement of Internet/ technology with the above. For music: South American and North American singer/songwriters with contemporary/pop/worldbeat original material. We fully finance one title per year at most, mostly we joint venture titles which meet our mission, editorial, and involvement requirements. Submissions: *'one page query letter only, with a paragraph on who will buy a copy of your work and your resume of previous publications or releases. No unsolicited manuscripts or tapes- we simply pitch them in the trash.'* SASP for confirmation of receipt. We request samples or demos if interested.'' avg. press run 1000 units print/CD, 500 units cassette. Expects 2 titles 2006, 2 titles 2007. Discounts: Quantity discounts are for resellers providing a sales tax license number and 501 (c) institutional buyers. Quantity: 2-4 units, 20%;5-50 units, 40%; 51+ units, 60%. Cash discount of 5% and shipping at no charge applicable to orders paid in full. No special discounts. Discounts are fortified for orders not paid in full within 90 days. No returns after 90 days. 100pp. Reporting time: 3 months. We accept simultaneous submissions only within our strict submission guidelines. Publishes less than 2% of manuscripts submitted. Payment: royalties quarterly. If we finance a publication, author royalties are approximately 10% of net revenue collected. On joint ventures, consultations and subsidy projects, we retain a royalty percentage of net ranging from 10 to 50%. Copyrights for author. Subjects: The Americas, Culture, Great Lakes, Immigration, Internet, Language, Latin America, Michigan, Midwest, Multicultural, Music, Native American, North America, Performing Arts, Poetry.

PALO ALTO REVIEW, Ellen Shull, 1400 West Villaret Blvd., San Antonio, TX 78224, 210-921-5017. 1992. Poetry, fiction, articles, art, photos, interviews, satire, reviews, letters, news items. ''Diane Glancy (Native American Poet), Victor Villasenor (author of *Rain of Gold*). Interview: Richard Rodriguez (author, scholar). Generally, not more than 15pp. in length, we are looking for good, clear writing that makes a point.'' circ. 700. 2/yr. Pub'd 2 issues 2005; expects 2 issues 2006, 2 issues 2007. sub. price $10; per copy $5; sample $5. Back issues: $5. 64pp. Reporting time: maximum of 3 months. Simultaneous submissions accepted, if noted as such. Percent of mss submitted which are published: articles/essays 40%, poems 2%, stories 2-3%. Payment: 2 copies. Copyrighted. Pub's reviews: 3 in 2005. §Not interested in children's, gay & lesbian. Ads: $100/$50/$35 1/4 page. Subjects: Autobiography, Book Reviewing, Education, Essays, Fiction, Humor, Interviews, Journals, Memoirs, Poetry.

The Pamphleeter's Press, Rabia Ali, PO Box 3374, Stony Creek, CT 06405, 203-483-8820, Fax 203-483-1429, E-mail pamphpress@aol.com. 1991. Articles, photos, interviews, non-fiction. ''The Pamphleeter's Press publishes books and pamphlets on politics, history & culture that address some of the most urgent functions of our times - which the major publishing houses have no time for.'' avg. press run 4M. Pub'd 3 titles 2005; expects 3 titles 2006, 3-4 titles 2007. Discounts: various discounts offered. Trade book orders are handled by our distributor: Inbook at 800-243-0138. 350pp. Reporting time: 4-6 weeks. Simultaneous submissions accepted: yes. Publishes 25% of manuscripts submitted. Payment: 6-1/2% to 7-1/2%. Copyrights for author. Subjects: Culture, Current Affairs, Global Affairs, History, Politics, Public Affairs, Translation.

Pancake Press, Patrick Smith, 163 Galewood Circle, San Francisco, CA 94131, 415-665 9215. 1973. Poetry, long-poems. ''Not presently accepting unsolicited mss.'' avg. press run 1M. Expects 1 title 2006. Discounts: 40%. 35-50pp. Reporting time: 1 month. Payment: arranged by mutual consent. Does not copyright for author. Subjects: Arts, Poetry.

PANDA, Esmond Jones, Editor, 46 First Avenue, Clase, Swansea, W. Glam SA6 7LL, United Kingdom. 2000. circ. 300. Quarterly. sub. price UK: £10 .. USA: $18; per copy UK: £4 .. USA: $6.

Pangaea, 226 South Wheeler Street, Saint Paul, MN 55105-1927, 651-690-3320 tel/fax, info@pangaea.org, http://pangaea.org. 1991. ''No unsolicited submissions accepted at this time.'' avg. press run 7.5M. Pub'd 3 titles 2005; expects 3 titles 2006, 3 titles 2007. Discounts: bookstores 1-4 20%, 5-9 25% 10-14 30% 15-24 35% 25+ 40%; wholesalers: Baker & Taylor, Follett, Quality, Lectorum, YBP, Blackwell's. 200pp. Copyrights for author. Subjects: African Literature, Africa, African Studies, The Americas, Animals, Anthropology, Archaelogy, Bilingual, Biology, Caribbean, Children, Youth, Conservation, Cuba, Earth, Natural History, Latin America, Nature, Puerto Rico, Travel.

PANIC STRIPS, Shannon D. Harle, Publisher, Shannon D. Harle, PO Box 1005, Swannanoa, NC 28778-1005. 1997. Cartoons, satire. ''Subscription includes all the zines I do= *Panic Strips, T.V. Heads*, and also *Rotten Pepper*.'' circ. 100-150. 2 or 3. Pub'd 2 issues 2005; expects 2 issues 2006, 3 issues 2007. sub. price $5; per copy $1.55; sample $1.55. Back issues: 2 for $1.55. 20pp. Reporting time: 1 month. Simultaneous submissions accepted: no. Payment: no. Copyrighted, reverts to author. §no. Subjects: Cartoons, Comics.

•**Panther Books (see also GOODIE),** Romy Ashby, 197 Seventh Avenue 4C, New York, NY 10011, www.goodie.org. 2001. Poetry, fiction, photos, interviews, letters. ''Please see our website http://www.goodie.org. Authors include: Ira Cohen, Edgar Oliver, Marty Matz.'' avg. press run 1500. Pub'd 1 title 2005; expects 1 title 2006, 2 titles 2007. Discounts: 2-10 copies 40%11+ copies 50%. 150pp. Copyrights for author. Subjects: Beat, Fiction, Interviews, New York, Novels, Photography, Storytelling, Surrealism.

Panther Creek Press (see also TOUCHSTONE LITERARY JOURNAL), Guida Jackson, Publisher; Ted Walthen, Acquisitions Editor; William Laufer, Associate Editor; Jerry Cooke, Editorial Assistant; Tucker Jackson, Webmaster; W. A. Jackson, Publicity Director; Adam Murphy, Graphic Designer, PO Box 130233,

Panther Creek Stn., Spring, TX 77393, panthercreek3@hotmail.com, www.panthercreekpress.com. 1999. Poetry, fiction, non-fiction. "Fiction: 50,000-80,000 words, nonfiction same. Poetry: 100-200 pages. Recent authors: Paul Christensen, Robb Jackson, Dodie Meeks, Eric Muirhead, Omar Pound, Christopher Woods. We do not read unsolicited mss. We read queries only. If we request the manuscript, chances are good we will publish it." avg. press run 1M. Pub'd 4 titles 2005; expects 5 titles 2006, 4-5 titles 2007. Discounts: trade 5+ 40%. 230pp. Reporting time: 3 weeks, queries only. We accept simultaneous submissions on queries only. If we request the manuscript, we expect an exclusive submission for 2 months. We do not accept unsolicited manuscripts. Publishes 1% of manuscripts submitted. Payment: 10% on list price, paid annually, no advance against royalties will be paid. Copyrights for author. Subjects: African Literature, Africa, African Studies, Classical Studies, Essays, Fiction, Genealogy, Latin America, Literature (General), Memoirs, Myth, Mythology, Native American, Novels, Poetry, Reference, Texas, Third World, Minorities.

PAPERBACK PARADE, Gryphon Books, Gary Lovisi, PO Box 209, Brooklyn, NY 11228-0209. 1986. Articles, photos, interviews, criticism, reviews, letters, news items, non-fiction. "A quarterly digest magazine devoted to collectible vintage, rare paperbacks with articles, interviews, lists, on famous paperback authors, artists, publishers, and dozens of cover reproductions of scarce/rare books. Now with *color* covers!" circ. 1M. 5/yr. Pub'd 6 issues 2005; expects 6 issues 2006, 5 issues 2007. sub. price $35, $55 outside USA; per copy $10 + postage; sample $10 + postage. Back issues: $10 per issue + postage. Discounts: 40% on 5 or more of each issue. 100-110pp. Reporting time: 2-4 weeks. Simultaneous submissions accepted: no. Payment: copies and other arrangements. Copyrighted, reverts to author. Pub's reviews: dozens in 2005. §Non-fiction. Ads: $50/$25. Subjects: Arts, Bibliography, Book Arts, Book Collecting, Bookselling, Collectibles, Crime, Fantasy, Sherlock Holmes, H.P. Lovecraft, Mystery, Science Fiction, Writers/Writing.

PAPERPLATES, Bernard Kelly, Editor and Publisher; Tim Conley, Reviews Editor; Colleen Flood, Poetry Editor; Bethany Gibson, Fiction Editor, 19 Kenwood Avenue, Toronto, ON M6C 2R8, Canada. 1991. Poetry, fiction, articles, art, photos, cartoons, interviews, satire, criticism, reviews, letters, parts-of-novels, plays, non-fiction. "Online only. Average length for secondary pieces (reviews, opinions, etc.) is 2,500 words. Maximum length for feature articles is 5,000 words. Maximum length for poetry is 1,500 words." 4/yr. Pub'd 2 issues 2005; expects 4 issues 2006, 4 issues 2007. 40pp. Reporting time: 3-4 months. Simultaneous submissions accepted: no. Publishes 25% of manuscripts submitted. Payment: none. Copyrighted, reverts to author. Pub's reviews: 6 in 2005. §Fiction, poetry, essays. Ads: $300/$150/$100 1/3 page/$75 1/4 page/$50 1/6 page. Subjects: Book Reviewing, Essays, Fiction, Literary Review, Poetry, Short Stories, Storytelling.

Paperweight Press, L. H. Selman, 123 Locust Street, Santa Cruz, CA 95060-3907, 831-427-1177 or 1 800 538-0766. 1975. Art. avg. press run 3M. Pub'd 1 title 2005; expects 2 titles 2006, 3 titles 2007. Discounts: 6 or more copies, 40%; Distributor 200 or more, 60%. 200pp. Reporting time: 4-6 weeks. Payment: TBA. Copyrights for author. Subjects: Antiques, Arts.

Para Publishing (see also PUBLISHING POYNTERS), Dan Poynter, Publisher, PO Box 8206 - Q, Santa Barbara, CA 93118-8206, 805-968-7277, Fax 805-968-1379, info@parapublishing.com, www.parapublishing.com. 1969. Photos, cartoons, news items, non-fiction. "Para Publishing specializes in non-fiction books on parachutes/skydiving and book writing/publishing/marketing. The technical parachute books and popular skydiving books have always been sold through non-traditional outlets. Publisher Dan Poynter is the author of 100+ books, 51 monographs and over 500 magazine articles, most of them on publishing. He serves as a consultant to the mail order and publishing industries and conducts workshops in Santa Barbara on book marketing, promotion and distribution. Poynter is a past Vice-President of the Publishers Marketing Association. No manuscripts, query first. Query regarding parachute and publishing books only. When offering a parachute manuscript, we want to know how many jumps you have made." avg. press run 5M-10M. Pub'd 7 titles 2005; expects 8 titles 2006, 8 titles 2007. Discounts: 6-199 40%, 200-499 50%, 500+ 55%. 250pp. Reporting time: 1 week. Simultaneous submissions accepted: yes. We publish 60% of manuscripts submitted, but we screen before submission. Payment: 6-8% of list price. Copyrights for author. Subjects: Publishing, Sports, Outdoors, Writers/Writing.

PARABOLA MAGAZINE, Natalie Baan, Managing Editor, 135 East 15 Street, New York, NY 10003-3557, 212-505-6200, Fax 212-979-7325, parabola@panix.com, www.parabola.org. 1976. Fiction, articles, art, photos, interviews, criticism, reviews, letters, non-fiction. "*Parabola* publishes articles (2M-3M words), retellings of traditional myths and stories (to 1500 words), and reviews (500-600 words). We look for material that explores the myth, symbol, ritual, and art of the world's religious and spiritual traditions. Past contributors have included Robert Thurman, Kathleen Norris, Helen Luke, Seyyed Hossein Nasr, Robert Aitken, P.L. Travers, Joseph Campbell, Ursula K. LeGuin. Issues are thematic: Addiction, Creative Response, Sense of Humor, Repetition and Renewal, Money, etc. Visit our website for guidelines, themes, and hints." circ. 24M. 4/yr. Pub'd 4 issues 2005; expects 4 issues 2006, 4 issues 2007. sub. price $26; per copy $7.50; sample $6.00. Back issues: $9.95, for 5+ $8.95 each. Discounts: 15% for agencies. 128pp. Reporting time: 3 months average. We prefer not to receive simultaneous submissions. Publishes 5-10% of manuscripts submitted. Payment: upon publication.

Copyrighted, reverts to author. Pub's reviews: 35 in 2005. §Mythology, comparative religion, anthropology, folklore, children's books,. Ads: $1075 full/$725 half/$415 1/4 page, rates go down w/multiple placement. Subjects: Folklore, Metaphysics, Myth, Mythology, Philosophy, Religion, Spiritual.

PARADIDOMI, Adrienne Lewis, PO Box 5648, Saginaw, MI 48603-0648, 989-529-5283; alewis@mayapple-press.com; www.mayapplepress.com. 1978. Poetry, fiction, reviews. "(par-ad-id'-o-mee); to deliver up treacherously by betrayal It is said that sometimes that our thoughts betray us. The poet George Herbert described his thoughts as "all a case of knives." How do thoughts betray? What is their modus operandi? Language. Our words are capable of delivering us into the hands of our rivals with all the finesse of a well-placed kiss. With this in mind, a creative writer must learn to use language responsibly. Poetry and fiction need to be fresh linguistically. The concrete and abstract elements of life that we are all intimately familiar with must be made new, must intentionally be comprised of many levels of language, and must cause the salubrious effect of engaging the reader.The Paradidomi Review is a semi-annual literary publication of Mayapple Press. Submissions are accepted on an ongoing basis. Please visit www.mayapplepress.com for more information on this and other Mayapple titles." circ. 250. 2/yr. Pub'd 1 issue 2005; expects 2 issues 2006, 2 issues 2007. sub. price $16.00; per copy $8.00; sample $5.00. Back issues: $5.00. Discounts: Bookstores, libraries, and classroom discounts: 1-5 Copies; 20% no returns, mixed titles OK 6 or more 3Copies; 0% consignment, mixed titles OK 6 or more Copies, 40% returnable, mixed titles OK 6 or more Copies; 50% non-returnable, mixed titles OK Any number, prepaid add 5% to discount above any order type Review publications may query for a review copy of latest titles.Wholesalers and Retailers may order from our website or through Partners Distributing. 100pp. Reporting time: 8 weeks. Simultaneous submissions accepted: Yes. Publishes 10% of manuscripts submitted. Payment: 2 copies of the publication. Copyrighted, reverts to author. Pub's reviews: 3 in 2005. §Poetry, Fiction, Creative NonFiction. Subjects: Creativity, Fiction, Poetry, Reviews.

Paradigm Publications, Robert L. Felt, Acquisitions Editor; Sabina Wilms Ph.D., Senior Editor; Nigel Wisemabn Ph.D., Senior Linguist; Eric Brand LAC, Clinical Editor, 202 Bendix Drive, Taos, NM 87571, 505 758 7758, Fax 505 758 7768, info@paradigm-pubs.com, www.paradigm-pubs.com. 1981. Non-fiction. "Scholarship and clinical excellence in acupuncture and oriental medicine." avg. press run 2M. Pub'd 4 titles 2005; expects 4 titles 2006, 4 titles 2007. Discounts: 40% net 30, library 20%. 500pp. Reporting time: 4-8 months. Simultaneous submissions accepted: yes. Publishes 1% of manuscripts submitted. Payment: 10%/15%/18% on net. Does not copyright for author. Subjects: Acupuncture, Alternative Medicine.

Paradise Publications, Christie Stilson, 8110 SW Wareham, Portland, OR 97223, 503-246-1555. 1983. Non-fiction. avg. press run 10M. Pub'd 2 titles 2005; expects 3 titles 2006, 3 titles 2007. 320pp. Reporting time: 2 months. Payment: negotiable. Copyrights for author. Subjects: Hawaii, Reference, Transportation.

Paradise Research Publications, Inc., Kenneth C. Burns, Box 837, Kihei, HI 96753-0837, 808-874-4876, dickb@dickb.com. 1994. avg. press run 3M. Pub'd 4 titles 2005; expects 4 titles 2006, 4 titles 2007. Discounts: 20% for 1 book, 40% for all over 1. 250pp. Reporting time: 1 week. Simultaneous submissions accepted: yes. Publishes 10% of manuscripts submitted. Does not copyright for author. Subject: Alcohol, Alcoholism.

PARADOXISM, Dr. Florentin Smarandache, Editor, 200 College Road, University of New Mexico, Gallup, NM 87301, 505-863-7647, fax 505-863-7532, smarand@unm.edu, www.gallup.unm.edu/~smarandache/a/paradoxism.htm. 1990. "*Paradoxism,* (formerly *The Paradoxist Literary Movement Journal*), is an annual journal of 'avant-garde poetry, experiments, poems without verses, literature beyond the words, anti-language, non-literature and its literature, as well as the sense of the non-sense; revolutionary forms of poetry.' We want avant-garde poetry, 1-2 pages, any subject, any style (lyrical experiments). *Paradoxism* was set up by the editor in 1980's as an anti-totalitarian protest, and it is based on an excessive use of contradictions, antitheses, antinomies, paradoxes in creation. No classical, fixed forms. We have published poetry by Paul Georgelin, Titu Popescu, Ion Rotaru, Michele de LaPlante, Claude LeRoy. Do not submit mss. in the summer." circ. 500. 1/yr. Pub'd 1 issue 2005; expects 1 issue 2006, 1 issue 2007. 52pp. Reporting time: 3-6 months. Simultaneous submissions accepted: no. Payment: 1 copy.

Paragon House Publishers, Rosemary Yokoi, 1925 Oakcrest Avenue, Suite 7, St. Paul, MN 55113-2619, Tel: (651) 644-3087, Fax: (651) 644-0997, www.paragonhouse.com. 1962. Non-fiction. avg. press run 3000. Pub'd 12 titles 2005; expects 11 titles 2006, 10-15 titles 2007. 280pp. Simultaneous submissions accepted: Yes. Publishes 2% of manuscripts submitted. Payment: Royalty payment twice yearly. Advance $1000. Copyrights for author. Subjects: Ethics, Holocaust, New Age, Philosophy, Political Science, Spiritual, Textbooks.

Parallax Press, Travis Masch Mr., Publisher; Rachel Neumann Mrs., Senior Editor, 2236B 6th St., Berkeley, CA 94710-2219, 510-525-0101; e-Mail info@parallax.org; web address http://www.parallax.org. 1986. "Buddhist and related books-especially how Buddhism might become more engaged in peace and social justice work. Primary author: Thich Nhat Hanh." avg. press run 4M. Pub'd 9 titles 2005; expects 8 titles 2006, 9 titles 2007. Discounts: standard. 200pp. Reporting time: 2 months. Publishes small % of manuscripts submitted. Payment: no advance, royalty. Copyrights for author. Subjects: Buddhism, Children, Youth, Non-Violence,

352

Religion, Zen.

PARENT TALK NEWSLETTER, Family Learning Association, Inc., Carl B. Smith, Director, 3925 Hagan Street, Suite 101, Bloomington, IN 47401, 812-322-9862, 800-759-4723, Fax 812-331-2776.

PARENTEACHER MAGAZINE, Carmen McGuinness, Editor-in-Chief; Michelle Banks, Managing Editor; Jennifer Bair, Managing Editor, PO Box 1246, Mount Dora, FL 32756, 352-385-1877, 800-732-3868, Fax 352-385-9424, rachat@aol.com. 1997. Poetry, fiction, articles, photos, interviews, criticism, reviews, letters, news items, non-fiction. "500-1500 words. Mail or e-mail submissions attention Carmen McGuinness." circ. 50M. 6/yr. Pub'd 4 issues 2005; expects 6 issues 2006, 6 issues 2007. sub. price $9.99; per copy $2.50; sample free. Back issues: none. Discounts: $1 per copy, minimum of 50 copies. 30pp. Reporting time: 1 month. Simultaneous submissions accepted: yes. Publishes 85% of manuscripts submitted. Payment: negotiable. Copyrighted, rights reverting to author negotiable. Pub's reviews: 10 in 2005. §Literacy, education, family, children, health, nutrition, children's books. Ads: $675/$510/$585 2/3 page/$330 1/3 page/$280 1/4 page/$160 1/8 page. Subjects: Adolescence, Children, Youth, Education, How-To, Language, Literature (General), Non-Fiction, Parenting, Reading, Young Adult.

Parenting Press, Inc., Carolyn Threadgill, Publisher, PO Box 75267, Seattle, WA 98175-0267, 206-364-2900, Fax 206-364-0702. 1979. Non-fiction. "Non-fiction; parent education." avg. press run 5M. Pub'd 1 title 2005; expects 3 titles 2006, 3 titles 2007. Discounts: contact publisher. 32pp childrens, 198pp parenting. Reporting time: 1-6 months. Simultaneous submissions accepted: yes. Publishes 1% of manuscripts submitted. Payment: case-by-case. Copyrights for author. Subjects: Children, Youth, Education, Family, Non-Fiction, Parenting, Picture Books, Sexual Abuse.

Pariah Press (see also HEELTAP/Pariah Press), Richard David Houff, 604 Hawthorne Avenue East, St. Paul, MN 55101-3531. 1992. Poetry. "Pariah Press is a non-profit chapbook publisher. Strictly solicited. We've lost most of our funding under the currentadministration (Bush); future projects will be limited." avg. press run 500. Pub'd 2-4 titles 2005. Discounts: none as yet. 24pp. Reporting time: we now *solicit*, only if money permits. Simultaneous submissions accepted: yes. Publishes 1% of manuscripts submitted. Payment: 50 copies. Copyrights for author. Subjects: Anarchist, Avant-Garde, Experimental Art, Beat, Dada, Humor.

Parissound Publishing, 30 Tamalpais Avenue, Larkspur, CA 94939, Fax 415-924-5379, parissound@aol.com, www.parissound.com. 1995. Fiction, non-fiction. avg. press run 10M. Pub'd 2 titles 2005; expects 3 titles 2006, 5 titles 2007. 175pp. Reporting time: 30 days. Simultaneous submissions accepted: yes. Publishes 30% of manuscripts submitted. Payment: negotiable. Copyrights for author. Subjects: Alternative Medicine, Fiction, Health, How-To.

Parity Press, Kim Anderson, 1450 W. Horizon Ridge Pkwy, B304-226, Henderson, NV 89012, 877-260-8989, 702-364-8988 fax, www.paritypress.biz, www.shiftingrings.com,. 2005. Fiction. "As a new small press, our goal is to provide books that ecourage and empower young people. We are actively seeking titles that provide a positve message to children - on up to young adult. Fiction novels preferred, but will consider others." avg. press run 4000. Expects 1 title 2006, 1 title 2007. Discounts: Distributor/Wholesaler discount = 55%Bookstore discount for 2-4 copies = 20% 5-99 copies = 40% 100+ = 50%. 175pp. Reporting time: 8-10 weeks. Simultaneous submissions accepted: Yes. Publishes 1% of manuscripts submitted. Payment: usual standard terms, depends on work. Subjects: Juvenile Fiction, Non-Fiction, Novels.

Park Place Publications, Kedron Bryson, 591 Lighthouse Ave #20, Pacific Grove, CA 93950-0829, 831-649-6640, Fax 831-649-6649, publishingbiz@sbcglobal.net, www.parkplacepublications.com. 1991. Art, non-fiction. avg. press run 1M. Pub'd 4 titles 2005; expects 4 titles 2006, 4 titles 2007. Discounts: 40% bookstores; 20% single title. 150pp. Reporting time: 30 days. Simultaneous submissions accepted: yes. Publishes 1% of manuscripts submitted. Payment: varies. Copyrights for author. Subjects: Aging, Autobiography, Business & Economics, Children, Youth, Genealogy, Horticulture, Medicine, Pets, Travel.

Parkway Publishers, Inc., Rao Aluri, PO Box 3678, Boone, NC 28607, 828-265-3993. 1992. Non-fiction. "Book on the history, culture and tourism of western North Carolina; 250-400 pages double spaced; emphasis on marketability to tourists." avg. press run 1M. Pub'd 10 titles 2005; expects 15 titles 2006, 20 titles 2007. Discounts: bookstores 5+ copies 40%. 200pp. Reporting time: 6 weeks. Simultaneous submissions accepted: no. Publishes 25% of manuscripts submitted. Payment: 10% on first 1,000 copies, 15% afterward. Copyrights for author. Subjects: Appalachia, Autobiography, Biology, Civil War, Education, History.

PARNASSUS LITERARY JOURNAL, Michele Leslie, Kudzu Press, 433 South 7th St., Suite 1508, Minneapolis, MN 55415. 1975. Poetry, articles, reviews. "We are open to all poets. Also open to any subject or style, but please keep it clean. Short poetry has a better chance. Will not accept over 24 lines. Recent contributors include: H.F. Noyes, Ruth Schuler, Eugene Bofelho, and Diana Rubin." circ. 150+. 3/yr. Pub'd 3 issues 2005; expects 3 issues 2006, 3 issues 2007. sub. price $18 for US and Canada, $25 overseas, make checks payable to Denver Stull; per copy $7; sample $3. Back issues: $3 (when available). Discounts: 20% to schools, libraries, and order of 5 or more. 50-75pp. Reporting time: 30 days. Simultaneous submissions accepted: yes. Publishes 10% of manuscripts submitted. Payment: due to increasing expenses, we are now asking that our contributors purchase a subscription or a copy of the issue they are in. Not copyrighted. Subjects: Haiku, Humor, Literature (General), Poetry.

PARNASSUS: Poetry in Review, Herbert Leibowitz, Editor & Publisher; Ben Downing, Co-Editor, 205 West 89th Street #8F, New York, NY 10024-1835, 212-362-3492, Fax 212-875-0148, parnew@aol.com, website www.parnassuspoetry.com. 1972. "Length varies from four pages to forty. Editorial policy is intentionally eclectic. Recent and forthcoming contributors: Adrienne Rich, David Barbe, Marilyn Chin, Tom Disch, Judith Gleason, Marjorie Perloff, Rafael Campo, Carl Phillips, Rikki Duconnet, Wayne Koestenbaum, Hayden Carruth, Seamus Heaney, Helen Vendler, William Logan, Eric Ormsby. Publish one or two unsolicited poems per year." circ. 1.75M. 2/yr. Pub'd 2 issues 2005; expects 2 issues 2006, 2 issues 2007. sub. price $24 individuals, $46 institutions; per copy $12-$15; sample $12-$15. Back issues: $10 per issue (indiv.), $20/issue (libraries). Discounts: 10% to magazine subscription agencies, 30% to bookstores. 350pp. Reporting time: 3 weeks to 2 months. Simultaneous submissions accepted: yes. Publishes 10% of manuscripts submitted. Payment: Essays: $200-$500; poems: $30/page. Copyrighted, rights revert to author on request. Pub's reviews: 60-80 in 2005. §Poetry, poetic fiction, non-academic poetry criticism. Ads: $250/$150. Subjects: Literary Review, Poetry.

Parthian, Gwen Davies, Publishing Editor, The Old Surgery, Napier Street, Cardigan SA43 1ED, United Kingdom, parthianbooks@yahoo.co.uk, www.parthianbooks.co.uk. 1993. Fiction. ""While Parthian has only been publishing for a relatively short period, it has made a significant impact on the contemporary English language literary scene in Wales."World Literature Today." avg. press run 1000. Pub'd 8 titles 2005; expects 10 titles 2006, 12 titles 2007. Discounts: Negotiable. 150pp. Reporting time: Eight weeks. Simultaneous submissions accepted: Yes. Publishes 10% of manuscripts submitted. Payment: 10% of cover price. Copyrights for author. Subjects: Drama, Fiction, Gay, Writers/Writing.

PARTING GIFTS, March Street Press, Robert Bixby, 3413 Wilshire Drive, Greensboro, NC 27408-2923, www.marchstreetpress.com. 1988. Poetry, fiction. "Poems any length—prefer up to 20 lines. Fiction to 1,000 words, but stress is on highly imagistic language." circ. 100. 2/yr. Pub'd 2 issues 2005; expects 2 issues 2006, 2 issues 2007. sub. price $18; per copy $9; sample $9. Back issues: $9. Discounts: write. 93pp. Reporting time: usually within 24 hours. Payment: 1 copy. Copyrighted, reverts to author. Subjects: Alcohol, Alcoholism, Anarchist, Avant-Garde, Experimental Art, Fiction, Poetry, Women, Zen.

Partisan Press (see also BLUE COLLAR REVIEW), Al Markowitz, PO Box 11417, Norfolk, VA 23517, e-mail: red-ink@earthlink.net, website: http:www.Partisanpress.org. 1993. Poetry, fiction, long-poems. "Looking for working class poetry or short stories-mostly poetry. Social/political focus but with a broad range. High quality writing, no polemics or screed." avg. press run 350. Pub'd 4 titles 2005; expects 3-4 titles 2006. 40-60pp. Reporting time: 3-6 weeks. Simultaneous submissions accepted: yes. Publishes 10% of manuscripts submitted. Payment: 40 copies. Does not copyright for author. Subjects: Communism, Marxism, Leninism, Culture, Feminism, Labor, Multicultural, Peace, Race, Socialist, Society, Worker.

PASSAGER, Kendra Kopelke, Mary Azrael, Christina Gay, Jessica Schultheis, 1420 N. Charles Street, Baltimore, MD 21201-5779, www.passagerpress.com. 1989. Poetry, fiction, parts-of-novels, long-poems, non-fiction. "Fiction and memoir: 4,000 words maximum. Poetry: 40 lines max per poem, 5 poems maximum. No reprints. Please visit Web site or contact us for current guidelines. *Passager* publishes fiction, poetry, and memoir that give voice to human experience. We provide exposure for older writers, with a special interest in those who have recently discovered their creative self. We also act as a literary community for writers of all ages who are not connected to academic institutions or other organized groups." circ. 1500. 2/yr. Pub'd 2 issues 2005; expects 2 issues 2006, 2 issues 2007. sub. price $20 for 2 years (4 issues); overseas US $25; libraries/institutions $34; per copy $8-$6; sample $6. 32pp. Reporting time: 3 months. Simultaneous submissions accepted: OK; Please notify if work is accepted elsewhere. Payment: 2 copies of issue in which work appears. Copyrighted, reverts to author. No ads. Subjects: Aging, Americana, Arts, Autobiography, Book Arts, Creativity, Language, Literature (General), Memoirs, Translation, Women.

PASSAGES NORTH, Kate Myers Hanson, Editor-in-Chief, English Dept., N. Michigan Univ., 1401 Presque Isle Avenue, Marquette, MI 49855, 906-227-1203, Fax 906-227-1096, passages@nmu.edu, http://myweb.nmu.edu/~passages. 1979. Poetry, fiction, interviews, parts-of-novels, long-poems, non-fiction. "*Passages North*'s primary interest is high quality poetry and short fiction, interviews and creative non-fiction. Contributors: Established and emerging writers; encourages students in writing programs. Recently published Tess Gallagher, Mark Halliday, Tony Hoagland, Jorie Graham, Jack Driscoll, Frances Leftkowitz, W.P. Kinsella, Jack Gantos, and Bonnie Campbell. Send SASE for submission guidelines. Submit all prose double-spaced with ample margins; use paper clips, not staples. Name and address on top right corner of top page; submissions returned only if an SASE (w/adequate postage) is included." circ. 1.5M. 1/yr. Pub'd 2 issues 2005; expects 2 issues 2006, 1 issue 2007. sub. price $13/yr, $25/2 yrs; per copy $13; sample $13. Back issues:

$2 (single back issues 1999 and earlier). Discounts: contact us. 225pp. Reporting time: 3 months. Simultaneous submissions accepted: yes. Publishes 5-10% of manuscripts submitted. Payment: 2 copies. Copyrighted, reverts to author. Ads: exchange ads only. Subjects: Communication, Journalism, Creativity, Fiction, Great Lakes, Humor, Literary Review, Literature (General), Michigan, Non-Fiction, Poetry, Prose, Short Stories, Surrealism.

PASSAIC REVIEW (MILLENNIUM EDITIONS), Richard P. Quatrone, c/o Ah! Sunflower Theater, 410-1/2 Morris Avenue, Spring Lake, NJ 07762-1320. 1979. Poetry, fiction, articles, art, photos, interviews, satire, criticism, reviews, long-poems. "No 'soviet poetry' please. Send real writing. Erotic work welcomed." circ. 100. 2-6/yr. Pub'd 15 titles 2005; expects 2-6 issues 2006, 2-6 issues 2007. sub. price $10; per copy $2 + 75¢ postage; sample $2 + 75¢ postage. Back issues: $2 + 75¢ postage. Discounts: inquire. Pages vary. Reporting time: immediate to indefinite. Simultaneous submissions accepted only if indicated. Payment: copies of magazine. Not copyrighted. Ads: $80/$40/$20/$10. Subjects: Literary Review, Poetry.

Passeggiata Press, Inc., Donald Herdeck, Editor and Publisher; Norman Ware, Int'l Editor, 420 West 14th Street, Pueblo, CO 81003-2708, 719-544-1038, Fax 719-546-7889, e-mail Passeggia@aol.com. 1997. Poetry, fiction, criticism, long-poems, plays. "Publishers of Third World literature (Africa, Caribbean, Middle East, Pacific, Asia), and the scholarship thereof: recently bio-lingual poetry collections (one poet per vol.) English language, English-Russian, English-Bulgaria, English-Hungarian and some architective books." avg. press run 1M-2M. Pub'd 15 titles 2005; expects 10-15 titles 2006. Discounts: 30% prepaid by retailers and wholesalers; 20% prepaid by libraries; 20% not prepaid, university bookstores. No discounts on single-copy orders 40% on prepaid 100 copies, 10 titles min. 175-250pp. Reporting time: 5-6 weeks, but often much longer or shorter. Simultaneous submissions accepted: yes. Publishes 3-5% of manuscripts submitted. Payment: usually 7.5% with small advance. Copyrights for author. Subjects: African Literature, Africa, African Studies, Architecture, Bibliography, Biography, Black, Business & Economics, Criticism, Drama, Fiction, Folklore, Indexes & Abstracts, Middle East, Music, Poetry, Theatre.

Passing Through Publications, Fiona Rock, 1918 23rd Street, San Francisco, CA 94107. 1996. Poetry, fiction, art, photos. "Our business is dedicated to publishing works of odd fiction." avg. press run 2M. Pub'd 1 title 2005; expects 2-3 titles 2006, 2-3 titles 2007. Discounts: 5+ copies 40%. 100pp. Reporting time: immediate. Simultaneous submissions accepted: no. Publishes less than 1% of manuscripts submitted. Payment: individual agreements. Copyrights for author. Subjects: Anarchist, Counter-Culture, Alternatives, Communes, Fiction, Lifestyles, Prose, Short Stories, Transportation, Women.

PASSION, Crescent Moon, Jeremy Robinson, PO Box 393, Maidstone, Kent ME14 5XU, United Kingdom. 1994. Poetry, articles, art, photos, interviews, criticism, reviews, music, letters, parts-of-novels. "Shortish mss. prefered; literature, media, cultural studies, feminism, arts topics." circ. 200. 4/yr. Pub'd 4 issues 2005; expects 4 issues 2006, 4 issues 2007. sub. price $17; per copy $4; sample $4. Back issues: $3 for 1, $2.50 for 2 or more. Discounts: Trade 20% on single order, 35% on 2+. 50pp. Reporting time: 2 months. Simultaneous submissions accepted: yes. Publishes 3% of manuscripts submitted. Payment: to be negotiated. Copyrighted, reverts to author. Pub's reviews: 100 in 2005. §Arts, literature, media, cultural studies, poetry. Ads: $20/$10/$5 1/4 page. Subjects: Arts, Biography, Book Reviewing, Creativity, Criticism, Culture, Emily Dickinson, Electronics, Feminism, Interviews, D.H. Lawrence, Literary Review, Literature (General), Magic, Media.

Passion Power Press, Inc, Jamie Binder, PO 127, Indianapolis, IN 46206-0127, 317-356-6885 or 317-357-8821. 2004. Poetry, fiction, satire, long-poems, non-fiction. "We specialize in first-time authors with a passion to communicate." avg. press run 5000. Pub'd 1 title 2005; expects 3 titles 2006, 5 titles 2007. Discounts: 40-55%. 300pp. Reporting time: 90 days. Simultaneous submissions accepted: Yes. Publishes 75% of manuscripts submitted. Payment: no advances, 12%-50% return to author based on sales volume. Copyrights for author. Subjects: Children, Youth, Erotica, Essays, Feminism, Fiction, Gay, Gender Issues, Lesbianism, Multicultural, Non-Fiction, Poetry, Sex, Sexuality, Social Work, Wine, Wineries, Women.

The Passion Profit Company, Walt Goodridge, PO Box 618, Church Street Station, New York, NY 10008-0618, (646)219-3565, info@passionprofit.com, www.passionprofit.com. 1992. Poetry, non-fiction. "We are interested in non-fiction. Primarily business "how to" which helps people discover, develop or profit from their passions." Pub'd 3 titles 2005; expects 3 titles 2006, 5 titles 2007. Discounts: 1 book15% discount2-4 books = 20% Discount5-9 books = 30% Discount1O + BOOKS = 40%. 200pp. Reporting time: 120 days. Simultaneous submissions accepted: Yes. Publishes 20% of manuscripts submitted. Payment: Varies. Call for details. Does not copyright for author. Subjects: African-American, Business & Economics, Caribbean, Entertainment, Finances, Inspirational, New Age, Poetry, Public Relations/Publicity, Publishing.

Passport Press, Jack Levesque, Miranda d'Hauteville, PO Box 2543, Champlain, NY 12919-2543, 514-937-3868, Fax 514-931-0871, e-mail travelbook@bigfoot.com. 1976. "Travel and children's items." avg. press run 10M. Pub'd 4 titles 2005; expects 6 titles 2006, 4 titles 2007. Discounts: 20% with payment (small orders); 6 copies, 40%. 400pp. Payment: as negotiated. Does not copyright for author. Subjects: Children, Youth, Latin America, Transportation.

Past Times Publishing Co., Jordan R. Young, Editorial Director, PO Box 661, Anaheim, CA 92815, 714-997-1157; jyoung@fea.net, www.oldtimeshowbiz.com. 1980. "Formerly Moonstone Press. Although we're not soliciting manuscripts, Past Times Publishing is not strictly a self-publishing operation. Have been in business 18 years and have titles by four authors, with books in the works." Pub'd 1 title 2005; expects 1 title 2006, 1 title 2007.

PAST TIMES: The Nostalgia Entertainment Newsletter, Randy Skretredt, 7308 Fillmore Drive, Buena Park, CA 90620, 714-527-5845; skretved@ix.netcom.com. 1990. Articles, reviews, news items. "News and reviews regarding movies and music of the '20s, '30s and '40s; also old-time radio, early television and popular culture. Nothing contemporary. Nothing about history or events outside the entertainment field. Nothing on antiques. No poetry." circ. 5M. 4/yr. Pub'd 3 issues 2005; expects 4 issues 2006, 4 issues 2007. sub. price $11; per copy $2.75; sample $3. Back issues: $3-5. 32pp. Reporting time: varies. Publishes 75% of manuscripts submitted. Payment: copies. Copyrighted, reverts to author. Pub's reviews: 60+ in 2005. §movies, music of '20s, '30s, '40s; old-time radio; early '50s TV; classic reissues strips/comic books. $100/$60 (class. no longer available; we do have small ads as low as $10). Subjects: Cartoons, Electronics, Entertainment, Movies, Music, Radio, Tapes & Records, Theatre.

THE PASTOR'S WIFE NEWSLETTER, Janice Hildreth, 8731 Brynwood Drive, Boise, ID 83704, janicetpw@email.msn.com, www.pastorswife.com.

THE PATERSON LITERARY REVIEW, THE NEW JERSEY POETRY RESOURCE BOOK, The Poetry Center, Maria Mazziotti Gillan, Editor, Passaic County Community College, College Boulevard, Paterson, NJ 07505-1179, 973-684-6555. 1979. Poetry, fiction, art. "Stories should be short. Poems: under 60 lines preferred. Poetry, fiction, reviews. 6 x 9 size for art work. Clear photocopies acceptable. *No unsolicited reviews.*" circ. 1M. 1/yr. Pub'd 1 issue 2005; expects 1 issue 2006, 1 issue 2007. sub. price $14; per copy $14; sample $14. Back issues: $14. Discounts: 40% for orders of 10 or more. 320pp. Reporting time: 6 months. Simultaneous submissions accepted: yes. Publishes 5% of manuscripts submitted. Payment: contributor's copies. Copyrighted, reverts to author. Pub's reviews: 7 in 2005. §Poetry, short stories, novels (particularly African American, Latino, Asian American, Native American), critical books on literature. Ads: $200/$100/$50 1/4 page. Subjects: Literary Review, Poetry.

Path Press, Inc., Bennett J. Johnson, President, PO Box 2925, Chicago, IL 60690-2925, 847-424-1620, fax: 847-424-1623. 1969. Poetry, fiction, non-fiction. "Path Press, Inc. has merged its operations with Third World Press, Inc., 7822 South Dobson Avenue, Chicago, IL 60619." avg. press run 5M. Expects 1 title 2006, 6-10 titles 2007. Usual trade discounts. 300pp. Reporting time: 90-120 days. Payment: no advance, 10% royalty for first 5M copies, staggered rate to 15% after that. Copyrights for author. Subjects: African Literature, Africa, African Studies, Biography, Black, Chicago, Children, Youth, Civil Rights, Fiction, Literature (General), Non-Fiction, Non-Violence, Politics, Third World, Minorities, World War II.

Pathfinder Press (see also NEW INTERNATIONAL A magazine of Marxist politics and theory), Steve Clark, Editorial Director, Mary-Alice Waters, P.O. Box 162767, Atlanta, GA 30321-2767, www.pathfinder-press.com; orders@pathfinderpress.com (orders); pathfinder@pathfinderpress.com (editorial); permis-sions@pathfinderpress.com (permissions). 1928. "Publisher of books on current events, history, economics, Marxism, Black studies, labor, women's liberation, Cuba, South Africa. Authors include Malcolm X, Nelson Mandela, Che Guevara, Fidel Castro, V.I. Lenin, Karl Marx, and Leon Trotsky. Accounts by participants and leaders of the Cuban Revolution; primary source material on Marxism, Russian Revolution, working-class movement. Distributor of New International, a magazine of Marxist politics and theory." Pub'd 4 titles 2005; expects 8 titles 2006, 5 titles 2007. Discounts: retail bookstores 40-42%; textbooks 25%; libraries pay full price. 300pp. Subjects: African Literature, Africa, African Studies, The Americas, Black, Communism, Marxism, Leninism, Cuba, Current Affairs, History, Labor, Latin America, Political Science, Politics, Socialist, Third World, Minorities, U.S.S.R., Women.

Pathwise Press (see also BATHTUB GIN), Christopher Harter, PO Box 178, Erie, PA 16512, pathwisepress@hotmail.com. 1997. Poetry, fiction, articles, art, photos, interviews, satire, criticism, reviews, non-fiction. "Looking to publish poetry or short fiction chapbooks of around 40-48 pages. Strong imagery desired. Nothing overly academic or Bukowskiesque. Query first to see if accepting new manuscripts. If so, send manuscript and cover letter. Will work with author to match their ideas/design to ours. Submission time: June 1 to September 15." avg. press run 150-200 initial run. Expects 2 titles 2006, 2 titles 2007. Discounts: sliding scale. 48pp. Reporting time: 1-2 months. Simultaneous submissions accepted: yes. Payment: author receives 15 author copies up front, 10% royalties on sales over initial 100. Copyrights for author. Subjects: Absurdist, Dada, Literary Review, Literature (General), Poetry, Prose.

The Patrice Press, Gregory M. Franzwa, 319 Nottingham Drive, Tooele, UT 84074-2836, 602-882-0906, Fax 602-882-4161. 1967. Non-fiction. "Full-length books, usually on history, primary emphasis on emigration to the American West in the 19th century." avg. press run 2M. Pub'd 6 titles 2005; expects 8 titles 2006, 8 titles

2007. Discounts: 1-4 20%, 5-9 40%, 10-24 42%, 25+ 43%. 300pp. Reporting time: 30 days. Publishes 1% of manuscripts submitted. Payment: 12.5% net. Does not copyright for author. Subjects: Arizona, Aviation, Biography, History, Missouri.

PATTERNS OF CHOICE: A Journal of People, Land, and Money, Peter Donovan, Erin Donovan, 501 South Street, Enterprise, OR 97828, 541-426-6490; pdonovan@orednet.org; www.orednet.org/~pdonovan. 1997. Articles, art, photos, cartoons, reviews, news items, non-fiction. "*Patterns of Choice* provides firsthand, on-site reporting about situations where people have engaged in conscous efforts to manage wholes (people, land, money) rather than issues, problems, agendas, species, fragments, or 'parts.' Agriculture, resource management, communities." circ. 250. 4/yr. Pub'd 4 issues 2005; expects 4 issues 2006, 4 issues 2007. sub. price $25; per copy $7; sample $7. 24pp. Reporting time: 6 weeks. Simultaneous submissions accepted: yes. Publishes 30% of manuscripts submitted. Payment: 5¢/word. Not copyrighted. Pub's reviews: 2 in 2005. §Holistic management, economic development. Ads: $100/$50. Subjects: Agriculture, Biology, Business & Economics, Counter-Culture, Alternatives, Communes, Ecology, Foods, Management, Pacific Northwest, Water.

PAVEMENT SAW, Pavement Saw Press, David Baratier, Editor, PO Box 6291, Columbus, OH 43206, 614-445-0534, info@pavementsaw.org, www.pavementsaw.org. 1994. Poetry, art, photos, interviews, reviews, concrete art. "Five poems, clean photocopy (prefer type quality) with cover letter. One page prose or 1-2 pages short fiction, are acceptable also. Always send attention getting devices with submissions. *Pavement Saw* seeks unusual poetry and prose. Peruse a copy for further indications of style and content. *Pavement Saw* rarely accepts previously published material, simultaneous submissions, and letterless mass submissions. Named emotion and greeting cards will be returned in flaming envelopes. There is one featured writer or section (20 pages or so) each issue. #5 George Kalamaras, #6 Julie Otten, #7 Sean Cole #8 The all unfinished male author interview issue(where famous male poets, including the poet laureate of Canada, are interviewed then stopped before completion). Odd themes are sprung inside each issue including The Minty Fresh Pirate Issue, The Man Po(etry), The Whitey Issue, The Ultimate (superhero) Issue and so on. Issues 1-7 are sold out. We are one of the few journals who focus on the prose poem & letter boundaries. Guidelines are in issue #10." circ. 551. 1/yr. Pub'd 1 issue 2005; expects 1 issue 2006, 1 issue 2007. sub. price $15/2 issues; per copy $8; sample $8. Back issues: $8. Discounts: 40% for 5 copies. 88pp. Reporting time: 1-4 months, we only read from June 1st to the end of August. Simultaneous submissions accepted, only from writers who have not had their first full length collection published. Publishes less than 1% of manuscripts submitted. Payment: 4 or more copies. Copyrighted, reverts to author. Pub's reviews: 18 in 2005. §Books of poetry by contemporary authors, and anthologies. Subjects: Avant-Garde, Experimental Art, Construction, Dada, Labor, Poetry, Prose, Short Stories, Surrealism.

Pavement Saw Press (see also PAVEMENT SAW), David Baratier, Editor, PO Box 6291, Columbus, OH 43206, info@pavementsaw.org, www.pavementsaw.org. 1994. Poetry. "Often, material for the full length books are chosen from authors previously published in Pavement Saw. Reading the journal and submitting pieces before sending material to the press would be more than necessary for full length titles. We have an annual chapbook competition and our we are the only publisher to have our chapbooks recently reviewed in Poets & Writers and Publishers Weekly. We also have a full-length book competition in July and August. Previous judges include Judith Vollmer, Bin Ramke, David Bromige and others. The winner receives $1,000. Query before sending for guidelines or contest rules. The 2nd Edition of *Hands Collected: The Poems of Simon Perchik 1949-1999,* 612pp was released in 2003. *Drunk & Disorderly: Selected Poems* by Alan Catlin, 186pp, was also released in 2003.Our catalog also includes Errol Miller, Gordon Massman, Richard Blevins, Dana Curtis, Jeffrey Levine, Rachel Simon, Julie Otten, Garin Cycholl, Steve Davenport, Rodney Koeneke, Kaya Oakes, Sheila E. Murphy and 42 other books." avg. press run 1M for full length books, 400 copies for chapbooks. Pub'd 8 titles 2005; expects 7 titles 2006, 8 titles 2007. Discounts: 40% for 5 copies or more. 80-612pp books, 32-40pp chapbooks. Simultaneous submissions accepted: yes. Publishes less than 1% of manuscripts submitted. Payment: negotiable. Copyrights for author. Subjects: Avant-Garde, Experimental Art, Construction, Dada, Gender Issues, Handwriting/Written, Labor, Poetry, Prose, Sports, Outdoors, Surrealism.

Paycock Press (see also GARGOYLE), Richard Myers Peabody, Editor, 3819 N. 13th Street, Arlington, VA 22201, Fax 703-525-9296, hedgehog2@erols.com. 1976. Poetry, fiction, art, photos, satire, reviews, long-poems. "Poetry titles: *Collected Poems* by Ed Cox. Fiction titles: *In Praise of What Persists* by Joyce Renwick. Anthologies: *Grace and Gravity: Fiction by Washington Area Women* ed. by Richard Peabody. Nonfiction: *Mavericks: Nine Independent Publishers* ed. by Richard Peabody." avg. press run 1M. Expects 1 title 2006, 1 title 2007. Dealer discount available. 60-100pp. Reporting time: 1 month. Payment: 10% of press run plus 50/50 split on sales if/when we break even. Copyrights for author. Subjects: Fiction, Poetry.

PEACEWORK, Sara Burke, Co-Editor; Sam Diener, Co-Editor, 2161 Massachusetts Avenue, Cambridge, MA 02140, 617-661-6130. 1972. Articles, art, photos, cartoons, interviews, satire, reviews, letters, news items, non-fiction. "*Peacework* focuses on 'global thought and local action for nonviolent social change.'" circ. 2K.

10/yr. Pub'd 10 issues 2005; expects 10 issues 2006, 10 issues 2007. sub. price $23, $14 student-low income, $1 prisoners; per copy $2; sample free. 24pp. Reporting time: 2 weeks - 1 month. Payment: free subscription. Copyrighted under a Creative Commons Attribution-Noncommercial-ShareAlike License unless author wishes to retain copyright. Pub's reviews: 14 in 2005. §Peace and social justice. Paid advertising not accepted. Subjects: African-American, AIDS, Anarchist, Chicano/a, Civil Rights, Counter-Culture, Alternatives, Communes, Environment, Feminism, Gay, Global Affairs, Human Rights, Multicultural, Non-Violence, Peace, War.

Peachtree Publishers, Ltd., Helen Harris, Submissions Editor, 1700 Chattahoochee Avenue, Atlanta, GA 30318, 404-876-8761, www.peachtree-online.com. 1977. Non-fiction. "Peachtree Publishers, Ltd. is interested in quality childrens fiction and non-fiction for all ages, and adult non-fiction and guides for the Southeast. To submit a manuscript, send complete manuscript(required for children's picture books) or an outline and 3 sample chapters, along with biographical information on the author, and a SASE large enough to hold the material. Please mark to the attention of Helen Harriss." avg. press run 5M-25M. Pub'd 30 titles 2005; expects 35 titles 2006, 35 titles 2007. Discounts: retail 12+ copies 50% non-returnable; 1-4 20%, 5-10 40%, 11-24 42%, 25-49 43%, 50-199 44%, 200-499 45%, 500+ 46% returnable; jobbers 50% on 50 or more assorted. Pages vary. Reporting time: 4-6 months. Simultaneous submissions accepted: yes. Payment: individual basis subject to contractual terms. Copyrights for author. Subjects: Children, Youth, Health, Parenting, Picture Books, Self-Help, Young Adult.

Peanut Butter and Jelly Press, LLC, Alyza Harris, PO Box 239, Newton, MA 02459-0002, 617-630-0945 phone/fax, www.publishinggame.com. 1998. Non-fiction. "No unsolicited manuscripts." avg. press run 50M. Expects 5 titles 2006, 5 titles 2007. Discounts: 1 copy 40%, 2-9 45%, 10+ 50%. 300pp. Subject: Health.

PEARL, Pearl Editions, Joan Jobe Smith, Marilyn Johnson, Barbara Hauk, 3030 E. Second Street, Long Beach, CA 90803-5163, 562-434-4523 phone/fax or 714-968-7530, PearlMag@aol.com, www.pearlmag.com. 1987. Poetry, fiction, art, cartoons. "We are interested in accessible, humanistic poetry and short fiction that communicates and is related to real life. Humor and wit are welcome, along with the ironic and serious. No taboos stylistically or subject-wise. Prefer poems up to 35 lines and short stories up to 1200 words. Submissions accepted September through May *only*. Our purpose is to provide a forum for lively, readable poetry and prose that reflects a wide variety of contemporary voices, viewpoints, and experiences and that speaks to *real* people about *real* life in direct, living language, from the profane to the sublime. Have recently published poetry by Kim Addonizio, Jim Daniels, Gerald Locklin, Lisa Glatt, and David Hernandez." circ. 600. 2/yr. Pub'd 2 issues 2005; expects 2 issues 2006, 2 issues 2007. sub. price $21 (2 issues)+ 1 poetry book; per copy $10; sample $8. Discounts: 2+ 40%. 128pp. Reporting time: 6-8 weeks. Simultaneous submissions accepted: yes. Publishes 5% of manuscripts submitted. Payment: 1 copy. Copyrighted, reverts to author. Subjects: Poetry, Short Stories.

Pearl Editions (see also PEARL), Joan Jobe Smith, Marilyn Johnson, Barbara Hauk, 3030 E. Second Street, Long Beach, CA 90803-5163, 562-434-4523 phone/fax or 714-968-7530, PearlMag@aol.com, www.pearl-mag.com. 1989. Poetry. "Currently only publish solicited authors and winner of our annual poetry book contest." avg. press run 500. Pub'd 4 titles 2005; expects 2 titles 2006, 2 titles 2007. Discounts: 2+ 40%. 80pp. Reporting time: 4-5 months (contest). We accept simultaneous submissions for our contest. Publishes less than 1% of manuscripts submitted. Payment: $1,000 + 25 copies (contest winners), 25 copies (solicited authors). Copyrights for author. Subject: Poetry.

Pearl's Book'em Publisher, Pearlie Harris, Shonia Brown, Keisha Whitehorn, Yvette Appiah, 6300 Powers Ferry Road, Suite 600, #272, Atlanta, GA 30339-2961, 404-373-4603, Fax 419-828-8202, bookpearl@book-pearl.com, www.bookpearl.com. 2000. Poetry, art, photos, reviews, music, long-poems. Expects 2 titles 2006, 3 titles 2007. Discounts: bulk,library,wholesalers, institutions, classrooms. 100pp. Reporting time: 4 weeks. Simultaneous submissions accepted: Yes. Payment: advances, royalty. Copyrights for author. Subjects: African-American, Arts, Audio/Video, Children, Youth, Christianity, Comics, Creativity, Culture, English, Essays, Graphics, Haiku, Literature (General), Music.

Pearl-Win Publishing Co., Barbara Fitz Vroman, N4721 9th Drive, Hancock, WI 54943-7617, 715-249-5407. 1980. Poetry, fiction, non-fiction. "We are not enouraging submissions at this time since we have a backlog of good material." avg. press run 3M. Pub'd 2 titles 2005; expects 2 titles 2006. Discounts: 40% trade; 20% libraries. Poetry 64pp, prose 250pp. Reporting time: reasonable. Payment: 10% hard, 7.5% paper. Copyrights for author. Subjects: Fiction, Poetry.

Peartree Books & Music, Barbara Birenbaum, PO Box 14533, Clearwater, FL 33766-4533, P/ F 727-531-4973. 1985. "No pre-k picture books. Accept manuscripts and queries for GRL-S that lend themselves to pen + ink drawings. Also subsidy works w/full color illustrations all levels Pre K-Gr. 8." avg. press run 1M-3M. Expects 5 titles 2006, 5+ titles 2007. Discounts: 20% libraries, retail 40% paper, 30% cloth, jobbers 50%+. 50pp. Reporting time: 6 weeks. Simultaneous submissions accepted: yes. Payment: percent of sales of book based on profit margin. Copyrights for author. Subjects: Animals, Animals, Birds, Children, Youth,

Fiction, History, Law, Magazines, Multicultural, Nature, Sports, Outdoors.

Pebble Press, Inc., Robert Piepenburg, 1610 Longshore Drive, Ann Arbor, MI 48105. 1957. Art, photos. avg. press run 4M. Expects 1 title 2006, 1 title 2007. Discounts: 40%. 159pp. Reporting time: 2 months. Payment: to be arranged. Copyrights for author. Subjects: Arts, Crafts, Hobbies.

Pecan Grove Press, H. Palmer Hall, St. Mary's University, 1 Camino Santa Maria, San Antonio, TX 78228, 210-436-3441. 1985. Poetry. "Pecan Grove Press publishes contemporary poetry with an emphasis on first book poets and with roots grounded in its origins in Texas, though not limited to regional authors." avg. press run 375. Pub'd 4 titles 2005; expects 5 titles 2006, 5 titles 2007. Discounts: 30% Discount to Booksellers40% Discount to Baker and Taylor. 60-70pp. Reporting time: 2-3 months. Simultaneous submissions accepted: Yes. Publishes 3% of manuscripts submitted. Payment: 50% after cost of printing is recovered. Copyrights for author. Subject: Poetry.

THE PEDESTAL MAGAZINE.COM, John Amen, Editor in Chief; Nathan Leslie, Fiction Editor, 704-889-2787, pedestalmagazine@aol.com, www.thepedestalmagazine.com. 2000. Poetry, fiction, art, photos, interviews, non-fiction. "On-line only journal. Previously featured writers include Maxime Kumin, Sharon Olds, W.S. Merwin, Ai, and Thomas Lux. Other prominent features include an interactive Forum, an online Art Gallery and Bookstore." circ. 11,000 per month. 6/yr. Expects 6 issues 2006, 6 issues 2007. sub. price free. Back issues: archived on the website, no charge. 30pp. Reporting time: 1-2 months. Simultaneous submissions accepted: yes. Publishes 2% of manuscripts submitted. Payment: poetry: $30/poem, Fiction and Nonfiction: 5¢/word, 6,000 word max. Copyrighted, rights revert to author, however we retain the right to republish in subsequent issue or anthology. Pub's reviews: 2 in 2005. §See submit page on website for instructions. Ads: banner ads $150 per month on prominent pages. Subjects: Arts, Fiction, Internet, Interviews, Magazines, Non-Fiction, Poetry, Visual Arts.

Pedestal Press, Deborah Cardile, PO Box 6093, Yorkville Station, New York, NY 10128, 212-876-5119. 1991. Non-fiction. "Office address: 170 East 89th Street, New York, NY 10128." avg. press run 5M. Expects 2 titles 2006, 2-3 titles 2007. Discounts: 2-4 20%, 5-99 40%, 100+ 50%. 250pp. Reporting time: 60-90 days. Payment: 10% of retail price on first 5M copies sold, 12.5% on next 5M, 15% on copies sold over 10M. Copyrights for author. Subjects: Cooking, Health, Non-Fiction, Psychology, Romance, Self-Help.

PEDIATRICS FOR PARENTS, Richard J. Sagall, PO Box 63716, Philadelphia, PA 19147-7516, 215-625-9609, richsagall@pedsforparents.com, www.pedsforparents.com. 1981. Non-fiction. "*Pediatrics for Parents* is the newsletter for parents and others who care for children." circ. 35M. 12/yr. Pub'd 12 issues 2005; expects 12 issues 2006, 12 issues 2007. sub. price $20; per copy $3; sample $3. Back issues: $5. Discounts: write for details. 12pp. Reporting time: 30-60 days. Simultaneous submissions accepted: yes. Publishes 50% of manuscripts submitted. Payment: $25-$50. Copyrighted, reverts to author. Ads: none. Subjects: Health, Parenting.

PEGASUS, M.E. Hildebrand, Pegasus Publishing, PO Box 61324, Boulder City, NV 89006-1324. 1986. Poetry. circ. 200. 4/yr. Pub'd 4 issues 2005; expects 4 issues 2006, 4 issues 2007. sub. price $20, int'l add $5 postage; per copy $6 includes postage; sample $6 includes postage. Back issues: $6 includes postage. 32pp. Reporting time: 2 weeks. Simultaneous submissions accepted: no. Publishes 10-15% of manuscripts submitted. Payment: publication. Copyrighted, reverts to author. §Poetry publishing. Subject: Poetry.

Pegasus Communications, Inc., Janice Molloy, Content Director; Kali Saposnick, Publications Editor, 1 Moody Street, Waltham, MA 02453-5339. 1989. Non-fiction. "Specific articles/books related to organizational learning and systems thinking (a management science). Not general management. Contributors include Daniel Kim, Peter Senge, Russell Ackoff, Jay Forrester, Margaret Wheatley, Chris Argyris. Work in dialogue, Appreciative Inquiry, Servant Leadership." avg. press run 4M. Pub'd 4 titles 2005; expects 2 titles 2006, 3 titles 2007. Discounts: bulk, resale. 75pp. Reporting time: 3 months. Simultaneous submissions accepted: yes. Publishes 5% of manuscripts submitted. Payment: usually sliding scale based on quantities sold, starts at 10%. Copyrights for author. Subjects: Leadership, Management.

THE PEGASUS REVIEW, Art Bounds, PO Box 88, Henderson, MD 21640-0088, 410-482-6736. 1980. Poetry, fiction, art, cartoons, satire. "Upon publication writer will receive two copies of *The Pegasus Review*. Occasional book awards throughout the year. Recommend purchasing a sample copy to better understand format ($2.50) for 2003 themes - request by SASE. Upcoming 2003 themes: Jan./Feb. Books/Music/Art, Mar./Apr. Humor, May/June Memories/Dreams, July/Aug. Nature, Sept./Oct. Men & Women, Nov./Dec. The Written Word. Occasionally comments on returned manuscripts. Publishes 10 new writers a year. Recently published work by Jane Stuart, Peggy Fitzgerald, Michael Keshigian, and Robert Deluty, to mention a few. Advice: Read and write; write and read. Read what has been written in the past as well as what is current. Keep your work circulating. Get involved with a 'critiquing' group. Persevere." circ. 130. 6/yr + special issues. Pub'd 6 issues 2005; expects 6 issues 2006, 6 issues 2007. sub. price $12; per copy $2.50; sample $2.50. Back issues: $2.50. 10-12pp. Reporting time: 4-10 weeks. Simultaneous submissions accepted: yes. Publishes 35% of manuscripts submitted. Payment: 2 copies and additional book awards (throughout year). Copyrighted, reverts to author. Subjects: Fiction, Poetry.

Pella Publishing Co. (see also THE CHARIOTEER; JOURNAL OF THE HELLENIC DIASPORA), Leandros Papathanasiou, Publisher, President, 337 West 36th Street, New York, NY 10018, 212-279-9586. 1976. Poetry, fiction, articles, art, criticism, reviews, letters, plays, non-fiction. "We are interested in Modern Greek studies and culture, but also have a general list composed of new fiction and poetry by young writers and books on contemporary society and politics. We also publish books on the work of young artists." avg. press run 3M. Pub'd 4 titles 2005; expects 10 titles 2006, 10 titles 2007. Discounts: jobbers 30%, bookstores 20%. 176pp. Reporting time: 4-6 weeks. Simultaneous submissions accepted: no. Publishes 1% of manuscripts submitted. Payment: standard royalty arrangements. Copyrights for author. Subject: Greek.

Pellingham Casper Communications (see also THE ART OF ABUNDANCE), Paula Langguth Ryan, 1121 Annapolis Road, Suite 120, Odenton, MD 21113, 800-507-9244; 208-545-8164 (fax), www.ArtOfAbundance.com. 1998. Non-fiction. "Personal finance self-help inspirational titles." avg. press run 10000. Pub'd 1 title 2005; expects 2 titles 2006, 4 titles 2007. Discounts: 2-10 copies 25% bookstores/retailersdistributors 55% no returnsdistributors 40% returns allowed. 176-224pp. Reporting time: 3 months on queries, does not accept unsolicited manuscripts. Query first. Simultaneous submissions accepted: Yes. Publishes 25% of manuscripts submitted. Payment: 12%-15% royalty, paid quarterly. Does not copyright for author. Subjects: Finances, Inspirational, Marketing, Spiritual.

PEMBROKE MAGAZINE, Shelby Stephenson, Editor; Norman Macleod, Founding Editor, UNCP, Box 1510, Pembroke, NC 28372-1510, 919-521-4214 ext 433. 1969. Poetry, fiction, articles, art, photos, criticism, reviews. "Contributors: Felix Pollak, Fred Chappell, A.R. Ammons, Betty Adcock, Robert Morgan, Barbara Guest, Fleda Jackson, Judson Crews, Reinhold Grimm, Gerald Barrax, Ronald H. Bayes, Lee Smith, John Ehle, Michael Martin, and Jill McCorkle." circ. 500. 1/yr. Pub'd 2 issues 2005; expects 1 issue 2006. sub. price $10; per copy $10 (overseas $14.03); sample $8. Discounts: 40% bookstores. 275pp. Reporting time: 1-4 months. Simultaneous submissions accepted: no. Payment: copy. Copyrighted, rights revert to author, except for right of editor to reprint the magazine and to issue a *PM* anthology. Pub's reviews: 6 in 2005. §Native American poetry and novels. Ads: $40/$25. Subjects: Fiction, Literary Review, Poetry.

PEMMICAN, Pemmican Press, Robert Edwards, Co-editor; Ben Howard, Co-editor, PO Box 2692, Kirkland, WA 98083-2692, www.pemmicanpress.com. 1992. Poetry, articles, interviews, criticism, reviews, long-poems. "Our bias is toward literature that directly confronts the political and social issues of our time. We also would like to see poetry of imagery and imagination. We have published Sherman Alexie, Al Markowitz, and Marilyn Zuckerman." circ. 1000 approx. 2/yr. Pub'd 2 issues 2005; expects 2 issues 2006, 2 issues 2007. sub. price internet magazine. Reporting time: 1 month. Simultaneous submissions accepted: yes. Payment: none. yes/yes. Pub's reviews: 8 in 2005. §Political, poetry of "witness", social, feminist, working class, blue collar, erotica, prose poems, poetry of imagination, revolutionary. Also collections of essays, short fiction and creative non-fiction that are working class or political in nature. Ads: none. Subjects: Civil Rights, Communism, Marxism, Leninism, Erotica, Experimental, Literary Review, Literature (General), Pacific Northwest, Poetry, Politics, Socialist, Surrealism.

Pemmican Press (see also PEMMICAN), Robert Edwards, Ben Howard, PO Box 2692, Kirkland, WA 98083, thebenhoward@yahoo.com, www.pemmicanpress.com. 1992. Poetry, long-poems. avg. press run 300. Pub'd 2 titles 2005; expects 1 title 2006, 1 title 2007. Discounts: varies. Pages vary. Reporting time: 1 month, approximately. Simultaneous submissions accepted: yes. Publishes less than 5% of manuscripts submitted. Payment: none. Copyrights for author. Subject: Poetry.

PEN AMERICA: A Journal for Writers & Readers, 588 Broadway, Room 303, New York, NY 10012-3229, 212-334-1660 x115, Fax 212-334-2181, journal@pen.org, www.pen.org/journal. 2000. Poetry, fiction, articles, art, photos, interviews, criticism, letters, parts-of-novels, long-poems, plays, non-fiction. "*PA* publishes transcripts of PEN events and forums, as well as the work of PEN's award winners and members. *PA* does not accept unsolicited submissions except from members of PEN American Center." circ. 4M. 2/yr. Pub'd 1 issue 2005; expects 2 issues 2006, 2 issues 2007. sub. price $18 individual, $28 institute; per copy $10. Discounts: bookstore/classroom 40%. 240pp. Copyrighted, reverts to author. Ads: $600/$300.

Pendant Publishing Inc., Cathie Jorgenson, PO Box 2933, Grand Junction, CO 81502, 970-243-6465. 1982. Non-fiction. avg. press run 5M+. Pub'd 3 titles 2005; expects 3 titles 2006, 6 titles 2007. 300pp. Reporting time: 3 months. Simultaneous submissions accepted: no. Publishes 3% of manuscripts submitted. Payment: 10% net. Copyrights for author. Subjects: Business & Economics, Crafts, Hobbies, Motivation, Success, Public Affairs, Travel.

Pen-Dec Press (see also RAINBOWS WITH RED REMOVED; THE RAM'S CHIN'S GOATEE; SHEAR-CROPPER SALON (FOR THE HAIR-BRAINED)), Jim DeWitt, Editor, 2526 Chatham Woods, Grand Rapids, MI 49546. 1978. "No unsolicited mss. Poetry only: juiced, with zip. Must include letter of purpose, brief bio, SASE.'' Expects 1 title 2006, 1 title 2007. 24pp. Reporting time: 3 months. Simultaneous submissions accepted: yes. Publishes 1% of manuscripts submitted. Copyrights for author.

Pendragonian Publications (see also PENNY DREADFUL: Tales and Poems of Fantastic Terror; SONGS OF INNOCENCE), Michael Pendragon, PO Box 719, New York, NY 10101-0719, mmpendragon@aol.com. 1995. Poetry, fiction, articles, art, interviews, criticism, reviews, letters, long-poems, non-fiction. ''Poetry up to 5 pages (rhymed, metered, lyrical preferred), stories set in the 19th century or earlier. *Penny Dreadful* publishes tales and poems which celebrate the darker aspects of Man, the World and their Creator (Gothic/Romantic Horror). *Songs of Innocence* publishes tales and poems which celebrate the nobler aspects of mankind and the human experience. Recent contributors to *Penny Dreadful* include: John B. Ford, Laurel Robertson, Scott Thomas, Paul Bradshaw, Nancy Bennett, K.S. Hardy, Louise Webster, Karen R. Porter, James S. Dorr, Kevin N. Roberts, Charlee Jacob, Tamera Latham, Dennis Saleh, Ann K. Schwader, and Susan E. Abramski.'' avg. press run 200. Pub'd 4 titles 2005; expects 3 titles 2006, 2 titles 2007. Discounts: 1 year subscription (3 issues) $25. 200+pp. Reporting time: up to 1 year. Simultaneous submissions accepted: yes. Publishes 5% of manuscripts submitted. Payment: 1 copy. Does not copyright for author. Subjects: Essays, Fantasy, Fiction, Literary Review, Literature (General), Myth, Mythology, Poetry, Reviews, Short Stories.

PENNINE INK MAGAZINE, Laura Sheridan, Editor, The Gallery, Yorke Street, Burnley, Lancs. BB11 1HD, England, sheridansdandl@yahoo.co.uk. 1983. Poetry, fiction, articles, parts-of-novels, non-fiction. ''Quality poetry up to 40 lines. Prose/short stories up to 1,000 words. We publish once a year around December, so please do not send material until around August/September.'' circ. 400. 1/yr. price per copy £3, $6; sample £3, $6. Back issues: £2, $4. 48pp. Reporting time: 2 months. Simultaneous submissions accepted: yes. Publishes 10% of manuscripts submitted. Payment: free copy of magazine. Copyrighted, reverts to author. Ads: none. Subjects: Fiction, Poetry, Prose.

PENNINE PLATFORM, Nicholas Bielby, Editor, Frizingley Hall, Frizinghall Road, Bradford BD9 4LD, England, 01274 541015, nicholas.bielby@virgin.net, www.pennineplatform.co.uk. 1966. Poetry, criticism, reviews. ''The magazine depends entirely on subscriptions. Tries to keep a high standard. Copyrighted for contributors who retain copyright. Submit hard copy with SAE and/or email. No email submissions. Any poetry but concrete, prose poems or haiku. Religious (but not religiose) poetry accepted. Craft and intelligence preferred. Crit. given.'' circ. 300. 2/yr. Pub'd 2 issues 2005; expects 2 issues 2006, 2 issues 2007. sub. price £8.50 UK, £10 Europe, £12 elsewhere in world. Payable only in sterling. Payment by Paypal possible; per copy £4.50 UK, £6 abroad; sample £4.50 UK, £6 abroad. Back issues: £2.50 UK, £4 abroad. Discounts: bulk orders by agreement. 60pp. Reporting time: submissions usually considered Sept-Oct and Jan-March. Simultaneous submissions accepted: no. Publishes 10% of manuscripts submitted. Payment: contributor copy. Copyrighted. Pub's reviews: 8 in 2005. §Poetry. Subjects: Literary Review, Poetry, Reviews, Translation.

Pennsylvania State University Press (see also SHAW: THE ANNUAL OF BERNARD SHAW STUDIES), Fred D. Crawford, Penn State Press, Suite C, 820 N. University Drive, University Park, PA 16802-1711, 814-865-1327. 1951. Articles. avg. press run 2M. Pub'd 1 title 2005; expects 1 title 2006, 1 title 2007. Discounts: short-20%. 265pp. Reporting time: 2 months. Payment: 1 copy of the volume. Copyrights for author in name of publisher. Subjects: English, Literary Review, G.B. Shaw.

PENNY DREADFUL: Tales and Poems of Fantastic Terror, Pendragonian Publications, Michael Pendragon, PO Box 719, New York, NY 10101-0719, mmpendragon@aol.com. 1996. Poetry, fiction, articles, art, interviews, criticism, reviews, letters, long-poems, non-fiction. ''Art: black and white line art only. All must be in the Gothic/Horror genre.'' circ. 200. 1-2/yr. Pub'd 1 issue 2005; expects 1 issue 2006, 1 issue 2007. sub. price $25/3 issues; per copy $10; sample $10. Back issues: usually sells out the first month. 200+pp. Reporting time: up to 1 year. Simultaneous submissions accepted: yes. Publishes 5% of manuscripts submitted. Payment: 1 free issue. Not copyrighted. Pub's reviews: 30 in 2005. §Gothic, horror, romantic, literary. Subjects: Essays, Fantasy, Fiction, Literary Review, Literature (General), Myth, Mythology, Poetry, Reviews, Short Stories.

PENNY-A-LINER, Redrosebush Press, Ella M. Dillon, PO Box 2163, Wenatchee, WA 98807-2163, 509-662-7858. 1995. Poetry, fiction, articles, art, photos, cartoons, interviews, satire, criticism, reviews, letters, non-fiction. ''Prefer poetry 30 lines or less, other writings 500-1,500 words. Short stories, anecdotes, articles, essays, some poetry, puzzles, word games, jokes, cartoons all being accepted now. No pornography. Original work only. Please put name and address on each page. Please type all submissions, double-spaced. Send SASE if you desire an answer.'' circ. 1M+. 3/yr. Pub'd 3 issues 2005; expects 3 issues 2006, 3 issues 2007. sub. price $21; per copy $7.50; sample free. Back issues: $3.25. 52pp. Reporting time: when published. Simultaneous submissions accepted: yes. Payment: 1¢/word and copy. Copyrighted, reverts to author. Pub's reviews: 5 in 2005. §No pornography. Ads: $300/$200/$25 and up.

Pennycorner Press (see also THE INCLUSION NOTEBOOK), Gayle Kranz, Publisher, PO Box 8, Gilman, CT 06336, 860-873-3545, Fax 860-873-1311. 1994. Fiction, articles, photos, interviews, reviews, non-fiction. avg. press run 500-5M. Pub'd 2 titles 2005; expects 3 titles 2006, 3 titles 2007. Discounts: negotiated. 250pp.

Reporting time: 2 months. Publishes 1% of manuscripts submitted. Payment: negotiated. Copyrights for author. Subjects: Disabled, Education, Electronics, Health, How-To, Newsletter, Novels.

Penthe Publishing, Arthur Ward, PO Box 1066, Middletown, CA 95461-1066, 800-649-5954, 707-987-3470, penthpub@earthlink.net, penthepub.com. 1996. Poetry, fiction. avg. press run 5000. Expects 1 title 2006. Discounts: Retailers/Bookstores 40%Distributors 65%. 350pp. Reporting time: We are not accepting unsolicited mss at this time. Subjects: Birds, Birth, Birth Control, Population, Counter-Culture, Alternatives, Communes, Earth, Natural History, Ecology, Foods, Environment, Fiction, Humor, Literature (General), Men, Religion, Science Fiction, Singles, Sports, Outdoors, Women.

The People's Press, Shirley Richburg, 4810 Norwood Avenue, Baltimore, MD 21207-6839, (410)448-0254 phone/fax, (800)517-4475, biblio@talkamerica.net. Poetry, fiction, non-fiction. "We aim to move readers to try and make the world a better place than when we inherited it. "Excellence" with a human rights/dignity theme is the major criterion for publication. FAMILIAR, published in 2005, is our most recent work; this anthology includes submissions from Ken Anderson, Claudette Bass, Randolph R. Bridgeman, Jaclyn Brown, Tammie Burnsed, Carme'l Carrillo, Dane Cervine, Marcus Colasurdo, Larry Crist, F. Anthony D'Alessandro, donnarkevic, Maureen Tolman Flannery, Elisabeth Fogt, William Freedman, Elizabeth Gauffreau, Stephen Gibson, John Gilgun, etal." Discounts: 40%. Reporting time: Usually within a month or two. Simultaneous submissions accepted: Yes. Payment: Royalties are paid, along with copies of author's publication(s). Copyrights for author. Subjects: Adolescence, Aging, Community, Family, Fiction, Human Rights, Humanism, Lifestyles, Multicultural, Non-Fiction, Non-Violence, Novels, Peace, Poetry, Society.

PEREGRINE, Amherst Writers & Artists Press, Inc., Nancy Rose, Editor; Nancy Rose, Managing Editor, 190 University Drive, Amherst, MA 01002-3818, 413-253-3307 phone, awapress@aol.com, www.amherstwriters.com. 1981. Poetry, fiction, reviews. "*Peregrine* has provided a forum for national and international writers since 1981 and is committed to finding excellent work by new writers as well as established authors. We seek poetry and fiction that is fresh, imaginative, human, and memorable." circ. 1M. 1/yr. Pub'd 1 issue 2005; expects 1 issue 2006, 1 issue 2007. sub. price $25/3 years; per copy $12 postpaid; sample $10 postpaid. Back issues: varies. Discounts: call for info. 100pp. Reporting time: we read January to June and report on mss. within 4-6 months of deadlines. Simultaneous submissions accepted: yes. Publishes 1% of manuscripts submitted. Payment: 2 copies. Copyrighted, reverts to author. Subjects: Essays, Fiction, Poetry, Reviews.

Perikles Publishing, PO Box 5367, Naperville, IL 60567-5367, 630-244-2263, www.periklespublishing.com.

PERIPHERAL VISION, Ken Schroeder, Apartado 240, Portalegre, 7300, Portugal. 1998. Poetry, fiction, art, photos, cartoons, satire, parts-of-novels, long-poems, collages, plays. "A wretched little bilingual zine for semi-brilliant stray dog heroes wandering the Iberian plenitudes. 3000 word limit, more or less." circ. 100-200. 2-4/yr. Pub'd 2 issues 2005; expects 2 issues 2006, 4 issues 2007. sub. price $6; per copy $3. 40-50pp. Reporting time: fast. Simultaneous submissions accepted: yes. Publishes 25% of manuscripts submitted. Payment: copies. Not copyrighted. Subjects: Absurdist, Avant-Garde, Experimental Art, Beat, Bilingual, Dada, English, Erotica, Europe, Haiku, Journals, Portugal, Spain, T'ai Chi, Zen.

The Permanent Press/The Second Chance Press, Martin Shepard, Judith Shepard, 4170 Noyac Road, Sag Harbor, NY 11963, 631-725-1101. 1979. Fiction, satire, news items. "We publish original material and specialize in quality fiction." avg. press run 2M. Expects 12 titles 2006, 12 titles 2007. Discounts: 20-50%. 250pp. Reporting time: 8-12 weeks. Simultaneous submissions accepted: yes. Publishes .17% of manuscripts submitted. Payment: 10% net, small standard advances, for all writers. Copyrights for author. Subjects: Fiction, Literature (General).

Perpetual Press, Matthew Lucas, PO Box 3956, Seattle, WA 98124-3956, 800-807-3030. 1993. Photos, non-fiction. avg. press run 5-7M. Pub'd 2 titles 2005; expects 3 titles 2006. 300pp. Simultaneous submissions accepted: yes. Subjects: Business & Economics, Careers, Guidance, How-To, Japan, Non-Fiction, Pacific Northwest, Self-Help, Sports, Outdoors, Transportation.

Perrin Press, David Moncur, 1700 W Big Beaver Rd Ste 315, Troy, MI 48084, 248.649.8071, fax 248.649.8087, www.perrinpress.com. 2004. Fiction. "At Perrin Press, we believe that children's creativity is limitless, and our goal is to encourage this creativity by producing wonderful books that fuel young minds and let imaginations soar. We are committed to publishing well-written books that can be enjoyed by children and the adults who read to them." avg. press run 5000. Pub'd 1 title 2005; expects 2 titles 2006, 5 titles 2007. Discounts: 2-4 copies 20%5-9 copies 30%10-24 copies 40%25-49 copies 42%50-99 copies 44%100-199 copies 48%200+ copies 50%. 32pp. Reporting time: 2-3 weeks. Simultaneous submissions accepted: Yes. Copyrights for author. Subjects: Adolescence, Children, Youth, Dreams, Family, Fantasy, Fiction, Folklore, Magic, Myth, Mythology, Picture Books, Reading, Storytelling.

Persephone Press (see also Scots Plaid Press), Tom Tolnay, Editor-Publisher, PO Box 81, Delhi, NY 13753. 1987. Poetry, art, photos, long-poems. "Persephone Press is now an adjunct to Birch Brook Press, PO Box 81,

Delhi, NY 13753 and is exclusively for poetry. Poetry Book Publication Award Endowment series is for up coming workshop leaders or career poets who have published but no more than 2 books or chapbooks. No entry fee, no application process; must be nominated 24pg. ms. recommended *by university instructors or editors.*" avg. press run 250-500-1000. Pub'd 2 titles 2005; expects 5 titles 2006, 4 titles 2007. Discounts: orders of 5 copies 30%; of 10 copies 40%. 32-64-320pp. Reporting time: 1-6 months. Simultaneous submissions accepted: yes. Publishes 10% of manuscripts submitted. Payment: Persephone Press Award Series now endowed; no entry fee; 80-90% of edition paid as royalties in advance. Copyrights for author. Subjects: Haiku, Poetry.

PERSONAL EXCELLENCE, Executive Excellence Publishing, Ken Shelton, 1366 E. 1120 S., Provo, UT 84606, 800-304-9782; editorial@eep.com; www.eep.com.

Personhood Press, Cathy Winch, PO Box 370, Fawnskin, CA 92333-0370, 909-866-2912,Fax 909-866-2961, 800 429 1192, www.personhoodpress.com. 2003. Non-fiction. "Personhood Press publishes "Books for All that You ARE", primarily focusing on personal and/or spiritual growth and development. Recent publications include "Parenting Well in a Media Age" which provides parents with tools to teach kids to be discerning media viewers; "Coming Home: Community, Creativity and Consciousness" describes the value of "community" and how to create a healthy communities at work, locally, etc. "The Gentle Art of Blessing" offers lessons for living your spirituality in everyday life. "Modern Medicine: The New World Religion" shows how beliefs secretly influence medical dogmas and practices. "Love is Not a Game, But You Should Know the Odds" shows you how to search for a quality love relationship. "I Thought I Was the Crazy One" 201 ways to identify and deal with toxic people." avg. press run 2000. Pub'd 17 titles 2005; expects 2 titles 2006, 4 titles 2007. Discounts: 50% prepaid non-returnable Bookstores purchase through IPG (exclusive distributor for trade sales). 200-300pp. Reporting time: 1-4 weeks. Simultaneous submissions accepted: Yes. Publishes 10% of manuscripts submitted. Payment: 10% royalties, no advances usually, payment bi-annually. Copyrights for author. Subject: Non-Fiction.

Perugia Press, Susan Kan, PO Box 60364, Florence, MA 01062-0364, info@perugiapress.com, www.perugiapress.com. 1997. Poetry. "Perugia Press Prize: An award of $1000 and publication is given annually for a first or second unpublished poetry collection by a woman. Submit 48 to 72 pages with a $20 entry fee between August 1 and November 15. Send an e-mail, SASE, or visit the web site for complete guidelines. The winner of the contest is the only book we publish each year." avg. press run 800. Pub'd 1 title 2005; expects 1 title 2006, 1 title 2007. Discounts: standard. Reporting time: by April 1 for the annual contest. Simultaneous submissions accepted: yes. Copyrights for author. Subjects: Poetry, Women.

Petroglyph Press, Ltd., 160 Kamehameha Avenue, Hilo, HI 96720-2834, 808-935-6006, Fax 808-9335-1553, BBinfo@BasicallyBooks.com, www.BasicallyBooks.com. 1962. Non-fiction. avg. press run 2M. Pub'd 2 titles 2005; expects 2 titles 2006, 2 titles 2007. Discounts: 40% trade, 50% jobber, 55% 500+ books. 90pp. Payment: 10% author, 5% illustrator; paid quarterly. Does not copyright for author. Subjects: Crafts, Hobbies, Ecology, Foods, Folklore, Gardening, Hawaii, Health, Language.

Phantom Press Publications (see also MYSTERIES MAGAZINE), Kim Guarnaccia, Editor-in-Chief, 13 Appleton Road, Nantucket, MA 02554-2705. 1989. Fiction, non-fiction. "Will consider any length material - always include an SASE with submission." Expects 1 title 2006, 1 title 2007. Discounts: 40% thru distributor. 144pp. Reporting time: 3-6 weeks. Simultaneous submissions accepted: yes. Publishes 10% of manuscripts submitted. Payment: contributors copies only. Does not copyright for author. Subjects: Environment, Fiction, New Age, Science Fiction, Short Stories.

Phelps Publishing Company, PO Box 22401, Cleveland, OH 44122, 216-433-2531, 216-752-4938. 1993. Art, cartoons, non-fiction. avg. press run 3M. Expects 2 titles 2006, 3 titles 2007. Discounts: jobber 50-55%, trade 30-40%, bulk 65-70%. 80pp. Reporting time: 6-8 weeks. We Publish art instruction books and graphic novels. Send non-returnable samples for consideration. Copyrights for author. Subjects: African-American, Arts, Asian-American, Book Arts, Children, Youth, Comics, Fantasy, How-To, Multicultural, Native American, Visual Arts.

PHILADELPHIA POETS, Rosemary Cappello, 1919 Chestnut Street, Apartment 1721, Philadelphia, PA 19103-3430, redrose108@comcast.net. 1980. Poetry, art, reviews. "*Philadelphia Poets* does not publish poets from Philadelphia only. The editor believes in the humanistic ideals of those who founded Philadelphia, and since it originates from that city, thus the name. Although it seeks to provide a venue for current poets, tribute is paid to those of the past as well. Volume 9 Number 2 featured a special section on Writers and Readers Showcase, a group that was active in Philadelphia in the early 1980's. Volume 10 Number 1 contains ten pages of poetry by the late Jim Marinell. Volume 10 Number 2 pays homage to the late Almitra David with 12 pages of her poetry. Contributors have been Gerald Stern, Kate Northrop, Louis McKee, Ann Menebroker, Joan Jobe Smith, Fred Voss, Eileen Spinelli, Mbali Umoja, Beth Philips Brown, Lamont Steptoe, Aschak, Tommi Avicolli Mecca, Janet Mason and many other fine poets, approximately 40 poets per issue. Cover artists have been the late Sid Shupak, Sean Wholey, Barbara Barasch Rosin, Peter Quarracino, Lynn Liberman, Clifford Ward and

Nina Nocella.'' circ. 250. 2/yr. Pub'd 2 issues 2005; expects 2 issues 2006, 2 issues 2007. sub. price $25; per copy $10; sample $10. Back issues: $10. Discounts: Negotiable. 124pp. Reporting time: Six weeks. Simultaneous submissions accepted: No. Publishes 50% of manuscripts submitted. Payment: Two copies. Copyrighted, reverts to author. Pub's reviews: 6 in 2005. §Poetry and creative non-fiction. No advertising.

Philokalia Books, Sam Torode, 102 West Grove Street, South Wayne, WI 53587, 608-439-1763 phone/Fax (call first), storode@philokaliabooks.com, www.philokaliabooks.com. 2002. Fiction, non-fiction. ''Not currently accepting unsolicited manuscripts.'' avg. press run 3M. Expects 4 titles 2006, 4 titles 2007. Discounts: trade (terms - net 30) 1 copy 0%, 2-4 20%, 5-24 40%, 25+ 42%; wholesale (terms - 90 days) 25+ 50%, less than 25 subject to trade discount; catalogs (terms - 30 days) 46%. 200pp. Simultaneous submissions accepted: no. Copyrights for author. Subject: Religion.

Philomel Books, Patricia Lee Gauch, Vice President and Editor at Large; Michael Green, Associate Publisher and Editorial Director; Emily Heath, Editor; Courtenay Lewis, Associate Editor, 345 Hudson Street, New York, NY 10014, 212-414-3610. 1980. Poetry, fiction, non-fiction. ''We are a hardcover children's trade book list. Our primary emphasis is on picturebooks, with a small number of young adult novels and middle grade novels. We publish some poetry. We look for fresh and innovative books imbued with a child's spirit and crafted with fine writing and art. Recent selections include *Mister Seahorse* by Eric Carle, *Rakkety Tam* by Brian Jacques, *An Orange for Frankie* by Patricia Polacco, and *Eagle Strike* by Anthony Horowitz.'' avg. press run 5M-10M. Expects 25 titles 2006. Novels 200pp, picturebooks 32pp. Reporting time: 2 months on queries, 3 months on manuscripts. Simultaneous submissions accepted: yes. Publishes 1% of manuscripts submitted. Payment: varies. Does not copyright for author. Subject: Children, Youth.

Philopsychy Press, Stephen Palmquist, PO Box 1224, Shatin Central, N.T., Hong Kong, Contact us by phone (852-3411-7289), fax (852-3411-7379), email (ppp@net1.hkbu.edu.hk), or by visiting our web site (www.hkbu.edu.hk/~ppp/ppp/intro.html). First book published in September 1992; formally registered as a company in February of 1993. Non-fiction. ''Philopsychy Press exists for the purpose of encouraging and promoting scholarly author-publishing. Scholars (or scholarly-minded non-academics) who have a book they would like to publish themselves, but do not wish to bother setting up their own company, are invited to contact us for information about how we can assist you. Terms are negotiable, but normally a small percentage fee is charged in return for assigning an ISBN and (if necessary) arranging a printer in and shipping from Hong Kong.'' avg. press run 1500. Pub'd 1 title 2005; expects 1 title 2007. Discounts: bookstores 25% on consignment sales; 40% on advance payment. 250pp. Reporting time: 1 month. Simultaneous submissions accepted: yes. Publishes 10% of manuscripts submitted. Payment: negotiable. Copyrights for author. Subjects: Christianity, Dreams, Earth, Natural History, Human Rights, Law, Metaphysics, Non-Violence, Philosophy, Politics, Psychology, Religion, Self-Help, Textbooks.

Phi-Psi Publishers, Sean O'Connell, Box 75198, Ritchie P.O., Edmonton, AB T6E 6K1, Canada, phipsibk@netscape.net. 1999. Plays. avg. press run 500. Pub'd 2 titles 2005; expects 2 titles 2006, 1 title 2007. Discounts: 20-40%. 110pp. Reporting time: 2-3 months. Simultaneous submissions accepted: yes. Publishes 10-20% of manuscripts submitted. Payment: 10-15% of net. Copyrights for author. Subjects: Drama, Philosophy.

PHOEBE: A Journal of Literature and Art, Kati Fargo, Editor; Shawn Flanagan, Poetry Editor; Kelli Ford, Fiction Editor, MSN 2D6, 4400 University Drive, George Mason University, Fairfax, VA 22030, www.gmu.edu.pubs/phoebe/. 1971. Poetry, fiction, art, interviews, reviews. circ. 1.5M. 2/yr. Pub'd 2 issues 2005; expects 2 issues 2006, 2 issues 2007. sub. price $12; per copy $6; sample $6. Back issues: $6. Discounts: none. 128pp. Reporting time: 3-5 months, longer during summer. Simultaneous submissions accepted: yes. Publishes 3% of manuscripts submitted. Payment: two copies or subscription. Copyrighted, reverts to author. Pub's reviews: 2 in 2005. Ads: exchange ads accepted. Subjects: Avant-Garde, Experimental Art, Fiction, Literature (General), Poetry.

Phoenix Illusion, Shay Phoenix R, Publisher; Lynnet Decoteau S, Editor, PO Box 2268, New York, NY 10027, (917) 577-8499. 2005. Poetry, fiction, parts-of-novels, long-poems. ''Currently we only publish poetry and fiction (novels).'' avg. press run 500. Expects 2 titles 2006, 5 titles 2007. Discounts: 1 book No discoun t2-4 books 20% off 5-9 books 30% off 10-24 books 40% off 25-49 books 42% off 50-74 books 44% off 100-199 books 48% off 200 Or more books 50% off. 200pp. Reporting time: 1 to 2 months. Simultaneous submissions accepted: No. Publishes 10% of manuscripts submitted. Copyrights for author. Subjects: Fiction, Novels, Reviews, Short Stories.

PhoeniX in Print, Patricia Arnold, P. O. Box 81234, Chicago, IL 60681-0234, 877-560-0330, 312-946-9698 fax, info@phoenixinprint.com, www.phoenixinprint.com. 2004. Non-fiction. ''PhoeniX in Print publishes "books that make the spirit soar". Seeking uplifting, empowering, superbly written prose that is not preachy and does not promote fear.'' avg. press run 5000. Expects 1 title 2006, 2 titles 2007. Discounts: General 40% discount on orders placed directly with publisher. 300pp. Reporting time: One month. Simultaneous submissions accepted: Yes. Payment: Varies. Does not copyright for author. Subjects: African-American, Inspirational, Metaphysics, New Age, Non-Fiction, Relationships, Spiritual, Women.

Phony Lid Publications (see also PICK POCKET BOOKS), K. Vaughn Dessaint, PO Box 29066, Los Angeles, CA 90029, phonylid@fyuocuk.com, www.fyuocuk.com. 1998. Poetry, fiction, articles, art, photos, cartoons, interviews, satire, music, letters, non-fiction. "We accept manuscripts of any length with a focus on post punk urban gore." avg. press run 300 poetry, 500 fiction. Pub'd 16 titles 2005; expects 20 titles 2006, 20 titles 2007. Discounts: 25%. 36pp. Reporting time: 2 months. Simultaneous submissions accepted: no. Publishes 5% of manuscripts submitted. Payment: 25%. Copyrights for author. Subjects: Beat, Charles Bukowski, Culture, Drugs, Henry Miller, Short Stories.

Phrygian Press (see also ZYX), Arnold Skemer, 58-09 205th Street, Bayside, NY 11364, PhrygianZYX @ AOL.COM. 1984. Fiction. "Focus is on innovative fiction. Presently engaged in long term project: Arnold Skemer's *ABCDEFGHIJKLMNOPQRSTUVWXYZ*, a novella-continuum (=a series of novellae constituting a unity). Approximate completion in 2020. This and other works published in microeditions of 100. Binding done in house. In 1997, published Skemer's *Momus*, a novella-in-a-box, an unbound text to be read in random order. A chapbook series has now begun. Published *Metafictions* by Richard Kostelanetz and *E.S.P.* by Alan Catlin in 2001. Published Skemer's *E* in 2003.This is a spartan micropress with stark covers, low overhead, no frills, accepting no subsidies or grants, in full samizdat spirit of publishing." avg. press run 100. Pub'd 1 title 2005; expects 1 title 2006, 1 title 2007. Discounts: libraries and institutions 20%; wholesalers and bookstores 1-4 30%. 60pp; chapbooks 20pp. Reporting time: timely. Simultaneous submissions accepted: no. Payment: negotiable. Does not copyright for author. Subjects: Avant-Garde, Experimental Art, Dada, Fiction, Poetry, Surrealism.

Piano Press, Elizabeth C. Axford, PO Box 85, Del Mar, CA 92014-0085, pianopress@pianopress.com, www.pianopress.com, 619-884-1401. 1998. Poetry, fiction, music, long-poems, non-fiction. "Publish songbooks and CD's for music teachers and students, music teaching materials and some poetry. All work is original and/or public domain. All manuscripts are computer typeset." avg. press run 500-1M. Pub'd 13 titles 2005; expects 12 titles 2006, 10 titles 2007. Discounts: 40%-55% wholesale. 36-112pp. Reporting time: 2-3 months. Simultaneous submissions accepted: yes. Publishes 25% of manuscripts submitted. Payment: copies of chapbook or anthology for poetry, short stories and essays, standard print music and/or mechanical royalty for sheet music, songbooks and/or CDs. Copyrights for author. Subjects: Children, Youth, Music, Poetry, Tapes & Records, Technology.

Piccadilly Books, Ltd., Leslie Fife, PO Box 25203, Colorado Springs, CO 80936, 719-550-9887. 1985. Non-fiction. "Email orders to: orders@piccadillybooks.com." avg. press run 3M. Pub'd 4 titles 2005; expects 3 titles 2006, 3 titles 2007. Discounts: 6-23 45%, 24-99 50%, 100-199 55%, 200+ 60%. 150pp. Reporting time: 8 weeks. Simultaneous submissions accepted: NO. Payment: negotiable. Copyrights for author. Subjects: Alternative Medicine, Business & Economics, Health, How-To, Non-Fiction, Nutrition.

PICK POCKET BOOKS, Phony Lid Publications, K. Vaughn Dessaint, PO Box 29066, Los Angeles, CA 90029, phonylid@fyuocuk.com, www.fyuocuk.com. 1998. Poetry, fiction, articles, art, photos, cartoons, satire, reviews, music, letters, non-fiction. "We accept manuscripts of any length with a focus on post punk, urban gore." circ. 500. 2/yr. Pub'd 2 issues 2005; expects 2 issues 2006, 2 issues 2007. sub. price none; per copy $2; sample $3 previous, $5 current. Back issues: $2. Discounts: 25% over 20. 36pp. Reporting time: 2 months. Simultaneous submissions accepted: no. Publishes 5% of manuscripts submitted. Payment: copies and subscription. Copyrighted, reverts to author. Pub's reviews: 50+ in 2005. §Fiction, underground, post beat/punk poetry. Ads: none. Subjects: Beat, Charles Bukowski, Culture, Drugs, Henry Miller, Short Stories.

Pictorial Histories Pub. Co., Stan Cohen, 713 S. 3rd Street, Missoula, MT 59801, 406-549-8488, www.pictorialhistoriespublishing.com, fax 406-718-9280. 1976. Non-fiction. "Only do history books, mainly military." avg. press run 2-3M. Pub'd 6 titles 2005; expects 5 titles 2006, 5 titles 2007. Discounts: trade 40%, distributor 55%. 180pp. Reporting time: 1 month. Simultaneous submissions accepted: no. Publishes 10% of manuscripts submitted. Payment: 10%. Copyrights for author. Subject: History.

Pierian Press, C. Edward Wall, PO Box 1808, Ann Arbor, MI 48106, 734-434-5530, Fax 734-434-5582. 1968. "Biographies, reference books, resources on information literacy."

PIG IRON, Pig Iron Press, Jim Villani, Editor, 26 North Phelps Street, PO Box 237, Youngstown, OH 44501-0237, 330-747-6932, Fax 330-747-0599. 1974. Poetry, fiction, articles, art, photos, cartoons, criticism, parts-of-novels, long-poems, collages, plays, concrete art, non-fiction. "Compiled creative and investigative examinations of popular social themes. Energetic and inclusive of marginal insight. Length: open. Style/bias: open. Recent contributors: Winona Baker, Jeanne Carney, Joel Harris, Lyn Lifshin, Ed Meek, Leonard Moskovit, Dirk van Nouhuys, Julia Older, Jack Remick, Ed Schwartz, Laurel Speer, Karl Tierney." circ. 1M. 1/yr. Pub'd 1 issue 2005; expects 1 issue 2006, 1 issue 2007. price per copy $18.95; sample $5.00. Back issues: write for backlist. Discounts: 20% for 1 or 2copies, 40% for 3+ copies. 175pp. Reporting time: 90 days.

Simultaneous submissions accepted: no. Publishes 2% of manuscripts submitted. Payment: 2 copies, $5 per page fiction, $5 per poem. Copyrighted, reverts to author. §Forthcoming: Jazz Tradition; Frontier: Custom & Archetype; Years of Rage: 1960s; Religion in Modernity; 20th Century. No ads. Subjects: Arts, Avant-Garde, Experimental Art, Comics, Counter-Culture, Alternatives, Communes, Criticism, Culture, Culture, Dada, Design, Family, Feminism, Fiction, Graphics, Photography, Poetry.

Pig Iron Press (see also PIG IRON), Jim Villani, Publisher, 26 North Phelps Street, PO Box 237, Youngstown, OH 44501, 330-747-6932, Fax 330-747-0599. 1973. Poetry, fiction, art, photos, collages, non-fiction. "Want marginal and emphatic voices. We sponsor the Kenneth Patchen Competition -reading fee = $5." avg. press run 1M. Pub'd 1 title 2005; expects 2 titles 2006, 2 titles 2007. Discounts: 20%/40% for 3+ copies. Pages vary. Reporting time: 4 months. Simultaneous submissions accepted: no. Payment: 10% annually. Copyrights for author. Subjects: Anarchist, Arts, Dada, Fiction, Poetry, Politics, Science Fiction.

PIKEVILLE REVIEW, Sydney England, Editor, Humanities Department, Pikeville College, Pikeville, KY 41501, 606-218-5002. 1987. Poetry, fiction, articles, interviews, reviews. "We publish contemporary fiction and poetry, interviews, creative essays and book reviews." circ. 500. 1/yr. Pub'd 1 issue 2005; expects 1 issue 2006, 1 issue 2007. sub. price $4; per copy $4; sample $3. Back issues: $2. 112pp. Reporting time: 4 months. Simultaneous submissions accepted: no. Payment: copies. Copyrighted, reverts to author. Pub's reviews: 2 in 2005. Subjects: Appalachia, Criticism, Kentucky, Literary Review, Men, Multicultural, South, Women.

Pilgrims Book House, Rama Nand Tiwari, Founder, MD; John Snyder, Executive Editor; Christopher N Burchett, Editor, Thamel, PO Box 3872, Kathmandu, Nepal, 977-1-4700942, Fax 977-1-4700943, pilgrims@wlink.com.np, www.pilgrimsbooks.com. 2000. Non-fiction. avg. press run 1.5-3M. Expects 60 titles 2006. Discounts: 40%. 350pp. Reporting time: 60 days. Simultaneous submissions accepted: yes. Publishes 15% of manuscripts submitted. Payment: 10% annually in July. Does not copyright for author. Subjects: Asia, Indochina, Buddhism, Non-Fiction, Religion, Third World, Minorities, Transportation.

The Pin Prick Press, Roberta Mendel, 23511 Chagrin Boulevard #519, Beachwood, OH 44122-5539, 216-378-2253, Fax 216-378-2275. 1978. Poetry. "Published one index to all its publications 1978-80; only *books* published are those by Roberta Mendel. Re: Serial Publications: We copyright the issue, but not each individual submission used *within* each issue; copyright reverts to author on *written* request. *The Pin Prick Press* welcomes an exchange program with other small presses/magazines, involving its literary publications. We, as a service to other presses and self-publishers, will enclose promo material with its own promo literature. Send SASE for further details. We will continue to publish literature, but are also branching out into the travel field. See *Travel Planners* $3.00 each/$40.00 set. We published two literary titles in 1984; *War Poems* and *Jewish Poems*. Publication of our three literary serial publications: *Phantasmagoria, Journey Into The Surreal, Pastiche, Poems Of Place*, and *Snippets, A Melange Of Woman*, have been temporarily suspended. However, back copies are available, and a new generation of these publications will soon be in print." avg. press run 100-poetry; 1M-travel titles. Pub'd 1 title 2005; expects 2 titles 2006, 1 title 2007. Discounts: Available only on current travel publications of 2 or more copies/sets and only to distributors. 24pp (literary titles only). Reporting time: ASAP. Simultaneous submissions accepted: no. Publishes a variable % of manuscripts submitted. Payment: 1 contributor copy in which author's work appears. We copyright the issue, not the individual submission. Subjects: Bibliography, Haiku, How-To, Indexes & Abstracts, Judaism, Literature (General), Mathematics, Medieval, Philosophy, Poetry, Printing, Psychology, Reference, Religion, Reprints, Society, Transportation, Women.

Pinchgut Press, Marjorie Pizer, 6 Oaks Avenue, Cremorne, Sydney, N.S.W. 2090, Australia, 02-9908-2402. 1948. Poetry, fiction, non-fiction. "Australian poetry in particular, psychology (i.e., self help)." avg. press run 1.2M-3M. Pub'd 1 title 2005. Usual trade discounts. Reporting time: quite quickly. Payment: 10% retail price. Subjects: Children, Youth, Fiction, Poetry.

PINE ISLAND JOURNAL OF NEW ENGLAND POETRY, Linda Porter, PO Box 317, West Springfield, MA 01090. 1998. Poetry. "Submissions limited to poets currently residing in New England. Up to thirty lines, haiku and other forms welcome, no horror, no erotica, no previously published material. Please include cover letter with current bio. and SASE." circ. 200. 2/yr. Pub'd 2 issues 2005; expects 2 issues 2006, 2 issues 2007. sub. price $10; per copy $5; sample $5. Discounts: library discount available. 50pp. Reporting time: 6-8 weeks. Simultaneous submissions accepted: no. Publishes 10% of manuscripts submitted. Payment: $1 per poem, plus one copy. Copyrighted, reverts to author. Pub's reviews. §books of poetry by New England poets/editors published within the last twelve months. Subjects: Haiku, New England, Poetry.

Pine Publications, 2947 Jerusalem Avenue, Wantagh, NY 11793-2020. 1997. Non-fiction. avg. press run 3M. Pub'd 1 title 2005; expects 1 title 2007. 400pp. Simultaneous submissions accepted: no. Copyrights for author. Subjects: Education, Health, Medicine, Non-Fiction, Reference, Textbooks.

Pineapple Press, Inc., June Cussen, PO Box 3889, Sarasota, FL 34230-3889, 941-739-2219, FAX: 941-739-2296. 1982. Fiction, non-fiction. "We publish hard and soft cover adult trade fiction and nonfiction, as well as hard and soft cover books for children and young adults—all with a focus on the Southeast, and in particular, Florida." avg. press run 3M+. Pub'd 20 titles 2005; expects 21 titles 2006, 20 titles 2007. Discounts: trade 1-3 copies 20%, 4-15 40%, 16-49 42%, 50-99 43%, 100-199 44%, 200+ 46%. 300pp. Reporting time: 3 months. Simultaneous submissions accepted: yes. Publishes less than 1% of manuscripts submitted. Payment: negotiable. Copyrights for author. Subjects: Animals, Birds, Conservation, Cooking, Environment, Fiction, Florida, Gardening, Ernest Hemingway, History, Nature, Reference, Senior Citizens, Travel, Young Adult.

PINYON, Randy Phillis, Editor; Carol Christ, Poetry Editor; John Nizalowski, Fiction Editor, Dept. of Languages, Lit., & Comm., Mesa State College, 1100 North Ave., Grand Junction, CO 81502-2647, 970-248-1740. 1996. Poetry, fiction, long-poems. "No bias other than quality, though we appreciate a strong voice." circ. 300. 1/yr. Pub'd 1 issue 2005; expects 1 issue 2006, 1 issue 2007. sub. price $8; per copy $9; sample $3.50. Back issues: $3.50. Discounts: standard. 120pp. Reporting time: reading period Aug. 1 to Dec. 1, report in February. Simultaneous submissions accepted: Okay with notification. Publishes 5% of manuscripts submitted. Payment: copies. Copyrighted, reverts to author. Subjects: Colorado, Fiction, Poetry, Prose.

PIPERS MAGAZINE, Aircraft Owners Group, Jodi Lindquist, Editor, PO Box 5000, Iola, WI 54945, 715-445-5000; e-mail piper@aircraftownergroup.com. Articles, photos, interviews. "Aimed at owners and pilots of Piper aircraft." circ. 3,978. 12/yr. Pub'd 12 issues 2005; expects 12 issues 2006, 12 issues 2007. sub. price $42, includes membership in Piper Owner Society; per copy $4; sample free on request. Back issues: $3. Discounts: subscription only. 48pp. Reporting time: varies. Payment: 5¢/word and up, on publication. Copyrighted, rights revert to author after 30 days. Pub's reviews: 6 in 2005. §Aviation, pilot's skills and experiences. Ads: call for media kit. Subjects: Airplanes, Aviation.

Pirate Publishing International, Sarah Jane Kaserman, 6323 St. Andrews Circle South, Fort Myers, FL 33919-1719, 239-939-4845 phone/Fax, superK@juno.com. 1999. Fiction, articles, non-fiction. avg. press run 5M. Pub'd 2 titles 2005; expects 1 title 2006, 1 title 2007. Discounts: 45-55%. 300+pp. Reporting time: 3 months. Simultaneous submissions accepted: yes. Publishes 3% of manuscripts submitted. Payment: varies. Copyrights for author. Subjects: Children, Youth, Fiction, History.

PITCHFORK POETRY MAGAZINE, Pitchfork Press, Chris Gibson, Editor, 2002A Guadalupe #461, Austin, TX 78705.

PivotPoint Press, Robert Logan, PO Box 577468, Chicago, IL 60657-7468, 773-561-1512 phone/Fax, info@PivotPointPress.com, www.PivotPointPress.com. 2003. Non-fiction. avg. press run 5M. Expects 1 title 2006, 2 titles 2007. Discounts: standard. 264pp. Reporting time: 3 months. Simultaneous submissions accepted: no. Publishes 5% of manuscripts submitted. Payment: standard. Copyrights for author. Subjects: Business & Economics, Family.

The Place In The Woods (see also READ, AMERICA!), Roger A. Hammer, Editor & Publisher, 3900 Glenwood Avenue, Golden Valley, MN 55422-5302, Tel: 763-374-2120. 1980. Poetry, fiction, photos, interviews, criticism, reviews, letters, news items, non-fiction. "SAN 689-058X. Primarily interested in short biographies (and art) on significant achievements by American minorities—African-American, Women, Native People, Seniors, Handicapped/Disabled, Hispanic, War Vets, Gay/Lesbians, Young Achievers, Business Person, Asian/Pacific, other minority persons with significant but *little-known* contributions to the American culture. Well-documented personalities (such as African-Americans in sports or entertainment) are unacceptable. Interested in developing role models for minorities (adults and children). Need talented illustrators at whatever level, age who speak for their minority. Bios can run 50 to 500 words. Pays for completed work or leads. Queries recommended. Also looking for new material with themes appealing to elementary through seconday educational levels. Should be creative and original—subjects not found in general textbooks, yet of interest to mainstream Americans, young and adult." avg. press run 2M. Pub'd 1 title 2005; expects 2 titles 2006, 4 titles 2007. Discounts: 40% wholesaler/distributor; 40% to RIF programs; quantity rates on request. 30-80pp. Reporting time: 1 week-1 month. Simultaneous submissions accepted: no. Publishes 10% of manuscripts submitted. Payment: royalties vary with material, buys all rights with liberal reprint permission. Does not copyright for author. Subjects: African-American, Asian-American, Biography, Black, Book Reviewing, Chicano/a, Children, Youth, Civil Rights, Disabled, Education, Handicapped, Native American, Poetry, Third World, Minorities, Women.

PLAIN BROWN WRAPPER (PBW), Richard Freeman, 513 N. Central Avenue, Fairborn, OH 45324-5209, 513-878-5184. 1988. Poetry, fiction, articles, art, criticism, reviews, parts-of-novels, long-poems, non-fiction. "*PBW* comes out on floppy disc for Macintosh computers, so the only limitation is what can go onto a floppy disc. However, I can put in computer art if sent to me via floppy disc, and can print very long pieces if sent on floppy. Some contributors: Lisa B. Herskovits, Jennifer Blowdryer, Marie Markoe, Art Snyder, Danielle Willis, Anni Roberts." circ. 80 + several computer bulletin boards. 2/yr. Pub'd 2 issues 2005; expects 2 issues 2006, 2 issues 2007. price per copy $2. Back issues: $2. Discounts: none. 5-600pp. Reporting time: 1 week. Payment: 1 copy. Not copyrighted. Pub's reviews: 60 in 2005. §I will send material to my reviewers; prefer underground zines. Will trade. Subjects: Arts, Autobiography, Avant-Garde, Experimental Art, Book Reviewing, Computers, Calculators, Culture, Dada, Diaries, Dreams, Electronics, Erotica, Humor, James Joyce, Jack Kerouac, Los Angeles.

•**Plain Philosophy Center,** Mark Plain, 310 - 8870 Citation Drive, Richmond, BC V6Y 3A3, Canada, 1-604-276-8272. 1998. Non-fiction. "General Philosophy, Christian Philosophy, Philosophy of Science." avg. press run 2000. Expects 2 titles 2006, 5 titles 2007. Discounts: please contact us. 150pp. Reporting time: 3 months. Simultaneous submissions accepted: Yes. Publishes 2% of manuscripts submitted. Payment: please contact us. Copyrights for author. Subjects: Philosophy, Religion, Self-Help.

Plain View Press, Susan Bright, PO Box 42255, Austin, TX 78704, 512 441 2452. 1975. Poetry, fiction, art, photos, letters, long-poems, plays, non-fiction. "Plain View Press is an issue-based literary publishing house which has published 170 titles since it began in 1975. Our issue orientation began with feminism and has expanded to peace and justice, environment, and fair trade. We publish established and new writers. Please read publication guidelines at: http://www.plainviewpress.net/." avg. press run 700, offset, 100 POD. Pub'd 12 titles 2005; expects 24 titles 2006, 24 titles 2007. Discounts: library discounts vary, standard bookstore rates, call for more information, 512 441 2452, new titles filed with Lightning Source. 100pp. Reporting time: varies. Simultaneous submissions accepted: Yes. Publishes 5% of manuscripts submitted. Payment: Non-traditional profit and cost structure. We copyright in author's name. Subjects: Adolescence, Aging, Arts, Environment, Experimental, Family, Fantasy, Feminism, Fiction, Futurism, Global Affairs, Indigenous Cultures, Non-Violence, Poetry, Women.

Plains Press, David R. Pichaske, PO Box 6, Granite Falls, MN 56241, 507-537-6463. 1984. "We focus on material from the Minnesota/Iowa/South Dakota region—poetry, fiction and prose/critism/scholarship." avg. press run 1M. Pub'd 1 title 2005; expects 1 title 2006, 1 title 2007. Discounts: 2-5 20%, 6+ 40%, STOP 40% and add shipping. 176pp.

Planning/Communications, Daniel Lauber, 7215 Oak Avenue, River Forest, IL 60305-1935, 708-366-5200, fax: 708-366-5280, email: dl@planningcommunications.com, website: http://jobfindersonline.com. 1976. Non-fiction. "Prefer to publish books that help people: career books, dream fulfillment, business, politics, urban affairs, housing. Particularly interested in manuscripts that cut through ideological biases to deal with causes and solutions to problems. Interested in career books on subjects that have not already been exhausted by other authors. Length of material: at least 150 pages final book. Manuscripts should be prepared in a Windows-based word processor *without formatting* other than bold and italics." avg. press run 6M. Pub'd 1 title 2005; expects 3 titles 2006, 3 titles 2007. Discounts: trade standards (40%; standard return policy); bulk 10-29 copies 20%, 30-50 25%, 51+ 30%; write for classroom, jobber discounts. 280pp. Reporting time: 4 months. Simultaneous submissions accepted: yes. Publishes 5% of manuscripts submitted. Payment: contact us, varies with author, but better than industry standards. Does not copyright for author. Subjects: Business & Economics, Careers, Employment, Government, Public Affairs.

Plantagenet Productions (see also PLANTAGENET PRODUCTIONS, Libraries of Spoken Word Recordings and of Stagescripts), Westridge (Open Centre), Highclere, Nr. Newbury, Berkshire RG20 9PJ, England. Pub'd 1 title 2005; expects 1 title 2007.

PLANTAGENET PRODUCTIONS, Libraries of Spoken Word Recordings and of Stagescripts, Plantagenet Productions, Dorothy Rose Gribble, Director of Productions, Westridge (Open Centre), Star Lane, Highclere, Newbury RG20 9PJ, England. 1964. "Recordings of poetry, philosophy, narrative and light work on cassette, tape, LP. Family history: *Gribble Annals 1* by Charles Besly Gribble, Captain East India Company, Besly 1986, £2.25 plus postage; *Gribble Annals 2* by Henry Gribble, Captain, East India Company, 1988, £4.50 + p/h. *Milton Traditions,* compiled by F.G.M. Milton and D.R. Gribble, £10.50 + p/h (direct sales), 1990. *Gribble Annals 3: Family Letters 1822-1940,* 1992, £12.75 + p/h (direct sales). *Gribble Annals 4: Kinship* £16.50 + p/h (direct sales)." Erratic. Pub'd 1 issue 2005; expects 3 issues 2006. price per copy LP-£2.25, £2, £1 cassette £2.25, £1.75 postage extra. Subject: Tapes & Records.

THE PLASTIC TOWER, Carol Dyer, Roger Kyle-Keith, PO Box 702, Bowie, MD 20718. 1989. Poetry, art, reviews. "Prefer poems of two pages or shorter. No style or subject biases; our only 'no-no' is fiction. We just don't have the space to print stories right now! We read throughout the year, but typically are slowest in December." circ. 200. 4/yr. Pub'd 4 issues 2005; expects 4 issues 2006, 4 issues 2007. sub. price $8; per copy $2.50; sample $2.50. Back issues: free for large SASE with 3 stamps postage. Discounts: schools, libraries and bulk; write for details. 48pp. Reporting time: 5 months. Simultaneous submissions accepted: yes. Publishes 5% of manuscripts submitted. Payment: in copies. Copyrighted, reverts to author. Pub's reviews: 20 in 2005. §Poetry chapbooks and literary magazines. Subject: Poetry.

•**Platinum Dreams Publishing,** Jactesha Childress, P.O. Box 320693, Flint, MI 48532, jkash@platinum-dreamspublishing.com, (810)720-3390, www.platinumdreamspublishing.com. 2006. Fiction, music, non-fiction. Expects 1 title 2006, 3 titles 2007. 250pp. Reporting time: 6-8 weeks. Simultaneous submissions accepted: No.

368

Copyrights for author. Subjects: African-American, Fiction, Juvenile Fiction, Motivation, Success, Non-Fiction, Novels, Self-Help, Spiritual.

Platinum One Publishing, J. Shailander, Copy Editor; Jean Church, Editor Advisor, 30 Cooper Lake Road Suite A7, Mableton, GA 30126, www.platinumonepublishing.com, fax:1-203-651-1825, Email:customerservice@platinumonepublishing.com. 2003. Fiction, non-fiction. "Fiction or non Fiction, we tend to focus on the market for a particular manuscript first, its feasability and the companys' ROI. Once we acknowledge the solicited manuscript market we will partner with the author. There will be a collaborative effort on the entire project." avg. press run 3000. Pub'd 1 title 2005; expects 1 title 2006, 2 titles 2007. Discounts: 3-10-20% or 55% for no returns and net 60. 250-350pp. Reporting time: two weeks. Simultaneous submissions accepted: No. Publishes 100% of manuscripts submitted. Payment: Royalty payments will consist of 15% of net sales asside from the resources allocated in the project. Copyrights for author. Subjects: Advertising, Self-Promotion, Children, Youth, Consulting, Cooking, Creativity, Divorce, Drama, Fiction, Health.

Platonic 3way Press (see also FIGHT THESE BASTARDS), Don Winter, Co-editor and Co-publisher; Oren Wagner, Co-editor and Co-publisher; Steve Henn, Co-editor and Co-publisher, PO Box 844, Warsaw, IN 46581. 2005.

Platte Purchase Publishers, Alberto Meloni, PO Box 8096, 3406 Frederick Ave., St. Joseph, MO 64508-8096, (816) 232-8471,fax.(816) 232-8482, sjm@stjosephmuseum.org. 1992. Pub'd 2 titles 2005; expects 4 titles 2006, 4 titles 2007. Discounts: 40% discount for wholesale customers and educational institutions. Subjects: Book Collecting, Bookselling, Civil War, Research, The West.

Players Press, Inc., Robert W. Gordon, Vice President Editorial, PO Box 1132, Studio City, CA 91614-0132, 818-789-4980. 1965. Plays, non-fiction. avg. press run 2M-15M. Pub'd 28 titles 2005; expects 35 titles 2006, 35-50 titles 2007. Discounts: 20%-45% trade. 200pp. Reporting time: 3-6 months. Simultaneous submissions accepted: no. Publishes performing arts 12%, general 3% of manuscripts submitted. Payment: varies, dependent on material. Copyrights for author. Subjects: Arts, Avant-Garde, Experimental Art, Drama, Education, Entertainment, Shakespeare, Theatre.

PLEASANT LIVING, Brandylane Publishers, Inc., Robert H. Pruett, Editor; Mary A. Tobey, Associate Editor, 5 South 1st St., Richmond, VA 23219-3716, 804-644-3091. 1989. Poetry, fiction, articles, photos, reviews, letters, non-fiction. "Material must be regionally oriented. Read a copy of our publication before submitting. Our readers are a diverse group, from 30-80 years of age, educated, interested in the Bay and its preservation and interested in reading clear, readable prose." circ. 5M. 6/yr. Pub'd 6 issues 2005; expects 6 issues 2006, 6 issues 2007. sub. price $15; sample free. Back issues: $5. Discounts: 50%. 40pp. Reporting time: 6 weeks. Simultaneous submissions accepted: yes. Publishes 25% of manuscripts submitted. Payment: varies. Copyrighted, reverts to author. Pub's reviews: 8 in 2005. §Nonfiction, fiction, poetry. Ads: $700/$400. Subjects: Environment, Family, Gardening, Lifestyles, Non-Fiction, Poetry, Reviews, Short Stories, Virginia.

Pleasure Boat Studio: A Literary Press, Jack Estes, 201 West 89 Street, New York, NY 10024-1848, 212-362-8563 telephone, 888-810-5308 fax, pleasboat@nyc.rr.com, www.pleasureboatstudio.com. 1996. Poetry, fiction, satire, criticism, non-fiction. "Pleasure Boat Studio is a publisher, primarily in trade paperback editions (occasional chapbooks), of the best poetry, fiction, and non-fiction (in English language original and translation) that it can find. Query via email only with sample and cover letter. But please read what we publish before submitting a query. So much of what we get really doesn't fit. Also a new imprint: Aequitas Books. Also a new division: Empty Bowl Press." avg. press run 1-5M. Pub'd 5 titles 2005; expects 6 titles 2006, 6 titles 2007. Discounts: 1 copy 0%, 2-4 20%, 5+ 40%. Poetry 64-96pp, fiction and non-fiction 150-225pp. Reporting time: Not always very fast. Sometimes six months or longer. Much better if you submit electronically. Simultaneous submissions accepted: yes. We are a very small press. Chances of publication with us are correspondingly small. Payment: standard royalty contract. Copyrights for author. Subjects: African-American, Alaska, Buddhism, China, Culture, Environment, Fiction, Gay, Non-Fiction, Novels, Philosophy, Poetry, Satire, Sociology, Translation.

PLEIADES MAGAZINE-Philae-Epic Journal-Thoughts Journal, John L. Moravec, Editor-in-Chief, PO Box 140213, Edgewater, CO 80214-9998, fax: 303-237-1019. 1983; Philae founded 1947; Thoughts Magazine 1996. Poetry, fiction, articles, music, plays, non-fiction. "Short-shorts from 500-800 words." circ. 1.2M. 2/yr. Pub'd 2 issues 2005. sub. price $9; per copy $3; sample $3. Back issues: $2. 75pp. Reporting time: 2 weeks. Payment: copies or cash awards. Copyrighted, reverts to author. Pub's reviews: 2 in 2005. §General humanitarian and social. Ads: $1 per word/block ads 3 X 2-1/2 $25 two issues/customer furnishes ad (illustrations) black + white.

Plexus Publishing, Inc. (see also BIOLOGY DIGEST), Thomas H. Hogan, 143 Old Marlton Pike, Medford, NJ 08055, 609-654-6500. 1977. Non-fiction. "Publish a limited number of books on biology and natural history." avg. press run 2M. Expects 4 titles 2006, 4 titles 2007. Discounts: 40%. 200pp. Reporting time: 60 days. Payment: $500 advance against royalty of 10-15%. Copyrights for author. Subject: Science.

PLOPLOP, Geekspeak Unique Press, John Clark; Kit Andis, Contributing Editor, ploplopt@yahoo.com. 1991. Poetry, fiction, articles, art, cartoons, interviews, satire, reviews, music, letters, parts-of-novels, collages, plays, concrete art, non-fiction. "Bukowski, Vonnegut, Fielding, Dawson, Eileen Myles, Kit Andis, Gerald Locklin, Edward Field, Hal Sirowitz, Ferlinghetti, Kuda LaBranch, and Dan Grossman. pLopLop prefers poetry that is witty and brief, concise and with impact. Open to most forms except for the extremely conventional and academic. Future issues will focus on surrealist collaborations, also known as Flap Action Brain Splashes." circ. 300-500. 1/yr. Pub'd 1 issue 2005; expects 1 issue 2006, 1 issue 2007. sub. price $10; per copy $5; sample $5. Discounts: 20%. 50pp. Reporting time: 6-8 weeks. Simultaneous submissions accepted: yes. Publishes 5% of manuscripts submitted. Payment: 1 copy. Copyrighted. Pub's reviews. §Avant-garde, experimental, humor, music-pop/rock, surrealist collaborations, dada experiments, fluxus elaborations. Subjects: Book Arts, Jack Kerouac, Henry Miller, Surrealism.

PLOUGHSHARES, Don Lee, Editor; David Daniel, Poetry Editor, Emerson College, 120 Boylston Street, Boston, MA 02116, 617-824-8753. 1971. Poetry, fiction, parts-of-novels, long-poems. "Maximum length for prose 6M words. Read an issue or two before submitting. In the past, we announced specific themes for issues, but we no longer restrict submissions to thematic topics. Recent contributors: Joseph Brodsky, Rita Dove, Garrett Kaoru Hongo, Seamus Heaney, Carol Frost, Sharon Olds, Joyce Carol Oates, Michael S. Harper, Mary Oliver, Phillip Lopate, Sue Miller, Gerald Stern. Reading period: August 1 to March 31 (Postmark dates)." circ. 6M. 3/yr. Pub'd 3 issues 2005; expects 3 issues 2006, 3 issues 2007. sub. price $24/3 issues (individual), $27/3 issues (institutional), Add $12/yr for international.; per copy $10.95; sample $10.95. Back issues: prices vary. Discounts: 40% trade (6 copies or more); 10% agent. 224pp. Reporting time: 3-5 months. Simultaneous submissions accepted: yes. Publishes 1% of manuscripts submitted. Payment: $25/page prose, $50 minimum, $250 max. per author. Copyrighted, rights released on publication. Pub's reviews: 11 in 2005. §Quality literary poetry, fiction, non-fiction. Ads: $400/$275. Subjects: Criticism, Fiction, Literary Review, Poetry.

PLS, Chris Juhasz, 3605 W. Pioneer Pkwy. Ste. C, Pantego, TX 76013-4500, 800-328-3757, cjuhasz@plsweb.com.

Pluma Productions, PO BOX 1138, Los Angeles, CA 90078-1138, email pluma@earthlink.net. 1992. Poetry. "Will only consider works by Southern Dominicans - a Roman Catholic Order of Religious priests and brothers." avg. press run 1.5M. Expects 1 title 2006, 1 title 2007. Discounts: 40%. 96pp. Simultaneous submissions accepted: no. Copyrights for author. Subject: Poetry.

Plus Publications, Maria Rhinesmith, Managing Editor, 208 Bass Road, PO Box 265, Scotland, CT 06264, 860-456-0646, 800-793-0666, fax 860-456-2803, e-mail haelix@neca.com, http://plusyoga.necaweb.com. 1988. Non-fiction. "No submissions accepted currently." Discounts: trade 40%, wholesale 50%-60%. 200pp. Simultaneous submissions accepted: no. Subjects: Channelling, Feminism, New Age, Psychology, Religion, Self-Help, Spiritual, Women, Yoga.

Plympton Press International, Muriel Rile, 58 Christopher Drive, Princeton, NJ 08540-2321, 609-279-9184, Fax 609-279-9185, rilemuriel@cs.com. 1993. Non-fiction. "Books on Japan and other countries, especially relating to business/economics." avg. press run 20M. Expects 1 title 2006, 1 title 2007. Discounts: available upon request. 300pp. Reporting time: 1 month. Publishes 10% of manuscripts submitted. Payment: negotiated. Copyrights for author. Subjects: Adolescence, Business & Economics, Education, Japan, Sociology.

PMS POEMMEMOIRSTORY, Linda Frost, Editor-in-Chief, English Dept., HB 217, 1530 3rd Avenue South, Birmingham, AL 35294-1260, 205-934-5380, Fax 205-975-8125, lfrost@uab.edu, www.pms-journal.org. 2001. Poetry, fiction, non-fiction. "Our three principle genres are those listed in our title: poetry, memoir, and short stories. We publish exclusively work by women (and those posing as women), and look simply for the best and most catchy work we receive to print. We are *not* a goddess-promoting, menses-celebrating, chick-flick revering publication; we do *not* favor work *about* PMS. On the other hand, we're not afraid to be politicized. In an attempt to enhance the arts in our home state, we make it a point to publish at least some work by writers from Alabama, although we are by no means a regional journal. In each issue, we feature one memoir that we solicit (although suggestions here are welcome) from a woman who would not describe herself as a writer, but who has experienced something of national and historic significance (e.g., our first issue featured a memoir by Emily Lyons, the nurse critically injured in the 1998 bombing of the women's clinic in Birmingham). Writers we have published include Cathleen Calbert, Vicki Covington, Denise Duhamel, Elaine Equi, Amy Gerstler, Honoree Fanonne Jeffers, Allison Joseph, MaryJo Mahoney, Kat Meads, Lucia Perillo, Molly Peacock, Paisley Rekdal, Carly Sachs, Sonia Sanchez, Lori Soderlind, Ruth Stone, Natasha Trethewey, and Harriet Zinnes. We love the up-and-coming as much as we do the established and famous. Work from PMS has been republished in Best American Poetry (twice), Best American Essays, New Stories from the South, and has recieved honorable mention in the Pushcart Prize. PMS is distributed by Bernhard DeBoer, Inc. and Ingram Periodicals, Inc. We ask that submitters send up to five poems *or* fifteen pages of prose; not both. Our reading period each year is from September 1 through November 30." circ. 1000. 1/yr. Pub'd 1 issue 2005; expects 1 issue 2006, 1 issue 2007. sub. price $7; per copy $5; sample $6. Back issues: $6. 120pp. Reporting time: 2-8 weeks. Simultaneous submissions accepted: yes. Publishes 12% of manuscripts submitted. Payment: 2 copies and a 1-year subscription. Copyrighted, reverts to author. Subject: Poetry.

Pocahontas Press, Inc., Mary C. Holliman, President & Publisher, PO Drawer F, Blacksburg, VA 24063-1020, 540-951-0467, 800-446-0467. 1984. Poetry, fiction, non-fiction. "Our first trade book was the true story of the Golden Hill Indians of Connecticut told in the words of Chief Big Eagle. We are publishing a series of books for middle-school age children and teen-agers, short story length, in both Spanish and English with black-and-white illustrations; these are historical and biographical topics and most will be in the series Tales of the Virginia Wilderness. We are also interested in memoirs, family histories, poetry collections, and scientific monographs. We do not publish fiction unless it is closely tied to historical events and real people are main characters." avg. press run poetry 500, other 1M-3M. Pub'd 6 titles 2005; expects 3 titles 2006, 3 titles 2007. Discounts: for prepayment 5%, wholesalers: 1 20%, 2-50 40%, 51+ 50%. 80-180pp. Reporting time: 3 months or more. Simultaneous submissions accepted: yes. Publishes probally no more than 1% of manuscripts submitted. Payment: 10% royalty. Copyrights for author. Subjects: Americana, Appalachia, Bilingual, Biography, Chicano/a, Children, Youth, Communication, Journalism, Fiction, Folklore, History, Literature (General), Maine, Native American, New England, Third World, Minorities.

POCKETS, Lynn Gilliam, 1908 Grand Avenue, Nashville, TN 37203-0004, 615-340-7333,pockets@upper-room.org,www.pockets.org. 1978. Poetry, fiction, articles, art, photos, non-fiction. "The purpose of Pockets is the help children, ages six through eleven, grow in their relationship with God. Pockets is an interdenominational devotional magazine, with readers representing many cultures and ethnic backgrounds. Content reflects a variety of cultural backgrounds, rural and urban settings, and a variety of family units.The magazine presents an understanding of God that is whole and mature. We want to help children wrap themselves in Christian tradition and envision themselves in the light of that tradition. Through scripture, fiction, poetry, prayer, art, graphics, and activities, children see a Christian lifestyle that portrays an openness to the continuing revelation of God's will. The magazine emphasizes that God loves us and that God's grace calls us into community. Through this commuinty of God's people we experience God's love in our daily lives.Content encompasses a wide variety of concerns and needs. Each issue is thematic, based on issues faced by today's children. Pockets affirms children as persons created and loved by God. We strive to provide ways for them to experience God's love, to communicate with God, and to enable them to relate to people, to make decisions, and to learn how to show the love of God to others." 11/yr. Pub'd 11 issues 2005; expects 11 issues 2006, 11 issues 2007. sub. price $19.95; per copy $3.00; sample 9x12 SASE w/4 first-class stamps. Back issues: 9x12 SASE with 4 1st class stamps. Discounts: 10 copies $15.00/issue20 copies $30.00/issue30 copies $45.00/issue. 48pp. Reporting time: maximum of 6 weeks. Simultaneous submissions accepted: No. Publishes 5% of manuscripts submitted. Payment: made at the time of acceptance. Copyrighted, rights are returned to author one year after publication and upon request of rights from the author. No advertising. Subject: Children, Youth.

Pocol Press, J. Thomas Hetrick, 6023 Pocol Drive, Clifton, VA 20124-1333, 703-830-5862, chrisand-tom@erols.com, www.pocolpress.com. 1999. Fiction, art, photos, interviews, non-fiction. "Pocol Press is the leader in short fiction collections and baseball history from first-time, non-agented authors. Expert storytellers welcome. Recent fiction contributors include Colin Pip Dixon with *...in God's Flower Garden*, Nathan Leslie with *Believers* and *Playing Mac* by Grant Tracey. Most recent baseball books are *Foul Ball in Beantown* by G.S. Rowe and *Early Dreams* by David Nemec. Please see our website for more details, especially on purchasing and submissions. No electronic submissions, please. Distributed by Baker & Taylor." avg. press run 500. Pub'd 6 titles 2005; expects 6 titles 2006, 4 titles 2007. Discounts: 55% for bulk purchase from bookstores, 70% for classroom. 200pp. Reporting time: 1-3 months. Simultaneous submissions accepted: no. Payment: 1-2 payments per annum, 10% net. Copyrights for author. Subjects: Family, Fiction, Genealogy, Homelessness, Horror, India, Judaism, Memoirs, Poetry, Religion, San Francisco, Short Stories, Sports, Outdoors, Vietnam, World War II.

POEM, Rebecca Harbor, Editor; Georgette Perry, Assistant Editor; Nancy Compton Williams, Assistant Editor, P.O. Box 2006, Huntsville, AL 35804. 1967. Poetry. circ. 500. 2/yr. Pub'd 2 issues 2005; expects 2 issues 2006, 2 issues 2007. sub. price $20; per copy $10. Back issues: $7. 85pp. Reporting time: 1-2 months. Simultaneous submissions accepted: no. Publishes 5-6 % of manuscripts submitted. Payment: 2 copies. Copyrighted, reverts to author. Ads: none. Subject: Poetry.

POEMS & PLAYS, Gaylord Brewer, Department of English, Middle Tennessee State University, Murfreesboro, TN 37132, 615-898-2712. 1993. Poetry, art, plays. "Recent contributors include Rane Arroyo, Nancy Naomi Carlson, and Robert Collins. Short plays (10-15 pgs.) have a better chance of publication. We *read* for this spring annual from Oct. 1-Dec. 31, either open submissions or 20-24 page manuscripts for the Tennessee Chapbook Prize. Contest entries can be any combo of poetry and drama. Winner is published as interior chapbook in *Poems & Plays*. Recent winners are Laura Maria Censabella (drama) and Julie Lechevsky (poetry). Author receives 50 copies of issue. For contest, SASE and $10 (for reading fee and one copy of issue) required. *Poems & Plays* was awarded a Pipistrelle, Best of the Small Presses Award in 2000.'' circ. 800. 1/yr. Pub'd 1 issue 2005; expects 1 issue 2006, 1 issue 2007. sub. price $10/2 issues; per copy $6; sample $6. Back issues: please call or write for availability. Discounts: please call/write. 80+pp. Reporting time: 1-2 months. Publishes 2% of manuscripts submitted. Payment: 1 copy. Copyrighted, reverts to author. Ads: none. Subjects: Drama, Poetry.

POESIA, Jay Ross, Editor in Chief, Executive Square, One West Mountain Street, Fayetteville, AR 72701, Telephone 479.444.9323,Fax 479.444.9326, www.indianbaypress.com. 2003. Poetry. ''We provide a forum featuring previously unpublished poets.'' circ. 2000. 4/yr. Pub'd 1000 issues 2005; expects 2000 issues 2006, 3000 issues 2007. sub. price 12.00; per copy 3.75; sample free. Back issues: inquire. Discounts: 50%. 60pp. Reporting time: 1 week. Simultaneous submissions accepted: No. Publishes 40% of manuscripts submitted. Payment: $ 10.00 per poem plus 2 free contributor copies of the issue in which the work appears. Copyrighted, reverts to author. Pub's reviews: 4 in 2005. §poetry. Ads: full page $ 450.00. Subject: Poetry.

POESY MAGAZINE, Brian Morrisey, Doug Holder, P.O. Box 7823, Santa Cruz, CA 95061, www.poesy.org, info@poesy.org. 1990. Poetry, articles, art, photos, interviews, criticism, reviews. ''POESY MAGAZINE IS AN ANTHOLOGY for poets across the country. Poesy's main concentration is Boston, MA and Santa Cruz, CA, two thriving homesteads for poets and artists. Eastern and western poets rarely collaborate on publications. Our goal is to unite the two scenes, updating poets on what's happening across the country. Poesy is based in Santa Cruz, we have a Boston editor, Doug Holder, covering the Boston area. We publish inspirational poetry, reviews, interviews, articles, readings, and whatever fits best. Poesy is published seasonally... with the change of climate comes earthquakes of emotion outlet into poetry. Newsprint became the chosen media of Poesy, not only because its low-cost printing expense, but also because it is accessible to the general public. The idea is not to overwhelm your reader with fancy paper and cardstock covers, but we want to remain true to the original intentions of Poesy and bring a lighter notion to the table that promotes interesting and active verse that strays away from the dark and dry stereotypes that exist when referring to poetry by society. To achieve this goal, we have incorporated photography throughout our pages of each issue, that not only relate to the poems, but draw the eye into the page while discovering the words. The poems and photos compliment one another. Poesy strives to be the best literary journal on the market while remaining true to publishing poetry and art that pushes the creative aura to its limits. Poetry is a breathtaking, artistic venture into the world of the unknown. It is about finding your voice and letting it be heard through outlets like Poesy.'' circ. 4,000. 4/yr. Pub'd 4 issues 2005; expects 4 issues 2006, 4 issues 2007. sub. price $12.00; per copy $1; sample $1. Back issues: $3.00. 16pp. Reporting time: 6-8 weeks. Simultaneous submissions accepted: no. Publishes 10% of manuscripts submitted. Payment: 3 copies. Copyrighted, reverts to author. Pub's reviews: 15 in 2005. §Poetry. Ads: $85 Full /$50 Half /$35 Quarter. Subjects: Photography, Poetry.

POET LORE, The Writer's Center, Jody Bolz, Executive Editor; E. Ethelbert Miller, Executive Editor; Jason DeYoung, Managing Editor, The Writer's Center, 4508 Walsh Street, Bethesda, MD 20815-6006, 301-654-8664. 1889. Poetry, reviews. ''All material submitted for possible publication must include a stamped, self-addressed envelope.'' circ. 650. 2/yr. Pub'd 4 issues 2005; expects 4 issues 2006, 4 issues 2007. sub. price $18 indiv., $28 instit.; per copy $9, $5 foreign postage; sample $5.50 plus $1 shipping. Back issues: $9 for double issues; $4.50 for earlier single issues. Discounts: agency 5%. 144pp. Reporting time: 2-4 months. Simultaneous submissions accepted: yes *indicate in cl*. Publishes 5% of manuscripts submitted. Payment: 2 copies of issue. Copyrighted, reverts to author. Pub's reviews: 14 in 2005. §Small press poetry books, and poetry books published by major publishers & university presses. Ads: full pg$100/half pg$55. Subjects: Poetry, Reviews.

Poet Tree Press, Tom Worthen PhD, 1488 North 200 West, Logan, UT 84341-6803, 888-618-8444, Fax 435-713-4422, editor@poettreepress.com, www.poettreepress.com. 2000. Poetry. avg. press run 15M. Expects 2 titles 2006, 2 titles 2007. Discounts: 40% trade. 248pp. Simultaneous submissions accepted: no. Publishes 10% of manuscripts submitted. Copyrights for author. Subjects: Children, Youth, Poetry.

POETALK, Bay Area Poets Coalition, Maggie Morley, Editor, PO Box 11435, Berkeley, CA 94712-2435, poetalk@aol.com, http://hometown.aol.com/poetalk/myhomepage/index.html. 1974. Poetry. ''SASE required.'' circ. 400. 4/yr. Pub'd 3 issues 2005; expects 4 issues 2006, 4 issues 2007. sub. price $15 membership (includes yearly anthology); $8 subscription (write for foreign rates); per copy $3; sample free (SASE, business size) 83¢ postage required. Back issues: most issues available. 36pp. Reporting time: 2-4 months. Simultaneous submissions accepted: yes. Publishes 20-30% of manuscripts submitted. Payment: copy. Copyrighted, reverts to author. Ads: none. Subject: Poetry.

POETIC SPACE: Poetry & Fiction, Don Hildenbrand, Editor; Thomas Strand, Fiction Editor, PO Box 11157, Eugene, OR 97440. 1983. Poetry, fiction, articles, art, photos, interviews, criticism, reviews, news items. ''Short to medium length poems, short fiction, short essays, articles, reviews, contemporary, modern poetry, film, video, drama reviews and B&W photography. Artwork (line drawings, sketches), graphics. Open to beginners. Open to experimental. Recent contributors: Poetry: John M. Bennett, Chan Yong, Albert Huffstickler, Peter

Kime, Pete Lee, Walt Phillips, Crawdad Nelson, Lyn Lifshin, Simon Perchik, Albert Huffsmichlin, Sherman Alexie, Paul Weineman. Fiction: Laten Carter, John Lipton, Seamus O'Bannion. Essays; Sesshu Foster, Maggie Jaffre. Chinese translations: Scott Francis. Art: Albert Huffsticklan. Shakespeare Reviews: Don Hildenbrand. Interview with Diane Ann-Jabar: Arabian Jazz author.'' circ. 500-600. 2/yr plus one chapbook (poetry and fiction). Pub'd 2 issues 2005; expects 2 issues 2006, 2 issues 2007. sub. price $7/2 issues, $13.50/4 issues, $5 anthology, 1987-1991; per copy $4; sample $3. Back issues: $5 per issue. 30-40pp. Reporting time: 1-2 months. Payment: in copies depending on budget (as to number). Copyrighted, rights revert to author, but reserve right to include in anthology. Pub's reviews: 2 in 2005. §Poetry, novels, plays, film. Ads: $150/$80/$40 1/4 page/$30 3 X 4/$25 business card. Subjects: Awards, Foundations, Grants, Book Reviewing, Fiction, Newsletter, Pacific Northwest, Poetry.

POETICA MAGAZINE, Reflections of Jewish Thought, Michal Mahgerefteh, P.O.Box 11014, Norfolk, VA 23517, www.poeticamagazine.com. 2003. Poetry, fiction, art, photos, long-poems, non-fiction. ''The goal of Poetica is to publish poetry, essays, and short stories (2-3 pages if well written) pertaining to Jewish subjects or presenting a Jewish point of view. We like poetry that builds around real experiences, and real characters, and that avoids abstractions and over philosophizing. Recent contributors are Ronald Pies, Rachel Barenblat, Judy Belsky, and Gilda Kreuter.'' circ. 150. 3/yr. Pub'd 3 issues 2005; expects 3 issues 2006, 3 issues 2007. sub. price $5.00; per copy $14.00; sample no charge. Back issues: inquire. 50pp. Reporting time: 1 month. Simultaneous submissions accepted: Yes. Payment: 1 copy per published piece. writers retain all rights to their work. Ads: $36.00 half page $54.00 full page. Subjects: Fiction, History, Holocaust, Humor, Judaism, Memoirs, Non-Fiction, Poetry, Prose, Religion, Short Stories, Spiritual, Theosophical, Writers/Writing.

POETRY, Christian Wiman, Editor, 444 North Michigan Ave., Suite 1850, Chicago, IL 60611-4034, tel 312-787-7070, fax 312-787-6650, email poetry@poetrymagazine.org, www.poetrymagazine.org. 1912. Poetry, articles, photos, criticism, reviews, letters, long-poems. circ. 10,000. 12/yr. Pub'd 12 issues 2005; expects 12 issues 2006, 12 issues 2007. sub. price individuals $35, $46 outside USA, institutions $38, $49 outside USA; per copy $3.75 plus $1.75 post; sample $3.75 plus $1.75 postage. Back issues: $4.25 plus $1.75 post. 64pp. Reporting time: 8 weeks. Simultaneous submissions accepted: no. Publishes less than 1% of manuscripts submitted. Payment: $150/page prose, $10/line verse. Copyrighted, reverts to author per author's request. Pub's reviews: 67 in 2005. §Poetry, Criticism/Essays, and poetry-related novels and non-fiction. Ads: $387/$238. Subject: Poetry.

•**The Poetry Center (see also THE PATERSON LITERARY REVIEW),** Maria Mazziotti Gillan, Passaic Community College, One College Boulevard, Paterson, NJ 07505-1179, 973-684-6555. 1977. Poetry, fiction, long-poems. Simultaneous submissions accepted: YES. Subjects: Arts, Essays, Juvenile Fiction, Literary Review, Literature (General), Magazines, Multicultural, Poetry, Short Stories, Writers/Writing.

The Poetry Center Press/Shoestring Press, P.M. Morrison; Bill Johnson, Associate Editor, 3 Monte Vista Road, Orinda, CA 94563, 925-254-6639. 1986. Poetry, fiction, non-fiction. ''Have published fine limited letter-press editions as well as modest chapbooks and hardcover and perfect bound editions. Professional consultation and assistance to self-publishers.'' avg. press run 250-5M. Pub'd 5 titles 2005; expects 6 titles 2006, 8 titles 2007. Discounts: trade, wholesale. Payment: negotiated. Copyrights for author. Subjects: Book Arts, How-To, Humor, Inspirational, Motivation, Success, Poetry, Printing, Self-Help, Senior Citizens.

POETRY DEPTH QUARTERLY, Joyce Odam, Editor; G. Elton Warrick, Publisher, 5836 North Haven Drive, North Highlands, CA 95660, 916-331-3512, e-mail: poetrydepthquarterly.com NO download or attached files accepted. Prefers postal submissions with S.A.S.E. Magazine established in 1995. For Art guidelines and submissions of photographs and original art,: Art Editors, Carol and Gerald Wheeler, e mail: csw@houston.rr.com Postal address: 1811 Brookchester Street, Katy, Texas 77450. Poetry, art. ''Cover letter *required* with short 3-10 line biography. All poems must be in English, typewritten and presented exactly as you would like them to appear. Due to the page size, only 52 characters will fit across the page, including spaces. Poems of any length are considered, but each work must be the original property of the submitting poet. Send 3-5 poems. Your name and address must appear on each page submitted. For non e-mail submissions: include an SASE.'' circ. 200. 4/yr. Pub'd 4 issues 2005; expects 4 issues 2006, 4 issues 2007. sub. price $20/yr; $38/2 years, $56/3 years; add $12 a year for foreign postage; per copy $5.50; sample $5.50. Back issues: $5.50. 35-60pp. Reporting time: 2 weeks to 3 months. Simultaneous submissions accepted: no. Publishes 5-10% of manuscripts submitted. Payment: author/contributor receives 1 copy. Copyrighted, reverts to author.

Poetry Direct, Brian Levison, Rip Bulkeley, 6 Princes Street, Oxford, OX4 1DD, United Kingdom, ++44-1865791202 :: editors@poetry-direct.com :: http://www.poetry-direct.com. 2003. Poetry, long-poems. ''Poetry Direct is a regionally focussed 'not-for-loss' publisher (central southern England) and we do not read or respond to totally unsolicited complete MSS. That said, we are already building a reputation for good poetry and very high production values. So if you really are the next Derek Walcott, by all means send us a sample of your work by email (maximum 6 shortish poems) and we will certainly get back to you.'' avg. press run 200. Pub'd 3 titles 2005; expects 1-2 titles 2006, 1-2 titles 2007. Discounts: Retailers - 33%. 90pp. Reporting time:

Eight weeks. Simultaneous submissions accepted: No. Publishes 25% of manuscripts submitted. Payment: Informal - profits will be shared equitably if there are any, and authors have access to our accounts. Does not copyright for author. Subject: Poetry.

POETRY EAST, Richard Jones, Editor; Beth Townsend Davila, Assistant Editor, Dept. of English, DePaul Univ., 802 West Belden Avenue, Chicago, IL 60614-3214, 773-325-7487, http://condor.depaul.edu/~poetryea/home.html. 1980. Poetry, fiction, articles, art, photos, interviews, criticism, reviews, letters, collages, concrete art, news items. "The journal is published twice each year, in the spring and autumn. We are open to all subject areas - the political, the spiritual, the personal. Our only criterion for selection is excellence, but we are partial to poems that have some fire to them." circ. 1.5M. 2/yr. Pub'd 2 issues 2005; expects 2 issues 2006, 2 issues 2007. sub. price $15; per copy $10, $15 for anthologies; sample $8. Back issues: #9/10 *Art & Guns: Political Poetry* $20; #19 *The Inward Eye: the Photographs of Ed Roseberry* $10; #43 *Origins* $15. Discounts: bookstores 20%. 200pp for single issue, 300pp for double issue. Reporting time: 4 months. Simultaneous submissions accepted: no. Publishes less than 5% of manuscripts submitted. Payment: copies, honorariums. Copyrighted, reverts to author. Ads: none. Subjects: Fiction, Literary Review, Literature (General), Poetry, Translation.

THE POETRY EXPLOSION NEWSLETTER (THE PEN), Arthur C. Ford, PO Box 4725, Pittsburgh, PA 15206-0725, 1-866-234-0297,arthurford@hotmail.com. 1985. Poetry. "We use poetry of max. length 30 lines, and prose max. 200-300 words. Rhyme and non-rhyme. Submit a max. of 5 poems, SASE and $1 reading fee." circ. 850. 4/yr. Pub'd 4 issues 2005; expects 4 issues 2006, 4 issues 2007. sub. price $20; sample $4. Back issues: $4. 10-15pp. Reporting time: 2-4 weeks. Simultaneous submissions accepted: yes. Publishes 10-15% of manuscripts submitted. Payment: copies. Copyrighted, reverts to author. Pub's reviews: 2 in 2005. §Poetry, prose. Ads: $100/$50/$25 1/4 page/$10 bus. card. Subject: Poetry.

POETRY FLASH, Joyce Jenkins, Publisher & Editor; Richard Silberg, Associate Editor, 1450 Fourth Street #4, Berkeley, CA 94710, 510-525-5476, Fax 510-525-6752. 1972. Poetry, articles, art, photos, interviews, criticism, reviews, collages, news items. "*Poetry Flash*, A Poetry Review & Literary Calendar for the West, publishes reviews, essays, interviews, poems, and calls for submissions. Our primary editorial focus is poetry, but we do review literary and experimental fiction, interview fiction writers, and cover every genre and kind of literary event in our event calendar. The intention is to review and publish high quality work of interest to writers in California, the Northwest, Southwest and beyond. We publish established and emerging poets and writers who may live in any geographical location. Queries should be made for reviews and interviews; poems may be sent with SASE. Occasional double-numbered issues." circ. 22M. 4/yr. Pub'd 4 issues 2005; expects 4 issues 2006, 4 issues 2007. sub. price $12 for four issues, $22 for eight.; per copy free at bookstores, libraries, cafes, art centers or by subscription; sample one copy free on request. Back issues: $2-$5 depending on year. 52-60pp. Reporting time: 4 months. Simultaneous submissions accepted: Yes, with notification. Publishes 10% of manuscripts submitted. Payment: 2-year subscription for poems, payment for articles. Copyrighted, reverts to author. Pub's reviews: 150 in 2005. §Poetry, experimental or literary fiction, criticism or biography, especially poetry related. Ads: $630/$315/$15.75 column inch. Subjects: Book Reviewing, Criticism, Poetry.

Poetry Harbor (see also NORTH COAST REVIEW), Patrick McKinnon, Ellie Schoenfeld, PO Box 202, Kailua Kona, HI 96745-0202. 1992. avg. press run 1M. Pub'd 2 titles 2005; expects 2 titles 2006, 2 titles 2007. Discounts: 40% booksellers; 55% wholesalers. 56pp. Reporting time: 1-6 months. Simultaneous submissions accepted: yes. Publishes 20% of manuscripts submitted. Payment: $10 + copies. Copyrights for author. Subjects: Michigan, Minnesota, Native American, The North, Poetry, Wisconsin.

Poetry Ireland (see also POETRY IRELAND REVIEW), Biddy Jenkinson, Bermingham Tower, Upper Yard, Dublin Castle, Dublin 2, Ireland. 1981. Poetry, reviews. avg. press run 1,100. Pub'd 4 titles 2005; expects 4 titles 2006, 4 titles 2007. Discounts: agencies 10%. 136pp. Reporting time: 3 months max. Simultaneous submissions accepted: no. Publishes 5-10% of manuscripts submitted. Payment: poems in copies, articles/reviews by arrangement IR £10 per contributor or 1 year subscription. Copyrights for author. Subjects: Gaelic, Ireland, Poetry.

POETRY IRELAND REVIEW, Poetry Ireland, Biddy Jenkinson, Bermingham Tower, Upper yard, Dublin Castle, Dublin 2, Ireland, 6714632 + 353-1, fax 6714634 + 353-1. 1981. Poetry, interviews, criticism. "*Poetry Ireland Review* accepts material from outside Ireland. The themes do not have to be necessarily Irish. We prefer if they are not Irish. We publish both established and lesser-known poets." circ. 1,100. 4/yr. Pub'd 4 issues 2005; expects 4 issues 2006, 4 issues 2007. sub. price airmail IRT 44.00, US$70; surface IRT 24.00, US$50; per copy IR £5.99; sample IR £5.99. Back issues: IR £5.99. Discounts: agencies 10%; bulk discount by arrangement. 136pp. Reporting time: 3 months max. Simultaneous submissions accepted: no. Publishes 5-10% of manuscripts submitted. Payment: IR£10 per contribution or subscription. Copyrighted, reverts to author. Pub's reviews: 50 in 2005. §New major collections of international interest and Irish collections. Ads: by arrangement. Subjects: Gaelic, Ireland, Poetry.

POETRY KANTO, Alan Botsford, Co-editor; Nishihara Katsumasa, Co-editor, Kanto Gakuin University, Kamariya Minami 3-22-1, Kanazawa-Ku, Yokohama 236-8502, Japan. 1984. Poetry. "PK has a cross-cultural as well as literary mission. Seeks well-crafted original poems in English, as well as Japanese poems in English translation (query first: alan@kanto-gakuin.ac.jp). Some recent contributors include (among Westerners); Gwyneth Lewis, Vijay Seshadri, Harryette Mullen, Rigoberto Gonzalez, Ellen Bass, Bruce A. Jacobs, Ilya Kaminsky. Reads between September through May." circ. 1000. 1/yr. Pub'd 1 issue 2005; expects 1 issue 2006, 1-2 issues 2007. Back issues: send reply coupons to cover air mail or sea mail. 100pp. Simultaneous submissions accepted: no. Publishes 10% of manuscripts submitted. Payment: 3 contributor's copies. Not copyrighted. Ads: none. Subject: Poetry.

THE POETRY MISCELLANY, Richard Jackson, English Dept. Univ of Tennessee, Chattanooga, TN 37403, 423-425-4238. 1971. Poetry, interviews, criticism, reviews, long-poems. "David Wagoner, Denise Levertov, Tomaz Salamun, Mark Strand, Laura Jensen, Richard Wilbur, Donald Justice, James Tate, Dara Wier, Carol Muske, Maxine Kumin, Robert Penn Warren, Marvin Bell, Jean Valentine, David St. John, A.R. Ammons, Stanley Kunitz, Charles Simic, John Hollander, Linda Pastan, William Stafford, John Haines, Pamela Stewart, Galway Kinnell, W. S. Merwin, William Meredith, Laurence Raab, Cynthia MacDonald, Robert Pack, Carolyn Forche, Anthony Hecht, John Ashbery, Donald Finkel, Michael Harper, Robert Creeley, David Ignatow, Donald Hall, Heather McHugh, Sharon Olds, Stanley Plumly, William Matthews. Review essays 1M words must be assigned/approved in advance. We use translations too. Send translations with originals to John Duval, Translation Workshop, University of Arkansas, Fayetteville, AK 72701." circ. 500. 1/yr. Pub'd 1 issue 2005; expects 1 issue 2006, 1 issue 2007. sub. price $10; per copy $10; sample $10. Back issues: same price as current issues. Discounts: 30% for orders of ten or more to groups and individuals. 50pp. Reporting time: 6 months. Simultaneous submissions accepted: no. Publishes 1% of manuscripts submitted. Payment: copies. Copyrighted, rights revert to author upon request as for re-publication. Pub's reviews: 4 in 2005. §Poetry, poetics. Ads: $50 1/2 page. Subjects: Criticism, Poetry, Translation.

POETRY NOW, Sacramento's Literary Review and Calendar, Heather Hutcheson, 1719 25th St., Sacramento, CA 95816, 916-441-7395, poetrynow@sacramentopoetrycenter.org, www.sacramentopoetry-center.org. 1994. Poetry, articles, photos, interviews, criticism, reviews. circ. 1M + website. 12/yr. Pub'd 12 issues 2005; expects 12 issues 2006, 12 issues 2007. sub. price $25; per copy $3; sample $3. Back issues: n/a. Discounts: call for information. 8pp. Reporting time: 1-3 months. Simultaneous submissions accepted: yes. Publishes 20% of manuscripts submitted. Payment: none. Not copyrighted. Pub's reviews: 4+ in 2005. §Poetry, performance or reading of poetry. Ads: call for information/3 X 5=$20/month. Subjects: Poetry, Reviews.

POETRY NZ, Alistair Paterson, 37 Margot Street, Epsom, Auckland 3, New Zealand, 64-9-524-5656. 1990. Poetry. "U.S. office (sales only): 1040 Paseo El Mirador, Palm Springs, CA 92262. Work submitted for publication may be sent to the editor at 34B Methuen Road, Avondale, Auckland, New Zealand." circ. 1M. 2/yr. Pub'd 2 issues 2005; expects 2 issues 2006, 2 issues 2007. sub. price $35, $16.50 US; per copy $16.95, $8.95 US. Back issues: $16.95, $8.95 US. Discounts: trade 35% on single copies, 10% sub. agency, net for sub. libraries. 92pp. Reporting time: 4 weeks. Simultaneous submissions accepted: no. Publishes 10% of manuscripts submitted. Payment: $25 per issue. Copyrighted, reverts to author. Pub's reviews: 15+ in 2005. §Poetry. Ads: none. Subject: Poetry.

The Poetry Project (see also THE POETRY PROJECT NEWSLETTER; THE WORLD), Editorial Staff, St. Mark's Church, 131 East 10th Street, New York, NY 10003, 212-674-0910, poproj@thorn.net. 1966. Poetry, fiction, art, photos, long-poems, non-fiction. "We mainly publish solicited work." avg. press run 4,000'/800 respectively. Pub'd 1 title 2005; expects 1 title 2006, 1 title 2007. Discounts: none. 128pp. Reporting time: 6 months. Simultaneous submissions accepted: yes. Publishes 5% of manuscripts submitted. Payment: copies. Does not copyright for author. Subject: Poetry.

THE POETRY PROJECT NEWSLETTER, The Poetry Project, St. Mark's Church, 131 East 10th Street, New York, NY 10003, 212-674-0910, poproj@thorn.net. 1966. Poetry, fiction, articles, art, interviews, criticism, reviews, letters. "We also list events scheduled at the Poetry Project and publications received." circ. 4M. 5/yr. Pub'd 5 issues 2005; expects 5 issues 2006, 5 issues 2007. sub. price $20; per copy $5; sample $5. Back issues: $5 if available. Discounts: none. 32pp. Reporting time: 2 months. Simultaneous submissions accepted: no. Publishes 5% of manuscripts submitted. Payment: copies. Copyrighted, reverts to author. Pub's reviews: 40 in 2005. §Poetry. Ads: $250/$160/$60-250. Subjects: Avant-Garde, Experimental Art, Literary Review, Literature (General), Poetry.

POETRY REVIEW, Fiona Sampson Dr, 22 Betterton Street, London WC2H 9BX, England. 1912. Poetry, articles, photos, interviews, criticism, reviews, letters, long-poems. circ. 5M. 4/yr. Pub'd 4 issues 2005; expects 4 issues 2006. sub. price $56 individuals, $70 institutions, all airmail; per copy $10 surface; $15 airmail; sample $10 surface, $15 airmail. Back issues: $10 surface, $15 airmail. Discounts: 1/3 to trade. 128pp. Reporting time: 3 months. Payment: £40- £120 per poem, up to £250 per esay, dependent on length. Copyrighted, reverts to author. Pub's reviews: 120 in 2005. §Poetry, criticism, relevant novels, biographies/autobiographies, belle-lettres, etc. Ads: £250/£170/£300 back page/£85 1/4 page/£275 3,500 loose inserts. Subject: Poetry.

POETRY USA, National Poetry Association Publishers, Herman Berlandt, Editor, 934 Brannan Street, 2nd floor, San Francisco, CA 94103, 415-552-9261, Fax 415-552-9271, www.nationalpoetry.org. 1985. Poetry, reviews. "Submission: Send no more than three poems, SASE, and e-mail address. *Poetry USA*, published by the National Poetry Association based in San Francisco, is a quarterly journal that aims to provide a common space for the diversity of voices that make up the American experience. Each issue usually includes poems from all over the country, and often includes sections from young people, people without a home, and people in prison. Our preference tends to be for shorter poems (under 50 lines, please) accessible to the non-literary general public. Poets from the community are invited to serve as guest editors, choosing different themes for each issue. The National Poetry Association, an all-volunteer organization founded in 1975, is committed to promoting the written, spoken and visual use of language in new and traditional ways." circ. 3M. 3-4/yr. Pub'd 4 issues 2005; expects 4 issues 2006, 4 issues 2007. sub. price $15; per copy $3; sample $4 ppd. Back issues: $4 ppd. Discounts: 50%. 36pp. Reporting time: 2-6 months. Simultaneous submissions accepted: yes. Publishes 5% of manuscripts submitted. Payment: 2 copies. Copyrighted, reverts to author. Pub's reviews: 4 in 2005. §Poetry and poetry anthologies. Ads: $200/$125/$50 1/8 page/$25 card. Subject: Poetry.

POETS & WRITERS MAGAZINE, Poets & Writers, Inc., Mary Gannon, Editor, 72 Spring Street, New York, NY 10012, 212-226-3586, Fax 212-226-3963, www.pw.org. 1973. Articles, photos, letters, concrete art, news items. "Subscription orders: Poets & Writers Magazine, PO Box 543, Mount Morris, IL 61054, 815-734-1123, email poet@kable.com. *Poets & Writers Magazine* publishes factual articles of interest to writers, editors, publishers, and all others interested in contemporary American literature. It also publishes essays, interviews with writers, and news and comments on publishing, political issues, grants and awards, and requests for submissions. Most articles are written by freelance writers. Always send a letter of inquiry to the editor prior to submitting a manuscript. *Poets & Writers Magazine* has a Letters column and encourages comment from readers. *Poets & Writers Magazine* does not review poetry or fiction." circ. 71M. 6/yr. Pub'd 6 issues 2005; expects 6 issues 2006, 6 issues 2007. sub. price $19.95, $38/2 yrs for individuals; per copy $4.95; sample $4.95. Back issues: $3.95 prior to 1999, after $4.95. Discounts: bookstores, min. 10 copies, 40%; to distributors, min. 10 copies, 50%; to teachers, for bulk subscriptions, min. 20, 20% to one address. 120pp. Reporting time: 2 months. Simultaneous submissions accepted: no. Publishes 10% of manuscripts submitted. Payment: $100-$300. Copyrighted, reverts to author. Ads: $2,080/$1,120, less 20% at 6X rate; classifieds $120 up to 50 words, over 50 $2.50 per add'l word. Subjects: Fiction, Poetry.

Poets & Writers, Inc. (see also POETS & WRITERS MAGAZINE), Thesese Eiben, Editor, 72 Spring Street, New York, NY 10012, 212-226-3586, Fax 212-226-3963, www.pw.org. 1970. Articles, photos, interviews, letters, concrete art, news items, non-fiction. "Poets & Writers publishes *A Directory of American Poets and Fiction Writers*, 2001-2002 Edition, a listing of contact names, addresses, phone numbers, e-mail and website addresses and publications for over 7,400 poets, fiction writers, and performance writers." avg. press run 3M. Expects 1 title 2006. Discounts: distributed through Small Press Distribution, 1341 7th Street, Berkeley, CA 94710-1403, 510-524-1668. Pages vary. Subjects: Fiction, Literature (General), Poetry, Reference.

POETS AT WORK, Jessee Poet Publications, Jessee Poet, PO Box 232, Lyndora, PA 16045. 1985. Poetry. "Length—about 20 lines and under. I publish everyone who writes in good taste. William Middleton, Ralph Hammond, Ann Gasser, and at least 300 other poets. I am a marvelous market for unpublished poets." circ. 300+. 6/yr. Pub'd 6 issues 2005; expects 6 issues 2006, 6 issues 2007. sub. price $23; per copy $4; sample $4. Back issues: $4 when available. 40pp. Reporting time: 2 weeks. Simultaneous submissions accepted and I accept previously published material (poetry). Publishes nearly 100% of manuscripts submitted. Payment: none. Copyrighted, reverts to author. Ads: negotiable. Subject: Poetry.

POETS ON THE LINE, Linda Lerner, PO Box 20292, Brooklyn NY 11202-0007, Brooklyn, NY 11202-0007, 718-596-0137. 1995. Poetry, interviews, non-fiction. "*No unsolicited manuscripts*. Nos. 9&10 came out 1/2000 (double millennium issue) and will be the last regular issue to come out. There may be an occasional special issue of *POTL*, no plans as of yet. In this issue are: W.D. Ehrhart, Lynne Savitt, Kell Robertson, Janine Pommy Vega, Tony Moffat, Jack Micheline, Todd Moore, and others.)." 2/yr. Pub'd 1-2 issues 2005; expects 1 issue 2006, 1 issue 2007. 31pp. Payment: none. Copyrighted, reverts to author. Subject: Poetry.

POETS' ROUNDTABLE, Esther Alman, 826 South Center Street, Terre Haute, IN 47807, 812-234-0819. 1939. Poetry, news items. "*Poets' Rountable* is a bulletin published bimonthly for members of Poets' Study Club. It is not an open market for poetry. Open contests: One annual open competition—The International Contest, with awards of $25 and $15 in three categories: serious poems, light verse, traditional haiku. No entry fees. Deadline is February 1st each year. Send entries to Annual International Contest, Esther Alman, 826 South Center Street, Terre Haute, IN 47807. We use *only* material by members for publication, but annual contest is open to everyone. We keep manuscripts in a file, but will return on request, for publication of poems *by members only*." circ. 2M. 6/yr. Pub'd 6 issues 2005; expects 6 issues 2006, 6 issues 2007. sub. price $15 membership; sample free. 12pp. Payment: none. Copyrighted, reverts to author. Pub's reviews: 25 in 2005. No ads. Subjects: Haiku, Magazines, Poetry.

POETSWEST ONLINE, Barbara A. Evans, Editor; J. Glenn Evans, Poetry Editor, 1011 Boren Avenue #155, Seattle, WA 98104, 206-682-1268, info@poetswest.com, www.poetswest.com. 1988. Poetry. "General poetry published online. Submit 6 poems not to exceed 50 lines each. Poetry changes quarterly. Unscheduled hard copy anthology of poems selected from previously published online poems from time to time. Author contacted for permission. Publishes 25% of poems submitted. Simultaneous and previous published poems okay. Include previous publication credits. Publish one to four book reviews per year. No payment other than exposure. Reporting time two months. Copyright reverts to author." Back issues: 1998-2002 issues in print: 3 or more $4 each. Simultaneous submissions accepted: yes. Publishes 25% of manuscripts submitted. Copyrighted, reverts to author. Pub's reviews: 3 in 2005. §Poetry books and chapbooks. Ads: none. Subject: Poetry.

Pogo Press, Incorporated, Moira F. Harris, 4 Cardinal Lane, St. Paul, MN 55127, 651-483-4692, fax 651-483-4692, E-mail pogopres@minn.net. 1986. Art, non-fiction. "Submission by prearrangement only." avg. press run 3M. Pub'd 3 titles 2005; expects 3 titles 2006, 3 titles 2007. Discounts: query. Pages vary. Reporting time: 60 days. Simultaneous submissions accepted: no. Payment: negotiable. Copyrights for author. Subjects: Architecture, Arts, Culture, Essays, Florida, History, Humor, Military, Veterans, Minnesota, Music, Native American, Theatre, Travel.

POGO STICK, Lillian Kopaska-Merkel, 1300 Kicker Road, Tuscaloosa, AL 35404, 553-2284, uniquewish@juno.com. 2004. Poetry, fiction, art, cartoons. "Only work by people under 17." circ. 100. 4/yr. Expects 1 issue 2006, 4 issues 2007. sub. price $12; per copy $4; sample $4. Back issues: $4. 19pp. Reporting time: up to 2 months. Simultaneous submissions accepted: yes. Publishes 70% of manuscripts submitted. Payment: 1 copy of magazine. Not copyrighted. Ads: $2/$1.50/$1. Subjects: Fantasy, Fiction, Juvenile Fiction, Poetry, Science Fiction, Short Stories, Visual Arts, Young Adult.

POINT OF CONTACT, The Journal of Verbal & Visual Arts, Pedro Cuperman, Owen Shapiro, 216 H.B. Crouse Building, Syracuse University, Syracuse, NY 13244-1160, 315-443-2247, Fax 315-443-5376, cfawcett@syr.edu, www.pointcontact.org. 1975. Poetry, photos, interviews, criticism, parts-of-novels, long-poems, concrete art, non-fiction. "Journal of creative scholarship in the arts. Some recent contributors include: Robert Ashley, Alicia Borinsky, Trisha Brown, Pedro Cuperman, Elka Krajewska, Marco Maggi, Jeffrey Mehlman, Nam June Paik, Raimon Panikkar, Liliana Porter, Izhar Patkin, Ana Tiscornia, Owen Shapiro, Andy Waggoner, Wayne Wang. Text and art contributions by invitation only." circ. 200. 2/yr. Expects 2 issues 2006, 2 issues 2007. sub. price $40; $60 institutions; per copy $20; sample $10. Back issues: $20. Discounts: negotiable. 100pp. Reporting time: 3-6 months. Simultaneous submissions accepted: no. Payment: none. Copyrighted, does not revert to author. Ads: $300/$175. Subjects: Arts, Avant-Garde, Experimental Art, Caribbean, Culture, Electronics, English, Feminism, Language, Latin America, Latino, Literature (General), Multicultural, Puerto Rico, Translation, U.S. Hispanic.

Poisoned Pen Press, 6962 E. First Avenue #103, Scottsdale, AZ 85251, 480-945-3375, Fax 480-949-1707, info@poisonedpenpress.com. 1997. Fiction. "Only interested in mystery-fiction." Copyrights for author.

Polar Bear & Company, Paul du Houx, PO Box 311, Solon, ME 04979-0311, 207-643-2795, solon@tds.net, www.polarbearandco.com. 1991. Poetry, fiction, articles, art, photos, cartoons, satire, criticism, letters, long-poems, news items, non-fiction. "The theme of our Web site is: Mythology for Modern Democracy Brings Variety to Everyday Life. This is a way of understanding how truth is projected by fiction and how nonfiction can develop the imagination. The theme is as broad as the author's vision can be, but there is a sense of direction, focus, and clarity that tends to enhance the natural environment and our sense of equal opportunity. For example, we have published books for young people such as: "Martin McMillan and the Lost Inca City" by Elaine Russell where Martin takes his skateboard on an archaeological dig in Peru and rides down a secret path to adventure. He and his new friend Isabel gain insight into the modern adult world, the Incan world, and their own world, while becoming immersed in a new culture where meetings and clashes between richly diverse civilizations lead to a web of secret activity. "This is the best novel about two teens brought together with a mystery to solve that I have read." (Judy Bean, "Maine in Print.") And for adults, "The Proud and the Immortal" by Oswald Rivera: "Rivera proves that the great American novel can be written in our times. With compelling insight the reader is brought underground to live in disused Amtrak tunnels with a family community existing on the edge day by day. Meanwhile millions are being made literally above their heads. I couldn't put it down." (James Curtis, "The Maine Times.") And, "Letters From a Civil War Surgeon," by Dr. William Child of the Fifth New Hampshire Volunteers, the entire collection published for the first time." avg. press run 2,000. Pub'd 4 titles 2005; expects 5 titles 2006, 5 titles 2007. 200pp. Simultaneous submissions accepted: Yes. Payment: individual. Copyrights for author. Subjects: Autobiography, Biography, Crime, Essays, Fiction, Juvenile Fiction, Literature (General), Maine, Memoirs, Mystery, Myth, Mythology, Non-Fiction, Novels, Poetry, Short Stories.

Polebridge Press (see also FORUM; THE FOURTH R), PO Box 7268, Santa Rosa, CA 95407-0268, 707-523-1323, fax 707-523-1350. 1981. Articles, interviews, criticism, reviews. Subject: Religion.

Polka Dot Publishing, Stanley F. Schmidt, PO Box 8458, Reno, NV 89507-8458, 775-852-2690 phone, LifeofFred@yahoo.com. 2001. Non-fiction. avg. press run 2M. Pub'd 3 titles 2005; expects 3 titles 2006, 2 titles 2007. 544pp. Reporting time: 1 month. Simultaneous submissions accepted: yes. Publishes about 20% of manuscripts submitted. Payment: to be arranged. Copyrights to be arranged. Subjects: Christianity, Mathematics.

Poltroon Press, Alastair Johnston, PO Box 5476, Berkeley, CA 94705-0476, 510-845-8097. 1974. Poetry, fiction, art, photos, interviews, satire, criticism, concrete art, non-fiction. "Do not read unsolicited work. Recent books: Mark Coggins, Vulture Capital (Detective fiction, 2002) ISBN: 0-918395-21-6; Philip Whalen, Prose [Out] Takes (poetry, 2002); Alastair Johnston, Zephyrus Image: A Bibliography, with photos by Rob Rusk, illustrated by Michael Myers (2003) ISBN: 0-918395-22-4." avg. press run 200-1000. Pub'd 4 titles 2005; expects 5 titles 2006, 4 titles 2007. Discounts: distributor: Small Press Distribution, or visit us on line at www.poltroonpress.com. 64pp. Payment: 15%. Copyrights for author. Subjects: African Literature, Africa, African Studies, Bibliography, Design, Poetry, Printing.

Polygonal Publishing House, Michael Weinstein, PO Box 357, Washington, NJ 07882, 908-689-3894. 1976. Non-fiction. "We publish books on mathematics." avg. press run 1M. Expects 1 title 2006, 1 title 2007. Discounts: 20% trade & bulk. 200pp. Payment: 17%. Subject: Mathematics.

Pomegranate Communications, PO Box 808022, Petaluma, CA 94975-8022, info@pomegranate.com. 1965. Art, photos. avg. press run 5M-15M. Pub'd 24 titles 2005; expects 20 titles 2006, 20 titles 2007. Discounts: 50% non-returnable. 110pp. Reporting time: 6 weeks. Simultaneous submissions accepted: yes. Publishes a small % of manuscripts submitted. Does not copyright for author. Subjects: African-American, Arts, Photography, Women.

Poor Souls Press/Scaramouche Books, Paul Fericano, Editor; Charlie Chase, Executive Editor; Bruce Pryor, Managing Editor; Kate Noel, Art Editor, PO Box 236, Millbrae, CA 94030. 1974. Satire. "Sorry, but Poor Souls Press cannot accept unsolicited material. If you're a satirist, we encourage self-publishing and close contact with others involved in the genre. Poor Souls Press is the book publishing subsidiary of Yossarian Universal (YU) News Service, the world's only parody news and disinformation syndicate with bureaus in 37 cities worldwide. We publish broadsides, postcards, chapbooks, pamphlets, and dispatches. Visit us online at: www.yunews.com." avg. press run 3. Pub'd 3 titles 2005; expects 3 titles 2006, 3 titles 2007. 1 page. Payment: usually pay our authors with half the print run. Copyrights for author. Subject: Satire.

•PORCUPINE LITERARY ARTS MAGAZINE, W.A. Reed, PO Box 259, Cedarburg, WI 53012, 262-376-9178, ppine259@aol.com, www.porcupineliteraryarts.com. 1996. Poetry, fiction, art. "Porcupine Literary Arts Magazine is a highly regarded journal dedicated to the publication of quality poetry, short fiction, essays, and visual artwork. In addition to featuring the work of emerging and well-known writers, each issue profiles artists or writers of national and international prominence through color portfolios and interviews. Unsolicited manuscripts and art work are welcomed throughout the year. There are no restrictions as to theme or style. Prose should be readable, professional, and of a high quality. Make us care about the characters. Poetry should be accessible and highly selective. If a submission is not timely for one issue, it will be considered for another. Past issues have included the poetry of Antler, James Grabill, George Wallace, and S. M. Page, the essays and short fiction of Ward Kelley and Richard Thieme, and the visual artwork of Terese Agnew, Ladislav Hanka, and Dale Chihuly." circ. 1000. 2/yr. Pub'd 2 issues 2005; expects 2 issues 2006, 2 issues 2007. sub. price $15.95; per copy $9; sample $5. Back issues: $5. Discounts: distributors-15%, bookstores-40%. 170pp. Reporting time: 90 days. Simultaneous submissions accepted: No. Publishes 5% of manuscripts submitted. Payment: 1 contributor's copy. Copyrighted, reverts to author. Ads: full page color- $400, full page b&w- $250.

PORTALS, Redrosebush Press, Ella M. Dillon, PO Box 2163, Wenatchee, WA 98807-2163, 509-662-7858. 1991. Poetry, fiction, articles, art, photos, cartoons, interviews, satire, criticism, reviews, letters, non-fiction. "Prefer poetry 30 lines or less, other writings 500-1,500 words." circ. 1M+. 4/yr. Pub'd 4 issues 2005; expects 4 issues 2006, 4 issues 2007. sub. price $18; per copy $6; sample free. Back issues: $2.50. Discounts: none. 52pp. Reporting time: when published. Simultaneous submissions accepted: yes. Payment: none. Copyrighted, reverts to author. Pub's reviews: 5 in 2005. §No pornography. Ads: $300/$200/$25 and up.

Portals Press, John P. Travis, 4411 Fontainebleau Drive, New Orleans, LA 70125, 504-821-7723, travport@bellsouth.net, www.portalspress.com. 1992. Poetry, fiction, long-poems. "Authors we have published: Kay Murphy, Ralph Adamo, John Gery, Maxine Cassin, Richard Katrovas, Tom Whalen, William S. Maddox, Nancy Harris, Grace Bauer, Brad Richard, Yictove, Chris Chandler, and H.R. Stoneback." avg. press run 500-1M. Pub'd 1 title 2005; expects 1 title 2006, 1 title 2007. Discounts: 40%. 128pp. Reporting time: 1 month. Simultaneous submissions accepted: okay. Publishes 1% of manuscripts submitted. Payment: 10-20%. Copyrights for author. Subjects: Fiction, Poetry, Science Fiction.

PORTLAND REVIEW, Kevin Friedman, Editor, PO Box 347, Portland, OR 97207-0347, 503-725-4533. 1956. Poetry, fiction, art, photos, parts-of-novels, long-poems, collages. *"Portland Review* is a literary journal that seeks the innovative. Works published combine excellent writing, compelling story and unique voice." circ. 500. 3/yr. Pub'd 3 issues 2005; expects 3 issues 2006, 3 issues 2007. sub. price $28; per copy $9; sample $8. Back issues: $6. Discounts: $54 two year subscription. 120pp. Reporting time: 4-6 months. Not accepting submissions from June 1 - Agust 31, 2005. Simultaneous submissions accepted: yes. Publishes 3% of manuscripts submitted. Payment: copies and exposure. Copyrighted, reverts to author. Pub's reviews. §Broad areas of interest. Ads: $100/$60/$30 1/4 page. Subjects: Avant-Garde, Experimental Art, Beat, Cuba, Erotica, Experimental, Fiction, Journals, Literary Review, Literature (General), Poetry, Post Modern, Prose, Surrealism.

Portmanteau Editions, Harry H. Barlow, Jennifer M. Thornton, PO Box 665, Somers, NY 10589. 1987. Poetry, fiction, satire, non-fiction. "Publishing schedule filled. The editors, in the depressive phase of their manic-depression, can't consider new manuscripts or proposals at present." Pub'd 2 titles 2005; expects 2 titles 2006, 3 titles 2007. Discounts: standard. Reporting time: 4 months. Payment: standard royalties. Copyrights for author. Subjects: Fiction, Humor, Poetry, Satire.

PORTRAIT, Susan T. Landry, Melissa Shook, 11 Robeson St., Jamaica Plain, MA 02130. 2003. Art, photos, long-poems, non-fiction. "PORTRAIT is a quarterly publication that explores the realm of biography through art and literature. Each issue features one artist and one writer in an intimate 5 x 7 portable format. PORTRAIT continues under new editors to function as a collectible publication as well as a forum for the ongoing discussion of our interests in one another." 4/yr. Pub'd 6 issues 2005; expects 4 issues 2006, 4 issues 2007. sub. price $18.00; per copy $5.00; sample $5.00. Back issues: inquire. Discounts: inquire. 15pp. Reporting time: 4-5 weeks. Simultaneous submissions accepted: Yes. Payment: Complimentary issues. Copyrighted, reverts to author.

The Post-Apollo Press, Simone Fattal, 35 Marie Street, Sausalito, CA 94965, 415-332-1458, fax 415-332-8045. 1982. Poetry, fiction. Pub'd 4 titles 2005; expects 4 titles 2006, 4 titles 2007. Discounts: Bookstores: 20% returnable (+10% restocking fee); 40% non-returnable. Reporting time: 2 months. Simultaneous submissions accepted: no. Payment: percentage after all expenses are met. Copyrights for author. Subjects: Fiction, History, Literature (General), Middle East, Poetry, Visual Arts.

POSTCARD CLASSICS (formerly DELTIOLOGY), Dr. James Lewis Lowe, Deltiologists of America, PO Box 8, Norwood, PA 19074-0008, 610-485-8572. 1960. "No hardcopy. See www.Deltiologists-America.com." Back issues: 10 *POSTCARD CLASSICS* back issues: $10; 50 *DELTIOLOGY* $30 + shipping. *??? Write.* Copyrighted. Pub's reviews: 2 in 2005. §Books about picture postcards and postcard collecting only. Ads: No. Subject: Postcards.

POTOMAC REVIEW, Myrna Goldenberg, Executive Editor; Christa Watters, Senior Editor; Eli Flam, Editor; Hilary Tham, Poetry Editor, Paul Peck Humanities Institute, Montgomery College, 51 Mannakee St., Rockville, MD 20850, 301-610-4100, www.montgomerycollege.edu/potomacreview. 1994. Poetry, fiction, articles, art, photos, interviews, satire, reviews, letters, parts-of-novels, plays, non-fiction. "Prose submissions should be no more than 3,000 words. We carry first-timers as well as the previous published. Regionally based, we seek up to three poems to total five pages. A challenging mix of poets, writers (fiction-nonfiction) and artwork. Our aim is to provide thought-provoking, literary material that challenges the intellect and gives voice to our shared humanity." circ. 1.7M. 2/yr. Pub'd 2 issues 2005; expects 2 issues 2006, 2 issues 2007. sub. price $18; per copy $10; sample $10. Back issues: $3 depending on availability. Discounts: on ads 20% for a year's worth. 248pp. Reporting time: within 90 days. Simultaneous submissions accepted, but should be noted. Publishes approx. 5% of manuscripts submitted. Payment: 1 copy, modest sum for assigned nonfiction. Copyrighted, reverts to author. Pub's reviews: about 30 in 2005. §From regionally-relevant fiction, non-fiction, poetry outward. Ads: $250/$150. Subjects: Appalachia, Arts, Book Reviewing, Culture, Drama, Environment, Ethics, Humanism, Humor, Literature (General), Memoirs, Non-Fiction, Poetry, Prose, Public Affairs.

Pottersfield Press, Lesley Choyce, 83 Leslie Road, East Lawrencetown, NS, B2Z 1P8, Canada, 1-800-Nimbus 9 (for orders). 1979. Fiction, photos, cartoons, satire, non-fiction. "Interest in Canadian, Nova Scotian material, especially non-fiction right now. U.S. orders to: Nimbus Publishing, Box 9301, Station A, Halifax, NS Canada B3K 5N5." avg. press run 1M-2M. Pub'd 6 titles 2005; expects 6 titles 2006, 6 titles 2007. Discounts: 20% 1-5 books, 40% 6+ mixed titles. 192pp. Reporting time: 3 months. Payment: 10% list. Copyrights for author. Subjects: Canada, Counter-Culture, Alternatives, Communes, Fiction, Literature (General), Science Fiction.

Power Potentials Publishing, PO Box 187, Cascade, CO 80809, sagejno@earthlink.net.

The Power Within Institute, Inc., John Maki, 439 So. Buncombe Rd, #932, Greer, SC 29650, 864-877-4990. 1987.

PowerPartners USA, 1155 Camino Del Mar, Ste. 209, Del Mar, CA 92014, info@themagicseed.com.

THE POWYS JOURNAL, The Powys Society, Prof. J. Lawrence Mitchell, 82 Linden Road, Gloucester GL1

5HD, England, 01452-304539. 1991. Articles, reviews. "*The Powys Journal* is a refereed journal published by the Powys Society to promote the understanding and appreciation of the lives and works of the members of the Powys family, principally John Cowper Powys, Theodore Francis Powys and Llewelyn Powys. Scholarly and critical articles, memoirs and unpublished works by the Powys family are welcomed." circ. 500. 1/yr. Pub'd 1 issue 2005; expects 1 issue 2006, 1 issue 2007. sub. price £7.50; per copy £7.50; sample £7.50. Back issues: 1991 £6, 1992 £7. Discounts: by arrangement. 230pp. Reporting time: 1 month. Payment: 2 copies of journal on publication. Copyrighted, reverts to author. Pub's reviews: 5 in 2005. §All material related to Powys family and their circle. Ads: by arrangement. Subjects: Arts, Criticism, Literature (General).

The Powys Society (see also THE POWYS JOURNAL), Dr. Peter Foss, Louis De Bruin, Hamilton's, Kilmersdon, Bath, Somerset BH3 5TE, United Kingdom, 01452-304539. avg. press run 500. Pub'd 3 titles 2005; expects 2 titles 2006, 2 titles 2007. Discounts: by arrangement. Pages vary.

THE PRAIRIE JOURNAL OF CANADIAN LITERATURE, Prairie Journal Press, A. Burke, PO Box 61203 Brentwood P.O., 217, 3630 Brentwood Road N.W., Calgary, Alberta T2L 2K6, Canada, prairiejournal@yahoo.com, www.geocities.com/prairiejournal. 1983. Poetry, fiction, interviews, criticism, reviews, long-poems. "Recent contributors: Laurie Anne Whitt, Fred Cogswell, interviews with poet Lorna Crozier, playwright James Reaney. Literary biases for reviews of Canadian prairie literature; also one act plays. Poems of the Month is a feature being launched by our brand-new website. Submit up to 4 poems with $1 reading fee by snail mail, reply by e-mail or return with SASE." circ. 500+. 2/yr. Pub'd 2 issues 2005; expects 2 issues 2006, 2 issues 2007. sub. price $6, $12 institutions; per copy $6; sample $3. Back issues: $5. Discounts: negotiable. 40-60pp. Reporting time: 2 weeks. Payment: copies and honoraria. Copyrighted. Pub's reviews: 6 in 2005. §Western, prairie, literary, Canadian. Ads: $50/$25/exchange. Subjects: Canada, Criticism, English, Fiction, Great Plains, Humor, Libraries, Literary Review, Literature (General), Magazines, Midwest, Poetry, Theatre, Women.

Prairie Journal Press (see also THE PRAIRIE JOURNAL OF CANADIAN LITERATURE), A. Burke, Brentwood P.O., Calgary, Alberta T2L 2K6, Canada, prairiejournal@yahoo.com, www.geocities.com/ prairiejournal. 1983. Poetry, fiction, interviews, criticism, reviews, long-poems, plays. "Recent publication of an anthology of short fiction by six authors and a collection of poetry by one author. *Prairie Journal Fiction* $6 and for $6 *A Vision of Birds* by Ronald Kurt. Potential contributors please send samples of work with IRC and envelope for reply, covering letter." avg. press run 600+. Pub'd 1 title 2005; expects 2 titles 2006, 1 title 2007. Discounts: negotiable. 40-60pp. Reporting time: 2 weeks - 6 months. Publishes 20% of manuscripts submitted. Payment: copies. Copyrights for author. Subjects: Canada, Criticism, English, Fiction, Humor, Literature (General), Poetry, Women.

•PRAIRIE MARGINS, Amanda Papenfus, Department of English, Bowling Green State University, Bowling Green, OH 43403, debrab@bgnet.bgsu.edu http://www.bgsu.edu/departments/creative-writing/home.html (under BFA).

PRAIRIE SCHOONER, Hilda Raz, Editor-in-Chief; Kelly Grey Carlisle, Managing Editor, 201 Andrews Hall, PO Box 880334, Univ. of Nebraska, Lincoln, NE 68588-0334, 402-472-0911. 1926. Poetry, fiction, art, interviews, reviews, parts-of-novels, long-poems, non-fiction. "Manuscripts are read from September 1st through May 31st only." circ. 2.0M. 4/yr. Pub'd 4 issues 2005; expects 4 issues 2006, 4 issues 2007. sub. price $26; per copy $9; sample $6. Write for information on back issue prices. Write for information on discounts. 200pp. Reporting time: 3-4 months. Simultaneous submissions accepted: no. Publishes 1% of manuscripts submitted. Payment: copies of magazine, and annual prizes; payments depend on grants rec'd. Copyrighted, rights revert to author upon request. Pub's reviews: 20 in 2005. §Current literature. Ads: $200 for full page, 30% discount to university presses. Subjects: Essays, Fiction, Literary Review, Poetry, Reviews, Short Stories.

PRAIRIE WINDS, Katie Jarabek, Editor, Dakota Wesleyan University, DWU Box 536, Mitchell, SD 57301, 605-995-2814. 1946. Poetry, fiction, art, photos, long-poems, plays. "Annual literary review. All submissions must have SASE. Art and photos—preferably black and white; deadline end of January." circ. 500. 1/yr. Pub'd 1 issue 2005; expects 1 issue 2006, 1 issue 2007. sub. price $7; per copy $7; sample $7. Back issues: $10. 50-70pp. Reporting time: 2 months from deadline. Simultaneous submissions accepted: no. Publishes 18% of manuscripts submitted. Payment: 2 copies each. Copyrighted, reverts to author. Ads: none. Subjects: Arts, Fiction, Photography, Poetry.

Prakalpana Literature (see also KOBISENA; PRAKALPANA SAHITYA/PRAKALPANA LITERA-TURE), Vattacharja Chandan, Dilip Gupta, P-40 Nandana Park, Calcutta-700034, West Bengal, India, (91) (033) 478-2347. 1974. Poetry, articles. "Biases: we invite in English or in Bengali: 1) only avant garde experimental poem, story having definitely visual, sonorous & mathematical dimensions—which we call Sarbangin poetry/story; 2) Prakalpana (=P for prose, poetry + R for story + A for art, essay + K for kinema, kinetic + L for play + N for song, novel...)—which is a composition using the above forms appropriately; 3) also articles on Prakalpana literature. If selected, at first we publish the work (if possible with translation) in our mags, then we include it in our future anthology. Submissions not returnable. Length of material: in any case within 2,400 words. USA Distributor: 1025 Thorn Run Road, Moon Township, PA 15108-2817.'' avg. press run 500. Discounts: 20%. 48pp. Simultaneous submissions accepted: no. Payment: none. Does not copyright for author. Subjects: Literature (General), Poetry.

PRAKALPANA SAHITYA/PRAKALPANA LITERATURE, Prakalpana Literature, Vattacharja Chandan, P-40 Nandana Park, Calcutta-700034, West Bengal, India, (91) (033) 478-2347. 1977. Poetry, articles, reviews, letters, news items. ''Biases: we invite in English or in Bengali: 1) only avant garde/experimental poem, story having definitely visual, sonorous & mathematical dimensions—which we call Sarbangin poetry/story; 2) Prakalpana (=P for prose, poetry + R for story + A for art, essay + K for kinema, kinetic + L for play + N for song, novel...)—which is a composition using the above forms appropriately; 3) also criticism, essay & letters on Prakalpana literature. Submissions not returnable. Length of material: in any case within 2,400 words. Some recent contributors: Dilip Gupta, Vattacharja Chandan, Norman J. Olson, Shyamali Mukhopadhyay Bhattacharya, Sheila Murphy, and Jessica Manack.'' circ. 1M. 1/yr. Pub'd 1 issue 2005; expects 1 issue 2006, 1 issue 2007. sub. price 6 rupees; per copy 20 rupees. Overseas: 6 IRCs or exhcnage of little mags; sample 20 rupees. Overseas: 6 IRCs or exchange of little mags. Back issues: 20 rupees. Discounts: 20%. 120pp. Simultaneous submissions accepted: no. Payment: none. Not copyrighted. §Experimental/avant garde/alternative literary & art books and magazines. Ads: 500 rupees/300 rupees/800 rupees (2nd, 3rd, 4th cover pages). Subjects: Literary Review, Literature (General), Poetry.

Prakken Publications (see also THE EDUCATION DIGEST; TECH DIRECTIONS), George F. Kennedy, Publisher, PO Box 8623, Ann Arbor, MI 48107-8623, 734-975-2800, Fax 734-975-2787, publisher@techdirections.com. 1935. Articles, photos, cartoons, letters, news items, non-fiction. ''*Prakken Publications* publishes reference books, textbooks, magazines, workbooks, software and video primarily in career-technical and technology education. Recently published works include: *Machinists Ready Reference, 9th Edition*; *Technology's Past: American's Industrial Revolution and the People Who Delivered the Goods*; *Winning Ways: Best Practices in Work-Based Learning*; *Workforce Education: Issues for the New Century*; *Outdoor Power Equipment*; *Shopform* (software for machinists), *Technology's Past, Vol. 2: More Heroes of Invention and Innovation*, *Workforce Preparation: An International Perspective.*'' avg. press run 3M. Pub'd 2 titles 2005; expects 3 titles 2006, 4 titles 2007. Discounts: 20% educational; bookstores, jobbers call for pricing. 225pp. Reporting time: 2 months *if* reply requested and SASE furnished. Simultaneous submissions accepted: yes. Publishes 20% of manuscripts submitted. Payment: negotiable royalty; generally 10% of receipts, payable June 30, Dec. 30, for books. Copyrights for author. Subjects: Education, Employment, Magazines, Reference, Technology, Textbooks, Worker.

Preludium Publishers (see also LIFTOUTS), Barry Casselman, 520 5th Street SE #4, Minneapolis, MN 55414-1628, 612-321-9044, Fax 612-305-0655, barcass@mr.net. 1971. Poetry, fiction, criticism, plays. ''Preludium Publishers is interested in experimental work in poetry and fiction, and in the translation of new writing which has not previously been published in English. *Unsolicited manuscripts are not considered at this time.* Translators should make inquiry before sending any manuscript, and must include an SASE for a reply.'' avg. press run 1M. Expects 2 titles 2007. Payment: negotiable; some payment to all authors. Copyrights for author. Subjects: Fiction, Poetry, Theatre, Translation.

Premier Publishers, Inc. (see also BOOK NEWS & BOOK BUSINESS MART), Neal Michaels, Owen Bates, PO Box 330309, Fort Worth, TX 76163, 817-293-7030. 1971. Non-fiction. ''We reprint and publish books on success, self-help, how-to, business success and the mail order industry.'' avg. press run 5M. Pub'd 6 titles 2005; expects 10 titles 2006, 8 titles 2007. Discounts: sold primarily through mail order trade. 50% discount to mail order dealers with quantity discounts averaging 60% and 70%. 96pp. Reporting time: 4-12 weeks. Payment: negotiable; small royalty advances possible; outright royalties generally percentage of retail; amount dependent upon author and subject matter. Copyrights for author. Subjects: Book Collecting, Bookselling, How-To, Printing.

Premium Press America, George Schnitzer Jr., 2606 Eugenia Avenue, Suite C, Nashville, TN 37211, 615-256-8484. 1986. Fiction, photos, non-fiction. ''Specialize in gift/souvenir books to gift shops, book stores and speciality outlets—state and federal parks, souvenir stores, museums, historical sites and the like.Added romance novels (352 pgs)in 2006.'' avg. press run 10,000-20,000. Pub'd 6 titles 2005; expects 9 titles 2006, 9 titles 2007. Discounts: 55-60% to distributors and wholesalers, 12 copies, 45-50% to retailers. 128pp. Reporting time: 2 to 3 weeks. Simultaneous submissions accepted: Yes. Payment: Small advance against 15% of collected money paid quarterly. Copyrights for author. Subjects: Arkansas, Children, Youth, Christmas, Civil War, Florida, Inspirational, Native American, Romance, South Carolina, Sports, Outdoors, Tennessee, Texas, Virginia, Wine, Wineries, Women.

PREMONITIONS, Tony Lee, 13 Hazely Combe, Arreton, Isle of Wight, PO30 3AJ, United Kingdom, http://www.pigasuspress.co.uk. 1992. Poetry, fiction, art, cartoons, satire, long-poems. ''The most important piece of advice we can offer is - study copies of our magazine first! Because reading what we have already published is the best way to learn what sort of writings may be suitable for Premonitions." 1/yr. Pub'd 1 issue 2005. price per copy $13; sample $13. Back issues: 4.10. 60pp. Reporting time: 1 to 6 months. Simultaneous submissions accepted: No. Payment: 5 or US$5 per 1,000 words, for stories + copy of the magazine, copy only for poetry, artwork, and shorter fiction or prose. Copyrighted. §cutting-edge science fiction and fantasy. Subjects: Absurdist, Artificial Intelligence, Experimental, Fantasy, Fiction, Futurism, Poetry, Science Fiction, Short Stories.

PREP Publishing, Anne McKinney, 1110 1/2 Hay Street, Suite C, Fayetteville, NC 28305, 910-483-6611, Fax 910-483-2439. 1994. Fiction, non-fiction. "Street address: 1110-1/2 Hay Street, Fayetteville, NC 28305." avg. press run 5M+. Pub'd 6 titles 2005; expects 6 titles 2006, 8 titles 2007. Discounts: 20%-50%. 250-350pp. Reporting time: 12 weeks. Simultaneous submissions accepted: yes. Publishes 5% of manuscripts submitted. Payment: 6%. Copyrights for author. Subjects: Careers, Caribbean, Fiction, How-To, Inspirational, Management, Motivation, Success, North Carolina, Novels, Religion, Romance, Spiritual.

PRESA, Presa Press, Larry Hill, PO Box 792, Rockford, MI 49341, presapress@aol.com. 2005. Poetry, art, photos, criticism, reviews. "Imagistic bias. If it's political, it better be more than just bitching. Surrealism, experimental & personal poetry. We don't think that cutting prose into lines necessarily makes it a good poem. Something magical, some kind of intuitive leap in the last line is preferred. Imagery is essential. Contributors include Harry Smith, Kirby Condgon, Hugh Fox, Eric Greinke, A. D. Winans, Lynne Savitt, David Cope, Jim Cohn, Brian Adam, Ronnie M. Lane." circ. 1000. 2/yr. Expects 1 issue 2006, 2 issues 2007. sub. price $15.00; per copy $8.50; sample $8.50. Back issues: N/A. Discounts: 50% discount to the trade. 48-60pp. Reporting time: Up to one month. Simultaneous submissions accepted: No. Payment: Pays in copies. Copyright, reverts to author on publication, except we retain the right to reprint. Pub's reviews. §Poetry books & chapbooks. Ads: half page - $35.00full page - $60.00. Subjects: Avant-Garde, Experimental Art, Essays, Experimental, Poetry, Reviews, Surrealism.

Presa Press (see also PRESA), Larry Hill, PO Box 792, Rockford, MI 49341, presapress@aol.com. 2002. Poetry, non-fiction. "Prefers imagistic poetry where form is extension of content. Biases against overtly political or didactic material." Pub'd 3 titles 2005; expects 5 titles 2006. Discounts: Library: 1-5 c opies 10%; 6+ copies 20%Bookstores: Softcovers 50%; Hardcovers 20%Wholesalers: 1-4 copies 20%; 5-10 copies 25%. 100-200pp. Reporting time: varies. Simultaneous submissions accepted: No. Payment: flat fee or copies. Individual works in author's name, anthologies in publisher's name. Acquires perpetual rights to print works in anthologies. Subjects: Avant-Garde, Experimental Art, Experimental, Memoirs.

The Preservation Foundation, Inc., J. Richard Loller, Editor, 2213 Pennington Bend Road, Nashville, TN 37214, 800-228-8517, 615-269-2433, preserve@storyhouse.org, www.storyhouse.org. 1976. Non-fiction.

THE PRESIDENTS' JOURNAL, Cottontail Publications, Ellyn R. Kern, 79 Drakes Ridge, Bennington, IN 47011-1802, 812-427-3921. 1984. Articles, art, photos, reviews, letters, news items, non-fiction. "This newsletter provides a glimpse at the personal and not the political side of the presidents and their families. By doing so we can learn more about the times they represented and the roots of our past as individuals in this great United States of America. Looking for columnists interested in writing for future issues on related topics. Submit ideas and sample of writing and qualifications." circ. 100. 4/yr. Pub'd 2 issues 2005; expects 5 issues 2006, 4 issues 2007. sub. price $14; per copy $3.50; sample free for 1st class stamp. Back issues: $2.50. 6pp. Reporting time: 6 weeks. Payment: $5 for articles accepted for publication that review a presidentially related tourist site (not a home). Describe details of location, theme, cost, authenticity, and impressions. Enclose SASE for return of manuscript. Pay in subscription copies for 750 word articles. (Query) Up to $10 for reprints. Copyrighted, publisher keeps reprint and web site rights. Pub's reviews: 2 in 2005. §Related to presidents. Ads: none. Subjects: Americana, Collectibles, Crafts, Hobbies, Presidents, Travel.

The Press at Foggy Bottom, Mike Rosenthal, 35 Linden Lane, 2nd Floor, Princeton, NJ 08540, 609-921-1782. 1994. Fiction, cartoons, criticism, music, plays. "The Press at Foggy Bottom publishes, on an ongoing basis, short run, reprintable trade books of anthologies of interest to children, young adults and the young at heart. Selected materials are also expressed as examples of the Book Arts in limited editions. We are interested in the whole range of literary expression including but not necessarily limited to short stories, humor, folk tales, plays, music, poetry, picture books, cartoons and even literary criticism which can be enjoyed by everyone including adults who are concerned with what children and young adults read. Our efforts, produced in either trade book or Book Art form, are intended to contain offerings children, young adults and parents can share, if not together, than separately within each volume. Great emphasis is placed on non-violence, where characters think up clever ways of besting the tribulations of any and all types of injustice and unfairness using the mental agility of matching wits and the understanding of people coupled with a concomitant, unstated message of ethical conduct. Lightheartedness, humor and good, clean fun are certainly always welcome! As always, we are interested in good secular material, but we are also more focused now, in Judaism. To this purpose, The Havurah for Jewish Storypeople: Tellers, Writers, Illustrators, & Scholars is performing free outreach services. We seek to help those who would like to publish while enjoying the benefits of a supportive, social, scholary and religious extended community. Please write to the Editor for details.'' avg. press run 500. Pub'd 1 title 2005; expects 3 titles 2006, 3-4 titles 2007. Discounts: by agreement. 100pp. Reporting time: 1-2 months. Simultaneous submissions accepted: yes. Publishes 25% of manuscripts submitted. Payment: by agreement. We copyright for author by agreement. Subjects: Cartoons, Children, Youth, Education, Fiction, Folklore, Humor, Judaism, Non-Violence, Religion, Short Stories, Social Work, Storytelling, Theatre.

Press Here (see also TUNDRA), Michael Dylan Welch, Editor & Publisher, 22230 NE 28th Place, Sammamish, WA 98074-6408, WelchM@aol.com. 1989. Poetry, articles, interviews, satire, criticism. ''Press Here publishes books of poetry, primarily haiku and related forms. Query before sending manuscripts. Authors include Paul O. Williams, William J. Higginson, Lee Gurga, Edward J. Rielly, Randy Brooks, Jeanne Emrich, Michael Dylan Welch and others. Books have won ten Merit Book Awards from the Haiku Society of America (including two first-place prizes). Manuscripts preferred only by those widely published in the leading haiku magazines. Especially interested in books of criticism on or about haiku, or small-book-length interviews with established haiku poets.'' avg. press run 200-1M. Pub'd 1 title 2005; expects 2 titles 2006, 3 titles 2007. Discounts: at least 10% for 5-9 books (all one title); discounts negotiable. 28-112pp. Reporting time: usually 1-4 weeks for queries, 2-6 months for manuscripts (query first please). Simultaneous submissions accepted: no. Publishes 5% of manuscripts submitted. Payment: usually in copies. Copyrights for author. Subjects: Anthology, Lewis Carroll, Criticism, Haiku, Japan, Nature, Poetry, Zen.

The Press of Appletree Alley, Barnard Taylor, 138 South 3rd Street, Lewisburg, PA 17837-1910. 1982. avg. press run 150. Pub'd 2 titles 2005; expects 1 title 2006, 2 titles 2007. Discounts: 30% dealers, 10% standing orders. 48-60pp. Payment: 10 copies of the limited edition. Does not copyright for author. Subjects: D.H. Lawrence, Poetry, Prose, G.B. Shaw, Short Stories.

THE PRESSED PRESS, Kara Harris, PO Box 6039, Baltimore, MD 21231-0039. 1997. Articles, art, cartoons, interviews, satire, reviews, music, news items, non-fiction. ''Essays or work submitted, preferably under 5 pages or 5,000 words.'' circ. 1M. 2/yr. Pub'd 2 issues 2005; expects 2 issues 2006, 2 issues 2007. sub. price $4; per copy $2. Discounts: bulk (10+) sold for 50¢ each. 60pp. Reporting time: 2 weeks. Simultaneous submissions accepted: yes. Publishes ~40% of manuscripts submitted. Not copyrighted. Pub's reviews. §Political. Ads: $50/$25/$15 1/4 page. Subjects: Absurdist, Avant-Garde, Experimental Art, Culture, Music, Politics.

PRESSED WAFER: A Boston Review, 9 Columbus Square, Boston, MA 02116.

PRETEXT, Pen & Inc Press, Katri Skala, Managing Editor; Jon Cook, General Editor, Pen & Inc Press, School of Literature & Creative Writing, Norwich, Norfolk NR4 7TJ, United Kingdom, +44 (0)1603 592783, Fax + 44 (0)1603 507728, info@penandinc.co.uk, www.inpressbooks.co.uk/penandinc. 1999. Poetry, fiction, photos, interviews, criticism, letters, parts-of-novels, long-poems, plays. ''Recent contributors include: Michle Roberts, Patricia Duncker, Christopher Hope, Paul Bailey, J G Ballard, Maureen Duffy, Michael Holroyd, Blake Morrison, Seamus Heaney, Iain Sinclair.'' circ. 700. 2/yr. Pub'd 2 issues 2005; expects 2 issues 2006, 3 issues 2007. sub. price £14 UK, £16 Europe, £18 ROW; per copy £7.99 UK, £8.99 Europe, £9.99 Rest of World. Back issues: £7.99 UK, £8.99 Europe, £9.99 ROW. 200pp. Reporting time: 3 months. Simultaneous submissions accepted: yes. Publishes 2% of manuscripts submitted. Payment: £50 per contribution. Copyrighted, reverts to author. Ads: apply for details. Subjects: Arts, Essays, Fiction, Literature (General), Non-Fiction, Photography, Poetry, Prose, Writers/Writing.

Primal Publishing, Lauren Leja, PO Box 1179, Allston, MA 02134-0007, Fax 617-787-5406, e-mail primal@primalpub.com. 1986. Fiction, art, photos, satire, letters, parts-of-novels, non-fiction. ''Modern literature for primitive people.'' avg. press run e-book. Expects 10 titles 2006, 25 titles 2007. 80pp. Reporting time: 1-3 months. Publishes 25% of manuscripts submitted. Payment: 50%. Does not copyright for author. Subjects: Crime, Fiction, Literature (General), Novels.

PRIMARY WRITING, Phyllis Rosenzweig, Diane Ward, 2009 Belmont Road NW #203, Washington, DC 20009. 1995. Poetry. circ. 500. 2-4/yr. Pub'd 3 issues 2005; expects 4 issues 2006, 3-4 issues 2007. sub. price $10; per copy $5; sample $5. Back issues: $5-$6. 1-6pp. Reporting time: varies. Simultaneous submissions accepted: Yes. Payment: none. Copyrighted, reverts to author. Subject: Poetry.

PRIMAVERA, Karen Choy, Co-editor; Valerie Harris, Co-editor; Erin Rhodes, Co-editor, PO Box 37-7547, Chicago, IL 60637-7547, 773-324-5920. 1974. Poetry, fiction, art, photos, satire. ''*Primavera* publishes work expressing the perspectives and experiences of women. We are interested equally in established and in unknown writers and artists. We will be happy to comment on your work in a personal letter *if you ask us to*. Please do not ask unless you are genuinely receptive to constructive, candid criticism. All submissions must be typed (double-spaced) and accompanied by a SASE of sufficient size, bearing sufficient postage. Try to keep a top limit of 3600 words. No simultaneous submissons or previously published material, print or on-line. Recent contributors: Marie Mutsuki Mockett, Ray Jones, Bonnie Stanard, and Sharma Shields.'' circ. 1M. 1/yr. Pub'd 1 issue 2005; expects 1 issue 2006. sub. price $10; per copy $10; sample $5. Back issues: #1-#29 $5. Discounts:

10% off for orders of 3 or more. 144pp. Reporting time: up to 6 months, usually 2 weeks. Simultaneous submissions accepted: no. Publishes 2.5% of manuscripts submitted. Payment: 2 copies. Copyrighted, reverts to author. No ads. Subjects: Fiction, Poetry, Women.

Princess Publishing, Cecile Hammill, Editor; Cheryl A. Matschek, Publisher, PO Box 25406, Portland, OR 97298, 503-297-1565. 1987. Non-fiction. avg. press run 5M. Pub'd 1 title 2005; expects 2 titles 2006, 2 titles 2007. 150-200pp. Reporting time: 1 month. Simultaneous submissions accepted: no. Publishes 1-5% of manuscripts submitted. Payment: variable. Copyrights for author. Subjects: Alternative Medicine, Business & Economics, Christianity, Food, Eating, Health, Leadership, Motivation, Success, Nutrition, Pets, Self-Help, Vegetarianism.

Princess Tides Publishing LLC, Carol Heston, 3 Gerry Street, Marblehead, MA 01945-3029, www.princesstides.com. 2004. Fiction. "Princess Tides Publishing was formed to publish selected works of fiction and non-fiction for readers who seek creative, stimulating entertainment, knowledge and insight. As a woman-owned business, we are particularly interested in works that portray strong women in challenging roles. On February 1, 2005, we released our first book, Absolute Values, a novel by Andrew R Menard (HC, 386 pages, $24.95). See www.princesstides.com." avg. press run 5000. Expects 2-3 titles 2006, 4-6 titles 2007. Discounts: Normal discount structure by distribution channel. 400pp. Reporting time: 4 to 8 weeks. Simultaneous submissions accepted: Yes. Payment: TBA. Copyrights for author.

Princeton Book Company, Publishers, Charles H. Woodford, President, 614 U.S. Hwy 130, Suite 1E, Hightstown, NJ 08520-2651, 609-426-0602, Fax 609-426-1344. 1975. Music, non-fiction. "Princeton Book Company, Publishers is a publisher of books on dance. Most of our books have a text as well as a trade market. Elysian Editions was started as a new imprint in 2000 to publish books nonfiction unrelated to dance." avg. press run 3M. Pub'd 5 titles 2005; expects 4 titles 2006, 4 titles 2007. Discounts: 40% trade, 20% text. 200pp. Reporting time: 6-8 weeks. Payment: 10% on net receipts; usually no advance. Copyrights for author. Subjects: Dance, Health, Performing Arts, Textbooks, Travel, Yoga.

Printed Matter Press (Tokyo), Hillel Wright, Taylor Mignon, Joseph Zanghi, Yagi Bldg. 4F, 2-10-13 Shitaya,, Taito-ku, Tokyo, Japan, 110-0004, Japan, Fax: 81-03-3871-4964 email:info@printedmatterpress.com, http://www.printedmatterpress.com. 1976. Poetry, fiction. "Recent contributors: Cid Corman, Kazuko Shiraishi, Shuntaro Tanikawa, Malinda Markham, Ralph Alfonso, Crad Kilodney, and Donald Richie." avg. press run 1M. Pub'd 1 title 2005; expects 1 title 2006, 2 titles 2007. 212pp. Reporting time: 3 months. Simultaneous submissions accepted: no. Publishes 25% of manuscripts submitted. Payment: case by case. Copyrights for author. Subjects: Fiction, Poetry.

PRISM INTERNATIONAL, Carla Elm Clement, Executive Editor; Regan Taylor, Executive Editor; Bren Simmers, Poetry Editor; Ben Hart, Fiction Editor, E462-1866 Main Mall, University of British Columbia, Vancouver BC V6T 1Z1, Canada, 604-822-2514, Fax 604-822-3616, prism@interchange.ubc.ca, www.prism.arts.ubc.ca. 1959. Poetry, fiction, art, parts-of-novels, long-poems, plays, non-fiction. "*Prism* publishes translations of poetry and fiction from languages other than English. No reviews or scholarly essays." circ. 1.25M. 4/yr. Pub'd 4 issues 2005; expects 4 issues 2006, 4 issues 2007. sub. price $25 indiv., $32 libraries, outside Canada pay US funds.; per copy $9 (bookstores and in person); sample $10 (covers mailing costs). Back issues: varies. 80pp. Reporting time: 12-16 weeks. Simultaneous submissions accepted: no. Publishes 3-5% of manuscripts submitted. Payment: per page: $40 poetry, $20 prose, $10 web + 1-year subscription. Selected authors get an additional $10/printed page for publication on the World Wide Web;. Copyrighted, reverts to author. Ads: $300/$200. Subjects: Drama, Fiction, Literature (General), Non-Fiction, Poetry, Translation, Visual Arts.

PRISON LEGAL NEWS, Paul Wright, 2400 NW 80th Street, PMB 148, Seattle, WA 98117, 206-246-1022, Fax 206-505-94499, pln@prisonlegalnews.org. 1990. Articles, interviews, satire, criticism, reviews, letters, news items, non-fiction. "*PLN* reports on court decisions affecting the rights of prisoners, we cover news and analysis of prisons from around the world. The majority of each issue is written by prisoners and former prisoners and is uncensored by prison officials. *PLN* has a progressive point of view and seeks to educate its readers concerning racism, homophobia and sexism within the prison community and organize its readers into a force for progressive change within the penal system." circ. 4,500. 12/yr. Pub'd 12 issues 2005; expects 12 issues 2006, 12 issues 2007. sub. price $25 individuals, $60 institutions; per copy $5; sample $2. Back issues: $60 per year for 12 issues. $5 single issues. Discounts: contact editors to make special arrangements. 48pp. Reporting time: 6-8 weeks depending on timeliness. Simultaneous submissions accepted: yes. Publishes 20% of manuscripts submitted. Payment: $40 for articles over 1,500 words, $10 for anything under 1,500 words. Not copyrighted. Pub's reviews: 60 in 2005. §Prisons, criminal justice, revolutionary struggle/politics, law, etc. Ads: $495/$295, classified rates are $50 for two months, 185 characters. Subjects: Civil Rights, Crime, Government, Human Rights, Immigration, Law, Prison.

Pristine Publishing, Liliana Monteil Doucette, 7586 Lochinvar Court, Highland, CA 92346, 909-862-1991 phone/Fax, www.pristinepublishing.com. 2001. Fiction, non-fiction. avg. press run 5M. Expects 2 titles 2006, 4 titles 2007. Discounts: upon request. 300pp. Reporting time: 3 months. Simultaneous submissions accepted: yes. Payment: as per contract. Copyrights for author. Subjects: Finances, Romance.

PRIVACY JOURNAL, Robert Ellis Smith, PO Box 28577, Providence, RI 02908, 401-274-7861, 401-274-4747, orders@privacyjournal.net, www.privacyjournal.net. 1974. Articles, cartoons, reviews, letters, news items. 12/yr. Pub'd 12 issues 2005; expects 12 issues 2006, 12 issues 2007. sub. price $125/$165 overseas; per copy $10; sample free. Back issues: $70 per whole year. Discounts: $35 to individuals if paid in advance. 8pp. Reporting time: 1 month. Publishes 25% of manuscripts submitted. Payment: negotiable. Copyrights negotiable. Pub's reviews. §Privacy, computers and society, surveillance. No ads. Subjects: Computers, Calculators, Consumer, Law, Newsletter.

Pro musica press, Edward Foreman, 2501 Pleasant Ave, Minneapolis, MN 55404-4123. 1967. Criticism, music, non-fiction. ''We specialize in vocal pedagogy, translations of classics and reprints of important more recent contributions to the field. Author submissions are welcome.'' avg. press run 500. Expects 2 titles 2006. Discounts: Trade: 10%. 300pp. Reporting time: 2-4 weeks. Payment: Usual royalty 10% of published price. Negotiable. Most of our titles are copyrighted for the press. Subject: Music.

Profile Press, Ann & Deidre Woodward, Silhouettes, How to Cut for Fun and Money, 6051 Greenway Court, Manassas, VA 20112-3049, 703-730-0642. 1988. Non-fiction. avg. press run 5M. Pub'd 1 title 2005. Discounts: 5-20 copies, 40% - all over 50%. 100pp. Reporting time: 3 months. Simultaneous submissions accepted: no. Copyrights for author. Subject: Crafts, Hobbies.

Progressive Education (see also PROGRESSIVE PERIODICALS DIRECTORY/UPDATE), Craig T. Canan, 115 Nashboro Boulevard, Nashville, TN 37217. 1980. Art, cartoons, reviews, concrete art. avg. press run 1.5M. Discounts: over 5 $9 each. 36pp. Reporting time: 1 month. Payment: none. Copyrights for author. Subjects: Counter-Culture, Alternatives, Communes, Magazines, Media, Newsletter, Newspapers, Public Affairs, Reference, Reviews.

PROGRESSIVE PERIODICALS DIRECTORY/UPDATE, Progressive Education, Craig T. Canan, 115 Nashboro Boulevard, Nashville, TN 37217. 1980. Art, cartoons, reviews, concrete art. circ. 1.5M. Expects 1 issue 2006. sub. price $16; per copy $16; sample $16. Back issues: $16. Discounts: over 5, $9 each. 36pp. Reporting time: 4 weeks. Payment: none. Copyrighted, reverts to author. Pub's reviews: 600 in 2005. §Progressive periodicals on social concerns in U.S. Ads: $200/$100. Subjects: Counter-Culture, Alternatives, Communes, Magazines, Media, Newsletter, Newspapers, Public Affairs, Reference, Reviews.

Prologue Press, 375 Riverside Drive #14-C, New York, NY 10025.

Proof Press (see also RAW NERVZ HAIKU), D. Howard, 67 Court Street, Aylmer, QC J9H 4M1, Canada, dhoward@aix1.uottawa.ca. 1994. Poetry. ''Haiku, renga.'' avg. press run 200. Pub'd 7 titles 2005; expects 10 titles 2006, 10 titles 2007. 6-40pp. Reporting time: 6 weeks to 3 months. Simultaneous submissions accepted: no. Publishes 10% of manuscripts submitted. Payment: 10% of run. Copyrights for author.

PROP, 31 Central Avenue, Farnworth, Bolton BL4 0AU, England.

Propeller Press, John Gravdahl, PO Box 729, Fort Collins, CO 80522, 970-482-8807, Fax 970-493-1240, john@propellerpress.com, www.propellerpress.com. 1998. ''We are an independent children's book publisher.'' avg. press run 5M. Pub'd 1 title 2005; expects 1 title 2006, 1 title 2007. Discounts: 40% to resellers, 55% to distributors. 32pp. Reporting time: asap. Payment: none yet. Copyrights for author. Subjects: Children, Youth, Picture Books.

PROSE AX, Jhoanna Salazar, USS Emory S. Land Repair Dept., FPO, AE 09545, prose_ax@att.net, www.proseax.com. 2000. Poetry, fiction, art, photos, parts-of-novels, concrete art, non-fiction. ''We don't really like rhyming poems. Please only send up to 2000 words of a story. We only print in black and white so send art that will look OK in b&w. Recent contributors include Justin Barrett, Richard Jordan, and Nathalie Chicha.'' circ. 600. 3/yr. Pub'd 3 issues 2005; expects 3 issues 2006, 3 issues 2007. sub. price $6; per copy $2; sample $2. 36pp. Reporting time: 2-4 months. Simultaneous submissions accepted: yes. Publishes 20% of manuscripts submitted. Payment: 2 copies. Copyrighted, reverts to author. Subject: Journals.

PROSODIA, George Mattingly, Faculty Advisor, New College of California/Poetics, 766 Valencia Street, San Francisco, CA 94110, 415-437-3479, Fax 415-437-3702. 1990. Poetry, fiction, photos, plays, concrete art. ''Each issue has a different staff and different theme. Invitations to submit are based on taste of particular staff. Issues contain 20-25% student work.'' circ. 500. 1/yr. Pub'd 1 issue 2005; expects 1 issue 2006, 1 issue 2007. sub. price $8; per copy $8. Back issues: order through SPD-Berkeley. Discounts: see SPD's schedule. 120pp. Reporting time: 5 months or less. Simultaneous submissions accepted: yes. Publishes 50% of manuscripts submitted. Payment: copies. Copyrighted, reverts to author. Ads: $120 negotiable. Subject: Poetry.

Prospect Press (see also SPARROWGRASS POETRY NEWSLETTER), Helen McInnis, Jerome Welch,

1000 West London Street, El Reno, OK 73036-3426, www.tinplace.com/prospect. 1997. Poetry, fiction, long-poems, non-fiction. "We are a full-service press committed to publishing the many talented writers and poets, both new and experienced, many of whom do not wish to work with commercial publishers. Whether volumes are done as subsidy/self-published or non-subsidy, we work closely with authors, offering personal, professional service in producing and marketing high quality, finely designed books with unique covers, many 4-color. Almost all of our books receive positive reviews in the media, for example, Gary West's (of the *Dallas Morning News*) book, *Razoo At The Races*, was widely reviewed." avg. press run 750-2M. Pub'd 10 titles 2005; expects 15 titles 2006, 25 titles 2007. Discounts: standard trade and jobber. 128pp. Reporting time: 4-6 weeks. Simultaneous submissions accepted: yes. Publishes 65% of manuscripts submitted. Payment: royalty from 5% on up, self published and subsidy authors receive all proceeds. Copyrights for author. Subjects: Autobiography, Fiction, Non-Fiction, Poetry.

Prospect Press (see also CELEBRATION), William Sullivan, 2707 Lawina Road, Baltimore, MD 21216-1608, (410) 542-8785. 1975. Poetry. "Seldom use poems that rhyme, otherwise we are open to most forms. Sheila E. Murphy; Lyn Lifshin; Laurie Calhoun; George Gott; David Sapp; Timothy Houghton; Austin Straus." avg. press run 300. Expects 1 title 2006, 1 title 2007. 25pp. Reporting time: six months. Simultaneous submissions accepted: No. Publishes 5% of manuscripts submitted. Payment: one copy of issue in which work appears. Each issue is copyrighted by the editor. Subject: Poetry.

Protean Press, Terry Horrigan, 287-28th Avenue, San Francisco, CA 94121, fax 415-386-4980. 1982. Poetry, articles, art, letters, non-fiction. "Recent publications: Portfolio of 25 photographs, Digressions on a Door; soft-cover essay with etching and bibliography, Quipu." avg. press run 60. Pub'd 1 title 2005; expects 3 titles 2006, 2 titles 2007. Discounts: 1-4 25%, 5-9 35%. Pages vary. Simultaneous submissions accepted: no. Publishes 0% of manuscripts submitted. Payment: varies. Copyrights for author. Subjects: The Americas, Anthropology, Archaelogy, Biography, History, Language, Poetry.

PROVINCETOWN ARTS, Provincetown Arts Press, Christopher Busa, 650 Commercial Street, Provincetown, MA 02657, 508-487-3167, web: www.provincetownarts.com. 1985. Poetry, fiction, articles, art, photos, cartoons, interviews, criticism, reviews, collages, non-fiction. "Published annually in July, *Provincetown Arts* focuses broadly on the artists and writers, emerging and established, who inhabit or visit the tip of Cape Cod. Previous cover subjects have included Norman Mailer, Robert Motherwell, and Annie Dillard, Stanley Kunitz, Mark Doty, Mary Oliver, and Karen Finley. Placing contemporary creative activity in a context that draws upon a 75-year tradition of literature, visual art, and theatre, *Provincetown Arts* seeks to consolidate the voices and images of the nation's foremost summer art colony. Some recent contributors include Olga Broumas, Douglas Huebler, Michael Klein, Susan Mitchell, Martha Rhodes, and Anne-Marie Levine." circ. 8M. 1/yr. Pub'd 1 issue 2005; expects 1 issue 2006, 1 issue 2007. sub. price $10; per copy $10; sample $10. Back issues: $10. Discounts: 40% for resale. 184pp. Reporting time: 2 months. Simultaneous submissions discouraged. Publishes 2% of manuscripts submitted. Payment: prose $100-300, poetry $25-125, art $25-300. Copyrighted, reverts to author. Pub's reviews: 20 in 2005. §Biographies of artists, exhibition catalogues, poetry, fiction. Ads: $950/$550/color available. Subjects: Arts, Literature (General), Poetry, Visual Arts.

Provincetown Arts Press (see also PROVINCETOWN ARTS), Christopher Busa, Editorial Director, PO Box 35, 650 Commercial Street, Provincetown, MA 02657, 508-487-3167; FAX 508-487-8634. "A non-profit press for artists and poets." avg. press run artbooks-3M, poetry-1.5M. Pub'd 3 titles 2005; expects 4 titles 2006, 4 titles 2007. Discounts: 40%. Art books 150pp, poetry 70pp. Reporting time: 4 months. Simultaneous submissions accepted: no. Publishes 2% of manuscripts submitted. Payment: $500 advance, 10% royalties.

Pruett Publishing Company, Jim Pruett, Publisher, PO Box 2140, Boulder, CO 80306-2140, 303-449-4919, toll free: 1-800-247-8224. 1959. Art, photos, non-fiction. "Publisher of books pertaining to outdoor travel and recreation, fishing, and the West. Books include *A Climbing Guide to Colorado's Fourteeners: 20th Anniversry Edition, Colorado Nature Almanac,* and *The Earth is Enough.*" avg. press run varies per book. Pub'd 6 titles 2005; expects 12 titles 2006, 7-10 titles 2007. Discounts: write for a copy of our complete schedule. Pages vary. Reporting time: 4-6 weeks. Simultaneous submissions accepted: yes. Publishes about 10% of manuscripts submitted. Payment: generally a royalty basis for authors. Copyrights for author. Subjects: Alaska, Anthropology, Archaelogy, Arizona, Bicycling, Colorado, Cooking, Environment, History, Montana, Nature, New Mexico, Southwest, Sports, Outdoors, Wine, Wineries, Wyoming.

PSI Research/The Oasis Press/Hellgate Press, Emmett Ramey, Editor, PO Box 3727, Central Point, OR 97502, 800-228-2275. 1975. "Small business-oriented. Successful Business Library is a series of how-to business guides designed for entrepreneurs and small businesspersons. Hellgate is military history and adventure travel." avg. press run based on demand. Pub'd 29 titles 2005; expects 32 titles 2006, 35 titles 2007. Discounts: 20%-40% bookstores, 15% libraries. 250pp. Reporting time: 2 months for expression of interest. Publishes 1-2% of manuscripts submitted. Payment: as per licensing agreement. Does not copyright for author. Subjects: Business & Economics, Consulting, How-To, Liberal Arts, Marketing, Public Relations/Publicity, Taxes, Trade.

386

PSYCHE, Eros Books, Mary Nicholaou, 463 Barlow Avenue, Staten Island, NY 10308, 718-317-7484. 2002. Fiction, articles, cartoons, criticism, reviews, letters, parts-of-novels, non-fiction. "*Psyche* is a postmodern newsletter of literary fiction and nonfiction. We provide a forum for experiments in open forms that interrogate the canon." 4/yr. Expects 4 issues 2006, 4 issues 2007. sub. price $3; per copy 75¢; sample 50¢. Back issues: 50¢. Discounts: 25%-40%. 16-20pp. Reporting time: 2 months. Simultaneous submissions accepted: yes. Publishes 50% of manuscripts submitted. Payment: currently 10 contributor's copies. Copyrighted, reverts to author. Pub's reviews. §Postmodern novellas, novels, short stories, graphic novels, nonfiction and romance. Ads: $15/$10/$5 1/3 page. Subjects: Biography, Criticism, Education, Essays, Gender Issues, Language, Lifestyles, Literary Review, Myth, Mythology, New Age, Philosophy, Post Modern, Psychology, Relationships.

PSYCHOANALYTIC BOOKS: A QUARTERLY JOURNAL OF REVIEWS, Joseph Reppen, Editor, 211 East 70th Street, New York, NY 10021, 212-628-8792, Fax 212-628-8453, psabooks@datagram.com. 1990. Reviews. "Book reviews of books in the *broad* field of psychoanalysis including clinical and theoretical psychoanalysis, Freud studies, history of psychoanalysis, psychobiography, psychohistory, and the psychoanalytic study of literature and the arts. News and notes on books and journals in psychoanalysis. ISSN 1044-2103. By invitation only." circ. 1M. 4/yr. Pub'd 4 issues 2005; expects 4 issues 2006, 4 issues 2007. sub. price $55, $105 institutions; per copy $15. Back issues: $15. 160pp. Payment: none. Copyrighted, does not revert to author. Pub's reviews: 150 in 2005. §Psychoanalysis, Freud studies, history of psychoanalysis, psychobiography, psychohistory, psychoanalytic study of literature and the arts. Ads: $200/$125. Subjects: Book Reviewing, Criticism, Psychiatry, Psychology, Reviews, Science.

Psychohistory Press (see also THE JOURNAL OF PSYCHOHISTORY), Lloyd deMause, Editor, 140 Riverside Drive, New York, NY 10024, 212-799-2294. 1973. Articles. avg. press run 3M. Pub'd 2 titles 2005; expects 3 titles 2006. Discounts: 20%. 300pp. Reporting time: 4 weeks. Copyrights for author. Subjects: Anthropology, Archaelogy, History, Psychology.

PSYCHOPOETICA, Geoff Lowe, Trevor Millum, Department of Psychology, University of Hull, Hull HU6 7RX, United Kingdom, website www.fernhse.demon.co.uk/eastword/psycho. 1980. Poetry, reviews. "Psychologically based poetry published on the website only. Visit the site to see what we like." Updated as new material is available. Reporting time: 6-8 weeks. Simultaneous submissions accepted: yes. Payment: none. Copyrighted. Subjects: Experimental, Poetry, Psychology.

PTOLEMY/BROWNS MILLS REVIEW, David C. Vajda, PO Box 252, Juliustown, NJ 08042. 1979. Poetry, fiction, articles, satire, criticism, parts-of-novels, long-poems, concrete art. circ. 100-250. 1-2/yr. Expects 3-4 issues 2006, 2 issues 2007. sub. price $4; per copy $2; sample $1-$2. Back issues: $1-$2. No discounts per se. 16pp. Reporting time: 1 week to 1 month. Payment: 5 copies per acceptance. Copyrighted, rights revert to author with permission. No ads. Subjects: Fiction, Poetry.

THE PUBLIC HISTORIAN, University of California Press, Ann Plane, Editor; Lindsey Reed, Managing Editor, University of California Press, 2000 Center Street, Suite 303, Berkeley, CA 94704-1223, 510-643-7154. 1978. Articles, interviews, reviews, news items, non-fiction. "Editorial address: Dept. of History, University of California, Santa Barbara, CA 93106." circ. 1514. 4/yr. Pub'd 4 issues 2005; expects 4 issues 2006, 4 issues 2007. sub. price $60 indiv., $128 instit., $25 students (+ $20 air freight); per copy $15 indiv.; $38 instit., $15 students; sample free. Back issues: same as single copy price. Discounts: foreign subs. agents 10%, one-time orders 10+ 30%, standing orders (bookstores): 1-99 40%, 100+ 50%. 144pp. Reporting time: 2-3 months. Copyrighted, does not revert to author. Pub's reviews: 50 in 2005. §History. Ads: $295/$220. Subject: History.

THE PUBLIC RELATIONS QUARTERLY, Howard Penn Hudson, Editor-in-Chief, PO Box 311, Rhinebeck, NY 12572, 845-876-2081, Fax 845-876-2561. 1955. Articles, interviews, reviews. circ. 5M. 4/yr. Pub'd 4 issues 2005; expects 4 issues 2006, 4 issues 2007. sub. price $65; per copy $16.25. 48pp. Reporting time: 1 month. Publishes 60% of manuscripts submitted. Payment: in copies. Copyrighted, reverts to author. Pub's reviews: 6-8 in 2005. §Public relations, writing, management. Ads: $800/$400/$35-inch. Subjects: Communication, Journalism, Public Affairs.

THE PUBLICITY HOUND, Joan Stewart, 3434 County Road KK, Port Washington, WI 53074-9638, www.publicityhound.com. 1998. Articles, photos, interviews, reviews, letters, news items. "Welcomes how-to articles and success stories regarding free publicity." 6/yr. Pub'd 6 issues 2005; expects 6 issues 2006, 6 issues 2007. sub. price $9.95 a year (6 issues); per copy $7; sample free sample online at www.publicityhound.com. Back issues: $7 each. Discounts: write for details. 8pp. Reporting time: 1 week. Simultaneous submissions accepted: yes. Publishes 75% of manuscripts submitted. Payment: none. Copyrighted, reverts to author. Pub's reviews: 12 in 2005. §Publicity, public relations, marketing, crisis communications. Ads: none. Subjects: Advertising, Self-Promotion, Magazines, Marketing, Media, Newspapers, Radio, Television.

PublishAmerica, LLLP., Miranda Prather, Editorial Director; Rebecca Embree, Acquisitions Editor; Sarah Andrews, Acquisitions Editor; Sarah Becker, Text Production Manager, PO Box 151, Frederick, MD 21705-0151, 240-529-1031, Fax 301-631-9073, writers@publishamerica.com, www.publishamerica.com. 1999.

Poetry, fiction, articles, satire, parts-of-novels. "Publish America, Inc. is interested in submissions from talented new authors. Manuscripts should be a minimum of 20,000 words. We pay special attention to authors, plots, and subjects overcoming challenges and obstacles. Mailed or emailed submissions are both acceptable." avg. press run print on demand. Pub'd 500 titles 2005; expects 800 titles 2006, 800 titles 2007. Discounts: 40% to retailers, 55% to wholesalers. 200pp. Reporting time: 1-2 months. Simultaneous submissions accepted: yes. Publishes 60% of manuscripts submitted. Payment: 8% minimum on royalties. Does not copyright for author. Subjects: Biography, Christianity, Drama, Fiction, Humor, Juvenile Fiction, Military, Veterans, Mystery, Philosophy, Poetry, Romance, Science Fiction, Short Stories, Spiritual.

PUBLISHING POYNTERS, Para Publishing, Dan Poynter, PO Box 8206-Q, Santa Barbara, CA 93118-8206, 805-968-7277, Fax 805-968-1379, info@parapublishing.com, www.parapublishing.com. 1986. News items. "Book marketing news and ideas from Dan Poynter. *Publishing Poynters* is full of non-fiction book marketing, promotion and distribution leads." circ. 16,000+. 26/yr. Pub'd 26 issues 2005; expects 26 issues 2006, 26 issues 2007. sub. price $9.95/2 years; sample free. Back issues: free. 20pp. Reporting time: 2 weeks. Simultaneous submissions accepted: yes. Payment: none. Copyrighted. Pub's reviews: 15 in 2005. §Non-fiction book marketing, promotion or distribution *only*. Subjects: Printing, Publishing.

Publishing Works, Jeremy Townsend, 60 Winter St., Exeter, NH 03833-2029, 603-778-9883, Fax 603-772-1980, 800-333-9883, email: jeremy@publishingworks.com. 2003. Fiction, photos, non-fiction. "250-300 words, usually reviews of animal books or personal experience essays preferred (for mags)." avg. press run 1M. Pub'd 25 titles 2005. Discounts: 40%-55%. 56pp. Reporting time: 14 days. Simultaneous submissions accepted: yes. Publishes 90% of manuscripts submitted. Payment: varies. Copyrights for author. Subjects: Animals, Children, Youth, Literature (General), Nature, Pets.

Pudding House Publications (see also PUDDING MAGAZINE: The International Journal of Applied Poetry), Jennifer Bosveld, Editor,President; Fred Kirchner, Publications Director; Steve Abbott, Associate Editor; Kathleen Burgess, Associate Editor; Doug Swisher, Assistant Editor; Bob Pringle, Associate Editor; Mark Hartenbach, Associate Editor; Carol Schott Martino, Columnist, Assistant Editor; Bennett Rader, Assistant Editor; Sandra Feen-Diehl, Assistant Editor, 81 Shadymere Lane, Columbus, OH 43213-1568, 614-986-1881, info@puddinghouse.com, www.puddinghouse.com. 1979. Poetry, non-fiction. "Will not return manuscripts for which SASE is not enclosed. $10.00 reading fee for chapbooks, outside of competition 10-40 pages, $15 over 40 pages." avg. press run 400 chapbooks (that might be several reprints); 3000 anthologies. Pub'd 130 titles 2005; expects 130 titles 2006, 130 titles 2007. Discounts: 10% for single copies to classrooms, teachers, bookstores, non-profit or charity organizations; 35% on 10 or more copies 40% 25 or more, 50% on 50+. 24-32pp for chapbooks; 200pp for anthologies. Reporting time: 2 weeks except for competition submissions; sometimes overnight. Simultaneous submissions accepted: no. Publishes less than 1% of manuscripts submitted. Payment: 20 copies of the book; deep discount on additionals, but no expectations for authors to buy extras. Copyrights for author, but we don't register the copyright. Subjects: Poetry, Psychology.

PUDDING MAGAZINE: The International Journal of Applied Poetry, Pudding House Publications, Jennifer Bosveld, Editor; Steve Abbott, Associate Editor; Doug Swisher, Associate Editor; Kathleen Burgess, Associate Editor; Mark Hartenbach, Associate Editor; Robert Pringle, Associate Editor, 81 Shadymere Lane, Columbus, OH 43213-1568, 614-986-1881, info@puddinghouse.com, www.puddinghouse.com. 1979. Poetry, articles, art, photos, cartoons, interviews, criticism, reviews, letters, non-fiction. "All styles and forms of poetry considered. Looking for the wildly different and the subtly profound. We recommend: reflections of intense human situations, conflict, and closure poems on popular culture, politics, social concern, quirky character, and the contemporary scene; concrete images and specific detail; artful expressions of unique situations; or the shock of recognition in things perhaps felt before (or almost felt) but never spoken. No trite comparisons, please. No cliches. No religious verse or sentimentality. Mini-Articles: by poets who share their craft in the human services; about *applied poetry* experiences either from clients/patients or from psychiatrists, teachers, or other professionals and paraprofesionals who put the art of poetry to use in helping others. Reviews of poetry books and chapbooks, how-to-write-poetry books, methodology books, and other relevant publications that would be beneficial to groups or individual readers. Likes dense, rich short stories, 1-2 pages." circ. 1M. Irregular. Pub'd 2 issues 2005; expects 2 issues 2006, 2 issues 2007. sub. price $29.95/4 issues; per copy $8.95; sample $8.95. Back issues: $8.95, $455 for back set. Discounts: 20% on 5+ copies to classrooms, teachers, independent bookstores, non-profit or charity organizations; 35% on 10-49, 50% on 50+. 45-95pp. Reporting time: usually overnight; if held, we're traveling. Simultaneous submissions accepted: no. Publishes way less than 1% of manuscripts submitted. Payment: 1 copy, featured poets receive 4 copies and $10. Copyrighted, rights revert to author, with Pudding House retaining permission to reprint. Pub's reviews: 15 in 2005. §Poetry, 'applied poetry', popular culture and the arts, social justice. Ads: $200/$135 only in our priorties no classifieds. Subjects: Poetry, Psychology.

Puddin'head Press, David Gecic, PO Box 477889, Chicago, IL 60647, 708-656-4900. 1985. Poetry, fiction. "We publish two or three books a year and have many submissions. We get to choose from high quality material. Please only submit work if you are a serious writer. Visit www.puddinheadpress.com.''

PUERTO DEL SOL, Kevin McIlvoy, Fiction Editor; Kathleen West, Poetry Editor; Gail Lavender, Essay Editor, MSC 3E, PO Box 30001, New Mexico State University, Las Cruces, NM 88003, 505-646-2345. 1961. Poetry, fiction, art, photos, interviews, reviews, parts-of-novels, long-poems, plays, non-fiction. ''Emphasis on Southwestern Chicano, Nat. Am. The primary emphasis, however, is on *top quality writing*, wherever it comes from. Some Latin American with trans.'' circ. 1M. 2/yr. Pub'd 2 issues 2005; expects 2 issues 2006, 2 issues 2007. sub. price $10; per copy $8; sample $8. Back issues: complete set $200 (vol 1 no. 1-vol 27 no. 2). Discounts: 40% general, 50% jobber. 200pp. Reporting time: 18 weeks. Simultaneous submissions accepted: yes. Publishes 3-5% of manuscripts submitted. Payment: copies. Copyrighted, reverts to author. Pub's reviews: 8 in 2005. §Chicano, Native American, poetry, fiction, Southwestern, anthologies. Ads: $120/$75. Subjects: Fiction, Poetry.

PULSAR POETRY MAGAZINE, David Pike, 34 Lineacre, Grange Park, Swindon, Wiltshire SN5 6DA, United Kingdom, 01793-875941, e-mail pulsar.ed@btopenworld.com, web: www.pulsarpoetry.com. 1994. Poetry, articles, art, photos, cartoons, reviews, long-poems, news items. ''The U.S. subscription price covers and includes the cost of mailing. £ Sterling cheques - UK £8 only. US equivalent $18.00 Not keen on religious poetry. Will not advertise vanity press.'' circ. 300. 2/yr. Pub'd 4 issues 2005; expects 2 issues 2006, 2 issues 2007. sub. price $18; per copy $9; sample Free UK. Back issues: $9.00/copy. Discounts: Special subscription price to colleges/universities: price on application. 40pp. Reporting time: If accepted, may not appear for two issues. Simultaneous submissions accepted: No. Publishes 1 in 40?% of manuscripts submitted. Payment: None, but receive free copy of magazine. Copyrighted, reverts to author. Pub's reviews: 20 in 2005. §Poetry only, also poetry CDs. Ads: $10/$5. Subjects: Arts, Book Reviewing, England, Language, Literary Review, Literature (General), Poetry, Quotations, Tapes & Records, Writers/Writing.

•**Puna Press,** Lesli Bandy, Marketing Director, P.O. Box 7790, San Diego, CA 92107, 619.278.8089, www.punapress.com. 1995. Poetry, art. avg. press run 500. Pub'd 2 titles 2005; expects 2 titles 2006, 4 titles 2007. Discounts: 40%-50%. 50-200pp. Reporting time: 4 to 6 months. Simultaneous submissions accepted: Yes. Does not copyright for author. Subjects: Arts, Poetry, Visual Arts.

Royal Purcell, Publisher, Royal Purcell, 806 West Second Street, Bloomington, IN 47403, 812-336-4195. 1985. Non-fiction. ''Submit query first, preferably with specific outline of nonfiction subject and SASE.'' avg. press run 1M. Expects 1 title 2006, 1 title 2007. Discounts: 1-5 20%, 6-24 30%, 25-49 40%, 50-99 45%, 100 up 50%. 150pp. Reporting time: 2 weeks for query. Payment: 10-15%. Copyrights for author. Subjects: Anthropology, Archaelogy, Culture, Ecology, Foods, Education, Humanism, Sociology.

Purple Finch Press, Nancy Benson, 109 Warwick Road, Syracuse, NY 13214-2219, 315-445-8087. 1992. Poetry, fiction, art, photos, interviews, reviews, non-fiction. ''We are not considering unsolicited manuscripts at this time. Additional address: 109 Warwick Road, Dewitt, NY 13214. Length of material: 100-300 pages. Biases: sensitive, literary prose, poetry, cookbooks, mystery novels—adult and juvenile.'' avg. press run 500-2M. Pub'd 1 title 2005; expects 2 titles 2006, 3 titles 2007. Discounts: 1 book 10%, 2-10 20%, 11+ 25%. 101pp. Reporting time: 2 months. Simultaneous submissions accepted: yes. Publishes 20% of manuscripts submitted. Payment: 4-7.5% of net price. Copyrights for author. Subjects: Arts, Children, Youth, Computers, Calculators, Dance, Education, English, Fiction, Interviews, Mystery, Non-Fiction, Parenting, Poetry, Short Stories, Visual Arts.

Purple Mouth Press (see also IT GOES ON THE SHELF), Ned Brooks, 4817 Dean Lane, Lilburn, GA 30047-4720, nedbrooks@sprynet.com, http://home.sprynet.com/~nedbrooks/home.htm. 1975. Fiction, art, satire. avg. press run 500. Discounts: 40% for 5 or more. 60pp. Reporting time: 1 week. Payment: yes. Copyrights for author. Subjects: Fantasy, Science Fiction.

PURPLE PATCH, Geoff Stevens, 25 Griffiths Road, West Bromwich, B71 2EH, England. 1976. Poetry, fiction, articles, art, reviews, news items. ''Mainly poetry. Fiction should be short.'' circ. 200. 3/yr. Pub'd 3 issues 2005; expects 5 issues 2006, 3 issues 2007. sub. price £5.60 for 3, includes 100th issue (2001); per copy £1.50; $5 bill or £2 sterling cheque (due to postage/exchange charges etc.); sample £1.50, $5 bill. 24+pp. Reporting time: 1 month. Simultaneous submissions accepted: yes. Publishes 5% of manuscripts submitted. Payment: none. Copyrighted, reverts to author. Pub's reviews: 150 in 2005. §Poetry, short stories, biographies of writers, art. Ads: inquire. Subjects: Fiction, Literary Review, Poetry.

Pushcart Press, Bill Henderson, PO Box 380, Wainscott, NY 11975, 631-324-9300, www.pushcartprize.com. 1973. ''Each year we will publish *The Pushcart Prize: Best of the Small Presses*, with the help of our distinguished contributing editors. We also sponsor the annual Editors' Book Award for manuscripts overlooked by commercial publishers. (All manuscripts must be nominated by an editor.).'' avg. press run varies. Pub'd 8 titles 2005; expects 8 titles 2006, 9 titles 2007. Discounts: 1-9, 20%; 10+, 40%. 200-600pp. Reporting time: varies. Payment: 10%. Copyrights for author. Subjects: How-To, Literature (General).

Pussywillow, Sasha Briar Newborn, 1212 Punta Gorda Street #13, Santa Barbara, CA 93103-3568, 805-899-2145 phone/Fax. 2002. Poetry, fiction, art, photos, music, parts-of-novels. "Material for Pussywillow must be erotic. Our audience is primarily women, who feel good about sexuality." avg. press run 1M. Expects 1 title 2006, 2 titles 2007. None, no returns. 80pp. Reporting time: 2 months. Simultaneous submissions accepted: yes. Publishes 3% of manuscripts submitted. Payment: by agreement. Copyrights for author. Subjects: Autobiography, Bisexual, Erotica, Gay, Gender Issues, Lesbianism, Memoirs, Relationships, Romance, Sex, Sexuality.

Pussywillow Publishing House, Inc., 844 South Park View Circle, Mesa, AZ 85208-4782. "We publish for authors if the book is good." avg. press run 2.5M-5M. Discounts: 40% stores; 15-20% reps; distributors 60%. 36pp. Copyrights for author. Subject: Biography.

Putting Up Books, LC, T.J. Flynn, P.O. Box J * 6079 Avenue F, McIntosh, FL 32664, phone 3525914535, fax 3525914626. 2001. Art, non-fiction. "We seek works fitting identifiable and quantifiable niches where there are no current titles." Pub'd 1 title 2005; expects 1 title 2006, 2 titles 2007. Discounts: 40% trade discount / 55% for 100 or more copies. 125pp. Reporting time: 30 days. Simultaneous submissions accepted: No. Publishes 25% of manuscripts submitted. Payment: No advances, 50-50 split after expenses are recovered. Does not copyright for author. Subjects: Crafts, Hobbies, Florida, Management, Military, Veterans.

Pygmy Forest Press, Leonard Cirino, 1125 Mill St, Springfield, OR 97477-3729, 541-747-9734. 1987. Poetry, fiction, art, reviews, non-fiction. "Query with 10-15 pages." avg. press run 200. Pub'd 2 titles 2005; expects 3 titles 2006, 4 titles 2007. Discounts: 1/3 off to retail and institutional prisoners; libraries full price. 20-80pp. Reporting time: immediate to 1 month. Simultaneous submissions accepted: yes. Publishes 3-5% of manuscripts submitted. Payment: new format is that author must subsidy 90% of printing costs and will receive like in copies. Copyrights for author. Subjects: Anarchist, Arts, Asian-American, John Berryman, Black, California, Chicano/a, Fiction, Native American, Pacific Northwest, Poetry, Prison, Short Stories, Tapes & Records, Translation.

Pyncheon House, David Rhodes, 6 University Drive, Suite 105, Amherst, MA 01002. 1991. Poetry, fiction, criticism. "Recent contributors: F.D. Reeve, Jonathan Edward, Rebecca Scott and James Cole." avg. press run 2M-3M. Pub'd 4 titles 2005; expects 4 titles 2006, 4 titles 2007. Discounts: 1-5 10%, 6-15 15%, 16-25 20%; direct to library 20%, 26-100 30% 101+ negotiable. 150pp. Reporting time: 3-6 months. Publishes 5% of manuscripts submitted. Payment: 10% and/or free books. Copyrights for author. Subjects: Criticism, Fiction, Literature (General), Novels, Poetry, Short Stories.

Q

QED Press, Cynthia Frank, President, Managing Editor; Joe Shaw, Editor, 155 Cypress Street, Fort Bragg, CA 95437, 707-964-9520, Fax 707-964-7531, qedpress@mcn.org. 1986. Fiction, art, non-fiction. "QED Press is a small, Mendocino-based publishing house whose vision is to publish fiction and non-fiction that inspires readers to transcend national, racial and ethnic boundaries through appreciation of world literature and art. Each year QED publishes selected titles of uncommon interest and quality." avg. press run 3M. Pub'd 1 title 2005; expects 5 titles 2006, 5 titles 2007. Discounts: 1-2 books list, 3-5 33%, 6+ 40%. 224pp. Reporting time: 3 months. Simultaneous submissions accepted: yes. Publishes less than 3% of manuscripts submitted. Payment: varies. Copyrights for author. Subjects: African-American, Biography, Careers, Fiction, Health, History, How-To, Literature (General), Memoirs, Mental Health, Pacific Northwest, Political Science, Printing, Self-Help, Women.

QP Publishing (see also QUALITY QUIPS NEWSLETTER), Nancy Sue Swoger, PO Box 18281, Pittsburgh, PA 15236-0281, phone/Fax. 1990. Non-fiction. "Primary focus is quality/technical non-fiction. Will consider other works in the non-fiction field. Also interested in any business publications." avg. press run 1M. Pub'd 2 titles 2005; expects 3 titles 2006. Discounts: 1-4 books 20%, 5-9 30%, 10-24 40%, 25-49 45%, 50+ 50%. 184pp. Publishes 50% of manuscripts submitted. Payment: negotiable. Copyrights for author. Subject: Business & Economics.

QRL POETRY SERIES, Quarterly Review of Literature Press, Theodore Weiss, Renee Weiss, Princeton University, 185 Nassau Street, Princeton, NJ 08540, 609-258-4703. 1943. Poetry, long-poems. "4-6 books under one cover and listed by volume number." sub. price 2 volumes paper $20, single $12, $20 institutional & hardback per volume; per copy $20/cl, $10/pa, anniversary double volume $20/pa, $25/cl; sample $10. Back issues: roughly $20 per volume, cloth; $10 per volume paper; write for catalog for complete list. Discounts: non-returnable—bookstores 40% on 5+ copies, 10% on 1 copy; agency 10%; 20% for returnable arrangements.

390

250-350pp. Copyrighted, does not revert to author. Subjects: Poetry, Translation.

Quail Ridge Press, PO Box 123, Brandon, MS 39043, kgrissom@quailridge.com.

Quale Press, Gian Lombardo, 93 Main Street, Florence, MA 01062, 413-587-0776 phone/Fax, central@quale.com. 1997. "No unsolicited work. Press will only publish prose poetry, experimental fiction and literary criticism on a solicited basis only. Also interested mainly in scientific, engineering and computer-related books emphasizing the humanistic aspect and effects of technology. Query first. Occasionally will publish reprints of exceptional but overlooked literary work currently not in print." avg. press run Titles being published print-on-demand. Advance copies number from 75 to 125. Pub'd 5 titles 2005; expects 5 titles 2006, 5 titles 2007. Discounts: 20% agent/jobber on more than 10 copies. 64-152pp. Payment: Author receives net sales royalty. Copyrights for author. Subjects: Computers, Calculators, Criticism, Engineering, Experimental, Fiction, Literature (General), Poetry, Science, Socialist, Surrealism.

QUALITY QUIPS NEWSLETTER, QP Publishing, Nancy Sue Swoger, PO Box 18281, Pittsburgh, PA 15236-0281, phone/Fax. 1991. "This quarterly newsletter deals with quality, customer service and team issues (non-fiction business). Book reviews are a regular feature (6-8 reviews per issue). Distribution is to quality managers, customer service managers and representatives, and quality engineers, to companies of all sizes." circ. 5M. 4/yr. Pub'd 4 issues 2005; expects 4 issues 2006, 4 issues 2007. sub. price $30. 10pp. Payment: free 1 year subscription. Pub's reviews: 24-32 in 2005. Subject: Business & Economics.

Quality Sports Publications, Susan Smith, 24 Buysse Drive, Coal Valley, IL 61240, 800-464-1116, Fax 309-234-5019, www.qualitysportsbooks.com. 1993. Art, photos, interviews, reviews, non-fiction. "We only publish non-fiction sports related titles. Team histories, biographies, instructional sports books, etc." avg. press run 3-5M. Pub'd 3 titles 2005; expects 3 titles 2006, 3 titles 2007. Discounts: 1 book 20%, 2-24 40%, 25-99 43%, 100-199 45%, 200-499 46%, 500-1999 48%, 2000+ 50%. 200pp. Reporting time: 1 month of less. Simultaneous submissions accepted: yes. Publishes 10% of manuscripts submitted. Payment: it varies on authors. Copyrights for author. Subjects: History, Sports, Outdoors.

Quality Words in Print, PO Box 2704, Costa Mesa, CA 92628-2704, 714-436-5700, fax: 714-668-9448, web: www.qwipbooks.com, email: custserv@nbnbooks.com.

Quantum Leap S.L.C. Publications, Rev. RaDine Amen-ra, 2740 Greenbriar Parkway, Ste. 201, Atlanta, GA 30331, 877-571-9788, www.blackamericanhandbook.com. 2000. Articles, photos, interviews, letters, news items, non-fiction. avg. press run 3M. Pub'd 1 title 2005; expects 3 titles 2006, 3 titles 2007. Discounts: go to website. 200pp. Payment: 30%. Copyrights for author. Subjects: African-American, Anthropology, Archaelogy, Black, Culture, Genealogy, North America, Race.

QUARTER AFTER EIGHT, Kelley Evans, Editor-in-Chief, Ellis Hall, Ohio University, Athens, OH 45701. 1993. Fiction, articles, interviews, satire, criticism, letters, parts-of-novels, plays, non-fiction. "QAE seeks dynamic prose works—short fiction, prose-poetry, letters, drama, essays, memoirs, translations—that eschew the merely prosaic across a range of genres. Although *QAE* does not publish traditional verse and/or lyric poetry, the editors do welcome work that provocatively explores—even challenges—the prose/poetry distinction." circ. 1M. 1/yr. Pub'd 1 issue 2005; expects 1 issue 2006, 1 issue 2007. sub. price $10; per copy $10; sample $10. Back issues: sold out. Discounts: 25+ copies 30%, distributed by Bernhard DeBoer, Ingram. 300pp. Reporting time: 3-4 months. We accept simultaneous submissions if stated in cover letter. Publishes 7% of manuscripts submitted. Payment: 2 copies of upcoming issue. Copyrighted, reverts to author. Pub's reviews: 3 in 2005. §Cutting edge prose and poetry books. Subjects: Criticism, Culture, Essays, Fiction, Interviews, Prose.

Quarterly Committee of Queen's University (see also QUEEN'S QUARTERLY: A Canadian Review), Boris Castel, Queen's University, Kingston, Ontario K7L 3N6, Canada, 613-533-2667, qquarter@post.queensu.ca, http://info.queensu.ca/quarterly. 1893. Poetry, fiction, articles, interviews, satire, criticism, parts-of-novels, plays. "Articles: 20-25 double-spaced pages plus copy on disk in Wordperfect. Recent contributors: Marlene Brant Castellano, Jerry S. Grafstein, Sylvia Ostry, Janice Gross Stein, Michael Ignatieff, Conor Cruise O'Brien." avg. press run 3.5M. Expects 1 title 2006. 224pp. Reporting time: 2-3 months. Payment: yes. Copyrights for author. Subjects: Arts, Biography, Book Reviewing, Business & Economics, Criticism, Earth, Natural History, Education, History, Literature (General), Philosophy, Politics, Psychology, Science.

Quarterly Review of Literature Press (see also QRL POETRY SERIES), Theodore Weiss, Renee Weiss, 900 Hollingshead Spring Road, Apt J-300, Skillman, NJ 08558-2075, 609-921-6976, Fax 609-258-2230, qrl@princeton.edu. 1943. Poetry. avg. press run 3M-5M. Pub'd 4-6 titles 2005. Discounts: 10%. 350pp. Reporting time: 1-3 months. Simultaneous submissions accepted: yes. Payment: $1000 and 100 copies for each manuscript printed. Copyright by QRL. Subject: Poetry.

QUARTERLY WEST, Mike White, Editor; Paul Ketzle, Editor, 255 South Central Campus Drive, Dept. of

English, LNCO 3500/University of Utah, Salt Lake City, UT 84112-9109, 801-581-3938. 1976. Poetry, fiction, interviews, criticism, reviews, parts-of-novels, long-poems, non-fiction. "We publish quality fiction, poetry, nonfiction and reviews in experimental or traditional forms, by new or established writers. We solicit our reviews but do read unsolicited ones. Since 1982 we have sponsored a biennial novella competition with cash prizes for the two winners. We read unsolicited MSS from *Sept. 1-May 1 only* and will accept simultaneous submissions (make this clear in your cover letter). Contributors: Ai, Kate Braverman, Ron Carlson, Andre Dubus, Stephen Dunn, Allen Ginsberg, Albert Goldbarth, Eamon Grennan, Barry Hannah, Tess Gallagher, Patricia Goedicke, Philip Levine, Larry Levis, Lynne McMahon, Lucia Perillo, Francine Prose, Dave Smith, George Saunders, Eleanor Wilner." circ. 1700. 2/yr. Pub'd 2 issues 2005; expects 2 issues 2006, 2 issues 2007. sub. price $14.00; per copy $8.50; sample $7.50. Back issues: $5. Discounts: agents 25%, bookstores 40%. 144pp. Reporting time: 3-6 months. Simultaneous submissions accepted: yes. Publishes less than 1% of manuscripts submitted. Payment: 2 copies; $25-$100 fiction, $25-100 poetry, $500 novella competition. Copyrighted, does not revert to author. Pub's reviews: 5 in 2005. §Fiction, poetry, and non-fiction. Ads: $150/$85. Subjects: Fiction, Poetry, Reviews.

QUARTZ HILL JOURNAL OF THEOLOGY:A Journal of Bible and Contemporary Theological Thought, Quartz Hill Publishing House, R.P. Nettelhorst, Editor; Dandi Moyers, Assistant Editor, 43543 51st Street West, Quartz Hill, CA 93536, 661-722-0891, 661-943-3484, E-mail robin@theology.edu. 1993. Poetry, articles, interviews, criticism, reviews, non-fiction. *"Quartz Hill Journal of Theology* is the official journal of Quartz Hill School of Theology, a ministry of Quartz Hill Community Church. Quartz Hill Community Church is associated with the Southern Baptist Convention. We accept as our doctrinal statement *The Baptist Faith and Message,* adopted by the SBC in 1963. Length: 25,000 words max.; prefer 5,000-10,000. Submit complete manuscript. Enclose SASE for response. Submissions without SASE will be disposed of unread." circ. 200. 4/yr. Pub'd 2 issues 2005; expects 4 issues 2006, 4 issues 2007. sub. price $40; per copy $10.95; sample $10.95. Back issues: $10.95. Discounts: none. 100pp. Reporting time: 30 days. Simultaneous submissions accepted: yes. Publishes 10% of manuscripts submitted. Payment: 1 contributor's copy. Copyrighted, does not revert to author. Pub's reviews: 12 in 2005. §Bible, theology, science, literature, poetry. Ads: $50/$25/will trade ads with other publishers. Subjects: Christianity, Religion.

Quartz Hill Publishing House (see also QUARTZ HILL JOURNAL OF THEOLOGY:A Journal of Bible and Contemporary Theological Thought), R.P. Nettelhorst, Editor; Dandi Moyers, Assistant Editor, 43543 51st Street West, Quartz Hill, CA 93536, 661-722-0891, 661-943-3484, E-mail robin@theology.edu. 1993. Non-fiction. "Quartz Hill Publishing House is the official publishing arm of Quartz Hill School of Theology, a ministry of Quartz Hill Community Church. Quartz Hill Community Church is associated with the Southern Baptist Convention. We accept as our doctrinal statement *The Baptist Faith and Message,* adopted by the SBC in 1963. Length: 500,000 words max. for books. Query first. Must enclose SASE for response. Submissions without SASE will be disposed of unread." avg. press run 200. Pub'd 5 titles 2005; expects 5 titles 2006, 5 titles 2007. 200pp. Reporting time: 30 days. Publishes 1% of manuscripts submitted. Payment: no advance; 10% royalty. Copyrights for author. Subjects: Christianity, Religion.

QUEEN OF ALL HEARTS, Montfort Publications, J. Patrick Gaffney, Editor; Roger M. Charest, Managing Editor, 26 South Saxon Avenue, Bay Shore, NY 11706, info@montfortmissionaries.com, www.montfortmissionaries.com. 1950. Poetry, fiction, articles, art, non-fiction. *"Queen of all Hearts* Magazine promotes knowledge of and devotion to the Mother of God, by explaining the Scriptural basis as well as the traditional teaching of the Church concerning the Mother of Jesus; her place in theology, the apostolate and spiritual life of the Roman Catholic Church; to make known her influence, over the centuries, in the fields of history, literature, art, music, poetry, etc., and to keep our readers informed of the happenings and recent developments in all fields of Marian endeavors around the world. Length of article: 1500 to 2500 words. Authors: Roman Ginn, o.c.s.o., Viola Ward, Joseph Tusiani, etc." circ. 1.5M. 6/yr. Pub'd 6 issues 2005; expects 6 issues 2006, 6 issues 2007. sub. price $22; per copy $2; sample $2. Back issues: 50% discount plus postage. Discounts: schedules upon request. 48pp. Reporting time: less than a month. Simultaneous submissions accepted: no. Publishes approx. 25% of manuscripts submitted. Payment: yes, most of the time. Not copyrighted. Pub's reviews: about 18 in 2005. §Marian topics. Ads: none. Subject: Religion.

QUEEN'S QUARTERLY: A Canadian Review, Quarterly Committee of Queen's University, Boris Castel, Queen's University, Kingston, Ontario K7L 3N6, Canada, 613-533-2667, qquarter@post.queensu.ca, http:/info.queensu.ca/quarterly. 1893. Poetry, fiction, articles, interviews, satire, criticism, parts-of-novels, plays. "Articles 2000 - 3000 words by email or regular mail. Recent contributors include Michael Ignatieff, Mavis Gallant, Mark Kingwell, Leslie Millin, Michael Posner." circ. 3.5M. 4/yr. Pub'd 4 issues 2005; expects 4 issues 2006, 4 issues 2007. sub. price $20 Canada, $25 U.S.; per copy $6.50; sample $6.50. Back issues: depends on age, min. $4, max. $6. Discounts: none. 160pp. Reporting time: 1 month. Simultaneous submissions accepted: no. Payment: up to $300 (short stories), $80 per poem, copies, subscriptions. Copyrighted, reverts to author. Pub's reviews: 60 in 2005. §Serious books only, history, science, politics, philosophy, social science, literary studies, music, art, etc. Not interested in unsolicited reviews. Ads: none. Subjects: Arts, Biography,

Book Reviewing, Business & Economics, Criticism, Earth, Natural History, Education, History, Literature (General), Philosophy, Politics, Psychology, Science.

QUERCUS REVIEW, Sam Pierstorff, Modesto Junior College, 435 College Avenue, Modesto, CA 95350, 209-575-6183, pierstorffs@mjc.edu, www.quercusreview.com. 2000. Poetry, fiction, art, photos. ''Established in 1999, *Quercus Review (QR)* has quickly become a prominent literary arts journal, publishing numerous nationally recognized, award-winning authors and artists from all across the nation. Additionally, *QR* continues to discover new voices and reflect the lyricism of California's Great Central Valley. However, our main goal has always been simply to publish the best work we can find. Recent contributors: X.J. Kennedy, Amiri Baraka, Gerald Locklin, Lawrence Raab, Naomi Shihab Nye, Steve Kowit, Alan Catlin, Lyn Lifshin, Charles Harper Webb, Stellasue Lee, Wilma McDaniel. In addition to publishing our annual literary arts journal, Quercus Review Press publishes one full-length collection of poetry by a single author every year through our annual book award contest. More info about the Quercus Review Press Poetry Series can be found at our website.'' circ. 500. 2/yr. Pub'd 1 issue 2005; expects 2 issues 2006, 2 issues 2007. sub. price $17 for 1yr. (2 books); $35 for 2 yrs. (4 books); per copy $8; sample $8. Back issues: $6. Discounts: Additional contributor copies are $5. Other discounts available for orders of 10 or more. 124pp. Reporting time: 3 weeks to 6 months. Simultaneous submissions accepted: no. Publishes 10% of manuscripts submitted. Payment: 1 copy + $5 for additional copies. Copyrighted, reverts to author. Subjects: Fiction, Poetry.

THE QUEST, Quest Books: Theosophical Publishing House, John Algeo, PO Box 270, Wheaton, IL 60189, 630-668-1571. 1988. Articles, art, photos, interviews, reviews, non-fiction. ''*The Quest* is a wholistic metaphysical magazine, with articles on philosophy, comparative religion, science, arts, and psychology.'' circ. 10M+. 6/yr. Pub'd 6 issues 2005; expects 6 issues 2006, 6 issues 2007. sub. price $17.97; per copy $3.95; sample $4. Back issues: $5. Discounts: sold by subscription only. 40pp. Reporting time: 3 months. Simultaneous submissions accepted: no. Payment: on publication. Copyrighted. Pub's reviews. §Wholistic perspective, comparative philosophy, science, religion, and the arts. Ads: none. Subjects: Arts, Metaphysics, Philosophy, Psychology, Religion, Science, Spiritual, Theosophical.

Quest Books: Theosophical Publishing House (see also THE QUEST), Sharron Dorr, Publishing Manager, 306 W. Geneva Rd., PO Box 270, Wheaton, IL 60189-0270, 630-665-0130, Fax 630-665-8791, questoperations@theosmail.net. 1968. Art, non-fiction. ''Esoteric, comparative religion, psychology, philosophy, health, holistic healing, astrology, meditation, holistic living.'' avg. press run 5M. Pub'd 12 titles 2005; expects 6 titles 2006, 6 titles 2007. 200pp. Reporting time: 1-6 months. Payment: paid once a year. Copyrights for author. Subjects: Buddhism, Environment, Health, Inspirational, Metaphysics, Myth, Mythology, Native American, Non-Fiction, Philosophy, Psychology, Religion, Spiritual, Theosophical, Yoga, Zen.

QUEST: AN INTERDISCIPLINARY JOURNAL FOR ASIAN CHRISTIAN SCHOLARS, The Chinese University Press, David K.S. Suh, Editor in Chief; Wendy Chan, Managing Editor; Salvador T. Martinez, Book Review Editor, The Chinese University of Hong Kong, Sha Tin, New Territories, Hong Kong, Hong Kong, 852-26096500, 852-26037355, cup@cuhk.edu.hk, www.chineseupress.com. 2002. 2/yr. Pub'd 2 issues 2005; expects 2 issues 2006, 2 issues 2007. sub. price $40 (Institution), $24 (Individual); per copy $20 (Institution), $12 (Individual). Back issues: $20 (Institution), $12 (Individual). Simultaneous submissions accepted: No. Pub's reviews: 6 in 2005. §Religion. Subjects: Christianity, Religion.

Questex Consulting Ltd., K. Slater, 8 Karen Drive, Guelph, Ontario N1G 2N9, Canada, 519-824-7423. 1978. ''Currently accepting only Canadian plays (i.e. plays written by a resident of Canada, or by a Canadian living abroad, or with significant recognisable Canadian setting, content, etc.) for the CAPCAT series. CAPCAT (Canadian Amateur Playwrights' Catalogue) is a collective arrangement in which all members pay a fee (up to $200 per play, depending on the length of play submitted) for guaranteed publication if literary, etc., standards are met. Arrangements can be made for payment to be waived for high-quality plays in selected cases.'' Pub'd 5 titles 2005; expects 5 titles 2006, 6 titles 2007. Discounts: 20% for libraries and multiple orders. 70pp. Reporting time: 1 month. Simultaneous submissions accepted: yes. Publishes members 90%, non-members 20% of manuscripts submitted. Payment: 10% sales, 50% performance. Copyrights for author. Subjects: Drama, Environment, Fiction, History, Humor, Mystery, Short Stories, Theatre.

Quicksilver Productions, Jim Maynard, P.O.Box 340, 559 S Mountain Avenue, Ashland, OR 97520-3241, 541-482-5343, Fax 541-482-0960. 1973. ''Not accepting manuscripts at this time.'' avg. press run 30M. Pub'd 5 titles 2005; expects 6 titles 2006, 6 titles 2007. Discounts: trade and jobbers, (trade from 40% at 5 copies to 50% at 1,000 mixed titles). Prepaid orders receive 5% extra discount plus free shipping. Copyrights for author. Subjects: Astrology, Cooking, Occult.

THE QUIET FEATHER, Taissa Csaky, Dominic Hall, Tim Major, St. Mary's Cottage, Church Street, Dalton-In-Furness, Cumbria, LA15 8BA, ENGLAND, United Kingdom. 2004. Poetry, fiction, articles, art, photos, cartoons, interviews, music, plays, non-fiction. circ. 200. 4/yr. Pub'd 3 issues 2005; expects 4 issues

2006, 4 issues 2007. sub. price 9; per copy 2.50; sample 2.50. Back issues: 2.50. 24pp. Reporting time: 2 weeks. Simultaneous submissions accepted: Yes. Publishes 5% of manuscripts submitted. Payment: Profit-sharing when circulation gets larger - see http://www.thequietfeather.co.uk/QFworks.htm. Not copyrighted. Subjects: Arts, Cartoons, Creativity, Current Affairs, Environment, Fiction, Non-Fiction, Poetry, Politics, Prose, Short Stories, Travel.

Quiet Storm Books, Clint Gaige, PO Box 1666, Martinsburg, WV 25402, 361-992-5587, Fax 208-498-9259, management@quietstormbooks.com, www.quietstormbooks.com. 2002. Fiction, non-fiction. "Quiet Storm Books is an independent publisher featuring the work of emerging authors in a variety of genres." Expects 9 titles 2006, 12 titles 2007. 280pp. Reporting time: 60 days. Payment: royalty, no advances. Does not copyright for author. Subjects: Fantasy, Fiction, Mystery, Non-Fiction.

Quiet Tymes, Inc., Roger J. Wannell, Founder, 1400 Downing Street, Denver, CO 80218, 303-839-8628, Fax 720-488-2682. 1979. "Quiet Tymes, Inc. holds trademark for The Baby Soother." We sometimes copyright for author. Subjects: Family, Parenting, Tapes & Records.

Quill Driver Books, Stephen Blake Mettee, Publisher, 1254 Commerce Way, Sanger, CA 93657-8731, 559-876-2170, Fax 559-876-2180, 800-497-4909. 1993. Non-fiction. "Additional imprint is Word Dancer Press. Quill Driver Books publishes hardcover and trade paperback originals and reprints with national appeal. Word Dancer Press imprint is used for regional and special market hardcover and trade paperback books. Unagented submissions welcome. Please query before submitting manuscripts. Send SASE." avg. press run 2.5M-5M. Pub'd 6 titles 2005; expects 6 titles 2006, 8 titles 2007. Discounts: retailers 1 book 20%, 2-9 40%, 10-49 43%, 50+ 46% libraries and schools 20%. Special discounts apply to reference titles, please inquire. 200pp. Reporting time: 30 days. Simultaneous submissions accepted: yes. Publishes 1/4 of 1% of manuscripts submitted. Payment: royalties negotiated. Copyrights for author. Subjects: California, History, How-To, Self-Help, Senior Citizens, Writers/Writing.

Quincannon Publishing Group, Alan Quincannon, Editor-in-Chief; Holly Benedict, Editor, Compass Point Mysteries, Patricia Drury, Loretta Bolger, Jeanne Wilcox, PO Box 8100, Glen Ridge, NJ 07028, 973-669-8367, editors@quincannongroup.com, www.quincannongroup.com. 1990. "Imprints: Compass Point Mysteries and Tory Corner Editions." avg. press run 2.5M. Pub'd 5 titles 2005; expects 5 titles 2006, 5 titles 2007. Copyrights for author.

•**Quinn Entertainment,** 7535 Austin Harbour Drive, Cumming, GA 30041, Phone (770) 356-3847, Fax (770) 886-1475, info@quinnentertainment.com, www.quinnentertainment.com. Fiction, plays, non-fiction. "Quinn Entertainment is dedicated to the promotion of fun and educational books that enrich the lives of children." Discounts: 55% Discount. 150pp.

R

R & M Publishing Company, Dillard Haley, Editor; Barbara G. Blackwell, Editor, Mack B. Morant; McGorine Cassell, Editor, PO Box 1276, Holly Hill, SC 29059, 803-279-2262. 1978. "We will look at any subject of quality work. However, we are most interested in historical documentations, educational and how-to materials." avg. press run 1M-2M. Expects 1-3 titles 2006. Discounts: 20-55%. 42-110pp. Reporting time: 6-12 weeks or less. Publishes less than 1% of manuscripts submitted. Payment: negotiable. Copyrights for author. Subjects: Arts, Ecology, Foods, Education, Genealogy, How-To, Sociology.

Rabeth Publishing Company, Raymond Quigley, Elizabeth Quigley, 3515 NE 61st St., Gladstone, MO 64119-1931, email: qurabeth@kvmo.net. 1990. Poetry, fiction, non-fiction. avg. press run 400-2M. Pub'd 2 titles 2005; expects 3 titles 2006, 3-4 titles 2007. Discounts: 40% to trade. 100-125pp. Reporting time: 2-4 weeks. Simultaneous submissions accepted: yes. Publishes 30-50% of manuscripts submitted. Payment: negotiable. Copyrights for author. Subjects: Fiction, Non-Fiction, Poetry, Religion.

Rada Press, Inc., Daisy Pellant, 1277 Fairmount Avenue, St. Paul, MN 55105-7052, phone: 651-554-7645; fax: 651-455-6975. 1975. Non-fiction. "Our publishing focus is education. We produce books for students in their middle and high school years. Our special area is history." avg. press run 500. Pub'd 13 titles 2005; expects 1 title 2006, 1 title 2007. 100pp. Reporting time: 30 days. Simultaneous submissions accepted: Yes. Payment: 10% of cover price; no advances. Subjects: Communication, Journalism, Education, Geography, History, Media, Non-Fiction, Political Science, Technology.

Radiant Press, Rabia Harris, P.O. Box 20017, NYC, NY 10025-9992, 212-592-1765. 2004. Fiction, parts-of-novels. "The Radiant Press publishes fiction, metafiction, science fiction, pulp fiction, cyberpunk, hard-boiled detective stories, soft-boiled detective stories, elegiac reveries, nocturnal fugues, surreal adventure stories, random observations, odd speculations, vagrant fantasies, and other forms of the written word that may or may not fit in any of the above categories.'' avg. press run 4000. Expects 1-2 titles 2006, 3-4 titles 2007. Discounts: 2-10 copies 33% 11-49 copies 40% 50-99 copies 42%100-249 copies 44%250-999 copies 50%1000+ 55%. 300-400pp. Reporting time: Two or three months. Simultaneous submissions accepted: Yes. Payment: At the moment, our author's share equally in the profits (if and when they occur). Does not copyright for author. Subjects: Absurdist, Anarchist, Crime, Fantasy, Fashion, Fiction, Gender Issues, Horror, Humor, Mystery, Novels, Post Modern, Science Fiction, Storytelling.

Ragged Edge Press, Harold E. Collier, Acquisitions Editor, PO Box 708, 73 West Burd Street, Shippensburg, PA 17257, 717-532-2237, Fax 717-532-6110. 1994. Non-fiction. ''Ragged Edge Press makes a difference in people's lives with topics that focus on religion and relationships.'' avg. press run 2M-3M. Expects 4 titles 2006, 10 titles 2007. Discounts: available on request. 200pp. Reporting time: 30 days for proposals, 90 days for full manuscripts, proposal guidelines upon request. Simultaneous submissions accepted: yes. Payment: twice yearly. Copyrights for author. Subjects: Christianity, Non-Fiction, Religion, Society.

Ragged Raven Press (see also IOTA), Bob Mee, Janet Murch, 1 Lodge Farm, Snitterfield, Stratford-upon-Avon, Warwickshire CV37 0LR, England, 44-1789-730320, raggedravenpress@aol.com, www.raggedraven.co.uk. 1998. Poetry, non-fiction. ''Poetry - Submissions welcome for individual collections. Annual anthology linked to international competition. Nonfiction - schedule currently full.'' avg. press run 400. Pub'd 2 titles 2005; expects 2 titles 2006, 2 titles 2007. Discounts: 33%. 84pp. Reporting time: 1 month. Simultaneous submissions accepted: no. Publishes 5% of manuscripts submitted. Payment: negotiated individually with authors of collections, 1 free copy for anthology. Copyrights for author. Subjects: Non-Fiction, Poetry.

RAIN TAXI REVIEW OF BOOKS, Eric Lorberer, PO Box 3840, Minneapolis, MN 55403, 612-825-1528 tel/Fax, info@raintaxi.com, www.raintaxi.com. 1995. Articles, interviews, reviews. ''Book reviews run from 400 words to 1500 words. Interview lengths vary widely. Feature articles from 850 to 3000 words. Manuscripts are usually solicited.'' circ. 18,000. 4/yr. Pub'd 4 issues 2005; expects 4 issues 2006, 4 issues 2007. sub. price $12 domestic/ $20 Canada or Mexico/$28 overseas international; per copy $4. Back issues: $4. Discounts: distributed free of charge in bookstores & literary centers. 56pp. Reporting time: 30 days. Simultaneous submissions accepted: no. Publishes 10% of manuscripts submitted. Payment: copies of magazine, otherwise none. Copyrighted, reverts to author. Pub's reviews: 200 in 2005. §Books and audio- literary fiction & nonfiction, poetry, cultural studies, art. Ads: $800full/$400half/$300 1/3 page/$250 1/4 page/$150 1/8 page. Contract pricing available. Subjects: Avant-Garde, Experimental Art, Book Reviewing, Essays, Interviews, Literary Review, Reviews.

Rainbow Books, Inc., Betsy Wright-Lampe, PO Box 430, Highland City, FL 33846-0430, 863-648-4420, 863-647-5951, rbibooks@aol.com, www.rainbowbooksinc.com. 1979. Fiction, non-fiction. ''Writers' guide-lines for first-class, self-addressed, stamped envelope; No work under 64 pages. No religious material; no biographies/autobiographies unless a celebrity or marketable, no diet books or business books at all. Looking for how-to and self-help books for adults; self-help books for kids—both adult and children's nonfiction by credentialled authors, please. Being the parent of a successful child does NOT qualify as credentials for a parenting book. We seek active authors who give lectures, seminars and who otherwise assist in promotion of themselves and their books. We enjoy discovering first-time authors. Please be professional in your approach. If you haven't already done so, research and learn about being an author and working with a publisher. Read The Writer magazine, read The Self-Publishing Manual by Dan Poynter and 1001 Ways to Market Your Books by John Kremer. Understand the industry through those two books. We do not offer big advances, and we do not contract on incomplete works. Please, no email queries.'' avg. press run 10M. Pub'd 10 titles 2005; expects 16 titles 2006, 20 titles 2007. Discounts: Single-copy orders must be pre-paid, you pay S&H. Our wholesale terms are 50% (returnable), 55% (nonreturnable), no minimum order. Our VOR is Ingram, but we also work with Baker & Taylor, Book Clearing House and a boatload of jobbers. Our titles are available new through Amazon.com's Advantage Program and used (bookstore returns) through the Marketplace Program. Our 1-800 order number (Book Clearing House) is 1-800-431-1579 (all major cards accepted). We cannot process credit card orders at our editorial offices; those orders must go through Book Clearing House. 250pp. Reporting time: 4 weeks (only with SASE). Simultaneous submissions accepted: yes. Publishes 5% of manuscripts submitted. Payment: Contract depends on material, usually $500 advance, 6% royalty, but we are flexible. We can go with no advance for a higher royalty. Payment twice yearly. Copyrights for author. Subjects: Appalachia, Armenian, Aviation, Black, Children, Youth, How-To, Men, Mystery, Native American, Non-Fiction, Parenting, Psychology, Relationships, Science, Self-Help.

RAINBOW CURVE, Julianne Bonnet, Poetry Editor; Daphne Young, Fiction Editor, P.O. Box 93206, Las Vegas, NV 89193-3206, rainbowcurve@sbcglobal.net, www.rainbowcurve.com. 2002. Poetry, fiction, photos, parts-of-novels, long-poems. ''Rainbow Curve is a segment of highway which bridges two halves of the city of

Las Vegas - the affluence of the "new" Las Vegas with their sparkling new developments, to the old downtown and the struggles of an aging tradition. Similarly, Rainbow Curve hopes to uphold the fundamentals of some old literary traditions while, at the same time, paving the way for work that speaks to a new and diverse audience. Recent contributors include: Catherine Ryan Hyde, Virgil Suarez, Terry Ehret and Rob Carney.'' circ. 250. 2/yr. Pub'd 2 issues 2005; expects 2 issues 2006, 2 issues 2007. sub. price $16; per copy $8; sample $6. Back issues: inquire. Discounts: inquire. 100pp. Reporting time: Maximum of three months. Simultaneous submissions accepted: Yes. Publishes 2% of manuscripts submitted. Payment: One contributor copy upon publication. Copyrighted, reverts to author. Ads: Advertise for trade. Subjects: Absurdist, Arts, Avant-Garde, Experimental Art, Essays, Experimental, Feminism, Haiku, Humor, Memoirs, Poetry, Post Modern, Prose, Satire, Short Stories, Storytelling.

RAINBOWS WITH RED REMOVED, Pen-Dec Press, 2526 Chatham Woods, Grand Rapids, MI 49546. 2002. ''No fiction. No unsolicited mss. Poetry only: juiced, with zip. Must include letter of purpose, brief bio, SASE.'' Irregular. sample price $4. 24pp.

Raised Barn Press, 3300 Powell St., Apt. 327, Emeryville, CA 94608-4909, info@raisedbarnpress.com.

RALPH'S REVIEW, Ralph Cornell, 129 Wellington Avenue, #A, Albany, NY 12203-2637. 1988. Poetry, fiction, art, cartoons, letters. ''No heavy racial, political, rape stories. No slasher stories. Up to 1,000 words; poems to 2 pages. Recent contributors: R. Cornell, Dan Buck, Frederick Zydek, Joseph Danoski, Joyce Frohn, Brendan J. McDonald, and Joanne Tolson. There is now a $2 reading fee for all stories and $.50 each for poems.'' circ. 100+. 2+. Pub'd 3 issues 2005; expects 3 issues 2006, 3 issues 2007. sub. price $15; per copy $5; sample $3. Back issues: varies. 35pp. Reporting time: 2-4 weeks. Simultaneous submissions accepted: yes. Publishes 50-60% of manuscripts submitted. Payment: 1 copy. Copyrighted, reverts to author. Ads: $18/$10/$3 1''/$7 3x5/$5 business card. Subjects: Anthropology, Archaelogy, Antiques, Artificial Intelligence, Birds, Book Collecting, Bookselling, Collectibles, Conservation, Dreams, Folklore, Gardening, H.P. Lovecraft, Occult, Philately, Poetry, Science Fiction.

Ram Press (see also CATAMARAN SAILOR), Amelia Norlin, PO Box 2060, Key Largo, FL 33037, 305-451-3287, Fax 305-453-0255, rick@catsailor.comt, www.rambooks.com, www.catsailor.com. 1991. Fiction, non-fiction. Expects 4 titles 2006, 6 titles 2007. Discounts: 2-4 20%, 5-99 40%, 100+ 60%. 352pp. Reporting time: 60 days. Payment: standard. Subjects: Fiction, How-To, Non-Fiction, Sports, Outdoors, Water.

Rama Publishing Co., Richard Aschwanden, Charles Aschwanden, 3598 S. Chapel Road, Carthage, MO 64836-4082, 417-358-1093. 1983. Fiction, articles, non-fiction. ''In 40 years of married life Richard and Maria Aschwanden of Carthage, MO, have reared 10 healthy children and never have had a doctor's or dentist's bill because of illness. They attribute this to a philosophy of healthy living which includes preventative family nutrition. Rama Publishing Co. is interested in editing and publishing booklets and books dealing with regeneration of mankind in the physical, mental, and spiritual aspects.'' avg. press run 500-2M. Expects 3 titles 2006, 5 titles 2007. Discounts: 5-25, 25%; 26-50, 40%; 51+, 50%. 150pp. Reporting time: 5 weeks. Payment: 10-15% on net receipts; no advance. Copyrights for author. Subjects: Children, Youth, Ecology, Foods, Education, Health, Women.

RAMBUNCTIOUS REVIEW, Richard Goldman, Co-Editor; Nancy Lennon, Co-Editor; Elizabeth Hausler, Co-Editor, Rambunctious Press, Inc., 1221 West Pratt Blvd., Chicago, IL 60626. 1984. Poetry, fiction, art, photos, satire, plays. ''*Rambunctious Review* accepts submissions from September through May. Length of material: poems 100 lines, fiction 12 pages. No biases. Recent contributors: Maureen Flannery, B.Z. Niditch, Hugh Fox, and Glenna Holloway.'' circ. 600. 1/yr. Pub'd 1 issue 2005; expects 1 issue 2006, 1 issue 2007. sub. price $12/3 issues; per copy $4; sample $4. Back issues: $4. Discounts: none. 48pp. Reporting time: 9 months. Publishes 10% of manuscripts submitted. Payment: 2 free copies of the magazine. Copyrighted, reverts to author. Ads: none. Subjects: Drama, Fiction, Poetry.

THE RAM'S CHIN'S GOATEE, Pen-Dec Press, 2526 Chatham Woods, Grand Rapids, MI 49546. 2002. ''No fiction. No unsolicited mss. Poetry only: juiced, with zip. Must include letter of purpose, brief bio, SASE.'' Irregular. sample price $4. 24pp.

Peter E. Randall Publisher, Deirdre Randall, PO Box 4726, Portsmouth, NH 03802-4726, 603-431-5667deidre @ perpublisher.com www.perpublisher.com. 1970. Poetry, photos, non-fiction. ''We are subsidy publishers, working with many communities, historical societies, businesses, and individuals to produce quality cloth and paperbound books. Catalogue at perpublisher.com.'' avg. press run varies from 500 up. Pub'd 20 titles 2005; expects 20 titles 2006, 20 titles 2007. Reporting time: one month. Copyrights for author. Subjects: Biography, History, Maine, New England, New Hampshire, Photography, Picture Books.

RANDEE, Josh Schollmeyer, P.O. Box 578660, Chicago, IL 60657-8660. 2003. Photos, cartoons, interviews, satire, reviews, letters. ''Part social criticism, part silliness (we think of ourselves as cleverly stupid), Randee raises a big middle finger to popular culture and the modern media. In the vein of Spy and National Lampoon, it holds nothing sacred and lambasts any and everything worth lambasting. Recent contributors include: Nick Rogers, Jesus Christ, Josh Schollmeyer, Ronald Reagan, Nathan J. Stange and Bob Green.'' circ. 500. 2/yr. Pub'd 1 issue 2005; expects 2 issues 2006, 3 issues 2007. price per copy $6; sample $4. Back issues: $7.50. Discounts: 10-20 copies 20 percent21-30 copies 30 percent31-50 copies 35 percent51-250 copies 40 percent251-1,000 copies 45 percent. 52pp. Reporting time: Four to six weeks. Simultaneous submissions accepted: No. Publishes 5% of manuscripts submitted. Payment: Free copy of the magazine. Copyrighted, does not revert to author. §Off-beat and quirky bits of popular culture. Subjects: Humor, Satire.

Rarach Press, Ladislav R. Hanka, 1005 Oakland Drive, Kalamazoo, MI 49008. 1981. Poetry, art, long-poems. ''This is essentially a vehicle for my art and rather personal and idiosyncratic notions of what I wish to print: i.e. occasional small books, poems set into an etching, wood engravings, handbills, posters for exhibitions, and one substantial book of 100 pp. containing 5 long poems in Czech. This is labor-intensive hand-done bibliophilia. My bread and butter is printing my own artwork often as suites of etchings or wood engravings sometimes with a bit of type-set commentary, titles or description. The bibliophilia is an amusement appearing irregularly. I am essentially uninterested in unsolicited manuscripts, unless someone wants me to illustrate something I like.'' avg. press run 20-30. Pub'd 1 title 2005; expects 1 title 2006, 1 title 2007. Discounts: 40% off for dealers. 10-100pp. Payment: done individually, generally in copies of print. Does not copyright for author. Subjects: Book Arts, Folklore, Poetry.

RARITAN: A Quarterly Review, Jackson Lears, Editor-in-Chief; Stephanie Volmer, Managing Editor, 31 Mine Street, New Brunswick, NJ 08903, 732-932-7887, Fax 732-932-7855, rqr@rci.rutgers.edu. 1981. Poetry, articles, interviews, criticism, reviews, non-fiction. ''*Raritan* specializes in literary and cultural criticism. In addition to essays, *Raritan* prints a *small* quantity of poetry and fiction. Contributors include Adam Phillips, Richard Rorty, Victoria Nelson, Richard White, Marina Warner, John Hollander, and Georgina Kleege.'' circ. 3.5M. 4/yr. Pub'd 4 issues 2005; expects 4 issues 2006. sub. price $24 individuals, $35 institutions; per copy $8; sample $8 where applicable. Back issues: $6 per copy. Discounts: available for bookstores, distributors, and subscription agencies. 160pp. Reporting time: 4-6 months. Simultaneous submissions accepted: no. Payment: $100. Copyrighted. Pub's reviews: 23 in 2005. §Literary criticism, philosophy, pol. sci., fine arts, history. Ads: $275/$180. Subjects: Arts, Book Reviewing, Criticism, Literature (General).

Raspberry Press Limited, Betty J. Schultz, PO Box 1, Dixon, IL 61021-0001, 815-288-4910, email: raspberrypresslimited@yahoo.com, Url: www.raspberrypresslimited.com. 1988. ''Additional address: 1989 Grand Detour Road, Dixon, IL 61021.'' Reporting time: 3 weeks. Simultaneous submissions accepted: yes. Subject: Children, Youth.

RATTAPALLAX, Marilyn Hacker, Editor; Alan Cheuse, Fiction Editor; Willie Perdomo, Editor; Idra Novey, Editor; Flavia Rocha, Editor, 532 La Guardia Place, Suite 353, New York, NY 10012, info@rattapallax.com. 1998. Poetry, fiction, art, photos, satire, criticism, long-poems, concrete art, non-fiction. ''Some recent contributors: Martin Espada, Anthony Hecht, Billy Collins, MC Solaar, Lou Reed, Marilyn Hacker, Glyn Maxwell, and Yusef Komunyakaa.'' circ. 2M. 2/yr. Pub'd 2 issues 2005; expects 2 issues 2006, 2 issues 2007. price per copy $7.95; sample $7.95. Back issues: $7.95. 128pp. Reporting time: 2 weeks. Simultaneous submissions accepted: no. Copyrighted, reverts to author. Ads: $300/$150. Subjects: Arts, Criticism, Essays, Fiction, Haiku, Literature (General), Non-Fiction, Poetry, Prose, Short Stories, Visual Arts.

RATTLE, Alan Fox, Editor-in-Chief; Timothy Green, Associate Editor, 12411 Ventura Blvd., Studio City, CA 91604, 818-505-6777. 1993. Poetry, interviews, criticism, reviews. ''Essays on writing 2500 words or less.'' circ. 4000. 2/yr. Pub'd 2 issues 2005; expects 2 issues 2006, 2 issues 2007. sub. price $16; per copy $10; sample $10. Back issues: $5. Discounts: Half-off for Libraries, otherwise negotiable. 196pp. Reporting time: 6-8 weeks. Simultaneous submissions accepted: Yes. Publishes 1% of manuscripts submitted. Payment: 2 copies. Copyrighted, reverts to author. Pub's reviews: 8 in 2005. §Poetry essays on craft, process. No advertising. Subject: Poetry.

Rattlesnake Press (see also RATTLESNAKE REVIEW; SNAKELETS; VYPER), Kathy Kieth, P.O. Box 1647, Orangevale, CA 95662, 916-966-8620.

RATTLESNAKE REVIEW, Rattlesnake Press, Kathy Kieth, P.O. Box 1647, Orangevale, CA 95662, 916-966-8620. 2004. Poetry, articles, art, photos, interviews, reviews, letters. ''Preference given to submissions from Northern California.'' circ. approx. 200. Quarterly. Expects 4 issues 2006, 4 issues 2007. sub. price $15 for 4 issues of Rattlesnake Review, 3 issues of Snakelets, 2 issues of VYPER, assorted broadsides; per copy free; sample free. Back issues: $2. 40pp. Reporting time: 3 months. Simultaneous submissions accepted: no. Payment: checks to Kathy Kieth. Copyrighted, reverts to author. Pub's reviews: 6 in 2005. §No. Cal. poetry. Subject: Poetry.

RAVEN - A Journal of Vexillology, Edward Kaye, Editor, 1977 N. Olden Ave. Ext., PMB 225, Trenton, NJ 08618-2193. 1994. Articles, art, photos, non-fiction. ''The North American Vexillological Association (NAVA) is a nonprofit organization dedicated to the promotion of vexillology, which is the scientific and scholarly study of flags and their history and symbolism." circ. 435. 1/yr. Pub'd 1 issue 2005; expects 1 issue 2006, 1 issue 2007. sub. price $20; per copy $20, $30 double issue; sample $20. Back issues: $20/$30. Discounts: available. 96pp. Reporting time: 40-60 days. Simultaneous submissions accepted: no. Publishes 50% of manuscripts submitted. Payment: copies. Copyrighted, negotiate rights reverting to author. Ads: none.

THE RAVEN CHRONICLES, Phoebe Bosche, Managing Editor & Co-Publisher; Phil Red Eagle, Co-Publisher; Athena Stevens, Contributing Editor; Jeannine Hall Gailey, Contributing Editor; Kathleen Alcala, Contributing Editor; Beth Myhr, Contributing Editor; Holly Yasui, Contributing Editor; Paul Hunter, Contributing Editor; Jody Aliesan, Contributing Editor, Richard Hugo House, 1634 11th Avenue, Seattle, WA 98122-2419, 206-364-2045, editors@ravenchronicles.org, www.ravenchronicles.org. 1991. Poetry, fiction, articles, art, photos, cartoons, interviews, satire, criticism, reviews, music, letters, parts-of-novels, long-poems, plays, concrete art, non-fiction. "Raven Chronicles publishes and promotes work which documents the profound contribution of art and literature created at the community level. Raven publications reflect the cultural diversity and multitude of viewpoints of writers from the Pacific Northwest, the US, and beyond. SASE required. Check web site for submission periods and themes. Recent contributors include: Diane Glancy, Dina Ben-Lev, Carolyn Lei-lani Lau, Abe Blashko, Charles Johnson, Elizabeth Woody, Sherman Alexie, Rita Chavez, Stacey Levine." circ. 1-2,000. 2-4/yr. Pub'd 2 issues 2005; expects 3 issues 2006, 3 issues 2007. sub. price $20, $30 foreign; per copy $6-$7; sample $5 plus $2.00 postage. Email or write for back issues pricing. Discounts: 50% to distributors; 50% to educators ordering 40 or more. 80-96pp. Reporting time: 2-6 months. Simultaneous submissions accepted: A few: but write editors first. Publishes 7-9% of manuscripts submitted. Payment: $0-$40 and/or copies. Copyrighted, reverts to author. Pub's reviews: 30 in 2005. §Poetry, Fiction, Non-fiction, essays: reviews published in print and on our web site. Ads: $300/$100/$25 business card. Subjects: Bilingual, Experimental, Fiction, Indigenous Cultures, Literary Review, Literature (General), Multicultural, Non-Fiction, Poetry, Reviews, Short Stories, Storytelling, Translation, Young Adult.

Raven Publishing, Inc. (see also ALONE TOGETHER), Janet Hill, P.O. Box 2866, Norris, MT 59745, 406-685-3545, 866-685-3545, fax: 406-685-3599. 2001. Fiction. "We also publish books, but are not taking book proposals at this time as our schedule is full through 2008. However, submissions for Alone Together are always welcome and will be considered." Pub'd 2 titles 2005; expects 3 titles 2006, 3 titles 2007. Reporting time: usually report in one month. Simultaneous submissions accepted: Yes. Copyrights for author.

Raven Rocks Press, John Morgan, 53650 Belmont Ridge Road, Beallsville, OH 43716, 614-926-1705. 1972. Fiction, non-fiction. "In addition to re-publishing classic children's books by Ethel Cook Eliot, Raven Rocks Press has published Warren Stetzel's book, *School for the Young* (explores some of our assumptions about our human nature and the nature of our world), and reprinted *Hollingsworth's Vision*, a first-person account by a 19th-century Quaker. We expect to publish materials which touch on a variety of fields: education, economics and social organization, environmental issues, solar and underground construction. Those involved in Raven Rocks Press are members of Raven Rocks, Inc., an organization which is engaged in these and other fields, and much of what we publish will be out of our own experience. We will hope, too, to publish relevant material from elsewhere. No exact price is set for *School for the Young*. Rather, contributions are accepted from those able to make them. With this policy, it has been possible for some to secure the book at little or no cost. Others have been able to contribute enough to make up the difference." avg. press run 5M. Expects 1 title 2006, 1 title 2007. Discounts: bookstores & jobbers 1 copy 15%, 2-3 copies 30%, 4+ 40%. 244pp. Copyrights for author. Subjects: Children, Youth, Education, Environment, Psychology.

Raven Tree Press, LLC, Amy Crane Johnson, 200 S. Washington St., Suite 306, Green Bay, WI 54301, 920-438-1605, 920-438-1607, 877-256-0579, raven@raventreepress.com, www.raventreepress.com. 2000. "Raven Tree Press publishes children's bilingual (English/Spanish) picture books." Expects 10 titles 2007. Discounts: See web site for distributor and wholesaler information.Contact raven@raventreepress.com for more info on discounts. 32pp. Submission information can be obtained from the web site, ww.raventreepress.com. Payment: Advance and royalties are contracted on a title-by-title basis. Copyrights for author. Subjects: Bilingual, Picture Books.

RavenHaus Publishing, Dolores Dowd, Karrie Zukowski, 227 Willow Grove Road, Stewartsville, NJ 08886, 908-859-4331, Fax 908-859-3088. 1997. Fiction, non-fiction. avg. press run 3M. Pub'd 4 titles 2005; expects 3 titles 2006, 5 titles 2007. Discounts: 50%. 220pp. Reporting time: 3 months. Simultaneous submissions accepted: yes. Publishes 20% of manuscripts submitted. Payment: min. $1,000 advance, 10% net. Does not copyright for author. Subjects: Cooking, Fantasy, Fiction, Games, Mystery, Non-Fiction, Supernatural.

Ravenhawk Books, Hans Jr. Shepherd, Carl Lasky, 7739 E. Broadway Boulevard #95, Tucson, AZ 85710, 520-296-4491, Fax 520-296-4491, ravenhawk6dof@yahoo.com. 1999. Fiction, non-fiction. "No unsolicited materials are accepted at this time." avg. press run 2.5M. Expects 5 titles 2006, 6 titles 2007. Discounts: 55% off cover retail. 65% off if title is ordered 60 days prior to publication date. 320pp. Simultaneous submissions accepted: no. Publishes .005% of manuscripts submitted. Payment: graduated royalty schedule 35%-45%-55% calculated from gross profits. Copyrights for author. Subjects: Anthology, Fiction, Non-Fiction, Novels,

398

Self-Help.

Raven's Eye Press, Inc., PO Box 4351, Durango, CO 81302, 970-247-4233, Fax 970-259-3238, ravenseye@frontier.net, www.ravenseyepress.com. 1999. Non-fiction. "Raven's Eye Press is a small niche publisher that accepts original works of nonfiction pertinent to the Colorado Plateau. We want work that informs, provides insight, and emphasizes social responsibility for sustaining the biological diversity of this planet." avg. press run 3-5M. Expects 1 title 2006, 2 titles 2007. Discounts: based on order quantity, large orders based on simplified discount schedule. 300pp. Reporting time: queries 1 month, proposals 2 months, manuscripts 3 months. Simultaneous submissions accepted: no. Payment: 5-12% net. Does not copyright for author. Subjects: Environment, Family, Psychology, Sociology.

Ravenwood Publishing, Dee Linton, Danette Mulrine, 4421 Ravenwood Ave., Sacramento, CA 95821-6726, 916-215-0765, Fax 916-972-9312, http://www.ravenwoodpub.com. 1997. Non-fiction. Pub'd 2 titles 2005; expects 3 titles 2006, 5 titles 2007. 150pp. Reporting time: 60 days. Simultaneous submissions accepted: no. Publishes 10% of manuscripts submitted. Copyrights for author. Subjects: Acupuncture, AIDS, Alternative Medicine, Arts, California, Military, Veterans, Poetry.

Raw Dog Press, R. Gerry Fabian, 151 S. West Street, Doylestown, PA 18901, 215-345-6838. 1977. Poetry. "We are now doing only our Post Poem Series. We publish in the summer. Submit any time. The type of poetry that we are looking for is short (2-10) lines. We want 'people-oriented' work. We'll send samples for $4.00. You MUST enclose a short note and a SASE. Neatness and professionalism really count with us. Visit web page http://rawdogpress.bravehost.com/Index.html1." avg. press run 100. Pub'd 1 title 2005; expects 1 title 2006, 1 title 2007. Discounts: will negotiate and haggle with anyone; will exchange. 12-15pp. Reporting time: 1 month. Simultaneous submissions accepted: no. Publishes 10% of manuscripts submitted. Payment: varies with the material but we will work something out (copies +). Copyright is agreed upon. Subjects: Humor, Poetry.

RAW NERVZ HAIKU, Proof Press, Dorothy Howard, 67 Court Street, Aylmer, QC J9H 4M1, Canada, dhoward@aix1.uottawa.ca. 1994. Poetry, fiction, articles, art, reviews, letters, collages. "Haiku, senryu, renga, tanka, haibun, haiga." circ. 260. 4/yr. Pub'd 4 issues 2005; expects 4 issues 2006, 4 issues 2007. sub. price Canada $25, US US$22, elsewhere US$24; per copy Canada $7, US US$6, elsewhere US$7; sample Canada $7, US US$6, elsewhere US$7. Back issues: $5 to contributors. 52pp. Reporting time: 4-6 weeks. Simultaneous submissions accepted: no. Payment: none. Copyrighted, reverts to author. Pub's reviews: 3 in 2005. §Haiku, etc.

Rayve Productions Inc., Norm Ray, Barbara Ray, PO Box 726, Windsor, CA 95492, 707-838-6200, Fax 707-838-2220, E-mail rayvepro@aol.com. 1989. Pub'd 3 titles 2005; expects 5 titles 2006, 5 titles 2007. Subjects: African Literature, Africa, African Studies, Business & Economics, California, Careers, Folklore, Genealogy, Health, History, How-To, Journals, Newsletter, Parenting, Reference, Senior Citizens, Transportation.

•Razor7 Publishing, Coleman Andre, PO Box 6746, Altadena, CA 91003-6746, (626) 205-3154. 2005. Poetry, fiction, satire. "Books with a cutting edge that are not afraid to cross genres. We like stuff that is not afraid to say "Here I am, now think about what I am saying."Fiction, we expect big things from Blackbirds a our volume fictional series wrapped around real events in 2006. Check out our first title "A Liar's Tale."." avg. press run 1500. Expects 1 title 2006, 3 titles 2007. Discounts: 1- No discount2-4 20%5-9 30%10-24 40%25-49 42%50-74 44%75-99-46%100-199-48%200 or more 50%. 300pp. Does not copyright for author. Subjects: African-American, Fantasy, Fiction, Political Science, Science Fiction.

REACH, Ronnie Goodyer Mr, The Manacles, Predannack, The Lizard, Cornwall TR12 7AU, United Kingdom, reachmagazine@indigodreams.plus.com. 1987. Poetry, reviews, letters. "A welcoming and friendly established magazine that has lively letters page and unique 'family' feel. All forms of poetry published by subscription including free and formal verse. A monthly 50 award to the most popular poem voted for by subscribers. A series of mini-competitions also on verse forms or themes. Submission of poetry restricted to 3 per issue with form supplied by magazine. No submission forms supplied with back copies." circ. 300. 12/yr. Pub'd 12 issues 2005; expects 12 issues 2006, 12 issues 2007. sub. price 54; per copy 4.50; sample 4.50. Back issues: 4.50. 68pp. Reporting time: one month maximum. Simultaneous submissions accepted: No. Publishes 50% of manuscripts submitted. Pub's reviews: 36 in 2005. §poetry. Ads: 30 page. Subject: Poetry.

Reach Productions Publishing, PO Box 18495, Anaheim, CA 92807, 714-693-1800, publishing@reachpro-ductions.com, www.reachproductions.com. 2002. Fiction, articles, art, cartoons, interviews, criticism, plays, non-fiction. avg. press run 3M. Pub'd 2 titles 2005; expects 10 titles 2006, 15 titles 2007. Discounts: trade, bulk, classroom, etc. 144pp. Simultaneous submissions accepted: yes. Publishes 15-25% of manuscripts submitted. Payment: varies on work. Copyrights for author. Subjects: Civil Rights, Creativity, Education, Fiction, Government, Literature (General), Non-Fiction, Political Science, Research, Science Fiction.

REACTIONS, Pen & Inc Press, Clare Pollard, Editor, Pen & Inc Press, School of Literature & Creative Writing, Norwich, Norfolk NR4 7TJ, United Kingdom. 1999. Poetry. "*Reactions* is an annual anthology of contemporary poetry, which is published in book format. It is a specific national and international showcase for up-and-coming poets who have had a first collection published or who are about to reach that stage. It includes the work of around 20 new poets every year, and provides an exclusive preview of the next generation of poetry stars. Any theme/format allowed, we just want *good poetry*." 1/yr. Pub'd 1 issue 2005; expects 1 issue 2006, 1 issue 2007. price per copy £7.99; sample £7.99. 200pp. Reporting time: 3 months. Simultaneous submissions accepted: yes. Payment: £50. Copyrighted. Subject: Poetry.

•**Read Press LLC,** Philip Simms, 305 Madison Ave., Suite 449, New York, NY 10165. 2006. Non-fiction. "Middle school writing only. Biased against constructivist texts. Prefer Behaviorist/Direct Instruction models. Know what you're writing about and write about it clearly." avg. press run 2500. Expects 2 titles 2006, 4 titles 2007. 300pp. Reporting time: 3-4 months. Simultaneous submissions accepted: No. Payment: Per negotiation. Copyrights for author. Subjects: English, Language, Textbooks, Writers/Writing.

READ, AMERICA!, The Place In The Woods, Roger A. Hammer, Editor & Publisher, 3900 Glenwood Avenue, Golden Valley, MN 55422. 1982. Reviews. "A quarterly newsletter to Libraries, Reading Is Fundamental, Head Start, and migrant education programs. ISSN-0891-4214. Looking for professional children's librarians to do regular reviews. Three feature sections: powtry for children and adults, short stories for children, trends and case histories in education, literacy." circ. 10M. 4/yr. Pub'd 4 issues 2005; expects 4 issues 2006, 4 issues 2007. sub. price $25; per copy $7.50; sample $7.50. Back issues: $5. Discounts: 15% to qualified book suppliers & librarians. 16pp. Reporting time: 1 week to 6 months. Simultaneous submissions accepted: no. Publishes 20% of manuscripts submitted. Payment: 50 per review or article. Copyrighted, does not revert to author. Pub's reviews: 8 in 2005. §Children's books, P/K - 12, stories on trends, ideas, problem solving. Ads: use flier inserts—rates on request. Subjects: Bilingual, Book Collecting, Bookselling, Chicano/a, Children, Youth, Publishing, Reading, Reviews.

READERS SPEAK OUT!, Ron Richardson, 4003 - 50th Avenue SW, Seattle, WA 98116. 1997. Non-fiction. "Runs responses (50-150 words) to pertinent and controversial questions. Query first. Many contributors are teen homeschoolers. Publishing procedures internships (by mail) offered to young adults. ISSN 1523-7451. Member of American Civil Liberties Union. Donated subscription of zine offered to any academic library. Will help any young adult launch her own zine. If you are a teenager who wants someone to critique your writing (stories, poems, essays), you may contact me. At no charge to you, I will critique your writing - but please ask me first before sending me your writing. Also, I critique contemporary fine art photography (4x6 prints only, please)." circ. 150. 4/yr. Pub'd 4 issues 2005; expects 4 issues 2006, 4 issues 2007. sub. price free; per copy free; sample free. Back issues: free. 2pp. Reporting time: 1 month. Publishes 65% of manuscripts submitted. Payment: 2 copies. Copyrighted, reverts to author. Ads: free classifieds for contributors who have their own zines. Subjects: Adolescence, Amish Culture, Architecture, Buddhism, Communication, Journalism, Co-ops, Counter-Culture, Alternatives, Communes, Current Affairs, Editing, Essays, Feminism, Lesbianism, Networking, Young Adult, Zines.

Reading Connections, Mary Howard Ms., P.O. Box 52426, Tulsa, OK 74152-0426, 818-902-0278 contact number of Marketing Manager. 2003. Non-fiction. "Educational products; reading, literacy. Dr. Mary Howard is a passionate advocate for the struggling reader and provides clear strategies in her books (one with 4 CDs, one with DVD) for building effective elementary-school literacy programs." avg. press run 10000. Pub'd 3 titles 2005; expects 1 title 2006. Discounts: 2-4 copies 10%5-9 copies 20%10-14 copies 30%15+ copies 40%for book with CD. 152pp. Reporting time: 7 days. Simultaneous submissions accepted: Yes. Publishes 5% of manuscripts submitted. Does not copyright for author. Subjects: Education, Non-Fiction, Reading.

REAL PEOPLE, Alex Polner, 900 Oak Tree Avenue, Suite C, c/o Hochman, South Plainfield, NJ 07080-5118. 1988. Articles, photos, interviews, non-fiction. "1000-1500 words, articles about *celebrities and very interesting people*; articles about issues (e.g., entertainment world, TV, people and their "interesting" occupations)." circ. 100M. 6/yr. Pub'd 6 issues 2005; expects 6 issues 2006, 6 issues 2007. sub. price $24; per copy $4; sample $4. Back issues: $3. Discounts: negotiable. 64pp. Reporting time: 4 weeks. Simultaneous submissions accepted: no. Publishes 10% of manuscripts submitted. Payment: $50-$300. Copyrighted, we buy all rights. Pub's reviews: 15 in 2005. §Celebrities/biographies, autobiographies, memoirs, showbusiness, TV, fiction. Ads: color $2400, b&w $2000/color $1440, b&w $1200/75¢ per word (25 word minimum). Subjects: Americana, Biography, Electronics, Entertainment, Interviews.

Really Great Books, Mari Florence, Nina Wiener, PO Box 86121, Los Angeles, CA 90086-0121, 213-624-8555, fax 213-624-8666, www.reallygreatbooks.com. 1998. Fiction, photos, non-fiction. "*Really Great Books* is publishing an ecclectic list of books inspired by Los Angeles. Most titles have a popular culture leaning. RGB is also the publisher of *The Glovebox Guides*, your roadmap to the city's best places to eat, drink, unwind, and play. We are accepting absolutely no submissions at this time." avg. press run 2M. Pub'd 4 titles 2005; expects 3 titles 2006, 4 titles 2007. 256pp. Reporting time: 6 weeks. Simultaneous submissions accepted: yes. Publishes 5% of manuscripts submitted. Payment: no advance, competetive royalties paid quarterly. Does not copyright for author. Subjects: Architecture, Arts, California, Counter-Culture, Alternatives, Communes,

Crime, Electronics, Fiction, Los Angeles, Multicultural, Photography.

RealPeople Press, Box F, Moab, UT 84532.

Rebekah Publishing, PO Box 713, Gunnison, CO 81230, 877-790-4588, Rebekahbooks@adelphia.net, www.rebekahbooks.com.

Recon Publications, Chris Robinson, Editor; Lewis Bellis, Business Manager, PO Box 14602, Philadelphia, PA 19134. 1973. avg. press run 2M.

Red Alder Books, David Steinberg, Box 2992, Santa Cruz, CA 95063, 831-426-7082, eronat@aol.com. 1974. Poetry, fiction, art, photos, letters, long-poems, non-fiction. "Our present emphasis is fine art sexual photography." avg. press run 3M. Expects 1 title 2006, 1 title 2007. Discounts: 2-4 books 20%, 5+ 40%. 150pp. Reporting time: 2-6 weeks. Simultaneous submissions accepted: yes. Publishes a very small % of manuscripts submitted. Payment: varies. Copyrights for author. Subjects: Biography, Community, Drugs, Erotica, Feminism, Fiction, Men, Photography, Poetry, Psychology, Sex, Sexuality, Society, Women.

RED AND BLACK, Jack Grancharoff, PO Box 12, Quaama, NSW 2550, Australia. 1964. Reviews, non-fiction. circ. 200. 1-2/yr. Expects 1 issue 2006, 2 issues 2007. sub. price £6; per copy £3; sample free. Back issues: not a set price; depends on buyer's circumstances. 35-40pp. Reporting time: variable. Simultaneous submissions accepted: yes. Publishes 75% of manuscripts submitted. Payment: none. Not copyrighted. Pub's reviews: 1 in 2005. §Anarchism, libertarianism, feminism, any other anti-statist positions. None. Subject: Anarchist.

Red Candle Press (see also CANDELABRUM POETRY MAGAZINE), M.L. McCarthy, Mr, 1 Chatsworth Court, Outram Rd., Southsea PO5 1RA, England, 02392753696, rcp@poetry7.fsnet.co.uk, www.members.tri-pod.com/redcandlepress. 1970. Poetry. "Poetry. The Red Candle Press is a fringe-press. It provides a (free) service to poets and does not aim to make a profit. Contributors to *Candelabrum Poetry Magazine* receive one free copy." avg. press run 1M for magazine. Discounts: 1/3 to booksellers. Reporting time: 1-2 months. Simultaneous submissions accepted: no. Payment: free copy to magazine contributors. Copyrights for author. Subject: Poetry.

Red Cedar Press (see also RED CEDAR REVIEW), Douglas Dowland, Editor, 17C Morrill Hall, Michigan State University, E. Lansing, MI 48824, 517-355-9656, rcreview@msu.edu. 1963. avg. press run 500. Pub'd 2 titles 2005; expects 2 titles 2006, 2 titles 2007. 100pp. Reporting time: 3 months. Simultaneous submissions accepted: no. Payment: in copies. Subjects: Arts, Book Reviewing, Fiction, Graphics, Poetry, Short Stories.

RED CEDAR REVIEW, Red Cedar Press, Douglas Dowland, General Editor, 17C Morrill Hall, English Dept., Michigan State Univ., E. Lansing, MI 48824, 517-355-9656, rcreview@msu.edu. 1963. Poetry, fiction, art, photos, interviews, criticism, reviews, parts-of-novels, long-poems. "We have no particular editorial bias—clarity is appreciated, sentimentality isn't. Some recent contributors: William Stafford, Diane Wakoski, Hugh Fox, Judith McCombs, Barbara Drake, Charles Edward Eaton, Dan Gerber, Herbert Scott, Lyn Lifshin. We're also open to new writers; we generally try to comment on promising work that we don't accept. In some cases, we ask for resubmissions-no guarantees, of course. Our two annual issues come out around March/April and Oct/Nov, but submissions are considered year-round. Reporting time longer in summer. No simultaneous submissions, please." circ. 700. 2/yr. Pub'd 2 issues 2005; expects 2 issues 2006, 2 issues 2007. sub. price $10; per copy $5; sample $3. Back issues: $3. Discounts: library $4/$8. 80pp. Reporting time: 8-12 weeks. Simultaneous submissions accepted: no. Publishes 5% of manuscripts submitted. Payment: 2 copies. Copyrighted, reverts to author. Ads: $100/$50/$25. Subjects: Arts, Book Reviewing, Fiction, Graphics, Poetry, Short Stories.

Red Dragon Press, 433 Old Town Court, Alexandria, VA 22314, 703-683-5877. 1993. Poetry, fiction. "Red Dragon Press is undertaking to promote authors of innovative, progressive, and experimental works, who aspire to evoke the emotions of the reader by stressing the symbolic value of language, and in the creation of meaningful new ideas, forms, and methods. We are proponents of works that represent the nature of man as androgynous, as in the fusing of male and female symbolism, and we support works that deal with psychological and parapsychological topics." avg. press run 500. Expects 2 titles 2006, 2 titles 2007. Discounts: retail 40%. 64pp. Reporting time: 6 months or less. Simultaneous submissions accepted: yes. Publishes 5% of manuscripts submitted. Payment: none. Does not copyright for author. Subjects: Poetry, Short Stories.

Red Dust, Joanna Gunderson, PO Box 630, Gracie Station, New York, NY 10028, 212-348-4388. 1963. Poetry, fiction. "Short works, once accepted, must be sent on disk. In general, authors get 30 copies. There is no advance." avg. press run 300 short works. Pub'd 2 titles 2005; expects 2 titles 2006, 2 titles 2007. Discounts: libraries 20%; wholesalers & booksellers 1 copy-30%, 2 or more-40%, paperback 1-4 copies-20%, 5 or more-40%. 140pp, short works 16-32pp. Reporting time: 2 months. Simultaneous submissions accepted: yes. Publishes 10% of manuscripts submitted. Payment: $300 advance against royalty for full-length works, for short works we pay nothing and claim no rights. Copyrights for author. Subjects: Drama, Fiction, Poetry, Translation.

Red Eye Press, James Goodwin, Richard Kallan, PO Box 65751, Los Angeles, CA 90065-0751, 323-225-3805. 1988. Art, photos, non-fiction. "We do not accept unsolicited manuscripts or proposals." avg. press run 5M-18M. Pub'd 2 titles 2005; expects 2 titles 2006, 1 title 2007. Discounts: 37%-63%. 360pp. Reporting time: 8 weeks. Simultaneous submissions accepted: yes. Publishes 5% of manuscripts submitted. Payment: 10%. Copyrights for author. Subjects: Counter-Culture, Alternatives, Communes, Drugs, Horticulture, How-To, Quotations, Reference.

Red Hand Press (see also CLARA VENUS), Marie Kazalia, ATTN: Marie Kazalia, 6160 Stoddard Hayes Road, Farmdale, OH 44417-9773, phone: 415-447-7334 E-mail: RedHandPress@hotmail.com http:/ /ClaraVenus.BlogSpot.com http://RedHandPress.BlogSpot.com. 2004. Poetry, fiction, art, photos, long-poems, collages. "Only interested in submissions of very short prose, AKA flash fiction, flash memoir or other flash 500 words or less." avg. press run 450. Pub'd 4 titles 2005; expects 8 titles 2006, 12 titles 2007. 50pp. Reporting time: Faster by regular mail slower response to e-mail submissions. Simultaneous submissions accepted: Yes. Publishes 34% of manuscripts submitted. ISSN #'s on annuals. Subjects: Anarchist, Arts, Asia, Indochina, Asian-American, Black, Dada, Folklore, Gay, Humanism, Humor, Literature (General), Photography, Poetry, Psychology, Socialist.

RED HAWK, Suburban Wilderness Press, Linda Erickson, Patrick McKinnon, Bud Backen, 75-6100 Alii Drive, Apt. B28, Kailua-Kona, HI 96740-2308. 1984. Poetry, fiction, art, photos, interviews, satire, criticism, long-poems, collages. "We tend toward work that brings an interesting story. We prefer characters other than 'you' & 'me' & 'I.' We consider rhythm the element lacking in most of the work we pass up. We have published Ron Androla, Adrian C. Louis, Todd Moore, Albert Huffstickler and Linda Wing recently." circ. 900. Published every 260 days. Pub'd 2 issues 2005; expects 1 issue 2006, 2 issues 2007. sub. price $26/3 issues, $99 lifetime sub.; per copy $9.95; sample $9.95. Back issues: not available. Discounts: none. 36pp. Reporting time: 1 week to never. Simultaneous submissions accepted: yes. Publishes a variable % of manuscripts submitted. Payment: varies. Copyrighted, reverts to author. Ads: none. Subjects: Arts, Fiction, Literary Review, Literature (General), Magazines, Minnesota, Poetry.

Red Hen Press, Mark Cull, PO Box 3537, Granada Hills, CA 91394, Fax 818-831-6659, E-mail editors@redhen.org. 1994. Poetry, fiction, non-fiction. avg. press run 1M. Pub'd 10 titles 2005; expects 10 titles 2006, 20 titles 2007. Discounts: 40% bookstores, 20% classroom. 100pp. Reporting time: 2 months. Simultaneous submissions accepted: yes. Publishes 5% of manuscripts submitted. Payment: 10%. Copyrights for author. Subjects: Essays, Fiction, Poetry.

RED LAMP, Brad Evans, Editor, 5 Kahana Court, Mountain Creek, Queensland 4557, Australia, evans-baj@hotmail.com. "Additional address: Brad Evans (Ed.), 61 Glenmere Close, Cherry Hinton, Cambs. CB1 8EF U.K. *Red Lamp* publishes realist, socialist, and humanitarian poetry. Subscriptions should be made out in cheque to Brad Evans (Editor). The deadlines for forthcoming issues are June 30 and Nov. 30." 2/yr. Pub'd 2 issues 2005; expects 2 issues 2006, 2 issues 2007. price per copy $5 Aust.

Red Letter Press, Helen Gilbert, Managing Editor, 4710 University Way NE #100, Seattle, WA 98105-4427, 206-985-4621, Fax 206-985-8965, redletterpress@juno.com. 1990. Non-fiction. "No unsolicited manuscripts." avg. press run 3M. Pub'd 1 title 2005; expects 1 title 2006, 1-2 titles 2007. Discounts: bookstores 40%, wholesalers/distributors negotiable, classes 20%. 200pp. Subjects: Feminism, Gay, Labor, Lesbianism, Poetry, Politics, Socialist, Third World, Minorities.

RED OWL, Edward O. Knowlton, 35 Hampshire Road, Portsmouth, NH 03801-4815, 603-431-2691, RedOwlMag@aol.com. 1995. Poetry, art. "No stories or reviews are used. Send the best poetry you can spare. There's a spring/summer edition, which I look for cheerful poems. Try to look ahead! Think of the fact that Pres. Kennedy was born in May. The other edition is autumn/winter. For that I'll use some grim poems, yet still it's harvest time and Christmas. I don't want email subs. Inquire before sending any artwork or photographs. Deadlines: Dec. 21st for spring/summer; June 21st for autumn/winter. I don't read well when it's hot or cold. Add name and address to every sheet. Don't forget SASE for full return. Interested in new and unpublished poets. Submission quantity: 2-4. Special interests: Seasonal as described above. Find a harmony between nature and industry. International subs. appreciated." circ. 200. 2/yr. Pub'd 2 issues 2005; expects 2 issues 2006, 2 issues 2007. sub. price $20; per copy $10; sample $10. 70pp. Reporting time: 2 weeks - 2 months. Simultaneous submissions accepted: yes. Publishes 7% of manuscripts submitted. Payment: contributor's copy. Not copyrighted. Ads: none. Subjects: Aging, Ancient Astronauts, Animals, Astronomy, Birth, Birth Control, Population, Bisexual, Botany, Business & Economics, Conservation, Dreams, Ecology, Foods, Energy, England, Environment, Erotica.

Red Rock Press, Ilene Barth, Creative Director, 459 Columbus Avenue, Ste. 114, New York, NY 10024, 212-362-8304, Fax 212-362-6216, redrockprs@aol.com, www.redrockpress.com. 1999. Poetry, concrete art, non-fiction. "We have one series, Virtue Victorious, that publishes 1500-2000 word first person essays and poems. Each volume has its own editor; please check *www.virtuevictorious.com* for submission guidelines and addresses. At our New York office, we review submissions for nonfiction books only. Each submission must be accompanied by sophisticated marketing plan. We are particularly interested in books with crossover potential to the gift market. Most of our authors have previously published books; some are very well known.'' avg. press run 5M-8M. Pub'd 2 titles 2005; expects 3 titles 2006, 3 titles 2007. Discounts: contact Richard Barth at above addresses for schedules. Reporting time: 4-6 weeks. Simultaneous submissions accepted: no. Publishes 10% of manuscripts submitted. Payment: varies. Copyrights for author. Subjects: Dining, Restaurants, Fashion, Food, Eating, Humor, Inspirational, Literature (General), Memoirs, Sex, Sexuality.

RED ROCK REVIEW, Richard Logsdon, Todd Moffet, English Dept J2A/Com. College S. NV, 3200 E. Cheyenne Avenue, N. Las Vegas, NV 89030, www.ccsn.nevada.edu/english/redrockreview/default.html. 1996. Poetry, fiction, articles, reviews, non-fiction. ''Each issue is 100-125 pages in length. Short stories no more than 10,000 words. Poems should be one page max. Essays to be no more than 5,000. No biases. Recent contributors: Kim Addonizio, Dorianne Luax, Tony Barnstone, Aliki Barnstone, Catherine Ryan Hyde, Cynthia Hogue, and Ellen Bass.'' 2/yr. Pub'd 2 issues 2005; expects 2 issues 2006, 2 issues 2007. sub. price $9.50; per copy $5.50. Back issues: $2. Discounts: $2.50 per copy to distributor, bookstores, etc. 120pp. Reporting time: 4 months. Simultaneous submissions accepted: yes. Publishes 5-10% of manuscripts submitted. Payment: 2 copies of current issue. Copyrighted, reverts to author. Pub's reviews: 6 in 2005. §New small literary magazines, collections of poetry, short stories, etc. Subjects: Essays, Poetry, Reviews, Short Stories.

•**Red Tiger Press (see also ARTISTIC RAMBLINGS),** A.D. Beache, P.O. Box 2907, Thomasville, NC 27361, PH: 832-634-7012, Fax: 530-323-8251, email: RedTigerPress@gmail.com. 2005. Poetry, fiction, articles, art, photos, interviews, satire, music, letters, long-poems, concrete art, non-fiction. Expects 2 titles 2006, 8 titles 2007. Discounts: 3-10 copies 25%. Simultaneous submissions accepted: Yes. Subjects: Creativity, Erotica, Fantasy, Feminism, Fiction, Folklore, Futurism, Non-Fiction, Occult, Performing Arts, Photography, Poetry, Prose, Short Stories, Writers/Writing.

RED WHEELBARROW, Randolph Splitter, 21250 Stevens Creek Blvd., De Anza College, Cupertino, CA 95014, Fax 408-864-5629, splitterrandolph@fhda.edu. 1976. Poetry, fiction, art, photos, cartoons, interviews, reviews, non-fiction. ''Seeks diversity and authenticity. Formerly known as *Bottomfish*. Recent contributors include Mark Brazaitis, Gaylord Brewer, Christopher Buckley, Walter Griffin, George Keithley, Walt McDonald, Virgil Suarez, Amber Coverdale Sumrall, and Mario Susko. Interviews with Chitra Divakaruni, James D. Houston, Al Young, Morton Marcus, Alfredo Vea, Adrienne Rich, Khaled Hosseini, Tracy Kidder. Submissions accepted between Sept. 1 and Jan. 31 only.'' circ. 250-500. 1/yr. Pub'd 1 issue 2005; expects 1 issue 2006, 1 issue 2007. price per copy $10 (current issue); sample $10/2.50. Back issues: $2.50. 100-350pp. Reporting time: 3-6 months. Simultaneous submissions accepted: yes. Publishes 5-10% of manuscripts submitted. Payment: 2 copies of magazine. Copyrighted, reverts to author. Ads: $100/$50. Subjects: California, Drama, Essays, Fiction, Interviews, Literature (General), Poetry, Short Stories.

REDACTIONS: Poetry & Poetics, Tom Holmes, Michelle Bonczek, Mike Dockins, 24 College St., Apt. 1, Brockport, NY 14420, Email: poetry@redactions.com, Web: www.redactions.com. 2002. Poetry, interviews, reviews, long-poems. ''We are a journal dedicated to poetry and poetics. We now accept submissions only by email. Either attach submissions as a Word, wordpad, notepad, .rtf, or .txt document or cut and paste submissions into body of e-mail. Please include a brief bio and your mailing address. Also indicate if submissions are being considered elsewhere. We publish poems, book reviews, translations, interviews, manifestos, and essays about poetry, poetics, poetry movements, poets, or a group of poets. We have published: Naomi Shihab Nye, Bob Hicok, Christopher Buckley, Kurt Brown, Natasha Saje, Stan Sanvel Rubin, Matthew Rohrer, Paisley Rekdal, Gerry LaFemina, Louis Jenkins, Christopher Howell, John Hodgen, William Heyen, James Grabill, Denise Duhamel, and others.'' circ. 350. Every 9 months. Pub'd 1 issue 2005; expects 1 issue 2006, 2 issues 2007. sub. price $15; per copy $8; sample $8. Make any checks payable to "Tom Holmes". 104pp. Reporting time: 2-3 months. Simultaneous submissions accepted: Yes, if notified immediately if accepted elsewhere. Publishes 10% of manuscripts submitted. Payment: 2 copies. Not copyrighted, rights revert to author upon publication. Pub's reviews: 10 in 2005. §Poetry. Subject: Poetry.

RedBone Press, Lisa C. Moore, PO Box 15571, Washington, DC 20003-0571, 202-667-0392, Fax 301-559-5239. 1997. Fiction, non-fiction. ''Accepts ms celebrating culture of black lesbians and gay men, and work that promotes understanding between black gays/lesbians and black mainstream.'' avg. press run 2M. Pub'd 1 title 2005; expects 6 titles 2006, 4 titles 2007. Discounts: 40% trade. 215pp. Reporting time: 3-6 months. Simultaneous submissions accepted: yes. Publishes 1% of manuscripts submitted. Payment: varies. Copyrights for author. Subjects: Black, Gay, Lesbianism.

Redfield Publishers, Ellie Brown, PO Box 888870, Atlanta, GA 30356, 770-698-0561; 877-438-5469; Fax 770-396-8175; redfieldpubs@bellsouth.net; www.redfieldjinx.com.

Redgreene Press (see also RC Anderson Books; Spring Grass), R.C. Anderson, Editor, PO Box 22322, Pittsburgh, PA 15222. 1990. Poetry, long-poems. ''Always reading for the REDGREENE POETRY PRIZE

($100): enclose SASE for reply and $10 reading fee; send up to 24 pages of poetry—any style or subject plus table of contents and bio; no manuscripts returned. Entrants will receive a free copy of a previous winner's chapbook. Future ANTHOLOGIES are planned on subjects such as America (all viewpoints), portraits (people, places, things), art/color/artists, seasons and nature, animals, life and death, music, parent/child/primal experiences, spiritual/religion, women, sex, and on writing/writers. I like quality poetry, and remain open to new writers, subjects, and styles. Authors include John Sokol, Samuel Hazo, Andrew T. Roy (Collected Poems), Jay Udall, Marjorie Maddox. Spring Grass Press has published unknown poets and handsewn haiku books (Andrew T. Roy: My Chinese Haiku). RC Anderson Books has also published selected books in which the author bears half or all of the costs. *Fine editing and accuracy are valued by all imprints.* Query first with self-addressed stamped envelope and three pages of book. Genealogies & biographies welcome, along with fiction and nonfiction.'' Discounts: standard. Simultaneous submissions accepted: Yes. Can copyright for author if requested. Subjects: Anthology, Autobiography, Biography, Book Arts, Desktop Publishing, Editing, Fiction, Genealogy, Haiku, Non-Fiction, Novels, Poetry, Printing, Psychology, Writers/Writing.

REDISCOVER MUSIC CATALOG, Allan Shaw, 705 South Washington, Naperville, IL 60540-6654, 630-305-0770, Fax 630-305-0782, folkera@folkera.com. 1990. Photos, interviews, reviews, music, news items. ''Generally short.'' circ. 25M-50M. 6/yr. Pub'd 6 issues 2005; expects 6 issues 2006, 6 issues 2007. sub. price free; per copy free; sample free. 32pp. Reporting time: varies. Publishes 1% of manuscripts submitted. Payment: none. Not copyrighted. Subject: Music.

REDIVIDER, Dara Cerv, Department of Writing, Literature, and Publishing, Emerson College, 120 Boylston Street, Boston, MA 02116. 2003. Poetry, fiction, art, photos, parts-of-novels, collages, plays, concrete art, non-fiction. ''Redivider, a journal of international literature and art, is run by the graduate students of the Writing, Literature, and Publishing Department of Emerson College in Boston. The journal, formerly known as the Beacon Street Review, made its debut at the 2004 AWP Conference in Chicago, and features a fresh and eclectic selection of poetry, fiction, creative non-fiction, plays and art by both emerging and established artists. Dorianne Laux, Joe Wenderoth, Randall Mann, Anne Lambert and others have graced our pages over past issues.'' 2/yr. Pub'd 2 issues 2005; expects 2 issues 2006, 2 issues 2007. sub. price $10; per copy $6; sample $6. Back issues: inquire. 150pp. Reporting time: 1-5 months. Simultaneous submissions accepted: Yes. Payment: Two copies of the issue in which a contributor appears. Copyrighted, reverts to author. Subjects: Absurdist, Arts, Experimental, Fiction, Non-Fiction, Photography, Poetry.

RedJack, Heidi Lampietti, P.O. Box 633, Bayside, CA 95524, (707) 825-7817, heidi@redjack.us. 1998. Fiction. ''RedJack publishes books of science fiction, humor, humorous science fiction, and science-fiction-related blank notebooks. Our fiction titles to date include: *The Adventures of Damion Koehkh, MD, Space Doctor (Original Scripts and Photos from the Series); X and Y, and Other Like Stories* (Sept. 2005); and the Liquid Laughter Collaborative Writing Project. At this time, we are not accepting unsolicited manuscripts.'' avg. press run 1000. Pub'd 1 title 2005; expects 1 title 2006, 1 title 2007. Discounts: 45%. 200pp. Subjects: Absurdist, Biography, Experimental, Fiction, Humor, Science Fiction, Self-Help, Space, Television.

Redrosebush Press (see also PENNY-A-LINER; PORTALS), Ella M. Dillon, PO Box 2163, Wenatchee, WA 98807-2163, 509-662-7858. 1991. Poetry, fiction, articles, art, photos, cartoons, interviews, satire, criticism, reviews, letters, non-fiction. avg. press run 500-3.1M. Pub'd 3 titles 2005; expects 1-3 titles 2006, 1-3 titles 2007. 60-260pp. Reporting time: asap. Simultaneous submissions accepted: yes. Publishes 100% of manuscripts submitted. Payment: customer pays printing costs, retains all proceeds. Copyrights for author.

Reed Press, Sally Smith, P.O. Box 701, Montrose, CA 91021, 818-248-6433, fax 818-248-6561 www.Mer-Folk.com. 1998. Fiction. ''Reeds Press is a new imprint of Victirian Essence Press. Our new imprint is concentrating on publishing general adult fiction with a romance element. We like romantic comedy, romantic thrillers, comedy and romantic fantasy. Although we like general adult fiction with a romance element and stories about love, we are not interested in category or formula romance novels. * We have several projects lined up for 2005 right now and are only considering well-written polished manuscripts in the genres listed above. Our goal is to develop a new line of uncommon romantic fiction.'' avg. press run 3000. Expects 1 title 2006, 2 titles 2007. Discounts: 1 - no discount2-4 - 20%5-9 - 30%10-24 - 40%25-49 - 42%50-99 - 44%100-199 - 48%200 or more - 50%. 325pp. Reporting time: 1 month for queries, synopsis and first 3 chapters - no manuscripts unless requested please. Simultaneous submissions accepted: Yes. Publishes 1% of manuscripts submitted. Payment: offers no advance, offers standard royalies and pays every 6 months. Does not copyright for author. Subjects: Celtic, Fantasy, Fiction, Romance.

Reference Service Press, R. David Weber, Sandra Hirsh, 5000 Windplay Drive, Suite 4, El Dorado Hills, CA 95762, (916) 939-9620, fax: (916) 939-9626, email: info@rspfunding.com, web site: www.rspfunding.com. 1975. Non-fiction. ''Reference Service Press is a library-oriented reference publishing company. We specialize in the development of directories of financial aid for special needs groups (e.g. women, minorities, the disabled).'' avg. press run 5M. Pub'd 10 titles 2005; expects 14 titles 2006, 6 titles 2007. Discounts: up to 20%. 350pp. Reporting time: 60 days or less. Payment: 10% and up, depending upon sales; royalties paid annually.

Copyrights for author. Subjects: Asian-American, Awards, Foundations, Grants, Black, Chicano/a, Education, Native American, Reference, Women.

REFERENCE SERVICES REVIEW, MCB University Press, Dr. Ilene Rockman, MCB University Press, 60/62 Toller Lane, Bradford, W. Yorkshire BD8 9BY, England, 01274-777700, Fax 01274-785200 or 785201, www.mcb.co.uk. 1972. Articles, reviews. "Library/reference." 4/yr. Pub'd 4 issues 2005; expects 4 issues 2006, 4 issues 2007. sub. price $169; per copy $42; sample free. 96pp. Reporting time: 4 weeks. Simultaneous submissions accepted: no. Payment: none. We request that authors assign copyright to publisher. Pub's reviews. §All subjects in reference format. Ads: none. Subject: Reference.

REFLECTIONS LITERARY JOURNAL, Ernest L Avery, PO Box 1197, Roxboro, NC 27573, 336-599-1181, reflect@piedmontcc.edu. 1999. Poetry, fiction, non-fiction. "Volume VIII will appear in 2006, publication has been suspended for 2007; will resume with Volume IX in 2008. No submissions accepted until 01/01/2007; will consider submissions from North Carolina authors only. Poetry (each poem one page or less), short fiction and personal essays (up to 4000 words) by established and emerging writers at all levels. Local, regional, international (in English). Submit 1-5 poems, or 1 story, or 1 essay. Send two copies of ms, one with name and address, one without. Include biog information in brief cover letter. Will consider all accessible forms of poetry, including traditional forms. Annual deadline Dec. 31. Recent contributors: J. Dixon Hearne, Peter Rennebohm, Maureen Sherbondy, Shari O'Brien, Betsy Humphreys. Vern Cowles Short Fiction Award: publication, $600 award, 5 contributor's copies. Winners notified in Mar.-Apr." circ. 200. 1/yr. Pub'd 1 issue 2005; expects 1 issue 2006. price per copy $7; sample $7. Back issues: $3. 120pp. Reporting time: up to 12 months, we read Sept.-Feb. and notify writers Mar.-Apr. We accept simultaneous submissions if notified immediately upon acceptance elsewhere. Publishes 5-10% of manuscripts submitted. Payment: contributor's copy. Copyrighted, reverts to author. Subjects: Essays, Fiction, Poetry, Short Stories, South.

Regent Press (see also Defiant Times Press), Mark B. Weiman, 6020-A Adeline, Oakland, CA 94608, 510-547-7602. 1978. Poetry, fiction, non-fiction. avg. press run 300 - 1,000. Pub'd 10 titles 2005; expects 10 titles 2006, 10 titles 2007. Discounts: 1 copy 20%, 2-3 30%, 4+ 40%. 200pp. Reporting time: varies. Payment: varies, % of gross. Copyrights for author. Subject: Literature (General).

Re-invention UK Ltd, Stephen Kuta Mr, Primrose Cottage, Lakes Farm, Braintree Green, Rayne, Braintree, United Kingdom, (0044) 1245 332147. 2004. Poetry, fiction, art, photos, cartoons, parts-of-novels, long-poems, plays, concrete art, non-fiction. "Our mission is to challenge important issues and target controversial topics. All of our publications help raise money for charity." avg. press run 1000. Pub'd 4 titles 2005; expects 15 titles 2006, 25 titles 2007. Discounts: Trade discounts: 2 - 25 copies 25%26 copies or more - 35%. 200pp. Reporting time: 2 - 4 weeks. Simultaneous submissions accepted: Yes. Payment: We don't necessarily pay an advance but on a royalty basis we allow 25%, unless arranged otherwise. Subjects: Abstracts, Adolescence, African Literature, Africa, African Studies, AIDS, Avant-Garde, Experimental Art, Bisexual, Creativity, Disabled, Erotica, Gay, Juvenile Fiction, Lesbianism, Memoirs, Photography, Poetry.

Reliance Books, Sarah Webber, 208 E. Oak Crest Drive, Ste. 250, Wales, WI 53183-9700, 262-968-9857, Fax 262-968-9854, contact@reliancebooks.com, www.reliancebooks.com. 2002. Non-fiction. "Please see website for more information. Query required prior to submission." avg. press run 5M. Expects 2 titles 2006, 4-6 titles 2007. Discounts: quantity discounts available by volume. 200pp. Reporting time: 90 days. Simultaneous submissions accepted: yes. Publishes a variable % of manuscripts submitted. Payment: by agreement. Copyrights for author. Subjects: Business & Economics, Ethics, Finances, Leadership, Management.

RELIGION & AMERICAN CULTURE, University of California Press, Thomas J. Davis, Managing Editor, University of California Press, 2000 Center St., Suite 303, Berkeley, CA 94704-1223, 510-643-7154. 1990. Articles. "Editorial address: CSRAC, 425 University Blvd., Room 341, Indiana University-Purdue University, Indianapolis, IN 46202-5140. Copyrighted by the Center for the Study of Religion and American Culture." circ. 726. 2/yr. Pub'd 2 issues 2005; expects 2 issues 2006, 2 issues 2007. sub. price $29 indiv., $88 inst., $18 student; per copy $15 indiv., $51 inst., $15 student; sample same as single copy. Discounts: foreign subs. agents 10%, 10+ one-time orders 30%. 130pp. Copyrighted, does not revert to author. Ads: $295/$220. Subjects: Culture, History, Literature (General), Religion, Sociology.

•**REMARK,** Kathleen Paul-Flanagan, PO Box 880493, Port Saint Lucie, FL 34986, www.remarkpoetry.net remarkpoetry@gmail.com. 1998. Poetry. ""remark." contains mostly poetry, with a flash fiction piece once in a while. (Submissions for fiction are not taken. I find pieces of flash fiction on my own.) I prefer free verse over traditional rhymed forms. Email submissoins only. The PO Box is for subscription payments only. "remark." is handmade. No two issues are alike. Some recent contributors- Lyn Lifshin, Christopher Cunningham, Brian McGettrick, Sheila Knowles, William Taylor, Jr. and Nescher Pyscher." circ. 55. 10/yr. Pub'd 10 issues 2005; expects 10 issues 2006, 10 issues 2007. sub. price $30; per copy $6; sample $4. Back issues: inquire. Discounts: 5 or more copies drops the prices to $4 an issue. 40pp. Reporting time: Three weeks. Simultaneous submissions accepted: Yes. Publishes 10% of manuscripts submitted. Payment: one copy of the issue the poet appears in.

Not copyrighted. Pub's reviews: approx. 8 in 2005. §Poetry Chapbooks. Ads: A removable postcard ad costs $25 for three issues.

REMS Publishing & Publicity, Dr. Maureen Stephenson, 25852 McBean Parkway #714, Valencia, CA 91355-2004, 800-915-0048, 661-287-3309, Fax 661-287-4443, remesbookdoctor@comcast.net, www.remspublishingpublicity.com, www.maureenstephenson.com, www.makemoneywritingsite.com. 1998. Fiction, satire, non-fiction. "If manuscript is over 150 pages, please send only story line, synopsis, and chapter headings for consideration. In addition, we also accept 'teen' age group books published under our Books for Young People division. Send all manuscripts with SASE." avg. press run 50-500. Pub'd 4 titles 2005; expects 3 titles 2006, 2 titles 2007. 150pp. Reporting time: 6-12 weeks. Simultaneous submissions accepted: yes. Publishes 5% of manuscripts submitted. Payment: negotiated per author. Copyrights for author. Subjects: Advertising, Self-Promotion, Autobiography, Avant-Garde, Experimental Art, Biography, Business & Economics, Careers, Inspirational, Inspirational, Ireland, Non-Fiction.

RENDITIONS, Research Centre for Translation, Chinese University of Hong Kong, Eva Hung, Editor, Chinese University of Hong Kong, Shatin, NT, Hong Kong, 852-26097407; fax 852-26035110; e-mail renditions@cuhk.hk. 1973. "A Chinese-English translation magazine. Publishes translations only of Chinese poetry, prose and fiction, classical and contemporary. Also welcomes articles on related topics dealing with Chinese language, literature and arts, or on translation. All submitted translations must be accompanied by Chinese text; require *pinyin* romanization. Special issues include: Contemporary Women Writers; Hong Kong Writing; Middlebrow Fiction; Drama; Classical Prose; Taiwan literature." 2/yr. price per copy US $17. Back issues: same as current prices. Discounts: trade discount for agents and bookstores. 160pp. Simultaneous submissions accepted: no. Payment: honoraria and 2 free copies to contributors. Copyrighted, does not revert to author. Ads: full page $280 US/1/2 page $170 US/inside back cover (full page only) $380 US. Subjects: Literature (General), Translation.

REPORTS OF THE NATIONAL CENTER FOR SCIENCE EDUCATION, Andrew Petto, Editor, NCSE, Box 9477, Berkeley, CA 94709, 510-601-7203, Fax 510-601-7204. 1980. Articles, criticism, reviews, letters, news items, non-fiction. "Scientists review creationist arguments and also report on developments in evolutionary science." circ. 3.5M. 6/yr. Pub'd 6 issues 2005; expects 6 issues 2006, 6 issues 2007. sub. price $30, foreign $37, foreign air $39; per copy $5; sample same. Back issues: $5 each. Discounts: complete set $450 (all pubs), $150 *Creation Evolution Journal* only. 44pp. Reporting time: 1 month. Simultaneous submissions accepted: yes. Payment: none; free issues are provided. Copyrighted, reverts to author. Pub's reviews: 12 in 2005. §The creation/evolution controversy. Ads: contact editor. Subjects: Anthropology, Archaelogy, Education, Humanism, Philosophy, Religion, Science.

REPRESENTATIONS, University of California Press, Catherine Gallagher, Co-Chair; Tom Laqueur, Co-Chair; Jean Day, Managing Editor, University of California Press, 2000 Center Street, Suite 303, Berkeley, CA 94704-1223, 510-643-7154. 1982. Art, photos, criticism, non-fiction. "Editorial address: *Representations*, 322 Wheeler Hall, MC 1030, University of California, Berkeley, CA 94720." circ. 1244. 4/yr. Pub'd 4 issues 2005; expects 4 issues 2006, 4 issues 2007. sub. price $42 individual, $173 institution, $28 students (+ $20 air freight); per copy $12 indiv.; $46 instit., $12 students (+ $20 air freight); sample free. Back issues: same as single copy price. Discounts: foreign subs. agent 10%, one-time orders 10+ 30%, standing orders (bookstores): 1-99 40%, 100+ 50%. 96pp. Reporting time: 1 month. Copyrighted, does not revert to author. Ads: $325/$225. Subjects: Anthropology, Archaelogy, Arts, Criticism, Culture, English, History.

Research Centre for Translation, Chinese University of Hong Kong (see also RENDITIONS), Eva Hung, General Editor, Research Centre for Translation, Chinese University of Hong Kong, Shatin, NT, Hong Kong, 852-26097407; e-Mail renditions@cuhk.hk. 1973. Poetry, articles, long-poems, plays. avg. press run 2M. Discounts: trade discount to distributors and bookstores. 160pp. Reporting time: 3 months. Simultaneous submissions accepted: no. Publisher owns copyright. Subjects: Literature (General), Translation.

RESEARCH IN YORUBA LANGUAGE & LITERATURE, Technicians of the Sacred, Lawrence O. Adewole, 1317 N. San Fernando Blvd., Suite 310, Burbank, CA 91504. Articles, interviews, reviews, music, non-fiction. circ. 2M. 4/yr. price per copy $30; sample $30. 110pp. Pub's reviews. Ads: $300.

Resource Publications, Inc. (see also LITURGICAL CATECHESIS; MINISTRY & LITURGY), William Burns, Publisher; Denise Anderson, Editorial Director, 160 East Virginia Street #290, San Jose, CA 95112-5876, 408-286-8505, Fax 408-287-8745, info@rpinet.com, www.rpinet.com, www.safe-learning.com. 1973. Poetry, fiction, articles, art, photos, cartoons, interviews, criticism, reviews, music, letters, plays, concrete art, news items, non-fiction. "Interested primarily in imaginative resources for worship, counseling, ministry, and education. In-house graphics and typography." avg. press run 2M-5M. Pub'd 20 titles 2005; expects 12 titles 2006, 20 titles 2007. Discounts: standard trade. 120pp. Reporting time: 8 weeks. Simultaneous submissions accepted: no. Publishes (unsolicited) 5% of manuscripts submitted. Payment: editorial fee or royalty on sales. Copyrights for author. Subjects: Arts, Dance, Drama, Education, Ethics, Humor, Medieval,

Mentoring/Coaching, Music, Parenting, Religion, Safety, Spiritual, Tapes & Records, Theatre.

RESOURCES FOR FEMINIST RESEARCH/DOCUMENTATION SUR LA RECHERCHE FEMIN-ISTE, Philinda Masters, Editor, 252 Bloor Street W., Toronto, Ontario M5S 1V6, Canada, 416-923-6641, ext. 2278, Fax 416-926-4725, E-mail rfrdrf@oise.utoronto.ca. 1972. Articles, interviews, criticism, reviews. "Articles, abstracts, bibliographies, resource guides. Thematic issues regularly. Bilingual (English and French)." circ. 2M. 2/yr. Pub'd 2 issues 2005; expects 2 issues 2006, 2 issues 2007. sub. price $38 Canadian, $58 foreign, $77 institution (Canada), $94 institution (outside Canada); per copy $15 individual; sample free to institutions and libraries. Back issues: individuals: $7-15 each, $38 volume, $58 outside Canada/vol; institutions: $20 each, $77 vol./Canada, $94 outside Canada. Discounts: write for details. 250pp. Reporting time: 1 week. Simultaneous submissions accepted: no. Publishes 50% of manuscripts submitted. Payment: none. Copyrighted. Pub's reviews: 30 in 2005. §Women's studies, feminist research. Ads: $300 full page/$150 1/2 page. Subjects: Book Reviewing, Education, Feminism, Women.

RESOURCES FOR RADICALS, THE LONG ARC, Brian Burch, PO Box 73620, 509 St. Clair Avenue West, Toronto, ON M6C 1C0, Canada, 416-651-5800, burch@web.ca. 1998. *"Resources for Radicals* is an annual annotated bibliography of print resources for use by those active in movements for non-violent social change. From info on civil disobedience to starting a community garden, a wide spectrum of material is presented in min review format. Review material is always wanted. Not open to submissions." 1/yr. Pub'd 1 issue 2005; expects 1 issue 2006, 1 issue 2007. sub. price $12 Canada, $13 US (US funds), $15 rest of the world (US funds). 115pp.

Rest of Your Life Publications, 118 East Palomino Drive, Tempe, AZ 85284-2354, 203-853-0303, Fax 203-853-0307, www.restofyourlife.com. 1999. Non-fiction. "We create and produce audio tapes and market them." avg. press run 1M. Pub'd 1 title 2005; expects 2 titles 2006, 3 titles 2007. Simultaneous submissions accepted: no. Publishes 50% of manuscripts submitted. Payment: negotiable. Copyrights for author. Subject: Self-Help.

Reveal (see also THE AFFILIATE), Peter Riden, 4322 Cleroux, Chomedey, Laval, Quebec H7T 2E3, Canada, 514-687-8966. 1976. "Contact us way in advance if interested to get anything being printed. We are making use of photocopiers for the present times." avg. press run as requested. Discounts: 5% to all our Affiliates Members ($75/year '94). 40+pp. Reporting time: 1 month prior to due date(s). Simultaneous submissions accepted: yes. Publishes at least 25% of manuscripts submitted. Payment: complimentary copy. Copyrights are usually a mutual agreement. Subjects: Health, Holography, Human Rights, Humanism, Inspirational, Libertarian, Magazines, Medicine, Missouri, Music, Mystery, Myth, Mythology, Newsletter, Newspapers, Non-Fiction.

THE REVIEW OF CONTEMPORARY FICTION, Dalkey Archive Press, John O'Brien, ISU Campus Box 8905, Normal, IL 61790-8905, 309-438-7555. 1981. Articles, interviews, criticism, reviews. "No unsolicited manuscripts. First twenty issues devoted to Gilbert Sorrentino, Paul Metcalf, Hubert Selby, Douglas Woolf, Wallace Markfield, William Gaddis, Coleman Dowell, Nicholas Mosley, Paul Bowles, William Eastlake, Aidan Higgins, Jack Kerouac, Robert Pinget, Julio Cortazar, John Hawkes, William S. Burroughs, Ishmael Reed, Juan Goytisolo, Camilo Jose Cela, Charles Bukowski. Recent contributors: Gilbert Sorrentino, Robert Creeley, William S. Burroughs, Carlos Fuentes, Paul Metcalf, Edward Dorn, Edmund White, Thom Gunn, Luisa Valenzuela, Juan Goytisolo, Samuel Beckett, Gabriel Garcia Marquez." circ. 3.5k. 3/yr. Pub'd 3 issues 2005; expects 3 issues 2006, 3 issues 2007. sub. price $17 indiv., $26 instit.; per copy $8; sample $8. Back issues: $8. Discounts: 10% to agencies; 45% to bookstores with a minimum order of 5 units. 180pp. Payment: copy. Copyrighted, reverts to author. Pub's reviews: 150 in 2005. §Fiction, criticism. Ads: $250/exchange. Subjects: Fiction, Literary Review.

RFD, RFD Collective, PO Box 68, Liberty, TN 37095, 615-536-5176. 1974. Poetry, fiction, articles, art, photos, cartoons, interviews, reviews, letters, news items, non-fiction. *"RFD* is a country journal by gay men, for gay men. Any material relevant to building our community is considered. A networking tool for radical faeries." circ. 2.5M. 4/yr. Pub'd 4 issues 2005; expects 4 issues 2006, 4 issues 2007. sub. price $25 2nd Class mailing, $37 1st Class, $30 foreign; per copy $7.75; sample $7.75. Back issues: $2 each when available over 1 year old. Discounts: bookstores 40%. 52pp. Reporting time: 3 months minimum. Payment: 1 copy of the issue in which their work appears. Copyrighted, reverts to author. Pub's reviews: 33 in 2005. §Country concerns, spiritual realities, gay men, poetry, alternatives (new age), radical faeries. Ads: $350/$175. Subjects: Agriculture, Community, Counter-Culture, Alternatives, Communes, Fiction, Gardening, Gay, Health, Men, New Age, Peace, Poetry, Politics, Prison, Spiritual.

RFF Press / Resources for the Future, Don Reisman, 1616 P Street NW, Washington, DC 20036-1400, 202-328-5086, 202-328-5002, 1-800-537-5487, rffpress@rff.org, www.rffpress.org. 1999. Non-fiction. "RFF Press extends the mission of Resources for the Future by publishing books that make a distinct and original contribution to scholarship, teaching, debate, and decisionmaking about important issues in environmental and natural resource policy and in risk analysis. Since its founding, Resources for the Future has published groundbreaking works about natural resources and the environment. Works of economic analysis such as Allen Kneese's *Measuring the Benefits of Clean Air and Water* and Krutilla and Fisher's *The Economics of Natural Environments* helped establish the identity of RFF. They influenced a generation of scholarship outside of RFF and had an important impact on public policy. Created as a new publishing imprint in late 1999, RFF Press expands upon this tradition by producing books that present a broad range of social science approaches to the study of natural resources and the environment. Authors of RFF Press books include RFF staff and leading researchers at universities and NGOs around the world. To ensure their quality and objectivity, publications are subject to a peer review process equal to that employed by the most rigorous university presses. RFF Press books are issued in both print and electronic (e-book) formats. They are marketed by the Press itself, by a distribution arrangement with Johns Hopkins University Press, and by select, overseas partners.'' avg. press run 1000. Pub'd 15 titles 2005; expects 18 titles 2006, 20 titles 2007. Discounts: Contact Meg Keller keller@rff.org for complete discount schedules. 250pp. Reporting time: 1-3 months. Simultaneous submissions accepted: No. Publishes 10% of manuscripts submitted. Payment: Varies; contact us for more information. Copyright varies; contact us for more information. Subjects: Agriculture, Business & Economics, Conservation, Earth, Natural History, Ecology, Foods, Environment, Nature, Non-Fiction, Political Science, Public Affairs, Textbooks.

RGA Publishing, 224 Cindyann Drive, East Greenwich, RI 02818-2429, rgapub@gallilaw.com.

RHETORICA: A Journal of the History of Rhetoric, University of California Press, Harvey Yunis, Editor, Univ of California Press, 2000 Center Street, Suite 303, Berkeley, CA 94704-1223, 510-643-7154. ''Publication of and copyrighted by the International Society for the History of Rhetoric. Editorial address: Dept. of Classical Studies, Rice University, 6100 Main Street, Houston, TX 77005-1892.'' circ. 1062. 4/yr. Pub'd 4 issues 2005; expects 4 issues 2006, 4 issues 2007. sub. price $44 indiv., $140 instit., $18 students; per copy $12 indiv., $37 instit., $12 students; sample free. Back issues: same as single copy price. Discounts: foreign subs. agents 10%, one-time orders 10+ 30%, standing orders (bookstores): 1-99 40%, 100+ 50%. 112pp. Reporting time: 2 months. Payment: none. Copyrighted, does not revert to author. Ads: $295/$220. Subject: Language.

Rhiannon Press, Mary Sue Koeppel, Editor, P.O. Box 140310, Gainesville, FL 32614, skoeppel@fccj.edu ; contact@writecorner.com. 1977. Poetry, long-poems. ''New editor as of 2003. Concentration on women's poetry. Line up new chapbook authors on my own. *See Writecorner.com for other chances to work with this new editor.''* avg. press run 500. Pub'd 1 title 2005; expects 1 title 2006, 1 title 2007. 25-35pp. Payment: copies of work or percentage of copies. Copyrights for author. Subjects: Poetry, Women.

Rhinecliff Press, Ltd., Dr. Rita E. Kirsch, PO Box 333, Rhinecliff, NY 12574, rkirsch@hvc.rr.com.

RHINO: THE POETRY FORUM, Alice George, Deborah Nodler Rosen, Kathleen Kirk, Helen Degen Cohen, PO Box 591, Evanston, IL 60204, www.rhinopoetry.org. 1976. Poetry, fiction, art, collages. ''RHINO is looking for compelling poetry, short-short fiction (2-3 pp), and translations. We encourage regional talent while listening to voices from around the world. Editors are partial to adventurous work in love with language. Submit 3-5 poems with SASE between April-October 1 only. Read excerpts on website at www.rhinopoetry.org.'' circ. 1M. 1/yr. Pub'd 1 issue 2005; expects 1 issue 2006, 1 issue 2007. sub. price $10/1year; $18/2yrs; per copy $10; sample $5. Back issues: $5. 150pp. Reporting time: 4-6 months. Simultaneous submissions accepted: yes. Publishes 5% of manuscripts submitted. Payment: 2 copies. Copyrighted, reverts to author. Subjects: African-American, Asian-American, Experimental, Fiction, Poetry, Third World, Minorities, Translation, U.S. Hispanic, Women.

Ridge Times Press, Guest Editors, PO Box 14, Caspar, CA 95420, 707-964-0463. 1981. ''We are not currently accepting new titles.'' avg. press run 3.5M. Discounts: 40% off cover price. 160pp. Reporting time: 2 months. Payment: $15 + 2 copies. Copyrights negotiable. Subjects: Earth, Natural History, Third World, Minorities.

Ridgeway Press of Michigan, M.L. Liebler, PO Box 120, Roseville, MI 48066, 313-577-7713, Fax to M.L. Liebler 586-296-3303, E-mail mlliebler@aol.com. 1973. ''No unsolicited manuscripts.'' avg. press run 300-1M. Pub'd 1 title 2005; expects 1 title 2006, 1 title 2007. Discounts: 20% to college bookstores, 40% to others. 30-60pp. Simultaneous submissions accepted: no. Publishes less than 5% of manuscripts submitted. Payment: authors get 50 copies of book. Does not copyright for author. Subjects: Christianity, Drama, Fiction, Labor, Poetry, Surrealism.

Rio Nuevo Publishers, W. Ross Humphreys, PO Box 5250, Tucson, AZ 85703, 520-623-9558, Fax 520-624-5888. 1975. avg. press run 10M. Pub'd 5 titles 2005; expects 9 titles 2006, 12 titles 2007. Pages vary. Reporting time: 90 days. Payment: semi-annual. Copyrights for author. Subjects: Anthropology, Archaelogy, Arizona, Chicano/a, Children, Youth, Colorado, Comics, Earth, Natural History, Folklore, History, Indians, Native American, Nature, New Mexico, Southwest, The West.

Rising Star Publishers (see also ORACLE POETRY; ORACLE STORY), Obi Harrison Ekwonna, 7510

Lake Glen Drive, Glenn Dale, MD 20769, 301-352-2533, Fax 301-352-2529. "We are fulltime book publishers: fiction and non-fiction: novels, criticisms, biographies, memoirs histories etc." Simultaneous submissions accepted: Send your submissions in hard copies and file(s)in diskette and or CDs or file attachment(s).

Rising Tide Press New Mexico, Pamela Tree, Publisher; Eva Correlli, Assoc. Publisher, PO Box 6136, Santa Fe, NM 87502-6136, 505-983-8484, Fax 505-983-8484. 1991. Poetry. "We publish environmental books plus belle lettres plus prose poetry. A division of American-Canadian Publishers, Inc., a non-profit corporation. Our latest book title says it all: *Every Person's Little Book of P=L=U=T=O=N=I=U=M* by Stanley Berne with Arlene Zekowski. This popular book, written for just plain folks, is a study of the Department of Energy and the Nuclear Power Industry, which demonstrates a U.S. Government out of control. Why should our own government agency poison us all? We are going to be hammering away on environmental issues, before it's too late! Please do *not* send unsolicited materials." avg. press run 6M. Expects 2 titles 2006, 2 titles 2007. Discounts: 40% to all bookstores, 50% on 10—not one bookstore has returned this book. 200pp. Payment: yes. Copyrights for author. Subjects: Environment, Nuclear Energy.

RIVER CITY, Mary Leader, Editor, University of Memphis, Department of English, Memphis, TN 38152, 901-678-4591, www.people.memphis.edu/~rivercity. 1980. Poetry, fiction, articles, interviews. "*River City* publishes fiction, poetry, photographs, and essays. Please do not send unsolicited manuscripts during the summer. Essays, interviews/profile, personal experience. Query. Length 1000-5000 words. Inquire as to upcoming themes. No genre fiction. Send complete mss. Length 1000-5000 words. Poetry: free verse, traditional, experimental. Submit maximum of 5 poems. Annual fiction contest: $1500 first place, $350 second, $150 third. Annual poetry contest: $1,000 first place. Send SASE for guidelines. It's a good idea to see an issue of *River City* before submitting." circ. 1M. 2/yr. Pub'd 2 issues 2005; expects 2 issues 2006, 2 issues 2007. sub. price $12, $24/3 years; per copy $7; sample $7. Back issues: $7. 150pp. Reporting time: 2 weeks to 3 months. Simultaneous submissions accepted: no. Publishes 5% of manuscripts submitted. Payment: 2 copies. Copyrighted, reverts to author. Ads: exchange ads for other publications. Subjects: Fiction, Literature (General), Poetry.

RIVER KING POETRY SUPPLEMENT, Wayne Lanter, Co-Editor; Donna Biffar, Co-Editor; Emily Lambeth-Climaco, Associate Editor; Phil Miller, Art Editor, PO Box 122, Freeburg, IL 62243. 1995. circ. 6M. 2/yr. Pub'd 2 issues 2005; expects 2 issues 2006, 2 issues 2007. sub. price free; per copy free; sample free. Back issues: none. 12pp. Reporting time: 6 months. Simultaneous submissions accepted: no. Publishes 10% of manuscripts submitted. Payment: 10 copies. Copyrighted, reverts to author. Ads: none. Subject: Poetry.

River Press, Paul Marks, 499 Islip Avenue, Islip, NY 11751-1826, 631-277-8618, Fax 631-277-8660, rivpress@aol.com. 1995. Non-fiction. "We publish self-help and self-improvement books and a/c tapes." avg. press run 5M. Expects 4 titles 2006, 6 titles 2007. 200pp. Reporting time: 60 days. Simultaneous submissions accepted: yes. Payment: to be determined. Copyrights for author. Subjects: Divorce, Marriage, Psychology, Relationships, Self-Help.

THE RIVER REVIEW/LA REVUE RIVIERE, Tammie Fleeger, Virginia Lausier, University of Maine-Fort Kent, 23 University Drive, Fort Kent, ME 04743-1292, 207-834-7542, river@maine.edu. 1995. Poetry, fiction, articles, photos, interviews, satire, criticism, reviews, parts-of-novels, long-poems, non-fiction. "We are international and bilingual (English/French) and publish in the language of composition. We focus on North New England and Eastern Canada, and are especially interested in the Franco-American and French Canadian experience." circ. 750. 1/yr. Pub'd 1 issue 2005; expects 1 issue 2006, 1 issue 2007. sub. price $6 US, $8.50 Canada; sample $5 US. Back issues: $4 US. Discounts: available on individual basis. 150pp. Reporting time: varies, up to a year, usually less. Simultaneous submissions accepted: no. Payment: copies. Copyrighted, reverts to author. Pub's reviews: 1 in 2005. §Anything gearing on the French experience in North America. Subjects: Canada, Culture, Earth, Natural History, English, Environment, Essays, Fiction, Folklore, France, French, History, Literature (General), Maine, Multicultural, Native American, Nature.

RIVER STYX, Richard Newman, Editor; Michael Nye, Managing Editor, 3547 Olive St., Suite 107, St. Louis, MO 63103-1014, 314-533-4541, www.riverstyx.org. 1975. Poetry, fiction, art, photos, interviews, parts-of-novels, long-poems, non-fiction. "*River Styx* is an award-winning multi-cultural publication of literature and art. Recent issues have featured Alan Shapiro, Yusef Komunyakaa, Julia Alvarez, Andrew Hudgins, R.S. Gwynn, Reginald Shepherd, Catherine Bowman, Marilyn Hacker, Ha Jin, and Rodney Jones. Art/photography by Deborah Luster, Tim Rollins, and K.O.S." circ. 3M. 3/yr. Pub'd 3 issues 2005; expects 3 issues 2006, 3 issues 2007. sub. price $20 individuals, $28 institutions; per copy $7; sample $7. Back issues: complete set, issues 5-52: $7-30. Discounts: 33% to stores, 40% with orders of 10 or more. 108pp. Reporting time: 3-5 months. We accept simultaneous submissions, but not enthusiastically. Publishes 1% of manuscripts submitted. Payment: 2 contributor's copies, 1 year subscription, $8/page if funds available. Copyrighted, reverts to author. Ads: $250/$175. Subjects: Arts, Fiction, Graphics, Literature (General), Photography, Poetry, Translation.

RIVER TEETH: A Journal of Nonfiction Narrative, University of Nebraska Press, Joe Mackall, Dan Lehman, University of Nebraska Press, 1111 Lincoln Mall #400, Lincoln, NE 68588-0630, www.nebraska-press.unl.edu. 1999. Articles, interviews, criticism, non-fiction. "The editors seek the best creative nonfiction, including narrative reporting, essay, memoir, and critical essays on nonfiction. Recent contributors include Kim Barnes, David James Duncan, Madeleine Blais, Philip Gerard, Jon Franklin, Nancy Mairs, Leon Dash, Susan Sheehan, Mark Kramer, and Wil Haygood." circ. 1M. 2/yr. Pub'd 2 issues 2005; expects 2 issues 2006, 2 issues 2007. sub. price Individuals: $20 per year; Institutions $55 per year; Foreign Subscriptions add $15; per copy $15; sample $15. Back issues: $15. 190pp. Reporting time: 2-4 months. Simultaneous submissions accepted: yes. Publishes 1-5 percent% of manuscripts submitted. Payment: 2 copies. Copyrighted, reverts to author. Ads: Contact University of Nebraska Press. Subjects: Communication, Journalism, Essays, Memoirs, Non-Fiction, Storytelling.

Rivercross Publishing, Inc., Josh Furman, 6214 Wynfield Court, Orlando, FL 32819, 407-876-7720. 1945. "Query first before submitting." avg. press run 1M. Expects 12 titles 2006, 30 titles 2007. Discounts: 1-4 books 25%, 5-49 33%, 50-250 40%, 250-500 46%. Simultaneous submissions accepted: Yes. Payment: mostly subsidy and custom publishing. Copyrights for author. Subjects: African Literature, Africa, African Studies, Autobiography, Aviation, Biography, Broadcasting, Fiction, Humor, Medicine, Native American, Occult, Poetry, Real Estate, Science Fiction, Weather, Yoga.

RIVERSEDGE, The University of TX-Pan American Press, Desirae Aguirre, TheUniversity of Texas Pan American, 1201 W. University, Lamar Bldg., Room 9A, Edinburg, TX 78541, 956-381-3638, bookworm@panam.edu. 1983. Poetry, fiction, art, photos, non-fiction. circ. 400. 2/yr. Pub'd 2 issues 2005; expects 2 issues 2006, 2 issues 2007. sub. price $12; per copy $6. Back issues: $6. 120pp. Reporting time: 6-9 months. Simultaneous submissions accepted: yes. Payment: 2 complimentary copies. Copyrighted, reverts to author. Subjects: Arts, Fiction, Non-Fiction, Poetry.

Riverstone Publishing, PO Box 270852, St. Paul, MN 55127, 651-762-1323, Fax 651-204-0063, contact@americanyouth.net, www.AmericanYouth.net. 2002. News items, non-fiction. "Recent title: *Battle Scars* by Tim Hutchinson, The True Story of How One Teen Nearly Became The Biggest Mass Murderer Ever." avg. press run 5M. Pub'd 1 title 2005; expects 3 titles 2006, 5 titles 2007. Discounts: libraries 30%, bookstores 45%, jobber (Ingram, B&T, etc.) 45%. 250pp. Reporting time: 4 weeks. Simultaneous submissions accepted: yes. Publishes 25% of manuscripts submitted. Payment: 20% paid monthly. Copyrights for author. Subject: Non-Fiction.

Riverstone, A Press for Poetry, PO Box 1421, Carefree, AZ 85377-1421. 1992. Poetry. "We are a chapbook press only. Any style. Please submit in April or May only up until June 1st postmark deadline. Enclose $10 reading fee and SASE for results (includes a copy of the winning chapbook). Manuscripts will not be returned. Please include one cover page with contact information and one cover page with title only. The annual contest is our only submission time. No further guidelines." avg. press run 300. Pub'd 1 title 2005; expects 1 title 2006, 1 title 2007. Discounts: 40% to the author and to bookstores. 20-36pp. Reporting time: 2 months from deadline. Simultaneous submissions accepted: yes. Publishes 1% of manuscripts submitted. Payment: copies (50) and award of $100. Copyrights for author. Subject: Poetry.

RIVERWIND, Bonnie Proudfoot, Editor; Kris Williams, Editor, Arts & Sciences, Oakley 312, Hocking College, Nelsonville, OH 45764. 1975. Poetry, fiction, art, photos, interviews, reviews, plays, non-fiction. "Open to new and established writers. Story/play/interview length: not to exceed 15 manuscript pages, double-spaced. On poetry: batches of 3-6, any subject, any length, but typed. We enjoy both imagistic and lyric poems. We do not read manuscripts during the summer. Recent contributors include Gerald Wheeler, Larry Smith, Roy Bentley, Jill Rosser, and Mark Halliday." circ. 400. 1/yr. Pub'd 1 issue 2005; expects 1 issue 2006, 1 issue 2007. sub. price $10; per copy $5; sample $5. Back issues: $5. 112-156pp. Reporting time: 1-3 months. Simultaneous submissions accepted: no. Payment: 2 copies. Copyrighted, reverts to author. Pub's reviews: none in 2005. §Contemporary American poetry and fiction. Ads: open. Subjects: Literary Review, Midwest, Ohio.

•**Riverwinds Publishing,** John Bond, 109 Cromwell Court, Woodbury, NJ 08096, 856-845-1250. 2005. Non-fiction. avg. press run 1500. Expects 1 title 2006, 1 title 2007. 160pp. Simultaneous submissions accepted: No. Copyrights for author. Subjects: How-To, Writers/Writing.

RIVET MAGAZINE, Leah Baltus, 3518 Fremont Avenue N. #118, Seattle, WA 98103, editor@rivetmaga-zine.org, www.rivetmagazine.org. 2001. Poetry, fiction, articles, art, photos, cartoons, interviews, satire, reviews, parts-of-novels, long-poems, plays, non-fiction. "Rivet is a panoramic magazine that uses themes to reveal intersections of art and culture. Literary and glossy at once, Rivet turns the notion of niche inside out: Its broad collection of ideas, styles and forms favors a big-picture perspective rooted in a way of thinking, rather than a specific interest. Recent contributors include Elizabeth Knaster, Kelly Igoe, Kynan Antos, Rain Grimes, Melissa Sands, Jeremy Richards, Matt Neyens, Emily Mannion, Michael Dylan Welch." circ. 1500. 4/yr. Pub'd 4 issues 2005; expects 4 issues 2006, 4 issues 2007. sub. price $16; per copy $5; sample $3. Back issues:

inquire. Discounts: Distributors: 10%; Wholesalers, retailers, bookstores: 40%; Other: negotiable. 72pp. Reporting time: 1-3 months. Simultaneous submissions accepted: No. Publishes 10% of manuscripts submitted. Payment: Pro-bono. Copyrighted, rights revert to author on publication. Rivet reserves the right, however, to re-publish all work on its Web site and in future collections or anthologies. Pub's reviews: 20 in 2005. §Independent music, writing, art, film, etc. Ads: $225 full/$150 half. Subjects: Arts, Autobiography, Bibliography, Cities, Culture, Essays, Experimental, Fiction, Humor, Liberal Arts, Lifestyles, Multicultural, Non-Fiction, Photography, Poetry.

THE ROANOKE REVIEW, Paul Hanstedt, Roanoke College, 221 College Lane, Salem, VA 24153, 540-375-2380. 1968. Poetry, fiction. "Poems to 100 lines, fiction to 7,500 words. Recent contributors include Robert Morgan, Charles Wright, and Lucy Ferriss." circ. 200-300. 1/yr. Pub'd 1 issue 2005; expects 1 issue 2006, 1 issue 2007. sub. price $13/2 years; per copy $8; sample $5. Back issues: $5. Discounts: $5 to libraries and agencies. 176pp. Reporting time: 12-16 weeks. Simultaneous submissions accepted: yes. Payment: 2 copies. Copyrighted, rights revert to author but acknowledgement of original publisher demanded.

Roaring Lion Press, Katja Morgenstern, 415 Highland Square Drive NE, Atlanta, GA 30306-2285.

Roblin Press, 388 Tarrytown Road, Upper Level, White Plains, NY 10607, 914-220-6509. 1979. Non-fiction. "Looking for non-fiction—primarily 'how-to' and self-help and money making type book manuscripts." avg. press run 25M. Pub'd 3 titles 2005; expects 6 titles 2006. Discounts: 4-10 copies 25%, 10-499 copies 40%, 500+ 50%. 200pp. Reporting time: 30 days. Payment: flexible, prefer outright purchase. Copyrights for author. Subjects: Consumer, How-To, Writers/Writing.

•**ROCK & SLING: A Journal of Literature, Art and Faith,** Susan Cowger, Kris Christensen, Laurie Klein, P. O. Box 30865, Spokane, WA 99223, editors@rockandsling.org, www.rockandsling.org. 2004. Poetry, fiction, articles, art, photos, interviews, reviews, non-fiction. "The editors of Rock & Sling like ardent, edgy, vibrant explorations of faith and experience. We publish literary prose and poetry with broad or explicit associations to Christian faith or its history. We seek complexity of thought and emotion. No genre writing or didacticism, no devotions or testimonies. Recent contributors include: Christopher Howell, Laurie Lamon, Susanna Childress, Lisa Knopp, Michelle Bitting, John Hodgen, and Luci Shaw." circ. 300. 2/yr. Pub'd 2 issues 2005; expects 2 issues 2006, 2 issues 2007. sub. price $18.00; per copy $10.00; sample $10.00. Back issues: $10.00. No discounts. 140pp. Reporting time: Responds in 6 weeks (up to 4 months if held for consideration). Simultaneous submissions accepted: Yes. Pays 2 copies for 1st rights. Copyrighted, reverts to author. Pub's reviews: 2 in 2005. §books, music and film.

•**Rock Island Press,** Louis Skipper, 3411 West Circle Drive, Pearland, TX 77581. 2006. Poetry, fiction, non-fiction. avg. press run 200. Expects 2 titles 2006, 3 titles 2007. 150pp. Reporting time: two weeks. Simultaneous submissions accepted: No. Publishes 100% of manuscripts submitted. Copyrights for author.

Rock Spring Press Inc., Alice Platt, 6015 Morrow Street East Suite 106, Jacksonville, FL 32217, editor@rockspringpress.com. 2004. Non-fiction. "Rock Spring Press is interested in publishing non-fiction writing about the outdoors, nature, the environment, and travel - preferably travel in natural places. Historical is also acceptable if it is related to nature/environment. Manuscripts covering regions east of the Mississippi River in the United States are preferred. Anthologies and/or essay collections will not be considered." avg. press run 2000. Expects 2 titles 2006, 3 titles 2007. 275pp. Reporting time: Three months. Simultaneous submissions accepted: Yes. Publishes 10% of manuscripts submitted. Payment: 12-14% of the wholesale price. Small advance possible. Royalties paid biannually. Copyrights for author. Subjects: Adirondacks, Americana, Appalachia, Biography, Conservation, Culture, Earth, Natural History, Ecology, Foods, Environment, Florida, History, Kentucky, Louisiana, Nature, South Carolina.

RockBySea Books, Henrik F Christensen Dr, Guldberg Hus, Guldbergsgade 9, Copenhagen, 2200 Copenhagen N, Denmark, + 45 35 35 44 80. 1997. Fiction. "We publish in two categories : Historical novel (fiction) and Modern Thrillers." avg. press run 1500. Pub'd 1 title 2005; expects 1 title 2006, 1 title 2007. Discounts: 45-50 % is the maximum discountrate. 450pp. Reporting time: 4-6 weeks. Simultaneous submissions accepted: No. Payment: 15 %. Copyrights for author. Subjects: Christianity, Christmas, Fiction, History, North America, Prison.

THE ROCKFORD REVIEW, David Ross, PO Box 858, Rockford, IL 61105-0858, dragonldy@prodigy.net. 1971. Poetry, fiction, art, satire, plays. "*Rockford Review*, a literary arts magazine, is published by the Rockford Writers' Guild each summer and winter as a 100-page perfectbound book. *Review* seeks experimental or traditional poetry of up to 50 lines (shorter works are preferred). Short fiction, essays, and satire are welcome—in the 250 to 1300-word range. We also publish one-acts and other dramatic forms (1300 words). We are always on the lookout for black and white illustrations and glossy photos in a vertical format. We look for writing that explores the range of human emotions and that would appeal to a general readership." circ. 350. 2/yr. Pub'd 3 issues 2005; expects 3 issues 2006, 3 issues 2007. sub. price $20 (includes monthly newsletter *Write Away*); per copy $6; sample $6. Discounts: none. 52pp. Reporting time: 6-8 weeks for poetry, longer for prose. Simultaneous submissions accepted: yes. Publishes 5-10% of manuscripts submitted. Payment: copies, Editor's Choice $25 prizes 1) prose, 2) poetry. Copyrighted, reverts to author. Ads: none. Subjects: Avant-Garde, Experimental Art, Drama, Fiction, Poetry, Prose, Satire.

ROCKY MOUNTAIN KC NEWS, Rocky Mountain KC Publishing Co., John Frea, 9574 Buttonwood Drive #A, Sandy, UT 84092, 801-298-6869, getproducts@juno.com. 1993. Fiction, satire, reviews, parts-of-novels, news items. ''Subsidiary: Excaliber Publishing. *Enclose self-addressed stamped envelope for return. If none is supplied, then manuscript will not be returned and will be destroyed.'' circ. 242M. 6/yr. Pub'd 6 issues 2005; expects 6 issues 2006, 6 issues 2007. sub. price $36; per copy $6; sample $5. Back issues: $5 each. Discounts: 2% off the top. 50pp. Reporting time: 60 days. Simultaneous submissions accepted: no. Publishes 25% of manuscripts submitted. Payment: $20-$100 per submission, based on content and length. Copyrighted, does not revert to author. Pub's reviews: 6 in 2005. §Animals, business, how-to, pets, self-help, adventure. Ads: $2,500/$1,250/$625 1/4 page. Subjects: Animals, Business & Economics, Fiction, Folklore, Pets, Publishing, Supernatural.

Rocky Mountain KC Publishing Co. (see also ROCKY MOUNTAIN KC NEWS), John Frea, 9574 Buttonwood Drive #A, Sandy, UT 84092, 801-298-6869, getproducts@juno.com. 1993. Fiction, satire, reviews, parts-of-novels, news items. ''Subsidiary: Excaliber Publishing Co. * Enclose self-addressed stamped envelope for return. If none is supplied, then manuscript will not be returned and will be destroyed.'' Pub'd 23 titles 2005; expects 20 titles 2006, 25 titles 2007. Discounts: 2% off the top. 50pp. Reporting time: 60 days. Simultaneous submissions accepted: no. Publishes 25% of manuscripts submitted. Payment: based on projected sales. We copyright for author, if needed. Subjects: Animals, Business & Economics, Fiction, Folklore, Pets, Publishing, Supernatural.

ROCTOBER COMICS AND MUSIC, Jake Austen, 1507 East 53rd Street #617, Chicago, IL 60615, 773 875 6470. 1992. Fiction, articles, photos, cartoons, interviews, reviews, music, collages, news items, non-fiction. ''*Roctober* is commited to a joyful exploration into the history of popular music and it's most colorful characters.'' circ. 5,000. 3/yr. Pub'd 3 issues 2005; expects 3 issues 2006, 3 issues 2007. sub. price $10; per copy $4; sample $4. Back issues: $4. 96pp. Reporting time: 2 weeks from receipt. Publishes 10% of manuscripts submitted. Payment: lifetime subscription. Copyrighted, reverts to author. Pub's reviews: 1500 in 2005. §Music, film, baseball related themes, monsters. Ads: $170/$90. Subjects: Americana, Chicago, Comics, Counter-Culture, Alternatives, Communes, Fantasy, Feminism, Folklore, Movies, Music, Storytelling, Television.

Rodnik Publishing Co., Robert Powers, Senior Editor; Lidiya Zabokritskaya, Editor; Lillian Levy Guevara, Editor; Steve Pallady, Editor, PO Box 46956, Seattle, WA 98146-0956, Tel 206-937-5189 Fax 206-937-3554, URL: www.rodnikpublishing.com. 1994. avg. press run 3-5M. Pub'd 1 title 2005; expects 2 titles 2006, 2 titles 2007. Discounts: max. 55%. 400pp. Simultaneous submissions accepted: yes. Payment: by contract. Copyrights for author. Subjects: Dictionaries, English, Language, Relationships, Russia, Sex, Sexuality, Vietnam.

ROGER, Renee Soto, Roger Williams University, Department of English Lit & Creative Writing, Bristol, RI 02809, 401 254 5350.

Rollaway Bay Publications, Inc., Rick Elliott, 6334 S. Racine Circle, Suite 100, Centennital, CO 80111-6404, Tel=303 799-8320, Fax=303 799-4220, email publisher@rollawaybay.com. 2003. Non-fiction. ''We at Rollaway Bay Publications are dedicated to independent production of high stanard interesting (not boring) business titles. We expect our readers to enjoy reading our books while learning something new and valuable in the process.'' avg. press run 3000. Expects 2-5 titles 2006, 5-10 titles 2007. Discounts: Bookstores & Libraries - Credit card or prepaid orders = 45% discount; invoiced order (with approved credit) = 40% discount. 350pp. Reporting time: 3 to 4 weeks. Simultaneous submissions accepted: Yes. Publishes 5% of manuscripts submitted. Copyrights for author. Subject: Business & Economics.

Rolling Hills Publishing, Michael Gray, P.O. Box 724, New Windsor, MD 21776, 410-635-3233, info@rollinghillspublishing.com, www.rollinghillspublishing.com. 2003. Non-fiction. ''Educational and How to books.'' avg. press run 5000. Pub'd 1 title 2005; expects 2 titles 2007. 112pp. Reporting time: 10 days. Simultaneous submissions accepted: Yes. Subjects: Autos, Construction, Consumer, Crafts, Hobbies, Education, Finances, How-To, Marriage, Non-Fiction, Real Estate, Wood Engraving/Woodworking.

Ronin Publishing, Inc., Beverly A. Potter, Publisher, Box 22900, Oakland, CA 94609, 510-420-3669, Fax 510-420-3672, ronin@roninpub.com, www.roninpub.com. 1983. Non-fiction. ''No unsolicited material.'' avg. press run 5-7,000. Pub'd 5 titles 2005; expects 5 titles 2006, 5 titles 2007. Discounts: less than 5 25%, up to 50 40%, 51+ 50%,. Pages vary, average is 192. Simultaneous submissions accepted: yes. Payment: 10% net, some advances. Copyrights for author. Subjects: Business & Economics, How-To, Humor.

Ronsdale Press, R. Hatch, Director, 3350 West 21st Avenue, Vancouver, B.C. V6S 1G7, Canada, 604-738-4688, toll free 888-879-0919, Fax 604-731-4548. 1988. Poetry, fiction, art, photos, satire, parts-of-novels, long-poems, collages, plays, concrete art, non-fiction. avg. press run 1.2M-2M. Pub'd 10 titles 2005; expects 11 titles 2006, 9 titles 2007. Discounts: trade 40%, libraries 20%, wholesale (bulk) 50%. 108pp. Reporting time: 1 month to 6 weeks. Simultaneous submissions accepted, but must be stated so. Publishes 10% of manuscripts submitted. Payment: 10% of retail, royalties negotiated at contract signing. Copyrights for author. Subjects: Autobiography, Bilingual, Biography, British Columbia, British Columbia, Canada, Children, Youth, Criticism, Drama, Fiction, History, Literature (General), Non-Fiction, Photography, Poetry.

ROOM, John Perlman, 38 Ferris Place, Ossining, NY 10562-2818. 1987. Poetry. "*Room* will publish single author chapbooks when and if a ms. so impresses the editor that he would be remiss in returning the work." circ. 150. Frequency varies. sub. price gratis. Pages vary. Reporting time: ASAP. Simultaneous submissions accepted: no. Publishes 1% of manuscripts submitted. Payment: copies. Not copyrighted. Subject: Poetry.

ROOM OF ONE'S OWN, PO Box 46160, Station D, Vancouver, BC V6J 5G5, Canada. 1975. Poetry, fiction, art, photos, cartoons, interviews, reviews, parts-of-novels, long-poems, plays. "Good quality literary material by, for and about women. Payment in Canadian funds only." circ. 3000. 4/yr. Pub'd 4 issues 2005; expects 4 issues 2006, 4 issues 2007. sub. price individuals - $27 Canada, CDN$39 US CDN$49.50 foreign, institutions - $36 Canada, CDN$48 US and CDN$58.50 foreign; per copy $9 Canada, US$10 US and foreign; sample $5 Canada, US$5 US and foreign. Back issues: In Canada: $10; In the US: $13; Outside North America: $18. 112pp. Reporting time: 9 months. Simultaneous submissions accepted: no. Publishes 8% of manuscripts submitted. Payment: $50-$75, plus 1-year sub. Copyrighted, reverts to author. Pub's reviews: 8-10 in 2005. §Literature, women. Ads: $60/$30/$20 1/3 page. Subjects: Literary Review, Literature (General), Women.

Rose Alley Press, David D. Horowitz, 4203 Brooklyn Avenue NE #103A, Seattle, WA 98105-5911, 206-633-2725, rosealleypress@juno.com, www.rosealleypress.com. 1995. Poetry, non-fiction. "Rose Alley Press primarily publishes books of rhymed metrical verse and an annually updated booklet about writing and promotion. We have published books by poets Victoria Ford, William Dunlop, Michael Spence, David D. Horowitz, Douglas Schuder, Joannie K. Stangeland, and Donald Kentop. We do *not* accept or read unsolicited manuscripts." avg. press run 1M. Pub'd 1 title 2005; expects 1 title 2006, 1 title 2007. Discounts: bookstores 40%, libraries 10%, distributors 55%; possible discount for bulk purchase. 28-104pp. Payment: 10 copies, percentage of profit from sales of book after earning back printing and marketing expenses. Copyrights for author. Subjects: Poetry, Writers/Writing.

Rose Publishing Co., Walter Nunn, 2723 Foxcroft Road, #208, Little Rock, AR 72227-6513, 501-227-8104; Fax 501-227-8338. 1973. Art, photos, cartoons. "Primarily books of nonfiction about Arkansas. Typical titles are 150-250 pp, usually cloth or trade paperback." avg. press run 1M. Pub'd 7 titles 2005; expects 6 titles 2006, 6 titles 2007. Discounts: trade, 5-24 copies, 40%; classroom, 10% for college and public schools. 200pp. Reporting time: 6 weeks. Publishes 1% of manuscripts submitted. Payment: 10% of gross. Copyrights for author. Subjects: Arkansas, History, South.

Rose Shell Press, Rochelle L. Holt, Publisher & Editor, Rochelle L. Holt, 15223 Coral Isle Court, Fort Myers, FL 33919-8434, www.angelfire.com/blues2/rlynnholt, RochelleL317@copper.net. 1992. Poetry, fiction, articles, art, photos, cartoons, interviews, criticism, reviews, letters, news items. "Only consider people who have purchased one of our books. Send SASE for current flyer. Primarily by invitation but also accept author as producer (low rates) projects. Check amazon.com as well as our web site to see varied books published." avg. press run 100-300. Pub'd 5 titles 2005; expects 3 titles 2006, 2 titles 2007. Discounts: 40% bookstores & classrooms & bulk over 10. 60-80pp. Reporting time: 2 weeks. Simultaneous submissions accepted: yes. Publishes 50% of manuscripts submitted. Payment: contributors copies, and arrangement with author/producer. Does not copyright for author. Subjects: Fiction, Poetry, Women.

ROSEBUD, Roderick Clark, N 3310 Asje Rd., Cambridge, WI 53523, 608-423-4750. 1993. Poetry, fiction, articles, art, interviews, satire, parts-of-novels, long-poems, plays, non-fiction. "*Rosebud* is a magazine designed 'for people who enjoy good writing.' Each issue features five rotating themes, such as 'Songs of Suburbia' and 'Mothers Daughters, Wives.' Stories, articles, profiles and poems of love, alienation, travel, humor, nostalgia, and unexpected revelation. Send a SASE for guidelines or check www.rsbd.net. *Rosebud* is looking for interesting voices and discerning readers." circ. 12M. 4/yr. Expects 3 issues 2006, 4 issues 2007. sub. price $20/3 issues; per copy $7.95; sample $7.95. Back issues: $7.95 or 3 for $18. Discounts: upon request. 136pp. Reporting time: 14 weeks. Simultaneous submissions accepted: yes. Publishes 5% of manuscripts submitted. Payment: $15 per piece. Copyrighted, reverts to author. Ads: $500/$300. Subjects: Fiction, Literary Review, Poetry, Prose, Writers/Writing.

ROTTEN PEPPER, Shannon D. Harle, Publisher, Shannon D. Harle, PO Box 1005, Swannanoa, NC 28778-1005. 1997. Cartoons, satire. "Subscription includes all the zines I do= *T.V. Heads, Rotten Pepper, Panic Strips.*" circ. 100-150. 2-3/yr. Pub'd 2 issues 2005; expects 2 issues 2006, 3 issues 2007. sub. price $5; per copy $1.55; sample $1.55. Back issues: 2 for $1.55. 20pp. Reporting time: 1 month. Simultaneous submissions accepted: no. Payment: no. Copyrighted, reverts to author. §no. Subjects: Cartoons, Comics.

THE ROUND TABLE: A Journal of Poetry and Fiction, Alan Lupack, Barbara Tepa Lupack, PO Box 18673, Rochester, NY 14618. 1984. Poetry, fiction. "We look for quality and craftsmanship rather than any particular form. We read poetry and fiction year-round. In 1987 we adopted an annual format, combining poetry & fiction. In 1989, we did another issue of the theme of King Arthur & the Knights of the Round Table. In 1990 we returned to general poetry and fiction. Now we will publish Arthurian chapbooks almost exclusively (with only occasional issues on other themes). We will publish volumes of Arthurian poetry or fiction by one author instead of an issue of the journal, as we did in 1991." Irregular. Expects 1 issue 2006, 1 issue 2007. sub. price varies; sample $7.50. Back issues: $6-$10. Discounts: arranged on request. 64pp. Reporting time: we try for 2 months, usually longer. Payment: 5 copies of chapbook. Copyrighted, reverts to author. Subjects: Fiction, Poetry.

Rowan Mountain Press (see also SISTERS IN CRIME BOOKS IN PRINT), PO Box 10111, Blacksburg, VA 24062-0111, 540-449-6178, e-mail faulkner@bev.net, web www.rowanmountain.com. 1988. Poetry, non-fiction. "Appalachian poetry and short stories. Manuscript submission by invitation. Recent authors: R. Franklin Pate, Jim Wayne Miller, Sharyn McCrumb, Bennie Lee Sinclair, Harry Dean, Earl S. Zehr, Norman M. Bowman." avg. press run 300. Pub'd 1 title 2005; expects 2 titles 2006, 1 title 2007. Discounts: 2-4 copies 20%, 5+ 40%; 40% any quantity and s/h if prepaid. 75pp. Payment: 10% of press run. Copyrights for author. Subjects: Appalachia, Education, Mystery, Poetry, Scotland, Short Stories, Vietnam, War.

Rowan Press, Inc., Joan Robinson-Blumit, Editor, PO Box 80954, Phoenix, AZ 85060-0954, 602-954-5638, jvblumit@extremezone.com. 1997. Poetry, fiction. ""The Wheel" is published quarterly for the Neopagan market. Poetry, short fiction: 3,000-6,000 words. Speculative fiction featuring Pagan/fantasy themes including short stories, poems, and line art. Integrate how to ideas with creative expression. Imaginative thought is emphasized daily subject matter expressed in magickal circumstance will be given priority. Also, think seasonally when submitting. Articulate your muse in context with your spirituality and practice. Be inspirational, be clever. Any tradition involving Paganism, (traditions, rituals), incorporated into real world settings are encouraged. Integrate a Pagan lifestyle with contemporary issues facing and concerning Pagans. Be educational and be creative—stress who we are as individuals yet show that we're not different. For example, write about topics that show tolerance and understanding between Pagans and non-Pagans. No science fiction. No essays or opinion articles. Submission guidelines: SASE or visit website www.rowanpress.com." 32pp. Reporting time: 4-6 weeks. Simultaneous submissions accepted: yes. Payment: $5-$10 for stories, depending on length. Copy of issue in which published for poems. Copyright: One time rights only. Subject: Fiction.

Rowhouse Press (see also JACK MACKEREL MAGAZINE), Greg Bachar, PO Box 23134, Seattle, WA 98102-0434. 1992. Poetry, fiction, art, photos, criticism, music, parts-of-novels, long-poems, non-fiction. "Send money orders (cash only) to Greg Bachar." avg. press run varies. Pub'd 1 title 2005; expects 3-4 titles 2006, 7-8 titles 2007. Pages vary. Reporting time: 2-4 weeks. Payment: copies. Copyrights for author. Subjects: Arts, Biography, Book Reviewing, Comics, Criticism, Dada, Dance, Electronics, Fiction, History, Holography, Language, Literature (General), Music, Philosophy.

R-Squared Press, Dan Romanchik, Brenda Romanchik, 1325 Orkney Drive, Ann Arbor, MI 48103-2966, 313-930-6564 phone/Fax. 1994. Non-fiction. "We publish books in areas that interest us personally, including adoption, cooking, and bicycle touring. Our first book, *A Birthmother's Book of Memories* was published in spring of 1994. Our latest book, *How to Open An Adoption*, appeared in the Spring of 1998." Expects 3 titles 2006, 3 titles 2007. Discounts: write for information. Payment: standard. Copyrights for author. Subjects: Adoption, Bicycling, Cooking.

RUBBERSTAMPMADNESS, Roberta Sperling, PO Box 610, Corvallis, OR 97330-0610. 1980. Articles, art, photos, interviews, reviews, letters. circ. 18M. 6/yr. Pub'd 6 issues 2005; expects 6 issues 2006, 6 issues 2007. sub. price $24.95; per copy $5.99; sample $5.99. Back issues: $6 USA/Canada $9 overseas. Discounts: $7. 108pp. Payment: $100-$200 depending on size of article. Copyrighted. Pub's reviews: 36 in 2005. §Rubberstamping, paper arts, creative ideas, book arts, mail art. Ads: $1270/$780/$1.75 per word. Subjects: Arts, Visual Arts.

RUBIES IN THE DARKNESS, Peter Geoffrey Paul Thompson, Editor, 41 Grantham Road, Manor Park, London E12 5LZ, England. 1991. Poetry. "Traditional, romantic and spiritually inspired poetry (international). Recent contributors include Pamela Constantine, Peter Geoffrey Paul Thompson, Philip Higson, Pamela Harvey, Jack Clubb (USA), Dr. K. Ikeda (Japan), Tim Cloudsley (Columbia), and Dr. A. Schedchikov (Russia)." circ. 250. 2/yr. Expects 2 issues 2006, 2 issues 2007. sub. price £10, $20; per copy £5, $10; sample £5, $10. Back issues: £5, $10. Discounts: none. 36pp. Reporting time: 1 month maximum. Simultaneous submissions accepted: no. Publishes 20% of manuscripts submitted. Payment: by arrangement for individual anthologies; mag: one free copy only. Copyrighted. Small ads free for subscribers, no other ads accepted. Subject: Poetry.

Ruby Sky Publishing, 16055 SW Walker Road #225, Beaverton, OR 97006-4942, 503-372-5824, Fax

503-629-5505, kay@rubyskypublishing.com, www.rubyskypublishing.com.

THE RUE BELLA, Nigel Bird, Geoff Bird, 40, Jordangate, Macclesfield SK10 1EW, England, www.ruebella.co.uk. 1998. Poetry, fiction. circ. 350-400. 2/yr. Pub'd 2 issues 2005; expects 2 issues 2006, 2 issues 2007. sub. price £10/4 issues; per copy £3.50. Back issues: £1.50. 120pp. Reporting time: 6-8 weeks. Simultaneous submissions accepted: yes. Publishes 10% of manuscripts submitted. Payment: free copy. Copyrighted, reverts to author. Subjects: Poetry, Short Stories.

RUMINATIONS: The Nigerian Dwarf & Mini Dairy Goat Magazine, Cheryl K Smith, 22705 Hwy 36, Cheshire, OR 97419, 541 998-6081. 1993. Poetry, fiction, articles, photos, cartoons, interviews, reviews, letters, news items, non-fiction. "Ruminations is dedicated to the free exchange of ideas, knowledge and opinions relevant to Nigerian Dwarf and other miniature dairy goats." circ. 350. 4/yr. Pub'd 6 issues 2005; expects 4 issues 2006, 4 issues 2007. sub. price $18; per copy $5.00; sample $5.00. Back issues: $4.00. 32pp. Reporting time: 1 day to 4 weeks. Simultaneous submissions accepted: No. Payment: No payment; ad exchanges. Copyrighted. Pub's reviews: approx 6 in 2005. §goats, poison plants, videos, livestock, health. Ads: Classified—$25/wordDisplay—$25/%30/$40/$60/$80/$100/$115. Subjects: Agriculture, Book Reviewing, How-To, Pets, Reviews.

The Runaway Spoon Press, Bob Grumman, 1708 Hayworth Road, Port Charlotte, FL 33952, 941-629-8045. 1987. Poetry, art, cartoons, satire, criticism, reviews, long-poems, collages, plays, non-fiction. "My press is in its second decade and slowing down. I'm no longer as open to new authors as I once was. I'm definitely not interested in the kind of thing commercial and academic presses publish. I've recently published Clemente Padin, Karl Kempton and Carla Bertola." avg. press run 100. Pub'd 4 titles 2005; expects 5 titles 2006, 6 titles 2007. Discounts: 40% off for purchase of 5 or more copies of a book, 40% retailers' discount. 48pp. Reporting time: indefinite. Simultaneous submissions accepted: yes. Publishes 10% of manuscripts submitted. Payment: author gets 25% of each printing. Does not copyright for author. Subjects: Arts, Avant-Garde, Experimental Art, Comics, Criticism, Drama, Graphics, Humor, Poetry, Psychology, Visual Arts.

RUNES, A Review of Poetry, Arctos Press, CB Follett, Susan Terris, PO Box 401, Sausalito, CA 94966-0401, 415-331-2503, Fax 415-331-3092, runesrev@aol.com, http://members.aol.com/runes. 2000. Poetry. "A themed annual poetry anthology. Seeking poems that have passion, originality, and conviction. We are looking for narrative and lyric poetry that is well-crafted and has something surprising to say. No greeting card verse. Prefer poems under 100 lines. Theme for 2006 is Hearth. Theme for 2007 is Connection. Robert Hass & Brenda Hillman are the judges for the 2007 RUNES Award Competition (deadline May 31st 2007)!" circ. 1M. 1/yr. Pub'd 1 issue 2005; expects 1 issue 2006, 1 issue 2007. sub. price $12 for one year, $21 for two years; per copy $12; sample $10. Back issues: Available for $10. Includes shipping and tax. 160pp. Reporting time: 4 months. We accept simultaneous submissions if notified. Publishes 2-3% of manuscripts submitted. Payment: 1 copy. Copyrighted, reverts to author. §Poetry. Ads: none. Subject: Poetry.

Running Press, Stuart Teacher, President and Publishers; Al Struzinski, Vice President and COO; Carlo DeVito, Associate Publisher; Mike Ward, Editorial Director; Sam Caggiula, Director of Publicity; Lucy Pappas, Contract Department, 125 South 22nd Street, Philadelphia, PA 19103, 215-567-5080, www.runningpress.com. 1973. Non-fiction. avg. press run 30M. Pub'd 66 titles 2005; expects 90 titles 2006, 100 titles 2007. Discounts: 1-4 20%, 5-24 40%, 25-49 42%, 50-99 43%, 100-249 44%, 250-599 45%, 600-1499 46%, 1500+ 47%, 50% wholesale. Reporting time: 1 month. Payment: negotiable. Copyrights for author. Subjects: Arts, Children, Youth, Cooking, Gardening, How-To, Literature (General), Miniature Books, Postcards, Reference, Sports, Outdoors.

RURAL HERITAGE, Gail Damerow, 281 Dean Ridge Lane, Gainesboro, TN 38562-5039, 931-268-0655, editor@ruralheritage.com, www.ruralheritage.com. 1976. Articles, photos, cartoons. "900-1200 words re: draft horses, mules, and oxen including implements, vehicles, uses, hitching methods, auction prices, logging, farming, how-to, etc. (SASE for guidelines or visit the Business Office at ruralheritage.com). Contributors: Drew Conroy PhD, Sam Moore, Beth A. Valentine DVM PhD. We do not pay for reviews, reviewer gets to keep the book." circ. 5M. 6/yr. Pub'd 6 issues 2005; expects 6 issues 2006, 6 issues 2007. sub. price $26; per copy $6.25; sample $8 includes S/H. Discounts: agent 30%. 108pp. Reporting time: 1-3 months. Simultaneous submissions rarely accepted. Publishes 10% of manuscripts submitted. Copyrighted, reverts to author. Pub's reviews: 42 in 2005. §Draft animals, gardening, country topics (construction, crafts, etc.). Ads: $285/$160/35¢ per word, send for rate card or visit the Business Office at ruralheritage.com. Subjects: Agriculture, Amish Culture, Animals.

Russell Dean and Company, Bradd Hopkins, Executive Editor, Anne Schroeder, 17110 1'2 408th Ave. SE, Gold Bar, WA 98251, toll free: 888-205-0004, 360-793-4919, fax: 360-793-7579, email: topdogrdc@peo-plepc.com, , www.RDandCo.com. 1997. Fiction, non-fiction. "2004 release: *Down to the Wire: The Lives of the Triple Crown Champions* by Robert Shoop (nonfiction). 2003 release: *Wolf's Rite* by Terry Person (fiction). 2002 releases: *Scent of Cedars*, edited by Anne Schroeder (anthology of emerging writers)." avg. press run 3M.

Pub'd 2 titles 2005; expects 2 titles 2006, 2 titles 2007. Discounts: industry standard/as negotiated in bulk. 230pp. Reporting time: 3-6 months. Simultaneous submissions accepted: no. Publishes less than 1% of manuscripts submitted. Payment: industry standard with signing bonus. Copyrights for author. Subjects: Anthology, Fiction, Non-Fiction.

Russet Press, Kathleen Millman, 3442 Capland Ave., Clermont, FL 34711-5738. 1995.

Russian Information Services (see also RUSSIAN LIFE), Paul Richardson, Stephanie Ratmeyer, PO Box 567, Montpelier, VT 05601-0567, 802-223-4955. 1990. Non-fiction. "Publish Russian Life magazine, plus a few maps and even fewer books." avg. press run 5M. Pub'd 5 titles 2005; expects 5 titles 2006, 5+ titles 2007. Discounts: case by case. 200pp. Reporting time: 1 month. Payment: case by case. Copyrights for author. Subjects: Business & Economics, Russia, Travel, U.S.S.R.

RUSSIAN LIFE, Russian Information Services, Paul Richardson, Publisher & Editorial Director, PO Box 567, Montpelier, VT 05601-0567. 1956. Photos, non-fiction. "Bi-monthly magazine on Russian history, culture, travel." 6/yr. Pub'd 6 issues 2005; expects 6 issues 2006, 6 issues 2007. sub. price $33 US, $38 foreign; per copy $8. Back issues: $8. 64pp. Reporting time: 1 month. Publishes less than 10% of manuscripts submitted. Copyrighted, rights do not revert if WFH. Pub's reviews: 6-8 in 2005. §History, culture. Ads: contact for rates. Subject: Russia.

Ryrich Publications, Barbara Gladding, 825 South Waukegan Road, PMB 183 A-8, Lake Forest, IL 60045, 847-234-7967, Fax 847-234-7967, ryrichpub@aol.com. 1996. Fiction. "Children's fiction to 30,000 words. Prefer middle-grade, 8-12 years, and young adult." avg. press run 1-5M. Expects 1 title 2006, 3 titles 2007. Discounts: universal. 100-200pp. Reporting time: 6-8 weeks. Simultaneous submissions accepted: yes. Payment: policy varies. Copyrighting for author available. Subjects: Animals, Children, Youth, Fiction, Juvenile Fiction.

S

•**Saber Press,** Michael Conti, 268 Main Street, PMB 138, North Reading, MA 01864, Tel. 978-749-3731, Fax 978-475-5420, Email: admin@sabergroup.com, Website: www.saber-press.com. Non-fiction. "We are currently accepting manuscripts for consideration. All submissions will be handled with great care to ensure your privacy. We are interested in non-fiction training and informational material that will be of interest to our particular audience, the law enforcement, military, and corporate security sectors.We offer full publishing services as well as consultation services to assist you in making your project a reality." Special discounts are available. Contact Booksales@sabergroup.com for more information! 150-400pp. Reporting time: 1-2 weeks. Simultaneous submissions accepted: Yes. Payment: Industry standard (and better) arrangements are available. Copyrights for author. Subject: Non-Fiction.

The Sacred Beverage Press, Amelie Frank, Matthew Niblock, PO Box 10312, Burbank, CA 91510-0312, Fax 818-780-1912, sacredbev@aol.com. 1994. Poetry, art, long-poems. "The press is currently on hiatus. Sole editorial bias: Quality. Contributors: The Carma Bums, The Valley Contemporary Poets, FrancEyE, Nelson Gary, Richard Osborn Hood, and Diane DiPrima." avg. press run 500-1M. Pub'd 3 titles 2005; expects 3 titles 2006, 4 titles 2007. Discounts: 40% retail. 100pp. Reporting time: 2-3 months. Simultaneous submissions accepted: no. Publishes 5% of manuscripts submitted. Payment: % of sales after costs are met; 40% of consignment sales; 25 free author's copies; author's expenses. Copyrights for author. Subject: Poetry.

Sacred Spaces Press, Ruth King, PO Box 7812, Berkeley, CA 94707, 510-559-9341, inquiries@sacredspaces-press.com, www.sacredspacespress.com. 2004. Non-fiction. "We are a new, non-traditional publisher interested in supporting self-help authors self-publish. We offer: * individual coaching to conceptualize and/or outline your manuscript. * educational workshops and personal coaching on the various stages of self publishing. * support that foster inspiration, stimulation, momentum, and commitment. * editorial, layout, cover design, and printing referral. * advise on distribution options. * marketing tips, and much more.We desire subjects that include psychospiritual works, wisdom traditions, self-discovery, creativity, health and healing, relationships, women's and men's issues, mythology, aging, grief and loss, and other subjects for the inner life. We welcome topics of both spiritual and intellectual value, with an everyday application in our lives." Expects 1 title 2006, 4 titles 2007. 240pp. Reporting time: 3 months. Simultaneous submissions accepted: yes. Payment: to be arranged. Copyrights for author. Subjects: Psychology, Self-Help, Spiritual.

SACS Consulting, Timothy A. Dimoff, 520 South Main St., Suite 2512, Akron, OH 44311-1073, tadimoff@sacsconsulting.com, www.sacsconsulting.com 330-255-1101. 1990. Non-fiction. "Focus on business topics including high risk and security issues,human resource issues, and entrepreneurship.'' avg. press run 3M. Pub'd 3 titles 2005; expects 1 title 2006, 2 titles 2007. Discounts: 40% to bookstores, 50% wholesale/distributors, 20% libraries & schools, 2-4 quantities 20%, 5-99 40%, 100+ 50%. 125pp. Simultaneous submissions accepted: yes. Payment: negotiable. Copyrights for author. Subjects: Business & Economics, Careers, Management.

Sadorian Publications, PO Box 2443, Durham, NC 27715-2443, 919-599-3038, Fax 309-431-4387, sadorianllc@aol.com, www.Sadorianonline.com. 2000. Poetry, fiction, art, non-fiction. ''The preferred range for novels is from 60,000 to 80,000 words. We do not publish hate-related, pornographic material. Submissions are not returned, they are shred, please do not send your only copy. All submissions must include a SASE and a stamped postcard for confirmation of receipt. Due to the volume of submissions we receive, we cannot discuss or provide the status of your manuscript via email or telephone. Please include a SASE to be notified with regards to your submission. No SASE, no response.'' avg. press run 3000. Pub'd 12 titles 2005; expects 12 titles 2006, 18 titles 2007. Discounts: less than 10 units 0%, 10-49 40%, 50-249 45%, 250+ 50%. 275pp. Reporting time: 2-3 months. Simultaneous submissions accepted: yes. Publishes 5-10% of manuscripts submitted. Copyrights for author. Subjects: African-American, Children, Youth, Fiction, Inspirational, Memoirs, Poetry.

Sagamore Publishing, Doug Sanders, 804 N. Neil St, Champaign, IL 61820, 800-327-5557, 217-359-5940, 217-359-5975 (fax), HTTP://www.sagamorepub.com. 1974. Non-fiction. ''For the past 31 years, Sagamore Publishing has been doing materials for the parks, recreation and leisure industry. Each quarter, we publish the prestigious Journal of the Parks and Recreation Administration. Well-known in their respective fields, some of our recent authors are: Ruth V. Russell, Ted Cable, Tom Griffiths, Chris Edginton, Thomas Sawyer, Linda Jean Carpenter, David Austin, Norma Stumbo H. Ken Cordell and Joseph J. Bannon.'' Pub'd 8 titles 2005; expects 8 titles 2006, 8 titles 2007. Discounts: Trade discounts are negotiable. Standard volume discounts are: 1-9 10%, 10-49 20%, 50-99 30%, 100+ 35%. Add 5% if books are non-returnable. 345pp. Reporting time: 1-2 months. Payment: We pay royalties every six months. Subjects: Business & Economics, Children, Youth, Conservation, Education, Environment, Health, Journals, Music, Psychology, Reference, Self-Help, Senior Citizens, Sports, Outdoors, Storytelling, Third World, Minorities.

Sagapress, Inc., Ngaere Macray, Box 21, 30 Sagaponack Road, Sagaponack, NY 11962, 516-537-3717; Fax 516-537-5415. 1982. Non-fiction. ''Distributed by Timber Press, 9999 SW Wilshire, Portland, OR 97225, 1-800-327-5680.'' avg. press run 5M. Pub'd 4 titles 2005; expects 5 titles 2006, 5 titles 2007. Discounts: trade. 300pp. Subjects: Biography, Gardening, History.

Sage Hill Press, Thomas Caraway, 3725 University Ave., Apt.101, Grand Forks, ND 58203-0523, 701-777-9605, sagehillpress@yahoo.com. 2004. Poetry, criticism, long-poems, non-fiction. ''I tend to favor non-experimental writing, environmental themes, narrative, meditative, or dramatic lyric poetry, but above all, good writing. Also interested in poetry in translation.'' avg. press run 500-1000. Expects 1 title 2006, 3 titles 2007. Discounts: 40% wholesale. 88pp. Reporting time: 3 months. Simultaneous submissions accepted: Yes, if notified. Copyrights for author. Subjects: Criticism, Environment, Poetry, Surrealism, Translation, Writers/Writing.

SAGE OF CONSCIOUSNESS E-ZINE, Michelle Williams, PO Box 1209, Ocala, FL 34478-1209, sageofcon@gmail.com http://www.sageofcon.org. 2004. Poetry, fiction, articles, art, photos, interviews, satire, parts-of-novels, long-poems, collages, plays, concrete art, non-fiction. ''ISSN 1555-192X. We look for innovative, ground breaking—perhaps even touching the edges of the taboo—poetry, short stories, photography, plays, digital media, and art that speaks to a reader's soul in some fashion. Our mission is to publish art, photography, short fiction and non-fiction, poetry, essay, articles, plays, paintings, digital media, and to give artists and writers an outlet to present their work. Sage of Consciousness editors are from different backgrounds, upbringings, and have different tastes, points of view, and political affiliations; we do not select pieces based on political, religious, or geographical bias. Each piece submitted stands on its own merits. We also delve further into the writing and art world by offering helpful articles for writers and artists, links to writing communities, and offer to put links to artists and writers' web sites. Artists and writers who have published in Sage of Consciousness E-Zine include: Marianne Vincent, SuzAnne C. Cole, Rob Rosen, Corey Mesler, Robyn Rose, Ivan D. Young, Chris Woods, and Nano Boye Nagle.'' circ. 1369. 4/yr. Expects 4 issues 2006, 4 issues 2007. sub. price free; per copy free; sample free. Back issues: free. Discounts: free. 60pp. Reporting time: Notification of submission received within 14 days. Simultaneous submissions accepted: Yes. Publishes 47% of manuscripts submitted. Payment: Yes. Copyrighted, reverts to author. Subjects: Arts, Avant-Garde, Experimental Art, Essays, Fiction, Graphic Design, Haiku, Internet, Non-Fiction, Photography, Poetry, Prose, Short Stories, Visual Arts, Writers/Writing, Zines.

SAGEWOMAN, Anne Newkirk Niven, Editor in Chief; Cristina Eisenberg, Managing Editor, PO Box 641, Point Arena, CA 95468. 1986. Articles, art, photos, interviews, reviews, music. circ. 21M. 4/yr. Pub'd 4 issues 2005; expects 4 issues 2006, 4 issues 2007. sub. price $21; per copy $6; sample $6. Back issues: $6. Discounts:

none. 96pp. Reporting time: 1-2 months. We rarely accept simultaneous submissions. Publishes 20% of manuscripts submitted. Payment: minimum 2¢ per word, sometimes higher. Copyrighted, reverts to author. Pub's reviews: 12 in 2005. §Women's spirituality, ecology, feminism. Ads: $625/$325/$1.50 per word. Subjects: Astrology, Celtic, Metaphysics, Myth, Mythology, New Age, Occult, Spiritual, Tarot, Women.

St. Andrews College Press (see also CAIRN: The New ST. ANDREWS REVIEW), L.W. Johns, Editor, 1700 Dogwood Mile, Laurinburg, NC 28352-5598, 910-277-5310. 1969. Poetry, fiction, interviews, reviews, long-poems, plays, non-fiction. *"Cairn* is especially interested in fiction and poetry by new writers. We have no particular editorial biases, but in general we do not accept genre work, childrens lit , or literary criticism. Recent contributors include Dana Gioia, Robert Creeley, and Virgil Suarez. Submissions are read between June 1 and November 1, and *Cairn* is published in late spring." avg. press run 500. Pub'd 5 titles 2005; expects 5 titles 2006, 5 titles 2007. Discounts: 40%. 100pp. Reporting time: 3-4 months, usually sooner. Simultaneous submissions accepted: yes, with notification of simultaneous submission and acceptance elsewhere. Publishes 2% of manuscripts submitted. Payment: 2 copies, 50% discount on extra copies. Copyrights for author. Subjects: Drama, Fiction, Literary Review, Poetry.

ST. CROIX REVIEW, Angus MacDonald, Publisher; Barry Myles MacDonald, Editor, Box 244, Stillwater, MN 55082, 651-439-7190, Fax 651-439-7017. 1968. Articles, criticism, reviews, letters. "19th century liberalism." circ. 2M. 6/yr. Pub'd 6 issues 2005; expects 6 issues 2006, 6 issues 2007. sub. price $30 1-year membership price; per copy $5; sample $5 postage & handling. Back issues: $5. Discounts: 50% for bulk orders, of 10. 64pp. Reporting time: 14 days. Simultaneous submissions accepted: yes. Publishes 10% of manuscripts submitted. Payment: none. Copyrighted, does not revert to author. Pub's reviews: 25 in 2005. §Social commentary. Ads: none. Subjects: Book Reviewing, Business & Economics, Criticism, Culture, Education, Political Science, Politics, Religion.

St. John's Publishing, Inc., Timothy Montgomery, Editor-in-Chief; Donna L. Montgomery, President, 6824 Oaklawn Avenue, Edina, MN 55435, 952-920-9044. 1986. Fiction, non-fiction. "Trade paperback publisher of quality nonfiction. No manuscripts accepted for review without prior approval based on query letter and synopsis with SASE." avg. press run 5M. Pub'd 1 title 2005; expects 3 titles 2006, 3 titles 2007. Discounts: per quantity for individuals, schools, libraries, government agencies; up to 42% for bookstores; 50% for wholesalers and jobbers. 200pp. Reporting time: 3 weeks or less. Payment: standard royalty; minimal advance; payments semi-annual. Copyrights for author. Subject: Parenting.

St Kitts Press, Elizabeth Whitaker, PO Box 8173, Wichita, KS 67208, 888-705-4887, 316-685-3201, Fax 316-685-6650, ewhitaker@skpub.com. 1998. Fiction. "Imprint of SK Publications. 70,000-90,000 words of material length. Biases: mystery and suspense fiction. Recent contributors: Radine Trees Nehring, Ellen Edwards Kennedy, Laurel Schunk, Ralph Allen, and N.J. Lindquist." avg. press run 1.5M hardbacks, 2M paperbacks. Pub'd 2 titles 2005; expects 2 titles 2006, 2 titles 2007. Discounts: trade - distributors and booksellers. 300pp. Reporting time: 3 months. Simultaneous submissions accepted: yes. Publishes 15% of manuscripts submitted. Payment: 500 advances, 12-15% royalty, paid quarterly. Copyrights for author. Subject: Mystery.

ST. LOUIS JOURNALISM REVIEW, Charles L. Klotzer, Editor-Publisher Emeritus; Ed Bishop, Editor, 470 E. Lockwood Ave., WH 414, St. Louis, MO 63119, 314-968-5905. 1970. Articles, photos, cartoons, interviews, satire, criticism, reviews, letters, news items. circ. 4M. 10/yr. Pub'd 10 issues 2005; expects 10 issues 2006, 10 issues 2007. sub. price $47; per copy $5; sample $5. Back issues: $5. Discounts: $6 off to subscription agencies, 50% split to stores & outlets. 32pp. Reporting time: 2-3 weeks. We accept simultaneous submissions if so indicated. Payment: $40-$200 (or more). Copyrighted, reverts to author. Pub's reviews: 20 in 2005. §Critique of print and broadcast media, journalism, particularly St Louis area, media, communications, press, broadcasting, cable, and items not covered by media. Ads: $900 for a full-page—8 1/2" by 11;" Write for additional rates. Subjects: Book Reviewing, Communication, Journalism, Criticism, Current Affairs, Illinois, Journals, Literary Review, Magazines, Media, Midwest, Missouri, Newspapers, Radio, Television.

Saint Mary's Press, Lorraine Kilmartin, 702 Terrace Heights, Winona, MN 55987, 800-533-8095, http://www.smp.org, smpress@smp.org. 1943. Fiction, non-fiction. "We publish books on the following subjects: prayer, reflection, spiritual memoirs, family spirituality, healing, grieving, caregiving, understanding Christian faith and practice, spiritual poetry, fiction for young adults, high school religion textbooks." avg. press run 7.5M. Pub'd 20 titles 2005; expects 20 titles 2006, 20 titles 2007. 150pp. Reporting time: 3 months. Simultaneous submissions accepted: yes. Copyrights for author. Subjects: Adolescence, Catholic, Children, Youth, Christianity, Fiction, Guidance, Non-Fiction, Religion, Short Stories, Spiritual, Textbooks, Young Adult.

ST. VITUS PRESS & POETRY REVIEW, Theron Moore, Editor; Todd Moore, Editor, 7408 Estes Park Avenue NW, Albuquerque, NM 87114. "Outlaw poetry." 2/yr. sub. price $10/YEAR.

SAKANA, Johanne LePage, 11 Bangor Mall Blvd #114, Bangor, ME 04401. 2004. Poetry, fiction, art, photos, cartoons, interviews, criticism, reviews, long-poems. "We revel in "discovering" writers yet unread and publishing these new writers alongside those more seasoned. There seems to be, at any given time, a handful of writing styles in vogue. Don't worry if your work doesn't seem particularly commercial, popular, or esteemed. Sakana is aware of the climate, but doesn't scale its publishing trends to reflect what other magazines are doing. We are our own fish. Always, always include a cover letter regardless of what type of work you are submitting to us and provide a SASE. For the most current and comprehensive information on us, visit: http://www.geocities.com/sakanamag. Recent contributors include Joyce Odam, Troy Casa, Catherine Munch, Anselm Brocki, and John N. Miller." circ. 100. 4/yr. Pub'd 1 issue 2005; expects 4 issues 2006, 4 issues 2007. sub. price $16; per copy $4; sample $4. Back issues: $3. Discounts: 2-14 copies 25%, 15-30 copies 40%. 48pp. Reporting time: usually two weeks, never more than two months. Publishes 15% of manuscripts submitted. Payment: one copy. Copyrighted, reverts to author. Pub's reviews: 3 in 2005. §Poetry collections, other small literary magazines, literary novels. Subjects: Abstracts, Absurdist, Avant-Garde, Experimental Art, Dada, Dreams, Essays, Experimental, Haiku, Language, Literary Review, Memoirs, Philosophy, Poetry, Surrealism, Translation.

SALAMANDER, Jennifer Barber, Salamander/Suffolk University English Dept., 41 Temple Street, Boston, MA 02114. 1992. Poetry, fiction, art, photos, parts-of-novels. "We publish outstanding new and established writers, and works in translation. Recent contributors: Rachel Hadas, Paul Yoon, Frannie Lindsay, Judith Baumel, Susan Rich, Yiyun Li, Bill Bukovsan." circ. 1M. 2/yr. Pub'd 2 issues 2005; expects 2 issues 2006, 2 issues 2007. sub. price $12; per copy $6; sample $3. Back issues: $3 when available. Discounts: write for details. 120pp. Reporting time: 4 months. Publishes 5% of manuscripts submitted. Payment: 2 copies of magazine; $200 per story; $25 per poem honoraria. Copyrighted, reverts to author. Pub's reviews: 6 in 2005. §primarily poetry. Ads: $150. Subjects: Fiction, Memoirs, Poetry, Short Stories, Translation.

SALMAGUNDI, Robert Boyers, Editor; Peggy Boyers, Executive Editor; Marc Woodworth, Associate Editor; Tom Lewis, Associate Editor, Skidmore College, 815 North Broadway, Saratoga Springs, NY 12866-1632, 518-584-5186. 1965. Poetry, fiction, articles, photos, interviews, satire, criticism, reviews, letters, parts-of-novels, non-fiction. "Recent contributors: George Steiner, Seamus Heaney, Robert Pinsky, Bernard-Henri Levi, Ben Barber, Martha Nussbaum, Peter Singer, Jean Elshtain, Mary Gordon, Orlando Patterson. Pur reading persio begins on October 15th and ends on April 1. Any mss. received outside that oersiod will not be returned." circ. 4500- 6M. 4/yr. Pub'd 4 issues 2005; expects 4 issues 2006, 4 issues 2007. sub. price $20-1 year $30-2 yrs $40-3 yrs $60-5 yrs Inquire for institutional rates; per copy $8; sample $5. Back issues: send SASE for the list. Discounts: 40% to stores/ 2 yr. sub.: $30./ 5 yr. sub.: $60. 200pp. Reporting time: 6-9 months. Simultaneous submissions accepted: yes. Payment: none. Copyrighted, reverts to author. Pub's reviews: 12 in 2005. §Politics, social sciences, literary crit, poetry, fiction, essays. Ads: $150/$200/$250 cover. Subjects: Arts, Biography, Book Reviewing, Communism, Marxism, Leninism, Criticism, Culture, Dance, Electronics, Electronics, English, Fiction, Judaism, Latin America, Philosophy, Poetry.

Salmon Poetry Ltd., Jessie Lendennie, Knockeven, Cliffs of Moher, Co. Clare, Ireland, 011-353-65-7081941, info@salmonpoetry.com, www.salmonpoetry.com. 1981. Poetry, non-fiction. "Salmon has an extensive list of Irish, American, Canadian and British poets." avg. press run 1,000. Pub'd 10 titles 2005; expects 10 titles 2006, 10 titles 2007. Discounts: distributed in the U.S. by Dufour Editions, who have their own pricing system. 80pp. Reporting time: 6 months. Simultaneous submissions accepted: yes. Publishes 1% of manuscripts submitted. Payment: 10% of retail cover price. Copyrights for author. Subjects: Non-Fiction, Poetry, Publishing.

Salmon Run Press, John E. Smelcer, Chief Editor, PO Box 671236, Chugiak, AK 99567-1236. 1991. Poetry, fiction, art, non-fiction. "Recently published work by X.J. Kennedy, Joy Harjo, Denise Duhamel, John Haines, Ursula K. LeGuin, Molly Peacock, R.L. Barth, Phillip Levine, Denise Levertov, and Moore Moran." avg. press run 500-1M. Pub'd 5 titles 2005; expects 3-5 titles 2006, 3-5 titles 2007. Discounts: 40% to retailers, 50-55% to distributors, 30% to libraries. 68-156pp. Reporting time: 1-3 months. Simultaneous submissions accepted: yes. Publishes 1-2% of manuscripts submitted. Payment: 5-10% royalties and copies. Copyrights for author.

SALT HILL, English Department, Syracuse University, Syracuse, NY 13244-1170. 1994. Poetry, fiction, articles, art, interviews, criticism, reviews, parts-of-novels, long-poems, non-fiction. "Address your submission to specific genre editor: Poetry Editor, Fiction Editor, etc. Fiction: 6,000 word maximum; poems - send 3-5. Recent contributers include: Dean Young, Brian Evenson, Kim Addonizio, Terese Svoboda, James Tate, Steve Almond, and Nin Andrews. We hold annual poetry and short short fiction contests. Deadline - January 15th. For more information visit our web site at http://students.syr.edu/salthill." circ. 1M. 2/yr. Pub'd 2 issues 2005; expects 2 issues 2006, 2 issues 2007. sub. price $15; per copy $8; sample $8. Back issues: $5. 120-150pp. Reporting time: 2-6 months. Simultaneous submissions accepted: yes. Publishes 5% of manuscripts submitted. Payment: 2 copies. Copyrighted, reverts to author. Pub's reviews: 4 in 2005. §Poetry, short story, fiction, hypertext. Ads: $125/$75. Ad swaps welcome.

•**Salt Publishing,** Chris Hamilton-Emery, PO Box 937, Great Wilbraham, Cambridge, United Kingdom, +44 (0)1223 882220 chris@saltpublishing.com. 2002. Poetry, fiction, criticism. "The list includes a widening range of internationally-acclaimed authors, including major works by leading British poets John James, Tony Lopez, Peter Robinson and John Wilkinson, landmark titles by American poets Charles Bernstein, Maxine Chernoff, Forrest Gander, Peter Gizzi, Paul Hoover, Ron Silliman and Susan Wheeler, and new work by prize-winning Australian authors Pam Brown, Jill Jones, Kate Lilley, Peter Rose, Tom Shapcott and John Tranter. Salts authors appear at festivals and conferences the world over and their work continues to receive major critical attention." avg. press run 200. Pub'd 28 titles 2005; expects 40 titles 2006, 50 titles 2007. Discounts: 1-4 copies 20%5-249 copies 45%250-499 copies 46%500+ copies 47%. 144pp. Reporting time: Four months. Simultaneous submissions accepted: Yes. Publishes 5% of manuscripts submitted. Payment: 5%-7.5%, no advance, paid annually in June, first full year after publication on amounts exceeding $75. Does not copyright for author. Subjects: Black, Essays, Experimental, Feminism, Gay, Indigenous Cultures, Interviews, Latin America, Literature (General), Poetry, Short Stories, Women, Writers/Writing.

•THE SALT RIVER REVIEW, James Cervantes, 448 N. Matlock, Mesa, AZ 85203-7222, http://www.poetserv.org/. 1997. Poetry, fiction, articles, criticism, reviews, letters, long-poems, non-fiction. "The Salt River Review is an eclectic and high-quality online publication. We have published work by Tess Gallagher, David Graham, Laura Jensen, Dara Wier, Carlos Reyes, Paul Howell, Halvard Johnson, Wendy Taylor Carlisle, Greg Simon, and John Morgan." circ. 500. 3/yr. Pub'd 3 issues 2005; expects 3 issues 2006, 3 issues 2007. sample price $0. 50pp. Reporting time: Three days to three months. Simultaneous submissions accepted: Yes. Publishes 2% of manuscripts submitted. Payment: None. Copyrighted, reverts to author. Pub's reviews: 2 in 2005. §These are done in-house.

Samuel Powell Publishing Company, 2201 I Street, Sacramento, CA 95816, 916-443-1161. 1978. Fiction. avg. press run 750. Expects 1-2 titles 2006, 1-2 titles 2007. Discounts: 55% distributors, 40% bookstores. 105pp. Copyrights for author. Subject: Fiction.

•**Sand and Sable Publishing,** Joyce Hyndman, Publisher; Brandy Wilson, Editor; Ronald Hyndman, Creative Designer, P.O. Box 744, Jonesboro, GA 30237, 404-509-3352. 2005. Non-fiction. "Sand and Sable publishing offers adult fictional romances, ppetry and romantic. Within the next year we are expecting to expand our publishing capacity to include children and teen self awarness books, puzzles and straight talk informationals. Our focus is tapping into talent from varied backgrounds and experiences. All writtenn work is a form of self expression and art. We cater to individuals who have a story to tell, but lack the platform to do so." avg. press run 5000. Expects 2 titles 2006, 5 titles 2007. Discounts: For independant bookstores, a 30% discount for orders over 5. For wholesalers, a 40% discount for orders over 20 and 30% for orders under 20. 304pp. Reporting time: the average reporting time is three weeks. Simultaneous submissions accepted: Yes. Publishes 50% of manuscripts submitted. Payment: All contracts are negotiable based on the type of involvement and creative control author wants to have with publishing thier product. Based on the needs of the author. Subjects: Adolescence, Advertising, Self-Promotion, African Literature, Africa, African Studies, Black, Family, Fantasy, Fashion, Feminism, Festivals, Fiction, Gaelic, Magazines, Novels, Nursing, Peace.

Sand River Press, Bruce W. Miller, 1319 14th Street, Los Osos, CA 93402, 805-543-3591. 1987. Non-fiction. avg. press run 3M. Pub'd 2 titles 2005; expects 3 titles 2006, 1 title 2007. Discounts: 3+ 40%, 100+ 42%, 200+ 43%. 132pp. Reporting time: 8 weeks, must send return postage. Payment: standard. Copyrights for author. Subjects: California, Earth, Natural History, History, Literature (General), Native American, The West.

SANDPOINT MAGAZINE, Keokee Co. Publishing, Inc., Billie Jean Plaster, Editor; Chris Bessler, Publisher, PO Box 722, Sandpoint, ID 83864, 208-263-3573, info@keokee.com. 1990. Fiction, articles, art, photos, cartoons, interviews, criticism, reviews, parts-of-novels, long-poems, news items, non-fiction. "Physical Address: 307 N. 2nd Avenue, Sandpoint, ID 83864. *Sandpoint Magazine* is a regional magazine for North Idaho." circ. 25M. 2/yr. Pub'd 2 issues 2005; expects 2 issues 2006, 2 issues 2007. sub. price $7; per copy $3; sample $3.50. Back issues: $3.50. Discounts: negotiable. 48pp. Reporting time: 2 months. Simultaneous submissions accepted: yes. Publishes 25% of manuscripts submitted. Payment: negotiable. Copyrighted. Ads: 1720/110/$45 for 25 words. Subjects: Conservation, Entertainment, Essays, Idaho, Lifestyles, Pacific Northwest, Sports, Outdoors, Travel.

Sanguinaria Publishing, Selma Miriam, Betsey Beaven, Noel Furie, 85 Ferris Street, Bridgeport, CT 06605, 203-576-9168. 1980. "We will publish material of interest to feminists." avg. press run 5M. Pub'd 1 title 2005; expects 1 title 2007. Discounts: 40% for 5 or more copies; single copies, net. 348pp. Payment: 10% royalty fees. Copyrights for author. Subjects: Ecology, Foods, Feminism, Health, Lesbianism, Women.

Santa Ana River Press, Jack Robinson, PO Box 5473, Norco, CA 92860-8016, 877-822-9623, editorial@santaanariverpress.com, www.santaanariverpress.com. 2003. Fiction, non-fiction. "In our early days, we are focusing on publishing high-quality new editions of forgotten early works about California, with thoughtful forewords and annotation. We expect to begin accepting novels and nonfiction about California by 2007; initially our strong bias will be in favor of works about California history, or historical fiction set in California. We plan to add California travel books to our catalog beginning in 2008." avg. press run 1M. Pub'd

3 titles 2005; expects 3 titles 2006, 3 titles 2007. 250pp. Reporting time: 1 month. Simultaneous submissions accepted: Yes. Publishes approx. 10% of manuscripts submitted. Payment: will vary. Copyrights for author. Subjects: California, Fiction, History, Travel.

Santa Fe Writers Project, Andrew Gifford, PMB 170, 3509 Connecticut Avenue NW, Washington, DC 20008-2470, info@sfwp.com, www.sfwp.com. 1998. Fiction, satire, criticism, non-fiction. avg. press run 500. Expects 2 titles 2006, 4 titles 2007. 330pp. Reporting time: 60 days. Simultaneous submissions accepted: Yes. Subjects: Americana, Anarchist, Counter-Culture, Alternatives, Communes, Erotica, Fantasy, Fiction, History, Literature (General), Memoirs, Mystery, Occult, Prose, Satire, Science Fiction, Southwest.

Santa Monica Press, PO Box 1076, Santa Monica, CA 90406-1076, 310-230-7759, Fax 310-230-7761. 1991. Photos, non-fiction. "At Santa Monica Press, we're not afraid to cast a wide editorial net. Our vision extends from lively and modern how-to books to offbeat looks at popular culture, from film history to literature. Recent titles include "Elvis Presley Passed Here," "Atomic Wedgies, Wet Willies, & Other Acts of Roguery," "L.A. Noir," "Calculated Risk," "Loving Through Bars," and "Can a Dead Man Strike Out?" Please see the "Author Guidelines" page on our website (www.santamonicapress.com) for submission instructions." Pub'd 14 titles 2005; expects 10 titles 2006, 12 titles 2007. Reporting time: 2-3 months. Simultaneous submissions accepted: yes. Payment: 4%-10% net royalty; $0-$2500 advance. Copyrights for author. Subjects: Arts, Culture, Entertainment, Folklore, How-To, Humor, Los Angeles, Movies, Music, Non-Fiction, Performing Arts, Reference, Theatre, Travel, Visual Arts.

THE SANTA MONICA REVIEW, Andrew Tonkovich, 1900 Pico Boulevard, Santa Monica, CA 90405, www.smc.edu/sm_review. 1988. Fiction, parts-of-novels, non-fiction. "Recent contributors: Amy Gerstler, Judith Grossman, Jim Krusoe, Bernard Cooper, Michelle Latiolais. Looking for literary fiction and creative nonfiction." circ. 1M. 2/yr. Pub'd 1 issue 2005; expects 2 issues 2006, 2 issues 2007. sub. price $12; per copy $7; sample $7. Back issues: varies. 200pp. Reporting time: 1 month. Simultaneous submissions accepted: yes. Publishes 1% of manuscripts submitted. Payment: 2 copies plus subscription. Copyrighted, reverts to author. Ads: $200/$100. Subject: Literary Review.

Saqi Books Publisher, 26 Westbourne Grove, London W2 5RH, England, 020 7221 9347, fax 020 7229 7492. 1983. "Main focus is on works dealing with the Middle East, Islam and the Third World. Saqi's authors include some of the major European experts on the Middle East, as well as writers from the region itself: Germaine Tillion, Jacques Berque, Maxime Rodinson." avg. press run 3.5M. Pub'd 8 titles 2005; expects 8 titles 2006, 10 titles 2007. Discounts: as arranged by U.S. distributors—St. Martin's Press, Scholarly & Reference Div., 175 Fifth Avenue, New York, NY 10010, tel: 212-982-3900, Fax: 212-777-6359. 224pp. Reporting time: 8 weeks. Payment: annually (March). Copyrights for author. Subjects: Arts, Bibliography, Bilingual, Biography, Fiction, History, Language, Literature (General), Middle East, Poetry, Political Science, Politics, Religion, Reprints, Third World, Minorities.

Sarabande Books, Sarah Gorham, Editor-in-Chief; Kirby Gann, Managing Editor; Kristina McGrath, Associate Editor, 2234 Dundee Road Suite 200, Louisville, KY 40205, www.sarabandebooks.org. 1994. Poetry, fiction, non-fiction. avg. press run 2500. Pub'd 10 titles 2005; expects 10 titles 2006, 10 titles 2007. Discounts: contact Consortium Book Sales and Distribution: 800/283-3572. 224pp. Reporting time: Three months. Simultaneous submissions accepted: Yes. Publishes 1% of manuscripts submitted. Payment: standard royalty contract. Copyrights for author. Subjects: Essays, Fiction, Literature (General), Poetry.

Saskatchewan Writers Guild (see also GRAIN MAGAZINE), Elizabeth Philips, Editor; Marlis Wesseler, Fiction Editor; Sean Virgo, Poetry Editor, PO Box 67, Saskatoon, SK S7K 3K1, Canada, 306-244-2828, grainmag@sasktel.net. 1973. Poetry, fiction, art, parts-of-novels, long-poems, plays, non-fiction. avg. press run 1.3M. Pub'd 4 titles 2005; expects 4 titles 2006, 4 titles 2007. 128pp. Reporting time: 3 months. Simultaneous submissions accepted: no. Publishes 7% of manuscripts submitted. Payment: $40/page up to $175, payment upon publication plus 2 contributors copies. Copyrights for author. Subjects: Arts, Drama, Fiction, Language, Poetry.

Sasquatch Books, Chad Haight, Publisher, 119 S. Main Street, Suite 400, Seattle, WA 98104-2555, 206-467-4300, 800-775-0817, Fax 206-467-4301, books@SasquatchBooks.com. 1986. Pub'd 34 titles 2005; expects 41 titles 2006, 45 titles 2007. Reporting time: 6-8 weeks. Simultaneous submissions accepted: yes. Copyrights for author. Subjects: Alaska, California, Children, Youth, Cooking, Cooking, Earth, Natural History, Gardening, Native American, Native American, Nature, Nature, Pacific Northwest, Transportation, Travel.

SAT SANDESH: THE MESSAGE OF THE MASTERS, Arthur Stein PhD, Vinod Sena PhD, 680 Curtis Corner Road, Wakefield, RI 02879, (401) 783-0662. 1968. Articles, photos, interviews, reviews, letters, parts-of-novels, long-poems. "Subscription address: Route 1, Box 24, Bowling Green, VA 22427. *Sat Sandesh: The Message of Truthful Living* is published for the purpose of sharing the teachings of Sant Rajinder Singh (the living spiritual guide of the Science of Spirituality), Sant Darshan Singh Ji, Param Sant Kirpal Singh Ji, and Hazur Baba Sawan Singh Ji, and earlier teachers of Surat Shabd Yoga (meditation on inner light and celestial sound). Includes poetry, experiences with spiritual teachers, responses to questions, children's corner, and other features." circ. 938. 12/yr. Pub'd 12 issues 2005; expects 12 issues 2006, 12 issues 2007. sub. price $23; per copy $2.50; sample free. Back issues: $2.50. Discounts: bookstores & libraries 40%; distributors, contact for information. 32pp. Payment: none. Not copyrighted. Pub's reviews: 2 in 2005. §Books of Sawan Kirpal Publications. Ads: none. Subjects: Philosophy, Religion, Spiritual, Yoga.

Saturday Press, Charlotte Mandel, Editor, PO Box 43534, Upper Montclair, NJ 07043, 973-239-0436, fax: 973-239-0427. 1975. Poetry. "Sponsor of Eileen W. Barnes Award for women poets over forty. Not reading new submissions at this time." avg. press run 1M. Discounts: 40% to bookstores and jobbers. 64-102pp. Reporting time: responds to queries in 2 weeks. Publishes less than 1% of manuscripts submitted. Payment: individual arrangement. Copyrights for author. Subject: Poetry.

The Saunderstown Press, Allen A. Johnson, 54 Camp Avenue, North Kingstown, RI 02852, 401-295-8810; Fax 401-294-9939. 1985. Poetry, fiction, satire, non-fiction. "We publish from 2-4 titles per year. Always interested in new authors but no unsolicited manuscripts. Current books in production include medicine, careers, religion cooking, and philosophy." avg. press run 1M. Expects 1 title 2006, 2 titles 2007. Discounts: 50% trade, 20% educational and library. 50-100pp. Reporting time: 2-3 weeks from receipt. Simultaneous submissions accepted: no. Publishes 2% of manuscripts submitted. Payment: 20% (25% for exceptional) on sales (or 50% of profit). Copyrights for author. Subjects: Careers, Disabled, Education, Employment, Guidance, Handicapped, How-To, Humanism, Inspirational, Interviews, Philosophy, Prison, Psychology, Self-Help, Textbooks.

Savant Garde Workshop, Vilna Jorgen II, Publisher & Editor-in-Chief; Artemis Smith, Artistic Director, PO Box 1650, Sag Harbor, NY 11963-0060, 631-725-1414; website www.savantgarde.org. 1964. Poetry, fiction, criticism, long-poems, plays, concrete art, non-fiction. "We have suspended operations waiting upon major funding for expansion. Don't expect a reply unless your SASE query is accepted. DO NOT SEND MS until invited upon query, as it will be returned unopened. Focus on multinational intelligentsia. Looking for people who have eventual Nobel Prize potential. Publish limited signed editions and their overruns, ON DEMAND." On Demand. Expects 1 title 2006, 1 title 2007. Discounts: 25% rare bookdealers, bookdealers, wholesalers, art galleries & print shops. 300pp. Simultaneous submissions accepted: no. Publishes 1+% of manuscripts submitted. Payment: varies. Copyrights for author. Subjects: Arts, Atheism, Creativity, Dada, Drama, Ethics, Fiction, Humanism, Literature (General), Music, Philosophy, Poetry, Science, Science Fiction, Society.

Savor Publishing House, Inc., Carol Anderson, 6020 Broken Bow Dr., Citrus Heights, CA 95621, 916 729-3664, 866 762-7898. 2002. Poetry, fiction, non-fiction. "Savor Publishing House is the creator of the Smarties series. This is a medically based multicultural picture book series designed to develop early readers and educate in the field of medicine." avg. press run 3000. Expects 2 titles 2006, 1 title 2007. Discounts: Trade discounts are based on the number of books purchased.1-5 books 20%6-25 books 30%26 or more books 40%. 33pp. Reporting time: We do not accept submissions. Simultaneous submissions accepted: No. Payment: $3000 to $5000 advance with 10% royalty. Copyrights for author. Subjects: Health, Medicine, Multicultural, Picture Books, Storytelling.

SB&F (SCIENCE BOOKS & FILMS), Heather Malcomson, Editor, 1200 New York Avenue NW, Washington, DC 20005, 202-326-6646. 1965. Articles, interviews, reviews, news items. "Reviews books, films, videos, and software in all the sciences for all ages. We do not accept unsolicited reviews or articles." circ. 4.5M. 6/yr. Pub'd 6 issues 2005; expects 6 issues 2006, 6 issues 2007. sub. price $45; per copy $7 + $1.50 p/h; sample free. Back issues: $7, plus $1.50 p/h. Discounts: agents 10%. 48pp. Payment: none. Copyrighted, reverts to author. Pub's reviews: 898 in 2005. §Sciences. Ads: $900/$635. Subject: Science.

SCANDINAVIAN REVIEW, Edward P. Gallagher, Publisher; Adrienne Gyongy, Editor, 58 Park Avenue, New York, NY 10016-3007, 212-879-9779. 1913. Poetry, fiction, articles, art, photos, interviews, satire, criticism, reviews, letters, parts-of-novels, long-poems, plays, non-fiction. "Suggested length of articles: 1500-2000 words. Include return postage and SAE. Recent contributors: R. Jeffrey Smith, Leslie Eliason, Ulla Tarres-Wahlberg, Jan-Erik Lundstrom. Focus: Scandinavian culture and society." circ. 5M. 3/yr. Pub'd 3 issues 2005; expects 3 issues 2006, 3 issues 2007. sub. price $15, $20 foreign; per copy $4; sample $4. Back issues: available. Discounts: negotiable. 96-104pp. Reporting time: 3 months to publish. Payment: poetry $10 p.(a/t); articles $100-$200, fiction $75-$125 (a/t). Copyrighted, reverts to author. Pub's reviews: several in 2005. Ads: $400/$250/$150 1/4 page. Subjects: Literature (General), Politics, Scandinavia, Society, Translation.

Scarecrow Press (see also VOYA (Voice of Youth Advocate)), Edward Kurdyla, Publisher and Editorial Director; Melissa Ray, Assistant Managing Editor, 4501 Forbes Blvd., Suite 200, Lanham, MD 20706, 301-459-3366; Fax 301-429-5747. 1950. Criticism, non-fiction. "Very varied list. Emphasis on reference books, scholarly monographs, some professional textbooks. Dominant subject areas include: Cinema, women, minorities, music, literature, library science, parapsychology, religion." avg. press run 750. Expects 165 titles 2006. Discounts: net to libraries, etc; 22% to bookstores. 390pp. Reporting time: 2 months. We accept simultaneous submissions if they are marked as such. Publishes 35% of manuscripts submitted. Payment: 10% first 1M copies; 15% thereafter; 15% on all copies for camera ready mss. Copyrights for author. Subjects: Arts, Education, Libraries, Music, Reference.

Scarlet Tanager Books, Lucille L. Day, PO Box 20906, Oakland, CA 94620, 510-763-3874. 1999. Poetry, fiction, long-poems, non-fiction. "Length of material: 64-160 pages. West Coast writers only (California, Oregon, Washington, Alaska, Hawaii). Recent contributors: Daniel Hawkes, Judy Wells, Naomi Ruth Lowinsky, Lucille Lang Day, Jack Foley, Marc Elihu Hofstadter, and Risa Kaparo." avg. press run 1M. Pub'd 3 titles 2005. Discounts: bookstores 40%, wholesalers 55%. 100pp. Reporting time: 3 months. Simultaneous submissions accepted: yes. Publishes 1% of manuscripts submitted. Payment: 10% of press run. Copyrights for author. Subjects: Fiction, Non-Fiction, Poetry.

Scars Publications (see also CHILDREN, CHURCHES AND DADDIES, A Non Religious, Non Familial Literary Magazine; DOWN IN THE DIRT LITERARY MAGAZINE, the prose & poetry magazine revealing all your dirty little secrets; FREEDOM AND STRENGTH PRESS FORUM), Janet Kuypers, Attn: Janet Kuypers, 829 Brian Court, Gurnee, IL 60031-3155, Editor@scars.tv, http://scars.tv. 1993. Poetry, fiction, art, photos, letters, long-poems, collages, non-fiction. "Scars Publications was created originally for the magazine *Children, Churches and Daddies*, and the magazine *Down In the Dirt*, but now extends itself to printing perfect bound paperback collection volumes from the magazine and also for publishing an occasional book or 24-page special highlighting one or two authors alone. If you submit work, please let me know whether you want a single piece published in the magazine or are looking for a collection of your own work being published. A cover letter is appreciated. If you're published in a book, please be prepared to try to sell copies to your friends and in stores in your area. That's how we succeed. Otherwise, look at the guidelines for *Children, Churches and Daddies*. We also run a book/chapbook contest. Contact Sears for more infomation. Electronic submissions (e-mail or text format, Macintash prefered) appreciated. Issues are available in print only as books (paid only), electronic format, and on the World Wide Web at above address." avg. press run determined individually. Pub'd 6 titles 2005; expects 12 titles 2006, 12 titles 2007. Books 200pp, chapbooks 24-32pp. Reporting time: We'll get back to you in a week if there is a SASE in it; if not, you'll never hear from us. Simultaneous submissions accepted: yes. Publishes 40% of manuscripts submitted. Payment: none for collection volumes; contact me about printing larger volumes of individual artist's works. Does not copyright for author. Subjects: Arts, Beat, Book Arts, Chicago, Counter-Culture, Alternatives, Communes, Culture, Feminism, Fiction, Graphics, Language, Literature (General), Magazines, Photography, Poetry, Women.

Scentouri, Publishing Division, A.C. Doyle, c/o Prosperity + Profits Unlimited, PO Box 416, Denver, CO 80201-0416, 303-575-5676, Fax 303-575-1187. 1982. avg. press run 1.5M. Discounts: 25% to libraries, bookstores, etc. 60pp. Reporting time: 6 weeks. Subjects: Biography, Crafts, Hobbies, Education, How-To, Reference, Textbooks.

SCHOLAR-PRACTITIONER QUARTERLY, Caddo Gap Press, Patrick Jenlink Dr., Coeditor; Raymond Horn Dr., Co-editor, 3145 Geary Blvd. PMB 275, San Francisco, CA 94118, 415 666-3012. sub. price $60 individuals, $120 institutions. 96pp.

SCHOOL MATES, U.S. Chess Federation, Beatriz Marinello, 3054 NYS Route 9W, New Windsor, NY 12553, 914-562-8350; Fax 914-561-2437; schoolmates@uschess.org. 1987. Poetry, fiction, articles, art, photos, cartoons, interviews, collages. "Length: 500-750 words; i.e., short articles for grades 3-6 about chess and chessplayers. Games, puzzles, artwork relating to chess also welcome." circ. 21M. 6/yr. Pub'd 4 issues 2005; expects 6 issues 2006, 6 issues 2007. sub. price $12.50 ($12 for Scholastic members - $7); per copy $2.25; sample free. Back issues: $2.25. 20pp. Reporting time: 2 months lead time. Payment: $40/1,000-word mss. Copyrighted. Ads: $1500/$800/$80 per inch. Subjects: Children, Youth, Games.

School of American Research Press, James Brooks, Director of Publications, PO Box 2188, Santa Fe, NM 87504-2188, 505-954-7206, Fax 505-954-7241, bkorders@sarsf.org. Subject: Anthropology, Archaelogy.

Schreiber Publishing, Morry Schreiber, 51 Monroe Street, Suite 101, Rockville, MD 20850-4193, 301-424-7737, Fax 301-424-2336, spbooks@aol.com, www.schreiberNet.com. 1957. "Languages, Judaica." Expects 10 titles 2006. Pages vary. Reporting time: 30-90 days. Simultaneous submissions accepted: yes. Publishes 20% of manuscripts submitted. Payment: negotiable. Copyrights for author.

Schuylkill Living (see also SCHUYLKILL LIVING MAGAZINE), Erica Ramus, 115 S Centre St., Pottsville, PA 17901-3000, 570-622-8625. 1997. Fiction, articles, photos, interviews, reviews, news items, non-fiction. "Must be related to Schuylkill County Pennsylvania. This is a regional title." avg. press run 5000. Pub'd 1 title 2005; expects 1 title 2006, 1 title 2007. Discounts: 20% discount to bookstores & distributors. 64pp. Reporting time: 4 weeks. Simultaneous submissions accepted: No. Payment: Pays upon publication. Does not copyright for author.

SCHUYLKILL LIVING MAGAZINE, Schuylkill Living, Erica Ramus, 115 S. Centre Street, Pottsville, PA

17901, 570-622-8625, Fax 570-622-2143, eramus@comcast.net, www.schuylkillliving.com. 1997. Poetry, articles, art, photos, interviews, reviews, news items, non-fiction. circ. 5M. 4/yr. Pub'd 4 issues 2005; expects 4 issues 2006, 4 issues 2007. sub. price $20; per copy $4.95; sample $5. Back issues: $5. 64pp. Reporting time: 3 weeks. Simultaneous submissions accepted: no. Publishes 25% of manuscripts submitted. Payment: $50-100. Copyrighted, reverts to author. Pub's reviews: 2 in 2005. §Only publishes LOCAL INTEREST information and poetry. Ads: $1600/$800. Subject: Gardening.

SCHUYLKILL VALLEY JOURNAL OF THE ARTS, Peter Krok, Editor; John Capista, Managing Editor, 419 Green Lane (rear), Philadelphia, PA 19128, Fax 215-483-5661, max@manayunkartcenter.org, macpoet1@aol.com, www.manayunkartcenter.org. 1991. Poetry, fiction, articles, photos, criticism, non-fiction. ''The journal will include poetry, a featured poet from the region, accessible criticism, articles on contemporary artists in the region, short essays, pieces on a kind of regional but not currently popular themes, tips on the craft of writing, and painting, etc.'' circ. 200. 2/yr. Pub'd 2 issues 2005; expects 2 issues 2006, 2 issues 2007. sub. price $12; per copy $6; sample $5. 100pp. Reporting time: varies. Publishes a variable % of manuscripts submitted. Payment: 2 copies. Copyrighted, reverts to author. Subjects: Non-Fiction, Poetry.

SCIENCE & SOCIETY, Guilford Publications, Inc., David Laibman, 72 Spring Street, New York, NY 10012, 212-431-9800. 1936. Articles, interviews, criticism, reviews, non-fiction. ''The journal presents scholarship in political economy and the economic analysis of capitalist and socialist societies; in philosophy and methodology of the natural and social sciences; in history, labor, Black and women's studies; in aesthetics, literature and the arts.'' circ. 2.5M. 4/yr. Pub'd 4 issues 2005; expects 4 issues 2006, 4 issues 2007. sub. price $35 indiv., $185 instit.; per copy $10 ($7 on newsstand); sample free. Back issues: $10. Discounts: 5% subscription agents, 50% distributors. 128pp. Payment: none. Copyrighted, reverts to author. Pub's reviews. §Economic analysis, socialism, social sciences, history, women's studies. Ads: $250/$125/$350 back cover/$300 3rd cover. Subjects: Book Reviewing, Counter-Culture, Alternatives, Communes, Criticism, Culture, History, Journals, Politics, Socialist, Women.

SCIENCE AND TECHNOLOGY, Univelt, Inc., R.H. Jacobs, Series Editor, PO Box 28130, San Diego, CA 92198, 760-746-4005, Fax 760-746-3139, sales@univelt.com, www.univelt.com. 1964. ''Space and related fields. An irregular serial. Publishers for the American Astronautical Society. Standing orders accepted. Vols. 1-110 published.'' circ. 400. Irregular. Pub'd 5 issues 2005; expects 5 issues 2006, 5 issues 2007. sub. price varies. Back issues: no. Discounts: 20%, or more by arrangement; special prices for classroom use. 200-700pp. Reporting time: 60 days. Payment: 10% (if the volume author). Copyrighted, authors may republish material with appropriate credits given and authorization from publishers. Ads: none. Subjects: Engineering, Political Science, Science, Sociology, Space.

SCIENCE/HEALTH ABSTRACTS, Phylis Austin, PO Box 553, Georgetown, GA 31754. 1980. News items, non-fiction. circ. 1M. 6/yr. Pub'd 6 issues 2005; expects 6 issues 2006, 6 issues 2007. sub. price $6; per copy $1; sample $1. Back issues: $1/issue. 4pp. Reporting time: none needed. Payment: none. Copyrighted, reverts to author. Pub's reviews: 50 in 2005. §Health, computers, science, gardening, alternative medicine. Ads: none. Subjects: Birth, Birth Control, Population, Counter-Culture, Alternatives, Communes, Drugs, Ecology, Foods, Family, Gardening, Health, How-To, Massage, Medicine, New Age, Parenting, Science, Self-Help, Vegetarianism.

Scienter Press, David Leightty, 1304 Highland Avenue, Louisville, KY 40204-2027, Fax 502-583-5608, dleightty@earthlink.net. 2003. Poetry. ''Scienter is a publisher of small books, chiefly by invitation. The goal of the press is to publish poems that manifest meaning—poems that show the poet had something in mind. Our strong preference is for poems having measure.'' avg. press run 100. Pub'd 5 titles 2005; expects 5 titles 2006, 5 titles 2007. 16pp. Payment: copies only. Copyrights for author. Subject: Poetry.

Scientia Publishing, LLC, Cynthia McNeill, P. O. Box 5495, Chatsworth, CA 91313, 1-818-620-0433, www.scientiapublishingllc.com. 2001. Non-fiction. ''Scientia Publishing, LLC welcomes fresh and innovative ideas for the subjects of our nonfiction books. We prefer natural history, environment, and subjects of general science for consideration.'' Expects 1-2 titles 2007. Discounts: Provided upon request. 300pp. Reporting time: We respond within 72 hours upon receipt of a manuscript. Simultaneous submissions accepted: No. Payment: These are determined individually. Copyrights for author. Subjects: Alaska, Anthropology, Archaelogy, Artificial Intelligence, Astronomy, Biology, Biotechnology, Birds, Earth, Natural History, Ecology, Foods, Environment, Nature, Non-Fiction, Oceanography, Research, Science.

Score (see also SPORE), Crag Hill, 1111 E. Fifth Street, Moscow, ID 83843. 1983. Poetry, fiction, art, photos, interviews, criticism, reviews, music, letters, parts-of-novels, long-poems, collages, plays, concrete art, non-fiction. ''Presently, because of other publishing commitments (a magazine, a broadside series), we are only able to publish 2 books per year. Please query.'' avg. press run 200. Pub'd 2 titles 2005; expects 2 titles 2006, 2 titles 2007. 20-30pp. Reporting time: 3 minutes to 3 months. Simultaneous submissions accepted: yes. Publishes 5% of manuscripts submitted. Payment: 1/4 of first edition then copies at cost. Does not copyright for author.

Subjects: Arts, Avant-Garde, Experimental Art, Interviews, Language, Literature (General), Poetry.

Scots Plaid Press (see also Persephone Press), Jeff Farr, President, 600 Kelly Road, Carthage, NC 28327, 910-947-2587; Fax 910-947-5112. 1987. Poetry. "Archival handbound chapbook. *Query first*; describe MS & PC include bio/vita, SASE. *Do not submit ms.* no more than 3 page sample. Accept no unsolicited ms." avg. press run 500-1.5M. Pub'd 9 titles 2005; expects 12 titles 2006, 24 titles 2007. Discounts: 30% on orders of 5 copies; 40% for 10 copies. 40pp. Reporting time: 1 day to 1 month. Simultaneous submissions accepted: yes. Publishes 1% of manuscripts submitted. Payment: 10%. Does not copyright for author. Subject: Poetry.

Andrew Scott Publishers, E.S. Lev, 15023 Tierra Alta, Del Mar, CA 92014, 858-755-0715 phone/Fax, e-mail andrewscottpublishers@juno.com. 1998. Fiction. "Dedicated to advance informative, realistic mysteries. *Prescription for Terror* is our debut novel." avg. press run 2M. Expects 2 titles 2006, 1 title 2007. Discounts: 50% non-returnable, 40% returnable plus freight. 240pp. Reporting time: 2 weeks. Simultaneous submissions accepted: no. Publishes 1% of manuscripts submitted. Copyrights for author. Subject: Mystery.

Scottwall Associates, Publishers, James Heig, 95 Scott Street, San Francisco, CA 94117, 415-861-1956. 1982. Non-fiction. "We publish books on California history, biographies." avg. press run 5M-10M. Pub'd 2 titles 2005; expects 2 titles 2006, 2-3 titles 2007. Discounts: 40% to bookstores in quantity orders; 40% to prepaid STOP orders; 30% single copy orders; 20% to schools & libraries. 200-500pp. Reporting time: indefinite. Payment: 8% royalty on all books sold and paid for. Copyrights for author. Subjects: Airplanes, Americana, Biography, California, History, Ireland, Native American, San Francisco.

SCP JOURNAL, Tal Brooke, President and Editor, PO Box 4308, Berkeley, CA 94704. 1975. Articles, interviews, reviews, letters, news items, non-fiction. "*SCP* is a non-profit organization that researches and publishes information on new religious cult movements and spiritual trends. No unsolicited Mss." circ. 18M. 4 journals, 4 newsletters published per year. Pub'd 4 issues 2005; expects 4 issues 2006, 4 issues 2007. sub. price $25/year; per copy $5; sample free - newsletter only. Back issues: $5-6. Discounts: 40% for retailers. 40pp single journals; 60pp for double journals. Reporting time: 3-6 weeks, only after telephone approval, do not submit before phone inquiry. Payment: varies. Copyrighted, does not revert to author. Pub's reviews: 4 in 2005. §Religion, metaphysics, cults, sociology and psychology of religion. Subjects: Religion, Spiritual.

SCRAWL MAGAZINE, Sam Lahoz, PO Box 205, New York, NY 10012, e-mail scrawl@bigfoot.com. 1995. Reviews, music. circ. 5M. 2/yr. Expects 2 issues 2006, 2 issues 2007. sub. price $10; per copy $2.95; sample $4 ppd. Back issues: $4 ppd. 56pp. Reporting time: 2 months. Payment: none. Copyrighted, does not revert to author. Pub's reviews: 12 in 2005. §Music, art, photography, politics, feminism, films; no poetry. Ads: $235/$150/$90 1/4 page. Subjects: Arts, Music.

THE SCRIBIA, Danielle B. Otero, Uju Ifeanyi, PO Box 68, Grambling State University, Grambling, LA 71245, 318-274-2190, oterod@gram.,edu. 1966. Poetry, fiction, articles, art, interviews, criticism, reviews, letters, parts-of-novels, long-poems, plays, concrete art, non-fiction. "Emphasis on GSU student and alumni work, multi-culturalism, southern culture. Recent contributors: X.J. Kennedy, Pinkie Gordon Lane, Errol Miller, Mary Winters, Christopher Pressfield, Maitaika Favorite." circ. 800. 1/yr. Pub'd 1 issue 2005; expects 1 issue 2006, 1 issue 2007. sub. price cops; per copy cops; sample cops. Back issues: cops. Discounts: none. 72pp. Reporting time: 3-6 months. Simultaneous submissions accepted with notices. Publishes 20% of manuscripts submitted. Payment: 2 copies. Copyrighted, reverts to author. Pub's reviews: 2 in 2005. §Contemparary literature, multi-cultural issues. Ads: trade. Subjects: African-American, Literature (General), Poetry.

Scripta Humanistica, Bruno Damiani, Editor, 1383 Kersey Lane, Potomac, MD 20854, 301-294-7949, 301-340-1095. avg. press run 500. Pub'd 15 titles 2005. Discounts: 20%. 200pp. Reporting time: 4 weeks. Simultaneous submissions accepted: no. Publishes 35% of manuscripts submitted. Payment: 5% of gross sales. Does not copyright for author. Subjects: James Joyce, Poetry.

SCRIVENER, Meredith Needham, Coordinating Editor; Anca Szilagyi, Coordinating Editor; Matthew Frassica, Fiction Editor; Kristie LeBlanc, Fiction Editor; Addy Litfin, Poetry Editor; Dan Huffateer, Poetry Editor; Kristie LeBlanc, Book Review Editor; Lukas Rieppel, Photography Editor; Pablo Rodriguez, Photography Editor, McGill University, 853 Sherbrooke Street W., Montreal, P.Q. H3A 2T6, Canada, scrivenermag@hotmail.com. 1980. Poetry, fiction, art, photos, interviews, criticism, reviews, non-fiction. "Recent book reviews only. Prose less than 30 pages typed; creative shorts. Poetry 5-10 pages. Black & white photos and graphics. Please send international reply coupon (not U.S. stamps) + self-addressed envelopes. New material only—no reprints. Does not report from May to August." circ. 500. 1/yr. Pub'd 1 issue 2005; expects 1 issue 2006, 1 issue 2007. sub. price $7 + $2 p/h; per copy same; sample same. Back issues: same. Discounts: 40% commission for 10 or more copies. 100pp. Reporting time: 4-6 months. We accept simultaneous submissions, but submitters must list the other journals to which they have made submissions. Payment: 1 free copy, more upon request. Copyrighted, reverts to author. Pub's reviews: 3 in 2005. §Canadian and American prose, poetry, criticism. Ads: currently under review. Subjects: Arts, Book Reviewing, Criticism, English, Fiction, Literature (General), Poetry.

Scrivenery Press, Ed Williams, Leila Joiner, PO Box 740969-1003, Houston, TX 77274-0969, 713-665-6760, fax 713-665-8838, e-mail books@scrivenery.com, website www.scrivenery.com. 1998. Fiction, non-fiction. "We are a royalty publisher of book-length fiction and nonfiction. Complete guidelines for #10 SASE. Needs: fiction-literary, mainstream, historical (no romance or fantasy), and literate thriller/suspense/mystery; nonfiction-humanities, pre-WWII history and biography, some how-to subjects. Query first with sample chapters; no unsolicited manuscripts. Open to unagented or new writers." avg. press run 1-3M. Pub'd 2 titles 2005; expects 14 titles 2006, 20 titles 2007. Discounts: distribution through Ingram Books; write with inquiries about bulk purchases. 250pp. Reporting time: queries: 4-8 weeks; ms: 8-16 weeks. Simultaneous submissions accepted: yes. Publishes 20% of manuscripts submitted. Payment: 10% to 12-1/2% of retail price. Copyrights for author. Subjects: Anthology, Biography, Creativity, English, Fiction, How-To, Literature (General), Mystery, Non-Fiction, Novels.

SCULPTURAL PURSUIT MAGAZINE, Nancy DeCamillis, P.O. Box 749, Littleton, CO 80160, 303-738-9892, www.sculpturalpursuit.com, speditor@sculpturalpursuit.com. 2002. Poetry, articles, art, photos, interviews, criticism, reviews, letters, long-poems, concrete art, news items, non-fiction. "Sculptural Pursuit is a quarterly publication that explores the world of sculpture and its creative and technical processes in order to enlighten, inform, and entertain sculptors, collectors, and the curious. While Sculptural Pursuit emphasizes three-dimensional art, it also features poetry, prose and two-dimensional art. Articles providing information on the world of sculpture include: art history, techniques and processes, health and safety issues, and interviews with current three-dimensional artists. These enhance the readers' knowledge base; allow the reader to envision what a career in art entails; and provide motivation and encouragement, regardless of the creative endeavors undertaken by the reader. HPP offers a free monthly e-newsletter to persons who are interested in art." circ. 7500. 4/yr. Pub'd 4 issues 2005; expects 4 issues 2006, 4 issues 2007. sub. price $28.00; per copy $8.00; sample $8. Back issues: $8.00. Discounts: Distributors - 50%Bulk sales - no returns:5 - 15 copies 38%16-35 copies 41%36-55 copies 44%56-75 copies 47%over 75 copies 50%. 84pp. Reporting time: 4-6 weeks. Simultaneous submissions accepted: Yes. Publishes 30% of manuscripts submitted. Payment is done with ad space, or variable fee. Copyrighted, reverts to author one year following publication. Pub's reviews: 6 in 2005. §Art books & magazines, particularly ones that focus on three-dimensional art and artists. Ads: Color: $1620/$978/$568/$1999/$2278(full/half/quarter/inside front & back covers/back cover). Subjects: Abstracts, Advertising, Self-Promotion, Architecture, Arts, Book Arts, Design, Inspirational, Interviews, Liberal Arts, Motivation, Success, Photography, Poetry, Renaissance, Visual Arts, Writers/Writing.

Sea Challengers, Inc., 4 Sommerset Rise, Monterey, CA 93940, 831-373-6306, Fax 831-373-4566. 1977. avg. press run 5M. Pub'd 1 title 2005; expects 2 titles 2006, 2 titles 2007. Discounts: STOP 20%; 2-9 40%, 10-19 42%, 20-99 45%, 100+ 50%. 112pp. Reporting time: 30 days. Simultaneous submissions accepted: yes. Publishes 10% of manuscripts submitted. Payment: 10% of net sales. Copyrights for author. Subjects: Earth, Natural History, Education, Marine Life, Science.

Sea Fog Press (see also HARMONY: Voices for a Just Future), Rose Evans, 447 20th Avenue, San Francisco, CA 94121, 415-221-8527. 1982. Non-fiction. "2 children's books published, 1 bimonthly magazine." avg. press run 5M. Expects 1 title 2006. Discounts: bookstores 4+ copies, 40%. 200pp. Reporting time: 1 month. Simultaneous submissions accepted: yes. Publishes .03% of manuscripts submitted. Payment: standard. Copyrights for author. Subjects: Children, Youth, Education.

SEA KAYAKER, Christopher Cunningham, Editor; Leslie Forsberg, Executive Editor, PO Box 17029, Seattle, WA 98107-0729, 206-789-1326, Fax 206-781-1141, mail@seakayakermag.com. 1984. Fiction, articles, art, photos, cartoons, interviews, reviews, letters, non-fiction. "1M-3M words; specializing in sea kayaking; bias towards education and environmental." circ. 27M+. 6/yr. Pub'd 6 issues 2005; expects 6 issues 2006, 6 issues 2007. sub. price $23.95; per copy $4.95; sample $7.30. Back issues: 1-2 issues $7.30, 3+ $6.30 each. Discounts: 5-9 copies 35%, 10+ 45%, no returns. 82+pp. Reporting time: 2 months. Simultaneous submissions rarely accepted. Publishes 15% of manuscripts submitted. Payment: approx. $120 per publ. page, on publication. Copyrighted, reverts to author. Pub's reviews: 6 in 2005. §Sea kayaking. Ads: call for current rates 206-789-6413. Subjects: Environment, Geology, How-To, Marine Life, Sports, Outdoors, Travel, Water.

Search Institute, Bill Kauffmann, 615 First Ave. NE, Ste. 125, Minneapolis, MN 55413-2254, 612-692-5527 direct phone, 612-692-5553 fax, 877-240-7251 toll free orders. 1958. Non-fiction. "Search Institute publishes practical and hope-filled books to create a world where all young people are valued and thrive. At the heart of the institute's work is the 40 Developmental Assets. Search Institute has surveyed more than 1,000,000 students in grades 6 -12 in more than 2,000 communities. This scientific research is the basis for the creation of our framework for healthy youth development known as the 40 Developmental Assets. "Assets," as they are commonly known, represent simple wisdom about the kinds of positive experiences and characteristics young people need to succeed." avg. press run 4,000. Pub'd 14 titles 2005; expects 14 titles 2006, 15 titles 2007. Discounts: Distributed to the trade by Independent Publishers Group; toll free 800-888-4741; www.ipg-book.com. 225pp. Reporting time: 10 -12 weeks. Simultaneous submissions accepted: Yes. Publishes 10% of manuscripts submitted. Subjects: Adolescence, Adoption, Awards, Foundations, Grants, Children, Youth, Family, Mentoring/Coaching, Non-Fiction, Parenting, Relationships, Trade.

Seaside Publishing, PO Box 979, St. Petersburg, FL 33731-0979, sales@famousflorida.com. 1992. avg. press run 20M. Pub'd 10 titles 2005; expects 10 titles 2006, 10 titles 2007. Discounts: 20-40%. 200pp. Reporting time: 60 days. Simultaneous submissions accepted: no. Publishes 5% of manuscripts submitted. Payment: varies. Copyrights for author.

Second Aeon Publications, Peter Finch, 19 Southminster Road, Roath, Cardiff, Wales CF23 5AT, Great Britain, 029-2049-3093, secondaeon@peterfinch.co.uk. 1967. Poetry, art, long-poems, collages, concrete art. avg. press run 300-1M. Pub'd 1 title 2005. Discounts: by arrangement. 50pp. Reporting time: 2 weeks. Payment: by arrangement. Does not copyright for author. Subject: Poetry.

Second Coming Press, A.D. Winans, PO Box 31249, San Francisco, CA 94131. 1972. Poetry, fiction. avg. press run 1M-1.5M. Pub'd 1 title 2005; expects 1 title 2007. Discounts: 20% library only if this listed source is quoted; bookstores 5+ books 40%. 64-72pp, anthologies 200-240pp. Reporting time: 30 days. Payment: 10% of press run, 50% of any profit after expenses are met. Only copyrights for author upon arrangement. Subjects: Literature (General), Poetry.

SECOND GUESS, Bob Conrad, PO Box 9382, Reno, NV 89507, www.secondguess.net. 1991. Articles, photos, interviews, satire, criticism, reviews, music, letters, news items, non-fiction. "Mostly a punk slant or revolving issues relevant to punk rock." circ. 1M-2M. 1/yr. Pub'd 1 issue 2005; expects 1 issue 2006, 1 issue 2007. sub. price $15; per copy $3.50; sample $3.50. Back issues: $2. Discounts: none. 80pp. Publishes 0% of manuscripts submitted. Payment: none. Copyrighted, reverts to author. Pub's reviews: 50 in 2005. §Alternative living, music, anarchist politics, non-mainstream, sustainability. Ads: none. Subjects: Agriculture, Alternative Medicine, Anarchist, Anthropology, Archaelogy, Birth, Birth Control, Population, Business & Economics, Education, Environment, Futurism, Interviews, Mental Health, Metaphysics, Multicultural, Nature, Zines.

See Sharp Press, Charles Bufe, Publisher, PO Box 1731, Tucson, AZ 85702-1731, 520-628-8720, Fax 520-628-8720, info@seesharppress.com, www.seesharppress.com. 1984. Non-fiction. "Length is unimportant—quality is the deciding factor; our published works range from a 4,000 word pamphlet to a 200,000-word classic reprint. Biases are towards works with anarchist and/or atheist views and toward works providing practical information, especially in the area of music." avg. press run 2M for pamphlets, 4M for books. Pub'd 1 title 2005; expects 6 titles 2006, 4 titles 2007. Discounts: books exclusively distributed by Independent Publisher Group, pamphlets distributed by AK Press in U.S. and by Freedom Press and Active Distribution in the UK. Books 192pp, pamphlets 32pp. Reporting time: 1 month. Simultaneous submissions accepted: no. Publishes 1% to 2% of manuscripts submitted. Payment: for books - normally 7% of cover first run, 8.5% to 10% thereafter; quarterly payments; for pamphlets - 10% of press run in lieu of royalties. Sometimes copyright for author if author overseas, otherwise no, but will provide info to authors on how to do it. Subjects: Alcohol, Alcoholism, Anarchist, Atheism, Biography, H.L. Mencken, Music, Non-Fiction, Philosophy, Politics, Psychology, Quotations.

SEED SAVERS EXCHANGE, Kent Whealy, 3094 North Winn Road, Decorah, IA 52101, 563-382-5990, Fax 563-382-5872. 1975. Articles, photos, interviews, letters, non-fiction. "Seed Exchange of Heirloom Vegetable & Fruit Varieties." circ. 8M. 3/yr. Pub'd 3 issues 2005; expects 3 issues 2006, 3 issues 2007. sub. price $35 US, $40 Canada and Mexico, $50 overseas. Back issues: not available. 200pp. Payment: none. Copyrighted. Ads: none accepted. Subjects: Conservation, Gardening.

SEEMS, Karl Elder, Editor, c/o Lakeland College, Box 359, Sheboygan, WI 53082-0359. 1971. Poetry, fiction, parts-of-novels, long-poems, non-fiction. "No. 14, *What Is the Future of Poetry?*, in its third printing, contains essays by Cutler, Dacey, Dunn, Evans, Elliott, Etter, Flaherty, Gildner, Hathaway, Heffernan, Hershon, Heyen, Hilton, Matthews, McKeown, Morgan, Oliphant, Rice, Scott, Sobin, Stryk, and Zimmer. ($5) Samples of back issues, detailed guidelines, etc., are available at www1.lakeland.edu/seems/. For insight concerning the editor's own work and aesthetic inclinations see pages and links at www.karlelder.com." circ. 500. Irregular. Pub'd 1 issue 2005; expects 2 issues 2006, 2 issues 2007. sub. price $16/4 issues; per copy $4; sample $4. Discounts: 25%. 40pp. Reporting time: 1-4 months. Simultaneous submissions accepted: no. Publishes less than .5% of manuscripts submitted. Payment: copies. Copyrighted, reverts to author. Subjects: Fiction, Non-Fiction, Poetry.

The Seer Press, Alexander J Cuthbert; Suzanne Muir Scott, Dr, PO Box 29313, Glasgow, Lanarkshire, Scotland, G20 2AE, United Kingdom. 2004. Poetry. avg. press run 200. Expects 2 titles 2006, 2 titles 2007. Discounts: 0-10 35%11-100% 40%. 28-40pp. Simultaneous submissions accepted: No. Copyrights for author. Subject: Poetry.

The Sektor Co., Joseph Crest, PO Box 501005, San Diego, CA 92150, 858-485-6616, fax 858-485-6572. 1994. Non-fiction. "Inspirational biography, patriotic and American heritage, military history." avg. press run 3M-10M. Pub'd 1 title 2005; expects 3 titles 2006, 6 titles 2007. Discounts: 20-55%. 250pp. Reporting time: 1

month. Simultaneous submissions accepted: yes. Publishes 20% of manuscripts submitted. Payment: flexible. Does not copyright for author. Subjects: Americana, Biography, History, Military, Veterans, Vietnam, World War II.

Selah Publishing Co. Inc., David P. Schaap, 4143 Brownsville Rd #2, Pittsburgh, PA 15227-3306, 845-338-2816, Fax 845-338-2991, customerservice@selahpub.com. 1988. Poetry, music. "Publish primarily in the field of Church Music and Hymnology. Books vary in length from small to large publications." avg. press run 5M. Pub'd 2 titles 2005; expects 2 titles 2006, 3-4 titles 2007. Discounts: trade 1-3 copies 20%, 4-up 40%. 200pp. Reporting time: 1-2 months. Simultaneous submissions accepted: yes. Payment: generally 10% of retail sales price. Copyrights for author. Subjects: Music, Reference.

Select Press (see also JOURNAL OF SOCIAL BEHAVIOR AND PERSONALITY), Roderick P. Crandall Ph.D., PO Box 37, Corte Madera, CA 94925, 415-209-9838. 1986. "Academic reserch, psychology, speech, business, sociology, etc." Pub'd 7 titles 2005; expects 6 titles 2006, 6 titles 2007.

SelectiveHouse Publishers, Inc., Gerilynne Seigneur, PO Box 10095, Gaithersburg, MD 20898, 301-990-2999; email sr@selectivehouse.com; www.selectivehouse.com. 1997. Fiction, non-fiction. "See our web page for the types of books published. Primarily mainstream fiction with science fiction and/or spiritual overtones." avg. press run 2M. Pub'd 2 titles 2005; expects 2 titles 2006, 3 titles 2007. 300pp. Reporting time: 6-8 weeks. Simultaneous submissions accepted: yes. Publishes less than 1% of manuscripts submitted. Copyrights for author. Subjects: Christianity, Fiction, Mystery, New Age, Novels, Religion, Science Fiction, Spiritual.

Selous Foundation Press, 325 Pennsylvania Avenue, SE, Washington, DC 20001. 1987. avg. press run 3M. Pub'd 2 titles 2005; expects 4 titles 2006, 6 titles 2007. Discounts: bookstores-prorated by # of copies, discounters/sales reps—60%/60 days, 55%/90 days. 250pp. Reporting time: 90 days. Payment: negotiable. Copyrights for author. Subject: Political Science.

Semiotext Foreign Agents Books Series (see also SEMIOTEXT(E)), Jim Fleming, Sylvere Lotringer, PO Box 568, Brooklyn, NY 11211, 718-963-2603; E-mail semiotexte@aol.com. 1983. "Small books under 250 pages; politics, philosophy and culture." avg. press run 5M. Pub'd 3 titles 2005; expects 5 titles 2006, 7 titles 2007. Discounts: trade, 40%, distributors 50%. 200pp. Reporting time: 6 weeks. Payment: arranged per title. Copyrights for author. Subjects: African Literature, Africa, African Studies, Anarchist, Avant-Garde, Experimental Art, Communism, Marxism, Leninism, Counter-Culture, Alternatives, Communes, Criticism, Culture, Philosophy, Politics, Sex, Sexuality, U.S.S.R.

SEMIOTEXT(E), Autonomedia, Inc., Semiotext Foreign Agents Books Series, Sylvere Lotringer, Jim Fleming, PO Box 568, Brooklyn, NY 11211, 718-963-2603, e-Mail semiotexte@aol.com. 1974. "Do not solicit submissions." circ. 6M. 2/yr. Pub'd 2 issues 2005; expects 2 issues 2006, 2 issues 2007. sub. price $16; per copy varies; sample $12. Discounts: trade 40%, distributors 50%. 350pp. Publishes 2% of manuscripts submitted. Payment: varies. Copyrighted, reverts to author. Pub's reviews. Subjects: African Literature, Africa, African Studies, Anarchist, Avant-Garde, Experimental Art, Communism, Marxism, Leninism, Counter-Culture, Alternatives, Communes, Criticism, Culture, Folklore, Philosophy, Politics, Sex, Sexuality.

SENECA REVIEW, Deborah Tall, Editor; John D'Agata, Associate Editor for Creative Nonfiction, Hobart & William Smith Colleges, Geneva, NY 14456, 315-781-3392, Fax 315-781-3348, senecareview@hws.edu. 1970. Poetry, long-poems, non-fiction. "We publish a great number of translations and are always happy to receive submissions of them. We favor innovative poems and lyrical nonfiction. Recent contributors: Anne Carson, Yusef Komunyakaa, Fanny Howe, Jorie Graham, Reginald Shepherd." circ. 1M. 2/yr. Pub'd 2 issues 2005; expects 2 issues 2006, 2 issues 2007. sub. price $11, $20/2 years; per copy $7; sample $7. Back issues: $7. Discounts: 40% trade for stores. 100pp. Reporting time: 10-14 weeks. Simultaneous submissions accepted: No. And please make only one submission during annual reading period. Publishes 1% of manuscripts submitted. Payment: 2 copies and a 2-year subscription. Copyrighted, reverts to author. Ads: $75, special small press rates, exchange. Subjects: Criticism, Essays, Non-Fiction, Poetry, Translation.

SENSATIONS MAGAZINE, Snake Hill Press, David Messineo, Publisher and Executive Editor, P.O. Box 90, Glen Ridge, NJ 07028. 1987. Poetry, fiction, photos, criticism, reviews, long-poems. "Three-time winner, American Literary Magazine Awards, celebrating 20th anniversary without grant funding in 2007. Go to www.sensationsmag.com for details ("Join" button to subscribe, "Learn" button for history/general information, "Attend" button for upcoming events, "Submit" button for submission requirements). Theme: "The 2004 Presidential Election, One Year Later." Deadline: Oct 1, 2005. Theme: "Retro" (see website for details in Jan 2006). Deadline: June 15, 2006." 2/yr. Pub'd 4 issues 2005; expects 2 issues 2006, 2 issues 2007. sub. price $40; per copy $20; sample $20. Back issues: inquire. Discounts: None. Per issue, 100-200pp. Reporting time: Two months from deadline. Simultaneous submissions accepted: Yes. Publishes 15% of manuscripts submitted. Payment: $100 for #1 poem, $50 for #2 poem, $100 for #1 story. Copyrighted, reverts to author. Pub's reviews: approx. 4 in 2005. §Only review poetry books published by our active subscribers. No advertising accepted within magazine. Subjects: Americana, Bisexual, Civil Rights, Fiction, Gay, History, Literary Review, Literature (General), Mystery, Performing Arts, Poetry, Prose, Research, Science Fiction, Short Stories.

THE $ENSIBLE SOUND, Karl Nehring, 403 Darwin Drive, Snyder, NY 14226, 716-833-0930. 1976. Articles, art, photos, cartoons, interviews, satire, criticism, reviews, music, letters, news items, non-fiction. "We run mainly audio equipment reviews, musical recording reviews, audio semi-technical articles, and audio and music industry news." circ. 14M. 6/yr. Pub'd 6 issues 2005; expects 6 issues 2006, 6 issues 2007. sub. price $29; per copy $6; sample $3. Back issues: 5 each $3 each after one year old. Discounts: 5 or more 20%. 96pp. Reporting time: 2 weeks. Simultaneous submissions accepted: no. Publishes 30% of manuscripts submitted. Payment: yes. Copyrighted, reverts to author. Pub's reviews: 14 in 2005. §Technical, music related, audio related, Hi Fi, Stereo, Home theater. Ads: b&w $1200/$750, color $1500/$900, no classifieds. Subjects: Crafts, Hobbies, Music.

Sentient Publications, LLC, Connie Shaw, 1113 Spruce Street, Boulder, CO 80302, 303-443-2188, Fax 303-381-2538, www.sentientpublications.com. 2001. Non-fiction. "Sentient Publications, LLC publishes books on cultural creativity, experimental education, transformative spirituality, holistic health, new science, ecology, and a variety of other topics, approached from an integral viewpoint. Our authors are intensely interested in exploring the nature of life from fresh perspectives, addressing life's great questions, and fostering the full expression of the human potential. Sentient Publication's books arise from the spirit of inquiry and the richness of the inherent dialogue between writer and reader.Our Culture Tools series is designed to give social catalyzers and cultural entrepreneurs the essential information, technology, and inspiration to forge a sustainable, creative, and compassionate world." avg. press run 3M. Pub'd 13 titles 2005; expects 15 titles 2006, 18 titles 2007. Discounts: Trade discounts are through our distributor, National Book Network. 200pp. Reporting time: 1-2 months. Simultaneous submissions accepted: yes. Publishes 3% of manuscripts submitted. Payment: varies. Copyrights for author. Subjects: Aging, Alternative Medicine, Culture, Current Affairs, Education, Health, How-To, Non-Fiction, Parenting, Psychology, Publishing, Relationships, Sex, Sexuality, Spiritual, Theatre.

SEQUENTIAL, Paul Hornschemeier, 2324 W. Walton Street #3F, Chicago, IL 60622-7101, feedback@sequentialcomics.com, www.sequentialcomics.com. 1999. Art, photos, cartoons, interviews, reviews. "Experimental comics from Paul Hornschemeier, author of Forlorn Funnies and "Mother, Come Home"." circ. 2M. 4/yr. Pub'd 4 issues 2005; expects 4 issues 2006, 4 issues 2007. price per copy $7. Discounts: retails 50%, for nonretailers order 3+ issues, get 25% off the cover price (applies to all issues ordered in qualifying purchase). 128pp. Reporting time: within 2 weeks. Simultaneous submissions accepted: yes. Publishes a variable % of manuscripts submitted. Payment: copies of that issue. Copyright is stated, not federally registered. Subjects: Avant-Garde, Experimental Art, Comics.

Seraphic Press, Karen Singer, 1531 Cardiff Avenue, Los Angeles, CA 90035, 310 557-0132, seraphicpress@aol.com, seraphicpressblogspot.com.

Serpent & Eagle Press, Jo Mish, 10 Main Street, Laurens, NY 13796, 607-432-2990. 1981. Poetry, fiction, art, photos, non-fiction. "I've shifted emphasis to short book-length work on historical & folk-lore oriented subjects. I'll put out an occasional book of poetry. Not accepting submissions during 2002-03." avg. press run 200. Expects 1 title 2007. Discounts: 40%. 30pp. Simultaneous submissions accepted: no. Payment: varies. Does not copyright for author. Subjects: Folklore, Poetry.

Set Sail Productions, LLC, Eric Holmes, 621 Wills Point, Allen, TX 75013, 469 951 7245, www.setsailmotivation.com, eric@setsailforsuccess.com. 2003. Non-fiction. "Set Sail Productions specializes in personal development, self-help and motivation." avg. press run 5500. Pub'd 1 title 2005; expects 5 titles 2006, 10 titles 2007. 152pp. Reporting time: 2-4 weeks. Simultaneous submissions accepted: Yes. Publishes 20% of manuscripts submitted. Copyrights for author. Subjects: Careers, Current Affairs, Ethics, Finances, Health, Inspirational, Leadership, Management, Marketing, Mentoring/Coaching, Motivation, Success, Non-Fiction, Quotations, Sports, Outdoors, Taxes.

Seven Arrows Publishing, Inc., David Findley, 8721 Santa Monica Boulevard #532, Los Angeles, CA 90069, 310-360-9474, Fax 310-289-9474, office@sevenarrowsonline.com, www.sevenarrowsonline.com. 2001. Non-fiction. "Recent release: *Romantic Stability* by Dane." avg. press run 5M. Expects 1 title 2006, 1 title 2007. 195pp. Reporting time: usually less than 3 months. Simultaneous submissions accepted: yes. Publishes 5% of manuscripts submitted. Payment: authors get $1 for each book sold, period. Subjects: Non-Fiction, Self-Help, Spiritual.

Seven Buffaloes Press (see also THE AZOREAN EXPRESS; THE BADGER STONE CHRONICLES; BLACK JACK & VALLEY GRAPEVINE; THE BREAD AND BUTTER CHRONICLES; HILL AND HOLLER), Art Coelho, Box 249, Big Timber, MT 59011. 1973. Poetry, fiction, art, photos, interviews, reviews, parts-of-novels, long-poems, collages. "Book-length manuscripts are not being accepted at this time. I do publish some books, even novels, but the authors are those that have had work in my magazines." avg. press run 750. Pub'd 8 titles 2005; expects 2 titles 2006. Discounts: 1-4 0%, 5 copies or more 30%. 80pp. Reporting time: within a week; sometimes same day. Payment: negotiable. Copyrights for author. Subjects: Fiction, Poetry.

SevenStar Communications, 13315 Washington Blvd., Ste. 200, Los Angeles, CA 90066, 310-302-1207, Fax 310-302-1208, taostar@taostar.com, www.sevenstarcom.com. 1976. Non-fiction. "We only publish titles on Chinese medicine and/or Taoism." avg. press run 3M. Pub'd 2 titles 2005; expects 1 title 2006, 4 titles 2007. 120pp. Reporting time: 2 months. Simultaneous submissions accepted: yes. Publishes 50% of manuscripts submitted. Payment: royalty on sales, no advance. Copyrights for author. Subjects: Alternative Medicine, T'ai Chi.

74th Street Productions, L.L.C., Nigel Loring, Editor, 350 North 74th Street, Seattle, WA 98103, 206-781-1447, info@74thstreet.com, www.74thstreet.com, www.writersatthepodium.com. 1996. Fiction, art, photos, non-fiction. "*No* unsolicited manuscripts - e-mail for guidelines. Shakespeare For Young Adults (7-14) plays retold in story form. Theatre oriented topics for young people. Presentation skills for writers." avg. press run 3M. Pub'd 1 title 2005; expects 1 title 2006, 1 title 2007. 100pp. Reporting time: varies. Simultaneous submissions accepted: yes. Subjects: Marketing, Motivation, Success, Performing Arts, Prose, Shakespeare, Speaking, Theatre, Theatre, Writers/Writing.

SEWANEE REVIEW, George Core, Editor; Leigh Anne Couch, Managing Editor, University of the South, 735 University Avenue, Sewanee, TN 37383-1000, 931-598-1246, email:lcouch@sewanee.edu. 1892. Poetry, fiction, articles, criticism, reviews, letters, non-fiction. "Publish book reviews, but books and reviewers are selected by editor. No electronic submissions or queries are accepted at this time. Our reading period extends from September 1 to June 1." circ. 2.5M. 4/yr. Pub'd 4 issues 2005; expects 4 issues 2006, 4 issues 2007. sub. price $33 instit., $25 indiv.; per copy $8.50; sample $8.50. Back issues: $9 for issues 1964-2002 (some vary); before 1964 inquire. Discounts: 5% to subscription agents. 192pp. Reporting time: 3-6 weeks after receipt. Simultaneous submissions accepted: no. Publishes less than .5% of manuscripts submitted. Payment: $10-$12/printed page for prose; 60¢/line for poetry. Copyrighted, reverts to author. Pub's reviews: 89 in 2005. §New fiction & poetry; literary criticism; biography, memoirs, and general nonfiction. Ads: $350/$245. Subjects: Book Reviewing, Criticism, English, Essays, Fiction, Literary Review, Literature (General), Memoirs, Non-Fiction, Poetry, Reviews, Short Stories, Writers/Writing.

•**Shadow Poetry (see also SP QUILL QUARTERLY MAGAZINE; WHITE LOTUS),** Marie Summers, 1209 Milwaukee Street, Excelsior Springs, MO 64024, Fax: (208) 977-9114, shadowpoetry@shadow-poetry.com, http://www.shadowpoetry.com. 2000.

THE SHAKESPEARE NEWSLETTER, John W. Mahon, Thomas A. Pendleton, English Department, Iona College, New Rochelle, NY 10801. 1951. Poetry, articles, criticism, reviews, letters, news items. circ. 2.5M. 4/yr. Pub'd 4 issues 2005; expects 4 issues 2006, 4 issues 2007. sub. price indiv. $15, instit. $15, $17 foreign; per copy $4; sample $4. Back issues: $4. Discounts: none. 20pp. Reporting time: 1-2 months. Payment: 3 copies. Not copyrighted. Pub's reviews: 30+ in 2005. §Scholarly and any interesting Shakespeareana and related material. Ads: $210/$125, discounts for multiple insertions. Subjects: Criticism, Drama, English, Shakespeare, Theatre.

SHAMAN'S DRUM: A Journal of Experiential Shamanism, Timothy White, PO Box 270, Williams, OR 97544, 541-846-1313. 1985. Poetry, articles, art, photos, interviews, reviews, letters, news items, non-fiction. "We seek contributions directed to a general but well-informed audience. Past contributors have included Jeanne Achterberg, Brooke Medicine Eagle, Richard Erdoes. We see *Shaman's Drum* as an ongoing effort to expand, challenge, and refine our readers' and our own understanding of shamanism in practice. In the process, we cover a wide range of related topics—from indigenous medicineway practices to contemporary shamanic psychotherapies, from transpersonal healing ceremonies to ecstatic spiritual practices. Our focus is on experiential shamanism. We prefer original material that is based on, or illustrated with, firsthand knowledge and personal experience. Articles should, however, be well documented with descriptive examples and pertinent background information. We are looking for examples of not only how shamanism has transformed individual lives but also practical ways it can help ensure the survival of life on this planet. We want material that captures the heart and feeling of shamanism and that can inspire people to direct action and participation." circ. 12M. 4/yr. Pub'd 4 issues 2005; expects 4 issues 2006, 4 issues 2007. sub. price $19; per copy $6.95; sample $7. Back issues: $7 each or 4 for $19. Discounts: retail 30%, classroom 30%, wholesale 50%. 80+pp. Reporting time: 3 months. Simultaneous submissions accepted: no. Publishes 5% of manuscripts submitted. Payment: 5¢ per word. Copyrighted, rights reverting to author is optional. Pub's reviews: 24 in 2005. §Shamanism, Native American spirituality, Entheogens. Ads: $990/$450/$330 1/3 page. Subjects: Anthropology, Archaelogy, Dreams, Native American, Religion, Spiritual.

•**Shambling Gate Press,** Lawrence Paulson, 3314 Rosemary Lane, Hyattsville, MD 20782-1032, 301-779-6863, 301-779-9263. 1995. Poetry, fiction, non-fiction. avg. press run 2000. Expects 1 title 2006, 1 title 2007. Discount to bookstores and other retailers 50% on 2 copies or more. 100-400pp. Copyrights for author.

Shangri-La Publications, Sheldon Gosline, Publisher; Lester Ness, Chief Editor, #3 Coburn Hill Rd., Warren Center, PA 18851-0065, telephone 570-395-3423, fax 570-395-0146, toll free 866-966-6288, email shangrila@egypt.net, web http://shangri-la.0catch.com. 1998. Fiction, articles, art, photos, cartoons, criticism, music, long-poems, plays, news items, non-fiction. "We publish advanced academic research with a cross cultural focus in our Marco Polo Monographs Series. The most recent volume is #9, *FUNDING EXPLORATION*. We publish political topics, such as *MUSLIMS IN THE WEST* and mystery novels such as *LILAC MOON*. We have a children's book series under the imprint Panda Print, with *ZOONAUTS: THE SECRET OF ANIMALVILLE*. In 2004, we are beginning a new joint venture with a number of Chinese universities and research institutes to publish the latest Chinese scientific research. In 2004 we are beginning a new journal called *Chinese Agriculture and Life Sciences (CALS)*. We have an Egyptian Language series called *HIERATIC PALEOGRAPHY*." avg. press run 2000 to 5000. Pub'd 4 titles 2005; expects 3 titles 2006, 12 titles 2007. Discounts: 20 academic / 45 trade. 200 to 400pp. Reporting time: 1 to 2 months. Simultaneous submissions accepted: no. Publishes 12% of manuscripts submitted. Payment: 7% royalty. Copyrights for author. Subjects: African Literature, Africa, African Studies, Anthropology, Archaelogy, Antiques, Architecture, Bibliography, Biography, Book Collecting, Bookselling, Book Reviewing, Classical Studies, Communism, Marxism, Leninism, Community, Computers, Calculators, Conservation, Crafts, Hobbies, Dada.

SHARE INTERNATIONAL, Benjamin Creme, PO Box 971, North Hollywood, CA 91603, 818-785-6300, Fax 818-904-9132, share@shareintl.org, www.shareintl.org/. 1982. Articles, photos, interviews, reviews, letters, news items, non-fiction. "Combines socially-conscious and spiritual perspectives on world events and news about emergence of Maitreya, the World Teacher." circ. 5M. 10/yr. Pub'd 10 issues 2005; expects 10 issues 2006, 10 issues 2007. sub. price $30; per copy $3.50; sample $3.50. Back issues: $3.50. Discounts: library $20, volume discount on back issues 20%. 24-40pp. Payment: none. Copyrighted, does not revert to author. Pub's reviews: 4 in 2005. §Subjects we cover. Ads: none. Subjects: Birth, Birth Control, Population, Book Reviewing, Business & Economics, Environment, Futurism, Humanism, Hunger, Inspirational, Interviews, New Age, Peace, Politics, Society, Spiritual, Third World, Minorities.

SHARING & CARING, Halbar Publishing, Bill Halbert, Mary Barnes, 309 VZ County Road 3224, Wills Point, TX 75169-9732. 1994. Poetry, fiction, articles, art, photos, cartoons, interviews, satire, criticism, reviews, music, letters, long-poems, news items, non-fiction. "Will publish long or continued material and furnish extra pages if paid for, our cost. Marian Ford Park, Linda Hutton, Uncle Mickey (Mickey H. Clarke), Terri Warden, Mary Kraft, Victoria Widry, Robert R. Hentz, Ni Nichi, Charles H. Thornton, Thomas Lynn, Joe Sharp, Jeff Klein, Betty Webster Bishop, Jani Johe Webster, Bruce Ellison (archives), many of the best too numorous to list." circ. 100+. 4/yr. Pub'd 4 issues 2005; expects 4 issues 2006, 4 issues 2007. sub. price $55; per copy $9; sample $9. Discounts: commensurate with inquiry, ours run $2.16 to mail, multiples would cut this down. 80pp. Reporting time: with SASE, next day's mail usually. Simultaneous submissions accepted: yes. Publishes 90% of manuscripts submitted. Payment: lots of cash contests w/cash award for best voted poetry and prose each quarter. Not copyrighted. Pub's reviews: 8 in 2005. §All except porn, occult, excess sex and profanity. Ads: $22/$15/25¢ per word classifieds.

SHARING IDEAS FOR PROFESSIONAL SPEAKERS, Dorothy M. Walters, PO Box 398, Glendora, CA 91740, 626-335-8069; fax 626-335-6127. 1978. "Our newsmagazine is to the world of paid speaking what Variety is to show business. We feature stories, news, announcements about speakers, their books, cassette albums, meeting planners and all elements of the world of paid speaking. We restrict material: by and about speakers. Submissions by subscribers only." circ. 6M. 4/yr. Pub'd 6 issues 2005; expects 6 issues 2006, 4 issues 2007. sub. price $95 2/yr, includes free *Directory of Agents & Bureaus* and *How to Be Booked by Speakers Bureaus* album; Canada and Mexico $124 2/yr (includes book in Mexico); all other foreign $179 2/yr, includes book; sample $10 one time only. Back issues: varies as to availability, $10. 48+pp. Reporting time: 2 months. Payment: none. Copyrighted, reverts to author. Pub's reviews: 90 in 2005. §We are interested in anything on the subject of paid speaking. Must be advertiser or subscriber. Ads: $539/$350/$600 outside back cover/$570 inside cover.

SHATTERED WIG REVIEW, Sonny Bodkin, 425 East 31st Street, Baltimore, MD 21218, 410-243-6888. 1988. Poetry, fiction, articles, art, cartoons, satire, letters, parts-of-novels, collages, concrete art. "Do you take medicine? I take 3 "Joan Crawfords In a Wheelchair". Like Gertrude said it's in the telling, not necessarily what's told. Or as Serge Gainsbourg said: "Beauty ages and fades, while ugliness endures" (or words to that effect). We have a penchant for hardboiled surreal absurdity, but will accept anything that hits the target with a solid twang." circ. 500. 2/yr. Pub'd 2 issues 2005; expects 2 issues 2006, 2 issues 2007. sub. price $12.00; per copy $6; sample $5. Back issues: $5. Discounts: 10%. 66pp. Reporting time: 4 months. Simultaneous submissions accepted: Yes. Payment: One contributor's copy. Not copyrighted. Subjects: Alcohol, Alcoholism, Anarchist, Arts, Biography, William Blake, Lewis Carroll, Cities, Comics, Dada, Folklore, James Joyce, Literature (General), H.P. Lovecraft, Music, Poetry.

‡**SHAW: THE ANNUAL OF BERNARD SHAW STUDIES, Pennsylvania State University Press,** Fred D.

Crawford, Penn State Press, Suite C, 820 N. University Drive, University Park, PA 16802-1711, 814-865-1327. 1951. Articles, interviews, criticism, reviews, letters. circ. 2M. 1/yr. Pub'd 1 issue 2005; expects 1 issue 2006, 1 issue 2007. sub. price $35; per copy $35. 265pp. Reporting time: 2 months. Simultaneous submissions accepted: no. Publishes 25-30% of manuscripts submitted. Payment: 1 copy of the volume. Copyrighted, does not revert to author. Pub's reviews: 3 in 2005. §Shaw. Ads: none. Subjects: English, Literary Review, G.B. Shaw.

SHEAR-CROPPER SALON (FOR THE HAIR-BRAINED), Pen-Dec Press, 2526 Chatham Woods, Grand Rapids, MI 49546. 2002. "No fiction. No unsolicited mss. Poetry only: juiced, with zip. Must include letter of purpose, brief bio, SASE." Irregular. sample price $4. 24pp.

Shearer Publishing, Katherine Shearer, President, 406 Post Oak Road, Fredericksburg, TX 78624, 830-997-6529. 1981. Non-fiction. avg. press run 2M-40M. Pub'd 2 titles 2005; expects 4 titles 2006, 4 titles 2007. 250pp. Reporting time: average is 3 months. Payment: depends on book. Copyrights for author. Subjects: Fiction, Gardening, Texas.

SHEMP! The Lowlife Culture Magazine, Lawrence K. Yoshida, 593 Waikala Street, Kahului, HI 96732-1736, e-mail shempzine@yahoo.com. 1993. Articles, photos, criticism, reviews, letters. "Not for artsy types! No submissions. We are pro-choice carnivores. We are low-life scum, slackers, and shemps. We accept cash donations and money orders (made out to Lawrence Yoshida)." circ. 400. 6/yr. Expects 6 issues 2006, 6 issues 2007. price per copy $1 + 2 stamps; sample $1 + 2 stamps. Back issues: same (when available). 12pp. Publishes 0% of manuscripts submitted. Not copyrighted. Pub's reviews: 18 in 2005. §Punk rock, cocktail music, soundtracks, B-movies, Asian/Asian related films, true crime books. Subjects: Asian-American, Crime, Electronics, Movies, Music, Elvis Presley, Tapes & Records.

SHENANDOAH NEWSLETTER, Scan Doa, 736 West Oklahoma Street, Appleton, WI 54914. 1973. Poetry, articles, criticism, reviews, letters, news items, non-fiction. "All material must relate to American Indian by Indians. Editor holds strict rights on this." circ. 1M. 12/yr. Pub'd 12 issues 2005; expects 12 issues 2006, 12 issues 2007. sub. price $17.50; per copy $1.75; sample $1.75. 21pp. Reporting time: material must be into office by 24th of previous month. Payment: none. Not copyrighted. Pub's reviews: 30 in 2005. §Material relating to Native Peoples and their struggles/history. Ads: none. Subjects: Indians, Native American, Third World, Minorities.

SHENANDOAH: THE Washington and Lee University Review, R.T. Smith, Editor; Lynn L. Leech, Managing Editor, Mattingly House / 2 Lee Avenue, Lexington, VA 24450-0303, 540-458-8765; http://shenandoah.wlu.edu. 1950. Poetry, fiction, art, reviews, non-fiction. "For over half a century *Shenandoah* has published splendid poems, stories, essays and reviews that display passionate understanding, formal accomplishment and serious mischief. Reading period Sept through May; work received June through August will be returned unread. Upcoming special issues in 2005-06: Winter, 2005: featuring The Robert Penn Warren Centennial Prize winning essay. Send mss. attn: The Robert Penn Warren Centennial Prize; postmark deadline 8/15/05; Spring, 2006: featuring traditional music. Send mss. attn: Traditional Music feature; postmark deadline 12/1/05; Winter, 2006: essays on Tom Wolfe, along with related memoirs, poems, stories, reviews. Also articles on William Hoffman and Cy Twombly. Send mss. attn: Wolfe feature; postmark deadline 5/1/06). 2006 Glasgow Prize for Emerging Writers $2,500. Open to all writers of short fiction with only one published book in that genre. The Prize includes cash award, publication of new work in *Shenandoah* and a reading at Washington and Lee University. To apply, send first book, samples of new work (1 or 2 unpublished stories), vita and check for $22 (which brings a year's subscription to *Shenandoah*) between March 15 and March 31, 2006 to R. T. Smith, The Glasgow Prize, Mattingly House, 2 Lee Avenue, Washington and Lee University, Lexington, VA 24450-0303." circ. 1.3M. 3/yr. Pub'd 4 issues 2005; expects 3 issues 2006, 3 issues 2007. sub. price $22 individual, $25 institution; foreign subscribers add $8/yr for postage; per copy $10; sample $10. Back issues: $10. Discounts: 50% bulk rate to bookstores. 200pp. Reporting time: 3 weeks. Publishes less than 1% of manuscripts submitted. Payment: $25/page prose; $2.50/line poetry; $300/cover art + 1 free copy of issue in which work appears and 1 year free subscription. Copyrighted, rights revert to author. Pub's reviews: 7 in 2005. §Short fiction/poetry—solicited reviews only. Ads: $300/$200. Subjects: Book Reviewing, Essays, Fiction, Literary Review, Literature (General), Non-Fiction, Poetry.

Shen's Books, 40951 Fremont Boulevard, Fremont, CA 94538, 510-668-1898, www.shens.com.

SHERLOCKIAN TIDBITS, Arnold Korotkin, 36 Hawthorne Place #2Q, Montclair, NJ 07042-3279. 1987. Photos, cartoons, news items. "Our publication contains article, graphics, reviews, etc., pertaining to the master detective, Sherlock Holmes." circ. 221. 4/yr. Pub'd 4 issues 2005; expects 4 issues 2006, 4 issues 2007. sub. price $8; per copy $2; sample $2. 13pp. Not copyrighted. Pub's reviews: 4 in 2005. §Mystery books, magazines, etc. Subject: Mystery.

Sherman Asher Publishing, Jim Mafchir, P.O. Box 31725, Santa Fe, NM 87501-0172, 505-988-7214, Fax 505-988-7214, westernedge@santa-fe.net, www.shermanasher.com. 1994. Poetry, fiction, non-fiction. avg. press run 1.5M. Pub'd 1 title 2005; expects 3 titles 2006, 2 titles 2007. Discounts: 20% library, 40% trade, 50%

bulk. Book length. Reporting time: 4 months. Simultaneous submissions accepted: Only if advised. Publishes a variable % of manuscripts submitted. Copyrights for author. Subjects: Bilingual, Fiction, Memoirs, Poetry.

•**shift 4 Publishing,** Aaron Voorhees, Editor; Daniel Fleenor, Editor, PO Box 18916, Denver, CO 80218, editor@shift4publishing.com. 2006. Non-fiction. ''At shift 4 Publishing, our mission is to creatively deliver specific information that will better peoples lives and help them to fulfill their dreams. Our current focus is in the areas of medical school and residency training.Our most recent work is "The Medical School Interview: Secrets and a System for Success".'' avg. press run 500. Expects 4 titles 2006, 5 titles 2007. Discounts: 25% discount. 110pp. Reporting time: 3 weeks. Simultaneous submissions accepted: No. Publishes 30% of manuscripts submitted. Payment: 7%, standard royalty advancement and payment schedule. Copyrights for author. Subjects: Interviews, Medicine, Nursing.

Shining Mountain Publishing, 2268 Spinnaker Circle, Longmont, CO 80503, Telephone 303-651-6230, email info@shiningmountain.net, website www.shiningmountain.net. 2002. Pub'd 1 title 2005; expects 2 titles 2006, 2 titles 2007. 175pp.

•**Shipyard Press, LC,** Marilyn Brown, Editor; Ana Melisa Brown, Publisher, 191 Brightwater Falls Road, Henderson, NC 28739-7171, 239-822-9964. 2005. avg. press run 1085. Expects 1 title 2006, 2 titles 2007. Discounts: 2-10 copies 20%case of 32 40%10+cases 50%. 212pp. Subjects: Architecture, Aviation, Fiction, Florida.

SHIRIM, Marc Steven Dworkin, 259 Saint Joseph Avenue, Long Beach, CA 90803-1733. 1982. Poetry. ''*Shirim* seeks poetry (original + translated) of Jewish reference. Such known poets as Yehuda Amichai, Robert Mezey, Deena Metzger, Karl Shapiro, Irving Layton, Jerome Rothenberg, and Howard Schwartz have had poetry appear in the magazine. All submissions are welcome.'' circ. 250. 2/yr. Expects 1 issue 2006, 2 issues 2007. sub. price $7; per copy $4; sample $4. 36pp. Reporting time: 2 months. Payment: copies. Copyrighted, reverts to author. Pub's reviews: 2 in 2005. Subjects: Judaism, Poetry.

SHO, Johnny Cordova, Editor, PO Box 31, Prescott, AZ 86302. 2002. Poetry. ''We are slightly partial to street poetry, but are open to anything well-written. Step on our toes, grab us by the throat, kiss us on the mouth, get our attention.'' circ. 500. 2/yr. Pub'd 1 issue 2005; expects 1 issue 2006, 2 issues 2007. sub. price $20; per copy $10; sample $10. Back issues: none. Discounts: none at this time. 80-120pp. Reporting time: 1-4 months. Simultaneous submissions accepted: yes. Publishes 5% of manuscripts submitted. Payment: 1 copy. Copyrighted, reverts to author. Ads: none. Subjects: Anarchist, Beat, Buddhism, Native American, Poetry, Sex, Sexuality, Zen.

THE SHOP: A Magazine of Poetry, John Wakeman, Editor; Hilary Wakeman, Editor, c/o Skeagh, Schull, County Cork, Ireland.

SHORT FUSE, Holden, PO Box 90436, Santa Barbara, CA 93190. 1983. Poetry, fiction, articles, art, photos, cartoons, interviews, satire, criticism, music, letters, parts-of-novels, long-poems, collages, plays, concrete art, non-fiction. ''Some recent contributors: Lyn Lifshin, Blair Wilson, Richard Kostelanetz, Hector, Frank Moore, Annie Sprinkle, Dragon Mangan, and Bob Zark. *Short Fuse* is open to anyone's participation and material from people from all walks of life is included. The physical form of the magazine is adaptable to the requirements of the pieces included. Its sociological and ideological context is antiauthoritarian-populist. Esthetically, there's an openness to the avant-garde and experimental but no single aesthetic theory is endorsed to the exclusion of others. However, some ideas derived from dada, surrealism, and punk are of lingering interest.'' circ. 500+. 4/yr. Pub'd 4 issues 2005; expects 4 issues 2006, 4 issues 2007. sub. price free to institutionalized persons, $9 for 6 issues otherwise; per copy $1; sample $1. Back issues: $1. 20pp. Reporting time: 1 week. Payment: copies. Copyrighted, reverts to author. Subjects: Anarchist, Arts, Avant-Garde, Experimental Art, Cartoons, Counter-Culture, Alternatives, Communes, Creativity, Criticism, Dada, Dreams, Erotica, Essays, Fiction, Folklore, Haiku, Libertarian.

SHORTRUNS, Shirley Copperman, Sr.Editor; Dana Sigmund, Editor, 720 Wesley Ave. #10, Tarpon Springs, FL 34689, 727-942-2218. 1986. Fiction, articles, cartoons, interviews, satire, criticism, music, parts-of-novels, news items, non-fiction. ''We read ALL submitted work. You must be flexible if we require additional editing by you/us. Only material with return postage included will be returned.'' circ. 18M & several special issues. 4/yr. Pub'd 4 issues 2005; expects 4 issues 2006, 4 issues 2007. sub. price Only sent to qualified user. 32-64pp. Reporting time: 2 weeks. Simultaneous submissions accepted: Yes. Publishes 15% of manuscripts submitted. Payment: By copies. Copyrighted, reverts to author. Pub's reviews: 15-20 in 2005. §We review @ 50 music CD's. Ads: We will add this to our new music edition. Subjects: Book Reviewing, Comics, Cooking, Crafts, Hobbies, Experimental, Festivals, Fiction, Food, Eating, Magazines, Music, Newsletter, Occult, Sex, Sexuality, Singles, Tapes & Records.

Sibyl Publications, Inc, Miriam Selby, 2505 Reuben Boise road, Dallas, OR 97338, 503-623-3438, fax 503-623-2943. 1993. Non-fiction. ''Not accepting mss. at this time. Small press of women's books. Nonfiction, positive themes. No poetry or fiction. Topics are: cooking, women and change, aging, women in midlife, mythology, spirituality, health, other women's issues. No manuscripts accepted. *Inventing Ourselves Again: Woman Face Middle Age, Sacred Myths: Stories of World Religion, The Goddess Speaks*, revised edition and *Mythmaking: Heal Your Past, Claim Your Future, Spirited Threads, Oh Boy, Oh Boy, Oh Boy!, Love, Loss & Healing: A Woman's Guide to Transforming Grief, Food No Matter What! Stories & Recipes for Perfect Dining in an Imperfect World*, and *Classic Liqueurs*." avg. press run 7.5M. Pub'd 2 titles 2005; expects 5 titles 2006, 5 titles 2007. Discounts: trade 40%, schools 25%. 200pp. Payment: 10-12% of net (minus discounts and returns). Copyrights for author. Subjects: Cooking, Feminism, Myth, Mythology, Parenting, Psychology, Spiritual, Women.

Sidran Institute, 200 E. Joppa Road, Suite 207, Towson, MD 21286, 410-825-8888, Fax 410-337-0747, sidran@sidran.org, www.sidran.org. 1991. Non-fiction. "Division of Sidran Traumatic Stress Foundation. Our focus is on mental health, primarily in the area of trauma (sexual abuse, child abuse, war, violent crime, etc.)." avg. press run 1M-2M. Pub'd 4 titles 2005; expects 4 titles 2006, 2 titles 2007. Discounts: trade 1-2 copies 20%, 3-49 40%, 50-99 41%, 100+ 42%. 300pp. Simultaneous submissions accepted: no. Payment: varies. Subjects: Mental Health, Psychology, Self-Help, Sexual Abuse.

Sierra Outdoor Products Co., Joseph F. Petralia, PO Box 2497, San Francisco, CA 94126-2497, 415-258-0777 phone/Fax, www.sierraoutdoorproducts.com. 1979. Non-fiction. "*Publisher looking for additional manuscripts.*" avg. press run 2M-5M. Pub'd 2 titles 2005; expects 1 title 2006, 2 titles 2007. Discounts: 40-55%. 250pp. Reporting time: 90 days. Simultaneous submissions accepted: yes. Publishes 5-10% of manuscripts submitted. Payment: negotiable. Copyrights for author. Subjects: Crafts, Hobbies, Sports, Outdoors.

Signpost Press Inc. (see also BELLINGHAM REVIEW), Brenda Miller, Editor-in-Chief, Mail Stop 9053, WWU, Bellingham, WA 98225, 360-650-4863. 1975. Poetry, fiction, non-fiction. "Not accepting book mss. at present." avg. press run 500. Discounts: 40% on 5 or more copies. 24-68pp. Reporting time: 1-3 months. Payment: varies. Copyrights for author. Subject: Poetry.

•**SIGNS, University of Chicago Press,** Mary Hawkesworth, Rutgers University, Voorhees Chapel, Room 8, 5 Chapel Drive, New Brunswick, NJ 08901, 732-932-2841 (main #), 732-932-5732 (fax), http://www.journals.uchicago.edu/Signs/home.html. "Founded in 1975, *Signs* is recognized as the leading international journal in women's studies. *Signs* publishes articles from a wide range of disciplines in a variety of voices, articles engaging gender, race, culture, class, sexuality, and / or nation. The focus of essays ranges from cross-disciplinary theorizing and methodologies to specific disciplinary issues, framed to enter conversations of interest across disciplines." 4/yr. Pub's reviews.

SIGNS: JOURNAL OF WOMEN IN CULTURE AND SOCIETY, Sandra Harding, Kathryn Norberg, UCLA, Box 957122, 1400H Public Policy Building, Los Angeles, CA 90095-7122, 310-206-2562, Fax 310-206-1261, signs@signs.ucla.edu. 1975. Articles, interviews, criticism, reviews, letters, non-fiction. circ. 7M. 4/yr. Pub'd 4 issues 2005; expects 4 issues 2006, 4 issues 2007. sub. price $38 indiv., $140 instit., $27 students; per copy $8.50 indiv.; $35 instit. Back issues: contact business office, University of Chicago Press, Journals Division, PO Box 37005, Chicago IL 60637, for this information. Discounts: standard agencies. 265pp. Reporting time: 3-6 months, contact editorial office for this information. Payment: 10 copies of journal issue or 1/yr subscription. Copyrighted, does not revert to author. Pub's reviews: 40 in 2005. §Women, feminist studies. Subjects: Feminism, Women.

Silk Pages Publishing, PO Box 385, Deerwood, MN 56444, Fax 218-534-3949.

THE SILT READER, Temporary Vandalism Recordings, Robert Roden, Barton M. Saunders, PO Box 6184, Orange, CA 92863-6184. 1999. Poetry. "Recent contributors: George Gott, Lyn Lifshin, Gerald Locklin, Edward M. O'Durr Supranowicz, Donna Pucciani, and Mather Schneider." circ. 500. 2/yr. Pub'd 2 issues 2005; expects 2 issues 2006, 2 issues 2007. price per copy $2; sample $2. 32pp. Reporting time: 3-6 months. Simultaneous submissions accepted: yes. Publishes 3% of manuscripts submitted. Payment: 2 copies. Copyrighted, reverts to author. Ads: $50 full page. Subjects: Haiku, Journals, Poetry.

THE SILVER WEB, Ann Kennedy, PO Box 38190, Tallahassee, FL 32315. 1989. Poetry, fiction, articles, art, photos, cartoons, interviews, satire, reviews. "*The Silver Web* is a semi-annual publication featuring new fiction, poetry and art. The Editor is looking for thought-provoking works ranging from speculative fiction to dark fantasy and all weirdness in between. FICTION: Short stories of 8000 words or less (don't send anything longer w/o a query first, or it will be returned unread). Looking for a twist of the bizarre. This could be classified as horror, dark fantasy, speculative fiction or science fiction. No S & S or fantasy/quest stories. Also, please, please, PLEASE no typical revenge stories. Give me strong believable characters and a solid imaginative story that surprises me, not merely shocks me. I'd like to see works that may possibly fall between the cracks of other magazines. Above all, the writing must be good. POETRY: Use above descriptions. The poetry must be well-written and provide good imagery. ART: Pen & Ink, Black & White photography, charcoals, pencils (if dark enough and clearly defined). Separate guidelines for artists available. NON-FICTION: Please query about specific articles. Interested in interviews with writers, poets, artists, publishers, editors and other people in the industry. Satire and humor also invited and I love Letters to the Editor. Reprints considered (include info on prior publication). Simultaneous submissions accepted, but please no multiple submissions. Give me time to respond to one manuscript before sending me another. Cover letters are enjoyed but not essential. Please don't explain your story in the cover letter. Let the work speak for itself. You must provide an SASE with proper postage to insure a response. If the postage is not enough to return the work, it will be considered disposable.'' circ. 2M. 2/yr. Pub'd 2 issues 2005; expects 2 issues 2006, 2 issues 2007. sub. price $12; per copy $5.95 + $1.25 p/h; sample $5.95 + $1.25 p/h. Back issues: all sold out. Discounts: $3.57 @ wholesale, $4 to contributors. 80+pp. Reporting time: 4-6 weeks. Simultaneous submissions accepted: yes. Publishes less than 1% of manuscripts submitted. Payment: 2-3¢ a word. Copyrighted, reverts to author. Pub's reviews: 4 in 2005. §Horror, speculative fiction, science fiction, experimental, surreal, slipstream. Ads: $100/$50/$25 1/4 page/$35 digest. Subjects: Fantasy, Science Fiction, Supernatural, Surrealism.

SILVER WINGS, Jackson Wilcox, PO Box 2340, Clovis, CA 93613-2340, 661-264-3726. 1983. Poetry. ''Poems with Christian foundation focusing on the realities of faith.'' circ. 250-300. 6/yr. Pub'd 6 issues 2005; expects 6 issues 2006, 6 issues 2007. sub. price $10; per copy $2; sample $2. Back issues: $2 as available. Discounts: 20%. 16-32pp. Reporting time: 4 weeks. We rarely accept simultaneous submissions. Publishes 10% of manuscripts submitted. Payment: 1 copy. Not copyrighted. Pub's reviews: 4 in 2005. §Poetry books only. Ads: none. Subjects: Community, Family, Reference.

Silverfish Review Press, Rodger Moody, Editor, PO Box 3541, Eugene, OR 97403, 503-344-5060. 1979. Poetry. ''Guidelines for the annual Gerald Cable Book Award for a first book by a poet and the Open Submission Period for Poetry are available from the website: www.silverfishreviewpress.com.'' avg. press run 1M. Pub'd 2 titles 2005; expects 3 titles 2006, 3 titles 2007. Discounts: 40% wholesale for bookstores. 80pp. Reporting time: 16-20 weeks. Simultaneous submissions accepted: yes. Payment: $1,000 to winner of annual poetry book contest (for author who has yet to publish a book) plus publication by Silverfish Review Press and 100 copies of the book. See the website for contract details for the Open Submission Period for Poetry. Copyrights for author. Subject: Poetry.

Silverstone Press, PO Box 8429, Tacoma, WA 98418-0429, (253)472-6707, fax (253)276-0233, email info@silverstonepress.com. 2003.

SIMPLYWORDS, Ruth Niehaus, 605 Collins Avenue #23, Centerville, GA 31028, simplywords@hotmail.com. 1991. Poetry, fiction, articles, letters, non-fiction. 4/yr. Pub'd 4 issues 2005; expects 4 issues 2006, 4 issues 2007. sub. price $18.50; per copy $5; sample $5. Back issues: none. Discounts: none. 38pp. Reporting time: 2-3 weeks. Simultaneous submissions accepted: no. Publishes 80% of manuscripts submitted. Payment: none. Not copyrighted, all rights revert to author on publication. Pub's reviews: 1-2 in 2005. Ads: must write for rates.

SING OUT! Folk Music & Folk Songs, Mark Moss, Editor; Scott Atkinson, Managing Editor, PO Box 5460, Bethlehem, PA 18015-0460, 610-865-5366; Fax 610-865-5129; info@singout.org. 1950. Articles, art, photos, interviews, reviews, music, letters, news items. ''No unsolicited submissions. We print music and lyrics of folk songs.'' circ. 12.5M. 4/yr. Pub'd 4 issues 2005; expects 4 issues 2006, 4 issues 2007. sub. price $25 indiv., $30 institution; per copy $6.95; sample $7. Back issues: $3 to $8 depending on the issue, write to Circulation Department for complete list. 216pp. Reporting time: variable. Simultaneous submissions accepted: no. Payment: 7¢ per word. Copyrighted, does not revert to author. Pub's reviews: 750 in 2005. §Music, folklore, politics, arts, third world, ethnic materials, etc., women history labor, folk music records. Ads: $570/$350/60¢. Subjects: Folklore, Music.

SINISTER WISDOM, Fran Day, Editor; Susan Levinkind, Administrator, PO Box 3252, Berkeley, CA 94703. 1976. Poetry, fiction, articles, art, photos, cartoons, interviews, satire, criticism, reviews, letters, parts-of-novels, long-poems, collages, plays, concrete art, non-fiction. ''*Sinister Wisdom* is a magazine for the lesbian imagination in the arts and politics. Contributors range from 'famous' writers to first-time submitters—quality and original voice are what count. Subject matter may be anything that expresses depth of vision. Multi-cultural: writing by lesbians of color, Jewish, disabled, fat, ethnic, working class, older and younger lesbians encouraged.'' circ. 3M. 3/yr. Pub'd 3 issues 2005; expects 3 issues 2006, 3 issues 2007. sub. price $20, $25 foreign, $33 institutions and libraries; per copy $7.50 (pp); sample $7.50 (pp). Back issues: $5-$6. Discounts: 40% to bookstores, 45-50% for bulk sales of 50 or more. 128-144pp. Reporting time: 3-9 months. We prefer not to receive simultaneous submissions. Payment: 2 copies. Copyrighted, reverts to author. Pub's reviews: 10 in 2005. §Lesbian poetry, fiction, theatre, arts and non-fiction, especially with radical emphasis. Ads: $200/$100/$50 1/4/write for classified. Subjects: Feminism, Lesbianism, Literature (General), Women.

SISTERS IN CRIME BOOKS IN PRINT, Rowan Mountain Press, Vicki Cameron, Editor, PO Box 10111,

Blacksburg, VA 24062-0111, 540-449-6178, e-mail faulkner@bev.net, web www.rowanmountain.com. 1989. Fiction, non-fiction. "Compendium of information on current mystery titles by women authors." circ. 10M. 1/yr. Pub'd 1 issue 2005; expects 1 issue 2006, 1 issue 2007. price per copy $2.50 includes s/h, free to bookstores and libraries. Back issues: none available. Discounts: 2-4 20%, 5+ 40%; 40% if prepaid and s/h any quantity. 80pp. Payment: none. Copyrighted. Ads: none. Subjects: Crime, Feminism, German, Mystery, Non-Fiction, Short Stories, Women, Writers/Writing, Young Adult.

Sisyphus Press (see also BABEL MAGAZINE), PO Box 10495, State College, PA 16805-0495, www.babelmagazine.com.

Six Strings Music Publishing, PO Box 7718-155, Torrance, CA 90504-9118, 800-784-0203, Fax 310-362-8864, www.sixstringsmusicpub.com. 1997. avg. press run 3-5M. Pub'd 2 titles 2005; expects 5 titles 2006, 10 titles 2007. Discounts: contact us for details. Copyrights for author. Subjects: How-To, Music.

Sixteen Rivers Press, Valerie Berry, Founding Member; Jackie Kudler, Founding Member; Terry Ehret, Founding Member; Margaret Kaufman, Founding Member; Carolyn Miller, Founding Member; Susan Sibbet, Founding Member; Gerald Fleming, Author Member; Maria Benet, Author Member; Sharon Olson, Author Member; Murray Silverstein, Author Member; Nina Lindsay, Author Member; Helen Wickes, Author Member, PO Box 640663, San Francisco, CA 94164-0663, 415-273-1303, www.sixteenrivers.org. 2001. Poetry. "Sixteen Rivers is a shared-work regional poetry collective. Authors must live in the San Francisco Bay Area and be willing to make a three year commitment of 10 hours/month to help run the press if a manuscript is selected for publication. Book-length poetry manuscripts 60-80 pages are considered from January 1 to March 1. Please review our submission guidelines at our website www.sixteenrivers.org." avg. press run 1000. Pub'd 3 titles 2005; expects 2 titles 2006, 2 titles 2007. 80-96pp. Reporting time: 4-5 months. Simultaneous submissions accepted: yes. Publishes 10-20% of manuscripts submitted. Payment: Authors receive 25 copies of their books. All profits are returned to the press to support the next publications. Copyrights for author.

SKANKY POSSUM, 2925 Higgins Street, Austin, TX 78722.

SKEPTICAL INQUIRER, Kendrick Frazier, PO Box 703, Amherst, NY 14226, 716-636-1425, Skeptinq@aol.com. 1976. Articles, art, photos, cartoons, criticism, reviews, letters, news items, non-fiction. "Articles 2,000-3,500 words, reviews 600-1,200 words, news and comments 250-1,000 words, letters and forum 250-1,000 words. Contributors: Martin Gardner, Stephen Jay Gould, James Randi and Richard Dawkins. We investigate science, paranormal, and pseudo science claims from a skeptical point of view." circ. 40M. 6/yr. Pub'd 6 issues 2005; expects 6 issues 2006, 6 issues 2007. sub. price $35; per copy $4.95; sample free. Back issues: $4.95. Discounts: 50% off 10 or more copies. 68pp. Reporting time: 2 months. Simultaneous submissions accepted: no. Payment: issues. Copyrighted, does not revert to author. Pub's reviews: 25-30 in 2005. §Science, paranormal, psychology, popular culture, fringe science. Ads: none. Subjects: Education, Newsletter, Psychology, Science.

SKIDROW PENTHOUSE, Rob Cook, Stephanie Dickinson, 44 Four Corners Road, Blairstown, NJ 07825, 212-614-9505 (hm). 1998. Poetry, fiction, articles, art, photos, cartoons, interviews, parts-of-novels, long-poems, collages, non-fiction. "Skidrow Penthouse is published to give emerging and idiocyncratic writers a new forum. We're looking for authentic voices, surreal, experimental, New York School, formal or free verse. We want poets and fiction writers who sound like themselves, not workshop professionals. We showcase a poet in each issue by publishing a full-length collection within the magazine. We have published poetry by Andrew Kaufman, Maya Hebert, Gil Fagiani, John Colburn, Lisa Jarnot, Aase Berg, Johannes Goransson, Marc DePalo, Hilary Melton, Ronald Wardall, and James Grinwis." circ. 500. 1/yr. Pub'd 1 issue 2005; expects 1 issue 2006, 1 issue 2007. sub. price $20; per copy $12.50. Back issues: Inquire. Discounts: 2-10 copies 25%. 275pp. Reporting time: Three to four months. Simultaneous submissions accepted: Yes. Payment: Contributor's copy. Copyrighted, reverts to author. Pub's reviews. §Poetry, fiction, non-fiction collections, criticism. Ads: Full page $90Half page $45. Subjects: Arts, Experimental, Fiction, Non-Fiction, Photography, Poetry, Post Modern.

SKINNYDIPPING, Peter Kacalanos, Nakeditor, 51-04 39th Avenue, Woodside, NY 11377-3145, 718-651-4689, FAX 718-424-1883. 1990. Poetry, fiction, articles, art, photos, cartoons, interviews, satire, criticism, reviews, letters, plays, news items, non-fiction. "Skinnydipping is published by a large nudist social organization, The Skinnydippers, covering all the northeastern states. The club schedules many non-sexual clothing-optional activities every weekend. All submissions must be about nudism (health benefits, social opportunities, back-to-nature movement, loss of body shame, nudist resorts, nude beaches, legal hassles, etc.). Satire and parody are especially welcome. Length can range from 50 to 1,500 words. Illustrations can be anatomically correct; Skinnydipping's readers are nudes, not prudes. Write for free sample." circ. 3M-5M. 4/yr. Pub'd 4 issues 2005; expects 4 issues 2006, 4 issues 2007. sub. price $20, including membership; sample free. Back issues: free. Discounts: call for details. 12pp. Reporting time: 1 week or less. Simultaneous submissions accepted: yes. Publishes 25% of manuscripts submitted. Payment: no money; many free copies of magazine. Copyrighted, reverts to author. Pub's reviews: 6 in 2005. §All must be about social nudism or body acceptance, at least reviewed part must be. Ads: $130/$70/$90 2/3 page/$50 1/3/$30 1/6/$20 1/12. Subjects: Clothing, Counter-Culture, Alternatives, Communes, Erotica, Family, Feminism, Health, Libertarian, Massage, Men, New Age, Sex, Sexuality, Singles, Sociology, Sports, Outdoors, Women.

SKS Press, George Augustus Stallings Jr., 5000 Pennsylvania Avenue Suites D & E, Suitland, MD 20746-1062, 301.669.6550, 301.669.6528, 1.888.800.3360. 2003. Non-fiction. avg. press run 5,000. Pub'd 1 title 2005; expects 2-4 titles 2006, 12-20 titles 2007. Discounts: 5-10 copies 40%. 176-225pp. Reporting time: 6-8 weeks. Simultaneous submissions accepted: Yes. Publishes 25% of manuscripts submitted. Copyrights for author. Subjects: Christianity, Euthanasia, Death, Family, Grieving, Inspirational, Peace, Religion, Spiritual, Weddings.

SKYDIVING, Michael Truffer, 1725 North Lexington Avenue, DeLand, FL 32724, 904-736-9779, fax 904-736-9786. 1979. Articles, photos, cartoons, interviews, news items, non-fiction. "Contributors must be knowledgeable about sport parachuting." circ. 14,250. 12/yr. Pub'd 12 issues 2005; expects 12 issues 2006, 12 issues 2007. sub. price $20; per copy $4; sample $5. Back issues: $5. Discounts: depends, inquire. 64pp. Reporting time: 3 weeks. Copyrighted, rights revert to author, but depends. Pub's reviews: 10 in 2005. §Aviation, parachuting, skydiving. Ads: $817/$482/50¢ per word. Subjects: Aviation, Sports, Outdoors.

SKYLARK, Pamela Hunter, Editor-in-Chief, 2200 169th Street, Purdue University Calumet, Hammond, IN 46323, 219-989-2273, Fax 219-989-2165, poetpam49@yahoo.com. 1972. Poetry, fiction, articles, art, photos, interviews, satire, criticism, plays, non-fiction. "*Skylark* is the fine arts annual of Purdue University Calumet. We are equally interested in the works of known and unknown authors. All submissions must be accompanied by an S.A.S.E. with sufficient postage. Cover letter must state that submission is not simultaneous. We do not publish work that has been previously published in any form." circ. 800-1M. 1/yr. Pub'd 1 issue 2005; expects 1 issue 2006, 1 issue 2007. sub. price $8; per copy $8; sample $6.50 back issues. Discounts: orders of 10+ at $4.50/copy. 100pp. Reporting time: 3-6 months (do not read May 1 to November 1). Simultaneous submissions accepted: no. Publishes 20% of manuscripts submitted. Payment: copy of publication per poem, up to 3 copies for prose. Copyrighted, reverts to author. Ads: $120/$60/$30 1/4 page (rates subject to change). Subjects: Arts, Avant-Garde, Experimental Art, Drama, Essays, Fiction, Folklore, Graphics, Haiku, Humor, Non-Fiction, Poetry, Prose, Satire, Short Stories, Visual Arts.

Skyline West Press/Wyoming Almanac, Philip J. Roberts, 1409 Thomes, Laramie, WY 82072, 307-745-8205. 1982. Non-fiction. "Considers only manuscripts dealing with history, politics and culture of Wyoming or reference works on that geographic area." avg. press run 2M. Pub'd 1 title 2005; expects 1 title 2006, 2 titles 2007. Discounts: 40% to recognized dealers. 140-576pp. Reporting time: 4-5 weeks. Simultaneous submissions accepted: no. Publishes 10% of manuscripts submitted. Payment: varies with author (negotiable). Copyrights vary. Subjects: Great Plains, The West, Wyoming.

SLANT: A Journal of Poetry, James Fowler, University of Central Arkansas, PO Box 5063, Conway, AR 72035-5000, 501-450-5107. 1987. Poetry. "We use traditional and 'modern' poetry, even experimental, moderate length, any subject on approval of Board of Readers. Our purpose is to publish a journal of fine poetry from all regions. No haiku, no translations. No previously published poems. No multiple submissions. Recent contributors include Kaye Bache-Snyder, Anselm Brocki, Maureen Tolman Flannery, Paul Hostovsky, Barbara F. Lefcowitz, and Charles Harper Webb. Submission deadline is November 15 for annual spring publication." circ. 175. 1/yr. Pub'd 1 issue 2005; expects 1 issue 2006, 1 issue 2007. sub. price $10; per copy $10; sample $10. Back issues: $6. Discounts: negotiable. 120pp. Reporting time: 3-4 months from deadline. Simultaneous submissions accepted: no. Publishes 5% of manuscripts submitted. Payment: 1 copy on publication. Copyrighted, reverts to author. Ads: none. Subject: Poetry.

Slapering Hol Press, Margo Stever, Ann Lauinger, 300 Riverside Drive, Sleepy Hollow, NY 10591-1414, 914-332-5953, Fax 914-332-4825, info@writerscenter.org, www.writerscenter.org. 1990. Poetry. "We publish emerging poets who have never published in book form, and thematic anthologies. 2005, *A House That Falls*, Sean Nevin; 2004, *Juliet As Herself*, Nancy Taylor Everett; 2003, *Days When Nothing Happens*, David Tucker; *Water Stories*, Brighde Mullins; 2002, *The Scottish Cafe*, Susan H. Case; 2001, *The Landscape of Mind*, Jianqing Zheng; 1998, *The Last Campaign*, Rachel Loden; 1994, 1999, *What's Become of Eden: Poems of Family at Century's End*; 1992, *River Poems*. Annual chapbook competition deadline May 15th; send SASE or see website for guidelines." avg. press run 500. Pub'd 1 title 2005; expects 1 title 2006, 1 title 2007. Discounts: standard. 28-36pp. Reporting time: 3-4 months. Simultaneous submissions accepted: yes. Annual chapbook competition winner is paid $1000 plus 10 copies. Copyrights for author. Subject: Poetry.

SLEAZOID EXPRESS, Bill Landis, PO Box 620, Old Chelsea Station, New York, NY 10011. 1998. Articles, photos, interviews, criticism, reviews, non-fiction. "Recent contributor: Michelle Clifford." circ. 5M. 4/yr. Expects 4 issues 2006, 4 issues 2007. price per copy $7; sample $7. Back issues: on request. Discounts: none. 65pp. Simultaneous submissions accepted: no. Publishes a slim to 0% of manuscripts submitted. Payment: none. Copyrighted, reverts to author. Pub's reviews. §Film, biography, sex. Ads: $250 full page. Subjects: Arts,

Electronics, Erotica, Fantasy.

Sligo Press, 4 Willow Drive, Apt. 2, Provincetown, MA 02657-1638, 508-487-5113, Fax 508-487-5113, dplennon@comcast.net. 2000. Fiction, criticism. "Sligo Press was established to publish scholarly/critical work on Norman Mailer. *Norman Mailer: Works and Days* by J. Michael & Donna Pedro Lennon, a bio-bibliography, illus., 280 pp., published Fall 2000. *Norman Mailer's Letters on An American Dream, 1963-69* consisting of 76 letters, a critical introduction, appendices, bibliography and index published June 2004 in a limited edition of 110 copies. Edited by J. Michael Lennon. Norman Mailer's Provincetown: The Wild West of the East, published in a limited edition August 2005." avg. press run 500. Pub'd 1 title 2005; expects 1 title 2006, 2 titles 2007. 295pp. Simultaneous submissions accepted: yes. Payment: yes. Copyrights for author. Subjects: Bibliography, Biography, Criticism, Literature (General).

SLIPSTREAM, Slipstream Productions, Dan Sicoli, Robert Borgatti, Livio Farallo, Box 2071, New Market Station, Niagara Falls, NY 14301, 716-282-2616 (after 5 p.m., E.S.T.). 1980. Poetry, art, photos, parts-of-novels, long-poems, collages, concrete art. "Submissions are completely open. Query for themes. Reading through 2007 for a general issue. NO LONGER READING FICTION. Some recent contributors are Gerald Locklin, Martin Vest, Eric Gansworth, David Lawrence, Michelle Bitting, Christopher Walsh, Lori Jakiela, Khan Wong." circ. 600. 1/yr. Pub'd 1 issue 2005; expects 1 issue 2006, 1 issue 2007. sub. price $20; per copy $7; sample $7. Back issues: available upon request. 100pp. Reporting time: 2-8 weeks. Payment: presently only in copies. Copyrighted, reverts to author. Subjects: Arts, Graphics, Photography, Poetry.

Slipstream Productions (see also SLIPSTREAM), Dan Sicoli, Robert Borgatti, Livio Farallo, Box 2071, New Market Station, Niagara Falls, NY 14301. 1980. Poetry, fiction, art, photos, long-poems, collages. avg. press run 500. Pub'd 2 titles 2005; expects 3 titles 2006, 2 titles 2007. 40pp. Simultaneous submissions accepted: yes.

SLUG & LETTUCE, Christine Boarts, PO Box 26632, Richmond, VA 23261-6632. 1986. Photos, reviews, music. "Networking newspaper for communication and contacts within the underground punk scene. Includes photographs and reviews of zines and music." circ. 9M. 4/yr. Pub'd 4 issues 2005; expects 4 issues 2006, 4 issues 2007. sub. price 4 60¢ stamps; per copy SASE-60¢; sample SASE-60¢. Back issues: 60¢ stamp per issue. 20pp. Not copyrighted. Pub's reviews: tons in 2005. §Punk, alternative music, alternative culture, environmental, political left. Ads: 2-1/2 X 5 $25, 5 X 5 $50, 5 X 7-1/2 $75. Subject: Networking.

THE SMALL BUSINESS ADVISOR, Joseph Gelb, PO Box 436, Woodmere, NY 11598, 516-374-1387, Fax 516-374-1175, smalbusadv@aol.com, www.smallbusinessadvice.com. 1974. Poetry, articles, cartoons, reviews, letters. "Length of material 900-1500 words." circ. 1M. 12/yr. Pub'd 2 issues 2005; expects 12 issues 2006, 12 issues 2007. sub. price $45; per copy $7.25; sample $3. Back issues: $8. Discounts: Bulk rate to be negotiated. 16pp. Reporting time: 2 months. Simultaneous submissions accepted: yes. Publishes 60% of manuscripts submitted. Payment: copies 2 times. Copyrighted. Pub's reviews: 1 in 2005. §Business management, marketing, human resources, cash management. Subjects: Business & Economics, Insurance, Labor, Law, Management.

Small Dogs Press, Susan Sabo, PO Box 4127, Seal Beach, CA 90740, 562-673-8488, email: susan@smalldogspress.com, www.smalldogspress.com. 2003. Fiction. "Looking for unusual, full-length, literary novels. Visit our website for more information." avg. press run 3M. Expects 2 titles 2006. Discounts: write to discuss. 300pp. Reporting time: 4-6 weeks. Simultaneous submissions accepted: yes. Payment: to be discussed. Copyrights for author. Subject: Fiction.

SMALL FRUITS REVIEW, David G. Himelrick, D. Himelrick, Horticulture Dept., 137 Julian C. Miller Hall, Baton Rouge, LA 70803-2120, 334-844-3042, dhimelri@acesag.auburn.edu. 2000. Art, photos, reviews, non-fiction. "This is a refereed scientific journal covering all aspects of small fruit production. Contains research, reviews and extension educational materials." 4/yr. Expects 4 issues 2006, 4 issues 2007. sub. price $40; per copy $10; sample free. Discounts: yes. Reporting time: 9 months. Simultaneous submissions accepted: no. Publishes 85% of manuscripts submitted. Payment: none. Copyrighted. Pub's reviews. §Fruit. Ads: none. Subjects: Gardening, Horticulture.

Small Helm Press, Pearl Evans, 4235 Porte de Palmas, Unit 182, San Diego, CA 92122-5123, 707-763-5757, smallhelm@comcast.net. 1986. Non-fiction. "Small Helm Press is unable to receive unsolicited manuscripts at this time." Expects 1 title 2007. Discounts: 3 up 40%, 25 up 50% for bookstores. 128pp. Payment: individual basis. Copyrights for author. Subjects: China, Christianity, Culture, Education, Non-Fiction, Public Affairs.

THE SMALL PRESS BOOK REVIEW, Henry Berry, Editor, PO Box 176, Southport, CT 06890, 203-332-7629. 1985. Reviews, news items. "Reviews: 150-200 words, plus annotation books also received. Electronically published for libraries and on-line computer networks, including the Internet and America Online." 10/yr. Pub'd 10 issues 2005; expects 10 issues 2006, 10 issues 2007. Reporting time: 2 months. Not copyrighted. Pub's reviews: 800 in 2005. §Interested in all areas. Subjects: Book Reviewing, Magazines.

THE SMALL PRESS REVIEW/SMALL MAGAZINE REVIEW, Dustbooks, Len Fulton, Editor-Publisher; Bob Grumman, Contributing Editor (Experioddica); Michael Andre, Contributing Editor (New York

Letter); Richard Lauson, Associate Editor, PO Box 100, Paradise, CA 95967-9999, 530-877-6110, 800-477-6110, fax: 530-877-0222, email: publisher@dustbooks.com, Website: http://www.dustbooks.com. 1966. Articles, cartoons, interviews, reviews, letters, news items. "The *Small Press Review* seeks to study and promulgate the small press and little magazine (i.e. the *independent* publisher) worldwide. It was started in 1966 as part of an effort by its publisher to get a grip on small press/mag information since no one at the time (or for some years thereafter) seemed interested in doing it. It is also designed to promote the small press in a variety of ways. *SPR/SMR* publishes reviews, guest editorials and other material related to BOTH books and magazines published by small publishers. We are always on the lookout for competently written reviews (yes, we have a 'style sheet'), as long as they hold to a page in length and review a title published by a small press or magazine. *SPR/SMR* has regular 'News Notes' sections which give info about small press activities, manuscript needs (*and there are many!*), contests, prizes and so on. We print full-info listings bi-monthly on many new small presses and many new magazines which come into our database throughout the year. A particularly popular feature of the magazine is the 'Free Sample Mart' which lists about two dozen free samples of small magazines and books available each issue." circ. 3.5M. 6/yr. Pub'd 6 issues 2005; expects 6 issues 2006, 6 issues 2007. sub. price individuals $25/yr, $33/2 yrs, $36/3 yrs, $39/4 yrs; institutions $29/yr, $39/2 yrs, $47/3 yrs, $52/4 yrs; per copy $2.50; sample free. Back issues: inquire. Discounts: schedule available for agents. 24pp. Reporting time: 3-6 weeks. Publishes 75% of manuscripts submitted. Not copyrighted. Pub's reviews: 200 in 2005. §Anything published by a small press. Ads: $150/$90/$75/$50/(display). Subjects: Book Reviewing, Magazines, Publishing, Reference, Reviews.

SMARANDACHE NOTIONS JOURNAL, American Research Press, Dr. Sabin Tabirca, J. McGray, Box 141, Rehoboth, NM 87322, m_l_perez@yahoo.com, http://www.gallup.unm.edu/~smarandache/. 1990. Articles. "Research papers on Smarandache Notions such as: Smarandache type functions, sequences, numbers, primes, constants, classes of paradoxes and quantum paradoxes, paradoxist geometries (partially Euclidean and partially non-Euclidean), manifolds, algebraic structures and neutrosophic algebraic structures, neutrosophy (a generalization of dialectics), neutrosophic logic (generalization of fuzzy logic), neutrosophic set (generalization of fuzzy set), neutrosophic probability and statistics (generalization of classical and imprecise probabilities), Smarandache hypothesis that there is no speed barrier in the universe, unmatter (a new form of matter), tautologies, Dezert-Smarandache Theory of plausible and paradoxist reasoning in information fusion (DSmT), etc." circ. 5M. 1-2/yr. Pub'd 1 issue 2005; expects 1 issue 2006, 1-2 issues 2007. sub. price $39.95; per copy $39.95; sample $39.95. Back issues: none available. 250-300pp. Reporting time: 1 month. Simultaneous submissions accepted: yes. Publishes 80% of manuscripts submitted. Payment: free copies of the magazine. Copyrighted, reverts to author. Pub's reviews: 4 in 2005. §Papers, books, etc. about Smarandache Notions. Ads: $20/page. Subject: Mathematics.

SMARTISH PACE, Stephen Reichert, PO Box 22161, Baltimore, MD 21203, www.smartishpace.com. 1999. Poetry, reviews, long-poems. "Recent contributors: Paul Muldoon, Stephen Dunn, Maxine Kumin, Carl Dennis, Diane Wakoski, Campbell McGrath, and Carol Muske-Dukes." circ. 500. 2/yr. Pub'd 2 issues 2005; expects 2 issues 2006, 2 issues 2007. sub. price $20; per copy $10; sample $10. Back issues: $10 Issue 1, $6 Issues 2-9. Discounts: none. 145pp. Reporting time: 2-8 months. Simultaneous submissions accepted: yes. Publishes 1-3% of manuscripts submitted. Payment: copies of issue. Copyrighted, reverts to author. Pub's reviews: 10-20 in 2005. §Recent books of poetry. Ads: inquire. Subjects: Book Reviewing, Haiku, Journals, Literary Review, Literature (General), Magazines, Poetry, Reviews, Translation, Writers/Writing.

The Smith (subsidiary of The Generalist Assn., Inc.), Harry Smith, Publisher, 69 Joralemon Street, Brooklyn, NY 11201-4003. 1964. Poetry, fiction. "Not currently reading unsolicited mss. For book orders only please contact: Arts End Books, POB 441, W. Dover VT 05356 or marshallbrooks.com." avg. press run 1.5M. Discounts: varies to bookstores and wholesalers. 80pp. Copyrights for author. Subjects: Essays, Fiction, Non-Fiction, Novels, Poetry, Prose, Short Stories.

Genny Smith Books, Genny Smith, Editor, Publisher, 23100 Via Esplendor, Villa 44, Cupertino, CA 95014, 650-964-4071, www.liveoakpress.com. 1976. Articles, photos, non-fiction. "I specialize in publications on the Eastern Sierra region of California—to date, guidebooks, natural history, regional history, and sets of historic postcards. My guidebooks (I edit and coauthor them) to this mountain-and-desert vacation area include chapters on roads, trails, natural history and history. Best known localities in this region are Owens Valley and Mammoth Lakes. These guidebooks are for sightseers, campers, hikers, fishermen, nature lovers and history buffs. Alternate address: PO Box 1060, Mammoth Lakes, CA 93546 (summer only). All my books are now published by The Live Oak Press, LLC PO Box 60036, Palo Alto, CA 94306, (650) 853-0197." avg. press run 7M. Pub'd 1 title 2005; expects 1 title 2006, 1 title 2007. 224pp. Payment: Varies from sharing of royalties to flat payment for material. Copyrights for author. Subjects: Americana, Autobiography, California, Conservation, Earth, Natural History, Geology, History, Native American, Non-Fiction, Sports, Outdoors, Mark Twain, Water, The West, Women.

Richard W. Smith Military Books, 114 Gates Drive, Hendersonville, TN 37075-4840. avg. press run 1.5M.

Pub'd 1 title 2005; expects 1 title 2006. 200pp. Payment: yes. Copyrights for author.

Smith-Johnson Publisher, Irwin Gray, 175-14 73rd Avenue, Flushing, NY 11366-1502, 718-969-3825, fax 718-591-0227. 2001. Non-fiction. "Business/management/entrepreneurial." avg. press run 4500. Pub'd 1 title 2005. Discounts: 50% discount to the trade. 300pp. Reporting time: 2 months. Simultaneous submissions accepted: Yes. Publishes 10% of manuscripts submitted. Payment: individual arrangements. Copyright: individual arrangements. Subjects: Business & Economics, Consulting, Education, Engineering, Leadership, Management, Motivation, Success.

SMOKE, Windows Project, Dave Ward, Liver House, 96 Bold Street, Liverpool L1 4HY, England. 1974. Poetry, fiction, art, photos, cartoons, long-poems, collages, concrete art. "Tom Pickard, Jim Burns, Dave Calder, Roger McGough, Frances Horovitz." circ. 500. 2/yr. sub. price £3/6 issues incl. postage; per copy 50p plus post; sample 50p plus post. 24pp. Reporting time: as quickly as possible. Publishes 1.28% of manuscripts submitted. Payment: none. Not copyrighted. No ads. Subjects: Fiction, Poetry.

Smyrna Press, Dan Georgakas, Barbara Saltz, Box 1151, Union City, NJ 07087, Fax 201-617-0203, smyrnapress@hotmail.com. 1964. Poetry, fiction, art, parts-of-novels, collages, plays, non-fiction. "We try to publish 1-3 books a year which combine the latest technical breakthroughs with a concern for social change that is essentially Marxist but undogmatic. Our current projects combine art and politics as well as themes of sexual liberation. We can use good line drawings or woodcuts. We also distribute books for Intervention Press, Pella Publishing, and some titles of Lake View Press. Query before sending any material. Sample copies of literary books, $2; sample copies of art books, $3." avg. press run 2M. Pub'd 2 titles 2005; expects 2 titles 2006, 2 titles 2007. Discounts: 40% bookstores, 10% education, bulk by arrangement, 30% prepaid bookstores. 60-250pp. Reporting time: 2-3 weeks, query before submitting. Simultaneous submissions accepted: no. Publishes 1% of manuscripts submitted. Payment: copies and 10% net. Copyrights for author. Subjects: Anarchist, Arts, Bibliography, Bilingual, Cuba, Drama, Feminism, Fiction, Graphics, Labor, Middle East, Poetry, Socialist, Third World, Minorities, Women.

Snake Hill Press (see also SENSATIONS MAGAZINE), David Messineo J, P.O. Box 90, Glen Ridge, NJ 07028. 1999. Poetry. "Manuscript submissions by invitation only. Prospective authors should start by submitting poetry to Sensations Magazine (www.sensationsmag.com, "Submit" button, then "Poetry" button - deadlines Oct 1, 2005 and June 15, 2006)." avg. press run 500. Expects 1 title 2007. Discounts: None. Book 1: 52 pgs. Book 2: 264 pgs. Book 3: 20 pgs. Book 4 (hardcover): 200 pgs. Book 5 (hardcover): 100 pgs (est.). Reporting time: Varies. Simultaneous submissions accepted: No. Publishes 1% of manuscripts submitted. Payment: Varies. Copyrights for author. Subjects: Americana, Civil Rights, Culture, History, Human Rights, Italian-American, Lifestyles, Marketing, Poetry, Politics, Publishing, Research, Sex, Sexuality, Technology, Young Adult.

SNAKE NATION REVIEW, Roberta George, Founding Editor; Jean Arambula, Managing Editor, 110 #2 West Force, Valdosta, GA 31601, 912-249-8334. 1989. Poetry, fiction, art, photos. circ. 1M. 3/yr. Pub'd 3 issues 2005; expects 3 issues 2006, 3 issues 2007. sub. price $20; per copy $6; sample $6 (includes mailing). Back issues: $6 (includes mailing). Discounts: 40% to bookstores, jobbers. 110pp. Reporting time: 3-6 months. Simultaneous submissions accepted: yes. Publishes 10% of manuscripts submitted. Payment: 2 copies or prize money. Copyrighted, reverts to author. Ads: $100/$50/$25.

SNAKELETS, Rattlesnake Press, Kathy Kieth, P.O. Box 1647, Orangevale, CA 95662, 916-966-8620, kathykieth@hotmail.com. 2004. Poetry, art, photos, cartoons, reviews. "Poetry by CHILDREN ages 0-12." circ. approx. 100. 3 times/yr: Oct., Feb., May. Pub'd 2 issues 2005; expects 3 issues 2006, 3 issues 2007. sub. price free; per copy free; sample free. Back issues: $2. 30pp. Reporting time: a week. Simultaneous submissions accepted: no. Copyrighted, reverts to author.

Snapshot Press, John Barlow, PO Box 132, Waterloo, Liverpool L22 8WZ, United Kingdom, info@snapshotpress.co.uk, www.snapshotpress.co.uk. 1997. Poetry. "Snapshot Press specializes in haiku, tanka and short poetry, publishing anthologies, individual collections, and *The Haiku Calendar*. It runs two established annual contests: 'The Snapshot Press Collection Competition' for unpublished collections of haiku or tanka, and 'The Haiku Calendar Competition'. Please see the website for further details. (N.B. Publication of the journals *Snapshots* (haiku) and *Tangled Hair* (tanka) ceased in 2006.)." Expects 12 titles 2006, 6 titles 2007. Discounts: 33%. 64-224pp. Simultaneous submissions accepted: no. Publishes 3% of manuscripts submitted. Payment: Royalties paid annually on individual collections. Subjects: Haiku, Poetry.

SNIPER LOGIC, Campus Box 226, University of Colorado, Boulder, CO 80309.

Snow Group, PO Box 10864, Bainbridge Island, WA 98110, patrick@createyourowndestiny.com.

SNOW LION NEWSLETTER & CATALOG, Snow Lion Publications, Inc., PO Box 6483, Ithaca, NY 14851, www.snowlionpub.com. 1985. "News, announcements and products on Tibetan culture." circ. 30M. 4/yr. Pub'd 4 issues 2005; expects 4 issues 2006, 4 issues 2007. price per copy free. 60pp. Payment: none.

Copyrighted, reverts to author. Ads: see website. Subject: Magazines.

Snow Lion Publications, Inc. (see also SNOW LION NEWSLETTER & CATALOG), Jeffrey M. Cox, PO Box 6483, Ithaca, NY 14851, 607-273-8519, Fax 607-273-8508, www.snowlionpub.com. 1980. Non-fiction. "180 titles in print." avg. press run 5M. Pub'd 17 titles 2005; expects 15 titles 2006, 15 titles 2007. Discounts: 40% average. 250pp. Publishes 30% of manuscripts submitted. Payment: 8% average. Copyrights for author. Subject: Buddhism.

SNOW MONKEY, Kathryn Rantala, Christiel Cottrell, PO Box 127, Edmonds, WA 98020, www.ravenna-press.com/snowmonkey. 1999. Poetry, fiction, art, photos. "We prefer poetry limited to 2 pages, fiction under 2,000 words, prose poems, flash fiction. Experimental work highly encouraged, as long as it is interesting and displays craft. Bias against overt violence gratuitous to art. Send 3-5 poems, 3 prose poems per submission. Email ok, no html please." circ. 150. 2/yr. Pub'd 2 issues 2005; expects 2 issues 2006, 2 issues 2007. sub. price $10; per copy $6; sample $6. Back issues: $3 + postage. Discounts: standard. 90-100pp. Reporting time: varies, try for no longer than 1 month. We accept simultaneous submissions if advised. Publishes 10-20% of manuscripts submitted. Payment: 1 copy of the issue. Copyrighted, reverts to author. Subjects: Avant-Garde, Experimental Art, Fiction, Poetry, Translation, Visual Arts, Washington (state).

SNOWY EGRET, Philip Repp, Editor; Karl Barnebey, Publisher, PO Box 29, Terre Haute, IN 47808. 1922. Poetry, fiction, articles, art, interviews, satire, criticism, reviews, letters, parts-of-novels, long-poems, non-fiction. "Emphasis on natural history and human beings in relation to nature from literary, artistic, philosophical, and historical points of view. Prose generally not more than 3M words but will consider up to 10M; poetry generally less than page although long poems will be considered. Interested in works that celebrate the abundance and beauty of nature and examine the variety of ways, both positive and negative, through which human beings connect psychologically and spiritually with the natural world and living things. Looking for nature-oriented original graphics (offset prints, lithographs, woodcuts, etc) that can be editioned as part of an issue. Review copies of books desired. Originality of material or originality of treatment and literary quality and readability important. Payment on publication plus 2 contributor's copies. Recent contributors: Conrad Hilberry, David Abrams, James Armstrong, Justin D'Ath, Patricia Hooper. Send #10 SASE for writer's guidelines." circ. 500. 2/yr. Pub'd 2 issues 2005; expects 2 issues 2006, 2 issues 2007. sub. price $15/1 year, $25/2 years; per copy $8; sample $8. Back issues: available on request. 56pp. Reporting time: 2 months. Simultaneous submissions accepted: yes. Publishes less than 5% of manuscripts submitted. Payment: prose, $2 mag page; poetry, $4/poem, $4 mag page. Copyrighted, reverts to author. Pub's reviews: none in 2005. §Review essays only. Ads: none. Subjects: Animals, Biology, Birds, Earth, Natural History, Fiction, Nature, Poetry.

SO TO SPEAK: A Feminist Journal of Language & Art, Heather Holliger, Editor, So To Speak, George Mason University, 4400 University Drive, MS 2D6, Fairfax, VA 22030-4444, sts@gmu.edu, www.gmu.edu/org/sts. 1991. Poetry, fiction, art, photos, interviews, reviews, long-poems, plays, non-fiction. "*So to Speak* aims to feature work that addresses issues of significance to women's lives and movements for women's equality. We are especially interested in pieces that explore issues of race, class, and sexuality in relation to gender. We publish work by emerging and established writers that lives up to a high standard of language, form, and meaning. *So to Speak* offers annual Poetry, Fiction, and Nonfiction Contests (see our website for details)." circ. 1.3M. 2/yr. Pub'd 2 issues 2005; expects 2 issues 2006, 2 issues 2007. sub. price $12; per copy $7; sample $7. Back issues: $3. 100pp. Reporting time: 3-4 months. Simultaneous submissions accepted: yes. Publishes 10% of manuscripts submitted. Payment: 2 copies. Copyrighted, reverts to author. Ads: $50/$25-negotiable, also exchange ads. Subjects: Arts, Book Reviewing, Creativity, Feminism, Fiction, Interviews, Lesbianism, Multicultural, Non-Fiction, Photography, Poetry, Visual Arts, Women, Writers/Writing.

SO YOUNG!, Anti-Aging Press, Julia M. Busch, PO Box 142174, Coral Gables, FL 33114, 305-662-3928, Fax 305-661-4123. 1996. Poetry, articles, reviews, letters, news items, non-fiction. "Positive, very up-paced. 200-500 words. Aromatherapy, cosmetics, acupressure, short subjects also, short *up* poetry. Recent contributors: Nancy Dahlberg, Joe Polansky, astrologers, experts in fields, Phil Breman investigative reporter. Milton Feher, Relaxation/Dance, therapist, Lisa Curtis, president Sophrological Society." 4/yr. Pub'd 6 issues 2005; expects 4 issues 2006, 4 issues 2007. sub. price $35 USA, Canada; per copy $9 USA, Canada; sample same. Back issues: $6 before issue #45, #45 and after $9. Discounts: 25-49 20%, 50-100 30%, 100-499 40%, 500-999 50%, 1000+ 55%. 12pp. Reporting time: 1 month. Simultaneous submissions accepted: yes. Payment: newsletter copies. Copyrighted, reverts to author. Pub's reviews: 30+ in 2005. §Anti-aging, positive thought, holistic health, spiritual, cutting-edge medical breakthrough. Subjects: Alcohol, Alcoholism, Conservation, Energy, Health, How-To, Humor, Men, Poetry, Safety, Self-Help, Senior Citizens, Singles, Spiritual, Tapes & Records, Women.

SOCIAL ANARCHISM: A Journal of Practice and Theory, Howard J. Ehrlich, 2743 Maryland Avenue, Baltimore, MD 21218, 410-243-6987. 1980. Fiction, articles, art, photos, cartoons, interviews, satire, criticism, reviews, letters, non-fiction. "Essays should be between 1,000 and 15,000 words. Book reviews: 500-2,000 words. Recent contributors: Neala Schleuning, Kingsley Widmer, Brian Martin, Colin Ward, Elaine Leeder,

Gaetano Piluso, David Bouchier, Murray Bookchin, Jane Myerding." circ. 1.2M. 2/yr. Pub'd 2 issues 2005; expects 2 issues 2006, 2 issues 2007. sub. price $16 for 4 issues; per copy $5; sample $5. Back issues: $5. Discounts: 40%. 96pp. Reporting time: 6 weeks. Payment: 3 copies. Not copyrighted. Pub's reviews: 40 in 2005. §Anarchism, feminism, ecology, radical arts and culture. Subjects: Anarchist, Community, Counter-Culture, Alternatives, Communes, Environment, Feminism, Non-Violence.

SOCIAL JUSTICE: A JOURNAL OF CRIME, CONFLICT, & WORLD ORDER, Global Options, Gregory Shank, PO Box 40601, San Francisco, CA 94140, 415-550-1703, socialjust@aol.com, www.socialjusticejournal.org. 1974. Poetry, articles, interviews, satire, reviews, news items, non-fiction. "Maximum length: 30 double-spaced ms pages, including footnotes. Recent authors: Edward Herman, Tony Platt, Samir Amin, Elaine Kim, Nancy Sheper-Hughes. A journal of progressive criminology, international law, human rights, and social conflicts." circ. 3M. 4/yr. Pub'd 4 issues 2005; expects 4 issues 2006, 4 issues 2007. sub. price $40 individual, $80 institution; per copy $12.95 individual, $20 institutions; sample $10. Back issues: same as single copy price or available from University Microfilms, Ann Arbor, MI. Discounts: agency 15%, trade discount to stores, distribution handled through De Boer, Ingram, Ubiquity. 180-200pp. Reporting time: 90 days. Simultaneous submissions accepted: no. Payment: none. Copyrighted, does not revert to author. Pub's reviews: 3 in 2005. §Criminology, international law, civil liberties, minority issues, pedagogy, women, human rights. Ads: $125/$75. Subjects: Book Reviewing, Civil Rights, Community, Crime, Drugs, Human Rights, Labor, Law, Prison, Race, Socialist, Society, Sociology, Third World, Minorities.

SOCIAL POLICY, Michael J. Miller, Editor; Renee Miller, Managing Editor, c/o Organize Training Center, 442 Vicksburg Street, San Francisco, CA 94114-3831, 650-557-9720, Fax 650-355-1299, sclplcy@aol.com. 1970. Articles, art, photos, interviews, criticism, reviews, letters, non-fiction. "Articles run 2M-5M words, on contemporary social thought and policy analysis (environmental, economics, community development, community organizing, labor movements, social movements, education). Recent special issues dealt with self-help, campaign finance reform, national service, welfare reform, labor, school reform. *Social Policy* is the magazine of progressive ideas for the 21st century." circ. 3M. 4/yr. Pub'd 4 issues 2005; expects 4 issues 2006. sub. price $45 individuals, $185 institutions; sample $5. Back issues: $10. Discounts: $18.50 subscription agent. 64pp. Reporting time: 2-4 weeks. Simultaneous submissions accepted: no. Publishes 50% of manuscripts submitted. Payment: none. Copyrighted, rights do not revert to author unless requested. Pub's reviews: 2 in 2005. §Nonfiction, social policy materials, esp. in area of economics and human services, sociology, social change, community organizing, social movements, labor movements. Ads: none. Subjects: Community, Education, Labor, Society, Sociology.

SOCIAL PROBLEMS, University of California Press, James Holstein, Editor; Stephen L. Franzois, Associate Editor, University of California Press, 2000 Center Street, Suite 303, Berkeley, CA 94704-1223, 510-643-7154. 1953. Articles, reviews, non-fiction. "Editorial address: P.O. Box 1881, Milwaukee WI, 53201-1881. Copyrighted by Society for the Study of Social Problems." circ. 3747. 4/yr. Pub'd 4 issues 2005; expects 4 issues 2006, 4 issues 2007. sub. price $136 (+ $20 air freight); per copy $36; sample free. Back issues: same as single copy price. Discounts: foreign subs. agent 10%, one-time order 10+ 30%, standing orders (bookstores): 1-99 40%, 100+ 50%. 160pp. Copyrighted, does not revert to author. Ads: $295/$220. Subjects: Society, Sociology.

SOCIETE, Technicians of the Sacred, Courtney Willis, 1317 N. San Fernando Blvd., Suite 310, Burbank, CA 91504. 1983. Poetry, fiction, articles, art, photos, interviews, reviews, music, non-fiction. "Related to African, neo-African systems, religion, magic, hermetic, etc." circ. 500. 3/yr. Pub'd 3 issues 2005; expects 3 issues 2006, 3 issues 2007. sub. price $15; per copy $10; sample $10. Back issues: $10. 130pp. Reporting time: 4 weeks. Payment: copy of issue. Copyrighted. Pub's reviews: 1 in 2005. §Voodoo-neo African, African religions, magic, occult, religion, gnosticism, hermetics. Subjects: Caribbean, Cuba, Cults, Folklore, Latin America, H.P. Lovecraft, Myth, Mythology, Networking, Occult, Religion, Reprints, Spiritual.

SOCIOLOGICAL PERSPECTIVES, University of California Press, Peter M. Nardi, Editor, University of California Press, 2000 Center St., Suite 303, Berkeley, CA 94704-1223, 510-643-7154. 1957. Articles. "Editorial Address: Sociology Dept., Pitzer College, The Claremont Colleges, 1050 N. Mills Ave., Claremont, CA 91711. Copyrighted by the Pacific Sociological Association." circ. 1736. 4/yr. Pub'd 4 issues 2005; expects 4 issues 2006, 4 issues 2007. sub. price Inst. $251; per copy Inst. $67. Discounts: foreign subs. agents 10%, 10+ one-time orders 30%. 170pp. Copyrighted, does not revert to author. Ads: $295/$220. Subject: Sociology.

THE SOCIOLOGICAL QUARTERLY, University of California Press, Kevin Leicht, Editor; Beth Lyman, Managing Editor, University of California Press, 2000 Center St., Suite 303, Berkeley, CA 94704-1223, 510-643-7154. 1959. Articles. "Editorial address: Dept. of Sociology, Univ. of Iowa, W505 Seashore Hall, Iowa City, IA 52242. Copyrighted by the Midwest Sociological Society." circ. 2214. 4/yr. Pub'd 4 issues 2005; expects 4 issues 2006, 4 issues 2007. sub. price $75 indiv., $255 inst.; per copy $25 indiv., $67 inst.; sample same as single copy. Discounts: foreign subs. agents 10%, 10+ one-time orders 30%. 192pp. Copyrighted, does not revert to author. Ads: $295/$220. Subjects: Education, Psychology, Research, Social Work, Sociology.

A SOFT DEGRADE, Chad Schultz, 58 2nd Street NE, Medicine Hat, AB T1A 5K7, Canada, diefortheflag@hotmail.com, www.asoftdegrade.com. 1999. Poetry, fiction, articles, art, photos, satire, criticism, letters, collages, news items, non-fiction. ''"This is a stylish zine with a bitter self reflective interior like the inside of a seedy motel: 'Kamloops. First motel I've stayed in alone. Am I supposed to call for a prostitute.' Poems and grainy black and white pictures. It's about finding a way to live that isn't everybody else's way to live, though nobody here wants to end up alone in that motel room again." - Hal Niedzviecki. Canada's only current AD FREE magazine. New 8.5x5.5 size format and glorious full color artwork.'' circ. 100-200+. 1-2/yr. Expects 2 issues 2006, 2-4 issues 2007. price per copy $6; sample $2 digital sample. Back issues: $2 b/w. 55pp. Simultaneous submissions accepted: Yes. Publishes 75% of manuscripts submitted. Payment: to be negotiated. Not copyrighted. Subjects: Anarchist, Arts, Avant-Garde, Experimental Art, Canada, Color, Counter-Culture, Alternatives, Communes, Creativity, Design, Dreams, Non-Fiction, Photography, Poetry, Satire, Surrealism, Visual Arts.

Soft Skull Press, Sander Hicks, Nick Mamatas, 55 Washington Street, Ste. 804, Brooklyn, NY 11201-1066, 212-673-2502, Fax 212-673-0787, sander@softskull.com, www.softskull.com. 1992. Poetry, fiction, art, photos, cartoons, satire, music, plays, news items, non-fiction. ''Seeking radical, sharp, punk, intelligent, avant pop, fiction, and explosive, radical, political nonfiction. Writers under 35 especially welcome. No bourgeois boredom or middle-class whining. Recent books: *No More Prisons* by William Upski Winsatt, *What the Fuck? The Avant Porn Anthology* by Michael Hemmingson.'' avg. press run 3M. Pub'd 10 titles 2005; expects 12 titles 2006, 18 titles 2007. Discounts: distributed wholesale for fundraisers, 55% for 10+ copies. 120pp. Reporting time: 3 weeks. Simultaneous submissions accepted: no. Publishes 3% of manuscripts submitted. Payment: advance negotiable (most under $1,000), 7/8/9% royalty per 5,000 sold. Copyrights for author. Subjects: Absurdist, African-American, AIDS, Anarchist, Artificial Intelligence, Avant-Garde, Experimental Art, Beat, Biotechnology, Bisexual, Business & Economics, Civil Rights, Communism, Marxism, Leninism, Counter-Culture, Alternatives, Communes, Culture, Zines.

SOJOURN: A Journal of the Arts, Desiree Ward, Editor; Susan Rushing-Adams, Managing Editor; Solana DeLamont, Managing Editor, Office of Arts & Humanities, JO 31, Box 830688, Univ. of Texas-Dallas, Dallas, TX 75083-0688, Email: sojourn@utdallas.edu Web site: www.sojournjournal.org. 1986. Poetry, fiction, art, photos, satire, parts-of-novels, long-poems, collages, plays, non-fiction. circ. 500. 1/yr. Pub'd 1 issue 2005; expects 1 issue 2006, 1 issue 2007. No subscriptions yet. Back issues: Send SASE, or donate online to receive a copy of our latest issue while in stock. 160pp. Reporting time: May-June. Simultaneous submissions accepted: no. Publishes 5-10% of manuscripts submitted. Payment: 1 copy. Not copyrighted. Ads: yes-see website. Subjects: Drama, Fiction, Non-Fiction, Photography, Poetry, Translation.

SOLAS Press, Dominic Colvert, PO Box 4066, Antioch, CA 94531, 925-978-9781, Fax 925-978-2599, info@solaspress.com. 1998. Non-fiction. ''Book-length philosophy and religion.'' avg. press run 1.5M. Pub'd 1 title 2005; expects 2 titles 2006, 3 titles 2007. Discounts: 40% bookstores, 20% libraries. 300pp. Reporting time: 2 months. Simultaneous submissions accepted: no. Publishes a variable % of manuscripts submitted. Payment: 10%. Copyrights for author. Subjects: Arts, Catholic, History, Humanism, Philosophy, Religion, Science.

Solcat Publishing, Cristiano Nogueira, Rua Visconde de Piraja 82 sala 508, Ipanema - Rio de Janeiro - RJ Cep: 22411-000, Brazil, +55-21-3813-6740. 2003. Non-fiction. ''Editor of Rio for Partiers, the most visual guide to Rio de JaneiroEditor of Advanced Macking , the shy man's guide to one-night stands.'' avg. press run 4000. Pub'd 2 titles 2005; expects 4 titles 2006, 8 titles 2007. Discounts: 1-10 14$11-20 13$31-5 12$51-100 11$101-500 10$500 9$. 160pp. Reporting time: 4 days. Simultaneous submissions accepted: Yes. Publishes 80% of manuscripts submitted. Payment: to be agreed. Copyright: to be agreed. Subjects: Cartoons, Chicago, English, Language, Latin America, Marketing, Men, Music, Nature, Newsletter, Science, Singles, Sports, Outdoors, Translation, Visual Arts.

SOLO, Glenna Luschei, Founding Editor & Editor-in-Chief; David Oliveira, Co-Editor; Jackson Wheeler, Co-Editor, 5146 Foothill, Carpinteria, CA 93013, berrypress@aol.com. 1996. Poetry, criticism, reviews, long-poems. ''Recent contributors include: Fred Chappell, Jane Hirshfield, Carolyn Kizer, Linda Pastan, Carol Muske, Ronald Bayes, Forest Gander, Ron Koertge, Robert Creeley, Robert Bly, and Sherman Alexie.'' circ. 1M. 2/yr. Pub'd 2 issues 2005; expects 2 issues 2006, 2 issues 2007. sub. price $16/2 issues; per copy $9; sample $9. Back issues: $5 for old *Cafe Solo*. Discounts: tradition. 130pp. Reporting time: 1 month. Simultaneous submissions accepted: no. Publishes 75% of manuscripts submitted. Payment: copies. Copyrighted, rights reverting negotiable. Pub's reviews: 1 book of poetry review, 4 small book review(s) notes in 2005. §Poetry, criticism. Subjects: Criticism, Poetry.

SOLO FLYER, David B. McCoy, 1112 Minuteman Avenue NW, Massillon, OH 44646. 1979. Poetry. ''Three or more 4-page flyers will be published a year, each by an individual author. For the near future, we will be publishing prose poetry only. Also, accepting only email submissions. dbmccoy@eudoramail.com.'' circ. 100. 3/yr. Pub'd 3 issues 2005; expects 3 issues 2006, 3 issues 2007. sample price free with SASE. 4pp. Reporting time: 1-3 months. Simultaneous submissions accepted: yes. Publishes 5-10% of manuscripts submitted. Payment: 20-25 copies. Copyrighted, reverts to author. Subject: Poetry.

$olvency International Inc., Publishing, Olga Favrow, Rod Griffin, PO Box 17802, Clearwater, FL 33762, 727-536-2779, Fax 727-507-8320, solv1@juno.com, www.solvencyinternational.com. 1996. Fiction, non-fiction. Pub'd 3 titles 2005; expects 4 titles 2006, 5 titles 2007. Discounts: book trade 55%. 250pp. Reporting time: 60 days. Simultaneous submissions accepted: yes. Publishes 1% of manuscripts submitted. Payment: 10% of list price. Copyrights for author. Subjects: Fiction, Non-Fiction.

SOM Publishing, division of School of Metaphysics (see also THRESHOLDS JOURNAL), Dr. Barbara Condron, CEO & Editor-in-Chief, 163 Moon Valley Road, Windyville, MO 65783, 417-345-8411, www.som.org. 1973. "Educational, inspirational, uplifting books designed to raise the consciousness of humanity." avg. press run 5M. Pub'd 1 title 2005; expects 4 titles 2006, 4 titles 2007. Discounts: 40% trade, 50% jobbers, 20% organizations, churches, groups without sales tax number. 180-224pp. Payment: none. SOM holds copyright. Subjects: Dreams, Health, How-To, Metaphysics, New Age, Science Fiction, Spiritual.

SOMETHING TO READ, Carolyn Frances, PO Box 810, Livermore, CA 94551, smalltown@ldsliving.com, http://altlmiss.tripod.com/smalltown. 2003. Poetry, fiction, long-poems. "A celebration of nature, life, home, and humanity, *Something to Read* seeks to bring uplifting and moving writing to the reader. We appreciate vibrant writing and beautiful, lyric language. We look for strongly defined characters and delightful or clever images." circ. 100. 4/yr. Expects 2 issues 2006, 4 issues 2007. sub. price $16; per copy $5. 20pp. Reporting time: 3-5 months. Simultaneous submissions accepted: no. Payment: contributor copy. Not copyrighted. Subjects: Community, Fantasy, Fiction, Literature (General), Medieval, Mormon, Mystery, Nature, Poetry.

SONGS OF INNOCENCE, Pendragonian Publications, Michael Pendragon, Editor & Publisher, PO Box 719, New York, NY 10101-0719, mmpendragon@aol.com. 1999. Poetry, fiction, articles, art, interviews, criticism, reviews, letters, long-poems, non-fiction. "Poetry, short stories (3,500 word maximum), essays and b/w artwork which celebrate the nobler aspects of mankind and the human experience. Rhymed, metered, lyrical verse preferred. Publishes literary poetry and prose in the tradition of Blake, Shelley, Keats, Whitman, Emerson, Wordsworth, Thoreau and Twain." circ. 200. 1-2/yr. Pub'd 2 issues 2005; expects 2 issues 2006, 2 issues 2007. sub. price $25/3 issues; per copy $10; sample $10. Back issues: $5. 150+pp. Reporting time: up to 1 year. Simultaneous submissions accepted: yes. Publishes 5% of manuscripts submitted. Payment: 1 copy. Not copyrighted. Pub's reviews: 25 in 2005. §Romantic poetry, the Bardic tradition, prophetic verse. Subjects: Essays, Fantasy, Fiction, Literary Review, Literature (General), Myth, Mythology, Poetry, Reviews, Short Stories.

SONORA REVIEW, David James Poissant; Mark Polansak, Editors-in-Chief, Dept. of English, University of Arizona, Tucson, AZ 85721, 520-624-9192. 1980. Poetry, fiction, articles, interviews, satire, criticism, reviews, letters, parts-of-novels, non-fiction. "We publish poetry, fiction, and creative non-fiction, as well as interviews and book reviews. Submissions should be accompanied by an SASE. Editors change every year. Please address work to the appropriate genre editor: Fiction, Poetry, etc. Business or subscription matters and any questions or forms should be addressed to the Managing Editor. Revisions only upon editorial request. Simultaneous submissions accepted." circ. 800. 2/yr. Pub'd 2 issues 2005; expects 2 issues 2006, 2 issues 2007. sub. price $16; per copy $8; sample $6. Discounts: 40% to bookstores. 120pp. Reporting time: 3-6 months. Simultaneous submissions accepted: yes. Publishes 1% of manuscripts submitted. Payment: 2 contributor's copies. Copyrighted, reverts to author. Pub's reviews: 2 in 2005. Ads: $90/$45. Subject: Literary Review.

Sonoran Publishing, George A. Fathauer, 6700 W. Chicago Street, Suite 1, Chandler, AZ 85226-3337, 480-961-5176. 1994. Art, non-fiction. "Books on history of radio and electronics, for historians and collectors of radios. Purchased existing inventory and publishing rights to several titles from another publisher." avg. press run 3M. Pub'd 1 title 2005; expects 2 titles 2006, 1 title 2007. Discounts: 6-24 copies 40%, 25-49 copies 42%, 50-99 44%, 100+ 46%. 250pp. Reporting time: 60 days. Simultaneous submissions accepted: yes. Publishes 20% of manuscripts submitted. Payment: usually 10% royalty. Does not copyright for author. Subjects: Antiques, Collectibles, Electronics, History, Radio.

•Soul (see also SOUL), Aisha Johnson, 806 8th Street Thomas, Birmingham, AL 35214, Soul@delimaehowar.org. 2003. Poetry, fiction, art, long-poems, non-fiction. avg. press run 250. Pub'd 1 title 2005; expects 2 titles 2006, 5 titles 2007. Discounts: 5 copes or more 10 copies. 100-150pp. Reporting time: varies. Payment: varies. Copyrights for author. Subjects: African Literature, Africa, African Studies, Black, Community, Creativity, Culture, Education, Essays, Fiction, Memoirs, Non-Fiction, Peace, Poetry, Short Stories, Spiritual, Writers/Writing.

•SOUL, Soul, Aisha Johnson, 806 8th Street Thomas, Birmingham, AL 35214, Soul@delimaehowar.org. 2006. Poetry, fiction, long-poems, non-fiction. circ. 500. 1000/yr. Expects 2 issues 2007. sub. price 20.00; per copy 10.00; sample 10.00. Back issues: inquire. Discounts: 5 copies of 10% off. 125pp. Reporting time: varies. Simultaneous submissions accepted: No. Publishes 25% of manuscripts submitted. Payment: varies.

Copyrighted. Ads: 25.00 half50.00 whole page.

Sound View Publishing, Inc., James Green, P.O. Box 696, Shoreham, NY 11786-0696, 631-899-2481, Fax 631-899-2487, 1-888-529-3496, info@SoundViewPublishing.com, www.SoundViewPublishing.com. 2003. Non-fiction. "We deal in Self Help books designed to serve as platforms for speakers." avg. press run 3000. Expects 1 title 2006, 1 title 2007. Discounts: Distributors/Wholesalers—55%.Institutions/Classrooms— 40%.Retail Bookstores—2-4 20%, 5-99 40%, 100+ 50%.Libraries—3 or more 20%.Outside Sales—3 or more 20%, even case lots 40%. 280pp. Reporting time: We do not take unsolicited manuscripts. Simultaneous submissions accepted: No. Publishes 0% of manuscripts submitted. Does not copyright for author. Subjects: Inspirational, Non-Fiction, Self-Help.

Soundboard Books, 933 Exmoor Way, Sunnyvale, CA 94087, 408-738-1705, sboardbooks@sbcglobal.net. 1990. Non-fiction. avg. press run 2M. Expects 1 title 2006, 1 title 2007. Discounts: 2-15 20%, 16+ 40%. 48pp. Copyrights for author. Subject: Biography.

SOUNDINGS EAST, J.D. Scrimgeour, Advisory Editor; Todd Doehner, Prose Editor; Jeremy Lakazcyck, Poetry Editor, English Dept., Salem State College, Salem, MA 01970, 978-542-6205. 1973. Poetry, fiction, non-fiction. "Publishes poetry, fiction and creative non-fiction. We read Sept. 1-March 1. For 2006-07, in addition to general submissions, we are calling for submissions in poetry, fiction, and nonfiction for a special section: The War in Iraq." circ. 1.5M. 1/yr. Pub'd 1 issue 2005; expects 1 issue 2006, 1 issue 2007. sub. price $10; per copy $5; sample $3. Back issues: usually $3 per copy. 80pp. Reporting time: 2-3 months. Simultaneous submissions accepted: yes. Publishes 5% of manuscripts submitted. Payment: 2 free copies. Not copyrighted. Subjects: Fiction, Poetry.

Sourcebooks, Inc., Mark Warda, Todd Stocke, 1935 Brookdale Road, Ste. 139, Naperville, IL 60563, 630-961-3900; Fax 630-961-2168. 1987. Non-fiction. "Shipping Address: 1725 Clearwater/Largo Rd. S., Clearwater, FL 33756. Also publish under the imprint of Sphinx Publishing." Pub'd 15 titles 2005; expects 65 titles 2006, 65 titles 2007. 130pp. Reporting time: 3 months. Copyrights for author. Subjects: Business & Economics, How-To, Law, Real Estate.

•Sources (see also THE SOURCES HOTLINK), Ulli Diemer, 489 College Street, Suite 305, Toronto ON M6G 1A5, Canada, Phone: 416-964-7799. Fax: 416-964-8763. 1977. Articles, reviews, news items, non-fiction. "We publish materials related to journalism, media, media criticism, research, skepticism, propaganda, public relations, public speaking, communications.Recent contributors include Dean Tudor, Lynn Fenske, Allan Bonner, Ann Douglas, Cathleen Fillmore, Mark LaVigne, Barbara Florio Graham, Ulli Diemer, Steve Slaunwhite, Peter Urs Bender, Barrie Zwicker." avg. press run 3000. Pub'd 5 titles 2005; expects 6 titles 2006, 6 titles 2007. Discounts: Distributors 50%Retailers & Bookstores 40%Insitutions & classrooms - negotiated. 280pp. Reporting time: 1 month. Simultaneous submissions accepted: Yes. Publishes 50% of manuscripts submitted. Payment: Royalty varies per title. No advances. Payments quarterly. Copyrights for author. Subjects: Awards, Foundations, Grants, Canada, Communication, Journalism, Marketing, Media, Public Relations/ Publicity, Reference.

•THE SOURCES HOTLINK, Sources, Ulli Diemer, 489 College Street, Suite 305, Toronto ON M6G 1A5, Canada, Phone: 416-964-7799. Fax: 416-964-8763. 1996. Articles, interviews, reviews, news items, non-fiction. "Articles, interviews, case studies, reviews, personal experiences related to media relations, public relations, and getting publicity." circ. 1200. 4/yr. Pub'd 4 issues 2005; expects 4 issues 2006, 4 issues 2007. sub. price $20; per copy $5; sample $2. Back issues: inquire. 8pp. Reporting time: 1 month. Simultaneous submissions accepted: Yes. Publishes 70% of manuscripts submitted. Copyrighted, reverts to author. Pub's reviews: 12 in 2005. §Books, periodicals and Web sites related to media, public relations, communications, self-promotion, public speaking, publicity. Ads: Full page $6752/3 page $5401/2 page $4351/3 page $3501/4 page $2901/6 page $195. Subjects: Advertising, Self-Promotion, Communication, Journalism, Internet, Media, Public Relations/Publicity, Reviews.

SOUTH AMERICAN EXPLORER, Don Montague, 126 Indian Creek Road, Ithaca, NY 14850, 607-277-0488, Fax 607-277-6122, explorer@samexplo.org. 1977. Articles, photos, interviews, reviews, letters, news items, non-fiction. circ. 7M. 4/yr. Pub'd 4 issues 2005; expects 4 issues 2006, 4 issues 2007. sub. price $22/4 issues; subs included in $40 Club membership; per copy $4; sample $3. Back issues: $4. Discounts: $1 per issue. 65pp. Reporting time: 8 weeks. Simultaneous submissions accepted: yes. Publishes 80% of manuscripts submitted. Payment: negotiable. Copyrighted, reverts to author. Pub's reviews: 16 in 2005. §Latin America, natural history, field sciences, adventure, folk art, outdoor sports, travel, South American history. Ads: $775/$395/25, also color $975/$495. Subjects: Earth, Natural History, Latin America.

SOUTH CAROLINA REVIEW, Wayne Chapman, Editor, Ctr. for Electronic & Digital Publishing, Clemson University, 611 Strode Tower, Box 340522, Clemson, SC 29634-0522, 864-656-3151; 864-656-5399. 1968. Poetry, fiction, articles, interviews, satire, criticism, reviews, non-fiction. "Past contributors: Steve Almond, Alberto Rios, Jane Marcus, George Will, Mary Gordon, Tim O'Brien, Richard Rodriguez, Christopher

Dickey.'' circ. 500. 2/yr. Pub'd 2 issues 2005. sub. price $22 + $3 s/h; per copy $14; sample $14. Back issues: $14. 192-256pp. Reporting time: 4-9 weeks. Simultaneous submissions accepted: no. Payment: copies. Copyrighted. Pub's reviews: 18 in 2005. §Poetry, literary history, criticism, contemporary fiction. Subjects: Fiction, Poetry.

SOUTH DAKOTA REVIEW, Brian Bedard, Editor, Department of English / University of South Dakota, 414 East Clark St., Vermillion, SD 57069, 605-677-5184, 605-677-5966, email: sdreview@usd.edu, website: http://www.usd.edu/sdreview. 1963. Poetry, fiction, articles, art, interviews, criticism, parts-of-novels, non-fiction. ''Issues vary in content; not every type of material will be in each issue. Still committed to Western subjects and focuses as primary interest, though all regions considered if awareness of natural world is reflected.'' circ. 550. 4/yr. Pub'd 4 issues 2005; expects 4 issues 2006, 4 issues 2007. sub. price $30, $45/2 years; international: $38, $61/2 years; per copy $10; sample $8. Back issues: some are available, send for price list. Discounts: 40% to bookstores. 120-150pp. Reporting time: 8-10 weeks, except during summer. Simultaneous submissions accepted: yes, as long as noted on cover letter. Publishes 3%-5% of manuscripts submitted. Payment: 2 copies plus 1 year subscription. We reserve first and reprint rights, all others revert to writer upon publication. Ads: none. Subjects: Biography, Criticism, Essays, Fiction, Great Plains, Literature (General), Midwest, Native American, Nature, Non-Fiction, Poetry, Short Stories, Southwest, The West.

South End Press, Loie Hayes, Jill Petty, Joey Fox, Alexander Dwinnell, Jocelyn Burrell, Asha Tall, 7 Brookline Street #1, Cambridge, MA 02139-4146, 617-547-4002, email: southend@southendpress.org. 1977. Criticism, non-fiction. ''At South End Press—a collectively managed, non-profit publisher of non-fiction—our goal is to provide books that encourage critical thinking and constructive action, thereby helping to create fundamental social change. Since 1977, we have released over 200 titles addressing the key issues of the day, focusing on political, economic, cultural, gender, race, and ecological dimensions of life in the United States and the world.'' avg. press run 3M. Pub'd 6 titles 2005; expects 10 titles 2006, 11 titles 2007. Discounts: bookstores 20-50%. 250pp. Reporting time: 6-8 weeks. Simultaneous submissions accepted: yes. Publishes 1-5% of manuscripts submitted. Payment: 11% of discount price. Copyrights for author. Subjects: Anarchist, Environment, Feminism, Labor, Peace, Politics, Race, Socialist.

Southeast Missouri State University Press (see also BIG MUDDY: Journal of the Mississippi River Valley), Susan Swartwout, MS 2650, One University Plaza, Cape Girardeau, MO 63701, (573) 651-2044, fax (573)651-5188, upress@semo.edu, www6.semo.edu/universitypress. 2002. Poetry, fiction, articles, art, photos, interviews, reviews, news items, non-fiction. ''We don't publish children's literature, romance, westerns. We do have a special fondness for material from or about the Mississippi River Valley, but have and will publish good literature outside that focus. Recent authors include Linda Busby Parker, William Trowbridge, Morley Swingle, Robert Hamblin.'' avg. press run 2500. Pub'd 4 titles 2005; expects 4 titles 2006, 4 titles 2007. Discounts: Distributors 55%Bookstores 40%Classrooms 40%. 300pp. Reporting time: book manuscript: 6 - 9 months. Simultaneous submissions accepted: Yes. Publishes 8% of manuscripts submitted. Payment: We pay royalties. Copyrights for author. Subjects: African-American, Americana, Biography, Civil Rights, Civil War, Essays, Fiction, History, Kentucky, Multicultural, Non-Fiction, Novels, Poetry, Reviews, Short Stories.

THE SOUTHERN CALIFORNIA ANTHOLOGY, James Ragan, Editor-in-Chief, Master of Prof. Writing Program, WPH 404/Univ. of Southern Calif., Los Angeles, CA 90089-4034, 213-740-3252. 1983. Poetry, fiction. ''Fiction submissions - 25 pp. maximum. Poetry submissions - limited to 5 poems. Please enclose SASE. Recent contributors include John Updike, James Merrill, Robert Bly, Joyce Carol Oates, James Ragan, Marge Piercy, Doris Grumbach, Amiri Baraka, Czeslaw Milosz, Andrei Voznesensky, Yevgeny Yevtushenko, Donald Hall, Denise Levertov, X.J. Kennedy, and W.S. Merwin.'' circ. 1M. 1/yr. Pub'd 1 issue 2005; expects 1 issue 2006, 1 issue 2007. sub. price $9.95; per copy $9.95; sample $5. Back issues: $5. Discounts: Bookstores 40%. 140pp. Reporting time: 3 months. Simultaneous submissions accepted: no. Publishes 10% of manuscripts submitted. Payment: 3 copies. Copyrighted, reverts to author. Subjects: Fiction, Poetry.

SOUTHERN HUMANITIES REVIEW, Dan R. Latimer, Co-Editor; Virginia M. Kouidis, Co-Editor, 9088 Haley Center, Auburn University, AL 36849, 334-844-9088, www.auburn.edu/english/shr/home.htm. 1967. Poetry, fiction, articles, interviews, satire, criticism, reviews, parts-of-novels, non-fiction. ''No e-mail submissions. Recent contributors: Andrew Hudgins, Walt McDonald, R.T. Smith, Patricia Foster, Paul Crenshaw, and Stephen Dunn.'' circ. 700. 4/yr. Pub'd 4 issues 2005; expects 4 issues 2006, 4 issues 2007. sub. price $15 U.S., $20 foreign; per copy $5 U.S.; $7 foreign; sample $5 U.S.; $7 foreign. Back issues: same as single copy price/or complete volumes, $15 US $20 foreign. Discounts: none. 100pp. Reporting time: 1-3 months. Simultaneous submissions accepted: no. Publishes poetry 2%, fiction 1%, essays 12% of manuscripts submitted. Payment: $100 best essay, $100 best story, $50 best poem *published* each volume. Copyrighted, reverts to author. Pub's reviews: 26 in 2005. §Criticism, fiction, poetry. Ads: $100 inside back cover, full page only, arranged well in advance. Subjects: Book Reviewing, Criticism, Fiction, Literary Review, Poetry.

Southern Illinois University Press, John Stetter, PO Box 3697, Carbondale, IL 62902, 618-453-6615 (phone) 618-453-1221 (FAX). 1955. Poetry, non-fiction. ''SIU Press publishes books in rhetoric and composition, poetry, Civil War and regional history, film studies, theater studies, criminology, aviation, and related fields. All poetry should be submitted to Allison Joseph, Editor, The Crab Orchard Review, English Dept. Southern Illinois University, Carbondale, IL 62902. Please query Dr. Joseph before submitting poetry manuscripts. As a scholarly publisher SIU Press follows the standard external peer review process for all manuscripts." avg. press run 800. Pub'd 50 titles 2005; expects 56 titles 2006, 58 titles 2007. Discounts: Standard trade discounts apply. 300-500pp. Reporting time: 2 - 4 months. Simultaneous submissions accepted: No. Payment: Depends on the kind of book submitted. We will copyright in the name of the author on request, otherwise in the name of the university. Subjects: African-American, Audio/Video, Aviation, Botany, Crime, Great Plains, History, Illinois, Jack Kerouac, Movies, Nature, Non-Fiction, Performing Arts, Scandinavia.

SOUTHERN INDIANA REVIEW, Ron Mitchell, Editor, College of Liberal Arts, Univ. of Southern Indiana, 8600 University Blvd., Evansville, IN 47712, 812-461-5202, Fax 812-465-7152, email sir@usi.edu. 1994. Poetry, fiction, articles, art, photos, interviews, criticism, reviews, letters, parts-of-novels, long-poems, plays, non-fiction. circ. 1000. 2/yr. Pub'd 2 issues 2005; expects 2 issues 2006, 2 issues 2007. sub. price $16; per copy $10; sample $10. Back issues: $6. 150pp. Reporting time: 2 months. Simultaneous submissions accepted: yes. Publishes 10% of manuscripts submitted. Payment: 2 copies of magazine. Copyrighted, reverts to author. Pub's reviews: 6 in 2005. §Midwestern themes.

Southern Methodist University Press, Kathryn Lang, PO Box 750415, Dallas, TX 75275-0415, 214-768-1433, 214-768-1428 (fax), 800-826-8911 (orders), klang@mail.smu.edu, www.tamu.edu/upress. 1937. Fiction, non-fiction. "The SMU Press is known nationally as a publisher of books of the highest quality for the "educated general reader." We publish 10-12 titles a year in the areas of creative nonfiction, ethics and human values, literary fiction, medical humanities, performing arts, Southwestern studies, and sport." Pub'd 6 titles 2005; expects 9 titles 2006, 12 titles 2007. Discounts: Wholesale discounts (returnable accounts): 1 or more copies 50%.Wholesale discounts (non-returnable accounts): 1 or more 55%.Retail discounts (returnable accounts): 1 or more copies 45%.Retail discounts (non-returnable accounts): 50%. 288pp. Reporting time: 6-8 months. Simultaneous submissions accepted: Yes. Publishes 10% of manuscripts submitted. Payment: 10% net royalties; $500 advance; annual payment. Copyrights for author. Subjects: Medicine, Non-Fiction, Novels, Short Stories, Southwest, Sports, Outdoors, Texas.

SOUTHERN POETRY REVIEW, Robert Parham, Editor; James Smith, Associate Editor, Armstrong Atlantic State University, Dept. of LLP, 11935 Abercorn Street, Savannah, GA 31419-1997, 912-921-5633, Fax 912-927-5399, smithjam@mail.armstrong.edu, www.spr.armstrong.edu. 1958. Poetry. "No restrictions on form, style or content." 2/yr. Pub'd 2 issues 2005; expects 2 issues 2006, 2 issues 2007. sub. price $12, individual; $15 institutional; per copy $6; sample $6. Back issues: $6. 80pp. Reporting time: 6-8 weeks. Simultaneous submissions accepted: Yes, but please indicate. Publishes 5% of manuscripts submitted. Payment: publication; 2 contributor copies. Copyrighted, reverts to author. Ads: none. Subject: Poetry.

THE SOUTHERN QUARTERLY: A Journal of the Arts in the South, Douglas Chambers, Editor; Ann Branton, Managing Editor, 118 College Drive #5078, The University of Southern Mississippi, Hattiesburg, MS 39406-5078, 601-266-4350, Fax 601-266-6393, www.usm.edu/soq. 1962. Articles, art, photos, interviews, criticism, reviews, music, letters. "We are commited to the interdisciplinary study of southern culture through reasoned consideration of the arts. We define "the arts" broadly to include literature, poetry, folklore, anthropology and history, as well as the traditional arts. Likewise, we take an expansive view of "the South" to incorporate the circum-Caribbean. We will continue to publish articles based on original research or new critical analysis, and will seek to address the wide range of interests of our audience. We are continuing the annual "Bibliography of the Visual Arts and Architecture in the South," and will feature more extensive reviews of recent books and films. The *Quarterly* encourages submissions from all disciplines, though you will see a slight shift in emphasis from literature to history. Inquiries and manuscripts should be addressed to *The Southern Quarterly* at the above address." circ. 650. 4/yr. Expects 4 issues 2006, 4 issues 2007. sub. price $18/yr, $32/2 yr individual; $35/yr institutions, add $5 for international mailing; per copy $10. plus shipping; sample upon request. Back issues: vary, price list available. Discounts: subscription agency $15/individual subscriptions; $30 institutional subscriptions, add $5 for int'l mailing. 160pp. Reporting time: 3-5 months. Simultaneous submissions accepted: no. Payment: 2 copies of journal and 1 yr. subscription. Copyrighted, does not revert to author. Pub's reviews. §Studies of the arts in the South: literature, history, music, art, architecture, popular and folk arts, theatre and dance. Ads: 100/$75 or exchange free. Subjects: African-American, Anthropology, Archaelogy, Architecture, Arts, Book Reviewing, Criticism, Dance, Drama, Folklore, History, Memoirs, Music, South, Theatre, Visual Arts.

THE SOUTHERN REVIEW, Bret Lott, Editor, Old Presidents' House, Louisiana State University, Baton Rouge, LA 70803-5005, 225-578-5108. 1965 new series (1935 original series). Poetry, fiction, articles, art, photos, interviews, criticism, reviews, letters, parts-of-novels, non-fiction. "We emphasize craftsmanship and intellectual content. We favor articles on contemporary literature and on the history and culture of the South. Recent contributors: Lewis P. Simpson, W.D. Snodgrass, Seamus Heaney, Reynolds Price, Lee Smith, Mary

Oliver, Medbh McGuckian, Eavan Boland, Andrea Barrett, Ann Beattie, and B.H. Fairchild." circ. 3.1M. 4/yr. Pub'd 4 issues 2005; expects 4 issues 2006, 4 issues 2007. sub. price $25 ind., $50 inst.; per copy $8 ind., $16 inst.; sample $8 ind., $16 inst. Back issues: same. 250pp. Reporting time: 6-8 weeks. Publishes 1% or less of manuscripts submitted. Payment: $30 per page. Copyrighted, reverts to author. Pub's reviews: 12 in 2005. §Contemporary literature, fiction, poetry, culture of the South. Ads: $250/$150. Subjects: Fiction, Literary Review, Literature (General), Poetry.

•**SOUTHWEST COLORADO ARTS PERSPECTIVE,** Heather Leavitt, Art Director, Publisher; Sonja Horoshko, Editor, P.O. Box 843, Mancos, CO 81328-0843, 970-739-3200, 970-533-0642, www.artsperspective.com. 2004. Poetry, articles, art, photos, cartoons, interviews, music, letters, collages. "Arts Perspective is a venue for artists in Southwest Colorado. We strive to share the lives of artists with our readers by bringing them into the artists' life, their studio, share their vision, their passion and their world. We use freelance writers and do not have a staff. We have published works by Leanne Goebel, Sonja Horoshko, Jeff Mannix and Jonathan Thompson. Each issue features 2-4 in-depth articles about artists, a studio visit, poem, exhibition and events listings, an opinion, resources for artists and an image gallery of fine artworks." circ. 8,000-10,000 per quarter. Quarterly. Pub'd 4 issues 2005; expects 4 issues 2006, 4 issues 2007. sub. price $20; sample Free. Back issues: $5. 32pp. Reporting time: 2-14 days. Simultaneous submissions accepted: No. Payment: $75 for 750-1000 words, $15 for poetry. Copyrighted. §Fine art of Southwest Colorado communities. Ads: $700/$400/$250/$85/$25/(display). Subjects: Arts, Avant-Garde, Experimental Art, Awards, Foundations, Grants, Book Arts, Calligraphy, Festivals, Graphics, Haiku, Music, Performing Arts, Photography, Poetry, Politics, Prose, Theatre.

Southwest Research and Information Center (see also VOICES FROM THE EARTH), Annette Aguayo, Editor, PO Box 4524, Albuquerque, NM 87196-4524, 505-262-1862; Fax 505-262-1864; Info@sric.org; www.sric.org. 1974. Articles, reviews, news items. "Resource information for citizen action of all kinds. Review of small and 'alternative' press publications in more than 30 categories of environmental justice and social change issues." avg. press run 2.5M. Pub'd 4 titles 2005; expects 4 titles 2006, 4 titles 2007. Discounts: 40% to distributors. 48pp. Reporting time: 1 month. Payment: occasional funding secured. Does not copyright for author. Subjects: Book Reviewing, Energy, Environment, Health, Indigenous Cultures, New Mexico, Newsletter, Nuclear Energy, Society, Southwest, Water.

SOUTHWEST REVIEW, Willard Spiegelman, Editor-in-Chief; Jennifer Cranfill, Managing Editor, Southern Methodist University, P.O. Box 750374, Dallas, TX 75275-0374, 214-768-1037, www.southwestreview.org. 1915. Poetry, fiction, articles, criticism, parts-of-novels, long-poems, non-fiction. "The fourth oldest, continuously published literary quarterly in the country. The *Southwest Review* tries to discover works by new writers and publish them beside those of more established authors. All submissions should be typed neatly on white paper. Manuscripts must be accompanied by a stamped, self-addressed envelope for reply, and will not be returned unless SASE includes sufficient postage. *SWR* prefers not to receive simultaneous, email, or fax submissions, and does not consider work that has been published previously. Manuscripts are not accepted during the months of June, July, and August. We have no specific limitations as to theme. Preferred length for articles and fiction is 3,500 to 7,000 words. We demand very high quality in poetry; we accept both traditional and experimental writing; we place no arbitrary limits on length. Morton Marr Poetry Prize contest awards $1,000, first prize, and $500, second prize, to poem by a writer who has not yet published a first book. See web site for entry fee and contest guidelines." circ. 1,500. 4/yr. Pub'd 4 issues 2005; expects 4 issues 2006, 4 issues 2007. sub. price 1 yr $24; 2 yrs $42; 3 yrs $65.; per copy $6; sample $6. Back issues: Available on request. Discounts: 15% to agencies. 144pp. Reporting time: 3 months. Simultaneous submissions accepted: no. Publishes 3% of manuscripts submitted. Payment: Yes. Amount varies. Copyrighted, reverts to author. Ads: Full page: $250; Half Page: $150; Covers 2 & 3: $300; Cover 4: $400. Subjects: Essays, Fiction, Literature (General), Non-Fiction, Poetry.

SOU'WESTER, Allison Funk, Co-Editor; Geoff Schmidt, Co-Editor, Southern Illinois University, Edwardsville, IL 62026-1438. 1960. Poetry, fiction, interviews, reviews, long-poems, non-fiction. "We have no particular editorial biases or taboos. We publish the best poetry and fiction we can find." circ. 500. 2/yr. Pub'd 2 issues 2005; expects 2 issues 2006, 2 issues 2007. sub. price $12; per copy $6; sample $6. Back issues: price varies. 128pp. Reporting time: 3 months. Simultaneous submissions accepted: yes. Publishes 2% of manuscripts submitted. Payment: 2 copies; 1 year subscription. Copyrighted, reverts to author. Pub's reviews: §Books of poems and short fiction. Ads: $90/$50. Subjects: Fiction, Poetry.

THE SOW'S EAR POETRY REVIEW, The Sow's Ear Press, Errol Hess, Managing Editor; Kristin Camitta Zimet, Editor, 355 Mt Lebanon Rd, Donalds, SC 29638-9115, errol@kitenet.net. 1989. Poetry, art, photos, interviews, reviews. "No length limits on poems. We try to be eclectic. We look for work which 'makes the familiar strange, or the strange familiar,' which shines the light of understanding on the particular, and which uses sound and rhythms to develop meaning. Recent contributors: Penelope Scambly Schott, Virgil Suarez, Susan Terris, Madeline Tiger, and Steven Lautermilch." circ. 500. 4/yr. Pub'd 4 issues 2005; expects 4 issues 2006, 4 issues 2007. sub. price $15; per copy $5; sample $5. Discounts: trade 30%. 32pp. Reporting time: 3-4 months. Simultaneous submissions accepted: yes. Publishes 5% of manuscripts submitted. Payment: 2 copies. Copyrighted, reverts to author. Pub's reviews: 3 in 2005. §Any poetry. Ads: none. Subjects: Poetry, Visual Arts.

The Sow's Ear Press (see also THE SOW'S EAR POETRY REVIEW), Kristin Zimet, Editor; Errol Hess, Managing Editor, 355 Mt Lebanon Rd, Donalds, SC 29638-9115, errol@kitenet.net. 1989. Poetry. "Our present activity is restricted to publishing *The Sow's Ear Poetry Review*. Our book publication may be resumed later.We look for poems that are carefully crafted, keenly felt, and freshly perceived. We like poems with voice, a sense of place, delight in language, and a meaning that unfolds. Recent contributors: Lynne Knight, Jeanne Emmons, Emily Rosko, Jeffrey Ethan Lee, Susan Terris, Peter Meinke. We sponsor two contests annually, in Sept.-Oct. for individual poems and March-April for chapbooks. SASE or e-mail request for complete guidelines." avg. press run 600. Reporting time: 3 months for non-contest submissions, varied for contest submissions. Simultaneous submissions accepted: yes. Publishes 5% of manuscripts submitted. Copyrights for author. Subject: Poetry.

•**SP QUILL QUARTERLY MAGAZINE, Shadow Poetry,** Marie Summers, 1209 Milwaukee Street, Excelsior Springs, MO 64024, Fax: (208) 977-9114, spquill@shadowpoetry.com, http://www.shadow-poetry.com/magazine/spquill.html. 2004. Poetry, fiction, articles, art, interviews, reviews, letters. "Wants high-quality poetry, short stories, quotes, and artwork. Does not want anything in poor taste, or poorly crafted poetry." Quarterly. Pub'd 4 issues 2005; expects 4 issues 2006, 4 issues 2007. sub. price $20 yr/USA, $24 yr/Canada, $28 yr/International; per copy $7.95 USA, $8.95 Canada, $9.95 International; sample $7.95 USA, $8.95 Canada, $9.95 International. 52-60pp. Reporting time: Three weeks before printing or sooner. Simultaneous submissions accepted: No. Publishes 8% of manuscripts submitted. Copyrighted, reverts to author. Pub's reviews: 12 in 2005. §Poetry. Ads: Line Ads: (up to three lines), $5.00; Business Card, $15.00; Quarter Page (2.25" x 3.5"), $25.00; Half Page: (4.5" x 3.5"), $50.00; Full Page (4.5" x 7"): $100.00; Back Cover (4.5" x 7"), $200.00. Subjects: Arts, Creativity, Essays, Literary Review, Literature (General), Poetry, Short Stories.

SPACE AND TIME, Space and Time Press, Gordon Linzner, Editor-in-Chief; Gerard Houarner, Fiction Editor; Linda D. Addison, Poetry Editor, 138 West 70th Street 4-B, New York, NY 10023-4432. 1966. Poetry, fiction, art, cartoons. "*Space and Time* is a fantasy and science fiction magazine, we have a very broad definition of fantasy (which includes SF) and we aren't fussy about sub-genre barriers, but we want nothing that obviously falls outside of fantasy (i.e. straight mystery, mainstream, etc.). Prefer under 10M words." circ. 2M. 2/yr. Pub'd 2 issues 2005; expects 2 issues 2006, 2 issues 2007. sub. price $10; per copy $5 + 1.50 p/h; sample $5 + 1.50 p/h. Discounts: 40% off on orders of 5 or more copies of an issue. 48pp. Reporting time: 6-8 weeks. Simultaneous submissions accepted: no. Publishes 1% of manuscripts submitted. Payment: 1¢ per word on acceptance. Copyrighted, reverts to author. Ads: $150/$75/50¢ per word ($10 min.). Subjects: Fantasy, Science Fiction.

Space and Time Press (see also SPACE AND TIME), Gordon Linzner, Publisher & Editor, 138 West 70th Street 4-B, New York, NY 10023-4468. 1984. Fiction. "Not actively soliciting at this time (overstocked). Fantasy and science fiction novels—preferably ones that don't fit neatly into a sub-genre. Interested in seeing borderline fantasy-mysteries, along lines of George Chesbro's *Mongo* series. We are still overstock and not considering new book proposals for the indefinite future. We *are* looking for short stories for the magazine." avg. press run 1M. Expects 1 title 2006, 1 title 2007. Discounts: 1 30%, 2-4 35%, 5-24 40%. 160pp. Payment: 10% of cover price, based on print run, within 3 months of publication. Copyrights for author. Subjects: Fantasy, Science Fiction.

SPARE CHANGE NEWS, Marc D. Goldfinger, Editor; Cynthia Baron, Assistant Editor, 1151 Massachusetts Avenue, Cambridge, MA 02138, 617-497-1595, scnews@homelessempowerment.org. 1992. circ. 10M. 26/yr. Pub'd 26 issues 2005; expects 26 issues 2006, 26 issues 2007. sub. price $25; per copy $1; sample $1. 16pp. Payment: 3 free copies and stipend under $50. Rights revert to author but articles are available for NASNA members. Pub's reviews: 8 in 2005. §Issues regarding homelessness or ecological degradation. Ads: contact us.

Sparkplug Press, Daniel Farrands, 636 N. Kilkea Dr., Los Angeles, CA 90048-2214, Phone: 323-632-9826, Fax: 323-658-7379, website: www.sparkplugpress.com. 2003. avg. press run 5000. Pub'd 1 title 2005; expects 1 title 2006, 3 titles 2007. Discounts: 55%. 250-350pp.

SPARROWGRASS POETRY NEWSLETTER, Prospect Press, Helen McInnis, PO box 247, El Reno, OK 73036-0247. 1993. Poetry. "*Sparrowgrass Poetry Newsletter* provides articles of interest to poets of all kinds and levels of experience on writing, markets, other poets and events. In addition, we sponsor two Contests each year for subscribers, awarding prizes of $100, $50, and $25 to the top three poets, and publication in the *Newsletter* for winners and 7 honorable mentions. Other special contests on occasion. Reading fee of $2 per poem for contests." circ. 1M. 4/yr. Pub'd 4 issues 2005; expects 4 issues 2006, 4 issues 2007. sub. price $21.95; per copy $4.50; sample $4.50. 6pp. Reporting time: 6 months (for contest winners). Simultaneous submissions accepted: yes. Publishes 5% of manuscripts submitted. Payment: $100, $50, $25 to top three contest winners, books awarded in other occasional contests. Copyrighted, reverts to author. Pub's reviews: 1-2 in 2005. §Only those on writing poetry. Ads: none. Subject: Poetry.

SPEAK UP, Speak Up Press, PO Box 100506, Denver, CO 80250, 303-715-0837, Fax 303-715-0793, speakupres@aol.com, www.speakuppress.org. 1999. Poetry, fiction, art, photos, plays, non-fiction. "Original work by young people 13-19 years old only. Written work: 2500 words max. See web site for submission information or contact Speak Up Press for required submission forms." circ. 2M. 1/yr. Pub'd 1 issue 2005; expects 1 issue 2006, 1 issue 2007. sub. price $10; per copy $10; sample free. Discounts: classroom 50%, bookstores 50%, libraries 50%. 128pp. Reporting time: up to 4 months. Simultaneous submissions accepted: yes. Publishes 10% of manuscripts submitted. Payment: 2 copies. Copyrighted, reverts to author. Ads: none. Subjects: Arts, Fiction, Young Adult.

Speak Up Press (see also SPEAK UP), G.J. Bryant, PO Box 100506, Denver, CO 80250, 303-715-0837, Fax 303-715-0793, speakupres@aol.com, www.speakuppress.org. 1999. Fiction, non-fiction. "Not currently accepting submissions." avg. press run 1M. Reporting time: 2 months. Simultaneous submissions accepted: yes. Payment: negotiable. Copyrights for author. Subject: Young Adult.

SPEAKEASY, Bart Schneider, 1011 Washington Avenue South, Ste 200, Minneapolis, MN 55415, 612-215-2575, speakeasy@loft.org, www.speakeasymagazine.org. 2002. Poetry, criticism, reviews, letters, non-fiction. "*Speakeasy* is a quarterly literary culture magazine published by the Loft Literary Center. Offering a literary look at life, each theme-based issue of *Speakeasy* features topical essays, new poetry, original fiction and/or creative nonfiction, contributions from the magazines readers, and reviews of new books. The mission of *Speakeasy* is that of its publisher, The Loft Literary Center: to foster a writing community, the artistic development of writers, and an audience for literature. The magazine features well-known contributors like Naomi Shihab Nye, Chuck Palahniuk, Rosellen Brown, and Li-Young Lee, along with emerging writers. *Speakeasy* also includes the voices of its community of readers and writers through postcards, verbal Rorschachs, and questionnaires. Fiction and poetry submissions are accepted, as are queries for essays or book reviews. Additionally, the annual *Speakeasy* Prize in Poetry and Prose awards two $1000 prizes (one in each category) plus publication in the magazine. All guidelines are at www.speakeasymagazine.org." 4/yr. Pub'd 5 issues 2005; expects 4 issues 2006, 4 issues 2007. sub. price $19.99; per copy $5.95; sample $5.95. Back issues: Available at www.speakeasymagazine.org. Discounts: Internet offer $14.99. 56pp. Simultaneous submissions accepted: no. Copyrighted, reverts to author. Pub's reviews: approx. 50 in 2005. §literary fiction, nonfiction, and poetry. Ads: Full Page BW $1210; 1/2 Page BW $770; 1/4 Page BW $525; Adlet $125; Classified $50. 4-color add 15%. Frequency discounts available. Subjects: Book Reviewing, Fiction, Literary Review, Literature (General), Non-Fiction, Poetry, Society, Writers/Writing.

SPECIALTY TRAVEL INDEX, Risa Weinreb, Editor, PO BOX 458, San Anselmo, CA 94979-0458, 415-455-1643, Fax 415-455-1648, shansen@specialtytravel.com, www.specialtytravel.com. 1980. Articles, photos, non-fiction. "The Special Interest and Adventure Travel Directory." circ. 25K. 2/yr. Pub'd 2 issues 2005; expects 2 issues 2006, 2 issues 2007. sub. price $10; per copy $6; sample $6. Back issues: $10. Discounts: 50% distributors. 130pp. Reporting time: 30 days. Simultaneous submissions accepted: yes. Publishes 5% of manuscripts submitted. Payment: yes. Copyrighted. Ads: $2,990/$1,900. Subjects: Sports, Outdoors, Transportation, Travel.

Speck Press, Susan Hill Newton, Editor; Derek Lawrence, Publisher, PO Box 102004, Denver, CO 80250, 303-744-1478, 800-996-9783, FAX 800-996-9783, books@speckpress.com, www.speckpress.com. 2002. Fiction, non-fiction. avg. press run 5-10M. Pub'd 7 titles 2005; expects 6 titles 2006, 7 titles 2007. 200+pp. Reporting time: 3-5 months. Simultaneous submissions accepted: yes. Publishes less than 1% of manuscripts submitted. Payment: varies. Copyrights for author. Subjects: Culture, Law, Music, Mystery, Performing Arts, Publishing, Sex, Sexuality.

Spectrum Press, Daniel Vian, Editor-in-Chief; Kristi Sprinkle, Senior Editor, 3023 N Clark Street, #109, Chicago, IL 60657. 1991. Poetry, fiction, criticism, plays, non-fiction. "We publish electronic books only, text-file format. We no longer accept unsolicited manuscripts." Pub'd 50 titles 2005; expects 50 titles 2006, 50 titles 2007. Reporting time: 2 weeks. Simultaneous submissions accepted: yes. Publishes 1% of manuscripts submitted. Payment: 30%, author retains print media rights. Does not copyright for author. Subjects: Criticism, Erotica, Feminism, Fiction, Gay, Lesbianism, Literature (General), Non-Fiction, Novels, Poetry, Short Stories.

Spectrum Productions, Nick Starbuck, 979 Casiano Road, Los Angeles, CA 90049. 1974. Plays. "We are interested in receiving inquiries (not mss.) in the field of translations of European drama before the twentieth century." Copyrights for author. Subject: Drama.

The Speech Bin, Inc., Jan J. Binney, Senior Editor, PO Box 922668, Norcross, GA 30010-2668, 772-770-0007, FAX 772-770-0006; website: www.speechbin.com. 1984. "The Speech Bin publishes educational materials and books in speech-language pathology, audiology, occupational and physical therapy, special education, and treatment of communication disorders in children and adults. One publication is *Getting*

Through: Communicating When Someone You Care For Has Alzheimer's Disease, a unique book written for caregivers (both family members and professionals) of Alzheimer's victims. Most Speech Bin authors are specialists in communication disorders, rehabilitation, or education although we are eager to receive queries for new books and materials from all authors who write for our specialized market. Please study our market before submitting fiction. The Speech Bin also publishes educational card sets and games plus novelties. We do not accept faxed submissions or telephone inquiries." avg. press run varies. Pub'd 8-10 titles 2005; expects 10-12 titles 2006, 10-12 titles 2007. Discounts: 20%. 40-400pp. Reporting time: 2-3 months. Simultaneous submissions accepted: no. Publishes 2-5% of manuscripts submitted. Payment: varies. Copyrights for author. Subjects: Bilingual, Communication, Journalism, Education.

SPEX (SMALL PRESS EXCHANGE), Margaret Speaker Yuan, PO Box E, Corte Madera, CA 94976, 866-622-1325. 1979. Articles, reviews, letters, news items. "This is the newsletter of the Bay Area Independent Publishers Association, a non-profit public benefit organization." circ. 300. 10/yr. Pub'd 12 issues 2005; expects 10 issues 2006, 10 issues 2007. sub. price Included in membership in BAIPA, $40 yearly; sample SASE. 8pp. Payment: none. Copyrighted, reverts to author. Ads: $80/$60/$40 1/4 page/$20 1/8 page/classifieds $3 per 4 lines. Subjects: Book Collecting, Bookselling, Book Reviewing, How-To, Printing.

SPIDER, Marianne Carus, Editor-in-Chief; Heather Delabre, Associate Editor, PO Box 300, Peru, IL 61354, 815-224-5803, ext 656, Fax 815-224-6615, mmiklavcic@caruspub.com. 1994. "Word limit for fiction - 1000 words, nonfiction - 800 words. Include bibliography with nonfiction. SASE required for response." circ. 80M. 12/yr. Pub'd 12 issues 2005; expects 12 issues 2006, 12 issues 2007. sub. price $35.97; per copy $5; sample $5. Back issues: $5. 34pp. Reporting time: approx. 3 months. We accept simultaneous submissions, but please indicate as such. Publishes 1% of manuscripts submitted. Payment: stories and articles up to 25¢ per word, poems up to $3 per line. Copyrighted, does not revert to author. Pub's reviews: 8 in 2005. §Chapter books, middle grade fiction, poetry, younger nonfiction, joke, craft, or puzzle collections. Ads: none. Subjects: Children, Youth, Literature (General), Magazines.

SPIKED, 7 Swansea Road, Norwich NR2 5HU, England.

SPILLWAY, Tebot Bach, Mifanwy Kaiser, Editor; J.D. Lloyd, Editor; Catherine Turner, Associate Editor, Box 7887, Huntington Beach, CA 92615-7887, 714-968-0905. 1993. Poetry, photos, criticism, reviews, long-poems. "Recent contributors: John Balaban, Eleanor Wilner, Richard Jones, David St. John, M.L. Liebler, Allison Joseph, Sam Hamill, Jody Azzouni, Jan Wesley, Jeanette Clough, Amy Uyematsu, and Susan Terris.Eleanor Wilner, Pushcart Winner for her poem *Sidereal* in *Spillway 10*." 2/yr. Pub'd 2 issues 2005; expects 2 issues 2006, 2 issues 2007. sub. price $16; per copy $10 postpaid; sample $10 postpaid. Back issues: $8 postpaid. Discounts: by arrangement. 176pp. Reporting time: 2 weeks to 6 months. Simultaneous submissions accepted, must be stated in cover letter. Publishes 2% of manuscripts submitted. Payment: 1 copy. Copyrighted, reverts to author. Pub's reviews. §Poetry related material. Subjects: Criticism, Photography, Poetry.

SPIN, Owen Bullock, PO Box 13-533, Grey Street, Tauranga, New Zealand, 07 576 1886. 1986. Poetry. "*Spin* accepts contributions from subscribers mainly." circ. 150. 3/yr. Pub'd 3 issues 2005; expects 3 issues 2006, 3 issues 2007. sub. price $US15, includes airmail p/h outside New Zealand; per copy $US5; sample $US3. Back issues: none available. Discounts: refer EBSCO. 60pp. Reporting time: 4 months max. - usually less. Simultaneous submissions accepted: no. Publishes 50% of manuscripts submitted. Payment: nil. Copyrighted, reverts to author. Pub's reviews: 3 in 2005. §Poetry and criticism. Ads: gratis to subscribers. Subject: Poetry.

•**Spinifex Press,** Susan Hawthorne, PO Box 212, North Melbourne VIC 3051, Australia, +61-3-9329 6088, Fax +61-3-9329 9238. 1991. Poetry, fiction, art, photos, cartoons, long-poems, plays, non-fiction. "Our mission is to publish innovatiive and controversial feminist books with an optimistic edge. Our range is diverse and includes authors from Australia, USA, Canada, Botswana, India, Bangladesh, Lebanon, Japan, Philippines, New Zealand, Germany and elsewhere." avg. press run 3000. Pub'd 10 titles 2005; expects 5 titles 2006, 4 titles 2007. All books sold in North America go through our distributors, Independent Publishers Group (IPG). We offer standard trade discounts in Australia of 40% to booksellers. Book with prices in Australian dollars are not available in the USA through IPG, but can be ordered directly over our website: www.spinifexpress.com.au. 250pp. Reporting time: We are currently not accepting unsolicited manuscripts. Simultaneous submissions accepted: No. Publishes 1% of manuscripts submitted. Copyrights for author. Subjects: Arts, Crime, Feminism, Health, Indigenous Cultures, Lesbianism, Literature (General), Memoirs, Multicultural, Myth, Mythology, Non-Violence, Peace, Poetry, Theatre, Women.

SPINNING JENNY, Black Dress Press, C.E. Harrison, P.O. Box 1373, New York, NY 10276-1373, www.spinning-jenny.com. 1994. Poetry, fiction, plays. circ. 1M. 1/yr. Pub'd 1 issue 2005; expects 1 issue 2006, 1 issue 2007. sub. price $15/2 years; per copy $8; sample $8. Back issues: $8, if available. Discounts: refer to DeBoer Distributors. 96pp. Reporting time: 1-4 months. Simultaneous submissions accepted: no. Publishes Less than 5% of manuscripts submitted. Payment: contributors' copies. Copyrighted, reverts to author. Ads: none.

Subjects: Drama, Fiction, Poetry.

The Spinning Star Press, Carl Tate, Bob Starr, 1065 E. Fairview Blvd., Inglewood, CA 90302. 1986. Music. "We may slow down on some submitted materials, but will be more active soon. Length of material: 108 pages. Biases: cataloging and chronicle of recording artists from the South and West. Recent contributors: Bob Starr, Carl Tate, The All-Star Band, etc. We are inactive as of now on #18, 19, 20, 25., science fiction, biography, music." avg. press run 1M. Pub'd 1 title 2005; expects 1 title 2006, 2 titles 2007. Discounts: bulk, classroom, agents, jobbers, libraries, cultural events. 108pp. Reporting time: indefinite. Subject: Music.

Spire Press (see also SPIRE MAGAZINE), Shelly Reed, 532 LaGuardia Place, Ste. 298, New York, NY 10012, www.spirepress.org. 2002. Poetry, fiction, non-fiction. "Poetry chapbooks, poetry full-length, fiction and nonfiction. Fiction/nonfiction accepted only through contests and in August. Please read guidelines first!" avg. press run 1M. Pub'd 4 titles 2005; expects 5 titles 2006, 5 titles 2007. Discounts: 3+ copies 40% if ordered from press directly. Full-length Poetry 60, Poetry chapbooks 20-40, fiction 250. Reporting time: depends on contest deadline. Simultaneous submissions accepted: yes, if notified. Publishes 1-2% of manuscripts submitted. Payment: contest and/or contract, copies for first 150 copies sold, 15% net thereafter. Copyrights for author. Subjects: Culture, Fiction, Memoirs, Non-Fiction, Poetry.

Spirit Press, Suzanne Deakins, Publisher; Larry Foltz, Editor-in-Chief; Aaron Yeagle, Art Director, Spirit Press, PO Box 12346, Portland, OR 97212, spiritpress@onespiritfoundation.org, www.onespiritfoundation.org 877-906-5381. 1997. Poetry, fiction, articles, art, photos, letters, long-poems. avg. press run 3M. Pub'd 3 titles 2005; expects 10 titles 2006, 15 titles 2007. Discounts: 40% to bookstores quanity discounts. 200pp. Reporting time: 30 days. Simultaneous submissions accepted: yes. Publishes 2% of manuscripts submitted. Payment: e-books every other month, paperbacks 2X a year. Copyrights for author. Subjects: Astrology, Buddhism, China, Creativity, Crystals, Gay, Jewelry, Gems, Lesbianism, Metaphysics, Philosophy, Sex, Sexuality, Spiritual, Sufism, Theosophical, Zen.

SPIRIT TALK, Spirit Talk Press, Bear Chief, PO Box 390, Browning, MT 59417, 406-338-2882; E-mail blkfoot4@3rivers.net. 1993. Poetry, fiction, articles, art, photos, cartoons, interviews, satire, criticism, reviews, music, letters, parts-of-novels, long-poems, collages, plays, concrete art, news items, non-fiction. "This is a specialty periodic book which focuses on Native American cultures, especially the Plains Indian." circ. 10M. 4/yr. Pub'd 4 issues 2005; expects 4 issues 2006, 4 issues 2007. sub. price $25; per copy $7.95; sample $4.95. Back issues: $25 - 4 issues. Discounts: 40% to bookstores, 50% to distributors. 64pp. Reporting time: 1 month. Simultaneous submissions accepted: yes. Publishes 80% of manuscripts submitted. Payment: negotiable. Copyrighted, does not revert to author. Pub's reviews: 4 in 2005. §All materials pertaining to American Indians, including video and audio cassettes.

Spirit Talk Press (see also SPIRIT TALK), Bear Chief, PO Box 390, Browning, MT 59417-0390, 406-338-2882; E-mail: LongStandingBearChief@blackfoot.org, web: www.blackfoot.org. 1992. Poetry, fiction, articles, art, photos, cartoons, interviews, satire, criticism, reviews, music, letters, parts-of-novels, long-poems, collages, plays, concrete art, news items, non-fiction. "We publish only books and other media by and about Native American culture." avg. press run 6M. Pub'd 1 title 2005; expects 2 titles 2006, 6 titles 2007. Discounts: 40% stores, 50% book distributor. Reporting time: 4 weeks. Simultaneous submissions accepted: yes. Publishes 20% of manuscripts submitted. Payment: negotiable. Copyrights for author. Subjects: Animals, Arts, Bilingual, Montana, Native American, The West.

The Spirit That Moves Us Press, Inc., Morty Sklar, Editor, Publisher; Marcela Bruno, Technical Consultant, PO Box 720820-DB, Jackson Heights, Queens, NY 11372-0820, 718-426-8788, msklar@mindspring.com. 1974. Poetry, fiction, art, photos, parts-of-novels, long-poems, collages, concrete art, non-fiction. "We are in limbo at present. Please query with a SASE or call before sending work, for our needs and time-frames. Catalog available for the asking. We have two series going: the *Editor's Choice* series, which contains selections from other small press books and magazines, and the Ethnic Diversity Series, the latest of which is *Patchwork of Dreams: Voices from the Heart of the New America.* Sample copies: *Editor's Choice III* $10 (reg $15); *Patchwork of Dreams* $11, (reg. $15)." avg. press run 1M-4.2M. Pub'd 1 title 2005. Discounts: 50% making-space sale. 208-504pp. Reporting time: 3 months after deadline date, or 1 week if no deadline. Publishes 1.5% poetry, fiction 2% of manuscripts submitted. Payment: cash for single author book; cash and clothbound copy for anthologies, 40% off paperback copies and 25% off extra clothbounds. Copyrights for author. Subjects: Anthology, Essays, Multicultural, Photography, Poetry, Short Stories.

Spirit, Nature and You, Suzanne Strisower, PO Box 559, Oroville, CA 95965, www.spiritandnature.com. 2000. Non-fiction. "Not currently open to others materials. Query first. Focus on environmental sustainability, solar, spiritual and divination." Expects 1 title 2006, 2 titles 2007. Reporting time: 8 weeks. Simultaneous submissions accepted: no. Payment: varies. Copyrights for author. Subjects: The Americas, New Age, Spiritual.

SPIRITCHASER, Elizabeth Hundley, 3183 Sharon-Copley Road, Medina, OH 44256, 330-722-1561. 1994. Articles. "After my sister and her husband died of cancer 23 days apart, I began my spiritual search. I interview people I am drawn to, of different faiths. Naomi Judd was my first subscriber. I've interviewed Deepak Chopra, Bernie Siegel, Cece Winans, Dave Dravecky, Dr. Joyce Brothers, Sonya Friedman.'' circ. 20. Pub'd 1 issue 2005; expects 3 issues 2006, 3 issues 2007. sub. price $20; per copy $5; sample $5. Back issues: $5. Discounts: none. 8pp. Publishes 0% of manuscripts submitted. Copyrighted, reverts to author. Subjects: Inspirational, Newsletter, Spiritual.

Spiritual Understanding Network, LLC, Elizabeth Barberi, P.O.Box 48, Salisbury, CT 06068-0048, www.matterofspirit.com. 2003. Non-fiction. ''S.U.N., LLC publishes religious / spiritual books that describe personal spiritual experience and (without being preachy)invite individuals to deepen spiritual life. The books recognize that God may be found through more than one religion and encourage respect between religious paths. Books accepted for publication avoid scholarly language, but retain academic precision and are grammatically correct.'' avg. press run 2600. Expects 1 title 2006, 1 title 2007. Discounts: Bookstores 40% (1-5 books)Bookstores 42% (6-47 books)Wholesalers/distributors 55%Institutions/Classrooms 42%. 200pp. Reporting time: one year. Simultaneous submissions accepted: No. Publishes 1% of manuscripts submitted. Payment: No advances; Negotiated royalties; Annual payments. Does not copyright for author. Subjects: Biography, Catholic, Edgar Cayce, Creativity, Dreams, Inspirational, Multicultural, Native American, Parenting, Religion, Self-Help, Society, Spiritual, Theosophical, Zen.

SPITBALL: The Literary Baseball Magazine, Mike Shannon, Editor-in-Chief; William J. McGill, Managing Editor & Poetry Editor; Mark Schraf, Fiction Editor; Tom Eckel, Contributing Editor, 5560 Fox Road, Cincinnati, OH 45239-7271, 513-385-2268. 1981. Poetry, fiction, articles, art, cartoons, interviews, satire, criticism, reviews, parts-of-novels, long-poems, collages, plays, concrete art, non-fiction. ''*Spitball* is a unique litarary magazine devoted to baseball. We publish primarily poetry & fiction, with no biases concerning style or technique or genre. We strive to publish only what we consider to be good work, however, and using baseball as subject matter does not guarantee acceptance. We have no big backlog of accepted material, nevertheless, and good baseball poetry and fiction submitted to us can be published reasonably quickly. If one has never written about baseball, it would probably help a great deal to read the magazine or our book, *The Best of Spitball*, an anthology, published by Pocket Books, March 1988. We try to give considerate fair treatment to everything we receive. We occasionally publish special issues. First issue of 1989 was devoted entirely to David Martin's sequence of poems connecting one-time Milwaukee Brewers outfielder Gorman Thomas to Wisconsin lorre and mythology. A $6 payment must accompany submissions from writers submitting to *Spitball* for the first time. We will send a sample copy in return. The $6 is a one-time charge. Once you have paid it, you may submit additional material as often as you like at no charge.'' circ. 1M. 2/yr. Pub'd 2 issues 2005; expects 2 issues 2006, 2 issues 2007. sub. price $12; per copy $6; sample $6. Back issues: many sold out, write for prices and availability. Discounts: can be negotiated. 96pp. Reporting time: from 1 week to 3 months. Simultaneous submissions accepted: no. Payment: copies. Not copyrighted. Pub's reviews: 60 in 2005. §We would love to receive review copies of any small press publications dealing with baseball, especially baseball poetry and fiction. Ads: $100/$60. Subjects: Fiction, Kentucky, Poetry, Sports, Outdoors.

Spoon River Poetry Press, David R. Pichaske, PO Box 6, Granite Falls, MN 56241. 1976. Poetry. ''We do not, as a rule, solicit book-length manuscripts. Mostly we favor Midwest writers working with Midwest subjects and themes.'' avg. press run 1.5M. Pub'd 6 titles 2005; expects 3 titles 2006, 3 titles 2007. Discounts: 2-5 20%, 6+ 40% to bookstores; textbook orders 20%; 20% if payment accompanies order to individuals and libraries. 32-400+pp. Payment: 50% of receipts over set, print, bind costs. Copyrights for author.

SPOON RIVER POETRY REVIEW, Lucia Getsi, Editor, Department of English 4240, Illinois State University, Normal, IL 61790-4240, 309-438-7906, 309-438-3025. 1976. Poetry. circ. 1.5M. 2/yr. Pub'd 2 issues 2005; expects 2 issues 2006, 2 issues 2007. sub. price $15 ($18 institutions); per copy $10; sample $10. Back issues: $5-$10. Discounts: 30%. 128pp. Reporting time: 3 months. We reluctantly accept simultaneous submissions. Publishes 1% of manuscripts submitted. Payment: year's subscription. Copyrighted, reverts to author. Pub's reviews: 2 in 2005. §Books of poems, poetry translations, anthologies of poems, criticism and poetics. Ads: $150/$75. Subjects: Poetry, Reviews.

SPORE, Score, Crag Hill, 1111 E. Fifth Street, Moscow, ID 83843, schneider-hill@adelphia.com, http://scorecard.typepad.com/spore/. 1983. Articles, art, photos, interviews, criticism, reviews, letters, concrete art. ''Our primary focus is the visual poem—creative, historical, theoretical—but we're also interested in any work pushing back boundaries, verse or prose. Subscription price includes 1 issues of *SPORE* plus occasional publications such as broadsides and postcards that I can fit into the envelope.'' circ. 150-250. 1/yr. Pub'd 1 issue 2005; expects 1 issue 2006, 1 issue 2007. sub. price $12 per issue; per copy $12; sample $12. Back issues: query. 80pp. Reporting time: 2 weeks to 6 months. Simultaneous submissions accepted: Yes, but make sure to let us know. Publishes 5-10% of manuscripts submitted. Payment: 1 copy. Not copyrighted. Pub's reviews: 1 in 2005. §We would be interested in books and magazines with a visual/literal basis. Ads: none. Subjects: Arts, Avant-Garde, Experimental Art, Language, Literature (General), Poetry.

SPOUT, Spout Press, John Colburn, Chris Watercott, Michelle Filkins, PO BOX 581067, Minneapolis, MN

55458-1067, http://www.spoutpress.com. 1989. Poetry, fiction, articles, art, cartoons, interviews, letters, collages, non-fiction. "Accepts poetry, prose, and fiction for publication. Submission should include SASE. Looking for the unique voice, for someone with something to say in an offbeat way." circ. 200+. 2-3/yr. Pub'd 3 issues 2005; expects 2 issues 2006, 3 issues 2007. sub. price $12; per copy $4; sample $4. Back issues: $3. 56pp. Reporting time: 2-6 months. Simultaneous submissions accepted: yes. Publishes 10% of manuscripts submitted. Payment: copy. Copyrighted, reverts to author. Subjects: Essays, Fiction, Non-Fiction, Poetry.

Spout Press (see also SPOUT), John Colburn, Michelle Filkins, Chris Watercott, PO Box 581067, Minneapolis, MN 55458-1067. 1996. Poetry, fiction, non-fiction. "Recent anthology includes Jim Northrup, Jonis Agee, and Alison McGhee. Tend to put out calls for anthologies or theme-related books rather than publish single-author manuscripts." avg. press run 500. Expects 2 titles 2006, 2 titles 2007. 110pp. Reporting time: 2-3 months. Simultaneous submissions accepted: yes. Publishes 5% of manuscripts submitted. Payment: varies. Copyrights for author. Subjects: Essays, Fiction, Non-Fiction, Poetry.

Spring Grass (see also Redgreene Press), RC Anderson, PO Box 22322, Pittsburgh, PA 15222.

Spring Harbor Press, Margaret Black, Director, Box 346, Delmar, NY 12054, 518-478-7817, 518-478-7817, springharbor@verizon.net, www.springharborpress.com. 1985. avg. press run 1M. Pub'd 1 title 2005; expects 2 titles 2006, 2 titles 2007. Copyrights for author. Subject: Fiction.

Spring Publications Inc., James Hillman, Publisher; Klaus Ottmann, Editor-in-Chief, 28 Front Street #3, Putnam, CT 06260-1927, Fax 203-974-3195, www.springpublications.com. 1941. Non-fiction. "Jungian background but critical reflection on Jungian tradition; intellectual but neither academic nor new age. Psychology, mythology, religion, eco-psychology." avg. press run 1M. Pub'd 5 titles 2005; expects 10 titles 2006, 20 titles 2007. Discounts: Continuum is our distributor. 196pp. Reporting time: 3-6 months. Simultaneous submissions accepted: no. Publishes 1% of manuscripts submitted. Payment: varies. Copyrights for author. Subjects: Classical Studies, Myth, Mythology, Philosophy, Psychology, Religion.

SPRING: A Journal of Archetype and Culture, Jay Livernois, Senior Editor; Nancy Cater, Managing Editor, P.O. Box 207, Woodstock, CT 06281-0207. 1941. Articles, interviews, criticism, reviews, non-fiction. "Approx. 192 pages, 12 page articles in magazine." circ. 2M. 1/yr. Pub'd 2 issues 2005; expects 2 issues 2006, 2 issues 2007. sub. price $30 + shipping if billed, no shipping charge if prepaid; per copy $20; sample free. Back issues: $20; $10 if a subscriber. Discounts: classroom 40%, jobbers & trade 20% 1-4 copies (30% if prepaid), 40% 5-10, 45% 11-99. 192pp. Reporting time: 3 months. Simultaneous submissions accepted: no. Publishes 10% of manuscripts submitted. Payment: none. Copyrighted, does not revert to author. Pub's reviews: 22 in 2005. §Depth psychology, mythology, art, architecture, Renaissance, philosophy, the occult, classical studies, religion. Ads: $200/$135. Subjects: Literature (General), Psychology.

SPROUTLETTER, Michael Linden, Box 62, Ashland, OR 97520. 1980. Articles, interviews, reviews, letters, news items, non-fiction. "*Sproutletter* publishes articles, book reviews, recipes and news items relating to sprouting, algae (blue-green), Amazonian healing herbs, indoor live food growing, live foods, vegetarianism, holistic health and nutrition. Query requested before submitting works. Articles should be no more than 1M words." circ. 3.1M. 4/yr. Pub'd 4 issues 2005; expects 4 issues 2006, 4 issues 2007. sub. price $12 USA, $14 Canada and Mexico, $14 foreign surface, $25 foreign airmail; per copy $3, $4.50 Can/Mex, $4.50 surf, $5.50 air; sample same. Back issues: 20% off 1-45. Discounts: 10-50 40%, 51-100 45%, 101-200 50%. 12pp. Reporting time: 4 weeks. Payment: $25-$100. Copyrighted, reverts to author. Pub's reviews: 20 in 2005. §Sprouting, algae, raw foods, indoor gardening, holistic health, nutrition. Ads: $160/$90/25¢. Subjects: Cooking, Counter-Culture, Alternatives, Communes, Disease, Ecology, Foods, Gardening, Health, Networking, New Age, Water.

•SQUARE ONE, Jennifer Dunbar Dorn, Campus Box 226, University of Colorado, Boulder, CO 80309-0001, 303-492-8890, square1@colorado.edu, http://www.colorado.edu/English/squareone/index.htm. 2003. circ. 600. 1/yr. Pub'd 1 issue 2005; expects 1 issue 2006, 1 issue 2007. sub. price $10; per copy $7; sample $7 or free. Back issues: $10. Discounts: 2-10 copies 25%. 100pp.

Square One Publishers, Inc., Rudy Shur, Publisher, 115 Herricks Road, Garden City Park, NY 11040, 516-535-2010, Fax 516-535-2014, sq1info@aol.com, www.squareonepublishers.com. 1999. Non-fiction. "Here at Square One Publishers, we produce books that provide reliable information on a range of meaningful, as well as intriguing, topics. Square One is the best place to start! When submitting a proposal, please include only: a cover letter that includes some biographical info on the author and indicates the book's potential audience; 2-3 page overview of the book; table of contents; and SASE for return of your material." avg. press run 8-10M. Pub'd 20 titles 2005; expects 25 titles 2006, 25 titles 2007. Discounts: trade 20%-45%. 225pp. Reporting time: 4 weeks. Simultaneous submissions accepted: yes. Publishes 2% of manuscripts submitted. Payment: 10% of net, paid semi-annually. Copyrights for author. Subjects: Alternative Medicine, Collectibles, Cooking, Crafts, Hobbies, Environment, Finances, Grieving, Health, How-To, New Age, Non-Fiction, Parenting, Religion, Vegetarianism, Writers/Writing.

454

SRLR Press (see also SULPHUR RIVER LITERARY REVIEW), James Michael Robbins, PO Box 19228, Austin, TX 78760. 1997. Poetry, fiction, articles, art, photos, interviews, satire, criticism, non-fiction. "We have published books by Errol Miller, Frances Neidhardt, James Scofield, Albert Huffstickler, Nola Perez, Willie James King, Ben Norwood, Lee Slonimsky, and Joe Ahearn. We publish by invitation only. No unsolicited manuscripts are accepted." avg. press run 250-500. Pub'd 1 title 2005; expects 2 titles 2006, 2 titles 2007. Discounts: varies. 80pp. Payment: 50/50 split once printing is paid for. Copyrights for author. Subjects: Fiction, Poetry.

STAND MAGAZINE, Michael Hulse, John Kinsella, School of English, Univeristy of Leeds, Leeds LS2 9JT, England. 1952. Poetry, interviews, criticism, reviews, letters. circ. 4.5M. 4/yr. Pub'd 4 issues 2005; expects 4 issues 2006. sub. price $49.50; per copy $13; sample $5. Back issues: $10. 120pp. Reporting time: 1-2 months. Simultaneous submissions accepted: no. Publishes 5% of manuscripts submitted. Payment: $45/poem, $45/1,000 words prose. Copyrighted, reverts to author. Pub's reviews: 30 in 2005. §Literature. Ads: $225/$112/$56 1/4 page. Subject: Literary Review.

Standard Publications, Inc., PO Box 2226, Champaign, IL 61825, 217-898-7825, spi@standardpublications.com.

Standish Press, Olga Rothschild, 105 Standish Street, Duxbury, MA 02332-5027, 781-934-9570, Fax 781-934-9570,duxroth@verizon.net. 1999. Non-fiction. "Publishes health and fitness, self-help, medical care, writing, home improvement, humor, business, travel for an educated adult audience. Recent title: *Better Health, Simple, Sensible Strategies* by Dick Rothschild. *No poetry, please.*" avg. press run 3M-5M. Expects 1 title 2007. Discounts: 2-4 books 20%, 5-99 40%, 100+ 50%; short 20%. 192pp. Reporting time: 1 month, query before submitting. We accept simultaneous submissions, but please query before submission. Publishes 10% of manuscripts submitted. Payment: 5-10% royalty on retail price. Does not copyright for author. Subjects: Business & Economics, Construction, Health, How-To, Humor, Medicine, Nursing, Travel, Writers/Writing.

Stanford Oak Press, Inc., John Breitly, P.O. Box 30349, Bethesda, MD 20824, 301 652 8444, mbaker@stanfordoak.com.

THE STAR BEACON, Earth Star Publications, Ann Ulrich Miller, Publisher, PO Box 117, Paonia, CO 81428, 970-527-3257, fax (866) 882-1346, earthstar@tripod.net, http://earthstar.tripod.com/. 1987. Poetry, articles, art, photos, cartoons, interviews, reviews, letters, long-poems, news items, non-fiction. "*Star Beacon* readers are looking for the latest information on UFOs and related phenomena, as most of them are UFO percipients of various degrees, searching for answers. Because science, for the most part, has rejected them, *Star Beacon* readers are turning to metaphysics (the science of higher mind) for such answers as why are we here, where are we going, how can we make our world and the universe better." circ. 500+. 12/yr. Pub'd 8 issues 2005; expects 12 issues 2006, 12 issues 2007. sub. price $27 print US, $30 Canada, $36 foreign, $12 PDF; per copy $2.50; sample $2. Back issues: $1.50. Discounts: 50% to retailers. 16pp. Reporting time: 2 weeks. Simultaneous submissions accepted: yes. Publishes 80% of manuscripts submitted. Payment: copies, subscription, small honorarium in some cases. Copyrighted, reverts to author. Pub's reviews: 12 in 2005. §UFOs, metaphysics, psychic phenomena, New Age living, astrology, shamanism. Ads: $80/$40/$20 1/4 page/$10 1/8 page/$3 per column inch/20 cents per word classifieds. Subjects: Newsletter, Space, Spiritual.

Starbooks Press/FLF Press, P.J. Powers, Founder, 1391 Boulevard of the Arts, Sarasota, FL 34236-2904, 941-957-1281, Fax 941-955-3829, starxxx@gte.net. 1980. Poetry, fiction, art, photos, long-poems, collages, plays, non-fiction. avg. press run 5M. Pub'd 10 titles 2005; expects 12 titles 2006. Discounts: 55% distributors, 40% booksellers. 512pp. Reporting time: 2-3 months. Payment: negotiable. Copyrights for author. Subjects: Crime, Electronics, Entertainment, Erotica, Fiction, Florida, Gay, Interviews, Movies, Non-Fiction, Poetry, Prison, Psychology, Sex, Sexuality, Writers/Writing.

Starcherone Books, PO Box 303, Buffalo, NY 14201-0303, www.starcherone.com. 2000. Fiction. "Looking for innovative fiction, new stuff, work which renews our faith in the form. Best chance for consideration is to enter our annual contest, which has a deadline of January 31. We only consider unsolicited work during the months of August and September. Do not send manuscripts during our contest period, from October through July. Please query first." avg. press run 1000. Pub'd 2 titles 2005; expects 4 titles 2006, 4 titles 2007. Discounts: wholesale 40%. 200pp. Reporting time: 6-8 months. We accept simultaneous submissions if author makes it clear it is under consideration elsewhere. Publishes 1% of manuscripts submitted. Payment: $500 advance; 15% royalties. Copyrights for author. Subjects: Fiction, Post Modern, Prose, Storytelling, Surrealism.

Stardate Publishing Company, John Cothran, P. O. Box 112302, Carrollton, TX 75011-2302, voice-972-898-8349,fax-1-800-521-0633, jcothran@stardatepublishing.com, www.stardatepublishing.com. 1984. Art, photos, non-fiction. "I am interested in culture." avg. press run 4000. Expects 1 title 2006. Discounts: 2-10 copies 25%. 382pp. Reporting time: A week. Simultaneous submissions accepted: No. Publishes 50% of manuscripts submitted. Payment: Varies. Copyrights for author. Subjects: Adolescence, African-American, The Americas, Avant-Garde, Experimental Art, Civil Rights, Civil War, Culture, Education,

Entertainment, Literature (General), Military, Veterans, Movies, Music, Non-Fiction, World War II.

StarLance Publications, James B. King, 5104 Cooperstown Lane, Pasco, WA 99301-8984. 1987. Fiction, art, cartoons. "All currently planned books are collections of cartoons, science fiction and fantasy illustration, illustrated science fiction and fantasy short fiction, and graphic novels. Desired art is black line and all mediums that reproduce well in b/w halftone. Books aimed at mainstream market, including young adults. Profanity, nudity, and sexually explicit material are not desired." avg. press run 5M. Pub'd 1 title 2005; expects 1 title 2006, 1 title 2007. Discounts: 20-55% based on quantity. 128pp. Reporting time: 2-6 weeks. Simultaneous submissions accepted: no. Publishes 5% of manuscripts submitted. Payment: per word, upon publication, sometimes royalties. Does not copyright for author. Subjects: Cartoons, Fantasy, Fiction, Science Fiction, Short Stories.

Starlight Press, Ira Rosenstein, Box 3102, Long Island City, NY 11103. 1980. Poetry. "Anthology published in 1992. No immediate publishing plans." avg. press run 300. Discounts: normal trade. 35pp. Reporting time: 2 months. Payment: 2 free copies & 50% discount on further Starlight copies (any title). Copyrights for author. Subject: Poetry.

•Starry Night Publishing, Richard Goldstein, 904 Broad Street, Collingdale, PA 19023, www.starrynightpublishing.com. 2005. Satire, non-fiction. "Our primary focus is non-fiction." avg. press run 1000. Pub'd 1 title 2005; expects 6 titles 2006, 25 titles 2007. 200-300pp. Reporting time: 2 weeks. Simultaneous submissions accepted: Yes. Publishes 5% of manuscripts submitted. Payment: Varies on material, level of expertise, amount of work required and type of market. Varies on Situation. Subjects: Family, History, Humor, Non-Fiction, Nutrition, Public Affairs, Relationships, Self-Help, Senior Citizens, Women.

STATE AND LOCAL GOVERNMENT REVIEW, Michael J. Scicchitano, Editor; Ann Allen, Contact Person, Carl Vinson Institute of Government, 201 N. Milledge Ave., Univ. of GA, Athens, GA 30602, 706-542-2736. 1968. "A journal of research and viewpoints on state, local, and intergovernmental issues." circ. 1.4M. 3/yr. Pub'd 3 issues 2005; expects 3 issues 2006, 3 issues 2007. sub. price $22 individual, $35 library, new electronic subscription: $18 individual, $32 library; per copy $6. Back issues: volumes 1-7 $1/copy, all other $5/copy. 72pp. Reporting time: 10 weeks. Publishes 25% of manuscripts submitted. Copyrighted. Pub's reviews. Subject: Political Science.

STATE OF CALIFORNIA LABOR, University of California Press, Ruth Milkman, Editor; Rebecca Frazier, Managing Editor, University of California Press, 2000 Center St., Suite 303, Berkeley, CA 94704-1223, 510-634-7154. 2001. Articles. "Editorial address: UC Institute for Labor and Employment, 2310 Hershey Hall, UCLA, Box 951478, Los Angeles, CA 90095-1478. Copyrighted by the Regents of the University of California." circ. 2500. 1/yr. Pub'd 1 issue 2005; expects 1 issue 2006, 1 issue 2007. sub. price $25 indiv., $70 inst., $25 student; per copy $25 indiv., $70 inst., $25 student; sample same as single copy. Discounts: foreign subs. agents 10%, one-time orders 30%. 236pp. Copyrighted, does not revert to author. Ads: $295/$220. Subjects: Labor, Research.

State University of New York Press, James Peltz, Director; Jane Bunker, Editor in Chief, 194 Washington Avenue Suite 305, Albany, NY 12210, main editorial 518-472-5000, orders 800-666-2211, website www.sunypress.edu. 1966. Non-fiction. "Editorial Program: Scholarly titles and serious works of general interest in most areas of the humanities and the social sciences, with special interest in African-American studies; anthropology; Asian studies; communication; cultural studies; education; environmental studies; film studies; Holocaust studies; Jewish studies; literature and literary theory and criticism; Middle Eastern studies; philosophy; political science; psychology; religious studies; rhetoric and composition; sociology; sports studies; and womens studies." avg. press run 750. Pub'd 170 titles 2005; expects 175 titles 2006, 175 titles 2007. Discounts: Trade Titles-Hardcover & Paper: T follows price, 40%; Short Titles-Cloth & Paper: 20%;Prepaid and "STOP" orders-Paper and Trade: 40%, Cloth: 20%Classroom adoption: 20%Trade sales may earn higher discount on short paperbacks if placed through sales reps or through SUNY Press Sales Manager. 288pp. Reporting time: one to two months. Simultaneous submissions accepted: Yes. Publishes 5% of manuscripts submitted. Payment: royalties after 1000 sold depending on contract. Copyrights for author. Subjects: African-American, Anthropology, Archaeology, Criticism, Culture, Education, Environment, Holocaust, Literature (General), Middle East, Philosophy, Political Science, Psychology, Religion, Sociology, Women.

Steel Balls Press, R. Don Steele, Box 807, Whittier, CA 90608, E-mail don@steelballs.com. 1986. Non-fiction. "No unsolicited m/s! 1 page. Query letters only. Specialize in controversial how-to/self help. *Absolutely* no New Age, poetry, fiction." avg. press run 20M. Pub'd 2 titles 2005; expects 2 titles 2006, 2 titles 2007. Discounts: normal trade; STOP 25%. 224pp. Reporting time: 6 weeks. Simultaneous submissions accepted: yes. Publishes 2% of manuscripts submitted. Payment: 10% retail cover price after 500 copies. Does not copyright for author. Subjects: Drugs, Health, How-To, Men, Romance, Self-Help, Sex, Sexuality, Singles.

Steel Toe Books, Tom C. Hunley Ph.D., English Department / 20C Cherry Hall, Western Kentucky University / 1 Big Red Way, Bowling Green, KY 42101-3576, (270) 745-5769 tom.hunley@wku.edu www.steeltoebooks.com. 2003. Poetry. ''Our titles are Einstein Considers a Sand Dune by James Doyle, winner of the 2003 Steel Toe Books Prize in Poetry, selected by David Kirby, Diary of a Cell by Jennifer Gresham, winner of the 2004 Steel Toe Books Prize in Poetry, selected by Charles Harper Webb, Blue Positive by Martha Silano, Becoming the Villainess by Jeannine Hall Gailey, and Conditions and Cures by Ken Waldman. In the future, rather than running a contest, we will hold open reading periods every year during the month of June. There is no fee, but we ask that everyone submitting to us purchase one of our books ($12).'' avg. press run 500. Pub'd 1 title 2005; expects 3 titles 2006, 2 titles 2007. Discounts: 40%. 90pp. Reporting time: one to three months. Simultaneous submissions accepted: Yes. Publishes 1% of manuscripts submitted. Payment: Authors receive 20% royalties, plus 10 copies. Copyrights for author. Subject: Poetry.

Steerforth Press, L.C., Thomas Powers, Senior Editor; Michael Moore, Senior Editor; Alan Lelchuk, Senior Editor; Chip Fleischer, Publisher, 25 Lebanon St., Hanover, NH 03755-2143, 603-643-4787. 1993. Fiction, non-fiction. ''No unsolicited manuscripts accepted.'' avg. press run 5M. Pub'd 15 titles 2005; expects 15 titles 2006, 20 titles 2007. 275pp. Reporting time: query first. Payment: standard cuts for clothbound and paperbacks. Copyrights for author. Subjects: Biography, Essays, History, Literature (General), Memoirs, Novels.

Stellaberry Press, Edward Cervinski, P.O. Box 18217, St. Paul, MN 55118, http://www.stellaberry.com. 2005. Poetry, fiction, cartoons, music, parts-of-novels, non-fiction. avg. press run 3000. Expects 3 titles 2006, 3 titles 2007. 50-300pp. Reporting time: We respond to an author immediately that we've received their manuscript...acceptance, editing, and publishing times varies with each manuscript. Simultaneous submissions accepted: Yes. Subjects: Children, Youth, Fiction, Music, Non-Fiction, Poetry.

Stemmer House Publishers, Inc., Barbara Holdridge, 4 White Brook Road, Gilsum, NH 03448. 1975. Fiction, non-fiction. avg. press run 5M. Pub'd 20 titles 2005; expects 15 titles 2006, 15 titles 2007. Discounts: 42% for 5 assorted titles or more to retailers. 170pp. Reporting time: 4 weeks. Simultaneous submissions accepted: yes. Publishes .1% of manuscripts submitted. Payment: royalty and advance. Copyrights for author. Subjects: Arts, Design, Earth, Natural History, Fiction.

SterlingHouse Publisher, Cynthia Sterling, Publisher & CEO; Jennifer Himes, Managing Editor; Megan Davidson, Editor; Chelley Lenkner, Production Manager; Jeff Butler, Production; Jennifer Piemme Movie, Foreign & Domestic Rights Agent; Danielle Chiotti, Public Relations, 7436 Washington Ave., Ste. 200, Pittsburgh, PA 15218, 412-821-6211, ordering line 1-888-542-BOOK (2665), Fax 412-821-6997, sterlingho@aol.com or ceshor@aol.com, www.sterlinghousepublisher.com or www.ceshore.com. 1998. Poetry, fiction, non-fiction. avg. press run 3M-3.5M. Pub'd 64 titles 2005; expects 50 titles 2006, 50 titles 2007. Discounts: call distributor for trade and bookstore discounts: Partners (800) 336-3137; direct sales and special sales call for pricing: (888) 542-BOOK. 245pp. Reporting time: 2-6 months. Simultaneous submissions accepted: yes. Publishes less than 10% of manuscripts submitted. Payment: 10-12% royalty, royalties paid bi-yearly. Copyrights for author. Subjects: Biotechnology, Christianity, Essays, Fantasy, Fiction, Holocaust, Memoirs, Metaphysics, Mystery, New Age, Poetry, Politics, Religion, Science Fiction, Sex, Sexuality.

•**Chuck Stewart,** Chuck Stewart, 3722 Bagley Ave. #19, Los Angeles, CA 90034-4113, www.StewartEducationServices.com. 2000. Non-fiction. ''Eclectic mix from "Bankrupt Your Student Loans," "Lead Hazards in Residential Real Estate," "Mold Hazards in Residential Real Estate," to "Queer Word Puzzles," "Queer History and Politics Word Games," and "Queer Pop Culture Word Games."'' avg. press run 500. Pub'd 3 titles 2005; expects 3 titles 2006, 2 titles 2007. Discounts: negotiated. 300pp. Reporting time: 30 days. Simultaneous submissions accepted: No. Publishes 1% of manuscripts submitted. Payment: 10%. Copyrights for author. Subjects: Environment, Finances, Gay, Lesbianism, Safety.

Stewart Publishing & Printing, Robert Stewart, 17 Sir Constantine Drive, Markham, ON L3P 2X3, Canada, www.stewartbooks.com 905-294-4389; FAX 905-294-8718; robert@stewartbooks.com. 1992. Poetry, fiction, letters, non-fiction. Pub'd 33 titles 2005; expects 40 titles 2006, 45 titles 2007. Copyrights for author. Subjects: Biography, Business & Economics, England, Genealogy, History, How-To, Ireland, Miniature Books, New Age, Printing, Scotland, Self-Help, Spiritual, Textbooks.

Still Waters Press, Shirley Lake, 459 South Willow Avenue, Galloway, NJ 08205-4633. 1985. Poetry, non-fiction. ''Still Waters Press of Galloway, New Jersey, is on publishing hiatus for an, as yet, undetermined but lengthy period of time, due to the editor's long illness. No manuscripts will be read, accepted, or invited for at least two years. Chapbooks on the SWP booklist remain in print and are available until further notice. Authors of SWP chapbooks are invited to contact the editor to arrange for acquisition or disposition of the "masters" of their chapbooks. Gratitude to all poets, now, and always.'' avg. press run 300. Pub'd 2 titles 2005. Discounts: 40%. 32pp. Reporting time: Please do not submit manuscripts. If submitted, expect long delay in response. Simultaneous submissions accepted: No. Publishes 0% of manuscripts submitted. Payment: No longer publishing new works.

The Stillwater Press, PO Box 265, Stillwater, NJ 07875, umperrin@palace.net.

THE STINGING FLY, Declan Meade, Publisher-Editor; Eabhan Ni Shuileabhain, Poetry Editor, PO Box 6016, Dublin 8, Ireland, stingingfly@gmail.com, www.stingingfly.org. 1997. Poetry, fiction, articles, art, photos, cartoons, interviews, criticism, reviews, letters, parts-of-novels, long-poems, collages, plays, news items, non-fiction. "The Stinging Fly is dedicated to promoting new Irish and international writing. It has a particular interest in discovering and fostering new writing talent. We operate an open submission policy, with specific reading periods for each issue posted on our web site. No email submissions are accepted but we can respond to international postal submissions by email. Full submission guidelines on our web site." circ. 1000. 3/yr. Pub'd 2 issues 2005; expects 3 issues 2006, 3 issues 2007. sub. price 22 euro (International); per copy 8 euro (International); sample 8 euro (International). 96pp. Reporting time: 3 months. Simultaneous submissions accepted: No. Publishes 10% of manuscripts submitted. Payment: Two copies plus 25 euro. Copyrighted, reverts to author. Pub's reviews: 10 in 2005. §Fiction and poetry, Irish and international. Ads: Full Page 250 euro, half page 150 euro. Subjects: Interviews, Ireland, Literary Review, Literature (General), Poetry, Prose, Reviews, Short Stories, Translation, Writers/Writing.

•**Stone and Scott, Publishers,** Les Boston, PO Box 56419, Sherman Oaks, CA 91413-1419, 818-904-9088 Fax 818-787-1431 www.StoneandScott.com. 1990. Poetry, fiction, non-fiction. "Also publish wordplay: sponnerisms, puns, and such. *Stoopnagle's Tale Is Twisted: Spoonerisms Run Amok* has been a staple for four years. *The Giant Book of Animal Jokes: Beastly Humor for Grownups* by Richard Lederer and James Ertner with Illustrations by James McLean is new for 2006. *Hawk,* a novel by William Wallis, won PMA's 2006 Benjamin Franklin Award in Fiction. We have too much work in process to consider new material." avg. press run 2,000 - 3,000.

Stone Bridge Press, Peter Goodman, Publisher, PO Box 8208, Berkeley, CA 94707, 510-524-8732. 1989. Fiction, non-fiction. "Interested in material on Japan and Japanese culture: 1) Language—classroom texts and self-study, especially intermediate level. 2) Japanese fiction in translation—novels and short story collections, fine literature primarily, but will consider mysteries and science fiction. 3) Design—especially gardens and architecture. 4) Current affairs and business. Do *not* want cliched treatments of Japan, *haiku* diaries, or books based entirely on second sources and outdated studies/translations. Wish to present contemporary portrait of Japan of use to people who need to interact or deal with Japan. Also distributes software for learning Japanese." avg. press run 3M. Pub'd 9 titles 2005; expects 5 titles 2006, 5 titles 2007. Discounts: available through distributor (Weatherhill, Inc.). 160pp. Reporting time: 2-3 months, 3 weeks if proposal only. Simultaneous submissions accepted: yes. Publishes less than 5% of manuscripts submitted. Payment: advance vs. royalties. Copyrights for author. Subjects: Business & Economics, Design, Japan, Language, Translation, Transportation.

STONE SOUP, The Magazine By Young Writers and Artists, Gerry Mandel, William Rubel, Box 83, Santa Cruz, CA 95063, 831-426-5557, Fax 831-426-1161, e-mail editor@stonesoup.com, www.stonesoup.com. 1973. Poetry, fiction, art, photos, reviews, letters, parts-of-novels, long-poems, plays. "All material written & drawn by children 8-13." circ. 20M. 6/yr. Pub'd 6 issues 2005; expects 6 issues 2006, 6 issues 2007. sub. price $34; per copy $5.75; sample $5.75. Back issues: prices upon request. Discounts: schedule available upon request. 48pp. Reporting time: 4 weeks. Simultaneous submissions accepted: no. Publishes .5% of manuscripts submitted. Payment: 2 copies, $40 plus certificate. Copyrighted, does not revert to author. Pub's reviews: 12 in 2005. §Children's books. Ads: none. Subjects: Children, Youth, Education, Magazines.

Stonehorse Publishing, LLC, Rainer Kohrs Ph.D., Marketing Director, 10632 S. Memorial Ave., Ste 245, Tulsa, OK 74133, 1.888.867.1927, Fax: 1.888.867.1927, generalinfo@stonehorsepublishing.com, www.stone-horsepublishing.com. 2004. Fiction, non-fiction. avg. press run 7500. Expects 1 title 2006, 2 titles 2007. Discounts: 1 copy 40%, 2-100 copies 50%, 101 or more 55%. 55% Nonreturn option: If a buyer is willing to purchase nonreturnable books, discount is a flat 55% for 10 or more books, plus free freight. 32pp. Copyrights for author. Subjects: Children, Youth, Fantasy, Fiction, Non-Fiction, Picture Books.

•**Stony Meadow Publishing,** Stan Swanson, 2262 Ridge Drive, Broomfield, CO 80020, 303-960-9072 / stan@stonymeadowpublishing.com / www.stonymeadowpublishing.com. 2005. Fiction, non-fiction. "We publish children's books (fiction and non-fiction) and adult non-fiction titles at this time." avg. press run 1000. Expects 3 titles 2006, 4 titles 2007. Discounts: 25% discount to distributors, bookstores, retailers and institutions regardless of quantity. 200pp. Reporting time: 30-60 days. Simultaneous submissions accepted: Yes. Payment: We do not have a set royalty. Royalty is based on book's potential, number of pages, price, etc. Copyrights for author. Subjects: Advertising, Self-Promotion, Book Collecting, Bookselling, Collectibles, Creativity, Dictionaries, Fantasy, Fiction, How-To, Music, Non-Fiction, Novels, Parenting, Publishing, Writers/Writing, Young Adult.

Storm Publishing Group, Debarkes Johnson, 8117 Birchfield Dr, Indianapolis, IN 46268, stormpublishing@sbcglobal.net, www.stormpublishinggroup.com. 2005. Non-fiction. "we publish NONFICTION: How-to, cookbooks, gardening, travel guides and travel related books." avg. press run 3000. Expects 16 titles 2006, 30 titles 2007. 150pp. Reporting time: 2-6 months. Simultaneous submissions accepted: Yes. Publishes 55% of manuscripts submitted. Payment: 5-7% of retail for royalties, advances very from book to book. Copyrights for author. Subjects: Animals, Cooking, Finances, Gardening, How-To, Non-Fiction, Parenting, Pets, Publishing, Quilting, Sewing, Real Estate, Travel, Wood Engraving/Woodworking.

Stormline Press, Inc., Raymond Bial S., P. O. Box 593, Urbana, IL 61801, 217-328-2665. 1985. Poetry, fiction, art, photos, satire, non-fiction. "Stormline Press publishes works of literary and artistic distinction, with emphasis upon rural and small town life in the American Midwest. Notable titles include Living With Lincoln by Dan Guillory and Silent Friends by Margaret Lacey. No unsolicited queries or manuscripts are accepted. Stormline Press publishes by invitation only." avg. press run 1. Expects 1 title 2006, 1 title 2007. Discounts: 40% discount; no charge for shipping on orders of five or more books. 100-250pp. Reporting time: One month. Simultaneous submissions accepted: No. Payment: 15% of net sales price. 1. Subjects: Agriculture, Americana, Amish Culture, Fiction, History, Humor, Indiana, Literature (General), Mystery, Non-Fiction, North America, Photography, Short Stories, Storytelling, Writers/Writing.

STORMWARNING!, PO Box 21604, Seattle, WA 98111, 206-374-2215 phone/Fax, vvawai@oz.net, www.oz.net/~vvawai/. 1986. Poetry, articles, art, photos, cartoons, criticism, reviews, letters, news items, non-fiction. "Vets, Vietnam veterans especially encouraged. Anti-war, peace, justice issues, revolution, people's struggles. Veterans of all eras. Young people. Radical thinking." circ. 3M. 2-3/yr. Pub'd 2 issues 2005; expects 2 issues 2006, 2 issues 2007. sub. price $10; per copy $2; sample free. Back issues: 1/2 cover price. Discounts: bookstores/newstands 50%, outposts 3+ 70%. 16pp. Simultaneous submissions accepted: yes. Payment: none. Not copyrighted. Pub's reviews: 4 in 2005. §Books, Vietnam War, history, fiction by Nam vets, Gulf War, social issues. Ads: none. Subjects: Book Reviewing, Civil Rights, Communism, Marxism, Leninism, Counter-Culture, Alternatives, Communes, Crime, Criticism, Current Affairs, History, Human Rights, Military, Veterans, Peace, Politics, Vietnam, War, Young Adult.

Story County Books, Theresa Pappas, Co-Editor; Michael Martone, Co-Editor, PO Box 21179, Tuscaloosa, AL 35402-1179. 1984. Fiction. "Story County Books was published in Story County, Iowa. We publish one story chapbooks in formats that vary with each story. We publish cheap chapbooks, and we try to keep the price under $1. Our first book was Michael Wilkerson's *Can This Story Be Saved?* a take-off of the *Ladies Home Journal* piece. We chose a Dell Purse Book format to complement the 'self-improvement' parody of the piece. We are interested in clever stories, regional stories, stories with a voice." avg. press run 100. Pub'd 1 title 2005; expects 1 title 2006, 1 title 2007. Discounts: 50%. Pages vary. Reporting time: 14 months. Simultaneous submissions accepted: no. Publishes 1% of manuscripts submitted. Payment: by arrangement. Copyrights for author. Subject: Fiction.

Story Line Press, Robert McDowell, Three Oaks Farm, PO Box 1240, Ashland, OR 97520-0055, 541-512-8792, Fax 541-512-8793, mail@storylinepress.com, www.storylinepress.com. 1985. Poetry, fiction, criticism, long-poems, plays, non-fiction. avg. press run 2.5M. Pub'd 15 titles 2005; expects 15 titles 2006, 15 titles 2007. Discounts: bookstores 1-4 20%, 5-24 40%, 25-99 43%, 100+ 45%. 140pp. Payment: standard author's contract. Copyrights for author. Subject: Poetry.

STORYBOARD, Robert Alan Burns, General Editor, Christopher S. Lobban, Division of English, University of Guam, Mangilao, GU 96923, storybd@uog.edu, rburns@uog9.uog.edu. 1991. Poetry, fiction, art, photos, interviews, parts-of-novels, long-poems, non-fiction. "Material should have Pacific regional focus or be written by a resident of this region." circ. 200. 1/yr. Pub'd 1 issue 2005; expects 1 issue 2006, 1 issue 2007. sub. price $7.50; per copy $7.50; sample $4. Back issues: $5. Discounts: 30% retail; 50% distributor. 100pp. Reporting time: 4-6 months, SASE required. Simultaneous submissions accepted: no. Publishes 30% of manuscripts submitted. Payment: 2 copies. Copyrighted, reverts to author. Ads: $150/$100/$50 1/3 page. Subject: Pacific Region.

Storycraft Publishing (see also JUNIOR STORYTELLER; THE KIDS' STORYTELLING CLUB WEBSITE), Vivian Dubrovin, PO Box 205, Masonville, CO 80541, 970-669-3755 phone/Fax, Vivian@storycraft.com, www.storycraft.com. 1993. Fiction, articles, non-fiction. "Shipping address: 8600 Firethorn Drive, Loveland, CO 80538. We are a narrow niche publisher of books and periodicals for young (age 9-12) storytellers. Interested in feature articles on young tellers and programs for young storytellers. We are expanding into related areas. Query only. No unsolicited material accepted." avg. press run 3M. Pub'd 1 title 2005; expects 1 title 2006, 1-3 titles 2007. Discounts: library 20%, bookstore 40%, distributor 50%, other by contract. 80-204pp. Reporting time: query only. Simultaneous submissions accepted: no. Payment: varies. Copyrights for author vary. Subjects: Children, Youth, Crafts, Hobbies, Education, Storytelling, Young Adult.

STORYQUARTERLY, M. M. M. Hayes, Editor & Co-Publisher; Will Hayes, Co-Publisher, 431 Sheridan Road, Kenilworth, IL 60043-1220, www.storyquarterly.com; storyquarterly@yahoo.com; 847-256-6998;. 1975. Fiction, photos, interviews, satire, parts-of-novels, non-fiction. "Accept submissions only online, as of Oct 1, 2003. Read only between Oct 1 and January 31. Needs: Literary stories of any type or style, serious or humorous. No preferred length. Short-shorts as well as longer. Accept transl. of contemporary authors, looking especially for Spanish translations in both languages. No genre work. Publish prominent and first-time authors in each issue. Recently published: Chris Abani, Steve Almond, Richard Bausch, T.C. Boyle, Robert Olen Butler, John Casey, J.M. Coetzee, Rebecca Curtis, Stephen Dixon, Andre Dubus, Stuart Dybek, Richard Ford, Reginald Gibbons, Robert Hellenga, Alice Hoffman, Charles Johnson, David Michael Kaplan, James McManus, Angeles Mastretta, Pamela Painter, Emily Raboteau, Mark Strand, Mark Winegardner, and Nancy Zafris. Robie Macauley Award given to one story already selected for publication. Meticulous editing and author-approval of galleys. Publish 35-50 stories per year, three publications online and one large print anthology annually.'' circ. 6,000. One large print anthology published annually; Three quarters published online. Pub'd 1 issue 2005; expects 2 issues 2006, 4 issues 2007. sub. price one year $9; two years $16; five years $40; life subscription $250.; per copy $9; sample $6; foreign orders add $6 for postage. Back issues: $6; foreign orders add $6 for postage. Discounts: contact Editor. 550pp. Reporting time: 2-4 months. Simultaneous submissions accepted: yes. Publishes .05% of manuscripts submitted. Payment: 10 copies and life subscription. Copyrighted, reverts to author. Ads: $175/90/50. Subjects: Fiction, Literature (General), Translation.

Storytime Ink International, Christine Petrell Kallevig, PO Box 470505, Cleveland, OH 44147-0505, 440-838-4881; fax 408-580-5967; e-mail storytimeink@att.net. 1991. ''Looking for material that combines storytelling with a tangible art form, i.e. cutting stories, drawing stories, folding stories. Should be less than 1,000 words with an ironic twist at the end. No violence. Should be appropriate for children, but entertaining for adults.'' avg. press run 5M. Expects 2 titles 2006, 2 titles 2007. Discounts: usual trade. 100pp. Reporting time: 1 month. Payment: negotiable. Copyrights for author. Subjects: Children, Youth, Crafts, Hobbies, Education, Storytelling.

•THE STRANGE FRUIT, Jessica Star Rockers, 300 Lenora Street #250, Seattle, WA 98121, phone 206-780-1921, fax 309-273-8112, www.thestrangefruit.com, submissions@thestrangefruit.com. 2005. Poetry, fiction, parts-of-novels, non-fiction. ''the strange fruit reveres authenticity, preferring plain-spoken, straightforward language over obscure, verbose imagery. We aim to present poetry and prose that examines personal experiences for their commonly strange synchronicity. We gravitate towards work that demonstrates the profundity of what appears casual, that which usually goes unspoken, capturing those small moments whose meaning speaks loudest when we are most quiet.'' circ. 500. 2/yr. Expects 2 issues 2006, 2 issues 2007. sub. price $11; per copy $6; sample $6. Back issues: inquire. 100pp. Reporting time: 1-3 months. Simultaneous submissions accepted: Yes. Payment: contributors receive two copies of the issue in which their work appears. Copyrighted, reverts to author. Subjects: Essays, Fiction, Non-Fiction, Poetry, Short Stories.

Strata Publishing, Inc., Kathleen Domenig, PO Box 1303, State College, PA 16804, 814-234-8545, Fax 814-238-7222, www.stratapub.com. 1990. Non-fiction. ''We publish mid-and upper-level textbooks for college courses, as well as scholarly and professional books that might be used extensively in such courses.'' Pub'd 4 titles 2005; expects 1 title 2006, 3 titles 2007. Reporting time: 1-3 months. Simultaneous submissions accepted: yes. Payment: varies. Copyrights for author. Subjects: Civil Rights, Communication, Journalism, Communication, Journalism, Criticism, Editing, Language, Law, Media, Media, Political Science, Speaking, Writers/Writing.

Strawberry Patchworks, Susan A. McCreary, Box 3, Green Mansion, North, VA 23128, 804-725-7560, berrybooks@villagepop.com. 1982. Non-fiction. ''We specialize in one subject cookbooks, softcover using 4 color process on cover. Emphasis on originality of subject and exploring every aspect of the subject. Poetry, art and history are incorporated throughout books.'' avg. press run 2M-4M. Pub'd 1 title 2005; expects 1 title 2006, 1 title 2007. Discounts: trade 40%, wholesaler 50%. 100-200pp. Reporting time: 1 month or less. Payment: negotiable, no advances. Copyrights for author. Subjects: Cooking, Ecology, Foods.

STRINGTOWN, Polly Buckingham, Editor; Jenny Heard, Associate Editor, PO Box 1406, Medical Lake, WA 99022-1406, stringtown@earthlink.net, http://www.home.earthlink.net/~stringtown/index.html. 1998. Poetry, fiction, parts-of-novels, long-poems, plays, non-fiction. ''Submissions determine the content. We prefer to read manuscripts Sept.-April. We've published work from Peter Meinke, Judith Skillman, James Bertolino, and James Nolan.'' circ. 1M. 1/yr. Pub'd 1 issue 2005; expects 1 issue 2006, 1 issue 2007. sub. price $6.00; per copy $6.00; sample $6.00 or $3.00 for any back issue. Back issues: $3. Discounts: $4 wholesale or $4.50 consignment for independent bookstores. 56pp. Average reporting time is three to six months. We accept simultaneous submissions with notification upon acceptance elsewhere. Publishes 10-15% of manuscripts submitted. Payment: 5 copies. Copyrighted, reverts to author. Subjects: Fiction, Poetry.

STRUGGLE: A Magazine of Proletarian Revolutionary Literature, Tim Hall, PO Box 13261, Detroit, MI 48213-0261. 1985. Poetry, fiction, articles, art, cartoons, satire, criticism, reviews, music, letters, collages, plays. ''We want literature and art of rebellion against the ruling class.'' 4/yr. Pub'd 2 issues 2005; expects 4 issues 2006, 4 issues 2007. sub. price $10, $12 to institutions, $15 overseas, $5 to prisoners, trades ok; per copy $2; sample $3.00 via mail. Back issues: by arrangement (vol. 1 available, photocopied at extra charge), $120 for full set (19 years). Discounts: by arrangement. 36pp. Reporting time: 3 months. We encourage simultaneous submissions. Publishes 10% of manuscripts submitted. Payment: 1 copy. Not copyrighted. Ads: none. Subjects: Astronomy, Black, Chicano/a, Communism, Marxism, Leninism, Drama, Fiction, Humor, Labor, Native

American, Poetry, Satire, Short Stories, Socialist, Third World, Minorities, Women.

STUDENT LAWYER, Ira Pilchen, Editor, ABA Publishing, Ira Pilchen, 321 North Clark St., Ste. LL2, Chicago, IL 60610-4772. 1972. Articles. *"Student Lawyer* is a monthly legal affairs magazine circulated to members of the American Bar Association's Law Student Division. It is a features magazine, not a legal journal, competing for a share of law students' limited spare time, so the articles we publish must be informative, lively 'good reads.' We have no interest whatsoever in footnoted, academic articles. *Student Lawyer* has 4 feature articles in each issue, ranging from 2,500 to 4,000 words apiece. We also have 5 to 6 departments , 1,200-1,800 word articles covering innovative legal programs, commentary, and brief law school and legal world news items. Writers should write according to the amount of their material and not beyond. We are interested in professional and legal education issues, sociolegal phenomena, legal career features, profiles of lawyers who are making an impact on the profession. We do not accept poetry." circ. 30M. 9/yr. Pub'd 9 issues 2005; expects 9 issues 2006, 9 issues 2007. sub. price $22; per copy $8; sample same. Discounts: included in membership to ABA's Law Student Division. 48pp. Reporting time: 4 weeks. Payment: varies. Copyrighted, reverts to author. Ads: $2,070/$1,345/$23.75 first 20 words, $1.05/word thereafter. Subject: Law.

STUDIA CELTICA, University Of Wales Press, J. Beverley Smith, Chief Editor, Miranda Aldhouse-Green, Frances Lynch, W. J. Mahon, Dafydd Johnston, 10 Columbus Walk, Brigantine Place, Cardiff CF10 4UP, Wales, 44-029-2049-6899, Fax 44-029-2049-6108, press@press.wales.ac.uk, www.wales.ac.uk/press. 1966. Articles. "Devoted mainly to philological and linguistic studies of the Celtic languages." circ. 300. 1/yr. sub. price £25 individuals, £40 institutions; per copy £25 individuals, £40 institutions; sample same. Back issues: £20 per double issue. Discounts: 10%. 350pp. Payment: none. Pub's reviews: 9 in 2005. §Celtic. Ads: none. Subject: Celtic.

Studio 4 Productions, Karen Ervin-Pershing, PO Box 280400, Northridge, CA 91328-0400, 888publish (782-5474), Fax 314-993-4485, www.studio4productions.com. 1972. "Length: +/-200 pages. Most recent publications: *The Wisdom to Choose* and *Shadowdad*." avg. press run 3M-6M. Pub'd 3 titles 2005; expects 3 titles 2006, 3 titles 2007. Discounts: varies 30-65% (quantity based). 200pp. Reporting time: 30 days. Simultaneous submissions accepted: yes. Publishes 5% of manuscripts submitted. Payment: 10% list paid annually. We hold copyrights on most books. Subjects: Parenting, Self-Help, Senior Citizens, Social Work, Travel.

STUDIO - A Journal of Christians Writing, Paul Grover, Managing Editor, Robert Leighton-Jones, Kate Lumley, 727 Peel Street, Albury, N.S.W. 2640, Australia, email: pgrover@bigpond.com,www: www.studio-journal.net. 1980. Poetry, fiction, articles, reviews, letters. "Published poets by reputable Australian publishing houses have been represented. Material varies from short poems to short stories of 2M to 5M words." circ. 300. 4/yr. Pub'd 4 issues 2005; expects 4 issues 2006, 4 issues 2007. sub. price $AUD60; per copy $AUD15; sample $AUD10 (air mail). Discounts: order of 20 or more in advance of printing receives 10%. 36pp. Reporting time: 3 months. Simultaneous submissions accepted: yes. Publishes 20% of manuscripts submitted. Payment: for contests $AUD50, no payment for ordinary submissions but free copy posted for submissions. Copyrighted, reverts to author. Pub's reviews: 30 in 2005. §Poetry, fiction, books for children. Ads: $AUD100/$AUD50/no classified. Subjects: Australia, Book Reviewing, Fiction, Graphics, Literary Review, Literature (General), Poetry, Religion.

STUDIO ONE, College of St. Benedict, Haehn Campus Center, St. Joseph, MN 56374. 1976. Poetry, fiction, art, photos, satire, long-poems. "Short fiction should generally be fewer than 5,000 words. *Studio One* accepts submissions of literary and visual art from across the nation, but contributors from the Midwest are especially encouraged to submit. Art should reproduce well in black and white. Now accept color visual art." circ. 900. 1/yr. Pub'd 1 issue 2005; expects 1 issue 2006, 1 issue 2007. sub. price $6 check or money order with SASE. 70-100pp. Reporting time: we try to send out acceptance/rejection letters within 1 month of the deadline. Simultaneous submissions accepted: no. Publishes 10% of manuscripts submitted. Payment: none. Copyrighted, reverts to author. Subjects: Arts, Essays, Fiction, Photography, Poetry, Short Stories.

Stunt Publishing, Michael Kewley, 22287 Mulholland Hwy, #281, Calabasas, CA 91302, ph:818-312-5157, fax:818-312-5157, www.stuntpublishing.com, stuntpublishing@stuntpublishing.com. 2003. Fiction, art, collages. "children's books." Pub'd 1 title 2005; expects 1-2 titles 2006, 1-2 titles 2007. 32pp. Simultaneous submissions accepted: Yes. Subjects: Children, Youth, Family, Picture Books.

SUBSYNCHRONOUS PRESS, THE LAUGHING DOG, Hillary Lyon, Co-editor; Warren Andrle, Co-editor, 4729 E. Sunrise #326, Tucson, AZ 85718. 2000. "Submit no more than 3 poems, 30 lines each, with SASE." circ. 150. Twice a year. Pub'd 2 issues 2005; expects 2 issues 2006, 2 issues 2007. price per copy $3; sample $2. 30pp. Reporting time: 2-6 months. Simultaneous submissions accepted: *No*. Payment: Contributors recieve one free copy of the issue their poem(s) appears in. Copyrighted, reverts to author.

SUB-TERRAIN, Anvil Press, Brian Kaufman, Managing Editor, P.O. Box 3008, Main Post Office, Vancouver, BC V6B 3X5, Canada, 604-876-8710, subter@portal.ca, www.subterrain.ca. 1988. Poetry, fiction,

461

articles, photos, interviews, satire, criticism, reviews, non-fiction. "subTerrain no longer accepts unsolicited poetry submissions." circ. 4M. 3/yr. Pub'd 3 issues 2005; expects 3 issues 2006, 3 issues 2007. sub. price $15; per copy $4.95 Can., $3.95 US; sample $5 to cover post. Back issues: $5. 56pp. Reporting time: 4-6 months. Simultaneous submissions are accepted, but please inform us if the work has been accepted for publication elsewhere. Publishes 5% of manuscripts submitted. Payment: Prose: $25 per page; Poetry: $20 per poem; photography/illustration: $25 - $100; plus complimentary 1-year subscription + 5 contributor copies of issue in which your work appears. Copyrighted, reverts to author. Pub's reviews: 30 in 2005. §Poetry, fiction, social issues (primarily releases from small to med. size publishers not receiving attention they deserve). Send review copies Attn: Review Column. Ads: $750 (full col., back cover); $575 (full col. inside front/back); $450 (full page b/w); $250 1/2 page; Publishing industry, bookstores, literary related *only*. Subjects: Avant-Garde, Experimental Art, Erotica, Experimental, Fiction, Non-Fiction, Prose, Satire, Socialist, Theatre.

Suburban Wilderness Press (see also RED HAWK), PO Box 202, Kailua-Kona, HI 96745. 1984. Poetry, fiction, art, photos, collages. "Broadsides." avg. press run 150. Pub'd 40 titles 2005; expects 40 titles 2006, 40 titles 2007. Discounts: none. 1 page broadsides. Reporting time: 1 week to never. Publishes a variable % of manuscripts submitted. Payment: varies. Copyrights for author. Subjects: Minnesota, Poetry.

Success Publishing, Allan H. Smith, 3419 Dunham Drive, Box 263, Warsaw, NY 14569. 1978. Non-fiction. "How to make money. How to start in business. How to market your product. How to publish. Sewing, craft, business." avg. press run 2M-5M. Pub'd 6 titles 2005; expects 4 titles 2006, 6 titles 2007. Discounts: 1 10%, 2-6 25%, 7-15 40%, 16-50 50%, 50-100 53%; library 25%. 150pp. Reporting time: 90-120 days. Payment: varies. Copyrights for author. Subjects: Crafts, Hobbies, Education, Family, How-To, Printing, Quilting, Sewing.

Sugar Loaf Press, 4160 Racoon Valley Road, Alexandria, OH 43001, 740-924-9335. 2000. Pub'd 1 title 2005; expects 2 titles 2006, 2 titles 2007. Reporting time: 1 month.

Sherwood Sugden & Company, Publishers, Sherwood Sugden, 315 Fifth Street, Peru, IL 61354, 815-224-6651, Fax 815-223-4486, philomon1@netscape.net www.geocities.com/sugdenpublishers/ (or) www.sugdenpublishers.com. 1975. Non-fiction. avg. press run 3M. Pub'd 3 titles 2005; expects 3 titles 2006, 3 titles 2007. Discounts: 40% STOP; otherwise 20%-1 copy, 25% 2-3 copies, 40%-5+ copies. 300pp. Reporting time: 2-3 months. Payment: 8%-12%. Copyrights for author. Subjects: Biography, Christianity, Criticism, Education, English, History, History, Literature (General), Philosophy, Religion, Reprints, South, Textbooks.

SULPHUR RIVER LITERARY REVIEW, SRLR Press, James Michael Robbins, PO Box 19228, Austin, TX 78760-9228, 512-292-9456. 1978. Poetry, fiction, articles, art, photos, interviews, satire, criticism, non-fiction. circ. 200. 2/yr. Pub'd 2 issues 2005; expects 2 issues 2006, 2 issues 2007. sub. price $12; per copy $7; sample $7. Back issues: $7. 145pp. Reporting time: 1 month. Simultaneous submissions accepted: yes. Publishes 1% of manuscripts submitted. Payment: 2 contributor's copies. Copyrighted, reverts to author. Subjects: Arts, Essays, Fiction, Language, Literary Review, Literature (General), Myth, Mythology, Non-Fiction, Poetry, Prose, Short Stories, Visual Arts.

SUMMER ACADEME: A Journal of Higher Education, Caddo Gap Press, David Schejbal, Editor, 3145 Geary Boulevard #275, San Francisco, CA 94118, 415-392-1911. 1997. Articles. "An annual journal of college and university summer session administrators." circ. 1M. 1/yr. Pub'd 1 issue 2005; expects 1 issue 2006, 1 issue 2007. sub. price $30 indiv., $60 instit.; per copy $30. 96pp. Reporting time: 2 months. Publishes 25% of manuscripts submitted. Payment: none. Copyrighted, reverts to author. Ads: none. Subject: Education.

Summer Stream Press, David Duane Frost, Editor, PO Box 6056, Santa Barbara, CA 93160-6056, 805-962-6540. 1978. Poetry, non-fiction. "This press is now producing and marketing a series of cassette tapes under the general title: Poetic Heritage. #102180 Elinor Wylie/Amy Lowell; #103010 Sara Teadsale/Margaret Widdemer; #103150 Edna St. Vincent Millay; #103290 Emily Dickinson/Lizette Woodworth Reese." avg. press run 5M. Expects 1 title 2007. Discounts: 50% no returns. 450pp. Reporting time: 6 months to 1 year. Simultaneous submissions accepted: yes. Publishes 2% of manuscripts submitted. Payment: 15% - paid annually January 1st. Copyrights for author. Subjects: Non-Fiction, Poetry.

Summerset Press, Brooks Robards, Jim Kaplan, 20 Langworthy Road, Northampton, MA 01060, 413-586-3394 phone/FAX, BrooksRoba@aol.com. 1994. avg. press run 1M. Expects 1 title 2006. Discounts: 60-40%. 100pp. Reporting time: 30 days. Simultaneous submissions accepted: yes. Payment: individually negotiated. Does not copyright for author. Subjects: Poetry, Sports, Outdoors, Travel.

Summit Crossroads Press, Eileen Haavik, 3154 Gracefield Road - Suite T13, Silver Spring, MD 20904, 301-890-1647, Fax 301-890-1647, SumCross@aol.com, www.parentsuccess.com. 1993. Non-fiction. "Publishes books relating to parenting, family and school." avg. press run 5M. Discounts: wholesaler/distributor 55%, bookstores 40%. 250pp. Reporting time: 2 weeks. Simultaneous submissions accepted: yes. Payment: 10% of net receipts. Copyrights for author. Subjects: Children, Youth, Family, Parenting.

462

Sun Books (see also THE TOWNSHIPS SUN), Patricia Ball, Box 28, Lennoxville, Quebec J1M 1Z3, Canada. "Books published only for clients to their specs. They hold all rights, etc." Subject: History.

Sun Designs, PO Box 6, Oconomowoc, WI 53066, 262-567-4255. 1979. Photos. "These are books of designs, with some plans, some books have a short history, toy book has children's story." avg. press run 20M. Pub'd 2 titles 2005; expects 1 title 2006, 1 title 2007. 96pp. Copyrights for author. Subjects: Crafts, Hobbies, Design.

Sun Dog Press, Al Berlinski, 22058 Cumberland Drive, Northville, MI 48167, 248-449-7448, Fax 248-449-4070, sundogpr@voyager.net. 1987. Poetry, fiction, letters. "Hard-edged and innovative fiction, poetry, letters. Book length manuscripts considered." avg. press run 500-1M. Pub'd 2 titles 2005; expects 2 titles 2006, 2 titles 2007. Discounts: 20%-48%. 250pp. Reporting time: 8 weeks. Simultaneous submissions accepted: yes. Payment: royalty on sales. Copyrights for author. Subjects: Fantasy, Fiction, Memoirs, Poetry.

•**Sun Rising Press,** Smock Donette, 724 Felix Street, St Joseph, MO 64501, 816-676-0122. 2003. Poetry, fiction, non-fiction. "There are actually three imprints The Sun Rising Poetry Press authors such as Anastasia Clark, CE Laines and many of the greats in poetry today. The Sun Rising Press- South of Mainstree- Robert Gately nominated for pulizer. The Mandala Press self help and metaphysical books. Gordon banta books, Rochelle Morore, Jessica Taylor and many other well knowns." avg. press run 1000. Pub'd 20 titles 2005; expects 50 titles 2006, 100 titles 2007. Discounts: 35% 5-50 copies 40% 50+-all sales returnable. 150pp. Reporting time: with in two days if submitted electronically. Simultaneous submissions accepted: Yes. Payment: 10-20%. Copyrights for author. Subjects: Acupuncture, Alcohol, Alcoholism, Alternative Medicine, Aromatherapy, Astrology, Buddhism, Edgar Cayce, Crime, Crystals, Cults, Culture, Mental Health, Myth, Mythology, New Age, Zen.

THE SUN, A Magazine of Ideas, Sy Safransky, 107 North Roberson Street, Chapel Hill, NC 27516, 919-942-5282. 1974. Poetry, fiction, articles, art, photos, cartoons, interviews, satire, letters, parts-of-novels, long-poems, collages, non-fiction. "A monthly magazine of ideas in its twenty-eighth year of publication, *The Sun* celebrates good writing—and the warmth of shared intimacies—in essays, fiction, interviews, and poetry. People write in the magazine of their struggle to understand their lives, often baring themselves with remarkable candor. Recent contributors: Poe Ballantine, Derrick Jensen, Alison Luterman, Stephen J. Lyons, and Sybil Smith." circ. 50M. 12/yr. Pub'd 12 issues 2005; expects 12 issues 2006, 12 issues 2007. sub. price $34; per copy $3.95; sample $5. Back issues: complete set of all available back issues for $300. Discounts: 50% for distributors. 48pp. Reporting time: 3 months. Simultaneous submissions accepted: no. Publishes 1% of manuscripts submitted. Payment: essays and interviews $300-$1,000; short stories $300-$500; poetry $50-$200; photos $50-$300. Copyrighted, reverts to author. Ads: none. Subjects: Essays, Fiction, Interviews, Journals, Non-Fiction, Photography, Poetry.

Sunbelt Publications, Lowell Lindsay, 1256 Fayette Street, El Cajon, CA 92020-1511, 619-258-4911, Fax 619-258-4916, mail@sunbeltpub.com, www.sunbeltbooks.com. 1988. Fiction, non-fiction. "We accept proposals for nonfiction books with camera-ready supporting materials (e.g., photos, maps, artwork) that would have a broad, general market appeal in our genre of 'Adventures in the Cultural Heritage and Natural History of the Californias.'" avg. press run 3M-5M. Pub'd 14 titles 2005; expects 6 titles 2006, 6 titles 2007. Discounts: 40% to booksellers with resale #, 55% to AWBA-listed wholesalers. 250-300pp. Reporting time: 1 month. Simultaneous submissions accepted: yes. Payment: royalties based on net sales. Copyright will be registered for author, but may assigned to author or publisher. Subjects: Bicycling, California, Dictionaries, Earth, Natural History, Folklore, Geology, History, Maps, Mexico, Native American, Non-Fiction, Sports, Outdoors, Travel, U.S. Hispanic, The West.

Sunlight Publishers, Joseph Kent, Poetry Editor, PO Box 640545, San Francisco, CA 94109, 415-776-6249. 1989. Poetry. "Some bias toward poetic consciousness of an evolutionary nature and organic poetry in the modernist vein based on experience of the perceiver." avg. press run 700. Expects 3 titles 2006. Discounts: 2-4 30%, 5-100 40%. 64pp. Reporting time: 1 month. Payment: 10% royalty on all sales, paid twice yearly. Copyrights for author. Subject: Poetry.

•**sunnyoutside,** David McNamara, P.O. Box 441429, Somerville, MA 02144, www.sunnyoutside.com. Poetry, fiction, non-fiction. Simultaneous submissions accepted: No. Does not copyright for author.

Sunnyside Press, Richard Triumpho, 297 Triumpho Road, St. Johnsville, NY 13452-4003, 518-568-7853 phone/Fax, triglade@telenet.net. 2001. Non-fiction. avg. press run 1M. Pub'd 2 titles 2005; expects 2 titles 2006, 4 titles 2007. Discounts: trade 40%. 248pp. Reporting time: 6 weeks. Simultaneous submissions accepted: yes. Publishes 10% of manuscripts submitted. Payment: negotiable. Copyrights for author. Subjects: Adirondacks, Agriculture, Alaska, Americana, Amish Culture, Business & Economics, Folklore, Non-Fiction.

•**Sunrise Health Coach Publications,** Jan DeCourtney, PO Box 21132, Boulder, CO 80308, Phone and fax: 303-527-2886, info@sunrisehealthcoach.com, http://sunrisehealthcoach.com. 1996. Non-fiction. "Alternative medicine books for symptom relief, pain relief, natural healing, physical, emotional, and mental health. Books focusing on self-help for chronic illness and optimal health.'' avg. press run 3000. Expects 1 title 2006, 2 titles 2007. Discounts: See website at http://sunrisehealthcoach.com. 100-440pp. Reporting time: 2 months. Simultaneous submissions accepted: Yes. Payment: TBA. TBA. Subjects: Alternative Medicine, Health, Self-Help.

SunShine Press Publications, Inc., Jackie Hofer, Publisher, 6 Gardner Court, Longmont, CO 80501, 303-772-3556, jlhof1@yahoo.com, www.sunshinepress.com. 1986. Poetry, photos, non-fiction. ''Will be publishing books and chapbooks in CD format *only* for reading and viewing in Adobe Reader. All will be in full color including any photographs, art or illustrations. They will be sold primarily on the Internet and other online sources. Recent publication: *Tree Magic: Nature's Antennas* 450 pages in full color, 169 authors (poems and short stories) and 115 photos and paintings. Authors include Kirby Congdon, Jim Fisher, John Fitzpatrick, Laurie Klein, Jacqueline Marcus, Reg Saner, Howard Rheingold and others. (see www.sunshinepress.com) Currently working on a CD of nature poems, photographs and paintings. Watch *Small Press Review* and *Poets and Writers* for requests for submissions.'' avg. press run 1,000. Pub'd 1 title 2005; expects 2 titles 2006, 3 titles 2007. 200pp. Reporting time: 3 months SASE. Simultaneous submissions accepted: yes. Copyrights for author. Subjects: Animals, Anthology, Arts, Color, Essays, Nature, Non-Fiction, Poetry, Prose, Short Stories, Spiritual.

Sunstone Press, James Clois Smith Jr., President, PO Box 2321, Santa Fe, NM 87504-2321, 505-988-4418, fax 505-988-1025, jsmith@sunstonepress.com. 1971. Fiction, non-fiction. ''Primarily southwestern US subjects; prefers non-fiction.'' avg. press run 3M. Pub'd 24 titles 2005; expects 24 titles 2006, 30 titles 2007. Discounts: standard. 160pp. Reporting time: 90 days or less. Simultaneous submissions accepted: no. Payment: royalty only. Copyrights for author. Subjects: Crafts, Hobbies, History, Southwest.

SUPERIOR CHRISTIAN NEWS, Superior Christian Press, Ed Chaberek, Guna Chaberek, PO Box 424, Superior, MT 59872. 1995. Poetry, articles. ''Recent contributors include Arthur Winfield Knight, Robert Kimm, Simon Perchik, John Grey, and Ronald Scott. Poetry, 40 lines or less, emphasis on originality. Very important - we want translations of poetry from any language. Magazine is now a Christian publication, please consider this when submitting.'' circ. 100-150. 4/yr. Pub'd 4 issues 2005; expects 4 issues 2006, 4 issues 2007. sub. price $6; per copy $6; sample $6. Back issues: none. Discounts: classroom 10 copies $50. 24-40pp. Reporting time: within 6 months. Simultaneous submissions accepted: yes. Publishes 10% of manuscripts submitted. Payment: 1 copy. Not copyrighted, all rights except 1st always with author. No ads. Subjects: Poetry, Translation.

Superior Christian Press (see also SUPERIOR CHRISTIAN NEWS), Ed Chaberek, Guna Chaberek, PO Box 424, Superior, MT 59872. 1995. Poetry, articles. ''We are looking for more inspirational, factual, research-oriented prose (nonfiction) pieces of a Christian nature. No biases. But must be sound intellectually. Though we believe in Jesus absolutely and in the literal Resurrection we, like the writers of the Gospels and Paul, maintain that faith must be supported by intellect.'' avg. press run 100-150. Pub'd 4 titles 2005; expects 4 titles 2006, 4 titles 2007. 24-40pp. Reporting time: within 6 months. We accept simultaneous submissions, but want to be informed. Publishes less than 10% of manuscripts submitted. Payment: 1 copy on publication. Does not copyright for author. Subjects: Philosophy, Poetry, Religion, Sociology.

George Suttton Publishing Co., Sutton George, 54 Crawford Drive, Aurora, Ontario, Canada L4G 4R4, Canada, georgesutton2005@yahoo.com. 2004. Fiction, articles, interviews, criticism, reviews, letters, parts-of-novels. ''Some recent contributors:1. Recently re-discovered works/letters/diaries by Leo Tolstoy, one of the world 's best novelists2. Seniors Yearbook and Directory with many Health, Longevity, Retirement Tips, etc.'' avg. press run 500. Pub'd 2 titles 2005; expects 5 titles 2006, 10 titles 2007. Discounts: 2-10 copies 25%. 250pp. Reporting time: 2 months. Simultaneous submissions accepted: No. Publishes 1% of manuscripts submitted. Payment: 10 percent. Does not copyright for author. Subjects: Family, Health, Language, Literature (General).

Swallow's Tale Press (see also Livingston Press), Joe Taylor, Editor, c/o LU Press, Station 22, University of West Alabama, Livingston, AL 35470. 1983. Poetry, fiction. avg. press run 1M. Expects 1 title 2007. Discounts: 20-50%. 88pp. Reporting time: 6 months. Publishes 1% of manuscripts submitted. Payment: percentage of books. Copyrights for author. Subjects: Fiction, Poetry.

Swamp Press (see also TIGHTROPE), Ed Rayher, 15 Warwick Avenue, Northfield, MA 01360-1105. 1975. Poetry, art, long-poems. ''We make limited edition letterpress books which live up to the standards of the fine-crafted poem. We're open to almost anything, as long as it's the best...to last 1,000 years. Recent contributors: Chuck Zerby, L.A. Davidson, vincent tripi, Robert Bensen.'' avg. press run 300. Pub'd 2 titles 2005; expects 2 titles 2006, 2 titles 2007. Discounts: dealers and booksellers 40%, continuing collectors 40%, libraries 20%. 60pp. Reporting time: 8 weeks. Simultaneous submissions accepted: no. Publishes 1% of manuscripts submitted. Payment: 10% press run. Does not copyright for author. Subject: Poetry.

Swan Duckling Press (see also THE BLUE MOUSE), Mark Bruce, PO Box 586, Cypress, CA 90630. 1999.

Poetry. avg. press run 300. Pub'd 3 titles 2005. 40pp. Reporting time: 3-6 months. Simultaneous submissions accepted: no. Publishes 20% of manuscripts submitted. Payment: authors retain copyright, pays in copies. We do not copyright for author unless chapbook.

Swan Publishing Company, Sharon Davis, Hal Davidson, Pete Billac, Debra Merry, Quinn Brown, 1059 County Road 100, Burnet, TX 78611-3535, 512-756-6800, swanbooks@ghg.net, www.swan-pub.com. 1987. Fiction, non-fiction. "Our first two books have been successful; *How Not To Be Lonely* is approaching 400,000 copies in print in 13 months. Our authors work with us to promote their books and we work under an unusual arrangement. We are not a vanity publisher but we sought investors for the authors and worked the arrangements to mutual satisfaction." avg. press run 5M. Pub'd 12 titles 2005; expects 15 titles 2006, 20 titles 2007. Discounts: call for rates. 96pp. Reporting time: 1 month maximum. Payment: 10%, more with volume sales. Copyrights for author. Subjects: Advertising, Self-Promotion, Autos, Construction, Family, Fiction, Gardening, Health, How-To, Medicine, Men, Parenting, Real Estate, Self-Help, Self-Help, Sex, Sexuality.

Swan Raven & Company, Amy Owen, Managing Editor, PO Box 1429, Columbus, NC 28722. 1992. "We do books in the areas of shamanisn/indigevous; alternative healthy positive speculations for the future, and men/women issues." avg. press run 5M. Pub'd 2 titles 2005; expects 2 titles 2006, 3 titles 2007. Discounts: 40% wholesale. 220pp. Reporting time: 1 month-45 days. Simultaneous submissions accepted: no. Publishes 1% of manuscripts submitted. Payment: 8%-15% at 7,500 increments. Copyrights for author. Subjects: Autobiography, Children, Youth, Counter-Culture, Alternatives, Communes, Futurism, Health, Indians, Metaphysics, Native American, New Age, Psychology, Spiritual, Women.

Swedenborg Foundation, Deborah Forman, 320 North Church Street, West Chester, PA 19380, (610) 430-3222 (Phone), (610) 430-7982 Fax, 1-800-355-3222 (Phone), info@swedenborg.com, www.swedenborg.com. 1850. Fiction, articles, interviews, non-fiction. "We only accept for publication books that contain Swedenborgian content consistent with out mission. Most of our books are by or about Swedenborg's life and work. Our annual Chrysalis Reader is an anthology of short prose pieces and poems." Pub'd 4 titles 2005; expects 4 titles 2006, 7 titles 2007. Discounts: Retail discount schedule:(all books combine for discounts whether single or assorted titles)1- 4 copies 20%5- 24 copies 40%25-99 copies 42%. 220pp. Reporting time: three months. Simultaneous submissions accepted: Yes. Publishes 5% of manuscripts submitted. Copyrights for author. Subjects: Non-Fiction, Religion, Self-Help, Spiritual.

SWEET ANNIE & SWEET PEA REVIEW, Sweet Annie Press, Beverly A. Clark, 7750 Highway F-24 West, Baxter, IA 50028, 641-792-3578, Fax 641-792-1310. 1995. Poetry, fiction, photos, reviews. "Short stories, poems of short to medium length. No violence." circ. 30. 4/yr. Pub'd 4 issues 2005; expects 4 issues 2006, 4 issues 2007. sub. price $24; per copy $6; sample $6 + $1 shipping. 34pp. Reporting time: 4-6 months or shorter. We prefer not to accept simultaneous submissions. Publishes 25% of manuscripts submitted. Payment: 1 copy. Copyrighted, reverts to author. Pub's reviews: 1 in 2005. §Environmental (land, sea), women's issues, natural living, health, food, stress reduction, simplified living, solitude, meditation. Subjects: Poetry, Short Stories.

Sweet Annie Press (see also SWEET ANNIE & SWEET PEA REVIEW), Beverly A. Clark, 7750 Highway F-24 West, Baxter, IA 50028, 641-417-0020. 1995. Poetry, fiction, photos, reviews, letters, long-poems, non-fiction. "$5 reading fee." avg. press run 30. Expects 4 titles 2006, 4 titles 2007. Discounts: none. 34pp. Reporting time: 4-6 months, will be shorter in future. We prefer not to accept simultaneous submissions. Publishes 25% of manuscripts submitted. Payment: 1 copy. Does not copyright for author. Subjects: Poetry, Short Stories.

Swing-Hi Press, Lara Kilgore, 16213 East Mercer Circle, Aurora, CO 80013, 303-766-3153, fax:303-766-2989, toll free:1-866-828-8725, barbara@naturalbodyshape.com, www.naturalbodyshape.com. 2003. Expects 1 title 2006, 1 title 2007. Subject: Yoga.

SWINK, Leelila Strogov, 244 Fifth Ave. #2722, New York, NY 10001, 212-591-1651, 212-658-9995, www.swinkmag.com. 2004. Poetry, fiction, art, photos, cartoons, parts-of-novels, long-poems, non-fiction. "Swink is a biannual print magazine dedicated to identifying and promoting literary talent in both established and emerging writers. We're interested in writing that pushes the boundaries of the traditionalwriting that is new in concept, form or execution; that reflects a diversity of thought, experience or perspective; that provokes or entertains. Recent authors include Amy Bloom, Charles D'Ambrosio, Neal Pollack, Chris Offutt, Jonathan Ames, Steve Almond, Bob Hicok, Lucia Perillo, Beckian Fritz Goldberg and D. Nurkse, among others.Swink publishes fiction, non-fiction, poetry and interviews, and sponsors frequent readings and events in New York City and Los Angeles. Online theme issues of fiction, essays and poetry will also be available exclusively on our website." circ. 3000. 2/yr. Expects 2 issues 2006, 2 issues 2007. sub. price $16; per copy $10; sample $10. Back issues: $10. Discounts: 40% discount. 224pp. Reporting time: 3 months. Simultaneous submissions accepted: Yes. Publishes 1% of manuscripts submitted. Payment: $100 for fiction; $25 for poetry. Copyrighted, reverts to author. §Fiction, essays, poetry, artwork, photography. Ads: $400 full page. Subjects: Arts, Cartoons,

Essays, Experimental, Fiction, Non-Fiction, Photography, Poetry, Short Stories.

SYCAMORE REVIEW, Rebekah Silverman, Editor-in-Chief, Department of English, Purdue University, West Lafayette, IN 47907, 765-494-3783. 1988. Poetry, fiction, art, photos, cartoons, interviews, satire, criticism, reviews, letters, parts-of-novels, long-poems, plays, non-fiction. *"Sycamore Review* accepts personal essays, short fiction, translations, drama (one act or standalone pieces) and quality poetry in any form. We are a journal devoted to contemporary literature, publishing both traditional and experimental forms. Submissions read between Aug. 1 and March 1 (the academic year).Please remember *SR*'s WABASH PRIZE FOR POETRY. $1000 prize for the winning poem, plus publication in SR. Final contest judge: Tony Hoagland. Send 3 poems per $10 entry fee. DEADLINE: September, 24 2005. Visit http://www.sla.purdue.edu/sycamore for more information." circ. 1M. 2/yr. Pub'd 2 issues 2005; expects 2 issues 2006, 2 issues 2007. sub. price $12, $14 foreign; per copy $7; sample $7. Back issues: 20% off cover. Discounts: call for info. 160pp. Reporting time: 4 months maximum. Simultaneous submissions accepted: yes. Publishes 5% of manuscripts submitted. Payment: 2 copies. Copyrighted, reverts to author. Pub's reviews: approx. 10 in 2005. §Poetry collections, short story and essay collections, novels, nonfiction that would appeal to readers of literature. Ads: Will participate in adswaps. Contact for paid advertisements. Subjects: Arts, Book Reviewing, Drama, English, Essays, Fiction, Indiana, Interviews, Literary Review, Literature (General), Non-Fiction, Poetry, Reviews, Short Stories, Writers/Writing.

Sylvan Books, Thomas Duncan, PO Box 772876, Steamboat Springs, CO 80477-2876, 970-870-6071. 1984. Subjects: Business & Economics, Crafts, Hobbies, Women.

Symbios, Sanford R. Wilbur, 4367 S.E. 16th, Gresham, OR 97080-9178, 503-667-0633, home.netcom.com/ ~symbios. 1994. Expects 1 title 2006. Discounts: 1 copy 20%; 2-9 copies 40%; 10+ 60%.

SYMBOLIC INTERACTION, University of California Press, Simon Gottschalk, Editor, University of California Press, 2000 Center St., Suite 303, Berkeley, CA 94704-1223, 510-643-7154. 1977. Articles. "Editorial address: Dept of Sociology, University of Nevada, Las Vegas, 4505 Maryland Parkway, Las Vegas, NV 89154-5033. Copyrighted by the Society for the Study of Symbolic Interaction." circ. 787. 4/yr. Pub'd 4 issues 2005; expects 4 issues 2006, 4 issues 2007. sub. price $80 indiv., $251 inst., $27 student; per copy $21 indiv., $67 inst., $21 student; sample same as single copy. Discounts: foreign subs. agents 10%, 10+ one-time orders 30%. 170pp. Copyrighted, does not revert to author. Ads: $295/$220. Subjects: Social Work, Sociology.

SYMPLOKE: A Journal for the Intermingling of Literary, Cultural and Theoretical Scholarship, Jeffrey R. Di Leo, c/o J. Di Leo, Univ. of Houston, 3007 N. Ben Wilson, Victoria, TX 77901, Fax 361-570-4207, editor@symploke.org. 1993. Articles, interviews, criticism, non-fiction. *"Symploke* has no theoretical bias, and supports scholarship on any aspect of the intermingling of discourses and/or disciplines." circ. 650. 2/yr. Pub'd 2 issues 2005; expects 2 issues 2006, 2 issues 2007. sub. price $30; per copy $15; sample $10. Back issues: $40 per volume (2 issues). 130pp. Reporting time: 3 months. Simultaneous submissions accepted: yes. Publishes 10% of manuscripts submitted. Payment: none. Copyrighted, does not revert to author. Pub's reviews: 30 in 2005. §literary theory and criticism; cultural studies; philosophy; contemporary fiction. Ads: $100/$75/ exchanges. Subjects: Arts, Criticism, Culture, English, Ethics, Feminism, Fiction, History, Humanism, Non-Fiction, Novels, Philosophy, Politics, Race, Reading.

SYMPOSIUM, Augustus Pallotta, Editor; Elizabeth Foxwell, Managing Editor, Heldref Publications, 1319 18th St NW, Washington, DC 20036-1802, 202-296-6267 X275, Fax 202-293-6130, www.heldref.org. 1946. Articles, criticism, reviews. *"Symposium,* a journal in modern foreign literatures, includes research on authors, themes, periods, genres, works, and theory, frequently through comparative studies. Works are cited, and often discussed, in the original language. Submissions are approx. 15-25 double-spaced pages." circ. 500. 4/yr. Pub'd 4 issues 2005; expects 4 issues 2006, 4 issues 2007. sub. price $51; per copy $27; sample $27. 56pp. Simultaneous submissions accepted: no. Payment: 2 contributor's copies. Copyrighted, does not revert to author. Pub's reviews: 11 in 2005. §Books pertaining to modern foreign literatures. Ads: $155 full page. Subjects: Biography, France, French, Italy, Journals, Latin America, Literature (General), Spain.

synaesthesia press, Jim Camp, PO Box 1763, Tempe, AZ 85280, jim@chapbooks.org, www.chapbooks.org. 1995. Poetry, fiction, letters, parts-of-novels, long-poems, non-fiction. "Query first, always, no matter what. SASE gets replies." avg. press run 125. Pub'd 4 titles 2005; expects 3-4 titles 2006, 4 titles 2007. Discounts: contact me. 16pp. Reporting time: 6 months. Simultaneous submissions accepted: yes. Publishes 1% of manuscripts submitted. Payment: usually $200 and 6 copies. We can copyright for author. Subjects: Fiction, Poetry.

Synapse-Centurion, Jeff Curry, 1211 Berkeley St., Suite 3, Santa Monica, CA 90404, 310-829-2752, www.synapse-centurion.com. 1992. "High quality fiction and non-fiction. Mostly Green thinking. No unsolicited submissions." avg. press run 3M. Pub'd 1 title 2005; expects 2 titles 2006, 2 titles 2007. Discounts: normal trade. 250pp. Payment: 8-10% paid bi-yearly. Copyrights for author. Subjects: Earth, Natural History, Ecology, Foods, Environment, Fiction, Humor, Martial Arts, Mystery, Nature.

466

Synergetic Press, Deborah Parrish Snyder, 1 Bluebird Court, Santa Fe, NM 87508-1531, Tel. 505-424-0237 Fax. 505 424 3336 e-mail: tango@synergeticpress.com website: www.synergeticpress.com. 1971. Poetry, fiction, art, cartoons, long-poems, plays, non-fiction. ''50-350 pages in length. New and classic works in biospherics, Biosphere 2, ethnobotany, feng-shui, drama, fiction, culturology, and poetry.'' avg. press run 2M. Pub'd 4 titles 2005; expects 3 titles 2006, 3 titles 2007. Discounts: bookstores: 1-4 20% + postage, 5-10 40% + postage, 11-25 42% postage-free, 26-50 43%, 51-99 44%. 200pp. Reporting time: 1-3 months. Payment: 10% authors royalty. Sometimes copyrights for author. Subjects: Arts, Avant-Garde, Experimental Art, China, Comics, Drama, Earth, Natural History, Metaphysics, Poetry, Visual Arts.

Synergistic Press, Bud Johns, 3965 Sacramento St., San Francisco, CA 94118, 415-EV7-8180, Fax 415-751-8505; website www.synergisticbooks.com; e-mail goodreading@synergisticbooks.com. 1968. Articles, art, letters, non-fiction. ''Synergistic Press focuses its activity on nonfiction but in 2000 published its first novel, *Baby's Breath*. Its eclectic list of nonfiction shows the firm's wide-ranging interests including *Old Dogs Remembered* (an anthology of nonfiction and poems by 46 writers reminiscing about a much-loved dog), *Dying Unafraid* (the stories of people who did just that, told without pop psychology or religious intonations), *My ABC Book of Cancer* (written and drawn by a 10-year-old cancer patient, with supplemental text about her and childhood cancer), and art-focused titles such as *Not a Station But a Place, Paris Alive, Last Look at the Old Met* and *The Ecotopian Sketchbook*. Most of our titles have been developed internally and that probably will continue to be the case.'' avg. press run 3M-5M. Pub'd 2 titles 2005; expects 1 title 2006, 1 title 2007. Discounts: trade: single copies, 20%; 2-5, 35%, 6-11, 37%; 12-49, 40%, 50 or more, 44%; wholesaler/jobber discounts upon request. Pages vary, have published from 52-240pp. Reporting time: 1 month. Payment: varies with title. Copyrights for author. Subjects: Architecture, Arts, Bilingual, Biography, Fiction, France, French, Humor, Literature (General), Sports, Outdoors, Transportation.

•**Synergy Press,** Sally Miller, POB 8, Flemington, NJ 08822-0008, 908.782.7101, 908.237.1491, Synergy@SynergyBookService, www.SynergyBookService.com. 1985. Fiction, non-fiction. ''Our main subjects are health and sexuality. With a several-year hiatus for personal health reasons, we're back with a cookbook, a memoir, and in 2006, a newly discovered author of short fiction (12,000 words) Mykola Dementiuk will be featured. Prefer unorthodox sexual topics.'' avg. press run 100-2500. Pub'd 1 title 2005; expects 6 titles 2006, 8 titles 2007. Discounts: varies with book, 40-50%. 70-100pp. Reporting time: 1-2 weeks if phone number included. Simultaneous submissions accepted: Yes. Publishes 75% of manuscripts submitted. Payment: Varies with chapbook. $1-200 plus $1/book sold. Does not copyright for author. Subjects: Adolescence, Alternative Medicine, Bisexual, Erotica, Fiction, Gay, Gender Issues, Health, Libertarian, Nutrition, Relationships, Sex, Sexuality, Sexual Abuse, Short Stories, Spiritual.

SYNERJY: A Directory of Renewable Energy, Jeff Twine, Box 1854/Cathedral Station, New York, NY 10025, 212-865-9595, jtwine@synerjy.com. 1974. ''Bibliographic directory of renewable energy: solar, biomass, hydrogen, wind, water, geothermal, and energy storage. Thousands of publications, products, facilities and conferences. Summer/Fall issues are yearly cumulations.'' circ. 200. 2/yr. Pub'd 2 issues 2005; expects 2 issues 2006, 2 issues 2007. sub. price $65 institution, $30 individual; per copy $30 winter issue; $40 summer cumulation. Back issues: $150 for any 10 cumulative back issues. Discounts: $60/yr for standing order. 70pp. Copyrighted, reverts to author. Subjects: Bibliography, Energy.

Syracuse Cultural Workers/Tools for Change, Dik Cool, Publisher, PO Box 6367, Syracuse, NY 13217, 315-474-1132, free fax 877-265-5399, scw@syrculturalworkers.org. 1982. Art, photos, cartoons, collages. ''SCW publishes and distributes the annual Peace Calendar, the Women Artists Datebook, posters, notecards, postcards, T-shirts, and selected books. We are a multicultural, visual arts publisher and distributor. Our images, in general, relate to peace and social justice, personal or social liberation and feminism. We sell wholesale and by direct mail.'' avg. press run 5-17M. Pub'd 20 titles 2005; expects 25 titles 2006, 25 titles 2007. Discounts: 40% returnable, 50% nonreturnable calendars; posters and cards 50%; books 40%, t-shirts 40%. 28pp. Reporting time: 3-6 months. Simultaneous submissions accepted: yes. Payment: 6%, one time calendar payment $100-200, cover $400. Does not copyright for author. Subjects: Arts, Black, Counter-Culture, Alternatives, Communes, Feminism, Feminism, Gay, Human Rights, Labor, Latin America, Lesbianism, Native American, Peace, Peace, Politics, Visual Arts.

Syukhtun Editions, Theo Radic, Odengatan 8, 114 24 Stockholm, Sweden, (468)6124988, theoradic@yahoo.com, http://www.syukhtun.net. 1987. Poetry, art, satire, music, long-poems, collages, plays, non-fiction. ''Syukhtun Editions publishes non-fiction, poetry, plays, sheet music for guitar and fine arts prints. We give special emphasis to Native Californian cultures, and view the arts of writing and reading as ways to better understand Reality. Translations of prose and poetry from other languages are also of special interest, as in our bilingual Swedish-English edition, Selected Poetry of Edith Sodergran. Please contact us by regular mail or email before submitting anything.'' avg. press run 300. Pub'd 3 titles 2005; expects 3 titles 2006, 5 titles 2007. Discounts: 5-10 copies 20%. 200pp. Reporting time: 2 weeks. Simultaneous submissions accepted: No. Payment: negotiable. Copyrights for author. Subjects: Arts, Autobiography, California, Drama, Music, Myth,

Mythology, Native American, Non-Fiction, Poetry, Prose, Satire, T'ai Chi, Visual Arts.

T

T.V. HEADS, Shannon D. Harle, Publisher, Shannon D. Harle, PO Box 1005, Swannanoa, NC 28778-1005. 1997. Cartoons, satire. "Subscription includes all the zines I do= *Panic Strips, T.V. Heads,* and also *Rotten Pepper.*" circ. 100-150. 2-3/yr. Pub'd 2 issues 2005; expects 2 issues 2006, 3 issues 2007. sub. price $5; per copy $1.55; sample $1.55. Back issues: 2 for $1.55. 20pp. Reporting time: 1 month. Simultaneous submissions accepted: no. Payment: no. Copyrighted, reverts to author. §no. Subjects: Cartoons, Comics.

THE TABBY: A CHRONICLE OF THE ARTS AND CRAFTS MOVEMENT, Bruce Smith, 3085 Buckingham Drive SE, Port Orchard, WA 98366, (360) 871-7707. 1996. Articles, criticism, reviews, non-fiction. "Letterpress printed and hand bound, THE TABBY chronicles both the historic Arts & Crafts movement and its current-day revival. It provides a forum for new research, for analysis and thoughtful historical narrative, for well-founded criticism, and the occasional wandering contemplation. Past articles can be seen on the website at www.artsandcraftspress.com/tabby." circ. 480. 4/yr. Pub'd 1 issue 2005; expects 4 issues 2006, 4 issues 2007. sub. price $65; per copy $20; sample $20. Back issues: inquire. Discounts: three or more copies: 40%. 108pp. Reporting time: two weeks. Simultaneous submissions accepted: Yes. Publishes 40% of manuscripts submitted. Payment: payment upon publication; $100 to $500 per piece. Copyrighted, reverts to author. Pub's reviews: approx. 8 in 2005. §Any essays, theses, books, or catalogues relating to the turn-of-the-century Arts and Crafts movement. No advertising. Subjects: Antiques, Architecture, Arts, Book Arts, Culture, History.

TABOO: Journal of Education & Culture, Caddo Gap Press, Shirley R. Steinberg, Editor, 3145 Geary Boulevard #275, San Francisco, CA 94118, 415-392-1911. 1995. Poetry, articles, art, reviews. "Articles, commentary, research, opinion about education and culture." circ. 300. 2/yr. Pub'd 2 issues 2005; expects 2 issues 2006, 2 issues 2007. sub. price $50 ind., $100 inst.; per copy $25. Back issues: $20 each. Discounts: 15% to subscription agencies. 150pp. Reporting time: 2 months. Simultaneous submissions accepted: no. Publishes 50% of manuscripts submitted. Payment: none. Copyrighted, reverts to author. Pub's reviews. §Education and culture. Ads: $200 full page. Subject: Education.

TAI CHI, Wayfarer Publications, Marvin Smalheiser, Editor, PO Box 39938, Los Angeles, CA 90039, 323-665-7773, www.tai-chi.com. 1977. Articles, interviews, reviews, letters, news items. "Articles about T'ai Chi Ch'uan, Chinese internal martial arts, Chi kung, meditation, health about 700-5M words each." circ. 50M. 6/yr. Pub'd 6 issues 2005; expects 6 issues 2006, 6 issues 2007. sub. price $20; per copy $3.95; sample $3.95. 92pp. Reporting time: 3 weeks. Simultaneous submissions accepted: no. Publishes 80% of manuscripts submitted. Payment: up to $500. Copyrighted. Ads: $825 BW Full Page/$1,030 for 4 color. Subjects: Health, New Age, Philosophy, Spiritual.

TAKAHE, Cassandra Fusco, Victoria Broome, Bernadette Hall, Isa Moynihan, Mark Johnstone, James Norcliffe, Tony Scanlan, PO Box 13-335, Christchurch 1, New Zealand, 03-5198133. 1989. Poetry, fiction, art, cartoons, long-poems. "*Takahe* is a literary magazinewhich has no preconceived biases as to length or form. It aims to introduce young writers to a larger readership than they might otherwise enjoy by publishing them along side established figures (e.g. Kapka Kassabova, David Eggleton, David Hill, Mike Johnson). *Takahe* is interested in translation in addition to original fiction/poetry." circ. 340. 3-4/yr. Pub'd 3 issues 2005; expects 3 issues 2006, 3 issues 2007. sub. price $24NZ/4 issues within New Zealand, $32NZ/4 issues foreign countries; per copy $6NZ; sample $7.50NZ. 60pp. Reporting time: 1-4 months. Simultaneous submissions accepted if advised. Publishes 15% of manuscripts submitted. Payment: complimentary copy, plus small increment at editor's discretion. Copyrighted, reverts to author. Pub's reviews: 7 in 2005. Ads: $80NZ/$40NZ. Subjects: Fiction, Literary Review, Literature (General), Poetry.

Talent House Press, Paul Hadella, 1306 Talent Avenue, Talent, OR 97540, talhouse@mcleodusa.net. 1992. Poetry, fiction, art, photos, cartoons, satire, non-fiction. "Projects vary but never stem from unsolicited mss." avg. press run 150-300. Pub'd 5 titles 2005; expects 5 titles 2006, 5 titles 2007. 40pp. Reporting time: 6 weeks. Payment: varies. Does not copyright for author.

Talisman House, Publishers, Edward Foster, PO Box 3157, Jersey City, NJ 07303-3157, 201-938-0698. 1993. Poetry, fiction, interviews, criticism. avg. press run 1M-2M. Pub'd 2 titles 2005; expects 7 titles 2006, 7 titles 2007. Discounts: negotiated individually. 60-250pp. Reporting time: 3 months. Payment: negotiated individually. Copyrights for author. Subjects: Criticism, Fiction, Interviews, Literature (General), Novels, Poetry.

468

TALKING RIVER REVIEW, Lewis-Clark State College, 500 8th Avenue, Lewiston, ID 83501, Email: triver@lcsc.edu, www.lcsc.edu/TalkingRiverReview/. 1994. Poetry, fiction, art, photos, parts-of-novels, long-poems, non-fiction. *"The Talking River Review* may cease publication after the Winter 2002 issue, but a final decision has not been made. Please see our website for updated information. Maximum length of prose is 7,500 words. Up to 5 poems may be submitted, any length or style. Recent contributers include: William Kittredge, Pattiann Rogers, Stephen Dunn, and Dorianne Laux." circ. 500. 2/yr. Pub'd 2 issues 2005; expects 2 issues 2006, 2 issues 2007. sub. price $14; per copy $5; sample $5. Back issues: $5. Discounts: 40% to bookstores. 140pp. Reporting time: 3 months. We accept simultaneous submissions with notification. Publishes 2% of manuscripts submitted. Payment: 2 copies and a year's subscription. Copyrighted, reverts to author. Ads: none. Subject: Literature (General).

TalSan Publishing/Distributors, Sandi J. Lloyd, 7614 W. Bluefield Avenue, Glendale, AZ 85308, 602-843-1119, fax 602-843-3080. 1995. Fiction, non-fiction. "Mysteries, sci-fi, fantasy, history, romance, etc. All categories, all genres no poetry." avg. press run 1M. Expects 10 titles 2006, 20 titles 2007. Discounts: returnable: 1-4 20%, 5-24 40%, 25-49 42%, 50-99 43%, 100-999 45%, 1000+ 57%. Libraries: 1-9 10%, 10+ 15%. Reporting time: 2-3 weeks. Payment: standard 7-10%. Copyrights for author. Subjects: Fiction, Non-Fiction.

Tamal Vista Publications, Wayne de Fremery, 19A Forest St. #31, Cambridge, MA 02140, www.tamalvista.com, 617-492-7234. 1976. Poetry, fiction, criticism, non-fiction. "Tamal Vista Publications is a family-run business with roots in the book printing and publishing industry that go back three generations. Tamal Vista's publications have always reflected the passions of the family members running the company. Founder Peter de Fremery brought together his knowledge of printing, gained while working for his father as a printer's representative, with a passion for woodworking and the outdoors to create Tamal Vista's original line of books on woodworking and boatbuilding. Now owned by his son Wayne de Fremery, Tamal Vista reflects both the company's history and Wayne's passion for East Asian literature, particularly Korean poetry." Discounts: 1-4 copies 20%, must have CWO; 5+ 40%. Reporting time: 1 month. Copyrights for author. Subjects: Asia, Indochina, Bilingual, Botany, Buddhism, California, Crafts, Hobbies, How-To, Pacific Region, Poetry, Sports, Outdoors, Translation.

Tameme, C.M. Mayo, 199 First Street, Los Altos, CA 94022, www.tameme.org. 1999. Poetry, fiction, parts-of-novels, long-poems, non-fiction. *"Tameme* is now publishing bilingual (Spanish/English) chapbooks of new writing from North America: Canada, the US, and Mexico. Please do not submit without first consulting the guidelines on the website. Tameme is the Nahautl word for messenger or porter. Pronounced 'ta-may-may.'" Discounts: please contact us for more info. Reporting time: varies. Simultaneous submissions accepted: yes. Publishes 2% of manuscripts submitted. Payment: varies depending on funding. We are now a press. Depends on contract. Subjects: Bilingual, Canada, Fiction, Mexico, Non-Fiction, Poetry, Translation.

TAMPA REVIEW, University of Tampa Press, Richard B. Mathews, Editor; Elizabeth Winston, Nonfiction Editor; Don Morrill, Poetry Editor; Lisa Birnbaum, Fiction Editor; Martha Serpas, Poetry Editor; Kathleen Ochshorn, Fiction Editor, 401 W. Kennedy Boulevard, University of Tampa-19F, Tampa, FL 33606-1490, (813) 253-6266, Email: utpress@ut.edu, http://utpress.ut.edu, http://tampareview.ut.edu. 1988. Poetry, fiction, art, photos, interviews, non-fiction. *"Tampa Review*Tampa Review is a literary magazine dedicated to the integration of contemporary literature and visual arts. Each issue features contemporary writing and art from Florida and the world, emphasizing connections between the Tampa Bay region and the international literary community. Publishing in a hardcover format, the editors strive to produce a physically beautiful magazine that presents words in meaningful aesthetic relationship with world-class visual art. We consider submission between September 1 and December 31 each year. The annual Tampa Review Prize for Poetry awards $1,000 plus book publication in hardcover and quality paperback. Reading fee: $20; submission deadline, Dec. 31. See guidelines at *http://tampareview.ut.edu.* Recent contributors: Peter Meinke, Naomi Nye, Richard Chess, Julia B. Levine, Dionisio D. Martnez, Lola Haskins, and Richard Terrill." circ. 750. 2/yr. Pub'd 2 issues 2005; expects 2 issues 2006, 2 issues 2007. sub. price $15; per copy $9.95; sample $6. Back issues: $9.95. Discounts: retail booksellers: cash, 1-4 copies 20% off cover price, 5 or more 40%. 80-96pp. Reporting time: we read from September through December; report January through March. Simultaneous submissions accepted: NO. Publishes 4% of manuscripts submitted. Payment: $10 per printed page. Copyrighted, reverts to author. Exchange ads only.

Tantalus Books, Rick Griggs, 4529 Idledale Drive, Fort Collins, CO 80526-5152, www.tantalusbooks.com. 1989. "Special emphasis on *Balanced Mastery* for combining life balance with career achievement. Tantalus Books provides titles for the 10-Month *Mastery Academy* leadership training series." avg. press run 5M. Pub'd 3 titles 2005; expects 3 titles 2006, 3 titles 2007. Simultaneous submissions accepted: no. Publishes 1-2% of manuscripts submitted.

TAPROOT LITERARY REVIEW, Taproot Press Publishing Co., Tikvah Feinstein, Editor Publisher; Tina Forbes, Associate Editor; Marc and Amy Rosenberg, Technology; Candace Austin, Publicity Editor; Monte

Wilkinson, Consulting Editor, PO Box 204, Ambridge, PA 15003, 724-266-8476, taproot10@aol.com. 1984. Poetry, fiction, art, photos, reviews. "International Literary Review looking for the best quality poetry and short fiction available. We enjoy diversity and multinational themes and varied formats by both new and established writers. We also conduct an annual writing contest and publish winners and best of entries and submissions alike." circ. 500. 1/yr. Pub'd 2 issues 2005; expects 2 issues 2006, 3 issues 2007. sub. price $7.50; per copy $8.95; sample $5. Back issues: $6.50. Discounts: contributor copy $6.50 each, plus $2 p/h. 94pp. Reporting time: 6-8 months. Simultaneous submissions accepted: no. Publishes 30% of manuscripts submitted. Payment: copies. Copyrighted, reverts to author. Pub's reviews: 2 in 2005. §Ask us first if we are interested. Ads: ask for rates. Subjects: Fiction, Literary Review, Literature (General), Poetry, Short Stories, Storytelling.

Taproot Press Publishing Co. (see also TAPROOT LITERARY REVIEW), Tikvah Feinstein, Editor Publisher; Tina Forbes, Associate Editor; Candace Austin, Publicity Editor, Box 204, Ambridge, PA 15003, taproot10@aol.com. 1985. Poetry, fiction, art, photos. "Taproot Press is a subsidiary of Taproot Writer's Workshop Inc., a non-profit group with its goal to assist fine writers. We sponsor an annual contest. Recently published: Ran Huntsberry, B.Z. Niditch, Zan Gay, Lila Julius, Lyn Lifshin, and T. Anders Carson." avg. press run 500-1M. Pub'd 3 titles 2005; expects 3 titles 2006, 4 titles 2007. Discounts: 50% retailers, libraries, schools. 98pp. Reporting time: 3-6 months. Simultaneous submissions accepted: no. Publishes 10-20% of manuscripts submitted. Payment: books. Copyrights for author. Subjects: Poetry, Short Stories.

TAPROOT, a journal of older writers, Philip W. Quigg, Editor; Joan Martin, Associate Editor, PO Box 841, University at Stony Brook, Stony Brook, NY 11790-0841, 631-689-0668. 1974. Poetry, articles, art, photos, non-fiction. "Poetry, prose and art by elder writers. Publication limited to Taproot Workshop members." circ. 1M. 2/yr. Pub'd 2 issues 2005; expects 2 issues 2006, 2 issues 2007. sub. price $18; per copy $8; sample $8. Back issues: variable $3-$6. Discounts: please inquire. 100pp. Reporting time: 2 months. Payment: 1 copy. Copyrighted, reverts to author. Ads: $1,000/$500/negotiable. Subjects: Aging, Literature (General), Poetry, Public Affairs, Senior Citizens.

TAR RIVER POETRY, Luke Whisnant, Editor, Department of English, East Carolina University, Greenville, NC 27858-4353, 252-328-6046. 1978. Poetry, reviews. "Among recent featured contributors have been Laurence Lieberman, Tom Reiter, Leslie Norris, Brendan Galvin, Betty Adcock, Louis Simpson, Julie Suk, Mark Jarman, Deborah Cummins, Elizabeth Dodd, Susan Elizabeth Howe, Henry Taylor, Mark Cox, Debra Kang Dean, Thom Ward, David Mason, Gray Jacobik, Jeffrey Harrison, Robert Cording, Larry Woiwode, Kimberly Meyer, Fred Chappell, Natasha Saje, Susan Cohen, Jonathan Holden, James Harms, Bruce Bennett, and Al Maginnes." circ. 700. 2/yr. Pub'd 2 issues 2005; expects 2 issues 2006, 2 issues 2007. sub. price $12, $20/2 yrs; per copy $6.50; sample $6.50. Back issues: $6.50. Discounts: 40% to bookstores. 64pp. Reporting time: 4-6 weeks. Simultaneous submissions accepted: no. Publishes 15-20% of manuscripts submitted. Payment: contributor's copies. Rights reassigned to author upon request. Pub's reviews: 6 in 2005. §Poetry. Ads: we swap ads. Subject: Poetry.

THE TARPEIAN ROCK, Arx Publishing LLC, PO Box 1333, Merchantville, NJ 08109. 2003. Poetry, fiction, cartoons, reviews. Annual. 16pp. Simultaneous submissions accepted: No. Publishes Less than 10% of manuscripts submitted. Ads: Back cover: $250, Inside front/back cover: $200, Full page: $150, 1/2 page: $80, 1/4 page: $60, 1/8 page: $40. Subjects: Arts, Cartoons, Essays, Fantasy, Fiction, Literature (General), Poetry, Science Fiction, Short Stories.

Taurean Horn Press, Bill Vartnaw, PO Box 641097, San Francisco, CA 94164. 1974. Poetry. "Publications in print: *In Concern: for Angels* by Bill Vartnaw, *From Spirit to Matter* by Carol Lee Sanchez, *Spectacles* by Tom Sharp, *Bone Songs* by Gail Mitchell, *On the Good Red Interstate, Truck Stop Tellings and Other Poems* by Lee Francis, *Whose Really Blues* by Q. R. Hand, Jr. No submissions accepted." avg. press run 500. Expects 1 title 2006, 1 title 2007. Discounts: 40% to book trade. 100pp. Publishes 0% of manuscripts submitted. Payment: copies and/or other arrangements agreed upon prior to publication. Copyrights for author. Subject: Poetry.

Tax Property Investor, Inc., F. Marea, PO Box 4602, Winter Park, FL 32793, 407-671-0004. 1989. Non-fiction. "Publishing for real estate investors." avg. press run 5M. Expects 1 title 2006, 3 titles 2007. Discounts: trade 3-99 40%; 100-199 45%; 200499 50%, 500+ 55%. 160pp. Reporting time: 30 days. Payment: to be negotiated. Subjects: How-To, Real Estate, Taxes.

TEACHER EDUCATION QUARTERLY, Caddo Gap Press, Thomas Nelson, Editor, 3145 Geary Boulevard #275, San Francisco, CA 94118, 415-392-1911. 1971. Articles. "The quarterly journal of the California Council on the Education of Teachers." circ. 900. 4/yr. Pub'd 4 issues 2005; expects 4 issues 2006, 4 issues 2007. sub. price $75 indiv., $150 instit., $50 students; per copy $25. 96pp. Reporting time: 2 months. Publishes 25% of manuscripts submitted. Payment: none. Copyrighted, reverts to author. Ads: $200 full page. Subject: Education.

TEACHER LIBRARIAN: The Journal for School Library Professionals, Kim Tabor, Managing Editor, Scarecrow Press Inc., Bldg B, 15200 NBN Way, Blue Ridge Summit, PA 17214-1069, 717-794-3800 X3597.

470

1973. Articles, art, criticism, reviews, letters, news items. "Emphasis on library service to children and young adults." circ. 7,500-10,000. 5/yr. Pub'd 5 issues 2005; expects 5 issues 2006, 5 issues 2007. sub. price $59 billed, $54 prepaid; per copy $9.80; sample free on request. Back issues: on request. Discounts: on request. 72pp. Reporting time: 2 months. Payment: $100/article. Not copyrighted. Pub's reviews: 250 in 2005. §Professional materials for librarians, magazines for young people, new paperbacks for children, new paperbacks for young adults. Ads: $720/$400. Subjects: Education, Libraries.

Teachers & Writers Collaborative (see also TEACHERS & WRITERS MAGAZINE), Christopher Edgar, 5 Union Square West, New York, NY 10003, 212-691-6590, 212-675-0171. 1967. Articles, interviews, reviews. "No poetry." avg. press run 3M. Pub'd 3 titles 2005; expects 3 titles 2006, 4 titles 2007. Discounts: varies. 230pp. Reporting time: varies. Simultaneous submissions accepted: no. Publishes 2% of manuscripts submitted. Payment: varies. Copyrights for author. Subjects: Arts, Education.

TEACHERS & WRITERS MAGAZINE, Teachers & Writers Collaborative, Christopher Edgar; Christina Davis, Editor, 5 Union Square West, New York, NY 10003, 212-691-6590, www.twc.org. 1967. Articles, interviews, reviews, letters. "No poetry." circ. 3M. 5/yr. Pub'd 5 issues 2005; expects 5 issues 2006. sub. price $20; per copy $4; sample same. Back issues: $4. Discounts: none. 32pp. Reporting time: varies. Simultaneous submissions accepted: no. Publishes 5% of manuscripts submitted. Payment: varies. Copyrighted, reverts to author. Pub's reviews: 5 in 2005. §Education and writing. Ads: none. Subjects: Arts, Education.

Tears in the Fence (see also TEARS IN THE FENCE), David Caddy, 38 Hod View Stourpaine, Blandford Forum, Dorset DT11 8TN, United Kingdom. 1995. Poetry, fiction. "Recent contributors include: Damian Furniss, Gerald Locklin, Gregory Warren Wilson, K.V. Skene, Joan-Jobe Smith." avg. press run 300. Pub'd 8 titles 2005; expects 6 titles 2006, 10 titles 2007. 48pp. Reporting time: no unsolicited submissions. Payment: yes. Copyrights for author. Subjects: Poetry, Prose.

TEARS IN THE FENCE, Tears in the Fence, David Caddy, Sarah Hopkins, 38 Hod View, Stourpaine, Blandford Forum, Dorset DT11 8TN, England. 1985. Poetry, fiction, art, interviews, criticism, reviews. circ. 1.5M. 3/yr. Pub'd 3 issues 2005; expects 3 issues 2006, 3 issues 2007. sub. price £12, $20 cash including postage; per copy £5, $7 cash including postage; sample same. Back issues: sold out. 112pp. Reporting time: 2-3 weeks. Simultaneous submissions accepted: no. Publishes 1-2% of manuscripts submitted. Payment: 1 copy. Copyrighted, reverts to author. Pub's reviews: 42 in 2005. Subjects: Criticism, Poetry, Prose.

Tebot Bach (see also SPILLWAY), Mifanwy Kaiser, Editor, Box 7887, Huntington Beach, CA 92615-7887, 714-968-0905. 1998. Poetry. "*The Way In* by Robin Chapman, winner of the 1999 Posner Book Length Poetry Award from The Council for Wisconsin Writers. *Written in Pain* by M.L. Liebler, winner of Wayne State University Board of Governors Award, *Cantatas* by Jeanette Clough." Pub'd 3 titles 2005; expects 3 titles 2006, 3 titles 2007. Discounts: by arrangement. 96pp. Reporting time: 3-6 months. Simultaneous submissions accepted: no. Payment: contract for individual poet's books. Subject: Poetry.

TECH DIRECTIONS, Prakken Publications, Susanne Peckham, Managing Editor, PO Box 8623, Ann Arbor, MI 48107, 734-975-2800 ext. 206, Fax 734-975-2787, susanne@techdirections.com. 1941. Articles, cartoons, collages, news items, non-fiction. "*Tech Directions* serves the fields of industrial education, technology education and career-technical education, which includes automotive, drafting, general shop, graphic arts, electronics, machine shop, welding, woodworking, computer technology and other subjects of interest to teachers in junior highs, senior highs, vocational-technical schools, and community colleges." circ. 38M. 10/yr. Pub'd 10 issues 2005; expects 10 issues 2006, 10 issues 2007. sub. price $30; per copy $5; sample free (note: qualified individuals receive the mag free on request). Back issues: $5. Discounts: agent= 10%, individual multi-year rates= 2 yr, $55, 3 yr $80 (US). 50pp. Reporting time: 2 months. Accept simultaneous submissions only in exceptional cases. Publishes 20% of manuscripts submitted. Payment: honorarium $25-$250, depends on length, illustrations. Copyrighted, does not revert to author. Pub's reviews: 40 in 2005. §Industrial/technical/vocational education, technology, crafts. Ads: $3976/$2408/$215 col. inch. Subjects: Careers, Education, Worker.

Technicians of the Sacred (see also RESEARCH IN YORUBA LANGUAGE & LITERATURE; SOCIETE), Courtney Willis, 1317 N. San Fernando Boulevard, Suite 310, Burbank, CA 91504. 1983. Non-fiction. avg. press run 500. Pub'd 3 titles 2005; expects 4 titles 2006. 130pp. Reporting time: 4 weeks. Copyrights for author. Subjects: Occult, Religion.

•**Technics Publications, LLC,** Steve Hoberman, PO Box 161, Bradley Beach, NJ 07720, dbooks@technics-pub.com. 2005. Non-fiction. "We focus on business and computer books." avg. press run 5000. Expects 1 title 2006, 2 titles 2007. Discounts: 2-10 copies 25%10-20 copies 35%More than 20 40%. 150pp. Subject: Computers, Calculators.

Tecolote Publications, Carol Bowers, 4918 Del Monte Avenue, San Diego, CA 92107, telephone (619)222-6066, e-mail tecopubs@earthlink.net, website tecolotepublications.com. 1986. Poetry, fiction, non-fiction. "Main publications are local history books (San Diego County) nature books, novels, poetry; author - subsidize." avg. press run 1-5M. Pub'd 11 titles 2005; expects 10 titles 2006, 10 titles 2007. Discounts: trade - 40%; wholesalers - 50%. 150pp. Copyrights for author.

TEEN VOICES MAGAZINE, Alison Amoroso, Editor-in-Chief; Ellyn Ruthstrom, Managing Editor, 80 Summer St. #300, Boston, MA 02110-1218, 617-426-5505, Fax 617-426-5577, womenexp@teenvoices.com, www.teenvoices.com. 1988. Poetry, fiction, articles, art, photos, cartoons, interviews, satire, criticism, reviews, music, letters, news items, non-fiction. "Additional address: PO Box 120-027, Boston, MA 02112-0027. We publish the writing of teenage girls *only.*" circ. 60M. 4/yr. Pub'd 4 issues 2005; expects 4 issues 2006, 4 issues 2007. sub. price $19.95; per copy $2.95 US, $3.95 Canada; sample $5. Back issues: $5-$10 depending on issue. Discounts: bulk, human service agencies, classrooms. 68pp. Reporting time: 6 months. Simultaneous submissions accepted: yes. Publishes 40% of manuscripts submitted. Payment: 5 copies of magazine. Copyrighted, non-exclusive rights revert to author. Pub's reviews: 12 in 2005. §Teenage girls or teenagers in general might want to know about. Ads: b+w: $1,200/$750/$2.50 word if it runs only 1 issue; color: $2000/$1,230/$1.75 per word if it runs 4 issues (10 word min.). Subjects: Poetry, Race, Sexual Abuse, Women, Young Adult.

The Teitan Press, Inc., Franklin C. Winston, President, PO Box 1972, Bolingbrook, IL 60440, e-mail editor@teitanpress.com, http://www.teitanpress.com. 1985. Fiction, non-fiction. "We only use in-house material; we do not accept submissions." avg. press run 1M. Expects 1 title 2006, 1 title 2007. Discounts: 50% to wholesalers, 20%-40% to retail outlets depending on quantity; 10% to libraries postpaid. 200pp. Copyrights for author. Subjects: History, Occult, Poetry, Short Stories, Theosophical.

Telephone Books, Maureen Owen, 2358 South Bannnock St., Denver, CO 80223, (303) 698-7837, pomowen@ix.netcom.com. 1971. Poetry, fiction, plays. "Press will do 2 books a year, but titles remain available. Books: *The Amerindian Coastline Poem* by Fanny Howe; *Hot Footsteps* by Yuki Hartman; *Ciao Manhattan* by Rebecca Wright; *Delayed: Not Postponed* by Fielding Dawson; *The Secret History of the Dividing Line* by Susan Howe; *The Temple* by Janet Hamill; *No More Mr. Nice Guy* by Sam Kashner; *Audrey Hepburn's Symphonic Salad and the Coming of Autumn* by Tom Weigel; *The Telephone Book* by Ed Friedman; *3-Way Split* by Rebecca Brown; *Hot* by Joe Johnson; *The Celestial Splendor Shining Forth From Geometric Thought* and *On the Motion of the Apparently Fixed Stars* by Britt Wilkie. No unsolicited ms." avg. press run 750-1M. Pub'd 2 titles 2005. 40-80pp. Simultaneous submissions accepted: no. Payment: in copies. Copyrights for author. Subject: Poetry.

TELOS, Telos Press, Russell Berman, Editor; David Pan, Review Editor; Robert Richardson, Managing Editor, 431 East 12th Street, New York, NY 10009, 212-228-6479. 1968. Articles, criticism, reviews, non-fiction. "For additional information, please visit our website, www.telospress.com." circ. 1000. 4/yr. Pub'd 4 issues 2005; expects 4 issues 2006, 4 issues 2007. sub. price Invididuals: $60/year; Institutions: $180/year; per copy $15 US; $18 International. Back issues: Individuals: $20/each; Institutions: $50/each. Discounts: 30% bulk orders, 10% agent, 30% bookstores. 192pp. Reporting time: 3-6 months. Payment: none. Copyrighted. Pub's reviews: approx. 12 in 2005. §Politics, philosophy, critical and social theory, law, religion, culture, and the arts. Ads: Please inquire. Subjects: Arts, Criticism, Current Affairs, Europe, Global Affairs, Government, History, Journals, Law, Literature (General), Philosophy, Political Science, Politics, Religion.

Telos Press (see also TELOS), Russell Berman, Editor; David Pan, Review Editor; Robert Richardson, Managing Editor, 431 East 12th Street, New York, NY 10009, 212-228-6479. 1968. Articles, criticism, reviews, non-fiction. "For more information, please visit our website, www.telospress.com." Discounts: usual is 30%, other can be arranged. Reporting time: 6 months. Payment: Negotiated. Subjects: Arts, Criticism, Culture, Europe, Journals, Law, Literature (General), Philosophy, Politics, Post Modern, Translation.

Temple Inc., Charles Potts, PO Box 1773, Walla Walla, WA 99362-0033, info@thetemplebookstore.com. 1995. Poetry, non-fiction. "The Temple has suspended publication. Back issues available for $5. Do not send unsolicited manuscripts." avg. press run 500-1.2M. Pub'd 2 titles 2005; expects 3 titles 2006, 4 titles 2007. Discounts: 40% trade. 120pp. Reporting time: varies. Simultaneous submissions accepted: No submissions of any kind. Publishes 1% of manuscripts submitted. Payment: 10%. Copyrights for author. Subjects: History, Poetry, Political Science.

Temporary Vandalism Recordings (see also THE SILT READER), Robert Roden, Barton M. Saunders, PO Box 6184, Orange, CA 92863-6184, tvrec@yahoo.com. 1991. Poetry. "Have never published unsolicited manuscripts for our chapbooks. Suggest a ten poem sample with SASE for reply. We only publish 1-2 chapbooks per year." 100 first run, optional reprinting if needed. Pub'd 2 titles 2005; expects 1 title 2006, 2 titles 2007. Discounts: 40%. 40pp. Reporting time: 3-6 months. Simultaneous submissions accepted: yes. Publishes 1% of manuscripts submitted. Payment: 5 copies, 50% of net sales. Does not copyright for author. Subject: Poetry.

Ten Penny Players, Inc. (see also WATERWAYS: Poetry in the Mainstream), Barbara Fisher, Co-Editor;

Richard Spiegel, Co-Editor, 393 St. Pauls Avenue, Staten Island, NY 10304-2127, 718-442-7429, www.tenpennyplayers.org. 1975. Poetry, fiction, plays. "Books: Age range is child to adult. Varying lengths: 8pp-150pp. We stress an integration of language and picture so that the material can be used either as a book to read or a book to perform. Also child + young adult poets published monthly in literary magazines and picture books from NYC elementary & high schools including incarcerated youths. No unsolicited manuscripts, please." avg. press run 200. Pub'd 2 titles 2005; expects 2 titles 2006, 3 titles 2007. Discounts: standard 60/40. 60pp. Simultaneous submissions accepted: no. Payment: negotiable. Copyrights for author. Subjects: Arts, Drama, Poetry.

Ten Star Press, D. Millhouse, 2860 Plaza Verde, Santa Fe, NM 87507, 505-473-4813 phone/Fax, dorbil@rt66.com. 1988. Poetry, fiction, criticism, reviews, parts-of-novels, plays, non-fiction. "Primarily fiction (novels and novellas), non-fiction and collections of various types of material. Radical left and socialist oriented. All orders go to Ten Star." avg. press run 2M-3M. Pub'd 2 titles 2005; expects 1 title 2006. Discounts: can be arranged. 250-350pp. Reporting time: 1 month. Simultaneous submissions accepted: yes. Payment: to be arranged. Does not copyright for author. Subjects: Fiction, Health, Non-Fiction, Novels, Poetry, Yoga.

•**Tendre Press,** Ann Kreilkamp, 134 N. Overhill Dr., Bloomington, IN 47408, 812-334-1987, www.tendrepress.com. 2006. Non-fiction. avg. press run 5000. Expects 1 title 2007. 250pp. Subjects: Aging, Astrology, Autobiography, Biography, Dreams, Euthanasia, Death, Inspirational, Memoirs, Metaphysics, New Age, Non-Fiction, Philosophy, Psychology, Society, Spiritual.

Terra Nova Press, Susan Curry, 1309 Redwood Lane, Davis, CA 95616, 530-756-7417. 1984. Non-fiction. "Not accepting manuscripts at present." avg. press run 5M. Discounts: trade 1-4 20%, 5-24 40%, 25-49 43% and up; wholesalers and jobbers 1-4 20%, 5-49 45%, 50-99 50% and up; bulk on request. 250pp. Payment: reporting twice/year, accompanied by check. Copyrights for author. Subjects: Children, Youth, Family, Non-Fiction, Self-Help.

Tesseract Publications, Janet Leih, PO Box 164, Canton, SD 57013-0164, 605-987-5070, Fax same, call ahead, it is a one-liner information@tesseractpublications.com, www.tesseractpublications.com. 1981. Poetry, fiction, non-fiction. "Prefer feminist, non-fiction, poetry." avg. press run 300-500. Pub'd 1 title 2005; expects 2 titles 2006, 2 titles 2007. Discounts: available on request. 60pp. Reporting time: 3 months. Simultaneous submissions accepted: yes. Payment: subsidized publications only. Copyrights for author if asked. Subjects: Feminism, Poetry.

TEXAS POETRY JOURNAL, Smith Steven Ray, P.O. Box 90635, Austin, TX 78709-0635, 512-779-6202, www.texaspoetryjournal.com, submissions@texaspoetryjournal.com. 2004. Poetry, interviews, criticism, non-fiction. "Texas Poetry Journal publishes poetry and poets from around the world in a quality and affordable format, perfect for readers at home or on-the-go. Our goal is to add poetry to the lives of busy people, to bring a touch of extraordinary language to each day.Texas Poetry Journal publishes poetry, interviews with poets, criticism for a general audience, and black and white photography. The print edition is published semi-annually. We also publish a Feature Poem on our web site each week." circ. 400. 2/yr. Expects 2 issues 2006, 2 issues 2007. sub. price 12; per copy 7.50; sample 7.50. Back issues: 7.50. Discounts: Bookstores 40%Jobbers 5%Distributors 55%. 100pp. Reporting time: 3 months. Simultaneous submissions accepted: Yes. Publishes 8% of manuscripts submitted. Payment: One copy. Copyrighted, reverts to author. Ads: Half Page $40Full Page $75. Subjects: Interviews, Photography, Poetry.

THE TEXAS REVIEW, Texas Review Press, Paul Ruffin, Editor, English Department, Sam Houston State University, Huntsville, TX 77341-2146. 1976. Poetry, fiction, articles, photos, interviews, reviews. "Because of the size of our magazine, we do not encourage the submission of long poems or exceptionally long short stories. Now accept photography, critical essays on literature and culture, etc. Each year we publish the *The Texas Review* Poetry Award Chapbook. We will no longer read during June through August." circ. 750-1M. 2/yr. Pub'd 2 issues 2005; expects 2 issues 2006. sub. price $20; 2 years $35; 3 years $50; per copy $10; sample $5. Back issues: $5. Discounts: 40% to libraries. 160pp. Reporting time: 8 weeks-6 months. Simultaneous submissions accepted: no. Publishes 2% of manuscripts submitted. Payment: copies, subscription (1 year). Copyrighted, rights revert to author on request. Pub's reviews: 24 in 2005. §Poetry, fiction, history, art, literary criticism, informal essays. Ads: exchange ads only. Subject: Literary Review.

Texas Review Press (see also THE TEXAS REVIEW), Paul Ruffin, Editor, English Department, Sam Houston State University, Huntsville, TX 77341-2146. 1976. "We do not read June-August." avg. press run 500. Pub'd 3 titles 2005. 160pp. Reporting time: 2-6 months. Simultaneous submissions accepted: no. Publishes 1% of manuscripts submitted. Payment: copies plus 1 year subscription. Copyrights for author.

Texas Tech University Press, Noel Parsons, Judith Keeling, Box 41037, Lubbock, TX 79409-1037, 806-742-2982, fax 806-742-2979. 1971. Fiction, art, photos, letters, non-fiction. "Publish scholarly, trade, and crossover books in the natural sciences and natural history; environmental studies and literature of place;

regional history and culture; Western Americana; Vietnam War and Southeast Asian studies; eighteenth-century studies; Joseph Conrad studies; costume and textile history and conservation; regional fiction.'' avg. press run 1500. Pub'd 18 titles 2005; expects 24 titles 2006, 24 titles 2007. Discounts: 1-2 copies 20%3-9 copies 40%10-24 copies 41%25-49 copies 42%50-99 copies 44%100+ copies 45%1-9 nonreturnable copies 40%10+ nonreturnable copies 50%. 250pp. Reporting time: queries, 1 week; proposals, 1 month; manuscripts, 2 months. Simultaneous submissions accepted: No. Publishes 6% of manuscripts submitted. Payment: 10% of net on trade and promising crossover titles. Copyrights for author. Subjects: Asia, Indochina, Biography, Botany, Clothing, Environment, Fiction, Great Plains, Literature (General), Native American, Nature, Photography, Texas, Textiles, Vietnam, The West.

TFG Press, 244 Madison Avenue, #254, New York, NY 10016, floatingal@aol.com.

THALIA: Studies in Literary Humor, Jaqueline Tavernier, Editor, English Dept.,University of Ottawa, 70 Laurier East, Ottawa, Ontario, K1N 6N5, Canada, thaliahumor@hotmail.com. 1978. Articles, art, cartoons, interviews, satire, criticism, reviews, letters, collages, non-fiction. ''the last volume published is vol 21 (2004).'' circ. 500. 2/yr or 1 double issue. sub. price $25 individuals, $30 libraries, discounts for 2 or 3 year subs.; sample varies with the issue requested. Back issues: varies with the issues requested. Discounts: by direct query only. 75-125pp. Reporting time: varies with ms. content. We accept simultaneous submissions, but we must know about it and get first copyrights. Publishes 25-30% of manuscripts submitted. Payment: none. Copyrighted, copyrights contract signed prior to publication. Pub's reviews: 2 in 2005. §Any area connected to humor. Ads: $150/$75. Subjects: Criticism, Humor, Literary Review, Literature (General).

Thatch Tree Publications, K. Jones, Kathy Alba PhD, 2250 N. Rock Road, Suite 118-169, Wichita, KS 67226, 316-687-6629, thatchtreepub@aol.com, www.kathyalba.com, www.thatchtreepublications.com. 2001. Fiction, art, photos, non-fiction. ''Full length novels - generally wholesome or Christian. Nonfiction works of any subject except the occult or negative.'' avg. press run 1M. Pub'd 2 titles 2005; expects 2 titles 2006, 2 titles 2007. Discounts: 10-20% for bulk, 50% for distributors. 220pp. Reporting time: 2-3 weeks. Payment: the authors pay for everything and retain total rights. Copyrights for author. Subjects: Arts, Christianity, Crafts, Hobbies, Education, English, Fiction, Futurism, Health, How-To, Inspirational, Interviews, Language, Literature (General), Medicine, Non-Fiction.

THE2NDHAND, Todd Dills, 2543 W. Walton #3, Chicago, IL 60647, 773-278-7034. 2000. Fiction, articles, art, cartoons, interviews, satire, reviews, letters, news items, non-fiction. ''We accept prose for our print edition, a broadsheet that focuses on the work of a single writer, of up to 5000 words in length and pay a nominal fee. Our online magazine publishes weekly and accepts work of up to 2500 words in length. Recent contributors include Al Burian, Anne Elizabeth Moore, Todd Dills, Jeb Gleason-Allured, Elizabeth Crane, Joe Meno, Doug Milam, Brian Costello, Paul A. Toth, and many more. . . .'' circ. 2M. 4/yr. Pub'd 4 issues 2005; expects 4 issues 2006, 4 issues 2007. We offer lifetime subscriptions to the printed broadsheet for a donation of $30 or more; price per copy $1 or 2 stamps; sample write us. Back issues: write and send $1. Four pages, or 1 large 11"-by-17" page printed both sides.pp. Reporting time: 3 weeks. Simultaneous submissions accepted: yes. Publishes 50% of manuscripts submitted. Payment: We pay up to $200 for our single-author broadsheets. Copyrighted, reverts to author. Pub's reviews: 2 in 2005. §Editor Todd Dills publishes reviews of books and other work in his twice-monthly online column, "Wing and Fly" (the2ndhand.com/wingandfly). Please send materials to his attention. Ads: none. Subjects: Absurdist, Comics, Hypnosis, Storytelling, T'ai Chi, Taxes.

THEATER, Duke University Press, Erika Munk, 222 York Street, New Haven, CT 06520, 203-432-1568, Fax 203-432-8336, e-mail theater.magazine@yale.edu. 1968. Articles, photos, interviews, satire, criticism, reviews, letters, plays. ''For more than thirty years, *Theater* has published the finest new writing by and about contemporary theater artists. The magazine's perspectives are different from those of any other American theater publication: at once practical, creative, and scholarly. Published three times annually, *Theater* focuses on modern and contemporary theater, with an emphasis on what's new, experimental, even radical.'' circ. 3M. 3/yr. Pub'd 3 issues 2005; expects 3 issues 2006, 3 issues 2007. sub. price $22 individuals, $45 libraries; per copy $8; sample $8. Back issues: $5/$8. Discounts: agents 8%; bookstores 20%-25%; bulk 10-15% (back issues only). 121pp. Reporting time: 8 weeks. Simultaneous submissions accepted: yes. Payment: $50-$150. Copyrighted, playwrights retain copyright. Pub's reviews: 4 per issue in 2005. §New books on theater, new plays, production. Ads: $250/$150. Subjects: Book Reviewing, Drama, Essays, Interviews, Martial Arts, Theatre.

THEATRE DESIGN AND TECHNOLOGY, United States Institute for Theatre Technology, Inc., David Rodger, Editor; Deborah Hazlett, Art Editor, 6443 Ridings Road, Syracuse, NY 13206-1111. 1965. Articles, photos, interviews, reviews, letters, news items. ''The magazine covers the art and technology of producing live performing arts and entertainment. Articles discuss historical scene design as well as contemporary design. Pieces on lighting and sound focus on both the artistic effects of these elements and the newest, most effective ways to use these elements. Costume design and designers are often highlighted. Reports on newly created standards in the industry, health and safety issues, new facilities, and new products appear regularly.

Interpretative articles as well as technical research findings all combine to make *TD&T* an important and one-of-a-kind source for practitioners of theatre design, theatre building, and theatre technology.'' circ. 4M. 4/yr. Pub'd 4 issues 2005; expects 4 issues 2006, 4 issues 2007. sub. price $48 domestic, $58 foreign (libraries only). Back issues: $6 members; $9 non-members. Discounts: none. 76pp. Reporting time: 6 weeks. Payment: none. Copyrighted, rights held by magazine after publication unless author wishes separate copyright. Pub's reviews: 13 in 2005. §Books only, scenography, scene design, engineering, architecture, costume. Ads: $890/$535 for black/white; color available at additional cost. Subjects: Architecture, Arts, Book Reviewing, Dance, Drama, Electronics, Holography, Theatre.

THEECLECTICS, Creative With Words Publications (CWW), Brigitta Geltrich, Editor & Publisher; Bert Hower, Editor, PO Box 223226, Carmel, CA 93922, fax 831-655-8627; e-mail cwwpub@usa.net; website http://members.tripod.com/~CreativeWithWords. 1998. Poetry, fiction, cartoons, satire. ''On any topic, written by adults only (20 and older), poetry preferred.'' 2/yr. Pub'd 2 issues 2005; expects 2 issues 2006, 2 issues 2007. price per copy $6. Discounts: authors 20%; offices, schools, libraries, clubs 10%; legitimate shutins get a one time only free copy. 16+pp. Reporting time: 2-4 weeks after set deadline. Simultaneous submissions accepted: no. Publishes 90% of manuscripts submitted. Payment: 20% discount. Copyrighted, reverts to author. Ads: $125/$70/$35/$16. Subject: Poetry.

THEMA, Virginia Howard, PO Box 8747, Metairie, LA 70011-8747, Telephone: 504-887-1263; e-mail: thema@cox.net; website address: http://members.cox.net/thema. 1988. Poetry, fiction, art, cartoons. ''Each issue is related to a unique central premise. Publication dates and themes (submission deadline in brackets): Sept. 2007, *Written in Stone* [11-1-06]; Feb. 2008, *Everybody Quit* [3-1-07]; May 2008, *Henry's Fence* [7-1-07].'' circ. 300. 3/yr. Pub'd 3 issues 2005; expects 3 issues 2006, 3 issues 2007. sub. price $16; per copy $8; sample $8. Back issues: $8. Discounts: 10%. 180pp. Reporting time: 5-6 months after manuscript submission deadline of specific issue. Simultaneous submissions accepted: yes, but must fit upcoming theme. Publishes 10% of manuscripts submitted. Payment: $25 short stories, $10 poetry, $10 b/w artwork, $25 color cover art, $10 short-short pieces. Copyrighted, reverts to author. §Fiction. Ads: $150/$100/$50 1/4 page. Subjects: Fiction, Literature (General).

Theytus Books Ltd., Greg Young-Ing, Manager, Green Mountain Road, Lot 45, RR #2, Site 50, Comp. 8, Penticton, B.C. V2A 6J7, Canada. 1980. Poetry, fiction, photos, non-fiction. ''Recent contributors: Jeannette Armstrong, Beth Cuthand, Douglas Cardinal, Ruby Slipperjack, Lee Maracle, and Drew Hayden Taylor.'' avg. press run 4M. Pub'd 4 titles 2005; expects 4 titles 2006, 4 titles 2007. 150pp. Reporting time: 6 months to 1 year. Payment: 8-10% 2 times a year. Copyrights for author. Subjects: Anthropology, Archaelogy, Children, Youth, Electronics, Fiction, History, Native American, Poetry.

THIN COYOTE, Lost Prophet Press, Christopher Jones, 221 Stanford Drive SE #2, Albuquerque, NM 87106-3586, 505.256.4589 knucklemerchant@hotmail.com. 1992. Poetry, fiction, art, photos, interviews, satire, collages, plays. ''When we are able to stop guzzling whiskey long enough to read submissions, we tend to favor the work of scofflaws, muleskinners, seers, witchdoctors, maniacs, alchemists, giant-slayers, and their ilk.'' circ. 200-300. 3/yr. Pub'd 2 issues 2005; expects 3 issues 2006, 3 issues 2007. sub. price $18; per copy $6; sample $7. Back issues: available on request. Discounts: on request. 45pp. Reporting time: 1 month. Simultaneous submissions accepted: yes. Publishes 2-3% of manuscripts submitted. Payment: 1 copy of issue in which they appear. Copyrighted, reverts to author. Pub's reviews. §Poetry, fiction, artwork. Ads: $100/$50/$25. Subjects: Arts, Celtic, Fiction, Photography, Poetry.

Think Tank Press, Inc. (see also MAGAZINE), Heidi Peite, Monique Verdin, PO Box 2228, New Orleans, LA 70176, www.thinktankpress.com. 2002. Poetry, fiction, art, photos, collages, plays, non-fiction. avg. press run 250. Pub'd 8 titles 2005; expects 8 titles 2006, 10 titles 2007. Discounts: 40%. 100pp. Simultaneous submissions accepted: yes. Publishes 35% of manuscripts submitted. Payment: yes. Copyrights for author. Subjects: Arts, Fiction, Non-Fiction, Novels, Photography, Poetry.

•**thinkBiotech,** Yali Friedman, 3909 Witmer Rd #416, Niagara Falls, NY 14305. 2003. Non-fiction. ''Publishing books on biotechnology and business.'' avg. press run 2000. Expects 1 title 2006, 2 titles 2007. Discounts: 1-5 copies 20%6+ copies 50% (wholesalers only). 300pp. Reporting time: 4 weeks. Subjects: Business & Economics, Science.

THINKERMONKEY, John Yotko J, Gurnee, IL 60031-3155, editor@thinkermonkey.com. 2005. Articles, letters, non-fiction. ''We publigh essays, commentaries, and prose about pertinent topics - anything form state and government rights, political topics such as welfare or social security, personal topics such as abortion, and more. See our site, http://www.thinkermonkey.com, for information on what we look for.'' Expects 4 issues 2006, 12 issues 2007. Reporting time: probably within 2 weeks. Simultaneous submissions accepted: Yes. Publishes 55% of manuscripts submitted. Payment: payment is the publication of your work. The rights to the writing are always retained by the author. You only grant us permission to print your work. Subjects: Adoption, AIDS, Anarchist, Civil Rights, Essays, Ethics, Non-Fiction, Non-Violence, Political Science, Politics,

Psychology, Public Affairs, Social Security, Society.

THIRD COAST, Glenn Deutsch, Editor, Department of English, Western Michigan University, Kalamazoo, MI 49008-5331, 269-387-2675, Fax 269-387-2562, www.wmich.edu/thirdcoast. 1995. Poetry, fiction, interviews, parts-of-novels, long-poems, non-fiction. *"Third Coast* publishes poetry, fiction (including traditional and experimental fiction, shorts, and novel excerpts, but not genre fiction), creative nonfiction (including reportage, essay, memoir, and fragments) and translations. We encourage new as well as established writers. We recommend you look at an issue before submitting. You may order single issues (a current issue is $8; a back issue is $6) by sending a check made out to *Third Coast.* Write Sample Current Issue or Sample Back Issue on the envelope. *Third Coast* does not consider previously published work. We accept simultaneous submissions but ask that you notify us immediately if your piece is accepted elsewhere. Please include a self-addressed, stamped envelope (SASE). Submissions without SASEs or international reply coupons cannot be acknowledged or returned. Direct your submission to the appropriate editors: Fiction, Creative Nonfiction, or Poetry. Send poetry and prose submissions separately. With fiction and nonfiction, we ask that you send one piece at a time. We consider pieces ranging up to 9,000 words; authors wishing to submit longer manuscripts should query with an SASE or international reply coupons. As for shorts, we accept up to five at a time. Fiction and nonfiction submissions should be typed, double-spaced, openly margined, and printed clearly. The authors name, address, email address, and phone number should be included on the first page. Each subsequent page should have a page number and the authors name or title of the piece. Poetry should be typed and single-spaced, with the authors name or a shortened title on each page. Stanza breaks should be double-spaced. Please send no more than five poems at a time (with a maximum of fifteen pages total per submission). Reading period: The editors invite submissions of unsolicited manuscripts all year long. Payment is two contributor's copies and a one-year subscription. All rights revert to the author upon publication.Submissions generally will be returned or accepted within four months. Please do not phone or email about the status of your submission. Please wait a minimum of three months to send follow-up inquiries, and if you choose to do so, use regular mail only; write Submission Inquiry-Fiction, Submission Inquiry-Poetry, or Submission Inquiry-Creative Nonfiction on the envelope; and enclose an SASE or international reply coupons. Recent contributors include: Keith Banner, Moira Crone, Sean Thomas Dougherty, Albert Goldbarth, Mark Halliday, Terrance Hayes, Bob Hicok, Major Jackson, Trudy Lewis, John McNally, Mary Morris, Peter Orner, Tim Seibles, and Nance Van Winckel. Authors whose work in *Third Coast* has been recently anthologized: Ted Kooser, *Best American Poetry 2003,* Alan Shapiro, *Best American Poetry 2003,* Sharon Dilworth, 2002 Pushcart Prize in Fiction." circ. 3000. 2/yr. Pub'd 2 issues 2005; expects 2 issues 2006, 2 issues 2007. sub. price $14; per copy $8; sample $8. Back issues: $6. Discounts: classroom - $6/issue. 176pp. Reporting time: 12 weeks. Simultaneous submissions accepted: yes. Publishes 1% of manuscripts submitted. Payment: 2 copies, year subscription, discounted copies. Not copyrighted, rights revert to author upon publication. Pub's reviews: 20 in 2005. §Poetry, fiction, creative nonfiction. Ads: negotiable; will consider ad swaps. Subjects: Essays, Fiction, Poetry, Short Stories.

Third Dimension Publishing, Teri Washington, 930 Thomas Avenue, North Brunswick, NJ 08902, 732-832-5387. 2003. Poetry, non-fiction. "Spirituality, Christian Living, Empowerment books. christian Greeting Cards." avg. press run 2000. Pub'd 1 title 2005; expects 2 titles 2006, 5 titles 2007. Discounts: 25%. 100pp. Reporting time: 4-6 Weeks. Simultaneous submissions accepted: No. Publishes 5% of manuscripts submitted. Copyrights for author. Subjects: Family, Relationships, Religion, Women.

THIRD WAY, Third Way Publications Ltd., PO Box 1243, London, SW7 3PB, England, 44(0)20-7-373-3432 phone/Fax, thirdway@dircon.co.uk, www.thirdway.org. 1990. Articles, art, photos, cartoons, interviews, criticism, reviews, music, concrete art. "1,000-2,000 words of decentralist, green, radical comment." circ. 1K. 4/yr. Pub'd 4 issues 2005; expects 4 issues 2006, 4 issues 2007. sub. price UK £5, Europe £6, rest of world (air) £9, $15US; per copy £1, $2US; sample £1.25, $3US. Back issues: none. Discounts: none. 16pp. Simultaneous submissions accepted: no. Publishes 30% of manuscripts submitted. Payment: none. Copyrighted, reverts to author. Pub's reviews: 20 in 2005. §Politics, economics, stake-holding, direct democracy, green issues. Ads: on application. Subjects: Book Reviewing, Political Science.

Third Way Publications Ltd. (see also COUNTER CULTURE; MOTHER EARTH; THIRD WAY), PO Box 1243, London, SW7 3PB, England, 44(0)20-7-373-3432 phone/Fax, thirdway@dircon.co.uk, www.thirdway.org. 1990. Music, letters, non-fiction. "Our main area of interest is in de-centralist, nationalist and co-operative alternatives to Capitalism." avg. press run 500. 16pp. Reporting time: 1 month. Copyrights for author. Subject: Political Science.

Thirsty Turtle Press, Daniel Rogers, CEO; Nina B. Rogers, Editor, PO Box 402, Maggie Valley, NC 28751, Phone 828-926-6472, FAX 828-926-8851, dan@thirstyturtlepress.com, www.thirstyturtlepress.com. 2003. Fiction, non-fiction. avg. press run 500 - 1000. Expects 1 title 2006, 2 titles 2007. 225pp. Reporting time: 10 Days. Simultaneous submissions accepted: Yes. Publishes 90% of manuscripts submitted. Copyrights for author. Subjects: Autobiography, History, Non-Fiction, Ohio, Outdoor Adventure, Travel.

Thirteen Colonies Press, John F. Millar, 710 South Henry Street, Williamsburg, VA 23185, 757-229-1775.

1986. Art, music, non-fiction. "We specialize in popular history (non-fiction) from the period of the Renaissance up to 1800." avg. press run 3M. Pub'd 2 titles 2005; expects 3 titles 2006, 3 titles 2007. Discounts: retailer 40% up to 24 copies, 45% 24+ copies; wholesaler 20% up to 6 copies, 50% up to 24 copies, 60% 24+ copies; libraries 10% 1 book, 2+ books 30%. 200pp. Payment: 10% gross sales, paid quarterly on previous quarter's sales. Copyrights for author. Subjects: Americana, The Americas, Architecture, Biography, Canada, Christianity, Crafts, Hobbies, Dance, Europe, History, Music, New England, Religion.

‡13TH MOON, Judith E. Johnson, Editor, 1400 Washington Avenue, SUNY, English Department, Albany, NY 12222-0001, 518-442-5593. 1973. Poetry, fiction, articles, art, photos, interviews, criticism, reviews, parts-of-novels, long-poems, plays, news items, non-fiction. "Current issues include work by Josephine Jacobsen, Lyn Lifshin, Lori Anderson, Kim Vaseth, Carolyn Beard Whitlow, Nell Altizer, Toi Derricotte, Judith Barrington, Ethel Schwabacher, Sallie Bingham, Lavonne Mueller, Star Olderman, Cassandra Medley, Courtland Jessup, Alicia Ostriker, Laurel Speer, Kathleene West, Ursula K. LeGuin, Chitra Divakaruni, E.M. Broner, Susan Montez and Frances Sherwood. Volume XI, Nos. 1 & 2, features translations of the work of Italian women writers and a special sectin on Feminist Fiction(s). Future issues will feature work by Eastern European and Caribbean women writers and feminist politics." circ. 1.5M. 1 double-issue per year. Pub'd 1 issue 2005; expects 1 issue 2006. sub. price $10 for 1 double issue; per copy $10; sample $10. Back issues: $10. Discounts: varies. 275pp. Reporting time: 2 weeks to 4 months. Payment: copies. Copyrighted, reverts to author. Pub's reviews: 3 in 2005. §Poetry by women small press books by women/literature by women/women's literary history by women. Ads: $200/$125. Subjects: Criticism, Essays, Feminism, Fiction, Graphics, Journals, Lesbianism, Literary Review, Literature (General), Magazines, Poetry, Reviews, Short Stories, Visual Arts, Women.

THIS IS IMPORTANT, F.A. Nettelbeck, Editor, PO Box 69, Beatty, OR 97621, 541-533-2486, www.aftermathbooks.com. 1980. Poetry. "Patterned after a religious tract and features one poem from six different poets each issue. The pamphlets are distributed on buses, subways, toilet floors, in laundromats, bars, theaters, etc., with the aim being to get poetry out to non-literary types and others. Some of the featured poets have included: William S. Burroughs, Richard Kostelanetz, Wanda Coleman, Todd Moore, Tom Clark, John Giorno, Lyn Lifshin, David Fisher, James Bertolino, John M. Bennett, Jack Micheline, Ann Menebroker, Judson Crews, Anselm Hollo, Flora Durham, Charles Bernstein, Robin Holcomb, Michael McClure, Douglas Blazek, James Grauerholz, Nila Northsun, Allen Ginsberg...as well as many others. Send poems. We want it *all* as long as it's *small*...but, *make me cry*. Make checks payable to F.A. Nettelbeck." circ. 1M. 4/yr. Pub'd 2 issues 2005; expects 2 issues 2006, 2 issues 2007. sub. price $10; per copy SASE; sample $1. Back issues: individual issues vary in price, when available. Limited complete sets of Issues #1-#16 are available for $100 per set. Discounts: none. 8pp. Reporting time: immediate. Simultaneous submissions accepted: yes. Publishes 20% of manuscripts submitted. Payment: 50 copies. Copyrighted, reverts to author. Subject: Poetry.

This New World Publishing, LLC, Diana Luce, 13500 SW Pacific Highway, Ste. 129, Tigard, OR 97223, 503-670-1153, Fax 503-213-5889, diana@thisnewworld.com, www.thisnewworld.com. 2002. Fiction, non-fiction. "Children's book material only." avg. press run 5000. Pub'd 1 title 2005; expects 2 titles 2006, 2 titles 2007. Discounts: 60% to Biblio (our distributor)non-book stores may order in bulk from 33% to 85% off. See http://www.naptimeadventures.com/bulk.html for current schedule. 32pp. Reporting time: 2 months. Simultaneous submissions accepted: yes. Publishes .1% of manuscripts submitted. Payment: Flat fee from $500 to $5000. Copyrights for author. Subjects: Children, Youth, Non-Fiction, Picture Books, Young Adult.

Thorp Springs Press, Paul Foreman, Foster Robertson, 1400 Cullen Avenue, Austin, TX 78757-2527. 1971. Poetry, fiction, plays. "Looking for quality poetry. SASE required." avg. press run 1M. Pub'd 2 titles 2005; expects 2 titles 2006, 1 title 2007. Discounts: bookstores 40%, 10 or more copies; jobbers 10%, 3-10 copies; 20%, 11-50 copies. 150-200pp. Reporting time: 3 months. Payment: standard royalty. Copyrights for author. Subjects: English, Language, Literature (General), Poetry, Public Affairs.

THOUGHT BOMBS, Anthony Rayson, PO Box 721, Homewood, IL 60430, 708-534-1334, anthonyrayson@hotmail.com. 1998. Poetry, fiction, articles, art, photos, cartoons, satire, criticism, reviews, letters, parts-of-novels, collages, news items, non-fiction. "*Thought Bombs* is a literary anarchist, activist, 60-paged digest-sized zine. I also write other zines and edit still others. I mostly include the work of myself, prisoners, and activists." circ. 500. 3/yr. Pub'd 3 issues 2005; expects 3 issues 2006, 3 issues 2007. sub. price donation; per copy $2; sample $2. Back issues: 20% off orders over $5. Discounts: willing to entertain offers. 60pp. We will possibly accept simultaneous submissions. Publishes 50% of manuscripts submitted. Payment: do not pay contributors. Not copyrighted. Pub's reviews: a few in 2005. Ads: none. Subjects: Anarchist, Feminism, Prison.

THOUGHTS FOR ALL SEASONS: The Magazine of Epigrams, Michel Paul Richard, Editor-in-Chief, 86 Leland Road, Becket, MA 01223, 413-623-0174. 1976. Poetry, satire. "Dedicated to preserving the epigram as a literary form. Guidelines for writing epigrams available on request without charge (with SASE). Poetry: rhyming quatrains, limericks; nonsense verse with good imagery; no haiku." circ. 1M. Irregular, special issues. Expects 1 issue 2006. sub. price $4.75 + $1.25 p/h; per copy $4.75 + $1.25 p/h; sample $4.75 + $1.25 p/h. Back issues: Vol. 2,3 & 4 available $3.75 + $1.25 p/h. Discounts: none. 80pp. Reporting time: 1 week. Simultaneous submissions accepted: yes. Publishes 15% of manuscripts submitted. Payment: 1 free copy of magazine. Copyrighted, reverts to author. Ads: $125/$80. Subjects: Humor, Society.

Three Bean Press, Seneca Clark, Editor, Author, Publisher, Owner; Julie Decedue, Illustrator, Publisher, Owner; Sandy Giardi, Editor, Author, Publisher, Owner, P.O. Box 15386, Boston, MA 02215, phone: 617.584.5759, fax: 617.266.3446, email: info@threebeanpress.com, web: www.threebeanpress.com. 2005. Fiction. "Three Bean Press publishes children's books. "Lily + the Imaginary Zoo" by Seneca Clark and Sandy Giardi, illustrated by Julie Decedue." avg. press run 3000. Expects 2 titles 2006, 6 titles 2007. Discounts: 1-2 copies no discount3-5 copies 25%6-20 copies 40%21-300 copies 50%301-up copies 55%. 32pp. Reporting time: 1 week. Subject: Children, Youth.

Three Bears Publishing, Ashley, 690 Community Row, Winnipeg, Manitoba Canada R3R 1H7, Canada, Tel. 1 (204) 783-7966, Email: info@ThreeBearsPublishing.com, Website: www.ThreeBearsPublishing.com. 2005. Fiction, art. "Publishes Children's books for ages 5 and up." Expects 1 title 2006, 3 titles 2007. 32pp. Reporting time: Due to the large number of submissions we receive, we may only respond to manuscripts we are interested in publishing. Simultaneous submissions accepted: Yes. Subjects: Children, Youth, Fiction, Humor.

Three House Publishing, Ray Goldman, P.O. Box 6672, Chesterfield, MO 63006-6672, 314-277-4560. 2005. Fiction. "Three House Publishing is a small independent publishing company. We specialize in helping teachers transform years of original course materials into custom published books. Three House Publishing is dedicated to publishing the work of teachers who want to explore alternative ways of teaching. Three House Publishing also publishes a few novels and short story collections. We like writers who have found innovative ways to use fiction to motivate people to change their lives. Our mission is to discover and to publish the works of those teachers and writers who have found imaginative ways to craft books that have a beneficial impact on the audiences for whom they are written." avg. press run 500. Expects 2 titles 2006, 1-3 titles 2007. Discounts: 1-10 40%11-19 44%20+ 47%. 150-250pp. Reporting time: 3 to 4 months. Simultaneous submissions accepted: No. Payment: 10% Royalty. No advances. Payments Sent Twice a Year. Copyrights for author. Subjects: African Literature, Africa, African Studies, African-American, Biology, Business & Economics, English, Feminism, Fiction, How-To, Latino, Novels, Psychology, Reading, Research, Science.

Three Mile Harbor, PO Box 1951, East Hampton, NY 11937.

Three Pyramids Publishing, John F. Simone, 6512 Nathans Landing Drive, Raleigh, NC 27603-7914, 813-426-3334, E-mail JFS999@mindspring.com. 1989. Non-fiction. "Trade paperbacks on New Age, occult, metaphysics, tarot, spiritual and associated topics. Practical advice, how-to information. 64-200 pages average. Manuscripts must be on IBM-compatible disks. Will read submissions, prefer query letter & sample chapter first." avg. press run 500-3M. Pub'd 1 title 2005; expects 3 titles 2006, 3 titles 2007. Discounts: trade 3-299 40%, 300-499 50%, 500+ 55%. 200pp. Reporting time: 2 weeks to 1 month. We accept simultaneous submissions if noted when submitting. Payment: 5-10% net; no advance. Copyrights for author. Subjects: Astrology, Crystals, Dreams, England, How-To, Magic, Metaphysics, Myth, Mythology, New Age, Occult, Spiritual, Supernatural, Tarot.

THE THREEPENNY REVIEW, Wendy Lesser, Editor; John Berger, Consulting Editor; Frank Bidart, Consulting Editor; Anne Carson, Consulting Editor; Jonathan Franzen, Consulting Editor; Elizabeth Hardwick, Consulting Editor; Grace Paley, Consulting Editor; Gore Vidal, Consulting Editor; Lawrence Weschler, Consulting Editor; Ian McEwan, Consulting Editor; Gideon Lewis-Kraus, Deputy Editor, PO Box 9131, Berkeley, CA 94709-0131, 510-849-4545. 1979. Poetry, fiction, art, interviews, criticism, reviews. "Length of material: Reviews should be 1M-3M words, covering several books or an author in depth, or dealing with a whole topic (e.g., the current theater season in one city, or the state of jazz clubs in another). Fiction should be under 5M words; poems should be under 100 lines. Special features: Though primarily a literary and performing arts review, *The Threepenny Review* will contain at least one essay on a topic of current social or political concern in each issue. Interested essayists should first submit a letter of inquiry. Recent Contributors: John Berger, Thom Gunn, Amy Tan. *SASE must accompany all manuscripts.*" circ. 10M. 4/yr. Pub'd 4 issues 2005; expects 4 issues 2006, 4 issues 2007. sub. price $25, $45/2 years, $50/yr foreign; per copy $7; sample $12 (includes shipping). Back issues: variable (price list available). 36pp. Reporting time: 1 to 2 months (but we do NOT read in the fall months). Simultaneous submissions accepted: No. Payment: $200-$400. Copyrighted, reverts to author. Pub's reviews: 20 in 2005. §Fiction, poetry, essays, philosophy, social theory, visual arts and architecture, history, criticism. Ads: $1200/$900/$500 (full/half/quarter page). Subjects: Arts, Criticism, Electronics, Fiction, Literary Review, Literature (General), Poetry, Theatre.

THRESHOLDS JOURNAL, SOM Publishing, division of School of Metaphysics, Dr. Barbara Condron, Editor-in-Chief, 163 Moon Valley Road, Windyville, MO 65783, 417-345-8411, www.som.org. 1975. "Print version is an annual publication which serves as a voice for School of Metaphysics teachings. Educational, inspirational, and visionary. On-line publication accepts articles that are uplifting, educational, inspirational, and visionary. Need sort pieces, under 1000 words. Includes on-line interviews with well-known people who are successful in their fields. Recent interviews with Bernie Siegel, Diane Stein, Fred Pryor, Raymond Moody, Deena Metzger, Barbara Max Hubbard, Swami Beyondananda, Dalai Lama." circ. 5M+. 1/yr. Pub'd 1 issue 2005; expects 1 issue 2006, 1 issue 2007. sub. price online publication only. Back issues: $5 for available issues. Discounts: available only through SOMA. Reporting time: 5 weeks-3 months. Payment: if accepted, international exposure, membership to SOMA ($60 value). Copyrighted, does not revert to author. Classified only, by donation to School of Metaphysics. Subjects: Arts, Dreams, Education, Fiction, Health, Humor, Inspirational, Magazines, Metaphysics, Religion, Science Fiction, Spiritual.

Thunder Rain Publishing Corp., Katherine (Rhi) Tracy, Editor, PO Box 87, Alamogordo, NM 88311-0087, 985-320-8484, rhi@thunder-rain.com, www.thunder-rain.com, www.lintrigue.org. 1996. Poetry, fiction, articles, art, photos, satire, criticism, reviews, long-poems, non-fiction. "Thunder-Rain Award Contest $100 each year for winning submission published in L'Intrigue WebZine. See www.lintrigue.org for details." Publishes 3 online issues a year. Reporting time: 3-6 months. Simultaneous submissions accepted: yes. Copyrights for author. Subjects: Essays, Experimental, Fiction, Literary Review, Louisiana, Non-Fiction, Photography, Poetry, Prose, Reviews, Short Stories, Zines.

Thundercloud Books, Laurel Tesoro, Press Contact, PO Box 97, Aspen, CO 81612, (970) 925-1588, fax (970) 920-9361, web: www.ThundercloudBooks.com, www.WakingThe Ancients.com. 2003. Fiction. "Novels for adults involving southwestern United States, prehistoric civilizations, outdoors and recreation, women's concerns." Expects 1 title 2007. Copyrights for author. Subjects: Arizona, Colorado, Fiction, History, Indigenous Cultures, Literature (General), Native American, New Mexico, Society, Travel, Utah.

Tia Chucha Press, Luis J. Rodriguez, PO Box 328, San Fernando, CA 91341, 818-898-0013. 1989. Poetry, fiction. "A project of Tia Chucha's Centro Cultural, a not-for-profit corporation. Distributed by: Northwestern University Press, 625 Colfax, Evanston, IL 60208; 800-621-2736; FAX 800-621-8476." avg. press run 1M. Pub'd 1 title 2005; expects 2 titles 2006, 3 titles 2007. 64pp. Reporting time: 6 weeks to 6 months. We accept simultaneous submissions, but we must be informed if another publisher is interested. Publishes .05% of manuscripts submitted. Payment: 10% royalties, discount on books. Copyrights for author. Subjects: Literature (General), Multicultural, Poetry.

TIFARA, Sandrine Roland, 08 BP 28 Cidex 02 Abidjan 08, Cocody Lycee Technique 150 Logts Bat N Appt 107, Abidjan Ivory Coast, East Africa, +225 07 67 81 98. 2004. Articles, interviews, music, letters, non-fiction. circ. 50000. 12/yr. Expects 12 issues 2007. sub. price Fcfa 15000; per copy Fcfa 1500; sample free. Back issues: Fcfa 1000. Discounts: 2-10 copies 5%. 24pp. Reporting time: 1 week. Simultaneous submissions accepted: Yes. Publishes 50% of manuscripts submitted. Payment: none. Copyrighted, does not revert to author. Pub's reviews: none in 2005. Subjects: African Literature, Africa, African Studies, Book Reviewing, Business & Economics, Careers, Children, Youth, Community, Crafts, Hobbies, Education, Health, Literary Review, Literature (General), Religion, Spiritual, Sports, Outdoors, Women.

TIFERET: A Journal of Spiritual Literature, Eryon Press, Cynthia Brown, PO Box 659, Peapack, NJ 07977-0659, 908-781-2556.

Tiger Moon, Terry Reis Kennedy, 3-882 Coconut Grove, Prasanthi Nilayam A.P.515134, India. 1991. "We publish poetry, fiction, and literary essays, biography, Tibetan-related material, and doctoral dissertations. For more information contact Terry Reis Kennedy by email at cosmicpowrepress@yahoo.co.in." avg. press run 1M. 100-200pp. Reporting time: 2 months. Simultaneous submissions accepted: yes. Payment: copies. Copyrights for author.

TIGHTROPE, Swamp Press, Ed Rayher, 15 Warwick Avenue, Northfield, MA 01360. 1975. Poetry, art, long-poems. "Fine poetry and graphic art printed by letterpress in artistic and sometimes unconventional formats. Recent contributors: Greg Joly, Chuck Zerby, Carolyn Cushing." circ. 350. 2/yr. Pub'd 2 issues 2005; expects 2 issues 2006, 2 issues 2007. sub. price $10; per copy $6; sample $6. Back issues: $6. Discounts: bookstores and dealers 40%. 60pp. Reporting time: 8 weeks. Simultaneous submissions accepted: No. Publishes 1% of manuscripts submitted. Payment: copies. Copyrighted, reverts to author. Subjects: Graphics, Haiku, Poetry.

TIMBER CREEK REVIEW, J.M. Freiermuth, Editor; Celestine Woo, Associate Editor, c/o J.M. Freiermuth, PO Box 16542, Greensboro, NC 27416. 1994. Poetry, fiction, articles, photos, cartoons, interviews, satire, letters, non-fiction. "*Timber Creek Review* is a quarterly collection of short stories with a few poems. Contributors in the fourth year include Renee Coleman, Lucille Bellucci, Bill McGill, Lynn V. Sadler, Matt Briggs, and Tim Poland. Send all correspondence and make all checks payable to: J.M. Freiermuth. Published 40 stories in 2000-2001. We do not accept reprints." circ. 140-170. 4/yr. Pub'd 4 issues 2005; expects 4 issues 2006, 4 issues 2007. sub. price $15 individuals, $16 institutions and Canada, $22 international; per copy $4.25; sample $4.25. Discounts: 50% for creative writing classes and groups. 76-88pp. Reporting time: from the next mail to 4 months. Simultaneous submissions accepted: yes. Publishes 8-12% of manuscripts submitted. Payment: 1 year subscription for first story, 1 copy for poems, additional short stories and short-short stories to 2 pages. Pays $25 to $50 for stories, including annual subscription. Not copyrighted, rights revert to author upon publication. Pub's reviews: none in 2005. §Books of short stories. Ads: none.

Timber Press, Dale Johnson, Acquisitions Editor, Botany; Neal Maillet, Aquisitions Editor, Horticulture & Fine Gardening; Eve Goodman, Acquisitions Editor, Regional, 133 SW Second Avenue, Suite 450, Portland, OR 97204-3527. 1976. Non-fiction. ''Main emphasis is Northwestern subject matter, horticulture, botany, and natural history.'' avg. press run 5M. Pub'd 60 titles 2005; expects 60 titles 2006, 60 titles 2007. Discounts: 1 20%, 5 40%, 25 42%, 50 44%, 100 46%, 150 48%. 275pp. Reporting time: 2 months. Simultaneous submissions accepted: no. Publishes 15% of manuscripts submitted. Payment: by arrangement. Copyrights for author. Subjects: Biology, Birds, Botany, Earth, Natural History, Environment, Gardening, Horticulture, Marine Life, Nature, Oregon, Pacific Northwest, Pacific Region, Science, Wine, Wineries.

TIMBER TIMES, Steven R. Gatke, PO Box 219, Hillsboro, OR 97123. 1992. Articles, photos, cartoons, interviews, reviews, news items, non-fiction. circ. 2.7M. 4/yr. Pub'd 4 issues 2005; expects 4 issues 2006, 4 issues 2007. sub. price $19; per copy $4.75; sample $6. Back issues: $6. Discounts: 40% on minimum quantity of 5 to all retailers. 52pp. Simultaneous submissions accepted: no. Publishes 90+% of manuscripts submitted. Payment: 1 yr. subscription. Copyrighted, reverts to author. Pub's reviews: 20 in 2005. §Railroad, logging, lumbering, forestry. Ads: $125/$65/$35 1/4 page/$20 1/8 page. Subjects: Crafts, Hobbies, Pacific Northwest, Transportation.

Timberline Press, Clarence Wolfshohl, 6281 Red Bud, Fulton, MO 65251, 573-642-5035. 1975. Poetry, non-fiction. ''Print chapbooks of 20-50 pages (prefer shorter 20-30 pp). We look at all poetry sent, but lean toward nature poetry with a sense of place or good lyrical, imagistic poetry. Actually, our taste is eclectic with quality being our primary criterion. We also publish short essays of natural history (under 20 pages) which will be printed in a reduced size format (not miniature). No set preference, but possible contributors should be familiar with better contemporary writers of natural history.'' avg. press run 200. Pub'd 4 titles 2005; expects 4 titles 2006, 2 titles 2007. Discounts: 1-4 books 25%, 5+ 40%. 25-45pp. Reporting time: 30 days. Payment: 50-50 split after expenses. Does not copyright for author. Subjects: Earth, Natural History, Poetry.

Time Barn Books, Klyd Watkins, 529 Barrywood Drive, Nashville, TN 37220-1636, www.thetimegarden.com. 2000. Poetry, music. ''I publish stuff that I believe in that might not get out there otherwise, much of it my own work. I am not seeking manuscripts and have a short pile on hand that I may never get around to reading.'' avg. press run 100. Pub'd 2 titles 2005; expects 3 titles 2006. Discounts: 40%. 40pp. Reporting time: My first response will be quick but my final answer may never come. Simultaneous submissions accepted: No. Publishes 33% of manuscripts submitted. Payment: The authors pay the publishing costs and own all the books. I take 40% for any that I sell. I add the symbol for the author but do not send to Library of Congress. Subject: Poetry.

TIME FOR RHYME, Richard W. Unger, Editor, c/o Richard Unger, PO Box 1055, Battleford SK S0M 0E0, Canada, 306-445-5172. 1995. Poetry. ''This is a handcrafted, pocket-sized quarterly magazine that publishes *only* rhyming poetry. Writer's guidelines or advertisers guidelines available with SASE (IRC or $1US acceptable from non-Canadians without Canadian postage).'' circ. 83. 4/yr. Pub'd 4 issues 2005; expects 4 issues 2006, 4 issues 2007. sub. price $12 Cdn. for Canadians, $12US for Americans, $19 Cdn. for overseas; per copy $3.25 with SASE, Americans use either Canadian postage or IRCs, $5 Cdn. overseas; sample $3.25 Cdn. for Canadians, $3.25 US for Americans, $5 Cdn. overseas. Back issues: same. 32pp. Reporting time: as quickly as possible. Simultaneous submissions accepted: no. Publishes less than 1% of manuscripts submitted. Payment: 1 copy (when financially viable, will consider cash payment). Copyrighted, reverts to author. Pub's reviews: 4 in 2005. §Those mostly or entirely containing rhyming poetry (either new or old with artwork). Ads: classifieds 15¢/word. Subject: Poetry.

Timeless Books (see also ASCENT), Clea McDougall, Editor, 3 MacDonell Ave, Suite 300, Toronto, ON M6R 2A3, Canada, 1-800-661-8711, (416) 645-6747, contact@timeless.org, www.timeless.org. 1977. Non-fiction. ''Timeless publications are for those who seek a deeper meaning and purpose to their lives. Our focus is on the ancient teachings of yoga and Buddhism. Inspiration is combined with practical tools for living a life of quality and to bring out the best in ourselves and others.'' avg. press run 2000. Pub'd 4 titles 2005; expects 4 titles 2006, 4/ titles 2007. Discounts: 1-5 titles 20%, 5 or more 40%. 250pp. Reporting time: one to three months. Copyrights for author. Subjects: Autobiography, Biography, Buddhism, Inspirational, Memoirs, Metaphysics, Non-Fiction, Religion, Self-Help, Spiritual, Tapes & Records, Yoga.

The Times Journal Publishing Co., Darlene Melville, Managing Editor, PO Box 1286, Puyallup, WA 98371, 253-848-2779. 1946. Fiction, photos, non-fiction. ''We are a subsidy publisher only and prefer a query letter. We will work closely with the author on editing, page layouts, cover design and promoting distribution.'' avg. press run 1200. Pub'd 1 title 2005; expects 2 titles 2006, 4 titles 2007. Discounts: standard. 290pp. Reporting time: 3 months. Payment: individually negotiated. Copyrights for author. Subjects: Airplanes, Aviation,

480

Biography, Editing, Fiction, Non-Fiction, Photography.

Timson Edwards, Co. (see also FOTOTEQUE; The Leaping Frog Press; THE WILDWOOD READER), PO Box 55-0898-DB, Jacksonville, FL 32255-0898, 904-705-6806, gonz2171@bellsouth.net, www.short-fiction.com. 1998. Poetry, fiction, articles, photos, interviews, reviews, news items. "Although we concentrate our efforts on publishing the short fiction work of new and emerging authors, we are also interested in publishing previously published short fiction collections that have gone out of print. Our main focus still remains publishing traditional photo and essay layouts for our photography monographs. We need short 400 to 1800 word articles about health and wellness for our localized magazine "First Health Magazine" published in various cities by associate publishers. We have our associate publishers are local independent business owners that help make it easier for local residents to live a healthy lifestyle. Our Leaping Frog press is dedicated to publishing short fiction for children, and the Wildwood Reader is a literary short fiction journal. We are working on an anthology project that will publish 2 to 4 times a year. We hope to receive good work from new writers, our guidelines are on our site. Please remember to always - always include a self addressed stamped envelope for notices and return of your materials. Visit www.short-fiction.com or www.timsonedwards.com for additional information, good luck and thanks for your time." avg. press run Varies with project; min 50 maximum 2,500. 148pp. Reporting time: Varies with project, usually 6 to 8 weeks. Simultaneous submissions accepted: Yes, however, it is up to the author to figure out what needs to be done if there is a conflict. We will always bow out gracefully if there is a problem! Payment: Varies with the project. We always pay an advance and negotiate royalties; sometimes pay with books; a web page on one of our sites; a complete web site for a year. Due to the fact that we are primarily interested in new or emerging writers, when we do pay it can be as little as $45.00 for the story to as high as $275.00. Though to be honest it is usually on the lower side. If we make money, we have paid additional bonuses. We will always share the wealth! Copyrights always revert back to the author....

•**TIN HOUSE MAGAZINE,** Win McCormack, Publisher, PO Box 469049, Escondido, CA 92046. "A journal of sex, saints and satellite convulsions! Each issue includes fiction, non-fiction, New Voices, Author Interviews, Lost and Found (underappreciated books), profound Pilgrimages, a Readable Feast (memorable dishes and the events that inspired them), Blithe Spirits (signature drinks). We set out to capture the energy and vitality of the best new writers in fiction and poetry from around the world and showcase their work in a format that's elegant, inspired and inviting."

TINY LIGHTS: A Journal of Personal Essay, Susan Bono, PO Box 928, Petaluma, CA 94953, 707-762-3208, sbono@tiny-lights.com, www.tiny-lights.com. 1995. Non-fiction. "*Tiny Lights* celebrates the power of personal essay with a biannual journal in newsletter format devoted to short essay. The annual essay contest, which offers $1000 in prizes, provides the material for the summer issue and various issues of *Lights on Line*, *TL*'s online journal. The winter issue is by invitation only. Past contributors include Gerald Haslam, Jean Hegland, Robin Beeman, Ron Franscell, Pat Schneider, Dan Coshnear, Sheila Bender." circ. approx. 500. 2/yr. Pub'd 2 issues 2005; expects 2 issues 2006, 2 issues 2007. sub. price $10; per copy $5. Back issues: $3. Discounts: contact us. 16pp. Reporting time: 3 months. Simultaneous submissions accepted: yes. Publishes 10% of manuscripts submitted. Payment: contest issue only. Not copyrighted. Ads: Go to "Literary Services Directory" at www.tiny-lights.com for rates. Subjects: Essays, Memoirs.

Titan Press, Stephani Wilson, Publisher, PO Box 17897, Encino, CA 91416-7897. 1980. Poetry, fiction, photos, non-fiction. "We look only at high quality manuscripts. If it also embodies socially redeeming commentary, terrific. Very 'current' styles are preferred. We have strong liaisons in the entertainment industry and are thusly somewhat media oriented. Only strong writers with some sort of track record should submit. We sponsor the 'Masters Literary Award', and publish the results, et al. Professionalism, style and quality are the keys to submission here. We are not interested in simply the good, but rather the great. To know us, read something by: Milan Kundera, Scott Alixander Sonders, Tom Robbins, Chaim Potok, or John Irving." avg. press run 3K-10K poetry, 50K calendars, 5-50K novels. Pub'd 6 titles 2005; expects 6 titles 2006, 6 titles 2007. Discounts: trade 2-4 20%, 5-9 30%, 10-24 40%, 25-49 45%, 50-99 50%; schools and libraries less added 5%. 112pp. Reporting time: 2-6 months. Payment: 5-10% on sales + guarantee and expenses, see Standard Writers Union Contract. Copyrights for author. Subjects: Awards, Foundations, Grants, Fiction, Health, Photography, Poetry, Science, Sex, Sexuality, Spiritual.

Titlewaves Publishing; Writers Direct, Rob Sanford, Cathy Crary, 4-1579 Kuhio Hwy, Ste 104, Kapaa, HI 96746-1859, orders 800-867-7323. 1989. Fiction, articles, photos, cartoons, interviews, satire, news items, non-fiction. avg. press run print-on-demand (200). Pub'd 1 title 2005; expects 3 titles 2006, 4 titles 2007. Discounts: 3-299 40%, 300-499 50%, 500+ 55%, STOP orders 40% + $2.75/order. 235pp. Reporting time: 30 days. Simultaneous submissions accepted: yes. Publishes 2% of manuscripts submitted. Payment: varies; better than standard. Copyrights for author. Subjects: Ecology, Foods, Ethics, Finances, Hawaii, Health, How-To, Humor, Inspirational, Marketing, Motivation, Success, Nature, Non-Fiction, Quotations, Spiritual, Travel.

•**Titus Home Publishing,** Carolena Lapierre, 204 N. Main, Rogersville, MO 65742-6574, 417-753-3449. 2006.

Photos, non-fiction. "Titus Home Publishing "Books to Pass On" Wholesome books on Family History, Life Stories, Cookbooks, Special family helps and advice, Children's books." Expects 2 titles 2006, 2 titles 2007. Discounts: 2-10 copies 20%11+ copies 40%. 130pp. Reporting time: 60 Days. Copyrights for author. Subjects: Adoption, Aging, Amish Culture, Autobiography, Biography, Children, Youth, Cooking, Family, Genealogy, History, Journals, Memoirs, Picture Books, Poetry, Storytelling.

TMC Books LLC (see also WILDERNESS MEDICINE NEWSLETTER), Peter Lewis, 731 Tasker Hill Rd., Conway, NH 03818, 603-447-5589,info@tmcbooks.com www.tmcbooks.com. 2002. Articles, non-fiction. "TMC Books is a specialty publisher, we supply textbooks to Stonehearth Open Learning Opportunities (SOLO), the well known education school in the White Mountains of New Hampshire, we also publish the online magazine Wilderness Medicine Newsletter, guide books, and some non-fiction titles." avg. press run 8000. Pub'd 1 title 2005; expects 1 title 2006, 1 title 2007. 120pp. Reporting time: Due to a baglog of projects we are not looking for manuscrip submissions at this time. Simultaneous submissions accepted: No. Does not copyright for author. Subjects: Architecture, Education, Medicine, Nature, New England, Non-Fiction.

TnT Classic Books, Linda Reynolds, Francine L. Trevens, 360 West 36 Street #2NW, New York, NY 10018-6412, 212-736-6279, Fax 212-695-3219, tntclassics@aol.com, www.tntclassicbooks.com. 1994. Fiction, plays. "We handle old JH Press gay play series and their gay novels. We are moving into a children's line called the Happy Task Series. Overstocked and not reading until mid-2005." avg. press run 2M. Expects 1 title 2006, 1 title 2007. Discounts: 40% commercial bookstores, 30% college bookstores, none for orders under 5 books. 100pp. Simultaneous submissions accepted: no. Payment: 10% semi-annually. Copyrights for author. Subjects: Drama, Fiction, Gay, Lesbianism, Novels.

Toad Hall Press (see also Toad Hall, Inc.), Sharon Jarvis, President, RR 2 Box 2090, Laceyville, PA 18623, 717-869-1031. 1995. Non-fiction. "We primarily are consultants for book-length works only. Send a query letter first. Will read and provide written analysis of first 3 chapters plus synopsis of a manuscript or the complete self-published book for $50. Will work with self-publishers before and after publication. Toad Hall Press (as opposed to Toad Hall, Inc., the parent company)publishes non-fiction only." avg. press run 4M. Pub'd 1 title 2005; expects 2 titles 2006, 2 titles 2007. 224pp. Reporting time: 3 months. Payment: We publish by co-op arrangement only. Copyrights for author. Subjects: Health, Publishing.

Toad Hall, Inc. (see also Belfry Books; The Bradford Press; Hands & Heart Books; Toad Hall Press), Sharon Jarvis, RR 2 Box 2090, Laceyville, PA 18623, 570-869-2942; Fax 570-869-1031. 1995. Non-fiction. "We primarily are consultants for book-length works only. Send a query letter first. Will read and provide written analysis of first 3 chapters plus synopsis of a manuscript or the complete self-published book for $50. Will work with self-publishers before and after publication." avg. press run Suggested runs of 300. Pub'd 2 titles 2005; expects 4 titles 2006, 4 titles 2007. Discounts: Books sold through New Leaf and other wholesalers. 224pp. Reporting time: 3 months. Simultaneous submissions accepted: no. Payment: We publish by co-op arrangement only. Copyrights for author. Subjects: Metaphysics, New Age, Occult, Supernatural.

•**Toad Press International Chapbook Series,** Genevieve Kaplan, Sean Bernard, 4985 West 7th Street #18, Reno, NV 89503, www.toadpress.blogspot.com, toadpress@hotmail.com. 2003. Poetry, fiction, letters, long-poems. "We publish literary translations only." avg. press run 200. Pub'd 1 title 2005; expects 2 titles 2006, 2 titles 2007. 35pp. Reporting time: see website for submission period. Simultaneous submissions accepted: Yes. Payment: pays in copies only. Subjects: Absurdist, Danish, Experimental, Fiction, Literature (General), Poetry, Post Modern, Translation, Writers/Writing.

•**Toadlily Press,** Myrna Goodman Editor, Maxine Silverman Editor, Meredith Trede Editor, Jennifer Wallace Editor, P O. Box 2, Chappaqua, NY 10514, mgoodman@toadlilypress.com, www.toadlilypress.com. 2005. Poetry. "The Quartet Series presents four poets each represented by a chapbook, in one handsome, perfect-bound volume. Toadlily publications are as artful and imaginative as the words within them." avg. press run 1000. Pub'd 1 title 2005; expects 1 title 2006, 1 title 2007. Discounts: 30-40%. 80pp. Reporting time: 2-3 months. Simultaneous submissions accepted: Yes. Payment: cash and copies of book. Author retains rights of his/her individual work, we copyright the Quartet Series. Subject: Poetry.

Tolling Bell Books, Lea Thomas, 5555 Oakbrook Parkway, Suite 330, Norcross, GA 30093, 770-757-2934, Fax 770-448-0130, info@tollingbellbooks.com, www.tollingbellbooks.com. 2003. Fiction. "Do not call regarding manuscript submission. See our website for genres accepted, submission requirements, and/or how to email a query." Pub'd 2 titles 2005; expects 2 titles 2006, 2 titles 2007. Reporting time: 3 months. Simultaneous submissions accepted: yes. Publishes 1-2% of manuscripts submitted. Payment: varies. Does not copyright for author. Subjects: Children, Youth, Fiction, Mystery, Science Fiction.

Tomart Publications, Tom Tumbusch; Jack Wade, Customer Service; Rebecca Trissel, Assistant to Publisher, 3300 Encrete Lane, Dayton, OH 45439-1944, 937-294-2250; Fax 937-294-1024. 1977. Non-fiction. "We publishers of antique & collectible photo price guides for Disneyana (any Disney product), radio premiums, character glasses, space adventure collectibles, etc. Other non-fiction on related subjects. Books on musical theatre.'' avg. press run 6M-10M. Pub'd 3 titles 2005; expects 6 titles 2006, 5 titles 2007. Discounts: booksellers 40%, distributors up to 60%. 220pp. Reporting time: 30 days. Payment: 10% advance. Copyrights for author. Subjects: Antiques, Biography, Book Collecting, Bookselling, Collectibles, Crafts, Hobbies, Disney, Theatre.

Tombouctou Books, Michael Wolfe, 1472 Creekview Lane, Santa Cruz, CA 95062, 831-476-4144. 1975. Poetry, fiction, interviews, long-poems. ''No unsolicited manuscripts will be returned. Distributed to the trade by Small Press Distribution, 1341 Seventh StreetBerkeley, CA 94710-1409.'' avg. press run 500-2M. Pub'd 4 titles 2005; expects 4 titles 2006, 4 titles 2007. Discounts: inquire publisher. 48-200pp. Simultaneous submissions accepted: no. Publishes 1% of manuscripts submitted. Payment: varies. Copyrights for author. Subjects: African Literature, Africa, African Studies, Fiction, Poetry.

•**Top 20 Press,** Paul Bernabei, 1873 Standord Avenue, St. Paul, MN 55105, 651-690-5758. 2003. Non-fiction. ''To provide books and materials to help people develop their potential.'' Expects 1 title 2007. Discounts: 2-10 copies 25%. 230pp. Subjects: Adolescence, Children, Youth, Family, Leadership, Non-Fiction, Relationships, Self-Help, Young Adult.

Top Shelf Productions, Inc., Chris Staros, Publisher; Brett Warnock, Publisher, PO Box 1282, Marietta, GA 30061-1282, 770-425-0551, Fax: 770-427-6395, Email: chris@topshelfcomix.com. 1997. ''Top Shelf Productions is the graphic novel and comics publisher best known for its ability to discover and showcase the vanguard of the alternative comics scene. Since forming in 1997, Top Shelf Productions has published over one-hundred graphic novels and comic books that have helped to revitalize interest in comics as a literary art form. Most notably, Craig Thompsons *Blankets* and Alan Moore & Eddie Campbell's *From Hell*, both of which have garnered critical accolades from the likes of Time Magazine, Entertainment Weekly, Publishers Weekly, The New Yorker, and the New York Times Book Review. Perennial favorites also include: Craig Thompson's *Good-bye, Chunky Rice*; Alan Moore's *Voice of the Fire*, Jeffrey Brown's *Clumsy* and *Unlikely*; James Kochalka's *Monkey vs. Robot*; Doug TenNapel's *Creature Tech*; Alex Robinsons *Box Office Poison*; Rich Koslowski's *Three Fingers*, Scott Morse's *The Barefoot Serpent*; and Jon B. Cooke's award-winning *Comic Book Artist* magazine.''

Topping International Institute, Inc., Wayne W. Topping, 2505 Cedarwood Avenue, Ste. 3, Bellingham, WA 98225, 360-647-2703, Fax 360-647-0164, topping2@gte.net. 1984. Non-fiction. ''Wholistic health area only. Alternative health care. Stress management.'' avg. press run 2M+. Pub'd 1 title 2005; expects 1 title 2006, 1 title 2007. Discounts: 10+ 40%, 200+ 50%, 500+ 40%-25%. 150pp. Reporting time: 3 months. Payment: 8-10% royalty. Copyrights for author. Subjects: Health, Psychology.

TORQUERE: Journal of the Canadian Lesbian and Gay Studies Association, University of Calgary Press, Lee Easton, Editor, University of Calgary Press, 2500 University Drive NW, Calgary, AB T2N 1N4, Canada, 403-220-3514, Fax 403-282-0085, ucpmail@ucalgary.ca, www.uofcpress.com. 1999. ''*torquere* seeks to publicize scholarly and creative work on topics concerning queer aspects of Canada and its social, political, material, and textual culture, or on queer topics outside Canadian Studies by scholars conducting queer research in Canada. A diversity of approaches is welcomed from a wide spectrum of areas including previously unpublished creative writing and visual art by and about Canadian queer, lesbian, gay, bisexual, and transgendered peple. *torquere* is particularly interested in work that seeks to play with conventional forms and genres in ways that are innovative and challenging.'' circ. 250. 1/yr. Pub'd 1 issue 2005; expects 1 issue 2006, 1 issue 2007. sub. price $60 CAD for regular CLGSA members, $30 CAD for student CLGSA members, $75 CAD for institutions, outside Canada, price in USD. 200pp. Pub's reviews. Ads: contact the editor. Subjects: Bisexual, Gay, Lesbianism.

TORRE DE PAPEL, Eduardo Guizar Alvarez, 111 Phillips Hall, The University of Iowa, Iowa City, IA 52242, 319-335-0487. 1991. Poetry, fiction, articles, art, interviews, criticism, reviews. circ. 400. 3/yr. Pub'd 2 issues 2005; expects 3 issues 2006, 3 issues 2007. sub. price $30; per copy $10; sample $10. Back issues: $15. 110pp. Reporting time: 2 months (may vary). Payment: none. Copyrighted, rights revert to author and publisher. Pub's reviews. §Latin American literature (Hispanic and Brazilian), Caribbean literature, Spanish literature, Portuguese literature, Chicano/Puerto Rican/Cuban American/Afro-American literature, translations and linguistics. Subjects: Caribbean, Criticism, Journals, Latin America, Latino, Literary Review, Literature (General), Portugal, Puerto Rico, Spain, Translation, Women, Writers/Writing.

Tortuga Books, Carolyn Gloeckner, PO Box 420564, Summerland Key, FL 33042, 800-345-6665 (orders), 305-745-8709, Fax 305-745-2704, www.tortugabooks.com. 1998. Non-fiction. avg. press run 5M. Pub'd 3 titles 2005; expects 1 title 2006, 2 titles 2007. Discounts: 2-3 10%, 4-10 20%, 11-20 30%, 21-100 40%, 100+ 50%. 200pp. Reporting time: 2 months. Simultaneous submissions accepted: no. Payment: cash. Does not copyright for author. Subjects: Caribbean, Children, Youth, Environment, Florida, Marine Life, Non-Fiction, Picture Books, Puerto Rico, Sports, Outdoors, Travel.

•**Total Cardboard Publishing,** John Mansfield, 70 Mount Barker Road, Stirling, SA 5152, Australia, www.totalcardboard.com. 2003. Poetry, fiction, articles. "Total Cardboard focuses on aesthetics too subtle for the mainstream press." avg. press run 300. Pub'd 3 titles 2005; expects 2 titles 2006, 3 titles 2007. Discounts: 40% trade discount. 200pp. Reporting time: 1 month. Simultaneous submissions accepted: Yes. Publishes 20% of manuscripts submitted. Payment: Split all profits 50-50. Copyrights for author. Subjects: Anarchist, Australia, Avant-Garde, Experimental Art, Experimental, Fiction, Gaelic, Genealogy, Paper, Psychiatry, Zen.

TOUCHSTONE, Old Stage Publishing, Dan Culberson, PO Box 17446, Boulder, CO 80308-0446, 303-444-3363, danculberson@juno.com. 1996. Articles, interviews, criticism, news items, non-fiction. "*Touchstone* is an e-mail distributed free newsletter that is also published on the Internet at http://www.forums.delphiforums.com/touchstone and is concerned with political activism." circ. 300. 12/yr. Pub'd 12 issues 2005; expects 12 issues 2006, 12 issues 2007. sub. price free; per copy free; sample free. Back issues: $1. 10pp. Reporting time: 1 week. Simultaneous submissions accepted: yes. Publishes 25% of manuscripts submitted. Payment: 2 copies. Copyrighted, reverts to author. Pub's reviews: none in 2005. §Politics, elections, political activism, government. Ads: none. Subjects: Birth, Birth Control, Population, Black, Business & Economics, Civil Rights, Colorado, Communism, Marxism, Leninism, Community, Conservation, Counter-Culture, Alternatives, Communes, Crime, Cuba, Culture, Current Affairs, Earth, Natural History, Education.

Touchstone Adventures, Jane Heim, Publisher, PO Box 177, Paw Paw, IL 61353. 1996. Non-fiction. avg. press run 2M. Pub'd 2 titles 2005. Discounts: 20-60%. 224pp. Reporting time: 3-6 months. Simultaneous submissions accepted: no. Publishes a small % of manuscripts submitted. Payment: open. Does not copyright for author. Subjects: Agriculture, Astrology, Autos, Christmas, Conservation, Counter-Culture, Alternatives, Communes, Creativity, Culture, Ecology, Foods, Environment, Gardening, Health, Homelessness, How-To, Human Rights.

Touchstone Center Publications, 141 East 88th Street, New York, NY 10128, rlewis212@aol.com. 1969. "At present Touchstone Center Publications is primarily concerned with documenting and publishing the work of the The Touchstone Center - particularly its work with children and teachers in the area of arts education, poetry and the nature of the imaginative experience."

TOUCHSTONE LITERARY JOURNAL, Panther Creek Press, Guida Jackson, Publisher & Editor; William Laufer, Poetry Editor; Julia Mercedes Gomez-Rivas, Fiction Editor; T.E. Walthen, Poetry Editor, PO Box 130233, The Woodlands, TX 77393-0233. 1976. Poetry, fiction, interviews, criticism, reviews, non-fiction. "No line limit for good poetry, prose." circ. 1M. 1/yr, plus book-length collections. Pub'd 2 issues 2005; expects 2 issues 2006, 2 issues 2007. sub. price contribution: 1 book postage stamps; per copy same; sample same. Back issues: same. 80pp. Reporting time: 6 weeks. Payment: 1 copy. Copyrighted, reverts to author. Pub's reviews: 6 in 2005. §Poetry, short story collections. Subjects: Fiction, Poetry, Reviews, Translation.

TOWER, Tower Poetry Society, Joanna Lawson, c/o McMaster University, 1280 Main Street W Box 1021, Hamilton, Ontario, L8S ICO, Canada. 1950. Poetry. "Length of material should be up to 40 lines." circ. 250. 2/yr. Pub'd 2 issues 2005; expects 2 issues 2006, 2 issues 2007. sub. price $8 Canada and US, $9.50 abroad plus $2 p/h (Can. funds); per copy $3 + $1p/h (Can. Funds); sample $2+ $1p/h (Can. funds). Back issues: $3. Discounts: 40%. 44pp. Reporting time: 2 months if submitted in February or August. Simultaneous submissions accepted: no. Publishes 15-20% of manuscripts submitted. Payment: 1 copy. Copyrighted, reverts to author.

Tower Poetry Society (see also TOWER), Joanna Lawson, c/o McMaster University, 1280 Main Street W. Box 1021, Hamilton, Ontario, L8S 1CO, Canada. 1950. Poetry. avg. press run 250. Pub'd 100 titles 2005; expects 100 titles 2006. 44pp. Reporting time: 2 months for submissions in Feb. + Aug. Simultaneous submissions accepted: no. Publishes 20% of manuscripts submitted. Payment: none. Does not copyright for author.

THE TOWNSHIPS SUN, Sun Books, Patricia Ball, Editor; Marion Greenlay, Business Manager; Patricia Ball, Advertising Manager, Box 28, Lennoxville, Quebec J1M 1Z3, Canada. 1972. Articles, photos, interviews, letters, news items, non-fiction. "*The Townships Sun* is Quebec's only rural English-language alternative newspaper. We cover agriculture, ecology, folklore, arts & crafts, how-to, and anything else of importance or interest to the people of Quebec's Eastern Townships. Because the English speaking popluation of Quebec is declining, we are broadening our circulation to reach adjacent parts of New England, the Maritimes, and Ontario; thus articles pertaining to these regions may also be welcome. We do use reprints from other periodicals, providing that they do not have substantial circulation in the Eastern Townships." circ. 1M. 12/yr. Pub'd 12 issues 2005; expects 12 issues 2006, 12 issues 2007. sub. price $16, $21 outside Canada; per copy $1.50; sample $1.50. Back issues: $2. 16pp. Reporting time: 1 month. Payment: $1 per inch. Copyrighted, reverts to author. Pub's reviews: 12 in 2005. §Agriculture, back-to-earth alternative philosophy, folklore, Canadiana, ecology, regional history, topics current interest - drugs, travel, etc. Ads: 55¢ MAL or $15 CNU. Subjects: Agriculture, Canada, Earth, Natural History, Ecology, Foods.

TRADICION REVISTA, LPD Press, Paul Rhetts, Barbe Awalt, 925 Salamanca NW, Los Ranchos de

Albuquerque, NM 87107-5647, 505-344-9382, Fax 505-345-5129, info@nmsantos.com. 1995. Articles, art, photos, non-fiction. "A journal on contemporary and traditional Spanish Colonial art and culture." circ. 5-10M per issue. 2/yr; Summer (July) and Winter (December). Pub'd 4 issues 2005; expects 4 issues 2006, 4 issues 2007. sub. price $15; per copy $10; sample $10. Back issues: $10. 64-72pp. Reporting time: 1-2 months. Simultaneous submissions accepted: yes. Publishes 80% of manuscripts submitted. Payment: negotiable. Copyrighted. Pub's reviews: 40 in 2005. §Southwest art and culture; Hispanic topics. Ads: b/w: $360/$240/$160, 4-color: $975/$650/$475. Subjects: Anthropology, Archaelogy, Arizona, Arts, Catholic, Colorado, Latin America, Latino, New Mexico, Southwest, Texas, Textiles, Weaving.

TRADITION MAGAZINE, Bob Everhart, Editor, PO Box 492, Anita, IA 50020, 712-762-4363 phone/Fax, bobeverhart@yahoo.com. 1976. "*Tradition Magazine* is the voice of traditional acoustic music in America. *Must* deal with traditional country, bluegrass, and folk music." circ. 3M. 6/yr. Pub'd 6 issues 2005; expects 6 issues 2006, 6 issues 2007. sub. price $20; per copy $3.50; sample $3.50. Back issues: $4. 56pp. Reporting time: 6 weeks. Simultaneous submissions accepted: yes. Publishes 2-10% of manuscripts submitted. Payment: yes, determined. Copyrighted, reverts to author. Pub's reviews: 35 in 2005. §Traditional country-bluegrass-faith music, old-time music and their players. Ads: $100/$75/$50. Subjects: Americana, Appalachia, Arts, Book Reviewing, Crafts, Hobbies, Culture, Dance, Entertainment, Folklore, Great Plains, Midwest, Music, South, Weaving.

Trafford Publishing, 6E-2333 Government Street, Victoria, BC V8T 4P4, Canada, 888-232-4444, Fax 250-383-6804, sales@trafford.com, www.trafford.com. 1995. "Trafford Publishing has provided self-publishing services to thousands of authors worldwide since 1995. If you have finished manuscript you can now have it published and available worldwide in just weeks!" Pub'd 2200 titles 2005; expects 3100 titles 2006, 4500 titles 2007. Discounts: 40% for booksellers, 15% for libraries and colleges and 60% for our authors. 50-700pp. Simultaneous submissions accepted: yes. Publishes 99% of manuscripts submitted. Payment: author makes 60% of gross margin. Subjects: Fiction, Non-Fiction.

Trafton Publishing, Rick Singer, 109 Barcliff Terrace, Cary, NC 27511-8900. 1993. Cartoons, satire, music. "We look for well conceived how to manuals/books/cassettes or videos for music lovers. Also, we need clean and original humor of any length, from a joke to a complete book." avg. press run 10M. Pub'd 3 titles 2005; expects 3-5 titles 2006, 3-5 titles 2007. Discounts: 30%-65%, depending on book and quantity. 150pp. Reporting time: 1-3 months. Publishes 5% of manuscripts submitted. Payment: varies. Does not copyright for author. Subjects: Aging, Erotica, How-To, Humor, Music.

TRANSCENDENT VISIONS, CRAZED NATION, David Kime, Beth Greenspan, 251 South Olds Boulevard, 84-E, Fairless Hills, PA 19030-3426, 215-547-7159. 1992. Poetry, fiction, art, photos, cartoons. "We publish fiction under ten pages. Typed, double spaced. All material published is by psychiatric survivors (ex-mental patients). Past contributors include Beth Greenspan, Dean Patrick Carvin and Warren F. Stewart. We publish poetry also." circ. 200. 1/yr. Pub'd 3 issues 2005; expects 2 issues 2006, 1 issue 2007. sub. price $3; per copy $3; sample $3. Back issues: $2. Discounts: will trade for zine with 20-30 pages. 26pp. Reporting time: 3 months. Simultaneous submissions accepted: yes. Publishes 25% of manuscripts submitted. Payment: 1 issue. Not copyrighted. Pub's reviews: 10 in 2005. §Psychiatric survivor magazines primarily. Ads: if we like an ad, we'll print it free. Subject: Literary Review.

Transcending Mundane, Inc., Tommy Kirchhoff, Kat Kirchhoff, Andy Baillargeon, PO Box 1241, Park City, UT 84060-1241, 435-615-9609, tommy@paracreative.com, www.paracreative.com. 1998. Poetry, fiction, articles, art, photos, cartoons, satire, reviews, letters, plays, concrete art, non-fiction. "Our policy is "no news." It must either be funny, witty, off the wall or out of the norm. We accept unsolicited work, but can't always read all of it; we only respond to the stuff that really tickles us." avg. press run 15-3M. Pub'd 1 title 2005; expects 1-3 titles 2006, 3-5 titles 2007. Discounts: commercial-40% off all orders over five books. 150pp. Reporting time: not set yet. Simultaneous submissions accepted: yes. Payment: not set yet. Copyrights for author. Subjects: Arts, Colorado, Counter-Culture, Alternatives, Communes, Humor, Philosophy, Satire, Sex, Sexuality, Surrealism.

TRANSITIONS ABROAD: The Guide to Living, Learning, and Working Overseas, Sherry Schwarz, Editor & Publisher, PO Box 745, Bennington, VT 05201, 802-442-4827, info@transitionsabroad.com, www.transitionsabroad.com. 1977. Articles, art, photos, letters, news items, non-fiction. "We like material with detailed practical information on long-stay educational, low-budget, and socially responsible travel abroad." circ. 12M. 6/yr. Pub'd 6 issues 2005; expects 6 issues 2006, 6 issues 2007. sub. price $28; per copy $4.95; sample $6.45 postpaid. Discounts: 50%. 64pp. Reporting time: 1 month. Simultaneous submissions accepted: yes. Publishes 25% of manuscripts submitted. Payment: at publication. Copyrighted, reverts to author. Pub's reviews: 50 in 2005. §Literary travel material, travel books, language study, resource material on work, international careers, study and travel abroad. Ads: $1,056/$799/$2 per word. Subjects: Asia, Indochina, Danish, Disabled, Ecology, Foods, Environment, France, French, German, Ireland, Italy, Japan, Portugal, Romanian Studies, Scandinavia, Third World, Minorities, Transportation.

TRANSLATION REVIEW, Rainer Schulte, Editor; Dennis Kratz, Editor, Univ. of Texas-Dallas, Box 830688 - JO51, Richardson, TX 75083-0688, 972-883-2093, Fax 972-883-6303. 1978. Articles, interviews, criticism, reviews, news items, non-fiction. "The *Translation Review* is a publication of the American Literary Translators Association and is distributed to members and subscribing libraries. The *Review* deals exclusively with the theory, application and evaluation of literary works in translation." circ. 1,000. 2/yr. Pub'd 2 issues 2005; expects 2 issues 2006, 2 issues 2007. Subscription by membership to ALTA only; $75 for US and Canada Libraries, $100 for International Libraries, $60 for US & Canada Individuals, $70 Individual International, $80 Joint Household(one TR), $20 Students and $150 institutions.; price per copy N/A; sample $20. Back issues: $20 each. 90pp. Reporting time: 8-12 weeks. Simultaneous submissions accepted: no. Publishes 30% of manuscripts submitted. Payment: copies. Copyrighted. Pub's reviews: 2 in 2005. §Any literary work in recent English translation. Ads: $250 Full Page, $160 Half Page, $95 Quarter Page. Subjects: Literary Review, Translation.

TRAVEL BOOKS WORLDWIDE, Travel Keys, Peter Manston, Publisher; Robert Bynum, Editor, PO Box 160691, Sacramento, CA 95816-0691, 916-452-5200. 1991. "A review of travel books and related maps, etc. No submissions please; 100% staff written." circ. 1.4M. 10/yr. Pub'd 10 issues 2005; expects 10 issues 2006, 10 issues 2007. sub. price $36 US, $48 Canada, US$72 or £42 elsewhere; per copy $4; sample $4. 16pp. Simultaneous submissions accepted: no. Copyrighted, does not revert to author. Pub's reviews: 264 in 2005. §Travel, cooking, maps & globes, nonfiction travel narratives. Ads: none accepted. Subjects: Book Reviewing, Transportation.

Travel Keys (see also TRAVEL BOOKS WORLDWIDE), Peter B. Manston, Publisher; Robert Bynum, Associate Editor, PO Box 160691, Sacramento, CA 95816-0691, 916-452-5200. 1984. Reviews, non-fiction. "Practical, succinct travel and antique guides. Staff-written or sometimes work for hire." avg. press run 5M-12M. Pub'd 4 titles 2005; expects 5 titles 2006, 4 titles 2007. Discounts: bookstores 40% less than 30 books, 46% 31+ books. 320pp. Reporting time: 1 month. We accept simultaneous submissions if mentioned as such in cover letter. Publishes 10% of manuscripts submitted. Payment: variable. Copyrights for author, but copyright fee charged against author's royalty account. Subjects: Europe, How-To, Transportation.

TRAVEL NATURALLY, Bernard J. Loibl, PO Box 317, Newfoundland, NJ 07435, 973-697-3552, Fax 973-697-8313, naturally@internaturally.com. 1981. Fiction, articles, art, photos, cartoons, interviews, reviews, news items, non-fiction. "*Travel Naturally* focuses on wholesome nude family recreation it is a glossy full-color magazine that includes many informative articles and photos on travel and upscale nudist resorts around the world." circ. 35M. 4/yr. Pub'd 4 issues 2005; expects 4 issues 2006, 4 issues 2007. sub. price $28.00; per copy $11.00 ppd.; sample $11.00 ppd. Back issues: $11.00 ppd. Discounts: 50% distributors, 40% retailers. 68pp. Reporting time: 6 weeks. Simultaneous submissions accepted: yes. Publishes 30% of manuscripts submitted. Payment: $80 per published page. Copyrighted, reverts to author. Pub's reviews: 4 in 2005. §naturism, nudism, clothes-free vacation destinations, nudist resorts. Ads: $600/$380/$280 1/3 page/$160 1/6 page/$15 (25 words or less). Subjects: Arts, Avant-Garde, Experimental Art, Civil Rights, Counter-Culture, Alternatives, Communes, Human Rights, Humanism, Lifestyles, Nature, Travel, Visual Arts.

Tree of Life Books. Imprints: Progressive Press, Banned Books, John Leonard, PO Box 126, Joshua Tree, CA 92252, 760-366-3695, fax 760-366-2937. 1972. Non-fiction. "New mission is political protest literature exposing neo-con agenda. Backlist is new age books on the Essene Jesus, holistic health, and inspirational." avg. press run 5000. Expects 4 titles 2006, 3 titles 2007. Discounts: 40%. 300pp. Reporting time: A few days. Simultaneous submissions accepted: Yes. Publishes 10% of manuscripts submitted. Payment: approx. 10 - 15% of net selling price, advance negotiable. Copyrights for author. Subjects: African-American, Alternative Medicine, Animals, Christianity, Ecology, Foods, New Age, Politics, Sufism, Translation, War.

Trellis Publishing, Inc., Mary Koski, Rachel Ellen, PO Box 16141-D, Duluth, MN 55816. 1997. "We will be taking on a few, high-quality children's picture books; however, we need to wait a year before taking submissions." avg. press run 10M. Pub'd 1 title 2005; expects 2 titles 2006, 2 titles 2007. Discounts: yes. Cloth 32pp, workbooks 16pp. Simultaneous submissions accepted: yes. Payment: 10% paid to author/illustrator on retail price. Copyrights for author. Subjects: Children, Youth, Picture Books, Public Relations/Publicity.

Trentham Books (see also THE JOURNAL OF DESIGN AND TECHNOLOGY EDUCATION; MCT - MULTICULTURAL TEACHING), Westview House, 734 London Road, Oakhill, Stoke-on-Trent, Staffordshire ST4 5NP, England, 01782-745567, Fax 01782-745553. 1982. Articles. avg. press run 2M. Pub'd 27 titles 2005. Discounts: usual trade. 56-280pp. Reporting time: 1 month. Simultaneous submissions accepted: no. Publishes 25% of manuscripts submitted. Payment: 7-1/2% on price. Copyrights for author. Subjects: Community, Education, Labor.

Tres Picos Press, Jim Brumfield, 116 Martinelli Street, Suite #1, Watsonville, CA 95076, 831 254-7447; email: submissions@trespicospress.com. 2003. Fiction, non-fiction. "We are new and small but will consider anything that we think can successfully be marketed. Before submitting anything, ask yourself one question: can you convince me that your book will sell at least 3,000 copies?'' avg. press run 3000. Discounts: Our books are distributed by Biblio distribution, a sister company of the National Book Network. email orders@trespicospress.com for information on discounts. 320pp. Reporting time: 1 - 2 months. Simultaneous submissions accepted: Yes. Publishes 1% of manuscripts submitted. Payment: negotiable. Does not copyright for author. Subjects: Agriculture, Anthropology, Archaelogy, Australia, California, Caribbean, Fiction, Libertarian, Mexico, New Zealand, Old West, Real Estate, Sports, Outdoors, Mark Twain, The West, Yosemite.

Trickle Creek Books, Toni Albert, 500 Andersontown Rd, Mechanicsburg, PA 17055, 717-766-2638, fax 717-766-1343, 800-353-2791. 1994. Fiction, non-fiction. ''We publish books that teach kids to care for the Earth. Our books are used by teachers in classrooms across the nation, as well as by parents and homeschoolers. All of our books are written by Toni Albert, M.Ed., author of more than forty books that help children explore nature and love our environment.'' avg. press run 4000. Pub'd 1 title 2005; expects 1 title 2007. Discounts: Retailers - 2 copies 20%, 3-4 copies 30%, 5-99 copies 40%; Wholesalers - 50%; Distributors - 65%; Libraries - 20%. 48pp. Subjects: Animals, Biology, Birds, Education, Environment, Gardening, Marine Life, Nature, Non-Fiction, Oceanography, Science.

TRICYCLE: The Buddhist Review, James Shaheen, 92 Vandam Street, New York, NY 10013-1007. 1991. Poetry, fiction, articles, art, photos, cartoons, interviews, satire, letters, parts-of-novels, news items, non-fiction. circ. 50M. 4/yr. Pub'd 4 issues 2005; expects 4 issues 2006, 4 issues 2007. sub. price $24; per copy $7.95; sample $7.95. Back issues: $15.95. 104pp. Reporting time: 3 months. Simultaneous submissions accepted: no. Publishes 10% of manuscripts submitted. Payment: varies. Copyrighted, reverts to author. Pub's reviews: 32 in 2005. §Buddhism, religion, philosophy, Asian studies. Ads: Contact Goodfellows at: 510-548-1680. Subject: Buddhism.

Triple Tree Publishing, Liz Cratty, PO Box 5684, Eugene, OR 97405, 541-338-3184, Fax 541-484-5358, www.tripletreepub.com. 1997. Fiction. ''Publishes uncommon fiction. Elizabeth Engstrom/Alan Clark collaboration in limited edition, Barry Shannon irreverent adventure/mystery in trade pb.'' avg. press run varies. Pub'd 2 titles 2005; expects 4 titles 2006, 4 titles 2007. Discounts: 30% on limited editions, standard 40% elsewhere. 320pp. Reporting time: 2 weeks. Simultaneous submissions accepted: yes. Publishes a small % of manuscripts submitted. Payment: varies. Copyrights for author. Subjects: Fiction, Humor, Literature (General), Mystery.

TRIQUARTERLY, Northwestern University Press, Susan Betz, 629 Noyes Street, Evanston, IL 60208, (847) 491-2046; fax (847)491-8150; www.nupress.northwestern.edu. 1958. Poetry, fiction. circ. 2000. 3/yr. Pub'd 3 issues 2005; expects 3 issues 2006, 3 issues 2007. sub. price $24; per copy 11.95; sample free. Back issues: inquire. 288pp. Ads: inquire for advertising rates.

•**Triskelion Publishing,** Terese Ramin, Print & Media Liaison; Kristi Studts, Publisher; Gail Northman, Executive Editor; Kathi Troyer, Inspiration Editor; Brynna Ramin, SF&F Editor, 15508 W. Bell Road #101, PMB #205, Surprise, AZ 85374, Contact: 517-294-0765, Sales: 602-509-8582, Fax: 623-561-0250, sales@triskelionpublishing.com, www.triskelionpublishing.net. 2004. Fiction. ''Triskelion Publishing is: All about women. All about extraordinary. We publish fiction for and about women, including romance, sf/f, futuristic, paranormal, gothic-horror, erotic romance in our Sister O imprint, inspirational romance fiction, action-adventure, suspense-thriller, mystery, etc. Romance is an element in almost all of our fiction, but doesn't necessarily always play in the forefront.We publish full-length novels (45,000 words to 80,000 words), as well as anthologies, and we also publish some novellas in our e-publishing products (where we publish over 100 novels, anthologies & novellas every year.) We also do novel reprints. Submission guidelines are available at the website: www.triskelionpublishing.net. Queries should be made in the body of an email to submissions@triskelionpublishing.com. Inspirational submissions should be made to submissions@triskelion-publishing.com ATTN: Kathi Troyer.'' avg. press run 750-2500. Pub'd 10 titles 2005; expects 36-50 titles 2006, 50-75 titles 2007. 300-350pp. Reporting time: 14 - 45 days. Simultaneous submissions accepted: No. Publishes 50% of manuscripts submitted. Payment: ebook royalties are paid monthly beginning 45 days after the work's first appearance; print royalties are paid quarterly as soon as the distributors pay us. Does not copyright for author. Subjects: Erotica, Fantasy, Fiction, Gay, Inspirational, Lesbianism, Mystery, Occult, Romance, Science Fiction, Supernatural.

Triumvirate Publications, Vladimir Chernozemsky, Publisher, 497 West Avenue 44, Los Angeles, CA 90065-3917, 818-340-6770 Phone/Fax, Triumpub@aol.com, www.Triumpub.com. 1985. Fiction. ''Publisher of genre fiction: Science Fiction/Fantasy, Mystery, Thriller/Suspense, Horror/Occult, Adventure.'' avg. press run 8M. Pub'd 3 titles 2005; expects 3 titles 2006, 5 titles 2007. Discounts: retail: 1 copy 20%, 2-3 30%, 4+ 40%, wholesale: 1-2 copies 30%, 3-4 40%, 5+ 50%, quantity stocking orders 55%. 500pp. Reporting time: 2 months. Simultaneous submissions accepted: yes. Payment: trade standard. Copyrights for author. Subjects: Crime, Fantasy, Fiction, Horror, Mystery, Science Fiction.

Tropical Press, Gordon Witherspoon, PO Box 161174, Miami, FL 33116, www.tropicalpress.com. 1998.

Fiction. "Recent contributors: Michael Largo, Russ Hall, and Michael Rothenberg." avg. press run 2.5M. Pub'd 3 titles 2005; expects 3 titles 2006, 3 titles 2007. Discounts: 40%. 300pp. Reporting time: 4 months. Simultaneous submissions accepted: yes. Publishes 3% of manuscripts submitted. Payment: royalty only. Copyrights for author. Subject: Fiction.

Trost Publishing, Katherine Moody, 509 Octavia St., New Orleans, LA 70115, 504-680-6754, www.trostpublishing.com,. 2004. Non-fiction. avg. press run 20000. Expects 1 title 2006, 2 titles 2007. 150-200pp. Simultaneous submissions accepted: Yes. Does not copyright for author. Subject: Business & Economics.

TRUE POET MAGAZINE, Michelle True. 2003. Poetry, articles. "We are a webzine dedicated to publishing the best in poetry by new or published writers. Our mission is to help promote poetry and provide a voice for gifted poets." circ. 10,000. 12/yr. Pub'd 12 issues 2005; expects 12 issues 2006, 12 issues 2007. 10pp. Reporting time: 3-4 weeks. Simultaneous submissions accepted: Yes. Publishes 3% of manuscripts submitted. We do not currently have advertising. Subjects: Poetry, Publishing, Writers/Writing.

Truebekon Books, Antonio Nunes, Anne Tarr, PO Box 353, American Fork, UT 84003, 801-796-3730. 2000. Fiction. "We are not actively pursuing submissions, but rather contact authors who are known to us. We do not accept unsolicited manuscripts. However, this may change in the future. We publish adult and children's fiction only. No nonfiction." avg. press run 2M-10M. Expects 1 title 2006, 2 titles 2007. Discounts: distributors 55%, bookstores 40%. 36-200pp. Reporting time: 3 months. Simultaneous submissions accepted: no. Publishes 0% of manuscripts submitted. Payment: varies. Copyrights for author. Subjects: Children, Youth, Fiction.

Truly Fine Press, Jerry Madson, PO Box 891, Bemidji, MN 56619. 1973. "Truly Fine Press has in the past published a pamphlet series, and also published Minnesota's first tabloid novel. Must query first. Only publish ulra limited edition visual poetry that gravitates toward art." avg. press run varies. Pages vary. Reporting time: 2 weeks to 6 months. Copyrights for author.

Truman Press, Inc., d/b/a "Hannover House", Eric Parkinson, President, Publisher; Cathy Gaccione, New Product Acquisitions Editor, 163 Amsterdam Ave. #303, New York, NY 10023, 866-227-2628; Fax 479-587-0857; www.HannoverHouse.com. 1993. avg. press run 25,000. Pub'd 8 titles 2005; expects 12 titles 2006, 10 titles 2007. Discounts: standard. 250-750pp. Reporting time: varies. We sometimes accept simultaneous submissions. Publishes less than 10% of manuscripts submitted. Payment: advances against standard rates. We copyright for author if necessary.

Truman State University Press, Nancy Rediger, Director-Editor in Chief, 100 East Normal Street, Kirksville, MO 63501, 660-785-7336, Fax 660-785-4480, http://tsup.truman.edu. 1986. Poetry, art, photos, criticism, non-fiction. "Early modern studies, American studies, poetry series." avg. press run 1000. Pub'd 10 titles 2005; expects 10 titles 2006, 10 titles 2007. Discounts: 20%, 2-9 copies 30%, 10+ 40%, 100+ 50%. 300pp. Reporting time: 3 months. Simultaneous submissions accepted: no. Publishes 10% of manuscripts submitted. Payment: 6%-10%. Copyrights for author. Subjects: Civil War, Environment, History, Midwest, Non-Fiction, North America, Poetry, Presidents, Religion, Renaissance.

TRUTH SEEKER, Bonnie Lange, Publisher-Editor, 239 S. Juniper Street, Escondido, CA 92025-0550, 760-489-5211, Fax 760-489-5311, tseditor@aol.com, www.truthseeker.com. 1873. Articles, interviews, criticism, news items. "Length of material: 400-1,600 words. Past contributors: Steve Allen, Gerald LaRue, Howard Blume, Arthur Melville, David Icke, Jon Rappoport, Louis Turi, Zecharia Sitchin, and Angela Brown Miller." circ. 1M. 1/yr. Pub'd 1 issue 2005; expects 1 issue 2006, 1 issue 2007. sub. price $20; per copy $10; sample $10. Back issues: $20. 40-220pp. Simultaneous submissions accepted: yes. Publishes 20% of manuscripts submitted. Payment: $75 per article plus 1 year subscription. Copyrighted, reverts to author. Pub's reviews: 10 in 2005. §Freethought, religion, government. Ads: none. Subjects: Atheism, Education, Ethics, Euthanasia, Death, Government, History, Human Rights, Metaphysics, New Age, Philosophy, Religion, Reviews, Shaker, Taxes, Women.

•TU REVIEW, Sherry Ph.D Truffin, Advisor-Editor, Tiffin University, 155 Miami St., Tiffin, OH 44883, 419-448-3299, Fax 419-443-5009, TUReview@tiffin.edu, http://bruno.tiffin.edu/tureview/. 2004. Poetry, fiction, non-fiction. "We are an online literary journal that accepts both poetry and prose. Fiction, essays, prose poems, or any type of poetry, all should be characterized by being original and using vivid, specific imagery. Submission guidelines and more specific writing tips can be found at our website. Submissions accepted Sept. 1 to April 1, maximum length 4,500 words." 2/yr. Simultaneous submissions accepted: no. Payment: satisfaction and byline. Copyrighted, reverts to author.

THE TULE REVIEW, Jane Blue, Sacramento Poetry Center, 1719 25th St., Sacramento, CA 95816-5813, 916-441-7395, blueattule@yahoo.com, www.sacramentopoetrycenter.org. 1998. Poetry. "Regional magazine published by Sacramento Poetry Center. Recent contributors: Doug Blazek, Ann Menebroker, Dennis Schmitz, and Muriel Zeller. Revived in 1998 in chapbook format. Sacramento-San Joaquin bias, but consider others."

488

circ. 500. 2/yr. Pub'd 2 issues 2005; expects 2 issues 2006, 2 issues 2007. sub. price w/SPC membership; per copy $5; sample $5. 28-32pp. Reporting time: 2-4 months. Simultaneous submissions accepted: no. Payment: 2 copies. Copyrighted, reverts to author. Subject: Poetry.

TULSA STUDIES IN WOMEN'S LITERATURE, University of Tulsa, Holly Laird, Editor; Sarah Theobald-Hall, Managing Editor, 600 S. College, Tulsa, OK 74104-3189, 918-631-2503, Fax 918-631-2065, sarah-theobald-hall@utulsa.edu. 1982. Articles, criticism, reviews, letters. circ. 1M. 2/yr. Pub'd 2 issues 2005; expects 2 issues 2006, 2 issues 2007. sub. price U.S. individuals $12/1 yr, $23/2 yrs, $34/3 yrs, institutions $14/$27/$40, other individuals $15/$29/$43, institutions $16/$31/$46, U.S. students $10/$19/$28, elsewhere students $12/$23/$34, airmail surcharge $10; per copy $7 US/$8 elsewhere; sample $7US/$8 elsewhere. Back issues: $10. 150pp. Reporting time: 6 months. Simultaneous submissions accepted: no. Payment: none. Copyrighted, does not revert to author. Pub's reviews: 25 in 2005. §Women's literature—critical studies. Ads: $150/$75. Subjects: Literary Review, Women.

TUNDRA, Press Here, Michael Dylan Welch, 22230 NE 28th Place, Sammamish, WA 98074-6408, welchm@aol.com. 1999. Poetry, interviews, criticism, reviews. "*Tundra* is a journal for short poetry, 13 lines or fewer in length (especially, but not limited to, haiku, senryu, and tanka)." circ. 650. 3/yr. Expects 1 issue 2006, 2 issues 2007. sub. price $21; per copy $10; sample $10. Back issues: Available at the single copy price. 128pp. Reporting time: 1-4 weeks. Simultaneous submissions accepted: no. Publishes 0.5% of manuscripts submitted. Payment: 1 contributor's copy. Copyrighted, reverts to author. Pub's reviews: 2-4 in 2005. §Short poetry or criticism about short poetry. Ads: none. Subjects: Criticism, Haiku, Poetry.

Tuns Press, Faculty of Architecture and Planning, Dalhousie University, Box 1000 Central Station, Halifax, Nova Scotia B3J 2X4, Canada, 902-494-3925, Fax 902-423-6672, tuns.press@dal.ca, tunspress.dal.ca. 1989. Non-fiction. "Faculty press. Publishes books on architecture and planning." avg. press run 1M-2M. Discounts: trade. Subjects: Architecture, Canada, Design, History.

Tupelo Press, Jeffrey Levine, Editor-in-Chief; Margaret Donovan, Managing Editor; Susan Williamson, Associate Publisher, PO Box 539, Dorset, VT 05251, Telephone 802-366-8185,Fax 802-362-1883. 1999. Poetry, fiction, letters, non-fiction. avg. press run 5000. Pub'd 9 titles 2005; expects 14 titles 2006, 15 titles 2007. Reporting time: 3 months. Simultaneous submissions accepted: yes. Payment: standard royalty contract and some advances. Copyrights for author. Subjects: Memoirs, Non-Fiction, Novels, Poetry, Prose, Short Stories.

TURNING THE TIDE: Journal of Anti-Racist Action, Research & Education, Michael Novick, PO Box 1055, Culver City, CA 90232-1055, 310-495-0299, antiracistaction_la@yahoo.com. 1987. Poetry, articles, photos, cartoons, interviews, satire, criticism, reviews, news items, non-fiction. "Prefer short pieces, 1-2 poems each issue." circ. 10M. 6/yr. Pub'd 5 issues 2005; expects 6 issues 2006, 6 issues 2007. sub. price $16 individuals, $26 institutions (payable to Michael Novick); per copy $2.95 newsstands; sample $4. Back issues: $5, inquire on availability. 8pp. Reporting time: 1-2 months. Simultaneous submissions accepted: yes. Publishes 6-8% of manuscripts submitted. Payment: 5 free copies. Not copyrighted. Pub's reviews: 2-3 in 2005. §Racism, sexism, homophobia, liberation movements. Ads: $100/$65/$35 1/4 page. Subjects: African-American, Anarchist, Chicano/a, Children, Youth, Ecology, Foods, Feminism, Gay, Hawaii, Human Rights, Native American, Prison, Puerto Rico, Race, Third World, Minorities, War.

TURNING WHEEL, Susan Moon, PO Box 3470, Berkeley, CA 94703. 1980. Poetry, articles, art, photos, cartoons, interviews, criticism, reviews, letters, news items, non-fiction. "*Turning Wheel* is about 'engaged' Buddhism, or Buddhism and social activism. We print articles, art, poetry, etc. about nonviolent protest, about issues of activism, sexism, human rights, etc. in American Buddhist communities and Asian Buddhist countries. We print Gary Snyder, Thich Nhat Hanh, grassroots activists." circ. 7M. 4/yr. Pub'd 4 issues 2005; expects 4 issues 2006, 4 issues 2007. sub. price $45 membership, $20 low-income; per copy $5 newstand; sample $6 by mail. 48pp. Reporting time: about 1 month. Simultaneous submissions accepted: yes. Publishes 20% of manuscripts submitted. Payment: 2 copies of magazine, one year subscription. Copyrighted, reverts to author. Pub's reviews: about 20 in 2005. §Buddhism and social activism, engaged spirituality, deep ecology, social ecology. Ads: $345/$190/50¢. Subjects: Asian-American, Buddhism, Community, Ecology, Foods, Education, Euthanasia, Death, Human Rights, Non-Violence, Spiritual, Zen.

TurnKey Press, Michael Odom, 2100 Kramer Lane Suite 300, Austin, TX 78758-4094, 512.478.2028. 2002.

TURNROW, Jack Heflin, William Ryan, Univ. of Louisiana at Monroe, English Dept., 700 University Ave., Monroe, LA 71209, 318-342-1520, Fax 318-342-1491, ryan@ulm.edu, heflin@ulm.edu, http://turn-row.ulm.edu. 2001. Poetry, fiction, articles, art, photos, cartoons, criticism, letters, parts-of-novels, long-poems, plays, non-fiction. "Seeks nonfiction of a general interest. Interested also in publishing the works of authors written in genres different from what they usually publish." circ. 1M. 2/yr. Pub'd 2 issues 2005; expects 2 issues 2006, 2 issues 2007. sub. price $12; per copy $7; sample $7. 200pp. Reporting time: 2 months. Simultaneous submissions accepted: no. Publishes .01% of manuscripts submitted. Payment: $50 poem,

$15/page for prose, $150-$250 features. Copyrighted, reverts to author. Ads: $200 full page. Subjects: Arts, Essays, Fiction, Non-Fiction, Photography, Poetry, Translation.

Turnstone Press, Todd Besant, Managing Editor; Kelly Stifora, Marketing Director, 607-100 Arthur Street, Winnipeg R3B 1H3, Canada, 204-947-1555, info@turnstonepress.com. 1976. Poetry, fiction, criticism, long-poems. "Contemporary Canadian writing." avg. press run 1M. Pub'd 12 titles 2005; expects 12 titles 2006, 12 titles 2007. Discounts: bookstores 1-9 copies 20%, 10+ 40%; schools & libraries 40%; wholesalers 45%. Poetry 80pp, fiction & criticism 220pp. Reporting time: 4 months. Query first before sending simultaneous submissions. Publishes .8% of manuscripts submitted. Payment: 10% paid annually. Copyrights for author. Subjects: Criticism, Fiction, Literature (General), Memoirs, Mystery, Novels, Poetry, Short Stories, Travel.

Turtle Press, division of S.K. Productions Inc., Cynthia Kim, PO Box 290206, Wethersfield, CT 06129-0206, 860-721-1198. 1990. Non-fiction. "We publish primarily non-fiction titles of interest to martial artists and those readers interested in self-protection. We are especially interested in new, unique or previously unpublished facets of the arts. Will also consider topics related to Asian culture, such as Zen, philosophy, etc." avg. press run 3M-4M. Pub'd 4 titles 2005; expects 5 titles 2006, 5 titles 2007. 300pp. Reporting time: 1 month. Simultaneous submissions accepted: yes. Publishes 2-3% of manuscripts submitted. Payment: 10% on gross (royalties), advance of $500-$1000. Copyrights for author. Subjects: Martial Arts, Philosophy, Zen.

Tuumba Press, Lyn Hejinian, Editor, 2639 Russell Street, Berkeley, CA 94705-2131, 510-548-1817,510-704-8350. 1976. Poetry, fiction, articles, long-poems, plays. "In its current manifestation, Tuumba Press publishes work by invitation only." avg. press run 750.

24th Street Irregular Press, Richard Hansen, 1008 24th Street, Sacramento, CA 95816. 2000.

TWENTY-EIGHT PAGES LOVINGLY BOUND WITH TWINE, Christoph Meyer, PO Box 106, Danville, OH 43014. 2001. Poetry, fiction, art, photos, cartoons, letters, collages, non-fiction. "No unsolicited submissions except art. I do use illustrators and artist and cartoonist. Anyone interested in doing art for *28PLBWT* should write w/samples of drawings (b/w only)." circ. 756. 2-5/yr. Pub'd 3 issues 2005; expects 4 issues 2006, 3-4 issues 2007. sub. price $10/6 issues; per copy $2; sample $2. Back issues: $2, $3 for 5. 28pp. Payment: subscription, contributor's copies, a little bit of $. Not copyrighted. Ads: no ads. Subjects: Autobiography, Non-Fiction, Ohio.

The Twickenham Press, Nancy Bogen, 31 Jane Street, New York, NY 10014, 212-741-2417. 1980. Fiction. "Our orientation has been and will remain literary, feminist, and politically liberal. We have been dormant for a long time but hope to begin starting up operations very soon, beginning with a website. We are looking into e-books in the long term as a viable alternative to paper-waste. For novels, queries should include a paragraph about yourself, a brief description of the work you would like to submit, and a word-count—nothing else. An SASE would be appreciated. Agents and other strictly commercial types need NOT apply." avg. press run 1M. Expects 1 title 2006, 1-2 titles 2007. Discounts: 20% to libraries; 40-50% to dealers; returns to 99 years. 250pp. Reporting time: long. Simultaneous submissions accepted: yes. Payment: 10-15% of list. Copyrights for author. Subjects: Feminism, Fiction, Gay, Lesbianism, Literature (General), Poetry.

Twilight Times Books, Lida E. Quillen, PO Box 3340, Kingsport, TN 37664-0340, 423-323-0183 phone/Fax, publisher@twilighttimesbooks.com, www.twilighttimesbooks.com. 1999. Fiction, non-fiction. "Open to submissions July 15 to August 5th. Be sure to check the web site for current submission guidelines." Pub'd 12 titles 2005; expects 12 titles 2006, 10 titles 2007. 250pp. Reporting time: 2 months. Simultaneous submissions accepted: no. Publishes 10% of manuscripts submitted. Payment: standard. Does not copyright for author. Subjects: Fantasy, Fiction, Humor, Mystery, New Age, Non-Fiction, Science Fiction, Self-Help, Translation, Vietnam, Women, Writers/Writing, Young Adult.

Twin Sisters Productions, 2680 West Market Street, Akron, OH 44333-4206, 800-248-TWIN, 330-864-3000, Fax 800-480-TWIN, 330-864-3200. 1987. avg. press run 10M. Pub'd 4 titles 2005; expects 4 titles 2006, 4 titles 2007. 24-64pp. Reporting time: 4-6 weeks. Simultaneous submissions accepted: yes. Copyrights for author.

Twin Souls Publications (see also MIDNIGHT SHOWCASE: Romance Digest, Erotic-ahh Digest, Special Digest), Jewel Adams, P.O. Box 726, Lusk, WY 82225, 307-334-3165, 727-848-5962, publisher@midnight-showcase.com, http://www.midnightshowcase.com. 2005. Fiction. "Midnight Showcase publishes Romance and Erotic-ahh Romance Digest, which are themed collections of short stories to 25,000 word novellas in each digest. We also publish full novels as Special Editions in all the Romance and Erotic-ahh Romance genres." Expects 15 titles 2006, 30 titles 2007. 250pp. Reporting time: Three to Four Weeks. Simultaneous submissions accepted: No. Publishes 25% of manuscripts submitted. Payment: Royalty is based on word count and is the same for print and ebook formats. Author retains the copyright of their work, contract is for exclusive rights for one year with renewal, contract is on site to review. Subjects: Erotica, History, Romance.

TWINSWORLD, Raymond W. Brandt, PO Box 980481, Ypsilanti, MI 48198-0481, twinworld1@aol.com.

1989. Poetry, fiction, articles, art, photos, cartoons, criticism, reviews, letters, collages, news items, non-fiction. "The only magazine published *for twins by twins* worldwide." circ. 4M. 4/yr. Pub'd 4 issues 2005; expects 6 issues 2006, 8 issues 2007. sub. price $20; per copy $5; sample $3. Back issues: all issues in archives, $4/each. Discounts: none. 42pp. Reporting time: 90 days. Simultaneous submissions accepted: yes. Publishes 68% of manuscripts submitted. Payment: none. Copyrighted, reverts to author. Pub's reviews: 14 in 2005. §Twins or high order multiples. Ads: $100/$60/$25 1/4 page.

Twisted Spoon Press, Howard Sidenberg, PO Box 21, Preslova 12, Prague 5, 150 00, Czech Republic, www.twistedspoon.com. 1992. Poetry, fiction, art, photos, letters, non-fiction. "No unsolicited manuscripts." avg. press run 1.5M-2M. Pub'd 4 titles 2005; expects 5 titles 2006, 6 titles 2007. Discounts: distributor takes care of this. 200pp. Reporting time: 6 months. Simultaneous submissions accepted: no. Payment: by contract. Copyrights for author. Subjects: Dada, Essays, Fiction, Poetry, Prose, Surrealism, Translation.

Two Dog Press, Karen Kaiser, PO Box 164, Brooklin, ME 04616-0164, email human@twodogpress.com. 1997. Poetry, fiction, art, photos, non-fiction. "We publish books about dogs. Our preference is for material that features dogs without getting sentimental. We're looking for fresh, innovative prose and poetry, art and interesting non-fiction about dogs." avg. press run 8M. Pub'd 1 title 2005; expects 1 title 2006, 1 title 2007. Discounts: jobber 55%, bookstores: 1 10%, 2-4 20%, 5 or more 40%. 100pp. Reporting time: 3 months. Simultaneous submissions accepted: no. Publishes 2% of manuscripts submitted. Payment: varies. Copyrights for author. Subjects: Animals, Folklore, Pets, Poetry.

Two Eagles Press International, Dr. Paul E. Huntsberger, 1029 Hickory Drive, Las Cruces, NM 88005, 505-523-7911, Fax 505-523-1953, Cell 505-644-5436, twoeaglespress@comcast.net, twoeaglespress.com. 1991. Non-fiction. "Additional address: 1029 Hickory Drive, Las Cruces, NM 88005. Multicultural/ international oriented materials prferred; book length 50-200 pages; will consider bilingual English/Spanish submissions." avg. press run 3.0M. 240pp. Reporting time: 6 weeks. Simultaneous submissions accepted: No. Payment: 10%, payable biannually. Copyrights for author. Subjects: Bilingual, Business & Economics, Chicano/a, Culture, Latin America, Latino, Management, Mexico, Multicultural, New Mexico, Non-Fiction, Southwest, Texas, U.S. Hispanic.

TWO LINES: A Journal of Translation, Zack Rogow, Editor-Artistic Director, Center for the Art of Translation, 35 Stillman Street, Suite 201, San Francisco, CA 94107, 415-512-8812 (phone) /415-512-8824 (fax), web: www.catranslation.org. 1995. Poetry, fiction, articles, art, interviews, satire, criticism, letters, parts-of-novels, long-poems, plays, non-fiction. "*Two Lines* is a forum for translation. We seek the best of international literature in translation from any language into English. Each submission must be accompanied by a translator's introduction regarding the original work, the author, and the translation process. A copy of the original text must be included as well. All genres of literature in translation will be considered. Submission guidelines are announced at the end of the summer. Read submission guidelines carefully before submitting. Published annually in the spring. Email submissions to: submissions@catranslation.org." circ. 1500. 1/yr. Pub'd 1 issue 2005; expects 1 issue 2006, 1 issue 2007. price per copy $10.95 + $2.50 s/h domestic, $4 Canada/Mexico, $6 s/h int'l; sample same. Back issues: $5-11. Discounts: 20% libraries, 40% bookstores/agent. 250pp. Reporting time: 3 months after submission deadline. Simultaneous submissions accepted: no. Publishes 15% of manuscripts submitted. Payment: $35. Copyrighted, rights revert to author but journal requests rights to single reprint as well. Ads: contact us. Subjects: Literature (General), Translation.

•2River Chapbook Series (see also 2River), Richard Long, 7474 Drexel DR, University City, MO 63130, long@2River.org. 1996. Poetry. "2River occasionally publishes individual authors in the 2River Chapbook Series. Each chapbook appears online at www.2River.org, as well as in print." Reporting time: One to two months. Publishes 1% of manuscripts submitted. Copyrights for author.

Two Thousand Three Associates, 4180 Saxon Drive, New Smyrna Beach, FL 32169-3851, 386-427-7876, Fax 386-423-7523. 1994. Non-fiction. "No unsolicited manuscripts. *Proposals only.*" avg. press run 5M. Pub'd 2 titles 2005; expects 4 titles 2006, 4 titles 2007. Discounts: IPG (Independent Publishers Group) distributes our books and sets discount rate. 144pp. Reporting time: 1 month. Simultaneous submissions accepted: yes. Payment: per author/individual basis. Copyrights for author. Subjects: Aging, Caribbean, Caribbean, Children, Youth, Family, Florida, Florida, Humor, Humor, Romance, Sports, Outdoors, Sports, Outdoors, Travel.

2.13.61 Publications, 7510 Sunset Boulevard #602, Los Angeles, CA 90046, 323-969-8791. 1984. Pub'd 1 title 2005; expects 1 title 2006, 1 title 2007. Publishes 0% of manuscripts submitted. Copyrights for author.

2River (see also 2River Chapbook Series; THE 2RIVER VIEW), Richard Long, 7474 Drexel Dr., University City, MO 63130, 314-721-7393, www.2River.org. 1996. Poetry. "Since 1996, 2River has been a site of poetry, art, and theory, quarterly publishing The 2River View and occasionally publishing individual authors in the 2River Chapbook Series. All publications appear online and afterwards in print." avg. press run 100. Pub'd 4 titles 2005; expects 4 titles 2006, 4 titles 2007. 32pp. Reporting time: A couple of months at most for submissions to The 2River View, and a few week for submissions to the 2River Chapbook Series. Simultaneous submissions accepted: No. Publishes 1% of manuscripts submitted. Payment: Copies. Does not copyright for author. Subject: Poetry.

THE 2RIVER VIEW, 2River, Richard Long, 7474 Drexel Dr., University City, MO 63130, 314-721-7393, www.2River.org, long@2River.org. 1996. Poetry. "Since 1996, 2River has been a site of poetry, art, and theory, quarterly publishing The 2River View and occasionally publishing individual authors in the 2River Chapbook Series. All publications appear online and afterwards in print." circ. 200. 4/yr. Pub'd 4 issues 2005; expects 4 issues 2006, 4 issues 2007. sub. price Free; per copy Free; sample PDF is online. Back issues: None. 32pp. Reporting time: A couple of months at most. Simultaneous submissions accepted: No. Publishes 1% of manuscripts submitted. Payment: Copy. Copyrighted, reverts to author. Ads: None. Subject: Poetry.

Twynz Publishing, Dianna Williams, Dana Williams, PO Box 1084, Florissant, MO 63031-1948, 314-995-1551, Fax 314-831-6214, twynzpub@aol.com, www.twynzpub.com. 1999. Fiction, art. "New small press in St. Louis, Mo. First title *The Red Squeaky Nose* by Barbara J. Seeley." avg. press run 3M. Expects 3-7 titles 2006, 5-7 titles 2007. Discounts: 2-9 books 10%, 10-24 20%, 25-49 30%, 50-74 40%, 75-199 45%, 200+ 50%. 24pp. Reporting time: 4-8 weeks. Simultaneous submissions accepted: yes. Publishes a variable % of manuscripts submitted. Payment: 7-15% royalty, no advances. Copyrights for author. Subjects: Children, Youth, Entertainment, Fiction, Juvenile Fiction, Multicultural, Picture Books, Storytelling.

•**Typographia Press,** Leon Lozner, 1269 Rand Rd, Des Plaines, IL 60016, 847-635-8311. 2004. Poetry, fiction, parts-of-novels, non-fiction. avg. press run 1000. Pub'd 1 title 2005; expects 12 titles 2006, 24 titles 2007. Discounts: Special 15% Discount on all titles printed small numbers of copies (250-1000)Including design, printing and publishing. 268pp. Reporting time: Week. Simultaneous submissions accepted: Yes. Copyrights for author. Subjects: Americana, The Americas, Arts, Bilingual, Chicago, Family, Fiction, Food, Eating, Holocaust, Immigration, Printing, Surrealism, U.S.S.R., War, World War II.

Tyr Publishing, Paul Massell, PO Box 9189, Santa Rosa, CA 95405-1189, 623-298-7235, Fax 480-323-2177, info@tyrpublishing.com, www.tyrpublishing.com. 2002. Fiction, non-fiction. "We are looking for high quality materials from authors with an enthusiasm to promote their work over the long haul. We are especially interested in working with authors who are considered experts on their subject matter and/or have a target audience with whom they have a special way to reach." avg. press run 10M. Pub'd 1 title 2005; expects 2 titles 2006, 5 titles 2007. 325pp. Simultaneous submissions accepted: no. Copyrights for author. Subjects: Catholic, Christianity, Cooking, Cosmology, Non-Fiction, Philosophy, Religion, Science, Spiritual, J.R.R. Tolkien.

Tyrannosaurus Press (see also THE ILLUMINATA), Roxanne Reiken, 5624 Fairway Dr., Zachary, LA 70791, 225.287.8885, Fax 206-984-0448, info@tyrannosauruspress.com, www.tyrannosauruspress.com. 2002. Fiction. "We are interested in novel length speculative fiction (science fiction, fantasy, and horror)." avg. press run 2000. Pub'd 2 titles 2005; expects 1 title 2006, 1 title 2007. 400pp. Reporting time: Due to hurricane Katrina, we are not accepting queries until 8/1/2006. Simultaneous submissions accepted: yes. Payment: varies. Copyrights for author. Subjects: Fantasy, Science Fiction.

Tzipora Publications, Inc., Dina Grossman, P.O. Box 633, New York, NY 10035, www.tziporapub.com. 2002. Poetry, art, non-fiction. "We do not review unsolicited manuscripts." Expects 1 title 2006, 2 titles 2007. Discounts: Negotiable. 200-250pp. Does not copyright for author. Subjects: Arts, Avant-Garde, Experimental Art, Judaism, Middle East, Non-Fiction, Poetry, Russia, Translation, U.S.S.R., Visual Arts.

U

THE U*N*A*B*A*S*H*E*D LIBRARIAN, THE "HOW I RUN MY LIBRARY GOOD" LETTER, Maurice J. Freedman, Publisher & Editor-in-Chief, PO Box 325, Mount Kisco, NY 10549, Fax 914-244-0941. 1971. Poetry, fiction, articles, photos, cartoons, interviews, satire, criticism, reviews, letters, non-fiction. "*U*L* seeks long (and especially short) articles on innovative library procedures; forms and book lists. Articles should be complete to enable the reader to 'do it' with little or no research. Single paragraph 'articles' are ok with *U*L*. We ask for non-exclusive rights. Also humorous library situations, library poetry, library fiction, library cartoons." 4/yr. Pub'd 4 issues 2005; expects 4 issues 2006. sub. price $57.50 foreign & Canadian postage add $8, payable in US funds on US bank; per copy $14.50 foreign + Canadian postage add $2, airmail $5; sample free to libraries and librarians (send address label). Back issues: (most are in print) are $14.50 each, add $2 foreign + Canadian p/h. 32pp. Simultaneous submissions accepted: yes. Publishes 5-10% of manuscripts submitted. Payment: none. Copyrighted. Pub's reviews: 10 in 2005. §Library subjects only. Ads: none. Subject: Libraries.

U.S. Chess Federation (see also CHESS LIFE; SCHOOL MATES), Glenn Petersen, (CL); Beatriz Marinello, (SM), 3054 NYS Route 9W, New Windsor, NY 12553, 914-562-8350. 1939. Articles, photos, cartoons, news items, non-fiction.

UBC Press, R. Peter Milroy, 2029 West Mall, Vancouver, BC V6T 1Z2, Canada, Phone 604-822-5959, 1-877-377-9378; Fax 604-822-6083, 1-800-668-0821; info@ubcpress.ca; www.ubcpress.ca. 1971. Non-fiction. "Publisher, distributor of scholarly books, some general trade and text, non-fiction. Canadian agent for US, Canadian and British academic publishers." Pub'd 54 titles 2005; expects 55-60 titles 2006, 55-60 titles 2007. Reporting time: One month or less. Simultaneous submissions accepted: No. Subjects: Agriculture, Anthropology, Archaelogy, Architecture, Asia, Indochina, Canada, Education, Health, History, Language, Law, Native American, Political Science, Politics, Public Affairs, Society.

Uccelli Press (see also BRANCHES), PO Box 85394, Seattle, WA 98145-1394, 206-240-0075, Fax 206-361-5001, editor@uccellipress.com, www.uccellipress.com.

UCLA Chicano Studies Research Center Press (see also AZTLAN: A Journal of Chicano Studies), Chon A. Noriega, Editor; Wendy Belcher, Managing Editor, University of California-Los Angeles, 193 Haines Hall, Los Angeles, CA 90095-1544, 310-825-2642, press@chicano.ucla.edu, www.chicano.ucla.edu. 1970. Articles, criticism, reviews, letters, non-fiction. "Original research and analysis related to Mexican Americans." avg. press run 1M. Pub'd 1 title 2005; expects 4 titles 2006, 2 titles 2007. Discounts: for classroom use only. 300pp. Reporting time: 6 months. Simultaneous submissions accepted: no. Publishes 15% of manuscripts submitted. Payment: books in quantity. Copyrights for author. Subjects: Chicano/a, Society.

•THE UGLY TREE, Mucusart Publications, Paul Neads, Mucusart Publications, 6 Chiffon Way, Trinity Riverside, Gtr Manchester M3 6AB, England, paul@mucusart.co.uk, www.mucusart.co.uk/press.htm. 2002. Poetry. "Open theme but with a penchant for the relationship of the spoken word to the page. Poets featured in back issues include Duane Locke, Todd Swift, Aoife Mannix, Helen Thomas, Joolz Denby, Tony Walsh, Jackie Hagan, Conor Aylward, Robert D. Hogge, Tim Lucas & John G. Hall." circ. 100. 3/yr. Pub'd 3 issues 2005; expects 3 issues 2006, 3 issues 2007. sub. price 10.00; per copy 3.50; sample 3.50. Back issues: 2.00. Discounts: 10-19 copies 10%, 20+ copie 15%. 40pp. Reporting time: 4-8 weeks. Simultaneous submissions accepted: No. Publishes 5% of manuscripts submitted. Copyrighted, reverts to author. Pub's reviews: 5 in 2005. §New poetry collections/live events. Ads: 5.00 per issue/10.00 per annum. Limitede space available. Subject: Poetry.

UglyTown, Tom Fassbender, Jim Pascoe, PO Box 411655, Los Angeles, CA 90041-8655, 213-484-8334, Fax 213-484-8333, www.uglytown.com. 1996. Fiction. avg. press run 3M-5M. Pub'd 3 titles 2005; expects 9 titles 2006, 8 titles 2007. 288pp. Reporting time: varies, no longer than 12 months. Simultaneous submissions accepted: yes. Publishes 3% of manuscripts submitted. Payment: varies, usually percentage of cover price. Copyrights for author. Subjects: Fiction, Mystery, Reprints, Supernatural.

Ultramarine Publishing Co., Inc., Christopher P. Stephens, PO Box 303, Hastings-on-Hudson, NY 10706, 914-478-1339. 1965. Poetry, fiction. "We rescue books. We primarily distribute titles for authors (a major publisher has remaindered). The author buys some of the stock and we sell it for the author and split the proceeds." avg. press run 500-2.5M. Pub'd 20 titles 2005; expects 25 titles 2006, 30 titles 2007. Discounts: 1-4 20%; 5-9 30%; 10+ 40%. 250pp. Reporting time: 60 days. We have never published an unsolicited manuscript. Payment: varies. Copyrights for author. Subjects: Fantasy, Fiction, Poetry, Science Fiction.

Ulysses Books, Carlos Labbate, P O Box 937, Oregon House, CA 95962, 530-692-9393, 888-644-4425. 1995. Letters, non-fiction. "Inspirational works." avg. press run 1500. Pub'd 3 titles 2005; expects 3 titles 2006, 3 titles 2007. 300pp. Subjects: Inspirational, Metaphysics, Philosophy, Quotations, Spiritual.

•UmbraProjects, Ltd., Samuel Peterson, Editor, 3616 Jamestown Lane, Jacksonville, FL 32223-7497, up_admin@juno.com. 2004. Poetry, fiction, articles, cartoons, satire, parts-of-novels, long-poems, plays. "Manuscripts submitted by e-mail are exceptable and will be seen as a normal submission. We prefer fiction (fiction, sci-fi and fantasy). It can be as macabre as you want to write it, or not, your choice. Tell us if another publishing house won't publish you because you are writing abou vampires and we'll give you special interest. We also publish comics (perferably in Japanese manga style)." avg. press run 100. Pub'd 2 titles 2005; expects 5 titles 2006, 20 titles 2007. Discounts: Authors receive a 20% discount upon ordering the first 10 copies and 40% for off orders with more than 10 copies. 30-350pp. Reporting time: Two weeks. Simultaneous submissions accepted: yes. Publishes 80% of manuscripts submitted. Payment: Author receives 15% royalties. Will create a Copyright for the author, but wil not register the Copyright (so people will leave you alone, but it may not stand in a court of law). Subjects: Cartoons, Fantasy, Fiction, Graphic Design, Japan, Juvenile Fiction, Magazines, Medieval, Miniature Books, Myth, Mythology, Picture Books, Romance, Writers/Writing, Young Adult, Zines.

UMBRELLA Online, Judith A. Hoffberg, PO Box 3640, Santa Monica, CA 90408, 310-399-1146, Fax 310-399-5070, umbrella@ix.netcom.com. 1978. Articles, art, photos, cartoons, interviews, criticism, reviews, news items, non-fiction. "News and reviews of artists' books & artists' periodicals." circ. 1M. 3-4/yr. Pub'd 3 issues 2005; expects 3 issues 2006, 3 issues 2007. sub. price $15 for individuals; $20 for institutions. Back issues: $8 and above. Discounts: none. 36pp. Reporting time: 4 weeks. Payment: none. Copyrighted, reverts to author. Pub's reviews: 200 in 2005. §Contemporary art, photography, bookworks by artists, new artists' publications like periodicals, pamphlets, audioworks by artists, records by artists, copy art. Subjects: Arts, Book Arts, Book Collecting, Bookselling, Book Reviewing, Photography, Printing, Tapes & Records, Visual Arts.

UNBOUND, Rick Henry, Dept. of English & Communication, SUNY-Potsdam, Potsdam, NY 13676, unbound@potsdam.edu. 2001. Fiction, parts-of-novels, collages, concrete art. "Fiction that exceeds the page." circ. 100. 1/yr. Expects 1 issue 2007. sub. price $10; per copy $10. 48pp. Reporting time: 4 months. Simultaneous submissions accepted: yes. Payment: copies. Not copyrighted. Subjects: Avant-Garde, Experimental Art, Fiction, Post Modern.

UND Press (see also NORTH DAKOTA QUARTERLY), Robert W. Lewis, Editor; William Borden, Fiction Editor; Jay Meek, Poetry Editor, University of North Dakota, PO Box 7209, Grand Forks, ND 58202, 701-777-3321. 1910. Poetry, fiction, articles, art, photos, interviews, satire, criticism, reviews, long-poems, non-fiction. Pub'd 80 titles 2005; expects 80 titles 2006, 80 titles 2007. 175pp. Reporting time: 1-4 months. We accept simultaneous submissions for fiction and essays if noted in cover letter, but not for poetry. Publishes 5% of manuscripts submitted. Payment: in copies. Copyrights for author. Subjects: Book Reviewing, Criticism, Culture, Great Plains, Ireland, Literary Review, Literature (General), Native American.

UNDER THE SUN, Heidemarie Z. Weidner, Editor, English Dept., Box 5053, Tennessee Technological University, Cookeville, TN 38505, 931-372-3768;hweidner@tntech.edu;www.tntech.edu/underthesun. 1995. Non-fiction. "'An essay,' it has been said, 'is a short piece of prose in which the author reveals himself in relation to any subject under the sun.' Hence, the name of our magazine. It is devoted exclusively to the publication of a form that began with Montaigne and that continues, despite neglect, to thrive today. No academic articles, reviews, feature stories, or excerpts. An essay from our inauguual issue was chosen for inclusion in the 1997 volume of Best American Essays. We have had "Notables" every year since then." 1/yr. Pub'd 1 issue 2005; expects 1 issue 2006, 1 issue 2007. sub. price $12.00; per copy $12.00; sample $7.00. Back issues: From $7.00 to $2.00, depending on the year. 200-250pp. Reporting time: 1-4 months. Simultaneous submissions accepted: no. Publishes 10% of manuscripts submitted. Payment: 1 copy, 50% for additional copies. Copyrighted, reverts to author. Ads: none.

UNDER THE VOLCANO, Richard Black, PO Box 236, Nesconset, NY 11767, www.underthevolcano.net. 1991. Articles, reviews, music. circ. 7M. 6/yr. Pub'd 6 issues 2005; expects 6 issues 2006, 6 issues 2007. sub. price $20; per copy $5; sample $5. Back issues: $5. Discounts: Distributors get a 50% discount off the cover price. 60pp. Reporting time: 120 days. Simultaneous submissions accepted: no. Payment: none. Not copyrighted. §Underground music. Ads: Full page: $400 / Half page: $275 / Quarter page: $160. Subjects: Culture, Current Affairs, Entertainment, Music, Reviews, Zines.

UNDERSTANDING MAGAZINE, Dionysia Press Ltd., Denise Smith, Thom Nairn, 20 A Montgomery Street, Edinburgh, EH7 5JS, United Kingdom, 0131-4780680. 1989. Poetry, fiction, articles, art, photos, satire, criticism, reviews, parts-of-novels, long-poems, plays. circ. 500. 1/yr. Pub'd 1 issue 2005; expects 1 issue 2006, 1 issue 2007. sub. price £10 overseas; per copy £3.50 + £1.50 p/h; sample £2.50 + £1.50 p/h. Back issues: same. Discounts: 2 mags for £8. 150pp. Reporting time: 8 months. Simultaneous submissions accepted: no. Publishes 20% of manuscripts submitted. Payment: free copy. Not copyrighted. Pub's reviews: 4 in 2005. §Poetry, short stories, novels. Ads: £100/£50/25pp per word. Subjects: African Literature, Africa, African Studies, African-American, William Blake, Lewis Carroll, Classical Studies, Criticism, Kafka, Rudyard Kipling, Literature (General), Philosophy, Reviews, Satire, Surrealism, Tennessee, Writers/Writing.

Underwhich Editions, Paul Dutton, Steven Smith, PO Box 262, Adelaide Street Station, Toronto, Ontario M5C 2J4, Canada, 536-9316. 1978. Poetry, fiction, art, interviews, music, long-poems, collages, plays, concrete art, non-fiction. "Dedicated to presenting, in diverse and appealing physical formats, new works by contemporary creators, focusing on formal invention and encompassing the expanded frontiers of literary and musical endeavor. Recent contributors include: Bob Cobbing, Gerry Gilbert, Gerry Shikatani, Lia Pas." avg. press run 200-500. Expects 2 titles 2006, 3 titles 2007. Discounts: 40% to resellers, 20% to educational institutions and libraries, 20% to radio stations on audiocassettes only. 30-50pp. Payment: 10% (copies or sales). Copyright remains with author. Subjects: Avant-Garde, Experimental Art, Literature (General), Music, Poetry, Short Stories, Tapes & Records.

THE UNDERWOOD REVIEW, Hanover Press, Faith Vicinanza, Linda Yuhas, PO Box 596, Newtown, CT 06470-0596, 203-426-3388, Fax 203-426-3398, hanoverpress@faithvicinanza.com. 1997. Poetry, fiction, long-poems, non-fiction. circ. 500. 1/yr. Pub'd 1 issue 2005; expects 1 issue 2006, 1 issue 2007. sub. price $12; per copy $12; sample $12. Back issues: $10. 160pp. Reporting time: 6-12 months. Simultaneous submissions accepted: yes. Publishes 3% of manuscripts submitted. Payment: 2 copies. Copyrighted, reverts to author. Pub's

494

reviews: 1 in 2005. §Poetry. Ads: none.

Unfinished Monument Press, James Deahl, 237 Prospect Street South, Hamilton, Ontario L8M 2Z6, Canada, 905-312-1779, james@meklerdeahl.com, www.meklerdeahl.com. 1978. Poetry, long-poems. "At the moment we have a large backlog and are not looking for new material. UnMon has published Milton Acorn, Raymond Souster, Robert Priest, Linda Rogers, and Tanis MacDonald. We like People's Poetry." avg. press run 500. Pub'd 4 titles 2005. Discounts: 40% trade and libraries. 126pp. Reporting time: 1 year. Simultaneous submissions accepted: yes. Payment: 10% in cash or copies. Copyrights for author. Subject: Poetry.

United Lumbee Nation (see also UNITED LUMBEE NATION TIMES), Silver Star Reed, PO Box 512, Fall River Mills, CA 96028, 916-336-6701. 1977. Art. "We have 3 copyrighted books out: *United Lumbee Indian Ceremonies*, an Indian cookbook, *Over The Cooking Fires*, and *United Lumbee Deer Clan Cook Book*, all edited and compiled by Princess Silver Star Reed." avg. press run 100. Pub'd 1 title 2005; expects 1 title 2007. Discounts: 20% per copy. 20-25pp. Payment: none. Does not copyright for author. Subjects: Ecology, Foods, Folklore, Native American.

UNITED LUMBEE NATION TIMES, United Lumbee Nation, Silver Star Reed, P.O. Box 512, Fall River Mills, CA 96028, 530-336-6701. 1979. circ. 2M. 3-4/yr. Pub'd 3 issues 2005; expects 3 issues 2006, 4 issues 2007. sub. price $8/4 issues; per copy $2; sample $2. 8-12pp. Reporting time: no set time, write for press time of next issue. Payment: none. Not copyrighted. Pub's reviews: 1-3 in 2005. §Native American Indian Heritage and Native American Indians today. Ads: $120/$60/Business card size $12/10% discount if put in four issues. Subjects: Book Reviewing, Crafts, Hobbies, Ecology, Foods, Education, Folklore, Native American, Reprints.

United Nations University Press, Gareth Johnston, United Nations University, 53-70 Jingumae 5-chome, Shibuya-ku, Tokyo, Japan, Tel: +81-3499-2811, Fax: +81-3-3406-7345, sales@hq.unu.edu, http://www.unu.edu/unupress. 1990. Articles. "scholary publications in the fields of political science and international relations, environment and sustainable development." avg. press run 1500. Pub'd 16 titles 2005; expects 17 titles 2006, 18 titles 2007. Discounts: 2-10 copies 25%11-25 copies 30%26- 35%. 350pp. Reporting time: 6 weeks. Simultaneous submissions accepted: No. Publishes 33% of manuscripts submitted. Payment: no royalty payments are made to authors/editors. UN University holds copyright to all publications. Subjects: African Literature, Africa, African Studies, Asia, Indochina, Business & Economics, Education, Environment, Ethics, Europe, Finances, Geography, Japan, Multicultural, Non-Fiction, Peace, Political Science, Politics.

United States Institute for Theatre Technology, Inc. (see also THEATRE DESIGN AND TECHNOLOGY), David Rodger, Editor; Deborah Hazlett, Art Director, 6443 Ridings Road, Syracuse, NY 13206-1111. 1965. Articles, interviews, criticism, reviews. avg. press run 4M. 76pp. Reporting time: 6-10 weeks. Payment: none.

Unity House (see also DAILY WORD; UNITY MAGAZINE), 1901 NW Blue Parkway, Unity Village, MO 64065, 816-524-3550, fax 816-251-3552. 1889. Poetry, non-fiction. "Types of books sought: spiritual, metaphysical, Christian, self-help, motivational, healing, mysticism." Pub'd 16 titles 2005; expects 18 titles 2006, 18 titles 2007. Discounts: wholesalers 52%, retailers 40%. 200pp. Reporting time: 6 months. Simultaneous submissions accepted: no. Publishes 1% of manuscripts submitted. Payment: upon acceptance. Copyrights for author. Subjects: Children, Youth, Health, History, Inspirational, Metaphysics, Motivation, Success, Non-Fiction, Religion, Self-Help, Spiritual, Young Adult.

UNITY MAGAZINE, Unity House, 1901 NW Blue Parkway, Unity Village, MO 64065-0001, 816-524-3550. 1889. Poetry, articles, photos, non-fiction. "Types of materials sought: spiritual, metaphysical, Christian, self-help, motivational, healing, mysticism." circ. 40M. 6/yr. Pub'd 6 issues 2005; expects 6 issues 2006, 6 issues 2007. sub. price $19.95; per copy $3.50; sample free. 48pp. Reporting time: 3 months. Simultaneous submissions accepted: no. Payment: upon acceptance. Copyrighted, reverts to author. Pub's reviews: 4 in 2005. Ads: none. Subjects: Health, History, Metaphysics, Motivation, Success, Non-Fiction, Religion, Self-Help, Spiritual.

Univelt, Inc. (see also AAS HISTORY SERIES; ADVANCES IN THE ASTRONAUTICAL SCIENCES; SCIENCE AND TECHNOLOGY), Robert H. Jacobs, Series Editor, PO Box 28130, San Diego, CA 92198-0130, voice:760-746-4005; Fax:760-746-3139; Email:sales@univelt.com, Web Site: http://www.uni-velt.com. 1970. "We are publishing books on space, astronomy, veterinary medicine (esp. first aid for animals). *To Catch a Flying Star: A Scientific Theory of UFOs*; *Realm of the Long Eyes* (astronomy); *General First Aid for Dogs* (veterinary medicine); *The Case for Mars*; *Spacecraft Tables 1957-1990*; *The Human Quest in Space* (space). Publishers for the American Astronautical Society." avg. press run 500-2M. Pub'd 10 titles 2005; expects 10 titles 2006, 10 titles 2007. Discounts: 20%; special discounts for classroom use; larger discounts by arrangement. 100-700pp. Reporting time: 60 days. Payment: 10% for a volume author. Copyright held by Society or Univelt but obtained by Univelt. Subjects: Adirondacks, Animals, Astronomy, Communication, Journalism, Engineering, Graphics, Indexes & Abstracts, Language, Political Science, Printing, Reference, Science, Science Fiction, Sociology.

Universal Unity, Dr. S. Karipineni, 1860 Mowry Avenue #400, Fremont, CA 94538-1730. 1992. avg. press run 20M. Pub'd 3 titles 2005; expects 2 titles 2006. Discounts: 40% 1-4, 50% 5 or more. 300pp. Reporting time: varies. Publishes 1-10% of manuscripts submitted. Payment: varies. Copyrights for author. Subjects: New Age, Non-Fiction, Religion, Spiritual, Theosophical, Translation, Women.

University of Alabama Press (see also ALABAMA HERITAGE), Donna Cox, Box 870342, 500 Margaret Drive, Tuscaloosa, AL 35487-0342, 205-348-7434, www.AlabamaHeritage.com.

University of Alaska Press, Erica Hill, Editor, PO Box 756240, Fairbanks, AK 99775-6240, 907.474.5831, 907.474.5502 fax, 888.252.6657, fypress@uaf.edu. www.uaf.edu/uapress. 1969. Non-fiction. "University of Alaska Press publishes scholarly nonfiction about Alaska and the circumpolar North." avg. press run 1500. Pub'd 11 titles 2005; expects 10 titles 2006. 300pp. Simultaneous submissions accepted: Yes. Publishes 10% of manuscripts submitted. Subjects: Alaska, Anthropology, Archaelogy, Native American, The North, Pacific Region.

University of Arkansas Press, Larry Malley, McIlroy House, 201 Ozark Avenue, Fayetteville, AR 72701, 1-479-575-3246. 1980. Poetry, non-fiction. "The Press has a Poetry Series edited by Enid Shomer that publishes four poetry collections each year, two in the fall, two in the spring. Check our website for submission requirements:www.uapress.com." avg. press run 1500. Pub'd 10 titles 2005; expects 12 titles 2006, 12 titles 2007. Discounts: 1-2 copiies 20%3-24 copies 40%25-49 copies 41%50-99 copies 42%100-249 copies 44%250+ 46%. 240pp. Reporting time: Usually around 4-6 months. Simultaneous submissions accepted: Yes. Publishes 3% of manuscripts submitted. Payment: No advance, standard royalty rates. Copyrights for author. Subjects: African-American, Americana, Arkansas, Biography, Civil War, Communication, Journalism, Criticism, Folklore, History, Middle East, Non-Fiction, Poetry, Political Science, South, Trade.

University of Calgary Press (see also ARIEL, A Review of International English Literature; CANADIAN JOURNAL OF COUNSELLING; CANADIAN JOURNAL OF LATIN AMERICAN AND CARIBBEAN STUDIES/Revue canadienne des etudes latino-americaines et caraibes; CANADIAN JOURNAL OF PHILOSOPHY; CANADIAN JOURNAL OF PROGRAM EVALUATION; CURRENTS: New Scholarship in the Human Services; INTERNATIONAL ADDICTION; INTERNATIONAL ELEC-TRONIC JOURNAL FOR LEADERSHIP IN LEARNING; MOUSEION, Journal of the Classical Association of Canada/Revue de la Societe Canadienne des Etudes Classiques; TORQUERE: Journal of the Canadian Lesbian and Gay Studies Association), John King, Senior Editor, 2500 University Drive NW, Calgary, Alberta T2N 1N4, Canada, 403-220-7578, Fax 403-282-0085, www.uofcpress.com. 1981. Poetry, non-fiction. "The University of Calgary Press (UC Press) is a non-profit, scholarly publisher committed to producing high-calibre academic and trade books and journals on a wide range of subjects, including art and architecture, the Canadian North, and international topics such as African studies and Latin American studies. As the heartland publisher, we are also particularly known for our focus on Alberta and the North American west. The University of Calgary Press seeks to: publish works that give voice to the heartland of the continent, with a special emphasis on Alberta; publish works that are innovative, experimental, and offer alternative perspectives; publish works that offer diverse views on international themes; help new writers break into academic and trade markets and nurture their careers; and link the creation and dissemination of new knowledge. Orders and inquiries: IN CANADA: Canada uniPRESSES, Georgetown Terminal Warehouses, 34 Armstrong Ave., Georgetown, ON, L7G 4R9. Telephone: 877-864-8477, Fax 877-864-4272, e-mail orders@gtwcanada.com IN THE U.S.: Michigan State University Press, 1405 S. Harrison Road, Ste. 25, Manly Miles Bldg., E. Lansing, MI 48823-5245. Phone 517-355-9543, Fax 517-432-2611, e-mail msupress@msu.edu IN THE U.K. AND EUROPE: Gazelle Book Services, White Cross Mills, High Town, Lancaster LA1 4XS, U.K.. Phone 1524-68765, Fax 1524-63232, e-mail sales@gazellebooks.co.uk." Pub'd 31 titles 2005; expects 30 titles 2006, 30 titles 2007. Discounts: Booksellers: 20-46% Libraries: 10% College and University bookstores: 20-46%. 250pp. Simultaneous submissions accepted: no. Payment: No advances, royalties 5% net sales after costs are recovered. Copyrights for author. Subjects: African Literature, Africa, African Studies, Anthropology, Archaelogy, Arts, Biography, Canada, Environment, History, Holocaust, Indigenous Cultures, Native American, The North, North America, Political Science, The West, Women.

University of California Press (see also AGRICULTURAL HISTORY; ASIAN SURVEY; CLASSICAL ANTIQUITY; CONTEXTS: UNDERSTANDING PEOPLE IN THEIR SOCIAL WORLDS; FEDERAL SENTENCING REPORTER; FILM QUARTERLY; GASTRONOMICA: The Journal of Food and Culture; HISTORICAL STUDIES IN THE PHYSICAL & BIOLOGICAL SCIENCES; HUNTINGTON LIBRARY QUARTERLY; INDEX TO FOREIGN LEGAL PERIODICALS; JOURNAL OF MUSICOLOGY; JOURNAL OF PALESTINE STUDIES; JOURNAL OF THE AMERICAN MUSICOLOGICAL SOCIETY; LAW AND LITERATURE; MEXICAN STUDIES/ESTUDIOS MEXICANOS; MUSIC PERCEPTION; MUSIC THEORY SPECTRUM; 19TH-CENTURY LITERA-TURE; 19TH-CENTURY MUSIC; NOVA RELIGIO; ORAL HISTORY REVIEW; PACIFIC HISTORICAL REVIEW; THE PUBLIC HISTORIAN; RELIGION & AMERICAN CULTURE;

REPRESENTATIONS; RHETORICA: A Journal of the History of Rhetoric; SOCIAL PROBLEMS; SOCIOLOGICAL PERSPECTIVES; THE SOCIOLOGICAL QUARTERLY; STATE OF CALI-FORNIA LABOR; SYMBOLIC INTERACTION), Rebecca Simon, Assistant Director, Journals, 2000 Center Street, Suite 303, Berkeley, CA 94704-1223, 510-643-7154, e-mail journals@ucpress.edu. 1893. Articles, photos, interviews, criticism, reviews. avg. press run varies. Pub'd 28 titles 2005; expects 31 titles 2006, 31 titles 2007. Pages vary. Reporting time: varies widely. Payment: none. Copyrights in the name of Regents of the University of California (see individual listings).

University of Chicago Press (see also CRITICAL INQUIRY; INTERNATIONAL JOURNAL OF AMERICAN LINGUISTICS; JOURNAL OF BRITISH STUDIES; THE LIBRARY QUARTERLY; MODERN PHILOLOGY; OCEAN YEARBOOK; SIGNS), Paula Barker Duffy, Director, 1427 E. 60th Street, Chicago, IL 60437-2954, 773-702-7700,http://www.press.uchicago.edu/. 1891. Poetry, fiction, art, photos, criticism, music, long-poems, news items, non-fiction. "The University of Chicago Press, a non-profit university publisher founded in 1891, publishes ground breaking books and cutting edge journals in the humanities, sciences, and social sciences for a global community of scholars, researchers, professionals, and educated readers. Often ranked as the largest university press in the United States, Chicago has developed an internationally respected list of academic, professional, and writing reference books, as well as a premier list of Chicago regional titles. Through its Chicago Distribution Services division, the Press also distributes books for more than four dozen not-for-profit scholarly presses and maintains the Chicago Digital Distribution Center with its unique digital printing center adjacent to the warehouse and the BiblioVault repository for book files. Also, the Journals Division of the Press currently distributes nearly 50 journals and hardcover serials, presenting original research from international scholars in the social sciences, humanities, education, biological and medical sciences, and physical sciences. A complete list of books and journals published by Chicago can be found at: www.press.uchicago.edu." Pub'd 210 titles 2005; expects 188 titles 2006, 200 titles 2007. Payment: Once a year, after fiscal close. Copyright is usually in the name of the Press. Subjects: African Literature, Africa, African Studies, Agriculture, Anthropology, Archaelogy, Architecture, Arts, Bibliography, Cities, Conservation, Criticism, Earth, Natural History, Education, Gay, History, Labor, Lesbianism.

University of Illinois Press, 1325 South Oak Street, Champaign, IL 61820-6903, 217-333-0950. 1918. "Poetry manuscripts considered in February ONLY. $25.00 nonrefundable reading fee, payable by check or money order to the University of Illinois Press. Manuscripts will NOT be returned unless you also provide a stamped, self-addressed, manuscript-size mailer." avg. press run 1000-1500.

University of Massachusetts Press, Bruce Wilcox, Director; Clark Dougan, Senior Editor; Paul Wright, Editor, Box 429, Amherst, MA 01004, 413-545-2217; fax 413-545-1226; orders 1-800-537-5487. 1963. Poetry, fiction, criticism, non-fiction. "Scholarly books and serious nonfiction, with an emphasis on American studies, broadly construed. We also publish the annual winners of the Juniper Prize for Poetry, the AWP Grace Paley Prize in Short Fiction, and the Juniper Prize for Fiction. Information is available at our website—www.umass.edu/umpress." Pub'd 36 titles 2005; expects 34 titles 2006, 35 titles 2007. Discounts: For discount terms, please contact our distributor, Hopkins Fulfillment Service, at 1-800-537-5487. Reporting time: preliminary response within two weeks, followed by formal review process. Simultaneous submissions accepted: Yes. Payment: royalties vary. Copyrights for author. Subjects: African-American, Architecture, Arts, Biography, Civil Rights, Criticism, Current Affairs, Environment, History, Memoirs, Multicultural, New England, Non-Fiction, Vietnam.

University of Michigan Press, LeAnn Fields, 839 Greene Street, Ann Arbor, MI 48104-3209, Phone 734-764-4388, Fax 734-615-1540, http://www.press.umich.edu/. 1930. Pub'd 160 titles 2005; expects 160 titles 2006, 160 titles 2007.

University of Nebraska Press (see also RIVER TEETH: A Journal of Nonfiction Narrative), Ladette Randolph Ms, 1111 Lincoln Mall #400, Lincoln, NE 68508-3905, 402 472 3581, 402 472 6214, 800 755 1105, pressmail@unl.edu, www.nebraskapress.unl.edu, www.bisonbooks.com. 1941. "The University of Nebraska Press, founded in 1941, seeks to encourage, develop, publish, and disseminate research, literature, and the publishing arts. The Press is the largest academic publisher in the Great Plains and a major publisher of books about that region. It is the states largest repository of the knowledge, arts, and skills of publishing and advises the University and the people of Nebraska about book publishing. Reporting to the Vice-Chancellor for Research and having a faculty advisory board, the Press maintains scholarly standards and fosters innovations guided by refereed evaluations." avg. press run 2000. Pub'd 141 titles 2005; expects 160 titles 2006, 170 titles 2007. Discounts: Discount schedule available on request or through ABA Handbook. 280pp. Reporting time: 1-2 weeks. Simultaneous submissions accepted: No. Publishes 20% of manuscripts submitted. Payment: varies. Copyrights for author. Subjects: African-American, Anthropology, Archaelogy, Civil War, Feminism, Great Plains, History, Indigenous Cultures, Literature (General), Midwest, Native American, Nebraska, Non-Fiction, The North, Old West, World War II.

University of Nevada Press, Joanne O'Hare, MS 166, Reno, NV 89557-0076, 775-784-6573, www.nvbooks.nevada.edu.

University of Pittsburgh Press, 3400 Forbes Avenue, 5th Floor, Eureka Bldg., Pittsburgh, PA 15260, 412-383-2456. 1936.

University of Scranton Press, Patricia Mecadon, 445 Madison Ave., Scranton, PA 18510, 1-800-941-3081, 1-800-941-8804, www.scrantonpress.com.

University of South Carolina Press, Linda Fogle, Assistant Director for Operations; Alex Moore, Acquisitions Editor, 1600 Hampton Street, 5th Floor, Columbia, SC 29208, 803-777-5245; 803-777-0160; www.sc.edu/uscpress. 1944. Art, photos, criticism, letters, non-fiction. avg. press run 1000. Pub'd 39 titles 2005; expects 42 titles 2006, 44 titles 2007. 200-500pp. Reporting time: 3-6 months for full proposal or manuscript. Simultaneous submissions accepted: Yes. Publishes 15% of manuscripts submitted. Payment: Varies widely. Copyright in name of university negotiable. Subjects: African-American, Architecture, Arts, Civil Rights, Civil War, Cooking, Folklore, Food, Eating, Gardening, History, Literature (General), Memoirs, Nature, Religion, South Carolina.

University of Tampa Press (see also TAMPA REVIEW), Richard Mathews, 401 W Kennedy Blvd, Tampa, FL 33606, (813) 253-6266, Email: utpress@ut.edu, http://utpress.ut.edu, http://tampareview.ut.edu. 1952. Poetry, photos, interviews, criticism, letters, plays, non-fiction. "The University of Tampa Press publishes a limited number of books related to local and regional history as well as hardcover and quality paperback books by the annual winners of the Tampa Review Prize for Poetry. Recent poetry winners are Jordan Smith, Julia B. Levine, Sarah Maclay, and Lance Larsen. Other UT Press poets are Jenny Browne, Richard Chess, Kathleen Jesme, Lisa Steinman, and Richard Terrill, winner of the 2004 Minnesota Book Award for poetry. Winners in drama are Brian Silberman (MANIFEST), Susan Miller (A MAP OF DOUBT AND RESCUE) and J.T. Rogers (MADAGASCAR). The press also publishes two journals, TAMPA REVIEW, a hardcover literary magazine issued twice yearly, and PINTER REVIEW, a scholarly annual collection of essays on the work of Harold Pinter.The press does not currently accept unsolicited work except through its annual book award competitions and by direct submission to each journal, following published guidelines." avg. press run 750. Pub'd 7 titles 2005; expects 6-8 titles 2006, 6-8 titles 2007. Discounts: 1-4 copies 20%5+ copies 40%Some titles are on short discount. 88-450pp. Reporting time: Poetry and drama are accepted only via contest submission (see guidelines at http://pinter.ut.edu and http://tampareview.ut.edu/tr_prize.html). Simultaneous submissions accepted: No. Publishes 1% of manuscripts submitted. Payment: varies. Copyrights for author. Subjects: Book Arts, Criticism, Drama, English, Essays, Florida, History, Interviews, Literary Review, Literature (General), Non-Fiction, Poetry, Printing, Prose, Theatre.

University of Tulsa (see also JAMES JOYCE QUARTERLY; TULSA STUDIES IN WOMEN'S LITERATURE), Robert Spoo, Editor, 600 South College, Tulsa, OK 74104, 918-631-2501, Fax 918-584-0623, carol-kealiher@utulsa.edu, www.utulsa.edu/JJoyceQtrly. 1963. Articles, criticism, reviews. avg. press run 1.9M. Pub'd 4 titles 2005; expects 4 titles 2006, 4 titles 2007. 150pp. Reporting time: 5-6 months. Simultaneous submissions accepted: no. Publishes 40% of manuscripts submitted. Payment: contributor's copies and offprints. Copyrights for author. Subjects: Ireland, James Joyce, Literary Review.

The University of TX-Pan American Press (see also RIVERSEDGE), Desirae Aguirre Ms., Editor, The University of TX-Pan American Press, 1201 W. Univ. Drive, Lamar Bldg., Room 9A, Edinburg, TX 78541, 956-381-3638, Fax 956-381-3697, bookworm@panam.edu. 120pp. Payment: Payment is 2 complimentary copies. After printing copyrights revert to the author.

University of Utah Press, 1795 E. South Campus Drive #101, Salt Lake City, UT 84112, 800-621-2736, Fax 800-621-8471, UofUpress.com. 1949. Pub'd 26 titles 2005; expects 23 titles 2006, 30 titles 2007. Subjects: The Americas, Anthropology, Archaelogy, Language, Memoirs, Middle East, Mormon, Native American, Non-Fiction, Southwest, Trade, Utah, The West, Women, World War II.

University of Virginia Press, Richard Holway, Acquisitions Editor; Boyd Zenner, Acquisitions Editor; Cathie Brettschneider, Acquisitions Editor, P.O. Box 400318, Charlottesville, VA 22904-4318, 800-831-3406, 877-288-6400, vapress@virginia.edu, www.upress.virginia.edu. 1963. Poetry, art, photos, criticism, letters, non-fiction. "The University of Virginia Press was founded in 1963 to advance the intellectual interests not only of the University of Virginia, but of institutions of higher learning throughout the state. A member of the Association of American University Presses, UVaP currently publishes fifty to sixty new titles annually. New titles are approved by the Board of Directors after a rigorous process of peer review. The UVaP editorial program focuses primarily on the humanities and social sciences with special concentrations in American history, African American studies, southern studies, literature, ecocriticism, and regional books. While it continuously pursues new titles, UVaP also maintains a backlist of over 1,000 titles in print. Some recent titles are *Pocahontas, Powhatan, Opechancanough, Equity and Excellence in American Higher Education, Bitter Fruits of Bondage* and *Schooling and Riding the Sport Horse.*" avg. press run 1,500. Pub'd 57 titles 2005; expects 53 titles 2006, 60 titles 2007. Discounts: 1:20% 2-25:40% 26-100:42% 101-200:43% 201 or more:46%.

256pp. Reporting time: Anywhere from 2 months to a year if the author is still revising the manuscript. Simultaneous submissions accepted: Yes. Payment: Royalty is only given under special arrangements for certain books. We maintain copyright of all books unless there is a special case. Subjects: African Literature, Africa, African Studies, Architecture, Biography, Caribbean, Civil War, France, French, Gardening, History, Thomas Jefferson, Literature (General), Non-Fiction, Poetry, Sports, Outdoors, Translation, Virginia.

University Of Wales Press (see also ALT-J: Association for Learning Technology Journal; BORDERLINES: Studies in American Culture; CONTEMPORARY WALES; EFRYDIAU ATHRON-YDDOL; JOURNAL OF CELTIC LINGUISTICS; KANTIAN REVIEW; LLEN CYMRU; STUDIA CELTICA; WELSH HISTORY REVIEW; WELSH JOURNAL OF EDUCATION; WELSH MUSIC HISTORY), 10 Columbus Walk, Brigantine Place, Cardiff CF10 4UP, Wales, +44-02-2049-6899, Fax +44-029-2049-6108, press@press.wales.ac.uk, www.wales.ac.uk/press. 1922. Articles, criticism, non-fiction. "Available in North America from Paul & Company Publishers Consortium." avg. press run 500. Pub'd 8 titles 2005; expects 8 titles 2006, 8 titles 2007. Discounts: 10%. 100pp. Payment: none. Does not copyright for author. Subject: Celtic.

‡UNIVERSITY OF WINDSOR REVIEW, Alistair MacLeod, Fiction Editor; John Ditsky, Poetry Editor; Susan Gold Smith, Art Editor; Simon Watson, Editorial Assistant, Department of English, University of Windsor, Windsor, Ontario N9B3P4, Canada, 519-293-4232 X2332; Fax 519-973-7050; uwrevu@uwindsor.ca. 1965. Poetry, fiction, articles, art, photos, cartoons, interviews, satire, criticism, parts-of-novels, long-poems, collages, plays, concrete art, non-fiction. "We try to offer a balance of fiction and poetry distinguished by excellence—among those who have appeared are: W.D. Valgardson, Joyce Carol Oates, Tom Wayman, etc." circ. 250. 2/yr. Pub'd 2 issues 2005; expects 2 issues 2006, 2 issues 2007. sub. price $19.95 CDN. (+ 7% GST) and $19.95 U.S. per year; per copy $10 Cdn. and $7 U.S. per year; sample $8 Cdn. and $7 U.S. per year. Back issues: please write. Discounts: n/a at present. 100pp. Reporting time: 6 weeks. Simultaneous submissions accepted: no. Payment: $50 for story or essay, $15 for poem. Copyrighted, reverts to author. Ads: no paid ads at present, though possibly in near future; same for exchange ads—please write. Subjects: Arts, Fiction, Literary Review, Poetry.

University of Wisconsin Press, Andrea Christofferson, Marketing Manager; Raphael Kadushin, Humanities Acquisitions Editor; Robert Mandel, Press Director and Acquisitions Editor, 1930 Monroe Street, 3rd Floor, Madison, WI 53711-2059, (608)263-0814, fax (608)263-1132. 1947. Fiction, criticism, non-fiction. "UW Press publishes books and journals valued by a world-wide scholarly community, which are an extension of the university's teaching and research missions. We also publish books that serve to doument the regional heritage of the Great Lakes region. Areas of special inerest include: Jewish Studies, African Studies, Gay & Lesbian Studies, Environmental Studies, Anthropology, and History.UW Press publishes a few poetry and fiction titles each season." Pub'd 85 titles 2005; expects 75 titles 2006, 70 titles 2007.

University Press of Colorado, Darrin Pratt, 5589 Arapahoe Avenue, Suite 206C, Boulder, CO 80303, Orders: 800-627-7377, Editorial: 720-406-8849, Fax: 720-406-3443. 1965. Non-fiction. "We publish non-fiction books with a focus on anthropology, archaeology, history, natural history, and the state of Colorado and Rocky Mountain Region." avg. press run 750. Pub'd 34 titles 2005; expects 20 titles 2006, 20 titles 2007. 268-340pp. Reporting time: 2-4 weeks. Simultaneous submissions accepted: Yes. Publishes less than 5% of manuscripts submitted. Copyrights for author. Subjects: The Americas, Animals, Anthropology, Archaelogy, Astronomy, Biology, Birds, Botany, Colorado, History, Law, Mexico, Non-Fiction, Political Science, South America, The West.

UnKnownTruths.com Publishing Company, Walter Parks, 8815 Conroy Windermere Rd., Suite 190, Orlando, FL 32835, Ph 407-929-9207, Fax 407-876-3933, info@unknowntruths.com. 2003. Fiction, non-fiction. "Publishes books and produces Television Programing of true stories of the unusual or of the previously unexplained. The 56 stories currently in development or already published are grouped into seven catagories: Religious and Philosophical, Health and Medical, Historical, Psychic, Children-Young Adults-Nature, Travel and Leisure, and Fact Based Novels." avg. press run 5000. Pub'd 1 title 2005; expects 4 titles 2006, 9 titles 2007. Discounts: Standard. 304pp. Simultaneous submissions accepted: no. Copyrights for author. Subjects: Aging, Christianity, Earth, Natural History, History, Metaphysics, Myth, Mythology, Philosophy, Physics, Religion, Science, Spiritual, Supernatural, Technology, Treasure.

•Unlimited Publishing LLC, P.O. Box 3007, Bloomington, IN 47402, Please see http://www.unlimitedpub-lishing.com for contact info. 2000. Fiction, non-fiction. "Specializing in re-publishing out-of-print books and short nonfiction by professional writers." Discounts: Typically 50% non-returnable from Ingram, 40% returnable from B&T, lower in bulk. Call for details. 250pp. Reporting time: Prompt. Simultaneous submissions accepted: No. Publishes 10% of manuscripts submitted. Payment: Modest advances possible, royalties of $1.50 per book or better.

UNMUZZLED OX, ZerOX Books, Michael Andre, 105 Hudson St., New York, NY 10013, 718-448-3395,

212-226-7170, MAndreOX@aol.com. 1971. Poetry, fiction, articles, art, photos, interviews, criticism, reviews, music, letters, parts-of-novels. "It's helpful if contributors already understand pre-anti-post-modernism. Tabloid. We do not publish reviews, but we review books elsewhere and love to get them. We become ever more esoteric. Following the editing and publication of W.H. Auden's translation of an 18th century opera libretto, we plan an *Ox* of neo-baroque comapct disks." circ. 20M. 2/yr. sub. price $20; per copy $12; sample $12. Back issues: 1-6: $20 each 7-21 cover price. Discounts: 40%. 140pp. Reporting time: 2 weeks. Payment: none. Copyrighted. §Art, literature, music, politics. Ads: $65/$35. Subjects: Arts, Literary Review.

UNO MAS MAGAZINE, Jim Saah, 3007 Weller Road, Silver Spring, MD 20906-3888, Fax 301-770-3250, unomasmag@aol.com, http://www.unomas.com/. Poetry, fiction, articles, art, photos, cartoons, interviews, satire, criticism, reviews, music, long-poems, non-fiction. "Recent features: T.C. Boyle, Harvey Pekar, Larry Brown, Suzie Bright. Bands: Sugar, Lucinda Williams, Sebadoh, Fugazi, Uncle Tufelo, John Zorn." circ. 3.5M. 4/yr. Pub'd 3 issues 2005; expects 4 issues 2006, 4 issues 2007. sub. price $11; per copy $3.50 ppd; sample $3.50. Back issues: $3.50. 50pp. Reporting time: varies. Payment: in copies (will pay for art or photo supplies). Copyrighted, reverts to author. Pub's reviews: 3 in 2005. §Fiction, poetry, music, art, photography. Ads: $200/150/100-new ad rates. Subjects: Arts, Book Arts, Cartoons, Literature (General), Music, Photography, Reviews, Satire, Sex, Sexuality.

UnTechnical Press, Michael Bremer, 16410 Gibboney Lane, Grass Valley, CA 95949, 530-271-7129; 888-59-BOOKS; Fax 530-271-7129; michael@untechnicalpress.com; www.untechnicalpress.com. 1999. Non-fiction. "Only publishing books that fit into our existing lines. See website for more info. Query by e-mail first." avg. press run 5M-19M. Pub'd 3 titles 2005; expects 5 titles 2006, 7 titles 2007. Discounts: to be determined. 150-300pp. Reporting time: 60 days. Simultaneous submissions accepted: no. Payment: to be determined. Copyrights to be determined. Subjects: Computers, Calculators, Self-Help, Writers/Writing.

UNWOUND, Lindsay Wilson, P.O. Box 3193, Moscow, ID 83843-1907, unwoundmagazine@excite.com, www.fyuocuk.com/unwound.htm. 1998. "I want writing on modern life. I like writing that is informal, honest and identifiable and has concerns for the image, leaning more and more to the surreal image. Looking for poetry based on poet's life that knows what has been said before to avoid cliches and is struggling, yes, struggling, to say something new and fresh. I do *not* like private poetry - poetry is there to communicate - not destroy communication. If I had to be there to understand it, don't send it. I want work that considers the reader. What I'm primarily interested in is new modes of thought within contemporary themes and myths, which takes those themes and myths and recreates them or makes them new. I could care less about traditional forms and old ways of thought - rhyme will be rejected immediately! The poet is here to create new ways of thought not say what's already been said before. Each issue has two featured writers that receive 3-6 pages of space each, with picture and long bio. The last eight have been: C.C. Russell, Dan Crocker, John Grey, August Bleed, Jon Cone, Laura Joy Lustig, Mark Terrill and john sweet. The genres that have the best chance of getting accepted into *Unwound* are: b&w art, intelligent cartoons, fiction, essays, reviews and prose (not necessarily in that order). *Must* send SASE for reply. Send *only* questions (no submissions) via email. Keep fiction, essays, and creative nonfiction under 2,500 words and check out the website for more info." circ. 200. 2/yr. Pub'd 5 issues 2005; expects 2 issues 2006, 2 issues 2007. sub. price $5; per copy $3; sample $3. Back issues: $3. Discounts: varies, write for info. 48pp. Reporting time: 4 weeks-4 months. Simultaneous submissions accepted: no. Publishes 5% of manuscripts submitted. Payment: 1 copy. Not copyrighted. Pub's reviews: 20 in 2005. §Poetry, chapbooks, music, raves, magazines. Ads: $15/$7.50/trade with like magazines. Subjects: Absurdist, African-American, Arts, Australia, Beat, Book Reviewing, Cartoons, Dada, Dreams, Drugs, Pacific Northwest, Poetry, Surrealism, The West, Wyoming.

Upper Access Inc., Steve Carlson, 87 Upper Access Road, Hinesburg, VT 05461, 800-310-8320 (orders only), 802-482-2988, Fax 802-304-1005, info@upperaccess.com. 1987. Non-fiction. "*No* genre focus. We are looking for unique non-fiction to improve the quality of life. We also publish business software for the book publishing industry. Our primary software programs are *Publishers' Assistant* (Invoicing and office management) and *Couplet* (title and contact management, including creating ONIX databases)." avg. press run 8M. Pub'd 3 titles 2005; expects 1 title 2006, 3 titles 2007. Discounts: Most of our trade sales are now through our distributor, Midpoint Trade, so their discount schedule prevails. 195-603pp. Reporting time: 2 weeks, usually. We accept simultaneous submissions, but inquire first. Publishes a very small % of manuscripts submitted. Payment: 10% of net sales to 5,000 books, 15% thereafter, modest advance for finished mss. Copyrights for author. Subjects: Consumer, Ecology, Foods, Environment, Ethics, Food, Eating, Grieving, Health, Non-Fiction, Peace, Politics, Real Estate, Reference, Self-Help, Taxes.

•**UPSTAIRS AT DUROC,** Barbara Beck, Co-editor, 20 Boulevard du Montparnasse, 75015 Paris, France, wice@wice-paris.org (attention:Upstairs at Duroc submissions). 1999. Poetry, fiction, art, photos, parts-of-novels, concrete art, non-fiction. "We publish poetry of all kinds, fiction and nonfiction and a few pages of artwork/photography. New as well as established writers from the Paris, France area, Europe, and all English-speaking countries. Recent issues contain work by Alice Notley, David Lehman, Mark Tursi, Jennifer

500

K. Dick, and Albert Flynn DeSilver." circ. 170. 1/yr. Pub'd 1 issue 2005; expects 1 issue 2006, 2 issues 2007. price per copy Euros 7; sample Euros 7. Back issues: inquire. No discounts. 100pp. Reporting time: 4 months. Simultaneous submissions accepted: Yes. Publishes 10% of manuscripts submitted. Payment: 1 contributor's copy. Not copyrighted. Ads: no advertising. Subjects: Americana, Avant-Garde, Experimental Art, Europe, Experimental, Fiction, Literary Review, Non-Fiction, North America, Poetry, Prose, Short Stories.

Urban Legend Press (see also THE URBANITE), Mark McLaughlin, Editor & Publisher, PO Box 4737, Davenport, IA 52808. 1991. Poetry, fiction, reviews, parts-of-novels, long-poems, non-fiction. "Writers must request our guidelines (w/SASE) if interested in submitting to *The Urbanite*, and must query (again, w/SASE) before submitting book projects." avg. press run 750-1M. Pub'd 4 titles 2005; expects 5 titles 2006, 5 titles 2007. Discounts: interested companies should inquire. 60-92pp. Reporting time: 2-3 months. Simultaneous submissions accepted: no. Publishes less than 5% of manuscripts submitted. Payment: for anthologies, we pay 'per word,' varies for chapbooks (negotiable). Does not copyright for author. Subjects: Arts, Dada, Fantasy, Gay, Humor, Poetry, Reviews, Science Fiction, Short Stories, Surrealism.

The Urbana Free Library, Frederick A. Schlipf, 210 West Green Street, Urbana, IL 61801, 217-367-4057. 1874. Articles, photos, non-fiction. "Currently, all the library's publications are on the history and people of east central Illinois." avg. press run 500-1,500. Discounts: retail and wholesale schedules are available on request. *History of Champaign County; Combined 1893, 1913, and 1929 Atlases of Champaign County*, and *From Salt Fork to Chickamauga* are short-discounted. Pages vary. Payment: usually 15% of net. Subjects: Genealogy, Geography, Government, History, Illinois, Indexes & Abstracts, Libraries, Midwest, Military, Veterans, Photography, Transportation.

THE URBANITE, Urban Legend Press, Mark McLaughlin, Editor & Publisher, PO Box 4737, Davenport, IA 52808. 1991. Poetry, fiction, reviews, parts-of-novels, non-fiction. "Stories to 3,000 words; poetry up to 2 typed pages. Submitters must write for guidelines (and include a SASE) prior to sending us material. Fiction and poetry must concern the surreal; plus, we have theme issues. Recent contributors: Pamela Briggs, M.R. Scofidio, John Pelan, Jeffrey Osier, Alexa de Monterice, Michael McCarty, and Rain Graves." circ. 750-1M. 3/yr. Pub'd 2 issues 2005; expects 3 issues 2006, 3 issues 2007. sub. price $13.50/3 issues; per copy $5; sample $5. Back issues: #2,#5 $5 ea. Discounts: interested companies should inquire. 60-92pp. Reporting time: 2-3 months. Simultaneous submissions accepted: no. Publishes less than 5% of manuscripts submitted. Payment: 2¢ to 3¢/word for fiction and nonfiction, $10 per poem; for first N. American serial rights and non-exclusive rights for public readings (we give public readings on a local/regional level). Copyrighted, reverts to author. Pub's reviews: none in 2005. §Publications (books=story collections and novels) with surreal content. Ads: inquire. Subjects: Arts, Dada, Fantasy, Gay, Humor, Poetry, Reviews, Science Fiction, Short Stories, Surrealism.

Urion Press, Alan Rosenus, PO Box 10085, San Jose, CA 95157, 408-867-7695 phone/Fax. 1972. Fiction. "Reprints, fiction, history. Please send letter of inquiry first." avg. press run 2.5M. Expects 1 title 2006. Discounts: bookstores 40% on orders over 3, jobbers 50% on orders over 10. 250pp. Reporting time: 1 month. Copyrights for author. Subjects: Fiction, History, Literature (General).

Urthona Press, David Hopes, Lily Lightman, 62 LakeShore Drive, Asheville, NC 28804-2436. 1995. Poetry, fiction, art, photos, plays, non-fiction. "Book length only." avg. press run 750-1M. Expects 4 titles 2006, 4 titles 2007. Pages vary. Reporting time: 5 months or less. Simultaneous submissions accepted: yes. Publishes 10% of manuscripts submitted. Payment: case by case. Copyrights for author. Subjects: Arts, Non-Fiction, Poetry, Prose.

US1 Poets' Cooperative (see also US1 WORKSHEETS), Rotating board, PO Box 127, Kingston, NJ 08528-0127, www.princetononline.org/us1poets/. 1973. Poetry, fiction. "Reading period May 15-June 30. Single issue $7." avg. press run 500. Pub'd 1 title 2005; expects 1 title 2006, 1 title 2007. Discounts: inquire. 76pp. Reporting time: three-four months after June 30. Simultaneous submissions accepted: yes, but must notify if accepted elsewhere. Publishes 30% of manuscripts submitted. Payment: 1 copy. Copyrights for author. Subjects: Fiction, Poetry.

US1 WORKSHEETS, US1 Poets' Cooperative, Rotating panel, PO Box 127, Kingston, NJ 08528-0127, www.princetononline.org/us1poets/. 1973. Poetry, fiction, satire, long-poems. "We primarily publish poetry, but will consider exceptional fiction up to 2000 words. Submit up to five poems, single or double-spaced, but not more than five pages. A wide range of tastes represented in the rotating panel of editors. No restriction on subject or point of view. We read unsolicited mss. Reading period May 15 through June 30. All inquiries and mss should be sent to U.S.1 Worksheets, P.O. Box 127, Kingston, NJ 08528." circ. 500. 1/yr. Pub'd 1 issue 2005; expects 1 issue 2006, 1 issue 2007. sub. price $7 (one year) $12 (two years); per copy $7; sample $5. Back issues: inquire. No. 1 and No. 2 have become quite rare, several issues sold out. Discounts: inquire. 76pp. Reporting time: three-four months, after June 30. Simultaneous submissions accepted: yes, but must notify if accepted elsewhere. Publishes 30% of manuscripts submitted. Payment: 1 copy. Copyrighted, reverts to author. Ads: none. Subjects: Fiction, Poetry.

Utah State University Press, Michael Spooner, John Alley, 7800 Old Main Hill, Logan, UT 84322-7800, 435-797-1362, Fax 435-797-0313, kathleen.kingsbury@usu.edu (marketing) web: www.usu.edu/usupress. 1972. "Scholarly books." avg. press run 1-2K. Pub'd 20 titles 2005; expects 20 titles 2006, 20 titles 2007. Discounts: retail, wholesale, educ. 200pp. Reporting time: 6 weeks. Simultaneous submissions accepted: no. Publishes 10% of manuscripts submitted. Payment: yes. Does not copyright for author. Subjects: Education, English, Environment, Folklore, History, Native American, Nature.

•**The Utility Company LLC,** Kenneth Massie, 15893 Northgate Drive, Dumfries, VA 22025-1704, 703 583.4408. 2002. Non-fiction. Expects 1 title 2006, 1 title 2007. 100-250pp. Simultaneous submissions accepted: No. Publishes 1% of manuscripts submitted. Does not copyright for author. Subjects: Business & Economics, Consulting, Energy, Leadership, Management, Mentoring/Coaching, Motivation, Success.

UTNE READER, Nina Utne, Chair; David Schimke, Executive Editor; Keith Goetzman, Senior Editor; Julie Hanus, Assistant Editor; Hannah Lobel, Assistant Editor, 1624 Harmon Place #330, Minneapolis, MN 55403, 612-338-5040, www.utne.com. 1984. Articles, art, photos, cartoons, interviews, satire, criticism, reviews, letters, news items, non-fiction. "*Utne Reader* is a digest of alternative ideas and material reprinted from alternative and independent media. We don't accept unsolicited reviews, but we do accept unsolicited essays and cartoons." circ. 228M. 6/yr. Pub'd 6 issues 2005; expects 6 issues 2006, 6 issues 2007. sub. price $19.97; per copy $4.99; sample $7 (includes p/h). Back issues: $7, some older issues are $25. Discounts: inquire. 104pp. Reporting time: 2 months. Payment: varies. Copyrighted, reverts to author. Pub's reviews: 60-80 in 2005. §All independently-published books and periodicals welcome. Ads: $16,080/$9,650/$4.70 classified word. Subjects: Culture, Current Affairs, Society.

V

V52 Press, Jesse Post, 52 Mt. Vernon Street, #3, Somerville, MA 02145-3401. 2002. Poetry, fiction, cartoons, satire, criticism, letters, plays, non-fiction. "V52 Press is a partnership devoted to encouraging and promoting excellence in self-published writing. We set high standards for quality of writing and attractive production in hopes that we can get some of the most urgent and inspiring writing out there to readers without any corporate hassle. We only publish writing that makes us feel refreshed after turning the last page of the manuscript. We are interested in any manuscript that sounds like you wrote it, not your influences; that has a clear, consistent theme; and that keeps the pages turning. All poetry, prose, comics, personal essay, and other non-fiction welcome. We do have a bias against elaborate memoirs or novels, though you are still welcome to submit those types of things if you feel it will hold our attention." avg. press run 500. Pub'd 2 titles 2005; expects 3 titles 2006, 3 titles 2007. Discounts: 2-10 copies 30%10 + 40%Consignment terms also available. 100pp. Reporting time: Immediate response on arrival, two months for a full review of the manuscript. Simultaneous submissions accepted: Yes. Publishes 30% of manuscripts submitted. Payment: Author and publisher split expenses and profits 70-30 (author-publisher). More traditional advance/royalty arrangements possible depending on the marketability of the project. Copyrights for author. Subjects: Absurdist, Autobiography, Essays, Experimental, Fiction, Folklore, Food, Eating, Literature (General), Non-Fiction, Poetry, Politics, Prose, Travel, Zines.

VACATION PLACE RENTALS, J. Mark Press, Barbara Morris Fischer, PO Box 24-3474, Boynton Beach, FL 33424, www.VacationPlaceRentals.com. 2005. Articles, letters, non-fiction. "We publish brief vacation rental experiences online." circ. page views 16,500 mo. Ongoing. Reporting time: Same day, only if your essay, max. 300 words, is accepted. Simultaneous submissions accepted: yes. Publishes 60% of manuscripts submitted. Copyrighted, reverts to author. Subjects: Advertising, Self-Promotion, The Americas, Asia, Indochina, Australia, Cities, Dining, Restaurants, Entertainment, Europe, Festivals, Leisure/Recreation, Lighthouses, Portugal, Reviews, Shipwrecks, Travel.

Vagabond Press, John Bennett, 605 East 5th Avenue, Ellensburg, WA 98926-3201, 509-962-8471, vagabond@eburg.com, www.eburg.com/~vagabond. 1966. Fiction, articles, art, photos, interviews, reviews, letters, parts-of-novels, plays. "Query before submitting." avg. press run 1M. Pub'd 1 title 2005; expects 1 title 2006, 1 title 2007. Discounts: 20% trade; orders over $75 40%; 20% book jobbers. 200pp. Reporting time: 3-4 weeks. Simultaneous submissions accepted: yes. Payment: by agreement. Copyrights for author. Subjects: Literature (General), Magazines.

Vagabond Press, Richard Kendrick, PO Box 4830, Austin, TX 78765-4830, (512) 343-1540, vagabondpress@sbcglobal.net, vagabondpress.com. 2004. Poetry, fiction. "Publishing vital, innovative literary works." avg. press run 1000. Pub'd 1 title 2005; expects 3 titles 2006, 2 titles 2007. Reporting time: 3-4 weeks. Simultaneous submissions accepted: Yes. Copyrights for author. Subjects: Fiction, Poetry.

VALLUM: CONTEMPORARY POETRY, Joshua Auerbach, Helen Zisimatos, PO Box 48003, Montreal, QC H2V 4S8, Canada, vallummag@sympatico.ca, www.vallummag.com. 2000. Poetry, articles, art, photos, interviews, criticism, reviews, long-poems, concrete art, non-fiction. "We publish poetry that's fresh and edgy, contemporary and well-crafted. Send 4-7 unpublished poems. Recent contributors: Paul Muldoon, Stephen Dunn, John Kinsella, Anne Simpson, Charles Bernstein, Erin Moure." circ. 2500. 2/yr. Pub'd 2 issues 2005; expects 2 issues 2006, 2 issues 2007. sub. price $17.50 CDN (Canada); $15.50 US (United States); $23 USD (outside North America); per copy $9 CDN (Canada); $7.95 US (United States); $12 USD (outside North America). 100pp. Reporting time: 6 - 12 months. Simultaneous submissions accepted: no. Publishes less than 2% of manuscripts submitted. Payment: rates vary, honorarium and 1 copy. Copyrighted, reverts to author. Pub's reviews: 10 in 2005. §Poetry books, chapbooks, essays on poetry and poetics. Ads: $225 (CDN) full page, $125 (CDN) half page. Subjects: Arts, Book Reviewing, Essays, Interviews, Literary Review, Photography, Poetry, Reviews, Translation, Visual Arts, Writers/Writing.

Van Cleave Publishing, Erik Fortman, 1712 Riverside Dr. #93, Austin, TX 78741, 5126655451. 2004. Fiction, non-fiction. "Van Cleave Publishing seeks to promote two types of books. Fiction books will be creative and progressive. We appreciate the work of the Lost Generation forward.Non-Fiction books will be the base of the company. We are concentrating on books concerning politics, World & American History, and government. VCP concentrates on conspiracy theory and history revision." avg. press run 10000. Expects 3 titles 2006, 10 titles 2007. Discounts: 2-4 copies 20%5-9 copies 30%10-19 copies 40%20-49 copies 50%100+ copies 60%. 300pp. Reporting time: 6-12 weeks. Simultaneous submissions accepted: No. Publishes 10% of manuscripts submitted. Payment: Up to $500 in advance, and 15% of net. Copyrights for author. Subjects: Anarchist, Beat, Civil War, Communism, Marxism, Leninism, Counter-Culture, Alternatives, Communes, Drugs, History, Holocaust, Libertarian, Literature (General), Military, Veterans, Political Science, Politics, Science Fiction, Texas.

Vanderbilt University Press, Sue Havlish, VU Station B #351813, 2301 Vanderbilt Place, Nashville, TN 37235-1813, 615-343-2446. 1940. Criticism, letters, non-fiction. "The Press's primary mission is to select, produce, market, and disseminate scholarly publications of outstanding quality and originality. In conjunction with the long-term development of its editorial program, the Press draws on and supports the intellectual activities of the University and its faculty. Although its main emphasis falls in the area of scholarly publishing, the Press also publishes books of substance and significance that are of interest to the general public, including regional books. In this regard, the Press also supports Vanderbilt's service and outreach to the larger local and national community." Pub'd 15 titles 2005; expects 20 titles 2006, 30 titles 2007. Reporting time: 1 month. Simultaneous submissions accepted: Yes. Publishes 5% of manuscripts submitted. Payment: small royalties. We usually copyright in the name of the press, but will copyright in the name of the author if asked. Subjects: Arts, Black, Chicano/a, Children, Youth, Cities, Criticism, English, Folklore, Health, Labor, Language, Latin America, Literary Review, Literature (General), Men.

VanderWyk & Burnham, PO Box 2789, Acton, MA 01720, 978-263-7595, FAX:978-263-0696, email:info@VandB.com, www.VandB.com. 1994. Non-fiction. avg. press run 3M. Pub'd 2 titles 2005; expects 6 titles 2006, 4 titles 2007. 182pp. Reporting time: 1-6 months. Simultaneous submissions accepted: yes. Publishes 2% of manuscripts submitted. Payment: advances $500-2000; royalty 5-10%. Copyrights for author. Subjects: Aging, Autobiography, Education, Family, Humanism, Non-Fiction, Psychology, Self-Help, Social Work, Women.

Vanessapress, Janet Baird, Vice President, PO Box 82761, Fairbanks, AK 99708, 907-488-5079; jrb@mosquitonet.com. 1984. Poetry, fiction, art, long-poems, non-fiction. "Vanessapress offers publication opportunity to Alaskan women authors for their stories and dreams of life in the Great Land. Publications include poetry, short stories, adventure, cancer journal, pioneer and homestead family experiences. All titles are in stock. Manuscripts or sample chapters are to be typed, double spaced, four copies with SASE if manuscript is to be returned." avg. press run 1.25M. Pub'd 1 title 2005; expects 1 title 2006, 1 title 2007. Discounts: 40% to retail bookstores, (order through Vanessapress); special orders prepay required on single copy. 125pp. Reporting time: 3 months. Simultaneous submissions accepted: no. Payment: arranged by contract. Does not copyright for author. Subjects: Feminism, Women.

•VANITAS, Vincent Katz, 211 West 19th Street, #5, New York, NY 10011-4001, vanitas@el.net. 2005. Poetry, fiction, art, photos, criticism, parts-of-novels. "VANITAS was founded to add a voice in a time of crisis; also as a means of collective inquiry or discovery into current problems, using primarily voices of artists. A conversation among the arts is stimulated, with authors who are not usually writers solicited for statements, poems, etc. Contributors to the first issue include: Daniel Bouchard, Alvin Curran, Jordan Davis, Jim Dine, Nada Gordon, Richard Hell, Ann Lauterbach, Judith Malina, Ange Mlinko, Nick Piombino, Jerome Sala, Anne Waldman." circ. 1000. 1/yr. Expects 1 issue 2006, 1 issue 2007. price per copy $15. Discounts: case sensitive. 140pp. Copyrighted, reverts to author. Pub's reviews: approx. 2 in 2005. §poetry, literary history. Subjects: Experimental, Performing Arts, Poetry.

Vantage Press, Inc., Richard Fairbanks, 419 Park Ave. S., New York, NY 10016, Ph:212-736-1767, F: 212-736-2273, 1-800-882-3273. 1949. Poetry, fiction, satire, criticism, parts-of-novels, long-poems, plays, non-fiction. avg. press run 450. Simultaneous submissions accepted: Yes. Copyrights for author.

VARIOUS ARTISTS, Tony Lewis-Jones, 24, Northwick Road, Bristol BS7 0UG, England. 1992. Poetry, fiction, articles, interviews, music, letters, non-fiction. "Circulation is by email to a select list of subscribers, including the ground-breaking publishers Rattapallax of New York and nthposition of London. We also have good links with Haiku Ireland & Poetry Scotland. Subscriptions are US $12/year, $20 Canadian etc., cheques please to A Lewis-Jones. Please send no more than 6 poems in the body of an email to: tonylj@firewater.fsworld.co.uk." Pub'd 150 issues 2005. Reporting time: 1 week. Payment: Some commissioned work by arrangement. Copyrighted, reverts to author. Pub's reviews: 5 in 2005. §Any poetry which meets the criteria above. Ads: none. Subjects: Arts, Culture, Haiku, Literary Review, Literature (General), Media, Poetry, Wales, Women, Writers/Writing.

Varro Press, Michael Nossaman, PO Box 8413, Shawnee Mission, KS 66208, 913-385-2034, Fax 913-385-2039, varropress@aol.com. 1992. Non-fiction. "Additional address: 4507 W. 90th Street, Shawnee Mission, KS 66207. Publisher of law enforcement, security, executive protection training manuals, handbooks, etc." avg. press run 2M. Pub'd 1 title 2005; expects 5 titles 2006, 5 titles 2007. Discounts: 1-9 20%, 10-19 30%, 20+ 40%. Pages vary. Reporting time: 60 days. Simultaneous submissions accepted: yes. Publishes 50% of manuscripts submitted. Payment: yes. Copyrights for author. Subjects: Safety, Weapons.

Vedanta Press, R. Adjemian, 1946 Vedanta Place, Hollywood, CA 90068-3996, 323-960-1728,e-mail address: bob@vedanta.org,web address:www.vedanta.com,web page shows our online catalog. Note that titles with an asterisk by the title in the catalog are not wholesale titles. 1947. Non-fiction. "Although I am open to 'that special title', we generally do not print from outside our organization. As a matter of fact, we are mainly keeping our previous titles in print. Rarely is a 'new' title published." avg. press run 3M. Pub'd 2 titles 2005; expects 1 title 2006, 3 titles 2007. Discounts: 5+ 40%. 150pp. Payment: no royalty to authors - no payments. Copyrights are usually to Vedanta Society or Vedanta Press. Subject: Religion.

VEGETARIAN JOURNAL, The Vegetarian Resource Group, Keryl Cryer, PO Box 1463, Baltimore, MD 21203, 410-366-VEGE (8343). 1982. Articles, art, cartoons, interviews, reviews, letters, news items, non-fiction. circ. 20M. 4/yr. Pub'd 4 issues 2005; expects 4 issues 2006, 4 issues 2007. sub. price $20; per copy $4.50; sample $4. Back issues: inquire. Discounts: inquire. 36pp. Reporting time: 1 month. Simultaneous submissions accepted: no. Payment: inquire. Copyrighted, we retain reprint rights. Pub's reviews: 16 in 2005. §Vegetarianism, animal rights, scientific nutrition, recipes. Ads: none. Subjects: Animals, Consumer, Cooking, Ecology, Foods, Health, Vegetarianism.

The Vegetarian Resource Group (see also VEGETARIAN JOURNAL), Debra Wasserman, Charles Stahler, PO Box 1463, Baltimore, MD 21203, 410-366-8343. 1982. avg. press run 8M. Pub'd 3 titles 2005; expects 3 titles 2006, 3 titles 2007. Discounts: 40% bookstores. 224pp. Subjects: Cooking, Ecology, Foods, Vegetarianism.

Vehicule Press, Simon Dardick, General Editor; Carmine Starnino, Poetry Editor; Andrew Steinmetz, Fiction Editor, PO Box 125, Place du Parc Station, Montreal, Quebec H2X 4A3, Canada, 514-844-6073, FAX 514-844-7543, vp@vehiculepress.com, www.vehiculepress.com. 1973. Poetry, fiction, non-fiction. "Publishers of Canadian literary works with occasional titles in the area of urban social history and feminism. Actively publish fiction in translation (French [Quebec] to English). Recent publications: *The Rent Collector* by B. Glen Rotchin, *The New Canon: An Anthology of Canadian Poetry* edited by Carmine Starnino, *How We All Swiftly: The First Six Books* by Don Coles, *Out to Dry in Cape Breton* by Anita Lahey, *Dr. Delicious: Memoirs of a Life in CanLit* by Robert Lecker." avg. press run 1M-1.5M. Pub'd 12 titles 2005; expects 12 titles 2006, 12 titles 2007. Discounts: jobbers 20%; bookstores 40%; occasional short-discounted title 20%; please inquire. Poetry 76pp, other 300pp. Reporting time: 3 months. Simultaneous submissions accepted: no. Payment: generally 10-12%. Copyrights for author. Subjects: Canada, Cities, Dining, Restaurants, Fiction, Multicultural, Non-Fiction, Poetry, Short Stories, Translation.

Velazquez Press, Claudia P. Huesca, 9682 Telstar Ave. Suite 110, El Monte, CA 91731, 626-448-3448, 626-602-3817, info@academiclearningcompany.com, www.velazquezpress.com. 2003. Non-fiction. "Velazquez Press prides itself on publishing bilingual reference and language education material." avg. press run 10,000. Pub'd 4 titles 2005; expects 3 titles 2006, 12 titles 2007. Discounts: 40-55%. Reporting time: 1 month. Simultaneous submissions accepted: Yes. Publishes 10% of manuscripts submitted. Payment: The author usually receives 10 % of the retail sales of the book. Copyrights for author. Subjects: Bilingual, Dictionaries, Education, Language, Reference.

VELONEWS, John Wilcockson, Editorial Director; Kip Mikler, Editor, 1830 North 55th Street, Boulder, CO 80301. 1972. Articles, photos, cartoons, interviews, reviews, letters, news items, non-fiction. "We now do color editorial." circ. 50M. 20/yr. Pub'd 20 issues 2005; expects 20 issues 2006, 20 issues 2007. sub. price $49.97;

per copy $4.99; sample free (followed by subscription). Back issues: $6 each. Discounts: none. 120pp. Reporting time: several weeks. Simultaneous submissions accepted: no. Publishes 30% of manuscripts submitted. Payment: flat fee with penalty if story not modemed or sent on disk; $19.80-$120 for photos, $100-$300 for color cover. Copyrighted, reverts to author. Pub's reviews: 5 in 2005. §Competitive cycling. Ads: $4840/$3360/$1 (4-color rates). Subject: Bicycling.

Venus Communications, PO Box 48822, Athens, GA 30604, 706-369-1547, fax 706-369-8598, email venus@venuscomm.com, www.venuscomm.com. 1996. Art, photos, non-fiction. avg. press run 2M-10M. Pub'd 1 title 2005; expects 2 titles 2006. Simultaneous submissions accepted: yes. Payment: to be negotiated. Copyrights negotiable. Subjects: Animals, Arts, Asian-American, Botany, China, Crafts, Hobbies, Culture, Dreams, Gardening, German, Horticulture, Native American, Nature, Old West, T'ai Chi.

Verbatim Books, Laurence Urdang, 4 Laurel Drive, Old Lyme, CT 06371-1462, 860-434-2104, www.verbatimbooks.com. 1974. Non-fiction. "Language (English) mainly." avg. press run 3M. Discounts: 20% for 1-4 copies, 40% for 1-4 copies paid with order, 50% ppd for +4 copies, 55% ppd for +4 payment with order. 360pp. Reporting time: 6 weeks. Publishes practically 0% of manuscripts submitted. Payment: 10% of list price on trade sales; 5% on mail order; 50% of subsidiary rights sales. Copyrights for author. Subject: Language.

Verona Publishing, PO Box 24071, Edina, MN 55424, 612-991-5467 www.veronapublishing.com. 1998. Fiction, art, photos, letters, non-fiction. avg. press run 25m. Expects 5 titles 2006, 7/7 titles 2007. 160pp. Reporting time: 1-2 months. Simultaneous submissions accepted: yes. Payment: 5% to 15% of gross.

VERSAL, Megan M. Garr, Cralan Kelder, Robert Glick, Amsterdam, Holland, versal@wordsinhere.com (queries only), http://versal.wordsinhere.com. 2002. Poetry, fiction, art, photos, letters, long-poems, plays. "We look for writers with an instinct for language and line break, for the urgent, involved, and unexpected. Recent contributors include Helen Degen Cohen, Russell Edson, Marilyn Hacker, Omar Perez, Aleida Rodrguez, Larry Sawyer, Naomi Shihab Nye, Mark Terrill, and Ellen Wehle. Reading Period: Sept 15-Jan 15. We only accept submissions sent by email. Please check the website during the submission period for the correct email address to which to send your submission." 1/yr. Pub'd 1 issue 2005; expects 1 issue 2006, 1 issue 2007. price per copy 8 euro. 100pp. Reporting time: 1-4 months. Simultaneous submissions accepted: yes. Publishes 4% of manuscripts submitted. Payment: copy. Copyrighted, reverts to author. Subjects: Fiction, Literature (General), Multicultural, Poetry, Prose, Short Stories, Visual Arts.

VERSE, Andrew Zawacki, Brian Henry, Department of English, University of Georgia, Athens, GA 30602. 1984. Poetry, articles, interviews, criticism, reviews. "Articles on contemporary, 10 to 20 pages long, most suitable. We publish a large number of translations of poetry, and poetry by British, American, Australian and international writers. Recent contributors: Kenneth Koch, Allen Grossman, Peter Porter, Medbh McGuckian, Charles Wright, Kevin Hart, Karen Volkman, James Tate, August Kleinzahler, John Kinsella, Penelope Shuttle, Charles Bernstein, and John Ashbery. Translations of Tomaz Salamun, Ales Debeljak, Eugen Jebeleanu." circ. 1M. 3/yr. Pub'd 3 issues 2005; expects 3 issues 2006, 3 issues 2007. sub. price $18 individual, $30 institution; per copy $8; sample $6. Back issues: $5. 128-256pp. Reporting time: 3-6 months. Simultaneous submissions accepted: yes. Publishes about 1% of manuscripts submitted. Payment: 2 copies and 1-year subscription. Copyrighted, reverts to author. Pub's reviews: 60 in 2005. §Poetry, poetry criticism, interviews with poets. Ads: $150 full page.

Versus Press, Don Waters, John Dewitt, PO Box 475307, San Francisco, CA 94147-5307. Fiction, non-fiction. "Versus Press is an independent small press with the primary goal of providing a literary forum for emerging and recognized writers who carry messages that are at once renegade, progressive, urgent, political, but altogether needed." avg. press run 2M. Pub'd 2 titles 2005; expects 1 title 2006. Discounts: wholesale of 3+ get 40%. Pages vary. Reporting time: 1-2 months. Simultaneous submissions accepted: yes. Publishes 1% of manuscripts submitted. Payment: varies by contract. Copyrights for author. Subjects: Avant-Garde, Experimental Art, Erotica, Fiction, Non-Fiction, Novels, Satire, Sex, Sexuality.

The Vertin Press (see also THE CLIFFS "sounding"), Kilgore Splake T., P.O. Box 7, 220 Sixth Street, Calumet, MI 49913, 906-337-5970. 2005. Poetry, fiction, art, letters, non-fiction. "THE CLIFFS "sounding is published four times a year: winter, spring, summer and fall Short poems short stores and black and white art." avg. press run 100. Expects 6 titles 2006, 8 titles 2007. Discounts: 20%. 50pp. Reporting time: within 4 weeks. Simultaneous submissions accepted: No. Does not copyright for author. Subjects: Anarchist, Anthropology, Archaelogy, Antiques, Architecture, Arts, Biography, Black, Book Reviewing, Community, Criticism, Dada, Dance, Earth, Natural History, Ecology, Foods, Fiction.

Verve Press, Glyn Goldfisher, Assistant Editor, PO Box 1997, Huntington Beach, CA 92647, fax: 714-840-8335. 1986. avg. press run 4M. Pub'd 1 title 2005; expects 1 title 2006, 1 title 2007. Discounts: bookstores less than 4 20%, more 50% non-returnable; 40% returnable, 20% college textbook stores. 216pp. Does not copyright for author. Subjects: Creativity, Writers/Writing.

Vesta Publications Limited (see also WRITER'S LIFELINE), Stephen Gill, Editor-in-Chief, PO Box 1641, Cornwall, Ont. K6H 5V6, Canada, 613-932-2135, FAX 613-932-7735. 1974. Poetry, fiction, criticism, plays. avg. press run 1M. Pub'd 11 titles 2005; expects 10 titles 2006, 20 titles 2007. Discounts: wholesalers 50%, libraries 10%, no shipping charges to American customers or other customers outside Canada. 120pp. Reporting time: 4-6 weeks. Simultaneous submissions accepted: yes. Publishes 1% of manuscripts submitted. Payment: 10% paid annually. Copyrights for author. Subjects: Asia, Indochina, Asian-American, Criticism, Drama, Fiction, Poetry, Religion.

Vestibular Disorders Association, Lisa Haven PhD, PO Box 13305, Portland, OR 97213-0305, 503-229-7705, Fax 503-229-8064, toll-free 1-800-837-8428, veda@vestibular.org, www.vestibular.org. 1983. Articles, interviews, reviews, news items, non-fiction. "Please do not send unsolicited manuscripts." Pub'd 3 titles 2005; expects 3 titles 2006, 3 titles 2007. Discounts: none. Simultaneous submissions accepted: no. Payment: negotiated. Copyrights for author. Subjects: Aging, Disabled, Disease, Health, Medicine, Newsletter, Psychology, Research, Social Security.

Via Dolorosa Press (see also ERASED, SIGH, SIGH), Hyacinthe L. Raven, 701 East Schaaf Road, Cleveland, OH 44131-1227, viadolorosapress@sbcglobal.net. 1994. Poetry, fiction, criticism, long-poems, non-fiction. "We do not accept submissions by phone, fax, or e-mail. Please view our submission guidelines at www.angelfire.com/oh2/dolorosa/index.html - we have a specific tone, style, and theme that we do not veer from. Do not send floppy disks or CD-ROMS. Include SASE for response; we do not reply by e-mail." avg. press run 500-1M, reprinted when supply runs out. Pub'd 4 titles 2005; expects 9 titles 2006, 5-10 titles 2007. Discounts: rates available upon request for bookstores. 30pp. Reporting time: 2 months. Simultaneous submissions accepted: no. Publishes 10% of manuscripts submitted. Payment: 10% copies of print run and 25% royalties. Does not copyright for author. Subjects: Anarchist, Atheism, Criticism, English, Ethics, Euthanasia, Death, Fiction, Grieving, Haiku, Humanism, Literature (General), Philosophy, Poetry, Post Modern, Zines.

Via Media Publishing Company (see also JOURNAL OF ASIAN MARTIAL ARTS), Michael A. DeMarco, 941 Calle Mejia #822, Santa Fe, NM 87501, 505-983-1919; fax 814-526-5262; e-mail info@goviamedia.com; website www.goviamedia.com. 1991. Fiction, articles, art, photos, interviews, non-fiction. "Asian martial arts, European martial arts, Asia-related topics. Length is open. First publication, "Martial Musings: A Portrayal of Martial Arts in the 20th Century" by Robert W. Smith." avg. press run 10M. Expects 2 titles 2006, 5 titles 2007. Discounts: regular discounts offered. Reporting time: 1-2 months. Simultaneous submissions accepted: no. Publishes 10% of manuscripts submitted. Payment: standard. Copyrights for author. Subjects: Asia, Indochina, Martial Arts, T'ai Chi.

Victory Press, 543 Lighthouse Avenue, Monterey, CA 93940-1422, (831) 883-1725, Fax (831)883-8710. 1988. "We do not accept freelance submissions." avg. press run 2.5-5M. Expects 2 titles 2007. Discounts: 40% for 5 or more, 50% 50 or more. 100+pp. Simultaneous submissions accepted: no. Publishes 1% of manuscripts submitted. Payment: 10%. Copyrights for author. Subjects: Folklore, Multicultural, New Age.

VINEGAR CONNOISSEURS INTERNATIONAL NEWSLETTER, Lawrence Diggs, PO Box 41, Roslyn, SD 57261, 605-486-4536; vinegar@itctec.com. 1996. Non-fiction. "All articles related to vinegar." circ. 20M. 4/yr. Expects 4 issues 2006, 4 issues 2007. sub. price $10; per copy $3; sample $3. Back issues: $3. Discounts: 50% over 10 copies. 8pp. Reporting time: 3 months. Simultaneous submissions accepted: yes. Publishes 10% of manuscripts submitted. Payment: none. Copyrighted, reverts to author. Pub's reviews: 4 in 2005. §Vinegar. Subjects: Biology, Cooking, Crafts, Hobbies, Ecology, Foods, Health, Homemaking, How-To, Lifestyles, Wine, Wineries.

Vintage Romance Publishing, LLC, Dawn Carrington, Editor and Business Manager, 107 Clearview Circle, Goose Creek, SC 29445, (843) 270-3742, www.vrpublishing.com, submissions@vrpublishing.com. 2004. Poetry, fiction, non-fiction. "Vintage Romance Publishing is interested in publishing nostalgic romances set anytime before 1969. We have several lines of historical romance including romantic suspense, era romances, comedy, inspirational, and coming soon, we will debut our Mystique line specifically for African-American historicals and Spanish Eyes specifically for Hispanic historicals. We publish a select amount of non-fiction dealing with romance, i.e., true love stories, and we will be publishing anthologies each year with different types of short stories." Expects 5-10 titles 2006, 10-15 titles 2007. Discounts: 2-10 copies 25%11-15 copies 27%. 200pp. Reporting time: Within one week for query, one month for partial submission and three months for full. Simultaneous submissions accepted: No. Publishes 5% of manuscripts submitted. Payment: Authors receive 40% of the download price and we pay royalties every three months. Does not copyright for author. Subjects: Family, Fiction, History, Non-Fiction, Novels, Poetry, Prose, Romance, Vietnam, World War II.

Virginia Pines Press, 7092 Jewell North, Kinsman, OH 44428, virginiapines@nlc.net, www.virginiapines.com. 2000. Fiction, non-fiction. "Full-length creative nonfiction - spiritual warfare, Christian viewpoint." avg. press run 10M. Pub'd 1 title 2005; expects 2 titles 2006, 9 titles 2007. Discounts: listed at bowkerlink.com. 250pp. Reporting time: 8-10 weeks. Simultaneous submissions accepted: yes. Payment: contract. Copyrights for author.

Subjects: Christianity, Inspirational, Non-Fiction.

THE VIRGINIA QUARTERLY REVIEW, Ted Genoways, Editor, One West Range, University of Virginia, PO Box 400223, Charlottesville, VA 22904-4223, Email: vqreview@virginia.edu, ph: 434-924-3124, web: www.vqronline.org. 1925. Poetry, fiction, articles, art, photos, satire, criticism, reviews, long-poems, non-fiction. "Recent contributors include Diane Ackerman, Isabel Allende, Margaret Atwood, Tom Bissell, Michael Chabon, Robert Creeley, E. L. Doctorow, Rita Dove, Stuart Dybek, Jane Jacobs, Galway Kinnell, John McNally, Toni Morrison, Thisbe Nissen, Joyce Carol Oates, Salman Rushdie, and Art Spiegelman." circ. 5,000+. 4/yr. Pub'd 4 issues 2005; expects 4 issues 2006, 4 issues 2007. sub. price $25 individual, $28 institution; per copy $11; sample $11. 288pp. Reporting time: 3 months. Simultaneous submissions accepted: no. Publishes less than 10% of manuscripts submitted. Payment: Fiction & Nonfiction: $100/typeset page; Poetry: $5/line, $200 minimum per poem. Exclusive first serial rights in North America. Pub's reviews: 200 in 2005. §All. Ads: $300 full-page, $180 half-page. Subjects: Book Reviewing, Culture, Current Affairs, Fiction, Global Affairs, Government, History, Literature (General), Poetry, Politics, Reprints, Short Stories.

Visibility Unlimited Publications, Trevor A. Freeman, 30605 Curzulla Road, Menifee Valley, CA 92584, 909-926-5125, lithic1@linkline.com. 2003. Fiction, non-fiction. "Visibility Unlimited is a micro press interested in a large range of topics ranging from archaeological/historic studies to science fiction and horror. We are particularly interested in short story collections for chapbook length projects, and novella lengths of 15,000 to 25,000 words. Query before submittal." avg. press run 200. Expects 2 titles 2006, 4 titles 2007. Discounts: bookstores and others who order 5+ copies receive a 40% discount. 60pp. Reporting time: 3 weeks. Simultaneous submissions accepted: yes. Payment: variable. Copyrights for author. Subjects: Advertising, Self-Promotion, Animals, Anthropology, Archaelogy, Architecture, Fantasy, Fiction, Food, Eating, History.

Vision (see also Vision, Vision Paperbacks and Fusion Press), Charlotte Cole, 101 Southwark Street, London SE1 OJF, United Kingdom, 020-7928-5599, Fax 020-7928-8822, editorial@visionpaperbacks.co.uk, www.visionpaperbacks.co.uk. Non-fiction. "We publish non-fiction books for a general audience, including investigative journalism, current affairs, biography and autobiography, popular culture, relationships, sexuality and alternative lifestyle. Recent titles include *Forget You Had A Daughter* by Sandra Gregory with Michael Tierney, *Human Traffic* by Craig McGill and *CQ: Learn the Secret of Lasting Love* by Glenn D Wilson and Jon Cousins. We are an independent publisher. Send brief synopsis and 3 sample chapters, by post or e-mail." avg. press run varies. Pub'd 19 titles 2005; expects 18 titles 2006, 20 titles 2007. Discounts: varies. 288pp. Reporting time: 2 months. Simultaneous submissions accepted: yes. Publishes 5% of manuscripts submitted. Payment: varies. Copyrights for author. Subjects: Autobiography, Biography, Bisexual, Counter-Culture, Alternatives, Communes, Culture, Current Affairs, Gay, Gender Issues, Human Rights, Lesbianism, Memoirs, Non-Fiction, Politics, Prison, Sex, Sexuality.

Vision Works Publishing, Dr. Joseph Rubino, PO Box 217, Boxford, MA 01921, 888-821-3135, Fax 630-982-2134, visionworksbooks@email.com. 1999. Fiction, non-fiction. "We focus on personal development, leadership, self-improvement titles that champion the human spirit and enhance productivity and communication." avg. press run 4M. Pub'd 4 titles 2005; expects 4 titles 2006, 4 titles 2007. 180pp. Reporting time: 60 days. Simultaneous submissions accepted: yes. Publishes 10% of manuscripts submitted. Payment: negotiable. Will copyright for author if desired. Subjects: Business & Economics, Self-Help, Young Adult.

Vision, Vision Paperbacks and Fusion Press (see also Vision), Charlotte Cole, Editor, 101 Southwark Street, London SE1 0JF, United Kingdom, info@visionpaperbacks.co.uk. 1996. "Vision and Vision Paperbacks publish quality investigative titles covering current affairs, investigative journalism and biography. We only publish *nonfiction titles only*. Our imprint, Fusion Press, was founded in 1999 to provide a forum for challenging prevailing cultural attitudes. Fusion seeks to push boundaries predominantly in the realm of popular culture, gender issues and sexuality, but also alongside autobiography and psychology. No fiction, poetry, childrens or MBS/new age please." Pub'd 25 titles 2005; expects 25 titles 2006, 25 titles 2007.

VISIONHOPE NEWSLETTER, CHRISTIAN CONNECTION PEN PAL NEWSLETTER, Annagail Lynes, PO Box 45305, Phoenix, AZ 85064-5305, 602-852-9774, visionhopemag@netzero.net, http://www.angelfire.com/biz2/buswriting/. 2000. Articles, non-fiction. "Although geared toward young adults, it is enjoyed by those young and those more mature alike." 6/yr. Pub'd 6 issues 2005; expects 6 issues 2006, 6 issues 2007. sub. price $15; per copy $3; sample $3. Back issues: $3. 12pp. Reporting time: 1 month. Simultaneous submissions accepted: yes. Publishes 50% of manuscripts submitted. Payment: complimentary copy. Copyrighted, reverts to author. Subject: Young Adult.

Visions Communications, 200 E. 10th Street #714, New York, NY 10003, 212-529-4029 phone/Fax. 1995. Non-fiction. avg. press run 3M. Pub'd 4 titles 2005; expects 4 titles 2006, 5 titles 2007. Discounts: 20% w/flexibility. 150pp. Reporting time: 2 months. Simultaneous submissions accepted: yes. Publishes 5% of manuscripts submitted. Payment: 10-25%. Copyrights for author. Subjects: Astronomy, Business & Economics, Current Affairs, Energy, Engineering, Leadership, Lifestyles, Non-Fiction, Psychology, Spiritual, Sports,

Outdoors, Textbooks, War, Women, Young Adult.

VISIONS-INTERNATIONAL, The World Journal of Illustrated Poetry, Black Buzzard Press, Bradley R. Strahan, Publisher, Poetry Editor; Shirley G. Sullivan, Associate Editor; Melissa Bell, Review Editor; Jeff Minor, Art Editor; Lane Jennings, Circulation, 3503 Ferguson Lane, Austin, TX 78754. 1979. Poetry, art, photos, reviews. "We are looking for poetry that excites the imagination, that says things in fascinating new ways (even if they are the same old things), that hits people 'where they live.' We are open minded about poetry styles but send us *only your best*. You may include matching pen and ink illustrations. We don't care if you're a big name but we do expect poetry that is well worked (no poetasters please). We are always looking for good translations, particularly of work not previously rendered into English and from unusual languages such as Catalan, Celtic languages, Malayan (please include original language version when submitting). Prefer poems under 60 lines (but will consider longer). Recent contributors: Louis Simpson, Naomi Shihab-Nye, Lawrence Ferlinghetti, Marilyn Hacker, Michael Mott, Ai, Sharon Olds, Charles Wright, Miller Williams, Eamon Grennan, Andrei Codrescu, T. Alan Broughton and Marilyn Krysl. Please don't submit more than 6, or less than 3 poems at a time (not more than once a year unless requested). Strongly recommend getting a sample copy (cost \$4.95) before submitting material. *Submissions without SASE will be trashed!* We are indexed in *The Index of American Periodical Verse*, the *Roths Periodical Index, the American Humanities Index*, and *Roths Index of Poetry Periodicals*. We are also in *Ulrich's* periodicals listings." circ. 750. 2/yr. Pub'd 2 issues 2005; expects 2 issues 2006, 2 issues 2007. We now only offer a 4 issue subscription for \$25. Special LIBRARY rates, Please inquire; price per copy \$6.50. add \$3 per copy for Europe Airmail, \$4 for airmail to Asia, Africa and the South Pacific or \$2.50 for Airmail to Latin America and the Carribean; sample \$4.95 plus same postage as single copy. Back issues: quoted on request (a full backrun is still available). Discounts: bulk 30+ copies 30%. 48pp. Reporting time: 3 days to 3 weeks, unless we are out of the country. Publishes 1% of manuscripts submitted. Payment: 1 contributor's copy, we hope to get money to pay contributors at least \$5 per poem in future. Copyrighted, reverts to author. Ads: none. Subjects: Literary Review, Poetry, Translation.

Vista Mark Publications, Gene Hines, 4528 S. Sheridan, Suite 114, Tulsa, OK 74145, 918-665-6030, Fax 918-665-6039. 1989. Articles, interviews. avg. press run 2.5M-5M. Pub'd 1 title 2005; expects 3 titles 2006, 5 titles 2007. Discounts: prepay 2-4 20%, 5-9 30%, 10-24 40%, 25-49 42%, 50-74 44%, 75-99 46%, 100-199 48%, 200+ 50%. 78pp. Copyrights for author. Subject: How-To.

Vista Publishing, Inc., Carolyn S. Zagury, 151 Delaware Ave, Oakhurst, NJ 07755, sales@vistapubl.com, www.vistapubl.com. 1991. Poetry, fiction, non-fiction. "We focus on nurse authors." avg. press run 1M. Pub'd 12 titles 2005; expects 12 titles 2006, 15 titles 2007. Discounts: offered. Pages vary. Reporting time: 90 days. Simultaneous submissions accepted: yes. Payment: based on project. Copyrights for author. Subjects: Alternative Medicine, Business & Economics, Health, Medicine, Non-Fiction, Nursing, Women.

Visual Studies Workshop (see also AFTERIMAGE), Joan Lyons, Cordinator, VSW Press, 31 Prince Street, Rochester, NY 14607, 585-442-8676, www.vsw.org. 1972. Art, photos, interviews, criticism, reviews, concrete art, news items. avg. press run 1M. Pub'd 12 titles 2005; expects 12 titles 2006, 12 titles 2007. Discounts: 20% to bookstores. Pages vary. Payment: varies. Copyrights for author. Subjects: Arts, Book Arts, Photography.

VITAE SCHOLASTICAE: The Journal of Educational Biography, Caddo Gap Press, Patricia Inman, Editor; Naomi Norquay, Editor, 3145 Geary Boulevard #275, San Francisco, CA 94118, 415-392-1911. 1980. Articles. "The annual journal of the International Society of Educational Biography." circ. 200. 2/yr. Pub'd 2 issues 2005; expects 2 issues 2006, 2 issues 2007. sub. price \$50 indiv., \$100 instit.; per copy \$50. 96pp. Reporting time: 2 months. Publishes 25% of manuscripts submitted. Payment: none. Copyrighted, reverts to author. Ads: \$200 per page. Subject: Education.

VLQ (Verse Libre Quarterly), Artisan Studio Design, C.E. Laine, PO Box 185, Falls Church, VA 22040-0185, Fax 703-852-3906, editor@vlqpoetry.com, http://vlqpoetry.com. 2000. Poetry, art, photos, long-poems. "*VLQ* looks for quality poetry of any length or style (except rhymed poetry). Past contributors include Janet Buck, Dorothy D. Mienko, Michael Meyerhofer, Ward Kelley, Lyn Lifshin, Pris Campbell, Nick Antosca, T.E. Ballard, Kristy Bown, kris t kahn, Erin Elizabeth, Michelle Cameron, David Mascellani, Jane Fenton Keane, Brett Hursey, Debrah Kayla Sterling and contributing editor C.E. Laine. *VLQ* nominates for the Pushcart Prize." circ. electronic, POD. Pub'd 4 issues 2005; expects 4 issues 2006, 4 issues 2007. price per copy free; sample free. 20pp. Reporting time: 60 days. Simultaneous submissions accepted: yes. Publishes 5% of manuscripts submitted. Payment: none. Not copyrighted. Subjects: Experimental, Photography, Poetry.

VOICES FROM THE EARTH, Southwest Research and Information Center, Annette Aguayo, Editor, PO Box 4524, Albuquerque, NM 87196, 505-262-1862, Fax 505-262-1864. 2000. Articles, reviews, news items. "Activist oriented. Environmental views, news and reviews on issues primarily, but not limited to, the Southwest." circ. 2.5M. 4/yr. Pub'd 4 issues 2005; expects 4 issues 2006, 4 issues 2007. sub. price \$10.00 students and senior citizens, \$15 individuals, \$30 institutions; per copy \$4.50; sample \$2. Back issues: \$2.50. Discounts: 40% to distributors. 12pp. Reporting time: 1 month. Payment: occasional. Copyrighted by Southwest

Research & Information Center. Pub's reviews: 14 in 2005. §Environmental, consumer & social problems. Subjects: Book Reviewing, Energy, Environment, Health, New Mexico, Nuclear Energy, Southwest, Water.

VOICES - ISRAEL, Helen Bar-Lev, 11, Haefroni Street, Mevaseret Zion, 90805, Israel, +972-2-5342451. 1972. Poetry. "*Voices Israel* is the only magazine in Israel devoted entirely to poetry in English. It calls for the submission of intelligible and feeling poetry concerned with the potentialities of the human spirit, and the dangers confronting it. Copyright to all poems is vested in the poets themselves; the only request of the Editorial Board is that if a poem is first printed in *Voices Israel*, that fact should be made known in any subsequent publications of it. No more than four poems to be submitted to each issue (one a year), preferably 40 lines or less in seven copies, to reach the Editor by the first of September each year." circ. 350. 1/yr. Expects 1 issue 2006, 1 issue 2007. sub. price $15 postpaid; per copy $15 postpaid; sample $10 postpaid. Back issues: $10 as available. Discounts: 33-1/3% off to recognized booksellers only. No library discounts. 125pp. Reporting time: report in fall/winter each year. Simultaneous submissions accepted: no. Payment: none. Copyrighted, reverts to author. Subjects: Beat, Humor, Judaism, Middle East, Non-Violence, Peace, Poetry, Religion, Vegetarianism.

Volcano Press, Inc, Ruth Gottstein, Publisher; Adam Gottstein, Associate Publisher, PO Box 270, Volcano, CA 95689, 209-296-4991, fax 209-296-4995, Credit card or check orders only: 1-800-879-9636, e-mail sales@volcanopress.com, website http://www.volcanopress.com. 1976. News items, non-fiction. "All materials published in book form, posters, audio tapes." avg. press run 3M-5M. Pub'd 2 titles 2005; expects 4 titles 2006, 4 titles 2007. Discounts: 1-9 copies: full price, 10-24 copies: 20% discount, 25-49 copies: 25%, 50-99 copies: 30%, 100+ copies: 35%. Reporting time: 3 months. Payment: Royalties. Copyrights for author. Subjects: Asian-American, Chicano/a, Children, Youth, Community, Folklore, Health, History, Indexes & Abstracts, Lesbianism, Psychology, Public Affairs, Reference, Religion, Society, Tapes & Records.

THE VOLUNTARYIST, Carl Watner, Box 1275, Gramling, SC 29348, 864-472-2750. 1982. Articles, cartoons, interviews, criticism, letters. circ. 300. 4/yr. Pub'd 4 issues 2005; expects 4 issues 2006, 4 issues 2007. sub. price 6 issues: $20, $25 overseas; per copy $4; sample $1. Back issues: 10 different issues $30. 8pp. Reporting time: 2 weeks. Payment: free subscription. Not copyrighted. Pub's reviews: 4 in 2005. Ads: $50 business card. Subjects: Anarchist, Libertarian, Non-Violence.

Vonpalisaden Publications Inc., 60 Saddlewood Drive, Hillsdale, NJ 07642-1336, 201-664-4919. 1986. Non-fiction. "Currently pet/hobby (dogs) animal book publisher (so far non-fiction only). *The Rottweiler: An International Study of the Breed*, by Dr. Dagmar Hodinar." avg. press run 5M. Pub'd 1 title 2005. Discounts: for resale: 1-9 copies 20%, 10-25 30%, 26-50 40%, 51-99 45%, 100+ 50% plus addit. 10% on net if displayed in catalogue. 350+pp. Subjects: Animals, Pets.

THE VORTEX, Axios Newletter, Inc., David Gorham, 30-32 Macaw Avenue, PO Box 279, Belmopan, Belize, 501-8-23284. 1981. Fiction, articles, art, photos, cartoons, interviews, satire, criticism, reviews, letters, parts-of-novels, collages, concrete art, news items, non-fiction. "A historical + wargamers journal. Articles needed on politics and battles and wars, in the period between 1812 and 1930—especially Europe and America. Also articles on wargames, the people into wargames, and photos, art and cartoons on the same. Write for an intelligent lay reader rather than a professional historian, length 400-2.5M words. By-line given. Emphasis on articles that would interest wargamers!! Some poetry (on our subject matter)." circ. 2.33M. 13/yr. Pub'd 13 issues 2005; expects 13 issues 2006, 13 issues 2007. sub. price $15; $25/2 years; per copy $2; sample $2. Back issues: $2. Discounts: write for information (about 40% discount). 12pp. Reporting time: 6-8 weeks. Payment: $20-$100 depending on article. Copyrighted, reverts to author. Pub's reviews: 16 in 2005. §Wargames, military history. Ads: $160/$87.50/5¢. Subjects: Caribbean, History, Libertarian, Society, War.

VOYA (Voice of Youth Advocate), Scarecrow Press, Cathi Dunn MacRae, Editor, 4720 Boston Way, Lanham, MD 20706, 301-459-3366. 1978. circ. 4M. 6/yr. Pub'd 6 issues 2005; expects 6 issues 2006, 6 issues 2007. sub. price $38.50; per copy $6.42; sample write for info. Back issues: $10. Discounts: write for info. 70pp. Payment: yes, varies. Copyrighted. Pub's reviews: 2500 in 2005. §Young adult. Ads: write for info. Subjects: Children, Youth, Young Adult.

Voyageur Publishing Co.,Inc., Nathaniel Kenton, Managing Editor, 1012 Greenwich Park, Nashville, TN 37215-2415, 615-463-3179. 1986. Fiction, non-fiction. "Query first with SASE, address to Nathaniel Kenton, Managing Editor." avg. press run 3,000. Expects 1 title 2006, 2 titles 2007. 360pp. Publishes about 10% of manuscripts submitted. Copyrights for author. Subjects: Biography, Crime, Fiction, Forensic Science, Global Affairs, History, Italian-American, Italy, Language, Martial Arts, Medieval, Michigan, Midwest, Old West, Scandinavia.

•**VYPER, Rattlesnake Press,** Kathy Kieth, P.O. Box 1647, Orangevale, CA 95662, 916-966-8620. 2005. Poetry. "Poetry by young people only, ages 13-19 years." circ. 150. 3/yr. Pub'd 1 issue 2005; expects 4 issues 2006, 2 issues 2007. sub. price $15; sample free. Back issues: $2. 20pp. Reporting time: 1 week. Simultaneous submissions accepted: No. Publishes 99% of manuscripts submitted. Payment: contributor's copy. Copyrighted, reverts to author. Subject: Poetry.

W

W.W. Norton, 500 Fifth Avenue, New York, NY 10110, 212-354-5500. 1923.

W.W. Publications (see also MINAS TIRITH EVENING-STAR), Philip W. Helms, PO Box 373, Highland, MI 48357-0373, 727-585-0985 phone/Fax. 1967. Poetry, fiction, articles, art, photos, cartoons, interviews, satire, criticism, reviews, music, letters, long-poems, news items, non-fiction. "Send questions to: Paul S. Ritz, PO Box 901, Clearwater, FL 33757." avg. press run 200-500. Pub'd 2 titles 2005; expects 1 title 2006, 3 titles 2007. 200pp. Reporting time: 2 months. Payment: 5 free copies. Copyrights for author. Subject: J.R.R. Tolkien.

•John Wade, Publisher, John Wade, P. O. Box 303, Phillips, ME 04966, 1-888-211-1381. 1989. Poetry, fiction, art, non-fiction. avg. press run 3000. Pub'd 1 title 2005; expects 1 title 2006, 1 title 2007. Discounts: 50% booksellers, 55% wholesalers, No minimum copies. 250pp. Subjects: Animals, Arts, Biography, Crafts, Hobbies, Fiction, Geology, Handicapped, How-To, D.H. Lawrence, Maine, New Age, Occult, Poetry, Sports, Outdoors.

Wafer Mache Publications, Donna Horn, 16 Elmgate Road, Marlton, NJ 08053-2402, (856)983-5360 http://www.WaferMache.com. 1982. Non-fiction. "publish confectionery art, cake decorating how-to articles, and how-to craft books and articles on edible sculpture, edible party and holiday decorations." avg. press run 3000. Pub'd 2 titles 2005; expects 3 titles 2006, 3 titles 2007. Discounts: 2-10 copies 25%. 100pp. Reporting time: 4-6 weeks. Simultaneous submissions accepted: No. Publishes 5% of manuscripts submitted. Payment: varies. Copyrights for author. Subjects: Arts, Food, Eating, How-To.

THE WAKING, Ethan Lewis, 488 Brookens Hall, UIS, Springfield, IL 62792-9243, elewis@uis.edu, www.geocities.com/uis_the_waking/. 2003. Poetry. "New on-line journal to begin-print journal in near future. See website for guidelines." 6/yr. Expects 6 issues 2006, 12 issues 2007. Reporting time: 6-8 weeks. Simultaneous submissions accepted: yes. Publishes 1% of manuscripts submitted. Payment: free copy. Copyrighted, reverts to author. Pub's reviews. §Poetry, fiction and art. Subject: Poetry.

THE WALLACE STEVENS JOURNAL, The Wallace Stevens Society Press, John N. Serio, Editor; Joseph Duemer, Poetry Editor, Clarkson University, Box 5750, Potsdam, NY 13699-5750, 315-268-3987, serio@clarkson.edu, www.wallacestevens.com. 1977. Poetry, articles, criticism, reviews, letters, news items. "*The Wallace Stevens Journal* publishes criticism on the poetry of Wallace Stevens. It also publishes archival material, Stevensesque poems, a current bibliography, and book reviews. Recent contributors have been: Eleanor Cook, Alan Filreis, Diane Wakoski, B.J. Leggett, Albert Gelpi, Helen Vendler, and Milton Bates." circ. 600. 2/yr. Pub'd 2 issues 2005; expects 2 issues 2006, 2 issues 2007. sub. price $30 for individuals ($50 2-years), $38 for institutions, $45 for foreign; per copy $10; sample $5 (postage). Back issues: $7 per number. 120pp. Reporting time: 6 weeks. Simultaneous submissions accepted: no. Publishes 25% of manuscripts submitted. Payment: copies. Copyrighted, reverts to author. Pub's reviews: 5 in 2005. §Wallace Stevens. Ads: $200/$150. Subjects: Biography, Criticism, Culture, Literature (General), Philosophy, Poetry, Post Modern.

The Wallace Stevens Society Press (see also THE WALLACE STEVENS JOURNAL), John N. Serio, Series Editor, Box 5750 Clarkson University, Potsdam, NY 13699-5750, 315-268-3987, Fax 268-3983, serio@clarkson.edu, www.wallacestevens.com. 1992. Poetry. "We initiated a poetry series with the publication of *Inhabited World: New & Selected Poems 1970-1995* by John Allman (166pp). We hope to publish a book of poetry each year." avg. press run 900. Pub'd 1 title 2005; expects 1 title 2006, 1 title 2007. Discounts: 20-30% depending on quantity. 80pp. Reporting time: 6-8 weeks. Simultaneous submissions accepted: no. Publishes 5% of manuscripts submitted. Payment: 10%. Copyrights for author. Subject: Poetry.

WALT WHITMAN QUARTERLY REVIEW, Ed Folsom, 308 EPB The University of Iowa, Iowa City, IA 52242-1492, 319-335-0454, 335-0592, Fax 319-335-2535, wwqr@uiowa.edu. 1983. Articles, criticism, letters, non-fiction. "The *Walt Whitman Quarterly Review* is a literary quarterly begun in the summer of 1983. *WWQR* features previously unpublished letters and documents written by Whitman, critical essays dealing with Whitman's work and its place in American literature, thorough reviews of Whitman-related books, and an ongoing Whitman bibliography—one of the standard reference sources for Whitman studies. The journal is edited by Ed Folsom and published at The University of Iowa and the editorial board is made up of some of the most distinguished Whitman scholars including Betsy Erkkila, Harold Aspiz, Arthur Golden, Jerome Loving, James E. Miller Jr., Roger Asselineau, and M. Wynn Thomas. We also offer for sale selected back issues of the *Walt Whitman Review* (1955-1982). Please write for details." circ. 1M. 4/yr. Pub'd 4 issues 2005; expects 4

510

issues 2006, 4 issues 2007. sub. price $12 individuals, $15 institutions ($3 postage charge on foreign subs); per copy $3; sample $3. Back issues: $3 each. Discounts: 10% to agencies for subscriptions, 40% to bookstores, 25% to classroom. 56pp. Reporting time: 1-3 months. Payment: contributor copies. Copyrighted, reverts to author. Pub's reviews: 8 in 2005. §Whitman scholarship, 19th and 20th American and World literature that discusses Whitman, poetry collections that reveal Whitman influences. Ads: $100/$50. Subjects: Criticism, Walt Whitman.

WAR, LITERATURE & THE ARTS: An International Journal of the Humanities, Donald Anderson, 2354 Fairchild Drive, Suite 6D149, Department of English & Fine Arts, United States Air Force Academy, CO 80840, 719-333-8465, website: WLAjournal.com. 1989. Poetry, fiction, articles, art, photos, interviews, satire, criticism, reviews, letters, parts-of-novels, long-poems, plays, concrete art, non-fiction. "From time immemorial, war and art have reflected one another. It is this intersection of war and art that WLA seeks to illuminate. If one of the functions of art is to disturb the status quo, to force us to view the world anew, to consider our capacities to build or tear down, then we welcome those disturbances. Before we made fire, before we made tools, before we made weapons, we made images. Art, at its deepest level is about preserving the world. Recent contributors include Paul West, Philip Caputo, Robert Pinsky, Dana Gioia, Carolyn Forche, Wendy Bishop, Robert Morgan, Ellen Bass." circ. 600. 1/yr. Pub'd 1 issue 2005; expects 1 issue 2006, 1 issue 2007. Journal provided free of charge to libraries and serious scholars. Back issues: free if in print. 350pp. Reporting time: 6 months. Simultaneous submissions accepted: No. Publishes 25% of manuscripts submitted. Payment: Two copies of the journal. Public Domain. Pub's reviews: 20 in 2005. §Works from any time or culture that explore the intersection of war and art. Subjects: Arts, Biography, Book Reviewing, Civil War, Fiction, Holocaust, Literary Review, Literature (General), Memoirs, Photography, Poetry, Vietnam, Visual Arts, War, Weapons.

Warthog Press, Patricia Fillingham, 77 Marlboro St., Belmont, MA 02478. 1979. Poetry, art, photos, music. "Warthog Press is interested in poetry that will bring poetry back to people, rather than using it as an academic exercise. We are interested in poetry that says something, and says it well." avg. press run 1M. Pub'd 2 titles 2005. 64pp. Reporting time: 1 month. Simultaneous submissions accepted: yes. Does not copyright for author. Subject: Poetry.

WASCANA REVIEW OF CONTEMPORARY POETRY AND SHORT FICTION, Michael Trussler, Editor; Marcel De Coste, Fiction Editor; Nick Ruddick, Poetry Editor, Department of English, University of Regina, Regina, Sask S4S 0A2, Canada, 584-4302. 1966. Poetry, fiction, articles, reviews. circ. 300-500. 2/yr. Pub'd 2 issues 2005; expects 2 issues 2006, 2 issues 2007. sub. price $12 ($10 Canadian); per copy $5; sample $5. Discounts: 20% for subscription agencies. 90pp. Reporting time: 2-3 months. Simultaneous submissions accepted: no. Publishes 10% of manuscripts submitted. Payment: poetry $10 per page; fiction, reviews, critical articles $3 per page. Copyrighted, reverts to author. Pub's reviews: 2 in 2005. §Canadian literature, modern literature,contemporary world literature in English, short fiction, poetry.

THE WASHINGTON MONTHLY, Paul Glastris, Editor-in-Chief; Charles Peters, Founding Editor; Joshua Green, Editor; Stephanie Mencimer, Editor, 733 15th Street NW, Suite 1000, Washington, DC 20005-6014, 202-393-5155. 1969. Articles, art, photos, satire, reviews, letters, non-fiction. "Art & photos commissioned to accompany articles." circ. 18M. 10/yr (combined Jan/Feb and July/Aug). Pub'd 10 issues 2005; expects 10 issues 2006, 10 issues 2007. sub. price $29.95; per copy $4.50; sample $5. Back issues: $5. 64pp. Reporting time: 2 months. Payment: 10¢/word. Copyrighted, does not revert to author. Pub's reviews: 60 in 2005. §Government, politics, public affairs, education, media, society, culture. Ads: $4000/$2500/rates are lower for publishers. Subjects: Book Reviewing, Communication, Journalism, Education, Government, Labor, Media, Non-Fiction, Political Science, Politics, Public Affairs, Society, Washington, D.C.

Washington State University Press, Glen Lindeman, PO Box 645910, Pullman, WA 99164-5910, 509-335-7880, 509-335-8568 (fax), 800-354-7360, wsupress@wsu.edu, wsupress.wsu.edu.

WASHINGTON TRAILS, Andrew Engelson, Managing Editor, 2019 3rd Ave., Suite #100, Seattle, WA 98121-2430, 206-625-1367, www.wta.org. 1966. Articles, art, photos, cartoons, interviews, reviews, letters, news items, non-fiction. "Editorial content is heavily weighted for *Pacific Northwest backpackers*, ski tourers, snow shoers, etc. We frequently purchase outside material, but pay not more than $25.00 per manuscript." circ. 6,000. 10/yr. Pub'd 10 issues 2005; expects 10 issues 2006, 10 issues 2007. sub. price $35; per copy $3.50; sample n/c. Back issues: $3.50. 40pp. Reporting time: 2 months. Copyrighted, reverts to author. Pub's reviews: 6 in 2005. §Hiking, backpacking, cross-country skiing, snowshoeing, nature study and related activities—all with NW focus where applicable. Ads: $285/$143/50¢-wd. $12 min. Subjects: Environment, Nature, Pacific Northwest, Sports, Outdoors.

Washington Writers' Publishing House, Moira Egan, President; Elisavietta Ritchie, Fiction Coordinator; Theresa Galvin, Treasurer; Sid Gold, Distribution Coordinator; Piotr Gwiazda, Publicity and Distribution, PO Box 15271, Washington, DC 20003, 301-652-5636, website: www.wwph.org, Megan@bcps.org (Egan), gwiazda@umbc.edu (Gwiazda), elisavietta@xchesapeake.net (Ritchie). 1975. Poetry, fiction. "Open to poets and fiction writers in the Greater Washington and Baltimore area only (a 60-mile radius from the Capitol). A *cooperative* press. Minimum of two year commitment to Press required. Annual deadline is November 1." avg. press run 750. Pub'd 3 titles 2005; expects 3 titles 2006, 3 titles 2007. Discounts: bulk orders-5 or more titles 40%; bookstores 20%. 64-72pp (poetry), 250pp (fiction). Reporting time: about 3-4 months, submissions are accepted only during submission period, July 1 to October 15, decisions made by end of year. Simultaneous submissions accepted: yes. Publishes 2-3% of manuscripts submitted. Payment: authors receive 50 copies and $500. Does not copyright for author. Subjects: Fiction, Poetry.

Water Mark Press, Coco Gordon, 138 Duane Street, New York, NY 10013, 212-285-1609, 914-238-6549, cocogord@mindspring.com, http://www.galerie.kultur.at/coco/base/core.htm. 1978. Poetry, art, photos, music, long-poems, collages, concrete art. "Works that are artist-book based with the artist book concept - merging avant garde writing with avant garde art and other avant garde visuals, photos, music, poetry. 2003 did an anthology of 45 artists and bioregionalists from 16 nations in *Visioning Life Systems* as an artist book in edition of 144 copies.TIKYSK (Things I Know You Should Know) now a subdivision of Water Mark Press for Permaculture/Bioregionally based projects and art." avg. press run 100. Pub'd 1 title 2005; expects 3 titles 2007. Discounts: 40% more than 2 copies of for 1980's series, 20% on handmade paper and special editions for more than 3 copies. Pages vary. Simultaneous submissions accepted: no. Payment: varies. varies. Subjects: Audio/Video, Avant-Garde, Experimental Art, Dada, Ecology, Foods, Environment, Poetry, Visual Arts, Zen.

Water Row Press (see also WATER ROW REVIEW), Cisco Harland, PO Box 438, Sudbury, MA 01776. 1985. Poetry, fiction, interviews, criticism, plays. "Our main focus are books and broadsides relative to the understanding and appreciation of the writings and times of 'Beat' writers. We are also seeking poetry and fiction from second generation 'Beats' and 'Outsiders'. Editions include signed limitations. Some recent contributors include Tom Clark, Arthur Knight, R. Crumb, Joy Walsh, William Burroughs. Any manuscripts which add to the understanding of Kerouac, Ginsberg, Bukowski are welcome. Tributes, poetry, dissertations, artwork. New poets' submissions always welcome." avg. press run 500-1M. Pub'd 5 titles 2005; expects 10 titles 2006, 10 titles 2007. Discounts: 2-5 copies 25%, 6 or more 40%, distributors inquire. Reporting time: 4-8 weeks. Payment: copies of work and additional payment on publication to be arranged. Copyrights for author. Subjects: Fiction, Jack Kerouac, Poetry.

WATER ROW REVIEW, Water Row Press, Cisco Harland, PO Box 438, Sudbury, MA 01776. 1986. Poetry, fiction, articles, interviews, criticism, reviews, parts-of-novels. "Recent contributors: William Burroughs, Charles Bukowski, Jeffrey Weinberg." circ. 2.5M. 4/yr. Pub'd 4 issues 2005; expects 4 issues 2006, 4 issues 2007. sub. price $24; per copy $6; sample $6. Discounts: 2-10 20%, 11 or more 40%. 100pp. Copyrighted. Pub's reviews: 12 in 2005. §Literature, fiction, poetry. Subjects: Jack Kerouac, Literary Review, Literature (General), Poetry.

WATER~STONE REVIEW, Mary Rockcastle, Editor; Sheila O'Connor, Prose Editor; Patricia Kirkpatrick, Poetry Editor, MS-A1730, 1536 Hewitt Avenue, Saint Paul, MN 55104-1284, water-stone@gw.hamline.edu. 1998. Poetry, fiction, interviews, reviews, non-fiction. circ. 2,000. 1/yr. sub. price $14; per copy $14. 275pp. Simultaneous submissions accepted: Yes. Pub's reviews: 2 in 2005. §We review poetry and creative nonfiction. We have our own reviewers and do not accept submissions for reviews. Ads: Full page, $250Half page, $150.

WATERFRONT WORLD SPOTLIGHT, 1622 Wisconsin Ave. N.W., Washington, DC 20007, 202-337-0356. 1981. Photos, news items. "No longer published as a magazine, only as electronic newsletter." circ. 1M-1.2M. 4/yr. Pub'd 4 issues 2005; expects 4 issues 2006, 4 issues 2007. Copyrighted. Pub's reviews: 20 in 2005. §Urban design, architecture, city planning, economic development, real estate, boating. Ads: none.

Waters Edge Press, 98 Main Street #527, Tiburon, CA 94920, 415-435-2837, Fax 415-435-2404, JAG@WatersEdgePress.com, www.WatersEdgePress.com. 1996. Art, photos, non-fiction. avg. press run 2.5M-10M. Expects 1 title 2006, 2 titles 2007. Discounts: 55% gift stores, (bookstores, libraries, gift stores through distributors), also Amazon.com, Barnes and Noble.com, Borders.com. 64pp. Simultaneous submissions accepted: yes. Copyrights for author.

Watershed Books, Joy Riley, Publisher, 9413 Southgate Drive, Cincinnati, OH 45241-3340, publisher@watershedbooks.com. 1995. Fiction, non-fiction. "Not accepting submissions." avg. press run varies. Expects 1 title 2006, 3 titles 2007. Discounts: wholesalers 55%, dealers 40%, 45% for unopened box of 48. Pages vary.

WATERWAYS: Poetry in the Mainstream, Bard Press, Ten Penny Players, Inc., Barbara Fisher, Co-Editor; Richard Spiegel, Co-Editor, 393 St. Pauls Avenue, Staten Island, NY 10304-2127, 718-442-7429, www.tenpennyplayers.org, bfisher@si.rr.com or rspiegel@si.rr.com. 1978. Poetry. "Our themes and sample issues are posted at our web site and should be used as guides before submitting. e-mail submissions can be sent as text and usually are answered more quickly. Recently published poets include Richard Kostelanetz, Ida Fasel, Sylvia Manning & John Grey." circ. 100-200. 11/yr. Pub'd 11 issues 2005; expects 11 issues 2006, 11 issues 2007. sub. price $33; per copy $3.50; sample $3.50. Back issues: $3.50 (includes postage). 40pp. Reporting time: 1 month. Simultaneous submissions accepted: yes. Publishes 50% of manuscripts submitted. Payment: copies. Copyrighted, reverts to author.

WAV MAGAZINE: Progressive Music Art Politics Culture, Wasim Muklashy, 3253 S. Beverly Dr., Los Angeles, CA 90034, (310) 876-0490. 2004. Poetry, fiction, articles, art, photos, cartoons, interviews, satire, criticism, reviews, music, non-fiction. "we're very interested in socially conscious artists in the fields of rock, hip-hop and electronic music, as well as artists, poets and writers with similar themes. We're trying to help build and nurture an environmentally conscious and globally cooperative society." circ. 20000. 4/yr. Pub'd 2 issues 2005; expects 4 issues 2006, 6 issues 2007. sub. price $14.99; per copy $3.99; sample free. Back issues: inquire. Discounts: inquire. 68pp. Reporting time: within a month. Simultaneous submissions accepted: Yes. Publishes 15% of manuscripts submitted. Payment: inquire. Copyrighted, reverts to author. Pub's reviews: approx. 20 in 2005. §books, music, dvds of a progressive nature. Ads: inquire. Subjects: Alternative Medicine, Anarchist, Arts, Audio/Video, Comics, Environment, Feminism, Global Affairs, Government, Human Rights, Humor, Media, Music, Non-Violence, Photography.

Wave Books, Joshua Beckman, Editor; Matthew Zapruder, Editor, 1938 Fairview Avenue East, Seattle, WA 98102, info@wavepoetry.com, www.wavepoetry.com. 2000. Poetry. "Wave Books is an independent poetry press based in Seattle, Washington. Dedicated to publishing the best in American poetry by new and established authors, Wave Books was founded in 2005, joining forces with already-established publisher Verse Press. Wave Books seeks to build on and expand the mission of Verse Press by publishing strong innovative work and encouraging our authors to expand and interact with their readership through nationwide readings and events, affirming our belief that the audience for poetry is larger and more diverse than commonly thought." avg. press run varies. Pub'd 6 titles 2005; expects 8 titles 2006, 8 titles 2007. Reporting time: 4 months. Payment: varies. Copyrights for author. Subject: Poetry.

Wave Publishing, Carol Doumani, 4 Yawl Street, Marina del Rey, CA 90292-7159, 310-306-0699. 1994. Fiction, non-fiction. "Our goal is to create the highest quality hardcover books." avg. press run 4M. Pub'd 1 title 2005; expects 1 title 2007. Discounts: 1-2 books 0%, 3-9 books 40%, 10-19 books 45%, 20+ books 50%. 360pp. Simultaneous submissions accepted: no. Publishes 0% of manuscripts submitted. Subjects: Cooking, Fiction.

WAVELENGTH: A Magazine of Poetry in Prose and Verse, Dr. David Rogers, 1753 Fisher Ridge Road, Horse Cave, KY 42749. 2000. Poetry. "I've published Robert Cooperman, Lyn Lifshin, Louis Phillips, Simon Perchik, others. Don't care for rhymed verse, but will consider it if good. Don't care for religious unless they challenge convention somehow. Odd spacing that bounces all over the page is usually a turn-off. Above all, however, the publishable poem is exciting, entertaining *and* thought-provoking for the reader. More poets should ask themselves what the reader will find attractive in their work before sending it out. Longer poems (2-3 pages, up to 100 lines) ok if good." circ. 100. 3/yr. Pub'd 3 issues 2005; expects 3 issues 2006, 3 issues 2007. sub. price $15; per copy $6; sample $6. Back issues: $6. Discounts: none. 25-75pp. Reporting time: 3-4 months. I accept simultaneous submissions, but I consider publishing rights to be granted by submitting the poem; thus I will not reprint the entire magazine if someone tries to withdraw a simultaneous submission after it's printed. Publishes 10% of manuscripts submitted. Payment: 1 copy. Copyrighted, reverts to author. Pub's reviews: 2 in 2005. §Poetry only. Ads: $25/$15. Subject: Poetry.

Wayfarer Publications (see also TAI CHI), Marvin Smalheiser, PO Box 39938, Los Angeles, CA 90039, 323-665-7773. 1981. Articles, interviews, reviews, letters, news items, non-fiction. avg. press run 20M. Pub'd 1 title 2005; expects 2 titles 2006, 3 titles 2007. Simultaneous submissions accepted: no. Subjects: Health, Spiritual.

Wayfinder Press, Marcus E. Wilson, PO Box 217, Ridgway, CO 81432, 970-626-5452. 1980. Non-fiction. "We specialize in history and guide books about the Southwest." avg. press run 3M. Pub'd 2 titles 2005; expects 2 titles 2006, 2 titles 2007. Discounts: bookstores 40%, jobbers 50%. 150pp. Reporting time: 10 days. Simultaneous submissions accepted: yes. Publishes 1% of manuscripts submitted. Payment: quarterly. Does not copyright for author. Subjects: History, Sports, Outdoors.

Wayside Publications, N. Nottingham, PO Box 318, Goreville, IL 62939, n.nott@waysidepub.com, www.waysidepub.com. 2004. Articles. "Wayside publishes 'Teacher Tips' books for religious teachers of children, ages 4-11. Each book is a collection of ideas from several authors. These books feature all aspects of children's worship (i.e. Bible lessons, puzzles, games, activities, crafts, puppets, songs, prayer, discipline, and more). Submissions must be original, unpublished material, written in a clear, concise manner. Artistic ability is not required, but rough sketches are encouraged, if necessary to portray an idea. We are looking for fresh, easy, fun activities and lessons that are not limited to a specific denomination. Email submission preferred. Payment is made in copies of the published book. This is a great opportunity for new authors to obtain writing credits. Recent contributor: Violet Toler." avg. press run 1000. Expects 6 titles 2006, 4-6 titles 2007. Discounts: 40% retail bookstore, 20% libraries, 50% dealers (200+ books), 30% STOP orders. 55pp. Reporting time: 4 weeks.

Payment: $10 and one copy of the book for each published idea. Does not copyright for author. Subjects: Children, Youth, Crafts, Hobbies, How-To, Religion.

Weber State University (see also WEBER STUDIES: Voices and Viewpoints of the Contemporary West), Brad L. Roghaar, Weber State University, 1214 University Circle, Ogden, UT 84408-1214, 801-626-6616, 801-262-6473, weberstudies@weber.edu, http://weberstudies.weber.edu.

WEBER STUDIES: Voices and Viewpoints of the Contemporary West, Weber State University, Brad L. Roghaar, Editor; Michael Wutz, Associate Editor; Kathryn MacKay, Associate Editor, Weber State University, 1214 University Circle, Ogden, UT 84408-1214, 801-626-6473 or 6616. 1984. Poetry, fiction, articles, art, photos, interviews, parts-of-novels, long-poems, non-fiction. "Recent Contributors: Robert Dana, Ken Burns, Robert Pinsky, Waddie Mitchell, Ken Brewer, Michael Schumacher, Gary Gildner, Maxine Hong Kingston, Carlos Fuentes, Amy Ling, William Kloefkorn, Dipti Ranjan Pattanaik, David James Duncan, Max Oelschlaeger, James Welch, Janice Gould, Louis Owens, Robin Cohen, David Lee, Katharine Coles, Raquel Valle-Senties, Robert Hodgson Wagoner, Linda Sillito, Stephen Trimble, Wayne C. Booth, Virgil Suarez, Robert Olmstead, Kate Wheeler, Nancy Kline, David Quammen, Peggy Shumaker, Pattiann Rogers, Terry Tempest Williams, Joseph M. Ditta, Ron McFarland, Daniel R. Schwarz, Barry Lopez, and Chitra Banervee Divakaruni. Length of articles: 2,000 to 5,000 words. We are known for our fiction/interview series in which we feature original work by an author followed by an interview with her/him in the same issue. We like to publish 2-3 pages of poetry per poet in order to give a genuine flavor of the poet to our readers. Generally we ask for about 3-5 poems for submission. We like manuscripts that inform the culture and environment (both broadly defined) of the contemporary Western United States." circ. 1K-1.2K. 3/yr. Pub'd 3 issues 2005; expects 3 issues 2006, 3 issues 2007. sub. price $30 institutions, $20 individuals; per copy $8; sample $8. Back issues: $10. Discounts: 15%. 132pp. Reporting time: 3-4 months. Simultaneous submissions accepted: yes. Publishes 5% of manuscripts submitted. Payment: $100-$300 or more depending on our grant monies and length of mss. Copyrighted, reverts to author. Ads: none. Subjects: Conservation, Environment, Essays, Fiction, History, Interviews, Multicultural, Native American, Nature, Non-Fiction, Poetry, Short Stories, Southwest, Utah, The West.

WEIRD TALES, George Scithers, Editor; Darrell Schweitzer, Editor, 6644 Rutland St., Philadelphia, PA 19149-2128. 1923. Poetry, fiction. "Weird fiction up to 10K words. We're looking for the best in fantasy-based horror, heroic fantasy, and exotic mood pieces plus the occasional odd story that won't fit anywhere else." circ. 9M. 4/yr. Pub'd 4 issues 2005; expects 4 issues 2006, 4 issues 2007. sub. price $16; per copy $5.95; sample $6. Discounts: inquire. 58pp. Reporting time: 1-2 months. Simultaneous submissions accepted: no. Publishes 5% of manuscripts submitted. Payment: 3¢-6¢ on acceptance. Copyrighted. Pub's reviews. §Horror, fantasy, related criticism.

Wellcome Institute for the History of Medicine (see also MEDICAL HISTORY), 210 Euston Road, London NW1 2BE, England. Subjects: Alternative Medicine, Disease, Health, History, Medicine, Nursing, Society.

The Wellsweep Press, John Cayley, Harold Wells, Unit 3 Ashburton Centre276 Cortis Road, 276 Cortis Road, London SW15 3AY, United Kingdom, ws@shadoof.net. 1988. Poetry, fiction, non-fiction. "Specializes in literary translation from Chinese literature." avg. press run 750-1M. Pub'd 4 titles 2005; expects 5 titles 2006, 5-6 titles 2007. Discounts: trade 35%. 96pp. Reporting time: can be 2 months. Payment: by arrangement, up to 6%. Subjects: China, Essays, Fiction, Literature (General), Non-Fiction.

WELSH HISTORY REVIEW, University Of Wales Press, Kenneth O. Morgan, Editor; Ralph A. Griffiths, Assistant Editor, 10 Columbus Walk, Brigantine Place, Cardiff CF10 4UP, Wales, 44-029-2049-6899, Fax 44-029-2049-6108, press@press.wales.ac.uk, www.wales.ac.uk/press. 1960. Articles. "Articles in English on various aspects of Welsh history." circ. 500. 2/yr. Pub'd 2 issues 2005; expects 2 issues 2006, 2 issues 2007. sub. price £13; per copy £6.50; sample £6.50. Back issues: £6.50. Discounts: 10%. 120pp. Payment: none. Copyrighted, does not revert to author. Pub's reviews: 20 in 2005. §History, esp. Welsh history. Ads: £75/£37.50. Subject: History.

WELSH JOURNAL OF EDUCATION, University Of Wales Press, John Fitz, Editor; Sian Rhiannon Williams, Reviews Editor; Gareth Elwyn Jones, Consultant Editor, 10 Columbus Walk, Brigantine Place, Cardiff CF10 4UP, Wales, 44-029-2049-6899, Fax 44-029-2049-6108, press@press.wales.ac.uk, www.wales.ac.uk/press. Articles, reviews. circ. 500. Pub'd 2 issues 2005. sub. price £30 institutions, £20 individuals; per copy £15. Discounts: 10%. 64pp. Payment: none. Copyrighted, reverts to author. Pub's reviews. §Education. Ads: £75/£37.50. Subject: Education.

WELSH MUSIC HISTORY, University Of Wales Press, John Harper, Editor; Wyn Thomas, Welsh Editor, 10 Columbus Walk, Brigantine Place, Cardiff CF10 4UP, Wales, 44-029-2049-6899, Fax 44-029-2049-6108, press@press.wales.ac.uk, www.wales.ac.uk/press. 1996. Articles. circ. 300. 1/yr. Pub'd 1 issue 2005; expects 1 issue 2006, 1 issue 2007. sub. price £15. Discounts: 10%. 220pp. Subject: Music.

Wesleyan University Press, Suzanna Tamminen, Director, Editor-in-Chief; Eric Levy, Acquisitions Editor, 215 Long Lane, Middletown, CT 06459, 860-685-7711. 1957. avg. press run 1500. Pub'd 38 titles 2005; expects 25 titles 2006, 24 titles 2007. 256pp. Reporting time: 3-4 months. We only occasionally accept simultaneous submissions. Publishes 5% of manuscripts submitted. Payment: dependent on author. Copyrights for author.

The Wessex Collective, Sandra Shwayder Sanchez, P.O. Box 1088, Nederland, CO 80466, 303-258-3004. 2005. Fiction. ''Wessex Collective is a non-profit publisher committed to publishing fiction of social significance. Authors of 2005 titles include Peter Burnham, Sandra Shwayder Sanchez, Ita Willen, Brian Backstrand and William Davey.'' avg. press run 500. Expects 6 titles 2006, 6 titles 2007. Discounts: 40% to bookstoresall others 12 or more copies 10%. 125-300pp. Reporting time: We are not taking submissions. We read mss. by invitation only. Simultaneous submissions accepted: No. Payment: This is a non-profit collective and authors are not paid for first publication rights. Proceeds from sale of subsidiary rights goes to the author. Authors are expected to do own copyright applications.

WEST BRANCH, Paula Closson Buck, Editor; Andrew Ciotola, Managing Editor, Bucknell Hall, Bucknell University, Lewisburg, PA 17837, 570-577-1853, westbranch@bucknell.edu. 1977. Poetry, fiction, articles, criticism, reviews, parts-of-novels, long-poems, non-fiction. ''*West Branch* publishes fiction, poetry, nonfiction, and reviews in a range of styles from the traditional to the innovative. We are open to work from both new and established writers.'' circ. 1M. 2/yr. Pub'd 2 issues 2005; expects 2 issues 2006, 2 issues 2007. sub. price $10; per copy $6; sample $3. Back issues: $4. Discounts: 20-40% to bookstores. 118-140pp. Reporting time: 6-10 weeks. We accept simultaneous submissions if marked as such. Publishes 5% of manuscripts submitted. Payment: $10/page ($20 min./$100 max.) and 2 copies. Copyrighted, reverts to author. Pub's reviews: 4 in 2005. §Contemporary fiction, poetry, all modes of literary nonfiction. Ads: exchange ads only. Subjects: Essays, Fiction, Literary Review, Non-Fiction, Poetry.

WEST COAST LINE: A Journal of Contemporary Writing and Criticism, Miriam Nichols, Editor; Roger Farr, Managing Editor, 2027 EAA, Simon Fraser University, Burnaby, B.C. V5A 1S6, Canada. 1990. Interviews, criticism. ''Criticism, bibliography, reviews, and interviews concerned with contemporary writing, poetry and short fiction.'' circ. 500. 3/yr. Pub'd 3 issues 2005; expects 3 issues 2006, 3 issues 2007. sub. price $25 individuals, $40 libraries; per copy $10; sample $10. Back issues: $8. Discounts: $7 agents & jobbers. 128-144pp. Reporting time: 6-8 months. Simultaneous submissions accepted: no. Publishes 20% of manuscripts submitted. Payment: 2 contributor's copies & modest royalty fee. Copyrighted, reverts to author. Pub's reviews: 3 in 2005. §Experimental postmodern poetry, prose, criticism, cultural studies, art history, poetics, aesthetics. Subjects: Avant-Garde, Experimental Art, Canada, Criticism, Language, Multicultural, Poetry, Post Modern, Race.

West Coast Paradise Publishing, Robert G. Anstey, PO Box 2093, Sardis Sta. Main, Sardis, B.C. V2R 1A5, Canada, 604-824-9528, Fax 604-824-9541, web:http://rg.anstey.ca/. 1993. Poetry, fiction, non-fiction. avg. press run 100. Pub'd 12 titles 2005; expects 12 titles 2006, 12 titles 2007. Reporting time: 1 week. Simultaneous submissions accepted: yes. Publishes 90% of manuscripts submitted. Copyrights for author. Subjects: Autobiography, Biography, Fiction, Music, Non-Fiction, Poetry.

West End Press, PO Box 27334, Albuquerque, NM 87125. 1976. Poetry, fiction, art, music, long-poems, plays, non-fiction. ''Politically progressive material favored.'' avg. press run 1M-2M. Pub'd 4 titles 2005; expects 2 titles 2006, 3 titles 2007. Discounts: write for info. 48-192pp. Reporting time: 2 to 3 months. Simultaneous submissions accepted: no. Publishes 1% of manuscripts submitted. Payment: in copies, 10% of run; 6% cash payment for initial print run; rest is negotiable. Copyrights for author. Subjects: African-American, Asian-American, Chicano/a, Feminism, Humanism, Native American, Politics, Socialist, Women, Worker.

West Virginia University Press, Patrick Conner, P.O. Box 6295, G3 White Hall, Morgantown, WV 26506, Office (304) 293-8400, Toll free for orders (866) 988-7737, Fax (304) 293-6585. 1963. Poetry, fiction, art, photos, criticism, music, parts-of-novels, non-fiction. ''The mission of the WVU Press is to publish scholary works on a wide variety of subjects and to publish books of interest to the general reader with a focus on Appalachia.'' avg. press run 3000. Pub'd 7 titles 2005; expects 12 titles 2006, 12-14 titles 2007. Discounts: Retail trade discounts 1-4 copies 20%, 5+ 40% except short discount titles (s) which are 20% regardless of quantity. 300pp. Reporting time: One month. Simultaneous submissions accepted: No. Publishes 25% of manuscripts submitted. Payment: Varies. Copyrights for author. Subjects: African Literature, Africa, African Studies, Agriculture, Arts, Black, Civil War, Classical Studies, Fiction, Gay, Literature (General), Music, Native American, Poetry, Political Science, Politics, Race.

WESTERN AMERICAN LITERATURE, Melody Graulich, Editor; Evelyn Funda, Book Review Editor, English Dept., Utah State Univ., 3200 Old Main Hill, Logan, UT 84322-3200, 435-797-1603, Fax 435-797-4099, wal@cc.usu.edu. 1966. Articles, art, photos, cartoons, interviews, criticism, reviews. ''Send books for review to Book Review Editor. No unsolicited reviews.'' circ. 1M+. 4/yr. Pub'd 4 issues 2005;

expects 4 issues 2006, 4 issues 2007. sub. price $22 individuals, $65 institutions, $30 for individuals who want to be members of the Western Literature Association, $25 students; per copy $7.50 indiv., $13 libraries; sample free back issues (based on availability). Back issues: $7.50 indiv., $13 libraries. Discounts: 20% agency. 112pp. Reporting time: 2 months. Simultaneous submissions accepted: no. Publishes 10% of manuscripts submitted. Payment: 1 copy, tear sheets (for articles); tear sheets only for reviewers. Copyrighted, does not revert to author. Pub's reviews: 100-120 in 2005. §Books by western authors, about western authors or western literature, or books that focus on the West. Ads: $150/$90/no classifieds. Subjects: Folklore, Great Plains, Robinson Jeffers, Jack Kerouac, Literary Review, Literature (General), Jack London, Southwest, Texas, Visual Arts, The West.

WESTERN HUMANITIES REVIEW, Barry Weller, Editor; Karen Brennan, Fiction Editor; Richard Howard, Poetry Editor; David McGlynn, Managing Editor, University of Utah, Salt Lake City, UT 84112, 801-581-6070. 1947. Poetry, fiction, articles, art, interviews, satire, criticism, reviews, music, letters, parts-of-novels, long-poems, plays, concrete art, non-fiction. "We prefer 2-3M words; We print articles in the humanities, fiction, poetry, and film and book reviews. Recent contributors: Joseph Brodsky, Jeanette Haien, Deborah Eisenberg, Tom Disch, Allen Grossman, Debora Greger, Bin Ramke, Nicholas Christopher, Lucie Brock-Broido, James McManus, Richard Pairier, Helen Vendler." circ. 1.5M. 4/yr. Pub'd 4 issues 2005; expects 4 issues 2006. sub. price $20 (institutions) $20 (individuals); per copy $10; sample $10. Back issues: $10. Discounts: 25% to agents. 150pp. Reporting time: 3-6 months. Simultaneous submissions accepted: yes. Publishes less than 1% of manuscripts submitted. Payment: $5 per printed page, $10 minimum. Copyrighted, rights revert to author on request. We don't use ads. Subjects: Literary Review, Literature (General).

Western New York Wares, Inc., Brian S. Meyer, PO Box 733, Ellicott Station, Buffalo, NY 14205, 716-832-6088, www.wnybooks.com. 1984. Non-fiction. "We specialize in publishing regional books that focus on western New York's people, attractions, architecture, and rich history." Pub'd 2 titles 2005; expects 3 titles 2006, 3 titles 2007. Discounts: 40% to authorized vendors on orders of 12+, 10% for small orders. 96pp. Reporting time: 6 weeks. Simultaneous submissions accepted: no. Publishes 3% of manuscripts submitted. Payment: 50% of net profits. Does not copyright for author. Subjects: Architecture, History, Nature, Travel.

Westgate Press, Lorraine Chandler, Editor, 2137 Alexandria Hwy, Leesville, LA 71446-7355. 1979. Art, photos, collages, non-fiction. "Metaphysical material, occult science and philosophy, esoteric mss. in related areas. Presently we are publishing *The Book Of Azrael* by Leilah Wendell, 'an intimate and first person encounter with the True Personification of Death! This dark and melancholy Angel is revealed through the writings of His Earthbound 'Bride' as well as direct communications with the Angel of Death Himself! Never before and never again will a book of this nature be offered. *This is not fiction.* But rather an account of the journey of an ancient spirit from the beginning of time to the present and beyond!...A Divine Dance Macabre!' That should give you an idea of what we are interested in. We request that *only queries* be sent at this time with appropriate SASE." avg. press run 500-5M. Pub'd 3 titles 2005; expects 3 titles 2006, 5 titles 2007. Discounts: 1-5 books 20%, 6-25 40%, 26-50 43%, 51-100 46%, 100+ 50%, discount applies to booksellers and others. 200+pp. Reporting time: 1 month on ms., 2 weeks on query. Simultaneous submissions accepted: yes. Publishes 20% of manuscripts submitted. Payment: negotiable on a project to project basis; no advance at present. Copyrights for author. Subjects: Arts, Euthanasia, Death, Fantasy, Folklore, Graphics, Metaphysics, New Age, Non-Fiction, Occult, Philosophy, Postcards, Prose, Supernatural, Surrealism, Visual Arts.

Westhampton Publishing, Jessica Lay, 3540 Crain Highway, PMB #162, Bowie, MD 20716, 301-249-8733, fax 301-249-4119, web: www.WesthamptonPublishing.com.

WESTVIEW, James Silver, Editor; Kevin Collins, Managing Editor; John Bradshaw, Assistant Editor; Joel Kendall, Publications Manager; Joyce Stoffers, Non-Fiction Editor, SW Oklahoma State University, Language Arts Dept, 100 Campus Dr., Weatherford, OK 73096, 580-774-3242, Fax 580-774-7111, james.silver@swosu.edu. 1981. Poetry, fiction, articles, art, photos, interviews, criticism, reviews, parts-of-novels, long-poems, plays, non-fiction. "*Westview* publishes fiction, poetry, drama, nonfiction, book reviwes, scholarly work, literary criticism, and artwork. *Westview* holds only the first rights for all works published unless otherwise specified. Recent contributors: Miller Williams, Carolyne Wright, Walter McDonald, and Alicia Ostriker." circ. 300. 2/yr. Pub'd 2 issues 2005; expects 2 issues 2006, 2 issues 2007. sub. price $15/2 years within US, $25 all others; per copy $5; sample $5. Back issues: $5. Discounts: inquire. 76pp. Reporting time: 3-6 months. Simultaneous submissions accepted if notified should poem be taken elsewhere. Publishes 5% of manuscripts submitted. Payment: copies. Copyrighted, reverts to author. Pub's reviews. §Regional topics, poetry, art related. Ads: $450/$300/$150 1/4 page/$75 1/8 page (all prices are for 4 issues).

Westview Press, 11 Cambridge Center, Cambridge, MA 02142, j.mccrary@perseusbooks.com, www.westviewpress.com.

WeWrite LLC, Delores Palmer, Publisher, 11040 Alba Road, Ben Lomond, CA 95005-9220, dpalmer@wewrite.net, www.wewrite.net. 1993. Poetry, fiction, art, cartoons. "Physical address: 11040 Alba Rd, Ben Lomond, California 95005. Publisher: specializing in books by kids, for kids called WeWrite Kids.

Created within a workshop setting. An illustrator sketches while children brainstorm and act out story ideas." avg. press run 1M-15M. Pub'd 1 title 2005; expects 4 titles 2006, 20 titles 2007. Discounts: jobber 40%. 60pp. Reporting time: Less than 6 months. Simultaneous submissions accepted: yes. Publishes 80% of manuscripts submitted. Payment: none, prepaid by client quantity purchase. Copyright for author, and we own most copyrights. Subjects: Business & Economics, Cartoons, Children, Youth, Education, Finances, Marketing, Prison.

Whalesback Books, W.D. Howells, Box 9546, Washington, DC 20016, 202-333-2182. 1988. Art, photos, non-fiction. "Books of interest to museums: art, architecture and graphic presentations." avg. press run 2M-5M. Pub'd 1 title 2005; expects 1-2 titles 2006, 2 titles 2007. Discounts: standard. 200-300pp. Payment: negotiable. Copyrights for author. Subjects: Anthropology, Archaelogy, Antiques, Architecture, Arts, Photography.

Wharton Publishing, Inc., T. Losasso, 2683 Via De La Valle, Suite G #210, Del Mar, CA 92014, 760-931-8977, Fax 858-759-7097, e-mail marketingtina@aol.com. 1991. Non-fiction. "Effective and easy to apply information that impacts people's wealth, health, relationships, time or attitude. Books with commercial tie-ins to products or services." Pub'd 1 title 2005; expects 2 titles 2006, 4 titles 2007. 140pp. Reporting time: 30 days or less. Simultaneous submissions accepted: no. Payment: varies. Copyrights for author. Subjects: Health, How-To, Non-Fiction.

WHAT IS ENLIGHTENMENT?, Enlighten Next, Andrew Cohen, Editor in Chief; Craig Hamilton, Managing Editor; Carter Phipps, Editor, PO Box 2360, Lenox, MA 01240-5360, 413-637-6000, Fax 413-637-6015, wie@wie.org. 1991. Articles, photos, cartoons, interviews, criticism, reviews, letters, non-fiction. "Recent contributors: Ken Wilber, Dalai Lama, Howard Bloom." circ. 65K. 4/yr. Pub'd 2 issues 2005; expects 4 issues 2006, 4 issues 2007. sub. price $19.95; per copy $7.50; sample $7.50. Back issues: $9. Discounts: 40%. 140pp. Simultaneous submissions accepted: No. Copyrighted, rights possibly revert to author on publication. Pub's reviews: 10 in 2005. §Spirituality. Ads: $1340/$820 color; $970/600 B&W. Subjects: Book Reviewing, Environment, Ethics, Futurism, Inspirational, Judaism, Philosophy, Politics, Post Modern, Psychology, Religion, Science, Spiritual, Theosophical, Zen.

What The Heck Press, Jenny Stein, PO Box 149, Ithaca, NY 14851-0149, 607-275-0806, Fax 607-275-0702. 1992. Poetry, fiction, non-fiction. "Childrens audio. Currently not accepting submissions." avg. press run 5M. Discounts: trade 40%, call or write for discounts on large or special orders. 100pp. Payment: confidential. Copyrights for author. Subject: Children, Youth.

Wheatmark Book Publishing, Atilla Vekony, Publishing Consultant, 610 East Delano Street, Suite 104, Tucson, AZ 85705-5210, 888-934-0888, 520-798-0888, 520-798-3394 (fax), http://www.bookpublisher.com. 1999. Poetry, fiction, long-poems, plays, non-fiction. "Print-on-demand (POD) and short run book publisher offering personalized publishing services, including design, editing, distribution and self-publishing." Discounts: Booksellers = 40% Wholesalers = 55% Fully returnable. Reporting time: Quickly. Payment: 20% royalties are paid quarterly, no advances offered. Will officially copyright as per author's wishes. Subjects: Advertising, Self-Promotion, Arizona, Business & Economics, Christianity, Literature (General), Management, Memoirs, Non-Fiction, Parenting, Politics, Real Estate, Religion, Research, Self-Help, Speaking.

Whelks Walk Press, Marianne Mitchell, Publisher; Joan Peternel, Editor, 37 Harvest Lane, Southampton, NY 11968, whelkswalk@aol.com. 1995. Poetry, fiction, articles, art, photos, interviews, criticism, reviews. "The *Whelks Walk Review* has ceased publication. Two books were published by the Press: *Howl and Hosanna*, poems (1997) and *Nintotem: Indiana Stories* (1999), both by Joan Peternel. The Press has been inactive since 2000, but do check us again in 2006." Copyrights for author. Subjects: Arts, Culture, Fiction, Movies, Performing Arts, Poetry, Prose, Television.

which press, Jonathan Miller, P.O. Box 10159, San Jose, CA 95157, info@whichpress.com / www.whichpress.com / (866) 830-0924. 2000. Poetry, fiction, articles, art, photos, cartoons, interviews, satire, criticism, reviews, music, parts-of-novels, long-poems, collages, concrete art, news items, non-fiction. "Which Press was created for those who grapple with the one word question: *which?* To which category, which segment, which nation, which group - if any - do I belong? The press is meant to provide a voice for individuals whose identities and/or creative work lie *between* the accepted categories most take for granted. As such, we seek authors who identify personally with this mission. We look for instructive, inspiring, and entertaining works that contain their unique voice. Which Press publishes literary novels, full-length short story collections, poetry, visual artwork and essays year-round. We also publish individual short fiction pieces, poetry, essays, visual artwork, book and film reviews, commentary and interviews biannually in our literary magazine called Be Which. *Please visit www.whichpress.com for submission instructions.*" Reporting time: 4-6 weeks. Simultaneous submissions accepted: No. Payment: For full-length books: Author receives a royalty on the net revenues of 80%; Non-binding in the event that an author is approached by a larger publisher; Advances of up to $1,000 as the work is prepared for publication; Author takes a significant role in the marketing and sale of the work once published. For Be Which Magazine contributions: payment in the form of copies. Copyrights for author. Subjects: Avant-Garde, Experimental Art, Book Reviewing, Fiction, Gay, Gender Issues, Interviews, Multicultural, Non-Fiction, Poetry, Race, Short Stories.

Whiskey Creek Press, Debra Womack, Publisher & Executive Editor; Jan Janssen, Executive Editor - Torrid Romance Division; Marsha Briscoe, Senior Editor; Chere Gruver, Senior Editor - Torrid Romance Division, P.O. Box 51052, Casper, WY 82605-1052, 307-265-8585 (fax only), email: publisher@whiskeycreek-press.com, websites: www.whiskeycreekpress.com, www.whiskeycreekpresstorrid.com. 2003. Fiction, non-fiction. "Our editorial mission is to bring quality works of Fiction and Non-Fiction by outstanding authors to our reading public." Pub'd 100 titles 2005; expects 150 titles 2006, 150 titles 2007. Discounts: Up to 40% for qualified wholesale orders. 280pp. Reporting time: 90-120 days, depending on the number of received submissions. Simultaneous submissions accepted: No. Publishes 10% of manuscripts submitted. Payment: 2 year contract required, royalties paid to authors quarterly at 30% for ebooks and 7.5% for paperbacks. No advances. Does not copyright for author. Subjects: Anthology, Erotica, Fantasy, Fiction, Horror, Humor, Inspirational, Mystery, Non-Fiction, Old West, Romance, Science Fiction, Self-Help, Supernatural, Young Adult.

Whispering Pine Press, Matthew Wilson, Director of Marketing and Sales, 507 N. Sullivan Rd. Ste. A-7, Spokane Valley, WA 99037-8531, Phone: (509) 927-0404, Fax: (509) 927-1550, Web: www.whisperingpine-press.com, E-Mail: whisperingpinepressinc@hotmail.com. 2000. Poetry, non-fiction. "We specialize in publication of wholesome, family-oriented reading material. Our line of titles includes cookbooks, regional humor, children's literature, Christian-themed books and journals, books about and for foster and adopted children, juvenile horse-themed activity and coloring books, etc..." avg. press run 500. Pub'd 5 titles 2005; expects 10 titles 2006, 12 titles 2007. Discounts: 2 copies 40%. 300pp. Simultaneous submissions accepted: No. Subjects: Adolescence, Adoption, African Literature, Africa, African Studies, African-American, Americana, Animals, Cooking, Family, Folklore, Gardening, Gender Issues, Pacific Northwest, Picture Books, Poetry, Washington (state).

WHISPERING WIND MAGAZINE, Jack B. Heriard, PO Box 1390, Folsom, LA 70437-1390, 504-796-5433, whiswind@i-55.com, www.whisperingwind.com. 1967. Articles, art, photos, cartoons, interviews, reviews, letters, news items. "Magazine for those interested in the American Indian; the traditions and crafts, past and present." circ. 24M. 6/yr. Pub'd 6 issues 2005; expects 6 issues 2006, 6 issues 2007. sub. price $21; per copy $4.50; sample $6. Back issues: included in each issue. Discounts: 5-20 $2.70 each. 56pp. Reporting time: 4-8 weeks. Simultaneous submissions accepted: yes. Publishes 80% of manuscripts submitted. Payment: copies and subscription. Copyrighted, does not revert to author. Pub's reviews: 25 in 2005. §American Indian. Ads: $362/$186/60¢. Subjects: Crafts, Hobbies, Culture, How-To, Indians, Native American.

White Buck Publishing, David J. Thomas, Editor-in-Chief; Rebekka K. Nielson, Poetry Editor, 5187 Colorado Avenue, Sheffield Village, OH 44054-2338, 440-934-7117 phone/fax, submissions@whitebuckpublishing.com. 1996. Poetry, art, photos, criticism, long-poems, non-fiction. "Accept only material which reflect Christian theology, ethics, and morals. Work with book length manuscripts only. Poetry, non-fiction, apologetics, etc. are solicited." avg. press run 10-25M. Expects 2 titles 2006, 4 titles 2007. Discounts: retail base 40%, wholesale 50-55%, distribution 60-65%; sliding scale on basis of single order quantity. 225pp. Reporting time: 12-18 months. Simultaneous submissions accepted: yes. Publishes 1-3% of manuscripts submitted. Payment: as circumstances dictate. Copyrights for author if requested. Subjects: Catholic, Christianity, Grieving, Poetry, Religion, Spiritual, Theosophical.

White Cliffs Media, Inc., Lawrence Aynesmith, PO Box 6083, Incline Village, NV 89450. 1985. Poetry, art, photos, music. "Current emphasis is on innovative publications in world and popular music. Compact Discs, cassettes often included. General trade titles also considered. Current title: *The Healing Power of the Drum* by Robert Lawrence Friedman." avg. press run varies. Pub'd 12 titles 2005; expects 3 titles 2006, 10 titles 2007. Discounts: follow industry standards. 180pp. Reporting time: 1-3 months. Publishes 10% of manuscripts submitted. Payment: varies. Copyrights for author. Subjects: African Literature, Africa, African Studies, Anthropology, Archaelogy, Arts, Biography, Black, Caribbean, Chicano/a, Computers, Calculators, Cults, Folklore, Music, Third World, Minorities.

•**White Crosslet Publishing Co,** Marc Anthony Hatsis, 456 West Lake Road, tuxedo park, NY 10987, 845 351 3345 (fax&telephone). 2006. Poetry, fiction, articles, art, photos, interviews, satire, criticism, reviews, parts-of-novels, collages, plays, non-fiction. "White Crosslet Publishing Co is committed to publishing works which combine an aesthetic foundation (art, poetry, fiction, contemporary artist monographs), with a marked esoteric or symbolic element. For 2006 White Crosslet is publishing two cookbooks on raw foods which are heavily illustrated throughout with symbolic line drawings by Marc-Anthony Hatsis. Other titles deal with esoteric vegetarianism, the tarot, and elaborately illustrated limited edition books of poetry. One forthcoming work of poetry entitled "tempestad" is by Spanish poet and critic Ilia Galan, the book will be illustrated by Marc

Anthony Hatsis.'' avg. press run 15000. Expects 10 titles 2006, 15 titles 2007. Discounts: 2-10 copies 25%10-49 copies 40%50-99 copies 46%100+copies 50%. 200pp. Reporting time: one week. Simultaneous submissions accepted: Yes. Payment: we usually purchase works on a "work for hire" basis, but could entertain possible royalty contract arrangements. Copyrights for author. Subjects: Absurdist, Arts, Astrology, Avant-Garde, Experimental Art, Cults, Dada, Drama, Experimental, Hypnosis, Magic, New Age, Non-Fiction, Occult, Tarot, Vegetarianism.

WHITE CROW, Osric Publishing, Christopher Herdt, PO Box 4501, Ann Arbor, MI 48106. 1994. Poetry, fiction, art, photos. ''Send fiction submissions to fiction@wcrow.com; poetry submissions to poetry@wcrow.com. Guidelines available on Web site: www.wcrow.com.'' circ. 200. 2/yr. Pub'd 4 issues 2005; expects 4 issues 2006, 4 issues 2007. sub. price $8; per copy $2.50; sample $2. Discounts: 50% to libraries and teachers. 32pp. Reporting time: 6 months. Simultaneous submissions accepted: yes. Publishes 2% of manuscripts submitted. Payment: negotiable, copies. Not copyrighted. Pub's reviews: none in 2005. §Literature, zines. Ads: $20/$10. Subjects: Fiction, Poetry.

White Eagle Coffee Store Press (see also FRESH GROUND), Rotating, PO Box 383, Fox River Grove, IL 60021, 708-639-9200. 1992. Poetry, fiction. ''Poetry and fiction chapbooks by invitation and by competition. Literary only.'' avg. press run 400+. Pub'd 2 titles 2005; expects 6 titles 2006, 6 titles 2007. Discounts: negotiable, usually 40%. 28pp. Reporting time: 8-10 weeks. Payment: copies. Copyrights for author. Subjects: Fiction, Poetry.

•WHITE LOTUS, Shadow Poetry, Marie Summers, Editor, 1209 Milwaukee Street, Excelsior Springs, MO 64024, (208) 977-9114. 2005. Poetry, photos, interviews, reviews. ''White Lotus accepts high quality submissions of these forms: haiku and senryu. Haiga, sumi-e, and haiku related articles and/or book reviews are welcome. Send up to ten pieces per poet for review with the appropriate seasonal theme in accordance with the next issue to be released by mail, email to whitelotus@shadowpoetry.com, or submit via online forms. Originality is a requirement. We reserve the right to reject submissions as a whole that do not contain original pieces or thoughts. Name of the poet, address, and email address (if applicable) must accompany all submissions, no exceptions. If submitting by mail, please supply a #10 SASE, no postcards. All work, if accepted, must be the original work(s) of the poet/author/artist and previously unpublished. No web published material permitted.'' 2/yr. Pub'd 2 issues 2005; expects 2 issues 2006, 2 issues 2007. sub. price $14.00/year US; $16.00/year Canadian; $18.00/year International; per copy $7.95/US; $8.95/Canadian; $9.95/International; sample $7.95/US; $8.95/Canadian; $9.95/International. Back issues: $7.95/US; $8.95/Canadian; $9.95/International. 32-60pp. Reporting time: 2-3 weeks. Simultaneous submissions accepted: No. Publishes 2-5% of manuscripts submitted. Payment: None. Copyrighted, reverts to author. Pub's reviews: 4 in 2005. §haiku, tanka, haibun, haiga. Ads: None.

White Mane Publishing Company, Inc., Harold Collier, Acquisitions Editor, 73 West Burd Street, PO Box 708, Shippensburg, PA 17257, 717-532-2237, Fax 717-532-6110, email:marketing@whitemane.com. 1987. Non-fiction. ''White Mane Books emphasizes the importance of fine quality non-fiction adult military history. White Mane Kids is historically based fiction for children and young adults.'' avg. press run 3M-5M. Pub'd 30 titles 2005; expects 40 titles 2006, 50 titles 2007. Discounts: available on request. 200-300pp. Reporting time: 120 days with guideline and manuscript, proposal guidelines available on request. Simultaneous submissions accepted: yes. Payment: twice yearly statements. Copyrights for author. Subjects: Americana, Biography, Children, Youth, Civil War, History, Military, Veterans, Non-Fiction, War, Women, World War II.

White Pine Press, Dennis Maloney, Editor; Elaine LaMattina, Editor, PO Box 236, Buffalo, NY 14201-0236, 716-627-4665 phone/Fax, wpine@whitepine.org, www.whitepine.org. 1973. Poetry, fiction, long-poems, non-fiction. ''Do not send unsolicited ms without querying first. We read unsolicited American poetry only as part of our annual competition. White Pine Press has published fine works of poetry, fiction, essays, non-fiction, and literature in translation from many languages. We are not presently reading new American fiction.'' avg. press run 1M-2M. Pub'd 10 titles 2005; expects 12 titles 2006, 12 titles 2007. Discounts: 2-4 copies 20%, 5+ 40%. 150-250pp. Reporting time: 1-3 months. Simultaneous submissions accepted: yes. Publishes 1% of manuscripts submitted. Payment: copies, honorarium, royalties. Does not copyright for author. Subjects: Asia, Indochina, Essays, Fiction, Latin America, Novels, Poetry, Short Stories, Translation, Zen.

White Thread Press, Abdur Mangera R, 480 Whitman Street #102, Goleta, CA 93117, 805 968 4666. 2004. Non-fiction. ''We publish classical and traditional works by Muslim scholars on Islam and related sciences.'' avg. press run 4000. Expects 5 titles 2006, 5 titles 2007. Discounts: 2-4 copies 35%5-9 copies 40%10-99 copies 42%100-499 copies 45%500+ copies call for priceExceptions are possible. 145pp. Copyrights for author. Subjects: Autobiography, Biography, Ethics, History, Law, Philosophy, Spiritual, Sufism.

White Urp Press (see also ABBEY), 5360 Fallriver Row Court, Columbia, MD 21044. avg. press run 200. 15-20pp. Simultaneous submissions accepted: no. Does not copyright for author.

WHITEWALL OF SOUND, Jim Clinefelter, 411 NE 22nd #21, Portland, OR 97232-3270, jcline@teleport.com. 1983. Poetry, fiction, articles, art, photos, interviews, criticism, long-poems, collages, concrete art, non-fiction. "This magazine originated in NE Ohio, and is reflective of publications that have been produced in that area. And please note that it's *Whitewall* not *White Wall*. The title is a reference to automobile tires. Please request a sample issue before submitting your work or check the listings on www.printedmatter.org." circ. 100-250. 1-4/yr. Pub'd 1 issue 2005; expects 3 issues 2006, 3 issues 2007. price per copy varies; sample $10 ink-jet printer. Back issues: varies. Discounts: Special prices available to libraries and schools, please inquire via e-mail. 30pp. Simultaneous submissions accepted: yes. Publishes a variable % of manuscripts submitted. Payment: 1 copy. Copyrighted, reverts to author. Ads: none. Subjects: Avant-Garde, Experimental Art, Bibliography, Ohio, Pacific Northwest.

WHITEWALLS: A Journal of Language and Art, Anthony E. Elms, Managing Editor, PO Box 8204, Chicago, IL 60680, email aeelms@aol.com. 1978. Articles, art, photos, concrete art. "Recent contributers: Luis Camnitzer, Gregg Bordowitz, Christoph Fink, Julia Fish, Laurie Palmer." circ. 2,000 and up. 2/yr. Pub'd 1 issue 2005; expects 2 issues 2006, 2 issues 2007. sub. price $15, overseas $25, institutions $20, $25 overseas inst., $35 overseas air inst.; per copy $8; sample $8 except museums and libraries. Back issues: $8 for most issues, some are $10. Negotiable price for complete set. 120-150pp. Reporting time: 6-12 months. We accept simultaneous submissions on occasion. Payment: none. Copyrighted, does not revert to author. §Art, critical theory. Ads: $250 1x, $400 per year/$150 1x, $250 per year. Subjects: Arts, Avant-Garde, Experimental Art, Book Arts, Photography, Visual Arts.

Whitford Press, Ellen Taylor, Editor, 4880 Lower Valley Road, Atglen, PA 19310, 610-593-1777, Fax 610-593-2002, www.schifferbooks.com. 1987. Non-fiction. "Whitford Press distributes for the Donning Company." avg. press run 5M. Pub'd 2 titles 2005; expects 3 titles 2006, 3 titles 2007. Discounts: 1 10%, 2-4 20%, 5-24 40%, 25-49 42%, 50-99 43%, 100-249 44%, 250-499 45%, 500+ 46%. 200pp. Reporting time: usually 1 month. Simultaneous submissions accepted: no. Payment: royalties paid twice yearly. Copyrights for author. Subjects: Astrology, Health, Native American, New Age, Non-Fiction, Occult, Philosophy, Psychology, Spiritual, Sports, Outdoors.

Whitston Publishing Co., 1717 Central Avenue, Suite 201, Albany, NY 12205. 1969. Pub'd 15 titles 2005; expects 15 titles 2006, 15 titles 2007. Reporting time: 120-180 days. Copyrights for author. Subjects: African Literature, Africa, African Studies, Architecture, Bibliography, Biography, Business & Economics, Charles Dickens, Emily Dickinson, English, Indexes & Abstracts, Literary Review, Medieval, Native American, Poetry, Political Science, Sports, Outdoors.

Whole Notes Press (see also WHOLE NOTES), Nancy Peters Hastings, PO Box 1374, Las Cruces, NM 88004, 505-382-7446. 1988. Poetry. "Each year Whole Notes Press features the work of a single poet in a chapbook. Submissions to the Whole Notes Chapbook Series are welcomed. Send a sampler of 3-8 poems along with a stamped, self-addressed envelope. Recent chapbooks by Roy Scheele and Dan Stryk." avg. press run 400. Pub'd 1 title 2005; expects 1 title 2006, 1 title 2007. Discounts: available upon request. 20pp. Reporting time: 1 month. Simultaneous submissions accepted: no. Publishes 1% of manuscripts submitted. Payment: author will receive 25 copies of the chapbook. Copyrights for author. Subject: Poetry.

Whole Person Associates Inc., Susan Gustafson, 210 West Michigan Street, Duluth, MN 55802-1908, 218-727-0500, Fax 218-727-0505. 1977. avg. press run 5M-10M. Pub'd 5 titles 2005. Discounts: normal trade for some books/professional discounts. 192pp. Simultaneous submissions accepted: yes. Copyrights for author. Subjects: Canada, Feminism, Health, Men, Minnesota, Psychology, Psychology, Sports, Outdoors, Wisconsin.

WHOLE TERRAIN - REFLECTIVE ENVIRONMENTAL PRACTICE, Rowland Russell, Managing Editor, 40 Avon Street, Antioch University New England, Keene, NH 03431-3552, 603-357-3122 ex. 272. 1992. Poetry, fiction, art, interviews, non-fiction. "Fiction, nonfiction, and personal essay manuscripts on specific yearly themes should be no longer than 2,000 words. Poetry submissions also accepted. Recent contributors include: Terry Tempest Williams, Thomas Moore, Simon Ortiz, David James Duncan, and Ann Zwinger. New theme guidelines are posted each summer on our website (www.wholeterrain.org); they may also be requested from our office via phone or email." circ. 2000. 1/yr. Pub'd 1 issue 2005; expects 1 issue 2006, 1 issue 2007. sub. price $7; per copy $7. Back issues: $7. Discounts: Discounts are offered on multiple-year subscriptions, and to wholesalers. 52pp. Reporting time: 6-8 weeks after annual submission deadline. We are not able to reply to unsolicited material that is off theme. Simultaneous submissions accepted: yes. Publishes 15% of manuscripts submitted. Payment: None. Contributors are compensated with copies of their issue, and a lifetime subscription to Whole Terrain. Copyrighted, reverts to author. §Environmental topics, nature related fiction and non-fiction. Subjects: Environment, Essays, Fiction, Nature, Non-Fiction, Poetry.

Wide World Publishing/TETRA, Elvira Monroe, PO Box 476, San Carlos, CA 94070, 650-593-2839, Fax 650-595-0802. 1976. Articles, photos, non-fiction. "Imprint—Math Products Plus.wegsite: http://www.wideworldpublishing.com." avg. press run varies. Pub'd 10 titles 2005; expects 8 titles 2006, 8 titles 2007. Discounts: 2-4 books 20%, 5-49 40%, 25-49 42%, 50-99 44%, 100+ 48%. 200 to 300pp. Reporting time: 30

days. Payment: 10%. Copyrights for author. Subjects: Australia, California, Ecology, Foods, Greek, Hawaii, Mathematics, Transportation.

WILD DUCK REVIEW, Casey Walker, P.O. Box 335, Davenport, CA 95017, 831.471.9246 casey@wildduckreview.com. 1994. Poetry, fiction, articles, art, photos, interviews, satire, criticism, reviews, letters, news items, non-fiction. "Recent contributors include: Jim Dodge, Jerry Martien, Gary Snyder, Galway Kinnell, Bill Joy, Nelson Foster, Florence Shepard, Ed Casey, Marilynne Robinson, Wendell Berry, Martha Herbert, Stuart Newman, Richard Strohman, David Noble, Jim Harrison, Jack Turner, Terry Tempest Williams, Freeman House, Keekok Lee, Bill McKibben, Elizabeth Herron, Lewis Lapham, Todd Gitlin, Suzanne Romaine, Catherine Keller. Does not read unsolicited manuscripts." circ. 8M. sub. price $24; per copy $6; sample $6. Back issues: If in stock, $6. each. Discounts: 30% discount on orders of 15 copies or more of each issue used for educational purposes. 44 10x14" pp. Payment: copies. Copyrighted, reverts to author. Subjects: Arts, Biology, Environment, Interviews, Literary Review, Nature, Philosophy, Physics, Politics, Writers/ Writing.

THE WILD FOODS FORUM, Eco Images, Vickie Shufer, P.O. Box 61413, Virginia Beach, VA 23466-1413, 757-421-3929, 757-421-3929, wildfood@infionline.net, http://wildfood.home.infionline.net. Articles, non-fiction. "nature related publications; provide information on how to identify and use wild plants for food, medicine, crafts." circ. 500. 4/yr. Pub'd 4 issues 2005; expects 4 issues 2006, 4 issues 2007. sub. price $15; per copy $3.00; sample $3.00 or free. Back issues: Inquire. Discounts: 40%. 16pp. Reporting time: 1-2 months. Simultaneous submissions accepted: Yes. Publishes 60% of manuscripts submitted. Payment: individual basis. Copyrighted, reverts to author. Pub's reviews: approx. 6 in 2005. §ethnobotanyedible plantsmedicinal plants. Ads: $85 (full page)$35 (half page)$15 (quarter page)$10 (business card size). Subjects: Alternative Medicine, Botany, Cooking, Ecology, Foods, Gardening, Nature, Newsletter, Non-Fiction.

WILD PLUM, Constance Campbell, Founding Editor, PO Box 4282, Austin, TX 78765. 2003. Poetry. 1/yr. Pub'd 1 issue 2005; expects 1 issue 2006, 1 issue 2007. sub. price $9; per copy $9; sample $9. 48pp. Reporting time: 2 months, unless work is under consideration. Simultaneous submissions accepted: no. Publishes 5% of manuscripts submitted. Payment: 1 copy. Copyrighted, reverts to author. Subject: Poetry.

•Wild West Publishing House, Burton H. Wolfe, P.O. Box 642836, San Francisco, CA 94164-2836, Telephone and fax: 415/921-5629. e-mail: bhwolfe@msn.com. 1972. Fiction, satire. "The purpose of this publishing house, inactive from 1975 until 2006, is to provide a means for authors who are blacklisted everywhere, or whose books are banned because the material in them is so sensitive or controversial, to get their work into print. It is our intention to publish books of any kind that meet that criteria. Until a financial angel is found, however, or until the house makes a substantial profit on its own, authors will have to bear all costs of production and promotion." Expects 1 title 2006, 2 titles 2007. Discounts: 40 percent discount on all for all only if ordered from BookSurge.com.No discount if ordered directly from this small press. 200pp. Reporting time: One month. Simultaneous submissions accepted: No. Publishes 1% of manuscripts submitted. Payment: No advances. For the time being, 50-50 profit split. Payment every six months. Copyrights for author. Subjects: Americana, Anarchist, Atheism, Biography, Birth, Birth Control, Population, Communication, Journalism, Counter-Culture, Alternatives, Communes, Culture, Current Affairs, Essays, Humor, Myth, Mythology, Non-Fiction, Religion, Satire.

Zelda Wilde Publishing, John Lehman F., 315 Water St., Cambridge, WI 53523, 608-423-9609. 2003. Poetry, non-fiction. "We specialize in literary and business books that have clearly defined audiences and efficient means to reach them." avg. press run 2000. Pub'd 1 title 2005; expects 2 titles 2006, 2 titles 2007. Discounts: 2-10 copies 25%. 136pp. Reporting time: We are currently not accepting unsolicited manuscripts. Simultaneous submissions accepted: No. Publishes 1% of manuscripts submitted. Payment: Authors receive a percent of sales. Copyrights for author. Subjects: Biography, Buddhism, How-To, Leadership, Liberal Arts, Non-Fiction, North America, Prose, Public Relations/Publicity, Trade, Wisconsin, Zen.

Wilderness Adventure Books, Erin Sims Howarth, Po Box 856, Manchester, MI 48158-0856, www.wildernessbooks.org. 1983. Photos, non-fiction. "We publish mostly how to guides of the Great Lakes outdoors. Recent books include: *Edible Medicinal Plants of the Great Lakes Region.*" avg. press run 3M. Pub'd 4 titles 2005; expects 4 titles 2006, 4 titles 2007. Discounts: 30-50%. 300pp. Reporting time: 6 weeks. Simultaneous submissions accepted: yes. Publishes 5% of manuscripts submitted. Payment: 5-10% of retail/every 6 months. Copyrights for author. Subjects: Bicycling, Botany, Great Lakes, How-To, Michigan, Shipwrecks, Sports, Outdoors.

WILDERNESS MEDICINE NEWSLETTER, TMC Books LLC, Peter Lewis, 731 Tasker Hill Rd., Conway, NH 03818, 603-447-5589, info@tmcbooks.com www.tmcbooks.com. 2002. Non-fiction. "ISSN-1059-6518." 6/yr. Pub'd 6 issues 2005; expects 6 issues 2006, 6 issues 2007. sub. price $15; sample Free Online at www.tmcbooks.com. Back issues: can be ordered through TMC Books either by phone or email info@tmcbooks.com. 10pp. Payment: Check or online c/c. Copyrighted. Subject: Medicine.

Wilderness Ministries, Paul L. Prough Jr., PO Box 225, Mount Union, PA 17066, 814-542-8668. 1975. Fiction, photos, non-fiction. avg. press run 2M. Pub'd 3 titles 2005; expects 3 titles 2006, 4 titles 2007. 75pp. Reporting time: 6-12 months. Simultaneous submissions accepted: no. Publishes 1% of manuscripts submitted. Payment: negotiated. Does not copyright for author. Subjects: Christianity, Inspirational, Juvenile Fiction, Motivation, Success, Religion, Spiritual.

Wilderness Press, Caroline Winnett, Publisher, 1200 5th Street, Berkeley, CA 94710-1306, 510-843-8080; fax 510-548-1355; e-mail mail@wildernesspress.com. 1966. Non-fiction. "Conservation, environmental bias. Bias for accuracy. Bias against sloppy writing." avg. press run 5M. Pub'd 10 titles 2005; expects 15 titles 2006, 15 titles 2007. 180pp. Reporting time: 2 weeks. Simultaneous submissions accepted: yes. Publishes 5% of manuscripts submitted. Payment: competitive royalty paid quarterly or semi-annually. Copyrights for author. Subject: Sports, Outdoors.

Wildflower Press, Jeanne Shannon, PO Box 4757, Albuquerque, NM 87196-4757, 505-296-0691, Fax 505-296-6124, jspoetry@aol.com. 1981. Poetry. "Additional address: 1217 Espejo Street NE, Albuquerque, NM 87112-5215." avg. press run 800. Pub'd 3 titles 2005; expects 1 title 2006, 1 title 2007. Discounts: 40% to bookstores. 110pp. Reporting time: 2-3 weeks. Simultaneous submissions accepted: yes. Publishes 25% of manuscripts submitted. Payment: copies. Copyrights for author. Subjects: Appalachia, Essays, Experimental, Memoirs, Metaphysics, Nature, Poetry, Short Stories.

THE WILDWOOD READER, Timson Edwards, Co., Marlene McLauglin, Alex Gonzalez, PO Box 55-0898, Jacksonville, FL 32255-0898, 904-705-6806; gonz2171@bellsouth.net; www.short-fiction.com. 1995. Fiction, photos. "Short short fiction, essays, stream of conscience prose and anything creative - especially if the material matches the photography. We would prefer writings in the traditional literary realm. However, any material may be sent except erotica, western, sci-fi and horror. We would like to see collaborations of new or emerging writers and new fine art photographers." circ. 500. 4/yr. Pub'd 2 issues 2005; expects 4 issues 2006, 4 issues 2007. sub. price $15; per copy $6; sample $8. Discounts: trade 30% no returns; bulk 50% no returns; agents 5-10% commission on any sale; bonafide school/classroom orders 50%. 48pp. Reporting time: 3 months. Simultaneous submissions accepted: yes. Publishes 60% of manuscripts submitted. Payment: $10-$25. Copyrighted, reverts to author. Pub's reviews: 1-4 in 2005. §Short fiction, essays, photography. Ads: $250/$100/$25. Subjects: Essays, Fiction, Interviews, Literature (General), Magazines, New Age, Photography, Satire.

WILLIAM AND MARY REVIEW, Editors rotate yearly, Campus Center, PO Box 8795, Williamsburg, VA 23187-8795, 757-221-3290, Fax 757-221-3451. 1962. Poetry, fiction, art, photos, satire, criticism, long-poems, non-fiction. "The Review is an internationally circulated literary magazine published by The College of William and Mary. In our recent issues, we have published works by Cornelius Eady, Dana Gioia, Eric Paul Shaffer, David Bergman, Walta Borawski, Forest Gander, Minnie Bruce Pratt, Dan Bellm, Forrest Gander, among others." circ. 5M. 1/yr. Pub'd 1 issue 2005; expects 1 issue 2006, 1 issue 2007. sub. price $5.50; per copy $5.50; sample $5.50. Back issues: $5.50 per issue. Discounts: 40% off list for trade. 102pp. Reporting time: 4-5 months. We accept simultaneous submissions, but not preferred. Publishes 1% of manuscripts submitted. Payment: 5 copies of issue. Copyrighted, reverts to author. Subject: Literary Review.

Willis Publishing, PO Box 7002, Piscataway, NJ 08854-7002.

WILLOW REVIEW, Michael Latza, College of Lake County, 19351 W. Washington, Grayslake, IL 60030, 847-543-2956, com426@clcillinois.edu, www.clcillinois.edu/community/willowreview.asp. 1969. Poetry, fiction, interviews, reviews, non-fiction. "Willow Review is a non-profit journal published annually at the College of Lake County and partially supported by a grant from the Illinois Arts Council (a state agency), College of Lake County Publications, and private contributions and sales. Submissions are invited Sept. 1st to May 1st. Send a maximum of five poems or short fiction and creative non-fiction up to 7,000 words. All work should be unpublished and accompanied by a self-addressed stamped envelope. Manuscripts will not be returned unless requested. We will accept simultaneous submissions if indicated in the cover letter. At this time we are not accepting electronic submissions. As part of our mission Willow Review also publishes reviews of books written by Midwestern writers or published by Midwestern presses. Recent Contributors: Patricia Smith, Lisel Mueller, Li-Young Lee." circ. 1000. 1/yr. Pub'd 1 issue 2005; expects 1 issue 2006, 1 issue 2007. sub. price one year, $7 / 3 years, $18 / 5 years, $30.; per copy $7; sample $5. Back issues: inquire. 110pp. Reporting time: 12-16 weeks. Simultaneous submissions accepted: Yes. Publishes 5% of manuscripts submitted. Payment: 2 copies of magazine. Copyrighted, reverts to author. Pub's reviews: 1 in 2005. §Poetry Books. Subjects: Fiction, Non-Fiction, Poetry.

WILLOW SPRINGS, Samuel Ligon, Editor; O'Connor Rodriguez Adam, Managing Editor, Willow Springs, Eastern Washington University, 705 West First Avenue, Spokane, WA 99201, 509-623-4349. 1977. Poetry, fiction, interviews, criticism, reviews, parts-of-novels, long-poems, non-fiction. "Michael Burkard, Russell Edson, Alison Baker, Thomas Lux, Alberto Rios, Carolyn Kizer, Madeline DeFrees, Peter Cooley, Yusef

Komunyakaa, Donald Revell, William Stafford, Lee Upton, Paisley Rekdal, and Robert Gregory. We encourage the submissions of translations from all languages and periods, as well as essays and essay-reviews.'' circ. 1,700. 2/yr. Pub'd 2 issues 2005; expects 2 issues 2006, 2 issues 2007. sub. price $13.00; per copy $7; sample $5. Back issues: varies. Discounts: 40%. 144pp. Reporting time: 1-3 months. Simultaneous submissions accepted: Yes. Publishes .5% of manuscripts submitted. Payment: 2 contributor copies. Copyrighted, reverts to author. Pub's reviews: none in 2005. §Poetry, fiction, nonfiction. Ads: Exchange only. Subjects: Criticism, Essays, Fiction, Interviews, Non-Fiction, Poetry, Prose, Translation.

Willow Tree Press, Inc. (see also Criminal Justice Press), Richard S. Allinson, PO Box 249, Monsey, NY 10952, 845-354-9139. 1983. Non-fiction. avg. press run 750. Pub'd 6 titles 2005; expects 13 titles 2006, 10 titles 2007. Discounts: 1-9 books 30%, 10-99 40%. 300pp. Reporting time: 2 months. Simultaneous submissions accepted: yes. Payment: 10%. Subjects: Crime, Law, Sociology.

Willowgate Press, Robert B. Tolins, Editor-in-Chief; Robert I. Katz, Managing Editor, 120 Brook Road, Port Jefferson, NY 11777-1665, willowgatepress@yahoo.com, www.willowgatepress.com. 1999. Fiction. ''We publish book-length fiction in all genres.'' avg. press run 3M. Expects 2 titles 2006, 2-3 titles 2007. Discounts: negotiable to the trade. 240pp. Reporting time: 2 months initially, then 6 months for entire manuscript. However, we are currently closed to new submissions and expect to remain so until January 2005. Simultaneous submissions accepted: yes. Publishes 1-2% of manuscripts submitted. Payment: $500 advance, standard royalty. Does not copyright for author. Subjects: Fantasy, Fiction, Literature (General), Mystery, Novels, Science Fiction.

Willowood Press, Judith Greenwood, Publisher, PO Box 1846, Minot, ND 58702, 701-838-0579. 1980. Non-fiction. ''Guides to library research for undergraduate and graduate university students specialized by subject and level of difficulty. University reference-bibliography; art.'' avg. press run 1M+. 180pp. Subjects: Libraries, Reference.

WillowTree Press LLC, PO Box 142414, St. Louis, MO 63114-0414, 314-423-3634. 1999. Fiction, non-fiction. ''Publisher of Pagan oriented fiction and non-fiction books, as well as educational DVD's. Unsolicited submissions are recycled unread.'' Discounts: Wholesalers 55% Retailers 40%. Copyrights for author. Subjects: Fiction, Mystery, Non-Fiction, Novels, Occult, WICCA.

Wilshire Books Inc., 9731 Variel Ave., Chatsworth, CA 91311-4315, 818-700-1522 [tel], 818-700-1527 [fax], website: www.mpowers.com. 1947. avg. press run 5M. Pub'd 25 titles 2005; expects 25 titles 2006, 25 titles 2007. 224pp. Reporting time: 2 months. Simultaneous submissions accepted: yes. Publishes a variable % of manuscripts submitted. Payment: varies. Copyrights for author. Subjects: How-To, Humor, Hypnosis, Magic, Marketing, Metaphysics, Motivation, Success, Non-Fiction, Psychology, Publishing, Self-Help, Sex, Sexuality.

Wilton Place Publishing, Michele C. Osterhout, PO Box 291, La Canada, CA 91012, 818-790-5601. 1982. Fiction. avg. press run 5M. Expects 2 titles 2006, 3 titles 2007. Discounts: 3-199 40%, 200-499 50%. 301pp. Reporting time: 6 months. Payment: case by case. Copyrights for author.

WIN NEWS, Fran P. Hosken, Editor & Publisher, 187 Grant Street, Lexington, MA 02173, 781-862-9431, Fax 781-862-1734. 1975. ''*WIN News (Women's International Network)* has ongoing columns on women and health, women and development, women and media, environment, violence, united nations and more. International career opportunities are listed; an investigation on genital/sexual mutilations regularly reports; news from Africa, the Middle East, Asia & Pacific, Europe and the Americas are featured in every issue! You are invited to send news and participate! *WIN* is a non-profit organization. Contributions tax-deductible. We hope to hear from you soon. Deadline (next issue): July.'' circ. 1M-1.1M. 4/yr. Pub'd 4 issues 2005; expects 4 issues 2006, 4 issues 2007. sub. price $48 institution, $35 individual, add $4/yr postage abroad, add $10/yr air abroad; per copy $5; sample $5. Back issues: $15/year. Discounts: available on request. 80pp. Simultaneous submissions accepted, but must be 1-2 pages of facts, documented reports, and no fiction. Payment: none. Copyrighted. Pub's reviews: 18-20+ in 2005. §Women and international development, women's right world-wide. Ads: $300/$150/$75 1/4 page. Subjects: Health, Women.

WIND, Chris Green, Editor; Rebecca Howell, Poetry Editor; Arwen Donahue, Fiction Editor, PO Box 24548, Lexington, KY 40524, 859-277-6849, www.wind.wind.org. 1971. Poetry, fiction, articles, interviews, criticism, reviews, news items, non-fiction. ''No set length on poetry. 4,000 words on fiction. No biases.'' circ. 425. 3/yr. Pub'd 3 issues 2005; expects 3 issues 2006, 3 issues 2007. sub. price $15 individual, $20 institutional, $22 foreign; per copy $6; sample $4.50. Back issues: $4.50. Discounts: extra copies available to contributors at cost. 120pp. Reporting time: 3-5 months. Simultaneous submissions accepted reluctantly. Publishes 1% of manuscripts submitted. Payment: 1 contributor's copy. Copyrighted, reverts to author. Pub's reviews: 5 in 2005. §Small presses only. Ads: $150/$75. Subjects: Appalachia, Essays, Fiction, Kentucky, Literature (General), Multicultural, Poetry, Reviews.

•**Wind Publications,** 600 Overlook Drive, Nicholasville, KY 40356.

Wind River Institute Press/Wind River Broadcasting, Jim McDonald, 117 East 11th, Loveland, CO 80537, 970-669-3442, Fax 970-663-6081, 800-669-3993. 1985. Non-fiction. "Technical regulatory in broadcast industry." avg. press run 5M. Pub'd 1 title 2005; expects 2 titles 2006, 2 titles 2007. Discounts: 2+ 20%. 200pp. Subjects: Engineering, Government, Law, Radio.

Wind River Press, 254 Dogwood Drive, Hershey, PA 17033, promotions@windriverpress.com.

WINDHOVER: A Journal of Christian Literature, Donna Walker-Nixon, PO Box 8008, UMHB, Belton, TX 76513, 254-295-4565. 1995. Poetry, interviews, reviews, parts-of-novels, long-poems, plays, non-fiction. circ. 500. 1/yr. Pub'd 1 issue 2005; expects 1 issue 2006, 1 issue 2007. sub. price $8; per copy $8; sample $5. Back issues: $5. 148pp. Reporting time: 3 months, sometimes longer. Simultaneous submissions accepted: yes. Publishes 10% of manuscripts submitted. Payment: 2 copies. Copyrighted, reverts to author. Pub's reviews: 4 in 2005. §Collections of stories or poetry by Christian writers. Subject: Literary Review.

Windows Project (see also SMOKE), Dave Ward, Liver House, 96 Bold Street, Liverpool L1 4HY, England. 1974. Poetry, fiction, art, photos, cartoons, long-poems, collages, concrete art. avg. press run 500. Pub'd 1 title 2005; expects 1 title 2006. Discounts: 33%. 24pp. Reporting time: as quickly as possible. Publishes 1.28% of manuscripts submitted. Payment: 1 copy. Subject: Poetry.

Windstorm Creative, Cris Newport MS, 7419 Ebbert Drive SE, Port Orchard, WA 98367, www.windstorm-creative.com. 1989. Poetry, fiction, art, photos, cartoons, satire, long-poems, collages, plays, non-fiction. "You must visit website for guidelines and mandatory mailing label." avg. press run 10,000 copies. Pub'd 100 titles 2005; expects 200 titles 2006, 200 titles 2007. Discounts: For bookstores, libraries, schools, and other retail outlets we offer a 50% off retail, payment in 60 days; returns accepted within 60 day period. Late accounts will have discounts reduced to 10%. Distributor discounts are arranged individually. 250pp. Reporting time: Can be up to 6 months for full manuscripts. 3 months for queries. We accept simultaneous submissions with notification. Publishes 2-5% of manuscripts submitted. Payment: We do not offer advances. We pay a 15% royalty of gross monies received. We issue royalty statements twice a year in March and September. Does not copyright for author. Subjects: Anthropology, Archaeology, Arts, Black, Children, Youth, Comics, Crafts, Hobbies, Fiction, Folklore, Gay, How-To, Lesbianism, Literature (General), Medieval, Native American, Occult.

Windward Publishing, An Imprint of Finney Company (see also Finney Company, Inc.), Alan Krysan, President, 8075 215th Street West, Lakeville, MN 55044, (952) 469-6699, Fax: (952) 469-1968, (800) 846-7027, Fax: (800) 330-6232, feedback@finney-hobar.com, www.finney-hobar.com. 1973. Non-fiction. "This imprint of Finney Company offers trade books for both children and adults with and educational base. Most recent releases are Wild Beach, Space Station Science, Daddy Played Music for the Cows, and Nightlight." avg. press run 5000. Pub'd 5 titles 2005; expects 2-7 titles 2006, 5-10 titles 2007. Discounts: 1-9 copies 20%10-49 copies 40%50 or more copies 50%. Reporting time: 8-10 weeks. Simultaneous submissions accepted: Yes. Payment: varies. Subjects: Animals, Children, Youth, Florida, Leisure/Recreation, Marine Life, Nature, Non-Fiction, Picture Books, Space, Trade, Travel, Whaling.

Wineberry Press, Elisavietta Ritchie, 3207 Macomb Street, NW, Washington, DC 20008-3327, 410-586-3086, 202-363-8036, elisavietta@chesapeake.net. 1983. Poetry. "To order books: Wineberry Press, PO Box 298, Broomes Island, MD 20615, 410-586-3086. Send check or money order. Press formed as collaborative to publish anthology *Finding The Name*, 1983. *Get With It, Lord*, chapbook by Beatrice Murphy, 1990; *Horse and Cart: Stories from the Country*, fiction by Elisabeth Stevens, 1990; *Listening For Wings* by Maxine Combs, 2002. Can't handle unsolicited manuscripts—already have plenty I'd like to publish." avg. press run 500-2M. Pub'd 2 titles 2005; expects 1 title 2006, 1 title 2007. Discounts: 40% to booksellers. 32-200pp. Reporting time: ASAP. Simultaneous submissions accepted: no. Publishes 1% of manuscripts submitted. Payment: copies (as many as they need), some free, some discounted. Does not copyright for author. Subjects: Conservation, Fiction, Poetry.

WinePress Publishing, Athena Dean, Acquisitions, PO Box 428, Enumclaw, WA 98022, 360-802-9758, Fax 360-802-9992, info@winepresspub.com. 1993. "Most titles are Christian based messages." avg. press run 2.5M. Pub'd 77 titles 2005; expects 90 titles 2006, 100 titles 2007. Discounts: 1-5 books 30%, 6+ 40%, case lots 50%. 168pp. Reporting time: 2-3 days. Simultaneous submissions accepted: yes. Publishes 25% of manuscripts submitted. Payment: author pays for production, keeps all profits from sales. Copyrights for author. Subjects: Christianity, Inspirational, Religion.

Wings Press, Bryce Milligan, 627 E. Guenther, San Antonio, TX 78210, 210-271-7805 (phone and fax). 1975. Poetry, fiction, art, plays, non-fiction. "Wings Press publishes a wide array of multicultural literature. We very very rarely accept unsolicited submissions, and we never publish "poets" who do not read poetry. *The Bloomsbury Review* called Wings Press "the best little publishing house in Texas."." avg. press run 3000. Pub'd 12 titles 2005; expects 14 titles 2006, 8 titles 2007. Discounts: trade—40%distributors—55%textbook use—20%. 150pp. Reporting time: avg 3 months. Simultaneous submissions accepted: Yes. Publishes 2% of manuscripts submitted. Payment: Royalties but no advances. Copyrights for author. Subjects: African-American, Anthology, Bilingual, Black, Celtic, Chicano/a, Fiction, Latino, Literature (General), Native American, Non-Fiction, Poetry, Texas, U.S. Hispanic, Young Adult.

Winslow Publishing, Michelle West, Box 38012, 550 Eglinton Avenue West, Toronto, Ontario M5N 3A8, Canada, 416-789-4733, winslow@interlog.com, www.winslowpublishing.com. 1981. Non-fiction. "After publishing for mail order only since 1981, we moved into book stores in 1986. Title range from *The Complete Guide To Companion Advertising* to *The No-Bull Guide To Getting Published And Making It As A Writer*. At present, most business is still in mail order, and we are always looking for new reps to drop ship for. Please send *Queries only* (no mss)—non-fiction only, which can be marketed through the mail. Books do *not* have to have Canadian content - we are well represented in the U.S., and will be expanding greatly in the next couple of years. (Someday we'll be a *Big* Press!) We are completely computerized, and would appreciate mss on disk." avg. press run 1M-5M (mail order), 5M (bookstore). Pub'd 4 titles 2005; expects 4 titles 2006, 4 titles 2007. Discounts: 40% on 5 or more copies of a title. 160pp. Reporting time: 1-2 weeks. Payment: usual royalties, or purchase ms. outright. Copyrights for author. Subjects: Business & Economics, Communication, Journalism, Consumer, How-To, Printing.

WISCONSIN ACADEMY REVIEW, Joan Fischer, Editor, 1922 University Ave., Madison, WI 53705, 608-263-1692. 1954. Poetry, fiction, articles, art, photos, interviews, criticism, reviews. "We use poetry, short fiction, art and literary history, and book reviews that have Wisconsin connected author or subject, as well as scientific articles or political essays which have Wisconsin tie-in. Quarterly journal of the Wisconsin Academy of Sciences, Arts and Letters. If not Wisconsin return address, include Wisconsin connection with submission or query. Include SASE." circ. 1.5M. 4/yr. Pub'd 4 issues 2005; expects 4 issues 2006, 4 issues 2007. sub. price none available, free to members or available for $5 purchase; per copy $5; sample $5. Back issues: none. Discounts: none. 56pp. Reporting time: 8-10 weeks. Simultaneous submissions accepted: no. Payment: 2 copies. Copyrighted. Pub's reviews: 24 in 2005. §Wisconsin connected books by author or subject. Ads: none. Subjects: Culture, Wisconsin.

WISCONSIN TRAILS, Scott Klug, Publisher & CEO; Harriet Brown, Editor; Laura Kearney, Managing Editor, PO Box 317, Black Earth, WI 53515-0317, e-mail editor@wistrails.com. 1960. Poetry, articles, art, photos, interviews, satire, criticism, reviews, letters, news items, non-fiction. "*Wisconsin Trails* at present is interested in articles about Wisconsin: nature and the environment, heritage, folklore, travel, art and the arts, personality profiles, history, food and restaurants, outdoor sports. Magazine submissions should contain detailed outline plus clips. No phone calls please." circ. 40-45M. 6/yr. Pub'd 6 issues 2005; expects 6 issues 2006, 6 issues 2007. sub. price $24.95; per copy $4.95; sample $4.95 + $3 p/h. Back issues: $7. Discounts: subscription agency, all other universal schedule. 84+pp. Reporting time: 1-3 months. We accept simultaneous submissions, but must be clearly indicated. Publishes 5% of manuscripts submitted. Payment: on publication. Copyrighted, rights revert to author after 60 days. Pub's reviews: 6 in 2005. §Outdoor sports, activities, food and restaurants, travel, arts events, anything dealing w/Wisconsin, photography. Ads: frequency discounts available; contact Dennis Parker, dparker@wistrails.com, for information. Subjects: Agriculture, Animals, Arts, Bicycling, Conservation, Cooking, Environment, Essays, Folklore, History, Non-Fiction, Performing Arts, Sports, Outdoors, Travel, Wisconsin.

Wisdom Publications, Inc., Timothy McNeill, Publisher; David Kittelstrom, Editor; Josh Bartok, Editor, 199 Elm Street, Somerville, MA 02144-3129, 617-776-7416; Fax 617-776-7841. 1975. Non-fiction. "Wisdom Publications is dedicated to making available authentic Buddhist works for the benefit of all. We publish translations of the sutras and tantras, commentaries and teachings of past and contemporary Buddhist masters, and original works by the world's leading Buddhist scholars. We publish our titles with the appreciation of Buddhism as a living philosophy and with the special commitment to preserve and transmit important works from all the major Buddhist traditions.Wisdom Publications is a 501(c)3 nonprofit charitable organization, and all profits are reinvested into the creation of new works. Our titles are distributed worldwide and have been translated into more than thirty foreign languages. We have a backlist of over two hundred titles in print, with over twenty new titles appearing each year." avg. press run 5M. Pub'd 12 titles 2005; expects 12 titles 2006, 14 titles 2007. Discounts: Trade sales thru Publishers Group West. 224pp. Reporting time: 3 months. Simultaneous submissions accepted: yes. Publishes 5% of manuscripts submitted. Payment: once a year based on net sales. We sometimes copyright for author. Subjects: Asia, Indochina, Buddhism, Philosophy, Psychology, Religion, Self-Help, Spiritual.

Wise Press, Line Wise, 8794 Rolling Acres Trail, Fair Oaks, TX 78015-4015, Fax 619-437-4160, lwise@san.rr.com, www.wisepress.com. 1999. Long-poems, non-fiction. avg. press run 5M. Expects 1 title 2006, 2 titles 2007. Discounts: 40%, buyer pays shipping. 188pp. Reporting time: 3 months. Simultaneous submissions accepted: yes. Publishes 5-10% of manuscripts submitted. Payment: 2 books. Copyrights for author. Subjects: Grieving, Poetry, Senior Citizens, Short Stories.

THE WISE WOMAN, Ann Forfreedom, 2441 Cordova Street, Oakland, CA 94602, 510-536-3174. 1980.

Poetry, articles, art, photos, cartoons, interviews, reviews, music, news items, non-fiction. "No longer accepting unsolicited submissions. Focus of *The Wise Woman*: feminist spirituality, feminist witchcraft, feminist issues. Includes articles, columns (such as *The War Against Women* and *The Rising of Women*). Annotated songs appropriate to subject, interviews, poems, art, wise sayings, cartoons by Bulbul, photos. Also available on microfilm through University Microfilms International." circ. small but influential. 4/yr. Pub'd 2 issues 2005; expects 2 issues 2006, 4 issues 2007. sub. price $15; per copy $4; sample $4. Back issues: $4. 20pp. Reporting time: varies, try to reply promptly when SASE is included. Simultaneous submissions accepted: no. Payment: copy of the issue. Copyrighted, rights revert to author, but TWW reserves the right to reprint. Subjects: Feminism, Occult, Spiritual.

Wish Publishing, Holly Kondras, President, PO Box 10337, Terra Haute, IN 47801, 812-299-5700, email:holly@wishpublishing.com. 1999. Non-fiction. "We are a women's sports publishing company. We publish books by and for women in sports." avg. press run 3M. Pub'd 8 titles 2005; expects 8 titles 2006, 8 titles 2007. 224pp. Reporting time: 6-8 weeks. Simultaneous submissions accepted: yes. Publishes 10% of manuscripts submitted. Payment: arranged on a title by title basis. Copyrights for author. Subjects: Health, Sports, Outdoors, Women.

THE WISHING WELL, Laddie Hosler, Editor and Publisher, PO Box 178440, San Diego, CA 92177-8440, 858-695-3139, laddiewww@aol.com, www.wishingwellwomen.com. 1974. Poetry, articles, art, photos, criticism, reviews, letters, news items, non-fiction. "*The Wishing Well* is a national correspondence magazine featuring current self-descriptions, some with photos, (by code number) of loving women wishing to safely write/meet one another...a sincere, dignified, loving publication. *Free info.*" 6/yr. Pub'd 6 issues 2005; expects 6 issues 2006, 6 issues 2007. Memberships: 2-4 mo $25; 4-6 mo $40; 6-8 mo. $60; 10-12 mo $80 U.S.; optional photo published $5-$10 extra; price per copy $5; sample $5. Back issues: $5. *The List* 25pp, *Complete Edition* 30pp. Copyrighted. Pub's reviews: 15 in 2005. §Women, book reviews (relating to readership), human rights, relating to women, bi-sexual women, human relationships, growth, lesbian. Ads: query, $10 per inch one time (3-1/4'' wide) $8 per inch 3 insertions or more. $1 word one time; 80¢ word 3 times in one year. Subjects: Gay, Humanism, Lesbianism, Newsletter, Poetry, Women.

•**WISTERIA: A Journal of Haiku, Senryu, and Tanka,** Tony Thompson, P.O. Box 150932, Lufkin, TX 75915-0932. 2006. Poetry. "We accept haiku, senryu, and tanka poetry only. Recent contributors include Michael McClintock, Pamela Miller Ness, Kirsty Karkow, and Michael Dylan Welch." circ. 200. 4/yr. Expects 4 issues 2006, 4 issues 2007. sub. price $10; per copy $3; sample $3. Back issues: $3. 24pp. Reporting time: 2 weeks. Simultaneous submissions accepted: No. Publishes 10% of manuscripts submitted. Payment: $1.00 maximum per poet and one copy of issue. Copyrighted, reverts to author. Ads: no ads accepted. Subject: Haiku.

Wizard Works, Jan O'Meara, PO Box 1125, Homer, AK 99603, 907-235-8757 phone/Fax, toll free 877-210-2665, wizard@xyz.net. 1988. Poetry, fiction, art, photos, cartoons, reviews, non-fiction. "Alaska subjects only. No unsolicited manuscripts without query first." avg. press run 1M. Pub'd 2 titles 2005; expects 2 titles 2006, 2 titles 2007. Discounts: library 20%, wholesale 1-5 20%, 6-99 40%, 100+ 50%. 130pp. Payment: negotiable. Copyrights for author. Subject: Alaska.

WOMAN'S ART JOURNAL, Elsa Honig Fine, 1711 Harris Road, Laverock, PA 19038-7208, 215-233-0639. 1980. Articles, art, reviews. "*WAJ* is a semiannual publication devoted to women and issues related to women in all areas of the visual arts. It is concerned with recovering a lost heritage and with documenting the lives and work of contemporary women in the arts, many of whom have been neglected previously because of their sex. *WAJ* represents sound scholarship presented with clarity, and it is open to all ideas and encourages research from all people." circ. 2M. 2/yr. Pub'd 2 issues 2005; expects 2 issues 2006, 2 issues 2007. sub. price $20 indiv., $38 instit.; per copy $18; sample $18. Back issues: $18. Discounts: trade $5.50 per issue plus mailing. 64pp. Reporting time: 1 month. Simultaneous submissions accepted: no. Publishes 50% of manuscripts submitted. Payment: none. Copyrighted, reverts to author. Pub's reviews: 50 in 2005. §Women in all areas of visual arts, images of women. Ads: $475/$325/$625 full back color cover/$275 1/3 page. Subjects: Arts, Women.

WOMEN AND LANGUAGE, Anita Taylor, Executive Editor, Communication Dept, George Mason University, Fairfax, VA 22030. 1975. Articles, cartoons, interviews, criticism, reviews, news items, non-fiction. "*Women and Language* is an interdisciplinary research periodical. WL attends to communication, language, gender and women's issues. It reports books, journals, articles and research in progress; publishes short articles and speeches." circ. 500+. 2/yr. Pub'd 2 issues 2005; expects 2 issues 2006, 2 issues 2007. sub. price $30 all US institutions; $15 U.S., Canadian and Mexican individuals; $25 other international individuals; $40 all international institutions (US funds only).; per copy $7.50. Back issues: $180 for Vols 1-28, plus postage, some are photocopies. 70pp. Reporting time: 2-3 months. Publishes 35% of manuscripts submitted. Payment: none. Copyrighted, does not revert to author. Pub's reviews: 4 in 2005. §Women's studies, language, gender, linguistics, communication, speech, public address. No ads. Subjects: Communication, Journalism, Feminism, Gender Issues, Language, Speaking, Women.

526

Women In Print, Brigitte Thompson, PO Box 1527, Williston, VT 05495, 802-288-8040, fax 802-288-8041, www.WomenInPrint.com, womeninprint@surfglobal.net,. 2004. Fiction, non-fiction. "Exclusive publisher of books written by women." avg. press run 5000. Expects 3 titles 2006, 3 titles 2007. Discounts: 1-4 copies 10%5-10 15%11-25 20%26-99 25%100+ 35%. 375pp. Reporting time: 1 month. Simultaneous submissions accepted: Yes. Publishes 15% of manuscripts submitted. Payment: 25% of net proceeds go to authors - paid quarterly. Copyrights for author. Subjects: Fiction, Non-Fiction.

WOMEN IN THE ARTS BULLETIN/NEWSLETTER, Women In The Arts Foundation, Inc., Erin Butler, 32-35 30th Street #D24, Astoria, NY 11106, 718-545-9337. 1971. Articles, photos, interviews, letters, news items. "Length: 200 to 1,000 words—must be on women's art movement or topics relevant to women artists." circ. 1M. 3/yr. Pub'd 3 issues 2005; expects 3 issues 2006, 3 issues 2007. sub. price $9, $15 institution, $19 foreign; per copy $1; sample free. 6pp. Reporting time: 2-3 months. Payment: none. Copyrighted, reverts to author. Pub's reviews: 1 in 2005. §Women's visual art & writing. Ads: $110/$60. Subjects: Arts, Women.

Women In The Arts Foundation, Inc. (see also WOMEN IN THE ARTS BULLETIN/NEWSLETTER), Erin Butler, Editor, 32-35 30th Street #D24, Astoria, NY 11106. 1971. Payment: none. Does not copyright for author.

Women of Diversity Productions, Inc., 5790 Park Street, Las Vegas, NV 89149-2304, 702-341-9807; fax 702-341-9828; E-mail dvrsty@aol.com. 1995. Art, photos, cartoons, non-fiction. avg. press run 3.5M. Pub'd 1 title 2005; expects 1 title 2006, 2 titles 2007. Discounts: 40% trade; 50% for 100 or more bulk, agent, author; 20% classroom. 150pp. Reporting time: 1-2 months. Simultaneous submissions accepted: yes. Publishes less than 50% of manuscripts submitted. Payment: 8% first 1000, increasing increments. Copyrights for author. Subjects: Health, Mental Health, Parenting, Psychology, Self-Help, Self-Help, Women.

WOMEN'S REVIEW OF BOOKS, Amy Hoffman, 628 North 2nd Street, Philadelphia, PA 19123, 215-925-4390. 1983. Poetry, fiction, articles, art, photos, cartoons, interviews, criticism, reviews, letters, news items. circ. 7500. 6/yr. Pub'd 11 issues 2005; expects 3 issues 2006, 6 issues 2007. sub. price $33; per copy $5; sample free. Back issues: $5. Discounts: 5% to subscription agents on instituional subscriptions. 32pp. Reporting time: Contact Editor. Simultaneous submissions accepted: No. Payment: Contact Editor. Copyrighted. Pub's reviews: 50 in 2005. §Books by and about women. Ads: Contact publisher for rate card information.

Women's Studies Librarian, University of Wisconsin System (see also FEMINIST COLLECTIONS: A QUARTERLY OF WOMEN'S STUDIES RESOURCES; FEMINIST PERIODICALS: A CURRENT LISTING OF CONTENTS; NEW BOOKS ON WOMEN & FEMINISM), Phyllis Holman Weisbard, JoAnne Lehman, Linda Fain, Ingrid Markhardt, 430 Memorial Library, 728 State Street, Madison, WI 53706, 608-263-5754. 1977. Articles, interviews, criticism, reviews, non-fiction. "In addition to the three periodicals listed above, we publish a series *Wisconsin Bibliographies in Women's Studies.*" avg. press run 1.1M. Pub'd 1 title 2005. Reporting time: 1-2 weeks. Simultaneous submissions accepted: no. Payment: none. Does not copyright for author. Subjects: Bibliography, Book Collecting, Bookselling, Book Reviewing, Feminism, Indexes & Abstracts, Lesbianism, Libraries, Printing, Wisconsin, Women.

Wood River Publishing, Gary H. Schwartz, 9 Stevens Court, Tiburon, CA 94920, 415-256-9300, Fax 415-256-9400, info@picturesnow.com. 1989. avg. press run 10M. Discounts: standard. Subjects: Bibliography, Sports, Outdoors.

Wood Thrush Books, Walt McLaughlin, Publisher, Editor; Judy Ashley, Associate Editor, 85 Aldis Street, St. Albans, VT 05478, 802-524-6606. 1985. Non-fiction. "Currently looking at booklength collections of nature-related essays and non-fiction narratives. No longer publishing chapbooks of poetry." avg. press run 200. Pub'd 3 titles 2005; expects 1 title 2006, 2 titles 2007. Discounts: 40%. 72-128pp. Reporting time: 3 months. Publishes 2% of manuscripts submitted. Payment: copies. Copyrights for author. Subjects: Earth, Natural History, Essays, Nature, Non-Fiction, Philosophy, Sports, Outdoors.

Wood Works, Paul Hunter, 4131 Greenwood Ave. N., Seattle, WA 98103-7017, www.woodworkspress.com. 1994. Poetry, fiction, long-poems. avg. press run 400-500. Pub'd 3 titles 2005; expects 3 titles 2006, 3 titles 2007. Discounts: 40% on trade paper, no discount on signed hardbound. 32pp. Reporting time: 3-6 months. Simultaneous submissions accepted: no. Publishes 1-5% of manuscripts submitted. Payment: 50 copies plus the first signed hardback. Copyrights for author. Subject: Poetry.

Woodbine House, Susan Stokes, Editor; Nancy Gray Paul, Acquisitions Editor, 6510 Bells Mill Road, Bethesda, MD 20817-1636, 301-947-3440. 1985. Non-fiction. "Full length mss - non-fiction, children's fiction." avg. press run 5M-10M. Pub'd 10 titles 2005; expects 12 titles 2006, 11 titles 2007. Discounts: available on request. 300pp. Reporting time: 1-3 months. Simultaneous submissions accepted: yes. Publishes less than 1% of manuscripts submitted. Payment: on an individual basis. Does not copyright for author. Subject: Disabled.

Woodland Press, LLC and Woodland Gospel Publishing, Cheryl Davis, Editor, Aquisitions; Tim Fortune, CFO; Davis Keith, CEO, 118 Woodland Drive, Chapmanville, WV 25508, 304-752-7500, Fax 304-752-9002; kdavis@woodlandpress.com; tfortune@woodlandpress.com; www.woodlandpress.com. 2002. Non-fiction. ''We focus on Appalachian History. We also emphasize inspirational titles through our Woodland Gospel Publishing Division.'' avg. press run 5000. Pub'd 6 titles 2005; expects 6 titles 2006, 10 titles 2007. Discounts: 40% -55% based upon quantity. Simultaneous submissions accepted: Yes. Publishes 10% of manuscripts submitted. Payment: 60 - 90-days.

WOODWORKER'S JOURNAL, Larry Stoiaken, Editor-in-Chief; Rob Johnstone, Editor; Joanna Takes, Senior Editor, 4365 Willow Drive, Medina, MN 55340, 763-478-8306, Fax 763-478-8396, editor@woodworkersjournal.com. 1976. Articles. ''Woodworking articles.'' circ. 243,716. 6/yr. Pub'd 6 issues 2005; expects 6 issues 2006, 6 issues 2007. sub. price $19.95; per copy $5.99. 98pp. Reporting time: 6 months. Simultaneous submissions accepted: no. Publishes less than 5% of manuscripts submitted. Payment: 25¢/word. Copyrighted, does not revert to author. Pub's reviews. §Woodworking. Ads: full-page $9,880 4-color 1X, $7,870 4-color 12X; half-page $5,145 4-color 1X, half-page $4,125 4-color 12X. Subjects: Crafts, Hobbies, Wood Engraving/Woodworking.

THE WORCESTER REVIEW, Rodger Martin, 1 Ekman St., Worcester, MA 01607-1513, 603-924-7342, 978-797-4770. 1973. Poetry, fiction, art, photos, satire, criticism. ''Submit up to five poems. Fiction to 4,000 words maximum. Literary articles and criticism should have a central New England connection. Photography: black and white glossy, minimum 5''x 7''. Graphic art: black and white, minimum 5''x 7''. Author's name should appear in upper left of each page. We permit simultaneous submissions.'' circ. 1M. 1/yr. Pub'd 1 issue 2005; expects 1 issue 2006, 1 issue 2007. sub. price $25 membership in Worcester County Poetry Assoc.; per copy $12; sample $6 plus $2.50 shipping and handling. Back issues: see website listing. Discounts: 20% on orders of 10 or more of current issues. 150pp. Reporting time: 9-12 months. Simultaneous submissions accepted: yes. Payment: 2 contributor's copies. Copyrighted, reverts to author. Pub's reviews: 1 in 2005. §Central-New England writers. Ads: $150 benefactors/$75 patrons; Full page per issue $250/1/2 pg. $150. Subjects: Criticism, Fiction, Graphics, Literary Review, New England, Photography, Poetry.

Word Association Publishers, 205 5th Avenue, Tarentum, PA 15084, publish@wordassociation.com, www.wordassociation.com.

The Word Doctor Online Publishing, Linda L. Labin PhD, 3448 S. Winding Path, Inverness, FL 34450-7518, 352-726-2829, doclabin@theworddoctoronline.com, http://theworddoctoronline.com. 2002. Fiction, articles, art, photos, satire, criticism, reviews, parts-of-novels, plays, non-fiction. ''Small publisher of fine fiction, literary criticism, humor/satire, art/photos/computer graphics, nonfiction how-to's (e.g. resumes, web design). Currently publishing 3-D E-books (DigitalWebBooks) created using DeskTopAuthor; planning paperback launch in 2003. Titles: *The Metaphor: A Collage Novel*, by Stephen Granger, *The ABCs of Resumes: Everything You Need to Know to Write Winning Resumes*, by Linda L. Labin. No unsolicited mss.'' Expects 2-3 titles 2006, 7-10 titles 2007. 200+pp. Reporting time: 2 months. Simultaneous submissions accepted: no. Publishes 25% of manuscripts submitted. Payment: up to 30% royalty for e-book authors. Copyrights for author. Subjects: Advertising, Self-Promotion, Experimental, Fiction, Graphic Design, Graphics, Non-Fiction, Prose, Self-Help.

•**Word Forge Books,** Mary Shafer, PO Box 97, Ferndale, PA 18921, Tel 610-847-2456, email info@wordforgebooks.com, URL www.wordforgebooks.com. 2005. Fiction, art, non-fiction. ''Word Forge Books is an independent publisher of quality nonfiction and fiction titles about the following subjects: Regional history, folkways & folklore, weather & the environment, nature, animals & habitat, alternative health & wellness, non-religious inspiration & spirituality, creativity & personal empowerment. More than ever, our world can be a dangerous and frightening place. People are bombarded daily with dark, scary and cynical messages and images. We believe what's really needed now are messages of hope, of positive vision, and of genuine caring for all living creatures. Our mission is to provide a platform for some of today's most forward-thinking, constructive voices in ideas and literature. We seek out authors and artists whose sincere wish is to help make a better world for us all. Many of our products carry a give-back, meaning that a portion of the sale of each item is donated to a related charity or independent project. Word Forge Books is constantly searching for products that will help our customers adopt and live with such constructive ideas and visions. Our lines include: BOOKS, Audiobooks, Interactive titles on DVD, eBooks; ARTWORK: Original 2D & 3D works, Limited edition prints, Stationery, greeting & blank note cards; RELATED PRODUCTS: Calendars, Tins, licensed character figures and other unique gift items. We hope readers find Word Forge Books an oasis of what's best about our world, and a sense of comfort and connectedness in our community of readers and doers.'' avg. press run 2500. Expects 1 title 2006, 2 titles 2007. Discounts: All: 5 copy min.; shipping via media mail $2.50 ist copy, $0.75 ea. add'l, all prepaidBooksellers: 40% returnable, 50% non-returnableRetailers: 50% non-returnableClassrooms & Libraries: 1-4 copies full retail; 5-9 copies 10%; 10+ 15%wholesalers & jobbers: negotiable. 450pp. Reporting time: 3 months. Simultaneous submissions accepted: Yes. Publishes 30% of manuscripts submitted. Payment: At this point, everything is negotiable, depending on the needs of the creator and our needs as a publisher. We register our books and other products with the copyright office, in whose name the contract stipulates holds the copyright. That could be us or the author, depending on our negotiations. Subjects: Alternative Medicine, Americana, Animals, Anthology, Arts, Creativity, Fiction, Gay, Grieving, Health, History, Nature, Photography, Picture Books, Weather.

WORD IS BOND, Aaron Counts, PO Box 18304, Seattle, WA 98118, submissions@unblind.com, www.unblind.com. 2003. Poetry, fiction, long-poems. "Word is Bond is working to bridge the gap between spoken word, traditional poetry and urban fiction with a literary bent. We want to create a forum for underrepresented voices that show the true diversity of urban America." circ. 1000. 2/yr. Expects 2 issues 2006, 2 issues 2007. sub. price $12; per copy $7; sample $7. Back issues: $5. Discounts: 5+ copies, 40% to distributors, retailers, bookstores. Bulk discounts for classroom use. Please contact with specific details. 96pp. Reporting time: 4-8 weeks. Simultaneous submissions accepted: Yes. Publishes 10% of manuscripts submitted. Payment: Two contributor's copies. Copyrighted, reverts to author 90 days after publication. Ads: $50 per half page. Subjects: African-American, Asian-American, Black, Chicano/a, Children, Youth, Feminism, Fiction, Music, Native American, North America, Poetry, Politics, Prose, Third World, Minorities, Women.

Word Press, PO Box 541106, Cincinnati, OH 45254-1106, 513-474-3761, Fax 513-474-9034, www.word-press.com.

The Word Works, Karren Alenier, PO Box 42164, Washington, DC 20015, fax: 301-581-9443, editor@wordworksdc.com, www.wordworksdc.com. 1974. Poetry. "Generally, The Word Works publishes contemporary poetry in single author volumes. Our Washington Prize books includes such authors as Enid Shomer, Christopher Bursk, Fred Marchant, Nathalie Anderson, Michael Atkinson, Ron Mohring, Richard Lyons." avg. press run 1000. Pub'd 4 titles 2005; expects 3 titles 2006, 2 titles 2007. Discounts: 5+ copies 40% but buyer pays shipping. 72pp. Reporting time: three months. we only accept unsolicited manuscripts through our Washington Prize. Simultaneous submissions accepted: Yes. Publishes 5% of manuscripts submitted. Payment: Authors get 15% of the run. Does not copyright for author. Subjects: Experimental, Literature (General), Translation.

WordFarm, Cindy Bunch, Mark Eddy Smith, 2010 Michigan Avenue, La Porte, IN 46350, info@wordfarm.net, www.wordfarm.net. 2002. Poetry, fiction, non-fiction. "We are interested in a mix of new and classic, traditional and experimental, poetry and prose, print and digital. We print 2-4 titles per year, and we devote significant time to design, marketing and publicity for those. We also offer nonprint publication opportunities such as audio books, books on CD-ROM and online/downloadable books." avg. press run 500-2M. Pub'd 3 titles 2005; expects 2 titles 2006, 3 titles 2007. Discounts: please inquire. 128pp. Reporting time: 1-3 months. Simultaneous submissions accepted: yes. Publishes 5% of manuscripts submitted. Payment: $100 advance; 10-15% on net receipts. Copyrights for author. Subjects: Essays, Fiction, Memoirs, Novels, Poetry, Short Stories, Writers/Writing.

WORDS OF WISDOM, Mikhammad Abdel-Ishara, Editor; Roslyn Willett, Associate Editor, Mikhammad Abdel-Ishara, Editor, PO Box 16542, Greensboro, NC 27416, e-mail wowmail@hoopsmail.com. 1981. Poetry, fiction, articles, photos, cartoons, interviews, satire, letters, non-fiction. "*Words of Wisdom* is a quarterly collection of short stories, personal essays, one-act plays, and satire with a few poems. Prefer prose in the 1,500 to 4,000 word range, and poems to thirty lines including stanza breaks. We published 49 stories by 44 authors, and 52 poems in 2004. Contributors in the last three years include Roger Coleman, Dennis Vannata, Mary Stuart, Patrick O'Neill." circ. 120-140. 4/yr. Pub'd 4 issues 2005; expects 4 issues 2006, 4 issues 2007. sub. price $17 individuals, $18 institutions, $18US Canada, and $24 international Air Mail; per copy $4.75; sample $4.75. Back issues: $4.75. Discounts: 50% for creative writing classes and groups. 76-84pp. Reporting time: usually 2 weeks to 4 months. Simultaneous submissions accepted, but no reprints please. Publishes 10-15% of manuscripts submitted. Payment: 1 year subscription for first story, 1 copy for poems, additional stories, and short-shorts. Not copyrighted, rights revert to author upon publication. Pub's reviews: none in 2005. §Books of short stories that include a story that first appeared in WoW. None. Subjects: Asia, Indochina, Essays, Fiction, Haiku, Humor, Non-Fiction, Satire, Short Stories, Travel.

WordWorkers Press, Linda Bishop, 502 Pleasant Hill Road, Sebastopol, CA 95472-4024, 707-824-4307, 800-357-6016, Fax 707-829-7159, info@independenteye.org. 1989. Plays. "Devoted to publication of plays of high literary merit in progressive forms, both in anthologies and acting editions." avg. press run 2M. Pub'd 1 title 2005; expects 1 title 2006, 2 titles 2007. Discounts: text 35%, bookstores 40%, wholesalers 55%. 50-208pp. Reporting time: 4 months. Payment: negotiable. Copyrights for author. Subjects: Drama, Theatre.

Wordwrights Canada, Susan Ioannou, PO Box 456, Station O, Toronto, Ontario M4A 2P1, Canada, wordwrights@sympatico.ca, www.wordwrights.ca. 1985. avg. press run 500-1M. Pub'd 2 titles 2005; expects 1 title 2007. Discounts: please request schedule. 28-160pp. Reporting time: 1 month. Simultaneous submissions accepted: no. Publishes less than 1% of manuscripts submitted. Payment/honorarium on publication plus copies. Author owns copyright. Subjects: Creativity, Criticism, Editing, Poetry, Writers/Writing.

WORDWRIGHTS MAGAZINE, Argonne House Press, R.D. Baker, 1620 Argonne Place NW, Washington, DC 20009-5901, 202-328-9769, www.wordwrights.com, publisher@wordwrights.com. 1995. Poetry, fiction, interviews, satire, parts-of-novels, long-poems, non-fiction. "We prefer fiction between 2,500-5,000 words in length. We prefer to publish several poems by each poet we publish. Contact us by letter or e-mail for a FREE SAMPLE COPY of WordWrights." circ. 2M. 2/yr. Pub'd 2 issues 2005; expects 2 issues 2006, 2 issues 2007. sub. price $25; per copy $8; sample $4. Back issues: $3 each. Discounts: 50%. 32pp. Reporting time: up to 6 months. Simultaneous submissions accepted: yes. Publishes 10% of manuscripts submitted. Payment: free copy. Copyrighted, reverts to author. Ads: $500/$300. Subjects: Fiction, Poetry.

WORKING WRITER, Maggie Frisch, PO Box 6943, Libertyville, IL 60048, workingwriters@aol.com. 2000. Articles, criticism, letters, non-fiction. "*Working Writer Newsletter* is for writers of all genres, at all levels. Submissions on writing topics (how-to, how-not-to, tips, shared experience) are always welcome. Request guidelines by e-mail, or simply e-mail article to workingwriters@aol.com (not as attachment). *WW* offers "solid information with a sense of humor and a spirit of writing camraderie." circ. 200. 6/yr. Pub'd 6 issues 2005; expects 6 issues 2006, 6 issues 2007. sub. price $12.95 by mail, $24.95/2 years, $6 by e-mail (PDF); per copy $2.00 regular mail, $1.00 by e-mail; sample free by e-mail, on request. Back issues: $2 by regular mail, $1 by e-mail. Discounts: $11.95/year for seniors, students; quantities provided at cost for conferences, classrooms, etc. 12pp. Reporting time: immediate (upon receipt). Simultaneous submissions accepted: yes. Publishes 90% of manuscripts submitted. Payment: byline, short bio with plug for books, copies of article, link to WW website. Copyrighted, reverts to author. Ads: none. Subject: Writers/Writing.

WorkLife Publishing, 14925 E. Morning Vista Lane, Scottsdale, AZ 85262-6891, 602-992-0144. 1996. Non-fiction. avg. press run 3M. Pub'd 1 title 2005; expects 2 titles 2006, 2 titles 2007. 200pp. Subjects: Business & Economics, Worker.

THE WORLD, The Poetry Project, Staff of the Poetry Project, St. Marks Church/The Poetry Project, 131 East 10th Street, New York, NY 10003, poproj@thorn.net. 1966. Poetry, fiction, interviews, long-poems. "Recent contributors: Alice Notley, John Ashbery, Amiri Baraka, Diane de Prima, Wang Ping, Ron Padgett, Paul Beatty, Eric Bogosian, Wanda Coleman, Harryette Mullen, Brenda Coultas, Tracie Morris, Jamie Manrique." circ. 750. 1/yr. Pub'd 1 issue 2005; expects 1 issue 2006, 1 issue 2007. sub. price $25/4 issues; per copy $7; sample $7. Back issues: on request. Discounts: none. 128pp. Reporting time: 6 months. Simultaneous submissions accepted: yes. Publishes 5% of manuscripts submitted. Payment: copies. Copyrighted, reverts to author. Ads: $125/$75. Subjects: Fiction, Poetry.

World Changing Books, Jason Wolf, Justin Pahio, PO Box 5491, Hilo, HI 96720, 808-934-7942. 1993. Non-fiction. "Second address: 489 Ocean View Dr., Hilo, HI 96720. Our primary concern this year is with the book *Never 'Old': The Ultimate Success Story* by Jesse Anson Dawn. This book is the product of 24 years of study and research, and presents unprecedented breakthroughs in health and anti-aging - all presented in a lively and delightful style." avg. press run 5M. Pub'd 1 title 2005; expects 3-4 titles 2006, 1 title 2007. Discounts: 40-50% for wholesale and bookstores. 250pp. Reporting time: 1-2 weeks. Payment: negotiable. Copyrights for author. Subjects: Aging, Health, Human Rights, Humor.

World Gumbo Publishing, Douglas Barkley, 7801 Alma Suite 105-323, Plano, TX 75025-3483, 1-888-318-2911, dbarkley@worldgumbo.com, www.worldgumbo.com. 2004. Non-fiction. "Information is Yummy!!! At World Gumbo Publishing, we are commited to providing vital, hip, and fresh business and personal growth information to savvy readers. Think COOL Business Books.Publishers of Cracking the Networking CODE - 4 Steps to Priceless Business Relationships by Dean Lindsay." avg. press run 10,000. Expects 3 titles 2007. Discounts: Special Trade Discounts Available!!! contact Toll Free: 1-800-346-5566. 160-192pp. Reporting time: 6 weeks. Simultaneous submissions accepted: Yes. Publishes 2% of manuscripts submitted. Payment: Varies Greatly. Copyrighting is available but not a deal breaker. Subjects: Advertising, Self-Promotion, Business & Economics, Consulting, Humor, Inspirational, Leadership, Mentoring/Coaching, Multicultural, Networking, Non-Fiction, Public Relations/Publicity, Scandinavia, Self-Help, Speaking, Trivia.

World Love Press Publishing, Dan S. Leyrer, 1028 Joliet Street, New Orleans, LA 70118, 504-866-4476 phone/Fax, worldlovepress@aol.com. 2000. Poetry, fiction, satire, non-fiction. avg. press run 3M. Expects 1 title 2006, 2 titles 2007. Discounts: 2-4 books 20%, 5-9 30%, 10-24 40%, 25-49 42%, 50-74 44%, 75-199 48%, 200+ 50%, classroom 1-12 books 20%, 13+ 40%. 112pp. Reporting time: 30 days. Publishes -30% of manuscripts submitted. Payment: varies. Copyrights for author. Subjects: Fiction, Humor, Metaphysics, Poetry, The West, Zen.

World Music Press, Judith Cook Tucker, Publisher, Editor-in-Chief; Claudia Chapman, Art Director, Assoc. Editor, PO Box 2565, Danbury, CT 06813-2565, 203-748-1131; fax 203-748-3432; e-mail info@worldmusic-press.com; website www.worldmusicpress.com. 1985. Photos, music, non-fiction. "We are looking for manuscripts of traditional music from non-Western cultures with in-depth annotation, prepared with the participation and knowledge of the indigenous musicians from whose repertoires the material is drawn. Slant is definitely for use by educators, and should be accurate and authentic but not dry or scholarly in tone. Range: grades 3-12 in particular. Current authors include Ghanaian master musician Abraham Kobena Adzenyah, Dumisani Maraire (ethnomusicologist/musician from Zimbabwe), Nick Page. *Vocal Traditions* choral series (choral pieces for school use inspired by or drawn from traditional music of many cultures, including Italy, Cuba, Africa, Latin America, the rural south (US), Israel, Native America). Composers/arrangers include Carlos Abril, Pete Seeger, Dumisani Maraire, and Alejandro Jimenez.'' avg. press run 1.5M books, 3M-10M choral pieces. Pub'd 2 titles 2005; expects 3 titles 2006, 3 titles 2007. Discounts: 40% 1-50; 45% 51-100, 50% 101+ mixed titles ok; mixed books/tapes ok; S.T.O.P. orders ok; *non-returnable*. 135pp. Reporting time: 1 month. Payment: 10% net (nego.) royalty; small advance; annual payments. Copyrights for author. Subjects: African Literature, Africa, African Studies, Asia, Indochina, Audio/Video, Caribbean, Cuba, Dance, Education, Folklore, Latin America, Multicultural, Music, Native American, Poland, Tapes & Records, Vietnam.

WORLD OF FANDOM MAGAZINE, Allen Shevy, PO Box 9421, Tampa, FL 33604, 813-933-7424. 1987. Fiction, articles, art, photos, cartoons, interviews, criticism, reviews, music, non-fiction. ''Physical address: 2525 W. Knollwood Street, Tampa, FL 33614-4334. We will run anything as long as it has to do with comic books, movies, music, or TV. Art is also acceptable.'' circ. 70M+. 4/yr. Pub'd 4 issues 2005; expects 4 issues 2006, 4 issues 2007. sub. price $14, $35 foreign; per copy $4.25, $7.50 foreign; sample same. Back issues: upon request, based on copies in stock. Discounts: will trade with mags; wholesale 60% non-returnable, 40% returnable. 108pp. Payment: depends on content but usually complimentary copies. Copyrighted, reverts to author. Pub's reviews. §SciFi, horror, movie, music, TV, review comic books. Ads: $400/$225/$125 1/4 page/discounts for more than 1 issue. Subjects: Book Reviewing, Cartoons, Comics, Criticism, Disney, Electronics, Entertainment, Fantasy, Interviews, Magazines, Media, Movies, Music, Reviews, Science Fiction.

World Travel Institute, Inc., Gladson I. Nwanna Ph.D, 8268 Streamwood Drive, PO Box 32674, Baltimore, MD 21208, 410-922-4903; website www.worldtravelinstitute.com. 1992. Articles, news items, non-fiction. avg. press run 10M. Expects 2 titles 2006, 4 titles 2007. Discounts: available (standard trade). 400pp. Reporting time: 4 weeks. Simultaneous submissions accepted: no. Copyrights for author. Subject: Transportation.

World Wisdom,Inc., PO Box 2682, Bloomington, IN 47402, 812-330-3232, e-mail customers@worldwisdom.com. 1981. Non-fiction. avg. press run 3M. Pub'd 18 titles 2005; expects 16 titles 2006, 18 titles 2007. Discounts: trade 40% no minimum; libraries 50%. 350pp. Reporting time: 3-6 months. Publishes 2% of manuscripts submitted. Copyrights for author. Subjects: Philosophy, Religion.

WRESTLING - THEN & NOW, Evan Ginzburg, PO Box 640471, Oakland Gdns. Station, Flushing, NY 11364. 1990. Articles, interviews, satire, reviews, letters, news items, non-fiction. ''Explores history of professional wrestling. Features warm reminisces, where are they now type features, interviews, clippings, etc.'' circ. 275. 12/yr + annual. Pub'd 11 issues 2005; expects 12 issues 2006, 12 issues 2007. sub. price $25; per copy $2.50; sample free. Back issues: $2. 16pp. Reporting time: varies. Simultaneous submissions accepted: yes. Publishes 75% of manuscripts submitted. Payment: copies. Copyrighted, reverts to author. Pub's reviews: 20 in 2005. §Book, video, fanzine reviews. Ads: $40/$25/15¢ per word to subscribers, 75¢ non-subscribers. Subjects: Entertainment, Newsletter.

Writecorner.com Press, Robert B. Gentry, Mary Sue Koeppel, P.O. Box 140310, Gainesville, FL 32614-0310, www.writecorner.com. 2002. Fiction, criticism, reviews, parts-of-novels, non-fiction. ''Writecorner Press at www.writecorner.com features the annual E.M. Koeppel Short Fiction Award - first prize $1,100; Editors' choices - $100; and the P.L. Titus Short Fiction Scholarship - $500. Contest submissions postmarked between Oct. 1 and April 30. See website for guidelines. Site also features Fresh & Ripe pages of short fiction as well as book reviews. Send books for review on the site. (Editors - Mary Sue Koeppel is the 17 year editor of *Kalliope* and Robert B. Gentry is an award-winning fiction writer.).'' Payment: $1,100.00 annual E.M. Koeppel Short Fiction Award. Copyrights for author. Subjects: Fiction, Literary Review, Literature (General).

The Writers Block, Inc., Sandra Thomas Wales, President, POB 821, Franklin, KY 42135-0821, cell: 270-791-6252, fax: 270-586-9840; HEGwritersbl@aol.com, HaleyElizabethGarwood.com. 1994. Fiction. ''Historical novels run about 450 pages. That is our main interest, but we do publish good mystery novels, very little romance, and some mainstream in the works. We are operating slowly to remain debt free. Note: No unsolicited or unagented materials.'' avg. press run 5-10M. Pub'd 1 title 2005; expects 2 titles 2006, 3 titles 2007. Discounts: 2-4 20%, 5-99 40%, 100+ in even case lots 55%. 450pp. Reporting time: 3 months. Simultaneous submissions accepted: yes. Publishes 1% of manuscripts submitted. Payment: 10%, no advance. Copyrights for author. Subject: Fiction.

WRITER'S CAROUSEL, The Writer's Center, Rick Walter, Managing Editor, 4508 Walsh Street, Bethesda, MD 20815-6006, 301-654-8664. 1976. Articles, art, cartoons, interviews, reviews, letters, news items. ''We are a writer's journal featuring articles and forums on the practice of writing and the writing trade, book reviews, literary journal reviews and a list of markets.'' circ. 6M. 6/yr. Pub'd 6 issues 2005; expects 6 issues 2006, 6 issues 2007. sub. price $40. 24pp. Reporting time: 30 days. Simultaneous submissions accepted:

no. Payment: copies. Copyrighted. Pub's reviews: 24 in 2005. §Books about writing, new poetry, fiction and drama. Ads: write for rate sheet. Subjects: Book Reviewing, Communication, Journalism, Creativity, Editing, English, Interviews, Publishing.

The Writer's Center (see also POET LORE; WRITER'S CAROUSEL), 4508 Walsh Street, Bethesda, MD 20815-6006, 301-654-8664, www.writer.org. 1977.

WRITER'S CHRONICLE, David Fenza, Editor-in-Chief; Supriya Bhatnagar, Editor, Mail Stop 1E3, George Mason University, Fairfax, VA 22030-4444, 703-993-4301, http://awpwriter.org. 1967. Articles, interviews, criticism, news items. "Articles pertaining to contemporary literature, writing, and the teaching of writing welcome. News items, grants & awards, magazine submission notices. Interviews in every issue." circ. 26M. 6 issues each academic year. Pub'd 6 issues 2005; expects 6 issues 2006, 6 issues 2007. sub. price $20-6 editions/$34-12 issues. Contact the office for international rates.; per copy $4.95; sample $5.00. Back issues: $5.00. 72pp. Reporting time: 3 months. Simultaneous submissions accepted: yes/please notify if accepted elsewhere. Publishes 5% of manuscripts submitted. Payment: honorarium and copies, $10/100 words, no kill fees. Copyrighted, reverts to author. Ads: Display - $1,040 - Full Page/$695 - Half Page/$590 - Junior Page/$485 - Third Page/$375 - Quarter Page/$250 - Ninth Page/Classifieds: $70 for up to 50 words, $1 per each additional word. Subjects: Criticism, Editing, Education, Essays, Fiction, Literature (General), Non-Fiction, Poetry, Women, Writers/Writing.

WRITERS CORNER, T.L. Dorn, 142 Camelot Drive, Castle Rock, WA 98611-9471. 1998. Fiction, non-fiction. "Stories 1-7 pages mostly excepted. Exceptional stories up to 23 pages have been published." circ. 300. 6/yr. sub. price $17; per copy $5; sample $5. Back issues: $6. 80pp. Reporting time: 2 months. Simultaneous submissions accepted: yes. Publishes 85% of manuscripts submitted. Payment: free copy. Copyrighted, reverts to author. Pub's reviews. Ads: $30/$17/bus card $7.

WRITER'S EXCHANGE, Gene Boone, 129 Thurman Lane, Clinton, TN 37716-6611, E-mail eboone@aol.com, www.users.aol.com/writernet. 1986. Poetry, articles, art, cartoons, interviews, letters. "Poetry, to 24 lines, various subjects/forms. Articles on writing-related topics, to 1200 words. Interviews, to 1200 words with writers/poets or publishers. Art-small drawings (ink), any subject: nature, etc. Cartoons-writing-related cartoons." circ. 250-300. 4/yr. Pub'd 4 issues 2005; expects 4 issues 2006, 4 issues 2007. sub. price $12; per copy $2; sample $2. Back issues: $1 and SASE. 40pp. Reporting time: 2-4 weeks. Publishes 80% of manuscripts submitted. Payment: contributors copy. Copyrighted, reverts to author. Pub's reviews: 250-300 in 2005. §Literary and commercial fiction, poetry, nonfiction, art, books on writing. Ads: $50/$25/$5 small display ad. Subjects: Creativity, Literary Review, Poetry, Reviews, Writers/Writing.

Writers' Haven Press (see also HA!), Sharon E. Svendsen, Nancy Ryan, P. O. Box 368, Seabeck, WA 98380-0368, (360) 830-5772. 2002. Poetry, fiction, art, cartoons, satire, parts-of-novels, long-poems, non-fiction. "We publish poetry books by women, contest-winners chapbooks, and HA!, a humor magazine with fiction, poetry, cartoons, and humorous prose." avg. press run 500. Pub'd 2 titles 2005; expects 8 titles 2006, 10 titles 2007. Discounts: 5-10 copies 25%. 100pp. Reporting time: three to six months. Simultaneous submissions accepted: Yes. Publishes 5% of manuscripts submitted. Payment: 50 copies of book and 15% royalty after production costs have been met. Copyrights for author. Subjects: Cartoons, Civil Rights, Comics, Cooking, Essays, Food, Eating, Haiku, Humor, Poetry, Prose, Satire, Self-Help, Short Stories, Women.

WRITERS INK, Writers Ink Press, Writers Unlimited Agency, Inc, David B. Axelrod, PO Box 2344, Selden, NY 11784, 631-451-0478, Fax 631-451-0478, http://www.writersunlimited.org. 1975. Articles, art, photos, cartoons, interviews, satire, criticism, reviews, collages. "We have changed to an on-line format. Consult our website and contact us to suggest material. http://www.writersunlimited.org." circ. 2M. 0-4/yr. Pub'd 1 issue 2005; expects 2 issues 2006, 1 issue 2007. sub. price $6; per copy $1; No samples. Back issues: specific issues by request, free if available. Discounts: none-but free to worthy folks or groups—sold, $6 yearly rate direct by 1st class mail from WI. 4-12pp. Reporting time: immediate (maximum 2 weeks) only if we are interested; no reply means "no thanks" Payment: 50¢/col. inch or $2/photo. Copyrighted, reverts to author. Pub's reviews: 1 in 2005. §All aids to writers, general interest and of course, L.I. works, mags, books. Ads: $15/$8/25¢. Subject: Book Reviewing.

Writers Ink Press (see also WRITERS INK), David B. Axelrod, 233 Mooney Pond, PO Box 2344, Selden, Long Island, NY 11784-2344, 631-451-0478, Fax 631-451-0478, axelrodthepoet@yahoo.com. 1975. Poetry. "No unsolicited mss. at this time." avg. press run 800. Pub'd 2 titles 2005; expects 3 titles 2006, 3 titles 2007. Discounts: 30% bookstores & distributors. Chapbooks 24-48pp, perfectbound 72-128pp. Payment: 50% profit over cost, varies. Copyrights for author. Subject: Poetry.

WRITERS' JOURNAL, Leon Ogroske, Editor; John Ogroske, Publisher-Managing Editor, PO Box 394, Perham, MN 56573-0394, Phone 218-346-7921, Fax 218-346-7924, E-mail writersjournal@writersjournal.com, Web site www.writersjournal.com. 1980. Poetry, fiction, articles, photos, reviews. "Articles on the art of writing - inspirational and informative - 500-2000 words. Especially interested in articles discussing unusual freelance writing markets. Markets Report. *Writers' Journal* is a bi-monthly journal for writers and poets. We sponsor a 5000 word Fiction contest, 2000 word Short Story, Romance, Travel Writing, and Horror/Ghost contests with cash prizes up to $500.00. We also sponsor three Poetry contests and two Photo contests each year. We have six 'Write to Win!' contests where a starter phrase is given. See our Web site www.writersjournal.com or send an SASE for contest guidelines.'' circ. 26M. 6/yr. Pub'd 6 issues 2005; expects 6 issues 2006, 6 issues 2007. sub. price $19.97; per copy $5.99; sample $5. Back issues: $5. Discounts: varies. 64pp. Reporting time: Up to six months. Simultaneous submissions accepted: yes. Publishes 20% of manuscripts submitted. Payment: $10-$50 and copies. Copyrighted, reverts to author. Ads: $750-900/$420-500/ $1.50 per word. Subjects: Desktop Publishing, Editing, Fiction, Poetry, Publishing, Writers/Writing.

WRITER'S LIFELINE, Vesta Publications Limited, Stephen Gill, Editor, PO Box 1641, Cornwall, Ont. K6H 5V6, Canada. 1974. circ. 2M. 3/yr. Pub'd 3 issues 2005; expects 3 issues 2006, 3 issues 2007. sub. price $18; per copy $3; sample $8 for 3 issues. Back issues: $1.50. Discounts: 30%. 36pp. Reporting time: 4-6 weeks. Payment: in copies at present. Copyrighted. Pub's reviews: 80 in 2005. §All, but particularly about writing and publishing. Ads: $150/$100/$15. Subjects: African Literature, Africa, African Studies, Arts, Awards, Foundations, Grants, Book Reviewing, Communication, Journalism, Fiction, Libraries, Literature (General), Poetry.

Writers Unlimited Agency, Inc (see also WRITERS INK), David B. Axelrod, PO Box 2344, Selden, NY 11784, 631-451-0478, Fax 631-451-0478, writersunlimitedagency@yahoo.com http://www.writersunlimited.org. 1975. ''We keep an active file of poets' work and can sometimes provide referals for publication and/or readings. No unsolicited mss.'' avg. press run 800. Pub'd 2 titles 2005; expects 3 titles 2006, 3 titles 2007. Discounts: 30% distributor/bookseller. 40pp. Payment: varies. Copyrights for author. Subject: Poetry.

Writer's World Press, Lavern Hall, Publisher, PO Box 284, Aurora, OH 44202-0284, Writers-World@juno.com, www.writersworldpress.com. 1991. Non-fiction. ''Resources for writers and publishers (reference books/directories). Query with book proposal including overview, TOC, chapter-by-chapter outline, market and competition, sample chapter, bio, SASE (or if you do not want the proposal returned, #10 SASE for response). Reporting time 4-6 weeks. Identify simultaneous submissions. Publishes a very selective % of manuscripts submitted. Payment: flat fee. Copyrights for author.Through our consulting division, Books by Design, we offer consulting and editorial services for writers seeking publication, authors who wish to self-publish, or those wanting to produce family histories/memoirs. We specialize in nonfiction books, but will edit fiction (including historical and contemporary romance).''

WRITING FOR OUR LIVES, Janet M. McEwan, 647 N. Santa Cruz Ave., The Annex, Los Gatos, CA 95030, 408-354-8604. 1991. Poetry, fiction, letters, parts-of-novels, non-fiction. ''This periodical serves as a vessel for poems, short fiction, stories, letters, autobiographies, and journal excerpts from the life-stories, experiences, and spiritual journeys of women. Please observe maximum word/page limit: approx. 2100 words (7 pages). Please send 2 SASEs. Women writers only, please.'' circ. 500. Irregular, no more than 1/yr. Expects 1 issue 2007. sub. price 2 issues $15.50 U.S., $21 overseas; per copy $8, $11 overseas; sample $6-$8, $9-$11 overseas. Back issues: $6-$8, $9-$11 overseas; any 4 copies for $20, $25 overseas. Discounts: trade 40%. 80pp. Reporting time: first report immediate, second varies. Simultaneous submissions accepted: yes. Publishes fewer than 5% of manuscripts submitted. Payment: 2 copies, plus discount on copies and subscription. Copyrighted, reverts to author. Subjects: Autobiography, Feminism, Fiction, Poetry, Short Stories, Women.

WSQ (formerly WOMEN'S STUDIES QUARTERLY), The Feminist Press at the City University of New York, Florence Howe, Publisher; Anjoli Roy, Managing Editor; Cindi Katz, General Editor; Nancy Miller, General Editor, The Feminist Press at CUNY, 365 Fifth Avenue, Suite 5406, New York, NY 10016, 212-817-7915, 212-817-1593, aroy@gc.cuny.edu, www.feministpress.org/wsq. 1972. Poetry, fiction, articles, art, photos, cartoons, interviews, satire, criticism, reviews, letters, collages, news items, non-fiction. circ. 1200. 2/yr. Pub'd 2 issues 2005; expects 2 issues 2006, 2 issues 2007. sub. price $40 individuals, $60 institutions, foreign $55 individuals, $75 institutions; per copy $22 (double issue). Back issues: $18 per copy. Discounts: See Consortium or our catalog on line at www.feministpress.org. 400pp. Pub's reviews: 8 in 2005. §Women's studies. Ads: $175/$100/$75. Subjects: Criticism, Education, Essays, Feminism, Gender Issues, History, Lesbianism, Reviews, Sociology, Third World, Minorities, Women.

Wynn Publishing, Edward Wincentsen, PO Box 1491, Pickens, SC 29671, 864-878-6469, Fax 864-878-6267, jack@wynnco.com. 1994. Articles, photos, interviews, criticism, reviews, music. avg. press run 5M. Pub'd 1 title 2005; expects 2 titles 2006, 4 titles 2007. Discounts: 20-55%. 122pp. Reporting time: 2-4 weeks. Simultaneous submissions accepted: yes. Payment: varies. Copyrights for author. Subjects: Biography, Entertainment, Music.

Wytherngate Press, Pamela Mogen, P O Box 3134, Couer d Alene, ID 83816, 208-818-3078, 208-661-4566, wytherngatepress@gmail.com, after 4/30/2006: info@wytherngate.com. 2003. Fiction. ''Fiction and non-fiction written for the discerning reader. Mild "language" acceptable if appropriate for context. No explicit sexual descriptions." Pub'd 1 title 2005; expects 3 titles 2006, 3 titles 2007. Discounts: 35%. Reporting time: 1 month. Simultaneous submissions accepted: Yes. Payment: 55% profit after editing, production, shipping costs. $200 reading fee for edited manuscripts. Unedited manuscripts will be edited at $25 per hour. Does not copyright for author. Subjects: Christianity, Fantasy, Fiction, History, Inspirational, Mystery, Religion, Romance.

X

•**Xavier House Publishing,** James Bilodeau, PO BOX 1103, Franklin, KY 42135, james@xavier-house.com, www.xavier-house.com, 502-212-9314. 2005. Satire, criticism, non-fiction. Expects 1 title 2006, 2 titles 2007. 180pp. Reporting time: 4-6 weeks. Simultaneous submissions accepted: yes. Publishes 50% of manuscripts submitted. Copyrights for author. Subjects: Americana, Amish Culture, Biography, Government, Humor, Kentucky, Midwest, Non-Fiction, Politics, Tennessee.

XAVIER REVIEW, Richard Collins, Editor; Robert E. Skinner, Managing Editor, Box 110C, Xavier University, New Orleans, LA 70125, 504-520-7549 Collins, 483-7303 Skinner, Fax 504-485-7917. 1980. Poetry, fiction, photos, criticism, reviews, parts-of-novels. circ. 300. 2/yr. Pub'd 2 issues 2005; expects 2 issues 2006, 2 issues 2007. sub. price $10 individuals, $15 institutions; per copy $5; sample $5. Back issues: inquire. Discounts: inquire. 75pp. Reporting time: 1 month. Simultaneous submissions accepted: Yes, if notified. Publishes 5% of manuscripts submitted. Payment: 2 copies of issue. Copyrighted, rights reassigned to author upon request. Pub's reviews: 10 in 2005. §Southern ethnic, and Latin-American culture, African-American. Ads: $40/$20. Subjects: The Americas, Black, Book Reviewing, Caribbean, Essays, Fiction, Literary Review, Literature (General), Louisiana, Poetry, Short Stories, South.

XCP: CROSS-CULTURAL POETICS, Mark Nowak, College of St. Catherine, 601 25th Avenue South, Minneapolis, MN 55454, website http://bfn.org/~xcp. 1997. "Seeks to address the increasingly untenable boundaries between poetry, politics, and cultural studies. Recent contributors: Amiri Baraka, Kimiko Hahn, George Marcus, Adrienne Rich." circ. 850. 2/yr. sub. price $18 indivduals, $40 institutions, foreign add $5; checks payable to College of St. Catherine.; per copy $10; sample $9. 176pp. Reporting time: 1-2 months. Simultaneous submissions accepted: no. Payment: 2 copies. Copyrighted, reverts to author. Pub's reviews: 30 in 2005. §Marxism; Cultural and Performance Studies; Labor History; Anti-globalization; International and Intercultural Poetry and Poetics; Politics. Ads: $125. Subjects: African-American, Anthropology, Archaelogy, Asian-American, Avant-Garde, Experimental Art, Culture, Folklore, Multicultural, Native American.

Xenos Books, Karl Kvitko, Box 52152, Riverside, CA 92517, 909-370-2229, E-mail info@xenosbooks.com, www.xenosbooks.com. 1986. Poetry, fiction, art, satire, long-poems, plays, non-fiction. avg. press run 300-500. Pub'd 3 titles 2005; expects 3 titles 2006, 3 titles 2007. Discounts: 20-40%. 120-200pp. Reporting time: 1-3 months. Simultaneous submissions accepted: yes. Publishes 5% of manuscripts submitted. Payment: individual agreements. Copyrights for author if requested. Subjects: Autobiography, Bilingual, Drama, Fiction, Non-Fiction, Novels, Poetry, Prose, Surrealism, Translation, U.S.S.R.

X-RAY, Johnny Brewton, Po Box 2234, Pasadena, CA 91102, johnny@xraybookco.com. 1993. Poetry, fiction, art, photos, cartoons, interviews, satire, music, collages, concrete art. "*X-Ray* is an Art/ literary magazine or sorts. Sometimes bound like a book and sometimes loose leaf in a letterpress box. Recent contributors include Ruth Weiss, Wanda Gleman, Dan Fante, Bern Porter, A.D. Winans, Allen Ginsberg, Jaime Hernandez, Charles Bukowski, August Kleinzahler, Neeli Cherkovski, Jack Micheline and Hunter S. Thompson. Correspondence artists are encouraged to contribute. Accepting short fiction, poetry, erotica, prose, found poems, experimental poetry, found objects, assemblage, original art, comics, interviews, photography, etc. Materials range from Chinese telephone directory, sheet music from the early 1900's to hemp and colored craft paper. Every page a different paper. Chapbooks can be found within the pages stuffed into envelopes and fold-out broadsides also grace the pages. Guidelines vary depending upon the issue. Send one completed suggested piece for approval. After approval send at least 126 pieces as the edition is limited to 126. 100 numbered and 26 lettered copies + 4 proofs. Send SASE for exact guideline information." circ. 126. 100 numbered copies and 26 lettered A-Z and signed. 2/yr. Pub'd 2 issues 2005; expects 2 issues 2006, 2 issues 2007. sub. price none; per copy $55. Back issues: none. 80pp. Reporting time: 2 weeks. Simultaneous submissions accepted: no. Publishes 25% of manuscripts submitted. Payment: 1 copy. Copyrighted, reverts to author. Pub's reviews. §Novels, poetry, music, zines, art, whatever... Ads: none. Subjects: Arts, Literature (General).

X-Ray Book Co. (see also BAGAZINE), Johnny Brewton, P.O. Box 2234, Pasadena, CA 91102. 2005. Poetry, fiction, articles, art, photos, cartoons, interviews, letters, parts-of-novels, collages, concrete art. "X-Ray seeks original work and ideas. We discourage those who embarrassingly emulate poorly the style of Charles

534

Bukowski. Influence is great but remember, there's only one Bukowski. Contributors include: Billy Childish, Charles Bukowski, Hunter S. Thompson, Allen Ginsberg, Thurston Moore, Michael Montfort, Mark Faigenbaum, Johnny Brewton, Michael Napper, F.N. Wright, Timothy Leary and more." avg. press run 126. Expects 2 titles 2006, 2 titles 2007. Discounts: contact publisher for more information. 50pp. Reporting time: 10 Days. Simultaneous submissions accepted: No. Payment: (1) copy unless specifed in mutual agreement. Copyright reverts to authors with permission to reprint all works in collection of past issues book. Subjects: Abstracts, Absurdist, Architecture, Avant-Garde, Experimental Art, Beat, Charles Bukowski, Chicano/a, Experimental, Jack Kerouac, Music, Photography, Poetry, Short Stories, Tapes & Records, Zines.

XTANT, xtant.anabasis, Thomas Taylor, 814 - 318 Place, Ocean Park, WA 98640, (360) 665-3248. 2000. Poetry, fiction, art, photos, criticism, reviews, collages, concrete art. "rcent contributors, John M. Bennett, Jim Leftwich, Thomas Lowe Taylor, Jukka Lehmus, Sheila Murphy, Scott MacLeod, John Crouse, Vincent Ferrini." circ. 151. 1/yr. Pub'd 1 issue 2005; expects 1 issue 2006, 1 issue 2007. sub. price $25; per copy $25. Back issues: n/a. Discounts: none given. 200pp. Reporting time: 7 days with SASE. Simultaneous submissions accepted: Yes. Publishes 5% of manuscripts submitted. Payment: no payment, one copy per contributor. Not copyrighted. Pub's reviews: approx 3 in 2005. §experimental writing, visual poetry. Ads: 300/pg; 150/half pg. Subjects: Abstracts, Absurdist, Bilingual, Erotica, Fiction, Folklore, Futurism, Graphics, Literary Review, Occult, Poetry, Spiritual, Sufism, Surrealism, Writers/Writing.

xtant.anabasis (see also XTANT), Thomas Taylor, 814 - 318 Place, Ocean Park, WA 98640, (360) 665-3248. 1976. Poetry, fiction, art, photos, cartoons, criticism, reviews, long-poems, collages, concrete art. "publish post post-modern, abstract-exprressionist with a spiritual bent, visual poetry, post language school, neo-superflat, graffiti, asemic writing." avg. press run 151. Pub'd 11 titles 2005; expects 2-6 titles 2006, 2-6 titles 2007. Discounts: no discounts offered. 40-900pp. Reporting time: response within 7 days with SASE. Simultaneous submissions accepted: Yes. Publishes 5% of manuscripts submitted. Payment: no. sales to date. Copyrights for author. Subjects: Avant-Garde, Experimental Art, Experimental, Futurism, Graphics, Poetry, Prose, Spiritual, Writers/Writing.

XTRAS, From Here Press, William J. Higginson, Penny Harter, PO Box 1402, Summit, NJ 07902-1402. 1975. Poetry, fiction, criticism, parts-of-novels, long-poems, plays, non-fiction. "*Xtras*, a cooperative chapbook series, features writing in both verse and prose. Issues of *Xtras* are devoted to the work of one or a related group of writers who cooperate in publishing their own chapbooks, and receive a substantial number of copies in payment. Individual *Xtras* chapbooks feature poems by Penny Harter, W.J. Higginson, and Ruth Stone, haiku and sequences by Alan Pizzarelli, W.J. Higginson, Adele Kenny, and Elizabeth Searle Lamb, workshop writings by teens and elderly, haiku and short poems by Allen Ginsberg, diary in haiku-prose by Rod Tulloss, essays and long poems by WJH. Not reading unsolicited mss now." circ. 200-500. 0-1/yr. Expects 1 issue 2007. price per copy $3-$4.95. Discounts: 40% to trade (5 mixed titles; titles can be mixed with From Here Press books). 28-72pp. Reporting time: 1 month. Payment: a substantial number of copies. Copyrighted, reverts to author. No ads. Subjects: Haiku, Poetry.

Y

THE YALE REVIEW, J.D. McClatchy, Editor; Susan Bianconi, Managing Editor, Yale University, PO Box 208243, New Haven, CT 06520-8243. 1911. Poetry, fiction, articles, criticism, reviews, letters, long-poems, plays, non-fiction. "Advertising, subscription office: Blackwell Publishers, 350 Main Street, Malden, MA 02148." circ. 6M. 4/yr. Pub'd 4 issues 2005; expects 4 issues 2006. sub. price $65 institutions, $27 individuals; per copy $10 (includes postage and handling); sample $10 (includes postage and handling). Back issues: on request. Discounts: distributor, 50%, agent 20% bookstores 10%. 160pp plus 16-24pp front matter. Reporting time: 1-2 months. Simultaneous submissions accepted: no. Publishes less than 5% of manuscripts submitted. Payment: on publication. Copyright Yale University, remaining so on publication by agreement with author or transfer of copyright to author. Pub's reviews: 12 in 2005. §Literature, history, fiction, poetry, economics, biography, arts & architecture, politics, foreign affairs. Ads: on request. Subjects: Criticism, English, Literary Review.

YALE REVIEW OF BOOKS, PO Box 206560, New Haven, CT 06520, joanna.neborsky@yale.edu, cesar.garza@yale.edu.

Yale University Press, Jonathan Brent, Larisa Heimert, John Kulka, Mary Jane Peluso, Jean Thompson Black, Patricia Fidler, Michael O'Malley, Lauren Shapiro, Keith Condon, PO Box 209040, New Haven, CT 06520, 203-432-0960, 203-432-0948 [fax], www.yalebooks.com. 1908. Poetry, art, photos, criticism, music, letters, plays, non-fiction. "By publishing serious works that contribute to a global understanding of human affairs, Yale University Press aids in the discovery and dissemination of light and truth, lux et veritas, which is a central purpose of Yale University. The publications of the Press are books and other materials that further scholarly investigation, advance interdisciplinary inquiry, stimulate public debate, educate both within and outside the classroom, and enhance cultural life. Through the distribution of works that combine excellence in scholarship with skillful editing, design, production, and marketing, the Press demonstrates its commitment to increasing the range and vigor of intellectual pursuits within the university and elsewhere. With an innovative and entrepreneurial spirit, Yale University Press continually extends its horizons to embody university press publishing at its best."

THE YALOBUSHA REVIEW, Neal Walsh, Editor, English Dept, Univ. of Mississippi, PO Box 1848, University, MS 38677-1848, 662-915-3175, yalobusha@olemiss.edu, www.olemiss.edu/yalobusha. 1995. Poetry, fiction, art, photos, interviews, parts-of-novels, long-poems, plays, non-fiction. "*The Yalobusha Review* is an annual small-press publication whose main goal is promoting quality writing, regardless of subject matter, genre, or type. Each year we feature prominent or emerging writers alongside new and often unpublished writers. Previous editions have featured stories and poems by Barry Hannah, Charles Wright, Tom Chandler, George Singleton, Janisse Ray, Shay Youngblood, Alan Michael Parker, and National Book Award finalist Dan Chaon, as well as interviews with Lee Smith (*Saving Grace, The Last Girls*), Jill McCorkle Youngblood (*Black Girl in Paris*), and Steve Almond (*My Life in Heavy Metal, Candy Freak*). Reading period: July 15 - Nov. 15. Please see the website for full submissions guidelines. CONTEST: Second Annual Barry Hannah Fiction Prize. Winner receives $500 & publication in 2005 *Yalobusha Review*. Deadline is September 30. Include SASE and $10 reading fee (cash or check made out to Yalobusha Review). Please see our website for full details." circ. 1000. 1/yr. Pub'd 1 issue 2005; expects 1 issue 2006, 1 issue 2007. sub. price $8/yr for multiple years; per copy $10; sample $5. Back issues: $5. Discounts: Please contact us for bulk discount information. 125pp. Reporting time: 1-3 months to manuscripts. Simultaneous submissions accepted: no. Publishes 3-5% of manuscripts submitted. Payment: Small honorarium & 2 contributor's copies. Copyrighted, reverts to author. Ads: for swap.

YA'SOU/Skyline Productions, David D. Bell, Editor, PO Box 77463, Columbus, OH 43207. Poetry. "No profanity, no excess violence. Poetry 26 lines or less. Reading fee: $1.50 per poem." circ. 60. 4/yr. Pub'd 4 issues 2005; expects 4 issues 2006, 4 issues 2007. Publishes 80% of manuscripts submitted. Payment: free copy. Not copyrighted. Ads: none.

Ye Olde Font Shoppe, Victoria Rivas, PO Box 8328, New Haven, CT 06530, e-mail yeolde@webcom.com; website www.webcom.com/yeolde. 1995. Poetry. "Chapbooks and perfect bound poetry books. Recent authors: Linda Lerner, A.D. Winana, Lynne Savitt, Tony Moffeit." avg. press run 500. Pub'd 8 titles 2005; expects 15 titles 2006, 30 titles 2007. Discounts: 40% off author and reseller. 40 and 80pp. Reporting time: 6-8 weeks. Simultaneous submissions accepted: no. Publishes 25% of manuscripts submitted. Payment: 10% of retail, once a year. Copyrights for author. Subject: Poetry.

YE OLDE NEWES, Jim Smith, Po Box 151107, Lufkin, TX 75915-1107, 936-637-7475. 1981. "Magazine about the Scarborough Faire." circ. 30M. 1/yr. Pub'd 2 issues 2005; expects 1 issue 2006, 1 issue 2007. price per copy $4; sample $5. Back issues: not available. 156pp. Reporting time: done in March each year. Simultaneous submissions accepted: yes. Publishes less than 5% of manuscripts submitted. Payment: none. Copyrighted, reverts to author. Ads: none accepted. Subjects: Crafts, Hobbies, Entertainment, Fantasy, Festivals, Medieval, Renaissance.

Years Press, F. Richard Thomas, Editor, Publisher; Leonora H. Smith, Associate Editor, Dept. of ATL, EBH, Michigan State University, E. Lansing, MI 48824-1033. 1973. Poetry. "Occasional publisher of chapbooks, usually solicited after hearing a reading. *Centering Magazine* has become a series of one-author chapbooks." avg. press run 300-400. Pub'd 1 title 2005; expects 1 title 2006, 1 title 2007. 12-24pp. Reporting time: 1 month. Payment: 5 copies. Subjects: Magazines, Poetry, Scandinavia.

Yellow Moon Press, Robert B. Smyth, PO Box 381316, Cambridge, MA 02238-0001, 617-776-2230, Fax 617-776-8246, E-mail story@yellowmoon.com, www.yellowmoon.com. 1978. Poetry, music, non-fiction. "Authors/Storytellers include: Coleman Barks, Robert Bly, Rafe Martin, Michael Meade, Elizabeth McKim, Lorraine Lee Hammond, Doug Lipman, Maggi Peirce, Ruth Stone, and Dovie Thomason. *Yellow Moon* is committed to publishing material related to the oral tradition. It is our goal to make available material that explores the history of the oral tradition while breathing new life into it." avg. press run varies with title. Pub'd 3 titles 2005; expects 3 titles 2006, 3-4 titles 2007. Distributed to the trade through Ingram, Baker & Taylor, and Amazon. 32-56pp. Reporting time: 6-8 weeks. Simultaneous submissions accepted: no. Publishes 1% of manuscripts submitted. Payment: varies according to book. Copyrights for author. Subjects: Folklore, Men, Music, Myth, Mythology, Native American, New England, Poetry, Storytelling, Tapes & Records, Translation, Women.

Yes International Publishers (see also HIMALAYAN PATH), Theresa King, 1317 Summit Avenue, St.

Paul, MN 55105, 651-645-6808, Fax 651-645-7935, yes@yespublishers.com, www.yespublishers.com. 1988. Non-fiction. "Books for self-transformation. Yoga, wellness, spirituality, personal transformation, yoga psychology." avg. press run 2M. Pub'd 1 title 2005; expects 3 titles 2006, 2 titles 2007. Discounts: 40% no returns. 200pp. Reporting time: 2 weeks to 2 months. Simultaneous submissions accepted: no. Publishes 1% of manuscripts submitted. Copyrights for author. Subjects: Autobiography, Catholic, Christianity, Health, Poetry, Self-Help, Spiritual, Women, Yoga.

YMAA Publication Center, James O'Leary, Editor; Jwing-Ming Yang, President; David Ripianzi, Director, 4354 Washington Street, Roslindale, MA 02131, 617-323-7215, Fax 617-323-7417, ymaa@aol.com, www.ymaa.com. 1982. Non-fiction. "Publication categories: Traditional Asian martial arts, Taijiquan, Qigong, Eastern thought, Oriental healing, East/West synthesis, Fitness grounded in an Asian tradition." avg. press run 4M. Pub'd 8 titles 2005; expects 10 titles 2006, 10 titles 2007. 180pp. Reporting time: 3 months. Simultaneous submissions accepted: yes. Publishes 20% of manuscripts submitted. Payment: no advance, royalty on books sold. Copyrights for author. Subjects: Alternative Medicine, Asia, Indochina, Health, How-To, Martial Arts, Spiritual, Sports, Outdoors, T'ai Chi.

Yo San Books, Barbara Wolff, Project Coordinator, 13315 W. Washington Blvd, Ste. 200, Los Angeles, CA 90066. 1976. Non-fiction. avg. press run 1M-1.5M. Pub'd 2 titles 2005; expects 2 titles 2006, 4 titles 2007. 200pp. Reporting time: 2 months. Simultaneous submissions accepted: yes. Payment: royalty. Copyrights for author. Subjects: Acupuncture, New Age, T'ai Chi.

YogaVidya.com, Brian Dana Akers, PO Box 569, Woodstock, NY 12498-0569, 845-679-2313, Fax 586-283-4680, info@yogavidya.com, www.yogavidya.com. 2001. Photos, non-fiction. "YogaVidya.com is dedicated to publishing excellent and affordable books about Yoga. It is independent of all other commercial, governmental, educational, and religious institutions." Reporting time: Less than 48 hours. Simultaneous submissions accepted: No. Payment: Royalties paid quarterly. Copyrights for author. Subject: Yoga.

Dan Youra Studios, Inc. (see also FERRY TRAVEL GUIDE), Dan Youra, PO Box 1169, Port Hadlock, WA 98339-1169. 1980. Articles, photos, non-fiction. "We are generally self-publishers. We do publish on a co-operative basis with others." avg. press run 50M. Pub'd 3 titles 2005; expects 3 titles 2006, 3 titles 2007. Discounts: 3-12 40%, 13-50 45%, 51-150 50%, 151+ 55%. 128pp. Reporting time: fast. Payment: varies, co-operative.

•YUKHIKA—LATUHSE, Jim Stevens, P.O. Box 365, Oneida Nation Arts Program, Oneida, WI 54155-0365, jstevens@ez-net.com. 2005. Poetry, fiction, articles, criticism, parts-of-novels, plays, non-fiction. "Editorial board: Jim Stevens, Richie Plass, Jennifer Stevens. Ed Two Rivers, Editor-at-Large. We publish work by Native American writers only. Our mission is to publish as wide a range of writing by Native American writers as we can. Recent contibutors: Kim Blaeser, Jose Boner, Bruce King, Richie Plass, Denise Sweet, Ed Two Rivers." circ. 500. 1/yr. Pub'd 1 issue 2005; expects 1 issue 2006, 1 issue 2007. sub. price $5.00; per copy $5.00; sample $5.00. Back issues: inquire. 48pp. Reporting time: 1 month. Simultaneous submissions accepted: No. Publishes 90% of manuscripts submitted. Payment in copies. Not copyrighted. Pub's reviews: none in 2005. Subjects: Essays, Fiction, Native American, Non-Fiction, Poetry.

Z

Zagier & Urruty Publicaciones, Sergio Zagier, Dario Urruty, PO Box 94 Sucursal 19, Buenos Aires 1419, Argentina, 541-572-1050. 1985. Articles, photos, reviews, letters, news items, non-fiction. "We publish basically about travel and tourism (books, maps, guides, magazines) and about science. Manuscripts about traveling through South America and Antarctica are welcome. Spanish, English, German and French. We also are interested in photographies travel and adventour-oriented. Any length of manuscripts are considered." avg. press run 5M. Pub'd 6 titles 2005; expects 6 titles 2006, 12 titles 2007. Discounts: 50% distributor, 30% bookstores, 20% travel companies. 128pp. Reporting time: 6 weeks. Payment: on an individual basis depending on the kind of work. Copyrights for author. Subjects: The Americas, Animals, Anthropology, Archaelogy, Birds, Book Reviewing, Conservation, Earth, Natural History, Ethics, Geography, History, Judaism, Latin America, Native American, Physics, Sports, Outdoors.

ZAHIR, Unforgettable Tales, Sheryl Tempchin, 315 South Coast Hwy. 101 Suite U8, Encinitas, CA 92024, stempchin@zahirtales.com, http://www.zahirtales.com. 2003. Fiction. "Speculative fiction, perhaps more than any other type of literature, gives voice to the collective, mythic dream that is at the center of human existence. Zahir's goal is twofold: to find and bring to light new speculative fiction of literary quality, and to encourage emerging writers by providing them with an audience for their work. Since Zahir's debut in 2003 we have published a wide variety of speculative short stories, from science fiction to fantasy to magical realism and beyond. Each 80 page issue includes eight to ten stories, some by established writers, but many by those with few or no publishing credits. We are always thrilled and honored to be the first to publish the work of a promising new writer." circ. 150. 3/yr. Pub'd 3 issues 2005; expects 3 issues 2006, 3 issues 2007. sub. price $15; per copy $6.50; sample $6.50. Back issues: $6.50. Discounts: inquire. 80pp. Reporting time: 4 to 8 weeks. Simultaneous submissions accepted: No. Publishes 6% of manuscripts submitted. Payment: $10 flat fee upon publication. Copyrighted, reverts to author. Subjects: Fantasy, Science Fiction, Supernatural, Surrealism.

Zante Publishing, Steve Johnson, P.O. Box 35404, Greensboro, NC 27425, (336) 605-7900. 2004. Non-fiction. "We specialize in high quality titles, heavily promoted for the national market. Authors must commit to taking active participation in promoting their titles." avg. press run 5000. Pub'd 1 title 2005; expects 2 titles 2006, 2 titles 2007. 200pp. Reporting time: 30 days. Simultaneous submissions accepted: No. Publishes 30% of manuscripts submitted. Copyrights for author. Subjects: Europe, Travel.

ZAUM - The Literary Review of Sonoma State University, Julie Reid, Senior Editor; Kay Elliott, Assistant Editor, English Department, SSU, 1801 E. Cotati Avenue, Rohnert Park, CA 94928, 707-664-2140. 1996. Poetry, fiction, art, photos, criticism, collages. "All prose max. 10 pages, 5 poems max. All color artwork in slide form, b&w prints ok. We only accept submissions from students currently enrolled in an undergraduate or graduate degree program." circ. 500. 1/yr. Pub'd 1 issue 2005; expects 1 issue 2006, 1 issue 2007. sub. price $9.50; per copy $7.51 + p/h; sample $7.51 + p/h. Back issues: 4 for $20, 5 for $25. 100pp. Reporting time: 3-6 months. We accept simultaneous submissions, but let us know. Publishes 7% of manuscripts submitted. Payment: 1 copy. Copyrighted, reverts to author. Ads: none. Subject: Avant-Garde, Experimental Art.

ZAWP, Rabah Seffal, PO Box 411, Mossville, IL 61552-0411, 309-310-7709. 2005. Fiction, criticism. "Ethnic ProfilingNorth African literatureHistory of North Africa." avg. press run 1000. Expects 1 title 2006, 2 titles 2007. Discounts: 2-10 copies 10%11-20 copies 15%20-50 copies 20%. 70pp. Reporting time: One week. Simultaneous submissions accepted: No. Publishes 1% of manuscripts submitted. Payment: 15%. Copyrights for author. Subjects: African Literature, Africa, African Studies, Criticism, Indigenous Cultures, Literature (General), Non-Fiction, Translation.

•**Zebra Press,** Kevin Orr, PO box 915, Monticello, FL 32345. 2005. Fiction. "Zebra Press publishers fiction literature that captures the narrative southern voice." avg. press run 3000. Expects 1 title 2007. Discounts: 1-25 copies 10% discount25-99 copies 20% discount100-499 copies 40% discount500-999 copies 50% discount1000-14999 60% discountTerms: Non-returnable, net 30 days, FOB warehouse/ printing plant, freight collectFree shipping on any pre publication orders. 275pp. Reporting time: 4-6 months. Simultaneous submissions accepted: No. Copyrights for author. Subjects: Fiction, Juvenile Fiction, South.

Paul Zelevansky, Lynn Zelevansky, Paul Zelevansky, 1455 Clairidge Drive, Beverly Hills, CA 90210-2214. 1975. "Material used: work that mixes visual and verbal forms." avg. press run 500-1M. Pub'd 1 title 2005; expects 1 title 2006, 1 title 2007. Discounts: bookstores 40%. 80pp. Author has copyright of work; we have copyright of book.

Zephyr Press, J. Kates, Co-Director; Leora Zeitlin, Co-Director; Christopher Mattison, Managing Editor, 50 Kenwood Street, Brookline, MA 02446, 617-713-2813. 1980. Poetry, fiction, non-fiction. "We publish literary fiction, non-fiction and poetry, with an emphasis on contemporary literature in translation. We do not read unsolicited manuscripts, but will consider a query (must include a brief summary of publications and professional credits, and a sample of the proposed work no longer than 10 pages)." avg. press run 2-3M. Pub'd 1 title 2005; expects 4 titles 2006, 7 titles 2007. Discounts: trade 30%; libaries and individuals 20% if pre-paid; distributed by Consortium, 800-626-4330. 300pp. Reporting time: 2-12 weeks. Simultaneous submissions accepted: yes. Payment: 8-10% of publisher's net. Copyrights for author. Subjects: Asia, Indochina, Culture, Europe, Novels, Poetry, Russia, Translation, Women.

ZerOX Books (see also UNMUZZLED OX), Michael Andre, 105 Hudson Street, #311, New York, NY 10013. 1971. "ZerOx Books is an occasional imprint of Unmuzzled Ox Books." avg. press run 105.

Zerx Press, Mark Weber, 725 Van Buren Place SE, Albuquerque, NM 87108, zerxpress@aol.com, www.zerxrecords.com. 1983. Poetry, fiction, art, photos. "50 chapbooks since 1983. Contributors: Gerald Locklin, Judson Crews, Todd Moore, Ann Menebroker, Ron Androla, Hugh Fox, Kurt Nimmo, Kell Robertson, Cheryl Townsend, and Brent Leake. Am not really in the market financially for unsolicited mss." avg. press run 200-500. Pub'd 5 titles 2005; expects 6 titles 2006, 2+ titles 2007. 44pp. Reporting time: less than a week. Payment: we've never made back initial printing costs but think it'd be like 10% or 15% after 1000 sold; author usually gets 25-35 copies and is able to buy extra at Zerx cost. Copyrights for author. Subjects: Poetry, Prose, Short Stories.

ZINE WORLD: A Reader's Guide to the Underground Press, Jerianne Thompson, PO Box 330156, Murfreesboro, TN 37133-0156, www.undergroundpress.org. 1996. Art, reviews, letters, news items. "Short reviews of underground or alternative lit, books, newsletters, etc.'' circ. 1.2M. 3/yr. Pub'd 3 issues 2005; expects 3 issues 2006, 3 issues 2007. sub. price $14; per copy $4; sample $4. 64pp. Reporting time: staff only. Simultaneous submissions accepted: no. Publishes 0% of manuscripts submitted. Payment: none. Copyrighted, reverts to author. Pub's reviews: 1,200+ in 2005. §Self-published and/or counterculture, "anything that's not mainstream corporate-controlled crap'' Ads: $130/$65. Subjects: Counter-Culture, Alternatives, Communes, Publishing, Reviews, Writers/Writing, Zines.

ZINE-ON-A-TAPE, Andrew Savage, 35 Kearsley Road, Sheffield, S2 4TE, United Kingdom, www.andy-sav.free-online.co.uk/. 1985. Poetry, reviews, music, news items. "Formerly *Super Trouper*. The magazine is produced on cassette.'' circ. 100. 1/yr. Pub'd 1 issue 2005; expects 1 issue 2006, 1 issue 2007. sub. price £3 or $8 postpaid. Back issues: £2 or $6 postpaid. Reporting time: 3 months. Simultaneous submissions accepted: yes. Publishes 15% of manuscripts submitted. Payment: 1 copy of it that hasn't already been eaten. Rights revert to author. Pub's reviews: 5 in 2005. §Poetry and music. Subjects: Biology, Dreams, Humor, Hypnosis, Music, Occult, Poetry, Tapes & Records.

ZOETROPE: ALL-STORY, Michael Ray, Editor, 916 Kearny Street, San Francisco, CA 94133-5107, 415-788-7500, www.all-story.com. 1997. Fiction, plays. "Short stories and one-act plays under 7,000 words. Submissions must be accompanied by an SASE. Recent contributors: Richard Powers, ZZ Packer, Dave Eggers, Mary Gaitskill, John Sayles, Ryu Murakami, Neil Jordan, A. M. Homes.'' circ. 25,000. 4/yr. Pub'd 4 issues 2005; expects 4 issues 2006, 4 issues 2007. sub. price $19.95; per copy $6.95; sample $6.95 with $2 p/h. 108pp. Reporting time: 6 months. Simultaneous submissions accepted: yes. Publishes 0.3% of manuscripts submitted. Payment: $1,000 and 5 copies of magazine. Copyrighted, buy 1st serial rights. Ads: $3,500 full page, $1,725 half, with discounts for multi-issue commitments. Subject: Fiction.

Zoilita Grant MS CCHt., Attn: Zoilita Grant, 200 Lincoln Street, Longmont, CO 80501, 303-776-6103, Fax 303-682-2384, info@selfhealing.com, www.selfhealing.com. 1997. avg. press run 2.7M. Pub'd 7 titles 2005; expects 5 titles 2006, 5 titles 2007. 175pp. Simultaneous submissions accepted: yes. Payment: yes. Copyrights for author. Subjects: New Age, Psychology, Self-Help.

Zon International Publishing Co., William Manns, PO Box 6459, Santa Fe, NM 87502, 505-995-0102, Fax 505-995-0103, e-mail zon@nets.com. 1985. Art. "We publish photo books on Americana.'' avg. press run 15M. Pub'd 1 title 2005; expects 3 titles 2006, 6 titles 2007. Discounts: 4-9 40%, 10-49 45%, 50+ 50%. 250pp. Publishes almost 0% of manuscripts submitted. Payment: flat fee and royalty. Does not copyright for author. Subjects: Armenian, Arts, Photography, The West.

ZONE, Zone Books, Michel Feher, Jonathan Crary, 1226 Prospect Ave., Brooklyn, NY 11218-1304, 212-625-0048, Fax 212-625-9772, urzone@aol.com. 1985. Articles, art, photos, non-fiction. "*Zone* explores critical developments in modern culture. Each issue examines a single theme from a transdisciplinary perspective, with texts on art, literature, economics, history and philosophy, as well as photographic essays, historical and technical dossiers, artists projects and formal questionnaires. The theme of the first issue was the contemporary city. Future issues will explore the human body and technology, pragmatics, the global West, politics and time.'' circ. 7M. 0/yr. sub. price varies; per copy varies; sample varies. Back issues: vary. Discounts: sold to trade through The MIT Press. 450pp. Copyrighted, rights reverting to author varies. Subjects: Anthropology, Archaelogy, Architecture, Avant-Garde, Experimental Art, Design, History, Philosophy, Religion, Sociology, Translation.

ZONE 3, Blas Falconer, Poetry Editor; Barry Kitterman, Fiction Editor; Susan Wallace, Mg. Editor, Austin Peay State University, Box 4565, Clarksville, TN 37044, 931-221-7031/7891. 1986. Poetry. "*Zone 3* is a poetry and fiction journal published in Tennessee but seeking submissions and readership nationwide and beyond. For title, see the planting zone map on back of seed package. Editors want poems that are deeply rooted in place, mind, heart, experience, rage, imagination, laughter, etc. Published fall and spring. Issues include work by Stafford, Coleman Barks, Julia Alvarez, Jared Carter, Bruchac, Orr, Burkard, Michael Blumenthal, Kloefkorn, Piercy, Budy, Bowers, Al Young, McBrearty, Kristine Somerville, Gina Ochsner, Virgil Suarez, Joan Frank, Gerry LaFemina, Jim Daniels, Beth Martinelli, and Antonio Jocson.'' circ. 1M. 2/yr. Pub'd 1 issue 2005; expects 2 issues 2006, 2 issues 2007. sub. price $10/yr, $12 to libraries & institutions; per copy $5; sample $5. Back issues: $4. Discounts: 33%. 125pp. Payment: copies. Copyrighted, reverts to author. Pub's reviews. §Poetry, fiction, and creative nonfiction. Subjects: Fiction, Non-Fiction, Poetry, Translation.

Zone Books (see also ZONE), Meighan Gale, 1226 Prospect Ave., Brooklyn, NY 11218, NY 11218, 718 686 0048, 718 686 9045. 1985. Non-fiction. "Zone Books is an independent non-profit publishing house that produces a small but select list of titles in the arts and humanities. Its publishing program includes philosophy, history, cultural studies, art history, critical theory, anthropology, literature, political science, and Asian and classical studies. Zone Books is also committed to the translation of important works by contemporary European authors.'' avg. press run 3000. Pub'd 4 titles 2005; expects 4 titles 2006, 5 titles 2007. 250-500pp. Reporting time: 3 months. Simultaneous submissions accepted: Yes. Publishes 0% of manuscripts submitted.

Copyrights for author.

Zoo Press (see also THE NEBRASKA REVIEW), Neil Azevedo, Publisher; K. Caitlin Phelps, Assistant Editor, PO Box 3528, Omaha, NE 68103, 402-770-8104, editors@zoopress.org, http://zoopress.org. 2000. Poetry, fiction, criticism, plays. "We currently publish The Paris Review Prize in Poetry, The Kenyon Review Prize in Poetry for a First Book, The Angela Marie Ortiz Award for the Novel, The Zoo Press Award for Short Fiction and The Parnassus Prize in Poetry Criticism. See our website for submission guidelines. Recent authors include Christopher Cessac, Eric Charles LeMay, Kate Light and Judith Taylor." avg. press run varies. Pub'd 3 titles 2005; expects 8 titles 2006, 12 titles 2007. Discounts: standard discounts set by our distributor, the Univ. of Nebraska Press (800) 755-1105. 80pp. Reporting time: varies. Simultaneous submissions accepted: yes. Publishes 1% of manuscripts submitted. Payment: standard. Copyrights for author. Subjects: Criticism, Drama, Fiction, Literature (General), Poetry.

Zookeeper Publications, Allan Falk, Jacqueline DeRouin, 2010 Cimarron Drive, Okemos, MI 48864-3908, 517-347-4697. 1991. Non-fiction. avg. press run 1.5M. Pub'd 3 titles 2005; expects 2 titles 2006. Discounts: 50% wholesale, 40% consignment. 165-240pp. Reporting time: 1 month. Payment: negotiable; principally self-funded. Copyrights for author. Subject: Games.

Zumaya Publications, Elizabeth Burton, P.O. Box 2146, Garibaldi Highlands, B.C. V0N 1T0, Canada, 512-707-2694, 235-660-2009. 2000. Fiction, non-fiction. "Zumaya publishes full-length works of fiction and nonfiction. Preferred minimum word count for adult fiction is 65,000 words, with preference for 85,000-135,000 words. We will read works of 40,000 words and up; however, the author will likely be encouraged to expand it or combine it with other short works before the manuscript will be accepted. For Young Adult, teen fiction and childrens chapter books, minimum word count is 35,000 with a preferred maximum of 60,000 words.In fiction, we look for well-written, professional presented manuscripts that extend the boundaries of the usual genre definitions. We want the kind of books people cant put down and cant get enough of. While we dont necessarily turn down well-crafted stories that fall into the standard formulas for their genre, our first choice will always be the one that moves beyond those formulas, whether because of unique characters or new plot twists. Books for children and young adults should first and foremost be first-rate stories, with lessons and morals implicit rather than explicit. We do not publish childrens picture books at this time. However, we do publish illustrated books for middle readers and young adults.In nonfiction, we look for books that will potentially have or develop a wide audience in the areas of paranormal phenomena, true crime, self-help, history/cultural and inspirational/New Age. While we have no objection to Christian works, we don't feel we are suited to properly marketing them, and encourage Christian writers to exhaust those publishers noted for that area first. We will consider memoirs if they contain a self-help element or if the author has a unique view that has broad appeal.For our eXtasy erotica line, we want good stories in which the erotic elements fit smoothly and are a vital part of the plot and/or development of character. Erotica submissions should be sent to extasybooks@telus.net. For submission guidelines specific to eXtasy Books, go to http://www.extasy-books.com." avg. press run 1. Pub'd 20 titles 2005; expects 37 titles 2006, 34 titles 2007. Discounts: 1-20 copies, 35% prepaid; 20+ copies, 40% prepaid by special order. 250pp. Reporting time: Average response time is 4-5 months. Simultaneous submissions accepted: Yes. Publishes 2% of manuscripts submitted. Payment: We do not pay advances at this time. Authors receive 40% of net on all retail and third-party sales and 20 copies of the book at straight wholesale. They may purchase additional copies at wholesale plus $2. Royalties are paid twice annually in February and August provided a minimum of $50 is attained. All royalties due in a calendar year are paid the following February. Does not copyright for author. Subjects: Anthology, Dreams, Fiction, History, Inspirational, Literature (General), Memoirs, Native American, Occult, Reprints, Science Fiction, Self-Help, Spiritual, Tarot, WICCA.

ZUZU'S PETALS: QUARTERLY ONLINE, T. Dunn, Editor, 1836 Ashley River Road, Ste. E, Charleston, SC 29407-4761, info@zuzu.com, www.zuzu.com. 1992. Poetry, fiction, articles, art, cartoons, satire, criticism, reviews, parts-of-novels, collages, concrete art, non-fiction. "Closed for submissions until 12/2006. High quality writing about the human experience. We provide a showcase for some of America's finest writing and publish talented and relatively undiscovered writers. No sing song verse or amateur stuff please. We also run a poetry contest which helps fund the publication of our magazine. Write for guidelines. We are proudly ad-free. *Library Journal* calls us 'An exciting new little.'" circ. unlimited. 4/yr. Pub'd 4 issues 2005; expects 4 issues 2006, 4 issues 2007. price per copy Availible on the World Wide Web; sample $5 for our print poetry sample. 200pp. Reporting time: 2 weeks - 2 months. Simultaneous submissions accepted: yes. Publishes 5% of manuscripts submitted. Payment: none, the magazine is free through the net. Copyrighted, reverts to author. Subjects: Arts, Criticism, Culture, Essays, Fiction, Humor, Literary Review, Literature (General), Poetry, Publishing, Reference, Short Stories, Sociology, Visual Arts, Writers/Writing.

Zygote Publishing, Tate Young, PO Box #4049, 10467 80 Ave NW, Edmonton, AB T6E 4S8, Canada, (780)439-7580, (780)439-7529, www.zygotepublishing.com. 2004. Poetry, fiction, long-poems. "Zygote Publishing is a collective of highly motivated, like-minded, literature-loving, Western Canadian individuals who are dedicated to presenting literary works in a manner that captivates and entices new audiences.Our first book, Nunt, is the shocking story of a man who walks out on his wife and embarks on a ferocious two year odyssey of womanizing and alcohol-fuelled violence. Tourette roars across a barbaric America in this savage tale of murderous fist fights and molotov cocktails, doing battle with malevolent priests, falling in love with obsessed prostitutes, and desperately trying to exorcise the ghosts of his failed marriage.'' avg. press run 2000. Expects 1 title 2006, 1 title 2007. Discounts: 46% to distributors, jobbers, wholesalers40% to bookstores20% to institutions. 112pp. Reporting time: 6 weeks. Simultaneous submissions accepted: Yes. Publishes 1% of manuscripts submitted. Payment: No advances so far. Does not copyright for author. Subjects: Charles Bukowski, Erotica, Fiction, Haiku, Ernest Hemingway, James Joyce, Kafka, Jack Kerouac, Henry Miller, Anais Nin, Poetry, Religion, Sex, Sexuality, Weapons, Zen.

ZYX, Phrygian Press, Arnold Skemer, 58-09 205th Street, Bayside, NY 11364-1712, PhrygianZYX @ AOL.COM, 718-428-9368. 1990. Criticism, reviews. ''Essays and commentary on innovative/experimental fiction. We are interested in tendencies in avant-garde fiction, useful techniques and stratagems that a fictioneer can avail himself of, author resources (self-publishing, technological changes and publishing empowerment). Some reviews. Accepting original fiction, but make it compact, ideally 1-2 pages. Poetry accepted. Recent contributors: Christopher Mulrooney, James Chapman, Spencer Selby, Luis Cuauhtemoc Berriozabal, Richard Kostelanetz, Geoff Huth, Randall Brock, John Crouse, T. Kilgore Splake, Leonard J. Cirino, Florentin Smarandache, Jon Cone, Jonathan Hayes, John Grey, Thomas Lowe Taylor, Crag Hill, Alan Catlin, Nathan Whiting, Normal, Kevin Higgins, Jonathan Hayes, Doreen King, Bob Grumman, Guy R. Beining, Mark Sonnenfeld, Daneen Wardrop, Jnana Hodson, Robert Michael O'Hearn, Edward Mycue, Michael S. Begnal, Gerald England, B.Z. Niditch, Susan Maurer, Spiel, Louis E. Bourgeois, R.W. Watkins, Cardinal Cox, Robert Pomerhn, Dan Weber, George Kuntzman, David Madgalene.'' circ. 333. 3/yr. Pub'd 3 issues 2005; expects 3 issues 2006, 3 issues 2007. Subscriptions in multiples of the then prevailing 1st class base rate if you wish issues periodically. Will send up to one pound of back issues for $2.00 which would contain approximately 15 issues; up to 2 pounds, $3.00.; price per copy gratis; send return postage appropriate for 39¢, 63¢, etc; sample same. Back issues: Send $2.00 for just under one pound of back issues. Send $3.00 for just under 2 pounds. 10pp. Reporting time: 4-5 months. Simultaneous submissions accepted: no. Payment: copies. Copyrighted, reverts to author. Pub's reviews: 20 in 2005. §Innovative fiction and criticism. Subjects: Avant-Garde, Experimental Art, Book Reviewing, Dada, Post Modern, Surrealism, Writers/Writing.

ZYZZYVA, Howard Junker, Editor; Amanda Field, Managing Editor, PO Box 590069, San Francisco, CA 94159-0069, Tel 415-752-4393 Fax 415-752-4391, editor@zyzzyva.org, www.zyzzyva.org. 1985. Poetry, fiction, art, photos, satire, letters, plays, concrete art, non-fiction. ''Only writers who live on West Coast.'' circ. 3M. 3/yr. Pub'd 3 issues 2005; expects 3 issues 2006, 3 issues 2007. sub. price $24/44; per copy $11; sample $6. Back issues: $10. 192pp. Reporting time: prompt. Simultaneous submissions accepted: no. Publishes 1% of manuscripts submitted. Payment: $50. Copyrighted, reverts to author. Ads: $500 full/$300 half/$200 quarter page.

Regional Index

flesh_on_bone@yahoo.com, http://almostnormalcomics.tripod.com

Blue Planet Books Inc., 4619 W. McRae Way, Glendale, AZ 85308, Fax 623-780-0468, www.blueplanetbooks.net

Delaney Day Press, 14014 North 64th Drive, Glendale, AZ 85306-3706, Tel:623-810-7590, Fax:623-878-2084, books@delaneydaypress.com, www.delaneydaypress.com

FLUENT ASCENSION, c/o FIERCE Concepts, PO Box 6407, Glendale, AZ 85312, submissions@fluentascension.com, www.fluentascension.com

Ho Logos Press, 7007 W Tonto Dr, Glendale, AZ 85308-5535, 877-407-7744,623-566-6104,fax 623-566-6105, hlpressmarketing@yahoo.com, www.hlpress.com

TalSan Publishing/Distributors, 7614 W. Bluefield Avenue, Glendale, AZ 85308, 602-843-1119, fax 602-843-3080

THE ILLUSTRATOR COLLECTOR'S NEWS, PO Box 6433, Kingman, AZ 86402-6433, 360-452-3810; ticn@olypen.com

CREOSOTE: A Journal of Poetry and Prose, Mohave Community College—Dept. of English, 1977 W. Acoma Blvd., Lake Havasu City, AZ 86403, 928-505-3375

Andros Books, P. O. Box 2887, Mesa, AZ 85204, androsbks@aol.com

NEW THOUGHT, International New Thought Alliance, 5003 East Broadway Road, Mesa, AZ 85206, 480-830-2461

Pussywillow Publishing House, Inc., 844 South Park View Circle, Mesa, AZ 85208-4782

THE SALT RIVER REVIEW, 448 N. Matlock, Mesa, AZ 85203-7222, http://www.poetserv.org/

THE NEW SUPERNATURAL MAGAZINE, PO Box 3641, Page, AZ 86040-3641, MorrisPublish2@aol.com, http://hometown.aol.com/morrispublish2/

R. E. FARRELLBOOKS, LLC, P.O. Box 6507, Peoria, AZ 85385-6507, (623) 640-7915

Arizona Master Gardener Press, 4341 E. Broadway Road, Phoenix, AZ 85040-8807, 602-470-8086 ext. 312, Fax 602-470-8092

CHRISTIAN CONNECTION PEN PAL NEWSLETTER, PO Box 45305, Phoenix, AZ 85064-5305, 602-852-9774, christpals@netzero.net, www.angelfire.com/az/ChristianPals/

FIREBREEZE PUBLISHING, 11666 N. 28th. Dr. #255, Phoenix, AZ 85029-5625, 602-547-3946

GRAY AREAS, 4212 West Cactus Rd. #1110, PMB 195, Phoenix, AZ 85029-2902, www.grayarea.com

Hunter Publishing, Co., PO Box 9533, Phoenix, AZ 85068, 602-944-1022

Integra Press, 1702 W. Camelback Road, Suite 13, PMB 119, Phoenix, AZ 85015, 602-841-4911, Fax 602-242-5745, info@integra.com

Rowan Press, Inc., PO Box 80954, Phoenix, AZ 85060-0954, 602-954-5638, jvblumit@extremezone.com

VISIONHOPE NEWSLETTER, PO Box 45305, Phoenix, AZ 85064-5305, 602-852-9774, visionhopemag@netzero.net, http://www.angelfire.com/biz2/buswriting/

Native West Press, PO Box 12227, Prescott, AZ 86304, 928-771-8376, nativewestpres@cableone.net, www.nativewest-press.com

SHO, PO Box 31, Prescott, AZ 86302

EMERGING, 7119 East Shea Blvd., Suite 109, PMB 418, Scottsdale, AZ 85254, 480-948-1800, Fax 480-948-1870, teleosinst@aol.com

Footsteps Media, #621, 6929 N. Hayden Road, Suite C4, Scottsdale, AZ 85250, footstepsadventures@cox.net

LP Publications (Teleos Institute), 7119 East Shea Boulevard, Suite 109, PMB 418, Scottsdale, AZ 85254, 480-948-1800, Fax 480-948-1870

Poisoned Pen Press, 6962 E. First Avenue #103, Scottsdale, AZ 85251, 480-945-3375, Fax 480-949-1707, info@poisonedpenpress.com

WorkLife Publishing, 14925 E. Morning Vista Lane, Scottsdale, AZ 85262-6891, 602-992-0144

Big Mouth Publications, 560 Concho Dr., Sedona, AZ 86351-7957

In Print Publishing, PO Box 20765, Sedona, AZ 86341, 928-284-5298, Fax 928-284-5283

Doral Publishing, 16080 West Wildflower Drive, Surprise, AZ 85374-5053, (623) 875-2057, (623) 875-2059, (800) 633-5385

Triskelion Publishing, 15508 W. Bell Road #101, PMB #205, Surprise, AZ 85374, Contact: 517-294-0765, Sales: 602-509-8582, Fax: 623-561-0250, sales@triskelionpublishing.com, www.triskelionpublishing.net

Bilingual Review Press, Hispanic Research Center, Arizona State Univ., Box 875303, Tempe, AZ 85287-5303

BILINGUAL REVIEW/Revista Bilingue, Hispanic Research Center, Arizona State Univ., Box 872702, Tempe, AZ 85287-2702

BRB Publications, Inc., PO Box 27869, Tempe, AZ 85285-7869, 800-929-3811, Fax 800-929-4981, brb@brbpub.com, www.brbpub.com

CHASQUI, Dept of Languages and Literature, Arizona State University, Tempe, AZ 85207-0202, 480-965-3752, fax: 480-965-0135, web: www.public.asu.edu/~atdwf.

Facts on Demand Press, PO Box 27869, Tempe, AZ 85285-7869, 800-929-3811, Fax 800-929-4981, brb@brbpub.com, www.brbpub.com

HAYDEN'S FERRY REVIEW, Box 871502, Arizona State University, Tempe, AZ 85287-1502, 480-965-1243

New Falcon Publications, 1739 E. Broadway Road, Suite 1-277, Tempe, AZ 85282, 602-708-1409 (phone),602-708-1410 (fax),info@newfalcon.com (email),http://www.newfalcon.com (website)

Rest of Your Life Publications, 118 East Palomino Drive, Tempe, AZ 85284-2354, 203-853-0303, Fax 203-853-0307, www.restofyourlife.com

synaesthesia press, PO Box 1763, Tempe, AZ 85280, jim@chapbooks.org, www.chapbooks.org

California Bill's Automotive Handbooks, PO Box 91858, Tucson, AZ 85752-1858, 520-547-2462, Fax 888-511-1501, web: www.californiabills.com, www.goodyearbooks.com www.nononsenseguides.com

Dream Street Publishing, PO Box 65355, Tucson, AZ 85728-5355, Fax 520-529-3911

Galen Press, Ltd., PO Box 64400, Tucson, AZ 85728-4400, 520-577-8363, Fax 520-529-6459

Imago Press, 3710 East Edison Street, Tucson, AZ 85716, 520-327-0540, ljoiner@dakotacom.net, www.ImagoBooks.com

THE LAUGHING DOG, #326, 4729 E. Sunrise, Tucson, AZ 85718, LaughingDogAZ@cs.com

THE MATCH, PO Box 3488, Tucson, AZ 85722

Microdex Bookshelf, 1212 N. Sawtelle, Suite 120, Tucson, AZ 85716, 520-326-3502

Ravenhawk Books, 7739 E. Broadway Boulevard #95, Tucson, AZ 85710, 520-296-4491, Fax 520-296-4491, ravenhawk6dof@yahoo.com

Rio Nuevo Publishers, PO Box 5250, Tucson, AZ 85703, 520-623-9558, Fax 520-624-5888

See Sharp Press, PO Box 1731, Tucson, AZ 85702-1731, 520-628-8720, Fax 520-628-8720, info@seesharppress.com, www.seesharppress.com

SONORA REVIEW, Dept. of English, University of Arizona, Tucson, AZ 85721, 520-624-9192

SUBSYNCHRONOUS PRESS, 4729 E. Sunrise #326, Tucson, AZ 85718

Wheatmark Book Publishing, 610 East Delano Street, Suite 104, Tucson, AZ 85705-5210, 888-934-0888, 520-798-0888, 520-798-3394 (fax), http://www.bookpublisher.com

ARKANSAS

HEROES FROM HACKLAND, 1225 Evans St., Arkadelphia, AR 71923, 870-246-6223
THE OXFORD AMERICAN, 201 Donaghey Ave., #107, Conway, AR 72035-5001, www.oxfordamericanmag.com
SLANT: A Journal of Poetry, University of Central Arkansas, PO Box 5063, Conway, AR 72035-5000, 501-450-5107
AQUATERRA, METAECOLOGY & CULTURE, 5473 Highway 23N, Eureka Springs, AR 72631
Emerald Wave, 13828 White Oak Circle #R, Fayetteville, AR 72704-8422, 479-575-0019, Fax 479-575-0807, emeraldwave33@aol.com
POESIA, Executive Square, One West Mountain Street, Fayetteville, AR 72701, Telephone 479.444.9323,Fax 479.444.9326, www.indianbaypress.com
University of Arkansas Press, McIlroy House, 201 Ozark Avenue, Fayetteville, AR 72701, 1-479-575-3246
Rose Publishing Co., 2723 Foxcroft Road, #208, Little Rock, AR 72227-6513, 501-227-8104; Fax 501-227-8338
Lancer Militaria, Box 1188, Mt. Ida, AR 71957-1188, 870-867-2232; www.warbooks.com
NEBO, Department of English, Arkansas Tech University, Russellville, AR 72801, 479-968-0256

ARMED FORCES EUROPE

PROSE AX, USS Emory S. Land Repair Dept., FPO, AE 09545, prose_ax@att.net, www.proseax.com

CALIFORNIA

Hunter House Inc., Publishers, PO Box 2914, Alameda, CA 94501, 510-865-5282, Fax 510-865-4295, info@hunterhouse.com, www.hunterhouse.com
Latham Foundation, Latham Plaza, 1826 Clement Avenue, Alameda, CA 94501-1397, 510-521-0920, www.latham.org
THE LATHAM LETTER, Latham Found., Latham Plaza Bldg., 1826 Clement Avenue, Alameda, CA 94501-1397, 415-521-0920, www.latham.org
Razor7 Publishing, PO Box 6746, Altadena, CA 91003-6746, (626) 205-3154
Past Times Publishing Co., PO Box 661, Anaheim, CA 92815, 714-997-1157; jyoung@fea.net, www.oldtimeshowbiz.com
Reach Productions Publishing, PO Box 18495, Anaheim, CA 92807, 714-693-1800, publishing@reachproductions.com, www.reachproductions.com
SOLAS Press, PO Box 4066, Antioch, CA 94531, 925-978-9781, Fax 925-978-2599, info@solaspress.com
Munchweiler Press, 13940 Okesa Road, Apple Valley, CA 92307-7220, 760-245-9215, Fax 760-245-9418, tedlish@munchwei-lerpress.com, www.munchweilerpress.com
THE AMERICAN POETRY JOURNAL, PO Box 2080, Aptos, CA 95001-2080, editor@americanpoetryjournal.com, www.americanpoetryjournal.com
Chatoyant, PO Box 832, Aptos, CA 95003, 831-662-3047 phone/Fax, books@chatoyant.com, www.chatoyant.com
Dream Horse Press, PO Box 2080, Aptos, CA 95001-2080, dreamhorsepress@yahoo.com, www.dreamhorsepress.com
CULTURE CHANGE, PO Box 4347, Arcata, CA 95518, 707-826-7775
Impact Publishers, Inc., PO Box 6016, Atascadero, CA 93423-6016, 805-466-5917, Fax 805-466-5919, info@impactpub-lishers.com, www.impactpublishers.com
Barney Press, 3807 Noel Place, Bakersfield, CA 93306, 805-871-9118
Ballena Press, PO Box 578, Banning, CA 92220, (951)849-7289, Fax (951)849-3549, E-mail: malkipress@aol.com, www.malkimuseum.com
THE JOURNAL OF CALIFORNIA AND GREAT BASIN ANTHROPOLOGY, P.O. Box 578, Banning, CA 92220, 951-849-7289,951-849-3549, malkipress@aol.com, malkimuseum.org
Malki Museum Press, P.O. Box 578, Banning, CA 92220, 951-849-7289, Fax 951-849-3549, E-Mail: malkipress@aol.com, www.malkimuseum.org
ARCATA ARTS, P.O.B. 800, Bayside, CA 95524, 707 822 5839, 707 826 2002, 888 687 8962, pub@arcata-arts.com, http://arcata-arts.com
RedJack, P.O. Box 633, Bayside, CA 95524, (707) 825-7817, heidi@redjack.us
Cadmus Editions, PO Box 126, Belvedere-Tiburon, CA 94920-0126, 707-762-0510
WeWrite LLC, 11040 Alba Road, Ben Lomond, CA 95005-9220, dpalmer@wewrite.net, www.wewrite.net
AGRICULTURAL HISTORY, University of California Press, 2000 Center Street, Suite 303, Berkeley, CA 94704-1223, 510-643-7154
ANARCHY: A Journal of Desire Armed, PO Box 3448, Berkeley, CA 94703, editors@anarchymag.org
ASIAN SURVEY, University of California Press, 2000 Center Street, Suite 303, Berkeley, CA 94704-1223, 510-643-7154
Bay Area Poets Coalition, POETALK, PO Box 11435, Berkeley, CA 94712-2435, poetalk@aol.com, www.bayareapoetscoali-tion.org
Bay Tree Publishing, 721 Creston Road, Berkeley, CA 94708, telephone 510-526-2916, fax 510-525-0842
THE BERKELEY REVIEW OF BOOKS, 1731 10th Street, Apt. A, Berkeley, CA 94710
Carousel Press, PO Box 6038, Berkeley, CA 94706-0038, 510-527-5849, carous4659@aol.com, www.carousel-press.com
CC. Marimbo, PO Box 933, Berkeley, CA 94701-0933
THE CHEROTIC (r)EVOLUTIONARY, PO Box 11445, Berkeley, CA 94712, 510-526-7858, FAX 510-524-2053, fmoore@eroplay.com
CLASSICAL ANTIQUITY, Univ of California Press, 2000 Center Street, Suite 303, Berkeley, CA 94704-1223, 510-643-7154
Command Performance Press, 1755 Hopkins St., Berkeley, CA 94707-2714, 510-524-1191
CONTEXTS: UNDERSTANDING PEOPLE IN THEIR SOCIAL WORLDS, University of California Press, 2000 Center St., Suite 303, Berkeley, CA 94704-1223, 510-643-7154
Creative Arts Book Company, 833 Bancroft Way, Berkeley, CA 94710, staff@creativeartsbooks.com
Dharma Publishing, 2910 San Pablo Avenue, Berkeley, CA 94702, 510-548-5407 ext. 20, fax: 510-548-2230, web:dharmapublishing.com
The Dibble Fund for Marriage Education, PO Box 7881, Berkeley, CA 94707-0881, 800-695-7975, Fax 510-528-1956, e-mail dibblefund@aol.com, www.buildingrelationshipskills.org
FEDERAL SENTENCING REPORTER, University of California Press, 2000 Center Street, Suite 303, Berkeley, CA 94704-1223, 510-643-7154
FILM QUARTERLY, University of California Press, 2000 Center Street, Suite 303, Berkeley, CA 94704-1223, 510-643-7154
GASTRONOMICA: The Journal of Food and Culture, 2000 Center Street, Suite 303, Journals Division, Berkeley, CA 94704-1223, 510-643-7154, Fax 510-642-9917, journals@ucpress.edu
GESAR-Buddhism in the West, 2910 San Pablo Avenue, Berkeley, CA 94702, 415-548-5407
The Gutenberg Press, c/o Fred Foldvary, 1920 Cedar Street, Berkeley, CA 94709, 510-843-0248, e-mail gutenbergpress@po-

box.com
Heyday Books, PO Box 9145, Berkeley, CA 94709, 510-549-3564, Fax 510-549-1889
HISTORICAL STUDIES IN THE PHYSICAL & BIOLOGICAL SCIENCES, University of California Press, 2000 Center Street, Suite 303, Berkeley, CA 94704-1223, 510-643-7154
HUNTINGTON LIBRARY QUARTERLY, University of California Press, 2000 Center St., Suite 303, Berkeley, CA 94704-1223, 626-405-2174
INDEX TO FOREIGN LEGAL PERIODICALS, University of California Press, 2000 Center Street, Suite 303, Berkeley, CA 94704-1223, 510-643-7154
JOURNAL OF MUSICOLOGY, University of California Press, 2000 Center Street, Suite 303, Berkeley, CA 94704-1223, 510-643-7154
JOURNAL OF PALESTINE STUDIES, University of California Press, 2000 Center St., Suite 303, Berkeley, CA 94704-1223, 510-643-7154
JOURNAL OF THE AMERICAN MUSICOLOGICAL SOCIETY, University of California Press, 2000 Center St., Suite 303, Berkeley, CA 94704-1223, 510-643-7154
Judah Magnes Museum Publications, 2911 Russell Street, Berkeley, CA 94705
Kelsey St. Press, 2824 Kelsey St., Berkeley, CA 94705, 510-845-2260, Fax 510-548-9185, info@kelseyst.com, www.kelseyst.com
LAW AND LITERATURE, University of California Press, 2000 Center St., Suite 303, Berkeley, CA 94704-1223, 510-643-7154
MEXICAN STUDIES/ESTUDIOS MEXICANOS, University of California Press, 2000 Center Street, Suite 303, Berkeley, CA 94704-1223, 510-643-7154
THE MONTHLY INDEPENDENT TRIBUNE TIMES JOURNAL POST GAZETTE NEWS CHRONICLE BULLETIN, 80 Fairlawn Drive, Berkeley, CA 94708-2106
MUSIC PERCEPTION, Univ of CA Press, 2000 Center Street, Suite 303, Berkeley, CA 94704-1223, 510-643-7154
MUSIC THEORY SPECTRUM, University of California Press, 2000 Center St., Suite 303, Berkeley, CA 94704-1223, 510-643-7154
MYSTERY READERS JOURNAL, PO Box 8116, Berkeley, CA 94707-8116, 510-845-3600, www.mysteryreaders.org
NEWS FROM NATIVE CALIFORNIA, PO Box 9145, Berkeley, CA 94709, 510-549-3564; FAX 510-549-1889
19TH-CENTURY LITERATURE, University of California Press, 2000 Center Street, Suite 303, Berkeley, CA 94704-1223, 510-643-7154
19TH-CENTURY MUSIC, University of California Press, 2000 Center Street, Suite 303, Berkeley, CA 94704-1223, 510-643-7154
Nolo Press, 950 Parker Street, Berkeley, CA 94710, 510-549-1976, Fax 510-548-5902
North Atlantic Books, PO Box 12327, Berkeley, CA 94712, 800-337-2665, 510-559-8277, fax 510-559-8272, www.northatlanticbooks.com
NOVA RELIGIO, University of California Press, 2000 Center St., Suite 303, Berkeley, CA 94704-1223, 510-643-7154
Omni Books, 2342 Shattuck Avenue, Berkeley, CA 94704
ORAL HISTORY REVIEW, University of California Press, 2000 Center St., Suite 303, Berkeley, CA 94704-1223, 510-643-7154
PACIFIC HISTORICAL REVIEW, Univ of California Press, 2000 Center Street, Suite 303, Berkeley, CA 94704-1223, 510-643-7154
Pacific View Press, PO Box 2897, Berkeley, CA 94702, Fax 510-843-5835, pvp@mindspring.com
Parallax Press, 2236B 6th St., Berkeley, CA 94710-2219, 510-525-0101; e-Mail info@parallax.org; web address http://www.parallax.org
POETALK, PO Box 11435, Berkeley, CA 94712-2435, poetalk@aol.com, http://hometown.aol.com/poetalk/myhomepage/index.html
POETRY FLASH, 1450 Fourth Street #4, Berkeley, CA 94710, 510-525-5476, Fax 510-525-6752
Poltroon Press, PO Box 5476, Berkeley, CA 94705-0476, 510-845-8097
THE PUBLIC HISTORIAN, University of California Press, 2000 Center Street, Suite 303, Berkeley, CA 94704-1223, 510-643-7154
RELIGION & AMERICAN CULTURE, University of California Press, 2000 Center St., Suite 303, Berkeley, CA 94704-1223, 510-643-7154
REPORTS OF THE NATIONAL CENTER FOR SCIENCE EDUCATION, NCSE, Box 9477, Berkeley, CA 94709, 510-601-7203, Fax 510-601-7204
REPRESENTATIONS, University of California Press, 2000 Center Street, Suite 303, Berkeley, CA 94704-1223, 510-643-7154
RHETORICA: A Journal of the History of Rhetoric, Univ of California Press, 2000 Center Street, Suite 303, Berkeley, CA 94704-1223, 510-643-7154
Sacred Spaces Press, PO Box 7812, Berkeley, CA 94707, 510-559-9341, inquiries@sacredspacespress.com, www.sacredspacespress.com
SCP JOURNAL, PO Box 4308, Berkeley, CA 94704
SINISTER WISDOM, PO Box 3252, Berkeley, CA 94703
SOCIAL PROBLEMS, University of California Press, 2000 Center Street, Suite 303, Berkeley, CA 94704-1223, 510-643-7154
SOCIOLOGICAL PERSPECTIVES, University of California Press, 2000 Center St., Suite 303, Berkeley, CA 94704-1223, 510-643-7154
THE SOCIOLOGICAL QUARTERLY, University of California Press, 2000 Center Street, Suite 303, Berkeley, CA 94704-1223, 510-643-7154
STATE OF CALIFORNIA LABOR, University of California Press, 2000 Center St., Suite 303, Berkeley, CA 94704-1223, 510-634-7154
Stone Bridge Press, PO Box 8208, Berkeley, CA 94707, 510-524-8732
SYMBOLIC INTERACTION, University of California Press, 2000 Center St., Suite 303, Berkeley, CA 94704-1223, 510-643-7154
THE THREEPENNY REVIEW, PO Box 9131, Berkeley, CA 94709-0131, 510-849-4545
TURNING WHEEL, PO Box 3470, Berkeley, CA 94703
Tuumba Press, 2639 Russell Street, Berkeley, CA 94705-2131, 510-548-1817,510-704-8350
University of California Press, 2000 Center Street, Suite 303, Berkeley, CA 94704-1223, 510-643-7154, e-mail journals@ucpress.edu
Wilderness Press, 1200 5th Street, Berkeley, CA 94710-1306, 510-843-8080; fax 510-548-1355; e-mail mail@wildernesspress.com

Four Continents Press, 256 S. Robertson #3194, Beverly Hills, CA 90211-2898, 310-276-6525, Fax 310-276-6595, fourcontpress@hotmail.com
Laredo Publishing Co., Inc./Renaissance House, 9400 Lloydcrest Drive, Beverly Hills, CA 90210-2528
Milk Mug Publishing, 9190 W. Olympic Blvd., Ste. 253, Beverly Hills, CA 90212, info@milkmugpublishing.com, www.thehoopsterbook.com
Museon Publishing, PO Box 17095, Beverly Hills, CA 90209-2095, 310-788-0228
Paul Zelevansky, 1455 Clairidge Drive, Beverly Hills, CA 90210-2214
PAST TIMES: The Nostalgia Entertainment Newsletter, 7308 Fillmore Drive, Buena Park, CA 90620, 714-527-5845; skretved@ix.netcom.com
Ascension Publishing, 920 East Cedar Avenue, Burbank, CA 91501-1528, 818-848-8145
Nateen Publishing, 730 North Naomi Street, Burbank, CA 91505, 818-567-1987, Fax 818-567-0829
RESEARCH IN YORUBA LANGUAGE & LITERATURE, 1317 N. San Fernando Blvd., Suite 310, Burbank, CA 91504
The Sacred Beverage Press, PO Box 10312, Burbank, CA 91510-0312, Fax 818-780-1912, sacredbev@aol.com
SOCIETE, 1317 N. San Fernando Blvd., Suite 310, Burbank, CA 91504
Technicians of the Sacred, 1317 N. San Fernando Boulevard, Suite 310, Burbank, CA 91504
Buddhist Text Translation Society, 1777 Murchison Drive, Burlingame, CA 94010-4504, (707) 468-9112, e-mail EileenHu@drba.org
Stunt Publishing, 22287 Mulholland Hwy, #281, Calabasas, CA 91302, ph:818-312-5157, fax:818-312-5157, www.stuntpublishing.com, stuntpublishing@stuntpublishing.com
American Carriage House Publishing, P.O. Box 1130, Nevada City, California, CA 95959, 530.470.0720
LIFETIME MAGAZINE, P.O. Box 1130, Nevada City, California, CA 95959, 530.470.0720
THE INDENTED PILLOW, PO Box 3502, Camarillo, CA 93011, rjones@mymailstation.com
Macrocosm USA, Inc., PO Box 185, Cambria, CA 93428, 805-927-2515, e-Mail brockway@macronet.org, www.macronet.org
Borden Publishing Co., 300 Carlsbad Village Drive, Suite 108A #110, Carlsbad, CA 92008, 760-594-0918, Fax 760-967-6843, bordenpublishing@sbcglobal.net, www.bordenpublishing.com
Craftsman Book Company, 6058 Corte Del Cedro, Carlsbad, CA 92011, 760-438-7828
French Bread Publications, P.O. Box 56, Carlsbad, CA 92018
Gurze Books, PO Box 2238, Carlsbad, CA 92018, 760-434-7533, Fax 760-434-5476, gurze@aol.com
Magnus Press Imprint: Canticle Books, PO Box 2666, Carlsbad, CA 92018, 760-806-3743, Fax 760-806-3689, toll free 800-463-7818, magnuspres@aol.com www.magnuspress.com
PACIFIC COAST JOURNAL, PO Box 56, Carlsbad, CA 92018-0056, e-mail paccoastj@frenchbreadpublications.com
Creative With Words Publications (CWW), PO Box 223226, Carmel, CA 93922-3226, Fax: 831-655-8627; e-mail: cwwpub@usa.net; http://members.tripod.com/~creativewithwords
THEECLECTICS, PO Box 223226, Carmel, CA 93922, fax 831-655-8627; e-mail cwwpub@usa.net; website http://members.tripod.com/~CreativeWithWords
Brown Fox Books, 1090 Eugenia Place, Carpinteria, CA 93013, 805-684-5951, Fax 805-684-1628, Manager@Brownfoxbooks.com, www.Brownfoxbooks.com
SOLO, 5146 Foothill, Carpinteria, CA 93013, berrypress@aol.com
Ridge Times Press, PO Box 14, Caspar, CA 95420, 707-964-0463
The Infinity Group, 22516 Charlene Way, Castro Valley, CA 94546, 510-581-8172; kenandgenie@yahoo.com
THE MOUNTAIN ASTROLOGER, PO Box 970, Cedar Ridge, CA 95924-0970, 530-477-8839, www.mountainastrologer.com
GOLDEN ISIS MAGAZINE, PO Box 4263, Chatsworth, CA 91313-4263, 775-417-0737 phone/Fax, golden.isis@prodigy.net
Golden Isis Press, PO Box 4263, Chatsworth, CA 91313
Scientia Publishing, LLC, P. O. Box 5495, Chatsworth, CA 91313, 1-818-620-0433, www.scientiapublishingllc.com
Wilshire Books Inc., 9731 Variel Ave., Chatsworth, CA 91311-4315, 818-700-1522 [tel], 818-700-1527 [fax]; website: www.mpowers.com
Flume Press, California State University, Chico, 400 W. First Street, Chico, CA 95929-0830, 530-898-5983
Heidelberg Graphics, 2 Stansbury Court, Chico, CA 95928-9410, 530-342-6582
MACROBIOTICS TODAY, PO Box 3998, Chico, CA 95927-3998, 530-566-9765, Fax 530-566-9768, foundation@gomf.macrobiotic.net
MAGICAL BLEND/NATURAL BEAUTY & HEALTH/TRANSITIONS, PO Box 600, Chico, CA 95927-0600, 888-296-2442, Fax 530-893-9076, editor@magicalblend.com
MB Media, Inc., PO Box 600, Chico, CA 95927, 888-296-2442, Fax 530-893-9076, editor@magicalblend.com
George Ohsawa Macrobiotic Foundation, PO Box 3998, Chico, CA 95927-3998, 530-566-9765, Fax 530-566-9768, foundation@gomf.macrobiotic.net
LifeThread Publications, 7541 Wooddale Way, Citrus Heights, CA 95610-2621, 916-722-3452, E-mail sosborn@ix.netcom.com
LITVISION, 7711 Greenback Lane #156, Citrus Heights, CA 95610
Savor Publishing House, Inc., 6020 Broken Bow Dr., Citrus Heights, CA 95621, 916 729-3664, 866 762-7898
SILVER WINGS, PO Box 2340, Clovis, CA 93613-2340, 661-264-3726
Bear Star Press, 185 Hollow Oak Drive, Cohasset, CA 95973, 530-891-0360, www.bearstarpress.com
C & T Publishing, 1651 Challenge Drive, Concord, CA 94520-5206, 925-677-0377
JOURNAL OF SOCIAL BEHAVIOR AND PERSONALITY, PO Box 37, Corte Madera, CA 94925, 415-209-9838
Select Press, PO Box 37, Corte Madera, CA 94925, 415-209-9838
SPEX (SMALL PRESS EXCHANGE), PO Box E, Corte Madera, CA 94976, 866-622-1325
Quality Words in Print, PO Box 2704, Costa Mesa, CA 92628-2704, 714-436-5700, fax: 714-668-9448, web: www.qwipbooks.com, email: custserv@nbnbooks.com
THE KERF, 883 W. Washington Boulevard, Crescent City, CA 95531, 707-465-2360, Fax 707-464-6867
EquiLibrium Press, 10736 Jefferson Blvd. #680, Culver City, CA 90230, 310-417-8217, Fax 310-417-8122, equipress@equipress.com
TURNING THE TIDE: Journal of Anti-Racist Action, Research & Education, PO Box 1055, Culver City, CA 90232-1055, 310-495-0299, antiracistaction_la@yahoo.com
Happy About, 21265 Stevens Creek Blvd, Suite 205, Cupertino, CA 95014, 408-257-3000, dustbooks-publisher@happyabout.info, http://www.happyabout.info
RED WHEELBARROW, 21250 Stevens Creek Blvd., De Anza College, Cupertino, CA 95014, Fax 408-864-5629, splitterrandolph@fhda.edu
Genny Smith Books, 23100 Via Esplendor, Villa 44, Cupertino, CA 95014, 650-964-4071, www.liveoakpress.com
THE BLUE MOUSE, PO Box 586, Cypress, CA 90630

546

Swan Duckling Press, PO Box 586, Cypress, CA 90630

WILD DUCK REVIEW, P.O. Box 335, Davenport, CA 95017, 831.471.9246 casey@wildduckreview.com

Terra Nova Press, 1309 Redwood Lane, Davis, CA 95616, 530-756-7417

Piano Press, PO Box 85, Del Mar, CA 92014-0085, pianopress@pianopress.com, www.pianopress.com, 619-884-1401

PowerPartners USA, 1155 Camino Del Mar, Ste. 209, Del Mar, CA 92014, info@themagicseed.com

Andrew Scott Publishers, 15023 Tierra Alta, Del Mar, CA 92014, 858-755-0715 phone/Fax, e-mail andrewscottpublishers@juno.com

Wharton Publishing, Inc., 2683 Via De La Valle, Suite G #210, Del Mar, CA 92014, 760-931-8977, Fax 858-759-7097, e-mail marketingtina@aol.com

Front Row Experience, 540 Discovery Bay Boulevard, Discovery Bay, CA 94514, 925-634-5710

Sunbelt Publications, 1256 Fayette Street, El Cajon, CA 92020-1511, 619-258-4911, Fax 619-258-4916, mail@sunbeltpub.com, www.sunbeltbooks.com

The Glencannon Press, PO Box 1428, El Cerrito, CA 94530-4428, 707-745-3933, fax 707-747-0311

THE ACORN, PO Box 1266, El Dorado, CA 95623, acorn@mail2world.com

Reference Service Press, 5000 Windplay Drive, Suite 4, El Dorado Hills, CA 95762, (916) 939-9620, fax: (916) 939-9626, email: info@rspfunding.com, web site: www.rspfunding.com

New Win Publishing, 9682 Telstar Ave. Suite 110, El Monte, CA 91731, 626-448-3448, 626-602-3817, info@academiclearningcompany.com, www.newwinpublishing.com

Velazquez Press, 9682 Telstar Ave. Suite 110, El Monte, CA 91731, 626-448-3448, 626-602-3817, info@academiclearningcompany.com, www.velazquezpress.com

Raised Barn Press, 3300 Powell St., Apt. 327, Emeryville, CA 94608-4909, info@raisedbarnpress.com

ZAHIR, Unforgettable Tales, 315 South Coast Hwy. 101 Suite U8, Encinitas, CA 92024, stempchin@zahirtales.com, http://www.zahirtales.com

Titan Press, PO Box 17897, Encino, CA 91416-7897

TIN HOUSE MAGAZINE, PO Box 469049, Escondido, CA 92046

TRUTH SEEKER, 239 S. Juniper Street, Escondido, CA 92025-0550, 760-489-5211, Fax 760-489-5311, tseditor@aol.com, www.truthseeker.com

FINE BOOKS & COLLECTIONS, PO Box 106, Eureka, CA 95502, 707-443-9562, Fax 707-443-9572, scott@finebooksmagazine.com, www.finebooksmagazine.com

Miles & Miles, 3420 M Street, Eureka, CA 95503-5462

Adams-Blake Publishing, 8041 Sierra Street, Fair Oaks, CA 95628, 916-962-9296

GINOSKO, PO Box 246, Fairfax, CA 94978, GinoskoEditor@aol.com

African Ways Publishing, 3112 Estates Drive, Fairfield, CA 94533-9721, 925-631-0630, Fax 925-376-1926

United Lumbee Nation, PO Box 512, Fall River Mills, CA 96028, 916-336-6701

UNITED LUMBEE NATION TIMES, P.O. Box 512, Fall River Mills, CA 96028, 530-336-6701

Jalmar Press/Innerchoice Publishing, PO Box 370, Fawnskin, CA 92333, Fax 909 866 2961 Email: info@jalmarpress.com

Personhood Press, PO Box 370, Fawnskin, CA 92333-0370, 909-866-2912,Fax 909-866-2961, 800 429 1192, www.personhoodpress.com

THE NATIONAL POETRY REVIEW, PO Box 4041, Felton, CA 95018-1196, nationalpoetryreview@yahoo.com, www.nationalpoetryreview.com

Floreant Press, 6195 Anderson Rd, Forestville, CA 95436, 7078877868

Floreant Press, 6195 Anderson Rd, Forestville, CA 95436, 707 887 7868

Cypress House, 155 Cypress Street, Fort Bragg, CA 95437, 707-964-9520, Fax 707-964-7531, publishing@cypresshouse.com

Lost Coast Press, 155 Cypress Street, Fort Bragg, CA 95437, 800-773-7782, fax 707-964-7531, www.cypresshouse.com, joeshaw@cypresshouse.com

QED Press, 155 Cypress Street, Fort Bragg, CA 95437, 707-964-9520, Fax 707-964-7531, qedpress@mcn.org

CURL MAGAZINE, 39270 Paseo Padre Parkway #142, Fremont, CA 94538-1616, 877-854-3850, Fax 510-429-9659, bayareafitness@excite.com, www.CurlMagazine.com

Shen's Books, 40951 Fremont Boulevard, Fremont, CA 94538, 510-668-1898, www.shens.com

Universal Unity, 1860 Mowry Avenue #400, Fremont, CA 94538-1730

Adventure Books Inc., PO Box 5196, Fresno, CA 93755, 559-294-8781, adventurebooks@juno.com

East West Discovery Press, PO Box 2393, Gardena, CA 90247, 310-532-1115, Fax 310-768-8926, info@eastwestdiscovery.com, web www.eastwestdiscovery.com

Balcony Media, Inc., 512 E. Wilson Avenue, Suite 213, Glendale, CA 91206, 818-956-5313(T), 818-956-5904(F), web: www.laarch.com, email: diana@balconypress.com

SHARING IDEAS FOR PROFESSIONAL SPEAKERS, PO Box 398, Glendora, CA 91740, 626-335-8069; fax 626-335-6127

White Thread Press, 480 Whitman Street #102, Goleta, CA 93117, 805 968 4666

Red Hen Press, PO Box 3537, Granada Hills, CA 91394, Fax 818-831-6659, E-mail editors@redhen.org

Comstock Bonanza Press, 18919 William Quirk Drive, Grass Valley, CA 95945-8611, 530-263-2906

UnTechnical Press, 16410 Gibboney Lane, Grass Valley, CA 95949, 530-271-7129; 888-59-BOOKS; Fax 530-271-7129; michael@untechnicalpress.com; www.untechnicalpress.com

BIG BRIDGE: A Webzine of Poetry and Everything Else, 16083 Fern Way, Guerneville, CA 95446, www.bigbridge.org

KALDRON, An International Journal Of Visual Poetry, PO Box 7164, Halcyon, CA 93421-7164, 805-489-2770, www.thing.net/~grist/l&d/kaldron.htm

BLOODJET LITERARY MAGAZINE, 20 Driftwood Trail, Half Moon Bay, CA 94019-2349, 650-726-5939; Fax 415-921-3730

New World Press, 20 Driftwood Trail, Half Moon Bay, CA 94019-2349, 650-726-5939; Fax 415-921-3730

Mille Grazie Press, 967 Clover Lane, Hanford, CA 93230-2255

Naturegraph Publishers, PO Box 1047, 3543 Indian Creek Road, Happy Camp, CA 96039, 530-493-5353, 530-493-5240, 1-800-390-5353. nature@isqtel.net, www.naturegraph.com

Pristine Publishing, 7586 Lochinvar Court, Highland, CA 92346, 909-862-1991 phone/Fax, www.pristinepublishing.com

Acting World Books, PO Box 3044, Hollywood, CA 90078, 818-905-1345, Fax 800-210-1197

THE AGENCIES-WHAT THE ACTOR NEEDS TO KNOW, PO Box 3044, Hollywood, CA 90078, 818-905-1345

THE HOLLYWOOD ACTING COACHES AND TEACHERS DIRECTORY, PO Box 3044, Hollywood, CA 90078, 818-905-1345

Hollywood Film Archive, 8391 Beverly Boulevard, PMB 321, Hollywood, CA 90048-2633

Vedanta Press, 1946 Vedanta Place, Hollywood, CA 90068-3996, 323-960-1728,e-mail address: bob@vedanta.org,web address:www.vedanta.com,web page shows our online catalog. Note that titles with an asterisk by the title in the catalog are not wholesale titles.

SPILLWAY, Box 7887, Huntington Beach, CA 92615-7887, 714-968-0905

Tebot Bach, Box 7887, Huntington Beach, CA 92615-7887, 714-968-0905

Verve Press, PO Box 1997, Huntington Beach, CA 92647, fax: 714-840-8335

The Spinning Star Press, 1065 E. Fairview Blvd., Inglewood, CA 90302

CALIFORNIA QUARTERLY (CQ), CSPS/CQ, 21 Whitman Court, Irvine, CA 92617, 949-854-8024, jipalley@aol.com

Level 4 Press, 13518 Jamul Drive, Jamul, CA 91935-1635, 619-669-3100, 619-374-7311 fax, sales@level4Press.com, www.level4press.com

Tree of Life Books. Imprints: Progressive Press, Banned Books, PO Box 126, Joshua Tree, CA 92252, 760-366-3695, fax 760-366-2937

BLUE UNICORN, 22 Avon Road, Kensington, CA 94707, 510-526-8439

Oyez, 212 Colgate Avenue, Kensington, CA 94708-1122

Wilton Place Publishing, PO Box 291, La Canada, CA 91012, 818-790-5601

International University Line (IUL), PO Box 2525, La Jolla, CA 92038, Tel 858-457-0595, Fax 858-581-9073, email info@iul-press.com, http://www.iul-press.com

A Melody from an Immigrant's Soul, 5712 Baltimore Dr. #461, La Mesa, CA 91942, (619) 667-0925 E-mail: dorishka1@sbcglobal.net

Laguna Wilderness Press, P.O. Box 149, Laguna Beach, CA 92652, Phone: 951-827-1571, Fax: 951-827-5685, info@lagunawildernesspress.com, www.lagunawildernesspress.com

Frontline Publications, PO Box 1104, Lake Forest, CA 92609, 949-837-6258

Info Net Publishing, 21142 Canada Road #1C, Lake Forest, CA 92630-6714, 949-458-9292, Fax 949-462-9595, herb@infonetpublishing.com

Parissound Publishing, 30 Tamalpais Avenue, Larkspur, CA 94939, Fax 415-924-5379, parissound@aol.com, www.paris-sound.com

SOMETHING TO READ, PO Box 810, Livermore, CA 94551, smalltown@ldsliving.com, http://altlmiss.tripod.com/smalltown

Auromere Books and Imports, 2621 W. US Highway 12, Lodi, CA 95242-9200, 800-735-4691, 209-339-3710, Fax 209-339-3715, books@auromere.com, www.auromere.com

FMA Publishing, 1920 Pacific Ave, #16152, Long Beach, CA 90746, (T)310-438-3483, (F)310-438-3486, (E)info@fmapublishing.com, www.fmapublishing.com

Intelligenesis Publications, 6414 Cantel Street, Long Beach, CA 90815, 562-598-0034, www.bookmasters.com/marktplc/00337.htm

KT Publishing, 111 West Ocean Blvd., 10th Floor, Long Beach, CA 90801

Mama Incense Publishing, PO Box 4635, Long Beach, CA 90804-9998, 310-490-9097, www.mamaincense.com

PEARL, 3030 E. Second Street, Long Beach, CA 90803-5163, 562-434-4523 phone/fax or 714-968-7530, PearlMag@aol.com, www.pearlmag.com

Pearl Editions, 3030 E. Second Street, Long Beach, CA 90803-5163, 562-434-4523 phone/fax or 714-968-7530, PearlMag@aol.com, www.pearlmag.com

SHIRIM, 259 Saint Joseph Avenue, Long Beach, CA 90803-1733

Tameme, 199 First Street, Los Altos, CA 94022, www.tameme.org

AAIMS Publishers, 11000 Wilshire Boulevard, PO Box 241777, Los Angeles, CA 90024-0777, 213-968-1195, 888-490-2276, fax 213-931-7217, email aaims1@aol.com

AMERICAN INDIAN CULTURE AND RESEARCH JOURNAL, 3220 Campbell Hall, Box 951548, Los Angeles, CA 90095-1548, 310-825-7315, Fax 310-206-7060, www.sscnet.ucla.edu/esp/aisc/index.html

American Indian Studies Center, 3220 Campbell Hall, Box 951548, UCLA, Los Angeles, CA 90095-1548, 310-825-7315, Fax 310-206-7060, www.sscnet.ucla.edu/esp/aisc/index.html

Ariko Publications, 8513 Venice Blvd #201, Los Angeles, CA 90034

AZTLAN: A Journal of Chicano Studies, University of California-Los Angeles, 193 Haines Hall, Los Angeles, CA 90095-1544, 310-825-2642, press@chicano.ucla.edu, www.chicano.ucla.edu

Black Diamond Book Publishing, PO Box 492299, Los Angeles, CA 90049-8299, 800-962-7622, Fax 310-472-9833, nancy_shaffron@compuserve.com

BLACK LACE, PO Box 83912, Los Angeles, CA 90083, 310-410-0808, fax 310-410-9250, e-mail newsroom@blk.com

BLACKFIRE, PO Box 83912, Los Angeles, CA 90083, 310-410-0808, fax 310-410-9250, e-mail newsroom@blk.com

BLK, PO Box 83912, Los Angeles, CA 90083, 310-410-0808, fax 310-410-9250, e-mail newsroom@blk.com

BLK Publishing Company, PO Box 83912, Los Angeles, CA 90083, 310-410-0808, Fax 310-410-9250, newsroom@blk.com

Bombshelter Press, P.O Box 481266, Bicentennial Station, Los Angeles, CA 90048, 310-651-5488, jgrapes@bombshelterpress.com, http://www.bombshelterpress.com

Cloverfield Press, 429 North Ogden Drive, Apt.1, Los Angeles, CA 90036-1730, submissions@cloverfieldpress.com, www.cloverfieldpress.com

Cotsen Institute of Archaeology Publications, Univ. of California-Los Angeles, A210 Fowler, Los Angeles, CA 90095-1510, 310-825-7411

Dablond Publishing, 6733 Colgate Avenue, Los Angeles, CA 90048, dablondpublish@aol.com

THE DUCKBURG TIMES, 3010 Wilshire Blvd., #362, Los Angeles, CA 90010-1146, 213-388-2364

Everflowing Publications, PO Box 191536, Los Angeles, CA 90019, 323-993-8577, everflowing@nycmail.com

FRAN MAGAZINE, PO Box 291459, Los Angeles, CA 90029, 213.250.3788

Heat Press, PO Box 26218, Los Angeles, CA 90026, 213-482-8902, heatpresseditions@yahoo.com

Hollywood Creative Directory, 5055 Wilshire Blvd., Los Angeles, CA 90036, 800-815-0503, 323-525-2369, Fax 323-525-2393, www.hcdonline.com

Ignite! Entertainment, P.O. Box 641131, Los Angeles, CA 90064-1980, ignite-entertainment@earthlink.net

International Jewelry Publications, PO Box 13384, Los Angeles, CA 90013-0384, 626-282-3781, Fax 626-282-4807

Jamenair Ltd., PO Box 241957, Los Angeles, CA 90024-9757, 310-470-6688

KABBALAH, 1062 S. Robertson Boulevard, Los Angeles, CA 90035, 310-657-5404, Fax 310-657-7774, kabmag@kabbalah.dymp.com, www.kabbalah.com

KUUMBA, PO Box 83912, Los Angeles, CA 90083, 310-410-0808, fax 310-410-9250, e-mail newsroom@blk.com

Les Figues Press, PO Box 35628, Los Angeles, CA 90035, trose@olywa.net

LOS, 150 N. Catalina St., No. 2, Los Angeles, CA 90004, website: http://home.earthlink.net/~lospoesy, email: lospoesy@earthlink.net

Middle Passage Press, 5517 Secrest Drive, Los Angeles, CA 90043, 213-298-0266

MOMMY AND I ARE ONE, 2218 Princeton Ave., Los Angeles, CA 90026-2014, 323-960-0358, jjcrashcourse@hotmail.com

548

NEW GERMAN REVIEW: A Journal of Germanic Studies, Dept of Germanic Languages, UCLA, 212 Royce Hall, Los Angeles, CA 90095-1539, 310-825-3955

Nova Press, 11659 Mayfield Ave, Suite 1, Los Angeles, CA 90049, 310-207-4078, E-mail novapress@aol.com

ONTHEBUS, Bombshelter Press, P.O. Box 481266, Bicentennial Station, Los Angeles, CA 90048, http://www.bombshelter-press.com or http://www.jackgrapes.com

Phony Lid Publications, PO Box 29066, Los Angeles, CA 90029, phonylid@fyuocuk.com, www.fyuocuk.com

PICK POCKET BOOKS, PO Box 29066, Los Angeles, CA 90029, phonylid@fyuocuk.com, www.fyuocuk.com

Pluma Productions, PO BOX 1138, Los Angeles, CA 90078-1138, email pluma@earthlink.net

Really Great Books, PO Box 86121, Los Angeles, CA 90086-0121, 213-624-8555, fax 213-624-8666, www.reallygreat-books.com

Red Eye Press, PO Box 65751, Los Angeles, CA 90065-0751, 323-225-3805

Seraphic Press, 1531 Cardiff Avenue, Los Angeles, CA 90035, 310 557-0132, seraphicpress@aol.com, seraphicpressblogs-pot.com

Seven Arrows Publishing, Inc., 8721 Santa Monica Boulevard #532, Los Angeles, CA 90069, 310-360-9474, Fax 310-289-9474, office@sevenarrowsonline.com, www.sevenarrowsonline.com

SevenStar Communications, 13315 Washington Blvd., Ste. 200, Los Angeles, CA 90066, 310-302-1207, Fax 310-302-1208, taostar@taostar.com, www.sevenstarcom.com

SIGNS: JOURNAL OF WOMEN IN CULTURE AND SOCIETY, UCLA, Box 957122, 1400H Public Policy Building, Los Angeles, CA 90095-7122, 310-206-2562, Fax 310-206-1261, signs@signs.ucla.edu

THE SOUTHERN CALIFORNIA ANTHOLOGY, Master of Prof. Writing Program, WPH 404/Univ. of Southern Calif., Los Angeles, CA 90089-4034, 213-740-3252

Sparkplug Press, 636 N. Kilkea Dr., Los Angeles, CA 90048-2214, Phone: 323-632-9826, Fax: 323-658-7379, website: www.sparkplugpress.com

Spectrum Productions, 979 Casiano Road, Los Angeles, CA 90049

Chuck Stewart, 3722 Bagley Ave. #19, Los Angeles, CA 90034-4113, www.StewartEducationServices.com

TAI CHI, PO Box 39938, Los Angeles, CA 90039, 323-665-7773, www.tai-chi.com

Triumvirate Publications, 497 West Avenue 44, Los Angeles, CA 90065-3917, 818-340-6770 Phone/Fax, Triumpub@aol.com, www.Triumpub.com

2.13.61 Publications, 7510 Sunset Boulevard #602, Los Angeles, CA 90046, 323-969-8791

UCLA Chicano Studies Research Center Press, University of California-Los Angeles, 193 Haines Hall, Los Angeles, CA 90095-1544, 310-825-2642, press@chicano.ucla.edu, www.chicano.ucla.edu

UglyTown, PO Box 411655, Los Angeles, CA 90041-8655, 213-484-8334, Fax 213-484-8333, www.uglytown.com

WAV MAGAZINE: Progressive Music Art Politics Culture, 3253 S. Beverly Dr., Los Angeles, CA 90034, (310) 876-0490

Wayfarer Publications, PO Box 39938, Los Angeles, CA 90039, 323-665-7773

Yo San Books, 13315 W. Washington Blvd, Ste. 200, Los Angeles, CA 90066

WRITING FOR OUR LIVES, 647 N. Santa Cruz Ave., The Annex, Los Gatos, CA 95030, 408-354-8604

Sand River Press, 1319 14th Street, Los Osos, CA 93402, 805-543-3591

The Bieler Press, 4216-1/4 Glencoe Avenue, Marina del Rey, CA 90292

The Dragon Press, 4230 Del Rey Avenue, Marina del Rey, CA 90292, 1-877-907-5400, Fax 626-398-7450

Wave Publishing, 4 Yawl Street, Marina del Rey, CA 90292-7159, 310-306-0699

Fithian Press, PO Box 2790, McKinleyville, CA 95519-2790, 805-962-1780, Fax 805-962-8835, dandd@danielpublishing.com

Visibility Unlimited Publications, 30605 Curzulla Road, Menifee Valley, CA 92584, 909-926-5125, lithic1@linkline.com

Penthe Publishing, PO Box 1066, Middletown, CA 95461-1066, 800-649-5954, 707-987-3470, penthpub@earthlink.net, penthepub.com

NEW AMERICAN WRITING, 369 Molino Avenue, Mill Valley, CA 94941, 415-389-1877, Fax 415-384-0364

Poor Souls Press/Scaramouche Books, PO Box 236, Millbrae, CA 94030

QUERCUS REVIEW, Modesto Junior College, 435 College Avenue, Modesto, CA 95350, 209-575-6183, pierstorffs@mjc.edu, www.quercusreview.com

NEROUP REVIEW, 202 Spencer St., Apt. #5, Monterey, CA 93940-1859, www.neroupreview.com, submissions@neroupre-view.com

Sea Challengers, Inc., 4 Sommerset Rise, Monterey, CA 93940, 831-373-6306, Fax 831-373-4566

Victory Press, 543 Lighthouse Avenue, Monterey, CA 93940-1422, (831) 883-1725, Fax (831)883-8710

Reed Press, P.O. Box 701, Montrose, CA 91021, 818-248-6433, fax 818-248-6561 www.Mer-Folk.com

Myriad Press, 12535 Chandler Blvd. #3, N. Hollywood, CA 91607, 818-508-6296

Blue Dolphin Publishing, Inc., PO Box 8, Nevada City, CA 95959, 530-265-6925

Crystal Clarity, Publishers, 14618 Tyler Foote Road, Nevada City, CA 95959, 1-800-424-1055; 530-478-7600; fax 530-478-7610

Dawn Publications, 12402 Bitney Springs Rd., Nevada City, CA 95959, 530-274-7775, toll free 800-545-7475, fax 530-274-7778, nature@dawnpub.com

Gateways Books And Tapes, Box 370, Nevada City, CA 95959-0370, 530-477-8101, fax 800-869-0658, info@gatewaysbook-sandtapes.com, www.gatewaysbooksandtapes.com

Lexikos, PO Box 1289, Nevada City, CA 95959

THE JOURNAL OF HISTORICAL REVIEW, PO Box 2739, Newport Beach, CA 92659, 949-631-1490, ihr@ihr.org

Noontide Press, PO Box 2719, Newport Beach, CA 92659, 949-631-1490, e-mail editor@noontidepress.com

ORANGE COAST MAGAZINE, 3701 Birch Street, Suite 100, Newport Beach, CA 92660-2618, 949-862-1133

Santa Ana River Press, PO Box 5473, Norco, CA 92860-8016, 877-822-9623, editorial@santaanariverpress.com, www.santaanariverpress.com

CHECKER CAB MAGAZINE - THE LITTLE 'ZINE THAT COULD! Fiction That Takes The Long Way Home, P. O. Box 1464, North Highlands, CA 95660-1464, checkercab@sbcglobal.net, www.checkercabmagazine.com

POETRY DEPTH QUARTERLY, 5836 North Haven Drive, North Highlands, CA 95660, 916-331-3512, e-mail: poetrydepthquarterly.com NO download or attached files accepted. Prefers postal submissions with S.A.S.E.

SHARE INTERNATIONAL, PO Box 971, North Hollywood, CA 91603, 818-785-6300, Fax 818-904-9132, share@shar-eintl.org, www.shareintl.org/

Lord John Press, 19073 Los Alimos Street, Northridge, CA 91326, 818-360-5804

Studio 4 Productions, PO Box 280400, Northridge, CA 91328-0400, 888publish (782-5474), Fax 314-993-4485, www.studio4productions.com

BIGFOOT TIMES, 10926 Milano Avenue, Norwalk, CA 90650, www.bigfoottimes.net

Chandler & Sharp Publishers, Inc., 11 Commercial Blvd.Suite A, Novato, CA 94949, 415-883-2353, FAX 415-440-5004,

www.chandlersharp.com
New World Library, 14 Pamaron Way, Novato, CA 94949-6215
THE BLACK SCHOLAR: Journal of Black Studies and Research, PO Box 2869, Oakland, CA 94609, 510-547-6633
Broken Shadow Publications, 472 44th Street, Oakland, CA 94609-2136, 510 594-2200
Burning Bush Publications, PO Box 9636, Oakland, CA 94613-0636, 510-482-9996, www.bbbooks.com, editors@bbbooks.com
COLORLINES, 4096 Piedmont Avenue, PMB 319, Oakland, CA 94611, 510-653-3415, Fax 510-653-3427, colorlines@arc.org, www.colorlines.com
Defiant Times Press, 6020-A Adeline, Oakland, CA 94608, defianttimespress@lycos.com
580 SPLIT, Mills College, P.O. Box 9982, Oakland, CA 94613-0982
Food First Books, 398 60th Street, Oakland, CA 94618, 510-654-4400, FAX 510-654-4551, foodfirst@foodfirst.org
GRASSROOTS FUNDRAISING JOURNAL, 1904 Franklin St Ste 705, Oakland, CA 94612, 510-452-4520, Fax 510-452-2122, info@grassrootsfundraising.org, www.grassrootsfundraising.org
IN OUR OWN WORDS, PO Box 9636, Oakland, CA 94613, www.bbbooks.com
The Independent Institute, 100 Swan Way, Oakland, CA 94621-1428, 510-632-1366, fax 510-568-6040, email info@independent.org, www.independent.org
THE INDEPENDENT REVIEW: A Journal of Political Economy, 100 Swan Way, Oakland, CA 94621-1428, 510-632-1366, fax 510-568-6040, email review@independent.org, www.independent.org/review
Institute for Contemporary Studies, 3100 Harrison Street, Oakland, CA 94611-5526
LAUNDRY PEN, 3132 Harrison St.,, Oakland, CA 94611, laundrypen@yahoo.com, www.geocities.com/laundrypen
LEFT CURVE, PO Box 472, Oakland, CA 94604, E-mail editor@leftcurve.org
Regent Press, 6020-A Adeline, Oakland, CA 94608, 510-547-7602
Ronin Publishing, Inc., Box 22900, Oakland, CA 94609, 510-420-3669, Fax 510-420-3672, ronin@roninpub.com, www.roninpub.com
Scarlet Tanager Books, PO Box 20906, Oakland, CA 94620, 510-763-3874
THE WISE WOMAN, 2441 Cordova Street, Oakland, CA 94602, 510-536-3174
Angel Power Press, PO Box 3327, Oceanside, CA 92051, 760-721-6666
THE SILT READER, PO Box 6184, Orange, CA 92863-6184
Temporary Vandalism Recordings, PO Box 6184, Orange, CA 92863-6184, tvrec@yahoo.com
Rattlesnake Press, P.O. Box 1647, Orangevale, CA 95662, 916-966-8620
RATTLESNAKE REVIEW, P.O. Box 1647, Orangevale, CA 95662, 916-966-8620
SNAKELETS, P.O. Box 1647, Orangevale, CA 95662, 916-966-8620, kathykieth@hotmail.com
VYPER, P.O. Box 1647, Orangevale, CA 95662, 916-966-8620
Ulysses Books, P O Box 937, Oregon House, CA 95962, 530-692-9393, 888-644-4425
The Poetry Center Press/Shoestring Press, 3 Monte Vista Road, Orinda, CA 94563, 925-254-6639
Spirit, Nature and You, PO Box 559, Oroville, CA 95965, www.spiritandnature.com
Park Place Publications, 591 Lighthouse Ave #20, Pacific Grove, CA 93950-0829, 831-649-6640, Fax 831-649-6649, publishingbiz@sbcglobal.net, www.parkplacepublications.com
OYSTER BOY REVIEW, PO Box 299, Pacifica, CA 94044, email@oysterboyreview.com, www.oysterboyreview.com
ETC Publications, 1456 Rodeo Road, Palm Springs, CA 92262, 760-325-5352, fax 760-325-8841
Event Horizon Press, PO Box 2006, Palm Springs, CA 92263, 760-329-3950
Lexicus Press, PO Box 1691, Palo Alto, CA 94301, 6507995602
The Live Oak Press, LLC, PO Box 60036, Palo Alto, CA 94306-0036, 650-853-0197, info@liveoakpress.com, www.liveoakpress.com
Dustbooks, PO Box 100, Paradise, CA 95967-0100, 530-877-6110, 1-800-477-6110, Fax 530-877-0222, email: publisher@dustbooks.com, Website: http://www.dustbooks.com
THE SMALL PRESS REVIEW/SMALL MAGAZINE REVIEW, PO Box 100, Paradise, CA 95967-9999, 530-877-6110, 800-477-6110, fax: 530-877-0222, email: publisher@dustbooks.com, Website: http://www.dustbooks.com
BAGAZINE, Po Box 2234, Pasadena, CA 91102
Hope Publishing House, PO Box 60008, Pasadena, CA 91116, 626-792-6123; fax 626-792-2121
INDEFINITE SPACE, PO Box 40101, Pasadena, CA 91114
X-RAY, Po Box 2234, Pasadena, CA 91102, johnny@xraybookco.com
X-Ray Book Co., P.O. Box 2234, Pasadena, CA 91102
North Star Books, PO Box 589, Pearblossom, CA 93553-0589, 661-944-1130, NorthStarBooks@avradionet.com
R.L. Crow Publications, P.O. Box 262, Penn Valley, CA 95946, Fax and Message: (530) 432-8195, info@rlcrow.com
THE BOOKWATCH, 12424 Mill Street, Petaluma, CA 94952, 415-437-5731
ON PARAGUAY, 1724 Burgundy Court, Petaluma, CA 94954, 707-763-6835; E-mail paraguay@wco.com
Pomegranate Communications, PO Box 808022, Petaluma, CA 94975-8022, info@pomegranate.com
TINY LIGHTS: A Journal of Personal Essay, PO Box 928, Petaluma, CA 94953, 707-762-3208, sbono@tiny-lights.com, www.tiny-lights.com
Jupiter Scientific Publishing, c/o Weng, 415 Moraga Avenue, Piedmont, CA 94611-3720, 510-420-1015, admin@jupiterscientific.org, www.jupiterscientific.org
Bluestocking Press, PO Box 1014, Dept. D, Placerville, CA 95667-1014, 530-622-8586, Fax 530-642-9222, 1-800-959-8586 (orders only), website: www.bluestockingpress.com
Blueprint Books, PO Box 10757, Pleasanton, CA 94588, 925-425-9513, Fax 1-800-605-2914, 1-800-605-2913, editor@blueprintbooks.com, blueprintbooks.com
CKO UPDATE, PO Box 10757, Pleasanton, CA 94588, 925-425-9513, Fax 1-800-605-2914, 1-800-605-2913, editor@blueprintbooks.com, blueprintbooks.com
LANGUAGEANDCULTURE.NET, 4000 Pimlico Drive, Ste. 114-192, Pleasanton, CA 94588, 925-462-0490 info@languageandculture.net
NEWWITCH, P.O. Box 641, Point Arena, CA 95468, Phone:888-724-3966, Fax:707-882-2793, website http://www.newwitch.com
SAGEWOMAN, PO Box 641, Point Arena, CA 95468
QUARTZ HILL JOURNAL OF THEOLOGY:A Journal of Bible and Contemporary Theological Thought, 43543 51st Street West, Quartz Hill, CA 93536, 661-722-0891, 661-943-3484, E-mail robin@theology.edu
Quartz Hill Publishing House, 43543 51st Street West, Quartz Hill, CA 93536, 661-722-0891, 661-943-3484, E-mail robin@theology.edu
DREAM FANTASY INTERNATIONAL, 411 14th Street #H1, Ramona, CA 92065-2769

Dramaline Publications, 36851 Palm View Road, Rancho Mirage, CA 92270-2417, 760-770-6076, FAX 760-770-4507, drama.line@verizon.net

Mills Custom Services Publishing, P.O. Box 866, Rancho Mirage, CA 92270, 760-250-1897, fax 760-406-6280, vamills@aol.com, www.aonestopmall.com, www.buybookscds.com

Noble Porter Press, 36-851 Palm View Road, Rancho Mirage, CA 92270, 760-770-6076, fax 760-770-4507

Mission Press, PO Box 9586, Rancho Santa Fe, CA 92067, e-mail MissionPress@compuserve.com

Over the Wall Inc. Publishing & Productions, 1035 Jackson Street, Red Bluff, CA 96080, 888-267-1418

DayDream Publishing, 808 Vincent ST, Redondo Beach, CA 90277, www.daydreampublishers.com

Brason-Sargar Publications, PO Box 872, Reseda, CA 91337, 818-994-0089, Fax 305-832-2604, sonbar@bigfoot.com

EPICENTER: A LITERARY MAGAZINE, PO Box 367, Riverside, CA 92502, www.epicentrermagazine.org

LATIN AMERICAN PERSPECTIVES, PO Box 5703, Riverside, CA 92517-5703, 951-827-1571, fax 951-827-5685, laps@mail.ucr.edu, www.latinamericanperspectives.com

Xenos Books, Box 52152, Riverside, CA 92517, 909-370-2229, E-mail info@xenosbooks.com, www.xenosbooks.com

THE COMPLEAT NURSE, 3615 Villa Serena Circle, Rocklin, CA 95765-5547, www.drybones.com

ZAUM - The Literary Review of Sonoma State University, English Department, SSU, 1801 E. Cotati Avenue, Rohnert Park, CA 94928, 707-664-2140

FINANCIAL FOCUS, 2140 Professional Drive Ste. 105, Roseville, CA 95661-3734, 916-791-1447, Fax 916-791-3444, jeverett@quiknet.com

ASIA FILE, PO Box 277193, Sacramento, CA 95827-7193, E-mail asiafile@earthlink.net, www.EroticTravel.com

Athanor Books (a division of ETX Seminars), P.O.Box 222201, Sacramento, CA 95820, 916-424-4355

Bronze Girl Productions, Inc., 1341 Helmsman Way, Sacramento, CA 95833-3419, fax 916-922-1989, bronzegirl.com,

Casperian Books LLC, PO Box 161026, Sacramento, CA 95816-1026

EKPHRASIS, PO Box 161236, Sacramento, CA 95816-1236, http://hometown.aol.com/ekphrasisl

Fingerprint Press, PO Box 278075, Sacramento, CA 95827, 877-807-4509, info@fingerprintpress.com, www.fingerprint-press.com

Frith Press, PO Box 161236, Sacramento, CA 95816-1236, http://hometown.aol.com/ekphrasisl

FUCK DECENCY, 5960 S. Land Park Drive #253, Sacramento, CA 95822, www.asstr.org/~roller/index.html, ftp://ftp.asstr.org/pub/authors/roller/

Jullundur Press, 1001 G St., Suite 301, Sacramento, CA 95814, 866-449-1600, fax 916-449-1320, web: www.TheLawyersClas-sof69.com

MGW (Mom Guess What) Newsmagazine, 1123 21st St., Suite 200, Sacramento, CA 95814-4225, 916-441-6397, fax:916-441-6422, info@mgwnews.com, www.mgwnews.com

MYSTERY ISLAND MAGAZINE, Mystery Island, 384 Windward Way, Sacramento, CA 95831-2420, blacksharkpress@mys-teryisland.net www.mysteryisland.net

Mystery Island Publications, 384 Windward Way, Sacramento, CA 95831-2420, blacksharkpress@mysteryisland.net www.mysteryisland.net

POETRY NOW, Sacramento's Literary Review and Calendar, 1719 25th St., Sacramento, CA 95816, 916-441-7395, poetrynow@sacramentopoetrycenter.org, www.sacramentopoetrycenter.org

Ravenwood Publishing, 4421 Ravenwood Ave., Sacramento, CA 95821-6726, 916-215-0765, Fax 916-972-9312, http://www.ravenwoodpub.com

Samuel Powell Publishing Company, 2201 I Street, Sacramento, CA 95816, 916-443-1161

TRAVEL BOOKS WORLDWIDE, PO Box 160691, Sacramento, CA 95816-0691, 916-452-5200

Travel Keys, PO Box 160691, Sacramento, CA 95816-0691, 916-452-5200

THE TULE REVIEW, Sacramento Poetry Center, 1719 25th St., Sacramento, CA 95816-5813, 916-441-7395, blueattule@yahoo.com, www.sacramentopoetrycenter.org

24th Street Irregular Press, 1008 24th Street, Sacramento, CA 95816

SPECIALTY TRAVEL INDEX, PO BOX 458, San Anselmo, CA 94979-0458, 415-455-1643, Fax 415-455-1648, shansen@specialtytravel.com, www.specialtytravel.com

THE PACIFIC REVIEW, Department of English, Calif State University, San Bernardino, CA 92407

Medusa Press, PO Box 458, San Carlos, CA 94070, info@medusapress.net, www.medusapress.nes

Wide World Publishing/TETRA, PO Box 476, San Carlos, CA 94070, 650-593-2839, Fax 650-595-0802

AAS HISTORY SERIES, PO Box 28130, San Diego, CA 92198, 760-746-4005, Fax 760-746-3139, sales@univelt.com, www.univelt.com

ADOLESCENCE, 3089C Clairemont Dr., Suite 383, San Diego, CA 92117, 619-571-1414

ADVANCES IN THE ASTRONAUTICAL SCIENCES, PO Box 28130, San Diego, CA 92198, 760-746-4005, Fax 760-746-3139, sales@univelt.com, www.univelt.com

Altair Publications, PO Box 221000, San Diego, CA 92192-1000, 858-453-2342, e-mail altair@astroconsulting.com

Always Productions, PO Box 33836, San Diego, CA 92163

Birdalone Books, 2212 32nd St., San Diego, CA 92104-5602, Fax 812-337-0118

Birth Day Publishing Company, PO Box 7722, San Diego, CA 92167

Blue Dove Press, 4204 Sorrento Valley Blvd, Ste. K, San Diego, CA 92121, 858-623-3330, orders 800-691-1008, FAX 858-623-3325, mail@bluedove.org, www.bluedove.org

Brenner Information Group, PO Box 721000, San Diego, CA 92172-1000, 858-538-0093

Caernarvon Press, 4435 Marlborough Ave. #3, San Diego, CA 92116, (619) 284-0411, terryh@cts.com

Cedar Hill Books, 3730 Arnold Avenue, San Diego, CA 92104, www.cedarhillbooks.org

CEDAR HILL REVIEW, 3730 Arnold Avenue, San Diego, CA 92104, www.cedarhillbooks.org

THE CHRISTIAN LIBRARIAN, Ryan Library, PLNU, 3900 Lomaland Drive, San Diego, CA 92106

THE CRAPSHOOTER, PO Box 421440, San Diego, CA 92142, larryedell@aol.com

Culturelink Press, PO. Box 3538, San Diego, CA 92163, Tel. (619) 501-9873, www.culturelinkpress.com; Fax purchase and school orders: Tel(619) 501-1369

Dawn Sign Press, 6130 Nancy Ridge Drive, San Diego, CA 92121-3223

E & D Publishing, Inc., PO Box 740536, San Diego, CA 92174, edpub@pacbell.net, www.eandpublishing.com

FAMILY THERAPY, 3089C Clairemont Dr., Suite 383, San Diego, CA 92117, 619-571-1414

GRASSLIMB, P.O. Box 420816, San Diego, CA 92142-0816, valerie@grasslimb.com, www.grasslimb.com

Hungry Tiger Press, 5995 Dandridge Lane, Suite 121, San Diego, CA 92115-6575

LadyePress USA, LLC, 230 West Laurel Street #705, San Diego, CA 92101-1467

Leaf Press, PO Box 421440, San Diego, CA 92142, leafpress@aol.com

Libra Publishers, Inc., 3089C Clairemont Dr., Suite 383, San Diego, CA 92117, 619-571-1414

Mho & Mho Works, Box 16719, San Diego, CA 92176, 619-280-3488
OmegaRoom Press, 4041 Louisiana St #1, San Diego, CA 92104, omegaroom@yahoo.com
Puna Press, P.O. Box 7790, San Diego, CA 92107, 619.278.8089, www.punapress.com
SCIENCE AND TECHNOLOGY, PO Box 28130, San Diego, CA 92198, 760-746-4005, Fax 760-746-3139, sales@univelt.com, www.univelt.com
The Sektor Co., PO Box 501005, San Diego, CA 92150, 858-485-6616, fax 858-485-6572
Small Helm Press, 4235 Porte de Palmas, Unit 182, San Diego, CA 92122-5123, 707-763-5757, smallhelm@comcast.net
Tecolote Publications, 4918 Del Monte Avenue, San Diego, CA 92107, telephone (619)222-6066, e-mail tecopubs@earthlink.net, website tecolotepublications.com
Univelt, Inc., PO Box 28130, San Diego, CA 92198-0130, voice:760-746-4005; Fax:760-746-3139; Email:sales@univelt.com, Web Site: http://www.univelt.com
THE WISHING WELL, PO Box 178440, San Diego, CA 92177-8440, 858-695-3139, laddiewww@aol.com, www.wishingwellwomen.com
Tia Chucha Press, PO Box 328, San Fernando, CA 91341, 818-898-0013
AK Press, PO Box 40682, San Francisco, CA 94140, 415-864-0892, FAX 415-864-0893, akpress@org.org
Alan Wofsy Fine Arts, PO Box 2210, San Francisco, CA 94126, 415-292-6500, www.art-books.com, alanwolfsyfinearts@art-books.com
Androgyne Books, 930 Shields, San Francisco, CA 94132, 415-586-2697
ART BUREAU, PO Box 225221, San Francisco, CA 94122, 415-759-1788, info@artbureau.org, www.artbureau.org
Aspermont Press, 1249 Hayes Street, San Francisco, CA 94117, 415-863-2847
Aunt Lute Books, PO Box 410687, San Francisco, CA 94141, 415-826-1300; FAX 415-826-8300
BALLOT ACCESS NEWS, PO Box 470296, San Francisco, CA 94147, 415-922-9779, fax 415-441-4268, e-Mail ban@igc.apc.org, www.ballot-access.org
BOOKS TO WATCH OUT FOR, PO Box 882554, San Francisco, CA 94188-2554, 415-642-9993, editor at BooksToWatchOutFor dot com, www.BooksToWatchOutFor.com
Caddo Gap Press, 3145 Geary Boulevard, Suite 275, San Francisco, CA 94118, 415-666-3012 telephone,415-666-3552 fax,caddogap@aol.com,www.caddogap.com
CALLBOARD, 870 Market Street #375, San Francisco, CA 94102, 415-430-1140; www.theatrebayarea.org
Card Publishing, 3450 Sacramento Street #405, San Francisco, CA 94118-1914, cardpublishing.com
Carrier Pigeon Press, PO Box 460141, San Francisco, CA 94146-0141, 415-821-2090
Carol Anne Carroll Communications, PO Box 410333, San Francisco, CA 94141-0333, 415-839-6310, WritingandBeyond@aol.com
Children's Book Press, 2211 Mission Street, San Francisco, CA 94110-1811, 415-995-2200, FAX 415-995-2222, cbookpress@cbookpress.org
City Lights Books, Attn: Bob Sharrard, Editor, 261 Columbus Avenue, San Francisco, CA 94133, 415-362-8193
CLAMOUR: A Dyke Zine, 144 Albion Street, San Francisco, CA 94110
CLARA VENUS, Attn: Marie Kazalia, PO BOX 422344, San Francisco, CA 94142, E-mail: RedHandPress@hotmail.com, http://ClaraVenus.BlogSpot.com, http://RedHandPress.BlogSpot.com
ClearPoint Press, PO Box 170658, San Francisco, CA 94117, 415-386-5377 phone/Fax
Cleis Press, PO Box 14684, San Francisco, CA 94114-0684, cleis@cleispress.com; www.cleispress.com
The Communication Press, PO Box 22541, San Francisco, CA 94122, 415-386-0178
CREEPY MIKE'S OMNIBUS OF FUN, PO Box 401026, San Francisco, CA 94140-1026, creepymike@hotmail.com
Down There Press, 938 Howard St., #101, San Francisco, CA 94103-4100, 415-974-8985 x 205, fax 415-974-8989, 800-289-8423, downtherepress@excite.com, www.goodvibes.com/dtp/dtp.html
EDUCATIONAL FOUNDATIONS, 3145 Geary Boulevard, Suite 275, San Francisco, CA 94118, 415-666-3012
EDUCATIONAL LEADERSHIP & ADMINISTRATION, 3145 Geary Boulevard #275, San Francisco, CA 94118, 415-392-1911
FOURTEEN HILLS: The SFSU Review, Creative Writing Dept., SFSU, 1600 Holloway Avenue, San Francisco, CA 94132, 415-338-3083, fax 415-338-0504, E-mail hills@sfsu.edu
Gay Sunshine Press, Inc., PO Box 410690, San Francisco, CA 94141, 415-626-1935; Fax 415-626-1802
GIRLFRIENDS MAGAZINE, PMB 30, 3101 Mission St., San Francisco, CA 94110-4515, 415-648-9464, fax 415-648-4705, e-mail staff@girlfriendsmag.com, website www.girlfriendsmag.com
GLB Publishers, 1028 Howard Street #503, San Francisco, CA 94103-2868, 415-621-8307, www.GLBpubs.com
Global Options, PO Box 40601, San Francisco, CA 94140, 415-550-1703
HAIGHT ASHBURY LITERARY JOURNAL, 558 Joost Avenue, San Francisco, CA 94127
Haight-Ashbury Publications, 856 Stanyan Street, San Francisco, CA 94117, 415-752-7601, Fax 415-933-8674
HARMONY: Voices for a Just Future, PO Box 210056, San Francisco, CA 94121-0056, 415-221-8527
Heritage House Publishers, PO Box 194242, San Francisco, CA 94119, 415-776-3156
INTERNATIONAL JOURNAL OF EDUCATIONAL POLICY, RESEARCH, AND PRACTICE, 3145 Geary Blvd. PMB 275, San Francisco, CA 94118, 415-666-3012, fax 415-666-3552, caddogap@aol.com, www.caddogap.com
ISSUES, PO Box 424885, San Francisco, CA 94142-4885, 415-864-4800 X136
ISSUES IN TEACHER EDUCATION, 3145 Geary Blvd. PMB 275, San Francisco, CA 94118, 415 666-3012
Ithuriel's Spear, 730 Eddy St., #304, San Francisco, CA 94109, (415) 440-3204 / http://www.ithuriel.com
JOURNAL FRANCAIS, 944 Market Street, Suite 210, San Francisco, CA 94102, 415-981-9088 ext. 705, Fax 415-981-9177, fprecourt@journalfrancais.com, www.journalfrancais.com
JOURNAL OF CURRICULUM THEORIZING, 3145 Geary Boulevard, PMB 275, San Francisco, CA 94118
JOURNAL OF PSYCHOACTIVE DRUGS, 612 Clayton Street, San Francisco, CA 94117, 415-565-1904, Fax 415-864-6162
JOURNAL OF THOUGHT, 3145 Geary Boulevard #275, San Francisco, CA 94118, 415-392-1911
King Publishing, 1801 Bush Street, Suite 300, San Francisco, CA 94109, Fax 415-563-1467
Leyland Publications, PO Box 410690, San Francisco, CA 94141, 415-626-1935
MacAdam/Cage Publishing Inc., 155 Sansome Street, Ste. 550, San Francisco, CA 94104-3615, 415-986-7502, Fax 415-986-7414, info@macadamcage.com
Meridien PressWorks, J. Powell, PO Box 640024, San Francisco, CA 94164, 415-928-8904
MOTHER EARTH JOURNAL: An International Quarterly, 934 Brannan St., San Francisco, CA 94103, 415-868-8865, 415-552-9261, info@internationalpoetrymuseum.org
MULTICULTURAL EDUCATION, 3145 Geary Boulevard, Ste. 275, San Francisco, CA 94118, 415-392-1911
National Poetry Association Publishers, 934 Brannan Street, 2nd Floor, San Francisco, CA 94103, 415-776-6602, Fax 415-552-9271, www.nationalpoetry.org

Night Horn Books, PO Box 424906, San Francisco, CA 94142-4906, 415-440-2442; nighthornb@aol.com

No Starch Press, 555 De Haro Street, Suite 250, San Francisco, CA 94107-2365, 415-863-9900

Norton Coker Press, PO Box 640543, San Francisco, CA 94164-0543, 415-922-0395

NOTES AND ABSTRACTS IN AMERICAN AND INTERNATIONAL EDUCATION, 3145 Geary Boulevard #275, San Francisco, CA 94118, 415-392-1911

Pancake Press, 163 Galewood Circle, San Francisco, CA 94131, 415-665 9215

Passing Through Publications, 1918 23rd Street, San Francisco, CA 94107

POETRY USA, 934 Brannan Street, 2nd floor, San Francisco, CA 94103, 415-552-9261, Fax 415-552-9271, www.nationalpoetry.org

PROSODIA, New College of California/Poetics, 766 Valencia Street, San Francisco, CA 94110, 415-437-3479, Fax 415-437-3702

Protean Press, 287-28th Avenue, San Francisco, CA 94121, fax 415-386-4980

SCHOLAR-PRACTITIONER QUARTERLY, 3145 Geary Blvd. PMB 275, San Francisco, CA 94118, 415 666-3012

Scottwall Associates, Publishers, 95 Scott Street, San Francisco, CA 94117, 415-861-1956

Sea Fog Press, 447 20th Avenue, San Francisco, CA 94121, 415-221-8527

Second Coming Press, PO Box 31249, San Francisco, CA 94131

Sierra Outdoor Products Co., PO Box 2497, San Francisco, CA 94126-2497, 415-258-0777 phone/Fax, www.sierraoutdoorproducts.com

Sixteen Rivers Press, PO Box 640663, San Francisco, CA 94164-0663, 415-273-1303, www.sixteenrivers.org

SOCIAL JUSTICE: A JOURNAL OF CRIME, CONFLICT, & WORLD ORDER, PO Box 40601, San Francisco, CA 94140, 415-550-1703, socialjust@aol.com, www.socialjusticejournal.org

SOCIAL POLICY, c/o Organize Training Center, 442 Vicksburg Street, San Francisco, CA 94114-3831, 650-557-9720, Fax 650-355-1299, sclplcy@aol.com

SUMMER ACADEME: A Journal of Higher Education, 3145 Geary Boulevard #275, San Francisco, CA 94118, 415-392-1911

Sunlight Publishers, PO Box 640545, San Francisco, CA 94109, 415-776-6249

Synergistic Press, 3965 Sacramento St., San Francisco, CA 94118, 415-EV7-8180, Fax 415-751-8505; website www.synergisticbooks.com; e-mail goodreading@synergisticbooks.com

TABOO: Journal of Education & Culture, 3145 Geary Boulevard #275, San Francisco, CA 94118, 415-392-1911

Taurean Horn Press, PO Box 641097, San Francisco, CA 94164

TEACHER EDUCATION QUARTERLY, 3145 Geary Boulevard #275, San Francisco, CA 94118, 415-392-1911

TWO LINES: A Journal of Translation, Center for the Art of Translation, 35 Stillman Street, Suite 201, San Francisco, CA 94107, 415-512-8812 (phone) /415-512-8824 (fax), web: www.catranslation.org.

Versus Press, PO Box 475307, San Francisco, CA 94147-5307

VITAE SCHOLASTICAE: The Journal of Educational Biography, 3145 Geary Boulevard #275, San Francisco, CA 94118, 415-392-1911

Wild West Publishing House, P.O. Box 642836, San Francisco, CA 94164-2836, Telephone and fax: 415/921-5629. e-mail: bhwolfe@msn.com

ZOETROPE: ALL-STORY, 916 Kearny Street, San Francisco, CA 94133-5107, 415-788-7500, www.all-story.com

ZYZZYVA, PO Box 590069, San Francisco, CA 94159-0069, Tel 415-752-4393 Fax 415-752-4391, editor@zyzzyva.org, www.zyzzyva.org

ABLE MUSE, 467 Saratoga Avenue #602, San Jose, CA 95129, www.ablemuse.com, editor@ablemuse.com

Anancybooks, PO Box 28677, San Jose, CA 95159-8677, 408-286-0726, Fax 408-947-0668, info@anancybooks.com, www.anancybooks.com

Asylum Arts, c/o Leaping Dog Press, PO Box 3316, San Jose, CA 95156-3316, Phone/fax: (877) 570-6873 E-mail: editor@leapingdogpress.com, Web: www.leapingdogpress.com, Chapbooks and ephemera: www.cafepress.com/ldp/

Backbeat Press, 123 E San Carlos # 306, San Jose, CA 95112, 408-464-6715, tazz@backbeatpress.com, www.backbeatpress.com

R.J. Bender Publishing, PO Box 23456, San Jose, CA 95153, 408-225-5777, Fax 408-225-4739, order@bender-publishing.com

Ibexa Press, P.O. Box 611732, San Jose, CA 95161, www.ibexa.com, info@ibexa.com

INDIA CURRENTS, Box 21285, San Jose, CA 95151, 408-274-6966, Fax 408-274-2733, e-Mail editor@indiacurrents.com

Leaping Dog Press / Asylum Arts Press, PO Box 3316, San Jose, CA 95156-3316, Phone/fax: (877) 570-6873 E-mail: editor@leapingdogpress.com, Web: www.leapingdogpress.com, Chapbooks and ephemera: www.cafepress.com/ldp/

Library Research Associates, PO Box 32234, San Jose, CA 95152-2234, Fax 408-926-2207

LITURGICAL CATECHESIS, 160 E. Virginia Street #290, San Jose, CA 95112-5876, 408-286-8505, Fax 408-287-8748

MINISTRY & LITURGY, 160 East Virginia Street, #290, San Jose, CA 95112-5876, 408-286-8505, Fax 408-287-8748, E-mail mleditor@rpinet.com, www.rpinet.com

Resource Publications, Inc., 160 East Virginia Street #290, San Jose, CA 95112-5876, 408-286-8505, Fax 408-287-8745, info@rpinet.com, www.rpinet.com, www.safe-learning.com

Urion Press, PO Box 10085, San Jose, CA 95157, 408-867-7695 phone/Fax

which press, P.O. Box 10159, San Jose, CA 95157, info@whichpress.com / www.whichpress.com / (866) 830-0924

Five Fingers Press, PO Box 4, San Leandro, CA 94577-0100

FIVE FINGERS REVIEW, PO Box 4, San Leandro, CA 94577-0100

EZ Nature Books, PO Box 4206, San Luis Obispo, CA 93403

ORNAMENT, PO Box 2349, San Marcos, CA 92079, 760-599-0222, Fax 760-599-0228

Golden West Books, PO Box 80250, San Marino, CA 91118-8250, 626-458-8148

Huntington Library Press, 1151 Oxford Road, San Marino, CA 91108, 626-405-2172, Fax 626-585-0794, e-mail booksales@huntington.org

Fast Foot Forward Press, 7 West 41st Ave, #302, San Mateo, CA 94403-5105, 650-483-7007, info@fastfootforwardpress.com, www.fastfootforwardpress.com

DUFUS, Lummox, PO Box 5301, San Pedro, CA 90733-5301, www.geocities.com/lumoxraindog/index.html

LUMMOX JOURNAL, PO Box 5301, San Pedro, CA 90733-5301, 562-331-4351, e-mail raindog@lummoxpress.com http://www.lummoxpress.com

Lummox Press, PO Box 5301, San Pedro, CA 90733-5301, 562-439-9858, email: lumoxraindog@earthlink.net, http://home.earthlink.net/~lumoxraindog/ http://www.geocities.com/lumoxraindog/dufus.html

Oma Books of the Pacific, PO Box 9095, San Pedro, CA 90734-9095, publisher@omabooks.com, www.omabooks.com

Mandala Publishing, 17 Paul Drive, Suite 104, San Rafael, CA 94903-2043, 415.526.1380; 800.688.2218; Fax: 415.532.3281; info@mandala.org; www.mandala.org

The Crazy Pet Press, 231 Market Place #283, San Ramon, CA 94583, 888-877-7737, Fax 925-242-0199,

mail@crazypetpress.com, www.crazypetpress.com
Origin Press, PO Box 151117, San Raphael, CA 94915
Quill Driver Books, 1254 Commerce Way, Sanger, CA 93657-8731, 559-876-2170, Fax 559-876-2180, 800-497-4909
Aegean Publishing Company, PO Box 6790, Santa Barbara, CA 93160, 805-964-6669
Bandanna Books, 1212 Punta Gorda Street #13, Santa Barbara, CA 93103-3568, 805-899-2145 phone/Fax
CAMERA OBSCURA: Feminism, Culture, and Media Studies, c/o Department of Film Studies, University of California, Santa Barbara, CA 93106-9430, 805-893-7069; fax 805-893-8630; e-Mail cameraobscura@filmstudies.ucsb.edu
FREEBIES MAGAZINE, PO Box 21957, Santa Barbara, CA 93121-1957, freebies@aol.com
Green River Press, PO Box 6454, Santa Barbara, CA 93160, 805-964-4475, Fax 805-967-6208, narob@cox.net
INTO THE TEETH WIND, College of Creative Studies, University of California, Santa Barbara, Santa Barbara, CA 93106, www.ccs.ucsb.edu/windsteeth
Joelle Publishing, PO Box 91229, Santa Barbara, CA 93190, 805-962-9887
Allen A. Knoll Publishers, 200 W. Victoria Street, 2nd Floor, Santa Barbara, CA 93101-3627, 805-564-3377, Fax 805-966-6657, bookinfo@knollpublishers.com
Para Publishing, PO Box 8206 - Q, Santa Barbara, CA 93118-8206, 805-968-7277, Fax 805-968-1379, info@parapublishing.com, www.parapublishing.com
PUBLISHING POYNTERS, PO Box 8206-Q, Santa Barbara, CA 93118-8206, 805-968-7277, Fax 805-968-1379, info@parapublishing.com, www.parapublishing.com
Pussywillow, 1212 Punta Gorda Street #13, Santa Barbara, CA 93103-3568, 805-899-2145 phone/Fax
SHORT FUSE, PO Box 90436, Santa Barbara, CA 93190
Summer Stream Press, PO Box 6056, Santa Barbara, CA 93160-6056, 805-962-6540
Amethyst & Emerald, 1556 Halford Avenue, Suite 124, Santa Clara, CA 95051-2661, 408-244-6864, Fax 408-249-7646
COLLEGE ENGLISH, Dept. of English, U Mass/Boston, Santa Clara University, Santa Clara, CA 95053
Aristata Publishing, 16429 Lost Canyon Rd., Santa Clarita, CA 91387, Ph (661) 600-5011, Fx (661) 299-9478, general@aristatapublishing.com, www.aristatapublishing.com
Alcatraz Editions, 3965 Bonny Doon Road, Santa Cruz, CA 95060
GAMBARA MAGAZINE, PO Box 3887, Santa Cruz, CA 95063-3887, editor@gambara.org
GREENHOUSE REVIEW, 3965 Bonny Doon Road, Santa Cruz, CA 95060
Greenhouse Review Press, 3965 Bonny Doon Road, Santa Cruz, CA 95060-9706, 831-426-4355
Moving Parts Press, 10699 Empire Grade, Santa Cruz, CA 95060-9474, 408-427-2271
Nolo Press Occidental, 501 Mission Street, Suite 2, Santa Cruz, CA 95060, 831-466-9922, 800-464-5502, Fax: 831-466-9927, E-mail: inbox@nolotech.com, Website: http://www.nolotech.com
Paperweight Press, 123 Locust Street, Santa Cruz, CA 95060-3907, 831-427-1177 or 1 800 538-0766
POESY MAGAZINE, P.O. Box 7823, Santa Cruz, CA 95061, www.poesy.org, info@poesy.org
Red Alder Books, Box 2992, Santa Cruz, CA 95063, 831-426-7082, eronat@aol.com
STONE SOUP, The Magazine By Young Writers and Artists, Box 83, Santa Cruz, CA 95063, 831-426-5557, Fax 831-426-1161, e-mail editor@stonesoup.com, www.stonesoup.com
Tombouctou Books, 1472 Creekview Lane, Santa Cruz, CA 95062, 831-476-4144
Archer Books, PO Box 1254, Santa Maria, CA 93456, 805-878-8279 phone, email: jtc@archer-books.com, web site: www.archer-books.com
Bonus Books, Inc., 1223 Wilshire Blvd., #597, Santa Monica, CA 90403-5400, www.bonusbooks.com
Clover Park Press, PO Box 5067, Santa Monica, CA 90409-5067, 310-452-7657, info@cloverparkpress.com, http://www.cloverparkpress.com
Global Sports Productions, Ltd., 1223 Broadway, Suite 102, Santa Monica, CA 90404, 310-454-9480, Fax 253-874-1027, globalnw@earthlink.net, www.sportsbooksempire.com
Key Publications, PO Box 1064, Santa Monica, CA 90406, 818-613-7348
Middleway Press, 606 Wilshire Boulevard, Attention: Mwende May, Marketing Associate, Santa Monica, CA 90401-1502, (310) 309-3208 ofc, (310) 260-8910 fax, middlewaypress@sgi-usa.org, www.middlewaypress.com
Santa Monica Press, PO Box 1076, Santa Monica, CA 90406-1076, 310-230-7759, Fax 310-230-7761
THE SANTA MONICA REVIEW, 1900 Pico Boulevard, Santa Monica, CA 90405, www.smc.edu/sm_review
Synapse-Centurion, 1211 Berkeley St., Suite 3, Santa Monica, CA 90404, 310-829-2752, www.synapse-centurion.com
UMBRELLA Online, PO Box 3640, Santa Monica, CA 90408, 310-399-1146, Fax 310-399-5070, umbrella@ix.netcom.com
Clamshell Press, 160 California Avenue, Santa Rosa, CA 95405
FORUM, PO Box 6144, Santa Rosa, CA 95406, 707-532-1323, fax 707-523-1350
THE FOURTH R, PO Box 6144, Santa Rosa, CA 95406, 707-523-1325, fax 707-523-1350
Golden Door Press, 6450 Stone Bridge Road, Santa Rosa, CA 95409, (707) 538-5018
IN OUR OWN WORDS, P. O. Box 4658, Santa Rosa, CA 95402, http://www.bbbooks.com
Maledicta Press, PO Box 14123, Santa Rosa, CA 95402-6123, Phone: (707) 795-8178 E-mail: aman@sonic.net Web site: http://www.sonic.net/maledicta/
MALEDICTA: The International Journal of Verbal Aggression, PO Box 14123, Santa Rosa, CA 95402-6123, Telephone: 707-795-8178 E-mail: aman@sonic.net Web site: http://www.sonic.net/maledicta/
NEONATAL NETWORK: The Journal of Neonatal Nursing, 2270 Northpoint Parkway, Santa Rosa, CA 95407-7398, www.neonatalnetwork.com
NICU Ink, 2270 Northpoint Parkway, Santa Rosa, CA 95407-7398, 888-642-8465, www.neonatalnetwork.com
Polebridge Press, PO Box 7268, Santa Rosa, CA 95407-0268, 707-523-1323, fax 707-523-1350
Tyr Publishing, PO Box 9189, Santa Rosa, CA 95405-1189, 623-298-7235, Fax 480-323-2177, info@tyrpublishing.com, www.tyrpublishing.com
Arctos Press, PO Box 401, Sausalito, CA 94966-0401, 415-331-2503, Fax 415-331-3092, runes@aol.com, http://members.aol.com/runes
E & E Publishing, 1001 Bridgeway, No. 227, Sausalito, CA 94965, Tel: 415-331-4025, Fax: 415-331-4023, www.EandEGroup.com/Publishing
In Between Books, PO Box 790, Sausalito, CA 94966, 415 383-8447
The Post-Apollo Press, 35 Marie Street, Sausalito, CA 94965, 415-332-1458, fax 415-332-8045
RUNES, A Review of Poetry, PO Box 401, Sausalito, CA 94966-0401, 415-331-2503, Fax 415-331-3092, runesrev@aol.com, http://members.aol.com/runes
Small Dogs Press, PO Box 4127, Seal Beach, CA 90740, 562-673-8488, email: susan@smalldogspress.com, www.smalldogspress.com
KMT, A Modern Journal of Ancient Egypt, PO Box 1475, Sebastopol, CA 95473, 707-823-6079 phone/Fax

WordWorkers Press, 502 Pleasant Hill Road, Sebastopol, CA 95472-4024, 707-824-4307, 800-357-6016, Fax 707-829-7159, info@independenteye.org
Brooke-Richards Press, 15030 Ventura Blvd., #19-415, Sherman Oaks, CA 91403, 818-205-1266, fax: 818-906-7867
Life Energy Media, 15030 Ventura Blvd, Suite 908, Sherman Oaks, CA 91403, 818-995-3263
Stone and Scott, Publishers, PO Box 56419, Sherman Oaks, CA 91413-1419, 818-904-9088 Fax 818-787-1431 www.StoneandScott.com
Crystal Press, 4212 E. Los Angeles Avenue # 42, Simi Valley, CA 93063-3308, 805-527-4369, Fax 805-527-3949, crystalpress@aol.com
NMD Books, 2828 Cochran Street, Ste. 285, Simi Valley, CA 93065
Hot Pepper Press, PO Box 39, Somerset, CA 95684
The Madson Group, Inc., 13775 A Mono Way, Suite 224, Sonora, CA 95370, 360-446-5348, fax 360-446-5234, email madsongroup@earthlink.net, www.petgroomer.com
Dakota Books, 2801 Daubenbiss #1, Soquel, CA 95073, 831-477-7174
NEW AMERICAN IMAGIST, PO Box 124, South Pasadena, CA 91031-0124
China Books & Periodicals, Inc., 360 Swift Ave., Suite #48, South San Francisco, CA 94080-6220, 800-818-2017 [tel], 650-872-7808 [fax], email: orders@chinabooks.com, website: www.chinabooks.com
Hoover Institution Press, Stanford University, Stanford, CA 94305-6010, 650-723-3373, e-mail baker@hoover.stanford.edu
Abigon Press, 12135 Valley Spring Lane, Studio City, CA 91604, ascap@pacbell.net
Empire Publishing Service, PO Box 1344, Studio City, CA 91614-0344
Gaslight Publications, PO Box 1344, Studio City, CA 91614-0344
Players Press, Inc., PO Box 1132, Studio City, CA 91614, 818-789-4980
RATTLE, 12411 Ventura Blvd., Studio City, CA 91604, 818-505-6777
Jireh Publishing Company, P.O. Box 1911, Suisun City, CA 94585-1911, (510) 276-3322, (FAX: 425-645-0423), www.jirehpublishing.com
Accendo Publishing, 355 N Wolfe Road # 237, Sunnyvale, CA 94085, 408-406-6697 phone, 408-733-1444 fax
Soundboard Books, 933 Exmoor Way, Sunnyvale, CA 94087, 408-738-1705, sboardbooks@sbcglobal.net
Lahontan Images, PO Box 1592, Susanville, CA 96130-1592, 530-257-6747
dreamslaughter, PO Box 571454, Tarzana, CA 91357, 8183216708, http://www.dreamslaughter.com
Beacon Light Publishing (BLP), PO Box 1612, Thousand Oaks, CA 91358, 805-583-2002, toll free 888-771-1197
The Center Press, PO Box 6936, Thousand Oaks, CA 91361, 818-889-7071, Fax 818-889-7072
CRIMINAL JUSTICE ABSTRACTS, 2455 Teller Road, Thousand Oaks, CA 91320
Waters Edge Press, 98 Main Street #527, Tiburon, CA 94920, 415-435-2837, Fax 415-435-2404, JAG@WatersEdgePress.com, www.WatersEdgePress.com
Wood River Publishing, 9 Stevens Court, Tiburon, CA 94920, 415-256-9300, Fax 415-256-9400, info@picturesnow.com
Six Strings Music Publishing, PO Box 7718-155, Torrance, CA 90504-9118, 800-784-0203, Fax 310-362-8864, www.sixstringsmusicpub.com
Acton Circle Publishing Company, PO Box 1564, Ukiah, CA 95482, 707-463-3921, 707-462-2103, Fax 707-462-4942; actoncircle@pacific.net
Kosmos Books, 991 St. Andrews Drive, Ste. 138, Upland, CA 91784, ellesawatzky@earthlink.net
Delta Press, 27460 Avenue Scott, Valencia, CA 91355, Fax 661-294-2208
REMS Publishing & Publicity, 25852 McBean Parkway #714, Valencia, CA 91355-2004, 800-915-0048, 661-287-3309, Fax 661-287-4443, remesbookdoctor@comcast.net, www.remspublishingpublicity.com, www.maureenstephenson.com, www.makemoneywritingsite.com
Apples & Oranges, Inc., PO Box 2296, Valley Center, CA 92082
4AM POETRY REVIEW, 13213 Oxnard #7, Van Nuys, CA 91401, fourampoetryreview@gmail.com http://fourampoetryre-view.i8.com
Gain Publications, PO Box 2204, Van Nuys, CA 91404, 818-981-1996
Acrobat Books, PO Box 870, Venice, CA 90294, 310-578-1055, Fax 310-823-8447
88: A Journal of Contemporary American Poetry, PO Box 2872, Venice, CA 90294, 310-712-1238, Fax 310-828-4860, t88ajournal@aol.com, guidelines at www.hollyridgepress.com
Hollyridge Press, PO Box 2872, Venice, CA 90294, 310-712-1238, Fax 310-828-4860, hollyridgepress@aol.com, http://www.hollyridgepress.com
Monroe Press, 362 Maryville Avenue, Ventura, CA 93003-1912
Lemon Shark Press, 1604 Marbella Drive, Vista, CA 92081-5463, 760-727-2850, lemonsharkpress@yahoo.com, www.lemonsharkpress.com
Volcano Press, Inc, PO Box 270, Volcano, CA 95689, 209-296-4991, fax 209-296-4995, Credit card or check orders only: 1-800-879-9636, e-mail sales@volcanopress.com, website http://www.volcanopress.com
Massey-Reyner Publishing, PO Box 323, Wallace, CA 95254, phone/fax 209-763-2590, e-mail learning@goldrush.com
Kiva Publishing, Inc., 21731 East Buckskin Drive, Walnut, CA 91789, 909-595-6833, fax 909-860-5424
AltaMira Press, 1630 N. Main Street #367, Walnut Creek, CA 94596, 925-938-7243, Fax 925-933-9720
Devil Mountain Books, PO Box 4115, Walnut Creek, CA 94596, 925-939-3415, Fax 925-937-4883, cbsturges@aol.com
Tres Picos Press, 116 Martinelli Street, Suite #1, Watsonville, CA 95076, 831 254-7447; email: submissions@trespicos-press.com
Film-Video Publications/Circus Source Publications, 7944 Capistrano Avenue, West Hills, CA 91304
THE GREAT AMERICAN POETRY SHOW, A SERIAL POETRY ANTHOLOGY, P.O. Box 69506, West Hollywood, CA 90069-0506, 1-323-969-4905
The Muse Media, PO Box 69506, West Hollywood, CA 90069, 323-969-4905, www.tgaps.com
Steel Balls Press, Box 807, Whittier, CA 90608, E-mail don@steelballs.com
Rayve Productions Inc., PO Box 726, Windsor, CA 95492, 707-838-6200, Fax 707-838-2220, E-mail rayvepro@aol.com
The Owl Press, PO Box 126, Woodacre, CA 94973-0126, 415-438-1539, asisowl@mindspring.com, www.theowlpress.com
The Heyeck Press, 25 Patrol Court, Woodside, CA 94062, 650-851-7491, Fax 650-851-5039, heyeck@ix.netcom.com
Infinite Corridor Publishing, 6633 Yount St., Youtville, CA 94599-1280, 415-292-5639; Fax 415-931-5639; E-mail corridor@slip.net

COLORADO

Thundercloud Books, PO Box 97, Aspen, CO 81612, (970) 925-1588, fax (970) 920-9361, web: www.Thundercloud-Books.com, www.WakingThe Ancients.com
Swing-Hi Press, 16213 East Mercer Circle, Aurora, CO 80013, 303-766-3153, fax:303-766-2989, toll free:1-866-828-8725,

barbara@naturalbodyshape.com, www.naturalbodyshape.com

CLARK STREET REVIEW, PO Box 1377, Berthoud, CO 80513, clarkreview@earthlink.net, http://home.earthlink.net/~clarkreview/

Howling Dog Press / Brave New World Order Books, P.O. Box 853, Berthoud, CO 80513-0853, WritingDangerously@msn.com, www.howlingdogpress.com, www.howlingdogpress.com/OMEGA

OMEGA, P.O. Box 853, Berthoud, CO 80513-0853, WritingDangerously@msn.com, www.howlingdogpress.com, www.howlingdogpress.com/OMEGA

Blue Poppy Press, 5441 Western Avenue #2, Boulder, CO 80301-2733, 800-487-9296

THE BOOMERPHILE, PO Box 17446, Boulder, CO 80308-0446, 303-444-3363, www.forums.delphiforums.com/boomer

BOULDER HERETIC, PO Box 17446, Boulder, CO 80308-0446, 303-444-3363, danculberson@juno.com

Cassandra Press, Inc., PO Box 228, Boulder, CO 80306, 303 444 2590

Devenish Press, P.O. Box 17007, Boulder, CO 80308-0007, 303-926-0378 phone/fax, books@devenishpress.com, www.devenishpress.com

DIVIDE Creative Responses to Contemporary Social Questions, Univ. of Colorado, Boulder / UCB 317, Boulder, CO 80309, www.colorado.edu/journals/divide

Gemstone House Publishing, PO Box 19948, Boulder, CO 80308, sthomas170@aol.com

LOVING MORE, PO Box 4358, Boulder, CO 80306, 303-543-7540, lmm@lovemore.com

Old Stage Publishing, PO Box 17446, Boulder, CO 80308-0446, 303-444-3363, danculberson@juno.com

Paladin Enterprises, Inc., Gunbarrel Tech Center, 7077 Winchester Circle, Boulder, CO 80301, 303-443-7250, Fax 303-442-8741, www.paladin-press.com

Pruett Publishing Company, PO Box 2140, Boulder, CO 80306-2140, 303-449-4919, toll free: 1-800-247-8224

Sentient Publications, LLC, 1113 Spruce Street, Boulder, CO 80302, 303-443-2188, Fax 303-381-2538, www.sentientpublications.com

SNIPER LOGIC, Campus Box 226, University of Colorado, Boulder, CO 80309

SQUARE ONE, Campus Box 226, University of Colorado, Boulder, CO 80309-0001, 303-492-8890, square1@colorado.edu, http://www.colorado.edu/English/squareone/index.htm

Sunrise Health Coach Publications, PO Box 21132, Boulder, CO 80308, Phone and fax: 303-527-2886, info@sunrisehealthcoach.com, http://sunrisehealthcoach.com

TOUCHSTONE, PO Box 17446, Boulder, CO 80308-0446, 303-444-3363, danculberson@juno.com

University Press of Colorado, 5589 Arapahoe Avenue, Suite 206C, Boulder, CO 80303, Orders: 800-627-7377, Editorial: 720-406-8849, Fax: 720-406-3443

VELONEWS, 1830 North 55th Street, Boulder, CO 80301

Clearwater Publishing Co., PO Box 778, Broomfield, CO 80038-0778, 303-436-1982, fax 917-386-2769, e-mail kenn@clearwaterpublishing.com OR wordguise@aol.com

Stony Meadow Publishing, 2262 Ridge Drive, Broomfield, CO 80020, 303-960-9072 / stan@stonymeadowpublishing.com / www.stonymeadowpublishing.com

Communication Creativity, 425 Cedar, PO Box 909, Buena Vista, CO 81211, 719-395-8659, Marilyn@CommunicationCreativity.com, www.communicationcreativity.com

Nicholas Lawrence Books, 932 Clover Avenue, Canon City, CO 81212, 719-276-0152, Fax 719-276-0154, icareinc@webtv.net

Power Potentials Publishing, PO Box 187, Cascade, CO 80809, sagejno@earthlink.net

Glenbridge Publishing Ltd., 19923 E. Long Avenue, Centennial, CO 80016-1969, 720-870-8381, fax: 720-870-5598, website: www.glenbridgepublishing.com, email: glenbridge@qwest.net

Rollaway Bay Publications, Inc., 6334 S. Racine Circle, Suite 100, Centennial, CO 80111-6404, Tel=303 799-8320, Fax=303 799-4220, email publisher@rollawaybay.com

Aaron Communications III, P.O. Box 63270, Colorado Springs, CO 80962-3270, 719-487-0342

Arjuna Library Press, 1025 Garner St., D, Space 18, Colorado Springs, CO 80905-1774, Email address pfuphoff@earthlink.net Website address http://home.earthlink.net/~pfuphoff/

THE ELEVENTH MUSE, PO Box 2413, Colorado Springs, CO 80901, poetrywest@yahoo.com, http://www.poetrywest.org/muse.htm

Gauntlet Press, 5307 Arroyo Street, Colorado Springs, CO 80922-3825, info@gauntletpress.com, www.gauntletpress.com

HANG GLIDING, U.S. Hang Gliding Assoc., Inc., PO Box 1330, Colorado Springs, CO 80901-1330, 719-632-8300, fax 719-632-6417

INTERLIT, Cook Communications Ministries International, 4050 Lee Vance View, Colorado Springs, CO 80918-7100, 719-536-0100, Fax 719-536-3266

JOURNAL OF REGIONAL CRITICISM, 1404 East Bijou Street, Colorado Springs, CO 80909-5520

LrnIT Publishing Div. ICFL, Inc., 1122 Samuel Pt., Colorado Springs, CO 80906-6310, 800-584-1080, Fax 925-476-0707, icfl@lrnit.org, www.lrnit.org

Mountain Automation Corporation, 6090 Whirlwind Dr, Colorado Springs, CO 80918-7560, 719-598-8256, Fax 719-598-8516, Order 800-345-6120, Order Fax 970-493-8781, Order Email mac@intrepidgroup.com, Order Web http://www.railwayshop.com/mountain.shtml, Order Address POB 2324 Ft Collins CO 80522-2324

Piccadilly Books, Ltd., PO Box 25203, Colorado Springs, CO 80936, 719-550-9887

Affinity Publishers Services, c/o Continuous, PO Box 416, Denver, CO 80201-0416, 303-575-5676, email: mail@contentprovidermedia.com

Arden Press, Inc., PO Box 418, Denver, CO 80201, 303-697-6766

THE BLOOMSBURY REVIEW, 1553 Platte Street, Suite 206, Denver, CO 80202-1167, 303-455-3123, Fax 303-455-7039

Center For Self-Sufficiency, PO Box 416, Denver, CO 80201-0416, 305-575-5676

City Life Books, LLC, P.O. Box 371136, Denver, CO 80237, 303-773-9353

THE CLIMBING ART, 6390 E. Floyd Dr., Denver, CO 80222-7638

DENVER QUARTERLY, University of Denver, Denver, CO 80208, 303-871-2892

ELIXIR, PO Box 27029, Denver, CO 80227, www.elixirpress.com

Elixir Press, PO Box 27029, Denver, CO 80227-0029, www.elixirpress.com

END OF LIFE CHOICES, PO Box 101810, Denver, CO 80250-1810, Fax 303-639-1224, davidgoldberg@endoflifechoices.org, www.endoflifechoices.org

Face to Face Press, 3419 Fillmore St., Denver, CO 80205-4257, slevart@face2facepress.com, www.face2facepress.com

HEARTLODGE: Honoring the House of the Poet, P.O. Box 370627, Denver, CO 80237, heartlodgepoets@gmail.com

Lamp Light Press, Publishing Division, PO Box 416, Denver, CO 80201-0416, 303-575-5676, Fax 303-575-1187

MANY MOUNTAINS MOVING, 1136 South University Blvd., Denver, CO 80210-1907, 303-545-9942, Fax 303-444-6510

Nunciata, Publishing Division, PO Box 416, Denver, CO 80201-0416, 303-575-5676, Fax 303-575-1187

Quiet Tymes, Inc., 1400 Downing Street, Denver, CO 80218, 303-839-8628, Fax 720-488-2682

Scentouri, Publishing Division, c/o Prosperity + Profits Unlimited, PO Box 416, Denver, CO 80201-0416, 303-575-5676, Fax 303-575-1187

shift 4 Publishing, PO Box 18916, Denver, CO 80218, editor@shift4publishing.com

SPEAK UP, PO Box 100506, Denver, CO 80250, 303-715-0837, Fax 303-715-0793, speakupres@aol.com, www.speakup-press.org

Speak Up Press, PO Box 100506, Denver, CO 80250, 303-715-0837, Fax 303-715-0793, speakupres@aol.com, www.speakuppress.org

Speck Press, PO Box 102004, Denver, CO 80250, 303-744-1478, 800-996-9783, FAX 800-996-9783, books@speckpress.com, www.speckpress.com

Telephone Books, 2358 South Bannnock St., Denver, CO 80223, (303) 698-7837, pomowen@ix.netcom.com

Alpine Guild, Inc., PO Box 4848, Dillon, CO 80435, Fax 970-262-9378, information@alpineguild.com

CUTTHROAT, A JOURNAL OF THE ARTS, P.O. Box 2414, Durango, CO 81302, 970-903-7914, www.cutthroatmag.com, cutthroatmag@gmail.com

Raven's Eye Press, Inc., PO Box 4351, Durango, CO 81302, 970-247-4233, Fax 970-259-3238, ravenseye@frontier.net, www.ravenseyepress.com

Kali Press, PO Box 5324, Eagle, CO 81631-5324, sales@kalipres.com

PLEIADES MAGAZINE-Philae-Epic Journal-Thoughts Journal, PO Box 140213, Edgewater, CO 80214-9998, fax: 303-237-1019

Advanced Learning Press, 317 Inverness Way South, Suite 150, Englewood, CO 80112, 303-504-9312, 303-504-9417, 800-844-6599

Center for Literary Publishing, Colorado Review / Dept of English, Colorado State University, Fort Collins, CO 80523, 970-491-5449, creview@colostate.edu, http://coloradoreview.colostate.edu

COLORADO REVIEW, Colorado Review / Dept of English, Colorado State University, Fort Collins, CO 80523, 970-491-5449, creview@colostate.edu, http://coloradoreview.colostate.edu

Cottonwood Press, Inc., 109-B Cameron Drive, Fort Collins, CO 80525, 970-204-0715

Paul Dilsaver, Publisher, 2802 Clydesdale Court, Fort Collins, CO 80526-1155

Propeller Press, PO Box 729, Fort Collins, CO 80522, 970-482-8807, Fax 970-493-1240, john@propellerpress.com, www.propellerpress.com

Tantalus Books, 4529 Idledale Drive, Fort Collins, CO 80526-5152, www.tantalusbooks.com

Fulcrum, Inc., 16100 Table Mountain Pkwy #300, Golden, CO 80403-1672, 303-277-1623

The Love and Logic Press, Inc., 2207 Jackson Street, Golden, CO 80401, 303-278-7552

Pendant Publishing Inc., PO Box 2933, Grand Junction, CO 81502, 970-243-6465

PINYON, Dept. of Languages, Lit., & Comm., Mesa State College, 1100 North Ave., Grand Junction, CO 81502-2647, 970-248-1740

C & G Publishing, Inc., 2706 West 18th St. Rd, Greeley, CO 80634-5772, 970-356-9622, ccgcook@aol.com

Cladach Publishing, P.O. Box 336144, Greeley, CO 80633, 970-371-9530 phone, 970-351-8240 fax, info@cladach.com, www.cladach.com

Rebekah Publishing, PO Box 713, Gunnison, CO 81230, 877-790-4588, Rebekahbooks@adelphia.net, www.rebekahbooks.com

GLASS ART, PO Box 260377, Highlands Ranch, CO 80163-0377, 303-791-8998

Mapletree Publishing Company, 6233 Harvard Lane, Highlands Ranch, CO 80130-3773, 800-537-0414, mail@mapletreepublishing.com, www.mapletreepublishing.com

Anchor Cove Publishing, Inc., PO Box 270588, Littleton, CO 80128, Tel 303-972-0099, Fax 303-265-9119

SCULPTURAL PURSUIT MAGAZINE, P.O. Box 749, Littleton, CO 80160, 303-738-9892, www.sculpturalpursuit.com, speditor@sculpturalpursuit.com

THE AMERICAN DRIVEL REVIEW, 1425 Stuart Street #1, Longmont, CO 80501, 720-494-8719 info@americandrivelreview.com www.americandrivelreview.com

Shining Mountain Publishing, 2268 Spinnaker Circle, Longmont, CO 80503, Telephone 303-651-6230, email info@shiningmountain.net, website www.shiningmountain.net

SunShine Press Publications, Inc., 6 Gardner Court, Longmont, CO 80501, 303-772-3556, jlhof1@yahoo.com, www.sunshinepress.com

Zoilita Grant MS CCHt., Attn: Zoilita Grant, 200 Lincoln Street, Longmont, CO 80501, 303-776-6103, Fax 303-682-2384, info@selfhealing.com, www.selfhealing.com

Alpine Publications, Inc., 225 S. Madison Avenue, Loveland, CO 80537, 970-667-9317, Fax 970-667-9157, alpinepubl@aol.com, www.alpinepub.com

Wind River Institute Press/Wind River Broadcasting, 117 East 11th, Loveland, CO 80537, 970-669-3442, Fax 970-663-6081, 800-669-3993

SOUTHWEST COLORADO ARTS PERSPECTIVE, P.O. Box 843, Mancos, CO 81328-0843, 970-739-3200, 970-533-0642, www.artsperspective.com

JUNIOR STORYTELLER, PO Box 205, Masonville, CO 80541, 970-669-3755 phone/Fax, vivdub@aol.com, www.storycraft.com

THE KIDS' STORYTELLING CLUB WEBSITE, PO Box 205, Masonville, CO 80541, 970-669-3755 phone/Fax, vivdub@aol.com, www.storycraft.com

Storycraft Publishing, PO Box 205, Masonville, CO 80541, 970-669-3755 phone/Fax, Vivian@storycraft.com, www.storycraft.com

The Wessex Collective, P.O. Box 1088, Nederland, CO 80466, 303-258-3004

Earth Star Publications, PO Box 117, Paonia, CO 81428, 970-527-3257, earthstar@tripod.net, http://earthstar.tripod.com/

HIGH COUNTRY NEWS, PO Box 1090, Paonia, CO 81428, 970-527-4898, editor@hcn.org

THE STAR BEACON, PO Box 117, Paonia, CO 81428, 970-527-3257, fax (866) 882-1346, earthstar@tripod.net, http://earthstar.tripod.com/

National Writers Press, 17011 Lincoln Ave., #421, Parker, CO 80134, 720-851-1944, Fax 303-841-2607, www.nationalwriters.com

Outskirts Press, Inc., 10940 S. Parker Road - 515, Parker, CO 80134, 1-888-OP-BOOKS, info@outskirtspress.com, www.outskirtspress.com

Passeggiata Press, Inc., 420 West 14th Street, Pueblo, CO 81003-2708, 719-544-1038, Fax 719-546-7889, e-mail Passeggia@aol.com

Wayfinder Press, PO Box 217, Ridgway, CO 81432, 970-626-5452

Bardsong Press, PO Box 775396, Steamboat Springs, CO 80477, 970-870-1401, Fax 970-879-2657, bard@bardsongpress.com,

www.bardsongpress.com
Sylvan Books, PO Box 772876, Steamboat Springs, CO 80477-2876, 970-870-6071
WAR, LITERATURE & THE ARTS: An International Journal of the Humanities, 2354 Fairchild Drive, Suite 6D149, Department of English & Fine Arts, United States Air Force Academy, CO 80840, 719-333-8465, website: WLAjournal.com
Earth-Love Publishing House LTD, 3440 Youngfield Street #353, Wheatridge, CO 80033, 303-233-9660
Journal of Pyrotechnics, 1775 Blair Rd, Whitewater, CO 81527, 970-245-0692
JOURNAL OF PYROTECHNICS, 1775 Blair Rd, Whitewater, CO 81527, 970-245-0692

CONNECTICUT

Institute of Healing Arts & Sciences, 2 Wintonbury Mall, Bloomfield, CT 06002-2466, healing@anguillanet.com
Kumarian Press, Inc., 1294 Blue Hills Avenue, Bloomfield, CT 06002, 860-243-2098, FAX 860-243-2867, ordering 1-800-289-2667, kpbooks@kpbooks.com, www.kpbooks.com
The Intrepid Traveler, PO Box 531, Branford, CT 06405, 203-488-5341, Fax 203-488-7677, admin@intrepidtraveler.com
DRAMA GARDEN, PO Box 1158, Bridgeport, CT 06601-1158, 203-455-7285
New Creature Press, PO Box 1158, Bridgeport, CT 06601-1158, 203-455-7285
Sanguinaria Publishing, 85 Ferris Street, Bridgeport, CT 06605, 203-576-9168
World Music Press, PO Box 2565, Danbury, CT 06813-2565, 203-748-1131; fax 203-748-3432; e-mail info@worldmusic-press.com; website www.worldmusicpress.com
FRESHWATER, 170 Elm Street, Enfield, CT 06082-3873, 860-253-3105, freshwater@acc.commnet.edu, www.acc.comm-net.edu/freshwater.htm
THE INCLUSION NOTEBOOK, PO Box 8, Gilman, CT 06336, 860-873-3545; Fax 860-873-1311
Pennycorner Press, PO Box 8, Gilman, CT 06336, 860-873-3545, Fax 860-873-1311
Chicory Blue Press, Inc., 795 East Street North, Goshen, CT 06756, 860-491-2271, Fax 860-491-8619
Higganum Hill Books, PO Box 666, Higganum, CT 06441, rcdebold@connix.com
Hastings Art Reference, PO Box 833, Madison, CT 06443, 203-245-2246, Fax 203-245-5116, pfalk@cshore.com, www.falkart.com
Wesleyan University Press, 215 Long Lane, Middletown, CT 06459, 860-685-7711
Benchmark Publications Inc., PO Box 1594, New Canaan, CT 06840-1594, 203-966-6653, Fax 203-972-7129, www.benchpress.com
New Canaan Publishing Company Inc., PO Box 752, New Canaan, CT 06840, 203-966-3408 phone,203-548-9072 fax
CONNECTICUT REVIEW, SCSU, 501 Crescent Street, New Haven, CT 06515, 203-392-6737, Fax 203-392-5748
Cooper Hill Press, 1440 Whalley Avenue #232, New Haven, CT 06515, 203-387-7236 phone/Fax, editor@cooperhill.com, www.cooperhill.com
THEATER, 222 York Street, New Haven, CT 06520, 203-432-1568, Fax 203-432-8336, e-mail theater.magazine@yale.edu
THE YALE REVIEW, Yale University, PO Box 208243, New Haven, CT 06520-8243
YALE REVIEW OF BOOKS, PO Box 206560, New Haven, CT 06520, joanna.neborsky@yale.edu, cesar.garza@yale.edu
Yale University Press, PO Box 209040, New Haven, CT 06520, 203-432-0960, 203-432-0948 [fax], www.yalebooks.com
Ye Olde Font Shoppe, PO Box 8328, New Haven, CT 06530, e-mail yeolde@webcom.com; website www.webcom.com/yeolde
THE CONNECTICUT POET, PO Box 596, Newtown, CT 06470-0596, 203-426-3388, Fax 203-426-3398, hanover-press@faithvicinanza.com, www.poetz.com/connecticut
Hanover Press, PO Box 596, Newtown, CT 06470-0596, 203-426-3388, Fax 203-426-3398, hanoverpress@faithvicinanza.com
THE UNDERWOOD REVIEW, PO Box 596, Newtown, CT 06470-0596, 203-426-3388, Fax 203-426-3398, hanoverpress@faithvicinanza.com
Verbatim Books, 4 Laurel Drive, Old Lyme, CT 06371-1462, 860-434-2104, www.verbatimbooks.com
Biographical Publishing Company, 35 Clark Hill Road, Prospect, CT 06712-1011, 203-758-3661, Fax 253-793-2618, biopub@aol.com
Spring Publications Inc., 28 Front Street #3, Putnam, CT 06260-1927, Fax 203-974-3195, www.springpublications.com
Spiritual Understanding Network, LLC, P.O.Box 48, Salisbury, CT 06068-0048, www.matterofspirit.com
Plus Publications, 208 Bass Road, PO Box 265, Scotland, CT 06264, 860-456-0646, 800-793-0666, fax 860-456-2803, e-mail haelix@neca.com, http://plusyoga.necaweb.com
The Benefactory, Inc., 2 Klarides Village Drive, Seymour, CT 06483-2737
FRIENDS OF PEACE PILGRIM, PO Box 2207, Shelton, CT 06484
Newmark Publishing Company, PO Box 603, South Windsor, CT 06074
THE SMALL PRESS BOOK REVIEW, PO Box 176, Southport, CT 06890, 203-332-7629
Hannacroix Creek Books, Inc, 1127 High Ridge Road, #110, Stamford, CT 06905-1203, 203-321-8674, Fax 203-968-0193, hannacroix@aol.com
The Kenneth G. Mills Foundation, 65 High Ridge Road, Suite 103, Stamford, CT 06905, 800-437-1454, fax: 905-951-9712, email: info@kgmfoundation.org, www:kgmfoundation.org
THE CONNECTICUT POETRY REVIEW, PO Box 818, Stonington, CT 06378
The Pamphleeter's Press, PO Box 3374, Stony Creek, CT 06405, 203-483-8820, Fax 203-483-1429, E-mail pamphpress@aol.com
Grayson Books, PO Box 270549, W. Hartford, CT 06127, 860-523-1196 phone/Fax, GraysonBooks@aol.com, www.GraysonBooks.com
CONNECTICUT RIVER REVIEW: A National Poetry Journal, PO Box 4053, Waterbury, CT 06704, http://pages.prodigy.net/mmwalker/cpsindex.html
Fine Tooth Press, PO Box 11512, Waterbury, CT 06703, kolchak@snet.net, http://www.finetoothpress.com
The Bold Strummer Ltd., 110-C Imperial Avenue, PO Box 2037, Westport, CT 06880-2037, 203-227-8588, toll free 866-518-9991 (orders only),Fax 203-227-8775, theboldstrummer@msn.com, www.boldstrummerltd.com
Turtle Press, division of S.K. Productions Inc., PO Box 290206, Wethersfield, CT 06129-0206, 860-721-1198
SPRING: A Journal of Archetype and Culture, P.O. Box 207, Woodstock, CT 06281-0207

DELAWARE

BOTTLE, 50 Loch Lomond St., Bear, DE 19701-4714, bill@bospress.net, www.bospress.net
Bottle of Smoke Press, 902 Wilson Drive, Dover, DE 19904-2437, bill@bospress.net, www.bospress.net
Birdsong Books, 1322 Bayview Road, Middletown, DE 19709, 302-378-7274, Fax 302-378-0339, birdsongbooks@del-aware.net
Oak Knoll Press, 310 Delaware Street, New Castle, DE 19720-5038, 800-996-2556, 302-328-7232, fax 302-328-7274, oakknoll@oakknoll.com, www.oakknoll.com

BLADES, Poporo Press, 335 Paper Mill Road, Newark, DE 19711-2254

DISTRICT OF COLUMBIA

AERIAL, PO Box 25642, Washington, DC 20007, 202-362-6418, aerialedge@aol.com

AMERICAN FORESTS, PO Box 2000, Washington, DC 20013, 202-737-1944

Americans for the Arts, 1000 Vermont Ave. NW, Washington, DC 20005, To order publications, call 1.800.321.4510. For information on Americans for the Arts and membership, call 202.371.2830.

ANQ: A Quarterly Journal of Short Articles, Notes, and Reviews, 1319 18th Street NW, Washington, DC 20036, 202-296-6267 x275, Fax 202-293-6130, www.heldref.org

Argonne House Press, 1620 Argonne Place NW, Washington, DC 20009-5901, 202-328-9769, www.wordwrights.com, publisher@wordwrights.com

ARTSLINK, 1000 Vermont Avenue NW, 6th Floor, Washington, DC 20005, 202-371-2830

Avocus Publishing, Inc., 1223 Potomac Street NW, Washington, DC 20007, 202-333-8190

The Compass Press, Box 9546, Washington, DC 20016, 202-333-2182, orders 212-564-3730

CONSCIENCE: The Newsjournal of Catholic Opinion, Catholics for a Free Choice, 1436 U Street NW #301, Washington, DC 20009-3997, 202-986-6093, Fax 202-332-7995, conscience@catholicsforchoice.org, www.conscience-magazine.org

E. S. Publishers & Distributors, P.O. Box 75074, Washington, DC 20013, 202 302-7211

FOLIO: A Literary Journal of American University, Dept. of Literature, American University, Washington, DC 20016, NO PHONE CALLS PLEASE, folio_editors@yahoo.com, www.foliojournal.org

Gallaudet University Press, 800 Florida Avenue NE, Washington, DC 20002-3695, 202-651-5488

HAND PAPERMAKING, PO Box 77027, Washington, DC 20013-7027, 800-821-6604, Fax 301-220-2394, info@handpaper-making.org

THE HUMANIST, 1777 T st. NW, Washington, DC 20009-7125, 800-837-3792, 202-238-9003 fax, www.americanhuman-ist.org, aha@americanhumanist.org

Island Press, 1718 Connecticut Avenue NW #300, Washington, DC 20009, 202-232-7933; FAX 202-234-1328; e-mail info@islandpress.org; Website www.islandpress.org

KEREM: Creative Explorations in Judaism, 3035 Porter Street, NW, Washington, DC 20008, 202-364-3006, langner@erols.com, www.kerem.org

Maisonneuve Press, P.O. Box 2980, Washington, DC 20013-2980, 301-277-7505, Fax 301-277-2467

OFF OUR BACKS, 2337B 18th Street NW, 2nd Floor, Washington, DC 20009-2003, 202-234-8072

PRIMARY WRITING, 2009 Belmont Road NW #203, Washington, DC 20009

RedBone Press, PO Box 15571, Washington, DC 20003-0571, 202-667-0392, Fax 301-559-5239

RFF Press / Resources for the Future, 1616 P Street NW, Washington, DC 20036-1400, 202-328-5086, 202-328-5002, 1-800-537-5487, rffpress@rff.org, www.rffpress.org

Santa Fe Writers Project, PMB 170, 3509 Connecticut Avenue NW, Washington, DC 20008-2470, info@sfwp.com, www.sfwp.org

SB&F (SCIENCE BOOKS & FILMS), 1200 New York Avenue NW, Washington, DC 20005, 202-326-6646

Selous Foundation Press, 325 Pennsylvania Avenue, SE, Washington, DC 20001

SYMPOSIUM, Heldref Publications, 1319 18th St NW, Washington, DC 20036-1802, 202-296-6267 X275, Fax 202-293-6130, www.heldref.org

THE WASHINGTON MONTHLY, 733 15th Street NW, Suite 1000, Washington, DC 20005-6014, 202-393-5155

Washington Writers' Publishing House, PO Box 15271, Washington, DC 20003, 301-652-5636, website: www.wwph.org, Megan@bcps.org (Egan), gwiazda@umbc.edu (Gwiazda), elisavietta@xchesapeake.net (Ritchie)

WATERFRONT WORLD SPOTLIGHT, 1622 Wisconsin Ave. N.W., Washington, DC 20007, 202-337-0356

Whalesback Books, Box 9546, Washington, DC 20016, 202-333-2182

Wineberry Press, 3207 Macomb Street, NW, Washington, DC 20008-3327, 410-586-3086, 202-363-8036, elisavietta@chesa-peake.net

The Word Works, PO Box 42164, Washington, DC 20015, fax: 301-581-9443, editor@wordworksdc.com, www.wordworksdc.com

WORDWRIGHTS MAGAZINE, 1620 Argonne Place NW, Washington, DC 20009-5901, 202-328-9769, www.wordwrights.com, publisher@wordwrights.com

FLORIDA

Infinite Possibilities Publishing Group, Inc., PO Box 150823, Altamonte Springs, FL 32715-0823, (407) 699-6603 office (407) 331-3926 fax

HARP-STRINGS, PO Box 640387, Beverly Hills, FL 34464

Garrett Publishing, Inc., 2500 N. Military Trail, Suite 260, Boca Raton, FL 33431-6320, 561-953-1322, Fax 561-953-1940

New Paradigm Books, 22491 Vistawood Way, Boca Raton, FL 33428, 561-482-5971, 800-808-5179, Fax 561-852-8322, darbyc@earthlink.net, www.newpara.com

J. Mark Press, PO Box 24-3474, Boynton Beach, FL 33424, www.worldtv3.com/jmark.htm

VACATION PLACE RENTALS, PO Box 24-3474, Boynton Beach, FL 33424, www.VacationPlaceRentals.com

Byte Masters International, PO Box 3805, Clearwater, FL 33767, 727-593-3717, FAX 727-593-3605, Email BernieByte@aol.com

Peartree Books & Music, PO Box 14533, Clearwater, FL 33766-4533, P/ F 727-531-4973

$olvency International Inc., Publishing, PO Box 17802, Clearwater, FL 33762, 727-536-2779, Fax 727-507-8320, solv1@juno.com, www.solvencyinternational.com

Russet Press, 3442 Capland Ave., Clermont, FL 34711-5738

Anti-Aging Press, Box 142174, Coral Gables, FL 33114, 305-662-3928, 305-661-2802, Fax 305-661-4123, julia2@gate.net

MANGROVE MAGAZINE, Dept. of English, Univ. of Miami, PO Box 248145, Coral Gables, FL 33124, 305-284-2182

SO YOUNG!, PO Box 142174, Coral Gables, FL 33114, 305-662-3928, Fax 305-661-4123

AuthorsOmniscient Publishers, 11325 SW 1st Street, Coral Springs, FL 33071, (954)340-8845, authors@authors-sell-book.com, http://www.authors-sell-book.com

Liberty Publishing Company, Inc., PO Box 4248, Deerfield Beach, FL 33442-4248, 561-395-3750

The Lighthouse Press, PO Box 910, Deerfield Beach, FL 33443-0910, thelighthousepress@attbi.net, www.lighthouseedi-tion.com, fax:954-360-9994

Missing Man Press, 1313 S. Military Trail, #193, Deerfield Beach, FL 33442, 954 263-5416, mmp@missingmanpress.com, http://missingmanpress.com

SKYDIVING, 1725 North Lexington Avenue, DeLand, FL 32724, 904-736-9779, fax 904-736-9786

BEACHCOMBER MAGAZINE, PO Box 2255, Delray Beach, FL 33445, 561-734-5428, Fax 561-276-0931, Autelitano@aol.com, www.AuteliMedia.com

Kotzig Publishing, Inc., 109 NW 16th St., Delray Beach, FL 33444-3029, 800-589-7989, Fax 561-819-0207, susan@kotzigpublishing.com, www.kotzigpublishing.com

Denlinger's Publishers Ltd., PO Box 1030, Edgewater, FL 32132-1030, 386-416-0009, 386-236-0517 (fax), editor@thebook-den.com, acquisitions@thebookden.com, www.thebookden.com

NUTHOUSE, c/o Twin Rivers Press, PO Box 119, Ellenton, FL 34222

Ocean Publishing, P.O. Box 1080, Flagler Beach, FL 32136-1080, 386-517-1600, Fax 386-517-2564, oceanpub-lisher@cfl.rr.com, www.ocean-publisher.com

Consumer Press, 13326 SW 28th Street, Ste. 102, Fort Lauderdale, FL 33330-1102, 954-370-9153, info@consumerpress.com

GULF & MAIN Southwest Florida Lifestyle, 2235 First St., Suite 217, Fort Myers, FL 33901, 239-791-7900, 239 791-7974, www.gulfandmain.net

Pirate Publishing International, 6323 St. Andrews Circle South, Fort Myers, FL 33919-1719, 239-939-4845 phone/Fax, superK@juno.com

Rose Shell Press, Rochelle L. Holt, 15223 Coral Isle Court, Fort Myers, FL 33919-8434, www.angelfire.com/blues2/rlynnholt, RochelleL317@copper.net

Children Of Mary, PO Box 350333, Ft. Lauderdale, FL 33335-0333, 954-583-5108 phone/fax, mascmen8@bellsouth.net, www.catholicbook.com

FIDELIS ET VERUS, PO Box 350333, Ft. Lauderdale, FL 33335-0333

InterMedia Publishing, Inc., 2120 Southwest 33 Avenue, Ft. Lauderdale, FL 33312-3750, intermediapub@juno.com

COUNTERPOISE: For Social Responsibilities, Liberty and Dissent, 1716 SW Williston Road, Gainesville, FL 32608-4049, 352-335-2200

Florida Academic Press, PO Box 540, Gainesville, FL 32602-0540, 352-332-5104, Fax 352-331-6003, FAPress@gmail.com, web: www.FloridaAcademicPress.com

INDY MAGAZINE, 503 NW 37th Avenue, Gainesville, FL 32609-2204, 352-373-6336, jmason@gator.net, www.indy-world.com

LIBRARIANS AT LIBERTY, 1716 SW Williston Road, Gainesville, FL 32608, 352-335-2200

Maupin House Publishing, Inc., PO Box 90148, Gainesville, FL 32607, 1-800-524-0634, Fax 352-373-5546

Rhiannon Press, P.O. Box 140310, Gainesville, FL 32614, skoeppel@fccj.edu ; contact@writecorner.com

Writecorner.com Press, P.O. Box 140310, Gainesville, FL 32614-0310, www.writecorner.com

Aglob Publishing, PO Box 4036, Hallandale, FL 33008, 954-456-1476, Fax 954-456-3903, aglobpubl1@aol.com

Athena Press, 5956 W 16th Ave, Hialeah, FL 33012-6814

Good Life Products, PO Box 170070, Hialeah, FL 33017-0070, 305-362-6998, Fax 305-557-6123

Rainbow Books, Inc., PO Box 430, Highland City, FL 33846-0430, 863-648-4420, 863-647-5951, rbibooks@aol.com, www.rainbowbooksinc.com

The Word Doctor Online Publishing, 3448 S. Winding Path, Inverness, FL 34450-7518, 352-726-2829, doclabin@theworddoc-toronline.com, http://theworddoctoronline.com

Dumouriez Publishing, PO Box 12849, Jacksonville, FL 32209, 904.536.8910, http://www.dpublishing1.com ,admin@dpub-lishing1.com, tocca@dpublishing1.com

Famaco Publishers (Qalam Books), PO Box 440665, Jacksonville, FL 32244-0665, 904-434-5901, Fax 904-777-5901, famapub@aol.com

FOTOTEQUE, PO Box 55-0898, Jacksonville, FL 32255-0898, 904-705-6806, htpp://www.fototeque.com (must inquire prior to adding portfolios)

KALLIOPE, A Journal of Women's Literature and Art, FCCJ - South Campus, 11901 Beach Blvd., Jacksonville, FL 32246, 904-646-2081, www.fccj.org/kalliope

The Leaping Frog Press, PO Box 55-0898, Jacksonville, FL 32255-0898, Write to us (we all still write letters right?) PO Box 55-0898 Jacksonville, FL 32255-0898. http://www.short-fiction.com, www.timsonedwards.com, publisher@bellsouth.net if you need to send email, do not send attachments, we will request the attachment.

MUDLARK, English Department, University of North Florida, Jacksonville, FL 32224-2645, mudlark@unf.edu, www.unf.edu/mudlark

Rock Spring Press Inc., 6015 Morrow Street East Suite 106, Jacksonville, FL 32217, editor@rockspringpress.com

Timson Edwards, Co., PO Box 55-0898-DB, Jacksonville, FL 32255-0898, 904-705-6806, gonz2171@bellsouth.net, www.short-fiction.com

UmbraProjects, Ltd., 3616 Jamestown Lane, Jacksonville, FL 32223-7497, up_admin@juno.com

THE WILDWOOD READER, PO Box 55-0898, Jacksonville, FL 32255-0898, 904-705-6806; gonz2171@bellsouth.net; www.short-fiction.com

CATAMARAN SAILOR, PO Box 2060, Key Largo, FL 33037, 05-451-3287, Fax 305-453-0255, rick@catsailor.comt, www.catsailor.com

Foodnsport Press, 609 N Jade Drive, Key Largo, FL 33037, 541-688-8809, www.foodnsport.com

Ram Press, PO Box 2060, Key Largo, FL 33037, 305-451-3287, Fax 305-453-0255, rick@catsailor.comt, www.rambooks.com, www.catsailor.com

Galt Press, PO Box 186, Lake Wales, FL 33859-0186, 863-678-0011, galt@galtpress.com, www.galtpress.com

Bolton Press, 3600 Oak Manor Lane, Apt. #42, Largo, FL 33774-1220, 727-489-3628

Putting Up Books, LC, P.O. Box J * 6079 Avenue F, McIntosh, FL 32664, phone 3525914535, fax 3525914626

THE GREAT BLUE BEACON, 1425 Patriot Drive, Melbourne, FL 32940, ajircc@juno.com

AE-TU Publishing, P O Box 960246, Miami, FL 33296-0246, (305)408-3817, Fax on demand, aetupub@hotmail.com, www.aetupublishing.com

Comparative Sedimentology Lab., University of Miami, RSMAS/MGG, 4600 Rickenbacker Cswy., Miami, FL 33149

Costa Rica Books, PO Box 025216, Suite 1, SJO 981, Miami, FL 33102-5216, 619-461-6131, crbooks@racsa.co.cr, www.costaricabooks.com

Tropical Press, PO Box 161174, Miami, FL 33116, www.tropicalpress.com

THE FURNACE REVIEW, 905 Michigan Ave., Apt. 3, Miami Beach, FL 33139-5352, submissions@thefurnacereview.com, http://www.thefurnacereview.com

Cantadora Press, 5406 Persimmon Hollow Rd., Milton, FL 32583-6700

COGNITIO: A Graduate Humanities Journal, 5406 Persimmon Hollow Rd., Milton, FL 32583-6700

Zebra Press, PO box 915, Monticello, FL 32345

PARENTEACHER MAGAZINE, PO Box 1246, Mount Dora, FL 32756, 352-385-1877, 800-732-3868, Fax 352-385-9424, rachat@aol.com

Admiral House Publishing, 4281 7th Avenue SW, Naples, FL 34119-4029, email AdmHouse@swfla.rr.com
Albion Press, 14100 Tamiami Trail E., Lot 348, Naples, FL 34114-8485, 314-962-7808 phone/Fax, e-mail albionpr@stlnet.com
Morgen Publishing Incorporated, PO Box 754, Naples, FL 34106, Fax 239-263-8472
Bookhome Publishing/Panda Publishing, PO Box 5900, Navarre, FL 32566, E-mail bookhome@gte.net; www.bookhome.com
Luthers Publishing, 1009 North Dixie Freeway, New Smyrna Beach, FL 32168-6221, 386-423-1600 phone/Fax, www.lutherspublishing.com
Two Thousand Three Associates, 4180 Saxon Drive, New Smyrna Beach, FL 32169-3851, 386-427-7876, Fax 386-423-7523
Atlantic Publishing Group, Inc., 1210 SW 23rd Place, Ocala, FL 34474-7014, 800-555-4037, Fax 352-622-5836, sales@atlantic-pub.com, www.atlantic-pub.com
SAGE OF CONSCIOUSNESS E-ZINE, PO Box 1209, Ocala, FL 34478-1209, sageofcon@gmail.com http://www.sageof-con.org
Bandido Books, 9806 Heaton Court, Orlando, FL 32817, 407-657-9707, Fax 407-677-9796, publish@bandidobooks.com, www.bandidobooks.com
THE FLORIDA REVIEW, English Department, University of Central Florida, Orlando, FL 32816-1346, 407-823-2038
Rivercross Publishing, Inc., 6214 Wynfield Court, Orlando, FL 32819, 407-876-7720
UnKnownTruths.com Publishing Company, 8815 Conroy Windermere Rd., Suite 190, Orlando, FL 32835, Ph 407-929-9207, Fax 407-876-3933, info@unknowntruths.com
Carnifex Press, PO Box 1686, Ormond Beach, FL 32175, armand@carnifexpress.net, http://www.carnifexpress.net
Boulevard Books, Inc. Florida, 1016 Buena Vista Boulevard, Panama City, FL 32401-2157
BAYOU, Department of English, University of West Florida, Pensacola, FL 32514, 850-474-2900
BAYOU, The University of West Florida/English Dept., 11000 University Parkway, Pensacola, FL 32514-5751, 904-474-2923
Ethos Publishing, 4224 Spanish Trail Place, Pensacola, FL 32504-8561
The Runaway Spoon Press, 1708 Hayworth Road, Port Charlotte, FL 33952, 941-629-8045
REMARK, PO Box 880493, Port Saint Lucie, FL 34986, www.remarkpoetry.net remarkpoetry@gmail.com
Orage Publishing, 1460 Wren Ct, Punta Gorda, FL 33950, p-941-639-6144, fax-941-639-4144
THE NAUTILUS, PO Box 1580, Sanibel, FL 33957, 941-395-2233, Fax 941-395-6706, jleal@shellmuseum.org
A Cappela Publishing, Inc., PO Box 3691, Sarasota, FL 34230-3691, phone: 941-351-2050 fax: 941-351-4735 email: acappub@aol.com website: www.acappela.com
Ageless Press, 3759 Collins St., Sarasota, FL 34232-3201, 941-365-1367, irishope@comcast.net
Barefoot Press, 1012 Danny Drive, Sarasota, FL 34243-4409, 941-751-3200, fax 941-751-3244
LegacyForever, 4930 Capri Avenue, Sarasota, FL 34235-4320, 941-358-3339
Pineapple Press, Inc., PO Box 3889, Sarasota, FL 34230-3889, 941-739-2219, FAX: 941-739-2296
Starbooks Press/FLF Press, 1391 Boulevard of the Arts, Sarasota, FL 34236-2904, 941-957-1281, Fax 941-955-3829, starxxx@gte.net
MIDWEST POETRY REVIEW, 7443 Oak Tree Lane, Spring Hill, FL 34607-2324
Kings Estate Press, 870 Kings Estate Road, St. Augustine, FL 32086, 800-249-7485, rmkkep@bellsouth.net
Seaside Publishing, PO Box 979, St. Petersburg, FL 33731-0979, sales@famousflorida.com
Tortuga Books, PO Box 420564, Summerland Key, FL 33042, 800-345-6665 (orders), 305-745-8709, Fax 305-745-2704, www.tortugabooks.com
Anhinga Press, PO Box 10595, Tallahassee, FL 32302, 850-442-1408, Fax 850-442-6323, info@anhinga.org, www.anhinga.org
Azreal Publishing Company, 1226 High Road, Tallahassee, FL 32304-1833, (850) 222-7425, www.azrealpublishing.com, info@azrealpublishing.com
Fiction Collective Two (FC2), Dept. of English, Florida State University, Tallahassee, FL 32306-1580, 850-644-2260, Fax 850-644-6808
THE LIBRARY QUARTERLY, Florida State University, School of Information Studies, 101 Shores Building, Tallahassee, FL 32306-2100
THE SILVER WEB, PO Box 38190, Tallahassee, FL 32315
Llumina Press, 7915 W. McNab Road, Tamarac, FL 33321, 954 726-0902
TAMPA REVIEW, 401 W. Kennedy Boulevard, University of Tampa-19F, Tampa, FL 33606-1490, (813) 253-6266, Email: utpress@ut.edu, http://utpress.ut.edu, http://tampareview.ut.edu
University of Tampa Press, 401 W Kennedy Blvd, Tampa, FL 33606, (813) 253-6266, Email: utpress@ut.edu, http://utpress.ut.edu, http://tampareview.ut.edu
WORLD OF FANDOM MAGAZINE, PO Box 9421, Tampa, FL 33604, 813-933-7424
SHORTRUNS, 720 Wesley Ave. #10, Tarpon Springs, FL 34689, 727-942-2218
Four Seasons Publishers, PO Box 51, Titusville, FL 32781, phone 321-632-2932,fax 321-632-2935,fseasons@bellsouth.net
Heritage Global Publishing, 908 Innergary Place, Valrico, FL 33594, 813-643-6029
Eurotique Press, 3109 45th Street, Suite 300, West Palm Beach, FL 33407-1915, 561-687-0455; 800-547-4326
Common Boundaries, 2895 Luckie Road, Weston, FL 33331-3047, 954-385-8434, Fax 954-385-8652, www.commonboundar-ies.com, info@commonboundaries.com
Tax Property Investor, Inc., PO Box 4602, Winter Park, FL 32793, 407-671-0004

GEORGIA

A Child Called Poor, P O Box 5716, Albany, GA 31706, 229-291-7556, 229-439-9061, ACHILDCALLEDPOOR.COM
THE GEORGIA REVIEW, 012 Gilbert Hall, University of Georgia, Athens, GA 30602-9009, 706-542-3481
THE LANGSTON HUGHES REVIEW, Department of English, 254 Park Hall, Univ. of Georgia, Athens, GA 30602-6205, 706-542-1261
LITERARY IMAGINATION: The Review of the Association of Literary Scholars and Critics, Dept. of Classics, 221 Park Hall, University of Georgia, Athens, GA 30602-6203, 706-542-0417, Fax 706-542-8503, litimag@uga.edu, www.bu.edu/literary
STATE AND LOCAL GOVERNMENT REVIEW, Carl Vinson Institute of Government, 201 N. Milledge Ave., Univ. of GA, Athens, GA 30602, 706-542-2736
Venus Communications, PO Box 48822, Athens, GA 30604, 706-369-1547, fax 706-369-8598, email venus@venuscomm.com, www.venuscomm.com
VERSE, Department of English, University of Georgia, Athens, GA 30602
ART PAPERS, PO Box 5748, Atlanta, GA 31107-5748, 404-588-1837, Fax 404-588-1836, editor@artpapers.org, www.artpapers.org
ATLANTA REVIEW, PO Box 8248, Atlanta, GA 31106
The Chicot Press, Box 53198, Atlanta, GA 30355, 770-640-9918, Fax 770-640-9819, info@cypressmedia.net
Clarity Press, Inc., 3277 Roswell Road NE, Suite 469, Atlanta, GA 30305, Editorial: 877-613-1495 Fax 877-613-7868,

clarity@islandnet.com, editorial: claritypress@usa.net, www.claritypress.com

FIVE POINTS, P.O. Box 3999, Georgia State University, Atlanta, GA 30302-3999, 404-463-9484, Fax 404-651-3167

LULLWATER REVIEW, Box 22036, Emory University, Atlanta, GA 30322, 404-727-6184

NEW INTERNATIONAL A magazine of Marxist politics and theory, P.O. Box 162767, Atlanta, GA 30321-2767, www.pathfinderpress.com

Pathfinder Press, P.O. Box 162767, Atlanta, GA 30321-2767, www.pathfinderpress.com; orders@pathfinderpress.com (orders); pathfinder@pathfinderpress.com (editorial); permissions@pathfinderpress.com (permissions)

Peachtree Publishers, Ltd., 1700 Chattahoochee Avenue, Atlanta, GA 30318, 404-876-8761, www.peachtree-online.com

Pearl's Book'em Publisher, 6300 Powers Ferry Road, Suite 600, #272, Atlanta, GA 30339-2961, 404-373-4603, Fax 419-828-8202, bookpearl@bookpearl.com, www.bookpearl.com

Quantum Leap S.L.C. Publications, 2740 Greenbriar Parkway, Ste. 201, Atlanta, GA 30331, 877-571-9788, www.blackamericanhandbook.com

Redfield Publishers, PO Box 888870, Atlanta, GA 30356, 770-698-0561; 877-438-5469; Fax 770-396-8175; redfieldpubs@bell-south.net; www.redfieldjinx.com

Roaring Lion Press, 415 Highland Square Drive NE, Atlanta, GA 30306-2285

BLUE HORSE, P.O. Box 6061, Augusta, GA 30906, 706-798-5628

Blue Horse Publications, PO Box 6061, Augusta, GA 30906, 706-798-5628

Harbor House, 111 Tenth Street, Augusta, GA 30901, 706-738-0354(phone), 706-823-5999(fax), harborhouse@harborhouse-books.com, www.harborhousebooks.com

SIMPLYWORDS, 605 Collins Avenue #23, Centerville, GA 31028, simplywords@hotmail.com

Brentwood Christian Press, 4000 Beallwood Avenue, Columbus, GA 31904

Dream Catcher Publishing, 3260 Keith Bridge Road #343, Cumming, GA 30041-4058, 770-887-7058, fax 888-771-2800, dcp@dreamcatcherpublishing.net, www.dreamcatcherpublishing.net

Quinn Entertainment, 7535 Austin Harbour Drive, Cumming, GA 30041, Phone (770) 356-3847, Fax (770) 886-1475, info@quinnentertainment.com, www.quinnentertainment.com

Maryland Historical Press, 2364 Sandell Drive, Dunnwoody, GA 30338, 770-671-0740

THE CHATTAHOOCHEE REVIEW, Georgia Perimeter College, 2101 Womack Road, Dunwoody, GA 30338-4497, 770-274-5145

GoldenIsle Publishers, Inc., 2395 Hawkinsville Highway, Eastman, GA 31023, 478-374-5806(5841), Fax 478-374-9720

New World Press, Inc, 5626 Platte Dr., Ellenwood, GA 30294, (404)512-6760

SCIENCE/HEALTH ABSTRACTS, PO Box 553, Georgetown, GA 31754

Sand and Sable Publishing, P.O. Box 744, Jonesboro, GA 30237, 404-509-3352

IT GOES ON THE SHELF, 4817 Dean Lane, Lilburn, GA 30047-4720, nedbrooks@sprynet.com

Purple Mouth Press, 4817 Dean Lane, Lilburn, GA 30047-4720, nedbrooks@sprynet.com, http://home.sprynet.com/~nedbrooks/home.htm

Platinum One Publishing, 30 Cooper Lake Road Suite A7, Mableton, GA 30126, www.platinumonepublishing.com, fax:1-203-651-1825, Email:customerservice@platinumonepublishing.com

Mercer University Press, 1400 Coleman Ave., Macon, GA 31207, (478) 301-2880, (478) 301-2585 fax

Cherokee Publishing Company, PO Box 1730, Marietta, GA 30061, 404-467-4189

Fitness Press, P O Box 4912, Marietta, GA 30061, 770-578-8207; Fax 770-973-2154

Franklin-Sarrett Publishers, 3761 Vineyard Trace, Marietta, GA 30062, 770-578-9410, Fax 770-973-4243, info@franklin-sarrett.com, www.franklin-sarrett.com

J&W Publishers, Inc., PO Box 7238, Marietta, GA 30065, (770) 374-2990

Top Shelf Productions, Inc., PO Box 1282, Marietta, GA 30061-1282, 770-425-0551, Fax: 770-427-6395, Email: chris@topshelfcomix.com

P.R.A. Publishing, P.O. Box 211701, Martinez, GA 30917-1701, (706) 855-6173, (630) 597-0548, fax(s)(706) 855-8794, (425)669-3833 www.prapublishing.com, submissions@phoenixrisingarts.com

ARTS & LETTERS: Journal of Contemporary Culture, Georgia College & State University, Campus Box 89, Milledgeville, GA 31061-0490, 478-445-1289, al@gcsu.edu, http://al.gcsu.edu

The Speech Bin, Inc., PO Box 922668, Norcross, GA 30010-2668, 772-770-0007, FAX 772-770-0006; website: www.speechbin.com

Tolling Bell Books, 5555 Oakbrook Parkway, Suite 330, Norcross, GA 30093, 770-757-2934, Fax 770-448-0130, info@tollingbellbooks.com, www.tollingbellbooks.com

Gallopade International, 665 Highway 74 South #600, Peachtree City, GA 30269-3036

THE OLD RED KIMONO, Social & Cultural Studies,, Floyd College, Rome, GA 30162, 706-368-7623

SOUTHERN POETRY REVIEW, Armstrong Atlantic State University, Dept. of LLP, 11935 Abercorn Street, Savannah, GA 31419-1997, 912-921-5633, Fax 912-927-5399, smithjam@mail.armstrong.edu, www.spr.armstrong.edu

5th Street Books, 1691 Norris landing Drive, Suite A, Snellville, GA 30039-0028, 770-483-0431, www.5thstreetbooks.com

Brook Street Press, PO Box 20284, St. Simons Island, GA 31522, 912-638-0264, Fax 912-638-0265, info@brookstreet-press.com, www.brookstreetpress.com

Old Sport Publishing Company, PO Box 2757, Stockbridge, GA 30281, 770-914-2237, Fax 770-914-9261, info@oldsportpublishing.com, www.oldsportpublishing.com

Aspen Mountain Publishing, 5885 Cumming Highway Suite 108, PMB 254, Sugar Hill, GA 30518, www.aspenmtnpublishing.com

Anvil Publishers, Inc., PO Box 2694, Tucker, GA 30085-2694, 770-938-0289, Fax 770-493-7232, anvilpress@aol.com, www.anvilpub.com

HOGTOWN CREEK REVIEW, 4736 Hummingbird Lane, Valdosta, GA 31602-6701, tel:229-219-1122, www.hogtown-creek.org

SNAKE NATION REVIEW, 110 #2 West Force, Valdosta, GA 31601, 912-249-8334

GUAM

STORYBOARD, Division of English, University of Guam, Mangilao, GU 96923, storybd@uog.edu, rburns@uog9.uog.edu

HAWAII

Aardwolfe Books, PO Box 471, Aiea, HI 96701-0471, publisher@aardwolfe.com, www.aardwolfe.com

LifeQuest Publishing Group, PO Box 760, Hana, HI 96713-0760, fax 425-392-1854, e-mail lifequest@usa.net

Petroglyph Press, Ltd., 160 Kamehameha Avenue, Hilo, HI 96720-2834, 808-935-6006, Fax 808-9335-1553, BBinfo@BasicallyBooks.com, www.BasicallyBooks.com

World Changing Books, PO Box 5491, Hilo, HI 96720, 808-934-7942
Bamboo Ridge Press, PO Box 61781, Honolulu, HI 96839-1781, 808-626-1481 phone/Fax, brinfo@bambooridge.com
BAMBOO RIDGE, Journal of Hawai'i Literature and Arts, PO Box 61781, Honolulu, HI 96839-1781
The Bess Press, 3565 Harding Avenue, Honolulu, HI 96816, 808-734-7159
CHINA REVIEW INTERNATIONAL, Center for Chinese Studies, Univ of Hawaii, 1890 East-West Road, Rm. 417, Honolulu, HI 96822-2318, 808-956-8891, Fax 808-956-2682
HAWAI'I REVIEW, c/o Dept. of English, 1733 Donaghho Road, Honolulu, HI 96822, 808-956-3030
HAWAII PACIFIC REVIEW, 1060 Bishop Street, Hawai'i Pacific University, Honolulu, HI 96813, 808-544-1108
Island Style Press, 6950 Hawaii Kai Drive Apt. 403, Honolulu, HI 96825-4149
MANOA: A Pacific Journal of International Writing, Univ. of Hawaii English Department, 1733 Donaghho Road, Honolulu, HI 96822, 808-956-3070, Fax 808-956-3083, mjournal-l@hawaii.edu, manoajournal.hawaii.edu
Mo'omana'o Press, 3030 Kalihi St., Honolulu, HI 96818, 808-843-2502; (fax) 808-843-2572; email: clear@maui.net
SHEMP! The Lowlife Culture Magazine, 593 Waikala Street, Kahului, HI 96732-1736, e-mail shempzine@yahoo.com
Poetry Harbor, PO Box 202, Kailua Kona, HI 96745-0202
RED HAWK, 75-6100 Alii Drive, Apt. B28, Kailua-Kona, HI 96740-2308
Suburban Wilderness Press, PO Box 202, Kailua-Kona, HI 96745
Titlewaves Publishing; Writers Direct, 4-1579 Kuhio Hwy, Ste 104, Kapaa, HI 96746-1859, orders 800-867-7323
Good Book Publishing Company, PO Box 837, Kihei, HI 96753-0837, 808-874-4876, dickb@dickb.com, www.dickb.com/index.shtml
Paradise Research Publications, Inc., Box 837, Kihei, HI 96753-0837, 808-874-4876, dickb@dickb.com
Pacific Isle Publishing Company, PO Box 827, Makawao, HI 96768, 808-572-9232 phone, books@bromes.com, www.bromes.com
BLACK SHEETS MAGAZINE, 33-3313 Moku St., Pahoa, HI 96778-8305, 415-431-0173; Fax 415-431-0172; blacksheets@blackbooks.com
Maui arThoughts Co., PO Box 967, Wailuku, HI 96793-0967, 808-244-0156 phone/Fax, booksmaui@hawaii.rr.com, www.booksmaui.com

IDAHO

Ahsahta Press, Boise State University, Department of English, Boise, ID 83725-1525, 208-426-2195, ahsahta@boisestate.edu, http://ahsahtapress.boisestate.edu
COLD-DRILL, 1910 University Drive, Boise, ID 83725, 208-426-3862
Cold-Drill Books, Dept. of English, Boise State University, Boise, ID 83725
Idaho Center for the Book, 1910 University Drive, Boise, ID 83725-1525, 208-426-1999, Fax 208-426-4373, www.lili.org/icb
THE IDAHO REVIEW, Boise State University, 1910 University Drive/English Dept., Boise, ID 83725, 208-426-1002, http://english.boisestate.edu/idahoreview/
Limberlost Press, 17 Canyon Trail, Boise, ID 83716
THE PASTOR'S WIFE NEWSLETTER, 8731 Brynwood Drive, Boise, ID 83704, janicetpw@email.msn.com, www.pastorswife.com
The Caxton Press, 312 Main Street, Caldwell, ID 83605, 208-459-7421
Wytherngate Press, P O Box 3134, Couer d Alene, ID 83816, 208-818-3078, 208-661-4566, wytherngatepress@gmail.com, after 4/30/2006: info@wytherngate.com
Mountain Meadow Press, PO Box 447, Kooskia, ID 83539, phone 208-926-7875; fax 208-926-7579; email: mmp@cybrquest.com
TALKING RIVER REVIEW, Lewis-Clark State College, 500 8th Avenue, Lewiston, ID 83501, Email: triver@lcsc.edu, www.lcsc.edu/TalkingRiverReview/
ELECTRONIC GREEN JOURNAL, University of Idaho Library, Moscow, ID 83844-2360, 208-885-6631, e-mail majanko@uidaho.edu, www.egj.lib.uidaho.edu/index.html
THE FRANK REVIEW, Lindsay Wilson & Nathan Graziano, P.O. Box 3193, Moscow, ID 83843-1907, frankreview@ex-cite.com
FUGUE, Brink Hall, Room 200, Engl. Dept., University of Idaho, Moscow, ID 83844-1102, 208-885-6156
Score, 1111 E. Fifth Street, Moscow, ID 83843
SPORE, 1111 E. Fifth Street, Moscow, ID 83843, schneider-hill@adelphia.com, http://scorecard.typepad.com/spore/
UNWOUND, P.O. Box 3193, Moscow, ID 83843-1907, unwoundmagazine@excite.com, www.fyuocuk.com/unwound.htm
Blue Scarab Press, PO Box 4966, Pocatello, ID 83205-4966
The Great Rift Press, 1135 East Bonneville, Pocatello, ID 83201, 208-232-6857, orders 800-585-6857, Fax 208-233-0410
Howling Wolf Publishing, PO Box 1045, Pocatello, ID 83204, 208-233-2708 phone e-mail kirby@kirbyjonas.com
Keokee Co. Publishing, Inc., PO Box 722, Sandpoint, ID 83864, 208-263-3573, www.keokeebooks.com
Lost Horse Press, 105 Lost Horse Lane, Sandpoint, ID 83864, 208-255-4410, Fax 208-255-1560, losthorse-press@mindspring.com
SANDPOINT MAGAZINE, PO Box 722, Sandpoint, ID 83864, 208-263-3573, info@keokee.com

ILLINOIS

The Teitan Press, Inc., PO Box 1972, Bolingbrook, IL 60440, e-mail editor@teitanpress.com, http://www.teitanpress.com
CRAB ORCHARD REVIEW, SIUC Dept. of English - Mail Code 4503, 1000 Faner Drive, Carbondale, IL 62901, 618-453-6833, www.siu.edu/~crborchd
Southern Illinois University Press, PO Box 3697, Carbondale, IL 62902, 618-453-6615 (phone) 618-453-1221 (FAX)
Sagamore Publishing, 804 N. Neil St, Champaign, IL 61820, 800-327-5557, 217-359-5940, 217-359-5975 (fax), HTTP://www.sagamorepub.com
Standard Publications, Inc., PO Box 2226, Champaign, IL 61825, 217-898-7825, spi@standardpublications.com
University of Illinois Press, 1325 South Oak Street, Champaign, IL 61820-6903, 217-333-0950
KARAMU, Department of English, Eastern Illinois Univ., Charleston, IL 61920, 217-581-6297
ACM (ANOTHER CHICAGO MAGAZINE), 3709 N. Kenmore, Chicago, IL 60613, 312-248-7665, www.anotherchicago-mag.com
African American Images, 1909 West 95th Street, Chicago, IL 60643-1105, 312-445-0322, Fax 312-445-9844
Black Light Fellowship, PO Box 5369, Chicago, IL 60680, 773-826-7790, Fax 773-826-7792
CHICAGO REVIEW, 5801 South Kenwood, Chicago, IL 60637
Chicago Review Press, 814 North Franklin Street, Chicago, IL 60610, 312-337-0747
CORNERSTONE, 939 W. Wilson Avenue, Chicago, IL 60640, 773-561-2450 ext. 2080, Fax 773-989-2076

CRITICAL INQUIRY, University of Chicago, Wieboldt Hall 202, 1050 East 59th Street, Chicago, IL 60637, Telephone: (773) 702-8477; Fax: (773) 702-3397, http://www.journals.uchicago.edu/CI/home.html
EbonyEnergy Publishing, Inc. (NFP), P.O. Box 43476, Chicago, IL 60643-0476, 773-851-5159
EUPHONY, 5706 S University Ave, Room 001, Chicago, IL 60615
GEM Literary Foundation Press, P.O. Box 43476, Chicago, IL 60643-0476, 773-445-4946
Kedzie Press, 2647 N. Western Ave., Ste #8042, Chicago, IL 60647-2034, (773)252-7220, www.kedziepress.com, info@kedziepress.com
Lake Claremont Press, 4650 N. Rockwell Street, Chicago, IL 60625, 773-583-7800, Fax 773-583-7877, lcp@lakeclaremont.com, www.lakeclaremont.com
LIGHT: The Quarterly of Light Verse, PO Box 7500, Chicago, IL 60680, 800-285-4448 (Charge Orders only), 708-488-3188 (voice), www.lightquarterly.com (no submissions via fax or e-mail)
Lyceum Books, Inc., 5758 S. Blackstone, Chicago, IL 60637, 773-643-1902, Fax 773-643-1903, lyceum@lyceumbooks.com, www.lyceumbooks.com
Merl Publications, 1658 N Milwaukee Ave # 242, Chicago, IL 60647, (708)445 8385 contact@merlpublications.com www.merlpublications.com
MODERN PHILOLOGY, University of Chicago, Wieboldt Hall 106, 1050 E. 59th Street, Chicago, IL 60637, 773-702-7600 (main #), 773-702-0694 (fax), http://www.journals.uchicago.edu/index.html
Open Court Publishing Company, 140 South Dearborn St., #1450, Chicago, IL 60605-5203, 312-939-1500, Fax 312-939-8150
Oracle Press, PO Box 5491, Chicago, IL 60680
OTHER VOICES, Univ. of Illinois, English Dept., 601 S. Morgan Street, M/C 162, Chicago, IL 60607, 312-413-2209, othervoices@listserv.uic.edu. www.othervoicesmagazine.org
OYEZ REVIEW, Dept. of Literature & Languages, 430. S. Michigan Ave, Chicago, IL 60605, www.roosevelt.edu/oyezreview
Path Press, Inc., PO Box 2925, Chicago, IL 60690-2925, 847-424-1620, fax: 847-424-1623
PhoeniX in Print, P. O. Box 81234, Chicago, IL 60681-0234, 877-560-0330, 312-946-9698 fax, info@phoenixinprint.com, www.phoenixinprint.com
PivotPoint Press, PO Box 577468, Chicago, IL 60657-7468, 773-561-1512 phone/Fax, info@PivotPointPress.com, www.PivotPointPress.com
POETRY, 444 North Michigan Ave., Suite 1850, Chicago, IL 60611-4034, tel 312-787-7070, fax 312-787-6650, email poetry@poetrymagazine.org, www.poetrymagazine.org
POETRY EAST, Dept. of English, DePaul Univ., 802 West Belden Avenue, Chicago, IL 60614-3214, 773-325-7487, http://condor.depaul.edu/~poetryea/home.html
PRIMAVERA, PO Box 37-7547, Chicago, IL 60637-7547, 773-324-5920
Puddin'head Press, PO Box 477889, Chicago, IL 60647, 708-656-4900
RAMBUNCTIOUS REVIEW, Rambunctious Press, Inc., 1221 West Pratt Blvd., Chicago, IL 60626
RANDEE, P.O. Box 578660, Chicago, IL 60657-8660
ROCTOBER COMICS AND MUSIC, 1507 East 53rd Street #617, Chicago, IL 60615, 773 875 6470
SEQUENTIAL, 2324 W. Walton Street #3F, Chicago, IL 60622-7101, feedback@sequentialcomics.com, www.sequentialcomics.com
Spectrum Press, 3023 N Clark Street, #109, Chicago, IL 60657
STUDENT LAWYER, ABA Publishing, Ira Pilchen, 321 North Clark St., Ste. LL2, Chicago, IL 60610-4772
THE2NDHAND, 2543 W. Walton #3, Chicago, IL 60647, 773-278-7034
University of Chicago Press, 1427 E. 60th Street, Chicago, IL 60437-2954, 773-702-7700,http://www.press.uchicago.edu/
WHITEWALLS: A Journal of Language and Art, PO Box 8204, Chicago, IL 60680, email aeelms@aol.com
Quality Sports Publications, 24 Buysse Drive, Coal Valley, IL 61240, 800-464-1116, Fax 309-234-5019, www.qualitysportsbooks.com
Brooks Books, 3720 N. Woodridge Drive, Decatur, IL 62526, (217) 877-2966
MAYFLY, 3720 N. Woodridge Drive, Decatur, IL 62526, (217) 877-2966
Northern Illinois University Press, 310 N. Fifth Street, DeKalb, IL 60115, (815) 753-1826 phone; (815) 753-1845 fax
Ara Pacis Publishers, PO Box 1202, Des Plaines, IL 60017-1202
BRIDAL CRAFTS, 2400 Devon, Suite 375, Des Plaines, IL 60018, 847-635-5800
Clapper Publishing Co., 2400 Devon, Suite 375, Des Plaines, IL 60018, 847-635-5800, 800-444-0441
CRAFTS 'N THINGS, 2400 Devon, Suite 375, Des Plaines, IL 60018, 847-635-5800
THE CROSS STITCHER, 2400 Devon, Suite 375, Des Plaines, IL 60018, 847-635-5800
PACK-O-FUN, 2400 Devon, Suite 375, Des Plaines, IL 60018, 847-635-5800
PAINTING, 2400 Devon, Suite 375, Des Plaines, IL 60018, 847-635-5800
Typographia Press, 1269 Rand Rd, Des Plaines, IL 60016, 847-635-8311
Raspberry Press Limited, PO Box 1, Dixon, IL 61021-0001, 815-288-4910, email: raspberrypresslimited@yahoo.com, Url: www.raspberrypresslimited.com
DRUMVOICES REVUE, Southern Illinois University, English Dept., Box 1431, Edwardsville, IL 62026-1431, 618-650-2060; Fax 618-650-3509
SOU'WESTER, Southern Illinois University, Edwardsville, IL 62026-1438
MARQUEE, York Theatre Building, 152 N. York Road, Suite 200, Elmhurst, IL 60126, 630-782-1800, Fax 630-782-1802, thrhistsoc@aol.com
MODERN HAIKU, PO Box 7046, Evanson, IL 60204-7046
BRILLIANT STAR, Baha'i National Center, 1233 Central Street, Evanston, IL 60201
Northwestern University Press, 629 Noyes Street, Evanston, IL 60208-4170, (847) 491-2046; fax (847)491-8150; www.nupress.northwestern.edu
RHINO: THE POETRY FORUM, PO Box 591, Evanston, IL 60204, www.rhinopoetry.org
TRIQUARTERLY, 629 Noyes Street, Evanston, IL 60208, (847) 491-2046; fax (847)491-8150; www.nupress.northwestern.edu
FRESH GROUND, PO Box 383, Fox River Grove, IL 60021, 708-639-9200
White Eagle Coffee Store Press, PO Box 383, Fox River Grove, IL 60021, 708-639-9200
RIVER KING POETRY SUPPLEMENT, PO Box 122, Freeburg, IL 62243
FREE LUNCH, PO Box 717, Glenview, IL 60025-0717, www.poetsfreelunch.org
Wayside Publications, PO Box 318, Goreville, IL 62939, n.nott@waysidepub.com, www.waysidepub.com
WILLOW REVIEW, College of Lake County, 19351 W. Washington, Grayslake, IL 60030, 847-543-2956, com426@clcillinois.edu, www.clcillinois.edu/community/willowreview.asp
NATURE SOCIETY NEWS, PO Box 390, Griggsville, IL 62340-0390, 217-833-2323, Fax 217-833-2123, natsoc@adams.net,

www.naturesociety.org
CHILDREN, CHURCHES AND DADDIES, A Non Religious, Non Familial Literary Magazine, Attn: Janet Kuypers, 829 Brian Court, Gurnee, IL 60031-3155, ccandd96@scars.tv, http://scars.tv
DeerTrail Books, 637 Williams Court, Gurnee, IL 60031-3136, 847-367-0014
DOWN IN THE DIRT LITERARY MAGAZINE, the prose & poetry magazine revealing all your dirty little secrets, Scars Publications, 829 Brian Court, Gurnee, IL 60031-3155, AlexRand@scars.tv, http://scars.tv
FREEDOM AND STRENGTH PRESS FORUM, Scars Publications, 829 Brian Court, Gurnee, IL 60031-3155, Editor@scars.tv, http://scars.tv
Scars Publications, Attn: Janet Kuypers, 829 Brian Court, Gurnee, IL 60031-3155, Editor@scars.tv, http://scars.tv
THINKERMONKEY, Gurnee, IL 60031-3155, editor@thinkermonkey.com
Airplane Books, 831 Ridge Road, Highland Park, IL 60035-3835
December Press, Box 302, Highland Park, IL 60035
THOUGHT BOMBS, PO Box 721, Homewood, IL 60430, 708-534-1334, anthonyrayson@hotmail.com
STORYQUARTERLY, 431 Sheridan Road, Kenilworth, IL 60043-1220, www.storyquarterly.com; storyquarterly@yahoo.com; 847-256-6998;
Ryrich Publications, 825 South Waukegan Road, PMB 183 A-8, Lake Forest, IL 60045, 847-234-7967, Fax 847-234-7967, ryrichpub@aol.com
WORKING WRITER, PO Box 6943, Libertyville, IL 60048, workingwriters@aol.com
Mayhaven Publishing, PO Box 557, 803 Buckthorn Circle, Mahomet, IL 61853-0557, 217-586-4493; fax 217-586-6330
AIM MAGAZINE, PO Box 1174, Maywood, IL 60153-8174
ZAWP, PO Box 411, Mossville, IL 61552-0411, 309-310-7709
Perikles Publishing, PO Box 5367, Naperville, IL 60567-5367, 630-244-2263, www.periklespublishing.com
REDISCOVER MUSIC CATALOG, 705 South Washington, Naperville, IL 60540-6654, 630-305-0770, Fax 630-305-0782, folkera@folkera.com
Sourcebooks, Inc., 1935 Brookdale Road, Ste. 139, Naperville, IL 60563, 630-961-3900; Fax 630-961-2168
AMERICAN BOOK REVIEW, Illinois State University, Campus Box 4241, Normal, IL 61790-4241, 309-438-3026, Fax 309-438-3523
Dalkey Archive Press, ISU Campus Box 8905, Normal, IL 61790-8905, 309-438-7555
MANDORLA: New Writing from the Americas / Nueva escritura de las Americas, ISU, Dept. of English, Campus Box 4240, Normal, IL 61790-4240, Publications Unit tel (309) 438-3025, Fax (309) 438-5414, email to mandorla-magazine@ilstu.edu, website at http://www.litline.org/Mandorla/
THE REVIEW OF CONTEMPORARY FICTION, ISU Campus Box 8905, Normal, IL 61790-8905, 309-438-7555
SPOON RIVER POETRY REVIEW, Department of English 4240, Illinois State University, Normal, IL 61790-4240, 309-438-7906, 309-438-3025
The P. Gaines Co., Publishers, PO Box 2253, Oak Park, IL 60303
Touchstone Adventures, PO Box 177, Paw Paw, IL 61353
AFTERTOUCH: New Music Discoveries, 1024 West Willcox Avenue, Peoria, IL 61604-2675, 309-685-4843
Bollix Books, 1609 W. Callender, Peoria, IL 61606, 309-453-4903, Fax 309-676-6557, editor@bollixbooks.com, www.bollisbooks.com
DOWNSTATE STORY, 1825 Maple Ridge, Peoria, IL 61614, 309-688-1409, email ehopkins@prairienet.org, http://www.wiu.edu/users/mfgeh/dss
CRICKET, PO Box 300, Peru, IL 61354, 815-224-5803, ext. 656, Fax 815-224-6615, mmiklavcic@caruspub.com
LADYBUG, the Magazine for Young Children, 315 5th Street, PO Box 300, Peru, IL 61354, 815-224-5803, ext. 656, Fax 815-224-6615, mmiklavcic@caruspub.com
THE MONIST: An International Quarterly Journal of General Philosophical Inquiry, 315 Fifth Street, Peru, IL 61354, (815)224-6651,(815)223-4486,philomon1@netscape.net,http//monist.buffalo.edu
SPIDER, PO Box 300, Peru, IL 61354, 815-224-5803, ext 656, Fax 815-224-6615, mmiklavcic@caruspub.com
Sherwood Sugden & Company, Publishers, 315 Fifth Street, Peru, IL 61354, 815-224-6651, Fax 815-223-4486, philomon1@netscape.net www.geocities.com/sugdenpublishers/ (or) www.sugdenpublishers.com
The Hosanna Press, 203 Keystone, River Forest, IL 60305, 708-771-8259
Planning/Communications, 7215 Oak Avenue, River Forest, IL 60305-1935, 708-366-5200, fax: 708-366-5280, email: dl@planningcommunications.com, website: http://jobfindersonline.com
juel house publishers and literary services, P.O.Box 415, Riverton, IL 62561, (217)629-9026 juelhouse@familyonline.com
Helm Publishing, 3923 Seward Ave., Rockford, IL 61108-7658, work: 815-398-4660, dianne@publishersdrive.com, www.publishersdrive.com
THE ROCKFORD REVIEW, PO Box 858, Rockford, IL 61105-0858, dragonldy@prodigy.net
THE WAKING, 488 Brookens Hall, UIS, Springfield, IL 62792-9243, elewis@uis.edu, www.geocities.com/uis_the_waking/
Oak Tree Press, 140 E. Palmer St., Taylorville, IL 62568, 217-824-6500, Fax 217-824-2040, oaktreepub@aol.com, www.oaktreebooks.com
NINTH LETTER, 234 English Bldg., University of Illinois, 608 S. Wright St., Urbana, IL 61801, (217) 244-3145, fax (217)244-4147, www.ninthletter.com, ninthletter@uiuc.edu
Stormline Press, Inc., P. O. Box 593, Urbana, IL 61801, 217-328-2665
The Urbana Free Library, 210 West Green Street, Urbana, IL 61801, 217-367-4057
Amnos Publications, 2501 South Wolf Road, Westchester, IL 60154, 312-562-2744
Crossway Books, 1300 Crescent Street, Wheaton, IL 60187, 630-682-4300
My Heart Yours Publishing, PO Box 4975, Wheaton, IL 60187, (630) 452-2809, www.myheartyours.com, tanya@myheartyours.com, jeannine@myheartyours.com
THE QUEST, PO Box 270, Wheaton, IL 60189, 630-668-1571
Quest Books: Theosophical Publishing House, 306 W. Geneva Rd., PO Box 270, Wheaton, IL 60189-0270, 630-665-0130, Fax 630-665-8791, questoperations@theosmail.net
NEW STONE CIRCLE, 1185 E 1900 N Road, White Heath, IL 61884
The Design Image Group Inc., 7000 South Adams St., Suite 111, Willowbrook, IL 60527-7565, 630-789-8991, Fax 630-789-9013
BLACKBOOK PRESS, THE POETRY ZINE, 1608 Wilmette Avenue, Wilmette, IL 60091, 847-302-9547, krvanheck@noctrl.edu
NoteBoat, Inc., PO Box 6155, Woodridge, IL 60517, 630-697-7229,630-910-4553

INDIANA

Cottontail Publications, 79 Drakes Ridge, Bennington, IN 47011-1802, 812-427-3921, cot202@netscape.net
THE PRESIDENTS' JOURNAL, 79 Drakes Ridge, Bennington, IN 47011-1802, 812-427-3921
Banta & Pool Literary Properties, 1020 Greenwood Avenue, Bloomington, IN 47401, writerpool@aol.com
DWAN, 915 West Second St. #7, Bloomington, IN 47403, e-mail dwanzine@hotmail.com
Family Learning Association, Inc., 3925 Hagan Street, Suite 101, Bloomington, IN 47401, 812-323-9862, 1-800-759-4723, Fax 812-331-2776
FROZEN WAFFLES, The Writer's Group, 329 West 1st St., Apt. 5, Bloomington, IN 47403-2474, 812-333-6304 c/o Rocky
Frozen Waffles Press/Shattered Sidewalks Press; 45th Century Chapbooks, The Writer's Group, 329 West 1st Street #5, Bloomington, IN 47403-2474
INDIANA REVIEW, Ballantine Hall 465, Indiana University, 1020 E. Kirkwood Avenue, Bloomington, IN 47405-7103, 812-855-3439
PARENT TALK NEWSLETTER, 3925 Hagan Street, Suite 101, Bloomington, IN 47401, 812-322-9862, 800-759-4723, Fax 812-331-2776
Royal Purcell, Publisher, 806 West Second Street, Bloomington, IN 47403, 812-336-4195
Tendre Press, 134 N. Overhill Dr., Bloomington, IN 47408, 812-334-1987, www.tendrepress.com
Unlimited Publishing LLC, P.O. Box 3007, Bloomington, IN 47402, Please see http://www.unlimitedpublishing.com for contact info.
World Wisdom,Inc., PO Box 2682, Bloomington, IN 47402, 812-330-3232, e-mail customers@worldwisdom.com
THE DROOD REVIEW OF MYSTERY, 484 E. Carmel Drive #378, Carmel, IN 46032, Fax 317-705-1402, info@droodreview.com, www.droodreview.com
Outrider Press, 2036 Northwinds Drive, Dyer, IN 46311-1874, 708-672-6630, Fax 708-672-5820, outriderPr@aol.com, www.outriderpress.com, 800-933-4680 code 03.
Filibuster Press, 5 Kim Ct., Elkhart, IN 46514-4009, 574-266-6622, publisher@filibusterpress.com, www.filibusterpress.com
METAL CURSE, PO Box 302, Elkhart, IN 46515-0302, email: cursed@sbinet.com
EVANSVILLE REVIEW, Univ. of Evansville, English Dept., 1800 Lincoln Avenue, Evansville, IN 47722, 812-488-1042
SOUTHERN INDIANA REVIEW, College of Liberal Arts, Univ. of Southern Indiana, 8600 University Blvd., Evansville, IN 47712, 812-461-5202, Fax 812-465-7152, email sir@usi.edu
FIRST CLASS, PO Box 86, Friendship, IN 47021, christopherm@four-sep.com, www.four-sep.com
Four-Sep Publications, PO Box 86, Friendship, IN 47021, christopherm@four-sep.com, www.four-sep.com
SKYLARK, 2200 169th Street, Purdue University Calumet, Hammond, IN 46323, 219-989-2273, Fax 219-989-2165, poetpam49@yahoo.com
AIS Publications, PO Box 42603, Indianapolis, IN 46242-0603, Office: (317) 856-8942, Cell: (317) 292-2615
BRANCHES, PO Box 30348, Indianapolis, IN 46230, 317-255-5594, editor@branches.com, www.branches.com
GENRE: WRITER AND WRITINGS, PO Box 42603, Indianapolis, IN 46242-0603, Office: (317) 856-8942, Cell: (317) 292-2615
NANNY FANNY, 008 Pin Oak Court, Indianapolis, IN 46260-1530, email: nightpoet@prodigy.net
Passion Power Press, Inc, PO 127, Indianapolis, IN 46206-0127, 317-356-6885 or 317-357-8821
Storm Publishing Group, 8117 Birchfield Dr, Indianapolis, IN 46268, stormpublishing@sbcglobal.net, www.stormpublishing-group.com
WordFarm, 2010 Michigan Avenue, La Porte, IN 46350, info@wordfarm.net, www.wordfarm.net
Bordighera, Inc., PO Box 1374, Lafayette, IN 47902-1374, 818-205-1266, via1990@aol.com
Etaoin Shrdlu Press, Fandom House, 30 N. 19th Street, Lafayette, IN 47904
PABLO LENNIS, Fandom House, 30 N. 19th Street, Lafayette, IN 47904
Marathon International Book Company, Department SPR, PO Box 40, Madison, IN 47250-0040, 812-273-4672 phone/Fax, jwortham@seidata.com
COOKING CONTEST CHRONICLE, PO Box 10792, Merrillville, IN 46411-0792
NOTRE DAME REVIEW, 840 Flanner Hall, University of Notre Dame, Notre Dame, IN 46556, 574-631-6952, Fax 574-631-4795
Friends United Press, 101 Quaker Hill Drive, Richmond, IN 47374, 765-962-7573
Wish Publishing, PO Box 10337, Terra Haute, IN 47801, 812-299-5700, email:holly@wishpublishing.com
POETS' ROUNDTABLE, 826 South Center Street, Terre Haute, IN 47807, 812-234-0819
SNOWY EGRET, PO Box 29, Terre Haute, IN 47808
FIGHT THESE BASTARDS, P.O. Box 844, Warsaw, IN 46581, 317-457-3505 email address for publication: evilgenius@platonic3waypress.com web site address: Platonic3WayPress.com
Platonic 3way Press, PO Box 844, Warsaw, IN 46581
SYCAMORE REVIEW, Department of English, Purdue University, West Lafayette, IN 47907, 765-494-3783

IOWA

FLYWAY, 206 Ross Hall, Iowa State University, Ames, IA 50011, 515-294-8273, FAX 515-294-6814, flyway@iastate.edu
TRADITION MAGAZINE, PO Box 492, Anita, IA 50020, 712-762-4363 phone/Fax, bobeverhart@yahoo.com
SWEET ANNIE & SWEET PEA REVIEW, 7750 Highway F-24 West, Baxter, IA 50028, 641-792-3578, Fax 641-792-1310
Sweet Annie Press, 7750 Highway F-24 West, Baxter, IA 50028, 641-417-0020
LifeCircle Press, PO Box 805, Burlington, IA 52601, www.lifecircleent.com
CESUM MAGAZINE, 1903 Merner Avenue, Cedar Falls, IA 50613, 319-210-0951, cesiummagazine@gmail.com, www.cesium-online.com
NORTH AMERICAN REVIEW, University Of Northern Iowa, 1222 W. 27th Street, Cedar Falls, IA 50614-0516, 319-273-6455
COE REVIEW, 1220 1st Ave NE, Cedar Rapids, IA 52402
Urban Legend Press, PO Box 4737, Davenport, IA 52808
THE URBANITE, PO Box 4737, Davenport, IA 52808
SEED SAVERS EXCHANGE, 3094 North Winn Road, Decorah, IA 52101, 563-382-5990, Fax 563-382-5872
MASSEY COLLECTORS NEWS—WILD HARVEST, Box 529, Denver, IA 50622, 319-984-5292
Islewest Publishing, 4242 Chavenelle Drive, Dubuque, IA 52002, 319-557-1500, Fax 319-557-1376
BOOK MARKETING UPDATE, PO Box 205, Fairfield, IA 52556-0205, 641-472-6130, Fax 641-472-1560, e-mail johnkremer@bookmarket.com
Open Horizons Publishing Company, PO Box 205, Fairfield, IA 52556-0205, 641-472-6130, Fax 641-472-1560, e-mail

566

johnkremer@bookmarket.com
FARMER'S DIGEST, 1003 Central Avenue, Fort Dodge, IA 50501-0624, 800-673-4763
Mountaintop Books, 21708 Eastman Road, Glenwood, IA 51534-6221
HOR-TASY, PO Box 158, Harris, IA 51345
THE ANNALS OF IOWA, 402 Iowa Avenue, Iowa City, IA 52240, 319-335-3931, fax 319-335-3935, e-mail marvin-bergman@uiowa.edu
IOWA HERITAGE ILLUSTRATED, State Historical Society of Iowa, 402 Iowa Avenue, Iowa City, IA 52240, 319-335-3916, Fax 319-335-3935, ginalie-swaim@uiowa.edu
THE IOWA REVIEW, 308 EPB, Univ. Of Iowa, Iowa City, IA 52242, 319-335-0462
TORRE DE PAPEL, 111 Phillips Hall, The University of Iowa, Iowa City, IA 52242, 319-335-0487
WALT WHITMAN QUARTERLY REVIEW, 308 EPB The University of Iowa, Iowa City, IA 52242-1492, 319-335-0454, 335-0592, Fax 319-335-2535, wwqr@uiowa.edu
Ice Cube Press, 205 North Front Street, North Liberty, IA 52317, 1-319-626-2055, fax 1-413-451-0223, steve@icecube-press.com, www.icecubepress.com
THE BRIAR CLIFF REVIEW, 3303 Rebecca St., Sioux City, IA 51104, 712-279-1651
Five Bucks Press, PO Box 31, Stacyville, IA 50476-0031, 641-710-9953, fivebuckspress@omnitelcom.com, www.fivebucks-press.com

KANSAS

NSR Publications, 1482 51st Road, Douglass, KS 67039, 620-986-5472, e-mail: nsrpublications@englishthrough.com, website: nsrpublications.com
FREETHOUGHT HISTORY, Box 5224, Kansas City, KS 66119, 913-588-1996
COTTONWOOD, Room 400, Kansas Union, 1301 Jayhawk Blvd., University of Kansas, Lawrence, KS 66045, 785-864-2528 (Lorenz), 785-864-3777 (Wedge)
Cottonwood Press, 400 Kansas Union, Box J, Univ. of Kansas, Lawrence, KS 66045, 785-864-2528
FIRST INTENSITY, PO Box 665, Lawrence, KS 66044-0665, e-mail leechapman@aol.com
First Intensity Press, PO Box 665, Lawrence, KS 66044, e-mail leechapman@aol.com
GROWING FOR MARKET, PO Box 3747, Lawrence, KS 66046, 785-748-0605, 800-307-8949, growing4market@earth-link.net, www.growingformarket.com
JOURNAL OF SCIENTIFIC EXPLORATION, 810 E. 10th Street, Lawrence, KS 66044-3018, e-mail sims@jse.com
Mica Press - Paying Our Dues Productions, 1508 Crescent Road, Lawrence, KS 66044-3120, Only contact by E-mail jgrant@bookzen.com; website www.bookzen.com
Morgan Quitno Corporation, PO Box 1656, Lawrence, KS 66044, 785-841-3534, 800-457-0742, mqpr@midusa.net
Nonetheless Press, 20332 W. 98th Street, Lenexa, KS 66220-2650, 913-254-7266, Fax 913-393-3245, info@nonetheless-press.com
ENVIRONMENTAL & ARCHITECTURAL PHENOMENOLOGY NEWSLETTER, 211 Seaton Hall, Architecture Dept., Kansas State University, Manhattan, KS 66506-2901, 913-532-1121
Editorial Research Service, 1009 East Layton Drive, Olathe, KS 66061-2933, 913-829-0609
McGavick Field Publishing, 118 North Cherry, Olathe, KS 66061, 913-782-1700, Fax 913-782-1765, fran@abcnanny.com, colleen@nationwidemedia.net, www.abcnanny.com
THE MIDWEST QUARTERLY, Pittsburg State University, History Department, Pittsburg, KS 66762, 620-235-4369
Varro Press, PO Box 8413, Shawnee Mission, KS 66208, 913-385-2034, Fax 913-385-2039, varropress@aol.com
MOUTH: Voice of the Dis-Labeled Nation, Mouth Magazine, 4201 SW 30th Street, Topeka, KS 66614-3203, Fax 785-272-7348
Al-Galaxy Publishing Corporation, PO Box 2591, Wichita, KS 67201, 316-651-0464, Fax 316-651-0461, email: sales@algalaxypress.com
St Kitts Press, PO Box 8173, Wichita, KS 67208, 888-705-4887, 316-685-3201, Fax 316-685-6650, ewhitaker@skpub.com
Thatch Tree Publications, 2250 N. Rock Road, Suite 118-169, Wichita, KS 67226, 316-687-6629, thatchtreepub@aol.com, www.kathyalba.com, www.thatchtreepublications.com

KENTUCKY

MEDUSA'S HAIRDO, 2631 Seminole Avenue, Ashland, KY 41102, 606-325-7203, medusashairdo@yahoo.com
APPALACHIAN HERITAGE, CPO 2166, Berea, KY 40404-3699, 859-985-3699, 859-985-3903, george_brosi@berea.edu, www.berea.edu/appalachianheritage
DOVETAIL: A Journal by and for Jewish/Christian Families, 775 Simon Greenwell Ln., Boston, KY 40107, 502-549-5440, Fax 502-549-3543, 800-530-1596, DI-IFR@Bardstown.com, carolw44@aol.com, www.dovetailinstitute.org
Steel Toe Books, English Department / 20C Cherry Hall, Western Kentucky University / 1 Big Red Way, Bowling Green, KY 42101-3576, (270) 745-5769 tom.hunley@wku.edu www.steeltoebooks.com
The Writers Block, Inc., POB 821, Franklin, KY 42135-0821, cell: 270-791-6252, fax: 270-586-9840; HEGwritersbl@aol.com, HaleyElizabethGarwood.com
Xavier House Publishing, PO BOX 1103, Franklin, KY 42135, james@xavier-house.com, www.xavier-house.com, 502-212-9314
Finishing Line Press, PO Box 1626, Georgetown, KY 40324, 859-514-8966, finishingbooks@aol.com, www.finishingline-press.com
HORTIDEAS, 750 Black Lick Road, Gravel Switch, KY 40328, 859-332-7606
THE LICKING RIVER REVIEW, Department of Literature and Language, Northern Kentucky University, Highland Heights, KY 41099
GENIE: POEMS: JOKES: ART, 1753 Fisher Ridge, Horse Cave, KY 42749
WAVELENGTH: A Magazine of Poetry in Prose and Verse, 1753 Fisher Ridge Road, Horse Cave, KY 42749
APEX SCIENCE FICTION & HORROR DIGEST, PO Box 2223, Lexington, KY 40588, 859-312-3974, http://www.apexdigest.com, submission@apexdigest.com
LIMESTONE: A Literary Journal, English Dept., Univ. of Kentucky, 1215 Patterson Office Tower, Lexington, KY 40506-0027, 859-257-6981, www.uky.edu/AS/English/Limestone
WIND, PO Box 24548, Lexington, KY 40524, 859-277-6849, www.wind.wind.org
Aran Press, 1036 S. Fifth Street, Louisville, KY 40203, aranpres@aye.net
Chicago Spectrum Press, 4824 Brownsboro Center, Louisville, KY 40207-2342, 502-899-1919; Fax 502-896-0246; evanstonpb@aol.com
Green River Writers, Inc./Grex Press, 103 Logsdon Court, Louisville, KY 40243-1161, 502-245-4902

KWC Press, 851 S. 4th Street #207, Louisville, KY 40203, eaugust@insightbb.com
THE LOUISVILLE REVIEW, Spalding University, 851 S. 4th Street, Louisville, KY 40203, 502-585-9911 ext. 2777, louisvillereview@spalding.edu, www.louisvillereview.org
Millennium Vision Press, 401 West Main St., Suite 706, Louisville, KY 40202-2937, phone 502 5892607 fax 502 5896123
Orpheus Press, 3221 Tara Gale Drive, Louisville, KY 40216
Sarabande Books, 2234 Dundee Road Suite 200, Louisville, KY 40205, www.sarabandebooks.org
Sciener Press, 1304 Highland Avenue, Louisville, KY 40204-2027, Fax 502-583-5608, dleightty@earthlink.net
THE MAD HATTER, 320 S. Seminary Street, Madisonville, KY 42431, 270-825-6000, Fax 270-825-6072, rwatson@hopkins.k12.ky.us, www.hopkins.k12.us/gifted/mad_hatter.htm
Wind Publications, 600 Overlook Drive, Nicholasville, KY 40356
PIKEVILLE REVIEW, Humanities Department, Pikeville College, Pikeville, KY 41501, 606-218-5002

LOUISIANA

Claitor's Law Books & Publishing Division, Inc., 3165 S. Acadian, PO Box 261333, Baton Rouge, LA 70826-1333, 225-344-0476; FAX 225-344-0480; claitors@claitors.com; www.claitors.com
Gothic Press, 1701 Lobdell Ave. No. 32, Baton Rouge, LA 70806, 225, 925, 2917 www.gothicpress.com gothicpt12@aol.com
Louisiana State University Press, PO Box 25053, Baton Rouge, LA 70894-5053, 225-578-6294, Fax 225-578-6461
NEW DELTA REVIEW, New Delta Review, Louisiana State University, Department of English, 249 Allen Hall, Baton Rouge, LA 70803, 225-578-4079
SMALL FRUITS REVIEW, D. Himelrick, Horticulture Dept., 137 Julian C. Miller Hall, Baton Rouge, LA 70803-2120, 334-844-3042, dhimelri@acesag.auburn.edu
THE SOUTHERN REVIEW, Old Presidents' House, Louisiana State University, Baton Rouge, LA 70803-5005, 225-578-5108
THE LOUISIANA REVIEW, Liberal Arts Div. PO Box 1129, Louisiana State Univ., Eunice, LA 70535
WHISPERING WIND MAGAZINE, PO Box 1390, Folsom, LA 70437-1390, 504-796-5433, whiswind@i-55.com, www.whisperingwind.com
THE SCRIBIA, PO Box 68, Grambling State University, Grambling, LA 71245, 318-274-2190, oterod@gram.,edu
Westgate Press, 2137 Alexandria Hwy, Leesville, LA 71446-7355
DESIRE STREET, 257 Bonnabel Boulevard, Metairie, LA 70005-3738, 504-835-8472 (Andrea), 504-467-9034 (Jeanette), Fax 504-834-2005, ager80@worldnet.att.net, Fax 504-832-1116, neworleanspoetryforum@yahoo.com
Lycanthrope Press, PO Box 9028, Metairie, LA 70005-9028, 504-866-9756
THEMA, PO Box 8747, Metairie, LA 70011-8747, Telephone: 504-887-1263; e-mail: thema@cox.net; website address: http://members.cox.net/thema
TURNROW, Univ. of Louisiana at Monroe, English Dept., 700 University Ave., Monroe, LA 71209, 318-342-1520, Fax 318-342-1491, ryan@ulm.edu, heflin@ulm.edu, http://turnrow.ulm.edu
H-NGM-N, 715 College Avenue, Natchitoches, LA 71457, nathanpritts@hotmail.com
H_NGM_N B_ _KS, NSU/Dept. of Language & Communication, Natchitoches, LA 71497, editor@h-ngm-n.com
The American Zen Association, 5500 Prytania St., #20, New Orleans, LA 70115
Garrett County Press, 828 Royal Street #248, New Orleans, LA 70116, 504-598-4685, www.gcpress.com
HERE AND NOW, 5500 Prytania St #201, New Orleans, LA 70130, info@nozt.org, www.nozt.org
THE ILLUMINATA, PO Box 8337, New Orleans, LA 70182-8337, Illuminata@tyrannosauruspress.com, www.Tyrannosaurus-usPress.com
Light of New Orleans Publishing, 828 Royal Street #307, New Orleans, LA 70116, 504-523-4322, Fax 504-522-0688, editor@frenchquarterfiction.com, www.frenchquarterfiction.com
Margaret Media, Inc., 425 Manasses Place, New Orleans, LA 70119, using cell phone temporarily: (601)918-8240, orders@margaretmedia.com
THE NEW LAUREL REVIEW, 828 Lesseps Street, New Orleans, LA 70117, 504-947-6001
NEW ORLEANS REVIEW, Box 195, Loyola University, New Orleans, LA 70118, 504-865-2475
NOLA-MAGICK, 828 Royal Street # 214, New Orleans, LA 70116, 504-301-1080, (fax) 504-309-9004, info@nolamagick.org, www.nolamagick.org
Portals Press, 4411 Fontainebleau Drive, New Orleans, LA 70125, 504-821-7723, travport@bellsouth.net, www.portals-press.com
Think Tank Press, Inc., PO Box 2228, New Orleans, LA 70176, www.thinktankpress.com
Trost Publishing, 509 Octavia St., New Orleans, LA 70115, 504-680-6754, www.trostpublishing.com,
World Love Press Publishing, 1028 Joliet Street, New Orleans, LA 70118, 504-866-4476 phone/Fax, worldlovepress@aol.com
XAVIER REVIEW, Box 110C, Xavier University, New Orleans, LA 70125, 504-520-7549 Collins, 483-7303 Skinner, Fax 504-485-7917
4AllSeasons Publishing, P.O. Box 6473, Shreveport, LA 71136, 504-715-3094
Tyrannosaurus Press, 5624 Fairway Dr., Zachary, LA 70791, 225.287.8885, Fax 206-984-0448, info@tyrannosauruspress.com, www.tyrannosauruspress.com

MAINE

Laureate Press, PO Box 8125, Bangor, ME 04402-8125, 800-946-2727
SAKANA, 11 Bangor Mall Blvd #114, Bangor, ME 04401
Nicolas-Hays, Inc., PO Box 1126, Berwick, ME 03901-1126
Heartsong Books, PO Box 370, Blue Hill, ME 04614-0370, publishers/authors phone: 207-266-7673, e-mail maggie@downeast.net, http://heartsongbooks.com
ME MAGAZINE, PO Box 182, Bowdoinham, ME 04008, 207-666-8453
Brook Farm Books, PO Box 246, Bridgewater, ME 04735, 506-375-4680
Two Dog Press, PO Box 164, Brooklin, ME 04616-0164, email human@twodogpress.com
Coyote Books, PO Box 629, Brunswick, ME 04011
Downeast Books, PO Box 679, Camden, ME 04843, 207-594-9544, Fax 207-594-0147, books@downeast.com, www.downeastbooks.com, www.countrysportpress.com
Clamp Down Press, PO Box 7270, Cape Porpoise, ME 04014-7270, 207-967-2605
Alice James Books, University of Maine at Farmington, 238 Main Street, Farmington, ME 04938-1911, 207-778-7071 phone/Fax, ajb@umf.maine.edu
THE AUROREAN, PO Box 187, Farmington, ME 04938, 207-778-0467
BELOIT POETRY JOURNAL, P.O. Box 151, Farmington, ME 04938, (207)778-0020, sharkey@maine.edu, www.bpj.org
THE RIVER REVIEW/LA REVUE RIVIERE, University of Maine-Fort Kent, 23 University Drive, Fort Kent, ME

04743-1292, 207-834-7542, river@maine.edu
The Latona Press, 24 Berry Cove Road, Lamoine, ME 04605
Haunted Rowboat Press, 162 Longley Road, Madison, ME 04950
MONKEY'S FIST, P.O. Box 316, Madison, ME 04950
Common Courage Press, Box 702, Monroe, ME 04951, 207-525-0900, 800-497-3207, Fax 207-525-3068
John Wade, Publisher, P. O. Box 303, Phillips, ME 04966, 1-888-211-1381
THE CAFE REVIEW, c/o Yes Books, 589 Congress Street, Portland, ME 04101, caferevieweditors@mailcity.com, www.thecafereview.com
MAINE IN PRINT, PO Box 9301, Portland, ME 04104-9301, 207-386-1400, Fax 207-386-1401, www.mainewriters.org
Harvest Hill Press, PO Box 55, Salisbury Cove, ME 04672, 207-288-8900; fax 207-288-3611
Leete's Island Books, Box 1, Sedgewick, ME 04676, 212-748-8678; e-mail PNeill@compuserve.com
Polar Bear & Company, PO Box 311, Solon, ME 04979-0311, 207-643-2795, solon@tds.net, www.polarbearandco.com
Century Press, PO Box 298, Thomaston, ME 04861, 207-354-0998, cal@americanletters.org, www.americanletters.org
Conservatory of American Letters, PO Box 298, Thomaston, ME 04861-0298, 207-354-0998, cal@americanletters.org, www.americanletters.org
Dan River Press, PO Box 298, Thomaston, ME 04861-0298, 207-354-0998, cal@americanletters.org, www.americanletters.org
NORTHWOODS JOURNAL, A Magazine for Writers, PO Box 298, Thomaston, ME 04861-0298, 207-345-0998, cal@americanletters.org, www.americanletters.org
Northwoods Press, PO Box 298, Thomaston, ME 04861-0298, 207-354-0998, cal@americanletters.org, www.americanletters.org
Goose River Press, 3400 Friendship Road, Waldoboro, ME 04572, Telephone & Fax: 207-832-6665, e mail: gooseriverpress@adelphia.net, web:www.gooseriverpress.com
Off the Grid Press, P.O. Box 84, Weld, ME 04285, www.offthegridpress.net
Moon Mountain Publishing, PO Box 188, West Rockport, ME 04865-0188, www.moonmountainpub.com
Moon Pie Press, 16 Walton Street, Westbrook, ME 04092, www.moonpiepress.com
Abernathy House Publishing, PO Box 1109, Yarmouth, ME 04096-1109, 207-838-6170, info@abernathyhousepub.com, www.abernathyhousepub.com

MARYLAND

Back House Books, 1703 Lebanon Street, Adelphi, MD 20783
CAFE NOIR REVIEW, 1703 Lebanon Street, Adelphi, MD 20783
The Bunny & The Crocodile Press/Forest Woods Media Productions, Inc, 1821 Glade Court, Annapolis, MD 21403-1945, 304-754-8847
Abecedarian books, Inc., 2817 Forest Glen Drive, Baldwin, MD 21013, 410-692-6777, fax 410-692-9175, toll free 877-782-2221, books@abeced.com, www.abeced.com
ALTERNATIVE PRESS INDEX, Alternative Press Center, Inc., PO Box 33109, Baltimore, MD 21218, 410-243-2471, altpress@altpress.org
AMBIT : JOURNAL OF POETRY AND POETICS, 19 Murdock Road, Baltimore, MD 21212, 410.718.6574
American Literary Press, 8019 Belair Road #10, Baltimore, MD 21236, 410-882-7700, Fax 410-882-7703, amerlit@americanliterarypress.com, www.americanliterarypress.com
Bancroft Press, PO Box 65360, Baltimore, MD 21209-9945, 410-358-0658, Fax 410-764-1967
BLACKBIRD, PO Box 16235, Baltimore, MD 21210, e-mail chocozzz2@aol.com
BrickHouse Books, Inc., 306 Suffolk Road, Baltimore, MD 21218, 410-235-7690, 410-704-2869
CELEBRATION, 2707 Lawina Road, Baltimore, MD 21216-1608, (410) 542-8785
DIRTY LINEN, PO Box 66600, Baltimore, MD 21239-6600, 410-583-7973, Fax 410-337-6735
C.H. Fairfax Co., Inc., PO Box 7047, Baltimore, MD 21216, www.yougetpublished.com
furniture_press, 19 Murdock Road, Baltimore, MD 21212, 410.718.6574
Icarus Press, 1015 Kenilworth Drive, Baltimore, MD 21204, 410-821-7807, www.icaruspress.com
PASSAGER, 1420 N. Charles Street, Baltimore, MD 21201-5779, www.passagerpress.com
The People's Press, 4810 Norwood Avenue, Baltimore, MD 21207-6839, (410)448-0254 phone/fax, (800)517-4475, biblio@talkamerica.net
THE PRESSED PRESS, PO Box 6039, Baltimore, MD 21231-0039
Prospect Press, 2707 Lawina Road, Baltimore, MD 21216-1608, (410) 542-8785
SHATTERED WIG REVIEW, 425 East 31st Street, Baltimore, MD 21218, 410-243-6888
SMARTISH PACE, PO Box 22161, Baltimore, MD 21203, www.smartishpace.com
SOCIAL ANARCHISM: A Journal of Practice and Theory, 2743 Maryland Avenue, Baltimore, MD 21218, 410-243-6987
VEGETARIAN JOURNAL, PO Box 1463, Baltimore, MD 21203, 410-366-VEGE (8343)
The Vegetarian Resource Group, PO Box 1463, Baltimore, MD 21203, 410-366-8343
World Travel Institute, Inc., 8268 Streamwood Drive, PO Box 32674, Baltimore, MD 21208, 410-922-4903; website www.worldtravelinstitute.com
THE BOOK ARTS CLASSIFIED, PO Box 1209, Beltsville, MD 20704-1209, 800-821-6604, Fax 800-538-7549, pagetwo@bookarts.com, www.bookarts.com
Gryphon House, Inc., PO Box 207, Beltsville, MD 20704-0207, 301-595-9500
THE FUTURIST, World Future Society, 7910 Woodmont Avenue, Suite 450, Bethesda, MD 20814-3032, 301-656-8274
IBEX Publishers, Inc., PO Box 30087, Bethesda, MD 20824, toll free 888-718-8188, 301-718-8188, Fax 301-907-8707
POET LORE, The Writer's Center, 4508 Walsh Street, Bethesda, MD 20815-6006, 301-654-8664
Stanford Oak Press, Inc., P.O. Box 30349, Bethesda, MD 20824, 301 652 8444, mbaker@stanfordoak.com
Woodbine House, 6510 Bells Mill Road, Bethesda, MD 20817-1636, 301-947-3440
WRITER'S CAROUSEL, 4508 Walsh Street, Bethesda, MD 20815-6006, 301-654-8664
The Writer's Center, 4508 Walsh Street, Bethesda, MD 20815-6006, 301-654-8664, www.writer.org
THE PLASTIC TOWER, PO Box 702, Bowie, MD 20718
Westhampton Publishing, 3540 Crain Highway, PMB #162, Bowie, MD 20716, 301-249-8733, fax 301-249-4119, web: www.WesthamptonPublishing.com
Cornell Maritime Press, Inc., PO Box 456, Centreville, MD 21617, 410-758-1075, www.cmptp.com
FEMINIST STUDIES, 0103 Taliaferro, University of Maryland, College Park, MD 20742-7726, 301-405-7415, Fax 301-405-8395, creative@feministstudies.org; www.feministstudies.org
ABBEY, 5360 Fall River Row Court, Columbia, MD 21044-1910, e-mail at greisman@aol.com
White Urp Press, 5360 Fallriver Row Court, Columbia, MD 21044

Nightsun Books, 823 Braddock Road, Cumberland, MD 21502-2622, 301-722-4861

A COMPANION IN ZEOR, 1622-B Swallow Crest Drive, Sunrise Villas Apartments, Edgewood, MD 21040-1751, Fax 410-676-0164, Klitman323@aol.com, cz@simegen.com www.simegen.com/sgfandom/rimonslibrary/cz/

PublishAmerica, LLLP., PO Box 151, Frederick, MD 21705-0151, 240-529-1031, Fax 301-631-9073, writers@publishamerica.com, www.publishamerica.com

NIGHTSUN, Department of English, Frostburg State University, Frostburg, MD 21532-1099, nightsun@frostburg.edu

Bob & Bob Publishing, Bob & Bob Associates, Inc., P.O. Box 10246, Gaithersburg, MD 20898-0246, 301-518-9835, Fax 301-515-0962, bobandbobinc@comcast.net, www.bobandbob.com

SelectiveHouse Publishers, Inc., PO Box 10095, Gaithersburg, MD 20898, 301-990-2999; email sr@selectivehouse.com; www.selectivehouse.com

IWAN: INMATE WRITERS OF AMERICA NEWSLETTER, Box 1673, Glen Burnie, MD 21060, e-mail inwram@netscape.com

Rising Star Publishers, 7510 Lake Glen Drive, Glenn Dale, MD 20769, 301-352-2533, Fax 301-352-2529

ANTIETAM REVIEW, 14 West Washington St., Hagerstown, MD 21740-5512, 301-791-3132

LISTEN, 55 West Oak Ridge Drive, Hagerstown, MD 21740

THE PEGASUS REVIEW, PO Box 88, Henderson, MD 21640-0088, 410-482-6736

Open University of America Press, 3916 Commander Drive, Hyattsville, MD 20782-1027, 301-779-0220 phone/Fax, openuniv@aol.com

Shambling Gate Press, 3314 Rosemary Lane, Hyattsville, MD 20782-1032, 301-779-6863, 301-779-9263

Daedal Press, 257 Foster Knoll Drive, Joppa, MD 21085-4756

ORACLE POETRY, PO Box 7413, Langley Park, MD 20787

ORACLE STORY, PO Box 7413, Langley Park, MD 20787

Scarecrow Press, 4501 Forbes Blvd., Suite 200, Lanham, MD 20706, 301-459-3366; Fax 301-429-5747

VOYA (Voice of Youth Advocate), 4720 Boston Way, Lanham, MD 20706, 301-459-3366

GERMAN LIFE, 1068 National Highway, LaVale, MD 21502-7501, 301-729-6190, Fax 301-729-1720, editor@germanlife.com

Rolling Hills Publishing, P.O. Box 724, New Windsor, MD 21776, 410-635-3233, info@rollinghillspublishing.com, www.rollinghillspublishing.com

THE ART OF ABUNDANCE, 1121 Annapolis Road, Suite 120, Odenton, MD 21113, 800-507-9244; 208-545-8164 (fax), www.ArtOfAbundance.com

Pellingham Casper Communications, 1121 Annapolis Road, Suite 120, Odenton, MD 21113, 800-507-9244; 208-545-8164 (fax), www.ArtOfAbundance.com

Scripta Humanistica, 1383 Kersey Lane, Potomac, MD 20854, 301-294-7949, 301-340-1095

POTOMAC REVIEW, Paul Peck Humanities Institute, Montgomery College, 51 Mannakee St., Rockville, MD 20850, 301-610-4100, www.montgomerycollege.edu/potomacreview

Schreiber Publishing, 51 Monroe Street, Suite 101, Rockville, MD 20850-4193, 301-424-7737, Fax 301-424-2336, spbooks@aol.com, www.schreiberNet.com

ART CALENDAR, PO Box 2675, Salisbury, MD 21802, 410-749-9625, Fax 410-749-9626, carolyn@artcalendar.com, www.artcalendar.com

AMERICAN HIKER, 1422 Fenwick Lane, Silver Spring, MD 20910-2160, 301-565-6704

American Hiking Society, 1422 Fenwick Lane, Silver Spring, MD 20910-2160, 301-565-6704

Beckham Publications Group, PO Box 4066, Silver Spring, MD 20914, phone: 301-384-7995; fax: 413-702-5632; editor@beckhamhouse.com, jv@beckhamhouse.com; www.beckhamhouse.com

Summit Crossroads Press, 3154 Gracefield Road - Suite T13, Silver Spring, MD 20904, 301-890-1647, Fax 301-890-1647, SumCross@aol.com, www.parentsuccess.com

UNO MAS MAGAZINE, 3007 Weller Road, Silver Spring, MD 20906-3888, Fax 301-770-3250, unomasmag@aol.com, http://www.unomas.com/

SKS Press, 5000 Pennsylvania Avenue Suites D & E, Suitland, MD 20746-1062, 301.669.6550, 301.669.6528, 1.888.800.3360

THE BALTIMORE REVIEW, PO Box 36418, Towson, MD 21286, www.BaltimoreReview.org

Sidran Institute, 200 E. Joppa Road, Suite 207, Towson, MD 21286, 410-825-8888, Fax 410-337-0747, sidran@sidran.org, www.sidran.org

Affirmative Publishing LC, 104 Colton Street, Upper Marlboro, MD 20774

The Galileo Press Ltd., 3637 Black Rock Road, Upperco, MD 21155-9322

Nanticoke Books, Box 333, Vienna, MD 21869-0333, 410-376-2144

ACME Press, PO Box 1702, Westminster, MD 21158, 410-848-7577

Heritage Books, Inc., 65 E. Main Street, Westminster, MD 21157-5026, 301-390-7708, Fax 301-390-7153, info@heritage-books.com

MINIATURE DONKEY TALK INC, 1338 Hughes Shop Road, Westminster, MD 21158, 410-875-0118, Fax 410-857-9145, minidonk@qis.net, www.miniaturedonkey.net

MASSACHUSETTS

VanderWyk & Burnham, PO Box 2789, Acton, MA 01720, 978-263-7595, FAX:978-263-0696, email:info@VandB.com, www.VandB.com

Primal Publishing, PO Box 1179, Allston, MA 02134-0007, Fax 617-787-5406, e-mail primal@primalpub.com

Amherst Writers & Artists Press, Inc., PO Box 1076, Amherst, MA 01004, 413-253-7764 phone/Fax, awapress@aol.com, www.amherstwriters.com

JUBILAT, English Dept., Bartlett Hall, University of Massachusetts, Amherst, MA 01003-0515, jubilat@english.umass.edu, www.jubilat.org

THE MASSACHUSETTS REVIEW, South College, University of Massachusetts, Amherst, MA 01003-7140, 413-545-2689

PEREGRINE, 190 University Drive, Amherst, MA 01002-3818, 413-253-3307 phone, awapress@aol.com, www.amherstwriters.com

Pyncheon House, 6 University Drive, Suite 105, Amherst, MA 01002

University of Massachusetts Press, Box 429, Amherst, MA 01004, 413-545-2217; fax 413-545-1226; orders 1-800-537-5487

THE LONG TERM VIEW: A Journal of Informed Opinion, Massachusetts School of Law, 500 Federal Street, Andover, MA 01810, 978-681-0800

THE NEW RENAISSANCE, an international magazine of ideas & opinions, emphasizing literature & the arts, 26 Heath Road #11, Arlington, MA 02474-3645

Haley's, PO Box 248, Athol, MA 01331, marcia@haleysantiques.com, www.haleysantiques.com

History Compass, LLC, 25 Leslie Rd., Auburndale, MA 02466, www.historycompass.com, 617 332 2202 (O), 617 332 2210 (F)

THOUGHTS FOR ALL SEASONS: The Magazine of Epigrams, 86 Leland Road, Becket, MA 01223, 413-623-0174

Warthog Press, 77 Marlboro St., Belmont, MA 02478

AGNI, Boston University Writing Program, 236 Bay State Road, Boston, MA 02215, 617-353-7135, agni@bu.edu

APPALACHIA JOURNAL, 5 Joy Street, Boston, MA 02108, 617-523-0636

Appalachian Mountain Club Books, 5 Joy Street, Boston, MA 02108, 617-523-0636

ASSEMBLAGE: A Critical Journal of Architecture and Design Culture, 1140 Washington St. Apt. 6, Boston, MA 02118-4502, email assmblag@gsd.harvard.edu

BAY WINDOWS, 631 Tremont Street, Boston, MA 02118, 617-266-6670, X211

Beacon Press, 25 Beacon Street, Boston, MA 02108, 617-742-2110

D.B.A. Books, 291 Beacon Street #8, Boston, MA 02116, 617-262-0411

THE EUGENE O'NEILL REVIEW, Department of English, Suffolk University, Boston, MA 02114-4280, 617-573-8272

Harvard Common Press, 535 Albany Street, Boston, MA 02118, 617-423-5803; 888-657-3755

Intercultural Press, Inc., 100 City Hall Plaza, Suite 501, Boston, MA 02108-2105, 617.523.3801, e-mail books@intercultural-press.com

THE NEW ENGLAND QUARTERLY, c/o Massachusetts Historical Society, 1154 Boylston St., Boston, MA 02215, 617-646-0543, fax: 617-859-0074, website: www.newenglandquarterly.org

PLOUGHSHARES, Emerson College, 120 Boylston Street, Boston, MA 02116, 617-824-8753

PRESSED WAFER: A Boston Review, 9 Columbus Square, Boston, MA 02116

REDIVIDER, Department of Writing, Literature, and Publishing, Emerson College, 120 Boylston Street, Boston, MA 02116

SALAMANDER, Salamander/Suffolk University English Dept., 41 Temple Street, Boston, MA 02114

TEEN VOICES MAGAZINE, 80 Summer St. #300, Boston, MA 02110-1218, 617-426-5505, Fax 617-426-5577, womenexp@teenvoices.com, www.teenvoices.com

Three Bean Press, P.O. Box 15386, Boston, MA 02215, phone: 617.584.5759, fax: 617.266.3446, email: info@threebean-press.com, web: www.threebeanpress.com

Vision Works Publishing, PO Box 217, Boxford, MA 01921, 888-821-3135, Fax 630-982-2134, visionworksbooks@email.com

Brookline Books, 34 University Rd, Brookline, MA 02445, 617-834-6772

Hermes House Press, 113 Summit Avenue, Brookline, MA 02446-2319, 617-566-2468

KAIROS, A Journal of Contemporary Thought and Criticism, 113 Summit Avenue, Brookline, MA 02446-2319

Zephyr Press, 50 Kenwood Street, Brookline, MA 02446, 617-713-2813

Circlet Press, Inc., 1770 Mass Avenue #278, Cambridge, MA 02140, 617-864-0492, Fax 617-864-0663, circlet-info@circlet.com

THE HARVARD ADVOCATE, 21 South Street, Cambridge, MA 02138, Fax 617-496-9740, contact@theharvardadvocate.com

HARVARD REVIEW, Lamont Library, Harvard University, Cambridge, MA 02138, 617-495-9775

HARVARD WOMEN'S LAW JOURNAL, Publications Center, Harvard Law School, Cambridge, MA 02138, 617-495-3726

JLA Publications, A Division Of Jeffrey Lant Associates, Inc., 50 Follen Street #507, Cambridge, MA 02138, 617-547-6372, drjlant@worldprofit.com, www.worldprofit.com and www.jeffreylant.com

Life Lessons, PO Box 382346, Cambridge, MA 02238, 617-576-2546, fax 617-576-3234, e-mail walkingwm@aol.com, website www.mindwalks.com

The MIT Press, 55 Hayward Street, Cambridge, MA 02142-1315, 617-253-5646, 617-258-6779, 800-405-1619

PEACEWORK, 2161 Massachusetts Avenue, Cambridge, MA 02140, 617-661-6130

South End Press, 7 Brookline Street #1, Cambridge, MA 02139-4146, 617-547-4002, email: southend@southendpress.org

SPARE CHANGE NEWS, 1151 Massachusetts Avenue, Cambridge, MA 02138, 617-497-1595, scnews@homelessempowerment.org

Tamal Vista Publications, 19A Forest St. #31, Cambridge, MA 02140, www.tamalvista.com, 617-492-7234

Westview Press, 11 Cambridge Center, Cambridge, MA 02142, j.mccrary@perseusbooks.com, www.westviewpress.com

Yellow Moon Press, PO Box 381316, Cambridge, MA 02238-0001, 617-776-2230, Fax 617-776-8246, E-mail story@yellowmoon.com, www.yellowmoon.com

Earthwinds Editions, P.O. 505319, Chelsea, MA 02150, 617-889-0253

THE AMERICAN DISSIDENT, 1837 Main Street, Concord, MA 01742-3811, todslone@yahoo.com

OSIRIS, Box 297, Deerfield, MA 01342-0297

Pagan Press, 11 Elton St., Dorchester, MA 02125-1412, 617-282-2133, john_lauritsen@post.harvard.edu

Standish Press, 105 Standish Street, Duxbury, MA 02332-5027, 781-934-9570, Fax 781-934-9570,duxroth@verizon.net

Ash Lad Press, PO Box 294, East Orleans, MA 02643, 508-255-2301 phone/Fax

Adastra Press, 16 Reservation Road, Easthampton, MA 01027-1227, gmetras@rcn.com

Perugia Press, PO Box 60364, Florence, MA 01062-0364, info@perugiapress.com, www.perugiapress.com

Quale Press, 93 Main Street, Florence, MA 01062, 413-587-0776 phone/Fax, central@quale.com

THE ART HORSE, 2 Mason Street, Gloucester, MA 01930-5902, http://kathywer.homepage.com/index.html

Atlantic Path Publishing, PO Box 1556, Gloucester, MA 01931-1556, 978-283-1531, Fax 866-640-1412, contactus@atlantic-pathpublishing.com, www.atlanticpathpublishing.com

THE NOISE, 74 Jamaica Street, Jamaica Plain, MA 02130, 617-524-4735, tmax@thenoise-boston.com

PORTRAIT, 11 Robeson St., Jamaica Plain, MA 02130

THE LONG STORY, 18 Eaton Street, Lawrence, MA 01843, 978-686-7638, rpburnham@mac.com, http://homepage.mac.com/rpburnham/longstory.html

Enlighten Next, PO Box 2360, Lenox, MA 01240-5182, 413-637-6000, Fax 415-637-6015, info@enlightennext.org

WHAT IS ENLIGHTENMENT?, PO Box 2360, Lenox, MA 01240-5360, 413-637-6000, Fax 413-637-6015, wie@wie.org

WIN NEWS, 187 Grant Street, Lexington, MA 02173, 781-862-9431, Fax 781-862-1734

Loom Press, Box 1394, Lowell, MA 01853

Blanket Fort Publishing, 117 Lakeview Avenue, Lynn, MA 01904, 781-632-1824

Magnolia Publishing, PO Box 5537, Magnolia, MA 01930

Micah Publications Inc., 255 Humphrey Street, Marblehead, MA 01945, 617-631-7601

Princess Tides Publishing LLC, 3 Gerry Street, Marblehead, MA 01945-3029, www.princesstides.com

Bliss Publishing Company, Inc., PO Box 920, Marlboro, MA 01752

IDM Press, 51 Mystic St, Medford, MA 02155-3643, 781.391.2361

MYSTERIES MAGAZINE, 13 Appleton Road, Nantucket, MA 02554-2705

Phantom Press Publications, 13 Appleton Road, Nantucket, MA 02554-2705

Coastal 181, 29 Water Street, Newburyport, MA 01950, 978-462-2436, 978 462-9198 (fax), 877-907-8181, www.coastal181.com

Focus Publishing/R. Pullins Co., PO Box 369, Newburyport, MA 01950, 800-848-7236, Fax 978-462-9035, pullins@pullins.com, www.pullins.com

Peanut Butter and Jelly Press, LLC, PO Box 239, Newton, MA 02459-0002, 617-630-0945 phone/fax, www.publishing-game.com

Heartsome Publishing, PO Box 129, Norfolk, MA 02056

New England Cartographics, Inc., PO Box 9369, North Amherst, MA 01059-9369, 413-549-4124, toll free 888-995-6277, Fax 413-549-3621, email: geolopes@crocker.com URL: www.necartographics.com

AT-HOME DAD, 61 Brightwood Avenue, North Andover, MA 01845, athomedad@aol.com, www.athomedad.com

Saber Press, 268 Main Street, PMB 138, North Reading, MA 01864, Tel. 978-749-3731, Fax 978-475-5420, Email: admin@sabergroup.com, Website: www.saber-press.com

BUST DOWN THE DOOR AND EAT ALL THE CHICKENS: A Journal of Absurd and Surreal Fiction, 57 Cherry Street, Northampton, MA 01060, (413) 320-4173/ http://www.absurdistjournal.com

Interlink Publishing Group, Inc., 46 Crosby Street, Northampton, MA 01060, 413 582 7054 tel, 413 582 7057 fax, www.interlinkbooks.com, info@interlinkbooks.com

MEAT FOR TEA: THE NORTHAMPTON REVIEW, 23 Orchard Street, Northampton, MA 01060, 413-585-5795, 323-547-4101

Summerset Press, 20 Langworthy Road, Northampton, MA 01060, 413-586-3394 phone/FAX, BrooksRoba@aol.com

Swamp Press, 15 Warwick Avenue, Northfield, MA 01360-1105

TIGHTROPE, 15 Warwick Avenue, Northfield, MA 01360

Annedawn Publishing, PO Box 247, Norton, MA 02766-0247, 508-222-9069

The Larcom Press, PO Box 161, Prides Crossing, MA 01965, 978-927-8707, Fax 978-927-8904, amp@larcompress.com, www.larcompress.com

LARCOM REVIEW, PO Box 161, Prides Crossing, MA 01965, 978-927-8707, Fax 978-927-8904, amp@larcompress.com, www.larcompress.com

OUTLANDER, PO Box 1546, Provincetown, MA 02657

PROVINCETOWN ARTS, 650 Commercial Street, Provincetown, MA 02657, 508-487-3167, web: www.provincetownarts.com

Provincetown Arts Press, PO Box 35, 650 Commercial Street, Provincetown, MA 02657, 508-487-3167; FAX 508-487-8634

Sligo Press, 4 Willow Drive, Apt. 2, Provincetown, MA 02657-1638, 508-487-5113, Fax 508-487-5113, dplennon@comcast.net

Walter H. Baker Company (Baker's Plays), PO Box 699222, Quincy, MA 02269-9222, 617-745-0805, Fax 617-745-9891, www.bakersplays.com

NIGHT TRAIN, 212 Bellingham Ave., #2, Revere, MA 02151-4106, rustybarnes@nighttrainmagazine.com, www.nighttrainmagazine.com

Mad River Press, State Road, Richmond, MA 01254, 413-698-3184

YMAA Publication Center, 4354 Washington Street, Roslindale, MA 02131, 617-323-7215, Fax 617-323-7417, ymaa@aol.com, www.ymaa.com

SOUNDINGS EAST, English Dept., Salem State College, Salem, MA 01970, 978-542-6205

Little Pear Press, PO Box 343, Seekonk, MA 02771, Martha@LittlePearPress.com, www.LittlePearPress.com

HAPPENINGNOW!EVERYWHERE, P.O. Box 45204, Somerville, MA 02145, happeningmagazine@yahoo.com, www.happeningnoweverywhere.com

IBBETSON ST. PRESS, 25 School Street, Somerville, MA 02143, dougholder@post.harvard.edu

Ibbetson St. Press, 25 School Street, Somerville, MA 02143-1721, dougholder@post.harvard.edu

sunnyoutside, P.O. Box 441429, Somerville, MA 02144, www.sunnyoutside.com

V52 Press, 52 Mt. Vernon Street, #3, Somerville, MA 02145-3401

Wisdom Publications, Inc., 199 Elm Street, Somerville, MA 02144-3129, 617-776-7416; Fax 617-776-7841

Harvest Shadows Publications, PO Box 378, Southborough, MA 01772-0378, Prefer contact by email. dbharvest@harvestshadows.com, www.harvestshadows.com

Anthony Publishing Company, Inc., 206 Gleasondale Road, Stow, MA 01775-1356, 978-897-7191

Water Row Press, PO Box 438, Sudbury, MA 01776

WATER ROW REVIEW, PO Box 438, Sudbury, MA 01776

Agityne Corp, PO Box 690, Upton, MA 01568, 508-529-4135, www.agityne.com/

Pegasus Communications, Inc., 1 Moody Street, Waltham, MA 02453-5339

EASTGATE QUARTERLY REVIEW OF HYPERTEXT, 134 Main Street, Watertown, MA 02472, 617-924-9044, info@eastgate.com, www.eastgate.com

Eastgate Systems, Inc., 134 Main Street, Watertown, MA 02472, 617-924-9044, info@eastgate.com, www.eastgate.com

Branden Books, PO Box 812094, Wellesley, MA 02482, 781-235-3634, Fax 781-790-1056, branden@brandenbooks.com, www.brandenbooks.com

KLIATT, 33 Bay State Road, Wellesley, MA 02481, 781-237-7577 phone/fax, kliatt@aol.com

Leapfrog Press, PO Box 1495, Wellfleet, MA 02667-1495, 508-349-1925, fax 508-349-1180, email books@leapfrogpress.com, www.leapfrogpress.com

The B & R Samizdat Express, 33 Gould Street, West Roxbury, MA 02132, 617-469-2269, seltzer@samizdat.com, main content site http://www.samizdat.com online store http://store.yahoo.com/samizdat

Cervena Barva Press, P. O. Box 440357, West Somerville, MA 02144-3222, editor@cervenabarvapress.com, http://www.cervenabarvapress.com

PINE ISLAND JOURNAL OF NEW ENGLAND POETRY, PO Box 317, West Springfield, MA 01090

BUTTON, PO Box 77, Westminster, MA 01473, sally@moonsigns.net, www.moonsigns.net

One Less Press, 6 Village Hill Road, Williamsburg, MA 01096-9706, (413) 586-7921, onelessartontherange@yahoo.com, onelessmag.blogspot.com

ONE LESS: Art on the Range, 6 Village Hill Road, Williamsburg, MA 01096-9706, 413-268-7370, onelessartontherange@yahoo.com, onelessmag.blogspot.com

New Voices Publishing, PO Box 560, Wilmington, MA 01887, 978-658-2131, Fax 978-988-8833, rschiano@kidsterrain.com, www.kidsterrain.com

DINER a journal of poetry, P.O. Box 60676, Greendale Station, Worcester, MA 01606, 508-853-4143, www.spokenword.to/diner

Metacom Press, 1 Tahanto Road, Worcester, MA 01602-2523, 508-757-1683

THE WORCESTER REVIEW, 1 Ekman St., Worcester, MA 01607-1513, 603-924-7342, 978-797-4770

MICHIGAN

aatec publications, PO Box 7119, Ann Arbor, MI 48107, 800-995-1470, Fax 734-995-1471, e-mail aatecpub@mindspring.com
Affable Neighbor Press, 110 Felch St., Ann Arbor, MI 48103-3330
Axiom Information Resources, PO Box 8015, Ann Arbor, MI 48107, 734-761-4824
BRIDGES: A Journal for Jewish Feminists and Our Friends, PO Box 1206, Ann Arbor, MI 48106-1206, 888-359-9188, E-mail clare@bridgesjournal.org
Center for Japanese Studies, 105 S. State St. #1085, Ann Arbor, MI 48109-1285, 734-647-8885, Fax 734-647-8886
Department of Romance Languages, University of Michigan, 4108 MLB, Ann Arbor, MI 48109-1275, 734-764-5344; fax 734-764-8163; e-mail kojo@umich.edu
THE EDUCATION DIGEST, PO Box 8623, Ann Arbor, MI 48107, 734-975-2800 ext. 207, Fax 734-975-2787, kschroeder@eddigest.com
HOBART, PO Box 1658, Ann Arbor, MI 48103, info@hobartpulp.com, submit@hobartpulp.com, http://www.hobartpulp.com
MICHIGAN FEMINIST STUDIES, 1122 Lane Hall, Univ. of Michigan, 204 South State Street, Ann Arbor, MI 48109-1290, 734-761-4386, Fax 734-647-4943, e-mail mfseditors@umich.edu
MICHIGAN QUARTERLY REVIEW, 3574 Rackham, University of Michigan, 915 E. Washington St., Ann Arbor, MI 48109-1070, 734-764-9265
Moondance Press, 4830 Dawson Drive, Ann Arbor, MI 48103, 734-426-1641, maser@mac.com, http://www.blessingway.net
The Olivia and Hill Press, Inc., PO Box 7396, Ann Arbor, MI 48107, 734-663-0235 (voice), Fax 734-663-6590, theOHPress@aol.com, www.oliviahill.com
ORCHID: A Literary Review, P.O. BOX 131457, Ann Arbor, MI 48113-1457
Palladium Communications, 320 South Main Street, PO Box 8403, Ann Arbor, MI 48107-8403, 734-668-4646; FAX 734-663-9361
Pebble Press, Inc., 1610 Longshore Drive, Ann Arbor, MI 48105
Pierian Press, PO Box 1808, Ann Arbor, MI 48106, 734-434-5530, Fax 734-434-5582
Prakken Publications, PO Box 8623, Ann Arbor, MI 48107-8623, 734-975-2800, Fax 734-975-2787, publisher@techdirections.com
R-Squared Press, 1325 Orkney Drive, Ann Arbor, MI 48103-2966, 313-930-6564 phone/Fax
TECH DIRECTIONS, PO Box 8623, Ann Arbor, MI 48107, 734-975-2800 ext. 206, Fax 734-975-2787, susanne@techdirections.com
University of Michigan Press, 839 Greene Street, Ann Arbor, MI 48104-3209, Phone 734-764-4388, Fax 734-615-1540, http://www.press.umich.edu/
WHITE CROW, PO Box 4501, Ann Arbor, MI 48106
AMERICAN HARMONICA, 104 Highland Avenue, Battle Creek, MI 49015
Mayapple Press, 408 N. Lincoln St., Bay City, MI 48708, 989-892-1429 (voice/fax), jbkerman@mayapplepress.com, www.mayapplepress.com
NewPages, PO Box 1580, Bay City, MI 48706
NEWPAGES: Alternatives in Print & Media, PO Box 1580, Bay City, MI 48706, 989-671-0081, www.newpages.com
Gazelle Publications, 11560 Red Bud Trail, Berrien Springs, MI 49103, 269-471-4717, info@gazellepublications.com, www.gazellepublications.com
LIGHTWORKS MAGAZINE, PO Box 1202, Birmingham, MI 48012-1202, 248-626-8026, lightworks_mag@hotmail.com
THE CLIFFS "sounding", P.O. Box 7, 220 Sixth Street, Calumet, MI 49913, 906-337-5970
The Vertin Press, P.O. Box 7, 220 Sixth Street, Calumet, MI 49913, 906-337-5970
Christian Traditions Publishing, 7728 Springborn Road, Casco, MI 48064-3910, 810-765-4805; searcher@in-gen.net
Gravity Presses (Lest We All Float Away), Inc., 27030 Havelock, Dearborn Heights, MI 48127, 313-563-4683, e-mail mikeb5000@yahoo.com
NOW HERE NOWHERE, 27030 Havelock, Dearborn Heights, MI 48127, 313-563-4683, e-mail kingston@gravitypresses.com
ABSINTHE: New European Writing, P.O. Box 11445, Detroit, MI 48211-1445, www.absinthenew.com, dhayes@absinthenew.com
Lotus Press, Inc., PO Box 21607, Detroit, MI 48221, 313-861-1280, fax 313-861-4740, lotuspress@aol.com
MOTORBOOTY MAGAZINE, PO Box 02007, Detroit, MI 48202
STRUGGLE: A Magazine of Proletarian Revolutionary Literature, PO Box 13261, Detroit, MI 48213-0261
THE CENTENNIAL REVIEW, 312 Linton Hall, Mich. State Univ., E. Lansing, MI 48824-1044, 517-355-1905
Red Cedar Press, 17C Morrill Hall, Michigan State University, E. Lansing, MI 48824, 517-355-9656, rcreview@msu.edu
RED CEDAR REVIEW, 17C Morrill Hall, English Dept., Michigan State Univ., E. Lansing, MI 48824, 517-355-9656, rcreview@msu.edu
Years Press, Dept. of ATL, EBH, Michigan State University, E. Lansing, MI 48824-1033
FOURTH GENRE: EXPLORATIONS IN NONFICTION, Dept. of Writing, Rhetoric, & American Cultures, 229 Bessey, Michigan State University, East Lansing, MI 48824, 517-432-2556; fax 517-353-5250; e-mail fourthgenre@cal.msu.edu
Grand River Press, PO Box 1342, East Lansing, MI 48826, 517-332-8181
HYPATIA: A Journal of Feminist Philosophy, 503 South Kedzie Hall, Michigan State University, East Lansing, MI 48824
Michigan State University Press, 1405 S. Harrison Road, #25, East Lansing, MI 48823-5202, 517-355-9543; fax 517-432-2611; E-mail msp07@msu.edu
FIFTH ESTATE, PO Box 201016, Ferndale, MI 48220-9016
JAM RAG, Box 20076, Ferndale, MI 48220-0076, 248-336-9243
BlackBerry Literary Services, 2956 Mackin Road, Flint, MI 48504, 810-234-0899, fax: 810-234-8593, toll-free:1-877-266-5705, web:www.bblit.bravehost.com, email:bblit@bravehost.com
Platinum Dreams Publishing, P.O. Box 320693, Flint, MI 48532, jkash@platinumdreamspublishing.com, (810)720-3390, www.platinumdreamspublishing.com
Blue Mouse Studio, 26829 37th Street, Gobles, MI 49055, 616-628-5160; fax 616-628-4970
THE BANNER, 2850 Kalamazoo SE, Grand Rapids, MI 49560, 616-224-0819
CRC Publications, 2850 Kalamazoo SE, Grand Rapids, MI 49560
Wm.B. Eerdmans Publishing Co., 255 Jefferson Avenue, S.E., Grand Rapids, MI 49503, 616-459-4591
Pen-Dec Press, 2526 Chatham Woods, Grand Rapids, MI 49546
RAINBOWS WITH RED REMOVED, 2526 Chatham Woods, Grand Rapids, MI 49546
THE RAM'S CHIN'S GOATEE, 2526 Chatham Woods, Grand Rapids, MI 49546
SHEAR-CROPPER SALON (FOR THE HAIR-BRAINED), 2526 Chatham Woods, Grand Rapids, MI 49546
BIG SCREAM, 2782 Dixie S.W., Grandville, MI 49418, 616-531-1442

Nada Press, 2782 Dixie S.W., Grandville, MI 49418, 616-531-1442
Dream Publishing Co., 1304 Devonshire, Grosse Pointe Park, MI 48230, 313-882-6603, Fax 313-882-8280
Avery Color Studios, 511 D Avenue, Gwinn, MI 49841, 800-722-9925
W.W. Publications, PO Box 373, Highland, MI 48357-0373, 727-585-0985 phone/Fax
Kelton Press, PO Box 4236, Jackson, MI 49204, 517-788-8542; 888-453-5880
Flowerfield Enterprises, LLC, 10332 Shaver Road, Kalamazoo, MI 49024, 269-327-0108, www.wormwoman.com
LITERALLY HORSES/REMUDA, 208 Cherry Hill Street, Kalamazoo, MI 49006-4221, 616-345-5915, literally-horses@aol.com
New Issues Poetry & Prose, Western Michigan University, 1903 W. Michigan Avenue, Kalamazoo, MI 49008-5331, 269-387-8185, Fax 269-387-2562, new-issues@wmich.edu, www.wmich.edu/newissues
Rarach Press, 1005 Oakland Drive, Kalamazoo, MI 49008
THIRD COAST, Department of English, Western Michigan University, Kalamazoo, MI 49008-5331, 269-387-2675, Fax 269-387-2562, www.wmich.edu/thirdcoast
National Woodlands Publishing Company, 8846 Green Briar Road, Lake Ann, MI 49650-9532, 231-275-6735, phone/Fax, nwoodpc@chartermi.net
Black Pearl Enterprises LLC, PO Box 14304, Lansing, MI 48901, 517-204-4197, 18884829797, 5174829522, www.divineblackpearls.com
Medi-Ed Press, 523 Hunter Boulevard, Lansing, MI 48910, 800-500-8205, fax 517-882-0554. Medi.EdPress@verizon.net; www.Medi-EdPress.com.
THE MACGUFFIN, Schoolcraft College, 18600 Haggerty Road, Livonia, MI 48152, (734) 462-4400 Ext. 5327, Fax: (734) 462-4679, Email: macguffin@schoolcraft.edu, Website: www.macguffin.org
Wilderness Adventure Books, Po Box 856, Manchester, MI 48158-0856, www.wildernessbooks.org
PASSAGES NORTH, English Dept., N. Michigan Univ., 1401 Presque Isle Avenue, Marquette, MI 49855, 906-227-1203, Fax 906-227-1096, passages@nmu.edu, http://myweb.nmu.edu/~passages
AMERICAN ROAD, PO Box 46519, Mont Clemens, MI 48046, Orders 1-877-285-5434. General information 425-774-6135, fax 586-468-7483, sales@mockturtlepress.com, www.mockturtlepress.com, General Manager Becky Repp 206-369-5782.
Mock Turtle Press, PO Box 46519, Mount Clemens, MI 48046, Orders 1-877-285-5434. General information 586-468-7299, fax 586-468-7483, sales@mockturtlepress.com, www.mockturtlepress.com
Sun Dog Press, 22058 Cumberland Drive, Northville, MI 48167, 248-449-7448, Fax 248-449-4070, sundogpr@voyager.net
Mehring Books, Inc., PO Box 48377, Oak Park, MI 48237-5977, 248-967-2924, 248-967-3023, sales@mehring.com
Zookeeper Publications, 2010 Cimarron Drive, Okemos, MI 48864-3908, 517-347-4697
PageFree Publishing, Inc., 109 South Farmer Street, Otsego, MI 49078, 269-692-3926
PRESA, PO Box 792, Rockford, MI 49341, presapress@aol.com
Presa Press, PO Box 792, Rockford, MI 49341, presapress@aol.com
CONTROLLED BURN, KCC, 10775 N. St. Helen Road, Roscommon, MI 48653, 989-275-5000, Fax 989-275-8745, crockerd@kirtland.edu
Ridgeway Press of Michigan, PO Box 120, Roseville, MI 48066, 313-577-7713, Fax to M.L. Liebler 586-296-3303, E-mail mlliebler@aol.com
ALARM CLOCK, PO Box 1551, Royal Oak, MI 48068, 248-442-8634
DEAD FUN, PO Box 752, Royal Oak, MI 48068-0752
PARADIDOMI, PO Box 5648, Saginaw, MI 48603-0648, 989-529-5283; alewis@mayapplepress.com; www.mayapple-press.com
INKY TRAIL NEWS, 50416 Schoenharr #111, Shelby Twp., MI 48315, e-mail inkytrails@comcast.net
LOGIC LETTER, 13957 Hall Road, #185, Shelby Twp., MI 48315
Gearhead Press, Attn: Bruce Rizzon, 53 Nash Street, Sparta, MI 49345-1217
Innisfree Press, 908 Wolcott Ave., St. Joseph, MI 49085-1717, 215-518-6688, Fax 215 247-2343, InnisfreeP@aol.com
Arbutus Press, 2364 Pinehurst Trail, Traverse City, MI 49686, phone 231-946-7240, FAX 231-946-4196, editor@arbutus-press.com, www.Arbutuspress
Book Marketing Solutions, 10300 E. Leelanau Court, Traverse City, MI 49684, p. 231-939-1999, f. 231-929-1993, info@bookmarketingsolutions.com
Eighth Sea Books, PO Box 1925, Traverse City, MI 49685-1925, 231-946-0678, info@8thSeaBooks.com, www.8thSea-Books.com
INDEPENDENT PUBLISHER ONLINE, 1129 Woodmere Ave., Ste. B, Traverse City, MI 49686, 231-933-0445, Fax 231-933-0448, jimb@bookpublisher.com, www.independentpublisher.com
Perrin Press, 1700 W Big Beaver Rd Ste 315, Troy, MI 48084, 248.649.8071, fax 248.649.8087, www.perrinpress.com
Ladyslipper Press, 15075 County Line Road, Tustin, MI 49688, 231-775-9455, www.ladyslipperpress.com
AFFABLE NEIGHBOR, 43 Margaret Street, Whitmore Lake, MI 48189-9502
OUT YOUR BACKDOOR: The Magazine of Do-It-Yourself Adventure and Homegrown Culture, 4686 Meridian Road, Williamston, MI 48895, 517-347-1689; jeff@outyourbackdoor.com; outyourbackdoor.com
JOURNAL OF NARRATIVE THEORY, Eastern Michigan University, 614J Pray-Harrold Hall, Eng. Dept., Ypsilanti, MI 48197, 734-487-3175, Fax 734-483-9744, website www.emich.edu/public/english/JNT/JNT.html
TWINSWORLD, PO Box 980481, Ypsilanti, MI 48198-0481, twinworld1@aol.com

MINNESOTA

Focus Publications, Inc., PO Box 609, Bemidji, MN 56601, 218-751-2183; focus@paulbunyan.net
Loonfeather Press, P.O. Box 1212, Bemidji, MN 56619, 218-444-4869 www.loonfeatherpress.com
Truly Fine Press, PO Box 891, Bemidji, MN 56619
Little Leaf Press, 5902 Hummingbird Road, Braham, MN 55006-2742, 304-638-0173, Fax 304-523-7212, littleleaf@max-minn.com, www.littleleafpress.com
Knife in the Toaster Publishing Company, LLC, PO Box 399, Cedar, MN 55011-0399, 763-434-2422, Fax 763-413-1181, ericmjs@aol.com
BTW Press, LLC, PO Box 554, Chanhassen, MN 55317, 1-866-818-8029, www.btwpress.com
Silk Pages Publishing, PO Box 385, Deerwood, MN 56444, Fax 218-534-3949
Holy Cow! Press, PO Box 3170, Mount Royal Station, Duluth, MN 55803, 218-724-1653 phone/Fax
LAKE SUPERIOR MAGAZINE, Lake Superior Port Cities Inc., P.O. Box 16417, Duluth, MN 55816-0417, 218-722-5002, fax 218-722-4096, www.lakesuperior.com, e-mail: edit@lakesuperior.com.
Lake Superior Port Cities Inc., P.O. Box 16417, Duluth, MN 55816-0417, 888-244-5253, 218-722-5002, FAX 218-722-4096, www.lakesuperior.com, reader@lakesuperior.com.

Trellis Publishing, Inc., PO Box 16141-D, Duluth, MN 55816

Whole Person Associates Inc., 210 West Michigan Street, Duluth, MN 55802-1908, 218-727-0500, Fax 218-727-0505

Beaver's Pond Press, Inc., 7104 Ohms Lane, Suite 216, Edina, MN 55439-2129, 952-829-8818, email: BeaversPondPress@integra.net, www.beaverspondpress.com

St. John's Publishing, Inc., 6824 Oaklawn Avenue, Edina, MN 55435, 952-920-9044

Verona Publishing, PO Box 24071, Edina, MN 55424, 612-991-5467 www.veronapublishing.com

THE LIBERATOR, 17854 Lyons Street, Forest Lake, MN 55025, 651-464-7663, Fax 651-464-7135, E-mail rdoyle@mensdefense.org

The Place In The Woods, 3900 Glenwood Avenue, Golden Valley, MN 55422-5302, Tel: 763-374-2120

READ, AMERICA!, 3900 Glenwood Avenue, Golden Valley, MN 55422

Ellis Press, PO Box 6, Granite Falls, MN 56241, Fax 507-537-6815

Plains Press, PO Box 6, Granite Falls, MN 56241, 507-537-6463

Spoon River Poetry Press, PO Box 6, Granite Falls, MN 56241

NEW UNIONIST, 1301 Cambridge St., Ste. 102, Hopkins, MN 55343-1925, 651-646-5546, nup@minn.net

Anacus Press, An Imprint of Finney Company, 8075 215th Street West, Lakeville, MN 55044, (952) 469-6699, Fax: (952) 469-1968, (800) 326-9272, Fax: (800) 330-6232 feedback@finney-hobar.com, www.anacus.com

Ecopress, An Imprint of Finney Company, 8075 215th Street West, Lakeville, MN 55044, Phone: 952-469-6699 or (800) 846-7027, Fax: 952-469-1968 or (800) 330-6232, ecopress@peak.org, www.ecopress.com

Finney Company, Inc., 8075 215th Street West, Lakeville, MN 55044, (952) 469-6699, Fax: (952) 469-1968, (800)846-7027, Fax: (800) 330-6232, feedback@finney-hobar.com, www.finney-hobar.com

Galde Press, Inc., PO Box 460, Lakeville, MN 55044, telephone: 952-891-5991, email: phyllis@galdepress.com web: www.galdepress.com

Hobar Publications, A Division of Finney Company, 8075 215th Street West, Lakeville, MN 55044, (952) 469-6699, Fax:(952) 469-1968, (800)846-7027, Fax: (800) 330-6232, feedback@finney-hobar.com, www.finney-hobar.com

Windward Publishing, An Imprint of Finney Company, 8075 215th Street West, Lakeville, MN 55044, (952) 469-6699, Fax: (952) 469-1968, (800) 846-7027, Fax: (800) 330-6232, feedback@finney-hobar.com, www.finney-hobar.com

The Creative Company, PO Box 227, Mankato, MN 56002

WOODWORKER'S JOURNAL, 4365 Willow Drive, Medina, MN 55340, 763-478-8306, Fax 763-478-8396, editor@woodworkersjournal.com

Blue Raven Press, 219 S.E. Main St., Suite 506, Minneapolis, MN 55414, 612-331-8039, 612-331-8115, www.blueravenpress.com

Coffee House Press, 27 N. 4th Street, Minneapolis, MN 55401, 612-338-0125, Fax 612-338-4004, fish@coffeehousepress.org, www.coffeehousepress.org

CONDUIT, 510 Eighth Avenue NE, Minneapolis, MN 55413, www.conduit.org, info@conduit.org

Contemax Publishers, 17815 24th Ave N., Suite 100, Minneapolis, MN 55447

Eckankar, Attn: John Kulick, PO Box 27300, Minneapolis, MN 55427-0300, 952-380-2300, Fax 952-380-2395

INDUSTRY MINNE-ZINE, 12 Vincent Avenue South, Minneapolis, MN 55405, 612.308.2467

JOURNAL OF BRITISH STUDIES, University of Minnesota, Dept. of History, 614 Soc Sci Tower, 267 19th Ave., S., Minneapolis, MN 55445, http://www.journals.uchicago.edu/JBS/home.html

KARAWANE, 402 S. Cedar Lake Road, Minneapolis, MN 55405, 612-381-1229, karawane@prodigy.net, www.karawane.org, www.karawane.homestead.com

Kar-Ben Publishing, Inc., c/o Lerner Publishing Group, 241 First Avenue North, Minneapolis, MN 55401, 800-4KARBEN (in USA)

LIFTOUTS, 520 5th Street SE #4, Minneapolis, MN 55414-1628, (612) 321-9044 barcass@mr.net

LUNA, Dept. of English, Univ. of Minnesota, 207 Lind Hall, 207 Church St., Minneapolis, MN 55455

METROPOLITAN FORUM, PO Box 582165, Minneapolis, MN 55458, 612-328-4177, info@metropolitanforum.com, www.metropolitanforum.com

Mid-List Press, 4324 12th Avenue South, Minneapolis, MN 55407-3218, 612-822-3733, Fax 612-823-8387, guide@midlist.org, www.midlist.org

Milkweed Editions, 1011 Washington Ave. S., Ste. 300, Minneapolis, MN 55415, 612-332-3192, Fax 612-215-2550, www.milkweed.org

MINNESOTA LITERATURE, 3723 Glendal Terrace, Minneapolis, MN 55410-1340, mnlit@aol.com

MIP Company, PO Box 27484, Minneapolis, MN 55427, 763-544-5915, Fax 612-871-5733, mp@mipco.com, www.mipco.com

North Stone Editions, PO Box 14098, Minneapolis, MN 55414

THE NORTH STONE REVIEW, PO Box 14098, Minneapolis, MN 55414

PAJ NTAUB VOICE, Hmong American Institute for Learning (HAIL), 2654 Logan Avenue North, Minneapolis, MN 55411, Phone (651) 214-0955, Fax (612) 588-1534, mainengmoua@mn.rr.com

PARNASSUS LITERARY JOURNAL, Kudzu Press, 433 South 7th St., Suite 1508, Minneapolis, MN 55415

Preludium Publishers, 520 5th Street SE #4, Minneapolis, MN 55414-1628, 612-321-9044, Fax 612-305-0655, barcass@mr.net

Pro musica press, 2501 Pleasant Ave, Minneapolis, MN 55404-4123

RAIN TAXI REVIEW OF BOOKS, PO Box 3840, Minneapolis, MN 55403, 612-825-1528 tel/Fax, info@raintaxi.com, www.raintaxi.com

Search Institute, 615 First Ave. NE, Ste. 125, Minneapolis, MN 55413-2254, 612-692-5527 direct phone, 612-692-5553 fax, 877-240-7251 toll free orders

SPEAKEASY, 1011 Washington Avenue South, Ste 200, Minneapolis, MN 55415, 612-215-2575, speakeasy@loft.org, www.speakeasymagazine.org

SPOUT, PO BOX 581067, Minneapolis, MN 55458-1067, http://www.spoutpress.com

Spout Press, PO Box 581067, Minneapolis, MN 55458-1067

UTNE READER, 1624 Harmon Place #330, Minneapolis, MN 55403, 612-338-5040, www.utne.com

XCP: CROSS-CULTURAL POETICS, College of St. Catherine, 601 25th Avenue South, Minneapolis, MN 55454, website http://bfn.org/~xcp

ASCENT, Department of English, Concordia College, Moorhead, MN 56562, E-mail Ascent@cord.edu

New Rivers Press, Inc., c/o MSUM, 1104 7th Avenue South, Moorhead, MN 56563-0178, contact@newriverspress.org, www.newriverspress.org

MeteoritePress.com, 1730 New Brighton Blvd. #104-271, NE Minneapolis, MN 55413, meteoritepress@aol.com, www.meteoritepress.com

WRITERS' JOURNAL, PO Box 394, Perham, MN 56573-0394, Phone 218-346-7921, Fax 218-346-7924, E-mail writersjournal@writersjournal.com, Web site www.writersjournal.com

KUMQUAT MERINGUE, PO Box 736, Pine Island, MN 55963-0736, Telephone 507-367-4430, moodyriver@aol.com, www.kumquatcastle.com
GREAT RIVER REVIEW, PO Box 406, Red Wing, MN 55066, 651-388-2009, info@andersoncenter.org, www.anderson-center.org
Blue Sky Marketing Inc., PO Box 21583, Saint Paul, MN 55121-0583, 651-687-9835
THE FIREFLY (A Tiny Glow In a Forest of Darkness), 211 7th Street East #503, Saint Paul, MN 55101-2390
Pangaea, 226 South Wheeler Street, Saint Paul, MN 55105-1927, 651-690-3320 tel/fax, info@pangaea.org, http://pangaea.org
WATER~STONE REVIEW, MS-A1730, 1536 Hewitt Avenue, Saint Paul, MN 55104-1284, water-stone@gw.hamline.edu
STUDIO ONE, College of St. Benedict, Haehn Campus Center, St. Joseph, MN 56374
Ally Press, 524 Orleans St., St. Paul, MN 55107, 651-291-2652, pferoe@comcast.net
Brighton Publications, Inc., PO Box 120706, St. Paul, MN 55112-0706, 651-636-2220
Fieldstone Alliance, 60 Plato Boulevard East, Suite 150, St. Paul, MN 55107, 800-274-6024, Fax 651-556-4517, books@fieldstonealliance.org, www.fieldstonealliance.org
Graywolf Press, 2402 University Avenue #203, St. Paul, MN 55114, 651-641-0077, 651-641-0036
HEELTAP/Pariah Press, c/o Richard D. Houff, 604 Hawthorne Ave. East, St. Paul, MN 55101-3531
HIMALAYAN PATH, 1317 Summit Ave., St. Paul, MN 55105, 651-645-6808,fax 651-645-7935,yes@yespublishers.com, www.yespublishers.com
Midwest Villages & Voices, PO Box 40214, St. Paul, MN 55104, 612-822-6878 or e-mail: midwestvillages@yahoo.com (e-mail preferred)
Minnesota Historical Society Press, 345 Kellogg Blvd. West, St. Paul, MN 55102-1906, 651-297-2221
MINNESOTA HISTORY, Minnesota Historical Society Press, 345 Kellogg Blvd., St. Paul, MN 55102, 1651-297-2221
Paragon House Publishers, 1925 Oakcrest Avenue, Suite 7, St. Paul, MN 55113-2619, Tel: (651) 644-3087, Fax: (651) 644-0997, www.paragonhouse.com
Pariah Press, 604 Hawthorne Avenue East, St. Paul, MN 55101-3531
Pogo Press, Incorporated, 4 Cardinal Lane, St. Paul, MN 55127, 651-483-4692, fax 651-483-4692, E-mail pogopres@minn.net
Rada Press, Inc., 1277 Fairmount Avenue, St. Paul, MN 55105-7052, phone: 651-554-7645; fax: 651-455-6975
Riverstone Publishing, PO Box 270852, St. Paul, MN 55127, 651-762-1323, Fax 651-204-0063, contact@americanyouth.net, www.AmericanYouth.net
Stellaberry Press, P.O. Box 18217, St. Paul, MN 55118, http://www.stellaberry.com
Top 20 Press, 1873 Standord Avenue, St. Paul, MN 55105, 651-690-5758
Yes International Publishers, 1317 Summit Avenue, St. Paul, MN 55105, 651-645-6808, Fax 651-645-7935, yes@yespublishers.com, www.yespublishers.com
ST. CROIX REVIEW, Box 244, Stillwater, MN 55082, 651-439-7190, Fax 651-439-7017
MOTHERVERSE: A Journal of Contemporary Motherhood, 2663 Hwy 3, Two Harbors, MN 55616, website www.motherverse.com, email editor@motherverse.com, submissions email submissions@motherverse.com, ordering email order@motherverse.com, advertising email ads@motherverse.com
J-Press Publishing, 4796 126th St. N., White Bear Lake, MN 55110, 651-429-1819, 651-429-1819 fax, 888-407-1723, sjackson@jpresspublishing.com, http://www.jpresspublishing.com
MAIN CHANNEL VOICES: A Dam Fine Literary Magazines, P.O. Box 492, Winona, MN 55987-0492, http://www.mainchannelvocies.com
Saint Mary's Press, 702 Terrace Heights, Winona, MN 55987, 800-533-8095, http://www.smp.org, smpress@smp.org

MISSISSIPPI

Quail Ridge Press, PO Box 123, Brandon, MS 39043, kgrissom@quailridge.com
Good News Publishing Ministries, 690 Mount Airey Church Road, Columbus, MS 39701-9712, 662-245-1376, 1-877-59-GOODNEWS, Fax 662-245-1343, dapoet1@bellsouth.net, www.dgoodnews.com
MISSISSIPPI REVIEW, 118 College Dr., #5144, Hattiesburg, MS 39406-0001, 601-266-5600, www.mississippireview.com
THE SOUTHERN QUARTERLY: A Journal of the Arts in the South, 118 College Drive #5078, The University of Southern Mississippi, Hattiesburg, MS 39406-5078, 601-266-4350, Fax 601-266-6393, www.usm.edu/soq
LIFE 101, 1739 University Avenue, Oxford, MS 38655, 662-513-0159, Fax 662-234-9266, neilwhite@elife101.com, www.nautiluspublishing.com
THE YALOBUSHA REVIEW, English Dept, Univ. of Mississippi, PO Box 1848, University, MS 38677-1848, 662-915-3175, yalobusha@olemiss.edu, www.olemiss.edu/yalobusha

MISSOURI

BIG MUDDY: Journal of the Mississippi River Valley, MS 2650, One University Plaza, Cape Girardeau, MO 63701, (573) 651-2044, fax (573)651-5188, upress@semo.edu, www6.semo.edu/universitypress
THE CAPE ROCK, English Dept, Southeast Missouri State Univ., Cape Girardeau, MO 63701, 314-651-2500
Southeast Missouri State University Press, MS 2650, One University Plaza, Cape Girardeau, MO 63701, (573) 651-2044, fax (573)651-5188, upress@semo.edu, www6.semo.edu/universitypress
Rama Publishing Co., 3598 S. Chapel Road, Carthage, MO 64836-4082, 417-358-1093
Three House Publishing, P.O. Box 6672, Chesterfield, MO 63006-6672, 314-277-4560
AFRO-HISPANIC REVIEW, Romance Languages, Univ. of Missouri, 143 Arts & Science Building, Columbia, MO 65211, 573-882-5040 or 573-882-5041
CENTER: A Journal of the Literary Arts, 202 Tate Hall, Columbia, MO 65211, 573-884-7775
Columbia Alternative Library Press, PO Box 1446, Columbia, MO 65205-1446, 573-442-4352 jmcquinn@calpress.org
THE MISSOURI REVIEW, 1507 Hillcrest Hall, University of Missouri-Columbia, Columbia, MO 65211, 573-882-4474, Fax 573-884-4671, umcastmr@missouri.edu
Shadow Poetry, 1209 Milwaukee Street, Excelsior Springs, MO 64024, Fax: (208) 977-9114, shadowpoetry@shadowpoetry.com, http://www.shadowpoetry.com
SP QUILL QUARTERLY MAGAZINE, 1209 Milwaukee Street, Excelsior Springs, MO 64024, Fax: (208) 977-9114, spquill@shadowpoetry.com, http://www.shadowpoetry.com/magazine/spquill.html
WHITE LOTUS, 1209 Milwaukee Street, Excelsior Springs, MO 64024, (208) 977-9114
Twynz Publishing, PO Box 1084, Florissant, MO 63031-1948, 314-995-1551, Fax 314-831-6214, twynzpub@aol.com, www.twynzpub.com
Timberline Press, 6281 Red Bud, Fulton, MO 65251, 573-642-5035
Rabeth Publishing Company, 3515 NE 61st St., Gladstone, MO 64119-1931, email: qurabeth@kvmo.net
OVERLAND JOURNAL, Oregon-California Trails Association, PO Box 1019, Independence, MO 64051-0519, 816-252-2276,

Fax 816-836-0989, octa@indepmo.org

Acorn Books, 7337 Terrace, Suite 200, Kansas City, MO 64114-1256, 816-523-8321, fax 816-333-3843, e-mail jami.parkison@micro.com, www.acornbks.com

ADVENTURES, 6401 The Paseo, Kansas City, MO 64131, 816-333-7000

BkMk Press, University of Missouri-Kansas City, 5101 Rockhill, University House, Kansas City, MO 64110, 816-235-2558, FAX 816-235-2611, bkmk@umkc.edu

Compact Clinicals, 7205 NW Waukomis Drive, Kansas City, MO 64151, 816-587-0044 or 800-408-8830, Fax 816-587-7198

DISC GOLF WORLD, 509 E 18th St, Kansas City, MO 64108-1508, 816-471-3472, fax 816-471-4653, email info@discgolfworld.com

Helicon Nine Editions, Box 22412, Kansas City, MO 64113, 816-753-1095, Fax 816-753-1016, helicon9@aol.com, www.heliconnine.com

IRISH FAMILY JOURNAL, Box 7575, Kansas City, MO 64116

Irish Genealogical Foundation, Box 7575, Kansas City, MO 64116, 816-454-2410, mike@irishroots.com

LIVING CHEAP NEWS, PO Box 8178, Kansas City, MO 64112, 816-523-0224, livcheap@aol.com, www.livingcheap.com

NEW LETTERS, Univ. of Missouri - Kansas City; University House, 5101 Rockhill Road, Kansas City, MO 64110, 816-235-1168, Fax 816-235-2611, www.newletters.org

THE GREEN HILLS LITERARY LANTERN, Truman State University, Division of Language and Literature, McClain Hall, Kirksville, MO 63501-4221, 660-785-4487, adavis@truman.edu, jksmith@grm.net, jbeneven@truman.edu, ll.truman.edu/ghllweb

Truman State University Press, 100 East Normal Street, Kirksville, MO 63501, 660-785-7336, Fax 660-785-4480, http://tsup.truman.edu

THE FUNNY PAPER, 615 NW Jacob Drive #206, Lees Summit, MO 64081-1215, felix22557@aol.com

Images Unlimited and Snaptail Press, a Division of Images Unlimited Publishing, PO Box 305, Maryville, MO 64468, 660-582-4279, Fax 775-871-7829, info@imagesunlimitedpub.com, www.imagesunlimitedpub.com

THE LAUREL REVIEW, Department of English, Northwest Missouri State University, Maryville, MO 64468, 816-562-1265

HandyCraft Media Productions, P.O. Box 222, Republic, MO 65738-0222, 417-234-8373

BOULEVARD, 6614 Clayton Road, PMB 325, Richmond Heights, MO 63117, 314-862-2643

Titus Home Publishing, 204 N. Main, Rogersville, MO 65742-6574, 417-753-3449

LOST GENERATION JOURNAL, Route 5 Box 134, Salem, MO 65560, 314-729-2545, Fax 314-729-2545

Heartland Publishing, PO Box 402, Seymour, MO 65746-0402, Tel. (417) 848-7946, Tel/Fax (417) 935-9146, www.goheartland.com

Sun Rising Press, 724 Felix Street, St Joseph, MO 64501, 816-676-0122

Platte Purchase Publishers, PO Box 8096, 3406 Frederick Ave., St. Joseph, MO 64508-8096, (816) 232-8471,fax.(816) 232-8482, sjm@stjosephmuseum.org

AFRICAN AMERICAN REVIEW, Saint Louis University, Humanities 317, 3800 Lindell Boulevard, St. Louis, MO 63108-3414, 314-977-3688, FAX 314-977-1514, moodyjk@slu.edu, keenanam@slu.edu, http://aar.slu.edu

EFG, Inc., 2207 South 39th Street, St. Louis, MO 63110-4019, 314-647-6788, FAX 314-647-1609

Epoch Press, 8356 Olive Boulevard, St. Louis, MO 63132-2814, Phone: 314-991-8758, Fax: 314-997-1788, Web Site: www.epoch-press.net, E-Mail: whgreen@inlink.com, keenanam@slu.edu, http://aar.slu.edu

KAJ-MAHKAH: EARTH OF EARTH, St. Louis, MO 63110, http://geocities.com/kajmahkah/

NATURAL BRIDGE, English Dept., Univ. of Missouri, One University Blvd., St. Louis, MO 63121, natural@umsl.edu, www.umsl.edu/~natural

ONE Health Publishing, LLC, PO Box 31073, St. Louis, MO 63131-1073, www.onehealthpublishing.com, publishers@onehealthpublishing.com, phone: 314-822-3774, fax: 314-821-5463

RIVER STYX, 3547 Olive St., Suite 107, St. Louis, MO 63103-1014, 314-533-4541, www.riverstyx.org

ST. LOUIS JOURNALISM REVIEW, 470 E. Lockwood Ave., WH 414, St. Louis, MO 63119, 314-968-5905

WillowTree Press LLC, PO Box 142414, St. Louis, MO 63114-0414, 314-423-3634

Gorilla Convict Publications, PO Box 492, St. Peters, MO 63376, www.gorillaconvict.com

DAILY WORD, 1901 NW Blue Parkway, Unity Village, MO 64065, 816-524-3550, fax 816-251-3553

Unity House, 1901 NW Blue Parkway, Unity Village, MO 64065, 816-524-3550, fax 816-251-3552

UNITY MAGAZINE, 1901 NW Blue Parkway, Unity Village, MO 64065-0001, 816-524-3550

2River Chapbook Series, 7474 Drexel DR, University City, MO 63130, long@2River.org

2River, 7474 Drexel Dr., University City, MO 63130, 314-721-7393, www.2River.org

THE 2RIVER VIEW, 7474 Drexel Dr., University City, MO 63130, 314-721-7393, www.2River.org, long@2River.org

SOM Publishing, division of School of Metaphysics, 163 Moon Valley Road, Windyville, MO 65783, 417-345-8411, www.som.org

THRESHOLDS JOURNAL, 163 Moon Valley Road, Windyville, MO 65783, 417-345-8411, www.som.org

MONTANA

THE AZOREAN EXPRESS, PO Box 249, Big Timber, MT 59011

THE BADGER STONE CHRONICLES, PO Box 249, Big Timber, MT 59011

BLACK JACK & VALLEY GRAPEVINE, Box 249, Big Timber, MT 59011

THE BREAD AND BUTTER CHRONICLES, PO Box 249, Big Timber, MT 59011

HILL AND HOLLER, Box 249, Big Timber, MT 59011

Seven Buffaloes Press, Box 249, Big Timber, MT 59011

Cattpigg Press, PO Box 565, Billings, MT 59103, 406-248-4875, e-mail starbase@mcn.net, website www.mcn.net/~starbase/dawn

Council For Indian Education, 1240 Burlington Avenue, Billings, MT 59102-4224, 406-248-3465 phone, 1-5 pm Mtn.time, FAX: (406)-248-1297 www.cie-mt.org., cie@cie-mt.org.

GoldenHouse Publishing Group, 290 Energy Boulevard, Billings, MT 59102-6806, 406-655-1224, groadifer@msn.com

CORONA, Dept. of Hist. & Phil., Montana State Univ., PO Box 172320, Bozeman, MT 59717-2320, 406-994-5200

Magic Circle Press, PO Box 1123, Bozeman, MT 59771

SPIRIT TALK, PO Box 390, Browning, MT 59417, 406-338-2882; E-mail blkfoot4@3rivers.net

Spirit Talk Press, PO Box 390, Browning, MT 59417-0390, 406-338-2882; E-mail: LongStandingBearChief@blackfoot.org, web: www.blackfoot.org

American & World Geographic Publishing, PO Box 5630, Helena, MT 59601, 406-443-2842

AMERICAN JUROR (formerly FIJACTIVIST, 1989-2004), PO Box 5570, Helena, MT 59604-5570, 406-442-7800

Farcountry Press, 2222 Washington Street, Helena, MT 59604, lisa.juvik@farcountrypress.com

CRONE CHRONICLES: A Journal of Conscious Aging, 319 West 3rd St., Laurel, MT 59044
Cave Books, 2870 Sol Terra Lane, Missoula, MT 59803-1803, 314-862-7646
CUTBANK, English Dept., University of Montana, Missoula, MT 59812
Mountain Press Publishing Co., PO Box 2399, Missoula, MT 59806, 406-728-1900
Pictorial Histories Pub. Co., 713 S. 3rd Street, Missoula, MT 59801, 406-549-8488, www.pictorialhistoriespublishing.com, fax 406-718-9280
ALONE TOGETHER, PO Box 2885, Norris, MT 59745, 406-685-3545, Fax 406-685-3599, at@ravenpublishing.net, toll free: 866-685-3545
Raven Publishing, Inc., P.O. Box 2866, Norris, MT 59745, 406-685-3545, 866-685-3545, fax: 406-685-3599
SUPERIOR CHRISTIAN NEWS, PO Box 424, Superior, MT 59872
Superior Christian Press, PO Box 424, Superior, MT 59872
THE BLIND MAN'S RAINBOW, PO Box 1190, Troy, MT 59935-1190, editor@theblindpress.com, www.theblindpress.com
The Blind Press, PO Box 1190, Troy, MT 59935

NEBRASKA

Night Howl Productions, PO Box 1, Clay Center, NE 68933
Morris Publishing, PO Box 2110, Kearney, NE 68848, 800-650-7888
Black Oak Press, PO Box 4663, University Place Stn., Lincoln, NE 68504, 402-467-4608
Foundation Books, PO Box 22828, Lincoln, NE 68542-2828, 402-438-7080, Fax 402-438-7099, www.foundationbooks.com
PRAIRIE SCHOONER, 201 Andrews Hall, PO Box 880334, Univ. of Nebraska, Lincoln, NE 68588-0334, 402-472-0911
RIVER TEETH: A Journal of Nonfiction Narrative, University of Nebraska Press, 1111 Lincoln Mall #400, Lincoln, NE 68588-0630, www.nebraskapress.unl.edu
University of Nebraska Press, 1111 Lincoln Mall #400, Lincoln, NE 68508-3905, 402 472 3581, 402 472 6214, 800 755 1105, pressmail@unl.edu, www.nebraskapress.unl.edu, www.bisonbooks.com
Addicus Books, Inc., PO Box 45327, Omaha, NE 68145, 402-330-7493
The Backwaters Press, 3502 North 52nd Street, Omaha, NE 68104-3506, 402-451-4052e-mail: gkosmicki@cox.net..comWebsite: www.thebackwaterspress.homestead.com
Holmes House, 530 North 72nd Avenue, Omaha, NE 68114
Lone Willow Press, PO Box 31647, Omaha, NE 68131-0647, 402-551-9=0343
THE NEBRASKA REVIEW, FA 212, University of Nebraska-Omaha, Omaha, NE 68182-0324, 402-554-3159
Zoo Press, PO Box 3528, Omaha, NE 68103, 402-770-8104, editors@zoopress.org, http://zoopress.org

NEVADA

PEGASUS, Pegasus Publishing, PO Box 61324, Boulder City, NV 89006-1324
America West Publishers, PO Box 2208, Carson City, NV 89702, 800-729-4131
Juniper Creek Publishing, Inc., P.O. Box 2205, Carson City, NV 89702, 775 849-1637 (voice), 775 849-1707 (fax), jcpi@junipercreekpubs.com, www.junipercreekpubs.com
Juniper Creek Press, 208 Glen Vista Drive, Dayton, NV 89403, 775-246-3427, junipercreekpres@aol.com
Parity Press, 1450 W. Horizon Ridge Pkwy, B304-226, Henderson, NV 89012, 877-260-8989, 702-364-8988 fax, www.paritypress.biz, www.shiftingrings.com,
White Cliffs Media, Inc., PO Box 6083, Incline Village, NV 89450
ART:MAG, PO Box 70896, Las Vegas, NV 89170, 702-734-8121
Cascada Corporation / Scherf Books, MegaGrace Books, PO Box 80180, Las Vegas, NV 89180-0180, ds@scherf.com, www.scherf.com, www.megagrace.com, www.cascada.cc
Crystal Publishers, Inc., 3460 Lost Hills Drive, Las Vegas, NV 89122, 702-434-3037 phone/Fax
Dash-Hill, LLC, 3540 W. Sahara Avenue #O94, Las Vegas, NV 89102-5816, 212-591-0384, www.dashhillpress.com
Huntington Press, 3665 S. Procyon Avenue, Las Vegas, NV 89103, 702-252-0655; Fax 702-252-0675; editor@huntington-press.com; http://www.huntingtonpress.com; http://www.lasvegasadvisor.com
Long & Silverman Publishing, Inc., 800 North Rainbow Boulevard, Suite 208, Las Vegas, NV 89107, Phone (702) 948-5073, Fax (702) 447-9733, www.lspub.com
Mountain Media, 3172 N. Rainbow Boulevard, Suite 343, Las Vegas, NV 89108, voice 702-656-3285, publisher@TheLibertarian.us, Web site http://www.LibertyBookShop.us
RAINBOW CURVE, P.O. Box 93206, Las Vegas, NV 89193-3206, rainbowcurve@sbcglobal.net, www.rainbowcurve.com
Women of Diversity Productions, Inc., 5790 Park Street, Las Vegas, NV 89149-2304, 702-341-9807; fax 702-341-9828; E-mail dvrsty@aol.com
New American Publishing Co., 3033 Waltham Way, McCarran, NV 89434, napc@pocketmail.com
RED ROCK REVIEW, English Dept J2A/Com. College S. NV, 3200 E. Cheyenne Avenue, N. Las Vegas, NV 89030, www.ccsn.nevada.edu/english/redrockreview/default.html
Beagle Bay Books, 3040 June Meadow Road, Reno, NV 89509, 775-827-8654, Fax 775-827-8633, info@beaglebay.com, www.beaglebay.com
CALIFORNIA EXPLORER, 1135 Terminal Way, Suite 209, Reno, NV 89502
Delta-West Publishing, Inc., 507 Casazza Drive, Suite D, Reno, NV 89502-3346, 775-828-9398, 888-921-6788 (outside of NV), fax 775-828-9163, info@deltawest.com
Gold Standard Press, Corporate Service Center, 5190 Neil Road, Suite 430, Reno, NV 89502-8535, contact@kokobono.com
JetKor, PO Box 33238, Reno, NV 89533, 775-846-1185, Fax 775-746-4649, sdelsol@gbis.com, www.jetkor.com
Polka Dot Publishing, PO Box 8458, Reno, NV 89507-8458, 775-852-2690 phone, LifeofFred@yahoo.com
SECOND GUESS, PO Box 9382, Reno, NV 89507, www.secondguess.net
Toad Press International Chapbook Series, 4985 West 7th Street #18, Reno, NV 89503, www.toadpress.blogspot.com, toadpress@hotmail.com
University of Nevada Press, MS 166, Reno, NV 89557-0076, 775-784-6573, www.nvbooks.nevada.edu

NEW HAMPSHIRE

Concrete Wolf Press, PO Box 730, Amherst, NH 03031-0730, editors@concretewolf.com, http://concretewolf.com
Genesis Publishing Company, Inc., 36 Steeple View Drive, Atkinson, NH 03811-2467
Igneus Press, 310 N. Amherst Road, Bedford, NH 03110, 603-472-3466
Hobblebush Books, 17-A Old Milford Road, Brookline, NH 03033, Ph./Fax: 603-672-4317, E-mail: hobblebush@charter.net, Web: www.hobblebush.com
COMPASS ROSE, 40 Chester Street, Chester, NH 03036, 603-887-7428, compassrose@chestercollege.edu, http:/

578

/compassrose.chestercollege.edu

AMERICAN JONES BUILDING & MAINTENANCE, 15 Maple St., #2, Concord, NH 03301-4202, Tel:206-218-5437; Email: vonb1@excite.com

Missing Spoke Press, PO Box 1314, Concord, NH 03302, 603-724-4010, Email:vonb1@excite.com

TMC Books LLC, 731 Tasker Hill Rd., Conway, NH 03818, 603-447-5589,info@tmcbooks.com www.tmcbooks.com

WILDERNESS MEDICINE NEWSLETTER, 731 Tasker Hill Rd., Conway, NH 03818, 603-447-5589, info@tmcbooks.com www.tmcbooks.com

William L. Bauhan, Publisher, PO Box 443, Dublin, NH 03444-0443, 603-563-8020

Oyster River Press, 36 Oyster River Road, Durham, NH 03824-3029, 603-868-5006, oysterriverpress@comcast.net, www.oysterriverpress.com

Publishing Works, 60 Winter St., Exeter, NH 03833-2029, 603-778-9883, Fax 603-772-1980, 800-333-9883, email: jeremy@publishingworks.com

LightLines Publishing, 12 Wilson Street, Farmington, NH 03835-3428, 603-755-3091, Fax 603-755-3748, lightlinespublishing@yahoo.com, www.lightlinespublishing.com

Stemmer House Publishers, Inc., 4 White Brook Road, Gilsum, NH 03448

Chase Publishing, PO Box 1200, Glen, NH 03838-1200, 603-383-4166, Fax 603-383-8162, achase@chasepublishing.com, www.chasepublishing.com

Nicolin Fields Publishing, Inc., 861 Lafayette Rd Unit 2A, Hampton, NH 03842-1232, 603-758-6363, Fax 603-758-6366, nfp@rcn.com

Steerforth Press, L.C., 25 Lebanon St., Hanover, NH 03755-2143, 603-643-4787

Fantail, PO Box 462, Hollis, NH 03049-0462, http://www.fantail.com, mail@fantail.com, phone: (603) 880-3539

WHOLE TERRAIN - REFLECTIVE ENVIRONMENTAL PRACTICE, 40 Avon Street, Antioch University New England, Keene, NH 03431-3552, 603-357-3122 ex. 272

The Ark, 51 Pleasant Street, Marlborough, NH 03455-2532, 603-876-4160, anarkiss@mindspring.com

FLASH!POINT, PO Box 540, Merrimack, NH 03054-0540, flashpointlit@yahoo.com

ACCCA Press, 149 Cannongate III, Nashua, NH 03063-1953

THE NEW HAMPSHIRE REVIEW: A Journal of Poetry & Politics, P.O. Box 322, Nashua, NH 03060-0322, www.newhampshirereview.com

FREELANCE WRITER'S REPORT, PO Box A, North Stratford, NH 03590, 603-922-8338, fwr@writers-editors.com, www.writers-editors.com

APPLESEEDS, 30 Grove Street, Suite C, Peterborough, NH 03458, 603-924-7209, Fax 603-924-7380, custsvc@cobblestone.mv.com

AUDIO EXPRESS, PO Box 876, Peterborough, NH 03458, 603-924-9464, www.audioxpress.com

CALLIOPE: Exploring World History, 30 Grove Street, Suite C, Peterborough, NH 03458, 603-924-7209, Fax 603-924-7380, custsvc@cobblestone.mv.com

Cobblestone Publishing Company, 30 Grove Street, Suite C, Peterborough, NH 03458, 603-924-7209, Fax 603-924-7380, custsvc@cobblestone.mv.com

COBBLESTONE: Discover American History, 30 Grove Street, Suite C, Peterborough, NH 03458, 603-924-7209, Fax 603-924-7380, custsvc@cobblestone.mv.com

FACES: People, Places, and Culture, 30 Grove Street, Suite C, Peterborough, NH 03458, 603-924-7209, Fax 603-924-7380, custsvc@cobblestone.mv.com

Follow Me! Guides, PO Box 525, Peterborough, NH 03458, 1-800-862-5042 ext. 23, hillarydavis@mac.com

FOOTSTEPS: African American History, 30 Grove Street, Suite C, Peterborough, NH 03458, 603-924-7209, Fax 603-924-7380, custsvc@cobblestone.mv.com

ODYSSEY: Adventures in Science, 30 Grove Street, Suite C, Peterborough, NH 03458, 603-924-7209, Fax 603-924-7380, custsvc@cobblestone.mv.com

Peter E. Randall Publisher, PO Box 4726, Portsmouth, NH 03802-4726, 603-431-5667deidre @ perpublisher.com www.perpublisher.com

RED OWL, 35 Hampshire Road, Portsmouth, NH 03801-4815, 603-431-2691, RedOwlMag@aol.com

COLOR WHEEL, 36 West Main Street, Warner, NH 03278, info@colorwheeljournal.net www.colorwheeljournal.net

NEW JERSEY

SKIDROW PENTHOUSE, 44 Four Corners Road, Blairstown, NJ 07825, 212-614-9505 (hm)

Technics Publications, LLC, PO Box 161, Bradley Beach, NJ 07720, dbooks@technicspub.com

The Midknight Club, PO Box 25, Browns Mills, NJ 08015, info@midknightclub.net, www.midknightclub.net

Next Decade, Inc., 39 Old Farmstead Road, Chester, NJ 07930-2732, 908-879-6625, Fax 908-879-2920

CHRISTIAN*NEW AGE QUARTERLY, PO Box 276, Clifton, NJ 07015-0276, www.christiannewage.com, info@christiannewage.com

Homa & Sekey Books, PO Box 103, Dumont, NJ 07628, 201-384-6692, Fax 201-384-6055, info@homabooks.com, www.homabooks.com

Marymark Press, 45-08 Old Millstone Drive, East Windsor, NJ 08520, 609-443-0646

The Fire!! Press, 241 Hillside Road, Elizabeth, NJ 07208-1432, 908-289-3714 phone/Fax, fire.press@verizon.net

Grand Slam Press, Inc., 2 Churchill Road, Englewood Cliffs, NJ 07632

EXIT 13 MAGAZINE, PO Box 423, Fanwood, NJ 07023, Exit13magazine@yahoo.com (no attachments)

Synergy Press, POB 8, Flemington, NJ 08822-0008, 908.782.7101, 908.237.1491, Synergy@SynergyBookService, www.SynergyBookService.com

Still Waters Press, 459 South Willow Avenue, Galloway, NJ 08205-4633

Edin Books, Inc., 102 Sunrise Drive, Gillette, NJ 07933-1944

ASPHODEL, Department of Composition & Rhetoric, Rowan University, Glassboro, NJ 08028

Quincannon Publishing Group, PO Box 8100, Glen Ridge, NJ 07028, 973-669-8367, editors@quincannongroup.com, www.quincannongroup.com

SENSATIONS MAGAZINE, P.O. Box 90, Glen Ridge, NJ 07028

Snake Hill Press, P.O. Box 90, Glen Ridge, NJ 07028

Lincoln Springs Press, 40 Post Avenue, Hawthorne, NJ 07506-1809

Princeton Book Company, Publishers, 614 U.S. Hwy 130, Suite 1E, Hightstown, NJ 08520-2651, 609-426-0602, Fax 609-426-1344

Vonpalisaden Publications Inc., 60 Saddlewood Drive, Hillsdale, NJ 07642-1336, 201-664-4919

LONG SHOT, PO Box 6238, Hoboken, NJ 07030, www.longshot.org

Abaton Book Company, 100 Gifford Avenue, Jersey City, NJ 07304-1704, fax 201-369-0297

Talisman House, Publishers, PO Box 3157, Jersey City, NJ 07303-3157, 201-938-0698

PTOLEMY/BROWNS MILLS REVIEW, PO Box 252, Juliustown, NJ 08042

US1 Poets' Cooperative, PO Box 127, Kingston, NJ 08528-0127, www.princetononline.org/us1poets/

US1 WORKSHEETS, PO Box 127, Kingston, NJ 08528-0127, www.princetononline.org/us1poets/

Broken Rifle Press, 33 Morton Drive, Lavallette, NJ 08735-2826, 732-830-7014, jerrkate@erols.com

THE LITERARY REVIEW, Fairleigh Dickinson University, 285 Madison Avenue, Madison, NJ 07940, 973-443-8564, Fax 973-443-8364

BIG HAMMER, Dave Roskos, PO Box 54, Manasquan, NJ 08736, 732-295 9920, iniquitypress@hotmail.com www.iniquitypress.com (no email submissions)

Iniquity Press/Vendetta Books, PO Box 54, Manasquan, NJ 08736, 732 295 9920, iniquitypress@hotmail.com

Branch Redd Books, 9300 Atlantic Avenue, Apt. 218, Margate City, NJ 08402-2340

BRANCH REDD REVIEW, 9300 Atlantic Ave, Apt 218, Margate City, NJ 08402-2340

Wafer Mache Publications, 16 Elmgate Road, Marlton, NJ 08053-2402, (856)983-5360 http://www.WaferMache.com

Fountainhead Productions, Inc., 514 Morristown Road, Matawan, NJ 07747-3580, 732-583-2211; Fax 732-583-4123; topgun@skyweb.net

BIOLOGY DIGEST, 143 Old Marlton Pike, Medford, NJ 08055, 609-654-6500

Plexus Publishing, Inc., 143 Old Marlton Pike, Medford, NJ 08055, 609-654-6500

Arx Publishing LLC, PO Box 1333, Merchantville, NJ 08109, 856-486-1310, Fax 856-665-0170, info@arxpub.com, www.arxpub.com

Evolution Publishing, PO Box 13333, Merchantville, NJ 08109, 856-486-1310, Fax 856-665-0170, info@evolpub.com, www.evolpub.com

THE TARPEIAN ROCK, PO Box 1333, Merchantville, NJ 08109

Montemayor Press, PO Box 526, Millburn, NJ 07041, 973-761-1341, Fax 973-378-9749, mail@montemayorpress.com, montemayorpress.com

SHERLOCKIAN TIDBITS, 36 Hawthorne Place #2Q, Montclair, NJ 07042-3279

The Middle Atlantic Press, 10 Twosome Drive, Box 600, Moorestown, NJ 08057, 856-235-4444, orders 800-257-8481, fax 800-225-3840

Advantage World Press, 1625 Nottingham Way, Mountainside, NJ 07092-1340, 973-324-0034, Fax 973-324-1951, info@advantageworldpress.com, www.advantageworldpress.com

RARITAN: A Quarterly Review, 31 Mine Street, New Brunswick, NJ 08903, 732-932-7887, Fax 732-932-7855, rqr@rci.rutgers.edu

SIGNS, Rutgers University, Voorhees Chapel, Room 8, 5 Chapel Drive, New Brunswick, NJ 08901, 732-932-2841 (main #), 732-932-5732 (fax), http://www.journals.uchicago.edu/Signs/home.html

THE (LIBERTARIAN) CONNECTION, 10 Hill Street #22-L, Newark, NJ 07102, 973-242-5999

TRAVEL NATURALLY, PO Box 317, Newfoundland, NJ 07435, 973-697-3552, Fax 973-697-8313, naturally@internaturally.com

Third Dimension Publishing, 930 Thomas Avenue, North Brunswick, NJ 08902, 732-832-5387

Vista Publishing, Inc., 151 Delaware Ave, Oakhurst, NJ 07755, sales@vistapubl.com, www.vistapubl.com

NWI National Writers Institute, PO Box 305, Palmyra, NJ 08065-0305, E-mail cust@top100online.com

THE NEW JERSEY POETRY RESOURCE BOOK, The Poetry Center at Passaic County Community College, One College Blvd., Paterson, NJ 07505-1179, (973) 684-6555

THE PATERSON LITERARY REVIEW, Passaic County Community College, College Boulevard, Paterson, NJ 07505-1179, 973-684-6555

The Poetry Center, Passaic Community College, One College Boulevard, Paterson, NJ 07505-1179, 973-684-6555

Eryon Press, PO Box 659, Peapack, NJ 07977-0659, 908-781-2556

TIFERET: A Journal of Spiritual Literature, PO Box 659, Peapack, NJ 07977-0659, 908-781-2556

Hug The Earth Publications, 42 Greenwood Avenue, Pequannock, NJ 07440

HUG THE EARTH, A Journal of Land and Life, 42 Greenwood Avenue, Pequannock, NJ 07440

Willis Publishing, PO Box 7002, Piscataway, NJ 08854-7002

Amadeus Press, 512 Newark Pompton Tpke., Pompton Plains, NJ 07444, 973-835-6375 x204, fax 973-835-6504, www.amadeuspress.com

Limelight Editions, 512 Newark Pompton Turnpike, Pompton Plains, NJ 07444, 718-381-0421, 973-835-6375, fax 973-835-6504, info@limelighteditions.com, www.limelighteditions.com

ONTARIO REVIEW, 9 Honey Brook Drive, Princeton, NJ 08540

Ontario Review Press, 9 Honey Brook Drive, Princeton, NJ 08540

Plympton Press International, 58 Christopher Drive, Princeton, NJ 08540-2321, 609-279-9184, Fax 609-279-9185, rilemuriel@cs.com

The Press at Foggy Bottom, 35 Linden Lane, 2nd Floor, Princeton, NJ 08540, 609-921-1782

QRL POETRY SERIES, Princeton University, 185 Nassau Street, Princeton, NJ 08540, 609-258-4703

JOURNAL OF NEW JERSEY POETS, County College of Morris, 214 Center Grove Road, Randolph, NJ 07869-2086, 973-328-5471, szulauf@ccm.edu

FotoArt International, 5 Courtney Way, Red Bank, NJ 07701-0770, fotoart@usamailbox.com

Crandall, Dostie & Douglass Books, Inc., 245 West 4th Avenue, Roselle, NJ 07203-1135, Phone: 908.241.5439, Fax: 908.245.4972, Email: Publisher@CDDbooks.com, www.CDDbooks.com

DEVIL BLOSSOMS, PO Box 5122, Seabrook, NJ 08302

Quarterly Review of Literature Press, 900 Hollingshead Spring Road, Apt J-300, Skillman, NJ 08558-2075, 609-921-6976, Fax 609-258-2230, qrl@princeton.edu

BLACK BOUGH, 188 Grove Street #1, Somerville, NJ 08876

Martinez Press, 769 Mosswood Ave., South Orange, NJ 07079-2440, raymond@flatironsystems.com, www.flatironsystems.com

REAL PEOPLE, 900 Oak Tree Avenue, Suite C, c/o Hochman, South Plainfield, NJ 07080-5118

PASSAIC REVIEW (MILLENNIUM EDITIONS), c/o Ah! Sunflower Theater, 410-1/2 Morris Avenue, Spring Lake, NJ 07762-1320

RavenHaus Publishing, 227 Willow Grove Road, Stewartsville, NJ 08886, 908-859-4331, Fax 908-859-3088

The Stillwater Press, PO Box 265, Stillwater, NJ 07875, umperrin@palace.net

OTTN Publishing, 16 Risler Street, Stockton, NJ 08559, 609-397-4005, 609-397-4007 (fax), inquiries@ottnpublishing.com, www.ottnpublishing.com

From Here Press, PO Box 1402, Summit, NJ 07902-1402
XTRAS, PO Box 1402, Summit, NJ 07902-1402
FIRSTHAND, PO Box 1314, Teaneck, NJ 07666, 201-836-9177
THE KELSEY REVIEW, Mercer County Community College, PO Box B, Trenton, NJ 08690, 609-586-4800 ext. 3326, kelsey.review@mccc.edu
RAVEN - A Journal of Vexillology, 1977 N. Olden Ave. Ext., PMB 225, Trenton, NJ 08618-2193
Smyrna Press, Box 1151, Union City, NJ 07087, Fax 201-617-0203, smyrnapress@hotmail.com
THE CLASSICAL OUTLOOK, Department of Classics and General Humanities, Dickson Hall, Montclair State University, Upper Montclair, NJ 07043
Saturday Press, PO Box 43534, Upper Montclair, NJ 07043, 973-239-0436, fax: 973-239-0427
Polygonal Publishing House, PO Box 357, Washington, NJ 07882, 908-689-3894
Down The Shore Publishing, PO Box 100, West Creek, NJ 08092, 609-978-1233; fax 609-597-0422
Riverwinds Publishing, 109 Cromwell Court, Woodbury, NJ 08096, 856-845-1250

NEW MEXICO

Thunder Rain Publishing Corp., PO Box 87, Alamogordo, NM 88311-0087, 985-320-8484, rhi@thunder-rain.com, www.thunder-rain.com, www.lintrigue.org
Amador Publishers, 607 Isleta Blvd. SW, Albuquerque, NM 87105-3827, 505-877-4395, 800-730-4395, Fax 505-877-4395, harry@nmia.com, www.amadorbooks.com
BLUE MESA REVIEW, Creative Writing Center/Univ. of New Mexico, MSCO3-2170, Humanities 274, Albuquerque, NM 87131-0001, 505-277-6347, fax 505-277-0021, bluemesa@unm.edu, www.unm.edu/~bluemesa (web)
Central Avenue Press, PO Box 144, 2132-A Central SE, Albuquerque, NM 87106, (505) 323-9953 www.centralavepress.com
FICTION WRITER'S GUIDELINE, 2511 Schell Court NE, Albuquerque, NM 87106-2531, 505-352-9490, bcamenson@aol.com, www.fictionwriters.com
Health Press, PO Box 37470, Albuquerque, NM 87176-7470, goodbooks@healthpress.com
KNUCKLE MERCHANT - The Journal of Naked Literary Aggression, 221 Stanford Drive SE #2, Albuquerque, NM 87106-3586, 505.256.4589 knucklemerchant@hotmail.com
La Alameda Press, 9636 Guadalupe Trail NW, Albuquerque, NM 87114, 505-897-0285, www.laalamedapress.com
Lost Prophet Press, 221 Stanford Drive SE #2, Albuquerque, NM 87106-3586, 505.256.4589
ST. VITUS PRESS & POETRY REVIEW, 7408 Estes Park Avenue NW, Albuquerque, NM 87114
Southwest Research and Information Center, PO Box 4524, Albuquerque, NM 87196-4524, 505-262-1862; Fax 505-262-1864; Info@sric.org; www.sric.org
THIN COYOTE, 221 Stanford Drive SE #2, Albuquerque, NM 87106-3586, 505.256.4589 knucklemerchant@hotmail.com
VOICES FROM THE EARTH, PO Box 4524, Albuquerque, NM 87196, 505-262-1862, Fax 505-262-1864
West End Press, PO Box 27334, Albuquerque, NM 87125
Wildflower Press, PO Box 4757, Albuquerque, NM 87196-4757, 505-296-0691, Fax 505-296-6124, jspoetry@aol.com
Zerx Press, 725 Van Buren Place SE, Albuquerque, NM 87108, zerxpress@aol.com, www.zerxrecords.com
The Heather Foundation, 713 W. Spruce #48, Deming, NM 88030, 915-261-0502, sm@look.net
Gallery West Associates, PO Box 1272, El Prado, NM 87529, 505-751-0073
OUTER-ART, University of New Mexico, 200 College Road, Gallup, NM 87301, smarand@unm.edu, www.gallup.unm.edu/~smarandache/a/outer-art.htm
PARADOXISM, 200 College Road, University of New Mexico, Gallup, NM 87301, 505-863-7647, fax 505-863-7532, smarand@unm.edu, www.gallup.unm.edu/~smarandache/a/paradoxism.htm
BEATLICK NEWS, 940 1/2 W Van Patten, Las Cruces, NM 88005, 505-496-8729
BEATLICK NEWS POETRY & ARTS NEWSLETTER, 940 1/2 Van Patten Ave., Las Cruces, NM 88005-2222, 505-496-8729
Canonymous Press, PO Box 1478, Las Cruces, NM 88004-1478, e-mail press@canonymous.com, www.canonymous.com
PUERTO DEL SOL, MSC 3E, PO Box 30001, New Mexico State University, Las Cruces, NM 88003, 505-646-2345
Two Eagles Press International, 1029 Hickory Drive, Las Cruces, NM 88005, 505-523-7911, 505-523-1953, Cell 505-644-5436, twoeaglespress@comcast.net, twoeaglespress.com
Whole Notes Press, PO Box 1374, Las Cruces, NM 88004, 505-382-7446
LPD Press, 925 Salamanca NW, Los Ranchos de Albuquerque, NM 87107-5647, 505-344-9382, Fax 505-345-5129, info@nmsantos.com
TRADICION REVISTA, 925 Salamanca NW, Los Ranchos de Albuquerque, NM 87107-5647, 505-344-9382, Fax 505-345-5129, info@nmsantos.com
Noemi Press, P.O. Box 1330, Mesilla Park, NM 88047
Crones Unlimited, PO Box 433, Peralta, NM 87042, M5799@cronesunlimited.com, www.cronesunlimited.com
Duende Press, Box 571, Placitas, NM 87043, 505-867-5877
American Research Press, Box 141, Rehoboth, NM 87322, m_l_perez@yahoo.com, www.gallup.unm.edu/~smarandache/eBooks-otherformats.htm and www.gallup.unm.edu/~smarandache/eBooksLiterature.htm
SMARANDACHE NOTIONS JOURNAL, Box 141, Rehoboth, NM 87322, m_l_perez@yahoo.com, http://www.gallup.unm.edu/~smarandache/
Kivaki Press, 96 Paa Ko Drive, Sandia Park, NM 87047-0501, 828-274-7941, info@kivakipress.com, www.kivakipress.com
American Canadian Publishers, Inc., PO Box 4595, Santa Fe, NM 87502-4595, 505-983-8484, Fax 505-983-8484
Ancient City Press, 3101 Old Pecos Trail, Unit 244, Santa Fe, NM 87505-9088, 505-982-8195
Azro Press, PMB 342, 1704 Llano Street B, Santa Fe, NM 87505, gae@nets.com, www.azropress.com
Burning Books, PO Box 2638, Santa Fe, NM 87504, Fax 505-820-6216, brnbx@nets.com, burningbooks.org
BUSINESS SPIRIT JOURNAL, 4 Camino Azul, Santa Fe, NM 87508, 505-474-7604, Fax 505-471-2584, message@bizspirit.com, www.bizspirit.com
COALITION FOR PRISONERS' RIGHTS NEWSLETTER, PO Box 1911, Santa Fe, NM 87504, 505-982-9520
The Message Company, 4 Camino Azul, Santa Fe, NM 87508, 505-474-0998, Fax 505-471-2584
New Atlantean Press, PO Box 9638, Santa Fe, NM 87504, 505-983-1856 phone/Fax, global@thinktwice.com, www.thinktwice.com
Rising Tide Press New Mexico, PO Box 6136, Santa Fe, NM 87502-6136, 505-983-8484, Fax 505-983-8484
School of American Research Press, PO Box 2188, Santa Fe, NM 87504-2188, 505-954-7206, Fax 505-954-7241, bkorders@sarsf.org
Sherman Asher Publishing, P.O. Box 31725, Santa Fe, NM 87501-0172, 505-988-7214, Fax 505-988-7214, westernedge@santa-fe.net, www.shermanasher.com

Sunstone Press, PO Box 2321, Santa Fe, NM 87504-2321, 505-988-4418, fax 505-988-1025, jsmith@sunstonepress.com
Synergetic Press, 1 Bluebird Court, Santa Fe, NM 87508-1531, Tel. 505-424-0237 Fax. 505 424 3336 e-mail: tango@synergeticpress.com website: www.synergeticpress.com
Ten Star Press, 2860 Plaza Verde, Santa Fe, NM 87507, 505-473-4813 phone/Fax, dorbil@rt66.com
Via Media Publishing Company, 941 Calle Mejia #822, Santa Fe, NM 87501, 505-983-1919; fax 814-526-5262; e-mail info@goviamedia.com; website www.goviamedia.com
Zon International Publishing Co., PO Box 6459, Santa Fe, NM 87502, 505-995-0102, Fax 505-995-0103, e-mail zon@nets.com
Alamo Square Press, 103 FR 321, Tajique, NM 87016, 503-384-9766, alamosquare@earthlink.net
Paradigm Publications, 202 Bendix Drive, Taos, NM 87571, 505 758 7758, Fax 505 758 7768, info@paradigm-pubs.com, www.paradigm-pubs.com
Oscura Press, PO 835, Tijeras, NM 87059-0835, 505-384-2792, press@thewestern.net, books.thewestern.net

NEW YORK

A & U AMERICA'S AIDS MAGAZINE, 25 Monroe Street, Suite 205, Albany, NY 12210-2729, 518-426-9010, Fax 518-436-5354, mailbox@aumag.org
THE LITTLE MAGAZINE, Department of English, State Univ. of New York, University of Albany, Albany, NY 12222, website www.albany.edu/~litmag.
Mount Ida Press, 152 Washington Avenue, Albany, NY 12210-2203, Tel: 518-426-5935, Fax: 518-426-4116
RALPH'S REVIEW, 129 Wellington Avenue, #A, Albany, NY 12203-2637
State University of New York Press, 194 Washington Avenue Suite 305, Albany, NY 12210, main editorial 518-472-5000, orders 800-666-2211, website www.sunypress.edu
13TH MOON, 1400 Washington Avenue, SUNY, English Department, Albany, NY 12222-0001, 518-442-5593
Whitston Publishing Co., 1717 Central Avenue, Suite 201, Albany, NY 12205
Amherst Media, Inc., P.O. Box 586, Amherst, NY 14226, 716-874-4450; www.amherstmedia.com
FREE INQUIRY, Council For Secular Humanism, PO Box 664, Amherst, NY 14226-0664, 716-636-7571
SKEPTICAL INQUIRER, PO Box 703, Amherst, NY 14226, 716-636-1425, Skeptinq@aol.com
AXES & ALLEYS, 25-26 44th Street #A1, Astoria, NY 11103, 718-204-0313, jeremy@danielbester.com
CRITICAL REVIEW, 32-26 35th Street, Astoria, NY 11106-1102, 203-270-8103; fax 203-270-8105; e-mail info@criticalreview.com
WOMEN IN THE ARTS BULLETIN/NEWSLETTER, 32-35 30th Street #D24, Astoria, NY 11106, 718-545-9337
Women In The Arts Foundation, Inc., 32-35 30th Street #D24, Astoria, NY 11106
Aspicomm Media, PO Box 1212, Baldwin, NY 11510, Phone (516) 642-5976, Fax (516) 489-1199, www.aspicomm.com
Barrytown/Station Hill Press, 124 Station Hill Road, Barrytown, NY 12507, 845-340-4300, fax: 845-339-0780, web: www.stationhill.org, email: publisher@stationhill.org
INVESTMENT COLUMN QUARTERLY (newsletter), PO Box 233, Barryville, NY 12719, 914-557-8713
NAR Publications, PO Box 233, Barryville, NY 12719, 914-557-8713
Montfort Publications, 26 South Saxon Avenue, Bay Shore, NY 11706, 516-665-0726, FAX 516-665-4349
QUEEN OF ALL HEARTS, 26 South Saxon Avenue, Bay Shore, NY 11706, info@montfortmissionaries.com, www.montfortmissionaries.com
BEGINNINGS - A Magazine for the Novice Writer, PO Box 214-R, Bayport, NY 11705-0214, 631-472-1143, jenineb@optonline.net, www.scbeginnings.com
L D A Publishers, 42-46 209 Street, Suite B-11, Bayside, NY 11361, 718-224-9484, Fax 718-224-9487, 888-388-9887
Phrygian Press, 58-09 205th Street, Bayside, NY 11364, PhrygianZYX @ AOL.COM
ZYX, 58-09 205th Street, Bayside, NY 11364-1712, PhrygianZYX @ AOL.COM, 718-428-9368
Nightboat Books, PO Box 656, Beacon, NY 12508, editor@nightboat.org, www.nightboat.org
THE LEDGE POETRY & FICTION MAGAZINE, 40 Maple Avenue, Bellport, NY 11713-2011, www.theledgemagazine.com
HARPUR PALATE, English Dept., PO Box 6000, Binghamton University, Binghamton, NY 13902-6000, http://harpurpalate.binghamton.edu
Harrington Park Press, 10 Alice Street, Binghamton, NY 13904-1580, Tel.:(607) 722-5857, Fax (607)722-8465, Web: http://www.HaworthPress.com
The Haworth Press, 10 Alice Street, Binghamton, NY 13904-1580, Tel.: (607)722-5857, Fax: (607)722-8465, Web: http://www.HaworthPress.com
REDACTIONS: Poetry & Poetics, 24 College St., Apt. 1, Brockport, NY 14420, Email: poetry@redactions.com, Web: www.redactions.com
FARMING UNCLE, c/o Toro, PO Box 427, Bronx, NY 10458-0711
Fordham University Press, 2546 Belmont Avenue, University Box L, Bronx, NY 10458, 718-817-4781
Inner City Press, P.O. Box 580188, Mount Carmel Station, Bronx, NY 10458, Web: InnerCityPress.org Tel: 718-716-3540
INNER CITY PRESS, P.O. Box 580188, Mount Carmel Station, Bronx, NY 10458, Web: InnerCityPress.org Tel: 718-716-3540
JOURNAL OF MENTAL IMAGERY, c/o Brandon House, PO Box 240, Bronx, NY 10471
ABRAMELIN: a Journal of Poetry and Magick, Box 337, Brookhaven, NY 11719, 631 803-2211
Actium Publishing, Inc., 1375 Coney Island Avenue #122, Brooklyn, NY 11230, 718-382-2129, fax 718-621-0402, email home@actium1.com
ADVANCES IN THANATOLOGY, 391 Atlantic Ave., Brooklyn, NY 11217-1708, 718-858-3026, 718-852-1846,no 800,rhalporn@pipeline.com, thanatology.org
Autonomedia, Inc., PO Box 568, Brooklyn, NY 11211, 718-936-2603, e-Mail autonobook@aol.com
BOMB MAGAZINE, 80 Hanson Place #703, Brooklyn, NY 11217-1505, 212-431-3943, Fax 212-431-5880
Center for Thanatology Research & Education, Inc., 391 Atlantic Ave., Brooklyn, NY 11217-1708, 718-858-3026, 718-852-1846,no 800,rhalporn@pipeline.com, thanatology.org
DOWNTOWN BROOKLYN: A Journal of Writing, English Department; Long Island Univ., Brooklyn, Campus, 1 University Plaza, Brooklyn, NY 11201
THE EAST VILLAGE INKY, 122 Dean Street, Brooklyn, NY 11201, inky@erols.com
Gryphon Books, PO Box 209, Brooklyn, NY 11228-0209
HANGING LOOSE, 231 Wyckoff Street, Brooklyn, NY 11217, www.hangingloosepress.com
Hanging Loose Press, 231 Wyckoff Street, Brooklyn, NY 11217, www.hangingloosepress.com
HARDBOILED, PO Box 209, Brooklyn, NY 11228
IAMBS & TROCHEES, 6801 19th Avenue #5H, Brooklyn, NY 11204, 718-232-9268
INSURANCE, 132 N. 1st Street #11, Brooklyn, NY 11211, ctokar@hotmail.com

KOJA, PO Box 140083, Brooklyn, NY 11214
Lunar Offensive Publications, 1910 Foster Avenue, Brooklyn, NY 11230-1902
LUNGFULL! MAGAZINE, 316 23rd Street, Brooklyn, NY 11215-6409, lungfull@rcn.net
Malafemmina Press, 4211 Fort Hamilton Parkway, Brooklyn, NY 11219
Merkos Publications, 291 Kingston Ave., Brooklyn, NY 11213, 718-778-0226, fax: 718-778-4148, email: orders@kehoton-line.com
PAPERBACK PARADE, PO Box 209, Brooklyn, NY 11228-0209
POETS ON THE LINE, PO Box 20292, Brooklyn NY 11202-0007, Brooklyn, NY 11202-0007, 718-596-0137
Semiotext Foreign Agents Books Series, PO Box 568, Brooklyn, NY 11211, 718-963-2603; E-mail semiotexte@aol.com
SEMIOTEXT(E), PO Box 568, Brooklyn, NY 11211, 718-963-2603, e-Mail semiotexte@aol.com
The Smith (subsidiary of The Generalist Assn., Inc.), 69 Joralemon Street, Brooklyn, NY 11201-4003
Soft Skull Press, 55 Washington Street, Ste. 804, Brooklyn, NY 11201-1066, 212-673-2502, Fax 212-673-0787, sander@softskull.com, www.softskull.com
ZONE, 1226 Prospect Ave., Brooklyn, NY 11218-1304, 212-625-0048, Fax 212-625-9772, urzone@aol.com
Zone Books, 1226 Prospect Ave., Brooklyn, NY 11218, NY 11218, 718 686 0048, 718 686 9045
Blowtorch Press, 55 Lark Street, Buffalo, NY 14211, webmaster@blowtorchpress.com
BUCKLE &, PO Box 1653, Buffalo, NY 14205
BUFFALO SPREE, 6215 Sheridan Drive, Buffalo, NY 14221-4837, 716-634-0820, fax 716-810-0075
EARTH'S DAUGHTERS: Feminist Arts Periodical, PO Box 41, Central Park Station, Buffalo, NY 14215-0041, 716-627-9825, http://bfn.org/~edaught
LIVING FREE, Box 29, Hiler Branch, Buffalo, NY 14223
THE NARROW ROAD: A Haibun Journal, 73 Constance Lane, Buffalo, NY 14227-1361, kujira@buffalo.com
Starcherone Books, PO Box 303, Buffalo, NY 14201-0303, www.starcherone.com
Western New York Wares, Inc., PO Box 733, Ellicott Station, Buffalo, NY 14205, 716-832-6088, www.wnybooks.com
White Pine Press, PO Box 236, Buffalo, NY 14201-0236, 716-627-4665 phone/Fax, wpine@whitepine.org, www.whitepine.org
Brookview Press, 901 Western Road, Castleton-on-Hudson, NY 12033, 518-732-7093 phone/Fax, info@brookviewpress.com, www.brookviewpress.com
Passport Press, PO Box 2543, Champlain, NY 12919-2543, 514-937-3868, Fax 514-931-0871, e-mail travelbook@bigfoot.com
Toadlily Press, P O. Box 2, Chappaqua, NY 10514, mgoodman@toadlilypress.com, www.toadlilypress.com
Beach & Company, Box 303, Cherry Valley, NY 13320
Cherry Valley Editions, PO Box 303, Cherry Valley, NY 13320, cveds@cherryvalley.com
Chicken Soup Press, Inc., PO Box 164, Circleville, NY 10919-0164, 845-692-6320, Fax 845-692-7574, poet@hvc.rr.com
NightinGale Resources, PO Box 322, Cold Spring, NY 10516, 212-753-5383
Berry Hill Press, 2349 State Route 12-B, Deansboro, NY 13328, 315-821-6188 phone/fax; dls@berryhillbookshop.com
Birch Brook Press, PO Box 81, Delhi, NY 13753, phone/fax orders & sales inquiries 607-746-7453, email birchbrook@usadatanet.net, www.birchbrookpress.info
Persephone Press, PO Box 81, Delhi, NY 13753
Spring Harbor Press, Box 346, Delmar, NY 12054, 518-478-7817, 518-478-7817, springharbor@verizon.net, www.springhar-borpress.com
Moody Street Irregulars, Inc., 2737 Dodge Road, East Amherst, NY 14051-2113
MOODY STREET IRREGULARS: A Jack Kerouac Magazine, 2737 Dodge Road, East Amherst, NY 14051-2113
Three Mile Harbor, PO Box 1951, East Hampton, NY 11937
Callawind Publications / Custom Cookbooks / Children's Books, 2059 Hempstead Turnpike, PMB 355, East Meadow, NY 11554-1711, 514-685-9109, Fax 514-685-7952, info@callawind.com
MOBILE BEAT: The DJ Magazine, PO Box 309, East Rochester, NY 14445, 585-385-9920, Fax 585-385-3637, webmaster@mobilebeat.com
Marsh Hawk Press, PO Box 206, East Rockaway, NY 11518-0206, Fax 212-598-4353, marshhawkpress@cs.com, www.marshhawkpress.org
BITTER OLEANDER, 4983 Tall Oaks Drive, Fayetteville, NY 13066-9776, Fax 315-637-5056, info@bitteroleander.com, www.bitteroleander.com
Smith-Johnson Publisher, 175-14 73rd Avenue, Flushing, NY 11366-1502, 718-969-3825, fax 718-591-0227
WRESTLING - THEN & NOW, PO Box 640471, Oakland Gdns. Station, Flushing, NY 11364
Ironweed Press, PO Box 754208, Parkside Station, Forest Hills, NY 11375, Ph 718-544-1120 Fax 718-268-2394
Howln Moon Press, 7222 State Highway 357, Franklin, NY 13775-3100, 607-829-2187 (office), 888-349-9438 (ordering), email: bmueller@hmpress.com
Athanata Arts, Ltd., P.O. Box, Garden City, NY 11530-0321
Square One Publishers, Inc., 115 Herricks Road, Garden City Park, NY 11040, 516-535-2010, Fax 516-535-2014, sq1info@aol.com, www.squareonepublishers.com
SENECA REVIEW, Hobart & William Smith Colleges, Geneva, NY 14456, 315-781-3392, Fax 315-781-3348, senecareview@hws.edu
The Greenfield Review Press, PO Box 308, Greenfield Center, NY 12833-0308, (518) 583-1440
CONFRONTATION, English Department, C.W. Post of Long Island Univ., Greenvale, NY 11548, 516-299-2720
Ultramarine Publishing Co., Inc., PO Box 303, Hastings-on-Hudson, NY 10706, 914-478-1339
Black Dome Press Corp., 1011 Route 296, Hensonville, NY 12439, 518-734-6357, Fax 518-734-5802
HOME PLANET NEWS, PO Box 455, High Falls, NY 12440, 845-687-4084, homeplanetnews@yahoo.com
Home Planet Publications, PO Box 455, High Falls, NY 12440, 845-687-4084, homeplanetnews@yahoo.com
The Groundwater Press, PO Box 704, Hudson, NY 12534, 516-767-8503
The Foundation for Economic Education, Inc., 30 South Broadway, Irvington, NY 10533, 914-591-7230; Fax 914-591-8910; E-mail freeman@fee.org
THE FREEMAN: Ideas On Liberty, 30 South Broadway, Irvington, NY 10533, 914-591-7230; Fax 914-591-8910; E-mail freeman@fee.org
River Press, 499 Islip Avenue, Islip, NY 11751-1826, 631-277-8618, Fax 631-277-8660, rivpress@aol.com
EPOCH MAGAZINE, 251 Goldwin Smith Hall, Cornell University, Ithaca, NY 14853-3201, 607-255-3385, Fax 607-255-6661
McBooks Press, Inc., I. D. Booth Bldg, 520 North Meadow Street #2, Ithaca, NY 14850-3229, 607-272-2114, FAX 607-273-6068, mcbooks@mcbooks.com, www.mcbooks.com
SNOW LION NEWSLETTER & CATALOG, PO Box 6483, Ithaca, NY 14851, www.snowlionpub.com
Snow Lion Publications, Inc., PO Box 6483, Ithaca, NY 14851, 607-273-8519, Fax 607-273-8508, www.snowlionpub.com
SOUTH AMERICAN EXPLORER, 126 Indian Creek Road, Ithaca, NY 14850, 607-277-0488, Fax 607-277-6122,

explorer@samexplo.org
What The Heck Press, PO Box 149, Ithaca, NY 14851-0149, 607-275-0806, Fax 607-275-0702
The Spirit That Moves Us Press, Inc., PO Box 720820-DB, Jackson Heights, Queens, NY 11372-0820, 718-426-8788, msklar@mindspring.com
House of Hits, Inc., North American Airlines Bldg 75, Suite 250, JFK International Airport, Jamaica, NY 11430, 718-656-2650
ARTELLA: the waltz of words and art, P.O. Box 78, Johnson, NY 10933, www.ArtellaWordsandArt.com
Ausable Press, 1026 Hurricane Road, Keene, NY 12942, 518-576-9273, 518-576-9227 fax, www.ausablepress.org
Labor Arts Books, 215 East Hazeltine Ave.., Kenmore, NY 14217-2828, 716-873-4131
Left Hand Books, 85A Fairmont Avenue, Kingston, NY 12401, 845-340-9892, lefthandb@ulster.net
McPherson & Company Publishers, PO Box 1126, 148 Smith Avenue, Kingston, NY 12402, 845-331-5807, toll free order #800-613-8219
ADIRONDAC, 814 Goggins Road, Lake George, NY 12845-4117, 518-668-4447, e-mail ADKinfo@adk.org
Adirondack Mountain Club, Inc., 814 Goggins Road, Lake George, NY 12845-4117, 518-668-4447, FAX 518-668-3746, e-mail pubs@adk.org
Serpent & Eagle Press, 10 Main Street, Laurens, NY 13796, 607-432-2990
The Edwin Mellen Press, PO Box 450, Lewiston, NY 14092, 716-754-2266
Mellen Poetry Press, PO Box 450, 415 Ridge Street, Lewiston, NY 14092-0450, 716-754-2266, Fax 716-754-4056, mellen@wzrd.com, www.mellenpress.com
Starlight Press, Box 3102, Long Island City, NY 11103
Cross-Cultural Communications, 239 Wynsum Ave., Merrick, NY 11566-4725, Tel: 516-868-5635 Fax: 516-379-1901 E: cccpoetry@aol.com, www.cross-culturalcommunications.com
Lintel, 24 Blake Lane, Middletown, NY 10940, 845-342-5224
BOOK/MARK SMALL PRESS REVIEW, PO Box 516, Miller Place, NY 11764-0516, 631-331-4118, cyberpoet@msn.com, www.writernetwork.com
THE ICONOCLAST, 1675 Amazon Road, Mohegan Lake, NY 10547-1804
Library Research Associates, Inc., 254 Nininger Road, Monroe, NY 10950-3977, 914-783-1144
Criminal Justice Press, PO Box 249, Monsey, NY 10952, Fax 845-362-8376
Willow Tree Press, Inc., PO Box 249, Monsey, NY 10952, 845-354-9139
THE U*N*A*B*A*S*H*E*D LIBRARIAN, THE "HOW I RUN MY LIBRARY GOOD" LETTER, PO Box 325, Mount Kisco, NY 10549, Fax 914-244-0941
ART TIMES, PO Box 730, Mount Marion, NY 12456-0730, 845-246-6944, info@arttimesjournal.com, www.arttimesjournal.com
FROGPOND: Quarterly Haiku Journal, PO Box 122, Nassau, NY 12123-0122, ithacan@earthlink.net
Haiku Society of America, PO Box 122, Nassau, NY 12123, 518-766-2039
UNDER THE VOLCANO, PO Box 236, Nesconset, NY 11767, www.underthevolcano.net
Obsessive Compulsive Anonymous, PO Box 215, New Hyde Park, NY 11040, 516-739-0662, Fax 212-768-4679, www.hometown.aol.com/west24th
CROSS CURRENTS, College of New Rochelle, New Rochelle, NY 10805-2339, 914-235-1439, Fax 914-235-1584, aril@ecunet.org
THE SHAKESPEARE NEWSLETTER, English Department, Iona College, New Rochelle, NY 10801
CHESS LIFE, United States Chess Federation, 3054 NYS Route 9W, New Windsor, NY 12553, 914-562-8350; Fax 914-236-4852; cleditor@uschess.org
SCHOOL MATES, 3054 NYS Route 9W, New Windsor, NY 12553, 914-562-8350; Fax 914-561-2437; schoolmates@us-chess.org
U.S. Chess Federation, 3054 NYS Route 9W, New Windsor, NY 12553, 914-562-8350
Akashic Books, PO Box 1456, New York, NY 10009, 212-433-1875, 212-414-3199, Akashic7@aol.com, www.akashic-books.com
ALIMENTUM - The Literature of Food, P. O. Box 776, New York, NY 10163, info@alimentumjournal.com www.alimentumjournal.com
Allworth Press, 10 East 23rd Street, Suite 510, New York, NY 10010, 212-777-8395, Fax 212-777-8261, Pub@allworth.com, www.allworth.com
AMERICA, 106 West 56th Street, New York, NY 10019, 212-581-4640
American Poet, The Academy of American Poets, 584 Broadway, Suite 604, New York, NY 10012, 212-274-0343, fax 212-274-9427, www.poets.org
ARARAT, 55 E 59th Street, New York, NY 10022-1112
THE ASIAN PACIFIC AMERICAN JOURNAL, 16 West 32nd Street, Suite 10A, New York, NY 10001-3814, 212-494-0061
Authors of Unity Publishing, 575 Madison Ave., 10th Floor, New York, NY 10022, 212 605 0407 or 646 286 0166
BARROW STREET, PO Box 1831, Murray Hill Stn., New York, NY 10156, 212-937-1970, www.barrowstreet.org
Barrow Street Press, PO Box 1831, Murray Hill Stn., New York, NY 10156, 212-937-1970, info@barrowstreet.org, www.barrowstreet.org
Bellevue Literary Press, Dept. of Medicine, NYU School of Medicine, 550 First Avenue OBV 612, New York, NY 10016, 212-263-7802, FAX:212-263-7803, egoldman@BLReview.org
BELLEVUE LITERARY REVIEW, NYU School of Medicine, Dept. of Medicine, 550 First Avenue, OBV-A612, New York, NY 10016, www.BLReview.org, info@BLReview.org
Biblio Press, PO Box 20195, London Terrace Stn., New York, NY 10011-0008, 212-989-2755, bibook@aol.com
BIGNEWS MAGAZINE, 484 West 43rd St., Apt. 24D, New York, NY 10036-6341, 212-679-4535, Fax 212-679-4573, bignewsmag@aol.com, www.mainchance.org
Black Dress Press, P.O. Box 1373, New York, NY 10276-1373, www.blackdresspress.com
Box Turtle Press, 184 Franklin Street, New York, NY 10013
Buenos Books America, 1133 Broadway, Suite 706, New York, NY 10010, www.buenosbooks.us
Calliope Press, PO Box 2408, New York, NY 10108-2408, 212-564-5068
Cantarabooks LLC, 204 East 11th Street 171, New York, NY 10003, 917.674.7560, editor@cantarabooks.com, www.cantarabooks.com
THE CHARIOTEER, 337 West 36 Street, New York, NY 10018, 212-279-9586
CHELSEA, PO Box 773, Cooper Station, New York, NY 10276-0773
Cheshire House Books, Attn: Joanna Rees, PO Box 2484, New York, NY 10021, 212-861-5404 phone/Fax, publisher@samthecat.com
CINEASTE MAGAZINE, 243 Fifth Ave., #706, New York, NY 10016-8703, 212-366-5720, Fax 212-366-5724

584

CONCRETE JUNGLE JOURNAL, 163 Third Avenue #130, New York, NY 10003, 718-465-8573 URL: www.concretejungle-press.com

Concrete Jungle Press, 163 Third Avenue #130, New York, NY 10003, Tel: 718-465-8573, Fax: 718-468-3007, URL: www.concretejunglepress.com

CONJUNCTIONS, 21 East 10th Street #3E, New York, NY 10003-5924, Phone: 845-758-1539, fax: 845-758-2660, e-mail: conjunctions@bard.edu, URL: www.conjunctions.com

Creative Roots, Inc., 140 Riverside Drive, New York, NY 10024, 212-799-2294

Crime and Again Press, 245 Eighth Avenue, Ste. 283, New York, NY 10011, 212-727-0151; crimepress@aol.com

CULTUREFRONT, 150 Broadway, Room #1700, New York, NY 10038-4401, 212-233-1131, fax 212-233-4607, e-mail hum@echonyc.com

Dancing Bridge Publishing, 370 Central Park West, Ste. 610, New York, NY 10025, 212-749-0029, Fax 212-280-4177, Erodenz@worldnet.att.net

THE DRAMATIST, The Dramatists Guild of America Inc., 1501 Broadway Suite 701, New York, NY 10036

Edgewise Press, 24 Fifth Avenue #224, New York, NY 10011, 212-982-4818, Fax 212-982-1364

Encounter Books, 900 Broadway, Ste.400, New York, NY 10003-1239, 415-538-1460, Fax 415-538-1461, read@encounter-books.com, www.encounterbooks.com

Falls Media, 1 Astor Place, PH K, New York, NY 10003, 917-667-2269, www.wouldyourather.com

The Feminist Press at the City University of New York, The Graduate Center, 365 Fifth Avenue, Suite 5406, New York, NY 10016, 212-817-7915, Fax 212-817-1593, www.feministpress.org

FICTION, c/o Dept. of English, City College, 138th Street & Convent Ave., New York, NY 10031, 212-650-6319

FISH DRUM MAGAZINE, PO Box 966, Murray Hill Station, New York, NY 10156, www.fishdrum.com

Fotofolio, Inc., 561 Broadway, 2nd Floor, New York, NY 10012-3918, 212-226-0923

Fouque Publishers, 244 5th Avenue #M220, New York, NY 10001-7604, 646-486-1061, Fax 646-486-1091, fouquepublishers@earthlink.net

Four Walls Eight Windows, 245 West 17th St., Apt. 11, New York, NY 10011-5373, e-mail edit@4w8w.com, www.4w8w.com

Four Way Books, PO Box 535, Village Station, New York, NY 10014, www.fourwaybooks.com four_way_editors@yahoo.com

Fugue State Press, PO Box 80, Cooper Station, New York, NY 10276, 212-673-7922

A GATHERING OF THE TRIBES, PO Box 20693, Tompkins Square, New York, NY 10009, 212-674-3778, Fax 212-674-5576, info@tribes.org, www.tribes.org

GAYELLOW PAGES, Box 533 Village Station, New York, NY 10014-0533, 646-213-0263 http://gayellowpages.com, gayellowpages@earthlink.net

GOODIE, 197 7th Avenue #4C, New York, NY 10011, www.goodie.org, romy@goodie.org, foxy@goodie.org

Greekworks, 337 West 36th St., New York, NY 10018-6401

Green Bean Press, PO Box 237, New York, NY 10013, 718-965-2076 phone/Fax, ian@greenbeanpress.com, www.greenbeanpress.com

Guarionex Press Ltd., 201 West 77th Street, New York, NY 10024, 212-724-5259

Guilford Publications, Inc., 72 Spring Street, New York, NY 10012

Hard Press, 632 East 14th Street, #18, New York, NY 10009, 212-673-1152

Emma Howard Books, Attn: Armando H. Luna, PO Box 385, Planetarium Stn., New York, NY 10024-0385, 212-996-2590 phone/Fax, emmahowardbooks@verizon.net, www.eelgrassgirls.com

THE HUDSON REVIEW, 684 Park Avenue, New York, NY 10021, 212-650-0020, Fax 212-774-1911

Ikon Inc., 151 First Ave. #46, New York, NY 10003

THE INDEPENDENT SHAVIAN, The Bernard Shaw Society, PO Box 1159 Madison Square Stn., New York, NY 10159-1159, 212-982-9885

The Institute of Mind and Behavior, PO Box 522, Village Station, New York, NY 10014, 212-595-4853

International Publishers Co. Inc., 239 West 23 Street, New York, NY 10011, 212-366-9816, Fax 212-366-9820

INTERNATIONAL WOMEN'S WRITING GUILD, Box 810, Gracie Station, New York, NY 10028, 212-737-7536, Fax 212-737-9469, iwwg@iwwg.org, www.iwwg.org

Italica Press, Inc., 595 Main Street, #605, New York, NY 10044, 212-935-4230; fax 212-838-7812; inquiries@italicapress.com

John James Company, 79 Worth Street, New York, NY 10013, 212-431-3235, Fax 212-625-9823, jjpublishing@msn.com

JEWISH CURRENTS, 45 E 33 Street 4th floor, New York, NY 10016, 212-889-2523, Fax 212-532-7518

JEWISH WOMEN'S LITERARY ANNUAL, National Council of Jewish Women NY Section, 820 Second Ave., New York, NY 10017-4504, 212-687-5030 ext.33/fax212-687-5032

THE JOURNAL OF MIND AND BEHAVIOR, PO Box 522, Village Station, New York, NY 10014, 212-595-4853

JOURNAL OF POLYMORPHOUS PERVERSITY, PO Box 1454, Madison Square Station, New York, NY 10159-1454, 212-689-5473, info@psychhumor.com, www.psychhumor.com

THE JOURNAL OF PSYCHOHISTORY, 140 Riverside Drive, New York, NY 10024, 212-799-2294

JOURNAL OF THE HELLENIC DIASPORA, 337 West 36th Street, New York, NY 10018, 212-279-9586

Junction Press, PO Box F, New York, NY 10034-0246, 212-942-1985

LEFT BUSINESS OBSERVER, 38 Greene Street, 4th Floor, New York, NY 10013-3505, phone 212-219-0010, fax 212-219-0098, dhenwood@panix.com, www.leftbusinessobserver.com

Libellum, 211 West 19th Street, #5, New York, NY 10011-4001, libellum@el.net

LILIES AND CANNONBALLS REVIEW, P.O. Box 702, Bowling Green Station, New York, NY 10274-0702, info@liliesandcannonballs.com, www.liliesandcannonballs.com

LILITH, 250 West 57th, #2432, New York, NY 10107, 212-757-0818

Ludlow Press, PO Box 2612, New York, NY 10009-9998, FAX: 1 (212) 937-3625, editor@LudlowPress.com, www.ludlowpress.com

THE MANHATTAN REVIEW, c/o Philip Fried, 440 Riverside Drive, #38, New York, NY 10027, 212-932-1854, phfried@aol.com

MICROWAVE NEWS, PO Box 1799, Grand Central Station, New York, NY 10163, 212-517-2800

MUDFISH, 184 Franklin Street, New York, NY 10013, 212-219-9278

NAMBLA BULLETIN, PO Box 174, Midtown Station, New York, NY 10018, 212-631-1194, arnoldschoen@yahoo.com

NBM Publishing Company, 555 8th Avenue, Ste. 1202, New York, NY 10018-4364, 212-643-5407, Fax 212-643-1545

New Concept Press, 425 West 57th Street Suite 2J, New York, NY 10019, 212-265-6284, Fax: 212-265-6659

THE NEW YORK QUARTERLY, PO Box 693, Old Chelsea Station, New York, NY 10113, info@nyquarterly.com, www.nyquarterly.com

Nightjar Press, P.O. Box 583, New York, NY 10002

NIGHTJAR REVIEW, P.O. Box 583, New York, NY 10002

THE NONVIOLENT ACTIVIST, War Resisters League, 339 Lafayette Street, New York, NY 10012, 212-228-0450, fax 212-228-6193, e-Mail wrl@igc.apc.org

NOON, 1369 Madison Avenue, PMB 298, New York, NY 10128, noonannual@yahoo.com

ON EARTH, 40 West 20th Street, New York, NY 10011, 212-727-2700

The Overlook Press, 141 Wooster Street #4, New York, NY 10012-3163, 914-679-8571

Panther Books, 197 Seventh Avenue 4C, New York, NY 10011, www.goodie.org

PARABOLA MAGAZINE, 135 East 15 Street, New York, NY 10003-3557, 212-505-6200, Fax 212-979-7325, parabola@panix.com, www.parabola.org

PARNASSUS: Poetry in Review, 205 West 89th Street #8F, New York, NY 10024-1835, 212-362-3492, Fax 212-875-0148, parnew@aol.com, website www.parnassuspoetry.com

The Passion Profit Company, PO Box 618, Church Street Station, New York, NY 10008-0618, (646)219-3565, info@passionprofit.com, www.passionprofit.com

Pedestal Press, PO Box 6093, Yorkville Station, New York, NY 10128, 212-876-5119

Pella Publishing Co., 337 West 36th Street, New York, NY 10018, 212-279-9586

PEN AMERICA: A Journal for Writers & Readers, 588 Broadway, Room 303, New York, NY 10012-3229, 212-334-1660 x115, Fax 212-334-2181, journal@pen.org, www.pen.org/journal

Pendragonian Publications, PO Box 719, New York, NY 10101-0719, mmpendragon@aol.com

PENNY DREADFUL: Tales and Poems of Fantastic Terror, PO Box 719, New York, NY 10101-0719, mmpendragon@aol.com

Philomel Books, 345 Hudson Street, New York, NY 10014, 212-414-3610

Phoenix Illusion, PO Box 2268, New York, NY 10027, (917) 577-8499

Pleasure Boat Studio: A Literary Press, 201 West 89 Street, New York, NY 10024-1848, 212-362-8563 telephone, 888-810-5308 fax, pleasboat@nyc.rr.com, www.pleasureboatstudio.com

The Poetry Project, St. Mark's Church, 131 East 10th Street, New York, NY 10003, 212-674-0910, poproj@thorn.net

THE POETRY PROJECT NEWSLETTER, St. Mark's Church, 131 East 10th Street, New York, NY 10003, 212-674-0910, poproj@thorn.net

POETS & WRITERS MAGAZINE, 72 Spring Street, New York, NY 10012, 212-226-3586, Fax 212-226-3963, www.pw.org

Poets & Writers, Inc., 72 Spring Street, New York, NY 10012, 212-226-3586, Fax 212-226-3963, www.pw.org

Prologue Press, 375 Riverside Drive #14-C, New York, NY 10025

PSYCHOANALYTIC BOOKS: A QUARTERLY JOURNAL OF REVIEWS, 211 East 70th Street, New York, NY 10021, 212-628-8792, Fax 212-628-8453, psabooks@datagram.com

Psychohistory Press, 140 Riverside Drive, New York, NY 10024, 212-799-2294

RATTAPALLAX, 532 La Guardia Place, Suite 353, New York, NY 10012, info@rattapallax.com

Read Press LLC, 305 Madison Ave., Suite 449, New York, NY 10165

Red Dust, PO Box 630, Gracie Station, New York, NY 10028, 212-348-4388

Red Rock Press, 459 Columbus Avenue, Ste. 114, New York, NY 10024, 212-362-8304, Fax 212-362-6216, redrockprs@aol.com, www.redrockpress.com

SCANDINAVIAN REVIEW, 58 Park Avenue, New York, NY 10016-3007, 212-879-9779

SCIENCE & SOCIETY, 72 Spring Street, New York, NY 10012, 212-431-9800

SCRAWL MAGAZINE, PO Box 205, New York, NY 10012, e-mail scrawl@bigfoot.com

SLEAZOID EXPRESS, PO Box 620, Old Chelsea Station, New York, NY 10011

SONGS OF INNOCENCE, PO Box 719, New York, NY 10101-0719, mmpendragon@aol.com

SPACE AND TIME, 138 West 70th Street 4-B, New York, NY 10023-4432

Space and Time Press, 138 West 70th Street 4-B, New York, NY 10023-4468

SPINNING JENNY, P.O. Box 1373, New York, NY 10276-1373, www.spinning-jenny.com

Spire Press, 532 LaGuardia Place, Ste. 298, New York, NY 10012, www.spirepress.org

SWINK, 244 Fifth Ave. #2722, New York, NY 10001, 212-591-1651, 212-658-9995, www.swinkmag.com

SYNERJY: A Directory of Renewable Energy, Box 1854/Cathedral Station, New York, NY 10025, 212-865-9595, jtwine@synerjy.com

Teachers & Writers Collaborative, 5 Union Square West, New York, NY 10003, 212-691-6590, 212-675-0171

TEACHERS & WRITERS MAGAZINE, 5 Union Square West, New York, NY 10003, 212-691-6590, www.twc.org

TELOS, 431 East 12th Street, New York, NY 10009, 212-228-6479

Telos Press, 431 East 12th Street, New York, NY 10009, 212-228-6479

TFG Press, 244 Madison Avenue, #254, New York, NY 10016, floatingal@aol.com

TnT Classic Books, 360 West 36 Street #2NW, New York, NY 10018-6412, 212-736-6279, Fax 212-695-3219, tntclassics@aol.com, www.tntclassicbooks.com

Touchstone Center Publications, 141 East 88th Street, New York, NY 10128, rlewis212@aol.com

TRICYCLE: The Buddhist Review, 92 Vandam Street, New York, NY 10013-1007

Truman Press, inc., d/b/a "Hannover House", 163 Amsterdam Ave. #303, New York, NY 10023, 866-227-2628; Fax 479-587-0857; www.HannoverHouse.com

The Twickenham Press, 31 Jane Street, New York, NY 10014, 212-741-2417

Tzipora Publications, Inc., P.O. Box 633, New York, NY 10035, www.tziporapub.com

UNMUZZLED OX, 105 Hudson St., New York, NY 10013, 718-448-3395, 212-226-7170, MAndreOX@aol.com

VANITAS, 211 West 19th Street, #5, New York, NY 10011-4001, vanitas@el.net

Vantage Press, Inc., 419 Park Ave. S., New York, NY 10016, Ph:212-736-1767, F: 212-736-2273, 1-800-882-3273

Visions Communications, 200 E. 10th Street #714, New York, NY 10003, 212-529-4029 phone/Fax

W.W. Norton, 500 Fifth Avenue, New York, NY 10110, 212-354-5500

Water Mark Press, 138 Duane Street, New York, NY 10013, 212-285-1609, 914-238-6549, cocogord@mindspring.com, http://www.galerie.kultur.at/coco/base/core.htm

THE WORLD, St. Marks Church/The Poetry Project, 131 East 10th Street, New York, NY 10003, poproj@thorn.net

WSQ (formerly WOMEN'S STUDIES QUARTERLY), The Feminist Press at CUNY, 365 Fifth Avenue, Suite 5406, New York, NY 10016, 212-817-7915, 212-817-1593, aroy@gc.cuny.edu, www.feministpress.org/wsq

ZerOX Books, 105 Hudson Street, #311, New York, NY 10013

Midmarch Arts Press, 300 Riverside Drive, New York City, NY 10025, 212-666-6990

LIFE LEARNING, PO Box 112, Niagara Falls, NY 14304-0112, (416) 260-0303, email: publisher@lifelearningmagazine.com, Website: www.lifelearningmagazine.com

NATURAL LIFE, Box 112, Niagara Falls, NY 14304-0112, 416-260-0303, email: natural@life.ca, web: www.NaturalLifeMa-

gazine.com
SLIPSTREAM, Box 2071, New Market Station, Niagara Falls, NY 14301, 716-282-2616 (after 5 p.m., E.S.T.)
Slipstream Productions, Box 2071, New Market Station, Niagara Falls, NY 14301
thinkBiotech, 3909 Witmer Rd #416, Niagara Falls, NY 14305
Radiant Press, P.O. Box 20017, NYC, NY 10025-9992, 212-592-1765
ROOM, 38 Ferris Place, Ossining, NY 10562-2818
Avocet Press Inc., 19 Paul Court, Pearl River, NY 10965, 212-754-6300, oopc@interport.net, www.avocetpress.com
Manifold Press, 102 Bridge Street, Plattsburgh, NY 12901, editormanifoldpress@msn.com, www.manifoldpress.com
Willowgate Press, 120 Brook Road, Port Jefferson, NY 11777-1665, willowgatepress@yahoo.com, www.willowgatepress.com
Chatterley Press International, 19 Dorothy Street, Port Jefferson Station, NY 11776, 631-928-9074 phone/Fax, info@chatterleypress.com
Odysseus Enterprises Ltd., PO Box 1548, Port Washington, NY 11050-0306, 516-944-5330, Fax 516-944-7540
BLUELINE, State University College, English Dept., Potsdam, NY 13676, 315-267-2043
UNBOUND, Dept. of English & Communication, SUNY-Potsdam, Potsdam, NY 13676, unbound@potsdam.edu
THE WALLACE STEVENS JOURNAL, Clarkson University, Box 5750, Potsdam, NY 13699-5750, 315-268-3987, serio@clarkson.edu, www.wallacestevens.com
The Wallace Stevens Society Press, Box 5750 Clarkson University, Potsdam, NY 13699-5750, 315-268-3987, Fax 268-3983, serio@clarkson.edu, www.wallacestevens.com
INKWELL, Manhattanville College, 2900 Purchase Street, Purchase, NY 10577, www.inkwelljournal.org
Aletheia Publications, Inc., 46 Bell Hollow Road, Putnam Valley, NY 10579-1426, 845-526-2873, Fax 845-526-2905
Honors Group, Adirondack Community College, SUNY, Queensbury, NY 12804
CADENCE: The Review of Jazz & Blues: Creative Improvised Music, Cadence Building, Redwood, NY 13679, 315-287-2852, Fax 315-287-2860
Black Spring Press, 63-89 Saunders Street #6G, Rego Park, NY 11374
BLACK SPRING REVIEW, 63-89 Saunders Street #6G, Rego Park, NY 11374
INNOVATING, The Rensselaerville Institute, Rensselaerville, NY 12147, 518-797-3783
Great Elm Press, 1205 County Route 60, Rexville, NY 14877
Monkfish Book Publishing Company, 27 Lamoree Road, Rhinebeck, NY 12572, 845-876-4861, www.monkfishpublishing.com
THE PUBLIC RELATIONS QUARTERLY, PO Box 311, Rhinebeck, NY 12572, 845-876-2081, Fax 845-876-2561
Rhinecliff Press, Ltd., PO Box 333, Rhinecliff, NY 12574, rkirsch@hvc.rr.com
AFTERIMAGE, 31 Prince Street, Rochester, NY 14607, 585/442.8676, fax 585.442.1992, afterimage@vsw.org, www.vsw.org/afterimage/
BOA Editions, Ltd., 260 East Avenue, Rochester, NY 14604, 585-546-3410, www.boaeditions.org
Lion Press, PO Box 92541, Rochester, NY 14692, phone 585-381-6410; fax 585-381-7439; for orders only 800-597-3068
THE ROUND TABLE: A Journal of Poetry and Fiction, PO Box 18673, Rochester, NY 14618
Visual Studies Workshop, 31 Prince Street, Rochester, NY 14607, 585-442-8676, www.vsw.org
Butcher Shop Press, 529 Beach 132nd St., Rockaway Park, NY 11694-1413
FULLOSIA PRESS, RPPS, PO Box 280, Ronkonkoma, NY 11779, deanofrpps@aol.com, http://rpps_fullosia_press.tripod.com
ALTERNATIVE EDUCATION RESOURCE ORGANIZATION, 417 Roslyn Road, Roslyn Heights, NY 11577, 516-621-2195, Fax 516-625-3257, jerryaero@aol.com
Bone World Publishing, 3700 County Road 24, Russell, NY 13684
MuscleHead Press, 3700 County Route 24, Russell, NY 13684
The Bookman Press, PO Box 1892, Sag Harbor, NY 11963, 631-725-1115
The Permanent Press/The Second Chance Press, 4170 Noyac Road, Sag Harbor, NY 11963, 631-725-1101
Savant Garde Workshop, PO Box 1650, Sag Harbor, NY 11963-0060, 631-725-1414; website www.savantgarde.org
Sagapress, Inc., Box 21, 30 Sagaponack Road, Sagaponack, NY 11962, 516-537-3717; Fax 516-537-5415
SALMAGUNDI, Skidmore College, 815 North Broadway, Saratoga Springs, NY 12866-1632, 518-584-5186
Autelitano Media Group (AMG), 1036 Dean St., Schenectady, NY 12309-5720, 561-350-1923, Fax 561-276-0931, Autelitano@aol.com, www.AuteliMedia.com
WRITERS INK, PO Box 2344, Selden, NY 11784, 631-451-0478, Fax 631-451-0478, http://www.writersunlimited.org
Writers Unlimited Agency, Inc, PO Box 2344, Selden, NY 11784, 631-451-0478, Fax 631-451-0478, writersunlimited-agency@yahoo.com http://www.writersunlimited.org
Writers Ink Press, 233 Mooney Pond, PO Box 2344, Selden, Long Island, NY 11784-2344, 631-451-0478, Fax 631-451-0478, axelrodthepoet@yahoo.com
HELIOTROPE, A JOURNAL OF POETRY, P.O Box 456, Shady, NY 12409, www.heliopoems.com
Sound View Publishing, Inc., P.O. Box 696, Shoreham, NY 11786-0696, 631-899-2481, Fax 631-899-2487, 1-888-529-3496, info@SoundViewPublishing.com, www.SoundViewPublishing.com
Slapering Hol Press, 300 Riverside Drive, Sleepy Hollow, NY 10591-1414, 914-332-5953, Fax 914-332-4825, info@writerscenter.org, www.writerscenter.org
THE $ENSIBLE SOUND, 403 Darwin Drive, Snyder, NY 14226, 716-833-0930
Portmanteau Editions, PO Box 665, Somers, NY 10589
Whelks Walk Press, 37 Harvest Lane, Southampton, NY 11968, whelkswalk@aol.com
Sunnyside Press, 297 Triumpho Road, St. Johnsville, NY 13452-4003, 518-568-7853 phone/Fax, triglade@telenet.net
AMERICAN TANKA, PO Box 120-024, Staten Island, NY 10312-0024, editorsdesk@americantanka.com, www.american-tanka.com
Bard Press, 393 St. Pauls Avenue, Staten Island, NY 10304-2127, 718-442-7429
DESIRE, 463 Barlow Avenue, Staten Island, NY 10308, 718-317-7484, marynicholaou@aol.com, www.geocities.com/marynicholaou/classic_blue.html
Eros Books, 463 Barlow Avenue, Staten Island, NY 10308, 718-317-7484
PSYCHE, 463 Barlow Avenue, Staten Island, NY 10308, 718-317-7484
Ten Penny Players, Inc., 393 St. Pauls Avenue, Staten Island, NY 10304-2127, 718-442-7429, www.tenpennyplayers.org
WATERWAYS: Poetry in the Mainstream, 393 St. Pauls Avenue, Staten Island, NY 10304-2127, 718-442-7429, www.tenpennyplayers.org, bfisher@si.rr.com or rspiegel@si.rr.com
TAPROOT, a journal of older writers, PO Box 841, University at Stony Brook, Stony Brook, NY 11790-0841, 631-689-0668
Celebrity Profiles Publishing, PO Box 344, Stonybrook, NY 11790, 631-862-8555, Fax 631-862-0139, celebpro4@aol.com, rgrudens1@aol.com
THE COMSTOCK REVIEW, Comstock Writers' Group, Inc., 4956 St. John Drive, Syracuse, NY 13215, www.comstockreview.org

587

NEW ENVIRONMENT BULLETIN, 270 Fenway Drive, Syracuse, NY 13224, 315-446-8009
POINT OF CONTACT, The Journal of Verbal & Visual Arts, 216 H.B. Crouse Building, Syracuse University, Syracuse, NY 13244-1160, 315-443-2247, Fax 315-443-5376, cfawcett@syr.edu, www.pointcontact.org
Purple Finch Press, 109 Warwick Road, Syracuse, NY 13214-2219, 315-445-8087
SALT HILL, English Department, Syracuse University, Syracuse, NY 13244-1170
Syracuse Cultural Workers/Tools for Change, PO Box 6367, Syracuse, NY 13217, 315-474-1132, free fax 877-265-5399, scw@syrculturalworkers.org
THEATRE DESIGN AND TECHNOLOGY, 6443 Ridings Road, Syracuse, NY 13206-1111
United States Institute for Theatre Technology, Inc., 6443 Ridings Road, Syracuse, NY 13206-1111
Bright Hill Press, PO Box 193, Treadwell, NY 13846-0193, 607-829-5055, fax 607-829-5054, wordthur@stny.rr.com. web: www.brighthillpress.org
White Crosslet Publishing Co, 456 West Lake Road, tuxedo park, NY 10987, 845 351 3345 (fax&telephone)
North Country Books, Inc., 311 Turner Street, Utica, NY 13501, 315-735-4877
IRISH LITERARY SUPPLEMENT, 2592 N Wading River Road, Wading River, NY 11792-1404, 631-929-0224
Pushcart Press, PO Box 380, Wainscott, NY 11975, 631-324-9300, www.pushcartprize.com
Pine Publications, 2947 Jerusalem Avenue, Wantagh, NY 11793-2020
Beekman Books, Inc., 300 Old All Angels Hill Road, Wappingers Falls, NY 12590, 845-297-2690
Success Publishing, 3419 Dunham Drive, Box 263, Warsaw, NY 14569
HEAVEN BONE MAGAZINE, 62 Woodcock Mt. Dr., Washingtonville, NY 10992-1828, 845-496-4109
Heaven Bone Press, 62 Woodcock Mtn. Dr., Washingtonville, NY 10992, 845-496-4109
THE ADIRONDACK REVIEW, 305 Keyes Avenue, Watertown, NY 13601-3731, publisher@blacklawrencepress.com, editor@adkreview.com, www.blacklawrencepress.com, www.adkreview.com
Black Lawrence Press, 305 Keyes Avenue, Watertown, NY 13601-3731, publisher@blacklawrencepress.com, editor@adkreview.com, www.blacklawrencepress.com, www.adkreview.com
Gingerbread House, 602 Montauk A Highway, West Hampton Beach, NY 11978, 631-288-5119, Fax 631-288-5179, ghbooks@optonline.net, www.gingerbreadbooks.com
National Economic Research Associates, Inc., 50 Main Street, 14th Floor, White Plains, NY 10606, 617-621-6289
Roblin Press, 388 Tarrytown Road, Upper Level, White Plains, NY 10607, 914-220-6509
Alms House Press, PO Box 218, Woodbourne, NY 12788-0218
Career Advancement Center, Inc., PO Box 436, Woodmere, NY 11598-0436, 516-374-1387, Fax 516-374-1175, caradvctr@aol.com, www.smallbusinessadvice.com
THE SMALL BUSINESS ADVISOR, PO Box 436, Woodmere, NY 11598, 516-374-1387, Fax 516-374-1175, smalbusadv@aol.com, www.smallbusinessadvice.com
Celtic Heritage Books, PO Box 770637, Woodside, NY 11377-0637, Tel/Fax: 718-478-8162; Toll Free: 877-785-2610 (code 0236)
LULLABY HEARSE, 45-34 47th St. Apt. 6AB, Woodside, NY 11377, editor@lullabyhearse.com, www.lullabyhearse.com
SKINNYDIPPING, 51-04 39th Avenue, Woodside, NY 11377-3145, 718-651-4689, FAX 718-424-1883
Ash Tree Publishing, PO Box 64, Woodstock, NY 12498, 845-246-8081
Ceres Press, PO Box 87, Woodstock, NY 12498, tel/fax: 845-679-5573, web: www.HealthyHighways.com
Maverick Books, Box 897, Woodstock, NY 12498, 866-478-9266 phone/Fax, maverickbooks@aol.com
YogaVidya.com, PO Box 569, Woodstock, NY 12498-0569, 845-679-2313, Fax 586-283-4680, info@yogavidya.com, www.yogavidya.com
Lekon New Dimensions Publishing, PO Box 504, Yonkers, NY 10702, 914-965-5181, rcnfyle@aol.com

NORTH CAROLINA

Altamont Press, Inc., 67 Broadway Street, Asheville, NC 28801-2919, 704-253-0468
Black Mountain Press, PO Box 18912, Asheville, NC 28814, Tel; 828-350-8484,email. BlackMtnPress@aol.com
Brave Ulysses Books, 54 Fulton St., Asheville, NC 28801-1807, 828-713-8840, cecil@braveulysses.com, www.braveulysses.com
FIBERARTS, 67 Broadway Street, Asheville, NC 28801-2919, 704-253-0468
THE FRONT STRIKER BULLETIN, The Retskin Report, PO Box 18481, Asheville, NC 28814-0481, 828-254-4487
Shannon D. Harle, Publisher, 329 Merrills Cove Rd., Asheville, NC 28803-8527
THE INDIE, 61 Dunwell Ave., Asheville, NC 28806-3431, 828-225-5994, raindance60@hotmail.com
Urthona Press, 62 LakeShore Drive, Asheville, NC 28804-2436
COMMUNITIES, 1025 Camp Elliott Road, Black Mountain, NC 28711, 828-669-9702, communities@ic.org, www.ic.org, store.ic.org
Lorien House, Attn: David Wilson, PO Box 1112, Black Mountain, NC 28711, 828-669-6211, LorienHouseA1@aol.com
Appalachian Consortium Press, University Hall, Appalachian State University, Boone, NC 28608, 704-262-2064, fax 704-262-6564
CORRECTION(S): A Literary Journal for Inmate Writing, PO Box 1326, Boone, NC 28607-1326
Parkway Publishers, Inc., PO Box 3678, Boone, NC 28607, 828-265-3993
Celo Valley Books, 160 Ohle Road, Burnsville, NC 28714, 828-675-5918
Scots Plaid Press, 600 Kelly Road, Carthage, NC 28327, 910-947-2587; Fax 910-947-5112
Trafton Publishing, 109 Barcliff Terrace, Cary, NC 27511-8900
Blink Chapbooks, CB #3520, Greenlaw Hall, UNC, Chapel Hill, NC 27599-3520
THE CAROLINA QUARTERLY, CB# 3520 Greenlaw Hall, Univ of N. Carolina, Chapel Hill, NC 27599-3520, 919-962-0244, Fax 919-962-3520
THE JOURNAL OF AFRICAN TRAVEL-WRITING, PO Box 346, Chapel Hill, NC 27514
LEGAL INFORMATION MANAGEMENT INDEX, Legal Information Services, 6609 Glen Forest Drive, Chapel Hill, NC 27514, 919-419-8390
THE SUN, A Magazine of Ideas, 107 North Roberson Street, Chapel Hill, NC 27516, 919-942-5282
A. Borough Books, 3901 Silver Bell Drive, Charlotte, NC 28211, 704-364-1788, 800-843-8490 (orders only), humorbooks@aol.com
IODINE POETRY JOURNAL, PO Box 18548, Charlotte, NC 28218-0548
MAIN STREET RAG, 4416 Shea Lane, Charlotte, NC 28227-8245, 704-573-2516, editor@mainstreetrag.com
Granite Publishing Group, PO Box 1429, Columbus, NC 28722, 828-894-8444, Fax 828-894-8454, GraniteP@aol.com, www.5thworld.com
Swan Raven & Company, PO Box 1429, Columbus, NC 28722

588

New Native Press, PO Box 661, Cullowhee, NC 28723, 828-293-9237

Carolina Academic Press, 700 Kent Street, Durham, NC 27701, 919-489-7486, fax:919-493-5668

Carolina Wren Press/Lollipop Power Books, 120 Morris Street, Durham, NC 27701, 919-560-2738; www.carolinawren-press.org

Duke University Press, Box 90660, Durham, NC 27708-0660, 919-687-3600; Fax 919-688-4574, www.dukepress.edu

Horse & Buggy Press, 2016 Englewood Avenue, Durham, NC 27705-4113, 919-828-2514

MINESHAFT, P. O. Box 1226, Durham, NC 27702

Sadorian Publications, PO Box 2443, Durham, NC 27715-2443, 919-599-3038, Fax 309-431-4387, sadorianllc@aol.com, www.Sadorianonline.com

Bright Mountain Books, Inc., 206 Riva Ridge Drive, Fairview, NC 28730-9764, booksbmb@charter.net

GREEN PRINTS, ''The Weeder's Digest'', PO Box 1355, Fairview, NC 28730, 828-628-1902, www.greenprints.com, patstone@atlantic.net

Longleaf Press, Methodist College, English Dept., 5400 Ramsey Street, Fayetteville, NC 28311, 910-822-5403

PREP Publishing, 1110 1/2 Hay Street, Suite C, Fayetteville, NC 28305, 910-483-6611, Fax 910-483-2439

Avisson Press, Inc., 3007 Taliaferro Road, Greensboro, NC 27408, 336-288-6989 phone/FAX

BACKWARDS CITY REVIEW, P.O. Box 41317, Greensboro, NC 27404-1317

ELT Press, English Dept., Univ of N. Carolina, PO Box 26170, Greensboro, NC 27402-6170, 336-334-5446, Fax 336-334-3281, langenfeld@uncg.edu

ENGLISH LITERATURE IN TRANSITION, 1880-1920, English Department/U of North Carolina, P.O. Box 26170, Greensboro, NC 27402-6170, 336-334-5446, Fax 336-334-3281; langenfeld@uncg.edu

THE GREENSBORO REVIEW, PO Box 26170, Dept. of English, Univ. of North Carolina-Greensboro, Greensboro, NC 27402-6170, 336-334-5459, Fax 336-256-1470, jlclark@uncg.edu, www.uncg.edu/eng/mfa

INTERNATIONAL POETRY REVIEW, Dept of Romance Languages, Univ. of North Carolina, Greensboro, NC 27402-6170, 336-334-5655

LETTER ARTS REVIEW, PO Box 9986, Greensboro, NC 27429, 800-369-9598, 336-272-6139, Fax 336-272-9015, lar@johnnealbooks.com

March Street Press, 3413 Wilshire Drive, Greensboro, NC 27408-2923, www.marchstreetpress.com

Open Hand Publishing LLC, PO Box 20207, Greensboro, NC 27420, 336-292-8585, Fax 336-292-8588, 866-888-9229; info@openhand.com; www.openhand.com

PARTING GIFTS, 3413 Wilshire Drive, Greensboro, NC 27408-2923, www.marchstreetpress.com

TIMBER CREEK REVIEW, c/o J.M. Freiermuth, PO Box 16542, Greensboro, NC 27416

WORDS OF WISDOM, Mikhammad Abdel-Ishara, Editor, PO Box 16542, Greensboro, NC 27416, e-mail wowmail@hoops-mail.com

Zante Publishing, P.O. Box 35404, Greensboro, NC 27425, (336) 605-7900

NORTH CAROLINA LITERARY REVIEW, English Department, East Carolina University, Greenville, NC 27858, 252-328-1537; Fax 252-328-4889

TAR RIVER POETRY, Department of English, East Carolina University, Greenville, NC 27858-4353, 252-328-6046

Shipyard Press, LC, 191 Brightwater Falls Road, Henderson, NC 28739-7171, 239-822-9964

Myrtle Hedge Press, PO Box 705, Kernersville, NC 27285

MBA Publications, PO Box 50, Kitty Hawk, NC 27949, 252-261-7611

Herrmann International, 794 Buffalo Creek Road, Lake Lure, NC 28746, Fax 704-625-9153

CAIRN: The New ST. ANDREWS REVIEW, St. Andrews Prebyterian College, 1700 Dogwood Mile, Laurinburg, NC 28352, 910-277-5000, 910-277-9925

St. Andrews College Press, 1700 Dogwood Mile, Laurinburg, NC 28352-5598, 910-277-5310

Thirsty Turtle Press, PO Box 402, Maggie Valley, NC 28751, Phone 828-926-6472, FAX 828-926-8851, dan@thirstyturtle-press.com, www.thirstyturtlepress.com

Metallo House Publishers, 170 E. River Road, Moncure, NC 27559-9617, 919-542-2908, Fax 919-774-5611

Explorer Press, 1501 Edgewood Drive, Mount Airy, NC 27030-5215, 336-789-6005, Fax 336-789-6005, E-mail terryleecollins@hotmail.com

Mount Olive College Press, Mount Olive College, 634 Henderson Street, Mount Olive, NC 28365

MOUNT OLIVE REVIEW, Department of Language and Literature, 634 Henderson Street, Mount Olive, NC 28365, 919-658-2502

PEMBROKE MAGAZINE, UNCP, Box 1510, Pembroke, NC 28372-1510, 919-521-4214 ext 433

DRT Press, PO Box 427, Pittsboro, NC 27312-0427, 1-919-542-1763 (phone/fax), editorial@drtpress.com, www.drtpress.com

C & M Online Media Inc., 3905 Meadow Field Lane, Raleigh, NC 27606-4470, www.cmonline.com, cm@cmonline.com

Ivy House Publishing Group, 5122 Bur Oak Circle, Raleigh, NC 27612, 919-782-0281

OBSIDIAN III: Literature in the African Diaspora, Dept. of English, Box 8105, NC State University, Raleigh, NC 27695-8105, 919-515-4150

Three Pyramids Publishing, 6512 Nathans Landing Drive, Raleigh, NC 27603-7914, 813-426-3334, E-mail JFS999@mindspring.com

REFLECTIONS LITERARY JOURNAL, PO Box 1197, Roxboro, NC 27573, 336-599-1181, reflect@piedmontcc.edu

Harlan Publishing Company; Alliance Books; Diakonia Publishing (Christian Books), P.O. Box 397, Summerfield, NC 27358, 336-643-5849, harlan@northstate.net, www.harlanpublishing.com

PANIC STRIPS, PO Box 1005, Swannanoa, NC 28778-1005

ROTTEN PEPPER, PO Box 1005, Swannanoa, NC 28778-1005

T.V. HEADS, PO Box 1005, Swannanoa, NC 28778-1005

Ammons Communications, 29 Regal Ave, Amy, Sylva, NC 28779-2877, v.ammons@mchsi.com

ARTISTIC RAMBLINGS, P.O. Box 2907, Thomasville, NC 27361, PH: 832-634-7012, Fax: 530-323-8251, email: ArtisticRamblings@gmail.com

Red Tiger Press, P.O. Box 2907, Thomasville, NC 27361, PH: 832-634-7012, Fax: 530-323-8251, email: RedTiger-Press@gmail.com

Banks Channel Books, 2314 Waverly Drive, Wilmington, NC 28403-6040, Order phone 1-800-2229796, E-mail bankschan@ec.rr.com

ECOTONE: Reimagining Place, UNCW Dept. of Creative Writing, 601 South College Road, Wilmington, NC 28403-3297, 910-962-3070

LifeSkill Institute, Inc., P.O. Box 302, Wilmington, NC 28402, 910-251-0665,910-763-2494,800-570-4009,lifeskill@earth-link.net,www.lifeskillinstitute.org

CRUCIBLE, Office of the Vice President for Academic Affairs, Barton College, Wilson, NC 27893, 252-399-6344

John F. Blair, Publisher, 1406 Plaza Drive, Winston-Salem, NC 27103, 336-768-1374

NORTH DAKOTA

Ephemera Bound Publishing, 719 9th St N, Fargo, ND 58102, 701-306-6458
NORTH DAKOTA QUARTERLY, University of North Dakota, PO Box 7209, Grand Forks, ND 58202, 701-777-3322
Sage Hill Press, 3725 University Ave., Apt.101, Grand Forks, ND 58203-0523, 701-777-9605, sagehillpress@yahoo.com
UND Press, University of North Dakota, PO Box 7209, Grand Forks, ND 58202, 701-777-3321
HEALTHY WEIGHT JOURNAL, 402 South 14th Street, Hettinger, ND 58639, 701-567-2646, Fax 701-567-2602, e-mail fmberg@healthyweight.net
Willowood Press, PO Box 1846, Minot, ND 58702, 701-838-0579

OHIO

KALEIDOSCOPE: Exploring the Experience of Disability through Literature & the Fine Arts, United Disability Services, 701 S. Main Street, Akron, OH 44311-1019, 330-762-9755, 330-379-3349 (TDD), Fax 330-762-0912, mshiplett@udsakron.org, pboerner@udsakron.org, www.udsakron.org
SACS Consulting, 520 South Main St., Suite 2512, Akron, OH 44311-1073, tadimoff@sacsconsulting.com, www.sacsconsulting.com 330-255-1101
Twin Sisters Productions, 2680 West Market Street, Akron, OH 44333-4206, 800-248-TWIN, 330-864-3000, Fax 800-480-TWIN, 330-864-3200
Sugar Loaf Press, 4160 Racoon Valley Road, Alexandria, OH 43001, 740-924-9335
The Ashland Poetry Press, Ashland University, Ashland, OH 44805, 419-289-5110, FAX 419-289-5329
HOTEL AMERIKA, 360 Ellis Hall, Ohio University, Athens, OH 45701, 740-597-1360, editors@hotelamerika.net, www.hotelamerika.net
Ohio University Press/Swallow Press, The Ridges, Building 19, Athens, OH 45701, 740-593-1157, www.ohio.edu/oupress
QUARTER AFTER EIGHT, Ellis Hall, Ohio University, Athens, OH 45701
Writer's World Press, PO Box 284, Aurora, OH 44202-0284, WritersWorld@juno.com, www.writersworldpress.com
The Pin Prick Press, 23511 Chagrin Boulevard #519, Beachwood, OH 44122-5539, 216-378-2253, Fax 216-378-2275
Raven Rocks Press, 53650 Belmont Ridge Road, Beallsville, OH 43716, 614-926-1705
CONFLUENCE, PO Box 336, Belpre, OH 45714-0336, 304-295-6599, wilmaacree@charter.net
GRASSLANDS REVIEW, PO Box 626, Berea, OH 44017
Gabriel's Horn Publishing Co., Inc., Box 141, Bowling Green, OH 43402, 419-352-1338, fax 419-352-1488
MID-AMERICAN REVIEW, Dept of English, Bowling Green State University, Bowling Green, OH 43403-0191, 419-372-2725, www.bgsu.edu/midamericanreview
PRAIRIE MARGINS, Department of English, Bowling Green State University, Bowling Green, OH 43403, debrab@bgnet.bgsu.edu http://www.bgsu.edu/departments/creative-writing/home.html (under BFA)
Faded Banner Publications, PO Box 101, Bryan, OH 43506-0101, 419-636-3807,419-63603807 (fax), 888-799-3787, fadedbanner.com
THE LISTENING EYE, KSU Geauga Campus, 14111 Claridon-Troy Road, Burton, OH 44021, 440-286-3840, grace_butcher@msn.com
CYBERFICT, English Department, Wright State Univ - Lake Campus, 7600 State Routem 703, Celina, OH 45822, www.wright.edu/~martin.kich/
GRAND LAKE REVIEW, Wright State University-Lake Campus, 7600 State Route 703, Celina, OH 45822, 419-586-0374, Fax 419-586-0368, martin.kich@wright.edu, www.wright.edu/~martin.kich/
New Community Press, 2692 Madison Road N-1, #263, Cincinnati, OH 45208, 513-509-9352, newcommunitypress@cinci.rr.com
SPITBALL: The Literary Baseball Magazine, 5560 Fox Road, Cincinnati, OH 45239-7271, 513-385-2268
Watershed Books, 9413 Southgate Drive, Cincinnati, OH 45241-3340, publisher@watershedbooks.com
Word Press, PO Box 541106, Cincinnati, OH 45254-1106, 513-474-3761, Fax 513-474-9034, www.word-press.com
Chapultepec Press, 4222 Chambers, Cincinnati, Ohio 45223, OH 45223, chapultepecpress@hotmail.com http://www.tokyoroserecords.com
Cleveland State Univ. Poetry Center, 1983 East 24th Street, Cleveland, OH 44115-2400, 216-687-3986; Fax 216-687-6943; poetrycenter@popmail.csuohio.edu
deep cleveland press, PO Box 14248, Cleveland, OH 44114-0248, 216-706-3725, press@deepcleveland.com, www.deepcleveland.com
ERASED, SIGH, SIGH, 701 East Schaaf Road, Cleveland, OH 44131-1227, ViaDolorosaPress@sbcglobal.net, www.angelfire.com/oh2/dolorosa/erased.html
OHIO WRITER, 12200 Fairhill Road, Townhouse #3A, Cleveland, OH 44120-1058, website: www.pwlgc.com
Phelps Publishing Company, PO Box 22401, Cleveland, OH 44122, 216-433-2531, 216-752-4938
Storytime Ink International, PO Box 470505, Cleveland, OH 44147-0505, 440-838-4881; fax 408-580-5967; e-mail storytimeink@att.net
Via Dolorosa Press, 701 East Schaaf Road, Cleveland, OH 44131-1227, viadolorosapress@sbcglobal.net
THE FUNNY TIMES, PO Box 18530, Cleveland Heights, OH 44118, 216-371-8600, Fax 216-371-8696, www.funnytimes.com, info@funnytimes.com
Hailey-Grey Books, 2569 Fairmount Blvd, Cleveland Heights, OH 44106, 216-932-3235
Ecrivez!, PO Box 247491, Columbus, OH 43224-2002, 614-253-0773, Fax 614-253-0774
THE JOURNAL, OSU Dept. of English, 164 W. 17th Avenue, 421 Denney Hall, Columbus, OH 43210-1370, 614-292-4076, fax 614-292-7816, thejournal@osu.edu
Luna Bisonte Prods, 137 Leland Ave, Columbus, OH 43214, 614-846-4126
Ohio State University Press, 1050 Carmack Road, Columbus, OH 43210, 614-292-6930
OHIOANA QUARTERLY, 274 E. First Avenue, Columbus, OH 43201, 614-466-3831, Fax 614-728-6974, e-mail ohioana@sloma.state.oh.us
PAVEMENT SAW, PO Box 6291, Columbus, OH 43206, 614-445-0534, info@pavementsaw.org, www.pavementsaw.org
Pavement Saw Press, PO Box 6291, Columbus, OH 43206, info@pavementsaw.org, www.pavementsaw.org
Pudding House Publications, 81 Shadymere Lane, Columbus, OH 43213-1568, 614-986-1881, info@puddinghouse.com, www.puddinghouse.com
PUDDING MAGAZINE: The International Journal of Applied Poetry, 81 Shadymere Lane, Columbus, OH 43213-1568, 614-986-1881, info@puddinghouse.com, www.puddinghouse.com
YA'SOU/Skyline Productions, PO Box 77463, Columbus, OH 43207

590

TWENTY-EIGHT PAGES LOVINGLY BOUND WITH TWINE, PO Box 106, Danville, OH 43014
Blue Hot Books, 5818 Wilmington Pike #320, Dayton, OH 45459-7004, 937-416-2475, Fax 937-767-9933, www.bluehotbooks.com
Kettering Foundation Press, 200 Commons Road, Dayton, OH 45459-2799, 937-434-7300
KETTERING REVIEW, 200 Commons Road, Dayton, OH 45459-2799, 937-434-7300
Tomart Publications, 3300 Encrete Lane, Dayton, OH 45439-1944, 937-294-2250; Fax 937-294-1024
Kenyette Productions, 20131 Champ Drive, Euclid, OH 44117-2208, 216-486-0544
PLAIN BROWN WRAPPER (PBW), 513 N. Central Avenue, Fairborn, OH 45324-5209, 513-878-5184
Red Hand Press, ATTN: Marie Kazalia, 6160 Stoddard Hayes Road, Farmdale, OH 44417-9773, phone: 415-447-7334 E-mail: RedHandPress@hotmail.com http://ClaraVenus.BlogSpot.com http://RedHandPress.BlogSpot.com
THE KENYON REVIEW, 104 College Drive, Gambier, OH 43022, 740-427-5208, Fax 740-427-5417, kenyonreview@kenyon.edu
HIRAM POETRY REVIEW, Box 162, Hiram, OH 44234, 330-569-5331, Fax 330-569-5166, poetryreview@hiram.edu
Bottom Dog Press, PO Box 425, Huron, OH 44839, 419-433-5560, x20784 http://members.aol.com/lsmithdog/bottomdog
Cambric Press dba Emerald House, 208 Ohio Street, Huron, OH 44839-1514
HEARTLANDS: A Magazine of Midwest Life and Art, Firelands College, Huron, OH 44839, 419-433-5560 X20784, lsmithdog@aol.com, www.theheartlandstoday.net
The Kent State University Press, PO Box 5190, 307 Lowry Hall, Kent, OH 44242-0001, 330-672-7913, 330-672-3104
Virginia Pines Press, 7092 Jewell North, Kinsman, OH 44428, virginiapines@nlc.net, www.virginiapines.com
Lucky Press, LLC, 126 S. Maple Street, Lancaster, OH 43130, Phone: 740-689-2950, Fax: 740-689-2951, Website: www.luckypress.com, Email: books@luckypress.com
OBSCURITY UNLIMITED, 1884 Meadows Road, Madison, OH 44157-1835
SOLO FLYER, 1112 Minuteman Avenue NW, Massillon, OH 44646
SPIRITCHASER, 3183 Sharon-Copley Road, Medina, OH 44256, 330-722-1561
Equine Graphics Publishing Group: New Concord Press, SmallHorse Press, Parallel Press, 7270 Forest Lane, Nashport, OH 43830-9045, 800-659-9442, 740-588-0181, fax 740-588-0183, writerone@newconcordpress.com, http://www.newconcordpress.com
RIVERWIND, Arts & Sciences, Oakley 312, Hocking College, Nelsonville, OH 45764
FIELD: Contemporary Poetry and Poetics, 50 N. Professor St., Oberlin, OH 44074-1091, 440-775-8408, Fax 440-775-8124, oc.press@oberlin.edu
Oberlin College Press, 50 N. Professor St., Oberlin, OH 44074-1091, 440-775-8408, Fax 440-775-8124, E-mail oc.press@oberlin.edu
Interalia/Design Books, PO Box 404, Oxford, OH 45056-0404, 513-523-1553 phone/Fax
Miami University Press, English Dept., Miami University, Oxford, OH 45056, 513-529-5221, Fax 513-529-1392, E-mail tumakw@muohio.edu
Envirographics, 98 Levan Dr., Painesville, OH 44077-3324, 440-352-8135
NOBODADDIES, 2491 State Route 45 South, Salem, OH 44460, E-mail rice@salem.kent.edu
White Buck Publishing, 5187 Colorado Avenue, Sheffield Village, OH 44054-2338, 440-934-7117 phone/fax, submissions@whitebuckpublishing.com
Implosion Press, 4975 Comanche Trail, Stow, OH 44224, 216-688-5210 phone/Fax, E-mail impetus@aol.com
TU REVIEW, Tiffin University, 155 Miami St., Tiffin, OH 44883, 419-448-3299, Fax 419-443-5009, TUReview@tiffin.edu, http://bruno.tiffin.edu/tureview/
New Sins Press, 3925 Watson Avenue, Toledo, OH 43612-1113
Garden House Press, P.O. Box 321 Trenton, Ohio 45067, Trenton, OH 45067, 513-988-7183
OUT OF LINE, P.O. Box 321 Trenton, OH 45067, Trenton, OH 45067, 513-988-7183
Holy Macro! Books, 13386 Judy Avenue NW, PO Box 82, Uniontown, OH 44685-9310, 330-715-2875, Fax 707-220-4510, consult@MrExcel.com, www.HolyMacroBooks.com
Alegra House Publishers, PO Box 1443-D, Warren, OH 44482, 216-372-2951
ICON, Kent State University/ Trumbull campus, 4314 Mahoning Ave., Warren, OH 44483, 330-847-0571
ARTFUL DODGE, Department of English, College of Wooster, Wooster, OH 44691, www.wooster.edu/artfuldodge
THE BOOK REPORT: The Magazine for Secondary School Library Media & Technology Specialists, 480 East Wilson Bridge Road #L, Worthington, OH 43085-2372
LIBRARY TALK: The Magazine for Elementary School Library Media & Technology Specialists, 480 East Wilson Bridge Road #L, Worthington, OH 43085-2372, 614-436-7107, fax 614-436-9490
Linworth Publishing, Inc., 480 East Wilson Bridge Road #L, Worthington, OH 43085-2372, 614-436-7107, FAX 614-436-9490
THE ANTIOCH REVIEW, PO Box 148, Yellow Springs, OH 45387, 937-769-1365
Community Service, Inc., PO Box 243, Yellow Springs, OH 45387-0243, 937-767-2161, www.smallcommunity.org
NEW SOLUTIONS, PO Box 243, Yellow Springs, OH 45387, 937-767-2161, info@communitysolution.org
Etruscan Press, Youngstown State University, English Department, Youngstown, OH 44555
PIG IRON, 26 North Phelps Street, PO Box 237, Youngstown, OH 44501-0237, 330-747-6932, Fax 330-747-0599
Pig Iron Press, 26 North Phelps Street, PO Box 237, Youngstown, OH 44501, 330-747-6932, Fax 330-747-0599

OKLAHOMA

BYLINE, PO Box 5240, Edmond, OK 73083-5240, 405-348-5591
Prospect Press, 1000 West London Street, El Reno, OK 73036-3426, www.tinplace.com/prospect
SPARROWGRASS POETRY NEWSLETTER, PO box 247, El Reno, OK 73036-0247
Lakepointe Publishing, PO Box 767, Enid, OK 73702-0767
The Colbert House, 1005 N. Flood Avenue, Suite 138, PO Box 150, Norman, OK 73069, 405-329-7999,FAX 405-329-6977, 800-698-2644, customerservice@greatbargainbooks.com, www.greatbargainbooks.com
Devi Press, Inc., 126 W. Main, Norman, OK 73069, (405) 447-0364
Excelsior Cee Publishing, PO Box 5861, Norman, OK 73070, 405-329-3909, Fax 405-329-6886, ecp@oecadvantage.net, www.excelsiorcee.com
Horse Creek Publications, Inc., 4500 Highland Hills Drive, Norman, OK 73026, 405-364-9647, schrems@worldnet.att.net
New Horizons Publishing, 5830 NW Expressway, Suite 225, Oklahoma City, OK 73132-5236, 405-823-9538, Fax 405-848-8118,
CIMARRON REVIEW, 205 Morrill Hall, Oklahoma State University, Stillwater, OK 74078-4069, (405) 744-9476, cimarronreview@yahoo.com, http://cimarronreview.okstate.edu
COFFEESPOONS, 1104 E. 38th Place, Tulsa, OK 74105, 918-712-9278

Hawk Publishing Group, Inc., 7107 S. Yale Avenue, PMB 345, Tulsa, OK 74136-6308, 918-492-3677, Fax 918-492-2120, www.hawkpub.com

IMOCO Publishing, PO Box 471721, Tulsa, OK 74147-1721, 208-978-2261, imoco@officefunnies.com, www.officefunnies.com

JAMES JOYCE QUARTERLY, University of Tulsa, 600 S. College, Tulsa, OK 74104, phone 918-631-2501, fax 918-631-2065, www.utulsa.edu/JJoyceQtrly

NIMROD INTERNATIONAL, 600 South College Avenue, Tulsa, OK 74104-3126

Reading Connections, P.O. Box 52426, Tulsa, OK 74152-0426, 818-902-0278 contact number of Marketing Manager

Stonehorse Publishing, LLC, 10632 S. Memorial Ave., Ste 245, Tulsa, OK 74133, 1.888.867.1927, Fax: 1.888.867.1927, generalinfo@stonehorsepublishing.com, www.stonehorsepublishing.com

TULSA STUDIES IN WOMEN'S LITERATURE, 600 S. College, Tulsa, OK 74104-3189, 918-631-2503, Fax 918-631-2065, sarah-theobald-hall@utulsa.edu

University of Tulsa, 600 South College, Tulsa, OK 74104, 918-631-2501, Fax 918-584-0623, carol-kealiher@utulsa.edu, www.utulsa.edu/JJoyceQtrly

Vista Mark Publications, 4528 S. Sheridan, Suite 114, Tulsa, OK 74145, 918-665-6030, Fax 918-665-6039

WESTVIEW, SW Oklahoma State University, Language Arts Dept, 100 Campus Dr., Weatherford, OK 73096, 580-774-3242, Fax 580-774-7111, james.silver@swosu.edu

OREGON

HOME POWER, PO Box 520, Ashland, OR 97520, Order line 800-707-6585, 541-512-0201, Fax 541-512-0343

Home Power, Inc., PO Box 275, Ashland, OR 97520, 916-475-3179

Quicksilver Productions, P.O.Box 340, 559 S Mountain Avenue, Ashland, OR 97520-3241, 541-482-5343, Fax 541-482-0960

SPROUTLETTER, Box 62, Ashland, OR 97520

Story Line Press, Three Oaks Farm, PO Box 1240, Ashland, OR 97520-0055, 541-512-8792, Fax 541-512-8793, mail@storylinepress.com, www.storylinepress.com

The Bacchae Press, c/o The Brown Financial Group, 10 Sixth Street, Suite 215, Astoria, OR 97103-5315, 503-325-7972; FAX 503-325-7959; 800-207-4358; E-mail brown@pacifier.com

THIS IS IMPORTANT, PO Box 69, Beatty, OR 97621, 541-533-2486, www.aftermathbooks.com

Ruby Sky Publishing, 16055 SW Walker Road #225, Beaverton, OR 97006-4942, 503-372-5824, Fax 503-629-5505, kay@rubyskypublishing.com, www.rubyskypublishing.com

Heritage West Books, 54977 Hunting Road, Bend, OR 97707-2632, 661-823-1941, Fax 661-823-1888, buckeye@lightspeed.net

Backcountry Publishing, 3303 Dick George Road, Cave Junction, OR 97523-9623, 541-955-5650

PSI Research/The Oasis Press/Hellgate Press, PO Box 3727, Central Point, OR 97502, 800-228-2275

RUMINATIONS: The Nigerian Dwarf & Mini Dairy Goat Magazine, 22705 Hwy 36, Cheshire, OR 97419, 541 998-6081

Camp Colton, 30000 S Camp Colton Dr., Colton, OR 97017, 503-824-2267

Alta Research, 131 NW 4th Street #290, Corvallis, OR 97330-4702, 877-360-ALTA, 541-929-5738, alta@alta-research.com

Calyx Books, PO Box B, Corvallis, OR 97330, 541-753-9384, Fax 541-753-0515, calyx@calyxpress.com, www.calyxpress.com

CALYX: A Journal of Art and Literature by Women, PO Box B, Corvallis, OR 97339, 541-753-9384, Fax 541-753-0515, calyx@calyxpress.com, www.calyxpress.com

The Fiction Works, 2070 SW Whiteside Drive, Corvallis, OR 97333, 541-730-2044, 541-738-2648, fictionworks@comcast.com, http://www.fictionworks.com

THE GROWING EDGE MAGAZINE, PO Box 1027, Corvallis, OR 97339-1027, 514-757-8477

Master's Plan Publishing, 2727 NW Ninth Street, Corvallis, OR 97330, 541-758-3456, Fax 541-757-8250, mastersplanpublishing@earthlink.net, www.mastersplanpublishing.com

New Moon Publishing, Inc., PO Box 1027, Corvallis, OR 97339-1027, 514-757-8477

Oregon State University Press, 500 Kerr Administration Building, Corvallis, OR 97331-2122, 541-737-3166, OSU.Press@oregonstate.edu, http://oregonstate.edu/dept/press

RUBBERSTAMPMADNESS, PO Box 610, Corvallis, OR 97330-0610

BOOK DEALERS WORLD, PO Box 606, Cottage Grove, OR 97424-0026

North American Bookdealers Exchange, PO Box 606, Cottage Grove, OR 97424-0026

The Narrative Press, PO Box 145, Crabtree, OR 97335, 541-259-2154, Fax 541-259-2154, service@narrativepress.com, www.narrativepress.com

Sibyl Publications, Inc, 2505 Reuben Boise road, Dallas, OR 97338, 503-623-3438, fax 503-623-2943

PATTERNS OF CHOICE: A Journal of People, Land, and Money, 501 South Street, Enterprise, OR 97828, 541-426-6490; pdonovan@orednet.org, www.orednet.org/~pdonovan

ALL ROUND, PO Box 10193, Eugene, OR 97440-2193, 541-431-3390, nathen@allroundmagazine.com, www.allroundmagazine.com

ANT ANT ANT ANT ANT, PO Box 3158, Eugene, OR 97403

BIRTHKIT NEWSLETTER, PO Box 2672, Eugene, OR 97402, 503-344-7438

GREEN ANARCHY, PO Box 11331, Eugene, OR 97440, collective@greenanarchy.org, www.greenanarchy.org

MIDWIFERY TODAY, PO Box 2672, Eugene, OR 97402, 541-344-7438

Midwifery Today, PO Box 2672, Eugene, OR 97402, 541-344-7438; Fax 541-344-1422; editorial@midwiferytoday.com, www.midwiferytoday.com

NATIONAL MASTERS NEWS, PO Box 50098, 2791 Oak Alley Suite 5, Eugene, OR 97405, 541-343-7716, Fax 541-345-2436, natmanews@aol.com

NORTHWEST REVIEW, 369 P.L.C., University of Oregon, Eugene, OR 97403

One Horse Press/Rainy Day Press, 1147 East 26th, Eugene, OR 97403, 503-484-4626

POETIC SPACE: Poetry & Fiction, PO Box 11157, Eugene, OR 97440

Silverfish Review Press, PO Box 3541, Eugene, OR 97403, 503-344-5060

Triple Tree Publishing, PO Box 5684, Eugene, OR 97405, 541-338-3184, Fax 541-484-5358, www.tripletreepub.com

Symbios, 4367 S.E. 16th, Gresham, OR 97080-9178, 503-667-0633, home.netcom.com/~symbios

Beyond Words Publishing, Inc., 20827 NW Cornell Road, Ste. 500, Hillsboro, OR 97124-9808, 503-531-8700, Fax 503-531-8773, www.beyondword.com

TIMBER TIMES, PO Box 219, Hillsboro, OR 97123

THE MINDFULNESS BELL, 645 Sterling Street, Jacksonville, OR 97530, e-mail mindbell@internetcds.com

BASALT, School of Arts and Sciences, Eastern Oregon University, La Grande, OR 97850, 541-962-3633

592

The Bear Wallow Publishing Company, 809 South 12th Street, La Grande, OR 97850, 541-962-7864, bearwallow@uwtc.net, www.bear-wallow.com
The Apostolic Press, 547 NW Coast Street, Newport, OR 97365, 541 264-0452
Elderberry Press, LLC, 1393 Old Homestead Drive, Second Floor,, Oakland, OR 97462, 541-459-6043 phone/Fax, editor@elderberrypress.com, www.elderberrypress.com
CLACKAMAS LITERARY REVIEW, 19600 South Molalla Avenue, Oregon City, OR 97045
Moon Lake Media, 16519 S. Bradley Road, Oregon City, OR 97045-8734, info@moonlakebooks.com, www.moonlake-books.com
AB, PO Box 190-abd, Philomath, OR 97370
DWELLING PORTABLY, Light Living Library, Po Box 190—DB, Philomath, OR 97370
Alaska Northwest Books, PO Box 10306, Portland, OR 97296-0306, 503-226-2402, Fax 503-223-1410, editorial@gacpc.com
Artwork Publications, LLC, 8335 SW Fairway Drive, Portland, OR 97225-2755, 503-297-2045, Fax 503-297-5163, artwilsn@easystreet.com
THE BEAR DELUXE, PO Box 10342, Portland, OR 97296, 503-242-1047, Fax 503-243-2645, bear@orlo.org
Beynch Press Publishing Company, 1928 S.E. Ladd Avenue, Portland, OR 97214, 503-232-0433
Blue Unicorn Press, Inc., PO Box 40300, Portland, OR 97240-0300, 503-957-5609
BookPartners, Inc., 3739 SE 8th Ave. #1, Portland, OR 97202-3701, bpbooks@teleport.com, www.bookpartners.com
BURNSIDE REVIEW, P.O. BOX 1782, Portland, OR 97207, sid@burnsidereview.org, www.burnsidereview.org
Collectors Press, Inc., PO Box 230986, Portland, OR 97281, 503-684-3030, Fax 503-684-3777
Communicom Publishing Company, 19300 NW Sauvie Island Road, Portland, OR 97231, 503-621-3049
Continuing Education Press, Portland State University, Continuing Education Press, PO Box 1394, Portland, OR 97207-1394, www.cep.pdx.edu
The Eighth Mountain Press, 624 Southeast 29th Avenue, Portland, OR 97214, 503-233-3936, ruth@eighthmountain.com
First Books, 6750 SW Franklin, # A, Portland, OR 97223-2542, 503,968,6777
GERTRUDE, 7937 N Wayland Ave, Portland, OR 97203, www.gertrude-journal.com
GERTRUDE, PO Box 83948, Portland, OR 97283, www.gertrudepress.org
Gertrude Press, PO Box 83948, Portland, OR 97283, www.gertrudepress.org
Glimmer Train Press, Inc., 1211 NW Glisan St., Suite 207, Portland, OR 97209, Ph: 503/221-0836 Web site address: www.glimmertrain.org
GLIMMER TRAIN STORIES, 1211 NW Glisan St., Suite 207, Portland, OR 97209, Ph: 503/221-0836 Web site address: www.glimmertrain.org
Gloger Family Books, 2020 NW Northrup Street #311, Portland, OR 97209-1679
THE GROVE REVIEW, 1631 NE Broadway, PMB #137, Portland, OR 97232, editor@thegrovereview.org, www.thegrovere-view.org
HUBBUB, 5344 S.E. 38th Avenue, Portland, OR 97202, 503-775-0370
JOURNAL OF PROCESS ORIENTED PSYCHOLOGY, 2049 NW Hoyt Street, Portland, OR 97209-1260, 503-222-3395
Lao Tse Press, Ltd., 2049 NW Hoyt Street, Portland, OR 97209-1260, 503-222-3395; fax 503-222-3778
Lean Press, PO Box 80334, Portland, OR 97280-1334, 503-708-4415, Fax 503-626-9098, mike@leanpress.com, www.leanpress.com
LEO Productions LLC., PO Box 1333, Portland, OR 97207, 360-601-1379, Fax 360-210-4133
MUSIC NEWS, 5536 NE Hassalo, Portland, OR 97213, 503-281-1191
Paradise Publications, 8110 SW Wareham, Portland, OR 97223, 503-246-1555
PORTLAND REVIEW, PO Box 347, Portland, OR 97207-0347, 503-725-4533
Princess Publishing, PO Box 25406, Portland, OR 97298, 503-297-1565
Spirit Press, Spirit Press, PO Box 12346, Portland, OR 97212, spiritpress@onespiritfoundation.org, www.onespiritfounda-tion.org 877-906-5381
Timber Press, 133 SW Second Avenue, Suite 450, Portland, OR 97204-3527
Vestibular Disorders Association, PO Box 13305, Portland, OR 97213-0305, 503-229-7705, Fax 503-229-8064, toll-free 1-800-837-8428, veda@vestibular.org, www.vestibular.org
WHITEWALL OF SOUND, 411 NE 22nd #21, Portland, OR 97232-3270, jcline@teleport.com
Bonanza Publishing, PO Box 204, Prineville, OR 97754, bonanza@ricksteber.com
Dimi Press, 3820 Oak Hollow Lane, SE, Salem, OR 97302, 503-364-7698, Fax 503-364-9727
Idylls Press, PO Box 3566, Salem, OR 97302-3566, 503-363-3601, 503-345-0890, info@idyllspress.com, www.idyllspress.com
Flying Pencil Publications, 33126 SW Callahan Road, Scappoose, OR 97056, 503-543-7171, fax: 503-543-7172
Angst World Library, PO Box 593, Selma, OR 97538-0593
Health Plus Publishers, PO Box 1027, Sherwood, OR 97140, 503-625-0589, Fax 503-625-1525
Multnomah Publishers, Inc., 601 N. Larch St., Sisters, OR 97759-9320, 541-549-1144, Fax 541-549-8048
Pygmy Forest Press, 1125 Mill St, Springfield, OR 97477-3729, 541-747-9734
Firelight Publishing, Inc., Box 444, Sublimity, OR 97385-0444, 503-767-0444, Fax 503-769-8950, editor@firelightpublish-ing.com, www.firelightpublishing.com
Gilgal Publications, PO Box 3399, Sunriver, OR 97707, 541-593-8418
Talent House Press, 1306 Talent Avenue, Talent, OR 97540, talhouse@mcleodusa.net
Carpe Diem Publishing, 1705 E. 17th Street, #400, The Dalles, OR 97058, 541-296-1552, waconner@aol.com
This New World Publishing, LLC, 13500 SW Pacific Highway, Ste. 129, Tigard, OR 97223, 503-670-1153, Fax 503-213-5889, diana@thisnewworld.com, www.thisnewworld.com
NewSage Press, PO Box 607, Troutdale, OR 97060-0607, 503-695-2211 www.newsagepress.com info@newsagepress.com
Accent On Music, LLC, PMB 252, 19363 Willamette Drive, West Linn, OR 97068, (503)699-1814, (503)699-1813(FAX), (800)313-4406, info@accentonmusic.com
SHAMAN'S DRUM: A Journal of Experiential Shamanism, PO Box 270, Williams, OR 97544, 541-846-1313
Kodiak Media Group, PO Box 1029-DB, Wilsonville, OR 97070, Fax 503-625-4087
nine muses books, 3541 Kent Creek Road, Winston, OR 97496, 541-679-6674, mw9muses@teleport.com

PENNSYLVANIA

TAPROOT LITERARY REVIEW, PO Box 204, Ambridge, PA 15003, 724-266-8476, taproot10@aol.com
Taproot Press Publishing Co., Box 204, Ambridge, PA 15003, taproot10@aol.com
Merwood Books, 237 Merwood Lane, Ardmore, PA 19003, 215-947-3934, Fax 215-947-4229
Whitford Press, 4880 Lower Valley Road, Atglen, PA 19310, 610-593-1777, Fax 610-593-2002, www.schifferbooks.com
Kobalt Books, P.O. Box 1062, Bala Cynwyd, PA 19004, 314-503-5462

Chistell Publishing, 2500 Knights Road, Suite 19-01, Bensalem, PA 19020
SING OUT! Folk Music & Folk Songs, PO Box 5460, Bethlehem, PA 18015-0460, 610-865-5366; Fax 610-865-5129; info@singout.org
TEACHER LIBRARIAN: The Journal for School Library Professionals, Scarecrow Press Inc., Bldg B, 15200 NBN Way, Blue Ridge Summit, PA 17214-1069, 717-794-3800 X3597
BearManor Media, PO Box 750, Boalsburg, PA 16827, ben@ritzbros.com, www.bearmanormedia.com
Dufour Editions Inc., PO Box 7, Chester Springs, PA 19425-0007, 610-458-5005, Fax 610-458-7103
Starry Night Publishing, 904 Broad Street, Collingdale, PA 19023, www.starrynightpublishing.com
Black Bear Publications, 1916 Lincoln Street, Croydon, PA 19021-8026, bbreview@earthlink.net, www.blackbearreview.com
BLACK BEAR REVIEW, Black Bear Publications, 1916 Lincoln Street, Croydon, PA 19021, bbreview@earthlink.net, www.blackbearreview.com
THE AGUILAR EXPRESSION, 1329 Gilmore Avenue, Donora, PA 15033, 724-379-8019, www.wordrunner.com/xfaguilar
MATCHBOOK, 240 Edison Furlong Road, Doylestown, PA 18901-3013, Fax 215-340-3965
Raw Dog Press, 151 S. West Street, Doylestown, PA 18901, 215-345-6838
Mammoth Books, 7 Juniata Street, DuBois, PA 15801, avallone@psu.edu
BATHTUB GIN, PO Box 178, Erie, PA 16512, pathwisepress@hotmail.com
JOURNAL OF ASIAN MARTIAL ARTS, 821 West 24th Street, Erie, PA 16502, 814-455-9517; fax 814-526-5262; e-mail info@goviamedia.com; website www.goviamedia.com
LAKE EFFECT, Penn State Erie, 5091 Station Road, Erie, PA 16563-1501, 814-898-6281
Pathwise Press, PO Box 178, Erie, PA 16512, pathwisepress@hotmail.com
CRAZED NATION, 251 S. Olds Boulevard #84-E, Fairless Hills, PA 19030-3426
TRANSCENDENT VISIONS, 251 South Olds Boulevard, 84-E, Fairless Hills, PA 19030-3426, 215-547-7159
Word Forge Books, PO Box 97, Ferndale, PA 18921, Tel 610-847-2456, email info@wordforgebooks.com, URL www.wordforgebooks.com
THE GETTYSBURG REVIEW, Gettysburg College, Gettysburg, PA 17325, 717-337-6770
FAT TUESDAY, 560 Manada Gap Road, Grantville, PA 17028, 717-469-7159
MacDonald/Sward Publishing Company, 120 Log Cabin Lane, Greensburg, PA 15601, 724-832-7767
Libertarian Press, Inc./American Book Distributors, PO Box 309, Grove City, PA 16127-0309, 724-458-5861
EXPERIMENTAL FOREST, 2430 North 2nd St. #3, Harrisburg, PA 17110-1104, 717-730-2143, xxforest@yahoo.com, www.geocities.com/paris/salon/9699
Wind River Press, 254 Dogwood Drive, Hershey, PA 17033, promotions@windriverpress.com
Arts & Letters Press, 826 Walnut Street, Hollidaysburg, PA 16648
Himalayan Institute Press, 630 Main St Suite 350, Honesdale, PA 18431, 570-647-1531, fax 570-647-1552, 800-822-4547, hibooks@himalayaninstitute.org, www.HimalayanInstitute.org
Markowski International Publishers, 1 Oakglade Circle, Hummelstown, PA 17036-9525, 717-566-0468, Fax 717-566-6423
Belfry Books, RR 2 Box 2090, Laceyville, PA 18623, 717-869-2942; Fax 717-869-1031
The Bradford Press, RR 2 Box 2090, Laceyville, PA 18623, 717-869-2942; Fax 717-869-1031
Hands & Heart Books, RR 2 Box 2090, Laceyville, PA 18623, 717-869-2942; Fax 717-869-1031
Toad Hall Press, RR 2 Box 2090, Laceyville, PA 18623, 717-869-1031
Toad Hall, Inc., RR 2 Box 2090, Laceyville, PA 18623, 570-869-2942; Fax 570-869-1031
Avari Press, P.O. Box 11325, Lancaster, PA 17605, editor@avaripress.com, http://www.avaripress.com
Free Reign Press, Inc., 502 Valley Stream Circle, Langhorne, PA 19053, 215-891-8894 phone, www.freereignpress.com
WOMAN'S ART JOURNAL, 1711 Harris Road, Laverock, PA 19038-7208, 215-233-0639
The Press of Appletree Alley, 138 South 3rd Street, Lewisburg, PA 17837-1910
WEST BRANCH, Bucknell Hall, Bucknell University, Lewisburg, PA 17837, 570-577-1853, westbranch@bucknell.edu
Jessee Poet Publications, PO Box 232, Lyndora, PA 16045
POETS AT WORK, PO Box 232, Lyndora, PA 16045
Bookhaven Press, LLC, 249 Field Club Circle, McKees Rocks, PA 15136-1034, 412-494-6926, Fax 412-494-5749, bookhaven@aol.com, http://federaljobs.net
THE ALLEGHENY REVIEW, Box 32, Allegheny College, Meadville, PA 16335, 814-332-6553
Trickle Creek Books, 500 Andersontown Rd, Mechanicsburg, PA 17055, 717-766-2638, fax 717-766-1343, 800-353-2791
J & J Consultants, Inc., 603 Olde Farm Road, Media, PA 19063, 610-565-9692, Fax 610-565-9694, wjones13@juno.com, www.members.tripod.com/walterjones/
MAD POETS REVIEW, PO Box 1248, Media, PA 19063-8248
NEW ALTERNATIVES, 603 Ole Farm Road, Media, PA 19063, 610-565-9692, Fax 610-565-9694, wjones13@juno.com, www.members.tripod/walterjones
Nova House Press, 470 North Latch's Lane, Merion, PA 19066
The Merion Press, Inc., PO Box 144, Merion Station, PA 19066-0144, 610-617-8919, Fax 610-617-8929, rjstern@merion-press.com, www.merionpress.com
Wilderness Ministries, PO Box 225, Mount Union, PA 17066, 814-542-8668
Camel Press, Box 212, Needmore, PA 17238, 717-573-4526
DUST (From the Ego Trip), Box 212, Needmore, PA 17238, 717-573-4526
THE FREEDONIA GAZETTE: The Magazine Devoted to the Marx Brothers, 335 Fieldstone Drive, New Hope, PA 18938-1224, 215-862-9734
CAKETRAIN, 174 Carriage Drive, North Huntingdon, PA 15642, www.caketrain.org, caketrainjournal@hotmail.com
Caketrain Press, 174 Carriage Drive, North Huntingdon, PA 15642, www.caketrain.org, caketrainjournal@hotmail.com
Believe! Publishing, PO Box 55, Norwood, PA 19074-0055, 717-917-1399, Fax 419-781-7170, info@believepublishing.com, www.believepublishing.com
POSTCARD CLASSICS (formerly DELTIOLOGY), PO Box 8, Norwood, PA 19074-0008, 610-485-8572
AMERICAN POETRY REVIEW, 117 S. 17th Street, Ste. 910, Philadelphia, PA 19103-5009, 215-496-0439
AXE FACTORY REVIEW, PO Box 40691, Philadelphia, PA 19107
Banshee Press, PO Box 11186, Philadelphia, PA 19136-6186
THE CAIMAN (formerly THE WEIRD NEWS), 7393 Rugby Street, Philadelphia, PA 19138-1236, caimans@yahoo.com
Cornerstone Publishing, 100 Leverington Avenue, Suite 2, Philadelphia, PA 19127, 267-975-7676, books@cornerstonepublishing.com, www.cornerstonepublishing.com
CYNIC BOOK REVIEW, PO Box 40691, Philadelphia, PA 19107
Cynic Press, PO Box 40691, Philadelphia, PA 19107
Paul Dry Books, 117 S. 17th Street, Suite 1102, Philadelphia, PA 19103, 215-231-9939, fax:215-231-9942, website:

www.@pauldrybooks.com
HIDDEN OAK POETRY JOURNAL, 402 South 25th St, Philadelphia, PA 19146-1004, hidoak@att.net
HOLY ROLLERS, PO Box 40691, Philadelphia, PA 19107
Ika, LLC, 4630 Sansom Street, 1st Floor, Philadelphia, PA 19139-4630, 215-327-7341
Jewish Publication Society, 2100 Arch Street, Philadelphia, PA 19103-1308, 215-802-0600, Fax 215-568-2017
JOURNAL OF AESTHETICS AND ART CRITICISM, Dept of Philosophy, Anderson Hall, 7th Floor, Temple University, Philadelphia, PA 19122, 502-852-0458, FAX 502-852-0459, email jaac@blue.temple.edu
Locks Art Publications, 600 Washington Square South, Philadelphia, PA 19106, 215-629-1000
LOW BUDGET ADVENTURE, PO Box 40691, Philadelphia, PA 19107
LOW BUDGET SCIENCE FICTION, PO Box 40691, Philadelphia, PA 19107
MAGNET MAGAZINE, 1218 Chestnut Street, Suite 508, Philadelphia, PA 19107, 215-413-8570, fax 215-413-8569, magnetmag@aol.com
ONE TRICK PONY, 8460 Franford Ave., Philadelphia, PA 19136-2031
Osric Publishing, 235 South 15th St., Apt 202, Philadelphia, PA 19102-5026
Our Child Press, PO Box 4379, Philadelphia, PA 19118-8379, 610-308-8988
PEDIATRICS FOR PARENTS, PO Box 63716, Philadelphia, PA 19147-7516, 215-625-9609, richsagall@pedsforparents.com, www.pedsforparents.com
PHILADELPHIA POETS, 1919 Chestnut Street, Apartment 1721, Philadelphia, PA 19103-3430, redrose108@comcast.net
Recon Publications, PO Box 14602, Philadelphia, PA 19134
Running Press, 125 South 22nd Street, Philadelphia, PA 19103, 215-567-5080, www.runningpress.com
SCHUYLKILL VALLEY JOURNAL OF THE ARTS, 419 Green Lane (rear), Philadelphia, PA 19128, Fax 215-483-5661, max@manayunkartcenter.org, macpoet1@aol.com, www.manayunkartcenter.org
WEIRD TALES, 6644 Rutland St., Philadelphia, PA 19149-2128
WOMEN'S REVIEW OF BOOKS, 628 North 2nd Street, Philadelphia, PA 19123, 215-925-4390
RC Anderson Books, PO Box 22322, Pittsburgh, PA 15222
Autumn House Press, P.O. Box 60100, Pittsburgh, PA 15211, 412-381-4261, www.autumnhouse.org
Carnegie Mellon University Press, Carnegie Mellon University, English Department, Pittsburgh, PA 15213, 412-268-6446
CREATIVE NONFICTION, 5501 Walnut Street #202, Pittsburgh, PA 15232-2329, 412-688-0304, fax 412-683-9173
Fontanel Books, 4106 Saline St., Pittsburgh, PA 15217-2716, 505-471-4102, Fax 505-471-4202, fontanelbooks@earthlink.net, www.fontanelbooks.com
Harobed Publishing Creations, P.O.Box 8195, Pittsburgh, PA 15217-0915, 412-243-9299 fax/phone(if beeps redial fax in use)
LATIN AMERICAN LITERARY REVIEW, PO Box 17660, Pittsburgh, PA 15235-0860, 412-824-7903, www.lalrp.org, latinreview@hotmail.com
Latin American Literary Review Press, PO Box 17660, Pittsburgh, PA 15235-0860, 412-824-7903, www.lalrp.org, latinreview@hotmail.com
LILLIPUT REVIEW, 282 Main Street, Pittsburgh, PA 15201
THE MINNESOTA REVIEW, Dept. of English, Carnegie Mellon University, Baker Hall 259, Pittsburgh, PA 15213-3890, editors@theminnesotareview.org
THE POETRY EXPLOSION NEWSLETTER (THE PEN), PO Box 4725, Pittsburgh, PA 15206-0725, 1-866-234-0297,arthurford@hotmail.com
QP Publishing, PO Box 18281, Pittsburgh, PA 15236-0281, phone/Fax
QUALITY QUIPS NEWSLETTER, PO Box 18281, Pittsburgh, PA 15236-0281, phone/Fax
Redgreene Press, PO Box 22322, Pittsburgh, PA 15222
Selah Publishing Co. Inc., 4143 Brownsville Rd #2, Pittsburgh, PA 15227-3306, 845-338-2816, Fax 845-338-2991, customerservice@selahpub.com
Spring Grass, PO Box 22322, Pittsburgh, PA 15222
SterlingHouse Publisher, 7436 Washington Ave., Ste. 200, Pittsburgh, PA 15218, 412-821-6211, ordering line 1-888-542-BOOK (2665), Fax 412-821-6997, sterlingho@aol.com or ceshor@aol.com, www.sterlinghousepublisher.com or www.ceshore.com
University of Pittsburgh Press, 3400 Forbes Avenue, 5th Floor, Eureka Bldg., Pittsburgh, PA 15260, 412-383-2456
Schuylkill Living, 115 S Centre St., Pottsville, PA 17901-3000, 570-622-8625
SCHUYLKILL LIVING MAGAZINE, 115 S. Centre Street, Pottsville, PA 17901, 570-622-8625, Fax 570-622-2143, eramus@comcast.net, www.schuylkillliving.com
Hermitage (Ermitazh), PO Box 578, Schuylkill Haven, PA 17972, 570-739-1505, fax 570-739-2383, e-mail yefimovim@aol.com, web www.hermitagepublishers.com
University of Scranton Press, 445 Madison Ave., Scranton, PA 18510, 1-800-941-3081, 1-800-941-8804, www.scranton-press.com
Alpha Beat Press, 806 East Ridge Ave., Sellersville, PA 18960-2723
ALPHA BEAT SOUP, 806 E. Ridge Avenue, Sellersville, PA 18960, 215,534,9409, dave421165@verizon.net
Burd Street Press, PO Box 708, 73 W. Burd Street, Shippensburg, PA 17257, 717-532-2237, Fax 717-532-6110
Ragged Edge Press, PO Box 708, 73 West Burd Street, Shippensburg, PA 17257, 717-532-2237, Fax 717-532-6110
White Mane Publishing Company, Inc., 73 West Burd Street, PO Box 708, Shippensburg, PA 17257, 717-532-2237, Fax 717-532-6110, email:marketing@whitemane.com
5:AM, Box 205, Spring Church, PA 15686
GAUNTLET: Exploring the Limits of Free Expression, 309 Powell Road, Springfield, PA 19064, 610-328-5476
BABEL MAGAZINE, PO Box 10495, State College, PA 16805-0495, www.babelmagazine.com
Sisyphus Press, PO Box 10495, State College, PA 16805-0495, www.babelmagazine.com
Strata Publishing, Inc., PO Box 1303, State College, PA 16804, 814-234-8545, Fax 814-238-7222, www.stratapub.com
Word Association Publishers, 205 5th Avenue, Tarentum, PA 15084, publish@wordassociation.com, www.wordassocia-tion.com
Pennsylvania State University Press, Penn State Press, Suite C, 820 N. University Drive, University Park, PA 16802-1711, 814-865-1327
SHAW: THE ANNUAL OF BERNARD SHAW STUDIES, Penn State Press, Suite C, 820 N. University Drive, University Park, PA 16802-1711, 814-865-1327
Shangri-La Publications, #3 Coburn Hill Rd., Warren Center, PA 18851-0065, telephone 570-395-3423, fax 570-395-0146, toll free 866-966-6288, email shangrila@egypt.net, web http://shangri-la.0catch.com
ATS Publishing, 996 Old Eagle School Road, Suite 1105, Wayne, PA 19087, 610-688-6000
B.B. Mackey Books, PO Box 475, Wayne, PA 19087-0475, www.mackeybooks.com

THE CIRCLE MAGAZINE, 173 Grandview Road, Wernersville, PA 19565, 610-823-2707, Fax 610-670-7017, circlemag@aol.com, www.circlemagazine.com
COLLEGE LITERATURE, 210 East Rosedale Avenue, West Chester University, West Chester, PA 19383, 610-436-2901, fax 610-436-2275, collit@wcupa.edu, www.collegeliterature.org
Swedenborg Foundation, 320 North Church Street, West Chester, PA 19380, (610) 430-3222 (Phone), (610) 430-7982 Fax, 1-800-355-3222 (Phone), info@swedenborg.com, www.swedenborg.com
Infinity Publishing, 1094 New Dehaven St, Suite 100, West Conshohocken, PA 19428, info@infinitypublishing.com
Kallisti Publishing, 332 Center Street, Wilkes-Barre, PA 18702, 877-444-6188
BRILLIANT CORNERS: A Journal of Jazz & Literature, Lycoming College, Williamsport, PA 17701, 570-321-4279
THE ENTERTAINMENT REVIEW OF THE SUSQUEHANNA VALLEY, PO Box 964, Williamsport, PA 17703-0964, 800-747-0897

RHODE ISLAND

ROGER, Roger Williams University, Department of English Lit & Creative Writing, Bristol, RI 02809, 401 254 5350
RGA Publishing, 224 Cindyann Drive, East Greenwich, RI 02818-2429, rgapub@gallilaw.com
The Saunderstown Press, 54 Camp Avenue, North Kingstown, RI 02852, 401-295-8810; Fax 401-294-9939
THE ALEMBIC, Department of English, Providence College, Providence, RI 02918-0001
Burning Deck Press, 71 Elmgrove Avenue, Providence, RI 02906
Copper Beech Press, P O Box 2578, English Department, Providence, RI 02906, 401-351-1253
HURRICANE ALICE, Dept. of English, Rhode Island College, Providence, RI 02908
ITALIAN AMERICANA, University of Rhode Island, 80 Washington Street, Providence, RI 02903-1803
PRIVACY JOURNAL, PO Box 28577, Providence, RI 02908, 401-274-7861, 401-274-4747, orders@privacyjournal.net, www.privacyjournal.net
BRYANT LITERARY REVIEW, Faculty Suite F, Bryant University, Smithfield, RI 02917, website http://bryant2.bryant.edu/~blr/
SAT SANDESH: THE MESSAGE OF THE MASTERS, 680 Curtis Corner Road, Wakefield, RI 02879, (401) 783-0662

SOUTH CAROLINA

Palanquin Press, English Department, University of South Carolina-Aiken, Aiken, SC 29801, 803-648-6851 x3208, fax 803-641-3461, email phebed@aiken.edu, email scpoet@scescape.net
APOSTROPHE: USCB Journal of the Arts, 801 Carteret Street, Beaufort, SC 29902, 843-521-4158, sjtombe@gwm.sc.edu
CRAZYHORSE, Dept. of English College of Charleston, 66 George Street, Charleston, SC 29424, crazyhorse@cofc.edu, http://crazyhorse.cofc.edu
ILLUMINATIONS, English Dept., 66 George Street, College of Charleston, Charleston, SC 29424-0001, Tel: 843-953-1920, Fax: 843-953-1924, Web: www.cofc.edu/illuminations
ZUZU'S PETALS: QUARTERLY ONLINE, 1836 Ashley River Road, Ste. E, Charleston, SC 29407-4761, info@zuzu.com, www.zuzu.com
SOUTH CAROLINA REVIEW, Ctr. for Electronic & Digital Publishing, Clemson University, 611 Strode Tower, Box 340522, Clemson, SC 29634-0522, 864-656-3151; 864-656-5399
JAMES DICKEY NEWSLETTER, University of South Carolina, English Department, Columbia, SC 29208, 803-777-7073
University of South Carolina Press, 1600 Hampton Street, 5th Floor, Columbia, SC 29208, 803-777-5245; 803-777-0160; www.sc.edu/uscpress
THE SOW'S EAR POETRY REVIEW, 355 Mt Lebanon Rd, Donalds, SC 29638-9115, errol@kitenet.net
The Sow's Ear Press, 355 Mt Lebanon Rd, Donalds, SC 29638-9115, errol@kitenet.net
Vintage Romance Publishing, LLC, 107 Clearview Circle, Goose Creek, SC 29445, (843) 270-3742, www.vrpublishing.com, submissions@vrpublishing.com
THE VOLUNTARYIST, Box 1275, Gramling, SC 29348, 864-472-2750
EMRYS JOURNAL, PO Box 8813, Greenville, SC 29601, www.emrys.org
Emrys Press, PO Box 8813, Greenville, SC 29601, www.emrys.org
Homecourt Publishers, 2435 East North Street #245, Greenville, SC 29615-1442, 864-232-7108 phone/Fax, info@homecourt-publishers.com, www.homecourtpublishers.com
Ninety-Six Press, Furman University, 3300 Poinsett Highway, Greenville, SC 29613, 864-294-3152/6
The Power Within Institute, Inc., 439 So. Buncombe Rd, #932, Greer, SC 29650, 864-877-4990
R & M Publishing Company, PO Box 1276, Holly Hill, SC 29059, 803-279-2262
Mystic Toad Press, PO Box 401, Pacolet, SC 29372-0401, 864-948-1263, mystictoadbooks@yahoo.com
Wynn Publishing, PO Box 1491, Pickens, SC 29671, 864-878-6469, Fax 864-878-6267, jack@wynnco.com

SOUTH DAKOTA

Tesseract Publications, PO Box 164, Canton, SD 57013-0164, 605-987-5070, Fax same, call ahead, it is a one-liner information@tesseractpublications.com, www.tesseractpublications.com
PRAIRIE WINDS, Dakota Wesleyan University, DWU Box 536, Mitchell, SD 57301, 605-995-2814
VINEGAR CONNOISSEURS INTERNATIONAL NEWSLETTER, PO Box 41, Roslyn, SD 57261, 605-486-4536; vinegar@itctec.com
SOUTH DAKOTA REVIEW, Department of English / University of South Dakota, 414 East Clark St., Vermillion, SD 57069, 605-677-5184, 605-677-5966, email: sdreview@usd.edu, website: http://www.usd.edu/sdreview

TENNESSEE

THE POETRY MISCELLANY, English Dept. Univ of Tennessee, Chattanooga, TN 37403, 423-425-4238
ZONE 3, Austin Peay State University, Box 4565, Clarksville, TN 37044, 931-221-7031/7891
BABYSUE, PO Box 3360, Cleveland, TN 37320-3360
BABYSUE MUSIC REVIEW, PO Box 3360, Cleveland, TN 37320-3360
WRITER'S EXCHANGE, 129 Thurman Lane, Clinton, TN 37716-6611, E-mail eboone@aol.com, www.users.aol.com/writernet
Leadership Education and Development, Inc., 1116 West 7th Street, PMB 175, Columbia, TN 38401, 931-379-3799; 800-659-6135, www.leadershipdevelopment.com
UNDER THE SUN, English Dept., Box 5053, Tennessee Technological University, Cookeville, TN 38505, 931-372-3768;hweidner@tntech.edu;www.tntech.edu/underthesun
AC Projects, Inc., 7376 Walker Road, Fairview, TN 37062-8141, 615-799-8104, Fax 615-799-2017

Crane Press, P.O. Box 680367, Franklin, TN 37068, 615-599-2017, fax 615-599-2018, 800-745-6273, Info@CranePress.com
RURAL HERITAGE, 281 Dean Ridge Lane, Gainesboro, TN 38562-5039, 931-268-0655, editor@ruralheritage.com, www.ruralheritage.com
Richard W. Smith Military Books, 114 Gates Drive, Hendersonville, TN 37075-4840
NOW AND THEN, PO Box 70556, East Tennessee State University, Johnson City, TN 37614-0556, 423-439-5348; fax 423-439-6340; e-mail woodsidj@etsu.edu
The Overmountain Press, 325 West Walnut Street, PO Box 1261, Johnson City, TN 37605, 800-992-2691, Fax 423-232-1252, www.overmountainpress.com
Twilight Times Books, PO Box 3340, Kingsport, TN 37664-0340, 423-323-0183 phone/Fax, publisher@twilighttimes-books.com, www.twilighttimesbooks.com
NEW MILLENNIUM WRITINGS, PO Box 2463, Knoxville, TN 37901, mark@mach2.com, www.mach2.com
RFD, PO Box 68, Liberty, TN 37095, 615-536-5176
Epona Publishing, 6208 Hackberry Lane, Maryville, TN 37801-1160
Omonomany, 5050 Poplar Avenue Suite 1510, Memphis, TN 38157, 901-374-9027, Fax 901-374-0508, jimweeks12@msn.com
RIVER CITY, University of Memphis, Department of English, Memphis, TN 38152, 901-678-4591, www.people.memphis.edu/~rivercity
Black Forest Press, Belle Arden Run, 490 Mountain View Drive, Mosheim, TN 37818, 800-451-9404; FAX 619-482-8704; E-mail: inquiries@blackforestpress.com
COMICS REVUE, PO Box 336 -Manuscript Press, Mountain Home, TN 37684-0336, 432-926-7495
Manuscript Press, PO Box 336, Mountain Home, TN 37684-0336, 423-926-7495
POEMS & PLAYS, Department of English, Middle Tennessee State University, Murfreesboro, TN 37132, 615-898-2712
ZINE WORLD: A Reader's Guide to the Underground Press, PO Box 330156, Murfreesboro, TN 37133-0156, www.undergroundpress.org
The Battery Press, Inc., PO Box 198885, Nashville, TN 37219, 615-298-1401; E-mail battery@aol.com
Ion Imagination Publishing, Ion Imagination Entertainment, Inc., PO Box 210943, Nashville, TN 37221-0943, 615-646-3644, 800-335-8672, Fax 615-646-6276, flumpa@aol.com, www.flumpa.com
Land Yacht Press, 504 Holt Valley Road, Nashville, TN 37221-1602, 615-646-2186 phone/Fax, landyacht-press@mindspring.com
Music City Publishing, P.O. Box 41696, Nashville, TN 37204-1696, www.musiccitypublishing.com
POCKETS, 1908 Grand Avenue, Nashville, TN 37203-0004, 615-340-7333,pockets@upperroom.org,www.pockets.org
Premium Press America, 2606 Eugenia Avenue, Suite C, Nashville, TN 37211, 615-256-8484
The Preservation Foundation, Inc., 2213 Pennington Bend Road, Nashville, TN 37214, 800-228-8517, 615-269-2433, preserve@storyhouse.org, www.storyhouse.org
Progressive Education, 115 Nashboro Boulevard, Nashville, TN 37217
PROGRESSIVE PERIODICALS DIRECTORY/UPDATE, 115 Nashboro Boulevard, Nashville, TN 37217
Time Barn Books, 529 Barrywood Drive, Nashville, TN 37220-1636, www.thetimegarden.com
Vanderbilt University Press, VU Station B #351813, 2301 Vanderbilt Place, Nashville, TN 37235-1813, 615-343-2446
Voyageur Publishing Co.,Inc., 1012 Greenwich Park, Nashville, TN 37215-2415, 615-463-3179
Iris Publishing Group, Inc (Iris Press / Tellico Books), 969 Oak Ridge Turnpike, # 328, Oak Ridge, TN 37830-8832, Ph: 865-483-0837, Fx: 865-481-3793, rcumming@irisbooks.com, www.irisbooks.com
SEWANEE REVIEW, University of the South, 735 University Avenue, Sewanee, TN 37383-1000, 931-598-1246, email:lcouch@sewanee.edu
Journey Books Publishing, 3205 Highway 431, Spring Hill, TN 37174, 615-791-8006

TEXAS

Set Sail Productions, LLC, 621 Wills Point, Allen, TX 75013, 469 951 7245, www.setsailmotivation.com, eric@setsailforsuccess.com
Future Horizons, Inc., 721 West Abram Street, Arlington, TX 76013-6995, 817-277-0727, 1-800-4890727, Fax 817-277-2270, info@futurehorizons-autism.com
American Short Fiction, PO Box 301209, Austin, TX 78703, 512.538.1305 (voice), 512.538.1306 (fax), web: americanshortfiction.org, email: editors@americanshortfiction.org, subscriptions@americanshortfiction.org
Argo Press, PO Box 4201, Austin, TX 78765-4201, charspot01@austin.rr.com
Black Buzzard Press, 3503 Ferguson Lane, Austin, TX 78754
BORDERLANDS: Texas Poetry Review, PO Box 33096, Austin, TX 78764, borderlandspoetry@sbcglobal.net, www.borderlands.org
CHARLTON SPOTLIGHT, PO Box 4201, Austin, TX 78765-4201, charspot01@austin.rr.com
THE DIRTY GOAT, 2717 Wooldridge, Austin, TX 78703, 512-482-8229, jbratcher3@aol.com
Eakins Press, PO Drawer 90159, Austin, TX 78709-0159, www.eakinpress.com, sales@eakinpress.com
Erespin Press, 6906 Colony Loop Drive, Austin, TX 78724-3749
Host Publications, Inc., 2717 Wooldridge, Austin, TX 78703-1953, 512-482-8229, Fax 512-482-0580, jbratcher3@aol.com
Liquid Paper Press, PO Box 4973, Austin, TX 78765, www.eden.com/~jwhagins/nervecowboy
NERVE COWBOY, PO Box 4973, Austin, TX 78765, www.onr.com/user/jwhagins/nervecowboy.html
NOVA EXPRESS, PO Box 27231, Austin, TX 78755, E-mail lawrenceperson@jump.net
OFFICE NUMBER ONE, 2111 Quarry Road, Austin, TX 78703, 512-445-4489
PITCHFORK POETRY MAGAZINE, 2002A Guadalupe #461, Austin, TX 78705
Plain View Press, PO Box 42255, Austin, TX 78704, 512 441 2452
SKANKY POSSUM, 2925 Higgins Street, Austin, TX 78722
SRLR Press, PO Box 19228, Austin, TX 78760
SULPHUR RIVER LITERARY REVIEW, PO Box 19228, Austin, TX 78760-9228, 512-292-9456
TEXAS POETRY JOURNAL, P.O. Box 90635, Austin, TX 78709-0635, 512-779-6202, www.texaspoetryjournal.com, submissions@texaspoetryjournal.com
Thorp Springs Press, 1400 Cullen Avenue, Austin, TX 78757-2527
TurnKey Press, 2100 Kramer Lane Suite 300, Austin, TX 78758-4094, 512.478.2028
Vagabond Press, PO Box 4830, Austin, TX 78765-4830, (512) 343-1540, vagabondpress@sbcglobal.net, vagabondpress.com
Van Cleave Publishing, 1712 Riverside Dr. #93, Austin, TX 78741, 5126655451
VISIONS-INTERNATIONAL, The World Journal of Illustrated Poetry, 3503 Ferguson Lane, Austin, TX 78754
WILD PLUM, PO Box 4282, Austin, TX 78765
WINDHOVER: A Journal of Christian Literature, PO Box 8008, UMHB, Belton, TX 76513, 254-295-4565

THE CARETAKER GAZETTE, PO Box 4005, Bergheim, TX 78004-4005, 830-336-3939, www.caretaker.org
Benecton Press, 9001 Grassbur Road, Bryan, TX 77808, 979-589-2665
Swan Publishing Company, 1059 County Road 100, Burnet, TX 78611-3535, 512-756-6800, swanbooks@ghg.net, www.swan-pub.com
Stardate Publishing Company, P. O. Box 112302, Carrollton, TX 75011-2302, voice-972-898-8349,fax-1-800-521-0633, jcothran@stardatepublishing.com, www.stardatepublishing.com
GLOBAL ONE TRAVEL & AUTOMOTIVE MAGAZINE, P. O. Box 3084, Cedar Hill, TX 75105-3084, 972-223-1558
Knowledge Concepts Publishing, P. O. Box 3084, Cedar Hill, TX 75105-3084, 972-223-1558
BRAZOS GUMBO, P.O. Box 12290, College Station, TX 77842, BrazosGumbo@yahoo.com
Health Yourself, 1617 Cafe Dumonde, Conroe, TX 77304, 936 7608558
Historical Resources Press, 2104 Post Oak Court, Corinth / Denton, TX 76210-1900, 940-321-1066, fax 940-497-1313, www.booksonhistory.com
THE AFRICAN HERALD, PO Box 132394, Dallas, TX 75313-2394
Behavioral Sciences Research Press, Inc., 12803 Demetra Drive, Ste. 100, Dallas, TX 75234, 972-243-8543, Fax 972-243-6349
Brown Books Publishing Group, 16200 N. Dallas Parkway, Suite 170, Dallas, TX 75248-2616, 972-381-0009, fax: 972-248-4336, publishing@brownbooks.com, www.brownbooks.com
Good Hope Enterprises, Inc., PO Box 132394, Dallas, TX 75313-2394, 214-823-7666, fax 214-823-7373
Inspiring Teachers Publishing, Inc., 12655 N. Central Expressway, Suite 810, Dallas, TX 75243, 877-496-7633 (toll-free), 972-496-7633, Fax 972-763-0355, info@inspiringteachers.com, www.inspiringteachers.com
SOJOURN: A Journal of the Arts, Office of Arts & Humanities, JO 31, Box 830688, Univ. of Texas-Dallas, Dallas, TX 75083-0688, Email: sojourn@utdallas.edu Web site: www.sojournjournal.org
Southern Methodist University Press, PO Box 750415, Dallas, TX 75275-0415, 214-768-1433, 214-768-1428 (fax), 800-826-8911 (orders), klang@mail.smu.edu, www.tamu.edu/upress
SOUTHWEST REVIEW, Southern Methodist University, P.O. Box 750374, Dallas, TX 75275-0374, 214-768-1037, www.southwestreview.org
AMERICAN LITERARY REVIEW, PO Box 311307, University of North Texas, Denton, TX 76203-1307, 940-565-2755
RIVERSEDGE, TheUniversity of Texas Pan American, 1201 W. University, Lamar Bldg., Room 9A, Edinburg, TX 78541, 956-381-3638, bookworm@panam.edu
The University of TX-Pan American Press, The University of TX-Pan American Press, 1201 W. Univ. Drive, Lamar Bldg., Room 9A, Edinburg, TX 78541, 956-381-3638, Fax 956-381-3697, bookworm@panam.edu
LAUGHING BEAR NEWSLETTER, 1418 El Camino Real, Euless, TX 76040-6555, e-mail editor@laughingbear.com, www.laughingbear.com
Wise Press, 8794 Rolling Acres Trail, Fair Oaks, TX 78015-4015, Fax 619-437-4160, lwise@san.rr.com, www.wisepress.com
BOOK NEWS & BOOK BUSINESS MART, PO Box 330309, Fort Worth, TX 76163, 817-293-7030
DESCANT, English Department, TCU, Box 297270, Fort Worth, TX 76129, 817-257-6537
Premier Publishers, Inc., PO Box 330309, Fort Worth, TX 76163, 817-293-7030
Shearer Publishing, 406 Post Oak Road, Fredericksburg, TX 78624, 830-997-6529
Gemini Publishing Company, 3102 West Bay Area Blvd., Suite 707, Friendswood, TX 77546, Phone: 281-316-4276, Fax: 281-316-1024, email:getgirls@getgirls.com, website: http://www.getgirls.com
Armadillo Publishing Corporation, PO Box 2052, Georgetown, TX 78627-2052, 512-863-8660
Arte Publico Press, University of Houston, Houston, TX 77204-2090, 713-743-2841, fax 713-743-2847
Bear House Publishing, 14781 Memorial Drive #10, Houston, TX 77079-5210
CIRCLE INC., THE MAGAZINE, PO Box 670096, Houston, TX 77267-0096, 281-580-8634
Circle of Friends Books, PO Box 670096, Houston, TX 77267-0096, 281-580-8634
ELEMENTS, 2260 W. Holcombe Blvd., Ste. 418, Houston, TX 77030, 713-747-4934, bwashington53@hotmail.com
GULF COAST, Dept. of English, University of Houston, Houston, TX 77204-3013
Lazywood Press, 1908 Harold Street, Houston, TX 77098-1502, 713-529-5500, mytable@aol.com, www.my-table.com
LUCIDITY POETRY JOURNAL, 14781 Memorial Drive #10, Houston, TX 77079-5210, 281-920-1795, ted-badger1@yahoo.com
MY TABLE: Houston's Dining Magazine, 1908 Harold Street, Houston, TX 77098-1502, 713-529-5500, teresabyrne-dodge@my-table.com, www.my-table.com
New Vision Publishing, 5757 Westheimer Road, PMB 3-362, Houston, TX 77057-5749, Fax 480-563-0675, newvisionpub@aol.com
Scrivenery Press, PO Box 740969-1003, Houston, TX 77274-0969, 713-665-6760, fax 713-665-8838, e-mail books@scrivenery.com, website www.scrivenery.com
ANGEL FACE POETRY JOURNAL, PO Box 102, Huffman, TX 77336, MaryAnkaPress@cs.com, www.maryanka.com
THE TEXAS REVIEW, English Department, Sam Houston State University, Huntsville, TX 77341-2146
Texas Review Press, English Department, Sam Houston State University, Huntsville, TX 77341-2146
Camino Bay Books, 331 Old Blanco Road, Kendalia, TX 78027-1901, 830-336-3636, 800-463-8181
Falcon Publishing, LTD, P O Box 6099, Kingwood, TX 77345-6099, 713-417-7600,281-360-8284,sales@falconpublishing.com,www.falconpublishing.com
IRON HORSE LITERARY REVIEW, Texas Tech University, English Dept., PO Box 43091, Lubbock, TX 79409-3091, 806-742-2500 X234
Texas Tech University Press, Box 41037, Lubbock, TX 79409-1037, 806-742-2982, fax 806-742-2979
GIN BENDER POETRY REVIEW, PO Box 150932, Lufkin, TX 75915-0932, ginbender@yahoo.com, www.ginbender.com
WISTERIA: A Journal of Haiku, Senryu, and Tanka, P.O. Box 150932, Lufkin, TX 75915-0932
YE OLDE NEWES, Po Box 151107, Lufkin, TX 75915-1107, 936-637-7475
JPS Publishing Company, 1141 Polo Run, Midlothian, TX 76065, 214-533-5685 (telephone), 972-775-5367 (fax), info@jpspublishing.com
PLS, 3605 W. Pioneer Pkwy. Ste. C, Pantego, TX 76013-4500, 800-328-3757, cjuhasz@plsweb.com
Rock Island Press, 3411 West Circle Drive, Pearland, TX 77581
Blue Cubicle Press, P.O. Box 250382, Plano, TX 75025-0382, 972 824 0646
THE FIRST LINE, PO Box 250382, Plano, TX 75025-0382, 972-824-0646, submission@thefirstline.com, www.thefirstline.com
World Gumbo Publishing, 7801 Alma Suite 105-323, Plano, TX 75025-3483, 1-888-318-2911, dbarkley@worldgumbo.com, www.worldgumbo.com
Friendly Oaks Publications, 227 Bunker Hill, PO Box 662, Pleasanton, TX 78064-0662, 830-569-3586, Fax 830-281-2617, E-mail friendly@docspeak.com

TRANSLATION REVIEW, Univ. of Texas-Dallas, Box 830688 - JO51, Richardson, TX 75083-0688, 972-883-2093, Fax 972-883-6303
CONCHO RIVER REVIEW, English Department, Angelo State University, San Angelo, TX 76909, 915-942-2269, me.hartje@angelo.edu
AMERICAN LETTERS & COMMENTARY, P.O. Box 830365, San Antonio, TX 78283, amerletters@satx.rr.com, www.amleters.org
Candlestick Publishing, PO Box 39241, San Antonio, TX 78218-1241
Hill Country Books, PO Box 791615, San Antonio, TX 78279, 830-228-5424
LONE STARS MAGAZINE, 4219 Flinthill, San Antonio, TX 78230-1619
PALO ALTO REVIEW, 1400 West Villaret Blvd., San Antonio, TX 78224, 210-921-5017
Pecan Grove Press, St. Mary's University, 1 Camino Santa Maria, San Antonio, TX 78228, 210-436-3441
Wings Press, 627 E. Guenther, San Antonio, TX 78210, 210-271-7805 (phone and fax)
Absey & Co., 23011 Northcrest Drive, Spring, TX 77389, 888-412-2739, Fax 281-251-4676, abseyland@aol.com
Panther Creek Press, PO Box 130233, Panther Creek Stn., Spring, TX 77393, panthercreek3@hotmail.com, www.panthercreekpress.com
TOUCHSTONE LITERARY JOURNAL, PO Box 130233, The Woodlands, TX 77393-0233
BOTH SIDES NOW, 10547 State Highway 110 North, Tyler, TX 75704-3731, 903-592-4263; web site: www.bothsides-now.info
FAQs Press, PO Box 130115, Tyler, TX 75713, 903-565-6653 phone/Fax, www.FAQsPress.com
Free People Press, 10547 State Hwy 110 N, Tyler, TX 75704-3731
BOOKS OF THE SOUTHWEST, 2508 Garner Field Road, Uvalde, TX 78801-6250, e-mail richter@hilconet.com
SYMPLOKE: A Journal for the Intermingling of Literary, Cultural and Theoretical Scholarship, c/o J. Di Leo, Univ. of Houston, 3007 N. Ben Wilson, Victoria, TX 77901, Fax 361-570-4207, editor@symploke.org
Halbar Publishing, 309 VZ County Road 3224, Wills Point, TX 75169-9732
SHARING & CARING, 309 VZ County Road 3224, Wills Point, TX 75169-9732
HILL COUNTRY SUN, PO Box 1482, Wimberley, TX 78676, 512-847-5162, allan@hillcountrysun.com, www.hillcountry-sun.com

UTAH

Truebekon Books, PO Box 353, American Fork, UT 84003, 801-796-3730
American Legacy Media, 1544 W 1620 N STE 1-G, Clearfield, UT 84015-8243, 801-774-5472, info@americanlegacy-media.com, http://americanlegacymedia.com
Gibbs Smith, Publisher, PO Box 667, Layton, UT 84041, 801-544-9800, Fax 801-544-5582, info@GibbsSmith.com
Eagle's View Publishing, 6756 North Fork Road, Liberty, UT 84310, 801-393-4555 (orders), editorial phone 801-745-0905
ISOTOPE: A Journal of Literary Nature and Science Writing, Department of English, 3200 Old Main Hill, Logan, UT 84322-3200, 435-797-3697, fax 435-797-3797, http://isotope.usu.edu
Poet Tree Press, 1488 North 200 West, Logan, UT 84341-6803, 888-618-8444, Fax 435-713-4422, editor@poettreepress.com, www.poettreepress.com
Utah State University Press, 7800 Old Main Hill, Logan, UT 84322-7800, 435-797-1362, Fax 435-797-0313, kathleen.kingsbury@usu.edu (marketing) web: www.usu.edu/usupress
WESTERN AMERICAN LITERATURE, English Dept., Utah State Univ., 3200 Old Main Hill, Logan, UT 84322-3200, 435-797-1603, Fax 435-797-4099, wal@cc.usu.edu
DREAM NETWORK, PO Box 1026, Moab, UT 84532-3031, 435-259-5936; Publisher@DreamNetwork.net http:dreamne-twork.net http://DreamNetwork.com
RealPeople Press, Box F, Moab, UT 84532
Weber State University, Weber State University, 1214 University Circle, Ogden, UT 84408-1214, 801-626-6616, 801-262-6473, weberstudies@weber.edu, http://weberstudies.weber.edu
WEBER STUDIES: Voices and Viewpoints of the Contemporary West, Weber State University, 1214 University Circle, Ogden, UT 84408-1214, 801-626-6473 or 6616
CineCycle Publishing, P.O. Box 982216, Park City, UT 84098
Transcending Mundane, Inc., PO Box 1241, Park City, UT 84060-1241, 435-615-9609, tommy@paracreative.com, www.paracreative.com
CHARITON REVIEW, Brigham Young University, Department of English, Provo, UT 84602, 801 422-1503, jim_barnes@byu.edu, www.jimbarnes.org
EXECUTIVE EXCELLENCE, 1366 E. 1120 S., Provo, UT 84606, 800-304-9782; editorial@eep.com; www.eep.com
Executive Excellence Publishing, 1806 N. 1120 W., Provo, UT 84604-1179, 800-304-9782; editorial@eep.com; www.eep.com
PERSONAL EXCELLENCE, 1366 E. 1120 S., Provo, UT 84606, 800-304-9782; editorial@eep.com; www.eep.com
THE DEFENDER - Rush Utah's Newsletter, Eborn Books, Box 559, Roy, UT 84067
American Book Publishing, PO Box 65624, Salt Lake City, UT 84165, 801-486-8639, Fax 801-382-0881, nospam@american-book.com, www.american-book.com
Bedside Books, 325 East 2400 South, Salt Lake City, UT 84115, info@american-book.com, www.american-book.com
LAKE STREET LIT: Art and Words from the Bottom of Lake Bonneville, P.O. Box 581438, Salt Lake City, UT 84158-1438, www.lakestreetlit.com
Motom, 76 West 2100 South, Salt Lake City, UT 84115, (801)499-6021
QUARTERLY WEST, 255 South Central Campus Drive, Dept. of English, LNCO 3500/University of Utah, Salt Lake City, UT 84112-9109, 801-581-3938
University of Utah Press, 1795 E. South Campus Drive #101, Salt Lake City, UT 84112, 800-621-2736, Fax 800-621-8471, UofUpress.com
WESTERN HUMANITIES REVIEW, University of Utah, Salt Lake City, UT 84112, 801-581-6070
ROCKY MOUNTAIN KC NEWS, 9574 Buttonwood Drive #A, Sandy, UT 84092, 801-298-6869, getproducts@juno.com
Rocky Mountain KC Publishing Co., 9574 Buttonwood Drive #A, Sandy, UT 84092, 801-298-6869, getproducts@juno.com
The Patrice Press, 319 Nottingham Drive, Tooele, UT 84074-2836, 602-882-0906, Fax 602-882-4161
Academic Innovations, 1386 Rio Virgin Dr., Washington, UT 84780, 800-967-8016, 800-967-4027
Eborn Books, 3601 S. 2700 W. B120, West Valley City, UT 84119, 801-965-9410, ebornbk@doitnow.com

VERMONT

TRANSITIONS ABROAD: The Guide to Living, Learning, and Working Overseas, PO Box 745, Bennington, VT 05201, 802-442-4827, info@transitionsabroad.com, www.transitionsabroad.com.

Goats & Compasses, PO Box 524, Brownsville, VT 05037, 802-484-5169
Tupelo Press, PO Box 539, Dorset, VT 05251, Telephone 802-366-8185,Fax 802-362-1883
9N-2N-8N-NAA NEWSLETTER, PO Box 275, East Corinth, VT 05040-0275, www.n-news.com
Longhouse, 1604 River Road, Guilford, VT 05301, poetry@sover.net, www.sover.net/~poetry
Upper Access Inc., 87 Upper Access Road, Hinesburg, VT 05461, 800-310-8320 (orders only), 802-482-2988, Fax 802-304-1005, info@upperaccess.com
THE LYRIC, PO Box 110, Jericho, VT 05465-0110
GREEN MOUNTAINS REVIEW, Johnson State College, Johnson, VT 05656, 802-635-1350
THE MARLBORO REVIEW, PO Box 243, Marlboro, VT 05344, www.marlbororeview.com
Atrium Society Publications, PO Box 816, Middlebury, VT 05753, 802-462-3900, fax 802-462-2792, e-mail atrium@atriumsoc.org, www.atriumsoc.org
Middlebury College Publications, Middlebury College, Middlebury, VT 05753, 802-443-5075, Fax 802-443-2088, E-mail nereview@middlebury.edu
NEW ENGLAND REVIEW, Middlebury College, Middlebury, VT 05753, 802-443-5075, fax 802-443-2088, e-mail nereview@middlebury.edu, http://go.middlebury.edu/nereview
HUNGER MOUNTAIN, The Vermont College Journal of Arts & Letters, Vermont College, 36 College Street, Montpelier, VT 05602, 800-336-6794 x8633, Fax 802-828-8649, hungermtn@tui.edu, www.hungermtn.org
Russian Information Services, PO Box 567, Montpelier, VT 05601-0567, 802-223-4955
RUSSIAN LIFE, PO Box 567, Montpelier, VT 05601-0567
Black Thistle Press, 165 Wiswall Hill Road, Newfane, VT 05345-9548, 212-219-1898
New Victoria Publishers, PO Box 27, Norwich, VT 05055, 802-649-5297
Bear & Company, One Park Street, Rochester, VT 05767-0388, Tel: 802-767-3174, Toll Free: 1-800-246-8648, Fax: 802-767-3726, Email: info@innertraditions.com
Main Street Arts Press, PO Box 100, Saxtons River, VT 05154, 802-869-2960, msa@sover.net
Mountainside Press, PO Box 407, Shaftsbury, VT 05262, 802-447-7094, Fax 802-447-2611
Wood Thrush Books, 85 Aldis Street, St. Albans, VT 05478, 802-524-6606
Glad Day Books, PO Box 112, Thetford, VT 05074
Arts End Books, PO Box 441, West Dover, VT 05356-0441, marshallbrooks.com
NOSTOC MAGAZINE, PO Box 441, West Dover, VT 05356-0441
Chelsea Green Publishing Company, PO Box 428, White River Junction, VT 05001-0428, 802-295-6300
Datamaster Publishing, LLC, PO Box 1527, Williston, VT 05495, 802-288-8040, Fax 802-288-8041, datamaster@surfglobal.net, www.DatamasterPublishing.com
Women In Print, PO Box 1527, Williston, VT 05495, 802-288-8040, fax 802-288-8041, www.WomenInPrint.com, womeninprint@surfglobal.net,
THE ANTHOLOGY OF NEW ENGLAND WRITERS, PO Box 5, Windsor, VT 05089-0005, 802-674-2315, newvtpoet@aol.com, www.newenglandwriters.org
GemStone Press, LongHill Partners, Inc., PO Box 237, Woodstock, VT 05091, 802-457-4000

VIRGIN ISLANDS

THE CARIBBEAN WRITER, University of the Virgin Islands, RR 1, Box 10,000, Kingshill, St. Croix, VI 00850, Phone: 340-692-4152, Fax: 340-692-4026, e-mail: qmars@uvi.edu, website: www.TheCaribbeanWriter.com

VIRGINIA

CORRECTIONS TODAY, American Correctional Association, 206 North Washington Street, Suite 200, Alexandria, VA 22314, 703-224-0000
THE EDITORIAL EYE, 66 Canal Center Plaza, Suite 200, Alexandria, VA 22314, 703-683-0683
EDUCATION IN FOCUS, PO Box 2, Alexandria, VA 22313, 703-548-0457
EEI Press, 66 Canal Center Plaza #200, Alexandria, VA 22314, 703-683-0683
firefall editions, 3213 Arundel Ave., Alexandria, VA 22306, 5105492461, www.firefallmedia.com
Orchises Press, PO Box 20602, Alexandria, VA 22320-1602, 703-683-1243
Red Dragon Press, 433 Old Town Court, Alexandria, VA 22314, 703-683-5877
AD/VANCE, 1593 Colonial Terrace #206, Arlington, VA 22209-1430
ALTERNATIVE PRESS REVIEW, PO Box 6245, Arlington, VA 22206
American Homeowners Foundation Press, 6776 Little Falls Road, Arlington, VA 22213, 703-536-7776, www.americanhomeowners.org
Bogg Publications, 422 North Cleveland Street, Arlington, VA 22201
BOGG: A Journal of Contemporary Writing, 422 N Cleveland Street, Arlington, VA 22201
GARGOYLE, 3819 North 13th Street, Arlington, VA 22201-4922, Phone/Fax 703-525-9296, hedgehog2@erols.com, gargoylemagazine@comcast.com, www.gargoylemagazine.com
Gival Press, PO Box 3812, Arlington, VA 22203, 703-351-0079 phone, givalpress@yahoo.com, www.givalpress.com
Paycock Press, 3819 N. 13th Street, Arlington, VA 22201, Fax 703-525-9296, hedgehog2@erols.com
Pocahontas Press, Inc., PO Drawer F, Blacksburg, VA 24063-1020, 540-951-0467, 800-446-0467
Rowan Mountain Press, PO Box 10111, Blacksburg, VA 24062-0111, 540-449-6178, e-mail faulkner@bev.net, web www.rowanmountain.com
SISTERS IN CRIME BOOKS IN PRINT, PO Box 10111, Blacksburg, VA 24062-0111, 540-449-6178, e-mail faulkner@bev.net, web www.rowanmountain.com
BRUTARIAN, 9405 Ulysses Court, Burke, VA 22015-1605
Blackwater Publications, 80 Laurel Oaks Lane, Castleton, VA 22716-2523, 540/987-9536; www.blackwaterpublications.com
Bereshith Publishing, PO Box 2366, Centreville, VA 20122-2366, 703-222-9387, Fax 707-922-0875, info@bereshith.com
ARCHIPELAGO, PO Box 2485, Charlottesville, VA 22902-2485, editor@archipelago.org, www.archipelago.org
dbS Productions, PO Box 1894, University Station, Charlottesville, VA 22903-0594, 800-745-1581, Fax 434-293-5502, info@dbs-sar.com, www.dbs-sar.com
IRIS: A Journal About Women, PO Box 800588, University of Virginia, Charlottesville, VA 22904, 434-924-4500, Fax 434-982-2901, iris@virginia.edu, http://womenscenter.virginia.edu/iris.htm
University of Virginia Press, P.O. Box 400318, Charlottesville, VA 22904-4318, 800-831-3406, 877-288-6400, vapress@virginia.edu, www.upress.virginia.edu
THE VIRGINIA QUARTERLY REVIEW, One West Range, University of Virginia, PO Box 400223, Charlottesville, VA 22904-4223, Email: vqreview@virginia.edu, ph: 434-924-3124, web: www.vqronline.org

Pocol Press, 6023 Pocol Drive, Clifton, VA 20124-1333, 703-830-5862, chrisandtom@erols.com, www.pocolpress.com
Chrysalis Reader, Box 4510, Route 1, Dillwyn, VA 23936, 1-434-983-3021
The Utility Company LLC, 15893 Northgate Drive, Dumfries, VA 22025-1704, 703 583.4408
PHOEBE: A Journal of Literature and Art, MSN 2D6, 4400 University Drive, George Mason University, Fairfax, VA 22030, www.gmu.edu.pubs/phoebe/
SO TO SPEAK: A Feminist Journal of Language & Art, So To Speak, George Mason University, 4400 University Drive, MS 2D6, Fairfax, VA 22030-4444, sts@gmu.edu, www.gmu.edu/org/sts
WOMEN AND LANGUAGE, Communication Dept, George Mason University, Fairfax, VA 22030
WRITER'S CHRONICLE, Mail Stop 1E3, George Mason University, Fairfax, VA 22030-4444, 703-993-4301, http://awpwriter.org
ANCIENT PATHS, PO Box 7505, Fairfax Station, VA 22039, ssburris@msn.com http://www.editorskylar.com
Artisan Studio Design, PO BOx 185, Falls Church, VA 22040-0185, Fax 703-852-3906, editor@vlqpoetry.com, http://VLQpoetry.com
Cavalier Press, P O Box 6437, Falls Church, VA 22040, http://www.cavalierpress.com
EROSHA, PO Box 185, Falls Church, VA 22040-0185, Fax 703-852-3906, editor@erosha.net, http://erosha.net
Little Poem Press, PO Box 185, Falls Church, VA 22040-0185, www.celaine.com/LittlePoemPress
VLQ (Verse Libre Quarterly), PO Box 185, Falls Church, VA 22040-0185, Fax 703-852-3906, editor@vlqpoetry.com, http://vlqpoetry.com
Glen Allen Press, 4036-D Cox Road, Glen Allen, VA 23060, 804-747-1776, Fax 804-273-0500, mail@glenallenpress.com, www.glenallenpress.com
THE BEACON: Journal of Special Education Law & Practice, PO Box 480, Hartfield, VA 23071, 804-758-8400, Fax 202-318-3239, info@harborhouselaw.com, www.harborhouselaw.com
Harbor House Law Press, Inc., PO Box 480, Hartfield, VA 23071, 804-758-8400, Fax 202-318-3239, info@harborhouse-law.com, www.harborhouselaw.com
THE HOLLINS CRITIC, PO Box 9538, Hollins University, VA 24020
Brunswick Publishing Corporation, 1386 Lawrenceville Plank Road, Lawrenceville, VA 23868, 434-848-3865; Fax 434-848-0607; brunswickbooks@earthlink.net
SHENANDOAH: THE Washington and Lee University Review, Mattingly House / 2 Lee Avenue, Lexington, VA 24450-0303, 540-458-8765; http://shenandoah.wlu.edu
Gifted Education Press/The Reading Tutorium, PO Box 1586, 10201 Yuma Court, Manassas, VA 20109-1586, 703-369-5017, giftededpress@comcast.net, www.giftededpress.com
Profile Press, 6051 Greenway Court, Manassas, VA 20112-3049, 703-730-0642
CHANTEH, the Iranian Cross-Cultural Quarterly, 7229 Vistas Lane, McLean, VA 22101, saideh_pakravan@yahoo.com, www.saideh-pakravan.com
DOLLS UNITED INTERACTIVE MAGAZINE, 6360 Camille Drive, Mechanicsville, VA 23111, http://www.dollsunited.com, 804-339-8579, editor@dollsunited.com
August Press LLC, 108 Terrell Road, PO Box 6693, Newport News, VA 23606, wdawkins4bj@aol.com, www.augustpress.net
Gardenia Press, 17 Cale Circle, Newport News, VA 23606-3733, 866-861-9443, Fax 414-463-5032, pressgdp@goweb-way.com, www.gardeniapress.com
BLUE COLLAR REVIEW, PO Box 11417, Norfolk, VA 23517, 757-627-0952, redart@pilot.infi.net
Partisan Press, PO Box 11417, Norfolk, VA 23517, e-mail: red-ink@earthlink.net, website: http:www.Partisanpress.org
POETICA MAGAZINE, Reflections of Jewish Thought, P.O.Box 11014, Norfolk, VA 23517, www.poeticamagazine.com
Strawberry Patchworks, Box 3, Green Mansion, North, VA 23128, 804-725-7560, berrybooks@villagepop.com
BRIDGES: An Interdisciplinary Journal of Theology, Philosophy, History, and Science, PO Box 3075, Oakton, VA 22124-3075, 703-281-4722, Fax 703-734-1976, E-mail Bridges23@aol.com
THE EDGE CITY REVIEW, 10912 Harpers Square Court, Reston, VA 20191, E-mail terry17@aol.com, www.edge-city.com
Millennium Workshop Production, 11501 Maple Ridge Road, Reston, VA 20190, 703-925-0610 phone/Fax, vkrivorotov@yahoo.com, www.george-the-dragonslayer.com, www.lifemaker.com
Brandylane Publishers, Inc., 5 S. 1st St., Richmond, VA 23219-3716, 804-644-3090, Fax 804-644-3092
FOLK ART MESSENGER, PO Box 17041, Richmond, VA 23226, 804-285-4532, 1-800-527-3655, fasa@folkart.org
Palari Publishing, PO Box 9288, Richmond, VA 23227-0288, phone/fax 866-570-6724, info@palaribooks.com, www.palaribooks.com
PLEASANT LIVING, 5 South 1st St., Richmond, VA 23219-3716, 804-644-3091
SLUG & LETTUCE, PO Box 26632, Richmond, VA 23261-6632
JUST WEST OF ATHENS, 6624 Hidden Woods Court, Roanoke, VA 24018-7489, submissions@westofathens.net, http://westofathens.net
Briarwood Publications, Inc., 150 West College Street, Rocky Mount, VA 24151, 540-483-3606; website www.briar-woodva.com
THE ROANOKE REVIEW, Roanoke College, 221 College Lane, Salem, VA 24153, 540-375-2380
Golden Quill Press, 102 Keswick Farm Road, Troutville, VA 24175-7130, 845-627-0386, thewritesource@pobox.com, www.thewritesource.homestead.com www.tellittothefuture.homestead.com, www.writersint.homestead.com
JOURNAL OF COURT REPORTING, 8224 Old Courthouse Road, Vienna, VA 22182, 703-556-6272, fax 703-556-6291, email pwacht@ncrahq.org
National Court Reporters Association Press, 8224 Old Courthouse Road, Vienna, VA 22182, 703-556-6272, fax 703-556-6291, email pwacht@ncrahq.org
Eco Images, P.O. Box 61413, Virginia Beach, VA 23466-1413, 757-421-3929, 757-421-3929, wildfood@infionline.net, http://wildfood.home.infionline.net
Luminous Epinoia Press, P O Box 10188, Virginia Beach, VA 23450-0188, (435)867-9045 www.luminousepinoia.com
THE WILD FOODS FORUM, P.O. Box 61413, Virginia Beach, VA 23466-1413, 757-421-3929, 757-421-3929, wildfood@infionline.net, http://wildfood.home.infionline.net
Books for All Times, Inc., PO Box 202, Warrenton, VA 20188, 540-428-3175, staff@bfat.com
all nations press, po box 601, White Marsh, VA 23183, 757-581-4063, www.allnationspress.com
Thirteen Colonies Press, 710 South Henry Street, Williamsburg, VA 23185, 757-229-1775
WILLIAM AND MARY REVIEW, Campus Center, PO Box 8795, Williamsburg, VA 23187-8795, 757-221-3290, Fax 757-221-3451
The Invisible College Press, LLC, PO Box 209, Woodbridge, VA 22194-0209, 703-590-4005, editor@invispress.com, www.invispress.com

WASHINGTON

Corvus Publishing Company, 6021 South Shore Road, Anacortes, WA 98221-8915, 360-293-6068, DP@CorvusBooks.com, www.CorvusBooks.com

Fine Edge Productions, 13589 Clayton Lane, Anacortes, WA 98221-8477, 360-299-8500, Fax 360-299-0535, office@FineEdge.com

Island Publishers, PO Box 201, Anacortes, WA 98221-0201, 360-293-5398

MARGIN: Exploring Modern Magical Realism, 321 High School Road NE, PMB #204, Bainbridge Island, WA 98110, magicalrealismmaven@yahoo.com, www.magical-realism.com

Snow Group, PO Box 10864, Bainbridge Island, WA 98110, patrick@createyourowndestiny.com

ABLAZE Publishing, 2800 122nd Place NE, Bellevue, WA 98005-1520, 877-624-0230, Fax 509-275-5817, info@laugh-it-off.com, www.laugh-it-off.com

ARNAZELLA, 3000 Landerholm Circle SE, Bellevue, WA 98007, 206-641-2373

Illumination Arts, PO Box 1865, Bellevue, WA 98009, 425-644-7185

Online Training Solutions, Inc., PO Box 951, Bellevue, WA 98009-0951, 425-885-1441, Fax 425-881-1642, quickcourse@otsiweb.com

BELLINGHAM REVIEW, Mail Stop 9053, WWU, Bellingham, WA 98225, 360-650-4863, bhreview@cc.wwu.edu

Bright Ring Publishing, Inc., PO Box 31338, Bellingham, WA 98228-3338, 800-480-4278, www.brightring.com

Signpost Press Inc., Mail Stop 9053, WWU, Bellingham, WA 98225, 360-650-4863

Topping International Institute, Inc., 2505 Cedarwood Avenue, Ste. 3, Bellingham, WA 98225, 360-647-2703, Fax 360-647-0164, topping2@gte.net

Owl Creek Press, 2693 S. Camano Drive, Camano Island, WA 98282

WRITERS CORNER, 142 Camelot Drive, Castle Rock, WA 98611-9471

ANIMAL PEOPLE, PO Box 960, Clinton, WA 98236-0960

THE NEW FORMALIST, P.O. Box 251, Dayton, WA 99328, thenewformalist@lycos.com http://www.newformalist.com

The New Formalist Press, Box 251, Dayton, WA 99328-0251, thenewformalist@lycos.com

SNOW MONKEY, PO Box 127, Edmonds, WA 98020, www.ravennapress.com/snowmonkey

Vagabond Press, 605 East 5th Avenue, Ellensburg, WA 98926-3201, 509-962-8471, vagabond@eburg.com, www.eburg.com/~vagabond

Marmot Publishing, 4652 Union Flat Creek Road, Endicott, WA 99125-9764, 509-657-3359, editor@marmotpublishing.com, www.marmotpublishing.com

WinePress Publishing, PO Box 428, Enumclaw, WA 98022, 360-802-9758, Fax 360-802-9992, info@winepresspub.com

Lockhart Press, Inc., 1717 Wetmore Avenue, Everett, WA 98201, 425-252-8882, ral@ralockhart.com, www.ralockhart.com

Hamster Huey Press, 7627 84th Avenue Ct. NW, Gig Harbor, WA 98335-6237, Phone 253-851-7839 http://www.hamsterhueypress.com

Olympic Mountain School Press, P.O. Box 1114, Gig Harbor, WA 98335, 253-858-4448

Russell Dean and Company, 17110 1'2 408th Ave. SE, Gold Bar, WA 98251, toll free: 888-205-0004, 360-793-4919, fax: 360-793-7579, email: topdogrdc@peoplepc.com, , www.RDandCo.com

Dunamis House, 19801 SE 123rd Street, Issaquah, WA 98027, 425-255-5274, fax 425-277-8780

Nystrom Publishing Co., PO Box 378, Issaquah, WA 98027, 425-392-0451

Dixon-Price Publishing, PO Box 1360, Kingston, WA 98346-1360, 360-297-8702, Fax 360-297-1620, dixonpr@dixon-price.com, www.dixonprice.com

PEMMICAN, PO Box 2692, Kirkland, WA 98083-2692, www.pemmicanpress.com

Pemmican Press, PO Box 2692, Kirkland, WA 98083, thebenhoward@yahoo.com, www.pemmicanpress.com

Mike French Publishing, 1619 Front Street, Lynden, WA 98264, 360-354-8326

STRINGTOWN, PO Box 1406, Medical Lake, WA 99022-1406, stringtown@earthlink.net, http://www.home.earthlink.net/~stringtown/index.html

EDGZ, Edge Publications, PO Box 799, Ocean Park, WA 98640-0799

XTANT, 814 - 318 Place, Ocean Park, WA 98640, (360) 665-3248

xtant.anabasis, 814 - 318 Place, Ocean Park, WA 98640, (360) 665-3248

Country Messenger Press, 78D Cameron Lake Loop Road, Okanogan, WA 98840, siniff@ncidata.com

Blue Star Press, 5333 71st Way NE, Olympia, WA 98516-9199

StarLance Publications, 5104 Cooperstown Lane, Pasco, WA 99301-8984

Hartley & Marks, Publishers, PO Box 147, Point Roberts, WA 98281, (800) 277-5887

FERRY TRAVEL GUIDE, PO Box 1169, Port Hadlock, WA 98339-1169

Dan Youra Studios, Inc., PO Box 1169, Port Hadlock, WA 98339-1169

THE TABBY: A CHRONICLE OF THE ARTS AND CRAFTS MOVEMENT, 3085 Buckingham Drive SE, Port Orchard, WA 98366, (360) 871-7707

Windstorm Creative, 7419 Ebbert Drive SE, Port Orchard, WA 98367, www.windstormcreative.com

Breakout Productions, PO Box 1643, Port Townsend, WA 98368, 360-379-1965, Fax 360-379-3794

Copper Canyon Press, PO Box 271, Port Townsend, WA 98368, poetry@coppercanyonpress.org, www.coppercanyonpress.org, 360-385 4925 (tel)

THE HERON'S NEST, 816 Taft Street, Port Townsend, WA 98368, www.theheronsnest.com

LIBERTY, PO Box 1181, Port Townsend, WA 98368, 360-379-0242

Washington State University Press, PO Box 645910, Pullman, WA 99164-5910, 509-335-7880, 509-335-8568 (fax), 800-354-7360, wsupress@wsu.edu, wsupress.wsu.edu

The Times Journal Publishing Co., PO Box 1286, Puyallup, WA 98371, 253-848-2779

MEDIA SPOTLIGHT, Po Box 290, Redmond, WA 98073

Hexagon Blue, 19301 SE 16th Street, Sammamish, WA 98075, 425-890-5351, info@hexagonblue.com, www.hexagonblue.com

Press Here, 22230 NE 28th Place, Sammamish, WA 98074-6408, WelchM@aol.com

TUNDRA, 22230 NE 28th Place, Sammamish, WA 98074-6408, welchm@aol.com

HA!, P. O. Box 368, Seabeck, WA 98380-0368, (360)830-5772

Writers' Haven Press, P. O. Box 368, Seabeck, WA 98380-0368, (360) 830-5772

Aviation Book Company, 7201 Perimeter Road South, Seattle, WA 98108-2999

Balanced Books Publishing, PO Box 14957, Seattle, WA 98144, 206-328-3995, fax 206-328-1339, toll free 877-838-4858, info@balancedbookspub.com, www.balancedbookspub.com

BARNWOOD, 10553 2nd Ave. NW, Seattle, WA 98177-4805

The Barnwood Press, 10553 2nd Ave. NW, Seattle, WA 98177-4805

602

Bay Press, 1411 4th Avenue, Suite 830, Seattle, WA 98101-2225, 206-284-5913

Bellywater Press, P.O. Box 95125, Seattle, WA 98145-2125, www.bellywaterpress.com

BIRD DOG, 1535 32nd Avenue, Apt. C, Seattle, WA 98122, www.birddogmagazine.com

Black Heron Press, PO Box 95676, Seattle, WA 98145

BLINK & Blink Chapbooks, PO Box 95487, Seattle, WA 98145-2487, rabbm@u.washington.edu

BRANCHES, PO Box 85394, Seattle, WA 98145-1394, 206-240-0075, Fax 206-361-5001, editor@branchesquarterly.com, www.branchesquarterly.com

CHRYSANTHEMUM, 202 6th Avenue South #1105, Seattle, WA 98104-2303, 206-682-3851, nooknoow@aol.com

THE COMICS JOURNAL, 7563 Lake City Way, Seattle, WA 98115

CRAB CREEK REVIEW, PO Box 85088, Seattle, WA 98145-1088, editors@crabcreekreview.org, www.crabcreekreview.org

CRANKY LITERARY JOURNAL, 322 10th Avenue E. C-5, Seattle, WA 98102, 206.328.4518

CUNE MAGAZINES, PO Box 31024, Seattle, WA 98103, Fax (206) 782-1330; www.cunemagazines.com; www.cune-press.net; magazines@cunepress.com

Cune Press, PO Box 31024, Seattle, WA 98103, Fax 206-782-1330, www.cunepress.net, www.cunemagazines.com, cune@cunepress.com

EduCare Press, PO Box 17222, Seattle, WA 98127, 206 706-4105

Fantagraphics Books, 7563 Lake City Way, Seattle, WA 98115

FINE MADNESS, PO Box 31138, Seattle, WA 98103-1138, www.finemadness.org, finemadness@comcast.net

FIVE WILLOWS MAGAZINE, 202 6th Avenue South #1105, Seattle, WA 98104-2303, 202-682-3851

Floating Bridge Press, C/O Richard Hugo House, 1634 - 11th Avenue, Seattle, WA 98122, www.scn.org/arts/floatingbridge; email floatingbridgepress@yahoo.com

GLOBAL VEDANTA, 2716 Broadway Avenue East, Seattle, WA 98102-3909, 206-323-1228, Fax 206-329-1791, global@vedanta-seattle.org, www.vedanta-seattle.org

Goldfish Press, 202 6th Avenue South #1105, Seattle, WA 98104-2303, 206-682-3851, nooknoow@aol.com

Bruce Gould Publications, PO Box 16, Seattle, WA 98111

Green Stone Publications, PO Box 22052, Seattle, WA 98122-0052, 206-524-4744

IMAGE: ART, FAITH, MYSTERY, 3307 Third Avenue West, Seattle, WA 98119, phone 206-281-2988, fax 206-281-2335

Impassio Press, PO Box 31905, Seattle, WA 98103, 206-632-7675, Fax 775-254-4073, books@impassio.com, www.impassio.com

JACK MACKEREL MAGAZINE, PO Box 23134, Seattle, WA 98102-0434

LETTER X, Seattle, WA 98102, submit@letterxmag.com, www.letterxmag.com

LITRAG, PO Box 21066, Seattle, WA 98111-3066, www.litrag.com

The Mountaineers Books, 1001 SW Klickitat Way, Suite 201, Seattle, WA 98134-1161, 206-223-6303

Parenting Press, Inc., PO Box 75267, Seattle, WA 98175-0267, 206-364-2900, Fax 206-364-0702

Perpetual Press, PO Box 3956, Seattle, WA 98124-3956, 800-807-3030

POETSWEST ONLINE, 1011 Boren Avenue #155, Seattle, WA 98104, 206-682-1268, info@poetswest.com, www.poets-west.com

PRISON LEGAL NEWS, 2400 NW 80th Street, PMB 148, Seattle, WA 98117, 206-246-1022, Fax 206-505-94499, pln@prisonlegalnews.org

THE RAVEN CHRONICLES, Richard Hugo House, 1634 11th Avenue, Seattle, WA 98122-2419, 206-364-2045, editors@ravenchronicles.org, www.ravenchronicles.org

READERS SPEAK OUT!, 4003 - 50th Avenue SW, Seattle, WA 98116

Red Letter Press, 4710 University Way NE #100, Seattle, WA 98105-4427, 206-985-4621, Fax 206-985-8965, redletterpress@juno.com

RIVET MAGAZINE, 3518 Fremont Avenue N. #118, Seattle, WA 98103, editor@rivetmagazine.org, www.rivetmagazine.org

Rodnik Publishing Co., PO Box 46956, Seattle, WA 98146-0956, Tel 206-937-5189 Fax 206-937-3554, URL: www.rodnikpublishing.com

Rose Alley Press, 4203 Brooklyn Avenue NE #103A, Seattle, WA 98105-5911, 206-633-2725, rosealleypress@juno.com, www.rosealleypress.com

Rowhouse Press, PO Box 23134, Seattle, WA 98102-0434

Sasquatch Press, 119 S. Main Street, Suite 400, Seattle, WA 98104-2555, 206-467-4300, 800-775-0817, Fax 206-467-4301, books@SasquatchBooks.com

SEA KAYAKER, PO Box 17029, Seattle, WA 98107-0729, 206-789-1326, Fax 206-781-1141, mail@seakayakermag.com

74th Street Productions, L.L.C., 350 North 74th Street, Seattle, WA 98103, 206-781-1447, info@74thstreet.com, www.74thstreet.com, www.writersatthepodium.com

STORMWARNING!, PO Box 21604, Seattle, WA 98111, 206-374-2215 phone/Fax, vvawai@oz.net, www.oz.net/~vvawai/

THE STRANGE FRUIT, 300 Lenora Street #250, Seattle, WA 98121, phone 206-780-1921, fax 309-273-8112, www.thestrangefruit.com, submissions@thestrangefruit.com

Uccelli Press, PO Box 85394, Seattle, WA 98145-1394, 206-240-0075, Fax 206-361-5001, editor@uccellipress.com, www.uccellipress.com

WASHINGTON TRAILS, 2019 3rd Ave., Suite #100, Seattle, WA 98121-2430, 206-625-1367, www.wta.org

Wave Books, 1938 Fairview Avenue East, Seattle, WA 98102, info@wavepoetry.com, www.wavepoetry.com

Wood Works, 4131 Greenwood Ave. N., Seattle, WA 98103-7017, www.woodworkspress.com

WORD IS BOND, PO Box 18304, Seattle, WA 98118, submissions@unblind.com, www.unblind.com

BELLOWING ARK, PO Box 55564, Shoreline, WA 98155, 206-440-0791

Bellowing Ark Press, PO Box 55564, Shoreline, WA 98155, 206-440-0791

Clearbridge Publishing, PO Box 33772, Shoreline, WA 98133, 206-533-9357, Fax 206-546-9756, beckyw@clearbridge.com, www.clearbridge.com

Light, Words & Music, 19630 Sunnyside Drive N, Apt. M108, Shoreline, WA 98133-1209, 206-546-1498, Fax 206-546-2585, sisp@aol.com

Arthur H. Clark Co., PO Box 14707, Spokane, WA 99214, 509-928-9540

HELIOTROPE: A Writer's Summer Solstice, PO Box 9938, Spokane, WA 99209-9938, e-mail gribneal@comcast.net

Lynx House Press, 420 West 24th, Spokane, WA 99203

ROCK & SLING: A Journal of Literature, Art and Faith, P. O. Box 30865, Spokane, WA 99223, editors@rockandsling.org, www.rockandsling.org

WILLOW SPRINGS, Willow Springs, Eastern Washington University, 705 West First Avenue, Spokane, WA 99201, 509-623-4349

Whispering Pine Press, 507 N. Sullivan Rd. Ste. A-7, Spokane Valley, WA 99037-8531, Phone: (509) 927-0404, Fax: (509)

927-1550, Web: www.whisperingpinepress.com, E-Mail: whisperingpinepressinc@hotmail.com
Silverstone Press, PO Box 8429, Tacoma, WA 98418-0429, (253)472-6707, fax (253)276-0233, email info@silverstone-press.com
HOME EDUCATION MAGAZINE, PO Box 1083, Tonasket, WA 98855, 509-486-1351, hem-editor@home-ed-magazine.com
Intelligent Technologies, Inc., 10906 NE 39th St., #A4, Vancouver, WA 98682-6789, Fax 360-254-4151
DIFFERENT KIND OF PARENTING, PO Box 514, Vashon Island, WA 98070-0514
KotaPress, PO Box 514, Vashon Island, WA 98070-0514, editor@kotapress.com, www.kotapress.com
KOTAPRESS ONLINE JOURNALS, PO Box 514, Vashon Island, WA 98070-0514
Brooding Heron Press, Bookmonger Road, Waldron Island, WA 98297, 360-420-8181
Temple Inc., PO Box 1773, Walla Walla, WA 99362-0033, info@thetemplebookstore.com
Hearts That Care Publishing, 888 West X Street, Washougal, WA 98671-7432
Blue Raven Publishing, 9 South Wenatchee Avenue, Wenatchee, WA 98801-2210, 509-665-8353
PENNY-A-LINER, PO Box 2163, Wenatchee, WA 98807-2163, 509-662-7858
PORTALS, PO Box 2163, Wenatchee, WA 98807-2163, 509-662-7858
Redrosebush Press, PO Box 2163, Wenatchee, WA 98807-2163, 509-662-7858

WEST VIRGINIA

Woodland Press, LLC and Woodland Gospel Publishing, 118 Woodland Drive, Chapmanville, WV 25508, 304-752-7500, Fax 304-752-9002; kdavis@woodlandpress.com; tfortune@woodlandpress.com; www.woodlandpress.com
Mountain State Press, 2300 MacCorkle Avenue SE, Charleston, WV 25304-1099, 304-357-4767, mspl@newwave.net
COMBAT, the Literary Expression of Battlefield Touchstones, PO Box 3, Circleville, WV 26804-0003, majordomo@com-bat.ws, www.combat.ws/
BIBLIOPHILOS, 200 Security Building, Fairmont, WV 26554, 304-366-8107
KESTREL: A Journal of Literature and Art, Fairmont State University, 1201 Locust Avenue, Fairmont, WV 26554-2451, 304-367-4815, Fax 304-367-4896, e-mail kestrel@mail.fscwv.edu
ABZ A Magazine of Poetry, John McKernan, Editor Marshall University, One John Marshall Drive, Huntington, WV 25755-2646
ABZ Poetry Press, PO Box 2746, Huntington, WV 25727-2746
Enlightened Living Publishing, LLC, P O Box 7291, Huntington, WV 25775-7291, telephone 304-486-9000, fax 304-486-5815, toll free 866-896-2665, e-mail: info@enlightenedlivingpublishing.com, www.enlightenedlivingpublishing.com
Ogden Press, 105 Greenway Place, Huntington, WV 25705-2205, Telephone # 304/733-3576
Quiet Storm Books, PO Box 1666, Martinsburg, WV 25402, 361-992-5587, Fax 208-498-9259, management@quietstorm-books.com, www.quietstormbooks.com
West Virginia University Press, P.O. Box 6295, G3 White Hall, Morgantown, WV 26506, Office (304) 293-8400, Toll free for orders (866) 988-7737, Fax (304) 293-6585

WISCONSIN

Adams-Pomeroy Press, PO Box 189, Albany, WI 53502, 608-862-3645, Fax 608-862-3647, adamspomeroy@ckhnet.com
Green Hut Press, 1015 Jardin Street East, Appleton, WI 54911, 920-734-9728, janwfcloak@uspower.net
SHENANDOAH NEWSLETTER, 736 West Oklahoma Street, Appleton, WI 54914
BELOIT FICTION JOURNAL, Box 11, Beloit College, Beloit, WI 53511, 608-363-2308
Crystal Dreams Publishing, W1227 East County Rd A, Berlin, WI 54923, 920-361-0961
WISCONSIN TRAILS, PO Box 317, Black Earth, WI 53515-0317, e-mail editor@wistrails.com
Lessiter Publications, PO Box 624, Brookfield, WI 53008-0624, 262-782-4480, Fax 262-782-1252
ROSEBUD, N 3310 Asje Rd., Cambridge, WI 53523, 608-423-4750
Zelda Wilde Publishing, 315 Water St., Cambridge, WI 53523, 608-423-9609
Foremost Press, 7067 Cedar Creek Rd., Cedarburg, WI 53012, 262.377.3180,mary@foremostpress.com, http://foremost-press.com
PORCUPINE LITERARY ARTS MAGAZINE, PO Box 259, Cedarburg, WI 53012, 262-376-9178, ppine259@aol.com, www.porcupineliteraryarts.com
Michael E. Coughlin, Publisher, PO Box 205, Cornucopia, WI 54827
THE DANDELION, PO Box 205, Cornucopia, WI 54827
Blue Tiger Press, 2016 Hwy 67, Dousman, WI 53118, 262-965-2751
Wm Caxton Ltd, PO Box 220, Ellison Bay, WI 54210-0220
Midwestern Writers Publishing House, PO Box 8, Fairwater, WI 53931
Highsmith Press, PO Box 800, Ft. Atkinson, WI 53538, 920-563-9571, Fax 920-563-4801, hpress@highsmith.com, www.hpress.highsmith.com
Raven Tree Press, LLC, 200 S. Washington St., Suite 306, Green Bay, WI 54301, 920-438-1605, 920-438-1607, 877-256-0579, raven@raventreepress.com, www.raventreepress.com
Pearl-Win Publishing Co., N4721 9th Drive, Hancock, WI 54943-7617, 715-249-5407
Aircraft Owners Group, PO Box 5000, Iola, WI 54945, 800-331-0038, e-mail cessna@aircraftownergroup.com or piper@aircraftownergroup.com
CESSNA OWNER MAGAZINE, PO Box 5000, Iola, WI 54945, 715-445-5000; E-mail cessna@aircraftownergroup.com
PIPERS MAGAZINE, PO Box 5000, Iola, WI 54945, 715-445-5000; e-mail piper@aircraftownergroup.com
Big Valley Press, S2104 Big Valley Road, La Farge, WI 54639, 608 489 3525
ABRAXAS, PO Box 260113, Madison, WI 53726-0113, 608-238-0175, abraxaspress@hotmail.com, www.geocities.com/abraxaspress/
Bleak House Books, an imprint of Diversity Incorporated, 923 Williamson St., Madison, WI 53703-3549, Fax: 608.259.8370 , info@bleakhousebooks.com www.bleakhousebooks.com, www.diversityincorporated.com
CREATIVITY CONNECTION, Room 622 Lowell Hall, 610 Langdon Street, Madison, WI 53703, 608-262-4911
FEMINIST COLLECTIONS: A QUARTERLY OF WOMEN'S STUDIES RESOURCES, 430 Memorial Library, 728 State Street, Madison, WI 53706, 608-263-5754
FEMINIST PERIODICALS: A CURRENT LISTING OF CONTENTS, 430 Memorial Library, 728 State Street, Madison, WI 53706, 608-263-5754
Ghost Pony Press, PO Box 260113, Madison, WI 53726-0113, 608-238-0175, ghostponypress@hotmail.com, www.geoci-ties.com/abraxaspress, www.thing.net/~grist/l&d/dalevy/dalevy.htm, www.thing.net/~grist/ld/saiz/saiz.htm
THE MADISON REVIEW, Dept of English, H.C. White Hall, 600 N. Park Street, Madison, WI 53706, 263-3303
THE MODERN LANGUAGE JOURNAL, University of Wisconsin, Department of French and Italian, Madison, WI

604

53706-1558, 608-262-5010
Muse World Media Group, PO Box 55094, Madison, WI 53705, 608-238-6681
NEW BOOKS ON WOMEN & FEMINISM, 430 Memorial Library, 728 State Street, Madison, WI 53706, 608-263-5754
University of Wisconsin Press, 1930 Monroe Street, 3rd Floor, Madison, WI 53711-2059, (608)263-0814, fax (608)263-1132
WISCONSIN ACADEMY REVIEW, 1922 University Ave., Madison, WI 53705, 608-263-1692
Women's Studies Librarian, University of Wisconsin System, 430 Memorial Library, 728 State Street, Madison, WI 53706, 608-263-5754
Marsh River Editions, M233 Marsh Road, Marshfield, WI 54449
ANTHILLS, PO Box 170322, Milwaukee, WI 53217-8026, www.centennialpress.com, chuck@centennialpress.com
Centennial Press, PO Box 170322, Milwaukee, WI 53217-8026
THE CREAM CITY REVIEW, PO Box 413, English Dept, Curtin Hall, Univ. of Wisconsin, Milwaukee, WI 53201, 414-229-4708
Creative Writing and Publishing Company, PO Box 511848, Milwaukee, WI 53203-0311, (414)447-7810, same for fax, creatwritpub.com
Grip Publishing, PO Box 091882, Milwaukee, WI 53209, 414-807-6403
Lemieux International Ltd., PO Box 170134, Milwaukee, WI 53217, 414-962-2844, FAX 414-962-2844, lemintld@msn.com
Sun Designs, PO Box 6, Oconomowoc, WI 53066, 262-567-4255
YUKHIKA—LATUHSE, P.O. Box 365, Oneida Nation Arts Program, Oneida, WI 54155-0365, jstevens@ez-net.com
N: NUDE & NATURAL, PO Box 132, Oshkosh, WI 54903, 920-426-5009
MIDWEST ART FAIRS, PO Box 72, Pepin, WI 54759, 715-442-2022
THE PUBLICITY HOUND, 3434 County Road KK, Port Washington, WI 53074-9638, www.publicityhound.com
Britton Road Press, PO Box 044618, Racine, WI 53404, Fax 262-633-5503
LITERARY MAGAZINE REVIEW, Univ. of Wisconsin-River Falls, English Dept., 410 S. 3rd Street, River Falls, WI 54022, email: jennifer.s.brantley@uwrf.edu, web site: http://www.uwrf.edu/lmr/
SEEMS, c/o Lakeland College, Box 359, Sheboygan, WI 53082-0359
Philokalia Books, 102 West Grove Street, South Wayne, WI 53587, 608-439-1763 phone/Fax (call first), storode@philokalia-books.com, www.philokaliabooks.com
Colgate Press, P.O.Box 597, Sussex, WI 53089, 414-477-8686
Reliance Books, 208 E. Oak Crest Drive, Ste. 250, Wales, WI 53183-9700, 262-968-9857, Fax 262-968-9854, contact@reliancebooks.com, www.reliancebooks.com
Jackson Harbor Press, RR 1, Box 107AA, 845 Jackson Harbor Road, Washington Island, WI 54246-9048
The Film Instruction Company of America, 5928 W. Michigan Street, Wauwatosa, WI 53213-4248, 414-258-6492
AT THE LAKE MAGAZINE, 93 West Geneva St., P.O. Box 1080, Williams Bay, WI 53191, phone 262-245-1000; fax 262-245-2000; toll free 800-386-3228; e-mail media@ntmediagroup.com; web www.ntmediagroup.com

WYOMING

Jetbak Publishing, 1258 S. Fenway Street, Casper, WY 82601-4022
Whiskey Creek Press, P.O. Box 51052, Casper, WY 82605-1052, 307-265-8585 (fax only), email: publisher@whiskeycreek-press.com, websites: www.whiskeycreekpress.com, www.whiskeycreekpresstorrid.com
Crazy Woman Creek Press, 3073 Hanson, Cheyenne, WY 82001, 707-829-8568, www.jewsofwyoming.org
One Eyed Press, 272 Road 6Rt, Cody, WY 82414, one_eyed_press@yahoo.com, www.one-eyed-press.com
High Plains Press, Box 123, 539 Cassa Road, Glendo, WY 82213, 307-735-4370, Fax 307-735-4590, 800-552-7819
Agathon Books, PO Box 630, Lander, WY 82520-0630, 307-332-5252, Fax 307-332-5888, agathon@rmisp.com, www.rmisp.com/agathon/
OWEN WISTER REVIEW, PO Box 3625, Laramie, WY 82071-3625, 307-766-4027; owr@uwyo.edu
Skyline West Press/Wyoming Almanac, 1409 Thomes, Laramie, WY 82072, 307-745-8205
MIDNIGHT SHOWCASE: Romance Digest, Erotic-ahh Digest, Special Digest, P.O. Box 726, Lusk, WY 82225, 307-334-3165, 727-848-5962, publisher@midnightshowcase.com, http://www.midnightshowcase.com
Twin Souls Publications, P.O. Box 726, Lusk, WY 82225, 307-334-3165, 727-848-5962, publisher@midnightshowcase.com, http://www.midnightshowcase.com
Alpine Press, PO Box 1930, Mills, WY 82644, 307-234-1990
Andmar Press, PO Box 217, Mills, WY 82644, e-mail fjozwik@csi.com; www.andmarpress.com

EAST AFRICA

TIFARA, 08 BP 28 Cidex 02 Abidjan 08, Cocody Lycee Technique 150 Logts Bat N Appt 107, Abidjan Ivory Coast, East Africa, +225 07 67 81 98

ARGENTINA

Zagier & Urruty Publicaciones, PO Box 94 Sucursal 19, Buenos Aires 1419, Argentina, 541-572-1050

AUSTRALIA

STUDIO - A Journal of Christians Writing, 727 Peel Street, Albury, N.S.W. 2640, Australia, email: pgrover@big-pond.com,www: www.studiojournal.net
BLAST, PO Box 134, Campbell, ACT 2612, Australia
DARK ANIMUS, PO Box 750, Katoomba, NSW 2780, Australia, skullmnky@hotmail.com, www.darkanimus.com
DOTLIT: The Online Journal of Creative Writing, Queensland University of Technology, Creative Industry Facul, PO Box 2434, Kelvin Grove, QLD 4059, Australia, (07)3864 2976, FAX (07)3864 1810, http://www.dotlit.qut.edu.au
ART VISIONARY MAGAZINE, GPO Box 1536, Melbourne, Victoria 3001, Australia, artvisionary@optusnet.com.au
RED LAMP, 5 Kahana Court, Mountain Creek, Queensland 4557, Australia, evans-baj@hotmail.com
Spinifex Press, PO Box 212, North Melbourne VIC 3051, Australia, +61-3-9329 6088, Fax +61-3-9329 9238
RED AND BLACK, PO Box 12, Quaama, NSW 2550, Australia
HECATE, School of English, Media Studies & Art History, The University of Queensland, St. Lucia, Queensland 4072, Australia, phone: 07 336 53146, fax: 07 3365 2799, web: www.emsah.uq.edu.au/awsr, email: c.ferrier@mailbox.uq.edu.au
Hecate Press, School of English, Media Studies and Art History, The University of Queensland, St. Lucia, Queensland 4072, Australia
Total Cardboard Publishing, 70 Mount Barker Road, Stirling, SA 5152, Australia, www.totalcardboard.com
Pinchgut Press, 6 Oaks Avenue, Cremorne, Sydney, N.S.W. 2090, Australia, 02-9908-2402
LINQ, School of Humanities, James Cook Univ.-North Queensland, Townsville 4811, Australia, e-mail jcu.linq@jcu.edu.au

Galaxy Press, 71 Recreation Street, Tweed Heads, N.S.W. 2485, Australia, (07) 5536-1997

BELIZE

AXIOS, 30-32 Macaw Avenue, PO Box 279, Belmodan, Belize, 501-8-23284
GORHAM, 30-32 Macaw Avenue, PO Box 279, Belmopan, Belize, 501-8-23284
ORTHODOX MISSION, 30-32 Macaw Avenue, Belmopan, Belize, 011-501-8-23284
Orthodox Mission in Belize, 30-32 Macaw Avenue, PO Box 279, Belmopan, Belize, 501-8-23284, fax 501-8-23633
THE VORTEX, 30-32 Macaw Avenue, PO Box 279, Belmopan, Belize, 501-8-23284
Axios Newletter, Inc., 16 Maxi Street, PO Box 90, Santa Elena, Cayo, Belize, 501-8-23284

BRAZIL

Solcat Publishing, Rua Visconde de Piraja 82 sala 508, Ipanema - Rio de Janeiro - RJ Cep: 22411-000, Brazil, +55-21-3813-6740

CANADA

THE ANTIGONISH REVIEW, St Francis Xavier University, PO Box 5000, Antigonish, Nova Scotia B2G 2W5, Canada
George Suttton Publishing Co., 54 Crawford Drive, Aurora, Ontario, Canada L4G 4R4, Canada, georgesutton2005@yahoo.com
Proof Press, 67 Court Street, Aylmer, QC J9H 4M1, Canada, dhoward@aix1.uottawa.ca
RAW NERVZ HAIKU, 67 Court Street, Aylmer, QC J9H 4M1, Canada, dhoward@aix1.uottawa.ca
CANADIAN MONEYSAVER, Box 370, Bath, Ontario K0H 1G0, Canada, www.canadianmoneysaver.ca, moneyinfo@canadianmoneysaver.ca
TIME FOR RHYME, c/o Richard Unger, PO Box 1055, Battleford SK S0M 0E0, Canada, 306-445-5172
Bayhampton Publications, 54 Mozart Crescent, Brampton, ON L6Y 2W7, Canada, 905-455-7331, Fax 905-455-0207, www.bayhampton.com
WEST COAST LINE: A Journal of Contemporary Writing and Criticism, 2027 EAA, Simon Fraser University, Burnaby, B.C. V5A 1S6, Canada
ESPERANTIC STUDIES, 8888 University Drive, Faculty of Education, Burnaby, BC, V5A 1S6, Canada, Off: 604-291-4489, Fax: 604.434.2624, jclark@esperantic.org, www.esperantic.org
ALBERTA HISTORY, 95 Holmwood Ave NW, Calgary Alberta T2K 2G7, Canada, 403-289-8149
FREEFALL, Alexandra Writers Centre Society, 922 9th Avenue S.E., Calgary, AB T2G 0S4, Canada, Fax 403-264-4730, awcs@telusplanet.net, www.alexandrawriters.org
CANADIAN JOURNAL OF COUNSELLING, University of Calgary Press, 2500 University Drive NW, Calgary, AB T2N 1N4, Canada, 613-237-1099, toll-free 877-765-5565, Fax 613-237-9786, info@ccacc.ca, www.ccacc.ca/
CURRENTS: New Scholarship in the Human Services, Faculty of Social Work, Univ. of Calgary, 2500 University Drive NW, Calgary, AB T2N 1N4, Canada, 403-220-7550, Fax 403-282-7269, currents@ucalgary.ca, www.uofcpress.com/journals/currents
HISTORY OF INTELLECTUAL CULTURE, Faculty of Education, EDT 722, Univ. of Calgary, 2500 Univ. Drive NW, Calgary, AB T2N 1N4, Canada, 403-220-6296, Fax 403-282-8479, elpanayo@ucalgary.ca, pjstortz@ucalgary.ca, www.ucalgary.ca/hic/
INTERNATIONAL ELECTRONIC JOURNAL FOR LEADERSHIP IN LEARNING, Faculty of Education, Univ. of Calgary, 2500 University Drive NW, Calgary, AB T2N 1N4, Canada, 403-220-5675, Fax 403-282-3005, www.ucalgary.ca/~iejll/
TORQUERE: Journal of the Canadian Lesbian and Gay Studies Association, University of Calgary Press, 2500 University Drive NW, Calgary, AB T2N 1N4, Canada, 403-220-3514, Fax 403-282-0085, ucpmail@ucalgary.ca, www.uofcpress.com
INTERNATIONAL ADDICTION, Addiction Centre, Foothills Hospital, 1403 29th Street NW, Univ. of Calgary, Calgary, AB T2N 2T9, Canada, 403-670-2025, Fax 403-670-2056, nady.el-guebaly@crha-health.ab.ca, http://ahdp.lib.ucalgary.ca/IA/
EDGE Science Fiction and Fantasy Publishing, PO Box 1714, Calgary, AB T2P 2L7, Canada, 403-254-0160
Historical Society of Alberta, 95 Holmwood Ave. NW, Calgary, Alberta T2K 2G7, Canada
THE PRAIRIE JOURNAL OF CANADIAN LITERATURE, PO Box 61203 Brentwood P.O., 217, 3630 Brentwood Road N.W., Calgary, Alberta T2L 2K6, Canada, prairiejournal@yahoo.com, www.geocities.com/prairiejournal
Prairie Journal Press, Brentwood P.O., Calgary, Alberta T2L 2K6, Canada, prairiejournal@yahoo.com, www.geocities.com/prairiejournal
ARIEL, A Review of International English Literature, The University of Calgary, 2500 University Drive NW, Calgary, Alberta T2N 1N4, Canada, 403-220-4657, Fax 403-289-1123, ariel@ucalgary.ca, www.english.ucalgary.ca/ariel/
CANADIAN JOURNAL OF PHILOSOPHY, University of Calgary Press, Univ. of Calgary, 2500 University Dr. N.W., Calgary, Alberta T2N 1N4, Canada, 403-220-3514, Fax 403-282-0085, ucpmail@ucalgary.ca
MOUSEION, Journal of the Classical Association of Canada/Revue de la Societe Canadienne des Etudes Classiques, University of Calgary Press, Univ. of Calgary, 2500 University Dr. N.W., Calgary, Alberta T2N 1N4, Canada, 403-220-3514, Fax 403-282-0085, ucpmail@ucalgary.ca
University of Calgary Press, 2500 University Drive NW, Calgary, Alberta T2N 1N4, Canada, 403-220-7578, Fax 403-282-0085, www.uofcpress.com
Aardvark Enterprises (A Division of Speers Investments Ltd.), 204 Millbank Drive S.W., Calgary, Alberta T2Y 2H9, Canada, 403-256-4639
Reveal, 4322 Cleroux, Chomedey, Laval, Quebec H7T 2E3, Canada, 514-687-8966
THE MYSTERY REVIEW, PO Box 233, Colborne, Ont. K0K 1S0, Canada, 613-475-4440, Fax 613-475-3400, mystrev@reach.net, www.themysteryreview.com
Vesta Publications Limited, PO Box 1641, Cornwall, Ont. K6H 5V6, Canada, 613-932-2135, FAX 613-932-7735
WRITER'S LIFELINE, PO Box 1641, Cornwall, Ont. K6H 5V6, Canada
ARTISTAMP NEWS, 4426 Island Hwy S, Courtenay, BC V9N 9T1, Canada
Pottersfield Press, 83 Leslie Road, East Lawrencetown, NS, B2Z 1P8, Canada, 1-800-Nimbus 9 (for orders)
Kriya Yoga Publications, 196 Mountain Road, PO Box 90, Eastman, Quebec J0E 1P0, Canada
Zygote Publishing, PO Box #4049, 10467 80 Ave NW, Edmonton, AB T6E 4S8, Canada, (780)439-7580, (780)439-7529, www.zygotepublishing.com
ON SPEC, PO Box 4727, Edmonton, AB T6E 5G6, Canada, 403-413-0215, onspec@onspec.ca
Phi-Psi Publishers, Box 75198, Ritchie P.O., Edmonton, AB T6E 6K1, Canada, phipsibk@netscape.net
EXCEPTIONALITY EDUCATION CANADA, Department of Educational Psychology, 6-102 Education North, University of Alberta, Edmonton, AB T6G 2G5, Canada, Telephone: (780) 492-2198/7471, Fax: (780) 492-1318, E-mail: eecj@ualberta.ca, judy.lupart@ualberta.ca, christina.rinaldi@ualberta.ca
THE INTERNATIONAL FICTION REVIEW, Culture & Language Studies, UNB, PO Box 4400, Fredericton, N.B. E3B 5A3,

Canada, 506-453-4636, Fax 506-447-3166, e-mail ifr@unb.ca

THE FIDDLEHEAD, Campus House, PO Box 4400, University of New Brunswick, Fredericton, NB E3B 5A3, Canada, 506-453-3501

Broken Jaw Press, PO Box 596 Stn A, Fredericton, NB E3B 5A6, Canada, ph/fax 506-454-5127, jblades@nbnet.nb.ca, www.brokenjaw.com

NEW MUSE OF CONTEMPT, Box 596 Stn A, Fredericton, NB E3B 5A6, Canada, www.brokenjaw.com

Zumaya Publications, P.O. Box 2146, Garibaldi Highlands, B.C. V0N 1T0, Canada, 512-707-2694, 235-660-2009

BRADY MAGAZINE, 165 Old Muskoka Road, Suite 306, Gravenhurst, Ontario P1P 1N3, Canada, 705-687-3963 [phone], 705-687-8736 [fax], editor@bradymagazine.com [e-mail], http://www.bradymagazine.com [website]

Questex Consulting Ltd., 8 Karen Drive, Guelph, Ontario N1G 2N9, Canada, 519-824-7423

Canadian Children's Press, 4th Floor, MacKinnon Building, University of Guelph, Guelph, Ontario N1G 2W1, Canada

ATLANTIS: A Women's Studies Journal/Revue d'etudes sur les femmes, Institute for the Study of Women, Mt. Saint Vincent University, Halifax, N.S. B3M 2J6, Canada, 902-457-6319, Fax 902-443-1352, atlantis@msvu.ca, www.msvu.ca/atlantis

THE DALHOUSIE REVIEW, Dalhousie University, Halifax, Nova Scotia B3H 3J5, Canada, 902-494-2541, fax 902-494-3561, email dalhousie.review@dal.ca

OCEAN YEARBOOK, Dalhousie Law School, 6061 University Avenue, Halifax, Nova Scotia B3H 4H9, Canada, 902-494-2955 (main #), 902-494-1316 (fax), http://www.journals.uchicago.edu/OY/home.html

Tuns Press, Faculty of Architecture and Planning, Dalhousie University, Box 1000 Central Station, Halifax, Nova Scotia B3J 2X4, Canada, 902-494-3925, Fax 902-423-6672, tuns.press@dal.ca, tunspress.dal.ca

Unfinished Monument Press, 237 Prospect Street South, Hamilton, Ontario L8M 2Z6, Canada, 905-312-1779, james@meklerdeahl.com, www.meklerdeahl.com

Tower Poetry Society, c/o McMaster University, 1280 Main Street W. Box 1021, Hamilton, Ontario, L8S 1CO, Canada

TOWER, c/o McMaster University, 1280 Main Street W Box 1021, Hamilton, Ontario, L8S ICO, Canada

Nip & Tuck Publishing, 736 Wilson Avenue, Kelowna, BC V1Y 6X9, Canada, 250-762-7861, nipandtuck@shaw.ca,

Quarterly Committee of Queen's University, Queen's University, Kingston, Ontario K7L 3N6, Canada, 613-533-2667, qquarter@post.queensu.ca, http://info.queensu.ca/quarterly

QUEEN'S QUARTERLY: A Canadian Review, Queen's University, Kingston, Ontario K7L 3N6, Canada, 613-533-2667, qquarter@post.queensu.ca, http://info.queensu.ca/quarterly

APPLE VALLEY REVIEW: A Journal of Contemporary Literature, c/o Queen's Postal Outlet, Box 12, Kingston, Ontario K7L 3R9, Canada, http://www.applevalleyreview.com/

Multi-Media Publications Inc., R.R. #4B, Lakefield, ON K0L 2H0, Canada, 905-721-1540 phone/Fax, info@mmpubs.com, www.mmpubs.com

Oolichan Books, PO Box 10, Lantzville, B.C., V0R 2H0, Canada, 250-390-4839, oolichanbooks@telus.net, www.oolichan.com

Hochelaga Press, 8140 Ogilvie, LaSalle, QC H8P 3R4, Canada, 514-366-5655, Fax 514-364-5655, hochelaga@sympatico.ca

Sun Books, Box 28, Lennoxville, Quebec J1M 1Z3, Canada

THE TOWNSHIPS SUN, Box 28, Lennoxville, Quebec J1M 1Z3, Canada

INGLESIDE NEWS ZINE, 5591 St-Laurent, Levis, QC, G6V 3V6, Canada, ingleside_news_zine@yahoo.com, www.geocities.com/ingleside_news_zine

LITERARY RESEARCH/RECHERCHE LITTERAIRE, Dept. of Modern Languages & Lit., University of Western Ontario, London, ON N6A 3K7, Canada, 519-661-3196, 519-661-2111 X85862, Fax 519-661-4093, cmihails@uwo.ca, http://collection.nlc-bnc.ca/100/201/300/literary_research-ef, or www.uwo.ca/modlang/ailc

Stewart Publishing & Printing, 17 Sir Constantine Drive, Markham, ON L3P 2X3, Canada, www.stewartbooks.com 905-294-4389; FAX 905-294-8718; robert@stewartbooks.com

A SOFT DEGRADE, 58 2nd Street NE, Medicine Hat, AB T1A 5K7, Canada, diefortheflag@hotmail.com, www.asoftdegrade.com

Canadian Educators' Press, 100 City Centre Drive, PO Box 2094, Mississauga, ON L5B 3C6, Canada, 905-826-0578

Lyons Publishing Limited, 2704 Jerring Mews, Mississauga, Ontario L5L 2M8, Canada, info@judypowell.com

SCRIVENER, McGill University, 853 Sherbrooke Street W., Montreal, P.Q. H3A 2T6, Canada, scrivenermag@hotmail.com

GOOD GIRL, 837 rue Gilford, Montreal, QB H2J 1P1, Canada, 514-288-5626, Fax 514-499-3904, info@goodgirl.ca, www.goodgirl.ca

FISH PISS, Box 1232, Place d'Armes, Montreal, QB H2Y 3K2, Canada

ASCENT, 837 Rue Gilford, Montreal, QC H2J 1P1, Canada, 514-499-3999, Fax 514-499-3904, info@ascentmagazine.com, www.ascentmagazine.com

VALLUM: CONTEMPORARY POETRY, PO Box 48003, Montreal, QC H2V 4S8, Canada, vallummag@sympatico.ca, www.vallummag.com

CANADIAN JOURNAL OF LATIN AMERICAN AND CARIBBEAN STUDIES/Revue canadienne des etudes latino-americaines et caraibes, CALACS, CCASLS SB-115, Concordia University, 1455 de Maisonneuve Ouest, Montreal, QC H3G 1M8, Canada, calacs@concordia.ca

INTERCULTURE, Intercultural Institute of Montreal, 4917 St-Urbain, Montreal, Quebec H2T 2W1, Canada, 514-288-7229, FAX 514-844-6800

NIGHTLIFE MAGAZINE, 4200, Boulevard St. Laurent, Suite 1470, Montreal, Quebec H2W 2R2, Canada, 514.278.3222

Vehicule Press, PO Box 125, Place du Parc Station, Montreal, Quebec H2X 4A3, Canada, 514-844-6073, FAX 514-844-7543, vp@vehiculepress.com, www.vehiculepress.com

Black Rose Books Ltd., C.P. 1258, Succ. Place du Parc, Montreal, Quebec H2X 4A7, Canada, 514-844-4076, Fax 514-849-4797, blakrose@web.net, http://www.web.net/blackrosebooks

CELLAR, PO Box 111, Moreton's Harbour, NL A0G 3H0, Canada

CONTEMPORARY GHAZALS, PO Box 111, Moreton's Harbour, NL A0G 3H0, Canada

FIDDLER MAGAZINE, PO Box 101, N. Sydney, NS B2A 3M1, Canada, 650-948-4383

JOURNAL OF CHILD AND YOUTH CARE, Malaspina University-College, Human Services, 900 5th Street, Nanaimo, BC V9R 5S5, Canada, 250-753-3245 X2207, Fax 250-741-2224, conlin@mala.bc.ca

New Orphic Publishers, 706 Mill Street, Nelson, BC V1L 4S5, Canada, 250-354-0494, Fax 250-352-0743

THE NEW ORPHIC REVIEW, 706 Mill Street, Nelson, BC V1L 4S5, Canada, 250-354-0494, Fax 250-352-0743

EVENT, Douglas College, PO Box 2503, New Westminster, B.C. V3L 5B2, Canada, 604-527-5293, Fax 604-527-5095, event@douglas.bc.ca, http://event.douglas.bc.ca

THE CAPILANO REVIEW, 2055 Purcell Way, North Vancouver, B.C. V7J 3H5, Canada, 604-984-1712

CANADIAN REVIEW OF AMERICAN STUDIES, University of Toronto Press, 5201 Dufferin Street, North York, ON M3H 5T8, Canada

NEW GRAFFITI, Ontario, Canada, newgraffiti@hotmail.com

OUR SCHOOLS/OUR SELVES, Canadian Centre for Policy Alternatives, 410-75 Albert Street, Ottawa, ON K1P 5E7, Canada, 416-463-6978 phone/Fax, web: www.policyalternatives.ca

CANADIAN JOURNAL OF PROGRAM EVALUATION, Canadian Evaluation Society, 1485 Laperriere Avenue, Ottawa, ON K1Z 7S8, Canada, 613-725-2526, Fax 613-729-6206, ces@thewillowgroup.com

Borealis Press Limited, 110 Bloomingdale Street, Ottawa, Ont. K2C 4A4, Canada, 613-798-9299, Fax 379-897-4747

JOURNAL OF CANADIAN POETRY, 110 Bloomingdale Street, Ottawa, Ont. K2C 4A4, Canada, 613-797-9299, Fax 613-798-9747

BARDIC RUNES, 424 Cambridge Street South, Ottawa, Ontario K1S 4H5, Canada, 613-231-4311

Book Coach Press, 14 Moorside Private, Ottawa, Ontario K2C 3P4, Canada, (613) 226-4850, 1-877-GGR-RUNE, www.gentlegiantrunes.com, gentlegiantrunes@sympatico.ca

Canadian Library Association, 328 Frank Street, Ottawa, Ontario K2P 0X8, Canada, 613-232-9625 X322, fax: 613-563-9895, www.cla.ca

FELICITER, 328 Frank Street, Ottawa, Ontario K2P 0X8, Canada, 613-232-9625, ext. 322

THALIA: Studies in Literary Humor, English Dept.,University of Ottawa, 70 Laurier East, Ottawa, Ontario, K1N 6N5, Canada, thaliahumor@hotmail.com

Theytus Books Ltd., Green Mountain Road, Lot 45, RR #2, Site 50, Comp. 8, Penticton, B.C. V2A 6J7, Canada

WASCANA REVIEW OF CONTEMPORARY POETRY AND SHORT FICTION, Department of English, University of Regina, Regina, Sask S4S 0A2, Canada, 584-4302

Coteau Books, 2517 Victoria Ave., Regina, Sask. S4P 0T2, Canada, 306-777-0170, e-mail coteau@coteaubooks.com

Munsey Music, Box 511, Richmond Hill, Ontario L4C 4Y8, Canada, 905-737-0208; www.pathcom.com/~munsey

Plain Philosophy Center, 310 - 8870 Citation Drive, Richmond, BC V6Y 3A3, Canada, 1-604-276-8272

Creative Guy Publishing, 206-7600 Moffatt Rd, Richmond, BC V6Y 3V1, Canada

Liaison Press, 206-7600 Moffatt Rd, Richmond, BC V6Y 3V1, Canada

BANANA RAG, RR 22, 3747 Hwy. 101, Roberts Creek, B.C. V0N 2W2, Canada, 604-885-7156

Banana Productions, RR 22, 3747 Highway 101, Roberts Creek, BC V0N 2W2, Canada, 604-885-7156, Fax 604-885-7183

INTERNATIONAL ART POST, RR 22, 3747 Highway 101, Roberts Creek, BC V0N 2W2, Canada

West Coast Paradise Publishing, PO Box 2093, Sardis Sta. Main, Sardis, B.C. V2R 1A5, Canada, 604-824-9528, Fax 604-824-9541, web:http://rg.anstey.ca/

THE NEO-COMINTERN, 97 Maxwell Crescent, Saskatoon, Sask. S7L 3Y4, Canada, www.neo-comintern.com

CROSSCURRENTS, 516 Ave K South, Saskatoon, Sask. S7M 2E2, Canada, Fax 306-244-0795, green@webster.sk.ca—www.webster.sk.ca/greenwich/xc.htm

BLACKFLASH, 12-23rd Street East, 2nd Floor, Saskatoon, Saskatchewan S7K 0H5, Canada, 306-374-5115, Fax 306-665-6568, editor@blackflash.ca

GRAIN MAGAZINE, PO Box 67, Saskatoon, SK S7K 3K1, Canada, 306-244-2828, grainmag@sasktel.net

Saskatchewan Writers Guild, PO Box 67, Saskatoon, SK S7K 3K1, Canada, 306-244-2828, grainmag@sasktel.net

LABOUR/LE TRAVAIL, Arts Publications, FM 2005, Memorial University, St. John's, NF A1C 5S2, Canada, 709-737-2144

Canadian Committee on Labour History, Arts Publications, FM 2005, Memorial University, St. John's, NL A1C 5S7, Canada, 709-737-2144

CHALLENGING DESTINY, R.R. 6, St. Marys, ON N4X 1C8, Canada, csp@golden.net, http://challengingdestiny.com, Available in PDF and other electronic formats

OPEN MINDS QUARTERLY, 680 Kirkwood Drive, Bldg. 1, Sudbury, ON P3E 1X3, Canada, 705-675-9193 ext. 8286, Fax 705-675-3501, openminds@nisa.on.ca, www.nisa.on.ca

Higher Ground Press, P.O. Box 650, Summerland, British Columbia, Canada V0H 1Z0, Canada, Tel 250-496-6802, 866-496-6802, hgt@uniserve.com

BLUELINES, #202, 7027-134 Street, Surrey, BC V3W 4T1, Canada, 604-596-1601, lpwordsolutions@hotmail.com; www.lpwordsolutions.com

Sources, 489 College Street, Suite 305, Toronto ON M6G 1A5, Canada, Phone: 416-964-7799. Fax: 416-964-8763

THE SOURCES HOTLINK, 489 College Street, Suite 305, Toronto ON M6G 1A5, Canada, Phone: 416-964-7799. Fax: 416-964-8763

Betelgeuse Books, Suite 516, 3044 Bloor St. West, Toronto Ontario M8X 2Y8, Canada, betelg@idirect.com

DESCANT, PO Box 314, Station P, M5S 2S8, Toronto, ON, Canada, phone: 416 593 2557, fax: 416 593 9362, email general: info@descant.on.ca, email subscriptions/back issues: circulation@descant.on.ca, web: www.descant.on.ca

Annick Press Ltd., 15 Patricia Avenue, Toronto, ON M2M 1H9, Canada, 416-221-4802, Fax 416-221-8400, annickpress@annickpress.com

BRICK, A Literary Journal, Box 537, Station Q, Toronto, ON M4T 2M5, Canada, www.brickmag.com, info@brickmag.com, orders@brickmag.com, submissions@brickmag.com

Inner City Books, Box 1271, Station Q, Toronto, ON M4T 2P4, Canada, 416-927-0355, FAX 416-924-1814, icb@inforamp.net

Coach House Books, 401 Huron, on bpNichol Lane, Toronto, ON M5S 2G5, Canada, t: 800-367-6360, f: 416-977-1158, website: www.chbooks.com

BROKEN PENCIL, PO Box 203 Station P, Toronto, ON M5S 2S7, Canada, 416-538-2813, E-mail editor@brokenpencil.com

KISS MACHINE, POB 108, Station P, Toronto, ON M5S 2S8, Canada

THE LONG ARC, PO Box 73620, 509 St. Clair Avenue West, Toronto, ON M6C 1C0, Canada, 416-651-5800, tasc@web.ca

RESOURCES FOR RADICALS, PO Box 73620, 509 St. Clair Avenue West, Toronto, ON M6C 1C0, Canada, 416-651-5800, burch@web.ca

PAPERPLATES, 19 Kenwood Avenue, Toronto, ON M6C 2R8, Canada

Timeless Books, 3 MacDonell Ave, Suite 300, Toronto, ON M6R 2A3, Canada, 1-800-661-8711, (416) 645-6747, contact@timeless.org, www.timeless.org

CODA: The Jazz Magazine, PO Box 1002, Station O, Toronto, Ont. M4A 2N4, Canada, 416-465-9093

Life Untangled Publishing, Toronto, Ontario, Canada, http://www.lifeuntangled.com

CANADIAN WOMAN STUDIES/les cahiers de la femme, 212 Founders College, York Univ., 4700 Keele Street, Toronto, Ontario M3J 1P3, Canada, 416-736-5356, fax 416-736-5765, e-mail cwscf@yorku.ca

Wordwrights Canada, PO Box 456, Station O, Toronto, Ontario M4A 2P1, Canada, wordwrights@sympatico.ca, www.wordwrights.ca

JONES AV, 88 Dagmar Av, Toronto, Ontario M4M 1W1, Canada, www.interlog.com/~oel

Underwhich Editions, PO Box 262, Adelaide Street Station, Toronto, Ontario M5C 2J4, Canada, 536-9316

Life Media, 508-264 Queens Quay W, Toronto, Ontario M5J 1B5, Canada, 416-260-0303, email publisher@lifemedia.ca, web www.lifemedia.ca

Winslow Publishing, Box 38012, 550 Eglinton Avenue West, Toronto, Ontario M5N 3A8, Canada, 416-789-4733,

winslow@interlog.com, www.winslowpublishing.com
RESOURCES FOR FEMINIST RESEARCH/DOCUMENTATION SUR LA RECHERCHE FEMINISTE, 252 Bloor Street W., Toronto, Ontario M5S 1V6, Canada, 416-923-6641, ext. 2278, Fax 416-926-4725, E-mail rfrdrf@oise.utoronto.ca
Between The Lines, 720 Bathurst Street, Suite 404, Toronto, Ontario M5S 2R4, Canada, 416-535-9914, fax 416-535-1484, btlbooks@web.ca
INTERNATIONAL JOURNAL OF AMERICAN LINGUISTICS, University of Toronto, 130 St. George Street, Department of Linguistics, Toronto, Ontario M5S 3H1, Canada, http://www.journals.uchicago.edu/IJAL/home.html
CONNEXIONS DIGEST, 489 College Street, Suite 305, Toronto, Ontario M6G 1A5, Canada, 416-964-1511, www.connexions.org
Connexions Information Services, Inc., 489 College Street, Suite 305, Toronto, Ontario M6G 1A5, Canada, 416-964-1511, www.connexions.org
Gesture Press, 623 Christie St., #4, Toronto, Ontario M6G 3E6, Canada
Guernica Editions, Inc., 11 Mount Royal Avenue, Toronto, Ontario M6H 2S2, Canada, 416-658-9888, Fax 416-657-8885, guernicaeditions@cs.com
CANADIAN JOURNAL OF COMMUNICATION, Canadian Centre for Studies in Publishing, Simon Fraser Univ., 515 West Hastings St., Vancouver BC V6B 5K3, Canada, (604) 291-5116
PRISM INTERNATIONAL, E462-1866 Main Mall, University of British Columbia, Vancouver BC V6T 1Z1, Canada, 604-822-2514, Fax 604-822-3616, prism@interchange.ubc.ca, www.prism.arts.ubc.ca
New Star Books Ltd., #107, 3477 Commercial Street, Vancouver, B.C. V5N 4E8, Canada, 604-738-9429, Fax 604-738-9332
Anvil Press, 278 East First Avenue, Vancouver, B.C. V5T 1A6, Canada, 604-876-8710, info@anvilpress.com, www.anvilpress.com
Good Times Publishing Co., 2211 West 2nd Avenue #209, Vancouver, B.C. V6K 1H8, Canada, 604-736-1045
Ronsdale Press, 3350 West 21st Avenue, Vancouver, B.C. V6S 1G7, Canada, 604-738-4688, toll free 888-879-0919, Fax 604-731-4548
CANADIAN LITERATURE, University of British Columbia, Buchanan E158, 1866 Main Mall, Vancouver, B.C. V6T 1Z1, Canada, 604-822-2780, fax 604-822-5504
Iconoclast Press, 3495 Cambie Street, Suite 144, Vancouver, BC V5Z 4R3, Canada, 604-682-3269 X8832, admin@iconoclastpress.com
SUB-TERRAIN, P.O. Box 3008, Main Post Office, Vancouver, BC V6B 3X5, Canada, 604-876-8710, subter@portal.ca, www.subterrain.ca
ROOM OF ONE'S OWN, PO Box 46160, Station D, Vancouver, B.C. V6J 5G5, Canada
UBC Press, 2029 West Mall, Vancouver, BC V6T 1Z2, Canada, Phone 604-822-5959, 1-877-377-9378; Fax 604-822-6083, 1-800-668-0821; info@ubcpress.ca; www.ubcpress.ca
THE AFFILIATE, 777 Barb Road, #257, Vankleek Hill, Ontario K0B 1R0, Canada, 613-678-3453
Trafford Publishing, 6E-2333 Government Street, Victoria, BC V8T 4P4, Canada, 888-232-4444, Fax 250-383-6804, sales@trafford.com, www.trafford.com
EcceNova Editions, 308-640 Dallas Road, Victoria, BC V8V 1B6, Canada, Fax: 250-595-8401 email: info@eccenova.com URL: www.eccenova.com
Horned Owl Publishing, 4605 Bearwood Court, Victoria, BC V8Y 3G1, Canada, fax 250-414-4987; e-mail hornowl@islandnet.com
THE MALAHAT REVIEW, PO Box 1700, Stn. CSC, Victoria, British Columbia V8W 2Y2, Canada
LICHEN Arts & Letters Preview, 234-701 Rossland Road East, Whitby, Ontario L1N 9K3, Canada, info@lichenjour-nal.ca,www.lichenjournal.ca
UNIVERSITY OF WINDSOR REVIEW, Department of English, University of Windsor, Windsor, Ontario N9B3P4, Canada, 519-293-4232 X2332; Fax 519-973-7050; uwrevu@uwindsor.ca
CANADIAN CHILDREN'S LITERATURE, Dept. of English, University of Winnipeg, 515 Portage Ave., Winnipeg MB R3B 2E9, Canada, 519-824-4120 ext. 53189, Fax 519-837-1315, ccl@uoguelph.ca, http://www.uoguelph.ca/ccl/
Turnstone Press, 607-100 Arthur Street, Winnipeg R3B 1H3, Canada, 204-947-1555, info@turnstonepress.com
Three Bears Publishing, 690 Community Row, Winnipeg, Manitoba Canada R3R 1H7, Canada, Tel. 1 (204) 783-7966, Email: info@ThreeBearsPublishing.com, Website: www.ThreeBearsPublishing.com
CONTEMPORARY VERSE 2: the Canadian Journal of Poetry and Critical Writing, 207-100 Arthur Street, Winnipeg, Manitoba R3B 1H3, Canada, (204) 949-1365, cv2@mb.sympatico.ca, www.contemporaryverse2.ca

PEOPLE'S REPUBLIC OF CHINA

CHINESE LITERATURE, 24 Baiwanzhuang Road, Beijing 100037, People's Republic of China, 892554
Chinese Literature Press, 24 Baiwanzhuang Road, Beijing 100037, People's Republic of China

CZECH REPUBLIC

Twisted Spoon Press, PO Box 21, Preslova 12, Prague 5, 150 00, Czech Republic, www.twistedspoon.com

DENMARK

RockBySea Books, Guldberg Hus, Guldbergsgade 9, Copenhagen, 2200 Copenhagen N, Denmark, + 45 35 35 44 80

ENGLAND

Original Plus, 18 Oxford Grove,Flat 3,, England, 01271862708; e-mail smithsssj@aol.com
Immediate Direction Publications, 7 Mountview, Church Lane West, Aldershot, Hampshire GU11 3LN, England, tdenyer@ntlworld.com, www.midnightstreet.co.uk
MIDNIGHT STREET, 7 Mountview, Church Lane West, Aldershot, Hampshire GU11 3LN, England
FORESIGHT MAGAZINE, 44 Brockhurst Road, Hodge Hill, Birmingham B36 8JB, England, 021-783-0587
PENNINE PLATFORM, Frizingley Hall, Frizinghall Road, Bradford BD9 4LD, England, 01274 541015, nicholas.bielby@vir-gin.net, www.pennineplatform.co.uk
LIBRARY HI TECH, MCB University Press, 60/62 Toller Lane, Bradford, W. Yorkshire BD8 9BY, England, 01274-777700, Fax 01274-785200 or 785201, www.mcb.co.uk
LIBRARY HIGH TECH NEWS, MCB University Press, 60/62 Toller Lane, Bradford, W. Yorkshire BD8 9BY, England, 01274-777700, Fax 01274-785200 or 785201, www.mcb.co.uk
MCB University Press, 60/62 Toller Lane, Bradford, W. Yorkshire BD8 9BY, England
REFERENCE SERVICES REVIEW, MCB University Press, 60/62 Toller Lane, Bradford, W. Yorkshire BD8 9BY, England, 01274-777700, Fax 01274-785200 or 785201, www.mcb.co.uk

VARIOUS ARTISTS, 24, Northwick Road, Bristol BS7 0UG, England
PENNINE INK MAGAZINE, The Gallery, Yorke Street, Burnley, Lancs. BB11 1HD, England, sheridansdandl@yahoo.co.uk
THE NEW WRITER, PO Box 60, Cranbrook, Kent TN17 2ZR, England, 01580-212626 admin@thenewwriter.com www.thenewwriter.com
THE JOURNAL (once "of Contemporary Anglo-Scandinavian Poetry"), 18 Oxford Grove, Flat 3, Devon. EX34 9HQ, England, 01271862708; e-mail smithsssj@aol.com
TEARS IN THE FENCE, 38 Hod View, Stourpaine, Blandford Forum, Dorset DT11 8TN, England
THE JOURNAL OF COMMONWEALTH LITERATURE, Bowker-Saur, Windsor Court, East Grinstead House, E. Grinstead, W. Sussex RH19 1XA, England, +44(0)1342-336122, Fax +44(0)1342-336197
DANDELION ARTS MAGAZINE, Casa Alba, 24 Frosty Hollow, E. Hunsbury, Northants NN4 0SY, England, 01604-701730
Fern Publications, Casa Alba, 24 Frosty Hollow, E. Hunsbury, Northants NN4 0SY, England, 01604-701730
PROP, 31 Central Avenue, Farnworth, Bolton BL4 0AU, England
Hippopotamus Press, 22 Whitewell Road, Frome, Somerset BA11 4EL, England, 0373-466653
THE POWYS JOURNAL, 82 Linden Road, Gloucester GL1 5HD, England, 01452-304539
BALLISTA, 6 Chiffon Way, Trinity Riverside, Gtr Manchester M3 6AB, England, +4407814570441, paul@mucusart.co.uk, www.mucusart.co.uk/press.htm
Mucusart Publications, 6 Chiffon Way, Trinity Riverside, Gtr Manchester M3 6AB, England, +4407814570441, paul@mucusart.co.uk, www.mucusart.co.uk/press.htm
THE UGLY TREE, Mucusart Publications, 6 Chiffon Way, Trinity Riverside, Gtr Manchester M3 6AB, England, paul@mucusart.co.uk, www.mucusart.co.uk/press.htm
STAND MAGAZINE, School of English, Univeristy of Leeds, Leeds LS2 9JT, England
KRAX, 63 Dixon Lane, Leeds, Yorkshire LS12 4RR, England
SMOKE, Liver House, 96 Bold Street, Liverpool L1 4HY, England
Windows Project, Liver House, 96 Bold Street, Liverpool L1 4HY, England
BULLETIN OF HISPANIC STUDIES, Dept. Of Hispanic Studies, The University, PO Box 147, Liverpool L69 3BX, England, 051 794 2774/5
Liverpool University Press, Dept. of Hispanic Studies, The University, PO Box 147, Liverpool L69 3BX, England, 051 794 2774/5
BAD POETRY QUARTERLY, PO Box 6319, London E11 2EP, England
Menard Press, 8 The Oaks, Woodside Avenue, London N12 8AR, England
MEDICAL HISTORY, Welcome Trust Centre for the History of Medicine at UCL, 210 Euston Road, London NW1 2BE, England, +44 (0)20 7679 8107, fax +44 (0)20 7679 8194
Wellcome Institute for the History of Medicine, 210 Euston Road, London NW1 2BE, England
Hole Books, 2 Hailsham Avenue, London SW2 3AH, England, (0) 208 677 3121, fax (0) 208 677 3121, email holebooks@yahoo.co.uk, web www.holebooks.com
COUNTER CULTURE, PO Box 1243, London SW7 3PB, England, 44(0)20-7-373-3432 phone/Fax, thirdway@dircon.co.uk, www.thirdway.org
MOTHER EARTH, PO Box 1243, London SW7 3PB, England, 44(0)70-7-373-3432 phone/Fax, thirdway@dircon.co.uk, www.thirdway.org
Christoffel & Le Cordier, 401 Langham House, 302 Regent Street, London W1B 3HH, England, christoffel@regent-st.com, www.christoffel.co.uk
Saqi Books Publisher, 26 Westbourne Grove, London W2 5RH, England, 020 7221 9347, fax 020 7229 7492
AQUARIUS, Flat 4, Room B, 116 Sutherland Avenue, Maida-Vale, London W9, England
LONDON REVIEW OF BOOKS, 28-30 Little Russell Street, London WC1A 2HN, England, 020-7209-1141, fax 020-7209-1151
POETRY REVIEW, 22 Betterton Street, London WC2H 9BX, England
Mind Power Publishing, 57 Elsinge Road, Enfield, London, EN1 4NS, England, +44(0)1992851158
AMBIT, 17 Priory Gardens, London, N6 5QY, England, 0181-340-3566
THIRD WAY, PO Box 1243, London, SW7 3PB, England, 44(0)20-7-373-3432 phone/Fax, thirdway@dircon.co.uk, www.thirdway.org
Third Way Publications Ltd., PO Box 1243, London, SW7 3PB, England, 44(0)20-7-373-3432 phone/Fax, thirdway@dircon.co.uk, www.thirdway.org
THE RUE BELLA, 40, Jordangate, Macclesfield SK10 1EW, England, www.ruebella.co.uk
The Association of Freelance Writers, Sevendale House, 7 Dale Street, Manchester, M1 1JB, England, 0161-228-2362, Fax 0161-228-3533
FREELANCE MARKET NEWS, Sevendale House, 7 Dale Street, Manchester, M1 1JB, England, 0161-228-2362, Fax 0161-228-3533
RUBIES IN THE DARKNESS, 41 Grantham Road, Manor Park, London E12 5LZ, England
PLANTAGENET PRODUCTIONS, Libraries of Spoken Word Recordings and of Stagescripts, Westridge (Open Centre), Star Lane, Highclere, Newbury RG20 9PJ, England
SPIKED, 7 Swansea Road, Norwich NR2 5HU, England
NOTTINGHAM MEDIEVAL STUDIES, School of History, University Park, Nottingham NG7 2RD, England, +44 115-9-515929, fax +44 115-9-515948, e-mail michael.jones@nottingham.ac.uk
N-B-T-V, Narrow Bandwidth Television Association, 1 Burnwood Dr., Wollaton, Nottingham, Notts NG8 2DJ, England, 0115-9282896
Plantagenet Productions, Westridge (Open Centre), Highclere, Nr. Newbury, Berkshire RG20 9PJ, England
THE AFRICAN BOOK PUBLISHING RECORD, PO Box 56, Oxford OX13EL, England, +44-(0)1865-511428; fax +44-1865-311534
ARETE, 8 New College Lane, Oxford OX1 3BN, England
FOURTH WORLD REVIEW, 26 High Street, Purton, Wiltshire SN5 9AE, England, 01793-772214
LORE AND LANGUAGE, National Centre for Eng. Cultural Tradition, The University, Sheffield S10 2TN, England, Sheffield 0114-2226296
Applied Probability Trust, School of Mathematics and Statistics, University of Sheffield, Sheffield S3 7RH, England, tel: +44 (0)114 222-3920; fax: +44 (0)114 272-9782; email: apt@sheffield.ac.uk; web: http://www.appliedprobability.org
MATHEMATICAL SPECTRUM, School of Mathematics and Statistics, University of Sheffield, Sheffield S3 7RH, England, tel: +44 (0)114 222-3920, fax: +44 (0)114 272-9782, email: apt@sheffield.ac.uk, web: http://www.appliedprobability.org
CANDELABRUM POETRY MAGAZINE, 1 Chatsworth Court, Outram Rd., Southsea PO5 1RA, England, tel: 02392 753696, rcp@poetry7.fsnet.co.uk, www.members.tripod.com/redcandlepress

Red Candle Press, 1 Chatsworth Court, Outram Rd., Southsea PO5 1RA, England, 02392753696, rcp@poetry7.fsnet.co.uk, www.members.tripod.com/redcandlepress
THE JOURNAL OF DESIGN AND TECHNOLOGY EDUCATION, Westview House, 734 London Road, Oakhill, Stoke-on-Trent, Staffordshire ST4 5NP, England, 01782-745567, Fax 01782-745553
MCT - MULTICULTURAL TEACHING, Westview House, 734 London Road, Oakhill, Stoke-on-Trent, Staffordshire ST4 5NP, England, 01782-745567, Fax 01782-745553
Trentham Books, Westview House, 734 London Road, Oakhill, Stoke-on-Trent, Staffordshire ST4 5NP, England, 01782-745567, Fax 01782-745553
K.T. Publications, 16, Fane Close, Stamford, Lincs., PE9 1HG, England, (07180) 754193
IOTA, 1 Lodge Farm, Snitterfield, Stratford-on-Avon, Warks CV37 0LR, England, 44-1789-730320, iotapoetry@aol.com, www.iotapoetry.co.uk
Ragged Raven Press, 1 Lodge Farm, Snitterfield, Stratford-upon-Avon, Warwickshire CV37 0LR, England, 44-1789-730320, raggedravenpress@aol.com, www.raggedraven.co.uk
Comrades Press, 23 George Street, Stockton, Southam, Warwickshire CV47 8JS, England, editor@comrade.org.uk, www.comrade.org.uk/press
PURPLE PATCH, 25 Griffiths Road, West Bromwich, B71 2EH, England
Hilltop Press, 4 Nowell Place, Almondbury, Huddersfield, West Yorkshire HD5 8PB, England
JAMES JOYCE BROADSHEET, School of English, University of Leeds, West Yorkshire LS2 9JT, England, 0113-233-4739
ORBIS, 17 Greenhow Avenue, West Kirby, Wirral CH48 5EL, England, +44 (0)151 625 1446; e-mail carolebaldock@hotmail.com
IMPress, 26 Oak Road, Withington, Manchester M2O 3DA, England, +44(0)161-2837636, info@impressbooks.fsnet.co.uk, www.impressbooks.fsnet.co.uk

FINLAND

BOOKS FROM FINLAND, PO Box 259, FI-00171 Helsinki, Finland, 358 (0) 201 1313451357942, booksfromfinland@finlit.fi , www.finlit.fi/booksfromfinland

FRANCE

UPSTAIRS AT DUROC, 20 Boulevard du Montparnasse, 75015 Paris, France, wice@wice-paris.org (attention:Upstairs at Duroc submissions)
FRANK: AN INTERNATIONAL JOURNAL OF CONTEMPORARY WRITING AND ART, 32 rue Edouard Vaillant, 93100 Montreuil Sous Bois, France, (33) 1 48596658, e-mail david@paris-anglo.com
Handshake Editions, Atelier A2, 83 rue de la Tombe-Issoire, Paris 75014, France, 4327-1767
J'ECRIS, BP 101, Saint-Cloud 92216, France, (1) 47-71-79-63

GREAT BRITAIN

Second Aeon Publications, 19 Southminster Road, Roath, Cardiff, Wales CF23 5AT, Great Britain, 029-2049-3093, secondaeon@peterfinch.co.uk
Peter Marcan Publications, PO Box 3158, London SEI 4RA, Great Britain, (020) 7357 0368

GERMANY

Expanded Media Editions, Prinz Albert Str. 38, 53113 Bonn, Germany, 0228/22 95 83, FAX 0228/21 95 07
Edition Gemini, Juelichstrasse 7, Huerth-Efferen D-50354, Germany, 02233/63550, Fax 02233/65866

GREECE

Anagnosis, Deliyianni 3, Maroussi 15122, Greece, +302106254654, Fax:+302106254089, www.anagnosis.gr

HOLLAND

VERSAL, Amsterdam, Holland, versal@wordsinhere.com (queries only), http://versal.wordsinhere.com

HONG KONG

ASIAN ANTHROPOLOGY, The Chinese University of Hong Kong, Sha Tin, New Territories, Hong Kong, Hong Kong, 852-26096508, 852-26037355
ASIAN JOURNAL OF ENGLISH LANGUAGE TEACHING, The Chinese University of Hong Kong, Sha Tin, New Territories, Hong Kong, Hong Kong, 852-26096508, 852-26037355, cup@cuhk.edu.hk, www.chineseupress.com
THE CHINA REVIEW: AN INTERDISCIPLINARY JOURNAL ON GREATER CHINA, The Chinese University of Hong Kong, Sha Tin, New Territories, Hong Kong, Hong Kong, 852-26096508,852-26037355, cup@cuhk.edu.hk,www.chineseupress.com
JOURNAL OF PSYCHOLOGY IN CHINESE SOCIETIES, The Chinese University of Hong Kong, Sha Tin, New Territories, Hong Kong, Hong Kong, 852-26096508, 852-26037355, cup@cuhk.edu.hk, www.chineseupress.com
QUEST: AN INTERDISCIPLINARY JOURNAL FOR ASIAN CHRISTIAN SCHOLARS, The Chinese University of Hong Kong, Sha Tin, New Territories, Hong Kong, Hong Kong, 852-26096500, 852-26037355, cup@cuhk.edu.hk, www.chineseupress.com
The Chinese University Press, The Chinese University of Hong Kong, Sha Tin, New Territories, Hong Kong, 852-26096508,852-26037355
HONG KONG JOURNAL OF SOCIOLOGY, The Chinese University of Hong Kong, Sha Tin, New Territories, Hong Kong, 852-26096508,852-26037355, cup@cuhk.edu.hk, www.chineseupress.com
Philopsychy Press, PO Box 1224, Shatin Central, N.T., Hong Kong, Contact us by phone (852-3411-7289), fax (852-3411-7379), email (ppp@net1.hkbu.edu.hk), or by visiting our web site (www.hkbu.edu.hk/~ppp/ppp/intro.html).
RENDITIONS, Chinese University of Hong Kong, Shatin, NT, Hong Kong, 852-26097407; fax 852-26035110; e-mail renditions@cuhk.hk
Research Centre for Translation, Chinese University of Hong Kong, Research Centre for Translation, Chinese University of Hong Kong, Shatin, NT, Hong Kong, 852-26097407; e-Mail renditions@cuhk.hk

INDIA

KOBISENA, P40 Nandana Park, Calcutta 700 034, W.B., India
Book Faith India, 414-416 Express Tower, Azadpur Commercial Complex, Delhi 110033, India, 91-11-713-2459, Fax 91-11-724-9674 and 724-9664, e-mail pilgrim@del2.vsnl.net.in

ABOL TABOL, 7/1 d Kalicharan Ghosh Road, Kolkata, W. Bengal, India, 033-25571767, babychowin@yahoo.co.in
JAFFE INTERNATIONAL, Kunnuparambil Buildings, Kurichy, Kottayam 686549, India, 91-481-430470; FAX 91-481-561190
Jaffe Publishing Management Service, Kunnuparambil Buildings, Kurichy, Kottayam 686549, India, phone/fax 91-481-430470
Tiger Moon, 3-882 Coconut Grove, Prasanthi Nilayam A.P.515134, India
Prakalpana Literature, P-40 Nandana Park, Calcutta-700034, West Bengal, India, (91) (033) 478-2347
PRAKALPANA SAHITYA/PRAKALPANA LITERATURE, P-40 Nandana Park, Calcutta-700034, West Bengal, India, (91) (033) 478-2347

INDONESIA

NEW VERSE NEWS, THE, c/o Penha, Jakarta International School, PO Box 1078JKS, Jakarta 12010, Indonesia, editor@newversenews.com

IRELAND

DOPE FRIENDS, Ivy Shields, Ballagh, Bushypark, Galway, Ireland, e-mail mmtaylor@iol.ie
JOURNAL OF MUSIC IN IRELAND (JMI), Edenvale, Esplanade, Bray, Co Wicklow, Ireland, 00-353-1-2867292 phone/Fax, editor@thejmi.com, www.thejmi.com
Salmon Poetry Ltd., Knockeven, Cliffs of Moher, Co. Clare, Ireland, 011-353-65-7081941, info@salmonpoetry.com, www.salmonpoetry.com
THE SHOP: A Magazine of Poetry, c/o Skeagh, Schull, County Cork, Ireland
Poetry Ireland, Bermingham Tower, Upper Yard, Dublin Castle, Dublin 2, Ireland
POETRY IRELAND REVIEW, Bermingham Tower, Upper yard, Dublin Castle, Dublin 2, Ireland, 6714632 + 353-1, fax 6714634 + 353-1
THE STINGING FLY, PO Box 6016, Dublin 8, Ireland, stingingfly@gmail.com, www.stingingfly.org
THE MAINE EVENT, Rusheen, Firies, Co. Kerry, Ireland, 066-9763084 phone/Fax, maineevent@eircom.net, www.mainee-vent.net
CRANNOG, Roscam, Galway, Ireland, editor@crannogmagazine.com, www.crannogmagazine.com

ISRAEL

THE OTHER ISRAEL, PO Box 2542, Holon 58125, Israel, Israel, 972-3-5565804 phone/Fax
VOICES - ISRAEL, 11, Haefroni Street, Mevaseret Zion, 90805, Israel, +972-2-5342451
ARC, PO Box 39385, Tel Aviv 61393, Israel, iawe_mailbox@yahoo.com

ITALY

LO STRANIERO: The Stranger, Der Fremde, L'Etranger, Piazza Amedeo 8, Naples 80121, Italy, ITALY/81/426052

JAPAN

POETRY KANTO, Kanto Gakuin University, Kamariya Minami 3-22-1, Kanazawa-Ku, Yokohama 236-8502, Japan
United Nations University Press, United Nations University, 53-70 Jingumae 5-chome, Shibuya-ku, Tokyo, Japan, Tel: +81-3499-2811, Fax: +81-3-3406-7345, sales@hq.unu.edu, http://www.unu.edu/unupress
Printed Matter Press (Tokyo), Yagi Bldg. 4F, 2-10-13 Shitaya,, Taito-ku, Tokyo, Japan, 110-0004, Japan, Fax: 81-03-3871-4964 email:info@printedmatterpress.com, http://www.printedmatterpress.com

MALAWI

BWALO: A Forum for Social Development, PO Box 278, Zomba, Malawi, 265-524-916, Fax 265-524-578

MEXICO

O!!Zone, Mexico
O!!ZONE, A LITERARY-ART ZINE, Mexico

NEPAL

Pilgrims Book House, Thamel, PO Box 3872, Kathmandu, Nepal, 977-1-4700942, Fax 977-1-4700943, pil-grims@wlink.com.np, www.pilgrimsbooks.com
LAYALAMA ONLINE MAGAZINE, 320 Phurkesalla Marg, Dhimelohan Swoyambhu,, P. O. Box 5146, Kathmandu, Nepal, Kathmandu 71100, Nepal, Tel: + 977 1 4274815, Fax: + 977 1 4274815, email:layalama@layalama.com, Website: http://www.layalama.com

THE NETHERLANDS

THE LEDGE, 8011 CE, Zwolle, The Netherlands, info@the-ledge.com, www.the-ledge.com
Amsterdam University Press, Prinsengracht 747-751, 1017 JX, Amsterdam, The Netherlands, T 0031 (0)20 4200050, F 0031 (0)20 4203412, www.aup.nl

NEW ZEALAND

Hallard Press, 43 Landscape Rd, Papatoetoe, Auckland 1701, New Zealand, 64 09 2782731, 64 09 2782731
TAKAHE, PO Box 13-335, Christchurch 1, New Zealand, 03-5198133
POETRY NZ, 37 Margot Street, Epsom, Auckland 3, New Zealand, 64-9-524-5656
SPIN, PO Box 13-533, Grey Street, Tauranga, New Zealand, 07 576 1886
BRAVADO, PO Box 13-533, Grey Street, Tauranga 3001, New Zealand, 07 576 3040, fax:07 570 2446

REPUBLIC OF PANAMA

Caribbean Books-Panama, Apdo. 0301-01249, Colon, Republic of Panama, +507-433-0349, http://www.caribbeanbooks-pub.com, publisher@caribbeanbookspub.com

PORTUGAL

PERIPHERAL VISION, Apartado 240, Portalegre, 7300, Portugal
NEO: Literary Magazine, Departamento de Linguas e Literaturas, Universidade dos Acores, 9500 Ponta Delgada, Portugal, www.neomagazine.org

SCOTLAND

NORTHWORDS, The Stable, Long Road, Avoch, Ross-shire IV9 8QR, Scotland, e-mail northwords@demon.co.uk
CHAPMAN, 4 Broughton Place, Edinburgh EH1 3RX, Scotland, 0131-557-2207

SINGAPORE

Monsoon Books, 106 Jalan Hang Jebat #02-14, 139527, Singapore, tel: (+65) 6476 3955, Fax: (+65) 6476 8513, email: sales@monsoonbooks.com, web: www.monsoonbooks.com.sg

SWEDEN

Syukhtun Editions, Odengatan 8, 114 24 Stockholm, Sweden, (468)6124988, theoradic@yahoo.com, http://www.syukhtun.net

SWITZERLAND

BIBLIOTHEQUE D'HUMANISME ET RENAISSANCE, Librairie Droz S.A., 11r.Massot, 1211 Geneve 12, Switzerland
Librairie Droz S.A., 11r.Massot, 1211 Geneve 12, Switzerland

UNITED KINGDOM

THE INTERPRETER'S HOUSE, 38 Verne Drive, Ampthill, MK45 2PS, United Kingdom, 01525-403018
INTERCHANGE, English Dept., Univ. of Wales, Hugh Owen Bldg., Penglais, Aberystwyth, Ceredigion SY23 3DY, United Kingdom
LATERAL MOVES, 5 Hamilton Street, Astley Bridge, Bolton BL1 6RJ, United Kingdom, (01204) 596369
The Powys Society, Hamilton's, Kilmersdon, Bath, Somerset BH3 5TE, United Kingdom, 01452-304539
THE CANNON'S MOUTH, 22 Margaret Grove, Harborne, Birmingham B17 9JH, United Kingdom, [+44] 121 449 3866
CADENZA, 2 Coastguard Cottages, Shore Road,Freiston Shore, Boston, Lincs PE22 0LZ, United Kingdom, eds@cadenza-magazine.co.uk
Re-invention UK Ltd, Primrose Cottage, Lakes Farm, Braintree Green, Rayne, Braintree, United Kingdom, (0044) 1245 332147
THE ORPHAN LEAF REVIEW, 26 Grove Park Terrace, Fishponds, Bristol, BS16 2BN, United Kingdom, www.orphanleaf.co.uk orphanleaf@jpwallis.co.uk
Salt Publishing, PO Box 937, Great Wilbraham, Cambridge, United Kingdom, +44 (0)1223 882220 chris@saltpublishing.com
Parthian, The Old Surgery, Napier Street, Cardigan SA43 1ED, United Kingdom, parthianbooks@yahoo.co.uk, www.parthianbooks.co.uk
CAMBRENSIS: THE SHORT STORY QUARTERLY MAGAZINE OF WALES, 41 Heol Fach, Cornelly, Bridgend, Mid-Glamorgan, CF334LN South Wales, United Kingdom, 01656-741-994
Feel Free Press, 'The Flat', Yew Tree Farm, Sealand Road, Chester, Cheshire, CH1 6BS, United Kingdom
OPEN WIDE MAGAZINE, 'The Flat', Yew Tree Farm, Sealand Road, Chester, Cheshire, CH1 6BS, United Kingdom
PANDA, 46 First Avenue, Clase, Swansea, W. Glam SA6 7LL, United Kingdom
THE QUIET FEATHER, St. Mary's Cottage, Church Street, Dalton-In-Furness, Cumbria, LA15 8BA, ENGLAND, United Kingdom
Tears in the Fence, 38 Hod View Stourpaine, Blandford Forum, Dorset DT11 8TN, United Kingdom
Dionysia Press Ltd., 127 Milton Road West, 7, Duddingston House Courtyard, Edinburgh, EH15 1Jg, United Kingdom, 0131-6611153 [tel/fax, 0131 6614853 [tel]
UNDERSTANDING MAGAZINE, 20 A Montgomery Street, Edinburgh, EH7 5JS, United Kingdom, 0131-4780680
THE FROGMORE PAPERS, 42 Morehall Avenue, Folkestone, Kent CT19 4EF, United Kingdom
The Frogmore Press, 42 Morehall Avenue, Folkestone, Kent. CT19 4EF, United Kingdom
OUTPOSTS POETRY QUARTERLY, 22, Whitewell Road, Frome, Somerset BA11 4EL, United Kingdom
NEW HOPE INTERNATIONAL REVIEW, 20 Werneth Avenue, Gee Cross, Hyde, Cheshire SK14 5NL, United Kingdom, www.geraldengland.co.uk
PSYCHOPOETICA, Department of Psychology, University of Hull, Hull HU6 7RX, United Kingdom, website www.fernhse.demon.co.uk/eastword/psycho
PREMONITIONS, 13 Hazely Combe, Arreton, Isle of Wight, PO30 3AJ, United Kingdom, http://www.pigasuspress.co.uk
Lawrence & Wishart, 10 High Street, Knapwell, Cambridge CB3 8NR, United Kingdom, aj@erica.demon.co.uk
BLITHE SPIRIT, Hill House Farm, Knighton, Powys LD7 1NA, United Kingdom, 0154-752-8542, Fax 0154-752-0685
The Seer Press, PO Box 29313, Glasgow, Lanarkshire, Scotland, G20 2AE, United Kingdom
Deborah Charles Publications, 173 Mather Avenue, Liverpool L18 6JZ, United Kingdom, fax 44-151-729-0371 from outside UK
The Old Stile Press, Catchmays Court, Llandogo, Monmouthshire NP5 4TN, United Kingdom
Bad Press, 21 Portland Rise, Finsbury Park, London, United Kingdom, Email: badpress@gmail.com Web: http://badpress.infinology.net
BAD PRESS SERIALS, 21 Portland Rise, Finsbury Park, London, United Kingdom, Email: badpress@gmail.com Web: http://badpress.infinology.net
FEMINIST REVIEW, Women's Studies, Univ. of N. London, 116-220 Holloway Road, London N7 8D8, United Kingdom
Vision, Vision Paperbacks and Fusion Press, 101 Southwark Street, London SE1 0JF, United Kingdom, info@visionpaperbacks.co.uk
Vision, 101 Southwark Street, London SE1 OJF, United Kingdom, 020-7928-5599, Fax 020-7928-8822, editorial@visionpaperbacks.co.uk, www.visionpaperbacks.co.uk
The Wellsweep Press, Unit 3 Ashburton Centre276 Cortis Road, 276 Cortis Road, London SW15 3AY, United Kingdom, ws@shadoof.net
OASIS, 12 Stevenage Road, London SW6 6ES, United Kingdom
GREEN ANARCHIST, BM 1715, London WC1N 3XX, United Kingdom
DIALOGOS: Hellenic Studies Review, Dept. of Byzantine & Modern Greek, Attn: David Ricks, King's College, London WC2R 2LS, United Kingdom, fax 020-7848-873-2830
Oasis Books, 12 Stevenage Road, London, SW6 6ES, United Kingdom
Crescent Moon, PO Box 393, Maidstone, Kent ME14 5XU, United Kingdom
PAGAN AMERICA, PO Box 393, Maidstone, Kent ME14 5XU, United Kingdom
PASSION, PO Box 393, Maidstone, Kent ME14 5XU, United Kingdom
Abbey Press, Northern Ireland, Courtenay Hill, Newry, Country Down BT34 2ED, United Kingdom, 01693-63142, Fax 01693-62514, Molly71Freeman@aol.com, www.geocities.com/abbeypress/
PRETEXT, Pen & Inc Press, School of Literature & Creative Writing, Norwich, Norfolk NR4 7TJ, United Kingdom, +44

(0)1603 592783, Fax + 44 (0)1603 507728, info@penandinc.co.uk, www.inpressbooks.co.uk/penandinc

REACTIONS, Pen & Inc Press, School of Literature & Creative Writing, Norwich, Norfolk NR4 7TJ, United Kingdom

Poetry Direct, 6 Princes Street, Oxford, OX4 1DD, United Kingdom, ++44-1865791202 :: editors@poetry-direct.com :: http://www.poetry-direct.com

ZINE-ON-A-TAPE, 35 Kearsley Road, Sheffield, S2 4TE, United Kingdom, www.andysav.free-online.co.uk/

PULSAR POETRY MAGAZINE, 34 Lineacre, Grange Park, Swindon, Wiltshire SN5 6DA, United Kingdom, 01793-875941, e-mail pulsar.ed@btopenworld.com, web: www.pulsarpoetry.com

FIRE, Field Cottage, Old Whitehill, Tackley, Kidlington OXON OX5 3AB, United Kingdom

REACH, The Manacles, Predannack, The Lizard, Cornwall TR12 7AU, United Kingdom, reachmagazine@indigo-dreams.plus.com

Athena Press, Queen's House, 2 Holly Road, Twickenham TW1 4EG, United Kingdom, www.athenapress.com

Snapshot Press, PO Box 132, Waterloo, Liverpool L22 8WZ, United Kingdom, info@snapshotpress.co.uk, www.snapshot-press.co.uk

WALES

ALT-J: Association for Learning Technology Journal, 10 Columbus Walk, Brigantine Place, Cardiff CF10 4UP, Wales, 044-029-2049-6899, Fax 44-029-2049-6108, press@press.wales.ac.uk, www.wales.ac.uk/press

CONTEMPORARY WALES, 10 Columbus Walk, Brigantine Place, Cardiff CF10 4UP, Wales, 44-029-2049-6899, Fax 44-029-2049-6108, press@press.wales.ac.uk, www.wales.ac.uk/press

EFRYDIAU ATHRONYDDOL, 10 Columbus Walk, Brigantine Place, Cardiff CF10 4UP, Wales, 44-029-2049-6899, Fax 44-029-2049-6108, press@press.wales.ac.uk, www.wales.ac.uk/press

JOURNAL OF CELTIC LINGUISTICS, 10 Columbus Walk, Brigantine Place, Cardiff CF10 4UP, Wales, 44-029-2049-6899, Fax 44-029-2049-6108, press@press.wales.ac.uk, www.wales.ac.uk/press

KANTIAN REVIEW, 10 Columbus Walk, Brigantine Place, Cardiff CF10 4UP, Wales, 44-029-2049-6899, Fax 44-029-2049-6108, press@press.wales.ac.uk, www.wales.ac.uk/press

LLEN CYMRU, 10 Columbus Walk, Brigantine Place, Cardiff CF10 4UP, Wales, 44-029-2049-6899, Fax 44-029-2049-6108, press@press.wales.ac.uk, www.wales.ac.uk/press

STUDIA CELTICA, 10 Columbus Walk, Brigantine Place, Cardiff CF10 4UP, Wales, 44-029-2049-6899, Fax 44-029-2049-6108, press@press.wales.ac.uk, www.wales.ac.uk/press

University Of Wales Press, 10 Columbus Walk, Brigantine Place, Cardiff CF10 4UP, Wales, +44-02-2049-6899, Fax +44-029-2049-6108, press@press.wales.ac.uk, www.wales.ac.uk/press

WELSH HISTORY REVIEW, 10 Columbus Walk, Brigantine Place, Cardiff CF10 4UP, Wales, 44-029-2049-6899, Fax 44-029-2049-6108, press@press.wales.ac.uk, www.wales.ac.uk/press

WELSH JOURNAL OF EDUCATION, 10 Columbus Walk, Brigantine Place, Cardiff CF10 4UP, Wales, 44-029-2049-6899, Fax 44-029-2049-6108, press@press.wales.ac.uk, www.wales.ac.uk/press

WELSH MUSIC HISTORY, 10 Columbus Walk, Brigantine Place, Cardiff CF10 4UP, Wales, 44-029-2049-6899, Fax 44-029-2049-6108, press@press.wales.ac.uk, www.wales.ac.uk/press

BORDERLINES: Studies in American Culture, 6 Gwennyth Street, Cathays, Cardiff CF24 4YD, Wales, 44-029-2023-1919, Fax 44-029-2023-0908, press@press.wales.ac.uk

WEST INDIES

Jako Books, Gablewoods South, PO Box VF665, Vieux Fort, St. Lucia, West Indies, 758-454-7839, info@jakoproductions.com, www.jakoproductions.com

Subject Index

Mills Custom Services Publishing
Our Child Press
R-Squared Press
Search Institute
THINKERMONKEY
Titus Home Publishing
Whispering Pine Press

ADVERTISING, SELF-PROMOTION

AD/VANCE
THE AFFILIATE
THE ART HORSE
Autelitano Media Group (AMG)
Banana Productions
Bay Tree Publishing
BlackBerry Literary Services
Blueprint Books
Bonus Books, Inc.
BOOK MARKETING UPDATE
CHECKER CAB MAGAZINE - THE LITTLE 'ZINE
    THAT COULD! Fiction That Takes The Long Way
    Home
Communication Creativity
D.B.A. Books
The Dragon Press
EFG, Inc.
ELEMENTS
GEM Literary Foundation Press
Happy About
Info Net Publishing
Knowledge Concepts Publishing
Kobalt Books
Llumina Press
Mama Incense Publishing
MEAT FOR TEA: THE NORTHAMPTON REVIEW
METAL CURSE
METROPOLITAN FORUM
MOBILE BEAT: The DJ Magazine
Motom
THE NEW SUPERNATURAL MAGAZINE
Nunciata
Open Horizons Publishing Company
Platinum One Publishing
THE PUBLICITY HOUND
REMS Publishing & Publicity
Sand and Sable Publishing
SCULPTURAL PURSUIT MAGAZINE
THE SOURCES HOTLINK
Stony Meadow Publishing
Swan Publishing Company
VACATION PLACE RENTALS
Visibility Unlimited Publications
Wheatmark Book Publishing
The Word Doctor Online Publishing
World Gumbo Publishing

AFRICAN LITERATURE, AFRICA, AFRICAN STU-
DIES

AAIMS Publishers
AFRICAN AMERICAN REVIEW
THE AFRICAN BOOK PUBLISHING RECORD
African Ways Publishing
AIM MAGAZINE
Ariko Publications
Autonomedia, Inc.
The B & R Samizdat Express
Back House Books
Backbeat Press
Bandanna Books
THE BLACK SCHOLAR: Journal of Black Studies and
    Research
Brunswick Publishing Corporation
BWALO: A Forum for Social Development
Chicago Spectrum Press
Clover Park Press
COLLEGE LITERATURE
THE DIRTY GOAT
DRUMVOICES REVUE

E. S. Publishers & Distributors
Earthwinds Editions
EbonyEnergy Publishing, Inc. (NFP)
EPICENTER: A LITERARY MAGAZINE
Fantail
The Feminist Press at the City University of New York
FIREBREEZE PUBLISHING
Florida Academic Press
Four Walls Eight Windows
GEM Literary Foundation Press
Good Hope Enterprises, Inc.
Helm Publishing
Host Publications, Inc.
Infinite Possibilities Publishing Group, Inc.
Inner City Press
Interlink Publishing Group, Inc.
INTERNATIONAL POETRY REVIEW
International Publishers Co. Inc.
Jako Books
THE JOURNAL OF AFRICAN TRAVEL-WRITING
Kenyette Productions
Kobalt Books
Lekon New Dimensions Publishing
LOST GENERATION JOURNAL
Lotus Press, Inc.
Mama Incense Publishing
Mercer University Press
New World Press, Inc
OBSIDIAN III: Literature in the African Diaspora
Ohio University Press/Swallow Press
ORACLE STORY
Oyez
Pangaea
Panther Creek Press
Passeggiata Press, Inc.
Path Press, Inc.
Pathfinder Press
Poltroon Press
Rayve Productions Inc.
Re-invention UK Ltd
Rivercross Publishing, Inc.
Sand and Sable Publishing
Semiotext Foreign Agents Books Series
SEMIOTEXT(E)
Shangri-La Publications
Soul
Three House Publishing
TIFARA
Tombouctou Books
UNDERSTANDING MAGAZINE
United Nations University Press
University of Calgary Press
University of Chicago Press
University of Virginia Press
West Virginia University Press
Whispering Pine Press
White Cliffs Media, Inc.
Whitston Publishing Co.
World Music Press
WRITER'S LIFELINE
ZAWP

AFRICAN-AMERICAN

Abernathy House Publishing
African Ways Publishing
Aglob Publishing
all nations press
American Literary Press
Aspicomm Media
Azreal Publishing Company
Bancroft Press
BEATLICK NEWS
BIG MUDDY: Journal of the Mississippi River Valley
BLACK LACE
Black Pearl Enterprises LLC
BlackBerry Literary Services
BLACKFIRE
BLK

BRILLIANT CORNERS: A Journal of Jazz & Literature
Bronze Girl Productions, Inc.
Burning Bush Publications
Cantadora Press
Center for Thanatology Research & Education, Inc.
CIRCLE INC., THE MAGAZINE
Circle of Friends Books
Clarity Press, Inc.
COALITION FOR PRISONERS' RIGHTS NEWSLETTER
COGNITIO: A Graduate Humanities Journal
The Colbert House
Common Courage Press
Cornerstone Publishing
Creative Writing and Publishing Company
Dream Publishing Co.
DRUMVOICES REVUE
E. S. Publishers & Distributors
Earthwinds Editions
Ecrivez!
ELEMENTS
Everflowing Publications
The Feminist Press at the City University of New York
Fingerprint Press
The Fire!! Press
FIREBREEZE PUBLISHING
Fotofolio, Inc.
4AllSeasons Publishing
GEM Literary Foundation Press
GOOD GIRL
Gorilla Convict Publications
Grip Publishing
Hole Books
Ika, LLC
IN OUR OWN WORDS
Infinite Possibilities Publishing Group, Inc.
IRIS: A Journal About Women
IRON HORSE LITERARY REVIEW
J & J Consultants, Inc.
J&W Publishers, Inc.
Kobalt Books
KUUMBA
Lekon New Dimensions Publishing
Mama Incense Publishing
Margaret Media, Inc.
MEAT: A Journal of Writing and Materiality
Mercer University Press
Miami University Press
Millennium Vision Press
Minnesota Historical Society Press
New Rivers Press, Inc.
New World Press, Inc
Open Hand Publishing LLC
The Overmountain Press
P.R.A. Publishing
Palari Publishing
The Passion Profit Company
PEACEWORK
Pearl's Book'em Publisher
Phelps Publishing Company
PhoeniX in Print
The Place In The Woods
Platinum Dreams Publishing
Pleasure Boat Studio: A Literary Press
Pomegranate Communications
QED Press
Quantum Leap S.L.C. Publications
Razor7 Publishing
RHINO: THE POETRY FORUM
Sadorian Publications
THE SCRIBIA
Soft Skull Press
Southeast Missouri State University Press
Southern Illinois University Press
THE SOUTHERN QUARTERLY: A Journal of the Arts in the South
Stardate Publishing Company
State University of New York Press
Three House Publishing

Tree of Life Books. Imprints: Progressive Press, Banned Books
TURNING THE TIDE: Journal of Anti-Racist Action, Research & Education
UNDERSTANDING MAGAZINE
University of Arkansas Press
University of Massachusetts Press
University of Nebraska Press
University of South Carolina Press
UNWOUND
West End Press
Whispering Pine Press
Wings Press
WORD IS BOND
XCP: CROSS-CULTURAL POETICS

AGING

Abernathy House Publishing
Anti-Aging Press
Bay Tree Publishing
Blue Dolphin Publishing, Inc.
Bonus Books, Inc.
Bronze Girl Productions, Inc.
CRONE CHRONICLES: A Journal of Conscious Aging
Dunamis House
EduCare Press
END OF LIFE CHOICES
Ethos Publishing
Fitness Press
Imago Press
LifeCircle Press
New Paradigm Books
THE NEW SUPERNATURAL MAGAZINE
North Star Books
Park Place Publications
PASSAGER
The People's Press
Plain View Press
RED OWL
Sentient Publications, LLC
TAPROOT, a journal of older writers
Tendre Press
Titus Home Publishing
Trafton Publishing
Two Thousand Three Associates
UnKnownTruths.com Publishing Company
VanderWyk & Burnham
Vestibular Disorders Association
World Changing Books

AGRICULTURE

AFFABLE NEIGHBOR
Affable Neighbor Press
AGRICULTURAL HISTORY
Alpine Press
THE AZOREAN EXPRESS
BANANA RAG
Beekman Books, Inc.
BLACK JACK & VALLEY GRAPEVINE
THE BLOOMSBURY REVIEW
THE CARETAKER GAZETTE
The Chicot Press
China Books & Periodicals, Inc.
Elderberry Press, LLC
FARMER'S DIGEST
FARMING UNCLE
Food First Books
THE GROWING EDGE MAGAZINE
The Haworth Press
Helm Publishing
Hobar Publications, A Division of Finney Company
HORTIDEAS
The Independent Institute
THE JOURNAL OF CALIFORNIA AND GREAT BASIN ANTHROPOLOGY
Kumarian Press, Inc.
La Alameda Press
Lahontan Images

Lessiter Publications
LOST GENERATION JOURNAL
Malki Museum Press
MASSEY COLLECTORS NEWS—WILD HARVEST
MINIATURE DONKEY TALK INC
NEROUP REVIEW
NEW ENVIRONMENT BULLETIN
THE NEW SUPERNATURAL MAGAZINE
Oasis Books
PATTERNS OF CHOICE: A Journal of People, Land, and Money
RFD
RFF Press / Resources for the Future
RUMINATIONS: The Nigerian Dwarf & Mini Dairy Goat Magazine
RURAL HERITAGE
SECOND GUESS
Stormline Press, Inc.
Sunnyside Press
Touchstone Adventures
THE TOWNSHIPS SUN
Tres Picos Press
UBC Press
University of Chicago Press
West Virginia University Press
WISCONSIN TRAILS

AIDS

A & U AMERICA'S AIDS MAGAZINE
Abernathy House Publishing
Aglob Publishing
Bay Press
BIG HAMMER
Biographical Publishing Company
BLK
Brookline Books
CONSCIENCE: The Newsjournal of Catholic Opinion
Focus Publications, Inc.
GEM Literary Foundation Press
GERTRUDE
GERTRUDE
Gertrude Press
GOOD GIRL
GREEN ANARCHIST
Lone Willow Press
METROPOLITAN FORUM
PEACEWORK
Ravenwood Publishing
Re-invention UK Ltd
Soft Skull Press
THINKERMONKEY

AIRPLANES

Ancient City Press
R.J. Bender Publishing
CESSNA OWNER MAGAZINE
The Film Instruction Company of America
Foundation Books
GAMBARA MAGAZINE
GLOBAL ONE TRAVEL & AUTOMOTIVE MAGAZINE
Ho Logos Press
Maryland Historical Press
NORTHERN PILOT
PIPERS MAGAZINE
Scottwall Associates, Publishers
The Times Journal Publishing Co.

ALASKA

Alaska Native Language Center
Alaska Northwest Books
THE CLIMBING ART
Council For Indian Education
The Denali Press
Fathom Publishing Co.
Fireweed Press
Heyday Books
Light, Words & Music
Mountain Automation Corporation

The Mountaineers Books
THE NEW SUPERNATURAL MAGAZINE
NORTHERN PILOT
Northern Publishing
Pleasure Boat Studio: A Literary Press
Pruett Publishing Company
Sasquatch Books
Scientia Publishing, LLC
Sunnyside Press
University of Alaska Press
Wizard Works

ALCOHOL, ALCOHOLISM

Aglob Publishing
ALONE TOGETHER
Capalo Press
Denlinger's Publishers Ltd.
Devil Mountain Books
DOPE FRIENDS
FIGHT THESE BASTARDS
Four Seasons Publishers
FRAN MAGAZINE
GEM Literary Foundation Press
Good Book Publishing Company
Gurze Books
Haight-Ashbury Publications
Hope Publishing House
Iniquity Press/Vendetta Books
INTERNATIONAL ADDICTION
Islewest Publishing
Jalmar Press/Innerchoice Publishing
JOURNAL OF PSYCHOACTIVE DRUGS
METROPOLITAN FORUM
National Writers Press
THE NEW SUPERNATURAL MAGAZINE
OUT OF LINE
Over the Wall Inc. Publishing & Productions
Paradise Research Publications, Inc.
PARTING GIFTS
See Sharp Press
SHATTERED WIG REVIEW
SO YOUNG!
Sun Rising Press

ALTERNATIVE MEDICINE

Accendo Publishing
Aglob Publishing
ALONE TOGETHER
BRANCHES
Brookline Books
Capalo Press
Eco Images
Epoch Press
Fitness Press
GOOD GIRL
Granite Publishing Group
Himalayan Institute Press
Hunter House Inc., Publishers
IN OUR OWN WORDS
JPS Publishing Company
Lamp Light Press
LifeCircle Press
LightLines Publishing
Lucky Press, LLC
Luminous Epinoia Press
MEDICAL HISTORY
Midwifery Today
Paradigm Publications
Parissound Publishing
Piccadilly Books, Ltd.
Princess Publishing
Ravenwood Publishing
SECOND GUESS
Sentient Publications, LLC
SevenStar Communications
Square One Publishers, Inc.
Sun Rising Press
Sunrise Health Coach Publications

618

Synergy Press
Tree of Life Books. Imprints: Progressive Press, Banned
    Books
Vista Publishing, Inc.
WAV MAGAZINE: Progressive Music Art Politics Culture
Wellcome Institute for the History of Medicine
THE WILD FOODS FORUM
Word Forge Books
YMAA Publication Center

AMERICANA

AFFABLE NEIGHBOR
Affable Neighbor Press
AMERICAN JONES BUILDING & MAINTENANCE
AMERICAN ROAD
Ammons Communications
Ancient City Press
Anvil Publishers, Inc.
Aspen Mountain Publishing
Avery Color Studios
Bear & Company
BIBLIOPHILOS
BIG MUDDY: Journal of the Mississippi River Valley
Blackwater Publications
Blue Mouse Studio
THE BOOMERPHILE
BORDERLINES: Studies in American Culture
Bordighera, Inc.
Branden Books
CANADIAN REVIEW OF AMERICAN STUDIES
The Caxton Press
CESUM MAGAZINE
Cherokee Publishing Company
Command Performance Press
Cottontail Publications
Crazy Woman Creek Press
CREOSOTE: A Journal of Poetry and Prose
Culturelink Press
Devil Mountain Books
Down The Shore Publishing
Eagle's View Publishing
Eborn Books
EXIT 13 MAGAZINE
FIGHT THESE BASTARDS
firefall editions
Fotofolio, Inc.
Foundation Books
Four Seasons Publishers
FRAN MAGAZINE
Gabriel's Horn Publishing Co., Inc.
Gallery West Associates
Gallopade International
Glenbridge Publishing Ltd.
Harbor House
Heritage Books, Inc.
Huntington Library Press
Ice Cube Press
International Publishers Co. Inc.
Lexikos
LPD Press
MAIN STREET RAG
Maryland Historical Press
MBA Publications
Missing Spoke Press
Mock Turtle Press
Mountain Press Publishing Co.
Mountainside Press
Music City Publishing
Naturegraph Publishers
Noontide Press
NORTHWOODS JOURNAL, A Magazine for Writers
Ohio University Press/Swallow Press
Oregon State University Press
PASSAGER
Pocahontas Press, Inc.
THE PRESIDENTS' JOURNAL
REAL PEOPLE
Rock Spring Press Inc.

ROCTOBER COMICS AND MUSIC
Santa Fe Writers Project
Scottwall Associates, Publishers
The Sektor Co.
SENSATIONS MAGAZINE
Genny Smith Books
Snake Hill Press
Southeast Missouri State University Press
Stormline Press, Inc.
Sunnyside Press
Thirteen Colonies Press
TRADITION MAGAZINE
Typographia Press
University of Arkansas Press
UPSTAIRS AT DUROC
Waters Edge Press
Whispering Pine Press
White Mane Publishing Company, Inc.
Wild West Publishing House
Word Forge Books
Xavier House Publishing

THE AMERICAS

Cantadora Press
COGNITIO: A Graduate Humanities Journal
Culturelink Press
CUTTHROAT, A JOURNAL OF THE ARTS
THE DIRTY GOAT
E. S. Publishers & Distributors
EXIT 13 MAGAZINE
Host Publications, Inc.
LPD Press
MANDORLA: New Writing from the Americas / Nueva
    escritura de las Americas
ORTHODOX MISSION
Orthodox Mission in Belize
Palladium Communications
Pangaea
Pathfinder Press
Protean Press
Spirit, Nature and You
Stardate Publishing Company
Thirteen Colonies Press
Typographia Press
University of Utah Press
University Press of Colorado
VACATION PLACE RENTALS
XAVIER REVIEW
Zagier & Urruty Publicaciones

AMISH CULTURE

GAMBARA MAGAZINE
READERS SPEAK OUT!
RURAL HERITAGE
Stormline Press, Inc.
Sunnyside Press
Titus Home Publishing
Xavier House Publishing

ANARCHIST

ABRAMELIN: a Journal of Poetry and Magick
AFFABLE NEIGHBOR
Affable Neighbor Press
THE AFFILIATE
AK Press
THE AMERICAN DISSIDENT
THE AMERICAN DRIVEL REVIEW
ANARCHY: A Journal of Desire Armed
ASIA FILE
Autonomedia, Inc.
BIG HAMMER
Black Rose Books Ltd.
BLACKBOOK PRESS, THE POETRY ZINE
BOTH SIDES NOW
Breakout Productions
CAFE NOIR REVIEW
THE CAIMAN (formerly THE WEIRD NEWS)
Carpe Diem Publishing

619

CESUM MAGAZINE
THE CHEROTIC (r)EVOLUTIONARY
City Lights Books
Columbia Alternative Library Press
Common Courage Press
Michael E. Coughlin, Publisher
THE DANDELION
EPICENTER: A LITERARY MAGAZINE
FIGHT THESE BASTARDS
Fine Tooth Press
GOOD GIRL
GRAY AREAS
GREEN ANARCHIST
GREEN ANARCHY
The Heather Foundation
HEELTAP/Pariah Press
Hole Books
The Independent Institute
INGLESIDE NEWS ZINE
Iniquity Press/Vendetta Books
Lawrence & Wishart
Libellum
THE (LIBERTARIAN) CONNECTION
LIBERTY
Life Untangled Publishing
THE MATCH
MGW (Mom Guess What) Newsmagazine
Mountain Media
Muse World Media Group
Mystery Island Publications
NEROUP REVIEW
New Falcon Publications
THE OTHER ISRAEL
Paladin Enterprises, Inc.
Pariah Press
PARTING GIFTS
Passing Through Publications
PEACEWORK
Pig Iron Press
Pygmy Forest Press
Radiant Press
RED AND BLACK
Red Hand Press
Santa Fe Writers Project
SECOND GUESS
See Sharp Press
Semiotext Foreign Agents Books Series
SEMIOTEXT(E)
SHATTERED WIG REVIEW
SHO
SHORT FUSE
Smyrna Press
SOCIAL ANARCHISM: A Journal of Practice and Theory
A SOFT DEGRADE
Soft Skull Press
South End Press
THINKERMONKEY
THOUGHT BOMBS
Total Cardboard Publishing
TURNING THE TIDE: Journal of Anti-Racist Action,
    Research & Education
Van Cleave Publishing
The Vertin Press
Via Dolorosa Press
THE VOLUNTARYIST
WAV MAGAZINE: Progressive Music Art Politics Culture
Wild West Publishing House

ANCIENT ASTRONAUTS

EcceNova Editions
Gardenia Press
Granite Publishing Group
THE MONTHLY INDEPENDENT TRIBUNE TIMES
    JOURNAL POST GAZETTE NEWS CHRONICLE
    BULLETIN
MYSTERIES MAGAZINE
RED OWL

ANIMALS

Abernathy House Publishing
Alaska Northwest Books
Alpine Publications, Inc.
ANIMAL PEOPLE
THE ART HORSE
Avery Color Studios
The Benefactory, Inc.
Biographical Publishing Company
Birdsong Books
Brookline Books
Camino Bay Books
Chelsea Green Publishing Company
City Life Books, LLC
Corvus Publishing Company
Crones Unlimited
Dawn Publications
Dimi Press
Dixon-Price Publishing
Doral Publishing
E & E Publishing
Epona Publishing
Equine Graphics Publishing Group: New Concord Press,
    SmallHorse Press, Parallel Press
EZ Nature Books
FARMING UNCLE
First Books
FISH DRUM MAGAZINE
Flowerfield Enterprises, LLC
Fotofolio, Inc.
Foundation Books
Gibbs Smith, Publisher
Hobar Publications, A Division of Finney Company
Howln Moon Press
Ion Imagination Publishing, Ion Imagination Entertainment,
    Inc.
Island Publishers
THE JOURNAL OF CALIFORNIA AND GREAT BASIN
    ANTHROPOLOGY
Laguna Wilderness Press
THE LATHAM LETTER
LITERALLY HORSES/REMUDA
Lucky Press, LLC
The Madson Group, Inc.
Malki Museum Press
Micah Publications Inc.
MINIATURE DONKEY TALK INC
Moon Pie Press
Mountain Press Publishing Co.
Native West Press
NATURE SOCIETY NEWS
New Paradigm Books
NewSage Press
Outrider Press
Pangaea
Peartree Books & Music
Peartree Books & Music
Pineapple Press, Inc.
Publishing Works
RED OWL
ROCKY MOUNTAIN KC NEWS
Rocky Mountain KC Publishing Co.
RURAL HERITAGE
Ryrich Publications
SNOWY EGRET
Spirit Talk Press
Storm Publishing Group
SunShine Press Publications, Inc.
Tree of Life Books. Imprints: Progressive Press, Banned
    Books
Trickle Creek Books
Two Dog Press
Univelt, Inc.
University Press of Colorado
VEGETARIAN JOURNAL
Venus Communications
Visibility Unlimited Publications

Vonpalisaden Publications Inc.
John Wade, Publisher
Whispering Pine Press
Windward Publishing, An Imprint of Finney Company
WISCONSIN TRAILS
Word Forge Books
Zagier & Urruty Publicaciones

ANTHOLOGY

Accendo Publishing
ARC
Backbeat Press
Bancroft Press
CEDAR HILL REVIEW
Central Avenue Press
Coteau Books
Cross-Cultural Communications
Ika, LLC
Imago Press
In Print Publishing
Infinite Possibilities Publishing Group, Inc.
The Infinity Group
J. Mark Press
Kobalt Books
THE LEDGE
Light of New Orleans Publishing
Little Pear Press
Llumina Press
McPherson & Company Publishers
The Midknight Club
Native West Press
THE NEW FORMALIST
Nightsun Books
Outskirts Press, Inc.
P.R.A. Publishing
Press Here
Ravenhawk Books
Redgreene Press
Russell Dean and Company
Scrivenery Press
The Spirit That Moves Us Press, Inc.
SunShine Press Publications, Inc.
Whiskey Creek Press
Wings Press
Word Forge Books
Zumaya Publications

ANTHROPOLOGY, ARCHAELOGY

AB
Alaska Geographic Society
Anagnosis
Ancient City Press
Arjuna Library Press
ASIAN ANTHROPOLOGY
The B & R Samizdat Express
Ballena Press
Bear & Company
THE BLOOMSBURY REVIEW
Blue Dolphin Publishing, Inc.
Blue Unicorn Press, Inc.
Cave Books
Celtic Heritage Books
Center for Japanese Studies
Chandler & Sharp Publishers, Inc.
THE CLASSICAL OUTLOOK
The Compass Press
Cotsen Institute of Archaeology Publications
CROSSCURRENTS
THE DALHOUSIE REVIEW
The Denali Press
DIALOGOS: Hellenic Studies Review
DREAM NETWORK
Eborn Books
FACES: People, Places, and Culture
Faded Banner Publications
Fine Tooth Press
Galde Press, Inc.
Gardenia Press

Glenbridge Publishing Ltd.
The Heather Foundation
Horned Owl Publishing
The Independent Institute
INTERCULTURE
ITALIAN AMERICANA
THE JOURNAL OF CALIFORNIA AND GREAT BASIN
    ANTHROPOLOGY
KMT, A Modern Journal of Ancient Egypt
Kumarian Press, Inc.
Laguna Wilderness Press
Libellum
Life Untangled Publishing
Malki Museum Press
Maryland Historical Press
Mehring Books, Inc.
Menard Press
Minnesota Historical Society Press
MOUSEION, Journal of the Classical Association of
    Canada/Revue de la Societe Canadienne des Etudes
    Classiques
Naturegraph Publishers
NEROUP REVIEW
NightinGale Resources
Northland Publishing/Rising Moon/Luna Rising
Pangaea
Protean Press
Pruett Publishing Company
Psychohistory Press
Royal Purcell, Publisher
Quantum Leap S.L.C. Publications
RALPH'S REVIEW
REPORTS OF THE NATIONAL CENTER FOR SCIENCE
    EDUCATION
REPRESENTATIONS
Rio Nuevo Publishers
School of American Research Press
Scientia Publishing, LLC
SECOND GUESS
SHAMAN'S DRUM: A Journal of Experiential Shamanism
Shangri-La Publications
THE SOUTHERN QUARTERLY: A Journal of the Arts in
    the South
State University of New York Press
Theytus Books Ltd.
TRADICION REVISTA
Tres Picos Press
UBC Press
University of Alaska Press
University of Calgary Press
University of Chicago Press
University of Nebraska Press
University of Utah Press
University Press of Colorado
The Vertin Press
Visibility Unlimited Publications
Whalesback Books
White Cliffs Media, Inc.
Windstorm Creative
XCP: CROSS-CULTURAL POETICS
Zagier & Urruty Publicaciones
ZONE

ANTIQUES

C & T Publishing
Cattpigg Press
China Books & Periodicals, Inc.
Downeast Books
EbonyEnergy Publishing, Inc. (NFP)
GemStone Press
Helm Publishing
THE ILLUSTRATOR COLLECTOR'S NEWS
INGLESIDE NEWS ZINE
INKY TRAIL NEWS
LAKE SUPERIOR MAGAZINE
MASSEY COLLECTORS NEWS—WILD HARVEST
Oak Knoll Press
Paperweight Press

RALPH'S REVIEW
Shangri-La Publications
Sonoran Publishing
THE TABBY: A CHRONICLE OF THE ARTS AND
CRAFTS MOVEMENT
Tomart Publications
The Vertin Press
Whalesback Books

APPALACHIA

Ammons Communications
APPALACHIA JOURNAL
Appalachian Consortium Press
APPALACHIAN HERITAGE
APPLE VALLEY REVIEW: A Journal of Contemporary
Literature
THE AZOREAN EXPRESS
BIBLIOPHILOS
BLACK JACK & VALLEY GRAPEVINE
Bright Mountain Books, Inc.
THE CLIMBING ART
ECOTONE: Reimagining Place
Great Elm Press
Iris Publishing Group, Inc (Iris Press / Tellico Books)
KESTREL: A Journal of Literature and Art
Lucky Press, LLC
Mountain State Press
NORTH CAROLINA LITERARY REVIEW
NORTHWOODS JOURNAL, A Magazine for Writers
NOW AND THEN
Ohio University Press/Swallow Press
The Overmountain Press
Parkway Publishers, Inc.
PIKEVILLE REVIEW
Pocahontas Press, Inc.
POTOMAC REVIEW
Rainbow Books, Inc.
Rock Spring Press Inc.
Rowan Mountain Press
TRADITION MAGAZINE
Wildflower Press
WIND

ARCHITECTURE

Ancient City Press
ART PAPERS
ASSEMBLAGE: A Critical Journal of Architecture and
Design Culture
Balcony Media, Inc.
Bay Press
Beekman Books, Inc.
Black Dome Press Corp.
THE BLOOMSBURY REVIEW
China Books & Periodicals, Inc.
Clover Park Press
Craftsman Book Company
Downeast Books
ENVIRONMENTAL & ARCHITECTURAL PHENOMEN-
OLOGY NEWSLETTER
Gibbs Smith, Publisher
INGLESIDE NEWS ZINE
Interalia/Design Books
Italica Press, Inc.
Libellum
MARQUEE
Midmarch Arts Press
MINISTRY & LITURGY
Minnesota Historical Society Press
Mount Ida Press
NEROUP REVIEW
OUT YOUR BACKDOOR: The Magazine of Do-It-
Yourself Adventure and Homegrown Culture
Passeggiata Press, Inc.
Pogo Press, Incorporated
READERS SPEAK OUT!
Really Great Books
SCULPTURAL PURSUIT MAGAZINE
Shangri-La Publications

Shipyard Press, LC
THE SOUTHERN QUARTERLY: A Journal of the Arts in
the South
Synergistic Press
THE TABBY: A CHRONICLE OF THE ARTS AND
CRAFTS MOVEMENT
THEATRE DESIGN AND TECHNOLOGY
Thirteen Colonies Press
TMC Books LLC
Tuns Press
UBC Press
University of Chicago Press
University of Massachusetts Press
University of South Carolina Press
University of Virginia Press
The Vertin Press
Visibility Unlimited Publications
WATERFRONT WORLD SPOTLIGHT
Western New York Wares, Inc.
Whalesback Books
Whitston Publishing Co.
X-Ray Book Co.
ZONE

ARIZONA

Eborn Books
Fretwater Press
LPD Press
Mountain Automation Corporation
Northland Publishing/Rising Moon/Luna Rising
The Patrice Press
Pruett Publishing Company
Rio Nuevo Publishers
Thundercloud Books
TRADICION REVISTA
Wheatmark Book Publishing

ARKANSAS

Mountain Automation Corporation
Premium Press America
Rose Publishing Co.
University of Arkansas Press

ARMENIAN

ARARAT
INTERNATIONAL POETRY REVIEW
Rainbow Books, Inc.
Zon International Publishing Co.

AROMATHERAPY

THE ART OF ABUNDANCE
Knowledge Concepts Publishing
MEAT FOR TEA: THE NORTHAMPTON REVIEW
Sun Rising Press

ARTHURIAN

Bad Press
Carpe Diem Publishing
Idylls Press
LOW BUDGET SCIENCE FICTION

ARTIFICIAL INTELLIGENCE

Ageless Press
Bad Press
EcceNova Editions
PREMONITIONS
RALPH'S REVIEW
Scientia Publishing, LLC
Soft Skull Press

ARTS

A & U AMERICA'S AIDS MAGAZINE
Aaron Communications III
Acrobat Books
THE ADIRONDACK REVIEW
AERIAL
AFFABLE NEIGHBOR
Affable Neighbor Press

622

THE AFFILIATE
AFTERIMAGE
Airplane Books
AK Press
Alan Wofsy Fine Arts
ALL ROUND
Glen Allen Press
Allworth Press
Altamont Press, Inc.
American Canadian Publishers, Inc.
THE AMERICAN DISSIDENT
THE AMERICAN DRIVEL REVIEW
Americans for the Arts
Ammons Communications
APOSTROPHE: USCB Journal of the Arts
ARC
Aristata Publishing
Arjuna Library Press
ARNAZELLA
ART BUREAU
ART CALENDAR
THE ART HORSE
ART PAPERS
ART TIMES
ART:MAG
ARTELLA: the waltz of words and art
ARTS & LETTERS: Journal of Contemporary Culture
ARTSLINK
ASCENT
ASSEMBLAGE: A Critical Journal of Architecture and
    Design Culture
Asylum Arts
Athanata Arts, Ltd.
Autonomedia, Inc.
BABYSUE MUSIC REVIEW
Back House Books
Backbeat Press
BACKWARDS CITY REVIEW
Balcony Media, Inc.
THE BALTIMORE REVIEW
Banana Productions
BANANA RAG
Bancroft Press
Barrytown/Station Hill Press
William L. Bauhan, Publisher
Bay Press
BEACHCOMBER MAGAZINE
THE BEAR DELUXE
The Bear Wallow Publishing Company
BearManor Media
BEATLICK NEWS
Beekman Books, Inc.
Bellywater Press
BIGNEWS MAGAZINE
BIRD DOG
Birdalone Books
Black Dome Press Corp.
Black Dress Press
BLACK WARRIOR REVIEW
BLACKFLASH
THE BLIND MAN'S RAINBOW
Bliss Publishing Company, Inc.
THE BLOOMSBURY REVIEW
Blue Raven Publishing
BLUE UNICORN
BOMB MAGAZINE
BOOK/MARK SMALL PRESS REVIEW
Borden Publishing Co.
BORDERLANDS: Texas Poetry Review
BOULEVARD
Branden Books
THE BREAD AND BUTTER CHRONICLES
THE BRIAR CLIFF REVIEW
BRILLIANT CORNERS: A Journal of Jazz & Literature
Brookline Books
Burning Books
BURNSIDE REVIEW
C & T Publishing

THE CAIMAN (formerly THE WEIRD NEWS)
Camp Colton
THE CAPILANO REVIEW
Cedar Hill Books
CEDAR HILL REVIEW
THE CENTENNIAL REVIEW
Center for Thanatology Research & Education, Inc.
CESUM MAGAZINE
CHANTEH, the Iranian Cross-Cultural Quarterly
Chatoyant
THE CHEROTIC (r)EVOLUTIONARY
CHICAGO REVIEW
Chicago Review Press
CHILDREN, CHURCHES AND DADDIES, A Non
    Religious, Non Familial Literary Magazine
China Books & Periodicals, Inc.
CIMARRON REVIEW
CineCycle Publishing
Clamshell Press
CLARA VENUS
COLOR WHEEL
CONDUIT
CONJUNCTIONS
CORONA
Coteau Books
COTTONWOOD
Cottonwood Press
COUNTER CULTURE
Creative Writing and Publishing Company
Crescent Moon
CROSSCURRENTS
CULTUREFRONT
THE DALHOUSIE REVIEW
DANDELION ARTS MAGAZINE
Dawn Sign Press
Delta Press
DENVER QUARTERLY
DESCANT
THE DIRTY GOAT
THE DMQ REVIEW
DOLLS UNITED INTERACTIVE MAGAZINE
DOWN IN THE DIRT LITERARY MAGAZINE, the prose
    & poetry magazine revealing all your dirty little secrets
Downeast Books
Dumouriez Publishing
E & E Publishing
EbonyEnergy Publishing, Inc. (NFP)
THE EDGE CITY REVIEW
Edgewise Press
EKPHRASIS
ELEMENTS
Empire Publishing Service
ENVIRONMENTAL & ARCHITECTURAL PHENOMEN-
    OLOGY NEWSLETTER
EPICENTER: A LITERARY MAGAZINE
Epoch Press
Ethos Publishing
Fern Publications
FIBERARTS
Film-Video Publications/Circus Source Publications
FINE MADNESS
Fine Tooth Press
First Books
580 SPLIT
FIVE POINTS
FLUENT ASCENSION
Fotofolio, Inc.
Fountainhead Productions, Inc.
Four Walls Eight Windows
FRAN MAGAZINE
FRANK: AN INTERNATIONAL JOURNAL OF CON-
    TEMPORARY WRITING AND ART
FREEDOM AND STRENGTH PRESS FORUM
FREEFALL
Gallery West Associates
GASTRONOMICA: The Journal of Food and Culture
Gateways Books And Tapes
Gertrude Press

Gibbs Smith, Publisher
Glenbridge Publishing Ltd.
GOOD GIRL
GRAIN MAGAZINE
Green Hut Press
GULF & MAIN Southwest Florida Lifestyle
Hands & Heart Books
Hard Press
Hastings Art Reference
HAWAI'I REVIEW
HEAVEN BONE MAGAZINE
Heaven Bone Press
Helicon Nine Editions
Helm Publishing
HILL COUNTRY SUN
Hollywood Creative Directory
Homa & Sekey Books
The Hosanna Press
Host Publications, Inc.
THE HUDSON REVIEW
Huntington Library Press
HUNTINGTON LIBRARY QUARTERLY
THE ILLUSTRATOR COLLECTOR'S NEWS
IMAGE: ART, FAITH, MYSTERY
INDUSTRY MINNE-ZINE
The Infinity Group
INGLESIDE NEWS ZINE
Interalia/Design Books
Interlink Publishing Group, Inc.
INTERNATIONAL ART POST
ITALIAN AMERICANA
Italica Press, Inc.
Ithuriel's Spear
IWAN: INMATE WRITERS OF AMERICA NEWSLET-
   TER
JACK MACKEREL MAGAZINE
Jako Books
JONES AV
JOURNAL OF AESTHETICS AND ART CRITICISM
JOURNAL OF REGIONAL CRITICISM
JUBILAT
JUST WEST OF ATHENS
KAJ-MAHKAH: EARTH OF EARTH
KALDRON, An International Journal Of Visual Poetry
KALLIOPE, A Journal of Women's Literature and Art
Kelsey St. Press
KMT, A Modern Journal of Ancient Egypt
KNUCKLE MERCHANT - The Journal of Naked Literary
   Aggression
LAKE EFFECT
LAKE STREET LIT: Art and Words from the Bottom of
   Lake Bonneville
LAKE SUPERIOR MAGAZINE
LATERAL MOVES
Leaping Dog Press / Asylum Arts Press
LEFT CURVE
Left Hand Books
LEO Productions LLC.
Les Figues Press
LICHEN Arts & Letters Preview
Light, Words & Music
LIGHTWORKS MAGAZINE
LINQ
LITRAG
LITURGICAL CATECHESIS
Locks Art Publications
LPD Press
LULLWATER REVIEW
LUMMOX JOURNAL
Lummox Press
Luna Bisonte Prods
THE MACGUFFIN
Macrocosm USA, Inc.
Mandala Publishing
MANDORLA: New Writing from the Americas / Nueva
   escritura de las Americas
MANOA: A Pacific Journal of International Writing
Peter Marcan Publications

Maverick Books
McPherson & Company Publishers
ME MAGAZINE
MEDIA SPOTLIGHT
Mehring Books, Inc.
Meridien PressWorks
METAL CURSE
METROPOLITAN FORUM
MGW (Mom Guess What) Newsmagazine
Midmarch Arts Press
MIDWEST ART FAIRS
Miles & Miles
MINISTRY & LITURGY
MOMMY AND I ARE ONE
MOTHERVERSE: A Journal of Contemporary Motherhood
Mountainside Press
NEROUP REVIEW
NERVE COWBOY
NEW AMERICAN IMAGIST
THE NEW ENGLAND QUARTERLY
THE NEW FORMALIST
The New Formalist Press
NEW LETTERS
NEW ORLEANS REVIEW
NEWS FROM NATIVE CALIFORNIA
Night Horn Books
NIGHTLIFE MAGAZINE
THE NOISE
Nonetheless Press
NOON
Northland Publishing/Rising Moon/Luna Rising
Norton Coker Press
NWI National Writers Institute
Oak Knoll Press
OHIOANA QUARTERLY
OPEN WIDE MAGAZINE
ORNAMENT
OUTER-ART
The Overlook Press
OWEN WISTER REVIEW
THE PACIFIC REVIEW
PAGAN AMERICA
PAJ NTAUB VOICE
Pancake Press
PAPERBACK PARADE
Paperweight Press
PASSAGER
PASSION
Pearl's Book'em Publisher
Pebble Press, Inc.
THE PEDESTAL MAGAZINE.COM
Phelps Publishing Company
PIG IRON
Pig Iron Press
PLAIN BROWN WRAPPER (PBW)
Plain View Press
Players Press, Inc.
The Poetry Center
Pogo Press, Incorporated
POINT OF CONTACT, The Journal of Verbal & Visual
   Arts
Pomegranate Communications
POTOMAC REVIEW
THE POWYS JOURNAL
PRAIRIE WINDS
PRETEXT
PROVINCETOWN ARTS
PULSAR POETRY MAGAZINE
Puna Press
Purple Finch Press
Pygmy Forest Press
Quarterly Committee of Queen's University
QUEEN'S QUARTERLY: A Canadian Review
THE QUEST
THE QUIET FEATHER
R & M Publishing Company
RAINBOW CURVE
RARITAN: A Quarterly Review

624

RATTAPALLAX
Ravenwood Publishing
Really Great Books
Red Cedar Press
RED CEDAR REVIEW
Red Hand Press
RED HAWK
REDIVIDER
REPRESENTATIONS
Resource Publications, Inc.
RIVER STYX
RIVERSEDGE
RIVET MAGAZINE
Rowhouse Press
RUBBERSTAMPMADNESS
The Runaway Spoon Press
Running Press
SAGE OF CONSCIOUSNESS E-ZINE
SALMAGUNDI
Santa Monica Press
Saqi Books Publisher
Saskatchewan Writers Guild
Savant Garde Workshop
Scarecrow Press
Scars Publications
Score
SCRAWL MAGAZINE
SCRIVENER
SCULPTURAL PURSUIT MAGAZINE
SHATTERED WIG REVIEW
SHORT FUSE
SKIDROW PENTHOUSE
SKYLARK
SLEAZOID EXPRESS
SLIPSTREAM
Smyrna Press
SO TO SPEAK: A Feminist Journal of Language & Art
A SOFT DEGRADE
SOLAS Press
THE SOUTHERN QUARTERLY: A Journal of the Arts in the South
SOUTHWEST COLORADO ARTS PERSPECTIVE
SP QUILL QUARTERLY MAGAZINE
SPEAK UP
Spinifex Press
Spirit Talk Press
SPORE
Stemmer House Publishers, Inc.
STUDIO ONE
SULPHUR RIVER LITERARY REVIEW
SunShine Press Publications, Inc.
SWINK
SYCAMORE REVIEW
SYMPLOKE: A Journal for the Intermingling of Literary, Cultural and Theoretical Scholarship
Synergetic Press
Synergistic Press
Syracuse Cultural Workers/Tools for Change
Syukhtun Editions
THE TABBY: A CHRONICLE OF THE ARTS AND CRAFTS MOVEMENT
THE TARPEIAN ROCK
Teachers & Writers Collaborative
TEACHERS & WRITERS MAGAZINE
TELOS
Telos Press
Ten Penny Players, Inc.
Thatch Tree Publications
THEATRE DESIGN AND TECHNOLOGY
THIN COYOTE
Think Tank Press, Inc.
THE THREEPENNY REVIEW
THRESHOLDS JOURNAL
TRADICION REVISTA
TRADITION MAGAZINE
Transcending Mundane, Inc.
TRAVEL NATURALLY
TURNROW

Typographia Press
Tzipora Publications, Inc.
UMBRELLA Online
University of Calgary Press
University of Chicago Press
University of Massachusetts Press
University of South Carolina Press
UNIVERSITY OF WINDSOR REVIEW
UNMUZZLED OX
UNO MAS MAGAZINE
UNWOUND
Urban Legend Press
THE URBANITE
Urthona Press
VALLUM: CONTEMPORARY POETRY
Vanderbilt University Press
VARIOUS ARTISTS
Venus Communications
The Vertin Press
Visual Studies Workshop
John Wade, Publisher
Wafer Mache Publications
WAR, LITERATURE & THE ARTS: An International Journal of the Humanities
WATERWAYS: Poetry in the Mainstream
WAV MAGAZINE: Progressive Music Art Politics Culture
West Virginia University Press
Westgate Press
Whalesback Books
Whelks Walk Press
White Cliffs Media, Inc.
White Crosslet Publishing Co
WHITEWALLS: A Journal of Language and Art
WILD DUCK REVIEW
Windstorm Creative
WISCONSIN TRAILS
WOMAN'S ART JOURNAL
WOMEN IN THE ARTS BULLETIN/NEWSLETTER
Word Forge Books
WRITER'S LIFELINE
X-RAY
Zon International Publishing Co.
ZUZU'S PETALS: QUARTERLY ONLINE

ASIA, INDOCHINA

Anthony Publishing Company, Inc.
ASIA FILE
ASIAN SURVEY
Autonomedia, Inc.
AXE FACTORY REVIEW
Book Faith India
China Books & Periodicals, Inc.
Chinese Literature Press
The Chinese University Press
CLARA VENUS
Cross-Cultural Communications
Cynic Press
FIREBREEZE PUBLISHING
Florida Academic Press
Homa & Sekey Books
Hoover Institution Press
INDIA CURRENTS
INTERNATIONAL POETRY REVIEW
JOURNAL OF ASIAN MARTIAL ARTS
Mandala Publishing
MANOA: A Pacific Journal of International Writing
NEW AMERICAN IMAGIST
Open Court Publishing Company
THE OTHER ISRAEL
PACIFIC HISTORICAL REVIEW
Pacific View Press
PAJ NTAUB VOICE
Pilgrims Book House
Red Hand Press
Tamal Vista Publications
Texas Tech University Press
TRANSITIONS ABROAD: The Guide to Living, Learning, and Working Overseas

UBC Press
United Nations University Press
VACATION PLACE RENTALS
Vesta Publications Limited
Via Media Publishing Company
White Pine Press
Wisdom Publications, Inc.
WORDS OF WISDOM
World Music Press
YMAA Publication Center
Zephyr Press

ASIAN-AMERICAN

THE ASIAN PACIFIC AMERICAN JOURNAL
Azreal Publishing Company
Back House Books
Bamboo Ridge Press
BAMBOO RIDGE, Journal of Hawai'i Literature and Arts
The Bess Press
BRILLIANT STAR
Burning Bush Publications
Carolina Wren Press/Lollipop Power Books
Center for Thanatology Research & Education, Inc.
Chandler & Sharp Publishers, Inc.
China Books & Periodicals, Inc.
CLARA VENUS
Comstock Bonanza Press
Cynic Press
East West Discovery Press
Fine Tooth Press
FIREBREEZE PUBLISHING
FIVE WILLOWS MAGAZINE
FROZEN WAFFLES
Fulcrum, Inc.
Goldfish Press
HAWAI'I REVIEW
Heritage West Books
Homa & Sekey Books
INDIA CURRENTS
Inner City Press
JOURNAL OF NARRATIVE THEORY
Kelsey St. Press
MANOA: A Pacific Journal of International Writing
Miami University Press
NEW AMERICAN IMAGIST
New Rivers Press, Inc.
PACIFIC HISTORICAL REVIEW
PAJ NTAUB VOICE
Phelps Publishing Company
The Place In The Woods
Pygmy Forest Press
Red Hand Press
Reference Service Press
RHINO: THE POETRY FORUM
SHEMP! The Lowlife Culture Magazine
TURNING WHEEL
Venus Communications
Vesta Publications Limited
Volcano Press, Inc
West End Press
WORD IS BOND
XCP: CROSS-CULTURAL POETICS

ASTROLOGY

ABRAMELIN: a Journal of Poetry and Magick
THE AFFILIATE
Altair Publications
Bear & Company
Blue Dolphin Publishing, Inc.
BOTH SIDES NOW
Cassandra Press, Inc.
CRONE CHRONICLES: A Journal of Conscious Aging
GOLDEN ISIS MAGAZINE
Golden Isis Press
Granite Publishing Group
Himalayan Institute Press
Intelligenesis Publications
Lycanthrope Press

THE MOUNTAIN ASTROLOGER
Quicksilver Productions
SAGEWOMAN
Spirit Press
Sun Rising Press
Tendre Press
Three Pyramids Publishing
Touchstone Adventures
White Crosslet Publishing Co
Whitford Press

ASTRONOMY

ABRAMELIN: a Journal of Poetry and Magick
Granite Publishing Group
Malki Museum Press
MYSTERIES MAGAZINE
Naturegraph Publishers
ODYSSEY: Adventures in Science
RED OWL
Scientia Publishing, LLC
STRUGGLE: A Magazine of Proletarian Revolutionary
    Literature
Univelt, Inc.
University Press of Colorado
Visions Communications

ATHEISM

BLACKBOOK PRESS, THE POETRY ZINE
BOULDER HERETIC
Carpe Diem Publishing
FREE INQUIRY
Free Reign Press, Inc.
Lycanthrope Press
Savant Garde Workshop
See Sharp Press
TRUTH SEEKER
Via Dolorosa Press
Wild West Publishing House

AUDIO/VIDEO

ABLAZE Publishing
AFTERIMAGE
Athanata Arts, Ltd.
AUDIO EXPRESS
Big Mouth Publications
CineCycle Publishing
CKO UPDATE
COUNTERPOISE: For Social Responsibilities, Liberty and
    Dissent
The Fiction Works
Flowerfield Enterprises, LLC
GULF & MAIN Southwest Florida Lifestyle
HandyCraft Media Productions
Ion Imagination Publishing, Ion Imagination Entertainment,
    Inc.
Level 4 Press
LifeQuest Publishing Group
LOW BUDGET ADVENTURE
Multi-Media Publications Inc.
Pearl's Book'em Publisher
Southern Illinois University Press
Water Mark Press
WAV MAGAZINE: Progressive Music Art Politics Culture
World Music Press

AUSTRALIA

Galaxy Press
Kali Press
STUDIO - A Journal of Christians Writing
Total Cardboard Publishing
Tres Picos Press
UNWOUND
VACATION PLACE RENTALS
Wide World Publishing/TETRA

AUTOBIOGRAPHY

A Cappela Publishing, Inc.
Aaron Communications III

Accendo Publishing
AIS Publications
Alaska Native Language Center
Amador Publishers
American Legacy Media
American Literary Press
Ancient City Press
Bear & Company
BearManor Media
BIBLIOPHILOS
Biographical Publishing Company
Bonus Books, Inc.
BookPartners, Inc.
Bright Mountain Books, Inc.
Brunswick Publishing Corporation
Carrier Pigeon Press
Cave Books
Celo Valley Books
China Books & Periodicals, Inc.
Coastal 181
Coteau Books
Crane Press
Creative Arts Book Company
CRONE CHRONICLES: A Journal of Conscious Aging
Crystal Clarity, Publishers
DANDELION ARTS MAGAZINE
Devil Mountain Books
E. S. Publishers & Distributors
THE EAST VILLAGE INKY
Fast Foot Forward Press
The Feminist Press at the City University of New York
Fern Publications
Fingerprint Press
Fouque Publishers
Gallaudet University Press
Green River Press
Harbor House
Himalayan Institute Press
Historical Resources Press
Hobblebush Books
Impassio Press
In Print Publishing
IRIS: A Journal About Women
Kenyette Productions
KESTREL: A Journal of Literature and Art
THE LEDGE
Leyland Publications
Limelight Editions
Little Pear Press
Llumina Press
MANOA: A Pacific Journal of International Writing
Massey-Reyner Publishing
Minnesota Historical Society Press
Moon Pie Press
Music City Publishing
The Narrative Press
New Concept Press
New World Press, Inc
Nicholas Lawrence Books
NOLA-MAGICK Press
Nonetheless Press
North Country Books, Inc.
Northwestern University Press
OPEN MINDS QUARTERLY
Outskirts Press, Inc.
PALO ALTO REVIEW
Park Place Publications
Parkway Publishers, Inc.
PASSAGER
PLAIN BROWN WRAPPER (PBW)
Polar Bear & Company
Prospect Press
Pussywillow
Redgreene Press
REMS Publishing & Publicity
Rivercross Publishing, Inc.
RIVET MAGAZINE
Ronsdale Press

Genny Smith Books
Swan Raven & Company
Syukhtun Editions
Tendre Press
Thirsty Turtle Press
Timeless Books
Titus Home Publishing
TWENTY-EIGHT PAGES LOVINGLY BOUND WITH TWINE
V52 Press
VanderWyk & Burnham
Vision
West Coast Paradise Publishing
White Thread Press
WRITING FOR OUR LIVES
Xenos Books
Yes International Publishers

AUTOS

Brown Fox Books
California Bill's Automotive Handbooks
Coastal 181
CULTURE CHANGE
GLOBAL ONE TRAVEL & AUTOMOTIVE MAGAZINE
GULF & MAIN Southwest Florida Lifestyle
Rolling Hills Publishing
Swan Publishing Company
Touchstone Adventures

AVANT-GARDE, EXPERIMENTAL ART

A & U AMERICA'S AIDS MAGAZINE
ABRAMELIN: a Journal of Poetry and Magick
ABRAXAS
AD/VANCE
AFFABLE NEIGHBOR
Affable Neighbor Press
AFTERIMAGE
Androgyne Books
ARC
Arjuna Library Press
ARNAZELLA
ART CALENDAR
ART PAPERS
ARTELLA: the waltz of words and art
ARTSLINK
ASSEMBLAGE: A Critical Journal of Architecture and Design Culture
Asylum Arts
Autonomedia, Inc.
BAGAZINE
BANANA RAG
BATHTUB GIN
BIRD DOG
BLACK BEAR REVIEW
BLACKBIRD
BLACKBOOK PRESS, THE POETRY ZINE
Brookline Books
Burning Books
BUST DOWN THE DOOR AND EAT ALL THE CHICKENS: A Journal of Absurd and Surreal Fiction
Camp Colton
THE CAPILANO REVIEW
Cervena Barva Press
THE CHEROTIC (r)EVOLUTIONARY
CLARA VENUS
CONDUIT
COUNTER CULTURE
THE DIRTY GOAT
DOLLS UNITED INTERACTIVE MAGAZINE
Duende Press
Earthwinds Editions
ELIXIR
EROSHA
Everflowing Publications
EXPERIMENTAL FOREST
Fiction Collective Two (FC2)
FIGHT THESE BASTARDS
FINE MADNESS

Five Fingers Press
FIVE FINGERS REVIEW
FLUENT ASCENSION
FRAN MAGAZINE
FRANK: AN INTERNATIONAL JOURNAL OF CON-
TEMPORARY WRITING AND ART
GERTRUDE
Gertrude Press
Ghost Pony Press
GOOD GIRL
GULF & MAIN Southwest Florida Lifestyle
HAWAI'I REVIEW
HEAVEN BONE MAGAZINE
Heaven Bone Press
HEELTAP/Pariah Press
Helicon Nine Editions
Host Publications, Inc.
ILLUMINATIONS
Implosion Press
INDUSTRY MINNE-ZINE
KALDRON, An International Journal Of Visual Poetry
KARAWANE
Kelsey St. Press
KOJA
Laguna Wilderness Press
LAKE EFFECT
LAKE STREET LIT: Art and Words from the Bottom of
Lake Bonneville
LATERAL MOVES
Leaping Dog Press / Asylum Arts Press
LEFT CURVE
LIGHTWORKS MAGAZINE
LO STRANIERO: The Stranger, Der Fremde, L'Etranger
LULLABY HEARSE
Luna Bisonte Prods
MANDORLA: New Writing from the Americas / Nueva
escritura de las Americas
Marymark Press
McPherson & Company Publishers
MEAT FOR TEA: THE NORTHAMPTON REVIEW
METAL CURSE
MOMMY AND I ARE ONE
Muse World Media Group
NEW HOPE INTERNATIONAL REVIEW
New Sins Press
NIGHTJAR REVIEW
NOBODADDIES
Northwestern University Press
O!!ZONE, A LITERARY-ART ZINE
One Less Press
OPEN WIDE MAGAZINE
OUTER-ART
PACIFIC COAST JOURNAL
Pariah Press
PARTING GIFTS
PAVEMENT SAW
Pavement Saw Press
PERIPHERAL VISION
PHOEBE: A Journal of Literature and Art
Phrygian Press
PIG IRON
PLAIN BROWN WRAPPER (PBW)
Players Press, Inc.
THE POETRY PROJECT NEWSLETTER
POINT OF CONTACT, The Journal of Verbal & Visual
Arts
PORTLAND REVIEW
PRESA
Presa Press
THE PRESSED PRESS
RAIN TAXI REVIEW OF BOOKS
RAINBOW CURVE
Re-invention UK Ltd
REMS Publishing & Publicity
THE ROCKFORD REVIEW
The Runaway Spoon Press
SAGE OF CONSCIOUSNESS E-ZINE
SAKANA

Score
Semiotext Foreign Agents Books Series
SEMIOTEXT(E)
SEQUENTIAL
SHORT FUSE
SKYLARK
SNOW MONKEY
A SOFT DEGRADE
Soft Skull Press
SOUTHWEST COLORADO ARTS PERSPECTIVE
SPORE
Stardate Publishing Company
SUB-TERRAIN
Synergetic Press
Total Cardboard Publishing
TRAVEL NATURALLY
Tzipora Publications, Inc.
UNBOUND
Underwhich Editions
UPSTAIRS AT DUROC
Versus Press
Water Mark Press
WEST COAST LINE: A Journal of Contemporary Writing
and Criticism
which press
White Crosslet Publishing Co
WHITEWALL OF SOUND
WHITEWALLS: A Journal of Language and Art
XCP: CROSS-CULTURAL POETICS
X-Ray Book Co.
xtant.anabasis
ZAUM - The Literary Review of Sonoma State University
ZONE
ZYX

AVIATION

AB
Alaska Geographic Society
ALL ROUND
Alta Research
Aviation Book Company
The Bear Wallow Publishing Company
Beekman Books, Inc.
Bright Mountain Books, Inc.
Burd Street Press
CESSNA OWNER MAGAZINE
Denlinger's Publishers Ltd.
The Film Instruction Company of America
Focus Publications, Inc.
Foundation Books
GLOBAL ONE TRAVEL & AUTOMOTIVE MAGAZINE
HANG GLIDING
Helm Publishing
House of Hits, Inc.
Lucky Press, LLC
Maryland Historical Press
NORTHERN PILOT
The Overmountain Press
The Patrice Press
PIPERS MAGAZINE
Rainbow Books, Inc.
Rivercross Publishing, Inc.
Shipyard Press, LC
SKYDIVING
Southern Illinois University Press
The Times Journal Publishing Co.

AWARDS, FOUNDATIONS, GRANTS

Americans for the Arts
ART CALENDAR
Film-Video Publications/Circus Source Publications
POETIC SPACE: Poetry & Fiction
Reference Service Press
Search Institute
Sources
SOUTHWEST COLORADO ARTS PERSPECTIVE
Titan Press
WRITER'S LIFELINE

BEAT

ABRAMELIN: a Journal of Poetry and Magick
AFFABLE NEIGHBOR
Affable Neighbor Press
Alpha Beat Press
THE AMERICAN DISSIDENT
Androgyne Books
BEATLICK NEWS
Bottle of Smoke Press
THE CAFE REVIEW
THE CAIMAN (formerly THE WEIRD NEWS)
Casperian Books LLC
THE CHEROTIC (r)EVOLUTIONARY
CLARA VENUS
THE DIRTY GOAT
EXPERIMENTAL FOREST
Frozen Waffles Press/Shattered Sidewalks Press; 45th
  Century Chapbooks
Hanover Press
HEELTAP/Pariah Press
Hole Books
Host Publications, Inc.
KUMQUAT MERINGUE
LUMMOX JOURNAL
Marymark Press
MEAT FOR TEA: THE NORTHAMPTON REVIEW
NEW HOPE INTERNATIONAL REVIEW
OPEN WIDE MAGAZINE
Panther Books
Pariah Press
PERIPHERAL VISION
Phony Lid Publications
PICK POCKET BOOKS
PORTLAND REVIEW
Scars Publications
SHO
Soft Skull Press
UNWOUND
Van Cleave Publishing
VOICES - ISRAEL
X-Ray Book Co.

JOHN BERRYMAN

Pygmy Forest Press

BIBLIOGRAPHY

THE AFRICAN BOOK PUBLISHING RECORD
ANQ: A Quarterly Journal of Short Articles, Notes, and
  Reviews
Appalachian Consortium Press
Arden Press, Inc.
Arts End Books
Athanor Books (a division of ETX Seminars)
BIBLIOPHILOS
Bottle of Smoke Press
Cantadora Press
Center for Japanese Studies
THE CHRISTIAN LIBRARIAN
COUNTERPOISE: For Social Responsibilities, Liberty and
  Dissent
Crane Press
The Denali Press
Dustbooks
EbonyEnergy Publishing, Inc. (NFP)
Ecrivez!
Edition Gemini
ELEMENTS
ELT Press
ENGLISH LITERATURE IN TRANSITION, 1880-1920
FEMINIST COLLECTIONS: A QUARTERLY OF WO-
  MEN'S STUDIES RESOURCES
FEMINIST PERIODICALS: A CURRENT LISTING OF
  CONTENTS
The Great Rift Press
Gryphon Books
Helm Publishing
Hoover Institution Press

INGLESIDE NEWS ZINE
THE JOURNAL OF COMMONWEALTH LITERATURE
Library Research Associates, Inc.
LINQ
LOST GENERATION JOURNAL
Peter Marcan Publications
Minnesota Historical Society Press
NEW BOOKS ON WOMEN & FEMINISM
Norton Coker Press
NOSTOC MAGAZINE
NOVA EXPRESS
Oak Knoll Press
Open Horizons Publishing Company
Palari Publishing
PAPERBACK PARADE
Passeggiata Press, Inc.
The Pin Prick Press
Poltroon Press
RIVET MAGAZINE
Saqi Books Publisher
Shangri-La Publications
Sligo Press
Smyrna Press
SYNERJY: A Directory of Renewable Energy
University of Chicago Press
WHITEWALL OF SOUND
Whitston Publishing Co.
Women's Studies Librarian, University of Wisconsin
  System
Wood River Publishing

BICYCLING

AB
Anacus Press, An Imprint of Finney Company
CineCycle Publishing
CULTURE CHANGE
DWELLING PORTABLY
EZ Nature Books
Fast Foot Forward Press
Nicolin Fields Publishing, Inc.
Fine Edge Productions
GAMBARA MAGAZINE
Heyday Books
Info Net Publishing
Menasha Ridge Press
New England Cartographics, Inc.
Northland Publishing/Rising Moon/Luna Rising
OUT YOUR BACKDOOR: The Magazine of Do-It-
  Yourself Adventure and Homegrown Culture
Pruett Publishing Company
R-Squared Press
Sunbelt Publications
VELONEWS
Wilderness Adventure Books
WISCONSIN TRAILS

BIGOTRY

MOUTH: Voice of the Dis-Labeled Nation

BILINGUAL

Alaska Native Language Center
THE AMERICAN DISSIDENT
Azreal Publishing Company
BEATLICK NEWS
Bilingual Review Press
BILINGUAL REVIEW/Revista Bilingue
Branden Books
The Chicot Press
China Books & Periodicals, Inc.
The Chinese University Press
Cross-Cultural Communications
DANDELION ARTS MAGAZINE
Dawn Sign Press
THE DIRTY GOAT
DWAN
East West Discovery Press
EVANSVILLE REVIEW
Fern Publications

FLUENT ASCENSION
Helicon Nine Editions
Host Publications, Inc.
Interlink Publishing Group, Inc.
INTERNATIONAL POETRY REVIEW
Italica Press, Inc.
Latin American Literary Review Press
LEO Productions LLC.
Merl Publications
NIGHTLIFE MAGAZINE
The Olivia and Hill Press, Inc.
Oyster River Press
P.R.A. Publishing
Pangaea
PERIPHERAL VISION
Pocahontas Press, Inc.
THE RAVEN CHRONICLES
Raven Tree Press, LLC
READ, AMERICA!
Ronsdale Press
Saqi Books Publisher
Sherman Asher Publishing
Smyrna Press
The Speech Bin, Inc.
Spirit Talk Press
Synergistic Press
Tamal Vista Publications
Tameme
Two Eagles Press International
Typographia Press
Velazquez Press
Wings Press
Xenos Books
XTANT

BIOGRAPHY

Aaron Communications III
Acorn Books
AE-TU Publishing
Affinity Publishers Services
African Ways Publishing
AIS Publications
AK Press
Alaska Geographic Society
American Legacy Media
Androgyne Books
THE ANNALS OF IOWA
ANQ: A Quarterly Journal of Short Articles, Notes, and
  Reviews
Appalachian Consortium Press
Archer Books
Arden Press, Inc.
ARTISTAMP NEWS
ATLANTIS: A Women's Studies Journal/Revue d'etudes
  sur les femmes
Avisson Press, Inc.
Azreal Publishing Company
Backbeat Press
Bancroft Press
Banta & Pool Literary Properties
Bear & Company
BearManor Media
Beekman Books, Inc.
BELLOWING ARK
Black Dome Press Corp.
Blackwater Publications
THE BLOOMSBURY REVIEW
Blue Unicorn Press, Inc.
Blueprint Books
Bonus Books, Inc.
Branden Books
Brooke-Richards Press
Brown Fox Books
Brunswick Publishing Corporation
Burd Street Press
Calliope Press
Cambric Press dba Emerald House
Camel Press

Celebrity Profiles Publishing
Celo Valley Books
THE CENTENNIAL REVIEW
Chelsea Green Publishing Company
Cherokee Publishing Company
Chicago Spectrum Press
China Books & Periodicals, Inc.
Clover Park Press
Coastal 181
Community Service, Inc.
The Compass Press
Comstock Bonanza Press
Coteau Books
COTTONWOOD
Cottonwood Press
Crescent Moon
CRONE CHRONICLES: A Journal of Conscious Aging
Cypress House
DANDELION ARTS MAGAZINE
DESIRE
Devil Mountain Books
Downeast Books
DUST (From the Ego Trip)
Dustbooks
E. S. Publishers & Distributors
Earth Star Publications
EbonyEnergy Publishing, Inc. (NFP)
ELT Press
Encounter Books
ENGLISH LITERATURE IN TRANSITION, 1880-1920
ENGLISH LITERATURE IN TRANSITION, 1880-1920
Eros Books
ETC Publications
Explorer Press
EZ Nature Books
The Feminist Press at the City University of New York
Fern Publications
Fine Tooth Press
Foremost Press
Foundation Books
Four Walls Eight Windows
THE FREEDONIA GAZETTE: The Magazine Devoted to
  the Marx Brothers
Friends United Press
Fulcrum, Inc.
Galde Press, Inc.
Gallaudet University Press
Garden House Press
Gardenia Press
GENRE: WRITER AND WRITINGS
Gibbs Smith, Publisher
Glenbridge Publishing Ltd.
Good Book Publishing Company
THE GREAT BLUE BEACON
The Great Rift Press
Harbor House
Harlan Publishing Company; Alliance Books; Diakonia
  Publishing (Christian Books)
HAWAI'I REVIEW
Heidelberg Graphics
Helm Publishing
Heritage House Publishers
Heritage West Books
Himalayan Institute Press
Historical Resources Press
History Compass, LLC
Hole Books
Hope Publishing House
Hot Box Press / Southern Roots Publishing
Icarus Press
Iconoclast Press
In Print Publishing
The Independent Institute
THE INDEPENDENT REVIEW: A Journal of Political
  Economy
INGLESIDE NEWS ZINE
International Publishers Co. Inc.
Ironweed Press

Italica Press, Inc.
JACK MACKEREL MAGAZINE
KESTREL: A Journal of Literature and Art
Kobalt Books
LadyePress USA, LLC
The Latona Press
THE LEDGE
Lekon New Dimensions Publishing
Lemieux International Ltd.
Libertarian Press, Inc./American Book Distributors
Library Research Associates, Inc.
Life Untangled Publishing
Limelight Editions
LOST GENERATION JOURNAL
LUMMOX JOURNAL
Mandala Publishing
Margaret Media, Inc.
Martinez Press
Maryland Historical Press
Maverick Books
MCM Entertainment, Inc. Publishing Division
Mercer University Press
Midmarch Arts Press
Mills Custom Services Publishing
Minnesota Historical Society Press
Monkfish Book Publishing Company
The Mountaineers Books
Music City Publishing
NEROUP REVIEW
New Concept Press
New Falcon Publications
NEW HOPE INTERNATIONAL REVIEW
NEW SOLUTIONS
Nicholas Lawrence Books
NightinGale Resources
Nip & Tuck Publishing
Nonetheless Press
NORTH CAROLINA LITERARY REVIEW
North Country Books, Inc.
Northern Publishing
Northwestern University Press
Oak Knoll Press
Open Hand Publishing LLC
Oregon State University Press
THE ORPHAN LEAF REVIEW
OUT OF LINE
Outskirts Press, Inc.
The Overmountain Press
Passeggiata Press, Inc.
PASSION
Path Press, Inc.
The Patrice Press
The Place In The Woods
Pocahontas Press, Inc.
Polar Bear & Company
Protean Press
PSYCHE
PublishAmerica, LLLP.
Pussywillow Publishing House, Inc.
QED Press
Quarterly Committee of Queen's University
QUEEN'S QUARTERLY: A Canadian Review
Peter E. Randall Publisher
REAL PEOPLE
Red Alder Books
Redgreene Press
RedJack
REMS Publishing & Publicity
Rivercross Publishing, Inc.
Rock Spring Press Inc.
Ronsdale Press
Rowhouse Press
Sagapress, Inc.
SALMAGUNDI
Saqi Books Publisher
Scentouri, Publishing Division
Scottwall Associates, Publishers
Scrivenery Press

See Sharp Press
The Sektor Co.
Shangri-La Publications
SHATTERED WIG REVIEW
Sligo Press
Soundboard Books
SOUTH DAKOTA REVIEW
Southeast Missouri State University Press
Spiritual Understanding Network, LLC
Steerforth Press, L.C.
Stewart Publishing & Printing
Sherwood Sugden & Company, Publishers
SYMPOSIUM
Synergistic Press
Tendre Press
Texas Tech University Press
Thirteen Colonies Press
Timeless Books
The Times Journal Publishing Co.
Titus Home Publishing
Tomart Publications
University of Arkansas Press
University of Calgary Press
University of Massachusetts Press
University of Virginia Press
The Vertin Press
Vision
Voyageur Publishing Co.,Inc.
John Wade, Publisher
THE WALLACE STEVENS JOURNAL
WAR, LITERATURE & THE ARTS: An International
    Journal of the Humanities
West Coast Paradise Publishing
White Cliffs Media, Inc.
White Mane Publishing Company, Inc.
White Thread Press
Whitston Publishing Co.
Wild West Publishing House
Zelda Wilde Publishing
Wynn Publishing
Xavier House Publishing

BIOLOGY

Cave Books
dbS Productions
The Denali Press
Dimi Press
Flowerfield Enterprises, LLC
Genesis Publishing Company, Inc.
Hobar Publications, A Division of Finney Company
Ion Imagination Publishing, Ion Imagination Entertainment,
    Inc.
Island Press
Laguna Wilderness Press
THE LATHAM LETTER
The Latona Press
THE NAUTILUS
Oregon State University Press
Pangaea
Parkway Publishers, Inc.
PATTERNS OF CHOICE: A Journal of People, Land, and
    Money
Scientia Publishing, LLC
SNOWY EGRET
Three House Publishing
Timber Press
Trickle Creek Books
University Press of Colorado
VINEGAR CONNOISSEURS INTERNATIONAL NEWS-
    LETTER
WILD DUCK REVIEW
ZINE-ON-A-TAPE

BIOTECHNOLOGY

CONSCIENCE: The Newsjournal of Catholic Opinion
Hobar Publications, A Division of Finney Company
THE HUMANIST
International University Line (IUL)

Scientia Publishing, LLC
Soft Skull Press
SterlingHouse Publisher

BIRDS

Alaska Geographic Society
ALL ROUND
Annedawn Publishing
Birdsong Books
Chelsea Green Publishing Company
CONCRETE JUNGLE JOURNAL
Corvus Publishing Company
Dimi Press
Hobar Publications, A Division of Finney Company
Light, Words & Music
Lucky Press, LLC
Mountain Press Publishing Co.
Naturegraph Publishers
New England Cartographics, Inc.
Northland Publishing/Rising Moon/Luna Rising
Peartree Books & Music
Penthe Publishing
Pineapple Press, Inc.
RALPH'S REVIEW
Scientia Publishing, LLC
SNOWY EGRET
Timber Press
Trickle Creek Books
University Press of Colorado
Zagier & Urruty Publicaciones

BIRTH, BIRTH CONTROL, POPULATION

THE AFFILIATE
ALONE TOGETHER
AT-HOME DAD
Carpe Diem Publishing
Cassandra Press, Inc.
Ceres Press
Children Of Mary
China Books & Periodicals, Inc.
CONSCIENCE: The Newsjournal of Catholic Opinion
Emerald Wave
FIDELIS ET VERUS
FREE INQUIRY
GOOD GIRL
Harvard Common Press
THE HUMANIST
Hunter House Inc., Publishers
IRIS: A Journal About Women
Midwifery Today
MOTHERVERSE: A Journal of Contemporary Motherhood
OFF OUR BACKS
Penthe Publishing
RED OWL
SCIENCE/HEALTH ABSTRACTS
SECOND GUESS
SHARE INTERNATIONAL
TOUCHSTONE
Wild West Publishing House

BISEXUAL

Black Pearl Enterprises LLC
BOOKS TO WATCH OUT FOR
Broken Jaw Press
Circlet Press, Inc.
CLARA VENUS
DWAN
Epoch Press
GAYELLOW PAGES
GERTRUDE
GERTRUDE
Gertrude Press
GIRLFRIENDS MAGAZINE
GLB Publishers
Grip Publishing
Harrington Park Press
IRIS: A Journal About Women
MEAT: A Journal of Writing and Materiality

METROPOLITAN FORUM
New Sins Press
Pussywillow
RED OWL
Re-invention UK Ltd
SENSATIONS MAGAZINE
Soft Skull Press
Synergy Press
TORQUERE: Journal of the Canadian Lesbian and Gay Studies Association
Vision

BLACK

AAIMS Publishers
African American Images
AFRICAN AMERICAN REVIEW
AFRO-HISPANIC REVIEW
AIM MAGAZINE
Ariko Publications
Aspicomm Media
Back House Books
BLACK LACE
Black Light Fellowship
THE BLACK SCHOLAR: Journal of Black Studies and Research
BLACKFIRE
BLK
BRILLIANT STAR
CAFE NOIR REVIEW
Carolina Wren Press/Lollipop Power Books
Clarity Press, Inc.
CODA: The Jazz Magazine
COTTONWOOD
Cottonwood Press
Creative Arts Book Company
EbonyEnergy Publishing, Inc. (NFP)
The Edwin Mellen Press
Everflowing Publications
The Feminist Press at the City University of New York
Fingerprint Press
The Fire!! Press
Garden House Press
Gay Sunshine Press, Inc.
Goldfish Press
Gorilla Convict Publications
Grip Publishing
History Compass, LLC
International Publishers Co. Inc.
IRIS: A Journal About Women
Jako Books
KUUMBA
Lotus Press, Inc.
Lyons Publishing Limited
Middle Passage Press
Millennium Vision Press
OBSIDIAN III: Literature in the African Diaspora
OUT OF LINE
Passeggiata Press, Inc.
Path Press, Inc.
Pathfinder Press
The Place In The Woods
Pygmy Forest Press
Quantum Leap S.L.C. Publications
Rainbow Books, Inc.
Red Hand Press
RedBone Press
Reference Service Press
Salt Publishing
Sand and Sable Publishing
Soul
STRUGGLE: A Magazine of Proletarian Revolutionary Literature
Syracuse Cultural Workers/Tools for Change
TOUCHSTONE
Vanderbilt University Press
The Vertin Press
West Virginia University Press
White Cliffs Media, Inc.

Windstorm Creative
Wings Press
WORD IS BOND
XAVIER REVIEW

WILLIAM BLAKE

SHATTERED WIG REVIEW
UNDERSTANDING MAGAZINE

BOOK ARTS

THE AFFILIATE
AFTERIMAGE
ART CALENDAR
ART PAPERS
ARTELLA: the waltz of words and art
ARTISTIC RAMBLINGS
BAGAZINE
Bellywater Press
BIBLIOPHILOS
BIRD DOG
THE BOOK ARTS CLASSIFIED
BOOK MARKETING UPDATE
BOOK/MARK SMALL PRESS REVIEW
Branden Books
Bright Hill Press
Clamp Down Press
Cold-Drill Books
DANDELION ARTS MAGAZINE
Devenish Press
Earthwinds Editions
EEI Press
Fern Publications
FINE BOOKS & COLLECTIONS
Gryphon Books
HAND PAPERMAKING
The Hosanna Press
Idaho Center for the Book
THE ILLUSTRATOR COLLECTOR'S NEWS
Interalia/Design Books
IT GOES ON THE SHELF
KALDRON, An International Journal Of Visual Poetry
KotaPress
LETTER ARTS REVIEW
LIGHTWORKS MAGAZINE
LUMMOX JOURNAL
Lummox Press
MAINE IN PRINT
Mayapple Press
New Rivers Press, Inc.
Open Horizons Publishing Company
PAPERBACK PARADE
PASSAGER
Phelps Publishing Company
PLOPLOP
The Poetry Center Press/Shoestring Press
Rarach Press
Redgreene Press
Scars Publications
SCULPTURAL PURSUIT MAGAZINE
SOUTHWEST COLORADO ARTS PERSPECTIVE
THE TABBY: A CHRONICLE OF THE ARTS AND CRAFTS MOVEMENT
UMBRELLA Online
University of Tampa Press
UNO MAS MAGAZINE
Visual Studies Workshop
WHITEWALLS: A Journal of Language and Art

BOOK COLLECTING, BOOKSELLING

BIBLIOPHILOS
Black Pearl Enterprises LLC
Blackwater Publications
THE BOOK ARTS CLASSIFIED
BOOK DEALERS WORLD
BOOK MARKETING UPDATE
BOOK NEWS & BOOK BUSINESS MART
Bottle of Smoke Press
Chicago Spectrum Press

Children Of Mary
Earthwinds Editions
EbonyEnergy Publishing, Inc. (NFP)
FINE BOOKS & COLLECTIONS
Gallopade International
Gryphon Books
Harobed Publishing Creations
Helm Publishing
THE ILLUSTRATOR COLLECTOR'S NEWS
INDEPENDENT PUBLISHER ONLINE
INDY MAGAZINE
INGLESIDE NEWS ZINE
INTERLIT
JAFFE INTERNATIONAL
Jaffe Publishing Management Service
LIBRARIANS AT LIBERTY
Peter Marcan Publications
MYSTERY READERS JOURNAL
Oak Knoll Press
Open Horizons Publishing Company
ORTHODOX MISSION
Orthodox Mission in Belize
OUT YOUR BACKDOOR: The Magazine of Do-It-Yourself Adventure and Homegrown Culture
PAPERBACK PARADE
Platte Purchase Publishers
Premier Publishers, Inc.
RALPH'S REVIEW
READ, AMERICA!
Shangri-La Publications
SPEX (SMALL PRESS EXCHANGE)
Stony Meadow Publishing
Tomart Publications
UMBRELLA Online
Women's Studies Librarian, University of Wisconsin System

BOOK REVIEWING

THE ADIRONDACK REVIEW
AE-TU Publishing
AFRICAN AMERICAN REVIEW
AIM MAGAZINE
ALABAMA LITERARY REVIEW
THE ANNALS OF IOWA
ANQ: A Quarterly Journal of Short Articles, Notes, and Reviews
Anti-Aging Press
THE ANTIGONISH REVIEW
ARTISTAMP NEWS
Arts End Books
ASCENT
AT-HOME DAD
AXE FACTORY REVIEW
THE BALTIMORE REVIEW
Bancroft Press
THE BEAR DELUXE
BIBLIOPHILOS
BIBLIOTHEQUE D'HUMANISME ET RENAISSANCE
Black Pearl Enterprises LLC
Black Rose Books Ltd.
BLK
THE BLOOMSBURY REVIEW
Blueprint Books
BOOK MARKETING UPDATE
THE BOOK REPORT: The Magazine for Secondary School Library Media & Technology Specialists
BOOK/MARK SMALL PRESS REVIEW
BOOKS FROM FINLAND
THE BOOKWATCH
BORDERLANDS: Texas Poetry Review
BRIDGES: An Interdisciplinary Journal of Theology, Philosophy, History, and Science
BUZZWORDS
Cedar Hill Books
CHELSEA
Children Of Mary
THE CHRISTIAN LIBRARIAN
CKO UPDATE

634

UNITED LUMBEE NATION TIMES
UNWOUND
VALLUM: CONTEMPORARY POETRY
The Vertin Press
THE VIRGINIA QUARTERLY REVIEW
VOICES FROM THE EARTH
WAR, LITERATURE & THE ARTS: An International
    Journal of the Humanities
THE WASHINGTON MONTHLY
WHAT IS ENLIGHTENMENT?
which press
Women's Studies Librarian, University of Wisconsin
    System
WORLD OF FANDOM MAGAZINE
WRITER'S CAROUSEL
WRITERS INK
WRITER'S LIFELINE
XAVIER REVIEW
Zagier & Urruty Publicaciones
ZYX

BOTANY

AB
BANANA RAG
CONCRETE JUNGLE JOURNAL
Eco Images
Granite Publishing Group
Laguna Wilderness Press
Naturegraph Publishers
RED OWL
Southern Illinois University Press
Tamal Vista Publications
Texas Tech University Press
Timber Press
University Press of Colorado
Venus Communications
Waters Edge Press
THE WILD FOODS FORUM
Wilderness Adventure Books

BRITISH COLUMBIA

New Star Books Ltd.
Open Hand Publishing LLC
Ronsdale Press
Ronsdale Press

BROADCASTING

BearManor Media
Bonus Books, Inc.
D.B.A. Books
EEI Press
Rivercross Publishing, Inc.

BRONTES

Casperian Books LLC

BUDDHISM

ABRAMELIN: a Journal of Poetry and Magick
Beacon Press
Blue Dove Press
Book Faith India
BOULDER HERETIC
Center for Japanese Studies
China Books & Periodicals, Inc.
ClearPoint Press
Dharma Publishing
EXPERIMENTAL FOREST
FLUENT ASCENSION
Frozen Waffles Press/Shattered Sidewalks Press; 45th
    Century Chapbooks
GESAR-Buddhism in the West
Granite Publishing Group
HEAVEN BONE MAGAZINE
Heaven Bone Press
INDIA CURRENTS
Ithuriel's Spear
Middleway Press
THE MINDFULNESS BELL

nine muses books
Parallax Press
Pilgrims Book House
Pleasure Boat Studio: A Literary Press
Quest Books: Theosophical Publishing House
READERS SPEAK OUT!
SHO
Snow Lion Publications, Inc.
Spirit Press
Sun Rising Press
Tamal Vista Publications
Timeless Books
TRICYCLE: The Buddhist Review
TURNING WHEEL
Zelda Wilde Publishing
Wisdom Publications, Inc.

CHARLES BUKOWSKI

AMERICAN JONES BUILDING & MAINTENANCE
BOTTLE
Bottle of Smoke Press
Casperian Books LLC
Devenish Press
EXPERIMENTAL FOREST
KNUCKLE MERCHANT - The Journal of Naked Literary
    Aggression
LULLABY HEARSE
OPEN WIDE MAGAZINE
Phony Lid Publications
PICK POCKET BOOKS
X-Ray Book Co.
Zygote Publishing

BUSINESS & ECONOMICS

A Cappela Publishing, Inc.
Actium Publishing, Inc.
Acton Circle Publishing Company
Adams-Blake Publishing
Addicus Books, Inc.
Advantage World Press
Affinity Publishers Services
AIS Publications
ARTSLINK
Aspen Mountain Publishing
AT-HOME DAD
Autelitano Media Group (AMG)
Bay Tree Publishing
Beekman Books, Inc.
Behavioral Sciences Research Press, Inc.
Benchmark Publications Inc.
Black Rose Books Ltd.
Blueprint Books
Bluestocking Press
Book Marketing Solutions
BOOK MARKETING UPDATE
BOOK NEWS & BOOK BUSINESS MART
Bookhaven Press, LLC
Bookhome Publishing/Panda Publishing
THE BOOMERPHILE
Brenner Information Group
Brighton Publications, Inc.
BUSINESS SPIRIT JOURNAL
Byte Masters International
CANADIAN MONEYSAVER
Career Advancement Center, Inc.
Carol Anne Carroll Communications
Center for Japanese Studies
Center For Self-Sufficiency
The Chicot Press
China Books & Periodicals, Inc.
CKO UPDATE
Clearwater Publishing Co.
Communication Creativity
Community Service, Inc.
Craftsman Book Company
Crane Press
Crystal Press
D.B.A. Books

Dash-Hill, LLC
Datamaster Publishing, LLC
DOLLS UNITED INTERACTIVE MAGAZINE
EbonyEnergy Publishing, Inc. (NFP)
Encounter Books
Enlightened Living Publishing, LLC
ETC Publications
EXECUTIVE EXCELLENCE
Executive Excellence Publishing
Film-Video Publications/Circus Source Publications
FINANCIAL FOCUS
The Foundation for Economic Education, Inc.
Franklin-Sarrett Publishers
THE FREEMAN: Ideas On Liberty
Frontline Publications
Gain Publications
The P. Gaines Co., Publishers
Gallopade International
Gemstone House Publishing
GENRE: WRITER AND WRITINGS
Glenbridge Publishing Ltd.
Good Hope Enterprises, Inc.
Bruce Gould Publications
GULF & MAIN Southwest Florida Lifestyle
Happy About
Harvard Common Press
The Heather Foundation
Helm Publishing
Hobar Publications, A Division of Finney Company
Hoover Institution Press
IMOCO Publishing
The Independent Institute
THE INDEPENDENT REVIEW: A Journal of Political
    Economy
Info Net Publishing
Institute for Contemporary Studies
Intercultural Press, Inc.
International Publishers Co. Inc.
The Intrepid Traveler
INVESTMENT COLUMN QUARTERLY (newsletter)
J&W Publishers, Inc.
Jamenair Ltd.
JLA Publications, A Division Of Jeffrey Lant Associates,
    Inc.
JOURNAL OF COURT REPORTING
KABBALAH
Kumarian Press, Inc.
LAKE SUPERIOR MAGAZINE
Lamp Light Press
LATIN AMERICAN PERSPECTIVES
Leadership Education and Development, Inc.
LEFT BUSINESS OBSERVER
Libertarian Press, Inc./American Book Distributors
LIBERTY
Liberty Publishing Company, Inc.
Life Energy Media
Life Untangled Publishing
LifeThread Publications
Long & Silverman Publishing, Inc.
THE LONG TERM VIEW: A Journal of Informed Opinion
The Madson Group, Inc.
MBA Publications
Mind Power Publishing
Mountain Publishing
Multi-Media Publications Inc.
Nateen Publishing
NATURAL LIFE
NEW SOLUTIONS
New Win Publishing
New World Library
Nolo Press
Nonetheless Press
North American Bookdealers Exchange
North Star Books
Nunciata
Oak Tree Press
Open Horizons Publishing Company
Palari Publishing

Park Place Publications
Passeggiata Press, Inc.
The Passion Profit Company
PATTERNS OF CHOICE: A Journal of People, Land, and
    Money
Pendant Publishing Inc.
Perpetual Press
Piccadilly Books, Ltd.
PivotPoint Press
Planning/Communications
Plympton Press International
Princess Publishing
PSI Research/The Oasis Press/Hellgate Press
QP Publishing
QUALITY QUIPS NEWSLETTER
Quarterly Committee of Queen's University
QUEEN'S QUARTERLY: A Canadian Review
Rayve Productions Inc.
RED OWL
Reliance Books
REMS Publishing & Publicity
RFF Press / Resources for the Future
ROCKY MOUNTAIN KC NEWS
Rocky Mountain KC Publishing Co.
Rollaway Bay Publications, Inc.
Ronin Publishing, Inc.
Russian Information Services
SACS Consulting
Sagamore Publishing
ST. CROIX REVIEW
SECOND GUESS
SHARE INTERNATIONAL
THE SMALL BUSINESS ADVISOR
Smith-Johnson Publisher
Soft Skull Press
Sourcebooks, Inc.
Standish Press
Stewart Publishing & Printing
Stone Bridge Press
Sunnyside Press
Sylvan Books
thinkBiotech
Three House Publishing
TIFARA
TOUCHSTONE
Trost Publishing
Two Eagles Press International
United Nations University Press
The Utility Company LLC
Vision Works Publishing
Visions Communications
Vista Publishing, Inc.
WATERFRONT WORLD SPOTLIGHT
WeWrite LLC
Wheatmark Book Publishing
Whitston Publishing Co.
Winslow Publishing
WorkLife Publishing
World Gumbo Publishing

CALIFORNIA

THE ACORN
Androgyne Books
THE AZOREAN EXPRESS
Ballena Press
Borden Publishing Co.
Carousel Press
Cedar Hill Books
CEDAR HILL REVIEW
THE CLIMBING ART
Clover Park Press
Command Performance Press
Comstock Bonanza Press
Creative Arts Book Company
Devil Mountain Books
East West Discovery Press
EZ Nature Books
Fingerprint Press

Gibbs Smith, Publisher
Heritage House Publishers
Heritage West Books
Heyday Books
Huntington Library Press
Iconoclast Press
IN OUR OWN WORDS
Allen A. Knoll Publishers
Lahontan Images
Lexikos
The Live Oak Press, LLC
MCM Entertainment, Inc. Publishing Division
Midmarch Arts Press
Miles & Miles
The Mountaineers Books
Mystery Island Publications
Nolo Press Occidental
North Star Books
NORTHERN PILOT
ORANGE COAST MAGAZINE
Pygmy Forest Press
Quill Driver Books
Ravenwood Publishing
Rayve Productions Inc.
Really Great Books
RED WHEELBARROW
Sand River Press
Santa Ana River Press
Sasquatch Books
Scottwall Associates, Publishers
Genny Smith Books
Sunbelt Publications
Syukhtun Editions
Tamal Vista Publications
Tres Picos Press
Waters Edge Press
Wide World Publishing/TETRA

CALLIGRAPHY

THE BOOK ARTS CLASSIFIED
China Books & Periodicals, Inc.
The Chinese University Press
firefall editions
LETTER ARTS REVIEW
The Overlook Press
SOUTHWEST COLORADO ARTS PERSPECTIVE

CANADA

Aardvark Enterprises (A Division of Speers Investments Ltd.)
Alaska Geographic Society
ASCENT
Betelgeuse Books
Between The Lines
Black Rose Books Ltd.
Borealis Press Limited
Broken Jaw Press
BROKEN PENCIL
CANADIAN CHILDREN'S LITERATURE
Canadian Educators' Press
CANADIAN JOURNAL OF COMMUNICATION
CANADIAN LITERATURE
THE CAPILANO REVIEW
CONNEXIONS DIGEST
Connexions Information Services, Inc.
Coteau Books
Creative Guy Publishing
DESCANT
FREEFALL
Liaison Press
LICHEN Arts & Letters Preview
Mountain Automation Corporation
NEW MUSE OF CONTEMPT
New Star Books Ltd.
NIGHTLIFE MAGAZINE
NORTHERN PILOT
Oolichan Books
Pottersfield Press

THE PRAIRIE JOURNAL OF CANADIAN LITERATURE
Prairie Journal Press
THE RIVER REVIEW/LA REVUE RIVIERE
Ronsdale Press
A SOFT DEGRADE
Sources
Tameme
Thirteen Colonies Press
THE TOWNSHIPS SUN
Tuns Press
UBC Press
University of Calgary Press
Vehicule Press
WEST COAST LINE: A Journal of Contemporary Writing and Criticism
Whole Person Associates Inc.

CAREERS

Acton Circle Publishing Company
THE ART OF ABUNDANCE
Aspen Mountain Publishing
Backbeat Press
Believe! Publishing
Bluestocking Press
Bookhaven Press, LLC
Bookhome Publishing/Panda Publishing
Carol Anne Carroll Communications
Contemax Publishers
Crane Press
EXECUTIVE EXCELLENCE
Executive Excellence Publishing
Finney Company, Inc.
Galen Press, Ltd.
GLOBAL ONE TRAVEL & AUTOMOTIVE MAGAZINE
Global Sports Productions, Ltd.
Harvard Common Press
Herrmann International
Infinite Possibilities Publishing Group, Inc.
Innisfree Press
J&W Publishers, Inc.
The Madson Group, Inc.
Mind Power Publishing
Multi-Media Publications Inc.
Nateen Publishing
New Win Publishing
Nonetheless Press
P.R.A. Publishing
Perpetual Press
Planning/Communications
PREP Publishing
QED Press
Rayve Productions Inc.
REMS Publishing & Publicity
SACS Consulting
The Saunderstown Press
Set Sail Productions, LLC
TECH DIRECTIONS
TIFARA

CARIBBEAN

Aspicomm Media
CANADIAN JOURNAL OF LATIN AMERICAN AND CARIBBEAN STUDIES/Revue canadienne des etudes latino-americaines et caraibes
THE CARIBBEAN WRITER
Comparative Sedimentology Lab.
Department of Romance Languages
E. S. Publishers & Distributors
FIREBREEZE PUBLISHING
Jako Books
Lyons Publishing Limited
Mayapple Press
Pangaea
The Passion Profit Company
POINT OF CONTACT, The Journal of Verbal & Visual Arts
PREP Publishing
SOCIETE

TORRE DE PAPEL
Tortuga Books
Tres Picos Press
Two Thousand Three Associates
Two Thousand Three Associates
University of Virginia Press
THE VORTEX
White Cliffs Media, Inc.
World Music Press
XAVIER REVIEW

LEWIS CARROLL

THE MAD HATTER
MEAT FOR TEA: THE NORTHAMPTON REVIEW
Press Here
SHATTERED WIG REVIEW
UNDERSTANDING MAGAZINE

CARTOONS

ABLAZE Publishing
AFFABLE NEIGHBOR
Affable Neighbor Press
Allworth Press
THE AMERICAN DISSIDENT
THE AMERICAN DRIVEL REVIEW
ARNAZELLA
AXE FACTORY REVIEW
BACKWARDS CITY REVIEW
BANANA RAG
BLACK WARRIOR REVIEW
BLK
BUTTON
THE CHEROTIC (r)EVOLUTIONARY
Creative Writing and Publishing Company
CREEPY MIKE'S OMNIBUS OF FUN
DOPE FRIENDS
END OF LIFE CHOICES
THE FRANK REVIEW
THE FUNNY PAPER
THE GREAT BLUE BEACON
HEROES FROM HACKLAND
Ignite! Entertainment
INDUSTRY MINNE-ZINE
INDY MAGAZINE
LifeCircle Press
LIGHT: The Quarterly of Light Verse
LOW BUDGET SCIENCE FICTION
MEAT FOR TEA: THE NORTHAMPTON REVIEW
Mica Press - Paying Our Dues Productions
MINESHAFT
THE NOISE
OFFICE NUMBER ONE
PANIC STRIPS
PAST TIMES: The Nostalgia Entertainment Newsletter
The Press at Foggy Bottom
THE QUIET FEATHER
ROTTEN PEPPER
SHORT FUSE
Solcat Publishing
StarLance Publications
SWINK
T.V. HEADS
THE TARPEIAN ROCK
UmbraProjects, Ltd.
UNO MAS MAGAZINE
UNWOUND
WeWrite LLC
WORLD OF FANDOM MAGAZINE
Writers' Haven Press

CATHOLIC

Bear & Company
Blackwater Publications
BOULDER HERETIC
Cantadora Press
Central Avenue Press
COGNITIO: A Graduate Humanities Journal
CONSCIENCE: The Newsjournal of Catholic Opinion

EZ Nature Books
Fingerprint Press
Fountainhead Productions, Inc.
Gingerbread House
Idylls Press
LITURGICAL CATECHESIS
LPD Press
MCM Entertainment, Inc. Publishing Division
MINISTRY & LITURGY
MUSIC NEWS
Open University of America Press
Saint Mary's Press
SOLAS Press
Spiritual Understanding Network, LLC
TRADICION REVISTA
Tyr Publishing
White Buck Publishing
Yes International Publishers

CAVES

Cave Books
Dimi Press

EDGAR CAYCE

Granite Publishing Group
Spiritual Understanding Network, LLC
Sun Rising Press

CELTIC

AFFABLE NEIGHBOR
Affable Neighbor Press
THE AFFILIATE
Bardsong Press
Blackwater Publications
Carpe Diem Publishing
Celtic Heritage Books
DeerTrail Books
DIRTY LINEN
Dufour Editions Inc.
THE EDGE CITY REVIEW
Fountainhead Productions, Inc.
Horned Owl Publishing
IRISH FAMILY JOURNAL
Irish Genealogical Foundation
IRISH LITERARY SUPPLEMENT
KNUCKLE MERCHANT - The Journal of Naked Literary
    Aggression
LLEN CYMRU
MAGICAL BLEND/NATURAL BEAUTY & HEALTH/
    TRANSITIONS
Monkfish Book Publishing Company
NEW AMERICAN IMAGIST
The Overmountain Press
Reed Press
SAGEWOMAN
STUDIA CELTICA
THIN COYOTE
University Of Wales Press
Waters Edge Press
Wings Press

CHANNELLING

Dream Street Publishing
Emerald Wave
Granite Publishing Group
New Paradigm Books
Plus Publications

CHICAGO

BLACKBOOK PRESS, THE POETRY ZINE
Chicago Review Press
CHILDREN, CHURCHES AND DADDIES, A Non
    Religious, Non Familial Literary Magazine
DOWN IN THE DIRT LITERARY MAGAZINE, the prose
    & poetry magazine revealing all your dirty little secrets
FREEDOM AND STRENGTH PRESS FORUM
Inner City Press
Lake Claremont Press

Libellum
Northern Illinois University Press
Northwestern University Press
Path Press, Inc.
ROCTOBER COMICS AND MUSIC
Scars Publications
Solcat Publishing
Typographia Press

CHICANO/A

Arte Publico Press
AZTLAN: A Journal of Chicano Studies
Back House Books
Bilingual Review Press
BILINGUAL REVIEW/Revista Bilingue
THE BLOOMSBURY REVIEW
Bronze Girl Productions, Inc.
Burning Bush Publications
Carolina Wren Press/Lollipop Power Books
THE CREAM CITY REVIEW
The Denali Press
The Feminist Press at the City University of New York
FIREBREEZE PUBLISHING
IN OUR OWN WORDS
Inner City Press
IRIS: A Journal About Women
IRON HORSE LITERARY REVIEW
MEXICAN STUDIES/ESTUDIOS MEXICANOS
NEW AMERICAN IMAGIST
PEACEWORK
The Place In The Woods
Pocahontas Press, Inc.
Pygmy Forest Press
READ, AMERICA!
Reference Service Press
Rio Nuevo Publishers
STRUGGLE: A Magazine of Proletarian Revolutionary
    Literature
TURNING THE TIDE: Journal of Anti-Racist Action,
    Research & Education
Two Eagles Press International
UCLA Chicano Studies Research Center Press
Vanderbilt University Press
Volcano Press, Inc
West End Press
White Cliffs Media, Inc.
Wings Press
WORD IS BOND
X-Ray Book Co.

CHILDREN, YOUTH

Aaron Communications III
Abernathy House Publishing
Acorn Books
Adirondack Mountain Club, Inc.
ADVENTURES
Alegra House Publishers
ALL ROUND
American Carriage House Publishing
Amherst Writers & Artists Press, Inc.
Ancient City Press
Angel Power Press
Annick Press Ltd.
AT-HOME DAD
Auromere Books and Imports
Azreal Publishing Company
Azro Press
The B & R Samizdat Express
Beekman Books, Inc.
The Benefactory, Inc.
Beyond Words Publishing, Inc.
Birdsong Books
THE BLOOMSBURY REVIEW
Blue Mouse Studio
Bollix Books
Book Marketing Solutions
THE BOOKWATCH
Borealis Press Limited

Boulevard Books, Inc. Florida
Bright Ring Publishing, Inc.
BRILLIANT STAR
Britton Road Press
Bronze Girl Productions, Inc.
Callawind Publications / Custom Cookbooks / Children's
    Books
CANADIAN CHILDREN'S LITERATURE
Carolina Wren Press/Lollipop Power Books
Center for Thanatology Research & Education, Inc.
The Center Press
Chicago Review Press
Chicken Soup Press, Inc.
COBBLESTONE: Discover American History
The Colbert House
Cornerstone Publishing
Coteau Books
Council For Indian Education
Creative With Words Publications (CWW)
Creative Writing and Publishing Company
CRICKET
Crones Unlimited
Crystal Dreams Publishing
CURRENTS: New Scholarship in the Human Services
Dancing Bridge Publishing
Dawn Publications
Dawn Sign Press
Delaney Day Press
Dharma Publishing
Downeast Books
Dream Publishing Co.
Dream Street Publishing
Dufour Editions Inc.
E & E Publishing
Eagle's View Publishing
East West Discovery Press
EbonyEnergy Publishing, Inc. (NFP)
Ecrivez!
EduCare Press
Wm.B. Eerdmans Publishing Co.
ELEMENTS
Epona Publishing
EXCEPTIONALITY EDUCATION CANADA
Falcon Publishing, LTD
Family Learning Association, Inc.
Flowerfield Enterprises, LLC
Focus Publications, Inc.
Fontanel Books
Fotofolio, Inc.
Front Row Experience
Fulcrum, Inc.
Future Horizons, Inc.
Galde Press, Inc.
The Galileo Press Ltd.
Gallaudet University Press
Gallopade International
Gazelle Publications
Gifted Education Press/The Reading Tutorium
Gingerbread House
Goose River Press
Grand Slam Press, Inc.
Gryphon House, Inc.
Guarionex Press Ltd.
Hannacroix Creek Books, Inc
HAPPENINGNOW!EVERYWHERE
Harvest Hill Press
The Haworth Press
Heartsong Books
Helm Publishing
History Compass, LLC
HOME EDUCATION MAGAZINE
Horned Owl Publishing
Hungry Tiger Press
Hunter House Inc., Publishers
Illumination Arts
Images Unlimited and Snaptail Press, a Division of Images
    Unlimited Publishing
Impact Publishers, Inc.

639

Interlink Publishing Group, Inc.
Ion Imagination Publishing, Ion Imagination Entertainment, Inc.
Jalmar Press/Innerchoice Publishing
JetKor
JOURNAL OF CHILD AND YOUTH CARE
JUNIOR STORYTELLER
Kar-Ben Publishing, Inc.
Kenyette Productions
THE KIDS' STORYTELLING CLUB WEBSITE
KLIATT
Allen A. Knoll Publishers
Laredo Publishing Co., Inc./Renaissance House
THE LATHAM LETTER
Libertarian Press, Inc./American Book Distributors
Little Leaf Press
The Love and Logic Press, Inc.
Luminous Epinoia Press
THE MAD HATTER
Magic Circle Press
Magnolia Publishing
Mama Incense Publishing
Mandala Publishing
Margaret Media, Inc.
MGW (Mom Guess What) Newsmagazine
Mind Power Publishing
Monroe Press
Mo'omana'o Press
Motom
Mountain Automation Corporation
Munchweiler Press
MUSIC NEWS
My Heart Yours Publishing
NATURAL LIFE
NEW ALTERNATIVES
New Canaan Publishing Company Inc.
New Voices Publishing
New World Press, Inc
NightinGale Resources
No Starch Press
Nonetheless Press
North Country Books, Inc.
Northland Publishing/Rising Moon/Luna Rising
NSR Publications
Ocean Publishing
Oolichan Books
Open Hand Publishing LLC
Open Horizons Publishing Company
Pacific View Press
Pangaea
Parallax Press
PARENTEACHER MAGAZINE
Parenting Press, Inc.
Park Place Publications
Passion Power Press, Inc
Passport Press
Path Press, Inc.
Peachtree Publishers, Ltd.
Pearl's Book'em Publisher
Peartree Books & Music
Perrin Press
Phelps Publishing Company
Philomel Books
Piano Press
Pinchgut Press
Pirate Publishing International
The Place In The Woods
Platinum One Publishing
Pocahontas Press, Inc.
POCKETS
Poet Tree Press
Premium Press America
The Press at Foggy Bottom
Propeller Press
Publishing Works
Purple Finch Press
Rainbow Books, Inc.
Rama Publishing Co.

Raspberry Press Limited
Raven Rocks Press
READ, AMERICA!
Rio Nuevo Publishers
Ronsdale Press
Running Press
Ryrich Publications
Sadorian Publications
Sagamore Publishing
Saint Mary's Press
Sasquatch Books
SCHOOL MATES
Sea Fog Press
Search Institute
SPIDER
Stellaberry Press
STONE SOUP, The Magazine By Young Writers and Artists
Stonehorse Publishing, LLC
Storycraft Publishing
Storytime Ink International
Stunt Publishing
Summit Crossroads Press
Swan Raven & Company
Terra Nova Press
Theytus Books Ltd.
This New World Publishing, LLC
Three Bean Press
Three Bears Publishing
TIFARA
Titus Home Publishing
Tolling Bell Books
Top 20 Press
Tortuga Books
Trellis Publishing, Inc.
Truebekon Books
TURNING THE TIDE: Journal of Anti-Racist Action, Research & Education
Two Thousand Three Associates
Twynz Publishing
Unity House
Vanderbilt University Press
Volcano Press, Inc
VOYA (Voice of Youth Advocate)
Wayside Publications
WeWrite LLC
What The Heck Press
White Mane Publishing Company, Inc.
Windstorm Creative
Windward Publishing, An Imprint of Finney Company
WORD IS BOND

CHINA

China Books & Periodicals, Inc.
CHINA REVIEW INTERNATIONAL
THE CHINA REVIEW: AN INTERDISCIPLINARY JOURNAL ON GREATER CHINA
Cynic Press
FIREBREEZE PUBLISHING
Inner City Press
LEO Productions LLC.
Pleasure Boat Studio: A Literary Press
Small Helm Press
Spirit Press
Synergetic Press
Venus Communications
The Wellsweep Press

SRI CHINMOY

INDIA CURRENTS
MAGICAL BLEND/NATURAL BEAUTY & HEALTH/ TRANSITIONS
Monkfish Book Publishing Company

CHRISTIANITY

Aaron Communications III
ABLAZE Publishing
American Literary Press

640

ANCIENT PATHS
Azreal Publishing Company
Beacon Light Publishing (BLP)
Beacon Press
Bellywater Press
Blue Dolphin Publishing, Inc.
Blue Dove Press
Book Marketing Solutions
BOULDER HERETIC
Brentwood Christian Press
Candlestick Publishing
Carrier Pigeon Press
Cascada Corporation / Scherf Books, MegaGrace Books
Children Of Mary
CHRISTIAN CONNECTION PEN PAL NEWSLETTER
CHRISTIAN*NEW AGE QUARTERLY
Cladach Publishing
CORNERSTONE
Crossway Books
Delaney Day Press
DOVETAIL: A Journal by and for Jewish/Christian Families
Dunamis House
Eborn Books
Wm.B. Eerdmans Publishing Co.
Falcon Publishing, LTD
FIDELIS ET VERUS
Fingerprint Press
Four Seasons Publishers
Friends United Press
FULLOSIA PRESS
Galaxy Press
Genesis Publishing Company, Inc.
The Glencannon Press
Good Book Publishing Company
Goose River Press
Harlan Publishing Company; Alliance Books; Diakonia Publishing (Christian Books)
The Heather Foundation
Heidelberg Graphics
Ho Logos Press
Hope Publishing House
ISSUES
Jireh Publishing Company
The Leaping Frog Press
LPD Press
Lycanthrope Press
Magnus Press Imprint: Canticle Books
MEDIA SPOTLIGHT
Mountaintop Books
Multnomah Publishers, Inc.
MUSIC NEWS
My Heart Yours Publishing
New Canaan Publishing Company Inc.
NOLA-MAGICK Press
OFFICE NUMBER ONE
Origin Press
ORTHODOX MISSION
Orthodox Mission in Belize
Pearl's Book'em Publisher
Philopsychy Press
Polka Dot Publishing
Princess Publishing
PublishAmerica, LLLP.
QUARTZ HILL JOURNAL OF THEOLOGY:A Journal of Bible and Contemporary Theological Thought
Quartz Hill Publishing House
QUEST: AN INTERDISCIPLINARY JOURNAL FOR ASIAN CHRISTIAN SCHOLARS
Ragged Edge Press
Ridgeway Press of Michigan
RockBySea Books
Saint Mary's Press
SelectiveHouse Publishers, Inc.
SKS Press
Small Helm Press
SterlingHouse Publisher
Sherwood Sugden & Company, Publishers

Thatch Tree Publications
Thirteen Colonies Press
Tree of Life Books. Imprints: Progressive Press, Banned Books
Tyr Publishing
UnKnownTruths.com Publishing Company
Virginia Pines Press
Wheatmark Book Publishing
White Buck Publishing
Wilderness Ministries
WinePress Publishing
Wytherngate Press
Yes International Publishers

CHRISTMAS

City Life Books, LLC
Cladach Publishing
Innisfree Press
LPD Press
Mayhaven Publishing
Mo'omana'o Press
Motom
Premium Press America
RockBySea Books
Touchstone Adventures
Waters Edge Press

CITIES

AMERICAN HIKER
Americans for the Arts
ASSEMBLAGE: A Critical Journal of Architecture and Design Culture
Barney Press
Black Rose Books Ltd.
Cantarabooks LLC
Carousel Press
Chandler & Sharp Publishers, Inc.
Clover Park Press
CONCRETE JUNGLE JOURNAL
ENVIRONMENTAL & ARCHITECTURAL PHENOMEN-OLOGY NEWSLETTER
Gallopade International
Gemini Publishing Company
GREEN ANARCHY
Helm Publishing
Heritage House Publishers
INGLESIDE NEWS ZINE
Inner City Press
INNER CITY PRESS
Italica Press, Inc.
Lake Claremont Press
Maisonneuve Press
Peter Marcan Publications
Martinez Press
Mount Ida Press
RIVET MAGAZINE
SHATTERED WIG REVIEW
University of Chicago Press
VACATION PLACE RENTALS
Vanderbilt University Press
Vehicule Press
WATERFRONT WORLD SPOTLIGHT

CIVIL RIGHTS

AE-TU Publishing
THE AFFILIATE
AIS Publications
BALLOT ACCESS NEWS
Beacon Press
Between The Lines
BIG HAMMER
BLACKBOOK PRESS, THE POETRY ZINE
BLK
THE BOOMERPHILE
THE CAIMAN (formerly THE WEIRD NEWS)
Cantadora Press
Clarity Press, Inc.
COALITION FOR PRISONERS' RIGHTS NEWSLETTER

COLORLINES
GAUNTLET: Exploring the Limits of Free Expression
Global Options
IN OUR OWN WORDS
Inner City Press
INNER CITY PRESS
THE LIBERATOR
Macrocosm USA, Inc.
MGW (Mom Guess What) Newsmagazine
Millennium Vision Press
MOUTH: Voice of the Dis-Labeled Nation
Open Hand Publishing LLC
THE OTHER ISRAEL
Path Press, Inc.
PEACEWORK
PEMMICAN
The Place In The Woods
PRISON LEGAL NEWS
Reach Productions Publishing
SENSATIONS MAGAZINE
Snake Hill Press
SOCIAL JUSTICE: A JOURNAL OF CRIME, CONFLICT,
    & WORLD ORDER
Soft Skull Press
Southeast Missouri State University Press
Stardate Publishing Company
STORMWARNING!
Strata Publishing, Inc.
THINKERMONKEY
TOUCHSTONE
TRAVEL NATURALLY
University of Massachusetts Press
University of South Carolina Press
Writers' Haven Press

CIVIL WAR

Beacon Light Publishing (BLP)
Blackwater Publications
John F. Blair, Publisher
Bright Mountain Books, Inc.
Burd Street Press
Cherokee Publishing Company
Chicago Spectrum Press
Denlinger's Publishers Ltd.
Epoch Press
Faded Banner Publications
FULLOSIA PRESS
Galen Press, Ltd.
Harbor House
Heartland Publishing
Historical Resources Press
MacDonald/Sward Publishing Company
Mercer University Press
Northern Illinois University Press
Ohio University Press/Swallow Press
The Overmountain Press
Parkway Publishers, Inc.
Platte Purchase Publishers
Premium Press America
Southeast Missouri State University Press
Stardate Publishing Company
Truman State University Press
University of Arkansas Press
University of Nebraska Press
University of South Carolina Press
University of Virginia Press
Van Cleave Publishing
WAR, LITERATURE & THE ARTS: An International
    Journal of the Humanities
West Virginia University Press
White Mane Publishing Company, Inc.

CLASSICAL STUDIES

ABLAZE Publishing
APOSTROPHE: USCB Journal of the Arts
The B & R Samizdat Express
Bandanna Books
Barrytown/Station Hill Press

BIBLIOPHILOS
Bliss Publishing Company, Inc.
Branden Books
Cantadora Press
The Chinese University Press
CLASSICAL ANTIQUITY
THE CLASSICAL OUTLOOK
CONTEMPORARY GHAZALS
THE DALHOUSIE REVIEW
DIALOGOS: Hellenic Studies Review
Dufour Editions Inc.
EbonyEnergy Publishing, Inc. (NFP)
The Edwin Mellen Press
Erespin Press
Evolution Publishing
Focus Publishing/R. Pullins Co.
Horned Owl Publishing
Libellum
Mandala Publishing
Monkfish Book Publishing Company
MOUSEION, Journal of the Classical Association of
    Canada/Revue de la Societe Canadienne des Etudes
    Classiques
NEROUP REVIEW
Panther Creek Press
Shangri-La Publications
Spring Publications Inc.
UNDERSTANDING MAGAZINE
West Virginia University Press

CLOTHING

AB
Backbeat Press
Eagle's View Publishing
Ibexa Press
INDUSTRY MINNE-ZINE
ORNAMENT
SKINNYDIPPING
Texas Tech University Press

COLLECTIBLES

Borden Publishing Co.
C & T Publishing
Cattpigg Press
Celebrity Profiles Publishing
Cottontail Publications
Epoch Press
FOLK ART MESSENGER
Galt Press
GemStone Press
Gibbs Smith, Publisher
Gryphon Books
THE ILLUSTRATOR COLLECTOR'S NEWS
INKY TRAIL NEWS
New Win Publishing
ORNAMENT
PAPERBACK PARADE
THE PRESIDENTS' JOURNAL
RALPH'S REVIEW
Sonoran Publishing
Square One Publishers, Inc.
Stony Meadow Publishing
Tomart Publications

COLOR

DOLLS UNITED INTERACTIVE MAGAZINE
Green Hut Press
A SOFT DEGRADE
SunShine Press Publications, Inc.

COLORADO

City Life Books, LLC
Cladach Publishing
Cottonwood Press, Inc.
LPD Press
Montemayor Press
Mountain Automation Corporation
PINYON

Pruett Publishing Company
Rio Nuevo Publishers
Thundercloud Books
TOUCHSTONE
TRADICION REVISTA
Transcending Mundane, Inc.
University Press of Colorado

COMICS

Alan Wofsy Fine Arts
ALL ROUND
Allworth Press
ALMOST NORMAL COMICS and Other Oddities
THE AMERICAN DRIVEL REVIEW
Argo Press
BABYSUE
BABYSUE MUSIC REVIEW
BACKWARDS CITY REVIEW
Bogg Publications
BROKEN PENCIL
Carnifex Press
Carpe Diem Publishing
CHARLTON SPOTLIGHT
THE COMICS JOURNAL
COMICS REVUE
CREEPY MIKE'S OMNIBUS OF FUN
DOPE FRIENDS
THE DUCKBURG TIMES
EbonyEnergy Publishing, Inc. (NFP)
Explorer Press
Fantagraphics Books
FAT TUESDAY
Fine Tooth Press
FISH DRUM MAGAZINE
Fotofolio, Inc.
GAUNTLET: Exploring the Limits of Free Expression
Helm Publishing
HEROES FROM HACKLAND
Ignite! Entertainment
INDIANA REVIEW
INDY MAGAZINE
JACK MACKEREL MAGAZINE
Knowledge Concepts Publishing
Leyland Publications
LIGHT: The Quarterly of Light Verse
Manuscript Press
MINESHAFT
MOTORBOOTY MAGAZINE
Mystery Island Publications
Mystic Toad Press
NBM Publishing Company
PANIC STRIPS
Pearl's Book'em Publisher
Phelps Publishing Company
PIG IRON
Rio Nuevo Publishers
ROCTOBER COMICS AND MUSIC
ROTTEN PEPPER
Rowhouse Press
The Runaway Spoon Press
SEQUENTIAL
SHATTERED WIG REVIEW
SHORTRUNS
Synergetic Press
T.V. HEADS
THE2NDHAND
WAV MAGAZINE: Progressive Music Art Politics Culture
Windstorm Creative
WORLD OF FANDOM MAGAZINE
Writers' Haven Press

COMMUNICATION, JOURNALISM

THE AFFILIATE
Allworth Press
ALTERNATIVE PRESS REVIEW
Arjuna Library Press
ATS Publishing
Autonomedia, Inc.

Bay Tree Publishing
BEACHCOMBER MAGAZINE
Beekman Books, Inc.
Between The Lines
Blackwater Publications
Bonus Books, Inc.
BROKEN PENCIL
CANADIAN JOURNAL OF COMMUNICATION
Chicory Blue Press, Inc.
THE CHRISTIAN LIBRARIAN
CKO UPDATE
Communication Creativity
Communicom Publishing Company
D.B.A. Books
EbonyEnergy Publishing, Inc. (NFP)
THE EDGE CITY REVIEW
EEI Press
ELEMENTS
ESPERANTIC STUDIES
FRAN MAGAZINE
FREELANCE WRITER'S REPORT
Gallopade International
Global Sports Productions, Ltd.
THE GREAT BLUE BEACON
Guarionex Press Ltd.
Helm Publishing
THE INDIE
INGLESIDE NEWS ZINE
Intercultural Press, Inc.
INTERLIT
J&W Publishers, Inc.
JLA Publications, A Division Of Jeffrey Lant Associates, Inc.
KALDRON, An International Journal Of Visual Poetry
KETTERING REVIEW
Life Untangled Publishing
LIGHTWORKS MAGAZINE
LOST GENERATION JOURNAL
LUMMOX JOURNAL
Lummox Press
Maupin House Publishing, Inc.
MEDIA SPOTLIGHT
Mills Custom Services Publishing
NEWPAGES: Alternatives in Print & Media
NEWPAGES: Alternatives in Print & Media
OHIO WRITER
Open Horizons Publishing Company
PASSAGES NORTH
Pocahontas Press, Inc.
THE PUBLIC RELATIONS QUARTERLY
Rada Press, Inc.
READERS SPEAK OUT!
RIVER TEETH: A Journal of Nonfiction Narrative
ST. LOUIS JOURNALISM REVIEW
Sources
THE SOURCES HOTLINK
The Speech Bin, Inc.
Strata Publishing, Inc.
Strata Publishing, Inc.
Univelt, Inc.
University of Arkansas Press
THE WASHINGTON MONTHLY
Wild West Publishing House
Winslow Publishing
WOMEN AND LANGUAGE
WRITER'S CAROUSEL
WRITER'S LIFELINE

COMMUNISM, MARXISM, LENINISM

Autonomedia, Inc.
Back House Books
Bad Press
Beekman Books, Inc.
BLUE COLLAR REVIEW
Bordighera, Inc.
THE CAIMAN (formerly THE WEIRD NEWS)
Children Of Mary
EbonyEnergy Publishing, Inc. (NFP)

643

EXPERIMENTAL FOREST
FIDELIS ET VERUS
Hoover Institution Press
International Publishers Co. Inc.
JOURNAL OF NARRATIVE THEORY
LEFT BUSINESS OBSERVER
Life Untangled Publishing
Mehring Books, Inc.
Partisan Press
Pathfinder Press
PEMMICAN
SALMAGUNDI
Semiotext Foreign Agents Books Series
SEMIOTEXT(E)
Shangri-La Publications
Soft Skull Press
STORMWARNING!
STRUGGLE: A Magazine of Proletarian Revolutionary Literature
TOUCHSTONE
Van Cleave Publishing

COMMUNITY

THE AFFILIATE
AFRICAN AMERICAN REVIEW
AMERICAN JONES BUILDING & MAINTENANCE
Americans for the Arts
ARTELLA: the waltz of words and art
Bay Tree Publishing
Bear & Company
Bellywater Press
Black Rose Books Ltd.
Bottom Dog Press
Carrier Pigeon Press
THE CHEROTIC (r)EVOLUTIONARY
COMMUNITIES
Community Service, Inc.
CRONE CHRONICLES: A Journal of Conscious Aging
EbonyEnergy Publishing, Inc. (NFP)
FRIENDS OF PEACE PILGRIM
Garden House Press
Global Options
GOOD GIRL
Heartland Publishing
HEARTLANDS: A Magazine of Midwest Life and Art
The Heather Foundation
Helm Publishing
Ice Cube Press
INDUSTRY MINNE-ZINE
Innisfree Press
INNOVATING
INTERCULTURE
IRIS: A Journal About Women
JOURNAL OF CHILD AND YOUTH CARE
KETTERING REVIEW
Kivaki Press
LAKE STREET LIT: Art and Words from the Bottom of Lake Bonneville
Life Untangled Publishing
LifeCircle Press
MGW (Mom Guess What) Newsmagazine
Missing Spoke Press
Mo'omana'o Press
NATURAL LIFE
NEROUP REVIEW
NEW ENVIRONMENT BULLETIN
NEW SOLUTIONS
OUT OF LINE
OUT YOUR BACKDOOR: The Magazine of Do-It-Yourself Adventure and Homegrown Culture
The People's Press
Red Alder Books
RFD
Shangri-La Publications
SILVER WINGS
SOCIAL ANARCHISM: A Journal of Practice and Theory
SOCIAL JUSTICE: A JOURNAL OF CRIME, CONFLICT, & WORLD ORDER

SOCIAL POLICY
SOMETHING TO READ
Soul
TIFARA
TOUCHSTONE
Trentham Books
TURNING WHEEL
The Vertin Press
Volcano Press, Inc

COMPUTERS, CALCULATORS

Adams-Blake Publishing
THE AFFILIATE
Ageless Press
ALT-J: Association for Learning Technology Journal
Autonomedia, Inc.
Benchmark Publications Inc.
THE BOOKWATCH
Brenner Information Group
Byte Masters International
Carpe Diem Publishing
THE CHRISTIAN LIBRARIAN
THE COMPLEAT NURSE
Frontline Publications
Gallopade International
GRAY AREAS
Happy About
Holy Macro! Books
INGLESIDE NEWS ZINE
Jamenair Ltd.
Lion Press
Martinez Press
MGW (Mom Guess What) Newsmagazine
Microdex Bookshelf
Mills Custom Services Publishing
NEROUP REVIEW
No Starch Press
NWI National Writers Institute
Online Training Solutions, Inc.
Paladin Enterprises, Inc.
PLAIN BROWN WRAPPER (PBW)
PRIVACY JOURNAL
Purple Finch Press
Quale Press
Shangri-La Publications
Technics Publications, LLC
UnTechnical Press
White Cliffs Media, Inc.

CONSERVATION

ADIRONDAC
Adirondack Mountain Club, Inc.
THE AFFILIATE
Alaska Geographic Society
AMERICAN FORESTS
AMERICAN HIKER
American Hiking Society
AMERICAN JONES BUILDING & MAINTENANCE
APPALACHIA JOURNAL
AQUATERRA, METAECOLOGY & CULTURE
BANANA RAG
Beacon Press
Bear & Company
THE BEAR DELUXE
BIG MUDDY: Journal of the Mississippi River Valley
Bliss Publishing Company, Inc.
THE BLOOMSBURY REVIEW
Cave Books
Chelsea Green Publishing Company
Downeast Books
DWELLING PORTABLY
ECOTONE: Reimagining Place
Elderberry Press, LLC
ELECTRONIC GREEN JOURNAL
Envirographics
Fulcrum, Inc.
Garden House Press
Granite Publishing Group

HIGH COUNTRY NEWS
Hobar Publications, A Division of Finney Company
INGLESIDE NEWS ZINE
Island Press
Keokee Co. Publishing, Inc.
Kivaki Press
Kumarian Press, Inc.
Laguna Wilderness Press
THE LATHAM LETTER
The Latona Press
Lexikos
Life Untangled Publishing
Macrocosm USA, Inc.
Missing Spoke Press
The Mountaineers Books
New England Cartographics, Inc.
NORTHWOODS JOURNAL, A Magazine for Writers
Oak Knoll Press
Ocean Publishing
ON EARTH
Oregon State University Press
OUT OF LINE
OUT YOUR BACKDOOR: The Magazine of Do-It-Yourself Adventure and Homegrown Culture
Pangaea
Pineapple Press, Inc.
RALPH'S REVIEW
RED OWL
RFF Press / Resources for the Future
Rock Spring Press Inc.
Sagamore Publishing
SANDPOINT MAGAZINE
SEED SAVERS EXCHANGE
Shangri-La Publications
Genny Smith Books
SO YOUNG!
TOUCHSTONE
Touchstone Adventures
University of Chicago Press
WEBER STUDIES: Voices and Viewpoints of the Contemporary West
Wineberry Press
WISCONSIN TRAILS
Zagier & Urruty Publicaciones

CONSTRUCTION

Consumer Press
HandyCraft Media Productions
Hobar Publications, A Division of Finney Company
New Community Press
Northland Publishing/Rising Moon/Luna Rising
PAVEMENT SAW
Pavement Saw Press
Rolling Hills Publishing
Standish Press
Swan Publishing Company

CONSULTING

Adams-Blake Publishing
Blueprint Books
Book Marketing Solutions
CKO UPDATE
Finney Company, Inc.
Firelight Publishing, Inc.
Friendly Oaks Publications
Happy About
IDM Press
Multi-Media Publications Inc.
Nonetheless Press
Platinum One Publishing
PSI Research/The Oasis Press/Hellgate Press
Smith-Johnson Publisher
The Utility Company LLC
World Gumbo Publishing

CONSUMER

Affinity Publishers Services
Bay Tree Publishing

THE BOOKWATCH
Brenner Information Group
Brighton Publications, Inc.
CANADIAN MONEYSAVER
Center For Self-Sufficiency
Communication Creativity
Consumer Press
DWELLING PORTABLY
GemStone Press
Guarionex Press Ltd.
GULF & MAIN Southwest Florida Lifestyle
Happy About
Liberty Publishing Company, Inc.
Macrocosm USA, Inc.
New Community Press
Nonetheless Press
PRIVACY JOURNAL
Roblin Press
Rolling Hills Publishing
Upper Access Inc.
VEGETARIAN JOURNAL
Winslow Publishing

COOKING

ABLAZE Publishing
Airplane Books
Alaska Northwest Books
ALIMENTUM - The Literature of Food
Amador Publishers
Avery Color Studios
BANANA RAG
Banta & Pool Literary Properties
The Bess Press
Blue Dolphin Publishing, Inc.
BookPartners, Inc.
Bright Mountain Books, Inc.
Bronze Girl Productions, Inc.
C & G Publishing, Inc.
Callawind Publications / Custom Cookbooks / Children's Books
Chicago Review Press
Chicago Spectrum Press
CHRISTIAN CONNECTION PEN PAL NEWSLETTER
Cladach Publishing
COOKING CONTEST CHRONICLE
Crystal Clarity, Publishers
EZ Nature Books
Fantail
Nicolin Fields Publishing, Inc.
First Books
Follow Me! Guides
Gabriel's Horn Publishing Co., Inc.
Goose River Press
Hands & Heart Books
Harvard Common Press
Harvest Hill Press
Images Unlimited and Snaptail Press, a Division of Images Unlimited Publishing
Info Net Publishing
Island Publishers
Jackson Harbor Press
Kar-Ben Publishing, Inc.
Lamp Light Press
Lazywood Press
Lemieux International Ltd.
Liberty Publishing Company, Inc.
Life Lessons
Life Media
LifeCircle Press
A Melody from an Immigrant's Soul
MY TABLE: Houston's Dining Magazine
NATURAL LIFE
New Community Press
NightinGale Resources
Northland Publishing/Rising Moon/Luna Rising
George Ohsawa Macrobiotic Foundation
THE ORPHAN LEAF REVIEW
Outrider Press

Pedestal Press
Pineapple Press, Inc.
Platinum One Publishing
Pruett Publishing Company
Quicksilver Productions
RavenHaus Publishing
R-Squared Press
Running Press
Sasquatch Books
Sasquatch Books
SHORTRUNS
Sibyl Publications, Inc
SPROUTLETTER
Square One Publishers, Inc.
Storm Publishing Group
Strawberry Patchworks
Titus Home Publishing
Tyr Publishing
University of South Carolina Press
VEGETARIAN JOURNAL
The Vegetarian Resource Group
VINEGAR CONNOISSEURS INTERNATIONAL NEWS-
LETTER
Wave Publishing
Whispering Pine Press
THE WILD FOODS FORUM
WISCONSIN TRAILS
Writers' Haven Press

CO-OPS

Carousel Press
Hobar Publications, A Division of Finney Company
Life Media
Macrocosm USA, Inc.
READERS SPEAK OUT!

COSMOLOGY

BUSINESS SPIRIT JOURNAL
Dawn Publications
EcceNova Editions
Fontanel Books
Granite Publishing Group
Tyr Publishing

COUNTER-CULTURE, ALTERNATIVES, COM-
MUNES

ABRAMELIN: a Journal of Poetry and Magick
AFFABLE NEIGHBOR
Affable Neighbor Press
ALL ROUND
ALTERNATIVE PRESS REVIEW
THE AMERICAN DISSIDENT
ARTISTAMP NEWS
ASCENT
Bad Press
Bear & Company
BLACKBOOK PRESS, THE POETRY ZINE
THE BOOMERPHILE
BOTH SIDES NOW
Breakout Productions
BROKEN PENCIL
THE CAIMAN (formerly THE WEIRD NEWS)
Cantarabooks LLC
Carpe Diem Publishing
Carrier Pigeon Press
Cassandra Press, Inc.
THE CHEROTIC (r)EVOLUTIONARY
CHILDREN, CHURCHES AND DADDIES, A Non
Religious, Non Familial Literary Magazine
COMMUNITIES
COUNTER CULTURE
COUNTERPOISE: For Social Responsibilities, Liberty and
Dissent
CRONE CHRONICLES: A Journal of Conscious Aging
Crystal Clarity, Publishers
The Denali Press
DOWN IN THE DIRT LITERARY MAGAZINE, the prose
& poetry magazine revealing all your dirty little secrets

Down There Press
DWELLING PORTABLY
The Edwin Mellen Press
FIRST CLASS
Four-Sep Publications
FREEDOM AND STRENGTH PRESS FORUM
Granite Publishing Group
GRAY AREAS
THE GROWING EDGE MAGAZINE
Higganum Hill Books
INDY MAGAZINE
INTERNATIONAL ART POST
Leyland Publications
THE (LIBERTARIAN) CONNECTION
LIBRARIANS AT LIBERTY
LIGHTWORKS MAGAZINE
LULLWATER REVIEW
Macrocosm USA, Inc.
MAGICAL BLEND/NATURAL BEAUTY & HEALTH/
TRANSITIONS
Mandala Publishing
MB Media, Inc.
MEAT: A Journal of Writing and Materiality
MeteoritePress.com
NEW ENVIRONMENT BULLETIN
NEWWITCH
THE OTHER ISRAEL
OUT YOUR BACKDOOR: The Magazine of Do-It-
Yourself Adventure and Homegrown Culture
Outrider Press
Paladin Enterprises, Inc.
Passing Through Publications
PATTERNS OF CHOICE: A Journal of People, Land, and
Money
PEACEWORK
Penthe Publishing
PIG IRON
Pottersfield Press
Progressive Education
PROGRESSIVE PERIODICALS DIRECTORY/UPDATE
READERS SPEAK OUT!
Really Great Books
Red Eye Press
RFD
ROCTOBER COMICS AND MUSIC
Santa Fe Writers Project
Scars Publications
SCIENCE & SOCIETY
SCIENCE/HEALTH ABSTRACTS
Semiotext Foreign Agents Books Series
SEMIOTEXT(E)
SHORT FUSE
SKINNYDIPPING
SOCIAL ANARCHISM: A Journal of Practice and Theory
A SOFT DEGRADE
Soft Skull Press
SPROUTLETTER
STORMWARNING!
Swan Raven & Company
Syracuse Cultural Workers/Tools for Change
TOUCHSTONE
Touchstone Adventures
Transcending Mundane, Inc.
TRAVEL NATURALLY
Van Cleave Publishing
Vision
Wild West Publishing House
ZINE WORLD: A Reader's Guide to the Underground Press

CRAFTS, HOBBIES

Affinity Publishers Services
Allworth Press
Altamont Press, Inc.
Ancient City Press
ART CALENDAR
ARTELLA: the waltz of words and art
Backbeat Press
Backcountry Publishing

BAGAZINE
The Bess Press
BRIDAL CRAFTS
Bright Ring Publishing, Inc.
BUTTON
C & T Publishing
Camp Colton
Cattpigg Press
Center For Self-Sufficiency
CHESS LIFE
Chicago Review Press
Cottontail Publications
Council For Indian Education
CRAFTS 'N THINGS
THE CROSS STITCHER
DOLLS UNITED INTERACTIVE MAGAZINE
Downeast Books
DWELLING PORTABLY
Eagle's View Publishing
ETC Publications
FIBERARTS
THE FRONT STRIKER BULLETIN
GemStone Press
Global Sports Productions, Ltd.
Guarionex Press Ltd.
Hands & Heart Books
HandyCraft Media Productions
Hobar Publications, A Division of Finney Company
Hunter Publishing, Co.
Ibexa Press
INGLESIDE NEWS ZINE
INKY TRAIL NEWS
THE JOURNAL OF DESIGN AND TECHNOLOGY
    EDUCATION
JUNIOR STORYTELLER
THE KIDS' STORYTELLING CLUB WEBSITE
Life Lessons
LifeCircle Press
Little Leaf Press
MGW (Mom Guess What) Newsmagazine
Midmarch Arts Press
MIDWEST ART FAIRS
Miles & Miles
Naturegraph Publishers
N-B-T-V
New Win Publishing
NightinGale Resources
No Starch Press
Oak Knoll Press
ORNAMENT
OUT YOUR BACKDOOR: The Magazine of Do-It-
    Yourself Adventure and Homegrown Culture
PACK-O-FUN
PAINTING
Pebble Press, Inc.
Pendant Publishing Inc.
Petroglyph Press, Ltd.
THE PRESIDENTS' JOURNAL
Profile Press
Putting Up Books, LC
Rolling Hills Publishing
Scentouri, Publishing Division
THE $ENSIBLE SOUND
Shangri-La Publications
SHORTRUNS
Sierra Outdoor Products Co.
Square One Publishers, Inc.
Storycraft Publishing
Storytime Ink International
Success Publishing
Sun Designs
Sunstone Press
Sylvan Books
Tamal Vista Publications
Thatch Tree Publications
Thirteen Colonies Press
TIFARA
TIMBER TIMES

Tomart Publications
TRADITION MAGAZINE
UNITED LUMBEE NATION TIMES
Venus Communications
VINEGAR CONNOISSEURS INTERNATIONAL NEWS-
    LETTER
John Wade, Publisher
Wayside Publications
WHISPERING WIND MAGAZINE
Windstorm Creative
WOODWORKER'S JOURNAL
YE OLDE NEWES

CREATIVITY

AFFABLE NEIGHBOR
Affable Neighbor Press
Americans for the Arts
ARTELLA: the waltz of words and art
ARTISTIC RAMBLINGS
Athanata Arts, Ltd.
Bellywater Press
BUSINESS SPIRIT JOURNAL
THE CANNON'S MOUTH
Carpe Diem Publishing
COOKING CONTEST CHRONICLE
CREATIVITY CONNECTION
Crescent Moon
CRONE CHRONICLES: A Journal of Conscious Aging
DOLLS UNITED INTERACTIVE MAGAZINE
ECOTONE: Reimagining Place
Firelight Publishing, Inc.
Granite Publishing Group
Green Hut Press
Hanover Press
The Heather Foundation
Herrmann International
INDUSTRY MINNE-ZINE
Innisfree Press
IRIS: A Journal About Women
JOURNAL OF AESTHETICS AND ART CRITICISM
LAKE STREET LIT: Art and Words from the Bottom of
    Lake Bonneville
Lamp Light Press
LifeCircle Press
LIGHTWORKS MAGAZINE
LULLABY HEARSE
LULLWATER REVIEW
Luminous Epinoia Press
MB Media, Inc.
METAL CURSE
Mind Power Publishing
THE NEO-COMINTERN
New World Library
Oyster River Press
PARADIDOMI
PASSAGER
PASSAGES NORTH
PASSION
Pearl's Book'em Publisher
Platinum One Publishing
THE QUIET FEATHER
Reach Productions Publishing
Red Tiger Press
Re-invention UK Ltd
Savant Garde Workshop
Scrivenery Press
SHORT FUSE
SO TO SPEAK: A Feminist Journal of Language & Art
A SOFT DEGRADE
Soul
SP QUILL QUARTERLY MAGAZINE
Spirit Press
Spiritual Understanding Network, LLC
Stony Meadow Publishing
Touchstone Adventures
Verve Press
Word Forge Books
Wordwrights Canada

WRITER'S CAROUSEL
WRITER'S EXCHANGE

CRIME

Addicus Books, Inc.
BIG HAMMER
Bleak House Books, an imprint of Diversity Incorporated
Breakout Productions
CIRCLE INC., THE MAGAZINE
Circle of Friends Books
COALITION FOR PRISONERS' RIGHTS NEWSLETTER
CORRECTIONS TODAY
Creative Arts Book Company
CRIMINAL JUSTICE ABSTRACTS
Criminal Justice Press
Dash-Hill, LLC
The Dragon Press
FMA Publishing
Fountainhead Productions, Inc.
FULLOSIA PRESS
Global Options
Gorilla Convict Publications
GRASSLIMB
GRAY AREAS
Gryphon Books
HARDBOILED
Holbrook Street Press
Iniquity Press/Vendetta Books
Macrocosm USA, Inc.
MYSTERY ISLAND MAGAZINE
THE MYSTERY REVIEW
North Country Books, Inc.
Over the Wall Inc. Publishing & Productions
Paladin Enterprises, Inc.
PAPERBACK PARADE
Polar Bear & Company
Primal Publishing
PRISON LEGAL NEWS
Radiant Press
Really Great Books
SHEMP! The Lowlife Culture Magazine
SISTERS IN CRIME BOOKS IN PRINT
SOCIAL JUSTICE: A JOURNAL OF CRIME, CONFLICT, & WORLD ORDER
Southern Illinois University Press
Spinifex Press
Starbooks Press/FLF Press
STORMWARNING!
Sun Rising Press
TOUCHSTONE
Triumvirate Publications
Voyageur Publishing Co.,Inc.
Willow Tree Press, Inc.

CRITICISM

ABRAXAS
AFRICAN AMERICAN REVIEW
AFTERIMAGE
ALABAMA LITERARY REVIEW
American Canadian Publishers, Inc.
THE ANTIGONISH REVIEW
Arjuna Library Press
ASSEMBLAGE: A Critical Journal of Architecture and Design Culture
Autonomedia, Inc.
Barrytown/Station Hill Press
Bay Press
BIBLIOTHEQUE D'HUMANISME ET RENAISSANCE
Bilingual Review Press
BIRD DOG
BOOK/MARK SMALL PRESS REVIEW
BORDERLANDS: Texas Poetry Review
Borealis Press Limited
BOULEVARD
CANADIAN CHILDREN'S LITERATURE
CANADIAN LITERATURE
THE CANNON'S MOUTH
Center for Japanese Studies

CINEASTE MAGAZINE
Clamshell Press
COUNTERPOISE: For Social Responsibilities, Liberty and Dissent
Crescent Moon
CROSSCURRENTS
THE DALHOUSIE REVIEW
THE DALHOUSIE REVIEW
Department of Romance Languages
DESCANT
DESIRE
THE DIRTY GOAT
THE DROOD REVIEW OF MYSTERY
Edgewise Press
88: A Journal of Contemporary American Poetry
Elderberry Press, LLC
ELT Press
Encounter Books
ENGLISH LITERATURE IN TRANSITION, 1880-1920
FEMINIST STUDIES
FIGHT THESE BASTARDS
Fine Tooth Press
FREEFALL
From Here Press
FUGUE
Galaxy Press
THE GEORGIA REVIEW
Gothic Press
Graywolf Press
GREEN MOUNTAINS REVIEW
Hippopotamus Press
HOME PLANET NEWS
Host Publications, Inc.
INGLESIDE NEWS ZINE
Interalia/Design Books
THE INTERNATIONAL FICTION REVIEW
THE IOWA REVIEW
IRISH LITERARY SUPPLEMENT
Ironweed Press
Jako Books
JAMES JOYCE BROADSHEET
JOURNAL OF AESTHETICS AND ART CRITICISM
JOURNAL OF CANADIAN POETRY
JOURNAL OF NARRATIVE THEORY
JOURNAL OF REGIONAL CRITICISM
KALDRON, An International Journal Of Visual Poetry
KALEIDOSCOPE: Exploring the Experience of Disability through Literature & the Fine Arts
THE KENYON REVIEW
LAKE EFFECT
LEFT CURVE
Life Untangled Publishing
LIFTOUTS
Limelight Editions
LINQ
LITERARY IMAGINATION: The Review of the Association of Literary Scholars and Critics
LITERARY MAGAZINE REVIEW
LOGIC LETTER
Lord John Press
LUMMOX JOURNAL
Lummox Press
MAGNET MAGAZINE
Maisonneuve Press
McPherson & Company Publishers
MEAT: A Journal of Writing and Materiality
Menard Press
METAL CURSE
MID-AMERICAN REVIEW
THE MIDWEST QUARTERLY
Miles & Miles
MUDLARK
Myriad Press
NEROUP REVIEW
NEW AMERICAN IMAGIST
THE NEW ENGLAND QUARTERLY
New Falcon Publications
NEW GERMAN REVIEW: A Journal of Germanic Studies

THE NEW RENAISSANCE, an international magazine of ideas & opinions, emphasizing literature & the arts
NORTH DAKOTA QUARTERLY
North Stone Editions
NOVA EXPRESS
ONE TRICK PONY
OUTER-ART
OUTPOSTS POETRY QUARTERLY
Oyez
Passeggiata Press, Inc.
PASSION
PIG IRON
PIKEVILLE REVIEW
PLOUGHSHARES
POETRY FLASH
THE POETRY MISCELLANY
THE POWYS JOURNAL
THE PRAIRIE JOURNAL OF CANADIAN LITERATURE
Prairie Journal Press
Press Here
PSYCHE
PSYCHOANALYTIC BOOKS: A QUARTERLY JOURNAL OF REVIEWS
Pyncheon House
Quale Press
QUARTER AFTER EIGHT
Quarterly Committee of Queen's University
QUEEN'S QUARTERLY: A Canadian Review
RARITAN: A Quarterly Review
RATTAPALLAX
REPRESENTATIONS
Ronsdale Press
Rowhouse Press
The Runaway Spoon Press
Sage Hill Press
ST. CROIX REVIEW
ST. LOUIS JOURNALISM REVIEW
SALMAGUNDI
SCIENCE & SOCIETY
SCRIVENER
Semiotext Foreign Agents Books Series
SEMIOTEXT(E)
SENECA REVIEW
SEWANEE REVIEW
THE SHAKESPEARE NEWSLETTER
SHORT FUSE
Sligo Press
SOLO
SOUTH DAKOTA REVIEW
SOUTHERN HUMANITIES REVIEW
THE SOUTHERN QUARTERLY: A Journal of the Arts in the South
Spectrum Press
SPILLWAY
State University of New York Press
STORMWARNING!
Strata Publishing, Inc.
Sherwood Sugden & Company, Publishers
SYMPLOKE: A Journal for the Intermingling of Literary, Cultural and Theoretical Scholarship
Talisman House, Publishers
TEARS IN THE FENCE
TELOS
Telos Press
THALIA: Studies in Literary Humor
13TH MOON
THE THREEPENNY REVIEW
TORRE DE PAPEL
TUNDRA
Turnstone Press
UND Press
UNDERSTANDING MAGAZINE
University of Arkansas Press
University of Chicago Press
University of Massachusetts Press
University of Tampa Press
Vanderbilt University Press
The Vertin Press

Vesta Publications Limited
Via Dolorosa Press
THE WALLACE STEVENS JOURNAL
WALT WHITMAN QUARTERLY REVIEW
WEST COAST LINE: A Journal of Contemporary Writing and Criticism
WILLOW SPRINGS
THE WORCESTER REVIEW
Wordwrights Canada
WORLD OF FANDOM MAGAZINE
WRITER'S CHRONICLE
WSQ (formerly WOMEN'S STUDIES QUARTERLY)
THE YALE REVIEW
ZAWP
Zoo Press
ZUZU'S PETALS: QUARTERLY ONLINE

CRYSTALS

ELEMENTS
Granite Publishing Group
Spirit Press
Sun Rising Press
Three Pyramids Publishing

CUBA

ASIA FILE
FIREBREEZE PUBLISHING
Martinez Press
Pangaea
Pathfinder Press
PORTLAND REVIEW
Smyrna Press
SOCIETE
TOUCHSTONE
World Music Press

CULTS

AFFABLE NEIGHBOR
Affable Neighbor Press
THE AFFILIATE
BLACKBOOK PRESS, THE POETRY ZINE
BOULDER HERETIC
Carrier Pigeon Press
firefall editions
MYSTERY ISLAND MAGAZINE
Mystery Island Publications
OFFICE NUMBER ONE
SOCIETE
Sun Rising Press
White Cliffs Media, Inc.
White Crosslet Publishing Co

CULTURE

AERIAL
AFFABLE NEIGHBOR
Affable Neighbor Press
AFTERIMAGE
Alaska Native Language Center
Americans for the Arts
ARC
Archer Books
Ariko Publications
ART CALENDAR
ARTS & LETTERS: Journal of Contemporary Culture
ASSEMBLAGE: A Critical Journal of Architecture and Design Culture
Autonomedia, Inc.
Balcony Media, Inc.
Bandanna Books
Bay Press
Bellywater Press
Between The Lines
Birch Brook Press
BIRD DOG
Black Lawrence Press
BLUE COLLAR REVIEW
BOOK/MARK SMALL PRESS REVIEW
THE BOOMERPHILE

Borealis Press Limited
BRIDGES: An Interdisciplinary Journal of Theology, Philosophy, History, and Science
BROKEN PENCIL
Chandler & Sharp Publishers, Inc.
THE CHARIOTEER
THE CHEROTIC (r)EVOLUTIONARY
CHILDREN, CHURCHES AND DADDIES, A Non Religious, Non Familial Literary Magazine
COLORLINES
CONTEXTS: UNDERSTANDING PEOPLE IN THEIR SOCIAL WORLDS
CORONA
Coteau Books
Crescent Moon
CRONE CHRONICLES: A Journal of Conscious Aging
CULTUREFRONT
Culturelink Press
Dawn Sign Press
DESCANT
DESIRE
THE DIRTY GOAT
DOWN IN THE DIRT LITERARY MAGAZINE, the prose & poetry magazine revealing all your dirty little secrets
Down There Press
Dumouriez Publishing
East West Discovery Press
ECOTONE: Reimagining Place
Encounter Books
Everflowing Publications
FACES: People, Places, and Culture
Falls Media
Five Fingers Press
FIVE FINGERS REVIEW
Four Walls Eight Windows
FRAN MAGAZINE
FREEDOM AND STRENGTH PRESS FORUM
FULLOSIA PRESS
GASTRONOMICA: The Journal of Food and Culture
THE GEORGIA REVIEW
GIRLFRIENDS MAGAZINE
GREEN ANARCHY
GREEN MOUNTAINS REVIEW
Heartsong Books
HISTORY OF INTELLECTUAL CULTURE
Hope Publishing House
Host Publications, Inc.
HURRICANE ALICE
Ika, LLC
THE INDIE
Iniquity Press/Vendetta Books
INKY TRAIL NEWS
Intercultural Press, Inc.
INTERCULTURE
Interlink Publishing Group, Inc.
Jako Books
JOURNAL OF AESTHETICS AND ART CRITICISM
KALDRON, An International Journal Of Visual Poetry
THE KENYON REVIEW
Kivaki Press
KMT, A Modern Journal of Ancient Egypt
Kodiak Media Group
La Alameda Press
LAKE STREET LIT: Art and Words from the Bottom of Lake Bonneville
LAKE SUPERIOR MAGAZINE
The Leaping Frog Press
LEFT CURVE
LifeCircle Press
LO STRANIERO: The Stranger, Der Fremde, L'Etranger
LPD Press
LULLWATER REVIEW
Macrocosm USA, Inc.
Mandala Publishing
Margaret Media, Inc.
MEDIA SPOTLIGHT
Mehring Books, Inc.
Mercer University Press

Middleway Press
Mountainside Press
Myriad Press
THE NEW ENGLAND QUARTERLY
NEWS FROM NATIVE CALIFORNIA
NightinGale Resources
NORTH DAKOTA QUARTERLY
Northland Publishing/Rising Moon/Luna Rising
NOVA RELIGIO
Origin Press
OUT YOUR BACKDOOR: The Magazine of Do-It-Yourself Adventure and Homegrown Culture
PAGAN AMERICA
Palladium Communications
The Pamphleteer's Press
Partisan Press
PASSION
Pearl's Book'em Publisher
Phony Lid Publications
PICK POCKET BOOKS
PIG IRON
PIG IRON
PLAIN BROWN WRAPPER (PBW)
Pleasure Boat Studio: A Literary Press
Pogo Press, Incorporated
POINT OF CONTACT, The Journal of Verbal & Visual Arts
POTOMAC REVIEW
THE PRESSED PRESS
Royal Purcell, Publisher
Quantum Leap S.L.C. Publications
QUARTER AFTER EIGHT
RELIGION & AMERICAN CULTURE
REPRESENTATIONS
THE RIVER REVIEW/LA REVUE RIVIERE
RIVET MAGAZINE
Rock Spring Press Inc.
ST. CROIX REVIEW
SALMAGUNDI
Santa Monica Press
Scars Publications
SCIENCE & SOCIETY
Semiotext Foreign Agents Books Series
SEMIOTEXT(E)
Sentient Publications, LLC
Small Helm Press
Snake Hill Press
Soft Skull Press
Soul
Speck Press
Spire Press
Stardate Publishing Company
State University of New York Press
Sun Rising Press
SYMPLOKE: A Journal for the Intermingling of Literary, Cultural and Theoretical Scholarship
THE TABBY: A CHRONICLE OF THE ARTS AND CRAFTS MOVEMENT
Telos Press
TOUCHSTONE
Touchstone Adventures
TRADITION MAGAZINE
Two Eagles Press International
UND Press
UNDER THE VOLCANO
UTNE READER
VARIOUS ARTISTS
Venus Communications
THE VIRGINIA QUARTERLY REVIEW
Vision
THE WALLACE STEVENS JOURNAL
Whelks Walk Press
WHISPERING WIND MAGAZINE
Wild West Publishing House
WISCONSIN ACADEMY REVIEW
XCP: CROSS-CULTURAL POETICS
Zephyr Press
ZUZU'S PETALS: QUARTERLY ONLINE

650

CURRENT AFFAIRS

Archer Books
Bancroft Press
Black Lawrence Press
Bluestocking Press
Bonus Books, Inc.
BOOK/MARK SMALL PRESS REVIEW
Caribbean Books-Panama
Clarity Press, Inc.
CONSCIENCE: The Newsjournal of Catholic Opinion
Crandall, Dostie & Douglass Books, Inc.
Culturelink Press
THE EDGE CITY REVIEW
Encounter Books
EXPERIMENTAL FOREST
The Foundation for Economic Education, Inc.
THE FREEMAN: Ideas On Liberty
GREEN ANARCHY
Ho Logos Press
IN OUR OWN WORDS
Jako Books
NAMBLA BULLETIN
National Writers Press
THE NEW RENAISSANCE, an international magazine of
    ideas & opinions, emphasizing literature & the arts
NEW VERSE NEWS, THE
Nonetheless Press
The Pamphleeter's Press
Pathfinder Press
THE QUIET FEATHER
READERS SPEAK OUT!
ST. LOUIS JOURNALISM REVIEW
Sentient Publications, LLC
Set Sail Productions, LLC
STORMWARNING!
TELOS
TOUCHSTONE
UNDER THE VOLCANO
University of Massachusetts Press
UTNE READER
THE VIRGINIA QUARTERLY REVIEW
Vision
Visions Communications
Wild West Publishing House

DADA

AD/VANCE
AFFABLE NEIGHBOR
Affable Neighbor Press
AK Press
American Canadian Publishers, Inc.
THE AMERICAN DRIVEL REVIEW
Androgyne Books
Arjuna Library Press
Asylum Arts
BANANA RAG
Black Oak Press
BLADES
BLUE HORSE
Blue Horse Publications
BUST DOWN THE DOOR AND EAT ALL THE
    CHICKENS: A Journal of Absurd and Surreal Fiction
THE CHEROTIC (r)EVOLUTIONARY
CHILDREN, CHURCHES AND DADDIES, A Non
    Religious, Non Familial Literary Magazine
THE DIRTY GOAT
EXPERIMENTAL FOREST
FAT TUESDAY
FINE MADNESS
THE FRANK REVIEW
FREEFALL
FROZEN WAFFLES
Frozen Waffles Press/Shattered Sidewalks Press; 45th
    Century Chapbooks
HEELTAP/Pariah Press
Host Publications, Inc.
Iniquity Press/Vendetta Books

JACK MACKEREL MAGAZINE
JOURNAL OF AESTHETICS AND ART CRITICISM
JOURNAL OF REGIONAL CRITICISM
KALDRON, An International Journal Of Visual Poetry
LIGHTWORKS MAGAZINE
LOST GENERATION JOURNAL
Luna Bisonte Prods
Lunar Offensive Publications
THE NEO-COMINTERN
NEROUP REVIEW
NEW MUSE OF CONTEMPT
North Stone Editions
Pariah Press
Pathwise Press
PAVEMENT SAW
Pavement Saw Press
PERIPHERAL VISION
Phrygian Press
PIG IRON
Pig Iron Press
PLAIN BROWN WRAPPER (PBW)
Red Hand Press
Rowhouse Press
SAKANA
Savant Garde Workshop
Shangri-La Publications
SHATTERED WIG REVIEW
SHORT FUSE
Twisted Spoon Press
UNWOUND
Urban Legend Press
THE URBANITE
The Vertin Press
Water Mark Press
White Crosslet Publishing Co
ZYX

DANCE

AFRICAN AMERICAN REVIEW
Amherst Writers & Artists Press, Inc.
ARTSLINK
Backbeat Press
Emrys Press
Everflowing Publications
Ibexa Press
IMAGE: ART, FAITH, MYSTERY
INGLESIDE NEWS ZINE
JACK MACKEREL MAGAZINE
Life Energy Media
Limelight Editions
LITURGICAL CATECHESIS
MINISTRY & LITURGY
Princeton Book Company, Publishers
Purple Finch Press
Resource Publications, Inc.
Rowhouse Press
SALMAGUNDI
THE SOUTHERN QUARTERLY: A Journal of the Arts in
    the South
THEATRE DESIGN AND TECHNOLOGY
Thirteen Colonies Press
TRADITION MAGAZINE
The Vertin Press
World Music Press

DANISH

ABSINTHE: New European Writing
Blue Dolphin Publishing, Inc.
Toad Press International Chapbook Series
TRANSITIONS ABROAD: The Guide to Living, Learning,
    and Working Overseas

DESIGN

Aegean Publishing Company
Allworth Press
APOSTROPHE: USCB Journal of the Arts
ART CALENDAR
ASSEMBLAGE: A Critical Journal of Architecture and

Design Culture
Athanata Arts, Ltd.
Balcony Media, Inc.
Banana Productions
Bellywater Press
Brenner Information Group
Ceres Press
DeerTrail Books
DOLLS UNITED INTERACTIVE MAGAZINE
ENVIRONMENTAL & ARCHITECTURAL PHENOMEN-
   OLOGY NEWSLETTER
GemStone Press
Ibexa Press
INDUSTRY MINNE-ZINE
Interalia/Design Books
KALDRON, An International Journal Of Visual Poetry
OUT YOUR BACKDOOR: The Magazine of Do-It-
   Yourself Adventure and Homegrown Culture
The Overlook Press
PIG IRON
Poltroon Press
SCULPTURAL PURSUIT MAGAZINE
A SOFT DEGRADE
Stemmer House Publishers, Inc.
Stone Bridge Press
Sun Designs
Tuns Press
WATERFRONT WORLD SPOTLIGHT
ZONE

DESKTOP PUBLISHING

Allworth Press
Chicago Spectrum Press
CKO UPDATE
THE GREAT BLUE BEACON
INTERLIT
Redgreene Press
WRITERS' JOURNAL

DIARIES

Burd Street Press
Burning Bush Publications
Cold-Drill Books
FREEFALL
Impassio Press
In Between Books
KESTREL: A Journal of Literature and Art
LEO Productions LLC.
Magic Circle Press
THE ORPHAN LEAF REVIEW
OVERLAND JOURNAL
PLAIN BROWN WRAPPER (PBW)

CHARLES DICKENS

Whitston Publishing Co.

JAMES DICKEY

JAMES DICKEY NEWSLETTER

EMILY DICKINSON

BIBLIOPHILOS
THE CENTENNIAL REVIEW
Chatterley Press International
Crescent Moon
PASSION
Whitston Publishing Co.

DICTIONARIES

The Bess Press
Celo Valley Books
CHECKER CAB MAGAZINE - THE LITTLE 'ZINE
   THAT COULD! Fiction That Takes The Long Way
   Home
The Chinese University Press
Maledicta Press
Malki Museum Press
Minnesota Historical Society Press
Rodnik Publishing Co.

Stony Meadow Publishing
Sunbelt Publications
Velazquez Press

DINING, RESTAURANTS

The Bess Press
Callawind Publications / Custom Cookbooks / Children's
   Books
GULF & MAIN Southwest Florida Lifestyle
The Intrepid Traveler
Lazywood Press
MY TABLE: Houston's Dining Magazine
N-B-T-V
NIGHTLIFE MAGAZINE
NOLA-MAGICK Press
Red Rock Press
VACATION PLACE RENTALS
Vehicule Press

DISABLED

Alpine Guild, Inc.
Azreal Publishing Company
BIG HAMMER
Brookline Books
Common Courage Press
Future Horizons, Inc.
The Haworth Press
THE INCLUSION NOTEBOOK
KALEIDOSCOPE: Exploring the Experience of Disability
   through Literature & the Fine Arts
Kodiak Media Group
Lucky Press, LLC
Massey-Reyner Publishing
Mho & Mho Works
MOUTH: Voice of the Dis-Labeled Nation
Pennycorner Press
The Place In The Woods
Re-invention UK Ltd
The Saunderstown Press
TRANSITIONS ABROAD: The Guide to Living, Learning,
   and Working Overseas
Vestibular Disorders Association
Woodbine House

DISEASE

BELLEVUE LITERARY REVIEW
Carolina Wren Press/Lollipop Power Books
THE COMPLEAT NURSE
Flowerfield Enterprises, LLC
Kali Press
MEDICAL HISTORY
MOUTH: Voice of the Dis-Labeled Nation
OPEN MINDS QUARTERLY
SPROUTLETTER
Vestibular Disorders Association
Wellcome Institute for the History of Medicine

DISNEY

BearManor Media
CELLAR
THE DUCKBURG TIMES
HEROES FROM HACKLAND
The Intrepid Traveler
Tomart Publications
WORLD OF FANDOM MAGAZINE

DIVORCE

Galt Press
Hunter House Inc., Publishers
Impact Publishers, Inc.
J&W Publishers, Inc.
Jalmar Press/Innerchoice Publishing
THE LIBERATOR
MCM Entertainment, Inc. Publishing Division
Mo'omana'o Press
Nolo Press Occidental
Platinum One Publishing
River Press

DRAMA

Admiral House Publishing
ALASKA QUARTERLY REVIEW
THE ALEMBIC
THE ALLEGHENY REVIEW
ANQ: A Quarterly Journal of Short Articles, Notes, and Reviews
APOSTROPHE: USCB Journal of the Arts
Arjuna Library Press
Arte Publico Press
ARTS & LETTERS: Journal of Contemporary Culture
ARTSLINK
Asylum Arts
Athanata Arts, Ltd.
Azreal Publishing Company
The B & R Samizdat Express
Walter H. Baker Company (Baker's Plays)
Bandanna Books
BATHTUB GIN
Bilingual Review Press
Black Dress Press
BOMB MAGAZINE
Borealis Press Limited
Branden Books
C & M Online Media Inc.
Cavalier Press
Cottonwood Press, Inc.
Dablond Publishing
Dawn Sign Press
DESCANT
DIALOGOS: Hellenic Studies Review
THE DIRTY GOAT
Dramaline Publications
Empire Publishing Service
ENGLISH LITERATURE IN TRANSITION, 1880-1920
THE EUGENE O'NEILL REVIEW
EVANSVILLE REVIEW
Everflowing Publications
Fall Creek Press
The Fiction Works
Fouque Publishers
Gallopade International
GRAIN MAGAZINE
HARVARD REVIEW
Host Publications, Inc.
IRISH LITERARY SUPPLEMENT
JOURNAL OF AESTHETICS AND ART CRITICISM
KAJ-MAHKAH: EARTH OF EARTH
THE KENYON REVIEW
Labor Arts Books
Left Hand Books
LEO Productions LLC.
LICHEN Arts & Letters Preview
LINQ
LITURGICAL CATECHESIS
THE LOUISIANA REVIEW
Marathon International Book Company
MCM Entertainment, Inc. Publishing Division
Mellen Poetry Press
Midmarch Arts Press
MINISTRY & LITURGY
New Concept Press
New Sins Press
Nightsun Books
Northwestern University Press
NWI National Writers Institute
OBSIDIAN III: Literature in the African Diaspora
THE PACIFIC REVIEW
Parthian
Passeggiata Press, Inc.
Phi-Psi Publishers
Platinum One Publishing
Players Press, Inc.
POEMS & PLAYS
POTOMAC REVIEW
PRISM INTERNATIONAL
PublishAmerica, LLLP.

Questex Consulting Ltd.
RAMBUNCTIOUS REVIEW
Red Dust
RED WHEELBARROW
Resource Publications, Inc.
Ridgeway Press of Michigan
THE ROCKFORD REVIEW
Ronsdale Press
The Runaway Spoon Press
St. Andrews College Press
Saskatchewan Writers Guild
Savant Garde Workshop
THE SHAKESPEARE NEWSLETTER
SKYLARK
Smyrna Press
SOJOURN: A Journal of the Arts
THE SOUTHERN QUARTERLY: A Journal of the Arts in the South
Spectrum Productions
SPINNING JENNY
STRUGGLE: A Magazine of Proletarian Revolutionary Literature
SYCAMORE REVIEW
Synergetic Press
Syukhtun Editions
Ten Penny Players, Inc.
THEATER
THEATRE DESIGN AND TECHNOLOGY
TnT Classic Books
University of Tampa Press
Vesta Publications Limited
White Crosslet Publishing Co
WordWorkers Press
Xenos Books
Zoo Press

DREAMS

AE-TU Publishing
Asylum Arts
BRANCHES
CLARA VENUS
CRONE CHRONICLES: A Journal of Conscious Aging
DREAM FANTASY INTERNATIONAL
DREAM NETWORK
Iconoclast Press
In Between Books
Iniquity Press/Vendetta Books
Innisfree Press
Lao Tse Press, Ltd.
The Leaping Frog Press
Luminous Epinoia Press
Lunar Offensive Publications
MAGICAL BLEND/NATURAL BEAUTY & HEALTH/ TRANSITIONS
METAL CURSE
The Midknight Club
Perrin Press
Philopsychy Press
PLAIN BROWN WRAPPER (PBW)
RALPH'S REVIEW
RED OWL
SAKANA
SHAMAN'S DRUM: A Journal of Experiential Shamanism
SHORT FUSE
A SOFT DEGRADE
SOM Publishing, division of School of Metaphysics
Spiritual Understanding Network, LLC
Tendre Press
Three Pyramids Publishing
THRESHOLDS JOURNAL
UNWOUND
Venus Communications
ZINE-ON-A-TAPE
Zumaya Publications

DRUGS

Addicus Books, Inc.
AFFABLE NEIGHBOR

Affable Neighbor Press
THE AFFILIATE
Alegra House Publishers
BIG HAMMER
Consumer Press
Devil Mountain Books
DOPE FRIENDS
Fountainhead Productions, Inc.
FRAN MAGAZINE
GAMBARA MAGAZINE
Global Options
GRAY AREAS
Haight-Ashbury Publications
Health Press
Iniquity Press/Vendetta Books
INTERNATIONAL ADDICTION
Jalmar Press/Innerchoice Publishing
JOURNAL OF PSYCHOACTIVE DRUGS
METAL CURSE
Mountain Media
New Moon Publishing, Inc.
Over the Wall Inc. Publishing & Productions
Paladin Enterprises, Inc.
Phony Lid Publications
PICK POCKET BOOKS
Red Alder Books
Red Eye Press
SCIENCE/HEALTH ABSTRACTS
SOCIAL JUSTICE: A JOURNAL OF CRIME, CONFLICT,
    & WORLD ORDER
Steel Balls Press
UNWOUND
Van Cleave Publishing

BOB DYLAN

AMERICAN JONES BUILDING & MAINTENANCE
Casperian Books LLC
EXPERIMENTAL FOREST
GRAY AREAS
Limelight Editions
MAGICAL BLEND/NATURAL BEAUTY & HEALTH/
    TRANSITIONS

EARTH, NATURAL HISTORY

ADIRONDAC
Adirondack Mountain Club, Inc.
Alaska Geographic Society
Alaska Northwest Books
Alpine Publications, Inc.
America West Publishers
AMERICAN FORESTS
AMERICAN HIKER
American Hiking Society
APPALACHIA JOURNAL
Appalachian Mountain Club Books
AQUATERRA, METAECOLOGY & CULTURE
Beacon Press
Birdsong Books
Black Dome Press Corp.
Bliss Publishing Company, Inc.
THE BLOOMSBURY REVIEW
THE BOOKWATCH
Camino Bay Books
Caribbean Books-Panama
Chelsea Green Publishing Company
Clover Park Press
Dawn Publications
Dimi Press
Downeast Books
ETC Publications
EXIT 13 MAGAZINE
EZ Nature Books
Flowerfield Enterprises, LLC
Fulcrum, Inc.
Gibbs Smith, Publisher
Great Elm Press
GREEN ANARCHY
Heartsong Books

Heyday Books
Island Press
JetKor
Laguna Wilderness Press
The Latona Press
Light, Words & Music
Maisonneuve Press
Malki Museum Press
MANOA: A Pacific Journal of International Writing
Mayhaven Publishing
Milkweed Editions
Mountain Press Publishing Co.
The Mountaineers Books
The Narrative Press
Native West Press
NATURE SOCIETY NEWS
Naturegraph Publishers
THE NAUTILUS
NEROUP REVIEW
Northland Publishing/Rising Moon/Luna Rising
Oregon State University Press
Pangaea
Penthe Publishing
Philopsychy Press
Quarterly Committee of Queen's University
QUEEN'S QUARTERLY: A Canadian Review
RFF Press / Resources for the Future
Ridge Times Press
Rio Nuevo Publishers
THE RIVER REVIEW/LA REVUE RIVIERE
Rock Spring Press Inc.
Sand River Press
Sasquatch Books
Scientia Publishing, LLC
Sea Challengers, Inc.
Genny Smith Books
SNOWY EGRET
SOUTH AMERICAN EXPLORER
Stemmer House Publishers, Inc.
Sunbelt Publications
Synapse-Centurion
Synergetic Press
Timber Press
Timberline Press
TOUCHSTONE
THE TOWNSHIPS SUN
University of Chicago Press
UnKnownTruths.com Publishing Company
The Vertin Press
Wood Thrush Books
Zagier & Urruty Publicaciones

EASTERN EUROPE

Cross-Cultural Communications
Northern Illinois University Press
Northwestern University Press

ECOLOGY, FOODS

ADIRONDAC
THE AFFILIATE
ALL ROUND
AMERICAN FORESTS
APPALACHIA JOURNAL
AQUATERRA, METAECOLOGY & CULTURE
Ash Tree Publishing
Beacon Press
Bear & Company
Beekman Books, Inc.
Black Rose Books Ltd.
Bliss Publishing Company, Inc.
THE BLOOMSBURY REVIEW
Blue Dolphin Publishing, Inc.
THE BOOKWATCH
Cassandra Press, Inc.
Chelsea Green Publishing Company
City Lights Books
Common Courage Press
DWELLING PORTABLY

654

ENVIRONMENTAL & ARCHITECTURAL PHENOMEN-
OLOGY NEWSLETTER
ETC Publications
Fine Tooth Press
Flowerfield Enterprises, LLC
Food First Books
Garden House Press
GASTRONOMICA: The Journal of Food and Culture
Granite Publishing Group
Great Elm Press
GREEN ANARCHIST
Island Press
Kivaki Press
La Alameda Press
THE LATHAM LETTER
The Latona Press
Lexikos
Library Research Associates
Life Media
MACROBIOTICS TODAY
Macrocosm USA, Inc.
MAGICAL BLEND/NATURAL BEAUTY & HEALTH/
TRANSITIONS
Malki Museum Press
Monkfish Book Publishing Company
Mo'omana'o Press
The Mountaineers Books
NATURAL LIFE
NEROUP REVIEW
NEW ENVIRONMENT BULLETIN
NightinGale Resources
George Ohsawa Macrobiotic Foundation
Oregon State University Press
OUT OF LINE
OUT YOUR BACKDOOR: The Magazine of Do-It-
Yourself Adventure and Homegrown Culture
PATTERNS OF CHOICE: A Journal of People, Land, and
Money
Penthe Publishing
Petroglyph Press, Ltd.
Royal Purcell, Publisher
R & M Publishing Company
Rama Publishing Co.
RED OWL
RFF Press / Resources for the Future
Rock Spring Press Inc.
Sanguinaria Publishing
SCIENCE/HEALTH ABSTRACTS
Scientia Publishing, LLC
SPROUTLETTER
Strawberry Patchworks
Synapse-Centurion
Titlewaves Publishing; Writers Direct
Touchstone Adventures
THE TOWNSHIPS SUN
TRANSITIONS ABROAD: The Guide to Living, Learning,
and Working Overseas
Tree of Life Books. Imprints: Progressive Press, Banned
Books
TURNING THE TIDE: Journal of Anti-Racist Action,
Research & Education
TURNING WHEEL
United Lumbee Nation
UNITED LUMBEE NATION TIMES
Upper Access Inc.
VEGETARIAN JOURNAL
The Vegetarian Resource Group
The Vertin Press
VINEGAR CONNOISSEURS INTERNATIONAL NEWS-
LETTER
Water Mark Press
Wide World Publishing/TETRA
THE WILD FOODS FORUM

EDITING

Aletheia Publications, Inc.
BIG HAMMER
Brenner Information Group

Cooper Hill Press
THE EDITORIAL EYE
Firelight Publishing, Inc.
THE GREAT BLUE BEACON
INTERLIT
READERS SPEAK OUT!
Redgreene Press
Strata Publishing, Inc.
The Times Journal Publishing Co.
Wordwrights Canada
WRITER'S CAROUSEL
WRITER'S CHRONICLE
WRITERS' JOURNAL

EDUCATION

Academic Innovations
Adirondack Mountain Club, Inc.
Advanced Learning Press
African American Images
AFRICAN AMERICAN REVIEW
Alaska Geographic Society
Alaska Native Language Center
Alpine Guild, Inc.
AltaMira Press
ALTERNATIVE EDUCATION RESOURCE ORGANIZA-
TION
ALT-J: Association for Learning Technology Journal
THE AMERICAN DISSIDENT
Andros Books
Applied Probability Trust
AQUATERRA, METAECOLOGY & CULTURE
ARTSLINK
Ash Lad Press
Athanata Arts, Ltd.
ATLANTIS: A Women's Studies Journal/Revue d'etudes
sur les femmes
Avocus Publishing, Inc.
Bandanna Books
Bandido Books
Bayhampton Publications
THE BEACON: Journal of Special Education Law &
Practice
Beekman Books, Inc.
Between The Lines
BILINGUAL REVIEW/Revista Bilingue
Black Forest Press
Blue Dolphin Publishing, Inc.
THE BOOK REPORT: The Magazine for Secondary School
Library Media & Technology Specialists
Books for All Times, Inc.
Branden Books
Bright Ring Publishing, Inc.
Brook Farm Books
Brookline Books
Caddo Gap Press
THE CAIMAN (formerly THE WEIRD NEWS)
Canadian Educators' Press
Center for Thanatology Research & Education, Inc.
The Chinese University Press
THE CLASSICAL OUTLOOK
Clearwater Publishing Co.
Community Service, Inc.
Continuing Education Press
Cooper Hill Press
CORRECTIONS TODAY
Cottonwood Press, Inc.
Council For Indian Education
Crystal Press
D.B.A. Books
Dawn Publications
Dawn Sign Press
DESIRE
DREAM NETWORK
Dream Publishing Co.
dreamslaughter
East West Discovery Press
EduCare Press
THE EDUCATION DIGEST

656

Success Publishing
Sherwood Sugden & Company, Publishers
SUMMER ACADEME: A Journal of Higher Education
TABOO: Journal of Education & Culture
TEACHER EDUCATION QUARTERLY
TEACHER LIBRARIAN: The Journal for School Library
    Professionals
Teachers & Writers Collaborative
TEACHERS & WRITERS MAGAZINE
TECH DIRECTIONS
Thatch Tree Publications
THRESHOLDS JOURNAL
TIFARA
TMC Books LLC
TOUCHSTONE
Trentham Books
Trickle Creek Books
TRUTH SEEKER
TURNING WHEEL
UBC Press
UNITED LUMBEE NATION TIMES
United Nations University Press
University of Chicago Press
Utah State University Press
VanderWyk & Burnham
Velazquez Press
VITAE SCHOLASTICAE: The Journal of Educational
    Biography
THE WASHINGTON MONTHLY
WELSH JOURNAL OF EDUCATION
WeWrite LLC
World Music Press
WRITER'S CHRONICLE
WSQ (formerly WOMEN'S STUDIES QUARTERLY)

EGYPT

Mystic Toad Press
New World Press, Inc

ELECTRONICS

Acting World Books
AD/VANCE
THE AGENCIES-WHAT THE ACTOR NEEDS TO
    KNOW
ART CALENDAR
ART PAPERS
Autonomedia, Inc.
Axiom Information Resources
Bancroft Press
Beacon Light Publishing (BLP)
BLK
BOMB MAGAZINE
CAMERA OBSCURA: Feminism, Culture, and Media
    Studies
CELLAR
Children Of Mary
CINEASTE MAGAZINE
Communicom Publishing Company
Crescent Moon
CULTUREFRONT
dbS Productions
Elderberry Press, LLC
FIDELIS ET VERUS
Film-Video Publications/Circus Source Publications
Future Horizons, Inc.
GAUNTLET: Exploring the Limits of Free Expression
THE HOLLYWOOD ACTING COACHES AND
    TEACHERS DIRECTORY
Hollywood Film Archive
JACK MACKEREL MAGAZINE
JOURNAL OF AESTHETICS AND ART CRITICISM
THE LAS VEGAS INSIDER
Leyland Publications
LIGHTWORKS MAGAZINE
Limelight Editions
MEDIA SPOTLIGHT
METAL CURSE
Midmarch Arts Press

N-B-T-V
NOBODADDIES
Norton Coker Press
PASSION
PAST TIMES: The Nostalgia Entertainment Newsletter
Pennycorner Press
PLAIN BROWN WRAPPER (PBW)
POINT OF CONTACT, The Journal of Verbal & Visual
    Arts
REAL PEOPLE
Really Great Books
Rowhouse Press
SALMAGUNDI
SALMAGUNDI
SHEMP! The Lowlife Culture Magazine
SLEAZOID EXPRESS
Sonoran Publishing
Starbooks Press/FLF Press
THEATRE DESIGN AND TECHNOLOGY
Theytus Books Ltd.
THE THREEPENNY REVIEW
WORLD OF FANDOM MAGAZINE

EMPLOYMENT

Aspen Mountain Publishing
Black Forest Press
Bookhaven Press, LLC
THE CARETAKER GAZETTE
CORRECTIONS TODAY
Finney Company, Inc.
Galen Press, Ltd.
Global Sports Productions, Ltd.
Harvard Common Press
Jamenair Ltd.
McGavick Field Publishing
New Win Publishing
Planning/Communications
Prakken Publications
The Saunderstown Press

ENERGY

aatec publications
Accendo Publishing
Adams-Blake Publishing
ALL ROUND
AQUATERRA, METAECOLOGY & CULTURE
Blue Dolphin Publishing, Inc.
CULTURE CHANGE
DWELLING PORTABLY
The Film Instruction Company of America
HIGH COUNTRY NEWS
HOME POWER
Home Power, Inc.
Island Press
Life Media
Luminous Epinoia Press
MAGICAL BLEND/NATURAL BEAUTY & HEALTH/
    TRANSITIONS
The Message Company
NEROUP REVIEW
NEW ENVIRONMENT BULLETIN
RED OWL
SO YOUNG!
Southwest Research and Information Center
SYNERJY: A Directory of Renewable Energy
The Utility Company LLC
Visions Communications
VOICES FROM THE EARTH

ENGINEERING

Adams-Blake Publishing
ADVANCES IN THE ASTRONAUTICAL SCIENCES
Aegean Publishing Company
AE-TU Publishing
AQUATERRA, METAECOLOGY & CULTURE
AUDIO EXPRESS
LrnIT Publishing Div. ICFL, Inc.
Muse World Media Group

N-B-T-V
Quale Press
SCIENCE AND TECHNOLOGY
Smith-Johnson Publisher
Univelt, Inc.
Visions Communications
Wind River Institute Press/Wind River Broadcasting

ENGLAND

THE CANNON'S MOUTH
E. S. Publishers & Distributors
THE EDGE CITY REVIEW
GREEN ANARCHIST
NightinGale Resources
North Stone Editions
PULSAR POETRY MAGAZINE
RED OWL
Stewart Publishing & Printing
Three Pyramids Publishing

ENGLISH

ANQ: A Quarterly Journal of Short Articles, Notes, and Reviews
APOSTROPHE: USCB Journal of the Arts
ATLANTIS: A Women's Studies Journal/Revue d'etudes sur les femmes
Bandanna Books
Bliss Publishing Company, Inc.
Borealis Press Limited
THE CANNON'S MOUTH
Cantadora Press
THE CENTENNIAL REVIEW
Chatterley Press International
CIMARRON REVIEW
COGNITIO: A Graduate Humanities Journal
COLLEGE ENGLISH
Cooper Hill Press
Cottonwood Press, Inc.
CREATIVE NONFICTION
THE DALHOUSIE REVIEW
THE DIRTY GOAT
THE EDGE CITY REVIEW
THE EDITORIAL EYE
Elderberry Press, LLC
Fine Tooth Press
FREEFALL
FULLOSIA PRESS
Galaxy Press
Gallaudet University Press
Gallopade International
Green Stone Publications
Host Publications, Inc.
THE IOWA REVIEW
JOURNAL OF AESTHETICS AND ART CRITICISM
JOURNAL OF NARRATIVE THEORY
LICHEN Arts & Letters Preview
Light, Words & Music
LULLWATER REVIEW
Maupin House Publishing, Inc.
Miles & Miles
Mind Power Publishing
Mucusart Publications
THE NEBRASKA REVIEW
THE NEW ENGLAND QUARTERLY
Orpheus Press
Oyster River Press
Pearl's Book'em Publisher
Pennsylvania State University Press
PERIPHERAL VISION
POINT OF CONTACT, The Journal of Verbal & Visual Arts
THE PRAIRIE JOURNAL OF CANADIAN LITERATURE
Prairie Journal Press
Purple Finch Press
Read Press LLC
REPRESENTATIONS
THE RIVER REVIEW/LA REVUE RIVIERE
Rodnik Publishing Co.

SALMAGUNDI
SCRIVENER
Scrivenery Press
SEWANEE REVIEW
THE SHAKESPEARE NEWSLETTER
SHAW: THE ANNUAL OF BERNARD SHAW STUDIES
Solcat Publishing
Sherwood Sugden & Company, Publishers
SYCAMORE REVIEW
SYMPLOKE: A Journal for the Intermingling of Literary, Cultural and Theoretical Scholarship
Thatch Tree Publications
Thorp Springs Press
Three House Publishing
University of Tampa Press
Utah State University Press
Vanderbilt University Press
Via Dolorosa Press
Whitston Publishing Co.
WRITER'S CAROUSEL
THE YALE REVIEW

ENTERTAINMENT

Acting World Books
THE AGENCIES-WHAT THE ACTOR NEEDS TO KNOW
AK Press
THE AMERICAN DRIVEL REVIEW
Axiom Information Resources
BANANA RAG
BEACHCOMBER MAGAZINE
BLK
THE BOOMERPHILE
CADENCE: The Review of Jazz & Blues: Creative Improvised Music
Celebrity Profiles Publishing
CREEPY MIKE'S OMNIBUS OF FUN
DAVID McCALLUM UPDATES
Empire Publishing Service
Film-Video Publications/Circus Source Publications
Fotofolio, Inc.
Fountainhead Productions, Inc.
THE HOLLYWOOD ACTING COACHES AND TEACHERS DIRECTORY
JAM RAG
juel house publishers and literary services
Lake Claremont Press
MEDIA SPOTLIGHT
METAL CURSE
MOBILE BEAT: The DJ Magazine
MYSTERY ISLAND MAGAZINE
THE NEO-COMINTERN
NIGHTLIFE MAGAZINE
Open Horizons Publishing Company
The Passion Profit Company
PAST TIMES: The Nostalgia Entertainment Newsletter
Players Press, Inc.
REAL PEOPLE
SANDPOINT MAGAZINE
Santa Monica Press
Starbooks Press/FLF Press
Stardate Publishing Company
TRADITION MAGAZINE
Twynz Publishing
UNDER THE VOLCANO
VACATION PLACE RENTALS
WORLD OF FANDOM MAGAZINE
WRESTLING - THEN & NOW
Wynn Publishing
YE OLDE NEWES

ENVIRONMENT

ADIRONDAC
AK Press
AMERICAN HIKER
American Hiking Society
Bay Tree Publishing
THE BEAR DELUXE

The Benefactory, Inc.
Bookhaven Press, LLC
Brave Ulysses Books
Brookview Press
THE CARETAKER GAZETTE
Ceres Press
COLOR WHEEL
Common Courage Press
Comparative Sedimentology Lab.
THE CREAM CITY REVIEW
CROSSCURRENTS
CULTURE CHANGE
CUTTHROAT, A JOURNAL OF THE ARTS
Dawn Publications
DWELLING PORTABLY
Ecopress, An Imprint of Finney Company
ECOTONE: Reimagining Place
ELECTRONIC GREEN JOURNAL
Envirographics
ENVIRONMENTAL & ARCHITECTURAL PHENOMEN-
    OLOGY NEWSLETTER
FARMING UNCLE
Filibuster Press
FOURTH WORLD REVIEW
Fretwater Press
FRIENDS OF PEACE PILGRIM
Gibbs Smith, Publisher
GREEN ANARCHIST
GREEN ANARCHY
Heartland Publishing
Heartsong Books
HIGH COUNTRY NEWS
Hope Publishing House
Ice Cube Press
The Independent Institute
THE INDEPENDENT REVIEW: A Journal of Political
    Economy
Island Press
JAM RAG
Kali Press
Keokee Co. Publishing, Inc.
THE KERF
Kumarian Press, Inc.
Laguna Wilderness Press
LAKE SUPERIOR MAGAZINE
Life Media
LrnIT Publishing Div. ICFL, Inc.
MANOA: A Pacific Journal of International Writing
MB Media, Inc.
Milkweed Editions
MOTHER EARTH
The Mountaineers Books
NEW ENVIRONMENT BULLETIN
New Star Books Ltd.
NewSage Press
North Country Books, Inc.
PEACEWORK
Penthe Publishing
Phantom Press Publications
Pineapple Press, Inc.
Plain View Press
PLEASANT LIVING
Pleasure Boat Studio: A Literary Press
POTOMAC REVIEW
Pruett Publishing Company
Quest Books: Theosophical Publishing House
Questex Consulting Ltd.
THE QUIET FEATHER
Raven Rocks Press
Raven's Eye Press, Inc.
RED OWL
RFF Press / Resources for the Future
Rising Tide Press New Mexico
THE RIVER REVIEW/LA REVUE RIVIERE
Rock Spring Press Inc.
Sagamore Publishing
Sage Hill Press
Scientia Publishing, LLC

SEA KAYAKER
SECOND GUESS
SHARE INTERNATIONAL
SOCIAL ANARCHISM: A Journal of Practice and Theory
South End Press
Southwest Research and Information Center
Square One Publishers, Inc.
State University of New York Press
Chuck Stewart
Synapse-Centurion
Texas Tech University Press
Timber Press
Tortuga Books
Touchstone Adventures
TRANSITIONS ABROAD: The Guide to Living, Learning,
    and Working Overseas
Trickle Creek Books
Truman State University Press
United Nations University Press
University of Calgary Press
University of Massachusetts Press
Upper Access Inc.
Utah State University Press
VOICES FROM THE EARTH
WASHINGTON TRAILS
Water Mark Press
WAV MAGAZINE: Progressive Music Art Politics Culture
WEBER STUDIES: Voices and Viewpoints of the
    Contemporary West
WHAT IS ENLIGHTENMENT?
WHOLE TERRAIN - REFLECTIVE ENVIRONMENTAL
    PRACTICE
WILD DUCK REVIEW
WISCONSIN TRAILS

EROTICA

Abecedarian books, Inc.
ABRAMELIN: a Journal of Poetry and Magick
Accendo Publishing
Asylum Arts
AXE FACTORY REVIEW
THE BOOMERPHILE
CAFE NOIR REVIEW
THE CHEROTIC (r)EVOLUTIONARY
Circlet Press, Inc.
CLARA VENUS
Creative Arts Book Company
THE DIRTY GOAT
Ephemera Bound Publishing
EROSHA
Eurotique Press
FUCK DECENCY
Gay Sunshine Press, Inc.
GENIE: POEMS: JOKES: ART
GLB Publishers
Hanover Press
Host Publications, Inc.
THE INDENTED PILLOW
Leyland Publications
LONG SHOT
LUMMOX JOURNAL
Lummox Press
Lunar Offensive Publications
Lycanthrope Press
METROPOLITAN FORUM
MIP Company
NORTHWOODS JOURNAL, A Magazine for Writers
OPEN WIDE MAGAZINE
Passion Power Press, Inc
PEMMICAN
PERIPHERAL VISION
PLAIN BROWN WRAPPER (PBW)
PORTLAND REVIEW
Pussywillow
Red Alder Books
RED OWL
Red Tiger Press
Re-invention UK Ltd

659

Santa Fe Writers Project
SHORT FUSE
SKINNYDIPPING
SLEAZOID EXPRESS
Spectrum Press
Starbooks Press/FLF Press
SUB-TERRAIN
Synergy Press
Trafton Publishing
Triskelion Publishing
Twin Souls Publications
Versus Press
Whiskey Creek Press
XTANT
Zygote Publishing

ESSAYS

THE ACORN
AERIAL
AGNI
ALASKA QUARTERLY REVIEW
THE AMERICAN DISSIDENT
AMERICAN INDIAN CULTURE AND RESEARCH
    JOURNAL
American Indian Studies Center
AMERICAN JONES BUILDING & MAINTENANCE
AMERICAN LETTERS & COMMENTARY
AMERICAN LITERARY REVIEW
APPLE VALLEY REVIEW: A Journal of Contemporary
    Literature
ARCHIPELAGO
ART:MAG
ARTS & LETTERS: Journal of Contemporary Culture
ASPHODEL
Asylum Arts
Avocus Publishing, Inc.
AXE FACTORY REVIEW
BACKWARDS CITY REVIEW
THE BALTIMORE REVIEW
Bancroft Press
BATHTUB GIN
BEATLICK NEWS
BELLINGHAM REVIEW
Bellywater Press
BIG MUDDY: Journal of the Mississippi River Valley
BITTER OLEANDER
BkMk Press
BLACK WARRIOR REVIEW
BORDERLANDS: Texas Poetry Review
Bordighera, Inc.
Brave Ulysses Books
BRILLIANT CORNERS: A Journal of Jazz & Literature
Broken Shadow Publications
Brookview Press
THE CAIMAN (formerly THE WEIRD NEWS)
Cantarabooks LLC
CHANTEH, the Iranian Cross-Cultural Quarterly
CHAPMAN
CHECKER CAB MAGAZINE - THE LITTLE 'ZINE
    THAT COULD! Fiction That Takes The Long Way
    Home
CHELSEA
Chelsea Green Publishing Company
THE CHEROTIC (r)EVOLUTIONARY
CIMARRON REVIEW
Coffee House Press
COLORADO REVIEW
CONFLUENCE
CONNECTICUT REVIEW
THE CREAM CITY REVIEW
CREATIVE NONFICTION
CREOSOTE: A Journal of Poetry and Prose
CRONE CHRONICLES: A Journal of Conscious Aging
Culturelink Press
Cynic Press
DESIRE
Devil Mountain Books
THE DIRTY GOAT

DUFUS
EASTGATE QUARTERLY REVIEW OF HYPERTEXT
ECOTONE: Reimagining Place
THE EDGE CITY REVIEW
Edgewise Press
The Eighth Mountain Press
Emrys Press
EPICENTER: A LITERARY MAGAZINE
EROSHA
EVANSVILLE REVIEW
EXPERIMENTAL FOREST
Five Fingers Press
FIVE FINGERS REVIEW
FLUENT ASCENSION
FOLIO: A Literary Journal of American University
FOURTH GENRE: EXPLORATIONS IN NONFICTION
THE FRANK REVIEW
GAUNTLET: Exploring the Limits of Free Expression
Gay Sunshine Press, Inc.
THE GEORGIA REVIEW
THE GETTYSBURG REVIEW
Gival Press
GREEN ANARCHY
Hanover Press
HARVARD REVIEW
HAWAI'I REVIEW
HAWAII PACIFIC REVIEW
HEAVEN BONE MAGAZINE
Heaven Bone Press
Helicon Nine Editions
Honors Group
Host Publications, Inc.
IAMBS & TROCHEES
ICON
THE ICONOCLAST
Imago Press
Impassio Press
IMPress
THE INDIE
Iniquity Press/Vendetta Books
INKY TRAIL NEWS
INNOVATING
THE IOWA REVIEW
Iris Publishing Group, Inc (Iris Press / Tellico Books)
THE JOURNAL
THE JOURNAL OF AFRICAN TRAVEL-WRITING
KALEIDOSCOPE: Exploring the Experience of Disability
    through Literature & the Fine Arts
KARAMU
THE KENYON REVIEW
KESTREL: A Journal of Literature and Art
Laguna Wilderness Press
THE LAUREL REVIEW
The Leaping Frog Press
THE LEDGE
LEFT CURVE
Libellum
LIGHT: The Quarterly of Light Verse
THE LISTENING EYE
LITERARY IMAGINATION: The Review of the Associa-
    tion of Literary Scholars and Critics
Lost Horse Press
THE LOUISVILLE REVIEW
LUMMOX JOURNAL
Lummox Press
LUNGFULL! MAGAZINE
MacDonald/Sward Publishing Company
MAIN STREET RAG
MANY MOUNTAINS MOVING
McPherson & Company Publishers
MEAT: A Journal of Writing and Materiality
MID-AMERICAN REVIEW
MINESHAFT
Missing Spoke Press
MOMMY AND I ARE ONE
Mountain State Press
MUDLARK
My Heart Yours Publishing

MY TABLE: Houston's Dining Magazine
MYSTERY ISLAND MAGAZINE
NATURAL BRIDGE
NEO: Literary Magazine
NEW DELTA REVIEW
THE NEW FORMALIST
THE NEW RENAISSANCE, an international magazine of
  ideas & opinions, emphasizing literature & the arts
New World Press, Inc
NORTH CAROLINA LITERARY REVIEW
OASIS
Oasis Books
OFFICE NUMBER ONE
OPEN MINDS QUARTERLY
ORBIS
THE ORPHAN LEAF REVIEW
OUTER-ART
Outrider Press
PACIFIC COAST JOURNAL
PALO ALTO REVIEW
Panther Creek Press
PAPERPLATES
Passion Power Press, Inc
Pearl's Book'em Publisher
Pendragonian Publications
PENNY DREADFUL: Tales and Poems of Fantastic Terror
PEREGRINE
The Poetry Center
Pogo Press, Incorporated
Polar Bear & Company
PRAIRIE SCHOONER
PRESA
PRETEXT
PSYCHE
QUARTER AFTER EIGHT
RAIN TAXI REVIEW OF BOOKS
RAINBOW CURVE
RATTAPALLAX
READERS SPEAK OUT!
Red Hen Press
RED ROCK REVIEW
RED WHEELBARROW
REFLECTIONS LITERARY JOURNAL
THE RIVER REVIEW/LA REVUE RIVIERE
RIVER TEETH: A Journal of Nonfiction Narrative
RIVET MAGAZINE
SAGE OF CONSCIOUSNESS E-ZINE
SAKANA
Salt Publishing
SANDPOINT MAGAZINE
Sarabande Books
SENECA REVIEW
SEWANEE REVIEW
SHENANDOAH: THE Washington and Lee University
  Review
SHORT FUSE
SKYLARK
The Smith (subsidiary of The Generalist Assn., Inc.)
SONGS OF INNOCENCE
Soul
SOUTH DAKOTA REVIEW
Southeast Missouri State University Press
SOUTHWEST REVIEW
SP QUILL QUARTERLY MAGAZINE
The Spirit That Moves Us Press, Inc.
SPOUT
Spout Press
Steerforth Press, L.C.
SterlingHouse Publisher
THE STRANGE FRUIT
STUDIO ONE
SULPHUR RIVER LITERARY REVIEW
THE SUN, A Magazine of Ideas
SunShine Press Publications, Inc.
SWINK
SYCAMORE REVIEW
THE TARPEIAN ROCK
THEATER

THINKERMONKEY
THIRD COAST
13TH MOON
Thunder Rain Publishing Corp.
TINY LIGHTS: A Journal of Personal Essay
TURNROW
Twisted Spoon Press
University of Tampa Press
V52 Press
VALLUM: CONTEMPORARY POETRY
WEBER STUDIES: Voices and Viewpoints of the
  Contemporary West
The Wellsweep Press
WEST BRANCH
White Pine Press
WHOLE TERRAIN - REFLECTIVE ENVIRONMENTAL
  PRACTICE
Wild West Publishing House
Wildflower Press
THE WILDWOOD READER
WILLOW SPRINGS
WIND
WISCONSIN TRAILS
Wood Thrush Books
WordFarm
WORDS OF WISDOM
WRITER'S CHRONICLE
Writers' Haven Press
WSQ (formerly WOMEN'S STUDIES QUARTERLY)
XAVIER REVIEW
YUKHIKA—LATUHSE
ZUZU'S PETALS: QUARTERLY ONLINE

ETHICS

Aardvark Enterprises (A Division of Speers Investments
  Ltd.)
Glen Allen Press
THE AMERICAN DISSIDENT
Beacon Press
BUSINESS SPIRIT JOURNAL
Cantadora Press
THE CHEROTIC (r)EVOLUTIONARY
COGNITIO: A Graduate Humanities Journal
CRONE CHRONICLES: A Journal of Conscious Aging
Wm.B. Eerdmans Publishing Co.
END OF LIFE CHOICES
Epoch Press
FREE INQUIRY
Galen Press, Ltd.
Genesis Publishing Company, Inc.
Heartland Publishing
HYPATIA: A Journal of Feminist Philosophy
IDM Press
Jalmar Press/Innerchoice Publishing
KEREM: Creative Explorations in Judaism
LIBERTY
Mind Power Publishing
Motom
THE NEW FORMALIST
The New Formalist Press
Paragon House Publishers
POTOMAC REVIEW
Reliance Books
Resource Publications, Inc.
Savant Garde Workshop
Set Sail Productions, LLC
SYMPLOKE: A Journal for the Intermingling of Literary,
  Cultural and Theoretical Scholarship
THINKERMONKEY
Titlewaves Publishing; Writers Direct
TRUTH SEEKER
United Nations University Press
Upper Access Inc.
Via Dolorosa Press
WHAT IS ENLIGHTENMENT?
White Thread Press
Zagier & Urruty Publicaciones

EUROPE

ABSINTHE: New European Writing
Carousel Press
Department of Romance Languages
THE DIRTY GOAT
E. S. Publishers & Distributors
GERMAN LIFE
Heyday Books
Host Publications, Inc.
THE JOURNAL OF HISTORICAL REVIEW
The Mountaineers Books
NightinGale Resources
PERIPHERAL VISION
TELOS
Telos Press
Thirteen Colonies Press
Travel Keys
United Nations University Press
UPSTAIRS AT DUROC
VACATION PLACE RENTALS
Zante Publishing
Zephyr Press

EUTHANASIA, DEATH

ADVANCES IN THANATOLOGY
BLACKBOOK PRESS, THE POETRY ZINE
BOULDER HERETIC
Center for Thanatology Research & Education, Inc.
CRONE CHRONICLES: A Journal of Conscious Aging
EcceNova Editions
END OF LIFE CHOICES
ERASED, SIGH, SIGH
Galen Press, Ltd.
GENRE: WRITER AND WRITINGS
THE HUMANIST
Lunar Offensive Publications
Lycanthrope Press
THE MONTHLY INDEPENDENT TRIBUNE TIMES JOURNAL POST GAZETTE NEWS CHRONICLE BULLETIN
MOUTH: Voice of the Dis-Labeled Nation
NewSage Press
SKS Press
Tendre Press
TRUTH SEEKER
TURNING WHEEL
Via Dolorosa Press
Westgate Press

EXPERIMENTAL

THE AMERICAN DRIVEL REVIEW
AMERICAN LETTERS & COMMENTARY
ARTELLA: the waltz of words and art
ASPHODEL
AXES & ALLEYS
BACKWARDS CITY REVIEW
BAGAZINE
BANANA RAG
BIRD DOG
BITTER OLEANDER
BOGG: A Journal of Contemporary Writing
BUST DOWN THE DOOR AND EAT ALL THE CHICKENS: A Journal of Absurd and Surreal Fiction
THE CAPILANO REVIEW
Comrades Press
CONJUNCTIONS
CRANKY LITERARY JOURNAL
CUTTHROAT, A JOURNAL OF THE ARTS
ELIXIR
EPICENTER: A LITERARY MAGAZINE
EROSHA
EUPHONY
FINE MADNESS
580 SPLIT
THE FLORIDA REVIEW
FRAN MAGAZINE
Gertrude Press

GLASS TESSERACT
GRASSLIMB
HOBART
Hole Books
JOURNAL OF PYROTECHNICS
THE KENYON REVIEW
LAKE EFFECT
LAUNDRY PEN
Les Figues Press
Libellum
Little Pear Press
Llumina Press
LULLABY HEARSE
LUNGFULL! MAGAZINE
MANDORLA: New Writing from the Americas / Nueva escritura de las Americas
MEAT FOR TEA: THE NORTHAMPTON REVIEW
MEAT: A Journal of Writing and Materiality
Miami University Press
NEW ORLEANS REVIEW
New Sins Press
THE NEW SUPERNATURAL MAGAZINE
Noemi Press
Outskirts Press, Inc.
Oyster River Press
PEMMICAN
Plain View Press
PORTLAND REVIEW
PREMONITIONS
PRESA
Presa Press
PSYCHOPOETICA
Quale Press
RAINBOW CURVE
THE RAVEN CHRONICLES
REDIVIDER
RedJack
RHINO: THE POETRY FORUM
RIVET MAGAZINE
SAKANA
Salt Publishing
SHORTRUNS
SKIDROW PENTHOUSE
SUB-TERRAIN
SWINK
Thunder Rain Publishing Corp.
Toad Press International Chapbook Series
Total Cardboard Publishing
UPSTAIRS AT DUROC
V52 Press
VANITAS
VLQ (Verse Libre Quarterly)
White Crosslet Publishing Co
Wildflower Press
The Word Doctor Online Publishing
The Word Works
X-Ray Book Co.
xtant.anabasis

FAMILY

AAIMS Publishers
Aardvark Enterprises (A Division of Speers Investments Ltd.)
Abernathy House Publishing
Academic Innovations
THE ACORN
ADVANCES IN THANATOLOGY
African American Images
Alegra House Publishers
ALONE TOGETHER
American Carriage House Publishing
Ammons Communications
Angel Power Press
APPLE VALLEY REVIEW: A Journal of Contemporary Literature
Aspicomm Media
AT-HOME DAD
Avocus Publishing, Inc.

662

Big Valley Press
BlackBerry Literary Services
Bolton Press
THE BOOMERPHILE
BRAZOS GUMBO
Bright Ring Publishing, Inc.
Carousel Press
CHRISTIAN CONNECTION PEN PAL NEWSLETTER
City Life Books, LLC
Cold-Drill Books
Community Service, Inc.
Cornerstone Publishing
Creative Writing and Publishing Company
Crones Unlimited
CURRENTS: New Scholarship in the Human Services
CUTTHROAT, A JOURNAL OF THE ARTS
Datamaster Publishing, LLC
Delaney Day Press
DOVETAIL: A Journal by and for Jewish/Christian Families
Dream Publishing Co.
DRT Press
Excelsior Cee Publishing
Fingerprint Press
Friendly Oaks Publications
Front Row Experience
Future Horizons, Inc.
Gallopade International
Gingerbread House
GLOBAL ONE TRAVEL & AUTOMOTIVE MAGAZINE
Grayson Books
Guarionex Press Ltd.
Harrington Park Press
Harvard Common Press
HARVARD WOMEN'S LAW JOURNAL
HOME EDUCATION MAGAZINE
Hope Publishing House
Images Unlimited and Snaptail Press, a Division of Images Unlimited Publishing
Impact Publishers, Inc.
Infinite Possibilities Publishing Group, Inc.
IRIS: A Journal About Women
J&W Publishers, Inc.
J. Mark Press
JOURNAL OF CHILD AND YOUTH CARE
juel house publishers and literary services
KABBALAH
Kivaki Press
Lamp Light Press
The Leaping Frog Press
LEO Productions LLC.
LIFE LEARNING
Life Media
LifeCircle Press
The Love and Logic Press, Inc.
LOVING MORE
Mama Incense Publishing
MCM Entertainment, Inc. Publishing Division
Mills Custom Services Publishing
Monroe Press
Moondance Press
MOTHERVERSE: A Journal of Contemporary Motherhood
Music City Publishing
My Heart Yours Publishing
Myriad Press
NEW SOLUTIONS
THE NEW SUPERNATURAL MAGAZINE
NightinGale Resources
No Starch Press
Nolo Press Occidental
Nonetheless Press
NORTHWOODS JOURNAL, A Magazine for Writers
NSR Publications
Oma Books of the Pacific
Our Child Press
Outrider Press
P.R.A. Publishing
Parenting Press, Inc.

The People's Press
Perrin Press
PIG IRON
PivotPoint Press
Plain View Press
PLEASANT LIVING
Pocol Press
Quiet Tymes, Inc.
Raven's Eye Press, Inc.
Sand and Sable Publishing
SCIENCE/HEALTH ABSTRACTS
Search Institute
SILVER WINGS
SKINNYDIPPING
SKS Press
Starry Night Publishing
Stunt Publishing
Success Publishing
Summit Crossroads Press
George Suttton Publishing Co.
Swan Publishing Company
Terra Nova Press
Third Dimension Publishing
Titus Home Publishing
Top 20 Press
Two Thousand Three Associates
Typographia Press
VanderWyk & Burnham
Vintage Romance Publishing, LLC
Whispering Pine Press

FANTASY

Abecedarian books, Inc.
Adventure Books Inc.
Amador Publishers
American Literary Press
Argo Press
ARTISTIC RAMBLINGS
Arx Publishing LLC
Avari Press
AXE FACTORY REVIEW
BALLISTA
BARDIC RUNES
Bereshith Publishing
Blue Planet Books Inc.
THE BOOKWATCH
Boulevard Books, Inc. Florida
BRAZOS GUMBO
BUST DOWN THE DOOR AND EAT ALL THE CHICKENS: A Journal of Absurd and Surreal Fiction
Caernarvon Press
THE CAIMAN (formerly THE WEIRD NEWS)
Caribbean Books-Panama
Carnifex Press
Cavalier Press
CELLAR
Central Avenue Press
CHALLENGING DESTINY
Circlet Press, Inc.
Creative Guy Publishing
Creative Writing and Publishing Company
The Design Image Group Inc.
Dream Catcher Publishing
DREAM FANTASY INTERNATIONAL
DREAMS AND NIGHTMARES
EASTGATE QUARTERLY REVIEW OF HYPERTEXT
EDGE Science Fiction and Fantasy Publishing
Ephemera Bound Publishing
Equine Graphics Publishing Group: New Concord Press, SmallHorse Press, Parallel Press
The Fiction Works
Firelight Publishing, Inc.
Four Seasons Publishers
Gardenia Press
GAUNTLET: Exploring the Limits of Free Expression
Gothic Press
Gryphon Books
Harrington Park Press

Haunted Rowboat Press
HOR-TASY
Hungry Tiger Press
Idylls Press
THE ILLUMINATA
Imago Press
IT GOES ON THE SHELF
Journey Books Publishing
Lemieux International Ltd.
Llumina Press
LOW BUDGET SCIENCE FICTION
Lunar Offensive Publications
Merrimack Books
METROPOLITAN FORUM
Millennium Workshop Production
Montemayor Press
Mountain Media
Mucusart Publications
Munsey Music
Mystic Toad Press
THE NEW SUPERNATURAL MAGAZINE
NORTHWOODS JOURNAL, A Magazine for Writers
NOVA EXPRESS
NWI National Writers Institute
OmegaRoom Press
ON SPEC
PABLO LENNIS
PAPERBACK PARADE
Pendragonian Publications
PENNY DREADFUL: Tales and Poems of Fantastic Terror
Perrin Press
Phelps Publishing Company
Plain View Press
POGO STICK
PREMONITIONS
Purple Mouth Press
Quiet Storm Books
Radiant Press
RavenHaus Publishing
Razor7 Publishing
Red Tiger Press
Reed Press
ROCTOBER COMICS AND MUSIC
Sand and Sable Publishing
Santa Fe Writers Project
THE SILVER WEB
SLEAZOID EXPRESS
SOMETHING TO READ
SONGS OF INNOCENCE
SPACE AND TIME
Space and Time Press
StarLance Publications
SterlingHouse Publisher
Stonehorse Publishing, LLC
Stony Meadow Publishing
Sun Dog Press
THE TARPEIAN ROCK
Triskelion Publishing
Triumvirate Publications
Twilight Times Books
Tyrannosaurus Press
Ultramarine Publishing Co., Inc.
UmbraProjects, Ltd.
Urban Legend Press
THE URBANITE
Visibility Unlimited Publications
Westgate Press
Whiskey Creek Press
Willowgate Press
WORLD OF FANDOM MAGAZINE
Wytherngate Press
YE OLDE NEWES
ZAHIR, Unforgettable Tales

FASHION

Altamont Press, Inc.
BLK
CESUM MAGAZINE

FIBERARTS
Fotofolio, Inc.
GemStone Press
GLOBAL ONE TRAVEL & AUTOMOTIVE MAGAZINE
GULF & MAIN Southwest Florida Lifestyle
Harobed Publishing Creations
Ibexa Press
INDUSTRY MINNE-ZINE
NIGHTLIFE MAGAZINE
Radiant Press
Red Rock Press
Sand and Sable Publishing

FEMINISM

AK Press
ALONE TOGETHER
American Literary Press
ASPHODEL
ATLANTIS: A Women's Studies Journal/Revue d'etudes sur les femmes
Aunt Lute Books
Autonomedia, Inc.
Avocus Publishing, Inc.
Backbeat Press
Bad Press
Beacon Press
Bear & Company
Between The Lines
Black Pearl Enterprises LLC
Black Rose Books Ltd.
BLUE COLLAR REVIEW
Blue Dolphin Publishing, Inc.
BOOKS TO WATCH OUT FOR
THE BOOMERPHILE
Bordighera, Inc.
BRIDGES: A Journal for Jewish Feminists and Our Friends
CAMERA OBSCURA: Feminism, Culture, and Media Studies
CANADIAN WOMAN STUDIES/les cahiers de la femme
Center for Thanatology Research & Education, Inc.
THE CHEROTIC (r)EVOLUTIONARY
Chicory Blue Press, Inc.
CHILDREN, CHURCHES AND DADDIES, A Non Religious, Non Familial Literary Magazine
City Life Books, LLC
CLARA VENUS
Cleis Press
COLLEGE LITERATURE
Common Courage Press
CONSCIENCE: The Newsjournal of Catholic Opinion
Crescent Moon
DOWN IN THE DIRT LITERARY MAGAZINE, the prose & poetry magazine revealing all your dirty little secrets
THE EAST VILLAGE INKY
The Eighth Mountain Press
Ephemera Bound Publishing
FEMINIST COLLECTIONS: A QUARTERLY OF WO-MEN'S STUDIES RESOURCES
FEMINIST PERIODICALS: A CURRENT LISTING OF CONTENTS
The Feminist Press at the City University of New York
FEMINIST STUDIES
FIGHT THESE BASTARDS
Four Walls Eight Windows
FREEDOM AND STRENGTH PRESS FORUM
GAYELLOW PAGES
GERTRUDE
GERTRUDE
Gertrude Press
GIRLFRIENDS MAGAZINE
GLB Publishers
Golden Isis Press
GOOD GIRL
Harrington Park Press
HARVARD WOMEN'S LAW JOURNAL
Hope Publishing House
HURRICANE ALICE
HYPATIA: A Journal of Feminist Philosophy

Bancroft Press
Banks Channel Books
Bardsong Press
Barrytown/Station Hill Press
BAYOU
Beagle Bay Books
THE BEAR DELUXE
BEGINNINGS - A Magazine for the Novice Writer
Bellevue Literary Press
BELLEVUE LITERARY REVIEW
BELLINGHAM REVIEW
BELLOWING ARK
Bellowing Ark Press
BELOIT FICTION JOURNAL
BIBLIOPHILOS
BIG MUDDY: Journal of the Mississippi River Valley
BIG SCREAM
Big Valley Press
Bilingual Review Press
Birch Brook Press
Birdalone Books
BITTER OLEANDER
BkMk Press
Black Diamond Book Publishing
Black Dress Press
Black Forest Press
Black Heron Press
BLACK JACK & VALLEY GRAPEVINE
Black Lawrence Press
Black Pearl Enterprises LLC
Black Thistle Press
BLACK WARRIOR REVIEW
BlackBerry Literary Services
BLACKBOOK PRESS, THE POETRY ZINE
Bleak House Books, an imprint of Diversity Incorporated
Blowtorch Press
BLUE HORSE
Blue Horse Publications
Blue Hot Books
BLUE MESA REVIEW
BLUELINE
BOGG: A Journal of Contemporary Writing
BOMB MAGAZINE
Book Marketing Solutions
Books for All Times, Inc.
BOOKS FROM FINLAND
Borealis Press Limited
Bottle of Smoke Press
Bottom Dog Press
BOULEVARD
Boulevard Books, Inc. Florida
Branden Books
THE BRIAR CLIFF REVIEW
BrickHouse Books, Inc.
BRILLIANT CORNERS: A Journal of Jazz & Literature
Britton Road Press
BROKEN PENCIL
Brook Street Press
Brunswick Publishing Corporation
BRYANT LITERARY REVIEW
BUFFALO SPREE
Burning Books
Burning Deck Press
BUST DOWN THE DOOR AND EAT ALL THE CHICKENS: A Journal of Absurd and Surreal Fiction
BUTTON
BUZZWORDS
BYLINE
C & M Online Media Inc.
Cadmus Editions
Caernarvon Press
CAFE NOIR REVIEW
CAKETRAIN
Caketrain Press
Calyx Books
CALYX: A Journal of Art and Literature by Women
Cantarabooks LLC
Caribbean Books-Panama

Carnifex Press
THE CAROLINA QUARTERLY
Carolina Wren Press/Lollipop Power Books
Casperian Books LLC
Cavalier Press
Cave Books
Cedar Hill Books
CEDAR HILL REVIEW
Celo Valley Books
Center for Japanese Studies
CENTER: A Journal of the Literary Arts
Central Avenue Press
Cervena Barva Press
CHANTEH, the Iranian Cross-Cultural Quarterly
CHAPMAN
CHARITON REVIEW
Chase Publishing
Chatterley Press International
CHECKER CAB MAGAZINE - THE LITTLE 'ZINE THAT COULD! Fiction That Takes The Long Way Home
CHELSEA
THE CHEROTIC (r)EVOLUTIONARY
Cherry Valley Editions
Chicory Blue Press, Inc.
CHILDREN, CHURCHES AND DADDIES, A Non Religious, Non Familial Literary Magazine
CIMARRON REVIEW
CIRCLE INC., THE MAGAZINE
Circle of Friends Books
City Life Books, LLC
City Lights Books
Cladach Publishing
Clamp Down Press
CLARA VENUS
Clearwater Publishing Co.
Cleis Press
Coffee House Press
The Colbert House
COLD-DRILL
COLORADO REVIEW
Communication Creativity
Comrades Press
CONCRETE JUNGLE JOURNAL
CONFLUENCE
CONJUNCTIONS
CONNECTICUT REVIEW
Copper Beech Press
CORRECTIONS TODAY
COTTONWOOD
Cottonwood Press
CRAB CREEK REVIEW
CRAB ORCHARD REVIEW
Crane Press
CRANKY LITERARY JOURNAL
CRANNOG
CRAZYHORSE
THE CREAM CITY REVIEW
Creative Arts Book Company
Creative Guy Publishing
CREATIVITY CONNECTION
CREOSOTE: A Journal of Poetry and Prose
Crime and Again Press
Crossway Books
CRUCIBLE
CUTBANK
CUTTHROAT, A JOURNAL OF THE ARTS
CYBERFICT
Cynic Press
Cypress House
THE DALHOUSIE REVIEW
Dalkey Archive Press
Dan River Press
DARK ANIMUS
December Press
Delta-West Publishing, Inc.
Denlinger's Publishers Ltd.
DESCANT

666

DESCANT
Desert Bloom Press
The Design Image Group Inc.
DESIRE
DEVIL BLOSSOMS
DIALOGOS: Hellenic Studies Review
Paul Dilsaver, Publisher
THE DIRTY GOAT
DOTLIT: The Online Journal of Creative Writing
DOWN IN THE DIRT LITERARY MAGAZINE, the prose
    & poetry magazine revealing all your dirty little secrets
Down The Shore Publishing
Down There Press
Downeast Books
Dream Catcher Publishing
DREAM FANTASY INTERNATIONAL
Dufour Editions Inc.
E & D Publishing, Inc.
E. S. Publishers & Distributors
Earth Star Publications
EARTH'S DAUGHTERS: Feminist Arts Periodical
EASTGATE QUARTERLY REVIEW OF HYPERTEXT
ECOTONE: Reimagining Place
Ecrivez!
THE EDGE CITY REVIEW
EduCare Press
The Eighth Mountain Press
Elderberry Press, LLC
ELIXIR
Elixir Press
ELT Press
EMRYS JOURNAL
Emrys Press
Ephemera Bound Publishing
EPICENTER: A LITERARY MAGAZINE
EPOCH MAGAZINE
Equine Graphics Publishing Group: New Concord Press,
    SmallHorse Press, Parallel Press
Eros Books
Ethos Publishing
EUPHONY
Eurotique Press
EVANSVILLE REVIEW
EVENT
Event Horizon Press
Expanded Media Editions
Falcon Publishing, LTD
FAT TUESDAY
Feel Free Press
FICTION
Fiction Collective Two (FC2)
The Fiction Works
FICTION WRITER'S GUIDELINE
Filibuster Press
Fine Tooth Press
FIREBREEZE PUBLISHING
Firelight Publishing, Inc.
First Books
FIRST INTENSITY
FISH DRUM MAGAZINE
Fithian Press
580 SPLIT
Five Fingers Press
FIVE FINGERS REVIEW
FIVE POINTS
Floreant Press
THE FLORIDA REVIEW
FLUENT ASCENSION
Flume Press
FLYWAY
FMA Publishing
FOLIO: A Literary Journal of American University
Fontanel Books
Foremost Press
Fountainhead Productions, Inc.
Fouque Publishers
Four Seasons Publishers
Four Walls Eight Windows

FOURTEEN HILLS: The SFSU Review
FRANK: AN INTERNATIONAL JOURNAL OF CON-
    TEMPORARY WRITING AND ART
Free People Press
FREEDOM AND STRENGTH PRESS FORUM
FREEFALL
French Bread Publications
THE FROGMORE PAPERS
FROZEN WAFFLES
Frozen Waffles Press/Shattered Sidewalks Press; 45th
    Century Chapbooks
FUGUE
Fugue State Press
Galde Press, Inc.
The Galileo Press Ltd.
Gallaudet University Press
Gallopade International
Garden House Press
Gardenia Press
GARGOYLE
GAUNTLET: Exploring the Limits of Free Expression
Gay Sunshine Press, Inc.
GEM Literary Foundation Press
Genesis Publishing Company, Inc.
THE GEORGIA REVIEW
GERTRUDE
GERTRUDE
Gertrude Press
Gesture Press
THE GETTYSBURG REVIEW
Gibbs Smith, Publisher
GIN BENDER POETRY REVIEW
Gival Press
GLASS TESSERACT
GLB Publishers
The Glencannon Press
Glimmer Train Press, Inc.
GLIMMER TRAIN STORIES
Golden Quill Press
GoldenIsle Publishers, Inc.
Goose River Press
Gothic Press
GRAIN MAGAZINE
GRASSLIMB
Graywolf Press
THE GREAT BLUE BEACON
GREAT RIVER REVIEW
GREEN MOUNTAINS REVIEW
Green River Press
THE GREENSBORO REVIEW
Grip Publishing
Gryphon Books
GULF COAST
Hailey-Grey Books
Haley's
HANGING LOOSE
Hanging Loose Press
Hanover Press
HAPPENINGNOW!EVERYWHERE
Harlan Publishing Company; Alliance Books; Diakonia
    Publishing (Christian Books)
Harrington Park Press
HARVARD REVIEW
Harvest Shadows Publications
Haunted Rowboat Press
HAWAI'I REVIEW
HAWAII PACIFIC REVIEW
The Haworth Press
HAYDEN'S FERRY REVIEW
HEARTLANDS: A Magazine of Midwest Life and Art
HEAVEN BONE MAGAZINE
Heaven Bone Press
Heidelberg Graphics
Helicon Nine Editions
Hermes House Press
Hermitage (Ermitazh)
The Heyeck Press
Higher Ground Press

HOBART
Hole Books
Hollyridge Press
Homa & Sekey Books
HOME PLANET NEWS
HOR-TASY
Host Publications, Inc.
Howling Wolf Publishing
ICON
THE ICONOCLAST
THE IDAHO REVIEW
Idylls Press
ILLUMINATIONS
IMAGE: ART, FAITH, MYSTERY
Imago Press
Impassio Press
IMPress
IN OUR OWN WORDS
INDIANA REVIEW
Infinite Possibilities Publishing Group, Inc.
The Infinity Group
Interlink Publishing Group, Inc.
THE INTERNATIONAL FICTION REVIEW
THE IOWA REVIEW
Iris Publishing Group, Inc (Iris Press / Tellico Books)
IRIS: A Journal About Women
IRON HORSE LITERARY REVIEW
Ironweed Press
Italica Press, Inc.
Ithuriel's Spear
JACK MACKEREL MAGAZINE
Jako Books
John James Company
J'ECRIS
JetKor
Jireh Publishing Company
THE JOURNAL
JOURNAL OF AESTHETICS AND ART CRITICISM
JOURNAL OF NARRATIVE THEORY
Journey Books Publishing
J-Press Publishing
juel house publishers and literary services
K.T. Publications
KAJ-MAHKAH: EARTH OF EARTH
KALEIDOSCOPE: Exploring the Experience of Disability
   through Literature & the Fine Arts
KARAMU
KARAWANE
THE KELSEY REVIEW
Kelsey St. Press
THE KENYON REVIEW
KESTREL: A Journal of Literature and Art
Allen A. Knoll Publishers
KNUCKLE MERCHANT - The Journal of Naked Literary
   Aggression
KOJA
La Alameda Press
LAKE EFFECT
The Larcom Press
LARCOM REVIEW
LATERAL MOVES
LAUNDRY PEN
THE LAUREL REVIEW
Lean Press
Leapfrog Press
Leaping Dog Press / Asylum Arts Press
The Leaping Frog Press
THE LEDGE
THE LEDGE POETRY & FICTION MAGAZINE
LegacyForever
Lekon New Dimensions Publishing
LEO Productions LLC.
Les Figues Press
Leyland Publications
Library Research Associates, Inc.
LICHEN Arts & Letters Preview
LIFTOUTS
Light of New Orleans Publishing

LIGHT: The Quarterly of Light Verse
LINQ
THE LISTENING EYE
LITERALLY HORSES/REMUDA
LITERARY IMAGINATION: The Review of the Associa-
   tion of Literary Scholars and Critics
LITRAG
THE LITTLE MAGAZINE
Little Pear Press
Llumina Press
THE LONG STORY
Loonfeather Press
Lord John Press
Lost Horse Press
Lost Prophet Press
THE LOUISIANA REVIEW
THE LOUISVILLE REVIEW
LOW BUDGET ADVENTURE
LOW BUDGET SCIENCE FICTION
Lucky Press, LLC
LULLWATER REVIEW
Lunar Offensive Publications
LUNGFULL! MAGAZINE
Lynx House Press
Lyons Publishing Limited
MacAdam/Cage Publishing Inc.
THE MACGUFFIN
THE MADISON REVIEW
Mama Incense Publishing
MANDORLA: New Writing from the Americas / Nueva
   escritura de las Americas
MANGROVE MAGAZINE
MANOA: A Pacific Journal of International Writing
MANY MOUNTAINS MOVING
Mapletree Publishing Company
March Street Press
THE MARLBORO REVIEW
Martinez Press
Maui arThoughts Co.
Maverick Books
Mayhaven Publishing
McBooks Press, Inc.
McPherson & Company Publishers
MEAT FOR TEA: THE NORTHAMPTON REVIEW
Meridien PressWorks
Merrimack Books
Merwood Books
Metacom Press
Miami University Press
Micah Publications Inc.
MID-AMERICAN REVIEW
The Midknight Club
Mid-List Press
Milkweed Editions
Mills Custom Services Publishing
MINESHAFT
MIP Company
Missing Spoke Press
MISSISSIPPI REVIEW
MOMMY AND I ARE ONE
Montemayor Press
Mo'omana'o Press
Motom
Mountain Media
Mountain State Press
Multnomah Publishers, Inc.
Munsey Music
My Heart Yours Publishing
Myriad Press
MYSTERY ISLAND MAGAZINE
Mystery Island Publications
Mystic Toad Press
Nada Press
National Writers Press
NATURAL BRIDGE
NEBO
THE NEBRASKA REVIEW
NEO: Literary Magazine

Neshui Publishing
NEW AMERICAN WRITING
NEW DELTA REVIEW
NEW ENGLAND REVIEW
New Falcon Publications
New Issues Poetry & Prose
NEW LETTERS
NEW MUSE OF CONTEMPT
NEW ORLEANS REVIEW
New Orphic Publishers
THE NEW ORPHIC REVIEW
THE NEW RENAISSANCE, an international magazine of
  ideas & opinions, emphasizing literature & the arts
New Rivers Press, Inc.
New Star Books Ltd.
NEW STONE CIRCLE
THE NEW SUPERNATURAL MAGAZINE
THE NEW WRITER
Newmark Publishing Company
Nightsun Books
NIMROD INTERNATIONAL
NOBODADDIES
Noemi Press
NOLA-MAGICK Press
Nonetheless Press
NOON
NORTH AMERICAN REVIEW
NORTH CAROLINA LITERARY REVIEW
North Stone Editions
NORTHERN PILOT
NORTHWEST REVIEW
Northwestern University Press
Northwoods Press
NOTRE DAME REVIEW
NOVA EXPRESS
NOW AND THEN
NOW HERE NOWHERE
NSR Publications
NWI National Writers Institute
O!!ZONE, A LITERARY-ART ZINE
Oak Tree Press
OASIS
Oasis Books
OBSIDIAN III: Literature in the African Diaspora
Ocean Publishing
OFFICE NUMBER ONE
OFFICE NUMBER ONE
Ohio University Press/Swallow Press
THE OLD RED KIMONO
OmegaRoom Press
Omonomany
One Eyed Press
One Less Press
Oolichan Books
Oracle Press
ORBIS
ORCHID: A Literary Review
Orchises Press
THE ORPHAN LEAF REVIEW
Orpheus Press
Oscura Press
Osric Publishing
OTHER VOICES
OUT OF LINE
Outrider Press
Outskirts Press, Inc.
Owl Creek Press
THE OXFORD AMERICAN
OYEZ REVIEW
OYSTER BOY REVIEW
Oyster River Press
THE PACIFIC REVIEW
PAJ NTAUB VOICE
Palari Publishing
PALO ALTO REVIEW
Panther Books
Panther Creek Press
PAPERPLATES

PARADIDOMI
Parissound Publishing
Parthian
PARTING GIFTS
PASSAGES NORTH
Passeggiata Press, Inc.
Passing Through Publications
Passion Power Press, Inc
Path Press, Inc.
Paycock Press
Pearl-Win Publishing Co.
Peartree Books & Music
THE PEDESTAL MAGAZINE.COM
THE PEGASUS REVIEW
PEMBROKE MAGAZINE
Pendragonian Publications
PENNINE INK MAGAZINE
PENNY DREADFUL: Tales and Poems of Fantastic Terror
Penthe Publishing
The People's Press
PEREGRINE
The Permanent Press/The Second Chance Press
Perrin Press
Phantom Press Publications
PHOEBE: A Journal of Literature and Art
Phoenix Illusion
Phrygian Press
PIG IRON
Pig Iron Press
Pinchgut Press
Pineapple Press, Inc.
PINYON
Pirate Publishing International
Plain View Press
Platinum Dreams Publishing
Platinum One Publishing
Pleasure Boat Studio: A Literary Press
PLOUGHSHARES
Pocahontas Press, Inc.
Pocol Press
POETIC SPACE: Poetry & Fiction
POETICA MAGAZINE, Reflections of Jewish Thought
POETRY EAST
POETS & WRITERS MAGAZINE
Poets & Writers, Inc.
POGO STICK
Polar Bear & Company
Portals Press
PORTLAND REVIEW
Portmanteau Editions
The Post-Apollo Press
Pottersfield Press
THE PRAIRIE JOURNAL OF CANADIAN LITERATURE
Prairie Journal Press
PRAIRIE SCHOONER
PRAIRIE WINDS
Preludium Publishers
PREMONITIONS
PREP Publishing
The Press at Foggy Bottom
PRETEXT
Primal Publishing
PRIMAVERA
Printed Matter Press (Tokyo)
PRISM INTERNATIONAL
Prospect Press
PTOLEMY/BROWNS MILLS REVIEW
PublishAmerica, LLLP.
PUERTO DEL SOL
Purple Finch Press
PURPLE PATCH
Pygmy Forest Press
Pyncheon House
QED Press
Quale Press
QUARTER AFTER EIGHT
QUARTERLY WEST
QUERCUS REVIEW

669

Questex Consulting Ltd.
THE QUIET FEATHER
Quiet Storm Books
Rabeth Publishing Company
Radiant Press
Ram Press
RAMBUNCTIOUS REVIEW
RATTAPALLAX
THE RAVEN CHRONICLES
RavenHaus Publishing
Ravenhawk Books
Razor7 Publishing
Reach Productions Publishing
Really Great Books
Red Alder Books
Red Cedar Press
RED CEDAR REVIEW
Red Dust
RED HAWK
Red Hen Press
Red Tiger Press
RED WHEELBARROW
Redgreene Press
REDIVIDER
RedJack
Reed Press
REFLECTIONS LITERARY JOURNAL
THE REVIEW OF CONTEMPORARY FICTION
RFD
RHINO: THE POETRY FORUM
Ridgeway Press of Michigan
RIVER CITY
THE RIVER REVIEW/LA REVUE RIVIERE
RIVER STYX
Rivercross Publishing, Inc.
RIVERSEDGE
RIVET MAGAZINE
RockBySea Books
THE ROCKFORD REVIEW
ROCKY MOUNTAIN KC NEWS
Rocky Mountain KC Publishing Co.
Ronsdale Press
Rose Shell Press
ROSEBUD
THE ROUND TABLE: A Journal of Poetry and Fiction
Rowan Press, Inc.
Rowhouse Press
Russell Dean and Company
Ryrich Publications
Sadorian Publications
SAGE OF CONSCIOUSNESS E-ZINE
St. Andrews College Press
Saint Mary's Press
SALAMANDER
SALMAGUNDI
Samuel Powell Publishing Company
Sand and Sable Publishing
Santa Ana River Press
Santa Fe Writers Project
Saqi Books Publisher
Sarabande Books
Saskatchewan Writers Guild
Savant Garde Workshop
Scarlet Tanager Books
Scars Publications
SCRIVENER
Scrivenery Press
SEEMS
SelectiveHouse Publishers, Inc.
SENSATIONS MAGAZINE
Seven Buffaloes Press
SEWANEE REVIEW
Shearer Publishing
SHENANDOAH: THE Washington and Lee University
   Review
Sherman Asher Publishing
Shipyard Press, LC
SHORT FUSE

SHORTRUNS
SKIDROW PENTHOUSE
SKYLARK
Small Dogs Press
The Smith (subsidiary of The Generalist Assn., Inc.)
SMOKE
Smyrna Press
SNOW MONKEY
SNOWY EGRET
SO TO SPEAK: A Feminist Journal of Language & Art
SOJOURN: A Journal of the Arts
$olvency International Inc., Publishing
SOMETHING TO READ
SONGS OF INNOCENCE
Soul
SOUNDINGS EAST
SOUTH CAROLINA REVIEW
SOUTH DAKOTA REVIEW
Southeast Missouri State University Press
THE SOUTHERN CALIFORNIA ANTHOLOGY
SOUTHERN HUMANITIES REVIEW
THE SOUTHERN REVIEW
SOUTHWEST REVIEW
SOU'WESTER
SPEAK UP
SPEAKEASY
Spectrum Press
SPINNING JENNY
Spire Press
SPITBALL: The Literary Baseball Magazine
SPOUT
Spout Press
Spring Harbor Press
SRLR Press
Starbooks Press/FLF Press
Starcherone Books
StarLance Publications
Stellaberry Press
Stemmer House Publishers, Inc.
SterlingHouse Publisher
Stonehorse Publishing, LLC
Stony Meadow Publishing
Stormline Press, Inc.
Story County Books
STORYQUARTERLY
THE STRANGE FRUIT
STRINGTOWN
STRUGGLE: A Magazine of Proletarian Revolutionary
   Literature
STUDIO - A Journal of Christians Writing
STUDIO ONE
SUB-TERRAIN
SULPHUR RIVER LITERARY REVIEW
Sun Dog Press
THE SUN, A Magazine of Ideas
Swallow's Tale Press
Swan Publishing Company
SWINK
SYCAMORE REVIEW
SYMPLOKE: A Journal for the Intermingling of Literary,
   Cultural and Theoretical Scholarship
synaesthesia press
Synapse-Centurion
Synergistic Press
Synergy Press
TAKAHE
Talisman House, Publishers
TalSan Publishing/Distributors
Tameme
TAPROOT LITERARY REVIEW
THE TARPEIAN ROCK
Ten Star Press
Texas Tech University Press
Thatch Tree Publications
THEMA
Theytus Books Ltd.
THIN COYOTE
Think Tank Press, Inc.

THIRD COAST
13TH MOON
Three Bears Publishing
Three House Publishing
THE THREEPENNY REVIEW
THRESHOLDS JOURNAL
Thunder Rain Publishing Corp.
Thundercloud Books
The Times Journal Publishing Co.
Titan Press
TnT Classic Books
Toad Press International Chapbook Series
Tolling Bell Books
Tombouctou Books
Total Cardboard Publishing
TOUCHSTONE LITERARY JOURNAL
Trafford Publishing
Tres Picos Press
Triple Tree Publishing
Triskelion Publishing
Triumvirate Publications
Tropical Press
Truebekon Books
TURNROW
Turnstone Press
The Twickenham Press
Twilight Times Books
Twisted Spoon Press
Twynz Publishing
Typographia Press
UglyTown
Ultramarine Publishing Co., Inc.
UmbraProjects, Ltd.
UNBOUND
UNIVERSITY OF WINDSOR REVIEW
UPSTAIRS AT DUROC
Urion Press
US1 Poets' Cooperative
US1 WORKSHEETS
V52 Press
Vagabond Press
Vehicule Press
VERSAL
Versus Press
The Vertin Press
Vesta Publications Limited
Via Dolorosa Press
Vintage Romance Publishing, LLC
THE VIRGINIA QUARTERLY REVIEW
Visibility Unlimited Publications
Voyageur Publishing Co.,Inc.
John Wade, Publisher
WAR, LITERATURE & THE ARTS: An International
    Journal of the Humanities
Washington Writers' Publishing House
Water Row Press
Wave Publishing
WEBER STUDIES: Voices and Viewpoints of the
    Contemporary West
The Wellsweep Press
WEST BRANCH
West Coast Paradise Publishing
West Virginia University Press
Whelks Walk Press
which press
Whiskey Creek Press
WHITE CROW
White Eagle Coffee Store Press
White Pine Press
WHOLE TERRAIN - REFLECTIVE ENVIRONMENTAL
    PRACTICE
THE WILDWOOD READER
WILLOW REVIEW
WILLOW SPRINGS
Willowgate Press
WillowTree Press LLC
WIND
Windstorm Creative

Wineberry Press
Wings Press
Women In Print
THE WORCESTER REVIEW
The Word Doctor Online Publishing
Word Forge Books
WORD IS BOND
WordFarm
WORDS OF WISDOM
WORDWRIGHTS MAGAZINE
THE WORLD
World Love Press Publishing
Writecorner.com Press
The Writers Block, Inc.
WRITER'S CHRONICLE
WRITERS' JOURNAL
WRITER'S LIFELINE
WRITING FOR OUR LIVES
Wytherngate Press
XAVIER REVIEW
Xenos Books
XTANT
YUKHIKA—LATUHSE
Zebra Press
ZOETROPE: ALL-STORY
ZONE 3
Zoo Press
Zumaya Publications
ZUZU'S PETALS: QUARTERLY ONLINE
Zygote Publishing

FINANCES

Acton Circle Publishing Company
Advantage World Press
THE ART OF ABUNDANCE
Bancroft Press
Bay Tree Publishing
BlackBerry Literary Services
Bluestocking Press
CANADIAN MONEYSAVER
Career Advancement Center, Inc.
CKO UPDATE
Communication Creativity
Epoch Press
Fountainhead Productions, Inc.
GAMBARA MAGAZINE
Garrett Publishing, Inc.
Gemstone House Publishing
GENRE: WRITER AND WRITINGS
Happy About
Infinite Possibilities Publishing Group, Inc.
INNOVATING
LifeCircle Press
Llumina Press
Long & Silverman Publishing, Inc.
Mind Power Publishing
MOTHER EARTH JOURNAL: An International Quarterly
Music City Publishing
North Star Books
The Passion Profit Company
Pellingham Casper Communications
Pristine Publishing
Reliance Books
Rolling Hills Publishing
Set Sail Productions, LLC
Square One Publishers, Inc.
Chuck Stewart
Storm Publishing Group
Titlewaves Publishing; Writers Direct
United Nations University Press
WeWrite LLC

F. SCOTT FITZGERALD

FRAN MAGAZINE
Libellum
LOST GENERATION JOURNAL

FLORIDA

BEACHCOMBER MAGAZINE
Cantadora Press
COGNITIO: A Graduate Humanities Journal
Comparative Sedimentology Lab.
IN OUR OWN WORDS
The Intrepid Traveler
LegacyForever
Light, Words & Music
B.B. Mackey Books
The Mountaineers Books
THE NEW SUPERNATURAL MAGAZINE
Ocean Publishing
Pineapple Press, Inc.
Pogo Press, Incorporated
Premium Press America
Putting Up Books, LC
Rock Spring Press Inc.
Shipyard Press, LC
Starbooks Press/FLF Press
Tortuga Books
Two Thousand Three Associates
Two Thousand Three Associates
University of Tampa Press
Windward Publishing, An Imprint of Finney Company

FOLKLORE

THE ACORN
Alaska Native Language Center
Ammons Communications
Anagnosis
Ancient City Press
APPLE VALLEY REVIEW: A Journal of Contemporary
   Literature
Ariko Publications
Avery Color Studios
THE AZOREAN EXPRESS
Ballena Press
BALLISTA
Black Dome Press Corp.
John F. Blair, Publisher
THE BLOOMSBURY REVIEW
Borealis Press Limited
Celtic Heritage Books
Center for Thanatology Research & Education, Inc.
Children's Book Press
Council For Indian Education
Creative With Words Publications (CWW)
Elderberry Press, LLC
EXIT 13 MAGAZINE
Feel Free Press
Firelight Publishing, Inc.
Foundation Books
FREEFALL
Fulcrum, Inc.
Galde Press, Inc.
Harbor House
HEARTLANDS: A Magazine of Midwest Life and Art
Ice Cube Press
IRISH LITERARY SUPPLEMENT
JOURNAL OF AESTHETICS AND ART CRITICISM
Kar-Ben Publishing, Inc.
KESTREL: A Journal of Literature and Art
Lake Claremont Press
LAKE EFFECT
LAKE SUPERIOR MAGAZINE
Lexikos
Lockhart Press, Inc.
LORE AND LANGUAGE
Luna Bisonte Prods
Lycanthrope Press
Maledicta Press
MALEDICTA: The International Journal of Verbal Aggres-
   sion
Margaret Media, Inc.
The Middle Atlantic Press
The Midknight Club

Monkfish Book Publishing Company
Mo'omana'o Press
Mystery Island Publications
New Falcon Publications
THE NEW SUPERNATURAL MAGAZINE
NightinGale Resources
North Country Books, Inc.
NORTHWOODS JOURNAL, A Magazine for Writers
One Horse Press/Rainy Day Press
PARABOLA MAGAZINE
Passeggiata Press, Inc.
Perrin Press
Petroglyph Press, Ltd.
Pocahontas Press, Inc.
The Press at Foggy Bottom
RALPH'S REVIEW
Rarach Press
Rayve Productions Inc.
Red Hand Press
Red Tiger Press
Rio Nuevo Publishers
THE RIVER REVIEW/LA REVUE RIVIERE
ROCKY MOUNTAIN KC NEWS
Rocky Mountain KC Publishing Co.
ROCTOBER COMICS AND MUSIC
Santa Monica Press
SEMIOTEXT(E)
Serpent & Eagle Press
SHATTERED WIG REVIEW
SHORT FUSE
SING OUT! Folk Music & Folk Songs
SKYLARK
SOCIETE
THE SOUTHERN QUARTERLY: A Journal of the Arts in
   the South
Sunbelt Publications
Sunnyside Press
TRADITION MAGAZINE
Two Dog Press
United Lumbee Nation
UNITED LUMBEE NATION TIMES
University of Arkansas Press
University of South Carolina Press
Utah State University Press
V52 Press
Vanderbilt University Press
Victory Press
Volcano Press, Inc
Waters Edge Press
WESTERN AMERICAN LITERATURE
Westgate Press
Whispering Pine Press
White Cliffs Media, Inc.
Windstorm Creative
WISCONSIN TRAILS
World Music Press
XCP: CROSS-CULTURAL POETICS
XTANT
Yellow Moon Press

FOOD, EATING

ALIMENTUM - The Literature of Food
Atlantic Publishing Group, Inc.
BANANA RAG
BlackBerry Literary Services
Creative Writing and Publishing Company
DWELLING PORTABLY
Eco Images
GAMBARA MAGAZINE
Ika, LLC
Images Unlimited and Snaptail Press, a Division of Images
   Unlimited Publishing
IRIS: A Journal About Women
Knowledge Concepts Publishing
Lake Claremont Press
Lamp Light Press
Lazywood Press
Llumina Press

MY TABLE: Houston's Dining Magazine
NOLA-MAGICK Press
NORTH CAROLINA LITERARY REVIEW
Princess Publishing
Red Rock Press
SHORTRUNS
Typographia Press
University of South Carolina Press
Upper Access Inc.
V52 Press
Visibility Unlimited Publications
Wafer Mache Publications
Writers' Haven Press

FORENSIC SCIENCE

Galen Press, Ltd.
GENRE: WRITER AND WRITINGS
Journal of Pyrotechnics
JOURNAL OF PYROTECHNICS
Voyageur Publishing Co.,Inc.

FRANCE, FRENCH

ABSINTHE: New European Writing
THE ADIRONDACK REVIEW
Bandanna Books
Barrytown/Station Hill Press
Beacon Light Publishing (BLP)
Black Lawrence Press
The Chicot Press
Cross-Cultural Communications
Department of Romance Languages
FRANK: AN INTERNATIONAL JOURNAL OF CON-
    TEMPORARY WRITING AND ART
INTERNATIONAL POETRY REVIEW
John James Company
LEO Productions LLC.
LOST GENERATION JOURNAL
NightinGale Resources
OSIRIS
THE RIVER REVIEW/LA REVUE RIVIERE
SYMPOSIUM
Synergistic Press
TRANSITIONS ABROAD: The Guide to Living, Learning,
    and Working Overseas
University of Virginia Press

FUNDRAISING

Bonus Books, Inc.
GRASSROOTS FUNDRAISING JOURNAL

FUTURISM

AE-TU Publishing
Angst World Library
ARTISTIC RAMBLINGS
BAGAZINE
THE CAIMAN (formerly THE WEIRD NEWS)
Cambric Press dba Emerald House
CONJUNCTIONS
Crane Press
Crystal Press
THE FUTURIST
Gallopade International
Heartsong Books
THE HUMANIST
KALDRON, An International Journal Of Visual Poetry
LOVING MORE
NEW ENVIRONMENT BULLETIN
NOVA EXPRESS
Plain View Press
PREMONITIONS
Red Tiger Press
SECOND GUESS
SHARE INTERNATIONAL
Swan Raven & Company
Thatch Tree Publications
WHAT IS ENLIGHTENMENT?
XTANT
xtant.anabasis

GAELIC

Celtic Heritage Books
Fountainhead Productions, Inc.
NEW AMERICAN IMAGIST
NORTHWORDS
Poetry Ireland
POETRY IRELAND REVIEW
Sand and Sable Publishing
Total Cardboard Publishing

GALAPAGOS ISLANDS

GAMBARA MAGAZINE

GAMES

ALL ROUND
Carousel Press
CHESS LIFE
THE CRAPSHOOTER
Dawn Sign Press
DISC GOLF WORLD
East West Discovery Press
Falls Media
Fountainhead Productions, Inc.
Front Row Experience
Gallopade International
Gateways Books And Tapes
Guarionex Press Ltd.
Hunter House Inc., Publishers
Huntington Press
Leaf Press
Liberty Publishing Company, Inc.
MEAT: A Journal of Writing and Materiality
MEDIA SPOTLIGHT
RavenHaus Publishing
SCHOOL MATES
Zookeeper Publications

GARDENING

Acton Circle Publishing Company
Affinity Publishers Services
Alaska Northwest Books
ALL ROUND
Andmar Press
Annedawn Publishing
Arizona Master Gardener Press
Banks Channel Books
Blue Dolphin Publishing, Inc.
Center For Self-Sufficiency
Chelsea Green Publishing Company
Chicago Review Press
The Chicot Press
Cladach Publishing
Downeast Books
Eco Images
FARMING UNCLE
Fulcrum, Inc.
Gallopade International
Garden House Press
GREEN PRINTS, ''The Weeder's Digest''
THE GROWING EDGE MAGAZINE
GROWING FOR MARKET
Hobar Publications, A Division of Finney Company
HORTIDEAS
INKY TRAIL NEWS
JetKor
Allen A. Knoll Publishers
La Alameda Press
LAKE SUPERIOR MAGAZINE
Life Media
Loonfeather Press
Moon Pie Press
Natureraph Publishers
No Starch Press
Nonetheless Press
OUT YOUR BACKDOOR: The Magazine of Do-It-
    Yourself Adventure and Homegrown Culture
Petroglyph Press, Ltd.

Pineapple Press, Inc.
PLEASANT LIVING
RALPH'S REVIEW
RFD
Running Press
Sagapress, Inc.
Sasquatch Books
SCHUYLKILL LIVING MAGAZINE
SCIENCE/HEALTH ABSTRACTS
SEED SAVERS EXCHANGE
Shearer Publishing
SMALL FRUITS REVIEW
SPROUTLETTER
Storm Publishing Group
Swan Publishing Company
Timber Press
Touchstone Adventures
Trickle Creek Books
University of South Carolina Press
University of Virginia Press
Venus Communications
Waters Edge Press
Whispering Pine Press
THE WILD FOODS FORUM

GAY

AD/VANCE
Alamo Square Press
THE ALEMBIC
Avari Press
Back House Books
Bad Press
Banta & Pool Literary Properties
Bay Press
BAY WINDOWS
Beacon Press
Between The Lines
BLACK LACE
BLACKFIRE
BLK
BOOKS TO WATCH OUT FOR
Bordighera, Inc.
Broken Jaw Press
Burning Bush Publications
Carolina Wren Press/Lollipop Power Books
Cavalier Press
CESUM MAGAZINE
THE CHEROTIC (r)EVOLUTIONARY
Circlet Press, Inc.
Common Courage Press
THE CREAM CITY REVIEW
Down There Press
DWAN
Epoch Press
FIGHT THESE BASTARDS
The Fire!! Press
FIRSTHAND
FLUENT ASCENSION
Garden House Press
Gay Sunshine Press, Inc.
GAYELLOW PAGES
GERTRUDE
GERTRUDE
Gertrude Press
GIRLFRIENDS MAGAZINE
Gival Press
GLB Publishers
Golden Isis Press
GOOD GIRL
Grip Publishing
Hanover Press
Harrington Park Press
Holmes House
Ignite! Entertainment
IN OUR OWN WORDS
Ithuriel's Spear
JOURNAL OF NARRATIVE THEORY
KUUMBA

LadyePress USA, LLC
Lemieux International Ltd.
Leyland Publications
Life Untangled Publishing
Lone Willow Press
METROPOLITAN FORUM
MGW (Mom Guess What) Newsmagazine
Mho & Mho Works
NAMBLA BULLETIN
New Falcon Publications
New Sins Press
New Star Books Ltd.
Odysseus Enterprises Ltd.
OFF OUR BACKS
OUT OF LINE
Pagan Press
Palari Publishing
Parthian
Passion Power Press, Inc
PEACEWORK
Pleasure Boat Studio: A Literary Press
Pussywillow
Red Hand Press
Red Letter Press
RedBone Press
Re-invention UK Ltd
RFD
Salt Publishing
SENSATIONS MAGAZINE
Spectrum Press
Spirit Press
Starbooks Press/FLF Press
Chuck Stewart
Synergy Press
Syracuse Cultural Workers/Tools for Change
TnT Classic Books
TORQUERE: Journal of the Canadian Lesbian and Gay
    Studies Association
Triskelion Publishing
TURNING THE TIDE: Journal of Anti-Racist Action,
    Research & Education
The Twickenham Press
University of Chicago Press
Urban Legend Press
THE URBANITE
Vision
West Virginia University Press
which press
Windstorm Creative
THE WISHING WELL
Word Forge Books

GENDER ISSUES

ALONE TOGETHER
APPLE VALLEY REVIEW: A Journal of Contemporary
    Literature
AuthorsOmniscient Publishers
BIG HAMMER
BOOKS TO WATCH OUT FOR
CAMERA OBSCURA: Feminism, Culture, and Media
    Studies
Cantarabooks LLC
CESUM MAGAZINE
COLLEGE LITERATURE
CONSCIENCE: The Newsjournal of Catholic Opinion
CURRENTS: New Scholarship in the Human Services
DESIRE
Down There Press
DWAN
Ephemera Bound Publishing
Epoch Press
Eros Books
EROSHA
GERTRUDE
Gertrude Press
GREEN ANARCHY
Harrington Park Press
The Haworth Press

HYPATIA: A Journal of Feminist Philosophy
IRIS: A Journal About Women
Islewest Publishing
J&W Publishers, Inc.
Kumarian Press, Inc.
LAKE EFFECT
MEAT: A Journal of Writing and Materiality
METROPOLITAN FORUM
MOTHERVERSE: A Journal of Contemporary Motherhood
Passion Power Press, Inc
Pavement Saw Press
PSYCHE
Pussywillow
Radiant Press
Synergy Press
Vision
which press
Whispering Pine Press
WOMEN AND LANGUAGE
WSQ (formerly WOMEN'S STUDIES QUARTERLY)

GENEALOGY

Alaska Native Language Center
Cantadora Press
COGNITIO: A Graduate Humanities Journal
Cottontail Publications
Crazy Woman Creek Press
DeerTrail Books
Guarionex Press Ltd.
Heritage Books, Inc.
INKY TRAIL NEWS
IRISH FAMILY JOURNAL
Irish Genealogical Foundation
Land Yacht Press
ORAL HISTORY REVIEW
Outskirts Press, Inc.
The Overmountain Press
Panther Creek Press
Park Place Publications
Pocol Press
Quantum Leap S.L.C. Publications
R & M Publishing Company
Rayve Productions Inc.
Redgreene Press
Stewart Publishing & Printing
Titus Home Publishing
Total Cardboard Publishing
The Urbana Free Library

GEOGRAPHY

APPALACHIA JOURNAL
The Denali Press
EduCare Press
EXIT 13 MAGAZINE
THE JOURNAL OF AFRICAN TRAVEL-WRITING
Lexikos
New England Cartographics, Inc.
Rada Press, Inc.
United Nations University Press
The Urbana Free Library
Zagier & Urruty Publicaciones

GEOLOGY

America West Publishers
Black Dome Press Corp.
Cave Books
Comparative Sedimentology Lab.
GemStone Press
Mountain Press Publishing Co.
SEA KAYAKER
Genny Smith Books
Sunbelt Publications
John Wade, Publisher

GERMAN

ABSINTHE: New European Writing
THE ADIRONDACK REVIEW
R.J. Bender Publishing

Black Lawrence Press
Dufour Editions Inc.
The Edwin Mellen Press
GERMAN LIFE
Green Hut Press
Ignite! Entertainment
INTERNATIONAL POETRY REVIEW
NEW GERMAN REVIEW: A Journal of Germanic Studies
SISTERS IN CRIME BOOKS IN PRINT
TRANSITIONS ABROAD: The Guide to Living, Learning,
    and Working Overseas
Venus Communications

GLOBAL AFFAIRS

Accendo Publishing
Bad Press
Cantarabooks LLC
EXPERIMENTAL FOREST
FEMINIST STUDIES
Food First Books
GREEN ANARCHIST
Ho Logos Press
Hope Publishing House
The Independent Institute
THE INDEPENDENT REVIEW: A Journal of Political
    Economy
THE INDIE
Kumarian Press, Inc.
LifeCircle Press
MAIN STREET RAG
MOTHERVERSE: A Journal of Contemporary Motherhood
Nonetheless Press
Origin Press
The Pamphleteer's Press
PEACEWORK
Plain View Press
TELOS
THE VIRGINIA QUARTERLY REVIEW
Voyageur Publishing Co.,Inc.
WAV MAGAZINE: Progressive Music Art Politics Culture

GOVERNMENT

Aletheia Publications, Inc.
Benchmark Publications Inc.
BLACKBOOK PRESS, THE POETRY ZINE
Bluestocking Press
Bookhaven Press, LLC
Borealis Press Limited
BWALO: A Forum for Social Development
THE CAIMAN (formerly THE WEIRD NEWS)
CESUM MAGAZINE
Chandler & Sharp Publishers, Inc.
Children Of Mary
CKO UPDATE
Comstock Bonanza Press
EXPERIMENTAL FOREST
FIDELIS ET VERUS
Florida Academic Press
The Foundation for Economic Education, Inc.
FPMI Solutions, Inc.
THE FREEMAN: Ideas On Liberty
Ho Logos Press
The Independent Institute
THE INDEPENDENT REVIEW: A Journal of Political
    Economy
INNOVATING
KETTERING REVIEW
Kumarian Press, Inc.
LifeCircle Press
THE LONG TERM VIEW: A Journal of Informed Opinion
Maryland Historical Press
Origin Press
Planning/Communications
PRISON LEGAL NEWS
Reach Productions Publishing
TELOS
TRUTH SEEKER
The Urbana Free Library

THE VIRGINIA QUARTERLY REVIEW
THE WASHINGTON MONTHLY
WAV MAGAZINE: Progressive Music Art Politics Culture
Wind River Institute Press/Wind River Broadcasting
Xavier House Publishing

GRAPHIC DESIGN

Allworth Press
Britton Road Press
EEI Press
INDUSTRY MINNE-ZINE
NORTH CAROLINA LITERARY REVIEW
SAGE OF CONSCIOUSNESS E-ZINE
UmbraProjects, Ltd.
The Word Doctor Online Publishing

GRAPHICS

ABRAXAS
Banana Productions
Barefoot Press
BOOK MARKETING UPDATE
Brenner Information Group
BrickHouse Books, Inc.
Bright Hill Press
CHILDREN, CHURCHES AND DADDIES, A Non
    Religious, Non Familial Literary Magazine
DOWN IN THE DIRT LITERARY MAGAZINE, the prose
    & poetry magazine revealing all your dirty little secrets
EDGZ
FREEDOM AND STRENGTH PRESS FORUM
The Hosanna Press
INDUSTRY MINNE-ZINE
INTERNATIONAL ART POST
KALDRON, An International Journal Of Visual Poetry
Life Untangled Publishing
LIGHT: The Quarterly of Light Verse
LIGHTWORKS MAGAZINE
LOST GENERATION JOURNAL
Luna Bisonte Prods
MEAT: A Journal of Writing and Materiality
THE NEW RENAISSANCE, an international magazine of
    ideas & opinions, emphasizing literature & the arts
Oak Knoll Press
Oasis Books
Pearl's Book'em Publisher
PIG IRON
Red Cedar Press
RED CEDAR REVIEW
RIVER STYX
The Runaway Spoon Press
Scars Publications
SKYLARK
SLIPSTREAM
Smyrna Press
SOUTHWEST COLORADO ARTS PERSPECTIVE
STUDIO - A Journal of Christians Writing
13TH MOON
TIGHTROPE
Univelt, Inc.
Westgate Press
THE WORCESTER REVIEW
The Word Doctor Online Publishing
XTANT
xtant.anabasis

GREAT LAKES

Anacus Press, An Imprint of Finney Company
Arbutus Press
Cambric Press dba Emerald House
Wm.B. Eerdmans Publishing Co.
Jackson Harbor Press
Ladyslipper Press
Lake Claremont Press
LAKE SUPERIOR MAGAZINE
Mayapple Press
Ohio University Press/Swallow Press
Palladium Communications
PASSAGES NORTH

Wilderness Adventure Books

GREAT PLAINS

THE AZOREAN EXPRESS
Eagle's View Publishing
NORTH DAKOTA QUARTERLY
OVERLAND JOURNAL
THE PRAIRIE JOURNAL OF CANADIAN LITERATURE
Skyline West Press/Wyoming Almanac
SOUTH DAKOTA REVIEW
Southern Illinois University Press
Texas Tech University Press
TRADITION MAGAZINE
UND Press
University of Nebraska Press
WESTERN AMERICAN LITERATURE

GREEK

ABSINTHE: New European Writing
Anagnosis
Bandanna Books
THE CHARIOTEER
DIALOGOS: Hellenic Studies Review
EduCare Press
Focus Publishing/R. Pullins Co.
Horned Owl Publishing
INTERNATIONAL POETRY REVIEW
JOURNAL OF THE HELLENIC DIASPORA
Kelsey St. Press
Pella Publishing Co.
Wide World Publishing/TETRA

GRIEVING

Center for Thanatology Research & Education, Inc.
City Life Books, LLC
Dumouriez Publishing
ERASED, SIGH, SIGH
Galen Press, Ltd.
Impact Publishers, Inc.
Islewest Publishing
Jalmar Press/Innerchoice Publishing
KotaPress
NewSage Press
SKS Press
Square One Publishers, Inc.
Upper Access Inc.
Via Dolorosa Press
White Buck Publishing
Wise Press
Word Forge Books

GUIDANCE

A Cappela Publishing, Inc.
Aaron Communications III
THE ART OF ABUNDANCE
AuthorsOmniscient Publishers
Black Forest Press
END OF LIFE CHOICES
Hunter House Inc., Publishers
Impact Publishers, Inc.
Jalmar Press/Innerchoice Publishing
Mind Power Publishing
Nonetheless Press
Perpetual Press
Saint Mary's Press
The Saunderstown Press

HAIKU

AIS Publications
ANT ANT ANT ANT ANT
ASPHODEL
THE AUROREAN
BLACK BEAR REVIEW
BLACK BOUGH
BLITHE SPIRIT
BOGG: A Journal of Contemporary Writing
Brooks Books
THE CANNON'S MOUTH

CELLAR
CONCRETE JUNGLE JOURNAL
DREAM FANTASY INTERNATIONAL
Feel Free Press
FREEFALL
FROGPOND: Quarterly Haiku Journal
From Here Press
FROZEN WAFFLES
Frozen Waffles Press/Shattered Sidewalks Press; 45th
    Century Chapbooks
GENRE: WRITER AND WRITINGS
GIN BENDER POETRY REVIEW
Golden Isis Press
Haiku Society of America
Hanover Press
THE HERON'S NEST
J. Mark Press
Jackson Harbor Press
KAJ-MAHKAH: EARTH OF EARTH
Kenyette Productions
La Alameda Press
LILLIPUT REVIEW
MAYFLY
MODERN HAIKU
Mystery Island Publications
THE NARROW ROAD: A Haibun Journal
NEW AMERICAN IMAGIST
NEW HOPE INTERNATIONAL REVIEW
PARNASSUS LITERARY JOURNAL
Pearl's Book'em Publisher
PERIPHERAL VISION
Persephone Press
The Pin Prick Press
PINE ISLAND JOURNAL OF NEW ENGLAND POETRY
POETS' ROUNDTABLE
Press Here
RAINBOW CURVE
RATTAPALLAX
Redgreene Press
SAGE OF CONSCIOUSNESS E-ZINE
SAKANA
SHORT FUSE
THE SILT READER
SKYLARK
SMARTISH PACE
Snapshot Press
SOUTHWEST COLORADO ARTS PERSPECTIVE
TIGHTROPE
TUNDRA
VARIOUS ARTISTS
Via Dolorosa Press
WISTERIA: A Journal of Haiku, Senryu, and Tanka
WORDS OF WISDOM
Writers' Haven Press
XTRAS
Zygote Publishing

HANDICAPPED

ABLAZE Publishing
Alpine Guild, Inc.
CONCRETE JUNGLE JOURNAL
Creative Arts Book Company
Massey-Reyner Publishing
The Place In The Woods
The Saunderstown Press
John Wade, Publisher

HANDWRITING/WRITTEN

Continuing Education Press
Pavement Saw Press

HAWAII

Bamboo Ridge Press
BAMBOO RIDGE, Journal of Hawai'i Literature and Arts
CHECKER CAB MAGAZINE - THE LITTLE 'ZINE
    THAT COULD! Fiction That Takes The Long Way
    Home
HAWAI'I REVIEW

Island Style Press
Light, Words & Music
MANOA: A Pacific Journal of International Writing
A Melody from an Immigrant's Soul
Mo'omana'o Press
Mountain Automation Corporation
THE NEW SUPERNATURAL MAGAZINE
Paradise Publications
Petroglyph Press, Ltd.
Titlewaves Publishing; Writers Direct
TURNING THE TIDE: Journal of Anti-Racist Action,
    Research & Education
Wide World Publishing/TETRA

HEALTH

AB
Abecedarian books, Inc.
ABLAZE Publishing
Addicus Books, Inc.
Ageless Press
Aglob Publishing
Alpine Guild, Inc.
Amador Publishers
Anti-Aging Press
ARCATA ARTS
Ash Tree Publishing
Avocus Publishing, Inc.
Balanced Books Publishing
Bear & Company
Beekman Books, Inc.
Beyond Words Publishing, Inc.
Blue Poppy Press
Bonus Books, Inc.
BookPartners, Inc.
THE BOOMERPHILE
Branden Books
Cassandra Press, Inc.
Cladach Publishing
THE COMPLEAT NURSE
Consumer Press
Creative Writing and Publishing Company
Cypress House
DAILY WORD
Dash-Hill, LLC
Delaney Day Press
Dharma Publishing
Down There Press
Dream Publishing Co.
Emerald Wave
Enlightened Living Publishing, LLC
Envirographics
Nicolin Fields Publishing, Inc.
Fitness Press
Flowerfield Enterprises, LLC
Focus Publications, Inc.
Foodnsport Press
FORESIGHT MAGAZINE
Four Walls Eight Windows
Front Row Experience
Future Horizons, Inc.
Galde Press, Inc.
Galen Press, Ltd.
Garden House Press
Glenbridge Publishing Ltd.
Golden West Books
GoldenHouse Publishing Group
Good Book Publishing Company
GULF & MAIN Southwest Florida Lifestyle
Gurze Books
Haight-Ashbury Publications
Harrington Park Press
Health Plus Publishers
Health Press
Health Yourself
HEALTHY WEIGHT JOURNAL
Heritage Global Publishing
Hill Country Books
Himalayan Institute Press

Hope Publishing House
Howln Moon Press
Hunter House Inc., Publishers
Impact Publishers, Inc.
IN OUR OWN WORDS
Innisfree Press
Jireh Publishing Company
Joelle Publishing
JOURNAL OF PSYCHOACTIVE DRUGS
Kali Press
Kivaki Press
La Alameda Press
Lamp Light Press
Lao Tse Press, Ltd.
Lemieux International Ltd.
Library Research Associates
Life Energy Media
Lion Press
LISTEN
MACROBIOTICS TODAY
Master's Plan Publishing
MB Media, Inc.
MEDICAL HISTORY
Midwifery Today
MND Publishing, Inc.
N: NUDE & NATURAL
New Atlantean Press
New Falcon Publications
New Sins Press
New Win Publishing
New World Library
Newmark Publishing Company
Nicolas-Hays, Inc.
Nonetheless Press
North Star Books
Northland Publishing/Rising Moon/Luna Rising
OFF OUR BACKS
George Ohsawa Macrobiotic Foundation
Origin Press
OVERLAND JOURNAL
Pacific View Press
Palari Publishing
Parissound Publishing
Peachtree Publishers, Ltd.
Peanut Butter and Jelly Press, LLC
Pedestal Press
PEDIATRICS FOR PARENTS
Pennycorner Press
Petroglyph Press, Ltd.
Piccadilly Books, Ltd.
Pine Publications
Platinum One Publishing
Princess Publishing
Princeton Book Company, Publishers
QED Press
Quest Books: Theosophical Publishing House
Rama Publishing Co.
Rayve Productions Inc.
Reveal
RFD
Sagamore Publishing
Sanguinaria Publishing
Savor Publishing House, Inc.
SCIENCE/HEALTH ABSTRACTS
Sentient Publications, LLC
Set Sail Productions, LLC
SKINNYDIPPING
SO YOUNG!
SOM Publishing, division of School of Metaphysics
Southwest Research and Information Center
Spinifex Press
SPROUTLETTER
Square One Publishers, Inc.
Standish Press
Steel Balls Press
Sunrise Health Coach Publications
George Suttton Publishing Co.
Swan Publishing Company

Swan Raven & Company
Synergy Press
TAI CHI
Ten Star Press
Thatch Tree Publications
THRESHOLDS JOURNAL
TIFARA
Titan Press
Titlewaves Publishing; Writers Direct
Toad Hall Press
Topping International Institute, Inc.
Touchstone Adventures
UBC Press
Unity House
UNITY MAGAZINE
Upper Access Inc.
Vanderbilt University Press
VEGETARIAN JOURNAL
Vestibular Disorders Association
VINEGAR CONNOISSEURS INTERNATIONAL NEWS-
    LETTER
Vista Publishing, Inc.
VOICES FROM THE EARTH
Volcano Press, Inc
Wayfarer Publications
Wellcome Institute for the History of Medicine
Wharton Publishing, Inc.
Whitford Press
Whole Person Associates Inc.
WIN NEWS
Wish Publishing
Women of Diversity Productions, Inc.
Word Forge Books
World Changing Books
Yes International Publishers
YMAA Publication Center

ERNEST HEMINGWAY

Broken Jaw Press
THE CENTENNIAL REVIEW
KUMQUAT MERINGUE
LOST GENERATION JOURNAL
Pineapple Press, Inc.
Zygote Publishing

HISTORY

Aardvark Enterprises (A Division of Speers Investments
    Ltd.)
AAS HISTORY SERIES
THE ACORN
Acorn Books
AFRICAN AMERICAN REVIEW
African Ways Publishing
AK Press
Alaska Geographic Society
ALBERTA HISTORY
AltaMira Press
American Legacy Media
AMERICAN ROAD
Ammons Communications
Anagnosis
THE ANNALS OF IOWA
Anvil Publishers, Inc.
Appalachian Consortium Press
Arden Press, Inc.
ARTISTAMP NEWS
Artwork Publications, LLC
ATLANTIS: A Women's Studies Journal/Revue d'etudes
    sur les femmes
Autonomedia, Inc.
Avari Press
Avery Color Studios
Axios Newletter, Inc.
The B & R Samizdat Express
BANANA RAG
Bandanna Books
The Battery Press, Inc.
William L. Bauhan, Publisher

The Bear Wallow Publishing Company
Beekman Books, Inc.
R.J. Bender Publishing
Betelgeuse Books
Between The Lines
BIBLIOPHILOS
BIBLIOTHEQUE D'HUMANISME ET RENAISSANCE
BIG MUDDY: Journal of the Mississippi River Valley
Biographical Publishing Company
Black Dome Press Corp.
Blackwater Publications
THE BLOOMSBURY REVIEW
Blue Unicorn Press, Inc.
Bluestocking Press
BookPartners, Inc.
THE BOOMERPHILE
Borealis Press Limited
A. Borough Books
Branden Books
Brentwood Christian Press
THE BRIAR CLIFF REVIEW
BRIDGES: An Interdisciplinary Journal of Theology, Philosophy, History, and Science
Bright Mountain Books, Inc.
Broken Jaw Press
Broken Rifle Press
Brooke-Richards Press
Brookline Books
Buenos Books America
Burd Street Press
THE CAIMAN (formerly THE WEIRD NEWS)
CALLIOPE: Exploring World History
Camel Press
Canadian Committee on Labour History
CANADIAN REVIEW OF AMERICAN STUDIES
Candlestick Publishing
Celtic Heritage Books
Center for Japanese Studies
Center for Thanatology Research & Education, Inc.
Chelsea Green Publishing Company
Cherokee Publishing Company
CINEASTE MAGAZINE
Arthur H. Clark Co.
Coastal 181
COBBLESTONE: Discover American History
COGNITIO: A Graduate Humanities Journal
Command Performance Press
Communication Creativity
Comparative Sedimentology Lab.
The Compass Press
Comstock Bonanza Press
Cotsen Institute of Archaeology Publications
Cottontail Publications
Cottonwood Press, Inc.
Country Messenger Press
Creative Roots, Inc.
CROSSCURRENTS
CULTUREFRONT
Cypress House
DAILY WORD
THE DALHOUSIE REVIEW
DANDELION ARTS MAGAZINE
December Press
DeerTrail Books
The Denali Press
Denlinger's Publishers Ltd.
Dharma Publishing
Down The Shore Publishing
Downeast Books
Dufour Editions Inc.
DUST (From the Ego Trip)
Eagle's View Publishing
Earthwinds Editions
East West Discovery Press
Edition Gemini
EduCare Press
The Edwin Mellen Press
Wm.B. Eerdmans Publishing Co.

ELEMENTS
Ephemera Bound Publishing
Erespin Press
Event Horizon Press
Evolution Publishing
EZ Nature Books
Fantail
Feel Free Press
The Feminist Press at the City University of New York
FEMINIST STUDIES
Fern Publications
Florida Academic Press
Fotofolio, Inc.
Foundation Books
The Foundation for Economic Education, Inc.
Fouque Publishers
Four Walls Eight Windows
THE FREEMAN: Ideas On Liberty
Friends United Press
Fulcrum, Inc.
Galde Press, Inc.
Gallaudet University Press
Garden House Press
Gardenia Press
Gay Sunshine Press, Inc.
GERMAN LIFE
The Glencannon Press
Golden Quill Press
Golden West Books
Good Book Publishing Company
GORHAM
The Gutenberg Press
Heartsong Books
Heidelberg Graphics
Heritage Books, Inc.
Heritage House Publishers
Heritage West Books
Hermitage (Ermitazh)
Heyday Books
High Plains Press
Hill Country Books
Historical Resources Press
Historical Society of Alberta
HISTORICAL STUDIES IN THE PHYSICAL & BIOLO-GICAL SCIENCES
History Compass, LLC
HISTORY OF INTELLECTUAL CULTURE
Ho Logos Press
Homa & Sekey Books
Hoover Institution Press
Horned Owl Publishing
Horse Creek Publications, Inc.
Hot Box Press / Southern Roots Publishing
Hunter Publishing, Co.
Huntington Library Press
HUNTINGTON LIBRARY QUARTERLY
Icarus Press
THE INDEPENDENT REVIEW: A Journal of Political Economy
Info Net Publishing
Intelligenesis Publications
Interlink Publishing Group, Inc.
IOWA HERITAGE ILLUSTRATED
Iris Publishing Group, Inc (Iris Press / Tellico Books)
Ironweed Press
Island Publishers
Island Style Press
ITALIAN AMERICANA
Italica Press, Inc.
JACK MACKEREL MAGAZINE
Jackson Harbor Press
John James Company
JEWISH CURRENTS
THE JOURNAL OF HISTORICAL REVIEW
JOURNAL OF NARRATIVE THEORY
THE JOURNAL OF PSYCHOHISTORY
Keokee Co. Publishing, Inc.
KMT, A Modern Journal of Ancient Egypt

Allen A. Knoll Publishers
LABOUR/LE TRAVAIL
LadyePress USA, LLC
Lahontan Images
Lake Claremont Press
LAKE SUPERIOR MAGAZINE
Land Yacht Press
The Latona Press
Lemieux International Ltd.
LEO Productions LLC.
Lexikos
Library Research Associates, Inc.
Life Untangled Publishing
Little Leaf Press
Lorien House
Lucky Press, LLC
MacDonald/Sward Publishing Company
Maisonneuve Press
Peter Marcan Publications
Margaret Media, Inc.
Martinez Press
Maryland Historical Press
Mayhaven Publishing
MCM Entertainment, Inc. Publishing Division
MEDICAL HISTORY
Mehring Books, Inc.
Mercer University Press
THE MIDWEST QUARTERLY
Miles & Miles
Minnesota Historical Society Press
Mock Turtle Press
MOTHERVERSE: A Journal of Contemporary Motherhood
Mount Ida Press
Mountain Automation Corporation
Mountain Meadow Press
Mountain State Press
N: NUDE & NATURAL
The Narrative Press
New England Cartographics, Inc.
THE NEW ENGLAND QUARTERLY
New Star Books Ltd.
NEWS FROM NATIVE CALIFORNIA
NightinGale Resources
Nip & Tuck Publishing
Noontide Press
North Country Books, Inc.
NORTHWOODS JOURNAL, A Magazine for Writers
NOVA RELIGIO
NWI National Writers Institute
Oak Knoll Press
Ocean Publishing
Ohio University Press/Swallow Press
Open Hand Publishing LLC
Orage Publishing
ORAL HISTORY REVIEW
Oregon State University Press
THE OTHER ISRAEL
The Overmountain Press
Paladin Enterprises, Inc.
The Pamphleeter's Press
Parkway Publishers, Inc.
Pathfinder Press
The Patrice Press
Peartree Books & Music
Pictorial Histories Pub. Co.
Pineapple Press, Inc.
Pirate Publishing International
Pocahontas Press, Inc.
POETICA MAGAZINE, Reflections of Jewish Thought
Pogo Press, Incorporated
The Post-Apollo Press
Protean Press
Pruett Publishing Company
Psychohistory Press
THE PUBLIC HISTORIAN
QED Press
Quality Sports Publications
Quarterly Committee of Queen's University

QUEEN'S QUARTERLY: A Canadian Review
Questex Consulting Ltd.
Quill Driver Books
Rada Press, Inc.
Peter E. Randall Publisher
Rayve Productions Inc.
RELIGION & AMERICAN CULTURE
REPRESENTATIONS
Rio Nuevo Publishers
THE RIVER REVIEW/LA REVUE RIVIERE
Rock Spring Press Inc.
RockBySea Books
Ronsdale Press
Rose Publishing Co.
Rowhouse Press
Sagapress, Inc.
Sand River Press
Santa Ana River Press
Santa Fe Writers Project
Saqi Books Publisher
SCIENCE & SOCIETY
Scottwall Associates, Publishers
The Sektor Co.
SENSATIONS MAGAZINE
Genny Smith Books
Snake Hill Press
SOLAS Press
Sonoran Publishing
Southeast Missouri State University Press
Southern Illinois University Press
THE SOUTHERN QUARTERLY: A Journal of the Arts in the South
Starry Night Publishing
Steerforth Press, L.C.
Stewart Publishing & Printing
Stormline Press, Inc.
STORMWARNING!
Sherwood Sugden & Company, Publishers
Sherwood Sugden & Company, Publishers
Sun Books
Sunbelt Publications
Sunstone Press
SYMPLOKE: A Journal for the Intermingling of Literary, Cultural and Theoretical Scholarship
THE TABBY: A CHRONICLE OF THE ARTS AND CRAFTS MOVEMENT
The Teitan Press, Inc.
TELOS
Temple Inc.
Theytus Books Ltd.
Thirsty Turtle Press
Thirteen Colonies Press
Thundercloud Books
Titus Home Publishing
Truman State University Press
TRUTH SEEKER
Tuns Press
Twin Souls Publications
UBC Press
Unity House
UNITY MAGAZINE
University of Arkansas Press
University of Calgary Press
University of Chicago Press
University of Massachusetts Press
University of Nebraska Press
University of South Carolina Press
University of Tampa Press
University of Virginia Press
University Press of Colorado
UnKnownTruths.com Publishing Company
The Urbana Free Library
Urion Press
Utah State University Press
Van Cleave Publishing
Vintage Romance Publishing, LLC
THE VIRGINIA QUARTERLY REVIEW
Visibility Unlimited Publications

Volcano Press, Inc
THE VORTEX
Voyageur Publishing Co.,Inc.
Wayfinder Press
WEBER STUDIES: Voices and Viewpoints of the
    Contemporary West
Wellcome Institute for the History of Medicine
WELSH HISTORY REVIEW
Western New York Wares, Inc.
White Mane Publishing Company, Inc.
White Thread Press
WISCONSIN TRAILS
Word Forge Books
WSQ (formerly WOMEN'S STUDIES QUARTERLY)
Wytherngate Press
Zagier & Urruty Publicaciones
ZONE
Zumaya Publications

SHERLOCK HOLMES

AE-TU Publishing
ENGLISH LITERATURE IN TRANSITION, 1880-1920
Gryphon Books
KUMQUAT MERINGUE
THE MYSTERY REVIEW
Mystic Toad Press
PAPERBACK PARADE

HOLOCAUST

AIS Publications
BLACKBIRD
Book Marketing Solutions
BRIDGES: An Interdisciplinary Journal of Theology,
    Philosophy, History, and Science
Creative Arts Book Company
Cross-Cultural Communications
GENRE: WRITER AND WRITINGS
THE JOURNAL OF HISTORICAL REVIEW
New Concept Press
Noontide Press
Paragon House Publishers
POETICA MAGAZINE, Reflections of Jewish Thought
State University of New York Press
SterlingHouse Publisher
Typographia Press
University of Calgary Press
Van Cleave Publishing
WAR, LITERATURE & THE ARTS: An International
    Journal of the Humanities

HOLOGRAPHY

JACK MACKEREL MAGAZINE
Reveal
Rowhouse Press
THEATRE DESIGN AND TECHNOLOGY

HOMELESSNESS

Calyx Books
FIGHT THESE BASTARDS
Pocol Press
Touchstone Adventures

HOMEMAKING

THE ACORN
Affinity Publishers Services
Brighton Publications, Inc.
Center For Self-Sufficiency
COOKING CONTEST CHRONICLE
MOTHERVERSE: A Journal of Contemporary Motherhood
Nunciata
OUT YOUR BACKDOOR: The Magazine of Do-It-
    Yourself Adventure and Homegrown Culture
VINEGAR CONNOISSEURS INTERNATIONAL NEWS-
    LETTER

HORROR

APEX SCIENCE FICTION & HORROR DIGEST
ARTISTIC RAMBLINGS

AXE FACTORY REVIEW
BALLISTA
BUST DOWN THE DOOR AND EAT ALL THE
    CHICKENS: A Journal of Absurd and Surreal Fiction
Carnifex Press
Crystal Dreams Publishing
Ephemera Bound Publishing
The Fiction Works
Foremost Press
Gothic Press
Harbor House
Harvest Shadows Publications
LOW BUDGET SCIENCE FICTION
LULLABY HEARSE
MEAT FOR TEA: THE NORTHAMPTON REVIEW
Medusa Press
Merrimack Books
Mucusart Publications
MYSTERY ISLAND MAGAZINE
Pocol Press
Radiant Press
Triumvirate Publications
Whiskey Creek Press

HORTICULTURE

Andmar Press
Arizona Master Gardener Press
Bright Mountain Books, Inc.
Focus Publishing/R. Pullins Co.
Huntington Library Press
B.B. Mackey Books
Malki Museum Press
Pacific Isle Publishing Company
Park Place Publications
Red Eye Press
SMALL FRUITS REVIEW
Timber Press
Venus Communications

HOW-TO

AB
Acting World Books
Actium Publishing, Inc.
Addicus Books, Inc.
Affinity Publishers Services
Affinity Publishers Services
THE AGENCIES-WHAT THE ACTOR NEEDS TO
    KNOW
Aglob Publishing
Airplane Books
Alaska Native Language Center
Aletheia Publications, Inc.
Allworth Press
Altamont Press, Inc.
American Literary Press
Amherst Media, Inc.
Annedawn Publishing
Anti-Aging Press
Arden Press, Inc.
THE ART HORSE
ATS Publishing
AUDIO EXPRESS
AuthorsOmniscient Publishers
Backcountry Publishing
Barney Press
Benchmark Publications Inc.
The Bess Press
Beynch Press Publishing Company
Big Mouth Publications
Blue Dolphin Publishing, Inc.
Bonus Books, Inc.
BOOK NEWS & BOOK BUSINESS MART
Bookhaven Press, LLC
A. Borough Books
Breakout Productions
Brenner Information Group
Bright Ring Publishing, Inc.
Brighton Publications, Inc.

Bronze Girl Productions, Inc.
BYLINE
Byte Masters International
C & T Publishing
Camp Colton
Career Advancement Center, Inc.
Cassandra Press, Inc.
Center For Self-Sufficiency
Chelsea Green Publishing Company
Chicago Review Press
Chicago Spectrum Press
The Chicot Press
CineCycle Publishing
Communication Creativity
The Communication Press
Communicom Publishing Company
Consumer Press
Contemax Publishers
Costa Rica Books
Cottonwood Press, Inc.
Crandall, Dostie & Douglass Books, Inc.
Crane Press
Crystal Dreams Publishing
Cypress House
D.B.A. Books
Dash-Hill, LLC
Denlinger's Publishers Ltd.
Dixon-Price Publishing
DOLLS UNITED INTERACTIVE MAGAZINE
Downeast Books
The Dragon Press
Dunamis House
Dustbooks
DWELLING PORTABLY
Eagle's View Publishing
Ecrivez!
Envirographics
ETC Publications
Ethos Publishing
Excelsior Cee Publishing
Famaco Publishers (Qalam Books)
Fast Foot Forward Press
FIBERARTS
Fitness Press
Flowerfield Enterprises, LLC
Foremost Press
Fountainhead Productions, Inc.
Four Seasons Publishers
Four Walls Eight Windows
The P. Gaines Co., Publishers
Gazelle Publications
Gemini Publishing Company
GemStone Press
Gilgal Publications
Glenbridge Publishing Ltd.
GLOBAL ONE TRAVEL & AUTOMOTIVE MAGAZINE
Good Life Products
Good Times Publishing Co.
Guarionex Press Ltd.
Hands & Heart Books
HandyCraft Media Productions
Harvard Common Press
Heidelberg Graphics
THE HOLLYWOOD ACTING COACHES AND TEACHERS DIRECTORY
Howln Moon Press
Hunter Publishing, Co.
Ibexa Press
Images Unlimited and Snaptail Press, a Division of Images Unlimited Publishing
In Print Publishing
Infinite Possibilities Publishing Group, Inc.
Info Net Publishing
Islewest Publishing
J&W Publishers, Inc.
Jamenair Ltd.
Jireh Publishing Company
JLA Publications, A Division Of Jeffrey Lant Associates,

Inc.
Kali Press
Knowledge Concepts Publishing
Lamp Light Press
LAUGHING BEAR NEWSLETTER
Lemieux International Ltd.
Lexikos
Liberty Publishing Company, Inc.
Life Untangled Publishing
Lion Press
Microdex Bookshelf
Motom
The Mountaineers Books
Muse World Media Group
National Writers Press
N-B-T-V
New Community Press
New Win Publishing
Nightsun Books
Nolo Press Occidental
North American Bookdealers Exchange
North Star Books
Nunciata
Oak Tree Press
One Horse Press/Rainy Day Press
Open Horizons Publishing Company
Outskirts Press, Inc.
Paladin Enterprises, Inc.
PARENTEACHER MAGAZINE
Parissound Publishing
Pennycorner Press
Perpetual Press
Phelps Publishing Company
Piccadilly Books, Ltd.
The Pin Prick Press
The Poetry Center Press/Shoestring Press
Premier Publishers, Inc.
PREP Publishing
PSI Research/The Oasis Press/Hellgate Press
Pushcart Press
QED Press
Quill Driver Books
R & M Publishing Company
Rainbow Books, Inc.
Ram Press
Rayve Productions Inc.
Red Eye Press
Riverwinds Publishing
Roblin Press
Rolling Hills Publishing
Ronin Publishing, Inc.
RUMINATIONS: The Nigerian Dwarf & Mini Dairy Goat Magazine
Running Press
Santa Monica Press
The Saunderstown Press
Scentouri, Publishing Division
SCIENCE/HEALTH ABSTRACTS
Scrivenery Press
SEA KAYAKER
Sentient Publications, LLC
Six Strings Music Publishing
SO YOUNG!
SOM Publishing, division of School of Metaphysics
Sourcebooks, Inc.
SPEX (SMALL PRESS EXCHANGE)
Square One Publishers, Inc.
Standish Press
Steel Balls Press
Stewart Publishing & Printing
Stony Meadow Publishing
Storm Publishing Group
Success Publishing
Swan Publishing Company
Tamal Vista Publications
Tax Property Investor, Inc.
Thatch Tree Publications
Three House Publishing

Three Pyramids Publishing
Titlewaves Publishing; Writers Direct
Touchstone Adventures
Trafton Publishing
Travel Keys
VINEGAR CONNOISSEURS INTERNATIONAL NEWS-
LETTER
Vista Mark Publications
John Wade, Publisher
Wafer Mache Publications
Wayside Publications
Wharton Publishing, Inc.
WHISPERING WIND MAGAZINE
Zelda Wilde Publishing
Wilderness Adventure Books
Wilshire Books Inc.
Windstorm Creative
Winslow Publishing
YMAA Publication Center

HUMAN RIGHTS

AB
ABRAMELIN: a Journal of Poetry and Magick
AE-TU Publishing
AIS Publications
AMERICAN JONES BUILDING & MAINTENANCE
Archer Books
Beacon Press
Candlestick Publishing
CESUM MAGAZINE
Clarity Press, Inc.
COALITION FOR PRISONERS' RIGHTS NEWSLETTER
COUNTERPOISE: For Social Responsibilities, Liberty and
Dissent
Crandall, Dostie & Douglass Books, Inc.
CROSSCURRENTS
DREAM NETWORK
END OF LIFE CHOICES
EXPERIMENTAL FOREST
FEMINIST STUDIES
Food First Books
The Foundation for Economic Education, Inc.
FOURTH WORLD REVIEW
FREE INQUIRY
THE FREEMAN: Ideas On Liberty
FRIENDS OF PEACE PILGRIM
GENRE: WRITER AND WRITINGS
GLB Publishers
Global Options
The Independent Institute
THE INDEPENDENT REVIEW: A Journal of Political
Economy
Inner City Press
INNER CITY PRESS
INTERCULTURE
JAM RAG
LIBERTY
METAL CURSE
MOTHERVERSE: A Journal of Contemporary Motherhood
MOUTH: Voice of the Dis-Labeled Nation
PEACEWORK
The People's Press
Philopsychy Press
PRISON LEGAL NEWS
Reveal
Snake Hill Press
SOCIAL JUSTICE: A JOURNAL OF CRIME, CONFLICT,
& WORLD ORDER
STORMWARNING!
Syracuse Cultural Workers/Tools for Change
Touchstone Adventures
TRAVEL NATURALLY
TRUTH SEEKER
TURNING THE TIDE: Journal of Anti-Racist Action,
Research & Education
TURNING WHEEL
Vision
WAV MAGAZINE: Progressive Music Art Politics Culture

World Changing Books

HUMANISM

AIS Publications
ASCENT
ATLANTIS: A Women's Studies Journal/Revue d'etudes
sur les femmes
BELLEVUE LITERARY REVIEW
Black Rose Books Ltd.
BOULDER HERETIC
Cantarabooks LLC
COLOR WHEEL
Common Courage Press
CULTUREFRONT
Dharma Publishing
Dufour Editions Inc.
EMERGING
END OF LIFE CHOICES
Erespin Press
Feel Free Press
Fine Tooth Press
FOURTH WORLD REVIEW
FREE INQUIRY
Garden House Press
GENRE: WRITER AND WRITINGS
Green Hut Press
THE HUMANIST
THE LATHAM LETTER
Life Untangled Publishing
LOGIC LETTER
LP Publications (Teleos Institute)
Luminous Epinoia Press
Lycanthrope Press
Maisonneuve Press
METAL CURSE
Mountaintop Books
OUT OF LINE
The People's Press
POTOMAC REVIEW
Royal Purcell, Publisher
Red Hand Press
REPORTS OF THE NATIONAL CENTER FOR SCIENCE
EDUCATION
Reveal
The Saunderstown Press
Savant Garde Workshop
SHARE INTERNATIONAL
SOLAS Press
SYMPLOKE: A Journal for the Intermingling of Literary,
Cultural and Theoretical Scholarship
TRAVEL NATURALLY
VanderWyk & Burnham
Via Dolorosa Press
West End Press
THE WISHING WELL

HUMOR

Abecedarian books, Inc.
ACME Press
Ageless Press
ALL ROUND
THE AMERICAN DRIVEL REVIEW
American Literary Press
ARTISTIC RAMBLINGS
Aspen Mountain Publishing
ASPHODEL
AT-HOME DAD
ATLANTIS: A Women's Studies Journal/Revue d'etudes
sur les femmes
AuthorsOmniscient Publishers
The B & R Samizdat Express
BABYSUE
BANANA RAG
Bancroft Press
BEGINNINGS - A Magazine for the Novice Writer
The Bess Press
Big Mouth Publications
BLADES

Blue Dolphin Publishing, Inc.
BLUE HORSE
Blue Horse Publications
Blue Mouse Studio
Bogg Publications
THE BOOMERPHILE
A. Borough Books
Brave Ulysses Books
BRAZOS GUMBO
Bright Mountain Books, Inc.
Brook Farm Books
BUST DOWN THE DOOR AND EAT ALL THE CHICKENS: A Journal of Absurd and Surreal Fiction
THE CANNON'S MOUTH
The Center Press
The Communication Press
CONJUNCTIONS
Cottonwood Press, Inc.
Creative Guy Publishing
CREOSOTE: A Journal of Poetry and Prose
Crones Unlimited
Crystal Dreams Publishing
Dawn Sign Press
Denlinger's Publishers Ltd.
DOPE FRIENDS
Downeast Books
THE EAST VILLAGE INKY
Event Horizon Press
Excelsior Cee Publishing
Falls Media
FAT TUESDAY
FINE MADNESS
Firelight Publishing, Inc.
First Books
Fotofolio, Inc.
FRAN MAGAZINE
Free Reign Press, Inc.
THE FREEDONIA GAZETTE: The Magazine Devoted to the Marx Brothers
Fulcrum, Inc.
THE FUNNY PAPER
THE FUNNY TIMES
Gardenia Press
Gateways Books And Tapes
GLOBAL ONE TRAVEL & AUTOMOTIVE MAGAZINE
GoldenIsle Publishers, Inc.
Green Stone Publications
HA!
HEELTAP/Pariah Press
Hobblebush Books
Ignite! Entertainment
IMOCO Publishing
INDY MAGAZINE
JetKor
JOURNAL OF AESTHETICS AND ART CRITICISM
JOURNAL OF POLYMORPHOUS PERVERSITY
juel house publishers and literary services
KALEIDOSCOPE: Exploring the Experience of Disability through Literature & the Fine Arts
Allen A. Knoll Publishers
KRAX
KUMQUAT MERINGUE
Lazywood Press
The Leaping Frog Press
LegacyForever
Lemieux International Ltd.
Liaison Press
Little Pear Press
THE MAD HATTER
MAIN STREET RAG
MALEDICTA: The International Journal of Verbal Aggression
MB Media, Inc.
MEAT FOR TEA: THE NORTHAMPTON REVIEW
METAL CURSE
MeteoritePress.com
METROPOLITAN FORUM
Miles & Miles

Millennium Workshop Production
MINESHAFT
MOMMY AND I ARE ONE
THE MONTHLY INDEPENDENT TRIBUNE TIMES JOURNAL POST GAZETTE NEWS CHRONICLE BULLETIN
MOTORBOOTY MAGAZINE
Muse World Media Group
Music City Publishing
MY TABLE: Houston's Dining Magazine
Mystic Toad Press
NANNY FANNY
New Victoria Publishers
No Starch Press
North Star Books
NORTHERN PILOT
NUTHOUSE
NWI National Writers Institute
Oak Tree Press
OFFICE NUMBER ONE
ORBIS
Paladin Enterprises, Inc.
PALO ALTO REVIEW
Pariah Press
PARNASSUS LITERARY JOURNAL
PASSAGES NORTH
Penthe Publishing
PLAIN BROWN WRAPPER (PBW)
POETICA MAGAZINE, Reflections of Jewish Thought
The Poetry Center Press/Shoestring Press
Pogo Press, Incorporated
Portmanteau Editions
POTOMAC REVIEW
THE PRAIRIE JOURNAL OF CANADIAN LITERATURE
Prairie Journal Press
The Press at Foggy Bottom
PublishAmerica, LLLP.
Questex Consulting Ltd.
Radiant Press
RAINBOW CURVE
RANDEE
Raw Dog Press
Red Hand Press
Red Rock Press
RedJack
Resource Publications, Inc.
Rivercross Publishing, Inc.
RIVET MAGAZINE
Ronin Publishing, Inc.
The Runaway Spoon Press
Santa Monica Press
SKYLARK
SO YOUNG!
Standish Press
Starry Night Publishing
Stormline Press, Inc.
STRUGGLE: A Magazine of Proletarian Revolutionary Literature
Synapse-Centurion
Synergistic Press
THALIA: Studies in Literary Humor
THOUGHTS FOR ALL SEASONS: The Magazine of Epigrams
Three Bears Publishing
THRESHOLDS JOURNAL
Titlewaves Publishing; Writers Direct
Trafton Publishing
Transcending Mundane, Inc.
Triple Tree Publishing
Twilight Times Books
Two Thousand Three Associates
Two Thousand Three Associates
Urban Legend Press
THE URBANITE
VOICES - ISRAEL
WAV MAGAZINE: Progressive Music Art Politics Culture
Whiskey Creek Press
Wild West Publishing House

INSPIRATIONAL

Aaron Communications III
American Literary Press
Ammons Communications
THE ART OF ABUNDANCE
Ascension Publishing
ASCENT
THE AUROREAN
Azreal Publishing Company
Bandido Books
Beacon Light Publishing (BLP)
Believe! Publishing
Beyond Words Publishing, Inc.
Big Valley Press
Biographical Publishing Company
Blue Dove Press
Blue Star Press
THE CANNON'S MOUTH
Cascada Corporation / Scherf Books, MegaGrace Books
City Life Books, LLC
Cladach Publishing
Crane Press
Crones Unlimited
Delaney Day Press
Denlinger's Publishers Ltd.
Dharma Publishing
Dream Publishing Co.
Dumouriez Publishing
E & D Publishing, Inc.
Excelsior Cee Publishing
Nicolin Fields Publishing, Inc.
Fingerprint Press
Four Seasons Publishers
Friendly Oaks Publications
Good Book Publishing Company
Goose River Press
Harlan Publishing Company; Alliance Books; Diakonia Publishing (Christian Books)
Heartsong Books
The Heather Foundation
Higher Ground Press
Himalayan Institute Press
Hope Publishing House
Illumination Arts
In Print Publishing
Innisfree Press
J&W Publishers, Inc.
The Kenneth G. Mills Foundation
Lamp Light Press
Leadership Education and Development, Inc.
The Leaping Frog Press
Light, Words & Music
Long & Silverman Publishing, Inc.
Luminous Epinoia Press
MAGICAL BLEND/NATURAL BEAUTY & HEALTH/ TRANSITIONS
Mandala Publishing
MB Media, Inc.
A Melody from an Immigrant's Soul
Middleway Press
Millennium Vision Press
Mind Power Publishing
Missing Man Press
Motom
Munsey Music
Music City Publishing
New Paradigm Books
New World Library
Origin Press
Oyster River Press
The Passion Profit Company
Pellingham Casper Communications
PhoeniX in Print
The Poetry Center Press/Shoestring Press
Premium Press America
PREP Publishing
Quest Books: Theosophical Publishing House

Red Rock Press
REMS Publishing & Publicity
REMS Publishing & Publicity
Reveal
Sadorian Publications
The Saunderstown Press
SCULPTURAL PURSUIT MAGAZINE
Set Sail Productions, LLC
SHARE INTERNATIONAL
SKS Press
Sound View Publishing, Inc.
SPIRITCHASER
Spiritual Understanding Network, LLC
Tendre Press
Thatch Tree Publications
THRESHOLDS JOURNAL
Timeless Books
Titlewaves Publishing; Writers Direct
Triskelion Publishing
Ulysses Books
Unity House
Virginia Pines Press
WHAT IS ENLIGHTENMENT?
Whiskey Creek Press
Wilderness Ministries
WinePress Publishing
World Gumbo Publishing
Wytherngate Press
Zumaya Publications

INSURANCE

Bay Tree Publishing
GLOBAL ONE TRAVEL & AUTOMOTIVE MAGAZINE
THE MONTHLY INDEPENDENT TRIBUNE TIMES JOURNAL POST GAZETTE NEWS CHRONICLE BULLETIN
THE SMALL BUSINESS ADVISOR

INTERNET

Actium Publishing, Inc.
Brenner Information Group
C & T Publishing
COUNTER CULTURE
DOLLS UNITED INTERACTIVE MAGAZINE
EEI Press
THE FRANK REVIEW
Frontline Publications
Happy About
Highsmith Press
J. Mark Press
JUST WEST OF ATHENS
MAIN STREET RAG
MARGIN: Exploring Modern Magical Realism
Martinez Press
New Community Press
New World Press, Inc
Palladium Communications
THE PEDESTAL MAGAZINE.COM
SAGE OF CONSCIOUSNESS E-ZINE
THE SOURCES HOTLINK

INTERVIEWS

ARTISTIC RAMBLINGS
ASCENT
AXE FACTORY REVIEW
THE BALTIMORE REVIEW
BIG MUDDY: Journal of the Mississippi River Valley
BIRD DOG
BITTER OLEANDER
BLACKBOOK PRESS, THE POETRY ZINE
BLACKFIRE
THE BLIND MAN'S RAINBOW
BLK
BOGG: A Journal of Contemporary Writing
THE BRIAR CLIFF REVIEW
BRILLIANT CORNERS: A Journal of Jazz & Literature
Brookline Books
Celebrity Profiles Publishing

CONCRETE JUNGLE JOURNAL
CONJUNCTIONS
CRAB ORCHARD REVIEW
THE CREAM CITY REVIEW
Crescent Moon
DOLLS UNITED INTERACTIVE MAGAZINE
THE DRAMATIST
DREAM NETWORK
Edin Books, Inc.
ELEMENTS
EVANSVILLE REVIEW
Finney Company, Inc.
FIVE POINTS
FOLIO: A Literary Journal of American University
FRAN MAGAZINE
FREEFALL
Gay Sunshine Press, Inc.
Gertrude Press
GRAY AREAS
THE GREEN HILLS LITERARY LANTERN
GULF COAST
Happy About
Impassio Press
THE INDIE
INNOVATING
ISSUES
THE JOURNAL
JUBILAT
juel house publishers and literary services
JUST WEST OF ATHENS
THE KENYON REVIEW
KESTREL: A Journal of Literature and Art
THE LEDGE
THE LONG TERM VIEW: A Journal of Informed Opinion
MAIN STREET RAG
MANGROVE MAGAZINE
THE MARLBORO REVIEW
Maryland Historical Press
MB Media, Inc.
METAL CURSE
MOMMY AND I ARE ONE
MOTHERVERSE: A Journal of Contemporary Motherhood
MUDLARK
THE MYSTERY REVIEW
NEO: Literary Magazine
NEW DELTA REVIEW
NEW LETTERS
THE NEW YORK QUARTERLY
NOTRE DAME REVIEW
NOVA EXPRESS
THE ORPHAN LEAF REVIEW
PALO ALTO REVIEW
Panther Books
PASSION
THE PEDESTAL MAGAZINE.COM
Purple Finch Press
QUARTER AFTER EIGHT
RAIN TAXI REVIEW OF BOOKS
REAL PEOPLE
RED WHEELBARROW
Salt Publishing
The Saunderstown Press
Score
SCULPTURAL PURSUIT MAGAZINE
SECOND GUESS
SHARE INTERNATIONAL
shift 4 Publishing
SO TO SPEAK: A Feminist Journal of Language & Art
Starbooks Press/FLF Press
THE STINGING FLY
THE SUN, A Magazine of Ideas
SYCAMORE REVIEW
Talisman House, Publishers
TEXAS POETRY JOURNAL
Thatch Tree Publications
THEATER
University of Tampa Press
VALLUM: CONTEMPORARY POETRY

WEBER STUDIES: Voices and Viewpoints of the Contemporary West
which press
WILD DUCK REVIEW
THE WILDWOOD READER
WILLOW SPRINGS
WORLD OF FANDOM MAGAZINE
WRITER'S CAROUSEL

INVENTING

Missing Spoke Press

IOWA

THE ANNALS OF IOWA
Blackwater Publications
THE BRIAR CLIFF REVIEW
Coffee House Press
Foundation Books
IOWA HERITAGE ILLUSTRATED
MIDWEST ART FAIRS

IRELAND

ABSINTHE: New European Writing
Beacon Press
Blackwater Publications
Celtic Heritage Books
Devenish Press
DOPE FRIENDS
Dufour Editions Inc.
THE EDGE CITY REVIEW
EXIT 13 MAGAZINE
Fountainhead Productions, Inc.
IRISH FAMILY JOURNAL
Irish Genealogical Foundation
IRISH LITERARY SUPPLEMENT
JAMES JOYCE BROADSHEET
JOURNAL OF MUSIC IN IRELAND (JMI)
Miami University Press
NORTH DAKOTA QUARTERLY
Open Hand Publishing LLC
Poetry Ireland
POETRY IRELAND REVIEW
REMS Publishing & Publicity
Scottwall Associates, Publishers
Stewart Publishing & Printing
THE STINGING FLY
TRANSITIONS ABROAD: The Guide to Living, Learning, and Working Overseas
UND Press
University of Tulsa

ITALIAN-AMERICAN

BIBLIOPHILOS
Bordighera, Inc.
ITALIAN AMERICANA
Malafemmina Press
MCM Entertainment, Inc. Publishing Division
Open University of America Press
Snake Hill Press
Voyageur Publishing Co.,Inc.

ITALY

ABSINTHE: New European Writing
Blue Dolphin Publishing, Inc.
Bordighera, Inc.
Cross-Cultural Communications
Department of Romance Languages
Desert Bloom Press
Italica Press, Inc.
LO STRANIERO: The Stranger, Der Fremde, L'Etranger
MCM Entertainment, Inc. Publishing Division
SYMPOSIUM
TRANSITIONS ABROAD: The Guide to Living, Learning, and Working Overseas
Voyageur Publishing Co.,Inc.

JAMAICA

Lyons Publishing Limited

JAPAN

Center for Japanese Studies
KUMQUAT MERINGUE
THE NARROW ROAD: A Haibun Journal
Perpetual Press
Plympton Press International
Press Here
Stone Bridge Press
TRANSITIONS ABROAD: The Guide to Living, Learning, and Working Overseas
UmbraProjects, Ltd.
United Nations University Press

ROBINSON JEFFERS

WESTERN AMERICAN LITERATURE

THOMAS JEFFERSON

Bluestocking Press
Maryland Historical Press
Mount Ida Press
University of Virginia Press

JEWELRY, GEMS

Eagle's View Publishing
GemStone Press
GULF & MAIN Southwest Florida Lifestyle
HandyCraft Media Productions
International Jewelry Publications
Kiva Publishing, Inc.
MIDWEST ART FAIRS
ORNAMENT
ORNAMENT
Spirit Press

JOURNALS

ARCHIPELAGO
BORDERLANDS: Texas Poetry Review
Burning Bush Publications
Chatterley Press International
CHILDREN, CHURCHES AND DADDIES, A Non Religious, Non Familial Literary Magazine
CREATIVE NONFICTION
DREAM NETWORK
580 SPLIT
FLUENT ASCENSION
FREEDOM AND STRENGTH PRESS FORUM
Hanover Press
Harrington Park Press
The Haworth Press
Impassio Press
The Independent Institute
LULLWATER REVIEW
Magic Circle Press
My Heart Yours Publishing
NEO: Literary Magazine
NEW ORLEANS REVIEW
PALO ALTO REVIEW
PERIPHERAL VISION
PORTLAND REVIEW
PROSE AX
Rayve Productions Inc.
Sagamore Publishing
ST. LOUIS JOURNALISM REVIEW
SCIENCE & SOCIETY
THE SILT READER
SMARTISH PACE
THE SUN, A Magazine of Ideas
SYMPOSIUM
TELOS
Telos Press
13TH MOON
Titus Home Publishing
TORRE DE PAPEL

JAMES JOYCE

Barrytown/Station Hill Press
Casperian Books LLC

EXPERIMENTAL FOREST
JAMES JOYCE BROADSHEET
JAMES JOYCE QUARTERLY
NOBODADDIES
PLAIN BROWN WRAPPER (PBW)
Scripta Humanistica
SHATTERED WIG REVIEW
University of Tulsa
Zygote Publishing

JUDAISM

ARC
Beacon Press
Biblio Press
Blue Dove Press
BOULDER HERETIC
BRIDGES: A Journal for Jewish Feminists and Our Friends
Burning Bush Publications
THE CAIMAN (formerly THE WEIRD NEWS)
Chicago Spectrum Press
Cross-Cultural Communications
DOVETAIL: A Journal by and for Jewish/Christian Families
The Edwin Mellen Press
The Eighth Mountain Press
Florida Academic Press
Fontanel Books
Gloger Family Books
IN OUR OWN WORDS
ISSUES
JEWISH CURRENTS
Jewish Publication Society
Judah Magnes Museum Publications
Kar-Ben Publishing, Inc.
KEREM: Creative Explorations in Judaism
LILITH
Mayapple Press
Micah Publications Inc.
Mountaintop Books
New Concept Press
NightinGale Resources
No Starch Press
The Pin Prick Press
Pocol Press
POETICA MAGAZINE, Reflections of Jewish Thought
The Press at Foggy Bottom
SALMAGUNDI
SHIRIM
Tzipora Publications, Inc.
VOICES - ISRAEL
WHAT IS ENLIGHTENMENT?
Zagier & Urruty Publicaciones

JUVENILE FICTION

Aaron Communications III
Azreal Publishing Company
Bronze Girl Productions, Inc.
Cladach Publishing
Creative Arts Book Company
Creative Writing and Publishing Company
Delaney Day Press
Ecrivez!
Fontanel Books
Hungry Tiger Press
Illumination Arts
Images Unlimited and Snaptail Press, a Division of Images Unlimited Publishing
Journey Books Publishing
juel house publishers and literary services
THE LEDGE
Little Pear Press
Loonfeather Press
Millennium Workshop Production
Ocean Publishing
Parity Press
Platinum Dreams Publishing
The Poetry Center
POGO STICK

Polar Bear & Company
PublishAmerica, LLLP.
Re-invention UK Ltd
Ryrich Publications
Twynz Publishing
UmbraProjects, Ltd.
Wilderness Ministries
Zebra Press

KAFKA

BUST DOWN THE DOOR AND EAT ALL THE
    CHICKENS: A Journal of Absurd and Surreal Fiction
Casperian Books LLC
Honors Group
UNDERSTANDING MAGAZINE
Zygote Publishing

KANSAS

COTTONWOOD
Cottonwood Press

KENTUCKY

Chicago Spectrum Press
Iris Publishing Group, Inc (Iris Press / Tellico Books)
THE LICKING RIVER REVIEW
The Overmountain Press
PIKEVILLE REVIEW
Rock Spring Press Inc.
Southeast Missouri State University Press
SPITBALL: The Literary Baseball Magazine
WIND
Xavier House Publishing

JACK KEROUAC

Alpha Beat Press
THE BOOMERPHILE
Casperian Books LLC
Creative Arts Book Company
EXPERIMENTAL FOREST
FRANK: AN INTERNATIONAL JOURNAL OF CON-
    TEMPORARY WRITING AND ART
Frozen Waffles Press/Shattered Sidewalks Press; 45th
    Century Chapbooks
Mica Press - Paying Our Dues Productions
OPEN WIDE MAGAZINE
PLAIN BROWN WRAPPER (PBW)
PLOPLOP
Southern Illinois University Press
Water Row Press
WATER ROW REVIEW
WESTERN AMERICAN LITERATURE
X-Ray Book Co.
Zygote Publishing

RUDYARD KIPLING

ENGLISH LITERATURE IN TRANSITION, 1880-1920
Mystery Island Publications
UNDERSTANDING MAGAZINE

LABOR

AMERICAN JONES BUILDING & MAINTENANCE
Beekman Books, Inc.
Between The Lines
BIG HAMMER
Black Rose Books Ltd.
THE BLOOMSBURY REVIEW
BLUE COLLAR REVIEW
Brenner Information Group
Canadian Committee on Labour History
COLORLINES
Global Options
History Compass, LLC
International Publishers Co. Inc.
Labor Arts Books
LABOUR/LE TRAVAIL
Macrocosm USA, Inc.
Maisonneuve Press
Mehring Books, Inc.

Missing Spoke Press
New Star Books Ltd.
NEW UNIONIST
OFF OUR BACKS
Open Hand Publishing LLC
OUR SCHOOLS/OUR SELVES
Partisan Press
Pathfinder Press
PAVEMENT SAW
Pavement Saw Press
Red Letter Press
Ridgeway Press of Michigan
THE SMALL BUSINESS ADVISOR
Smyrna Press
SOCIAL JUSTICE: A JOURNAL OF CRIME, CONFLICT,
    & WORLD ORDER
SOCIAL POLICY
South End Press
STATE OF CALIFORNIA LABOR
STRUGGLE: A Magazine of Proletarian Revolutionary
    Literature
Syracuse Cultural Workers/Tools for Change
Trentham Books
University of Chicago Press
Vanderbilt University Press
THE WASHINGTON MONTHLY

LANGUAGE

AERIAL
Alaska Native Language Center
Ariko Publications
ASIAN JOURNAL OF ENGLISH LANGUAGE TEACH-
    ING
Autonomedia, Inc.
Bandanna Books
Bilingual Review Press
BILINGUAL REVIEW/Revista Bilingue
BULLETIN OF HISPANIC STUDIES
Center for Japanese Studies
The Chicot Press
The Chinese University Press
Clamshell Press
THE CLASSICAL OUTLOOK
COLLEGE LITERATURE
Department of Romance Languages
DESIRE
DOWN IN THE DIRT LITERARY MAGAZINE, the prose
    & poetry magazine revealing all your dirty little secrets
EEI Press
Elderberry Press, LLC
Eros Books
ESPERANTIC STUDIES
Evolution Publishing
Family Learning Association, Inc.
Focus Publishing/R. Pullins Co.
FREEDOM AND STRENGTH PRESS FORUM
Gallaudet University Press
GRAIN MAGAZINE
HEAVEN BONE MAGAZINE
Heaven Bone Press
IBEX Publishers, Inc.
INTERNATIONAL POETRY REVIEW
Iris Publishing Group, Inc (Iris Press / Tellico Books)
JACK MACKEREL MAGAZINE
THE JOURNAL OF CALIFORNIA AND GREAT BASIN
    ANTHROPOLOGY
JOURNAL OF CELTIC LINGUISTICS
JOURNAL OF COURT REPORTING
KALDRON, An International Journal Of Visual Poetry
Liverpool University Press
LORE AND LANGUAGE
LULLWATER REVIEW
Maledicta Press
MALEDICTA: The International Journal of Verbal Aggres-
    sion
Malki Museum Press
Margaret Media, Inc.
Merl Publications

THE MODERN LANGUAGE JOURNAL
Moon Pie Press
National Court Reporters Association Press
nine muses books
The Olivia and Hill Press, Inc.
Open Horizons Publishing Company
OSIRIS
Oyster River Press
Palladium Communications
PARENTEACHER MAGAZINE
PASSAGER
Petroglyph Press, Ltd.
POINT OF CONTACT, The Journal of Verbal & Visual
    Arts
Protean Press
PSYCHE
PULSAR POETRY MAGAZINE
Read Press LLC
RHETORICA: A Journal of the History of Rhetoric
Rodnik Publishing Co.
Rowhouse Press
SAKANA
Saqi Books Publisher
Saskatchewan Writers Guild
Scars Publications
Score
Solcat Publishing
SPORE
Stone Bridge Press
Strata Publishing, Inc.
SULPHUR RIVER LITERARY REVIEW
George Suttton Publishing Co.
Thatch Tree Publications
Thorp Springs Press
UBC Press
Univelt, Inc.
University of Utah Press
Vanderbilt University Press
Velazquez Press
Verbatim Books
Voyageur Publishing Co.,Inc.
WEST COAST LINE: A Journal of Contemporary Writing
    and Criticism
WOMEN AND LANGUAGE

LAPIDARY

Cynic Press
GemStone Press

LATIN AMERICA

AFRO-HISPANIC REVIEW
Autonomedia, Inc.
THE BLOOMSBURY REVIEW
CANADIAN JOURNAL OF LATIN AMERICAN AND
    CARIBBEAN STUDIES/Revue canadienne des etudes
    latino-americaines et caraibes
Cedar Hill Books
CEDAR HILL REVIEW
CHASQUI
Cleis Press
Costa Rica Books
Cross-Cultural Communications
Department of Romance Languages
Fine Tooth Press
FIREBREEZE PUBLISHING
Garden House Press
Gay Sunshine Press, Inc.
Hoover Institution Press
Hope Publishing House
Inner City Press
Interlink Publishing Group, Inc.
INTERNATIONAL POETRY REVIEW
Iris Publishing Group, Inc (Iris Press / Tellico Books)
LATIN AMERICAN LITERARY REVIEW
Latin American Literary Review Press
LATIN AMERICAN PERSPECTIVES
Martinez Press
Mayapple Press

Palladium Communications
Pangaea
Panther Creek Press
Passport Press
Pathfinder Press
POINT OF CONTACT, The Journal of Verbal & Visual
    Arts
SALMAGUNDI
Salt Publishing
SOCIETE
Solcat Publishing
SOUTH AMERICAN EXPLORER
SYMPOSIUM
Syracuse Cultural Workers/Tools for Change
TORRE DE PAPEL
TRADICION REVISTA
Two Eagles Press International
Vanderbilt University Press
White Pine Press
World Music Press
Zagier & Urruty Publicaciones

LATINO

Archer Books
Azreal Publishing Company
BILINGUAL REVIEW/Revista Bilingue
Dream Publishing Co.
Latin American Literary Review Press
LPD Press
Lummox Press
MANDORLA: New Writing from the Americas / Nueva
    escritura de las Americas
Martinez Press
Merl Publications
Miami University Press
New Sins Press
Northland Publishing/Rising Moon/Luna Rising
Northwestern University Press
POINT OF CONTACT, The Journal of Verbal & Visual
    Arts
Three House Publishing
TORRE DE PAPEL
TRADICION REVISTA
Two Eagles Press International
Wings Press

LAW

Allworth Press
AMERICAN JUROR (formerly FIJACTIVIST, 1989-2004)
ART CALENDAR
Athanata Arts, Ltd.
THE BEACON: Journal of Special Education Law &
    Practice
Bluestocking Press
Buenos Books America
Claitor's Law Books & Publishing Division, Inc.
CRIMINAL JUSTICE ABSTRACTS
Criminal Justice Press
Event Horizon Press
Fathom Publishing Co.
Frontline Publications
The P. Gaines Co., Publishers
Galt Press
Global Options
Grand River Press
GRAY AREAS
Harbor House Law Press, Inc.
HARVARD WOMEN'S LAW JOURNAL
The Independent Institute
THE INDEPENDENT REVIEW: A Journal of Political
    Economy
INDEX TO FOREIGN LEGAL PERIODICALS
JOURNAL OF COURT REPORTING
LAW AND LITERATURE
LEGAL INFORMATION MANAGEMENT INDEX
THE LONG TERM VIEW: A Journal of Informed Opinion
Merl Publications
Metallo House Publishers

690

Millennium Vision Press
Morgen Publishing Incorporated
MOUTH: Voice of the Dis-Labeled Nation
National Court Reporters Association Press
Nolo Press
Nolo Press Occidental
Northern Illinois University Press
Peartree Books & Music
Philopsychy Press
PRISON LEGAL NEWS
PRIVACY JOURNAL
THE SMALL BUSINESS ADVISOR
SOCIAL JUSTICE: A JOURNAL OF CRIME, CONFLICT,
    & WORLD ORDER
Sourcebooks, Inc.
Speck Press
Strata Publishing, Inc.
STUDENT LAWYER
TELOS
Telos Press
UBC Press
University Press of Colorado
White Thread Press
Willow Tree Press, Inc.
Wind River Institute Press/Wind River Broadcasting

D.H. LAWRENCE

Chatterley Press International
Crescent Moon
Hailey-Grey Books
PASSION
The Press of Appletree Alley
John Wade, Publisher

LEADERSHIP

Advanced Learning Press
Affirmative Publishing LC
Alpine Guild, Inc.
Book Marketing Solutions
BUSINESS SPIRIT JOURNAL
Common Boundaries
EXECUTIVE EXCELLENCE
Executive Excellence Publishing
Falcon Publishing, LTD
Famaco Publishers (Qalam Books)
Finney Company, Inc.
J&W Publishers, Inc.
Leadership Education and Development, Inc.
Mind Power Publishing
Multi-Media Publications Inc.
Pegasus Communications, Inc.
Princess Publishing
Reliance Books
Set Sail Productions, LLC
Smith-Johnson Publisher
Top 20 Press
The Utility Company LLC
Visions Communications
Zelda Wilde Publishing
World Gumbo Publishing

LEISURE/RECREATION

Anacus Press, An Imprint of Finney Company
Anchor Cove Publishing, Inc.
BEACHCOMBER MAGAZINE
Brookview Press
HEARTLANDS: A Magazine of Midwest Life and Art
Margaret Media, Inc.
Mountainside Press
New England Cartographics, Inc.
New Win Publishing
VACATION PLACE RENTALS
Windward Publishing, An Imprint of Finney Company

LESBIANISM

Alamo Square Press
ATLANTIS: A Women's Studies Journal/Revue d'etudes
    sur les femmes

Aunt Lute Books
Back House Books
BAY WINDOWS
Beacon Press
BLACK LACE
BLK
BOOKS TO WATCH OUT FOR
Bordighera, Inc.
Broken Jaw Press
Burning Bush Publications
Carolina Wren Press/Lollipop Power Books
Cavalier Press
Cleis Press
Common Courage Press
THE CREAM CITY REVIEW
Down There Press
DWAN
The Eighth Mountain Press
Ephemera Bound Publishing
Feel Free Press
FEMINIST COLLECTIONS: A QUARTERLY OF WO-
    MEN'S STUDIES RESOURCES
FEMINIST PERIODICALS: A CURRENT LISTING OF
    CONTENTS
The Feminist Press at the City University of New York
FEMINIST STUDIES
Fine Tooth Press
Garden House Press
GAYELLOW PAGES
GERTRUDE
GERTRUDE
Gertrude Press
GIRLFRIENDS MAGAZINE
GLB Publishers
Golden Isis Press
Hanover Press
Harrington Park Press
JOURNAL OF NARRATIVE THEORY
KUUMBA
LONG SHOT
METROPOLITAN FORUM
MGW (Mom Guess What) Newsmagazine
MOTHERVERSE: A Journal of Contemporary Motherhood
NEW BOOKS ON WOMEN & FEMINISM
New Falcon Publications
New Sins Press
New Victoria Publishers
OFF OUR BACKS
OUT OF LINE
Passion Power Press, Inc
Pussywillow
READERS SPEAK OUT!
Red Letter Press
RedBone Press
Re-invention UK Ltd
Sanguinaria Publishing
SINISTER WISDOM
SO TO SPEAK: A Feminist Journal of Language & Art
Spectrum Press
Spinifex Press
Spirit Press
Chuck Stewart
Syracuse Cultural Workers/Tools for Change
13TH MOON
TnT Classic Books
TORQUERE: Journal of the Canadian Lesbian and Gay
    Studies Association
Triskelion Publishing
The Twickenham Press
University of Chicago Press
Vision
Volcano Press, Inc
Windstorm Creative
THE WISHING WELL
Women's Studies Librarian, University of Wisconsin
    System
WSQ (formerly WOMEN'S STUDIES QUARTERLY)

LIBERAL ARTS

Athanata Arts, Ltd.
Bandanna Books
BURNSIDE REVIEW
THE CAIMAN (formerly THE WEIRD NEWS)
PSI Research/The Oasis Press/Hellgate Press
RIVET MAGAZINE
SCULPTURAL PURSUIT MAGAZINE
Zelda Wilde Publishing

LIBERTARIAN

ANARCHY: A Journal of Desire Armed
ASIA FILE
Axios Newletter, Inc.
Bluestocking Press
Books for All Times, Inc.
Candlestick Publishing
City Lights Books
Columbia Alternative Library Press
Michael E. Coughlin, Publisher
THE DANDELION
Elderberry Press, LLC
The Foundation for Economic Education, Inc.
Free Reign Press, Inc.
THE FREEMAN: Ideas On Liberty
Garden House Press
Handshake Editions
The Heather Foundation
Iconoclast Press
THE INDEPENDENT REVIEW: A Journal of Political
   Economy
THE (LIBERTARIAN) CONNECTION
Libertarian Press, Inc./American Book Distributors
LIBERTY
LIVING FREE
Lycanthrope Press
Mills Custom Services Publishing
Mountain Media
New Falcon Publications
OPEN WIDE MAGAZINE
Reveal
SHORT FUSE
SKINNYDIPPING
Synergy Press
Tres Picos Press
Van Cleave Publishing
THE VOLUNTARYIST
THE VORTEX

LIBRARIES

Big Valley Press
THE BOOK REPORT: The Magazine for Secondary School
   Library Media & Technology Specialists
Canadian Library Association
THE CHRISTIAN LIBRARIAN
COUNTERPOISE: For Social Responsibilities, Liberty and
   Dissent
The Denali Press
DWAN
FELICITER
FEMINIST COLLECTIONS: A QUARTERLY OF WO-
   MEN'S STUDIES RESOURCES
FEMINIST PERIODICALS: A CURRENT LISTING OF
   CONTENTS
Happy About
The Haworth Press
Highsmith Press
INDEPENDENT PUBLISHER ONLINE
KLIATT
L D A Publishers
LEGAL INFORMATION MANAGEMENT INDEX
LIBRARIANS AT LIBERTY
LIBRARY HI TECH
LIBRARY HIGH TECH NEWS
LIBRARY TALK: The Magazine for Elementary School
   Library Media & Technology Specialists
Linworth Publishing, Inc.

Mills Custom Services Publishing
NEW AMERICAN IMAGIST
NEW BOOKS ON WOMEN & FEMINISM
Oak Knoll Press
THE PRAIRIE JOURNAL OF CANADIAN LITERATURE
Scarecrow Press
TEACHER LIBRARIAN: The Journal for School Library
   Professionals
THE U*N*A*B*A*S*H*E*D LIBRARIAN, THE "HOW I
   RUN MY LIBRARY GOOD" LETTER
The Urbana Free Library
Willowood Press
Women's Studies Librarian, University of Wisconsin
   System
WRITER'S LIFELINE

LIFESTYLES

AB
Bookhome Publishing/Panda Publishing
Callawind Publications / Custom Cookbooks / Children's
   Books
COMMUNITIES
CURL MAGAZINE
DESIRE
DWELLING PORTABLY
GAYELLOW PAGES
GLOBAL ONE TRAVEL & AUTOMOTIVE MAGAZINE
GULF & MAIN Southwest Florida Lifestyle
Harrington Park Press
HEARTLANDS: A Magazine of Midwest Life and Art
Life Lessons
LifeThread Publications
N: NUDE & NATURAL
Origin Press
Palari Publishing
Passing Through Publications
The People's Press
PLEASANT LIVING
PSYCHE
RIVET MAGAZINE
SANDPOINT MAGAZINE
Snake Hill Press
TRAVEL NATURALLY
VINEGAR CONNOISSEURS INTERNATIONAL NEWS-
   LETTER
Visions Communications

LIGHTHOUSES

GAMBARA MAGAZINE
VACATION PLACE RENTALS

LITERARY REVIEW

ABRAMELIN: a Journal of Poetry and Magick
THE ADIRONDACK REVIEW
AFRICAN AMERICAN REVIEW
ALASKA QUARTERLY REVIEW
THE ALLEGHENY REVIEW
AMERICAN BOOK REVIEW
THE AMERICAN DISSIDENT
AMERICAN LETTERS & COMMENTARY
ANQ: A Quarterly Journal of Short Articles, Notes, and
   Reviews
THE ANTIGONISH REVIEW
APOSTROPHE: USCB Journal of the Arts
ARC
ARCHIPELAGO
ARIEL, A Review of International English Literature
ATLANTIS: A Women's Studies Journal/Revue d'etudes
   sur les femmes
AURA LITERARY ARTS REVIEW
Back House Books
THE BALTIMORE REVIEW
Bancroft Press
BEATLICK NEWS
BELLEVUE LITERARY REVIEW
BELLINGHAM REVIEW
BIG MUDDY: Journal of the Mississippi River Valley
Black Dress Press

692

THE BLIND MAN'S RAINBOW
BLUE MESA REVIEW
BOOK/MARK SMALL PRESS REVIEW
BOOKS FROM FINLAND
THE BRIAR CLIFF REVIEW
Brooding Heron Press
BUZZWORDS
CANADIAN LITERATURE
THE CAPILANO REVIEW
Cedar Hill Books
CEDAR HILL REVIEW
CENTER: A Journal of the Literary Arts
CHAPMAN
CHARITON REVIEW
CHASQUI
THE CHATTAHOOCHEE REVIEW
CHICAGO REVIEW
CONFRONTATION
THE CONNECTICUT POETRY REVIEW
CONTROLLED BURN
CORRECTIONS TODAY
COTTONWOOD
Cottonwood Press
CRAB ORCHARD REVIEW
THE CREAM CITY REVIEW
Crescent Moon
THE CRIMSON CRANE
CRUCIBLE
CUTBANK
THE DALHOUSIE REVIEW
DESCANT
DESIRE
DOWN IN THE DIRT LITERARY MAGAZINE, the prose
    & poetry magazine revealing all your dirty little secrets
THE DROOD REVIEW OF MYSTERY
THE EDGE CITY REVIEW
EVANSVILLE REVIEW
THE FIDDLEHEAD
FINE MADNESS
Five Fingers Press
FIVE FINGERS REVIEW
THE FLORIDA REVIEW
THE FRANK REVIEW
FRANK: AN INTERNATIONAL JOURNAL OF CON-
    TEMPORARY WRITING AND ART
FREEFALL
THE GEORGIA REVIEW
GRAND LAKE REVIEW
THE GREAT BLUE BEACON
THE GREEN HILLS LITERARY LANTERN
GULF COAST
Hanover Press
Harobed Publishing Creations
THE HARVARD ADVOCATE
HARVARD REVIEW
Haunted Rowboat Press
THE HOLLINS CRITIC
HOME PLANET NEWS
Home Planet Publications
THE HUDSON REVIEW
THE ICONOCLAST
THE IDAHO REVIEW
INDEPENDENT PUBLISHER ONLINE
INDIANA REVIEW
INTERNATIONAL POETRY REVIEW
THE IOWA REVIEW
IRISH LITERARY SUPPLEMENT
IRON HORSE LITERARY REVIEW
Jako Books
JAMES JOYCE BROADSHEET
JAMES JOYCE QUARTERLY
THE JOURNAL OF COMMONWEALTH LITERATURE
JOURNAL OF NARRATIVE THEORY
juel house publishers and literary services
JUST WEST OF ATHENS
KAJ-MAHKAH: EARTH OF EARTH
KALDRON, An International Journal Of Visual Poetry
THE KELSEY REVIEW

THE KENYON REVIEW
KotaPress
THE LANGSTON HUGHES REVIEW
Latin American Literary Review Press
LICHEN Arts & Letters Preview
THE LICKING RIVER REVIEW
Limberlost Press
LINQ
LITERARY IMAGINATION: The Review of the Associa-
    tion of Literary Scholars and Critics
LITERARY MAGAZINE REVIEW
THE LITERARY REVIEW
LULLWATER REVIEW
Maisonneuve Press
THE MALAHAT REVIEW
THE MASSACHUSETTS REVIEW
Mehring Books, Inc.
MICHIGAN QUARTERLY REVIEW
MID-AMERICAN REVIEW
Middlebury College Publications
THE MIDWEST QUARTERLY
Mills Custom Services Publishing
MINESHAFT
THE MISSOURI REVIEW
MYSTERY READERS JOURNAL
THE MYSTERY REVIEW
NANNY FANNY
NEO: Literary Magazine
NEW ENGLAND REVIEW
NEW GRAFFITI
NEW HOPE INTERNATIONAL REVIEW
NEW ORLEANS REVIEW
New Orphic Publishers
THE NEW ORPHIC REVIEW
NEWPAGES: Alternatives in Print & Media
NIGHTSUN
NOBODADDIES
NORTH CAROLINA LITERARY REVIEW
NORTH DAKOTA QUARTERLY
North Stone Editions
NOTRE DAME REVIEW
NOVA EXPRESS
Oak Knoll Press
OHIO WRITER
OHIOANA QUARTERLY
ORBIS
OSIRIS
OTHER VOICES
P.R.A. Publishing
THE PACIFIC REVIEW
PAPERPLATES
PARNASSUS: Poetry in Review
PASSAGES NORTH
PASSAIC REVIEW (MILLENNIUM EDITIONS)
PASSION
THE PATERSON LITERARY REVIEW
Pathwise Press
PEMBROKE MAGAZINE
PEMMICAN
Pendragonian Publications
PENNINE PLATFORM
Pennsylvania State University Press
PENNY DREADFUL: Tales and Poems of Fantastic Terror
PIKEVILLE REVIEW
PLOUGHSHARES
The Poetry Center
POETRY EAST
THE POETRY PROJECT NEWSLETTER
PORTLAND REVIEW
THE PRAIRIE JOURNAL OF CANADIAN LITERATURE
PRAIRIE SCHOONER
PRAKALPANA   SAHITYA/PRAKALPANA   LITERA-
    TURE
PSYCHE
PULSAR POETRY MAGAZINE
PURPLE PATCH
RAIN TAXI REVIEW OF BOOKS
THE RAVEN CHRONICLES

RED HAWK
THE REVIEW OF CONTEMPORARY FICTION
RIVERWIND
ROOM OF ONE'S OWN
ROSEBUD
St. Andrews College Press
ST. LOUIS JOURNALISM REVIEW
SAKANA
THE SANTA MONICA REVIEW
SENSATIONS MAGAZINE
SEWANEE REVIEW
SHAW: THE ANNUAL OF BERNARD SHAW STUDIES
SHENANDOAH: THE Washington and Lee University
  Review
SMARTISH PACE
SONGS OF INNOCENCE
SONORA REVIEW
SOUTHERN HUMANITIES REVIEW
THE SOUTHERN REVIEW
SP QUILL QUARTERLY MAGAZINE
SPEAKEASY
STAND MAGAZINE
THE STINGING FLY
STUDIO - A Journal of Christians Writing
SULPHUR RIVER LITERARY REVIEW
SYCAMORE REVIEW
TAKAHE
TAPROOT LITERARY REVIEW
THE TEXAS REVIEW
THALIA: Studies in Literary Humor
13TH MOON
THE THREEPENNY REVIEW
Thunder Rain Publishing Corp.
TIFARA
TORRE DE PAPEL
TRANSCENDENT VISIONS
TRANSLATION REVIEW
TULSA STUDIES IN WOMEN'S LITERATURE
UND Press
University of Tampa Press
University of Tulsa
UNIVERSITY OF WINDSOR REVIEW
UNMUZZLED OX
UPSTAIRS AT DUROC
VALLUM: CONTEMPORARY POETRY
Vanderbilt University Press
VARIOUS ARTISTS
VISIONS-INTERNATIONAL, The World Journal of Illus-
  trated Poetry
WAR, LITERATURE & THE ARTS: An International
  Journal of the Humanities
WATER ROW REVIEW
WEST BRANCH
WESTERN AMERICAN LITERATURE
WESTERN HUMANITIES REVIEW
Whitston Publishing Co.
WILD DUCK REVIEW
WILLIAM AND MARY REVIEW
WINDHOVER: A Journal of Christian Literature
THE WORCESTER REVIEW
Writecorner.com Press
WRITER'S EXCHANGE
XAVIER REVIEW
XTANT
THE YALE REVIEW
ZUZU'S PETALS: QUARTERLY ONLINE

LITERATURE (GENERAL)

A & U AMERICA'S AIDS MAGAZINE
THE ADIRONDACK REVIEW
AERIAL
AK Press
ALASKA QUARTERLY REVIEW
THE AMERICAN DISSIDENT
THE AMERICAN DRIVEL REVIEW
ANCIENT PATHS
Androgyne Books
Anhinga Press

ANQ: A Quarterly Journal of Short Articles, Notes, and
  Reviews
APOSTROPHE: USCB Journal of the Arts
Appalachian Consortium Press
ARC
ARIEL, A Review of International English Literature
ARTS & LETTERS: Journal of Contemporary Culture
ASCENT
Asylum Arts
Athanata Arts, Ltd.
AURA LITERARY ARTS REVIEW
AuthorsOmniscient Publishers
Bamboo Ridge Press
BAMBOO RIDGE, Journal of Hawai'i Literature and Arts
Bandanna Books
Banta & Pool Literary Properties
Barrytown/Station Hill Press
BASALT
BATHTUB GIN
Beacon Press
THE BEAR DELUXE
BEATLICK NEWS
Beekman Books, Inc.
Bellywater Press
BIBLIOPHILOS
BIGNEWS MAGAZINE
Birch Brook Press
BkMk Press
Black Dress Press
Black Heron Press
Black Lawrence Press
Black Spring Press
BLACK SPRING REVIEW
BLOODJET LITERARY MAGAZINE
Bolton Press
BOOK/MARK SMALL PRESS REVIEW
BORDERLANDS: Texas Poetry Review
Bordighera, Inc.
Borealis Press Limited
Bottle of Smoke Press
BOULEVARD
Branden Books
THE BRIAR CLIFF REVIEW
BRILLIANT STAR
Broken Jaw Press
BROKEN PENCIL
Brookline Books
Brookview Press
Burning Books
Burning Bush Publications
BUST DOWN THE DOOR AND EAT ALL THE
  CHICKENS: A Journal of Absurd and Surreal Fiction
BUZZWORDS
Caketrain Press
Calyx Books
CALYX: A Journal of Art and Literature by Women
THE CAROLINA QUARTERLY
Casperian Books LLC
Central Avenue Press
Chatterley Press International
Chicago Spectrum Press
CHILDREN, CHURCHES AND DADDIES, A Non
  Religious, Non Familial Literary Magazine
Chinese Literature Press
CIMARRON REVIEW
THE CIRCLE MAGAZINE
City Lights Books
Clamp Down Press
Coffee House Press
COLD-DRILL
COLLEGE LITERATURE
COMPASS ROSE
CONDUIT
CONFLUENCE
CONJUNCTIONS
Coteau Books
CRAB CREEK REVIEW
CRANNOG

CRAZYHORSE
Creative Arts Book Company
CREATIVE NONFICTION
CREOSOTE: A Journal of Poetry and Prose
Crescent Moon
CRICKET
CRUCIBLE
Cypress House
Dalkey Archive Press
Dan River Press
December Press
Department of Romance Languages
DESCANT
DESIRE
DIALOGOS: Hellenic Studies Review
DOTLIT: The Online Journal of Creative Writing
Down The Shore Publishing
Downeast Books
DRUMVOICES REVUE
Dufour Editions Inc.
EARTH'S DAUGHTERS: Feminist Arts Periodical
EASTGATE QUARTERLY REVIEW OF HYPERTEXT
ECOTONE: Reimagining Place
THE EDGE CITY REVIEW
Edition Gemini
ELT Press
ENGLISH LITERATURE IN TRANSITION, 1880-1920
Ephemera Bound Publishing
EPICENTER: A LITERARY MAGAZINE
Eros Books
EVANSVILLE REVIEW
Feel Free Press
The Feminist Press at the City University of New York
FICTION
Fiction Collective Two (FC2)
FINE MADNESS
Firelight Publishing, Inc.
FIRST CLASS
THE FIRST LINE
FISH DRUM MAGAZINE
Fithian Press
THE FLORIDA REVIEW
FOLIO: A Literary Journal of American University
Fontanel Books
Four Seasons Publishers
Four Walls Eight Windows
Four-Sep Publications
FOURTEEN HILLS: The SFSU Review
FREEFALL
The Galileo Press Ltd.
Gay Sunshine Press, Inc.
GERTRUDE
THE GETTYSBURG REVIEW
Glimmer Train Press, Inc.
GLIMMER TRAIN STORIES
GRASSLIMB
Graywolf Press
Great Elm Press
Green Bean Press
Guernica Editions, Inc.
GULF COAST
HAIGHT ASHBURY LITERARY JOURNAL
Harobed Publishing Creations
THE HARVARD ADVOCATE
Hermitage (Ermitazh)
Heyday Books
The Heyeck Press
Hobblebush Books
THE HOLLINS CRITIC
Hollyridge Press
Holy Cow! Press
Homa & Sekey Books
HOME PLANET NEWS
Huntington Library Press
HUNTINGTON LIBRARY QUARTERLY
HURRICANE ALICE
ICON
THE ICONOCLAST

Idylls Press
ILLUMINATIONS
Impassio Press
In Between Books
INKWELL
The Institute of Mind and Behavior
INSURANCE
THE IOWA REVIEW
ITALIAN AMERICANA
Italica Press, Inc.
Ithuriel's Spear
IWAN: INMATE WRITERS OF AMERICA NEWSLET-
    TER
JACK MACKEREL MAGAZINE
Jako Books
JAMES JOYCE BROADSHEET
J'ECRIS
THE JOURNAL OF MIND AND BEHAVIOR
JOURNAL OF NARRATIVE THEORY
JPS Publishing Company
JUBILAT
JUST WEST OF ATHENS
KALDRON, An International Journal Of Visual Poetry
Kedzie Press
Kelsey St. Press
THE KENYON REVIEW
KEREM: Creative Explorations in Judaism
Allen A. Knoll Publishers
La Alameda Press
LAKE STREET LIT: Art and Words from the Bottom of
    Lake Bonneville
LATERAL MOVES
LATIN AMERICAN LITERARY REVIEW
Latin American Literary Review Press
LAW AND LITERATURE
Leapfrog Press
The Leaping Frog Press
THE LEDGE
Leete's Island Books
LEFT CURVE
Lekon New Dimensions Publishing
Lemon Shark Press
Les Figues Press
Light of New Orleans Publishing
LIGHT: The Quarterly of Light Verse
LIMESTONE: A Literary Journal
Lincoln Springs Press
LITERARY IMAGINATION: The Review of the Associa-
    tion of Literary Scholars and Critics
LOST GENERATION JOURNAL
Lotus Press, Inc.
Lotus Press, Inc.
LULLWATER REVIEW
LUNGFULL! MAGAZINE
MAINE IN PRINT
Maisonneuve Press
MANDORLA: New Writing from the Americas / Nueva
    escritura de las Americas
THE MANHATTAN REVIEW
MANOA: A Pacific Journal of International Writing
Mayapple Press
Mayhaven Publishing
McPherson & Company Publishers
MEDIA SPOTLIGHT
MEDUSA'S HAIRDO
Menard Press
Merrimack Books
MICHIGAN QUARTERLY REVIEW
MID-AMERICAN REVIEW
Middlebury College Publications
Mid-List Press
Midwest Villages & Voices
Miles & Miles
Milkweed Editions
Mind Power Publishing
MINNESOTA LITERATURE
THE MINNESOTA REVIEW
Monkfish Book Publishing Company

Synergistic Press
TAKAHE
Talisman House, Publishers
TALKING RIVER REVIEW
TAPROOT LITERARY REVIEW
TAPROOT, a journal of older writers
THE TARPEIAN ROCK
TELOS
Telos Press
Texas Tech University Press
THALIA: Studies in Literary Humor
Thatch Tree Publications
THEMA
13TH MOON
Thorp Springs Press
THE THREEPENNY REVIEW
Thundercloud Books
Tia Chucha Press
TIFARA
Toad Press International Chapbook Series
TORRE DE PAPEL
Triple Tree Publishing
Turnstone Press
The Twickenham Press
TWO LINES: A Journal of Translation
UND Press
UNDERSTANDING MAGAZINE
Underwhich Editions
University of Nebraska Press
University of South Carolina Press
University of Tampa Press
University of Virginia Press
UNO MAS MAGAZINE
Urion Press
V52 Press
Vagabond Press
Van Cleave Publishing
Vanderbilt University Press
VARIOUS ARTISTS
VERSAL
Via Dolorosa Press
THE VIRGINIA QUARTERLY REVIEW
THE WALLACE STEVENS JOURNAL
WAR, LITERATURE & THE ARTS: An International
    Journal of the Humanities
WATER ROW REVIEW
The Wellsweep Press
West Virginia University Press
WESTERN AMERICAN LITERATURE
WESTERN HUMANITIES REVIEW
Wheatmark Book Publishing
THE WILDWOOD READER
Willowgate Press
WIND
Windstorm Creative
Wings Press
The Word Works
Writecorner.com Press
WRITER'S CHRONICLE
WRITER'S LIFELINE
XAVIER REVIEW
X-RAY
ZAWP
Zoo Press
Zumaya Publications
ZUZU'S PETALS: QUARTERLY ONLINE

LONDON

Peter Marcan Publications

JACK LONDON

Elderberry Press, LLC
The Live Oak Press, LLC
WESTERN AMERICAN LITERATURE

LOS ANGELES

Balcony Media, Inc.
Clover Park Press

East West Discovery Press
Allen A. Knoll Publishers
LUMMOX JOURNAL
Lummox Press
MCM Entertainment, Inc. Publishing Division
PLAIN BROWN WRAPPER (PBW)
Really Great Books
Santa Monica Press

LOUISIANA

The Chicot Press
Claitor's Law Books & Publishing Division, Inc.
DESIRE STREET
THE LOUISIANA REVIEW
Margaret Media, Inc.
NEW ORLEANS REVIEW
NOLA-MAGICK Press
Rock Spring Press Inc.
Thunder Rain Publishing Corp.
XAVIER REVIEW

H.P. LOVECRAFT

Carnifex Press
Gryphon Books
Harbor House
METAL CURSE
NOVA EXPRESS
PAPERBACK PARADE
RALPH'S REVIEW
SHATTERED WIG REVIEW
SOCIETE

MAGAZINES

ALTERNATIVE PRESS REVIEW
THE AMERICAN DISSIDENT
ARCHIPELAGO
BABYSUE
BOOK MARKETING UPDATE
CHAPMAN
CHILDREN, CHURCHES AND DADDIES, A Non
    Religious, Non Familial Literary Magazine
CONFRONTATION
COUNTERPOISE: For Social Responsibilities, Liberty and
    Dissent
CREEPY MIKE'S OMNIBUS OF FUN
CRICKET
DARK ANIMUS
DOWN IN THE DIRT LITERARY MAGAZINE, the prose
    & poetry magazine revealing all your dirty little secrets
DREAM NETWORK
EEI Press
Epona Publishing
FEMINIST PERIODICALS: A CURRENT LISTING OF
    CONTENTS
FIDELIS ET VERUS
FRANK: AN INTERNATIONAL JOURNAL OF CON-
    TEMPORARY WRITING AND ART
FREEDOM AND STRENGTH PRESS FORUM
GRAY AREAS
THE GREAT BLUE BEACON
Gryphon Books
Heidelberg Graphics
THE ICONOCLAST
THE ILLUSTRATOR COLLECTOR'S NEWS
INDY MAGAZINE
Info Net Publishing
LATERAL MOVES
LITERARY MAGAZINE REVIEW
LOST GENERATION JOURNAL
MEDIA SPOTLIGHT
METAL CURSE
NEO: Literary Magazine
NEW HOPE INTERNATIONAL REVIEW
NEWPAGES: Alternatives in Print & Media
OHIO WRITER
OTHER VOICES
Peartree Books & Music
THE PEDESTAL MAGAZINE.COM

The Poetry Center
POETS' ROUNDTABLE
THE PRAIRIE JOURNAL OF CANADIAN LITERATURE
Prakken Publications
Progressive Education
PROGRESSIVE PERIODICALS DIRECTORY/UPDATE
THE PUBLICITY HOUND
RED HAWK
Reveal
ST. LOUIS JOURNALISM REVIEW
Sand and Sable Publishing
Scars Publications
SHORTRUNS
THE SMALL PRESS BOOK REVIEW
THE SMALL PRESS REVIEW/SMALL MAGAZINE
  REVIEW
SMARTISH PACE
SNOW LION NEWSLETTER & CATALOG
SPIDER
STONE SOUP, The Magazine By Young Writers and
  Artists
13TH MOON
THRESHOLDS JOURNAL
UmbraProjects, Ltd.
Vagabond Press
THE WILDWOOD READER
WORLD OF FANDOM MAGAZINE
Years Press

MAGIC

ABRAMELIN: a Journal of Poetry and Magick
Carpe Diem Publishing
Crescent Moon
Horned Owl Publishing
MAGICAL BLEND/NATURAL BEAUTY & HEALTH/
  TRANSITIONS
The Midknight Club
NEWWITCH
nine muses books
NOLA-MAGICK Press
PASSION
Perrin Press
Three Pyramids Publishing
White Crosslet Publishing Co
Wilshire Books Inc.

MAINE

THE CLIMBING ART
The Latona Press
MAINE IN PRINT
Moon Pie Press
New England Cartographics, Inc.
NORTHWOODS JOURNAL, A Magazine for Writers
Pocahontas Press, Inc.
Polar Bear & Company
Peter E. Randall Publisher
THE RIVER REVIEW/LA REVUE RIVIERE
John Wade, Publisher

MANAGEMENT

Acton Circle Publishing Company
Adams-Blake Publishing
Alpine Guild, Inc.
Americans for the Arts
Autelitano Media Group (AMG)
Behavioral Sciences Research Press, Inc.
Benchmark Publications Inc.
Blueprint Books
BUSINESS SPIRIT JOURNAL
Canadian Educators' Press
Dash-Hill, LLC
EXECUTIVE EXCELLENCE
Executive Excellence Publishing
Famaco Publishers (Qalam Books)
Finney Company, Inc.
Frontline Publications
GoldenHouse Publishing Group
Happy About

IDM Press
INNOVATING
J&W Publishers, Inc.
JOURNAL OF COURT REPORTING
The Madson Group, Inc.
Mind Power Publishing
Multi-Media Publications Inc.
PATTERNS OF CHOICE: A Journal of People, Land, and
  Money
Pegasus Communications, Inc.
PREP Publishing
Putting Up Books, LC
Reliance Books
SACS Consulting
Set Sail Productions, LLC
THE SMALL BUSINESS ADVISOR
Smith-Johnson Publisher
Two Eagles Press International
The Utility Company LLC
Wheatmark Book Publishing

MAPS

CONCRETE JUNGLE JOURNAL
New England Cartographics, Inc.
THE ORPHAN LEAF REVIEW
Sunbelt Publications

MARINE LIFE

Abernathy House Publishing
Dixon-Price Publishing
The Narrative Press
Naturegraph Publishers
NewSage Press
Ocean Publishing
Sea Challengers, Inc.
SEA KAYAKER
Timber Press
Tortuga Books
Trickle Creek Books
Windward Publishing, An Imprint of Finney Company

MARKETING

A Cappela Publishing, Inc.
Adams-Blake Publishing
Americans for the Arts
Autelitano Media Group (AMG)
Bay Tree Publishing
Brenner Information Group
D.B.A. Books
Dash-Hill, LLC
DOLLS UNITED INTERACTIVE MAGAZINE
The Dragon Press
GoldenHouse Publishing Group
HandyCraft Media Productions
Happy About
The Haworth Press
Infinite Corridor Publishing
Info Net Publishing
JOURNAL OF COURT REPORTING
Long & Silverman Publishing, Inc.
MBA Publications
Pellingham Casper Communications
PSI Research/The Oasis Press/Hellgate Press
THE PUBLICITY HOUND
Set Sail Productions, LLC
74th Street Productions, L.L.C.
Snake Hill Press
Solcat Publishing
Sources
Titlewaves Publishing; Writers Direct
WeWrite LLC
Wilshire Books Inc.

MARRIAGE

APPLE VALLEY REVIEW: A Journal of Contemporary
  Literature
Blue Dolphin Publishing, Inc.
Brighton Publications, Inc.

Cladach Publishing
The Dibble Fund for Marriage Education
DOVETAIL: A Journal by and for Jewish/Christian Families
Harlan Publishing Company; Alliance Books; Diakonia Publishing (Christian Books)
Impact Publishers, Inc.
MCM Entertainment, Inc. Publishing Division
METROPOLITAN FORUM
Nolo Press Occidental
Oak Tree Press
River Press
Rolling Hills Publishing

MARTIAL ARTS

Arjuna Library Press
Carpe Diem Publishing
JOURNAL OF ASIAN MARTIAL ARTS
LOW BUDGET ADVENTURE
The Overlook Press
Paladin Enterprises, Inc.
Synapse-Centurion
THEATER
Turtle Press, division of S.K. Productions Inc.
Via Media Publishing Company
Voyageur Publishing Co.,Inc.
YMAA Publication Center

MASSAGE

GULF & MAIN Southwest Florida Lifestyle
SCIENCE/HEALTH ABSTRACTS
SKINNYDIPPING

MATHEMATICS

Applied Probability Trust
Arjuna Library Press
Clearwater Publishing Co.
First Books
Huntington Press
JOURNAL OF REGIONAL CRITICISM
LrnIT Publishing Div. ICFL, Inc.
MATHEMATICAL SPECTRUM
MUSIC PERCEPTION
The Pin Prick Press
Polka Dot Publishing
Polygonal Publishing House
SMARANDACHE NOTIONS JOURNAL
Wide World Publishing/TETRA

MEDIA

Bad Press
Bay Press
BOOK MARKETING UPDATE
CAMERA OBSCURA: Feminism, Culture, and Media Studies
CineCycle Publishing
Cottonwood Press, Inc.
Crescent Moon
D.B.A. Books
Film-Video Publications/Circus Source Publications
HAPPENINGNOW!EVERYWHERE
Hollywood Creative Directory
KETTERING REVIEW
LEFT BUSINESS OBSERVER
LEFT CURVE
Mho & Mho Works
Open Horizons Publishing Company
OPEN WIDE MAGAZINE
PASSION
Progressive Education
PROGRESSIVE PERIODICALS DIRECTORY/UPDATE
THE PUBLICITY HOUND
Rada Press, Inc.
ST. LOUIS JOURNALISM REVIEW
Sources
THE SOURCES HOTLINK
Strata Publishing, Inc.
Strata Publishing, Inc.

VARIOUS ARTISTS
THE WASHINGTON MONTHLY
WAV MAGAZINE: Progressive Music Art Politics Culture
WORLD OF FANDOM MAGAZINE

MEDICINE

Adams-Blake Publishing
Alpine Guild, Inc.
America West Publishers
Bellevue Literary Press
BELLEVUE LITERARY REVIEW
Blowtorch Press
Carolina Academic Press
THE COMPLEAT NURSE
Consumer Press
dbS Productions
Devil Mountain Books
firefall editions
Flowerfield Enterprises, LLC
Future Horizons, Inc.
Galen Press, Ltd.
GoldenIsle Publishers, Inc.
The Haworth Press
Health Press
Health Yourself
HEALTHY WEIGHT JOURNAL
INTERNATIONAL ADDICTION
JOURNAL OF POLYMORPHOUS PERVERSITY
JOURNAL OF SCIENTIFIC EXPLORATION
Kali Press
Library Research Associates
Master's Plan Publishing
MEDICAL HISTORY
Medi-Ed Press
MIDWIFERY TODAY
Midwifery Today
MOUTH: Voice of the Dis-Labeled Nation
New Paradigm Books
NICU Ink
Park Place Publications
Pine Publications
Reveal
Rivercross Publishing, Inc.
Savor Publishing House, Inc.
SCIENCE/HEALTH ABSTRACTS
shift 4 Publishing
Southern Methodist University Press
Standish Press
Swan Publishing Company
Thatch Tree Publications
TMC Books LLC
Vestibular Disorders Association
Vista Publishing, Inc.
Wellcome Institute for the History of Medicine
WILDERNESS MEDICINE NEWSLETTER

MEDIEVAL

Avari Press
BIBLIOPHILOS
Blue Planet Books Inc.
Blue Unicorn Press, Inc.
CONTEMPORARY GHAZALS
Elderberry Press, LLC
Erespin Press
Fine Tooth Press
Italica Press, Inc.
LEO Productions LLC.
Mystic Toad Press
NOTTINGHAM MEDIEVAL STUDIES
The Pin Prick Press
Resource Publications, Inc.
SOMETHING TO READ
UmbraProjects, Ltd.
Voyageur Publishing Co.,Inc.
Whitston Publishing Co.
Windstorm Creative
YE OLDE NEWES

MEMOIRS

A Cappela Publishing, Inc.
Accendo Publishing
THE ACORN
African Ways Publishing
AGNI
Alaska Native Language Center
ALASKA QUARTERLY REVIEW
all nations press
American Legacy Media
APPLE VALLEY REVIEW: A Journal of Contemporary
    Literature
Archer Books
Bancroft Press
Bright Mountain Books, Inc.
BRILLIANT CORNERS: A Journal of Jazz & Literature
Caketrain Press
Cantarabooks LLC
Chicory Blue Press, Inc.
Cladach Publishing
COLORADO REVIEW
Comstock Bonanza Press
THE CREAM CITY REVIEW
Creative Arts Book Company
Crystal Dreams Publishing
Cypress House
December Press
Delaney Day Press
Denlinger's Publishers Ltd.
DESIRE
Emrys Press
Eros Books
Fast Foot Forward Press
Fingerprint Press
First Books
Fithian Press
Foremost Press
Fouque Publishers
FOURTH GENRE: EXPLORATIONS IN NONFICTION
Ice Cube Press
IMAGE: ART, FAITH, MYSTERY
Imago Press
Impassio Press
John James Company
LAKE STREET LIT: Art and Words from the Bottom of
    Lake Bonneville
Leapfrog Press
Little Pear Press
MacAdam/Cage Publishing Inc.
B.B. Mackey Books
MANGROVE MAGAZINE
Mayhaven Publishing
Mercer University Press
Music City Publishing
My Heart Yours Publishing
NEO: Literary Magazine
New Concept Press
NewSage Press
North Star Books
Ocean Publishing
Omonomany
Orchises Press
PALO ALTO REVIEW
Panther Creek Press
PASSAGER
Pocol Press
POETICA MAGAZINE, Reflections of Jewish Thought
Polar Bear & Company
POTOMAC REVIEW
Presa Press
Pussywillow
QED Press
RAINBOW CURVE
Red Rock Press
Re-invention UK Ltd
RIVER TEETH: A Journal of Nonfiction Narrative
Sadorian Publications

SAKANA
SALAMANDER
Santa Fe Writers Project
SEWANEE REVIEW
Sherman Asher Publishing
Soul
THE SOUTHERN QUARTERLY: A Journal of the Arts in
    the South
Spinifex Press
Spire Press
Steerforth Press, L.C.
SterlingHouse Publisher
Sun Dog Press
Tendre Press
Timeless Books
TINY LIGHTS: A Journal of Personal Essay
Titus Home Publishing
Tupelo Press
Turnstone Press
University of Massachusetts Press
University of South Carolina Press
University of Utah Press
Vision
WAR, LITERATURE & THE ARTS: An International
    Journal of the Humanities
Wheatmark Book Publishing
Wildflower Press
WordFarm
Zumaya Publications

MEN

AFRICAN AMERICAN REVIEW
ASIA FILE
AT-HOME DAD
Beacon Light Publishing (BLP)
Beacon Press
Bear & Company
BLK
Crones Unlimited
Ecrivez!
Fine Tooth Press
FIRSTHAND
Gemini Publishing Company
GLB Publishers
Hunter House Inc., Publishers
Ika, LLC
Islewest Publishing
THE LIBERATOR
Penthe Publishing
PIKEVILLE REVIEW
Rainbow Books, Inc.
Red Alder Books
RFD
SKINNYDIPPING
SO YOUNG!
Solcat Publishing
Steel Balls Press
Swan Publishing Company
Vanderbilt University Press
Whole Person Associates Inc.
Yellow Moon Press

H.L. MENCKEN

FULLOSIA PRESS
The Independent Institute
THE INDEPENDENT REVIEW: A Journal of Political
    Economy
See Sharp Press

MENTAL HEALTH

ABLAZE Publishing
AIS Publications
Caketrain Press
Carolina Wren Press/Lollipop Power Books
Compact Clinicals
Consumer Press
CURRENTS: New Scholarship in the Human Services
Delaney Day Press

Gallaudet University Press
GENRE: WRITER AND WRITINGS
Haight-Ashbury Publications
The Haworth Press
Holbrook Street Press
JACK MACKEREL MAGAZINE
JOURNAL OF PSYCHOACTIVE DRUGS
The Leaping Frog Press
Lemieux International Ltd.
LifeQuest Publishing Group
NEW ALTERNATIVES
OPEN MINDS QUARTERLY
QED Press
SECOND GUESS
Sidran Institute
Sun Rising Press
Women of Diversity Productions, Inc.

MENTORING/COACHING

THE ART OF ABUNDANCE
Finney Company, Inc.
Harlan Publishing Company; Alliance Books; Diakonia
    Publishing (Christian Books)
Music City Publishing
Resource Publications, Inc.
Search Institute
Set Sail Productions, LLC
The Utility Company LLC
World Gumbo Publishing

METAPHYSICS

AE-TU Publishing
Altair Publications
Arjuna Library Press
THE ART OF ABUNDANCE
Ascension Publishing
AT-HOME DAD
Authors of Unity Publishing
Bear & Company
Beyond Words Publishing, Inc.
Borden Publishing Co.
BOTH SIDES NOW
BRANCHES
Devi Press, Inc.
Dharma Publishing
Dream Street Publishing
EcceNova Editions
Edin Books, Inc.
Emerald Wave
EMERGING
Fontanel Books
Free People Press
Galde Press, Inc.
Gardenia Press
Gateways Books And Tapes
GOLDEN ISIS MAGAZINE
Golden Isis Press
Heartsong Books
HEAVEN BONE MAGAZINE
Heaven Bone Press
Higher Ground Press
Himalayan Institute Press
Horned Owl Publishing
In Print Publishing
JOURNAL OF REGIONAL CRITICISM
The Kenneth G. Mills Foundation
LifeSkill Institute, Inc.
LightLines Publishing
LP Publications (Teleos Institute)
Lycanthrope Press
MYSTERY ISLAND MAGAZINE
New Native Press
New Paradigm Books
New Vision Publishing
New World Library
NOLA-MAGICK Press
OFFICE NUMBER ONE
Origin Press

PARABOLA MAGAZINE
Philopsychy Press
PhoeniX in Print
THE QUEST
Quest Books: Theosophical Publishing House
SAGEWOMAN
SECOND GUESS
SOM Publishing, division of School of Metaphysics
Spirit Press
SterlingHouse Publisher
Swan Raven & Company
Synergetic Press
Tendre Press
Three Pyramids Publishing
THRESHOLDS JOURNAL
Timeless Books
Toad Hall, Inc.
TRUTH SEEKER
Ulysses Books
Unity House
UNITY MAGAZINE
UnKnownTruths.com Publishing Company
Westgate Press
Wildflower Press
Wilshire Books Inc.
World Love Press Publishing

MEXICO

Common Courage Press
Montemayor Press
Sunbelt Publications
Tameme
Tres Picos Press
Two Eagles Press International
University Press of Colorado

MICHIGAN

Avery Color Studios
Wm.B. Eerdmans Publishing Co.
Grand River Press
JAM RAG
Mayapple Press
Palladium Communications
PASSAGES NORTH
Poetry Harbor
Voyageur Publishing Co.,Inc.
Wilderness Adventure Books

MIDDLE EAST

ARC
Bluestocking Press
Clarity Press, Inc.
CONTEMPORARY GHAZALS
CRITICAL REVIEW
Florida Academic Press
Hoover Institution Press
House of Hits, Inc.
IBEX Publishers, Inc.
Interlink Publishing Group, Inc.
JEWISH CURRENTS
THE JOURNAL OF HISTORICAL REVIEW
JOURNAL OF PALESTINE STUDIES
Judah Magnes Museum Publications
KMT, A Modern Journal of Ancient Egypt
Noontide Press
Passeggiata Press, Inc.
The Post-Apollo Press
Saqi Books Publisher
Smyrna Press
State University of New York Press
Tzipora Publications, Inc.
University of Arkansas Press
University of Utah Press
VOICES - ISRAEL

MIDWEST

Acorn Books
American & World Geographic Publishing

THE ANNALS OF IOWA
Avery Color Studios
BIG MUDDY: Journal of the Mississippi River Valley
Blackwater Publications
THE BRIAR CLIFF REVIEW
Britton Road Press
Wm Caxton Ltd
Chicago Review Press
CHILDREN, CHURCHES AND DADDIES, A Non Religious, Non Familial Literary Magazine
DRUMVOICES REVUE
Foundation Books
FREEDOM AND STRENGTH PRESS FORUM
Gabriel's Horn Publishing Co., Inc.
Laguna Wilderness Press
THE LICKING RIVER REVIEW
Mayapple Press
Ohio University Press/Swallow Press
Palladium Communications
THE PRAIRIE JOURNAL OF CANADIAN LITERATURE
RIVERWIND
ST. LOUIS JOURNALISM REVIEW
SOUTH DAKOTA REVIEW
TRADITION MAGAZINE
Truman State University Press
University of Nebraska Press
The Urbana Free Library
Voyageur Publishing Co.,Inc.
Xavier House Publishing

MILITARY, VETERANS

AAIMS Publishers
American Legacy Media
Artwork Publications, LLC
The Battery Press, Inc.
R.J. Bender Publishing
Bookhaven Press, LLC
Broken Rifle Press
Cantadora Press
COGNITIO: A Graduate Humanities Journal
COMBAT, the Literary Expression of Battlefield Touchstones
Denlinger's Publishers Ltd.
Faded Banner Publications
FULLOSIA PRESS
Galde Press, Inc.
Historical Resources Press
History Compass, LLC
Lancer Militaria
Lemieux International Ltd.
Leyland Publications
LOW BUDGET ADVENTURE MYSTERIES MAGAZINE
The Narrative Press
Omonomany
Paladin Enterprises, Inc.
Pogo Press, Incorporated
PublishAmerica, LLLP.
Putting Up Books, LC
Ravenwood Publishing
The Sektor Co.
Stardate Publishing Company
STORMWARNING!
The Urbana Free Library
Van Cleave Publishing
White Mane Publishing Company, Inc.

HENRY MILLER

Casperian Books LLC
OPEN WIDE MAGAZINE
Phony Lid Publications
PICK POCKET BOOKS
PLOPLOP
Zygote Publishing

MINIATURE BOOKS

Clamp Down Press
DWELLING PORTABLY

Epona Publishing
Mayhaven Publishing
Running Press
Stewart Publishing & Printing
UmbraProjects, Ltd.

MINNESOTA

Blackwater Publications
Blue Unicorn Press, Inc.
THE BRIAR CLIFF REVIEW
Galde Press, Inc.
INDUSTRY MINNE-ZINE
KUMQUAT MERINGUE
MIDWEST ART FAIRS
Minnesota Historical Society Press
Poetry Harbor
Pogo Press, Incorporated
RED HAWK
Suburban Wilderness Press
Whole Person Associates Inc.

MISSOURI

Heartland Publishing
The Patrice Press
Reveal
ST. LOUIS JOURNALISM REVIEW

MONTANA

CUTBANK
The Great Rift Press
Horse Creek Publications, Inc.
Keokee Co. Publishing, Inc.
KUMQUAT MERINGUE
Mountain Meadow Press
Mountain Press Publishing Co.
Pruett Publishing Company
Spirit Talk Press

MORMON

American Legacy Media
BOULDER HERETIC
THE DEFENDER - Rush Utah's Newsletter
Eborn Books
SOMETHING TO READ
University of Utah Press

MOTIVATION, SUCCESS

Aaron Communications III
Accendo Publishing
Arden Press, Inc.
Behavioral Sciences Research Press, Inc.
Big Mouth Publications
Bronze Girl Productions, Inc.
CHECKER CAB MAGAZINE - THE LITTLE 'ZINE THAT COULD! Fiction That Takes The Long Way Home
City Life Books, LLC
Contemax Publishers
DAILY WORD
DREAM NETWORK
Dumouriez Publishing
EXECUTIVE EXCELLENCE
Executive Excellence Publishing
Finney Company, Inc.
Gardenia Press
Jalmar Press/Innerchoice Publishing
KABBALAH
Knowledge Concepts Publishing
Kobalt Books
Lamp Light Press
The Leaping Frog Press
Life Lessons
LifeQuest Publishing Group
Long & Silverman Publishing, Inc.
LrnIT Publishing Div. ICFL, Inc.
Markowski International Publishers
Massey-Reyner Publishing
Millennium Vision Press

Multi-Media Publications Inc.
North Star Books
Open Horizons Publishing Company
Pendant Publishing Inc.
Platinum Dreams Publishing
The Poetry Center Press/Shoestring Press
PREP Publishing
Princess Publishing
SCULPTURAL PURSUIT MAGAZINE
Set Sail Productions, LLC
74th Street Productions, L.L.C.
Smith-Johnson Publisher
Titlewaves Publishing; Writers Direct
Unity House
UNITY MAGAZINE
The Utility Company LLC
Wilderness Ministries
Wilshire Books Inc.

MOVIES

Black Lawrence Press
Cantarabooks LLC
CELLAR
CineCycle Publishing
CREEPY MIKE'S OMNIBUS OF FUN
December Press
THE EAST VILLAGE INKY
Film-Video Publications/Circus Source Publications
Fotofolio, Inc.
THE FREEDONIA GAZETTE: The Magazine Devoted to the Marx Brothers
FULLOSIA PRESS
GAUNTLET: Exploring the Limits of Free Expression
HAPPENINGNOW!EVERYWHERE
HEROES FROM HACKLAND
Hollywood Film Archive
IMAGE: ART, FAITH, MYSTERY
THE INDIE
INDY MAGAZINE
Lake Claremont Press
LegacyForever
Mayhaven Publishing
MGW (Mom Guess What) Newsmagazine
MOMMY AND I ARE ONE
MYSTERY ISLAND MAGAZINE
Mystic Toad Press
NEW ORLEANS REVIEW
NWI National Writers Institute
Open Horizons Publishing Company
OPEN WIDE MAGAZINE
PAST TIMES: The Nostalgia Entertainment Newsletter
ROCTOBER COMICS AND MUSIC
Santa Monica Press
SHEMP! The Lowlife Culture Magazine
Southern Illinois University Press
Starbooks Press/FLF Press
Stardate Publishing Company
Whelks Walk Press
WORLD OF FANDOM MAGAZINE

MOVING/RELOCATION

ECOTONE: Reimagining Place
First Books
Intercultural Press, Inc.

MULTICULTURAL

Americans for the Arts
APPLE VALLEY REVIEW: A Journal of Contemporary Literature
ART PAPERS
ARTS & LETTERS: Journal of Contemporary Culture
Azreal Publishing Company
Bay Tree Publishing
BkMk Press
BLUE COLLAR REVIEW
BOOK/MARK SMALL PRESS REVIEW
Burning Bush Publications
Caketrain Press
Calyx Books
Carolina Wren Press/Lollipop Power Books
COLLEGE LITERATURE
Cornerstone Publishing
Coteau Books
Crandall, Dostie & Douglass Books, Inc.
Cross-Cultural Communications
Dawn Sign Press
DESIRE
DOVETAIL: A Journal by and for Jewish/Christian Families
Dream Publishing Co.
dreamslaughter
E. S. Publishers & Distributors
East West Discovery Press
Face to Face Press
Five Fingers Press
FIVE FINGERS REVIEW
A GATHERING OF THE TRIBES
GERTRUDE
GERTRUDE
Gertrude Press
HAWAI'I REVIEW
Ibexa Press
Ika, LLC
Illumination Arts
INDIA CURRENTS
THE INDIE
Intercultural Press, Inc.
INTERCULTURE
Jako Books
KAJ-MAHKAH: EARTH OF EARTH
THE KENYON REVIEW
MANDORLA: New Writing from the Americas / Nueva escritura de las Americas
Margaret Media, Inc.
Mercer University Press
Montemayor Press
MOTHERVERSE: A Journal of Contemporary Motherhood
Naturegraph Publishers
NEO: Literary Magazine
NewSage Press
NEWWITCH
Oma Books of the Pacific
Open Hand Publishing LLC
OUTER-ART
Palladium Communications
Partisan Press
Passion Power Press, Inc
PEACEWORK
Peartree Books & Music
The People's Press
Phelps Publishing Company
PIKEVILLE REVIEW
The Poetry Center
POINT OF CONTACT, The Journal of Verbal & Visual Arts
THE RAVEN CHRONICLES
Really Great Books
THE RIVER REVIEW/LA REVUE RIVIERE
RIVET MAGAZINE
Savor Publishing House, Inc.
SECOND GUESS
SO TO SPEAK: A Feminist Journal of Language & Art
Southeast Missouri State University Press
Spinifex Press
The Spirit That Moves Us Press, Inc.
Spiritual Understanding Network, LLC
Tia Chucha Press
Two Eagles Press International
Twynz Publishing
United Nations University Press
University of Massachusetts Press
Vehicule Press
VERSAL
Victory Press
WEBER STUDIES: Voices and Viewpoints of the Contemporary West

WEST COAST LINE: A Journal of Contemporary Writing
and Criticism
which press
WIND
World Gumbo Publishing
World Music Press
XCP: CROSS-CULTURAL POETICS

MUSIC

AD/VANCE
AFRICAN AMERICAN REVIEW
AFTERTOUCH: New Music Discoveries
ALARM CLOCK
THE ALEMBIC
ALL ROUND
Allworth Press
Amadeus Press
Athanata Arts, Ltd.
BABYSUE
BABYSUE MUSIC REVIEW
BAGAZINE
Barrytown/Station Hill Press
BIG HAMMER
Birdalone Books
Birdalone Books
Black Dress Press
Black Lawrence Press
BLACK SHEETS MAGAZINE
Bliss Publishing Company, Inc.
The Bold Strummer Ltd.
BRILLIANT CORNERS: A Journal of Jazz & Literature
Burning Books
BUTTON
CADENCE: The Review of Jazz & Blues: Creative
Improvised Music
Carpe Diem Publishing
Celebrity Profiles Publishing
Clearwater Publishing Co.
CODA: The Jazz Magazine
Creative Arts Book Company
CREEPY MIKE'S OMNIBUS OF FUN
CROSSCURRENTS
Crystal Publishers, Inc.
DIRTY LINEN
THE EDGE CITY REVIEW
The Edwin Mellen Press
FIDDLER MAGAZINE
Fouque Publishers
GAUNTLET: Exploring the Limits of Free Expression
Glenbridge Publishing Ltd.
GRAY AREAS
HAPPENINGNOW!EVERYWHERE
HILL COUNTRY SUN
Hollywood Creative Directory
IMAGE: ART, FAITH, MYSTERY
THE INDIE
Iniquity Press/Vendetta Books
Ironweed Press
ITALIAN AMERICANA
JACK MACKEREL MAGAZINE
JAM RAG
JOURNAL OF AESTHETICS AND ART CRITICISM
JOURNAL OF MUSIC IN IRELAND (JMI)
JOURNAL OF MUSICOLOGY
JOURNAL OF THE AMERICAN MUSICOLOGICAL
SOCIETY
LegacyForever
Leyland Publications
Light, Words & Music
LIGHTWORKS MAGAZINE
Limelight Editions
LUMMOX JOURNAL
Lummox Press
MAGNET MAGAZINE
Mama Incense Publishing
Peter Marcan Publications
MB Media, Inc.
MCM Entertainment, Inc. Publishing Division

McPherson & Company Publishers
Medi-Ed Press
Merwood Books
MGW (Mom Guess What) Newsmagazine
MINISTRY & LITURGY
MOBILE BEAT: The DJ Magazine
MOMMY AND I ARE ONE
MOTORBOOTY MAGAZINE
Muse World Media Group
MUSIC NEWS
MUSIC PERCEPTION
MUSIC THEORY SPECTRUM
Mystery Island Publications
THE NEW ENGLAND QUARTERLY
Nicolas-Hays, Inc.
NIGHTLIFE MAGAZINE
19TH-CENTURY MUSIC
THE NOISE
Norton Coker Press
NoteBoat, Inc.
OPEN WIDE MAGAZINE
THE OXFORD AMERICAN
Palladium Communications
Passeggiata Press, Inc.
PAST TIMES: The Nostalgia Entertainment Newsletter
Pearl's Book'em Publisher
Piano Press
Pogo Press, Incorporated
THE PRESSED PRESS
Pro musica press
REDISCOVER MUSIC CATALOG
Resource Publications, Inc.
Reveal
ROCTOBER COMICS AND MUSIC
Rowhouse Press
Sagamore Publishing
Santa Monica Press
Savant Garde Workshop
Scarecrow Press
SCRAWL MAGAZINE
See Sharp Press
Selah Publishing Co. Inc.
THE $ENSIBLE SOUND
SHATTERED WIG REVIEW
SHEMP! The Lowlife Culture Magazine
SHORTRUNS
SING OUT! Folk Music & Folk Songs
Six Strings Music Publishing
Solcat Publishing
THE SOUTHERN QUARTERLY: A Journal of the Arts in
the South
SOUTHWEST COLORADO ARTS PERSPECTIVE
Speck Press
The Spinning Star Press
Stardate Publishing Company
Stellaberry Press
Stony Meadow Publishing
Syukhtun Editions
Thirteen Colonies Press
TRADITION MAGAZINE
Trafton Publishing
UNDER THE VOLCANO
Underwhich Editions
UNO MAS MAGAZINE
WAV MAGAZINE: Progressive Music Art Politics Culture
WELSH MUSIC HISTORY
West Coast Paradise Publishing
West Virginia University Press
White Cliffs Media, Inc.
WORD IS BOND
World Music Press
WORLD OF FANDOM MAGAZINE
Wynn Publishing
X-Ray Book Co.
Yellow Moon Press
ZINE-ON-A-TAPE

MYSTERY

A Cappela Publishing, Inc.
Abecedarian books, Inc.
Accendo Publishing
Adventure Books Inc.
Ageless Press
Aspicomm Media
Avari Press
Avocet Press Inc.
BEGINNINGS - A Magazine for the Novice Writer
Bleak House Books, an imprint of Diversity Incorporated
Boulevard Books, Inc. Florida
Caribbean Books-Panama
Cavalier Press
CELLAR
Central Avenue Press
Creative Arts Book Company
Crime and Again Press
DESIRE
THE DROOD REVIEW OF MYSTERY
Ecrivez!
Falcon Publishing, LTD
The Fiction Works
Firelight Publishing, Inc.
FMA Publishing
Foremost Press
Gaslight Publications
GAUNTLET: Exploring the Limits of Free Expression
Gryphon Books
HARDBOILED
Harlan Publishing Company; Alliance Books; Diakonia Publishing (Christian Books)
Haunted Rowboat Press
Idylls Press
Imago Press
J-Press Publishing
Allen A. Knoll Publishers
The Larcom Press
The Leaping Frog Press
LegacyForever
Lemieux International Ltd.
LOW BUDGET ADVENTURE
Mayhaven Publishing
The Merion Press, Inc.
MYSTERIES MAGAZINE
MYSTERY ISLAND MAGAZINE
MYSTERY READERS JOURNAL
THE MYSTERY REVIEW
Mystic Toad Press
New Victoria Publishers
New World Press, Inc
Oak Tree Press
The Overmountain Press
PAPERBACK PARADE
Polar Bear & Company
PublishAmerica, LLLP.
Purple Finch Press
Questex Consulting Ltd.
Quiet Storm Books
Radiant Press
Rainbow Books, Inc.
RavenHaus Publishing
Reveal
Rowan Mountain Press
St Kitts Press
Santa Fe Writers Project
Andrew Scott Publishers
Scrivenery Press
SelectiveHouse Publishers, Inc.
SENSATIONS MAGAZINE
SHERLOCKIAN TIDBITS
SISTERS IN CRIME BOOKS IN PRINT
SOMETHING TO READ
Speck Press
SterlingHouse Publisher
Stormline Press, Inc.
Synapse-Centurion

Tolling Bell Books
Triple Tree Publishing
Triskelion Publishing
Triumvirate Publications
Turnstone Press
Twilight Times Books
UglyTown
Whiskey Creek Press
Willowgate Press
WillowTree Press LLC
Wytherngate Press

MYTH, MYTHOLOGY

Agathon Books
Arjuna Library Press
BALLISTA
Bear & Company
BOULDER HERETIC
Bright Mountain Books, Inc.
Caribbean Books-Panama
Carnifex Press
CONJUNCTIONS
Coteau Books
DESIRE
DREAM NETWORK
EcceNova Editions
Firelight Publishing, Inc.
Focus Publishing/R. Pullins Co.
Fontanel Books
Golden Isis Press
Hanover Press
Heyday Books
Horned Owl Publishing
In Between Books
THE JOURNAL OF CALIFORNIA AND GREAT BASIN ANTHROPOLOGY
Lycanthrope Press
Malki Museum Press
MEDUSA'S HAIRDO
The Midknight Club
Mucusart Publications
New Native Press
NEWWITCH
nine muses books
ORBIS
Oregon State University Press
PAGAN AMERICA
Panther Creek Press
PARABOLA MAGAZINE
Pendragonian Publications
PENNY DREADFUL: Tales and Poems of Fantastic Terror
Perrin Press
Polar Bear & Company
PSYCHE
Quest Books: Theosophical Publishing House
Reveal
SAGEWOMAN
Sibyl Publications, Inc
SOCIETE
SONGS OF INNOCENCE
Spinifex Press
Spring Publications Inc.
SULPHUR RIVER LITERARY REVIEW
Sun Rising Press
Syukhtun Editions
Three Pyramids Publishing
UmbraProjects, Ltd.
UnKnownTruths.com Publishing Company
Wild West Publishing House
Yellow Moon Press

NATIVE AMERICAN

Abernathy House Publishing
ABRAXAS
AIS Publications
Alaska Geographic Society
Alaska Native Language Center
Alaska Northwest Books

ALBERTA HISTORY
AMERICAN INDIAN CULTURE AND RESEARCH
  JOURNAL
American Indian Studies Center
Ancient City Press
Avery Color Studios
The B & R Samizdat Express
Backcountry Publishing
Ballena Press
The Bess Press
Between The Lines
BIG MUDDY: Journal of the Mississippi River Valley
Black Dome Press Corp.
Borealis Press Limited
THE BRIAR CLIFF REVIEW
Bright Hill Press
Bright Mountain Books, Inc.
BRILLIANT STAR
Burning Bush Publications
Cantadora Press
Carolina Wren Press/Lollipop Power Books
Cedar Hill Books
CEDAR HILL REVIEW
Clarity Press, Inc.
Comstock Bonanza Press
Coteau Books
Council For Indian Education
THE CREAM CITY REVIEW
Cross-Cultural Communications
The Denali Press
Dream Catcher Publishing
DREAM NETWORK
Eagle's View Publishing
ETC Publications
Evolution Publishing
EZ Nature Books
FROZEN WAFFLES
Frozen Waffles Press/Shattered Sidewalks Press; 45th
  Century Chapbooks
Fulcrum, Inc.
FULLOSIA PRESS
GENRE: WRITER AND WRITINGS
Golden Isis Press
Goldfish Press
Granite Publishing Group
Heartland Publishing
Heartsong Books
Heidelberg Graphics
Heyday Books
HIGH COUNTRY NEWS
Historical Society of Alberta
History Compass, LLC
INTERCULTURE
IRON HORSE LITERARY REVIEW
THE JOURNAL OF CALIFORNIA AND GREAT BASIN
  ANTHROPOLOGY
Kiva Publishing, Inc.
La Alameda Press
Laguna Wilderness Press
LAKE SUPERIOR MAGAZINE
Loonfeather Press
Malki Museum Press
Maryland Historical Press
Miami University Press
The Middle Atlantic Press
Minnesota Historical Society Press
Monkfish Book Publishing Company
Mountain Meadow Press
National Woodlands Publishing Company
Naturegraph Publishers
THE NEW ENGLAND QUARTERLY
New Native Press
New Star Books Ltd.
New World Library
NEWS FROM NATIVE CALIFORNIA
NEWWITCH
North Country Books, Inc.
NORTH DAKOTA QUARTERLY

Oregon State University Press
ORNAMENT
The Overmountain Press
Palladium Communications
Panther Creek Press
Phelps Publishing Company
The Place In The Woods
Pocahontas Press, Inc.
Poetry Harbor
Pogo Press, Incorporated
Premium Press America
Pygmy Forest Press
Quest Books: Theosophical Publishing House
Rainbow Books, Inc.
Reference Service Press
Rio Nuevo Publishers
THE RIVER REVIEW/LA REVUE RIVIERE
Rivercross Publishing, Inc.
Sand River Press
Sasquatch Books
Sasquatch Books
Scottwall Associates, Publishers
SHAMAN'S DRUM: A Journal of Experiential Shamanism
SHENANDOAH NEWSLETTER
SHO
Genny Smith Books
SOUTH DAKOTA REVIEW
Spirit Talk Press
Spiritual Understanding Network, LLC
STRUGGLE: A Magazine of Proletarian Revolutionary
  Literature
Sunbelt Publications
Swan Raven & Company
Syracuse Cultural Workers/Tools for Change
Syukhtun Editions
Texas Tech University Press
Theytus Books Ltd.
Thundercloud Books
TURNING THE TIDE: Journal of Anti-Racist Action,
  Research & Education
UBC Press
UND Press
United Lumbee Nation
UNITED LUMBEE NATION TIMES
University of Alaska Press
University of Calgary Press
University of Nebraska Press
University of Utah Press
Utah State University Press
Venus Communications
WEBER STUDIES: Voices and Viewpoints of the
  Contemporary West
West End Press
West Virginia University Press
WHISPERING WIND MAGAZINE
Whitford Press
Whitston Publishing Co.
Windstorm Creative
Wings Press
WORD IS BOND
World Music Press
XCP: CROSS-CULTURAL POETICS
Yellow Moon Press
YUKHIKA—LATUHSE
Zagier & Urruty Publicaciones
Zumaya Publications

NATURE

THE ACORN
Acton Circle Publishing Company
Adirondack Mountain Club, Inc.
AMERICAN FORESTS
Birdsong Books
Brookview Press
CALIFORNIA EXPLORER
Clover Park Press
CONCRETE JUNGLE JOURNAL
Concrete Jungle Press

Coteau Books
Crones Unlimited
Dawn Publications
Down The Shore Publishing
Eco Images
Ecopress, An Imprint of Finney Company
ECOTONE: Reimagining Place
Envirographics
EZ Nature Books
GIN BENDER POETRY REVIEW
Harvard Common Press
Hobar Publications, A Division of Finney Company
Ice Cube Press
Iris Publishing Group, Inc (Iris Press / Tellico Books)
JetKor
Laguna Wilderness Press
Loonfeather Press
Malki Museum Press
Mayhaven Publishing
A Melody from an Immigrant's Soul
The Narrative Press
National Woodlands Publishing Company
Native West Press
Naturegraph Publishers
New England Cartographics, Inc.
NEW ENVIRONMENT BULLETIN
New Win Publishing
NEWWITCH
North Country Books, Inc.
North Star Books
Oregon State University Press
Outrider Press
Pangaea
Peartree Books & Music
Pineapple Press, Inc.
Press Here
Pruett Publishing Company
Publishing Works
RFF Press / Resources for the Future
Rio Nuevo Publishers
THE RIVER REVIEW/LA REVUE RIVIERE
Rock Spring Press Inc.
Sasquatch Books
Sasquatch Books
Scientia Publishing, LLC
SECOND GUESS
SNOWY EGRET
Solcat Publishing
SOMETHING TO READ
SOUTH DAKOTA REVIEW
Southern Illinois University Press
SunShine Press Publications, Inc.
Synapse-Centurion
Texas Tech University Press
Timber Press
Titlewaves Publishing; Writers Direct
TMC Books LLC
TRAVEL NATURALLY
Trickle Creek Books
University of South Carolina Press
Utah State University Press
Venus Communications
WASHINGTON TRAILS
WEBER STUDIES: Voices and Viewpoints of the
    Contemporary West
Western New York Wares, Inc.
WHOLE TERRAIN - REFLECTIVE ENVIRONMENTAL
    PRACTICE
WILD DUCK REVIEW
THE WILD FOODS FORUM
Wildflower Press
Windward Publishing, An Imprint of Finney Company
Wood Thrush Books
Word Forge Books

NEBRASKA

THE BRIAR CLIFF REVIEW
Heartland Publishing

Holmes House
Lone Willow Press
Missing Spoke Press
University of Nebraska Press

NETWORKING

AQUATERRA, METAECOLOGY & CULTURE
Black Forest Press
THE CHRISTIAN LIBRARIAN
CONNEXIONS DIGEST
Connexions Information Services, Inc.
Finney Company, Inc.
INTERNATIONAL WOMEN'S WRITING GUILD
LIGHTWORKS MAGAZINE
Martinez Press
OUT YOUR BACKDOOR: The Magazine of Do-It-
    Yourself Adventure and Homegrown Culture
READERS SPEAK OUT!
SLUG & LETTUCE
SOCIETE
SPROUTLETTER
World Gumbo Publishing

NEW AGE

Al-Galaxy Publishing Corporation
Allworth Press
American Literary Press
Amethyst & Emerald
Ascension Publishing
Athanor Books (a division of ETX Seminars)
Authors of Unity Publishing
Balanced Books Publishing
BALLISTA
Big Mouth Publications
Black Diamond Book Publishing
BOTH SIDES NOW
BRANCHES
Brason-Sargar Publications
CHRISTIAN*NEW AGE QUARTERLY
COMMUNITIES
Crystal Clarity, Publishers
Crystal Dreams Publishing
Dablond Publishing
Devi Press, Inc.
DOWN IN THE DIRT LITERARY MAGAZINE, the prose
    & poetry magazine revealing all your dirty little secrets
DREAM NETWORK
Edin Books, Inc.
Emerald Wave
Fontanel Books
Foremost Press
Free People Press
Gardenia Press
GOLDEN ISIS MAGAZINE
Golden Isis Press
Guarionex Press Ltd.
Guarionex Press Ltd.
Heartland Publishing
HEAVEN BONE MAGAZINE
Heaven Bone Press
Higher Ground Press
Himalayan Institute Press
Ika, LLC
Imago Press
In Print Publishing
The Kenneth G. Mills Foundation
LifeQuest Publishing Group
LifeSkill Institute, Inc.
LOVING MORE
Lycanthrope Press
Macrocosm USA, Inc.
Mho & Mho Works
The Midknight Club
MOTHER EARTH
THE MOUNTAIN ASTROLOGER
N: NUDE & NATURAL
NEW ENVIRONMENT BULLETIN
New Paradigm Books

New World Library
NEWWITCH
NOLA-MAGICK Press
OFFICE NUMBER ONE
Paragon House Publishers
The Passion Profit Company
Phantom Press Publications
PhoeniX in Print
Plus Publications
PSYCHE
RFD
SAGEWOMAN
SCIENCE/HEALTH ABSTRACTS
SelectiveHouse Publishers, Inc.
SHARE INTERNATIONAL
SKINNYDIPPING
SOM Publishing, division of School of Metaphysics
Spirit, Nature and You
SPROUTLETTER
Square One Publishers, Inc.
SterlingHouse Publisher
Stewart Publishing & Printing
Sun Rising Press
Swan Raven & Company
TAI CHI
Tendre Press
Three Pyramids Publishing
Toad Hall, Inc.
Tree of Life Books. Imprints: Progressive Press, Banned
  Books
TRUTH SEEKER
Twilight Times Books
Universal Unity
Victory Press
John Wade, Publisher
Westgate Press
White Crosslet Publishing Co
Whitford Press
THE WILDWOOD READER
Yo San Books
Zoilita Grant MS CCHt.

NEW ENGLAND

AMERICAN JONES BUILDING & MAINTENANCE
THE AUROREAN
Bliss Publishing Company, Inc.
Chelsea Green Publishing Company
THE CLIMBING ART
COLOR WHEEL
Nicolin Fields Publishing, Inc.
Follow Me! Guides
The Latona Press
Midmarch Arts Press
The Mountaineers Books
New England Cartographics, Inc.
THE NEW ENGLAND QUARTERLY
THE NOISE
NORTHWOODS JOURNAL, A Magazine for Writers
Oyster River Press
PINE ISLAND JOURNAL OF NEW ENGLAND POETRY
Pocahontas Press, Inc.
Peter E. Randall Publisher
Thirteen Colonies Press
TMC Books LLC
University of Massachusetts Press
THE WORCESTER REVIEW
Yellow Moon Press

NEW HAMPSHIRE

AMERICAN JONES BUILDING & MAINTENANCE
COLOR WHEEL
Crystal Press
Nicolin Fields Publishing, Inc.
Follow Me! Guides
Missing Spoke Press
New England Cartographics, Inc.
Oyster River Press
Peter E. Randall Publisher

NEW MEXICO

Ancient City Press
BEATLICK NEWS
BLUE MESA REVIEW
Cave Books
firefall editions
Heartland Publishing
The Intrepid Traveler
Kiva Publishing, Inc.
KUMQUAT MERINGUE
La Alameda Press
Lao Tse Press, Ltd.
LPD Press
Pruett Publishing Company
Rio Nuevo Publishers
Southwest Research and Information Center
Thundercloud Books
TRADICION REVISTA
Two Eagles Press International
VOICES FROM THE EARTH

NEW YORK

Adirondack Mountain Club, Inc.
Black Dome Press Corp.
Chelsea Green Publishing Company
CONCRETE JUNGLE JOURNAL
Concrete Jungle Press
THE EAST VILLAGE INKY
Follow Me! Guides
Fotofolio, Inc.
Four Walls Eight Windows
Gibbs Smith, Publisher
IN OUR OWN WORDS
INNER CITY PRESS
Land Yacht Press
McBooks Press, Inc.
Mount Ida Press
New England Cartographics, Inc.
North Country Books, Inc.
Panther Books

NEW ZEALAND

Tres Picos Press

NEWSLETTER

Affinity Publishers Services
Anti-Aging Press
AQUATERRA, METAECOLOGY & CULTURE
ARTISTAMP NEWS
ASIA FILE
Black Forest Press
Blueprint Books
THE BOOKWATCH
THE BREAD AND BUTTER CHRONICLES
Center For Self-Sufficiency
Community Service, Inc.
THE CONNECTICUT POET
COOKING CONTEST CHRONICLE
Downeast Books
Eborn Books
Eco Images
THE EDITORIAL EYE
EEI Press
EFG, Inc.
THE EUGENE O'NEILL REVIEW
The Fiction Works
FIDELIS ET VERUS
THE GREAT BLUE BEACON
Hanover Press
Harobed Publishing Creations
Heidelberg Graphics
INKY TRAIL NEWS
INTERNATIONAL WOMEN'S WRITING GUILD
Knowledge Concepts Publishing
Kodiak Media Group
LAUGHING BEAR NEWSLETTER
Moody Street Irregulars, Inc.

MOODY STREET IRREGULARS: A Jack Kerouac Magazine
NEW SOLUTIONS
OHIO WRITER
Pennycorner Press
POETIC SPACE: Poetry & Fiction
PRIVACY JOURNAL
Progressive Education
PROGRESSIVE PERIODICALS DIRECTORY/UPDATE
Rayve Productions Inc.
Reveal
SHORTRUNS
SKEPTICAL INQUIRER
Solcat Publishing
Southwest Research and Information Center
SPIRITCHASER
THE STAR BEACON
Vestibular Disorders Association
THE WILD FOODS FORUM
THE WISHING WELL
WRESTLING - THEN & NOW

NEWSPAPERS

BOOK MARKETING UPDATE
Children Of Mary
FIDELIS ET VERUS
INKY TRAIL NEWS
KETTERING REVIEW
Allen A. Knoll Publishers
Knowledge Concepts Publishing
Moon Pie Press
Progressive Education
PROGRESSIVE PERIODICALS DIRECTORY/UPDATE
THE PUBLICITY HOUND
Reveal
ST. LOUIS JOURNALISM REVIEW

NICARAGUA

INNER CITY PRESS
Martinez Press

ANAIS NIN

Chatterley Press International
KotaPress
LOST GENERATION JOURNAL
Magic Circle Press
Zygote Publishing

NON-FICTION

A Cappela Publishing, Inc.
Aaron Communications III
Abecedarian books, Inc.
Accendo Publishing
THE ACORN
Advantage World Press
Adventure Books Inc.
AE-TU Publishing
Ageless Press
Aglob Publishing
AIS Publications
AK Press
Alaska Native Language Center
Alaska Northwest Books
ALASKA QUARTERLY REVIEW
all nations press
Glen Allen Press
THE AMERICAN DRIVEL REVIEW
American Legacy Media
AMERICAN ROAD
Anacus Press, An Imprint of Finney Company
Ancient City Press
Anti-Aging Press
Apples & Oranges, Inc.
Archer Books
ARCHIPELAGO
Arden Press, Inc.
Ariko Publications
ARNAZELLA

ARTS & LETTERS: Journal of Contemporary Culture
ASPHODEL
AuthorsOmniscient Publishers
Avari Press
Avery Color Studios
Avocus Publishing, Inc.
AXE FACTORY REVIEW
Azreal Publishing Company
BACKWARDS CITY REVIEW
Balanced Books Publishing
THE BALTIMORE REVIEW
Bancroft Press
Banks Channel Books
Bay Press
Bayhampton Publications
THE BEAR DELUXE
The Bear Wallow Publishing Company
BearManor Media
BEATLICK NEWS
Bellevue Literary Press
BELLEVUE LITERARY REVIEW
BELLINGHAM REVIEW
Bellywater Press
Benchmark Publications Inc.
R.J. Bender Publishing
Benecton Press
The Bess Press
Beyond Words Publishing, Inc.
Big Mouth Publications
BIG MUDDY: Journal of the Mississippi River Valley
Biographical Publishing Company
Birdsong Books
Black Dome Press Corp.
Black Forest Press
Black Lawrence Press
Black Thistle Press
BLACK WARRIOR REVIEW
BlackBerry Literary Services
John F. Blair, Publisher
Blowtorch Press
BLUE MESA REVIEW
Blueprint Books
Bluestocking Press
Bonus Books, Inc.
Book Faith India
Book Marketing Solutions
Bookhome Publishing/Panda Publishing
Books for All Times, Inc.
Breakout Productions
THE BRIAR CLIFF REVIEW
Bright Mountain Books, Inc.
BRILLIANT CORNERS: A Journal of Jazz & Literature
Britton Road Press
Broken Rifle Press
Bronze Girl Productions, Inc.
Brookview Press
Brunswick Publishing Corporation
Buenos Books America
BUFFALO SPREE
Burd Street Press
BYLINE
C & M Online Media Inc.
CAKETRAIN
Caketrain Press
Cantadora Press
Caribbean Books-Panama
Cascada Corporation / Scherf Books, MegaGrace Books
Cave Books
Wm Caxton Ltd
The Caxton Press
CEDAR HILL REVIEW
THE CENTENNIAL REVIEW
CENTER: A Journal of the Literary Arts
Central Avenue Press
CHAPMAN
Chase Publishing
CHECKER CAB MAGAZINE - THE LITTLE 'ZINE THAT COULD! Fiction That Takes The Long Way

Home

Chelsea Green Publishing Company
Chicago Spectrum Press
Children Of Mary
CIMARRON REVIEW
CineCycle Publishing
CKO UPDATE
Cladach Publishing
COGNITIO: A Graduate Humanities Journal
COLORADO REVIEW
Common Courage Press
Communication Creativity
Comrades Press
Comstock Bonanza Press
CONJUNCTIONS
Consumer Press
Continuing Education Press
Cornerstone Publishing
CORRECTIONS TODAY
Country Messenger Press
CRAB ORCHARD REVIEW
Crane Press
CRAZYHORSE
THE CREAM CITY REVIEW
CREATIVE NONFICTION
CREATIVITY CONNECTION
CREOSOTE: A Journal of Poetry and Prose
Crossway Books
Crystal Dreams Publishing
Culturelink Press
Dablond Publishing
DAILY WORD
Datamaster Publishing, LLC
Dawn Publications
Delaney Day Press
Delta-West Publishing, Inc.
Devenish Press
DOTLIT: The Online Journal of Creative Writing
Dream Catcher Publishing
dreamslaughter
Dufour Editions Inc.
Dumouriez Publishing
Dunamis House
E. S. Publishers & Distributors
Eagle's View Publishing
EcceNova Editions
Eco Images
Ecopress, An Imprint of Finney Company
Ecrivez!
EduCare Press
Wm.B. Eerdmans Publishing Co.
EMRYS JOURNAL
Emrys Press
Ephemera Bound Publishing
EPICENTER: A LITERARY MAGAZINE
Epoch Press
Eros Books
EUPHONY
Eurotique Press
EVENT
Evolution Publishing
Excelsior Cee Publishing
Fast Foot Forward Press
Fathom Publishing Co.
The Feminist Press at the City University of New York
The Fiction Works
FIDELIS ET VERUS
Nicolin Fields Publishing, Inc.
Finney Company, Inc.
First Books
FIVE POINTS
Florida Academic Press
THE FLORIDA REVIEW
FLUENT ASCENSION
FLYWAY
FMA Publishing
Focus Publishing/R. Pullins Co.
FOLIO: A Literary Journal of American University

Foremost Press
Fountainhead Productions, Inc.
Fouque Publishers
Four Seasons Publishers
FRAN MAGAZINE
Franklin-Sarrett Publishers
Fretwater Press
Front Row Experience
FUGUE
Galde Press, Inc.
Galen Press, Ltd.
The Galileo Press Ltd.
Gallaudet University Press
Gardenia Press
Gaslight Publications
Gateways Books And Tapes
GAUNTLET: Exploring the Limits of Free Expression
GENRE: WRITER AND WRITINGS
THE GEORGIA REVIEW
GERTRUDE
GERTRUDE
Gertrude Press
Gival Press
GLB Publishers
The Glencannon Press
GOLDEN ISIS MAGAZINE
Golden Isis Press
Good Book Publishing Company
Goose River Press
Graywolf Press
THE GREAT BLUE BEACON
The Great Rift Press
GREEN ANARCHY
THE GREEN HILLS LITERARY LANTERN
Green Hut Press
Green River Press
Gryphon Books
GULF COAST
Haley's
Hanover Press
Harbor House
HAWAI'I REVIEW
Heartsong Books
Heidelberg Graphics
Historical Resources Press
Hobar Publications, A Division of Finney Company
Holbrook Street Press
Hoover Institution Press
Horse Creek Publications, Inc.
Hot Box Press / Southern Roots Publishing
Howln Moon Press
Ibexa Press
ICON
Idylls Press
Ika, LLC
IMAGE: ART, FAITH, MYSTERY
Imago Press
Impact Publishers, Inc.
Impassio Press
INDIANA REVIEW
THE INDIE
Infinite Possibilities Publishing Group, Inc.
INKWELL
INNOVATING
Interlink Publishing Group, Inc.
International University Line (IUL)
The Intrepid Traveler
THE IOWA REVIEW
Iris Publishing Group, Inc (Iris Press / Tellico Books)
IRON HORSE LITERARY REVIEW
Island Press
Italica Press, Inc.
J & J Consultants, Inc.
Jako Books
Jalmar Press/Innerchoice Publishing
Jireh Publishing Company
THE JOURNAL OF AFRICAN TRAVEL-WRITING
JOURNAL OF PYROTECHNICS

JPS Publishing Company
JUBILAT
JUST WEST OF ATHENS
KAJ-MAHKAH: EARTH OF EARTH
KALEIDOSCOPE: Exploring the Experience of Disability through Literature & the Fine Arts
Kali Press
THE KELSEY REVIEW
The Kenneth G. Mills Foundation
THE KENYON REVIEW
Keokee Co. Publishing, Inc.
KESTREL: A Journal of Literature and Art
La Alameda Press
Lake Claremont Press
LAKE EFFECT
LAKE STREET LIT: Art and Words from the Bottom of Lake Bonneville
The Larcom Press
LARCOM REVIEW
THE LAUREL REVIEW
Lean Press
THE LEDGE
LegacyForever
Leyland Publications
Liberty Publishing Company, Inc.
LICHEN Arts & Letters Preview
LifeQuest Publishing Group
Limelight Editions
Little Pear Press
THE LOUISVILLE REVIEW
MacAdam/Cage Publishing Inc.
THE MACGUFFIN
MAIN STREET RAG
Malki Museum Press
Mama Incense Publishing
MANOA: A Pacific Journal of International Writing
Marmot Publishing
Massey-Reyner Publishing
Maui arThoughts Co.
Mayhaven Publishing
MCM Entertainment, Inc. Publishing Division
Merl Publications
MeteoritePress.com
Mica Press - Paying Our Dues Productions
Microdex Bookshelf
MID-AMERICAN REVIEW
The Midknight Club
Mid-List Press
Milkweed Editions
MINESHAFT
MINIATURE DONKEY TALK INC
Minnesota Historical Society Press
Mock Turtle Press
Monroe Press
Montemayor Press
Moondance Press
Motom
Mountain Meadow Press
Music City Publishing
My Heart Yours Publishing
MYSTERY ISLAND MAGAZINE
NAR Publications
The Narrative Press
National Woodlands Publishing Company
National Writers Press
NATURAL BRIDGE
NEO: Literary Magazine
NEW GRAFFITI
NEW LETTERS
NEW ORLEANS REVIEW
Newmark Publishing Company
NewSage Press
NEWWITCH
Nip & Tuck Publishing
Nolo Press Occidental
NORTH AMERICAN REVIEW
NORTH CAROLINA LITERARY REVIEW
North Country Books, Inc.

North Star Books
NORTHERN PILOT
Northwestern University Press
NSR Publications
NWI National Writers Institute
Oasis Books
Ocean Publishing
One Less Press
Oolichan Books
OPEN MINDS QUARTERLY
OPEN WIDE MAGAZINE
THE ORPHAN LEAF REVIEW
Outskirts Press, Inc.
The Overmountain Press
THE OXFORD AMERICAN
OYEZ REVIEW
Oyster River Press
PAJ NTAUB VOICE
Paladin Enterprises, Inc.
Palari Publishing
PARENTEACHER MAGAZINE
Parenting Press, Inc.
Parity Press
PASSAGES NORTH
Passion Power Press, Inc
Path Press, Inc.
THE PEDESTAL MAGAZINE.COM
Pedestal Press
The People's Press
Perpetual Press
Personhood Press
PhoeniX in Print
Piccadilly Books, Ltd.
Pilgrims Book House
Pine Publications
Platinum Dreams Publishing
PLEASANT LIVING
Pleasure Boat Studio: A Literary Press
POETICA MAGAZINE, Reflections of Jewish Thought
Polar Bear & Company
POTOMAC REVIEW
PRETEXT
PRISM INTERNATIONAL
Prospect Press
Purple Finch Press
Quest Books: Theosophical Publishing House
THE QUIET FEATHER
Quiet Storm Books
Rabeth Publishing Company
Rada Press, Inc.
Ragged Edge Press
Ragged Raven Press
Rainbow Books, Inc.
Ram Press
RATTAPALLAX
THE RAVEN CHRONICLES
RavenHaus Publishing
Ravenhawk Books
Reach Productions Publishing
Reading Connections
Red Tiger Press
Redgreene Press
REDIVIDER
REMS Publishing & Publicity
Reveal
RFF Press / Resources for the Future
RIVER TEETH: A Journal of Nonfiction Narrative
RIVERSEDGE
Riverstone Publishing
RIVET MAGAZINE
Rolling Hills Publishing
Ronsdale Press
Russell Dean and Company
Saber Press
SAGE OF CONSCIOUSNESS E-ZINE
Saint Mary's Press
Salmon Poetry Ltd.
Santa Monica Press

Scarlet Tanager Books
SCHUYLKILL VALLEY JOURNAL OF THE ARTS
Scientia Publishing, LLC
Scrivenery Press
Search Institute
See Sharp Press
SEEMS
SENECA REVIEW
Sentient Publications, LLC
Set Sail Productions, LLC
Seven Arrows Publishing, Inc.
SEWANEE REVIEW
SHENANDOAH: THE Washington and Lee University
  Review
SISTERS IN CRIME BOOKS IN PRINT
SKIDROW PENTHOUSE
SKYLARK
Small Helm Press
The Smith (subsidiary of The Generalist Assn., Inc.)
Genny Smith Books
SO TO SPEAK: A Feminist Journal of Language & Art
A SOFT DEGRADE
SOJOURN: A Journal of the Arts
$olvency International Inc., Publishing
Soul
Sound View Publishing, Inc.
SOUTH DAKOTA REVIEW
Southeast Missouri State University Press
Southern Illinois University Press
Southern Methodist University Press
SOUTHWEST REVIEW
SPEAKEASY
Spectrum Press
Spire Press
SPOUT
Spout Press
Square One Publishers, Inc.
Starbooks Press/FLF Press
Stardate Publishing Company
Starry Night Publishing
Stellaberry Press
Stonehorse Publishing, LLC
Stony Meadow Publishing
Storm Publishing Group
Stormline Press, Inc.
THE STRANGE FRUIT
SUB-TERRAIN
SULPHUR RIVER LITERARY REVIEW
Summer Stream Press
THE SUN, A Magazine of Ideas
Sunbelt Publications
Sunnyside Press
SunShine Press Publications, Inc.
Swedenborg Foundation
SWINK
SYCAMORE REVIEW
SYMPLOKE: A Journal for the Intermingling of Literary,
  Cultural and Theoretical Scholarship
Syukhtun Editions
TalSan Publishing/Distributors
Tameme
Ten Star Press
Tendre Press
Terra Nova Press
Thatch Tree Publications
Think Tank Press, Inc.
THINKERMONKEY
Thirsty Turtle Press
This New World Publishing, LLC
Thunder Rain Publishing Corp.
Timeless Books
The Times Journal Publishing Co.
Titlewaves Publishing; Writers Direct
TMC Books LLC
Top 20 Press
Tortuga Books
Trafford Publishing
Trickle Creek Books

Truman State University Press
Tupelo Press
TURNROW
TWENTY-EIGHT PAGES LOVINGLY BOUND WITH
  TWINE
Twilight Times Books
Two Eagles Press International
Tyr Publishing
Tzipora Publications, Inc.
United Nations University Press
Unity House
UNITY MAGAZINE
Universal Unity
University of Arkansas Press
University of Massachusetts Press
University of Nebraska Press
University of Tampa Press
University of Utah Press
University of Virginia Press
University Press of Colorado
Upper Access Inc.
UPSTAIRS AT DUROC
Urthona Press
V52 Press
VanderWyk & Burnham
Vehicle Press
Versus Press
Vintage Romance Publishing, LLC
Virginia Pines Press
Vision
Visions Communications
Vista Publishing, Inc.
THE WASHINGTON MONTHLY
Waters Edge Press
WEBER STUDIES: Voices and Viewpoints of the
  Contemporary West
The Wellsweep Press
WEST BRANCH
West Coast Paradise Publishing
Westgate Press
Wharton Publishing, Inc.
Wheatmark Book Publishing
which press
Whiskey Creek Press
White Crosslet Publishing Co
White Mane Publishing Company, Inc.
Whitford Press
WHOLE TERRAIN - REFLECTIVE ENVIRONMENTAL
  PRACTICE
THE WILD FOODS FORUM
Wild West Publishing House
Zelda Wilde Publishing
WILLOW REVIEW
WILLOW SPRINGS
WillowTree Press LLC
Wilshire Books Inc.
Windward Publishing, An Imprint of Finney Company
Wings Press
WISCONSIN TRAILS
Women In Print
Wood Thrush Books
The Word Doctor Online Publishing
WORDS OF WISDOM
World Gumbo Publishing
WRITER'S CHRONICLE
Xavier House Publishing
Xenos Books
YUKHIKA—LATUHSE
ZAWP
ZONE 3

NON-VIOLENCE

Aaron Communications III
Abernathy House Publishing
ALONE TOGETHER
Broken Rifle Press
Crandall, Dostie & Douglass Books, Inc.
dreamslaughter

Fotofolio, Inc.
Free People Press
FRIENDS OF PEACE PILGRIM
Friends United Press
HARMONY: Voices for a Just Future
Heartsong Books
Himalayan Institute Press
Hope Publishing House
Ika, LLC
THE INDEPENDENT REVIEW: A Journal of Political
    Economy
THE INDIE
Jalmar Press/Innerchoice Publishing
KotaPress
Libellum
THE MINDFULNESS BELL
MINISTRY & LITURGY
NEW ENVIRONMENT BULLETIN
NewSage Press
THE NONVIOLENT ACTIVIST
Parallax Press
Path Press, Inc.
PEACEWORK
The People's Press
Philopsychy Press
Plain View Press
The Press at Foggy Bottom
SOCIAL ANARCHISM: A Journal of Practice and Theory
Spinifex Press
THINKERMONKEY
TURNING WHEEL
VOICES - ISRAEL
THE VOLUNTARYIST
WAV MAGAZINE: Progressive Music Art Politics Culture

THE NORTH

Alaska Geographic Society
Betelgeuse Books
EUPHONY
Mountain Automation Corporation
Poetry Harbor
University of Alaska Press
University of Calgary Press
University of Nebraska Press

NORTH AMERICA

BearManor Media
GAYELLOW PAGES
MANDORLA: New Writing from the Americas / Nueva
    escritura de las Americas
Maryland Historical Press
Palladium Communications
Quantum Leap S.L.C. Publications
RockBySea Books
Stormline Press, Inc.
Truman State University Press
University of Calgary Press
UPSTAIRS AT DUROC
Zelda Wilde Publishing
WORD IS BOND

NORTH CAROLINA

Ammons Communications
Banks Channel Books
John F. Blair, Publisher
Bright Mountain Books, Inc.
C & M Online Media Inc.
Explorer Press
GAMBARA MAGAZINE
NORTH CAROLINA LITERARY REVIEW
OYSTER BOY REVIEW
PREP Publishing

NOVELS

A Cappela Publishing, Inc.
ACME Press
ALASKA QUARTERLY REVIEW
American Literary Press

Ammons Communications
Arx Publishing LLC
Asylum Arts
AuthorsOmniscient Publishers
Avari Press
BACKWARDS CITY REVIEW
THE BALTIMORE REVIEW
Banks Channel Books
Bardsong Press
Barney Press
Bayhampton Publications
BIG MUDDY: Journal of the Mississippi River Valley
Black Heron Press
Black Lawrence Press
Black Oak Press
BlackBerry Literary Services
Blanket Fort Publishing
Blue Hot Books
Blue Planet Books Inc.
Bordighera, Inc.
Boulevard Books, Inc. Florida
Brookline Books
Brunswick Publishing Corporation
Cambric Press dba Emerald House
Cantarabooks LLC
Caribbean Books-Panama
Casperian Books LLC
Cave Books
CEDAR HILL REVIEW
Celo Valley Books
Central Avenue Press
City Life Books, LLC
Cladach Publishing
Cleis Press
Coffee House Press
CONCRETE JUNGLE JOURNAL
Concrete Jungle Press
CREOSOTE: A Journal of Poetry and Prose
The Design Image Group Inc.
DOTLIT: The Online Journal of Creative Writing
E & D Publishing, Inc.
EduCare Press
Ephemera Bound Publishing
Eros Books
Firelight Publishing, Inc.
First Books
Fithian Press
Fontanel Books
Foremost Press
Fouque Publishers
Free Reign Press, Inc.
The Galileo Press Ltd.
GEM Literary Foundation Press
Gibbs Smith, Publisher
GoldenIsle Publishers, Inc.
Green Bean Press
Grip Publishing
Harbor House
Hole Books
Idylls Press
ILLUMINATIONS
Imago Press
IMPress
In Between Books
Italica Press, Inc.
Jackson Harbor Press
JetKor
Journey Books Publishing
Allen A. Knoll Publishers
THE LEDGE
Lekon New Dimensions Publishing
Leyland Publications
Little Pear Press
Llumina Press
Loonfeather Press
Ludlow Press
LULLWATER REVIEW
Lyons Publishing Limited

Mama Incense Publishing
MANOA: A Pacific Journal of International Writing
McPherson & Company Publishers
Montemayor Press
Motom
Mountain Media
Mountain State Press
Muse World Media Group
Myriad Press
NEO: Literary Magazine
New Concept Press
THE NEW FORMALIST
New Orphic Publishers
THE NEW ORPHIC REVIEW
New Victoria Publishers
NWI National Writers Institute
THE ORPHAN LEAF REVIEW
The Overmountain Press
Panther Books
Panther Creek Press
Parity Press
Pennycorner Press
The People's Press
Phoenix Illusion
Platinum Dreams Publishing
Pleasure Boat Studio: A Literary Press
Polar Bear & Company
PREP Publishing
Primal Publishing
Pyncheon House
Radiant Press
Ravenhawk Books
Redgreene Press
Sand and Sable Publishing
Scrivenery Press
SelectiveHouse Publishers, Inc.
The Smith (subsidiary of The Generalist Assn., Inc.)
Southeast Missouri State University Press
Southern Methodist University Press
Spectrum Press
Steerforth Press, L.C.
Stony Meadow Publishing
SYMPLOKE: A Journal for the Intermingling of Literary,
    Cultural and Theoretical Scholarship
Talisman House, Publishers
Ten Star Press
Think Tank Press, Inc.
Three House Publishing
TnT Classic Books
Tupelo Press
Turnstone Press
Versus Press
Vintage Romance Publishing, LLC
White Pine Press
Willowgate Press
WillowTree Press LLC
WordFarm
Xenos Books
Zephyr Press

NUCLEAR ENERGY

Rising Tide Press New Mexico
Southwest Research and Information Center
VOICES FROM THE EARTH

NUMISMATICS

C & M Online Media Inc.
GAMBARA MAGAZINE

NURSING

Adams-Blake Publishing
Bandido Books
Believe! Publishing
Bonus Books, Inc.
Center for Thanatology Research & Education, Inc.
THE COMPLEAT NURSE
Delaney Day Press
Dream Publishing Co.

Galen Press, Ltd.
MEDICAL HISTORY
Midwifery Today
North Star Books
Sand and Sable Publishing
shift 4 Publishing
Standish Press
Vista Publishing, Inc.
Wellcome Institute for the History of Medicine

NUTRITION

AB
Consumer Press
Delaney Day Press
Dream Publishing Co.
Foodnsport Press
GLOBAL ONE TRAVEL & AUTOMOTIVE MAGAZINE
Health Yourself
Hunter House Inc., Publishers
Infinite Possibilities Publishing Group, Inc.
Llumina Press
Luminous Epinoia Press
MND Publishing, Inc.
Muse World Media Group
New Win Publishing
Piccadilly Books, Ltd.
Princess Publishing
Starry Night Publishing
Synergy Press

OCCULT

Alamo Square Press
ALONE TOGETHER
ARTISTIC RAMBLINGS
Athanor Books (a division of ETX Seminars)
Auromere Books and Imports
The B & R Samizdat Express
BALLISTA
Barrytown/Station Hill Press
Borden Publishing Co.
BOTH SIDES NOW
Cassandra Press, Inc.
EcceNova Editions
EMERGING
Ephemera Bound Publishing
Free People Press
Galde Press, Inc.
GOLDEN ISIS MAGAZINE
Golden Isis Press
Harbor House
Heartsong Books
Iconoclast Press
LegacyForever
LifeQuest Publishing Group
Llumina Press
LP Publications (Teleos Institute)
Lummox Press
Lycanthrope Press
MAGICAL BLEND/NATURAL BEAUTY & HEALTH/
    TRANSITIONS
MB Media, Inc.
The Midknight Club
Monkfish Book Publishing Company
Mucusart Publications
Muse World Media Group
Mystery Island Publications
New Falcon Publications
New Paradigm Books
nine muses books
NOLA-MAGICK Press
NORTHWOODS JOURNAL, A Magazine for Writers
Origin Press
Outrider Press
Quicksilver Productions
RALPH'S REVIEW
Red Tiger Press
Rivercross Publishing, Inc.
SAGEWOMAN

Santa Fe Writers Project
SHORTRUNS
SOCIETE
Technicians of the Sacred
The Teitan Press, Inc.
Three Pyramids Publishing
Toad Hall, Inc.
Triskelion Publishing
John Wade, Publisher
Westgate Press
White Crosslet Publishing Co
Whitford Press
WillowTree Press LLC
Windstorm Creative
THE WISE WOMAN
XTANT
ZINE-ON-A-TAPE
Zumaya Publications

OCEANOGRAPHY

Scientia Publishing, LLC
Trickle Creek Books

OHIO

The Bacchae Press
Faded Banner Publications
Gabriel's Horn Publishing Co., Inc.
HEARTLANDS: A Magazine of Midwest Life and Art
ICON
THE JOURNAL
Kenyette Productions
Lucky Press, LLC
MID-AMERICAN REVIEW
Mountain Automation Corporation
Ohio University Press/Swallow Press
OHIO WRITER
RIVERWIND
Thirsty Turtle Press
TWENTY-EIGHT PAGES LOVINGLY BOUND WITH
    TWINE
WHITEWALL OF SOUND

OLD WEST

The Bear Wallow Publishing Company
The Fiction Works
Fretwater Press
Heartland Publishing
High Plains Press
Ho Logos Press
LITERALLY HORSES/REMUDA
LOW BUDGET ADVENTURE
Mountain Meadow Press
Ohio University Press/Swallow Press
Tres Picos Press
University of Nebraska Press
Venus Communications
Voyageur Publishing Co.,Inc.
Whiskey Creek Press

OREGON

BURNSIDE REVIEW
Firelight Publishing, Inc.
Flying Pencil Publications
Fretwater Press
LEO Productions LLC.
NORTHERN PILOT
Timber Press

OUTDOOR ADVENTURE

Thirsty Turtle Press

PACIFIC NORTHWEST

Alaska Geographic Society
Alaska Northwest Books
ALL ROUND
Anacus Press, An Imprint of Finney Company
Ballena Press
BookPartners, Inc.

Carpe Diem Publishing
THE CLIMBING ART
Continuing Education Press
Dunamis House
DWELLING PORTABLY
FERRY TRAVEL GUIDE
FINE MADNESS
Firelight Publishing, Inc.
Flying Pencil Publications
THE FRANK REVIEW
Iconoclast Press
Island Publishers
Keokee Co. Publishing, Inc.
KotaPress
Light, Words & Music
Lost Horse Press
Mountain Meadow Press
The Mountaineers Books
NORTHERN PILOT
Open Hand Publishing LLC
Oregon State University Press
PATTERNS OF CHOICE: A Journal of People, Land, and
    Money
PEMMICAN
Perpetual Press
POETIC SPACE: Poetry & Fiction
Pygmy Forest Press
QED Press
SANDPOINT MAGAZINE
Sasquatch Books
Timber Press
TIMBER TIMES
UNWOUND
WASHINGTON TRAILS
Whispering Pine Press
WHITEWALL OF SOUND

PACIFIC REGION

The Bess Press
Blueprint Books
CHECKER CAB MAGAZINE - THE LITTLE 'ZINE
    THAT COULD! Fiction That Takes The Long Way
    Home
HAWAI'I REVIEW
NORTHERN PILOT
STORYBOARD
Tamal Vista Publications
Timber Press
University of Alaska Press

PAPER

EEI Press
Total Cardboard Publishing

PARENTING

Glen Allen Press
Andros Books
Angel Power Press
APPLE VALLEY REVIEW: A Journal of Contemporary
    Literature
Ascension Publishing
AT-HOME DAD
Avocus Publishing, Inc.
Bancroft Press
Bayhampton Publications
THE BEACON: Journal of Special Education Law &
    Practice
Beyond Words Publishing, Inc.
BlackBerry Literary Services
Bright Ring Publishing, Inc.
Bronze Girl Productions, Inc.
Cladach Publishing
Consumer Press
Cornerstone Publishing
Datamaster Publishing, LLC
Delaney Day Press
DOVETAIL: A Journal by and for Jewish/Christian
    Families

Dumouriez Publishing
THE EAST VILLAGE INKY
East West Discovery Press
Family Learning Association, Inc.
Fingerprint Press
First Books
Future Horizons, Inc.
Gallaudet University Press
GLB Publishers
Green River Press
Gurze Books
Harbor House Law Press, Inc.
Harlan Publishing Company; Alliance Books; Diakonia
    Publishing (Christian Books)
Harvard Common Press
Heritage Global Publishing
Images Unlimited and Snaptail Press, a Division of Images
    Unlimited Publishing
Impact Publishers, Inc.
Islewest Publishing
J&W Publishers, Inc.
Jalmar Press/Innerchoice Publishing
Kivaki Press
Knowledge Concepts Publishing
Kodiak Media Group
LIFE LEARNING
Llumina Press
The Love and Logic Press, Inc.
Luminous Epinoia Press
Macrocosm USA, Inc.
Mapletree Publishing Company
McGavick Field Publishing
A Melody from an Immigrant's Soul
Metallo House Publishers
Monroe Press
Mo'omana'o Press
Moondance Press
MOTHERVERSE: A Journal of Contemporary Motherhood
New Atlantean Press
New Win Publishing
New World Library
NICU Ink
Over the Wall Inc. Publishing & Productions
PARENTEACHER MAGAZINE
Parenting Press, Inc.
Peachtree Publishers, Ltd.
PEDIATRICS FOR PARENTS
Purple Finch Press
Quiet Tymes, Inc.
Rainbow Books, Inc.
Rayve Productions Inc.
Resource Publications, Inc.
St. John's Publishing, Inc.
SCIENCE/HEALTH ABSTRACTS
Search Institute
Sentient Publications, LLC
Sibyl Publications, Inc
Spiritual Understanding Network, LLC
Square One Publishers, Inc.
Stony Meadow Publishing
Storm Publishing Group
Studio 4 Productions
Summit Crossroads Press
Swan Publishing Company
Wheatmark Book Publishing
Women of Diversity Productions, Inc.

PEACE

American Literary Press
Atrium Society Publications
Black Pearl Enterprises LLC
BLUE COLLAR REVIEW
BRANCHES
Branden Books
Broken Rifle Press
COLOR WHEEL
Common Courage Press
FINE MADNESS

Free People Press
FRIENDS OF PEACE PILGRIM
Friends United Press
HARMONY: Voices for a Just Future
Heartsong Books
The Heather Foundation
IN OUR OWN WORDS
THE INDIE
International Publishers Co. Inc.
Iris Publishing Group, Inc (Iris Press / Tellico Books)
Knowledge Concepts Publishing
KotaPress
Kumarian Press, Inc.
Middleway Press
THE MINDFULNESS BELL
Moon Pie Press
NEW ENVIRONMENT BULLETIN
NewSage Press
THE NONVIOLENT ACTIVIST
Origin Press
ORTHODOX MISSION
Orthodox Mission in Belize
Oyster River Press
Partisan Press
PEACEWORK
The People's Press
RFD
Sand and Sable Publishing
SHARE INTERNATIONAL
SKS Press
Soul
South End Press
Spinifex Press
STORMWARNING!
Syracuse Cultural Workers/Tools for Change
Syracuse Cultural Workers/Tools for Change
United Nations University Press
Upper Access Inc.
VOICES - ISRAEL

PERFORMING ARTS

Aaron Communications III
Americans for the Arts
Ammons Communications
Aran Press
ART PAPERS
BIRD DOG
BRILLIANT CORNERS: A Journal of Jazz & Literature
DAVID McCALLUM UPDATES
Everflowing Publications
GLOBAL ONE TRAVEL & AUTOMOTIVE MAGAZINE
GULF & MAIN Southwest Florida Lifestyle
Harobed Publishing Creations
Hollywood Creative Directory
IMAGE: ART, FAITH, MYSTERY
THE INDIE
INDUSTRY MINNE-ZINE
KARAWANE
Libellum
Limelight Editions
McPherson & Company Publishers
Mountainside Press
New Concept Press
nine muses books
Northwestern University Press
Palladium Communications
Princeton Book Company, Publishers
Red Tiger Press
Santa Monica Press
SENSATIONS MAGAZINE
74th Street Productions, L.L.C.
Southern Illinois University Press
SOUTHWEST COLORADO ARTS PERSPECTIVE
Speck Press
VANITAS
Whelks Walk Press
WISCONSIN TRAILS

PETS

Biographical Publishing Company
Bronze Girl Productions, Inc.
City Life Books, LLC
Creative Writing and Publishing Company
Howln Moon Press
Kali Press
Lucky Press, LLC
MINIATURE DONKEY TALK INC
Moon Pie Press
NewSage Press
Outrider Press
Park Place Publications
Princess Publishing
Publishing Works
ROCKY MOUNTAIN KC NEWS
Rocky Mountain KC Publishing Co.
RUMINATIONS: The Nigerian Dwarf & Mini Dairy Goat
   Magazine
Storm Publishing Group
Two Dog Press
Vonpalisaden Publications Inc.

PHILATELY

ARTISTAMP NEWS
Banana Productions
INTERNATIONAL ART POST
RALPH'S REVIEW

PHILOSOPHY

ABRAMELIN: a Journal of Poetry and Magick
Agathon Books
AK Press
Glen Allen Press
Anagnosis
Anthony Publishing Company, Inc.
THE ART OF ABUNDANCE
ASCENT
Auromere Books and Imports
The B & R Samizdat Express
Bad Press
Barrytown/Station Hill Press
Birdalone Books
Black Rose Books Ltd.
BOTH SIDES NOW
BOULDER HERETIC
Brason-Sargar Publications
BRIDGES: An Interdisciplinary Journal of Theology,
   Philosophy, History, and Science
Buenos Books America
Burning Books
Camino Bay Books
CANADIAN JOURNAL OF PHILOSOPHY
Cantadora Press
Cherry Valley Editions
Children Of Mary
Community Service, Inc.
CONDUIT
Crane Press
CRITICAL REVIEW
THE DALHOUSIE REVIEW
Dharma Publishing
dreamslaughter
Dufour Editions Inc.
Edition Gemini
EduCare Press
The Edwin Mellen Press
EFRYDIAU ATHRONYDDOL
EPICENTER: A LITERARY MAGAZINE
Epoch Press
Eros Books
FAT TUESDAY
Feel Free Press
FEMINIST STUDIES
FIDELIS ET VERUS
Focus Publishing/R. Pullins Co.
FREE INQUIRY

Free People Press
Free Reign Press, Inc.
FREETHOUGHT HISTORY
Gearhead Press
Genesis Publishing Company, Inc.
GESAR-Buddhism in the West
Gifted Education Press/The Reading Tutorium
Glenbridge Publishing Ltd.
Goldfish Press
The Gutenberg Press
Handshake Editions
The Heather Foundation
Himalayan Institute Press
Ho Logos Press
THE HUMANIST
HYPATIA: A Journal of Feminist Philosophy
Iconoclast Press
Impassio Press
THE INDEPENDENT REVIEW: A Journal of Political
   Economy
The Institute of Mind and Behavior
Intelligenesis Publications
INTERCULTURE
ITALIAN AMERICANA
JACK MACKEREL MAGAZINE
JOURNAL OF AESTHETICS AND ART CRITICISM
THE JOURNAL OF MIND AND BEHAVIOR
JOURNAL OF REGIONAL CRITICISM
JOURNAL OF SCIENTIFIC EXPLORATION
KAIROS, A Journal of Contemporary Thought and
   Criticism
Kallisti Publishing
KANTIAN REVIEW
The Kenneth G. Mills Foundation
The Kenneth G. Mills Foundation
Kivaki Press
LAKE EFFECT
THE LEDGE
THE (LIBERTARIAN) CONNECTION
Libertarian Press, Inc./American Book Distributors
LIBERTY
Llumina Press
Lucky Press, LLC
Lycanthrope Press
MACROBIOTICS TODAY
Maisonneuve Press
Maryland Historical Press
MB Media, Inc.
MEAT: A Journal of Writing and Materiality
Mercer University Press
The Midknight Club
Mind Power Publishing
THE MONIST: An International Quarterly Journal of
   General Philosophical Inquiry
Monkfish Book Publishing Company
THE MOUNTAIN ASTROLOGER
THE NEO-COMINTERN
NEW AMERICAN IMAGIST
New Atlantean Press
New Falcon Publications
New Paradigm Books
NEW SOLUTIONS
NEW THOUGHT
Nicolas-Hays, Inc.
Nightsun Books
Nightsun Books
OFFICE NUMBER ONE
Ohio University Press/Swallow Press
George Ohsawa Macrobiotic Foundation
Open Court Publishing Company
Origin Press
PARABOLA MAGAZINE
Paragon House Publishers
Philopsychy Press
Phi-Psi Publishers
The Pin Prick Press
Plain Philosophy Center
Pleasure Boat Studio: A Literary Press

PSYCHE
PublishAmerica, LLLP.
Quarterly Committee of Queen's University
QUEEN'S QUARTERLY: A Canadian Review
THE QUEST
Quest Books: Theosophical Publishing House
REPORTS OF THE NATIONAL CENTER FOR SCIENCE
    EDUCATION
Rowhouse Press
SAKANA
SALMAGUNDI
SAT SANDESH: THE MESSAGE OF THE MASTERS
The Saunderstown Press
Savant Garde Workshop
See Sharp Press
Semiotext Foreign Agents Books Series
SEMIOTEXT(E)
SOLAS Press
Spirit Press
Spring Publications Inc.
State University of New York Press
Sherwood Sugden & Company, Publishers
Superior Christian Press
SYMPLOKE: A Journal for the Intermingling of Literary,
    Cultural and Theoretical Scholarship
TAI CHI
TELOS
Telos Press
Tendre Press
Transcending Mundane, Inc.
TRUTH SEEKER
Turtle Press, division of S.K. Productions Inc.
Tyr Publishing
Ulysses Books
UNDERSTANDING MAGAZINE
UnKnownTruths.com Publishing Company
Via Dolorosa Press
THE WALLACE STEVENS JOURNAL
Westgate Press
WHAT IS ENLIGHTENMENT?
White Thread Press
Whitford Press
WILD DUCK REVIEW
Wisdom Publications, Inc.
Wood Thrush Books
World Wisdom,Inc.
ZONE

PHOTOGRAPHY

ACM (ANOTHER CHICAGO MAGAZINE)
AFTERIMAGE
ALABAMA LITERARY REVIEW
Alaska Geographic Society
THE ALLEGHENY REVIEW
Allworth Press
American & World Geographic Publishing
Amherst Media, Inc.
Ammons Communications
ANTIETAM REVIEW
Appalachian Consortium Press
Arjuna Library Press
ARNAZELLA
ART CALENDAR
ARTISTIC RAMBLINGS
ASCENT
Avery Color Studios
BACKWARDS CITY REVIEW
BAGAZINE
Banana Productions
Barefoot Press
Barrytown/Station Hill Press
BATHTUB GIN
Bay Press
Beacon Light Publishing (BLP)
The Bear Wallow Publishing Company
BLACKFLASH
THE BLIND MAN'S RAINBOW
THE BREAD AND BUTTER CHRONICLES

THE BRIAR CLIFF REVIEW
THE CAPE ROCK
CHILDREN, CHURCHES AND DADDIES, A Non
    Religious, Non Familial Literary Magazine
CIMARRON REVIEW
COTTONWOOD
Cottonwood Press
Crazy Woman Creek Press
Dawn Sign Press
DESCANT
DOLLS UNITED INTERACTIVE MAGAZINE
DOWN IN THE DIRT LITERARY MAGAZINE, the prose
    & poetry magazine revealing all your dirty little secrets
Down There Press
East West Discovery Press
EEI Press
EROSHA
Feel Free Press
Film-Video Publications/Circus Source Publications
firefall editions
580 SPLIT
FOLIO: A Literary Journal of American University
Fotofolio, Inc.
FOTOTEQUE
THE FRANK REVIEW
FREEDOM AND STRENGTH PRESS FORUM
FROZEN WAFFLES
Gesture Press
Ghost Pony Press
GLOBAL ONE TRAVEL & AUTOMOTIVE MAGAZINE
HandyCraft Media Productions
Historical Resources Press
ICON
Iconoclast Press
IMAGE: ART, FAITH, MYSTERY
INDEFINITE SPACE
INDUSTRY MINNE-ZINE
INTERNATIONAL ART POST
JOURNAL OF REGIONAL CRITICISM
KAJ-MAHKAH: EARTH OF EARTH
Kenyette Productions
KESTREL: A Journal of Literature and Art
Allen A. Knoll Publishers
Laguna Wilderness Press
LAKE SUPERIOR MAGAZINE
Land Yacht Press
The Larcom Press
LARCOM REVIEW
The Leaping Frog Press
LEFT CURVE
Lessiter Publications
LICHEN Arts & Letters Preview
Light, Words & Music
LIGHTWORKS MAGAZINE
Lincoln Springs Press
THE LISTENING EYE
LITRAG
LOST GENERATION JOURNAL
Lost Prophet Press
Lunar Offensive Publications
THE MAD HATTER
MANDORLA: New Writing from the Americas / Nueva
    escritura de las Americas
MBA Publications
Meridien PressWorks
Midmarch Arts Press
MINESHAFT
Missing Man Press
Motom
N: NUDE & NATURAL
NEW ORLEANS REVIEW
NIGHTJAR REVIEW
NORTH CAROLINA LITERARY REVIEW
North Country Books, Inc.
Northland Publishing/Rising Moon/Luna Rising
Olympic Mountain School Press
One Less Press
OYEZ REVIEW

718

Oyster River Press
Panther Books
PIG IRON
POESY MAGAZINE
Pomegranate Communications
PRAIRIE WINDS
PRETEXT
Peter E. Randall Publisher
Really Great Books
Red Alder Books
Red Hand Press
Red Tiger Press
REDIVIDER
Re-invention UK Ltd
RIVER STYX
RIVET MAGAZINE
Ronsdale Press
SAGE OF CONSCIOUSNESS E-ZINE
Scars Publications
SCULPTURAL PURSUIT MAGAZINE
SKIDROW PENTHOUSE
SLIPSTREAM
SO TO SPEAK: A Feminist Journal of Language & Art
A SOFT DEGRADE
SOJOURN: A Journal of the Arts
SOUTHWEST COLORADO ARTS PERSPECTIVE
SPILLWAY
The Spirit That Moves Us Press, Inc.
Stormline Press, Inc.
STUDIO ONE
THE SUN, A Magazine of Ideas
SWINK
TEXAS POETRY JOURNAL
Texas Tech University Press
THIN COYOTE
Think Tank Press, Inc.
Thunder Rain Publishing Corp.
The Times Journal Publishing Co.
Titan Press
TURNROW
UMBRELLA Online
UNO MAS MAGAZINE
The Urbana Free Library
VALLUM: CONTEMPORARY POETRY
Visual Studies Workshop
VLQ (Verse Libre Quarterly)
WAR, LITERATURE & THE ARTS: An International Journal of the Humanities
WAV MAGAZINE: Progressive Music Art Politics Culture
Whalesback Books
WHITEWALLS: A Journal of Language and Art
THE WILDWOOD READER
THE WORCESTER REVIEW
Word Forge Books
X-Ray Book Co.
Zon International Publishing Co.

PHYSICS

Adams-Blake Publishing
AE-TU Publishing
Al-Galaxy Publishing Corporation
THE ART OF ABUNDANCE
BUSINESS SPIRIT JOURNAL
Clearwater Publishing Co.
Genesis Publishing Company, Inc.
JetKor
JOURNAL OF PYROTECHNICS
JOURNAL OF REGIONAL CRITICISM
JOURNAL OF SCIENTIFIC EXPLORATION
UnKnownTruths.com Publishing Company
WILD DUCK REVIEW
Zagier & Urruty Publicaciones

PICTURE BOOKS

Accendo Publishing
Ammons Communications
Azreal Publishing Company
Barefoot Press

Bellywater Press
Birdsong Books
BlackBerry Literary Services
Book Marketing Solutions
Callawind Publications / Custom Cookbooks / Children's Books
Command Performance Press
Crazy Woman Creek Press
Creative Writing and Publishing Company
Dawn Publications
Dream Catcher Publishing
Dream Publishing Co.
E & E Publishing
Epona Publishing
FOTOTEQUE
GEM Literary Foundation Press
Harobed Publishing Creations
Ika, LLC
Images Unlimited and Snaptail Press, a Division of Images Unlimited Publishing
JetKor
Little Leaf Press
Llumina Press
Millennium Workshop Production
New Voices Publishing
Northland Publishing/Rising Moon/Luna Rising
Ocean Publishing
Oolichan Books
P.R.A. Publishing
Parenting Press, Inc.
Peachtree Publishers, Ltd.
Perrin Press
Propeller Press
Peter E. Randall Publisher
Raven Tree Press, LLC
Savor Publishing House, Inc.
Stonehorse Publishing, LLC
Stunt Publishing
This New World Publishing, LLC
Titus Home Publishing
Tortuga Books
Trellis Publishing, Inc.
Twynz Publishing
UmbraProjects, Ltd.
Waters Edge Press
Whispering Pine Press
Windward Publishing, An Imprint of Finney Company
Word Forge Books

POETRY

ABBEY
Abbey Press, Northern Ireland
Abecedarian books, Inc.
ABRAMELIN: a Journal of Poetry and Magick
ABRAXAS
ABZ A Magazine of Poetry
ABZ Poetry Press
ACM (ANOTHER CHICAGO MAGAZINE)
THE ACORN
Adastra Press
THE ADIRONDACK REVIEW
Adventure Books Inc.
AERIAL
AFRICAN AMERICAN REVIEW
Agathon Books
AGNI
THE AGUILAR EXPRESSION
Ahsahta Press
AIS Publications
ALABAMA LITERARY REVIEW
ALASKA QUARTERLY REVIEW
THE ALEMBIC
Alice James Books
all nations press
THE ALLEGHENY REVIEW
Ally Press
Alms House Press
ALONE TOGETHER

Alpha Beat Press
AMBIT
AMBIT : JOURNAL OF POETRY AND POETICS
THE AMERICAN DISSIDENT
THE AMERICAN DRIVEL REVIEW
AMERICAN INDIAN CULTURE AND RESEARCH
    JOURNAL
American Indian Studies Center
AMERICAN JONES BUILDING & MAINTENANCE
AMERICAN LETTERS & COMMENTARY
American Literary Press
AMERICAN LITERARY REVIEW
THE AMERICAN POETRY JOURNAL
AMERICAN POETRY REVIEW
AMERICAN TANKA
Amethyst & Emerald
Ammons Communications
ANCIENT PATHS
Androgyne Books
ANGEL FACE POETRY JOURNAL
Anhinga Press
ANT ANT ANT ANT ANT
THE ANTHOLOGY OF NEW ENGLAND WRITERS
Anti-Aging Press
ANTIETAM REVIEW
THE ANTIGONISH REVIEW
THE ANTIOCH REVIEW
APOSTROPHE: USCB Journal of the Arts
APPALACHIA JOURNAL
APPLE VALLEY REVIEW: A Journal of Contemporary
    Literature
AQUARIUS
ARC
ARCHIPELAGO
Arctos Press
Arjuna Library Press
The Ark
ARSENIC LOBSTER MAGAZINE
THE ART HORSE
ART:MAG
Arte Publico Press
ARTELLA: the waltz of words and art
ARTFUL DODGE
ARTISTIC RAMBLINGS
ARTS & LETTERS: Journal of Contemporary Culture
Arts End Books
The Ashland Poetry Press
ASPHODEL
Athanata Arts, Ltd.
ATLANTA REVIEW
AURA LITERARY ARTS REVIEW
Ausable Press
Autumn House Press
Avocet Press Inc.
AXE FACTORY REVIEW
THE AZOREAN EXPRESS
The B & R Samizdat Express
BABYSUE
The Bacchae Press
Back House Books
BACKWARDS CITY REVIEW
The Backwaters Press
THE BADGER STONE CHRONICLES
BAGAZINE
THE BALTIMORE REVIEW
Banshee Press
Banta & Pool Literary Properties
Bard Press
BARNWOOD
The Barnwood Press
BARROW STREET
Barrow Street Press
Barrytown/Station Hill Press
BASALT
BATHTUB GIN
Bay Area Poets Coalition
BAYOU
THE BEAR DELUXE

Bear House Publishing
Bear Star Press
BEGINNINGS - A Magazine for the Novice Writer
BELLEVUE LITERARY REVIEW
BELLINGHAM REVIEW
BELLOWING ARK
Bellowing Ark Press
BELOIT POETRY JOURNAL
BIG MUDDY: Journal of the Mississippi River Valley
BIG SCREAM
Bilingual Review Press
Biographical Publishing Company
Birch Brook Press
BIRD DOG
BIRMINGHAM POETRY REVIEW
BITTER OLEANDER
BkMk Press
Black Bear Publications
BLACK BEAR REVIEW
Black Buzzard Press
Black Dress Press
Black Forest Press
BLACK JACK & VALLEY GRAPEVINE
Black Lawrence Press
Black Oak Press
Black Thistle Press
BLACK WARRIOR REVIEW
BlackBerry Literary Services
BLACKBOOK PRESS, THE POETRY ZINE
BLADES
THE BLIND MAN'S RAINBOW
BLITHE SPIRIT
BLOODJET LITERARY MAGAZINE
BLUE HORSE
Blue Horse Publications
BLUE MESA REVIEW
Blue Scarab Press
Blue Star Press
Blue Tiger Press
BLUE UNICORN
Blue Unicorn Press, Inc.
BLUELINE
BOA Editions, Ltd.
Bogg Publications
BOGG: A Journal of Contemporary Writing
Bombshelter Press
Book Marketing Solutions
BOOKS FROM FINLAND
BORDERLANDS: Texas Poetry Review
Borealis Press Limited
BOTTLE
Bottle of Smoke Press
Bottom Dog Press
BOULEVARD
Branch Redd Books
BRANCH REDD REVIEW
Brentwood Christian Press
THE BRIAR CLIFF REVIEW
BrickHouse Books, Inc.
Bright Hill Press
BRILLIANT CORNERS: A Journal of Jazz & Literature
Broken Jaw Press
Broken Shadow Publications
Bronze Girl Productions, Inc.
Brooding Heron Press
Brookline Books
Brooks Books
Brunswick Publishing Corporation
BRYANT LITERARY REVIEW
BUCKLE &
The Bunny & The Crocodile Press/Forest Woods Media
    Productions, Inc
Burning Deck Press
BURNSIDE REVIEW
BUTTON
BYLINE
C & G Publishing, Inc.
C & M Online Media Inc.

Cadmus Editions
Caernarvon Press
CAKETRAIN
Caketrain Press
CALIFORNIA QUARTERLY (CQ)
Calyx Books
CALYX: A Journal of Art and Literature by Women
Cambric Press dba Emerald House
CANADIAN LITERATURE
CANDELABRUM POETRY MAGAZINE
THE CANNON'S MOUTH
THE CAPE ROCK
THE CAPILANO REVIEW
THE CAROLINA QUARTERLY
Carolina Wren Press/Lollipop Power Books
CC. Marimbo
Cedar Hill Books
CEDAR HILL REVIEW
CELEBRATION
CELLAR
Celo Valley Books
Center for Japanese Studies
Center for Literary Publishing
Center for Thanatology Research & Education, Inc.
CENTER: A Journal of the Literary Arts
Central Avenue Press
Cervena Barva Press
CHANTEH, the Iranian Cross-Cultural Quarterly
CHAPMAN
CHARITON REVIEW
Chase Publishing
Chatoyant
CHELSEA
Cherry Valley Editions
Chicago Spectrum Press
Chicory Blue Press, Inc.
CHILDREN, CHURCHES AND DADDIES, A Non
    Religious, Non Familial Literary Magazine
CHRISTIAN CONNECTION PEN PAL NEWSLETTER
CHRYSANTHEMUM
CIMARRON REVIEW
City Life Books, LLC
City Lights Books
Clamp Down Press
Clamshell Press
CLARK STREET REVIEW
Cleveland State Univ. Poetry Center
Coffee House Press
COLD-DRILL
COLOR WHEEL
COLORADO REVIEW
Comrades Press
THE COMSTOCK REVIEW
CONCRETE JUNGLE JOURNAL
Concrete Jungle Press
Concrete Wolf Press
CONDUIT
CONFLUENCE
CONJUNCTIONS
THE CONNECTICUT POET
THE CONNECTICUT POETRY REVIEW
CONNECTICUT REVIEW
CONNECTICUT RIVER REVIEW: A National Poetry
    Journal
CONTEMPORARY GHAZALS
Copper Beech Press
Copper Canyon Press
Coteau Books
COTTONWOOD
Cottonwood Press
Cottonwood Press, Inc.
CRAB CREEK REVIEW
CRAB ORCHARD REVIEW
CRANKY LITERARY JOURNAL
CRANNOG
CRAZYHORSE
THE CREAM CITY REVIEW
Creative With Words Publications (CWW)

Creative Writing and Publishing Company
CREOSOTE: A Journal of Poetry and Prose
Crones Unlimited
Cross-Cultural Communications
R.L. Crow Publications
CRUCIBLE
Crystal Dreams Publishing
CUTBANK
CUTTHROAT, A JOURNAL OF THE ARTS
Cynic Press
THE DALHOUSIE REVIEW
DANDELION ARTS MAGAZINE
DARK ANIMUS
deep cleveland press
Delta Press
DENVER QUARTERLY
DESCANT
DESCANT
DESIRE STREET
DEVIL BLOSSOMS
DIALOGOS: Hellenic Studies Review
Paul Dilsaver, Publisher
THE DMQ REVIEW
Doctor Jazz Press
DOTLIT: The Online Journal of Creative Writing
DOWN IN THE DIRT LITERARY MAGAZINE, the prose
    & poetry magazine revealing all your dirty little secrets
Dream Catcher Publishing
DREAM FANTASY INTERNATIONAL
Dream Horse Press
DREAM NETWORK
DREAMS AND NIGHTMARES
Dufour Editions Inc.
DUFUS
DWAN
EARTH'S DAUGHTERS: Feminist Arts Periodical
ECOTONE: Reimagining Place
THE EDGE CITY REVIEW
Edgewise Press
EDGZ
The Edwin Mellen Press
The Eighth Mountain Press
88: A Journal of Contemporary American Poetry
EKPHRASIS
THE ELEVENTH MUSE
ELIXIR
Elixir Press
ELT Press
EMRYS JOURNAL
Emrys Press
EPICENTER: A LITERARY MAGAZINE
EPOCH MAGAZINE
Equine Graphics Publishing Group: New Concord Press,
    SmallHorse Press, Parallel Press
Erespin Press
EROSHA
EVANSVILLE REVIEW
EVENT
Everflowing Publications
EXIT 13 MAGAZINE
Expanded Media Editions
FAT TUESDAY
Feel Free Press
Fern Publications
THE FIDDLEHEAD
FIELD: Contemporary Poetry and Poetics
FINE MADNESS
Fingerprint Press
Finishing Line Press
First Books
FIRST CLASS
FIRST INTENSITY
FISH DRUM MAGAZINE
Fithian Press
580 SPLIT
Five Fingers Press
FIVE FINGERS REVIEW
FIVE POINTS

FIVE WILLOWS MAGAZINE
Floating Bridge Press
THE FLORIDA REVIEW
FLUENT ASCENSION
Flume Press
FLYWAY
FOLIO: A Literary Journal of American University
Fontanel Books
Fouque Publishers
Four Seasons Publishers
Four Way Books
4AM POETRY REVIEW
Four-Sep Publications
FOURTEEN HILLS: The SFSU Review
FRANK: AN INTERNATIONAL JOURNAL OF CON-
    TEMPORARY WRITING AND ART
FREE LUNCH
FREEDOM AND STRENGTH PRESS FORUM
FREEFALL
French Bread Publications
FRESH GROUND
FRESHWATER
Frith Press
THE FROGMORE PAPERS
The Frogmore Press
From Here Press
FROZEN WAFFLES
Frozen Waffles Press/Shattered Sidewalks Press; 45th
    Century Chapbooks
FUGUE
THE FUNNY PAPER
furniture_press
Galaxy Press
The Galileo Press Ltd.
GARGOYLE
Gay Sunshine Press, Inc.
Gazelle Publications
Gearhead Press
Geekspeak Unique Press
GEM Literary Foundation Press
GENRE: WRITER AND WRITINGS
THE GEORGIA REVIEW
GERTRUDE
GERTRUDE
Gertrude Press
Gesture Press
THE GETTYSBURG REVIEW
Ghost Pony Press
GIN BENDER POETRY REVIEW
Gival Press
GLASS TESSERACT
GLB Publishers
Goats & Compasses
Golden Isis Press
Goldfish Press
Goose River Press
GRAIN MAGAZINE
GRASSLANDS REVIEW
GRASSLIMB
Gravity Presses (Lest We All Float Away), Inc.
Grayson Books
Graywolf Press
THE GREAT BLUE BEACON
Great Elm Press
GREAT RIVER REVIEW
Green Bean Press
THE GREEN HILLS LITERARY LANTERN
Green Hut Press
GREEN MOUNTAINS REVIEW
Green River Press
Green River Writers, Inc./Grex Press
The Greenfield Review Press
Greenhouse Review Press
THE GREENSBORO REVIEW
The Groundwater Press
GULF COAST
HAIGHT ASHBURY LITERARY JOURNAL
Haiku Society of America

Haley's
HANGING LOOSE
Hanging Loose Press
Hannacroix Creek Books, Inc
Hanover Press
HAPPENINGNOW!EVERYWHERE
Hard Press
HARP-STRINGS
HARVARD REVIEW
Haunted Rowboat Press
HAWAI'I REVIEW
HAWAII PACIFIC REVIEW
HAYDEN'S FERRY REVIEW
HEARTLANDS: A Magazine of Midwest Life and Art
Heat Press
HEAVEN BONE MAGAZINE
Heaven Bone Press
Heidelberg Graphics
Helicon Nine Editions
HELIOTROPE, A JOURNAL OF POETRY
Hermes House Press
The Heyeck Press
Higganum Hill Books
High Plains Press
Hippopotamus Press
HIRAM POETRY REVIEW
H-NGM-N
Hobblebush Books
Hole Books
Holmes House
Holy Cow! Press
HOLY ROLLERS
HOME PLANET NEWS
Home Planet Publications
Horse & Buggy Press
The Hosanna Press
HUBBUB
IAMBS & TROCHEES
IBBETSON ST. PRESS
Ibbetson St. Press
IBEX Publishers, Inc.
Icarus Press
ICON
THE ICONOCLAST
Iconoclast Press
THE IDAHO REVIEW
Igneus Press
ILLUMINATIONS
IMAGE: ART, FAITH, MYSTERY
Imago Press
Implosion Press
In Between Books
IN OUR OWN WORDS
IN OUR OWN WORDS
INDEFINITE SPACE
INDIANA REVIEW
INDUSTRY MINNE-ZINE
The Infinity Group
Iniquity Press/Vendetta Books
INKWELL
INSURANCE
INTERNATIONAL POETRY REVIEW
THE INTERPRETER'S HOUSE
INTO THE TEETH WIND
IODINE POETRY JOURNAL
IOTA
THE IOWA REVIEW
Iris Publishing Group, Inc (Iris Press / Tellico Books)
IRISH LITERARY SUPPLEMENT
IRON HORSE LITERARY REVIEW
Island Publishers
ISSUES
Ithuriel's Spear
J & J Consultants, Inc.
J. Mark Press
Jackson Harbor Press
Jako Books
JetKor

JONES AV
THE JOURNAL
JOURNAL OF CANADIAN POETRY
JOURNAL OF NEW JERSEY POETS
JUBILAT
Judah Magnes Museum Publications
Junction Press
K.T. Publications
KAJ-MAHKAH: EARTH OF EARTH
KALDRON, An International Journal Of Visual Poetry
KALEIDOSCOPE: Exploring the Experience of Disability
    through Literature & the Fine Arts
KARAMU
KARAWANE
THE KELSEY REVIEW
Kelsey St. Press
The Kenneth G. Mills Foundation
Kenyette Productions
THE KENYON REVIEW
THE KERF
KESTREL: A Journal of Literature and Art
Kings Estate Press
KNUCKLE MERCHANT - The Journal of Naked Literary
    Aggression
KOJA
KOJA
KotaPress
KRAX
KUMQUAT MERINGUE
KUUMBA
La Alameda Press
LAKE EFFECT
LAKE STREET LIT: Art and Words from the Bottom of
    Lake Bonneville
Lamp Light Press
LANGUAGEANDCULTURE.NET
LARCOM REVIEW
LATERAL MOVES
THE LAUGHING DOG
THE LAUREL REVIEW
Leapfrog Press
Leaping Dog Press / Asylum Arts Press
THE LEDGE
THE LEDGE POETRY & FICTION MAGAZINE
LEFT CURVE
Left Hand Books
Les Figues Press
Level 4 Press
Libellum
LICHEN Arts & Letters Preview
THE LICKING RIVER REVIEW
LIFTOUTS
LIGHT: The Quarterly of Light Verse
LILLIPUT REVIEW
Limberlost Press
Lincoln Springs Press
LINQ
Liquid Paper Press
THE LISTENING EYE
LITERALLY HORSES/REMUDA
LITERARY IMAGINATION: The Review of the Associa-
    tion of Literary Scholars and Critics
LITRAG
THE LITTLE MAGAZINE
Little Pear Press
Little Poem Press
Lockhart Press, Inc.
LONE STARS MAGAZINE
Lone Willow Press
Longhouse
Loom Press
Loonfeather Press
Lorien House
Lost Horse Press
Lost Prophet Press
Lotus Press, Inc.
Lotus Press, Inc.
THE LOUISIANA REVIEW

THE LOUISVILLE REVIEW
LUCIDITY POETRY JOURNAL
LULLABY HEARSE
LULLWATER REVIEW
LUMMOX JOURNAL
Lummox Press
Luna Bisonte Prods
Lunar Offensive Publications
LUNGFULL! MAGAZINE
Lynx House Press
THE LYRIC
THE MACGUFFIN
THE MAD HATTER
Mad River Press
THE MADISON REVIEW
Magic Circle Press
MAIN CHANNEL VOICES: A Dam Fine Literary
    Magazines
MAIN STREET RAG
THE MAINE EVENT
MANDORLA: New Writing from the Americas / Nueva
    escritura de las Americas
MANGROVE MAGAZINE
THE MANHATTAN REVIEW
Manifold Press
MANOA: A Pacific Journal of International Writing
MANY MOUNTAINS MOVING
Marathon International Book Company
March Street Press
THE MARLBORO REVIEW
Marsh Hawk Press
Marymark Press
MATCHBOOK
Maui arThoughts Co.
Mayapple Press
ME MAGAZINE
MEDUSA'S HAIRDO
Mellen Poetry Press
A Melody from an Immigrant's Soul
Menard Press
Meridien PressWorks
Merrimack Books
Merwood Books
Metacom Press
METROPOLITAN FORUM
Miami University Press
Mica Press - Paying Our Dues Productions
MID-AMERICAN REVIEW
Mid-List Press
Midmarch Arts Press
MIDWEST POETRY REVIEW
THE MIDWEST QUARTERLY
Midwest Villages & Voices
Milkweed Editions
Mille Grazie Press
Millennium Vision Press
MINESHAFT
MIP Company
Missing Spoke Press
MISSISSIPPI REVIEW
Montemayor Press
Moody Street Irregulars, Inc.
MOODY STREET IRREGULARS: A Jack Kerouac
    Magazine
Moon Pie Press
MOTHER EARTH JOURNAL: An International Quarterly
Motom
Moving Parts Press
Mucusart Publications
MUDFISH
MUDLARK
The Muse Media
MYSTERY ISLAND MAGAZINE
Mystery Island Publications
Nada Press
NANNY FANNY
THE NARROW ROAD: A Haibun Journal
National Poetry Association Publishers

THE NATIONAL POETRY REVIEW
NATURAL BRIDGE
NEBO
THE NEBRASKA REVIEW
NEO: Literary Magazine
NERVE COWBOY
NEW ALTERNATIVES
NEW AMERICAN IMAGIST
NEW AMERICAN WRITING
NEW DELTA REVIEW
NEW ENGLAND REVIEW
THE NEW FORMALIST
NEW GRAFFITI
THE NEW HAMPSHIRE REVIEW: A Journal of Poetry & Politics
NEW HOPE INTERNATIONAL REVIEW
New Issues Poetry & Prose
THE NEW JERSEY POETRY RESOURCE BOOK
THE NEW LAUREL REVIEW
NEW LETTERS
New Native Press
NEW ORLEANS REVIEW
New Orphic Publishers
THE NEW ORPHIC REVIEW
THE NEW RENAISSANCE, an international magazine of ideas & opinions, emphasizing literature & the arts
New Rivers Press, Inc.
NEW STONE CIRCLE
NEW VERSE NEWS, THE
New World Press
THE NEW WRITER
THE NEW YORK QUARTERLY
Night Horn Books
NIGHTJAR REVIEW
Nightsun Books
NIMROD INTERNATIONAL
nine muses books
Ninety-Six Press
Noemi Press
NORTH AMERICAN REVIEW
NORTH CAROLINA LITERARY REVIEW
North Stone Editions
NORTHWEST REVIEW
Northwestern University Press
NORTHWOODS JOURNAL, A Magazine for Writers
Northwoods Press
NORTHWORDS
NOSTOC MAGAZINE
NOTRE DAME REVIEW
Nova House Press
NOW AND THEN
NOW HERE NOWHERE
O!!Zone
O!!ZONE, A LITERARY-ART ZINE
OASIS
Oasis Books
Oberlin College Press
OBSIDIAN III: Literature in the African Diaspora
Ocean Publishing
Off the Grid Press
Ohio University Press/Swallow Press
THE OLD RED KIMONO
Oma Books of the Pacific
ON EARTH
One Eyed Press
One Less Press
ONE TRICK PONY
Oolichan Books
OPEN MINDS QUARTERLY
Open University of America Press
ORACLE POETRY
Oracle Press
ORBIS
Orchises Press
THE ORPHAN LEAF REVIEW
OSIRIS
Osric Publishing
OUT OF LINE

OUTPOSTS POETRY QUARTERLY
Outrider Press
Owl Creek Press
The Owl Press
THE OXFORD AMERICAN
Oyez
OYEZ REVIEW
OYSTER BOY REVIEW
P.R.A. Publishing
PACIFIC COAST JOURNAL
THE PACIFIC REVIEW
PAGAN AMERICA
PAJ NTAUB VOICE
Palanquin Press
Palladium Communications
PALO ALTO REVIEW
Pancake Press
Panther Creek Press
PAPERPLATES
PARADIDOMI
PARNASSUS LITERARY JOURNAL
PARNASSUS: Poetry in Review
PARTING GIFTS
PASSAGES NORTH
PASSAIC REVIEW (MILLENNIUM EDITIONS)
Passeggiata Press, Inc.
Passion Power Press, Inc
The Passion Profit Company
THE PATERSON LITERARY REVIEW
Pathwise Press
PAVEMENT SAW
Pavement Saw Press
Paycock Press
PEARL
Pearl Editions
Pearl-Win Publishing Co.
Pecan Grove Press
THE PEDESTAL MAGAZINE.COM
PEGASUS
THE PEGASUS REVIEW
PEMBROKE MAGAZINE
PEMMICAN
Pemmican Press
Pendragonian Publications
PENNINE INK MAGAZINE
PENNINE PLATFORM
PENNY DREADFUL: Tales and Poems of Fantastic Terror
The People's Press
PEREGRINE
Persephone Press
Perugia Press
PHOEBE: A Journal of Literature and Art
Phrygian Press
Piano Press
PIG IRON
Pig Iron Press
The Pin Prick Press
Pinchgut Press
PINE ISLAND JOURNAL OF NEW ENGLAND POETRY
PINYON
The Place In The Woods
Plain View Press
THE PLASTIC TOWER
PLEASANT LIVING
Pleasure Boat Studio: A Literary Press
PLOUGHSHARES
Pluma Productions
PMS POEMMEMOIRSTORY
Pocol Press
POEM
POEMS & PLAYS
POESIA
POESY MAGAZINE
POET LORE
Poet Tree Press
POETALK
POETIC SPACE: Poetry & Fiction
POETICA MAGAZINE, Reflections of Jewish Thought

POETRY
The Poetry Center
The Poetry Center Press/Shoestring Press
Poetry Direct
POETRY EAST
THE POETRY EXPLOSION NEWSLETTER (THE PEN)
POETRY FLASH
Poetry Harbor
Poetry Ireland
POETRY IRELAND REVIEW
POETRY KANTO
THE POETRY MISCELLANY
POETRY NOW, Sacramento's Literary Review and Calendar
POETRY NZ
The Poetry Project
THE POETRY PROJECT NEWSLETTER
POETRY REVIEW
POETRY USA
POETS & WRITERS MAGAZINE
Poets & Writers, Inc.
POETS AT WORK
POETS ON THE LINE
POETS' ROUNDTABLE
POETSWEST ONLINE
POGO STICK
Polar Bear & Company
Poltroon Press
Portals Press
PORTLAND REVIEW
Portmanteau Editions
The Post-Apollo Press
POTOMAC REVIEW
THE PRAIRIE JOURNAL OF CANADIAN LITERATURE
Prairie Journal Press
PRAIRIE SCHOONER
PRAIRIE WINDS
Prakalpana Literature
PRAKALPANA   SAHITYA/PRAKALPANA   LITERATURE
Preludium Publishers
PREMONITIONS
PRESA
Press Here
The Press of Appletree Alley
PRETEXT
PRIMARY WRITING
PRIMAVERA
Printed Matter Press (Tokyo)
PRISM INTERNATIONAL
PROSODIA
Prospect Press
Prospect Press
Protean Press
PROVINCETOWN ARTS
PSYCHOPOETICA
PTOLEMY/BROWNS MILLS REVIEW
PublishAmerica, LLLP.
Pudding House Publications
PUDDING MAGAZINE: The International Journal of Applied Poetry
PUERTO DEL SOL
PULSAR POETRY MAGAZINE
Puna Press
Purple Finch Press
PURPLE PATCH
Pygmy Forest Press
Pyncheon House
QRL POETRY SERIES
Quale Press
Quarterly Review of Literature Press
QUARTERLY WEST
QUERCUS REVIEW
THE QUIET FEATHER
Rabeth Publishing Company
Ragged Raven Press
RAINBOW CURVE
RALPH'S REVIEW

RAMBUNCTIOUS REVIEW
Rarach Press
RATTAPALLAX
RATTLE
RATTLESNAKE REVIEW
THE RAVEN CHRONICLES
Ravenwood Publishing
Raw Dog Press
REACH
REACTIONS
Red Alder Books
Red Candle Press
Red Cedar Press
RED CEDAR REVIEW
Red Dragon Press
Red Dust
Red Hand Press
RED HAWK
Red Hen Press
Red Letter Press
RED ROCK REVIEW
Red Tiger Press
RED WHEELBARROW
REDACTIONS: Poetry & Poetics
Redgreene Press
REDIVIDER
REFLECTIONS LITERARY JOURNAL
Re-invention UK Ltd
RFD
Rhiannon Press
RHINO: THE POETRY FORUM
Ridgeway Press of Michigan
RIVER CITY
RIVER KING POETRY SUPPLEMENT
RIVER STYX
Rivercross Publishing, Inc.
RIVERSEDGE
Riverstone, A Press for Poetry
RIVET MAGAZINE
THE ROCKFORD REVIEW
Ronsdale Press
ROOM
Rose Alley Press
Rose Shell Press
ROSEBUD
THE ROUND TABLE: A Journal of Poetry and Fiction
Rowan Mountain Press
RUBIES IN THE DARKNESS
THE RUE BELLA
The Runaway Spoon Press
RUNES, A Review of Poetry
The Sacred Beverage Press
Sadorian Publications
Sage Hill Press
SAGE OF CONSCIOUSNESS E-ZINE
St. Andrews College Press
SAKANA
SALAMANDER
SALMAGUNDI
Salmon Poetry Ltd.
Salt Publishing
Saqi Books Publisher
Sarabande Books
Saskatchewan Writers Guild
Saturday Press
Savant Garde Workshop
Scarlet Tanager Books
Scars Publications
SCHUYLKILL VALLEY JOURNAL OF THE ARTS
Scienter Press
Score
Scots Plaid Press
THE SCRIBIA
Scripta Humanistica
SCRIVENER
SCULPTURAL PURSUIT MAGAZINE
Second Aeon Publications
Second Coming Press

SEEMS
The Seer Press
SENECA REVIEW
SENSATIONS MAGAZINE
Serpent & Eagle Press
Seven Buffaloes Press
SEWANEE REVIEW
SHATTERED WIG REVIEW
SHENANDOAH: THE Washington and Lee University Review
Sherman Asher Publishing
SHIRIM
SHO
Signpost Press Inc.
THE SILT READER
Silverfish Review Press
SKIDROW PENTHOUSE
SKYLARK
SLANT: A Journal of Poetry
Slapering Hol Press
SLIPSTREAM
SMARTISH PACE
The Smith (subsidiary of The Generalist Assn., Inc.)
SMOKE
Smyrna Press
Snake Hill Press
Snapshot Press
SNOW MONKEY
SNOWY EGRET
SO TO SPEAK: A Feminist Journal of Language & Art
SO YOUNG!
A SOFT DEGRADE
SOJOURN: A Journal of the Arts
SOLO
SOLO FLYER
SOMETHING TO READ
SONGS OF INNOCENCE
Soul
SOUNDINGS EAST
SOUTH CAROLINA REVIEW
SOUTH DAKOTA REVIEW
Southeast Missouri State University Press
THE SOUTHERN CALIFORNIA ANTHOLOGY
SOUTHERN HUMANITIES REVIEW
SOUTHERN POETRY REVIEW
THE SOUTHERN REVIEW
SOUTHWEST COLORADO ARTS PERSPECTIVE
SOUTHWEST REVIEW
SOU'WESTER
THE SOW'S EAR POETRY REVIEW
The Sow's Ear Press
SP QUILL QUARTERLY MAGAZINE
SPARROWGRASS POETRY NEWSLETTER
SPEAKEASY
Spectrum Press
SPILLWAY
SPIN
Spinifex Press
SPINNING JENNY
Spire Press
The Spirit That Moves Us Press, Inc.
SPITBALL: The Literary Baseball Magazine
SPOON RIVER POETRY REVIEW
SPORE
SPOUT
Spout Press
SRLR Press
Starbooks Press/FLF Press
Starlight Press
Steel Toe Books
Stellaberry Press
SterlingHouse Publisher
THE STINGING FLY
Story Line Press
THE STRANGE FRUIT
STRINGTOWN
STRUGGLE: A Magazine of Proletarian Revolutionary Literature

STUDIO - A Journal of Christians Writing
STUDIO ONE
Suburban Wilderness Press
SULPHUR RIVER LITERARY REVIEW
Summer Stream Press
Summerset Press
Sun Dog Press
THE SUN, A Magazine of Ideas
Sunlight Publishers
SunShine Press Publications, Inc.
SUPERIOR CHRISTIAN NEWS
Superior Christian Press
Swallow's Tale Press
Swamp Press
SWEET ANNIE & SWEET PEA REVIEW
Sweet Annie Press
SWINK
SYCAMORE REVIEW
synaesthesia press
Synergetic Press
Syukhtun Editions
TAKAHE
Talisman House, Publishers
Tamal Vista Publications
Tameme
TAPROOT LITERARY REVIEW
Taproot Press Publishing Co.
TAPROOT, a journal of older writers
TAR RIVER POETRY
THE TARPEIAN ROCK
Taurean Horn Press
Tears in the Fence
TEARS IN THE FENCE
Tebot Bach
TEEN VOICES MAGAZINE
The Teitan Press, Inc.
Telephone Books
Temple Inc.
Temporary Vandalism Recordings
Ten Penny Players, Inc.
Ten Star Press
Tesseract Publications
TEXAS POETRY JOURNAL
THEECLECTICS
Theytus Books Ltd.
THIN COYOTE
Think Tank Press, Inc.
THIRD COAST
13TH MOON
THIS IS IMPORTANT
Thorp Springs Press
THE THREEPENNY REVIEW
Thunder Rain Publishing Corp.
Tia Chucha Press
TIGHTROPE
Timberline Press
Time Barn Books
TIME FOR RHYME
Titan Press
Titus Home Publishing
Toad Press International Chapbook Series
Toadlily Press
Tombouctou Books
TOUCHSTONE LITERARY JOURNAL
TRUE POET MAGAZINE
Truman State University Press
THE TULE REVIEW
TUNDRA
Tupelo Press
TURNROW
Turnstone Press
The Twickenham Press
Twisted Spoon Press
Two Dog Press
2River
THE 2RIVER VIEW
Tzipora Publications, Inc.
THE UGLY TREE

Ultramarine Publishing Co., Inc.
Underwhich Editions
Unfinished Monument Press
University of Arkansas Press
University of Tampa Press
University of Virginia Press
UNIVERSITY OF WINDSOR REVIEW
UNWOUND
UPSTAIRS AT DUROC
Urban Legend Press
THE URBANITE
Urthona Press
US1 Poets' Cooperative
US1 WORKSHEETS
V52 Press
Vagabond Press
VALLUM: CONTEMPORARY POETRY
VANITAS
VARIOUS ARTISTS
Vehicule Press
VERSAL
Vesta Publications Limited
Via Dolorosa Press
Vintage Romance Publishing, LLC
THE VIRGINIA QUARTERLY REVIEW
VISIONS-INTERNATIONAL, The World Journal of Illus-
    trated Poetry
VLQ (Verse Libre Quarterly)
VOICES - ISRAEL
VYPER
John Wade, Publisher
THE WAKING
THE WALLACE STEVENS JOURNAL
The Wallace Stevens Society Press
WAR, LITERATURE & THE ARTS: An International
    Journal of the Humanities
Warthog Press
Washington Writers' Publishing House
Water Mark Press
Water Row Press
WATER ROW REVIEW
WATERWAYS: Poetry in the Mainstream
Wave Books
WAVELENGTH: A Magazine of Poetry in Prose and Verse
WEBER STUDIES: Voices and Viewpoints of the
    Contemporary West
WEST BRANCH
WEST COAST LINE: A Journal of Contemporary Writing
    and Criticism
West Coast Paradise Publishing
West Virginia University Press
Whelks Walk Press
which press
Whispering Pine Press
White Buck Publishing
WHITE CROW
White Eagle Coffee Store Press
White Pine Press
Whitston Publishing Co.
Whole Notes Press
WHOLE TERRAIN - REFLECTIVE ENVIRONMENTAL
    PRACTICE
WILD PLUM
Wildflower Press
WILLOW REVIEW
WILLOW SPRINGS
WIND
Windows Project
Wineberry Press
Wings Press
Wise Press
THE WISHING WELL
Wood Works
THE WORCESTER REVIEW
WORD IS BOND
WordFarm
Wordwrights Canada
WORDWRIGHTS MAGAZINE

THE WORLD
World Love Press Publishing
WRITER'S CHRONICLE
WRITER'S EXCHANGE
Writers' Haven Press
Writers Ink Press
WRITERS' JOURNAL
WRITER'S LIFELINE
Writers Unlimited Agency, Inc
WRITING FOR OUR LIVES
XAVIER REVIEW
Xenos Books
X-Ray Book Co.
XTANT
xtant.anabasis
XTRAS
Ye Olde Font Shoppe
Years Press
Yellow Moon Press
Yes International Publishers
YUKHIKA—LATUHSE
Zephyr Press
Zerx Press
ZINE-ON-A-TAPE
ZONE 3
Zoo Press
ZUZU'S PETALS: QUARTERLY ONLINE
Zygote Publishing

POLAND

ABSINTHE: New European Writing
Ohio University Press/Swallow Press
World Music Press

POLITICAL SCIENCE

AE-TU Publishing
AK Press
Archer Books
ATLANTIS: A Women's Studies Journal/Revue d'etudes
    sur les femmes
The B & R Samizdat Express
Bad Press
BALLOT ACCESS NEWS
Between The Lines
Black Lawrence Press
Bluestocking Press
Branden Books
Brunswick Publishing Corporation
Cantadora Press
Caribbean Books-Panama
Chandler & Sharp Publishers, Inc.
Clarity Press, Inc.
COGNITIO: A Graduate Humanities Journal
The Compass Press
CRITICAL REVIEW
THE DALHOUSIE REVIEW
dreamslaughter
Florida Academic Press
Focus Publishing/R. Pullins Co.
The Foundation for Economic Education, Inc.
FOURTH WORLD REVIEW
THE FREEMAN: Ideas On Liberty
Glenbridge Publishing Ltd.
Harrington Park Press
The Haworth Press
The Heather Foundation
Hoover Institution Press
THE INDEPENDENT REVIEW: A Journal of Political
    Economy
Interlink Publishing Group, Inc.
ITALIAN AMERICANA
JOURNAL OF PALESTINE STUDIES
KETTERING REVIEW
Kumarian Press, Inc.
Libertarian Press, Inc./American Book Distributors
LIBERTY
THE LONG TERM VIEW: A Journal of Informed Opinion
Maisonneuve Press

Mercer University Press
MEXICAN STUDIES/ESTUDIOS MEXICANOS
MOTHER EARTH
New Falcon Publications
Northern Illinois University Press
Open Hand Publishing LLC
OUT OF LINE
Paragon House Publishers
Pathfinder Press
QED Press
Rada Press, Inc.
Razor7 Publishing
Reach Productions Publishing
RFF Press / Resources for the Future
ST. CROIX REVIEW
Saqi Books Publisher
SCIENCE AND TECHNOLOGY
Selous Foundation Press
STATE AND LOCAL GOVERNMENT REVIEW
State University of New York Press
Strata Publishing, Inc.
TELOS
Temple Inc.
THINKERMONKEY
THIRD WAY
Third Way Publications Ltd.
UBC Press
United Nations University Press
Univelt, Inc.
University of Arkansas Press
University of Calgary Press
University Press of Colorado
Van Cleave Publishing
THE WASHINGTON MONTHLY
West Virginia University Press
Whitston Publishing Co.

POLITICS

Aardvark Enterprises (A Division of Speers Investments Ltd.)
ACM (ANOTHER CHICAGO MAGAZINE)
African Ways Publishing
Glen Allen Press
America West Publishers
Archer Books
Arden Press, Inc.
ATLANTIS: A Women's Studies Journal/Revue d'etudes sur les femmes
BALLOT ACCESS NEWS
Banta & Pool Literary Properties
Bay Press
Bay Tree Publishing
Benchmark Publications Inc.
Between The Lines
Black Lawrence Press
Blackwater Publications
THE BOOMERPHILE
BORDERLANDS: Texas Poetry Review
BOTH SIDES NOW
BOULDER HERETIC
Brave Ulysses Books
BROKEN PENCIL
CANADIAN REVIEW OF AMERICAN STUDIES
Caribbean Books-Panama
Cassandra Press, Inc.
Cedar Hill Books
CESUM MAGAZINE
Chandler & Sharp Publishers, Inc.
Chelsea Green Publishing Company
Chicago Review Press
Children Of Mary
The Chinese University Press
CINEASTE MAGAZINE
City Lights Books
COLORLINES
Common Courage Press
The Compass Press
Comstock Bonanza Press

CONSCIENCE: The Newsjournal of Catholic Opinion
CRITICAL REVIEW
CUTTHROAT, A JOURNAL OF THE ARTS
dreamslaughter
Dufour Editions Inc.
Editorial Research Service
Encounter Books
EPICENTER: A LITERARY MAGAZINE
Feel Free Press
FEMINIST REVIEW
FIDELIS ET VERUS
FIFTH ESTATE
Filibuster Press
The Film Instruction Company of America
Four Walls Eight Windows
FOURTH WORLD REVIEW
Free People Press
Free Reign Press, Inc.
Frontline Publications
THE FUNNY TIMES
Gain Publications
Galt Press
Glenbridge Publishing Ltd.
Good Hope Enterprises, Inc.
GREEN ANARCHIST
GREEN ANARCHY
Guernica Editions, Inc.
Harlan Publishing Company; Alliance Books; Diakonia Publishing (Christian Books)
HARMONY: Voices for a Just Future
Heyday Books
History Compass, LLC
Ho Logos Press
Hoover Institution Press
Horse Creek Publications, Inc.
INDUSTRY MINNE-ZINE
International Publishers Co. Inc.
JAM RAG
JEWISH CURRENTS
JOURNAL OF NARRATIVE THEORY
Kettering Foundation Press
KETTERING REVIEW
Kumarian Press, Inc.
LATIN AMERICAN PERSPECTIVES
LEFT BUSINESS OBSERVER
LEFT CURVE
THE (LIBERTARIAN) CONNECTION
Library Research Associates, Inc.
LifeThread Publications
LO STRANIERO: The Stranger, Der Fremde, L'Etranger
THE LONG TERM VIEW: A Journal of Informed Opinion
Lunar Offensive Publications
Macrocosm USA, Inc.
MAIN STREET RAG
MEAT: A Journal of Writing and Materiality
Mehring Books, Inc.
Menard Press
Mercer University Press
MND Publishing, Inc.
Mountain Media
MOUTH: Voice of the Dis-Labeled Nation
Moving Parts Press
NAMBLA BULLETIN
THE NEO-COMINTERN
THE NEW ENGLAND QUARTERLY
THE NEW HAMPSHIRE REVIEW: A Journal of Poetry & Politics
THE NEW RENAISSANCE, an international magazine of ideas & opinions, emphasizing literature & the arts
New Star Books Ltd.
NEW VERSE NEWS, THE
NEWS FROM NATIVE CALIFORNIA
nine muses books
THE NONVIOLENT ACTIVIST
OFF OUR BACKS
OUT OF LINE
The Pamphleeter's Press
Path Press, Inc.

Pathfinder Press
PEMMICAN
Philopsychy Press
Pig Iron Press
THE PRESSED PRESS
Quarterly Committee of Queen's University
QUEEN'S QUARTERLY: A Canadian Review
THE QUIET FEATHER
Red Letter Press
RFD
ST. CROIX REVIEW
Saqi Books Publisher
SCANDINAVIAN REVIEW
SCIENCE & SOCIETY
See Sharp Press
Semiotext Foreign Agents Books Series
SEMIOTEXT(E)
SHARE INTERNATIONAL
Snake Hill Press
South End Press
SOUTHWEST COLORADO ARTS PERSPECTIVE
SterlingHouse Publisher
STORMWARNING!
SYMPLOKE: A Journal for the Intermingling of Literary,
    Cultural and Theoretical Scholarship
Syracuse Cultural Workers/Tools for Change
TELOS
Telos Press
THINKERMONKEY
Tree of Life Books. Imprints: Progressive Press, Banned
    Books
UBC Press
United Nations University Press
Upper Access Inc.
V52 Press
Van Cleave Publishing
THE VIRGINIA QUARTERLY REVIEW
Vision
THE WASHINGTON MONTHLY
West End Press
West Virginia University Press
WHAT IS ENLIGHTENMENT?
Wheatmark Book Publishing
WILD DUCK REVIEW
WORD IS BOND
Xavier House Publishing

PORTUGAL

INTERNATIONAL POETRY REVIEW
NEO: Literary Magazine
PERIPHERAL VISION
TORRE DE PAPEL
TRANSITIONS ABROAD: The Guide to Living, Learning,
    and Working Overseas
VACATION PLACE RENTALS

POST MODERN

AD/VANCE
all nations press
Asylum Arts
Bad Press
BOGG: A Journal of Contemporary Writing
C & M Online Media Inc.
THE CAPILANO REVIEW
CESUM MAGAZINE
COLLEGE LITERATURE
CONJUNCTIONS
ELIXIR
Eros Books
FIGHT THESE BASTARDS
FIRST CLASS
Four-Sep Publications
THE FRANK REVIEW
JOURNAL OF AESTHETICS AND ART CRITICISM
JOURNAL OF NARRATIVE THEORY
KOJA
LAKE EFFECT
LEFT CURVE

McPherson & Company Publishers
MEAT FOR TEA: THE NORTHAMPTON REVIEW
MEAT: A Journal of Writing and Materiality
Midmarch Arts Press
THE NEO-COMINTERN
New Native Press
NOBODADDIES
OUTER-ART
PORTLAND REVIEW
PSYCHE
Radiant Press
RAINBOW CURVE
SKIDROW PENTHOUSE
Starcherone Books
Telos Press
Toad Press International Chapbook Series
UNBOUND
Via Dolorosa Press
THE WALLACE STEVENS JOURNAL
WEST COAST LINE: A Journal of Contemporary Writing
    and Criticism
WHAT IS ENLIGHTENMENT?
ZYX

POSTCARDS

BAGAZINE
BANANA RAG
Barefoot Press
Fotofolio, Inc.
FREEFALL
Gesture Press
Harobed Publishing Creations
INKY TRAIL NEWS
POSTCARD CLASSICS (formerly DELTIOLOGY)
Running Press
Waters Edge Press
Westgate Press

PRESIDENTS

Blackwater Publications
CESUM MAGAZINE
THE PRESIDENTS' JOURNAL
Truman State University Press

ELVIS PRESLEY

The Bess Press
THE BOOMERPHILE
GAMBARA MAGAZINE
LONG SHOT
The Overmountain Press
SHEMP! The Lowlife Culture Magazine

PRINTING

THE BOOK ARTS CLASSIFIED
BOOK DEALERS WORLD
BOOK MARKETING UPDATE
BOOK NEWS & BOOK BUSINESS MART
Brenner Information Group
Chicago Spectrum Press
Communication Creativity
Feel Free Press
FEMINIST COLLECTIONS: A QUARTERLY OF WO-
    MEN'S STUDIES RESOURCES
Harobed Publishing Creations
J'ECRIS
Jessee Poet Publications
JLA Publications, A Division Of Jeffrey Lant Associates,
    Inc.
LOST GENERATION JOURNAL
NEWPAGES: Alternatives in Print & Media
Oak Knoll Press
OHIO WRITER
The Pin Prick Press
The Poetry Center Press/Shoestring Press
Poltroon Press
Premier Publishers, Inc.
PUBLISHING POYNTERS
QED Press

Redgreene Press
SPEX (SMALL PRESS EXCHANGE)
Stewart Publishing & Printing
Success Publishing
Typographia Press
UMBRELLA Online
Univelt, Inc.
University of Tampa Press
Winslow Publishing
Women's Studies Librarian, University of Wisconsin System

PRISON

Aaron Communications III
AIS Publications
ALONE TOGETHER
BlackBerry Literary Services
Cedar Hill Books
CEDAR HILL REVIEW
COALITION FOR PRISONERS' RIGHTS NEWSLETTER
CORRECTION(S): A Literary Journal for Inmate Writing
CORRECTIONS TODAY
Global Options
Gorilla Convict Publications
GREEN ANARCHY
IWAN: INMATE WRITERS OF AMERICA NEWSLETTER
Leyland Publications
Maisonneuve Press
Mystery Island Publications
PRISON LEGAL NEWS
Pygmy Forest Press
RFD
RockBySea Books
The Saunderstown Press
SOCIAL JUSTICE: A JOURNAL OF CRIME, CONFLICT, & WORLD ORDER
Starbooks Press/FLF Press
THOUGHT BOMBS
TURNING THE TIDE: Journal of Anti-Racist Action, Research & Education
Vision
WeWrite LLC

PROSE

ALASKA QUARTERLY REVIEW
THE ALEMBIC
THE AMERICAN DRIVEL REVIEW
AMERICAN LETTERS & COMMENTARY
Amethyst & Emerald
ANCIENT PATHS
Androgyne Books
ARC
ARCHIPELAGO
ARTELLA: the waltz of words and art
ARTISTIC RAMBLINGS
Asylum Arts
BACKWARDS CITY REVIEW
THE BALTIMORE REVIEW
Bear House Publishing
BELLEVUE LITERARY REVIEW
BIRD DOG
BkMk Press
BlackBerry Literary Services
BLACKBOOK PRESS, THE POETRY ZINE
BOGG: A Journal of Contemporary Writing
BOOKS FROM FINLAND
THE BRIAR CLIFF REVIEW
BRILLIANT CORNERS: A Journal of Jazz & Literature
BUST DOWN THE DOOR AND EAT ALL THE CHICKENS: A Journal of Absurd and Surreal Fiction
CAKETRAIN
Carolina Wren Press/Lollipop Power Books
Casperian Books LLC
Cedar Hill Books
CEDAR HILL REVIEW
Cervena Barva Press
CESUM MAGAZINE

CIMARRON REVIEW
CLARK STREET REVIEW
CONJUNCTIONS
Coteau Books
CRAZYHORSE
CREOSOTE: A Journal of Poetry and Prose
Crones Unlimited
DREAM FANTASY INTERNATIONAL
ECOTONE: Reimagining Place
THE EDGE CITY REVIEW
The Eighth Mountain Press
EPICENTER: A LITERARY MAGAZINE
EROSHA
EVANSVILLE REVIEW
THE FLORIDA REVIEW
FLUENT ASCENSION
FOLIO: A Literary Journal of American University
Fontanel Books
FOURTEEN HILLS: The SFSU Review
Galaxy Press
GERTRUDE
GERTRUDE
GIN BENDER POETRY REVIEW
GLASS TESSERACT
GRASSLIMB
Graywolf Press
THE GREAT BLUE BEACON
HAPPENINGNOW!EVERYWHERE
Harobed Publishing Creations
HARVARD REVIEW
HAWAI'I REVIEW
Impassio Press
INDIANA REVIEW
INKWELL
INSURANCE
THE IOWA REVIEW
Iris Publishing Group, Inc (Iris Press / Tellico Books)
KALEIDOSCOPE: Exploring the Experience of Disability through Literature & the Fine Arts
The Kenneth G. Mills Foundation
KOJA
Les Figues Press
LICHEN Arts & Letters Preview
LIGHT: The Quarterly of Light Verse
Lincoln Springs Press
LITERALLY HORSES/REMUDA
LONE STARS MAGAZINE
Lost Horse Press
LULLABY HEARSE
LULLWATER REVIEW
LUMMOX JOURNAL
Lummox Press
MANDORLA: New Writing from the Americas / Nueva escritura de las Americas
MANGROVE MAGAZINE
MID-AMERICAN REVIEW
Milkweed Editions
MINESHAFT
NATURAL BRIDGE
New Rivers Press, Inc.
NIGHTJAR REVIEW
Oasis Books
One Less Press
ORBIS
THE ORPHAN LEAF REVIEW
The Owl Press
PAGAN AMERICA
PASSAGES NORTH
Passing Through Publications
Pathwise Press
PAVEMENT SAW
Pavement Saw Press
PENNINE INK MAGAZINE
PINYON
POETICA MAGAZINE, Reflections of Jewish Thought
PORTLAND REVIEW
POTOMAC REVIEW
The Press of Appletree Alley

PRETEXT
QUARTER AFTER EIGHT
THE QUIET FEATHER
RAINBOW CURVE
RATTAPALLAX
Red Tiger Press
THE ROCKFORD REVIEW
ROSEBUD
SAGE OF CONSCIOUSNESS E-ZINE
Santa Fe Writers Project
SENSATIONS MAGAZINE
74th Street Productions, L.L.C.
SKYLARK
The Smith (subsidiary of The Generalist Assn., Inc.)
SOUTHWEST COLORADO ARTS PERSPECTIVE
Starcherone Books
THE STINGING FLY
SUB-TERRAIN
SULPHUR RIVER LITERARY REVIEW
SunShine Press Publications, Inc.
Syukhtun Editions
Tears in the Fence
TEARS IN THE FENCE
Thunder Rain Publishing Corp.
Tupelo Press
Twisted Spoon Press
University of Tampa Press
UPSTAIRS AT DUROC
Urthona Press
V52 Press
VERSAL
Vintage Romance Publishing, LLC
Westgate Press
Whelks Walk Press
Zelda Wilde Publishing
WILLOW SPRINGS
The Word Doctor Online Publishing
WORD IS BOND
Writers' Haven Press
Xenos Books
xtant.anabasis
Zerx Press

PSYCHIATRY

Black Pearl Enterprises LLC
Brookline Books
Compact Clinicals
Consumer Press
Himalayan Institute Press
Holbrook Street Press
Hole Books
INTERNATIONAL ADDICTION
JOURNAL OF PSYCHOACTIVE DRUGS
OPEN MINDS QUARTERLY
PSYCHOANALYTIC BOOKS: A QUARTERLY JOUR-
    NAL OF REVIEWS
Total Cardboard Publishing

PSYCHOLOGY

ADOLESCENCE
Alamo Square Press
Alegra House Publishers
Aletheia Publications, Inc.
Alpine Guild, Inc.
Altair Publications
America West Publishers
Anthony Publishing Company, Inc.
ART CALENDAR
THE ART OF ABUNDANCE
Ash Lad Press
ATLANTIS: A Women's Studies Journal/Revue d'etudes
    sur les femmes
Atrium Society Publications
Authors of Unity Publishing
The B & R Samizdat Express
Barrytown/Station Hill Press
Bay Tree Publishing
Bayhampton Publications

Behavioral Sciences Research Press, Inc.
Beynch Press Publishing Company
Beyond Words Publishing, Inc.
Birth Day Publishing Company
BOULDER HERETIC
Brason-Sargar Publications
Brookline Books
Brunswick Publishing Corporation
Celo Valley Books
Center for Thanatology Research & Education, Inc.
The Center Press
The Chinese University Press
Common Boundaries
Compact Clinicals
Consumer Press
CORRECTIONS TODAY
Creative Roots, Inc.
CRONE CHRONICLES: A Journal of Conscious Aging
Dancing Bridge Publishing
Denlinger's Publishers Ltd.
Dharma Publishing
Down There Press
DREAM FANTASY INTERNATIONAL
DREAM NETWORK
Emerald Wave
ETC Publications
FAMILY THERAPY
Friendly Oaks Publications
Gateways Books And Tapes
Gay Sunshine Press, Inc.
Gifted Education Press/The Reading Tutorium
Gilgal Publications
GLB Publishers
Glenbridge Publishing Ltd.
Green Hut Press
Gurze Books
Health Press
Himalayan Institute Press
Holbrook Street Press
Howln Moon Press
Hunter House Inc., Publishers
Ice Cube Press
Impact Publishers, Inc.
Infinite Possibilities Publishing Group, Inc.
INKY TRAIL NEWS
Inner City Books
Innisfree Press
The Institute of Mind and Behavior
International University Line (IUL)
Islewest Publishing
ITALIAN AMERICANA
J & J Consultants, Inc.
Joelle Publishing
JOURNAL OF MENTAL IMAGERY
THE JOURNAL OF MIND AND BEHAVIOR
JOURNAL OF POLYMORPHOUS PERVERSITY
JOURNAL OF PROCESS ORIENTED PSYCHOLOGY
JOURNAL OF PSYCHOACTIVE DRUGS
THE JOURNAL OF PSYCHOHISTORY
JOURNAL OF PSYCHOLOGY IN CHINESE SOCIETIES
Kallisti Publishing
Lao Tse Press, Ltd.
Libra Publishers, Inc.
Life Energy Media
LifeQuest Publishing Group
LifeSkill Institute, Inc.
Lockhart Press, Inc.
LOGIC LETTER
The Love and Logic Press, Inc.
Markowski International Publishers
Monkfish Book Publishing Company
Monroe Press
MUSIC PERCEPTION
Mystery Island Publications
NEW AMERICAN IMAGIST
New Falcon Publications
New World Library
Nicolas-Hays, Inc.

Nightsun Books
North Star Books
Obsessive Compulsive Anonymous
Open Court Publishing Company
Origin Press
Over the Wall Inc. Publishing & Productions
P.R.A. Publishing
Pedestal Press
Philopsychy Press
The Pin Prick Press
Plus Publications
PSYCHE
PSYCHOANALYTIC BOOKS: A QUARTERLY JOURNAL OF REVIEWS
Psychohistory Press
PSYCHOPOETICA
Pudding House Publications
PUDDING MAGAZINE: The International Journal of Applied Poetry
Quarterly Committee of Queen's University
QUEEN'S QUARTERLY: A Canadian Review
THE QUEST
Quest Books: Theosophical Publishing House
Rainbow Books, Inc.
Raven Rocks Press
Raven's Eye Press, Inc.
Red Alder Books
Red Hand Press
Redgreene Press
River Press
The Runaway Spoon Press
Sacred Spaces Press
Sagamore Publishing
The Saunderstown Press
See Sharp Press
Sentient Publications, LLC
Sibyl Publications, Inc
Sidran Institute
SKEPTICAL INQUIRER
THE SOCIOLOGICAL QUARTERLY
Spring Publications Inc.
SPRING: A Journal of Archetype and Culture
Starbooks Press/FLF Press
State University of New York Press
Swan Raven & Company
Tendre Press
THINKERMONKEY
Three House Publishing
Topping International Institute, Inc.
VanderWyk & Burnham
Vestibular Disorders Association
Visions Communications
Volcano Press, Inc
WHAT IS ENLIGHTENMENT?
Whitford Press
Whole Person Associates Inc.
Whole Person Associates Inc.
Wilshire Books Inc.
Wisdom Publications, Inc.
Women of Diversity Productions, Inc.
Zoilita Grant MS CCHt.

PUBLIC AFFAIRS

Americans for the Arts
THE ANTIOCH REVIEW
Archer Books
AXIOS
Bay Tree Publishing
Bellevue Literary Press
Blackwater Publications
Borealis Press Limited
Camel Press
CANADIAN JOURNAL OF PROGRAM EVALUATION
Chandler & Sharp Publishers, Inc.
CKO UPDATE
The Compass Press
CONSCIENCE: The Newsjournal of Catholic Opinion
Continuing Education Press

Crandall, Dostie & Douglass Books, Inc.
The Denali Press
DUST (From the Ego Trip)
Editorial Research Service
The Foundation for Economic Education, Inc.
FOURTH WORLD REVIEW
THE FREEMAN: Ideas On Liberty
Fulcrum, Inc.
Gain Publications
Hoover Institution Press
THE INDIE
Infinite Possibilities Publishing Group, Inc.
Institute for Contemporary Studies
International Publishers Co. Inc.
KETTERING REVIEW
LEFT BUSINESS OBSERVER
LOGIC LETTER
THE LONG TERM VIEW: A Journal of Informed Opinion
Maisonneuve Press
Noontide Press
THE OTHER ISRAEL
The Pamphleteer's Press
Pendant Publishing Inc.
Planning/Communications
POTOMAC REVIEW
Progressive Education
PROGRESSIVE PERIODICALS DIRECTORY/UPDATE
THE PUBLIC RELATIONS QUARTERLY
RFF Press / Resources for the Future
Small Helm Press
Starry Night Publishing
TAPROOT, a journal of older writers
THINKERMONKEY
Thorp Springs Press
UBC Press
Volcano Press, Inc
THE WASHINGTON MONTHLY

PUBLIC RELATIONS/PUBLICITY

ART CALENDAR
Blueprint Books
CKO UPDATE
D.B.A. Books
Info Net Publishing
Kobalt Books
P.R.A. Publishing
The Passion Profit Company
PSI Research/The Oasis Press/Hellgate Press
Sources
THE SOURCES HOTLINK
Trellis Publishing, Inc.
Zelda Wilde Publishing
World Gumbo Publishing

PUBLISHING

A Cappela Publishing, Inc.
AE-TU Publishing
THE AFRICAN BOOK PUBLISHING RECORD
Alpine Guild, Inc.
BlackBerry Literary Services
Blueprint Books
BOOK MARKETING UPDATE
Bookhome Publishing/Panda Publishing
BROKEN PENCIL
Communication Creativity
Cornerstone Publishing
COUNTERPOISE: For Social Responsibilities, Liberty and Dissent
Creative Writing and Publishing Company
CREATIVITY CONNECTION
Dumouriez Publishing
Dustbooks
THE EDITORIAL EYE
EEI Press
EFG, Inc.
Gemstone House Publishing
THE GREAT BLUE BEACON
Happy About

INDEPENDENT PUBLISHER ONLINE
INTERLIT
IWAN: INMATE WRITERS OF AMERICA NEWSLETTER
JAFFE INTERNATIONAL
Jaffe Publishing Management Service
juel house publishers and literary services
Kobalt Books
Lamp Light Press
LAUGHING BEAR NEWSLETTER
LIBRARIANS AT LIBERTY
Lucky Press, LLC
MAINE IN PRINT
Myriad Press
THE NEW JERSEY POETRY RESOURCE BOOK
North American Bookdealers Exchange
Open Horizons Publishing Company
Para Publishing
The Passion Profit Company
PUBLISHING POYNTERS
READ, AMERICA!
ROCKY MOUNTAIN KC NEWS
Rocky Mountain KC Publishing Co.
Salmon Poetry Ltd.
Sentient Publications, LLC
THE SMALL PRESS REVIEW/SMALL MAGAZINE REVIEW
Snake Hill Press
Speck Press
Stony Meadow Publishing
Storm Publishing Group
Toad Hall Press
TRUE POET MAGAZINE
Wilshire Books Inc.
WRITER'S CAROUSEL
WRITERS' JOURNAL
ZINE WORLD: A Reader's Guide to the Underground Press
ZUZU'S PETALS: QUARTERLY ONLINE

PUERTO RICO

Inner City Press
Iris Publishing Group, Inc (Iris Press / Tellico Books)
Pangaea
POINT OF CONTACT, The Journal of Verbal & Visual Arts
TORRE DE PAPEL
Tortuga Books
TURNING THE TIDE: Journal of Anti-Racist Action, Research & Education

QUILTING, SEWING

Altamont Press, Inc.
C & T Publishing
DOLLS UNITED INTERACTIVE MAGAZINE
Eagle's View Publishing
FIBERARTS
MIDWEST ART FAIRS
Miles & Miles
Naturegraph Publishers
Storm Publishing Group
Success Publishing

QUOTATIONS

AIS Publications
ARTISTIC RAMBLINGS
Brason-Sargar Publications
CKO UPDATE
dreamslaughter
Nicolin Fields Publishing, Inc.
Happy About
Impassio Press
Light, Words & Music
LrnIT Publishing Div. ICFL, Inc.
Miles & Miles
Music City Publishing
Open Horizons Publishing Company
PULSAR POETRY MAGAZINE
Red Eye Press

See Sharp Press
Set Sail Productions, LLC
Titlewaves Publishing; Writers Direct
Ulysses Books

RACE

Back House Books
BLK
BLUE COLLAR REVIEW
CAMERA OBSCURA: Feminism, Culture, and Media Studies
THE CAPILANO REVIEW
COLLEGE LITERATURE
COLORLINES
Common Courage Press
Comstock Bonanza Press
Crandall, Dostie & Douglass Books, Inc.
Ecrivez!
JOURNAL OF NARRATIVE THEORY
MacDonald/Sward Publishing Company
Margaret Media, Inc.
MCT - MULTICULTURAL TEACHING
New Sins Press
Partisan Press
Quantum Leap S.L.C. Publications
SOCIAL JUSTICE: A JOURNAL OF CRIME, CONFLICT, & WORLD ORDER
South End Press
SYMPLOKE: A Journal for the Intermingling of Literary, Cultural and Theoretical Scholarship
TEEN VOICES MAGAZINE
TURNING THE TIDE: Journal of Anti-Racist Action, Research & Education
WEST COAST LINE: A Journal of Contemporary Writing and Criticism
West Virginia University Press
which press

RADIO

BearManor Media
BOOK MARKETING UPDATE
THE NOISE
PAST TIMES: The Nostalgia Entertainment Newsletter
THE PUBLICITY HOUND
ST. LOUIS JOURNALISM REVIEW
Sonoran Publishing
Wind River Institute Press/Wind River Broadcasting

READING

Abernathy House Publishing
ARCHIPELAGO
THE ART OF ABUNDANCE
COLLEGE LITERATURE
EEI Press
Family Learning Association, Inc.
FINE MADNESS
GAMBARA MAGAZINE
Highsmith Press
Imago Press
THE LEDGE
Maupin House Publishing, Inc.
PARENTEACHER MAGAZINE
Perrin Press
READ, AMERICA!
Reading Connections
SYMPLOKE: A Journal for the Intermingling of Literary, Cultural and Theoretical Scholarship
Three House Publishing

REAL ESTATE

Adams-Blake Publishing
Ancient City Press
CANADIAN MONEYSAVER
Carol Anne Carroll Communications
Communication Creativity
Consumer Press
First Books
Gemstone House Publishing

733

GLOBAL ONE TRAVEL & AUTOMOTIVE MAGAZINE
GULF & MAIN Southwest Florida Lifestyle
HandyCraft Media Productions
Happy About
The Heather Foundation
Long & Silverman Publishing, Inc.
MBA Publications
New Community Press
Rivercross Publishing, Inc.
Rolling Hills Publishing
Sourcebooks, Inc.
Storm Publishing Group
Swan Publishing Company
Tax Property Investor, Inc.
Tres Picos Press
Upper Access Inc.
Wheatmark Book Publishing

REFERENCE

Affinity Publishers Services
Alan Wofsy Fine Arts
Alaska Geographic Society
Appalachian Consortium Press
Arden Press, Inc.
Ariko Publications
Axiom Information Resources
The Bess Press
Biblio Press
Black Forest Press
Blowtorch Press
Brenner Information Group
Brunswick Publishing Corporation
Carol Anne Carroll Communications
Center for Japanese Studies
Center For Self-Sufficiency
THE CHRISTIAN LIBRARIAN
CONNEXIONS DIGEST
Connexions Information Services, Inc.
Cooper Hill Press
COUNTERPOISE: For Social Responsibilities, Liberty and
    Dissent
Dash-Hill, LLC
Dawn Sign Press
The Denali Press
dreamslaughter
Dustbooks
Earth-Love Publishing House LTD
THE EDUCATION DIGEST
Family Learning Association, Inc.
The Fiction Works
Film-Video Publications/Circus Source Publications
Galen Press, Ltd.
Global Sports Productions, Ltd.
Good Book Publishing Company
Hastings Art Reference
The Haworth Press
Ho Logos Press
Hollywood Creative Directory
Hollywood Film Archive
Howln Moon Press
Infinite Possibilities Publishing Group, Inc.
Kali Press
L D A Publishers
Lake Claremont Press
Lexikos
LIBRARY HI TECH
LIBRARY HIGH TECH NEWS
Maledicta Press
Peter Marcan Publications
Menasha Ridge Press
Microdex Bookshelf
Muse World Media Group
National Court Reporters Association Press
National Woodlands Publishing Company
Next Decade, Inc.
Nolo Press
Nolo Press Occidental
Oak Knoll Press

Panther Creek Press
Paradise Publications
The Pin Prick Press
Pine Publications
Pineapple Press, Inc.
Poets & Writers, Inc.
Prakken Publications
Progressive Education
PROGRESSIVE PERIODICALS DIRECTORY/UPDATE
Rayve Productions Inc.
Red Eye Press
Reference Service Press
REFERENCE SERVICES REVIEW
Running Press
Sagamore Publishing
Santa Monica Press
Scarecrow Press
Scentouri, Publishing Division
Selah Publishing Co. Inc.
SILVER WINGS
THE SMALL PRESS REVIEW/SMALL MAGAZINE
    REVIEW
Sources
Univelt, Inc.
Upper Access Inc.
Velazquez Press
Volcano Press, Inc
Willowood Press
ZUZU'S PETALS: QUARTERLY ONLINE

RELATIONSHIPS

Abernathy House Publishing
Accendo Publishing
APPLE VALLEY REVIEW: A Journal of Contemporary
    Literature
THE ART OF ABUNDANCE
Aspicomm Media
Authors of Unity Publishing
AuthorsOmniscient Publishers
Black Pearl Enterprises LLC
Bronze Girl Productions, Inc.
Cantarabooks LLC
City Life Books, LLC
Cladach Publishing
Cornerstone Publishing
Defiant Times Press
The Dibble Fund for Marriage Education
DOVETAIL: A Journal by and for Jewish/Christian
    Families
Down There Press
DRAMA GARDEN
Ecrivez!
GIRLFRIENDS MAGAZINE
Harlan Publishing Company; Alliance Books; Diakonia
    Publishing (Christian Books)
Herrmann International
Hunter House Inc., Publishers
Impact Publishers, Inc.
Infinite Possibilities Publishing Group, Inc.
Innisfree Press
Islewest Publishing
J&W Publishers, Inc.
KABBALAH
LOVING MORE
Luminous Epinoia Press
Mo'omana'o Press
Moon Pie Press
Muse World Media Group
Music City Publishing
New Creature Press
Nolo Press Occidental
PhoeniX in Print
PSYCHE
Pussywillow
Rainbow Books, Inc.
River Press
Rodnik Publishing Co.
Search Institute

Sentient Publications, LLC
Starry Night Publishing
Synergy Press
Third Dimension Publishing
Top 20 Press

RELIGION

AAIMS Publishers
Aardvark Enterprises (A Division of Speers Investments Ltd.)
ADVENTURES
Al-Galaxy Publishing Corporation
ALONE TOGETHER
America West Publishers
Amnos Publications
ANCIENT PATHS
ANGEL FACE POETRY JOURNAL
The Apostolic Press
ASCENT
Authors of Unity Publishing
AXIOS
Axios Newletter, Inc.
The B & R Samizdat Express
Ballena Press
Bandanna Books
THE BANNER
Beacon Light Publishing (BLP)
Bellywater Press
Biblio Press
Birth Day Publishing Company
Black Light Fellowship
BlackBerry Literary Services
Blue Dove Press
Book Faith India
BOTH SIDES NOW
BOULDER HERETIC
BRANCHES
Branden Books
Brentwood Christian Press
BRIDGES: An Interdisciplinary Journal of Theology, Philosophy, History, and Science
Bronze Girl Productions, Inc.
Brunswick Publishing Corporation
BUSINESS SPIRIT JOURNAL
Caribbean Books-Panama
Celtic Heritage Books
THE CENTENNIAL REVIEW
Center for Japanese Studies
CESUM MAGAZINE
CHANTEH, the Iranian Cross-Cultural Quarterly
Children Of Mary
CHRISTIAN CONNECTION PEN PAL NEWSLETTER
THE CHRISTIAN LIBRARIAN
CHRISTIAN*NEW AGE QUARTERLY
The Colbert House
CONSCIENCE: The Newsjournal of Catholic Opinion
CONTEMPORARY GHAZALS
CORNERSTONE
CRC Publications
CRONE CHRONICLES: A Journal of Conscious Aging
CROSS CURRENTS
Crystal Clarity, Publishers
Cynic Press
DAILY WORD
Dharma Publishing
DIALOGOS: Hellenic Studies Review
DOVETAIL: A Journal by and for Jewish/Christian Families
DRAMA GARDEN
Dumouriez Publishing
Dunamis House
Eborn Books
EcceNova Editions
The Edwin Mellen Press
Wm.B. Eerdmans Publishing Co.
Elderberry Press, LLC
Encounter Books
Enlighten Next

Ephemera Bound Publishing
Famaco Publishers (Qalam Books)
Feel Free Press
FIDELIS ET VERUS
Fingerprint Press
FISH DRUM MAGAZINE
Focus Publications, Inc.
FORUM
Foundation Books
THE FOURTH R
FREE INQUIRY
Free People Press
FREETHOUGHT HISTORY
Friends United Press
Galaxy Press
Galde Press, Inc.
Genesis Publishing Company, Inc.
Gilgal Publications
GLOBAL VEDANTA
Gloger Family Books
Good Book Publishing Company
Harbor House
Harlan Publishing Company; Alliance Books; Diakonia Publishing (Christian Books)
Heidelberg Graphics
Heritage Global Publishing
Himalayan Institute Press
Ho Logos Press
HOLY ROLLERS
Hope Publishing House
Horned Owl Publishing
THE HUMANIST
Iconoclast Press
Idylls Press
IMAGE: ART, FAITH, MYSTERY
In Print Publishing
Innisfree Press
INTERCULTURE
ISSUES
J&W Publishers, Inc.
JOURNAL OF NARRATIVE THEORY
Kar-Ben Publishing, Inc.
Kenyette Productions
KEREM: Creative Explorations in Judaism
Kobalt Books
LAKE STREET LIT: Art and Words from the Bottom of Lake Bonneville
LITURGICAL CATECHESIS
Lone Willow Press
LPD Press
Lycanthrope Press
MacDonald/Sward Publishing Company
Peter Marcan Publications
Maryland Historical Press
Massey-Reyner Publishing
MB Media, Inc.
MEDIA SPOTLIGHT
Mercer University Press
The Midknight Club
MINISTRY & LITURGY
THE MONIST: An International Quarterly Journal of General Philosophical Inquiry
Monkfish Book Publishing Company
Mo'omana'o Press
Mountain Automation Corporation
Mountaintop Books
Multnomah Publishers, Inc.
MUSIC NEWS
My Heart Yours Publishing
Mystery Island Publications
NEW AMERICAN IMAGIST
New Concept Press
New Creature Press
New Falcon Publications
NEW THOUGHT
New World Library
NEWWITCH
NightinGale Resources

NOLA-MAGICK Press
Northern Illinois University Press
NOVA RELIGIO
OFFICE NUMBER ONE
Open Court Publishing Company
Origin Press
OUT OF LINE
PAGAN AMERICA
PARABOLA MAGAZINE
Parallax Press
Penthe Publishing
Philokalia Books
Philopsychy Press
Pilgrims Book House
The Pin Prick Press
Plain Philosophy Center
Plus Publications
Pocol Press
POETICA MAGAZINE, Reflections of Jewish Thought
Polebridge Press
PREP Publishing
The Press at Foggy Bottom
QUARTZ HILL JOURNAL OF THEOLOGY:A Journal of
  Bible and Contemporary Theological Thought
Quartz Hill Publishing House
QUEEN OF ALL HEARTS
THE QUEST
Quest Books: Theosophical Publishing House
QUEST: AN INTERDISCIPLINARY JOURNAL FOR
  ASIAN CHRISTIAN SCHOLARS
Rabeth Publishing Company
Ragged Edge Press
RELIGION & AMERICAN CULTURE
REPORTS OF THE NATIONAL CENTER FOR SCIENCE
  EDUCATION
Resource Publications, Inc.
ST. CROIX REVIEW
Saint Mary's Press
Saqi Books Publisher
SAT SANDESH: THE MESSAGE OF THE MASTERS
SCP JOURNAL
SelectiveHouse Publishers, Inc.
SHAMAN'S DRUM: A Journal of Experiential Shamanism
SKS Press
SOCIETE
SOLAS Press
Spiritual Understanding Network, LLC
Spring Publications Inc.
Square One Publishers, Inc.
State University of New York Press
SterlingHouse Publisher
STUDIO - A Journal of Christians Writing
Sherwood Sugden & Company, Publishers
Superior Christian Press
Swedenborg Foundation
Technicians of the Sacred
TELOS
Third Dimension Publishing
Thirteen Colonies Press
THRESHOLDS JOURNAL
TIFARA
Timeless Books
Truman State University Press
TRUTH SEEKER
Tyr Publishing
Unity House
UNITY MAGAZINE
Universal Unity
University of South Carolina Press
UnKnownTruths.com Publishing Company
Vedanta Press
Vesta Publications Limited
VOICES - ISRAEL
Volcano Press, Inc
Wayside Publications
WHAT IS ENLIGHTENMENT?
Wheatmark Book Publishing
White Buck Publishing

Wild West Publishing House
Wilderness Ministries
WinePress Publishing
Wisdom Publications, Inc.
World Wisdom,Inc.
Wytherngate Press
ZONE
Zygote Publishing

RENAISSANCE

Avari Press
Chatterley Press International
Italica Press, Inc.
SCULPTURAL PURSUIT MAGAZINE
Truman State University Press
YE OLDE NEWES

REPRINTS

Alan Wofsy Fine Arts
ALTERNATIVE PRESS REVIEW
Ancient City Press
Avery Color Studios
Bliss Publishing Company, Inc.
BOTH SIDES NOW
Carousel Press
Center for Japanese Studies
Cherokee Publishing Company
Dixon-Price Publishing
Dumouriez Publishing
Eagle's View Publishing
Ecrivez!
The Feminist Press at the City University of New York
Free People Press
Friends United Press
Harlan Publishing Company; Alliance Books; Diakonia
  Publishing (Christian Books)
Heidelberg Graphics
Heritage Books, Inc.
Irish Genealogical Foundation
Ironweed Press
JUBILAT
Allen A. Knoll Publishers
Libertarian Press, Inc./American Book Distributors
Loonfeather Press
McPherson & Company Publishers
Mid-List Press
Monkfish Book Publishing Company
Mountain Press Publishing Co.
NEW AMERICAN IMAGIST
Oregon State University Press
OUT YOUR BACKDOOR: The Magazine of Do-It-
  Yourself Adventure and Homegrown Culture
Paladin Enterprises, Inc.
The Pin Prick Press
Saqi Books Publisher
SOCIETE
Sherwood Sugden & Company, Publishers
UglyTown
UNITED LUMBEE NATION TIMES
THE VIRGINIA QUARTERLY REVIEW
Zumaya Publications

RESEARCH

Americans for the Arts
Benecton Press
Brenner Information Group
Buenos Books America
COGNITIO: A Graduate Humanities Journal
EEI Press
Eros Books
Frontline Publications
Happy About
Journal of Pyrotechnics
JOURNAL OF PYROTECHNICS
Platte Purchase Publishers
Reach Productions Publishing
Scientia Publishing, LLC
SENSATIONS MAGAZINE

736

Snake Hill Press
THE SOCIOLOGICAL QUARTERLY
STATE OF CALIFORNIA LABOR
Three House Publishing
Vestibular Disorders Association
Wheatmark Book Publishing

RESISTANCE

MOUTH: Voice of the Dis-Labeled Nation

REVIEWS

ACM (ANOTHER CHICAGO MAGAZINE)
THE ALEMBIC
ALTERNATIVE PRESS REVIEW
AMBIT : JOURNAL OF POETRY AND POETICS
THE AMERICAN DRIVEL REVIEW
Androgyne Books
APPALACHIA JOURNAL
ARCHIPELAGO
THE BALTIMORE REVIEW
BELOIT POETRY JOURNAL
BIRD DOG
BLACK SHEETS MAGAZINE
THE BLIND MAN'S RAINBOW
BLUE MESA REVIEW
Blueprint Books
BOGG: A Journal of Contemporary Writing
BOOK MARKETING UPDATE
BOOK/MARK SMALL PRESS REVIEW
BORDERLANDS: Texas Poetry Review
CEDAR HILL REVIEW
CESUM MAGAZINE
CHECKER CAB MAGAZINE - THE LITTLE 'ZINE
    THAT COULD! Fiction That Takes The Long Way
    Home
CIMARRON REVIEW
COGNITIO: A Graduate Humanities Journal
COLLEGE LITERATURE
CONCRETE JUNGLE JOURNAL
CORRECTIONS TODAY
COUNTERPOISE: For Social Responsibilities, Liberty and
    Dissent
THE CREAM CITY REVIEW
CREEPY MIKE'S OMNIBUS OF FUN
CYNIC BOOK REVIEW
DREAM NETWORK
DUFUS
Earthwinds Editions
THE EAST VILLAGE INKY
EEI Press
88: A Journal of Contemporary American Poetry
ENGLISH LITERATURE IN TRANSITION, 1880-1920
EPICENTER: A LITERARY MAGAZINE
THE FLORIDA REVIEW
The Foundation for Economic Education, Inc.
THE FRANK REVIEW
THE FREEMAN: Ideas On Liberty
GAUNTLET: Exploring the Limits of Free Expression
THE GEORGIA REVIEW
GOLDEN ISIS MAGAZINE
GRAY AREAS
THE GREAT BLUE BEACON
GREEN ANARCHY
THE GREEN HILLS LITERARY LANTERN
HAPPENINGNOW!EVERYWHERE
Haunted Rowboat Press
IAMBS & TROCHEES
ILLUMINATIONS
INDEPENDENT PUBLISHER ONLINE
INDIANA REVIEW
INNOVATING
IOTA
JAMES JOYCE BROADSHEET
THE JOURNAL
THE JOURNAL OF AFRICAN TRAVEL-WRITING
juel house publishers and literary services
KABBALAH
KALEIDOSCOPE: Exploring the Experience of Disability

through Literature & the Fine Arts
THE KENYON REVIEW
KLIATT
LAUGHING BEAR NEWSLETTER
LICHEN Arts & Letters Preview
LIGHT: The Quarterly of Light Verse
LITERARY MAGAZINE REVIEW
LITRAG
LUMMOX JOURNAL
Lummox Press
Lunar Offensive Publications
MAIN STREET RAG
THE MARLBORO REVIEW
MATCHBOOK
MEAT: A Journal of Writing and Materiality
Mica Press - Paying Our Dues Productions
MID-AMERICAN REVIEW
MINESHAFT
THE MYSTERY REVIEW
NEW DELTA REVIEW
THE NEW ENGLAND QUARTERLY
NEW HOPE INTERNATIONAL REVIEW
THE NEW RENAISSANCE, an international magazine of
    ideas & opinions, emphasizing literature & the arts
North Stone Editions
NORTHWORDS
NOTRE DAME REVIEW
OASIS
ONE TRICK PONY
OPEN WIDE MAGAZINE
OYSTER BOY REVIEW
P.R.A. Publishing
PACIFIC COAST JOURNAL
PARADIDOMI
Pendragonian Publications
PENNINE PLATFORM
PENNY DREADFUL: Tales and Poems of Fantastic Terror
PEREGRINE
Phoenix Illusion
PLEASANT LIVING
POET LORE
POETRY NOW, Sacramento's Literary Review and Calen-
    dar
PRAIRIE SCHOONER
PRESA
Progressive Education
PROGRESSIVE PERIODICALS DIRECTORY/UPDATE
PSYCHOANALYTIC BOOKS: A QUARTERLY JOUR-
    NAL OF REVIEWS
QUARTERLY WEST
RAIN TAXI REVIEW OF BOOKS
THE RAVEN CHRONICLES
READ, AMERICA!
RED ROCK REVIEW
RUMINATIONS: The Nigerian Dwarf & Mini Dairy Goat
    Magazine
SEWANEE REVIEW
THE SMALL PRESS REVIEW/SMALL MAGAZINE
    REVIEW
SMARTISH PACE
SONGS OF INNOCENCE
THE SOURCES HOTLINK
Southeast Missouri State University Press
SPOON RIVER POETRY REVIEW
THE STINGING FLY
SYCAMORE REVIEW
13TH MOON
Thunder Rain Publishing Corp.
TOUCHSTONE LITERARY JOURNAL
TRUTH SEEKER
UNDER THE VOLCANO
UNDERSTANDING MAGAZINE
UNO MAS MAGAZINE
Urban Legend Press
THE URBANITE
VACATION PLACE RENTALS
VALLUM: CONTEMPORARY POETRY
WIND

WORLD OF FANDOM MAGAZINE
WRITER'S EXCHANGE
WSQ (formerly WOMEN'S STUDIES QUARTERLY)
ZINE WORLD: A Reader's Guide to the Underground Press

ROBOTICS

firefall editions

ROMANCE

A Cappela Publishing, Inc.
Amador Publishers
BEGINNINGS - A Magazine for the Novice Writer
Blue Planet Books Inc.
Crystal Dreams Publishing
Ephemera Bound Publishing
Equine Graphics Publishing Group: New Concord Press, SmallHorse Press, Parallel Press
Eros Books
The Fiction Works
Foremost Press
Four Seasons Publishers
4AllSeasons Publishing
Gardenia Press
Gemstone House Publishing
Homa & Sekey Books
Idylls Press
Ika, LLC
J. Mark Press
JetKor
Kobalt Books
Llumina Press
Lyons Publishing Limited
Maverick Books
Mayhaven Publishing
MCM Entertainment, Inc. Publishing Division
Mills Custom Services Publishing
Oak Tree Press
Outrider Press
Pedestal Press
Premium Press America
PREP Publishing
Pristine Publishing
PublishAmerica, LLLP.
Pussywillow
Reed Press
Steel Balls Press
Triskelion Publishing
Twin Souls Publications
Two Thousand Three Associates
UmbraProjects, Ltd.
Vintage Romance Publishing, LLC
Whiskey Creek Press
Wytherngate Press

ROMANIAN STUDIES

BIBLIOPHILOS
THE MONTHLY INDEPENDENT TRIBUNE TIMES JOURNAL POST GAZETTE NEWS CHRONICLE BULLETIN
TRANSITIONS ABROAD: The Guide to Living, Learning, and Working Overseas

RUSSIA

ABSINTHE: New European Writing
all nations press
Mehring Books, Inc.
MIP Company
Rodnik Publishing Co.
Russian Information Services
RUSSIAN LIFE
Tzipora Publications, Inc.
Zephyr Press

SACRAMENTO

Fingerprint Press

SAFETY

AB

Dash-Hill, LLC
Future Horizons, Inc.
GLOBAL ONE TRAVEL & AUTOMOTIVE MAGAZINE
Resource Publications, Inc.
SO YOUNG!
Chuck Stewart
Varro Press

SAN FRANCISCO

Alamo Square Press
Androgyne Books
Carousel Press
CLARA VENUS
THE COMPLEAT NURSE
Devil Mountain Books
firefall editions
GIRLFRIENDS MAGAZINE
Heritage House Publishers
Ithuriel's Spear
Lexikos
The Live Oak Press, LLC
Pocol Press
Scottwall Associates, Publishers

SATIRE

Aardwolfe Books
ABRAXAS
ACME Press
THE ACORN
ART:MAG
AXE FACTORY REVIEW
BABYSUE
Black Oak Press
BLUE HORSE
Blue Horse Publications
BUST DOWN THE DOOR AND EAT ALL THE CHICKENS: A Journal of Absurd and Surreal Fiction
Casperian Books LLC
The Center Press
CONCRETE JUNGLE JOURNAL
CONJUNCTIONS
Creative Guy Publishing
CREOSOTE: A Journal of Poetry and Prose
Delta-West Publishing, Inc.
DREAM FANTASY INTERNATIONAL
EPICENTER: A LITERARY MAGAZINE
Erespin Press
EVANSVILLE REVIEW
FAT TUESDAY
FIGHT THESE BASTARDS
FINE MADNESS
FLUENT ASCENSION
FRAN MAGAZINE
THE FRANK REVIEW
Free Reign Press, Inc.
GAMBARA MAGAZINE
GAUNTLET: Exploring the Limits of Free Expression
GENIE: POEMS: JOKES: ART
HAWAII PACIFIC REVIEW
JOURNAL OF POLYMORPHOUS PERVERSITY
juel house publishers and literary services
The Leaping Frog Press
Liaison Press
Mayhaven Publishing
McPherson & Company Publishers
MeteoritePress.com
THE MONTHLY INDEPENDENT TRIBUNE TIMES JOURNAL POST GAZETTE NEWS CHRONICLE BULLETIN
MOTORBOOTY MAGAZINE
Pleasure Boat Studio: A Literary Press
Poor Souls Press/Scaramouche Books
Portmanteau Editions
RAINBOW CURVE
RANDEE
THE ROCKFORD REVIEW
Santa Fe Writers Project
SKYLARK

A SOFT DEGRADE
STRUGGLE: A Magazine of Proletarian Revolutionary
  Literature
SUB-TERRAIN
Syukhtun Editions
Transcending Mundane, Inc.
UNDERSTANDING MAGAZINE
UNO MAS MAGAZINE
Versus Press
Wild West Publishing House
THE WILDWOOD READER
WORDS OF WISDOM
Writers' Haven Press

SCANDINAVIA

ABSINTHE: New European Writing
Cross-Cultural Communications
Horned Owl Publishing
SCANDINAVIAN REVIEW
Southern Illinois University Press
TRANSITIONS ABROAD: The Guide to Living, Learning,
  and Working Overseas
Voyageur Publishing Co.,Inc.
World Gumbo Publishing
Years Press

SCIENCE

AAS HISTORY SERIES
AB
ADVANCES IN THE ASTRONAUTICAL SCIENCES
AE-TU Publishing
ALL ROUND
ATLANTIS: A Women's Studies Journal/Revue d'etudes
  sur les femmes
Bellevue Literary Press
Benecton Press
BIOLOGY DIGEST
THE BOOKWATCH
BRIDGES: An Interdisciplinary Journal of Theology,
  Philosophy, History, and Science
Buenos Books America
BUSINESS SPIRIT JOURNAL
THE CENTENNIAL REVIEW
Central Avenue Press
Chicago Review Press
Clearwater Publishing Co.
Clover Park Press
Comparative Sedimentology Lab.
CONDUIT
Continuing Education Press
CROSSCURRENTS
Dawn Publications
The Denali Press
EcceNova Editions
firefall editions
Flowerfield Enterprises, LLC
Fountainhead Productions, Inc.
FREE INQUIRY
Frontline Publications
Genesis Publishing Company, Inc.
The Heather Foundation
History Compass, LLC
International University Line (IUL)
Ion Imagination Publishing, Ion Imagination Entertainment,
  Inc.
Island Press
Island Publishers
JetKor
JOURNAL OF POLYMORPHOUS PERVERSITY
Journal of Pyrotechnics
JOURNAL OF PYROTECHNICS
JOURNAL OF SCIENTIFIC EXPLORATION
Jupiter Scientific Publishing
Library Research Associates
Lorien House
Medi-Ed Press
The Message Company
Mission Press

Mo'omana'o Press
Muse World Media Group
N-B-T-V
Orchises Press
PABLO LENNIS
Plexus Publishing, Inc.
PSYCHOANALYTIC BOOKS: A QUARTERLY JOUR-
  NAL OF REVIEWS
Quale Press
Quarterly Committee of Queen's University
QUEEN'S QUARTERLY: A Canadian Review
THE QUEST
Rainbow Books, Inc.
REPORTS OF THE NATIONAL CENTER FOR SCIENCE
  EDUCATION
Savant Garde Workshop
SB&F (SCIENCE BOOKS & FILMS)
SCIENCE AND TECHNOLOGY
SCIENCE/HEALTH ABSTRACTS
Scientia Publishing, LLC
Sea Challengers, Inc.
SKEPTICAL INQUIRER
SOLAS Press
Solcat Publishing
thinkBiotech
Three House Publishing
Timber Press
Titan Press
Trickle Creek Books
Tyr Publishing
Univelt, Inc.
UnKnownTruths.com Publishing Company
WHAT IS ENLIGHTENMENT?

SCIENCE FICTION

AAS HISTORY SERIES
Abecedarian books, Inc.
AE-TU Publishing
Angst World Library
APEX SCIENCE FICTION & HORROR DIGEST
Argo Press
ARTISTIC RAMBLINGS
Arx Publishing LLC
AXE FACTORY REVIEW
BALLISTA
Bereshith Publishing
Blue Planet Books Inc.
BOMB MAGAZINE
THE BOOKWATCH
The Bradford Press
BUST DOWN THE DOOR AND EAT ALL THE
  CHICKENS: A Journal of Absurd and Surreal Fiction
C & M Online Media Inc.
Cambric Press dba Emerald House
Caribbean Books-Panama
Casperian Books LLC
Central Avenue Press
CHALLENGING DESTINY
Circlet Press, Inc.
A COMPANION IN ZEOR
Creative Guy Publishing
Crystal Dreams Publishing
Denlinger's Publishers Ltd.
DREAM FANTASY INTERNATIONAL
DREAMS AND NIGHTMARES
Earth Star Publications
EASTGATE QUARTERLY REVIEW OF HYPERTEXT
Ecrivez!
EDGE Science Fiction and Fantasy Publishing
Elderberry Press, LLC
Event Horizon Press
R. E. FARRELLBOOKS, LLC
Feel Free Press
The Fiction Works
Firelight Publishing, Inc.
FISH DRUM MAGAZINE
Foremost Press
Fountainhead Productions, Inc.

Four Seasons Publishers
Four Walls Eight Windows
Free Reign Press, Inc.
Gardenia Press
Gateways Books And Tapes
GRASSLIMB
Gryphon Books
Idylls Press
THE ILLUMINATA
Imago Press
IMPress
IT GOES ON THE SHELF
Journey Books Publishing
Leyland Publications
LOW BUDGET SCIENCE FICTION
Manuscript Press
Mayapple Press
The Midknight Club
Mountain Media
Mucusart Publications
Munsey Music
MYSTERY ISLAND MAGAZINE
Mystery Island Publications
Mystic Toad Press
New Falcon Publications
New Victoria Publishers
NOVA EXPRESS
OmegaRoom Press
ON SPEC
PABLO LENNIS
PAPERBACK PARADE
Penthe Publishing
Phantom Press Publications
Pig Iron Press
POGO STICK
Portals Press
Pottersfield Press
PREMONITIONS
PublishAmerica, LLLP.
Purple Mouth Press
Radiant Press
RALPH'S REVIEW
Razor7 Publishing
Reach Productions Publishing
RedJack
Rivercross Publishing, Inc.
Santa Fe Writers Project
Savant Garde Workshop
SelectiveHouse Publishers, Inc.
SENSATIONS MAGAZINE
THE SILVER WEB
SOM Publishing, division of School of Metaphysics
SPACE AND TIME
Space and Time Press
StarLance Publications
SterlingHouse Publisher
THE TARPEIAN ROCK
THRESHOLDS JOURNAL
Tolling Bell Books
Triskelion Publishing
Triumvirate Publications
Twilight Times Books
Tyrannosaurus Press
Ultramarine Publishing Co., Inc.
Univelt, Inc.
Urban Legend Press
THE URBANITE
Van Cleave Publishing
Whiskey Creek Press
Willowgate Press
WORLD OF FANDOM MAGAZINE
ZAHIR, Unforgettable Tales
Zumaya Publications

SCOTLAND

ABSINTHE: New European Writing
Celtic Heritage Books
DeerTrail Books

Dufour Editions Inc.
Mystic Toad Press
NORTHWORDS
Rowan Mountain Press
Stewart Publishing & Printing

SCOUTING

dbS Productions
GAMBARA MAGAZINE

SELF-HELP

A Cappela Publishing, Inc.
Affirmative Publishing LC
Al-Galaxy Publishing Corporation
ALONE TOGETHER
Amethyst & Emerald
Anti-Aging Press
Arden Press, Inc.
Ascension Publishing
THE AUROREAN
Authors of Unity Publishing
AuthorsOmniscient Publishers
Balanced Books Publishing
Bayhampton Publications
Beagle Bay Books
Behavioral Sciences Research Press, Inc.
Beyond Words Publishing, Inc.
Big Mouth Publications
Black Diamond Book Publishing
Black Forest Press
Black Pearl Enterprises LLC
Book Marketing Solutions
BookPartners, Inc.
Brason-Sargar Publications
Brenner Information Group
Broken Jaw Press
Bronze Girl Productions, Inc.
CANADIAN MONEYSAVER
Capalo Press
Center for Thanatology Research & Education, Inc.
Chicago Spectrum Press
Common Boundaries
Communication Creativity
Contemax Publishers
Crane Press
CREATIVITY CONNECTION
Crystal Dreams Publishing
Cypress House
D.B.A. Books
DAILY WORD
Dakota Books
Dancing Bridge Publishing
Dash-Hill, LLC
Dawn Sign Press
Delaney Day Press
Denlinger's Publishers Ltd.
DOVETAIL: A Journal by and for Jewish/Christian Families
Down There Press
dreamslaughter
E & D Publishing, Inc.
Ecrivez!
Emerald Wave
Envirographics
Epoch Press
Equine Graphics Publishing Group: New Concord Press, SmallHorse Press, Parallel Press
Excelsior Cee Publishing
EXECUTIVE EXCELLENCE
Executive Excellence Publishing
Falcon Publishing, LTD
Fast Foot Forward Press
Nicolin Fields Publishing, Inc.
FMA Publishing
Foremost Press
Fouque Publishers
Four Seasons Publishers
Fulcrum, Inc.

Future Horizons, Inc.
GoldenHouse Publishing Group
Hannacroix Creek Books, Inc
Harbor House Law Press, Inc.
Health Press
Herrmann International
Himalayan Institute Press
Holbrook Street Press
Hunter House Inc., Publishers
IMOCO Publishing
Impact Publishers, Inc.
Innisfree Press
Islewest Publishing
J&W Publishers, Inc.
Jireh Publishing Company
JOURNAL OF PSYCHOACTIVE DRUGS
JPS Publishing Company
KABBALAH
Kallisti Publishing
Knowledge Concepts Publishing
Life Lessons
LifeSkill Institute, Inc.
LightLines Publishing
LIVING CHEAP NEWS
Long & Silverman Publishing, Inc.
The Love and Logic Press, Inc.
Luminous Epinoia Press
Markowski International Publishers
Master's Plan Publishing
Middleway Press
Millennium Vision Press
Mind Power Publishing
Monroe Press
Music City Publishing
New Paradigm Books
New Win Publishing
New World Library
New World Library
Nolo Press Occidental
North Star Books
Nunciata
Oak Tree Press
Obsessive Compulsive Anonymous
Origin Press
Peachtree Publishers, Ltd.
Pedestal Press
Perpetual Press
Philopsychy Press
Plain Philosophy Center
Platinum Dreams Publishing
Plus Publications
The Poetry Center Press/Shoestring Press
Princess Publishing
QED Press
Quill Driver Books
Rainbow Books, Inc.
Ravenhawk Books
RedJack
Rest of Your Life Publications
River Press
Sacred Spaces Press
Sagamore Publishing
The Saunderstown Press
SCIENCE/HEALTH ABSTRACTS
Seven Arrows Publishing, Inc.
Sidran Institute
SO YOUNG!
Sound View Publishing, Inc.
Spiritual Understanding Network, LLC
Starry Night Publishing
Steel Balls Press
Stewart Publishing & Printing
Studio 4 Productions
Sunrise Health Coach Publications
Swan Publishing Company
Swan Publishing Company
Swedenborg Foundation
Terra Nova Press

Timeless Books
Top 20 Press
Twilight Times Books
Unity House
UNITY MAGAZINE
UnTechnical Press
Upper Access Inc.
VanderWyk & Burnham
Vision Works Publishing
Wheatmark Book Publishing
Whiskey Creek Press
Wilshire Books Inc.
Wisdom Publications, Inc.
Women of Diversity Productions, Inc.
Women of Diversity Productions, Inc.
The Word Doctor Online Publishing
World Gumbo Publishing
Writers' Haven Press
Yes International Publishers
Zoilita Grant MS CCHt.
Zumaya Publications

SENIOR CITIZENS

AuthorsOmniscient Publishers
Country Messenger Press
Creative With Words Publications (CWW)
DeerTrail Books
Down There Press
Dunamis House
Equine Graphics Publishing Group: New Concord Press, SmallHorse Press, Parallel Press
Fitness Press
Guarionex Press Ltd.
Heritage West Books
LifeCircle Press
MAGICAL BLEND/NATURAL BEAUTY & HEALTH/ TRANSITIONS
Pineapple Press, Inc.
The Poetry Center Press/Shoestring Press
Quill Driver Books
Rayve Productions Inc.
Sagamore Publishing
SO YOUNG!
Starry Night Publishing
Studio 4 Productions
TAPROOT, a journal of older writers
Wise Press

SEX, SEXUALITY

Affirmative Publishing LC
AK Press
Al-Galaxy Publishing Corporation
ALONE TOGETHER
ASIA FILE
AuthorsOmniscient Publishers
BLACK LACE
BLACK SHEETS MAGAZINE
BLACKFIRE
CAMERA OBSCURA: Feminism, Culture, and Media Studies
Carpe Diem Publishing
CESUM MAGAZINE
Circlet Press, Inc.
CONSCIENCE: The Newsjournal of Catholic Opinion
Crystal Dreams Publishing
Cynic Press
DWAN
Enlightened Living Publishing, LLC
Ephemera Bound Publishing
FEMINIST STUDIES
FIGHT THESE BASTARDS
FLUENT ASCENSION
Garrett County Press
Gay Sunshine Press, Inc.
GEM Literary Foundation Press
GLB Publishers
GRAY AREAS
Harrington Park Press

741

HARVARD WOMEN'S LAW JOURNAL
The Haworth Press
HYPATIA: A Journal of Feminist Philosophy
Impact Publishers, Inc.
THE INDENTED PILLOW
Kivaki Press
Knowledge Concepts Publishing
KUMQUAT MERINGUE
LAKE STREET LIT: Art and Words from the Bottom of Lake Bonneville
Leyland Publications
LOVING MORE
Luminous Epinoia Press
Lunar Offensive Publications
MALEDICTA: The International Journal of Verbal Aggression
MEAT FOR TEA: THE NORTHAMPTON REVIEW
MEAT: A Journal of Writing and Materiality
A Melody from an Immigrant's Soul
METROPOLITAN FORUM
MGW (Mom Guess What) Newsmagazine
MIP Company
Muse World Media Group
NAMBLA BULLETIN
PAGAN AMERICA
Passion Power Press, Inc
Pussywillow
Red Alder Books
Red Rock Press
Rodnik Publishing Co.
Semiotext Foreign Agents Books Series
SEMIOTEXT(E)
Sentient Publications, LLC
SHO
SHORTRUNS
SKINNYDIPPING
Snake Hill Press
Speck Press
Spirit Press
Starbooks Press/FLF Press
Steel Balls Press
SterlingHouse Publisher
Swan Publishing Company
Synergy Press
Titan Press
Transcending Mundane, Inc.
UNO MAS MAGAZINE
Versus Press
Vision
Wilshire Books Inc.
Zygote Publishing

SEXUAL ABUSE

ALONE TOGETHER
Black Diamond Book Publishing
CURRENTS: New Scholarship in the Human Services
Denlinger's Publishers Ltd.
GEM Literary Foundation Press
Islewest Publishing
Jalmar Press/Innerchoice Publishing
JOURNAL OF CHILD AND YOUTH CARE
Kodiak Media Group
Metallo House Publishers
Parenting Press, Inc.
Sidran Institute
Synergy Press
TEEN VOICES MAGAZINE

SHAKER

TRUTH SEEKER

SHAKESPEARE

APOSTROPHE: USCB Journal of the Arts
Bandanna Books
Empire Publishing Service
Players Press, Inc.
74th Street Productions, L.L.C.
THE SHAKESPEARE NEWSLETTER

SHIPWRECKS

Bad Press
Caribbean Books-Panama
LAKE SUPERIOR MAGAZINE
VACATION PLACE RENTALS
Wilderness Adventure Books

G.B. SHAW

ENGLISH LITERATURE IN TRANSITION, 1880-1920
THE INDEPENDENT SHAVIAN
IRISH LITERARY SUPPLEMENT
Limelight Editions
Pennsylvania State University Press
The Press of Appletree Alley
SHAW: THE ANNUAL OF BERNARD SHAW STUDIES

SHORT STORIES

Abecedarian books, Inc.
THE ADIRONDACK REVIEW
Ageless Press
ALASKA QUARTERLY REVIEW
THE ALEMBIC
THE AMERICAN DRIVEL REVIEW
AMERICAN JONES BUILDING & MAINTENANCE
AMERICAN LETTERS & COMMENTARY
AMERICAN LITERARY REVIEW
ANCIENT PATHS
Androgyne Books
THE ANTHOLOGY OF NEW ENGLAND WRITERS
APPLE VALLEY REVIEW: A Journal of Contemporary Literature
ARCHIPELAGO
THE ART HORSE
ART:MAG
ARTISTIC RAMBLINGS
ASPHODEL
Asylum Arts
BALLISTA
THE BALTIMORE REVIEW
THE BEAR DELUXE
Bear Star Press
BEATLICK NEWS
BELOIT FICTION JOURNAL
BIG MUDDY: Journal of the Mississippi River Valley
Biographical Publishing Company
BITTER OLEANDER
BkMk Press
Black Forest Press
Black Heron Press
Black Lawrence Press
Boulevard Books, Inc. Florida
The Bradford Press
Brave Ulysses Books
Broken Jaw Press
Broken Shadow Publications
BUFFALO SPREE
Burning Books
BUZZWORDS
Cantarabooks LLC
Carnifex Press
Cedar Hill Books
Central Avenue Press
Cervena Barva Press
CHECKER CAB MAGAZINE - THE LITTLE 'ZINE THAT COULD! Fiction That Takes The Long Way Home
CIMARRON REVIEW
Coffee House Press
COLD-DRILL
CONFLUENCE
CONJUNCTIONS
CRAB CREEK REVIEW
CRAB ORCHARD REVIEW
THE CREAM CITY REVIEW
CREOSOTE: A Journal of Poetry and Prose
Crones Unlimited
Crystal Dreams Publishing

Culturelink Press
CUTBANK
CUTTHROAT, A JOURNAL OF THE ARTS
DANDELION ARTS MAGAZINE
December Press
December Press
The Design Image Group Inc.
Devil Mountain Books
DOTLIT: The Online Journal of Creative Writing
DOWNSTATE STORY
DREAM FANTASY INTERNATIONAL
ECOTONE: Reimagining Place
Ecrivez!
Eros Books
EVANSVILLE REVIEW
Fern Publications
FIRST INTENSITY
Fithian Press
Five Fingers Press
FIVE FINGERS REVIEW
THE FLORIDA REVIEW
FLUENT ASCENSION
Flume Press
FOLIO: A Literary Journal of American University
Fontanel Books
Fouque Publishers
Four Way Books
FOURTEEN HILLS: The SFSU Review
Free Reign Press, Inc.
THE FROGMORE PAPERS
THE FUNNY TIMES
The Galileo Press Ltd.
THE GEORGIA REVIEW
GERTRUDE
GERTRUDE
Gertrude Press
Gibbs Smith, Publisher
GIN BENDER POETRY REVIEW
GLASS TESSERACT
Goose River Press
Gorilla Convict Publications
GRASSLANDS REVIEW
GRASSLIMB
Graywolf Press
GULF COAST
Hanover Press
HARDBOILED
HAWAII PACIFIC REVIEW
Helicon Nine Editions
Homa & Sekey Books
Horse & Buggy Press
THE ICONOCLAST
Imago Press
IMPress
In Between Books
INKY TRAIL NEWS
THE INTERPRETER'S HOUSE
ITALIAN AMERICANA
Jako Books
JetKor
THE JOURNAL OF AFRICAN TRAVEL-WRITING
juel house publishers and literary services
KAJ-MAHKAH: EARTH OF EARTH
THE KENYON REVIEW
KESTREL: A Journal of Literature and Art
Kings Estate Press
Allen A. Knoll Publishers
KOJA
LAKE EFFECT
THE LEDGE
LEFT CURVE
Lekon New Dimensions Publishing
LEO Productions LLC.
Leyland Publications
THE LICKING RIVER REVIEW
Light of New Orleans Publishing
THE LISTENING EYE
Little Pear Press

Loonfeather Press
LULLWATER REVIEW
MAIN STREET RAG
MANGROVE MAGAZINE
MANOA: A Pacific Journal of International Writing
MANY MOUNTAINS MOVING
McPherson & Company Publishers
MEAT FOR TEA: THE NORTHAMPTON REVIEW
A Melody from an Immigrant's Soul
MID-AMERICAN REVIEW
Mid-List Press
MINESHAFT
MIP Company
Mountain State Press
Mucusart Publications
MYSTERY ISLAND MAGAZINE
NATURAL BRIDGE
NEO: Literary Magazine
THE NEW RENAISSANCE, an international magazine of
     ideas & opinions, emphasizing literature & the arts
New Rivers Press, Inc.
NORTH CAROLINA LITERARY REVIEW
NORTHWORDS
One Less Press
OPEN MINDS QUARTERLY
ORACLE STORY
THE ORPHAN LEAF REVIEW
OTHER VOICES
Oyster River Press
PACIFIC COAST JOURNAL
PAPERPLATES
PASSAGES NORTH
Passing Through Publications
PAVEMENT SAW
PEARL
Pendragonian Publications
PENNY DREADFUL: Tales and Poems of Fantastic Terror
Phantom Press Publications
Phoenix Illusion
Phony Lid Publications
PICK POCKET BOOKS
PLEASANT LIVING
Pocol Press
POETICA MAGAZINE, Reflections of Jewish Thought
The Poetry Center
POGO STICK
Polar Bear & Company
PRAIRIE SCHOONER
PREMONITIONS
The Press at Foggy Bottom
The Press of Appletree Alley
PublishAmerica, LLLP.
Purple Finch Press
Pygmy Forest Press
Pyncheon House
Questex Consulting Ltd.
THE QUIET FEATHER
RAINBOW CURVE
RATTAPALLAX
THE RAVEN CHRONICLES
Red Cedar Press
RED CEDAR REVIEW
Red Dragon Press
RED ROCK REVIEW
Red Tiger Press
RED WHEELBARROW
REFLECTIONS LITERARY JOURNAL
Rowan Mountain Press
THE RUE BELLA
SAGE OF CONSCIOUSNESS E-ZINE
Saint Mary's Press
SALAMANDER
Salt Publishing
SENSATIONS MAGAZINE
SEWANEE REVIEW
SISTERS IN CRIME BOOKS IN PRINT
SKYLARK
The Smith (subsidiary of The Generalist Assn., Inc.)

SONGS OF INNOCENCE
Soul
SOUTH DAKOTA REVIEW
Southeast Missouri State University Press
Southern Methodist University Press
SP QUILL QUARTERLY MAGAZINE
Spectrum Press
The Spirit That Moves Us Press, Inc.
StarLance Publications
THE STINGING FLY
Stormline Press, Inc.
THE STRANGE FRUIT
STRUGGLE: A Magazine of Proletarian Revolutionary
   Literature
STUDIO ONE
SULPHUR RIVER LITERARY REVIEW
SunShine Press Publications, Inc.
SWEET ANNIE & SWEET PEA REVIEW
Sweet Annie Press
SWINK
SYCAMORE REVIEW
Synergy Press
TAPROOT LITERARY REVIEW
Taproot Press Publishing Co.
THE TARPEIAN ROCK
The Teitan Press, Inc.
THIRD COAST
13TH MOON
Thunder Rain Publishing Corp.
Tupelo Press
Turnstone Press
Underwhich Editions
UPSTAIRS AT DUROC
Urban Legend Press
THE URBANITE
Vehicule Press
VERSAL
THE VIRGINIA QUARTERLY REVIEW
WEBER STUDIES: Voices and Viewpoints of the
   Contemporary West
which press
White Pine Press
Wildflower Press
Wise Press
WordFarm
WORDS OF WISDOM
Writers' Haven Press
WRITING FOR OUR LIVES
XAVIER REVIEW
X-Ray Book Co.
Zerx Press
ZUZU'S PETALS: QUARTERLY ONLINE

SINGLES

Affirmative Publishing LC
Aspicomm Media
AuthorsOmniscient Publishers
Down There Press
Jireh Publishing Company
JPS Publishing Company
Nunciata
Penthe Publishing
SHORTRUNS
SKINNYDIPPING
SO YOUNG!
Solcat Publishing
Steel Balls Press

SOCIAL MOVEMENTS

MOUTH: Voice of the Dis-Labeled Nation

SOCIAL SECURITY

CURRENTS: New Scholarship in the Human Services
The Foundation for Economic Education, Inc.
THINKERMONKEY
Vestibular Disorders Association

SOCIAL WORK

The Chinese University Press
CURRENTS: New Scholarship in the Human Services
The Haworth Press
INTERCULTURE
Islewest Publishing
JOURNAL OF CHILD AND YOUTH CARE
JOURNAL OF PSYCHOACTIVE DRUGS
Lyceum Books, Inc.
MGW (Mom Guess What) Newsmagazine
OPEN MINDS QUARTERLY
Passion Power Press, Inc
The Press at Foggy Bottom
THE SOCIOLOGICAL QUARTERLY
Studio 4 Productions
SYMBOLIC INTERACTION
VanderWyk & Burnham

SOCIALIST

AIM MAGAZINE
Between The Lines
BLUE COLLAR REVIEW
Children Of Mary
Clarity Press, Inc.
Dufour Editions Inc.
Elderberry Press, LLC
FIDELIS ET VERUS
Global Options
International Publishers Co. Inc.
JEWISH CURRENTS
JOURNAL OF NARRATIVE THEORY
LEFT CURVE
Maisonneuve Press
Mehring Books, Inc.
Missing Spoke Press
THE NEO-COMINTERN
NEW UNIONIST
Partisan Press
Pathfinder Press
PEMMICAN
Quale Press
Red Hand Press
Red Letter Press
SCIENCE & SOCIETY
Smyrna Press
SOCIAL JUSTICE: A JOURNAL OF CRIME, CONFLICT,
   & WORLD ORDER
South End Press
STRUGGLE: A Magazine of Proletarian Revolutionary
   Literature
SUB-TERRAIN
West End Press

SOCIETY

ADOLESCENCE
ATLANTIS: A Women's Studies Journal/Revue d'etudes
   sur les femmes
AZTLAN: A Journal of Chicano Studies
Back House Books
Between The Lines
BLUE COLLAR REVIEW
BORDERLANDS: Texas Poetry Review
Borealis Press Limited
Chelsea Green Publishing Company
Community Service, Inc.
Crandall, Dostie & Douglass Books, Inc.
DRAMA GARDEN
The Edwin Mellen Press
Epoch Press
ETC Publications
FAMILY THERAPY
FOURTH WORLD REVIEW
THE FRANK REVIEW
Frontline Publications
GLB Publishers
Global Options
The Heather Foundation

The Institute of Mind and Behavior
INTERCULTURE
THE JOURNAL OF MIND AND BEHAVIOR
Kettering Foundation Press
KETTERING REVIEW
LAKE STREET LIT: Art and Words from the Bottom of
Lake Bonneville
LIBERTY
Libra Publishers, Inc.
Life Media
LOGIC LETTER
THE LONG TERM VIEW: A Journal of Informed Opinion
MEDICAL HISTORY
THE MIDWEST QUARTERLY
New Creature Press
NEW SOLUTIONS
NIGHTLIFE MAGAZINE
Partisan Press
The People's Press
The Pin Prick Press
Ragged Edge Press
Red Alder Books
Savant Garde Workshop
SCANDINAVIAN REVIEW
SHARE INTERNATIONAL
SOCIAL JUSTICE: A JOURNAL OF CRIME, CONFLICT,
& WORLD ORDER
SOCIAL POLICY
SOCIAL PROBLEMS
Southwest Research and Information Center
SPEAKEASY
Spiritual Understanding Network, LLC
Tendre Press
THINKERMONKEY
THOUGHTS FOR ALL SEASONS: The Magazine of
Epigrams
Thundercloud Books
UBC Press
UCLA Chicano Studies Research Center Press
UTNE READER
Volcano Press, Inc
THE VORTEX
THE WASHINGTON MONTHLY
Wellcome Institute for the History of Medicine

SOCIOLOGY

African American Images
AIM MAGAZINE
Aletheia Publications, Inc.
Appalachian Consortium Press
THE ART OF ABUNDANCE
Bad Press
Black Rose Books Ltd.
Broken Rifle Press
Canadian Educators' Press
CANADIAN REVIEW OF AMERICAN STUDIES
Carrier Pigeon Press
Chandler & Sharp Publishers, Inc.
CINEASTE MAGAZINE
COLORLINES
Community Service, Inc.
The Compass Press
CONTEMPORARY WALES
CONTEXTS: UNDERSTANDING PEOPLE IN THEIR
SOCIAL WORLDS
CRIMINAL JUSTICE ABSTRACTS
Criminal Justice Press
CRITICAL REVIEW
DeerTrail Books
dreamslaughter
ESPERANTIC STUDIES
FEMINIST STUDIES
Frontline Publications
Gain Publications
Gallaudet University Press
Global Options
GRAY AREAS
Haight-Ashbury Publications

The Heather Foundation
HONG KONG JOURNAL OF SOCIOLOGY
IDM Press
The Institute of Mind and Behavior
INTERCULTURE
Interlink Publishing Group, Inc.
ITALIAN AMERICANA
THE JOURNAL OF MIND AND BEHAVIOR
JOURNAL OF PSYCHOACTIVE DRUGS
KAIROS, A Journal of Contemporary Thought and
Criticism
KETTERING REVIEW
Kumarian Press, Inc.
LO STRANIERO: The Stranger, Der Fremde, L'Etranger
The Love and Logic Press, Inc.
MOUTH: Voice of the Dis-Labeled Nation
THE NEW ENGLAND QUARTERLY
NEW SOLUTIONS
North Star Books
NOVA RELIGIO
Open Court Publishing Company
OPEN MINDS QUARTERLY
Pleasure Boat Studio: A Literary Press
Plympton Press International
Royal Purcell, Publisher
R & M Publishing Company
Raven's Eye Press, Inc.
RELIGION & AMERICAN CULTURE
SCIENCE AND TECHNOLOGY
SKINNYDIPPING
SOCIAL JUSTICE: A JOURNAL OF CRIME, CONFLICT,
& WORLD ORDER
SOCIAL POLICY
SOCIAL PROBLEMS
SOCIOLOGICAL PERSPECTIVES
THE SOCIOLOGICAL QUARTERLY
State University of New York Press
Superior Christian Press
SYMBOLIC INTERACTION
Univelt, Inc.
Willow Tree Press, Inc.
WSQ (formerly WOMEN'S STUDIES QUARTERLY)
ZONE
ZUZU'S PETALS: QUARTERLY ONLINE

SOLAR

The Film Instruction Company of America
Life Media
Lorien House
Macrocosm USA, Inc.
NATURAL LIFE

SOUTH

Anvil Publishers, Inc.
Appalachian Consortium Press
APPLE VALLEY REVIEW: A Journal of Contemporary
Literature
BIG MUDDY: Journal of the Mississippi River Valley
John F. Blair, Publisher
Bright Mountain Books, Inc.
Cherokee Publishing Company
Harbor House
Margaret Media, Inc.
Midmarch Arts Press
Ninety-Six Press
Old Sport Publishing Company
The Overmountain Press
PIKEVILLE REVIEW
REFLECTIONS LITERARY JOURNAL
Rose Publishing Co.
THE SOUTHERN QUARTERLY: A Journal of the Arts in
the South
Sherwood Sugden & Company, Publishers
TRADITION MAGAZINE
University of Arkansas Press
XAVIER REVIEW
Zebra Press

SOUTH AMERICA

FIREBREEZE PUBLISHING
Hope Publishing House
Inner City Press
Montemayor Press
ON PARAGUAY
University Press of Colorado

SOUTH CAROLINA

Harbor House
Iris Publishing Group, Inc (Iris Press / Tellico Books)
Premium Press America
Rock Spring Press Inc.
University of South Carolina Press

SOUTHWEST

Amador Publishers
Ancient City Press
APPLE VALLEY REVIEW: A Journal of Contemporary
    Literature
Balcony Media, Inc.
Ballena Press
BOOKS OF THE SOUTHWEST
BORDERLANDS: Texas Poetry Review
CONCHO RIVER REVIEW
Duende Press
FISH DRUM MAGAZINE
Fretwater Press
Gallery West Associates
Gibbs Smith, Publisher
Hill Country Books
Kiva Publishing, Inc.
KUMQUAT MERINGUE
La Alameda Press
LPD Press
Mountain Media
Naturegraph Publishers
Pruett Publishing Company
Rio Nuevo Publishers
Santa Fe Writers Project
SOUTH DAKOTA REVIEW
Southern Methodist University Press
Southwest Research and Information Center
Sunstone Press
TRADICION REVISTA
Two Eagles Press International
University of Utah Press
VOICES FROM THE EARTH
WEBER STUDIES: Voices and Viewpoints of the
    Contemporary West
WESTERN AMERICAN LITERATURE

SPACE

AAS HISTORY SERIES
ADVANCES IN THE ASTRONAUTICAL SCIENCES
EcceNova Editions
Mystic Toad Press
ODYSSEY: Adventures in Science
RedJack
SCIENCE AND TECHNOLOGY
THE STAR BEACON
Windward Publishing, An Imprint of Finney Company

SPAIN

ABSINTHE: New European Writing
Department of Romance Languages
INTERNATIONAL POETRY REVIEW
Latin American Literary Review Press
PERIPHERAL VISION
SYMPOSIUM
TORRE DE PAPEL

SPEAKING

Blueprint Books
Book Marketing Solutions
Crane Press
Family Learning Association, Inc.

Finney Company, Inc.
Foundation Books
HandyCraft Media Productions
Multi-Media Publications Inc.
Music City Publishing
74th Street Productions, L.L.C.
Strata Publishing, Inc.
Wheatmark Book Publishing
WOMEN AND LANGUAGE
World Gumbo Publishing

SPIRITUAL

ABRAMELIN: a Journal of Poetry and Magick
Affirmative Publishing LC
Alamo Square Press
Altair Publications
America West Publishers
Amethyst & Emerald
THE ART OF ABUNDANCE
Ascension Publishing
ASCENT
Ash Tree Publishing
Athanor Books (a division of ETX Seminars)
Auromere Books and Imports
Authors of Unity Publishing
Azreal Publishing Company
Balanced Books Publishing
BALLISTA
Barney Press
Barrytown/Station Hill Press
BEGINNINGS - A Magazine for the Novice Writer
Beyond Words Publishing, Inc.
Birth Day Publishing Company
Black Diamond Book Publishing
Black Pearl Enterprises LLC
Blue Dove Press
BOTH SIDES NOW
Brason-Sargar Publications
BRILLIANT STAR
Brunswick Publishing Corporation
Cassandra Press, Inc.
Children Of Mary
CHRISTIAN*NEW AGE QUARTERLY
CIRCLE INC., THE MAGAZINE
Circle of Friends Books
Clearwater Publishing Co.
COLOR WHEEL
Common Boundaries
Crones Unlimited
Crystal Clarity, Publishers
DAILY WORD
Delaney Day Press
Devi Press, Inc.
Dharma Publishing
DOVETAIL: A Journal by and for Jewish/Christian
    Families
DREAM FANTASY INTERNATIONAL
Dream Street Publishing
dreamslaughter
Dumouriez Publishing
Earth Star Publications
EMERGING
Enlighten Next
Fontanel Books
FORESIGHT MAGAZINE
Four Seasons Publishers
FRIENDS OF PEACE PILGRIM
Friends United Press
Galde Press, Inc.
Gateways Books And Tapes
Gloger Family Books
Golden Isis Press
Good Book Publishing Company
Guarionex Press Ltd.
Harbor House
Harlan Publishing Company; Alliance Books; Diakonia
    Publishing (Christian Books)
Heartland Publishing

Heartsong Books
HEAVEN BONE MAGAZINE
Heaven Bone Press
Higher Ground Press
Himalayan Institute Press
Ho Logos Press
Holmes House
HOLY ROLLERS
Hope Publishing House
Iconoclast Press
IMAGE: ART, FAITH, MYSTERY
In Print Publishing
THE INDENTED PILLOW
THE INDIE
Innisfree Press
J. Mark Press
KABBALAH
The Kenneth G. Mills Foundation
KEREM: Creative Explorations in Judaism
Kivaki Press
Lamp Light Press
The Leaping Frog Press
Lemieux International Ltd.
LEO Productions LLC.
Life Energy Media
Light, Words & Music
LightLines Publishing
LITURGICAL CATECHESIS
LP Publications (Teleos Institute)
MAGICAL BLEND/NATURAL BEAUTY & HEALTH/
  TRANSITIONS
MB Media, Inc.
MEDIA SPOTLIGHT
A Melody from an Immigrant's Soul
The Midknight Club
MINISTRY & LITURGY
Missing Man Press
Monkfish Book Publishing Company
Morgen Publishing Incorporated
Mucusart Publications
Munsey Music
My Heart Yours Publishing
New Atlantean Press
New Native Press
New Paradigm Books
NEW THOUGHT
New Vision Publishing
New World Library
NEWWITCH
Nicolas-Hays, Inc.
NOLA-MAGICK Press
Origin Press
OUT OF LINE
PARABOLA MAGAZINE
Paragon House Publishers
Pellingham Casper Communications
PhoeniX in Print
Platinum Dreams Publishing
Plus Publications
POETICA MAGAZINE, Reflections of Jewish Thought
PREP Publishing
PublishAmerica, LLLP.
THE QUEST
Quest Books: Theosophical Publishing House
Resource Publications, Inc.
RFD
Sacred Spaces Press
SAGEWOMAN
Saint Mary's Press
SAT SANDESH: THE MESSAGE OF THE MASTERS
SCP JOURNAL
SelectiveHouse Publishers, Inc.
Sentient Publications, LLC
Seven Arrows Publishing, Inc.
SHAMAN'S DRUM: A Journal of Experiential Shamanism
SHARE INTERNATIONAL
Sibyl Publications, Inc
SKS Press

SO YOUNG!
SOCIETE
SOM Publishing, division of School of Metaphysics
Soul
Spirit Press
Spirit, Nature and You
SPIRITCHASER
Spiritual Understanding Network, LLC
THE STAR BEACON
Stewart Publishing & Printing
SunShine Press Publications, Inc.
Swan Raven & Company
Swedenborg Foundation
Synergy Press
TAI CHI
Tendre Press
Three Pyramids Publishing
THRESHOLDS JOURNAL
TIFARA
Timeless Books
Titan Press
Titlewaves Publishing; Writers Direct
TURNING WHEEL
Tyr Publishing
Ulysses Books
Unity House
UNITY MAGAZINE
Universal Unity
UnKnownTruths.com Publishing Company
Visions Communications
Wayfarer Publications
WHAT IS ENLIGHTENMENT?
White Buck Publishing
White Thread Press
Whitford Press
Wilderness Ministries
Wisdom Publications, Inc.
THE WISE WOMAN
XTANT
xtant.anabasis
Yes International Publishers
YMAA Publication Center
Zumaya Publications

SPORTS, OUTDOORS

ADIRONDAC
Adirondack Mountain Club, Inc.
Alaska Geographic Society
AMERICAN HIKER
American Hiking Society
Anchor Cove Publishing, Inc.
APPALACHIA JOURNAL
Appalachian Mountain Club Books
Apples & Oranges, Inc.
Avery Color Studios
Avery Color Studios
Backcountry Publishing
Birch Brook Press
Black Dome Press Corp.
John F. Blair, Publisher
Bliss Publishing Company, Inc.
Bonus Books, Inc.
Brunswick Publishing Corporation
CATAMARAN SAILOR
Cave Books
Celo Valley Books
The Center Press
Chicago Review Press
CineCycle Publishing
Clearwater Publishing Co.
THE CLIMBING ART
Coastal 181
CURL MAGAZINE
dbS Productions
DISC GOLF WORLD
Dixon-Price Publishing
Dunamis House
DWELLING PORTABLY

Ecopress, An Imprint of Finney Company
ETC Publications
Fast Foot Forward Press
FERRY TRAVEL GUIDE
Nicolin Fields Publishing, Inc.
Fine Edge Productions
Flying Pencil Publications
Front Row Experience
Fulcrum, Inc.
The Glencannon Press
Global Sports Productions, Ltd.
Grand Slam Press, Inc.
The Great Rift Press
HANG GLIDING
Heyday Books
Hill Country Books
Iconoclast Press
Info Net Publishing
JOURNAL OF ASIAN MARTIAL ARTS
Keokee Co. Publishing, Inc.
Laureate Press
Liberty Publishing Company, Inc.
THE LISTENING EYE
McBooks Press, Inc.
Menasha Ridge Press
MGW (Mom Guess What) Newsmagazine
Mission Press
Mountain Press Publishing Co.
The Mountaineers Books
NATIONAL MASTERS NEWS
New England Cartographics, Inc.
New Win Publishing
Northern Publishing
Old Sport Publishing Company
OUT YOUR BACKDOOR: The Magazine of Do-It-Yourself Adventure and Homegrown Culture
Paladin Enterprises, Inc.
Para Publishing
Pavement Saw Press
Peartree Books & Music
Penthe Publishing
Perpetual Press
Pocol Press
Premium Press America
Pruett Publishing Company
Quality Sports Publications
Ram Press
Running Press
Sagamore Publishing
SANDPOINT MAGAZINE
SEA KAYAKER
Set Sail Productions, LLC
Sierra Outdoor Products Co.
SKINNYDIPPING
SKYDIVING
Genny Smith Books
Solcat Publishing
Southern Methodist University Press
SPECIALTY TRAVEL INDEX
SPITBALL: The Literary Baseball Magazine
Summerset Press
Sunbelt Publications
Synergistic Press
Tamal Vista Publications
TIFARA
Tortuga Books
Tres Picos Press
Two Thousand Three Associates
Two Thousand Three Associates
University of Virginia Press
Visions Communications
John Wade, Publisher
WASHINGTON TRAILS
Wayfinder Press
Whitford Press
Whitston Publishing Co.
Whole Person Associates Inc.
Wilderness Adventure Books

Wilderness Press
WISCONSIN TRAILS
Wish Publishing
Wood River Publishing
Wood Thrush Books
YMAA Publication Center
Zagier & Urruty Publicaciones

STORYTELLING

Aardvark Enterprises (A Division of Speers Investments Ltd.)
THE ACORN
Alaska Native Language Center
Ammons Communications
ARTELLA: the waltz of words and art
Caribbean Books-Panama
CHECKER CAB MAGAZINE - THE LITTLE 'ZINE THAT COULD! Fiction That Takes The Long Way Home
Country Messenger Press
Empire Publishing Service
Falcon Publishing, LTD
Foundation Books
Highsmith Press
Innisfree Press
JUNIOR STORYTELLER
KARAWANE
THE KIDS' STORYTELLING CLUB WEBSITE
LAKE STREET LIT: Art and Words from the Bottom of Lake Bonneville
LONG SHOT
Malki Museum Press
Music City Publishing
THE NEW FORMALIST
Panther Books
PAPERPLATES
Perrin Press
The Press at Foggy Bottom
Radiant Press
RAINBOW CURVE
THE RAVEN CHRONICLES
RIVER TEETH: A Journal of Nonfiction Narrative
ROCTOBER COMICS AND MUSIC
Sagamore Publishing
Savor Publishing House, Inc.
Starcherone Books
Stormline Press, Inc.
Storycraft Publishing
Storytime Ink International
TAPROOT LITERARY REVIEW
THE2NDHAND
Titus Home Publishing
Twynz Publishing
Yellow Moon Press

SUFISM

Blue Dove Press
CONTEMPORARY GHAZALS
IBEX Publishers, Inc.
THE MONTHLY INDEPENDENT TRIBUNE TIMES JOURNAL POST GAZETTE NEWS CHRONICLE BULLETIN
New Paradigm Books
Spirit Press
Tree of Life Books. Imprints: Progressive Press, Banned Books
White Thread Press
XTANT

SUPERNATURAL

Affirmative Publishing LC
Authors of Unity Publishing
BALLISTA
BEGINNINGS - A Magazine for the Novice Writer
Black Diamond Book Publishing
EcceNova Editions
The Fiction Works
Foundation Books

Galde Press, Inc.
GOLDEN ISIS MAGAZINE
Golden Isis Press
Harbor House
Harlan Publishing Company; Alliance Books; Diakonia Publishing (Christian Books)
Harvest Shadows Publications
Lake Claremont Press
LOW BUDGET SCIENCE FICTION
LULLABY HEARSE
Medusa Press
The Midknight Club
THE MONTHLY INDEPENDENT TRIBUNE TIMES JOURNAL POST GAZETTE NEWS CHRONICLE BULLETIN
Mucusart Publications
MYSTERY ISLAND MAGAZINE
NEWWITCH
North Country Books, Inc.
RavenHaus Publishing
ROCKY MOUNTAIN KC NEWS
Rocky Mountain KC Publishing Co.
THE SILVER WEB
Three Pyramids Publishing
Toad Hall, Inc.
Triskelion Publishing
UglyTown
UnKnownTruths.com Publishing Company
Westgate Press
Whiskey Creek Press
ZAHIR, Unforgettable Tales

SURREALISM

AK Press
Androgyne Books
Arjuna Library Press
Asylum Arts
BIG HAMMER
Biographical Publishing Company
BITTER OLEANDER
BUST DOWN THE DOOR AND EAT ALL THE CHICKENS: A Journal of Absurd and Surreal Fiction
GRASSLIMB
JOURNAL OF REGIONAL CRITICISM
Leaping Dog Press / Asylum Arts Press
Lunar Offensive Publications
Marymark Press
THE MONTHLY INDEPENDENT TRIBUNE TIMES JOURNAL POST GAZETTE NEWS CHRONICLE BULLETIN
New Native Press
O!!Zone
O!!ZONE, A LITERARY-ART ZINE
Panther Books
PASSAGES NORTH
PAVEMENT SAW
Pavement Saw Press
PEMMICAN
Phrygian Press
PLOPLOP
PORTLAND REVIEW
PRESA
Quale Press
Ridgeway Press of Michigan
Sage Hill Press
SAKANA
THE SILVER WEB
A SOFT DEGRADE
Starcherone Books
Transcending Mundane, Inc.
Twisted Spoon Press
Typographia Press
UNDERSTANDING MAGAZINE
UNWOUND
Urban Legend Press
THE URBANITE
Westgate Press
Xenos Books

XTANT
ZAHIR, Unforgettable Tales
ZYX

T'AI CHI

Abecedarian books, Inc.
JOURNAL OF ASIAN MARTIAL ARTS
MAGICAL BLEND/NATURAL BEAUTY & HEALTH/ TRANSITIONS
PERIPHERAL VISION
SevenStar Communications
Syukhtun Editions
THE2NDHAND
Venus Communications
Via Media Publishing Company
YMAA Publication Center
Yo San Books

TAPES & RECORDS

Affinity Publishers Services
Barrytown/Station Hill Press
BIG HAMMER
Black Forest Press
Center For Self-Sufficiency
CREEPY MIKE'S OMNIBUS OF FUN
Cynic Press
DIRTY LINEN
Duende Press
Feel Free Press
FISH DRUM MAGAZINE
Global Options
GRAY AREAS
Impact Publishers, Inc.
In Print Publishing
Ion Imagination Publishing, Ion Imagination Entertainment, Inc.
JAM RAG
Light, Words & Music
Lummox Press
MOBILE BEAT: The DJ Magazine
NEW HOPE INTERNATIONAL REVIEW
New World Library
nine muses books
North Country Books, Inc.
Norton Coker Press
PAST TIMES: The Nostalgia Entertainment Newsletter
Piano Press
PLANTAGENET PRODUCTIONS, Libraries of Spoken Word Recordings and of Stagescripts
PULSAR POETRY MAGAZINE
Pygmy Forest Press
Quiet Tymes, Inc.
Resource Publications, Inc.
SHEMP! The Lowlife Culture Magazine
SHORTRUNS
SO YOUNG!
Timeless Books
UMBRELLA Online
Underwhich Editions
Volcano Press, Inc
World Music Press
X-Ray Book Co.
Yellow Moon Press
ZINE-ON-A-TAPE

TAROT

Carpe Diem Publishing
GOLDEN ISIS MAGAZINE
Golden Isis Press
MB Media, Inc.
A Melody from an Immigrant's Soul
NEWWITCH
SAGEWOMAN
Three Pyramids Publishing
White Crosslet Publishing Co
Zumaya Publications

TAXES

CANADIAN MONEYSAVER
Claitor's Law Books & Publishing Division, Inc.
Costa Rica Books
Long & Silverman Publishing, Inc.
PSI Research/The Oasis Press/Hellgate Press
Set Sail Productions, LLC
Tax Property Investor, Inc.
THE2NDHAND
TRUTH SEEKER
Upper Access Inc.

TECHNOLOGY

AB
Adams-Blake Publishing
Aegean Publishing Company
Americans for the Arts
Brenner Information Group
Frontline Publications
GREEN ANARCHY
Hobar Publications, A Division of Finney Company
HOME POWER
Mission Press
Open University of America Press
Piano Press
Prakken Publications
Rada Press, Inc.
Snake Hill Press
UnKnownTruths.com Publishing Company

TELEVISION

BOOK MARKETING UPDATE
CineCycle Publishing
Creative Writing and Publishing Company
CREEPY MIKE'S OMNIBUS OF FUN
DAVID McCALLUM UPDATES
Explorer Press
Film-Video Publications/Circus Source Publications
THE FREEDONIA GAZETTE: The Magazine Devoted to
    the Marx Brothers
HEROES FROM HACKLAND
Hollywood Creative Directory
THE PUBLICITY HOUND
RedJack
ROCTOBER COMICS AND MUSIC
ST. LOUIS JOURNALISM REVIEW
Whelks Walk Press

TENNESSEE

Crane Press
Inner City Press
Iris Publishing Group, Inc (Iris Press / Tellico Books)
Land Yacht Press
Premium Press America
UNDERSTANDING MAGAZINE
Xavier House Publishing

TEXAS

BORDERLANDS: Texas Poetry Review
BRAZOS GUMBO
CONCHO RIVER REVIEW
HILL COUNTRY SUN
Historical Resources Press
IRON HORSE LITERARY REVIEW
Lazywood Press
LPD Press
Midmarch Arts Press
Nolo Press Occidental
Panther Creek Press
Premium Press America
Shearer Publishing
Southern Methodist University Press
Texas Tech University Press
TRADICION REVISTA
Two Eagles Press International
Van Cleave Publishing
WESTERN AMERICAN LITERATURE

Wings Press

TEXTBOOKS

Adams-Blake Publishing
Ariko Publications
Avocus Publishing, Inc.
Black Forest Press
Bonus Books, Inc.
Book Marketing Solutions
Brookline Books
Canadian Educators' Press
Canadian Educators' Press
Chandler & Sharp Publishers, Inc.
Chicago Spectrum Press
Children Of Mary
Claitor's Law Books & Publishing Division, Inc.
Clearwater Publishing Co.
Communicom Publishing Company
Crystal Publishers, Inc.
Fathom Publishing Co.
The Fiction Works
FIDELIS ET VERUS
Focus Publishing/R. Pullins Co.
Front Row Experience
Galen Press, Ltd.
Gallaudet University Press
Genesis Publishing Company, Inc.
Gibbs Smith, Publisher
Gival Press
Green Hut Press
The Haworth Press
Herrmann International
IDM Press
Jamenair Ltd.
Journal of Pyrotechnics
Lamp Light Press
Little Leaf Press
LrnIT Publishing Div. ICFL, Inc.
Microdex Bookshelf
Nunciata
THE ORPHAN LEAF REVIEW
Orpheus Press
Paragon House Publishers
Philopsychy Press
Pine Publications
Prakken Publications
Princeton Book Company, Publishers
Read Press LLC
RFF Press / Resources for the Future
Saint Mary's Press
The Saunderstown Press
Scentouri, Publishing Division
Stewart Publishing & Printing
Sherwood Sugden & Company, Publishers
Visions Communications

TEXTILES

DOLLS UNITED INTERACTIVE MAGAZINE
Mount Ida Press
NEW HOPE INTERNATIONAL REVIEW
ORNAMENT
Texas Tech University Press
TRADICION REVISTA

THEATRE

A & U AMERICA'S AIDS MAGAZINE
Acting World Books
AFRICAN AMERICAN REVIEW
THE AGENCIES-WHAT THE ACTOR NEEDS TO
    KNOW
Americans for the Arts
ANQ: A Quarterly Journal of Short Articles, Notes, and
    Reviews
Athanata Arts, Ltd.
Walter H. Baker Company (Baker's Plays)
BOMB MAGAZINE
Bordighera, Inc.
CALLBOARD

750

Cantarabooks LLC
Center for Japanese Studies
Cervena Barva Press
Creative Writing and Publishing Company
THE DALHOUSIE REVIEW
THE DRAMATIST
Empire Publishing Service
THE EUGENE O'NEILL REVIEW
Fall Creek Press
THE FREEDONIA GAZETTE: The Magazine Devoted to the Marx Brothers
HAWAI'I REVIEW
THE HOLLYWOOD ACTING COACHES AND TEACHERS DIRECTORY
Hollywood Creative Directory
HOME PLANET NEWS
IMAGE: ART, FAITH, MYSTERY
IRISH LITERARY SUPPLEMENT
Labor Arts Books
LEO Productions LLC.
Limelight Editions
Magic Circle Press
MARQUEE
MEDIA SPOTLIGHT
New Concept Press
THE NEW RENAISSANCE, an international magazine of ideas & opinions, emphasizing literature & the arts
Northwestern University Press
Open Hand Publishing LLC
Passeggiata Press, Inc.
PAST TIMES: The Nostalgia Entertainment Newsletter
Players Press, Inc.
Pogo Press, Incorporated
THE PRAIRIE JOURNAL OF CANADIAN LITERATURE
Preludium Publishers
The Press at Foggy Bottom
Questex Consulting Ltd.
Resource Publications, Inc.
Santa Monica Press
Sentient Publications, LLC
74th Street Productions, L.L.C.
74th Street Productions, L.L.C.
THE SHAKESPEARE NEWSLETTER
THE SOUTHERN QUARTERLY: A Journal of the Arts in the South
SOUTHWEST COLORADO ARTS PERSPECTIVE
Spinifex Press
SUB-TERRAIN
THEATER
THEATRE DESIGN AND TECHNOLOGY
THE THREEPENNY REVIEW
Tomart Publications
University of Tampa Press
WordWorkers Press

THEOSOPHICAL

Altair Publications
EcceNova Editions
Ho Logos Press
Luminous Epinoia Press
Lycanthrope Press
MAGICAL BLEND/NATURAL BEAUTY & HEALTH/ TRANSITIONS
New Paradigm Books
NOLA-MAGICK Press
POETICA MAGAZINE, Reflections of Jewish Thought
THE QUEST
Quest Books: Theosophical Publishing House
Spirit Press
Spiritual Understanding Network, LLC
The Teitan Press, Inc.
Universal Unity
WHAT IS ENLIGHTENMENT?
White Buck Publishing

THIRD WORLD, MINORITIES

Aunt Lute Books
Back House Books

Between The Lines
Book Faith India
BORDERLANDS: Texas Poetry Review
Bordighera, Inc.
BRILLIANT STAR
Broken Rifle Press
Children's Book Press
Clarity Press, Inc.
COLLEGE LITERATURE
The Feminist Press at the City University of New York
Florida Academic Press
FOURTH WORLD REVIEW
FROZEN WAFFLES
Frozen Waffles Press/Shattered Sidewalks Press; 45th Century Chapbooks
Gay Sunshine Press, Inc.
Global Options
Goldfish Press
Heyday Books
INDIA CURRENTS
INTERCULTURE
INTERLIT
Kumarian Press, Inc.
LEFT CURVE
Lotus Press, Inc.
Mehring Books, Inc.
OBSIDIAN III: Literature in the African Diaspora
OFF OUR BACKS
THE OTHER ISRAEL
Panther Creek Press
Path Press, Inc.
Pathfinder Press
Pilgrims Book House
The Place In The Woods
Pocahontas Press, Inc.
Red Letter Press
RHINO: THE POETRY FORUM
Ridge Times Press
Sagamore Publishing
Saqi Books Publisher
SHARE INTERNATIONAL
SHENANDOAH NEWSLETTER
Smyrna Press
SOCIAL JUSTICE: A JOURNAL OF CRIME, CONFLICT, & WORLD ORDER
STRUGGLE: A Magazine of Proletarian Revolutionary Literature
TRANSITIONS ABROAD: The Guide to Living, Learning, and Working Overseas
TURNING THE TIDE: Journal of Anti-Racist Action, Research & Education
White Cliffs Media, Inc.
WORD IS BOND
WSQ (formerly WOMEN'S STUDIES QUARTERLY)

DYLAN THOMAS

Missing Spoke Press
THE NEW FORMALIST

H.D. THOREAU

THE AMERICAN DISSIDENT
THE CLIMBING ART
CONCRETE JUNGLE JOURNAL

J.R.R. TOLKIEN

Avari Press
Carnifex Press
Idylls Press
Tyr Publishing
W.W. Publications

TRADE

Gallaudet University Press
Jireh Publishing Company
PSI Research/The Oasis Press/Hellgate Press
Search Institute
University of Arkansas Press
University of Utah Press

Zelda Wilde Publishing
Windward Publishing, An Imprint of Finney Company

TRANSLATION

ABRAXAS
ABSINTHE: New European Writing
THE ADIRONDACK REVIEW
AGNI
Alcatraz Editions
Ariko Publications
The Ark
ARTFUL DODGE
ARTS & LETTERS: Journal of Contemporary Culture
Ash Tree Publishing
Asylum Arts
AuthorsOmniscient Publishers
BASALT
BIRD DOG
Birdalone Books
Black Lawrence Press
BOA Editions, Ltd.
BUCKLE &
THE CAPILANO REVIEW
Cedar Hill Books
Center for Japanese Studies
CHARITON REVIEW
CHELSEA
The Chinese University Press
Clamshell Press
CONNECTICUT REVIEW
Copper Beech Press
COTTONWOOD
Cottonwood Press
CRAB CREEK REVIEW
THE CREAM CITY REVIEW
Cross-Cultural Communications
Cynic Press
DWAN
The Edwin Mellen Press
Erespin Press
Eros Books
EVANSVILLE REVIEW
FIELD: Contemporary Poetry and Poetics
FINE MADNESS
Five Fingers Press
FIVE FINGERS REVIEW
Focus Publishing/R. Pullins Co.
FOLIO: A Literary Journal of American University
Fouque Publishers
FRANK: AN INTERNATIONAL JOURNAL OF CON-
TEMPORARY WRITING AND ART
FROZEN WAFFLES
Frozen Waffles Press/Shattered Sidewalks Press; 45th
Century Chapbooks
Gay Sunshine Press, Inc.
Goats & Compasses
GULF COAST
Haunted Rowboat Press
HAWAI'I REVIEW
IAMBS & TROCHEES
ILLUMINATIONS
Impassio Press
INTERLIT
INTERNATIONAL POETRY REVIEW
Italica Press, Inc.
JAMES JOYCE BROADSHEET
THE KENYON REVIEW
KESTREL: A Journal of Literature and Art
KOJA
Leaping Dog Press / Asylum Arts Press
Leete's Island Books
LIFTOUTS
LILLIPUT REVIEW
LITERARY IMAGINATION: The Review of the Associa-
tion of Literary Scholars and Critics
Longhouse
MANDORLA: New Writing from the Americas / Nueva
escritura de las Americas

MANOA: A Pacific Journal of International Writing
THE MARLBORO REVIEW
MATCHBOOK
Mayapple Press
Mellen Poetry Press
Menard Press
MID-AMERICAN REVIEW
Moon Pie Press
MUDLARK
NATURAL BRIDGE
NEW AMERICAN IMAGIST
NEW AMERICAN WRITING
NEW HOPE INTERNATIONAL REVIEW
THE NEW RENAISSANCE, an international magazine of
ideas & opinions, emphasizing literature & the arts
New Rivers Press, Inc.
Norton Coker Press
Oberlin College Press
ORBIS
The Pamphleteer's Press
PASSAGER
PENNINE PLATFORM
Pleasure Boat Studio: A Literary Press
POETRY EAST
THE POETRY MISCELLANY
POINT OF CONTACT, The Journal of Verbal & Visual
Arts
Preludium Publishers
PRISM INTERNATIONAL
Pygmy Forest Press
QRL POETRY SERIES
THE RAVEN CHRONICLES
Red Dust
RENDITIONS
Research Centre for Translation, Chinese University of
Hong Kong
RHINO: THE POETRY FORUM
RIVER STYX
Sage Hill Press
SAKANA
SALAMANDER
SCANDINAVIAN REVIEW
SENECA REVIEW
SMARTISH PACE
SNOW MONKEY
SOJOURN: A Journal of the Arts
Solcat Publishing
THE STINGING FLY
Stone Bridge Press
STORYQUARTERLY
SUPERIOR CHRISTIAN NEWS
Tamal Vista Publications
Tameme
Telos Press
Toad Press International Chapbook Series
TORRE DE PAPEL
TOUCHSTONE LITERARY JOURNAL
TRANSLATION REVIEW
Tree of Life Books. Imprints: Progressive Press, Banned
Books
TURNROW
Twilight Times Books
Twisted Spoon Press
TWO LINES: A Journal of Translation
Tzipora Publications, Inc.
Universal Unity
University of Virginia Press
VALLUM: CONTEMPORARY POETRY
Vehicule Press
VISIONS-INTERNATIONAL, The World Journal of Illus-
trated Poetry
White Pine Press
WILLOW SPRINGS
The Word Works
Xenos Books
Yellow Moon Press
ZAWP
Zephyr Press

ZONE
ZONE 3

TRANSPORTATION

AB
Alaska Northwest Books
ALL ROUND
AMERICAN ROAD
Anacus Press, An Imprint of Finney Company
BLADES
John F. Blair, Publisher
Book Faith India
Brown Fox Books
Coastal 181
Comstock Bonanza Press
DWELLING PORTABLY
The Eighth Mountain Press
Elderberry Press, LLC
Fantail
FERRY TRAVEL GUIDE
The Glencannon Press
Golden West Books
Harvard Common Press
Heritage House Publishers
History Compass, LLC
Hot Box Press / Southern Roots Publishing
Italica Press, Inc.
THE JOURNAL OF AFRICAN TRAVEL-WRITING
Keokee Co. Publishing, Inc.
THE LAS VEGAS INSIDER
Lexikos
Lion Press
Mock Turtle Press
Mountain Automation Corporation
Mountain Press Publishing Co.
The Mountaineers Books
NORTHERN PILOT
The Olivia and Hill Press, Inc.
Paradise Publications
Passing Through Publications
Passport Press
Perpetual Press
Pilgrims Book House
The Pin Prick Press
Rayve Productions Inc.
Sasquatch Books
SPECIALTY TRAVEL INDEX
Stone Bridge Press
Synergistic Press
TIMBER TIMES
TRANSITIONS ABROAD: The Guide to Living, Learning,
    and Working Overseas
TRAVEL BOOKS WORLDWIDE
Travel Keys
The Urbana Free Library
Wide World Publishing/TETRA
World Travel Institute, Inc.

TRAVEL

AB
Adirondack Mountain Club, Inc.
all nations press
American & World Geographic Publishing
AMERICAN ROAD
Anacus Press, An Imprint of Finney Company
Anagnosis
Arbutus Press
Ash Lad Press
ASIA FILE
Beagle Bay Books
BEATLICK NEWS
Bellywater Press
The Bess Press
Blue Cubicle Press
Bright Mountain Books, Inc.
CALIFORNIA EXPLORER
Callawind Publications / Custom Cookbooks / Children's
    Books

The Center Press
Central Avenue Press
CHECKER CAB MAGAZINE - THE LITTLE 'ZINE
    THAT COULD! Fiction That Takes The Long Way
    Home
Clover Park Press
Costa Rica Books
Culturelink Press
Dimi Press
Dixon-Price Publishing
Dumouriez Publishing
Earthwinds Editions
ECOTONE: Reimagining Place
THE ENTERTAINMENT REVIEW OF THE SUSQUE-
    HANNA VALLEY
EXIT 13 MAGAZINE
Floreant Press
THE FLORIDA REVIEW
Follow Me! Guides
GERMAN LIFE
HILL COUNTRY SUN
Huntington Press
INKY TRAIL NEWS
Intercultural Press, Inc.
Interlink Publishing Group, Inc.
The Intrepid Traveler
THE JOURNAL OF AFRICAN TRAVEL-WRITING
Lake Claremont Press
LAKE SUPERIOR MAGAZINE
Lemieux International Ltd.
Lexicus Press
Liberty Publishing Company, Inc.
The Live Oak Press, LLC
Menasha Ridge Press
MINESHAFT
Mock Turtle Press
Moon Pie Press
Mountain Meadow Press
Museon Publishing
N: NUDE & NATURAL
The Narrative Press
NEO: Literary Magazine
NOLA-MAGICK Press
Northern Publishing
Nystrom Publishing Co.
THE OXFORD AMERICAN
Pangaea
Park Place Publications
Pendant Publishing Inc.
Pineapple Press, Inc.
Pogo Press, Incorporated
THE PRESIDENTS' JOURNAL
Princeton Book Company, Publishers
THE QUIET FEATHER
Russian Information Services
SANDPOINT MAGAZINE
Santa Ana River Press
Santa Monica Press
Sasquatch Books
SEA KAYAKER
SPECIALTY TRAVEL INDEX
Standish Press
Storm Publishing Group
Studio 4 Productions
Summerset Press
Sunbelt Publications
Thirsty Turtle Press
Thundercloud Books
Titlewaves Publishing; Writers Direct
Tortuga Books
TRAVEL NATURALLY
Turnstone Press
Two Thousand Three Associates
V52 Press
VACATION PLACE RENTALS
Western New York Wares, Inc.
Windward Publishing, An Imprint of Finney Company
WISCONSIN TRAILS

WORDS OF WISDOM
Zante Publishing

TREASURE

Foundation Books
UnKnownTruths.com Publishing Company

TRIVIA

East West Discovery Press
The Intrepid Traveler
Mayhaven Publishing
World Gumbo Publishing

MARK TWAIN

BOULDER HERETIC
Mercer University Press
Genny Smith Books
Tres Picos Press

U.S. HISPANIC

Aaron Communications III
Ancient City Press
Archer Books
Banta & Pool Literary Properties
BILINGUAL REVIEW/Revista Bilingue
Buenos Books America
Carolina Wren Press/Lollipop Power Books
LPD Press
MANDORLA: New Writing from the Americas / Nueva
    escritura de las Americas
POINT OF CONTACT, The Journal of Verbal & Visual
    Arts
RHINO: THE POETRY FORUM
Sunbelt Publications
Two Eagles Press International
Wings Press

U.S.S.R.

ABSINTHE: New European Writing
firefall editions
Hoover Institution Press
Mehring Books, Inc.
A Melody from an Immigrant's Soul
MIP Company
Pathfinder Press
Russian Information Services
Semiotext Foreign Agents Books Series
Typographia Press
Tzipora Publications, Inc.
Xenos Books

UTAH

American Legacy Media
Gibbs Smith, Publisher
LAKE STREET LIT: Art and Words from the Bottom of
    Lake Bonneville
Thundercloud Books
University of Utah Press
WEBER STUDIES: Voices and Viewpoints of the
    Contemporary West

VEGETARIANISM

Abecedarian books, Inc.
Affinity Publishers Services
ASCENT
Center For Self-Sufficiency
GREEN ANARCHIST
INDIA CURRENTS
JPS Publishing Company
Life Media
Macrocosm USA, Inc.
MB Media, Inc.
McBooks Press, Inc.
Micah Publications Inc.
Princess Publishing
SCIENCE/HEALTH ABSTRACTS
Square One Publishers, Inc.
VEGETARIAN JOURNAL

The Vegetarian Resource Group
VOICES - ISRAEL
White Crosslet Publishing Co

VIETNAM

Caernarvon Press
Cedar Hill Books
Galen Press, Ltd.
Islewest Publishing
Pocol Press
Rodnik Publishing Co.
Rowan Mountain Press
The Sektor Co.
STORMWARNING!
Texas Tech University Press
Twilight Times Books
University of Massachusetts Press
Vintage Romance Publishing, LLC
WAR, LITERATURE & THE ARTS: An International
    Journal of the Humanities
World Music Press

VIRGINIA

Brunswick Publishing Corporation
PLEASANT LIVING
Premium Press America
University of Virginia Press

VISUAL ARTS

A & U AMERICA'S AIDS MAGAZINE
AFTERIMAGE
Allworth Press
Altamont Press, Inc.
Americans for the Arts
ARCHIPELAGO
ART CALENDAR
ARTELLA: the waltz of words and art
ARTISTAMP NEWS
ASCENT
ASSEMBLAGE: A Critical Journal of Architecture and
    Design Culture
Athanata Arts, Ltd.
Bandanna Books
BIRD DOG
BLACKBIRD
BLADES
Blue Raven Publishing
BOMB MAGAZINE
Burning Books
THE CAPILANO REVIEW
Center for Thanatology Research & Education, Inc.
DOLLS UNITED INTERACTIVE MAGAZINE
Down There Press
Earthwinds Editions
ECOTONE: Reimagining Place
Edgewise Press
FIBERARTS
FISH DRUM MAGAZINE
FLUENT ASCENSION
FOLIO: A Literary Journal of American University
FOLK ART MESSENGER
GemStone Press
GERTRUDE
Gesture Press
Green Hut Press
GULF COAST
HAND PAPERMAKING
Harobed Publishing Creations
Helicon Nine Editions
Hollywood Creative Directory
Hollywood Film Archive
HOME PLANET NEWS
The Hosanna Press
IMAGE: ART, FAITH, MYSTERY
Interalia/Design Books
INTERNATIONAL ART POST
JAMES JOYCE BROADSHEET
JOURNAL OF AESTHETICS AND ART CRITICISM

JUBILAT
KALDRON, An International Journal Of Visual Poetry
KESTREL: A Journal of Literature and Art
Kiva Publishing, Inc.
Allen A. Knoll Publishers
KNUCKLE MERCHANT - The Journal of Naked Literary
  Aggression
KOJA
LAKE STREET LIT: Art and Words from the Bottom of
  Lake Bonneville
LEFT CURVE
LICHEN Arts & Letters Preview
LIGHTWORKS MAGAZINE
LO STRANIERO: The Stranger, Der Fremde, L'Etranger
Luna Bisonte Prods
THE MAD HATTER
MANDORLA: New Writing from the Americas / Nueva
  escritura de las Americas
MANOA: A Pacific Journal of International Writing
MEDIA SPOTLIGHT
Midmarch Arts Press
THE NEW RENAISSANCE, an international magazine of
  ideas & opinions, emphasizing literature & the arts
NIGHTLIFE MAGAZINE
Nightsun Books
Norton Coker Press
O!!ZONE, A LITERARY-ART ZINE
One Less Press
OUTER-ART
THE PEDESTAL MAGAZINE.COM
Phelps Publishing Company
POGO STICK
The Post-Apollo Press
PRISM INTERNATIONAL
PROVINCETOWN ARTS
Puna Press
Purple Finch Press
RATTAPALLAX
RUBBERSTAMPMADNESS
The Runaway Spoon Press
SAGE OF CONSCIOUSNESS E-ZINE
Santa Monica Press
SCULPTURAL PURSUIT MAGAZINE
SKYLARK
SNOW MONKEY
SO TO SPEAK: A Feminist Journal of Language & Art
A SOFT DEGRADE
Solcat Publishing
THE SOUTHERN QUARTERLY: A Journal of the Arts in
  the South
THE SOW'S EAR POETRY REVIEW
SULPHUR RIVER LITERARY REVIEW
Synergetic Press
Syracuse Cultural Workers/Tools for Change
Syukhtun Editions
13TH MOON
TRAVEL NATURALLY
Tzipora Publications, Inc.
UMBRELLA Online
VALLUM: CONTEMPORARY POETRY
VERSAL
WAR, LITERATURE & THE ARTS: An International
  Journal of the Humanities
Water Mark Press
WESTERN AMERICAN LITERATURE
Westgate Press
WHITEWALLS: A Journal of Language and Art
ZUZU'S PETALS: QUARTERLY ONLINE

WALES

ABSINTHE: New European Writing
VARIOUS ARTISTS

WAR

ALONE TOGETHER
BIG HAMMER
Burd Street Press
Cedar Hill Books

Crystal Dreams Publishing
The Glencannon Press
GREEN ANARCHIST
GREEN ANARCHY
Ho Logos Press
Iniquity Press/Vendetta Books
Lunar Offensive Publications
MacDonald/Sward Publishing Company
Mercer University Press
Open Hand Publishing LLC
Paladin Enterprises, Inc.
PEACEWORK
Rowan Mountain Press
STORMWARNING!
Tree of Life Books. Imprints: Progressive Press, Banned
  Books
TURNING THE TIDE: Journal of Anti-Racist Action,
  Research & Education
Typographia Press
Visions Communications
THE VORTEX
WAR, LITERATURE & THE ARTS: An International
  Journal of the Humanities
White Mane Publishing Company, Inc.

WASHINGTON (STATE)

AMERICAN JONES BUILDING & MAINTENANCE
Dunamis House
Light, Words & Music
Mountain Meadow Press
NORTHERN PILOT
SNOW MONKEY
Whispering Pine Press

WASHINGTON, D.C.

FOLIO: A Literary Journal of American University
Inner City Press
THE WASHINGTON MONTHLY

WATER

Accendo Publishing
AQUATERRA, METAECOLOGY & CULTURE
Envirographics
Island Press
Kali Press
LAKE SUPERIOR MAGAZINE
New England Cartographics, Inc.
Oregon State University Press
PATTERNS OF CHOICE: A Journal of People, Land, and
  Money
Ram Press
SEA KAYAKER
Genny Smith Books
Southwest Research and Information Center
SPROUTLETTER
VOICES FROM THE EARTH

WEAPONS

Lunar Offensive Publications
Paladin Enterprises, Inc.
Varro Press
WAR, LITERATURE & THE ARTS: An International
  Journal of the Humanities
Zygote Publishing

WEATHER

APPALACHIA JOURNAL
GAMBARA MAGAZINE
JetKor
Rivercross Publishing, Inc.
Word Forge Books

WEAVING

Altamont Press, Inc.
ART CALENDAR
FIBERARTS
THE JOURNAL OF CALIFORNIA AND GREAT BASIN
  ANTHROPOLOGY

Open Hand Publishing LLC
ORNAMENT
TRADICION REVISTA
TRADITION MAGAZINE

WEDDINGS

Biographical Publishing Company
First Books
SKS Press

THE WEST

THE ACORN
Acorn Books
Alta Research
American & World Geographic Publishing
Andmar Press
Ballena Press
The Bear Wallow Publishing Company
THE CLIMBING ART
Clover Park Press
Cold-Drill Books
Comstock Bonanza Press
Crazy Woman Creek Press
Devil Mountain Books
E. S. Publishers & Distributors
Eagle's View Publishing
Firelight Publishing, Inc.
Floreant Press
Flying Pencil Publications
Foundation Books
Fretwater Press
The Glencannon Press
Heartland Publishing
HIGH COUNTRY NEWS
High Plains Press
Horse Creek Publications, Inc.
Lahontan Images
LITERALLY HORSES/REMUDA
Mountain Automation Corporation
Mountain Meadow Press
Mountain Media
Mountain Press Publishing Co.
Native West Press
Nip & Tuck Publishing
Oregon State University Press
OVERLAND JOURNAL
PACIFIC COAST JOURNAL
PACIFIC HISTORICAL REVIEW
Platte Purchase Publishers
Rio Nuevo Publishers
Sand River Press
Skyline West Press/Wyoming Almanac
Genny Smith Books
SOUTH DAKOTA REVIEW
Spirit Talk Press
Sunbelt Publications
Texas Tech University Press
Tres Picos Press
University of Calgary Press
University of Utah Press
University Press of Colorado
UNWOUND
WEBER STUDIES: Voices and Viewpoints of the
    Contemporary West
WESTERN AMERICAN LITERATURE
World Love Press Publishing
Zon International Publishing Co.

WHALING

EZ Nature Books
FRAN MAGAZINE
NewSage Press
Windward Publishing, An Imprint of Finney Company

WALT WHITMAN

Gay Sunshine Press, Inc.
WALT WHITMAN QUARTERLY REVIEW

WICCA

Harvest Shadows Publications
Horned Owl Publishing
NEWWITCH
NOLA-MAGICK Press
WillowTree Press LLC
Zumaya Publications

WILDLIFE

Corvus Publishing Company

WINE, WINERIES

Ika, LLC
MY TABLE: Houston's Dining Magazine
Passion Power Press, Inc
Premium Press America
Pruett Publishing Company
Timber Press
VINEGAR CONNOISSEURS INTERNATIONAL NEWS-
    LETTER

WISCONSIN

AT THE LAKE MAGAZINE
Faded Banner Publications
FEMINIST COLLECTIONS: A QUARTERLY OF WO-
    MEN'S STUDIES RESOURCES
Jackson Harbor Press
MIDWEST ART FAIRS
Poetry Harbor
Whole Person Associates Inc.
Zelda Wilde Publishing
WISCONSIN ACADEMY REVIEW
WISCONSIN TRAILS
Women's Studies Librarian, University of Wisconsin
    System

WOMEN

AAIMS Publishers
Abecedarian books, Inc.
ABRAMELIN: a Journal of Poetry and Magick
Accendo Publishing
AFRICAN AMERICAN REVIEW
Alaska Native Language Center
Alice James Books
American Literary Press
Amethyst & Emerald
Andros Books
APPLE VALLEY REVIEW: A Journal of Contemporary
    Literature
Arden Press, Inc.
Ash Tree Publishing
ATLANTIS: A Women's Studies Journal/Revue d'etudes
    sur les femmes
Aunt Lute Books
Back House Books
Biblio Press
Biographical Publishing Company
Blanket Fort Publishing
BLK
Blue Poppy Press
BOOKS TO WATCH OUT FOR
Bordighera, Inc.
BRILLIANT STAR
Burning Bush Publications
Calyx Books
CALYX: A Journal of Art and Literature by Women
CAMERA OBSCURA: Feminism, Culture, and Media
    Studies
CANADIAN WOMAN STUDIES/les cahiers de la femme
Carolina Wren Press/Lollipop Power Books
Carrier Pigeon Press
THE CENTENNIAL REVIEW
Chandler & Sharp Publishers, Inc.
Chatterley Press International
Chicory Blue Press, Inc.
CHILDREN, CHURCHES AND DADDIES, A Non
    Religious, Non Familial Literary Magazine

13TH MOON
TIFARA
TORRE DE PAPEL
TRUTH SEEKER
TULSA STUDIES IN WOMEN'S LITERATURE
Twilight Times Books
Universal Unity
University of Calgary Press
University of Utah Press
VanderWyk & Burnham
Vanessapress
VARIOUS ARTISTS
Visions Communications
Vista Publishing, Inc.
West End Press
White Mane Publishing Company, Inc.
WIN NEWS
Wish Publishing
THE WISHING WELL
WOMAN'S ART JOURNAL
WOMEN AND LANGUAGE
WOMEN IN THE ARTS BULLETIN/NEWSLETTER
Women of Diversity Productions, Inc.
Women's Studies Librarian, University of Wisconsin
    System
WORD IS BOND
WRITER'S CHRONICLE
Writers' Haven Press
WRITING FOR OUR LIVES
WSQ (formerly WOMEN'S STUDIES QUARTERLY)
Yellow Moon Press
Yes International Publishers
Zephyr Press

WOOD ENGRAVING/WOODWORKING

Clamp Down Press
HandyCraft Media Productions
Hobar Publications, A Division of Finney Company
New Win Publishing
Rolling Hills Publishing
Storm Publishing Group
WOODWORKER'S JOURNAL

WORKER

AMERICAN JONES BUILDING & MAINTENANCE
Back House Books
Black Forest Press
BLUE COLLAR REVIEW
Blue Cubicle Press
THE CAIMAN (formerly THE WEIRD NEWS)
FIGHT THESE BASTARDS
Finney Company, Inc.
Garrett County Press
International Publishers Co. Inc.
Mehring Books, Inc.
Missing Spoke Press
Partisan Press
Prakken Publications
TECH DIRECTIONS
West End Press
WorkLife Publishing

WORLD WAR II

American Legacy Media
R.J. Bender Publishing
Black Forest Press
Bluestocking Press
A. Borough Books
Brunswick Publishing Corporation
Burd Street Press
Cypress House
EZ Nature Books
The Glencannon Press
Heidelberg Graphics
Historical Resources Press
Ho Logos Press
THE JOURNAL OF HISTORICAL REVIEW
MCM Entertainment, Inc. Publishing Division

A Melody from an Immigrant's Soul
Noontide Press
Path Press, Inc.
Pocol Press
The Sektor Co.
Stardate Publishing Company
Typographia Press
University of Nebraska Press
University of Utah Press
Vintage Romance Publishing, LLC
White Mane Publishing Company, Inc.

WRITERS/WRITING

A Cappela Publishing, Inc.
ALASKA QUARTERLY REVIEW
Allworth Press
ARCHIPELAGO
Arden Press, Inc.
ARTELLA: the waltz of words and art
AuthorsOmniscient Publishers
Bellywater Press
BIRD DOG
Blueprint Books
BOOK MARKETING UPDATE
BOOK/MARK SMALL PRESS REVIEW
Bookhome Publishing/Panda Publishing
Bordighera, Inc.
BRADY MAGAZINE
BUZZWORDS
BYLINE
THE CANNON'S MOUTH
THE CAPILANO REVIEW
CEDAR HILL REVIEW
The Center Press
Central Avenue Press
CHECKER CAB MAGAZINE - THE LITTLE 'ZINE
    THAT COULD! Fiction That Takes The Long Way
    Home
CIMARRON REVIEW
City Life Books, LLC
Clearwater Publishing Co.
Communication Creativity
CREATIVITY CONNECTION
THE DRAMATIST
Dumouriez Publishing
EEI Press
ELEMENTS
FICTION WRITER'S GUIDELINE
FINE MADNESS
THE FLORIDA REVIEW
THE FRANK REVIEW
Gryphon Books
HEARTLANDS: A Magazine of Midwest Life and Art
IMAGE: ART, FAITH, MYSTERY
Impassio Press
In Between Books
INKY TRAIL NEWS
INTERLIT
Ironweed Press
J'ECRIS
KARAWANE
Lost Horse Press
LULLWATER REVIEW
MAINE IN PRINT
MANGROVE MAGAZINE
A Melody from an Immigrant's Soul
Moon Pie Press
Muse World Media Group
Myriad Press
NEW HOPE INTERNATIONAL REVIEW
NEW VERSE NEWS, THE
THE NEW WRITER
North Stone Editions
OHIO WRITER
OPEN WIDE MAGAZINE
Oyster River Press
PAPERBACK PARADE
Para Publishing

Parthian
POETICA MAGAZINE, Reflections of Jewish Thought
The Poetry Center
PRETEXT
PULSAR POETRY MAGAZINE
Quill Driver Books
Read Press LLC
Red Tiger Press
Redgreene Press
Riverwinds Publishing
Roblin Press
Rose Alley Press
ROSEBUD
Sage Hill Press
SAGE OF CONSCIOUSNESS E-ZINE
Salt Publishing
SCULPTURAL PURSUIT MAGAZINE
74th Street Productions, L.L.C.
SEWANEE REVIEW
SISTERS IN CRIME BOOKS IN PRINT
SMARTISH PACE
SO TO SPEAK: A Feminist Journal of Language & Art
Soul
SPEAKEASY
Square One Publishers, Inc.
Standish Press
Starbooks Press/FLF Press
THE STINGING FLY
Stony Meadow Publishing
Stormline Press, Inc.
Strata Publishing, Inc.
SYCAMORE REVIEW
Toad Press International Chapbook Series
TORRE DE PAPEL
TRUE POET MAGAZINE
Twilight Times Books
UmbraProjects, Ltd.
UNDERSTANDING MAGAZINE
UnTechnical Press
VALLUM: CONTEMPORARY POETRY
VARIOUS ARTISTS
Verve Press
WILD DUCK REVIEW
WordFarm
Wordwrights Canada
WORKING WRITER
WRITER'S CHRONICLE
WRITER'S EXCHANGE
WRITERS' JOURNAL
XTANT
xtant.anabasis
ZINE WORLD: A Reader's Guide to the Underground Press
ZUZU'S PETALS: QUARTERLY ONLINE
ZYX

WYOMING

Andmar Press
The Bear Wallow Publishing Company
Devenish Press
firefall editions
THE FRANK REVIEW
The Great Rift Press
High Plains Press
Laguna Wilderness Press
Pruett Publishing Company
Skyline West Press/Wyoming Almanac
UNWOUND

YOGA

Airplane Books
Crystal Clarity, Publishers
INDIA CURRENTS
JetKor
LifeQuest Publishing Group
Mandala Publishing
Plus Publications
Princeton Book Company, Publishers
Quest Books: Theosophical Publishing House

Rivercross Publishing, Inc.
SAT SANDESH: THE MESSAGE OF THE MASTERS
Swing-Hi Press
Ten Star Press
Timeless Books
Yes International Publishers
YogaVidya.com

YOSEMITE

Clover Park Press
Laguna Wilderness Press
The Live Oak Press, LLC
Tres Picos Press

YOUNG ADULT

A Cappela Publishing, Inc.
Abecedarian books, Inc.
Abernathy House Publishing
Affirmative Publishing LC
Annick Press Ltd.
Avari Press
Avisson Press, Inc.
The Bess Press
Book Marketing Solutions
Central Avenue Press
Chicken Soup Press, Inc.
Concrete Jungle Press
Cornerstone Publishing
Crystal Dreams Publishing
Delaney Day Press
Desert Bloom Press
East West Discovery Press
Falls Media
The Fiction Works
Finney Company, Inc.
First Books
Flowerfield Enterprises, LLC
Fontanel Books
Gallaudet University Press
Harrington Park Press
Infinite Possibilities Publishing Group, Inc.
Jalmar Press/Innerchoice Publishing
juel house publishers and literary services
JUNIOR STORYTELLER
THE KIDS' STORYTELLING CLUB WEBSITE
LEO Productions LLC.
LISTEN
Little Pear Press
Lucky Press, LLC
Luminous Epinoia Press
THE MAD HATTER
Mayhaven Publishing
Montemayor Press
Mo'omana'o Press
Munsey Music
NAMBLA BULLETIN
Neshui Publishing
NIGHTLIFE MAGAZINE
NSR Publications
Ocean Publishing
ORBIS
PARENTEACHER MAGAZINE
Peachtree Publishers, Ltd.
Pineapple Press, Inc.
POGO STICK
THE RAVEN CHRONICLES
READERS SPEAK OUT!
Saint Mary's Press
SISTERS IN CRIME BOOKS IN PRINT
Snake Hill Press
SPEAK UP
Speak Up Press
Stony Meadow Publishing
STORMWARNING!
Storycraft Publishing
TEEN VOICES MAGAZINE
This New World Publishing, LLC
Top 20 Press

Twilight Times Books
UmbraProjects, Ltd.
Unity House
Vision Works Publishing
VISIONHOPE NEWSLETTER
Visions Communications
VOYA (Voice of Youth Advocate)
Whiskey Creek Press
Wings Press

ZEN

Abecedarian books, Inc.
Alamo Square Press
ASCENT
Athanata Arts, Ltd.
BLITHE SPIRIT
Bottom Dog Press
Brooks Books
FAT TUESDAY
FISH DRUM MAGAZINE
FROZEN WAFFLES
Frozen Waffles Press/Shattered Sidewalks Press; 45th
  Century Chapbooks
HERE AND NOW
Iconoclast Press
Ika, LLC
Ithuriel's Spear
La Alameda Press
LifeQuest Publishing Group
MAGICAL BLEND/NATURAL BEAUTY & HEALTH/
  TRANSITIONS
MB Media, Inc.
THE MINDFULNESS BELL
Motom
Parallax Press
PARTING GIFTS
PERIPHERAL VISION
Press Here
Quest Books: Theosophical Publishing House
SHO
Spirit Press
Spiritual Understanding Network, LLC
Sun Rising Press
Total Cardboard Publishing
TURNING WHEEL
Turtle Press, division of S.K. Productions Inc.
Water Mark Press
WHAT IS ENLIGHTENMENT?
White Pine Press
Zelda Wilde Publishing
World Love Press Publishing
Zygote Publishing

ZINES

ALMOST NORMAL COMICS and Other Oddities
ARTELLA: the waltz of words and art
BAGAZINE
BEATLICK NEWS
BIG HAMMER
BLACKBOOK PRESS, THE POETRY ZINE
THE BLIND MAN'S RAINBOW
Blue Cubicle Press
Blueprint Books
BROKEN PENCIL
Carnifex Press
CHECKER CAB MAGAZINE - THE LITTLE 'ZINE
  THAT COULD! Fiction That Takes The Long Way
  Home
DEAD FUN
DWAN
THE FRANK REVIEW
furniture_press
GIN BENDER POETRY REVIEW
GREEN ANARCHIST
GREEN ANARCHY
Gryphon Books
Iniquity Press/Vendetta Books
THE LEDGE

Mucusart Publications
READERS SPEAK OUT!
SAGE OF CONSCIOUSNESS E-ZINE
SECOND GUESS
Soft Skull Press
Thunder Rain Publishing Corp.
UmbraProjects, Ltd.
UNDER THE VOLCANO
V52 Press
Via Dolorosa Press
X-Ray Book Co.
ZINE WORLD: A Reader's Guide to the Underground Press

NOTES

NOTES